15/88

A CONCORDANCE
to the Sonnet Sequences of
DANIEL, DRAYTON, SHAKESPEARE, SIDNEY, and SPENSER

Herbert S. Donow

SOUTHERN ILLINOIS UNIVERSITY PRESS
Cardondale and Edwardsville
FEFFER & SIMONS, INC.
London and Amsterdam

To Ann

Copyright © 1969 by Southern Illinois University Press
All rights reserved
Printed by Offset Lithography in the
    United States of America
Standard Book Number 8093–0400–7
Library of Congress Catalog Card Number 72–76188

Contents

Preface

THE THINKING that underlies a concordance of sonnet sequences reflects two assumptions: one about the nature of style and the other about the Elizabethan sonnet. The critic of poetic style has, for a long time, viewed his subject as an occult phenomenon, a chimerical will-o-the-wisp that only the initiated can grasp. With his own artistry, the commentator manages to impart his revelation about style to his earthbound disciples, telling them of how poets evoke in their tempos the sensuality of the South or make meters move with ponderous dignity, and of how metaphor stuns with its brilliance and wit. But Sensibility is dead: *requiescat in pace*; and the intuitive, highly subjective approach to literary style seems less relevant to our generation of modern critics. More reasonable is the approach that recognizes style to be a complex of patterns that can be described and measured and, ultimately, understood. That is my first assumption.

The other assumption I make, and a fairly common one, is that the degree of homogeneity among sonnets is sufficiently high that, for purposes of establishing a broadly based description of the genre, the poems can be treated as a group, regardless of author. Through the use of the various techniques of statistical inference, it should be possible to develop a set of probable sonnet characteristics. Up to now in discussing sonnets we have limited ourselves to making some very general distinctions: is a sonnet English or Italian in structure, is it Petrarchan or anti-Petrarchan in convention, and so forth. What I am suggesting is that we can do better with empirical methods. Given the similarities among sonnets with respect to vocabulary and meter, the use of rhetorical figures, and line and poem structure, the critic can quickly focus upon the finer points of style, the idiosyncrasies that, when encountered in reading, seem too diminutive and patternless to pause over.

This concordance is an invitation to those who share these assumptions to observe poets working in a tight convention, manifesting their poetic personalities in a controlled environment. By examining poems in a situation where the effects of semantic difference are minimized, we can study style as an abstraction, apart from meaning. At the same time, it may be possible to discern the extent to which these poets were directed by influences outside themselves: Petrarchanism, anti-Petrarchanism, Elizabethan poetic conventions, etc.

Although I offer no prescriptions on the use of this book, in conception the concordance was designed to support the assumptions that I have just described. In order to make the close comparisons that are, therefore, demanded, the separate index to each sequence has been rejected in favor of a single merged index to all six sequences. For the same reason, I chose to do the index in modern, American spelling rather than in the old spelling. The latter would have involved many more entries and would have partially frustrated my desire to juxtapose the lines from each of the poets. Admittedly orthography might be considered a component of style, but in the case of the Elizabethans, for a number of reasons, spelling differences cannot be considered reliable indicators of a poet's intention. I have preserved all archaisms and regionalisms, and in those cases where the OED could not resolve my doubts, I left the original form unchanged. No editing or modernizing was done to the lines themselves. The lines that are printed under each index entry appear exactly as they are in the authoritative editions.

The procedure that I employed in producing a modernized version of the text deserves a brief explanation. In an effort to maximize consistency in the modification of spelling and in order to free me from tedious clerical labors, I changed the old text into a list (one word per record) and sorted this list alphabetically, retaining all numbers that identified the source of the words. My assistant was able to encode modern spellings next to their archaic counterparts. She did this for all cases that conformed to rules that I had previously established. If a word was ambiguous and could not be resolved by reference to the text of the poem or if it was not covered by one of my rules, she marked the word and left it to me. Since the vast majority of words on the list were spelled according to modern conventions, only a relatively small number needed to be changed. Eventually cards were punched which included the old and new spelling and these cards were used to generate a new list made up of words in modernized spelling. This list enabled me to create a modernized linear version of the poems. A reading of the new version was necessary to clear up unresolved ambiguities. For example, "then" is used indiscriminately in the original texts; consequently, "than" had to be substituted by hand wherever required. A genuine advantage of this technique is that working with lists is far less conducive to error than working with the text where the mind is often deflected from its proper course by the delights of poetry.

One consequence of the modernized index is that many variant spellings disappear from the index. In addition, textual variants have been excluded. Since multiple listings of lines showing all variants would have inflated the volume excessively, I would have been obliged to exercise a large measure of selectivity. That path, with its numerous difficulties, was fraught with as many dangers as complete omission. In addition, the text of the Daniel sonnet sequence cannot be considered authoritative, and hence, with or without variants, my text would necessarily be imperfect. Ultimately my reason for exclusion was an economic one. In a manually made concordance, the editor is free to respond to his material with complete flexibility. The spelling of index words, the amount of context to provide, the handling of homonyms— all can be decided *ad hoc*. In a machine-generated concordance, policies and procedures have to be established from the beginning, thus making alterations in special cases difficult and highly impractical. In view of the special nature of this concordance it did not seem that the inclusion of a selected group of variant readings could add sufficient value to the concordance to justify the cost in human and machine time.

To keep the volume within reasonable limits, only a few sequences could be indexed. In choosing the following, I was principally influenced by the reputation of the poets among modern scholars and the adherence of the sequences to the common conventions of the genre. The six sequences are Samuel Daniel's *Delia*, Michael Drayton's *Idea's Mirrour* and *Idea*, William Shakespeare's *Sonnets*, Sir Philip Sidney's *Astrophel and Stella* and Edmund Spenser's *Amoretti*.[1]

Although the scope of the book has been confined to five hundred twenty-five poems by five poets, one of the virtues of the computer-generated concordance is its remarkable elasticity. If a user of this volume found that he could make good use of an expanded concordance, say involving the addition of the sonnets of Constable and Lodge, or if another user wanted material that had been removed in producing this book, both could, without too much difficulty, be accommodated. My concordance system, which was designed to run on an IBM 7044[2], as well as my tapes of the unabridged concordance and the sonnet texts are available for any sort of custom job that one might desire. As generalized concordance systems become more accessible and machine-readable texts more abundant, the made-to-order concordance will be a commonplace, and because its composition and format will reflect the special needs of its maker, it will have particularly great value.

In compiling the list of "non-significant" words to be excluded, I tried to be as consistent as possible. Therefore, I elected to eliminate certain classes of high

[1]The texts of the sequences were obtained from the following editions: *The Complete Works in Verse and Prose of Samuel Daniel*, ed. A. B. Grosart, Vol. I (1885); *The Works of Michael Drayton*, ed. J. W. Hebel, Vols. I, II (Oxford, 1931–32); *A New Variorum Edition of Shakespeare: The Sonnets*, ed. Hyder E. Rollins, Vol. XXIV (Philadelphia, 1944); *The Poems of Sir Philip Sidney*, ed. William A. Ringler, Jr. (Oxford, 1962); *The Works of Edmund Spenser: A Variorum Edition: The Minor Poems*, ed. Charles Grosvenor Osgood and Henry Gibbons Lotspeich, Vol. VII (Baltimore, 1947).

[2]The programs are written in *FORTRAN IV* and by the time this book has gone to press will have been adapted to run on an IBM 360.

frequency function words and to avoid making more than a bare minimum of decisions on individual words. My policy was to be absolutely liberal in adjudging significance. The classes of words that I have not used in the final concordance are coordinating conjunctions, article adjectives, all forms of the verb "to be," auxiliary verbs, pronouns of various types, eight of the most frequent prepositions and twelve other words that fall outside these categories. Following is a list of these words, one hundred and six in number:

a	didst	him	or	thine	where
am	*do	his	our	this	which
an	does	how	shall	those	who
and	doest	I	shalt	thou	whom
are	*dost	if	she	though	whose
*art	*doth	in	should	thus	why
at	for	into	shouldst	thy	*will
be	from	is	so	tis	wilt
been	*had	it	that	to	with
but	*hadst	*may	the	too	would
by	*hast	mayst	thee	us	wouldst
can	*hath	me	their	was	ye
cannot	*have	my	theirs	wast	yet
canst	*having	nor	them	we	you
could	he	not	then	were	your
couldst	her	now	there	wert	yours
*did	here	of	these	what	
diddest	hers	on	they	when	

Some of the above words occur not only as function words but also as content words. In these instances (see words with asterisk) the words are indexed and only those lines edited from the text which contain the word as function word. In addition to this editing, I have suppressed in the final printing all end punctuation (except question marks).

It is inevitable that errors in judgment or execution have occurred in editing this concordance. One area in which I am sure mistakes may be detected is in the indexing of plurals and possessives. I would issue a caveat to the reader to be alert to cases where I have falsely attributed plurality to a possessive or vice versa.

Format and Coding

The text of the concordance includes an index word, beginning in the first print position, with an integer on the same line; beneath the index word and indented two print positions, is the listing of the line or lines. The integer on the first line of the entry represents the number of occurrences of the word in the total corpus of poetry. This frequency should be the same as the number of lines listed below. The appendix contains raw frequencies for the individual sequences and is somewhat easier to use for obtaining figures for computation. The frequencies in the text are unreliable because they reflect some repetitions in Drayton's two sequences.

Since the printer that was available to me when I produced this concordance did not include lower case alphabetic characters nor did it include punctuation marks other than periods and commas, I had to resort to some artificial contrivances. Capitals are not indicated at the beginnings of lines, but wherever else a word is capitalized a dollar sign ($) precedes the upper case letter. A semi-colon appears as a period followed by a comma; a colon is indicated by two periods in succession. The question mark was encoded on punch cards as a 12-0 punch but the printer reproduces it as a plus sign; the exclamation point was encoded as an 11-0 punch and appears as a dash (—).

To the right of each line in the listing is a set of numbers that serves as an identification for that line. The first digit is the author code. The next group of digits, following the first period, indicates the poem number used by the editor of each respective edition. The final set of numbers, after the second period, is the line reference.

The author codes, based on the alphabetic sequence of the poets' names, are Daniel (1), Drayton (2), Shakespeare (3), Sidney (4), Spenser (5). In the case of Drayton, who has two sequences indexed, the poem number indicates the sequence to which reference is being made. If the line is from *Idea* the poem number will be from 1 to 63, corresponding to the actual number used in volume two of the Hebel edition. If the line is from *Idea's Mirrour,* the numbering begins at 101 and proceeds to 151: i.e. one hundred is added to the actual sonnet number as it appears in volume one of the Hebel edition. Thus if the first line of the third sonnet from *Idea* were being listed, it would be written

TAKING MY $PENNE, WITH $WORDS TO CAST MY $WOE   2.3.1.

Appendix

The appendix provides a listing of words and frequencies for each sequence showing the words in their descending order of frequency. In the table below, the number of words used by each poet and the total number of occurrences is provided.

Name	Number of Different Words	Number of Running Occurrences
Daniel	1,613	6,920
Drayton		
Idea's Mirrour	1,622	5,768
Idea	1,905	7,139
Shakespeare	3,149	17,676
Sidney	2,591	12,791
Spenser	2,195	10,000
Cumulative	6,640	60,294

Acknowledgments

A project like a machine-generated concordance is not exactly the sort of opus that can erupt from a tortured genius in the isolation of a freezing garret. It requires cooperation on the part of many people and the employment of some very expensive facilities. In a general way, I am grateful to various members of the university community who are eager to see the computer become a useful tool in teaching and research. Southern Illinois University has been a most willing supporter of this project. More specifically, I wish to acknowledge the major contribution made by a number of individuals who, in the line of duty and beyond, willingly helped me throughout the preparation of this book. To Mrs. Mary Wildrick, who prepared the poetry for keypunching and who, with a keen eye, did virtually all the checking at every stage, and to Michael Bartlett, who gave freely of his time and counsel in helping me with program preparation and debugging, I owe my unqualified appreciation. The staff of the Southern Illinois University Computer Center also deserves my deepest thanks. Dr. Thomas Purcell, Director, and Colonel George Flummer, Assistant Director, Mr. Philip Spielmacher of Research and Instruction, and Mr. William Jones, head of Research and Development, were assiduous in my behalf, as was David Eagan, Manager of Operations, who has cheerfully endured my importunate pleas to find a twenty-fifth hour in the computer's day. Larry Kinley and Bill Webb, also of Operations, were particularly helpful in numerous ways.

I wish also to thank the Southern Illinois University Office of Research and Projects under Dr. Ronald Hansen for its financial support throughout this project. Without this aid, I could never have begun. And for helping me finish, my thanks go to the American Council of Learned Societies, which has most generously bestowed on me an Award for Computer-Oriented Research in the Humanities. This grant has enabled me to expedite completion of the Concordance and to proceed with studies in the style of the Elizabethan sonnet.

For their kind permission to allow me to use copyrighted materials, I thank Basil Blackwell, Publisher, for the use of J. W. Hebel's *The Works of Michael Drayton;* the Johns Hopkins Press for the use of *The Works of Edmund Spenser: A Variorum Edition* (edited by Charles Grosvenor Osgood and Henry Gibbons Lotspeich); the Clarendon Press of Oxford for the use of *The Poems of Sir Philip Sidney* (edited by William A. Ringler, Jr.) and to the University of Pennsylvania Press for the use of *A New Variorum Edition of Shakespeare: The Sonnets* (edited by Hyder E. Rollins).

March 12, 1969   Herbert S. Donow
Carbondale, Illinois

ABUSE   5
  WHY SHOULD'ST THOU, $NIGHT, ABUSE ME ONELY THUS   2.37.10
  THEN BEAUTIOUS NIGARD WHY DOOST THOU ABUSE   3.4.5
  AND FOR MY SAKE EVEN SO DOTH SHE ABUSE ME   3.42.7
  SO HIM I LOOSE THROUGH MY UNKINDE ABUSE   3.134.12
  AND CAN WITH FOULE ABUSE SUCH BEAUTIES BLOT   4.24.11
ABUSED   1
  WHERE CHEEKES NEED BLOOD, IN THEE IT IS ABUS'D   3.82.14
ABUSES   1
  AT MY ABUSES, RECKCN UP THEIR OWNE   3.121.10
ABYSM   1
  IN SO PROFOUND $ABISME I THROW ALL CARE   3.112.9
ACCENTS   7
  WITH INTERRUPTED ACCENTS OF DESPAIRE   1.2.6
  MY HUMBLE ACCENTS BEARE THE $OLIVE BOUGH   1.4.11
  ALTHOUGH MY CAREFULL ACCENTS NEVER MOOV'D THEE   1.44.13
  IN AGED ACCENTS, AND UNTIMELY WORDS   1.55.2
  REDOUBLING SIGHES THE ACCENTS OF MY GRIEFE   2.111.12
  THE MOURNFULL ACCENTS OF MY LOVES DISPAYRE   2.141.8
  IN OTHER ACCENTS DOE THIS PRAISE CONFOUND   3.69.7
ACCEPT   2
  THE WHICH VOUCHSAFE $O GODDESSE TO ACCEPT   5.22.13
  LET HER ACCEPT ME AS HER FAITHFULL THRALL   5.29.10
ACCEPTABLE   1
  WHAT ACCEPTABLE $AUDIT CAN'ST THOU LEAVE+   3.4.12
ACCEPTANCE   1
  AND IN MY WILL NO FAIRE ACCEPTANCE SHINE   3.135.8
ACCESSORY   2
  DOE QUIT THE DEAD, AND ME NOT ACCESSARIE   2.2.6
  THAT I AN ACCESSARY NEEDS MUST BE   3.35.13
ACCIDENT   1
  NO IT WAS BUYLDED FAR FROM ACCIDENT   3.124.5
ACCIDENTS   1
  BUT RECKENING TIME, WHOSE MILLIOND ACCIDENTS   3.115.5
ACCOMPANIED   1
  ACCOMPANYDE WITH ANGELICK DELIGHTES   5.84.8
ACCOMPLISHMENT   1
  DOE YE NOT THINCK TH'ACCOMPLISHMENT OF IT   5.33.6
ACCORD   2
  THOSE THAT I FOSTRED OF MINE OWNE ACCORD   1.5.13
  BUT DID SHE KNOW HOW ILL THESE TWO ACCORD   5.31.13
ACCORDING   2
  SO SOUNDS MY $MUSE ACCORDING AS SHE STRIKES   1.57.3
  ACCORDING TO MY $LORD $LOVE'S OWNE BEHEST   4.50.6
ACCOUMPT   1
  WHY THEN SHOULD I ACCOUMPT OF LITTLE PAINE   5.26.13
ACCOUMPTS   1
  ACCOUMPTS MY SELFE HER CAPTIVE QUITE FORLORNE   5.29.4
ACCOUNT   5
  BEGINNING TO ACCOUNT THE SUM OF ALL MY CARES   2.110.2
  THE SAD ACCOUNT OF FORE-BEMONED MONE   3.30.11
  OR AT YOUR HAND TH'ACCOUNT OF HOURES TO CRAVE   3.58.3
  NO SHAPE SO TRUE, NC TRUTH OF SUCH ACCOUNT   3.62.6
  THOUGH IN THY STORES ACCOUNT I ONE MUST BE   3.136.10
ACCOUNTS   1
  WHERE I HAVE CAST TH'ACCOUNTS OF ALL MY CARE   1.1.6
ACCUMULATE   1
  AND ON JUST PROOFE SURMISE, ACCUMILATE   3.117.10
ACCURSED   1
  UPON THEE FALL FOR THINE ACCURSED HYRE   5.86.6

ACCURST   1
  DELIGHT PROTESTS HE IS NOT FOR THE ACCURST   4.95.7
ACCUSE   3
  ACCUSE ME THUS, THAT I HAVE SCANTED ALL   3.117.1
  BUT WHY OF TWO OTHES BREACH DOE I ACCUSE THEE   3.152.5
  T'ACCUSE OF PRIDE, OR RASHLY BLAME FOR OUGHT   5.61.4
ACCUSING   1
  WITHOUT ACCUSING YOU OF INJURY   3.58.8
ACHERON   1
  I LYKE NOT $LIMBO, NOR BLACKE $ACHERON   2.118.8
ACHIEVE   3
  THAT SINNE BY HIM ADVANTAGE SHOULD ATCHIVE   3.67.3
  WHICH WAS NOT HARD T'ATCHIVE AND BRING TO END   5.51.8
  MOST HAPPY HE THAT CAN AT LAST ATCHYVE   5.63.9
ACKNOWLEDGE   1
  I MAY NOT EVER-MORE ACKNOWLEDGE THEE   3.36.9
ACQUAINT   2
  AND $FATES AND $FURIES, WITH THEIR WOES ACQUAINT   2.39.4
  AND HEAVEN, AND EARTH, DOE WITH THEIR
                              WOES ACQUAINT   2.118.4
ACQUAINTANCE   4
  TO TAKE A NEW ACQUAINTANCE OF THY MINDE   3.77.12
  I WILL ACQUAINTANCE STRANGLE AND LOOKE STRANGE   3.89.8
  AND HAPLIE OF OUR OLD ACQUAINTANCE TELL   3.89.12
  VOUCHSAFE OF ALL ACQUAINTANCE THIS TO TELL   4.32.9
ACQUAINTED   4
  A WOMANS GENTLE HART BUT NOT ACQUAINTED   3.20.3
  WITH MINE OWNE WEAKENESSE BEING BEST ACQUAINTED   3.88.5
  SURE, IF THAT LONG WITH $LOVE ACQUAINTED EYES   4.31.5
  THE COURTLY $NYMPHS, ACQUAINTED WITH THE MONE   4.54.5
ACQUIT   1
  TO BE ACQUIT FRO MY CONTINUALL SMART   5.42.6
ACT   3
  WISE IN $CONCEIT, IN $ACT A VERY SOT   2.62.6
  WISE IN CONCEITE, IN ACTE A VERY SOT   2.150.6
  IN ACT THY BED-VOW BROAKE AND NEW FAITH TORNE   3.152.3
ACTION   3
  WHOSE ACTION IS NO STRONGER THEN A FLOWER+   3.65.4
  IS LUST IN ACTION, AND TILL ACTION, LUST   3.129.2
  IS LUST IN ACTION, AND TILL ACTION, LUST   3.129.2
ACTIONS   1
  WHOSE GLORIOUS ACTIONS LUCKILY HAD GAIND   1.45.7
ACTIVE   1
  TO SEE HIS ACTIVE CHILDE DO DEEDS OF YOUTH   3.37.2
ACTOR   1
  AS AN UNPERFECT ACTOR ON THE STAGE   3.23.1
ACTORS   1
  IF THE VILE ACTORS OF THE HEYNOUS DEED   2.46.6
ADAMANT   1
  LET HER, YF PLEASE HER, BYND WITH ADAMANT CHAYNE   5.42.10
ADD   6
  BUT I MAY ADDE ONE FEATHER TO THY FAME   1.43.9
  TO ADDE MORE GRIEFE TO AGGRAVATE MY SORROW   1.54.12
  TO THY FAIRE FLOWER AD THE RANCKE SMELL OF WEEDS   3.69.12
  YOU TO YOUR BEAUTIOUS BLESSINGS ADDE A CURSE   3.84.13
  AND TO THE MOST OF PRAISE ADDE SOME-THING MORE   3.85.10
  SO THOU BEEING RICH IN $WILL ADDE TO THY $WILL   3.135.11
ADDED   2
  HAVE ADDED FETHERS TO THE LEARNEDS WING   3.78.7
  THEN WHEN IT HATH MY ADDED PRAISE BESIDE   3.103.4

```
ADDER'S                        2
  OF OTHERS VOYCES, THAT MY $ADDERS SENCE            3.112.10
  VENEMOUS TOUNG TIPT WITH VILE ADDERS STING          5.86.1
ADDETH                         3
  MY WORTHY, $ONE TO THESE $NINE $WORTHIES ADDETH     2.18.9
  MY $WORTHIE, ONE TO THESE NINE $WORTHIES, ADDETH    2.108.9
  AND IN ABOUNDANCE ADDETH TO HIS STORE              3.135.10
ADDING                         1
  BY ADDING ONE THING TO MY PURPOSE NOTHING           3.20.12
ADDITION                       2
  AND BY ADDITION ME OF THEE DEFEATED                 3.20.11
  TO THY SWEET WILL MAKING ADDITION THUS              3.135.4
ADDRESS                        3
  SOME THAT KNOW HOW MY SPRING I DID ADDRESSE          4.23.5
  AND YET TO BREAKE MORE STAVES DID ME ADDRESSE        4.53.2
  SHE CRUELL WARRIOUR DOTH HER SELFE ADDRESSE          5.11.3
ADIEU                          2
  WHEN YOU HAVE BID YOUR SERVANT ONCE ADIEUE           3.57.8
  AND BIDDING TH'OLD $ADIEU, HIS PASSED DATE            5.4.3
ADJUNCT                        2
  AND EVERY HUMOR HATH HIS ADJUNCT PLEASURE            3.91.5
  TO KEEPE AN ADJUNCKT TO REMEMBER THEE              3.122.13
ADMIRATION                     1
  WITH ADMIRATION, EVER LOOKING ON HER                2.138.8
ADMIRE                        18
  WHILST WE BOTH MAKE THE WORLD ADMIRE AT US          1.26.13
  THAT MAKES THE WORLD ADMIRE SO STRANGE EFFECTS       1.34.8
  WHOSE GLORIOUS BLAZE THE WORLD DOTH SO ADMIRE        1.38.6
  MARVELL NOT, $LOVE, THOUGH I THY POW'R ADMIRE        2.34.1
  MARVELL NOT, $LOVE, THOUGH I THY POW'R ADMIRE        2.34.5
  MARVELL NOT, $LOVE, THOUGH I THY POW'R ADMIRE        2.34.9
  COME THOU AND READE, ADMIRE, APPLAUD MY $LINES      2.49.14
  WHEN SHE HER OWNE PERFECTION WOULD ADMIRE            2.57.6
  I FIND OLD $POETS HYLLS AND FLOODS ADMIRE           2.120.2
  OUR DATES ARE BREEFE, AND THEREFOR WE ADMIRE        3.123.5
  SINCE BEST WITS THINKE IT WIT THEE TO ADMIRE         4.80.2
  THE SOVERAYNE BEAUTY WHICH I DOO ADMYRE              5.3.1
  THE THING WHICH I DOO MOST IN HER ADMIRE             5.5.3
  I HONOR AND ADMIRE THE MAKERS ART                   5.24.4
  THAT MANY NOW MUCH WORSHIP AND ADMIRE               5.27.8
  THE BEAME OF LIGHT, WHOM MORTAL EYES ADMYRE         5.61.10
  THAT MAY ADMIRE SUCH WORLDS RARE WONDERMENT         5.69.12
  ALL THAT THEY KNOW NOT, ENVY OR ADMYRE              5.85.6
ADMIRED                        4
  O MINE EYES $COMET, SO ADMYR'D BY LOVING            2.129.7
  MAKING HIS STILE ADMIRED EVERY WHERE               3.84.12
  THAT YOUR BRIGHT BEAMS OF MY WEAK EIES ADMYRED       5.7.11
  SUCH MERCY SHAL YOU MAKE ADMYRED TO BE             5.49.13
ADMIRES                        1
  THE FAIREST FORME, THAT ALL THE WORLD ADMIRES        1.13.7
ADMIRETH                       2
  DELIA, THESE EYES THAT SO ADMIRETH THINE            1.45.1
  COULD ALL CONCEITE CONCLUDE, WHICH PAST
                          CONCEITE ADMIRETH            2.117.5
ADMIRING                       1
  TO SUBJECTS WORSE HAVE GIVEN ADMIRING PRAISE        3.59.14
ADMIT                          1
  ADMIT IMPEDIMENTS, LOVE IS NOT LOVE                 3.116.2
ADMITTED                       2
  AND WILL THY SOULE KNOWES IS ADMITTED THERE         3.136.3
```

ADMITTED LATE BY YOUR BEST-GRACED GRACE   4.82.10
ADONIS   1
DESCRIBE $ADONIS AND THE COUNTERFET   3.53.5
ADOPTIVE   1
GALLEIN'S ADOPTIVE SONNES, WHO BY A BEATEN WAY   4.102.9
ADORE   9
  OF HER, WHOSE SWEETEST GRACE I DO ADORE   1.13.10
  YET DO I LOVE, ADORE, AND PRAYSE THE SAME   1.14.7
  BEQUEATH THE HEAVENS THE STARRES THAT I ADORE   1.19.3
  O BLESSED $BROOKE, WHOSE MILKE-WHITE $SWANS ADORE   2.53.3
  O BLESSED $BROOKE, WHOSE MILK-WHITE $SWANS ADORE   2.113.3
  O VERTUE, WHICH ALL VERTUES DOE ADORE   2.146.7
  YET MORTALL LOOKES ADORE HIS BEAUTY STILL   3.7.7
  AND, FOOLES, ADORE IN TEMPLE OF OUR HART   4.5.7
  SO DYING LIVE, AND LIVING DO ADORE HER   5.14.14
ADORED   1
  A SOULE, THAT EVER HATH ADOR'D HER NAME   2.138.10
ADORN   4
  DOE BOTH APPEARE T'ADORNE HER BEAUTIES GRACE+   5.21.4
  AND THEY THEREWITH DOE POETES HEADS ADORNE   5.29.7
  EACH OF WHICH DID HER WITH THEYR GUIFTS ADORNE   5.61.8
  FOR WHEN AS DAY THE HEAVEN DOTH ADORNE   5.87.5
ADORNED   4
  SHE THEN IS SCORND THAT LATE ADORND THE $FAYRE   1.39.7
  MY $FAIRE, HAD I NOT ERST ADORND MY $LUTE   2.104.1
  HER MIND ADORND WITH VERTUES MANIFOLD   5.15.14
  ADORN'D WITH HONOUR, LOVE, AND CHASTITY   5.69.8
ADORNS   1
  WHOSE SPRINGING GRACE ADORNS THY GLORY NOW   1.39.10
ADULTERATE   1
  FOR WHY SHOULD OTHERS FALSE ADULTERAT EYES   3.121.5
ADVANCE   2
  BUT THOU ART ALL MY ART, AND DOOST ADVANCE   3.78.13
  HORSEMEN MY SKILL IN HORSMANSHIP ADVAUNCE   4.41.5
ADVANCED   1
  SO $COMET-LIKE EACH STARRE ADVAUNC'D HER LYGHT   2.125.10
ADVANTAGE   3
  ADVANTAGE ON THE $KINGDOME OF THE SHOARE   3.64.6
  THAT SINNE BY HIM ADVANTAGE SHOULD ATCHIVE   3.67.3
  A MAIDE OF $DYANS THIS ADVANTAGE FOUND   3.153.2
ADVENTURED   1
  THE SHIPWRACKE OF MY ILL ADVENTRED YOUTH   1.54.6
ADVENTUROUS   1
  LIKE AN ADVENTUROUS $SEA-FARER AM I   2.1.1
ADVERSARIES   1
  ALTHOUGH HER EYES MY ADVERSARIES BE   1.49.14
ADVERSE   1
  THY ADVERSE PARTY IS THY $ADVOCATE   3.35.10
ADVISED   1
  CAULD TO THAT AUDITE BY ADVIS'D RESPECTS   3.49.4
ADVOCATE   1
  THY ADVERSE PARTY IS THY $ADVOCATE   3.35.10
ADVOCATES   1
  AND YOU MY $VERSE, THE $ADVOCATES OF $LOVE   1.8.9
AEOLS'   1
  AND FAINE THOSE $AEOLS' YOUTHES THERE
                         WOULD THEIR STAY   4.103.9
AETNA'S   1
  ANOTHER, MERVAILES $SULPHURE $AETNAS FIRE   2.120.4

```
AFFABLE                        1
  HE NOR THAT AFFABLE FAMILIAR GHOST                    3.86.9
AFFAIRS                        2
  WHERE YOU MAY BE, OR YOUR AFFAIRES SUPPOSE            3.57.10
  TO STAND IN THY AFFAIRES, FALL BY THY SIDE           3.151.12
AFFECT                         2
  AFFECT NO HONOR BUT WHAT SHE CAN GIVE                 1.12.6
  T'AFFECT THIS LIFE, AND YET THIS LIFE DISLEEKE        1.20.11
AFFECTED                       3
  AFFECTED EVER, BUT T'ETERNIZE THEE                    1.58.2
  I PASSE NOT, I, HOW $MEN AFFECTED BEE                 2.42.9
  I PASSE NOT I HOW MEN AFFECTED BE                     2.128.9
AFFECTION                      2
  TO HAVE AFFECTION STRONG, A BODY WEAKE                1.20.8
  THAT WHO INDEED INFELT AFFECTION BEARES               4.61.5
AFFECTIONS                     4
  OF MINE AFFECTIONS TAKEN BY HER EIES                  1.22.14
  MADE OLD OFFENCES OF AFFECTIONS NEW                   3.110.4
  SHOOT OUT HIS DARTS TO BASE AFFECTIONS WOUND+         5.8.6
  BUT PURE AFFECTIONS BRED IN SPOTLESSE BREST           5.84.5
AFFECTS                        2
  MY LOVE AFFECTS NO FAME, NOR STEEMES OF $ART          1.4.14
  WITH CHAST AFFECTS, THAT NAUGHT BUT DEATH
                             CAN SEVER                  5.6.12
AFFIRM                         1
  THAT IN ONE SPEECH TWO $NEGATIVES AFFIRME             4.63.14
AFFIRMING                      1
  WITH THIS AFFIRMING $NO, DENYING I                    2.5.4
AFFLICTED                      6
  COME TO THEIR VIEW, WHO LIKE AFFLICTED ARE            1.3.3
  WHY SHOULD M'AFFLICTED $MUSE SO MUCH ENDEVOUR         1.17.7
  OF SUCH AS SPOILE THY POORE AFFLICTED STATE           1.28.4
  PEN'D IN THE GRIEFE OF MINE AFFLICTED $GHOST          2.54.6
  PEND IN THE GRIEFE OF MYNE AFFLICTED GHOST            2.101.6
  AND WITH MEEKE HUMBLESSE AND AFFLICTED MOOD           5.2.11
AFFLICTION                     4
  TO CRAVE REDRESSE, YET HOLD AFFLICTION DEARE          1.20.7
  THERE DO THESE SMOAKES THAT FROM AFFLICTION RISE      1.47.9
  HOW LONG SHALL I IN MINE AFFLICTION MOURNE+           1.49.1
  TH'AFFLICTION HER UNKIND DISDAINE DOTH MOVE           1.60.8
AFFORD                         2
  WHICH THOSE FAYRE $ILANDS OF THY LOOKES AFFOORD       2.134.6
  AND FOUND IT IN THY CHEEKE.. HE CAN AFFOORD           3.79.11
AFFORDS                        7
  I HOLD THAT VILE, WHICH $VULGAR WIT AFFORDS           2.4.11
  AND $SIGHES AND $SIGNES A SILLY $HOPE AFFORDS         2.13.8
  THOUGH I GIVE MORE THEN WELL AFFORDS MY STATE         2.28.5
  AND SIGHES AND SIGNES A SILLY HOPE AFFOORDS           2.121.8
  TO EVERY $HIMNE THAT ABLE SPIRIT AFFORDS              3.85.7
  THREE THEAMS IN ONE, WHICH WONDROUS SCOPE
                             AFFORDS                    3.105.12
  TO SOME A SWEETEST PLAINT, A SWEETEST
                             STILE AFFORDS              4.6.9
AFRAID                         3
  GREAT SHAME IT IS TO LEAVE LIKE ONE AFRAYD            5.14.3
  HER SELFE ASSURD, AND IS OF NOUGHT AFFRAYD            5.58.4
  AFFRAYD OF EVERY DANGERS LEAST DISMAY                 5.88.4
AFRESH                         1
  COMES FORTH AFRESH CUT OF THEIR LATE DISMAY           5.40.11
```

AFRIKE   1
  OF HERBES OR BEASTES, WHICH $INDE OR $AFRIKE HOLD   4.3.8
AFTER   23
  AND STILL MUST HOLD HER DEARE TILL AFTER DEATH   1.21.11
  THOU MAIST IN AFTER AGES LIVE ESTEEM'D   1.44.9
  AND $IDEOTS STILL ARE RUNNING AFTER $BOYES   2.22.7
  IT AFTER THEE, IS LIKE AN $EAGLET FLOWNE   2.56.14
  YOU SELFE AGAIN AFTER YOUR SELFES DECEASE   3.13.7
  AFTER A THOUSAND VICTORIES ONCE FOILD   3.25.10
  IS POORELY IMMITATED AFTER YOU   3.53.6
  AND MOCKE YOU WITH ME AFTER I AM GON   3.71.14
  AFTER MY DEATH (DEARE LOVE) FOR GET ME QUITE   3.72.3
  AS AFTER $SUN-SET FADETH IN THE $WEST   3.73.6
  AND DOE NOT DROP IN FOR AN AFTER LOSSE   3.90.4
  LIKE WIDDOWED WOMBES AFTER THEIR $LORDS DECEASE   3.97.8
  DRAWNE AFTER YOU, YOU PATTERNE OF ALL THOSE   3.98.12
  SO RUNST THOU AFTER THAT WHICH FLIES FROM THEE   3.143.9
  IN VOWING NEW HATE AFTER NEW LOVE BEARING   3.152.4
  NE ANY THEN SHALL AFTER IT INQUIRE   5.27.9
  SOONE AFTER WHEN MY JOY TO SORROW FLITS   5.54.7
  HUNTS AFTER BLOUD, WHEN HE BY CHANCE DOTH FIND   5.56.3
  AFTER LONG STORMES AND TEMPESTS SAD ASSAY   5.63.1
  LYKE AS A HUNTSMAN AFTER WEARY CHACE   5.67.1
  SO AFTER LONG PURSUIT AND VAINE ASSAY   5.67.5
  AFTER SO LONG A RACE AS I HAVE RUN   5.80.1
  THEN AS A STEED REFRESHED AFTER TOYLE   5.80.5
AFTER-FOLLOWING   1
  WHO OFT FORE-JUDGE MY AFTER-FOLLOWING RACE   4.26.13
AFTERWARDS   1
  MY MOST FULL FLAME SHOULD AFTERWARDS BURNE
                    CLEERER   3.115.4
AFTER-WORLDS   1
  NOW PASSE ON $TIME, TO AFTER-WORLDS TELL THIS   2.107.9
AGAIN   41
  YEELD TO THE $MARBLE THY HARD HART AGAINE   1.19.13
  YET SOONE AGAINE I MUST HER BACKE RECALL   1.25.7
  BUT LOVE NOW WHILST THOU MAIST BE LOV'D AGAINE   1.39.14
  BUT LOVE WHILST THAT THOU MAIST BE LOV'D AGAINE   1.40.1
  GIVE $ME MY $SELFE, AND TAKE YOUR $SELFE AGAINE   2.11.9
  AGAINE INCREASING, AS YOU ARE CONSUMING   2.16.11
  THAT SHE IS GONE, HER LIKE AGAINE TO SEE   2.17.14
  BUT NOW AGAINE $YOU WILL THE SAME DENIE   2.19.3
  BUT WITH THOSE $DROPS, THE $FLAME AGAINE
                    REVIVING   2.40.11
  NOW DOE I CURSE $HER, THEN AGAINE I BLESSE $HER   2.41.14
  MEDEA-LIKE, I MAKE THEE YOUNG AGAINE   2.44.6
  AND WITH THEIR $BALMES RECURE THE $WOUNDS AGAINE   2.50.8
  TO TAKE ALL $MINE, AND GIVE ME NONE AGAINE+   2.52.2
  FAIRE WORDS MAKE $FOOLES, REPLYETH HE AGAINE   2.59.4
  FOOLES AS WE MET, SO $FOOLES AGAINE WE PARTED   2.59.14
  AND WHEN $WE MEET AT ANY TIME AGAINE   2.61.6
  SO FOR MY $PLEDGE THOU GIVE ME $PLEDGE AGAINE   2.63.8
  SHALT SPRING AGAINE FROM TH'ASHES OF THY FAME   2.106.12
  NOW DOE I CURSE HER, THEN AGAINE I BLESSE HER   2.143.14
  BUT WITH THOSE DROPS THE COLES AGAINE REVYVING   2.144.11
  YOU SELFE AGAIN AFTER YOUR SELFES DECEASE   3.13.7
  THOU GAV'ST ME THINE NOT TO GIVE BACKE AGAINE   3.22.14
  WHO EVEN BUT NOW COME BACK AGAINE ASSURED   3.45.11
  I SEND THEM BACK AGAINE AND STRAIGHT GROW SAD   3.45.14
  TOO MORROW SEE AGAINE, AND DOE NOT KILL   3.56.7

```
SPENDING AGAINE WHAT IS ALREADY SPENT               3.76.12
HE ROBS THEE OF, AND PAYES IT THEE AGAINE            3.79.8
AND SO MY PATTENT BACK AGAINE IS SWERVING            3.87.8
COMES HOME AGAINE, ON BETTER JUDGEMENT MAKING        3.87.12
LIKE HIM THAT TRAVELS I RETURNE AGAINE               3.109.6
CALD IT ANEW, AND WOOED SLEEPE AGAINE                4.38.13
LOOKE ON AGAINE, THE FAIRE TEXT BETTER TRIE          4.67.7
THAT $ANGER' SELFE I NEEDS MUST KISSE AGAINE         4.73.14
RETOURNE AGAYNE MY FORCES LATE DISMAYD               5.14.1
AND WITH STERNE COUNTENANCE BACK AGAIN DOTH CHACE    5.21.7
THE SAME AT NIGHT SHE DID AGAINE UNREAVE             5.23.4
WILL SHINE AGAIN, AND LOOKE ON ME AT LAST            5.34.11
MAY LIKEWISE LOVE THEE FOR THE SAME AGAINE           5.68.10
FOR NONE CAN CALL AGAINE THE PASSED TIME             5.70.14
AGAYNE I WROTE IT WITH A SECOND HAND                 5.75.3
THEY YDLY BACK RETURNE TO ME AGAYNE                  5.78.10
AGAINST              36
AND STILL AGAINST HER FROWNES FRESH VOWES
                     REPAIREST                       1.8.3
IF THIS BE LOVE, TO WARRE AGAINST MY SOULE           1.9.5
AND ALL THINGS FIT AGAINST HER COMMING THERE         1.30.8
THAT FORTIFIE THY NAME AGAINST OLD AGE               1.55.10
AGAINST THE DARKE AND TIMES CONSUMING RAGE           1.55.12
INTIC'D MY $THOUGHTS, AGAINST ME TO CONSPIRE         2.23.10
AGAINST THESE $FOLKES, THAT THINKE THEMSELVES
                     SO WISE                          2.28.3
MY $EYES WITH $TEARES AGAINST THE FIRE STRIVING      2.40.9
WHOSE $BREST IS PROOFE AGAINST $COMPLAINT
                     OR $PRAYER+                      2.52.10
AGAINST THE $FORTE WHERE $BEAUTIES $ARMY LIES        2.142.2
MYNE EYES WITH TEARES AGAINST THE FIRE STRYVING      2.144.9
AGAINST THIS CUMMING END YOU SHOULD PREPARE          3.13.3
AGAINST THE STORMY GUSTS OF WINTERS DAY              3.13.11
WORTHY PERUSAL STAND AGAINST THY SIGHT               3.38.6
AGAINST THAT TIME (IF EVER THAT TIME COME)           3.49.1
AGAINST THAT TIME WHEN THOU SHALT STRANGELY PASSE    3.49.5
AGAINST THAT TIME DO I INSCONCE ME HERE              3.49.9
AND THIS MY HAND, AGAINST MY SELFE UPREARE           3.49.11
AGAINST MY LOVE SHALL BE AS I AM NOW                 3.63.1
AGAINST CONFOUNDING $AGES CRUELL KNIFE               3.63.10
AGAINST THE WRACKFULL SIEDGE OF BATTRING DAYES       3.65.6
UPON THOSE BOUGHES WHICH SHAKE AGAINST THE COULD     3.73.3
UPON THY SIDE, AGAINST MY SELFE ILE FIGHT            3.88.3
AGAINST THY REASONS MAKING NO DEFENCE                3.89.4
FOR THEE, AGAINST MY SELFE ILE VOW DEBATE            3.89.13
WHEN I AGAINST MY SELFE WITH THEE PERTAKE            3.149.2
OR MADE THEM SWERE AGAINST THE THING THEY SEE        3.152.12
TO SWERE AGAINST THE TRUTH SO FOULE A LIE            3.152.14
AGAINST STRANG MALLADIES A SOVERAIGNE CURE           3.153.8
LET FOLKE ORECHARG'D WITH BRAINE AGAINST ME CRIE     4.64.4
AGAINST YOUR EIES THAT JUSTICE I MAY GAINE           5.12.14
THE WHICH MY SELFE AGAINST MY SELFE DOE MAKE         5.44.6
TO BATTAILE FRESH AGAINST MY SELFE TO FIGHT          5.44.12
AS WILLING ME AGAINST HER WILL TO STAY               5.46.4
YET LIVE FOR EVER, THOUGH AGAINST HER WILL           5.48.13
BUT BEND YOUR FORCE AGAINST YOUR ENEMYES             5.49.8
AGANIPPE             1
I NEVER DRANKE OF $AGANIPPE WELL                     4.74.1
AGE                  24
AND FROST OF AGE HATH NIPT THY BEAUTIES NEERE        1.42.2
```

```
THE DATE OF $AGE, THE $KALENDS OF OUR DEATH          1.50.12
THAT FORTIFIE THY NAME AGAINST OLD AGE               1.55.10
THERE'S NOTHING GRIEVES ME, BUT THAT $AGE
                         SHOULD HASTE                2.8.1
THY $LIPS, WITH AGE, AS ANY $WAFER THINNE            2.8.10
TIME HATH THY $BEAUTIE, WHICH WITH $AGE
                         WILL LEAVE THEE             2.10.12
FROM $AGE TO $AGE, WHAT THOU HAST SOUGHT TO SEE      2.17.2
FROM $AGE TO $AGE, WHAT THOU HAST SOUGHT TO SEE      2.17.2
AGE RULES MY $LINES WITH $WRINKLES IN MY $FACE       2.44.2
SO THOU THROUGH WINDOWES OF THINE AGE SHALT SEE      3.3.11
RESEMBLING STRONG YOUTH IN HIS MIDDLE AGE            3.7.6
LIKE FEEBLE AGE HE REELETH FROM THE DAY              3.7.10
WITHOUT THIS FOLLIE, AGE, AND COULD DECAY            3.11.6
THE AGE TO COME WOULD SAY THIS $POET LIES            3.17.7
SO SHOULD MY PAPERS (YELLOWED WITH THEIR AGE)        3.17.9
HAD MY FRIENDS $MUSE GROWNE WITH THIS
                         GROWING AGE                 3.32.10
PAINTING MY AGE WITH BEAUTY OF THY DAIES             3.62.14
THE RICH PROUD COST OF OUTWORNE BURIED AGE           3.64.2
DOUBTING THE FILCHING AGE WILL STEALE
                         HIS TREASURE                3.75.6
FOR FEARE OF WHICH, HEARE THIS THOU AGE UNBRED       3.104.13
AND PEACE PROCLAIMES $OLIVES OF ENDLESSE AGE         3.107.8
WAIGHES NOT THE DUST AND INJURY OF AGE               3.108.10
IN THE OULD AGE BLACKE WAS NOT COUNTED FAIRE         3.127.1
AND AGE IN LOVE, LOVES NOT T' HAVE YEARES TOLD       3.138.12
AGED                3
IN AGED ACCENTS, AND UNTIMELY WORDS                  1.55.2
LIKE GRIZZLED $MOSSE UPON SOME AGED $TREE            2.8.8
SLEEPES AGED COLDNES, WITH $BEAUTIES FIRE WARMED     2.136.7
AGENTS              1
AND YOU MINE EYES, THE AGENTS OF MY HART             1.8.5
AGES                4
THOU MAIST IN AFTER AGES LIVE ESTEEM'D               1.44.9
ENSUING $AGES YET MY $RIMES SHALL CHERISH            2.44.11
AND TO BE PRAISD OF AGES YET TO BE                   3.101.12
FOR THAT THEY SHOULD ENDURE THROUGH MANY AGES        5.51.3
AGE'S               2
HATH TRAVAILD ON TO $AGES STEEPIE NIGHT              3.63.5
AGAINST CONFOUNDING $AGES CRUELL KNIFE               3.63.10
AGGRAVATE           2
TO ADDE MORE GRIEFE TO AGGRAVATE MY SORROW           1.54.12
AND LET THAT PINE TO AGGRAVAT THY STORE              3.146.10
AGREE               4
IF $FRENCH CAN YET THREE PARTS IN ONE AGREE          4.30.5
WHERE $NATURE DOTH WITH INFINITE AGREE+              4.35.4
WHOM ALL THE $GODS IN COUNCELL DID AGREE             5.24.9
BUT MERCY DOTH WITH BEAUTIE BEST AGREE               5.53.13
AGREED              1
AT LENGTH TO $LOVE'S DECREES, I FORC'D, AGREED       4.2.7
AGREEMENT           1
OR MAKE AGREEMENT WITH HER THRILLING EYES            5.36.6
AH                  20
AH YOU, AND NONE BUT YOU MY SORROWES READE           1.3.11
BUT AH, WHAT GLORIE CAN SHE GET THEREBY              1.27.11
BUT AH- NO MORE, THIS MUST NOT BE FORETOLD           1.50.13
AH SPORT (SWEET $MAIDE) IN SEASON OF THESE YEARES    1.51.5
AH., IF THOU ISSULESSE SHALT HAP TO DIE              3.9.3
AH BUT THOSE TEARES ARE PEARLE WHICH THY
                         LOVE SHEEDS                 3.34.13
```

```
BUT AH, THOUGHT KILLS ME THAT I AM NOT THOUGHT        3.44.9
AH WHEREFORE WITH INFECTION SHOULD HE LIVE            3.67.1
AH DOE NOT, WHEN MY HEART HATH SCAPTE THIS SORROW     3.90.5
AH YET DOTH BEAUTY LIKE A $DYALL HAND                 3.104.9
LET ME EXCUSE THEE, AH MY LOVE WELL KNOWES            3.139.9
AND AH WHAT HOPE, THAT HOPE SHOULD ONCE SEE DAY       4.35.7
'BUT AH,' $DESIRE STILL CRIES, 'GIVE ME
                           SOME FOOD'                 4.71.14
MY HEART CRIES 'AH', IT BURNES, MINE EYES
                           NOW DAZLED BE              4.76.11
YET AH, MY $MAYD'N $MUSE DOTH BLUSH TO
                           TELL THE BEST              4.77.14
BUT AH POORE $NIGHT, IN LOVE WITH $PHOEBUS' LIGHT     4.97.5
AH BED, THE FIELD WHERE JOYE'S PEACE SOME DO SEE      4.98.1
AH, IS IT NOT ENOUGH, THAT I AM THENCE                4.104.5
AH WHAT DOTH $PHOEBUS' GOLD THAT WRETCH AVAILE        4.108.10
AH WHY HATH NATURE TO SO HARD A HART                  5.31.1
AID                       8
UNTO MINE AID I SUMMON'D EV'RY $SENSE                 2.29.2
AND THUS BY THOSE OF WHOM I HOP'D FOR AYD             2.29.13
THUS TO MY AID, I LASTLY CONJURE THEE                 2.36.4
EACH ONE OF THESE, DOTH AYDE UNTO THE
                           OTHER LENDE                2.133.14
WHILST I ALONE DID CALL UPON THY AYDE                 3.79.1
GIVING HIM AYDE, MY VERSE ASTONISHED                  3.86.8
MUSES, I OFT INVOKED YOUR HOLY AYDE                   4.55.1
IN HER OWNE POWRE, AND SCORNETH OTHERS AYDE           5.58.2
AIM                       2
OR COULD MINE EYE BUT AYME, HER OBJECTS
                           PAST PERFECTION            2.117.6
WITH IDLE PAINES, AND MISSING AYME, DO GUESSE         4.23.4
AIMING                    2
AYMING AT THINGS EXCEEDING ALL PERFECTION             2.34.6
AYMING HIS ARROW AT MY VERY HART                      5.16.10
AIR                       27
TO PAINT ON FLOODS, TILL THE SHORE CRIE TO TH'AIRE    1.9.2
THE AYRE WITH SIGHES, THE EARTH BELOW
                           WITH TEARES+               1.21.6
NO SOONER SPREADS HER GLORY IN THE AYRE               1.39.5
LIGHTEN FOORTH SMILES TO CLEERE THE CLOUDED AIRE      1.51.9
AND THUS AM I IMPRISON'D IN THE $AIRE                 2.26.12
WITH HEAVIE $SIGHES WHILST THUS I BREAKE
                           THE $AYRE                  2.45.3
TO SHEW, THAT I HAD HATCH'D IT FOR THE $AYRE          2.56.7
WHICH PROOV'D MY BIRDS DELIGHTED IN THE AYRE          2.103.3
MY SIGHES SHALL STOP THE PASSAGE OF THE AYRE          2.115.7
MUST PASSE BY AYRE, OR ELSE DYE IN EXILE              2.122.4
SOME MUZ'D TO SEE THE EARTH ENVY THE AYRE             2.125.5
NO CLOWDE WAS SEENE, BUT CHRISTALINE THE AYRE         2.125.13
THE AYRE, UNTO MY SIGHES, AS $EAGLE TO THE FLIE       2.127.7
ONELY MY SIGHES ARE BY THE AYRE EXPRESSED             2.127.11
YET FIRE, WATER, AYRE, OF NATURE NOT DEPRIVED         2.127.12
WHILST FIRE, WATER, AYRE, TWIXT HEAVEN
                           AND EARTH SHAL BE          2.127.13
AND THUS AM I IMPRISOND IN THE AYRE                   2.137.12
CAST MY DESARTS INTO THE OPEN AYRE                    2.142.10
THAT HEAVENS AYRE IN THIS HUGE RONDURE HEMS           3.21.8
AS THOSE GOULD CANDELLS FIXT IN HEAVENS AYER          3.21.12
THE OTHER TWO, SLIGHT AYRE, AND PURGING FIRE          3.45.1
A $CROW THAT FLIES IN HEAVENS SWEETEST AYRE           3.70.4
```

ALL   366

WHERE I HAVE CAST TH'ACCOUNTS OF ALL MY CARE	1.1.6
WHO CAN SHEW ALL HIS LOVE, DOTH LOVE BUT LIGHTLY	1.1.14
WITNESSE YOUR $FATHERS GRIEFE EXCEEDES ALL OTHER	1.2.4
DELIA HER SELFE, AND ALL THE WORLD MAY VIEW	1.4.7
ALL UNAWARES, A $GODDESSE CHASTE I FINDE	1.5.3
THE WONDER OF ALL EYES THAT LOOKE UPON HER	1.6.7
THOUGH MY SOULES $IDOLL SCORNETH ALL MY VOWES	1.11.10
THOUGH ALL MY PRAYERS BE TO SO DEAFE EARES	1.11.11
ALL MY LIVES SWEET CONSISTS IN HER ALONE	1.12.13
THE FAIREST FORME, THAT ALL THE WORLD ADMIRES	1.13.7
LET THIS SUFFICE, THAT ALL THE WORLD MAY SEE	1.15.13
AND ALL IN VAINE, HER PRIDE IS SO INNATED	1.18.11
SHE YEELDS NO PLACE AT ALL FOR PITTIES DWELLING	1.18.12
(AND THAT WITH TEARES) YET ALL THIS WILL NOT MOVE HER	1.18.14
AND THAT ALL THIS MOOVES NOT HER THOUGHTS A WHIT	1.21.12
WHICH CONQUERS ALL BUT THEE, AND THEE TOO STAIES	1.23.2
OFT WHEN I FINDE IN HER NO TRUTH AT ALL	1.25.5
AND THETHER ALL MY FORCES DOE TRANSPORTE	1.27.7
MY FREEDOMES TYRANTS CONQUERING ALL BY ARTE	1.27.10
FOR WHILST THEY STRIVE WHICH SHALL BE $LORD OF ALL	1.28.5
ALL MY POORE LIFE BY THEM IS TRODEN DOWNE	1.28.6
THEY ALL ERECT THEIR $TROPHIES ON MY FALL	1.28.7
AND SERVE ALL THREE, AND YET THEY SPOILE ME TOO	1.28.14
AND ALL THINGS FIT AGAINST HER COMMING THERE	1.30.8
AND THREW ME DOWNE TO PAINE IN ALL THIS FIRE	1.36.5
AND THOSE BRIGHT RAIES THAT KINDLE ALL THIS FIRE	1.38.3
MUST YEELD UP ALL TO TYRANT $TIMES DESIRE	1.38.7
THAT TELLS THE TRUTH, AND SAYES THAT ALL IS GONE	1.41.4
THAT FIRE CAN BURNE WHEN ALL THE MATTER'S SPENT	1.41.10
AND ALL LIES WITHRED THAT WAS HELD SO DEERE	1.42.4
LIMMED WITH A $PENSILL NOT ALL UNWORTHY	1.42.6
ME FROM THE VULGAR, THEE FROM ALL OBSCURENES	1.44.12
MAKE ME TO SAY, WHEN ALL MY GRIEFES ARE GONE	1.51.13
LEAVE HER AND ALL, AND ALL FOR HER THAT LEAVES	1.52.6
LEAVE HER AND ALL, AND ALL FOR HER THAT LEAVES	1.52.6
MY JOYFULL $NORTH, WHERE ALL MY FORTUNE LIES	1.53.3
KEPT FOR HIMSELFE, DEFENDED FROM ALL HARMES	1.53.12
ALL OTHER HONORS DOE MY HOPES REFUSE	1.58.3
AND HOW I LIVE CAST DOWNE FROM OFF ALL MYRTH	1.60.9
DUELY TO COUNT THE SUMME OF ALL MY CARES	2.3.2
WHICH BY $EXTORTICN GAINETH ALL THEIR LOCKES	2.3.10
THAT ALL THEIR $WEALTH LIES IN THY BEAUTIES $BOOKES	2.3.12
AND ALL IS $THINE WHICH HATH BEEN DUE TO $ME	2.3.13
LEAVES TO HIS $SONNE ALL HE HAD HEAP'D TOGETHER	2.10.4
I GIVE $THEE BACKE, WHEN ALL THE REST IS SPENT	2.10.14
AND IF WITH $TEARES I FIND THEM ALL TOO LIGHT	2.13.7
'MONGST ALL THE $CREATURES IN THIS SPACIOUS $ROUND	2.16.1
WITH SO RARE SWEETNESSE ALL THE $HEAV'NS PERFUMING	2.16.10
ONE, IN WHOM ALL THE $EXCELLENCIES BE	2.17.3
IN PERFECT HUMANE SHAPE, ALL HEAV'NLY $BLISSE	2.17.12
AND ALL THIS WHILE, I WAS MISTAKEN THERE	2.19.12
WHO DOTED ON THE $OCCLT BEYOND ALL MEASURE	2.21.10
AND RANSACKE ALL $APOLLOS GOLDEN $TREASURE	2.21.12
AND I LOSE YOU, FOR ALL MY $WIT AND $PAINES	2.21.14

YOU NOW SUPPOSE ME ALL THIS TIME IN SPORT	2.24.7
OR ALL MY $HOPE FCR $SORROW WILL BE DEAD	2.26.14
I SCORNE ALL $EARTHLY $DUNG-BRED $SCARABIES	2.31.14
AYMING AT THINGS EXCEEDING ALL PERFECTION	2.34.6
ALL UNCLEANE $THOUGHTS, FOULE $SPIRITS CAST OUT IN MEE	2.35.13
BY ALL TRUE $LOVERS $SIGHES, $VOWES, AND $DESIRES	2.36.11
BY ALL THE $WOUNDS THAT EVER THOU HAST GIV'N	2.36.12
I CONJURE THEE BY ALL THAT I HAVE NAM'D	2.36.13
WHEN NOW THE $NIGHT DOTH SUMMON ALL TO SLEEPE+	2.37.2
HOW HAPPY ARE ALL CTHER LIVING $THINGS	2.37.5
O, $THOU THAT ART SC COURTEOUS ELSE TO ALL	2.37.9
MY $BREST THE $FORGE, INCLUDING ALL THE HEATE	2.40.3
WITH ALL HIS $TORMENTS AND $INFERNALL TERROR+	2.41.4
MY $BRAINE IS DRIE WITH WEEPING ALL TOO LONG	2.41.6
WHERE, IN THE $MAP CF ALL MY $MISERIE	2.44.3
ALL THAT I SEEKE, IS TO ETERNIZE YOU	2.47.14
TO TAKE ALL $MINE, AND GIVE ME NONE AGAINE+	2.52.2
BESTOWING ALL HER $EXCELLENCE ON YOU	2.57.7
MOST OF ALL SHORT, WHEN I SHOULD SHEW YOU MOST	2.57.13
SHAKE HANDS FOR EVER, $CANCELL ALL OUR $VOWES	2.61.5
NOW IF THOU WOULD'ST, WHEN ALL HAVE GIVEN HIM OVER	2.61.13
WHERE MOST I $LOST, THERE MOST OF ALL I $WAN	2.62.3
UNTO THE WORLD HAD ALL MY JOYES BEEN MUTE	2.104.3
THAT BY THY FAME ALL FAME SHALL BE SURVIVED	2.104.14
WITH THINE OWNE SWEETNES AL THE HEAVENS PERFUMING	2.106.10
THAT WONDER NOW WHEREIN ALL WONDERS BE	2.107.3
BEAUTY SOMETIME IN ALL HER GLORY CROWNED	2.109.1
WHERE SHEE REMAINES FOR ALL EYES TO BEHOLD	2.109.14
BEGINNING TO ACCOUNT THE SUM OF ALL MY CARES	2.110.2
WHO BY EXTORTION GAINETH ALL THEYR LOOKES	2.110.10
THAT ALL HER WEALTH LYES IN THY $BEAUTIES BOOKES	2.110.12
AND ALL IS THINE WHICH HATH BEEN DUE TO MEE	2.110.13
ALL UNCLEANE THOUGHTS, FOULE SPIRITS CAST OUT IN MEE	2.112.13
WITH WITHERED BROWES, ALL WRINCKLED WITH DISPAIRES	2.114.3
MY SWEET, MY FAIRE, MY GOOD, MY BEST OF ALL	2.115.12
UNHAPPY $BORNE, OF ALL UNHAPPY DAY	2.116.5
COULD ALL CONCEITE CONCLUDE, WHICH PAST CONCEITE ADMIRETH	2.117.5
AND IF WITH TEARES, I FIND THEM ALL TOO LIGHT	2.121.7
OF ALL THINE HONOUR SHEE HATH ROBBED THEE	2.126.4
HER $MARRYNERS DOE LEAVE HER ALL FORLORNE	2.134.11
OR ALL MY HOPE FOR SORRCW WILL BE DEAD	2.137.14
IN WHOM ALL PURENES WITH PERFECTION STROVE	2.141.3
PLAC'D IN THE FORLCRNE HOPE OF ALL DISPAYRE	2.142.1
WITH ALL HIS TORMENTS AND INFERNALL TERRCR	2.143.4
MY BRAYNE IS DRY WITH WEEPING ALL TOO LONG	2.143.6
BY BREAST THE FORGE, INCLUDING ALL THE HEATE	2.144.3
O VERTUE, WHICH ALL VERTUES DCE ADORE	2.146.7
CHEEFE GOOD, FROM WHOM ALL GOOD THINGS WE DERIVE	2.146.8
CONCEITE OF $ANGELS, WHICH ALL WISDOM TEACHEST	2.146.10
O RICHEST $CASKET CF ALL HEAVENLY TREASURE	2.146.11
STILL NAMING HER, IN NAMING ALL DELIGHT	2.148.12
SO MAY HE GRACE ALL THESE IN HER ALONE	2.148.13

```
SUPERLATIVE IN ALL COMPARISON                               2.148.14
AND BY ALL MEANES, LET BLACK UNKINDNES PROVE                2.149.13
WHERE MOST I LOST, THERE MOST OF ALL I WAN                  2.150.3
FOR ALL MY WOES, THAT ONELY SHALL SUFFISE                   2.151.4
THEN BEING ASKT, WHERE ALL THY BEAUTIE LIES                 3.2.5
WHERE ALL THE TREASURE OF THY LUSTY DAIES                   3.2.6
WHO ALL IN ONE, ONE PLEASING NOTE DO SING                   3.8.12
IF ALL WERE MINDED SO, THE TIMES SHOULD CEASE               3.11.7
AND $SOMMERS GREENE ALL GIRDED UP IN SHEAVES                3.12.7
AND ALL IN WAR WITH $TIME FOR LOVE OF YOU                   3.15.13
AND IN FRESH NUMBERS NUMBER ALL YOUR GRACES                 3.17.6
AND $SOMMERS LEASE HATH ALL TOO SHORT A DATE                3.18.4
TO THE WIDE WORLD AND ALL HER FADING SWEETS                 3.19.7
A MAN IN HEW ALL $HEWS IN HIS CONTROWLING                   3.20.7
WITH $APRILLS FIRST BORNE FLOWERS AND
                  ALL THINGS RARE                           3.21.7
FOR ALL THAT BEAUTY THAT DOTH COVER THEE                    3.22.5
AND ALL THE REST FORGOT FOR WHICH HE TOILD                  3.25.12
IN THY SOULES THOUGHT (ALL NAKED) WILL BESTOW IT            3.26.8
I ALL ALONE BEWEEPE MY CUT-CAST STATE                       3.29.2
ALL LOSSES ARE RESTORD, AND SORROWES END                    3.30.14
THY BOSOME IS INDEARED WITH ALL HEARTS                      3.31.1
AND THERE RAIGNES $LOVE AND ALL $LOVES
                  LOVING PARTS                              3.31.3
AND ALL THOSE FRIENDS WHICH I THOUGHT BURIED                3.31.4
WHO ALL THEIR PARTS OF ME TO THEE DID GIVE                  3.31.11
AND THOU (ALL THEY) HAST ALL THE ALL OF ME                  3.31.14
AND THOU (ALL THEY) HAST ALL THE ALL OF ME                  3.31.14
AND THOU (ALL THEY) HAST ALL THE ALL OF ME                  3.31.14
WITH ALL TRIUMPHANT SPLENDOR ON MY BROW                     3.33.10
AND THEY ARE RITCH, AND RANSOME ALL ILL DEEDS               3.34.14
ALL MEN MAKE FAULTS, AND EVEN I IN THIS                     3.35.5
TAKE ALL MY COMFORT OF THY WORTH AND TRUTH                  3.37.4
OR ANY OF THESE ALL, OR ALL, OR MORE                        3.37.6
OR ANY OF THESE ALL, OR ALL, OR MORE                        3.37.6
AND BY A PART OF ALL THY GLORY LIVE                         3.37.12
WHEN THOU ART ALL THE BETTER PART OF ME+                    3.39.2
TAKE ALL MY LOVES, MY LOVE, YEA TAKE THEM ALL               3.40.1
TAKE ALL MY LOVES, MY LOVE, YEA TAKE THEM ALL               3.40.1
ALL MINE WAS THINE, BEFORE THOU HADST THIS MORE             3.40.4
ALTHOUGH THOU STEALE THEE ALL MY POVERTY                    3.40.10
LASCIVIOUS GRACE, IN WHOM ALL IL WEL SHOWES                 3.40.13
THAT THOU HAST HER IT IS NOT ALL MY GRIEFE                  3.42.1
FOR ALL THE DAY THEY VIEW THINGS UNRESPECTED                3.43.2
ALL DAYES ARE NIGHTS TO SEE TILL I SEE THEE                 3.43.13
A QUEST OF THOUGHTS, ALL TENNANTS TO THE HEART              3.46.10
ON $HELLENS CHEEKE ALL ART OF BEAUTIE SET                   3.53.7
IN ALL EXTERNALL GRACE YOU HAVE SOME PART                   3.53.13
GAINST DEATH, AND ALL OBLIVIOUS EMNITY                      3.55.9
EVEN IN THE EYES OF ALL POSTERITY                           3.55.11
I HAVE NO PRECIOUS TIME AT AL TO SPEND                      3.57.3
IN SEQUENT TOILE ALL FORWARDS DO CONTEND                    3.60.4
FROM ME FARRE OF, WITH OTHERS ALL TO NEERE                  3.61.14
SINNE OF SELFE-LOVE POSSESSETH AL MINE EIE                  3.62.1
AND ALL MY SOULE, AND AL MY EVERY PART                      3.62.2
AND ALL MY SOULE, AND AL MY EVERY PART                      3.62.2
AS I ALL OTHER IN ALL WORTHS SURMOUNT                       3.62.8
AS I ALL OTHER IN ALL WORTHS SURMOUNT                       3.62.8
AND ALL THOSE BEAUTIES WHEREOF NOW HE'S $KING               3.63.6
TYR'D WITH ALL THESE FOR RESTFULL DEATH I CRY               3.66.1
```

```
TYR'D WITH ALL THESE, FROM THESE WOULD I BE GONE        3.66.13
WITHOUT ALL ORNAMENT, IT SELFE AND TRUE                3.68.10
ALL TOUNGS (THE VOICE OF SOULES) GIVE
                            THEE THAT END               3.69.3
DEATHS SECOND SELFE THAT SEALS UP ALL IN REST          3.73.8
WITH OUT ALL BAYLE SHALL CARRY ME AWAY                 3.74.2
SOME-TIME ALL FUL WITH FEASTING ON YOUR SIGHT          3.75.9
OR GLUTTONING ON ALL, OR ALL AWAY                      3.75.14
OR GLUTTONING ON ALL, OR ALL AWAY                      3.75.14
WHY WRITE I STILL ALL ONE, EVER THE SAME               3.76.5
SO ALL MY BEST IS DRESSING OLD WORDS NEW               3.76.11
BUT THOU ART ALL MY ART, AND DOOST ADVANCE             3.78.13
MY VERSE ALONE HAD ALL THY GENTLE GRACE                3.79.2
AND IN THE PRAISE THEREOF SPENDS ALL HIS MIGHT         3.80.3
THOUGH I (ONCE GONE) TO ALL THE WORLD MUST DYE         3.81.6
WHEN ALL THE BREATHERS OF THIS WORLD ARE DEAD          3.81.12
AND PRECIOUS PHRASE BY ALL THE $MUSES FIL'D            3.85.4
BOUND FOR THE PRIZE OF (ALL TO PRECIOUS) YOU           3.86.2
MY BONDS IN THEE ARE ALL DETERMINATE                   3.87.4
FOR BENDING ALL MY LOVING THOUGHTS ON THEE             3.88.10
THAT FOR THY RIGHT, MY SELFE WILL BEARE
                            ALL WRONG                   3.88.14
ALL THESE I BETTER IN ONE GENERALL BEST                3.91.8
AND HAVING THEE, OF ALL MENS PRIDE I BOAST             3.91.12
ALL THIS AWAY, AND ME MOST WRETCHED MAKE               3.91.14
AND ALL THINGS TURNES TO FAIRE, THAT EIES
                            CAN SEE                     3.95.12
IF THOU WOULDST USE THE STRENGTH OF ALL
                            THY STATE+                  3.96.12
WHEN PROUD PIDE $APRILL (DREST IN ALL HIS TRIM)        3.98.2
DRAWNE AFTER YOU, YOU PATTERNE OF ALL THOSE            3.98.12
BUT FOR HIS THEFT IN PRIDE OF ALL HIS GROWTH           3.99.12
TO SPEAKE OF THAT WHICH GIVES THEE ALL
                            THY MIGHT+                  3.100.2
THE ARGUMENT ALL BARE IS OF MORE WORTH                 3.103.3
SINCE ALL ALIKE MY SONGS AND PRAISES BE                3.105.3
FAIRE, KINDE, AND TRUE, IS ALL MY ARGUMENT             3.105.9
SO ALL THEIR PRAISES ARE BUT PROPHESIES                3.106.9
OF THIS OUR TIME, ALL YOU PREFIGURING                  3.106.10
ALL FRAILTIES THAT BESIEGE ALL KINDES OF BLOOD         3.109.10
ALL FRAILTIES THAT BESIEGE ALL KINDES OF BLOOD         3.109.10
TO LEAVE FOR NOTHING ALL THY SUMME OF GOOD             3.109.12
SAVE THOU MY $ROSE, IN IT THOU ART MY ALL              3.109.14
A SCONCE AND STRANGELY.. $BUT BY ALL ABOVE             3.110.6
NOW ALL IS DONE, HAVE WHAT SHALL HAVE NO END           3.110.9
YOU ARE MY $ALL THE WORLD, AND I MUST STRIVE           3.112.5
IN SO PROFOUND $ABISME I THROW ALL CARE                3.112.9
THAT ALL THE WORLD BESIDES ME THINKES
                            Y'ARE DEAD                  3.112.14
ACCUSE ME THUS, THAT I HAVE SCANTED ALL                3.117.1
WHERETO AL BONDS DO TIE ME DAY BY DAY                  3.117.4
THAT I HAVE HOYSTED SAILE TO AL THE WINDES             3.117.7
ALL MEN ARE BAD AND IN THEIR BADNESSE RAIGNE           3.121.14
BEYOND ALL DATE EVEN TO ETERNITY                       3.122.4
BUT ALL ALONE STANDS HUGELY POLLITICK                  3.124.11
LOSE ALL, AND MORE BY PAYING TOO MUCH RENT             3.125.6
ALL THIS THE WORLD WELL KNOWES YET NONE
                            KNOWES WELL                 3.129.13
AND ALL THEY FOULE THAT THY COMPLEXION LACKE           3.132.14
PERFORCE AM THINE AND ALL THAT IS IN ME                3.133.14
```

```
THOU USURER THAT PUT'ST FORTH ALL TO USE          3.134.10
THE SEA ALL WATER, YET RECEIVES RAINE STILL       3.135.9
THINKE ALL BUT ONE, AND ME IN THAT ONE $WILL      3.135.14
BE ANCHORD IN THE BAYE WHERE ALL MEN RIDE         3.137.6
SETS DOWNE HER BABE AND MAKES ALL SWIFT DISPATCH  3.143.3
LOVES EYE IS NOT SO TRUE AS ALL MENS.. NO         3.148.8
AM OF MY SELFE, ALL TIRANT FOR THY SAKE+          3.149.4
WHEN ALL MY BEST DOTH WORSHIP THY DEFECT          3.149.11
THAT IN MY MINDE THY WORST ALL BEST EXCEEDS+      3.150.8
FOR ALL MY VOWES ARE OTHES BUT TO MISUSE THEE     3.152.7
AND ALL MY HONEST FAITH IN THEE IS LOST           3.152.8
TO MAKE MY SELFE BELEEVE, THAT ALL IS WELL        4.2.13
WHAT $LOVE AND $BEAUTIE BE, THEN ALL MY DEED      4.3.13
BUT THINKE THAT ALL THE $MAP OF MY STATE
                    I DISPLAY                     4.6.13
SHE EVEN IN BLACKE DOTH MAKE ALL BEAUTIES FLOW+   4.7.11
TO HONOR ALL THEIR DEATHS, WHO FOR HER BLEED      4.7.14
CRIE, '$VICTORIE, THIS FAIRE DAY ALL IS OURS'     4.12.11
THAT TO WIN IT, IS ALL THE SKILL AND PAINE        4.12.14
WHILE $LOVE ON ME DOTH ALL HIS QUIVER SPEND       4.14.4
A LOATHING OF ALL LOOSE UNCHASTITIE              4.14.13
OF ALL THOSE GOODS, WHICH HEAV'N TO ME HATH LENT  4.18.4
FOR THOUGH SHE PASSE ALL THINGS, YET WHAT IS ALL  4.19.9
FOR THOUGH SHE PASSE ALL THINGS, YET WHAT IS ALL  4.19.9
OF ALL MY THOUGHTS HATH NEITHER STOP NOR START    4.23.13
AS SACRED THINGS, FAR FROM ALL DAUNGER'S SHOW     4.24.8
BENDS ALL HIS POWERS, EVEN UNTO $STELLA'S GRACE   4.27.14
DO EASLY YEELD, THAT ALL THEIR COASTS MAY BE      4.29.3
USE ALL TO HELPE HIS OTHER CONQUERINGS            4.29.8
VOUCHSAFE OF ALL ACQUAINTANCE THIS TO TELL        4.32.9
IN ALL SWEETE STRATAGEMS SWEETE $ARTE CAN SHOW    4.36.11
RICH IN ALL BEAUTIES WHICH MAN'S EYE CAN SEE      4.37.6
TO LEAVE THE SCEPTER OF ALL SUBJECT THINGS        4.38.4
WHOSE BEAMES BE JOYES, WHOSE JOYES ALL VERTUES BE 4.42.2
FROM ALL THE WORLD, HER HEART IS THEN HIS ROME    4.43.13
OF ALL THE GRAVE CONCEITS YOUR BRAINE DOTH BREED  4.51.6
HER EYES, HER LIPS, HER ALL, SAITH $LOVE DO THIS  4.52.3
TH' ANATOMY OF ALL MY WOES I WRATE                4.58.10
WHERE ALL MY GOOD I DO IN $STELLA SEE             4.60.2
THAT WHOLLY HERS, ALL SELFNESSE HE FORBEARES      4.61.7
LET ALL THE EARTH WITH SCORNE RECOUNT MY CASE     4.64.7
AND YET AMID ALL FEARES A HOPE THERE IS           4.66.9
WILL SHE TAKE TIME, BEFORE ALL WRACKED BE+        4.67.4
AND ALL IN VAINE, FOR WHILE THY BREATH MOST SWEET 4.68.9
MY FRIEND, THAT OFT SAW THROUGH ALL MASKES MY WO  4.69.5
THERE SHALL HE FIND ALL VICES' OVERTHROW          4.71.5
THY SELFE, DOEST STRIVE ALL MINDS THAT
                    WAY TO MOVE                   4.71.10
BUT THOU $DESIRE, BECAUSE THOU WOULDST HAVE ALL   4.72.13
OF ALL THE KINGS THAT EVER HERE DID RAIGNE        4.75.1
LOATHING ALL LIES, DOUBTING THIS $FLATTERIE IS    4.80.11
BREATHING ALL BLISSE AND SWEETNING TO THE HEART   4.81.3
HOW FAINE WOULD I PAINT THEE TO ALL MEN'S EYES    4.81.7
NYMPH OF THE GARD'N, WHERE ALL BEAUTIES BE        4.82.1
WITH DOING ALL, LEAVE NOTHING DONE BUT PAINE      4.85.8
THOU BUT OF ALL THE KINGLY $TRIBUTE TAKE          4.85.14
BUT IF ALL FAITH, LIKE SPOTLESSE $ERMINE LY       4.86.5
THEN THOSE BLEST EYES, WHERE ALL MY HOPES
                    DO DWELL                      4.86.13
STELLA WHOSE EYES MAKE ALL MY TEMPESTS CLEERE     4.87.3
```

IF THOU PRAISE NOT, ALL OTHER PRAISE IS SHAME	4.90.4
SINCE ALL MY WORDS THY BEAUTY DOTH ENDITE	4.90.13
SAY ALL, AND ALL WELL SAYD, STILL SAY THE SAME	4.92.14
SAY ALL, AND ALL WELL SAYD, STILL SAY THE SAME	4.92.14
THAT ALL THY HURTS IN MY HART'S WRACKE I REEDE	4.93.13
THE FIELD WHERE ALL MY THOUGHTS TO WARRE BE TRAIND	4.98.2
ALL MIRTH FAREWELL, LET ME IN SORROW LIVE	4.100.14
ALL FOLKES PREST AT THY WILL THY PAINE TO 'SWAGE	4.101.11
WHERE RIGROWS EXILE LOCKES UP ALL MY SENSE+	4.104.8
OF ALL THE POWERS WHICH LIFE BESTOWES ON ME	4.107.2
BIDS ALL OLD THOUGHTS TO DIE IN DUMPISH SPRIGHT	5.4.4
SPREDS IN DEFIANCE OF ALL ENEMIES	5.5.12
NO EIES BUT JOYES, IN WHICH AL POWERS CONSPIRE	5.8.3
WHOSE LIGHT DOTH LIGHTEN ALL THAT HERE WE SEE	5.9.14
ALL THIS WORLDS PRIDE BOW TO A BASER MAKE	5.10.11
AND AL HER FAULTS IN THY BLACK BOOKE ENROLL	5.10.12
YET MY POORE LIFE, ALL SORROWES TO ASSOYLE	5.11.9
ALL PAINE HATH END AND EVERY WAR HATH PEACE	5.11.13
ALL FEARELESSE THEN OF SO FALSE ENIMIES	5.12.3
BRING THEREFORE ALL THE FORCES THAT YE MAY	5.14.9
ALL THIS WORLDS RICHES THAT MAY FARRE BE FOUND	5.15.6
THAT WARNES AL LOVERS WAYT UPON THEIR KING	5.19.3
THAT ALL THE WOODS THEYR ECCHOES BACK REBOUNDED	5.19.7
BUT MONGST THEM ALL, WHICH DID $LOVES HONOR RAYSE	5.19.9
IN WHICH THE WORKE THAT SHE ALL DAY DID MAKE	5.23.3
FOR ALL THAT I IN MANY DAYES DOO WEAVE	5.23.7
WHOM ALL THE $GODS IN COUNCELL DID AGREE	5.24.9
FOR ALL THEIR FAULTS WITH WHICH THEY DID OFFEND	5.24.12
THEN ALL THE WOES AND WRECKS WHICH I ABIDE	5.25.11
SITH ALL WORLDS GLORIE IS BUT DROSSE UNCLEANE	5.27.2
I MAY IN TRUMP OF FAME BLAZE OVER ALL	5.29.12
THAT FIRE WHICH ALL THING MELTS, SHOULD HARDEN YSE	5.30.10
THAT IT CAN ALTER ALL THE COURSE OF KYND	5.30.14
AND ALL THOSE PRETIOUS ORNAMENTS DEFACE	5.31.4
SITH TO ALL OTHER BEASTES OF BLOODY RACE	5.31.5
THAT WITH THEYR TERROUR AL THE REST MAY CHACE	5.31.7
YET CANNOT ALL THESE FLAMES IN WHICH I FRY	5.32.5
NE ALL THE PLAYNTS AND PRAYERS WITH WHICH I	5.32.7
WITH ALL THE PLAYNTS WHICH TO HER BE APPLYDE	5.32.12
AND SHE TO STONES AT LENGTH ALL FROSEN TURNE+	5.32.14
ALL WERE IT AS THE REST BUT RUDELY WRIT	5.33.8
ALL THIS WORLDS GLORY SEEMETH VAYNE TO ME	5.35.13
AND ALL THEIR SHOWES BUT SHADOWES SAVING SHE	5.35.14
BUT AL MY DAYES IN PINING LANGUOR SPEND	5.36.3
BUT WHEN YE HAVE SHEWED ALL EXTREMITYES	5.36.9
ALL CARELESSE HOW MY LIFE FOR HER DECAYSE	5.38.10
EXPRESSING ALL THY MOTHERS POWREFULL ART	5.39.2
WHEN ALL THE GODS HE THREATS WITH THUNDRING DART	5.39.4
THEN ALL HER NATURES GOODLY GUIFTS ARE LOST	5.41.8
THAT ALL THE MORE MY SORROW IT AUGMENTETH	5.42.3
AND FROM ALL WANDRING LOVES WHICH MOTE PERVART	5.42.11
THAT NETHER I MAY SPEAKE NOR THINKE AT ALL	5.43.7
BUT YE HIGH HEVENS, THAT ALL THIS SOROWE SEE	5.46.9
SITH ALL YOUR TEMPESTS CANNOT HOLD ME BACKE	5.46.10
WHOM SHE ALL CARELESSE OF HIS GRIEFE CONSTRAYNED	5.48.9
IS NOT THE HART OF ALL THE BODY CHIEFE+	5.50.7
OF ALL WORLDS GLADNESSE MORE MY TORMENT FEED	5.52.12

```
DOTH PLEASE ALL BEASTS BUT THAT HIS LOOKS
                         THEM FRAY                         5.53.2
BEHOLDING ME THAT ALL THE PAGEANTS PLAY                    5.54.3
BE LYKE IN MERCY AS IN ALL THE REST                        5.55.14
AS IS A STORME, THAT ALL THINGS DOTH PROSTRATE             5.56.6
FINDING A TREE ALONE ALL COMFORTLESSE                      5.56.7
THAT AL MY WOUNDS WIL HEALE IN LITTLE SPACE                5.57.14
ALL FLESH IS FRAYLE, AND ALL HER STRENGTH UNSTAYD          5.58.5
ALL FLESH IS FRAYLE, AND ALL HER STRENGTH UNSTAYD          5.58.5
THEN AL THOSE FOURTY WHICH MY LIFE OUTWENT                 5.60.8
AND ALL THESE STORMES WHICH NOW HIS BEAUTY BLEND           5.62.11
OF ALL THAT DEARE AND DAYNTY IS ALYVE                      5.63.8
REMEMBRANCE OF ALL PAINES WHICH HIM OPPREST                5.63.12
ALL PAINES ARE NOTHING IN RESPECT OF THIS                  5.63.13
ALL SORROWES SHORT THAT GAINE ETERNALL BLISSE              5.63.14
BUT HER SWEET ODOUR DID THEM ALL EXCELL                    5.64.14
TO ALL THOSE HAPPY BLESSINGS WHICH YE HAVE                 5.66.1
WHEN I ALL WEARY HAD THE CHACE FORSOOKE                    5.67.6
AND FOR THY SAKE THAT ALL LYKE DEARE DIDST BUY             5.68.11
AND TELL HER PRAYSE TO ALL POSTERITY                       5.69.11
ALL SORTS OF FLOWERS THE WHICH ON EARTH DO SPRING          5.70.3
BUT AS YOUR WORKE IS WOVEN ALL ABOVE                       5.71.9
AND ALL THENSFORTH ETERNALL PEACE SHALL SEE                5.71.13
TO SING YOUR NAME AND PRAYSES OVER ALL                     5.73.12
OF ALL ALIVE MOST WORTHY TO BE PRAYSED                     5.74.12
WHERE WHENAS DEATH SHALL ALL THE WORLD SUBDEW              5.75.13
ALL SPRED WITH JUNCATS, FIT TO ENTERTAYNE                  5.77.3
FOR ALL THE REST, HOW EVER FAYRE IT BE                     5.79.5
DERIV'D FROM THAT FAYRE $SPIRIT, FROM
                         WHOM AL TRUE                      5.79.11
ALL OTHER FAYRE LYKE FLOWRES UNTYMELY FADE                 5.79.14
THAT LITTLE THAT I AM, SHALL ALL BE SPENT                  5.82.11
ALL THIS WORLDS GLORY SEEMETH VAYNE TO ME                  5.83.13
AND ALL THEYR SHEWES BUT SHADOWES SAVING SHE               5.83.14
ALL THAT THEY KNOW NOT, ENVY OR ADMYRE                     5.85.6
LET ALL THE PLAGUES AND HORRID PAINES OF HELL              5.86.5
AND WANDRING HERE AND THERE ALL DESOLATE                   5.89.7
ALLAY                    1
  WHAT $NESTOR'S COUNSELL CAN MY FLAMES ALAY               4.35.5
ALLAYED                  1
  WHICH BUT TOO DAIE BY FEEDING IS ALAIED                  3.56.3
ALL-EATING               1
  WERE AN ALL-EATING SHAME, AND THRIFTLESSE PRAISE         3.2.8
ALLEGE                   1
  SINCE WHY TO LOVE, I CAN ALLEDGE NO CAUSE                3.49.14
ALLEGORY'S               1
  YOU THAT WITH ALLEGORIE'S CURIOUS FRAME                  4.28.1
ALLOW                    4
  OUR $LAWES ALOW NO $LAND TO BASTERDY                     2.140.11
  HIM IN THY COURSE UNTAINTED DOE ALLOW                    3.19.11
  SO YOU ORE-GREENE MY BAD, MY GOOD ALOW+                  3.112.4
  THAT YOU ALLOW ME THEM BY SO SMALL RATE+                 4.92.2
ALLOWS                   1
  NO FAVOUR THOUGH, THE CRUELL FAIRE ALLOWES               1.11.12
ALLURE                   3
  SHE TO HER LOVE DOTH LOCKERS EYES ALLURE                 5.21.6
  MOTE SOFTEN IT AND TO HIS WILL ALLURE                    5.51.10
  SHE DOTH ALLURE ME TO MINE OWNE DECAY                    5.53.7
ALLURED                  2
  ALLUR'D A $DOLPHIN HIM FROM DEATH TO EASE                5.38.4
```

```
    THAT NETHER WILL FOR BETTER BE ALLURED                5.59.3
ALLUREMENT                        1
    THROUGH SWEET ALLUREMENT OF HER LOVELY HEW            5.31.10
ALLURING                          1
    WHO WITH THY SWEET ALURING HARMONY                    2.130.10
ALMOST                            3
    YET IN THESE THOUGHTS MY SELFE ALMOST DESPISING       3.29.9
    THAT EVERY WORD DOTH ALMOST FEL MY NAME               3.76.7
    AND ALMOST THENCE MY NATURE IS SUBDU'D                3.111.6
ALMS                              3
    UPON THE $ALMES OF THY SUPERFLUOUS PRAYSE             2.6.8
    YET CRAV'D THE $ALMES OF SUCH AS PASSED BY            2.23.4
    MAY GET NO ALMES BUT SCORNE OF BEGGERIE               4.47.8
ALOFT                             2
    LOOKING ALOFT FROM TURRET OF HER PRIDE                1.47.6
    AND HEAVIE IGNORANCE ALOFT TO FLIE                    3.78.6
ALONE                            48
    ALL MY LIVES SWEET CONSISTS IN HER ALONE              1.12.13
    AND THOU WITH CAREFULL BROW SITTING ALONE             1.41.2
    PENSIVE ALONE, ONELY BUT WITH $DISPAIRE               1.60.10
    YOU NOT ALONE, WHEN $YOU ARE STILL ALONE              2.11.1
    YOU NOT ALONE, WHEN $YOU ARE STILL ALONE              2.11.1
    OF THE $BIRDS KIND, THE $PHOENIX IS ALONE             2.16.2
    SITTING ALONE, $LOVE BIDS ME GOE AND WRITE            2.38.1
    AND $LOVE ALONE PICKS REASON OUT OF LOVE              2.38.14
    FAIRE $ARDEN, THOU MY $TEMPE ART ALONE                2.53.13
    THUS FROM MY $BREST, WHERE IT WAS BRED ALONE          2.56.13
    EV'N AS THIS $SPIRIT, SO YOU ALONE DOE PLAY           2.58.11
    TILL THOU ALONE TO PAY THE HEAVENS THEIR DUTIE        2.105.5
    A $PHOENIX THOU, THIS $PHOENIX THEN ALONE             2.106.2
    FAYRE $ARDEN, THOU MY $TEMPE ART ALONE                2.113.13
    LEFT AS THAT SUNNE ALONE TO COMFORT US                2.129.3
    SITTING ALONE, LOVE BIDS ME GOE AND WRITE             2.131.1
    AND $LOVE ALONE FINDS REASON IN MY LOVE               2.131.14
    FOR THOU ALONE RENEW'ST THAT OLDE DESIRE              2.145.13
    SO MAY HE GRACE ALL THESE IN HER ALONE                2.148.13
    FOR HAVING TRAFFIKE WITH THY SELFE ALONE              3.4.9
    I ALL ALONE BEWEEPE MY OUT-CAST STATE                 3.29.2
    THAT DUE OF MANY, NOW IS THINE ALONE                  3.31.12
    WITHOUT THY HELPE, BY ME BE BORNE ALONE               3.36.4
    THAT DUE TO THEE WHICH THOU DESERV'ST ALONE           3.39.8
    SWEETE FLATTERY, THEN SHE LOVES BUT ME ALONE          3.42.14
    MY LIFE BEING MADE OF FOURE, WITH TWO ALONE           3.45.7
    SAVE THAT TO DYE, I LEAVE MY LOVE ALONE               3.66.14
    THEN THOU ALONE KINGDOMES OF HEARTS SHOULDST OWE      3.70.14
    NOW COUNTING BEST TO BE WITH YOU ALONE                3.75.7
    WHILST I ALONE DID CALL UPON THY AYDE                 3.79.1
    MY VERSE ALONE HAD ALL THY GENTLE GRACE               3.79.2
    THEN THIS RICH PRAISE, THAT YOU ALONE, ARE YOU        3.84.2
    WRETCHED IN THIS ALONE, THAT THOU MAIST TAKE          3.91.13
    FAIRE, KINDE, AND TRUE, HAVE OFTEN LIV'D ALONE        3.105.13
    BUT ALL ALONE STANDS HUGELY POLLITICK                 3.124.11
    ALTHOUGH I SWEARE IT TO MY SELFE ALONE                3.131.8
    I'ST NOT YNOUGH TO TORTURE ME ALONE                   3.133.3
    TO ANY SENSUALL FEAST WITH THEE ALONE                 3.141.8
    STELLA ALONE WITH FACE UNARMED MARCHT                 4.22.9
    SEEME MOST ALONE IN GREATEST COMPANIE                 4.27.2
    IF $LOVE LEARNE NOT ALONE TO LOVE AND SEE             4.46.7
    HE CANNOT LOVE.. NO, NO, LET HIM ALONE'               4.54.8
    HOPING THAT WHEN THEY MIGHT FIND $STELLA ALONE        4.57.5
```

```
LEAVES, LINES, AND RYMES, SEEKE HER TO
                    PLEASE ALONE                    5.1.13
THE STORMES, WHICH SHE ALONE ON ME DOTH RAINE       5.46.14
LONGWHILE ALONE IN LANGUOR TO REMAINE               5.52.8
FINDING A TREE ALONE ALL COMFORTLESSE               5.56.7
SO I ALONE NOW LEFT DISCONSOLATE                    5.89.5
ALONG                   1
  IN $LILLIES' NEAST, WHERE $LOVE'S SELFE
                    LIES ALONG                       4.83.8
ALPHABET                1
  THINE EYES TAUGHT MEE THE $ALPHABET OF LOVE        2.111.1
ALREADY                 3
  SPENDING AGAINE WHAT IS ALREADY SPENT              3.76.12
  YET SINCE MY DEATH-WOUND IS ALREADY GOT            4.48.12
  HIS TROMPET SHRILL HATH THRISE ALREADY SOUNDED     5.19.2
ALSO                    1
  AND ALSO TO SUSTAYNE THY SELFE WITH FOOD           5.2.8
ALTAR                   1
  WILL BUILDE AN ALTAR TO APPEASE HER YRE            5.22.10
ALTARS                  1
  SPENT ON THINE $ALTARS, FLAMING UP TO $HEAV'N      2.36.10
ALTER                   2
  WHICH THOUGH IT ALTER NOT LOVES SOLE EFFECT        3.36.7
  THAT IT CAN ALTER ALL THE COURSE OF KYND           5.30.14
ALTERATION              1
  WHICH ALTERS WHEN IT ALTERATION FINDES             3.116.3
ALTERED                 2
  MAY STILL SEEME LOVE TO ME, THOUGH ALTER'D NEW     3.93.3
  I HATE SHE ALTERD WITH AN END                      3.145.9
ALTERETH                1
  OR IN THIS $ILAND ALT'RETH WITH THE $FASHIONS+     2.27.4
ALTERING                1
  DIVERT STRONG MINDES TO TH'COURSE OF ALTRING
                    THINGS                           3.115.8
ALTERS                  2
  WHICH ALTERS WHEN IT ALTERATION FINDES             3.116.3
  LOVE ALTERS NOT WITH HIS BREEFE HOURES
                    AND WEEKES                       3.116.11
ALTHOUGH                17
  HER BROW SHADES FROWNES, ALTHOUGH HER
                    EYES ARE SUNNY                   1.6.2
  ALTHOUGH THIS WORLD MAY SEEME HER DEEDE TO BLAME   1.30.13
  HE NEVER HAD MORE FAITH, ALTHOUGH MORE RIME        1.43.7
  ALTHOUGH MY CAREFULL ACCENTS NEVER MOOV'D THEE     1.44.13
  ALTHOUGH HER EYES MY ADVERSARIES BE                1.49.14
  THE $FIRE HE STOLE, ALTHOUGH OF $HEAV'NLY KIND     2.14.5
  ALTHOUGH OUR UNDEVIDED LOVES ARE ONE               3.36.2
  ALTHOUGH THOU STEALE THEE ALL MY POVERTY           3.40.10
  NO MATTER THEN ALTHOUGH MY FOOTE DID STAND         3.44.5
  SO LOVE BE THOU, ALTHOUGH TOO DAIE THOU FILL       3.56.5
  THEN CHURLS THEIR THOUGHTS (ALTHOUGH THEIR
                    EIES WERE KIND)                  3.69.11
  ALTHOUGH IN ME EACH PART WILL BE FORGOTTEN         3.81.4
  WHOSE WORTHS UNKNOWNE, ALTHOUGH HIS HIGTH
                    BE TAKEN                         3.116.8
  ALTHOUGH I SWEARE IT TO MY SELFE ALONE             3.131.8
  ALTHOUGH SHE KNOWES MY DAYES ARE PAST THE BEST     3.138.6
  AND THEN, THINKE THUS, ALTHOUGH THY BEAUTIE BE     4.40.9
  ALTHOUGH LESSE GIFTS IMPE FEATHERS OFT ON $FAME    4.75.4
```

ALWAYS   1
  O KNOW SWEET LOVE I ALWAIES WRITE OF YOU   3.76.9
AMAZE   2
  THE WHILES MY STONISHT HART STOOD IN AMAZE   5.16.3
  MADE TO AMAZE WEAKE MENS CONFUSED SKIL   5.17.2
AMAZED   2
  AT HER OWN RARE PERFECTIONS SO AMAZED   2.109.8
  BUT LOOKING STILL ON HER I STAND AMAZED   5.3.7
AMAZEDLY   1
  LASTLY, MINE $EYES AMAZEDLY HAVE SEENE   2.51.5
AMAZEMENT   2
  IN THEIR AMAZEMENT LYKE $NARCISSUS VAINE   5.35.7
  IN THEYR AMAZEMENT LYKE $NARCISSUS VAYNE   5.83.7
AMAZETH   1
  WHICH STEALES MENS EYES AND WOMENS SOULES AMASETH 3.20.8
AMBASSADORS   1
  GOE YOU MY LYNES, $EMBASSADORS OF LOVE   2.151.1
AMBER   1
  SOME BEAUTIE'S PEECE, AS AMBER COLOURD HED   4.91.6
AMBITION   2
  HAVE SEENE THOSE WALLS WHICH PROUD AMBITION
                               REAR'D   1.45.2
  BUT ONE WORSE FAULT, $AMBITION, I CONFESSE   4.27.11
AMBITION'S   1
  BUT HARDER $JUDGES JUDGE AMBITION'S RAGE   4.23.9
AMBITIOUS   3
  M'AMBITIOUS THOUGHTS CONFINED IN HER FACE   1.12.5
  WHAT, DOTH HIGH PLACE AMBITIOUS THOUGHTS AUGMENT+ 4.83.9
  NOR SO AMBITIOUS AM I, AS TO FRAME   4.90.5
AMBROSIAL   1
  MORE SWEET THAN $NECTAR OR $AMBROSIALL MEAT   5.39.13
AMBROSIAN   1
  LET HEAVENS WITHDRAW THEIR SWEET $AMBROZIAN
                               BREATH   2.145.11
AMBUSH   3
  MY REBELL THOUGHT FOR ME IN $AMBUSHE LYES   2.142.7
  THOU HAST PAST BY THE AMBUSH OF YOUNG DAIES   3.70.9
  A WICKED AMBUSH WHICH LAY HIDDEN LONG   5.12.6
AMEN   1
  AND LIKE UNLETTERED CLARKE STILL CRIE $AMEN   3.85.6
AMEND   1
  CHAUNGE EEKE OUR MYNDS AND FORMER LIVES AMEND   5.62.6
AMENDS   1
  OH TRUANT $MUSE WHAT SHALBE THY AMENDS   3.101.1
AMERCED   1
  SHALL BE BY HIM AMEARST WITH PENANCE DEW   5.70.12
AMIABLE   1
  MARK WHEN SHE SMILES WITH AMIABLE CHEARE   5.40.1
AMID   1
  AND YET AMID ALL FEARES A HOPE THERE IS   4.66.9
AMIDST   5
  RAVISH'D WITH $JOY AMID'ST A HELL OF $WOE   2.62.7
  BURN'D IN A $SEA OF YCE, AND DROWN'D AMIDST
                               A FIRE   2.62.14
  RAVISHT WITH JOY, AMIDST A HELL OF WOE   2.150.7
  BURN'D IN A $SEA OF $ICE, AND DROWN'D
                               AMIDST A FIRE   2.150.14
  AS IS A ROCKE AMIDST THE RAGING FLOODS   5.56.10
AMISS   7
  WRITING HER PRAYSE, I CANNOT WRITE AMISSE   2.42.14

```
WHO WRITES MY $MISTRES PRAISE, CAN NEVER
                         WRITE AMISSE                      2.128.14
MY SELFE CORRUPTING SALVING THY AMISSE                     3.35.7
WHICH LABORING FOR INVENTION BEARE AMISSE                  3.59.3
THEN GENTLE CHEATER URGE NOT MY AMISSE                     3.151.3
AS OF A FRIEND THAT MEANT NOT MUCH AMISSE                  4.56.8
LYKE SACRED PRIESTS THAT NEVER THINKE AMISSE               5.22.8
AMONG               3
THAT THOU AMONG THE WASTES OF TIME MUST GOE                3.12.10
WEEDS AMONG WEEDS, OR FLOWERS WITH FLOWERS
                         GATHERD                           3.124.4
AMONG A NUMBER ONE IS RECKON'D NONE                        3.136.8
AMONGST             7
THEN HEERE HE RIOTS, YET AMONGST THE REST                  2.10.7
AMONGST THE REST OF $FOCLES AND $CHILDREN BE               2.22.4
AMONGST THE DAINTIE $DEW-IMPEARLED FLOWRES                 2.53.8
AMONGST THOSE DAINTY DEW-EMPEARLED FLOWERS                 2.113.8
AMONGST THY DEEREST RELICKS TO BE KEPT                     5.22.14
THRUGH STUBBORN PRIDE AMONGST THEMSELVES DID JAR           5.44.2
TO WAYT ON LOVE AMONGST HIS LOVELY CREW                    5.70.10
AMOROUS             1
WHILES DIVING DEEPE THROUGH AMOROUS INSIGHT                5.76.7
AMPHION'S           1
WITH VOICE MORE FIT TO WED $AMPHION'S $LYRE                4.68.6
AMPLE               1
SO AMPLE EARES AS NEVER GOOD NEWES KNOW                    4.78.13
ANATOMIZE           1
MY LIFE, MY YOUTH, MY LOVE, I HEERE ANOTAMIZE              2.114.14
ANATOMY             1
TH' ANATOMY OF ALL MY WOES I WRATE                         4.58.10
ANCHOR              8
ARDENS SWEET $ANKOR, LET THY GLORY BEE                     2.32.13
CLEERE $ANKOR, ON WHOSE $SILVER-SANDED SHORE               2.53.1
AND THOU, SWEET $ANKOR, ART MY $HELICON                    2.53.14
CLEERE $ANKOR, ON WHOSE SILVER-SANDED SHORE                2.113.1
AND THOU SWEET $ANKOR ART MY $HELICON                      2.113.14
ARDENS SWEET $ANKOR LET THY GLORY BE                       2.124.13
HER $CABLE BROKE, HER SUREST $ANCHOR LOST                  2.134.10
AND ANCHOR FAST MY SELFE ON $VERTUE'S SHORE                4.62.11
ANCHORED            1
BE ANCHORD IN THE BAYE WHERE ALL MEN RIDE                  3.137.6
ANCHOR-HOLD         1
COME $TIME THE ANCHOR-HOLD OF MY DESIRE                    1.22.1
ANCIENT             1
TH'ANCIENT $WOUNDS NO LONGER CAN CONTAINE                  2.46.11
ANEW                6
BUT ($PHAENIX-LIKE) SHALL MAKE HER LIVE ANEW               1.38.14
AND THEREFORE ART INFORC'D TO SEEKE ANEW                   3.82.7
AND RUIN'D LOVE WHEN IT IS BUILT ANEW                      3.119.11
CALD IT ANEW, AND WOOED SLEEPE AGAINE                      4.38.13
THE NEW BEGINS HIS COMPAST COURSE ANEW                     5.62.2
OUT OF MY PRISON I WILL BREAKE ANEW                        5.80.6
ANGEL               12
AND MY GOOD $ANGELL (IN MY $SOULE DIVINE)                  2.18.11
MY $MUSE, MY $WORTHY, AND MY $ANGEL THEN                   2.18.13
BY THIS GOOD WICKED $SPIRIT, SWEET $ANGELL
                         $DEVILL                           2.20.14
AND MY GOOD $ANGELL IN MY SOULE DIVINE                     2.108.11
MY $MUSE, MY $WORTHY, AND MY $ANGELL THEN                  2.108.13
AND THOU AN $ANGELL ART, AND FROM ABOVE                    2.140.6
```

```
        THE BETTER ANGELL IS A MAN RIGHT FAIRE            3.144.3
        TEMPTETH MY BETTER ANGEL FROM MY SIGHT            3.144.6
        AND WHETHER THAT MY ANGEL BE TURN'D FINDE         3.144.9
        I GESSE ONE ANGEL IN AN OTHERS HEL                3.144.12
        TILL MY BAD ANGEL FIRE MY GOOD ONE OUT            3.144.14
        WHEN MY GOOD $ANGELL GUIDES ME TO THE PLACE        4.60.1
ANGELIC                     1
        ACCOMPANYDE WITH ANGELICK DELIGHTES                5.84.8
ANGELS                      7
        NINE ORDERS FIRST OF $ANGELS BE IN $HEAVEN         2.18.5
        WHERE BLESSED $ANGELS SINGING DAY AND NIGHT       2.105.13
        NINE ORDERS FIRST OF $ANGELS BE IN HEAVEN         2.108.5
        AND SUMMOND $ANGELS TO THYS BLESSED SIGHT        2.125.12
        CONCEITE OF $ANGELS, WHICH ALL WISDOM TEACHEST   2.146.10
        BUT $ANGELS COME TO LEAD FRAILE MINDES TO REST     5.8.7
        AND OF THE BROOD OF $ANGELS HEVENLY BORNE          5.61.6
ANGEL'S                     4
        THE $ANGELS TRESSES, TO HER TRESSED HAYRE         2.148.9
        DRIV'N ELSE TO GRAUNT BY $ANGEL'S SOPHISTRIE      4.61.13
        WHEN YE BEHOLD THAT $ANGELS BLESSED LOOKE          5.1.11
        THE GLORIOUS POURTRAICT OF THAT $ANGELS FACE       5.17.1
ANGER                       3
        THAT SOME-TIMES ANGER THRUSTS INTO HIS HIDE       3.50.10
        ANGER INVESTS WITH SUCH A LOVELY GRACE            4.73.13
        THAT $ANGER' SELFE I NEEDS MUST KISSE AGAINE      4.73.14
ANGRY                       4
        LOVE GROWING ANGRY, VEXED AT THE $SPLEENE          2.38.5
        LOVE GROWING ANGRY, VEXED AT THE SPLEENE          2.131.5
        ANGRY THAT HIS PRESCRIPTIONS ARE NOT KEPT         3.147.6
        WITH WHICH SHE WONTS TO TEMPER ANGRY $JOVE         5.39.3
ANGUISH                     3
        MY JOYS BUT SHADOWES, TOUCH OF TRUTH, MY ANGUISH   1.16.3
        HOW TO BE PALE WITH ANGUISH, RED WITH FEARE        1.20.2
        TO UTTER FORTH THE ANGUISH OF HIS HART            5.48.10
ANNALS                      1
        TH'ETERNALL $ANNALS OF A HAPPY PEN                 1.45.8
ANNEXED                     1
        AND TO HIS ROBBRY HAD ANNEXT THY BREATH           3.99.11
ANNOY                       6
        THESE SORROWING SIGHES, THE SMOAKE OF MINE ANNOY   1.24.1
        OR ELSE RECEAV'ST WITH PLEASURE THINE ANNOY+       3.8.4
        SONETS BE NOT BOUND PRENTISE TO ANNOY              4.70.5
        OR IF SUCH HEAVENLY SIGNES MUST PROVE ANNOY       4.100.13
        AND IN MY JOYES FOR THEE MY ONLY ANNOY           4.108.14
        AND CHAUNGE OLD YEARES ANNOY TO NEW DELIGHT       5.62.14
ANNOYED                     1
        THAT THUS I LIVE BOTH DAY AND NIGHT ANNOYD         1.26.8
ANNOYS                      2
        WHICH FOR REWARD SPOILE IT WITH VAINE ANNOYES     4.18.11
        THAT ONCE COME THERE, THE SOBS OF MINE ANNOYES    4.44.13
ANON                        2
        ANON PERMIT THE BASEST CLOUDES TO RIDE             3.33.5
        NOW PROUD AS AN INJOYER, AND ANON                  3.75.5
ANOTHER                    11
        GRATEFULL T'ANOTHER, TO MY SELFE UNKINDE          1.20.12
        TO ONE $MAN GIVES, DOTH ON ANOTHER SPEND           2.10.6
        ANOTHER, MERVAILES $SULPHURE $AETNAS FIRE         2.120.4
        ERE BEAUTIES DEAD FLEECE MADE ANOTHER GAY          3.68.8
        ANOTHER HUMBLER WIT TO SHEPHEARD'S PIPE RETIRES    4.6.7
        NOR HOPE, NOR WISHE ANOTHER COURSE TO FRAME       4.64.12
```

```
AND WITH ANOTHER DOTH IT STREIGHT RECURE            5.21.11
HOW THEN SHOULD I WITHOUT ANOTHER WIT                5.33.9
OR LEND YOU ME ANOTHER LIVING BREST                  5.33.14
THEN NEEDS ANOTHER $ELEMENT INQUIRE                  5.55.9
WITH LOVE MAY ONE ANOTHER ENTERTAYNE                 5.68.12
ANOTHER'S               2
ONE ON ANOTHERS NECKE DO WITNESSE BEARE              3.131.11
I AM NO PICK-PURSE CF ANOTHER'S WIT                  4.74.8
ANSWER                  7
I SAY, I $LOVE, YCU SLEIGHTLY ANSWERE I              2.5.5
ANSWERE NO MORE, WITH $SILENCE MAKE REPLY            2.5.11
THEN ANSWERE $NO AND I, AND I AND $NO                2.5.14
IF THOU COULDST ANSWERE THIS FAIRE CHILD OF MINE     3.2.10
IF THY SWEET VERTLE ANSWERE NCT THY SHOW             3.93.14
MAKE ANSWERE $MUSE, WILT THOU NOT HAPLY SAIE         3.101.5
I, CUMBRED WITH GOCD MANERS, ANSWER DO              4.30.13
ANSWERED  ·             2
I TELL YEE ($FAIRE) ILE NOT BE ANSWERED SC           2.5.3
HER $AUDITE (THOUGH DELAYD) ANSWER'D MUST BE         3.126.11
ANSWERING               1
LYKE IDLE $ECCHOES EVER AUNSWERING.. SO              2.141.7
ANSWERS                 4
AND THOUGH TH'EVENT OFT ANSWERS NOT THE SAME         1.35.8
WHICH HEAVILY HE ANSWERS WITH A GRONE                3.50.11
WITH DEARTH OF WORDS, OR ANSWERS QUITE AWRIE         4.27.3
'FOOLE,' ANSWERS HE, 'NC $INDES SUCH TREASURES
                          HOLD                       4.32.12
ANTHEMS                 3
THESE FATALL $ANTHEAMES, SAD AND MORNEFULL $SONGS    1.3.2
THE DOLEFULL $ANTHEMS OF MY ENDLESSE CARE            2.141.6
THEIR ANTHEMES SWEET DEVIZED OF LOVES PRAYSE         5.19.6
ANTIC                   1
MAKING WITHALL SOME FILTHY $ANTIKE $FACE             2.31.4
ANTICIPATE              1
THUS POLLICIE IN LOVE T'ANTICIPATE                   3.118.9
ANTIQUE                 6
AND STRETCHED MITER OF AN $ANTIQUE SONG              3.17.12
NOR DRAW NOE LINES THERE WITH THINE ANTIQUE PEN      3.19.10
SHOW ME YOUR IMAGE IN SCME ANTIQUE BOOKE             3.59.7
IN HIM THOSE HOLY ANTIQUE HOWERS ARE SEENE           3.68.9
I SEE THEIR ANTIQUE $PEN WOULD HAVE EXPREST          3.106.7
THE FAMOUS WARRIORS OF THE ANTICKE WORLD             5.69.1
ANTIQUITY               2
BEATED AND CHOPT WITH TAND ANTIQUITIE                3.62.10
BUT MAKES ANTIQUITIE FOR AYE HIS PAGE                3.108.12
ANVIL                   3
MY $HEART THE $ANVILE, WHERE MY $THOUGHTS
                          DOE BEATE                  2.40.1
MY $HART THE $ANVILE WHERE MY THOUGHTS DOE BEATE     2.144.1
DOE BEAT ON TH'ANCUYLE CF HER STUBBERNE WIT          5.32.8
ANY                     36
BEARE NOT REPORT CF ANY SLENDER FIRE                 1.4.3
WHICH STILL IS CHAC'D, WHILE I HAVE ANY BREATH       1.5.10
YET NEVER ANY TRUE EFFECT I PROVE                    1.25.4
IF ANY ASKE ME WHY SO SCCNE I CAME                   1.30.9
THOU CANST NOT DIE WHILST ANY ZEALE ABOUND           1.43.1
(IF LOVE IN HER HATH ANY POWER TO MOVE)              1.49.10
SEEKE OUT SOME PLACE, AND SEE IF ANY PLACE           1.52.9
IF ANY PLEASING RELISH HERE I USE                    1.57.11
THY $LIPS, WITH AGE, AS ANY $WAFER THINNE            2.8.10
```

```
WHILST $MOONE SHALL SHINE, OR ANY $FIRE
                        SHALL BURNE                 2.13.12
AS ANY $MANS, THAT $MEMORY CAN BOAST                2.27.10
AND WHEN $WE MEET AT ANY TIME AGAINE                2.61.6
WHILST $MOONE SHALL SHYNE BY NIGHT, OR
                        ANY FIRE SHALL BURNE        2.121.12
FOR SHAME DENY THAT THOU BEAR'ST LOVE TO ANY        3.10.1
AS ANY MOTHERS CHILDE, THOUGH NOT SO BRIGHT         3.21.11
OR ANY OF THESE ALL, OR ALL, OR MORE                3.37.6
THEE HAVE I NOT LOCKT UP IN ANY CHEST               3.48.9
(THOUGH YOU DOE ANY THING) HE THINKES NO ILL        3.57.14
I WAS NOT SICK OF ANY FEARE FROM THENCE             3.86.12
COULD MAKE ME ANY SUMMERS STORY TELL                3.98.7
IF TIME HAVE ANY WRINCLE GRAVEN THERE               3.100.10
IF ANY, BE A $SATIRE TO DECAY                       3.100.11
AS ANY SHE BELI'D WITH FALSE COMPARE                3.130.14
TO ANY SENSUALL FEAST WITH THEE ALONE               3.141.8
SUCH SMART MAY PITIE CLAIME OF ANY HART             4.44.3
BY NO PRETENCE CLAIME ANY MANER PLACE               4.52.11
NOR THIS, NOR THAT, NOR ANY SUCH SMALL CAUSE        4.75.12
THAT ANY LAUD TO ME THEREOF SHOULD GROW             4.90.10
THENCE, SO FARRE THENCE, THAT SCARCELY
                        ANY SPARKE                  4.104.6
CANNOT EXPRESSED BE BY ANY ART                      5.17.12
NE ANY THEN SHALL AFTER IT INQUIRE                  5.27.9
NE ANY MENTION SHALL THEREOF REMAINE                5.27.10
FONDNESSE IT WERE FOR ANY BEING FREE                5.37.13
SOME DAINTY EARES, CANNOT WITH ANY SKILL            5.38.6
NE FEARD WITH WORSE TO ANY CHAUNCE TO START         5.59.4
WITHOUT CONSTRAYNT OR DREAD OF ANY ILL              5.65.6
APACE                   2
WHOSE HARVEST SEEMD TO HASTEN NOW APACE             5.76.10
BEGIN HIS WITLESSE NOTE APACE TO CLATTER            5.85.4
APART                   2
HAUNTING UNTRODDEN PATHS TO WAILE APART             1.9.10
AND KNOWING, LOVE, AND LOVING, LAY APART            4.24.7
APES                    1
OR $PINDARE'S $APES, FLAUNT THEY IN PHRASES FINE    4.3.3
APOLLO'S                3
AND RANSACKE ALL $APOLLOS GOLDEN $TREASURE          2.21.12
I STILL FEARE $BUG-BEARES IN $APOLLO'S $CELL        2.39.12
I STYLL FEARE BUGBEARES IN $APOLLOS $CELL           2.118.12
APPAREL                 1
AND PUTS APPARRELL ON MY TOTTERED LOVING            3.26.11
APPEAL                  3
MY LAST $RESORT WHERETO MY HOPES APPEALE            1.22.2
WHAT BOOTES TO LAWES OF $SUCCOR TO APPEALE+         1.31.11
SINCE MY APPEALE SAIES I DID STRIVE TO PROOVE       3.117.13
APPEAR                  18
WISH TO BE PRESENT, AND YET SHUN T'APPEARE          1.20.4
THOUGH TH'ERROR OF MY YOUTH IN THEM APPEARE         1.55.13
BUT IT NO SOONER SAW MY $SUNNE APPEARE              2.56.5
BUT THEY NO SOONER SAW MY $SUNNE APPEARE            2.103.5
AS INTEREST OF THE DEAD, WHICH NOW APPEARE          3.31.7
THE OTHER AS YOUR BOUNTIE DOTH APPEARE              3.53.11
ON YOUR BROAD MAINE DOTH WILFULLY APPEARE           3.80.8
I LOVE NOT LESSE, THOGH LESSE THE SHOW APPEARE      3.102.2
FEARE TO OFFEND, WILL WORTHIE TO APPEARE            4.72.10
BUT NO SCUSE SERVES, SHE MAKES HER WRATH APPEARE    4.73.9
I SAW THAT TEARES DID IN HER EYES APPEARE           4.87.6
```

```
STELLA, I SAY MY $STELLA, SHOULD APPEARE              4.106.4
DOE BOTH APPEARE T'ADORNE HER BEAUTIES GRACE+         5.21.4
WHEN ON EACH EYELID SWEETLY DOE APPEARE              5.40.3
CLEARER THEN CHRISTALL WOULD THEREIN APPERE         5.45.12
SO WEAKE MY POWRES, SO SORE MY WOUNDS APPEARE        5.57.5
THE WHICH DOTH LONGER UNTO ME APPEARE               5.60.7
AND IN MY DARKNESSE GREATER DOTH APPEARE            5.66.12
APPEARANCE            1
AND SAYES IN HIM THEIR FAIRE APPEARANCE LYES        3.46.8
APPEARETH             1
SLEEPE IN THY $BEAUTY, $BEAUTY IN SLEEPE
                    APPEARETH                       2.136.2
APPEARING            2
THEIR SWEET APPEARING STILL SUCH POWER INSPIRES     1.34.7
DOTH HOMAGE TO HIS NEW APPEARING SIGHT              3.7.3
APPEARS              8
AND THAT IN $BEAUTIES LEASE EXPIR'D, APPEARES       1.50.11
AND WHERE THE SWEETEST BLOSSOMES FIRST APPEARES     1.51.7
I $EVER LOVE, WHERE NEVER $HOPE APPEARES            2.26.1
I $EVER LOVE, WHERE NEVER HOPE APPEARES             2.137.1
LOOKE IN YOUR GLASSE AND THERE APPEARES A FACE      3.103.6
MY SPRING APPEARES, O SEE WHAT HERE DOTH GROW       4.69.8
BENIGHTED IN COLD WO, BUT NOW APPEARES MY DAY       4.76.3
FAYRE WHEN THE ROSE IN HER RED CHEEKES APPEARES     5.81.3
APPEASE              4
YET MUST THAT BLISSE MY HUNGRY THOUGHTS APPEASE     1.24.12
WILL BUILDE AN ALTAR TO APPEASE HER YRE            5.22.10
THE DREADFULL TEMPEST OF HER WRATH APPEASE         5.38.7
THEN WITH SOME CORDIALLS SEEKE FIRST TO APPEASE    5.50.9
APPETITE             3
THY EDGE SHOULD BLUNTER BE THEN APETITE            3.56.2
MINE APPETITE I NEVER MORE WILL GRIN'DE           3.110.10
TH'UNCERTAINE SICKLIE APPETITE TO PLEASE          3.147.4
APPETITES            1
LIKE AS TO MAKE OUR APPETITES MORE KEENE           3.118.1
APPLAUD              1
COME THOU AND READE, ADMIRE, APPLAUD MY $LINES     2.49.14
APPLAUSE             1
SADLY I SIT, UNMOV'D WITH THE $APPLAUSE            2.47.11
APPLE                1
HOW LIKE $EAVES APPLE DOTH THY BEAUTY GROW         3.93.13
APPLES               1
TWOO GOLDEN APPLES OF UNVALEWD PRICE              5.77.6
APPLIED              1
WITH ALL THE PLAYNTS WHICH TO HER BE APPLYDE       5.32.12
APPLIES              2
TOWNE-FOLKES MY STRENGTH.., A DAINTIER
                    JUDGE APPLIES                   4.41.6
WHO HIS OWNE JOY TO HIS OWNE HURT APPLIES          4.78.7
APPLY                4
TO THEIR GROSSE $SENSE APPLY HER SELFE SO ILL      2.43.10
SINCE TO HIMSELFE HE DOTH YOUR GIFTS APPLY         4.43.3
AND FASHION TO WHAT HE IT LIST APPLY               5.32.4
THERE CAME TO ME A LEACH THAT WOULD APPLY          5.50.3
APPLYING             1
APPLYING FEARES TO HOPES, AND HOPES TO FEARES      3.119.3
APPOINT              1
AND BUT APPOINT ME FOR HER $TORMENTOR              2.115.3
APPOINTED            1
THY SHAFTS BE SPENT, AND SHEE (TO WARRE
                    APPOINTED)                      2.126.9
```

```
APPREHENDING                    1
   IN WEAKENED MINDS, QUICKE APPREHENDING BREED          4.66.3
APPREHENSION                    1
   IN SPEEDIE APPREHENSION, IT IS $SENSE                 2.12.10
APPROACH                        4
   APPROACH NOT TO BEHOLD SO GREAT DISTRESSE             1.3.6
   THE NIGHT AS TEDIOUS, WOOES TH'APPROCH OF DAY         4.89.6
   DARE TO APPROCH, THAT MAY MY SOLACE BREED             5.52.10
   THERE PRIDE DARE NOT APPROCH, NOR DISCORD SPILL       5.65.9
APPROVE                         4
   NEVER LET RISING $SUNNE APPROVE YOU LIERS             1.54.11
   SUFFRING MY FRIEND FOR MY SAKE TO APPROOVE HER        3.42.8
   SO THOU BE GOOD, SLANDER DOTH BUT APPROVE             3.70.5
   HATH LEFT ME, AND I DESPERATE NOW APPROOVE            3.147.7
APRIL                           5
   TO SPEND THE $APRILL OF MY YEARES IN GRIEFE           1.32.2
   NO $APRILL CAN REVIVE THY WITHERED FLOWRES            1.39.9
   CALLS BACKE THE LOVELY $APRILL OF HER PRIME           3.3.10
   WHEN PROUD PIDE $APRILL (DREST IN ALL HIS TRIM)       3.98.2
   THREE $APRILL PERFUMES IN THREE HOT $JUNES
                               BURN'D                    3.104.7
APRIL'S                         1
   WITH $APRILLS FIRST BORNE FLOWERS AND
                               ALL THINGS RARE           3.21.7
APRIL-SPRINGING                 1
   OR GLORIE OF MY $APRILL-SPRINGING YEERES              2.138.2
APT                             5
   FOR I WAS APT A SCHOLLER LIKE TO PROVE                2.111.3
   IN NATURE APT TO LIKE WHEN I DID SEE                  4.16.1
   LEAST JOY, BY $NATURE APT SPRITES TO ENLARGE          4.85.3
   BUT GIVE APT SERVANTS THEIR DUE PLACE, LET EYES       4.85.9
   BY LOVE WERE MADE APT TO CONSORT WITH ME              4.95.11
ARABIAN                         1
   T'$ARABIAN ODORS GIVE THY BREATHING SWEETE            1.19.6
ARCHED                          1
   THAT LOVELY, ARCHED, YVORIE, POLLISH'D $BROW          2.8.5
ARCHER                          1
   THAT BUSIE ARCHER HIS SHARPE ARROWES TRIES+           4.31.4
ARCHERS                         1
   ONE OF THOSE ARCHERS CLOSELY I DID SPY                5.16.9
ARCHERY                         1
   OR IF THOU'LT NOT, THY $ARCHERIE FORBEARE             2.48.5
ARDEN                           4
   WHERE $NIGHTINGALES IN $ARDEN SIT AND SING            2.53.7
   FAIRE $ARDEN, THOU MY $TEMPE ART ALONE                2.53.13
   WHERE $NIGHTINGALS IN $ARDEN SIT AND SING             2.113.7
   FAYRE $ARDEN, THOU MY $TEMPE ART ALONE                2.113.13
ARDEN'S                         2
   ARDENS SWEET $ANKOR, LET THY GLORY BEE                2.32.13
   ARDENS SWEET $ANKOR LET THY GLORY BE                  2.124.13
AREAD                           1
   BUT LODWICK, THIS OF GRACE TO ME AREAD                5.33.5
ARGUE                           1
   THAT IS TRUE BEAUTIE.. THAT DOTH ARGUE YOU            5.79.9
ARGUMENT                        9
   AND SCORNING $REASON'S MAYMED $ARGUMENT               2.38.6
   AND SCORNING $REASONS MAYMED $ARGUMENT                2.131.6
   THINE OWNE SWEET ARGUMENT, TO EXCELLENT               3.38.3
   AND YOU AND LOVE ARE STILL MY ARGUMENT                3.76.10
   I GRANT (SWEET LOVE) THY LOVELY ARGUMENT              3.79.5
```

```
AND GIVES THY PEN BOTH SKILL AND ARGUMENT        3.100.8
THE ARGUMENT ALL BARE IS OF MORE WORTH           3.103.3
FAIRE, KINDE, AND TRUE, IS ALL MY ARGUMENT       3.105.9
WHOSE LOFTY ARGUMENT UPLIFTING ME                5.82.13
ARGUMENTS                  1
HAST THOU FOUND SUCH AND SUCH LIKE ARGUMENTS+    4.67.10
ARIGHT                     2
THAT CENSURES FALSELY WHAT THEY SEE ARIGHT+      3.148.4
THE RAGING WAVES AND KEEPES HER COURSE ARIGHT    5.59.6
ARION                      1
ARION, WHEN THROUGH TEMPESTS CRUEL WRACKE        5.38.1
ARISE                     10
AND CROSSE MY CARES ERE GREATER SUMMES ARISE     1.1.12
A $WORLD OF $VOLUMES SHALL THEREOF ARISE         2.55.2
MORE THEN WORLDS VOLUMES SHALL THEREOF ARISE     2.102.2
THUS MIDST A THOUSAND WOES, TEN THOUSAND
                         JOYES ARISE            2.114.8
THAT I MAY BLESSE MEE AT THY SWEET ARISE         2.129.14
SO TIL THE JUDGEMENT THAT YOUR SELFE ARISE       3.55.13
TO THEM THAT WOULD MAKE SPEECH OF SPEECH ARISE   4.27.4
STELLA, WHENCE DOTH THIS NEW ASSAULT ARISE       4.36.1
INFECTED BY THOSE VAPOURS, WHICH ARISE           4.78.2
SO DARKE WITH MISTY VAPORS, WHICH ARISE          4.94.2
ARISING                    1
(LIKE TO THE $LARKE AT BREAKE OF DAYE ARISING)   3.29.11
ARISTOTLE'S                1
I DO NOT ENVIE $ARISTOTLE'S WIT                  4.64.9
ARKS                       2
YEELD $CITHEREAS SONNE THOSE $ARKES OF LOVE      1.19.2
THESE ARE THE $ARKES, THE $TROPHIES I ERECT      1.55.9
ARMED                      3
SWEETE SLEEPE SO ARM'D WITH $BEAUTIES
                         ARROWES DARTING        2.136.1
ASSAYLD WITH DEATH, YET ARM'D WITH GASTLY FEARE  2.142.3
HER SOULE, ARM'D BUT WITH SUCH A DAINTY RIND     4.57.7
ARMIES                     2
PEOPLED WITH $ARMIES OF PALE JEALOUS EYES        2.122.2
WHOLE ARMIES OF THY BEAUTIES ENTRED IN           4.36.4
ARMOR                      3
HER FLESH HIS FOOD, HER SKIN HIS ARMOUR BRAVE    4.29.12
IF I BUT STARS UPON MINE ARMOUR BEARE            4.104.10
IN WHOSE COTE ARMOUR RICHLY ARE DISPLAYD         5.70.2
ARMORY                     1
CLOS'D WITH THEIR QUIVERS IN SLEEP'S ARMORY      4.99.4
ARMS                       6
NEPTUNES BEST DARLING, HELD BETWEENE HIS ARMES   1.53.10
OF THOSE THREE GODS, WHOSE ARMES THE FAIREST WERE 4.13.2
THINKE $NATURE ME A MAN OF ARMES DID MAKE        4.41.11
SINCE IN THINE ARMES, IF LEARND FAME TRUTH
                         HATH SPREAD            4.65.13
LET BREATH SUCKE UP THOSE SWEETES, LET
                         ARMES EMBRACE          4.85.12
DESPOYLD OF WARLIKE ARMES AND KNOWEN SHIELD      5.52.4
ARMY                       1
AGAINST THE $FORTE WHERE $BEAUTIES $ARMY LIES    2.142.2
AROUND                     1
THAT DAINTY ODOURS FROM THEM THREW AROUND        5.64.3
ARRAY                      2
MY SINFULL EARTH THESE REBBELL POWRES
                         THAT THEE ARRAY        3.146.2
```

```
TO WHOM NOR ART NOR NATURE GRAUNTETH LIGHT            4.99.2
TO THIS GREAT CAUSE, WHICH NEEDS BOTH
                             USE AND ART              4.107.8
CANNOT EXPRESSED BE BY ANY ART                        5.17.12
AND WHEN I SIGH, SHE SAYES I KNOW THE ART             5.18.11
WAS IT THE WORKE OF NATURE OR OF $ART                 5.21.1
SUCH ART OF EYES I NEVER READ IN BOOKES               5.21.14
I HONOR AND ADMIRE THE MAKERS ART                     5.24.4
EXPRESSING ALL THY MOTHERS POWREFULL ART              5.39.2
BUT SUCH SWEET CORDIALLS PASSE $PHYSITIONS ART        5.50.12
ARTS                      1
AND $ARTS WITH THY SWEETE GRACES GRACED BE            3.78.12
ART'S                     1
FAIRING THE FOULE WITH $ARTS FAULSE BORROW'D
                             FACE                     3.127.6
AS                      310
FAIRE IS MY $LOVE, AND CRUELL AS SHE'S FAIRE          1.6.1
DEALE WITH THOSE DAINTY CHEEKES AS SHE DOTH DEALE     1.22.7
AS IF SHE WERE EXEMPT FROM $SYETH OR $BOW             1.23.3
AS SHORT THAT BLISSE, SO IS THE COMFORT RARE          1.24.11
AS ONE THAT DIES WITHOUT HER COMPANY                  1.25.8
THUS OFTEN AS I CHASE MY HOPE FROM ME                 1.25.9
OF SUCH AS SPOILE THY POORE AFFLICTED STATE           1.28.4
LIKE AS THE SPOTLESSE $ERMELIN DISTREST               1.29.1
I SEARCH THE EARTH, THE EARTH I FINDE AS SKANT        1.29.7
THUS SHADES MY LIFE SO LONG AS WANTS ENDURE           1.29.14
DO FEELE MINE INWARD HEAT AS GREAT (I KNOW IT)        1.43.6
I LOVE AS WELL, THOUGH HE COULD BETTER SHOW IT        1.43.8
SUFFICE, THOU SHALT BE LOV'D AS WELL AS SHEE          1.43.14
SUFFICE, THOU SHALT BE LOV'D AS WELL AS SHEE          1.43.14
SERVE AS AN INCENSE TO A CRUELL $DAME                 1.47.10
AND LET HER TELL ME AS SHE IS A WOMAN                 1.49.11
AND STRAIGHT TIS GONE AS IT HAD NEVER BEENE           1.50.4
DIVIDED FROM THE WORLD, AS BETTER WORTH               1.53.11
AS TO THE $ROMAN THAT WOULD FREE HIS $LAND            1.56.1
LIKE AS THE $LUTE DELIGHTS OR ELS DISLIKES            1.57.1
AS IS HIS ART THAT PLAYES UPON THE SAME               1.57.2
SO SOUNDS MY $MUSE ACCORDING AS SHE STRIKES           1.57.3
AS HOW THE $POLE TO EV'RY PLACE WAS REAR'D            2.1.8
THY $LIPS, WITH AGE, AS ANY $WAFER THINNE             2.8.10
AS $OTHER $MEN, SO I MY SELFE DOE $MUSE               2.9.1
GIVES HER THAT $NAME, AS SHE THE $BODY MOVES          2.12.4
AS INTELLECTUALL, IT IS $MEMORIE                      2.12.8
WHICH STILL SHALT BE, AS LONG AS THERE IS $SUNNE      2.13.10
WHICH STILL SHALT BE, AS LONG AS THERE IS $SUNNE      2.13.10
YET STAND AS FREE AS ERE YOU DID BEFORE               2.14.12
YET STAND AS FREE AS ERE YOU DID BEFORE               2.14.12
AGAINE INCREASING, AS YOU ARE CONSUMING               2.16.11
IN WHOM, $HEAV'N LOOKES IT SELFE AS IN A $GLASSE      2.17.4
AS THE $WORLDS $BEAUTIE IN HIS $INFANCIE              2.17.7
INTREATED ME, AS E'R I WISH'D HIS GOOD                2.21.3
WHEN I, AS FAST AS E'R MY $PENNE COULD TROT           2.21.5
WHEN I, AS FAST AS E'R MY $PENNE COULD TROT           2.21.5
HE STILL AS YOUNG AS WHEN HE FIRST WAS BORNE          2.22.9
HE STILL AS YOUNG AS WHEN HE FIRST WAS BORNE          2.22.9
NO WISER I, THEN WHEN AS YOUNG AS HE                  2.22.10
NO WISER I, THEN WHEN AS YOUNG AS HE                  2.22.10
GIVE $NATURE THANKES, YOU ARE NOT SUCH AS WE          2.22.12
YET CRAV'D THE $ALMES OF SUCH AS PASSED BY            2.23.4
AS ONE THAT FAINE HIS $SORROWES WOULD BEGUILE         2.24.6
```

```
I LAUGH AT $FORTUNE, AS IN JEST TO DIE                      2.24.14
AS THEY CANNOT ASCEND TO MY $HOPES $SPHERE                  2.26.7
IS $NOT $LOVE HERE, AS 'TIS IN OTHER $CLYMES                2.27.1
AND DIFF'RETH IT, AS DOE THE SEV'RALL $NATIONS+             2.27.2
I AM SURE MY $SIGHES COME FROM A $HEART AS TRUE             2.27.9
AS ANY $MANS, THAT $MEMORY CAN BOAST                        2.27.10
TO $SUCH AS SAY, $THY $LOVE I OVER-PRIZE                    2.28.1
AS COVETOUS THE OTHERS USE TO HAVE                          2.33.10
THEY SAY ($AS $POETS DOE) I USE TO FAINE                    2.42.6
WOULD $GOD I WERE AS IGNORANT AS THEY                       2.43.11
WOULD $GOD I WERE AS IGNORANT AS THEY                       2.43.11
BUT FALL TO BLEEDING, AS THEY DID BEFORE                    2.46.12
AS THOUGH TO ME IT NOTHING DID BELONG                       2.47.12
OR BEING $BLIND (AS FITTEST FOR THE $TRADE)                 2.48.9
AS $IN SOME $COUNTRIES, FARRE REMOTE FROM HENCE             2.50.1
AS'T PLEASE THE $FATES, BY THEIR RESISTLESSE
                                           FORCE            2.51.4
WITH SO PURE $LOVE, AS $TIME COULD NEVER BOAST              2.54.8
EV'N AS A $MAN THAT IN SOME $TRANCE HATH SEENE              2.57.9
IN $FORMER TIMES, SUCH AS HAD STORE OF $COYNE               2.58.1
AND TO ATTEND IT, THEM AS STRONGLY TY'D                     2.58.5
SUCH AS BY $ART TO GET THE SAME HAVE TRY'D                  2.58.7
EV'N AS THIS $SPIRIT, SO YOU ALONE DOE PLAY                 2.58.11
AS $LOVE AND I, LATE HARBOUR'D IN ONE $INNE                 2.59.1
AS WELL (SAYTH HE) TOO FORWARD, AS TOO SLOW                 2.59.6
AS WELL (SAYTH HE) TOO FORWARD, AS TOO SLOW                 2.59.6
FOOLES AS WE MET, SO $FOOLES AGAINE WE PARTED               2.59.14
WITH SO PURE LOVE AS TYME COULD NEVER BOAST                 2.101.8
AND STIL INCREASING AS THOU ART CONSUMING                   2.106.11
GAVE MEE SWEET LOOKES WHEN AS I LEARNED WELL                2.111.4
IN THIS FAYRE LIMMED GROUND AS WHITE AS SNOW                2.114.10
IN THIS FAYRE LIMMED GROUND AS WHITE AS SNOW                2.114.10
SHE'ST QUENCH HER THIRST AS DULY AS THEY FALL               2.115.10
SHE'ST QUENCH HER THIRST AS DULY AS THEY FALL               2.115.10
WHICH STILL SHALT BE AS LONG AS THERE IS $SUNNE             2.121.10
WHICH STILL SHALT BE AS LONG AS THERE IS $SUNNE             2.121.10
AS THOUGH THE HEAVEN HAD NOW AWAK'D HER EYES                2.125.11
THE WATER, TO MY TEARES, AS DROPS TO $OCEANS BE             2.127.6
THE AYRE, UNTO MY SIGHES, AS $EAGLE TO THE FLIE             2.127.7
THEY SAY, (AS $POETS DOE) I USE TO FAYNE                    2.128.6
LEFT AS THAT SUNNE ALONE TO COMFORT US                      2.129.3
SMYLING, AS THOUGH HE GLORIED IN HIS DEATH                  2.135.12
AS THEY CANNOT ASCEND TO MY HOPES SPHEARE                   2.137.7
OR EYES THAT HAVE BEHELD HER AS THEYR SUNNE                 2.138.7
SO SHALL I BE, AS I HAD NEVER BEENE                         2.142.13
BUT AS THE RIPER SHOULD BY TIME DECEASE                     3.1.3
BE AS THY PRESENCE IS GRACIOUS AND KIND                     3.10.11
AS FAST AS THOU SHALT WANE SO FAST THOU GROW'ST             3.11.1
AS FAST AS THOU SHALT WANE SO FAST THOU GROW'ST             3.11.1
AND DIE AS FAST AS THEY SEE OTHERS GROW                     3.12.12
AND DIE AS FAST AS THEY SEE OTHERS GROW                     3.12.12
AS TRUTH AND BEAUTIE SHAL TOGETHER THRIVE                   3.14.11
WHEN I PERCEIVE THAT MEN AS PLANTS INCREASE                 3.15.5
AS HE TAKES FROM YOU, I INGRAFT YOU NEW                     3.15.14
THOUGH YET HEAVEN KNOWES IT IS BUT AS A TOMBE               3.17.3
SO LONG AS MEN CAN BREATH OR EYES CAN SEE                   3.18.13
MAKE GLAD AND SORRY SEASONS AS THOU FLEET'ST                3.19.5
WITH SHIFTING CHANGE AS IS FALSE WOMENS FASHION             3.20.4
TILL NATURE AS SHE WROUGHT THEE FELL A DOTINGE              3.20.10
SO IS IT NOT WITH ME AS WITH THAT $MUSE                     3.21.1
```

```
AND THEN BELEEVE ME, MY LOVE IS AS FAIRE            3.21.10
AS ANY MOTHERS CHILDE, THOUGH NOT SO BRIGHT         3.21.11
AS THOSE GOULD CANDELLS FIXT IN HEAVENS AYER        3.21.12
SO LONG AS YOUTH AND THOU ARE OF ONE DATE           3.22.2
WHICH IN THY BREST DOTH LIVE, AS THINE IN ME        3.22.7
AS I NOT FOR MY SELFE, BUT FOR THEE WILL            3.22.10
AS TENDER NURSE HER BABE FROM FARING ILL            3.22.12
AS AN UNPERFECT ACTOR ON THE STAGE                  3.23.1
BUT AS THE $MARYGOLD AT THE SUNS EYE                3.25.6
DUTY SO GREAT, WHICH WIT SO POORE AS MINE           3.26.5
WHICH I NEW PAY AS IF NOT PAYD BEFORE               3.30.12
AS INTEREST OF THE DEAD, WHICH NOW APPEARE          3.31.7
AS THOU BEING MINE, MINE IS THY GOOD REPORT         3.36.14
AS A DECREPIT FATHER TAKES DELIGHT                  3.37.1
AS SOONE AS THINKE THE PLACE WHERE HE WOULD BE      3.44.8
AS SOONE AS THINKE THE PLACE WHERE HE WOULD BE      3.44.8
AS THUS, MINE EYES DUE IS THEIR OUTWARD PART        3.46.13
WHEN AS THY LOVE HATH CAST HIS UTMOST SUMME         3.49.3
AS IF BY SOME INSTINCT THE WRETCH DID KNOW          3.50.7
SO AM I AS THE RICH WHOSE BLESSED KEY               3.52.1
SO IS THE TIME THAT KEEPES YOU AS MY CHEST          3.52.9
OR AS THE WARD-ROBE WHICH THE ROBE DOTH HIDE        3.52.10
THE OTHER AS YOUR BOUNTIE DOTH APPEARE              3.53.11
THE $CANKER BLOOMES HAVE FULL AS DEEPE A DIE        3.54.5
AS THE PERFUMED TINCTURE OF THE $ROSES              3.54.6
HANG ON SUCH THORNES, AND PLAY AS WANTONLY          3.54.7
AS CAL IT $WINTER, WHICH BEING FUL OF CARE          3.56.13
LIKE AS THE WAVES MAKE TOWARDS THE PIBLED SHORE     3.60.1
ME THINKES NO FACE SO GRATIOUS IS AS MINE           3.62.5
AS I ALL OTHER IN ALL WORTHS SURMOUNT               3.62.8
AGAINST MY LOVE SHALL BE AS I AM NOW                3.63.1
THIS THOUGHT IS AS A DEATH WHICH CANNOT CHOOSE      3.64.13
AS TO BEHOLD DESERT A BEGGER BORNE                  3.66.2
WHEN BEAUTY LIV'D AND DY'ED AS FLOWERS DO NOW       3.68.2
AND HIM AS FOR A MAP DOTH $NATURE STORE             3.68.13
UTTRING BARE TRUTH, EVEN SO AS FOES $COMMEND        3.69.4
DO NOT SO MUCH AS MY POORE NAME REHERSE             3.71.11
AS AFTER $SUN-SET FADETH IN THE $WEST               3.73.6
AS THE DEATH BED, WHEREON IT MUST EXPIRE            3.73.11
SO ARE YOU TO MY THOUGHTS AS FOOD TO LIFE           3.75.1
OR AS SWEET SEASON'D SHEWERS ARE TO THE GROUND      3.75.2
AS TWIXT A MISER AND HIS WEALTH IS FOUND            3.75.4
NOW PROUD AS AN INJOYER, AND ANON                   3.75.5
FOR AS THE $SUN IS DAILY NEW AND OLD                3.76.13
THESE OFFICES, SO OFT AS THOU WILT LOOKE            3.77.13
AS EVERY $ALIEN PEN HATH GOT MY USE                 3.78.3
AS HIGH AS LEARNING, MY RUDE IGNORANCE              3.78.14
AS HIGH AS LEARNING, MY RUDE IGNORANCE              3.78.14
BUT SINCE YOUR WORTH (WIDE AS THE $OCEAN IS)        3.80.5
THE HUMBLE AS THE PROUDEST SAILE DOTH BEARE         3.80.6
THOU ART AS FAIRE IN KNOWLEDGE AS IN HEW            3.82.5
THOU ART AS FAIRE IN KNOWLEDGE AS IN HEW            3.82.5
AS VICTORS OF MY SILENCE CANNOT BOAST               3.86.11
THUS HAVE I HAD THEE AS A DREAME DOTH FLATTER       3.87.13
AS ILE MY SELFE DISGRACE, KNOWING THY WIL           3.89.7
WHO MOVING OTHERS, ARE THEMSELVES AS STONE          3.94.3
AS ON THE FINGER OF A THRONED $QUEENE               3.96.5
AS THOU BEING MINE, MINE IS THY GOOD REPORT         3.96.14
AS WITH YOUR SHADDOW I WITH THESE DID PLAY          3.98.14
TO MAKE HIM SEEME LONG HENCE, AS HE SHOWES NOW      3.101.14
```

```
AS $PHILOMELL IN SUMMERS FRONT DOTH SINGE            3.102.7
FOR AS YOU WERE WHEN FIRST YOUR EYE I EYCE           3.104.2
NOR MY BELOVED AS AN $IDOLL SHOW                     3.105.2
EVEN SUCH A BEAUTY AS YCU MAISTER NOW                3.106.8
SUPPOSDE AS FORFEIT TO A CONFIN'D DOOME              3.107.4
EVEN AS WHEN FIRST I HALLOWED THY FAIRE NAME         3.108.8
AS EASIE MIGHT I FRCM MY SELFE DEPART                3.109.3
AS FROM MY SOULE WHICH IN THY BREST DOTH LYE         3.109.4
SUCH CHERUBINES AS YOUR SWEET SELFE RESEMBLE         3.114.6
AS FAST AS OBJECTS TO HIS BEAMES ASSEMBLE            3.114.8
AS FAST AS OBJECTS TO HIS BEAMES ASSEMBLE            3.114.8
LIKE AS TO MAKE OUR APPETITES MORE KEENE             3.118.1
AS TO PREVENT OUR MALLADIES UNSEENE                  3.118.3
DISTIL'D FROM $LYMBECKS FOULE AS HELL WITHIN         3.119.2
AS I BY YOURS, Y'HAVE PAST A HELL OF $TIME           3.120.6
AND SOONE TO YOU, AS YOU TO ME THEN TENDRED          3.120.11
OR AT THE LEAST, SC LONG AS BRAINE AND HEART         3.122.5
AS SUBJECT TO TIMES LOVE, OR TO TIMES HATE           3.124.3
THY LOVERS WITHERING, AS THY SWEET SELFE GROW'ST     3.126.4
AS THOU GOEST ONWARDS STILL WILL PLUCKE
                                THEE BACKE           3.126.6
PAST REASON HATED AS A SWOLLOWED BAYT                3.129.7
AND YET BY HEAVEN I THINKE MY LOVE AS RARE           3.130.13
AS ANY SHE BELI'D WITH FALSE COMPARE                 3.130.14
THOU ART AS TIRANCUS, SC AS THOU ART                 3.131.1
THOU ART AS TIRANCUS, SC AS THOU ART                 3.131.1
AS THOSE WHOSE BEAUTIES PROUDLY MAKE THEM CRUELL     3.131.2
AND THENCE THIS SLAUNDER AS I THINKE PROCEEDS        3.131.14
THINE EIES I LOVE, AND THEY AS PITTYING ME           3.132.1
AS THOSE TWO MORNING EYES BECOME THY FACE            3.132.9
O LET IT THEN AS WELL BESEEME THY HEART              3.132.10
UNDER THAT BOND THAT HIM AS FAST DOTH BINDE          3.134.8
BE WISE AS THOU ART CRUELL, DC NOT PRESSE            3.140.1
AS TESTIE SICK-MEN WHEN THEIR DEATHS BE NEERE        3.140.7
AND SEALD FALSE BCNDS OF LOVE AS OFT AS MINE         3.142.7
AND SEALD FALSE BCNDS OF LOVE AS OFT AS MINE         3.142.7
BE IT LAWFULL I LCVE THEE AS THOU LOV'ST THOSE       3.142.9
WHOME THINE EYES WOOE AS MINE IMPORTUNE THEE         3.142.10
LOE AS A CAREFULL HUSWIFE RUNNES TO CATCH            3.143.1
THAT FOLLOW'D IT AS GENTLE DAY                       3.145.10
MY LOVE IS AS A FEAVER LCNGING STILL                 3.147.1
MY THOUGHTS AND MY DISCCURSE AS MAD MENS ARE         3.147.11
WHO ART AS BLACK AS HELL, AS DARKE AS NIGHT          3.147.14
WHO ART AS BLACK AS HELL, AS DARKE AS NIGHT          3.147.14
WHO ART AS BLACK AS HELL, AS CARKE AS NIGHT          3.147.14
WHO ART AS BLACK AS HELL, AS DARKE AS NIGHT          3.147.14
LOVES EYE IS NOT SC TRUE AS ALL MENS.. NC            3.148.8
AS HIS TRIUMPHANT PRIZE, PROUD OF THIS PRIDE         3.151.10
I CAN SPEAKE WHAT I FEELE, AND FEELE AS
                                MUCH AS THEY          4.6.12
I CAN SPEAKE WHAT I FEELE, AND FEELE AS
                                MUCH AS THEY          4.6.12
FOR SOONE AS THEY STRAKE THEE WITH $STELLA'S
                                RAYES                 4.10.12
AS DO BEWRAY A WANT OF INWARD TUCH                   4.15.10
AS WHO BY BEING PCISOND DOTH POISON KNOW             4.16.14
AND YET MY WORDS, AS THEM MY PEN DOTH FRAME           4.19.7
AS THAT SWEETE BLACKE WHICH VAILES THE
                                HEAV'NLY EYE          4.20.7
HATH THIS WORLD OUGHT SC FAIRE AS $STELLA IS+        4.21.14
```

```
AS WHAT THEIR HANDS DO HOLD, THEIR HEADS DO KNOW      4.24.6
AS SACRED THINGS, FAR FROM ALL DAUNGER'S SHOW         4.24.8
ARE $BEAUTIES THERE AS PROUD AS HERE THEY BE+         4.31.11
ARE $BEAUTIES THERE AS PROUD AS HERE THEY BE+         4.31.11
A $POET EKE, AS HUMCURS FLY OR CREEPE                 4.32.4
HIM AS THY SLAVE, AND NCW LONG NEEDY $FAME            4.35.10
AND IF THESE THINGS, AS BEING THINE BY RIGHT          4.39.12
AS GOOD TO WRITE AS FOR TO LIE AND GRONE              4.40.1
AS GOOD TO WRITE AS FOR TO LIE AND GRONE              4.40.1
AS HIS MAINE FORCE, CHOISE SPORT, AND
                          EASEFULL STAY               4.43.4
AND YET AS SOONE AS THEY SO FORMED BE                 4.50.5
AND YET AS SOONE AS THEY SO FORMED BE                 4.50.5
AS OF A FRIEND THAT MEANT NOT MUCH AMISSE             4.56.8
BUT AS HE THEM MORE SHORT OR SLACKE DOTH RAINE        4.58.4
AS MY YOUNG $DOVE MAY IN YOUR PRECEPTS WISE           4.63.3
AS I MAY WELL RECCUNT, BUT NONE CAN PRIZE             4.65.4
TREBLES SING HIGH, AS WELL AS BASES DEEPE             4.70.6
TREBLES SING HIGH, AS WELL AS BASES DEEPE             4.70.6
HATH CHEEKES TO SMILE, AS WELL AS EYES TC WEEPE       4.70.8
HATH CHEEKES TO SMILE, AS WELL AS EYES TC WEEPE       4.70.8
AS FAST THY $VERTUE BENDS THAT LOVE TO GCOD           4.71.13
EDWARD NAMED FOURTH, AS FIRST IN PRAISE I NAME        4.75.2
AS CONSTERD IN TRUE SPEECH, THE NAME OF
                          HEAV'N IT BEARES            4.77.11
SO PIERCING PAWES, AS SPCYLE WHEN THEY EMBRACE        4.78.10
SO NIMBLE FEET AS STIRRE STILL, THOUGH
                          ON THORNES                  4.78.11
SO AMPLE EARES AS NEVER GOOD NEWES KNOW               4.78.13
AS THOUGH THAT FAIRE SOFT HAND DID YOU
                          GREAT WRONG                 4.83.4
(AS HIS SOLE OBJECT OF FELICITIE)                     4.86.7
THE NIGHT AS TEDICUS, WCOES TH'APPROCH OF DAY         4.89.6
NOR SO AMBITIOUS AM I, AS TO FRAME                    4.90.5
SOME BEAUTIE'S PEECE, AS AMBER COLOURD HED            4.91.6
AS OF A CAITIFE WCRTHY SC TO DIE                      4.94.10
BY BEING PLACED IN SUCH A WRETCH AS I                 4.94.14
BUT AS YOU WITH MY BREAST I OFT HAVE NURST            4.95.3
AS CAN REFRESH THE HELL WHERE MY SOULE FRIES          4.100.8
SWEETNESSE, THAT BREATHES AND PANTS AS
                          OFT AS SHE                  4.101.2
SWEETNESSE, THAT BREATHES AND PANTS AS
                          OFT AS SHE                  4.101.2
AS THY LOOKES STURRE, RUNS UP AND DOWNE TO MAKE       4.101.10
AS GRUDGING ME MY SCRROWE'S ELOQUENCE+                4.104.4
AS WHAT MY HART STILL SEES THOU CANST NOT SPIE+       4.105.4
SURE THEY PREVAILE AS MUCH WITH ME, AS HE             4.106.12
SURE THEY PREVAILE AS MUCH WITH ME, AS HE             4.106.12
WHICH PANTS AS THCUGH IT STILL SHOULD
                          LEAPE TO THEE               4.107.6
AND AS A $QUEENE, WHO FROM HER PRESENCE SENDS         4.107.9
BUT SOONE AS THOUGHT OF THEE BREEDS MY DELIGHT        4.108.5
HAPPY YE LEAVES WHEN AS THOSE LILLY HANDS             5.1.1
THEN DOE I DIE, AS CNE WITH LIGHTNING FYRED           5.7.8
LOOKE EVER LOVELY, AS BECOMES YOU BEST                5.7.10
AS SHE DOTH LAUGH AT ME AND MAKES MY PAIN
                          HER SPORT                   5.10.14
SO AS I THEN DISARMED DID REMAINE                     5.12.5
TREADING DOWNE EARTH AS LOTHSOME AND FORLCRNE         5.13.11
ONE DAY AS I UNWARILY DID GAZE                        5.16.1
```

```
YET AS IT WAS, I HARDLY SCAP'T WITH PAINE            5.16.14
WHILES SHE AS STEELE AND FLINT DOTH STILL
                              REMAYNE                5.18.14
AS IF THEY KNEW THE MEANING OF THEIR LAYES           5.19.8
THERE I TO HER AS TH'AUTHOR OF MY BLISSE             5.22.9
AS MEANES OF BLISSE I GLADLY WIL EMBRACE             5.25.12
AND BE FORGOT AS IT HAD NEVER BEENE                  5.27.7
YIELDED THEM BY THE VANQUISHT AS THEYR MEEDS         5.29.6
LET HER ACCEPT ME AS HER FAITHFULL THRALL            5.29.10
ALL WERE IT AS THE REST BUT RUDELY WRIT              5.33.8
LYKE AS A SHIP THAT THRCUGH THE $OCEAN WYDE          5.34.1
SWEET IS THY VERTUE AS THY SELFE SWEET ART           5.39.5
MY SOULE WAS RAVISHT QUITE AS IN A TRAUNCE           5.39.10
AN HUNDRED $GRACES AS IN SHADE TO SIT                5.40.4
AS BEING LONG IN HER LOVES TEMPEST TOST              5.41.11
AS WILLING ME AGAINST HER WILL TO STAY               5.46.4
BUT AS SHE WILL, WHOSE WILL MY LIFE DOTH SWAY        5.46.7
AND KILL WITH LOOKS, AS $COCKATRICES DOO             5.49.10
AND RULES THE MEMBERS AS IT SELFE DOTH PLEASE+       5.50.8
SO OFT AS HOMEWARD I FROM HER DEPART                 5.52.1
AS IN THEYR MAKER YE THEM BEST MAY SEE               5.53.14
SO OFT AS I HER BEAUTY DOE BEHOLD                    5.55.1
BE LYKE IN MERCY AS IN ALL THE REST                  5.55.14
AS IS A $TYGRE THAT WITH GREEDINESSE                 5.56.2
AS IS A STORME, THAT ALL THINGS DOTH PROSTRATE       5.56.6
AS IS A ROCKE AMIDST THE RAGING FLOODS               5.56.10
THAT SOONEST FALS WHEN AS SHE MOST SUPPOSETH         5.58.3
AS $MARS IN THREE SCORE YEARES DOTH RUN
                              HIS SPHEARE            5.60.4
FOR BEING AS SHE IS DIVINELY WROUGHT                 5.61.5
LYKE AS A HUNTSMAN AFTER WEARY CHACE                 5.67.1
SO LET US LOVE, DEARE LOVE, LYKE AS WE OUGHT         5.68.13
BUT AS YOUR WORKE IS WOVEN ALL ABOVE                 5.71.9
LYKE AS A BYRD THAT IN ONES HAND DOTH SPY            5.73.5
AFTER SO LONG A RACE AS I HAVE RUN                   5.80.1
THEN AS A STEED REFRESHED AFTER TOYLE                5.80.5
IN THIS AS IN THE REST, YE MOTE INVENT               5.82.6
WHICH WHEN AS FAME IN HER SHRILL TRUMP
                              SHAL THUNDER           5.85.13
FOR WHEN AS DAY THE HEAVEN DOTH ADORNE               5.87.5
AND WHEN AS NIGHT HATH US OF LIGHT FORLORNE          5.87.7
I WANDER AS IN DARKNESSE OF THE NIGHT                5.88.3
LYKE AS THE $CULVER ON THE BARED BOUGH               5.89.1
ASCEND                      4
AND WING'D BY $FAME, YOU TO THE $STARRES ASCEND      2.16.13
AS THEY CANNOT ASCEND TC MY $HOPES $SPHERE           2.26.7
AND MOUNTING UP, SHALT TC THE HEAVENS ASCEND         2.106.13
AS THEY CANNOT ASCEND TO MY HOPES SPHEARE            2.137.7
ASCENDANT                   1
SATURNE CHIEFE $LCRD OF THE $ASCENDANT LAY           2.116.7
ASCENDING                   2
BE MY STRONG $FAITH ASCENDING TO THY $FAME           2.54.10
BY MY STRONG FAYTH ASCENDING TO THY FAME             2.101.10
ASCENDS                     1
TO PROVE THE $PYNICNS, IT ASCENDS THE $SKYES         2.56.10
ASHAMED                     2
'ART NOT ASHAM'D TC PUBLISH THY DISEASE+'            4.34.5
FORST BY THEIR $LCRD, WHO IS ASHAM'D TO FIND         4.99.13
ASHES                       3
SHALT SPRING AGAINE FROM TH'ASHES OF THY FAME        2.106.12
```

```
   THAT ON THE ASHES CF HIS YOUTH DOTH LYE              3.73.10
   WHAT THEN REMAINES BUT I TO ASHES BURNE              5.32.13
ASIDE                       2
   WHY WITH THE TIME DC I NCT GLANCE ASIDE              3.76.3
   DEARE HEART FORBEARE TO GLANCE THINE EYE ASIDE       3.139.6
ASK                         3
   IF ANY ASKE ME WHY SO SCCNE I CAME                   1.30.9
   AND ASKE A $WORLD UPON MY $LIFE TO DWELL             2.60.4
   AND ASKE A WORLD UPCN MY LIFE TO DWELL               2.149.4
ASKANCE                     1
   ASCONCE AND STRANGELY.. $BUT BY ALL ABOVE            3.110.6
ASKED                       1
   THEN BEING ASKT, WHERE ALL THY BEAUTIE LIES          3.2.5
ASKEW                       1
   BUT WHEN YE LOWRE, CR LCCKE ON ME ASKEW              5.7.7
ASKS                        1
   TURNING MY $PAPERS, ASKES, $WHAT HAVE WE HEERE+      2.31.3
ASLAKE                      1
   NO SKILL CAN STINT NOR REASON CAN ASLAKE             5.44.8
ASLEEP                      1
   IN SPORT I SUCKT, WHILE SHE ASLEEPE DID LIE          4.73.6
ASPECT                      4
   YOUR SWEET ASPECT CN HIM THAT HONOURS YOU            1.34.14
   POINTS ON ME GRATICUSLY WITH FAIRE ASPECT            3.26.10
   YET FIELD AND BOWRE ARE FULL OF HER ASPECT           5.78.8
   WHOSE SWEET ASPECT BOTH $GOD AND MAN CAN MOVE        5.89.11
ASPECTS                     1
   AND CALME AND TEMPEST FCLLOW THEIR ASPECTS           1.34.6
ASPIRE                     11
   BUT THESE WEAKE WHINGS PRESUMING TO ASPIRE           1.32.6
   HER PRIDE BROOK'D NCT PCCRE SOULES SHOULC
                          SO ASPIRE                     1.36.8
   THAT FARRE BEYOND $PROMETHEUS DID ASPIRE             2.14.4
   DOE WHAT I COULD, IT NEEDSLY WOULD ASPIRE            2.56.11
   DOE WHAT I COULD MY $EAGLETS WOULD ASPIRE            2.103.11
   NOR DO ASPIRE TO $CAESAR'S BLEEDING FAME             4.64.10
   CHIEFE GOOD, WHERETC MY HOPE DOTH ONLY ASPIRE        4.68.3
   GREAT HEAT, AND MAKES HIS FLAMES TO HEAVEN ASPIRE    5.6.8
   FOR TO THE HEAVEN HER HAUGHTY LOOKES ASPIRE          5.55.11
   BASE THINGS THAT TC HER LOVE TOO BOLD ASPIRE+        5.61.12
   BUT NOT TO DEEME CF HER DESERT ASPYRE                5.85.8
ASPIRED                     1
   SO NEERE THYNE EYES CELESTIALL SUNNE ASPYRED         2.122.10
ASSAIL                      2
   WHEN CONQU'RING $LCVE DID FIRST MY $HEART ASSAYLE    2.29.1
   I $STELLA'S EYES ASSAYLL, INVADE HER EARES           4.61.3
ASSAILED                    3
   ASSAYLD WITH DEATH, YET ARM'D WITH GASTLY FEARE      2.142.3
   BEAUTIOUS THOU ART, THEREFORE TU BE ASSAILED         3.41.6
   EITHER NOT ASSAYLD, OR VICTOR BEEING CHARG'C         3.70.10
ASSAULT                     1
   STELLA, WHENCE DOTH THIS NEW ASSAULT ARISE           4.36.1
ASSAY                       4
   DISDAYNE TO YIELD UNTO THE FIRST ASSAY               5.14.8
   AFTER LONG STORMES AND TEMPESTS SAD ASSAY            5.63.1
   SO AFTER LONG PURSLIT AND VAINE ASSAY                5.67.5
   VAYNE MAN, SAYD SHE, THAT DOEST IN VAINE ASSAY       5.75.5
ASSAYED                     1
   SITH NEVER OUGHT WAS EXCELLENT ASSAYDE               5.51.7
```

ASSEMBLE   1
  AS FAST AS OBJECTS TO HIS BEAMES ASSEMBLE   3.114.8
ASSISTANCE   1
  AND FOUND SUCH FAIRE ASSISTANCE IN MY VERSE   3.78.2
ASSISTS   1
  FORTUNE ASSISTS THE BOLDEST, I REPLY   2.59.7
ASSOIL   2
  YET MY POORE LIFE, ALL SORROWES TO ASSOYLE   5.11.9
  AND STOUTLY WILL THAT SECOND WORKE ASSOYLE   5.80.7
ASSUAGE   1
  ASWAGE YOUR STORMES, OR ELSE BOTH YOU AND SHE   5.46.11
ASSUAGEMENT   1
  WITHOUT HOPE OF ASWAGEMENT OR RELEASE+   5.36.4
ASSURANCE   4
  HIS SAFE ASSURANCE, STRONGLY IT RESTRAYNE   5.42.12
  WEAKE IS TH'ASSURANCE THAT WEAKE FLESH REPOSETH   5.58.1
  BUT FAYLETH TRUSTING ON HIS OWNE ASSURANCE   5.58.10
  SUCH SELFE ASSURANCE NEED NOT FEARE THE SPIGHT   5.59.9
ASSURE   1
  PITTIE ME THEN DEARE FRIEND, AND I ASSURE YEE   3.111.13
ASSURED   8
  WHO EVEN BUT NOW COME BACK AGAINE ASSURED   3.45.11
  FOR TEARME OF LIFE THOU ART ASSURED MINE   3.92.2
  INCERTENTIES NOW CROWNE THEM-SELVES ASSUR'DE   3.107.7
  THE ILLS THAT WERE, NOT GREW TO FAULTS ASSURED   3.118.10
  HER SELFE ASSURD, AND IS OF NOUGHT AFFRAYD   5.58.4
  THAT TO YOUR SELFE YE MOST ASSURED ARRE+   5.58.14
  THRISE HAPPIE SHE, THAT IS SO WELL ASSURED   5.59.1
  MOST HAPPY SHE THAT MOST ASSURED DOTH REST   5.59.13
ASTONISHED   1
  GIVING HIM AYDE, MY VERSE ASTONISHED   3.86.8
ASTONISHMENT   2
  IT STOPPED IS WITH THOUGHTS ASTONISHMENT   5.3.10
  BUT THIS THE WORKE OF HARTS ASTONISHMENT   5.81.14
ASTRAEA   2
  I PASSE NOT FOR $MINERVA, NOR $ASTREA   2.39.13
  I PASSE NOT FOR $MINERVA NOR $ASTRAEA   2.118.13
ASTRAY   3
  OUT OF HER COURSE DOTH WANDER FAR ASTRAY   5.34.4
  AND MY FRAYLE THOUGHTS TOO RASHLY LED ASTRAY+   5.76.6
  THE WHICH WAS WONT TO LEAD MY THOUGHTS ASTRAY   5.88.2
ASTROLOGY   1
  THOUGH DUSTIE WITS DARE SCORNE $ASTROLOGIE   4.26.1
ASTRONOMY   1
  AND YET ME THINKES I HAVE $ASTRONOMY   3.14.2
ATALANTA   1
  OR THOSE WHICH $ATALANTA DID ENTICE   5.77.8
ATE   2
  MY MAN-HOOD DARES NOT WITH FOULE $ATE MELL   2.39.10
  MY MANHOOD DARES NOT WITH FOULE $ATE MELL   2.118.10
ATHEIST   1
  SOME $ATHIEST OR VILE $INFIDELL IN LOVE   2.112.1
ATLAS   2
  OF $ATLAS TYR'D, YOUR WISEDOME'S HEAV'NLY SWAY   4.51.8
  THAT HAND, WHICH WITHOUT TOUCH HOLDS MORE
               THEN $ATLAS MIGHT   4.77.5
ATTAIN   2
  WHEN SHALL MY FAITH THE HAPPINES ATTAINE   1.49.7
  THE WHICH MY SELFE COULD NEVER YET ATTAYNE   5.84.10

```
ATTAINED                        2
   TO HAVE ATTEMPTED, THOUGH ATTAIND THEE NOT         1.35.14
   YET NEVER FOUND THAT BARBAROUS HAND ATTAIND        1.45.5
ATTAINT                         1
   AND THEREFORE MAIEST WITHOUT ATTAINT ORE-LOOKE     3.82.2
ATTAINTED                       1
   OF FAULTS CONCEALD, WHEREIN I AM ATTAINTED         3.88.7
ATTEMPT                         4
   OR BLAME TH'ATTEMPT PRESUMING SO TO SORE           1.35.2
   BECAUSE TH'ATTEMPT WAS FARRE ABOVE MY ART          1.36.7
   AND MY DECEIV'D ATTEMPT, DESERV'D MORE FAME        1.56.6
   ATTEMPT TO WORK HER GENTLE MINDES UNREST           5.84.4
ATTEMPTED                       1
   TO HAVE ATTEMPTED, THOUGH ATTAIND THEE NOT         1.35.14
ATTEMPTS                        1
   SUFFICE THAT HIGH ATTEMPTS HAVE NEVER SHAME        1.35.9
ATTEND                          7
   TO ATTEND THE PRESENCE OF MY WORLDS $DEERE         1.30.6
   THE READY HANDMAYDS ON HER GRACE T'ATTEND          1.48.2
   TH'$OCEAN NEVER DID ATTEND MORE DULY               1.48.5
   AND TO ATTEND IT, THEM AS STRONGLY TY'D            2.58.5
   I MUST ATTEND, TIMES LEASURE WITH MY MONE          3.44.12
   ON WHICH MY THOUGHTS DOC DAY AND NIGHT ATTEND      5.22.7
   NE OUGHT SO HARD, BUT HE THAT WOULD ATTEND         5.51.9
ATTENDING                       4
   BASELY ATTENDING ON THE HOPES OF MEN               1.58.8
   NO $VIRGINE ONCE ATTENDING ON THAT LIGHT           2.105.3
   ATTENDING ON HIS GOULDEN PILGRIMAGE                3.7.8
   AND CAPTIVE-GOOD ATTENDING $CAPTAINE ILL           3.66.12
ATTENDS                         2
   ATTENDS THAT $LAMPE WITH EYE WHICH NEVER
                             SLEEPETH                 2.105.10
   TILL IT HAVE WROUGHT WHAT THY OWNE WILL ATTENDS    4.107.11
ATTENTION                       1
   WITH STRONG ENDEVOUR AND ATTENTION DEW             5.80.8
ATTIRE                          4
   IN BASE ATTIRE, YET CLEERLY $BEAUTY SHINES         1.43.4
   SHALL DOFFE HER FLESHES BOROWD FAYRE ATTYRE        5.27.6
   OF THAT PROUD MAYD, WHOM NOW THOSE LEAVES ATTYRE   5.28.8
   SHE DOTH ATTYRE UNDER A NET OF GOLD                5.37.2
ATTIRES                         1
   SOME ONE HIS SONG IN $JOVE, AND $JOVE'S
                             STRANGE TALES ATTIRES    4.6.5
ATTONCE                         2
   YET BETTER WERE ATTONCE TO LET ME DIE              5.25.5
   THE WHICH HER MADE ATTONCE SO CRUELL FAIRE         5.55.4
ATTRACTIVE                      1
   DRAWNE WITH TH'ATRACTIVE VERTUE OF HER EYES        1.53.1
AUDIT                           4
   WHAT ACCEPTABLE $AUDIT CAN'ST THOU LEAVE+          3.4.12
   CAULD TO THAT AUDITE BY ADVIS'D RESPECTS           3.49.4
   HER $AUDITE (THOUGH DELAYD) ANSWER'D MUST BE       3.126.11
   WHEN INTO $REASON'S AUDITE I DO GO                 4.18.2
AUGMENT                         3
   WHAT, DOTH HIGH PLACE AMBITIOUS THOUGHTS AUGMENT+  4.83.9
   AND DAYLY MORE AUGMENT MY MISERYES+                5.36.8
   THEN DOE I MORE AUGMENT MY FOES DESPIGHT           5.44.10
AUGMENTED                       1
   AND FEELE MY FLAMES AUGMENTED MANIFOLD+            5.30.8
```

AUGMENTETH   1
  THAT ALL THE MORE MY SORROW IT AUGMENTETH   5.42.3
AUGURS   1
  AND THE SAD $AUGURS MOCK THEIR OWNE PRESAGE   3.107.6
AURORA   3
  RESTORE THY BLUSH UNTO $AURORA BRIGHT   1.19.7
  SHE COMES WITH LIGHT AND WARMTH, WHICH
                  LIKE $AURORA PROVE   4.76.5
  BUT WHEN $AURORA LEADES OUT $PHOEBUS' DAUNCE   4.98.12
AURORA'S   1
  TOWARDES $AURORA'S $COURT A $NYMPH DOTH DWELL   4.37.5
AUTHENTIC   1
  AUTENTIQUE SHALL MY VERSE IN TIME TO COME   1.55.6
AUTHENTIQUE   1
  I PROVE MY VERSE AUTENTIQUE STILL IN THYS   2.128.13
AUTHOR   2
  NOR $FORTUNE OF THY FORTUNE AUTHOR IS   4.33.8
  THERE I TO HER AS TH'AUTHOR OF MY BLISSE   5.22.9
AUTHORITY   2
  AND ARTE MADE TUNG-TIDE BY AUTHORITIE   3.66.9
  AND THEREFORE BY HER $LOVE'S AUTHORITY   4.62.9
AUTHORIZING   1
  AUTHORIZING THY TRESPAS WITH COMPARE   3.35.6
AUTUMN   3
  MAKES $SUMMER $WINTER, $AUTUMNE IN THE $SPRING   2.147.11
  THE TEEMING $AUTUMNE BIG WITH RITCH INCREASE   3.97.6
  THREE BEAUTIOUS SPRINGS TO YELLOW $AUTUMNE
                  TURN'D   3.104.5
AVAIL   2
  NOT TO AVAILE YOU, NOR DOE OTHERS GOOD   2.58.14
  AH WHAT DOTH $PHOEBUS' GOLD THAT WRETCH AVAILE   4.108.10
AVENGE   1
  DID MAKE THE MATTER TO AVENGE HER YRE   5.48.2
AVISE   1
  AVISE THEMSELVES THAT THEY ARE VAINELY SPENT   4.19.8
AVOID   1
  YET NOBLEST $CONQUEROURS DO WRECKES AVOID   4.40.11
AVON   2
  BUT $AVON RICH IN FAME, THOUGH POORE IN WATERS   1.58.11
  AVON SHALL BE MY $THAMES, AND SHE MY $SONG   1.58.13
AVON'S   2
  AND $AVONS $FAME, TO $ALBIONS $CLIFFES IS RAYSED   2.32.4
  AND $AVONS FAME, TO $ALBYONS $CLIVES IS RAYSED   2.124.4
AWAIT   1
  IN CLOSE AWAYT TO CATCH HER UNAWARE   5.71.4
AWAKE   6
  THE HORNED $RAM DOTH IN HIS COURSE AWAKE   2.147.2
  IT IS MY LOVE THAT KEEPES MINE EIE AWAKE   3.61.10
  VERTUE AWAKE, $BEAUTIE BUT BEAUTIE IS   4.47.9
  WILS HIM AWAKE, AND SOONE ABOUT HIM DIGHT   5.4.7
  AND GRIEFE RENEW, AND PASSIONS DOE AWAKE   5.44.11
  YET IN HER WINTERS BOWRE NOT WELL AWAKE   5.70.6
AWAKED   1
  AS THOUGH THE HEAVEN HAD NOW AWAK'D HER EYES   2.125.11
AWAKES   1
  AWAKES MY HEART, TO HEARTS AND EYES DELIGHT   3.47.14
AWARDS   1
  THAT SHE THAT MAKES ME SINNE, AWARDS ME PAINE   3.141.14
AWARE   1
  THEYR WEAKER HARTS, WHICH ARE NOT WEL AWARE+   5.37.8

AWAY   38
   WHICH TAKING THENCE, YOU HAVE ESCAP'D AWAY   2.14.11
   WHO GAVE CONSENT TO STEALE AWAY MY $HEART   2.23.11
   IF WHEN $NIGHT COMES, YOU BID ME GOE AWAY   2.37.14
   NEERER $MEN COME, $THAT FURTHER FLYES AWAY   2.58.9
   (QUOTH I) $THE $MAINE LOST, CAST THE $BY AWAY   2.59.11
   AND THUS (MY FAIRE) MY THOUGHTS AWAY BE FLOWNE   2.103.13
   AND THREESCOORE YEARE WOULD MAKE THE WORLD AWAY   3.11.8
   TO GIVE AWAY YOUR SELFE, KEEPS YOUR SELFE STILL   3.16.13
   THY SEIFE AWAY, ARE PRESENT STILL WITH ME   3.47.10
   STEALING AWAY THE TREASURE OF HIS $SPRING   3.63.8
   THAT $TIME WILL COME AND TAKE MY LOVE AWAY   3.64.12
   THE RIGHT OF SEPULCHERS, WERE SHORNE AWAY   3.68.6
   WHICH BY AND BY BLACKE NIGHT DOTH TAKE AWAY   3.73.7
   WITH OUT ALL BAYLE SHALL CARRY ME AWAY   3.74.2
   OR GLUTTONING ON ALL, OR ALL AWAY   3.75.14
   THEN $IF HE THRIVE AND I BE CAST AWAY   3.80.13
   ALL THIS AWAY, AND ME MOST WRETCHED MAKE   3.91.14
   BUT DOE THY WORST TO STEALE THY SELFE AWAY   3.92.1
   HOW MANY GAZERS MIGHST THOU LEAD AWAY   3.96.11
   AND THOU AWAY, THE VERY BIRDS ARE MUTE   3.97.12
   YET SEEM'D IT $WINTER STILL, AND YOU AWAY   3.98.13
   ONE OF HER FETHERED CREATURES BROAKE AWAY   3.143.2
   FROM HEAVEN TO HELL IS FLOWNE AWAY   3.145.12
   I HATE, FROM HATE AWAY SHE THREW   3.145.13
   HE BURNT UNWARES HIS WINGS, AND CANNOT FLY AWAY   4.8.14
   WAS HELD, IN OPEND SENSE IT FLIES AWAY   4.38.10
   FROM MY DEARE $CAPTAINNESSE TO RUN AWAY+   4.88.2
   ONLY TRUE SIGHS, YOU DO NOT GO AWAY   4.95.12
   HER SMILE ME DRAWES, HER FROWNE ME DRIVES AWAY   5.21.12
   BUT WAST AND WEARE AWAY IN TERMES UNSURE   5.25.3
   THAT WHEN A DREADFULL STORME AWAY IS FLIT   5.40.7
   IS PRISONER LED AWAY WITH HEAVY HART   5.52.3
   SHALL TURNE TO CAULMES AND TYMELY CLEARE AWAY   5.62.12
   SEEING THE GAME FROM HIM ESCAPT AWAY   5.67.2
   AND HAVING HARROWD HELL DIDST BRING AWAY   5.68.3
   BUT CAME THE WAVES AND WASHED IT AWAY   5.75.2
   HER GOODLY LIGHT WITH SMILES SHE DRIVES AWAY   5.81.8
   BUT JOYOUS HOURES DOO FLY AWAY TOO FAST   5.87.14
AWFUL   2
   SO CHILDREN STILL READE YOU WITH AWFULL EYES   4.63.2
   MYLD HUMBLESSE MIXT WITH AWFULL MAJESTY   5.13.5
AWHILE   4
   THEN, SWEET $DESPAIRE, AWHILE HOLD UP THY HEAD   2.26.13
   AND HAVING THUS AWHILE EACH OTHER THWARTED   2.59.13
   THEN SWEET $DISPAIRE, AWHILE HOLD UP THY HEAD   2.137.13
   AND GATHER TO MY SELFE NEW BREATH AWHILE   5.80.4
AWHIT   1
   HER HART MORE HARDE THEN YRON SOFT AWHIT   5.32.6
AWRY   3
   CLEERE-SIGHTED YOU, SOONE NOTE WHAT IS AWRIE   1.3.7
   WITH DEARTH OF WORDS, OR ANSWERS QUITE AWRIE   4.27.3
   HOW FARRE THEY SHOOTE AWRIE— THE TRUE CAUSE IS   4.41.12
AYE   5
   AYE ME, BUT YET THOU MIGHST MY SEATE FORBEARE   3.41.9
   BUT MAKES ANTIQUITIE FOR AYE HIS PAGE   3.108.12
   (EXIL'D FOR AY FROM THOSE HIGH TREASURES, WHICH   4.24.13
   SO MANIE EYES AY SEEKING THEIR OWNE WOE   4.78.12
   WHICH AY MOST FAIRE, NOW MORE THEN MOST
                       FAIRE SHOW   4.100.3

BABE   4
  AS TENDER NURSE HER BABE FROM FARING ILL   3.22.12
  LOVE IS A $BABE, THEN MIGHT I NOT SAY SO   3.115.13
  SETS DOWNE HER BABE AND MAKES ALL SWIFT DISPATCH   3.143.3
  WHILST I THY BABE CHACE THEE A FARRE BEHIND   3.143.10
BABES   2
  I THOUGHT THOSE BABES OF SOME PINNE'S
                   HURT DID WHINE   4.16.7
  WHILE THOSE POORE BABES THEIR DEATH IN
                   BIRTH DO FIND   4.50.11
BABE'S   1
  SO LUCKLES WAS MY $BABES NATIVITY   2.116.6
BABIES   1
  STELLA, THOU STRAIGHT LOOKST BABIES IN HER EYES   4.11.10
BABY   1
  LOVE STILL A $BABY, PLAYES WITH $GAWDES
                   AND $TOYES   2.22.5
BACK   27
  AND THY SWEET VOICE GIVE BACK UNTO THE $SPHEARES   1.19.10
  YET SOONE AGAINE I MUST HER BACKE RECALL   1.25.7
  AND SO SENT BACKE, AND THUS MY FORTUNE LIES   1.25.12
  WHEN BACKE I LOOKE, I SIGH MY FREEDOME PAST   1.28.9
  NO PITTYING EYE LOOKES BACKE UPON MY FEARES   1.32.10
  I GIVE $THEE BACKE, WHEN ALL THE REST IS SPENT   2.10.14
  CALL BACKE THE STIFFE-NECK'D $REBELS FROM $EXILE   2.25.11
  REASON PLUCKS BACK, COMMANDING ME TO STAY   2.38.2
  REASON PUT BACK, DOTH OUT OF SIGHT REMOVE   2.38.13
  REASON PLUCKS BACKE, COMMAUNDING ME TO STAY   2.131.2
  REASON PUT BACK, DOTH OUT OF SIGHT REMOVE   2.131.13
  CALLS BACKE THE LOVELY $APRILL OF HER PRIME   3.3.10
  THOU GAV'ST ME THINE NOT TO GIVE BACKE AGAINE   3.22.14
  WHO EVEN BUT NOW COME BACK AGAINE ASSURED   3.45.11
  I SEND THEM BACK AGAINE AND STRAIGHT GROW SAD   3.45.14
  OR WHAT STRONG HAND CAN HOLD HIS SWIFT
                   FOOTE BACK   3.65.11
  AND SO MY PATTENT BACK AGAINE IS SWERVING   3.87.8
  AS THOU GOEST ONWARDS STILL WILL PLUCKE
                   THEE BACKE   3.126.6
  BUT IF THOU CATCH THY HOPE TURNE BACK TO ME   3.143.11
  IF THOU TURNE BACK AND MY LOUDE CRYING STILL   3.143.14
  BUT WHEN MINE EYES BACKE TO THEIR HEAV'N
                   DID MOVE   4.66.13
  THAT ALL THE WOODS THEYR ECCHOES BACK REBOUNCED   5.19.7
  AND WITH STERNE COUNTENANCE BACK AGAIN DOTH CHACE   5.21.7
  SITH ALL YOUR TEMPESTS CANNOT HOLD ME BACKE   5.46.10
  DRAWNE WITH SWEET PLEASURES BAYT, IT BACK
                   DOTH FLY   5.72.7
  TO FEED HIS FILL, FLYES BACKE UNTO YOUR SIGHT   5.73.8
  THEY YDLY BACK RETURNE TO ME AGAYNE   5.78.10
BACKWARD   2
  FLINGING THE $FISHES BACKWARD WITH HIS HEELES   2.147.4
  OH THAT RECORD COULD WITH A BACK-WARD LOCKE   3.59.5
BAD   16
  FROM CARE TO CARE THAT LEADES A LIFE SO BAD   1.26.2
  AND BAD MY $SENSES TO A SOLEMNE $FEAST   2.7.2
  BAD IS THE $MATCH, WHERE NEITHER PARTIE WONNE   2.63.4
  IN DAIES LONG SINCE, BEFORE THESE LAST SO BAD   3.67.14
  SO YOU ORE-GREENE MY BAD, MY GOOD ALOW+   3.112.4
  CREATING EVERY BAD A PERFECT BEST   3.114.7
  WHICH IN THEIR WILS COUNT BAD WHAT I THINK GOOD+   3.121.8

```
ALL MEN ARE BAD AND IN THEIR BADNESSE RAIGNE        3.121.14
NOW THIS ILL WRESTING WORLD IS GROWNE SO BAD        3.140.11
TILL MY BAD ANGEL FIRE MY GOOD ONE OUT              3.144.14
WHILE THAT BLACKE HUE FROM ME THE BAD GUEST HID     4.20.11
THAT MINE OWNE WRITINGS LIKE BAD SERVANTS SHOW      4.21.3
WITH SUCH BAD MIXTURE OF MY NIGHT AND DAY           4.89.12
CURST BE THE PAGE FROM WHOME THE BAD TORCH FELL     4.105.11
THAT BAD HIS FRIEND, BUT THEN NEW MAIM'D, TO BE     4.106.13
THEN SO BAD END FOR HERETICKS ORDAYNED              5.48.6
```

BADGE   4
```
SINCE THEY DO WEARE HIS BADGE, MOST FIRMELY PROVE   4.52.4
THAT HIS RIGHT BADGE IS BUT WORNE IN THE HART       4.54.12
THE HEIGHT OF HONOR IN THE KINDLY BADGE
                        OF SHAME+                   4.102.3
FOR SINCE IT IS THE BADG WHICH I DOE BEARE          5.28.3
```
BADGES   1
```
BUT HEAVIE TEARES, BADGES OF EITHERS WOE            3.44.14
```
BADNESS   1
```
ALL MEN ARE BAD AND IN THEIR BADNESSE RAIGNE        3.121.14
```
BAIL   2
```
WITH OUT ALL BAYLE SHALL CARRY ME AWAY              3.74.2
BUT THEN MY FRIENDS HEART LET MY POORE
                        HEART BALE                  3.133.10
```
BAIT   4
```
PAST REASON HATED AS A SWOLLOWED BAYT               3.129.7
IS BUT A BAYT SUCH WRETCHES TO BEGUILE              5.41.10
TO MAKE THE BAYTE HER GAZERS TO EMBREW              5.53.11
DRAWNE WITH SWEET PLEASURES BAYT, IT BACK
                        DOTH FLY                    5.72.7
```
BAITING   2
```
BAYTING THE $LYON IN HIS FURIOUS HEAT               2.147.7
THE BAITING PLACE OF WIT, THE BALME OF WOE          4.39.2
```
BAITS   1
```
THAT FROM THE FOOLISH FISH THEYR BAYTS DOE HYDE     5.47.4
```
BALANCE   2
```
WHILE HE EACH THING IN SENSE'S BALLANCE WAYES       4.25.6
THAT $BALLANCE WEIGH'D WHAT SWORD DID
                        LATE OBTAINE                4.75.8
```
BALE   1
```
OF TH'INWARD BALE OF MY LOVE PINED HART             5.2.2
```
BALEFUL   1
```
BUT WHEN I FEELE THE BITTER BALEFULL SMART          5.24.5
```
BALLAST   1
```
THEN SO TO CAST HER $BALLAST OVER BOORD             2.134.8
```
BALM   1
```
THE BAITING PLACE OF WIT, THE BALME OF WOE          4.39.2
```
BALMS   1
```
AND WITH THEIR $BALMES RECURE THE $WOUNDS AGAINE    2.50.8
```
BALMY   1
```
NOW WITH THE DROPS OF THIS MOST BALMIE TIME         3.107.9
```
BANDS   6
```
SHALL HANDLE YOU AND HOLD IN LOVES SOFT BANDS       5.1.3
HAVE EVER SINCE ME KEPT IN CRUELL BANDS             5.12.12
OUT OF HER BANDS YE BY NO MEANES SHALL GET          5.37.12
SWEET BE THE BANDS, THE WHICH TRUE LOVE DOTH TYE    5.65.5
IN WHOSE STREIGHT BANDS YE NOW CAPTIVED ARE         5.71.7
MY HART, WHOM NONE WITH SERVILE BANDS CAN TYE       5.73.2
```
BANE   2
```
THE MORE I LOVE AND DOE EMBRACE MY BANE             5.42.4
O MIGHTY CHARM WHICH MAKES MEN LOVE THEYR BANE      5.47.13
```

```
BANISH                          3
   I BANISH HER, AND BLAME HER TRECHERY               1.25.6
   FOR SHE PROTESTS TC BANISH THEE HER FACE           4.46.5
   FROM COMMING NEARE THOSE $CHERRIES BANISH ME       4.82.8
BANISHED                        2
   LOVE BANISH'D $HEAV'N, IN $EARTH WAS HELD
                              IN SCORNE               2.23.1
   NOW BANISHT ART, BUT YET ALAS HOW SHALL+           4.72.14
BANKROUT                        1
   AND BY JUST COUNTS MY SELFE A BANCKROUT KNOW       4.18.3
BANKRUPT                        3
   AND I A $BANKRUPT, QUITE UNDONE BY $THEE           2.3.14
   AND I A $BANCKRUPT QUITE UNDONE BY THEE            2.110.14
   WHY SHOULD HE LIVE, NOW NATURE BANCKROUT IS        3.67.9
BANKS                           4
   THE $PEAKE HER $DCVE, WHOSE $BANKES SO FERTILE BE  2.32.7
   POORE $BROOKES AND $BANKS HAD NO SUCH
                              WONDERS BEENE           2.120.14
   THE $PEAKE HER $DCVE, WHOSE BANCKS SO
                              FERTILL BEE             2.124.7
   COME DAILY TO THE BANCKES, THAT WHEN THEY SEE      3.56.11
BANNED                          1
   THOU WHICH HAST BANN'D THY $THOUGHTS,
                      AND CURST THY $BIRTH            2.49.11
BANNER                          2
   HOW THEIR BLACKE BANNER MIGHT BE BEST DISPLAID     4.55.8
   AND HER FAIRE COUNTENANCE LIKE A GOODLY BANNER     5.5.11
BANNERS                         1
   MY FORCES RAZDE, THY BANNERS RAISD WITHIN          4.36.6
BANQUET                         2
   AND AT THE $BANQUET, IN HIS $DRUNKENNESSE          2.7.11
   AND TO THE PAINTED BANQUET BIDS MY HEART           3.47.6
BAR                             2
   MINE EYE, MY HEART THEIR PICTURES SIGHT
                              WOULD BARRE             3.46.3
   THEN $ORPHEUS WITH HIS HARP THEYR STRIFE DID BAR   5.44.4
BARBAROUS
   YET NEVER FOUND THAT BARBAROUS HAND ATTAIND        1.45.5
BARD                            1
   NIGHT BARD FROM $SUN, THOU FROM THY OWNE
                              SUNNE'S LIGHT           4.96.4
BARDS                           1
   AND LET THE $BARDS WITHIN THAT $IRISH $ILE         2.25.9
BARE                            12
   AND IN BARE WORDS PAINT OUT MY $PASSIONS PAINE     2.42.7
   AND IN BARE WORDS PAYNT CUT MY PASSIONS PAYNE      2.128.7
   MAY MAKE SEEME BARE, IN WANTING WORDS TO SHEW IT   3.26.6
   UTTRING BARE TRUTH, EVEN SO AS FOES $COMMEND       3.69.4
   BARE RN'WD QUIERS, WHERE LATE THE SWEET
                              BIRDS SANG              3.73.4
   THE ARGUMENT ALL BARE IS OF MORE WORTH             3.103.3
   BUT IN $VERT FIELD $MARS BARE A GOLDEN SPEARE      4.13.5
   HER DAINTIEST BARE WENT FREE., THE CAUSE
                              WAS THIS                4.22.13
   BECAUSE THEIR FOREFRONT BARE SWEET $STELLA'S
                              NAME                    4.50.14
   I BARE (WITH $ENVIE) YET I BARE YOUR SONG          4.83.5
   I BARE (WITH $ENVIE) YET I BARE YOUR SONG          4.83.5
   BARE ME IN HAND, THAT IN THIS $ORPHANE PLACE       4.106.3
```

BARED   1
  LYKE AS THE $CULVER ON THE BARED BOUGH   5.89.1
BARENESS   2
  BEAUTY ORE-SNOW'D AND BARENES EVERY WHERE   3.5.8
  WHAT OLD $DECEMBERS BARENESSE EVERY WHERE+   3.97.4
BARGE   1
  BEWARE FULL SAILES DROWNE NOT THY TOTTRING BARGE   4.85.2
BARK   5
  WHERE MY POORE SOULE, THE $BARKE OF SORROW LYES   2.134.3
  MY SAWSIE BARKE (INFERIOR FARRE TO HIS)   3.80.7
  IT IS THE STAR TO EVERY WANDRING BARKE   3.116.7
  WITH WHICH MY SILLY BARKE WAS TOSSED SORE   5.63.4
  FAYRE WHEN HER BREST LYKE A RICH LADEN BARKE   5.81.5
BARKS   1
  HE BARKS, MY SONGS THINE OWNE VOYCE OFT
                              DOTH PROVE   4.59.6
BARREN   5
  WHEN LOFTY TREES I SEE BARREN OF LEAVES   3.12.5
  AND BARREN RAGE OF DEATHS ETERNALL COLD+   3.13.12
  WITH MEANES MORE BLESSED THEN MY BARREN RIME+   3.16.4
  WHY IS MY VERSE SO BARREN OF NEW PRIDE+   3.76.1
  THE BARREN TENDER OF A $POETS DEBT   3.83.4
BARRENLY   1
  HARSH, FEATURELESSE, AND RUDE, BARRENLY PERRISH   3.11.10
BARS   2
  WHILST I WHOME FORTUNE OF SUCH TRYUMPH BARS   3.25.3
  EACH TRIFLE UNDER TRUEST BARRES TO THRUST   3.48.2
BASE   17
  THE MEANE OBSERVER (WHOM BASE SAFETY KEEPS)   1.35.10
  IN BASE ATTIRE, YET CLEERLY $BEAUTY SHINES   1.43.4
  TO SOME BASE $RUSTICK DOE THY SELFE PREFERRE   2.48.6
  COMPARE MY $WORTH WITH OTHERS BASE $DESERT   2.60.6
  COMPARE MY WORTH WITH OTHERS BASE DESERT   2.149.6
  TO LET BACE CLOUDES ORE-TAKE ME IN MY WAY   3.34.3
  TO BASE OF THEE TO BE REMEMBRED   3.74.12
  BUT IF THAT FLOWRE WITH BASE INFECTION MEETE   3.94.11
  DARKNING THY POWRE TO LEND BASE SUBJECTS LIGHT   3.100.4
  NOR TENDER FEELING TO BASE TOUCHES PRONE   3.141.6
  RICH FOOLES THERE BE, WHOSE BASE AND FILTHY HART   4.24.1
  FROM BASE DESIRE ON EARTHLY CATES TO PRAY+   4.88.8
  BASE THING I CAN NO MORE ENDURE TO VIEW   5.3.6
  SCORN OF BASE THINGS, AND SDEIGNE OF FOULE
                              DISHONOR   5.5.6
  SHOOT OUT HIS DARTS TO BASE AFFECTIONS WOUND+   5.8.6
  BASE THING, AND THINKE HOW SHE TO HEAVEN
                              MAY CLIME   5.13.10
  BASE THINGS THAT TO HER LOVE TOO BOLD ASPIRE+   5.61.12
BASELY   1
  BASELY ATTENDING ON THE HOPES OF MEN   1.58.8
BASENESS   2
  IN MY FRAILE SPIRIT BY HER FROM BASENESSE RAYSED   5.3.4
  NOR UNTO GLASSE.. SUCH BASENESSE MOUGHT
                              OFFEND HER   5.9.12
BASER   3
  SUCH LOVE NOT LYKE TO LUSTS OF BASER KYND   5.6.3
  ALL THIS WORLDS PRIDE BOW TO A BASER MAKE   5.10.11
  NOT SO, (QUOD I) LET BASER THINGS DEVIZE   5.75.9
BASES   2
  OR LAYD GREAT BASES FOR ETERNITY   3.125.3
  TREBLES SING HIGH, AS WELL AS BASES DEEPE   4.70.6

BASEST   4
   ANON PERMIT THE BASEST CLOUDES TO RIDE   3.33.5
   THE BASEST WEED OUT-BRAVES HIS DIGNITY   3.94.12
   THE BASEST $JEWELL WIL BE WELL ESTEEM'D   3.96.6
   THAT HAST MY MIND, NONE OF THE BASEST, BROUGHT   4.40.3
BASHFUL   1
   HOW TO BE BOLD FAR OFF, AND BASHFULL NEARE   1.20.5
BASILISK   1
   THE $BASILISKE HIS NATURE TAKES FROM THEE   2.130.5
BASTARD   6
   A $BASTARD ON BOTH SIDES NEEDES MUST THOU BE   2.140.10
   BY NATURES $LAWES WE THEE A $BASTARD FINDE   2.140.12
   GOE $BASTARD GOE, FOR SURE OF THENCE THOU ART   2.140.14
   BEFORE THESE BASTARD SIGNES OF FAIRE WERE BORNE   3.68.3
   IT MIGHT FOR FORTUNES BASTERD BE UNFATHERED   3.124.2
   AND $BEAUTIE SLANDERD WITH A BASTARD SHAME   3.127.4
BASTARDY   1
   OUR $LAWES ALOW NO $LAND TO BASTERDY   2.140.11
BATE   1
   THOU SETST A BATE BETWEENE MY WILL AND WIT   4.4.2
BATH   6
   AND GREW A SEETHING BATH WHICH YET MEN PROVE   3.153.7
   I SICK WITHALL THE HELPE OF BATH DESIRED   3.153.11
   BUT FOUND NO CURE, THE BATH FOR MY HELPE LIES   3.153.13
   GROWING A BATH AND HEALTHFULL REMEDY   3.154.11
   THAT SHE THE BETTER MAY IN BLOODY BATH   5.31.11
   DOTH BATH IN BLISSE AND MANTLETH MOST AT EASE   5.72.10
BATHED   1
   AND HAPPY RYMES BATH'D IN THE SACRED BROOKE   5.1.9
BATTERED   1
   WHERETO LONG SINCE, THROUGH MY LONG BATTRED EYES   4.36.3
BATTERING   1
   AGAINST THE WRACKFULL SIEDGE OF BATTRING DAYES   3.65.6
BATTERY   2
   AND LAY INCESSANT BATTERY TO HER HEART   5.14.10
   NE YOUR INCESSANT BATTRY MORE TO BEARE   5.57.4
BATTLE   2
   TO BATTELL, AND THE WEARY WAR RENEW'TH   5.11.4
   TO BATTAILE FRESH AGAINST MY SELFE TO FIGHT   5.44.12
BAY   3
   BE ANCHORD IN THE BAYE WHERE ALL MEN RIDE   3.137.6
   AND BY THE BAY WHICH I UNTO HER GAVE   5.29.3
   THE BAY (QUOTH SHE) IS OF THE VICTOURS BORNE   5.29.5
BAYS   2
   NO $BAYES I SEEKE TO DECKE MY MOURNING BROW   1.4.9
   THEN WOULD I DECKE HER HEAD WITH GLORIOUS BAYES   5.29.13
BEAM   1
   THE BEAME OF LIGHT, WHOM MORTAL EYES ADMYRE   5.61.10
BEAMS   20
   CAUS'D BY THOSE CRUELL BEAMES THAT WERE
                              SO STRONG   1.32.14
   HER GOLDEN BEAMES HAD NOW DISCOVERED   2.125.3
   AS FAST AS OBJECTS TO HIS BEAMES ASSEMBLE   3.114.8
   OF FORCE OF HEAV'NLY BEAMES, INFUSING
                              HELLISH PAINE   4.6.3
   IN COLOUR BLACKE, WHY WRAPT SHE BEAMES SO BRIGHT+   4.7.2
   LONG SINCE FORC'D BY THY BEAMES, BUT STONE
                              NOR TREE   4.36.13
   SENT FORTH THE BEAMES, WHICH MADE SO FAIRE
                              MY RACE   4.41.14

```
WHOSE BEAMES BE JOYES, WHOSE JOYES ALL VERTUES BE        4.42.2
CAN THOSE BLACKE BEAMES SUCH BURNING MARKES
                              ENGRAVE                    4.47.2
MEANE WHILE MY HEART CONFERS WITH $STELLA'S
                              BEAMES                     4.51.12
STELLA'S EYES SENT TO ME THE BEAMES OF BLISSE           4.66.11
WITH SUCH A ROSIE MORNE, WHOSE BEAMES
                    MOST FRESHLY GAY                     4.76.7
PRAY THAT MY SUNNE GO DOWNE WITH MEEKER
                    BEAMES TO BED                        4.76.14
THOSE LOOKES, WHOSE BEAMES BE JOY, WHOSE
                    MOTION IS DELIGHT                    4.77.1
WHEN $SUN IS HID, CAN STARRES SUCH BEAMES
                    DISPLAY+                             4.88.6
WHERE MEMORY SETS FOORTH THE BEAMES OF LOVE             4.88.11
THAT YOUR BRIGHT BEAMS OF MY WEAK EIES ADMYRED           5.7.11
THRUGH YOUR BRIGHT BEAMES DOTH NOT THE
                    BLINDED GUEST                        5.8.5
THAT DEATH OUT OF THEYR SHINY BEAMES DOE DART            5.24.7
REMOVE THE CAUSE BY WHICH YOUR FAYRE BEAMES
                    DARKNED BE                           5.45.14
BEAMY                         3
  WOULD SHE IN BEAMIE BLACKE, LIKE PAINTER WISE          4.7.3
  WHOSE FAIRE SKIN, BEAMY EYES, LIKE MORNING
                    SUN ON SNOW                          4.8.9
  THAT THROUGH MY HEART THEIR BEAMIE DARTS BE GONE       4.48.10
BEAR                          29
  BEARE NOT REPORT OF ANY SLENDER FIRE                   1.4.3
  MY HUMBLE ACCENTS BEARE THE $OLIVE BOUGH               1.4.11
  WHICH STILL MUST BEARE THE TITLE OF MY WRONG           1.32.13
  LAYES DOWNE HIS $QUIVER, WHICH HE ONCE DID BEARE       2.4.6
  BEARE WITH $ME THEN, THOUGH TROUBLED BE
                    MY $BRAINE                           2.9.12
  THEN HONEST $PEOPLE, BEARE WITH $LOVE AND $ME          2.22.2
  HIS TENDER HEIRE MIGHT BEARE HIS MEMORY                3.1.4
  IN SINGLENESSE THE PARTS THAT THOU SHOULD'ST BEARE     3.8.8
  BORNE ON THE BEARE WITH WHITE AND BRISTLY BEARD        3.12.8
  WHEN YOUR SWEET ISSUE YOUR SWEET FORME
                    SHOULD BEARE                         3.13.8
  WITH VERTUOUS WISH WOULD BEARE YOUR LIVING
                    FLOWERS                              3.16.7
  TO BEARE LOVES WRONG, THEN HATES KNOWNE INJURY         3.40.12
  PLODS DULY ON, TO BEARE THAT WAIGHT IN ME              3.50.6
  WHICH LABORING FOR INVENTION BEARE AMISSE              3.59.3
  THE VACANT LEAVES THY MINDES IMPRINT WILL BEARE        3.77.3
  THE HUMBLE AS THE PROUDEST SAILE DOTH BEARE            3.80.6
  THAT FOR THY RIGHT, MY SELFE WILL BEARE
                    ALL WRONG                            3.88.14
  ONE ON ANOTHERS NECKE DO WITNESSE BEARE                3.131.11
  BEARE THINE EYES STRAIGHT, THOUGH THY
                    PROUD HEART GOE WIDE                 3.140.14
  JOVES GOLDEN SHIELD DID $EAGLE SABLES BEARE            4.13.3
  BUT FIND SOME $HERCULES TO BEARE, IN STEED             4.51.7
  OF THEM, WHO IN THEIR LIPS $LOVE'S STANDERD BEARE      4.54.6
  AND THEN WITH PATIENCE BID ME BEARE MY FIRE            4.56.14
  NOW BLESSED YOU, BEARE ONWARD BLESSED ME               4.84.5
  O HAPPIE $TEMS, THAT DIDST MY $STELLA BEARE            4.103.1
  IF I BUT STARS UPON MINE ARMOUR BEARE                  4.104.10
  FOR SINCE IT IS THE BADG WHICH I DOE BEARE             5.28.3
  NE YOUR INCESSANT BATTRY MORE TO BEARE                 5.57.4
```

TO BEARE THE MESSAGE OF HER GENTLE SPRIGHT   5.81.12
BEARD   1
  BORNE ON THE BEARE WITH WHITE AND BRISTLY BEARD   3.12.8
BEARER   1
  OF MY DULL BEARER, WHEN FROM THEE I SPEED   3.51.2
BEAREST   2
  FOR SHAME DENY THAT THOU BEAR'ST LOVE TO ANY   3.10.1
  THOU BEAR'ST THE ARROW, I THE ARROW HEAD   4.65.14
BEARING   5
  BEARING THE WOUND, I NEEDES MUST FEELE THE PAINE   1.52.14
  BEARING THY HEART WHICH I WILL KEEPE SO CHARY   3.22.11
  BEARING THE WANTON BURTHEN OF THE PRIME   3.97.7
  IN VOWING NEW HATE AFTER NEW LOVE BEARING   3.152.4
  YE BEARING IT DOE SEEME TO ME INCLIND   5.28.4
BEARS   11
  TO $HYRCAN $TYGRES, AND TO RUTHLES $BEARES   1.19.12
  NOW WHILST THY BEAUTY BEARES WITHOUT A STAINE   1.40.3
  WITH $FOOLES AND $CHILDREN GOOD $DISCRETION
                          BEARES   2.22.1
  LET $WOLVES AND $BEARES BE CHARMED WITH
                          MY $VERSE   2.25.14
  TO HIM THAT BEARES THE STRONG OFFENSES LOSSE   3.34.12
  THE BEAST THAT BEARES ME, TIRED WITH MY WOE   3.50.5
  BUT BEARES IT OUT EVEN TO THE EDGE OF DOOME   3.116.12
  THAT WHO INDEED INFELT AFFECTION BEARES   4.61.5
  AS CONSTERD IN TRUE SPEECH, THE NAME OF
                          HEAV'N IT BEARES   4.77.11
  YET GROWEST MORE WRETCHED THEN THY NATURE BEARES   4.94.13
  THAT BOLDNED INNOCENCE BEARES IN HIR EIES   5.5.10
BEAST   8
  THE BEAST THAT BEARES ME, TIRED WITH MY WOE   3.50.5
  O WHAT EXCUSE WILL MY POORE BEAST THEN FIND   3.51.5
  AND NOW MAN'S WRONGS IN ME, POORE BEAST, DESCRIE   4.49.4
  AND REIGNETH OVER EVERY BEAST IN FIELD   5.20.6
  AND EVERY BEAST THAT TO HIS DEN WAS FLED   5.40.10
  A FEEBLE BEAST, DOTH FELLY HIM OPPRESSE   5.56.4
  THAT SHIP, THAT TREE, AND THAT SAME BEAST AM I   5.56.13
  STRANGE THING ME SEEMD TO SEE A BEAST SO WYLD   5.67.13
BEASTS   3
  OF HERBES OR BEASTES, WHICH $INDE OR $AFRIKE HOLD   4.3.8
  SITH TO ALL OTHER BEASTES OF BLOODY RACE   5.31.5
  DOTH PLEASE ALL BEASTS BUT THAT HIS LOOKS
                          THEM FRAY   5.53.2
BEAT   8
  WHERE BEAT THESE TEARES WITH ZEALE, AND
                          FURY DRIVES   1.48.10
  ON WHICH THE $SUNNE MIGHT BY REFLECTION BEAT   2.30.6
  MY $HEART THE $ANVILE, WHERE MY $THOUGHTS
                          DOE BEATE   2.40.1
  MY $HART THE $ANVILE WHERE MY THOUGHTS DOE BEATE   2.144.1
  MY $FOE CAME ON, AND BEAT THE AIRE FOR ME   4.53.13
  THAT FOR MY FAULTS YE WILL ME GENTLY BEAT   5.24.14
  THAT WITH HIS HEAVY SLEDGE HE CAN IT BEAT   5.32.3
  DOE BEAT ON TH'ANDUYLE OF HER STUBBERNE WIT   5.32.8
BEATED   1
  BEATED AND CHOPT WITH TAND ANTIQUITIE   3.62.10
BEATEN   2
  GALLEIN'S ADOPTIVE SONNES, WHO BY A BEATEN WAY   4.102.9
  SO MY STORME BEATEN HART LIKEWISE IS CHEARED   5.40.13

BEATING   1
  BITING MY TREWAND PEN, BEATING MY SELFE FOR SPITE   4.1.13
BEATS   1
  BEATS ON IT STRONGLY IT TO RUINATE   5.56.8
BEAUTEOUS   9
  THEN BEAUTIOUS NIGARD WHY DOOST THOU ABUSE   3.4.5
  SEEKING THAT BEAUTIOUS ROOFE TO RUINATE   3.10.7
  MAKES BLACKE NIGHT BEAUTIOUS, AND HER
                  OLD FACE NEW   3.27.12
  WHY DIDST THOU PROMISE SUCH A BEAUTIOUS DAY   3.34.1
  BEAUTIOUS THOU ART, THEREFORE TO BE ASSAILED   3.41.6
  OH HOW MUCH MORE DOTH BEAUTIE BEAUTIOUS SEEME   3.54.1
  AND SO OF YOU, BEAUTIOUS AND LOVELY YOUTH   3.54.13
  YOU TO YOUR BEAUTIOUS BLESSINGS ADDE A CURSE   3.84.13
  THREE BEAUTIOUS SPRINGS TO YELLOW $AUTUMNE
                  TURN'D   3.104.5
BEAUTIES   18
  AND FROST OF AGE HATH NIPT THY BEAUTIES NEERE   1.42.2
  AND THEREFORE GRIEVE NOT IF THY BEAUTIES DIE   1.45.9
  WITH THOSE RICH $BEAUTIES $HEAV'N GIVES
                  YOU TO KEEPE   2.58.12
  SINCE SWEETS AND BEAUTIES DO THEM-SELVES FORSAKE   3.12.11
  AND ALL THOSE BEAUTIES WHEREOF NOW HE'S $KING   3.63.6
  THY GLASSE WILL SHEW THEE HOW THY BEAUTIES WERE   3.77.1
  AS THOSE WHOSE BEAUTIES PROUDLY MAKE THEM CRUELL   3.131.2
  SHE EVEN IN BLACKE DOTH MAKE ALL BEAUTIES FLOW+   4.7.11
  BEAUTIES, WHICH WERE OF MANIE $CARRETS FINE   4.16.2
  YET WERE THE HID AND MEANER BEAUTIES PARCHT   4.22.12
  AND CAN WITH FOULE ABUSE SUCH BEAUTIES BLOT   4.24.11
  ARE $BEAUTIES THERE AS PROUD AS HERE THEY BE+   4.31.11
  WHOLE ARMIES OF THY BEAUTIES ENTRED IN   4.36.4
  RICH IN ALL BEAUTIES WHICH MAN'S EYE CAN SEE   4.37.6
  BEAUTIES SO FARRE FROM REACH OF WORDS, THAT WE   4.37.7
  NYMPH OF THE GARD'N, WHERE ALL BEAUTIES BE   4.82.1
  BEAUTIES WHICH DO IN EXCELLENCIE PASSE   4.82.2
  WHILE WANTON WINDS WITH BEAUTIES SO DEVINE   4.103.6
BEAUTIFIER   1
  SWEETNER OF MUSICKE, WISEDOME'S BEAUTIFIER   4.80.6
BEAUTIFIES   1
  WHILE GRACEFULL PITTY BEAUTY BEAUTIFIES   4.100.4
BEAUTIFUL   1
  AND BEAUTIE MAKING BEAUTIFULL OLD RIME   3.106.3
BEAUTY   128
  UNTO THE BOUNDLESSE $OCEAN OF THY BEAUTIE   1.1.1
  EXAMINE WELL THY BEAUTIE WITH MY TRUTH   1.1.11
  CHASTITIE AND $BEAUTIE, WHICH WERE DEADLY FOES   1.6.9
  AND MADE THY PASSIONS WITH HER BEAUTIE EVEN   1.8.4
  IF BEAUTY THUS BE CLOWDED WITH A FROWNE   1.21.1
  ROB HER FAIRE $BROW, BREAKE IN ON $BEAUTY, STEALE   1.22.5
  BEAUTY AND YOUTH T'OPINION AND DISDAINE   1.23.12
  GAZING THY BEAUTY DEIGN'D THEE BY THE SKIES   1.37.2
  THEN BEAUTY (NOW THE BURTHEN OF MY SONG)   1.38.5
  THAT FULL OF BEAUTY, TIME BESTOWES UPON HER   1.39.4
  DISSOLVES THE BEAUTY OF THE FAIREST BROW   1.39.12
  NOW WHILST THY BEAUTY BEARES WITHOUT A STAINE   1.40.3
  IN BASE ATTIRE, YET CLEERLY $BEAUTY SHINES   1.43.4
  BEAUTIE (SWEET $LOVE) IS LIKE THE MORNING DEW   1.50.1
  WHOSE BEAUTY MADE HIM SPEAKE THAT ELSE WAS DOMBE   1.55.8
  THEN JUDGE THE WORLD HER BEAUTY GIVES THE SAME   1.57.12
  BRIGHT STARRE OF $BEAUTY, ON WHOSE EYE-LIDS SIT   2.4.1

```
TIME HATH THY $BEAUTIE, WHICH WITH $AGE
                        WILL LEAVE THEE          2.10.12
WHERE $VERTUE, $HONOUR, $WIT, AND $BEAUTIE LAY   2.14.10
YOUR $BEAUTIE IS THE HOT AND SPLEND'ROUS $SUNNE  2.16.5
AS THE $WORLDS $BEAUTIE IN HIS $INFANCIE         2.17.7
AN $EVILL SPIRIT YOUR BEAUTIE HAUNTS $ME STILL   2.20.1
BUT HE WITH $BEAUTIE FIRST CORRUPTED $SIGHT      2.29.5
O, WHY SHOULD $BEAUTIE ($CUSTOME TO OBEY)        2.43.9
FROM THAT PROUD $BEAUTY, WHICH WAS MY BETRAYER+  2.52.12
BY THOSE REFLECTING $SUN-BEAMES OF THY BEAUTIE   2.105.8
THEN WITH THY BEAUTIE SET THE SAME ON FIRE       2.106.7
BEHOLD WORLDS $BEAUTIE IN HER INFANCIE           2.107.7
BEAUTY SOMETIME IN ALL HER GLORY CROWNED         2.109.1
AND THUS WHILST $BEAUTIE ON HER BEAUTY GAZED     2.109.5
AND THUS WHILST $BEAUTIE ON HER BEAUTY GAZED     2.109.5
THY FAYREST YOUTH AND $BEAUTIE DOE I SEE         2.114.6
RARE BEAUTY, $NATURES JOY, PERFECTIONS $MOTHER   2.123.2
HER $BOWE IS BEAUTY, WITH TEN THOUSAND STRINGS   2.126.6
SLEEPE IN THY $BEAUTY, $BEAUTY IN SLEEPE
                        APPEARETH                2.136.2
SLEEPE IN THY $BEAUTY, $BEAUTY IN SLEEPE
                        APPEARETH                2.136.2
SLEEPE LIGHTNING $BEAUTY, $BEAUTY SLEEPES
                        DARKNES CLEERETH         2.136.3
SLEEPE LIGHTNING $BEAUTY, $BEAUTY SLEEPES
                        DARKNES CLEERETH         2.136.3
SLEEPES WONDER $BEAUTY, WONDERS TO WORLDS
                        IMPARTING                2.136.4
SLEEP WATCHING $BEAUTY, $BEAUTY WAKING,
                        SLEEPE GUARDING          2.136.5
SLEEP WATCHING $BEAUTY, $BEAUTY WAKING,
                        SLEEPE GUARDING          2.136.5
BEAUTY IN SLEEPE, SLEEPE IN $BEAUTY CHARMED      2.136.6
BEAUTY IN SLEEPE, SLEEPE IN $BEAUTY CHARMED      2.136.6
SLEEPE WITH DELIGHT, $BEAUTY WITH LOVE REWARDING 2.136.8
SLEEPE AND $BEAUTY, WITH EQUALL FORCES STRYVING  2.136.9
BEAUTY HER STRENGTH UNTO SLEEPES WEAKNES
                        LENDING                  2.136.10
SLEEPE WITH $BEAUTY, $BEAUTY WITH SLEEPE
                        CONTENDING               2.136.11
SLEEPE WITH $BEAUTY, $BEAUTY WITH SLEEPE
                        CONTENDING               2.136.11
AND LET $INVENTION OF HER BEAUTY VAUNT           2.151.9
THEN BEING ASKT, WHERE ALL THY BEAUTIE LIES      3.2.5
PROOVING HIS BEAUTIE BY SUCCESSION THINE         3.2.12
THY UNUS'D BEAUTY MUST BE TOMB'D WITH THEE       3.4.13
BEAUTY ORE-SNOW'D AND BARENES EVERY WHERE        3.5.8
BEAUTIES EFFECT WITH BEAUTY WERE BEREFT          3.5.11
YET MORTALL LOOKES ADORE HIS BEAUTY STILL        3.7.7
THAT BEAUTY STILL MAY LIVE IN THINE OR THEE      3.10.14
HEREIN LIVES WISDOME, BEAUTY, AND INCREASE       3.11.5
THEN OF THY BEAUTY DO I QUESTION MAKE            3.12.9
SO SHOULD THAT BEAUTY WHICH YOU HOLD IN LEASE    3.13.5
AS TRUTH AND BEAUTIE SHAL TOGETHER THRIVE        3.14.11
IF I COULD WRITE THE BEAUTY OF YOUR EYES         3.17.5
STIRD BY A PAINTED BEAUTY TO HIS VERSE           3.21.2
FOR ALL THAT BEAUTY THAT DOTH COVER THEE         3.22.5
FOR WHETHER BEAUTY, BIRTH, OR WEALTH, OR WIT     3.37.5
THY BEAUTIE, AND THY YEARES FULL WELL BEFITS     3.41.3
AND CHIDE THY BEAUTY, AND THY STRAYING YOUTH     3.41.10
```

```
HERS BY THY BEAUTY TEMPTING HER TO THEE              3.41.13
THINE BY THY BEAUTIE BEEING FALSE TO ME              3.41.14
ON $HELLENS CHEEKE ALL ART OF BEAUTIE SET            3.53.7
THE ONE DOTH SHADDOW OF YOUR BEAUTIE SHOW            3.53.10
OH HOW MUCH MORE DOTH BEAUTIE BEAUTIOUS SEEME        3.54.1
PAINTING MY AGE WITH BEAUTY OF THY DAIES             3.62.14
MY SWEET LOVES BEAUTY, THOUGH MY LOVERS LIFE         3.63.12
HIS BEAUTIE SHALL IN THESE BLACKE LINES BE SEENE     3.63.13
HOW WITH THIS RAGE SHALL BEAUTIE HOLD A PLEA         3.65.3
OR WHO HIS SPOILE OR BEAUTIE CAN FORBID+             3.65.12
WHY SHOULD POORE BEAUTIE INDIRECTLY SEEKE            3.67.7
WHEN BEAUTY LIV'D AND DY'ED AS FLOWERS DO NOW        3.68.2
ROBBING NO OULD TO DRESSE HIS BEAUTY NEW             3.68.12
TO SHEW FAULSE $ART WHAT BEAUTY WAS OF YORE          3.68.14
THEY LOOKE INTO THE BEAUTY OF THY MIND               3.69.9
THE ORNAMENT OF BEAUTY IS SUSPECT                    3.70.3
FROM THY BEHAVIOUR, BEAUTIE DOTH HE GIVE             3.79.10
FOR I IMPAIRE NOT BEAUTIE BEING MUTE                 3.83.11
HOW LIKE $EAVES APPLE DOTH THY BEAUTY GROW           3.93.13
DOTH SPOT THE BEAUTIE OF THY BUDDING NAME+           3.95.3
FOR THY NEGLECT OF TRUTH IN BEAUTY DI'D+             3.101.2
BOTH TRUTH AND BEAUTY ON MY LOVE DEPENDS             3.101.3
BEAUTIE NO PENSELL, BEAUTIES TRUTH TO LAY            3.101.7
SUCH SEEMES YOUR BEAUTIE STILL.. $THREE
                          $WINTERS COLDE             3.104.3
AH YET DOTH BEAUTY LIKE A $DYALL HAND                3.104.9
AND BEAUTIE MAKING BEAUTIFULL OLD RIME               3.106.3
EVEN SUCH A BEAUTY AS YOU MAISTER NOW                3.106.8
TAN SACRED BEAUTIE, BLUNT THE SHARP'ST INTENTS       3.115.7
AND $BEAUTIE SLANDERD WITH A BASTARD SHAME           3.127.4
SWEET BEAUTY HATH NO NAME NO HOLY BOURE              3.127.7
AT SUCH WHO NOT BORNE FAIRE NO BEAUTY LACK           3.127.11
THAT EVERY TOUNG SAIES BEAUTY SHOULD LOOKE SO        3.127.14
THEN WILL I SWEARE BEAUTY HER SELFE IS BLACKE        3.132.13
THE STATUTE OF THY BEAUTY THOU WILT TAKE             3.134.9
THEY KNOW WHAT BEAUTIE IS, SEE WHERE IT LYES         3.137.3
WHAT $LOVE AND $BEAUTIE BE, THEN ALL MY DEED         4.3.13
TRUE, THAT TRUE $BEAUTIE $VERTUE IS INDEED           4.5.9
WHEREOF THIS $BEAUTIE CAN BE BUT A SHADE             4.5.10
VERTUE'S GREAT BEAUTIE IN THAT FACE I PROVE          4.25.13
PRINCESSE OF $BEAUTIE, FOR WHOSE ONLY SAKE           4.28.6
AND THEN, THINKE THUS, ALTHOUGH THY BEAUTIE BE       4.40.9
O EYES, WHICH DO THE $SPHEARES OF BEAUTIE MOVE       4.42.1
VERTUE AWAKE, $BEAUTIE BUT BEAUTIE IS                4.47.9
VERTUE AWAKE, $BEAUTIE BUT BEAUTIE IS                4.47.9
AND THEREFORE, THOUGH HER BEAUTIE AND HER GRACE      4.52.9
HOW $VERTUE MAY BEST LODG'D IN BEAUTIE BE            4.71.2
SO WHILE THY BEAUTIE DRAWES THE HEART TO LOVE        4.71.12
THAT FACE, WHOSE LECTURE SHEWES WHAT PERFECT
                          BEAUTIE. IS                4.77.2
SINCE ALL MY WORDS THY BEAUTY DOTH ENDITE            4.90.13
WHILE GRACEFULL PITTY BEAUTY BEAUTIFIES              4.100.4
BEAUTY IS SICKE, BUT SICKE IN SO FAIRE GUISE         4.101.5
THE SOVERAYNE BEAUTY WHICH I DOO ADMYRE              5.3.1
IN CHAST DESIRES ON HEAVENLY BEAUTY BOUND            5.8.8
THAT SO FAYRE BEAUTY WAS SO FOWLY SHAMED             5.41.14
BUT MERCY DOTH WITH BEAUTIE BEST AGREE               5.53.13
SO OFT AS I HER BEAUTY DOE BEHOLD                    5.55.1
THE GLORIOUS IMAGE OF THE MAKERS BEAUTIE             5.61.1
AND ALL THESE STORMES WHICH NOW HIS BEAUTY BLEND     5.62.11
```

```
WHERE WHEN THAT SOVERAYNE BEAUTY IT DOTH SPY        5.72.5
ON THE SWEET SPOYLE OF BEAUTIE THEY DID PRAY        5.76.8
THAT IS TRUE BEAUTIE.. THAT DOTH ARGUE YOU          5.79.9
AND PERFECT BEAUTY DID AT FIRST PROCEED             5.79.12
BEAUTY'S               44
AND THAT IN $BEAUTIES LEASE EXPIR'D, APPEARES       1.50.11
THESE TRIBUTARY PASSIONS, BEAUTIES DUE              1.60.5
THAT ALL THEIR $WEALTH LIES IN THY BEAUTIES
                          $BOOKES                   2.3.12
ONELY TO SHEW HER $BEAUTIES $SOV'RAIGNE $POW'R      2.50.14
THAT ALL HER WEALTH LYES IN THY $BEAUTIES
                          BOOKES                    2.110.12
DOWNE FELL HE IN THY $BEAUTIES $OCEAN DRENCHED      2.122.13
SEE HOW MY $DEERE COMES TO THY $BEAUTIES STAND      2.135.5
SWEETE SLEEPE SO ARM'D WITH $BEAUTIES
                          ARROWES DARTING           2.136.1
SLEEPES AGED COLDNES, WITH $BEAUTIES FIRE WARMED    2.136.7
AGAINST THE $FORTE WHERE $BEAUTIES $ARMY LIES       2.142.2
THAT THEREBY BEAUTIES $ROSE MIGHT NEVER DIE         3.1.2
AND DIGGE DEEP TRENCHES IN THY BEAUTIES FIELD       3.2.2
HOW MUCH MORE PRAISE DESERV'D THY BEAUTIES USE      3.2.9
UPON THY SELFE THY BEAUTIES LEGACY+                 3.4.2
BEAUTIES EFFECT WITH BEAUTY WERE BEREFT             3.5.11
WITH BEAUTITS TREASURE ERE IT BE SELFE KIL'D        3.6.4
BUT BEAUTIES WASTE HATH IN THE WORLD AN END         3.9.11
THY END IS $TRUTHES AND $BEAUTIES DOOME AND DATE    3.14.14
FOR BEAUTIES PATTERNE TO SUCCEDING MEN              3.19.12
THY BEAUTIES FORME IN TABLE OF MY HEART             3.24.2
AND DELVES THE PARALELS IN BEAUTIES BROW            3.60.10
ERE BEAUTIES DEAD FLEECE MADE ANOTHER GAY           3.68.8
WHERE BEAUTIES VAILE DOTH COVER EVERY BLOT          3.95.11
BEAUTIE NO PENSELL, BEAUTIES TRUTH TO LAY           3.101.7
ERE YOU WERE BORNE WAS BEAUTIES SUMMER DEAD         3.104.14
THEN IN THE BLAZON OF SWEET BEAUTIES BEST           3.106.5
OR IF IT WEARE IT BORE NOT BEAUTIES NAME            3.127.2
BUT NOW IS BLACKE BEAUTIES SUCCESSIVE HEIRE         3.127.3
THAT WHEREAS BLACKE SEEMES $BEAUTIE'S CONTRARY      4.7.10
WHICH $CUPID'S SELFE FROM $BEAUTIE'S MYNE
                          DID DRAW                  4.9.13
WHERE $VERTUE IS MADE STRONG BY $BEAUTIE'S MIGHT    4.48.2
IN $BEAUTIE'S THRONE, SEE NOW WHO DARES
                          COME NEARE                4.73.10
BEAUTIE'S PLAGUE, $VERTUE'S SCOURGE, SUCCOUR
                          OF LIES                   4.78.6
WHERE $BEAUTIE'S BLUSH IN $HONOUR'S GRAINE
                          IS DIDE                   4.80.8
SEE $BEAUTIE'S TOTALL SUMME SUMM'D IN HER FACE      4.85.10
SOME BEAUTIE'S PEECE, AS AMBER COLOURD HED          4.91.6
O TEARES, NO TEARES, BUT RAINE FROM BEAUTIE'S
                          SKIES                     4.100.1
THAT IN THAT PALENESSE BEAUTIE'S WHITE WE SEE       4.101.6
WHILE BEAUTIE'S REDDEST INKE $VENUS FOR
                          HIM DOTH STURRE           4.102.14
DOE BOTH APPEARE T'ADORNE HER BEAUTIES GRACE+       5.21.4
WHEN I BEHOLD THAT BEAUTIES WONDERMENT              5.24.1
GIVEN SO GOODLY GIFTES OF BEAUTIES GRACE+           5.31.2
AND THAT SAME GLORICUS BEAUTIES YOLE BOAST          5.41.9
OF MY LOVES CONQUEST, PEERELESSE BEAUTIES PRISE     5.69.7
BECALMED               1
WHERE MOST BECALM'D, WHERE WITH FOULE
                          $WEATHER SPENT            2.1.11
```

BECAUSE   22
  AND THUS I LIVE BECAUSE I LOVE HER DEERLY   1.16.14
  BECAUSE TH'ATTEMPT WAS FARRE ABOVE MY ART   1.36.7
  BECAUSE THEIR POWER SERVE TO EXACT THE SAME   1.47.12
  BECAUSE I LOOSELY TRIFLE IN THIS SORT   2.24.5
  AND I GIVE MUCH, BECAUSE I GAINE THEREBY   2.28.10
  THOU DOOST LOVE HER, BECAUSE THOU KNOWST
                       I LOVE HER   3.42.6
  BECAUSE HE NEEDS NO PRAISE, WILT THOU BE DUMB+   3.101.9
  BECAUSE I WOULD NOT DULL YOU WITH MY SONGE   3.102.14
  CUPID, BECAUSE THOU SHIN'ST IN $STELLAS EYES   4.12.1
  BECAUSE THAT $MARS, GROWNE SLACKER IN HER LOVE   4.17.2
  OR CARELESSE OF THE WEALTH BECAUSE HER OWNE   4.22.11
  OTHERS, BECAUSE THE $PRINCE MY SERVICE TRIES   4.23.7
  BECAUSE I OFT IN DARKE ABSTRACTED GUISE   4.27.1
  AND I, BUT FOR BECAUSE MY PROSPECT LIES   4.29.13
  OTHERS, BECAUSE OF BOTH SIDES I DO TAKE   4.41.9
  BECAUSE THEIR FOREFRONT BARE SWEET $STELLA'S
                       NAME   4.50.14
  BECAUSE I BREATHE NOT LOVE TO EVERIE ONE   4.54.1
  BUT THOU $DESIRE, BECAUSE THOU WOULDST HAVE ALL   4.72.13
  AND YET MY $STARRE, BECAUSE A SUGRED KISSE   4.73.5
  BECAUSE IN BRAVE ARRAY HEERE MARCHETH SHE   4.88.3
  BUT WHY+ BECAUSE OF YOU THEY MODELS BE   4.91.10
  IS IT BECAUSE YOUR EYES HAVE POWRE TO KILL+   5.49.2
BECK   2
  OH LET ME SUFFER (BEING AT YOUR BECK)   3.58.5
  RULES WITH A BECKE, SO TYRANNIZETH THEE   4.46.3
BECLOUDED   1
  PAINTED IN MY BECLOWDED STORMIE FACE   4.45.2
BECOME   5
  SHE MAY BECOME MORE KINDE TO THEE OR ME   1.23.14
  AND BY THAT HAND WHOM SUCH DEEDS ILL BECOME   1.31.14
  PITTY AND SMILES DOE BEST BECOME THE FAIRE   1.51.11
  AS THOSE TWO MORNING EYES BECOME THY FACE   3.132.9
  NO DOOME SHOULD MAKE ONE'S HEAV'N BECOME
                       HIS HELL   4.86.14
BECOMES   7
  AND THINKE THE SAME BECOMES THY FADING BEST   1.40.11
  MY HOPE BECOMES A FRIEND TO MY DESIRE   2.132.9
  BUT THAT YOUR TRESPASSE NOW BECOMES A FEE   3.120.13
  BETTER BECOMES THE GRAY CHEEKS OF TH' $EAST   3.132.6
  WHOSE NECKE BECOMES SUCH YOKE OF TYRANNY+   4.47.4
  BECOMES A CLOG) WILL SOONE EASE ME OF IT   4.59.14
  LOOKE EVER LOVELY, AS BECOMES YOU BEST   5.7.10
BECOMETH   1
  ME THINKES THIS $TIME BECOMMETH $LOVERS BEST   2.37.3
BECOMING   2
  YET SO THEY MOURNE BECOMMING OF THEIR WOE   3.127.13
  WHENCE HAST THOU THIS BECOMMING OF THINGS IL   3.150.5
BED   9
  WHEN $FAITH IS KNEELING BY HIS BED OF $DEATH   2.61.11
  THE GLORIOUS SUNNE WENT BLUSHING TO HIS BED   2.125.1
  WEARY WITH TOYLE, I HAST ME TO MY BED   3.27.1
  AS THE DEATH BED, WHEREON IT MUST EXPIRE   3.73.11
  TAKE THOU OF ME SMOOTH PILLOWES, SWEETEST BED   4.39.9
  PRAY THAT MY SUNNE GO DOWNE WITH MEEKER
                   BEAMES TO BED   4.76.14
  AH BED, THE FIELD WHERE JOYE'S PEACE SOME DO SEE   4.98.1
  STELLA IS SICKE, AND IN THAT SICKE BED LIES   4.101.1

HER GOODLY BOSOME LYKE A $STRAWBERRY BED	5.64.9

BEDECKED   1

| | |
| WITH MANY DEARE DELIGHTS BEDECKED FYNE | 5.71.12 |

BEDIM   1

| | |
| LET CLOUDS BEDIMME MY FACE, BREAKE IN MINE EYE | 4.64.5 |

BEDLAM   2

THUS TALKING IDLY IN THIS $BEDLAM FIT	2.9.9
AND $BEDLAM LIKE THUS RAVING IN MY GRIEFE	2.143.10

BEDLAM-LIKE   1

| | |
| AND $BEDLAM-LIKE, THUS RAVING IN MY $GRIEFE | 2.41.10 |

BEDS   1

| | |
| ROBD OTHERS BEDS REVENUES OF THEIR RENTS | 3.142.8 |

BED-VOW   1

| | |
| IN ACT THY BED-VOW BROAKE AND NEW FAITH TORNE | 3.152.3 |

BEE   2

YOUR SELFE UNTO THE $BEE YE DOE COMPARE	5.71.2
BETWEENE THE $SPYDER AND THE GENTLE $BEE	5.71.14

BEFITS   1

| | |
| THY BEAUTIE, AND THY YEARES FULL WELL BEFITS | 3.41.3 |

BEFORE   38

I GOE BEFORE UNTO THE $MIRTLE SHADES	1.30.5
GLORY DOTH FOLLOW, COURAGE GOES BEFORE	1.35.7
NOW JOY THY TIME BEFORE THY SWEET BE DONE	1.40.7
I THAT HAVE LOV'D THEE THUS BEFORE THOU FADST	1.41.7
FLOWERS HAVE A TIME BEFORE THEY COME TO SEEDE	1.51.3
AND LEARNE TO GATHER FLOWERS BEFORE THEY WITHER	1.51.6
YET STAND AS FREE AS ERE YOU DID BEFORE	2.14.12
STAY, SPEEDY $TIME, BEHOLD, BEFORE THOU PASSE	2.17.1
WHAT IT WAS THEN, AND THOU BEFORE IT WAS	2.17.8
BEFORE MY $FACE, IT LAYES DOWNE MY $DESPAIRES	2.20.9
BUT FALL TO BLEEDING, AS THEY DID BEFORE	2.46.12
AND OF HYS BLESSED BIRTH BEFORE FORE-TOLD	2.119.4
NOW DOE I SWEARE BY HEAVENS, BEFORE WE PART	2.140.3
SETS YOU MOST RICH IN YOUTH BEFORE MY SIGHT	3.15.10
WHICH I NEW PAY AS IF NOT PAYD BEFORE	3.30.12
WHAT HAST THOU THEN MORE THEN THOU HADST BEFORE+	3.40.2
ALL MINE WAS THINE, BEFORE THOU HADST THIS MORE	3.40.4
HATH BEENE BEFORE, HOW ARE OUR BRAINES BEGUILD	3.59.2
EACH CHANGING PLACE WITH THAT WHICH GOES BEFORE	3.60.3
IN DAIES LONG SINCE, BEFORE THESE LAST SO BAD	3.67.14
BEFORE THESE BASTARD SIGNES OF FAIRE WERE BORNE	3.68.3
BEFORE THE GOULDEN TRESSES OF THE DEAD	3.68.5
(THOUGH WORDS COME HIND-MOST) HOLDS HIS	
RANKE BEFORE	3.85.12
TO MARRE THE SUBJECT THAT BEFORE WAS WELL	3.103.10
THOSE LINES THAT I BEFORE HAVE WRIT DOE LIE	3.115.1
THEN THINKE THAT WE BEFORE HAVE HEARD THEM TOULD	3.123.8
BEFORE A JOY PROPOSD BEHIND A DREAME	3.129.12
TO FOLLOW THAT WHICH FLIES BEFORE HER FACE	3.143.7
HAVING NO SCARFE OF CLOWDS BEFORE HIS FACE	4.22.3
BEFORE SHE COULD PREPARE TO BE UNKIND	4.57.6
WILL SHE TAKE TIME, BEFORE ALL WRACKED BE+	4.67.4
WHAT SIGHES STOLNE OUT, OR KILD BEFORE	
FULL BORNE+	4.67.9
THAT WHERE BEFORE HART LOVED AND EYES DID SEE	4.88.12
AND IF THOSE FAYLE FALL DOWNE AND DY BEFORE HER	5.14.13
AND DOE MYNE HUMBLED HART BEFORE HER POURE	5.20.2
BUT LOTHE THE THINGS WHICH THEY DID LIKE BEFORE	5.35.11
AND DOE ME NOT BEFORE MY TIME TO DY	5.42.14
BUT LOATH THE THINGS WHICH THEY DID LIKE BEFORE	5.83.11

```
BEFRIENDS                      1
   THAT YOU WERE ONCE UNKIND BE-FRIENDS MEE NOW        3.120.1
BEG                            2
   KNOCKE AT THAT HARD HART, BEGGE TILL YOU
                               HAVE MOV'D HER          1.2.13
   I BEG NO SUBJECT TO USE ELOQUENCE                   4.28.9
BEGAN                          4
   WHEN FIRST I $ENDED, THEN I FIRST $BEGAN            2.62.1
   TO SHEW THEIR KINDE, BEGAN TO CLIME THE SKIES       2.103.10
   WHEN FIRST I ENDED, THEN I FIRST BEGAN              2.150.1
   BEGAN IN ME TO MOVE, ONE YEARE IS SPENT             5.60.6
BEGGAR                         1
   AS TO BEHOLD DESERT A BEGGER BORNE                  3.66.2
BEGGARED                       1
   BEGGERD OF BLOOD TO BLUSH THROUGH LIVELY VAINES     3.67.10
BEGGARS                        1
   WELL, WELL, MY $FRIENDS, WHEN $BEGGERS
                               GROW THUS BOLD          2.23.13
BEGGARY                        3
   WAND'RING ABROAD IN $NEED AND $BEGGERIE             2.23.2
   MAY GET NO ALMES BUT SCORNE OF BEGGERIE             4.47.8
   OF $LOVE, NEW-COIND TO HELPE MY BEGGERY             4.62.13
BEGGED                         1
   BY $SURGEONS BEG'D, THEIR $ART ON HIM TO TRIE       2.50.4
BEGIN                          9
   IN $LOVE THERE IS NO LACK, THUS I BEGIN             2.59.3
   THAT MINE EYE LOVES IT AND DOTH FIRST BEGINNE       3.114.14
   STELLA BEHOLD, AND THEN BEGIN TO ENDITE             4.15.14
   BUT WILT NEW WARRE UPON THINE OWNE BEGIN+           4.36.8
   DOTH $STELLA NOW BEGIN WITH PITEOUS EYE             4.67.2
   YOU CALME THE STORME THAT PASSION DID BEGIN         5.8.11
   I MUST BEGIN AND NEVER BRING TO END                 5.23.10
   THIS JOYOUS DAY, DEARE $LORD, WITH JOY BEGIN        5.68.5
   BEGIN HIS WITLESSE NOTE APACE TO CLATTER            5.85.4
BEGINNING                      1
   BEGINNING TO ACCOUNT THE SUM OF ALL MY CARES        2.110.2
BEGINS                         3
   BUT THEN BEGINS A JOURNY IN MY HEAD                 3.27.3
   THIS NIGHT WHILE SLEEPE BEGINS WITH HEAVY WINGS     4.38.1
   THE NEW BEGINS HIS COMPAST COURSE ANEW              5.62.2
BEGONE                         1
   SO WHEN I THINKE TO END THAT I BEGONNE              5.23.9
BEGOT                          2
   BEGOT BY FANCY, ON SWEET HOPE EXHORTIVE             2.141.2
   OF HOPES BEGOT BY FEARE, OF WOT NOT WHAT DESIRES    4.6.2
BEGUILE                        6
   AS ONE THAT FAINE HIS $SORROWES WOULD BEGUILE       2.24.6
   READING SOMETYME, MY SORROWES TO BEGUILE            2.120.1
   THOU DOO'ST BEGUILE THE WORLD, UNBLESSE
                               SOME MOTHER             3.3.4
   IS BUT A BAYT SUCH WRETCHES TO BEGUILE              5.41.10
   AND DYING DOE THEM SELVES OF PAYNE BEGUYLE          5.47.12
   AND FAINE MY GRIEFE WITH CHAUNGES TO BEGUILE        5.87.10
BEGUILED                       4
   HATH BEENE BEFORE, HOW ARE OUR BRAINES BEGUILD      3.59.2
   WITH WHAT PASTIME, TIME'S JOURNEY SHE BEGUILDE      4.92.12
   WITH PANTING HOUNDS BEGUILED OF THEIR PRAY          5.67.4
   SO GOODLY WONNE WITH HER OWNE WILL BEGUYLD          5.67.14
BEGUN                          11
   THE WORKE OF RIGOR, FATALLY BEGUN                   1.33.7
```

```
YOUR $LIFE SO LIKE THE $PHOENIXS BEGUN                 2.16.8
THOSE $PRIESTS WHICH FIRST THE $VESTALL
                          $FIRE BEGUN                  2.30.1
CALLING TO MINDE SINCE FIRST MY $LOVE BEGUN            2.51.1
TELL $ME, IF EVER SINCE THE $WORLD BEGUNNE             2.60.11
ME THINKES 'TIS LONG SINCE FIRST THESE
                          $WARRES BEGUN                2.63.2
SO BY THY DEATH, THY LIFE SHALL BE BEGUNNE             2.106.8
VOWES WERE MY VOWELS WHEN I THEN BEGUN                 2.111.5
NOW HAST THOU END, AND NOW THOU WAST BEGUN             2.141.12
TELL MEE, IF EVER SINCE THE WORLD BEGUNNE              2.149.11
WITH SHEW OF MORNING MYLDE HE HATH BEGUN               5.62.3
```
BEHAVIOR   1
```
FROM THY BEHAVIOUR, BEAUTIE DOTH HE GIVE               3.79.10
```
BEHELD   3
```
MYNE EYES BEHELD THYS CONFLICT IN THY FACE             2.136.14
OR EYES THAT HAVE BEHELD HER AS THEYR SUNNE            2.138.7
MINE EYES (SHALL I SAY CURST OR BLEST) BEHELD          4.16.10
```
BEHEST   1
```
ACCORDING TO MY $LORD $LOVE'S OWNE BEHEST              4.50.6
```
BEHIND   5
```
THAT THOU NO FORME OF THEE HAST LEFT BEHIND            3.9.6
MY GREEFE LIES ONWARD AND MY JOY BEHIND                3.50.14
BEFORE A JOY PROPOSD BEHIND A DREAME                   3.129.12
WHILST I THY BABE CHACE THEE A FARRE BEHIND            3.143.10
YET OF THAT BEST THOU LEAV'ST THE BEST BEHIND          4.11.4
```
BEHOLD   36
```
APPROACH NOT TO BEHOLD SO GREAT DISTRESSE              1.3.6
BEHOLD WHAT HAP $PIGMALION HAD TO FRAME                1.13.1
BEHOLD THE MESSAGE OF A CHAST DESIRE                   1.60.3
ONELY TWO $LOOPE-HOLES, THEN I MIGHT BEHOLD            2.8.4
STAY, SPEEDY $TIME, BEHOLD, BEFORE THOU PASSE          2.17.1
YOU THAT BEHOLD US, LAUGH US NOT TO SCORNE             2.22.11
NOTE BUT MY $SIGHES, AND THINE $EYES SHALL BEHOLD      2.55.5
BEHOLD THE $CLOUDS WHICH HAVE ECLIPS'D MY $SUNNE       2.60.9
NOTE BUT MY SIGHES, AND THINE EYES SHAL BEHOLD         2.102.5
STAY, STAY, SWEET $TIME, BEHOLD OR ERE
                          THOU PASSE                   2.107.1
BEHOLD WORLDS $BEAUTIE IN HER INFANCIE                 2.107.7
WHERE SHEE REMAINES FOR ALL EYES TO BEHOLD             2.109.14
O $EYES, BEHOLD YOUR HAPPY $HESPERUS                   2.129.1
THRICE HAPPY BE THOSE EYES WHICH MAY BEHOLD
                          THEE                         2.129.10
BEHOLD, THEIR OBJECTS OVER-SOONE DEPART                2.133.6
BEHOLD THE $CLOWDES WHICH HAVE ECLIPS'D MY SUNNE       2.149.9
WHEN YOU $MINERVA IN THE SUNNE BEHOLD                  2.151.5
WHEN I BEHOLD THE VIOLET PAST PRIME                    3.12.3
BUT WHEN IN THEE TIMES FORRWES I BEHOULD               3.22.3
AS TO BEHOLD DESERT A BEGGER BORNE                     3.66.2
THAT TIME OF YEEARE THOU MAIST IN ME BEHOLD            3.73.1
FOR WE WHICH NOW BEHOLD THESE PRESENT DAYES            3.106.13
YET IN GOOD FAITH SOME SAY THAT THEE BEHOLD            3.131.5
THAT THEY BEHOLD AND SEE NOT WHAT THEY SEE             3.137.2
STELLA BEHOLD, AND THEN BEGIN TO ENDITE                4.15.14
AND SO NOR WILL, NOR CAN, BEHOLD THOSE SKIES           4.25.7
WHEN YE BEHOLD THAT $ANGELS BLESSED LOOKE              5.1.11
WELL IS HE BORNE, THAT MAY BEHOLD YOU EVER             5.8.14
BUT THAT WHICH FAIREST IS, BUT FEW BEHOLD              5.15.13
WHEN I BEHOLD THAT BEAUTIES WONDERMENT                 5.24.1
STILL TO BEHOLD THE OBJECT OF THEIR PAINE              5.35.2
```

```
MOST LIVELY LYKE BEHOLD YOUR SEMBLANT TREW         5.45.4
SO OFT AS I HER BEAUTY DCE BEHOLD                  5.55.1
AND LET MY THOUGHTS BEHCLD HER SELFE IN MEE        5.78.14
STILL TO BEHOLD THE OBJECT OF THEYR PAYNE          5.83.2
ONELY BEHOLD HER RARE PERFECTION                   5.84.13
BEHOLDER             1
AT EVERY RASH BEHCLDER PASSING BY                  5.16.8
BEHOLDING            4
BEHOLDING ME THAT ALL THE PAGEANTS PLAY            5.54.3
YET SHE BEHOLDING ME WITH CONSTANT EYE             5.54.9
THERE SHE BEHOLDING ME WITH MYLDER LOOKE           5.67.9
OF WHICH BEHOLDING THE $IDAEA PLAYNE               5.88.9
BEHOLDS              1
WHERE HEAVEN BEHOLDS HER IN A MORTALL GLASSE       2.107.4
BEING               55
FOR BEING FULL, SHCULD I NOT THEN HAVE SPOKEN      1.7.13
BEING MERCILES LIKE THEE THAT NO MAN WEIES+        1.23.8
I LOVE TH'EFFECT THE CAUSE BEING OF THIS POWRE     1.26.11
FAITH BEING WITH BLCOD, AND FIVE YEARES
                        WITNES SIGN'D              1.31.6
TRANSPORTED FROM MY $SELFE, INTO $YOUR BEING       2.11.5
THAT BEING CHID, DID NEVER WORD REPLIE             2.15.10
WHICH BEING KINDLEC BY THAT HEAV'NLY FIRE          2.16.7
BEING STEDFASTLY CPPOSED TO THE SAME               2.30.4
OR BEING $BLIND (AS FITTEST FOR THE $TRADE)        2.48.9
THEN BEING ASKT, WHERE ALL THY BEAUTIE LIES        3.2.5
AND BEING FRANCK SHE LENDS TO THOSE ARE FREE       3.4.4
WHOSE SPEECHLESSE SCNG BEING MANY, SEEMING ONE     3.8.13
AS THOU BEING MINE, MINE IS THY GOOD REPCRT        3.36.14
THINE BY THY BEAUTIE BEEING FALSE TO ME            3.41.14
MY LIFE BEING MADE CF FCURE, WITH TWO ALCNE        3.45.7
HIS RIDER LOV'D NCT SPEED BEING MADE FROM THEE     3.50.8
THEREFORE DESIRE (CF PERFECTS LOVE BEING MADE)     3.51.10
BEING HAD TO TRYUMPH, BEING LACKT TO HOPE          3.52.14
BEING HAD TO TRYUMPH, BEING LACKT TO HOPE          3.52.14
AS CAL IT $WINTER, WHICH BEING FUL OF CARE         3.56.13
BEING YOUR SLAVE WHAT SHOULD I DOE BUT TEND        3.57.1
BEING YOUR VASSAIL BOUND TO STAIE YOUR LEISURE     3.58.4
OH LET ME SUFFER (BEING AT YOUR BECK)              3.58.5
CRAWLES TO MATURITY, WHEREWITH BEING CROWN'D       3.60.6
THEIR WORTH THE GREATER BEEING WOO'D OF TIME       3.70.6
EITHER NOT ASSAYLD, OR VICTOR BEEING CHARG'D       3.70.10
THE PRAY OF WORMES, MY BCDY BEING DEAD             3.74.10
OR (BEING WRACKT) I AM A WORTHLESSE BOTE           3.80.11
AND TOUNGS TO BE, YCUR BEEING SHALL REHEARSE       3.81.11
THAT YOU YOUR SELFE BEING EXTANT WELL MIGHT SHOW   3.83.6
WHICH SHALL BE MOST MY GLORY BEING DOMBE           3.83.10
FOR I IMPAIRE NOT BEAUTIE BEING MUTE               3.83.11
BEING FOND ON PRAISE, WHICH MAKES YOUR
                        PRAISES WORSE              3.84.14
WITH MINE OWNE WEAKENESSE BEING BEST ACQUAINTED    3.88.5
AS THOU BEING MINE, MINE IS THY GOOD REPORT        3.96.14
OR WHETHER DOTH MY MINDE BEING CROWN'D WITH YOU    3.114.1
EVEN SO BEING FULL CF YCUR NERE CLOYING
                        SWEETNESSE                 3.118.5
WHEN NOT TO BE, RECEIVES REPROACH OF BEING         3.121.2
AND YET THOU WILT, FOR I BEING PENT IN THEE        3.133.13
SO THOU BEEING RICH IN $WILL ADDE TO THY $WILL     3.135.11
BUT BEING BOTH FRCM ME BCTH TO EACH FRIEND         3.144.11
AS WHO BY BEING PCISOND DOTH POISON KNOW           4.16.14
```

```
AND IF THESE THINGS, AS BEING THINE BY RIGHT        4.39.12
I LODG'D THEE IN MY HEART, AND BEING BLIND          4.65.7
BY BEING PLACED IN SUCH A WRETCH AS I               4.94.14
THAT BEING NOW WITH HER HUGE BRIGTNESSE DAZED        5.3.5
AND BEING CAUGHT MAY CRAFTILY ENFOLD                5.37.7
FONDNESSE IT WERE FOR ANY BEING FREE                5.37.13
AS BEING LONG IN HER LOVES TEMPEST TOST             5.41.11
WHOME BEING CAUGHT SHE KILLS WITH CRUELL PRYDE       5.47.7
FOR BEING AS SHE IS DIVINELY WROUGHT                 5.61.5
BEING WITH THY DEARE BLOOD CLENE WASHT FROM SIN      5.68.7
BEING MY SELFE CAPTYVED HERE IN CARE                 5.73.1
THE FIRST MY BEING TO ME GAVE BY KIND                5.74.5
GIVE LEAVE TO REST ME BEING HALFE FORDONNE           5.80.3
BELAY                        1
THEN THOSE SMALL FORTS WHICH YE WERE WONT BELAY      5.14.6
BELIED                       1
AS ANY SHE BELI'D WITH FALSE COMPARE               3.130.14
BELIEVE                      5
WHO WILL BELEEVE MY VERSE IN TIME TO COME            3.17.1
AND THEN BELEEVE ME, MY LOVE IS AS FAIRE            3.21.10
NEVER BELEEVE THOUGH IN MY NATURE RAIGN'D            3.109.9
I DO BELEEVE HER THOUGH I KNOW SHE LYES              3.138.2
TO MAKE MY SELFE BELEEVE, THAT ALL IS WELL           4.2.13
BELIEVED                     1
MADDE SLANDERERS BY MADDE EARES BELEEVED BE         3.140.12
BELL                         1
THEN YOU SHALL HEARE THE SURLY SULLEN BELL           3.71.2
BELLAMOURES                  1
HER SNOWY BROWES LYKE BUDDED $BELLAMOURES            5.64.7
BELLOWS                      2
MY $SIGHES THE $BELLOWES, WHICH THE $FLAME
                            ENCREASETH              2.40.5
MY SIGHES, THE BELLOWES WHICH THE FLAME
                            INCREASETH             2.144.5
BELONG                       3
AS THOUGH TO ME IT NOTHING DID BELONG               2.47.12
TO WHAT YOU WILL, TO YOU IT DOTH BELONG             3.58.11
SUCH IS MY LOVE, TO THEE I SO BELONG                3.88.13
BELONGS                      2
TO HEARE WIT EIES BELONGS TO LOVES FINE WIHT        3.23.14
I SEE, A BETTER STATE TO ME BELONGS                  3.92.7
BELOVED                      5
GRAUNT IF THOU WILT, THOU ART BELOV'D OF MANY        3.10.3
THEN HAPPY I THAT LOVE AND AM BELOVED               3.25.13
THY SWEET BELOVED NAME NO MORE SHALL DWELL           3.89.10
NOR MY BELOVED AS AN $IDOLL SHOW                     3.105.2
MORE WORTHY I TO BE BELOV'D OF THEE                 3.150.14
BELOW                        2
THE AYRE WITH SIGHES, THE EARTH BELOW
                            WITH TEARES+            1.21.6
THUS SORING STILL, NOT LOOKING ONCE BELOW            2.122.9
BEMOAN                       1
FOR THOUGH I OFT MY SELFE OF THEM BEMONE             4.48.9
BEMOANING                    2
IN GRIEVOUS $PASSIONS, MY $WOES STILL BEMONING       2.40.8
IN GREEVOUS PASSIONS MY WOES STYLL BEMONING         2.144.8
BEMOANS                      1
MY MIND BEMONES HIS SENSE OF INWARD SMART            4.44.2
BEND                         7
SHALT BEND THY WRINCKLES HOMEWARD TO THE EARTH       1.50.10
```

```
THOUGH MY $CONCEIT I FURTHER SEEME TO BEND          2.34.10
I SEE MY COURSE TO LOSE MY SELFE DOTH BEND          4.18.12
'SCHOLLER,' SAITH $LOVE, 'BEND HITHERWARD
                        YOUR WIT'                    4.19.14
SOULE'S JOY, BEND NOT THOSE MORNING STARRES
                        FROM ME                      4.48.1
BUT BEND YOUR FORCE AGAINST YOUR ENEMYES            5.49.8
SO DOE I HOPE HER STUBBORNE HART TO BEND            5.51.11
BENDING              2
FOR BENDING ALL MY LOVING THOUGHTS ON THEE          3.88.10
WITHIN HIS BENDING SICKLES COMPASSE COME            3.116.10
BENDS                5
YET HOW SHEE BENDS TOWARDS THAT BLESSED $COAST       2.134.12
OR BENDS WITH THE REMOVER TO REMOVE                 3.116.4
BENDS ALL HIS POWERS, EVEN UNTO $STELLA'S GRACE     4.27.14
AS FAST THY $VERTUE BENDS THAT LOVE TO GOOD          4.71.13
NETHER TO ONE HER SELFE NOR OTHER BENDS             5.59.12
BENEFIT              2
THAT AM DEBARD THE BENIFIT OF REST+                 3.28.2
O BENEFIT OF ILL, NOW I FIND TRUE                   3.119.9
BENIGHTED            1
BENIGHTED IN COLD WO, BUT NOW APPEARES MY DAY        4.76.3
BENT                 5
BEYOND THE BENT OF HIS UNKNOWING $SIGHT             2.43.8
NOW WHILE THE WORLD IS BENT MY DEEDS TO CROSSE      3.90.2
CRIES TO CATCH HER WHOSE BUSIE CARE IS BENT         3.143.6
ON $CUPID'S BOW HOW ARE MY HEART-STRINGS BENT       4.19.1
WAS NOT IN FAULT, WHO BENT THY DAZLING RACE         4.105.6
BEQUEATH             2
BEQUEATH THE HEAVENS THE STARRES THAT I ADORE       1.19.3
WITH ONE THRICE-MARRY'D'S $PRAY'RS, THAT
                        DID BEQUEATH                 2.15.11
BEQUEATHED           1
BEQUEATH'D HIS WARDSHIP TO MY SOVERAIGNES EYE       2.116.12
BEQUEST              1
NATURES BEQUEST GIVES NOTHING BUT DOTH LEND          3.4.3
BEREFT               2
THIS EARTH OF THOSE SWEET $PROPHETS HATH BEREFT     2.119.6
BEAUTIES EFFECT WITH BEAUTY WERE BEREFT             3.5.11
BESEECHERS           1
LET NO UNKINDE, NO FAIRE BESEECHERS KILL            3.135.13
BESEEM               1
O LET IT THEN AS WELL BESEEME THY HEART             3.132.10
BESEEN               1
THAT GOODLY $IDOLL NOW SO GAY BESEENE               5.27.5
BESET                1
THE SHORES BESET WITH THOUSAND SECRET SPYES         2.122.3
BESHREW              1
BESHREW THAT HEART THAT MAKES MY HEART TO GROANE    3.133.1
BESIDE               2
THEN WHEN IT HATH MY ADDED PRAISE BESIDE            3.103.4
YET MANY WONDROUS THINGS THERE ARE BESIDE           5.17.8
BESIDES              2
WHO WITH HIS FEARE IS PUT BESIDES HIS PART          3.23.2
THAT ALL THE WORLD BESIDES ME THINKES
                        Y'ARE DEAD                   3.112.14
BESIEGE              2
WHEN FORTIE $WINTERS SHALL BESEIGE THY BROW          3.2.1
ALL FRAILTIES THAT BESIEGE ALL KINDES OF BLOOD      3.109.10
```

BESMEARED   1
   THEN UNSWEPT STONE, BESMEER'D WITH SLUTTISH TIME   3.55.4
BEST   64
    YOU BEST CAN JUDGE THE WRONGS THAT SHE HATH DONE   1.3.12
    BEST IN MY FACE, HOW CARES HAVE TILD DEEPE
                    FORROWES   1.4.8
    IF THIS HER WORST, HOW SHOULD HER BEST INFLAME+   1.17.11
    WHOSE STATE BEST SHEWES THE FORCE OF MURDERING
                    EIES+   1.37.4
    UPON MY SELFE THOU BEST MAYST FINDE THE FORME   1.37.8
    FOR WHAT SHE WAS, SHE BEST SHALL FIND IN YOU   1.38.12
    AND THINKE THE SAME BECOMES THY FADING BEST   1.40.11
    OR THAT MY WITS HAVE SHEWED THE BEST THEY COULD   1.44.3
    PITTY AND SMILES DOE BEST BECOME THE FAIRE   1.51.11
    NEPTUNES BEST DARLING, HELD BETWEENE HIS ARMES   1.53.10
    WHICH BEST BY YOU, OF LIVING $THINGS, IS KNOWNE   2.16.3
    ME THINKES THIS $TIME BECOMMETH $LOVERS BEST   2.37.3
    YOU BEST DISCERN'D OF MY $MINDS INWARD $EYES   2.57.1
    MY SWEET, MY FAIRE, MY GOOD, MY BEST OF ALL   2.115.12
    LOOKE WHOM SHE BEST INDOW'D, SHE GAVE THE MORE   3.11.11
    AND PERSPECTIVE IT IS BEST $PAINTERS ART   3.24.4
    LOOKE WHAT IS BEST, THAT BEST I WISH IN THEE   3.37.13
    LOOKE WHAT IS BEST, THAT BEST I WISH IN THEE   3.37.13
    WHEN MOST I WINKE THEN DOE MINE EYES BEST SEE   3.43.1
    THOU BEST OF DEEREST, AND MINE ONELY CARE   3.48.7
    SHALL TIMES BEST $JEWELL FROM TIMES CHEST
                    LIE HID+   3.65.10
    NOW COUNTING BEST TO BE WITH YOU ALONE   3.75.7
    SO ALL MY BEST IS DRESSING OLD WORDS NEW   3.76.11
    WITH MINE OWNE WEAKENESSE BEING BEST ACQUAINTED   3.88.5
    ALL THESE I BETTER IN ONE GENERALL BEST   3.91.8
    BUT BEST IS BEST, IF NEVER INTERMIXT   3.101.8
    BUT BEST IS BEST, IF NEVER INTERMIXT   3.101.8
    THEN IN THE BLAZON OF SWEET BEAUTIES BEST   3.106.5
    AND WORSE ESSAIES PROV'D THEE MY BEST OF LOVE   3.110.8
    THEN GIVE ME WELCOME, NEXT MY HEAVEN THE BEST   3.110.13
    CREATING EVERY BAD A PERFECT BEST   3.114.7
    MIGHT I NOT THEN SAY NOW I LOVE YOU BEST   3.115.10
    YET WHAT THE BEST IS, TAKE THE WORST TO BE   3.137.4
    ALTHOUGH SHE KNOWES MY DAYES ARE PAST THE BEST   3.138.6
    O LOVES BEST HABIT IS IN SEEMING TRUST   3.138.11
    WHEN ALL MY BEST DOTH WORSHIP THY DEFECT   3.149.11
    THAT IN MY MINDE THY WORST ALL BEST EXCEEDS+   3.150.8
    IN OBJECT BEST TO KNIT AND STRENGTH OUR SIGHT   4.7.6
    WHICH DARE CLAIME FROM THOSE LIGHTS THE
                    NAME OF BEST   4.9.11
    THAT WHEN THE HEAV'N TO THEE HIS BEST DISPLAYES   4.11.3
    YET OF THAT BEST THOU LEAV'ST THE BEST BEHIND   4.11.4
    YET OF THAT BEST THOU LEAV'ST THE BEST BEHIND   4.11.4
    MY BEST WITS STILL THEIR OWNE DISGRACE INVENT   4.19.5
    AND NOT IN $NATURE FOR BEST FRUITS UNFIT   4.19.13
    THAT MAKES ME OFT MY BEST FRIENDS OVERPASSE   4.27.12
    TO PORTRAIT THAT WHICH IN THIS WORLD IS BEST   4.50.8
    HOW THEIR BLACKE BANNER MIGHT BE BEST DISPLAID   4.55.8
    IN WELL RAISDE NOTES, MY PEN THE BEST IT MAY   4.70.10
    WISE SILENCE IS BEST MUSICKE UNTO BLISSE   4.70.14
    HOW $VERTUE MAY BEST LODG'D IN BEAUTIE BE   4.71.2
    IN VERSE, AND THAT MY VERSE BEST WITS
                    DOTH PLEASE+   4.74.11
    MAKES ME IN MY BEST THOUGHTS AND QUIETST
                    JUDGEMENT SEE   4.77.12

```
YET AH, MY $MAYD'N $MUSE DOTH BLUSH TO
                          TELL THE BEST          4.77.14
BEST CHARGE, AND BRAVEST RETRAIT IN $CUPID'S
                          FIGHT                  4.79.5
SINCE BEST WITS THINKE IT WIT THEE TO ADMIRE     4.80.2
THAT SICKENESSE BRAGS IT SELFE BEST GRACED TO BE 4.101.4
LOOKE EVER LOVELY, AS BECOMES YOU BEST           5.7.10
THE HEAVENS KNOW BEST WHAT IS THE BEST FOR ME    5.46.6
THE HEAVENS KNOW BEST WHAT IS THE BEST FOR ME    5.46.6
FIT MEDICINES FOR MY BODIES BEST RELIEFE         5.50.4
BUT MERCY DOTH WITH BEAUTIE BEST AGREE           5.53.13
AS IN THEYR MAKER YE THEM BEST MAY SEE           5.53.14
THEN SITH TO HEAVEN YE LYKENED ARE THE BEST      5.55.13
BUT HE MOST HAPPY WHO SUCH ONE LOVES BEST        5.59.14
BEST-GRACED                   1
ADMITTED LATE BY YOUR BEST-GRACED GRACE          4.82.10
BESTOW                        2
  HE DID BESTOW IN TEMPER OF THE $MIND           2.14.8
  IN THY SOULES THOUGHT (ALL NAKED) WILL BESTOW IT  3.26.8
BESTOWEST                     1
  AND THAT FRESH BLOUD WHICH YONGLY THOU BESTOW'ST  3.11.3
BESTOWING                     1
  BESTOWING ALL HER $EXCELLENCE ON YOU           2.57.7
BESTOWS                       2
  THAT FULL OF BEAUTY, TIME BESTOWES UPON HER    1.39.4
  OF ALL THE POWERS WHICH LIFE BESTOWES ON ME    4.107.2
BETOKENING                    1
  BETOKENING PEACE AND PLENTY TO ENSEW           5.62.4
BETRAY                        2
  HOW MANY $LAMBS MIGHT THE STERNE $WOLFE BETRAY 3.96.9
  FOR THOU BETRAYING ME, I DOE BETRAY            3.151.5
BETRAYED                      2
  TO CRUELL $LOVE MY $SOULE WAS FIRST BETRAY'D   2.29.14
  WHAT, HAVE I THUS BETRAYED MY LIBERTIE+        4.47.1
BETRAYER                      1
  FROM THAT PROUD $BEAUTY, WHICH WAS MY BETRAYER+ 2.52.12
BETRAYING                     2
  TO MY LYVES FOE HER $CHIEFTAINE STILL BETRAYING 2.142.8
  FOR THOU BETRAYING ME, I DOE BETRAY            3.151.5
BETRAYS                       2
  AND PRODIGALL OF HOWERS AND YEARES BETRAIES    1.23.11
  HER VOYCE BETRAIES ME TO HER HAND AND EYE      1.27.9
BETTER                       35
  SO RARE A FAITH OUGHT BETTER BE REWARDED       1.11.8
  HOPING THEREBY TO FREE MY BETTER PART          1.27.4
  I LOVE AS WELL, THOUGH HE COULD BETTER SHOW IT 1.43.8
  FOR THOUGH THAT $LAURA BETTER LIMNED BE        1.43.13
  DIVIDED FROM THE WORLD, AS BETTER WORTH        1.53.11
  WHERE I INTOMB'D, MY BETTER PART SHALL SAVE    2.44.12
  THAT RAPT IN $SPIRIT, IN BETTER $WORLDS
                          HATH BEENE             2.57.11
NOR THOU, NOR I, THE BETTER YET CAN HAVE         2.63.3
TO MARCH IN RANCKES OF BETTER EQUIPAGE           3.32.12
BUT SINCE HE DIED AND $POETS BETTER PROVE        3.32.13
WHEN THOU ART ALL THE BETTER PART OF ME+         3.39.2
WHETHER WE ARE MENDED, OR WHERE BETTER THEY      3.59.11
MY SPIRIT IS THINE THE BETTER PART OF ME         3.74.8
KNOWING A BETTER SPIRIT DOTH USE YOUR NAME       3.80.2
AND THEIR GROSSE PAINTING MIGHT BE BETTER US'D   3.82.13
COMES HOME AGAINE, ON BETTER JUDGEMENT MAKING    3.87.12
```

```
ALL THESE I BETTER IN ONE GENERALL BEST              3.91.8
I SEE, A BETTER STATE TO ME BELONGS                  3.92.7
THAT DID NOT BETTER FOR MY LIFE PROVIDE              3.111.3
THAT BETTER IS, BY EVIL STILL MADE BETTER           3.119.10
THAT BETTER IS, BY EVIL STILL MADE BETTER           3.119.10
TIS BETTER TO BE VILE THEN VILE ESTEEMED            3.121.1
BETTER BECOMES THE GRAY CHEEKS OF TH' $EAST          3.132.6
IF I MIGHT TEACH THEE WITTE BETTER IT WEARE          3.140.5
THE BETTER ANGELL IS A MAN RIGHT FAIRE               3.144.3
TEMPTETH MY BETTER ANGEL FROM MY SIGHT               3.144.6
OF $STELLA'S BROWES MADE HIM TWO BETTER BOWES        4.17.10
I, SEEING BETTER SIGHTS IN SIGHT'S DECAY             4.38.12
THAT GIV'ST NO BETTER EARE TO MY JUST CRIES          4.65.2
LOOKE ON AGAINE, THE FAIRE TEXT BETTER TRIE          4.67.7
YET BETTER WERE ATTONCE TO LET ME DIE                5.25.5
WHOSE PRYDE DEPRAVES EACH OTHER BETTER PART          5.31.3
THAT SHE THE BETTER MAY IN BLOODY BATH               5.31.11
WELL WORTHY THOU TO HAVE FOUND BETTER HYRE           5.48.5
THAT NETHER WILL FOR BETTER BE ALLURED               5.59.3
BETTERED                1
THEN BETTERD THAT THE WORLD MAY SEE MY PLEASURE      3.75.8
BETTERING               2
COMPARE THEM WITH THE BETT'RING OF THE TIME          3.32.5
SOME FRESHER STAMPE OF THE TIME BETTERING DAYES      3.82.8
BETWEEN                 7
NEPTUNES BEST DARLING, HELD BETWEENE HIS ARMES       1.53.10
THOU SETST A BATE BETWEENE MY WILL AND WIT           4.4.2
PHOEBUS WAS $JUDGE BETWEENE $JOVE, $MARS,
                        AND $LOVE                    4.13.1
TH'INDIFFERENT $JUDGE BETWEENE THE HIGH AND LOW      4.39.4
A STRIFE IS GROWNE BETWEENE $VERTUE AND $LOVE        4.52.1
BETWEENE THE JAWES OF HELLISH $JEALOUSIE             4.78.4
BETWEENE THE $SPYDER AND THE GENTLE $BEE             5.71.14
BETWIXT                 2
WHAT WILL $YOU KEEPE A MEANE THEN BETWIXT EITHER+    2.19.7
BETWIXT MINE EYE AND HEART A LEAGUE IS TOOKE         3.47.1
BEVEL                   1
I MAY BE STRAIGHT THOUGH THEY THEM-SELVES
                        BE BEVEL                     3.121.11
BEWAIL                  1
MYNE EYES WANT TEARES THUS TO BEWAYLE MY WOE         2.143.5
BEWAILED                1
LEAST MY BEWAILED GUILT SHOULD DO THEE SHAME         3.36.10
BEWARE                  1
BEWARE FULL SAILES DROWNE NOT THY TOTTRING BARGE     4.85.2
BEWEEP                  1
I ALL ALONE BEWEEPE MY OUT-CAST STATE                3.29.2
BEWITCH                 1
YOU DOE BEWITCH $ME, $O THAT I COULD FLIE            2.11.13
BEWRAY                  4
LEAST MY SAD LOOKES BEWRAY ME HOW I FARE             1.29.12
BEWRAY UNTO THE WORLD HOW FAIRE THOU ART             1.44.2
AS DO BEWRAY A WANT OF INWARD TUCH                   4.15.10
BEWRAY IT SELFE IN MY LONG SETLED EYES               4.23.2
BEWRAYED                2
FOR HER NO SOONER HAD MINE EYES BEWRAID              1.5.5
NO $SUNNE MY BLUSH AND ERROR HAD BEWRAID             1.7.7
BEWRAYING               1
MY TONGUE IN PAYNE, MY HARTS COUNSELS BEWRAYING      2.142.6
```

BEWRAYS   1
    BEWRAIES MY LOVE, WITH BROKEN WORDS HALFE SPOKEN   1.15.6
BEYOND   7
    THAT FARRE BEYOND $PROMETHEUS DID ASPIRE   2.14.4
    SO YOU OF $TIME SHALL LIVE BEYOND THE $END   2.16.14
    WHO DOTED ON THE $OCLT BEYOND ALL MEASURE   2.21.10
    RAVISH'D A $WORLD BEYOND THE FARTHEST $THOUGHT   2.34.2
    BEYOND THE BENT OF HIS UNKNOWING $SIGHT   2.43.8
    BEYOND ALL DATE EVEN TO ETERNITY   3.122.4
    THEE TO THY WRACKE BEYOND THY LIMITS STRAINE   4.85.4
BID   5
    AND BID THEM MOURNE, NAY MORE, DESPAIRE
                            WITH THEE   2.17.13
    IF WHEN $NIGHT COMES, YOU BID ME GOE AWAY   2.37.14
    WHEN YOU HAVE BID YOUR SERVANT ONCE ADIEUE   3.57.8
    AND THEN WITH PATIENCE BID ME BEARE MY FIRE   4.56.14
    BID HER THEREFORE HER SELFE SOONE READY MAKE   5.70.9
BIDDEN   1
    BID'N, PERHAPS HE FETCHETH THEE A GLOVE   4.59.7
BIDDING   1
    AND BIDDING TH'OLD $ADIEU, HIS PASSED DATE   5.4.3
BIDE   4
    AND PATIENCE TAME, TO SUFFERANCE BIDE EACH CHECK   3.58.7
    IS MORE THEN MY ORE-PREST DEFENCE CAN BIDE+   3.139.8
    THE NEW $PERNASSUS, WHERE THE $MUSES BIDE   4.80.5
    SOUGHT NOT TO FLY, BUT FEARELESSE STILL DID BIDE   5.67.10
BIDS   6
    SITTING ALONE, $LOVE BIDS ME GOE AND WRITE   2.38.1
    SITTING ALONE, LOVE BIDS ME GOE AND WRITE   2.131.1
    AND TO THE PAINTED BANQUET BIDS MY HEART   3.47.6
    BIDS ALL OLD THOUGHTS TO DIE IN DUMPISH SPRIGHT   5.4.4
    BUT WHEN I PLEADE, SHE BIDS ME PLAY MY PART   5.18.9
    MY CRUELL FAYRE STREIGHT BIDS ME WEND MY WAY   5.46.2
BIG   1
    THE TEEMING $AUTUMNE BIG WITH RITCH INCREASE   3.97.6
BILLING   1
    BUT YOU MUST NEEDS WITH THOSE LIPS BILLING BE+   4.83.12
BIND   5
    ILE BINDE HER THEN WITH MY TORNE-TRESSED HAIRE   2.115.13
    UNDER THAT BOND THAT HIM AS FAST DOTH BINDE   3.134.8
    THE $ORATOUR SO FARRE MEN'S HARTS DOTH BIND   4.58.2
    THOU WHOM TO ME SUCH MY GOOD TURNES SHOULD BIND   4.65.3
    LET HER, YF PLEASE HER, BYND WITH ADAMANT CHAYNE   5.42.10
BIRD   6
    EACH $BIRD SINGS TO HER SELFE, AND SO WILL I   1.59.14
    WHILST $LOVE (MY $PHOENIX BIRD) IN HER
                            OWN FLAME IS DYING   2.117.12
    OF BIRD, OF FLOWRE, OR SHAPE WHICH IT DOTH LACK   3.113.6
    AT SIGHT WHEREOF EACH BIRD THAT SITS ON SPRAY   5.40.9
    THE GENTLE BIRDE FEELES NO CAPTIVITY   5.65.7
    LYKE AS A BYRD THAT IN ONES HAND DOTH SPY   5.73.5
BIRDS   6
    WHICH PROOV'D MY BIRDS DELIGHTED IN THE AYRE   2.103.7
    BARE RN'WD QUIERS, WHERE LATE THE SWEET
                            BIRDS SANG   3.73.4
    AND THOU AWAY, THE VERY BIRDS ARE MUTE   3.97.12
    YET NOR THE LAIES OF BIRDS, NOR THE SWEET SMELL   3.98.5
    BUT WHEN BIRDS CHARME, AND THAT SWEETE
                            AIRE, WHICH IS   4.99.9
    WITH NOYSE WHEREOF THE QUYRE OF $BYRDS RESOUNDED   5.19.5

```
BIRD'S                         1
  OF THE $BIRDS KIND, THE $PHOENIX IS ALONE          2.16.2
BIRTH                         11
  MY JOYES ABORTIVE, PERISH IN THEIR BYRTH           1.60.11
  THOU WHICH HAST BANN'D THY $THOUGHTS,
                      AND CURST THY $BIRTH           2.49.11
  AND OF HYS BLESSED BIRTH BEFORE FORE-TOLD          2.119.4
  A DEARER BIRTH THEN THIS HIS LOVE HAD BROUGHT      3.32.11
  FOR WHETHER BEAUTY, BIRTH, OR WEALTH, OR WIT       3.37.5
  SHEWING THEIR BIRTH, AND WHERE THEY DID PROCEED+   3.76.8
  SOME GLORY IN THEIR BIRTH, SOME IN THEIR SKILL     3.91.1
  THY LOVE IS BITTER THEN HIGH BIRTH TO ME           3.91.9
  SUCH COLTISH GYRES, THAT TO MY BIRTH I OWE         4.21.6
  WHILE THOSE POORE BABES THEIR DEATH IN
                      BIRTH DO FIND                  4.50.11
  FROM NOBLER COURSE, FIT FOR MY BIRTH AND MIND      4.62.8
BIRTHRIGHT                     2
  WHICH UNTO IT BY BIRTHRIGHT I DO OW                4.18.6
  TO HAVE FOR NO CAUSE BIRTHRIGHT IN THE SKIE        4.26.5
BIT                            5
  MY MOUTH TOO TENDER IS FOR THY HARD BIT            4.4.8
  HOW $ULSTER LIKES OF THAT SAME GOLDEN BIT          4.30.9
  ARE HUMBLED THOUGHTS, WHICH BIT OF $REVERENCE
                      MOVE                           4.49.6
  I CAUGHT AT ONE OF THEM A HUNGRIE BIT              4.82.11
  SEEMD EVERY BIT, WHICH THENCEFORTH I DID EAT       5.39.14
BITE                           1
  I WILL BUT KISSE, I NEVER MORE WILL BITE           4.82.14
BITING                         1
  BITING MY TREWAND PEN, BEATING MY SELFE FOR SPITE  4.1.13
BITTER                         6
  THY LOVE IS BITTER THEN HIGH BIRTH TO ME           3.91.9
  NO BITTERNESSE THAT I WILL BITTER THINKE           3.111.11
  TO BITTER SAWCES DID I FRAME MY FEEDING            3.118.6
  THUS WHILE TH' EFFECT MOST BITTER WAS TO ME        4.87.12
  BUT WHEN I FEELE THE BITTER BALEFULL SMART         5.24.5
  SWEET IS THE NUT, BUT BITTER IS HIS PILL           5.26.6
BITTERNESS                     2
  NOR THINKE THE BITTERNESSE OF ABSENCE SOWRE        3.57.7
  NO BITTERNESSE THAT I WILL BITTER THINKE           3.111.11
BLACK                         33
  I LYKE NOT $LIMBO, NOR BLACKE $ACHERON             2.118.8
  BLACKE PYTCHY $NIGHT, COMPANYON OF MY WOE          2.145.1
  PORTRAITE OF HELL, THE AYRES BLACK MOURNING WEED   2.145.6
  AND BY ALL MEANES, LET BLACK UNKINDNES PROVE       2.149.13
  MAKES BLACKE NIGHT BEAUTIOUS, AND HER
                      OLD FACE NEW                   3.27.12
  HIS BEAUTIE SHALL IN THESE BLACKE LINES BE SEENE   3.63.13
  THAT IN BLACK INCK MY LOVE MAY STILL SHINE
                      BRIGHT                         3.65.14
  WHICH BY AND BY BLACKE NIGHT DOTH TAKE AWAY        3.73.7
  IN THE OULD AGE BLACKE WAS NOT COUNTED FAIRE       3.127.1
  BUT NOW IS BLACKE BEAUTIES SUCCESSIVE HEIRE        3.127.3
  THEREFORE MY $MISTERSSE EYES ARE $RAVEN BLACKE     3.127.9
  IF HAIRES BE WIERS, BLACK WIERS GROW ON HER HEAD   3.130.4
  THY BLACKE IS FAIREST IN MY JUDGEMENTS PLACE       3.131.12
  IN NOTHING ART THOU BLACKE SAVE IN THY DEEDS       3.131.13
  HAVE PUT ON BLACK, AND LOVING MOURNERS BEE         3.132.3
  THEN WILL I SWEARE BEAUTY HER SELFE IS BLACKE      3.132.13
  WHO ART AS BLACK AS HELL, AS DARKE AS NIGHT        3.147.14
```

```
IN COLOUR BLACKE, WHY WRAPT SHE BEAMES SO BRIGHT+      4.7.2
WOULD SHE IN BEAMIE BLACKE, LIKE PAINTER WISE          4.7.3
THAT WHEREAS BLACKE SEEMES $BEAUTIE'S CONTRARY         4.7.10
SHE EVEN IN BLACKE DOTH MAKE ALL BEAUTIES FLOW+        4.7.11
AS THAT SWEETE BLACKE WHICH VAILES THE
                             HEAV'NLY EYE              4.20.7
WHILE THAT BLACKE HUE FROM ME THE BAD GUEST HID        4.20.11
BUT FOR TO SPANGLE THE BLACKE WEEDS OF NIGHT           4.26.6
CAN THOSE BLACKE BEAMES SUCH BURNING MARKES
                             ENGRAVE                   4.47.2
HOW THEIR BLACKE BANNER MIGHT BE BEST DISPLAID         4.55.8
SHALL PAINT OUT JOY, THOUGH BUT IN BLACKE
                             AND WHITE                 4.70.11
OR SEEING JETS, BLACKE, BUT IN BLACKNESSE BRIGHT       4.91.8
WHAT INKE IS BLACKE INOUGH TO PAINT MY WO+             4.93.3
BOTH SADLY BLACKE, BOTH BLACKLY DARKNED BE             4.96.3
WHILE THE BLACKE HORRORS OF THE SILENT NIGHT           4.98.9
PAINT WOE'S BLACKE FACE SO LIVELY TO MY SIGHT          4.98.10
AND AL HER FAULTS IN THY BLACK BOOKE ENROLL            5.10.12
BLACKEST                 4
PAYNTED THE BLACKEST $IMAGE OF MY WOE                  2.114.11
I SOUGHT FIT WORDS TO PAINT THE BLACKEST
                             FACE OF WOE               4.1.5
AND THIS I SWEARE BY BLACKEST BROOKE OF HELL           4.74.7
THAT LIVING THUS IN BLACKEST WINTER NIGHT              4.89.13
BLACKLY              1
BOTH SADLY BLACKE, BOTH BLACKLY DARKNED BE             4.96.3
BLACKNESS            1
OR SEEING JETS, BLACKE, BUT IN BLACKNESSE BRIGHT       4.91.8
BLACKS               1
COMMIT TO THESE WASTE BLACKS, AND THOU
                             SHALT FINDE               3.77.10
BLAME               17
MAY JUSTLY PRAISE, AND BLAME MY LOVELESSE $FAIRE       1.2.8
I BANISH HER, AND BLAME HER TRECHERY                   1.25.6
LOOKE IN MY GRIEFES, AND BLAME ME NOT TO MOURNE        1.26.1
ILE PRAISE HER FACE, AND BLAME HER FLINTY HEART        1.26.12
ALTHOUGH THIS WORLD MAY SEEME HER DEEDE TO BLAME       1.30.13
YET THEE I BLAME NOT, THOUGH FOR THEE TIS DONE         1.32.5
AND BLAME MY SELFE T'EXCUSE THAT HEART OF THINE        1.33.12
OR BLAME TH'ATTEMPT PRESUMING SO TO SORE               1.35.2
AND SO LIKEWISE, RENOWMED IS THY BLAME                 1.56.9
I CANNOT BLAME THEE, FOR MY LOVE THOU USEST            3.40.6
NOT BLAME YOUR PLEASURE BE IT ILL OR WELL              3.58.14
OH BLAME ME NOT IF I NO MORE CAN WRITE                 3.103.5
IS PERJURD, MURDROUS, BLOUDY FULL OF BLAME             3.129.3
YOUR WORDS MY FRIEND (RIGHT HEALTHFULL
                             CAUSTIKS) BLAME           4.21.1
ON SERVANTS' SHAME OFT $MAISTER'S BLAME
                             DOTH SIT                  4.107.12
HER HARDNES BLAME WHICH I SHOULD MORE COMMEND+         5.51.6
T'ACCUSE OF PRIDE, OR RASHLY BLAME FOR OUGHT           5.61.4
BLAMED               4
BUT YET BE BLAM'D, IF THOU THIS SELFE DECEAVEST        3.40.7
THAT THOU ARE BLAM'D SHALL NOT BE THY DEFECT           3.70.1
NOR BLAM'D FOR BLOUD, NOR SHAM'D FOR SINFULL
                             DEED                      4.84.11
THEN TO BE BLAM'D FOR SPILLING GUILTLESSE BLOOD        5.38.14
BLASPHEME            1
MAY BLASPHEME THUS, AND SAY, I FLATTER THEE            2.112.3
```

```
BLAZE                           4
   WHERE BLAZE THOSE LIGHTS FAIREST OF EARTHLY
                            THINGS                      1.12.3
   WHOSE GLORIOUS BLAZE THE WORLD DOTH SO ADMIRE        1.38.6
   TO BLAZE THESE LAST, AND SWARE DEVOUTLY THEN         4.13.13
   I MAY IN TRUMP OF FAME BLAZE OVER ALL                5.29.12
BLAZON                          1
   THEN IN THE BLAZON OF SWEET BEAUTIES BEST            3.106.5
BLEED                           5
   OFT 'T'ATH BEEN PROV'D, THE BREATHLESSE
                            $COARSE WILL BLEED          2.46.8
   LOVE GAVE THE WOUND, WHICH WHILE I BREATHE
                            WILL BLEED                  4.2.2
   TO HONOR ALL THEIR DEATHS, WHO FOR HER BLEED         4.7.14
   WHOSE CURELESSE WOUNDS EVEN NOW MOST FRESHLY
                            BLEED                       4.48.11
   I CRY THY SIGHS., MY DEERE, THY TEARES I BLEEDE      4.93.14
BLEEDING                        6
   BUT FALL TO BLEEDING, AS THEY DID BEFORE             2.46.12
   THEN STANCH THE BLEEDING, THEN TRANS-PIERCE
                            THE $COARSE                 2.50.7
   SEE HOW HEE LOOKES UPON HIS BLEEDING WOUND           2.135.9
   WHICH THROUGH A BLEEDING HEART HIS POINT
                            DID SHOVE                   4.13.6
   NOR DO ASPIRE TO $CAESAR'S BLEEDING FAME             4.64.10
   WRITTEN WITH TEARES IN HARTS CLOSE BLEEDING BOOK     5.1.8
BLENCHES                        1
   THESE BLENCHES GAVE MY HEART AN OTHER YOUTH          3.110.7
BLEND                           1
   AND ALL THESE STORMES WHICH NOW HIS BEAUTY BLEND     5.62.11
BLESS                           6
   NOW DOE I CURSE $HER, THEN AGAINE I BLESSE $HER      2.41.14
   SINCE SHE DISDAINES TO BLESSE MY HAPPIE $VERSE       2.45.5
   THAT I MAY BLESSE MEE AT THY SWEET ARISE             2.129.14
   NOW DOE I CURSE HER, THEN AGAINE I BLESSE HER        2.143.14
   I BLESSE MY LOT, THAT WAS SO LUCKY PLACED            5.82.2
   AND BLESSE YOUR FORTUNES FAYRE ELECTION              5.84.14
BLESSED                         34
   THAT WHICH THY SUCCRING MERCY SHOULD HAVE BLEST      1.31.4
   SINCE HE THAT BLESSED $PARADISE DID PROVE            2.4.7
   WITH WHAT MIGHT MAKE THE $MISERABLE BLEST            2.23.8
   AND TELLS THE OTHER, HOW THEY SHOULD BE BLEST        2.29.12
   THY BLESSED $EYES, THE $SUNNE WHICH LIGHTS
                            THIS $FIRE                  2.30.9
   THAT IT, LIKE THOSE, BY LOOKING MIGHT BE BLEST       2.33.4
   O BLESSED $BROOKE, WHOSE MILKE-WHITE $SWANS ADORE    2.53.3
   WHERE BLESSED $ANGELS SINGING DAY AND NIGHT          2.105.13
   O BLESSED $BROOKE, WHOSE MILK-WHITE $SWANS ADORE     2.113.3
   AND OF HYS BLESSED BIRTH BEFORE FORE-TOLD            2.119.4
   AND SUMMOND $ANGELS TO THYS BLESSED SIGHT            2.125.12
   O BLESSED FAYRE, NOW VAILE THOSE HEAVENLY EYES       2.129.13
   TO LOOKE ON HER BY WHOM MINE EYES ARE BLEST          2.133.4
   YET HOW SHEE BENDS TOWARDS THAT BLESSED $COAST       2.134.12
   HIS STONE-COLD LIPS DOTH KISSE THE BLESSED
                            SHAFT                       2.135.14
   WITH MEANES MORE BLESSED THEN MY BARREN RIME+        3.16.4
   HOW WOULD (I SAY) MINE EYES BE BLESSED MADE          3.43.9
   SO AM I AS THE RICH WHOSE BLESSED KEY                3.52.1
   TO MAKE SOME SPECIALL INSTANT SPECIALL BLEST         3.52.11
   BLESSED ARE YOU WHOSE WORTHINESSE GIVES SKOPE        3.52.13
```

```
AND YOU IN EVERY BLESSED SHAPE WE KNOW              3.53.12
RETURNE OF LOVE, MORE BLEST MAY BE THE VIEW         3.56.12
BUT WHATS SO BLESSED FAIRE THAT FEARES NO BLOT      3.92.13
WHILST IT HATH THOUGHT IT SELFE SO BLESSED
                           NEVER+                   3.119.6
UPON THAT BLESSED WOOD WHOSE MOTION SOUNDS          3.128.2
MAKING DEAD WOOD MORE BLEST THEN LIVING LIPS        3.128.12
MINE EYES (SHALL I SAY CURST OR BLEST) BEHELD       4.16.10
THAT IN NO MORE BUT THESE I MIGHT BE FULLY BLEST    4.77.13
NOW BLESSED YOU, BEARE ONWARD BLESSED ME            4.84.5
NOW BLESSED YOU, BEARE ONWARD BLESSED ME            4.84.5
THEN THOSE BLEST EYES, WHERE ALL MY HOPES
                           DO DWELL                 4.86.13
WHEN YE BEHOLD THAT $ANGELS BLESSED LOOKE           5.1.11
AND WITH THE CREW OF BLESSED $SAYNTS UPBROUGHT      5.61.7
WHICH OFT I WISHT, YET NEVER WAS SO BLEST           5.76.14
```

BLESSES   1
```
NAMING THY NAME, BLESSES AN ILL REPORT              3.95.8
```
BLESSING   1
```
OF THEIR FAIRE SUBJECT, BLESSING EVERY BOOKE        3.82.4
```
BLESSINGS   2
```
YOU TO YOUR BEAUTIOUS BLESSINGS ADDE A CURSE        3.84.13
TO ALL THOSE HAPPY BLESSINGS WHICH YE HAVE          5.66.1
```
BLIND   19
```
BLIND WERE MINE $EYES, TILL THEY WERE
                           SEENE OF THINE           2.35.9
OR BEING $BLIND (AS FITTEST FOR THE $TRADE)         2.48.9
THEY THAT ARE BLIND, ARE $MINSTRELS OFTEN MADE      2.48.11
THOU, HER BLIND $SONNE, MAY'ST SIT BY
                           THEM, AND PLAY           2.48.14
HOW E'RE BLIND $FORTUNE TURNE HER GIDDIE $WHEELE    2.51.12
BLIND WERE MINE EYES, TILL THEY WERE SEENE
                           OF THINE                 2.112.9
LOOKING ON DARKNES WHICH THE BLIND DOE SEE          3.27.8
DOTH PART HIS FUNCTION, AND IS PARTLY BLIND         3.113.3
SWEARE TO THY BLIND SOULE THAT I WAS THY $WILL      3.136.2
THOU BLINDE FOOLE LOVE, WHAT DOOST THOU
                           TO MINE EYES             3.137.1
O CUNNING LOVE, WITH TEARES THOU KEEPST
                           ME BLINDE                3.148.13
THOSE THAT CAN SEE THOU LOV'ST, AND I AM BLIND      3.149.14
BUT THAT RICH FOOLE, WHO BY BLIND $FORTUNE'S LOT    4.24.9
TEACHING BLIND EYES BOTH HOW TO SMILE AND WEEPE     4.32.8
A CHAMBER DEAFE TO NOISE, AND BLIND TO LIGHT        4.39.10
THAT LOVE SHE DID, BUT LOVED A $LOVE NOT BLIND      4.62.6
I LODG'D THEE IN MY HEART, AND BEING BLIND          4.65.7
SHE COULD NOT SHEW MY BLIND BRAINE WAIES OF JOY     4.97.13
I STARVE MY BODY AND MINE EYES DOE BLYND            5.88.14
```
BLINDED   3
```
WHILST BLINDED ONES MINE ERROURS NEVER GESSE        1.3.8
YOU BLINDED SOULES WHOM YOUTH AND ERROUR LEADE      1.3.9
THRUGH YOUR BRIGHT BEAMS DOTH NOT THE
                           BLINDED GUEST            5.8.5
```
BLIND-HITTING   1
```
BLIND-HITTING BOY, SINCE SHE THAT THEE AND ME       4.46.2
```
BLINDNESS   1
```
AND TO INLIGHTEN THEE GAVE EYES TO BLINDNESSE       3.152.11
```
BLISS   33
```
WHOSE ROWLING GRACE DEIGNE ONCE A TURNE OF BLIS     1.12.12
THAT PITTY SHINES NO COMFORT TO MY BLIS             1.21.2
```

```
AS SHORT THAT BLISSE, SO IS THE COMFORT RARE          1.24.11
YET MUST THAT BLISSE MY HUNGRY THOUGHTS APPEASE       1.24.12
I ONELY SOUGHT THE BLISSE TO HAVE HER SIGHT           1.36.12
IN PERFECT HUMANE SHAPE, ALL HEAV'NLY $BLISSE         2.17.12
AND HEAVEN MAY JOY TO THINK ON PAST WORLDS
                              BLISSE                   2.107.12
AND THOU $CONCEITE, THE SHADOW OF MY BLISSE           2.141.9
A BLISSE IN PROOFE AND PROUD AND VERY WO              3.129.11
AND THEN WOULD NOT, OR COULD NOT SEE MY BLISSE        4.33.2
WHICH MAKE THE PATENTS OF TRUE WORLDLY BLISSE         4.37.13
THOSE DAINTIE DORES UNTO THE $COURT OF BLISSE         4.44.11
THAT VERTUOUS SOULE, SURE HEIRE OF HEAV'NLY
                              BLISSE                   4.52.7
WHEN I MIGHT READE THOSE LETTERS FAIRE OF BLISSE      4.56.5
BLIST IN MY CURSE, AND CURSED IN MY BLISSE            4.60.14
STELLA'S EYES SENT TO ME THE BEAMES OF BLISSE         4.66.11
O BLISSE, FIT FOR A NOBLER STATE THEN ME              4.69.2
THIS REALME OF BLISSE, WHILE VERTUOUS
                              COURSE I TAKE            4.69.13
WISE SILENCE IS BEST MUSICKE UNTO BLISSE              4.70.14
THOSE WORDS, WHICH DO SUBLIME THE QUINTESSENCE
                              OF BLISSE                4.77.8
BREATHING ALL BLISSE AND SWEETNING TO THE HEART       4.81.3
OF HIGHEST WISH, I WISH YOU SO MUCH BLISSE            4.84.13
O FATE, O FAULT, O CURSE, CHILD OF MY BLISSE          4.93.1
CALS EACH WIGHT TO SALUTE THE FLOURE OF BLISSE        4.99.11
MY SOULES LONG LACKED FOODE, MY HEAVENS BLIS          5.1.12
THE WHILES SHE LORDETH IN LICENTIOUS BLISSE           5.10.3
THERE I TO HER AS TH'AUTHOR OF MY BLISSE              5.22.9
AS MEANES OF BLISSE I GLADLY WIL EMBRACE              5.25.12
ALL SORROWES SHORT THAT GAINE ETERNALL BLISSE         5.63.14
DOTH BATH IN BLISSE AND MANTLETH MOST AT EASE         5.72.10
BUT HERE ON EARTH TO HAVE SUCH HEVENS BLISSE          5.72.14
THE BOWRE OF BLISSE, THE PARADICE OF PLEASURE         5.76.3
AND DEAD MY LIFE THAT WANTS SUCH LIVELY BLIS          5.89.14
BLISSED                  2
WEALTH BREEDING WANT, MORE BLIST, MORE
                              WRETCHED GROW            4.24.4
BLIST IN MY CURSE, AND CURSED IN MY BLISSE            4.60.14
BLOOD                    27
SAY HER DISDAINE HATH DRYED UP MY BLOOD               1.2.9
FAITH BEING WITH BLOOD, AND FIVE YEARES
                              WITNES SIGN'D            1.31.6
DRAWNE WITH MY BLOOD, AND PAINTED WITH MY CARES       1.47.3
TO WRITE WITH $BLOOD, OF FORCE OFFENDS THE $SIGHT     2.13.6
AND THE OLD $LEA BRAGS OF THE $DANISH $BLOUD          2.32.12
IN HEAT OF $BLOUD, A MODEST $MIND MIGHT MOVE          2.47.8
WHOSE $GRIEFE HATH PARCH'D THY $BODY,
                              DRY'D THY $BLOOD         2.49.8
PITTIE SO LEFT, TO TH'COLDNESSE OF YOUR $BLOOD        2.58.13
WITH MURTHERING HANDS IMBRUD IN MINE OWN BLOOD        2.114.12
TO WRITE WITH BLOOD, OF FORCE OFFENDS THE SIGHT       2.121.6
AND OLD $LEGEA BRAGS OF $DANISH BLOOD                 2.124.12
AND WALLOWING IN HIS BLOOD, SOME LYFE YET LAFT        2.135.13
AND SEE THY BLOOD WARME WHEN THOU FEEL'ST
                              IT COULD                 3.2.14
AND THAT FRESH BLOUD WHICH YONGLY THOU BESTOW'ST      3.11.3
AND BURNE THE LONG LIV'D $PHAENIX IN HER BLOOD        3.19.4
WHEN HOURES HAVE DREIND HIS BLOOD AND
                              FILD HIS BROW            3.63.3
```

```
BEGGERD OF BLOOD TO BLUSH THROUGH LIVELY VAINES          3.67.10
WHERE CHEEKES NEED BLOOD, IN THEE IT IS ABUS'D           3.82.14
ALL FRAILTIES THAT BESIEGE ALL KINDES OF BLOOD           3.109.10
GIVE SALUTATION TO MY SPORTIVE BLOOD+                    3.121.6
YET HIDING ROYALL BLOUD FULL OFT IN RURALL VAINE         4.6.8
MY BLOUD FROM THEM, WHO DID EXCELL IN THIS               4.41.10
NOR BLAM'D FOR BLOUD, NOR SHAM'D FOR SINFULL
                                        DEED            4.84.11
SHAMES NOT TO BE WITH GUILTLESSE BLOUD DEFYLDE           5.20.11
THEN TO BE BLAM'D FOR SPILLING GUILTLESSE BLOOD          5.38.14
HUNTS AFTER BLOUD, WHEN HE BY CHANCE DOTH FIND           5.56.3
BEING WITH THY DEARE BLOOD CLENE WASHT FROM SIN          5.68.7
```
BLOODED   1
```
THAT YE WERE BLOODED IN A YEELDED PRAY                   5.20.14
```
BLOODY   9
```
MAKE WARRE UPPON THIS BLOUDIE TIRANT TIME+               3.16.2
THE BLOODY SPURRE CANNOT PROVOKE HIM ON                  3.50.9
IS PERJURD, MURDROUS, BLOUDDY FULL OF BLAME              3.129.3
TILL BLOUDIE BULLET GET HIM WRONGFULL PRAY               4.20.4
THOSE SCARLET JUDGES, THREATNING BLOUDY PAINE+           4.73.11
THOUGH STRONGLY HEDG'D OF BLOUDY $LYON'S PAWES           4.75.10
SITH TO ALL OTHER BEASTES OF BLOODY RACE                 5.31.5
THAT SHE THE BETTER MAY IN BLOODY BATH                   5.31.11
YET EVEN WHYLST HER BLOODY HANDS THEM SLAY               5.47.9
```
BLOOMING   1
```
I SACRIFISE MY YOUTH, AND BLOOMING YEARES                1.24.5
```
BLOOMS   1
```
THE $CANKER BLOOMES HAVE FULL AS DEEPE A DIE             3.54.5
```
BLOSSOM   1
```
THE BUD OF JOY, THE BLOSSOME OF THE MORNE                5.61.9
```
BLOSSOMED   1
```
HER NIPPLES LYKE YONG BLOSSOMD $JESSEMYNES               5.64.12
```
BLOSSOMS   1
```
AND WHERE THE SWEETEST BLOSSOMES FIRST APPEARES          1.51.7
```
BLOT   9
```
MY LIFE NOR DEATH SHAL NEVER BE HER BLOT                 1.30.12
AND THEREFORE $DELIA, TIS TO ME NO BLOT                  1.35.13
FOR $GOD FORBID I SHOULD MY $PAPERS BLOT                 1.58.5
NOR NEVER STOOD ONE WORD THEREOF TO BLOT                 2.21.7
CANCELL MY NAME, AND BLOT IT WITH DISPAYRE               2.142.12
AND DO'ST HIM GRACE WHEN CLOUDS DOE BLOT
                                    THE HEAVEN          3.28.10
BUT WHATS SO BLESSED FAIRE THAT FEARES NO BLOT           3.92.13
WHERE BEAUTIES VAILE DOTH COVER EVERY BLOT               3.95.11
AND CAN WITH FOULE ABUSE SUCH BEAUTIES BLOT              4.24.11
```
BLOTS   1
```
SO SHALL THOSE BLOTS THAT DO WITH ME REMAINE             3.36.3
```
BLOTTED   2
```
SMOAK'D WITH MY $SIGHES, AND BLOTTED WITH
                                    MY $TEARES          2.54.4
SMOK'D WITH MY SIGHES, AND BLOTTED WITH
                                    MY TEARES           2.101.4
```
BLOW   5
```
UNDER THE BLOW OF THRALLED DISCONTENT                    3.124.7
BUT TO MY SELFE MY SELFE DID GIVE THE BLOW               4.33.9
SINCE $REASON'S SELFE DOTH BLOW THE COLE IN ME+          4.35.6
WHILE EACH DOTH BLOW THE FIER OF MY HART                 4.72.4
WING'D WITH WHOSE BREATH, SO PLEASING
                                    $ZEPHIRES BLOW      4.100.7
```

```
BLOWN                          3
   LOOKE $DELIA HOW W'ESTEEME THE HALFE BLOWNE $ROSE      1.39.1
   BUT STRAIGHT HER WIDE BLOWNE POMP COMES
                               TO DECLINE                 1.39.6
   LIKE A VAINE BUBBLE BLOWEN UP WITH AYRE                5.58.6
BLOWS                          3
   INVENTION, $NATURE'S CHILD, FLED STEP-DAME
                               $STUDIE'S BLOWES           4.1.10
   TILL DOWNE-RIGHT BLOWES DID FOYLE THY
                               CUNNING FENCE              4.10.11
   THE FRIENDLY FRAY, WHERE BLOWES BOTH WOUND
                               AND HEALE                  4.79.10
BLUNT                          3
   DEVOURING TIME BLUNT THOU THE $LYONS PAWES             3.19.1
   THAT OVER-GOES MY BLUNT INVENTION QUITE                3.103.7
   TAN SACRED BEAUTIE, BLUNT THE SHARP'ST INTENTS         3.115.7
BLUNTER                        1
   THY EDGE SHOULD BLUNTER BE THEN APETITE                3.56.2
BLUNTING                       1
   FOR BLUNTING THE FINE PCINT OF SELDOME PLEASURE        3.52.4
BLUSH                          9
   A MODEST $MAIDE, DECKT WITH A BLUSH OF HCNOR           1.6.5
   NO $SUNNE MY BLUSH AND ERROR HAD BEWRAID               1.7.7
   RESTORE THY BLUSH UNTO $AURORA BRIGHT                  1.19.7
   THE IMAGE OF THY BLUSH AND $SOMMERS HONOR              1.39.2
   BEGGERD OF BLOOD TC BLUSH THROUGH LIVELY VAINES        3.67.10
   TILL THAT HER BLUSH TAUGHT ME MY SHAME TC SEE          4.53.14
   THEY FLED WITH BLUSH, WHICH GUILTIE SEEM'D
                               OF LOVE                    4.66.14
   YET AH, MY $MAYD'N $MUSE DOTH BLUSH TO
                               TELL THE BEST              4.77.14
   WHERE $BEAUTIE'S BLUSH IN $HONOUR'S GRAINE
                               IS DIDE                    4.80.8
BLUSHED                        1
   SHE SO DISCHEVELD, BLUSHT., FROM WINDOW I              4.103.12
BLUSHING                       7
   SHORT IS THE GLORY CF THE BLUSHING $ROSE               1.50.6
   THE GLORIOUS SUNNE WENT BLUSHING TO HIS BED            2.125.1
   OUR BLUSHING SHAME, AN CTHER WHITE DISPAIRE            3.99.9
   AT THE WOODS BOULDNES BY THEE BLUSHING STAND           3.128.8
   WHERE BLUSHING RED, THAT $LOVE'S SELFE
                               THEM DOTH LOVE             4.43.10
   WHAT BLUSHING NOTES DOEST THOU IN MARGINE SEE+         4.67.8
   BUT SHE FORBIDS, WITH BLUSHING WORDS, SHE SAYES        4.81.9
BOARD                          1
   THEN SO TO CAST HER $BALLAST OVER BOORD                2.134.8
BOAST                          13
   AS ANY $MANS, THAT $MEMCRY CAN BOAST                   2.27.10
   OUR $NORTHERNE $BCRCERS BOAST OF $TWEEDS
                               FAIRE $FLOUD               2.32.10
   ONELY COMPELL'D ON THIS POORE GOOD TO BOAST            2.43.13
   WITH SO PURE $LOVE, AS $TIME COULD NEVER BOAST         2.54.8
   WITH SO PURE LOVE AS TYME COULD NEVER BOAST            2.101.8
   OUR $NORTHERN BORDERS BCAST OF $TWEEDS
                               FAIRE FLOOD                2.124.10
   OF PUBLIKE HONOUR AND PROUD TITLES BOST                3.25.2
   THEN MAY I DARE TC BOAST HOW I DOE LOVE THEE           3.26.13
   AS VICTORS OF MY SILENCE CANNOT BOAST                  3.86.11
   AND HAVING THEE, OF ALL MENS PRIDE I BOAST             3.91.12
   NO- $TIME, THOU SHALT NCT BOST THAT I DOE CHANGE       3.123.1
```

```
WHAT NOW THE $DUTCH IN THEIR FULL DIETS BOAST        4.30.6
AND THAT SAME GLORIOUS BEAUTIES YOLE BOAST           5.41.9
BOASTING                2
BOASTING, THAT SHE DOTH STILL DIRECT THE WAY         2.38.3
BOASTING THAT SHEE DOTH STILL DIRECT THE WAY         2.131.3
BOAT                    2
OR (BEING WRACKT) I AM A WORTHLESSE BOTE             3.80.11
THE BOTE FOR JOY COULD NOT TO DAUNCE FORBEARE        4.103.5
BODIES                  1
AND KNOW THOSE $BODIES HIGH RAIGNE ON THE LOW        4.26.11
BODY                   16
TO HAVE AFFECTION STRONG, A BODY WEAKE               1.20.8
GIVES HER THAT $NAME, AS SHE THE $BODY MOVES         2.12.4
AND THOUGH THIS $EARTHLY $BODY FADE AND DIE          2.44.13
NEERE THE DEAD $BODY HAPPILY BE BROUGHT              2.46.7
WHOSE $GRIEFE HATH PARCH'D THY $BODY,
                             DRY'D THY $BLOOD        2.49.8
MY BODY IS THE FRAME WHEREIN TI'S HELD               3.24.3
MY NAME BE BURIED WHERE MY BODY IS                   3.72.11
THE PRAY OF WORMES, MY BODY BEING DEAD               3.74.10
MY SOULE DOTH TELL MY BODY THAT HE MAY               3.151.7
THAT $VERTUE BUT THAT BODY GRAUNT TO US              4.52.14
THEN SOME GOOD BODY TELL ME HOW I DO                 4.60.12
IS NOT THE HART OF ALL THE BODY CHIEFE+              5.50.7
AND THEN MY BODY SHALL HAVE SHORTLY EASE             5.50.11
AND WITH ONE SALVE BOTH HART AND BODY HEALE          5.50.14
WITH GUIFTS OF BODY, FORTUNE AND OF MIND             5.74.4
I STARVE MY BODY AND MINE EYES DOE BLYND             5.88.14
BODY'S                  6
TO WORKE MY MIND, WHEN BODDIES WORK'S EXPIRED        3.27.4
SOME IN THEIR WEALTH, SOME IN THEIR BODIES FORCE     3.91.2
EATE UP THY CHARGE+ IS THIS THY BODIES END+          3.146.8
MY NOBLER PART TO MY GROSE BODIES TREASON            3.151.6
OF MY HARTS WOUND AND OF MY BODIES GRIEFE            5.50.2
FIT MEDICINES FOR MY BODIES BEST RELIEFE             5.50.4
BOILED                  1
BOYL'D WITH HER $SIGHES, IN GIVING UP THE $GHOST     2.15.7
BOILING                 3
MY BOILING SPRITES DID THITHER SOONE INCLINE         4.16.3
MELTS DOWNE HIS LEAD INTO MY BOYLING BREST           4.108.2
BUT THAT I BURNE MUCH MORE IN BOYLING SWEAT          5.30.7
BOLD                    7
THEN HAD I WALKT WITH BOLD ERECTED FACE              1.7.9
HOW TO BE BOLD FAR OFF, AND BASHFULL NEARE           1.20.5
WELL, WELL, MY $FRIENDS, WHEN $BEGGERS
                             GROW THUS BOLD          2.23.13
THEREFORE TO GIVE THEM FROM ME WAS I BOLD            3.122.11
TO SAY THEY ERRE, I DARE NOT BE SO BOLD              3.131.7
IS IT THAT MENS FRAYLE EYES, WHICH GAZE TOO BOLD     5.37.5
BASE THINGS THAT TO HER LOVE TOO BOLD ASPIRE+        5.61.12
BOLDENED                1
THAT BOLDNED INNOCENCE BEARES IN HIR EIES            5.5.10
BOLDER                  1
OFT WHEN MY SPIRIT DOTH SPRED HER BOLDER WINGES      5.72.1
BOLDEST                 1
FORTUNE ASSISTS THE BOLDEST, I REPLY                 2.59.7
BOLDLY                  1
AND THERE TO REST THEMSELVES DID BOLDLY PLACE        5.76.12
BOLDNESS                1
AT THE WOODS BOULDNES BY THEE BLUSHING STAND         3.128.8
```

```
BOND                        4
   THE BOND, THE FLAME, THE WOUND THAT FESTRETH SO    1.14.10
   O RARE EFFECT, TRUE BOND OF FRIENDSHIPS MEASURE    2.146.9
   UNDER THAT BOND THAT HIM AS FAST DOTH BINDE        3.134.8
   AND MAKE HIM BOND THAT BONDAGE EARST DYD FLY        5.65.4
BONDAGE                     1
   AND MAKE HIM BOND THAT BONDAGE EARST DYD FLY        5.65.4
BONDS                       3
   MY BONDS IN THEE ARE ALL DETERMINATE               3.87.4
   WHERETO AL BONDS DO TIE ME DAY BY DAY              3.117.4
   AND SEALD FALSE BONDS OF LOVE AS OFT AS MINE       3.142.7
BONES                       1
   WHEN THAT CHURLE DEATH MY BONES WITH DUST
                              SHALL COVER              3.32.2
BOOK                       13
   HERE I UNCLASPE THE $BOOKE OF MY CHARG'D SOULE      1.1.5
   IS FROM THE BOOKE OF HONOUR RASED QUITE            3.25.11
   SHOW ME YOUR IMAGE IN SOME ANTIQUE BOOKE           3.59.7
   AND OF THIS BOOKE, THIS LEARNING MAIST THOU TASTE  3.77.4
   SHALL PROFIT THEE, AND MUCH INRICH THY BOOKE       3.77.14
   OF THEIR FAIRE SUBJECT, BLESSING EVERY BOOKE       3.82.4
   BOOKE BOTH MY WILFULNESSE AND ERRORS DOWNE         3.117.9
   FOR LIKE A CHILD THAT SOME FAIRE BOOKE DOTH FIND   4.11.5
   SO LONG (THOUGH HE FROM BOOKE MYCHE TO DESIRE)     4.46.13
   FAR FAR TOO LONG TO LEARNE IT WITHOUT BOOKE         4.56.2
   WHO WILL IN FAIREST BOOKE OF $NATURE KNOW           4.71.1
   WRITTEN WITH TEARES IN HARTS CLOSE BLEEDING BOOK    5.1.8
   AND AL HER FAULTS IN THY BLACK BOOKE ENROLL        5.10.12
BOOKS                       8
   THAT ALL THEIR $WEALTH LIES IN THY BEAUTIES
                              $BOOKES                  2.3.12
   I QUAKE TO LOOKE ON $HECAT'S CHARMING $BOOKES      2.39.11
   THAT ALL HER WEALTH LYES IN THY $BEAUTIES
                              BOOKES                  2.110.12
   I QUAKE TO LOOKE ON $HECATS CHARMING BOOKES       2.118.11
   O LET MY BOOKS BE THEN THE ELOQUENCE               3.23.9
   SUCH ART OF EYES I NEVER READ IN BOOKES           5.21.14
   THEN BY THAT COUNT, WHICH LOVERS BOOKS INVENT      5.60.9
   THROUGH $FAERY LAND, WHICH THOSE SIX BOOKS
                              COMPILE                  5.80.2
BOOT                        1
   AND $WILL TOO BOOTE, AND $WILL IN OVER-PLUS       3.135.2
BOOTLESS                    1
   AND TROUBLE DEAFE HEAVEN WITH MY BOOTLESSE CRIES   3.29.3
BOOTS                       1
   WHAT BOOTES TO LAWES OF $SUCCOR TO APPEALE+       1.31.11
BOPEEPE                     1
   AND IN HER BREAST BOPEEPE OR COUCHING LYES        4.11.12
BORDERS                     2
   OUR $NORTHERNE $BORDERS BOAST OF $TWEEDS
                              FAIRE $FLOUD            2.32.10
   OUR $NORTHERN BORDERS BOAST OF $TWEEDS
                              FAIRE FLOOD            2.124.10
BORE                        2
   WER'T OUGHT TO ME I BORE THE CANOPY               3.125.1
   OR IF IT WEARE IT BORE NOT BEAUTIES NAME          3.127.2
BORN                       28
   GRIEFES EVER SPRINGING, COMFORTS NEVER BORNE       1.16.4
   STILL NEW BORNE SORROWES OF HER FRESH DISCAINE    1.16.10
   TH'$ORPHAN OF $FORTUNE, BORNE TO BE HER SCORNE     1.26.3
```

AND I (THOUGH BORNE WITHIN A COLDER CLIME)   1.43.5
BROTHER TO DEATH, IN SILENT DARKNES BORNE   1.54.2
FALSE $FRIENDS THY KINDNESSE, BORNE BUT
                    TO DECEIVE $THEE   2.10.10
ONELY BY DYING, BORNE THE VERY SAME   2.16.12
HE STILL AS YOUNG AS WHEN HE FIRST WAS BORNE   2.22.9
AND WANTING $FRIENDS, THOUGH OF A $GODDESSE BORNE   2.23.3
UNHAPPY $BORNE, OF ALL UNHAPPY DAY   2.116.5
NOW WAST THOU BORNE, NOW IN THY CRADLE SLAYNE   2.141.14
WITH $APRILLS FIRST BORNE FLOWERS AND
                    ALL THINGS RARE   3.21.7
AS TO BEHOLD DESERT A BEGGER BORNE   3.66.2
BEFORE THESE BASTARD SIGNES OF FAIRE WERE BORNE   3.68.3
WHOSE INFLUENCE IS THINE, AND BORNE OF THEE   3.78.10
ERE YOU WERE BORNE WAS BEAUTIES SUMMER DEAD   3.104.14
AND RATHER MAKE THEM BORNE TO OUR DESIRE   3.123.7
AT SUCH WHO NOT BORNE FAIRE NO BEAUTY LACK   3.127.11
YET WHO KNOWES NOT CONSCIENCE IS BORNE OF LOVE   3.151.2
LOVE BORNE IN $GREECE, OF LATE FLED FROM
                    HIS NATIVE PLACE   4.8.1
WHERE ROSES GUEULS ARE BORNE IN SILVER FIELD   4.13.11
IN MY FREE SIDE+ OR AM I BORNE A SLAVE   4.47.3
BY $NATURE BORNE, I GAVE TO THEE MINE EYES   4.65.8
WHAT SIGHES STOLNE OUT, OR KILD BEFORE
                    FULL BORNE+   4.67.9
WELL IS HE BORNE, THAT MAY BEHOLD YOU EVER   5.8.14
FOR LOOKING ON THE EARTH WHENCE SHE WAS BORNE   5.13.6
AND OF THE BROOD OF $ANGELS HEVENLY BORNE   5.61.6
TO BE DIVINE AND BORNE OF HEAVENLY SEED   5.79.10
BORNE   6
  (SAITH HE) $LIGHT BURTHEN'S HEAVY, IF
                    FARRE BORNE   2.59.10
THAT LOVE DIVINE WHICH I HAVE BORNE TO YOU   2.139.10
BORNE ON THE BEARE WITH WHITE AND BRISTLY BEARD   3.12.8
WITHOUT THY HELPE, BY ME BE BORNE ALONE   3.36.4
GOOD BROTHER $PHILIP, I HAVE BORNE YOU LONG   4.83.1
THE BAY (QUOTH SHE) IS OF THE VICTOURS BORNE   5.29.5
BORROWED   4
  WHICH MIGHT BE BORROW'D FROM NO $EARTHLY FLAME   2.30.2
  FAIRING THE FOULE WITH $ARTS FAULSE BORROW'D
                    FACE   3.127.6
  WHICH BORROWD FROM THIS HOLIE FIRE OF LOVE   3.153.5
  SHALL DOFFE HER FLESHES BOROWD FAYRE ATTYRE   5.27.6
BOSOM   10
  IN WHOSE DEARE $BOSOME, SWEET DELICIOUS $LOVE   2.4.5
  EVER HENCEFORTH MY $BOSOME BE YOUR $HEARSE   2.45.7
  WHOSE DEARE REMEMBRANCE IN MY $BOSOME LYES   2.57.3
  NO LOVE TOWARD OTHERS IN THAT BOSOME SITS   3.9.13
  THY BOSOME IS INDEARED WITH ALL HEARTS   3.31.1
  YET WHILE I LANGUISH, HIM THAT BOSOME CLIPS   4.59.9
  HER GOODLY BOSOME LYKE A $STRAWBERRY BED   5.64.9
  DOE YOU HIM TAKE, AND IN YOUR BOSOME BRIGHT   5.73.9
  HIM LODGING IN YOUR BOSOME TO HAVE LENT   5.73.14
  FAYRE BOSOME FRAUGHT WITH VERTUES RICHEST TRESURE 5.76.1
BOSOMS   1
  THE HUMBLE SALVE, WHICH WOUNDED BOSOMES FITS   3.120.12
BOSOM'S   2
  WHICH IN MY BOSOMES SHOP IS HANGING STIL   3.24.7
  PRISON MY HEART IN THY STEELE BOSOMES WARDE   3.133.9

```
BOSS                            1
  CURB'D IN WITH FEARE, BUT WITH GUILT BOSSE ABOVE      4.49.7
BOTH                           58
  THAT THUS I LIVE BOTH DAY AND NIGHT ANNOYD            1.26.8
  WHILST WE BOTH MAKE THE WORLD ADMIRE AT US            1.26.13
  THEE AND THY $LOVE FORLORNE, AND BOTH DISDAINES       1.52.7
  AND OF BOTH, WRONGFULL DEEMES, AND ILL CONCEIVES      1.52.8
  ONE NUMBER OF THE $EARTH, THE OTHER BOTH $DIVINE      2.18.3
  THOUGH $HEAVEN AND $EARTH, PROVE BOTH
                        TO ME UNTRUE                    2.51.13
  ONE NUMBER OF THE EARTH, THE OTHER BOTH DIVINE        2.108.3
  A $BASTARD ON BOTH SIDES NEEDES MUST THOU BE          2.140.10
  CLOUDES AND ECLIPSES STAINE BOTH $MOONE
                        AND $SUNNE                      3.35.3
  BOTH FINDE EACH OTHER, AND I LOOSE BOTH TWAINE        3.42.11
  BOTH FINDE EACH OTHER, AND I LOOSE BOTH TWAINE        3.42.11
  AND BOTH FOR MY SAKE LAY ON ME THIS CROSSE            3.42.12
  FOR NIMBLE THOUGHT CAN JUMPE BOTH SEA AND LAND        3.44.7
  ARE BOTH WITH THEE, WHERE EVER I ABIDE                3.45.2
  THEN BOTH YOUR $POETS CAN IN PRAISE DEVISE            3.83.14
  BOTH GRACE AND FAULTS ARE LOV'D OF MORE AND LESSE     3.96.3
  A THIRD NOR RED, NOR WHITE, HAD STOLNE OF BOTH        3.99.10
  AND GIVES THY PEN BOTH SKILL AND ARGUMENT             3.100.8
  BOTH TRUTH AND BEAUTY ON MY LOVE DEPENDS              3.101.3
  BOOKE BOTH MY WILFULNESSE AND ERRORS DOWNE            3.117.9
  THY REGISTERS AND THEE I BOTH DEFIE                   3.123.9
  HIM HAVE I LOST, THOU HAST BOTH HIM AND ME            3.134.13
  ON BOTH SIDES THUS IS SIMPLE TRUTH SUPPREST           3.138.8
  BUT BEING BOTH FROM ME BOTH TO EACH FRIEND            3.144.11
  BUT BEING BOTH FROM ME BOTH TO EACH FRIEND            3.144.11
  BOTH SO AND THUS, SHE MINDING $LOVE SHOULD BE         4.7.12
  BUT THOU WOULDST NEEDS FIGHT BOTH WITH
                        LOVE AND SENCE                  4.10.9
  BUT IF (BOTH FOR YOUR LOVE AND SKILL) YOUR NAME       4.15.12
  THAT UNTO ME, WHO FARE LIKE HIM THAT BOTH             4.19.10
  TEACHING BLIND EYES BOTH HOW TO SMILE AND WEEPE       4.32.8
  THAT I RESPECTS FOR BOTH OUR SAKES MUST SHOW          4.33.11
  BOTH BY THE JUDGEMENT OF THE $ENGLISH EYES            4.41.3
  OTHERS, BECAUSE OF BOTH SIDES I DO TAKE               4.41.9
  PARDON MINE EARES, BOTH I AND THEY DO PRAY            4.51.1
  SO CAPTIVES TO HIS $SAINT BOTH SOULE AND SENCE        4.61.6
  THE FRIENDLY FRAY, WHERE BLOWES BOTH WOUND
                        AND HEALE                       4.79.10
  IN HART BOTH SIGHT AND LOVE NOW COUPLED BE            4.88.13
  SUFFERING THE EVILS BOTH OF THE DAY AND NIGHT         4.89.9
  SINCE KIND OR CHANCE GIVES BOTH ONE LIVERIE           4.96.2
  BOTH SADLY BLACKE, BOTH BLACKLY DARKNED BE            4.96.3
  BOTH SADLY BLACKE, BOTH BLACKLY DARKNED BE            4.96.3
  SILENCE IN BOTH DISPLAIES HIS SULLEN MIGHT            4.96.5
  SLOW HEAVINESSE IN BOTH HOLDS ONE DEGREE              4.96.6
  IN BOTH A MAZEFULL SOLITARINESSE                      4.96.9
  TO THIS GREAT CAUSE, WHICH NEEDS BOTH
                        USE AND ART                     4.107.8
  AND SEEKE SOME SUCCCUR BOTH TO EASE MY SMART          5.2.7
  YET IN MY HART I THEN BOTH SPEAKE AND WRITE           5.3.13
  THE WHICH BOTH LYFE AND DEATH FORTH FROM YOU DART     5.7.3
  OF HER FREEWILL, SCORNING BOTH THEE AND ME            5.10.4
  AND BOTH THE $INDIAS OF THEIR TREASURES SPOILE        5.15.3
  IF $PEARLES, HIR TEETH BE PEARLES BOTH
                        PURE AND ROUND                  5.15.9
```

```
DOE BOTH APPEARE T'ADORNE HER BEAUTIES GRACE+        5.21.4
WHAT TYRANNY IS THIS BOTH MY HART TO THRALL          5.43.5
ASWAGE YOUR STORMES, OR ELSE BOTH YOU AND SHE        5.46.11
WILL BOTH TOGETHER ME TCC SORELY WRACK               5.46.12
AND WITH ONE SALVE BOTH HART AND BODY HEALE          5.50.14
DOTH SUFFER WRECK BCTH CF HER SELFE AND GOODS        5.56.12
WHOSE SWEET ASPECT BOTH $GOD AND MAN CAN MOVE        5.89.11
BOUGH                    4
MY HUMBLE ACCENTS BEARE THE $OLIVE BOUGH             1.4.11
BUT THAT WILD MUSICK BURTHENS EVERY BOW              3.102.11
SWEET IS THE $JUNIPERE, BUT SHARPE HIS BCUGH         5.26.2
LYKE AS THE $CULVER ON THE BARED BOUGH               5.89.1
BOUGHS                   1
UPON THOSE BOUGHES WHICH SHAKE AGAINST THE COULD     3.73.3
BOUND                    6
IN $WARRES AT HOME, OR WHEN FCR $CONQUESTS BOUND     2.58.2
BEING YOUR VASSAIL BOUND TO STAIE YOUR LEISURE       3.58.4
BOUND FOR THE PRIZE OF (ALL TO PRECIOUS) YOU         3.86.2
SONETS BE NOT BOUND PRENTISE TO ANNOY                4.70.5
IN CHAST DESIRES CN HEAVENLY BEAUTY BOUND            5.8.8
THE LEAGUE TWIXT THEM, THAT LOYAL LOVE
                              HATH BOUND             5.65.10
BOUNDED                  3
BUT BOUNDED THUS, TC $SCCTLAND GET YOU FCRTH         2.25.5
YET THIS LARGE $ROCME IS BOUNDED WITH $DESPAIRE      2.26.9
YET THYS LARGE ROCME IS BOUNDED WITH DYSPAIRE        2.137.9
BOUNDLESS                2
UNTO THE BOUNDLESSE $OCEAN OF THY BEAUTIE            1.1.1
SINCE BRASSE, NOR STONE, NOR EARTH, NOR
                              BOUNDLESSE SEA         3.65.1
BOUNDS                   2
WITHIN WHAT BOUNDS CAN CNE HIS LIKING STAY           4.35.3
DARE NOT HENCEFORTH ABOVE THE BOUNDS OF CEWTIE       5.61.3
BOUNTEOUS                2
THE BOUNTIOUS LARGESSE GIVEN THEE TO GIVE+           3.4.6
WHICH BOUNTIOUS GUIFT THCU SHOULDST IN
                              BOUNTY CHERRISH        3.11.12
BOUNTY                   2
WHICH BOUNTIOUS GUIFT THCU SHOULDST IN
                              BOUNTY CHERRISH        3.11.12
THE OTHER AS YOUR BCUNTIE DOTH APPEARE               3.53.11
BOW                      10
AS IF SHE WERE EXEMPT FRCM $SYETH OR $BOW            1.23.3
POORE $ROGUE, GOE PAWNE THY $FASCIA AND THY $BOW     2.48.3
THY $BOWE HALFE BRCKE, IS PEEC'D WITH
                              OLDE DESIRE            2.126.5
HER $BOWE IS BEAUTY, WITH TEN THOUSAND STRINGS       2.126.6
JOYNE WITH THE SPIGHT OF FORTUNE, MAKE ME BOW        3.90.3
NEEDES MUST I UNDER MY TRANSGRESSION BOW             3.120.3
BRAKE BOW, BRAKE SHAFTS, WHILE $CUPID
                              WEEPING SATE           4.17.8
ON $CUPID'S BOW HCW ARE MY HEART-STRINGS BENT        4.19.1
AND MAKES ME THEN BCW DCWNE MY HEAD, AND SAY         4.108.9
ALL THIS WORLDS PRICE BCW TO A BASER MAKE            5.10.11
BOWER                    10
WHEN SHE WAS RAPT TC THE INFERNALL $BOWER            2.36.8
SWEET BEAUTY HATH NC NAME NO HOLY BOURE              3.127.7
FRESH LOVE, THAT LCNG HATH SLEPT IN CHEERLESSE
                              BOWER                  5.4.6
AND SPOTLESSE PLEASURE BUILDS HER SACRED BOWRE       5.65.14
```

```
      YET IN HER WINTERS BOWRE NOT WELL AWAKE          5.70.6
      THE BOWRE OF BLISSE, THE PARADICE OF PLEASURE    5.76.3
      I SEEKE HER BOWRE WITH HER LATE PRESENCE DECKT   5.78.6
      YET NOR IN FIELD NOR BOWRE I HER CAN FYND        5.78.7
      YET FIELD AND BOWRE ARE FULL OF HER ASPECT       5.78.8
      GOE VISIT HER IN HER CHAST BOWRE OF REST         5.84.7
BOWERS                1
      FOR DAMZELS FIT TO DECKE THEIR LOVERS BOWRES     5.64.4
BOWS                  1
      OF $STELLA'S BROWES MADE HIM TWO BETTER BOWES    4.17.10
BOY                   15
      AND IN YOUR $EYE, THE $BOY THAT DID THE $MURTHER 2.2.11
      THOU PURBLIND $BOY, SINCE THOU HAST BEENE
                            SO SLACKE                  2.36.1
      GOE HYRE THY SELFE SOME BUNGLING $HARPERS $BOY   2.48.10
      NOTHING SWEET BOY, BUT YET LIKE PRAYERS DIVINE   3.108.5
      O THOU MY LOVELY $BOY WHO IN THY POWER           3.126.1
      THE BOY FOR TRIALL NEEDES WOULD TOUCH MY BREST   3.153.10
      DECEIV'D THE QUAKING BOY, WHO THOUGHT
                            FROM SO PURE LIGHT         4.8.10
      THE BOY REFUSDE FOR FEARE OF $MARSE'S HATE       4.17.5
      SEE THERE THAT BOY, THAT MURTHRING BOY I SAY     4.20.2
      SEE THERE THAT BOY, THAT MURTHRING BOY I SAY     4.20.2
      BLIND-HITTING BOY, SINCE SHE THAT THEE AND ME    4.46.2
      FOR WHEN, NAK'D BOY, THOU COULDST NO HARBOUR FIND 4.65.5
      GRIEFE BUT $LOVE'S WINTER LIVERIE IS, THE $BOY   4.70.7
      LOVE STILL A BOY, AND OFT A WANTON IS            4.73.1
      OR HERS WHOM NAKED THE $TROJAN BOY DID SEE       4.82.4
BOYISH                1
      IN TRUTH, O $LOVE, WITH WHAT A BOYISH KIND       4.11.1
BOYS                  1
      AND $IDEOTS STILL ARE RUNNING AFTER $BOYES       2.22.7
BRABBLING             1
      WOULDST BRABLING BE WITH SENCE AND LOVE IN ME    4.10.2
BRAG                  2
      NOR SHALL DEATH BRAG THOU WANDR'ST IN HIS SHADE  3.18.11
      I CANNOT BRAG OF WORD, MUCH LESSE OF DEED        4.66.5
BRAGS                 3
      AND THE OLD $LEA BRAGS OF THE $DANISH $BLOUD     2.32.12
      AND OLD $LEGEA BRAGS OF $DANISH BLOOD            2.124.12
      THAT SICKENESSE BRAGS IT SELFE BEST GRACED TO BE 4.101.4
BRAIN                 19
      WHAT THEY LAST THOUGHT OF, WHEN THE $BRAINE
                            GREW SICKE                 2.9.7
      BEARE WITH $ME THEN, THOUGH TROUBLED BE
                            MY $BRAINE                 2.9.12
      MY $BRAINE IS DRIE WITH WEEPING ALL TOO LONG     2.41.6
      THOU $LEADEN $BRAINE, WHICH CENSUR'ST
                            WHAT I WRITE               2.49.1
      MY BRAYNE IS DRY WITH WEEPING ALL TOO LONG       2.143.6
      THOSE CHILDREN NURST, DELIVERD FROM THY BRAINE   3.77.11
      THAT DID MY RIPE THOUGHTS IN MY BRAINE INHEARCE  3.86.3
      WHAT'S IN THE BRAINE THAT $INCK MAY CHARACTER    3.108.1
      TTHY GUIFT,, THY TABLES, ARE WITHIN MY BRAINE    3.122.1
      OR AT THE LEAST, SO LONG AS BRAINE AND HEART     3.122.5
      SOME FRESH AND FRUITFULL SHOWERS UPON
                            MY SUNNE-BURN'D BRAINE     4.1.8
      HOLDS MY YOUNG BRAINE CAPTIV'D IN GOLDEN CAGE    4.23.11
      OF ALL THE GRAVE CONCEITS YOUR BRAINE DOTH BREED 4.51.6
      PRINTS HIS OWNE LIVELY FORME IN RUDEST BRAINE    4.58.8
```

```
    LET FOLKE ORECHARG'D WITH BRAINE AGAINST ME CRIE     4.64.4
    NOT FOR HIS FAIRE OUTSIDE, NOR WELL LINED BRAINE     4.75.3
    NOR DO LIKE $LORDS, WHOSE WEAKE CONFUSED BRAINE      4.85.5
    GRIEFE FIND THE WORDS, FOR THOU HAST MADE
                                     MY BRAINE           4.94.1
    SHE COULD NOT SHEW MY BLIND BRAINE WAIES OF JOY      4.97.13
BRAINS                 2
    HATH BEENE BEFORE, HOW ARE OUR BRAINES BEGUILD       3.59.2
    AND $MUSES SCORNE WITH VULGAR BRAINES TO DWELL       4.74.3
BRAKE                  2
    BRAKE BOW, BRAKE SHAFTS, WHILE $CUPID
                               WEEPING SATE              4.17.8
    BRAKE BOW, BRAKE SHAFTS, WHILE $CUPID
                               WEEPING SATE              4.17.8
BRANCHES               1
    SWEET IS THE FIRBLOOME, BUT HIS BRAUNCHES ROUGH      5.26.4
BRAND                  5
    THENCE COMES IT THAT MY NAME RECEIVES A BRAND        3.111.5
    $CUPID LAID BY HIS BRAND AND FELL A SLEEPE           3.153.1
    BUT AT MY MISTRES EIE LOVES BRAND NEW FIRED          3.153.9
    LAID BY HIS SIDE HIS HEART INFLAMING BRAND           3.154.2
    THIS BRAND SHE QUENCHED IN A COOLE $WELL BY          3.154.9
BRASS                  4
    AND BRASSE ETERNALL SLAVE TO MORTALL RAGE            3.64.4
    SINCE BRASSE, NOR STONE, NOR EARTH, NOR
                               BOUNDLESSE SEA            3.65.1
    WHEN TYRANTS CRESTS AND TOMBS OF BRASSE
                               ARE SPENT                 3.107.14
    UNLESSE MY $NERVES WERE BRASSE OR HAMMERED
                               STEELE                    3.120.4
BRAVE                  7
    AND RIGHTLY CAME FROM THAT BRAVE MOUNTING $BROOD     2.56.8
    AND SEE THE BRAVE DAY SUNCK IN HIDIOUS NIGHT         3.12.2
    SAVE BREED TO BRAVE HIM, WHEN HE TAKES
                               THEE HENCE                3.12.14
    AND WERE THEIR BRAVE STATE OUT OF MEMORY             3.15.8
    LEAST IF NO VAILE THOSE BRAVE GLEAMES DID DISGUISE   4.7.7
    HER FLESH HIS FOOD, HER SKIN HIS ARMOUR BRAVE        4.29.12
    BECAUSE IN BRAVE ARRAY HEERE MARCHETH SHE            4.88.3
BRAVELY                1
    THAT BRAVELY MASKT, THEIR FANCIES MAY BE TOLD        4.3.2
BRAVER                 1
    MY $SOULE IS OF A BRAVER $METTLE MADE                2.4.10
BRAVERY                1
    HIDING THY BRAV'RY IN THEIR ROTTEN SMOKE             3.34.4
BRAVEST                1
    BEST CHARGE, AND BRAVEST RETRAIT IN $CUPID'S
                               FIGHT                     4.79.5
BRAWL                  1
    OR FOR SOME BRAWLE, WHICH IN THAT CHAMBER HIE        4.26.7
BRAZEN                 2
    I LIST NOT DIG SO DEEPE FOR BRASEN FAME              4.28.4
    THERE FAYTH DOTH FEARLESSE DWELL IN BRASEN TOWRE     5.65.13
BREACH                 2
    BUT WHY OF TWO OTHES BREACH DOE I ACCUSE THEE        3.152.5
    HAVING GOT UP A BREACH BY FIGHTING WELL              4.12.10
BREACHES               1
    IN MY SWEET PEACE SUCH BREACHES TO HAVE BRED         5.86.12
BREAK                  15
    AND LIST NOT SEEKE TO BREAKE, TO QUENCH, TO HEALE    1.14.9
```

```
ROB HER FAIRE $BROW, BREAKE IN ON $BEAUTY, STEALE      1.22.5
TO BREAKE THE $ISE THAT HATH CONGEALD HER HEART+       1.49.8
WITH HEAVIE $SIGHES WHILST THUS I BREAKE
                               THE $AYRE               2.45.3
(LIKE TO THE $LARKE AT BREAKE OF DAYE ARISING)         3.29.11
TIS NOT ENOUGH THAT THROUGH THE CLOUDE
                               THOU BREAKE             3.34.5
WHERE THOU ART FORST TO BREAKE A TWO-FOLD TRUTH        3.41.12
WHEN I BREAKE TWENTY.. I AM PERJUR'D MOST              3.152.6
AND YET TO BREAKE MORE STAVES DID ME ADDRESSE          4.53.2
LET CLOUDS BEDIMME MY FACE, BREAKE IN MINE EYE         4.64.5
THANKE-WORTHIEST YET WHEN YOU SHALL BREAKE
                               MY HART                 4.95.14
BREAKE FORTH AT LENGTH OUT OF THE INNER PART           5.2.5
AND IF I SILENT BE, MY HART WILL BREAKE                5.43.3
OUT OF MY PRISON I WILL BREAKE ANEW                    5.80.6
BREAKE OUT, THAT MAY HER SACRED PEACE MOLEST           5.84.2
BREAKFAST               1
BREAKEFAST OF $LOVE, BUT LO, LO, WHERE SHE IS          4.79.13
BREAKING                2
THENCE BREAKING FORTH DID THICK ABOUT ME THRONG        5.12.8
BREAKING HIS PRISON FORTH TO YOU DOTH FLY              5.73.4
BREAST                      44
AND STILL I TOYLE, TO CHANGE THE $MARBLE BREST         1.13.9
INTO THE SACRED $REFUGE OF THY BREST                   1.31.2
AND SET MY $BREST, HIS $LODGING, ON A FIRE             2.23.12
MY $BREST'S THE $VESSELL, WHICH INCLUDES THE SAME      2.30.12
MY WOFULL $HEART, IMPRISON'D IN MY $BREST              2.33.2
MY $BREST THE $FORGE, INCLUDING ALL THE HEATE          2.40.3
WHOSE $BREST IS PROOFE AGAINST $COMPLAINT
                         OR $PRAYER+                   2.52.10
LOOKE $THOU INTO MY BREST, AND $THOU SHALT SEE         2.55.9
THUS FROM MY $BREST, WHERE IT WAS BRED ALONE           2.56.13
LOOKE THOU INTO MY BREAST, AND THOU SHALT SEE          2.102.9
AND FROM MY BREAST INTO THINE EYES BE GONE             2.103.14
MAKING THY BREAST THAT SACRED RELIQUES SHRYNE          2.105.12
MY WOFULL HART IMPRISOND IN MY BREAST                  2.133.2
ROUZ'D FROM MY BREAST, HIS SURE AND SAFEST LAYRE       2.135.2
BY BREAST THE FORGE, INCLUDING ALL THE HEATE           2.144.3
WHICH IN THY BREST DOTH LIVE, AS THINE IN ME           3.22.7
AND DOMB PRESAGERS OF MY SPEAKING BREST                3.23.10
ARE WINDOWES TO MY BREST, WHERE-THROUGH THE $SUN       3.24.11
WITHIN THE GENTLE CLOSURE OF MY BREST                  3.48.11
AS FROM MY SOULE WHICH IN THY BREST DOTH LYE           3.109.4
EVEN TO THY PURE AND MOST MOST LOVING BREST            3.110.14
THE BOY FOR TRIALL NEEDES WOULD TOUCH MY BREST         3.153.10
THY SCEPTER USE IN SOME OLD $CATOE'S BREST             4.4.5
AND IN HER BREAST BOPEEPE OR COUCHING LYES             4.11.12
THAT IN HER BREAST THY PAP WELL SUGRED LIES            4.12.5
UPON WHOSE BREAST A FIERCER $GRIPE DOTH TIRE           4.14.2
SO IN MY SWELLING BREAST THAT ONLY I                   4.27.7
MY MOUTH DOTH WATER, AND MY BREAST DOTH SWELL          4.37.1
PITIE THEREOF GATE IN HER BREAST SUCH PLACE            4.45.7
CANNOT BE STAID WITHIN MY PANTING BREAST               4.50.2
WITH THAT FAIRE BREAST MAKING WOE'S DARKNESSE
                               CLEARE                  4.57.11
BUT AS YOU WITH MY BREAST I OFT HAVE NURST             4.95.3
O HONIED SIGHS, WHICH FROM THAT BREAST DO RISE         4.100.5
MELTS DOWNE HIS LEAD INTO MY BOYLING BREST             4.108.2
IN GENTLE BREST THAT SHALL ENDURE FOR EVER             5.6.10
```

```
MAY KINDLE LIVING FIRE WITHIN MY BREST              5.7.12
BUT YET IF IN YOUR HARDNED BREST YE HIDE            5.25.9
LET IT LYKEWISE YOUR GENTLE BREST INSPIRE           5.28.6
BUT IN YOUR BREST HIS LEAFE AND LOVE EMBRACE        5.28.14
OR LEND YOU ME ANOTHER LIVING BREST                 5.33.14
HER BREST LYKE LILLYES, ERE THEYR LEAVES BE SHED    5.64.11
HER BREST THAT TABLE WAS SO RICHLY SPREDD           5.77.13
FAYRE WHEN HER BREST LYKE A RICH LADEN BARKE        5.81.5
BUT PURE AFFECTIONS BRED IN SPOTLESSE BREST         5.84.5
```

BREASTS   3
```
IF SNOW BE WHITE, WHY THEN HER BRESTS ARE DUN       3.130.3
YOU SEEKE TO NURSE AT FULLEST BREASTS OF $FAME      4.15.13
HER BREASTS HIS TENTS, LEGS HIS TRIUMPHALL CARRE    4.29.11
```

BREATH   30
```
WHICH STILL IS CHAC'D, WHILE I HAVE ANY BREATH      1.5.10
IF THIS BE LOVE, TO DRAW A WEARIE BREATH            1.9.1
THEN DOE I LOVE AND DRAW THIS WEARIE BREATH         1.9.14
THEN DOE I LOVE, AND DRAW THIS WEARIE BREATH        1.10.1
YET CANNOT FINDE HER BREATHE UNTO MY REST           1.13.11
IF I HAVE LOV'D HER DEARER THEN MY BREATH           1.21.9
MY BREATH THAT CALLS THE HEAVENS TO WITNES IT       1.21.10
AND WILL WHILST I SHALL DRAW THIS BREATH OF MINE    1.33.10
AND THEN IN SIGHING, TO GIVE UP MY BREATH           2.20.12
NOW AT THE LAST GASPE, CF $LOVES LATEST $BREATH     2.61.9
WHILST THUS HE PANTETH FOR HIS LATEST BREATH        2.135.10
LET HEAVENS WITHDRAW THEIR SWEET $AMBROZIAN
                              BREATH                 2.145.11
SO LONG AS MEN CAN BREATH OR EYES CAN SEE           3.18.13
WHILE THOU DOST BREATH THAT POOR'ST INTO MY VERSE   3.38.2
WHEN SOMMERS BREATH THEIR MASKED BUDS DISCLOSES     3.54.8
O HOW SHALL SUMMERS HUNNY BREATH HOLD OUT           3.65.5
WHERE BREATH MOST BREATHS, EVEN IN THE
                              MOUTHS OF MEN          3.81.14
THEN OTHERS, FOR THE BREATH OF WORDS RESPECT        3.85.13
IF NOT FROM MY LOVES BREATH, THE PURPLE PRIDE       3.99.3
AND TO HIS ROBBRY HAD ANNEXT THY BREATH             3.99.11
THEN IN THE BREATH THAT FROM MY $MISTRES REEKES     3.130.8
THAT HER SWEETE BREATH MAKES OFT THY FLAMES
                              TO RISE                4.12.4
THAT WHEN THE BREATH OF MY COMPLAINTS DOTH TUCH     4.44.10
STELLA'S SWEETE BREATH THE SAME TO ME DID REED      4.58.11
AND ALL IN VAINE, FOR WHILE THY BREATH MOST SWEET   4.68.9
BUT WITH SHORT BREATH, LONG LOOKES, STAID
                              FEET AND WALKING HED   4.76.13
LET BREATH SUCKE UP THOSE SWEETES, LET
                              ARMES EMBRACE          4.85.12
YET TRUTH (IF $CAITIF'S BREATH MIGHTE
                              CALL THEE) THIS        4.93.5
WING'D WITH WHOSE BREATH, SO PLEASING
                              $ZEPHIRES BLOW         4.100.7
AND GATHER TO MY SELFE NEW BREATH AWHILE            5.80.4
```

BREATHE   6
```
WHAT IT IS TO BREATHE AND LIVE WITHOUT LIFE         1.20.1
INTO THE SAME THEN LET A $WOMAN BREATHE             2.15.9
LOVE GAVE THE WOUND, WHICH WHILE I BREATHE
                              WILL BLEED            4.2.2
WHILE TEARES POWRE OUT HIS INKE, AND SIGHS
                              BREATHE OUT HIS WORDS  4.6.10
BREATHE OUT THE FLAMES WHICH BURNE WITHIN
                              MY HEART               4.28.13
```

```
    BECAUSE I BREATHE NOT LOVE TO EVERIE ONE          4.54.1
BREATHED                    3
    BREATH'D FORTH THE SOUND THAT SAID I HATE         3.145.2
    BUT THIS AT LAST IS HER SWEET BREATH'D DEFENCE    4.61.4
    AND MODEST THOUGHTS BREATHD FROM WEL TEMPRED
                            SPRITES                   5.84.6
BREATHER                    1
    BREATHER OF LIFE, AND FASTNER OF DESIRE           4.80.7
BREATHERS                   1
    WHEN ALL THE BREATHERS OF THIS WORLD ARE DEAD     3.81.12
BREATHES                    2
    WHERE BREATH MOST BREATHS, EVEN IN THE
                            MOUTHS OF MEN             3.81.14
    SWEETNESSE, THAT BREATHES AND PANTS AS
                            OFT AS SHE                4.101.2
BREATHING                   2
    T'$ARABIAN ODORS GIVE THY BREATHING SWEETE        1.19.6
    BREATHING ALL BLISSE AND SWEETNING TO THE HEART   4.81.3
BREATHLESS                  1
    OFT 'T'ATH BEEN PROV'D, THE BREATHLESSE
                            $COARSE WILL BLEED        2.46.8
BREATH'S                    2
    MY $SMELLING WONNE WITH HER $BREATHS $SPICERIE    2.29.8
    THE SWEET OF $EDEN, TO HER BREATHES PERFUME       2.148.6
BRED                        7
    THUS FROM MY $BREST, WHERE IT WAS BRED ALONE      2.56.13
    MY $THOUGHTS BRED UP WITH $EAGLE-BIRDS OF LOVE    2.103.1
    FINDING THE FIRST CONCEIT OF LOVE THERE BRED      3.108.13
    YOU ARE SO STRONGLY IN MY PURPOSE BRED            3.112.13
    UNQUIET THOUGHT, WHOM AT THE FIRST I BRED         5.2.1
    BUT PURE AFFECTIONS BRED IN SPOTLESSE BREST       5.84.5
    IN MY SWEET PEACE SUCH BREACHES TO HAVE BRED      5.86.12
BREED                       11
    THAT'S FOR THY SELFE TO BREED AN OTHER THEE       3.6.7
    SAVE BREED TO BRAVE HIM, WHEN HE TAKES
                            THEE HENCE                3.12.14
    WHICH ELEMENTS WITH MORTALL MIXTURE BREED         4.5.11
    IF THAT BE SINNE WHICH IN FIXT HEARTS DOTH BREED  4.14.12
    NAY, THAT MAY BREED MY FAME, IT IS SO RARE        4.34.6
    WRACKES $TRIUMPHS BE, WHICH $LOVE (HIGH
                            SET) DOTH BREED           4.42.14
    THOUGH FALSE, YET WITH FREE SCOPE MORE
                            GRACE DOTH BREED          4.45.10
    OF ALL THE GRAVE CONCEITS YOUR BRAINE DOTH BREED  4.51.6
    EVEN THOSE SAD WORDS EVEN IN SAD ME DID BREED     4.58.14
    IN WEAKENED MINDS, QUICKE APPREHENDING BREED      4.66.3
    DARE TO APPROCH, THAT MAY MY SOLACE BREED         5.52.10
BREEDING                    1
    WEALTH BREEDING WANT, MORE BLIST, MORE
                            WRETCHED GROW             4.24.4
BREEDS                      4
    MY NEVER-CERTAINE $JOY BREEDS EVER-CERTAINE
                            $FEARES                   2.26.4
    MY NEVER CERTAINE JOY, BREEDS EVER-CERTAINE
                            FEARES                    2.137.4
    THEN PUBLICK MEANES WHICH PUBLICK MANNERS BREEDS  3.111.4
    BUT SOONE AS THOUGHT OF THEE BREEDS MY DELIGHT    4.108.5
BRIAR                       1
    SWEET IS THE $ROSE, BUT GROWES UPON A BRERE       5.26.1
```

```
BRIBED                          1
  MY $HEARING BRIB'D WITH HER $TONGUES $HARMONIE      2.29.6
BRIDE                           1
  NOR AT $FIFTEENE NE'R LONG'D TO BE A $BRIDE         2.15.6
BRIEF                           3
  NOR CAN I FORTUNE TO BREEFE MYNUITS TELL            3.14.5
  LOVE ALTERS NOT WITH HIS BREEFE HOURES
                            AND WEEKES                3.116.11
  OUR DATES ARE BREEFE, AND THEREFOR WE ADMIRE        3.123.5
BRIGHT                         25
  RESTORE THY BLUSH UNTO $AURORA BRIGHT               1.19.7
  WHICH NOW ARE MELTED BY THINE EYES BRIGHT SUN       1.32.7
  AND THOSE BRIGHT RAIES THAT KINDLE ALL THIS FIRE    1.38.3
  BRIGHT STARRE OF $BEAUTY, ON WHOSE EYE-LIDS SIT     2.4.1
  THOSE $EYES TO MY $HEART SHINING EVER BRIGHT        2.55.13
  THOSE EYES TO MY HART SHINING EVER BRIGHT           2.102.13
  THE GLORIOUS SUN-BEAMES OF HER EYES BRIGHT
                            SHINING                   2.109.10
  BUT THOU CONTRACTED TO THINE OWNE BRIGHT EYES       3.1.5
  AN EYE MORE BRIGHT THEN THEIRS, LESSE
                            FALSE IN ROWLING          3.20.5
  AS ANY MOTHERS CHILDE, THOUGH NOT SO BRIGHT         3.21.11
  I TELL THE $DAY TO PLEASE HIM THOU ART BRIGHT       3.28.9
  AND DARKELY BRIGHT, ARE BRIGHT IN DARKE DIRECTED    3.43.4
  AND DARKELY BRIGHT, ARE BRIGHT IN DARKE DIRECTED    3.43.4
  THEN THOU WHOSE SHADDOW SHADDOWES DOTH
                            MAKE BRIGHT               3.43.5
  AND NIGHTS BRIGHT DAIES WHEN DREAMS DO
                            SHEW THEE ME              3.43.14
  BUT YOU SHALL SHINE MORE BRIGHT IN THESE CONTENTS   3.55.3
  THAT IN BLACK INCK MY LOVE MAY STILL SHINE
                            BRIGHT                    3.65.14
  FOR I HAVE SWORNE THEE FAIRE, AND THOUGHT
                            THEE BRIGHT               3.147.13
  IN COLOUR BLACKE, WHY WRAPT SHE BEAMES SO BRIGHT+   4.7.2
  OR SEEING JETS, BLACKE, BUT IN BLACKNESSE BRIGHT    4.91.8
  THAT YOUR BRIGHT BEAMS OF MY WEAK EIES ADMYRED      5.7.11
  THRUGH YOUR BRIGHT BEAMS DOTH NOT THE
                            BLINDED GUEST             5.8.5
  DARTING THEIR DEADLY ARROWES FYRY BRIGHT            5.16.7
  SO I WHOSE STAR, THAT WONT WITH HER BRIGHT RAY      5.34.5
  DOE YOU HIM TAKE, AND IN YOUR BOSOME BRIGHT         5.73.9
BRIGHTEST                       1
  WHICH CLEERE OUR CLOUDED WORLD WITH BRIGHTEST
                            FLAME                     1.12.4
BRIGHTNESS                      5
  AND CLOUDS OBSCURE HAD SHADED STILL HER
                            BRIGHTNESSE               1.7.4
  AND THAT THY BRIGHTNES SETS AT LENGTH TO $WEST      1.40.9
  AND SWERE THAT BRIGHTNESSE DOTH NOT GRACE
                            THE DAY+                  3.150.4
  THAT BEING NOW WITH HER HUGE BRIGTNESSE DAZED       5.3.5
  BUT WITH SUCH BRIGHTNESSE WHYLEST I FILL MY MIND    5.88.13
BRING                          16
  AND SINNE OF FROWNES BRING HONOUR TO THE FACE       1.56.12
  UNKINDLY, SUCH DISTEMPRATURE DOTH BRING             2.147.10
  FOR TO THY SENSUALL FAULT I BRING IN SENCE          3.35.9
  AND HE THAT CALLS ON THEE, LET HIM BRING FORTH      3.38.11
  WHAT CAN MINE OWNE PRAISE TO MINE OWNE
                            SELFE BRING               3.39.3
```

```
    CAN BRING HIM TO HIS SWEET UP-LOCKED TREASURE         3.52.2
    FOR I AM SHAMD BY THAT WHICH I BRING FORTH            3.72.13
    WHEN OTHERS WOULD GIVE LIFE, AND BRING A TOMBE        3.83.12
    SO THAT MY SELFE BRING WATER FOR MY STAINE            3.109.8
    BRING ME WITHIN THE LEVEL OF YOUR FROWNE              3.117.11
    YOU THAT DO $DICTIONARIE'S METHODE BRING              4.15.5
    A PRETY CASE- I HOPED HER TO BRING                    4.57.12
    BRING THEREFORE ALL THE FORCES THAT YE MAY            5.14.9
    I MUST BEGIN AND NEVER BRING TO END                   5.23.10
    WHICH WAS NOT HARD T'ATCHIVE AND BRING TO END         5.51.8
    AND HAVING HARROWD HELL DIDST BRING AWAY              5.68.3
BRINGING                         1
    BRINGING WITH HER THOSE STARRY $NIMPHS,
                          WHOSE CHACE                     4.97.3
BRINGS                           9
    THE QUIET $EV'NING YET TOGETHER BRINGS                2.37.7
    FOR THY SWEET LOVE REMEMBRED SUCH WELTH BRINGS        3.29.13
    ALACK WHAT POVERTY MY $MUSE BRINGS FORTH              3.103.1
    WHEN TREMBLING VOICE BRINGS FORTH THAT
                          I DO $STELLA LOVE               4.6.14
    MY YOUTH DOTH WASTE, MY KNOWLEDGE BRINGS
                          FORTH TOYES                     4.18.9
    SO $STELLA'S HEART, FINDING WHAT POWER
                          $LOVE BRINGS                    4.29.5
    THE FIRST THAT STRAIGHT MY FANCIE'S ERROR BRINGS      4.38.5
    THEN SERVANT'S WRACKE, WHERE NEW DOUBTS
                          HONOR BRINGS                    4.45.11
    AND HUMBLED HARTS BRINGS CAPTIVES UNTO THEE           5.10.7
BRISTLY                          1
    BORNE ON THE BEARE WITH WHITE AND BRISTLY BEARD       3.12.8
BROAD                            2
    ON YOUR BROAD MAINE DOTH WILFULLY APPEARE             3.80.8
    THRUGH THE BROAD WORLD DOTH SPRED HIS GOODLY RAY      5.40.8
BROAD-BRIMMED                    1
    NOW BROAD-BRYMD $INDUS, THEN OF $PINDUS HEIGHT        2.120.5
BROADERED                        1
    BROADRED WITH BULS AND SWANS, POWDRED
                          WITH GOLDEN RAINE               4.6.6
BROILS                           1
    AND BROILES ROOTE CUT THE WORKE OF MASONRY            3.55.6
BROKE                            6
    BUT YOU BROKE INTO $HEAV'NS IMMORTALL STORE           2.14.9
    THY $BOWE HALFE BROKE, IS PEEC'D WITH
                          OLDE DESIRE                     2.126.5
    HER $CABLE BROKE, HER SUREST $ANCHOR LOST             2.134.10
    ONE OF HER FETHERED CREATURES BROAKE AWAY             3.143.2
    IN ACT THY BED-VOW BROAKE AND NEW FAITH TORNE         3.152.3
    THE $DAMZELL BROKE HIS MISINTENDED DART               5.16.12
BROKEN                           5
    MY FENCE OPPRESS'D, HAD FAILD, AND HEART
                          HAD BROKEN                      1.7.14
    BEWRAIES MY LOVE, WITH BROKEN WORDS HALFE SPOKEN      1.15.6
    THE BROKEN TOPS OF LOFTY TREES DECLARE                1.37.5
    DOST THOU DESIRE MY SLUMBERS SHOULD BE BROKEN         3.61.3
    WHOSE FRUITLESSE WORKE IS BROKEN WITH LEAST WYND      5.23.14
BROOD                            5
    AND RIGHTLY CAME FROM THAT BRAVE MOUNTING $BROOD      2.56.8
    AND THAT THEY CAME OF THIS RARE KINGLIE BROOD         2.103.8
    AND MAKE THE EARTH DEVOURE HER OWNE SWEET BROOD       3.19.2
    IN WHICH THOU LURKEST LYKE TO VIPERS BROOD            5.2.6
```

```
AND OF THE BROOD CF $ANGELS HEVENLY BORNE          5.61.6
BROOK                   10
   O BLESSED $BROOKE, WHOSE MILKE-WHITE $SWANS ADORE   2.53.3
   SAY THUS FAIRE $BROCKE, WHEN THOU SHALT
                     SEE THY QUEENE                    2.53.9
   O BLESSED $BROOKE, WHOSE MILK-WHITE $SWANS ACORE   2.113.3
   SAY THUS FAYRE $BROCKE WHEN THOU SHALT
                     SEE THY $QUEENE                   2.113.9
   WHICH IN HER FACE TEACH VERTUE, I COULD BROOKE      4.56.6
   AND THIS I SWEARE BY BLACKEST BROOKE OF HELL        4.74.7
   AND HAPPY RYMES BATH'D IN THE SACRED BROCKE         5.1.9
   OF THAT FAIRE SIGHT, THAT NOTHING ELSE
                     THEY BROOKE                       5.35.10
   THINKING TO QUENCH HER THIRST AT THE NEXT BROOKE    5.67.8
   OF THAT FAYRE SIGHT, THAT NOTHING ELSE
                     THEY BROOKE                       5.83.10
BROOKED                 1
   HER PRIDE BROOK'D NCT PCCRE SOULES SHOULD
                     SO ASPIRE                         1.36.8
BROOKS                  2
   NO OTHER PROUDER $BROOKES SHALL HEARE MY WRONG      1.58.14
   POORE $BROOKES AND $BANKS HAD NO SUCH
                     WONDERS BEENE                     2.120.14
BROOM-FLOWER            1
   SWEET IS THE BROOME-FLOWRE, BUT YET SOWRE ENCUGH    5.26.7
BROTHER                 2
   BROTHER TO DEATH, IN SILENT DARKNES BORNE           1.54.2
   GOOD BROTHER $PHILIP, I HAVE BORNE YOU LCNG         4.83.1
BROUGHT                11
   MINERVA-LIKE, BROUGHT FCCRTH WITHOUT A MCTHER       1.2.2
   (NOT TOO FARRE PAST) MAY TO THEIR $WITS
                     BE BROUGHT                        2.9.14
   WHO HAVING NOW BRCUGHT CN HIS END WITH $CARE        2.10.3
   NEERE THE DEAD $BCDY HAPPILY BE BROUGHT             2.46.7
   WHERE FIRST MY $LOVE INTC THE WORLD WAS BROUGHT     2.116.4
   A DEARER BIRTH THEN THIS HIS LOVE HAD BROUGHT       3.32.11
   FOR THEN DISPIGHT CF SPACE I WOULD BE BRCUGHT       3.44.3
   AND BROUGHT TC MEDICINE A HEALTHFULL STATE          3.118.11
   DOTH FALL TO STRAY, AND MY CHIEFE POWRES
                     ARE BROUGHT                       4.38.3
   THAT HAST MY MIND, NONE CF THE BASEST, BRCUGHT      4.40.3
   SWEET FRUIT OF PLEASURE BRCUGHT FROM PARADICE       5.77.11
BROW                   21
   NO $BAYES I SEEKE TC DECKE MY MOURNING BROW         1.4.9
   HER BROW SHADES FRCWNES, ALTHOUGH HER
                     EYES ARE SUNNY                    1.6.2
   LIVE RECONCILED FRIENDS WITHIN HER BROW             1.6.10
   FOR HER THE CRUELL $FAIRE, WITHIN WHOSE BROW        1.10.2
   AND IF A BROW WITH CARES CHARACTERS PAINTED         1.15.5
   ROB HER FAIRE $BRCW, BREAKE IN ON $BEAUTY, STEALE   1.22.5
   TIME, CRUELL TIME, COME AND SUBDUE THAT $BROW       1.23.1
   WHOSE CLOUDED BROW DOTH MAKE MY DAIES SO SAD        1.26.4
   YET NO MILD COMFORT WOULD THY $BROW REVEALE         1.31.9
   DISSOLVES THE BEAUTY OF THE FAIREST BROW            1.39.12
   AND THOU WITH CAREFULL BROW SITTING ALONE           1.41.2
   WHEN SHAL HER TROUBLED BROW CHARG'D WITH DISCAINE   1.49.5
   THAT LOVELY, ARCHED, YVCRIE, POLLISH'D $BROW        2.8.5
   WHEN FORTIE $WINTERS SHALL BESEIGE THY BROW         3.2.1
   O CARVE NOT WITH THY HOWERS MY LOVES FAIRE BROW     3.19.9
   WITH ALL TRIUMPHANT SPLENDOR ON MY BROW             3.33.10
```

```
  AND DELVES THE PARALELS IN BEAUTIES BROW              3.60.10
  WHEN HOURES HAVE DREIND HIS BLOOD AND
                          FILD HIS BROW                 3.63.3
  OR DURST INHABIT ON A LIVING BROW                     3.68.4
  OF HAND, OF FOOTE, OF LIP, OF EYE, OF BROW            3.106.6
  WHICH VULGAR SCANDALL STAMPT UPON MY BROW             3.112.2
BROWS                    5
  NOR GRAVER BROWES HAVE JUDG'D MY $MUSE SO VAINE       1.7.6
  BE IT NOT SEENE IN EITHER OF OUR $BROWES              2.61.7
  WITH WITHERED BROWES, ALL WRINCKLED WITH
                          DISPAIRES                     2.114.3
  OF $STELLA'S BROWES MADE HIM TWO BETTER BOWES         4.17.10
  HER SNOWY BROWES LYKE BUDDED $BELLAMOURES             5.64.7
BRUNT                    1
  TOO FEEBLE I T'ABIDE THE BRUNT SO STRONG              5.12.9
BUBBLE                   1
  LIKE A VAINE BUBBLE BLOWEN UP WITH AYRE               5.58.6
BUBBLING                 1
  THAT POISON FOULE OF BUBLING PRIDE DOTH LIE           4.27.6
BUD                      4
  WHILST YET HER TENDER BUD DOTH UNDISCLOSE             1.39.3
  WITHIN THINE OWNE BUD BURIEST THY CONTENT             3.1.11
  AND LOATHSOME CANKER LIVES IN SWEETEST BUD            3.35.4
  THE BUD OF JOY, THE BLOSSOME OF THE MORNE             5.61.9
BUDDED                   1
  HER SNOWY BROWES LYKE BUDDED $BELLAMOURES             5.64.7
BUDDING                  1
  DOTH SPOT THE BEAUTIE OF THY BUDDING NAME+            3.95.3
BUDS                     4
  ROUGH WINDES DO SHAKE THE DARLING BUDS OF $MAIE       3.18.3
  WHEN SOMMERS BREATH THEIR MASKED BUDS DISCLOSES       3.54.8
  FOR $CANKER VICE THE SWEETEST BUDS DOTH LOVE          3.70.7
  AND BUDS OF MARJEROM HAD STOLNE THY HAIRE             3.99.7
BUGBEARS                 2
  I STILL FEARE $BUG-BEARES IN $APOLLO'S $CELL          2.39.12
  I STYLL FEARE BUGBEARES IN $APOLLOS $CELL             2.118.12
BUILD                    3
  I BUILD MY $HOPES A WORLD ABOVE THE $SKIE             2.62.9
  I BUILD MY HOPES, A WORLD ABOVE THE SKYE              2.150.9
  WILL BUILDE AN ALTAR TO APPEASE HER YRE               5.22.10
BUILDED                  1
  NO IT WAS BUYLDED FAR FROM ACCIDENT                   3.124.5
BUILDING                 1
  HE OF TALL BUILDING, AND OF GOODLY PRIDE              3.80.12
BUILDS                   2
  SHE BUILDS HER FAME ON HIGHER SEATED PRAISE           4.81.10
  AND SPOTLESSE PLEASURE BUILDS HER SACRED BOWRE        5.65.14
BUILT                    4
  AND RUIN'D LOVE WHEN IT IS BUILT ANEW                 3.119.11
  THY PYRAMYDS BUYLT UP WITH NEWER MIGHT                3.123.2
  HATH HIS FRONT BUILT OF $ALABASTER PURE               4.9.3
  HER TEMPLE FAYRE IS BUILT WITHIN MY MIND              5.22.5
BULLET                   1
  TILL BLOUDIE BULLET GET HIM WRONGFULL PRAY            4.20.4
BULLS                    1
  BROADRED WITH BULS AND SWANS, POWDRED
                          WITH GOLDEN RAINE             4.6.6
BUNCH                    1
  HER NECK LYKE TO A BOUNCH OF $CULLAMBYNES             5.64.10
```

```
BUNDLES                      1
  SINCE $SONNETS THUS IN $BUNDLES ARE IMPREST          2.31.9
BUNGLING                     1
  GOE HYRE THY SELFE SOME BUNGLING $HARPERS $BOY       2.48.10
BURDEN                      10
  THEN BEAUTY (NOW THE BURTHEN OF MY SONG)             1.38.5
  A BURDEN TO MY SELFE, DISTREST IN MINDE              1.49.2
  WHEN THOU SURCHARG'D WITH BURTHEN OF THY YEERES      1.50.9
  (SAITH HE) $LIGHT $BURTHEN'S HEAVY, IF
                             FARRE BORNE                2.59.10
  ORE-CHARG'D WITH BURTHEN OF MINE OWNE LOVES MIGHT    3.23.8
  THE SECOND BURTHEN CF A FORMER CHILD+                3.59.4
  BEARING THE WANTON BURTHEN OF THE PRIME              3.97.7
  ON SILLY ME DO NOT THE BURTHEN LAY                   4.51.5
  OR DOTH THE TEDIOUS BURD'N OF LONG WO                4.66.2
  AND CLOGD WITH BURDEN OF MORTALITY                   5.72.4
BURDENED                     1
  A BURTHNED HART. '$HOW CAN WORDS EASE, WHICH ARE     4.34.2
BURDENS                      1
  BUT THAT WILD MUSICK BURTHENS EVERY BOW              3.102.11
BURIED                       6
  AND IN THEM-SELVES THEIR PRIDE LIES BURIED           3.25.7
  AND ALL THOSE FRIENDS WHICH I THOUGHT BURIED         3.31.4
  THOU ART THE GRAVE WHERE BURIED LOVE DOTH LIVE       3.31.9
  THE RICH PROUD COST OF CUTWORNE BURIED AGE           3.64.2
  MY NAME BE BURIED WHERE MY BODY IS                   3.72.11
  IN TOMBE OF LIDS THEN BURIED ARE MINE EYES           4.99.12
BURIEST                      1
  WITHIN THINE OWNE BUD BURIEST THY CONTENT            3.1.11
BURN                        18
  THAT FIRE CAN BURNE WHEN ALL THE MATTER'S SPENT      1.41.10
  WHO WHILST I BURNE, SHE SINGS AT MY SOULES WRACK     1.47.5
  WHICH WITH MY $SIGHES THIS $EPICURE DOTH BURNE       2.7.7
  WHILST $MOONE SHALL SHINE, OR ANY $FIRE
                             SHALL BURNE                2.13.12
  DOE WHAT THOU CANST, RAZE, MASSACRE, AND BURNE       2.63.11
  WHILST $MOONE SHALL SHYNE BY NIGHT, OR
                        ANY FIRE SHALL BURNE           2.121.12
  QUENCHLES DESIRE, MAKES HOPE BURNE, DRYES
                             MY TEARES                  2.132.5
  AND BURNE THE LONG LIV'D $PHAENIX IN HER BLOCD       3.19.4
  NOR $MARS HIS SWORD, NOR WARRES QUICK
                        FIRE SHALL BURNE               3.55.7
  MY MOST FULL FLAME SHOULD AFTERWARDS BURNE
                             CLEERER                    3.115.4
  AND FIND TH'EFFECT, FOR I DO BURNE IN LOVE           4.25.14
  BREATHE OUT THE FLAMES WHICH BURNE WITHIN
                             MY HEART                   4.28.13
  IF HE DO LOVE, I BURNE, I BURNE IN LOVE              4.59.2
  IF HE DO LOVE, I BURNE, I BURNE IN LOVE              4.59.2
  BUT WHEN IT ONCE DOTH BURNE, IT DOTH DIVIDE          5.6.7
  BUT THAT I BURNE MUCH MORE IN BOYLING SWEAT          5.30.7
  WHAT THEN REMAINES BUT I TO ASHES BURNE              5.32.13
  NOT WATER., FOR HER LOVE DOTH BURNE LIKE FYRE        5.55.6
BURNED                       6
  YOUR SELFE THUS BURNED IN THAT SACRED FLAME          2.16.9
  BURN'D IN A $SEA OF YCE, AND DROWN'D AMIDST
                             A FIRE                     2.62.14
  THY SELFE THUS BURNED IN THIS SACRED FLAME           2.106.9
  BURN'D IN A $SEA CF $ICE, AND DROWN'D
                        AMIDST A FIRE                  2.150.14
```

```
   THREE $APRILL PERFUMES IN THREE HOT $JUNES
                        BURN'D                           3.104.7
   THE $SUNNE WHICH OTHERS BURN'D, DID HER
                        BUT KISSE                        4.22.14
BURNETH                   2
   STILL MORE AND MORE IT TO MY TORMENT BURNETH          2.40.12
   STILL MORE AND MORE UNTO MY TORMENT BURNETH           2.144.12
BURNING                   4
   WHICH STILL TORMENTS ME IN DAYES BURNING FIRE         2.145.14
   LIFTS UP HIS BURNING HEAD, EACH UNDER EYE             3.7.2
   CAN THOSE BLACKE BEAMES SUCH BURNING MARKES
                        ENGRAVE                          4.47.2
   BURNING IN FLAMES OF PURE AND CHAST DESYRE            5.22.12
BURNS                     4
   THAT HOLDS, THAT BURNES, THAT WOUNDS ME
                        IN THIS SORT                     1.14.8
   YET THERE HE BURNES, IN FIRE THATS NEVER
                        QUENCHED                         2.122.14
   MY HEART CRIES 'AH', IT BURNES, MINE EYES
                        NOW DAZLED BE                    4.76.11
   BUT MY HEART BURNES, I CANNOT SILENT BE               4.81.11
BURNT                     1
   HE BURNT UNWARES HIS WINGS, AND CANNOT FLY AWAY       4.8.14
BUSH                      2
   WHO LIKE A THEEFE, HID IN DARKE BUSH DOTH LY          4.20.3
   WITHIN A BUSH HIS DREADFULL HEAD DOTH HIDE            5.53.3
BUSY                      4
   CRIES TO CATCH HER WHOSE BUSIE CARE IS BENT           3.143.6
   THESE QUESTIONS BUSIE WITS TO ME DO FRAME             4.30.12
   THAT BUSIE ARCHER HIS SHARPE ARROWES TRIES+           4.31.4
   TIRED WITH THE DUSTY TOILES OF BUSIE DAY              4.89.7
BUY                       2
   BUY TEARMES DIVINE IN SELLING HOURES OF DROSSE        3.146.11
   AND FOR THY SAKE THAT ALL LYKE DEARE DIDST BUY        5.68.11
CABINET                   2
   WHEN MY SOULES SUNNE FROM HER FAYRE $CABYNET          2.125.2
   SO WHEN THOU SAW'ST IN $NATURE'S CABINET              4.11.9
CABINETS                  1
   I SEND THOSE EYES THE CABINETS OF LOVE                1.60.6
CABLE                     1
   HER $CABLE BROKE, HER SUREST $ANCHOR LOST             2.134.10
CAESAR'S                  1
   NOR DO ASPIRE TO $CAESAR'S BLEEDING FAME              4.64.10
CAGE                      2
   HOLDS MY YOUNG BRAINE CAPTIV'D IN GOLDEN CAGE         4.23.11
   WITHIN HER CAGE, BUT SINGES AND FEEDS HER FILL        5.65.8
CAITIFF                   1
   AS OF A CAITIFE WORTHY SO TO DIE                      4.94.10
CAITIFF'S                 1
   YET TRUTH (IF $CAITIF'S BREATH MIGHTE
                        CALL THEE) THIS                  4.93.5
CALL                     29
   IN $RIGHT OR $WRONG, THEY CALL HER $CONSCIENCE        2.12.11
   CALL BACKE THE STIFFE-NECK'D $REBELS FROM $EXILE      2.25.11
   THAT EV'RY $CREATURE TO HIS KIND DO'ST CALL           2.37.11
   SOME CALL ON $HEAVEN, SOME INVOCATE ON $HELL          2.39.3
   ONELY I CALL ON MY DIVINE $IDEA                       2.39.14
   NOW CALL HER $GODDESSE, THEN I CALL HER $THIEFE       2.41.12
   NOW CALL HER $GODDESSE, THEN I CALL HER $THIEFE       2.41.12
   BUT EVER CALL UPON DIVINE $IDEA                       2.118.14
```

NOW CALL HER $GODDESSE, THEN I CALL HER THIEFE   2.143.12
NOW CALL HER $GODDESSE, THEN I CALL HER THIEFE   2.143.12
THOU MAIST CALL THINE, WHEN THOU FROM
                            YOUTH CONVERTEST   3.11.4
NO LOVE, MY LOVE, THAT THOU MAIST TRUE LOVE CALL   3.40.3
AS CAL IT $WINTER, WHICH BEING FUL OF CARE   3.56.13
WHILST I ALONE DID CALL UPON THY AYDE   3.79.1
FOR NOTHING THIS WIDE $UNIVERSE I CALL   3.109.13
FORGOT UPON YOUR DEAREST LOVE TO CALL   3.117.3
TO THIS I WITNES CALL THE FOLES OF TIME   3.124.13
O CALL NOT ME TO JUSTIFIE THE WRONG   3.139.1
WHO HATETH THEE THAT I DOE CALL MY FRIEND   3.149.5
NO WANT OF CONSCIENCE HOLD IT THAT I CALL   3.151.13
I CALL IT PRAISE TO SUFFER $TYRANNIE   4.2.11
IT IS MOST TRUE, WHAT WE CALL $CUPID'S DART   4.5.5
QUEENE $VERTUE'S COURT, WHICH SOME CALL
                            $STELLA'S FACE   4.9.1
DO THEY CALL $VERTUE THERE UNGRATEFULNESSE+   4.31.14
LOVE BY SURE PROOFE I MAY CALL THEE UNKIND   4.65.1
IN JUSTICE PAINES COME NOT TILL FAULTS DO CALL   4.86.10
YET TRUTH (IF $CAITIF'S BREATH MIGHTE
                            CALL THEE) THIS   4.93.5
FOR NONE CAN CALL AGAINE THE PASSED TIME   5.70.14
MEN CALL YOU FAYRE, AND YOU DOE CREDIT IT   5.79.1
CALLED   5
AND CALL'D TO TELL OF HIS $DISCOVERIE   2.1.3
CAULD TO THAT AUDITE BY ADVIS'D RESPECTS   3.49.4
LET NOT MY LOVE BE CAL'D $IDOLATRIE   3.105.1
CALD IT ANEW, AND WOOED SLEEPE AGAINE   4.38.13
WITH RAGE OF $LOVE, I CALD MY $LOVE UNKIND   4.62.2
CALLING   2
CALLING TO MINDE SINCE FIRST MY $LOVE BEGUN   2.51.1
AND CALLING FORTH OUT OF SAD $WINTERS NIGHT   5.4.5
CALLS   8
MY BREATH THAT CALLS THE HEAVENS TO WITNES IT   1.21.10
THUS IN MY $LOVE, $TIME CALLS ME TO RELATE   2.1.13
CALLS BACKE THE LOVELY $APRILL OF HER PRIME   3.3.10
THEN HOW WHEN NATURE CALLS THEE TO BE GONE   3.4.11
AND HE THAT CALLS ON THEE, LET HIM BRING FORTH   3.38.11
FOR WHAT CARE I WHO CALLES ME WELL OR ILL   3.112.3
WHERETO TH'INVITING TIME OUR FASHION CALLS   3.124.8
CALS EACH WIGHT TO SALUTE THE FLOURE OF BLISSE   4.99.11
CALM   4
AND CALME AND TEMPEST FOLLOW THEIR ASPECTS   1.34.6
NOW SEND FORTH HOPE, FOR NOW CALME PITTY SAVES   1.46.4
AND CALME THE TEMPEST WHICH MY SIGHS DOO RAISE   1.51.10
YOU CALME THE STORME THAT PASSION DID BEGIN   5.8.11
CALMS   1
SHALL TURNE TO CAULMES AND TYMELY CLEARE AWAY   5.62.12
CAME   18
IF ANY ASKE ME WHY SO SOONE I CAME   1.30.9
POWR'D OUT WHAT FIRST FROM QUICKE $INVENTION CAME   2.21.6
BUT WHEN MY $TOUCHING CAME TO PLAY HIS PART   2.29.9
AND RIGHTLY CAME FROM THAT BRAVE MOUNTING $BROOD   2.56.8
TILL THEY RETURN'D.. $HOME WHEN THEY NEVER CAME   2.58.6
AND THAT THEY CAME OF THIS RARE KINGLIE BROOD   2.103.8
BY INSPIRATION, CAME CONCEAV'D WITH THOUGHT   2.116.2
WHO PROPHECIED OF $CHRIST OR ERE HE CAME   2.119.3
AND SUE A FRIEND, CAME DEBTER FOR MY SAKE   3.134.11
CAME TRIPPING BY, BUT IN HER MAIDEN HAND   3.154.4

```
CAME THERE FOR CURE AND THIS BY THAT I PROVE        3.154.13
BUT WORDS CAME HALTING FORTH, WANTING
                        $INVENTION'S STAY             4.1.9
MY $FOE CAME ON, AND BEAT THE AIRE FOR ME           4.53.13
ALAS, WHENCE CAME THIS CHANGE OF LOOKES+ $IF I       4.86.1
THERE CAME TO ME A LEACH THAT WOULD APPLY            5.50.3
BUT CAME THE WAVES AND WASHED IT AWAY                5.75.2
BUT CAME THE TYDE, AND MADE MY PAYNES HIS PRAY       5.75.4
FAR PASSING THOSE WHICH $HERCULES CAME BY            5.77.7
CAMPS                          1
READY TO STORE THEIR CAMPES OF NEEDFULL THINGS       4.29.4
CANCEL                         2
SHAKE HANDS FOR EVER, $CANCELL ALL OUR $VOWES        2.61.5
CANCELL MY NAME, AND BLCT IT WITH DISPAYRE          2.142.12
CANCELLED                      1
AND WEEPE A FRESH LOVES LONG SINCE CANCELD WOE       3.30.7
CANDLE                         1
IF THIS DARKE PLACE YET SHEW LIKE CANDLE LIGHT       4.91.5
CANDLES                        1
AS THOSE GOULD CANDELLS FIXT IN HEAVENS AYER         3.21.12
CANKER                         5
AND LOATHSOME CANKER LIVES IN SWEETEST BUD           3.35.4
THE $CANKER BLOOMES HAVE FULL AS DEEPE A DIE         3.54.5
FOR $CANKER VICE THE SWEETEST BUDS DOTH LOVE         3.70.7
WHICH LIKE A CANKER IN THE FRAGRANT $ROSE            3.95.2
A VENGFULL CANKER EATE HIM UP TO DEATH               3.99.13
CANKER'S                       2
METALS DOE WASTE, AND FRET WITH $CANKERS $RUST       2.13.2
METTLES DOE WASTE, AND FRET WITH CANKERS RUST       2.121.2
CANOPY                         2
WHICH ERST FROM HEAT DID CANOPIE THE HERD            3.12.6
WER'T OUGHT TO ME I BORE THE CANOPY                  3.125.1
CAPES                          1
WHAT $CAPES HE DOUBLED, OF WHAT $CONTINENT           2.1.9
CAPTAIN                        2
OR CAPTAINE $JEWELLS IN THE CARCONET                 3.52.8
AND CAPTIVE-GOOD ATTENDING $CAPTAINE ILL             3.66.12
CAPTAINNESS                    1
FROM MY DEARE $CAPTAINNESSE TO RUN AWAY+             4.88.2
CAPTIVE                        2
ACCOUMPTS MY SELFE HER CAPTIVE QUITE FORLORNE        5.29.4
CAPTIVITY THENCE CAPTIVE US TO WIN                   5.68.4
CAPTIVED                       4
HOLDS MY YOUNG BRAINE CAPTIV'D IN GOLDEN CAGE       4.23.11
AND YIELD FOR PLEDGE MY POORE CAPTYVED HART          5.42.8
IN WHOSE STREIGHT BANDS YE NOW CAPTIVED ARE          5.71.7
BEING MY SELFE CAPTYVED HERE IN CARE                 5.73.1
CAPTIVE-GOOD                   1
AND CAPTIVE-GOOD ATTENDING $CAPTAINE ILL             3.66.12
CAPTIVES                       3
SO CAPTIVES TO HIS $SAINT BOTH SOULE AND SENCE       4.61.6
LYKE CAPTIVES TREMBLING AT THE VICTORS SIGHT         5.1.4
AND HUMBLED HARTS BRINGS CAPTIVES UNTO THEE          5.10.7
CAPTIVING                      1
WHO ME CAPTIVING STREIGHT WITH RIGOROUS WRONG        5.12.11
CAPTIVITY                      2
THE GENTLE BIRDE FEELES NO CAPTIVITY                 5.65.7
CAPTIVITY THENCE CAPTIVE US TO WIN                   5.68.4
CAR                            2
BUT WHEN FROM HIGH-MOST PICH WITH WERY CAR           3.7.9
```

```
    HER BREASTS HIS TENTS, LEGS HIS TRIUMPHALL CARRE      4.29.11
CARATS                        1
    BEAUTIES, WHICH WERE OF MANIE $CARRETS FINE            4.16.2
CARCANET                      1
    OR CAPTAINE $JEWELLS IN THE CARCONET                   3.52.8
CARE                         36
    WHERE I HAVE CAST TH'ACCOUNTS OF ALL MY CARE           1.1.6
    IF SO IT HAP, THIS CF-SPRING OF MY CARE                1.3.1
    THE NEVER-RESTING STONE CF $CARE TO ROULE              1.9.7
    THIS HEART MADE NCW THE PROSPECTIVE OF CARE            1.22.9
    SHE THINKES A LOOKE MAY RECOMPENCE MY CARE             1.24.9
    FROM CARE TO CARE THAT LEADES A LIFE SO BAD            1.26.2
    FROM CARE TO CARE THAT LEADES A LIFE SO BAD            1.26.2
    A WAY THROUGH WANT TO FREE MY SOULE FROM CARE          1.29.10
    WITH DARKE FORGETTING OF MY CARE RETURNE               1.54.4
    MY GRIEFES LONG LIV'D, AND CARE SUCCEEDING CARE        1.60.12
    MY GRIEFES LONG LIV'D, AND CARE SUCCEEDING CARE        1.60.12
    WHO HAVING NOW BRCUGHT CN HIS END WITH $CARE           2.10.3
    YET $HOPE DRAWES CN MY NEVER-HOPING $CARE              2.26.2
    LIKE THEY THAT $LUST, I CARE NOT, I WILL NONE          2.39.8
    YET HOPE DRAWES ON MY NEVER-HOPING CARE                2.137.2
    THE DOLEFULL $ANTHEMS OF MY ENDLESSE CARE              2.141.6
    THE $INNE OF CARE, THE $NURSE OF DRERY SORROW          2.145.2
    RECORDER OF REVENGE, REMEMBRANCER OF CARE              2.145.7
    THOU BEST OF DEEREST, AND MINE ONELY CARE              3.48.7
    AS CAL IT $WINTER, WHICH BEING FUL OF CARE             3.56.13
    FOR WHAT CARE I WHO CALLES ME WELL OR ILL              3.112.3
    IN SO PROFOUND $ABISME I THROW ALL CARE                3.112.9
    CRIES TO CATCH HER WHOSE BUSIE CARE IS BENT            3.143.6
    PAST CURE I AM, NCW $REASON IS PAST CARE               3.147.9
    VERTUE OF LATE, WITH VERTUOUS CARE TO STER             4.25.9
    THE GLASSES OF THY DAYLY VEXING CARE+'                 4.34.3
    NOR OUGHT DO CARE, THOUGH SOME ABOVE ME SIT            4.64.11
    LABOUR TU KILL IN ME THIS KILLING CARE                 4.68.12
    CARE SHINING IN MINE EYES, FAITH IN MY SPRITE          4.72.11
    O $GOD, THINKE YOU THAT SATISFIES MY CARE+             4.92.8
    BUT WIT CONFUS'D WITH TCO MUCH CARE DID MISSE          4.93.8
    SO GRATEFUL NOW YCU WAITE UPON MY CARE                 4.95.4
    NATURE WITH CARE SWEATES FOR HER DARLING'S SAKE        4.101.12
    THAT WITH SUCH POYSCNOUS CARE MY LOOKES
                            YOU MARKE                      4.104.2
    WHOM IF YE PLEASE, I CARE FOR OTHER NONE               5.1.14
    BEING MY SELFE CAPTYVED HERE IN CARE                   5.73.1
CARE-CHARMER                  1
    CARE-CHARMER $SLEEPE, SCNNE OF THE SABLE NIGHT         1.54.1
CAREER                        1
    THEN TO THE $TROPICKE TAKES HIS FULL $CAREERE          2.147.5
CAREFUL                       7
    AND OFT WITH CAREFULL TURNES, WITH SILENT $ART         1.8.7
    AND THOU WITH CAREFULL BROW SITTING ALONE              1.41.2
    ALTHOUGH MY CAREFULL ACCENTS NEVER MOOV'C THEE         1.44.13
    SHEW'D IN THESE LINES, THE WORKE OF CAREFULL
                            HOURES                         1.59.7
    HOW CAREFULL WAS I WHEN I TOOKE MY WAY                 3.48.1
    LOE AS A CAREFULL HUSWIFE RUNNES TO CATCH              3.143.1
    TILL THEN I WANDER CAREFULL COMFORTLESSE               5.34.13
CAREFULLY                     1
    THE HEW WHICH THOU SO CAREFULLY DOST NORISH            1.50.7
CARELESS                      4
    OR CARELESSE OF THE WEALTH BECAUSE HER OWNE            4.22.11
```

```
    ALL CARELESSE HOW MY LIFE FOR HER DECAYSE            5.38.10
    WHOM SHE ALL CARELESSE OF HIS GRIEFE CONSTRAYNED     5.48.9
    GOE TO MY LOVE, WHERE SHE IS CARELESSE LAYD          5.70.5
CARELESSNESS                 1
    FROM CARELESNESSE DID IN NO MANER GROW               4.93.7
CARES                       18
    AND CROSSE MY CARES ERE GREATER SUMMES ARISE         1.1.12
    PRESENT THE $IMAGE OF THE CARES I PROVE              1.2.3
    BEST IN MY FACE, HOW CARES HAVE TILD DEEPE
                                        FORROWES         1.4.8
    IN UNKINDE $LETTERS., WROTE SHE CARES NOT HOW        1.10.4
    AND YET THE $HYDRA OF MY CARES RENUES                1.16.9
    CARES NOT FOR THEE, BUT LETS THEE WASTE IN VAINE     1.23.10
    LONG ARE THEIR NIGHTS WHOSE CARES DO NEVER SLEEPE    1.26.5
    MY CARES DRAW ON MINE EVERLASTING NIGHT              1.30.1
    WITH STILL FRESH CARES, SUPPLIDE WITH NO RELIEFE     1.32.4
    MY CEASLES CARES CONTINUALLY RUN ON                  1.33.2
    ONCE LET THE $OCEAN OF MY CARES FINDE SHORE          1.46.13
    DRAWNE WITH MY BLOOD, AND PAINTED WITH MY CARES      1.47.3
    DUELY TO COUNT THE SUMME OF ALL MY CARES             2.3.2
    THE DRERIE ABSTRACTS OF MY ENDLESSE $CARES           2.54.2
    THE DRERY ABSTRACTS OF MY ENDLES CARES               2.101.2
    BEGINNING TO ACCOUNT THE SUM OF ALL MY CARES         2.110.2
    MY CARES MY MUTES SO MUTE TO CRAVE RELIEFE           2.111.10
    I SEE THE UGLY FACE OF MY DEFORMED CARES             2.114.2
CARE'S                       4
    AND IF A BROW WITH CARES CHARACTERS PAINTED          1.15.5
    STEALE FROM THY SELFE, AND BE THY CARES
                            OWNE THIEFE                   1.52.12
    STILL EMPTY GORG'D, WITH CARES CONSUMPTION
                            PYNDE                         2.116.14
    WITH CARE'S HARD HAND) TO TURNE AND TOSSE IN THEE    4.98.8
CARLEGION                    2
    CARLEGION $CHESTER VAUNTS HER HOLY $DEE              2.32.5
    CARLEGION $CHESTER, VAUNTS HER HOLY $DEE             2.124.5
CAROUSES                     1
    QUAFFING $CAROWSES IN THIS COSTLY $WINE              2.7.8
CARRIED                      1
    EACH HAD HIS CREAST, $MARS CARIED $VENUS' GLOVE      4.13.7
CARRY                        3
    TH'EVIDENCE SO GREAT A PROOFE DOTH CARRIE            2.2.8
    WITH OUT ALL BAYLE SHALL CARRY ME AWAY               3.74.2
    WHOSE YMAGE YET I CARRY FRESH IN MYND                5.78.4
CARVE                        3
    AND CARVE HIS PROPER GRIEFE UPON A STONE             1.13.2
    O CARVE NOT WITH THY HOWERS MY LOVES FAIRE BROW      3.19.9
    AN IMAGE IS, WHICH FOR OUR SELVES WE CARVE           4.5.6
CARVED                       1
    SHE CARV'D THEE FOR HER SEALE, AND MENT THERBY       3.11.13
CASE                        15
    HAVE FOLLOWED HARD THE $PROCESSE OF MY CASE          1.8.10
    I VIEW MY SELFE, MY SELFE IN WOFULL CASE             1.29.8
    NARCISSUS CHANG'D T'A FLOWER IN SUCH A CASE          1.37.12
    THY CRUELTY, THY GLORY., $O STRANGE CASE             1.56.10
    THEY RESOLUTE+ SO STANDS THE CASE WITH ME            2.24.12
    SO THAT ETERNALL LOVE IN LOVES FRESH CASE            3.108.9
    CAN JUDGE OF $LOVE, THOU FEEL'ST A $LOVER'S CASE     4.31.6
    OF $LOVERS NEVER KNOWNE, A GRIEVOUS CASE             4.45.6
    I CURST THEE OFT, I PITIE NOW THY CASE               4.46.1
    A PRETTY CASE- I HOPED HER TO BRING                  4.57.12
```

```
SHEWES LOVE AND PITIE TO MY ABSENT CASE          4.60.8
LET ALL THE EARTH WITH SCORNE RECOUNT MY CASE    4.64.7
NO WIND, NO SHADE CAN COOLE, WHAT HELPE
                        THEN IN MY CASE          4.76.12
STELLA NOW LEARNES (STRANGE CASE) TO WEEPE
                        IN THEE                  4.101.8
THOU TOLDST MINE EYES SHOULD HELPE THEIR
                        FAMISHT CASE+            4.106.6
```
CASKET   1
```
O RICHEST $CASKET OF ALL HEAVENLY TREASURE       2.146.11
```
CAST   13
```
WHERE I HAVE CAST TH'ACCOUNTS OF ALL MY CARE     1.1.6
CAST WATER-COLD $DISDAINE UPON MY FACE           1.5.8
AND HOW I LIVE CAST DOWNE FROM OFF ALL MYRTH     1.60.9
AND ON WHAT $ROCKS IN PERILL TO BE CAST+         2.1.12
TAKING MY $PENNE, WITH $WORDS TO CAST MY $WOE    2.3.1
ALL UNCLEANE $THOUGHTS, FOULE $SPIRITS
                        CAST OUT IN MEE          2.35.13
(QUOTH I) $THE $MAINE LOST, CAST THE $BY AWAY    2.59.11
OFT TAKING PEN IN HAND, WITH WORDS TO
                        CAST MY WOES             2.110.1
ALL UNCLEANE THOUGHTS, FOULE SPIRITS CAST
                        OUT IN MEE               2.112.13
THEN SO TO CAST HER $BALLAST OVER BOORD          2.134.8
CAST MY DESARTS INTO THE OPEN AYRE               2.142.10
WHEN AS THY LOVE HATH CAST HIS UTMOST SUMME      3.49.3
THEN $IF HE THRIVE AND I BE CAST AWAY            3.80.13
```
CASTLES   1
```
GAYNST SUCH STRONG CASTLES NEEDETH GREATER MIGHT  5.14.5
```
CATCH   5
```
NOR HIS OWNE VISION HOULDS WHAT IT DOTH CATCH    3.113.8
LOE AS A CAREFULL HUSWIFE RUNNES TO CATCH        3.143.1
CRIES TO CATCH HER WHOSE BUSIE CARE IS BENT      3.143.6
BUT IF THOU CATCH THY HOPE TURNE BACK TO ME      3.143.11
IN CLOSE AWAYT TO CATCH HER UNAWARE              5.71.4
```
CATCHING   1
```
AND CATCHING HOLD ON THINE OWNE WICKED HED       5.86.10
```
CATES   1
```
FROM BASE DESIRE ON EARTHLY CATES TO PRAY+       4.88.8
```
CATO'S   1
```
THY SCEPTER USE IN SOME OLD $CATOE'S BREST       4.4.5
```
CAUCASE   1
```
PELION AND $OSSA, FROSTY $CAUCASE OLD            2.120.6
```
CAUGHT   4
```
I CAUGHT AT ONE OF THEM A HUNGRIE BIT            4.82.11
AND BEING CAUGHT MAY CRAFTILY ENFOLD             5.37.7
WHOME BEING CAUGHT SHE KILLS WITH CRUELL PRYDE   5.47.7
RIGHT SO YOUR SELFE WERE CAUGHT IN CUNNING SNARE  5.71.5
```
CAUSE   30
```
AND CAUSE HER LEAVE TO TRIUMPH IN THIS WISE      1.10.9
I WORKE ON FLINT, AND THATS THE CAUSE I MONE     1.13.4
CAUSE ONCE THE DATE OF HER DISDAINE T'EXPIRE     1.22.3
I LOVE TH'EFFECT THE CAUSE BEING OF THIS POWRE   1.26.11
WHEREIN NO SHEW GAVE CAUSE OF LEAST SUSPECT      1.31.7
HER TOUCH DOTH CAUSE THE WARBLE OF THE SOUND     1.57.5
OR $NATURE MUST BE PARTIALL IN MY $CAUSE         2.27.13
THUS FROM THY SELFE THE CAUSE IS THUS DERIVED    2.104.13
THUS WAS THE WANTON CAUSE OF HYS OWNE WOE        2.122.12
THUS DO I FEELE THE PAINE, THE CAUSE,
                        YET CANNOT SEE           2.130.8
```

```
SINCE WHY TO LOVE, I CAN ALLEDGE NO CAUSE          3.49.14
THE CAUSE OF THIS FAIRE GUIFT IN ME IS WANTING     3.87.7
THE MORE I HEARE AND SEE JUST CAUSE OF HATE        3.150.10
PLEASURE MIGHT CAUSE HER READE, READING
                MIGHT MAKE HER KNOW                4.1.3
HER DAINTIEST BARE WENT FREE., THE CAUSE
                WAS THIS                           4.22.13
TO HAVE FOR NO CAUSE BIRTHRIGHT IN THE SKIE        4.26.5
HOW FARRE THEY SHOOTE AWRIE- THE TRUE CAUSE IS     4.41.12
ALAS, WHAT CAUSE IS THERE SO OVERTHWART            4.44.7
NOT THOUGH THEREOF THE CAUSE HER SELFE SHE KNOW    4.45.4
AND DO I SEE SOME CAUSE A HOPE TO FEEDE            4.66.1
GUESSE WE THE CAUSE.. '$WHAT, IS IT THUS+'
                $FIE NO                            4.74.12
NOR THIS, NOR THAT, NOR ANY SUCH SMALL CAUSE       4.75.12
AND NOTHING THEN THE CAUSE MORE SWEET COULD BE     4.87.13
THOUGHT WITH GOOD CAUSE THOU LIKEST SO
                WELL THE NIGHT                     4.96.1
TO THIS GREAT CAUSE, WHICH NEEDS BOTH
                USE AND ART                        4.107.8
STRONG THRUGH YOUR CAUSE, BUT BY YOUR VERTUE WEAK  5.8.12
WILL TEACH TO SPEAKE, AND MY JUST CAUSE TO PLEAD   5.43.10
REMOVE THE CAUSE BY WHICH YOUR FAYRE BEAMES
                DARKNED BE                         5.45.14
AND ERE SHE COULD THY CAUSE WEL UNDERSTAND         5.48.3
BUT PLEAD THY MAISTERS CAUSE UNJUSTLY PAYNED       5.48.8
```
CAUSED   1
```
CAUS'D BY THOSE CRUELL BEAMES THAT WERE
                SO STRONG                          1.32.14
```
CAUSEFUL   1
```
YET WAILE THY SELFE, AND WAILE WITH CAUSEFULL
                TEARES                             4.94.11
```
CAUSES   1
```
AND KNOW GREAT CAUSES, GREAT EFFECTS PROCURE       4.26.10
```
CAUSTICS   1
```
YOUR WORDS MY FRIEND (RIGHT HEALTHFULL
                CAUSTIKS) BLAME                    4.21.1
```
CEASE   13
```
SO SHALT THOU CEASE TO PLAGUE, AND I TO PAINE      1.19.14
I SHALL FORGET OLD WRONGS, MY GRIEFES
                SHALL CEASE                        1.46.11
CEASE DREAMES, TH'$IMAGES OF DAY DESIRES           1.54.9
DISCHARGE OUR $FORCES, HERE LET $MALICE CEASE      2.63.7
IF ALL WERE MINDED SO, THE TIMES SHOULD CEASE      3.11.7
O MAKE IN ME THOSE CIVILL WARRES TO CEASE          4.39.7
CEASE EAGER $MUSE, PEACE PEN, FOR MY SAKE STAY     4.70.12
CEASE WE TO PRAISE, NOW PRAY WE FOR A KISSE        4.79.14
AND I, MAD WITH DELIGHT, WANT WIT TO CEASE         4.81.13
BUT CEASE MINE EYES, YOUR TEARES DO WITNESSE
                WELL                               4.105.9
CEASSE THEN, TILL SHE VOUCHSAFE TO GRAWNT
                ME REST                            5.33.13
OR SHALL THEIR RUTHLESSE TORMENT NEVER CEASE       5.36.2
CEASSE THEN MYNE EYES, TO SEEKE HER SELFE TO SEE   5.78.13
```
CEASELESS   1
```
MY CEASLES CARES CONTINUALLY RUN ON               1.33.2
```
CEASETH   3
```
WHICH CEASETH NOT TO TEMPT $ME TO EACH $ILL        2.20.3
TOYLING WITH $PAINE, MY $LABOUR NEVER CEASETH      2.40.7
TOYLING WITH PAINE, MY LABOUR NEVER CEASETH        2.144.7
```

```
CELESTIAL                     13
  INKINDLED BY HER EYES CELESTIALL FIRE              1.59.4
  CELESTIALL FIRE, AND UNRESPECTING POWRES           1.59.5
  THE $FUELL KINDLED WITH $CELESTIALL $HEAT          2.30.8
  TO MY $SOULES $SUNNE, THOSE TWO $CELESTIALL
                              $EYES                  2.56.12
  STRAIGHT MOUNTING UP TO THY CELESTIALL EYES        2.103.12
  HAD NOT MINE EYE SEENE THY $CELESTIALL EYE         2.104.5
  WITH THINE EYES KINDLING THAT $CELESTIAL FLAME     2.105.7
  NAY, LOOKE THEE $TIME IN THIS $CELESTIALL GLASSE   2.107.5
  SO NEERE THYNE EYES CELESTIALL SUNNE ASPYRED       2.122.10
  CELESTIALL $IMAGE, $LOAD-STONE OF DESIRE           2.123.6
  WITH OUGLY RACK ON HIS CELESTIALL FACE             3.33.6
  AT WONDROUS SIGHT CF SO CELESTIALL HEW             5.3.8
  THE FAYRE $IDEA OF YOUR CELESTIALL HEW             5.45.7
CELL                          2
  I STILL FEARE $BUG-BEARES IN $APOLLO'S $CELL       2.39.12
  I STYLL FEARE BUGBEARES IN $APOLLOS $CELL          2.118.12
CENSOR'S                      1
  THEN HAD NO $CENSORS EYE THESE LINES SURVAID       1.7.5
CENSURE                       1
  I FEARE NO CENSURE, NOR WHAT THOU CANST SAY        2.31.5
CENSURES                      2
  YEE SHALLOW $CENSURES, SOMETIME SEE YEE NOT        2.24.9
  THAT CENSURES FALSELY WHAT THEY SEE ARIGHT+        3.148.4
CENSUREST                     1
  THOU $LEADEN $BRAINE, WHICH CENSUR'ST
                              WHAT I WRITE           2.49.1
CENTER                        1
  POORE SOULE THE CENTER CF MY SINFULL EARTH         3.146.1
CEREMONY                      1
  THE PERFECT CEREMONY OF LOVES RIGHT                3.23.6
CERTAIN                       5
  FALSE $HOPE PROLONGS MY EVER CERTAINE GRIEFE       1.25.1
  HOPES ARE UNSURE, WHEN CERTAINE IS MY PAINE        1.25.14
  MY NEVER CERTAINE JOY, BREEDS EVER-CERTAINE
                              FEARES                 2.137.4
  WHEN I WAS CERTAINE ORE IN-CERTAINTY               3.115.11
  COME SLEEPE, O SLEEPE, THE CERTAINE KNOT OF PEACE  4.39.1
CHAFE                         1
  BUT SHE IN CHAFE HIM FROM HER LAP DID SHOVE        4.17.7
CHAIN                         2
  DOUBT THERE HATH BENE, WHEN WITH HIS GOLDEN
                              CHAINE                 4.58.1
  LET HER, YF PLEASE HER, BYND WITH ADAMANT CHAYNE   5.42.10
CHAINS                        1
  ILE FETTER HER IN CHAINES OF PUREST LOVE           2.115.6
CHAIR                         1
  MUSES WHICH SADLY SIT ABCUT MY $CHAYRE             2.45.1
CHALLENGE                     1
  BUT SITH SHE WILL THE CCNQUEST CHALLENG NEEDS      5.29.9
CHAMBER                       3
  OR FOR SOME BRAWLE, WHICH IN THAT CHAMBER HIE      4.26.7
  A CHAMBER DEAFE TO NOISE, AND BLIND TO LIGHT       4.39.10
  MORE OFT THEN TO A CHAMBER MELODIE                 4.84.4
CHANCE                        9
  NOW, OR BY CHAUNCE, OR HEAVENS HIE PROVIDENCE      2.116.9
  BY CHANCE, OR NATURES CHANGING COURSE UNTRIM'D     3.18.8
  SOME LUCKIE WITS IMPUTE IT BUT TO CHAUNCE          4.41.8
  SINCE KIND OR CHANCE GIVES BOTH ONE LIVERIE        4.96.2
```

```
    THOU CHANCE TO COME, FALL LOWLY AT HER FEET          5.2.10
    HUNTS AFTER BLOUD, WHEN HE BY CHANCE DOTH FIND       5.56.3
    DEVOURING TYME AND CHANGEFUL CHANCE HAVE PRAYD       5.58.7
    NE FEARD WITH WORSE TO ANY CHAUNCE TO START          5.59.4
    WITH THE LOOSE WYND YE WAVING CHANCE TO MARKE        5.81.2
CHANCING                    1
    HER SUN-SHINE FACE THERE CHAUNSING TO ESPY           2.109.3
CHANGE                     20
    (DIANA-LIKE) TO WORKE MY SUDDEN CHANGE                 1.5.4
    AND STILL I TOYLE, TO CHANGE THE $MARBLE BREST        1.13.9
    WHEN GOLDEN HAIRES SHALL CHANGE TO SILVER WIER        1.38.2
    THOUGH HAPPIER FAR IF THOU WOULDST CHANGE
                             THY MIND                     1.56.14
    O CHANGE THY THOUGHT, THAT I MAY CHANGE MY MINDE      3.10.9
    O CHANGE THY THOUGHT, THAT I MAY CHANGE MY MINDE      3.10.9
    TO CHANGE YOUR DAY OF YOUTH TO SULLIED NIGHT          3.15.12
    WITH SHIFTING CHANGE AS IS FALSE WOMENS FASHION       3.20.4
    THAT THEN I SKORNE TO CHANGE MY STATE
                             WITH $KINGS                  3.29.14
    SO FAR FROM VARIATION OR QUICKE CHANGE+               3.76.2
    TO SET A FORME UPON DESIRED CHANGE                    3.89.6
    THEREFORE IN THAT I CANNOT KNOW THY CHANGE            3.93.6
    AND IN THIS CHANGE IS MY INVENTION SPENT            3.105.11
    CREEPE IN TWIXT VOWES, AND CHANGE DECREES
                             OF $KINGS                   3.115.6
    NO- $TIME, THOU SHALT NOT BOST THAT I DOE CHANGE    3.123.1
    TO BE SO TIKLED THEY WOULD CHANGE THEIR STATE       3.128.9
    ALAS, WHENCE CAME THIS CHANGE OF LOOKES+ $IF I        4.86.1
    SO LET US, WHICH THIS CHAUNGE OF WEATHER VEW          5.62.5
    CHAUNGE EEKE OUR MYNDS AND FORMER LIVES AMEND         5.62.6
    AND CHAUNGE OLD YEARES ANNOY TO NEW DELIGHT          5.62.14
CHANGED                     4
    NARCISSUS CHANG'D T'A FLOWER IN SUCH A CASE          1.37.12
    AND YOU ARE CHANG'D, BUT NOT T'A $HIACINT            1.37.13
    HAVE CHANG'D DESERT, LET MINE OWNE CONSCIENCE BE      4.86.2
    NOR TO THE $MOONE.. FOR THEY ARE CHANGED NEVER         5.9.6
CHANGEFUL                   1
    DEVOURING TYME AND CHANGEFUL CHANCE HAVE PRAYD       5.58.7
CHANGELINGS                 1
    OF OTHER'S CHILDREN CHANGELINGS USE TO MAKE          4.28.2
CHANGES                     2
    THAT MY STEEL'D SENCE OR CHANGES RIGHT OR WRONG     3.112.8
    AND FAINE MY GRIEFE WITH CHAUNGES TO BEGUILE        5.87.10
CHANGING                    2
    BY CHANCE, OR NATURES CHANGING COURSE UNTRIM'D       3.18.8
    EACH CHANGING PLACE WITH THAT WHICH GOES BEFORE      3.60.3
CHANNELS                    1
    WITH TEARES OUT OF THE $CHANNELS OF MINE EYES       2.115.9
CHARACTER                   3
    SINCE MINDE AT FIRST IN CARRECTER WAS DONE           3.59.8
    RESERVE THEIR $CHARACTER WITH GOULDEN QUILL          3.85.3
    WHAT'S IN THE BRAINE THAT $INCK MAY CHARACTER       3.108.1
CHARACTERED                 1
    FULL CHARACTERD WITH LASTING MEMORY                 3.122.2
CHARACTERS                  1
    AND IF A BROW WITH CARES CHARACTERS PAINTED          1.15.5
CHARGE                      2
    EATE UP THY CHARGE+ IS THIS THY BODIES END+         3.146.8
    BEST CHARGE, AND BRAVEST RETRAIT IN $CUPID'S
                             FIGHT                        4.79.5
```

```
CHARGED                       4
   RUNNES THIS POORE $RIVER, CHARG'D WITH
                          STREAMES OF ZEALE        1.1.2
   HERE I UNCLASPE THE $BOCKE OF MY CHARG'D SOULE  1.1.5
   WHEN SHAL HER TROUBLED BROW CHARG'D WITH DISCAINE  1.49.5
   EITHER NOT ASSAYLD, OR VICTOR BEEING CHARG'D    3.70.10
CHARIOT                       1
   WHICH, COUPLING $DOVES, GUIDES $VENUS'
                          CHARIOT RIGHT            4.79.4
CHARITABLE                    1
   I, LIKE A $MAN DEVOUT, AND CHARITABLE           2.23.5
CHARITY                       2
   THEN IS SHE $LOVE, IMBRACING $CHARITIE          2.12.5
   NO MARVELL THEN THOUGH $CHARITIE GROW COLD      2.23.14
CHARM                         3
   BUT WHEN BIRDS CHARME, AND THAT SWEETE
                          AIRE, WHICH IS           4.99.9
   WHO MAY WITH CHARME OF CONVERSATION SWEETE      4.106.10
   O MIGHTY CHARM WHICH MAKES MEN LOVE THEYR BANE  5.47.13
CHARMED                       2
   LET $WOLVES AND $BEARES BE CHARMED WITH
                          MY $VERSE                2.25.14
   BEAUTY IN SLEEPE, SLEEPE IN $BEAUTY CHARMED     2.136.6
CHARMETH                      2
   DESIRE, MY LOVE, MY SOULE, MY HOPE, HART,
                          AND LIFE CHARMETH        2.132.8
   BUT FROM THY HEART, WHILE MY SIRE CHARMETH THEE 4.32.13
CHARMING                      3
   I QUAKE TO LOOKE ON $HECAT'S CHARMING $BOOKES   2.39.11
   I QUAKE TO LOOKE ON $HECATS CHARMING BOOKES     2.118.11
   THE CHARMING SMILES, THAT ROB SENCE FROM
                          THE HART                 5.17.10
CHARTER                       2
   BE WHERE YOU LIST, YOUR CHARTER IS SO STRONG    3.58.9
   THE $CHARTER OF THY WORTH GIVES THEE RELEASING  3.87.3
CHARY                         1
   BEARING THY HEART WHICH I WILL KEEPE SO CHARY   3.22.11
CHASE                         9
   THUS OFTEN AS I CHASE MY HOPE FROM ME           1.25.9
   WHILST HER NEGLECTED CHILD HOLDS HER IN CHACE   3.143.5
   WHILST I THY BABE CHACE THEE A FARRE BEHIND     3.143.10
   BRINGING WITH HER THOSE STARRY $NIMPHS,
                          WHOSE CHACE              4.97.3
   AND WITH STERNE COUNTENANCE BACK AGAIN DOTH CHACE  5.21.7
   THEN FLY NO MORE FAYRE LOVE FROM $PHEBUS CHACE  5.28.13
   THAT WITH THEYR TERROUR AL THE REST MAY CHACE   5.31.7
   LYKE AS A HUNTSMAN AFTER WEARY CHACE            5.67.1
   WHEN I ALL WEARY HAD THE CHACE FORSOOKE         5.67.6
CHASED                        2
   WHICH STILL IS CHAC'D, WHILE I HAVE ANY BREATH  1.5.10
   NOR CHASTE BY HOUND, NOR FORC'D BY $HUNTERS ARTE  2.135.3
CHASTE                       19
   ALL UNAWARES, A $GODDESSE CHASTE I FINDE        1.5.3
   IF A SWEET LANGUISH WITH A CHAST DESIRE         1.15.2
   THAT INTIMATE IN VAINE MY CHASTE DESIRE         1.59.2
   MY CHASTE DESIRE, WHICH FROM DARKE SORROW SHINES  1.59.3
   BEHOLD THE MESSAGE OF A CHAST DESIRE            1.60.3
   THE PRECIOUS $SPICES BE YOUR CHASTE $DESIRE     2.16.6
   THE PRECIOUS $ODORS BE MY CHASTE $DESIRE        2.30.11
   BY CHASTE $DESIRE, TRUE $LOVE, AND VERTUOUS
                          $PRAYSE                  2.54.14
```

CHASTE HOLY $VOWES FOR MY $SOULES SACRIFICE   2.55.10
BY CHAST DESIRE, TRUE LOVE, AND VERTUES PRAISE   2.101.14
CHASTE HOLY VOWES FOR MY SOULES SACRIFICE   2.102.10
SEE CHASTE $DIANA, WHERE MY HARMLES HART   2.135.1
IF $CHASTE AND PURE DEVOTION OF MY YOUTH   2.138.1
WHILST MANY $NYMPHES THAT VOU'D CHAST
                              LIFE TO KEEP   3.154.3
NOW SINCE HER CHAST MIND HATES THIS LOVE IN ME   4.61.9
WITH CHAST AFFECTS, THAT NAUGHT BUT DEATH
                              CAN SEVER   5.6.12
IN CHAST DESIRES ON HEAVENLY BEAUTY BOUND   5.8.8
BURNING IN FLAMES OF PURE AND CHAST DESYRE   5.22.12
GOE VISIT HER IN HER CHAST BOWRE OF REST   5.84.7
CHASTEN   1
USE SOMETHING ELSE TO CHAST'N ME WITHALL   4.86.12
CHASTENED   1
WITH CHASTNED MIND, I STRAIGHT MUST SHEW
                              THAT SHE   4.61.10
CHASTENESS   1
WHERE $LOVE IS CHASTNESSE, $PAINE DOTH
                              LEARNE DELIGHT   4.48.3
CHASTEST   1
(THE CHASTEST FLAME THAT EVER WARMED HART)   1.44.4
CHASTITY   5
CHASTITIE AND $BEAUTIE, WHICH WERE DEADLY FOES   1.6.9
HERE $CHASTITY THAT $VESTALL MOST DIVINE   2.105.9
WHERE $CUPID IS SWORNE PAGE TO $CHASTITY+   4.35.8
THE SCHOOLES WHERE $VENUS HATH LEARN'D $CHASTITIE   4.42.4
ADORN'D WITH HONOUR, LOVE, AND CHASTITY   5.69.8
CHATTERING   1
DUMBE $SWANNES, NOT CHATRING $PIES, DO
                              $LOVERS PROVE   4.54.13
CHEAP   1
GOR'D MINE OWN THOUGHTS, SOLD CHEAP WHAT
                              IS MOST DEARE   3.110.3
CHEAT   1
WHAT DO'ST THOU MEANE TO $CHEATE ME OF MY $HEART   2.52.1
CHEATER   1
THEN GENTLE CHEATER URGE NOT MY AMISSE   3.151.3
CHECK   3
TO CHECK THE WORLD, HOW THEY INTOMB'D HAVE LIEN   1.45.3
AND PATIENCE TAME, TO SUFFERANCE BIDE EACH CHECK   3.58.7
IF THY SOULE CHECK THEE THAT I COME SO NEERE   3.136.1
CHECKED   2
SAP CHECKT WITH FROST AND LUSTIE LEAV'S QUITE GON   3.5.7
CHEARED AND CHECKT EVEN BY THE SELFE-SAME SKIE   3.15.6
CHECKS   1
WITH WHAT SHARPE CHECKES I IN MY SELFE AM SHENT   4.18.1
CHEEK   7
THY $CHEEKE, NOW FLUSH WITH $ROSES, SUNKE,
                              AND LEANE   2.8.9
THE FAYRE $ELIZIA, TO HER FAYRER CHEEKE   2.148.7
ON $HELLENS CHEEKE ALL ART OF BEAUTIE SET   3.53.7
WHY SHOULD FALSE PAINTING IMMITATE HIS CHEEKE   3.67.5
THUS IS HIS CHEEKE THE MAP OF DAIES OUT-WORNE   3.68.1
AND FOUND IT IN THY CHEEKE.. HE CAN AFFOORD   3.79.11
WHICH ON THY SOFT CHEEKE FOR COMPLEXION DWELLS+   3.99.4
CHEEKS   13
DEALE WITH THOSE DAINTY CHEEKES AS SHE DOTH DEALE   1.22.7
SO FADE THE $ROSES OF THOSE CHEEKS OF THINE   1.39.8

```
YOUR $CHEEKES YET PALE, SINCE FIRST HE
                      GAVE THE $WOUND          2.2.12
WHERE CHEEKES NEED BLOOD, IN THEE IT IS ABUS'D  3.82.14
LOV'S NOT $TIMES FOOLE, THOUGH ROSIE LIPS
                      AND CHEEKS               3.116.9
BUT NO SUCH $ROSES SEE I IN HER CHEEKES        3.130.6
BETTER BECOMES THE GRAY CHEEKS OF TH' $EAST    3.132.6
WHOSE PORCHES RICH (WHICH NAME OF CHEEKES ENDURE)  4.9.7
HATH CHEEKES TO SMILE, AS WELL AS EYES TO WEEPE  4.70.8
MILKE HANDS, ROSE CHEEKS, OR LIPS MORE
                      SWEET, MORE RED          4.91.7
WHERE THOSE RED CHEEKS, WHICH OFT WITH
                      FAIRE ENCREASE DID FRAME  4.102.2
HER RUDDY CHEEKES LYKE UNTO $ROSES RED         5.64.6
FAYRE WHEN THE ROSE IN HER RED CHEEKES APPEARES  5.81.3
CHEEK'S                  1
IN HER CHEEKES PIT THOU DIDST THY PITFOULD SET  4.11.11
CHEER                    6
OR IF THEY SING, TIS WITH SO DULL A CHEERE     3.97.13
DIAN THAT FAINE WOULD CHEARE HER FRIEND
                      THE $NIGHT               4.97.1
WOULD FAINE DRIVE CLOUDES FROM OUT MY
                      HEAVY CHEERE             4.97.11
WHAT SAIST THOU NOW, WHERE IS THAT DAINTY CHEERE  4.106.5
MARK WHEN SHE SMILES WITH AMIABLE CHEARE       5.40.1
SO LIKEWISE LOVE CHEARE YOU YOUR HEAVY SPRIGHT  5.62.13
CHEERED                  2
CHEARED AND CHECKT EVEN BY THE SELFE-SAME SKIE  3.15.6
SO MY STORME BEATEN HART LIKEWISE IS CHEARED   5.40.13
CHEERFUL                 2
UPON THY CHEEREFULL FACE, JOYE'S LIVERY WEARE  4.103.3
FED ON THE FULNESSE OF THAT CHEAREFULL GLAUNCE  5.39.12
CHEERLESS                1
FRESH LOVE, THAT LONG HATH SLEPT IN CHEERLESSE
                      BOWER                    5.4.6
CHEERS                   1
CHEERES FOR A TIME, BUT TILL THE $SUNNE DOTH SHEW  1.50.3
CHERISH                  6
WHICH HAPPILY POSTERITY MAY CHERRISH           1.42.10
ENSUING $AGES YET MY $RIMES SHALL CHERISH      2.44.11
WHICH BOUNTIOUS GUIFT THOU SHOULDST IN
                      BOUNTY CHERRISH          3.11.12
AND ONELY CHERISH DOTH WITH INJURIE            4.78.8
WHICH IF SHE GRAUNT, THEN LIVE AND MY
                      LOVE CHERISH             5.2.13
BUT THAT WHICH SHAL YOU MAKE IMMORTALL, CHERISH  5.27.14
CHERISHED                1
FED BUT WITH SMOKE, AND CHERISHT BUT WITH FIRE  1.15.4
CHERRIES                 1
FROM COMMING NEARE THOSE $CHERRIES BANISH ME   4.82.8
CHERRY                   1
SWEET GARD'N $NYMPH, WHICH KEEPES THE
                      $CHERRIE TREE            4.82.5
CHERUBINS                1
SUCH CHERUBINES AS YOUR SWEET SELFE RESEMBLE   3.114.6
CHEST                    4
THIS NEW RICH $NOVICE, LAVISH OF HIS CHEST     2.10.5
THEE HAVE I NOT LOCKT UP IN ANY CHEST          3.48.9
SO IS THE TIME THAT KEEPES YOU AS MY CHEST     3.52.9
SHALL TIMES BEST $JEWELL FROM TIMES CHEST
                      LIE HID+                 3.65.10
```

CHESTER   2
  CARLEGION $CHESTER VAUNTS HER HOLY $DEE   2.32.5
  CARLEGION $CHESTER, VAUNTS HER HOLY $DEE   2.124.5
CHID   1
  THAT BEING CHID, DID NEVER WORD REPLIE   2.15.10
CHIDE   6
  THEY DO BUT SWEETLY CHIDE THEE, WHO CONFOUNDS   3.8.7
  AND CHIDE THY BEAUTY, AND THY STRAYING YOUTH   3.41.10
  NOR DARE I CHIDE THE WORLD WITHOUT END HOURE   3.57.5
  THE FORWARD VIOLET THUS DID I CHIDE   3.99.1
  O FOR MY SAKE DOE YOU WISH FORTUNE CHIDE   3.111.1
  DOTH LOWRE, NAY, CHIDE., NAY, THREAT FOR
                    ONLY THIS   4.73.7
CHIDING   1
  CHIDING THAT TONGUE THAT EVER SWEET   3.145.6
CHIEF   11
  SATURNE CHIEFE $LORD OF THE $ASCENDANT LAY   2.116.7
  CHEEFE GOOD, FROM WHOM ALL GOOD THINGS WE DERIVE   2.146.8
  WHICH TO REPAIRE SHOULD BE THY CHIEFE DESIRE   3.10.8
  THAT SHE HATH THEE IS OF MY WAYLING CHEEFE   3.42.3
  WHEN $NATURE MADE HER CHIEFE WORKE, $STELLA'S EYES 4.7.1
  BUT SHINING FORTH OF HEATE IN HIS CHIEFE PRIDE   4.22.4
  TO KEEPE THEMSELVES AND THEIR CHIEF CITIES FREE   4.29.2
  DOTH FALL TO STRAY, AND MY CHIEFE POWRES
               ARE BROUGHT   4.38.3
  CHIEFE GOOD, WHERETO MY HOPE DOTH ONLY ASPIRE   4.68.3
  HIGHWAY SINCE YOU MY CHIEFE $PERNASSUS BE   4.84.1
  IS NOT THE HART OF ALL THE BODY CHIEFE+   5.50.7
CHIEFEST   2
  INVITES MY $HEART TO BE THE CHIEFEST $GHEST   2.7.4
  PREPAR'D BY $NATURE'S CHIEFEST FURNITURE   4.9.2
CHIEFTAIN   1
  TO MY LYVES FOE HER $CHIEFTAINE STILL BETRAYING   2.142.8
CHILD   12
  IF THOU COULDST ANSWERE THIS FAIRE CHILD OF MINE   3.2.10
  RESEMBLING SIER, AND CHILD, AND HAPPY MOTHER   3.8.11
  BUT WERE SOME CHILDE OF YOURS ALIVE THAT TIME   3.17.13
  AS ANY MOTHERS CHILDE, THOUGH NOT SO BRIGHT   3.21.11
  TO SEE HIS ACTIVE CHILDE DO DEEDS OF YOUTH   3.37.2
  THE SECOND BURTHEN OF A FORMER CHILD+   3.59.4
  YF MY DEARE LOVE WERE BUT THE CHILDE OF STATE   3.124.1
  WHILST HER NEGLECTED CHILD HOLDS HER IN CHACE   3.143.5
  INVENTION, $NATURE'S CHILD, FLED STEP-DAME
              $STUDIE'S BLOWES   4.1.10
  THUS GREAT WITH CHILD TO SPEAKE, AND HELPLESSE
              IN MY THROWES   4.1.12
  FOR LIKE A CHILD THAT SOME FAIRE BOOKE DOTH FIND   4.11.5
  O FATE, O FAULT, O CURSE, CHILD OF MY BLISSE   4.93.1
CHILDREN   8
  WITH $FOOLES AND $CHILDREN GOOD $DISCRETION
              BEARES   2.22.1
  AMONGST THE REST OF $FOOLES AND $CHILDREN BE   2.22.4
  THEN $FOOLES AND $CHILDREN FITT'ST TO
              GOE TOGETHER   2.22.8
  YET $FOOLES AND $CHILDREN SOMETIMES TELL IN PLAY 2.22.13
  THOSE CHILDREN NURST, DELIVERD FROM THY BRAINE   3.77.11
  OF OTHER'S CHILDREN CHANGELINGS USE TO MAKE   4.28.2
  SO CHILDREN STILL READE YOU WITH AWFULL EYES   4.63.2
  KILS HIS OWNE CHILDREN, TEARES, FINDING
              THAT THEY   4.95.10

```
CHILDREN'S                    1
  BY CHILDRENS EYES, HER HUSBANDS SHAPE IN MINCE       3.9.8
CHILD'S                       1
  THEN HENCE TO HEAVEN UNKIND, FOR THY CHILDS
                            PART                       2.140.13
CHILLING                      1
  SCORTCH NOT, BUT CNELY DO DARKE CHILLING
                            SPRITES REMOVE             4.76.8
CHIN                          1
  THAT WHEN THOU FEED'ST, THY $NOSE SHALL
                            TOUCH THY $CHINNE          2.8.12
CHIPS                         1
  AND SITUATION WITH THOSE DANCING CHIPS               3.128.10
CHOICE                        4
  WHERE MY HARTS THEEFE TO VEXE ME MADE HER CHOICE     1.27.6
  YET HEAVY HEART TO MAKE SO HARD A CHOISE             1.28.3
  AS HIS MAINE FORCE, CHOISE SPORT, AND
                            EASEFULL STAY              4.43.4
  WITH CHOISE DELIGHTS AND RAREST COMPANY              4.97.10
CHOICEST                      3
  OR REACH THE FRUITE OF $NATURE'S CHOISEST TREE       4.10.4
  WITH CHOISEST FLOWERS MY SPEECH TO ENGARLAND SO      4.55.2
  WITH CHOISEST WORDS, THY WORDS WITH REASONS RARE     4.68.10
CHOIR                         1
  WITH NOYSE WHEREOF THE QUYRE OF $BYRDS RESOUNDED     5.19.5
CHOIRS                        1
  BARE RN'WD QUIERS, WHERE LATE THE SWEET
                            BIRDS SANG                 3.73.4
CHOKED                        1
  OR CHOKED BE WITH OVERFLOWING GALL                   5.43.4
CHOOSE                        5
  THIS THOUGHT IS AS A DEATH WHICH CANNOT CHOOSE       3.64.13
  SO THAT I CANNOT CHUSE BUT WRITE MY MIND             4.50.9
  AND CANNOT CHUSE BUT PUT OUT WHAT I WRITE            4.50.10
  CHOSE RATHER TO BE PRAYSD FOR DOOING GOOD            5.38.13
  LET THE WORLD CHOSE TO ENVY OR TO WONDER             5.85.14
CHOPPED                       1
  BEATED AND CHOPT WITH TAND ANTIQUITIE                3.62.10
CHOSE                         2
  YOU, IN WHOM $NATURE CHOSE HER SELFE TO VIEW         2.57.5
  WHICH FOR THEIR HABITATION CHOSE OUT THEE            3.95.10
CHRIST                        1
  WHO PROPHECIED OF $CHRIST OR ERE HE CAME             2.119.3
CHRISTIAN                     1
  TO FILL HIS HORNES THIS YEARE ON $CHRISTIAN COAST    4.30.2
CHRONICLE                     1
  WHEN IN THE $CHRONICLE OF WASTED TIME                3.106.1
CHURCH                        1
  TILL THAT GOOD $GOD MAKE $CHURCH AND $CHURCHMAN
                            STARVE                     4.5.8
CHURCHES                      1
  CHURCHES OR SCHOOLES ARE FOR THY SEATE MORE FIT      4.4.6
CHURCHMAN                     1
  TILL THAT GOOD $GOD MAKE $CHURCH AND $CHURCHMAN
                            STARVE                     4.5.8
CHURL                         2
  AND TENDER CHORLE MAKST WAST IN NIGGARDING           3.1.12
  WHEN THAT CHURLE DEATH MY BONES WITH DUST
                            SHALL COVER                3.32.2
```

```
CHURLS                          1
   THEN CHURLS THEIR THOUGHTS (ALTHOUGH THEIR
                          EIES WERE KIND)              3.69.11
CINDERS                         2
   WHOSE SCORCHING GLEED, MY HEART TO $CINDERS
                          TURNETH                      2.40.10
   WITH SCORCHING GLEED MY HART TO CYNDERS TURNETH    2.144.10
CIRCLE                          2
   MY FORTUNES WHEELES THE CIRCLE OF HER EIES          1.12.11
   THE CIRCLE OF MY SORROWES NEVER ENDING              1.18.4
CIRCLE'S                        1
   IN WHICH HER CIRCLES VOYAGE IS FULFILD              5.60.3
CIRCUIT                         1
   I IN THE $CIRCUIT FOR THE $LAWRELL STROVE           2.47.6
CIRCUMPASSED                    1
   CIRCUMPASS'D ROUND WITH FILTH AND LOTHSOME MUD      1.29.2
CIRCUMSTANCE                    1
   THE $CIRCUMSTANCE DOTH MAKE IT GOOD, OR ILL         2.28.14
CITADEL                         1
   O NO, HER HEART IS SUCH A $CITTADELL                4.12.12
CITIES                          1
   TO KEEPE THEMSELVES AND THEIR CHIEF CITIES FREE     4.29.2
CIVIL                           3
   SUCH CIVILL WAR IS IN MY LOVE AND HATE              3.35.12
   O MAKE IN ME THOSE CIVILL WARRES TO CEASE           4.39.7
   BUT THIS CONTINUALL CRUELL CIVILL WARRE             5.44.5
CLAIM                           3
   WHICH DARE CLAIME FROM THOSE LIGHTS THE
                          NAME OF BEST                 4.9.11
   SUCH SMART MAY PITIE CLAIME OF ANY HART             4.44.3
   BY NO PRETENCE CLAIME ANY MANER PLACE               4.52.11
CLAPS                           1
   WITH $SHOWTS AND $CLAPS AT EV'RY LITTLE PAWSE       2.47.9
CLATTER                         1
   BEGIN HIS WITLESSE NOTE APACE TO CLATTER            5.85.4
CLAY                            1
   WHEN I (PERHAPS) COMPOUNDED AM WITH CLAY            3.71.10
CLEAN                           4
   THY $PEARLY $TEETH CUT OF THY $HEAD SO CLEANE       2.8.11
   AND BY AND BY CLEANE STARVED FOR A LOOKE            3.75.10
   LEAVE LADY IN YOUR GLASSE OF CHRISTALL CLENE        5.45.1
   BEING WITH THY DEARE BLOOD CLENE WASHT FROM SIN     5.68.7
CLEANLY                         1
   THAT THUS SO CLEANLY, I MY $SELFE CAN FREE          2.61.4
CLEAR                          15
   WHICH CLEERE OUR CLOUDED WORLD WITH BRIGHTEST
                          FLAME                        1.12.4
   LIGHTEN FOORTH SMILES TO CLEERE THE CLOUDED AIRE    1.51.9
   THAT WHERE THOSE TWO CLEARE SPARKLING
                          $EYES ARE PLAC'D             2.8.3
   CLEERE $ANKOR, ON WHOSE $SILVER-SANDED SHORE        2.53.1
   PASSING BY THAT CLEERE FOUNTAINE OF THINE EYE       2.109.2
   CLEERE $ANKOR, ON WHOSE SILVER-SANDED SHORE         2.113.1
   TO THE CLEERE DAY WITH THY MUCH CLEERER LIGHT       3.43.7
   THE CLEERE EYES MOYITIE, AND THE DEARE
                          HEARTS PART                  3.46.12
   NOT MAKING WORSE WHAT NATURE MADE SO CLEERE         3.84.10
   THAT HER CLEARE VOYCE LIFTS THY FAME TO THE SKIES   4.12.8
   WITH THAT FAIRE BREAST MAKING WOE'S DARKNESSE
                          CLEARE                       4.57.11
```

STELLA WHOSE EYES MAKE ALL MY TEMPESTS CLEERE   4.87.3
WITH LOVELY LIGHT TO CLEARE MY CLOUDY GRIEF   5.34.12
SO SINCE THE WINGED $GOD HIS PLANET CLEARE   5.60.5
SHALL TURNE TO CAULMES AND TYMELY CLEARE AWAY   5.62.12
CLEARED   1
WITH THAT SUNSHINE WHEN CLOUDY LOOKS ARE CLEARED   5.40.14
CLEARER   3
TO THE CLEERE DAY WITH THY MUCH CLEERER LIGHT   3.43.7
MY MOST FULL FLAME SHOULD AFTERWARDS BURNE
                              CLEERER   3.115.4
CLEARER THEN CHRISTALL WOULD THEREIN APPERE   5.45.12
CLEAREST   .2
O CLEEREST DAY-STARRE, NEVER MORE DECLYNING   2.129.8
NE OUGHT I SEE, THOUGH IN THE CLEAREST DAY   5.88.5
CLEARETH   1
SLEEPE LIGHTNING $BEAUTY, $BEAUTY SLEEPES
                      DARKNES CLEERETH   2.136.3
CLEAR-EYED   1
O CLEERE-EYDE $RECTOR OF THE HOLY $HILL   1.4.10
CLEARLY   1
IN BASE ATTIRE, YET CLEERLY $BEAUTY SHINES   1.43.4
CLEARS   2
WHEN DARKE SHALL SEEME THY DAY THAT NEVER CLEARES   1.42.3
THE SUNNE IT SELFE SEES NOT, TILL HEAVEN
                      CLEERES   3.148.12
CLEAR-SIGHTED   1
CLEERE-SIGHTED YOU, SOONE NOTE WHAT IS AWRIE   1.3.7
CLERK   1
AND LIKE UNLETTERED CLARKE STILL CRIE $AMEN   3.85.6
CLIFFS   1
AND $AVONS $FAME, TO $ALBIONS $CLIFFES IS RAYSED   2.32.4
CLIMB   3
TO SHEW THEIR KINDE, BEGAN TO CLIME THE SKIES   2.103.10
I RATHER WISHT THEE CLIME THE $MUSES' HILL   4.10.3
BASE THING, AND THINKE HOW SHE TO HEAVEN
                      MAY CLIME   5.13.10
CLIMBED   1
AND HAVING CLIMB'D THE STEEPE UP HEAVENLY HILL   3.7.5
CLIMBEST   1
WITH HOW SAD STEPS, O $MOONE, THOU CLIMB'ST
                      THE SKIES   4.31.1
CLIMBING   1
SCOURGE OF IT SELFE, STILL CLIMING SLIPPRIE
                      PLACE   4.23.10
CLIME   1
AND I (THOUGH BORNE WITHIN A COLDER CLIME)   1.43.5
CLIMES   2
IS $NOT $LOVE HERE, AS 'TIS IN OTHER $CLYMES   2.27.1
BUT FINDING THESE $NORTH CLYMES DO COLDLY
                      HIM EMBRACE   4.8.5
CLINGS   1
AND OFT SO CLINGS TO MY PURE $LOVE, THAT I   4.72.2
CLIPS   3
NOT USDE TO FROZEN CLIPS, HE STRAVE TO
                      FIND SOME PART   4.8.6
YET WHILE I LANGUISH, HIM THAT BOSOME CLIPS   4.59.9
CLIPS STREIGHT MY WINGS, STREIGHT WRAPS
                      ME IN HIS NIGHT   4.108.8
CLIVES   1
AND $AVONS FAME, TO $ALBYONS $CLIVES IS RAYSED   2.124.4

CLOAK   1
  AND MAKE ME TRAVAILE FORTH WITHOUT MY CLOAKE   3.34.2
CLOCK   2
  WHEN I DOE COUNT THE CLOCK THAT TELS THE TIME   3.12.1
  WHILST I (MY SOVERAINE) WATCH THE CLOCK FOR YOU   3.57.6
CLODS   1
  OF LIVELESSE $CLODS, US LIVING $MEN TO MAKE   2.14.7
CLOG   1
  BECOMES A CLOG) WILL SOONE EASE ME OF IT   4.59.14
CLOGGED   1
  AND CLOGD WITH BURDEN OF MORTALITY   5.72.4
CLOSE   9
  WHEN THOU WILT CLOSE UP THAT WHICH NOW
                            THOU SHOW'ST   1.40.10
  TO MY CLOSE HEART, WHERE WHILE SOME FIREBRANDS
                            HE DID LAY   4.8.13
  THERE HIMSELFE WITH HIS SHOT HE CLOSE DOTH LAY   4.20.8
  THEN BE THEY CLOSE, AND SO NONE SHALL DISPLEASE   4.34.8
  WRITTEN WITH TEARES IN HARTS CLOSE BLEEDING BOOK   5.1.8
  FOR IN THOSE LOFTY LOOKES IS CLOSE IMPLIDE   5.5.5
  IN THE CLOSE COVERT OF HER GUILEFULL EYEN   5.12.7
  A CLOSE INTENT AT LAST TO SHEW ME GRACE   5.25.10
  IN CLOSE AWAYT TO CATCH HER UNAWARE   5.71.4
CLOSED   2
  I START, LOOKE, HEARKE, BUT WHAT IN CLOSDE
                            UP SENCE   4.38.9
  CLOS'D WITH THEIR QUIVERS IN SLEEP'S ARMORY   4.99.4
CLOSED-UP   1
  THAT NEVER I WITH CLOS'D-UP SENSE DO LIE   4.32.6
CLOSELY   1
  ONE OF THOSE ARCHERS CLOSELY I DID SPY   5.16.9
CLOSET   3
  STRONG LOCKE OF KINDNESSE, $CLOSET OF
                            LOVES STORE   2.146.5
  (A CLOSET NEVER PEARST WITH CHRISTALL EYES)   3.46.6
  DEEPE IN THE CLOSET OF MY PARTS ENTYRE   5.85.9
CLOSING   1
  AND $INNOCENCE IS CLOSING UP HIS $EYES   2.61.12
CLOSURE   1
  WITHIN THE GENTLE CLOSURE OF MY BREST   3.48.11
CLOTHE   2
  IF THIS BE LOVE, TO CLOATHE ME WITH DARKE THOUGHTS   1.9.9
  OF SUCH HEAVEN STUFFE, TO CLOATH SO HEAVENLY
                            MYNDE   4.101.14
CLOTHED   3
  CLOTHED THE $NAKED, LODG'D THIS WAND'RING $GHEST   2.23.6
  CLOTH'D WITH FINE TROPES, WITH STRONGEST
                            REASONS LIN'D   4.58.6
  HOW CLOTH'D, HOW WAITED ON, SIGHD SHE OR SMILDE   4.92.10
CLOUD   5
  MY FORTUNE MANTLED WITH A CLOWDE S'OBSCURE   1.29.13
  NO CLOWDE WAS SEENE, BUT CHRISTALINE THE AYRE   2.125.13
  THE REGION CLOUDE HATH MASK'D HIM FROM ME NOW   3.33.12
  TIS NOT ENOUGH THAT THROUGH THE CLOUDE
                            THOU BREAKE   3.34.5
  FAYRE WHEN THAT CLOUD OF PRYDE, WHICH
                            OFT DOTH DARK   5.81.7
CLOUDED   4
  WHICH CLEERE OUR CLOUDED WORLD WITH BRIGHTEST
                            FLAME   1.12.4

  IF BEAUTY THUS BE CLOWDED WITH A FROWNE   1.21.1

```
WHOSE CLOUDED BROW DOTH MAKE MY DAIES SO SAD        1.26.4
LIGHTEN FOORTH SMILES TC CLEERE THE CLOUDED AIRE    1.51.9
CLOUDS            14
     AND CLOUDS OBSCURE HAD SHADED STILL HER
                              BRIGHTNESSE            1.7.4
  IMBRACING CLOUDS BY NIGHT, IN DAY TIME MOURNE      1.16.2
  IN HORRORS SABLE CLCWDES SETS MY LIVES SUNNE       1.30.2
  STILL LET ME SLEEPE, IMBRACING CLOUDS IN VAINE     1.54.13
  BEHOLD THE $CLOUDS WHICH HAVE ECLIPS'D MY $SUNNE   2.60.9
  BEHOLD THE $CLOWDES WHICH HAVE ECLIPS'D MY SUNNE   2.149.9
  AND DO'ST HIM GRACE WHEN CLOUDS DOE BLOT
                              THE HEAVEN             3.28.10
  .ANON PERMIT THE BASEST CLOUDES TO RIDE            3.33.5
  TO LET BACE CLOUDES ORE-TAKE ME IN MY WAY          3.34.3
CLOUDES AND ECLIPSES STAINE BOTH $MOONE
                              AND $SUNNE             3.35.3
  HAVING NO SCARFE CF CLOWDS BEFORE HIS FACE         4.22.3
  LET CLOUDS BEDIMME MY FACE, BREAKE IN MINE EYE     4.64.5
  WOULD FAINE DRIVE CLOUDES FROM OUT MY
                              HEAVY CHEERE           4.97.11
  ME TO DIRECT, WITH CLOUDES IS OVERCAST             5.34.6
CLOUDY            3
  AND IN THYS $IMAGE HIS DARKE CLOWDY EYES           2.114.13
  WITH LOVELY LIGHT TC CLEARE MY CLOUDY GRIEF        5.34.12
  WITH THAT SUNSHINE WHEN CLOUDY LOOKS ARE CLEARED   5.40.14
CLOYING           1
  EVEN SO BEING FULL CF YCUR NERE CLOYING
                              SWEETNESSE             3.118.5
COACHES           1
  THAT NOW IN $COACHES TRCUBLE EV'RY $STREET         2.6.2
COACHMAN          1
  CURST BE THE $COCHMAN WHICH DID DRIVE SO FAST      4.105.13
COAL              1
  SINCE $REASON'S SELFE DCTH BLOW THE COLE IN ME+    4.35.6
COALS             3
  THOSE SIGHES WHICH COOLE MY HART, ARE
                              COLES UNTO MY LCVE     2.132.2
  BUT WITH THOSE DRCPS THE COLES AGAINE REVYVING     2.144.11
  IN MY TRUE LOVE DID STIRRE UP COLES OF YRE         5.86.8
COAST             3
  YET HOW SHEE BENDS TOWARDS THAT BLESSED $COAST     2.134.12
  UPON THAT COAST, AN GIV'N UP FOR A SLAVE           4.29.14
  TO FILL HIS HORNES THIS YEARE ON $CHRISTIAN COAST  4.30.2
COASTS            1
  DO EASLY YEELD, THAT ALL THEIR COASTS MAY BE       4.29.3
COAT              1
  IN WHOSE COTE ARMCUR RICHLY ARE DISPLAYD           5.70.2
COCKATRICE        1
  THAT DAUNGEROUS EYE-KILLING $COCKATRICE            2.130.2
COCKATRICES       1
  AND KILL WITH LOOKS, AS $COCKATRICES DOO           5.49.10
COIL              1
  YOU $WILL, AND $WILL NOT, WHAT A COYLE IS HERE+    2.19.10
COIN              1
  IN $FORMER TIMES, SLCH AS HAD STORE OF $CCYNE      2.58.1
COLD              17
  NO MARVELL THEN THCUGH $CHARITIE GROW COLD         2.23.14
  SLOW $ARRER, FRANTICK $GALLUS, $CYDNUS CCLD        2.120.8
  AND SEE THY BLOOD WARME WHEN THOU FEEL'ST
                              IT COULD,              3.2.14
WITHOUT THIS FOLLIE, AGE, AND COULD DECAY,           3.11.6
```

AND BARREN RAGE OF DEATHS ETERNALL COLD+	3.13.12
UPON THOSE BOUGHES WHICH SHAKE AGAINST THE COULD	3.73.3
UNMOVED, COULD, AND TO TEMPTATION SLOW..	3.94.4
SUCH SEEMES YOUR BEAUTIE STILL.. $THREE	
$WINTERS COLDE	3.104.3
IN A COULD VALLIE-FOUNTAINE OF THAT GROUND	3.153.4
BUT SHE MOST FAIRE, MOST COLD, MADE HIM	
THENCE TAKE HIS FLIGHT	4.8.12
TO WARME WITH ILL-MADE FIRE COLD $MOSCOVY	4.30.4
IN THY COLD STUFFE A FLEGMATIKE DELIGHT+	4.56.11
BENIGHTED IN COLD WO, BUT NOW APPEARES MY DAY	4.76.3
NATURE'S PRAISE, $VERTUE'S STALL, $CUPID'S	
COLD FIRE	4.80.3
HOW COMES IT THEN THAT THIS HER COLD SO GREAT	5.30.2
IS NOT DELAYD BY HER HART FROSEN COLD	5.30.6
AND YSE WHICH IS CONGEALD WITH SENCELESSE COLD	5.30.11

COLDER   1

AND I (THOUGH BORNE WITHIN A COLDER CLIME)	1.43.5

COLDLY   1

BUT FINDING THESE $NORTH CLYMES DO COLDLY	
HIM EMBRACE	4.8.5

COLDNESS   2

PITTIE SO LEFT, TO TH'COLDNESSE OF YOUR $BLOOD	2.58.13
SLEEPES AGED COLDNES, WITH $BEAUTIES FIRE WARMED	2.136.7

COLOR   5

BUT SWEET, OR CULLER IT HAD STOLNE FROM THEE	3.99.15
TRUTH NEEDS NO COLLOUR WITH HIS COLLOUR FIXT	3.101.6
TRUTH NEEDS NO COLLOUR WITH HIS COLLOUR FIXT	3.101.6
IN COLOUR BLACKE, WHY WRAPT SHE BEAMES SO BRIGHT+	4.7.2
HOW DOTH THE COLOUR VADE OF THOSE VERMILLION	
DIES	4.102.5

COLORED   4

THE WORSER SPIRIT A WOMAN COLLOUR'D IL	3.144.4
WITH GUILDED LEAVES OR COLOURD $VELUME PLAYES	4.11.6
SOME BEAUTIE'S PEECE, AS AMBER COLOURD HED	4.91.6
AND WARNES THE $EARTH WITH DIVERS COLORD FLOWRE	5.4.11

COLORS   8

FOR THAT NO COLOURS CAN DEPAINT MY SORROWES	1.4.6
THESE COLOURS WITH THY FADING ARE NOT SPENT	1.42.11
AND FRESHEST $COLOURS WITH FOULE STAYNES	
DISGRACED	2.13.4
WITH HEAVENLY COLOURS DIDE, WITH NATURES	
WONDER CROUND	2.106.4
AND FRESHEST COLOURS WITH FOULE STAINES	
DISGRACED	2.121.4
NOR DO NOT USE SET COLOURS FOR TO WEARE	4.54.2
FOR THOUGH HE COLOURS COULD DEVIZE AT WILL	5.17.5
IN GOODLY COLOURS GLORIOUSLY ARRAYD	5.70.4

COLTISH   1

SUCH COLTISH GYRES, THAT TO MY BIRTH I OWE	4.21.6

COLUMBINES   1

HER NECK LYKE TO A BOUNCH OF $CULLAMBYNES	5.64.10

COMB   1

THEYR SNAKY HEADS DOE COMBE, FROM WHICH A SPRING	5.86.3

COME   43

COME TO THEIR VIEW, WHO LIKE AFFLICTED ARE	1.3.3
COME $TIME THE ANCHOR-HOLD OF MY DESIRE	1.22.1
TIME, CRUELL TIME, COME AND SUBDUE THAT $BROW	1.23.1
THEN THERE I DIE FROM WHENCE MY LIFE SHOULD COME	1.31.13
FLOWERS HAVE A TIME BEFORE THEY COME TO SEEDE	1.51.3
AUTENTIQUE SHALL MY VERSE IN TIME TO COME	1.55.6

```
I AM SURE MY $SIGHES COME FROM A $HEART AS TRUE      2.27.9
I WILL NOT COME IN $STIX OR $PHLEGETON               2.39.6
COME THOU AND READE, ADMIRE, APPLAUD MY $LINES       2.49.14
NEERER $MEN COME, $THAT FURTHER FLYES AWAY           2.58.9
SINCE THER'S NO HELPE, $COME LET US KISSE
                            AND PART                  2.61.1
THE TIME IS COME DELIVERED SHE MUST BE               2.116.3
I WYLL NOT COME IN $STIXE NOR $PHLEGITON             2.118.6
WHO WILL BELEEVE MY VERSE IN TIME TO COME            3.17.1
THE AGE TO COME WOULD SAY THIS $POET LIES            3.17.7
WHO EVEN BUT NOW COME BACK AGAINE ASSURED            3.45.11
FROM WHENCE AT PLEASURE THOU MAIST COME AND PART     3.48.12
AGAINST THAT TIME (IF EVER THAT TIME COME)           3.49.1
COME DAILY TO THE BANCKES, THAT WHEN THEY SEE        3.56.11
THAT $TIME WILL COME AND TAKE MY LOVE AWAY           3.64.12
HOW FARRE A MODERNE QUILL DOTH COME TO SHORT         3.83.7
(THOUGH WORDS COME HIND-MOST) HOLDS HIS
                            RANKE BEFORE             3.85.12
COME IN THE REREWARD OF A CONQUERD WOE               3.90.6
BUT IN THE ONSET COME, SO STALL I TASTE              3.90.11
OF THE WIDE WORLD, DREAMING ON THINGS TO COME        3.107.2
WITHIN HIS BENDING SICKLES COMPASSE COME            3.116.10
IF THY SOULE CHECK THEE THAT I COME SO NEERE         3.136.1
STRAIGHT IN HER HEART DID MERCIE COME                3.145.5
AND SURE AT LENGTH STOLNE GOODS DO COME TO LIGHT     4.15.11
COME LET ME WRITE, '$AND TO WHAT END+' $TO EASE      4.34.1
COME SLEEPE, O SLEEPE, THE CERTAINE KNOT OF PEACE    4.39.1
WHERE WELL HE KNOWES, NO MAN TO HIM CAN COME         4.43.14
THAT ONCE COME THERE, THE SOBS OF MINE ANNOYES       4.44.13
HER COME, AND HEARE WITH PATIENCE MY DESIRE          4.56.13
COME, COME, AND LET ME POWRE MY SELFE ON THEE        4.69.6
COME, COME, AND LET ME POWRE MY SELFE ON THEE        4.69.6
COME THEN MY $MUSE, SHEW THOU HEIGHT OF DELIGHT      4.70.9
IN $BEAUTIE'S THRONE, SEE NOW WHO DARES
                            COME NEARE               4.73.10
IN JUSTICE PAINES COME NOT TILL FAULTS DO CALL       4.86.10
OF COMFORT DARE COME TO THIS DUNGEON DARKE           4.104.7
THOU CHANCE TO COME, FALL LOWLY AT HER FEET          5.2.10
IS READY TO COME FORTH HIM TO RECEIVE                5.4.10
BUT $ANGELS COME TO LEAD FRAILE MINDES TO REST       5.8.7
COMEDY                  2
AND IS EVEN IRKT THAT SO SWEET $COMEDIE              4.51.13
AND MASK IN MYRTH LYKE TO A $COMEDY                  5.54.6
COMES                  14
BUT STRAIGHT HER WIDE BLOWNE POMP COMES
                            TO DECLINE               1.39.6
IF WHEN $NIGHT COMES, YOU BID ME GOE AWAY            2.37.14
YET SEE HOW RIGHT HE COMES UNTO MY FAYRE             2.135.4
SEE HOW MY $DEERE COMES TO THY $BEAUTIES STAND       2.135.5
COMES HOME AGAINE, ON BETTER JUDGEMENT MAKING        3.87.12
THENCE COMES IT THAT MY NAME RECEIVES A BRAND        3.111.5
THE DOORE BY WHICH SOMETIMES COMES FORTH
                            HER $GRACE                4.9.5
LET HER GO. $SOFT, BUT HERE SHE COMES. $GO TO        4.47.12
SHE COMES, AND STREIGHT THEREWITH HER
                            SHINING TWINS DO MOVE     4.76.1
SHE COMES WITH LIGHT AND WARMTH, WHICH
                            LIKE $AURORA PROVE        4.76.5
NAY SORROW COMES WITH SUCH MAINE RAGE, THAT HE       4.95.9
HOW COMES IT THEN THAT THIS HER COLD SO GREAT        5.30.2
OR HOW COMES IT THAT MY EXCEEDING HEAT               5.30.5
```

COMES FORTH AFRESH CUT CF THEIR LATE DISMAY	5.40.11

COMET   1
O MINE EYES $COMET, SO ADMYR'D BY LOVING	2.129.7

COMET-LIKE   1
SO $COMET-LIKE EACH STARRE ADVAUNC'D HER LYGHT	2.125.10

COMFORT   16
I WEIGH NO COMFORT UNLESSE SHE RELIEVE	1.12.8
THAT PITTY SHINES NC COMFORT TO MY BLIS	1.21.2
AS SHORT THAT BLISSE, SC IS THE COMFORT RARE	1.24.11
YET NO MILD COMFORT WOULD THY $BROW REVEALE	1.31.9
ONELY MY COMFORT STILL CONSISTS IN THIS	2.42.13
LEFT AS THAT SUNNE ALONE TO COMFORT US	2.129.3
TAKE ALL MY COMFORT OF THY WORTH AND TRUTH	3.37.4
MOST WORTHY COMFORT, NOW MY GREATEST GRIEFE	3.48.6
THOU WILT RESTORE TC BE MY COMFORT STILL	3.134.4
TWO LOVES I HAVE CF COMFORT AND DISPAIRE	3.144.1
OF EVERIE IMAGE, WHICH MAY COMFORT SHOW+	4.66.4
OR ART THOU ELSE TC COMFORT ME FORSWORNE+	4.67.11
OF COMFORT DARE CCME TO THIS DUNGEON DARKE	4.104.7
DOTH MAKE ME MOST TC WISH THY COMFORT NEERE	4.106.8
SINCE I HAVE LACKT THE CCMFORT OF THAT LIGHT	5.88.1
CAN COMFORT ME, BUT HER CWNE JOYOUS SIGHT	5.89.10

COMFORTLESS   2
TILL THEN I WANDER CAREFULL COMFORTLESSE	5.34.13
FINDING A TREE ALCNE ALL COMFORTLESSE	5.56.7

COMFORTS   4
GRIEFES EVER SPRINGING, COMFORTS NEVER BCRNE	1.16.4
MY LIVES SWEET SUNNE, MY DEAREST COMFORTS LIGHT	1.30.3
BUT YET, WHAT COMFCRTS SHALL I HEREBY GAINE+	1.52.13
THAT CONVERSATION SWEET, WHERE SUCH HIGH COMFORTS BE	4.77.10

COMING   7
AND ALL THINGS FIT AGAINST HER COMMING THERE	1.30.8
SHE COMMING NEERE, THAT MY POORE $HEART HATH SLAINE	2.46.9
AGAINST THIS CUMMING END YOU SHOULD PREPARE	3.13.3
SINCE SILDOM COMMING IN THE LONG YEARE SET	3.52.6
FROM COMMING NEARE THOSE $CHERRIES BANISH ME	4.82.8
WHO NOW IS COMMING FORTH WITH GIRLAND CROUNED	5.19.4
COMMING TO KISSE HER LYPS, (SUCH GRACE I FOUND)	5.64.1

COMMAND   1
DEARE, WHY SHOULD YCU CCMMAND ME TO MY $REST	2.37.1

COMMANDED   1
COMMANDED BY THE MCTION CF THINE EYES	3.149.12

COMMANDING   2
REASON PLUCKS BACK, COMMANDING ME TO STAY	2.38.2
REASON PLUCKS BACKE, CCMMAUNDING ME TO STAY	2.131.2

COMMENCE   1
AND GAINST MY SELFE A LAWFULL PLEA COMMENCE	3.35.11

COMMEND   4
AND MUCH COMMEND THE STRANGENESSE OF MY $VAINE	2.42.2
NOR WHO COMMEND OR DISCCMMEND MY VERSE	2.128.10
UTTRING BARE TRUTH, EVEN SO AS FOES $COMMEND	3.69.4
HER HARDNES BLAME WHICH I SHOULD MORE COMMEND+	5.51.6

COMMENDS   3
COTSWOLD COMMENDS HER $ISIS TO THE $TAME	2.32.9
NOR WHO COMMENDS, CR DISCOMMENDS MY $VERSE	2.42.10
COTSWOOLD COMMENDS HER $ISIS AND HER $TAME	2.124.9

COMMENT   2
WHEREON THE $STARS IN SECRET INFLUENCE CCMMENT	3.15.4

AND I WILL COMMENT UPON THAT OFFENCE   3.89.2
COMMENTS   2
WHILE COMMENTS OF YOUR PRAISE RICHLY COMPIL'D   3.85.2
(MAKING LASCIVIOUS COMMENTS ON THY SPORT)   3.95.6
COMMIT   3
WHO SHOULD I THINKE THE $MURTHER SHOULD COMMIT+   2.2.2
COMMIT MY WORDS UNTO THE FLEETING WIND   2.142.11
COMMIT TO THESE WASTE BLACKS, AND THOU
    SHALT FINDE   3.77.10
COMMITS   2
THAT ON HIMSELFE SUCH MURDROUS SHAME COMMITS   3.9.14
THOSE PRETTY WRONGS THAT LIBERTY COMMITS   3.41.1
COMMITTED   1
WHAT WRETCHED ERRORS HATH MY HEART COMMITTED   3.119.5
COMMON   5
UP, TO MY $PITCH, NO COMMON $JUDGEMENT FLYES   2.31.13
THE SOLYE IS THIS, THAT THOU DOEST COMMON GROW   3.69.14
THE EARTH CAN YEELD ME BUT A COMMON GRAVE   3.81.7
AND SWEETS GROWNE COMMON LOOSE THEIR DEARE
    DELIGHT   3.102.12
WHICH MY HEART KNOWES THE WIDE WORLDS
    COMMON PLACE+   3.137.10
COMPANION   2
BLACKE PYTCHY $NIGHT, COMPANYON OF MY WOE   2.145.1
DESIRE, THOUGH THOU MY OLD COMPANION ART   4.72.1
COMPANY   5
AS ONE THAT DIES WITHOUT HER COMPANY   1.25.8
YET MORE TO GRACE THE $COMPANY WITHALL   2.7.3
WHAT 'TIS TO KEEPE A $DRUNKARD COMPANIE   2.7.14
SEEME MOST ALONE IN GREATEST COMPANIE   4.27.2
WITH CHOISE DELIGHTS AND RAREST COMPANY   4.97.10
COMPARE   15
TO $NOTHING FITTER CAN I $THEE COMPARE   2.10.1
COMPARE MY $WORTH WITH OTHERS BASE $DESERT   2.60.6
THE FIRE, UNTO MY LOVE, COMPARE A PAINTED FIRE   2.127.5
LET HIM COMPARE IT TO HER HEAVENLY EYE   2.148.2
PRAYSING THE FAYREST, COMPARE IT TO MY FAIRE   2.148.11
COMPARE MY WORTH WITH OTHERS BASE DESERT   2.149.6
SHALL I COMPARE THEE TO A $SUMMERS DAY+   3.18.1
MAKING A COOPELMENT OF PROUD COMPARE   3.21.5
COMPARE THEM WITH THE BETT'RING OF THE TIME   3.32.5
AUTHORIZING THY TRESPAS WITH COMPARE   3.35.6
AS ANY SHE BELI'D WITH FALSE COMPARE   3.130.14
O BUT WITH MINE, COMPARE THOU THINE OWNE STATE   3.142.3
LONG-WHILE I SOUGHT TO WHAT I MIGHT COMPARE   5.9.1
AND THEREWITH DOE HER CRUELTY COMPARE   5.55.2
YOUR SELFE UNTO THE $BEE YE DOE COMPARE   5.71.2
COMPARED   1
COMPAR'D WITH LOSSE OF THEE, WILL NOT SEEME SO   3.90.14
COMPARISON   1
SUPERLATIVE IN ALL COMPARISON   2.148.14
COMPASS   3
SHEWES BY HIS $COMPASSE, HOW HIS $COURSE
    HE STEER'D   2.1.6
WHERE, IN THE COMPASSE OF A $MARYGOLD   2.151.7
WITHIN HIS BENDING SICKLES COMPASSE COME   3.116.10
COMPASSED   1
THE NEW BEGINS HIS COMPAST COURSE ANEW   5.62.2
COMPEERS   1
NO, NEITHER HE, NOR HIS COMPIERS BY NIGHT   3.86.7

COMPELLED   2
  ONELY COMPELL'D ON THIS POORE GOOD TO BOAST   2.43.13
  THUS MUCH MY HEART COMPELD MY MOUTH TO SAY   4.80.9
COMPILE   2
  YET BE MOST PROUD OF THAT WHICH I COMPILE   3.78.9
  THROUGH $FAERY LAND, WHICH THOSE SIX BOOKS
                     COMPILE   5.80.2
COMPILED   1
  WHILE COMMENTS OF YOUR PRAISE RICHLY COMPIL'D   3.85.2
COMPLAIN   7
  STILL TO COMPLAINE MY GRIEFES, WHILST NONE RELIEVE 1.9.8
  AND IF I FINDE SUCH PLEASURE TO COMPLAINE   1.48.13
  THE ONE BY TOYLE, THE OTHER TO COMPLAINE   3.28.7
  DO THOU THEN (FOR THOU CANST) DO THOU COMPLAINE   4.94.5
  SO $LADIE NOW TO YOU I DOO COMPLAINE   5.12.13
  BUT HAVING PINE AND HAVING NOT COMPLAINE   5.35.4
  BUT HAVING PINE, AND HAVING NOT COMPLAYNE   5.83.4
COMPLAINED   1
  AND WOULD NOT HEARE, WHEN HE TO HER COMPLAYNED   5.48.11
COMPLAINT   4
  HER PRAISE FROM MY COMPLAINT I MAY NOT PART   1.26.10
  WHOSE $BREST IS PROOFE AGAINST $COMPLAINT
                OR $PRAYER+   2.52.10
  MY $LIVES COMPLAINT IN DOLEFULL $ELEGIES   2.54.7
  MY LIVES COMPLAINT IN DOLEFUL $ELEGIES   2.101.7
COMPLAINTS   1
  THAT WHEN THE BREATH OF MY COMPLAINTS DOTH TUCH   4.44.10
COMPLEMENT   1
  OF NATURES SKILL THE ONELY COMPLEMENT   5.24.3
COMPLEXION   3
  AND OFTEN IS HIS GOLD COMPLEXION DIMM'D   3.18.6
  WHICH ON THY SOFT CHEEKE FOR COMPLEXION DWELLS+   3.99.4
  AND ALL THEY FOULE THAT THY COMPLEXION LACKE   3.132.14
COMPLEXIONED   1
  SO FLATTER I THE SWART COMPLEXIOND NIGHT   3.28.11
COMPOSED   1
  TO THIS COMPOSED WONDER OF YOUR FRAME   3.59.10
COMPOSITION   1
  UNTILL LIVES COMPOSITION BE RECURED   3.45.9
COMPOUND   1
  FOR COMPOUND SWEET., $FORGOING SIMPLE SAVOR   3.125.7
COMPOUNDED   1
  WHEN I (PERHAPS) COMPOUNDED AM WITH CLAY   3.71.10
COMPOUNDS   2
  TO NEW FOUND METHODS, AND TO COMPOUNDS STRANGE+   3.76.4
  WITH EAGER COMPOUNDS WE OUR PALLAT URGE   3.118.2
COMPTROL   1
  AND THAT HIGH LOOK, WITH WHICH SHE DOTH
                COMPTROLL   5.10.10
CON   1
  TO CON MY $CROS-ROWE ERE I LEARN'D TO SPELL   2.111.2
CONCEALED   2
  BY DOOME CONCEALED TO THE HEAVENS ABOVE   2.139.11
  OF FAULTS CONCEALD, WHEREIN I AM ATTAINTED   3.88.7
CONCEIT   13
  AND PLEASE YOUR SELFE WITH THIS $CONCEIT
              THE WHILE   2.24.8
  THOUGH MY $CONCEIT I FURTHER SEEME TO BEND   2.34.10
  SOME, WHO NOT KINDLY RELLISH MY $CONCEIT   2.42.5
  WISE IN $CONCEIT, IN $ACT A VERY SOT   2.62.6

```
COULD ALL CONCEITE CONCLUDE, WHICH PAST
                        CONCEITE ADMIRETH          2.117.5
COULD ALL CONCEITE CONCLUDE, WHICH PAST
                        CONCEITE ADMIRETH          2.117.5
SOME, WHO REACH NOT THE HEIGHT OF MY CONCEITE      2.128.5
AND THOU $CONCEITE, THE SHADOW OF MY BLISSE        2.141.9
CONCEITE OF $ANGELS, WHICH ALL WISDOM TEACHEST     2.146.10
WISE IN CONCEITE, IN ACTE A VERY SOT               2.150.6
THEN THE CONCEIT OF THIS INCONSTANT STAY           3.15.9
BUT THAT I HOPE SOME GOOD CONCEIPT OF THINE         3.26.7
FINDING THE FIRST CONCEIT OF LOVE THERE BRED       3.108.13
```

CONCEITS   1
```
OF ALL THE GRAVE CONCEITS YOUR BRAINE DOTH BREED   4.51.6
```

CONCEIVE   5
```
IN FEELING HEARTS THAT CAN CONCEIVE THESE LINES    1.43.2
REASON AND I (YOU MUST CONCEIVE) ARE TWAINE        2.9.10
IS LONG ERE IT CONCEIVE THE KINDLING FYRE          5.6.6
SUCH SUBTILE CRAFT MY $DAMZELL DOTH CONCEAVE       5.23.5
WIL SOONE CONCEIVE, AND LEARNE TO CONSTRUE WELL    5.43.14
```

CONCEIVED   1
```
BY INSPIRATION, CAME CONCEAV'D WITH THOUGHT        2.116.2
```

CONCEIVES   1
```
AND OF BOTH, WRONGFULL DEEMES, AND ILL CONCEIVES   1.52.8
```

CONCLUDE   1
```
COULD ALL CONCEITE CONCLUDE, WHICH PAST
                        CONCEITE ADMIRETH          2.117.5
```

CONCLUSIONS   1
```
AND GRACE, SICKE TOO, SUCH FINE CONCLUSIONS
                        TRIES                      4.101.3
```

CONCORD   2
```
IF THE TRUE CONCORD OF WELL TUNED SOUNDS           3.8.5
THE WIRY CONCORD THAT MINE EARE CONFOUNDS          3.128.4
```

CONDEMNED   3
```
CONDEMN'D BY $JOVE TO ENDLESSE $TORMENT BEE        2.14.2
THE $LILLIE I CONDEMNED FOR THY HAND               3.99.6
YE SHALL CONDEMNED BE OF MANY A ONE                5.36.14
```

CONDEMNING   3
```
AND $LOVE CONTEMNING $REASONS REASON WHOLLY        2.38.11
AND $LOVE CONTEMNING $REASONS REASON WHOLY         2.131.11
A STILL FELT PLAGUE, TO SELFE CONDEMNING ME        4.86.3
```

CONDITIONLY   1
```
AND THOUGH SHE GIVE BUT THUS CONDITIONLY           4.69.12
```

CONDITIONS   1
```
I OFFER FREE $CONDITIONS OF FAIRE $PEACE           2.63.5
```

CONDUCT   2
```
LET LOVE AND YOUTH CONDUCT THY PLEASURES THITHER   1.51.8
BY CONDUCT OF SOME STAR DOTH MAKE HER WAY          5.34.2
```

CONFERS   1
```
MEANE WHILE MY HEART CONFERS WITH $STELLA'S
                        BEAMES                     4.51.12
```

CONFESS   8
```
NOW I DENY $HER, THEN I DOE CONFESSE $HER          2.41.13
WHERE, THE FULL $PRAYSE I FREELY MUST CONFESSE     2.47.7
NOW I DENY HER, THEN I DOE CONFESSE HER            2.143.13
LET ME CONFESSE THAT WE TWO MUST BE TWAINE         3.36.1
I DO CONFESSE, PARDON A FAULT CONFEST              4.4.7
BUT ONE WORSE FAULT, $AMBITION, I CONFESSE         4.27.11
WHILE WITH THE PEOPLE'S SHOUTS I MUST CONFESSE     4.53.3
THEY PLEASE I DO CONFESSE, THEY PLEASE MINE EYES   4.91.9
```

```
CONFESSED                     2
  SO NOW I HAVE CONFEST THAT HE IS THINE              3.134.1
  I DO CONFESSE, PARDON A FAULT CONFEST                 4.4.7
CONFINE                       1
  IN WHOSE CONFINE IMMURED IS THE STORE                3.84.3
CONFINED                      5
  M'AMBITIOUS THOUGHTS CONFINED IN HER FACE            1.12.5
  FROM OUT DISPAIRE, WHEREIN THEY LIVE CONFINDE+       1.49.4
  THEREFORE MY VERSE TO CONSTANCIE CONFIN'DE          3.105.7
  SUPPOSDE AS FORFEIT TO A CONFIN'D DOOME             3.107.4
  A $GOD IN LOVE, TO WHOM I AM CONFIN'D              3.110.12
CONFINES                      1
  THOU POWRE THAT RUL'ST THE CONFINES OF THE NIGHT    1.10.5
CONFIRM                       1
  BUT $GRAMMER'S FORCE WITH SWEET SUCCESSE
                              CONFIRME                4.63.11
CONFLICT                      1
  MYNE EYES BEHELD THYS CONFLICT IN THY FACE         2.136.14
CONFOUND                      2
  AND TIME THAT GAVE, DOTH NOW HIS GIFT CONFOUND      3.60.8
  IN OTHER ACCENTS DOE THIS PRAISE CONFOUND           3.69.7
CONFOUNDED                    1
  OR STATE IT SELFE CONFOUNDED, TO DECAY             3.64.10
CONFOUNDING                   1
  AGAINST CONFOUNDING $AGES CRUELL KNIFE             3.63.10
CONFOUNDS                     3
  TO HIDIOUS WINTER AND CONFOUNDS HIM THERE           3.5.6
  THEY DO BUT SWEETLY CHIDE THEE, WHO CONFOUNDS       3.8.7
  THE WIRY CONCORD THAT MINE EARE CONFOUNDS          3.128.4
CONFUSE                       1
  STELLA'S GREAT POWRS, THAT SO CONFUSE MY MIND      4.34.14
CONFUSED                      3
  NOR DO LIKE $LORDS, WHOSE WEAKE CONFUSED BRAINE     4.85.5
  BUT WIT CONFUS'D WITH TOO MUCH CARE DID MISSE       4.93.8
  MADE TO AMAZE WEAKE MENS CONFUSED SKIL             5.17.2
CONFUSION                     1
  TO THIS THOUGHTS-MAZE, TO MY CONFUSION TENDING      1.18.2
CONGEALED                     2
  TO BREAKE THE $ISE THAT HATH CONGEALD HER HEART+    1.49.8
  AND YSE WHICH IS CONGEALD WITH SENCELESSE COLD     5.30.11
CONJOIN                       1
  AND HAD SHE PITTY TO CONJOYNE WITH THOSE            1.6.11
CONJURE                       2
  THUS TO MY AID, I LASTLY CONJURE THEE               2.36.4
  I CONJURE THEE BY ALL THAT I HAVE NAM'D            2.36.13
CONQUER                       2
  WHO WHILE THEY MAKE $LOVE CONQUER, CONQUER $LOVE    4.42.3
  WHO WHILE THEY MAKE $LOVE CONQUER, CONQUER $LOVE    4.42.3
CONQUERED                     2
  COME IN THE REREWARD OF A CONQUERD WOE             3.90.6
  A CONQUERD, YELDEN, RANSACKT HEART TO WINNE+       4.36.2
CONQUERING                    4
  THAT SERVES A $TROPHEY TO HER CONQUERING EIES     1.10.11
  MY FREEDOMES TYRANTS CONQUERING ALL BY ARTE       1.27.10
  WHEN CONQU'RING $LOVE DID FIRST MY $HEART ASSAYLE  2.29.1
  WITH MY HARTS TRYBUTE TO HER CONQUERING EYES      2.151.2
CONQUERINGS                   1
  USE ALL TO HELPE HIS OTHER CONQUERINGS             4.29.8
CONQUEROR                     1
  NOW $LOVE, IF THOU WILT PROVE A $CONQUEROR        2.115.1
```

CONQUERORS   1
  YET NOBLEST $CONQUEROURS DO WRECKES AVOID   4.40.11
CONQUERS   1
  WHICH CONQUERS ALL BUT THEE, AND THEE TOO STAIES   1.23.2
CONQUEST   9
  THOU VANQUISHING, THE $CONQUEST IS MINE OWNE   2.63.14
  TO BE DEATHS CONQUEST AND MAKE WORMES THINE HEIRE 3.6.14
  HOW TO DEVIDE THE CONQUEST OF THY SIGHT   3.46.2
  THE COWARD CONQUEST OF A WRETCHES KNIFE   3.74.11
  TILL BY DEGREES IT HAD FULL CONQUEST GOT   4.2.4
  OF CONQUEST, DO NOT THESE EFFECTS SUFFICE   4.36.7
  THE RUINES OF HER CONQUEST TO ESPIE   4.67.3
  BUT SITH SHE WILL THE CONQUEST CHALLENG NEEDS   5.29.9
  OF MY LOVES CONQUEST, PEERELESSE BEAUTIES PRISE   5.69.7
CONQUESTS   1
  IN $WARRES AT HOME, OR WHEN FOR $CONQUESTS BOUND   2.58.2
CONSCIENCE   5
  IN $RIGHT OR $WRONG, THEY CALL HER $CONSCIENCE   2.12.11
  LOVE IS TOO YOUNG TO KNOW WHAT CONSCIENCE IS   3.151.1
  YET WHO KNOWES NOT CONSCIENCE IS BORNE OF LOVE   3.151.2
  NO WANT OF CONSCIENCE HOLD IT THAT I CALL   3.151.13
  HAVE CHANG'D DESERT, LET MINE OWNE CONSCIENCE BE   4.86.2
CONSECRATE   1
  THE VERY PART WAS CONSECRATE TO THEE   3.74.6
CONSENT   2
  WHO GAVE CONSENT TO STEALE AWAY MY $HEART   2.23.11
  DOE IN CONSENT SHAKE HANDS TO TORTURE ME   3.28.6
CONSERVED   1
  O PLAINTS CONSERV'D IN SUCH A SUGRED PHRAISE   4.100.9
CONSIDER   1
  WHEN I CONSIDER EVERY THING THAT GROWES   3.15.1
CONSISTS   2
  ALL MY LIVES SWEET CONSISTS IN HER ALONE   1.12.13
  ONELY MY COMFORT STILL CONSISTS IN THIS   2.42.13
CONSONANT   1
  WORDS CONSONANT, AND SOUNDING TO THY FAME   2.111.8
CONSONANTS   1
  MY CONSONANTS THE NEXT WHEN I HAD DONE   2.111.7
CONSORT   2
  PLEASINGST CONSORT, WHERE EACH SENCE HOLDS A PART 4.79.3
  BY LOVE WERE MADE APT TO CONSORT WITH ME   4.95.11
CONSPIRE   5
  INTIC'D MY $THOUGHTS, AGAINST ME TO CONSPIRE   2.23.10
  THAT GAINST THY SELFE THOU STICKST NOT
                            TO CONSPIRE   3.10.6
  NO EIES BUT JOYES, IN WHICH AL POWERS CONSPIRE   5.8.3
  YET HERESY NOR TREASON DIDST CONSPIRE   5.48.7
  CONSUME THEE QUITE, THAT DIDST WITH GUILE
                            CONSPIRE   5.86.11
CONSTANCY   3
  THEREFORE MY VERSE TO CONSTANCIE CONFIN'DE   3.105.7
  THE CONSTANCY AND VIRTUE OF YOUR LOVE   3.117.14
  OTHES OF THY LOVE, THY TRUTH, THY CONSTANCIE   3.152.10
CONSTANT   7
  YET TO MY $GODDESSE AM I CONSTANT EVER   2.51.11
  AND CONSTANT STARS IN THEM I READ SUCH ART   3.14.10
  BUT YOU LIKE NONE, NONE YOU FOR CONSTANT HEART   3.53.14
  STILL CONSTANT IN A WONDROUS EXCELLENCE   3.105.6
  IS CONSTANT $LOVE DEEM'D THERE BUT WANT OF WIT+   4.31.10
  YET SHE BEHOLDING ME WITH CONSTANT EYE   5.54.9

```
     WHICH HER TOO CONSTANT STIFFENESSE DOTH
                           CONSTRAYN                     5.84.12
CONSTELLATIONS            1
   THAT NEVER LEARN'D WHAT $CONSTELLATIONS ARE           2.43.7
CONSTERD                  1
   AS CONSTERD IN TRUE SPEECH, THE NAME OF
                           HEAV'N IT BEARES              4.77.11
CONSTRAIN                 1
   WHICH HER TOO CONSTANT STIFFENESSE DOTH
                           CONSTRAYN                     5.84.12
CONSTRAINED               2
   TO STEALE SOME REST, BUT WRETCH I AM CONSTRAIND       4.98.6
   WHOM SHE ALL CARELESSE CF HIS GRIEFE CONSTRAYNED      5.48.9
CONSTRAINT                1
   WITHOUT CONSTRAYNT CR DREAD OF ANY ILL                5.65.6
CONSTRUE.                 1
   WIL SOONE CONCEIVE, AND LEARNE TO CONSTRUE WELL       5.43.14
CONSUME                   5
   THAT THEY MAY HELPE THEE TO CONSUME OUR CAIES+        1.23.6
   THE $DIAMOND SHALL ONCE CONSUME TO $DUST              2.13.3
   THE $DIAMOND SHALL ONCE CONSUME TO DUST               2.121.3
   NOR TO THE FIRE.. FCR THEY CONSUME NOT EVER           5.9.8
   CONSUME THEE QUITE, THAT DIDST WITH GUILE
                           CONSPIRE                      5.86.11
CONSUMED                  2
   WITH THIS POORE HEART CCNSUMED WITH DISPAIRE          1.22.8
   CONSUM'D WITH THAT WHICH IT WAS NURRISHT BY           3.73.12
CONSUMEST                 1
   THAT THOU CONSUM'ST THY SELFE IN SINGLE LIFE+         3.9.2
CONSUMING                 3
   AGAINST THE DARKE AND TIMES CONSUMING RAGE            1.55.12
   AGAINE INCREASING, AS YCU ARE CONSUMING               2.16.11
   AND STIL INCREASING AS THOU ART CONSUMING             2.106.11
CONSUMPTION               1
   STILL EMPTY GORG'D, WITH CARES CONSUMPTICN
                           PYNDE                         2.116.14
CONTAIN                   4
   TH'ANCIENT $WOUNDS NO LCNGER CAN CONTAINE             2.46.11
   LOOKE WHAT THY MEMCRIE CANNOT CONTAINE                3.77.9
   I SEE THE HOUSE, MY HEART THY SELFE CONTAINE          4.85.1
   FOR LOE MY LOVE DOTH IN HER SELFE CONTAINE            5.15.5
CONTAINED                 1
   WHAT WONDROUS VERTUE IS CONTAYND IN YOU               5.7.2
CONTAINS                  2
   THE WORTH OF THAT, IS THAT WHICH IT CONTAINES         3.74.13
   THE SPHEARE OF $CUPID FCURTY YEARES CONTAINES         5.60.10
CONTEMPLATION
   THE CONTEMPLATION CF WHCSE HEAVENLY HEW               5.80.11
   THROUGH CONTEMPLATICN OF MY PUREST PART               5.88.10
CONTEND                   3
   AND THUS WHILST SIGHES AND TEARES TOGETHER
                           DOE CONTENDE                  2.133.13
   IN SEQUENT TOILE ALL FORWARDS DO CONTEND              3.60.4
   BUT WITH YOUR $RUBARB WCRDS YOW MUST CONTEND          4.14.5
CONTENDING                1
   SLEEPE WITH $BEAUTY, $BEAUTY WITH SLEEPE
                           CONTENDING                    2.136.11
CONTENT                   7
   HAPPY IN SLEEPE, WAKING CONTENT TO LANGUISH           1.16.1
   AND SO CONTENT ME THAT HER FROWNES SHOULD BE          1.59.11
```

```
WITHIN THINE OWNE BUD BURIEST THY CONTENT              3.1.11
SO I RETURNE REBUKT TO MY CONTENT                      3.119.13
AND NOT CONTENT TO BE $PERFECTION'S HEIRE              4.71.9
I WAS CONTENT YOU SHOULD IN FAVOUR CREEPE             4.83.2
CANNOT SUCH GRACE YCUR SILLY SELFE CONTENT            4.83.11
CONTENTED                      6
HER SIGHT CONTENTED THUS TO SEE ME SPILL             1.36.13
AND ONELY REST CONTENTED WITH THE $LIGHT             2.43.6
WITH WHAT I MOST INJOY CONTENTED LEAST               3.29.8
IF THOU SURVIVE MY WELL CONTENTED DAIE               3.32.1
BUT BE CONTENTED WHEN THAT FELL AREST                3.74.1
HE IS CONTENTED THY POORE DRUDGE TO BE               3.151.11
CONTENTMENT                    3
WITH NO CONTENTMENT CAN THEMSELVES SUFFIZE            5.35.3
HER HARTS DESIRE WITH MCST CONTENTMENT PLEASE         5.72.12
WITH NO CONTENTMENT CAN THEMSELVES SUFFIZE            5.83.3
CONTENTS                       2
BUT YOU SHALL SHINE MORE BRIGHT IN THESE CONTENTS     3.55.3
WELL, HOW SO THOU INTERPRET THE CONTENTS             4.67.12
CONTINENT                      1
WHAT $CAPES HE DOUBLED, CF WHAT $CONTINENT           2.1.9
CONTINUAL                      3
MADE MORE OR LES BY THY CONTINUALL HAST               3.123.12
TO BE ACQUIT FRO MY CONTINUALL SMART                 5.42.6
BUT THIS CONTINUALL CRUELL CIVILL WARRE              5.44.5
CONTINUALLY                    1
MY CEASLES CARES CCNTINUALLY RUN ON                  1.33.2
CONTINUANCE                    1
THE FIRMEST FLINT DOTH IN CONTINUANCE WEARE           5.18.4
CONTRACTED                     2
BUT THOU CONTRACTED TO THINE OWNE BRIGHT EYES         3.1.5
WHICH PARTS THE SHORE, WHERE TWO CONTRACTED NEW       3.56.10
CONTRARIES                     1
THIS CRUELL KNOWLEDGE OF THESE CONTRARIES             1.20.13
CONTRARY                       3
WITH TEARES, SIGHES, AND DISDAINE, THYS
                        CONTRARY I PROVE              2.132.4
MINE OWNE SELFE LCVE QUITE CONTRARY I READ            3.62.11
THAT WHEREAS BLACKE SEEMES $BEAUTIE'S CONTRARY        4.7.10
CONTROL                        3
I SHOULD IN THOUGHT CONTROULE YOUR TIMES
                        OF PLEASURE                   3.58.2
CAN YET THE LEASE CF MY TRUE LOVE CONTROULE           3.107.3
WHEN MOST IMPEACHT, STANDS LEAST IN THY
                        CONTROULE                     3.125.14
CONTROLLED                     1
BY THEYR TEN $SIBILS HAVE THE WORLD CONTROLD          2.119.2
CONTROLLING                    2
A MAN IN HEW ALL $HEWS IN HIS CONTROWLING             3.20.7
AND $FOLLY ($DOCTCR-LIKE) CONTROULING SKILL           3.66.10
CONVERSATION                   2
THAT CONVERSATION SWEET, WHERE SUCH HIGH
                        COMFORTS BE                   4.77.10
WHO MAY WITH CHARME OF CCNVERSATION SWEETE            4.106.10
CONVERSING                     2
WHERE SHE WITH $LCVE CONVERSING HATH NOT BEENE        2.38.8
WHERE SHEE WITH $LCVE CCNVERSING HATH NOT BEENE       2.131.8
CONVERT                        3
TEARES CANNOT SOFTEN FLINT, NOR VOWES CONVART         1.11.3
IF FROM THY SELFE, TO STCRE THOU WOULDST CONVERT      3.14.12
```

```
      THOSE ENGINS CAN THE PROUDEST LOVE CONVERT        5.14.12
CONVERTED                  2
   THE EYES (FORE DUTICUS) NOW CONVERTED ARE            3.7.11
   WHEN LOVE CONVERTED FROM THE THING IT WAS            3.49.7
CONVERTEST                 1
   THOU MAIST CALL THINE, WHEN THOU FROM
                           YOUTH CONVERTEST             3.11.4
CONVEY                     1
   CONVAY THEE FROM THE THOUGHT OF THY DISGRACE         1.52.11
CONVOY                     1
   A HAPPY CONVOY TO A HOLY $LAND                       1.46.6
COOL                       3
   THOSE SIGHES WHICH COOLE MY HART, ARE
                           COLES UNTO MY LOVE           2.132.2
   THIS BRAND SHE QUENCHED IN A COOLE $WELL BY          3.154.9
   NO WIND, NO SHADE CAN COOLE, WHAT HELPE
                           THEN IN MY CASE              4.76.12
COOLS                      1
   LOVES FIRE HEATES WATER, WATER COOLES NOT LOVE       3.154.14
COPARTNER                  1
   COPARTNER OF THE RICHES OF THAT SIGHT                4.48.6
COPY                       2
   THOU SHOULDST PRINT MORE, NOT LET THAT COPPY DIE     3.11.14
   LET HIM BUT COPPY WHAT IN YOU IS WRIT                3.84.9
COPYING                    1
   BUT $COPYING IS, WHAT IN HER $NATURE WRITES          4.3.14
CORAL                      1
   CURRALL IS FARRE MORE RED, THEN HER LIPS RED         3.130.2
CORDIALS                   2
   THEN WITH SOME CORDIALLS SEEKE FIRST TO APPEASE      5.50.9
   BUT SUCH SWEET CORDIALLS PASSE $PHYSITIONS ART       5.50.12
CORN                       1
   AND WHEN $CORNE'S SOWNE, OR GROWNE INTO THE $EARE    2.48.7
CORRECT                    1
   NOR DOUBLE PENNANCE TO CORRECT CORRECTION            3.111.12
CORRECTION                 2
   WITH $DIET AND $CORRECTION, $MEN DISTRAUGHT          2.9.13
   NOR DOUBLE PENNANCE TO CORRECT CORRECTION            3.111.12
CORRESPONDENCE             1
   WHICH HAVE NO CORRESPONDENCE WITH TRUE SIGHT         3.148.2
CORRUPT                    2
   IF EYES CORRUPT BY OVER-PARTIALL LOOKES              3.137.5
   AND WOULD CORRUPT MY SAINT TO BE A DIVEL             3.144.7
CORRUPTED                  1
   BUT HE WITH $BEAUTIE FIRST CORRUPTED $SIGHT          2.29.5
CORRUPTING                 1
   MY SELFE CORRUPTING SALVING THY AMISSE               3.35.7
CORRUPTION                 1
   FROM FRAYLE CORRUPTION, THAT DOTH FLESH ENSEW        5.79.8
CORSE                      2
   OFT 'T'ATH BEEN PROV'D, THE BREATHLESSE
                           $COARSE WILL BLEED           2.46.8
   THEN STANCH THE BLEEDING, THEN TRANS-PIERCE
                           THE $COARSE                  2.50.7
COST                       5
   MY TOUCHT HEART TURNES IT TO THAT HAPPY COST         1.53.2
   THE RICH PROUD COST OF OUTWORNE BURIED AGE           3.64.2
   RICHER THEN WEALTH, PROUDER THEN GARMENTS COST       3.91.10
   WHY SO LARGE COST HAVING SO SHORT A LEASE            3.146.5
   AND STRANGE THINGS COST TOO DEARE FOR
                           MY POORE SPRITES             4.3.11
```

```
COSTLY                        2
  QUAFFING $CAROWSES IN THIS COSTLY $WINE            2.7.8
  PAINTING THY OUTWARD WALLS SO COSTLIE GAY+         3.146.4
COTSWOLD                      2
  COTSWOLD COMMENDS HER $ISIS TO THE $TAME           2.32.9
  COTSWOOLD COMMENDS HER $ISIS AND HER $TAME         2.124.9
COUCHING                      1
  AND IN HER BREAST BOPEEPE OR COUCHING LYES         4.11.12
COUNCIL                       1
  WHOM ALL THE $GODS IN COUNCELL DID AGREE           5.24.9
COUNSEL                       2
  WHAT $NESTOR'S COUNSELL CAN MY FLAMES ALAY         4.35.5
  OUT TRAYTOUR ABSENCE, DAREST THOU COUNSELL ME      4.88.1
COUNSELS                      3
  MY TONGUE IN PAYNE, MY HARTS COUNSELS BEWRAYING    2.142.6
  SOMEWHAT THY LEAD'N COUNSELS, WHICH I TOCKE        4.56.7
  NO MORE, MY DEARE, NO MORE THESE COUNSELS TRIE     4.64.1
COUNT                         8
  YET COUNT IT NO DISGRACE THAT I HAVE LOV'D THEE    1.44.14
  DUELY TO COUNT THE SUMME OF ALL MY CARES           2.3.2
  SHALL SUM MY COUNT, AND MAKE MY OLD EXCUSE         3.2.11
  WHEN I DOE COUNT THE CLOCK THAT TELS THE TIME      3.12.1
  WHICH IN THEIR WILS COUNT BAD WHAT I THINK GOOD+   3.121.8
  ONELY MY PLAGUE THUS FARRE I COUNT MY GAINE        3.141.13
  AND JOY THEREIN, THOUGH $NATIONS COUNT IT SHAME    4.28.8
  THEN BY THAT COUNT, WHICH LOVERS BOOKS INVENT      5.60.9
COUNTED                       2
  IN THE OULD AGE BLACKE WAS NOT COUNTED FAIRE       3.127.1
  THAT TO THE WORLD NAUGHT ELSE BE COUNTED DEARE     5.8.4
COUNTENANCE                   5
  BUT WHEN YOUR COUNTINANCE FILD UP HIS LINE         3.86.13
  AND HER FAIRE COUNTENANCE LIKE A GOODLY BANNER     5.5.11
  BUT THAT SAME LOFTY COUNTENANCE SEEMES TO SCORNE   5.13.9
  AND WITH STERNE COUNTENANCE BACK AGAIN DOTH CHACE  5.21.7
  A DREADFULL COUNTENAUNCE SHE GIVEN HATH            5.31.6
COUNTERFEIT                   2
  MUCH LIKER THEN YOUR PAINTED COUNTERFEIT           3.16.8
  DESCRIBE $ADONIS AND THE COUNTERFET                3.53.5
COUNTERPART                   1
  AND SUCH A COUNTER-PART SHALL FAME HIS WIT         3.84.11
COUNTEST                      1
  THOU COUNTEST $STELLA THINE, LIKE THOSE
                          WHOSE POWERS               4.12.9
COUNTING                      3
  NOW COUNTING BEST TO BE WITH YOU ALONE             3.75.7
  COUNTING NO OLD THING OLD, THOU MINE, I THINE      3.108.7
  COUNTING BUT DUST WHAT IN THE WAY DID LIE          4.105.8
COUNTRIES                     2
  HOW FARRE HE SAYL'D, WHAT $COUNTRIES HE HAD SEENE  2.1.4
  AS $IN SOME $COUNTRIES, FARRE REMOTE FROM HENCE    2.50.1
COUNTRY                       1
  AND SHOULD IN SOULE UP TO OUR COUNTREY MOVE        4.5.13
COUNTS                        1
  AND BY JUST COUNTS MY SELFE A BANCKROUT KNOW       4.18.3
COUPLED                       1
  IN HART BOTH SIGHT AND LOVE NOW COUPLED BE         4.88.13
COUPLEMENT                    1
  MAKING A COOPELMENT OF PROUD COMPARE               3.21.5
COUPLING                      1
  WHICH, COUPLING $DOVES, GUIDES $VENUS'
                          CHARIOT RIGHT              4.79.4
```

```
COVERING                        1
   GOLD IS THE COVERING OF THAT STATELY PLACE          4.9.4
COVERT                          1
   IN THE CLOSE COVERT OF HER GUILEFULL EYEN           5.12.7
COVET                           1
   TO COVET FETTERS, THOUGH THEY GOLDEN BEE            5.37.14
COVETED                         1
   THAT MAKETH IT BE CCVETED THE MORE                  5.26.10
COVETIZE                        2
   MY HUNGRY EYES THROUGH GREEDY COVETIZE              5.35.1
   MY HUNGRY EYES, THROUGH GREEDY COVETIZE             5.83.1
COVETOUS                        2
   AS COVETOUS THE OTHERS USE TO HAVE                  2.33.10
   FOR THOU ART COVETCUS, AND HE IS KINDE              3.134.6
COWARD                          2
   THE COWARD CONQUEST OF A WRETCHES KNIFE             3.74.11
   FAINT COWARD JOY NC LONGER TARRY DARE               4.95.5
COY                             3
   REASON REPROCHED WITH THIS COY $DISDAINE            2.38.9
   AND MURTHER'ST $VERTUE WITH THY COY DISDAINE        2.44.8
   REASON REPROCHED WITH THIS COY DISDAINE             2.131.9
CRADLE                          2
   TO M'INFANT STILE THE $CRADLE, AND THE $GRAVE       1.59.12
   NOW WAST THOU BORNE, NOW IN THY CRADLE SLAYNE       2.141.14
CRAFT                           2
   I SEE $YOUR CRAFT, NOW I PERCEIVE $YOUR CRIFT       2.19.11
   SUCH SUBTILE CRAFT MY $DAMZELL DOTH CONCEAVE        5.23.5
CRAFTILY                        3
   WHICH FROM ABOVE HE CRAFTILY DID TAKE               2.14.6
   WHILE CRAFTILY YOU SEEM'D YOUR CUT TO KEEPE         4.83.3
   AND BEING CAUGHT MAY CRAFTILY ENFOLD                5.37.7
CRAFTSMAN'S                      1
   A GREATER CRAFTESMANS HAND THERETO DOTH NEEDE       5.17.13
CRAVE                           7
   TO CRAVE REDRESSE, YET HOLD AFFLICTION DEARE        1.20.7
   AND LET ME TAKE MY SELFE WHAT I DOE CRAVE           2.5.12
   THIS TO EACH OTHER MUTUALLY THEY CRAVE              2.33.12
   TRUCE, GENTLE $LOVE, A $PARLY NOW I CRAVE           2.63.1
   MY CARES MY MUTES SC MUTE TO CRAVE RELIEFE          2.111.10
   OR AT YOUR HAND TH'ACCOUNT OF HOURES TO CRAVE       3.58.3
   WHO FUR LONG FAITH, THO DAYLY HELPE I CRAVE         4.47.7
CRAVED                          2
   YET CRAV'D THE $ALMES OF SUCH AS PASSED BY          2.23.4
   I CRAV'D THE THING WHICH EVER SHE DENIES            4.63.6
CRAWLS                          1
   CRAWLES TO MATURITY, WHEREWITH BEING CROWN'D        3.60.6
CREAM                           1
   WHOSE PANTS DO MAKE UNSPILLING CREAME TO FLOW       4.100.6
CREATED                         2
   AND FOR A WOMAN WERT THCU FIRST CREATED             3.20.9
   WHICH EYES NOT YET CREATED SHALL ORE-READ           3.81.10
CREATING                        1
   CREATING EVERY BAD A PERFECT BEST                   3.114.7
CREATION                        2
   BUT HEAVEN IN THY CREATION DID DECREE               3.93.9
   SLANDRING $CREATICN WITH A FALSE ESTEEME            3.127.12
CREATURE                        4
   SINCE, BUT YOUR SELFE, THERE WAS NO $CREATURE BY    2.2.3
   THAT EV'RY $CREATURE TO HIS KIND DO'ST CALL         2.37.11
   THE WRETCHED $CREATURE, DESTINED TO DIE             2.50.2
```

THE MOST SWEET-FAVOR OR DEFORMEDST CREATURE	3.113.10

CREATURES   3
'MONGST ALL THE $CREATURES IN THIS SPACIOUS
                          $ROUND   2.16.1
FROM FAIREST CREATURES WE DESIRE INCREASE   3.1.1
ONE OF HER FETHERED CREATURES BROAKE AWAY   3.143.2

CREDIT   4
WHY DOOST THOU $DELIA CREDIT SO THY GLASSE   1.37.1
WONNE GRACE AND CREDIT IN THE $EARES OF $MEN   2.47.4
SIMPLY I CREDIT HER FALSE SPEAKING TONGUE   3.138.7
MEN CALL YOU FAYRE, AND YOU DOE CREDIT IT   5.79.1

CREEP   6
YET WITH THE $MOLE I CREEPE INTO THE $EARTH   2.62.10
YET WITH THE $MOLE, I CREEPE INTO THE EARTH   2.150.10
CREEPE IN TWIXT VOWES, AND CHANGE DECREES
                          OF $KINGS   3.115.6
A $POET EKE, AS HUMOURS FLY OR CREEPE   4.32.4
IF STILL I FORCE HER IN SAD RIMES TO CREEPE   4.70.2
I WAS CONTENT YOU SHOULD IN FAVOUR CREEPE   4.83.2

CREST   2
EACH HAD HIS CREAST, $MARS CARIED $VENUS' GLOVE   4.13.7
CUPID THEN SMILES, FOR ON HIS CREST THERE LIES   4.13.9

CRESTS   1
WHEN TYRANTS CRESTS AND TOMBS OF BRASSE
                          ARE SPENT   3.107.14

CREW   2
AND WITH THE CREW OF BLESSED $SAYNTS UPBROUGHT   5.61.7
TO WAYT ON LOVE AMONGST HIS LOVELY CREW   5.70.10

CRIED   1
WITH SIGHT THEREOF CRIDE OUT., O FAIRE DISGRACE   4.103.13

CRIES   8
WHY SHOULD I MORE MOLEST THE WORLD WITH CRIES+   1.21.5
CRYES IN HIS PANGS, $GOD HELPE THE MOTHERLESSE   2.116.18
AND TROUBLE DEAFE HEAVEN WITH MY BOOTLESSE CRIES   3.29.3
CRIES TO CATCH HER WHOSE BUSIE CARE IS BENT   3.143.6
NOR TRUMPETS SOUND I HEARD, NOR FRIENDLY CRIES   4.53.12
THAT GIV'ST NO BETTER EARE TO MY JUST CRIES   4.65.2
'BUT AH,' $DESIRE STILL CRIES, 'GIVE ME
                          SOME FOOD'   4.71.14
MY HEART CRIES 'AH', IT BURNES, MINE EYES
                          NOW DAZLED BE   4.76.11

CRIME   4
BUT I FORBID THEE ONE MOST HAINOUS CRIME   3.19.8
YOUR SELFE TO PARDON OF SELFE-DOING CRIME   3.58.12
TO WAIGH HOW ONCE I SUFFERED IN YOUR CRIME   3.120.8
WHICH DIE FOR GOODNES, WHO HAVE LIV'D FOR CRIME   3.124.14

CRIMSON   2
THE MORNINGS $CRIMSON, TO HER LYPS ALIKE   2.148.5
WHO HATH THE CRIMSON WEEDS STOLNE FROM
                          MY MORNING SKIES+   4.102.4

CRIPPLE   2
A CRIPPLE $HAND TO WRITE, YET LAME BY $KIND   2.35.7
A CRIPPLE HAND TO WRITE, YET LAME BY KIND   2.112.7

CRISPED   1
THY DAINTIE $HAYRE, SO CURL'D, AND CRISPED NOW   2.8.7

CRITIC   1
TO CRYTTICK AND TO FLATTERER STOPPED ARE   3.112.11

CROCODILE   2
THE WEEPING $CROCODILE.. THESE VILE PERNICIOUS
                          THREE   2.130.4

```
THOU $CROCODILE, WHO WHEN THOU HAST ME SLAINE      2.130.13
CROOKED                    3
  ME $THINKES I SEE SOME CROOKED $MIMICKE JEERE       2.31.1
  CROOKED ECLIPSES GAINST HIS GLORY FIGHT             3.60.7
  SO THOU PREVENST HIS SIETH, AND CROOKED KNIFE       3.100.14
CROSS                      5
  AND CROSSE MY CARES ERE GREATER SUMMES ARISE        1.1.12
  THE PAIMENTS OF MY $LOVE, I READ, AND CROSSE        2.3.6
  THE PAYMENTS OF MY LOVE I READ, AND READING
                              CROSSE                   2.110.6
  AND BOTH FOR MY SAKE LAY ON ME THIS CROSSE          3.42.12
  NOW WHILE THE WORLD IS BENT MY DEEDS TO CROSSE      3.90.2
CROSSED                    2
  MIX'D WITH HER $TEARES, THAT NE'R HER
                              TRUE-$LOVE CROST        2.15.5
  A TORMENT THRICE THREE-FOLD THUS TO BE CROSSED      3.133.8
CROSSES                    2
  AND VIEW THE $CROSSES WHICH MY COURSE DOE LET       2.60.10
  AND VIEW THE CROSSES WHICH MY COURSE DOTH LET       2.149.10
CROSSING                   1
  CROSSING SWEET NATURE BY UNRULY WILL                2.147.12
CROSS-ROW                  1
  TO CON MY $CROS-ROWE ERE I LEARN'D TO SPELL         2.111.2
CROW                       2
  A $CROW THAT FLIES IN HEAVENS SWEETEST AYRE         3.70.4
  THE $CROE, OR $DOVE, IT SHAPES THEM TO
                              YOUR FEATURE            3.113.12
CROW-KEEPER                1
  PRACTISE THY $QUIVER, AND TURNE $CROW-KEEPER        2.48.8
CROWN                      5
  AND CROWNE THE $PIRENS WITH MY LIVING $SONG         2.25.4
  O OUR WORLDS WONDER, CROWNE OF HEAVEN ABOVE         2.129.9
  INCERTENTIES NOW CROWNE THEM-SELVES ASSUR'DE        3.107.7
  RICH IN THOSE GIFTS WHICH GIVE TH'ETERNALL
                              CROWNE                   4.37.11
  TO LOSE HIS $CROWNE, RATHER THEN FAILE HIS $LOVE    4.75.14
CROWNED                   10
  OUR $FLOUDS-$QUEEN $THAMES, FOR $SHIPS
                    AND $SWANS IS CROWNED             2.32.1
  WITH HEAVENLY COLOURS DIDE, WITH NATURES
                    WONDER CROUND                     2.106.4
  BEAUTY SOMETIME IN ALL HER GLORY CROWNED            2.109.1
  OUR FLOODS-$QUEENE $THAMES, FOR SHYPS
                    AND $SWANS IS CROWNED             2.124.1
  INTITLED IN THEIR PARTS, DO CROWNED SIT             3.37.7
  CRAWLES TO MATURITY, WHEREWITH BEING CROWN'D        3.60.6
  THEIR OUTWARD THUS WITH OUTWARD PRAISE IS CROWND    3.69.5
  OR WHETHER DOTH MY MINDE BEING CROWN'D WITH YOU     3.114.1
  NO KINGS BE CROWN'D BUT THEY SOME COVENANTS MAKE    4.69.14
  WHO NOW IS COMMING FORTH WITH GIRLAND CROUNED       5.19.4
CROWNING                   1
  CROWNING THE PRESENT, DOUBTING OF THE REST          3.115.12
CROWS                      1
  O HOW FOR JOY HE LEAPES, O HOW HE CROWES            4.17.12
CRUCIFY                    1
  THUS WILL I CRUCIFIE MY CRUELL SHEE                 2.115.17
CRUEL                     45
  SIGH OUT A $STORIE OF HER CRUELL DEEDES             1.2.5
  FAIRE IS MY $LOVE, AND CRUELL AS SHE'S FAIRE        1.6.1
  DID TREATE THE CRUELL FAIRE TO YEELD RELIEFE        1.8.8
```

```
FOR HER THE CRUELL $FAIRE, WITHIN WHOSE BROW           1.10.2
NO FAVOUR THOUGH, THE CRUELL FAIRE ALLOWES            1.11.12
YET WILL I WEEPE, VOW, PRAY TO CRUELL SHEE            1.11.13
BUT YET RESTORE THY FIERCE AND CRUELL MIND           1.19.11
THIS CRUELL KNOWLEDGE OF THESE CONTRARIES            1.20.13
TIME, CRUELL TIME, COME AND SUBDUE THAT $BROW         1.23.1
CAUS'D BY THOSE CRUELL BEAMES THAT WERE
                              SO STRONG              1.32.14
SERVE AS AN INCENSE TO A CRUELL $DAME                1.47.10
TO CRUELL $LOVE MY $SOULE WAS FIRST BETRAY'D         2.29.14
OR $CRUELL, IF THOU CAN'ST NOT., LET US SCORSE        2.52.7
THUS WILL I CRUCIFIE MY CRUELL SHEE                 2.115.17
THE $MUSES NICE, THE $FURIES CRUELL BE              2.118.7
THY SELFE THY FOE, TO THY SWEET SELFE TOO CRUELL      3.1.8
PRAISING THY WORTH, DISPIGHT HIS CRUELL HAND        3.60.14
AGAINST CONFOUNDING $AGES CRUELL KNIFE              3.63.10
SAVAGE, EXTREAME, RUDE, CRUELL, NOT TO TRUST        3.129.4
AS THOSE WHOSE BEAUTIES PROUDLY MAKE THEM CRUELL    3.131.2
ME FROM MY SELFE THY CRUELL EYE HATH TAKEN          3.133.5
BE WISE AS THOU ART CRUELL, DO NOT PRESSE           3.140.1
CANST THOU $O CRUELL, SAY I LOVE THEE NOT           3.149.1
OFT CRUELL FIGHTS WELL PICTURED FORTH DO PLEASE      4.34.4
DEARE $KILLER, SPARE NOT THY SWEET CRUELL SHOT      4.48.13
BUT THAT WHICH ONCE MAY WIN THY CRUELL HART         4.64.13
STELLA, WHILE NOW BY HONOUR'S CRUELL MIGHT           4.91.1
SHE CRUELL WARRIOUR DOTH HER SELFE ADDRESSE          5.11.3
HAVE EVER SINCE ME KEPT IN CRUELL BANDS             5.12.12
BUT SHE MORE CRUELL AND MORE SALVAGE WYLDE           5.20.9
OF SUCH POORE THRALLS HER CRUELL HANDS EMBREW       5.31.12
ARION, WHEN THROUGH TEMPESTS CRUEL WRACKE            5.38.1
TO BE SO CRUELL TO AN HUMBLED FOE+                   5.41.2
BUT THIS CONTINUALL CRUELL CIVILL WARRE              5.44.5
MY CRUELL FAYRE STREIGHT BIDS ME WEND MY WAY         5.46.2
WHOME BEING CAUGHT SHE KILLS WITH CRUELL PRYDE       5.47.7
THAT THEY TAKE PLEASURE IN HER CRUELL PLAY          5.47.11
INNOCENT PAPER WHOM TOO CRUELL HAND                  5.48.1
FAYRE CRUELL, WHY ARE YE SO FIERCE AND CRUELL+       5.49.1
FAYRE CRUELL, WHY ARE YE SO FIERCE AND CRUELL+       5.49.1
RIGHT SO MY CRUELL FAYRE WITH ME DOTH PLAY           5.53.5
THE WHICH HER MADE ATTONCE SO CRUELL FAIRE           5.55.4
FAYRE YE BE SURE, BUT CRUELL AND UNKIND              5.56.1
BUT GLORY THINKE TO MAKE THESE CRUEL STOURES        5.57.10
YE CRUELL ONE, WHAT GLORY CAN BE GOT                5.57.11
CRUELEST                    2
BY LOVING HER, THE CRUELST $FAIRE THAT LIVES        1.22.10
THE CRUELST $FAYRE THAT SEES I PINE FOR HER         1.22.11
CRUELLY                     1
THE LOVE WHICH ME SO CRUELLY TORMENTETH              5.42.1
CRUELNESS                   1
BUT TAKETH GLORY IN HER CRUELNESSE                  5.20.12
CRUELTIES                   2
OR DOST THOU SPARE HER FOR HER CRUELTIES             1.23.7
LET THEM FEELE TH'UTMOST OF YOUR CRUELTYES           5.49.9
CRUELTY                    12
SUCH HONOUR UNTO CRUELTY TO GIVE+                    1.17.8
UPON THIS HEART, WHOM CRUELTY WILL KILL              1.33.8
THEN MINE UNTO HER CRUELTY HATH BEENE                1.48.8
THY CRUELTY, THY GLORY., $O STRANGE CASE            1.56.10
THAT $CRUELTY HER SELFE MIGHT GRIEVE TO VIEW         1.60.7
ONLY LOV'D $TYRANTS, JUST IN CRUELTY                 4.42.6
```

```
THEN TO TORMENT ME THUS WITH CRUELTY                          5.25.7
SUCH CRUELTY SHE WOULD HAVE SOONE ABHORD                      5.31.14
BUT THAT THEIR CRUELTY DOTH STILL INCREACE                    5.36.7
ONELY LET HER ABSTAINE FROM CRUELTY                           5.42.13
AND WERE IT NOT THAT THROUGH YOUR CRUELTY                     5.45.9
AND THEREWITH DOE HER CRUELTY COMPARE                         5.55.2
CRUSHED                    1
WITH TIMES INJURIOUS HAND CHRUSHT AND ORE-WORNE               3.63.2
CRY                       13
TO PAINT ON FLOODS, TILL THE SHORE CRIE TO TH'AIRE            1.9.2
AND IN MY FALL I CRYE FOR HELPE WITH SPEEDE                   1.32.9
SAVE MEE I $CRIE, YOU SIGH ME OUT A $NO                       2.5.8
WHERE OTHER $MEN IN DEPTH OF $PASSION CRIE                    2.24.13
TYR'D WITH ALL THESE FOR RESTFULL DEATH I CRY                 3.66.1
AND LIKE UNLETTERED CLARKE STILL CRIE $AMEN                   3.85.6
LET DAINTIE WITS CRIE ON THE $SISTERS NINE                    4.3.1
CRIE, '$VICTORIE, THIS FAIRE DAY ALL IS OURS'                 4.12.11
BUT MORE I CRIE, LESSE GRACE SHE DOTH IMPART                  4.44.6
BUT ON HER NAME INCESSANTLY TO CRIE                           4.55.11
LET FOLKE ORECHARG'D WITH BRAINE AGAINST ME CRIE              4.64.4
I CRY THY SIGHS., MY DEERE, THY TEARES I BLEEDE               4.93.14
BUT WHEN I LAUGH SHE MOCKS, AND WHEN I CRY                    5.54.11
CRYING                     3
WAKEN HER SLEEPING PITTY WITH YOUR CRYING                     1.2.12
GROWNE HOARCE WITH CRYING MERCY, MERCY GIVE                   1.16.6
IF THOU TURNE BACK AND MY LOUDE CRYING STILL                  3.143.14
CRYSTAL                   11
THE $DART TRANSPEARSING, WERE THOSE $CHRISTALL
                                  EIES                        1.14.4
THE $CRYSTALL $TRENT, FOR $FOORDS AND
                       $FISH RENOWNED                         2.32.3
THY $CRISTALL STREAME REFINED BY HER $EYES                    2.53.4
MY LIQUIDS THEN WERE LIQUID CHRISTALL TEARES                  2.111.9
THAT CHRISTALL STREAME REFINED BY HER EYES                    2.113.4
THE CHRISTALL $TRENT, FOR $FOORDS AND
                       FISHE RENOWNED                         2.124.3
HYDES IN THOSE CHRISTALL QUIVERS OF HER EYES                  2.126.10
(A CLOSET NEVER PEARST WITH CHRISTALL EYES)                   3.46.6
NOR UNTO $CHRISTALL.. FOR NOUGHT MAY THEM SEVER               5.9.11
LEAVE LADY IN YOUR GLASSE OF CHRISTALL CLENE                  5.45.1
CLEARER THEN CHRISTALL WOULD THEREIN APPERE                   5.45.12
CRYSTALLINE                1
NO CLOWDE WAS SEENE, BUT CHRISTALINE THE AYRE                 2.125.13
CUCKOO                     3
THE MERRY $CUCKOW, MESSENGER OF $SPRING                       5.19.1
ERE $CUCKOW END, LET HER A REBELL BE                          5.19.14
SO DOES THE $CUCKOW, WHEN THE $MAVIS SINGS                    5.85.3
CULVER                     1
LYKE AS THE $CULVER ON THE BARED BOUGH                        5.89.1
CUMAEA                     1
EXCELLING HER OF $DELPHOS OR $CUMAEA                          2.119.11
CUMBERED                   1
I, CUMBRED WITH GOOD MANERS, ANSWER DO                        4.30.13
CUNNING                    6
YET EYES THIS CUNNING WANT TO GRACE THEIR ART                 3.24.13
WHAT NEEDST THOU WOUND WITH CUNNING WHEN
                        THY MIGHT                             3.139.7
O CUNNING LOVE, WITH TEARES THOU KEEPST
                        ME BLINDE                             3.148.13
TILL DOWNE-RIGHT BLOWES DID FOYLE THY
                        CUNNING FENCE                         4.10.11
```

```
     IN $MARTIALL SPORTS I HAD MY CUNNING TRIDE          4.53.1
     RIGHT SO YOUR SELFE WERE CAUGHT IN CUNNING SNARE    5.71.5
CUNNINGEST                    1
     OF CUNNINGST FISHERS IN MOST TROUBLED STREAMES      4.51.10
CUNNINGLY                     1
     AND WITH SLY SKILL SO CUNNINGLY THEM DRESSES        5.37.3
CUP                           2
     AND TO HIS PALLAT DOTH PREPARE THE CUP              3.114.12
     NECTAR OF $MIRTH, SINCE I $JOVE'S CUP DO KEEPE      4.70.4
CUPID                        13
     TO MAKE HER LOVE, CR $CUPID BE THOU DAMN'D          2.36.14
     CUPID, I HATE THEE, WHICH $I'DE HAVE THEE KNOW      2.48.1
     CUPID, DUMBE $IDOLL, PEEVISH $SAINT OF LOVE         2.126.1
     $CUPID LAID BY HIS BRAND AND FELL A SLEEPE          3.153.1
     WHERE $CUPID GOT NEW FIRE., MY MISTRES EYE          3.153.14
     CUPID, BECAUSE THOU SHIN'ST IN $STELLAS EYES        4.12.1
     CUPID THEN SMILES, FOR CN HIS CREST THERE LIES      4.13.9
     HIS MOTHER DEARE $CUPID OFFENDED LATE               4.17.1
     BRAKE BOW, BRAKE SHAFTS, WHILE $CUPID
                              WEEPING SATE               4.17.8
     WHERE $CUPID IS SWCRNE PAGE TO $CHASTITY+           4.35.8
     WHEN $CUPID, HAVING ME HIS SLAVE DESCRIDE           4.53.5
     O $DOCTOR $CUPID, THOU FOR ME REPLY                 4.61.12
     THE SPHEARE OF $CUPID FCURTY YEARES CONTAINES       5.60.10
CUPID'S                       9
     WHILST FROM THEYR RAYES BY $CUPIDS SKILFULL HAND    2.135.7
     IT IS MOST TRUE, WHAT WE CALL $CUPID'S DART         4.5.5
     WHICH $CUPID'S SELFE FRCM $BEAUTIE'S MYNE
                              DID DRAW                   4.9.13
     ON $CUPID'S BOW HCW ARE MY HEART-STRINGS BENT       4.19.1
     COULD HOPE BY $CUPID'S HELPE CN YOU TO PRAY         4.43.2
     PROFESSE IN DEED I DO NCT $CUPID'S ART              4.54.10
     VERTUE'S GOLD NOW MUST HEAD MY $CUPID'S DART        4.72.8
     BEST CHARGE, AND BRAVEST RETRAIT IN $CUPID'S
                              FIGHT                      4.79.5
     NATURE'S PRAISE, $VERTUE'S STALL, $CUPID'S
                              COLD FIRE                  4.80.3
CUPS                          1
     WHERE, IN HIS $CUPS O'RCCME WITH FOULE $EXCESSE     2.7.9
CURBED                        1
     CURB'D IN WITH FEARE, BUT WITH GUILT BOSSE ABOVE    4.49.7
CURE                          6
     I HAVE A $MED'CINE THAT SHALL CURE MY $LCVE         2.15.2
     EVEN THAT YOUR PITTIE IS ENOUGH TO CURE MEE         3.111.14
     PAST CURE I AM, NCW $REASON IS PAST CARE            3.147.9
     AGAINST STRANG MALLADIES A SOVERAIGNE CURE          3.153.8
     BUT FOUND NO CURE, THE BATH FOR MY HELPE LIES       3.153.13
     CAME THERE FOR CURE AND THIS BY THAT I PROVE        3.154.13
CURED                         3
     MY $VICES CUR'D, BY $VERTUES SPRUNG FROM THEE       2.35.11
     MY VICES CUR'D, BY VERTUES SPRUNG FROM THEE         2.112.11
     WHICH RANCKE OF GCCDNESSE WOULD BY ILL BE CURED     3.118.12
CURELESS                      1
     WHOSE CURELESSE WCUNDS EVEN NOW MOST FRESHLY
                              BLEED                      4.48.11
CURES                         1
     THAT HEALES THE WCUND, AND CURES NOT THE DISGRACE   3.34.8
CURING                        1
     BY CURING ME, AND KILLING ME EACH $HOW'R            2.50.13
```

CURIOUS   5
   WHAT CURIOUS $PENSILL SERVES TO LIM THEE FORTH+   2.146.3
   IF MY SLIGHT $MUSE DOE PLEASE THESE CURICUS
                              DAIES   3.38.13
   THE CURIOUS WITS, SEEING DULL PENSIVENESSE   4.23.1
   YOU THAT WITH ALLEGORIE'S CURIOUS FRAME   4.28.1
   BY $LOVE'S OWNE SELFE, BUT WITH SO CURIOUS
                              DROUGHT   4.38.7
CURIOUSLY   1
   WHERE, WITH SWEET $WOOD, LAYD CURIOUSLY BY $ART   2.30.5
CURLED   1
   THY DAINTIE $HAYRE, SO CURL'D, AND CRISPED NOW   2.8.7
CURLS   1
   AND SABLE CURLS OR SILVER'D ORE WITH WHITE   3.12.4
CURSE   7
   NOW DOE I CURSE $HER, THEN AGAINE I BLESSE $HER   2.41.14
   NOW DOE I CURSE HER, THEN AGAINE I BLESSE HER   2.143.14
   AND LOOKE UPON MY SELFE AND CURSE MY FATE   3.29.4
   YOU TO YOUR BEAUTIOUS BLESSINGS ADDE A CURSE   3.84.13
   BLIST IN MY CURSE, AND CURSED IN MY BLISSE   4.60.14
   O FATE, O FAULT, O CURSE, CHILD OF MY BLISSE   4.93.1
   WITH NO WORSE CURSE THEN ABSENCE MAKES ME TAST   4.105.14
CURSED   7
   THOU WHICH HAST BANN'D THY $THOUGHTS,
                         AND CURST THY $BIRTH   2.49.11
   MINE EYES (SHALL I SAY CURST OR BLEST) BEHELD   4.16.10
   I CURST THEE OFT, I PITIE NOW THY CASE   4.46.1
   BLIST IN MY CURSE, AND CURSED IN MY BLISSE   4.60.14
   CURST BE THE PAGE FROM WHOME THE BAD TORCH FELL   4.105.11
   CURST BE THE NIGHT WHICH DID YOUR STRIFE RESIST   4.105.12
   CURST BE THE $COCHMAN WHICH DID DRIVE SO FAST   4.105.13
CURTAINS   1
   PHOEBUS DREW WIDE THE CURTAINES OF THE SKIES   4.13.12
CUSTOM   1
   O, WHY SHOULD $BEAUTIE ($CUSTOME TO OBEY)   2.43.9
CUT   2
   THAT HE SHALL NEVER CUT FROM MEMORY   3.63.11
   WHILE CRAFTILY YOU SEEM'D YOUR CUT TO KEEPE   4.83.3
CUTTED   1
   OR DO YOU CUTTED $SPARTANES IMITATE+   4.92.3
CYDNUS   1
   SLOW $ARRER, FRANTICK $GALLUS, $CYDNUS COLD   2.120.8
CYNTHUS   1
   THE $DELIAN $CYNTHUS, THEN $OLYMPUS WEIGHT   2.120.7
CYPRESS   1
   SWEET IS THE $CYPRESSE, BUT HIS RYND IS TOUGH   5.26.5
CYTHEREA'S   1
   YEELD $CITHEREAS SONNE THOSE $ARKES OF LOVE   1.19.2
DAILY   9
   BUT DAY DOTH DAILY DRAW MY SORROWES LONGER   3.28.13
   COME DAILY TO THE BANCKES, THAT WHEN THEY SEE   3.56.11
   FOR AS THE $SUN IS DAILY NEW AND OLD   3.76.13
   THE GLASSES OF THY DAYLY VEXING CARE+'   4.34.3
   WHO FOR LONG FAITH, THO DAYLY HELPE I CRAVE   4.47.7
   MOST RUDE DISPAIRE MY DAILY UNBIDDEN GUEST   4.108.7
   DAYLY WHEN I DO SEEKE AND SEW FOR PEACE   5.11.1
   AND DAYLY MORE AUGMENT MY MISERYES+   5.36.8
   FOR THAT YOUR SELFE YE DAYLY SUCH DOE SEE   5.79.2
DAINTIER   1
   TOWNE-FOLKES MY STRENGTH., A DAINTIER
                         JUDGE APPLIES   4.41.6

```
DAINTIEST                        2
  FRAME DAINTIEST LUSTRE, MIXT OF SHADES AND LIGHT+    4.7.4
  HER DAINTIEST BARE WENT FREE., THE CAUSE
                          WAS THIS                     4.22.13
DAINTY                          13
  VEXING WITH UNTUN'D MOANE HER DAINTY EARES           1.21.8
  DEALE WITH THOSE DAINTY CHEEKES AS SHE DOTH DEALE    1.22.7
  THY DAINTIE $HAYRE, SO CURL'D, AND CRISPED NOW       2.8.7
  AMONGST THE DAINTIE $DEW-IMPEARLED FLOWRES           2.53.8
  AMONGST THOSE DAINTY DEW-EMPEARLED FLOWERS           2.113.8
  THE DAINTY GRASSE MAKE MUSICKE WITH HER FEETE        2.125.8
  LET DAINTIE WITS CRIE ON THE $SISTERS NINE           4.3.1
  THOSE DAINTIE DORES UNTO THE $COURT OF BLISSE        4.44.11
  HER SOULE, ARM'D BUT WITH SUCH A DAINTY RIND         4.57.7
  WHAT SAIST THOU NOW, WHERE IS THAT DAINTY CHEERE     4.106.5
  SOME DAINTY EARES, CANNOT WITH ANY SKILL             5.38.6
  OF ALL THAT DEARE AND DAYNTY IS ALYVE                5.63.8
  THAT DAINTY ODOURS FROM THEM THREW AROUND            5.64.3
DAMASKED                         1
  I HAVE SEENE $ROSES DAMASKT, RED AND WHITE           3.130.5
DAME                             1
  SERVE AS AN INCENSE TO A CRUELL $DAME                1.47.10
DAMNED                           3
  TO MAKE HER LOVE, OR $CUPID BE THOU DAMN'D           2.36.14
  AND TURNE THE $WHEELE WITH DAMNED $IXION             2.40.14
  AND TURNE THE WHEELE WITH DAMNED $IXION              2.144.14
DAMNING                          1
  AND DAMNING THEIR OWNE SELVES TO $TANTAL'S SMART     4.24.3
DAMSEL                           3
  THE $DAMZELL BROKE HIS MISINTENDED DART              5.16.12
  SUCH SUBTILE CRAFT MY $DAMZELL DOTH CONCEAVE         5.23.5
  SEE HOW THE STUBBORNE DAMZELL DOTH DEPRAVE           5.29.1
DAMSELS                          1
  FOR DAMZELS FIT TO DECKE THEIR LOVERS BOWRES         5.64.4
DANCE                            3
  THEY SHOULD STILL DAUNCE TO PLEASE A GAZER'S
                          SIGHT                        4.26.8
  BUT WHEN $AURORA LEADES OUT $PHOEBUS' DAUNCE         4.98.12
  THE BOTE FOR JOY COULD NOT TO DAUNCE FORBEARE        4.103.5
DANCING                          1
  AND SITUATION WITH THOSE DANCING CHIPS               3.128.10
DANGER                           3
  DANGER HATH HONOR, GREAT DESIGNES THEIR FAME         1.35.6
  TO VIEW YOUR FORME TOO MUCH, MAY DANGER BEE          1.37.11
  AND WARNE TO SHUN THE DAUNGER OF THEYR WRATH         5.31.8
DANGEROUS                        3
  WHO HATH SOME LONG AND DANG'ROUS $VOYAGE BEENE       2.1.2
  THAT DAUNGEROUS EYE-KILLING $COCKATRICE              2.130.2
  IN DREAD OF DEATH AND DAUNGEROUS DISMAY              5.63.3
DANGER'S                         2
  AS SACRED THINGS, FAR FROM ALL DAUNGER'S SHOW        4.24.8
  AFFRAYD OF EVERY DANGERS LEAST DISMAY                5.88.4
DANISH                           2
  AND THE OLD $LEA BRAGS OF THE $DANISH $BLOUD         2.32.12
  AND OLD $LEGEA BRAGS OF $DANISH BLOOD                2.124.12
DAPHNE                           1
  PROUD $DAPHNE SCORNING $PHAEBUS LOVELY FYRE          5.28.9
DARE                            18
  AND SEEKE THAT WHICH I DARE NOT HOPE TO FINDE        1.20.10
  THEN MAY I DARE TO BOAST HOW I DOE LOVE THEE         3.26.13
```

```
NOR DARE I CHIDE THE WORLD WITHOUT END HOURE        3.57.5
NOR DARE I QUESTION WITH MY JEALIOUS THOUGHT        3.57.9
TO SAY THEY ERRE, I DARE NOT BE SO BOLD             3.131.7
WHICH DARE CLAIME FROM THOSE LIGHTS THE
                            NAME OF BEST            4.9.11
THOUGH DUSTIE WITS DARE SCORNE $ASTROLOGIE          4.26.1
FOR WHEN HE WILL SEE WHO DARE HIM GAINESAY          4.43.5
'WHAT HE+' SAY THEY OF ME, 'NOW I DARE SWEARE       4.54.7
OF GENTLE FORCE, SO THAT MINE EYES DARE
                            GLADLY PLAY             4.76.6
FAINT COWARD JOY NO LONGER TARRY DARE               4.95.5
OF COMFORT DARE COME TO THIS DUNGEON DARKE          4.104.7
THAT LOOSELY THEY NE DARE TO LOOKE UPON HER         5.5.8
YET FIND I NOUGHT ON EARTH TO WHICH I DARE          5.9.3
DARE TO APPROCH, THAT MAY MY SOLACE BREED           5.52.10
DARE NOT HENCEFORTH ABOVE THE BOUNDS OF DEWTIE      5.61.3
THEN DARE BE LOV'D BY MEN OF MEANE DEGREE           5.61.14
THERE PRIDE DARE NOT APPROCH, NOR DISCORD SPILL     5.65.9
DARES                       3
MY MAN-HOOD DARES NOT WITH FOULE $ATE MELL          2.39.10
MY MANHOOD DARES NOT WITH FOULE $ATE MELL           2.118.10
IN $BEAUTIE'S THRONE, SEE NOW WHO DARES
                            COME NEARE              4.73.10
DAREST                      1
OUT TRAYTOUR ABSENCE, DAREST THOU COUNSELL ME       4.88.1
DARK                        22
IF THIS BE LOVE, TO CLOATHE ME WITH DARKE THOUGHTS  1.9.9
WHEN DARKE SHALL SEEME THY DAY THAT NEVER CLEARES   1.42.3
WITH DARKE FORGETTING OF MY CARE RETURNE            1.54.4
AGAINST THE DARKE AND TIMES CONSUMING RAGE          1.55.12
MY CHASTE DESIRE, WHICH FROM DARKE SORROW SHINES    1.59.3
AND IN THYS $IMAGE HIS DARKE CLOWDY EYES            2.114.13
AND DARKELY BRIGHT, ARE BRIGHT IN DARKE DIRECTED    3.43.4
WHAT FREEZINGS HAVE I FELT, WHAT DARKE
                            DAIES SEENE+            3.97.3
WHO ART AS BLACK AS HELL, AS DARKE AS NIGHT         3.147.14
WHO LIKE A THEEFE, HID IN DARKE BUSH DOTH LY        4.20.3
BECAUSE I OFT IN DARKE ABSTRACTED GUISE             4.27.1
SCORTCH NOT, BUT ONELY DO DARKE CHILLING
                            SPRITES REMOVE          4.76.8
THAT PRESENCE, WHICH DOTH GIVE DARKE HEARTS
                            A LIVING LIGHT          4.77.3
WHILE NO NIGHT IS MORE DARKE THEN IS MY DAY         4.89.10
IF THIS DARKE PLACE YET SHEW LIKE CANDLE LIGHT      4.91.5
SO DARKE WITH MISTY VAPORS, WHICH ARISE             4.94.2
OF COMFORT DARE COME TO THIS DUNGEON DARKE          4.104.7
THROUGH THAT DARKE FORNACE TO MY HART OPPREST       4.108.3
DARK IS THE WORLD, WHERE YOUR LIGHT SHINED NEVER    5.8.13
THOSE POWREFULL EIES, WHICH LIGHTEN MY
                            DARK SPRIGHT            5.9.2
FAYRE WHEN THAT CLOUD OF PRYDE, WHICH
                            OFT DOTH DARK           5.81.7
DARK IS MY DAY, WHYLES HER FAYRE LIGHT I MIS        5.89.13
DARKENED                    3
BOTH SADLY BLACKE, BOTH BLACKLY DARKNED BE          4.96.3
SUCH LIGHT IN SENSE, WITH SUCH A DARKNED MIND       4.99.14
REMOVE THE CAUSE BY WHICH YOUR FAYRE BEAMES
                            DARKNED BE              5.45.14
DARKENING                   1
DARKNING THY POWRE TO LEND BASE SUBJECTS LIGHT      3.100.4
```

```
   AND BIDDING TH'OLD $ADIEU, HIS PASSED DATE          5.4.3
DATELESS                     2
   FOR PRECIOUS FRIENDS HID IN DEATHS DATELES NIGHT    3.30.6
   A DATELESSE LIVELY HEAT STILL TO INDURE             3.153.6
DATES                        1
   OUR DATES ARE BREEFE, AND THEREFOR WE ADMIRE        3.123.5
DAUGHTER                     1
   SWEET SMILE, THE DAUGHTER OF THE $QUEENE CF LOVE    5.39.1
DAY                         72
   IMBRACING CLOUDS BY NIGHT, IN DAY TIME MOURNE       1.16.2
   THAT THUS I LIVE BOTH DAY AND NIGHT ANNOYD          1.26.8
   WILL RISE NO MORE TO ME, WHOSE DAY IS DUNNE         1.30.4
   WHEN DARKE SHALL SEEME THY DAY THAT NEVER CLEARES   1.42.3
   AND LET THE DAY BE TIME ENOUGH TO MOURNE            1.54.5
   CEASE DREAMES, TH'$IMAGES OF DAY DESIRES            1.54.9
   WHICH THOUGH THE $DAY DIS-JOYNE BY SEV'RALL
                                      FLIGHT           2.37.6
   WELL COULD I WISH, IT WOULD BE EVER $DAY            2.37.13
   WHERE BLESSED $ANGELS SINGING DAY AND NIGHT         2.105.13
   UNHAPPY $BORNE, OF ALL UNHAPPY DAY                  2.116.5
   AND OF JUST LENGTH OUR NIGHT AND DAY DOTH MAKE      2.147.3
   LIKE FEEBLE AGE HE REELETH FROM THE DAY             3.7.10
   AND SEE THE BRAVE DAY SUNCK IN HIDIOUS NIGHT        3.12.2
   AGAINST THE STORMY GUSTS OF WINTERS DAY             3.13.11
   TO CHANGE YOUR DAY CF YOUTH TO SULLIED NIGHT        3.15.12
   SHALL I COMPARE THEE TO A $SUMMERS DAY+             3.18.1
   LOE THUS BY DAY MY LIMS, BY NIGHT MY MIND           3.27.13
   BUT DAY BY NIGHT AND NIGHT BY DAY OPREST            3.28.4
   BUT DAY BY NIGHT AND NIGHT BY DAY OPREST            3.28.4
   I TELL THE $DAY TO PLEASE HIM THOU ART BRIGHT       3.28.9
   BUT DAY DOTH DAILY DRAW MY SORROWES LONGER          3.28.13
   (LIKE TO THE $LARKE AT BREAKE OF DAYE ARISING)      3.29.11
   IF THOU SURVIVE MY WELL CONTENTED DAIE              3.32.1
   WHY DIDST THOU PROMISE SUCH A BEAUTIOUS DAY         3.34.1
   FOR ALL THE DAY THEY VIEW THINGS UNRESPECTED        3.43.2
   TO THE CLEERE DAY WITH THY MUCH CLEERER LIGHT       3.43.7
   BY LOOKING ON THEE IN THE LIVING DAY+               3.43.10
   WHICH BUT TOO DAIE BY FEEDING IS ALATED             3.56.3
   SO LOVE BE THOU, ALTHOUGH TOO DAIE THOU FILL        3.56.5
   IN ME THOU SEEST THE TWI-LIGHT OF SUCH DAY          3.73.5
   THUS DO I PINE AND SURFET DAY BY DAY                3.75.13
   THUS DO I PINE AND SURFET DAY BY DAY                3.75.13
   KINDE IS MY LOVE TO DAY, TO MORROW KINDE            3.105.5
   I MUST EACH DAY SAY ORE THE VERY SAME               3.108.6
   THE MOUNTAINE, OR THE SEA, THE DAY, OR NIGHT        3.113.11
   WHERETO AL BONDS DO TIE ME DAY BY DAY               3.117.4
   WHERETO AL BONDS DO TIE ME DAY BY DAY               3.117.4
   THAT FOLLOW'D IT AS GENTLE DAY                      3.145.10
   AND SWERE THAT BRIGHTNESSE DOTH NOT GRACE
                                    THE DAY+           3.150.4
   CRIE, '$VICTORIE, THIS FAIRE DAY ALL IS OURS'       4.12.11
   I FIND HOW HEAV'NLY DAY WRETCH I DID MISSE          4.33.4
   HOW FAIRE A DAY WAS NEARE, O PUNISHT EYES           4.33.13
   AND AH WHAT HOPE, THAT HOPE SHOULD ONCE SEE DAY     4.35.7
   HAVING THIS DAY MY HORSE, MY HAND, MY LAUNCE        4.41.1
   STOLNE TO MY HEART, SINCE LAST FAIRE NIGHT,
                                    NAY DAY            4.66.10
   BENIGHTED IN COLD WO, BUT NOW APPEARES MY DAY       4.76.3
   WITH DARKEST SHADE DOTH OVERCOME MY DAY             4.89.2
   SINCE $STELLA'S EYES, WONT TO GIVE ME MY DAY        4.89.3
```

```
EACH DAY SEEMES LONG, AND LONGS FOR LONG-STAID
                         NIGHT                          4.89.5
THE NIGHT AS TEDIOUS, WOOES TH'APPROCH OF DAY           4.89.6
TIRED WITH THE DUSTY TOILES OF BUSIE DAY               4.89.7
SUFFERING THE EVILS BOTH OF THE DAY AND NIGHT          4.89.9
WHILE NO NIGHT IS MORE DARKE THEN IS MY DAY            4.89.10
NOR NO DAY HATH LESSE QUIET THEN MY NIGHT              4.89.11
WITH SUCH BAD MIXTURE OF MY NIGHT AND DAY              4.89.12
I FEELE THE FLAMES OF HOTTEST SOMMER DAY               4.89.14
WHOM IRON DOORES DO KEEPE FROM USE OF DAY+             4.108.11
ONE DAY I SOUGHT WITH HER HART-THRILLING EIES          5.12.1
ONE DAY AS I UNWARILY DID GAZE                         5.16.1
THEREFORE, I LYKEWISE ON SO HOLY DAY                   5.22.3
ON WHICH MY THOUGHTS DOO DAY AND NIGHT ATTEND          5.22.7
IN WHICH THE WORKE THAT SHE ALL DAY DID MAKE           5.23.3
THE LAURELL LEAFE, WHICH YOU THIS DAY DOE WEARE        5.28.1
UNTO THE FAYRE SUNSHINE IN SOMERS DAY                  5.40.6
MOST GLORIOUS $LORD OF LYFE THAT ON THIS DAY           5.68.1
THIS JOYOUS DAY, DEARE $LORD, WITH JOY BEGIN           5.68.5
ONE DAY I WROTE HER NAME UPON THE STRAND               5.75.1
FOR WHEN AS DAY THE HEAVEN DOTH ADORNE                 5.87.5
I WISH THAT NIGHT THE NOYOUS DAY WOULD END             5.87.6
I WISH THAT DAY WOULD SHORTLY REASCEND                 5.87.8
NE OUGHT I SEE, THOUGH IN THE CLEAREST DAY             5.88.5
DARK IS MY DAY, WHYLES HER FAYRE LIGHT I MIS           5.89.13
DAY-NETS                 1
THAT FROM HER LOCKES, THY DAY-NETS, NONE
                         SCAPES FREE                    4.12.2
DAYS                    26
THAT THEY MAY HELPE THEE TO CONSUME OUR DAIES+         1.23.6
WHOSE CLOUDED BROW DOTH MAKE MY DAIES SO SAD           1.26.4
LOTHSOME THEIR DAIES, WHOM NO SUN EVER JOYD            1.26.6
WHEN NOTHING ELSE REMAYNETH OF THESE DAYES             2.6.6
THAT IN MY DAYES I MAY NOT SEE THEE OLD                2.8.2
WHERE ALL THE TREASURE OF THY LUSTY DAIES              3.2.6
THEN LOOK I DEATH MY DAIES SHOULD EXPIATE              3.22.4
IF MY SLIGHT $MUSE DOE PLEASE THESE CURIOUS
                         DAIES                          3.38.13
ALL DAYES ARE NIGHTS TO SEE TILL I SEE THEE            3.43.13
AND NIGHTS BRIGHT DAIES WHEN DREAMS DO
                         SHEW THEE ME                   3.43.14
OH SURE I AM THE WITS OF FORMER DAIES                  3.59.13
PAINTING MY AGE WITH BEAUTY OF THY DAIES               3.62.14
AGAINST THE WRACKFULL SIEDGE OF BATTRING DAYES         3.65.6
IN DAIES LONG SINCE, BEFORE THESE LAST SO BAD          3.67.14
THUS IS HIS CHEEKE THE MAP OF DAIES OUT-WORNE          3.68.1
THOU HAST PAST BY THE AMBUSH OF YOUNG DAIES            3.70.9
SOME FRESHER STAMPE OF THE TIME BETTERING DAYES        3.82.8
THAT TONGUE THAT TELLS THE STORY OF THY DAIES          3.95.5
WHAT FREEZINGS HAVE I FELT, WHAT DARKE
                         DAIES SEENE+                   3.97.3
AND STOPS HIS PIPE IN GROWTH OF RIPER DAIES            3.102.8
FOR WE WHICH NOW BEHOLD THESE PRESENT DAYES            3.106.13
ALTHOUGH SHE KNOWES MY DAYES ARE PAST THE BEST         3.138.6
FOR ALL THAT I IN MANY DAYES DOO WEAVE                 5.23.7
BUT AL MY DAYES IN PINING LANGUOR SPEND                5.36.3
THIS YEARE ENSUING, OR ELSE SHORT MY DAYES             5.60.14
MANY LONG WEARY DAYES I HAVE OUTWORNE                  5.87.2
DAY'S                    5
AND NEVER WAKE TO FEELE THE DAYES DISDAINE             1.54.14
```

```
  THE GRAVE OF JOY, PRYSON OF DAYES DELIGHT          2.145.10
  WHICH STILL TORMENTS ME IN DAYES BURNING FIRE      2.145.14
  WHO LIST TO PRAISE THE DAYES DELICIOUS LYGHT       2.148.1
  WHEN DAIES OPPRESSICN IS NOT EAZD BY NIGHT         3.28.3
DAY-STAR               1
  O CLEEREST DAY-STARRE, NEVER MORE DECLYNING        2.129.8
DAZED                  1
  THAT BEING NOW WITH HER HUGE BRIGTNESSE DAZED      5.3.5
DAZZLE                 1
  THEY SUN-LIKE SHOULD MORE DAZLE THEN DELIGHT+      4.7.8
DAZZLED                4
  YOU OUT-CAST $EAGLETS, DAZELED WITH YOUR $SUNNE    1.3.10
  MY HEART THEN QUAK'D, THEN DAZLED WERE MINE EYES   4.53.10
  MY HEART CRIES 'AH', IT BURNES, MINE EYES
                        NOW DAZLED BE                4.76.11
  WAS NOT IN FAULT, WHO BENT THY DAZLING RACE        4.105.6
DEAD                  26
  DOE QUIT THE DEAD, AND ME NOT ACCESSARIE           2.2.6
  THE POWDER OF HER $HEART DRY'D, WHEN SHE IS DEAD   2.15.3
  OR ALL MY $HOPE FCR $SORROW WILL BE DEAD           2.26.14
  NEERE THE DEAD $BCDY HAPPILY BE BROUGHT            2.46.7
  IT FURTHERS $JUSTICE, BUT HELPES NOT THE DEAD      2.46.14
  OR ALL MY HOPE FOR SORRCW WILL BE DEAD             2.137.14
  WHICH I BY LACKING HAVE SUPPOSED DEAD              3.31.2
  AS INTEREST OF THE DEAD, WHICH NOW APPEARE         3.31.7
  WHEN IN DEAD NIGHT THEIR FAIRE IMPERFECT SHADE     3.43.11
  AND STEALE DEAD SEEING CF HIS LIVING HEW+          3.67.6
  BEFORE THE GOULDEN TRESSES OF THE DEAD             3.68.5
  ERE BEAUTIES DEAD FLEECE MADE ANOTHER GAY          3.68.8
  NOE $LONGER MOURNE FOR ME WHEN I AM DEAD           3.71.1
  THE PRAY OF WORMES, MY BODY BEING DEAD             3.74.10
  WHEN ALL THE BREATHERS CF THIS WORLD ARE DEAD      3.81.12
  ABOVE A MORTALL PITCH, THAT STRUCK ME DEAD+        3.86.6
  ERE YOU WERE BORNE WAS BEAUTIES SUMMER DEAD        3.104.14
  IN PRAISE OF $LADIES DEAD, AND LOVELY $KNIGHTS     3.106.4
  WHERE TIME AND OUTWARD FORME WOULD SHEW IT DEAD    3.108.14
  THAT ALL THE WORLD BESIDES ME THINKES
                        Y'ARE DEAD                   3.112.14
  MAKING DEAD WOOD MCRE BLEST THEN LIVING LIPS       3.128.12
  AND DEATH ONCE DEAD, THER'S NO MORE DYING THEN     3.146.14
  DEAD GLASSE, DOOST THOU THY OBJECT SO IMBRACE      4.105.3
  WHICH HOLD MY LIFE IN THEIR DEAD DOING MIGHT       5.1.2
  THAT MOTE ENLARGE HER LIVING PRAYSES DEAD          5.33.4
  AND DEAD MY LIFE THAT WANTS SUCH LIVELY BLIS       5.89.14
DEADLY                 4
  CHASTITIE AND $BEAUTIE, WHICH WERE DEADLY FOES     1.6.9
  MORPHEUS, THE LIVELY SONNE OF DEADLY SLEEPE        4.32.1
  HIS WANTON WINGS AND DARTS OF DEADLY POWER         5.4.8
  DARTING THEIR DEADLY ARRCWES FYRY BRIGHT           5.16.7
DEAF                   6
  THOUGH ALL MY PRAYERS BE TO SO DEAFE EARES         1.11.11
  AND MINE $EARES DEAFE, BY THY $FAME HEALED BEE     2.35.10
  SITH SHE IS DEAFE, AND WILL NOT HEARE MY $MONES    2.45.10
  AND MINE EARES DEAFE, BY THY FAME HEALED BE        2.112.10
  AND TROUBLE DEAFE HEAVEN WITH MY BOOTLESSE CRIES   3.29.3
  A CHAMBER DEAFE TC NOISE, AND BLIND TO LIGHT       4.39.10
DEAL                   5
  BY KNIFE, BY LIQUCR, OR BY SALVE TO DEALE          1.14.11
  DEALE WITH THOSE DAINTY CHEEKES AS SHE DCTH DEALE  1.22.7
  DEALE WITH THOSE DAINTY CHEEKES AS SHE DCTH DEALE  1.22.7
```

```
LEAVE WHAT THOU LIKEST NOT, DEALE NOT THOU WITH IT    4.4.4
DEALE THOU WITH POWERS OF THOUGHTS, LEAVE
                          LOVE TO WILL                 4.10.8
```

DEAR   69

```
LOOKE ON THE DEERE EXPENCES OF MY YOUTH               1.1.9
THOSE SNARY LOCKS, ARE THOSE SAME NETS
                          (MY $DEERE)                  1.14.1
THESE SAD NEGLECTED NOTES FOR HER DEARE SAKE+         1.17.2
TO CRAVE REDRESSE, YET HOLD AFFLICTION DEARE          1.20.7
AND STILL MUST HOLD HER DEARE TILL AFTER DEATH        1.21.11
TO ATTEND THE PRESENCE OF MY WORLDS $DEERE            1.30.6
AND ALL LIES WITHRED THAT WAS HELD SO DEERE           1.42.4
SUFFICE, THEY SHEW I LIV'D AND LOV'D THEE DEARE       1.55.14
IN WHOSE DEARE $BOSOME, SWEET DELICIOUS $LOVE         2.4.5
SLEW HIS DEARE $FRIEND, MY KIND AND TRUEST $HEART     2.7.12
DEARE, WHY SHOULD YOU COMMAND ME TO MY $REST          2.37.1
AND IN THESE $SHADES, DEARE $NYMPH, HE
                          OFT HATH BEENE               2.53.11
WHOSE DEARE REMEMBRANCE IN MY $BOSOME LYES            2.57.3
AND IN THESE SHADES (DEER $NIMPHE) HE
                          OFT HATH BEEN                2.113.11
O NONE BUT UNTHRIFTS, DEARE MY LOVE YOU KNOW          3.13.13
THE DEARE REPOSE FOR LIMS WITH TRAVAILL TIRED         3.27.2
AND WITH OLD WOES NEW WAILE MY DEARE TIMES WASTE      3.30.4
BUT IF THE WHILE I THINKE ON THEE (DEARE FRIEND)      3.30.13
HATH DEARE RELIGIOUS LOVE STOLNE FROM MINE EYE        3.31.6
AND OUR DEARE LOVE LOOSE NAME OF SINGLE ONE           3.39.6
THE CLEERE EYES MOYITIE, AND THE DEARE
                          HEARTS PART                  3.46.12
FOR TRUTH PROOVES THEEVISH FOR A PRIZE SO DEARE       3.48.14
AFTER MY DEATH (DEARE LOVE) FOR GET ME QUITE          3.72.3
FAREWELL THOU ART TOO DEARE FOR MY POSSESSING         3.87.1
TAKE HEED (DEARE HEART) OF THIS LARGE PRIVILEDGE      3.95.13
AND SWEETS GROWNE COMMON LOOSE THEIR DEARE
                          DELIGHT                      3.102.12
THAT MAY EXPRESSE MY LOVE, OR THY DEARE MERIT+        3.108.4
GOR'D MINE OWN THOUGHTS, SOLD CHEAP WHAT
                          IS MOST DEARE                3.110.3
PITTIE ME THEN DEARE FRIEND, AND I ASSURE YEE         3.111.13
AND GIVEN TO TIME YOUR OWNE DEARE PURCHAS'D
                          RIGHT                        3.117.6
NOR NEED I TALLIES THY DEARE LOVE TO SKORE            3.122.10
YF MY DEARE LOVE WERE BUT THE CHILDE OF STATE         3.124.1
FOR WELL THOU KNOW'ST TO MY DEARE DOTING HART         3.131.3
DEARE HEART FORBEARE TO GLANCE THINE EYE ASIDE        3.139.6
LOVE IS MY SINNE, AND THY DEARE VERTUE HATE           3.142.1
HER LOVE, FOR WHOSE DEARE LOVE I RISE AND FALL        3.151.14
THAT THE DEARE $SHE MIGHT TAKE SOME PLEASURE
                          OF MY PAINE                  4.1.2
AND STRANGE THINGS COST TOO DEARE FOR
                          MY POORE SPRITES             4.3.11
OF LIVING DEATHS, DEARE WOUNDS, FAIRE
                          STORMES AND FREESING FIRES   4.6.4
HIS MOTHER DEARE $CUPID OFFENDED LATE                 4.17.1
O $STELLA DEARE, HOW MUCH THY POWER HATH WROUGHT      4.40.2
FAIRE EYES, SWEET LIPS, DEARE HEART, THAT
                          FOOLISH I                    4.43.1
THEN THINKE MY DEARE, THAT YOU IN ME DO REED          4.45.12
YET $DEARE, LET ME THIS PARDON GET OF YOU             4.46.12
DEARE $KILLER, SPARE NOT THY SWEET CRUELL SHOT        4.48.13
```

```
THAT $STELLA (O DEARE NAME) THAT $STELLA IS          4.52.6
DEARE, WHY MAKE YOU MORE OF A DOG THEN ME+           4.59.1
DEARE, LOVE ME NOT, THAT YOU MAY LOVE ME MORE        4.62.14
FOR $GRAMMER SAYES (O THIS DEARE $STELLA WEIGHE)     4.63.12
NO MORE, MY DEARE, NO MORE THESE COUNSELS TRIE       4.64.1
THESE THINGS ARE LEFT ME BY MY ONLY $DEARE           4.72.12
WHEN FOR SO SOFT A ROD DEARE PLAY HE TRIE+           4.73.4
THEN SINCE (DEARE LIFE) YOU FAINE WOULD
                        HAVE ME PEACE                4.81.12
WHEN I WAS FORST FROM $STELLA EVER DEERE             4.87.1
FROM MY DEARE $CAPTAINNESSE TO RUN AWAY+             4.88.2
DEERE, THEREFORE BE NOT JEALOUS OVER ME              4.91.12
I CRY THY SIGHS., MY DEERE, THY TEARES I BLEEDE      4.93.14
YET SIGHS, DEERE SIGHS, INDEEDE TRUE FRIENDS
                        YOU ARE                      4.95.1
RUDELY THOU WRONGEST MY DEARE HARTS DESIRE           5.5.1
THAT TO THE WORLD NAUGHT ELSE BE COUNTED DEARE       5.8.4
TO THAT MOST SACRED $EMPRESSE MY DEAR DRED           5.33.2
FROM PRESENCE OF MY DEAREST DEARE EXYLDE             5.52.7
OF ALL THAT DEARE AND DAYNTY IS ALYVE                5.63.8
THIS JOYOUS DAY, DEARE $LORD, WITH JOY BEGIN         5.68.5
BEING WITH THY DEARE BLOOD CLENE WASHT FROM SIN      5.68.7
AND FOR THY SAKE THAT ALL LYKE DEARE DIDST BUY       5.68.11
SO LET US LOVE, DEARE LOVE, LYKE AS WE OUGHT         5.68.13
OF A DEARE FOE, AND THRALLED TO HIS LOVE             5.71.6
WITH MANY DEARE DELIGHTS BEDECKED FYNE               5.71.12
DEARER                  3
IF I HAVE LOV'D HER DEARER THEN MY BREATH            1.21.9
A DEARER BIRTH THEN THIS HIS LOVE HAD BROUGHT        3.32.11
EVEN THOSE THAT SAID I COULD NOT LOVE YOU DEERER     3.115.2
DEAREST                 9
HOLDES IN HER FAIREST HAND WHAT DEAREST IS           1.12.10
MY LIVES SWEET SUNNE, MY DEAREST COMFORTS LIGHT      1.30.3
MY WORDS MIGHT IMITATE MY DEEREST THOUGHTS
                        DIRECTION                    2.117.7
RARE OF-SPRING OF MY THOUGHTS, MY DEEREST $LOVE      2.141.1
SO I, MADE LAME BY $FORTUNES DEAREST SPIGHT          3.37.3
THOU BEST OF DEEREST, AND MINE ONELY CARE            3.48.7
FORGOT UPON YOUR DEAREST LOVE TO CALL                3.117.3
AMONGST THY DEEREST RELICKS TO BE KEPT               5.22.14
FROM PRESENCE OF MY DEAREST DEARE EXYLDE             5.52.7
DEARLY                  3
AND TELL TH'UNKINDE, HOW DEARELY I HAVE LOV'D HER    1.2.14
AND THUS I LIVE BECAUSE I LOVE HER DEERLY            1.16.14
AND YET IT MAY BE SAID I LOV'D HER DEERELY           3.42.2
DEARTH                  4
AND YET I $SURFET IN THE GREATEST $DEARTH            2.62.12
AND YET I SURFET IN THE GREATEST DEARTH              2.150.12
WHY DOST THOU PINE WITHIN AND SUFFER DEARTH          3.146.3
WITH DEARTH OF WORDS, OR ANSWERS QUITE AWRIE         4.27.3
DEARTHS                 1
OF PLAGUES, OF DEARTHS, OR SEASONS QUALLITY          3.14.4
DEATH                   57
MY THOUGHTS (LIKE $HOUNDES) PURSUE ME TO MY DEATH    1.5.12
IF THIS BE LOVE, TO LIVE A LIVING DEATH              1.9.13
I WRITTEN FINDE THE SENTENCE OF MY DEATH             1.10.3
AND STILL MUST HOLD HER DEARE TILL AFTER DEATH       1.21.11
IN LIFE AND DEATH $ILE TENDER HER GOOD NAME          1.30.11
MY LIFE NOR DEATH SHAL NEVER BE HER BLOT             1.30.12
THE DATE OF $AGE, THE $KALENDS OF OUR DEATH          1.50.12
```

BROTHER TO DEATH, IN SILENT DARKNES BORNE	1.54.2
AND HASTES $ME ON UNTO A SUDDEN $DEATH	2.20.10
WHERE $FAME BY $DEATH IS ONELY TO BE GOT	2.24.11
BUT WHAT OF THIS+ $SHOULD SHE TO DEATH BE LED	2.46.13
THOU WHICH HAST SCORNED $LIFE, AND HATED $DEATH	2.49.9
WHEN $FAITH IS KNEELING BY HIS BED OF $DEATH	2.61.11
FROM $DEATH TO $LIFE, THOU MIGHT'ST HIM YET RECOVER	2.61.14
OR IF NO THING BUT $DEATH WILL SERVE THY TURNE	2.63.9
SO BY THY DEATH, THY LIFE SHALL BE BEGUNNE	2.106.8
AND YET IN DEATH, SOME HOPE OF LIFE ESPYING	2.109.7
LAMENT'ST MY DEATH, WITH TEARES OF THY DISDAINE	2.130.14
SMYLING, AS THOUGH HE GLORIED IN HIS DEATH	2.135.12
SO IN LOVES DEATH SHALL LOVES PERFECTION PROVE	2.139.9
THY $MOTHER DYD HER LYFE TO $DEATH RESIGNE	2.140.5
ASSAYLD WITH DEATH, YET ARM'D WITH GASTLY FEARE	2.142.3
DEATH LIKE TO THEE, SO LYVE THOU STILL IN DEATH	2.145.9
DEATH LIKE TO THEE, SO LYVE THOU STILL IN DEATH	2.145.9
THEN WHAT COULD DEATH DOE IF THOU SHOULD'ST DEPART	3.6.11
NOR SHALL DEATH BRAG THOU WANDR'ST IN HIS SHADE	3.18.11
THEN LOOK I DEATH MY DAIES SHOULD EXPIATE	3.22.4
WHEN THAT CHURLE DEATH MY BONES WITH DUST SHALL COVER	3.32.2
SINKES DOWNE TO DEATH, OPPREST WITH MELANCHOLIE	3.45.8
GAINST DEATH, AND ALL OBLIVIOUS EMNITY	3.55.9
THIS THOUGHT IS AS A DEATH WHICH CANNOT CHOOSE	3.64.13
TYR'D WITH ALL THESE FOR RESTFULL DEATH I CRY	3.66.1
AFTER MY DEATH (DEARE LOVE) FOR GET ME QUITE	3.72.3
AS THE DEATH BED, WHEREON IT MUST EXPIRE	3.73.11
FROM HENCE YOUR MEMORY DEATH CANNOT TAKE	3.81.3
A VENGFULL CANKER EATE HIM UP TO DEATH	3.99.13
MY LOVE LOOKES FRESH, AND DEATH TO ME SUBSCRIBES	3.107.10
SO SHALT THOU FEED ON DEATH, THAT FEEDS ON MEN	3.146.13
AND DEATH ONCE DEAD, THER'S NO MORE DYING THEN	3.146.14
DESIRE IS DEATH, WHICH $PHISICK DID EXCEPT	3.147.8
FLIE, FLY, MY FRIENDS, I HAVE MY DEATH WOUND., FLY	4.20.1
OPPRESSING MORTALL SENSE, MY DEATH PROCEED	4.42.13
WHILE THOSE POORE BABES THEIR DEATH IN BIRTH DO FIND	4.50.11
THE PRETTIE DEATH, WHILE EACH IN OTHER LIVE	4.79.11
HIS WHO TILL DEATH LOOKT IN A WATRIE GLASSE	4.82.3
THOUGH HARBENGERS OF DEATH LODGE THERE HIS TRAINE	4.94.8
WITH CHAST AFFECTS, THAT NAUGHT BUT DEATH CAN SEVER	5.6.12
THE WHICH BOTH LYFE AND DEATH FORTH FROM YOU DART	5.7.3
BUT SINCE THAT LYFE IS MORE THEN DEATH DESYRED	5.7.9
SUCH DEATH THE SAD ENSAMPLE OF YOUR MIGHT	5.7.14
THAT DEATH OUT OF THEYR SHINY BEAMES DOE DART	5.24.7
AND IN THE SHADE OF DEATH IT SELFE SHALL SHROUD	5.27.3
BUT BY HIS DEATH WHICH SOME PERHAPS WILL MONE	5.36.13
ALLUR'D A $DOLPHIN HIM FROM DEATH TO EASE	5.38.4
IN DREAD OF DEATH AND DAUNGEROUS DISMAY	5.63.3
DIDST MAKE THY TRIUMPH OVER DEATH AND SIN	5.68.2
WHERE WHENAS DEATH SHALL ALL THE WORLD SUBDEW	5.75.13

DEATHS   5

DESIRING YET A THOUSAND DEATHS TO PROVE	2.134.7
OF THEIR SWEET DEATHES, ARE SWEETEST ODORS MADE	3.54.12

```
AS TESTIE SICK-MEN WHEN THEIR DEATHS BE NEERE        3.140.7
OF LIVING DEATHS, DEARE WOUNDS, FAIRE
                        STORMES AND FREESING FIRES  4.6.4
TO HONOR ALL THEIR DEATHS, WHO FOR HER BLEED         4.7.14
```
DEATH'S   5
```
TO BE DEATHS CONQUEST AND MAKE WORMES THINE HEIRE    3.6.14
AND BARREN RAGE OF DEATHS ETERNALL COLD+             3.13.12
FOR PRECIOUS FRIENDS HID IN DEATHS DATELES NIGHT     3.30.6
DEATHS SECOND SELFE THAT SEALS UP ALL IN REST        3.73.8
THOSE LIPS, WHICH MAKE DEATH'S PAY A MEANE
                        PRICE FOR A KISSE            4.77.6
```
DEATH-WOUND   1
```
YET SINCE MY DEATH-WOUND IS ALREADY GOT              4.48.12
```
DEBARRED   1
```
THAT AM DEBARD THE BENIFIT OF REST+                  3.28.2
```
DEBATE   1
```
FOR THEE, AGAINST MY SELFE ILE VOW DEBATE            3.89.13
```
DEBATETH   1
```
WHERE WASTFULL TIME DEBATETH WITH DECAY              3.15.11
```
DEBT   1
```
THE BARREN TENDER CF A $POETS DEBT                   3.83.4
```
DEBTOR   3
```
AND THUS MINE $EIES A DEBTOR TO THINE $EYE           2.3.9
AND THUS MINE EYES, A DEBTOR TO THINE EYE            2.110.9
AND SUE A FRIEND, CAME DEBTER FOR MY SAKE            3.134.11
```
DECAY   13
```
WITHOUT THIS FOLLIE, AGE, AND COULD DECAY            3.11.6
WHO LETS SO FAIRE A HOUSE FALL TO DECAY              3.13.9
WHERE WASTFULL TIME DEBATETH WITH DECAY              3.15.11
AND FORTIFIE YOUR SELFE IN YOUR DECAY                3.16.3
AND IN MINE OWNE LCVES STRENGTH SEEME TO DECAY       3.23.7
OR STATE IT SELFE CCNFOUNDED, TO DECAY               3.64.10
BUT LET YOUR LOVE EVEN WITH MY LIFE DECAY            3.71.12
THE WORST WAS THIS, MY LOVE WAS MY DECAY             3.80.14
IF ANY, BE A $SATIRE TO DECAY                        3.100.11
I, SEEING BETTER SIGHTS IN SIGHT'S DECAY             4.38.12
UNTO HER LOVE, AND TEMPTE TO THEYR DECAY             5.47.6
SHE DOTH ALLURE ME TO MINE OWNE DECAY                5.53.7
FOR I MY SELVE SHALL LYKE TO THIS DECAY              5.75.7
```
DECAYED   1
```
BUT NOW MY GRACIOUS NUMBERS ARE DECAYDE              3.79.3
```
DECAYS   3
```
FROM LOVE OR YEARES UNSUBJECT TO DECAIES             1.23.4
NOR CATES OF STEELE SO STRONG BUT TIME DECAYES+      3.65.8
ALL CARELESSE HOW MY LIFE FOR HER DECAYSE            5.38.10
```
DECEASE   3
```
BUT AS THE RIPER SHCULD BY TIME DECEASE              3.1.3
YOU SELFE AGAIN AFTER YCUR SELFES DECEASE            3.13.7
LIKE WIDDOWED WOMBES AFTER THEIR $LORDS DECEASE      3.97.8
```
DECEASED   4
```
THAT FOR HER LATE DECEASED $HUSBAND DY'D             2.15.8
THESE POORE RUDE LINES CF THY DECEASED $LOVER        3.32.4
AND HANG MORE PRAISE UPCN DECEASED I                 3.72.7
YOU THAT POORE $PETRARCH'S LONG DECEASED WOES        4.15.7
```
DECEIVE   4
```
FALSE $FRIENDS THY KINDNESSE, BORNE BUT
                        TO DECEIVE $THEE             2.10.10
THOU OF THY SELFE THY SWEET SELFE DOST DECEAVE       3.4.10
WHICH TIME AND THCUGHTS SO SWEETLY DOST DECEIVE      3.39.12
DEVIZ'D A $WEB HER WOOERS TO DECEAVE                 5.23.2
```

DECEIVED   5
  AND MY DECEIV'D ATTEMPT, DESERV'D MORE FAME   1.56.6
  WHETHER ARE THESE DECEIVED THEN, OR I+   2.28.12
  LIKE A DECEIVED HUSBAND, SO LOVES FACE   3.93.2
  HATH MOTION, AND MINE EYE MAY BE DECEAVED   3.104.12
  DECEIV'D THE QUAKING BOY, WHO THOUGHT
                    FROM SO PURE LIGHT   4.8.10
DECEIVEST   1
  BUT YET BE BLAM'D, IF THOU THIS SELFE DECEAVEST   3.40.7
DECEMBER'S   1
  WHAT OLD $DECEMBERS BARENESSE EVERY WHERE+   3.97.4
DECIDE   1
  SOMETIMES WHAT $SCHOOLE-MEN SCARCELY CAN DECIDE   2.46.3
DECK   5
  NO $BAYES I SEEKE TO DECKE MY MOURNING BROW   1.4.9
  STILL LET DISARMED PEACE DECKE HER AND THEE   1.53.13
  TO DECKE HIR SELFE, AND HER FAIRE MANTLE WEAVE   5.4.12
  THEN WOULD I DECKE HER HEAD WITH GLORIOUS BAYES   5.29.13
  FOR DAMZELS FIT TO DECKE THEIR LOVERS BOWRES   5.64.4
DECKED   4
  A MODEST $MAIDE, DECKT WITH A BLUSH OF HONOR   1.6.5
  THEN FADE THOSE FLOWERS THAT DECKT HER
                    PRIDE SO LONG   1.38.8
  DECKT WITH HER YOUTH WHEREON THE WORLD DOTH SMILE   1.53.6
  I SEEKE HER BOWRE WITH HER LATE PRESENCE DECKT   5.78.6
DECLARE   3
  THE BROKEN TOPS OF LOFTY TREES DECLARE   1.37.5
  DECLARE WHAT $FATE UNLUCKY $STARRES HAVE GIVEN   2.60.3
  DECLARE WHAT FATE UNLUCKY STARRES HAVE GIVEN   2.149.3
DECLINE   4
  BUT STRAIGHT HER WIDE BLOWNE POMP COMES
                    TO DECLINE   1.39.6
  AND SINCE THE WORLD TO JUDGEMENT DOTH DECLYNE   2.119.7
  IF NOW THE $MAY OF MY YEARES MUCH DECLINE   4.21.10
  WHICH WOULD NOT LET ME, WHOM SHE LOVED, DECLINE   4.62.7
DECLINES   1
  AND EVERY FAIRE FROM FAIRE SOME-TIME DECLINES   3.18.7
DECLINING   2
  O CLEEREST DAY-STARRE, NEVER MORE DECLYNING   2.129.8
  DECLYNING WITH THE SETTING OF MY SUNNE   2.141.10
DECREASE   1
  VAUNT IN THEIR YOUTHFULL SAP, AT HEIGHT DECREASE   3.15.7
DECREE   1
  BUT HEAVEN IN THY CREATION DID DECREE   3.93.9
DECREED   1
  I LOVED, BUT STRAIGHT DID NOT WHAT $LOVE DECREED   4.2.6
DECREES   2
  CREEPE IN TWIXT VOWES, AND CHANGE DECREES
                    OF $KINGS   3.115.6
  AT LENGTH TO $LOVE'S DECREES, I FORC'D, AGREED   4.2.7
DECREPIT   1
  AS A DECREPIT FATHER TAKES DELIGHT   3.37.1
DEDICATED   1
  THE DEDICATED WORDS WHICH WRITERS USE   3.82.3
DEE   2
  CARLEGION $CHESTER VAUNTS HER HOLY $DEE   2.32.5
  CARLEGION $CHESTER, VAUNTS HER HOLY $DEE   2.124.5
DEED   8
  ALTHOUGH THIS WORLD MAY SEEME HER DEEDE TO BLAME   1.30.13
  IF THE VILE ACTORS OF THE HEYNOUS DEED   2.46.6

THE SHADOW AND THE VAILE OF EVERY SINFULL DEED   2.145.8
WHAT $LOVE AND $BEAUTIE BE, THEN ALL MY DEED   4.3.13
WELL STAID WITH TRUTH IN WORD AND FAITH CF DEED   4.14.10
PROFESSE IN DEED I DO NCT $CUPID'S ART   4.54.10
I CANNOT BRAG OF WCRD, MUCH LESSE OF DEED   4.66.5
NOR BLAM'D FOR BLCUD, NCR SHAM'D FOR SINFULL
                                            DEED   4.84.11
DEEDS   15
SIGH OUT A $STORIE CF HER CRUELL DEEDES   1.2.5
AND BY THAT HAND WHCM SUCH DEEDS ILL BECCME   1.31.14
WORDS, THOUGHTS, AND DEEDS, DEVOTED TO HER HCNOR   2.138.6
AND THEY ARE RITCH, AND RANSOME ALL ILL DEEDS   3.34.14
TO SEE HIS ACTIVE CHILDE DO DEEDS OF YOUTH   3.37.2
SO FARRE FROM HOME INTO MY DEEDS TO PRYE   3.61.6
AND THAT IN GUESSE THEY MEASURE BY THY DEEDS   3.69.10
NOW WHILE THE WORLD IS BENT MY DEEDS TO CROSSE   3.90.2
FOR SWEETEST THINGS TURNE SOWREST BY THEIR
                                          DEEDES   3.94.13
THE GUILTIE GODDESSE OF MY HARMFULL DEEDS   3.111.2
BY THEIR RANCKE THCUGHTES, MY DEEDES MUST
                               NOT BE SHOWN   3.121.12
IN NOTHING ART THCU BLACKE SAVE IN THY DEEDS   3.131.13
THAT IN THE VERY REFUSE CF THY DEEDS   3.150.6
TO SING THE GLORY CF THEIR FAMOUS DEEDES   5.29.8
OF THEYR GREAT DEEDS AND VALAROUS EMPRIZE   5.69.4
DEEM   5
THE $ROSE LOOKES FAIRE, BUT FAIRER WE IT DEEME   3.54.3
DEEME THAT MY $MUSE SOME FRUIT OF KNOWLECGE PLIES   4.23.6
THEY DEEME, AND OF THEIR DOOME THE RUMOUR FLIES   4.27.5
THE WORLD THAT CANNCT DEEME OF WORTHY THINGS   5.85.1
BUT NOT TO DEEME OF HER DESERT ASPYRE   5.85.8
DEEMED   4
WHO THEN YET LIVING, DEEMD SHE HAD BEEN DYING   2.109.6
TO TRUTHS TRANSLATED, AND FOR TRUE THINGS DEEM'D   3.96.8
AND THE JUST PLEASURE LCST, WHICH IS SO DEEMED   3.121.3
IS CONSTANT $LOVE DEEM'D THERE BUT WANT CF WIT+   4.31.10
DEEMS   1
AND OF BOTH, WRONGFULL DEEMES, AND ILL CONCEIVES   1.52.8
DEEP   20
BEST IN MY FACE, HCW CARES HAVE TILD DEEPE
                              FORROWES   1.4.8
DEEPE IS THE WOUND MY SIGHES CAN WELL REPORT   1.14.6
TH'IMPRESSION OF HER EYES DO PEARCE SO DEEPE   1.26.7
STRIVING TO HOLD IT STRCNGLY IN THE $DEEPE   2.58.10
AND DIGGE DEEP TRENCHES IN THY BEAUTIES FIELD   3.2.2
TO SAY WITHIN THINE OWNE DEEPE SUNKEN EYES   3.2.7
THE $CANKER BLOCMES HAVE FULL AS DEEPE A DIE   3.54.5
WHILST HE UPON YOUR SOUNDLESSE DEEPE DOTH RICE   3.80.10
NOR PRAISE THE DEEPE VERMILLION IN THE $ROSE   3.98.10
FOR THAT DEEPE WOUND IT GIVES MY FRIEND AND ME   3.133.2
FOR I HAVE SWORNE DEEPE OTHES OF THY DEEPE
                                   KINDNESSE   3.152.9
FOR I HAVE SWORNE DEEPE OTHES OF THY DEEPE
                                   KINDNESSE   3.152.9
DIG DEEPE WITH LEARNING'S SPADE, NOW TELL
                           ME THIS   4.21.13
I LIST NOT DIG SO DEEPE FOR BRASEN FAME   4.28.4
TREBLES SING HIGH, AS WELL AS BASES DEEPE   4.70.6
DEEPE IS THE WOUND, THAT DINTS THE PARTS ENTIRE   5.6.11
WHICH HER DEEP WIT, THAT TRUE HARTS THOUGHT
                            CAN SPEL   5.43.13

```
   IN DEEP DISCOVERY OF THE MYNDS DISEASE              5.50.6
   WHILES DIVING DEEPE THROUGH AMOROUS INSIGHT         5.76.7
   DEEPE IN THE CLOSET OF MY PARTS ENTYRE              5.85.9
DEEPEST                    1
   MY DEEPEST SENCE, HOW HARD TRUE SORROW HITS        3.120.10
DEER                       2
   SEE HOW MY $DEERE COMES TO THY $BEAUTIES STAND      2.135.5
   THE GENTLE DEARE RETURND THE SELFE-SAME WAY         5.67.7
DEFACE                     2
   THEN LET NOT WINTERS WRAGGED HAND DEFACE            3.6.1
   AND ALL THOSE PRETIOUS ORNAMENTS DEFACE             5.31.4
DEFACED                    4
   DEFAC'D WITH $WRINKLES, THAT I MIGHT BUT SEE        2.8.6
   LETTERS AND $LINES WE SEE ARE SOONE DEFACED         2.13.1
   LETTERS AND LYNES WE SEE ARE SOONE DEFACED          2.121.1
   WHEN I HAVE SEENE BY TIMES FELL HAND DEFACED        3.64.1
DEFEAT                     1
   MINE OWNE TRUE LOVE THAT DOTH MY REST DEFEAT        3.61.11
DEFEATED                   1
   AND BY ADDITION ME OF THEE DEFEATED                 3.20.11
DEFECT                     2
   THAT THOU ARE BLAM'D SHALL NOT BE THY DEFECT        3.70.1
   WHEN ALL MY BEST DOTH WORSHIP THY DEFECT           3.149.11
DEFECTS                    2
   IF HER DEFECTS HAVE PURCHAST HER THIS FAME          1.17.9
   WHEN I SHALL SEE THEE FROWNE ON MY DEFECTS          3.49.2
DEFENCE                    1
   BUT THIS AT LAST IS HER SWEET BREATH'D DEFENCE      4.61.4
DEFEND                     1
   MY WIT DOTH STRIVE THOSE PASSIONS TO DEFEND         4.18.10
DEFENDANT                  1
   BUT THE DEFENDANT DOTH THAT PLEA DENY               3.46.7
DEFENDED                   1
   KEPT FOR HIMSELFE, DEFENDED FROM ALL HARMES         1.53.12
DEFENSE                    3
   AND NOTHING GAINST $TIMES SIETH CAN MAKE DEFENCE   3.12.13
   AGAINST THY REASONS MAKING NO DEFENCE              3.89.4
   IS MORE THEN MY ORE-PREST DEFENCE CAN BIDE+        3.139.8
DEFIANCE                   2
   I SEND DEFIANCE, SINCE IF OVERTHROWNE              2.63.13
   SPREDS IN DEFIANCE OF ALL ENEMIES                  5.5.12
DEFILED                    1
   SHAMES NOT TO BE WITH GUILTLESSE BLOUD DEFYLDE     5.20.11
DEFINE                     4
   AND DOTH THE SEV'RALL $OFFICES DEFINE              2.12.3
   DEFINE MY $WEALE, AND TELL THE JOYES OF $HEAVEN    2.60.1
   DEFINE MY LOVE, AND TELL THE JOYES OF HEAVEN       2.149.1
   AND FOR MY SELFE MINE OWNE WORTH DO DEFINE         3.62.7
DEFORMED                   2
   I SEE THE UGLY FACE OF MY DEFORMED CARES           2.114.2
   WITH SORROW DIMMED AND DEFORMD IT WERE             5.45.10
DEFORMEDST                 1
   THE MOST SWEET-FAVOR OR DEFORMEDST CREATURE        3.113.10
DEFY                       1
   THY REGISTERS AND THEE I BOTH DEFIE                3.123.9
DEGRADED                   1
   BUT MY DEGRADED HOPES, WITH SUCH DISGRACE          1.7.11
DEGREE                     3
   SLOW HEAVINESSE IN BOTH HOLDS ONE DEGREE           4.96.6
   THEN DARE BE LOV'D BY MEN OF MEANE DEGREE          5.61.14
```

```
      SHALL LIFT YOU UP UNTO AN HIGH DEGREE              5.82.14
DEGREES                       1
      TILL BY DEGREES IT HAD FULL CONQUEST GOT            4.2.4
DEIFIED                       1
      AND IN MY VERSE THY SELFE ART DEIFIED            2.104.12
DEIGN                         2
      WHOSE ROWLING GRACE DEIGNE ONCE A TURNE OF BLIS    1.12.12
      THOSE LAMPING EYES WILL DEIGNE SOMETIMES TO LOOK    5.1.6
DEIGNED                       3
      GAZING THY BEAUTY DEIGN'D THEE BY THE SKIES         1.37.2
      IF HER LIPS DAIGND TO SWEETEN MY POORE NAME        4.92.13
      BUT SINCE YE DEIGND SO GOODLY TO RELENT            5.82.9
DEIGNS                        1
      THAT NEVER DEIGNES TO GIVE ME JOY TO LIVE+          1.17.6
DEITY                         1
      THAT SHRINES IN FLESH SO TRUE A $DEITIE            4.4.13
DELAYED                       2
      HER $AUDITE (THOUGH DELAYD) ANSWER'D MUST BE      3.126.11
      IS NOT DELAYD BY HER HART FROSEN COLD              5.30.6
DELIA                        15
      DELIA HER SELFE, AND ALL THE WORLD MAY VIEW         1.4.7
      GOOD $DELIA LOSE, QUENCH, HEALE ME NOW AT LENGTH   1.14.14
      DELIA MY HART HATH LEARND OUT OF THOSE EYES        1.20.14
      INJURIOUS $DELIA YET I LOVE THEE STILL             1.33.9
      AND THEREFORE $DELIA, TIS TO ME NO BLOT            1.35.13
      WHY DOOST THOU $DELIA CREDIT SO THY GLASSE          1.37.1
      LOOKE $DELIA HOW W'ESTEEME THE HALFE BLOWNE $ROSE   1.39.1
      AND ($DELIA) THINKE THY MORNING MUST HAVE NIGHT     1.40.8
      THINKE NOT (SWEET $DELIA) THIS SHALL BE THY SHAME   1.44.5
      DELIA, THESE EYES THAT SO ADMIRETH THINE           1.45.1
      MY $DELIA HATH THE WATERS OF MINE EIES             1.48.1
      THERE WHERE MY $DELIA FAIRER THEN THE $SUNNE       1.53.5
      SO $DELIA, HATH MINE ERROR MADE ME KNOWNE          1.56.5
      YET HAPPY $DELIA THAT THOU WAST UNKIND            1.56.13
      SHALL HAVE MY $SONG, WHERE $DELIA HATH HER SEAT   1.58.12
DELIAN                        1
      THE $DELIAN $CYNTHUS, THEN $OLYMPUS WEIGHT        2.120.7
DELIA'S                       3
      STRAIGHT-WAY SHE HASTS HER UNTO $DELIAS EIES      1.25.10
      OFT DO I MARVELL, WHETHER $DELIAS EIES             1.34.1
      THIS IS MY STATE, AND $DELIAS HEART IS SUCH       1.60.13
DELICIOUS                     2
      IN WHOSE DEARE $BOSOME, SWEET DELICIOUS $LOVE       2.4.5
      WHO LIST TO PRAISE THE DAYES DELICIOUS LYGHT      2.148.1
DELIGHT                      48
      THE MOUNTING VENTER FOR A HIGH DELIGHT             1.35.3
      LINES OF DELIGHT, WHEREON HER YOUTH MIGHT SMILE    1.51.2
      THESE $LINES THAT NOW THOU SCORN'ST, WHICH
                            SHOULD DELIGHT THEE          2.8.13
      MY $TASTE BY HER SWEET $LIPS DRAWNE WITH $DELIGHT  2.29.7
      WHILST YET MINE $EYES DOE SURFET WITH $DELIGHT     2.33.1
      I MARVELL NOT, THOU FEEL'ST NOT MY $DELIGHT        2.49.3
      THE SOULES DELIGHT, THE SENCES TRUE DIRECTION     2.123.7
      WHILST THUS MINE EYES DOE SURFET WITH DELIGHT     2.133.1
      SLEEPE WITH DELIGHT, $BEAUTY WITH LOVE REWARDING  2.136.8
      THE GRAVE OF JOY, PRYSON OF DAYES DELIGHT        2.145.10
      STILL NAMING HER, IN NAMING ALL DELIGHT          2.148.12
      YET DOTH IT STEALE SWEET HOURES FROM LOVES
                            DELIGHT                      3.36.8
      AS A DECREPIT FATHER TAKES DELIGHT                3.37.1
```

```
AWAKES MY HEART, TO HEARTS AND EYES DELIGHT          3.47.14
POSSESSING OR PURSUING NO DELIGHT                    3.75.11
OF MORE DELIGHT THEN $HAWKES OR $HORSES BEE          3.91.11
THEY WEARE BUT SWEET, BUT FIGURES OF DELIGHT         3.98.11
AND SWEETS GROWNE COMMON LOOSE THEIR DEARE
                                     DELIGHT         3.102.12
AND IN SOME PERFUMES IS THERE MORE DELIGHT           3.130.7
THEY SUN-LIKE SHOULD MORE DAZLE THEN DELIGHT+          4.7.8
NO FORCE, NO FRAUD, ROBD THEE OF THY DELIGHT          4.33.7
WHERE $LOVE IS CHASTNESSE, $PAINE DOTH
                          LEARNE DELIGHT              4.48.3
THAT IN THE $MANAGE MYSELFE TAKES DELIGHT            4.49.14
IN THY COLD STUFFE A FLEGMATIKE DELIGHT+             4.56.11
WHICH WOOED WO, MOST RAVISHING DELIGHT               4.58.13
ALAS, IF YOU GRAUNT ONLY SUCH DELIGHT                4.59.12
WORLD OF MY WEALTH, AND HEAV'N OF MY DELIGHT          4.68.4
WHAT $OCEANS OF DELIGHT IN ME DO FLOW                 4.69.4
COME THEN MY $MUSE, SHEW THOU HEIGHT OF DELIGHT       4.70.9
SERVICE AND $HONOR, WONDER WITH DELIGHT               4.72.9
THOSE LOOKES, WHOSE BEAMES BE JOY, WHOSE
                          MOTION IS DELIGHT           4.77.1
NEAST OF YOUNG JOYES, SCHOOLMASTER OF DELIGHT         4.79.8
AND I, MAD WITH DELIGHT, WANT WIT TO CEASE           4.81.13
AND I DO SWEARE EVEN BY THE SAME DELIGHT             4.82.13
DELIGHT PROTESTS HE IS NOT FOR THE ACCURST           4.95.7
VIEWING THE SHAPE OF DARKNESSE AND DELIGHT           4.99.6
TO WRITE THEREIN MORE FRESH THE STORY
                          OF DELIGHT                 4.102.13
BUT SOONE AS THOUGHT OF THEE BREEDS MY DELIGHT       4.108.5
DOTH SEEME TO PROMISE HOPE OF NEW DELIGHT             5.4.2
THROUGH SWEET ILLUSION OF HER LOOKES DELIGHT         5.16.4
AND TAKE DELIGHT T'ENCREASE A WRETCHES WOE           5.41.7
NE OUGHT FOR FAYRER WEATHERS FALSE DELIGHT           5.59.8
AND CHAUNGE OLD YEARES ANNOY TO NEW DELIGHT          5.62.14
WHOSE LEAST DELIGHT SUFFICETH TO DEPRIVE             5.63.11
THERE MY FRAILE FANCY FED WITH FULL DELIGHT          5.72.9
PERHAPS HE THERE MAY LEARNE WITH RARE DELIGHT        5.73.11
THE NEAST OF LOVE, THE LODGING OF DELIGHT            5.76.2
IN HER UNSPOTTED PLEASAUNS TO DELIGHT                5.89.12
DELIGHTED                    3
SHALL BE SO MUCH DELIGHTED WITH THY STORY            2.6.10
WHICH PROOV'D MY BIRDS DELIGHTED IN THE AYRE         2.103.7
NOR ARE MINE EARES WITH THY TOUNGS TUNE
                          DELIGHTED                  3.141.5
DELIGHTS                     7
LIKE AS THE $LUTE DELIGHTS OR ELS DISLIKES           1.57.1
SWEETS WITH SWEETS WARRE NOT, JOY DELIGHTS IN JOY     3.8.2
DELIGHTS TO PEEPE, TO GAZE THEREIN ON THEE          3.24.12
WITH CHOISE DELIGHTS AND RAREST COMPANY             4.97.10
DELIGHTS NOT IN MY MERTH NOR RUES MY SMART          5.54.10
WITH MANY DEARE DELIGHTS BEDECKED FYNE              5.71.12
ACCOMPANYDE WITH ANGELICK DELIGHTES                  5.84.8
DELIVERED                    2
THE TIME IS COME DELIVERED SHE MUST BE              2.116.3
THOSE CHILDREN NURST, DELIVERD FROM THY BRAINE      3.77.11
DELIVERS                     1
FOR IT NO FORME DELIVERS TO THE HEART              3.113.5
DELPHOS                      1
EXCELLING HER OF $DELPHOS OR $CUMAEA               2.119.11
```

DELVES   1
  AND DELVES THE PARALELS IN BEAUTIES BROW   3.60.10
DEMAND   1
  WHEN I DEMAUND OF $PHENIX $STELLA'S STATE   4.92.6
DEMUR   1
  WELL $LOVE, SINCE THIS DEMURRE OUR SUTE
                           DOTH STAY   4.52.12
DEN   3
  WHEN MY $HEART IS THE VERY $DEN OF $HORRCR   2.41.2
  WHEN MY HART IS THE VERY $DEN OF HORROR   2.143.2
  AND EVERY BEAST THAT TO HIS DEN WAS FLED   5.40.10
DENIED   1
  BY SELFE EXAMPLE MAI'ST THOU BE DENIDE   3.142.14
DENIES   3
  BUT FINDING $NATURE THEIR REQUEST DENYES   2.33.11
  I CRAV'D THE THING WHICH EVER SHE DENIES   4.63.6
  WHICH EVEN TO SENCE, SENCE OF IT SELFE DENIES   4.94.7
DENIZENED   1
  WITH NEW-BORNE SIGHES AND DENISEND WIT DO SING   4.15.8
DENOTE   1
  IF IT BE NOT, THEN LOVE DOTH WELL DENOTE   3.148.7
DENY   7
  BUT NOW AGAINE $YCU WILL THE SAME DENIE   2.19.3
  NOW I DENY $HER, THEN I DOE CONFESSE $HER   2.41.13
  NOW I DENY HER, THEN I DOE CONFESSE HER   2.143.13
  FOR SHAME DENY THAT THOU BEAR'ST LOVE TO ANY   3.10.1
  BUT THE DEFENDANT DCTH THAT PLEA DENY   3.46.7
  DO $STELLA LOVE. $FCOLES, WHO DOTH IT DENY+   4.104.14
  GREAT WRONG I DOE, I CAN IT NOT DENY   5.33.1
DENYING   2
  AND STARVED YOU, IN SUCCOURS STILL DENYING   1.2.10
  WITH THIS AFFIRMING $NO, DENYING I   2.5.4
DEPAINT   1
  FOR THAT NO COLOURS CAN DEPAINT MY SORROWES   1.4.6
DEPART   8
  FINDING THEIR $OBJECTS CVER-SOONE DEPART   2.33.6
  FROM THENCE (THEY VCW) THEY NEVER WILL DEPART   2.132.12
  BEHOLD, THEIR OBJECTS OVER-SOONE DEPART   2.133.6
  THEN WHAT COULD DEATH DOE IF THOU SHOULD'ST
                           DEPART   3.6.11
  AS EASIE MIGHT I FRCM MY SELFE DEPART   3.109.3
  BY IRON LAWES OF DUTY TC DEPART   4.87.4
  SO OFT AS HOMEWARD I FRCM HER DEPART   5.52.1
  NE OUGHT FOR TEMPEST DOTH FROM IT DEPART   5.59.7
DEPARTED   1
  LONG SINCE DEPARTED (TO THE $WORLD NO MORE)   2.46.10
DEPARTEST   1
  IN ONE OF THINE, FRCM THAT WHICH THOU DEPARTEST 3.11.2
DEPEND   1
  THEN THAT, WHICH CN THY HUMOR DOTH DEPEND   3.92.8
DEPENDING   1
  TWIXT FEARE AND HCPE DEPENDING DOUBTFULLY+   5.25.4
DEPENDS   2
  FOR IT DEPENDS UPCN THAT LOVE OF THINE   3.92.4
  BOTH TRUTH AND BEAUTY ON MY LOVE DEPENDS   3.101.3
DEPRAVE   1
  SEE HOW THE STUBBORNE DAMZELL DOTH DEPRAVE   5.29.1
DEPRAVES   1
  WHOSE PRYDE DEPRAVES EACH OTHER BETTER PART   5.31.3

```
DEPRIVE                        1
  WHOSE LEAST DELIGHT SUFFICETH TO DEPRIVE              5.63.11
DEPRIVED                       2
  YET FIRE, WATER, AYRE, OF NATURE NOT DEPRIVED         2.127.12
  LET HIM, DEPRIVED OF SWEET BUT UNFELT JOYES           4.24.12
DEPRIVES                       3
  AND $LIBERTY DEPRIVES HIM OF HIS $SCOPE               2.26.11
  AND LYBERTY DEPRIVES HYM OF HYS SCOPE                 2.137.11
  WHOSE THWARTING COURSE, DEPRIVES THE WORLD
                                     OF REASON          2.147.14
DEPTH                          1
  WHERE OTHER $MEN IN DEPTH OF $PASSION CRIE            2.24.13
DERIVE                         2
  CHEEFE GOOD, FROM WHOM ALL GOOD THINGS WE DERIVE      2.146.8
  BUT FROM THINE EIES MY KNOWLEDGE I DERIVE             3.14.9
DERIVED                        5
  THUS FROM THY SELFE THE CAUSE IS THUS DERIVED         2.104.13
  THAT, FROM THAT SEA DERIV'D, TEARS' SPRING
                                     DID FLOW           4.45.8
  OF $HELICON WHENCE SHE DERIVED IS                     5.1.10
  FROM MOTHERS WOMB DERIV'D BY DEW DESCENT              5.74.6
  DERIV'D FROM THAT FAYRE $SPIRIT, FROM
                                WHOM AL TRUE            5.79.11
DERIVETH                       1
  THE WATER, MOYSTURE FROM MY TEARES DERIVETH           2.127.2
DESCANT                        2
  A WAYLING DESCANT ON THE SWEETEST GROUND              1.57.7
  NOR HAD I LEARN'D TO DESCANT ON MY FAIRE              2.104.4
DESCENT                        1
  FROM MOTHERS WOMB DERIV'D BY DEW DESCENT              5.74.6
DESCRIBE                       1
  DESCRIBE $ADONIS AND THE COUNTERFET                   3.53.5
DESCRIED                       2
  AND THEN DESCRIED THE GLISTRING OF HIS DART           4.20.13
  WHEN $CUPID, HAVING ME HIS SLAVE DESCRIDE             4.53.5
DESCRIES                       2
  BUT FOR THAT MAN WITH PAINE THIS TRUTH DESCRIES       4.25.5
  TO ME THAT FEELE THE LIKE, THY STATE DESCRIES         4.31.8
DESCRIPTIONS                   1
  I SEE DISCRIPTIONS OF THE FAIREST WIGHTS              3.106.2
DESCRY                         5
  BUT BY THY WORKE MY $STELLA I DESCRIE                 4.32.7
  AND NOW MAN'S WRONGS IN ME, POORE BEAST, DESCRIE      4.49.4
  ONE FROM THE OTHER SCARCELY CAN DESCRIE               4.72.3
  MOST GOODLY TEMPERATURE YE MAY DESCRY                 5.13.4
  I DOE AT LENGTH DESCRY THE HAPPY SHORE                5.63.5
DESERT                         8
  BUT THIS UNGRATEFULL, FOR MY GOOD DESERT              2.23.9
  COMPARE MY $WORTH WITH OTHERS BASE $DESERT            2.60.6
  COMPARE MY WORTH WITH OTHERS BASE DESERT              2.149.6
  WITHIN THE KNOWLEDGE OF MINE OWNE DESART              3.49.10
  AS TO BEHOLD DESERT A BEGGER BORNE                    3.66.2
  TO DOE MORE FOR ME THEN MINE OWNE DESERT              3.72.6
  HAVE CHANG'D DESERT, LET MINE OWNE CONSCIENCE BE      4.86.2
  BUT NOT TO DEEME OF HER DESERT ASPYRE                 5.85.8
DESERTS                        3
  CAST MY DESARTS INTO THE OPEN AYRE                    2.142.10
  IF IT WERE FILD WITH YOUR MOST HIGH DESERTS+          3.17.2
  WHEREIN I SHOULD YOUR GREAT DESERTS REPAY             3.117.2
```

DESERVE   2
  THOUGH THESE, NOR THESE, DESERVE TO BE IMBRACED   2.138.13
  THY PITTY MAY DESERVE TC PITTIED BEE   3.142.12
DESERVED   6
  ILE TELL THE WORLD THAT I DESERV'D BUT ILL   1.33.11
  THE SPOYLE OF FAME DESERV'D BY VERTUOUS MEN   1.45.6
  WHETHER MY FAITH HATH NCT DESERV'D HER LCVE+   1.49.12
  AND MY DECEIV'D ATTEMPT, DESERV'D MORE FAME   1.56.6
  HOW MUCH MORE PRAISE DESERV'D THY BEAUTIES USE   3.2.9
  RICH IN THE TREASURE OF DESERV'D RENOWNE   4.37.9
DESERVES   1
  DESERVES THE TRAVAILE OF A WORTHIER PEN   3.79.6
DESERVEST   1
  THAT DUE TO THEE WHICH THOU DESERV'ST ALCNE   3.39.8
DESERVING   1
  AND FOR THAT RITCHES WHERE IS MY DESERVING+   3.87.6
DESIGNED   2
  SACRED ON EARTH, DESIGN'D A $SAINT ABOVE   1.6.8
  WITH WHICH THAT HAPPY NAME WAS FIRST DESYND   5.74.2
DESIGNS   2
  DANGER HATH HONOR, GREAT DESIGNES THEIR FAME   1.35.6
  PAINTING MY $PASSICNS IN THESE SAD $DESIGNES   2.45.4
DESIRE   64
  THESE PLAINTIVE $VERSE, THE $POSTES OF MY DESIRE   1.4.1
  IF A SWEET LANGUISH WITH A CHAST DESIRE   1.15.2
  COME $TIME THE ANCHCR-HCLD OF MY DESIRE   1.22.1
  THAT MAKES ME FALL FROM CFF MY HIE DESIRE   1.32.8
  RAISING MY HOPES CN HILLS OF HIGH DESIRE   1.36.1
  MUST YEELD UP ALL TC TYRANT $TIMES DESIRE   1.38.7
  THAT INTIMATE IN VAINE MY CHASTE DESIRE   1.59.2
  MY CHASTE DESIRE, WHICH FROM DARKE SORROW SHINES   1.59.3
  BEHOLD THE MESSAGE CF A CHAST DESIRE   1.60.3
  THE PRECIOUS $SPICES BE YOUR CHASTE $DESIRE   2.16.6
  THE PRECIOUS $ODORS BE MY CHASTE $DESIRE   2.30.11
  THAT I AM ONELY STARV'D IN MY DESIRE   2.34.4
  THAT I AM ONELY STARV'D IN MY DESIRE   2.34.8
  AND YET AM ONELY STARV'C IN MY DESIRE   2.34.12
  MY $WORDS THE $HAMMERS, FASHIONING MY DESIRE   2.40.2
  IN $PRIDE OF $WIT, WHEN HIGH DESIRE OF $FAME   2.47.1
  BY CHASTE $DESIRE, TRUE $LOVE, AND VERTUCUS
                $PRAYSE   2.54.14
  AND WHEN THE $PLUMES WERE SUMM'D WITH
                SWEET DESIRE   2.56.9
  I HAVE, I WANT, $DESPAIRE, AND YET $DESIRE   2.62.13
  BY CHAST DESIRE, TRLE LCVE, AND VERTUES PRAISE   2.101.14
  BUT NOW THEIR PLUMES FULL SUMD WITH SWEET DESIRE   2.103.9
  ON HEAVENLIE TOP CF THY DIVINE DESIRE   2.106.6
  CELESTIALL $IMAGE, $LOAD-STONE UF DESIRE   2.123.6
  THY $BOWE HALFE BRCKE, IS PEEC'D WITH
                OLDE DESIRE   2.126.5
  THE PASSIONS OF DISPAIRE, BUT JOYES TO MY DESIRE   2.127.8
  THOSE TEARES WHICH QUENCH MY HOPE, STILL
                KINDLE MY DESIRE 2.132.1
  QUENCHLES DESIRE, MAKES HOPE BURNE, DRYES
                MY TEARES   2.132.5
  DESIRE, MY LOVE, MY SOULE, MY HOPE, HART,
                AND LIFE CHARMETH 2.132.8
  MY HOPE BECOMES A FRIEND TO MY DESIRE   2.132.9
  DESIRE, MY LOVE, MY SOULE, MY HOPE, MY
                HART, MY LIFE 2.132.13

```
FOR THOU ALONE RENEW'ST THAT OLDE DESIRE              2.145.13
I HAVE, I WANT, DISPAYRE, AND YET DESIRE              2.150.13
FROM FAIREST CREATURES WE DESIRE INCREASE              3.1.1
WHICH TO REPAIRE SHOULD BE THY CHIEFE DESIRE           3.10.8
THE FIRST MY THOUGHT, THE OTHER MY DESIRE              3.45.3
THEN CAN NO HORSE WITH MY DESIRE KEEPE PACE            3.51.9
THEREFORE DESIRE (OF PERFECTS LOVE BEING MADE)         3.51.10
UPON THE HOURES, AND TIMES OF YOUR DESIRE+             3.57.2
DOST THOU DESIRE MY SLUMBERS SHOULD BE BROKEN          3.61.3
AND RATHER MAKE THEM BORNE TO OUR DESIRE               3.123.7
NOR TASTE, NOR SMELL, DESIRE TO BE INVITED             3.141.7
DESIRE IS DEATH, WHICH $PHISICK DID EXCEPT             3.147.8
AND SO THE $GENERALL OF HOT DESIRE                     3.154.7
TO GRIEVE ME WORSE, IN SAYING THAT $DESIRE             4.14.6
WITHOUT DESIRE TO FEED OF FURTHER GRACE                4.46.8
SO LONG (THOUGH HE FROM BOOKE MYCHE TO DESIRE)         4.46.13
MY HORSE, HE SPURRES WITH SHARPE DESIRE MY HART        4.49.11
HER COME, AND HEARE WITH PATIENCE MY DESIRE            4.56.13
DESIRE STILL ON THE STILTS OF FEARE DOTH GO            4.66.8
LIGHT OF MY LIFE, AND LIFE OF MY DESIRE                4.68.2
'BUT AH,' $DESIRE STILL CRIES, 'GIVE ME
                    SOME FOOD'                          4.71.14
DESIRE, THOUGH THOU MY OLD COMPANION ART               4.72.1
BUT THOU $DESIRE, BECAUSE THOU WOULDST HAVE ALL        4.72.13
BREATHER OF LIFE, AND FASTNER OF DESIRE                4.80.7
FOR THOUGH FULL OF DESIRE, EMPTIE OF WIT               4.82.9
FROM BASE DESIRE ON EARTHLY CATES TO PRAY+             4.88.8
RUDELY THOU WRONGEST MY DEARE HARTS DESIRE             5.5.1
SO HARD IT IS TO KINDLE NEW DESIRE                     5.6.9
BURNING IN FLAMES OF PURE AND CHAST DESYRE             5.22.12
TH'IMPORTUNE SUIT OF MY DESIRE TO SHONNE               5.23.6
IS NOT DISSOLV'D THROUGH MY SO HOT DESYRE              5.30.3
NOT FYRE., FOR SHE DOTH FRIESE WITH FAINT DESIRE       5.55.8
HER HARTS DESIRE WITH MOST CONTENTMENT PLEASE          5.72.12
NE ONE LIGHT GLANCE OF SENSUALL DESYRE                 5.84.3
DESIRED                6
  THE LEVELL OF MY HOPES DESIRED MOST                  1.53.4
  AND FOR THEIR VERTUES I DESIERD TO KNOW              2.103.2
  TO SET A FORME UPON DESIRED CHANGE                   3.89.6
  I SICK WITHALL THE HELPE OF BATH DESIRED             3.153.11
  BUT SINCE THAT LYFE IS MORE THEN DEATH DESYRED       5.7.9
  DESIRED FOOD, TO IT DOTH MAKE HIS FLIGHT             5.73.6
DESIRES                11
  FOR HAPLESSE LOE EVEN WITH MINE OWNE DESIRES         1.13.5
  STILL MUST I WHET MY YONG DESIRES ABATED             1.18.9
  STARRES SURE THEY ARE, WHOSE MOTIONS RULE DESIRES    1.34.5
  FRAM'D MY DESIRES FIT FOR HER EYES TO KILL           1.36.14
  CEASE DREAMES, TH'$IMAGES OF DAY DESIRES             1.54.9
  BY ALL TRUE $LOVERS $SIGHES, $VOWES, AND
                    $DESIRES                            2.36.11
  MY WORDS THE HAMMERS, FASHIONING MY DESIRES          2.144.2
  OF HOPES BEGOT BY FEARE, OF WOT NOT WHAT DESIRES     4.6.2
  NOBLER DESIRES, LEAST ELSE THAT FRIENDLY FOE         4.21.7
  THENCE HIS DESIRES HE LEARNES, HIS LIVE'S
                    COURSE THENCE                       4.61.8
  IN CHAST DESIRES ON HEAVENLY BEAUTY BOUND            5.8.8
DESIRETH                1
  AND MY SOULE THEN OBTAINE WHICH SO MY
                    SOULE DESIRETH                      2.117.8
```

```
     INJOYD NO SOONER BUT DISPISED STRAIGHT              3.129.5
     THAT IT, DESPISDE IN TRUE BUT NAKED SHEW            4.55.3
DESPISING                      1
     YET IN THESE THOUGHTS MY SELFE ALMOST DESPISING     3.29.9
DESPITE                        9
     THEN WOULD I MAKE THEE READ, BUT TO DESPIGHT THEE   2.8.14
     WHILST IN DESPITE CF TYRANNIZING $TIMES             2.44.5
     DISPIGHT OF WRINKLES THIS THY GOULDEN TIME          3.3.12
     YET DOE THY WORST CULD $TIME DISPIGHT THY WRCNG     3.19.13
     FOR THEN DISPIGHT CF SPACE I WOULD BE BRCUGHT       3.44.3
     PRAISING THY WORTH, DISPIGHT HIS CRUELL HAND        3.60.14
     I WILL BE TRUE DISPIGHT THY SYETH AND THEE          3.123.14
     WHO IN DISPIGHT OF VIEW IS PLEASD TO DOTE           3.141.4
     THEN DOE I MORE AUGMENT MY FOES DESPIGHT            5.44.10
DESPITETH                      2
     DESPITETH $LOVE, AND LAUGHETH AT HER $FOLLY         2.38.10
     DISPIGHTETH $LOVE, AND LAUGHETH AT HER FOLLY        2.131.10
DESPOILED                      1
     DESPOYLD OF WARLIKE ARMES AND KNOWEN SHIELD         5.52.4
DESTINED                       1
     THE WRETCHED $CREATURE, DESTINED TO DIE             2.50.2
DESTINY                        1
     AND SHEE ON HER OWNE DESTINY DIVINING               2.109.11
DESTROY                        1
     WHOM YE DOE WRECK, DOE RUINE, AND DESTROY           5.56.14
DESTROYED                      1
     O DO NOT LET THY $TEMPLE BE DESTROYD                4.40.14
DESTROYS                       1
     AND KEPT UNUSDE THE USER SO DESTROYES IT            3.9.12
DETAIN                         1
     SHE MAY DETAINE, BUT NOT STILL KEEPE HER
                              TRESURE                    3.126.10
DETERMINATE                    1
     MY BONDS IN THEE ARE ALL DETERMINATE                3.87.4
DETERMINATION                  1
     FIND NO DETERMINATION, THEN YOU WERE                3.13.6
DETERMINED                     1
     AND BY THEIR VERDICT IS DETERMINED                  3.46.11
DETEST                         1
     THOU THOUGH STILL TIRED, YET STILL DOOST
                              IT DETEST                  4.96.14
DEVICE                         1
     SHOULD KINDLE FYRE BY WCNDERFULL DEVYSE+            5.30.12
DEVIL                          4
     LITTLE ILE SAY, BUT THINKE THE $DEVILL'S IN ME      2.15.14
     BY THIS GOOD WICKED $SPIRIT, SWEET $ANGELL
                              $DEVILL                    2.20.14
     AND WOULD CORRUPT MY SAINT TO BE A DIVEL            3.144.7
     IS IT NOT EVILL THAT SUCH A $DEVILL WANTS
                              HORNES+                    4.78.14
DEVISE                         9
     FOR HOW COULD $NATURE EVER THUS DEVISE              1.34.3
     DEVISE SOME MEANES, BUT HOW I MAY FORSAKE $YCU      2.11.10
     KINDE WORDS UNKINDEST MEATE I CAN DEVISE            2.115.11
     UNLESSE YOU WOULD DEVISE SOME VERTUOUS LYE          3.72.5
     THEN BOTH YOUR $PCETS CAN IN PRAISE DEVISE          3.83.14
     OR DID SHE ELSE THAT SOBER HUE DEVISE               4.7.5
     FOR THOUGH HE COLOURS CCULD DEVIZE AT WILL          5.17.5
     WHAT TROPHEE THEN SHALL I MOST FIT DEVIZE           5.69.5
     NOT SO, (QUOD I) LET BASER THINGS DEVIZE            5.75.9
```

```
DEVISED                      4
  DEVIS'D A $VESSELL TO RECEIVE THE $SUNNE        2.30.3
  AND DO SO LOVE, YET WHEN THEY HAVE DEVISDE      3.82.9
  THEIR ANTHEMES SWEET DEVIZED OF LOVES PRAYSE    5.19.6
  DEVIZ'D A $WEB HER WOOERS TO DECEAVE            5.23.2
DEVOTED                      1
  WORDS, THOUGHTS, AND DEEDS, DEVOTED TO HER HONOR  2.138.6
DEVOTION                     2
  IF $CHASTE AND PURE DEVOTION OF MY YOUTH        2.138.1
  MEN TO DEVOTION OUGHT TO BE INCLYND             5.22.2
DEVOUR                       2
  AND MAKE THE EARTH DEVOURE HER OWNE SWEET BROOD  3.19.2
  IN HIS MOST PRIDE DISDEIGNETH TO DEVOURE        5.20.7
DEVOURING                    2
  DEVOURING TIME BLUNT THOU THE $LYONS PAWES      3.19.1
  DEVOURING TYME AND CHANGEFUL CHANCE HAVE PRAYD  5.58.7
DEVOUT                       1
  I, LIKE A $MAN DEVOUT, AND CHARITABLE           2.23.5
DEVOUTLY                     1
  TO BLAZE THESE LAST, AND SWARE DEVOUTLY THEN    4.13.13
DEW                          2
  BEAUTIE (SWEET $LOVE) IS LIKE THE MORNING DEW   1.50.1
  WITH STRONG ENDEVOUR AND ATTENTION DEW          5.80.8
DEW-EMPEARLED                2
  AMONGST THE DAINTIE $DEW-IMPEARLED FLOWRES      2.53.8
  AMONGST THOSE DAINTY DEW-EMPEARLED FLOWERS      2.113.8
DIAL                         2
  THY DYALL HOW THY PRETIOUS MYNUITS WASTE        3.77.2
  AH YET DOTH BEAUTY LIKE A $DYALL HAND           3.104.9
DIAL'S                       1
  THOU BY THY DYALS SHADY STEALTH MAIST KNOW      3.77.7
DIAMOND                      3
  THE $DIAMOND SHALL ONCE CONSUME TO $DUST        2.13.3
  THE $DIAMOND SHALL ONCE CONSUME TO DUST         2.121.3
  NOR TO THE $DIAMOND.. FOR THEY ARE MORE TENDER  5.9.10
DIAN                         1
  DIAN THAT FAINE WOULD CHEARE HER FRIEND
                             THE $NIGHT           4.97.1
DIANA                        1
  SEE CHASTE $DIANA, WHERE MY HARMLES HART        2.135.1
DIANA-LIKE                   1
  (DIANA-LIKE) TO WORKE MY SUDDEN CHANGE          1.5.4
DIAN'S                       3
  A MAIDE OF $DYANS THIS ADVANTAGE FOUND          3.153.2
  VENUS IS TAUGHT WITH $DIAN'S WINGS TO FLIE      4.72.6
  EVEN SO (ALAS) A $LADY $DIAN'S PEERE            4.97.9
DICTIONARY'S                 1
  YOU THAT DO $DICTIONARIE'S METHODE BRING        4.15.5
DID                          3
  AND IN YOUR $EYE, THE $BOY THAT DID THE $MURTHER  2.2.11
  I LOVED, BUT STRAIGHT DID NOT WHAT $LOVE DECREED  4.2.6
  AS THOUGH THAT FAIRE SOFT HAND DID YOU
                             GREAT WRONG          4.83.4
DIE                          41
  THEN THERE I DIE FROM WHENCE MY LIFE SHOULD COME  1.31.13
  THEY WILL REMAINE, AND SO THOU CANST NOT DIE    1.42.14
  THOU CANST NOT DIE WHILST ANY ZEALE ABOUND      1.43.1
  AND THEREFORE GRIEVE NOT IF THY BEAUTIES DIE    1.45.9
  I SAY, I $DIE, YOU $ECCHO ME WITH I             2.5.7
  I LAUGH AT $FORTUNE, AS IN JEST TO DIE          2.24.14
```

```
AND MY $LIVES $HOPE WOULD DIE, BUT FOR $DESPAIRE        2.26.3
AND THOUGH THIS $EARTHLY $BODY FADE AND DIE             2.44.13
THE WRETCHED $CREATURE, DESTINED TO DIE                2.50.2
MUST PASSE BY AYRE, OR ELSE DYE IN EXILE               2.122.4
AND MY LIVES HOPE WOULD DIE BUT FOR DYSPAIRE           2.137.3
DIE, DIE, MY SOULE, AND NEVER TASTE OF JOY             2.139.1
DIE, DIE, MY SOULE, AND NEVER TASTE OF JOY             2.139.1
THAT THEREBY BEAUTIES $ROSE MIGHT NEVER DIE            3.1.2
DIE SINGLE AND THINE $IMAGE DIES WITH THEE             3.3.14
AH., IF THOU ISSULESSE SHALT HAP TO DIE                3.9.3
THOU SHOULDST PRINT MORE, NOT LET THAT COPPY DIE       3.11.14
AND DIE AS FAST AS THEY SEE OTHERS GROW                3.12.12
FOR AT A FROWNE THEY IN THEIR GLORY DIE                3.25.8
THE $CANKER BLOOMES HAVE FULL AS DEEPE A DIE           3.54.5
DIE TO THEMSELVES. $SWEET $ROSES DOE NOT SO            3.54.11
SAVE THAT TO DYE, I LEAVE MY LOVE ALONE                3.66.14
THOUGH I (ONCE GONE) TO ALL THE WORLD MUST DYE         3.81.6
HAPPY TO HAVE THY LOVE, HAPPY TO DIE                   3.92.12
THOUGH TO IT SELFE, IT ONELY LIVE AND DIE              3.94.10
WHICH DIE FOR GOODNES, WHO HAVE LIV'D FOR CRIME        3.124.14
WITNESSE OF LIFE TO THEM THAT LIVING DIE               4.32.2
GLAD IF FOR HER HE GIVE THEM LEAVE TO DIE              4.43.8
O LOOKE, O SHINE, O LET ME DIE AND SEE                 4.48.8
AS OF A CAITIFE WORTHY SO TO DIE                       4.94.10
IF NOT, DIE SOONE, AND I WITH THEE WILL PERISH         5.2.14
BIDS ALL OLD THOUGHTS TO DIE IN DUMPISH SPRIGHT        5.4.4
THEN DOE I DIE, AS ONE WITH LIGHTNING FYRED            5.7.8
TO FORCE ME LIVE AND WILL NOT LET ME DY                5.11.12
AND IF THOSE FAYLE FALL DOWNE AND DY BEFORE HER        5.14.13
YET BETTER WERE ATTONCE TO LET ME DIE                  5.25.5
AND DOE ME NOT BEFORE MY TIME TO DY                    5.42.14
BUT LIKE A STUPID STOCK IN SILENCE DIE                 5.43.8
AND THINCK THEY DY WITH PLEASURE, LIVE
                            WITH PAYNE                 5.47.14
AND GRANT THAT WE FOR WHOM THOU DIDDEST DYE            5.68.6
TO DY IN DUST, BUT YOU SHALL LIVE BY FAME              5.75.10
DIED                5
THAT FOR HER LATE DECEASED $HUSBAND DY'D               2.15.8
HIS $MOTHER DIED, AND BY HER $LEGACIE                  2.116.10
BUT SINCE HE DIED AND $POETS BETTER PROVE              3.32.13
WHEN BEAUTY LIV'D AND DY'ED AS FLOWERS DO NOW          3.68.2
IN MY LOVES VEINES THOU HAST TOO GROSELY DIED          3.99.5
DIES                3
AS ONE THAT DIES WITHOUT HER COMPANY                   1.25.8
LIVES WITHOUT HONOUR, DIES WITHOUT A NAME              1.35.11
DIE SINGLE AND THINE $IMAGE DIES WITH THEE             3.3.14
DIEST               1
UNLOK'D ON DIEST UNLESSE THOU GET A SONNE              3.7.14
DIET                1
WITH $DIET AND $CORRECTION, $MEN DISTRAUGHT            2.9.13
DIETS               1
WHAT NOW THE $DUTCH IN THEIR FULL DIETS BOAST          4.30.6
DIFFERENCE          1
ONE THING EXPRESSING, LEAVES OUT DIFFERENCE            3.105.8
DIFFERENT           1
OF DIFFERENT FLOWERS IN ODOR AND IN HEW                3.98.6
DIFFERETH           1
AND DIFF'RETH IT, AS DOE THE SEV'RALL $NATIONS+        2.27.2
DIG                 3
AND DIGGE DEEP TRENCHES IN THY BEAUTIES FIELD          3.2.2
```

```
DIG DEEPE WITH LEARNING'S SPADE, NOW TELL
                     ME THIS                          4.21.13
I LIST NOT DIG SO DEEPE FOR BRASEN FAME               4.28.4
DIGHT                   3
SILENT AND SAD IN MOURNING WEEDES DOTH DIGHT          4.97.8
WILS HIM AWAKE, AND SOONE ABOUT HIM DIGHT             5.4.7
THE GATE WITH PEARLES AND RUBYES RICHLY DIGHT         5.81.10
DIGNIFIED               1
SO DOST THOU TOO, AND THEREIN DIGNIFI'D               3.101.4
DIGNIFIES               1
THAT YOU ARE YOU, SO DIGNIFIES HIS STORY              3.84.8
DIGNITY                 1
THE BASEST WEED OUT-BRAVES HIS DIGNITY                3.94.12
DILATE                  1
FOR NOW YOUR LIGHT DOTH MORE IT SELFE DILATE          5.66.11
DIM                     1
MY EYES MADE DIM WITH LOOKES, POURE DOWN
                     A FLOOD OF TEARS                 2.133.10
DIMMED                  3
AND OFTEN IS HIS GOLD COMPLEXION DIMM'D               3.18.6
WHENAS A STORME HATH DIMD HER TRUSTY GUYDE            5.34.3
WITH SORROW DIMMED AND DEFORMD IT WERE                5.45.10
DINED                   1
AND EVER-MORE WITH SIGHES HE SUPT AND DYNDE           2.116.16
DINTS                   1
DEEPE IS THE WOUND, THAT DINTS THE PARTS ENTIRE       5.6.11
DIPHTHONGS              1
MY DOLEFULL $DYPTHONGS WERE MY LIVES DISPAIRES        2.111.11
DIRECT                  4
BOASTING, THAT SHE DOTH STILL DIRECT THE WAY          2.38.3
BOASTING THAT SHEE DOTH STILL DIRECT THE WAY          2.131.3
ME TO DIRECT, WITH CLOUDES IS OVERCAST                5.34.6
BUT WHEN MYNE EYES I THEREUNTO DIRECT                 5.78.9
DIRECTED                1
AND DARKELY BRIGHT, ARE BRIGHT IN DARKE DIRECTED      3.43.4
DIRECTION               3
TO $WISEDOME'S SELFE TO MINISTER DIRECTION            2.34.7
MY WORDS MIGHT IMITATE MY DEEREST THOUGHTS
                     DIRECTION                        2.117.7
THE SOULES DELIGHT, THE SENCES TRUE DIRECTION         2.123.7
DIRECTLY                1
SUSPECT I MAY, YET NOT DIRECTLY TELL                  3.144.10
DIRECTS                 2
TH'ARERAGE OF MY JOYES, DIRECTS ME TO MY LOSSE        2.110.8
BUT MY FAIRE $PLANET, WHO DIRECTS ME STILL            2.147.9
DISABLED                1
AND STRENGTH BY LIMPING SWAY DISABLED                 3.66.8
DISARMED                3
STILL LET DISARMED PEACE DECKE HER AND THEE           1.53.13
WAS SLEEPING BY A $VIRGIN HAND DISARM'D               3.154.8
SO AS I THEN DISARMED DID REMAINE                     5.12.5
DISCERN                 1
CAN SCARCE DISCERNE THE SHAPE OF MINE OWNE PAINE      4.94.4
DISCERNED               1
YOU BEST DISCERN'D OF MY $MINDS INWARD $EYES          2.57.1
DISCHARGE               2
DISCHARGE OUR $FORCES, HERE LET $MALICE CEASE         2.63.7
WHILE EVERIE OFFICE THEMSELVES WILL DISCHARGE         4.85.7
DISCLOSES               1
WHEN SOMMERS BREATH THEIR MASKED BUDS DISCLOSES       3.54.8
```

```
DISCOMMEND                    1
  NOR WHO COMMEND OR DISCOMMEND MY VERSE              2.128.10
DISCOMMENDS                   1
  NOR WHO COMMENDS, OR DISCOMMENDS MY $VERSE          2.42.10
DISCONSOLATE                  1
  SO I ALONE NOW LEFT DISCONSOLATE                    5.89.5
DISCONTENT                    2
  UNDER THE BLOW OF THRALLED DISCONTENT               3.124.7
  NOT PRIZING HER POORE INFANTS DISCONTENT            3.143.8
DISCORD                       1
  THERE PRIDE DARE NOT APPROCH, NOR DISCORD SPILL     5.65.9
DISCOURSE                     2
  MY THOUGHTS AND MY DISCOURSE AS MAD MENS ARE        3.147.11
  FOR ME, WHILE YOU DISCOURSE OF COURTLY TIDES        4.51.9
DISCOVERED                    1
  HER GOLDEN BEAMES HAD NOW DISCOVERED                2.125.3
DISCOVERY                     2
  AND CALL'D TO TELL OF HIS $DISCOVERIE               2.1.3
  IN DEEP DISCOVERY OF THE MYNDS DISEASE              5.50.6
DISCRETION                    1
  WITH $FOOLES AND $CHILDREN GOOD $DISCRETION
                          BEARES                      2.22.1
DISDAIN                      34
  SAY HER DISDAINE HATH DRYED UP MY BLOOD             1.2.9
  WHO WHILST I LOVE, DOTH KILL ME WITH DISDAINE       1.3.14
  BUT WITH DISDAINE TO SEE ME IN THAT PLACE           1.5.6
  CAST WATER-COLD $DISDAINE UPON MY FACE              1.5.8
  NOR YET THE WORLD HAVE HEARD OF SUCH DISDAINE       1.7.8
  TIS NOT DISDAINE MUST MAKE ME LEAVE TO LOVE         1.8.14
  PRAYERS PREVAILE NOT WITH A QUAINT DISDAINE         1.11.4
  FLINT, FROST, DISDAINE, WEARES, MELTES,
                       AND YEELDES WE SEE             1.11.14
  STILL NEW BORNE SORROWES OF HER FRESH DISDAINE      1.16.10
  AND VAPOURS OF DISDAINE SO OVERGROWNE               1.21.3
  CAUSE ONCE THE DATE OF HER DISDAINE T'EXPIRE        1.22.3
  BEAUTY AND YOUTH T'OPINION AND DISDAINE             1.23.12
  HER FOR DISDAINE, AND ME FOR LOVING THUS            1.26.14
  I IN MY LOVE, OR THOU IN THY DISDAINE               1.33.14
  HER THUNDER OF DISDAINE FORST ME RETIRE             1.36.4
  WHEN SHAL HER TROUBLED BROW CHARG'D WITH DISDAINE   1.49.5
  AND NEVER WAKE TO FEELE THE DAYES DISDAINE          1.54.14
  WHICH LOVE DOTH PAY, AND HER DISDAINE EXTORTS       1.60.2
  TH'AFFLICTION HER UNKIND DISDAINE DOTH MOVE         1.60.8
  REASON REPROCHED WITH THIS COY $DISDAINE            2.38.9
  AND MURTHER'ST $VERTUE WITH THY COY DISDAINE        2.44.8
  LAMENT'ST MY DEATH, WITH TEARES OF THY DISDAINE     2.130.14
  REASON REPROCHED WITH THIS COY DISDAINE             2.131.9
  DISDAYNE $ICE TO MY LIFE, IS TO MY SOULE A FIRE     2.132.3
  WITH TEARES, SIGHES, AND DISDAINE, THYS
                       CONTRARY I PROVE               2.132.4
  WITH MY SOULES FIRE, MY LIFE DISDAINE OUT-WEARES    2.132.7
  WITH TEARES, SIGHES, AND DISDAINE, SHALL
                       HAVE IMMORTAL STRIFE           2.132.14
  KNOWING THY HEART TORMENT ME WITH DISDAINE          3.132.2
  MY TOUNG-TIDE PATIENCE WITH TOO MUCH DISDAINE       3.140.2
  SO FORTIFIED WITH WIT, STOR'D WITH DISDAINE         4.12.13
  OR SPRITE, DISDAINE OF SUCH DISDAINE TO HAVE+       4.47.6
  OR SPRITE, DISDAINE OF SUCH DISDAINE TO HAVE+       4.47.6
  DISDAYNE TO YIELD UNTO THE FIRST ASSAY              5.14.8
  BUT SUDDEN DUMPS AND DRERY SAD DISDAYNE             5.52.11
```

DISDAINETH   2
  YET HIM FOR THIS, MY LOVE NO WHIT DISDAINETH   3.33.13
  IN HIS MOST PRIDE DISDEIGNETH TO DEVOURE   5.20.7
DISDAINFUL   1
  MY SIMPLE MEANING WITH DISDAYNFULL SCORNE   5.29.2
DISDAINS   6
  AND HER DISDAINES ARE $GALL, HER FAVOURS $HUNNY   1.6.4
  HER EYES EXACT IT, THOUGH HER HART DISDAINES ME   1.18.6
  THEE AND THY $LOVE FORLCRNE, AND BOTH DISDAINES   1.52.7
  SINCE SHE DISDAINES TO BLESSE MY HAPPIE $VERSE   2.45.5
  DISDAINES THE TILLAGE OF THY HUSBANDRY+   3.3.6
  THUNDRED DISDAINES AND LIGHTNINGS OF DISGRACE   4.60.4
DISEASE   3
  FOR THAT WHICH LONGER NURSETH THE DISEASE   3.147.2
  'ART NOT ASHAM'D TC PUBLISH THY DISEASE+'   4.34.5
  IN DEEP DISCOVERY CF THE MYNDS DISEASE   5.50.6
DISEASED   2
  TO BE DISEAS'D ERE THAT THERE WAS TRUE NEEDING   3.118.8
  FOR MEN DISEASD, BUT I MY $MISTRISSE THRALL   3.154.12
DISGRACE   18
  BUT MY DEGRADED HOPES, WITH SUCH DISGRACE   1.7.11
  YET COUNT IT NO DISGRACE THAT I HAVE LOV'D THEE   1.44.14
  CONVAY THEE FROM THE THCUGHT OF THY DISGRACE   1.52.11
  IS MODEL'D OUT THE $WORLD OF MY $DISGRACE   2.44.4
  WHEN IN DISGRACE WITH $FORTUNE AND MENS EYES   3.29.1
  STEALING UNSEENE TC WEST WITH THIS DISGRACE   3.33.8
  THAT HEALES THE WCUND, AND CURES NOT THE DISGRACE   3.34.8
  THOU CANST NOT (LCVE) DISGRACE ME HALFE SO ILL   3.89.5
  AS ILE MY SELFE DISGRACE, KNOWING THY WIL   3.89.7
  DULLING MY LINES, AND DCING ME DISGRACE   3.103.8
  MAY TIME DISGRACE, AND WRETCHED MYNUIT KILL   3.126.8
  BUT IS PROPHAN'D, IF NOT LIVES IN DISGRACE   3.127.8
  MY BEST WITS STILL THEIR OWNE DISGRACE INVENT   4.19.5
  BUT CANNOT SKILL TC PITIE MY DISGRACE   4.45.3
  THUNDRED DISDAINES AND LIGHTNINGS OF DISGRACE   4.60.4
  LET $FORTUNE LAY CN ME HER WORST DISGRACE   4.64.3
  WITH SIGHT THEREOF CRIDE OUT., O FAIRE DISGRACE   4.103.13
  BUT THOU ART GONE, NOW THAT SELFE FELT DISGRACE   4.106.7
DISGRACED   4
  AND FRESHEST $COLCURS WITH FOULE STAYNES
                 DISGRACED   2.13.4
  AND FRESHEST COLOURS WITH FOULE STAINES
                 DISGRACED   2.121.4
  YET FAIRE UNKINDE, TO GCCD TO BE DISGRACED   2.138.14
  AND RIGHT PERFECTICN WRCNGFULLY DISGRAC'D   3.66.7
DISGRACES   1
  NOR MY DISGRACES TC THE WORLD BE SEENE   2.142.14
DISGUISE   1
  LEAST IF NO VAILE THOSE BRAVE GLEAMES DID DISGUISE   4.7.7
DISGUISING   1
  DISGUYSING DIVERSLY MY TROUBLED WITS   5.54.4
DISH   1
  MONGST WHICH THERE IN A SILVER DISH DID LY   5.77.5
DISHEVELED   1
  SHE SO DISCHEVELD, BLUSHT., FROM WINDOW I   4.103.12
DISHONOR   1
  SCORN OF BASE THINGS, AND SDEIGNE OF FOULE
                 DISHONOR   5.5.6
DISJOIN   1
  WHICH THOUGH THE $DAY DIS-JOYNE BY SEV'RALL
                 FLIGHT   2.37.6

DISLIKE   1
  T'AFFECT THIS LIFE, AND YET THIS LIFE DISLEEKE   1.20.11
DISLIKES   1
  LIKE AS THE $LUTE DELIGHTS OR ELS DISLIKES   1.57.1
DISMAY   6
  PLAYNTS, PRAYERS, VOWES, RUTH, SORROW,
                      AND DISMAY   5.14.11
  THAT WITH ONE LOOKE SHE DOTH MY LIFE DISMAY   5.21.10
  DOE WANDER NOW IN DARKNESSE AND DISMAY   5.34.7
  COMES FORTH AFRESH CUT OF THEIR LATE DISMAY   5.40.11
  IN DREAD OF DEATH AND DAUNGEROUS DISMAY   5.63.3
  AFFRAYD OF EVERY DANGERS LEAST DISMAY   5.88.4
DISMAYED   2
  BE NOUGHT DISMAYD THAT HER UNMOVED MIND   5.6.1
  RETOURNE AGAYNE MY FORCES LATE DISMAYD   5.14.1
DISMISS   1
  WHOM SHE IMPLOYES, DISMISSE FROM THEE MY WIT   4.107.10
DISOBEYS   2
  AND YET THOU SEEST THY POWRE SHE DISOBAYES   1.23.9
  BUT SHE HIS PRECEPT PROUDLY DISOBAYES   5.19.11
DISPARAGEMENT   1
  THIS ONE DISPARAGEMENT THEY TO YOU GAVE   5.66.3
DISPATCH   1
  SETS DOWNE HER BABE AND MAKES ALL SWIFT DISPATCH   3.143.3
DISPENSE   1
  MARKE HOW WITH MY NEGLECT I DOE DISPENCE   3.112.12
DISPERSE   2
  DISPERSE THEIR $RAYES ON EV'RY VULGAR $SPIRIT   2.43.2
  AND UNDER THEE THEIR POESIE DISPERSE   3.78.4
DISPLACE   1
  FOR WITH MILD PLEASANCE, WHICH DOTH PRIDE
                      DISPLACE   5.21.5
DISPLAY   5
  BUT THINKE THAT ALL THE $MAP OF MY STATE
                      I DISPLAY   4.6.13
  WHEN $SUN IS HID, CAN STARRES SUCH BEAMES
                      DISPLAY+   4.88.6
  FIRST DID WITH PUFFING KISSE THOSE LOCKES
                      DISPLAY   4.103.11
  THEY LOOSELY DID THEYR WANTON WINGES DISPLAY   5.76.11
  BUT FAYREST SHE, WHEN SO SHE DOTH DISPLAY   5.81.9
DISPLAYED   2
  HOW THEIR BLACKE BANNER MIGHT BE BEST DISPLAID   4.55.8
  IN WHOSE COTE ARMOUR RICHLY ARE DISPLAYD   5.70.2
DISPLAYING   1
  SHE LIGHTNING $LOVE, DISPLAYING $VENUS' SKIES   4.63.7
DISPLAYS   3
  THAT WHEN THE HEAV'N TO THEE HIS BEST DISPLAYES   4.11.3
  WHICH INWARD SUNNE TO $HEROICKE MINDE DISPLAIES   4.25.8
  SILENCE IN BOTH DISPLAIES HIS SULLEN MIGHT   4.96.5
DISPLEASE   1
  THEN BE THEY CLOSE, AND SO NONE SHALL DISPLEASE   4.34.8
DISPLEASED   1
  BE NOT DISPLEASD THAT THESE MY PAPERS SHOULD   1.44.1
DISPLEASURE   1
  LOE WHERE SHE DROWNES, IN STORMES OF THY
                      DISPLEASURE   2.134.13
DISPOSED   1
  WHEN THOU SHALT BE DISPODE TO SET ME LIGHT   3.88.1

```
DISPOSSESS                    1
  WAS NOT TO DISPOSSESSE HER OF HER RIGHT         1.36.10
DISPRAISE                     2
  CANNOT DISPRAISE, BUT IN A KINDE OF PRAISE       3.95.7
  WITH SWORD OF WIT, GIVING WOUNDS OF DISPRAISE    4.10.10
DISPROVE                      1
  BUT $VERTUE THUS THAT TITLE DOTH DISPROVE        4.52.5
DISSOLVED                     1
  IS NOT DISSOLV'D THROUGH MY SO HOT DESYRE        5.30.3
DISSOLVES                     1
  DISSOLVES THE BEAUTY OF THE FAIREST BROW         1.39.12
DISSUADE                      1
  DISWADE ONE FOOLISH HEART FROM SERVING THEE      3.141.10
DISTANCE                      1
  INJURIOUS DISTANCE SHOULD NOT STOP MY WAY        3.44.2
DISTANT                       1
  THOUGH EITHER DISTANT, PRESENT YET TO EITHER     2.11.6
DISTEMPERATURE                1
  UNKINDLY, SUCH DISTEMPRATURE DOTH BRING          2.147.10
DISTEMPERED                   1
  AND THETHER HIED A SAD DISTEMPERD GUEST          3.153.12
DISTILLATION                  1
  THEN WERE NOT SUMMERS DISTILLATION LEFT          3.5.9
DISTILLED                     3
  BUT FLOWERS DISTIL'D THOUGH THEY WITH
                        WINTER MEETE               3.5.13
  IN THEE THY SUMMER ERE THOU BE DISTIL'D          3.6.2
  DISTIL'D FROM $LYMBECKS FOULE AS HELL WITHIN     3.119.2
DISTILLING                    1
  BUT PRECIOUS $TEARES DISTILLING FROM MINE $EYNE  2.7.6
DISTILLS                      4
  THESE TEARES, WHICH HEATE OF SACRED FLAME DISTILS 1.24.2
  GENTLY DISTILLS HIS $NECTAR-DROPPING SHOWRES     2.53.6
  GENTLY DISTILS HIS $NECTAR-DROPPING SHOWERS      2.113.6
  WHEN THAT SHALL VADE, BY VERSE DISTILS
                        YOUR TRUTH                 3.54.14
DISTRACTED                    2
  BUT STILL DISTRACTED IN $LOVES $LUNACIE          2.41.9
  BUT STILL DISTRACTED IN LOVES $LUNACY            2.143.9
DISTRACTEDLY                  1
  SO MUST YOUR PRAYSE DISTRACTEDLY BE TOLD         2.57.12
DISTRACTION                   2
  IN MOST DISTRACTION THEY KEEPE THAT IN $MINDE    2.9.8
  IN THE DISTRACTION OF THIS MADDING FEVER+        3.119.8
DISTRAUGHT                    1
  WITH $DIET AND $CORRECTION, $MEN DISTRAUGHT      2.9.13
DISTRESS                      3
  APPROACH NOT TO BEHOLD SO GREAT DISTRESSE        1.3.6
  TO GOE FROM SORROW, AND THINE OWNE DISTRESSE+    1.52.2
  AND THUS (POORE $ORPHAN) LYING IN DISTRESSE      2.116.17
DISTRESSED                    2
  LIKE AS THE SPOTLESSE $ERMELIN DISTREST          1.29.1
  A BURDEN TO MY SELFE, DISTREST IN MINDE          1.49.2
DITCH                         1
  LOOKES TO THE SKIES, AND IN A DITCH DOTH FALL+   4.19.11
DITTIES                       1
  WHEN IN HER NECKE YOU DID $LOVE DITTIES PEEPE    4.83.6
DIVERS                        1
  AND WARNES THE $EARTH WITH DIVERS COLORD FLOWRE  5.4.11
```

DIVERSELY   1
  DISGUYSING DIVERSLY MY TROUBLED WITS   5.54.4
DIVERT   1
  DIVERT STRONG MINDES TO TH'COURSE OF ALTRING
                              THINGS   3.115.8
DIVIDE   2
  HOW TO DEVIDE THE CONQUEST OF THY SIGHT   3.46.2
  BUT WHEN IT ONCE DOTH BURNE, IT DOTH DIVIDE   5.6.7
DIVIDED   2
  DIVIDED FROM THE WORLD, AS BETTER WORTH   1.53.11
  EVEN FOR THIS, LET US DEVIDED LIVE   3.39.5
DIVIDING   2
  AND THUS DIVIDING OF MY FATALL $HOURES   2.3.5
  AND THUS DEVIDING OF MY FATALL HOWRES   2.110.5
DIVINE   22
  OF EARTH ON EARTH A SUBSTANCE SO DIVINE   1.34.4
  THE $SOULE OF $MAN IMMORTALL AND DIVINE   2.12.2
  ONE NUMBER OF THE $EARTH, THE OTHER BOTH $DIVINE   2.18.3
  AND MY GOOD $ANGELL (IN MY $SOULE DIVINE)   2.18.11
  ONELY I CALL ON MY DIVINE $IDEA   2.39.14
  AND YET YOUR $GRACES OUTWARDLY $DIVINE   2.57.2
  BUT THY DIVINE PERFECTIONS BY THEIR SKILL   2.104.9
  HERE $CHASTITY THAT $VESTALL MOST DIVINE   2.105.9
  ON HEAVENLIE TOP OF THY DIVINE DESIRE   2.106.6
  ONE NUMBER OF THE EARTH, THE OTHER BOTH DIVINE   2.108.3
  AND MY GOOD $ANGELL IN MY SOULE DIVINE   2.108.11
  BUT EVER CALL UPON DIVINE $IDEA   2.118.14
  THAT MAN-GOD NOW OF WHOM THEY DYD DIVINE   2.119.5
  THAT LOVE DIVINE WHICH I HAVE BORNE TO YOU   2.139.10
  YET THOU A $GODDESSE ART, AND SO DIVINE   2.140.8
  THE PATIENCE OF SO RARE DIVINE A LOVE   2.149.14
  NOTHING SWEET BOY, BUT YET LIKE PRAYERS DIVINE   3.108.5
  BUY TEARMES DIVINE IN SELLING HOURES OF CROSSE   3.146.11
  WHILE WANTON WINDS WITH BEAUTIES SO DEVINE   4.103.6
  THING SO DIVINE TO VEW OF EARTHLY EYE   5.45.6
  GREAT SHAME IT IS, THING SO DIVINE IN VIEW   5.53.9
  TO BE DIVINE AND BORNE OF HEAVENLY SEED   5.79.10
DIVINELY   1
  FOR BEING AS SHE IS DIVINELY WROUGHT   5.61.5
DIVING   1
  WHILES DIVING DEEPE THROUGH AMOROUS INSIGHT   5.76.7
DIVINING   2
  AND SHEE ON HER OWNE DESTINY DIVINING   2.109.11
  AND FOR THEY LOOK'D BUT WITH DEVINING EYES   3.106.11
DIVINITY   4
  MY SOULE HAD NE'R FELT THY $DIVINITIE   2.104.7
  WHEN I DOE SPEAKE OF THY DIVINITIE   2.112.2
  WONDER OF $HEAVEN, GLASSE OF DIVINITIE   2.123.1
  THE LIVELY $IMAGE OF $DIVINITIE   2.146.14
DO   39
  YET THOUGH I SEE, THAT NOUGHT WE DOE, CAN MOVE   1.8.13
  WHAT SHOULD HER VERTUES DO, HER SMILES,
                              HER LOVE+   1.17.10
  WHAT CAN I DO BUT YEELD+ AND YEELD I DOO   1.28.13
  POORE SOULE QUITE SPENT, WHOSE FORCE CAN
                              DO NO MORE   1.46.3
  WHAT SHOULD I DO THEN, IF I SHOULD OBTAINE+   1.48.14
  NOR $LOVE, NOR $HATE, HOW THEN+ WHAT WILL
                              $YOU DOE+   2.19.6
  AND DIFF'RETH IT, AS DOE THE SEV'RALL $NATIONS+   2.27.2

WHAT SHOULD I SAY+ WHAT YET REMAINES TO DOE+	2.41.5
DOE WHAT I COULD, IT NEEDSLY WOULD ASPIRE	2.56.11
NOT TO AVAILE YOU, NOR DOE OTHERS GOOD	2.58.14
DOE WHAT THOU CANST, RAZE, MASSACRE, AND BURNE	2.63.11
DOE WHAT I COULD MY $EAGLETS WOULD ASPIRE	2.103.11
THEN WHAT COULD DEATH DOE IF THOU SHOULD'ST DEPART	3.6.11
AND DO WHAT ERE THOU WILT SWIFT-FOOTED TIME	3.19.6
YET DOE THY WORST OULD $TIME DISPIGHT THY WRONG	3.19.13
LEAST MY BEWAILED GUILT SHOULD DO THEE SHAME	3.36.10
BUT DOE NOT SO, I LOVE THEE IN SUCH SORT	3.36.13
TO SEE HIS ACTIVE CHILDE DO DEEDS OF YOUTH	3.37.2
DIE TO THEMSELVES. $SWEET $ROSES DOE NOT SO	3.54.11
BEING YOUR SLAVE WHAT SHOULD I DOE BUT TEND	3.57.1
NOR SERVICES TO DOE TIL YOU REQUIRE	3.57.4
(THOUGH YOU DOE ANY THING) HE THINKES NO ILL	3.57.14
TO DOE MORE FOR ME THEN MINE OWNE DESERT	3.72.6
THE INJURIES THAT TO MY SELFE I DOE	3.88.11
LEAST I (TOO MUCH PROPHANE) SHOULD DO IT WRONG	3.89.11
BUT DO THY WORST TO STEALE THY SELFE AWAY	3.92.1
THEY THAT HAVE POWRE TO HURT, AND WILL DOE NONE	3.94.1
THAT DOE NOT DO THE THING, THEY MOST DO SHOWE	3.94.2
BUT DOE NOT SO, I LOVE THEE IN SUCH SORT	3.94.5
THEN DO THY OFFICE $MUSE, I TEACH THEE HOW	3.101.13
YET DO NOT SO, BUT SINCE I AM NEERE SLAINE	3.139.13
EITHER TO DO LIKE HIM, WHICH OPEN SHONE	4.22.10
I WILL GOOD TRIBUTE PAY IF THOU DO SO	4.39.8
HER EYES, HER LIPS, HER ALL, SAITH $LOVE DO THIS	4.52.3
PROFESSE IN DEED I DO NOT $CUPID'S ART	4.54.10
THEN SOME GOOD BODY TELL ME HOW I DO	4.60.12
NOR DO LIKE $LORDS, WHOSE WEAKE CONFUSED BRAINE	4.85.5
GREAT WRONG I DOE, I CAN IT NOT DENY	5.33.1
AND DOE ME NOT BEFORE MY TIME TO DY	5.42.14

DOCTOR   1

O $DOCTOR $CUPID, THOU FOR ME REPLY	4.61.12

DOCTOR-LIKE   1

AND $FOLLY ($DOCTOR-LIKE) CONTROULING SKILL	3.66.10

DOFF   1

SHALL DOFFE HER FLESHES BOROWD FAYRE ATTYRE	5.27.6

DOG   2

DEARE, WHY MAKE YOU MORE OF A DOG THEN ME+	4.59.1
IF HE BE FAIRE, YET BUT A DOG CAN BE	4.59.4

DOING   5

DOING THEE VANTAGE, DUBLE VANTAGE ME	3.88.12
DULLING MY LINES, AND DOING ME DISGRACE	3.103.8
WITH DOING ALL, LEAVE NOTHING DONE BUT PAINE	4.85.8
WHICH HOLD MY LIFE IN THEIR DEAD DOING MIGHT	5.1.2
CHOSE RATHER TO BE PRAYSD FOR DOOING GOOD	5.38.13

DOLEFUL   4

MY $LIVES COMPLAINT IN DOLEFULL $ELEGIES	2.54.7
MY LIVES COMPLAINT IN DOLEFUL $ELEGIES	2.101.7
MY DOLEFULL $DYPTHONGS WERE MY LIVES DISPAIRES	2.111.11
THE DOLEFULL $ANTHEMS OF MY ENDLESSE CARE	2.141.6

DOLPHIN   2

ALLUR'D A $DOLPHIN HIM FROM DEATH TO EASE	5.38.4
NOR MOVE THE $DOLPHIN FROM HER STUBBORNE WILL	5.38.8

DOLT   1

WHO DOTED ON THE $DOLT BEYOND ALL MEASURE	2.21.10

DONE   21

READE IT (SWEET MAIDE) THOUGH IT BE DONE BUT SLEIGHTLY	1.1.13

```
YOU BEST CAN JUDGE THE WRONGS THAT SHE HATH CONE        1.3.12
THAT SHE HATH DONE, THE MOTIVE OF MY PAINE              1.3.13
ONCE LET HER KNOW, SH'HATH DONE ENOUGH
                              TO PROVE ME               1.10.13
IF I HAVE DONE DUE HOMAGE TO HER EYES                   1.15.9
WILL RISE NO MORE TO ME, WHOSE DAY IS DUNNE             1.30.4
YET THEE I BLAME NCT, THOUGH FOR THEE TIS DONE          1.32.5
NOW JOY THY TIME BEFORE THY SWEET BE DONE               1.40.7
NOR WHILST THE $WORLD IS, NEVER SHALL BE DONE           2.13.11
NAY, I HAVE DONE.. $YOU GET NO MORE OF $ME              2.61.2
MY CONSONANTS THE NEXT WHEN I HAD DONE                  2.111.7
NOR WHILST THE WORLD IS, NEVER SHALL BE DONE            2.121.11
WHICH SCORNE THE HONOR THAT IS DONE TO THEE             2.123.10
OR IF A WORLD OF FAITHFULL SERVICE DONE                 2.138.5
NOW SEE WHAT GOOD-TURNES EYES FOR EIES HAVE DONE        3.24.9
NO MORE BEE GREEV'D AT THAT WHICH THOU HAST DONE        3.35.1
SINCE MINDE AT FIRST IN CARRECTER WAS DONE              3.59.8
WHEN OTHER PETTIE GRIEFES HAVE DONE THEIR SPIGHT        3.90.10
NOW ALL IS DONE, HAVE WHAT SHALL HAVE NO END            3.110.9
WITH DOING ALL, LEAVE NOTHING DONE BUT PAINE            4.85.8
HAD SHE NOT SO DOCN, SURE I HAD BENE SLAYNE             5.16.13
DOOM                        9
BY DOOME CONCEALED TO THE HEAVENS ABOVE                 2.139.11
THY END IS $TRUTHES AND $BEAUTIES DOOME AND DATE        3.14.14
THAT WEARE THIS WORLD OUT TO THE ENDING CCOME           3.55.12
SUPPOSDE AS FORFEIT TO A CONFIN'D DOOME                 3.107.4
BUT BEARES IT OUT EVEN TO THE EDGE OF DOCME             3.116.12
WAS USDE IN GIVING GENTLE DOME                          3.145.7
BY $PHOEBUS' DOOME, WITH SUGRED SENTENCE SAYES          4.25.2
THEY DEEME, AND OF THEIR DOOME THE RUMOUR FLIES         4.27.5
NO DOOME SHOULD MAKE ONE'S HEAV'N BECOME
                              HIS HELL                   4.86.14
DOOR                        1
THE DOORE BY WHICH SOMETIMES COMES FORTH
                              HER $GRACE                 4.9.5
DOORS                       2
THOSE DAINTIE DORES UNTO THE $COURT OF BLISSE           4.44.11
WHOM IRON DOORES DO KEEPE FROM USE OF DAY+              4.108.11
DORUS                       1
WHEN $DORUS SINGS HIS SWEET $PAMELAS LOVE               2.151.10
DOST                        2
THOU BLINDE FOOLE LOVE, WHAT DOOST THOU
                              TO MINE EYES               3.137.1
HART RENT THY SELFE, THOU DOEST THY SELFE
                              BUT RIGHT                  4.33.5
DOTE                        2
WHO IN DISPIGHT OF VIEW IS PLEASD TO DOTE               3.141.4
IF THAT BE FAIRE WHEREON MY FALSE EYES DOTE             3.148.5
DOTED                       1
WHO DOTED ON THE $DOLT BEYOND ALL MEASURE               2.21.10
DOTH                        4
SHE DOTH ME WRONG, TO GRIEVE SO TRUE A HEART            1.21.14
THAT $GRACE WHICH DOTH MORE THEN IN WOMAN THEE          1.45.13
DOTH HOMAGE TO HIS NEW APPEARING SIGHT                  3.7.3
AND EACH DOTH GOOD TURNES NOW UNTO THE OTHER            3.47.2
DOTING                      2
TILL NATURE AS SHE WROUGHT THEE FELL A DOTINGE          3.20.10
FOR WELL THOU KNOW'ST TO MY DEARE DOTING HART           3.131.3
DOUBLE                      5
AND GIVEN GRACE A DOUBLE $MAJESTIE                      3.78.8
```

```
DOING THEE VANTAGE, DUBLE VANTAGE ME                 3.88.12
NOR DOUBLE PENNANCE TO CORRECT CORRECTION            3.111.12
A DOUBLE KEY, WHICH OPENS TO THE HEART               4.79.6
LONG LANGUISHING IN DOUBLE MALADY                    5.50.1
DOUBLED          1
WHAT $CAPES HE DOUBLED, CF WHAT $CONTINENT           2.1.9
DOUBT            4
YET THIS SHAL I NERE KNCW BUT LIVE IN DOUBT          3.144.13
THUS WRITE I WHILE I DOUBT TO WRITE, AND WREAKE      4.34.12
DOUBT THERE HATH BENE, WHEN WITH HIS GOLDEN
                              CHAINE                 4.58.1
THE DOUBT WHICH YE MISDEEME, FAYRE LOVE, IS VAINE    5.65.1
DOUBTFULLY       1
TWIXT FEARE AND HOPE DEPENDING DOUBTFULLY+           5.25.4
DOUBTING         4
DOUBTING, IF THAT PROUD $TYRANT SHOULD PREVAYLE      2.29.3
DOUBTING THE FILCHING AGE WILL STEALE
                              HIS TREASURE           3.75.6
CROWNING THE PRESENT, DOUBTING OF THE REST           3.115.12
LOATHING ALL LIES, DOUBTING THIS $FLATTERIE IS       4.80.11
DOUBTS           2
THEN SERVANT'S WRACKE, WHERE NEW DOUBTS
                              HONOR BRINGS           4.45.11
THAT FULL OF DOUBTS, THCU OF PERPLEXITY              4.96.7
DOVE             5
THE $PEAKE HER $DCVE, WHCSE $BANKES SO FERTILE BE    2.32.7
THE $PEAKE HER $DCVE, WHCSE BANCKS SO
                              FERTILL BEE            2.124.7
THE $CROE, OR $DOVE, IT SHAPES THEM TO
                              YOUR FEATURE           3.113.12
AS MY YOUNG $DOVE MAY IN YOUR PRECEPTS WISE          4.63.3
SEEK WITH MY PLAYNTS TO MATCH THAT MOURNFUL COVE     5.89.8
DOVES            1
WHICH, COUPLING $DCVES, GUIDES $VENUS'
                              CHARIOT RIGHT          4.79.4
DOWDY            1
THAT EV'RY $DOWDY, EV'RY $TRULL DOTH WEARE+          2.31.12
DOWN             27
LIE DOWNE TO WAILE, RISE UP TO SIGH AND GRIEVE       1.9.6
ALL MY POORE LIFE BY THEM IS TRODEN DOWNE            1.28.6
AND THREW ME DOWNE TO PAINE IN ALL THIS FIRE         1.36.5
AND HOW I LIVE CAST DOWNE FROM OFF ALL MYRTH         1.60.9
LAYES DOWNE HIS $QUIVER, WHICH HE ONCE DID BEARE     2.4.6
BEFORE MY $FACE, IT LAYES DOWNE MY $DESPAIRES        2.20.9
A SECOND $FLOUD, DCWNE RAYNING FROM MINE $EYES       2.55.4
A SECOND FLOOD DOWNE RAYNING FRUM MINE EYES          2.102.4
DOWNE FELL HE IN THY $BEAUTIES $OCEAN DRENCHED       2.122.13
MY EYES MADE DIM WITH LCCKES, POURE DOWN
                              A FLOUD OF TEARS       2.133.10
SINKES DOWNE TO DEATH, CPPREST WITH MELANCHOLIE      3.45.8
WHEN SOMETIME LOFTIE TOWERS I SEE DOWNE RASED        3.64.3
UPON THY PART I CAN SET DOWNE A STORY                3.88.6
BOOKE BOTH MY WILFULNESSE AND ERRORS DOWNE           3.117.9
SETS DOWNE HER BABE AND MAKES ALL SWIFT CISPATCH     3.143.3
THEN DID ON HIM WHC FIRST STALE DOWNE THE FIRE       4.14.3
YET STILL ON ME, C EYES, DART DOWNE YOUR RAYES       4.42.11
THAT HEAV'N OF JOYES THROWES ONELY DOWNE ON ME       4.60.3
PRAY THAT MY SUNNE GO DCWNE WITH MEEKER
                              BEAMES TO BED          4.76.14
AS THY LOOKES STURRE, RUNS UP AND DOWNE TO MAKE      4.101.10
```

```
     MELTS DOWNE HIS LEAD INTO MY BOYLING BREST        4.108.2
     AND MAKES ME THEN BOW DOWNE MY HEAD, AND SAY      4.108.9
     TREADING DOWNE EARTH AS LOTHSOME AND FORLORNE     5.13.11
     AND IF THOSE FAYLE FALL DOWNE AND DY BEFORE HER   5.14.13
     AND TREAD MY LIFE DOWNE IN THE LOWLY FLOURE       5.20.4
     SITS DOWNE TO REST HIM IN SOME SHADY PLACE        5.67.3
     IT DOWN IS WEIGHD WITH THOGHT OF EARTHLY THINGS   5.72.3
DOWNCAST               1
     NO DOWNE-CAST LOOKE HAD SIGNIFIED MY MISSE        1.7.10
DOWNRIGHT              1
     TILL DOWNE-RIGHT BLOWES DID FOYLE THY
                         CUNNING FENCE                 4.10.11
DOWNWARD               1
     WITH DOWNEWARD LOCKES, STILL READING ON THE EARTH  1.9.3
DRAINED                1
     WHEN HOURES HAVE DREIND HIS BLOOD AND
                         FILD HIS BROW                 3.63.3
DRANK                  1
     I NEVER DRANKE OF $AGANIPPE WELL                  4.74.1
DRAW                   9
     IF THIS BE LOVE, TO DRAW A WEARIE BREATH          1.9.1
     THEN DOE I LOVE AND DRAW THIS WEARIE BREATH       1.9.14
     THEN DOE I LOVE, AND DRAW THIS WEARIE BREATH      1.10.1
     MY CARES DRAW ON MINE EVERLASTING NIGHT           1.30.1
     AND WILL WHILST I SHALL DRAW THIS BREATH OF MINE  1.33.10
     NOR DRAW NOE LINES THERE WITH THINE ANTIQUE PEN   3.19.10
     THEY DRAW BUT WHAT THEY SEE, KNOW NOT THE HART    3.24.14
     BUT DAY DOTH DAILY DRAW MY SORROWES LONGER        3.28.13
     WHICH $CUPID'S SELFE FROM $BEAUTIE'S MYNE
                         DID DRAW                      4.9.13
DRAWN                  9
     DRAWNE WITH MY BLOOD, AND PAINTED WITH MY CARES   1.47.3
     DRAWNE WITH TH'ATRACTIVE VERTUE OF HER EYES       1.53.1
     MY $TASTE BY HER SWEET $LIPS DRAWNE WITH $DELIGHT 2.29.7
     AND YOU MUST LIVE DRAWNE BY YOUR OWNE
                         SWEET SKILL                   3.16.14
     MINE EYES HAVE DRAWNE THY SHAPE, AND THINE
                         FOR ME                        3.24.10
     DRAWNE AFTER YOU, YOU PATTERNE OF ALL THOSE       3.98.12
     ALAS, IF $FANCY DRAWNE BY IMAG'D THINGS           4.45.9
     I JOY TO SEE HOW IN YOUR DRAWEN WORK              5.71.1
     DRAWNE WITH SWEET PLEASURES BAYT, IT BACK
                         DOTH FLY                      5.72.7
DRAWS                  4
     YET $HOPE DRAWES ON MY NEVER-HOPING $CARE         2.26.2
     YET HOPE DRAWES ON MY NEVER-HOPING CARE           2.137.2
     SO WHILE THY BEAUTIE DRAWES THE HEART TO LOVE     4.71.12
     HER SMILE ME DRAWES, HER FROWNE ME DRIVES AWAY    5.21.12
DREAD                  4
     UNCERTAINE $DREAD GIVES $WINGS UNTO MY $HOPE      2.26.5
     TO THAT MOST SACRED $EMPRESSE MY DEAR DRED        5.33.2
     IN DREAD OF DEATH AND DAUNGEROUS DISMAY           5.63.3
     WITHOUT CONSTRAYNT OR DREAD OF ANY ILL            5.65.6
DREADFUL               4
     A DREADFULL COUNTENAUNCE SHE GIVEN HATH           5.31.6
     THE DREADFULL TEMPEST OF HER WRATH APPEASE        5.38.7
     THAT WHEN A DREADFULL STORME AWAY IS FLIT         5.40.7
     WITHIN A BUSH HIS DREADFULL HEAD DOTH HIDE        5.53.3
DREADING               1
     THAT LEAVES LOOKE PALE, DREADING THE $WINTERS
                         NEERE                         3.97.14
```

DREAM   3
  THUS HAVE I HAD THEE AS A DREAME DOTH FLATTER   3.87.13
  BEFORE A JOY PROPOSD BEHIND A DREAME   3.129.12
  WAS IT A DREAME, CR DID I SEE IT PLAYNE   5.77.1
DREAMING   1
  OF THE WIDE WORLD, DREAMING ON THINGS TO COME   3.107.2
DREAMS   3
  CEASE DREAMES, TH'$IMAGES OF DAY DESIRES   1.54.9
  BUT WHEN I SLEEPE, IN DREAMES THEY LOOKE ON THEE   3.43.3
  AND NIGHTS BRIGHT DAIES WHEN DREAMS DO
                              SHEW THEE ME   3.43.14
DREARY   4
  THE DRERIE ABSTRACTS OF MY ENDLESSE $CARES   2.54.2
  THE DRERY ABSTRACTS OF MY ENDLES CARES   2.101.2
  THE $INNE OF CARE, THE $NURSE OF DRERY SORROW   2.145.2
  BUT SUDDEN DUMPS AND DRERY SAD DISDAYNE   5.52.11
DREGS   1
  SO THEN THOU HAST BUT LOST THE DREGS OF LIFE   3.74.9
DRENCHED   1
  DOWNE FELL HE IN THY $BEAUTIES $OCEAN DRENCHED   2.122.13
DRESS   1
  ROBBING NO OULD TO DRESSE HIS BEAUTY NEW   3.68.12
DRESSED   2
  THINK'ST THOU MY $LOVE SHALL IN THOSE
                            $RAGGES BE DREST   2.31.11
  WHEN PROUD PIDE $APRILL (DREST IN ALL HIS TRIM)   3.98.2
DRESSES   1
  AND WITH SLY SKILL SO CUNNINGLY THEM DRESSES   5.37.3
DRESSING   1
  SO ALL MY BEST IS DRESSING OLD WORDS NEW   3.76.11
DRESSINGS   1
  THEY ARE BUT DRESSINGS CF A FORMER SIGHT   3.123.4
DREW   1
  PHOEBUS DREW WIDE THE CURTAINES OF THE SKIES   4.13.12
DRIBBED   1
  NOT AT FIRST SIGHT, NOR WITH A DRIBBED SHOT   4.2.1
DRIED   4
  SAY HER DISDAINE HATH DRYED UP MY BLOOD   1.2.9
  THE POWDER OF HER $HEART DRY'D, WHEN SHE IS DEAD   2.15.3
  WHOSE $GRIEFE HATH PARCH'D THY $BODY,
                            DRY'D THY $BLOOD   2.49.8
  THE DUREFULL $OAKE, WHOSE SAP IS NOT YET DRICE   5.6.5
DRIES   1
  QUENCHLES DESIRE, MAKES HOPE BURNE, DRYES
                              MY TEARES   2.132.5
DRIFT   1
  I SEE $YOUR CRAFT, NOW I PERCEIVE $YOUR DRIFT   2.19.11
DRINK   5
  NO OTHER $DRINKE WOULD SERVE THIS $GLUTTONS TURNE 2.7.5
  SALT LUKE-WARME TEARES SHEE FOR HIS DRINKE
                            DID GIVE   2.116.15
  WHILST LIKE A WILLING PACIENT I WILL DRINKE   3.111.9
  DRINKE UP THE MONARKS PLAGUE THIS FLATTERY+   3.114.2
  AND THROUGH THOSE LIPS DRINKE $NECTAR
                            FROM THAT TOONG   4.83.13
DRINKS   1
  AND MY GREAT MINDE MOST KINGLY DRINKES IT UP   3.114.10
DRIVE   3
  AND WHEN BY $MEANES, TO DRIVE IT OUT I TRY   2.20.6
  WOULD FAINE DRIVE CLOUDES FROM OUT MY
                            HEAVY CHEERE   4.97.11

```
        CURST BE THE $COCHMAN WHICH DID DRIVE SO FAST      4.105.13
DRIVEN                      1
        DRIV'N ELSE TO GRAUNT BY $ANGEL'S SOPHISTRIE       4.61.13
DRIVES                      3
        WHERE BEAT THESE TEARES WITH ZEALE, AND
                                FURY DRIVES               1.48.10
        HER SMILE ME DRAWES, HER FROWNE ME DRIVES AWAY     5.21.12
        HER GOODLY LIGHT WITH SMILES SHE DRIVES AWAY       5.81.8
DRIZZLING                   1
        AND DRIZLING DROPS THAT OFTEN DOE REDOUND          5.18.3
DROOPING                    2
        AND KEEPE MY DROOPING EYE-LIDS OPEN WIDE           3.27.7
        AND TO THE LIGHT LIFT UP THEYR DROJPING HED        5.40.12
DROP                        1
        AND DOE NOT DROP IN FOR AN AFTER LOSSE             3.90.4
DROPPING                    1
        YET CANNOT I WITH MANY A DROPPING TEARE            5.18.5
DROPS                       6
        UPON YOUR $LIPS THE SCARLET DROPS ARE FOUND        2.2.10
        BUT WITH THOSE $DROPS, THE $FLAME AGAINE
                                REVIVING                  2.40.11
        THE WATER, TO MY TEARES, AS DROPS TO $OCEANS BE    2.127.6
        BUT WITH THOSE DROPS THE COLES AGAINE REVYVING     2.144.11
        NOW WITH THE DROPS CF THIS MOST BALMIE TIME        3.107.9
        AND DRIZLING DROPS THAT OFTEN DOE REDOUND          5.18.3
DROSS                       2
        BUY TEARMES DIVINE IN SELLING HOURES OF CROSSE     3.146.11
        SITH ALL WORLDS GLORIE IS BUT DROSSE UNCLEANE      5.27.2
DROSSY                      1
        THAT HINDERS HEAVENLY THOUGHTS WITH DROSSY SLIME   5.13.12
DROUGHT                     1
        BY $LOVE'S OWNE SELFE, BUT WITH SO CURIOUS
                                DROUGHT                   4.38.7
DROWN                       4
        MY HEATES MUST DROWNE IN TH'$OCEAN OF MY TEARES    1.32.12
        NOW TEMPTING $ME, TO DROWNE MY $SELFE IN TEARES    2.20.11
        THEN CAN I DROWNE AN EYE (UN-US'D TO FLOW)         3.30.5
        BEWARE FULL SAILES DROWNE NOT THY TOTTRING BARGE   4.85.2
DROWNED                     4
        DROWN'D IN THE $TEARES, EXTORTED BY MY $LINES      2.45.2
        BURN'D IN A $SEA CF YCE, AND DROWN'D AMIDST
                                A FIRE                    2.62.14
        FORGOT HERSELFE, AND THCUGHT SHE HAD BEEN
                                DROWNED                   2.109.4
        BURN'D IN A $SEA CF $ICE, AND DROWN'D
                                AMIDST A FIRE             2.150.14
DROWNING                    1
        THREW IN HERSELFE, TO SAVE HERSELFE BY DROWNING    2.109.12
DROWNS                      2
        LOE WHERE SHE DROWNES, IN STORMES OF THY
                                DISPLEASURE               2.134.13
        THAT IT NOR GROWES WITH HEAT, NOR DROWNES
                                WITH SHOWRES              3.124.12
DRUDGE                      2
        AND EV'RY $DRUDGE DOTH DULL OUR SATIATE $EARE      2.31.10
        HE IS CONTENTED THY POORE DRUDGE TO BE            3.151.11
DRUGS                       1
        DRUGS POYSON HIM THAT SO FELL SICKE OF YOU         3.118.14
DRUNK                       2
        WHAT POTIONS HAVE I DRUNKE OF $SYREN TEARES        3.119.1
```

```
    SHE OFT HATH DRUNKE MY TEARES, NOW HOPES TO ENJOY    4.70.3
DRUNKARD                    1
    WHAT 'TIS TO KEEPE A $DRUNKARD COMPANIE               2.7.14
DRUNKENNESS                 1
    AND AT THE $BANQUET, IN HIS $DRUNKENNESSE             2.7.11
DRY                         3
    MY $BRAINE IS DRIE WITH WEEPING ALL TOO LONG         2.41.6
    MY BRAYNE IS DRY WITH WEEPING ALL TOO LONG           2.143.6
    TO DRY THE RAINE CN MY STORME-BEATEN FACE            3.34.6
DUDGEON                     1
    THAT EV'RY $DUDGEN LOW $INVENTION GOES+              2.31.8
DUE                        17
    IF I HAVE DONE DUE HOMAGE TO HER EYES                1.15.9
    ARE THOSE DUE TRIBUTES THAT MY FAITH DOTH PAY        1.24.3
    WHOSE DUE REPORTS GIVE HCNOR TO HER EYES             1.57.8
    THESE TRIBUTARY PASSIONS, BEAUTIES DUE               1.60.5
    AND ALL IS $THINE WHICH HATH BEEN DUE TO $ME         2.3.13
    HAVING THE $JUDGEMENT DUE TO HIS $OFFENCE            2.50.3
    AND ALL IS THINE WHICH HATH BEEN DUE TO MEE         2.110.13
    TO EATE THE WORLDS DUE, BY THE GRAVE AND THEE        3.1.14
    THAT DUE OF MANY, NCW IS THINE ALONE                3.31.12
    THAT DUE TO THEE WHICH THOU DESERV'ST ALCNE          3.39.8
    AS THUS, MINE EYES CUE IS THEIR OUTWARD PART        3.46.13
    THE EARTH CAN HAVE BUT EARTH, WHICH IS HIS DUE       3.74.7
    BUT GIVE APT SERVANTS THEIR DUE PLACE, LET EYES      4.85.9
    SO WHEN MY TOUNG WCULD SPEAK HER PRAISES CEW         5.3.9
    SHALL BE BY HIM AMEARST WITH PENANCE DEW            5.70.12
    FROM MOTHERS WOMB CERIV'D BY DEW DESCENT             5.74.6
    DEW TO THY SELFE THAT IT FOR ME PREPARD             5.86.14
DULL                       11
    (YET HIS DULL $SPIRIT HER NOT ONE JOT COULD MOVE)    2.21.2
    AND EV'RY $DRUDGE DCTH DULL OUR SATIATE $EARE       2.31.10
    AND SAY'ST, MY $LINES BE DULL, AND DOE NCT MCVE      2.49.2
    IF THE DULL SUBSTANCE OF MY FLESH WERE THOUGHT       3.44.1
    OF MY DULL BEARER, WHEN FROM THEE I SPEEC            3.51.2
    SHALL NAIGH NOE DULL FLESH IN HIS FIERY RACE        3.51.11
    OR IF THEY SING, TIS WITH SO DULL A CHEERE          3.97.13
    BECAUSE I WOULD NCT DULL YOU WITH MY SONGE         3.102.14
    WHILE HE INSULTS CRE DULL AND SPEACHLESSE
                              TRIBES                    3.107.12
    THE CURIOUS WITS, SEEING DULL PENSIVENESSE           4.23.1
    SO DULL AM, THAT I CANNCT LOOKE INTO                4.60.10
DULLING                     1
    DULLING MY LINES, AND DCING ME DISGRACE             3.103.8
DULLNESS                    1
    THE SPIRIT OF $LOVE, WITH A PERPETUAL DULNESSE       3.56.8
DULY                        4
    TH'$UCEAN NEVER DID ATTEND MORE DULY                1.48.5
    DUELY TO COUNT THE SUMME OF ALL MY CARES             2.3.2
    SHE'ST QUENCH HER THIRST AS DULY AS THEY FALL      2.115.10
    PLUDS DULY ON, TO BEARE THAT WAIGHT IN ME            3.50.6
DUMB                       13
    TOLDE THE DUMBE MESSAGE CF MY HIDDEN GRIEFE          1.8.6
    AND THAT MAKES HAPPY $LCVERS EVER DOMBE             1.17.14
    WHOSE BEAUTY MADE HIM SPEAKE THAT ELSE WAS DCMBE     1.55.8
    CUPID, DUMBE $IDOLL, PEEVISH $SAINT OF LCVE         2.126.1
    AND DOMB PRESAGERS CF MY SPEAKING BREST             3.23.10
    FOR WHO'S SO DUMBE THAT CANNOT WRITE TO THEE         3.38.7
    THINE EYES, THAT TAUGHT THE DUMBE ON HIGH TO SING    3.78.5
    WHICH SHALL BE MOST MY GLORY BEING DOMBE            3.83.10
```

ME FOR MY DOMBE THOUGHTS, SPEAKING IN EFFECT   3.85.14
BECAUSE HE NEEDS NO PRAISE, WILT THOU BE DUMB+   3.101.9
DUMBE $SWANNES, NOT CHATRING $PIES, DO
                            $LOVERS PROVE   4.54.13
NOW WITH SLOW WORDS, NOW WITH DUMBE ELOQUENCE   4.61.2
TEACHING DUMBE LIPS A NOBLER EXERCISE   4.81.4
DUMB-BORN   2
A DUMBE-BORNE $MUSE MADE TO EXPRESSE THE $MIND   2.35.6
A DUMBE-BORNE $MUSE MADE TO EXPRESSE THE MIND   2.112.6
DUMPISH   1
BIDS ALL OLD THOUGHTS TO DIE IN DUMPISH SPRIGHT   5.4.4
DUMPS   1
BUT SUDDEN DUMPS AND DRERY SAD DISDAYNE   5.52.11
DUN   1
IF SNOW BE WHITE, WHY THEN HER BRESTS ARE DUN   3.130.3
DUNG-BRED   1
I SCORNE ALL $EARTHLY $DUNG-BRED $SCARABIES   2.31.14
DUNGEON   1
OF COMFORT DARE COME TO THIS DUNGEON DARKE   4.104.7
DUREFUL   1
THE DUREFULL $OAKE, WHOSE SAP IS NOT YET DRIDE   5.6.5
DURST   2
OR DURST INHABIT ON A LIVING BROW   3.68.4
BUT ONLY FOR THIS WORTHY KNIGHT DURST PROVE   4.75.13
DUST   7
THE $DIAMOND SHALL ONCE CONSUME TO $DUST   2.13.3
THE $DIAMOND SHALL ONCE CONSUME TO DUST   2.121.3
WHEN THAT CHURLE DEATH MY BONES WITH DUST
                            SHALL COVER   3.32.2
WAIGHES NOT THE DUST AND INJURY OF AGE   3.108.10
COUNTING BUT DUST WHAT IN THE WAY DID LIE   4.105.8
BY WHOM MY SPIRIT OUT OF DUST WAS RAYSED   5.74.10
TO DY IN DUST, BUT YOU SHALL LIVE BY FAME   5.75.10
DUSTY   2
THOUGH DUSTIE WITS DARE SCORNE $ASTROLOGIE   4.26.1
TIRED WITH THE DUSTY TOILES OF BUSIE DAY   4.89.7
DUTCH   2
WE AND THE $DUTCH AT LENGTH OUR $SELVES TO SEVER   2.51.9
WHAT NOW THE $DUTCH IN THEIR FULL DIETS BOAST   4.30.6
DUTEOUS   1
THE EYES (FORE DUTICUS) NOW CONVERTED ARE   3.7.11
DUTY   8
RETURNING THEE THE TRIBUTE OF MY DUTIE   1.1.3
TILL THOU ALONE TO PAY THE HEAVENS THEIR DUTIE   2.105.5
THY MERRIT HATH MY DUTIE STRONGLY KNIT   3.26.2
TO WITNESSE DUTY, NOT TO SHEW MY WIT   3.26.4
DUTY SO GREAT, WHICH WIT SO POORE AS MINE   3.26.5
MY $MUSE AND I MUST YOU OF DUTIE GREET   4.84.7
BY IRON LAWES OF DUTY TO DEPART   4.87.4
DARE NOT HENCEFORTH ABOVE THE BOUNDS OF DEWTIE   5.61.3
DWELL   14
AND ASKE A $WORLD UPON MY $LIFE TO DWELL   2.60.4
SOME OLD $PERNASSUS, WHERE THE $MUSES DWELL   2.120.11
IT IS THY HEAVEN WITHIN HER FACE TO DWELL   2.123.13
AND ASKE A WORLD UPON MY LIFE TO DWELL   2.149.4
THE LOVELY GAZE WHERE EVERY EYE DOTH DWELL   3.5.2
YOU LIVE IN THIS, AND DWELL IN LOVERS EIES   3.55.14
FROM THIS VILE WORLD WITH VILDEST WORMES TO DWELL   3.71.4
LEANE PENURIE WITHIN THAT $PEN DOTH DWELL   3.84.5
THY SWEET BELOVED NAME NO MORE SHALL DWELL   3.89.10

```
   THAT IN THY FACE SWEET LOVE SHOULD EVER DWELL       3.93.10
   TOWARDES $AURORA'S $COURT A $NYMPH DOTH DWELL        4.37.5
   AND $MUSES SCORNE WITH VULGAR BRAINES TO DWELL       4.74.3
   THEN THOSE BLEST EYES, WHERE ALL MY HOPES
                            DO DWELL                    4.86.13
   THERE FAYTH DOTH FEARLESSE DWELL IN BRASEN TOWRE     5.65.13
DWELLERS              1
   HAVE I NOT SEENE DWELLERS ON FORME AND FAVOR         3.125.5
DWELLING              2
   SHE YEELDS NO PLACE AT ALL FOR PITTIES DWELLING      1.18.12
   THAT THOU MUST WANT OR FOOD, OR DWELLING PLACE       4.46.4
DWELLS                1
   WHICH ON THY SOFT CHEEKE FOR COMPLEXION DWELLS+      3.99.4
DYED                  3
   WITH HEAVENLY COLOURS DIDE, WITH NATURES
                          WONDER CROUND                 2.106.4
   FOR THY NEGLECT OF TRUTH IN BEAUTY DI'D+             3.101.2
   WHERE $BEAUTIE'S BLUSH IN $HONOUR'S GRAINE
                          IS DIDE                       4.80.8
DYER'S                1
   TO WHAT IT WORKES IN, LIKE THE $DYERS HAND           3.111.7
DYES                  1
   HOW DOTH THE COLOUR VADE OF THOSE VERMILLION
                          DIES                          4.102.5
DYING                11
   ONELY BY DYING, BORNE THE VERY SAME                  2.16.12
   WHO THEN YET LIVING, DEEM'D SHE HAD BEEN DYING       2.109.6
   WHILST $LOVE (MY $PHOENIX BIRD) IN HER
                          OWN FLAME IS DYING            2.117.12
   MY DYING LOOKES AND THOUGHTS ARE PEIZ'D
                          IN EQUALL FEARES              2.133.12
   AND WITH THE $SWAN RECORD THY DYING SONG             2.139.7
   AND DEATH ONCE DEAD, THER'S NO MORE DYING THEN       3.146.14
   AND READE THE SORROWES OF MY DYING SPRIGHT           5.1.7
   SO DYING LIVE, AND LIVING DO ADORE HER               5.14.14
   HOW LONG SHALL THIS LYKE DYING LYFE ENDURE           5.25.1
   AND DYING DOE THEM SELVES OF PAYNE BEGUYLE           5.47.12
   THE PITEOUS PASSION OF HIS DYING SMART               5.48.12
EACH                 60
   EACH $BIRD SINGS TO HER SELFE, AND SO WILL I         1.59.14
   SENSELESSE WITH TOO MUCH $JOY, EACH OTHER SEEING     2.11.7
   WHICH CEASETH NOT TO TEMPT $ME TO EACH $ILL          2.20.3
   THIS TO EACH OTHER MUTUALLY THEY CRAVE               2.33.12
   AND EACH RETURNES UNTO HIS $LOVE AT $NIGHT+          2.37.8
   FIRST MAKE INCISION ON EACH MAST'RING $VEINE         2.50.6
   BY CURING ME, AND KILLING ME EACH $HOW'R             2.50.13
   WHEN $DARKNESSE HATH OBSCUR'D EACH OTHER $LIGHT      2.55.14
   WITH $PROVERBS THUS EACH OTHER INTERTAINE            2.59.2
   AND HAVING THUS AWHILE EACH OTHER THWARTED           2.59.13
   WHEN DARKNES HATH OBSCUR'D EACH OTHER LIGHT          2.102.14
   WHEREIN EACH FAYREST PART EXCELLETH OTHER            2.123.4
   SO $COMET-LIKE EACH STARRE ADVAUNC'D HER LYGHT       2.125.10
   THIS LOVE, TEARS, SIGHES, MAINTAINE EACH
                          ONE HIS ELEMENT               2.127.4
   AND WHILST MY HART AND EYE, ENVY EACH
                          OTHERS PRAISE                 2.133.11
   EACH ONE OF THESE, DOTH AYDE UNTO THE
                          OTHER LENDE                   2.133.14
   LIFTS UP HIS BURNING HEAD, EACH UNDER EYE            3.7.2
   STRIKES EACH IN EACH BY MUTUALL ORDERING             3.8.10
```

STRIKES EACH IN EACH BY MUTUALL ORDERING   3.8.10
POINTING TO EACH HIS THUNDER, RAINE AND WINDE   3.14.6
AND EACH (THOUGH ENIMES TO ETHERS RAIGNE)   3.28.5
BOTH FINDE EACH OTHER, AND I LOOSE BOTH TWAINE   3.42.11
AND EACH DOTH GOOD TURNES NOW UNTO THE OTHER   3.47.2
EACH TRIFLE UNDER TRUEST BARRES TO THRUST   3.48.2
AND PATIENCE TAME, TO SUFFERANCE BIDE EACH CHECK   3.58.7
EACH CHANGING PLACE WITH THAT WHICH GOES BEFORE   3.60.3
ALTHOUGH IN ME EACH PART WILL BE FORGOTTEN   3.81.4
I MUST EACH DAY SAY ORE THE VERY SAME   3.108.6
TIL EACH TO RAZ'D OBLIVION YEELD HIS PART   3.122.7
FOR SINCE EACH HAND HATH PUT ON $NATURES POWER   3.127.5
BUT BEING BOTH FROM ME BOTH TO EACH FRIEND   3.144.11
OR WITH STRANGE SIMILIES ENRICH EACH LINE   4.3.7
PLAYING AND SHINING IN EACH OUTWARD PART   4.11.13
EACH HAD HIS CREAST, $MARS CARIED $VENUS' GLOVE   4.13.7
YET EACH PREPAR'D, WITH FANNE'S WEL-SHADING GRACE   4.22.7
WHILE HE EACH THING IN SENSE'S BALLANCE WAYES   4.25.6
EACH SOULE DOTH AT $LOVE'S FEET HIS WEAPONS LAY   4.43.7
WHILE EACH PRETENDS THAT $STELLA MUST BE HIS   4.52.2
NOR GIVE EACH SPEECH A FULL POINT OF A GRONE   4.54.4
EACH SENCE OF MINE, EACH GIFT, EACH POWER OF MIND   4.57.2
EACH SENCE OF MINE, EACH GIFT, EACH POWER OF MIND   4.57.2
EACH SENCE OF MINE, EACH GIFT, EACH POWER OF MIND   4.57.2
WHILE EACH DOTH BLOW THE FIER OF MY HART   4.72.4
PLEASINGST CONSORT, WHERE EACH SENCE HOLDS A PART   4.79.3
THE PRETTIE DEATH, WHILE EACH IN OTHER LIVE   4.79.11
NOT POINTING TO FIT FOLKES EACH UNDERCHARGE   4.85.6
UNITED POWERS MAKE EACH THE STRONGER PROVE   4.88.14
EACH DAY SEEMES LONG, AND LONGS FOR LONG-STAID
                                   NIGHT   4.89.5
FROM HEAVENLY STANDING HITS EACH MORTALL WIGHT   4.97.4
THAT TEDIOUS LEASURE MARKS EACH WRINCKLED LINE   4.98.11
WHEN FAR SPENT NIGHT PERSWADES EACH MORTALL EYE   4.99.1
CALS EACH WIGHT TO SALUTE THE FLOURE OF BLISSE   4.99.11
THAT TO EACH WORD, NAY SIGH OF MINE YOU HARKE   4.104.3
AND RARE PERFECTION OF EACH GOODLY PART   5.24.2
WHOSE PRYDE DEPRAVES EACH OTHER BETTER PART   5.31.3
WHEN ON EACH EYELID SWEETLY DOE APPEARE   5.40.3
AT SIGHT WHEREOF EACH BIRD THAT SITS ON SPRAY   5.40.9
EACH OF WHICH DID HER WITH THEYR GUIFTS ADORNE   5.61.8
SEEKES WITH SWEET PEACE TO SALVE EACH
                              OTHERS WOUND   5.65.12
AND SEEKE EACH WHERE, WHERE LAST I SAWE HER FACE   5.78.3
EAGER   2
WITH EAGER COMPOUNDS WE OUR PALLAT URGE   3.118.2
CEASE EAGER $MUSE, PEACE PEN, FOR MY SAKE STAY   4.70.12
EAGLE   2
THE AYRE, UNTO MY SIGHES, AS $EAGLE TO THE FLIE   2.127.7
JOVES GOLDEN SHIELD DID $EAGLE SABLES BEARE   4.13.3
EAGLE-BIRDS   1
MY $THOUGHTS BRED UP WITH $EAGLE-BIRDS OF LOVE   2.103.1
EAGLE'S   2
IF THEY WERE OF THE $EAGLES KINDE OR NO   2.103.4
TILL HE HIMSELFE THYS $EAGLES ART HAD TAUGHT   2.122.8
EAGLET   2
WHEN LIKE AN $EAGLET I FIRST FOUND MY $LOVE   2.56.1
IT AFTER THEE, IS LIKE AN $EAGLET FLOWNE   2.56.14
EAGLETS   2
YOU OUT-CAST $EAGLETS, DAZELED WITH YOUR $SUNNE   1.3.10

```
     DOE WHAT I COULD MY $EAGLETS WOULD ASPIRE          2.103.11
EAR                      8
   AND EV'RY $DRUDGE DOTH DULL OUR SATIATE $EARE         2.31.10
   AND WHEN $CORNE'S SOWNE, OR GROWNE INTO THE $EARE     2.48.7
   BY UNIONS MARRIED DO OFFEND THINE EARE               3.8.6
   SING TO THE EARE THAT DOTH THY LAIES ESTEEME         3.100.7
   THE WIRY CONCORD THAT MINE EARE CONFOUNDS            3.128.4
   LISTEN THEN $LORDINGS WITH GOOD EARE TO ME           4.37.3
   SO SWEETE SOUNDS STRAIGHT MINE EARE AND
                        HEART DO HIT                    4.55.13
   THAT GIV'ST NO BETTER EARE TO MY JUST CRIES          4.65.2
EARED                    1
   WITHIN THEMSELVES, AND ON THEM PLOUGHS HAVE EAR'D     1.45.4
EARLY                    2
   EVEN SO MY $SUNNE ONE EARLY MORNE DID SHINE          3.33.9
   AND TWIXT HER PAPS LIKE EARLY FRUIT IN $MAY          5.76.9
EARS                    17
   THOUGH ALL MY PRAYERS BE TO SO DEAFE EARES          1.11.11
   VEXING WITH UNTUN'D MOANE HER DAINTY EARES          1.21.8
   AND MINE $EARES DEAFE, BY THY $FAME HEALED BEE       2.35.10
   FILLING MINE $EARES WITH $NOISE, AND $NIGHTLY
                        GRONING                         2.40.6
   WONNE GRACE AND CREDIT IN THE $EARES OF $MEN         2.47.4
   AND MINE EARES DEAFE, BY THY FAME HEALED BE          2.112.10
   FILLING MYNE EARES WITH NOYSE AND NIGHTLY
                        GRONING                         2.144.6
   MADDE SLANDERERS BY MADDE EARES BELEEVED BE         3.140.12
   NOR ARE MINE EARES WITH THY TOUNGS TUNE
                        DELIGHTED                       3.141.5
   PARDON MINE EARES, BOTH I AND THEY DO PRAY           4.51.1
   I $STELLA'S EYES ASSAYLL, INVADE HER EARES           4.61.3
   THAT VOYCE, WHICH MAKES THE SOULE PLANT
                        HIMSELFE IN THE EARES           4.77.9
   SO AMPLE EARES AS NEVER GOOD NEWES KNOW              4.78.13
   AND THAT MY $MUSE TO SOME EARES NOT UNSWEET          4.84.2
   LET EARES HEARE SPEECH, WHICH WIT TO WONDER TIES     4.85.11
   OR DO YOU MEANE MY TENDER EARES TO SPARE             4.92.4
   SOME DAINTY EARES, CANNOT WITH ANY SKILL             5.38.6
EARTH                   47
   SACRED ON EARTH, DESIGN'D A $SAINT ABOVE             1.6.8
   WITH DOWNEWARD LOCKES, STILL READING ON THE EARTH    1.9.3
   THE AYRE WITH SIGHES, THE EARTH BELOW
                        WITH TEARES+                    1.21.6
   I SEARCH THE EARTH, THE EARTH I FINDE AS SKANT       1.29.7
   I SEARCH THE EARTH, THE EARTH I FINDE AS SKANT       1.29.7
   HEAVEN NOR EARTH WILL NOT, MY SELFE CANNOT WAKE      1.29.9
   OF EARTH ON EARTH A SUBSTANCE SO DIVINE              1.34.4
   OF EARTH ON EARTH A SUBSTANCE SO DIVINE              1.34.4
   SHALT BEND THY WRINCKLES HOMEWARD TO THE EARTH       1.50.10
   ONE NUMBER OF THE $EARTH, THE OTHER BOTH $DIVINE     2.18.3
   LOVE BANISH'D $HEAV'N, IN $EARTH WAS HELD
                        IN SCORNE                       2.23.1
   THOUGH $HEAVEN AND $EARTH, PROVE BOTH
                        TO ME UNTRUE                    2.51.13
   THEY $HEAVEN AND $EARTH TO PITTY SHALL PROVOKE       2.55.8
   YET WITH THE $MOLE I CREEPE INTO THE $EARTH          2.62.10
   THEY HEAVEN AND EARTH TO PITTY SHALL PROVOKE         2.102.8
   ONE NUMBER OF THE EARTH, THE OTHER BOTH DIVINE       2.108.3
   AND HEAVEN, AND EARTH, DOE WITH THEIR
                        WOES ACQUAINT                   2.118.4
```

```
THIS EARTH OF THOSE SWEET $PROPHETS HATH BEREFT      2.119.6
SOME MUZ'D TO SEE THE EARTH ENVY THE AYRE            2.125.5
WHILST FIRE, WATER, AYRE, TWIXT HEAVEN
                    AND EARTH SHAL BE                2.127.13
YET WITH THE $MOLE, I CREEPE INTO THE EARTH          2.150.10
A HEAVEN ON EARTH, CN EARTH NO HEAVEN BUT THIS       2.151.14
A HEAVEN ON EARTH, CN EARTH NO HEAVEN BUT THIS       2.151.14
AND MAKE THE EARTH DEVOURE HER OWNE SWEET BROOD      3.19.2
WITH $SUNNE AND $MOONE, WITH EARTH AND
                    SEAS RICH GEMS                   3.21.6
FROM SULLEN EARTH SINGS HIMNS AT $HEAVENS GATE       3.29.12
UPON THE FARTHEST EARTH REMOOV'D FROM THEE           3.44.6
BUT THAT SO MUCH CF EARTH AND WATER WROUGHT          3.44.11
SINCE BRASSE, NOR STONE, NOR EARTH, NOR
                    BOUNDLESSE SEA                   3.65.1
THE EARTH CAN HAVE BUT EARTH, WHICH IS HIS DUE       3.74.7
THE EARTH CAN HAVE BUT EARTH, WHICH IS HIS DUE       3.74.7
OR YOU SURVIVE WHEN I IN EARTH AM ROTTEN             3.81.2
THE EARTH CAN YEELD ME BUT A COMMON GRAVE            3.81.7
POORE SOULE THE CENTER CF MY SINFULL EARTH           3.146.1
MY SINFULL EARTH THESE REBBELL POWRES
                    THAT THEE ARRAY                  3.146.2
TRUE, THAT ON EARTH WE ARE BUT PILGRIMS MADE         4.5.12
LET ALL THE EARTH WITH SCORNE RECOUNT MY CASE        4.64.7
AND WARNES THE $EARTH WITH DIVERS COLORD FLOWRE      5.4.11
YET FIND I NOUGHT CN EARTH TO WHICH I DARE           5.9.3
FOR LOOKING ON THE EARTH WHENCE SHE WAS BORNE        5.13.6
WHAT SO IS FAYREST SHALL TO EARTH RETURNE            5.13.8
TREADING DOWNE EARTH AS LOTHSOME AND FORLORNE        5.13.11
NOT EARTH., FOR HER HIGH THOGHTS MORE
                    HEAVENLY ARE                     5.55.5
FALS LOWEST.. FOR CN EARTH NOUGHT HATH
                    ENDURAUNCE                       5.58.12
COULD NOT ON EARTH HAVE FOUND ONE FIT FOR MATE       5.66.6
ALL SORTS OF FLOWERS THE WHICH ON EARTH DO SPRING    5.70.3
BUT HERE ON EARTH TC HAVE SUCH HEVENS BLISSE         5.72.14
EARTHLY                  8
WHERE BLAZE THOSE LIGHTS FAIREST OF EARTHLY
                    THINGS                           1.12.3
WHICH MIGHT BE BORROW'D FROM NO $EARTHLY FLAME       2.30.2
I SCORNE ALL $EARTHLY $CUNG-BRED $SCARABIES          2.31.14
AND THOUGH THIS $EARTHLY $BODY FADE AND DIE          2.44.13
SUCH HEAVENLY TOUCHES NERE TOUCHT EARTHLY FACES      3.17.8
FROM BASE DESIRE CN EARTHLY CATES TO PRAY+           4.88.8
THING SO DIVINE TC VEW CF EARTHLY EYE                5.45.6
IT DOWN IS WEIGHD WITH THOGHT OF EARTHLY THINGS      5.72.3
EARTH'S                  1
THE WANDRING $MOONE IN EARTHS TRIPLICITIE            2.116.8
EASE                    13
AND SO WITH LOOKES, PROLCNGS MY LONG-LOOKT EASE      1.24.10
DOTH TEACH THAT EASE AND THAT REPOSE TO SAY          3.50.3
IN THINGS OF GREAT RECEIT WITH EASE WE PROOVE        3.136.7
WHERE WITH MOST EASE AND WARMTH HE MIGHT
                    EMPLOY HIS ART                   4.8.7
COME LET ME WRITE, '$AND TO WHAT END+' $TO EASE      4.34.1
A BURTHNED HART. '$HOW CAN WORDS EASE, WHICH ARE     4.34.2
BECOMES A CLOG) WILL SOCNE EASE ME OF IT             4.59.14
HOW FALLES IT THEN, THAT WITH SO SMOOTH AN EASE      4.74.9
O EASE YOUR HAND, TREATE NOT SO HARD YOUR SLAVE      4.86.9
AND SEEKE SOME SUCCCUR BOTH TO EASE MY SMART         5.2.7
```

```
  ALLUR'D A $DOLPHIN HIM FROM DEATH TO EASE              5.38.4
  AND THEN MY BODY SHALL HAVE SHORTLY EASE               5.50.11
  DOTH BATH IN BLISSE AND MANTLETH MOST AT EASE          5.72.10
EASED                  2
  WHEN DAIES OPPRESSICN IS NOT EAZD BY NIGHT             3.28.3
  ONLY WITH PAINES MY PAINES THUS EASED BE               4.93.12
EASEFUL                1
  AS HIS MAINE FORCE, CHOISE SPORT, AND
                        EASEFULL STAY                    4.43.4
EASIEST                1
  WHICH YEELDS THEM NCTHING, AT THE EASIEST RATE         2.28.7
EASILY                 3
  READE BUT HIS $VERSE, AND IT WILL EAS'LY PROVE         2.24.3
  BY THY RARE PLUME THY KIND IS EASLY KNOWNE             2.106.3
  DO EASLY YEELD, THAT ALL THEIR COASTS MAY BE           4.29.3
EAST                   2
  WHEN $EAST, WHEN $WEST, WHEN $SOUTH, AND
                        WHEN BY $NORTH                   2.1.7
  BETTER BECOMES THE GRAY CHEEKS OF TH' $EAST            3.132.6
EASY                   2
  AS EASIE MIGHT I FRCM MY SELFE DEPART                  3.109.3
  FOR EASIE THINGS THAT MAY BE GOT AT WILL               5.26.11
EAT                    4
  TO EATE THE WORLDS DUE, BY THE GRAVE AND THEE          3.1.14
  A VENGFULL CANKER EATE HIM UP TO DEATH                 3.99.13
  EATE UP THY CHARGE+ IS THIS THY BODIES END+            3.146.8
  SEEMD EVERY BIT, WHICH THENCEFORTH I DID EAT           5.39.14
EBB                    1
  THAT NEVER FALL TC EBBE, BUT EVER RISE                 1.48.3
ECHO                   1
  I SAY, I $DIE, YOU $ECCHO ME WITH I                    2.5.7
ECHOES                 2
  LYKE IDLE $ECCHOES EVER AUNSWERING.. SO                2.141.7
  THAT ALL THE WOODS THEYR ECCHOES BACK REBOUNDED        5.19.7
ECLIPSE                2
  THE MORTALL $MOONE HATH HER ECLIPSE INDUR'DE           3.107.5
  TUSH ABSENCE, WHILE THY MISTES ECLIPSE THAT LIGHT      4.88.9
ECLIPSED               3
  BEHOLD THE $CLOUDS WHICH HAVE ECLIPS'D MY $SUNNE       2.60.9
  LIGHTNING THE WORLD, ECLIPSED BY HIS SET               2.125.4
  BEHOLD THE $CLOWDES WHICH HAVE ECLIPS'D MY SUNNE       2.149.9
ECLIPSES               2
  CLOUDES AND ECLIPSES STAINE BOTH $MOONE
                        AND $SUNNE                       3.35.3
  CROOKED ECLIPSES GAINST HIS GLORY FIGHT                3.60.7
EDEN                   1
  THE SWEET OF $EDEN, TO HER BREATHES PERFUME            2.148.6
EDGE                   3
  THY EDGE SHOULD BLUNTER BE THEN APETITE                3.56.2
  THE HARDEST KNIFE ILL US'D DOTH LOOSE HIS EDGE         3.95.14
  BUT BEARES IT OUT EVEN TO THE EDGE OF DOOME            3.116.12
EDWARD                 1
  EDWARD NAMED FOURTH, AS FIRST IN PRAISE I NAME         4.75.2
E'ER                   3
  INTREATED ME, AS E'R I WISH'D HIS GOOD                 2.21.3
  WHEN I, AS FAST AS E'R MY $PENNE COULD TROT            2.21.5
  HOW E'RE BLIND $FCRTUNE TURNE HER GIDDIE $WHEELE       2.51.12
EFFECT                 9
  YET NEVER ANY TRUE EFFECT I PROVE                      1.25.4
  I LOVE TH' EFFECT THE CAUSE BEING OF THIS POWRE        1.26.11
```

```
    O RARE EFFECT, TRUE BOND OF FRIENDSHIPS MEASURE      2.146.9
    BEAUTIES EFFECT WITH BEAUTY WERE BEREFT                3.5.11
    WHICH THOUGH IT ALTER NOT LOVES SOLE EFFECT           3.36.7
    ME FOR MY DOMBE THOUGHTS, SPEAKING IN EFFECT          3.85.14
    AND STILL TH'EFFECT OF THY PERSWASIONS PROVE           4.4.11
    AND FIND TH'EFFECT, FOR I DO BURNE IN LOVE            4.25.14
    THUS WHILE TH' EFFECT MOST BITTER WAS TO ME           4.87.12
EFFECTS                    4
    THAT MAKES THE WORLD ADMIRE SO STRANGE EFFECTS         1.34.8
    EFFECTS OF LIVELY HEAT, MUST NEEDS IN NATURE GROW      4.8.11
    AND KNOW GREAT CAUSES, GREAT EFFECTS PROCURE          4.26.10
    OF CONQUEST, DO NOT THESE EFFECTS SUFFICE             4.36.7
EFFECTUALLY                1
    SEEMES SEEING, BUT EFFECTUALLY IS OUT                 3.113.4
EGLANTINE                  2
    SWEET IS THE $EGLANTINE, BUT PRICKETH NERE            5.26.3
    WITH WOODBYND FLOWERS AND FRAGRANT $EGLANTINE         5.71.10
EISEL                      1
    POTIONS OF $EYSELL GAINST MY STRONG INFECTION        3.111.10
EITHER                     9
    THOUGH EITHER DISTANT, PRESENT YET TO EITHER          2.11.6
    THOUGH EITHER DISTANT, PRESENT YET TO EITHER          2.11.6
    WHAT WILL $YOU KEEPE A MEANE THEN BETWIXT EITHER+     2.19.7
    BE IT NOT SEENE IN EITHER OF OUR $BROWES              2.61.7
    SO EITHER BY THY PICTURE OR MY LOVE                   3.47.9
    EITHER NOT ASSAYLD, OR VICTOR BEEING CHARG'D          3.70.10
    EITHER TO DO LIKE HIM, WHICH OPEN SHONE               4.22.10
    WITH EITHER LIP HE DOTH THE OTHER KISSE               4.43.11
    THEN EITHER $LYON OR THE $LYONESSE                    5.20.10
EITHER'S                   2
    AND EACH (THOUGH ENIMES TO ETHERS RAIGNE)             3.28.5
    BUT HEAVIE TEARES, BADGES OF EITHERS WOE              3.44.14
EKE                        7
    A $POET EKE, AS HUMOURS FLY OR CREEPE                 4.32.4
    AND EKE HIS LEARNED HAND AT PLEASURE GUIDE            5.17.6
    AND EKE MY TOUNG WITH PROUD RESTRAINT TO TIE+         5.43.6
    AND EKE MINE EIES WITH MEEKE HUMILITY                 5.43.11
    AND EKE HER MIND IS PURE IMMORTALL HYE                5.55.12
    CHAUNGE EEKE OUR MYNDS AND FORMER LIVES AMEND         5.62.6
    AND EEK MY NAME BEE WYPED OUT LYKEWIZE                5.75.8
ELDER                      1
    HOW CAN I THEN BE ELDER THEN THOU ART+                3.22.8
ELECTION                   1
    AND BLESSE YOUR FORTUNES FAYRE ELECTION               5.84.14
ELEGIES                    2
    MY $LIVES COMPLAINT IN DOLEFULL $ELEGIES              2.54.7
    MY LIVES COMPLAINT IN DOLEFUL $ELEGIES               2.101.7
ELEMENT                    2
    THIS LOVE, TEARS, SIGHES, MAINTAINE EACH
                         ONE HIS ELEMENT                  2.127.4
    THEN NEEDS ANOTHER $ELEMENT INQUIRE                   5.55.9
ELEMENTS                   3
    RECEIVING NAUGHTS BY ELEMENTS SO SLOE                 3.44.13
    FOR WHEN THESE QUICKER $ELEMENTS ARE GONE             3.45.5
    WHICH ELEMENTS WITH MORTALL MIXTURE BREED             4.5.11
ELIZABETHS                 1
    YE THREE $ELIZABETHS FOR EVER LIVE                    5.74.13
ELIZIA                     2
    ELIZIA IS TOO HIE A SEATE FOR MEE                    2.118.5
    THE FAYRE $ELIZIA, TO HER FAYRER CHEEKE              2.148.7
```

```
ELIZIUM                      1
  ELIZIUM IS TOO HIGH A SEATE FOR $ME            2.39.5
ELOQUENCE                    7
  O LET MY BOOKS BE THEN THE ELOQUENCE           3.23.9
  I BEG NO SUBJECT TC USE ELOQUENCE              4.28.9
  LEAVING ME NOUGHT BUT WAILING ELOQUENCE        4.38.11
  THAT I WELL FIND NC ELOQUENCE LIKE IT          4.55.14
  NOW WITH SLOW WORDS, NOW WITH DUMBE ELOQUENCE  4.61.2
  THAT ELOQUENCE IT SELFE ENVIES YOUR PRAISE     4.100.10
  AS GRUDGING ME MY SCRROWE'S ELOQUENCE+         4.104.4
ELSE                         30
  ONCE LET HER LOVE INDEED, OR ELS EYE ME NEVER  1.24.14
  ARE EYES, OR ELS TWC RADIANT STARRES THAT SHINE 1.34.2
  WHOSE BEAUTY MADE HIM SPEAKE THAT ELSE WAS DCMBE 1.55.8
  LIKE AS THE $LUTE DELIGHTS OR ELS DISLIKES     1.57.1
  ELSE HARSH MY STILE, UNTUNABLE MY $MUSE        1.57.9
  FOR NO GROUND ELS CCULD MAKE THE MJSICKE SUCH  1.57.13
  WHEN NOTHING ELSE REMAYNETH OF THESE DAYES     2.6.6
  ELSE SHOULD MY $LINES GLIDE ON THE $WAVES
                          OF $RHENE              2.25.3
  O, $THOU THAT ART SC COURTEOUS ELSE TO ALL     2.37.9
  OR ELSE $LOVE WERE UNABLE TO INDITE            2.38.4
  MUST PASSE BY AYRE, OR ELSE DYE IN EXILE       2.122.4
  ELS SENCELES LOVE CCULD NEVER ONCE ENDITE      2.131.4
  PITTY THE WORLD, CR ELSE THIS GLUTTON BE       3.1.13
  OR ELSE RECEAV'ST WITH PLEASURE THINE ANNCY+   3.8.4
  OR ELSE OF THEE THIS I PROGNOSTICATE           3.14.13
  OR MEE TO WHOM THCU GAV'ST IT, ELSE MISTAKING  3.87.10
  NONE ELSE TO ME, NCR I TO NONE ALIVE           3.112.7
  OR ELSE LET THEM IN STATELIER GLORIE SHINE     4.3.5
  OR DID SHE ELSE THAT SOBER HUE DEVISE          4.7.5
  NOBLER DESIRES, LEAST ELSE THAT FRIENDLY FOE   4.21.7
  THAT NO PACE ELSE THEIR GUIDED STEPS CAN FIND  4.58.3
  OR ELSE PRONOUNCING GRACE, WHEREWITH HIS MIND  4.58.7
  DRIV'N ELSE TO GRAUNT BY $ANGEL'S SOPHISTRIE   4.61.13
  OR ART THOU ELSE TO COMFORT ME FORSWORNE+      4.67.11
  USE SOMETHING ELSE TO CHAST'N ME WITHALL       4.86.12
  THAT TO THE WORLD NAUGHT ELSE BE COUNTED DEARE 5.8.4
  OF THAT FAIRE SIGHT, THAT NOTHING ELSE
                          THEY BROOKE            5.35.10
  ASWAGE YOUR STORMES, OR ELSE BOTH YOU AND SHE  5.46.11
  THIS YEARE ENSUING, OR ELSE SHORT MY DAYES     5.60.14
  OF THAT FAYRE SIGHT, THAT NOTHING ELSE
                          THEY BROOKE            5.83.10
ELSEWHERE                    4
  FOR THEE WATCH I, WHILST THOU DOST WAKE
                          ELSEWHERE             3.61.13
  TELL ME THOU LOV'ST ELSE-WHERE., BUT IN MY SIGHT 3.139.5
  THAT THEY ELSE-WHERE MIGHT DART THEIR INJURIES 3.139.12
  LIVELIER THEN ELSE-WHERE, $STELLA'S IMAGE SEE  4.39.14
ELYSIAN                      1
  TH'$ELISIAN GHOSTS SHALL NEVER KNOW THE SAME   1.30.14
EMBASE                       1
  AND THIS WORLDS WCRTHLESSE GLORY TO EMBASE     5.17.3
EMBASED                      1
  THAT ARE SO MUCH BY SO MEANE LOVE EMBASED      5.82.4
EMBASETH                     1
  AND TO THE GROUND HER EIE LIDS LOW EMBASETH    5.13.3
EMBASSAGE                    1
  TO THEE I SEND THIS WRITTEN AMBASSAGE          3.26.3
```

```
EMBASSY                        1
  IN TENDER $EMBASSIE OF LOVE TO THEE              3.45.6
EMBRACE                        10
  MY HART IMBRACETH $LOVE, $LOVE DOTH IMBRACE
                       MY HART                2.132.10
  AND OTHERS FOE, THE OTHERS FOE IMBRACE           2.136.13
  BUT FINDING THESE $NORTH CLYMES DO COLDLY
                       HIM EMBRACE             4.8.5
  THAT SEE MY WRACKE, AND YET EMBRACE THE SAME+    4.19.2
  SO PIERCING PAWES, AS SPOYLE WHEN THEY EMBRACE   4.78.10
  LET BREATH SUCKE UP THOSE SWEETES, LET
                       ARMES EMBRACE          4.85.12
  DEAD GLASSE, DOOST THOU THY OBJECT SO IMBRACE    4.105.3
  AS MEANES OF BLISSE I GLADLY WIL EMBRACE         5.25.12
  BUT IN YOUR BREST HIS LEAFE AND LOVE EMBRACE     5.28.14
  THE MORE I LOVE AND DOE EMBRACE MY BANE          5.42.4
EMBRACED                       1
  THOUGH THESE, NOR THESE, DESERVE TO BE IMBRACED  2.138.13
EMBRACETH                      1
  MY HART IMBRACETH $LOVE, $LOVE DOTH IMBRACE
                       MY HART                2.132.10
EMBRACING                      3
  IMBRACING CLOUDS BY NIGHT, IN DAY TIME MOURNE    1.16.2
  STILL LET ME SLEEPE, IMBRACING CLOUDS IN VAINE   1.54.13
  THEN IS SHE $LOVE, IMBRACING $CHARITIE           2.12.5
EMBREW                         2
  OF SUCH POORE THRALLS HER CRUELL HANDS EMBREW    5.31.12
  TO MAKE THE BAYTE HER GAZERS TO EMBREW           5.53.11
EMBRYON                        1
  HURT IN THE $EMBRYON, MAKES MY JOYES ABHORTIVE   2.141.4
EMNITY                         1
  GAINST DEATH, AND ALL OBLIVIOUS EMNITY           3.55.9
EMPLOY                         2
  AND NOW EMPLOY THE REMNANT OF MY WIT             4.2.12
  WHERE WITH MOST EASE AND WARMTH HE MIGHT
                       EMPLOY HIS ART          4.8.7
EMPLOYS                        1
  WHOM SHE IMPLOYES, DISMISSE FROM THEE MY WIT     4.107.10
EMPRESS                        1
  TO THAT MOST SACRED $EMPRESSE MY DEAR DRED       5.33.2
EMPRISE                        1
  OF THEYR GREAT DEEDS AND VALAROUS EMPRIZE        5.69.4
EMPTY                          3
  STILL EMPTY GORG'D, WITH CARES CONSUMPTION
                       PYNDE                  2.116.14
  FOR THOUGH FULL OF DESIRE, EMPTIE OF WIT         4.82.9
  SICKE, THIRSTY, GLAD (THOUGH BUT OF EMPTY
                       GLASSE)                4.104.11
ENAMELED                       1
  MORNE'S MESSENGER, WITH ROSE ENAMELD SKIES       4.99.10
ENAMELING                      1
  ENAM'LING WITH PIED FLOWERS THEIR THOUGHTS OF GOLD  4.3.4
ENAMORED                       1
  A THOUSAND $NIMPH-LIKE AND INAMOR'D $GRACES      2.4.2
ENCAGE                         1
  GENTLY ENCAGE, THAT HE MAY BE YOUR THRALL        5.73.10
ENCHANTING                     1
  TH'INCHAUNTING $SYREN, WHICH DOTH SO ENTICE      2.130.3
ENCHASED                       1
  SOM HEVENLY WIT, WHOSE VERSE COULD HAVE ENCHASED  5.82.7
```

ENCLOSE   2
  INCLOSE MY $MUSIKE, YOU POORE SENSELESSE $WALLS   2.45.9
  OH IN WHAT SWEETS DOEST THOU THY SINNES INCLOSE   3.95.4
ENCROACHMENT   1
  BY NO ENCROCHMENT WRONGD, NOR TIME FORGOT   4.84.10
END   30
  FINDING NO END NOR PERIOD OF MY PAINE   1.16.12
  FOR TO THEIR FLOW SHE NEVER GRANTS AN END   1.48.4
  WHO HAVING NOW BROUGHT ON HIS END WITH $CARE   2.10.3
  SO YOU OF $TIME SHALL LIVE BEYOND THE $END   2.16.14
  THE QUIET END OF THAT $LONG-LIVING QUEENE   2.51.7
  SO MAIST THOU LIVE, PAST WORLD, PAST FAME,
                        PAST END   2.106.14
  NOW HAST THOU END, AND NOW THOU WAST BEGUN   2.141.12
  BUT BEAUTIES WASTE HATH IN THE WORLD AN END   3.9.11
  AGAINST THIS CUMMING END YOU SHOULD PREPARE   3.13.3
  THY END IS $TRUTHES AND $BEAUTIES DOOME AND DATE 3.14.14
  ALL LOSSES ARE RESTORD, AND SORROWES END   3.30.14
  WHEN WHAT I SEEKE (MY WEARIE TRAVELS END)   3.50.2
  NOR DARE I CHIDE THE WORLD WITHOUT END HOURE   3.57.5
  SO DO OUR MINUITES HASTEN TO THEIR END   3.60.2
  ALL TOUNGS (THE VOICE OF SOULES) GIVE
                    THEE THAT END   3.69.3
  WHEN IN THE LEAST OF THEM MY LIFE HATH END   3.92.6
  NOW ALL IS DONE, HAVE WHAT SHALL HAVE NO END   3.110.9
  I HATE SHE ALTERD WITH AN END   3.145.9
  EATE UP THY CHARGE+ IS THIS THY BODIES END+   3.146.8
  OF SINFULL THOUGHTS, WHICH DO IN RUINE END+   4.14.8
  COME LET ME WRITE, '$AND TO WHAT END+' $TO EASE 4.34.1
  ALL PAINE HATH END AND EVERY WAR HATH PEACE   5.11.13
  ERE $CUCKOW END, LET HER A REBELL BE   5.19.14
  SO WHEN I THINKE TO END THAT I BEGONNE   5.23.9
  I MUST BEGIN AND NEVER BRING TO END   5.23.10
  AND KNOW NO END OF HER OWNE MYSERY   5.25.2
  TELL ME WHEN SHALL THESE WEARIE WOES HAVE END   5.36.1
  THEN SO BAD END FOR HERETICKS ORDAYNED   5.48.6
  WHICH WAS NOT HARD T'ATCHIVE AND BRING TO END 5.51.8
  I WISH THAT NIGHT THE NOYOUS DAY WOULD END   5.87.6
ENDEARED   1
  THY BOSOME IS INDEARED WITH ALL HEARTS   3.31.1
ENDEAVOR   2
  WHY SHOULD M'AFFLICTED $MUSE SO MUCH ENDEVOUR 1.17.7
  WITH STRONG ENDEVOUR AND ATTENTION DEW   5.80.8
ENDED   3
  WHEN FIRST I $ENDED, THEN I FIRST $BEGAN   2.62.1
  WHEN FIRST I ENDED, THEN I FIRST BEGAN   2.150.1
  HIGH TIME IT IS, THIS WARRE NOW ENDED WERE   5.57.2
ENDING   2
  THE CIRCLE OF MY SORROWES NEVER ENDING   1.18.4
  THAT WEARE THIS WORLD OUT TO THE ENDING DOOME 3.55.12
ENDITE   5
  ELS SENCELES LOVE COULD NEVER ONCE ENDITE   2.131.4
  STELLA BEHOLD, AND THEN BEGIN TO ENDITE   4.15.14
  SWEET KISSE, THY SWEETS I FAINE WOULD
                    SWEETLY ENDITE   4.79.1
  SINCE ALL MY WORDS THY BEAUTY DOTH ENDITE   4.90.13
  THE WONDER THAT MY WIT CANNOT ENDITE   5.3.14
ENDLESS   7
  IN ENDLES ERRORS, WHENCE I CANNOT PART   1.34.12
  CONDEMN'D BY $JOVE TO ENDLESSE $TORMENT BEE   2.14.2

```
    THE DRERIE ABSTRACTS OF MY ENDLESSE $CARES          2.54.2
    THE DRERY ABSTRACTS OF MY ENDLES CARES              2.101.2
    THE DOLEFULL $ANTHEMS OF MY ENDLESSE CARE           2.141.6
    AND PEACE PROCLAIMES $OLIVES OF ENDLESSE AGE        3.107.8
    THAT ENDLESSE PLEASURE SHALL UNTO ME GAINE+         5.26.14
ENDLESSLY                   1
    AND ENDLESLY DISPAIRING OF HIS GRACE                4.97.6
ENDOWED                     1
    LOOKE WHOM SHE BEST INDOW'D, SHE GAVE THE MORE      3.11.11
ENDURANCE                   1
    FALS LOWEST.. FOR ON EARTH NOUGHT HATH
                                    ENDURAUNCE          5.58.12
ENDURE                      12
    THUS SHADES MY LIFE SO LONG AS WANTS ENDURE         1.29.14
    A DATELESSE LIVELY HEAT STILL TO INDURE             3.153.6
    WHOSE PORCHES RICH (WHICH NAME OF CHEEKES ENDURE)   4.9.7
    BASE THING I CAN NO MORE ENDURE TO VIEW             5.3.6
    IN GENTLE BREST THAT SHALL ENDURE FOR EVER          5.6.10
    HOW LONG SHALL THIS LYKE DYING LYFE ENDURE          5.25.1
    THINCK EVER TO ENDURE SO TAEDIOUS TOYLE+            5.33.10
    AND CAN NO MORE ENDURE ON THEM TO LOOKE             5.35.12
    FOR THAT THEY SHOULD ENDURE THROUGH MANY AGES       5.51.3
    AND THAT IT THEN MORE STEDFAST WILL ENDURE          5.51.12
    WHICH I NO LENGER CAN ENDURE TO SUE                 5.57.3
    AND CAN NO MORE ENDURE ON THEM TO LOOKE             5.83.12
ENDURED                     2
    THE MORTALL $MOONE HATH HER ECLIPSE INDUR'DE        3.107.5
    WHICH HARDLY I ENDURED HERETOFORE                   5.63.2
ENEMIES                     5
    AND EACH (THOUGH ENIMES TO ETHERS RAIGNE)           3.28.5
    HER PRETTIE LOOKES HAVE BEENE MINE ENEMIES          3.139.10
    SPREDS IN DEFIANCE OF ALL ENEMIES                   5.5.12
    ALL FEARELESSE THEN OF SO FALSE ENIMIES             5.12.3
    BUT BEND YOUR FORCE AGAINST YOUR ENEMYES            5.49.8
ENEMY                       1
    AND OF SOME SENT FROM THAT SWEET ENEMIE $FRAUNCE    4.41.4
ENFEEBLED                   1
    THEN LACKT I MATTER, THAT INFEEBLED MINE            3.86.14
ENFOLD                      1
    AND BEING CAUGHT MAY CRAFTILY ENFOLD                5.37.7
ENFORCED                    1
    AND THEREFORE ART INFORC'D TO SEEKE ANEW            3.82.7
ENGARLAND                   1
    WITH CHOISEST FLOWERS MY SPEECH TO ENGARLAND SO     4.55.2
ENGINES                     1
    THOSE ENGINS CAN THE PROUDEST LOVE CONVERT          5.14.12
ENGLISH                     1
    BOTH BY THE JUDGEMENT OF THE $ENGLISH EYES          4.41.3
ENGRAFT                     1
    AS HE TAKES FROM YOU, I INGRAFT YOU NEW             3.15.14
ENGRAFTED                   1
    I MAKE MY LOVE INGRAFTED TO THIS STORE              3.37.8
ENGRAINED                   1
    WHICH $NATURE' SELFE DID MAKE, AND SELFE
                                    ENGRAIND THE SAME+  4.102.6
ENGRAVE                     1
    CAN THOSE BLACKE BEAMES SUCH BURNING MARKES
                                    ENGRAVE             4.47.2
ENGRAVED                    1
    ONELY MY LOVE IS IN THE FIRE INGRAVED               2.127.9
```

ENGROSSED   1
  AND MY NEXT SELFE THOU HARDER HAST INGROSSED   3.133.6
ENJOY   4
  WITH WHAT I MOST INJOY CONTENTED LEAST   3.29.8
  IT IS, SO FAIRE A $VERTUE TO ENJOY   4.68.14
  SHE OFT HATH DRUNKE MY TEARES, NOW HOPES TO ENJOY   4.70.3
  WHILE I DISPAIRE BY $SUNNE'S SIGHT TO ENJOY   4.97.14
ENJOYED   1
  INJOYD NO SOONER BUT DISPISED STRAIGHT   3.129.5
ENJOYER   1
  NOW PROUD AS AN INJOYER, AND ANON   3.75.5
ENJOYS   2
  SHIFTS BUT HIS PLACE, FOR STILL THE WORLD
                         INJOYES IT   3.9.10
  THE RICHEST GEMME OF $LOVE AND LIFE ENJOYES   4.24.10
ENKINDLED   1
  INKINDLED BY HER EYES CELESTIALL FIRE   1.59.4
ENLARGE   3
  AND IF MY PEN COULD MORE ENLARGE THY NAME   1.43.11
  LEAST JOY, BY $NATURE APT SPRITES TO ENLARGE   4.85.3
  THAT MOTE ENLARGE HER LIVING PRAYSES DEAD   5.33.4
ENLARGED   1
  TO TYE UP ENVY, EVERMORE INLARGED   3.70.12
ENLIGHTEN   1
  AND TO INLIGHTEN THEE GAVE EYES TO BLINDNESSE   3.152.11
ENLUMINED   1
  YET SINCE YOUR LIGHT HATH ONCE ENLUMIND ME   5.66.13
ENNOBLING   1
  ENNOBLING NEW FOUND $TROPES WITH PROBLEMES OLD   4.3.6
ENOUGH   14
  ONCE LET HER KNOW, SH'HATH DONE ENOUGH
                       TO PROVE ME   1.10.13
  AND LET THE DAY BE TIME ENOUGH TO MOURNE   1.54.5
  TIS NOT ENOUGH THAT THROUGH THE CLOUDE
                       THOU BREAKE   3.34.5
  AND LIKE ENOUGH THOU KNOWST THY ESTIMATE   3.87.2
  THEY HAD NOT STILL ENOUGH YOUR WORTH TO SING   3.106.12
  EVEN THAT YOUR PITTIE IS ENOUGH TO CURE MEE   3.111.14
  I'ST NOT YNOUGH TO TORTURE ME ALONE   3.133.3
  MORE THEN ENOUGH AM I THAT VEXE THEE STILL   3.135.3
  ALAS HAVE I NOT PAINE ENOUGH MY FRIEND   4.14.1
  WHAT INKE IS BLACKE INOUGH TO PAINT MY WO+   4.93.3
  KNOWING WORLDS PASSE, ERE SHE ENOUGH CAN FIND   4.101.13
  AH, IS IT NOT ENOUGH, THAT I AM THENCE   4.104.5
  SWEET IS THE BROOME-FLOWRE, BUT YET SOWRE ENOUGH   5.26.7
  ENOUGH IT IS FOR ONE MAN TO SUSTAINE   5.46.13
ENRICH   2
  SHALL PROFIT THEE, AND MUCH INRICH THY BOOKE   3.77.14
  OR WITH STRANGE SIMILIES ENRICH EACH LINE   4.3.7
ENRICHED   1
  WHOSE WORTHY PRIZE SHOULD HAVE ENRITCHT
                       THY TREASURE   2.134.14
ENROLL   2
  HERE HAVE I SUMM'D MY SIGHS, HERE I INROLE   1.1.7
  AND AL HER FAULTS IN THY BLACK BOOKE ENROLL   5.10.12
ENROLLED   4
  AND IF BY $THEE MY $PRAYERS MAY BE ENROL'D   2.55.7
  AND IF BY THEE MY PRAYERS MAY BE ENROLD   2.102.7
  WHOSE GLORIOUS HAND IMMORTALL HATH ENROLD THEE   2.129.12
  IN WHICH THEY WOULD THE RECORDS HAVE ENROLD   5.69.3

ENSAMPLE   2
  SUCH DEATH THE SAD ENSAMPLE OF YOUR MIGHT   5.7.14
  AND SHEW THE LAST ENSAMPLE OF YOUR PRIDE   5.25.6
ENSCONCE   1
  AGAINST THAT TIME DO I INSCONCE ME HERE   3.49.9
ENSUE   3
  WHAT EVER MAY ENSUE, O LET ME BE   4.48.5
  BETOKENING PEACE AND PLENTY TO ENSEW   5.62.4
  FROM FRAYLE CORRUPTION, THAT DOTH FLESH ENSEW   5.79.8
ENSUING   2
  ENSUING $AGES YET MY $RIMES SHALL CHERISH   2.44.11
  THIS YEARE ENSUING, OR ELSE SHORT MY DAYES   5.60.14
ENTANGLE   1
  SHE MAY ENTANGLE IN THAT GOLDEN SNARE   5.37.6
ENTERED   2
  AND SHUT THOSE WAIES MY FRIENDLY FOE FIRST ENTRED   1.27.3
  WHOLE ARMIES OF THY BEAUTIES ENTRED IN   4.36.4
ENTERTAIN   9
  LET OTHERS STRIVE TO ENTERTAINE WITH $WORDS   2.4.9
  WITH $PROVERBS THUS EACH OTHER INTERTAINE   2.59.2
  TO ENTERTAINE THE TIME WITH THOUGHTS OF LOVE   3.39.11
  STUDYING INVENTIONS FINE, HER WITS TO ENTERTAINE   4.1.6
  SOME $LOVERS SPEAKE WHEN THEY THEIR $MUSES
                             ENTERTAINE   4.6.1
  PREPARE YOUR SELFE NEW LOVE TO ENTERTAINE   5.4.14
  TO MAKE A TRUCE AND TERMES TO ENTERTAINE   5.12.2
  WITH LOVE MAY ONE ANOTHER ENTERTAYNE   5.68.12
  ALL SPRED WITH JUNCATS, FIT TO ENTERTAYNE   5.77.3
ENTERTAINMENT   1
  TO THEM THAT DO SUCH ENTERTAINMENT NEED   4.51.3
ENTICE   2
  TH'INCHAUNTING $SYREN, WHICH DOTH SO ENTICE   2.130.3
  OR THOSE WHICH $ATALANTA DID ENTICE   5.77.8
ENTICED   1
  INTIC'D MY $THOUGHTS, AGAINST ME TO CONSPIRE   2.23.10
ENTIRE   3
  LO HERE THE IMPOST OF A FAITH ENTIRE   1.60.1
  DEEPE IS THE WOUND, THAT DINTS THE PARTS ENTIRE 5.6.11
  DEEPE IN THE CLOSET OF MY PARTS ENTYRE   5.85.9
ENTITLED   1
  INTITLED IN THEIR PARTS, DO CROWNED SIT   3.37.7
ENTOMB   2
  THESE SHALL INTOMBE THOSE EIES, THAT HAVE
                          REDEEM'D   1.44.11
  WHEREIN THE $WORLD SHALL NOW INTOMBE HER $NAME   2.45.8
ENTOMBED   3
  TO CHECK THE WORLD, HOW THEY INTOMB'D HAVE LIEN 1.45.3
  WHERE I INTOMB'D, MY BETTER PART SHALL SAVE   2.44.12
  WHEN YOU INTOMBED IN MENS EYES SHALL LYE   3.81.8
ENTRANCE   1
  THIS $KINGS FAIRE $ENTRANCE, AND OUR $PEACE
                          WITH $SPAINE   2.51.8
ENTRAP   1
  WHICH SOUGHT ME TO ENTRAP IN TREASONS TRAINE   5.12.4
ENTRAPPED   1
  IN WHICH IF EVER YE ENTRAPPED ARE   5.37.11
ENTREAT   2
  PARDON FOR THEE, AND GRACE FOR ME INTREAT   5.2.12
  BUT HARDER GROWES THE MORE I HER INTREAT+   5.30.4

```
   TO BE DISEAS'D ERE THAT THERE WAS TRUE NEEDING      3.118.8
   WHO ERE KEEPES ME, LET MY HEART BE HIS GARDE        3.133.11
   WHAT WORDS SO ERE SHE SPEAKES PERSWADES FOR THEE     4.12.7
   BUT ERE I COULD FLIE THENCE, IT PIERC'D MY HEART     4.20.14
   KNOWING WORLDS PASSE, ERE SHE ENOUGH CAN FIND       4.101.13
   THAT ERE BY THEM OUGHT UNDERTAKEN BE                 4.107.3
   IS LONG ERE IT CONCEIVE THE KINDLING FYRE             5.6.6
   ERE $CUCKOW END, LET HER A REBELL BE                 5.19.14
   AND ERE SHE COULD THY CAUSE WEL UNDERSTAND            5.48.3
   IN WHICH I HOPE ERE LONG FOR TO ARRYVE                5.63.6
   HER BREST LYKE LILLYES, ERE THEYR LEAVES BE SHED     5.64.11
ERECT                  4
   THEY ALL ERECT THEIR $TROPHIES ON MY FALL            1.28.7
   NO LIGHTNING LOOKES WHICH FALLING HOPES ERECT        1.31.10
   THESE ARE THE $ARKES, THE $TROPHIES I ERECT           1.55.9
   USED $TROPHEES TO ERECT IN STATELY WIZE               5.69.2
ERECTED                1
   THEN HAD I WALKT WITH BOLD ERECTED FACE               1.7.9
ERECTING               2
   ERECTING $TROPHIES TO THY $SACRED $EYES              2.55.12
   ERECTING $TROPHIES TO THY SACRED EYES               2.102.12
ERINYS                 2
   SPIGHTFULL $ERINNIS FRIGHTS $ME WITH HER $LOCKES     2.39.9
   SPIGHTFULL $ERRINIS FRIGHTS MEE WITH HER LOOKES     2.118.9
ERMELIN                1
   LIKE AS THE SPOTLESSE $ERMELIN DISTREST              1.29.1
ERMINE                 1
   BUT IF ALL FAITH, LIKE SPOTLESSE $ERMINE LY          4.86.5
ERR                    1
   TO SAY THEY ERRE, I DARE NOT BE SO BOLD              3.131.7
ERRED                  1
   IN THINGS RIGHT TRUE MY HEART AND EYES
                               HAVE ERRED               3.137.13
ERROR                 11
   YOU BLINDED SOULES WHOM YOUTH AND ERROUR LEADE       1.3.9
   WHILST YOUTH AND ERROR LED MY WANDRING MINDE         1.5.1
   NO $SUNNE MY BLUSH AND ERROR HAD BEWRAID             1.7.7
   SINCE THE FIRST LOCKE THAT LED ME TO THIS ERROR      1.18.1
   THOUGH TH'ERROR OF MY YOUTH IN THEM APPEARE          1.55.13
   HIS ERROR WAS HIS HONOUR AND RENOWNE                 1.56.2
   SO $DELIA, HATH MINE ERROR MADE ME KNOWNE            1.56.5
   IF THIS BE ERROR AND UPON ME PROVED                 3.116.13
   THE FIRST THAT STRAIGHT MY FANCIE'S ERROR BRINGS     4.38.5
   OF STRAYING WAYES, WHEN VALIANT ERROUR GUIDES        4.51.11
   I AM RESOLV'D THY ERROUR TO MAINTAINE               4.67.13
ERRORS                 8
   WHILST BLINDED ONES MINE ERROURS NEVER GESSE         1.3.8
   IN ENDLES ERRORS, WHENCE I CANNOT PART              1.34.12
   THAT ERRORS SHOULD BE GRAC'D THAT MERIT SHAME       1.56.11
   SO ARE THOSE ERRORS THAT IN THEE ARE SEENE           3.96.7
   BOOKE BOTH MY WILFULNESSE AND ERRORS DOWNE          3.117.9
   WHAT WRETCHED ERRORS HATH MY HEART COMMITTED        3.119.5
   FOR THEY IN THEE A THOUSAND ERRORS NOTE             3.141.2
   THINKE THAT I THINKE STATE ERROURS TO REDRESSE       4.23.8
ERST                   3
   MY $FAIRE, HAD I NOT ERST ADORND MY $LUTE            2.104.1
   WHICH ERST FROM HEAT DID CANOPIE THE HERD            3.12.6
   AND MAKE HIM BOND THAT BONDAGE EARST DYD FLY         5.65.4
ESCAPED                2
   WHICH TAKING THENCE, YOU HAVE ESCAP'D AWAY          2.14.11
```

```
   SEEING THE GAME FROM HIM ESCAPT AWAY              5.67.2
ESCAPES              1
   AND THUS HER HEART ESCAPES, BUT THUS HER EYES     4.29.9
ESCHEW               1
   THE OLD YEARES SINNES FOREPAST LET US ESCHEW      5.62.7
ESPERIAN             1
   WHOSE FRUIT DOTH FARRE TH'$ESPERIAN TAST SURPASSE  4.82.6
ESPY                 2
   HER SUN-SHINE FACE THERE CHAUNSING TO ESPY        2.109.3
   THE RUINES OF HER CONQUEST TO ESPIE               4.67.3
ESPYING              1
   AND YET IN DEATH, SOME HOPE OF LIFE ESPYING       2.109.7
ESSAYS               1
   AND WORSE ESSAIES PROV'D THEE MY BEST OF LOVE     3.110.8
ESSEX                1
   ESSEX GREAT FALL, $TYRONE HIS $PEACE TO GAINE     2.51.6
ESTEEM               3
   LOOKE $DELIA HOW W'ESTEEME THE HALFE BLOWNE $ROSE  1.39.1
   SING TO THE EARE THAT DOTH THY LAIES ESTEEME      3.100.7
   SLANDRING $CREATION WITH A FALSE ESTEEME          3.127.12
ESTEEMED             4
   THOU MAIST IN AFTER AGES LIVE ESTEEM'D            1.44.9
   IF FAYTH AND ZEALE BE BUT ESTEEMD A TOY           2.139.3
   THE BASEST $JEWELL WIL BE WELL ESTEEM'D           3.96.6
   TIS BETTER TO BE VILE THEN VILE ESTEEMED          3.121.1
ESTEEMING            1
   THAT LOVE IS MARCHANDIZ'D, WHOSE RITCH ESTEEMING  3.102.3
ESTIMATE             1
   AND LIKE ENOUGH THOU KNOWST THY ESTIMATE          3.87.2
ETERNAL              14
   AND IN ETERNALL DARKNESSE EVER SLEEPS             1.35.12
   TH'ETERNALL $ANNALS OF A HAPPY PEN                1.45.8
   LIVES IN MY LINES, AND MUST ETERNALL BEE          1.45.14
   TH'ETERNALL WONDER OF OUR HAPPY $ILE              1.53.8
   THAT LUCKIE $LOAD-STARRE OF ETERNALL LIGHT        2.129.2
   AND BARREN RAGE OF DEATHS ETERNALL COLD+          3.13.12
   BUT THY ETERNALL $SOMMER SHALL NOT FADE           3.18.9
   WHEN IN ETERNALL LINES TO TIME THOU GROW'ST       3.18.12
   ETERNAL NUMBERS TO CUT-LIVE LONG DATE             3.38.12
   AND BRASSE ETERNALL SLAVE TO MORTALL RAGE         3.64.4
   SO THAT ETERNALL LOVE IN LOVES FRESH CASE         3.108.9
   RICH IN THOSE GIFTS WHICH GIVE TH'ETERNALL
                              CROWNE                 4.37.11
   ALL SORROWES SHORT THAT GAINE ETERNALL BLISSE     5.63.14
   AND ALL THENSFORTH ETERNALL PEACE SHALL SEE       5.71.13
ETERNITY             7
   WHERE I TO THEE $ETERNITIE SHALL GIVE             2.6.5
   MY $NAME SHALL MOUNT UPON $ETERNITIE              2.44.14
   TIMES THEEVISH PROGRESSE TO ETERNITIE             3.77.8
   BEYOND ALL DATE EVEN TO ETERNITY                  3.122.4
   OR LAYD GREAT BASES FOR ETERNITY                  3.125.3
   WHOSE NUMBERS, WAYES, GREATNESSE, ETERNITIE       4.26.3
   EVEN THIS VERSE VOWD TO ETERNITY                  5.69.9
ETERNIZE             4
   AFFECTED EVER, BUT T'ETERNIZE THEE                1.58.2
   WHILST THUS MY $PEN STRIVES TO ETERNIZE THEE      2.44.1
   ALL THAT I SEEKE, IS TO ETERNIZE YOU              2.47.14
   MY VERSE YOUR VERTUES RARE SHALL ETERNIZE         5.75.11
EVEN                 57
   AND MADE THY PASSIONS WITH HER BEAUTIE EVEN       1.8.4
```

```
FOR HAPLESSE LOE EVEN WITH MINE OWNE DESIRES        1.13.5
ONE $WOMAN NOW, MAKES THREE ODDE $NUMBERS EVEN      2.18.4
EV'N SO MY $MISTRES WORKES UPON MY $ILL             2.50.12
EV'N AS A $MAN THAT IN SOME $TRANCE HATH SEENE      2.57.9
EV'N AS THIS $SPIRIT, SO YOU ALONE DOE PLAY         2.58.11
ONE WONDER WOMAN NOW MAKES THREE OD NUMBERS EVEN    2.108.4
CHEARED AND CHECKT EVEN BY THE SELFE-SAME SKIE      3.15.6
WHEN SPARKLING STARS TWIRE NOT THOU GUIL'ST
                                   TH'EAVEN         3.28.12
EVEN SO MY $SUNNE ONE EARLY MORNE DID SHINE         3.33.9
ALL MEN MAKE FAULTS, AND EVEN I IN THIS             3.35.5
EVEN FOR THIS, LET US DEVIDED LIVE                  3.39.5
WHO LEAD THEE IN THEIR RYOT EVEN THERE              3.41.11
AND FOR MY SAKE EVEN SO DOTH SHE ABUSE ME           3.42.7
WHO EVEN BUT NOW COME BACK AGAINE ASSURED           3.45.11
AND EVEN THENCE THOU WILT BE STOLNE I FEARE         3.48.13
EVEN IN THE EYES OF ALL POSTERITY                   3.55.11
THY HUNGRIE EIES, EVEN TILL THEY WINCK
                              WITH FULNESSE          3.56.6
EVEN OF FIVE HUNDRETH COURSES OF THE $SUNNE         3.59.6
UTTRING BARE TRUTH, EVEN SO AS FOES $COMMEND        3.69.4
BUT LET YOUR LOVE EVEN WITH MY LIFE DECAY           3.71.12
WHERE BREATH MOST BREATHS, EVEN IN THE
                              MOUTHS OF MEN          3.81.14
EVEN SUCH A BEAUTY AS YOU MAISTER NOW               3.106.8
EVEN AS WHEN FIRST I HALLOWED THY FAIRE NAME        3.108.8
EVEN TO THY PURE AND MOST MOST LOVING BREST         3.110.14
EVEN THAT YOUR PITTIE IS ENOUGH TO CURE MEE         3.111.14
EVEN THOSE THAT SAID I COULD NOT LOVE YOU DEERER    3.115.2
BUT BEARES IT OUT EVEN TO THE EDGE OF DOOME         3.116.12
EVEN SO BEING FULL OF YOUR NERE CLOYING
                              SWEETNESSE             3.118.5
BEYOND ALL DATE EVEN TO ETERNITY                    3.122.4
NOR THAT FULL $STARRE THAT USHERS IN THE $EAVEN     3.132.7
NOW EVEN THAT FOOTSTEP OF LOST LIBERTIE              4.2.9
HOW THEN+ EVEN THUS.. IN $STELLA'S FACE I REED       4.3.12
SHE EVEN IN BLACKE DOTH MAKE ALL BEAUTIES FLOW+      4.7.11
DOTH PLUNGE MY WEL-FORM'D SOULE EVEN IN THE MIRE     4.14.7
I NOW HAVE LEARN'D $LOVE RIGHT, AND LEARN'D
                              EVEN SO                4.16.13
UNABLE QUITE TO PAY EVEN $NATURE'S RENT              4.18.5
BENDS ALL HIS POWERS, EVEN UNTO $STELLA'S GRACE      4.27.14
WHAT, MAY IT BE THAT EVEN IN HEAV'NLY PLACE          4.31.3
THEN EV'N OF FELLOWSHIP, O $MOONE, TELL ME           4.31.9
DOTH EVEN GROW RICH, NAMING MY STELLA'S NAME         4.35.11
WHOSE CURELESSE WOUNDS EVEN NOW MOST FRESHLY
                              BLEED                  4.48.11
AND IS EVEN IRKT THAT SO SWEET $COMEDIE              4.51.13
YOUTH, LUCKE, AND PRAISE, EVEN FILD MY
                              VEINES WITH PRIDE      4.53.4
EVEN THOSE SAD WORDS EVEN IN SAD ME DID BREED       4.58.14
EVEN THOSE SAD WORDS EVEN IN SAD ME DID BREED       4.58.14
BUT I UNBID, FETCH EVEN MY SOULE TO THEE             4.59.8
LATE TYR'D WITH WO, EVEN READY FOR TO PINE           4.62.1
WHICH EVEN OF SWEETNESSE SWEETEST SWEETNER ART       4.79.2
O KISSE, WHICH SOULES, EVEN SOULES TOGETHER TIES     4.81.5
AND I DO SWEARE EVEN BY THE SAME DELIGHT             4.82.13
THROUGH ME, WRETCH ME, EVEN $STELLA VEXED IS         4.93.4
WHICH EVEN TO SENCE, SENCE OF IT SELFE DENIES        4.94.7
EVEN SO (ALAS) A $LADY $DIAN'S PEERE                 4.97.9
```

```
YET EVEN WHYLST HER BLOODY HANDS THEM SLAY          5.47.9
EVEN THIS VERSE VOWD TO ETERNITY                    5.69.9
EVEN SO MY HART, THAT WONT ON YOUR FAYRE EYE        5.73.7
EVENING                    2
THE QUIET $EV'NING YET TOGETHER BRINGS              2.37.7
THEYR SAD PROTRACT FROM EVENING UNTILL MORNE        5.87.4
EVENT                      1
AND THOUGH TH'EVENT OFT ANSWERS NOT THE SAME        1.35.8
EVER                          81
THE TRUEST LOVE THAT EVER YET WAS SEENE             1.10.8
GRIEFES EVER SPRINGING, COMFORTS NEVER BORNE        1.16.4
WHY SHOULD I STRIVE TO MAKE HER LIVE FOR EVER       1.17.5
AND THAT MAKES HAPPY $LOVERS EVER DOMBE             1.17.14
THUS SHE RETURNES MY HOPES SO FRUITLESSE EVER       1.24.13
FALSE $HOPE PROLONGS MY EVER CERTAINE GRIEFE        1.25.1
LOTHSOME THEIR DAIES, WHOM NO SUN EVER JOYD         1.26.6
AND SEE MY FORTUNE EVER LIKE TO LAST                1.28.11
FINDING MY FORTUNE EVER IN THE WAINE                1.32.3
SEEKING IN VAINE WHAT I HAVE EVER SOUGHT            1.33.3
FOR HOW COULD $NATURE EVER THUS DEVISE              1.34.3
AND IN ETERNALL DARKNESSE EVER SLEEPS               1.35.12
THE FAIREST FLOWRE THAT EVER SAW THE LIGHT          1.40.6
(THE CHASTEST FLAME THAT EVER WARMED HART)          1.44.4
THAT EVER YET COVERED MORTALITY                     1.45.11
THAT NEVER FALL TO EBBE, BUT EVER RISE              1.48.3
AFFECTED EVER, BUT T'ETERNIZE THEE                  1.58.2
AND EVER THIS IN $MAD-MEN YOU SHALL FINDE           2.9.6
THESE WITH THE $GODS ARE EVER RESIDENT              2.18.7
I $EVER LOVE, WHERE NEVER $HOPE APPEARES            2.26.1
AND KNOWING MORE THEN EVER HATH BEENE TAUGHT        2.34.3
BY ALL THE $WOUNDS THAT EVER THOU HAST GIV'N        2.36.12
WELL COULD I WISH, IT WOULD BE EVER $DAY            2.37.13
EVER HENCEFORTH MY $BOSOME BE YOUR $HEARSE          2.45.7
A NAKED $STARVELING EVER MAY'ST THOU BE             2.48.2
YET TO MY $GODDESSE AM I CONSTANT EVER              2.51.11
THAT WHAT $THEY GET, $THEY EVER DOE RETAINE         2.52.4
THOSE $EYES TO MY $HEART SHINING EVER BRIGHT        2.55.13
TELL $ME, IF EVER SINCE THE $WORLD BEGUNNE          2.60.11
SHAKE HANDS FOR EVER, $CANCELL ALL OUR $VOWES       2.61.5
THOSE EYES TO MY HART SHINING EVER BRIGHT           2.102.13
THESE WITH THE $GODS ARE EVER RESIDENT              2.108.7
SUBDUE THYS $TYRANT EVER MARTYRING MEE              2.115.2
IF EVER WONDER COULD REPORT A WONDER                2.117.1
OR EVER JOY EXPRESSE, WHAT PERFECT JOY
                            HATH TAUGHT             2.117.3
BUT EVER CALL UPON DIVINE $IDEA                     2.118.14
O $LAMPE OF VERTUE, SUN-BRIGHT, EVER SHYNING        2.129.6
I $EVER LOVE, WHERE NEVER HOPE APPEARES             2.137.1
WITH ADMIRATION, EVER LOOKING ON HER                2.138.8
A SOULE, THAT EVER HATH ADOR'D HER NAME             2.138.10
LYKE IDLE $ECCHOES EVER AUNSWERING.. SO             2.141.7
TELL MEE, IF EVER SINCE THE WORLD BEGUNNE           2.149.11
MY LOVE SHALL IN MY VERSE EVER LIVE YOUNG           3.19.14
ARE BOTH WITH THEE, WHERE EVER I ABIDE              3.45.2
AGAINST THAT TIME (IF EVER THAT TIME COME)          3.49.1
TO PLAIE THE WATCH-MAN EVER FOR THY SAKE            3.61.12
FOR SLANDERS MARKE WAS EVER YET THE FAIRE           3.70.2
WHY WRITE I STILL ALL ONE, EVER THE SAME            3.76.5
THEN HATE ME WHEN THOU WILT, IF EVER, NOW           3.90.1
THAT IN THY FACE SWEET LOVE SHOULD EVER DWELL       3.93.10
```

TO ONE, OF ONE, STILL SUCH, AND EVER SO	3.105.4
O NO, IT IS AN EVER FIXED MARKE	3.116.5
I NEVER WRIT, NOR NO MAN EVER LOVED	3.116.14
THIS I DOE VOW AND THIS SHALL EVER BE	3.123.13
WHO EVER HATH HER WISH, THOU HAST THY $WILL	3.135.1
CHIDING THAT TONGUE THAT EVER SWEET	3.145.6
PLACED EVER THERE, GAVE HIM THIS MOURNING WEED	4.7.13
KEEPE STILL MY $ZENITH, EVER SHINE ON ME	4.42.8
WHAT EVER MAY ENSUE, O LET ME BE	4.48.5
HE SITS ME FAST, HOW EVER I DO STURRE	4.49.12
WHAT, DOST THOU THINKE THAT I CAN EVER TAKE	4.56.10
I CRAV'D THE THING WHICH EVER SHE DENIES	4.63.6
NOR EVER DID IN SHADE OF $TEMPE SIT	4.74.2
OF ALL THE KINGS THAT EVER HERE DID RAIGNE	4.75.1
WHEN I WAS FORST FROM $STELLA EVER DEERE	4.87.1
IN GENTLE BREST THAT SHALL ENDURE FOR EVER	5.6.10
TO KNIT THE KNOT, THAT EVER SHALL REMAINE	5.6.14
LOOKE EVER LOVELY, AS BECOMES YOU BEST	5.7.10
WELL IS HE BORNE, THAT MAY BEHOLD YOU EVER	5.8.14
NOR TO THE FIRE.. FOR THEY CONSUME NOT EVER	5.9.8
HAVE EVER SINCE ME KEPT IN CRUELL BANDS	5.12.12
FAYRER THEN FAYREST LET NONE EVER SAY	5.20.13
HOW EVER NOW THEREOF YE LITTLE WEENE	5.27.4
THINCK EVER TO ENDURE SO TAEDIOUS TOYLE+	5.33.10
IN WHICH IF EVER YE ENTRAPPED ARE	5.37.11
BUT JOY HER THRALL FOR EVER TO REMAYNE	5.42.7
YET LIVE FOR EVER, THOUGH AGAINST HER WILL	5.48.13
MAY LIVE FOR EVER IN FELICITY	5.68.8
YE THREE $ELIZABETHS FOR EVER LIVE	5.74.13
THAT MANY SOUGHT YET NONE COULD EVER TASTE	5.77.10
FOR ALL THE REST, HOW EVER FAYRE IT BE	5.79.5

EVER-CERTAIN   2
MY NEVER-CERTAINE $JOY BREEDS EVER-CERTAINE	
$FEARES	2.26.4
MY NEVER CERTAINE JOY, BREEDS EVER-CERTAINE	
FEARES	2.137.4

EVERLASTING   1
MY CARES DRAW ON MINE EVERLASTING NIGHT	1.30.1

EVERMORE   8
NEVER TO FINDE, AND EVERMORE TO SEEKE	1.20.9
THUS THE $WORLD DOTH, AND EVERMORE SHALL $REELE	2.51.10
AND EVER-MORE WITH SIGHES HE SUPT AND DYNDE	2.116.16
I MAY NOT EVER-MORE ACKNOWLEDGE THEE	3.36.9
TO TYE UP ENVY, EVERMORE INLARGED	3.70.12
AND FRANTICK MADDE WITH EVER-MORE UNREST	3.147.10
YOUR GOODLY SELFE FOR EVERMORE TO VEW	5.45.2
SHE LAUGHES, AND HARDENS EVERMORE HER HART	5.54.12

EVERY   74
WHEN EVERY PLACE PRESENTS LIKE FACE OF WOE	1.52.3
AS HOW THE $POLE TO EV'RY PLACE WAS REAR'D	2.1.8
THAT NOW IN $COACHES TROUBLE EV'RY $STREET	2.6.2
THAT EV'RY THING WHENCE $SHADOW DOTH PROCEED	2.13.13
THREE $NINES THERE ARE, TO EVERY ONE A $NINE	2.18.2
MAKES EVERY $ONE OF THESE THREE $NINES A $TEN	2.18.14
THUS AM I STILL PROVOK'D, TO EVERY $EVILL	2.20.13
AND LIKE A $WANTON, SPORTS WITH EV'RY $FETHER	2.22.6
IN EV'RY THING I HOLD THIS $MAXIM STILL	2.28.13
UNTO MINE AID I SUMMON'D EV'RY $SENSE	2.29.2
RECEIVING STRENGTH FROM EV'RY SECRET PART	2.30.7
THAT EV'RY $DUDGEN LOW $INVENTION GOES+	2.31.8

```
AND EV'RY $DRUDGE DOTH DULL OUR SATIATE $EARE        2.31.10
THAT EV'RY $DOWDY, EV'RY $TRULL DOTH WEARE+          2.31.12
THAT EV'RY $DOWDY, EV'RY $TRULL DOTH WEARE+          2.31.12
THAT EV'RY $CREATURE TO HIS KIND DO'ST CALL          2.37.11
DISPERSE THEIR $RAYES ON EV'RY VULGAR $SPIRIT         2.43.2
SOFTEN YOUR SELVES WITH EV'RY $TEARE THAT FALLS      2.45.11
WITH $SHOWTS AND $CLAPS AT EV'RY LITTLE PAWSE         2.47.9
WHEN THE PROUD $ROUND ON EV'RY SIDE HATH RUNG        2.47.10
THREE NINES THERE ARE, TO EVERIE ONE A NINE          2.108.2
MAKES EVERY ONE OF THESE THREE NINES A TEN          2.108.14
THAT EVERY THING WHENCE SHADOW DOTH PROCEEDE        2.121.13
THE SHADOW AND THE VAILE OF EVERY SINFULL DEED       2.145.8
THE LOVELY GAZE WHERE EVERY EYE DOTH DWELL            3.5.2
BEAUTY ORE-SNOW'D AND BARENES EVERY WHERE             3.5.8
WHEN EVERY PRIVAT WIDDOW WELL MAY KEEPE               3.9.7
WHEN I CONSIDER EVERY THING THAT GROWES              3.15.1
AND EVERY FAIRE FROM FAIRE SOME-TIME DECLINES        3.18.7
AND EVERY FAIRE WITH HIS FAIRE DOTH REHERSE          3.21.4
AND THOUGH THEY BE CUT-STRIPT BY EVERY PEN           3.32.6
FOR EVERY VULGAR PAPER TO REHEARSE                   3.38.4
ART LEFT THE PREY OF EVERY VULGAR THEEFE             3.48.8
THE WHICH HE WILL NOT EV'RY HOWER SURVAY             3.52.3
SINCE EVERY ONE, HATH EVERY ONE, ONE SHADE           3.53.3
SINCE EVERY ONE, HATH EVERY ONE, ONE SHADE           3.53.3
AND YOU BUT ONE, CAN EVERY SHADDOW LEND              3.53.4
AND YOU IN EVERY BLESSED SHAPE WE KNOW              3.53.12
AND ALL MY SOULE, AND AL MY EVERY PART               3.62.2
THAT EVERY WORD DOTH ALMOST FEL MY NAME              3.76.7
AS EVERY $ALIEN PEN HATH GOT MY USE                  3.78.3
OF THEIR FAIRE SUBJECT, BLESSING EVERY BOOKE         3.82.4
MAKING HIS STILE ADMIRED EVERY WHERE                3.84.12
TO EVERY $HIMNE THAT ABLE SPIRIT AFFORDS             3.85.7
AND EVERY HUMOR HATH HIS ADJUNCT PLEASURE            3.91.5
WHERE BEAUTIES VAILE DOTH COVER EVERY BLOT          3.95.11
WHAT OLD $DECEMBERS BARENESSE EVERY WHERE+           3.97.4
HATH PUT A SPIRIT OF YOUTH IN EVERY THING            3.98.3
AND MAKE TIMES SPOILES DISPISED EVERY WHERE        3.100.12
THE OWNERS TONGUE DOTH PUBLISH EVERY WHERE          3.102.4
BUT THAT WILD MUSICK BURTHENS EVERY BOW            3.102.11
CREATING EVERY BAD A PERFECT BEST                   3.114.7
IT IS THE STAR TO EVERY WANDRING BARKE              3.116.7
THAT EVERY TOUNG SAIES BEAUTY SHOULD LOOKE SO      3.127.14
AND SUTE THY PITTY LIKE IN EVERY PART              3.132.12
YOU THAT DO SEARCH FOR EVERIE PURLING SPRING         4.15.1
AND EVERIE FLOURE, NOT SWEET PERHAPS,
                            WHICH GROWES             4.15.3
WHO THOUGH MOST RICH IN THESE AND EVERIE PART       4.37.12
BECAUSE I BREATHE NOT LOVE TO EVERIE ONE             4.54.1
OF EVERIE IMAGE, WHICH MAY COMFORT SHOW+             4.66.4
WHILE EVERIE OFFICE THEMSELVES WILL DISCHARGE        4.85.7
ALL PAINE HATH END AND EVERY WAR HATH PEACE         5.11.13
AT EVERY RASH BEHOLDER PASSING BY                    5.16.8
AND REIGNETH OVER EVERY BEAST IN FIELD               5.20.6
SO EVERY SWEET WITH SOURE IS TEMPRED STILL           5.26.9
A MELTING PLEASANCE RAN THROUGH EVERY PART           5.39.7
SEEMD EVERY BIT, WHICH THENCEFORTH I DID EAT        5.39.14
AND EVERY BEAST THAT TO HIS DEN WAS FLED            5.40.10
AND EVERY PART REMAINES IMMORTALLY                   5.45.8
SEEING MY HART THROUGH LAUNCHED EVERY WHERE          5.57.7
TO EVERY PLANET POINT HIS SUNDRY YEARE               5.60.2
```

WHERE EVERY ONE THAT MISSETH THEN HER MAKE	5.70.11
AND MAKETH EVERY MINUTE SEEME A MYLE	5.87.12
AFFRAYD OF EVERY DANGERS LEAST DISMAY	5.88.4

EVE'S   1
HOW LIKE $EAVES APPLE DOTH THY BEAUTY GROW	3.93.13

EVIDENCE   1
TH'EVIDENCE SO GREAT A PROOFE DOTH CARRIE	2.2.8

EVIDENT   1
BUT THAT THOU NONE LOV'ST IS MOST EVIDENT	3.10.4

EVIDENTLY   1
HER SIMPLE $FOLLOWERS EVIDENTLY SHEWES	2.46.2

EVIL   7
AN $EVILL SPIRIT YOUR BEAUTIE HAUNTS $ME STILL	2.20.1
THUS AM I STILL PROVOK'D, TO EVERY $EVILL	2.20.13
BUT NOT TO TELL OF GOOD, OR EVIL LUCKE	3.14.3
THAT BETTER IS, BY EVIL STILL MADE BETTER	3.119.10
UNLESSE THIS GENERALL EVILL THEY MAINTAINE	3.121.13
TO WIN ME SOONE TO HELL MY FEMALL EVILL	3.144.5
IS IT NOT EVILL THAT SUCH A $DEVILL WANTS	
HORNES+	4.78.14

EVILS   1
SUFFERING THE EVILS BOTH OF THE DAY AND NIGHT	4.89.9

EXACT   2
HER EYES EXACT IT, THOUGH HER HART DISDAINES ME	1.18.6
BECAUSE THEIR POWER SERVE TO EXACT THE SAME	1.47.12

EXAMINE   1
EXAMINE WELL THY BEAUTIE WITH MY TRUTH	1.1.11

EXAMPLE   3
AND BY EXAMPLE, TRUE REPENTANCE PREACH	2.119.14
WHICH SHOULD EXAMPLE WHERE YOUR EQUALL GREW	3.84.4
BY SELFE EXAMPLE MAI'ST THOU BE DENIDE	3.142.14

EXCEED   1
I FOUND (OR THOUGHT I FOUND) YOU DID EXCEED	3.83.3

EXCEEDED   1
EXCEEDED BY THE HIGHT OF HAPPIER MEN	3.32.8

EXCEEDING   3
AYMING AT THINGS EXCEEDING ALL PERFECTION	2.34.6
OR HOW COMES IT THAT MY EXCEEDING HEAT	5.30.5
EXCEEDING SWEET, YET VOYD OF SINFULL VICE	5.77.9

EXCEEDS   3
WITNESSE YOUR $FATHERS GRIEFE EXCEEDES ALL OTHER	1.2.4
THAT IN MY MINDE THY WORST ALL BEST EXCEEDS+	3.150.8
THAT HER GREAT TRIUMPH WHICH MY SKILL EXCEEDS	5.29.11

EXCEL   8
AND $KENT WILL SAY, HER $MEDWAY DOTH EXCELL	2.32.8
SOME SAY, $THAT IN MY $HUMOR I EXCELL	2.42.4
AND $KENT WILL SAY, HER $MEDWAY DOTH EXCELL	2.124.8
SOME SAY THAT IN MY HUMOR I EXCELL	2.128.4
AND THAT UNFAIRE WHICH FAIRELY DOTH EXCELL	3.5.4
ABASE HER PRAISE, SAYING SHE DOTH EXCELL	4.37.8
MY BLOUD FROM THEM, WHO DID EXCELL IN THIS	4.41.10
BUT HER SWEET ODOUR DID THEM ALL EXCELL	5.64.14

EXCELLENCE   3
BESTOWING ALL HER $EXCELLENCE ON YOU	2.57.7
OTHERS, BUT STEWARDS OF THEIR EXCELLENCE	3.94.8
STILL CONSTANT IN A WONDROUS EXCELLENCE	3.105.6

EXCELLENCIES   1
ONE, IN WHOM ALL THE $EXCELLENCIES BE	2.17.3

EXCELLENCY   1
BEAUTIES WHICH DO IN EXCELLENCIE PASSE	4.82.2

EXCELLENT   3
  THINE OWNE SWEET ARGUMENT, TO EXCELLENT   3.38.3
  SITH NEVER OUGHT WAS EXCELLENT ASSAYDE   5.51.7
  TO SPEAKE HER PRAYSE AND GLORY EXCELLENT   5.74.11
EXCELLETH   1
  WHEREIN EACH FAYREST PART EXCELLETH OTHER   2.123.4
EXCELLING   1
  EXCELLING HER OF $DELPHOS OR $CUMAEA   2.119.11
EXCEPT   1
  DESIRE IS DEATH, WHICH $PHISICK DID EXCEPT   3.147.8
EXCESS   2
  WHERE, IN HIS $CUPS O'RCOME WITH FOULE $EXCESSE   2.7.9
  SHALL WORMES INHERITORS OF THIS EXCESSE   3.146.7
EXCHANGED   1
  JUST TO THE TIME, NCT WITH THE TIME EXCHANG'D   3.109.7
EXCHEQUER   1
  FOR SHE HATH NO EXCHECKER NOW BUT HIS   3.67.11
EXCUSE   9
  AND BLAME MY SELFE T'EXCUSE THAT HEART OF THINE   1.33.12
  SHALL SUM MY COUNT, AND MAKE MY OLD EXCUSE   3.2.11
  LOVING OFFENDORS THUS I WILL EXCUSE YEE   3.42.5
  THUS CAN MY LOVE EXCUSE THE SLOW OFFENCE   3.51.1
  O WHAT EXCUSE WILL MY POORE BEAST THEN FIND   3.51.5
  BUT LOVE, FOR LOVE, THUS SHALL EXCUSE MY JADE   3.51.12
  EXCUSE NOT SILENCE SO, FOR'T LIES IN THEE   3.101.10
  LET ME EXCUSE THEE, AH MY LOVE WELL KNOWES   3.139.9
  AND WHICH IS WORSE, NO GOOD EXCUSE CAN SHOW   4.18.7
EXCUSING   1
  EXCUSING THEIR SINS MORE THEN THEIR SINS ARE   3.35.8
EXECUTE   1
  ILE EXECUTE HER WITH A THOUSAND KISSES   2.115.16
EXECUTOR   1
  WHICH USED LIVES TH'EXECUTOR TO BE   3.4.14
EXEMPT   1
  AS IF SHE WERE EXEMPT FROM $SYETH OR $BOW   1.23.3
EXEMPTED   1
  YET SPARE HER $TIME, LET HER EXEMPTED BE   1.23.13
EXERCISE   1
  TEACHING DUMBE LIPS A NOBLER EXERCISE   4.81.4
EXHALED   1
  WHICH FROM HER LYPS EXHALD REFINED SWEET   2.125.6
EXHORTIVE   1
  BEGOT BY FANCY, ON SWEET HOPE EXHORTIVE   2.141.2
EXILE   3
  CALL BACKE THE STIFFE-NECK'D $REBELS FROM $EXILE 2.25.11
  MUST PASSE BY AYRE, OR ELSE DYE IN EXILE   2.122.4
  WHERE RIGROWS EXILE LOCKES UP ALL MY SENSE+   4.104.8
EXILED   2
  (EXIL'D FOR AY FRCM THOSE HIGH TREASURES, WHICH   4.24.13
  FROM PRESENCE OF MY DEAREST DEARE EXYLDE   5.52.7
EXORDIUMS   2
  WITH $FLAMES AND $LIGHTNINGS THEIR $EXORDIUMS
                              PAINT   2.39.2
  WITH FLAMES AND LIGHTNING THEIR EXORDIUMS PAYNT   2.118.2
EXPECTATION   2
  GREAT EXPECTATION, WEARE A TRAINE OF SHAME   4.21.8
  THUS I THE TIME WITH EXPECTATION SPEND   5.87.9
EXPECTING   1
  AND STILL EXPECTING WHEN SHE WILL RELENT   1.16.5

```
EXPENSE                         4
   IN WHICH EXPENCE, THE MOST SUPPOSE ME VAINE        2.28.6
   AND MONE TH'EXPENCE OF MANY A VANNISHT SIGHT       3.30.8
   AND HUSBAND NATURES RITCHES FROM EXPENCE           3.94.6
   TH'EXPENCE OF $SPIRIT IN A WASTE OF SHAME          3.129.1
EXPENSES                        1
   LOOKE ON THE DEERE EXPENCES OF MY YOUTH            1.1.9
EXPERIENCE                      2
   PLAINE-PATH'D $EXPERIENCE, TH'UNLEARNEDS GUIDE     2.46.1
   BUT THEIR $EXPERIENCE TO INCREASE THE MORE         2.50.11
EXPIATE                         1
   THEN LOOK I DEATH MY DAIES SHOULD EXPIATE          3.22.4
EXPIRE                          3
   CAUSE ONCE THE DATE OF HER DISDAINE T'EXPIRE       1.22.3
   AS THE DEATH BED, WHERECN IT MUST EXPIRE           3.73.11
   BUT WHAT THIS VERSE, THAT NEVER SHALL EXPYRE       5.27.11
EXPIRED                         2
   AND THAT IN $BEAUTIES LEASE EXPIR'D, APPEARES      1.50.11
   TO WORKE MY MIND, WHEN BODDIES WORK'S EXPIRED      3.27.4
EXPRESS                        13
   WHO HAD LESSE $ART THEM LIVELY TO EXPRESSE+        2.27.6
   A DUMBE-BORNE $MUSE MADE TO EXPRESSE THE $MIND     2.35.6
   EXPRESSE MY $WOES, AND SHEW THE PAINES OF $HELL    2.60.2
   A DUMBE-BORNE $MUSE MADE TO EXPRESSE THE MIND      2.112.6
   OR EVER JOY EXPRESSE, WHAT PERFECT JOY
                            HATH TAUGHT               2.117.3
   AND I WANT WORDS FCR TO EXPRESSE MY WRONG          2.143.8
   EXPRESSE MY WOES, AND SHEW THE PAYNES OF HELL      2.149.2
   THAT MAY EXPRESSE MY LOVE, OR THY DEARE MERIT+     3.108.4
   LEAST SORROW LEND ME WORDS AND WORDS EXPRESSE      3.140.3
   WIT LEARNES IN THEE PERFECTION TO EXPRESSE         4.35.12
   THY TEARES EXPRESSE NIGHT'S NATIVE MOISTURE RIGHT  4.96.8
   WHAT PEN, WHAT PENCILL CAN EXPRESSE HER FILL+      5.17.4
   THAT CAN EXPRESSE THE LIFE OF THINGS INDEED        5.17.14
EXPRESSED                       7
   ONELY MY SIGHES ARE BY THE AYRE EXPRESSED          2.127.11
   WHOSE PURE $IDEA NEVER TONGUE EXPREST              2.139.13
   MORE THEN THAT TONGE THAT MORE HATH MORE EXPREST   3.23.12
   I SEE THEIR ANTIQUE $PEN WOULD HAVE EXPREST        3.106.7
   AT RANDON FROM THE TRUTH VAINELY EXPREST           3.147.12
   TILL THAT IN WORDS THY FIGURE BE EXPREST           4.50.4
   CANNOT EXPRESSED BE BY ANY ART                     5.17.12
EXPRESSING                      2
   ONE THING EXPRESSING, LEAVES OUT DIFFERENCE        3.105.8
   EXPRESSING ALL THY MOTHERS POWREFULL ART           5.39.2
EXTANT                          1
   THAT YOU YOUR SELFE BEING EXTANT WELL MIGHT SHOW   3.83.6
EXTEND                          2
   THEN POSSIBLY $INVENTION CAN EXTEND                2.34.11
   THAT FURTHER SEEMES HIS TERME STILL TO EXTEND      5.87.11
EXTERN                          1
   WITH MY EXTERN THE CUTWARD HONORING                3.125.2
EXTERNAL                        1
   IN ALL EXTERNALL GRACE YOU HAVE SOME PART          3.53.13
EXTINGUISHED                    2
   THE $GODS PURE FIRE HATH BEEN EXTINGUISHT QUITE    2.105.2
   MY LOVE, MY TEARES, MY SIGHES, EXTINGUISHT
                            CANNOT BE                 2.127.14
EXTOL                           2
   OUR $WESTERNE $PARTS EXTOLL THEIR $WILIS $FAME     2.32.11
```

```
   OUR $WESTERNE PARTS EXTOLL THEYR $WILYS FAME      2.124.11
EXTORTED                    1
   DROWN'D IN THE $TEARES, EXTORTED BY MY $LINES      2.45.2
EXTORTION                   2
   WHICH BY $EXTORTION GAINETH ALL THEIR LOOKES       2.3.10
   WHO BY EXTORTION GAINETH ALL THEYR LOOKES          2.110.10
EXTORTS                     1
   WHICH LOVE DOTH PAY, AND HER DISDAINE EXTORTS      1.60.2
EXTREME                     2
   SAVAGE, EXTREAME, RUDE, CRUELL, NOT TO TRUST       3.129.4
   HAD, HAVING, AND IN QUEST, TO HAVE EXTREAME        3.129.10
EXTREMEST                   1
   SO PLEASING IS IN MY EXTREAMEST PAINE              5.42.2
EXTREMITIES                 1
   BUT WHEN YE HAVE SHEWED ALL EXTREMITYES            5.36.9
EXTREMITY                   2
   AND TORTURES $ME IN MOST EXTREMITY                 2.20.8
   WHEN SWIFT EXTREMITY CAN SEEME BUT SLOW            3.51.6
EYE                        75
   BUT UNTOUCHT HEARTS, WITH UNAFFECTED EIE           1.3.5
   THEN HAD NO $CENSORS EYE THESE LINES SURVAID       1.7.5
   ONCE LET HER LOVE INDEED, OR ELS EYE ME NEVER      1.24.14
   HER VOYCE BETRAIES ME TO HER HAND AND EYE          1.27.9
   RAIGNE IN MY THOUGHTS FAIRE HAND, SWEETE
                        EYE, RARE VOICE               1.28.1
   NO PITTYING EYE LOOKES BACKE UPON MY FEARES        1.32.10
   I FEARE YOUR EYE HATH TURND YOUR HEART TO FLINT    1.37.14
   AND IN YOUR $EYE, THE $BOY THAT DID THE $MURTHER   2.2.11
   AND THUS MINE $EIES A DEBTOR TO THINE $EYE         2.3.9
   NOW RAILE UPON HER $HAIRE, THEN ON HER $EYE        2.41.11
   HAD NOT MINE EYE SEENE THY $CELESTIALL EYE         2.104.5
   HAD NOT MINE EYE SEENE THY $CELESTIALL EYE         2.104.5
   ATTENDS THAT $LAMPE WITH EYE WHICH NEVER
                        SLEEPETH                      2.105.10
   PASSING BY THAT CLEERE FOUNTAINE OF THINE EYE      2.109.2
   AND THUS MINE EYES, A DEBTOR TO THINE EYE          2.110.9
   BEQUEATH'D HIS WARDSHIP TO MY SOVERAIGNES EYE      2.116.12
   OR COULD MINE EYE BUT AYME, HER OBJECTS
                        PAST PERFECTION               2.117.6
   AND TO MY HART SEND'ST POYSON FROM THINE EYE       2.130.7
   AND WHILST MY HART AND EYE, ENVY EACH
                        OTHERS PRAISE                 2.133.11
   NOW RAYLE UPON HER HAYRE, NOW ON HER EYE           2.143.11
   LET HIM COMPARE IT TO HER HEAVENLY EYE             2.148.2
   THE LOVELY GAZE WHERE EVERY EYE DOTH DWELL         3.5.2
   LIFTS UP HIS BURNING HEAD, EACH UNDER EYE          3.7.2
   IS IT FOR FEARE TO WET A WIDDOWES EYE              3.9.1
   SOMETIME TOO HOT THE EYE OF HEAVEN SHINES          3.18.5
   AN EYE MORE BRIGHT THEN THEIRS, LESSE
                        FALSE IN ROWLING              3.20.5
   MINE EYE HATH PLAY'D THE PAINTER AND HATH STEELD   3.24.1
   BUT AS THE $MARYGOLD AT THE SUNS EYE               3.25.6
   THEN CAN I DROWNE AN EYE (UN-US'D TO FLOW)         3.30.5
   HATH DEARE RELIGIOUS LOVE STOLNE FROM MINE EYE     3.31.6
   FLATTER THE MOUNTAINE TOPS WITH SOVERAINE EIE      3.33.2
   MINE EYE AND HEART ARE AT A MORTALL WARRE          3.46.1
   MINE EYE, MY HEART THEIR PICTURES SIGHT
                        WOULD BARRE                   3.46.3
   MY HEART, MINE EYE THE FREEEDOME OF THAT RIGHT     3.46.4
   BETWIXT MINE EYE AND HEART A LEAGUE IS TOOKE       3.47.1
```

```
WHEN THAT MINE EYE IS FAMISHT FOR A LOOKE          3.47.3
WITH MY LOVES PICTURE THEN MY EYE DOTH FEAST       3.47.5
AN OTHER TIME MINE EYE IS MY HEARTS GUEST          3.47.7
AND SCARCELY GREETE ME WITH THAT SUNNE THINE EYE   3.49.6
IT IS MY LOVE THAT KEEPES MINE EIE AWAKE           3.61.10
SINNE OF SELFE-LOVE POSSESSETH AL MINE EIE         3.62.1
THOSE PARTS OF THEE THAT THE WORLDS EYE DOTH VIEW  3.69.1
BY SEEING FARTHER THEN THE EYE HATH SHOWNE         3.69.8
AND PLACE MY MERRIT IN THE EIE OF SKORNE           3.88.2
FOR THEIR CAN LIVE NO HATRED IN THINE EYE          3.93.5
FOR AS YOU WERE WHEN FIRST YOUR EYE I EYDE         3.104.2
HATH MOTION, AND MINE EYE MAY BE DECEAVED          3.104.12
OF HAND, OF FOOTE, OF LIP, OF EYE, OF BROW         3.106.6
SINCE I LEFT YOU, MINE EYE IS IN MY MINDE          3.113.1
OR WHETHER SHALL I SAY MINE EIE SAITH TRUE         3.114.3
MINE EIE WELL KNOWES WHAT WITH HIS GUST
                             IS GREEING            3.114.11
THAT MINE EYE LOVES IT AND DOTH FIRST BEGINNE      3.114.14
ME FROM MY SELFE THY CRUELL EYE HATH TAKEN         3.133.5
WOUND ME NOT WITH THINE EYE BUT WITH THY TOUNG     3.139.3
DEARE HEART FORBEARE TO GLANCE THINE EYE ASIDE     3.139.6
LOVES EYE IS NOT SO TRUE AS ALL MENS.. NO          3.148.8
HOW CAN IT+ $O HOW CAN LOVES EYE BE TRUE           3.148.9
FOR I HAVE SWORNE THEE FAIRE.. MORE PERJURDE
                             EYE                   3.152.13
BUT AT MY MISTRES EIE LOVES BRAND NEW FIRED        3.153.9
WHERE $CUPID GOT NEW FIRE., MY MISTRES EYE         3.153.14
AS THAT SWEETE BLACKE WHICH VAILES THE
                        HEAV'NLY EYE               4.20.7
RICH IN ALL BEAUTIES WHICH MAN'S EYE CAN SEE       4.37.6
UNKIND, I LOVE YOU NOT.. $O ME, THAT EYE           4.47.13
OF $HOPE, WHICH MAKES IT SEEME FAIRE TO THE EYE    4.49.8
LET CLOUDS BEDIMME MY FACE, BREAKE IN MINE EYE     4.64.5
DOTH $STELLA NOW BEGIN WITH PITEOUS EYE            4.67.2
SCHOOL'D ONELY BY HIS MOTHER'S TENDER EYE          4.73.2
LET WO GRIPE ON MY HEART, SHAME LOADE MINE EYE     4.86.4
WHEN FAR SPENT NIGHT PERSWADES EACH MORTALL EYE    4.99.1
AND TO THE GROUND HER EIE LIDS LOW EMBASETH        5.13.3
WHEN SUDDENLY WITH TWINCLE OF HER EYE              5.16.11
THING SO DIVINE TO VEW OF EARTHLY EYE              5.45.6
YET SHE BEHOLDING ME WITH CONSTANT EYE             5.54.9
EVEN SO MY HART, THAT WONT ON YOUR FAYRE EYE       5.73.7
WHEREOF SOME GLANCE DOTH IN MINE EIE REMAYNE       5.88.8
EYED                    1
FOR AS YOU WERE WHEN FIRST YOUR EYE I EYDE         3.104.2
EYE-GLANCES             1
THE SWEET EYE-GLAUNCES, THAT LIKE ARROWES GLIDE    5.17.9
EYE-KILLING             1
THAT DAUNGEROUS EYE-KILLING $COCKATRICE            2.130.2
EYELID                  1
WHEN ON EACH EYELID SWEETLY DOE APPEARE            5.40.3
EYELIDS                 3
BRIGHT STARRE OF $BEAUTY, ON WHOSE EYE-LIDS SIT    2.4.1
AND KEEPE MY DROOPING EYE-LIDS OPEN WIDE           3.27.7
MY HEAVY EIELIDS TO THE WEARY NIGHT+               3.61.2
EYEN                    2
BUT PRECIOUS $TEARES DISTILLING FROM MINE $EYNE    2.7.6
IN THE CLOSE COVERT OF HER GUILEFULL EYEN          5.12.7
EYES                  246
AND SEE HOW JUST I RECKON WITH THINE EIES          1.1.10
```

```
PRESSE TO HER EYES, IMPORTUNE ME SOME GOOD           1.2.11
FOR HER NO SOONER HAD MINE EYES BEWRAID              1.5.5
HER BROW SHADES FROWNES, ALTHOUGH HER
                            EYES ARE SUNNY           1.6.2
THE WONDER OF ALL EYES THAT LOOKE UPON HER           1.6.7
AND YOU MINE EYES, THE AGENTS OF MY HART             1.8.5
TEARES IN MINE EYES, AND SORROW AT MY HART           1.9.12
THAT SERVES A $TROPHEY TO HER CONQUERING EIES        1.10.11
MY FORTUNES WHEELES THE CIRCLE OF HER EIES           1.12.11
THE $DART TRANSPEARSING, WERE THOSE $CHRISTALL
                            EIES                      1.14.4
IF I HAVE DONE DUE HOMAGE TO HER EYES                1.15.9
HER EYES EXACT IT, THOUGH HER HART DISDAINES ME      1.18.6
DELIA MY HART HATH LEARND OUT OF THOSE EYES          1.20.14
SITH I LIVE HATEFULL TO THOSE RUTHLESSE EIES         1.21.7
POWRE FROM THOSE EYES, WHICH PITTY CANNOT SPARE      1.22.6
OF MINE AFFECTIONS TAKEN BY HER EIES                 1.22.14
OR ART THOU GROWNE IN LEAGUE WITH THOSE
                            FAIRE EIES                1.23.5
STRAIGHT-WAY SHE HASTS HER UNTO $DELIAS EIES         1.25.10
TH'IMPRESSION OF HER EYES DO PEARCE SO DEEPE         1.26.7
WHILST BY THY EIES PURSU'D, MY POORE HEART FLEW      1.31.1
OFT DO I MARVELL, WHETHER $DELIAS EIES               1.34.1
ARE EYES, OR ELS TWO RADIANT STARRES THAT SHINE      1.34.2
STARRES THEN, NOT EYES, MOVE YOU WITH
                            A MILDER VIEW             1.34.13
FRAM'D MY DESIRES FIT FOR HER EYES TO KILL           1.36.14
WHOSE STATE BEST SHEWES THE FORCE OF MURDERING
                            EIES+                     1.37.4
THESE SHALL INTOMBE THOSE EIES, THAT HAVE
                            REDEEM'D                  1.44.11
DELIA, THESE EYES THAT SO ADMIRETH THINE             1.45.1
AND WAST HIM TO THEE WITH THOSE LOVELY EIES          1.46.5
A SACRIFICE THRICE-GRATEFULL TO HER EIES             1.47.11
MY $DELIA HATH THE WATERS OF MINE EIES               1.48.1
ALTHOUGH HER EYES MY ADVERSARIES BE                  1.49.14
I MUST NOT GRIEVE MY $LOVE, WHOSE EIES
                            WOULD REEDE               1.51.1
DRAWNE WITH TH'ATRACTIVE VERTUE OF HER EYES          1.53.1
JOYES IN THAT HONOR WHICH HER EYES HAVE WONNE        1.53.7
LET WAKING EYES SUFFICE TO WAILE THEIR SCORNE        1.54.7
BUT I MUST SING OF THEE, AND THOSE FAIRE EIES        1.55.5
WHOSE DUE REPORTS GIVE HONOR TO HER EYES             1.57.8
I SEND THOSE EYES THE CABINETS OF LOVE               1.60.6
AND THUS MINE $EIES A DEBTOR TO THINE $EYE           2.3.9
THAT WHERE THOSE TWO CLEARE SPARKLING
                            $EYES ARE PLAC'D          2.8.3
THY BLESSED $EYES, THE $SUNNE WHICH LIGHTS
                            THIS $FIRE                2.30.9
WHILST YET MINE $EYES DOE SURFET WITH $DELIGHT       2.33.1
BUT WHILST MINE $EYES THUS GREEDILY DOE GAZE         2.33.5
THAT $EYES WERE $HEART, OR THAT THE $HEART
                            WERE EYES                 2.33.9
THAT $EYES WERE $HEART, OR THAT THE $HEART
                            WERE EYES                 2.33.9
THAT $EYES COULD THINKE OF THAT MY $HEART
                            COULD SEE                 2.33.14
BLIND WERE MINE $EYES, TILL THEY WERE
                            SEENE OF THINE            2.35.9
TO WOUND HER $HEART, WHOSE $EYES HAVE WOUNDED ME     2.36.2
```

MY $EYES WITH $TEARES AGAINST THE FIRE STRIVING	2.40.9
WHY SHOULD YOUR FAIRE $EYES WITH SUCH	
SOV'RAIGNE GRACE	2.43.1
LASTLY, MINE $EYES AMAZEDLY HAVE SEENE	2.51.5
OR HAVE THINE $EYES SUCH $MAGIKE, OR THAT $ART	2.52.3
THY $CRISTALL STREAME REFINED BY HER $EYES	2.53.4
A SECOND $FLOUD, DCWNE RAYNING FROM MINE $EYES	2.55.4
NOTE BUT MY $SIGHES, AND THINE $EYES SHALL BEHOLD	2.55.5
ERECTING $TROPHIES TO THY $SACRED $EYES	2.55.12
THOSE $EYES TO MY $HEART SHINING EVER BRIGHT	2.55.13
BUT ON HER $RAYES WITH CPEN $EYES IT STOCC	2.56.6
TO MY $SOULES $SUNNE, THCSE TWO $CELESTIALL	
$EYES	2.56.12
YOU BEST DISCERN'D CF MY $MINDS INWARD $EYES	2.57.1
AT WHOSE PURE $EYES, $LCVE LIGHTS HIS	
HALLOW'D $FIRE	2.57.8
AND $INNOCENCE IS CLOSING UP HIS $EYES	2.61.12
A SECOND FLOOD DOWNE RAYNING FROM MINE EYES	2.102.4
NOTE BUT MY SIGHES, AND THINE EYES SHAL BEHCLD	2.102.5
ERECTING $TROPHIES TO THY SACRED EYES	2.102.12
THOSE EYES TO MY HART SHINING EVER BRIGHT	2.102.13
BUT ON HER RAYES WITH GAZING EYES THEY STOOD	2.103.6
STRAIGHT MOUNTING UP TO THY CELESTIALL EYES	2.103.12
AND FROM MY BREAST INTO THINE EYES BE GONE	2.103.14
WITH THINE EYES KINCLING THAT $CELESTIAL FLAME	2.105.7
THE GLORIOUS SUN-BEAMES OF HER EYES BRIGHT	
SHINING	2.109.10
WHERE SHEE REMAINES FOR ALL EYES TO BEHOLD	2.109.14
AND THUS MINE EYES, A DEBTOR TO THINE EYE	2.110.9
THINE EYES TAUGHT MEE THE $ALPHABET OF LCVE	2.111.1
BLIND WERE MINE EYES, TILL THEY WERE SEENE	
OF THINE	2.112.9
THAT CHRISTALL STREAME REFINED BY HER EYES	2.113.4
THAT FOR MY MIS-SPENT YCUTH THE TEARS	
FEL FROM MY EYES	2.114.4
THEN IN THESE TEARES, THE MIRRORS OF THESE EYES	2.114.5
AND IN THYS $IMAGE HIS CARKE CLOWDY EYES	2.114.13
WITH TEARES OUT OF THE $CHANNELS OF MINE EYES	2.115.9
PEOPLED WITH $ARMIES OF PALE JEALOUS EYES	2.122.2
WHY SHOULD'ST THOU PLACE THY $TROPHIES	
IN THOSE EYES	2.123.9
AS THOUGH THE HEAVEN HAD NOW AWAK'D HER EYES	2.125.11
HYDES IN THOSE CHRISTALL QUIVERS OF HER EYES	2.126.10
O $EYES, BEHOLD YCLR HAPPY $HESPERUS	2.129.1
THRICE HAPPY BE THCSE EYES WHICH MAY BEHCLD	
THEE	2.129.10
O BLESSED FAYRE, NCW VAILE THUSE HEAVENLY EYES	2.129.13
WHILST THUS MINE EYES DCE SURFET WITH DELIGHT	2.133.1
TO LOOKE ON HER BY WHOM MINE EYES ARE BLEST	2.133.4
BUT WHILST MINE EYES THUS GREEDILY DOE GAZE	2.133.5
MY EYES MADE DIM WITH LCOKES, POURE DOWN	
A FLOOD OF TEARS	2.133.10
MY $FAYRE, LOOKE FRCM THCSE TURRETS OF	
THINE EYES	2.134.1
AND THERE STANDS GAZING CN THOSE DARTING EYES	2.135.6
MYNE EYES BEHELD THYS CCNFLICT IN THY FACE	2.136.14
OR EYES THAT HAVE BEHELD HER AS THEYR SUNNE	2.138.7
WOUNDED WITH $ARRCWES FROM THY LIGHTNING EYES	2.142.5
MYNE EYES WANT TEARES THUS TO BEWAYLE MY WOE	2.143.5
MYNE EYES WITH TEARES AGAINST THE FIRE STRYVING	2.144.9

```
WITH MY HARTS TRYBUTE TO HER CONQUERING EYES        2.151.2
BUT THOU CONTRACTED TO THINE OWNE BRIGHT EYES        3.1.5
TO SAY WITHIN THINE OWNE DEEPE SUNKEN EYES           3.2.7
THE EYES (FORE DUTIOUS) NOW CONVERTED ARE            3.7.11
BY CHILDRENS EYES, HER HUSBANDS SHAPE IN MINDE       3.9.8
BUT FROM THINE EIES MY KNOWLEDGE I DERIVE            3.14.9
CAN MAKE YOU LIVE YOUR SELFE IN EIES OF MEN          3.16.12
IF I COULD WRITE THE BEAUTY OF YOUR EYES             3.17.5
SO LONG AS MEN CAN BREATH OR EYES CAN SEE            3.18.13
WHICH STEALES MENS EYES AND WOMENS SOULES AMASETH    3.20.8
TO HEARE WIT EIES BELONGS TO LOVES FINE WIHT         3.23.14
THAT HATH HIS WINDOWES GLAZED WITH THINE EYES        3.24.8
NOW SEE WHAT GOOD-TURNES EYES FOR EIES HAVE DONE     3.24.9
NOW SEE WHAT GOOD-TURNES EYES FOR EIES HAVE DONE     3.24.9
MINE EYES HAVE DRAWNE THY SHAPE, AND THINE
                                    FOR ME           3.24.10
YET EYES THIS CUNNING WANT TO GRACE THEIR ART        3.24.13
WHEN IN DISGRACE WITH $FORTUNE AND MENS EYES         3.29.1
WHEN MOST I WINKE THEN DOE MINE EYES BEST SEE        3.43.1
WHEN TO UN-SEEING EYES THY SHADE SHINES SO+          3.43.8
HOW WOULD (I SAY) MINE EYES BE BLESSED MADE          3.43.9
THROUGH HEAVY SLEEPE ON SIGHTLESSE EYES
                                    DOTH STAY+       3.43.12
(A CLOSET NEVER PEARST WITH CHRISTALL EYES)          3.46.6
AS THUS, MINE EYES DUE IS THEIR OUTWARD PART         3.46.13
EVEN IN THE EYES OF ALL POSTERITY                    3.55.11
YOU LIVE IN THIS, AND DWELL IN LOVERS EIES           3.55.14
THY HUNGRIE EIES, EVEN TILL THEY WINCK
                                WITH FULNESSE        3.56.6
THEN CHURLS THEIR THOUGHTS (ALTHOUGH THEIR
                                EIES WERE KIND)      3.69.11
THINE EYES, THAT TAUGHT THE DUMBE ON HIGH TO SING    3.78.5
WHEN YOU INTOMBED IN MENS EYES SHALL LYE             3.81.8
WHICH EYES NOT YET CREATED SHALL ORE-READ            3.81.10
THERE LIVES MORE LIFE IN ONE OF YOUR FAIRE EYES      3.83.13
AND ALL THINGS TURNES TO FAIRE, THAT EIES
                                CAN SEE              3.95.12
AND FOR THEY LOOK'D BUT WITH DEVINING EYES           3.106.11
HAVE EYES TO WONDER, BUT LACK TOUNGS TO PRAISE       3.106.14
HOW HAVE MINE EIES OUT OF THEIR $SPHEARES
                                BENE FITTED          3.119.7
FOR WHY SHOULD OTHERS FALSE ADULTERAT EYES           3.121.5
THEREFORE MY $MISTERSSE EYES ARE $RAVEN BLACKE       3.127.9
HER EYES SO SUTED, AND THEY MOURNERS SEEME           3.127.10
MY $MISTRES EYES ARE NOTHING LIKE THE $SUNNE         3.130.1
THINE EIES I LOVE, AND THEY AS PITTYING ME           3.132.1
AS THOSE TWO MORNING EYES BECOME THY FACE            3.132.9
THOU BLINDE FOOLE LOVE, WHAT DOOST THOU
                                TO MINE EYES         3.137.1
IF EYES CORRUPT BY OVER-PARTIALL LOOKES              3.137.5
OR MINE EYES SEEING THIS, SAY THIS IS NOT            3.137.11
IN THINGS RIGHT TRUE MY HEART AND EYES
                                HAVE ERRED           3.137.13
BEARE THINE EYES STRAIGHT, THOUGH THY
                        PROUD HEART GOE WIDE         3.140.14
IN FAITH I DOE NOT LOVE THEE WITH MINE EYES          3.141.1
WHOME THINE EYES WOOE AS MINE IMPORTUNE THEE         3.142.10
O ME- WHAT EYES HATH LOVE PUT IN MY HEAD             3.148.1
IF THAT BE FAIRE WHEREON MY FALSE EYES DOTE          3.148.5
LEAST EYES WELL SEEING THY FOULE FAULTS
                                SHOULD FINDE         3.148.14
```

```
COMMANDED BY THE MOTION OF THINE EYES              3.149.12
AND TO INLIGHTEN THEE GAVE EYES TO BLINDNESSE      3.152.11
IT IS MOST TRUE, THAT EYES ARE FORM'D TO SERVE      4.5.1
WHEN $NATURE MADE HER CHIEFE WORKE, $STELLA'S EYES  4.7.1
WHOSE FAIRE SKIN, BEAMY EYES, LIKE MORNING
                                  SUN ON SNOW       4.8.9
STELLA, THOU STRAIGHT LOOKST BABIES IN HER EYES    4.11.10
CUPID, BECAUSE THOU SHIN'ST IN $STELLAS EYES        4.12.1
MINE EYES (SHALL I SAY CURST OR BLEST) BEHELD      4.16.10
AND IN HER EYES OF ARROWES INFINIT                 4.17.11
BEWRAY IT SELFE IN MY LONG SETLED EYES              4.23.2
BUT ONLY $STELLA'S EYES AND $STELLA'S HART         4.23.14
THAT $VERTUE, IF IT ONCE MET WITH OUR EYES          4.25.3
TO MORTALL EYES MIGHT SWEETLY SHINE IN HER         4.25.11
AND THUS HER HEART ESCAPES, BUT THUS HER EYES       4.29.9
SURE, IF THAT LONG WITH $LOVE ACQUAINTED EYES       4.31.5
TEACHING BLIND EYES BOTH HOW TO SMILE AND WEEPE     4.32.8
HOW FAIRE A DAY WAS NEARE, O PUNISHT EYES          4.33.13
WHERETO LONG SINCE, THROUGH MY LONG BATTRED EYES    4.36.3
TO HATCH MINE EYES, AND THAT UNBITTED THOUGHT       4.38.2
BOTH BY THE JUDGEMENT OF THE $ENGLISH EYES          4.41.3
O EYES, WHICH DO THE $SPHEARES OF BEAUTIE MOVE      4.42.1
O EYES, WHERE HUMBLE LOCKES MOST GLORIOUS PROVE     4.42.5
YET STILL ON ME, O EYES, DART DOWNE YOUR RAYES     4.42.11
FAIRE EYES, SWEET LIPS, DEARE HEART, THAT
                                  FOOLISH I         4.43.1
THEN WITH THOSE EYES HE LOOKES, LO BY AND BY        4.43.6
LET NOT MINE EYES BE HEL-DRIV'N FROM THAT LIGHT     4.48.7
WITH SAD EYES I THEIR WEAKE PROPORTION SEE          4.50.7
HER EYES, HER LIPS, HER ALL, SAITH $LOVE DO THIS    4.52.3
MY HEART THEN QUAK'D, THEN DAZLED WERE MINE EYES   4.53.10
I $STELLA'S EYES ASSAYLL, INVADE HER EARES          4.61.3
SHE IN WHOSE EYES $LOVE, THOUGH UNFELT,
                                  DOTH SHINE        4.62.3
SO CHILDREN STILL READE YOU WITH AWFULL EYES        4.63.2
FOR LATE WITH HEART MOST HIGH, WITH EYES MOST LOW   4.63.5
BY $NATURE BORNE, I GAVE TO THEE MINE EYES          4.65.8
MINE EYES, MY LIGHT, MY HEART, MY LIFE, ALAS        4.65.9
STELLA'S EYES SENT TO ME THE BEAMES OF BLISSE      4.66.11
BUT WHEN MINE EYES BACKE TO THEIR HEAV'N
                                  DID MOVE         4.66.13
ENVIE, PUT OUT THINE EYES, LEAST THOU DO SEE        4.69.3
HATH CHEEKES TO SMILE, AS WELL AS EYES TO WEEPE     4.70.8
THAT INWARD SUNNE IN THINE EYES SHINETH SO          4.71.8
CARE SHINING IN MINE EYES, FAITH IN MY SPRITE      4.72.11
OF GENTLE FORCE, SO THAT MINE EYES DARE
                                  GLADLY PLAY       4.76.6
MY HEART CRIES 'AH', IT BURNES, MINE EYES
                                  NOW DAZLED BE    4.76.11
SO MANIE EYES AY SEEKING THEIR OWNE WOE            4.78.12
HOW FAINE WOULD I PAINT THEE TO ALL MEN'S EYES      4.81.7
BUT GIVE APT SERVANTS THEIR DUE PLACE, LET EYES     4.85.9
THEN THOSE BLEST EYES, WHERE ALL MY HOPES
                                  DO DWELL         4.86.13
STELLA WHOSE EYES MAKE ALL MY TEMPESTS CLEERE       4.87.3
I SAW THAT TEARES DID IN HER EYES APPEARE           4.87.6
THAT WHERE BEFORE HART LOVED AND EYES DID SEE      4.88.12
SINCE $STELLA'S EYES, WONT TO GIVE ME MY DAY        4.89.3
THINE EYES MY PRIDE, THY LIPS MY HISTORY            4.90.3
THEY PLEASE I DO CONFESSE, THEY PLEASE MINE EYES    4.91.9
```

FROM OUT THY HEAVY MOULD, THAT INBENT EYES	4.94.3
MINE EYES THEN ONLY WINKE, FOR SPITE PERCHANCE	4.98.13
IN TOMBE OF LIDS THEN BURIED ARE MINE EYES	4.99.12
AND JOY, WHICH IS INSEPERATE FROM THOSE EYES	4.101.7
WHERE BE THOSE $ROSES GONE, WHICH SWEETNED	
SO OUR EYES+	4.102.1
BUT CEASE MINE EYES, YOUR TEARES DO WITNESSE WELL	4.105.9
THOU TOLDST MINE EYES SHOULD HELPE THEIR	
FAMISHT CASE+	4.106.6
THOSE LAMPING EYES WILL DEIGNE SOMETIMES TO LOOK	5.1.6
THRETNING RASH EIES WHICH GAZE ON HER SO WIDE	5.5.7
THAT BOLDNED INNOCENCE BEARES IN HIR EIES	5.5.10
FAYRE EYES, THE MYRROUR OF MY MAZED HART	5.7.1
THAT YOUR BRIGHT BEAMS OF MY WEAK EIES ADMYRED	5.7.11
NO EIES BUT JOYES, IN WHICH AL POWERS CONSPIRE	5.8.3
THOSE POWREFULL EIES, WHICH LIGHTEN MY	
DARK SPRIGHT	5.9.2
THE HUGE MASSACRES WHICH HER EYES DO MAKE	5.10.6
ONE DAY I SOUGHT WITH HER HART-THRILLING EIES	5.12.1
AGAINST YOUR EIES THAT JUSTICE I MAY GAINE	5.12.14
IF $SAPHYRES, LOE HER EIES BE $SAPHYRES PLAINE	5.15.7
ON THOSE FAYRE EYES MY LOVES IMMORTALL LIGHT	5.16.2
SHE TO HER LOVE DOTH LOCKERS EYES ALLURE	5.21.6
WITH SUCH STRANGE TERMES HER EYES SHE DOTH INURE	5.21.9
SUCH ART OF EYES I NEVER READ IN BOOKES	5.21.14
WHICH HER FAYRE EYES UNWARES DOE WORKE IN MEE	5.24.6
MY HUNGRY EYES THROUGH GREEDY COVETIZE	5.35.1
WHOSE EYES HIM STARV'D.. SO PLENTY MAKES ME POORE	5.35.8
YET ARE MINE EYES SO FILLED WITH THE STORE	5.35.9
OR MAKE AGREEMENT WITH HER THRILLING EYES	5.36.6
IS IT THAT MENS FRAYLE EYES, WHICH GAZE TOO BOLD	5.37.5
TAKE HEED THEREFORE, MYNE EYES, HOW YE DOE STARE	5.37.9
AND EKE MINE EIES WITH MEEKE HUMILITY	5.43.11
LOVE LEARNED LETTERS TO HER EYES TO READ	5.43.12
HER EYES LOOKE LOVELY AND UPON THEM SMYLE	5.47.10
IS IT BECAUSE YOUR EYES HAVE POWRE TO KILL+	5.49.2
TO SHEW THE POWRE OF YOUR IMPERIOUS EYES	5.49.6
WITH THOUSAND ARROWES, WHICH YOUR EIES HAVE SHOT	5.57.8
THE BEAME OF LIGHT, WHOM MORTAL EYES ADMYRE	5.61.10
HER LOVELY EYES LYKE $PINCKS BUT NEWLY SPRED	5.64.8
BUT WHEN MYNE EYES I THEREUNTO DIRECT	5.78.9
CEASSE THEN MYNE EYES, TO SEEKE HER SELFE TO SEE	5.78.13
OR IN HER EYES THE FYRE OF LOVE DOES SPARKE	5.81.4
MY HUNGRY EYES, THROUGH GREEDY COVETIZE	5.83.1
WHOSE EYES HIM STARV'D.. SO PLENTY MAKES ME PORE	5.83.8
YET ARE MYNE EYES SO FILLED WITH THE STORE	5.83.9
I STARVE MY BODY AND MINE EYES DOE BLYND	5.88.14

EYE'S OR EYES'   10

WHICH NOW ARE MELTED BY THINE EYES BRIGHT SUN	1.32.7
INKINDLED BY HER EYES CELESTIALL FIRE	1.59.4
MY $HEART SHOULD SUFFER FOR MINE $EYES $OFFENCE	2.29.4
SO NEERE THYNE EYES CELESTIALL SUNNE ASPYRED	2.122.10
O MINE EYES $COMET, SO ADMYR'D BY LOVING	2.129.7
IN THINE EYES TRYUMPH MURTHERING MY POORE HART	2.140.2
THE CLEERE EYES MOYITIE, AND THE DEARE	
HEARTS PART	3.46.12
AS THUS, MINE EYES DUE IS THEIR OUTWARD PART	3.46.13
AWAKES MY HEART, TO HEARTS AND EYES DELIGHT	3.47.14
WHY OF EYES FALSEHOOD HAST THOU FORGED HOOKES	3.137.7

```
EYE'S-SPEECH                    1
   HER EYE'S-SPEECH IS TRANSLATED THUS BY THEE        4.67.5
FABLE                           1
   YET HEARING LATE A FABLE, WHICH DID SHOW           4.45.5
FACE                           66
   BEST IN MY FACE, HOW CARES HAVE TILD DEEPE
                                FORROWES              1.4.8
   CAST WATER-COLD $DISDAINE UPON MY FACE             1.5.8
   THEN HAD I WALKT WITH BOLD ERECTED FACE            1.7.9
   M'AMBITIOUS THOUGHTS CONFINED IN HER FACE          1.12.5
   ILE PRAISE HER FACE, AND BLAME HER FLINTY HEART    1.26.12
   THAT $MIRROR SHEWES WHAT POWER IS IN THY FACE      1.37.10
   READ IN MY FACE, A VOLUME OF DISPAIRES             1.47.1
   WHEN EVERY PLACE PRESENTS LIKE FACE OF WOE         1.52.3
   AND SINNE OF FROWNES BRING HONOUR TO THE FACE      1.56.12
   BEFORE MY $FACE, IT LAYES DOWNE MY $DESPAIRES      2.20.9
   MAKING WITHALL SOME FILTHY $ANTIKE $FACE           2.31.4
   AGE RULES MY $LINES WITH $WRINKLES IN MY $FACE     2.44.2
   HER SUN-SHINE FACE THERE CHAUNSING TO ESPY         2.109.3
   I SEE THE UGLY FACE OF MY DEFORMED CARES           2.114.2
   IT IS THY HEAVEN WITHIN HER FACE TO DWELL          2.123.13
   MYNE EYES BEHELD THYS CONFLICT IN THY FACE         2.136.14
   LOOKE IN THY GLASSE AND TELL THE FACE THOU VEWEST  3.3.1
   NOW IS THE TIME THAT FACE SHOULD FORME AN OTHER    3.3.2
   A $WOMANS FACE WITH NATURES OWNE HAND PAINTED      3.20.1
   MAKES BLACKE NIGHT BEAUTIOUS, AND HER
                                OLD FACE NEW          3.27.12
   KISSING WITH GOLDEN FACE THE MEDDOWES GREENE       3.33.3
   WITH OUGLY RACK ON HIS CELESTIALL FACE             3.33.6
   TO DRY THE RAINE ON MY STORME-BEATEN FACE          3.34.6
   ME THINKES NO FACE SO GRATIOUS IS AS MINE          3.62.5
   LIKE A DECEIVED HUSBAND, SO LOVES FACE             3.93.2
   THAT IN THY FACE SWEET LOVE SHOULD EVER DWELL      3.93.10
   RISE RESTY $MUSE, MY LOVES SWEET FACE SURVAY       3.100.9
   LOOKE IN YOUR GLASSE AND THERE APPEARES A FACE     3.103.6
   FAIRING THE FOULE WITH $ARTS FAULSE BORROW'D
                                FACE                  3.127.6
   THY FACE HATH NOT THE POWER TO MAKE LOVE GRONE     3.131.6
   A THOUSAND GRONES BUT THINKING ON THY FACE         3.131.10
   AS THOSE TWO MORNING EYES BECOME THY FACE          3.132.9
   TO PUT FAIRE TRUTH UPON SO FOULE A FACE            3.137.12
   AND THEREFORE FROM MY FACE SHE TURNES MY FOES      3.139.11
   TO FOLLOW THAT WHICH FLIES BEFORE HER FACE         3.143.7
   I SOUGHT FIT WORDS TO PAINT THE BLACKEST
                                FACE OF WOE           4.1.5
   HOW THEN+ EVEN THUS.. IN $STELLA'S FACE I REED     4.3.12
   AT LENGTH HE PERCH'D HIMSELF IN $STELLA'S
                                JOYFULL FACE          4.8.8
   QUEENE $VERTUE'S COURT, WHICH SOME CALL
                                $STELLA'S FACE        4.9.1
   STELLA'S FAIRE HAIRE, HER FACE HE MAKES
                                HIS SHIELD            4.13.10
   HAVING NO SCARFE OF CLOWDS BEFORE HIS FACE         4.22.3
   STELLA ALONE WITH FACE UNARMED MARCHT              4.22.9
   VERTUE'S GREAT BEAUTIE IN THAT FACE I PROVE        4.25.13
   BY ONLY THOSE TWO STARRES IN $STELLA'S FACE        4.26.14
   HOW SILENTLY, AND WITH HOW WANNE A FACE            4.31.2
   STELLA LOOKT ON, AND FROM HER HEAVENLY FACE        4.41.13
   STELLA OFT SEES THE VERIE FACE OF WO               4.45.1
   PAINTED IN MY BECLOWDED STORMIE FACE               4.45.2
```

```
FOR SHE PROTESTS TO BANISH THEE HER FACE            4.46.5
HER FACE+ $O $LOVE, A $ROGUE THOU THEN
                          SHOULDST BE                4.46.6
WHICH IN HER FACE TEACH VERTUE, I COULD BROOKE       4.56.6
TO FEELE MY GRIEFES, AND SHE WITH FACE AND VOICE     4.57.13
O VOICE, O FACE, MAUGRE MY SPEECHE'S MIGHT           4.58.12
LET CLOUDS BEDIMME MY FACE, BREAKE IN MINE EYE       4.64.5
O HEAV'NLY FOOLE, THY MOST KISSE-WORTHIE FACE        4.73.12
THAT FACE, WHOSE LECTURE SHEWES WHAT PERFECT
                          BEAUTIE IS                 4.77.2
SEE $BEAUTIE'S TOTALL SUMME SUMM'D IN HER FACE       4.85.10
SHEWES HER OFT AT THE FULL HER FAIREST FACE          4.97.2
PAINT WOE'S BLACKE FACE SO LIVELY TO MY SIGHT        4.98.10
UPON THY CHEEREFULL FACE, JOYE'S LIVERY WEARE        4.103.3
ONELY UNTO THE HEAV'N OF $STELLA'S FACE              4.105.7
FALSE FLATTERING HOPE, THAT WITH SO FAIRE A FACE     4.106.2
WHILES HER FAIRE FACE SHE REARES UP TO THE SKIE      5.13.2
THE GLORIOUS POURTRAICT OF THAT $ANGELS FACE         5.17.1
WHICH TEMPRED SO THE FEATURE OF HER FACE             5.21.2
AND SEEKE EACH WHERE, WHERE LAST I SAWE HER FACE     5.78.3
FACES                 2
SUCH HEAVENLY TOUCHES NERE TOUCHT EARTHLY FACES      3.17.8
THEY ARE THE $LORDS AND OWNERS OF THEIR FACES        3.94.7
FACULTY               1
HAVE FACULTIE BY NATURE TO SUBSIST                   3.122.6
FADE                  8
THEN FADE THOSE FLOWERS THAT DECKT HER
                          PRIDE SO LONG              1.38.8
SO FADE THE $ROSES OF THOSE CHEEKS OF THINE          1.39.8
SOONE DOTH IT FADE THAT MAKES THE FAIREST FLORISH    1.50.5
AND THOUGH THIS $EARTHLY $BODY FADE AND DIE          2.44.13
BUT THY ETERNALL $SOMMER SHALL NOT FADE              3.18.9
THEY LIVE UNWOO'D, AND UNRESPECTED FADE              3.54.10
NE LET THEYR FAMOUS MONIMENTS TO FADE                5.51.4
ALL OTHER FAYRE LYKE FLOWRES UNTYMELY FADE           5.79.14
FADES                 1
AND THERE PREPARE HER FLOWRES THAT NEVER FADES       1.30.7
FADEST                1
I THAT HAVE LOV'D THEE THUS BEFORE THOU FADST        1.41.7
FADETH                1
AS AFTER $SUN-SET FADETH IN THE $WEST                3.73.6
FADING                5
AND THINKE THE SAME BECOMES THY FADING BEST          1.40.11
THESE COLOURS WITH THY FADING ARE NOT SPENT          1.42.11
SPRINGING WITH THAT, AND FADING STRAIGHT
                          WITH THIS                  2.141.11
TO THE WIDE WORLD AND ALL HER FADING SWEETS          3.19.7
DOST THOU UPON THY FADING MANSION SPEND+             3.146.6
FAIL                  4
SHALL FAILE IN FORCE, THEIR WORKING NOT SO STRONG    1.38.4
AND IF THESE RULES DID FAILE, PROOFE MAKES
                          ME SURE                    4.26.12
TO LOSE HIS $CROWNE, RATHER THEN FAILE HIS $LOVE     4.75.14
AND IF THOSE FAYLE FALL DOWNE AND DY BEFORE HER      5.14.13
FAILED                1
MY FENCE OPPRESS'D, HAD FAILD, AND HEART
                          HAD BROKEN                 1.7.14
FAILEST               1
BUT FAILST THOU NOT IN PHRASE SO HEAV'NLY HIE+       4.67.6
```

FAILETH   1
  BUT FAYLETH TRUSTING ON HIS OWNE ASSURANCE   5.58.10
FAILING   1
  WHEN HIS $PULSE FAYLING, $PASSION SPEECHLESSE
                                   LIES   2.61.10
FAIN   11
  AS ONE THAT FAINE HIS $SORROWES WOULD BEGUILE   2.24.6
  THEY SAY ($AS $POETS DOE) I USE TO FAINE   2.42.6
  THEY SAY, (AS $POETS DOE) I USE TO FAYNE   2.128.6
  LOVING IN TRUTH, AND FAINE IN VERSE MY
                             LOVE TO SHOW   4.1.1
  SWEET KISSE, THY SWEETS I FAINE WOULD
                       SWEETLY ENDITE   4.79.1
  HOW FAINE WOULD I PAINT THEE TO ALL MEN'S EYES   4.81.7
  THEN SINCE (DEARE LIFE) YOU FAINE WOULD
                     HAVE ME PEACE   4.81.12
  DIAN THAT FAINE WOULD CHEARE HER FRIEND
                     THE $NIGHT   4.97.1
  WOULD FAINE DRIVE CLOUDES FROM OUT MY
                  HEAVY CHEERE   4.97.11
  AND FAINE THOSE $AECLS' YOUTHES THERE
                WOULD THEIR STAY   4.103.9
  AND FAINE MY GRIEFE WITH CHAUNGES TO BEGUILE   5.87.10
FAINT   3
  O HOW I FAINT WHEN I OF YOU DO WRITE   3.80.1
  FAINT COWARD JOY NO LONGER TARRY DARE   4.95.5
  NOT FYRE., FOR SHE DOTH FRIESE WITH FAINT DESIRE   5.55.8
FAIR   196
  MAY JUSTLY PRAISE, AND BLAME MY LOVELESSE $FAIRE   1.2.8
  BY MINE OWNE THOUGHTS, SET ON ME BY MY $FAIRE   1.5.11
  FAIRE IS MY $LOVE, AND CRUELL AS SHE'S FAIRE   1.6.1
  FAIRE IS MY $LOVE, AND CRUELL AS SHE'S FAIRE   1.6.1
  FOR HAD SHE NOT BEENE FAIRE AND THUS UNKINDE   1.6.13
  FOR HAD SHE NOT BEENE FAIRE AND THUS UNKINDE   1.7.1
  DID TREATE THE CRUELL FAIRE TO YEELD RELIEFE   1.8.8
  FOR HER THE CRUELL $FAIRE, WITHIN WHOSE BROW   1.10.2
  NO FAVOUR THOUGH, THE CRUELL FAIRE ALLOWES   1.11.12
  ROB HER FAIRE $BROW, BREAKE IN ON $BEAUTY, STEALE   1.22.5
  BY LOVING HER, THE CRUELST $FAIRE THAT LIVES   1.22.10
  THE CRUELST $FAYRE THAT SEES I PINE FOR HER   1.22.11
  OR ART THOU GROWNE IN LEAGUE WITH THOSE
                   FAIRE EIES   1.23.5
  RAIGNE IN MY THOUGHTS FAIRE HAND, SWEETE
                EYE, RARE VOICE   1.28.1
  SHE THEN IS SCORND THAT LATE ADORND THE $FAYRE   1.39.7
  BEWRAY UNTO THE WORLD HOW FAIRE THOU ART   1.44.2
  MOST FAIRE AND LOVELY $MAIDE, LOOKE FROM
                 THE SHORE   1.46.1
  PITTY AND SMILES DOE BEST BECOME THE FAIRE   1.51.11
  FLORISH FAIRE $ALBION, GLORY OF THE $NORTH   1.53.9
  BUT I MUST SING OF THEE, AND THOSE FAIRE EIES   1.55.5
  I TELL YEE ($FAIRE) ILE NOT BE ANSWERED SO   2.5.3
  AND MY FAIRE $MUSE, ONE $MUSE UNTO THE $NINE   2.18.10
  OUR $NORTHERNE $BORDERS BOAST OF $TWEEDS
                FAIRE $FLOUD   2.32.10
  THAT FAIRE $IDEA ONELY LIVES BY THEE   2.32.14
  BY THY FAIRE $MOTHERS UNAVOIDED $POWER   2.36.6
  WHY SHOULD YOUR FAIRE $EYES WITH SUCH
               SOV'RAIGNE GRACE   2.43.1
  SO MAY'ST THOU LIVE, TO THY FAIRE $MOTHERS $JOY   2.48.12

```
THIS $KINGS FAIRE $ENTRANCE, AND OUR $PEACE
                    WITH $SPAINE                    2.51.8
MY $SOULE-SHRIN'D $SAINT, MY FAIRE $IDEA LIES       2.53.2
SAY THUS FAIRE $BROOKE, WHEN THOU SHALT
                    SEE THY QUEENE                  2.53.9
FAIRE $ARDEN, THOU MY $TEMPE ART ALONE              2.53.13
MY $FAIRE, IF THOU WILT REGISTER MY LOVE            2.55.1
FAIRE WORDS MAKE $FOOLES, REPLYETH HE AGAINE        2.59.4
YOU HAVE SPUNNE A FAIRE $THRED, HE REPLYES
                    IN SCORNE                       2.59.12
SO $FAIRE A RISING, HAD SO $FOULE A SET             2.60.12
I OFFER FREE $CONDITIONS OF FAIRE $PEACE            2.63.5
MY $FAYRE, IF THOU WILT REGISTER MY LOVE            2.102.1
AND THUS (MY FAIRE) MY THOUGHTS AWAY BE FLOWNE      2.103.13
MY $FAIRE, HAD I NOT ERST ADORND MY $LUTE           2.104.1
NOR HAD I LEARN'D TO DESCANT ON MY FAIRE            2.104.4
AND THY YOUTH PAST, IN THIS FAIRE MIRROR SEE        2.107.6
AND MY FAIRE $MUSE, ONE $MUSE UNTO THE NINE         2.108.10
MY SOULE-SHRINDE $SAINT, MY FAIRE $IDEA LYES        2.113.2
SAY THUS FAYRE $BROOKE WHEN THOU SHALT
                    SEE THY $QUEENE                 2.113.9
FAYRE $ARDEN, THOU MY $TEMPE ART ALONE              2.113.13
IN THIS FAYRE LIMMED GROUND AS WHITE AS SNOW        2.114.10
MY HART SHALL BE THE PRISON FOR MY FAYRE            2.115.5
MY SWEET, MY FAIRE, MY GOOD, MY BEST OF ALL         2.115.12
SOME $HELYCON, AND SOME FAIRE $SIMOIS               2.120.12
OUR $NORTHERN BORDERS BOAST OF $TWEEDS
                    FAIRE FLOOD                     2.124.10
THAT FAYRE $IDEA SHEE DOTH LIVE BY THEE             2.124.14
WHEN MY SOULES SUNNE FROM HER FAYRE $CABYNET        2.125.2
LAUGHING FOR JOY UPON MY LOVELY FAYRE               2.125.14
O STARRE OF STARRES, FAYRE $PLANET MILDLY
                    MOOVING                         2.129.5
O BLESSED FAYRE, NOW VAILE THOSE HEAVENLY EYES      2.129.13
MY $FAYRE, LOOKE FROM THOSE TURRETS OF
                    THINE EYES                      2.134.1
WHICH THOSE FAYRE $ILANDS OF THY LOOKES AFFOORD     2.134.6
YET SEE HOW RIGHT HE COMES UNTO MY FAYRE            2.135.4
YET FAIRE UNKINDE, TO GOOD TO BE DISGRACED          2.138.14
O $THOU UNKINDEST FAYRE, MOST FAYREST SHEE          2.140.1
BUT MY FAIRE $PLANET, WHO DIRECTS ME STILL          2.147.9
THE FAYRE $ELIZIA, TO HER FAYRER CHEEKE             2.148.7
PRAYSING THE FAYREST, COMPARE IT TO MY FAIRE        2.148.11
SO FAIRE A $MORNING HAD SO FOULE A SET +            2.149.12
IF THOU COULDST ANSWERE THIS FAIRE CHILD OF MINE    3.2.10
FOR WHERE IS SHE SO FAIRE WHOSE UN-EARD WOMBE       3.3.5
BE NOT SELFE-WILD FOR THOU ART MUCH TOO FAIRE       3.6.13
WHO LETS SO FAIRE A HOUSE FALL TO DECAY             3.13.9
NEITHER IN INWARD WORTH NOR OUTWARD FAIRE           3.16.11
AND EVERY FAIRE FROM FAIRE SOME-TIME DECLINES       3.18.7
AND EVERY FAIRE FROM FAIRE SOME-TIME DECLINES       3.18.7
NOR LOOSE POSSESSION OF THAT FAIRE THOU OW'ST       3.18.10
O CARVE NOT WITH THY HOWERS MY LOVES FAIRE BROW     3.19.9
AND EVERY FAIRE WITH HIS FAIRE DOTH REHERSE         3.21.4
AND EVERY FAIRE WITH HIS FAIRE DOTH REHERSE         3.21.4
AND THEN BELEEVE ME, MY LOVE IS AS FAIRE            3.21.10
GREAT $PRINCES FAVORITES THEIR FAIRE LEAVES
                    SPREAD                          3.25.5
POINTS ON ME GRATIOUSLY WITH FAIRE ASPECT           3.26.10
WHEN IN DEAD NIGHT THEIR FAIRE IMPERFECT SHADE      3.43.11
```

```
OF THEIR FAIRE HEALTH, RECOUNTING IT TO ME          3.45.12
AND SAYES IN HIM THEIR FAIRE APPEARANCE LYES         3.46.8
THE $ROSE LOOKES FAIRE, BUT FAIRER WE IT DEEME       3.54.3
BEFORE THESE BASTARD SIGNES OF FAIRE WERE BORNE      3.68.3
TO THY FAIRE FLOWER AD THE RANCKE SMELL OF WEEDS     3.69.12
FOR SLANDERS MARKE WAS EVER YET THE FAIRE            3.70.2
AND FOUND SUCH FAIRE ASSISTANCE IN MY VERSE          3.78.2
OF THEIR FAIRE SUBJECT, BLESSING EVERY BOOKE         3.82.4
THOU ART AS FAIRE IN KNOWLEDGE AS IN HEW             3.82.5
THOU TRULY FAIRE, WERT TRULY SIMPATHIZDE             3.82.11
AND THEREFORE TO YOUR FAIRE NO PAINTING SET          3.83.2
THERE LIVES MORE LIFE IN ONE OF YOUR FAIRE EYES      3.83.13
THE CAUSE OF THIS FAIRE GUIFT IN ME IS WANTING       3.87.7
BUT WHATS SO BLESSED FAIRE THAT FEARES NO BLOT       3.92.13
AND ALL THINGS TURNES TO FAIRE, THAT EIES
                                      CAN SEE        3.95.12
TO ME FAIRE FRIEND YOU NEVER CAN BE OLD              3.104.1
FAIRE, KINDE, AND TRUE, IS ALL MY ARGUMENT           3.105.9
FAIRE, KINDE AND TRUE, VARRYING TO OTHER WORDS       3.105.10
FAIRE, KINDE, AND TRUE, HAVE OFTEN LIV'D ALONE       3.105.13
EVEN AS WHEN FIRST I HALLOWED THY FAIRE NAME         3.108.8
IN THE OULD AGE BLACKE WAS NOT COUNTED FAIRE         3.127.1
AT SUCH WHO NOT BORNE FAIRE NO BEAUTY LACK           3.127.11
AND IN MY WILL NO FAIRE ACCEPTANCE SHINE             3.135.8
LET NO UNKINDE, NO FAIRE BESEECHERS KILL             3.135.13
TO PUT FAIRE TRUTH UPON SO FOULE A FACE              3.137.12
THE BETTER ANGELL IS A MAN RIGHT FAIRE               3.144.3
FOR I HAVE SWORNE THEE FAIRE, AND THOUGHT
                                   THEE BRIGHT       3.147.13
IF THAT BE FAIRE WHEREON MY FALSE EYES DOTE          3.148.5
FOR I HAVE SWORNE THEE FAIRE.. MORE PERJURDE
                                         EYE         3.152.13
OF LIVING DEATHS, DEARE WOUNDS, FAIRE
                         STORMES AND FREESING FIRES  4.6.4
WHOSE FAIRE SKIN, BEAMY EYES, LIKE MORNING
                                 SUN ON SNOW              4.8.9
BUT SHE MOST FAIRE, MOST COLD, MADE HIM
                            THENCE TAKE HIS FLIGHT   4.8.12
FOR LIKE A CHILD THAT SOME FAIRE BOOKE DOTH FIND     4.11.5
CRIE, '$VICTORIE, THIS FAIRE DAY ALL IS OURS'        4.12.11
STELLA'S FAIRE HAIRE, HER FACE HE MAKES
                                 HIS SHIELD          4.13.10
NOR SO FAIRE LEVELL IN SO SECRET STAY                4.20.6
HATH THIS WORLD OUGHT SO FAIRE AS $STELLA IS+        4.21.14
PROGRESSING THEN FROM FAIRE TWINNES' GOLD'N PLACE    4.22.2
WHEN SOME FAIRE $LADIES, BY HARD PROMISE TIED        4.22.5
HOW FAIRE A DAY WAS NEARE, O PUNISHT EYES            4.33.13
SENT FORTH THE BEAMES, WHICH MADE SO FAIRE
                                 MY RACE             4.41.14
FAIRE EYES, SWEET LIPS, DEARE HEART, THAT
                             FOOLISH I               4.43.1
OF $HOPE, WHICH MAKES IT SEEME FAIRE TO THE EYE      4.49.8
NOT THIS FAIRE OUTSIDE, WHICH OUR HEARTS
                             DOTH MOVE               4.52.8
BUT YOU FAIRE MAIDES, AT LENGTH THIS TRUE
                             SHALL FIND              4.54.11
WHEN I MIGHT READE THOSE LETTERS FAIRE OF BLISSE     4.56.5
WITH THAT FAIRE BREAST MAKING WOE'S DARKNESSE
                             CLEARE                  4.57.11
IF HE BE FAIRE, YET BUT A DOG CAN BE                 4.59.4
```

```
STOLNE TO MY HEART, SINCE LAST FAIRE NIGHT,
                          NAY DAY                     4.66.10
LOOKE ON AGAINE, THE FAIRE TEXT BETTER TRIE           4.67.7
IT IS, SO FAIRE A $VERTUE TO ENJOY                    4.68.14
STELLA, THOSE FAIRE LINES, WHICH TRUE
                          GOODNESSE SHOW              4.71.4
WHO MARKE IN THEE WHAT IS IN THEE MOST FAIRE          4.71.11
NOT FOR HIS FAIRE OUTSIDE, NOR WELL LINED BRAINE      4.75.3
AS THOUGH THAT FAIRE SOFT HAND DID YOU
                          GREAT WRONG                 4.83.4
BE YOU STILL FAIRE, HONOURD BY PUBLIKE HEED           4.84.9
AND THAT FAIRE YOU MY $SUNNE, THUS OVERSPRED          4.91.3
WHICH AY MOST FAIRE, NOW MORE THEN MOST
                          FAIRE SHOW                  4.100.3
WHICH AY MOST FAIRE, NOW MORE THEN MOST
                          FAIRE SHOW                  4.100.3
BEAUTY IS SICKE, BUT SICKE IN SO FAIRE GUISE          4.101.5
WHERE THOSE RED CHEEKS, WHICH OFT WITH
                          FAIRE ENCREASE DID FRAME    4.102.2
WHILE THOSE FAIRE PLANETS ON THY STREAMES
                          DID SHINE                   4.103.4
WITH SIGHT THEREOF CRIDE OUT., O FAIRE DISGRACE       4.103.13
FALSE FLATTERING HOPE, THAT WITH SO FAIRE A FACE      4.106.2
BUT HEERE I DO STORE OF FAIRE $LADIES MEETE           4.106.9
TO DECKE HIR SELFE, AND HER FAIRE MANTLE WEAVE        5.4.12
THEN YOU FAIRE FLOWRE, IN WHOM FRESH YOUTH
                          DOTH RAINE                  5.4.13
AND HER FAIRE COUNTENANCE LIKE A GOODLY BANNER        5.5.11
FAYRE EYES, THE MYRROUR OF MY MAZED HART              5.7.1
MORE THEN MOST FAIRE, FULL OF THE LIVING FIRE         5.8.1
WHILES HER FAIRE FACE SHE REARES UP TO THE SKIE       5.13.2
SO FAYRE A PEECE FOR ONE REPULSE SO LIGHT             5.14.4
IF SILVER, HER FAIRE HANDS ARE SILVER SHEENE          5.15.12
ON THOSE FAYRE EYES MY LOVES IMMORTALL LIGHT          5.16.2
HER TEMPLE FAYRE IS BUILT WITHIN MY MIND              5.22.5
WHICH HER FAYRE EYES UNWARES DOE WORKE IN MEE         5.24.6
FAIRE PROUD NOW TELL ME WHY SHOULD FAIRE BE PROUD     5.27.1
FAIRE PROUD NOW TELL ME WHY SHOULD FAIRE BE PROUD     5.27.1
SHALL DOFFE HER FLESHES BOROWD FAYRE ATTYRE           5.27.6
FAIRE BE NO LENGER PROUD OF THAT SHALL PERISH         5.27.13
THEN FLY NO MORE FAYRE LOVE FROM $PHEBUS CHACE        5.28.13
OF THAT FAIRE SIGHT, THAT NOTHING ELSE
                          THEY BROOKE                 5.35.10
UNTO THE FAYRE SUNSHINE IN SOMERS DAY                 5.40.6
O FAYREST FAYRE LET NEVER IT BE NAMED                 5.41.13
THAT SO FAYRE BEAUTY WAS SO FOWLY SHAMED              5.41.14
THE FAYRE $IDEA OF YOUR CELESTIALL HEW                5.45.7
REMOVE THE CAUSE BY WHICH YOUR FAYRE BEAMES
                          DARKNED BE                  5.45.14
MY CRUELL FAYRE STREIGHT BIDS ME WEND MY WAY          5.46.2
FAYRE CRUELL, WHY ARE YE SO FIERCE AND CRUELL+        5.49.1
RIGHT SO MY CRUELL FAYRE WITH ME DOTH PLAY            5.53.5
THE WHICH HER MADE ATTONCE SO CRUELL FAIRE            5.55.4
FAYRE YE BE SURE, BUT CRUELL AND UNKIND               5.56.1
FAYRE BE YE SURE, BUT PROUD AND PITTILESSE            5.56.5
FAYRE BE YE SURE, BUT HARD AND OBSTINATE              5.56.9
NE NONE SO RICH OR WISE, SO STRONG OR FAYRE           5.58.9
WHY THEN DOE YE PROUD FAYRE, MISDEEME SO FARRE        5.58.13
BUT LET MY LOVES FAYRE $PLANET SHORT HER WAYES        5.60.13
FAYRE SOYLE IT SEEMES FROM FAR AND FRAUGHT
                          WITH STORE                  5.63.7
```

```
THE DOUBT WHICH YE MISDEEME, FAYRE LOVE, IS VAINE    5.65.1
BUT THE FAYRE TRESSES OF YOUR GOLDEN HAYRE           5.73.3
EVEN SO MY HART, THAT WONT ON YOUR FAYRE EYE         5.73.7
FAYRE BOSOME FRAUGHT WITH VERTUES RICHEST TRESURE    5.76.1
MEN CALL YOU FAYRE, AND YOU DOE CREDIT IT            5.79.1
BUT THE TREW FAYRE, THAT IS THE GENTLE WIT           5.79.3
FOR ALL THE REST, HOW EVER FAYRE IT BE               5.79.5
DERIV'D FROM THAT FAYRE $SPIRIT, FROM
                             WHOM AL TRUE            5.79.11
HE ONELY FAYRE, AND WHAT HE FAYRE HATH MADE          5.79.13
HE ONELY FAYRE, AND WHAT HE FAYRE HATH MADE          5.79.13
ALL OTHER FAYRE LYKE FLOWRES UNTYMELY FADE           5.79.14
FAYRE IS MY LOVE, WHEN HER FAYRE GOLDEN HEARES       5.81.1
FAYRE IS MY LOVE, WHEN HER FAYRE GOLDEN HEARES       5.81.1
FAYRE WHEN THE ROSE IN HER RED CHEEKES APPEARES      5.81.3
FAYRE WHEN HER BREST LYKE A RICH LADEN BARKE         5.81.5
FAYRE WHEN THAT CLOUD OF PRYDE, WHICH
                             OFT DOTH DARK           5.81.7
OF THAT FAYRE SIGHT, THAT NOTHING ELSE
                             THEY BROOKE             5.83.10
AND BLESSE YOUR FORTUNES FAYRE ELECTION              5.84.14
DARK IS MY DAY, WHYLES HER FAYRE LIGHT I MIS         5.89.13
FAIRER                      7
THERE WHERE MY $DELIA FAIRER THEN THE $SUNNE         1.53.5
THE FAYRE $ELIZIA, TO HER FAYRER CHEEKE              2.148.7
SHALL HATE BE FAIRER LOG'D THEN GENTLE LOVE+         3.10.10
THE $ROSE LOOKES FAIRE, BUT FAIRER WE IT DEEME       3.54.3
GROWES FAIRER THEN AT FIRST, MORE STRONG,
                             FAR GREATER             3.119.12
FAYRER THEN FAYREST LET NONE EVER SAY                5.20.13
NE OUGHT FOR FAYRER WEATHERS FALSE DELIGHT           5.59.8
FAIREST                     32
WITH FAIREST HAND, THE SWEET UNKINDEST $MAID         1.5.7
THOU POORE HEART SACRIFIZ'D UNTO THE FAIREST         1.8.1
WHERE BLAZE THOSE LIGHTS FAIREST OF EARTHLY
                             THINGS                  1.12.3
HOLDES IN HER FAIREST HAND WHAT DEAREST IS           1.12.10
THE FAIREST FORME, THAT ALL THE WORLD ADMIRES        1.13.7
DISSOLVES THE BEAUTY OF THE FAIREST BROW             1.39.12
THE FAIREST FLOWRE THAT EVER SAW THE LIGHT           1.40.6
TO HELPE HER FLIGHT THROUGHOUT THE FAIREST $ILE      1.43.10
THOUGH TIME DO SPOYLE THEE OF THE FAIREST VAILE      1.45.10
TO SAVE THINE OWNE, STRETCH OUT THE FAIREST HAND     1.46.8
STRETCH OUT THE FAIREST HAND, A PLEDGE OF PEACE      1.46.9
THEN I WOULD JOY THE FAIREST SHE THAT LIVES          1.48.12
SOONE DOTH IT FADE THAT MAKES THE FAIREST FLORISH    1.50.5
THY FAYREST YOUTH AND $BEAUTIE DOE I SEE             2.114.6
WHEREIN EACH FAYREST PART EXCELLETH OTHER            2.123.4
O $THOU UNKINDEST FAYRE, MOST FAYREST SHEE           2.140.1
PRAYSING THE FAYREST, COMPARE IT TO MY FAIRE         2.148.11
FROM FAIREST CREATURES WE DESIRE INCREASE            3.1.1
I SEE DISCRIPTIONS OF THE FAIREST WIGHTS             3.106.2
THOU ART THE FAIREST AND MOST PRECIOUS $JEWELL       3.131.4
THY BLACKE IS FAIREST IN MY JUDGEMENTS PLACE         3.131.12
THE FAYREST VOTARY TOOKE UP THAT FIRE                3.154.5
OF THOSE THREE GODS, WHOSE ARMES THE FAIREST WERE    4.13.2
WHO WILL IN FAIREST BOOKE OF $NATURE KNOW            4.71.1
SHEWES HER OFT AT THE FULL HER FAIREST FACE          4.97.2
BUT IF IN PRESENCE OF THAT FAYREST PROUD             5.2.9
WHAT SO IS FAYREST SHALL TO EARTH RETURNE            5.13.8
```

```
BUT THAT WHICH FAIREST IS, BUT FEW BEHOLD          5.15.13
FAYRER THEN FAYREST LET NONE EVER SAY              5.20.13
O FAYREST FAYRE LET NEVER IT BE NAMED              5.41.13
DOE I NOT SEE THAT FAYREST YMAGES                  5.51.1
BUT FAYREST SHE, WHEN SO SHE DOTH DISPLAY          5.81.9
```
FAIRING   1
```
FAIRING THE FOULE WITH $ARTS FAULSE BORROW'D
                              FACE                 3.127.6
```
FAIRLY   1
```
AND THAT UNFAIRE WHICH FAIRELY DOTH EXCELL         3.5.4
```
FAIR-MAID   1
```
FAIRE-MAYD NO MORE, BUT $MAYR-MAID BE THY NAME     2.130.9
```
FAIR-SWEET   1
```
MOST SWEET-FAIRE, MOST FAIRE-SWEET, DO NOT ALAS    4.82.7
```
FAIRY   3
```
NOT FINISHING HER $QUEENE OF FAERY                 5.33.3
THROUGH $FAERY LAND, WHICH THOSE SIX BOOKS
                              COMPILE              5.80.2
FIT FOR THE HANDMAYD OF THE $FAERY $QUEENE         5.80.14
```
FAITH   36
```
MY FAITH SHOULD WIN, IF $JUSTICE MIGHT HAVE PLACE  1.8.12
I VOW MY FAITH, WHERE FAITH IS NOT REGARDED        1.11.6
I VOW MY FAITH, WHERE FAITH IS NOT REGARDED        1.11.6
SO RARE A FAITH OUGHT BETTER BE REWARDED           1.11.8
IF THAT A LOYALL HART AND FAITH UNFAINED           1.15.1
ARE THOSE DUE TRIBUTES THAT MY FAITH DOTH PAY      1.24.3
NO PRIVILEDGE OF FAITH COULD IT PROTECT            1.31.5
FAITH BEING WITH BLOOD, AND FIVE YEARES
                              WITNES SIGN'D         1.31.6
MY FAITH SHALL WAXE, WHEN THOU ARE IN THY WAINING  1.41.8
THEN WHAT MY FAITH HATH BENE THY SELFE SHALL SEE   1.41.11
HE NEVER HAD MORE FAITH, ALTHOUGH MORE RIME        1.43.7
WHEN SHALL MY FAITH THE HAPPINES ATTAINE           1.49.7
WHETHER MY FAITH HATH NOT DESERV'D HER LOVE+       1.49.12
LO HERE THE IMPOST OF A FAITH ENTIRE               1.60.1
IN $ME'S THAT $FAITH WHICH $TIME CANNOT INVADE     2.4.12
BE MY STRONG $FAITH ASCENDING TO THY $FAME         2.54.10
MAKE KNOWNE THE $FAITH, THAT $FORTUNE
                              COULD NOT MOVE        2.60.5
WHEN $FAITH IS KNEELING BY HIS BED OF $DEATH       2.61.11
BY MY STRONG FAYTH ASCENDING TO THY FAME           2.101.10
BY THY GREAT POWER, AND BY STRONG FAYTH IN THEE    2.112.14
A FAYTH, THAT TIME NOR FORTUNE COULD NOT MOVE      2.138.11
IF FAYTH AND ZEALE BE BUT ESTEEMD A TOY            2.139.3
MAKE KNOWNE THAT FAYTH, UNKINDNES COULD NOT MOVE   2.149.5
AND PUREST FAITH UNHAPPILY FORSWORNE               3.66.4
YET IN GOOD FAITH SOME SAY THAT THEE BEHOLD        3.131.5
IN FAITH I DOE NOT LOVE THEE WITH MINE EYES        3.141.1
IN ACT THY BED-VOW BROAKE AND NEW FAITH TORNE      3.152.3
AND ALL MY HONEST FAITH IN THEE IS LOST            3.152.8
REASON, IN FAITH THOU ART WELL SERV'D, THAT STILL  4.10.1
WELL STAID WITH TRUTH IN WORD AND FAITH OF DEED    4.14.10
WHO FOR LONG FAITH, THO DAYLY HELPE I CRAVE        4.47.7
FOR $STELLA HATH WITH WORDS WHERE FAITH
                              DOTH SHINE            4.69.9
CARE SHINING IN MINE EYES, FAITH IN MY SPRITE      4.72.11
BUT IF ALL FAITH, LIKE SPOTLESSE $ERMINE LY        4.86.5
IS FAITH SO WEAKE+ $OR IS SUCH FORCE IN THEE+      4.88.5
THERE FAYTH DOTH FEARLESSE DWELL IN BRASEN TOWRE   5.65.13
```

FAITHFUL   4
    TRAITOUR TO ME, AND FAITHFULL TO MY $LOVE   1.25.2
    OR IF A WORLD OF FAITHFULL SERVICE DONE   2.138.5
    LOVE MOVES THY PAINE, AND LIKE A FAITHFULL PAGE   4.101.9
    LET HER ACCEPT ME AS HER FAITHFULL THRALL   5.29.10
FALL   18
    THEY ALL ERECT THEIR $TROPHIES ON MY FALL   1.28.7
    THAT MAKES ME FALL FROM OFF MY HIE DESIRE   1.32.8
    AND IN MY FALL I CRYE FOR HELPE WITH SPEEDE   1.32.9
    DID MAKE THE HONOUR OF THE FALL THE MORE   1.35.4
    THAT NEVER FALL TO EBBE, BUT EVER RISE   1.48.3
    BUT FALL TO BLEEDING, AS THEY DID BEFORE   2.46.12
    ESSEX GREAT FALL, $TYRONE HIS $PEACE TO GAINE   2.51.6
    SHE'ST QUENCH HER THIRST AS DULY AS THEY FALL   2.115.10
    WHO LETS SO FAIRE A HOUSE FALL TO DECAY   3.13.9
    TO STAND IN THY AFFAIRES, FALL BY THY SIDE   3.151.12
    HER LOVE, FOR WHOSE DEARE LOVE I RISE AND FALL   3.151.14
    LOOKES TO THE SKIES, AND IN A DITCH DOTH FALL+   4.19.11
    THAT NOT MY SOULE, WHICH AT THY FOOT DID FALL   4.36.12
    DOTH FALL TO STRAY, AND MY CHIEFE POWRES
                                   ARE BROUGHT   4.38.3
    MAKES ME FALL FROM HER SIGHT, THEN SWEETLY SHE   4.60.6
    THOU CHANCE TO COME, FALL LOWLY AT HER FEET   5.2.10
    AND IF THOSE FAYLE FALL DOWNE AND DY BEFORE HER   5.14.13
    UPON THEE FALL FOR THINE ACCURSED HYRE   5.86.6
FALLING   1
    NO LIGHTNING LOOKES WHICH FALLING HOPES ERECT   1.31.10
FALLS   8
    HOW FALS IT OUT SO STRANGELY YOU REPLY+   2.5.2
    SOFTEN YOUR SELVES WITH EV'RY $TEARE THAT FALLS   2.45.11
    AND LOOKING ON THEE, FALLS UPON THE GROUND   2.135.11
    IT SUFFERS NOT IN SMILINGE POMP, NOR FALLS   3.124.6
    FALS TO SHREWD TURNES, AND I WAS IN HIS WAY   4.17.14
    HOW FALLES IT THEN, THAT WITH SO SMOOTH AN EASE   4.74.9
    THAT SOONEST FALS WHEN AS SHE MOST SUPPOSETH   5.58.3
    FALS LOWEST.. FOR ON EARTH NOUGHT HATH
                                   ENDURAUNCE   5.58.12
FALSE   26
    FALSE $HOPE PROLONGS MY EVER CERTAINE GRIEFE   1.25.1
    FALSE $FRIENDS THY KINDNESSE, BORNE BUT
                                TO DECEIVE $THEE   2.10.10
    WITH SHIFTING CHANGE AS IS FALSE WOMENS FASHION   3.20.4
    AN EYE MORE BRIGHT THEN THEIRS, LESSE
                                FALSE IN ROWLING   3.20.5
    THINE BY THY BEAUTIE BEEING FALSE TO ME   3.41.14
    WHY SHOULD FALSE PAINTING IMMITATE HIS CHEEKE   3.67.5
    TO SHEW FAULSE $ART WHAT BEAUTY WAS OF YORE   3.68.14
    O LEAST YOUR TRUE LOVE MAY SEEME FALCE IN THIS   3.72.9
    THOU MAIST BE FALCE, AND YET I KNOW IT NOT   3.92.14
    IN MANIES LOOKES, THE FALCE HEARTS HISTORY   3.93.7
    O NEVER SAY THAT I WAS FALSE OF HEART   3.109.1
    FOR WHY SHOULD OTHERS FALSE ADULTERAT EYES   3.121.5
    FAIRING THE FOULE WITH $ARTS FAULSE BORROW'D
                                   FACE   3.127.6
    SLANDRING $CREATION WITH A FALSE ESTEEME   3.127.12
    AS ANY SHE BELI'D WITH FALSE COMPARE   3.130.14
    AND TO BE SURE THAT IS NOT FALSE I SWEARE   3.131.9
    AND TO THIS FALSE PLAGUE ARE THEY NOW
                                   TRANSFERRED   3.137.14
    UNLEARNED IN THE WORLDS FALSE SUBTILTIES   3.138.4

SIMPLY I CREDIT HER FALSE SPEAKING TONGUE   3.138.7
AND SEALD FALSE BONDS OF LOVE AS OFT AS MINE   3.142.7
IF THAT BE FAIRE WHEREON MY FALSE EYES DOTE   3.148.5
THOUGH FALSE, YET WITH FREE SCOPE MORE
                 GRACE DOTH BREED   4.45.10
FALSE FLATTERING HOPE, THAT WITH SO FAIRE A FACE   4.106.2
ALL FEARELESSE THEN OF SO FALSE ENIMIES   5.12.3
NE OUGHT FOR FAYRER WEATHERS FALSE DELIGHT   5.59.8
THAT WITH FALSE FORGED LYES, WHICH THOU DIDST TEL   5.86.7

FALSEHOOD   2
FROM HANDS OF FALSEHOOD, IN SURE WARDS OF TRUST+   3.48.4
WHY OF EYES FALSEHOOD HAST THOU FORGED HOOKES   3.137.7

FALSELY   1
THAT CENSURES FALSELY WHAT THEY SEE ARIGHT+   3.148.4

FAME   46
MY LOVE AFFECTS NO FAME, NOR STEEMES OF $ART   1.4.14
IF HER DEFECTS HAVE PURCHAST HER THIS FAME   1.17.9
DANGER HATH HONOR, GREAT DESIGNES THEIR FAME   1.35.6
BUT I MAY ADDE ONE FEATHER TO THY FAME   1.43.9
THE SPOYLE OF FAME DESERV'D BY VERTUOUS MEN   1.45.6
AND MORE THE FAME OF HIS MISTAKING HAND   1.56.3
AND MY DECEIV'D ATTEMPT, DESERV'D MORE FAME   1.56.6
ON MY HEART-STRINGS HIGH TUN'D UNTO HER FAME   1.57.4
NONE OTHER FAME MINE UNAMBITIOUS $MUSE   1.58.1
BUT $AVON RICH IN FAME, THOUGH POORE IN WATERS   1.58.11
AND WING'D BY $FAME, YOU TO THE $STARRES ASCEND   2.16.13
WHERE $FAME BY $DEATH IS ONELY TO BE GOT   2.24.11
AND $AVONS $FAME, TO $ALBIONS $CLIFFES IS RAYSED   2.32.4
OUR $WESTERNE $PARTS EXTOLL THEIR $WILIS $FAME   2.32.11
AND MINE $EARES DEAFE, BY THY $FAME HEALED BEE   2.35.10
THE STRONG-BUILT $TROPHIES TO HER LIVING $FAME   2.45.6
IN $PRIDE OF $WIT, WHEN HIGH DESIRE OF $FAME   2.47.1
BE MY STRONG $FAITH ASCENDING TO THY $FAME   2.54.10
BY MY STRONG FAYTH ASCENDING TO THY FAME   2.101.10
NOR MY $MUSE BEEN THE TRUMPET OF THY FAME   2.104.8
THAT BY THY FAME ALL FAME SHALL BE SURVIVED   2.104.14
THAT BY THY FAME ALL FAME SHALL BE SURVIVED   2.104.14
SHALT SPRING AGAINE FROM TH'ASHES OF THY FAME   2.106.12
SO MAIST THOU LIVE, PAST WORLD, PAST FAME,
                 PAST END   2.106.14
WORDS CONSONANT, AND SOUNDING TO THY FAME   2.111.8
AND MINE EARES DEAFE, BY THY FAME HEALED BE   2.112.10
IF $THOSE TEN $REGICNS REGISTRED BY $FAME   2.119.1
AND $AVONS FAME, TO $ALBYONS $CLIVES IS RAYSED   2.124.4
OUR $WESTERNE PARTS EXTOLL THEYR $WILYS FAME   2.124.11
A $MUSE, THAT UNTO HEAVEN HATH RAISD HER FAME   2.138.12
TO MAKE ME TOUNG-TIDE SPEAKING OF YOUR FAME   3.80.4
AND SUCH A COUNTER-PART SHALL FAME HIS WIT   3.84.11
GIVE MY LOVE FAME FASTER THEN TIME WASTS LIFE   3.100.13
THAT HER CLEARE VOYCE LIFTS THY FAME TO THE SKIES   4.12.8
YOU SEEKE TO NURSE AT FULLEST BREASTS OF $FAME   4.15.13
I LIST NOT DIG SO DEEPE FOR BRASEN FAME   4.28.4
NAY, THAT MAY BREED MY FAME, IT IS SO RARE   4.34.6
HIM AS THY SLAVE, AND NOW LONG NEEDY $FAME   4.35.10
NOR DO ASPIRE TO $CAESAR'S BLEEDING FAME   4.64.10
SINCE IN THINE ARMES, IF LEARND FAME TRUTH
                 HATH SPREAD   4.65.13
ALTHOUGH LESSE GIFTS IMPE FEATHERS OFT ON $FAME   4.75.4
SHE BUILDS HER FAME ON HIGHER SEATED PRAISE   4.81.10
STELLA THINKE NOT THAT I BY VERSE SEEKE FAME   4.90.1

```
NO IT WAS BUYLDED FAR FROM ACCIDENT                    3.124.5
CURRALL IS FARRE MORE RED, THEN HER LIPS RED           3.130.2
THAT $MUSICKE HATH A FARRE MORE PLEASING SOUND         3.130.10
THUS FARRE FOR LOVE, MY LOVE-SUTE SWEET FULLFILL       3.136.4
ONELY MY PLAGUE THUS FARRE I COUNT MY GAINE            3.141.13
WHILST I THY BABE CHACE THEE A FARRE BEHIND            3.143.10
AS SACRED THINGS, FAR FROM ALL DAUNGER'S SHOW          4.24.8
BEAUTIES SO FARRE FROM REACH OF WORDS, THAT WE         4.37.7
SINCE THEN THOU HAST SO FARRE SUBDUED ME               4.40.12
HOW FARRE THEY SHOOTE AWRIE- THE TRUE CAUSE IS         4.41.12
FAR FAR TOO LONG TC LEARNE IT WITHOUT BOOKE            4.56.2
FAR FAR TOO LONG TC LEARNE IT WITHOUT BOOKE            4.56.2
THE $ORATOUR SO FARRE MEN'S HARTS DOTH BIND            4.58.2
WITHOUT HOW FARRE THIS PRAISE IS SHORT OF YOU          4.80.13
WHOSE FRUIT DOTH FARRE TH'$ESPERIAN TAST SURPASSE      4.82.6
WHEN FAR SPENT NIGHT PERSWADES EACH MORTALL EYE        4.99.1
THENCE, SO FARRE THENCE, THAT SCARCELY
                             ANY SPARKE                4.104.6
WHAT NEEDETH YOU TC SEEKE SO FARRE IN VAINE+           5.15.4
ALL THIS WORLDS RICHES THAT MAY FARRE BE FOUND         5.15.6
OUT OF HER COURSE DOTH WANDER FAR ASTRAY               5.34.4
WHY THEN DOE YE PROUD FAYRE, MISDEEME SO FARRE         5.58.13
FAYRE SOYLE IT SEEMES FROM FAR AND FRAUGHT
                             WITH STORE                5.63.7
FAR PASSING THOSE WHICH $HERCULES CAME BY              5.77.7
FARE                     2
  LEAST MY SAD LOOKES BEWRAY ME HOW I FARE             1.29.12
  THAT UNTO ME, WHO FARE LIKE HIM THAT BOTH            4.19.10
FAREWELL                 2
  FAREWELL THOU ART TCO DEARE FOR MY POSSESSING        3.87.1
  ALL MIRTH FAREWELL, LET ME IN SORROW LIVE            4.100.14
FAR-FET                  1
  YOU TAKE WRONG WAIES, THOSE FAR-FET HELPES
                             BE SUCH                   4.15.9
FARING                   1
  AS TENDER NURSE HER BABE FROM FARING ILL             3.22.12
FARTHER                  4
  HOW FAR I TOYLE, STILL FARTHER OFF FROM THEE         3.28.8
  FOR THOU NOR FARTHER THEN MY THOUGHTS CANST MOVE     3.47.11
  BY SEEING FARTHER THEN THE EYE HATH SHOWNE           3.69.8
  TRIUMPH IN LOVE, FLESH STAIES NO FARTHER REASON      3.151.8
FARTHEST                 3
  RAVISH'D A $WORLD BEYOND THE FARTHEST $THOUGHT       2.34.2
  UPON THE FARTHEST EARTH REMOOV'D FROM THEE           3.44.6
  WHICH SHOULD TRANSPCRT ME FARTHEST FROM
                             YOUR SIGHT                3.117.8
FASCIA                   1
  POORE $ROGUE, GOE PAWNE THY $FASCIA AND THY $BOW     2.48.3
FASHION                  4
  WITH SHIFTING CHANGE AS IS FALSE WOMENS FASHION      3.20.4
  WHERETO TH'INVITING TIME OUR FASHION CALLS           3.124.8
  YOU FRAME MY THOUGHTS AND FASHION ME WITHIN          5.8.9
  AND FASHION TO WHAT HE IT LIST APPLY                 5.32.4
FASHIONING               2
  MY $WORDS THE $HAMMERS, FASHIONING MY DESIRE         2.40.2
  MY WORDS THE HAMMERS, FASHIONING MY DESIRES          2.144.2
FASHIONS                 1
  OR IN THIS $ILAND ALT'RETH WITH THE $FASHIONS+       2.27.4
FAST                     13
  WHEN I, AS FAST AS E'R MY $PENNE COULD TROT          2.21.5
```

```
     AS FAST AS THOU SHALT WANE SO FAST THOU GROW'ST        3.11.1
     AS FAST AS THOU SHALT WANE SO FAST THOU GROW'ST        3.11.1
     AND DIE AS FAST AS THEY SEE OTHERS GROW                3.12.12
     AS FAST AS OBJECTS TO HIS BEAMES ASSEMBLE              3.114.8
     UNDER THAT BOND THAT HIM AS FAST DOTH BINDE            3.134.8
     GIRT FAST BY MEMORIE, AND WHILE I SPURRE               4.49.10
     HE SITS ME FAST, HOW EVER I DO STURRE                  4.49.12
     AND ANCHOR FAST MY SELFE ON $VERTUE'S SHORE            4.62.11
     AS FAST THY $VERTUE BENDS THAT LOVE TO GOOD            4.71.13
     CURST BE THE $COCHMAN WHICH DID DRIVE SO FAST          4.105.13
     THIS HOLY SEASON FIT TO FAST AND PRAY                  5.22.1
     BUT JOYOUS HOURES DOO FLY AWAY TOO FAST                5.87.14
FASTENER                     1
     BREATHER OF LIFE, AND FASTNER OF DESIRE                4.80.7
FASTER                       1
     GIVE MY LOVE FAME FASTER THEN TIME WASTS LIFE          3.100.13
FATAL                        3
     THESE FATALL $ANTHEAMES, SAD AND MORNEFULL $SONGS      1.3.2
     AND THUS DIVIDING OF MY FATALL $HOURES                 2.3.5
     AND THUS DEVIDING OF MY FATALL HOWRES                  2.110.5
FATALLY                      1
     THE WORKE OF RIGOR, FATALLY BEGUN                      1.33.7
FATE                         6
     MY TEDIOUS $TRAVELS, AND OFT-VARYING $FATE             2.1.14
     DECLARE WHAT $FATE UNLUCKY $STARRES HAVE GIVEN         2.60.3
     DECLARE WHAT FATE UNLUCKY STARRES HAVE GIVEN           2.149.3
     AND LOOKE UPON MY SELFE AND CURSE MY FATE              3.29.4
     NOW I, WIT-BEATEN LONG BY HARDEST $FATE                4.60.9
     O FATE, O FAULT, O CURSE, CHILD OF MY BLISSE           4.93.1
FATES                        2
     AND $FATES AND $FURIES, WITH THEIR WOES ACQUAINT       2.39.4
     AS'T PLEASE THE $FATES, BY THEIR RESISTLESSE
                                            FORCE           2.51.4
FATHER                       5
     THAT LEARNED $FATHER, WHICH SO FIRMELY PROVES          2.12.1
     THY FATHER WAS A MAN, THAT WILL I PROVE                2.140.7
     YOU HAD A $FATHER, LET YOUR $SON SAY SO                3.13.14
     AS A DECREPIT FATHER TAKES DELIGHT                     3.37.1
     WHEREWITH MY FATHER ONCE MADE IT HALFE TAME            4.30.10
FATHERS                      1
     OR IN OUR $FATHERS DID SHE MORE TRANSGRESSE+           2.27.8
FATHER'S                     1
     WITNESSE YOUR $FATHERS GRIEFE EXCEEDES ALL OTHER       1.2.4
FAULT                        11
     THE FAULT IS HERS, THOUGH MINE THE HURT MUST BE        1.15.14
     FOR TO THY SENSUALL FAULT I BRING IN SENCE             3.35.9
     SAY THAT THOU DIDST FORSAKE MEE FOR SOME FALT          3.89.1
     SOME SAY THY FAULT IS YOUTH, SOME WANTONESSE           3.96.1
     I DO CONFESSE, PARDON A FAULT CONFEST                  4.4.7
     BUT ONE WORSE FAULT, $AMBITION, I CONFESSE             4.27.11
     PARDON THAT FAULT, ONCE MORE GRAUNT ME THE PLACE       4.82.12
     O FATE, O FAULT, O CURSE, CHILD OF MY BLISSE           4.93.1
     THEIR JUDGEMENTS HACKNEY ON, THE FAULT
                                 ON SICKNESSE LAY           4.102.10
     WAS NOT IN FAULT, WHO BENT THY DAZLING RACE            4.105.6
     IN FINDING FAULT WITH HER TOO PORTLY PRIDE             5.5.2
FAULTS                       13
     ALL MEN MAKE FAULTS, AND EVEN I IN THIS                3.35.5
     OF FAULTS CONCEALD, WHEREIN I AM ATTAINTED             3.88.7
     BOTH GRACE AND FAULTS ARE LOV'D OF MORE AND LESSE      3.96.3
```

```
THOU MAKST FAULTS GRACES, THAT TO THEE RESORT      3.96.4
THE ILLS THAT WERE, NOT GREW TO FAULTS ASSURED     3.118.10
AND IN OUR FAULTS BY LYES WE FLATTERED BE          3.138.14
LEAST EYES WELL SEEING THY FOULE FAULTS
                              SHOULD FINDE          3.148.14
LEAST GUILTY OF MY FAULTS THY SWEET SELFE PROVE    3.151.4
IN JUSTICE PAINES COME NOT TILL FAULTS DO CALL     4.86.10
AND AL HER FAULTS IN THY BLACK BOOKE ENROLL        5.10.12
FOR ALL THEIR FAULTS WITH WHICH THEY DID OFFEND    5.24.12
THAT FOR MY FAULTS YE WILL ME GENTLY BEAT          5.24.14
AND FLY THE FAULTS WITH WHICH WE DID OFFEND        5.62.8
```

FAVOR   6
```
NO FAVOUR THOUGH, THE CRUELL FAIRE ALLOWES         1.11.12
SO TRUE AND LOYALL LOVE NO FAVOUR GAINES ME        1.18.8
LET THOSE WHO ARE IN FAVOR WITH THEIR STARS        3.25.1
HAVE I NOT SEENE DWELLERS ON FORME AND FAVOR       3.125.5
I WAS CONTENT YOU SHOULD IN FAVOUR CREEPE          4.83.2
OF GRUDGING FOES, NE FAVOUR SEEK OF FRIENDS        5.59.10
```
FAVORITES   1
```
GREAT $PRINCES FAVORITES THEIR FAIRE LEAVES
                              SPREAD               3.25.5
```
FAVORS   3
```
AND HER DISDAINES ARE $GALL, HER FAVOURS $HUNNY    1.6.4
WHAT PASSIONS WOULD HER MILDER FAVOURS MOVE+       1.17.12
FAVOURS (I THINKE) WOULD SENCE QUITE OVERCOME      1.17.13
```
FAWN   3
```
ON WHOM FROUN'ST THOU THAT I DOE FAUNE UPON        3.149.6
FAWNE ON MY SELF, AND OTHERS TO DESPISE            4.27.8
LYKE A YOUNG FAWNE THAT LATE HATH LOST THE HYND    5.78.2
```
FEAR   30
```
HOW TO BE PALE WITH ANGUISH, RED WITH FEARE        1.20.2
I FEARE YOUR EYE HATH TURND YOUR HEART TO FLINT    1.37.14
I SAY NO MORE, I FEARE I SAYD TOO MUCH             1.60.14
WELL, WELL, I FEARE IT WILL BE PROV'D BY YOU       2.2.7
YET MY $HOPES $WINGS ARE LADEN SO WITH $FEARE      2.26.6
THOUGH $FEARE GIVES THEM MORE THEN A $HEAV'NLY
                              $SCOPE               2.26.8
I FEARE NO CENSURE, NOR WHAT THOU CANST SAY        2.31.5
I STILL FEARE $BUG-BEARES IN $APOLLO'S $CELL       2.39.12
NOT THAT THEY FEARE THE HOPE-LESSE $MAN TO KILL    2.50.10
FOR FEARE THAT SOME THEIR $TREASURES SHOULD
                              PURLOYNE             2.58.3
I STYLL FEARE BUGBEARES IN $APOLLOS $CELL          2.118.12
YET MY HOPES WINGS ARE LODEN SO WITH FEARE         2.137.6
YET FEARE GYVES THEM MORE THEN A HEAVENLY SCOPE    2.137.8
ASSAYLD WITH DEATH, YET ARM'D WITH GASTLY FEARE    2.142.3
IS IT FOR FEARE TO WET A WIDDOWES EYE              3.9.1
WHO WITH HIS FEARE IS PUT BESIDES HIS PART         3.23.2
SO I FOR FEARE OF TRUST, FORGET TO SAY             3.23.5
AND EVEN THENCE THOU WILT BE STOLNE I FEARE        3.48.13
I WAS NOT SICK OF ANY FEARE FROM THENCE            3.86.12
THEN NEED I NOT TO FEARE THE WORST OF WRONGS       3.92.5
FOR FEARE OF WHICH, HEARE THIS THOU AGE UNBRED     3.104.13
YET FEAR HER $O THOU MINNION OF HER PLEASURE       3.126.9
OF HOPES BEGOT BY FEARE, OF WOT NOT WHAT DESIRES   4.6.2
THE BOY REFUSDE FOR FEARE OF $MARSE'S HATE         4.17.5
CURB'D IN WITH FEARE, BUT WITH GUILT BOSSE ABOVE   4.49.7
DESIRE STILL ON THE STILTS OF FEARE DOTH GO        4.66.8
FEARE TO OFFEND, WILL WORTHIE TO APPEARE           4.72.10
TWIXT FEARE AND HOPE DEPENDING DOUBTFULLY+         5.25.4
```

```
     SUCH SELFE ASSURANCE NEED NOT FEARE THE SPIGHT         5.59.9
     THAT FONDLY FEARE TO LOOSE YOUR LIBERTY                5.65.2
FEARED                      1
     NE FEARD WITH WORSE TO ANY CHAUNCE TO START            5.59.4
FEARFUL                     1          '
     O FEAREFULL MEDITATION, WHERE ALACK                    3.65.9
FEARFULLY                   1
     THE $ROSES FEAREFULLY ON THORNES DID STAND             3.99.8
FEARING                     3
     (FEARING THE STARS PRESAGED INFLUENCE)                 2.116.11
     ALAS WHY FEARING OF TIMES TIRANIE                      3.115.9
     READIE OF WIT AND FEARING NOUGHT BUT SHAME             4.14.11
FEARLESS                    3
     ALL FEARELESSE THEN OF SO FALSE ENIMIES                5.12.3
     THERE FAYTH DOTH FEARLESSE DWELL IN BRASEN TOWRE       5.65.13
     SOUGHT NOT TO FLY, BUT FEARELESSE STILL DID BIDE       5.67.10
FEARS                      11
     NO PITTYING EYE LOOKES BACKE UPON MY FEARES            1.32.10
     MY NEVER-CERTAINE $JOY BREEDS EVER-CERTAINE
                                     $FEARES                2.26.4
     MY DYING LOOKES AND THOUGHTS ARE PEIZ'D
                                 IN EQUALL FEARES           2.133.12
     MY NEVER CERTAINE JOY, BREEDS EVER-CERTAINE
                                     FEARES                 2.137.4
     BUT WEEPE TO HAVE, THAT WHICH IT FEARES TO LOOSE       3.64.14
     BUT WHATS SO BLESSED FAIRE THAT FEARES NO BLOT         3.92.13
     NOT MINE OWNE FEARES, NOR THE PROPHETICK SOULE         3.107.1
     APPLYING FEARES TO HOPES, AND HOPES TO FEARES          3.119.3
     APPLYING FEARES TO HOPES, AND HOPES TO FEARES          3.119.3
     IT FEARES NOT POLICY THAT $HERITICKE                   3.124.9
     AND YET AMID ALL FEARES A HOPE THERE IS                4.66.9
FEAST                       5
     AND BAD MY $SENSES TO A SOLEMNE $FEAST                 2.7.2
     PINED WITH $HUNGER, RISING FROM A $FEAST               2.62.4
     PYNED WITH HUNGER, RYSING FROM A FEAST                 2.150.4
     WITH MY LOVES PICTURE THEN MY EYE DOTH FEAST           3.47.5
     TO ANY SENSUALL FEAST WITH THEE ALONE                  3.141.8
FEASTING                    1
     SOME-TIME ALL FUL WITH FEASTING ON YOUR SIGHT          3.75.9
FEASTS                      1
     THEREFORE ARE FEASTS SO SOLLEMNE AND SO RARE           3.52.5
FEATHER                     2
     BUT I MAY ADDE ONE FEATHER TO THY FAME                 1.43.9
     AND LIKE A $WANTON, SPORTS WITH EV'RY $FETHER          2.22.6
FEATHERED                   2
     SWIFT SPEEDY $TIME, FEATHRED WITH FLYING HOURES        1.39.11
     ONE OF HER FETHERED CREATURES BROAKE AWAY              3.143.2
FEATHERS                    3
     HE FRAMD HIM WINGS WITH FEATHERS OF HIS THOUGHT        2.122.5
     HAVE ADDED FETHERS TO THE LEARNEDS WING                3.78.7
     ALTHOUGH LESSE GIFTS IMPE FEATHERS OFT ON $FAME        4.75.4
FEATURE                     2
     THE $CROE, OR $DOVE, IT SHAPES THEM TO
                                 YOUR FEATURE               3.113.12
     WHICH TEMPRED SO THE FEATURE OF HER FACE               5.21.2
FEATURED                    1
     FEATUR'D LIKE HIM, LIKE HIM WITH FRIENDS POSSEST       3.29.6
FEATURELESS                 1
     HARSH, FEATURELESSE, AND RUDE, BARRENLY PERRISH        3.11.10
```

```
FED                          9
   FED BUT WITH SMOKE, AND CHERISHT BUT WITH FIRE      1.15.4
   FED WITH SOME PLEASING LOOKE THERE SHALL SHE BE     1.25.11
   WITHIN BE FED, WITHOUT BE RICH NO MORE              3.146.12
   FED BY THY WORTH, AND KINDLED BY THY SIGHT+         4.68.8
   AND SITHENS HAVE WITH SIGHES AND SORROWES FED       5.2.3
   FED ON THE FULNESSE OF THAT CHEAREFULL GLAUNCE      5.39.12
   THERE MY FRAILE FANCY FED WITH FULL DELIGHT         5.72.9
   MY THOUGHTS THE GUESTS, WHICH WOULD THEREON
                           HAVE FEDD                   5.77.14
   I FYND MY SELFE BUT FED WITH FANCIES VAYNE          5.78.12
FEE                          1
   BUT THAT YOUR TRESPASSE NOW BECOMES A FEE           3.120.13
FEEBLE                       3
   LIKE FEEBLE AGE HE REELETH FROM THE DAY             3.7.10
   TOO FEEBLE I T'ABIDE THE BRUNT SO STRONG            5.12.9
   A FEEBLE BEAST, DOTH FELLY HIM OPPRESSE             5.56.4
FEED                         7
   LOOKES FEED MY $HOPE, $HOPE FOSTERS ME IN VAINE     1.25.13
   SO SHALT THOU FEED ON DEATH, THAT FEEDS ON MEN      3.146.13
   WITHOUT DESIRE TO FEED OF FURTHER GRACE             4.46.8
   AND DO I SEE SOME CAUSE A HOPE TO FEEDE             4.66.1
   OF ALL WORLDS GLADNESSE MORE MY TORMENT FEED        5.52.12
   TO FEED HIS FILL, FLYES BACKE UNTO YOUR SIGHT       5.73.8
   AND THEREON FEED MY LOVE-AFFAMISHT HART             5.88.12
FEEDEST                      2
   THAT WHEN THOU FEED'ST, THY $NOSE SHALL
                           TOUCH THY $CHINNE           2.8.12
   FEED'ST THY LIGHTS FLAME WITH SELFE SUBSTANTIALL
                           FEWELL                      3.1.6
FEEDING                      3
   WHICH BUT TOO DAIE BY FEEDING IS ALAIED             3.56.3
   TO BITTER SAWCES DID I FRAME MY FEEDING             3.118.6
   FEEDING ON THAT WHICH DOTH PRESERVE THE ILL         3.147.3
FEEDS                        4
   FEEDES ON THE RARITIES OF NATURES TRUTH             3.60.11
   SO SHALT THOU FEED ON DEATH, THAT FEEDS ON MEN      3.146.13
   AND FEEDS AT PLEASURE ON THE WRETCHED PRAY          5.47.8
   WITHIN HER CAGE, BUT SINGES AND FEEDS HER FILL      5.65.8
FEEL                         17
   DO FEELE MINE INWARD HEAT AS GREAT (I KNOW IT)      1.43.6
   BEARING THE WOUND, I NEEDES MUST FEELE THE PAINE    1.52.14
   AND NEVER WAKE TO FEELE THE DAYES DISDAINE          1.54.14
   THUS DO I FEELE THE PAINE, THE CAUSE,
                           YET CANNOT SEE              2.130.8
   I FEELE, YOU KNOW, THE HEAVENS CAN TELL
                           THE REST                    2.139.14
   SAVE WHERE THOU ART NOT, THOUGH I FEELE THOU ART    3.48.10
   AND FOR THAT SORROW, WHICH I THEN DIDDE FEELE       3.120.2
   I CAN SPEAKE WHAT I FEELE, AND FEELE AS
                           MUCH AS THEY                4.6.12
   I CAN SPEAKE WHAT I FEELE, AND FEELE AS
                           MUCH AS THEY                4.6.12
   WHEN MOST I GLORIE, THEN I FEELE MOST SHAME         4.19.3
   TO ME THAT FEELE THE LIKE, THY STATE DESCRIES       4.31.8
   OR WANT I SENSE TO FEELE MY MISERIE+                4.47.5
   TO FEELE MY GRIEFES, AND SHE WITH FACE AND VOICE    4.57.13
   I FEELE THE FLAMES OF HOTTEST SOMMER DAY            4.89.14
   BUT WHEN I FEELE THE BITTER BALEFULL SMART          5.24.5
   AND FEELE MY FLAMES AUGMENTED MANIFOLD+             5.30.8
```

```
            LET THEM FEELE TH'UTMOST OF YOUR CRUELTYES        5.49.9
FEELEST                        3
      I MARVELL NOT, THOU FEEL'ST NOT MY $DELIGHT             2.49.3
      AND SEE THY BLOOD WARME WHEN THOU FEEL'ST
                                IT COULD                      3.2.14
      CAN JUDGE OF $LOVE, THOU FEEL'ST A $LOVER'S CASE        4.31.6
FEELING                        6
      IN FEELING HEARTS THAT CAN CONCEIVE THESE LINES         1.43.2
      NOT BY OUR FEELING, BUT BY OTHERS SEEING                3.121.4
      NOR TENDER FEELING TO BASE TOUCHES PRONE                3.141.6
      WHILE WITH A FEELING SKILL I PAINT MY HELL              4.2.14
      BUT FEELING PROOFE MAKES ME SAY THEY MISTAKE
                                IT FURRE                      4.102.11
      AND FEELING THENCE NO MORE HER SOROWES SADNESSE         5.39.11
FEELS                          1
      THE GENTLE BIRDE FEELES NO CAPTIVITY                    5.65.7
FEET                          12
      WHOSE FEETE DOE TREAD GREENE PATHS OF
                                YOUTH AND LOVE                1.6.6
      TO $THETIS GIVE THE HONOUR OF THY FEETE                 1.19.8
      AT HER PROUD FEETE, AND SHE RESPECTS NOT IT             1.24.6
      THE DAINTY GRASSE MAKE MUSICKE WITH HER FEETE           2.125.8
      AND OTHERS' FEETE STILL SEEM'D BUT STRANGERS
                                IN MY WAY                     4.1.11
      EACH SOULE DOTH AT $LOVE'S FEET HIS WEAPONS LAY         4.43.7
      THY REASONS FIRMLY SET ON $VERTUE'S FEET                4.68.11
      BUT WITH SHORT BREATH, LONG LOOKES, STAID
                                FEET AND WALKING HED          4.76.13
      SO NIMBLE FEET AS STIRRE STILL, THOUGH
                                ON THORNES                    4.78.11
      TEMPERS HER WORDS TO TRAMPLING HORSES FEET              4.84.3
      HUNDREDS OF YEARES YOU $STELLA'S FEET MAY KISSE         4.84.14
      THOU CHANCE TO COME, FALL LOWLY AT HER FEET             5.2.10
FELICITY                       2
      (AS HIS SOLE OBJECT OF FELICITIE)                       4.86.7
      MAY LIVE FOR EVER IN FELICITY                           5.68.8
FELL                          10
      THAT FOR MY MIS-SPENT YOUTH THE TEARS
                                FEL FROM MY EYES              2.114.4
      DOWNE FELL HE IN THY $BEAUTIES $OCEAN DRENCHED          2.122.13
      TILL NATURE AS SHE WROUGHT THEE FELL A DOTINGE          3.20.10
      WHEN I HAVE SEENE BY TIMES FELL HAND DEFACED            3.64.1
      BUT BE CONTENTED WHEN THAT FELL AREST                   3.74.1
      DRUGS POYSON HIM THAT SO FELL SICKE OF YOU              3.118.14
      $CUPID LAID BY HIS BRAND AND FELL A SLEEPE              3.153.1
      CURST BE THE PAGE FROM WHOME THE BAD TORCH FELL         4.105.11
      BUT GREEDILY HER FELL INTENT POURSEWTH                  5.11.7
      OF THAT SELFE KYND WITH WHICH THE $FURIES FELL          5.86.2
FELLOWSHIP                     2
      THEN EV'N OF FELLOWSHIP, O $MOONE, TELL ME              4.31.9
      NOW FROM THY FELLOWSHIP I NEEDS MUST PART               4.72.5
FELLY                          1
      A FEEBLE BEAST, DOTH FELLY HIM OPPRESSE                 5.56.4
FELT                           5
      MY SOULE HAD NE'R FELT THY $DIVINITIE                   2.104.7
      WHAT FREEZINGS HAVE I FELT, WHAT DARKE
                                DAIES SEENE+                  3.97.3
      A STILL FELT PLAGUE, TO SELFE CONDEMNING ME             4.86.3
      CANNOT HEAVN'S FOOD, ONCE FELT, KEEPE
                                STOMAKES FREE                 4.88.7
```

```
        BUT THOU ART GONE, NOW THAT SELFE FELT DISGRACE    4.106.7
FELTEST                  1
        WHICH NEVER FELT'ST MY FIERIE TOUCH OF $LOVE        2.49.4
FEMALE                   1
        TO WIN ME SOONE TO HELL MY FEMALL EVILL            3.144.5
FENCE                    1
        TILL DOWNE-RIGHT BLOWES DID FOYLE THY
                              CUNNING FENCE                4.10.11
FERTILE                  2
        THE $PEAKE HER $DOVE, WHOSE $BANKES SO FERTILE BE  2.32.7
        THE $PEAKE HER $DOVE, WHOSE BANCKS SO
                              FERTILL BEE                  2.124.7
FERVENT                  3
        STRONG IS THE NET, AND FERVENT IS THE FLAME        1.14.5
        THE PAYNEFULL SMITH WITH FORCE OF FERVENT HEAT     5.32.1
        BUT STILL THE MORE SHE FERVENT SEES MY FIT         5.32.9
FESTER                   1
        LILLIES THAT FESTER, SMELL FAR WORSE THEN WEEDS    3.94.14
FESTERETH                1
        THE BOND, THE FLAME, THE WOUND THAT FESTRETH SO    1.14.10
FETCH                    1
        BUT I UNBID, FETCH EVEN MY SOULE TO THEE           4.59.8
FETCHETH                 1
        BID'N, PERHAPS HE FETCHETH THEE A GLOVE            4.59.7
FETTER                   1
        ILE FETTER HER IN CHAINES OF PUREST LOVE           2.115.6
FETTERED                 2
        SO MY $LOVE IS STILL FETT'RED WITH VAINE $HOPE     2.26.10
        SO MY LOVE IS STYLL FETTERED WITH VAINE HOPE       2.137.10
FETTERS                  1
        TO COVET FETTERS, THOUGH THEY GOLDEN BEE           5.37.14
FEVER                    2
        IN THE DISTRACTION OF THIS MADDING FEVER+          3.119.8
        MY LOVE IS AS A FEAVER LONGING STILL               3.147.1
FEW                      3
        FOR SOME FEW $RAGGES, WHEREWITH TO COVER THEE      2.48.4
        WHEN YELLOW LEAVES, OR NONE, OR FEW DOE HANGE      3.73.2
        BUT THAT WHICH FAIREST IS, BUT FEW BEHOLD          5.15.13
FICKLE                   1
        DOEST HOULD TIMES FICKLE GLASSE, HIS SICKLE,
                              HOWER                        3.126.2
FIE                      3
        FY, SCHOOLE OF $PATIENCE, $FY, YOUR LESSON IS      4.56.1
        FY, SCHOOLE OF $PATIENCE, $FY, YOUR LESSON IS      4.56.1
        GUESSE WE THE CAUSE.. '$WHAT, IS IT THUS+'
                              $FIE NO                      4.74.12
FIELD                    9
        AND DIGGE DEEP TRENCHES IN THY BEAUTIES FIELD       3.2.2
        BUT IN $VERT FIELD $MARS BARE A GOLDEN SPEARE      4.13.5
        WHERE ROSES GUEULS ARE BORNE IN SILVER FIELD       4.13.11
        AH BED, THE FIELD WHERE JOYE'S PEACE SOME DO SEE   4.98.1
        THE FIELD WHERE ALL MY THOUGHTS TO WARRE
                              BE TRAIND                    4.98.2
        AND REIGNETH OVER EVERY BEAST IN FIELD             5.20.6
        I GOE LYKE ONE THAT HAVING LOST THE FIELD          5.52.2
        YET NOR IN FIELD NOR BOWRE I HER CAN FYND          5.78.7
        YET FIELD AND BOWRE ARE FULL OF HER ASPECT         5.78.8
FIELDS                   1
        I SEEKE THE FIELDS WITH HER LATE FOOTING SYND      5.78.5
```

FIEND   2
   AND WHETHER THAT MY ANGEL BE TURN'D FINDE   3.144.9
   DOTH FOLLOW NIGHT WHO LIKE A FIEND   3.145.11
FIERCE   6
   BUT YET RESTORE THY FIERCE AND CRUELL MIND   1.19.11
   PLUCKE THE KEENE TEETH FROM THE FIERCE
                         $TYGERS YAWES   3.19.3
   OR SOME FIERCE THING REPLEAT WITH TOO MUCH RAGE 3.23.3
   OF THOSE FIERCE DARTS, DISPAIRE AT ME DOTH THROW 4.39.6
   THE GROUND OF THIS FIERCE $LOVE AND LOVELY HATE 4.60.11
   FAYRE CRUELL, WHY ARE YE SO FIERCE AND CRUELL+   5.49.1
FIERCER   1
   UPON WHOSE BREAST A FIERCER $GRIPE DOTH TIRE   4.14.2
FIERY   6
   YOUR FIRY HEATE LETS NOT HER GLORY PASSE   1.38.13
   TO WHOM MY $MUSE WITH FIERIE $WINGS SHALL PASSE 2.25.10
   WHICH NEVER FELT'ST MY FIERIE TOUCH OF $LOVE   2.49.4
   THE GOLDEN $SUNNE UPON HIS FIERY WHEELES   2.147.1
   SHALL NAIGH NOE DULL FLESH IN HIS FIERY RACE   3.51.11
   DARTING THEIR DEADLY ARROWES FYRY BRIGHT   5.16.7
FIFTEEN   1
   NOR AT $FIFTEENE NE'R LONG'D TO BE A $BRIDE   2.15.6
FIGHT   7
   CROOKED ECLIPSES GAINST HIS GLORY FIGHT   3.60.7
   UPON THY SIDE, AGAINST MY SELFE ILE FIGHT   3.88.3
   BUT THOU WOULDST NEEDS FIGHT BOTH WITH
                         LOVE AND SENCE   4.10.9
   ONE HAND FORGOTT TO RULE, TH'OTHER TO FIGHT   4.53.11
   BEST CHARGE, AND BRAVEST RETRAIT IN $CUPID'S
                         FIGHT   4.79.5
   SUCH HAUGHTY MYNDS ENUR'D TO HARDY FIGHT   5.14.7
   TO BATTAILE FRESH AGAINST MY SELFE TO FIGHT   5.44.12
FIGHTING   1
   HAVING GOT UP A BREACH BY FIGHTING WELL   4.12.10
FIGHTS   2
   OFT CRUELL FIGHTS WELL PICTURED FORTH DO PLEASE 4.34.4
   WO, HAVING MADE WITH MANY FIGHTS HIS OWNE   4.57.1
FIGURE   2
   STEALE FROM HIS FIGURE, AND NO PACE PERCEIV'D   3.104.10
   TILL THAT IN WORDS THY FIGURE BE EXPREST   4.50.4
FIGURED   2
   I FIGURDE ON THE TABLE OF MINE HART   1.13.6
   WHICH HATH NOT FIGUR'D TO THEE MY TRUE SPIRIT   3.108.2
FIGURES   1
   THEY WEARE BUT SWEET, BUT FIGURES OF DELIGHT   3.98.11
FILCHED   1
   IF $HE, FROM $HEAV'N THAT FILCH'D THAT
                         LIVING $FIRE   2.14.1
FILCHING   1
   DOUBTING THE FILCHING AGE WILL STEALE
                         HIS TREASURE   3.75.6
FILED   1
   AND PRECIOUS PHRASE BY ALL THE $MUSES FIL'D   3.85.4
FILL   11
   SO LOVE BE THOU, ALTHOUGH TOO DAIE THOU FILL   3.56.5
   YOUR LOVE AND PITTIE DOTH TH'IMPRESSION FILL   3.112.1
   I FILL IT FULL WITH WILS, AND MY WILL ONE   3.136.6
   TO FILL HIS HORNES THIS YEARE ON $CHRISTIAN COAST 4.30.2
   WHAT PEN, WHAT PENCILL CAN EXPRESSE HER FILL+   5.17.4
   AND FILL THE WORLD WITH HER VICTORIOUS PRAYSE   5.29.14

WITHIN HER CAGE, BUT SINGES AND FEEDS HER FILL   5.65.8
TO FEED HIS FILL, FLYES BACKE UNTO YOUR SIGHT   5.73.8
THERE FILL YOUR SELFE WITH THOSE MOST
                              JOYOUS SIGHTS   5.84.9
AND MY GLAD MOUTH WITH HER SWEET PRAYSES FILL   5.85.12
BUT WITH SUCH BRIGHTNESSE WHYLEST I'FILL MY MIND   5.88.13
FILLED   7
  NOW WHILST THY $MAY HATH FILD THY LAP
                              WITH FLOWERS   1.40.2
  IF IT WERE FILD WITH YOUR MOST HIGH DESERTS+   3.17.2
  WHEN HOURES HAVE DREIND HIS BLOOD AND
                              FILD HIS BROW   3.63.3
  BUT WHEN YOUR COUNTINANCE FILD UP HIS LINE   3.86.13
  YOUTH, LUCKE, AND PRAISE, EVEN FILD MY
                              VEINES WITH PRIDE   4.53.4
  YET ARE MINE EYES SO FILLED WITH THE STORE   5.35.9
  YET ARE MYNE EYES SO FILLED WITH THE STORE   5.83.9
FILLING   2
  FILLING MINE $EARES WITH $NOISE, AND $NIGHTLY
                              GRONING   2.40.6
  FILLING MYNE EARES WITH NOYSE AND NIGHTLY
                              GRONING   2.144.6
FILTH   1
  CIRCUMPASS'D ROUND WITH FILTH AND LOTHSOME MUD   1.29.2
FILTHY   3
  MAKING WITHALL SOME FILTHY $ANTIKE $FACE   2.31.4
  RICH FOOLES THERE BE, WHOSE BASE AND FILTHY HART   4.24.1
  LET NOT ONE SPARKE OF FILTHY LUSTFULL FYRE   5.84.1
FIND   68
  ALL UNAWARES, A $GODDESSE CHASTE I FINDE   1.5.3
  THE WORLD HAD NEVER KNOWNE WHAT I DOE FINDE   1.7.3
  I WRITTEN FINDE THE SENTENCE OF MY DEATH   1.10.3
  YET CANNOT FINDE HER BREATHE UNTO MY REST   1.13.11
  NEVER TO FINDE, AND EVERMORE TO SEEKE   1.20.9
  AND SEEKE THAT WHICH I DARE NOT HOPE TO FINDE   1.20.10
  OFT WHEN I FINDE IN HER NO TRUTH AT ALL   1.25.5
  I SEARCH THE EARTH, THE EARTH I FINDE AS SKANT   1.29.7
  NO SUCCOUR FINDE I NOW WHEN MOST I NEEDE   1.32.11
  UPON MY SELFE THOU BEST MAYST FINDE THE FORME   1.37.8
  FOR WHAT SHE WAS, SHE BEST SHALL FIND IN YOU   1.38.12
  WHEN ONCE THEY FIND HER FLOWRE HER GLORY PAS   1.40.14
  WHEN MEN SHALL FIND THY FLOWER, THY GLORY PASSE   1.41.1
  THE WORLD SHALL FINDE THIS MYRACLE IN ME   1.41.9
  ONCE LET THE $OCEAN OF MY CARES FINDE SHORE   1.46.13
  AND IF I FINDE SUCH PLEASURE TO COMPLAINE   1.48.13
  I FINDE, MY $GRIEFES INNUMERABLE GROWE   2.3.3
  AND EVER THIS IN $MAD-MEN YOU SHALL FINDE   2.9.6
  AND IF WITH $TEARES I FIND THEM ALL TOO LIGHT   2.13.7
  I FIND OLD $POETS HYLLS AND FLOODS ADMIRE   2.120.2
  AND IF WITH TEARES, I FIND THEM ALL TOO LIGHT   2.121.7
  BY NATURES $LAWES WE THEE A $BASTARD FINDE   2.140.12
  FIND NO DETERMINATION, THEN YOU WERE   3.13.6
  BY OFT PREDICT THAT I IN HEAVEN FINDE   3.14.8
  TO FINDE WHERE YOUR TRUE $IMAGE PICTUR'D LIES   3.24.6
  FOR THEE, AND FOR MY SELFE, NOE QUIET FINDE   3.27.14
  BOTH FINDE EACH OTHER, AND I LOOSE BOTH TWAINE   3.42.11
  SHALL REASONS FINDE OF SETLED GRAVITIE   3.49.8
  O WHAT EXCUSE WILL MY POORE BEAST THEN FIND   3.51.5
  SHALL YOU PACE FORTH, YOUR PRAISE SHALL
                              STIL FINDE ROOME   3.55.10

```
TO FIND OUT SHAMES AND IDLE HOURES IN ME          3.61.7
COMMIT TO THESE WASTE BLACKS, AND THOU
                         SHALT FINDE             3.77.10
OH WHAT A HAPPY TITLE DO I FINDE                 3.92.11
AND THOU IN THIS SHALT FINDE THY MONUMENT        3.107.13
BUT THENCE I LEARNE AND FIND THE LESSON TRUE     3.118.13
O BENEFIT OF ILL, NOW I FIND TRUE                3.119.9
AND THOU SHALT FINDE IT MERRITS NOT REPROOVING   3.142.4
LEAST EYES WELL SEEING THY FOULE FAULTS
                         SHOULD FINDE            3.148.14
NOT USDE TO FROZEN CLIPS; HE STRAVE TO
                         FIND SOME PART             4.8.6
LOOKS OVER THE WORLD, AND CAN FIND NOTHING SUCH    4.9.10
FOR LIKE A CHILD THAT SOME FAIRE BOOKE DOTH FIND   4.11.5
AND FIND TH'EFFECT, FOR I DO BURNE IN LOVE        4.25.14
I FIND HOW HEAV'NLY DAY WRETCH I DID MISSE        4.33.4
MY HARMES ON $INK'S POORE LOSSE, PERHAPS
                         SOME FIND               4.34.13
AND YET SHE HEARES, YET I NO PITTY FIND            4.44.5
I MUCH DO GUESSE, YET FIND NO TRUTH SAVE THIS      4.44.9
WHILE THOSE POORE BABES THEIR DEATH IN
                         BIRTH DO FIND           4.50.11
BUT FIND SOME $HERCULES TO BEARE, IN STEED        4.51.7
BUT YOU FAIRE MAIDES, AT LENGTH THIS TRUE
                         SHALL FIND              4.54.11
THAT I WELL FIND NO ELOQUENCE LIKE IT            4.55.14
GROWNE NOW HIS SLAVES, HE FORST THEM OUT TO FIND  4.57.3
HOPING THAT WHEN THEY MIGHT FIND $STELLA ALONE    4.57.5
THAT NO PACE ELSE THEIR GUIDED STEPS CAN FIND     4.58.3
SWEET SAID THAT I TRUE LOVE IN HER SHOULD FIND    4.62.4
FOR WHEN, NAK'D BOY, THOU COULDST NO HARBOUR FIND 4.65.5
THERE SHALL HE FIND ALL VICES' OVERTHROW          4.71.5
GRIEFE FIND THE WORDS, FOR THOU HAST MADE
                         MY BRAINE               4.94.1
FORST BY THEIR $LORD, WHO IS ASHAM'D TO FIND      4.99.13
KNOWING WORLDS PASSE, ERE SHE ENOUGH CAN FIND    4.101.13
YET FIND I NOUGHT ON EARTH TO WHICH I DARE         5.9.3
FOR MY SWEET $SAYNT SOME SERVICE FIT WILL FIND    5.22.4
IN ONE SHORT HOURE I FIND BY HER UNDONNE          5.23.8
SUCH LABOUR LIKE THE $SPYDERS WEB I FYND         5.23.13
THE POWRE THEREOF, WHICH OFTE IN ME I FIND        5.28.5
THE MORE I FYND THEIR MALICE TO INCREACE         5.44.14
HUNTS AFTER BLOUD, WHEN HE BY CHANCE DOTH FIND    5.56.3
YET NOR IN FIELD NOR BOWRE I HER CAN FYND         5.78.7
I FYND MY SELFE BUT FED WITH FANCIES VAYNE       5.78.12
FINDING                    13
FINDING NO END NOR PERIOD OF MY PAINE            1.16.12
FINDING ME RAIN'D WITH SUCH A HEAVY HAND         1.28.12
FINDING MY FORTUNE EVER IN THE WAINE              1.32.3
FINDING THEIR $OBJECTS OVER-SOONE DEPART          2.33.6
BUT FINDING $NATURE THEIR REQUEST DENYES         2.33.11
FINDING THY WORTH A LIMMIT PAST MY PRAISE         3.82.6
FINDING THE FIRST CONCEIT OF LOVE THERE BRED     3.108.13
BUT FINDING THESE $NORTH CLYMES DO COLDLY
                         HIM EMBRACE               4.8.5
BUT FINDING NOT THOSE RESTLESSE FLAMES IN ME      4.16.5
SO $STELLA'S HEART, FINDING WHAT POWER
                         $LOVE BRINGS             4.29.5
KILS HIS OWNE CHILDREN, TEARES, FINDING
                         THAT THEY               4.95.10
```

```
IN FINDING FAULT WITH HER TOO PORTLY PRIDE        5.5.2
FINDING A TREE ALONE ALL COMFORTLESSE             5.56.7
FINDS                 3
AND $LOVE ALONE FINDS REASON IN MY LOVE           2.131.14
WHEREIN IT FINDES A JOY ABOVE THE REST            3.91.6
WHICH ALTERS WHEN IT ALTERATION FINDES            3.116.3
FINE                  10
TO HEARE WIT EIES BELONGS TO LOVES FINE WIHT      3.23.14
FOR BLUNTING THE FINE POINT OF SELDOME PLEASURE   3.52.4
STUDYING INVENTIONS FINE, HER WITS TO ENTERTAINE  4.1.6
OR $PINDARE'S $APES, FLAUNT THEY IN PHRASES FINE  4.3.3
IS NO FIT MARKE TO PIERCE WITH HIS FINE
                    POINTED DART                  4.8.3
OR AT THE MOST ON SOME FINE PICTURE STAYES        4.11.7
BEAUTIES, WHICH WERE OF MANIE $CARRETS FINE       4.16.2
CLOTH'D WITH FINE TROPES, WITH STRONGEST
                    REASONS LIN'D                 4.58.6
AND GRACE, SICKE TOO, SUCH FINE CONCLUSIONS
                    TRIES                         4.101.3
WITH MANY DEARE DELIGHTS BEDECKED FYNE            5.71.12
FINEST                1
IF $GOLD, HER LOCKS ARE FINEST GOLD ON GROUND     5.15.11
FINGER                2
THEN HAD NO FINGER POINTED AT MY LIGHTNESSE       1.7.2
AS ON THE FINGER OF A THRONED $QUEENE             3.96.5
FINGERS               3
WITH THY SWEET FINGERS WHEN THOU GENTLY SWAYST    3.128.3
ORE WHOME THEIR FINGERS WALKE WITH GENTLE GATE    3.128.11
GIVE THEM THEIR FINGERS, ME THY LIPS TO KISSE     3.128.14
FINISHING             1
NOT FINISHING HER $QUEENE OF FAERY                5.33.3
FIRBLOOM              1
SWEET IS THE FIRBLOOME, BUT HIS BRAUNCHES ROUGH   5.26.4
FIRE                  73
BEARE NOT REPORT OF ANY SLENDER FIRE              1.4.3
FED BUT WITH SMOKE, AND CHERISHT BUT WITH FIRE    1.15.4
AND THREW ME DOWNE TO PAINE IN ALL THIS FIRE      1.36.5
AND THOSE BRIGHT RAIES THAT KINDLE ALL THIS FIRE  1.38.3
THAT FIRE CAN BURNE WHEN ALL THE MATTER'S SPENT   1.41.10
INKINDLED BY HER EYES CELESTIALL FIRE             1.59.4
CELESTIALL FIRE, AND UNRESPECTING POWRES          1.59.5
WHILST $MOONE SHALL SHINE, OR ANY $FIRE
                    SHALL BURNE                   2.13.12
IF $HE, FROM $HEAV'N THAT FILCH'D THAT
                    LIVING $FIRE                  2.14.1
THE $FIRE HE STOLE, ALTHOUGH OF $HEAV'NLY KIND    2.14.5
WHICH BEING KINDLED BY THAT HEAV'NLY FIRE         2.16.7
AND SET MY $BREST, HIS $LODGING, ON A FIRE        2.23.12
THOSE $PRIESTS WHICH FIRST THE $VESTALL
                    $FIRE BEGUN                   2.30.1
THY BLESSED $EYES, THE $SUNNE WHICH LIGHTS
                    THIS $FIRE                    2.30.9
LOVE IS THE $FEWELL, WHICH MAINTAINES THE FIRE    2.40.4
MY $EYES WITH $TEARES AGAINST THE FIRE STRIVING   2.40.9
THOU, THUS WHOSE $SPIRIT $LOVE IN HIS
                    FIRE REFINES                  2.49.13
AT WHOSE PURE $EYES, $LOVE LIGHTS HIS
                    HALLOW'D $FIRE                2.57.8
BURN'D IN A $SEA OF YCE, AND DROWN'D AMIDST
                    A FIRE                        2.62.14
```

THE $GODS PURE FIRE HATH BEEN EXTINGUISHT QUITE	2.105.2
PRAISE HIM WHICH MADE THAT FIRE, WHICH	
LENDS THAT LIGHT	2.105.14
THEN WITH THY BEAUTIE SET THE SAME ON FIRE	2.106.7
ANOTHER, MERVAILES $SULPHURE $AETNAS FIRE	2.120.4
WHILST $MOONE SHALL SHYNE BY NIGHT, OR	
ANY FIRE SHALL BURNE	2.121.12
YET THERE HE BURNES, IN FIRE THATS NEVER	
QUENCHED	2.122.14
SUNNE OF THE WORLD, THOU HART REVYVING FIRE	2.123.8
OF PUREST GOLD, TEMPRED WITH VERTUES FIRE	2.126.7
MY $LOVE MAKES HOTE THE FIRE WHOSE HEAT IS SPENT	2.127.1
THE FIRE, UNTO MY LOVE, COMPARE A PAINTED FIRE	2.127.5
THE FIRE, UNTO MY LOVE, COMPARE A PAINTED FIRE	2.127.5
ONELY MY LOVE IS IN THE FIRE INGRAVED	2.127.9
YET FIRE, WATER, AYRE, OF NATURE NOT DEPRIVED	2.127.12
WHILST FIRE, WATER, AYRE, TWIXT HEAVEN	
AND EARTH SHAL BE	2.127.13
DISDAYNE $ICE TO MY LIFE, IS TO MY SOULE A FIRE	2.132.3
WITH MY SOULES FIRE, MY LIFE DISDAINE OUT-WEARES	2.132.7
MY LIFE A $PHOENIX IS IN MY SOULES FIRE	2.132.11
SLEEPES AGED COLDNES, WITH $BEAUTIES FIRE WARMED	2.136.7
LOVE IS THE FUELL WHICH MAINTAINES THE FIRE	2.144.4
MYNE EYES WITH TEARES AGAINST THE FIRE STRYVING	2.144.9
WHICH STILL TORMENTS ME IN DAYES BURNING FIRE	2.145.14
BURN'D IN A $SEA OF $ICE, AND DROWN'D	
AMIDST A FIRE	2.150.14
THE OTHER TWO, SLIGHT AYRE, AND PURGING FIRE	3.45.1
NOR $MARS HIS SWORD, NOR WARRES QUICK	
FIRE SHALL BURNE	3.55.7
IN ME THOU SEEST THE GLOWING OF SUCH FIRE	3.73.9
TILL MY BAD ANGEL FIRE MY GOOD ONE OUT	3.144.14
AND HIS LOVE-KINDLING FIRE DID QUICKLY STEEPE	3.153.3
WHICH BORROWD FROM THIS HOLIE FIRE OF LOVE	3.153.5
WHERE $CUPID GOT NEW FIRE., MY MISTRES EYE	3.153.14
THE FAYREST VOTARY TOOKE UP THAT FIRE	3.154.5
WHICH FROM LOVES FIRE TOCKE HEAT PERPETUALL	3.154.10
LOVES FIRE HEATES WATER, WATER COOLES NOT LOVE	3.154.14
THEN DID ON HIM WHO FIRST STALE DOWNE THE FIRE	4.14.3
TO WARME WITH ILL-MADE FIRE COLD $MOSCOVY	4.30.4
TILL WITHOUT FEWELL YOU CAN MAKE HOT FIRE	4.46.14
AND THEN WITH PATIENCE BID ME BEARE MY FIRE	4.56.14
SEEKING TO QUENCH IN ME THE NOBLE FIRE	4.68.7
WHILE EACH DOTH BLOW THE FIER OF MY HART	4.72.4
NATURE'S PRAISE, $VERTUE'S STALL, $CUPID'S	
COLD FIRE	4.80.3
THE LIGHT WHEROF HATH KINDLED HEAVENLY FYRE	5.3.3
IS LONG ERE IT CONCEIVE THE KINDLING FYRE	5.6.6
MAY KINDLE LIVING FIRE WITHIN MY BREST	5.7.12
MORE THEN MOST FAIRE, FULL OF THE LIVING FIRE	5.8.1
NOR TO THE FIRE.. FOR THEY CONSUME NOT EVER	5.9.8
PROUD $DAPHNE SCORNING $PHAEBUS LOVELY FYRE	5.28.9
MY LOVE IS LYKE TO YSE, AND I TO FYRE	5.30.1
THAT FIRE WHICH ALL THING MELTS, SHOULD	
HARDEN YSE	5.30.10
SHOULD KINDLE FYRE BY WONDERFULL DEVYSE+	5.30.12
DID SACRIFIZE UNTO THE GREEDY FYRE	5.48.4
NOT WATER., FOR HER LOVE DOTH BURNE LIKE FYRE	5.55.6
NOT FYRE., FOR SHE DOTH FRIESE WITH FAINT DESIRE	5.55.8
OR IN HER EYES THE FYRE OF LOVE DOES SPARKE	5.81.4

```
LET NOT ONE SPARKE OF FILTHY LUSTFULL FYRE          5.84.1
THE SPARKES WHEREOF LET KINDLE THINE OWN FYRE       5.86.9
FIREBRANDS            1
TO MY CLOSE HEART, WHERE WHILE SOME FIREBRANDS
                     HE DID LAY                      4.8.13
FIRED                 4
LOVE WAS THE FLAME THAT FIRED ME SO NEERE            1.14.3
THAT WITH THE RAYES HIS WAFTING PYNEONS FIRED       2.122.11
BUT AT MY MISTRES EIE LOVES BRAND NEW FIRED          3.153.9
THEN DOE I DIE, AS ONE WITH LIGHTNING FYRED          5.7.8
FIRES                 2
BY THINE OWNE LOVED $PSYCHES, BY THE $FIRES          2.36.9
OF LIVING DEATHS, DEARE WOUNDS, FAIRE
                     STORMES AND FREESING FIRES  4.6.4
FIRE'S                1
WHEN SORROW (USING MINE OWNE FIER'S MIGHT)           4.108.1
FIRM                  1
AND THE FIRME SOILE WIN OF THE WATRY MAINE           3.64.7
FIRMER                1
THE HARDER WONNE, THE FIRMER WILL ABIDE              5.6.4
FIRMEST               1
THE FIRMEST FLINT DOTH IN CONTINUANCE WEARE          5.18.4
FIRMLY                5
THAT LEARNED $FATHER, WHICH SO FIRMELY PROVES        2.12.1
SINCE THEY DO WEARE HIS BADGE, MOST FIRMELY PROVE    4.52.4
THY REASONS FIRMLY SET ON $VERTUE'S FEET             4.68.11
AND WITH HER OWNE GOODWILL HIR FYRMELY TYDE          5.67.12
SO FIRMELY, THAT YE NEVER MAY REMOVE                 5.71.8
FIRST                53
SINCE THE FIRST LOCKE THAT LED ME TO THIS ERROR      1.18.1
AND SHUT THOSE WAIES MY FRIENDLY FOE FIRST ENTRED    1.27.3
AND WHERE THE SWEETEST BLOSSOMES FIRST APPEARES      1.51.7
YOUR $CHEEKES YET PALE, SINCE FIRST HE
                     GAVE THE $WOUND                  2.2.12
TIS NINE YEERES NOW SINCE FIRST I LOST MY $WIT       2.9.11
NINE ORDERS FIRST OF $ANGELS BE IN $HEAVEN           2.18.5
POWR'D OUT WHAT FIRST FROM QUICKE $INVENTION CAME    2.21.6
HE STILL AS YOUNG AS WHEN HE FIRST WAS BORNE         2.22.9
WHEN CONQU'RING $LOVE DID FIRST MY $HEART ASSAYLE    2.29.1
BUT HE WITH $BEAUTIE FIRST CORRUPTED $SIGHT          2.29.5
TO CRUELL $LOVE MY $SOULE WAS FIRST BETRAY'D         2.29.14
THOSE $PRIESTS WHICH FIRST THE $VESTALL
                     $FIRE BEGUN                      2.30.1
AND FIRST THE SOUND AND VERTUE OF MY $NAME           2.47.3
FIRST MAKE INCISION ON EACH MAST'RING $VEINE         2.50.6
CALLING TO MINDE SINCE FIRST MY $LOVE BEGUN          2.51.1
WHEN LIKE AN $EAGLET I FIRST FOUND MY $LOVE          2.56.1
WHEN FIRST I $ENDED, THEN I FIRST $BEGAN             2.62.1
WHEN FIRST I $ENDED, THEN I FIRST $BEGAN             2.62.1
ME THINKES 'TIS LONG SINCE FIRST THESE
                     $WARRES BEGUN                    2.63.2
NINE ORDERS FIRST OF $ANGELS BE IN HEAVEN            2.108.5
AT MY FIRST $LESSON IN THY SACRED NAME               2.111.6
WHERE FIRST MY $LOVE INTO THE WORLD WAS BROUGHT      2.116.4
WHEN FIRST I ENDED, THEN I FIRST BEGAN               2.150.1
WHEN FIRST I ENDED, THEN I FIRST BEGAN               2.150.1
AND FOR A WOMAN WERT THOU FIRST CREATED              3.20.9
WITH $APRILLS FIRST BORNE FLOWERS AND
                     ALL THINGS RARE                  3.21.7
THE FIRST MY THOUGHT, THE OTHER MY DESIRE            3.45.3
```

```
THAT $GOD FORBID, THAT MADE ME FIRST YOUR SLAVE      3.58.1
SINCE MINDE AT FIRST IN CARRECTER WAS DONE           3.59.8
AT FIRST THE VERY WCRST CF FORTUNES MIGHT            3.90.12
FOR AS YOU WERE WHEN FIRST YOUR EYE I EYCE           3.104.2
SINCE FIRST I SAW YCU FRESH WHICH YET ARE GREENE     3.104.8
EVEN AS WHEN FIRST I HALLOWED THY FAIRE NAME         3.108.8
FINDING THE FIRST CCNCEIT OF LOVE THERE BRED         3.108.13
OH TIS THE FIRST, TIS FLATRY IN MY SEEING            3.114.9
THAT MINE EYE LOVES IT AND DOTH FIRST BEGINNE        3.114.14
GROWES FAIRER THEN AT FIRST, MORE STRONG,
                           FAR GREATER                3.119.12
NOT AT FIRST SIGHT, NOR WITH A DRIBBED SHOT          4.2.1
THE FIRST, THUS MATCHT, WERE SCARCELY $GENTLEMEN     4.13.14
THEN DID ON HIM WHC FIRST STALE DOWNE THE FIRE       4.14.3
TO KEEPE THE PACE CF THEIR FIRST LOVING STATE        4.17.4
THE FIRST THAT STRAIGHT MY FANCIE'S ERROR BRINGS     4.38.5
EDWARD NAMED FOURTH, AS FIRST IN PRAISE I NAME       4.75.2
POORE HOPE'S FIRST WEALTH, OSTAGE OF PROMIST
                           WEALE                      4.79.12
SEEING HOPE YEELD WHEN THIS WO STRAKE HIM FURST      4.95.6
FIRST DID WITH PUFFING KISSE THOSE LOCKES
                           DISPLAY                    4.103.11
THEY FIRST RESORT UNTO THAT SOUERAIGNE PART          4.107.4
UNQUIET THOUGHT, WHCM AT THE FIRST I BRED            5.2.1
DISDAYNE TO YIELD UNTO THE FIRST ASSAY               5.14.8
THEN WITH SOME CORDIALLS SEEKE FIRST TO APPEASE      5.50.9
WITH WHICH THAT HAPPY NAME WAS FIRST DESYND          5.74.2
THE FIRST MY BEING TO ME GAVE BY KIND                5.74.5
AND PERFECT BEAUTY DID AT FIRST PROCEED              5.79.12
FISH                    3
THE $CRYSTALL $TRENT, FCR $FOORDS AND
                           $FISH RENOWNED             2.32.3
THE CHRISTALL $TRENT, FCR $FOORDS AND
                           FISHE RENOWNED             2.124.3
THAT FROM THE FOOLISH FISH THEYR BAYTS DOE HYDE      5.47.4
FISHERS                 1
OF CUNNINGST FISHERS IN MOST TROUBLED STREAMES       4.51.10
FISHES                  1
FLINGING THE $FISHES BACKWARD WITH HIS HEELES        2.147.4
FIT                     21
AND ALL THINGS FIT AGAINST HER COMMING THERE         1.30.8
FRAM'D MY DESIRES FIT FCR HER EYES TO KILL           1.36.14
THUS TALKING IDLY IN THIS $BEDLAM FIT                2.9.9
I SOUGHT FIT WORDS TO PAINT THE BLACKEST
                           FACE OF WOE                4.1.5
CHURCHES OR SCHOOLES ARE FOR THY SEATE MCRE FIT      4.4.6
IS NO FIT MARKE TC PIERCE WITH HIS FINE
                           POINTED DART               4.8.3
THE THOROWEST WORDS, FIT FOR WOE'S SELFE TO GRONE    4.57.4
FROM NOBLER COURSE, FIT FOR MY BIRTH AND MIND        4.62.8
WITH VOICE MORE FIT TO WED $AMPHION'S $LYRE          4.68.6
O BLISSE, FIT FOR A NOBLER STATE THEN ME             4.69.2
NOT POINTING TO FIT FOLKES EACH UNDERCHARGE          4.85.6
THIS HOLY SEASON FIT TO FAST AND PRAY                5.22.1
FOR MY SWEET $SAYNT SOME SERVICE FIT WILL FIND       5.22.4
BUT STILL THE MORE SHE FERVENT SEES MY FIT           5.32.9
SINS THAT THIS ONE IS TOST WITH TROUBLOUS FIT        5.33.11
FIT MEDICINES FOR MY BODIES BEST RELIEFE             5.50.4
FOR DAMZELS FIT TC DECKE THEIR LOVERS BOWRES         5.64.4
COULD NOT ON EARTH HAVE FOUND ONE FIT FOR MATE       5.66.6
```

```
WHAT TROPHEE THEN SHALL I MOST FIT DEVIZE          5.69.5
ALL SPRED WITH JUNCATS, FIT TO ENTERTAYNE          5.77.3
FIT FOR THE HANDMAYD OF THE $FAERY $QUEENE          5.80.14
FITS                2
THE HUMBLE SALVE, WHICH WOUNDED BOSOMES FITS        3.120.12
SOMETIMES I JOY WHEN GLAD OCCASION FITS             5.54.5
FITTED              1
HOW HAVE MINE EIES CUT CF THEIR $SPHEARES
                          BENE FITTED               3.119.7
FITTER              2
TO $NOTHING FITTER CAN I $THEE COMPARE              2.10.1
SO $TYRAN HE NO FITTER PLACE COULD SPIE             4.20.5
FITTEST             2
THEN $FOOLES AND $CHILDREN FITT'ST TO
                          GOE TOGETHER              2.22.8
OR BEING $BLIND (AS FITTEST FOR THE $TRACE)         2.48.9
FIVE                4
FAITH BEING WITH BLOOD, AND FIVE YEARES
                          WITNES SIGN'D             1.31.6
EVEN OF FIVE HUNDRETH CCURSES OF THE $SUNNE         3.59.6
BUT MY FIVE WITS, NCR MY FIVE SENCES CAN            3.141.9
BUT MY FIVE WITS, NCR MY FIVE SENCES CAN            3.141.9
FIXED               6
YET WHETHER FIXT CR WANDRING STARRES ARE THEY       1.34.9
FIXT SURE THEY ARE, BUT WANDRING MAKE ME STRAY      1.34.11
AS THOSE GOULD CANDELLS FIXT IN HEAVENS AYER        3.21.12
TRUTH NEEDS NO COLLOUR WITH HIS COLLOUR FIXT        3.101.6
O NO, IT IS AN EVER FIXED MARKE                     3.116.5
IF THAT BE SINNE WHICH IN FIXT HEARTS DOTH BREED    4.14.12
FLAME               19
WHICH CLEERE OUR CLOUDED WORLD WITH BRIGHTEST
                          FLAME                     1.12.4
LOVE WAS THE FLAME THAT FIRED ME SO NEERE           1.14.3
STRONG IS THE NET, AND FERVENT IS THE FLAME         1.14.5
THE BOND, THE FLAME, THE WOUND THAT FESTRETH SO     1.14.10
THESE TEARES, WHICH HEATE OF SACRED FLAME DISTILS   1.24.2
THOUGH SPENT THY FLAME, IN ME THE HEAT REMAINING    1.41.6
(THE CHASTEST FLAME THAT EVER WARMED HART)          1.44.4
YOUR SELFE THUS BURNED IN THAT SACRED FLAME         2.16.9
WHICH MIGHT BE BORRCW'D FROM NO $EARTHLY FLAME      2.30.2
MY HOLY $THOUGHTS, THEY BE THE $VESTALL FLAME       2.30.10
MY $SIGHES THE $BELLOWES, WHICH THE $FLAME
                          ENCREASETH                2.40.5
BUT WITH THOSE $DRCPS, THE $FLAME AGAINE
                          REVIVING                  2.40.11
WITH THINE EYES KINDLING THAT $CELESTIAL FLAME      2.105.7
THY SELFE THUS BURNED IN THIS SACRED FLAME          2.106.9
WHILST $LOVE (MY $PHOENIX BIRD) IN HER
                          OWN FLAME IS DYING        2.117.12
MY SIGHES, THE BELLCWES WHICH THE FLAME
                          INCREASETH                2.144.5
FEED'ST THY LIGHTS FLAME WITH SELFE SUBSTANTIALL
                          FEWELL                    3.1.6
THOUGH ABSENCE SEEM'D MY FLAME TO QUALLIFIE         3.109.2
MY MOST FULL FLAME SHOULD AFTERWARDS BURNE
                          CLEERER                   3.115.4
FLAMES              12
WITH $FLAMES AND $LIGHTNINGS THEIR $EXORCIUMS
                          PAINT                     2.39.2
WITH FLAMES AND LIGHTNING THEIR EXORDIUMS PAYNT     2.118.2
```

```
THAT HER SWEETE BREATH MAKES OFT THY FLAMES
                        TO RISE                         4.12.4
BUT FINDING NOT THOSE RESTLESSE FLAMES IN ME            4.16.5
STRANGE FLAMES OF $LOVE IT IN OUR SOULES
                        WOULD RAISE                     4.25.4
BREATHE OUT THE FLAMES WHICH BURNE WITHIN
                        MY HEART                        4.28.13
WHAT $NESTOR'S COUNSELL CAN MY FLAMES ALAY              4.35.5
I FEELE THE FLAMES OF HOTTEST SUMMER DAY                4.89.14
GREAT HEAT, AND MAKES HIS FLAMES TO HEAVEN ASPIRE       5.6.8
BURNING IN FLAMES OF PURE AND CHAST DESYRE              5.22.12
AND FEELE MY FLAMES AUGMENTED MANIFOLD+                 5.30.8
YET CANNOT ALL THESE FLAMES IN WHICH I FRY              5.32.5
FLAMING                 1
SPENT ON THINE $ALTARS, FLAMING UP TO $HEAV'N           2.36.10
FLAMY                   1
HER FLAMIE GLISTRING LIGHTS INCREASE WITH
                        TIME AND PLACE                  4.76.10
FLATTER                 6
MAY BLASPHEME THUS, AND SAY, I FLATTER THEE             2.112.3
SO FLATTER I THE SWART COMPLEXIOND NIGHT                3.28.11
FLATTER THE MOUNTAINE TOPS WITH SOVERAINE EIE           3.33.2
THUS HAVE I HAD THEE AS A DREAME DOTH FLATTER           3.87.13
HOPE, ART THOU TRUE, OR DOEST THOU FLATTER ME+          4.67.1
WHEN I DOE PRAISE HER, SAY I DOE BUT FLATTER            5.85.2
FLATTERED               2
MAY SAY, THAT THOU ART FLATTERED BY MEE                 2.35.3
AND IN OUR FAULTS BY LYES WE FLATTERED BE               3.138.14
FLATTERER               1
TO CRYTTICK AND TO FLATTERER STOPPED ARE                3.112.11
FLATTERING              2
FALSE FLATTERING HOPE, THAT WITH SO FAIRE A FACE        4.106.2
SO SHE WITH FLATTRING SMYLES WEAKE HARTS
                        DOTH GUYDE                      5.47.5
FLATTERY                5
SWEETE FLATTERY, THEN SHE LOVES BUT ME ALONE            3.42.14
DRINKE UP THE MONARKS PLAGUE THIS FLATTERY+             3.114.2
OH TIS THE FIRST, TIS FLATRY IN MY SEEING               3.114.9
WHERE TRUTH IT SELFE MUST SPEAKE LIKE FLATTERIE+        4.35.2
LOATHING ALL LIES, DOUBTING THIS $FLATTERIE IS          4.80.11
FLAUNT                  1
OR $PINDARE'S $APES, FLAUNT THEY IN PHRASES FINE        4.3.3
FLED                    6
GIVE WARNING TO THE WORLD THAT I AM FLED                3.71.3
OR IF THEY HAVE, WHERE IS MY JUDGMENT FLED              3.148.3
INVENTION, $NATURE'S CHILD, FLED STEP-DAME
                        $STUDIE'S BLOWES                4.1.10
LOVE BORNE IN $GREECE, OF LATE FLED FROM
                        HIS NATIVE PLACE                4.8.1
THEY FLED WITH BLUSH, WHICH GUILTIE SEEM'D
                        OF LOVE                         4.66.14
AND EVERY BEAST THAT TO HIS DEN WAS FLED                5.40.10
FLEE                    2
MEE THINKS I FLEE, YET WANT I LEGS TO GOE               2.150.5
ON THE $THESSALIAN SHORE FROM HIM DID FLEE              5.28.10
FLEECE                  2
ERE BEAUTIES DEAD FLEECE MADE ANOTHER GAY               3.68.8
FORGETFULL OF THE FAMOUS GOLDEN FLEECE                  5.44.3
FLEETEST                1
MAKE GLAD AND SORRY SEASONS AS THOU FLEET'ST            3.19.5
```

```
FLEETING                         2
  COMMIT MY WORDS UNTO THE FLEETING WIND                2.142.11
  FROM THEE, THE PLEASURE OF THE FLEETING YEARE+          3.97.2
FLESH                            8
  IF THE DULL SUBSTANCE OF MY FLESH WERE THOUGHT          3.44.1
  SHALL NAIGH NOE DULL FLESH IN HIS FIERY RACE           3.51.11
  TRIUMPH IN LOVE, FLESH STAIES NO FARTHER REASON        3.151.8
  THAT SHRINES IN FLESH SO TRUE A $DEITIE                 4.4.13
  HER FLESH HIS FOOD, HER SKIN HIS ARMOUR BRAVE          4.29.12
  WEAKE IS TH'ASSURANCE THAT WEAKE FLESH REPOSETH         5.58.1
  ALL FLESH IS FRAYLE, AND ALL HER STRENGTH UNSTAYD       5.58.5
  FROM FRAYLE CORRUPTION, THAT DOTH FLESH ENSEW           5.79.8
FLESH'S                          1
  SHALL DOFFE HER FLESHES BOROWD FAYRE ATTYRE             5.27.6
FLEW                             1
  WHILST BY THY EIES PURSU'D, MY POORE HEART FLEW         1.31.1
FLIES                           10
  UP, TO MY $PITCH, NO COMMON $JUDGEMENT FLYES           2.31.13
  NEERER $MEN COME, $THAT FURTHER FLYES AWAY              2.58.9
  INTO HIS HART THE PIERCING $ARROW FLYES                2.135.8
  A $CROW THAT FLIES IN HEAVENS SWEETEST AYRE             3.70.4
  TO FOLLOW THAT WHICH FLIES BEFORE HER FACE             3.143.7
  SO RUNST THOU AFTER THAT WHICH FLIES FROM THEE         3.143.9
  THEY DEEME, AND OF THEIR DOOME THE RUMOUR FLIES         4.27.5
  WAS HELD, IN OPEND SENSE IT FLIES AWAY                 4.38.10
  MY $ORPHAN SENCE FLIES TO THE INWARD SIGHT             4.88.10
  TO FEED HIS FILL, FLYES BACKE UNTO YOUR SIGHT           5.73.8
FLIGHT                           6
  AND YET I CANNOT REPREHEND THE FLIGHT                   1.35.1
  TO HELPE HER FLIGHT THROUGHOUT THE FAIREST $ILE        1.43.10
  WHICH THOUGH THE $DAY DIS-JOYNE BY SEV'RALL
                       FLIGHT                             2.37.6
  BUT SHE MOST FAIRE, MOST COLD, MADE HIM
                       THENCE TAKE HIS FLIGHT             4.8.12
  AND UNTO HEAVEN FORGETS HER FORMER FLIGHT               5.72.8
  DESIRED FOOD, TO IT DOTH MAKE HIS FLIGHT                5.73.6
FLINGING                         1
  FLINGING THE $FISHES BACKWARD WITH HIS HEELES          2.147.4
FLINT                            7
  TEARES CANNOT SOFTEN FLINT, NOR VOWES CONVART           1.11.3
  FLINT, FROST, DISDAINE, WEARES, MELTES,
                       AND YEELDES WE SEE                1.11.14
  I WORKE ON FLINT, AND THATS THE CAUSE I MONE            1.13.4
  UPON THE FLINT OF SUCH A HART REBELLING                1.18.10
  I FEARE YOUR EYE HATH TURND YOUR HEART TO FLINT        1.37.14
  THE FIRMEST FLINT DOTH IN CONTINUANCE WEARE             5.18.4
  WHILES SHE AS STEELE AND FLINT DOTH STILL
                       REMAYNE                           5.18.14
FLINTY                           2
  ILE PRAISE HER FACE, AND BLAME HER FLINTY HEART        1.26.12
  OR IF THOU HAST, IT IS A FLINTY ONE                    2.52.14
FLIT                             1
  THAT WHEN A DREADFULL STORME AWAY IS FLIT               5.40.7
FLITS                            1
  SOONE AFTER WHEN MY JOY TO SORROW FLITS                 5.54.7
FLOAT                            1
  YOUR SHALLOWEST HELPE WILL HOLD ME UP A FLOATE          3.80.9
FLOATS                           1
  SEE WHERE SHEE FLOTES, LADEN WITH PUREST LOVE          2.134.5
```

```
FLOOD                          5
   OUR $NORTHERNE $BORDERS BOAST OF $TWEEDS
                         FAIRE $FLOUD              2.32.10
   A SECOND $FLOUD, DOWNE RAYNING FROM MINE $EYES  2.55.4
   A SECOND FLOOD DOWNE RAYNING FROM MINE EYES     2.102.4
   OUR $NORTHERN BORDERS BOAST OF $TWEEDS
                         FAIRE FLOOD               2.124.10
   MY EYES MADE DIM WITH LOOKES, POURE DOWN
                         A FLOOD OF TEARS          2.133.10
FLOODS                         3
   TO PAINT ON FLOODS, TILL THE SHORE CRIE TO TH'AIRE  1.9.2
   I FIND OLD $POETS HYLLS AND FLOODS ADMIRE       2.120.2
   AS IS A ROCKE AMIDST THE RAGING FLOODS          5.56.10
FLOOD'S-QUEEN                  2
   OUR $FLOUDS-$QUEEN $THAMES, FOR $SHIPS
                         AND $SWANS IS CROWNED     2.32.1
   OUR FLOODS-$QUEENE $THAMES, FOR SHYPS
                         AND $SWANS IS CROWNED     2.124.1
FLOUREDELUCE                   1
   NOR THAT HE MADE THE $FLOUREDELUCE SO FRAID     4.75.9
FLOURISH                       3
   SOONE DOTH IT FADE THAT MAKES THE FAIREST FLORISH  1.50.5
   FLORISH FAIRE $ALBION, GLORY OF THE $NORTH      1.53.9
   TIME DOTH TRANSFIXE THE FLORISH SET ON YOUTH    3.60.9
FLOW                          10
   FOR TO THEIR FLOW SHE NEVER GRANTS AN END       1.48.4
   THEN CAN I DROWNE AN EYE (UN-US'D TO FLOW)      3.30.5
   OFT TURNING OTHERS' LEAVES, TO SEE IF
                         THENCE WOULD FLOW         4.1.7
   SHE EVEN IN BLACKE DOTH MAKE ALL BEAUTIES FLOW+ 4.7.11
   LIES HATCHING STILL THE GOODS WHEREIN THEY FLOW 4.24.2
   THAT, FROM THAT SEA DERIV'D, TEARS' SPRING
                         DID FLOW                  4.45.8
   WHAT $OCEANS OF DELIGHT IN ME DO FLOW           4.69.4
   MY THOUGHTS I SPEAKE, AND WHAT I SPEAKE
                         DOTH FLOW                 4.74.10
   FOR NOTHING FROM MY WIT OR WILL DOTH FLOW       4.90.12
   WHOSE PANTS DO MAKE UNSPILLING CREAME TO FLOW   4.100.6
FLOWER                        15
   MY FLOWER UNTIMELY'S WITHRED WITH MY TEARES     1.24.7
   NARCISSUS CHANG'D T'A FLOWER IN SUCH A CASE     1.37.12
   THE FAIREST FLOWRE THAT EVER SAW THE LIGHT      1.40.6
   WHEN ONCE THEY FIND HER FLOWRE HER GLORY PAS    1.40.14
   WHEN MEN SHALL FIND THY FLOWER, THY GLORY PASSE 1.41.1
   WHOSE ACTION IS NO STRONGER THEN A FLOWER+      3.65.4
   TO THY FAIRE FLOWER AD THE RANCKE SMELL OF WEEDS 3.69.12
   THE SOMMERS FLOWRE IS TO THE SOMMER SWEET       3.94.9
   BUT IF THAT FLOWRE WITH BASE INFECTION MEETE    3.94.11
   OF BIRD, OF FLOWRE, OR SHAPE WHICH IT DOTH LACK 3.113.6
   AND EVERIE FLOURE, NOT SWEET PERHAPS,
                         WHICH GROWES              4.15.3
   CALS EACH WIGHT TO SALUTE THE FLOURE OF BLISSE  4.99.11
   AND WARNES THE $EARTH WITH DIVERS COLORD FLOWRE 5.4.11
   THEN YOU FAIRE FLOWRE, IN WHOM FRESH YOUTH
                         DOTH RAINE                5.4.13
   AND TREAD MY LIFE DOWNE IN THE LOWLY FLOURE     5.20.4
FLOWERS                       23
   AND THERE PREPARE HER FLOWRES THAT NEVER FADES  1.30.7
   THEN FADE THOSE FLOWERS THAT DECKT HER
                         PRIDE SO LONG             1.38.8
```

NO $APRILL CAN REVIVE THY WITHERED FLOWRES   1.39.9
NOW WHILST THY $MAY HATH FILD THY LAP
                          WITH FLOWERS   1.40.2
FLOWERS HAVE A TIME BEFORE THEY COME TO SEEDE   1.51.3
AND LEARNE TO GATHER FLOWERS BEFORE THEY WITHER   1.51.6
AMONGST THE DAINTIE $DEW-IMPEARLED FLOWRES   2.53.8
AMONGST THOSE DAINTY DEW-EMPEARLED FLOWERS   2.113.8
BUT FLOWERS DISTIL'D THOUGH THEY WITH
                          WINTER MEETE   3.5.13
WITH VERTUOUS WISH WOULD BEARE YOUR LIVING
                          FLOWERS   3.16.7
WITH $APRILLS FIRST BORNE FLOWERS AND
                          ALL THINGS RARE   3.21.7
WHEN BEAUTY LIV'D AND DY'ED AS FLOWERS DO NOW   3.68.2
OF DIFFERENT FLOWERS IN ODOR AND IN HEW   3.98.6
MORE FLOWERS I NOTED, YET I NONE COULD SEE   3.99.14
WEEDS AMONG WEEDS, OR FLOWERS WITH FLOWERS
                          GATHERD   3.124.4
WEEDS AMONG WEEDS, OR FLOWERS WITH FLOWERS
                          GATHERD   3.124.4
ENAM'LING WITH PIED FLOWERS THEIR THOUGHTS OF GOLD   4.3.4
WITH CHOISEST FLOWERS MY SPEECH TO ENGARLAND SO   4.55.2
ME SEEMD I SMELT A GARDIN OF SWEET FLOWRES   5.64.2
SUCH FRAGRANT FLOWRES DOE GIVE MOST ODOROUS
                          SMELL   5.64.13
ALL SORTS OF FLOWERS THE WHICH ON EARTH DO SPRING   5.70.3
WITH WOODBYND FLOWERS AND FRAGRANT $EGLANTINE   5.71.10
ALL OTHER FAYRE LYKE FLOWRES UNTYMELY FADE   5.79.14
FLOWING   1
AND WHEN MY FLOWING $NUMBERS THEY REHEARSE   2.25.13
FLOWN   3
IT AFTER THEE, IS LIKE AN $EAGLET FLOWNE   2.56.14
AND THUS (MY FAIRE) MY THOUGHTS AWAY BE FLOWNE   2.103.13
FROM HEAVEN TO HELL IS FLOWNE AWAY   3.145.12
FLOWS   1
WHICH FROM THE RIBS OF OLD $PARNASSUS FLOWES   4.15.2
FLUENTLY   1
SO MAY YOUR TONGUE STILL FLUENTLY PROCEED   4.51.2
FLUSH   1
THY $CHEEKE, NOW FLUSH WITH $ROSES, SUNKE,
                          AND LEANE   2.8.9
FLUTTERS   1
AND MY YONG SOULE FLUTTERS TO THEE HIS NEST   4.108.6
FLY   26
SO SHALT THOU FLYE ABOVE THE VULGAR $THRONG   2.6.13
YOU DOE BEWITCH $ME, $O THAT I COULD FLIE   2.11.13
ME THINKES I $FLIE, YET WANT I LEGGES TO $GOE   2.62.5
AND WITH THE SAME HE PRACTISED TO FLYE   2.122.7
THE AYRE, UNTO MY SIGHES, AS $EAGLE TO THE FLIE   2.127.7
AND HEAVIE IGNORANCE ALOFT TO FLIE   3.78.6
HE BURNT UNWARES HIS WINGS, AND CANNOT FLY AWAY   4.8.14
FLIE, FLY, MY FRIENDS, I HAVE MY DEATH
                          WOUND., FLY   4.20.1
FLIE, FLY, MY FRIENDS, I HAVE MY DEATH
                          WOUND., FLY   4.20.1
FLIE, FLY, MY FRIENDS, I HAVE MY DEATH
                          WOUND., FLY   4.20.1
BUT ERE I COULD FLIE THENCE, IT PIERC'D MY HEART   4.20.14
A $POET EKE, AS HUMOURS FLY OR CREEPE   4.32.4
WILLD ME THESE TEMPESTS OF VAINE LOVE TO FLIE   4.62.10

```
BUT DO NOT WILL ME FROM MY $LOVE TO FLIE           4.64.8
OF REASON, FROM WHOSE LIGHT THOSE NIGHT-BIRDS
                              FLIE                  4.71.7
VENUS IS TAUGHT WITH $DIAN'S WINGS TO FLIE         4.72.6
WITH WINGS OF $LOVE IN AIRE OF WONDER FLIE         4.86.8
HAVE MADE, BUT FORST BY $NATURE STILL TO FLIE     4.103.10
LEGIONS OF LOVES WITH LITTLE WINGS DID FLY         5.16.6
THEN FLY NO MORE FAYRE LOVE FROM $PHEBUS CHACE     5.28.13
AND FLY THE FAULTS WITH WHICH WE DID OFFEND        5.62.8
AND MAKE HIM BOND THAT BONDAGE EARST DYD FLY       5.65.4
SOUGHT NOT TO FLY, BUT FEARELESSE STILL DID BIDE   5.67.10
DRAWNE WITH SWEET PLEASURES BAYT, IT BACK
                              DOTH FLY             5.72.7
BREAKING HIS PRISON FORTH TO YOU DOTH FLY          5.73.4
BUT JOYOUS HOURES DOO FLY AWAY TOO FAST            5.87.14
```
FLYING   3
```
SWIFT SPEEDY $TIME, FEATHRED WITH FLYING HOURES    1.39.11
OR MY SWIFT-WINGED $MUSE TYRED BY TOO
                              HIE FLYING           2.117.10
AND PLEASD WITH OUR SOFT PEACE, STAID
                              HERE HIS FLYING RACE    4.8.4
```
FOE   9
```
AND SHUT THOSE WAIES MY FRIENDLY FOE FIRST ENTRED  1.27.3
AND OTHERS FOE, THE OTHERS FOE IMBRACE             2.136.13
AND OTHERS FOE, THE OTHERS FOE IMBRACE             2.136.13
TO MY LYVES FOE HER $CHIEFTAINE STILL BETRAYING    2.142.8
THY SELFE THY FOE, TO THY SWEET SELFE TOO CRUELL   3.1.8
NOBLER DESIRES, LEAST ELSE THAT FRIENDLY FOE       4.21.7
MY $FOE CAME ON, AND BEAT THE AIRE FOR ME          4.53.13
TO BE SO CRUELL TO AN HUMBLED FOE+                 5.41.2
OF A DEARE FOE, AND THRALLED TO HIS LOVE           5.71.6
```
FOES   5
```
CHASTITIE AND $BEAUTIE, WHICH WERE DEADLY FOES     1.6.9
KILL ME WITH SPIGHTS YET WE MUST NOT BE FOES       3.40.14
UTTRING BARE TRUTH, EVEN SO AS FOES $COMMEND       3.69.4
AND THEREFORE FROM MY FACE SHE TURNES MY FOES      3.139.11
OF GRUDGING FOES, NE FAVOUR SEEK OF FRIENDS        5.59.10
```
FOE'S   2
```
FROM THAT FOE'S WOUNDS THEIR TENDER SKINNES
                              TO HIDE              4.22.8
THEN DOE I MORE AUGMENT MY FOES DESPIGHT           5.44.10
```
FOIL   1
```
TILL DOWNE-RIGHT BLOWES DID FOYLE THY
                              CUNNING FENCE        4.10.11
```
FOILED   1
```
AFTER A THOUSAND VICTORIES ONCE FOILD              3.25.10
```
FOISON   1
```
SPEAKE OF THE SPRING, AND FOYZON OF THE YEARE      3.53.9
```
FOIST   1
```
WHAT THOU DOST FOYST UPON US THAT IS OULD          3.123.6
```
FOLK   1
```
LET FOLKE ORECHARG'D WITH BRAINE AGAINST ME CRIE   4.64.4
```
FOLKS   3
```
AGAINST THESE $FOLKES, THAT THINKE THEMSELVES
                              SO WISE              2.28.3
NOT POINTING TO FIT FOLKES EACH UNDERCHARGE        4.85.6
ALL FOLKES PREST AT THY WILL THY PAINE
                              TO 'SWAGE            4.101.11
```
FOLLOW   4
```
AND CALME AND TEMPEST FOLLOW THEIR ASPECTS         1.34.6
```

```
GLORY DOTH FOLLOW, COURAGE GOES BEFORE                     1.35.7
TO FOLLOW THAT WHICH FLIES BEFORE HER FACE                 3.143.7
DOTH FOLLOW NIGHT WHO LIKE A FIEND                         3.145.11
FOLLOWED              2
HAVE FOLLOWED HARD THE $PROCESSE OF MY CASE                1.8.10
THAT FOLLOW'D IT AS GENTLE DAY                             3.145.10
FOLLOWERS             1
HER SIMPLE $FOLLOWERS EVIDENTLY SHEWES                     2.46.2
FOLLOWING             1
LEAVE FOLLOWING THAT, WHICH IT IS GAINE TO MISSE           4.47.11
FOLLOWS               1
FOR STILL TEMPTATION FOLLOWES WHERE THOU ART               3.41.4
FOLLY                 6
AND DOE NOT STICKE TO TERME MY $PRAYSES FOLLY              2.28.2
DESPITETH $LOVE, AND LAUGHETH AT HER $FOLLY                2.38.10
DISPIGHTETH $LOVE, AND LAUGHETH AT HER FOLLY               2.131.10
WITHOUT THIS FOLLIE, AGE, AND COULD DECAY                  3.11.6
AND $FOLLY ($DOCTOR-LIKE) CONTROULING SKILL                3.66.10
HE KNOWES NOT) GROW IN ONLY FOLLIE RICH                    4.24.14
FOND                  3
OR WHO IS HE SO FOND WILL BE THE TOMBE                     3.3.7
BEING FOND ON PRAISE, WHICH MAKES YOUR
                          PRAISES WORSE                    3.84.14
'BUT WILL NOT WISE MEN THINKE THY WORDS
                          FOND WARE+'                      4.34.7
FONDLY                1
THAT FONDLY FEARE TO LOOSE YOUR LIBERTY                    5.65.2
FONDNESS              1
FONDNESSE IT WERE FOR ANY BEING FREE                       5.37.13
FOOD                 10
WHOSE $STOMACK UNTO $GALL HATH TURN'D THY $FOOD            2.49.6
SO ARE YOU TO MY THOUGHTS AS FOOD TO LIFE                  3.75.1
HER FLESH HIS FOOD, HER SKIN HIS ARMOUR BRAVE              4.29.12
THAT THOU MUST WANT OR FOOD, OR DWELLING PLACE             4.46.4
'BUT AH,' $DESIRE STILL CRIES, 'GIVE ME
                          SOME FOOD'                       4.71.14
STELLA FOOD OF MY THOUGHTS, HART OF MY HART                4.87.2
CANNOT HEAVN'S FOOD, ONCE FELT, KEEPE
                          STOMAKES FREE                    4.88.7
MY SOULES LONG LACKED FOODE, MY HEAVENS BLIS               5.1.12
AND ALSO TO SUSTAYNE THY SELFE WITH FOOD                   5.2.8
DESIRED FOOD, TO IT DOTH MAKE HIS FLIGHT                   5.73.6
FOOL                 11
YET BY MY $FROTH, THIS $FOOLE HIS $LOVE OBTAINES           2.21.13
SO TRUE A FOOLE IS LOVE, THAT IN YOUR $WILL                3.57.13
LOV'S NOT $TIMES FOOLE, THOUGH ROSIE LIPS
                          AND CHEEKS                       3.116.9
THOU BLINDE FOOLE LOVE, WHAT DOOST THOU
                          TO MINE EYES                     3.137.1
'FOOLE,' SAID MY $MUSE TO ME, 'LOOKE IN
                          THY HEART AND WRITE'             4.1.14
BUT, FOOLE, SEEKST NOT TO GET INTO HER HART                4.11.14
BUT THAT RICH FOOLE, WHO BY BLIND $FORTUNE'S LOT           4.24.9
'FOOLE,' ANSWERS HE, 'NO $INDES SUCH TREASURES
                          HOLD                             4.32.12
'WHAT NOW SIR FOOLE,' SAID HE, 'I WOULD NO LESSE           4.53.7
O HEAV'NLY FOOLE, THY MOST KISSE-WORTHIE FACE              4.73.12
NAY, MORE FOOLE I, OFT SUFFERED YOU TO SLEEPE              4.83.7
FOOLISH               6
HOW MANY PALTRY, FOOLISH, PAINTED THINGS                   2.6.1
```

DISWADE ONE FOOLISH HEART FROM SERVING THEE   3.141.10
THAT I HAD BENE MORE FOOLISH OR MORE WISE   4.33.14
PEACE, FOOLISH WIT, WITH WIT MY WIT IS MARD   4.34.11
FAIRE EYES, SWEET LIPS, DEARE HEART, THAT
                                  FOOLISH I   4.43.1
THAT FROM THE FOOLISH FISH THEYR BAYTS DOE HYDE   5.47.4
FOOLS   17
    WITH $FOOLES AND $CHILDREN GOOD $DISCRETION
                                 BEARES   2.22.1
    AMONGST THE REST OF $FOOLES AND $CHILDREN BE   2.22.4
    THEN $FOOLES AND $CHILDREN FITT'ST TO
                              GOE TOGETHER   2.22.8
    YET $FOOLES AND $CHILDREN SOMETIMES TELL IN PLAY   2.22.13
    SOME WISE IN SHEW, MORE $FOOLES INDEED THEN THEY   2.22.14
    FAIRE WORDS MAKE $FOOLES, REPLYETH HE AGAINE   2.59.4
    FOOLES AS WE MET, SO $FOOLES AGAINE WE PARTED   2.59.14
    FOOLES AS WE MET, SO $FOOLES AGAINE WE PARTED   2.59.14
    A FOOLES THINKE I, HAD YOU $IDEA SEENE   2.120.13
    TO THIS I WITNES CALL THE FOLES OF TIME   3.124.13
    AND, FOOLES, ADORE IN TEMPLE OF OUR HART   4.5.7
    O FOOLES, OR OVER-WISE, ALAS THE RACE   4.23.12
    RICH FOOLES THERE BE, WHOSE BASE AND FILTHY HART   4.24.1
    YET TO THOSE FOOLES HEAV'N SUCH WIT DOTH IMPART   4.24.5
    AND FOOLES CAN THINKE THOSE $LAMPES OF
                              PUREST LIGHT   4.26.2
    DO $STELLA LOVE. $FOOLES, WHO DOTH IT DENY+   4.104.14
    O LET NOT FOOLES IN ME THY WORKES REPROVE   4.107.13
FOOL'S   1
    YET TO THOSE FOOLES HEAV'N SUCH WIT DOTH IMPART   4.24.5
FOOT   5
    NO MATTER THEN ALTHOUGH MY FOOTE DID STAND   3.44.5
    OR WHAT STRONG HAND CAN HOLD HIS SWIFT FOOTE BACK 3.65.11
    OF HAND, OF FOOTE, OF LIP, OF EYE, OF BROW   3.106.6
    THAT NOT MY SOULE, WHICH AT THY FOOT DID FALL   4.36.12
    THE WHILES HER FOOT SHE IN MY NECKE DOTH PLACE   5.20.3
FOOTING   1
    I SEEKE THE FIELDS WITH HER LATE FOOTING SYND   5.78.5
FOOTSTEP   1
    NOW EVEN THAT FOOTSTEP OF LOST LIBERTIE   4.2.9
FOOTSTOOL   1
    BUT HIM THAT AT YOUR FOOTSTOOLE HUMBLED LIES   5.49.11
FORAGING   1
    STRIVING ABROAD A FORAGING TO GO   4.55.6
FORBEAR   4
    OR IF THOU'LT NOT, THY $ARCHERIE FORBEARE   2.48.5
    AYE ME, BUT YET THOU MIGHST MY SEATE FORBEARE   3.41.9
    DEARE HEART FORBEARE TO GLANCE THINE EYE ASIDE   3.139.6
    THE BOTE FOR JOY COULD NOT TO DAUNCE FORBEARE   4.103.5
FORBEARS   2
    THAT WHOLLY HERS, ALL SELFNESSE HE FORBEARES   4.61.7
    OR IF THY LOVE OF PLAINT YET MINE FORBEARES   4.94.9
FORBID   4
    FOR $GOD FORBID I SHOULD MY $PAPERS BLOT   1.58.5
    BUT I FORBID THEE ONE MOST HAINOUS CRIME   3.19.8
    THAT $GOD FORBID, THAT MADE ME FIRST YOUR SLAVE   3.58.1
    OR WHO HIS SPOILE OR BEAUTIE CAN FORBID+   3.65.12
FORBIDDEN   1
    THAT USE IS NOT FORBIDDEN USERY   3.6.5
FORBIDS   1
    BUT SHE FORBIDS, WITH BLUSHING WORDS, SHE SAYES   4.81.9

FORCE   26
    DID FORCE ME GRONE OUT GRIEFES, AND UTTER THIS   1.7.12
    WHOSE STATE BEST SHEWES THE FORCE OF MURDERING
                                    EIES+   1.37.4
    AND OF WHAT FORCE THY WOUNDING GRACES ARE   1.37.7
    SHALL FAILE IN FORCE, THEIR WORKING NOT SO STRONG   1.38.4
    POORE SOULE QUITE SPENT, WHOSE FORCE CAN
                                    DO NO MORE   1.46.3
    TO WRITE WITH $BLOUD, OF FORCE OFFENDS THE $SIGHT   2.13.6
    AS'T PLEASE THE $FATES, BY THEIR RESISTLESSE
                                    FORCE   2.51.4
    FROM THE STRONG $SPIRIT BY NO MEANES FORCE
                                    THE SAME   2.58.8
    TO WRITE WITH BLOOD, OF FORCE OFFENDS THE SIGHT   2.121.6
    AND MY STRONG SIGHES, THE AYRES WEAKE
                                    FORCE REVIVETH   2.127.3
    YET OTHERS FORCE, THE OTHERS FORCE REVIVING   2.136.12
    YET OTHERS FORCE, THE OTHERS FORCE REVIVING   2.136.12
    SWEET LOVE RENEW THY FORCE, BE IT NOT SAID   3.56.1
    SOME IN THEIR WEALTH, SOME IN THEIR BODIES FORCE   3.91.2
    OF FORCE OF HEAV'NLY BEAMES, INFUSING
                                    HELLISH PAINE   4.6.3
    NO FORCE, NO FRAUD, ROBD THEE OF THY DELIGHT   4.33.7
    AS HIS MAINE FORCE, CHOISE SPORT, AND
                                    EASEFULL STAY   4.43.4
    BUT $GRAMMER'S FORCE WITH SWEET SUCCESSE
                                    CONFIRME   4.63.11
    IF STILL I FORCE HER IN SAD RIMES TO CREEPE   4.70.2
    NOT BY RUDE FORCE, BUT SWEETEST SOVERAIGNTIE   4.71.6
    OF GENTLE FORCE, SO THAT MINE EYES DARE
                                    GLADLY PLAY   4.76.6
    IS FAITH SO WEAKE+ $OR IS SUCH FORCE IN THEE+   4.88.5
    THAT HUE, WHOSE FORCE MY HART STILL UNTO
                                    THRALDOME TIES+   4.102.8
    TO FORCE ME LIVE AND WILL NOT LET ME DY   5.11.12
    THE PAYNEFULL SMITH WITH FORCE OF FERVENT HEAT   5.32.1
    BUT BEND YOUR FORCE AGAINST YOUR ENEMYES   5.49.8
FORCED   12
    HER THUNDER OF DISDAINE FORST ME RETIRE   1.36.4
    YET WHICH AT LENGTH THOU MUST BE FORC'D TO LOSE   1.50.8
    NOR CHASTE BY HOUND, NOR FORC'D BY $HUNTERS ARTE   2.135.3
    WHERE THOU ART FORST TO BREAKE A TWO-FOLD TRUTH   3.41.12
    AT LENGTH TO $LOVE'S DECREES, I FORC'D, AGREED   4.2.7
    FORC'D BY A TEDIOUS PROOFE, THAT $TURKISH
                                    HARDNED HART   4.8.2
    LONG SINCE FORC'D BY THY BEAMES, BUT STONE
                                    NOR TREE   4.36.13
    GROWNE NOW HIS SLAVES, HE FORST THEM OUT TO FIND   4.57.3
    WHEN I WAS FORST FROM $STELLA EVER DEERE   4.87.1
    FORST BY THEIR $LORD, WHO IS ASHAM'D TO FIND   4.99.13
    HAVE MADE, BUT FORST BY $NATURE STILL TO FLIE   4.103.10
    WAS FORST TO YEELD MY SELFE INTO THEIR HANDS   5.12.10
FORCES   7
    AND THETHER ALL MY FORCES DOE TRANSPORTE   1.27.7
    I THUS OPPOSE MY $REASONS FORCES WHOLLY   2.28.4
    DISCHARGE OUR $FORCES, HERE LET $MALICE CEASE   2.63.7
    SLEEPE AND $BEAUTY, WITH EQUALL FORCES STRYVING   2.136.9
    MY FORCES RAZDE, THY BANNERS RAISD WITHIN   4.36.6
    RETOURNE AGAYNE MY FORCES LATE DISMAYD   5.14.1
    BRING THEREFORE ALL THE FORCES THAT YE MAY   5.14.9

```
FORDS                       2
  THE $CRYSTALL $TRENT, FCR $FOORDS AND
                            $FISH RENOWNED              2.32.3
  THE CHRISTALL $TRENT, FCR $FOORDS AND
                            FISHE RENOWNED              2.124.3
FORE                        1
  THE EYES (FORE DUTICUS) NOW CONVERTED ARE            3.7.11
FOREBEMOANED                1
  THE SAD ACCOUNT OF FORE-BEMONED MONE                 3.30.11
FOREDONE                    1
  GIVE LEAVE TO REST ME BEING HALFE FORDONNE           5.80.3
FOREFRONT                   1
  BECAUSE THEIR FOREFRONT BARE SWEET $STELLA'S
                            NAME                        4.50.14
FOREGONE                    1
  THEN CAN I GREEVE AT GREEVANCES FORE-GON             3.30.9
FOREHEAD                    1
  IF $YVORIE, HER FORHEAD YVORY WEENE                  5.15.10
FOREIGN                     1
  THAT $FORAINE $NATICNS RELLISH NOT OUR $TCNGUE       2.25.2
FOREJUDGE                   1
  WHO OFT FORE-JUDGE MY AFTER-FOLLOWING RACE           4.26.13
FORELOCK                    1
  UNLESSE SHE DOE HIM BY THE FORELOCK TAKE             5.70.8
FOREPAST                    1
  THE OLD YEARES SINNES FOREPAST LET US ESCHEW         5.62.7
FORESEE                     1
  AND YET COULD NOT BY RISING $MORNE FORESEE           4.33.12
FORESTS                     1
  HAVE FROM THE FORRESTS SHOOKE THREE SUMMERS
                            PRIDE                       3.104.4
FORETELL                    1
  SHEE OF WHOM $MERLIN LONG TYME DID FORE-TELL         2.119.10
FORETOLD                    2
  BUT AH- NO MORE, THIS MUST NOT BE FORETOLD           1.50.13
  AND OF HYS BLESSED BIRTH BEFORE FORE-TOLD            2.119.4
FORFEIT                     2
  SUPPOSDE AS FORFEIT TO A CONFIN'D DOOME              3.107.4
  MY SELFE $ILE FORFEIT, SO THAT OTHER MINE            3.134.3
FORGE                       2
  MY $BREST THE $FORGE, INCLUDING ALL THE HEATE        2.40.3
  BY BREAST THE FORGE, INCLUDING ALL THE HEATE         2.144.3
FORGED                      2
  WHY OF EYES FALSEHOCD HAST THOU FORGED HCOKES        3.137.7
  THAT WITH FALSE FORGED LYES, WHICH THOU CIDST TEL    5.86.7
FORGET                      2
  I SHALL FORGET OLD WRONGS, MY GRIEFES
                            SHALL CEASE                 1.46.11
  SO I FOR FEARE OF TRUST, FORGET TO SAY               3.23.5
FORGETFUL                   2
  RETURNE FORGETFULL $MUSE, AND STRAIGHT REDEEME       3.100.5
  FORGETFULL OF THE FAMOUS GOLDEN FLEECE               5.44.3
FORGETFULNESS               1
  WERE TO IMPORT FORGETFULNESSE IN MEE                 3.122.14
FORGETS                     2
  MY LIFE FORGETS TC NOURISH LANGUISHT SPRITES         4.42.10
  AND UNTO HEAVEN FORGETS HER FORMER FLIGHT            5.72.8
FORGETST                    1
  WHERE ART THOU $MUSE THAT THOU FORGETST SO LCNG      3.100.1
```

```
FORGETTING                    1
  WITH DARKE FORGETTING OF MY CARE RETURNE            1.54.4
FORGING                       1
  FORGING A GRIEFE TO WINNE A FAMES REWARD            1.4.4
FORGIVE                       2
  I DOE FORGIVE THY ROBB'RIE GENTLE THEEFE            3.40.9
  THO WORLDS QUITE ME, SHALL I MY SELFE FORGIVE+      4.93.11
FORGO                         1
  IF WILL, THEN SHE AT WILL MAY WILL FORGOE           5.41.4
FORGOING                      1
  FOR COMPOUND SWEET., $FORGOING SIMPLE SAVOR         3.125.7
FORGOT                        8
  FORGOT HERSELFE, AND THOUGHT SHE HAD BEEN
                            DROWNED                    2.109.4
  AND ALL THE REST FORGOT FOR WHICH HE TOILD          3.25.12
  THAT I IN YOUR SWEET THOUGHTS WOULD BE FORGOT       3.71.7
  FORGOT UPON YOUR DEAREST LOVE TO CALL               3.117.3
  DOE I NOT THINKE ON THEE WHEN I FORGOT              3.149.3
  ONE HAND FORGOTT TO RULE, TH'OTHER TO FIGHT         4.53.11
  BY NO ENCROCHMENT WRONGD, NOR TIME FORGOT           4.84.10
  AND BE FORGOT AS IT HAD NEVER BEENE                 5.27.7
FORGOTTEN                     2
  SHALL BE FORGOTTEN, WHOM NO $POET SINGS             2.6.3
  ALTHOUGH IN ME EACH PART WILL BE FORGOTTEN          3.81.4
FORLORN                       7
  THEE AND THY $LOVE FORLORNE, AND BOTH DISDAINES     1.52.7
  HER $MARRYNERS DOE LEAVE HER ALL FORLORNE           2.134.11
  PLAC'D IN THE FORLORNE HOPE OF ALL DISPAYRE         2.142.1
  AND FROM THE FOR-LORNE WORLD HIS VISAGE HIDE        3.33.7
  TREADING DOWNE EARTH AS LOTHSOME AND FORLORNE       5.13.11
  ACCOUMPTS MY SELFE HER CAPTIVE QUITE FORLORNE       5.29.4
  AND WHEN AS NIGHT HATH US OF LIGHT FORLORNE         5.87.7
FORM                          15
  THE FAIREST FORME, THAT ALL THE WORLD ADMIRES       1.13.7
  UPON MY SELFE THOU BEST MAYST FINDE THE FORME       1.37.8
  TO VIEW YOUR FORME TOO MUCH, MAY DANGER BEE         1.37.11
  NOW IS THE TIME THAT FACE SHOULD FORME AN OTHER     3.3.2
  THAT THOU NO FORME OF THEE HAST LEFT BEHIND         3.9.6
  WHEN YOUR SWEET ISSUE YOUR SWEET FORME
                            SHOULD BEARE              3.13.8
  THY BEAUTIES FORME IN TABLE OF MY HEART             3.24.2
  HOW WOULD THY SHADOWES FORME, FORME HAPPY SHOW      3.43.6
  HOW WOULD THY SHADOWES FORME, FORME HAPPY SHOW      3.43.6
  IN POLISHT FORME OF WELL REFINED PEN                3.85.8
  TO SET A FORME UPON DESIRED CHANGE                  3.89.6
  WHERE TIME AND OUTWARD FORME WOULD SHEW IT DEAD     3.108.14
  FOR IT NO FORME DELIVERS TO THE HEART               3.113.5
  HAVE I NOT SEENE DWELLERS ON FORME AND FAVOR        3.125.5
  PRINTS HIS OWNE LIVELY FORME IN RUDEST BRAINE       4.58.8
FORMED                        2
  IT IS MOST TRUE, THAT EYES ARE FORM'D TO SERVE      4.5.1
  AND YET AS SOONE AS THEY SO FORMED BE               4.50.5
FORMER                        8
  IN $FORMER TIMES, SUCH AS HAD STORE OF $COYNE       2.58.1
  THAT $WE ONE JOT OF FORMER $LOVE RETEYNE            2.61.8
  TO MORROW SHARPNED IN HIS FORMER MIGHT              3.56.4
  THE SECOND BURTHEN OF A FORMER CHILD+               3.59.4
  OH SURE I AM THE WITS OF FORMER DAIES               3.59.13
  THEY ARE BUT DRESSINGS OF A FORMER SIGHT            3.123.4
  CHAUNGE EEKE OUR MYNDS AND FORMER LIVES AMEND       5.62.6
```

```
AND UNTO HEAVEN FORGETS HER FORMER FLIGHT              5.72.8
FORMS                          1
  SUCH HEAVENLY FORMES OUGHT RATHER WORSHIPT BE        5.61.13
FORSAKE                        3
  DEVISE SOME MEANES, BUT HOW I MAY FORSAKE $YOU       2.11.10
  SINCE SWEETS AND BEAUTIES DO THEM-SELVES FORSAKE     3.12.11
  SAY THAT THOU DIDST FORSAKE MEE FOR SOME FALT        3.89.1
FORSAKEN                       3
  AND WHITHER (POORE FORSAKEN) WILT THOU GOE           1.52.1
  YET GOE (FORSAKEN) LEAVE THESE $WOODS,
                          THESE PLAINES                1.52.5
  OF HIM, MY SELFE, AND THEE I AM FORSAKEN             3.133.7
FORSOOK                        1
  WHEN I ALL WEARY HAD THE CHACE FORSOOKE              5.67.6
FORSOOTH                       2
  WHILE TOO MUCH WIT (FORSOOTH) SO TROUBLED ME         4.33.10
  YOU SAY FORSOOTH, YOU LEFT HER WELL OF LATE          4.92.7
FORSWORN                       5
  AND PUREST FAITH UNHAPPILY FORSWORNE                 3.66.4
  AND PROVE THEE VIRTUOUS, THOUGH THOU ART
                          FORSWORNE                    3.88.4
  IN LOVING THEE THOU KNOW'ST I AM FORSWORNE           3.152.1
  BUT THOU ART TWICE FORSWORNE TO ME LOVE SWEARING     3.152.2
  OR ART THOU ELSE TO COMFORT ME FORSWORNE+            4.67.11
FORT                           2
  AND WHILST I GARDE THESE WINDOWES OF THIS FORTE      1.27.5
  AGAINST THE $FORTE WHERE $BEAUTIES $ARMY LIES        2.142.2
FORTH                         43
  MINERVA-LIKE, BROUGHT FOORTH WITHOUT A MOTHER        1.2.2
  AND CANNOT ISSUE FORTH TO SEEKE HER GOOD             1.29.4
  LOOKE TO THE HEAVENS., THE HEAVENS YEELDE
                          FORTH NO GRACE               1.29.6
  NOW SEND FORTH HOPE, FOR NOW CALME PITTY SAVES       1.46.4
  LIGHTEN FOORTH SMILES TO CLEERE THE CLOUDED AIRE     1.51.9
  TO MODELL FORTH THE PASSIONS OF THE MORROW           1.54.10
  PROCEEDING FROM THE $PORT WHENCE HE PUT FORTH        2.1.5
  BUT BOUNDED THUS, TO $SCOTLAND GET YOU FORTH         2.25.5
  UPON THE $NEST I SET IT FORTH, TO PROVE              2.56.3
  UPON THE NEST I SET THEM, FORTH TO PROVE             2.103.3
  WHAT CURIOUS $PENSILL SERVES TO LIM THEE FORTH+      2.146.3
  AND MAKE ME TRAVAILE FORTH WITHOUT MY CLOAKE         3.34.2
  AND HE THAT CALLS ON THEE, LET HIM BRING FORTH       3.38.11
  SHALL YOU PACE FORTH, YOUR PRAISE SHALL
                          STIL FINDE ROOME             3.55.10
  FOR I AM SHAMD BY THAT WHICH I BRING FORTH           3.72.13
  ALACK WHAT POVERTY MY $MUSE BRINGS FORTH             3.103.1
  THOU USURER THAT PUT'ST FORTH ALL TO USE             3.134.10
  BREATH'D FORTH THE SOUND THAT SAID I HATE            3.145.2
  BUT WORDS CAME HALTING FORTH, WANTING
                          $INVENTION'S STAY            4.1.9
  WHEN TREMBLING VOICE BRINGS FORTH THAT
                          I DO $STELLA LOVE            4.6.14
  THE DOORE BY WHICH SOMETIMES COMES FORTH
                          HER $GRACE                   4.9.5
  MY YOUTH DOTH WASTE, MY KNOWLEDGE BRINGS
                          FORTH TOYES                  4.18.9
  BUT SHINING FORTH OF HEATE IN HIS CHIEFE PRIDE       4.22.4
  OFT CRUELL FIGHTS WELL PICTURED FORTH DO PLEASE      4.34.4
  SENT FORTH THE BEAMES, WHICH MADE SO FAIRE
                          MY RACE                      4.41.14
```

```
MY WORDS I KNOW DO WELL SET FORTH MY MIND                    4.44.1
BUT THEY DO SWELL AND STRUGGLE FORTH OF ME                   4.50.3
WHO HARD BY MADE A WINDOW SEND FORTH LIGHT                   4.53.9
WHERE MEMORY SETS FOORTH THE BEAMES OF LOVE                  4.88.11
BREAKE FORTH AT LENGTH OUT OF THE INNER PART                 5.2.5
NEW YEARE FORTH LOOKING OUT OF JANUS GATE                    5.4.1
AND CALLING FORTH OUT OF SAD $WINTERS NIGHT                  5.4.5
IS READY TO COME FORTH HIM TO RECEIVE                        5.4.10
THE WHICH BOTH LYFE AND DEATH FORTH FROM YOU DART            5.7.3
THENCE BREAKING FORTH DID THICK ABOUT ME THRONG              5.12.8
WHO NOW IS COMMING FORTH WITH GIRLAND CROUNED                5.19.4
HE FORTH WAS THROWN INTO THE GREEDY SEAS                     5.38.2
COMES FORTH AFRESH OUT OF THEIR LATE DISMAY                  5.40.11
TO UTTER FORTH THE ANGUISH OF HIS HART                       5.48.10
THEN SHALL THE NEW YEARES JOY FORTH FRESHLY SEND             5.62.9
BREAKING HIS PRISON FORTH TO YOU DOTH FLY                    5.73.4
WITH PRETIOUS MERCHANDIZE SHE FORTH DOTH LAY                 5.81.6
IN SETTING YOUR IMMORTALL PRAYSES FORTH                      5.82.12
FORTIFIED                      1
SO FORTIFIED WITH WIT, STOR'D WITH DISDAINE                  4.12.13
FORTIFY                        3
THAT FORTIFIE THY NAME AGAINST OLD AGE                       1.55.10
AND FORTIFIE YOUR SELFE IN YOUR DECAY                        3.16.3
FOR SUCH A TIME DO I NOW FORTIFIE                            3.63.9
FORTS                          1
THEN THOSE SMALL FORTS WHICH YE WERE WONT BELAY              5.14.6
FORTUNE                        25
MY HEAVY FORTUNE IS MUCH LIKE THE SAME                       1.13.3
AND SO SENT BACKE, AND THUS MY FORTUNE LIES                  1.25.12
TH'$ORPHAN OF $FORTUNE, BORNE TO BE HER SCORNE               1.26.3
AND SEE MY FORTUNE EVER LIKE TO LAST                         1.28.11
MY FORTUNE MANTLED WITH A CLOWDE S'OBSCURE                   1.29.13
FINDING MY FORTUNE EVER IN THE WAINE                         1.32.3
MY JOYFULL $NORTH, WHERE ALL MY FORTUNE LIES                 1.53.3
I LAUGH AT $FORTUNE, AS IN JEST TO DIE                       2.24.14
HOW E'RE BLIND $FORTUNE TURNE HER GIDDIE $WHEELE             2.51.12
FORTUNE ASSISTS THE BOLDEST, I REPLY                         2.59.7
MAKE KNOWNE THE $FAITH, THAT $FORTUNE
                        COULD NOT MOVE                       2.60.5
A FAYTH, THAT TIME NOR FORTUNE COULD NOT MOVE                2.138.11
LOE THUS MY LOVE, MY LYFE, MY FORTUNE TRYES                  2.142.4
NOR CAN I FORTUNE TO BREEFE MYNUITS TELL                     3.14.5
WHILST I WHOME FORTUNE OF SUCH TRYUMPH BARS                  3.25.3
WHEN IN DISGRACE WITH $FORTUNE AND MENS EYES                 3.29.1
AND SHALT BY FORTUNE ONCE MORE RE-SURVAY                     3.32.3
JOYNE WITH THE SPIGHT OF FORTUNE, MAKE ME BOW                3.90.3
O FOR MY SAKE DOE YOU WISH FORTUNE CHIDE                     3.111.1
NOR $FORTUNE OF THY FORTUNE AUTHOR IS                        4.33.8
NOR $FORTUNE OF THY FORTUNE AUTHOR IS                        4.33.8
LET $FORTUNE LAY ON ME HER WORST DISGRACE                    4.64.3
FORTUNE WHEELES STILL WITH ME IN ONE SORT SLOW               4.66.6
HOW IS THY GRACE BY MY STRANGE FORTUNE STAIND                4.98.3
WITH GUIFTS OF BODY, FORTUNE AND OF MIND                     5.74.4
FORTUNE'S                      7
MY FORTUNES WHEELES THE CIRCLE OF HER EIES                   1.12.11
SO I, MADE LAME BY $FORTUNES DEAREST SPIGHT                  3.37.3
AT FIRST THE VERY WORST OF FORTUNES MIGHT                    3.90.12
IT MIGHT FOR FORTUNES BASTERD BE UNFATHERED                  3.124.2
BUT THAT RICH FOOLE, WHO BY BLIND $FORTUNE'S LOT             4.24.9
BUT WHEN THE RUGGEDST STEP OF $FORTUNE'S RACE                4.60.5
```

```
    AND BLESSE YOUR FORTUNES FAYRE ELECTION           5.84.14
FORTY                    3
    WHEN FORTIE $WINTERS SHALL BESEIGE THY BROW         3.2.1
    THEN AL THOSE FOURTY WHICH MY LIFE OUTWENT          5.60.8
    THE SPHEARE OF $CUPID FOURTY YEARES CONTAINES       5.60.10
FORWARD                  2
    AS WELL (SAYTH HE) TOO FORWARD, AS TOO SLOW         2.59.6
    THE FORWARD VIOLET THUS DID I CHIDE                 3.99.1
FORWARDS                 1
    IN SEQUENT TOILE ALL FORWARDS DO CONTEND            3.60.4
FOSTERED                 2
    THOSE THAT I FOSTRED OF MINE OWNE ACCORD            1.5.13
    AND $MUSE-FOE $MARS, ABROAD FARRE FOSTRED BEE       1.53.14
FOSTERS                  1
    LOOKES FEED MY $HOPE, $HOPE FOSTERS ME IN VAINE     1.25.13
FOUL                    21
    WHERE MOST BECALM'D, WHERE WITH FOULE
                           $WEATHER SPENT               2.1.11
    WHERE, IN HIS $CUPS O'RCOME WITH FOULE $EXCESSE     2.7.9
    AND FRESHEST $COLOURS WITH FOULE STAYNES
                           DISGRACED                    2.13.4
    ALL UNCLEANE $THOUGHTS, FOULE $SPIRITS
                           CAST OUT IN MEE              2.35.13
    MY MAN-HOOD DARES NOT WITH FOULE $ATE MELL         2.39.10
    SO $FAIRE A RISING, HAD SO $FOULE A SET            2.60.12
    ALL UNCLEANE THOUGHTS, FOULE SPIRITS CAST
                           OUT IN MEE                  2.112.13
    MY MANHOOD DARES NOT WITH FOULE $ATE MELL          2.118.10
    AND FRESHEST COLOURS WITH FOULE STAINES
                           DISGRACED                   2.121.4
    SO FAIRE A $MORNING HAD SO FOULE A SET+            2.149.12
    DISTIL'D FROM $LYMBECKS FOULE AS HELL WITHIN        3.119.2
    FAIRING THE FOULE WITH $ARTS FAULSE BORROW'D
                           FACE                         3.127.6
    AND ALL THEY FOULE THAT THY COMPLEXION LACKE        3.132.14
    TO PUT FAIRE TRUTH UPON SO FOULE A FACE             3.137.12
    WOOING HIS PURITY WITH HER FOWLE PRIDE              3.144.8
    LEAST EYES WELL SEEING THY FOULE FAULTS
                           SHOULD FINDE                 3.148.14
    TO SWERE AGAINST THE TRUTH SO FOULE A LIE           3.152.14
    AND CAN WITH FOULE ABUSE SUCH BEAUTIES BLOT         4.24.11
    THAT POISON FOULE OF BUBLING PRIDE DOTH LIE         4.27.6
    WITNESSE WITH ME, THAT MY FOULE STUMBLING SO        4.93.6
    SCORN OF BASE THINGS, AND SDEIGNE OF FOULE
                           DISHONOR                     5.5.6
FOULLY                   1
    THAT SO FAYRE BEAUTY WAS SO FOWLY SHAMED            5.41.14
FOUND                   23
    THOUGH THOU A $LAURA HAST NO $PETRARCH FOUND        1.43.3
    YET NEVER FOUND THAT BARBAROUS HAND ATTAIND         1.45.5
    UPON YOUR $LIPS THE SCARLET DROPS ARE FOUND         2.2.10
    NONE LIKE TO THAT, NONE LIKE TO YOU IS FOUND        2.16.4
    WHEN LIKE AN $EAGLET I FIRST FOUND MY $LOVE         2.56.1
    IN $ONE WHOLE WORLD IS BUT ONE $PHOENIX FOUND       2.106.1
    AND LOOSING HER, MY FRIEND HATH FOUND THAT LOSSE    3.42.10
    AS TWIXT A MISER AND HIS WEALTH IS FOUND            3.75.4
    TO NEW FOUND METHODS, AND TO COMPOUNDS STRANGE+     3.76.4
    AND FOUND SUCH FAIRE ASSISTANCE IN MY VERSE         3.78.2
    AND FOUND IT IN THY CHEEKE.. HE CAN AFFOORD         3.79.11
    I FOUND (OR THOUGHT I FOUND) YOU DID EXCEED         3.83.3
```

```
I FOUND (OR THOUGHT I FOUND) YOU DID EXCEED        3.83.3
AND SICKE OF WEL-FARE FOUND A KIND OF MEETNESSE     3.118.7
A MAIDE OF $DYANS THIS ADVANTAGE FOUND             3.153.2
BUT FOUND NO CURE, THE BATH FOR MY HELPE LIES      3.153.13
ENNOBLING NEW FOUND $TROPES WITH PROBLEMES OLD     4.3.6
HAST THOU FOUND SUCH AND SUCH LIKE ARGUMENTS+      4.67.10
ALAS I FOUND, THAT SHE WITH ME DID SMART           4.87.5
ALL THIS WORLDS RICHES THAT MAY FARRE BE FOUND     5.15.6
WELL WORTHY THOU TO HAVE FOUND BETTER HYRE         5.48.5
COMMING TO KISSE HER LYPS, (SUCH GRACE I FOUND)    5.64.1
COULD NOT ON EARTH HAVE FOUND ONE FIT FOR MATE     5.66.6
FOUNTAIN                 1
PASSING BY THAT CLEERE FOUNTAINE OF THINE EYE      2.109.2
FOUNTAINS                1
ROSES HAVE THORNES, AND SILVER FOUNTAINES MUD      3.35.2
FOUR                     1
MY LIFE BEING MADE OF FOURE, WITH TWO ALONE        3.45.7
FOURTH                   1
EDWARD NAMED FOURTH, AS FIRST IN PRAISE I NAME     4.75.2
FRAGRANT                 3
WHICH LIKE A CANKER IN THE FRAGRANT $ROSE          3.95.2
SUCH FRAGRANT FLOWRES DOE GIVE MOST ODOROUS
                                  SMELL            5.64.13
WITH WOODBYND FLOWERS AND FRAGRANT $EGLANTINE      5.71.10
FRAID                    1
NOR THAT HE MADE THE $FLOUREDELUCE SO FRAID        4.75.9
FRAIL                    7
IN MY FRAILE SPIRIT BY HER FROM BASENESSE RAYSED   5.3.4
BUT $ANGELS COME TO LEAD FRAILE MINDES TO REST     5.8.7
IS IT THAT MENS FRAYLE EYES, WHICH GAZE TOO BOLD   5.37.5
ALL FLESH IS FRAYLE, AND ALL HER STRENGTH UNSTAYD  5.58.5
THERE MY FRAILE FANCY FED WITH FULL DELIGHT        5.72.9
AND MY FRAYLE THOUGHTS TOO RASHLY LED ASTRAY+      5.76.6
FROM FRAYLE CORRUPTION, THAT DOTH FLESH ENSEW      5.79.8
FRAILER                  1
OR ON MY FRAILTIES WHY ARE FRAILER SPIES           3.121.7
FRAILTIES                2
ALL FRAILTIES THAT BESIEGE ALL KINDES OF BLOOD     3.109.10
OR ON MY FRAILTIES WHY ARE FRAILER SPIES           3.121.7
FRAME                    17
ABOUT THE $TEMPLE OF THE PROUDEST FRAME            1.12.2
BEHOLD WHAT HAP $PIGMALION HAD TO FRAME            1.13.1
WHY SHOULD I SING IN VERSE, WHY SHOULD I FRAME     1.17.1
THOSE HOWERS THAT WITH GENTLE WORKE DID FRAME      3.5.1
MY BODY IS THE FRAME WHEREIN TI'S HELD             3.24.3
TO THIS COMPOSED WONDER OF YOUR FRAME              3.59.10
TO BITTER SAWCES DID I FRAME MY FEEDING            3.118.6
FRAME DAINTIEST LUSTRE, MIXT OF SHADES AND LIGHT+  4.7.4
IF THAT BE SINNE WHICH DOTH THE MANERS FRAME       4.14.9
AND YET MY WORDS, AS THEM MY PEN DOTH FRAME        4.19.7
YOU THAT WITH ALLEGORIE'S CURIOUS FRAME            4.28.1
THESE QUESTIONS BUSIE WITS TO ME DO FRAME          4.30.12
NOR HOPE, NOR WISHE ANOTHER COURSE TO FRAME        4.64.12
NOR THAT HE COULD YOUNG-WISE, WISE-VALIANT FRAME   4.75.5
NOR SO AMBITIOUS AM I, AS TO FRAME                 4.90.5
WHERE THOSE RED CHEEKS, WHICH OFT WITH
                            FAIRE ENCREASE DID FRAME  4.102.2
YOU FRAME MY THOUGHTS AND FASHION ME WITHIN        5.8.9
FRAMED                   3
FRAM'D MY DESIRES FIT FOR HER EYES TO KILL         1.36.14
```

HE FRAMD HIM WINGS WITH FEATHERS OF HIS THOUGHT   2.122.5
MOST HAPPY LETTERS FRAM'D BY SKILFULL TRADE   5.74.1
FRANCE   1
AND OF SOME SENT FRCM THAT SWEET ENEMIE $FRAUNCE   4.41.4
FRANK   1
AND BEING FRANCK SHE LENDS TO THOSE ARE FREE   3.4.4
FRANTIC   2
SLOW $ARRER, FRANTICK $GALLUS, $CYDNUS COLD   2.120.8
AND FRANTICK MADDE WITH EVER-MORE UNREST   3.147.10
FRAUD   1
NO FORCE, NO FRAUD, ROBD THEE OF THY DELIGHT   4.33.7
FRAUGHT   2
FAYRE SOYLE IT SEEMES FRCM FAR AND FRAUGHT
                           WITH STORE   5.63.7
FAYRE BOSOME FRAUGHT WITH VERTUES RICHEST TRESURE   5.76.1
FRAY   2
THE FRIENDLY FRAY, WHERE BLOWES BOTH WOUND
                           AND HEALE   4.79.10
DOTH PLEASE ALL BEASTS BUT THAT HIS LOOKS
                           THEM FRAY   5.53.2
FREE   20
HOPING THEREBY TO FREE MY BETTER PART   1.27.4
A WAY THROUGH WANT TO FREE MY SOULE FROM CARE   1.29.10
AS TO THE $ROMAN THAT WCULD FREE HIS $LAND   1.56.1
I GREATLY MARVELL, HOW YOU STILL GOE FREE   2.14.3
YET STAND AS FREE AS ERE YOU DID BEFORE   2.14.12
THAT THUS SO CLEANLY, I MY $SELFE CAN FREE   2.61.4
I OFFER FREE $CONDITIONS OF FAIRE $PEACE   2.63.5
AND BEING FRANCK SHE LENDS TO THOSE ARE FREE   3.4.4
AND TAKE THOU MY OBLACICN, POORE BUT FREE   3.125.10
BUT THOU WILT NOT, NOR HE WILL NOT BE FREE   3.134.5
HE PAIES THE WHOLE, AND YET AM I NOT FREE   3.134.14
THAT FROM HER LOCKES, THY DAY-NETS, NONE
                           SCAPES FREE   4.12.2
HER DAINTIEST BARE WENT FREE., THE CAUSE
                           WAS THIS   4.22.13
TO KEEPE THEMSELVES AND THEIR CHIEF CITIES FREE   4.29.2
THOUGH FALSE, YET WITH FREE SCOPE MORE
                           GRACE DOTH BREED   4.45.10
IN MY FREE SIDE+ CR AM I BORNE A SLAVE   4.47.3
CANNOT HEAVN'S FOCD, ONCE FELT, KEEPE
                           STOMAKES FREE   4.88.7
SO NEERE, IN SO GOOD TIME, SO FREE A PLACE+   4.105.2
FONDNESSE IT WERE FCR ANY BEING FREE   5.37.13
BUT ONELY THAT IS PERMANENT AND FREE   5.79.7
FREEDOM   2
WHEN BACKE I LOOKE, I SIGH MY FREEDOME PAST   1.28.9
MY HEART, MINE EYE THE FREEEDOME OF THAT RIGHT   3.46.4
FREEDOM'S
MY FREEDOMES TYRANTS CONQUERING ALL BY ARTE   1.27.10
FREELY   1
WHERE, THE FULL $PRAYSE I FREELY MUST CONFESSE   2.47.7
FREEWILL   1
OF HER FREEWILL, SCCRNING BOTH THEE AND ME   5.10.4
FREEZE   1
NOT FYRE., FOR SHE DOTH FRIESE WITH FAINT DESIRE   5.55.8
FREEZETH   1
THE MORE SHE FRIESETH IN HER WILFULL PRYCE   5.32.10
FREEZING   1
OF LIVING DEATHS, DEARE WOUNDS, FAIRE
                           STORMES AND FREESING FIRES   4.6.4

```
FREEZINGS                    1
   WHAT FREEZINGS HAVE I FELT, WHAT DARKE
                             DAIES SEENE+           3.97.3
FRENCH                 1
   IF $FRENCH CAN YET THREE PARTS IN ONE AGREE      4.30.5
FREQUENT               3
   NINE $MUSES DOE WITH $LEARNING STILL FREQUENT    2.18.6
   NINE $MUSES DOE WITH LEARNING STILL FREQUENT     2.108.6
   THAT I HAVE FREQUENT BINNE WITH UNKNOWN MINDES   3.117.5
FRESH                 19
   AND STILL AGAINST HER FROWNES FRESH VOWES
                             REPAIREST              1.8.3
   STILL NEW BORNE SORROWES OF HER FRESH DISDAINE   1.16.10
   WITH STILL FRESH CARES, SUPPLIDE WITH NO RELIEFE 1.32.4
   FRESH SHALT THOU SEE IN ME THE WOUNDS THOU MADST 1.41.5
   THOU THAT ART NOW THE WORLDS FRESH ORNAMENT      3.1.9
   WHOSE FRESH REPAIRE IF NOW THOU NOT RENEWEST     3.3.3
   AND THAT FRESH BLOUD WHICH YONGLY THOU BESTOW'ST 3.11.3
   AND IN FRESH NUMBERS NUMBER ALL YOUR GRACES      3.17.6
   AND WEEPE A FRESH LOVES LONG SINCE CANCELD WOE   3.30.7
   SINCE FIRST I SAW YOU FRESH WHICH YET ARE GREENE 3.104.8
   MY LOVE LOOKES FRESH, AND DEATH TO ME
                             SUBSCRIBES             3.107.10
   SO THAT ETERNALL LOVE IN LOVES FRESH CASE        3.108.9
   SOME FRESH AND FRUITFULL SHOWERS UPON
                             MY SUNNE-BURN'D BRAINE  4.1.8
   TO WRITE THEREIN MORE FRESH THE STORY
                             OF DELIGHT             4.102.13
   FRESH LOVE, THAT LONG HATH SLEPT IN CHEERLESSE
                             BOWER                  5.4.6
   THEN YOU FAIRE FLOWRE, IN WHOM FRESH YOUTH
                             DOTH RAINE             5.4.13
   TO BATTAILE FRESH AGAINST MY SELFE TO FIGHT      5.44.12
   FRESH SPRING THE HERALD OF LOVES MIGHTY KING     5.70.1
   WHOSE YMAGE YET I CARRY FRESH IN MYND            5.78.4
FRESHER                1
   SOME FRESHER STAMPE OF THE TIME BETTERING DAYES  3.82.8
FRESHEST               2
   AND FRESHEST $COLOURS WITH FOULE STAYNES
                             DISGRACED              2.13.4
   AND FRESHEST COLOURS WITH FOULE STAINES
                             DISGRACED              2.121.4
FRESHLY                3
   WHOSE CURELESSE WOUNDS EVEN NOW MOST FRESHLY
                             BLEED                  4.48.11
   WITH SUCH A ROSIE MORNE, WHOSE BEAMES
                             MOST FRESHLY GAY       4.76.7
   THEN SHALL THE NEW YEARES JOY FORTH FRESHLY SEND 5.62.9
FRET                   2
   METALS DOE WASTE, AND FRET WITH $CANKERS $RUST   2.13.2
   METTLES DOE WASTE, AND FRET WITH CANKERS RUST    2.121.2
FRIEND                24
   SLEW HIS DEARE $FRIEND, MY KIND AND TRUEST $HEART 2.7.12
   HAPS TO LEND SOME TO ONE TRUE HONEST $FRIEND     2.10.8
   MY HOPE BECOMES A FRIEND TO MY DESIRE            2.132.9
   BUT IF THE WHILE I THINKE ON THEE (DEARE FRIEND) 3.30.13
   SUFFRING MY FRIEND FOR MY SAKE TO APPROOVE HER   3.42.8
   AND LOOSING HER, MY FRIEND HATH FOUND THAT LOSSE 3.42.10
   BUT HERE'S THE JOY, MY FRIEND AND I ARE ONE      3.42.13
   THUS FARRE THE MILES ARE MEASURDE FROM THY FRIEND 3.50.4
```

```
IN TRUE PLAINE WORDS, BY THY TRUE TELLING FRIEND      3.82.12
TO ME FAIRE FRIEND YOU NEVER CAN BE OLD               3.104.1
ON NEWER PROOFE, TO TRIE AN OLDER FRIEND              3.110.11
PITTIE ME THEN DEARE FRIEND, AND I ASSURE YEE         3.111.13
FOR THAT DEEPE WOUND IT GIVES MY FRIEND AND ME        3.133.2
BUT SLAVE TO SLAVERY MY SWEET'ST FRIEND MUST BE       3.133.4
AND SUE A FRIEND, CAME DEBTER FOR MY SAKE             3.134.11
BUT BEING BOTH FROM ME BOTH TO EACH FRIEND            3.144.11
WHO HATETH THEE THAT I DOE CALL MY FRIEND             3.149.5
ALAS HAVE I NOT PAINE ENOUGH MY FRIEND                4.14.1
YOUR WORDS MY FRIEND (RIGHT HEALTHFULL
                           CAUSTIKS) BLAME            4.21.1
AS OF A FRIEND THAT MEANT NOT MUCH AMISSE             4.56.8
MY FRIEND, THAT OFT SAW THROUGH ALL MASKES MY WO      4.69.5
THAT DO NOT LEAVE YOUR LEAST FRIEND AT THE WURST      4.95.2
DIAN THAT FAINE WOULD CHEARE HER FRIEND
                           THE $NIGHT                 4.97.1
THAT BAD HIS FRIEND, BUT THEN NEW MAIM'D, TO BE       4.106.13
```

FRIENDLY   4
```
AND SHUT THOSE WAIES MY FRIENDLY FOE FIRST ENTRED     1.27.3
NOBLER DESIRES, LEAST ELSE THAT FRIENDLY FOE          4.21.7
NOR TRUMPETS SOUND I HEARD, NOR FRIENDLY CRIES        4.53.12
THE FRIENDLY FRAY, WHERE BLOWES BOTH WOUND
                           AND HEALE                  4.79.10
```

FRIENDS   15
```
LIVE RECONCILED FRIENDS WITHIN HER BROW               1.6.10
A GENTLE WARNING ($FRIENDS) THUS MAY YOU SEE          2.7.13
FALSE $FRIENDS THY KINDNESSE, BORNE BUT
                           TO DECEIVE $THEE           2.10.10
AND WANTING $FRIENDS, THOUGH OF A $GODDESSE BORNE     2.23.3
WELL, WELL, MY $FRIENDS, WHEN $BEGGERS
                           GROW THUS BOLD             2.23.13
NIGHT WAS ORDAYN'D, TOGETHER $FRIENDS TO KEEPE        2.37.4
FEATUR'D LIKE HIM, LIKE HIM WITH FRIENDS POSSEST      3.29.6
FOR PRECIOUS FRIENDS HID IN DEATHS DATELES NIGHT      3.30.6
AND ALL THOSE FRIENDS WHICH I THOUGHT BURIED          3.31.4
HAD MY FRIENDS $MUSE GROWNE WITH THIS
                           GROWING AGE                3.32.10
BUT THEN MY FRIENDS HEART LET MY POORE
                           HEART BALE                 3.133.10
FLIE, FLY, MY FRIENDS, I HAVE MY DEATH
                           WOUND., FLY                4.20.1
THAT MAKES ME OFT MY BEST FRIENDS OVERPASSE           4.27.12
YET SIGHS, DEERE SIGHS, INDEEDE TRUE FRIENDS
                           YOU ARE                    4.95.1
OF GRUDGING FOES, NE FAVOUR SEEK OF FRIENDS           5.59.10
```

FRIENDSHIP'S   1
```
O RARE EFFECT, TRUE BOND OF FRIENDSHIPS MEASURE       2.146.9
```
FRIES   1
```
AS CAN REFRESH THE HELL WHERE MY SOULE FRIES          4.100.8
```
FRIGHTS   2
```
SPIGHTFULL $ERINNIS FRIGHTS $ME WITH HER $LOOKES      2.39.9
SPIGHTFULL $ERRINIS FRIGHTS MEE WITH HER LOOKES       2.118.9
```
FRO   1
```
TO BE ACQUIT FRO MY CONTINUALL SMART                  5.42.6
```
FRONT   2
```
AS $PHILOMELL IN SUMMERS FRONT DOTH SINGE             3.102.7
HATH HIS FRONT BUILT OF $ALABASTER PURE               4.9.3
```
FRONTIERS   1
```
DOTH WILLING GRAUNT, THAT IN THE FRONTIERS HE         4.29.7
```

```
FROST                        3
   FLINT, FROST, DISDAINE, WEARES, MELTES,
                         AND YEELDES WE SEE        1.11.14
   AND FROST OF AGE HATH NIPT THY BEAUTIES NEERE    1.42.2
   SAP CHECKT WITH FROST AND LUSTIE LEAV'S QUITE GON  3.5.7
FROSTY                       1
   PELION AND $OSSA, FROSTY $CAUCASE OLD           2.120.6
FROTH                        1
   YET BY MY $FROTH, THIS $FOOLE HIS $LOVE OBTAINES  2.21.13
FROWN                        5
   IF BEAUTY THUS BE CLOWDED WITH A FROWNE          1.21.1
   FOR AT A FROWNE THEY IN THEIR GLORY DIE          3.25.8
   WHEN I SHALL SEE THEE FROWNE ON MY DEFECTS       3.49.2
   BRING ME WITHIN THE LEVEL OF YOUR FROWNE        3.117.11
   HER SMILE ME DRAWES, HER FROWNE ME DRIVES AWAY   5.21.12
FROWNEST                     1
   ON WHOM FROUN'ST THOU THAT I DOE FAUNE UPON      3.149.6
FROWNING                     1
   TWIXT JOY AND GRIEFE, YET WITH A SMYLING
                         FROWNING                  2.109.9
FROWNS                       5
   HER BROW SHADES FROWNES, ALTHOUGH HER
                         EYES ARE SUNNY             1.6.2
   AND STILL AGAINST HER FROWNES FRESH VOWES
                         REPAIREST                  1.8.3
   AND SINNE OF FROWNES BRING HONOUR TO THE FACE    1.56.12
   AND SO CONTENT ME THAT HER FROWNES SHOULD BE     1.59.11
   IS WRIT IN MOODS AND FROWNES AND WRINCKLES
                         STRANGE                    3.93.8
FROZEN                       4
   MAKING MY $SIGHES TO THAW THE $FROZEN $SEAS      2.25.8
   NOT USDE TO FROZEN CLIPS, HE STRAVE TO
                         FIND SOME PART             4.8.6
   IS NOT DELAYD BY HER HART FROSEN COLD            5.30.6
   AND SHE TO STONES AT LENGTH ALL FROSEN TURNE+    5.32.14
FRUIT                        8
   BUT SINCE THE SWEETEST ROOTE YEELDS FRUITE
                         SO SOWRE                   1.26.9
   BUT HOPE OF $ORPHANS, AND UN-FATHERED FRUITE     3.97.10
   OR REACH THE FRUITE OF $NATURE'S CHOISEST TREE   4.10.4
   BUT NEVER HEEDS THE FRUIT OF WRITER'S MIND       4.11.8
   DEEME THAT MY $MUSE SOME FRUIT OF KNOWLEDGE PLIES 4.23.6
   WHOSE FRUIT DOTH FARRE TH'$ESPERIAN TAST SURPASSE 4.82.6
   AND TWIXT HER PAPS LIKE EARLY FRUIT IN $MAY      5.76.9
   SWEET FRUIT OF PLEASURE BROUGHT FROM PARADICE    5.77.11
FRUITFUL                     1
   SOME FRESH AND FRUITFULL SHOWERS UPON
                         MY SUNNE-BURN'D BRAINE     4.1.8
FRUITLESS                    2
   THUS SHE RETURNES MY HOPES SO FRUITLESSE EVER    1.24.13
   WHOSE FRUITLESSE WORKE IS BROKEN WITH LEAST WYND  5.23.14
FRUITS                       2
   AND NOT IN $NATURE FOR BEST FRUITS UNFIT         4.19.13
   OR GEMMES, OR FRUTES OF NEW-FOUND $PARADISE      4.81.2
FRY                          1
   YET CANNOT ALL THESE FLAMES IN WHICH I FRY       5.32.5
FUEL                         5
   THE $FUELL KINDLED WITH $CELESTIALL $HEAT        2.30.8
   LOVE IS THE $FEWELL, WHICH MAINTAINES THE FIRE   2.40.4
   LOVE IS THE FUELL WHICH MAINTAINES THE FIRE      2.144.4
```

```
FEED'ST THY LIGHTS FLAME WITH SELFE SUBSTANTIALL
                          FEWELL                        3.1.6
TILL WITHOUT FEWELL YOU CAN MAKE HOT FIRE              4.46.14
FULFILL                 3
  AND HAVE NO STARS BUT THOSE, THAT MUST FULFILL        1.33.6
  THUS FARRE FOR LOVE, MY LOVE-SUTE SWEET FULLFILL      3.136.4
  $WILL, WILL FULFILL THE TREASURE OF THY LCVE          3.136.5
FULFILLED               1
  IN WHICH HER CIRCLES VOYAGE IS FULFILD                5.60.3
FULL                   33
  FOR BEING FULL, SHCULD I NOT THEN HAVE SPOKEN          1.7.13
  THAT FULL OF BEAUTY, TIME BESTOWES UPON HER            1.39.4
  WHERE, THE FULL $PRAYSE I FREELY MUST CONFESSE         2.47.7
  BUT NOW THEIR PLUMES FULL SUMD WITH SWEET DESIRE       2.103.9
  THEN TO THE $TROPICKE TAKES HIS FULL $CAREERE          2.147.5
  FULL MANY A GLORICUS MORNING HAVE I SEENE              3.33.1
  THY BEAUTIE, AND THY YEARES FULL WELL BEFITS           3.41.3
  THE $CANKER BLOOMES HAVE FULL AS DEEPE A DIE           3.54.5
  AS CAL IT $WINTER, WHICH BEING FUL OF CARE            3.56.13
  SOME-TIME ALL FUL WITH FEASTING ON YOUR SIGHT          3.75.9
  WAS IT THE PROUD FULL SAILE OF HIS GREAT VERSE         3.86.1
  MY MOST FULL FLAME SHOULD AFTERWARDS BURNE
                          CLEERER                       3.115.4
TO GIVE FULL GROWTH TO THAT WHICH STILL
                          DOTH GROW                    3.115.14
  EVEN SO BEING FULL CF YCUR NERE CLOYING
                          SWEETNESSE                    3.118.5
  FULL CHARACTERD WITH LASTING MEMORY                   3.122.2
  IS PERJURD, MURDRCUS, BLCUDDY FULL OF BLAME           3.129.3
  NOR THAT FULL $STARRE THAT USHERS IN THE $EAVEN       3.132.7
  I FILL IT FULL WITH WILS, AND MY WILL ONE             3.136.6
  TILL BY DEGREES IT HAD FULL CONQUEST GOT               4.2.4
  YET HIDING ROYALL BLOUD FULL OFT IN RURALL VAINE       4.6.8
  THAT THOSE LIPS SWELL, SC FULL OF THEE THEY BEE       4.12.3
  AND, $LOVE, I THOUGHT THAT I WAS FULL OF THEE         4.16.4
  WHAT NOW THE $DUTCH IN THEIR FULL DIETS BOAST         4.30.6
  NOR GIVE EACH SPEECH A FULL POINT OF A GRONE          4.54.4
  WHAT SIGHES STOLNE CUT, OR KILD BEFORE
                          FULL BORNE+                   4.67.9
  FOR THOUGH FULL OF CESIRE, EMPTIE OF WIT              4.82.9
  BEWARE FULL SAILES DROWNE NOT THY TOTTRING BARGE      4.85.1
  THAT FULL OF DOUBTS, THCU OF PERPLEXITY               4.96.7
  SHEWES HER OFT AT THE FULL HER FAIREST FACE           4.97.2
  MORE THEN MOST FAIRE, FULL OF THE LIVING FIRE          5.8.1
  THERE MY FRAILE FANCY FED WITH FULL DELIGHT           5.72.9
  YET FIELD AND BOWRE ARE FULL OF HER ASPECT            5.78.8
  JOY OF MY LIFE, FULL OFT FOR LOVING YOU               5.82.1
FULLEST                 1
  YOU SEEKE TO NURSE AT FULLEST BREASTS OF $FAME        4.15.13
FULLNESS                3
  THY HUNGRIE EIES, EVEN TILL THEY WINCK
                          WITH FULNESSE                 3.56.6
  STELLA, THE FULNESSE OF MY THOUGHTS OF THEE           4.50.1
  FED ON THE FULNESSE OF THAT CHEAREFULL GLAUNCE        5.39.12
FULLY                   1
  THAT IN NO MORE BUT THESE I MIGHT BE FULLY BLEST      4.77.13
FUMES                   1
  WHENCE THOSE SAME FUMES OF MELANCHOLY RISE            4.23.3
FUNCTION                1
  DOTH PART HIS FUNCTION, AND IS PARTLY BLIND           3.113.3
```

FUNCTIONS   1
  THESE OF THE $SOULE THE SEV'RALL $FUNCTIONS BEE   2.12.13
FUR   2
  BUT, BUT (ALAS) NIGHT'S SIDE THE ODS HATH FUR   4.96.12
  BUT FEELING PROOFE MAKES ME SAY THEY MISTAKE
                IT FURRE   4.102.11
FURIES   3
  AND $FATES AND $FURIES, WITH THEIR WOES ACQUAINT   2.39.4
  THE $MUSES NICE, THE $FURIES CRUELL BE   2.118.7
  OF THAT SELFE KYND WITH WHICH THE $FURIES FELL   5.86.2
FURIOUS   2
  BAYTING THE $LYON IN HIS FURIOUS HEAT   2.147.7
  ON HORSEBACKE MET HIM IN HIS FURIOJS RACE   4.22.6
FURNACE   1
  THROUGH THAT DARKE FORNACE TO MY HART OPPREST   4.108.3
FURNISHING   1
  WITH $SIGHES AND $TEARES STILL FURNISHING
                HIS $TABLE   2.23.7
FURNITURE   1
  PREPAR'D BY $NATURE'S CHIEFEST FURNITURE   4.9.2
FURROWS   2
  BEST IN MY FACE, HOW CARES HAVE TILD DEEPE
                FORROWES   1.4.8
  BUT WHEN IN THEE TIMES FORRWES I BEHOULD   3.22.3
FURTHER   7
  BUT $O, SEE, SEE, WE NEED INQUIRE NO FURTHER   2.2.9
  THOUGH MY $CONCEIT I FURTHER SEEME TO BEND   2.34.10
  NEERER $MEN COME, $THAT FURTHER FLYES AWAY   2.58.9
  THEN MORE I $TRAVELD, FURTHER FROM MY $REST   2.62.2
  THE MORE I TRAVELL, FURTHER FROM MY REST   2.150.2
  WITHOUT DESIRE TO FEED CF FURTHER GRACE   4.46.8
  THAT FURTHER SEEMES HIS TERME STILL TO EXTENC   5.87.11
FURTHERS   1
  IT FURTHERS $JUSTICE, BUT HELPES NOT THE DEAD   2.46.14
FURY   6
  THE FURY OF A MERCY-WANTING STORME   1.37.6
  WHERE BEAT THESE TEARES WITH ZEALE, AND
                FURY DRIVES   1.48.10
  SPENDST THOU THY FURIE CN SOME WORTHLESSE SONGE   3.100.3
  BUT THAT THEY STOPT HIS FURIE FROM THE SAME   4.50.13
  SOME DO I HEARE OF $POETS' FURIE TELL   4.74.5
  THAT ME WITH HEAVENLY FURY DOTH INSPIRE   5.85.11
GAIN   16
  BUT YET, WHAT COMFCRTS SHALL I HEREBY GAINE+   1.52.13
  YET AT THIS PRICE RETURNES ME TREBLE GAINE   2.28.8
  AND I GIVE MUCH, BECAUSE I GAINE THEREBY   2.28.10
  ESSEX GREAT FALL, $TYRONE HIS $PEACE TO GAINE   2.51.6
  IF I LOOSE THEE, MY LOSSE IS MY LOVES GAINE   3.42.9
  WHEN I HAVE SEENE THE HUNGRY $OCEAN GAINE   3.64.5
  AND GAINE BY ILLS THRISE MORE THEN I HAVE SPENT   3.119.14
  ONELY MY PLAGUE THUS FARRE I COUNT MY GAINE   3.141.13
  LEAVE FOLLOWING THAT, WHICH IT IS GAINE TO MISSE   4.47.11
  WHETHER WITH WORDS THIS SOVERAIGNTY HE GAINE   4.58.5
  HIS $SIRE'S REVENGE, JOYN'D WITH A KINGDOME'S
                GAINE   4.75.6
  AGAINST YOUR EIES THAT JUSTICE I MAY GAINE   5.12.14
  DO SEEKE MOST PRETICUS THINGS TO MAKE YOUR GAIN   5.15.2
  THAT ENDLESSE PLEASURE SHALL UNTO ME GAINE+   5.26.14
  ALL SORROWES SHORT THAT GAINE ETERNALL BLISSE   5.63.14
  WHEN LOOSING ONE, TWO LIBERTIES YE GAYNE   5.65.3

GAINED   3
  WHOSE GLORIOUS ACTICNS LUCKILY HAD GAIND   1.45.7
  AND GAIN'D BY $MARS, COULD YET MAD $MARS SO TAME   4.75.7
  THEN THINKE HOW LITLE GLORY YE HAVE GAYNED   5.36.10
GAINER   1
  AND I BY THIS WIL BE A GAINER TOO   3.88.9
GAINETH   2
  WHICH BY $EXTORTICN GAINETH ALL THEIR LOCKES   2.3.10
  WHO BY EXTORTION GAINETH ALL THEYR LOOKES   2.110.10
GAINS   2
  SO TRUE AND LOYALL LOVE NO FAVOUR GAINES ME   1.18.8
  AND PROUD OF MANY, LIVES UPON HIS GAINES+   3.67.12
GAINSAY   1
  FOR WHEN HE WILL SEE WHC DARE HIM GAINESAY   4.43.5
GAINST   8
  THAT GAINST THY SELFE THOU STICKST NOT
                         TO CONSPIRE   3.10.6
  AND NOTHING GAINST $TIMES SIFTH CAN MAKE DEFENCE   3.12.13
  AND GAINST MY SELFE A LAWFULL PLEA COMMENCE   3.35.11
  GAINST DEATH, AND ALL OBLIVIOUS EMNITY   3.55.9
  CROOKED ECLIPSES GAINST HIS GLORY FIGHT   3.60.7
  POTICNS OF $EYSELL GAINST MY STRONG INFECTION   3.111.10
  GAYNST SUCH STRONG CASTLES NEEDETH GREATER MIGHT   5.14.5
  GAYNST WHICH A SHIP OF SUCCOUR DESOLATE   5.56.11
GAIT   1
  ORE WHOME THEIR FINGERS WALKE WITH GENTLE GATE   3.128.11
GALIXIA   1
  THE $GALIXIA, TO HER MORE THEN WHITE   2.148.10
GALL   3
  AND HER DISDAINES ARE $GALL, HER FAVOURS $HUNNY   1.6.4
  WHOSE $STOMACK UNTC $GALL HATH TURN'D THY $FCOD   2.49.6
  OR CHOKED BE WITH CVERFLCWING GALL   5.43.4
GALLANT   1
  A $WITLESSE $GALLANT, A YOUNG $WENCH THAT WOO'D   2.21.1
GALLED   1
  (SPURD WITH LOVE'S SPUR, THOUGH GALD AND
                       SHORTLY RAIND   4.98.7
GALLEIN'S   1
  GALLEIN'S ADOPTIVE SONNES, WHO BY A BEATEN WAY   4.102.9
GALLIGLASSE   1
  AND MOLLIFIE THE SLAUGHT'RING $GALLIGLASSE   2.25.12
GALLUS   1
  SLOW $ARRER, FRANTICK $GALLUS, $CYDNUS CCLD   2.120.8
GAME   2
  AND LIKE A $TYRANT MAK'ST MY GRIEFE THY GAME   2.130.12
  SEEING THE GAME FRCM HIM ESCAPT AWAY   5.67.2
GANGES   1
  SOME $GANGES, $ISTER, AND OF $TAGUS TELL   2.120.9
GANYMEDE   1
  WHUSE TALENTS HELD YOUNG $GANIMED ABOVE   4.13.4
GAPING   1
  FROM OUT THAT NOYSCME GULFE, WHICH GAPING LIES   4.78.3
GARDEN   4
  NYMPH OF THE GARD'N, WHERE ALL BEAUTIES BE   4.82.1
  SWEET GARD'N $NYMPH, WHICH KEEPES THE
                     $CHERRIE TREE   4.82.5
  ME SEEMD I SMELT A GARDIN OF SWEET FLOWRES   5.64.2
  BY $LOVE HIMSELFE AND IN HIS GARDEN PLASTE   5.77.12
GARDENS   1
  AND MANY MAIDEN GARDENS YET UNSET   3.16.6
GARLAND   2
  A ROSIE GARLAND, AND A WEARIE HED   4.39.11

```
      WHO NOW IS COMMING FORTH WITH GIRLAND CROUNED        5.19.4
GARMENTS              2
    SOME IN THEIR GARMENTS THOUGH NEW-FANGLED ILL          3.91.3
    RICHER THEN WEALTH, PROUDER THEN GARMENTS COST         3.91.10
GASP              1
    NOW AT THE LAST GASPE, OF $LOVES LATEST $BREATH        2.61.9
GATE              5
    FROM SULLEN EARTH SINGS HIMNS AT $HEAVENS GATE         3.29.12
    PITIE THEREOF GATE IN HER BREAST SUCH PLACE            4.45.7
    NEW YEARE FORTH LOCKING OUT OF JANUS GATE              5.4.1
    BUT YE THEREBY MUCH GREATER GLORY GATE                 5.66.9
    THE GATE WITH PEARLES AND RUBYES RICHLY DIGHT          5.81.10
GATES             1
    NOR GATES OF STEELE SO STRONG BUT TIME DECAYES+        3.65.8
GATHER            2
    AND LEARNE TO GATHER FLOWERS BEFORE THEY WITHER        1.51.6
    AND GATHER TO .MY SELFE NEW BREATH AWHILE              5.80.4
GATHERED          1
    WEEDS AMONG WEEDS, OR FLOWERS WITH FLOWERS
                            GATHERD                        3.124.4
GAUDS             1
    LOVE STILL A $BABY, PLAYES WITH $GAWDES
                            AND $TOYES                     2.22.5
GAUDY             1
    AND ONLY HERAULD TO THE GAUDY SPRING                   3.1.10
GAVE             19
    WHEREIN NO SHEW GAVE CAUSE OF LEAST SUSPECT            1.31.7
    AND THAT WHICH GAVE ME WOUNDS, $ILE GIVE
                            IT KISSES                      1.46.12
    YOUR $CHEEKES YET PALE, SINCE FIRST HE
                            GAVE THE $WOUND                2.2.12
    WHO GAVE CONSENT TO STEALE AWAY MY $HEART              2.23.11
    GAVE $LIFE AND $COURAGE TO MY LAB'RING $PEN            2.47.2
    GAVE IT TO KEEPE TO $SPIRITS WITHIN THE $GROUND        2.58.4
    GAVE MEE SWEET LOCKES WHEN AS I LEARNED WELL           2.111.4
    O SWEET'ST REVENGE THAT ERE THE HEAVENS GAVE           2.139.6
    LOOKE WHOM SHE BEST INDOW'D, SHE GAVE THE MORE         3.11.11
    WERE IT NOT THY SOURE LEISURE GAVE SWEET LEAVE         3.39.10
    AND TIME THAT GAVE, DOTH NOW HIS GIFT CONFOUND         3.60.8
    THESE BLENCHES GAVE MY HEART AN OTHER YOUTH            3.110.7
    AND TO INLIGHTEN THEE GAVE EYES TO BLINDNESSE          3.152.11
    LOVE GAVE THE WOUND, WHICH WHILE I BREATHE
                            WILL BLEED                     4.2.2
    PLACED EVER THERE, GAVE HIM THIS MOURNING WEED         4.7.13
    BY $NATURE BORNE, I GAVE TO THEE MINE EYES             4.65.8
    AND BY THE BAY WHICH I UNTO HER GAVE                   5.29.3
    THIS ONE DISPARAGEMENT THEY TO YOU GAVE                5.66.3
    THE FIRST MY BEING TO ME GAVE BY KIND                  5.74.5
GAVEST            3
    THOU GAV'ST ME THINE NOT TO GIVE BACKE AGAINE          3.22.14
    THY SELFE THOU GAV'ST, THY OWNE WORTH
                            THEN NOT KNOWING               3.87.9
    OR MEE TO WHOM THOU GAV'ST IT, ELSE MISTAKING          3.87.10
GAY              4
    ERE BEAUTIES DEAD FLEECE MADE ANOTHER GAY              3.68.8
    PAINTING THY OUTWARD WALLS SO COSTLIE GAY+             3.146.4
    WITH SUCH A ROSIE MORNE, WHOSE BEAMES
                            MOST FRESHLY GAY               4.76.7
    THAT GOODLY $IDOLL NOW SO GAY BESEENE                  5.27.5
```

GAZE   16
  THEN LEAVE THY GLASSE, AND GAZE THY SELFE ON ME   1.37.9
  WHEN, IF SHE GRIEVE TO GAZE HER IN HER GLASSE   1.38.9
  BUT WHILST MINE $EYES THUS GREEDILY DOE GAZE   2.33.5
  SO DOTH THE $PLOW-MAN GAZE THE WAND'RING $STARRE   2.43.5
  DID NOT PERFECTION STILL ON HER PERFECTION GAZE   2.117.11
  BUT WHILST MINE EYES THUS GREEDILY DOE GAZE   2.133.5
  AT HER PERFECTION STAND YOU THEN AND GAZE   2.151.6
  THE LOVELY GAZE WHERE EVERY EYE DOTH DWELL   3.5.2
  DELIGHTS TO PEEPE, TO GAZE THEREIN ON THEE   3.24.12
  THRETNING RASH EIES WHICH GAZE ON HER SO WIDE   5.5.7
  ONE DAY AS I UNWARILY DID GAZE   5.16.1
  AND HAVING IT THEY GAZE ON IT THE MORE   5.35.6
  IS IT THAT MENS FRAYLE EYES, WHICH GAZE TOO BOLD   5.37.5
  TO LET THEM GAZE WHYLEST HE ON THEM MAY PRAY   5.53.4
  AND SEEING IT, THEY GAZE ON IT THE MORE   5.83.6
  WHEN OTHERS GAZE UPON THEYR SHADOWES VAYNE   5.88.6
GAZED   2
  AND THUS WHILST $BEAUTIE ON HER BEAUTY GAZED   2.109.5
  THY YOUTHES PROUD LIVERY SO GAZ'D ON NOW   3.2.3
GAZERS   2
  HOW MANY GAZERS MIGHST THOU LEAD AWAY   3.96.11
  TO MAKE THE BAYTE HER GAZERS TO EMBREW   5.53.11
GAZER'S   1
  THEY SHOULD STILL DAUNCE TO PLEASE A GAZER'S
                                         SIGHT   4.26.8
GAZETH   1
  GILDING THE OBJECT WHERE-UPON IT GAZETH   3.20.6
GAZING   4
  GAZING THY BEAUTY DEIGN'D THEE BY THE SKIES   1.37.2
  BUT ON HER RAYES WITH GAZING EYES THEY STOOD   2.103.6
  AND THERE STANDS GAZING ON THOSE DARTING EYES   2.135.6
  PITTIFULL THRIVORS IN THEIR GAZING SPENT   3.125.8
GEM   1
  THE RICHEST GEMME OF $LOVE AND LIFE ENJOYES   4.24.10
GEMS   3
  WITH $SUNNE AND $MOONE, WITH EARTH AND
                              SEAS RICH GEMS   3.21.6
  O KISSE, WHICH DOEST THOSE RUDDIE GEMMES IMPART   4.81.1
  OR GEMMES, OR FRUTES OF NEW-FOUND $PARADISE   4.81.2
GENERAL   3
  ALL THESE I BETTER IN ONE GENERALL BEST   3.91.8
  UNLESSE THIS GENERALL EVILL THEY MAINTAINE   3.121.13
  AND SO THE $GENERALL OF HOT DESIRE   3.154.7
GENTLE   27
  A GENTLE WARNING ($FRIENDS) THUS MAY YOU SEE   2.7.13
  O, JUDGE NOT RASHLY (GENTLE $SIR) I PRAY   2.24.4
  TRUCE, GENTLE $LOVE, A $PARLY NOW I CRAVE   2.63.1
  THOSE HOWERS THAT WITH GENTLE WORKE DID FRAME   3.5.1
  SHALL HATE BE FAIRER LOG'D THEN GENTLE LOVE+   3.10.10
  A WOMANS GENTLE HART BUT NOT ACQUAINTED   3.20.3
  I DOE FORGIVE THY ROBB'RIE GENTLE THEEFE   3.40.9
  GENTLE THOU ART, AND THEREFORE TO BE WONNE   3.41.5
  WITHIN THE GENTLE CLOSURE OF MY BREST   3.48.11
  MY VERSE ALONE HAD ALL THY GENTLE GRACE   3.79.2
  YOUR MONUMENT SHALL BE MY GENTLE VERSE   3.81.9
  SOME SAY THY GRACE IS YOUTH AND GENTLE SPORT   3.96.2
  IN GENTLE NUMBERS TIME SO IDELY SPENT   3.100.6
  ORE WHOME THEIR FINGERS WALKE WITH GENTLE GATE   3.128.11
  WAS USDE IN GIVING GENTLE DOME   3.145.7

```
THAT FOLLOW'D IT AS GENTLE DAY                         3.145.10
THEN GENTLE CHEATER URGE NOT MY AMISSE                 3.151.3
OF GENTLE FORCE, SO THAT MINE EYES DARE
                              GLADLY PLAY              4.76.6
IN GENTLE BREST THAT SHALL ENDURE FOR EVER             5.6.10
LET IT LYKEWISE YOUR GENTLE BREST INSPIRE              5.28.6
SUCH IS THE POWRE OF LOVE IN GENTLE MIND               5.30.13
THE GENTLE BIRDE FEELES NO CAPTIVITY                   5.65.7
THE GENTLE DEARE RETURND THE SELFE-SAME WAY            5.67.7
BETWEENE THE $SPYDER AND THE GENTLE $BEE               5.71.14
BUT THE TREW FAYRE, THAT IS THE GENTLE WIT             5.79.3
TO BEARE THE MESSAGE OF HER GENTLE SPRIGHT             5.81.12
ATTEMPT TO WORK HER GENTLE MINDES UNREST               5.84.4
GENTLEMEN            1
THE FIRST, THUS MATCHT, WERE SCARCELY $GENTLEMEN       4.13.14
GENTLEST            1
FOR IF IT SEE THE RUD'ST OR GENTLEST SIGHT             3.113.9
GENTLY              5
GENTLY DISTILLS HIS $NECTAR-DROPPING SHOWRES           2.53.6
GENTLY DISTILS HIS $NECTAR-DROPPING SHOWERS            2.113.6
WITH THY SWEET FINGERS WHEN THOU GENTLY SWAYST         3.128.3
THAT FOR MY FAULTS YE WILL ME GENTLY BEAT              5.24.14
GENTLY ENCAGE, THAT HE MAY BE YOUR THRALL              5.73.10
GET                17
BUT AH, WHAT GLORIE CAN SHE GET THEREBY                1.27.11
WHAT THOUGH MY $MUSE NO HONOR GET THEREBY              1.59.13
BUT BOUNDED THUS, TO $SCOTLAND GET YOU FORTH           2.25.5
THERE LET MY $VERSE GET GLORY IN THE $NORTH            2.25.7
GET NOT ONE GLANCE, TO RECOMPENCE MY $MERIT+           2.43.4
THAT WHAT $THEY GET, $THEY EVER DOE RETAINE            2.52.4
SUCH AS BY $ART TO GET THE SAME HAVE TRY'D             2.58.7
NAY, I HAVE DONE.. $YOU GET NO MORE OF $ME             2.61.2
UNLOK'D ON DIEST UNLESSE THOU GET A SONNE              3.7.14
AFTER MY DEATH (DEARE LOVE) FOR GET ME QUITE           3.72.3
BUT, FOOLE, SEEKST NOT TO GET INTO HER HART            4.11.14
TILL BLOUDIE BULLET GET HIM WRONGFULL PRAY             4.20.4
YET $DEARE, LET ME THIS PARDON GET OF YOU              4.46.12
MAY GET NO ALMES BUT SCORNE OF BEGGERIE                4.47.8
RATHER THEN BY MORE TRUTH TO GET MORE PAINE            4.67.14
OUT OF HER BANDS YE BY NO MEANES SHALL GET             5.37.12
ONELY MY PAINES WIL BE THE MORE TO GET HER             5.51.13
GETS                1
FOR WHO GETS WEALTH THAT PUTS NOT FROM THE SHORE+      1.35.5
GHASTLINESS         1
IN THEE OR SPRITES OR SPIRITED GASTLINESSE             4.96.11
GHASTLY             3
ASSAYLD WITH DEATH, YET ARM'D WITH GASTLY FEARE        2.142.3
WHICH LIKE A JEWELL (HUNGE IN GASTLY NIGHT)            3.27.11
IN NIGHT OF SPRITES THE GASTLY POWERS STUR             4.96.10
GHOST               4
BOYL'D WITH HER $SIGHES, IN GIVING UP THE $GHOST       2.15.7
PEN'D IN THE GRIEFE OF MINE AFFLICTED $GHOST           2.54.6
PEND IN THE GRIEFE OF MYNE AFFLICTED GHOST             2.101.6
HE NOR THAT AFFABLE FAMILIAR GHOST                     3.86.9
GHOSTS              1
TH'$ELISIAN GHOSTS SHALL NEVER KNOW THE SAME           1.30.14
GIDDY               2
AND WHY THESE GIDDY $METAPHORS I USE                   2.9.3
HOW E'RE BLIND $FORTUNE TURNE HER GIDDIE $WHEELE       2.51.12
```

GIFT   6
    WHICH BOUNTIOUS GUIFT THOU SHOULDST IN
                          BOUNTY CHERRISH   3.11.12
    AND TIME THAT GAVE, DOTH NOW HIS GIFT CONFOUND   3.60.8
    THE CAUSE OF THIS FAIRE GUIFT IN ME IS WANTING   3.87.7
    SO THY GREAT GUIFT UPON MISPRISION GROWING   3.87.11
    TTHY GUIFT,, THY TABLES, ARE WITHIN MY BRAINE   3.122.1
    EACH SENCE OF MINE, EACH GIFT, EACH POWER OF MIND 4.57.2
GIFTS   11
    HERE SEE THE GIFTS THAT $GOD AND NATURE LENT THEE 1.42.7
    THY $GIFTS THOU IN $OBSCURITIE DOEST WASTE   2.10.9
    THEN OF YOUR GRACES AND YOUR GIFTS TO TELL   3.103.12
    RICH IN THOSE GIFTS WHICH GIVE TH'ETERNALL
                          CROWNE   4.37.11
    SINCE TO HIMSELFE HE DOTH YOUR GIFTS APPLY   4.43.3
    ALTHOUGH LESSE GIFTS IMPE FEATHERS OFT ON $FAME   4.75.4
    OR OF THY GIFTS AT LEAST SHADE OUT SOME PART   4.81.8
    GIVEN SO GOODLY GIFTES CF BEAUTIES GRACE+   5.31.2
    THEN ALL HER NATURES GOODLY GUIFTS ARE LOST   5.41.8
    EACH OF WHICH DID HER WITH THEYR GUIFTS ADORNE   5.61.8
    WITH GUIFTS OF BODY, FORTUNE AND OF MIND   5.74.4
GILDED   3
    NOT MARBLE, NOR THE GUILDED MONUMENT   3.55.1
    AND GILDED HONOR SHAMEFULLY MISPLAST   3.66.5
    TO MAKE HIM MUCH OUT-LIVE A GILDED TOMBE   3.101.11
GILDEST   1
    WHEN SPARKLING STARS TWIRE NOT THOU GUIL'ST
                          TH'EAVEN   3.28.12
GILDING   2
    GILDING THE OBJECT WHERE-UPON IT GAZETH   3.20.6
    GUILDING PALE STREAMES WITH HEAVENLY ALCUMY   3.33.4
GILLYFLOWERS   1
    HER LIPS DID SMELL LYKE UNTO $GILLYFLOWERS   5.64.5
GIRDED   1
    AND $SOMMERS GREENE ALL GIRDED UP IN SHEAVES   3.12.7
GIRT   1
    GIRT FAST BY MEMORIE, AND WHILE I SPURRE   4.49.10
GIVE   71
    AFFECT NO HONOR BUT WHAT SHE CAN GIVE   1.12.6
    GROWNE HOARCE WITH CRYING MERCY, MERCY GIVE   1.16.6
    THAT NEVER DEIGNES TO GIVE ME JOY TO LIVE+   1.17.6
    SUCH HONOUR UNTO CRUELTY TO GIVE+   1.17.8
    T'$ARABIAN ODORS GIVE THY BREATHING SWEETE   1.19.6
    TO $THETIS GIVE THE HONOUR OF THY FEETE   1.19.8
    AND THY SWEET VOICE GIVE BACK UNTO THE $SPHEARES 1.19.10
    AND THAT WHICH GAVE ME WOUNDS, $ILE GIVE
                          IT KISSES   1.46.12
    CAN GIVE THE LEAST RELEASE UNTO THY GRIEFE   1.52.10
    WHOSE DUE REPORTS GIVE HONOR TO HER EYES   1.57.8
    NOR OTHER HAND COULD GIVE SO TRUE A TOUCH   1.57.14
    WHERE I TO THEE $ETERNITIE SHALL GIVE   2.6.5
    I GIVE $THEE BACKE, WHEN ALL THE REST IS SPENT 2.10.14
    GIVE $ME MY $SELFE, AND TAKE YOUR $SELFE AGAINE 2.11.9
    AND THEN IN SIGHING, TO GIVE UP MY BREATH   2.20.12
    GIVE $NATURE THANKES, YOU ARE NOT SUCH AS WE   2.22.12
    THOUGH I GIVE MORE THEN WELL AFFORDS MY STATE   2.28.5
    AND I GIVE MUCH, BECAUSE I GAINE THEREBY   2.28.10
    TO TAKE ALL $MINE, AND GIVE ME NONE AGAINE+   2.52.2
    SO FOR MY $PLEDGE THOU GIVE ME $PLEDGE AGAINE   2.63.8
    SALT LUKE-WARME TEARES SHEE FOR HIS DRINKE
                          DID GIVE   2.116.15

```
THE BOUNTIOUS LARGESSE GIVEN THEE TO GIVE+            3.4.6
AND YOUR SWEET SEMBLANCE TO SOME OTHER GIVE          3.13.4
TO GIVE AWAY YOUR SELFE, KEEPS YOUR SELFE STILL      3.16.13
THOU GAV'ST ME THINE NOT TO GIVE BACKE AGAINE        3.22.14
WHO ALL THEIR PARTS OF ME TO THEE DID GIVE           3.31.11
NOR CAN THY SHAME GIVE PHISICKE TO MY GRIEFE         3.34.9
WHILST THAT THIS SHADOW DOTH SUCH SUBSTANCE GIVE     3.37.10
OH GIVE THY SELFE THE THANKES IF OUGHT IN ME         3.38.5
WHEN THOU THY SELFE DOST GIVE INVENTION LIGHT+       3.38.8
THAT BY THIS SEPERATION I MAY GIVE                   3.39.7
TOWARDS THEE ILE RUN, AND GIVE HIM LEAVE TO GOE      3.51.14
BY THAT SWEET ORNAMENT WHICH TRUTH DOTH GIVE         3.54.2
ALL TOUNGS (THE VOICE OF SOULES) GIVE
                          THEE THAT END              3.69.3
BUT THOSE SAME TOUNGS THAT GIVE THEE SO
                          THINE OWNE                 3.69.6
GIVE WARNING TO THE WORLD THAT I AM FLED             3.71.3
OF MOUTHED GRAVES WILL GIVE THEE MEMORIE             3.77.6
AND MY SICK $MUSE DOTH GIVE AN OTHER PLACE           3.79.4
FROM THY BEHAVIOUR, BEAUTIE DOTH HE GIVE             3.79.10
WHEN OTHERS WOULD GIVE LIFE, AND BRING A TOMBE       3.83.12
GIVE NOT A WINDY NIGHT A RAINIE MORROW               3.90.7
GIVE MY LOVE FAME FASTER THEN TIME WASTS LIFE        3.100.13
THEN GIVE ME WELCOME, NEXT MY HEAVEN THE BEST        3.110.13
TO GIVE FULL GROWTH TO THAT WHICH STILL
                          DOTH GROW                  3.115.14
GIVE SALUTATION TO MY SPORTIVE BLOOD+                3.121.6
THEREFORE TO GIVE THEM FROM ME WAS I BOLD            3.122.11
GIVE THEM THEIR FINGERS, ME THY LIPS TO KISSE        3.128.14
TO MAKE ME GIVE THE LIE TO MY TRUE SIGHT             3.150.3
BUT TO MY SELFE MY SELFE DID GIVE THE BLOW           4.33.9
RICH IN THOSE GIFTS WHICH GIVE TH'ETERNALL
                          CROWNE                      4.37.11
GLAD IF FOR HER HE GIVE THEM LEAVE TO DIE            4.43.8
DOTH MAKE MY HEART GIVE TO MY TONGUE THE LIE         4.47.14
NOR GIVE EACH SPEECH A FULL POINT OF A GRONE         4.54.4
O GIVE MY PASSIONS LEAVE TO RUN THEIR RACE           4.64.2
AND THOUGH SHE GIVE BUT THUS CONDITIONLY             4.69.12
I GIVE YOU HERE MY HAND FOR TRUTH OF THIS            4.70.13
'BUT AH,' $DESIRE STILL CRIES, 'GIVE ME
                          SOME FOOD'                  4.71.14
THAT PRESENCE, WHICH DOTH GIVE DARKE HEARTS
                          A LIVING LIGHT              4.77.3
TEACHING THE MEANE, AT ONCE TO TAKE AND GIVE         4.79.9
BUT GIVE APT SERVANTS THEIR DUE PLACE, LET EYES      4.85.9
SINCE $STELLA'S EYES, WONT TO GIVE ME MY DAY         4.89.3
WHAT SOBS CAN GIVE WORDS GRACE MY GRIEFE TO SHOW+    4.93.2
AND DO I THEN MY SELFE THIS VAINE SCUSE GIVE+        4.93.9
WHILE SOBD OUT WORDS A PERFECT $MUSIKE GIVE          4.100.11
SWEETE, FOR A WHILE GIVE RESPITE TO MY HART          4.107.5
AND ON MY THOUGHTS GIVE THY $LIEFTENANCY             4.107.7
WITH MERCIFULL REGARD, GIVE MERCY TOO                5.49.12
SUCH FRAGRANT FLOWRES DOE GIVE MOST ODOROUS
                          SMELL                       5.64.13
THAT THREE SUCH GRACES DID UNTO ME GIVE              5.74.14
GIVE LEAVE TO REST ME BEING HALFE FORDONNE           5.80.3
TILL THEN GIVE LEAVE TO ME IN PLEASANT MEW           5.80.9
GIVEN                     14
NINE WORTHIE $WOMEN TO THE $WORLD WERE GIVEN         2.18.8
BY ALL THE $WOUNDS THAT EVER THOU HAST GIV'N         2.36.12
```

```
DECLARE WHAT $FATE UNLUCKY $STARRES HAVE GIVEN        2.60.3
NOW IF THOU WOULD'ST, WHEN ALL HAVE GIVEN
                            HIM OVER                  2.61.13
NINE WORTHY MEN UNTO THE WORLD WERE GIVEN             2.108.8
DECLARE WHAT FATE UNLUCKY STARRES HAVE GIVEN          2.149.3
THE BOUNTIOUS LARGESSE GIVEN THEE TO GIVE+            3.4.6
TO SUBJECTS WORSE HAVE GIVEN ADMIRING PRAISE          3.59.14
AND GIVEN GRACE A DOUBLE $MAJESTIE                    3.78.8
AND GIVEN TO TIME YOUR OWNE DEARE PURCHAS'D
                            RIGHT                     3.117.6
UPON THAT COAST, AM GIV'N UP FOR A SLAVE              4.29.14
OF HER HIGH HEART GIV'N ME THE MONARCHIE              4.69.10
GIVEN SO GOODLY GIFTES OF BEAUTIES GRACE+             5.31.2
A DREADFULL COUNTENAUNCE SHE GIVEN HATH               5.31.6
GIVES                   21
AND NEVER MERCY TO THY MERIT GIVES                    1.22.12
AND YEELD ME NOUGHT THAT GIVES THEM THEIR RENOWNE     1.28.8
THEN JUDGE THE WORLD HER BEAUTY GIVES THE SAME        1.57.12
TO ONE $MAN GIVES, DOTH ON ANOTHER SPEND             2.10.6
GIVES HER THAT $NAME, AS SHE THE $BODY MOVES          2.12.4
NOR GIVES $ME ONCE, BUT ONE POORE MINUTES REST        2.20.4
UNCERTAINE $DREAD GIVES $WINGS UNTO MY $HOPE          2.26.5
THOUGH $FEARE GIVES THEM MORE THEN A $HEAV'NLY
                            $SCOPE                    2.26.8
WITH THOSE RICH $BEAUTIES $HEAV'N GIVES
                            YOU TO KEEPE              2.58.12
UNCERTAINE-DREAD, GYVES WINGS UNTO MY HOPE            2.137.5
YET FEARE GYVES THEM MORE THEN A HEAVENLY SCOPE       2.137.8
NATURES BEQUEST GIVES NOTHING BUT DOTH LEND           3.4.3
SO LONG LIVES THIS, AND THIS GIVES LIFE TO THEE       3.18.14
BLESSED ARE YOU WHOSE WORTHINESSE GIVES SKOPE         3.52.13
THE $CHARTER OF THY WORTH GIVES THEE RELEASING        3.87.3
TO SPEAKE OF THAT WHICH GIVES THEE ALL
                            THY MIGHT+                3.100.2
AND GIVES THY PEN BOTH SKILL AND ARGUMENT             3.100.8
NOR GIVES TO NECESSARY WRINCKLES PLACE                3.108.11
FOR THAT DEEPE WOUND IT GIVES MY FRIEND AND ME        3.133.2
SINCE KIND OR CHANCE GIVES BOTH ONE LIVERIE           4.96.2
GIVES ME GREAT HOPE OF YOUR RELENTING MYND            5.28.2
GIVEST                   1
THAT GIV'ST NO BETTER EARE TO MY JUST CRIES           4.65.2
GIVING                   5
BOYL'D WITH HER $SIGHES, IN GIVING UP THE $GHOST      2.15.7
GIVING HIM AYDE, MY VERSE ASTONISHED                  3.86.8
WAS USDE IN GIVING GENTLE DOME                        3.145.7
WITH SWORD OF WIT, GIVING WOUNDS OF DISPRAISE         4.10.10
SO SHALL YOU LIVE BY GIVING LIFE TO ME                5.49.14
GLAD                    10
AND $QUEENES HEREAFTER SHALL BE GLAD TO LIVE          2.6.7
AND IN A MOMENT $MAD, $SOBER, $GLAD, AND $SORRIE      2.49.10
AND I AM GLAD, YEA GLAD WITHALL MY HEART              2.61.3
AND I AM GLAD, YEA GLAD WITHALL MY HEART              2.61.3
MAKE GLAD AND SORRY SEASONS AS THOU FLEET'ST          3.19.5
THIS TOLD, I JOY, BUT THEN NO LONGER GLAD             3.45.13
GLAD IF FOR HER HE GIVE THEM LEAVE TO DIE             4.43.8
SICKE, THIRSTY, GLAD (THOUGH BUT OF EMPTY
                            GLASSE)                   4.104.11
SOMETIMES I JOY WHEN GLAD OCCASION FITS               5.54.5
AND MY GLAD MOUTH WITH HER SWEET PRAYSES FILL         5.85.12
```

GLADDETH   2
  WITH ONE MORE $ORDER, THESE NINE $ORDERS
                          GLADDETH   2.18.12
  WITH ONE MORE ORDER, THESE NINE ORDERS GLADDETH   2.108.12
GLADLY   4
  WHY LOV'ST THOU THAT WHICH THOU RECEAVST
                          NOT GLADLY   3.8.3
  OF GENTLE FORCE, SO THAT MINE EYES DARE
                          GLADLY PLAY   4.76.6
  AS MEANES OF BLISSE I GLADLY WIL EMBRACE   5.25.12
  IN SLAYING HIM THAT WOULD LIVE GLADLY YOURS+   5.57.12
GLADNESS   2
  AND ME REVIVED WITH HART ROBBING GLADNESSE   5.39.8
  OF ALL WORLDS GLADNESSE MORE MY TORMENT FEED   5.52.12
GLADSOME   1
  INTO THE GLOOMING WORLD HIS GLADSOME RAY   5.62.10
GLANCE   6
  GET NOT ONE GLANCE, TO RECOMPENCE MY $MERIT+   2.43.4
  WHY WITH THE TIME DO I NOT GLANCE ASIDE   3.76.3
  DEARE HEART FORBEARE TO GLANCE THINE EYE ASIDE   3.139.6
  FED ON THE FULNESSE OF THAT CHEAREFULL GLAUNCE   5.39.12
  NE ONE LIGHT GLANCE OF SENSUALL DESYRE   5.84.3
  WHEREOF SOME GLANCE DOTH IN MINE EIE REMAYNE   5.88.8
GLANCING   1
  I MOTE PERCEIVE HOW IN HER GLAUNCING SIGHT   5.16.5
GLASS   26
  WHY DOOST THOU $DELIA CREDIT SO THY GLASSE   1.37.1
  THEN LEAVE THY GLASSE, AND GAZE THY SELFE ON ME   1.37.9
  WHEN, IF SHE GRIEVE TO GAZE HER IN HER GLASSE   1.38.9
  RECEIVED HAST THIS MESSAGE FROM THY GLASSE   1.41.3
  IN WHOM, $HEAV'N LOCKES IT SELFE AS IN A $GLASSE   2.17.4
  TIME, LOOKE THOU TOO, IN THIS $TRALUCENT $GLASSE   2.17.5
  WHERE HEAVEN BEHOLDS HER IN A MORTALL GLASSE   2.107.4
  NAY, LOOKE THEE $TIME IN THIS $CELESTIALL GLASSE   2.107.5
  LOOKING INTO THE GLASSE OF MY YOUTHS MISERIES   2.114.1
  WONDER OF $HEAVEN, GLASSE OF DIVINITIE   2.123.1
  LOOKE IN THY GLASSE AND TELL THE FACE THOU VEWEST   3.3.1
  THOU ART THY MOTHERS GLASSE AND SHE IN THEE   3.3.9
  A LIQUID PRISONER PENT IN WALLS OF GLASSE   3.5.10
  MY GLASSE SHALL NOT PERSWADE ME I AM OULD   3.22.1
  BUT WHEN MY GLASSE SHEWES ME MY SELFE INDEED   3.62.9
  THY GLASSE WILL SHEW THEE HOW THY BEAUTIES WERE   3.77.1
  THE WRINCKLES WHICH THY GLASSE WILL TRULY SHOW   3.77.5
  LOOKE IN YOUR GLASSE AND THERE APPEARES A FACE   3.103.6
  YOUR OWNE GLASSE SHOWES YOU, WHEN YOU
                          LOOKE IN IT   3.103.14
  DOEST HOULD TIMES FICKLE GLASSE, HIS SICKLE,
                          HOWER   3.126.2
  WHICH LOOKES TOO OFT IN HIS UNFLATTRING GLASSE   4.27.10
  HIS WHO TILL DEATH LOOKT IN A WATRIE GLASSE   4.82.3
  SICKE, THIRSTY, GLAD (THOUGH BUT OF EMPTY
                          GLASSE)   4.104.11
  DEAD GLASSE, DOOST THOU THY OBJECT SO IMBRACE   4.105.3
  NOR UNTO GLASSE.. SUCH BASENESSE MOUGHT
                          OFFEND HER   5.9.12
  LEAVE LADY IN YOUR GLASSE OF CHRISTALL CLENE   5.45.1
GLASSES   1
  THE GLASSES OF THY DAYLY VEXING CARE+'   4.34.3
GLAZED   1
  THAT HATH HIS WINDOWES GLAZED WITH THINE EYES   3.24.8

GLEAMS   1
  LEAST IF NO VAILE THOSE BRAVE GLEAMES DID DISGUISE   4.7.7
GLEED   2
  WHOSE SCORCHING GLEED, MY HEART TO $CINDERS
                              TURNETH   2.40.10
  WITH SCORCHING GLEED MY HART TO CYNDERS TURNETH   2.144.10
GLIDE   2
  ELSE SHOULD MY $LINES GLIDE ON THE $WAVES
                              OF $RHENE   2.25.3
  THE SWEET EYE-GLAUNCES, THAT LIKE ARROWES GLIDE   5.17.9
GLISTERING   3
  AND THEN DESCRIED THE GLISTRING OF HIS DART   4.20.13
  HER FLAMIE GLISTRING LIGHTS INCREASE WITH
                              TIME AND PLACE   4.76.10
  MODELS SUCH BE WOOD-GLOBES OF GLISTRING SKIES   4.91.11
GLOBE   1
  THE GLOBE OF WEALE, LIPS $LOVE'S INDENTURES MAKE   4.85.13
GLOOMING   1
  INTO THE GLOOMING WORLD HIS GLADSOME RAY   5.62.10
GLORIED   1
  SMYLING, AS THOUGH HE GLORIED IN HIS DEATH   2.135.12
GLORIFIED   1
  AND BY INSPIRING, GLORIFIDE MY QUILL   2.104.11
GLORIOUS   17
  WHOSE GLORIOUS BLAZE THE WORLD DOTH SO ADMIRE   1.38.6
  WHOSE GLORIOUS ACTICNS LUCKILY HAD GAIND   1.45.7
  THE GLORIOUS SUN-BEAMES OF HER EYES BRIGHT
                              SHINING   2.109.10
  THE GLORIOUS SUNNE WENT BLUSHING TO HIS BED   2.125.1
  WHOSE GLORIOUS HAND IMMORTALL HATH ENROLD THEE   2.129.12
  FULL MANY A GLORICUS MORNING HAVE I SEENE   3.33.1
  O EYES, WHERE HUMBLE LOOKES MOST GLORIOUS PROVE   4.42.5
  THE GLORIOUS POURTRAICT OF THAT $ANGELS FACE   5.17.1
  IN WHICH HER GLORICUS YMAGE PLACED IS   5.22.6
  THEN WOULD I DECKE HER HEAD WITH GLORIOUS BAYES   5.29.13
  AND THAT SAME GLORICUS BEAUTIES YDLE BOAST   5.41.9
  THE GLORIOUS IMAGE CF THE MAKERS BEAUTIE   5.61.1
  MOST GLORIOUS $LORD OF LYFE THAT ON THIS DAY   5.68.1
  THE HAPPY PURCHASE CF MY GLORIOUS SPOILE   5.69.13
  AND IN THE HEVENS WRYTE YOUR GLORIOUS NAME   5.75.12
  SHALL TURNE TO NOUGHT AND LOOSE THAT GLORIOUS HEW   5.79.6
  YOUR GLORIOUS NAME IN GOLDEN MONIMENT   5.82.8
GLORIOUSLY   1
  IN GOODLY COLOURS GLORICUSLY ARRAYD   5.70.4
GLORY   43
  AND MUST THEIR GLORY TO THE WORLD IMPART   1.10.12
  BUT AH, WHAT GLORIE CAN SHE GET THEREBY   1.27.11
  GLORY DOTH FOLLOW, COURAGE GOES BEFORE   1.35.7
  YOUR FIRY HEATE LETS NOT HER GLORY PASSE   1.38.13
  NO SOONER SPREADS HER GLORY IN THE AYRE   1.39.5
  WHOSE SPRINGING GRACE ADORNS THY GLORY NOW   1.39.10
  WHEN ONCE THEY FIND HER FLOWRE HER GLORY PAS   1.40.14
  WHEN MEN SHALL FIND THY FLOWER, THY GLORY PASSE   1.41.1
  HOW MANY LIVE, THE GLORY OF WHOSE NAME   1.44.7
  SHORT IS THE GLORY OF THE BLUSHING $ROSE   1.50.6
  FLORISH FAIRE $ALBICN, GLORY OF THE $NORTH   1.53.9
  THY CRUELTY, THY GLCRY., $O STRANGE CASE   1.56.10
  TO HAVE SEENE THEE, THEIR $SEXES ONELY GLORY   2.6.12
  THERE LET MY $VERSE GET GLORY IN THE $NORTH   2.25.7
  ARDENS SWEET $ANKCR, LET THY GLORY BEE   2.32.13

```
AND SUFF'RED HER TO GLORY IN MY $WRACKE                    2.36.3
NO PUBLIKE $GLORIE VAINELY I PURSUE                        2.47.13
BEAUTY SOMETIME IN ALL HER GLORY CROWNED                   2.109.1
ARDENS SWEET $ANKOR LET THY GLORY BE                       2.124.13
OR GLORIE OF MY $APRILL-SPRINGING YEERES                   2.138.2
FOR AT A FROWNE THEY IN THEIR GLORY DIE                    3.25.8
AND BY A PART OF ALL THY GLORY LIVE                        3.37.12
CROOKED ECLIPSES GAINST HIS GLORY FIGHT                    3.60.7
WHICH SHALL BE MOST MY GLORY BEING DOMBE                   3.83.10
THAT TO HIS SUBJECT LENDS NOT SOME SMALL GLORY             3.84.6
THAT THOU IN LOOSING ME, SHALL WIN MUCH GLORY              3.88.8
SOME GLORY IN THEIR BIRTH, SOME IN THEIR SKILL             3.91.1
DOTH HALFE THAT GLORY TO THE SOBER $WEST                   3.132.8
OR ELSE LET THEM IN STATELIER GLORIE SHINE                 4.3.5
WHEN MOST I GLORIE, THEN I FEELE MOST SHAME                4.19.3
AND THIS WORLDS WORTHLESSE GLORY TO EMBASE                 5.17.3
BUT TAKETH GLORY IN HER CRUELNESSE                         5.20.12
SITH ALL WORLDS GLORIE IS BUT DROSSE UNCLEANE              5.27.2
TO SING THE GLORY OF THEIR FAMOUS DEEDES                   5.29.8
ALL THIS WORLDS GLORY SEEMETH VAYNE TO ME                 5.35.13
THEN THINKE HOW LITLE GLORY YE HAVE GAYNED                 5.36.10
AND GREATER GLORY THINKE TO SAVE, THEN SPILL               5.49.4
BUT GLORY THINKE TO MAKE THESE CRUEL STOURES               5.57.10
YE CRUELL ONE, WHAT GLORY CAN BE GOT                       5.57.11
BUT YE THEREBY MUCH GREATER GLORY GATE                     5.66.9
RESEMBLING HEAVENS GLORY IN HER LIGHT                      5.72.6
TO SPEAKE HER PRAYSE AND GLORY EXCELLENT                   5.74.11
ALL THIS WORLDS GLORY SEEMETH VAYNE TO ME                 5.83.13
GLORY'S                           1
  HER GLORIES PRIDE THAT NONE MAY IT REPAYRE               5.58.8
GLOVE                           3
  SEATED WITH $SOL, AND WEARES $MINERVAS GLOVE             2.151.12
  EACH HAD HIS CREAST, $MARS CARIED $VENUS' GLOVE          4.13.7
  BID'N, PERHAPS HE FETCHETH THEE A GLOVE                  4.59.7
GLOWING                         1
  IN ME THOU SEEST THE GLOWING OF SUCH FIRE                3.73.9
GLUTTON                         1
  PITTY THE WORLD, OR ELSE THIS GLUTTON BE                 3.1.13
GLUTTONING                      1
  OR GLUTTONING ON ALL, OR ALL AWAY                        3.75.14
GLUTTON'S                       1
  NO OTHER $DRINKE WOULD SERVE THIS $GLUTTONS TURNE        2.7.5
GO                             37
  GOE WAILING $VERSE, THE $INFANTS OF MY LOVE              1.2.1
  I GOE BEFORE UNTO THE $MIRTLE SHADES                     1.30.5
  GOE YOU MY VERSE, GO TELL HER WHAT SHE WAS               1.38.11
  GOE YOU MY VERSE, GO TELL HER WHAT SHE WAS               1.38.11
  AND WHITHER (POORE FORSAKEN) WILT THOU GOE               1.52.1
  TO GOE FROM SORROW, AND THINE OWNE DISTRESSE+            1.52.2
  YET GOE (FORSAKEN) LEAVE THESE $WOODS,
                         THESE PLAINES                     1.52.5
  LEAVING THE $PATH THE GREATER PART DOE GOE               2.9.4
  I GREATLY MARVELL, HOW YOU STILL GOE FREE                2.14.3
  THEN $FOOLES AND $CHILDREN FITT'ST TO
                         GO TOGETHER                       2.22.8
  IF WHEN $NIGHT COMES, YOU BID ME GOE AWAY                2.37.14
  SITTING ALONE, $LOVE BIDS ME GOE AND WRITE               2.38.1
  POORE $ROGUE, GOE PAWNE THY $FASCIA AND THY $BOW         2.48.3
  GOE HYRE THY SELFE SOME BUNGLING $HARPERS $BOY           2.48.10
  ME THINKES I $FLIE, YET WANT I LEGGES TO $GOE            2.62.5
```

```
SITTING ALONE, LOVE BIDS ME GOE AND WRITE           2.131.1
GOE $BASTARD GOE, FOR SURE OF THENCE THOU ART       2.140.14
GOE $BASTARD GOE, FOR SURE OF THENCE THOU ART       2.140.14
MEE THINKS I FLEE, YET WANT I LEGS TO GOE           2.150.5
GOE YOU MY LYNES, $EMBASSADORS OF LOVE              2.151.1
THAT THOU AMONG THE WASTES OF TIME MUST GOE         3.12.10
OR SAY WITH $PRINCES IF IT SHAL GO WEL              3.14.7
TOWARDS THEE ILE RUN, AND GIVE HIM LEAVE TO GOE     3.51.14
AND THAT WHICH GOVERNES ME TO GOE ABOUT             3.113.2
I GRAUNT I NEVER SAW A GODDESSE GOE                 3.130.11
BEARE THINE EYES STRAIGHT, THOUGH THY
                         PROUD HEART GOE WIDE        3.140.14
WHEN INTO $REASON'S AUDITE I DO GO                  4.18.2
LET HER GO. $SOFT, BUT HERE SHE COMES. $GO TO       4.47.12
LET HER GO. $SOFT, BUT HERE SHE COMES. $GO TO       4.47.12
STRIVING ABROAD A FORAGING TO GO                    4.55.6
DESIRE STILL ON THE STILTS OF FEARE DOTH GO         4.66.8
PRAY THAT MY SUNNE GO DOWNE WITH MEEKER
                         BEAMES TO BED              4.76.14
ONLY TRUE SIGHS, YOU DO NOT GO AWAY                 4.95.12
I GOE LYKE ONE THAT HAVING LOST THE FIELD           5.52.2
GOE TO MY LOVE, WHERE SHE IS CARELESSE LAYD         5.70.5
LACKYNG MY LOVE I GO FROM PLACE TO PLACE            5.78.1
GOE VISIT HER IN HER CHAST BOWRE OF REST            5.84.7
GOD                          14
HERE SEE THE GIFTS THAT $GOD AND NATURE LENT THEE   1.42.7
FOR $GOD FORBID I SHOULD MY $PAPERS BLOT            1.58.5
O $GOD FROM $YOU, THAT I COULD PRIVATE BE           2.11.2
IF IT MIGHT PLEASE $YOU, WOULD TO $GOD $YOU COULD   2.19.4
WOULD $GOD I WERE AS IGNORANT AS THEY               2.43.11
CRYES IN HIS PANGS, $GOD HELPE THE MOTHERLESSE      2.116.18
NO $GOD ART THOU, A $GODDESSE SHEE DOTH PROVE       2.126.3
THAT $GOD FORBID, THAT MADE ME FIRST YOUR SLAVE     3.58.1
A $GOD IN LOVE, TO WHOM I AM CONFIN'D               3.110.12
TILL THAT GOOD $GOD MAKE $CHURCH AND $CHURCHMAN
                         STARVE                     4.5.8
BUT ($GOD WOT) WOT NOT WHAT THEY MEANE BY IT        4.74.6
O $GOD, THINKE YOU THAT SATISFIES MY CARE+          4.92.8
SO SINCE THE WINGED $GOD HIS PLANET CLEARE          5.60.5
WHOSE SWEET ASPECT BOTH $GOD AND MAN CAN MOVE       5.89.11
GODDESS                      12
ALL UNAWARES, A $GODDESSE CHASTE I FINDE            1.5.3
LAUGHTER LOVING $GODDESSE, WORLDLY PLEASURES
                         $QUEENE                    1.10.6
AND WANTING $FRIENDS, THOUGH OF A $GODDESSE BORNE   2.23.3
THOU ART MY $VESTA, THOU MY $GODDESSE ART           2.30.13
NOW CALL HER $GODDESSE, THEN I CALL HER $THIEFE     2.41.12
YET TO MY $GODDESSE AM I CONSTANT EVER              2.51.11
NO $GOD ART THOU, A $GODDESSE SHEE DOTH PROVE       2.126.3
YET THOU A $GODDESSE ART, AND SO DIVINE             2.140.8
NOW CALL HER $GODDESSE, THEN I CALL HER THIEFE      2.143.12
THE GUILTIE GODDESSE OF MY HARMFULL DEEDS           3.111.2
I GRAUNT I NEVER SAW A GODDESSE GOE                 3.130.11
THE WHICH VOUCHSAFE $O GODDESSE TO ACCEPT           5.22.13
GODDESSES                    1
THE $GODDESSES OF $MEMORY AND $WIT                  2.4.3
GODS                         8
THESE WITH THE $GODS ARE EVER RESIDENT              2.18.7
THESE WITH THE $GODS ARE EVER RESIDENT              2.108.7
SOME INVOCATE THE $GODS, SOME SPIRITS OF $HELL      2.118.3
```

```
AND TELL THE $GODS, $MARS IS PREDOMINANT          2.151.11
 OF THOSE THREE GODS, WHOSE ARMES THE FAIREST WERE  4.13.2
 WHOM ALL THE $GODS IN COUNCELL DID AGREE           5.24.9
 FOR WHICH THE GODS IN THEYR REVENGEFULL YRE        5.28.11
 WHEN ALL THE GODS HE THREATS WITH THUNDRING DART   5.39.4
GOD'S            1
 WITH ME THOSE PAINES FOR $GOD'S SAKE DO NOT TAKE   4.28.3
GODS'            1
 THE $GODS PURE FIRE HATH BEEN EXTINGUISHT QUITE    2.105.2
GOD-WARD         1
 THE $SPIRIT, WHEN IT TO $GOD-WARD DOTH INFLAME     2.12.12
GOES             3
 GLORY DOTH FOLLOW, COURAGE GOES BEFORE             1.35.7
 THAT EV'RY $DUDGEN LOW $INVENTION GOES+            2.31.8
 EACH CHANGING PLACE WITH THAT WHICH GOES BEFORE    3.60.3
GOEST            1
 AS THOU GOEST ONWARDS STILL WILL PLUCKE
                             THEE BACKE            3.126.6
GOING            1
 SINCE FROM THEE GOING, HE WENT WILFULL SLOW        3.51.13
GOLD            14
 THAT $GOLD NOR $HONOUR NE'R HAD POW'R TO MOVE      2.15.4
 THE $WELL OF $NECTAR, PAV'D WITH PEARLE
                             AND GOLD              2.109.13
 OF PUREST GOLD, TEMPRED WITH VERTUES FIRE          2.126.7
 AND OFTEN IS HIS GOLD COMPLEXION DIMM'D            3.18.6
 AS THOSE GOULD CANDELLS FIXT IN HEAVENS AYER       3.21.12
 ENAM'LING WITH PIED FLOWERS THEIR THOUGHTS OF GOLD 4.3.4
 GOLD IS THE COVERING OF THAT STATELY PLACE         4.9.4
 WHENCE HAST THOU $IVORIE, $RUBIES, PEARLE
                             AND GOLD              4.32.10
 VERTUE'S GOLD NOW MUST HEAD MY $CUPID'S DART       4.72.8
 AH WHAT DOTH $PHOEBUS' GOLD THAT WRETCH AVAILE     4.108.10
 IF $GOLD, HER LOCKS ARE FINEST GOLD ON GROUND      5.15.11
 IF $GOLD, HER LOCKS ARE FINEST GOLD ON GROUND      5.15.11
 SHE DOTH ATTYRE UNDER A NET OF GOLD                5.37.2
 THAT WHICH IS GOLD OR HEARE, MAY SCARSE BE TOLD+   5.37.4
GOLDEN          30
 RESTORE THY TRESSES TO THE GOLDEN $ORE             1.19.1
 WHEN GOLDEN HAIRES SHALL CHANGE TO SILVER WIER     1.38.2
 AND RANSACKE ALL $APOLLOS GOLDEN $TREASURE         2.21.12
 WITH THOSE SWEET STRINGS STOLNE FROM THY
                             GOLDEN HAYRE          2.104.2
 HER GOLDEN BEAMES HAD NOW DISCOVERED               2.125.3
 THE GOLDEN $SUNNE UPON HIS FIERY WHEELES           2.147.1
 DISPIGHT OF WRINKLES THIS THY GOULDEN TIME         3.3.12
 ATTENDING ON HIS GOULDEN PILGRIMAGE                3.7.8
 KISSING WITH GOLDEN FACE THE MEDDOWES GREENE       3.33.3
 BEFORE THE GOULDEN TRESSES OF THE DEAD             3.68.5
 RESERVE THEIR $CHARACTER WITH GOULDEN QUILL        3.85.3
 BROADRED WITH BULS AND SWANS, POWDRED
                             WITH GOLDEN RAINE      4.6.6
 JOVES GOLDEN SHIELD DID $EAGLE SABLES BEARE        4.13.3
 BUT IN $VERT FIELD $MARS BARE A GOLDEN SPEARE      4.13.5
 SURE YOU SAY WELL, YOUR WISDOME'S GOLDEN MINE      4.21.12
 PROGRESSING THEN FROM FAIRE TWINNES' GOLD'N PLACE  4.22.2
 HOLDS MY YOUNG BRAINE CAPTIV'D IN GOLDEN CAGE      4.23.11
 HOW $ULSTER LIKES OF THAT SAME GOLDEN BIT          4.30.9
 DOUBT THERE HATH BENE, WHEN WITH HIS GOLDEN
                             CHAINE                4.58.1
```

RAVISHT, STAID NOT, TILL IN HER GOLDEN HAIRE   4.103.7
WHAT GUYLE IS THIS, THAT THOSE HER GOLDEN TRESSES   5.37.1
SHE MAY ENTANGLE IN THAT GOLDEN SNARE   5.37.6
TO COVET FETTERS, THOUGH THEY GOLDEN BEE   5.37.14
FORGETFULL OF THE FAMOUS GOLDEN FLEECE   5.44.3
FOR THEY ARE LYKE BUT UNTO GOLDEN HOOKES   5.47.3
BUT THE FAYRE TRESSES OF YOUR GOLDEN HAYRE   5.73.3
TWOO GOLDEN APPLES CF UNVALEWD PRICE   5.77.6
FAYRE IS MY LOVE, WHEN HER FAYRE GOLDEN HEARES   5.81.1
YOUR GLORIOUS NAME IN GOLDEN MONIMENT   5.82.8
HER WORTH IS WRITTEN WITH A GOLDEN QUILL   5.85.10

GONE   19
THAT TELLS THE TRUTH, AND SAYES THAT ALL IS GONE   1.41.4
AND STRAIGHT TIS GONE AS IT HAD NEVER BEENE   1.50.4
MAKE ME TO SAY, WHEN ALL MY GRIEFES ARE GONE   1.51.13
THAT SHE IS GONE, HER LIKE AGAINE TO SEE   2.17.14
AND FROM MY BREAST INTO THINE EYES BE GONE   2.103.14
THEN HOW WHEN NATURE CALLS THEE TO BE GONE   3.4.11
SAP CHECKT WITH FRCST AND LUSTIE LEAV'S QUITE GON   3.5.7
HUNG WITH THE TROPHEIS OF MY LOVERS GON   3.31.10
TO LEAPE LARGE LENGTHS CF MILES WHEN THOU
                                      ART GONE   3.44.10
FOR WHEN THESE QUICKER $ELEMENTS ARE GONE   3.45.5
TYR'D WITH ALL THESE, FROM THESE WOULD I BE GONE   3.66.13
AND MOCKE YOU WITH ME AFTER I AM GON   3.71.14
THOUGH I (ONCE GONE) TO ALL THE WORLD MUST DYE   3.81.6
ALAS 'TIS TRUE, I HAVE GONE HERE AND THERE   3.110.1
IS GONE, AND NOW LIKE SLAVE-BORNE $MUSCOVITE   4.2.10
THAT THROUGH MY HEART THEIR BEAMIE DARTS BE GONE   4.48.10
GONE IS THE WINTER CF MY MISERIE   4.69.7
WHERE BE THOSE $RCSES GCNE, WHICH SWEETNED
                          SO OUR EYES+   4.102.1
BUT THOU ART GONE, NOW THAT SELFE FELT DISGRACE   4.106.7

GOOD   58
PRESSE TO HER EYES, IMPCRTUNE ME SOME GOOD   1.2.11
GOOD $DELIA LOSE, QUENCH, HEALE ME NOW AT LENGTH   1.14.14
AND CANNOT ISSUE FORTH TO SEEKE HER GOOD   1.29.4
IN LIFE AND DEATH $ILE TENDER HER GOOD NAME   1.30.11
LET WHAT I PRAISE, BE STILL MADE GOOD BY YOU   2.4.13
AND MY GOOD $ANGELL (IN MY $SOULE DIVINE)   2.18.11
BY THIS GOOD WICKED $SPIRIT, SWEET $ANGELL
                              $DEVILL   2.20.14
INTREATED ME, AS E'R I WISH'D HIS GOOD   2.21.3
WITH $FOOLES AND $CHILDREN GOOD $DISCRETICN
                              BEARES   2.22.1
BUT THIS UNGRATEFULL, FCR MY GOOD DESERT   2.23.9
THE $CIRCUMSTANCE DCTH MAKE IT GOOD, OR ILL   2.28.14
ONELY COMPELL'D ON THIS POORE GOOD TO BOAST   2.43.13
NOT TO AVAILE YOU, NOR DCE OTHERS GOOD   2.58.14
AND MY GOOD $ANGELL IN MY SOULE DIVINE   2.108.11
YET IN THESE JOYES, THE SHADOWES OF MY GCOD   2.114.9
MY SWEET, MY FAIRE, MY GOOD, MY BEST OF ALL   2.115.12
YET FAIRE UNKINDE, TO GCCD TO BE DISGRACEC   2.138.14
CHEEFE GOOD, FROM WHOM ALL GOOD THINGS WE DERIVE   2.146.8
CHEEFE GOOD, FROM WHOM ALL GOOD THINGS WE DERIVE   2.146.8
BUT NOT TO TELL OF GOOD, OR EVIL LUCKE   3.14.3
BUT THAT I HOPE SCME GOCD CONCEIPT OF THINE   3.26.7
AS THOU BEING MINE, MINE IS THY GOOD REPORT   3.36.14
AND EACH DOTH GOOD TURNES NOW UNTO THE OTHER   3.47.2
SO THOU BE GOOD, SLANDER DOTH BUT APPROVE   3.70.5

```
I THINKE GOOD THOUGHTS, WHILST OTHER WRITE
                    GOOD WORDES                      3.85.5
I THINKE GOOD THOUGHTS, WHILST OTHER WRITE
                    GOOD WORDES                      3.85.5
AS THOU BEING MINE, MINE IS THY GOOD REPORT          3.96.14
TO LEAVE FOR NOTHING ALL THY SUMME OF GOOD           3.109.12
SO YOU ORE-GREENE MY BAD, MY GOOD ALOW+              3.112.4
WHICH IN THEIR WILS COUNT BAD WHAT I THINK GOOD+     3.121.8
YET IN GOOD FAITH SOME SAY THAT THEE BEHOLD          3.131.5
TILL MY BAD ANGEL FIRE MY GOOD ONE OUT               3.144.14
TILL THAT GOOD $GOD MAKE $CHURCH AND $CHURCHMAN
                    STARVE                           4.5.8
BY REASON GOOD, GOOD REASON HER TO LOVE              4.10.14
BY REASON GOOD, GOOD REASON HER TO LOVE              4.10.14
AND WHICH IS WORSE, NO GOOD EXCUSE CAN SHOW          4.18.7
HOW $HOLLAND HEARTS, NOW SO GOOD TOWNES BE LOST      4.30.7
I, CUMBRED WITH GOOD MANERS, ANSWER DO               4.30.13
LISTEN THEN $LORDINGS WITH GOOD EARE TO ME           4.37.3
I WILL GOOD TRIBUTE PAY IF THOU DO SO                4.39.8
AS GOOD TO WRITE AS FOR TO LIE AND GRONE             4.40.1
HIS PRAISE TO SLEIGHT, WHICH FROM GOOD
                    USE DOTH RISE                    4.41.7
NO $PATIENCE, IF THOU WILT MY GOOD, THEN MAKE        4.56.12
WHEN MY GOOD $ANGELL GUIDES ME TO THE PLACE          4.60.1
WHERE ALL MY GOOD I DO IN $STELLA SEE                4.60.2
THEN SOME GOOD BODY TELL ME HOW I DO                 4.60.12
THOU WHOM TO ME SUCH MY GOOD TURNES SHOULD BIND      4.65.3
CHIEFE GOOD, WHERETO MY HOPE DOTH ONLY ASPIRE        4.68.3
AS FAST THY $VERTUE BENDS THAT LOVE TO GOOD          4.71.13
SO AMPLE EARES AS NEVER GOOD NEWES KNOW              4.78.13
GOOD BROTHER $PHILIP, I HAVE BORNE YOU LONG          4.83.1
BE YOUR WORDS MADE (GOOD $SIR) OF $INDIAN WARE       4.92.1
THOUGHT WITH GOOD CAUSE THOU LIKEST SO
                    WELL THE NIGHT                    4.96.1
SO NEERE, IN SO GOOD TIME, SO FREE A PLACE+          4.105.2
CHOSE RATHER TO BE PRAYSD FOR DOOING GOOD            5.38.13
AND SPEAKE HER GOOD, THOUGH SHE REQUITE IT ILL       5.48.14
GOOD SHAMES TO BE TO ILL AN INSTRUMENT               5.53.12
BUT SIMPLE TRUTH AND MUTUALL GOOD WILL               5.65.11
GOODLY               19
HE OF TALL BUILDING, AND OF GOODLY PRIDE             3.80.12
AND HER FAIRE COUNTENANCE LIKE A GOODLY BANNER       5.5.11
RESEMBLE TH'YMAGE OF THEIR GOODLY LIGHT              5.9.4
IN THAT PROUD PORT, WHICH HER SO GOODLY GRACETH      5.13.1
MOST GOODLY TEMPERATURE YE MAY DESCRY                5.13.4
AND RARE PERFECTION OF EACH GOODLY PART              5.24.2
THAT GOODLY $IDOLL NOW SO GAY BESEENE                5.27.5
GIVEN SO GOODLY GIFTES OF BEAUTIES GRACE+            5.31.2
THRUGH THE BROAD WORLD DOTH SPRED HIS GOODLY RAY     5.40.8
THEN ALL HER NATURES GOODLY GUIFTS ARE LOST          5.41.8
YOUR GOODLY SELFE FOR EVERMORE TO VEW                5.45.2
THE GOODLY YMAGE OF YOUR VISNOMY                     5.45.11
FOR WITH THE GOODLY SEMBLANT OF HER HEW              5.53.6
HER GOODLY BOSOME LYKE A $STRAWBERRY BED             5.64.9
SO GOODLY WONNE WITH HER OWNE WILL BEGUYLD           5.67.14
IN GOODLY COLOURS GLORIOUSLY ARRAYD                  5.70.4
A GOODLY TABLE OF PURE YVORY                         5.77.2
HER GOODLY LIGHT WITH SMILES SHE DRIVES AWAY         5.81.8
BUT SINCE YE DEIGND SO GOODLY TO RELENT              5.82.9
```

```
GOODNESS                      3
   WHICH RANCKE OF GOODNESSE WOULD BY ILL BE CURED    3.118.12
   WHICH DIE FOR GOODNES, WHO HAVE LIV'D FOR CRIME    3.124.14
   STELLA, THOSE FAIRE LINES, WHICH TRUE
                          GOODNESSE SHOW              4.71.4
GOODS                         4
   AND SURE AT LENGTH STOLNE GOODS DO COME TO LIGHT   4.15.11
   OF ALL THOSE GOODS, WHICH HEAV'N TO ME HATH LENT   4.18.4
   LIES HATCHING STILL THE GOODS WHEREIN THEY FLOW    4.24.2
   DOTH SUFFER WRECK BOTH OF HER SELFE AND GOODS      5.56.12
GOOD-TURNS                    1
   NOW SEE WHAT GOOD-TURNES EYES FOR EIES HAVE DONE   3.24.9
GOODWILL                      1
   AND WITH HER OWNE GOODWILL HIR FYRMELY TYDE        5.67.12
GORED                         1
   GOR'D MINE OWN THOUGHTS, SOLD CHEAP WHAT
                          IS MOST DEARE               3.110.3
GORGED                        1
   STILL EMPTY GORG'D, WITH CARES CONSUMPTION
                          PYNDE                       2.116.14
GOT                          10   (SEE GATE)
   WHERE $FAME BY $DEATH IS ONELY TO BE GOT           2.24.11
   AS EVERY $ALIEN PEN HATH GOT MY USE                3.78.3
   OH WHAT A MANSION HAVE THOSE VICES GOT             3.95.9
   WHERE $CUPID GOT NEW FIRE., MY MISTRES EYE         3.153.14
   TILL BY DEGREES IT HAD FULL CONQUEST GOT           4.2.4
   HAVING GOT UP A BREACH BY FIGHTING WELL            4.12.10
   AND STRAIGHT THEREWITH, LIKE WAGS NEW
                          GOT TO PLAY                 4.17.13
   YET SINCE MY DEATH-WOUND IS ALREADY GOT            4.48.12
   FOR EASIE THINGS THAT MAY BE GOT AT WILL           5.26.11
   YE CRUELL ONE, WHAT GLORY CAN BE GOT               5.57.11
GOTTEN                        1
   GOTTEN AT LAST WITH LABOUR AND LONG TOYLE          5.69.14
GOVERNS                       1
   AND THAT WHICH GOVERNES ME TO GOE ABOUT            3.113.2
GRACE                        56
   MY HOPES DOE REST IN LIMITS OF HER GRACE           1.12.7
   WHOSE ROWLING GRACE DEIGNE ONCE A TURNE OF BLIS    1.12.12
   OF HER, WHOSE SWEETEST GRACE I DO ADORE            1.13.10
   LOOKE TO THE HEAVENS., THE HEAVENS YEELDE
                          FORTH NO GRACE              1.29.6
   WHOSE SPRINGING GRACE ADORNS THY GLORY NOW         1.39.10
   THAT $GRACE WHICH DOTH MORE THEN IN WOMAN THEE     1.45.13
   THE READY HANDMAYDS ON HER GRACE T'ATTEND          1.48.2
   YET MORE TO GRACE THE $COMPANY WITHALL             2.7.3
   AND TAXE MY $MUSE WITH THIS FANTASTICKE $GRACE     2.31.2
   WHY SHOULD YOUR FAIRE $EYES WITH SUCH
                          SOV'RAIGNE GRACE            2.43.1
   WONNE GRACE AND CREDIT IN THE $EARES OF $MEN       2.47.4
   SO MAY HE GRACE ALL THESE IN HER ALONE             2.148.13
   YET EYES THIS CUNNING WANT TO GRACE THEIR ART      3.24.13
   AND DO'ST HIM GRACE WHEN CLOUDS DOE BLOT
                          THE HEAVEN                  3.28.10
   LASCIVIOUS GRACE, IN WHOM ALL IL WEL SHOWES        3.40.13
   IN ALL EXTERNALL GRACE YOU HAVE SOME PART          3.53.13
   AND WITH HIS PRESENCE GRACE IMPIETIE               3.67.2
   AND GIVEN GRACE A DOUBLE $MAJESTIE                 3.78.8
   MY VERSE ALONE HAD ALL THY GENTLE GRACE            3.79.2
   SOME SAY THY GRACE IS YOUTH AND GENTLE SPORT       3.96.2
```

```
BOTH GRACE AND FAULTS ARE LOV'D OF MORE AND LESSE      3.96.3
TO MOURNE FOR ME SINCE MOURNING DOTH THEE GRACE        3.132.11
AND SWERE THAT BRIGHTNESSE DOTH NOT GRACE
                             THE DAY+                   3.150.4
KNOWLEDGE MIGHT PITIE WINNE, AND PITIE
                             GRACE OBTAINE              4.1.4
THE DOORE BY WHICH SOMETIMES COMES FORTH
                             HER $GRACE                 4.9.5
THAT HER $GRACE GRACIOUS MAKES THY WRONGS,
                             THAT SHE                   4.12.6
BUT STRAIGHT I SAW MOTIONS OF LIGHTNING GRACE          4.20.12
YET EACH PREPAR'D, WITH FANNE'S WEL-SHADING GRACE      4.22.7
BENDS ALL HIS POWERS, EVEN UNTO $STELLA'S GRACE        4.27.14
I READE IT IN THY LOOKES, THY LANGUISHT GRACE          4.31.7
MOVE NOT THY HEAVY GRACE, THOU SHALT IN ME             4.39.13
UPON A WRETCH, THAT LONG THY GRACE HATH SOUGHT         4.40.7
BUT MORE I CRIE, LESSE GRACE SHE DOTH IMPART           4.44.6
THOUGH FALSE, YET WITH FREE SCOPE MORE
                             GRACE DOTH BREED           4.45.10
WITHOUT DESIRE TO FEED OF FURTHER GRACE                4.46.8
A KIND OF GRACE IT IS TO SLAY WITH SPEED               4.48.14
AND THEREFORE, THOUGH HER BEAUTIE AND HER GRACE        4.52.9
MIGHT WINNE SOME GRACE IN YOUR SWEET SKILL ARRAID      4.55.4
OR ELSE PRONOUNCING GRACE, WHEREWITH HIS MIND          4.58.7
ANGER INVESTS WITH SUCH A LOVELY GRACE                 4.73.13
THAT GRACE, WHICH $VENUS WEEPES THAT SHE
                             HER SELFE DOTH MISSE       4.77.4
WHO SINCE HE HATH, BY $NATURE'S SPECIALL GRACE         4.78.9
ADMITTED LATE BY YOUR BEST-GRACED GRACE                4.82.10
CANNOT SUCH GRACE YOUR SILLY SELFE CONTENT             4.83.11
WHAT SOBS CAN GIVE WORDS GRACE MY GRIEFE TO SHOW+      4.93.2
AND ENDLESLY DISPAIRING OF HIS GRACE                   4.97.6
HOW IS THY GRACE BY MY STRANGE FORTUNE STAIND          4.98.3
AND GRACE, SICKE TOO, SUCH FINE CONCLUSIONS
                             TRIES                      4.101.3
PARDON FOR THEE, AND GRACE FOR ME INTREAT              5.2.12
IN VAINE I SEEKE AND SEW TO HER FOR GRACE              5.20.1
DOE BOTH APPEARE T'ADORNE HER BEAUTIES GRACE+          5.21.4
A CLOSE INTENT AT LAST TO SHEW ME GRACE                5.25.10
GIVEN SO GOODLY GIFTES OF BEAUTIES GRACE+              5.31.2
BUT LODWICK, THIS OF GRACE TO ME AREAD                 5.33.5
MAKE PEACE THEREFORE, AND GRAUNT ME TIMELY GRACE       5.57.13
COMMING TO KISSE HER LYPS, (SUCH GRACE I FOUND)        5.64.1
GRACED                    4
THAT ERRORS SHOULD BE GRAC'D THAT MERIT SHAME          1.56.11
AND $ARTS WITH THY SWEETE GRACES GRACED BE             3.78.12
THAT SICKENESSE BRAGS IT SELFE BEST GRACED TO BE       4.101.4
FOR HAD THE EQUALL HEVENS SO MUCH YOU GRACED           5.82.5
GRACEFUL                  1
WHILE GRACEFULL PITTY BEAUTY BEAUTIFIES                4.100.4
GRACES                   12
LET $VENUS HAVE THY GRACES, HER RESIGN'D               1.19.9
AND OF WHAT FORCE THY WOUNDING GRACES ARE              1.37.7
A THOUSAND $NIMPH-LIKE AND INAMOR'D $GRACES            2.4.2
AND YET YOUR $GRACES OUTWARDLY $DIVINE                 2.57.2
AND IN FRESH NUMBERS NUMBER ALL YOUR GRACES            3.17.6
AND $ARTS WITH THY SWEETE GRACES GRACED BE             3.78.12
THEY RIGHTLY DO INHERRIT HEAVENS GRACES                3.94.5
THOU MAKST FAULTS GRACES, THAT TO THEE RESORT          3.96.4
THEN OF YOUR GRACES AND YOUR GIFTS TO TELL             3.103.12
```

```
    WHENCE WORDS, NOT WORDS, BUT HEAV'NLY
                        GRACES SLIDE            4.80.4
    AN HUNDRED $GRACES AS IN SHADE TO SIT        5.40.4
    THAT THREE SUCH GRACES DID UNTO ME GIVE      5.74.14
GRACETH                    1
    IN THAT PROUD PORT, WHICH HER SO GOODLY GRACETH   5.13.1
GRACIOUS                   6
    LOE IN THE $ORIENT WHEN THE GRACIOUS LIGHT   3.7.1
    BE AS THY PRESENCE IS GRACIOUS AND KIND      3.10.11
    ME THINKES NO FACE SO GRATIOUS IS AS MINE    3.62.5
    BUT NOW MY GRACIOUS NUMBERS ARE DECAYDE      3.79.3
    SHALL WILL IN OTHERS SEEME RIGHT GRACIOUS    3.135.7
    THAT HER $GRACE GRACIOUS MAKES THY WRONGS,
                        THAT SHE                4.12.6
GRACIOUSLY                 1
    POINTS ON ME GRATICUSLY WITH FAIRE ASPECT    3.26.10
GRAIN                      3
    THOUGHT IT IN WEIGHT TOO LIGHT BY MANY A $GRAINE   2.38.12
    THOUGHT HER IN WEIGHT TCO LIGHT BY MANY
                        A GRAINE                2.131.12
    WHERE $BEAUTIE'S BLUSH IN $HONOUR'S GRAINE
                        IS DIDE                 4.80.8
GRAMMAR                    4
    O $GRAMMER RULES, C NOW YOUR VERTUES SHOW    4.63.1
    FOR $GRAMMER SAYES (O THIS DEARE $STELLA WEIGHE)   4.63.12
    FOR $GRAMMER SAYES (TO $GRAMMER WHO SAYES NAY)    4.63.13
    FOR $GRAMMER SAYES (TO $GRAMMER WHO SAYES NAY)    4.63.13
GRAMMAR'S                  1
    BUT $GRAMMER'S FORCE WITH SWEET SUCCESSE
                        CONFIRME                4.63.11
GRANDAME                   1
    TILL THAT HIS GRANDAME $NATURE PITTYING IT   4.17.9
GRANT                     16
    GRAUNT IF THOU WILT, THCU ART BELOV'D OF MANY   3.10.3
    I GRANT (SWEET LOVE) THY LOVELY ARGUMENT     3.79.5
    I GRANT THOU WERT NCT MARRIED TO MY $MUSE    3.82.1
    I GRAUNT I NEVER SAW A GODDESSE GOE          3.130.11
    DOTH WILLING GRAUNT, THAT IN THE FRONTIERS HE   4.29.7
    THAT $VERTUE BUT THAT BCDY GRAUNT TO US      4.52.14
    ALAS, IF YOU GRAUNT ONLY SUCH DELIGHT        4.59.12
    DRIV'N ELSE TO GRAUNT BY $ANGEL'S SOPHISTRIE   4.61.13
    HER GRAUNT TO ME, BY HER OWNE VERTUE KNOW    4.63.4
    PARDON THAT FAULT, CNCE MORE GRAUNT ME THE PLACE   4.82.12
    LET HONOR SELFE TC THEE GRAUNT HIGHEST PLACE   4.103.14
    WHICH IF SHE GRAUNT, THEN LIVE AND MY
                        LOVE CHERISH            5.2.13
    TO GRAUNT SMALL RESPIT TO MY RESTLESSE TCILE   5.11.6
    CEASSE THEN, TILL SHE VOUCHSAFE TO GRAWNT
                        ME REST                 5.33.13
    MAKE PEACE THEREFORE, AND GRAUNT ME TIMELY GRACE   5.57.13
    AND GRANT THAT WE FCR WHOM THOU DIDDEST DYE   5.68.6
GRANTETH                   1
    TO WHOM NOR ART NCR NATURE GRAUNTETH LIGHT   4.99.2
GRANTING                   1
    FOR HOW DO I HOLD THEE BUT BY THY GRANTING   3.87.5
GRANTS                     1
    FOR TO THEIR FLOW SHE NEVER GRANTS AN END    1.48.4
GRASS                      1
    THE DAINTY GRASSE MAKE MUSICKE WITH HER FEETE   2.125.8
```

```
GRATEFUL                        2
  GRATEFULL T'ANOTHER, TO MY SELFE UNKINDE          1.20.12
  SO GRATEFULL NOW YOU WAITE UPON MY CARE            4.95.4
GRAVE                          10
  TO M'INFANT STILE THE $CRADLE, AND THE $GRAVE      1.59.12
  MY $HOPES REVIV'D, WHICH LONG IN $GRAVE HAD LYNE   2.35.12
  TO KEEPE $THEE FROM $OBLIVION AND THE $GRAVE       2.44.10
  MY HOPES REVIV'D WHICH LONG IN GRAVE HAD LYNE      2.112.12
  AND PRAISE HER STILL TO THY UNTIMELY GRAVE         2.139.8
  THE GRAVE OF JOY, PRYSON OF DAYES DELIGHT          2.145.10
  TO EATE THE WORLDS DUE, BY THE GRAVE AND THEE      3.1.14
  THOU ART THE GRAVE WHERE BURIED LOVE DOTH LIVE     3.31.9
  THE EARTH CAN YEELD ME BUT A COMMON GRAVE          3.81.7
  OF ALL THE GRAVE CONCEITS YOUR BRAINE DOTH BREED   4.51.6
GRAVED                          2
  SHALL REST IN $ISE, WHEN THINE IS GRAV'D
                        IN $MARBLE                   1.44.8
  GRAVED IN MINE $EPITAPH A $POET'S NAME             4.90.8
GRAVEN                          1
  IF TIME HAVE ANY WRINCLE GRAVEN THERE              3.100.10
GRAVER                          1
  NOR GRAVER BROWES HAVE JUDG'D MY $MUSE SO VAINE    1.7.6
GRAVES                          1
  OF MOUTHED GRAVES WILL GIVE THEE MEMORIE           3.77.6
GRAVITY                         1
  SHALL REASONS FINDE OF SETLED GRAVITIE             3.49.8
GRAY                            1
  BETTER BECOMES THE GRAY CHEEKS OF TH' $EAST        3.132.6
GREAT                          35
  APPROACH NOT TO BEHOLD SO GREAT DISTRESSE          1.3.6
  DANGER HATH HONOR, GREAT DESIGNES THEIR FAME       1.35.6
  DO FEELE MINE INWARD HEAT AS GREAT (I KNOW IT)     1.43.6
  NOR SEEKES IT TO BE KNOWNE UNTO THE $GREAT         1.58.10
  TH'EVIDENCE SO GREAT A PROOFE DOTH CARRIE          2.2.8
  ESSEX GREAT FALL, $TYRONE HIS $PEACE TO GAINE      2.51.6
  BY THY GREAT POWER, AND BY STRONG FAYTH IN THEE    2.112.14
  SO GREAT A SUMME OF SUMMES YET CAN'ST NOT LIVE+    3.4.8
  GREAT $PRINCES FAVORITES THEIR FAIRE LEAVES
                        SPREAD                       3.25.5
  DUTY SO GREAT, WHICH WIT SO POORE AS MINE          3.26.5
  O NO, THY LOVE THOUGH MUCH, IS NOT SO GREAT        3.61.9
  WAS IT THE PROUD FULL SAILE OF HIS GREAT VERSE     3.86.1
  SO THY GREAT GUIFT UPON MISPRISION GROWING         3.87.11
  AND MY GREAT MINDE MOST KINGLY DRINKES IT UP       3.114.10
  WHEREIN I SHOULD YOUR GREAT DESERTS REPAY          3.117.2
  OR LAYD GREAT BASES FOR ETERNITY                   3.125.3
  IN THINGS OF GREAT RECEIT WITH EASE WE PROOVE      3.136.7
  THUS GREAT WITH CHILD TO SPEAKE, AND HELPLESSE
                        IN MY THROWES                4.1.12
  GREAT EXPECTATION, WEARE A TRAINE OF SHAME         4.21.8
  FOR SINCE MAD $MARCH GREAT PROMISE MADE OF ME      4.21.9
  VERTUE'S GREAT BEAUTIE IN THAT FACE I PROVE        4.25.13
  AND KNOW GREAT CAUSES, GREAT EFFECTS PROCURE       4.26.10
  AND KNOW GREAT CAUSES, GREAT EFFECTS PROCURE       4.26.10
  STELLA'S GREAT POWRS, THAT SO CONFUSE MY MIND      4.34.14
  IF SO GREAT SERVICES MAY SCORNED BE                4.65.10
  AS THOUGH THAT FAIRE SOFT HAND DID YOU
                        GREAT WRONG                  4.83.4
  TO THIS GREAT CAUSE, WHICH NEEDS BOTH
                        USE AND ART                  4.107.8
```

GREAT HEAT, AND MAKES HIS FLAMES TO HEAVEN ASPIRE	5.6.8
GREAT SHAME IT IS TO LEAVE LIKE ONE AFRAYD	5.14.3
GIVES ME GREAT HOPE OF YOUR RELENTING MYND	5.28.2
THAT HER GREAT TRIUMPH WHICH MY SKILL EXCEEDS	5.29.11
HOW COMES IT THEN THAT THIS HER COLD SO GREAT	5.30.2
GREAT WRONG I DOE, I CAN IT NOT DENY	5.33.1
GREAT SHAME IT IS, THING SO DIVINE IN VIEW	5.53.9
OF THEYR GREAT DEEDS AND VALAROUS EMPRIZE	5.69.4

GREATER   21

AND CROSSE MY CARES ERE GREATER SUMMES ARISE	1.1.12
SEE THEN WHO SINNES THE GREATER OF US TWAINE	1.33.13
LEAVING THE $PATH THE GREATER PART DOE GOE	2.9.4
THUS POORE $THEEVES SUFFER, WHEN THE GREATER SCAPE	2.14.14
WITH GREATER $TORMENTS, THEN IT $ME DOTH TAKE	2.20.7
(THE $KING OF $SENCES, GREATER THEN THE REST)	2.29.10
AND YET LOVE KNOWES IT IS A GREATER GRIEFE	3.40.11
THEIR WORTH THE GREATER BEEING WOO'D OF TIME	3.70.6
GROWES FAIRER THEN AT FIRST, MORE STRONG, FAR GREATER	3.119.12
I SEE AND YET NO GREATER SOROW TAKE	4.18.13
TILL GREATER THEN MY WOMBE THOU WOXEN ART	5.2.4
GAYNST SUCH STRONG CASTLES NEEDETH GREATER MIGHT	5.14.5
A GREATER CRAFTESMANS HAND THERETO DOTH NEEDE	5.17.13
AND WISH THAT MORE AND GREATER THEY MIGHT BE	5.25.13
THAT GREATER MEEDE AT LAST MAY TURNE TO MEE	5.25.14
BUT MY PROUD ONE DOTH WORKE THE GREATER SCATH	5.31.9
AND GREATER GLORY THINKE TO SAVE, THEN SPILL	5.49.4
BUT HAVING HER, MY JOY WIL BE THE GREATER	5.51.14
THAT SEEMD THE LONGER FOR MY GREATER PAINES	5.60.12
BUT YE THEREBY MUCH GREATER GLORY GATE	5.66.9
AND IN MY DARKNESSE GREATER DOTH APPEARE	5.66.12

GREATEST   6

IN GREATEST $PERILS SOME $MEN PLEASANT BE	2.24.10
AND YET I $SURFET IN THE GREATEST $DEARTH	2.62.12
AND YET I SURFET IN THE GREATEST DEARTH	2.150.12
MOST WORTHY COMFORT, NOW MY GREATEST GRIEFE	3.48.6
SEEME MOST ALONE IN GREATEST COMPANIE	4.27.2
THE GREATEST $PRINCE WITH POMPOUS ROIALTY+	5.77.4

GREATLY   1

I GREATLY MARVELL, HOW YOU STILL GOE FREE	2.14.3

GREATNESS   1

WHOSE NUMBERS, WAYES, GREATNESSE, ETERNITIE	4.26.3

GRECIAN   1

AND YOU IN $GRECIAN TIRES ARE PAINTED NEW	3.53.8

GREECE   2

LOVE BORNE IN $GREECE, OF LATE FLED FROM HIS NATIVE PLACE	4.8.1
WHEN THOSE RENOUMED NOBLE $PERES OF $GREECE	5.44.1

GREEDILY   3

BUT WHILST MINE $EYES THUS GREEDILY DOE GAZE	2.33.5
BUT WHILST MINE EYES THUS GREEDILY DOE GAZE	2.133.5
BUT GREEDILY HER FELL INTENT POURSEWTH	5.11.7

GREEDINESS   1

AS IS A $TYGRE THAT WITH GREEDINESSE	5.56.2

GREEDY   4

MY HUNGRY EYES THROUGH GREEDY COVETIZE	5.35.1
HE FORTH WAS THROWN INTO THE GREEDY SEAS	5.38.2
DID SACRIFIZE UNTO THE GREEDY FYRE	5.48.4
MY HUNGRY EYES, THROUGH GREEDY COVETIZE	5.83.1

```
GREEING                     1
  MINE EIE WELL KNOWES WHAT WITH HIS GUST
                        IS GREEING            3.114.11
GREEN                       7
  WHOSE FEETE DOE TREAD GREENE PATHS OF
                    YOUTH AND LOVE            1.6.6
  WHOSE SHORT REFRESH UPON THE TENDER GREENE  1.50.2
  AND $SOMMERS GREENE ALL GIRDED UP IN SHEAVES 3.12.7
  KISSING WITH GOLDEN FACE THE MEDDOWES GREENE 3.33.3
  AND THEY SHALL LIVE, AND HE IN THEM STILL GREENE 3.63.14
  MAKING NO SUMMER OF AN OTHERS GREENE        3.68.11
  SINCE FIRST I SAW YOU FRESH WHICH YET ARE GREENE 3.104.8
GREET                       4
  AND SCARCELY GREETE ME WITH THAT SUNNE THINE EYE 3.49.6
  WHEN I WAS WONT TO GREET IT WITH MY LAIES   3.102.6
  AND TOUGHT IT THUS A NEW TO GREETE          3.145.8
  MY $MUSE AND I MUST YOU OF DUTIE GREET      4.84.7
GREW                        6
  WHAT THEY LAST THOUGHT OF, WHEN THE $BRAINE
                        GREW SICKE            2.9.7
  WHICH SHOULD EXAMPLE WHERE YOUR EQUALL GREW 3.84.4
  MAKING THEIR TOMBE THE WOMBE WHEREIN THEY GREW+ 3.86.4
  OR FROM THEIR PROUD LAP PLUCK THEM WHERE
                        THEY GREW             3.98.8
  THE ILLS THAT WERE, NOT GREW TO FAULTS ASSURED 3.118.10
  AND GREW A SEETHING BATH WHICH YET MEN PROVE 3.153.7
GRIEF                      34
  WITNESSE YOUR $FATHERS GRIEFE EXCEEDES ALL OTHER 1.2.4
  FORGING A GRIEFE TO WINNE A FAMES REWARD    1.4.4
  TOLDE THE DUMBE MESSAGE OF MY HIDDEN GRIEFE 1.8.6
  AND CARVE HIS PROPER GRIEFE UPON A STONE    1.13.2
  STILL HAVE I LIV'D IN GRIEFE, IN HOPE, IN TERROR 1.18.3
  FALSE $HOPE PROLONGS MY EVER CERTAINE GRIEFE 1.25.1
  PINES IN HER GRIEFE, IMPRISONED IN HER NEST 1.29.3
  TO SPEND THE $APRILL OF MY YEARES IN GRIEFE 1.32.2
  CAN GIVE THE LEAST RELEASE UNTO THY GRIEFE  1.52.10
  TO ADDE MORE GRIEFE TO AGGRAVATE MY SORROW  1.54.12
  WHICH TELLS THE WORLD HOW MUCH MY GRIEFE IMPORTS 1.60.4
  AND $BEDLAM-LIKE, THUS RAVING IN MY $GRIEFE 2.41.10
  WHOSE $GRIEFE HATH PARCH'D THY $BODY,
                        DRY'D THY $BLOOD      2.49.8
  PEN'D IN THE GRIEFE OF MINE AFFLICTED $GHOST 2.54.6
  PEND IN THE GRIEFE OF MYNE AFFLICTED GHOST  2.101.6
  TWIXT JOY AND GRIEFE, YET WITH A SMYLING
                        FROWNING              2.109.9
  I WELL PERCEIVE MY GRIEFE INNUMERABLE GROWES 2.110.3
  REDOUBLING SIGHES THE ACCENTS OF MY GRIEFE  2.111.12
  AND LIKE A $TYRANT MAK'ST MY GRIEFE THY GAME 2.130.12
  MY SIGHES BE SPENT WITH GRIEFE AND SIGHING SO 2.143.7
  AND $BEDLAM LIKE THUS RAVING IN MY GRIEFE   2.143.10
  NOR CAN THY SHAME GIVE PHISICKE TO MY GRIEFE 3.34.9
  AND YET LOVE KNOWES IT IS A GREATER GRIEFE  3.40.11
  THAT THOU HAST HER IT IS NOT ALL MY GRIEFE  3.42.1
  MOST WORTHY COMFORT, NOW MY GREATEST GRIEFE 3.48.6
  MY GREEFE LIES ONWARD AND MY JOY BEHIND     3.50.14
  GRIEFE BUT $LOVE'S WINTER LIVERIE IS, THE $BOY 4.70.7
  WHAT SOBS CAN GIVE WORDS GRACE MY GRIEFE TO SHOW+ 4.93.2
  GRIEFE FIND THE WORDS, FOR THOU HAST MADE
                        MY BRAINE             4.94.1
  WITH LOVELY LIGHT TO CLEARE MY CLOUDY GRIEF 5.34.12
```

```
    AND GRIEFE RENEW, AND PASSIONS DOE AWAKE            5.44.11
    WHOM SHE ALL CARELESSE OF HIS GRIEFE CONSTRAYNED    5.48.9
    OF MY HARTS WOUND AND OF MY BODIES GRIEFE           5.50.2
    AND FAINE MY GRIEFE WITH CHAUNGES TO BEGUILE        5.87.10
GRIEFS            11
    DID FORCE ME GRONE OUT GRIEFES, AND UTTER THIS      1.7.12
    STILL TO COMPLAINE MY GRIEFES, WHILST NONE RELIEVE  1.9.8
    GRIEFES EVER SPRINGING, COMFORTS NEVER BORNE        1.16.4
    THIS IS MY STATE, MY GRIEFES DO TOUCH SO NEERLY     1.16.13
    LOOKE IN MY GRIEFES, AND BLAME ME NOT TO MOURNE     1.26.1
    I SHALL FORGET OLD WRONGS, MY GRIEFES
                                   SHALL CEASE          1.46.11
    MAKE ME TO SAY, WHEN ALL MY GRIEFES ARE GONE        1.51.13
    MY GRIEFES LONG LIV'D, AND CARE SUCCEEDING CARE     1.60.12
    I FINDE, MY $GRIEFES INNUMERABLE GROWE              2.3.3
    WHEN OTHER PETTIE GRIEFES HAVE DONE THEIR SPIGHT    3.90.10
    TO FEELE MY GRIEFES, AND SHE WITH FACE AND VOICE    4.57.13
GRIEF'S            1
    AND NIGHT DOTH NIGHTLY MAKE GREEFES LENGTH
                                   SEEME STRONGER       3.28.14
GRIEVANCES         1
    THEN CAN I GREEVE AT GREEVANCES FORE-GON            3.30.9
GRIEVE            10
    LIE DOWNE TO WAILE, RISE UP TO SIGH AND GRIEVE      1.9.6
    SHE DOTH ME WRONG, TO GRIEVE SO TRUE A HEART        1.21.14
    WHEN, IF SHE GRIEVE TO GAZE HER IN HER GLASSE       1.38.9
    AND THEREFORE GRIEVE NOT IF THY BEAUTIES DIE        1.45.9
    FOR WOMEN GRIEVE TO THINKE THEY MUST BE OLD         1.50.14
    I MUST NOT GRIEVE MY $LOVE, WHOSE EIES
                                   WOULD REEDE          1.51.1
    THAT $CRUELTY HER SELFE MIGHT GRIEVE TO VIEW        1.60.7
    THAT THEY SHALL GRIEVE, THEY LIV'D NOT.
                                   IN THESE $TIMES      2.6.11
    THEN CAN I GREEVE AT GREEVANCES FORE-GON            3.30.9
    TO GRIEVE ME WORSE, IN SAYING THAT $DESIRE          4.14.6
GRIEVED            1
    NO MORE BEE GREEV'D AT THAT WHICH THOU HAST DONE    3.35.1
GRIEVES            1
    THERE'S NOTHING GRIEVES ME, BUT THAT $AGE
                                   SHOULD HASTE         2.8.1
GRIEVOUS           5
    MY HEART HATH PAID SUCH GRIEVOUS $USURIE            2.3.11
    IN GRIEVOUS $PASSIONS, MY $WOES STILL BEMONING      2.40.8
    MY HART HATH PAYD SUCH GRIEVOUS USURY               2.110.11
    IN GREEVOUS PASSIONS MY WOES STYLL BEMONING         2.144.8
    OF $LOVERS NEVER KNOWNE, A GRIEVOUS CASE            4.45.6
GRIND             1
    MINE APPETITE I NEVER MORE WILL GRIN'DE             3.110.10
GRIPE             2
    UPON WHOSE BREAST A FIERCER $GRIPE DOTH TIRE        4.14.2
    LET WO GRIPE ON MY HEART, SHAME LOADE MINE EYE      4.86.4
GRIZZLED           1
    LIKE GRIZZLED $MOSSE UPON SOME AGED $TREE           2.8.8
GROAN             8
    DID FORCE ME GRONE OUT GRIEFES, AND UTTER THIS      1.7.12
    WHICH HEAVILY HE ANSWERS WITH A GRONE               3.50.11
    FOR THAT SAME GRONE DOTH PUT THIS IN MY MIND        3.50.13
    THY FACE HATH NOT THE POWER TO MAKE LOVE GRONE      3.131.6
    BESHREW THAT HEART THAT MAKES MY HEART TO GROANE    3.133.1
    AS GOOD TO WRITE AS FOR TO LIE AND GRONE            4.40.1
```

NOR GIVE EACH SPEECH A FULL POINT OF A GRONE   4.54.4
THE THOROWEST WORDS, FIT FOR WOE'S SELFE TO GRONE   4.57.4
GROANING   2
FILLING MINE $EARES WITH $NOISE, AND $NIGHTLY
                              GRONING   2.40.6
FILLING MYNE EARES WITH NOYSE AND NIGHTLY
                              GRONING   2.144.6
GROANS   1
A THOUSAND GRONES BUT THINKING ON THY FACE   3.131.10
GROSS   3
TO THEIR GROSSE $SENSE APPLY HER SELFE SO ILL   2.43.10
AND THEIR GROSSE PAINTING MIGHT BE BETTER US'D   3.82.13
MY NOBLER PART TO MY GROSE BODIES TREASON   3.151.6
GROSSLY   1
IN MY LOVES VEINES THOU HAST TOO GROSELY DIED   3.99.5
GROUND   11
A WAYLING DESCANT ON THE SWEETEST GROUND   1.57.7
FOR NO GROUND ELS COULD MAKE THE MUSICKE SUCH   1.57.13
GAVE IT TO KEEPE TO $SPIRITS WITHIN THE $GROUND   2.58.4
IN THIS FAYRE LIMMED GROUND AS WHITE AS SNOW   2.114.10
AND LOOKING ON THEE, FALLS UPON THE GROUND   2.135.11
OR AS SWEET SEASON'D SHEWERS ARE TO THE GROUND   3.75.2
MY $MISTRES WHEN SHEE WALKES TREADS ON
                              THE GROUND   3.130.12
IN A COULD VALLIE-FOUNTAINE OF THAT GROUND   3.153.4
THE GROUND OF THIS FIERCE $LOVE AND LOVELY HATE   4.60.11
AND TO THE GROUND HER EIE LIDS LOW EMBASETH   5.13.3
IF $GOLD, HER LOCKS ARE FINEST GOLD ON GROUND   5.15.11
GROUNDED   2
IT IS SO GROUNDED INWARD IN MY HEART   3.62.4
HATE OF MY SINNE, GROUNDED ON SINFULL LOVING   3.142.2
GROW   21
I FINDE, MY $GRIEFES INNUMERABLE GROWE   2.3.3
WELL, WELL, MY $FRIENDS, WHEN $BEGGERS
                              GROW THUS BOLD   2.23.13
NO MARVELL THEN THOUGH $CHARITIE GROW COLD   2.23.14
AND DIE AS FAST AS THEY SEE OTHERS GROW   3.12.12
I SEND THEM BACK AGAINE AND STRAIGHT GROW SAD   3.45.14
THE SOLYE IS THIS, THAT THOU DOEST COMMON GROW   3.69.14
SPEAKING OF WORTH, WHAT WORTH IN YOU DOTH GROW   3.83.8
HOW LIKE $EAVES APPLE DOTH THY BEAUTY GROW   3.93.13
TO GIVE FULL GROWTH TO THAT WHICH STILL
                              DOTH GROW   3.115.14
IF HAIRES BE WIERS, BLACK WIERS GROW ON HER HEAD   3.130.4
FOR IF I SHOULD DISPAIRE I SHOULD GROW MADDE   3.140.9
PHRASES AND $PROBLEMES FROM MY REACH DO GROW   4.3.10
EFFECTS OF LIVELY HEAT, MUST NEEDS IN NATURE GROW   4.8.11
WEALTH BREEDING WANT, MORE BLIST, MORE
                              WRETCHED GROW   4.24.4
HE KNOWES NOT) GROW IN ONLY FOLLIE RICH   4.24.14
DOTH EVEN GROW RICH, NAMING MY STELLA'S NAME   4.35.11
MY SPRING APPEARES, O SEE WHAT HERE DOTH GROW   4.69.8
THAT ANY LAUD TO ME THEREOF SHOULD GROW   4.90.10
FROM CARELESNESSE DID IN NO MANER GROW   4.93.7
MAKING THOSE $LILLIES AND THOSE $ROSES GROW   4.100.2
MAKE IN MY HEAVY MOULD NEW THOUGHTS TO GROW   4.106.11
GROWEST   4
AS FAST AS THOU SHALT WANE SO FAST THOU GROW'ST   3.11.1
WHEN IN ETERNALL LINES TO TIME THOU GROW'ST   3.18.12
THY LOVERS WITHERING, AS THY SWEET SELFE GROW'ST   3.126.4

```
      YET GROWEST MORE WRETCHED THEN THY NATURE BEARES      4.94.13
GROWETH                  1
      BUT LO, WHILE I DO SPEAKE, IT GROWETH
                        NOONE WITH ME                       4.76.9
GROWING                  5
   LOVE GROWING ANGRY, VEXED AT THE $SPLEENE                2.38.5
   LOVE GROWING ANGRY, VEXED AT THE SPLEENE                 2.131.5
   HAD MY FRIENDS $MUSE GROWNE WITH THIS
                        GROWING AGE                         3.32.10
   SO THY GREAT GUIFT UPON MISPRISION GROWING               3.87.11
   GROWING A BATH AND HEALTHFULL REMEDY                     3.154.11
GROWN                   12
   GROWNE HOARCE WITH CRYING MERCY, MERCY GIVE              1.16.6
   OR ART THOU GROWNE IN LEAGUE WITH THOSE
                        FAIRE EIES                          1.23.5
   IS $NATURE GROWNE LESSE POW'RFULL IN THEIR
                        $HEIRES                             2.27.7
   AND WHEN $CORNE'S SOWNE, OR GROWNE INTO THE $EARE        2.48.7
   HAD MY FRIENDS $MUSE GROWNE WITH THIS
                        GROWING AGE                         3.32.10
   AND SWEETS GROWNE COMMON LOOSE THEIR DEARE
                        DELIGHT                             3.102.12
   WHO HAST BY WAYNING GROWNE, AND THEREIN SHOU'ST          3.126.3
   NOW THIS ILL WRESTING WORLD IS GROWNE SO BAD             3.140.11
   BECAUSE THAT $MARS, GROWNE SLACKER IN HER LOVE           4.17.2
   A STRIFE IS GROWNE BETWEENE $VERTUE AND $LOVE            4.52.1
   GROWNE NOW HIS SLAVES, HE FORST THEM OUT TO FIND         4.57.3
   IN THIS OLD WORLD, GROWNE NOW SO TOO TOO WISE            4.65.6
GROWS                   10
   I WELL PERCEIVE MY GRIEFE INNUMERABLE GROWES             2.110.3
   WHEN I CONSIDER EVERY THING THAT GROWES                  3.15.1
   GROWES FAIRER THEN AT FIRST, MORE STRONG,
                        FAR GREATER                         3.119.12
   THAT IT NOR GROWES WITH HEAT, NOR DROWNES
                        WITH SHOWRES                        3.124.12
   ROOTE PITTIE IN THY HEART THAT WHEN IT GROWES            3.142.11
   AND EVERIE FLOURE, NOT SWEET PERHAPS,
                        WHICH GROWES                        4.15.3
   AND $HUMBLENESSE GROWES ONE WITH $MAJESTIE               4.48.4
   SWEET IS THE $ROSE, BUT GROWES UPON A BRERE              5.26.1
   BUT HARDER GROWES THE MORE I HER INTREAT+                5.30.4
   AND HARDER GROWES THE HARDER SHE IS SMIT                 5.32.11
GROWTH                   4
   BUT FOR HIS THEFT IN PRIDE OF ALL HIS GROWTH             3.99.12
   AND STOPS HIS PIPE IN GROWTH OF RIPER DAIES              3.102.8
   TO GIVE FULL GROWTH TO THAT WHICH STILL
                        DOTH GROW                           3.115.14
   O LET ME PROP MY MIND, YET IN HIS GROWTH                 4.19.12
GRUDGE                   1
   MY $MUSE MAY WELL GRUDGE AT MY HEAV'NLY JOY              4.70.1
GRUDGING                 2
   AS GRUDGING ME MY SORROWE'S ELOQUENCE+                   4.104.4
   OF GRUDGING FOES, NE FAVOUR SEEK OF FRIENDS              5.59.10
GUARD                    3
   AND WHILST I GARDE THESE WINDOWES OF THIS FORTE          1.27.5
   TO GUARD THE LAWFULL REASONS ON THY PART                 3.49.12
   WHO ERE KEEPES ME, LET MY HEART BE HIS GARDE             3.133.11
GUARDING                 1
   SLEEP WATCHING $BEAUTY, $BEAUTY WAKING,
                        SLEEPE GUARDING                     2.136.5
```

```
GUESS                        6
  WHILST BLINDED ONES MINE ERROURS NEVER GESSE        1.3.8
  AND THAT IN GUESSE THEY MEASURE BY THY DEEDS        3.69.10
  I GESSE ONE ANGEL IN AN OTHERS HEL                  3.144.12
  WITH IDLE PAINES, AND MISSING AYME, DO GUESSE       4.23.4
  I MUCH DO GUESSE, YET FIND NO TRUTH SAVE THIS       4.44.9
  GUESSE WE THE CAUSE.. '$WHAT, IS IT THUS+'
                         $FIE NO                      4.74.12
GUESSED                      1
  ONELY MY TEARES BY $OCEANS MAY BE GESSED            2.127.10
GUEST                        9
  INVITES MY $HEART TO BE THE CHIEFEST $GHEST         2.7.4
  CLOTHED THE $NAKED, LODG'D THIS WAND'RING $GHEST    2.23.6
  AN OTHER TIME MINE EYE IS MY HEARTS GUEST           3.47.7
  AND THETHER HIED A SAD DISTEMPERD GUEST             3.153.12
  THE WINDOWES NOW THROUGH WHICH THIS HEAV'NLY GUEST  4.9.9
  WHILE THAT BLACKE HUE FROM ME THE BAD GUEST HID     4.20.11
  BUT HIM HER HOST THAT UNKIND GUEST HAD SLAINE       4.38.14
  MOST RUDE DISPAIRE MY DAILY UNBIDDEN GUEST          4.108.7
  THRUGH YOUR BRIGHT BEAMS DOTH NOT THE
                         BLINDED GUEST                5.8.5
GUESTS                       1
  MY THOUGHTS THE GUESTS, WHICH WOULD THEREON
                         HAVE FEDD                    5.77.14
GUIDE                        6
  OF HER OWNE SEATE, WHEREOF I MADE HER GUIDE         1.47.8
  PLAINE-PATH'D $EXPERIENCE, TH'UNLEARNEDS GUIDE      2.46.1
  NOR IN HID WAYES TO GUIDE $PHILOSOPHIE              4.28.10
  AND EKE HIS LEARNED HAND AT PLEASURE GUIDE          5.17.6
  WHENAS A STORME HATH DIMD HER TRUSTY GUYDE          5.34.3
  SO SHE WITH FLATTRING SMYLES WEAKE HARTS
                         DOTH GUYDE                   5.47.5
GUIDED                       2
  GUIDED SO WELL, THAT I OBTAIN'D THE PRIZE           4.41.2
  THAT NO PACE ELSE THEIR GUIDED STEPS CAN FIND       4.58.3
GUIDES                       5
  SUCH IS THE SUNNE, WHO GUIDES MY YOUTHFULL
                         SEASON                       2.147.13
  TIL WHATSOEVER STAR THAT GUIDES MY MOVING           3.26.9
  OF STRAYING WAYES, WHEN VALIANT ERROUR GUIDES       4.51.11
  WHEN MY GOOD $ANGELL GUIDES ME TO THE PLACE         4.60.1
  WHICH, COUPLING $DOVES, GUIDES $VENUS'
                         CHARIOT RIGHT                4.79.4
GUILDED                      1
  WITH GUILDED LEAVES OR COLOURD $VELUME PLAYES       4.11.6
GUILE                        2
  WHAT GUYLE IS THIS, THAT THOSE HER GOLDEN TRESSES   5.37.1
  CONSUME THEE QUITE, THAT DIDST WITH GUILE
                         CONSPIRE                     5.86.11
GUILEFUL                     3
  IN THE CLOSE COVERT OF HER GUILEFULL EYEN           5.12.7
  HENCEFORTH TOO RASHLY ON THAT GUILEFULL NET         5.37.10
  UNTILL YE HAVE THEYR GUYLEFULL TRAYNES WELL TRYDE   5.47.2
GUILT                        2
  LEAST MY BEWAILED GUILT SHOULD DO THEE SHAME        3.36.10
  CURB'D IN WITH FEARE, BUT WITH GUILT BOSSE ABOVE    4.49.7
GUILTLESS                    4
  BUT ONELY I, GUILTLESSE OF MURTH'RING IT            2.2.4
  THAT YOU, GUILTLESSE THEREOF, YOUR $NECTAR MIST     4.105.10
  SHAMES NOT TO BE WITH GUILTLESSE BLOUD DEFYLDE      5.20.11
```

```
        THEN TO BE BLAM'D FOR SPILLING GUILTLESSE BLOOD       5.38.14
GUILTY                  3
   THE GUILTIE GODDESSE OF MY HARMFULL DEEDS                  3.111.2
   LEAST GUILTY OF MY FAULTS THY SWEET SELFE PROVE            3.151.4
   THEY FLED WITH BLUSH, WHICH GUILTIE SEEM'D
                             OF LOVE                          4.66.14
GUISE                   2
   BECAUSE I OFT IN DARKE ABSTRACTED GUISE                    4.27.1
   BEAUTY IS SICKE, BUT SICKE IN SO FAIRE GUISE               4.101.5
GULES                   1
   WHERE ROSES GUEULS ARE BORNE IN SILVER FIELD               4.13.11
GULF                    1
   FROM OUT THAT NOYSOME GULFE, WHICH GAPING LIES             4.78.3
GULFS                   1
   THE $GULPHES AND $STRAITS, THAT STRANGELY
                             HE HAD PAST                      2.1.10
GULLS                   1
   WHICH NIGHTLY GULLS HIM WITH INTELLIGENCE                  3.86.10
GUST                    1
   MINE EIE WELL KNOWES WHAT WITH HIS GUST
                             IS GREEING                       3.114.11
GUSTS                   1
   AGAINST THE STORMY GUSTS OF WINTERS DAY                    3.13.11
GYRES                   1
   SUCH COLTISH GYRES, THAT TO MY BIRTH I OWE                 4.21.6
HABIT                   1
   O LOVES BEST HABIT IS IN SEEMING TRUST                     3.138.11
HABITATION              1
   WHICH FOR THEIR HABITATION CHOSE OUT THEE                  3.95.10
HACKNEY                 1
   THEIR JUDGEMENTS HACKNEY ON, THE FAULT
                             ON SICKNESSE LAY                 4.102.10
HAD                    19
   AND HAD SHE PITTY TO CONJOYNE WITH THOSE                   1.6.11
   BEHOLD WHAT HAP $PIGMALION HAD TO FRAME                    1.13.1
   HE NEVER HAD MORE FAITH, ALTHOUGH MORE RIME                1.43.7
   THEM IF I HAD THE VICTORY MINE OWNE                        1.56.7
   THAT $GOLD NOR $HONOUR NE'R HAD POW'R TO MOVE              2.15.4
   WHO HAD LESSE $ART THEM LIVELY TO EXPRESSE+                2.27.6
   IN $FORMER TIMES, SUCH AS HAD STORE OF $COYNE              2.58.1
   SO $FAIRE A RISING, HAD SO $FOULE A SET                    2.60.12
   SO $FAIRE A RISING, HAD SO $FOULE A SET                    2.149.12
   YOU HAD A $FATHER, LET YOUR $SON SAY SO                    3.13.14
   BEING HAD TO TRYUMPH, BEING LACKT TO HOPE                  3.52.14
   O HIM SHE STORES, TO SHOW WHAT WELTH SHE HAD               3.67.13
   SAVE WHAT IS HAD, OR MUST FROM YOU BE TOOKE                3.75.12
   MY VERSE ALONE HAD ALL THE GENTLE GRACE                    3.79.2
   THUS HAVE I HAD THEE AS A DREAME DOTH FLATTER              3.87.13
   THEY HAD NOT STILL ENOUGH YOUR WORTH TO SING               3.106.12
   PAST REASON HUNTED, AND NO SOONER HAD                      3.129.6
   HAD, HAVING, AND IN QUEST, TO HAVE EXTREAME                3.129.10
   EACH HAD HIS CREAST, $MARS CARIED $VENUS' GLOVE            4.13.7
HADST                   2
   WHAT HAST THOU THEN MORE THEN THOU HADST BEFORE+           3.40.2
   ALL MINE WAS THINE, BEFORE THOU HADST THIS MORE            3.40.4
HAIR                   12
   THY DAINTIE $HAYRE, SO CURL'D, AND CRISPED NOW             2.8.7
   NOW RAILE UPON HER $HAIRE, THEN ON HER $EYE                2.41.11
   WITH THOSE SWEET STRINGS STOLNE FROM THY
                             GOLDEN HAYRE                     2.104.2
```

```
ILE BINDE HER THEN WITH MY TORNE-TRESSED HAIRE        2.115.13
NOW RAYLE UPON HER HAYRE, NOW ON HER EYE              2.143.11
THE $ANGELS TRESSES, TO HER TRESSED HAYRE             2.148.9
AND BUDS OF MARJEROM HAD STOLNE THY HAIRE             3.99.7
STELLA'S FAIRE HAIRE, HER FACE HE MAKES
                           HIS SHIELD                 4.13.10
NOR NOURISH SPECIALL LOCKES OF VOWED HAIRE            4.54.3
RAVISHT, STAID NOT, TILL IN HER GOLDEN HAIRE          4.103.7
THAT WHICH IS GOLD OR HEARE, MAY SCARSE BE TOLD+      5.37.4
BUT THE FAYRE TRESSES OF YOUR GOLDEN HAYRE            5.73.3
HAIRS                5
WHEN GOLDEN HAIRES SHALL CHANGE TO SILVER WIER        1.38.2
WHEN WINTER SNOWES UPON THY SABLE HAIRES              1.41.14
WHEN WINTER SNOWES UPON THY SABLE HAIRES              1.42.1
IF HAIRES BE WIERS, BLACK WIERS GROW ON HER HEAD      3.130.4
FAYRE IS MY LOVE, WHEN HER FAYRE GOLDEN HEARES        5.81.1
HALF                 9
BEWRAIES MY LOVE, WITH BROKEN WORDS HALFE SPOKEN      1.15.6
LOOKE $DELIA HOW W'ESTEEME THE HALFE BLOWNE $ROSE     1.39.1
THY $BOWE HALFE BROKE, IS PEEC'D WITH
                           OLDE DESIRE                2.126.5
WHICH HIDES YOUR LIFE, AND SHEWES NOT
                           HALFE YOUR PARTS           3.17.4
THOU CANST NOT (LOVE) DISGRACE ME HALFE SO ILL        3.89.5
DOTH HALFE THAT GLORY TO THE SOBER $WEST              3.132.8
WHEREWITH MY FATHER ONCE MADE IT HALFE TAME           4.30.10
TILL I IN HAND HER YET HALFE TREMBLING TOOKE          5.67.11
GIVE LEAVE TO REST ME BEING HALFE FORDONNE            5.80.3
HALF-SLAIN              1
MY HALFE-SLAINE HART SHALL TAKE REVENGE ON THEE       2.140.4
HALLOWED               3
THY HALLOW'D $TEMPLE ONELY IS MY $HEART               2.30.14
AT WHOSE PURE $EYES, $LOVE LIGHTS HIS
                           HALLOW'D $FIRE             2.57.8
EVEN AS WHEN FIRST I HALLOWED THY FAIRE NAME          3.108.8
HALT                   1
SPEAKE OF MY LAMENESSE, AND I STRAIGHT WILL HALT      3.89.3
HALTING                1
BUT WORDS CAME HALTING FORTH, WANTING
                           $INVENTION'S STAY          4.1.9
HAMMERED               1
UNLESSE MY $NERVES WERE BRASSE OR HAMMERED
                           STEELE                     3.120.4
HAMMERS                2
MY $WORDS THE $HAMMERS, FASHIONING MY DESIRE          2.40.2
MY WORDS THE HAMMERS, FASHIONING MY DESIRES           2.144.2
HAND                  54
WITH FAIREST HAND, THE SWEET UNKINDEST $MAID          1.5.7
HOLDES IN HER FAIREST HAND WHAT DEAREST IS            1.12.10
HER VOYCE BETRAIES ME TO HER HAND AND EYE             1.27.9
RAIGNE IN MY THOUGHTS FAIRE HAND, SWEETE
                           EYE, RARE VOICE            1.28.1
FINDING ME RAIN'D WITH SUCH A HEAVY HAND              1.28.12
AND BY THAT HAND WHOM SUCH DEEDS ILL BECOME           1.31.14
YET NEVER FOUND THAT BARBAROUS HAND ATTAIND           1.45.5
TO SAVE THINE OWNE, STRETCH OUT THE FAIREST HAND      1.46.8
STRETCH OUT THE FAIREST HAND, A PLEDGE OF PEACE       1.46.9
THAT HAND THAT DARTS SO RIGHT AND NEVER MISSES        1.46.10
WROUGHT BY HER HAND THAT I HAVE HONOUR'D SO           1.47.4
AND MORE THE FAME OF HIS MISTAKING HAND               1.56.3
```

```
NOR OTHER HAND COULD GIVE SO TRUE A TOUCH              1.57.14
A CRIPPLE $HAND TO WRITE, YET LAME BY $KIND            2.35.7
OFT TAKING PEN IN HAND, WITH WORDS TO
                        CAST MY WOES                   2.110.1
A CRIPPLE HAND TO WRITE, YET LAME BY KIND              2.112.7
WHOSE GLORIOUS HAND IMMORTALL HATH ENROLD THEE         2.129.12
WHILST FROM THEYR RAYES BY $CUPIDS SKILFULL HAND       2.135.7
THEN LET NOT WINTERS WRAGGED HAND DEFACE               3.6.1
A $WOMANS FACE WITH NATURES OWNE HAND PAINTED          3.20.1
AND THIS MY HAND, AGAINST MY SELFE UPREARE             3.49.11
OR AT YOUR HAND TH'ACCOUNT OF HOURES TO CRAVE          3.58.3
PRAISING THY WORTH, DISPIGHT HIS CRUELL HAND           3.60.14
WITH TIMES INJURIOUS HAND CHRUSHT AND ORE-WORNE        3.63.2
WHEN I HAVE SEENE BY TIMES FELL HAND DEFACED           3.64.1
OR WHAT STRONG HAND CAN HOLD HIS SWIFT
                        FOOTE BACK                     3.65.11
THE HAND THAT WRIT IT, FOR I LOVE YOU SO               3.71.6
THE $LILLIE I CONDEMNED FOR THY HAND                   3.99.6
AH YET DOTH BEAUTY LIKE A $DYALL HAND                  3.104.9
OF HAND, OF FOOTE, OF LIP, OF EYE, OF BROW             3.106.6
TO WHAT IT WORKES IN, LIKE THE $DYERS HAND             3.111.7
FOR SINCE EACH HAND HATH PUT ON $NATURES POWER         3.127.5
TO KISSE THE TENDER INWARD OF THY HAND                 3.128.6
THOSE LIPS THAT $LOVES OWNE HAND DID MAKE              3.145.1
CAME TRIPPING BY, BUT IN HER MAIDEN HAND               3.154.4
WAS SLEEPING BY A $VIRGIN HAND DISARM'D                3.154.8
HAVING THIS DAY MY HORSE, MY HAND, MY LAUNCE           4.41.1
AND NOW HATH MADE ME TO HIS HAND SO RIGHT              4.49.13
ONE HAND FORGOTT TO RULE, TH'OTHER TO FIGHT            4.53.11
I GIVE YOU HERE MY HAND FOR TRUTH OF THIS              4.70.13
THAT HAND, WHICH WITHOUT TOUCH HOLDS MORE
                        THEN $ATLAS MIGHT              4.77.5
AS THOUGH THAT FAIRE SOFT HAND DID YOU
                        GREAT WRONG                    4.83.4
O EASE YOUR HAND, TREATE NOT SO HARD YOUR SLAVE        4.86.9
AND LOVE DOTH HOLD MY HAND, AND MAKES ME WRITE         4.90.14
WITH CARE'S HARD HAND) TO TURNE AND TOSSE IN THEE      4.98.8
BARE ME IN HAND, THAT IN THIS $ORPHANE PLACE           4.106.3
AND EKE HIS LEARNED HAND AT PLEASURE GUIDE             5.17.6
A GREATER CRAFTESMANS HAND THERETO DOTH NEEDE          5.17.13
BUT WHEN IN HAND MY TUNELESSE HARP I TAKE              5.44.9
INNOCENT PAPER WHOM TOO CRUELL HAND                    5.48.1
WITH PLENTEOUS HAND BY HEAVEN UPON YOU THROWN          5.66.2
TILL I IN HAND HER YET HALFE TREMBLING TOOKE           5.67.11
LYKE AS A BYRD THAT IN ONES HAND DOTH SPY              5.73.5
AGAYNE I WROTE IT WITH A SECOND HAND                   5.75.3
HANDLE                  1
SHALL HANDLE YOU AND HOLD IN LOVES SOFT BANDS           5.1.3
HANDMAID                1
FIT FOR THE HANDMAYD OF THE $FAERY $QUEENE             5.80.14
HANDMAIDS               1
THE READY HANDMAYDS ON HER GRACE T'ATTEND              1.48.2
HANDS                   12
SHAKE HANDS FOR EVER, $CANCELL ALL OUR $VOWES          2.61.5
WITH MURTHERING HANDS IMBRUD IN MINE OWN BLOOD         2.114.12
DOE IN CONSENT SHAKE HANDS TO TORTURE ME               3.28.6
FROM HANDS OF FALSEHOOD, IN SURE WARDS OF TRUST+       3.48.4
AS WHAT THEIR HANDS DO HOLD, THEIR HEADS DO KNOW       4.24.6
LOOKE AT MY HANDS FOR NO SUCH QUINTESSENCE             4.28.11
MILKE HANDS, ROSE CHEEKS, OR LIPS MORE
                        SWEET, MORE RED                4.91.7
```

```
HAPPY YE LEAVES WHEN AS THOSE LILLY HANDS        5.1.1
WAS FORST TO YEELD MY SELFE INTO THEIR HANDS     5.12.10
IF SILVER, HER FAIRE HANDS ARE SILVER SHEENE     5.15.12
OF SUCH POORE THRALLS HER CRUELL HANDS EMBREW    5.31.12
YET EVEN WHYLST HER BLOODY HANDS THEM SLAY       5.47.9
HAND'S                    1
YEELD THY HANDS PRIDE UNTO TH'$IVORY WHITE       1.19.5
HANG                      3
HANG ON SUCH THORNES, AND PLAY AS WANTONLY       3.54.7
AND HANG MORE PRAISE UPON DECEASED I             3.72.7
WHEN YELLOW LEAVES, OR NONE, OR FEW DOE HANGE    3.73.2
HANGING                   1
WHICH IN MY BOSOMES SHOP IS HANGING STIL         3.24.7
HAP                       3
IF SO IT HAP, THIS OF-SPRING OF MY CARE          1.3.1
BEHOLD WHAT HAP $PIGMALION HAD TO FRAME          1.13.1
AH., IF THOU ISSULESSE SHALT HAP TO DIE          3.9.3
HAPLESS                   1
FOR HAPLESSE LOE EVEN WITH MINE OWNE DESIRES     1.13.5
HAPLY                     3
HAPLYE I THINKE ON THEE, AND THEN MY STATE       3.29.10
AND HAPLIE OF OUR OLD ACQUAINTANCE TELL          3.89.12
MAKE ANSWERE $MUSE, WILT THOU NOT HAPLY SAIE     3.101.5
HAPPIER                   4
THOUGH HAPPIER FAR IF THOU WOULDST CHANGE
                              THY MIND           1.56.14
OR TEN TIMES HAPPIER BE IT TEN FOR ONE           3.6.8
TEN TIMES THY SELFE WERE HAPPIER THEN THOU ART   3.6.9
EXCEEDED BY THE HIGHT OF HAPPIER MEN             3.32.8
HAPPIES                   1
WHICH HAPPIES THOSE THAT PAY THE WILLING LONE    3.6.6
HAPPILY                   2
WHICH HAPPILY POSTERITY MAY CHERRISH             1.42.10
NEERE THE DEAD $BODY HAPPILY BE BROUGHT          2.46.7
HAPPINESS                 3
WHEN SHALL MY FAITH THE HAPPINES ATTAINE         1.49.7
THESE NOW THE OTHERS $HAPPINESSE DOE PRAYSE      2.33.7
HART NEED NOT WISH NONE OTHER HAPPINESSE         5.72.13
HAPPY                    41
BUT HAPPY HE THAT JOY'D HIS STONE AND ART        1.13.13
HAPPY IN SLEEPE, WAKING CONTENT TO LANGUISH      1.16.1
AND THAT MAKES HAPPY $LOVERS EVER DOMBE          1.17.14
TH'ETERNALL $ANNALS OF A HAPPY PEN               1.45.8
A HAPPY CONVOY TO A HOLY $LAND                   1.46.6
HAPPY THE HEART THAT SIGH'D FOR SUCH A ONE       1.51.14
MY TOUCHT HEART TURNES IT TO THAT HAPPY COST     1.53.2
TH'ETERNALL WONDER OF OUR HAPPY $ILE             1.53.8
YET HAPPY $DELIA THAT THOU WAST UNKIND           1.56.13
HOW HAPPY ARE ALL OTHER LIVING $THINGS           2.37.5
SINCE SHE DISDAINES TO BLESSE MY HAPPIE $VERSE   2.45.5
YET HAPPY HE THATS ROBD OF SUCH A THIEFE         2.126.14
O $EYES, BEHOLD YOUR HAPPY $HESPERUS             2.129.1
THRICE HAPPY BE THOSE EYES WHICH MAY BEHOLD
                              THEE               2.129.10
RESEMBLING SIER, AND CHILD, AND HAPPY MOTHER     3.8.11
NOW STAND YOU ON THE TOP OF HAPPIE HOURES        3.16.5
THEN HAPPY I THAT LOVE AND AM BELOVED            3.25.13
HOW CAN I THEN RETURNE IN HAPPY PLIGHT           3.28.1
THIS WISH I HAVE, THEN TEN TIMES HAPPY ME        3.37.14
HOW WOULD THY SHADOWES FORME, FORME HAPPY SHOW   3.43.6
```

```
SAVE WHERE YOU ARE, HOW HAPPY YOU MAKE THOSE        3.57.12
OH WHAT A HAPPY TITLE DC I FINDE                    3.92.11
HAPPY TO HAVE THY LCVE, HAPPY TO DIE                3.92.12
HAPPY TO HAVE THY LCVE, HAPPY TO DIE                3.92.12
SINCE SAUSIE $JACKES SO HAPPY ARE IN THIS           3.128.13
O HAPPIE $TEMS, THAT DIOST MY $STELLA BEARE         4.103.1
BUT IF I BY A HAPPY WINDOW PASSE                    4.104.9
HAPPY YE LEAVES WHEN AS THOSE LILLY HANDS           5.1.1
AND HAPPY LINES, CN WHICH WITH STARRY LIGHT         5.1.5
AND HAPPY RYMES BATH'D IN THE SACRED BROCKE         5.1.9
THRISE HAPPIE SHE, THAT IS SO WELL ASSURED          5.59.1
MOST HAPPY SHE THAT MOST ASSURED DOTH REST          5.59.13
BUT HE MOST HAPPY WHO SUCH ONE LOVES BEST           5.59.14
I DOE AT LENGTH DESCRY THE HAPPY SHORE              5.63.5
MOST HAPPY HE THAT CAN AT LAST ATCHYVE              5.63.9
TO ALL THOSE HAPPY BLESSINGS WHICH YE HAVE          5.66.1
THE HAPPY PURCHASE CF MY GLORIOUS SPOILE            5.69.13
MOST HAPPY LETTERS FRAM'D BY SKILFULL TRADE         5.74.1
WITH WHICH THAT HAPPY NAME WAS FIRST DESYND         5.74.2
THE WHICH THREE TIMES THRISE HAPPY HATH ME MADE     5.74.3
SWEET THOUGHTS I ENVY YCUR SO HAPPY REST            5.76.13
HAPS                          1
HAPS TO LEND SOME TC ONE TRUE HONEST $FRIEND        2.10.8
HARBINGERS                    1
THOUGH HARBENGERS CF DEATH LODGE THERE HIS TRAINE   4.94.8
HARBOR                        2
FOR WHEN, NAK'D BOY, THCU COULDST NO HARBOUR FIND   4.65.5
THE SACRED HARBOUR CF THAT HEVENLY SPRIGHT          5.76.4
HARBORED                      1
AS $LOVE AND I, LATE HARBOUR'D IN ONE $INNE         2.59.1
HARD                         22
KNOCKE AT THAT HARD HART, BEGGE TILL YOU
                              HAVE MOV'D HER         1.2.13
HAVE FOLLOWED HARD THE $PROCESSE OF MY CASE         1.8.10
HARD IS HER HART, AND WCE IS ME THEREFORE           1.13.12
YEELD TO THE $MARBLE THY HARD HART AGAINE           1.19.13
YET HEAVY HEART TC MAKE SO HARD A CHOISE            1.28.3
ONE IN MY LOVE, AND HER HARD HART STILL CNE         1.33.4
YET NOUGHT THE ROCKE OF THAT HARD HEART CAN MOVE    1.48.9
AND THY HARD HEART HAD YEELDED UP THE SAME          1.56.8
MY DEEPEST SENCE, HCW HARD TRUE SORROW HITS         3.120.10
MY MOUTH TOO TENDER IS FCR THY HARD BIT             4.4.8
WHEN SOME FAIRE $LADIES, BY HARD PROMISE TIED       4.22.5
'WHAT IDLER THING, THEN SPEAKE AND NOT BE HARD+'    4.34.9
WHO HARD BY MADE A WINDCW SEND FORTH LIGHT          4.53.9
O EASE YOUR HAND, TREATE NOT SO HARD YOUR SLAVE     4.86.9
WITH CARE'S HARD HAND) TC TURNE AND TOSSE IN THEE   4.98.8
SO HARD IT IS TO KINDLE NEW DESIRE                  5.6.9
AND LONG INTREATY SCFTEN HER HARD HART              5.18.6
AH WHY HATH NATURE TO SC HARD A HART                5.31.1
HER HART MORE HARDE THEN YRON SOFT AWHIT            5.32.6
WHICH WAS NOT HARD T'ATCHIVE AND BRING TC ENC       5.51.8
NE OUGHT SO HARD, BUT HE THAT WOULD ATTEND          5.51.9
FAYRE BE YE SURE, BUT HARD AND OBSTINATE            5.56.9
HARDEN                        1
THAT FIRE WHICH ALL THING MELTS, SHOULD
                              HARDEN YSE             5.30.10
HARDENED                      2
FORC'D BY A TEDIOUS PROCFE, THAT $TURKISH
                              HARDNED HART           4.8.2
```

```
    BUT YET IF IN YOUR HARDNED BREST YE HIDE          5.25.9
HARDENS                    1
    SHE LAUGHES, AND HARDENS EVERMORE HER HART        5.54.12
HARDER                     7
    AND MY NEXT SELFE THOU HARDER HAST INGROSSED      3.133.6
    BUT HARDER $JUDGES JUDGE AMBITION'S RAGE          4.23.9
    WHAT HARDER THING THEN SMART, AND NOT TO SPEAKE+  4.34.10
    THE HARDER WONNE, THE FIRMER WILL ABIDE           5.6.4
    BUT HARDER GROWES THE MORE I HER INTREAT+         5.30.4
    AND HARDER GROWES THE HARDER SHE IS SMIT          5.32.11
    AND HARDER GROWES THE HARDER SHE IS SMIT          5.32.11
HARDEST                    6
    TEARES, VOWES, AND PRAYERS, WINNE THE
                              HARDEST HART            1.11.1
    THE HARDEST KNIFE ILL US'D DOTH LOOSE HIS EDGE    3.95.14
    NOW I, WIT-BEATEN LONG BY HARDEST $FATE           4.60.9
    THE HARDEST STEELE IN TRACT OF TIME DOTH TEARE    5.18.2
    THE HARDEST YRON SOON DOTH MOLLIFY                5.32.2
    OF HARDEST $MARBLE ARE OF PURPOSE MADE+           5.51.2
HARDLY                     3
    YET AS IT WAS, I HARDLY SCAP'T WITH PAINE         5.16.14
    WITHIN MY HART, THOUGH HARDLY IT CAN SHEW         5.45.5
    WHICH HARDLY I ENDURED HERETOFORE                 5.63.2
HARDNESS                   1
    HER HARDNES BLAME WHICH I SHOULD MORE COMMEND+    5.51.6
HARDY                      1
    SUCH HAUGHTY MYNDS ENUR'D TO HARDY FIGHT          5.14.7
HARK                       2
    I START, LOOKE, HEARKE, BUT WHAT IN CLOSDE
                              UP SENCE                4.38.9
    THAT TO EACH WORD, NAY SIGH OF MINE YOU HARKE     4.104.3
HARM                       1
    A MONSTER, OTHER'S HARME, SELFE-MISERIE           4.78.5
HARMED                     1
    I HAVE (LIVE I AND KNOW THIS) HARMED THEE         4.93.10
HARMFUL                    1
    THE GUILTIE GODDESSE OF MY HARMFULL DEEDS         3.111.2
HARMLESS                   1
    SEE CHASTE $DIANA, WHERE MY HARMLES HART          2.135.1
HARMONY                    3
    MY $HEARING BRIB'D WITH HER $TONGUES $HARMONIE    2.29.6
    WHO WITH THY SWEET ALURING HARMONY               2.130.10
    OF HIS MAZDE POWERS KEEPES PERFIT HARMONY         4.99.8
HARMS                      2
    KEPT FOR HIMSELFE, DEFENDED FROM ALL HARMES       1.53.12
    MY HARMES ON $INK'S POORE LOSSE, PERHAPS
                              SOME FIND               4.34.13
HARP                       3
    THROUGH THE SWEET MUSICK WHICH HIS HARP DID MAKE  5.38.3
    THEN $ORPHEUS WITH HIS HARP THEYR STRIFE DID BAR  5.44.4
    BUT WHEN IN HAND MY TUNELESSE HARP I TAKE         5.44.9
HARPER'S                   1
    GOE HYRE THY SELFE SOME BUNGLING $HARPERS $BOY    2.48.10
HARROWED                   1
    AND HAVING HARROWD HELL DIDST BRING AWAY          5.68.3
HARSH                      2
    ELSE HARSH MY STILE, UNTUNABLE MY $MUSE           1.57.9
    HARSH, FEATURELESSE, AND RUDE, BARRENLY PERRISH   3.11.10
HARVEST                    3
    WHILST MY POORE LIPS WHICH SHOULD THAT
                              HARVEST REAPE           3.128.7
```

WHAT CAN BE HOPED MY HARVEST TIME WILL BE+   4.21.11
WHOSE HARVEST SEEMD TO HASTEN NOW APACE   5.76.10

HAST   14
WHAT TALKE I OF A $HEART, WHEN THOU HAST NONE+   2.52.13
OR IF THOU HAST, IT IS A FLINTY ONE   2.52.14
NOW HAST THOU END, AND NOW THOU WAST BEGUN   2.141.12
HASTE THOU THE $MASTER $MISTRIS OF MY PASSION   3.20.2
AND THOU (ALL THEY) HAST ALL THE ALL OF ME   3.31.14
WHAT HAST THOU THEN MORE THEN THOU HADST BEFORE+   3.40.2
THAT THOU HAST HER IT IS NOT ALL MY GRIEFE   3.42.1
TO LEAVE POORE ME, THOU HAST THE STRENGTH
                        OF LAWES   3.49.13
HIM HAVE I LOST, THOU HAST BOTH HIM AND ME   3.134.13
WHO EVER HATH HER WISH, THOU HAST THY $WILL   3.135.1
OH FROM WHAT POWRE HAST THOU THIS POWREFULL
                        MIGHT   3.150.1
WHENCE HAST THOU THIS BECOMMING OF THINGS IL   3.150.5
WHENCE HAST THOU $IVORIE, $RUBIES, PEARLE
                        AND GOLD   4.32.10
VAYNE MAN (QUOD I) THAT HAST BUT LITTLE PRIEFE   5.50.5

HASTE   6
WHICH HASTE FOR SUCCOUR TO HER SLOW REGARD   1.4.2
THERE'S NOTHING GRIEVES ME, BUT THAT $AGE
                        SHOULD HASTE   2.8.1
WEARY WITH TOYLE, I HAST ME TO MY BED   3.27.1
FROM WHERE THOU ART, WHY SHOULLD I HAST ME THENCE   3.51.3
MADE MORE OR LES BY THY CONTINUALL HAST   3.123.12
MAKE HAST THEREFORE SWEET LOVE, WHILEST
                        IT IS PRIME   5.70.13

HASTEN   2
SO DO OUR MINUITES HASTEN TO THEIR END   3.60.2
WHOSE HARVEST SEEMD TO HASTEN NOW APACE   5.76.10

HASTES   2
STRAIGHT-WAY SHE HASTS HER UNTO $DELIAS EIES   1.25.10
AND HASTES $ME ON UNTO A SUDDEN $DEATH   2.20.10

HASTY   1
A HASTIE $MAN (QUOTH HE) NE'R WANTED $WOE   2.59.8

HATCH   1
TO HATCH MINE EYES, AND THAT UNBITTED THOUGHT   4.38.2

HATCHED   1
TO SHEW, THAT I HAD HATCH'D IT FOR THE $AYRE   2.56.7

HATCHING   1
LIES HATCHING STILL THE GOODS WHEREIN THEY FLOW   4.24.2

HATE   26
WHAT, WILL $YOU HATE+ NAY THAT $YOU WILL
                        NOT NEITHER   2.19.5
NOR $LOVE, NOR $HATE, HOW THEN+ WHAT WILL
                        $YOU DOE+   2.19.6
OR WILL $YOU LOVE $ME, AND YET HATE $ME TOO+   2.19.8
YOUR $LOVE AND $HATE IS THIS, I NOW DOE
                        PROVE $YOU   2.19.13
YOU LOVE IN $HATE, BY $HATE TO MAKE $ME
                        LOVE $YOU   2.19.14
YOU LOVE IN $HATE, BY $HATE TO MAKE $ME
                        LOVE $YOU   2.19.14
CUPID, I HATE THEE, WHICH $I'DE HAVE THEE KNOW   2.48.1
LET THE $WORLD SEE THE UTMOST OF THY HATE   2.63.12
FOR THOU ART SO POSSEST WITH MURDROUS HATE   3.10.5
SHALL HATE BE FAIRER LOG'D THEN GENTLE LOVE+   3.10.10
SUCH CIVILL WAR IS IN MY LOVE AND HATE   3.35.12

```
FOR I MUST NERE LOVE HIM WHOM THOU DOST HATE        3.89.14
THEN HATE ME WHEN THOU WILT, IF EVER, NOW           3.90.1
BUT SHOOTE NOT AT ME IN YOUR WAKENED HATE           3.117.12
AS SUBJECT TO TIMES LOVE, OR TO TIMES HATE          3.124.3
LOVE IS MY SINNE, AND THY DEARE VERTUE HATE         3.142.1
HATE OF MY SINNE, GROUNDED ON SINFULL LOVING        3.142.2
BREATH'D FORTH THE SOUND THAT SAID I HATE           3.145.2
I HATE SHE ALTERD WITH AN END                       3.145.9
I HATE, FROM HATE AWAY SHE THREW                    3.145.13
I HATE, FROM HATE AWAY SHE THREW                    3.145.13
BUT LOVE HATE ON FOR NOW I KNOW THY MINDE           3.149.13
THE MORE I HEARE AND SEE JUST CAUSE OF HATE         3.150.10
IN VOWING NEW HATE AFTER NEW LOVE BEARING           3.152.4
THE BOY REFUSDE FOR FEARE OF $MARSE'S HATE          4.17.5
THE GROUND OF THIS FIERCE $LOVE AND LOVELY HATE     4.60.11
```
HATED   2
```
THOU WHICH HAST SCORNED $LIFE, AND HATED $DEATH     2.49.9
PAST REASON HATED AS A SWOLLOWED BAYT               3.129.7
```
HATEFUL   3
```
YET CANNOT LEAVE HER LOVE THAT HOLDS ME HATEFULL    1.18.5
SITH I LIVE HATEFULL TO THOSE RUTHLESSE EIES        1.21.7
SO I INVIRON'D WITH A HATEFULL WANT                 1.29.5
```
HATES   2
```
NOW SINCE HER CHAST MIND HATES THIS LOVE IN ME      4.61.9
SHALL QUICKLY ME FROM WHAT SHE HATES REMOVE         4.61.11
```
HATE'S   1
```
TO BEARE LOVES WRONG, THEN HATES KNOWNE INJURY      3.40.12
```
HATETH   1
```
WHO HATETH THEE THAT I DOE CALL MY FRIEND           3.149.5
```
HATH   34
```
SEE WHAT REWARD HE HATH THAT SERVES THE
                         UNGRATEFULL                1.18.7
DANGER HATH HONOR, GREAT DESIGNES THEIR FAME        1.35.6
MY $DELIA HATH THE WATERS OF MINE EIES              1.48.1
(IF LOVE IN HER HATH ANY POWER TO MOVE)             1.49.10
SHALL HAVE MY $SONG, WHERE $DELIA HATH HER SEAT     1.58.12
TIME HATH THY $BEAUTIE, WHICH WITH $AGE
                         WILL LEAVE THEE            2.10.12
WHAT $MUSE HATH POWER, ABOVE THY HEIGHT
                         TO RAISE THEE+             2.146.4
BUT BEAUTIES WASTE HATH IN THE WORLD AN END         3.9.11
AND $SOMMERS LEASE HATH ALL TOO SHORT A DATE        3.18.4
THAT SHE HATH THEE IS OF MY WAYLING CHEEFE          3.42.3
SINCE EVERY ONE, HATH EVERY ONE, ONE SHADE          3.53.3
FOR SHE HATH NO EXCHECKER NOW BUT HIS               3.67.11
MY LIFE HATH IN THIS LINE SOME INTEREST             3.74.3
YOU STILL SHALL LIVE (SUCH VERTUE HATH MY $PEN)     3.81.13
AND EVERY HUMOR HATH HIS ADJUNCT PLEASURE           3.91.5
WHEN IN THE LEAST OF THEM MY LIFE HATH END          3.92.6
THEN WHEN IT HATH MY ADDED PRAISE BESIDE            3.103.4
HATH MOTION, AND MINE EYE MAY BE DECEAVED           3.104.12
OF HIS QUICK OBJECTS HATH THE MINDE NO PART         3.113.7
SWEET BEAUTY HATH NO NAME NO HOLY BOURE             3.127.7
THAT $MUSICKE HATH A FARRE MORE PLEASING SOUND      3.130.10
THY FACE HATH NOT THE POWER TO MAKE LOVE GRONE      3.131.6
WHO EVER HATH HER WISH, THOU HAST THY $WILL         3.135.1
HATH THIS WORLD OUGHT SO FAIRE AS $STELLA IS+       4.21.14
OF ALL MY THOUGHTS HATH NEITHER STOP NOR START      4.23.13
HATH NO MISFORTUNE, BUT THAT $RICH SHE IS           4.37.14
HATH CHEEKES TO SMILE, AS WELL AS EYES TO WEEPE     4.70.8
```

WHO SINCE HE HATH, BY $NATURE'S SPECIALL GRACE   4.78.9
NOR NO DAY HATH LESSE QUIET THEN MY NIGHT   4.89.11
BUT, BUT (ALAS) NIGHT'S SIDE THE ODS HATH FUR   4.96.12
HER SELFE (TO SHEW NO OTHER JOY HATH PLACE)   4.97.7
ALL PAINE HATH END AND EVERY WAR HATH PEACE   5.11.13
AH WHY HATH NATURE TO SO HARD A HART   5.31.1
FALS LOWEST.. FOR ON EARTH NOUGHT HATH
                                ENDURAUNCE   5.58.12
HATRED   1
FOR THEIR CAN LIVE NO HATRED IN THINE EYE   3.93.5
HAUGHTY   2
SUCH HAUGHTY MYNDS ENUR'D TO HARDY FIGHT   5.14.7
FOR TO THE HEAVEN HER HAUGHTY LOOKES ASPIRE   5.55.11
HAUNTING   1
HAUNTING UNTRODDEN PATHS TO WAILE APART   1.9.10
HAUNTS   1
AN $EVILL SPIRIT YOUR BEAUTIE HAUNTS $ME STILL   2.20.1
HAVE   68
WHICH STILL IS CHAC'D, WHILE I HAVE ANY BREATH   1.5.10
MY FAITH SHOULD WIN, IF $JUSTICE MIGHT HAVE PLACE   1.8.12
LET $VENUS HAVE THY GRACES, HER RESIGN'D   1.19.9
T'HAVE PEACE ABROAD, AND NOUGHT WITHIN BUT STRIFE   1.20.3
HOW TO THINKE MUCH, AND HAVE NO WORDS TO SPEAKE   1.20.6
AND HAVE NO STARS BUT THOSE, THAT MUST FULFILL   1.33.6
SUFFICE THAT HIGH ATTEMPTS HAVE NEVER SHAME   1.35.9
I ONELY SOUGHT THE BLISSE TO HAVE HER SIGHT   1.36.12
AND ($DELIA) THINKE THY MORNING MUST HAVE NIGHT   1.40.8
FLOWERS HAVE A TIME BEFORE THEY COME TO SEEDE   1.51.3
PRAISING VERTUES IN THEM THAT HAVE THEM NOT   1.58.7
SHALL HAVE MY $SONG, WHERE $DELIA HATH HER SEAT   1.58.12
ILE MONE MY SELFE, AND HIDE THE WRONG I HAVE   1.59.10
YET $HEAV'N WILL STILL HAVE $MURTHER OUT AT LAST   2.2.14
MUST $WOE AND I, HAVE NAUGHT BUT $NO AND I+   2.5.9
NO I, AM I, IF I NO MORE CAN HAVE   2.5.10
I HAVE A $MED'CINE THAT SHALL CURE MY $LOVE   2.15.2
IF THIS $RECEIT HAVE NOT THE POW'R TO WINNE ME   2.15.13
OR HAVE OUR $PASSIONS LESSER POW'R THEN THEIRS   2.27.5
TURNING MY $PAPERS, ASKES, $WHAT HAVE WE HEERE+   2.31.3
AS COVETOUS THE OTHERS USE TO HAVE   2.33.10
SOME SAY, I HAVE A PASSING PLEASING $STRAINE   2.42.3
OR HAVE THINE $EYES SUCH $MAGIKE, OR THAT $ART   2.52.3
I HAVE, I WANT, $DESPAIRE, AND YET $DESIRE   2.62.13
NOR THOU, NOR I, THE BETTER YET CAN HAVE   2.63.3
SOME SAY, I HAVE A PASSING PLEASING $STRAINE   2.128.3
WITH TEARES, SIGHES, AND DISDAINE, SHALL
                        HAVE IMMORTAL STRIFE   2.132.14
I HAVE, I WANT, $DESPAIRE, AND YET $DESIRE   2.150.13
AND YET ME THINKES I HAVE $ASTRONOMY   3.14.2
THOUGH THOU REPENT, YET I HAVE STILL THE LOSSE   3.34.10
ROSES HAVE THORNES, AND SILVER FOUNTAINES MUD   3.35.2
THIS WISH I HAVE, THEN TEN TIMES HAPPY ME   3.37.14
IN ALL EXTERNALL GRACE YOU HAVE SOME PART   3.53.13
THE $CANKER BLOOMES HAVE FULL AS DEEPE A DIE   3.54.5
I HAVE NO PRECIOUS TIME AT AL TO SPEND   3.57.3
BUT WEEPE TO HAVE, THAT WHICH IT FEARES TO LOOSE   3.64.14
O NONE, UNLESSE THIS MIRACLE HAVE MIGHT   3.65.13
THE EARTH CAN HAVE BUT EARTH, WHICH IS HIS DUE   3.74.7
YOUR NAME FROM HENCE IMMORTALL LIFE SHALL HAVE   3.81.5
HAPPY TO HAVE THY LOVE, HAPPY TO DIE   3.92.12
THEY THAT HAVE POWRE TO HURT, AND WILL DOE NONE   3.94.1

```
HAVE EYES TO WONDER, BUT LACK TOUNGS TO PRAISE      3.106.14
NOW ALL IS DONE, HAVE WHAT SHALL HAVE NO END         3.110.9
HAVE FACULTIE BY NATURE TO SUBSIST                   3.122.6
HAD, HAVING, AND IN QUEST, TO HAVE EXTREAME          3.129.10
IF THOU DOOST SEEKE TO HAVE WHAT THOU
                              DOOST HIDE             3.142.13
SO WILL I PRAY THAT THOU MAIST HAVE THY $WILL        3.143.13
TWO LOVES I HAVE CF COMFORT AND DISPAIRE             3.144.1
WHICH HAVE NO CORRESPONDENCE WITH TRUE SIGHT         3.148.2
OR IF THEY HAVE, WHERE IS MY JUDGMENT FLED           3.148.3
ALAS HAVE I NOT PAINE ENOUGH MY FRIEND                4.14.1
FLIE, FLY, MY FRIENDS, I HAVE MY DEATH
                              WOUND., FLY             4.20.1
TO HAVE FOR NO CAUSE BIRTHRIGHT IN THE SKIE          4.26.5
OR SPRITE, DISDAINE OF SUCH DISDAINE TO HAVE+        4.47.6
SO MAY YOU STILL HAVE SCME WHAT NEW TO SAY           4.51.4
LET $VERTUE HAVE THAT $STELLA'S SELFE., YET THUS     4.52.13
BUT THOU $DESIRE, BECAUSE THOU WOULDST HAVE ALL      4.72.13
THEN SINCE (DEARE LIFE) YOU FAINE WOULD
                              HAVE ME PEACE          4.81.12
OR IF I NEEDS (SWEET $JUDGE) MUST TORMENTS HAVE      4.86.11
THANKE MAY YOU HAVE FOR SUCH A THANKFULL PART        4.95.13
THAT WORMES SHOULD HAVE THEIR $SUN, AND
                              I WANT MINE            4.98.14
NOR TO THE $STARRES.. FCR THEY HAVE PURER SIGHT       5.9.7
TELL ME WHEN SHALL THESE WEARIE WOES HAVE END        5.36.1
IS IT BECAUSE YOUR EYES HAVE POWRE TO KILL+          5.49.2
AND THEN MY BODY SHALL HAVE SHORTLY EASE             5.50.11
SWEET WARRIOUR WHEN SHALL I HAVE PEACE WITH YOU+     5.57.1
TO ALL THOSE HAPPY BLESSINGS WHICH YE HAVE           5.66.1
BUT HERE ON EARTH TC HAVE SUCH HEVENS BLISSE         5.72.14
HAVING                 10
FOR HAVING TRAFFIKE WITH THY SELFE ALONE              3.4.9
AND HAVING THEE, CF ALL MENS PRIDE I BOAST           3.91.12
THAT HAVING SUCH A SKOPE TO SHOW HER PRICE           3.103.2
HAD, HAVING, AND IN QUEST, TO HAVE EXTREAME          3.129.10
WHY SO LARGE COST HAVING SO SHORT A LEASE            3.146.5
HAVING NO SCARFE CF CLOWDS BEFORE HIS FACE            4.22.3
BUT HAVING PINE AND HAVING NOT COMPLAINE              5.35.4
AND HAVING IT THEY GAZE CN IT THE MORE                5.35.6
BUT HAVING HER, MY JOY WIL BE THE GREATER            5.51.14
BUT HAVING PINE AND HAVING NOT COMPLAINE              5.83.4
HAWKS                   2
SOME IN THEIR $HAWKES AND $HOUNDS, SOME
                          IN THEIR $HORSE            3.91.4
OF MORE DELIGHT THEN $HAWKES OR $HORSES BEE          3.91.11
HEAD                   21
THY $PEARLY $TEETH CUT CF THY $HEAD SO CLEANE         2.8.11
THEN, SWEET $DESPAIRE, AWHILE HOLD UP THY HEAD       2.26.13
THEN SWEET $DISPAIRE, AWHILE HOLD UP THY HEAD        2.137.13
LIFTS UP HIS BURNING HEAD, EACH UNDER EYE             3.7.2
TIL THEN, NOT SHOW MY HEAD WHERE THOU
                          MAIST PROVE ME             3.26.14
BUT THEN BEGINS A JCURNY IN MY HEAD                  3.27.3
TO LIVE A SCOND LIFE ON SECOND HEAD                  3.68.7
IF HAIRES BE WIERS, BLACK WIERS GROW ON HER HEAD     3.130.4
O ME- WHAT EYES HATH LOVE PUT IN MY HEAD             3.148.1
TO SHEW HER SKIN, LIPS, TEETH AND HEAD SC WELL+      4.32.11
A ROSIE GARLAND, AND A WEARIE HED                    4.39.11
THOU BEAR'ST THE ARROW, I THE ARROW HEAD             4.65.14
```

```
VERTUE'S GOLD NOW MUST HEAD MY $CUPID'S DART        4.72.8
BUT WITH SHORT BREATH, LONG LOOKES, STAID
                       FEET AND WALKING HED          4.76.13
SOME BEAUTIE'S PEECE, AS AMBER COLOURD HED           4.91.6
AND MAKES ME THEN BOW DOWNE MY HEAD, AND SAY         4.108.9
THEN WOULD I DECKE HER HEAD WITH GLORIOUS BAYES      5.29.13
SUFFICIENT WORKE FOR ONE MANS SIMPLE HEAD            5.33.7
AND TO THE LIGHT LIFT UP THEYR DROUPING HED          5.40.12
WITHIN A BUSH HIS DREADFULL HEAD DOTH HIDE           5.53.3
AND CATCHING HOLD ON THINE OWNE WICKED HED           5.86.10
```
HEADS   3
```
AS WHAT THEIR HANDS DO HOLD, THEIR HEADS DO KNOW     4.24.6
AND THEY THEREWITH DOE POETES HEADS ADORNE           5.29.7
THEYR SNAKY HEADS DOE COMBE, FROM WHICH A SPRING     5.86.3
```
HEAL   5
```
AND LIST NOT SEEKE TO BREAKE, TO QUENCH, TO HEALE    1.14.9
GOOD $DELIA LOSE, QUENCH, HEALE ME NOW AT LENGTH     1.14.14
THE FRIENDLY FRAY, WHERE BLOWES BOTH WOUND
                       AND HEALE                     4.79.10
AND WITH ONE SALVE BOTH HART AND BODY HEALE          5.50.14
THAT AL MY WOUNDS WIL HEALE IN LITTLE SPACE          5.57.14
```
HEALED   2
```
AND MINE $EARES DEAFE, BY THY $FAME HEALED BEE       2.35.10
AND MINE EARES DEAFE, BY THY FAME HEALED BE          2.112.10
```
HEALS   1
```
THAT HEALES THE WOUND, AND CURES NOT THE DISGRACE    3.34.8
```
HEALTH   2
```
OF THEIR FAIRE HEALTH, RECOUNTING IT TO ME           3.45.12
NO NEWES BUT HEALTH FROM THEIR $PHISITIONS KNOW      3.140.8
```
HEALTHFUL   3
```
AND BROUGHT TO MEDICINE A HEALTHFULL STATE           3.118.11
GROWING A BATH AND HEALTHFULL REMEDY                 3.154.11
YOUR WORDS MY FRIEND (RIGHT HEALTHFULL
                       CAUSTIKS) BLAME               4.21.1
```
HEAP   1
```
HEAPE THINE OWN VERTUES SEASONED BY THEIR SUNNE      2.106.5
```
HEAPED   1
```
LEAVES TO HIS $SONNE ALL HE HAD HEAP'D TOGETHER      2.10.4
```
HEAR   18
```
NO OTHER PROUDER $BROOKES SHALL HEARE MY WRONG       1.58.14
I $HEARE SOME SAY, THIS $MAN IS NOT IN LOVE          2.24.1
SITH SHE IS DEAFE, AND WILL NOT HEARE MY $MONES      2.45.10
A WORLD TO SEE, YET HOW HE JOYD TO HEARE             2.125.7
MUSICK TO HEARE, WHY HEAR'ST THOU MUSICK SADLY       3.8.1
TO HEARE WIT EIES BELONGS TO LOVES FINE WIHT         3.23.14
THEN YOU SHALL HEARE THE SURLY SULLEN BELL           3.71.2
FOR FEARE OF WHICH, HEARE THIS THOU AGE UNBRED       3.104.13
I LOVE TO HEARE HER SPEAKE, YET WELL I KNOW          3.130.9
THE MORE I HEARE AND SEE JUST CAUSE OF HATE          3.150.10
HER COME, AND HEARE WITH PATIENCE MY DESIRE          4.56.13
SHE HEARD MY PLAINTS, AND DID NOT ONLY HEARE         4.57.9
SOME DO I HEARE OF $POETS' FURIE TELL                4.74.5
LET EARES HEARE SPEECH, WHICH WIT TO WONDER TIES     4.85.11
AND HER SAD WORDS MY SADDED SENCE DID HEARE          4.87.8
IF YOU HEARE THAT THEY SEEME MY HART TO MOVE         4.91.13
THAT SHE WILL ONCE VOUCHSAFE MY PLAINT TO HEARE      5.18.7
AND WOULD NOT HEARE, WHEN HE TO HER COMPLAYNED       5.48.11
```
HEARD   7
```
THEN WHO HAD HEARD THE PLAINTS I UTTER NOW+          1.6.12
NOR YET THE WORLD HAVE HEARD OF SUCH DISDAINE        1.7.8
```

```
THEN THINKE THAT WE BEFORE HAVE HEARD THEM TOULD      3.123.8
NOR TRUMPETS SOUND I HEARD, NOR FRIENDLY CRIES        4.53.12
SHE HEARD MY PLAINTS, AND DID NOT ONLY HEARE          4.57.9
LEAST ONCE SHOULD NOT BE HEARD, TWISE
                         SAID, $NO, $NO              4.63.8
NO WORD WAS HEARD OF HER THAT MOST IT OUGHT           5.19.10
HEAREST                 1
   MUSICK TO HEARE, WHY HEAR'ST THOU MUSICK SADLY     3.8.1
HEARING                 3
   MY $HEARING BRIB'D WITH HER $TONGUES $HARMONIE     2.29.6
   HEARING YOU PRAISD, I SAY 'TIS SO, 'TIS TRUE       3.85.9
   YET HEARING LATE A FABLE, WHICH DID SHOW           4.45.5
HEARS                   1
   AND YET SHE HEARES, YET I NO PITTY FIND            4.44.5
HEARSAY                 1
   LET THEM SAY MORE THAT LIKE OF HEARE-SAY WELL      3.21.13
HEARSE                  1
   EVER HENCEFORTH MY $BOSOME BE YOUR $HEARSE         2.45.7
HEART                 242
   KNOCKE AT THAT HARD HART, BEGGE TILL YOU
                         HAVE MOV'D HER               1.2.13
   THESE LINES I USE, T'UNBURTHEN MINE OWNE HART      1.4.13
   MY FENCE OPPRESS'D, HAD FAILD, AND HEART
                         HAD BROKEN                   1.7.14
THOU POORE HEART SACRIFIZ'D UNTO THE FAIREST          1.8.1
AND YOU MINE EYES, THE AGENTS OF MY HART              1.8.5
TEARES IN MINE EYES, AND SORROW AT MY HART            1.9.12
INTENERAT THAT HEART THAT SETS SO LIGHT               1.10.7
UPON THE PROSTRATE SPOYLE OF THAT POORE HART          1.10.10
TEARES, VOWES, AND PRAYERS, WINNE THE
                         HARDEST HART                 1.11.1
FOR SHE THAT CAN MY HEART IMPARADIZE                  1.12.9
I FIGURDE ON THE TABLE OF MINE HART                   1.13.6
HARD IS HER HART, AND WOE IS ME THEREFORE             1.13.12
UNHAPPY I, TO LOVE A STONY HART                       1.13.14
IF THAT A LOYALL HART AND FAITH UNFAINED              1.15.1
AND LAIES TO VIEW MY $VULTUR-GNAWNE HART OPEN         1.15.8
HER EYES EXACT IT, THOUGH HER HART DISDAINES ME       1.18.6
UPON THE FLINT OF SUCH A HART REBELLING               1.18.10
YEELD TO THE $MARBLE THY HARD HART AGAINE             1.19.13
DELIA MY HART HATH LEARND OUT OF THOSE EYES           1.20.14
SHE DOTH ME WRONG, TO GRIEVE SO TRUE A HEART          1.21.14
WITH THIS POORE HEART CONSUMED WITH DISPAIRE          1.22.8
THIS HEART MADE NOW THE PROSPECTIVE OF CARE           1.22.9
ILE PRAISE HER FACE, AND BLAME HER FLINTY HEART       1.26.12
TO STOP THE PASSAGE OF MY VANQUISHT HART              1.27.2
WITH THEE SUCH POWERS TO PLAGUE ONE SILLY HARTE       1.27.12
YET HEAVY HEART TO MAKE SO HARD A CHOISE              1.28.3
WHILST BY THY EIES PURSU'D, MY POORE HEART FLEW       1.31.1
ONE IN MY LOVE, AND HER HARD HART STILL ONE           1.33.4
UPON THIS HEART, WHOM CRUELTY WILL KILL               1.33.8
AND BLAME MY SELFE T'EXCUSE THAT HEART OF THINE       1.33.12
WHOSE INFLUENCE RULE THE $ORBE OF MY POORE HART+      1.34.10
THINKING TO SCALE THE HEAVEN OF HER HART              1.36.2
I FEARE YOUR EYE HATH TURND YOUR HEART TO FLINT       1.37.14
(THE CHASTEST FLAME THAT EVER WARMED HART)            1.44.4
YET NOUGHT THE ROCKE OF THAT HARD HEART CAN MOVE      1.48.9
TO BREAKE THE $ISE THAT HATH CONGEALD HER HEART+      1.49.8
I KNOW HER HEART CANNOT BUT JUDGE WITH ME             1.49.13
HAPPY THE HEART THAT SIGH'D FOR SUCH A ONE            1.51.14
```

```
MY TOUGHT HEART TURNES IT TO THAT HAPPY COST          1.53.2
AND THY HARD HEART HAD YEELDED UP THE SAME            1.56.8
THIS IS MY STATE, AND $DELIAS HEART IS SUCH           1.60.13
MY $HEART WAS SLAINE, AND NONE BUT YOU AND I          2.2.1
MY HEART HATH PAID SUCH GRIEVOUS $USURIE              2.3.11
INVITES MY $HEART TO BE THE CHIEFEST $GHEST           2.7.4
SLEW HIS DEARE $FRIEND, MY KIND AND TRUEST $HEART     2.7.12
WHICH MY $HEART, LIGHTNED BY THY $LOVE, COTH SEE      2.12.14
THE POWDER OF HER $HEART DRY'D, WHEN SHE IS CEAD      2.15.3
YOU CANNOT LOVE, MY PRETTIE $HEART, AND WHY+          2.19.1
WHO GAVE CONSENT TC STEALE AWAY MY $HEART             2.23.11
I AM SURE MY $SIGHES COME FROM A $HEART AS TRUE       2.27.9
WHEN CONQU'RING $LOVE DID FIRST MY $HEART ASSAYLE     2.29.1
MY $HEART SHOULD SUFFER FOR MINE $EYES $OFFENCE       2.29.4
HE YEELDS $LOVE UP THE $KEYES UNTO MY $HEART          2.29.11
THY HALLOW'D $TEMPLE ONELY IS MY $HEART               2.30.14
MY WOFULL $HEART, IMPRISON'D IN MY $BREST             2.33.2
WISHING THEMSELVES, THAT THEY HAD BEENE MY $HEART     2.33.8
THAT $EYES WERE $HEART, OR THAT THE $HEART
                             WERE EYES                2.33.9
THAT $EYES WERE $HEART, OR THAT THE $HEART
                             WERE EYES                2.33.9
THAT $EYES COULD THINKE OF THAT MY $HEART
                             COULD SEE                2.33.14
TO WOUND HER $HEART, WHOSE $EYES HAVE WOUNDED ME      2.36.2
MY $HEART THE $ANVILE, WHERE MY $THOUGHTS
                             DOE BEATE                2.40.1
WHOSE SCORCHING GLEED, MY HEART TO $CINDERS
                             TURNETH                  2.40.10
WHEN MY $HEART IS THE VERY $DEN OF $HORROR            2.41.2
SHE COMMING NEERE, THAT MY POORE $HEART
                             HATH SLAINE              2.46.9
WHAT DO'ST THOU MEANE TO $CHEATE ME OF MY $HEART      2.52.1
AND FOR ONE PIECE OF $THINE, MY WHOLE HEART TAKE      2.52.8
WHAT TALKE I OF A $HEART, WHEN THOU HAST NONE+        2.52.13
THOSE $EYES TO MY $HEART SHINING EVER BRIGHT          2.55.13
SO MAY THE $HEAVENS READ WONDERS IN MY $HEART         2.60.8
AND I AM GLAD, YEA GLAD WITHALL MY HEART              2.61.3
MY $HEART FOR $HOSTAGE THAT IT SHALL REMAINE          2.63.6
THOSE EYES TO MY HART SHINING EVER BRIGHT             2.102.13
NOR MY HART KNOWNE THE POWER OF THY NAME              2.104.6
MY HART HATH PAYD SUCH GRIEVOUS USURY                 2.110.11
MY HART SHALL BE THE PRISON FOR MY FAYRE              2.115.5
MY $HART IMPRISONEC IN A HOPELES $ILE                 2.122.1
SUNNE OF THE WORLD, THOU HART REVYVING FIRE           2.123.8
AND TO MY HART SEND'ST POYSON FROM THINE EYE          2.130.7
HAST PLAYD THE THIEFE, AND STOLNE MY HART
                             FROM ME                  2.130.11
THOSE SIGHES WHICH COOLE MY HART, ARE
                             COLES UNTO MY LOVE       2.132.2
LOVE HEATS MY HART, MY HART-HEAT MY SIGHES
                             WARMETH                  2.132.6
DESIRE, MY LOVE, MY SOULE, MY HOPE, HART,
                             AND LIFE CHARMETH        2.132.8
MY HART IMBRACETH $LOVE, $LOVE DOTH IMBRACE
                             MY HART                  2.132.10
MY HART IMBRACETH $LOVE, $LOVE DOTH IMBRACE
                             MY HART                  2.132.10
DESIRE, MY LOVE, MY SOULE, MY HOPE, MY
                             HART, MY LIFE            2.132.13
```

```
MY WOFULL HART IMPRISOND IN MY BREAST              2.133.2
WISH NOW TO BE TRANS-FORMD INTO MY HART            2.133.8
MY HART SURCHARG'D WITH THOUGHTS, SIGHES
                         IN ABUNDANCE RAISE        2.133.9
AND WHILST MY HART AND EYE, ENVY EACH
                         OTHERS PRAISE             2.133.11
SEE CHASTE $DIANA, WHERE MY HARMLES HART           2.135.1
INTO HIS HART THE PIERCING $ARROW FLYES            2.135.8
IN THINE EYES TRYUMPH MURTHERING MY POORE HART     2.140.2
MY HALFE-SLAINE HART SHALL TAKE REVENGE ON THEE    2.140.4
WHEN MY HART IS THE VERY $DEN OF HORROR            2.143.2
MY $HART THE $ANVILE WHERE MY THOUGHTS DOE BEATE   2.144.1
WITH SCORCHING GLEED MY HART TO CYNDERS TURNETH    2.144.10
SO MAY THE HEAVENS READE WONDERS IN MY HART        2.149.8
A WOMANS GENTLE HART BUT NOT ACQUAINTED            3.20.3
IS BUT THE SEEMELY RAYMENT OF MY HEART             3.22.6
BEARING THY HEART WHICH I WILL KEEPE SO CHARY      3.22.11
PRESUME NOT ON THY HEART WHEN MINE IS SLAINE       3.22.13
WHOSE STRENGTHS ABONDANCE WEAKENS HIS OWNE HEART   3.23.4
THY BEAUTIES FORME IN TABLE OF MY HEART            3.24.2
THEY DRAW BUT WHAT THEY SEE, KNOW NOT THE HART     3.24.14
WHEN I AM SOME-TIME ABSENT FROM THY HEART          3.41.2
MINE EYE AND HEART ARE AT A MORTALL WARRE          3.46.1
MINE EYE, MY HEART THEIR PICTURES SIGHT
                         WOULD BARRE               3.46.3
MY HEART, MINE EYE THE FREEEDOME OF THAT RIGHT     3.46.4
MY HEART DOTH PLEAD THAT THOU IN HIM DOOST LYE     3.46.5
A QUEST OF THOUGHTS, ALL TENNANTS TO THE HEART     3.46.10
AND MY HEARTS RIGHT, THEIR INWARD LOVE OF HEART    3.46.14
BETWIXT MINE EYE AND HEART A LEAGUE IS TOOKE       3.47.1
OR HEART IN LOVE WITH SIGHES HIMSELFE
                         DOTH SMOTHER              3.47.4
AND TO THE PAINTED BANQUET BIDS MY HEART           3.47.6
AWAKES MY HEART, TO HEARTS AND EYES DELIGHT        3.47.14
BUT YOU LIKE NONE, NONE YOU FOR CONSTANT HEART     3.53.14
IT IS SO GROUNDED INWARD IN MY HEART               3.62.4
AH DOE NOT, WHEN MY HEART HATH SCAPTE THIS SORROW  3.90.5
THY LOOKES WITH ME, THY HEART IN OTHER PLACE       3.93.4
TAKE HEED (DEARE HEART) OF THIS LARGE PRIVILEDGE   3.95.13
O NEVER SAY THAT I WAS FALSE OF HEART              3.109.1
THESE BLENCHES GAVE MY HEART AN OTHER YOUTH        3.110.7
FOR IT NO FORME DELIVERS TO THE HEART              3.113.5
WHAT WRETCHED ERRORS HATH MY HEART COMMITTED       3.119.5
OR AT THE LEAST, SO LONG AS BRAINE AND HEART       3.122.5
NOE, LET ME BE OBSEQUIOUS IN THY HEART             3.125.9
FOR WELL THOU KNOW'ST TO MY DEARE DOTING HART      3.131.3
KNOWING THY HEART TORMENT ME WITH DISDAINE         3.132.2
O LET IT THEN AS WELL BESEEME THY HEART            3.132.10
BESHREW THAT HEART THAT MAKES MY HEART TO GROANE   3.133.1
BESHREW THAT HEART THAT MAKES MY HEART TO GROANE   3.133.1
PRISON MY HEART IN THY STEELE BOSOMES WARDE        3.133.9
BUT THEN MY FRIENDS HEART LET MY POORE
                         HEART BALE                3.133.10
BUT THEN MY FRIENDS HEART LET MY POORE
                         HEART BALE                3.133.10
WHO ERE KEEPES ME, LET MY HEART BE HIS GARDE       3.133.11
WHERETO THE JUDGEMENT OF MY HEART IS TIDE+         3.137.8
WHY SHOULD MY HEART THINKE THAT A SEVERALL PLOT    3.137.9
WHICH MY HEART KNOWES THE WIDE WORLDS
                         COMMON PLACE+             3.137.10
```

```
IN THINGS RIGHT TRUE MY HEART AND EYES
                        HAVE ERRED                       3.137.13
THAT THY UNKINDNESSE LAYES UPON MY HEART                 3.139.2
DEARE HEART FORBEARE TO GLANCE THINE EYE ASIDE           3.139.6
BEARE THINE EYES STRAIGHT, THOUGH THY
                        PROUD HEART GOE WIDE             3.140.14
BUT 'TIS MY HEART THAT LOVES WHAT THEY DISPISE           3.141.3
DISWADE ONE FOOLISH HEART FROM SERVING THEE              3.141.10
ROOTE PITTIE IN THY HEART THAT WHEN IT GROWES            3.142.11
STRAIGHT IN HER HEART DID MERCIE COME                    3.145.5
WITH INSUFFICIENCY MY HEART TO SWAY                      3.150.2
LAID BY HIS SIDE HIS HEART INFLAMING BRAND               3.154.2
'FOOLE,' SAID MY $MUSE TO ME, 'LOOKE IN
                        THY HEART AND WRITE'             4.1.14
I SWEARE, MY HEART SUCH ONE SHALL SHEW TO THEE           4.4.12
AND, FOOLES, ADORE IN TEMPLE OF OUR HART                 4.5.7
FORC'D BY A TEDIOUS PROOFE, THAT $TURKISH
                        HARDNED HART                     4.8.2
TO MY CLOSE HEART, WHERE WHILE SOME FIREBRANDS
                        HE DID LAY                       4.8.13
BUT, FOOLE, SEEKST NOT TO GET INTO HER HART              4.11.14
O NO, HER HEART IS SUCH A $CITTADELL                     4.12.12
WHICH THROUGH A BLEEDING HEART HIS POINT
                        DID SHOVE                        4.13.6
BUT ERE I COULD FLIE THENCE, IT PIERC'D MY HEART         4.20.14
BUT ONLY $STELLA'S EYES AND $STELLA'S HART               4.23.14
RICH FOOLES THERE BE, WHOSE BASE AND FILTHY HART         4.24.1
BREATHE OUT THE FLAMES WHICH BURNE WITHIN
                        MY HEART                         4.28.13
SO $STELLA'S HEART, FINDING WHAT POWER
                        $LOVE BRINGS                     4.29.5
AND THUS HER HEART ESCAPES, BUT THUS HER EYES            4.29.9
BUT FROM THY HEART, WHILE MY SIRE CHARMETH THEE          4.32.13
HART RENT THY SELFE, THOU DOEST THY SELFE
                        BUT RIGHT                        4.33.5
A BURTHNED HART. '$HOW CAN WORDS EASE, WHICH ARE         4.34.2
A CONQUERD, YELDEN, RANSACKT HEART TO WINNE+             4.36.2
RICH IN THE RICHES OF A ROYALL HART                      4.37.10
THAT IN MY HEART I OFFER STILL TO THEE                   4.40.13
FAIRE EYES, SWEET LIPS, DEARE HEART, THAT
                        FOOLISH I                        4.43.1
FROM ALL THE WORLD, HER HEART IS THEN HIS ROME           4.43.13
SUCH SMART MAY PITIE CLAIME OF ANY HART                  4.44.3
HER HEART, SWEETE HEART, IS OF NO $TYGRE'S KIND          4.44.4
HER HEART, SWEETE HEART, IS OF NO $TYGRE'S KIND          4.44.4
DOTH MAKE MY HEART GIVE TO MY TONGUE THE LIE             4.47.14
THAT THROUGH MY HEART THEIR BEAMIE DARTS BE GONE         4.48.10
MY HORSE, HE SPURRES WITH SHARPE DESIRE MY HART          4.49.11
MEANE WHILE MY HEART CONFERS WITH $STELLA'S
                        BEAMES                           4.51.12
MY HEART THEN QUAK'D, THEN DAZLED WERE MINE EYES         4.53.10
THAT HIS RIGHT BADGE IS BUT WORNE IN THE HART            4.54.12
SO SWEETE SOUNDS STRAIGHT MINE EARE AND
                        HEART DO HIT                     4.55.13
FOR LATE WITH HEART MOST HIGH, WITH EYES MOST LOW        4.63.5
BUT THAT WHICH ONCE MAY WIN THY CRUELL HART              4.64.13
I LODG'D THEE IN MY HEART, AND BEING BLIND               4.65.7
MINE EYES, MY LIGHT, MY HEART, MY LIFE, ALAS             4.65.9
STOLNE TO MY HEART, SINCE LAST FAIRE NIGHT,
                        NAY DAY                          4.66.10
```

```
OF HER HIGH HEART GIV'N ME THE MONARCHIE                    4.69.10
SO WHILE THY BEAUTIE DRAWES THE HEART TO LOVE               4.71.12
WHILE EACH DOTH BLOW THE FIER OF MY HART                    4.72.4
MY HEART CRIES 'AH', IT BURNES, MINE EYES
                        NOW DAZLED BE                        4.76.11
A DOUBLE KEY, WHICH OPENS TO THE HEART                      4.79.6
THUS MUCH MY HEART COMPELD MY MOUTH TO SAY                  4.80.9
BUT NOW SPITE OF MY HEART MY MOUTH WILL STAY                4.80.10
BREATHING ALL BLISSE AND SWEETNING TO THE HEART            4.81.3
BUT MY HEART BURNES, I CANNOT SILENT BE                     4.81.11
TO HER, WHERE I MY HEART SAFELIEST SHALL MEET               4.84.6
I SEE THE HOUSE, MY HEART THY SELFE CONTAINE                4.85.1
LET WO GRIPE ON MY HEART, SHAME LOADE MINE EYE              4.86.4
STELLA FOOD OF MY THOUGHTS, HART OF MY HART                 4.87.2
STELLA FOOD OF MY THOUGHTS, HART OF MY HART                 4.87.2
THAT WHERE BEFORE HART LOVED AND EYES DID SEE               4.88.12
IN HART BOTH SIGHT AND LOVE NOW COUPLED BE                  4.88.13
IF YOU HEARE THAT THEY SEEME MY HART TO MOVE                4.91.13
THANKE-WORTHIEST YET WHEN YOU SHALL BREAKE
                        MY HART                              4.95.14
THAT HUE, WHOSE FORCE MY HART STILL UNTO
                        THRALDOME TIES+                      4.102.8
AS WHAT MY HART STILL SEES THOU CANST NOT SPIE+             4.105.4
SWEETE, FOR A WHILE GIVE RESPITE TO MY HART                 4.107.5
THROUGH THAT DARKE FORNACE TO MY HART OPPREST               4.108.3
OF TH'INWARD BALE OF MY LOVE PINED HART                     5.2.2
YET IN MY HART I THEN BOTH SPEAKE AND WRITE                 5.3.13
FAYRE EYES, THE MYRROUR OF MY MAZED HART                    5.7.1
YOU STOP MY TOUNG, AND TEACH MY HART TO SPEAKE              5.8.10
BUT HER PROUD HART DOE THOU A LITTLE SHAKE                  5.10.9
AND LAY INCESSANT BATTERY TO HER HEART                      5.14.10
THE WHILES MY STONISHT HART STOOD IN AMAZE                  5.16.3
AYMING HIS ARROW AT MY VERY HART                            5.16.10
THE CHARMING SMILES, THAT ROB SENCE FROM
                        THE HART                             5.17.10
AND LONG INTREATY SOFTEN HER HARD HART                      5.18.6
AND DOE MYNE HUMBLED HART BEFORE HER POURE                  5.20.2
AND ON THE SAME MY HART WILL SACRIFISE                      5.22.11
IS NOT DELAYD BY HER HART FROSEN COLD                       5.30.6
AH WHY HATH NATURE TO SO HARD A HART                        5.31.1
HER HART MORE HARDE THEN YRON SOFT AWHIT                    5.32.6
AND ME REVIVED WITH HART ROBBING GLADNESSE                  5.39.8
SO MY STORME BEATEN HART LIKEWISE IS CHEARED                5.40.13
AND YIELD FOR PLEDGE MY POORE CAPTYVED HART                 5.42.8
AND IF I SILENT BE, MY HART WILL BREAKE                     5.43.3
WHAT TYRANNY IS THIS BOTH MY HART TO THRALL                 5.43.5
YET I MY HART WITH SILENCE SECRETLY                         5.43.9
WITHIN MY HART, THOUGH HARDLY IT CAN SHEW                   5.45.5
TO UTTER FORTH THE ANGUISH OF HIS HART                      5.48.10
IS NOT THE HART OF ALL THE BODY CHIEFE+                     5.50.7
THE INWARD LANGUOR OF MY WOUNDED HART                       5.50.10
AND WITH ONE SALVE BOTH HART AND BODY HEALE                 5.50.14
SO DOE I HOPE HER STUBBORNE HART TO BEND                    5.51.11
IS PRISONER LED AWAY WITH HEAVY HART                        5.52.3
SHE LAUGHES, AND HARDENS EVERMORE HER HART                  5.54.12
SEEING MY HART THROUGH LAUNCHED EVERY WHERE                 5.57.7
UNTO HER SELFE AND SETLED SO IN HART                        5.59.2
HART NEED NOT WISH NONE OTHER HAPPINESSE                    5.72.13
MY HART, WHOM NONE WITH SERVILE BANDS CAN TYE               5.73.2
EVEN SO MY HART, THAT WONT ON YOUR FAYRE EYE                5.73.7
```

```
    AND THEREON FEED MY LOVE-AFFAMISHT HART         5.88.12
HEARTED                     1
    OR TO THY SELFE AT LEAST KIND HARTED PROVE      3.10.12
HEART-HEAT                  1
    LOVE HEATS MY HART, MY HART-HEAT MY SIGHES
                          WARMETH                   2.132.6
HEART-PIERCING              1
    MORE $ARROWES WITH HART-PIERCING METTEL POYNTED 2.126.11
HEARTS                     15
    BUT UNTOUCHT HEARTS, WITH UNAFFECTED EIE        1.3.5
    IN FEELING HEARTS THAT CAN CONCEIVE THESE LINES 1.43.2
    WITH THESE, SHE STEALES MENS HARTS FOR
                          HER RELIEFE               2.126.13
    THY BOSOME IS INDEARED WITH ALL HEARTS          3.31.1
    WANT NOTHING THAT THE THOUGHT OF HEARTS CAN MEND 3.69.2
    THEN THOU ALONE KINGDOMES OF HEARTS SHOULDST OWE 3.70.14
    WHICH MANY $LEGIONS OF TRUE HEARTS HAD WARM'D   3.154.6
    IF THAT BE SINNE WHICH IN FIXT HEARTS DOTH BREED 4.14.12
    HOW $HOLLAND HEARTS, NOW SO GOOD TOWNES BE LOST 4.30.7
    NOT THIS FAIRE OUTSIDE, WHICH OUR HEARTS
                          DOTH MOVE                 4.52.8
    THE $ORATOUR SO FARRE MEN'S HARTS DOTH BIND     4.58.2
    THAT PRESENCE, WHICH DOTH GIVE DARKE HEARTS
                          A LIVING LIGHT            4.77.3
    AND HUMBLED HARTS BRINGS CAPTIVES UNTO THEE     5.10.7
    THEYR WEAKER HARTS, WHICH ARE NOT WEL AWARE+    5.37.8
    SO SHE WITH FLATTRING SMYLES WEAKE HARTS
                          DOTH GUYDE                5.47.5
HEART'S                    20
    WHICH TURN'D MY SPORT INTO A $HARTS DISPAIRE    1.5.9
    WHERE MY HARTS THEEFE TO VEXE ME MADE HER CHOICE 1.27.6
    POSSESSE ME WHOLE, MY HEARTS TRIUMVIRATE        1.28.2
    MY TONGUE IN PAYNE, MY HARTS COUNSELS BEWRAYING 2.142.6
    HARTS $METHRIDATE, THE SCULES PRESERVATIVE      2.146.6
    WITH MY HARTS TRYBUTE TO HER CONQUERING EYES    2.151.2
    THE CLEERE EYES MOYITIE, AND THE DEARE
                          HEARTS PART               3.46.12
    AND MY HEARTS RIGHT, THEIR INWARD LOVE OF HEART 3.46.14
    AN OTHER TIME MINE EYE IS MY HEARTS GUEST       3.47.7
    AWAKES MY HEART, TO HEARTS AND EYES DELIGHT     3.47.14
    IN MANIES LOOKES, THE FALCE HEARTS HISTORY      3.93.7
    WHAT ERE THY THOUGHTS, OR THY HEARTS WORKINGS BE 3.93.11
    THY PROUD HEARTS SLAVE AND VASSALL WRETCH TO BE 3.141.12
    THAT ALL THY HURTS IN MY HART'S WRACKE I REEDE  4.93.13
    WRITTEN WITH TEARES IN HARTS CLOSE BLEEDING BOOK 5.1.8
    RUDELY THOU WRONGEST MY DEARE HARTS DESIRE      5.5.1
    WHICH HER DEEP WIT, THAT TRUE HARTS THOUGHT
                          CAN SPEL                  5.43.13
    OF MY HARTS WOUND AND OF MY BODIES GRIEFE       5.50.2
    HER HARTS DESIRE WITH MOST CONTENTMENT PLEASE   5.72.12
    BUT THIS THE WORKE OF HARTS ASTONISHMENT        5.81.14
HEART-STRINGS              2
    ON MY HEART-STRINGS HIGH TUN'D UNTO HER FAME    1.57.4
    ON $CUPID'S BOW HOW ARE MY HEART-STRINGS BENT   4.19.1
HEART-THRILLING            1
    ONE DAY I SOUGHT WITH HER HART-THRILLING EIES   5.12.1
HEAT                       19
    THESE TEARES, WHICH HEATE OF SACRED FLAME DISTILS 1.24.2
    YOUR FIRY HEATE LETS NOT HER GLORY PASSE        1.38.13
    THOUGH SPENT THY FLAME, IN ME THE HEAT REMAINING 1.41.6
```

```
DO FEELE MINE INWARD HEAT AS GREAT (I KNOW IT)           1.43.6
THE $FUELL KINDLED WITH $CELESTIALL $HEAT                 2.30.8
MY $BREST THE $FORGE, INCLUDING ALL THE HEATE            2.40.3
IN HEAT OF $BLOUD, A MODEST $MIND MIGHT MOVE             2.47.8
MY $LOVE MAKES HOTE THE FIRE WHOSE HEAT IS SPENT        2.127.1
BY BREAST THE FORGE, INCLUDING ALL THE HEATE           2.144.3
BAYTING THE $LYON IN HIS FURIOUS HEAT                  2.147.7
WHICH ERST FROM HEAT DID CANOPIE THE HERD               3.12.6
THAT IT NOR GROWES WITH HEAT, NOR DROWNES
                            WITH SHOWRES               3.124.12
A DATELESSE LIVELY HEAT STILL TO INDURE                3.153.6
WHICH FROM LOVES FIRE TOOKE HEAT PERPETUALL           3.154.10
EFFECTS OF LIVELY HEAT, MUST NEEDS IN NATURE GROW       4.8.11
BUT SHINING FORTH CF HEATE IN HIS CHIEFE PRIDE          4.22.4
GREAT HEAT, AND MAKES HIS FLAMES TO HEAVEN ASPIRE        5.6.8
OR HOW COMES IT THAT MY EXCEEDING HEAT                  5.30.5
THE PAYNEFULL SMITH WITH FORCE OF FERVENT HEAT          5.32.1
```
HEATS   3
```
MY HEATES MUST DROWNE IN TH'$OCEAN OF MY TEARES        1.32.12
LOVE HEATS MY HART, MY HART-HEAT MY SIGHES
                            WARMETH                     2.132.6
LOVES FIRE HEATES WATER, WATER COOLES NOT LOVE        3.154.14
```
HEAVEN   72
```
HAST SENT THE INCENSE OF THY SIGHS TO HEAVEN             1.8.2
HEAVEN NOR EARTH WILL NCT, MY SELFE CANNOT WAKE         1.29.9
THINKING TO SCALE THE HEAVEN OF HER HART                1.36.2
YET $HEAV'N WILL STILL HAVE $MURTHER OUT AT LAST        2.2.14
IF $HE, FROM $HEAV'N THAT FILCH'D THAT
                            LIVING $FIRE                2.14.1
IN WHOM, $HEAV'N LOCKES IT SELFE AS IN A $GLASSE       2.17.4
TO THIS OUR $WORLD, TO $LEARNING, AND TO $HEAVEN       2.18.1
NINE ORDERS FIRST CF $ANGELS BE IN $HEAVEN             2.18.5
BUT SEE, FOR YOU TC $HEAV'N FOR $PHRAZE I RUNNE       2.21.11
LOVE BANISH'D $HEAV'N, IN $EARTH WAS HELD
                            IN SCORNE                   2.23.1
SPENT ON THINE $ALTARS, FLAMING UP TO $HEAV'N         2.36.10
SOME CALL ON $HEAVEN, SCME INVOCATE ON $HELL           2.39.3
THOUGH $HEAVEN AND $EARTH, PROVE BOTH
                            TO ME UNTRUE                2.51.13
THEY $HEAVEN AND $EARTH TO PITTY SHALL PROVOKE         2.55.8
WITH THOSE RICH $BEAUTIES $HEAV'N GIVES
                            YOU TO KEEPE                2.58.12
DEFINE MY $WEALE, AND TELL THE JOYES OF $HEAVEN        2.60.1
WHICH NAME MY $MUSE TO HIGHEST HEAVEN
                            SHAL RAISE                  2.101.13
THEY HEAVEN AND EARTH TC PITTY SHALL PROVCKE          2.102.8
WHERE HEAVEN BEHOLDS HER IN A MORTALL GLASSE          2.107.4
AND HEAVEN MAY JOY TO THINK ON PAST WORLCS
                            BLISSE                      2.107.12
UNTO THE $WORLD, TC $LEARNING, AND TO $HEAVEN         2.108.1
NINE ORDERS FIRST CF $ANGELS BE IN HEAVEN             2.108.5
AND HEAVEN, AND EARTH, DOE WITH THEIR
                            WOES ACQUAINT               2.118.4
WONDER OF $HEAVEN, GLASSE OF DIVINITIE                2.123.1
IT IS THY HEAVEN WITHIN HER FACE TO DWELL            2.123.13
AND IN THY HEAVEN, THERE ONELY IS MY HELL            2.123.14
AS THOUGH THE HEAVEN HAD NOW AWAK'D HER EYES         2.125.11
WHILST FIRE, WATER, AYRE, TWIXT HEAVEN
                            AND EARTH SHAL BE           2.127.13
O OUR WORLDS WONDER, CRCWNE OF HEAVEN ABCVE           2.129.9
```

A $MUSE, THAT UNTO HEAVEN HATH RAISD HER FAME   2.138.12
THEN HENCE TO HEAVEN UNKIND, FOR THY CHILDS
                              PART   2.140.13
DEFINE MY LOVE, AND TELL THE JOYES OF HEAVEN   2.149.1
A HEAVEN ON EARTH, CN EARTH NO HEAVEN BUT THIS   2.151.14
A HEAVEN ON EARTH, CN EARTH NO HEAVEN BUT THIS   2.151.14
BY OFT PREDICT THAT I IN HEAVEN FINDE   3.14.8
THOUGH YET HEAVEN KNOWES IT IS BUT AS A TOMBE   3.17.3
SOMETIME TOO HOT THE EYE OF HEAVEN SHINES   3.18.5
WHO HEAVEN IT SELFE FOR ORNAMENT DOTH USE   3.21.3
AND DO'ST HIM GRACE WHEN CLOUDS DOE BLOT
                         THE HEAVEN   3.28.10
AND TROUBLE DEAFE HEAVEN WITH MY BOOTLESSE CRIES   3.29.3
BUT HEAVEN IN THY CREATION DID DECREE   3.93.9
THEN GIVE ME WELCOME, NEXT MY HEAVEN THE BEST   3.110.13
TO SHUN THE HEAVEN THAT LEADS MEN TO THIS HELL   3.129.14
AND YET BY HEAVEN I THINKE MY LOVE AS RARE   3.130.13
AND TRULY NOT THE MORNING $SUN OF $HEAVEN   3.132.5
FROM HEAVEN TO HELL IS FLOWNE AWAY   3.145.12
THE SUNNE IT SELFE SEES NOT, TILL HEAVEN
                         CLEERES   3.148.12
THAT WHEN THE HEAV'N TO THEE HIS BEST DISPLAYES   4.11.3
OF ALL THOSE GOODS, WHICH HEAV'N TO ME HATH LENT   4.18.4
IN HIGHEST WAY OF HEAV'N THE $SUNNE DID RIDE   4.22.1
YET TO THOSE FOOLES HEAV'N SUCH WIT DOTH IMPART   4.24.5
THAT HEAV'N OF JOYES THROWES ONELY DOWNE CN ME   4.60.3
BUT WHEN MINE EYES BACKE TO THEIR HEAV'N
                         DID MOVE   4.66.13
WORLD OF MY WEALTH, AND HEAV'N OF MY DELIGHT   4.68.4
AS CONSTERD IN TRUE SPEECH, THE NAME OF
                         HEAV'N IT BEARES   4.77.11
NO DOOME SHOULD MAKE ONE'S HEAV'N BECOME
                         HIS HELL   4.86.14
OF SUCH HEAVEN STUFFE, TC CLOATH SO HEAVENLY
                         MYNDE   4.101.14
ONELY UNTO THE HEAV'N OF $STELLA'S FACE   4.105.7
GREAT HEAT, AND MAKES HIS FLAMES TO HEAVEN ASPIRE   5.6.8
BASE THING, AND THINKE HCW SHE TO HEAVEN
                         MAY CLIME   5.13.10
INTO THIS SINFULL WCRLD FROM HEAVEN TO SEND   5.24.10
BUT THEN FROM HEAVEN MOST HIDEOUS STORMES
                         ARE SENT   5.46.3
WHOM THEN SHALL I CR HEAVEN OR HER OBAY+   5.46.5
MY LOWER HEAVEN, SC IT PERFORCE MUST BEE   5.46.8
FOR TO THE HEAVEN HER HAUGHTY LOOKES ASPIRE   5.55.11
THEN SITH TO HEAVEN YE LYKENED ARE THE BEST   5.55.13
WITH PLENTEOUS HAND BY HEAVEN UPON YOU THROWN   5.66.2
NE BUT IN HEAVEN MATCHABLE TO NONE   5.66.7
AND UNTO HEAVEN FCRGETS HER FORMER FLIGHT   5.72.8
NE THINKS OF OTHER HEAVEN, BUT HOW IT MIGHT   5.72.11
FOR WHEN AS DAY THE HEAVEN DOTH ADORNE   5.87.5
NE JOY OF OUGHT THAT UNDER HEAVEN DOTH HOVE   5.89.9
HEAVENLY   46
THE $FIRE HE STOLE, ALTHOUGH OF $HEAV'NLY KIND   2.14.5
WHICH BEING KINDLED BY THAT HEAV'NLY FIRE   2.16.7
IN PERFECT HUMANE SHAPE, ALL HEAV'NLY $BLISSE   2.17.12
THOUGH $FEARE GIVES THEM MORE THEN A $HEAV'NLY
                         $SCOPE   2.26.8
NOR YET THOSE HEAVENLY SECRETS ONCE RESPECTED   2.105.4
WITH HEAVENLY COLCURS DIDE, WITH NATURES
                         WONDER CROUND   2.106.4

```
ON HEAVENLIE TOP CF THY DIVINE DESIRE                  2.106.6
O BLESSED FAYRE, NCW VAILE THOSE HEAVENLY EYES         2.129.13
YET FEARE GYVES THEM MORE THEN A HEAVENLY SCOPE        2.137.8
O RICHEST $CASKET CF ALL HEAVENLY TREASURE             2.146.11
LET HIM COMPARE IT TO HER HEAVENLY EYE                 2.148.2
AND HAVING CLIMB'D THE STEEPE UP HEAVENLY HILL         3.7.5
SUCH HEAVENLY TOUCHES NERE TOUCHT EARTHLY FACES        3.17.8
GUILDING PALE STREAMES WITH HEAVENLY ALCUMY            3.33.4
THE INWARD LIGHT.. AND THAT THE HEAVENLY PART          4.5.2
OF FORCE OF HEAV'NLY BEAMES, INFUSING
                            HELLISH PAINE              4.6.3
THE WINDOWES NOW THROUGH WHICH THIS HEAV'NLY GUEST     4.9.9
AS THAT SWEETE BLACKE WHICH VAILES THE
                            HEAV'NLY EYE               4.20.7
WHAT, MAY IT BE THAT EVEN IN HEAV'NLY PLACE            4.31.3
I FIND HOW HEAV'NLY DAY WRETCH I DID MISSE             4.33.4
STELLA LOOKT ON, AND FRCM HER HEAVENLY FACE            4.41.13
THE HEAV'NLY NATURE OF THAT PLACE IS SUCH              4.44.12
OF $ATLAS TYR'D, YOUR WISEDOME'S HEAV'NLY SWAY         4.51.8
THAT VERTUOUS SOULE, SURE HEIRE OF HEAV'NLY
                            BLISSE                     4.52.7
BUT FAILST THOU NCT IN PHRASE SO HEAV'NLY HIE+         4.67.6
MY $MUSE MAY WELL GRUDGE AT MY HEAV'NLY JOY            4.70.1
O HEAV'NLY FOOLE, THY MCST KISSE-WORTHIE FACE          4.73.12
WHENCE WORDS, NOT WCRDS, BUT HEAV'NLY
                            GRACES SLIDE               4.80.4
FROM HEAVENLY STANDING HITS EACH MORTALL WIGHT         4.97.4
OR IF SUCH HEAVENLY SIGNES MUST PROVE ANNOY            4.100.13
OF SUCH HEAVEN STUFFE, TO CLOATH SO HEAVENLY
                            MYNDE                      4.101.14
THE LIGHT WHEROF HATH KINDLED HEAVENLY FYRE            5.3.3
IN CHAST DESIRES CN HEAVENLY BEAUTY BOUND              5.8.8
THAT HINDERS HEAVENLY THOUGHTS WITH DROSSY SLIME       5.13.12
WHYLEST RAPT WITH JOY RESEMBLING HEAVENLY MACNES       5.39.9
NOT EARTH., FOR HER HIGH THOGHTS MORE
                            HEAVENLY ARE               5.55.5
THEY THAT IN COURSE OF HEAVENLY SPHEARES
                            ARE SKILD                  5.60.1
AND OF THE BROOD CF $ANGELS HEVENLY BORNE              5.61.6
SUCH HEAVENLY FORMES OUGHT RATHER WORSHIPT BE          5.61.13
THE SACRED HARBOUR CF THAT HEVENLY SPRIGHT             5.76.4
TO BE DIVINE AND BCRNE CF HEAVENLY SEED                5.79.10
THE CONTEMPLATION CF WHCSE HEAVENLY HEW                5.80.11
SOM HEVENLY WIT, WHCSE VERSE COULD HAVE ENCHASED       5.82.7
BUT THEY THAT SKILL NOT OF SO HEAVENLY MATTER          5.85.5
THAT ME WITH HEAVENLY FURY DOTH INSPIRE                5.85.11
BUT TH'ONELY IMAGE CF THAT HEAVENLY RAY                5.88.7
HEAVENS                  22
BEQUEATH THE HEAVENS THE STARRES THAT I ADORE          1.19.3
MY BREATH THAT CALLS THE HEAVENS TO WITNES IT          1.21.10
LOOKE TO THE HEAVENS., THE HEAVENS YEELDE
                            FORTH NO GRACE             1.29.6
LOOKE TO THE HEAVENS., THE HEAVENS YEELDE
                            FORTH NO GRACE             1.29.6
WITH SO RARE SWEETNESSE ALL THE $HEAV'NS
                            PERFUMING                  2.16.10
HEAV'NS ARE NOT KIND TO THEM, THAT KNOW
                            THEM MOST                  2.43.14
WHICH $NAME MY $MUSE TO HIGHEST $HEAV'NS
                            SHALL RAYSE                2.54.13
```

```
SO MAY THE $HEAVENS READ WONDERS IN MY $HEART        2.60.8
TILL THOU ALONE TC PAY THE HEAVENS THEIR DUTIE       2.105.5
WITH THINE OWNE SWEETNES AL THE HEAVENS
                                  PERFUMING          2.106.10
AND MOUNTING UP, SHALT TC THE HEAVENS ASCEND         2.106.13
O SWEET'ST REVENGE THAT ERE THE HEAVENS GAVE         2.139.6
BY DOOME CONCEALED TO THE HEAVENS ABOVE              2.139.11
I FEELE, YOU KNOW, THE HEAVENS CAN TELL
                                  THE REST           2.139.14
NOW DOE I SWEARE BY HEAVENS, BEFORE WE PART          2.140.3
LET HEAVENS WITHDRAW THEIR SWEET $AMBROZIAN
                                  BREATH             2.145.11
SO MAY THE HEAVENS READE WONDERS IN MY HART          2.149.8
HEAV'NS ENVY NOT AT MY HIGH TRIUMPHING               4.63.10
THE HEAVENS KNOW BEST WHAT IS THE BEST FCR ME        5.46.6
BUT YE HIGH HEVENS, THAT ALL THIS SOROWE SEE         5.46.9
AND IN THE HEVENS WRYTE YOUR GLORIOUS NAME           5.75.12
FOR HAD THE EQUALL HEVENS SO MUCH YOU GRACED         5.82.5
HEAVEN'S                    14
BUT YOU BROKE INTC $HEAV'NS IMMORTALL STCRE          2.14.9
NOW, OR BY CHAUNCE, OR HEAVENS HIE PROVIDENCE        2.116.9
THAT HEAVENS AYRE IN THIS HUGE RONDURE HEMS          3.21.8
AS THOSE GOULD CANDELLS FIXI IN HEAVENS AYER         3.21.12
FROM SULLEN EARTH SINGS HIMNS AT $HEAVENS GATE       3.29.12
SUNS OF THE WORLD MAY STAINE, WHEN HEAVENS
                                  SUN STAINTEH       3.33.14
A $CROW THAT FLIES IN HEAVENS SWEETEST AYRE          3.70.4
THEY RIGHTLY DO INHERRIT HEAVENS GRACES              3.94.5
OR SEEKE HEAVN'S CCURSE, OR HEAVN'S INSICE TC SEE    4.10.5
HEAV'NS ENVY NOT AT MY HIGH TRIUMPHING               4.63.10
CANNOT HEAVN'S FOOD, ONCE FELT, KEEPE
                            STOMAKES FREE            4.88.7
MY SOULES LONG LACKED FCODE, MY HEAVENS BLIS         5.1.12
RESEMBLING HEAVENS GLORY IN HER LIGHT                5.72.6
BUT HERE ON EARTH TC HAVE SUCH HEVENS BLISSE         5.72.14
HEAVILY                     2
AND HEAVILY FROM WCE TO WOE TELL ORE                 3.30.10
WHICH HEAVILY HE ANSWERS WITH A GRONE                3.50.11
HEAVINESS                   1
SLOW HEAVINESSE IN BOTH HOLDS ONE DEGREE             4.96.6
HEAVY                       20
MY HEAVY FORTUNE IS MUCH LIKE THE SAME               1.13.3
YET HEAVY HEART TC MAKE SO HARD A CHOISE             1.28.3
FINDING ME RAIN'D WITH SUCH A HEAVY HAND             1.28.12
WHERE LOE I LANGUISH IN SO HEAVY SMART               1.36.6
WITH HEAVIE $SIGHES WHILST THUS I BREAKE
                                  THE $AYRE          2.45.3
(SAITH HE) $LIGHT $BURTHEN'S HEAVY, IF
                            FARRE BORNE              2.59.10
THROUGH HEAVY SLEEPE ON SIGHTLESSE EYES
                            DOTH STAY+               3.43.12
BUT HEAVIE TEARES, BADGES OF EITHERS WOE             3.44.14
HOW HEAVIE DOE I JCURNEY ON THE WAY                  3.50.1
MY HEAVY EIELIDS TC THE WEARY NIGHT+                 3.61.2
AND HEAVIE IGNORANCE ALCFT TO FLIE                   3.78.6
THAT HEAVIE $SATURNE LAUGHT AND LEAPT WITH HIM       3.98.4
THIS NIGHT WHILE SLEEPE BEGINS WITH HEAVY WINGS      4.38.1
MOVE NOT THY HEAVY GRACE, THOU SHALT IN ME           4.39.13
FROM OUT THY HEAVY MOULD, THAT INBENT EYES           4.94.3
WOULD FAINE DRIVE CLOUDES FROM OUT MY
                            HEAVY CHEERE             4.97.11
```

```
MAKE IN MY HEAVY MOULD NEW THOUGHTS TO GROW          4.106.11
THAT WITH HIS HEAVY SLEDGE HE CAN IT BEAT            5.32.3
IS PRISONER LED AWAY WITH HEAVY HART                 5.52.3
SO LIKEWISE LOVE CHEARE YOU YOUR HEAVY SPRIGHT       5.62.13
HECATE'S                  3
  BY $HECAT'S $NAMES, BY $PROSERPINE'S SAD $TEARES   2.36.7
  I QUAKE TO LOOKE ON $HECAT'S CHARMING $BOOKES      2.39.11
  I QUAKE TO LOOKE ON $HECATS CHARMING BOOKES        2.118.11
HEDGED                    1
  THOUGH STRONGLY HEDG'D OF BLOUDY $LYON'S PAWES     4.75.10
HEED                      3
  TAKE HEED (DEARE HEART) OF THIS LARGE PRIVILEDGE   3.95.13
  BE YOU STILL FAIRE, HONOURD BY PUBLIKE HEED        4.84.9
  TAKE HEED THEREFORE, MYNE EYES, HOW YE DOE STARE   5.37.9
HEEDLESS                  1
  AND SET MY THOUGHTS IN HEEDLESSE WAYES TO RANGE    1.5.2
HEEDS                     1
  BUT NEVER HEEDS THE FRUIT OF WRITER'S MIND         4.11.8
HEELS                     1
  FLINGING THE $FISHES BACKWARD WITH HIS HEELES      2.147.4
HEIGHT                    9
  NOW BROAD-BRYMD $INDUS, THEN OF $PINDUS HEIGHT     2.120.5
  SOME, WHO REACH NOT THE HEIGHT OF MY CONCEITE      2.128.5
  WHAT $MUSE HATH POWER, ABOVE THY HEIGHT
                        TO RAISE THEE+               2.146.4
  VAUNT IN THEIR YOUTHFULL SAP, AT HEIGHT DECREASE   3.15.7
  EXCEEDED BY THE HIGHT OF HAPPIER MEN               3.32.8
  WHOSE WORTHS UNKNOWNE, ALTHOUGH HIS HIGTH
                        BE TAKEN                     3.116.8
  ALAS, IF FROM THE HEIGHT OF $VERTUE'S THRONE       4.40.5
  COME THEN MY $MUSE, SHEW THOU HEIGHT OF DELIGHT    4.70.9
  THE HEIGHT OF HONOR IN THE KINDLY BADGE
                        OF SHAME+                    4.102.3
HEINOUS                   2
  IF THE VILE ACTORS OF THE HEYNOUS DEED             2.46.6
  BUT I FORBID THEE ONE MOST HAINOUS CRIME           3.19.8
HEIR                      5
  HIS TENDER HEIRE MIGHT BEARE HIS MEMORY            3.1.4
  TO BE DEATHS CONQUEST AND MAKE WORMES THINE HEIRE  3.6.14
  BUT NOW IS BLACKE BEAUTIES SUCCESSIVE HEIRE        3.127.3
  THAT VERTUOUS SOULE, SURE HEIRE OF HEAV'NLY
                        BLISSE                       4.52.7
  AND NOT CONTENT TO BE $PERFECTION'S HEIRE          4.71.9
HEIRS                     1
  IS $NATURE GROWNE LESSE POW'RFULL IN THEIR
                        $HEIRES                      2.27.7
HELD                      7
  AND ALL LIES WITHRED THAT WAS HELD SO DEERE        1.42.4
  NEPTUNES BEST DARLING, HELD BETWEENE HIS ARMES     1.53.10
  LOVE BANISH'D $HEAV'N, IN $EARTH WAS HELD
                        IN SCORNE                    2.23.1
  WIL BE A TOTTER'D WEED OF SMAL WORTH HELD          3.2.4
  MY BODY IS THE FRAME WHEREIN TI'S HELD             3.24.3
  WHOSE TALENTS HELD YOUNG $GANIMED ABOVE            4.13.4
  WAS HELD, IN OPEND SENSE IT FLIES AWAY             4.38.10
HELEN                     1
  NO LOVELY $PARIS MADE THY $HELLEN HIS              4.33.6
HELEN'S                   1
  ON $HELLENS CHEEKE ALL ART OF BEAUTIE SET          3.53.7
```

```
HELICE                          1
  MY $HELICE THE LODESTAR OF MY LYFE                    5.34.10
HELICON                         4
  AND THOU, SWEET $ANKOR, ART MY $HELICON               2.53.14
  AND THOU SWEET $ANKOR ART MY $HELICON                 2.113.14
  SOME $HELYCON, AND SOME FAIRE $SIMOIS                 2.120.12
  OF $HELICON WHENCE SHE DERIVED IS                     5.1.10
HELL                           25
  SOME CALL ON $HEAVEN, SOME INVOCATE ON $HELL          2.39.3
  AND IN MY $SOULE THE PAINES OF $HELL I PROVE          2.41.3
  EXPRESSE MY $WOES, AND SHEW THE PAINES OF $HELL       2.60.2
  RAVISH'D WITH $JOY AMID'ST A HELL OF $WOE             2.62.7
  SOME INVOCATE THE $GODS, SOME SPIRITS OF $HELL        2.118.3
  WHOSE LYFE DOTH SAVE A THOUSAND SOULES
                             FROM HELL                  2.119.12
  AND IN THY HEAVEN, THERE ONELY IS MY HELL             2.123.14
  AND IN MY SOULE THE PAYNES OF HELL I PROVE            2.143.3
  PORTRAITE OF HELL, THE AYRES BLACK MOURNING WEED      2.145.6
  EXPRESSE MY WOES, AND SHEW THE PAYNES OF HELL         2.149.2
  RAVISHT WITH JOY, AMIDST A HELL OF WOE                2.150.7
  I AM TO WAITE, THOUGH WAITING SO BE HELL              3.58.13
  DISTIL'D FROM $LYMBECKS FOULE AS HELL WITHIN          3.119.2
  AS I BY YOURS, Y'HAVE PAST A HELL OF $TIME            3.120.6
  TO SHUN THE HEAVEN THAT LEADS MEN TO THIS HELL        3.129.14
  TO WIN ME SOONE TO HELL MY FEMALL EVILL               3.144.5
  I GESSE ONE ANGEL IN AN OTHERS HEL                    3.144.12
  FROM HEAVEN TO HELL IS FLOWNE AWAY                    3.145.12
  WHO ART AS BLACK AS HELL, AS DARKE AS NIGHT           3.147.14
  WHILE WITH A FEELING SKILL I PAINT MY HELL            4.2.14
  AND THIS I SWEARE BY BLACKEST BROOKE OF HELL          4.74.7
  NO DOOME SHOULD MAKE ONE'S HEAV'N BECOME
                             HIS HELL                   4.86.14
  AS CAN REFRESH THE HELL WHERE MY SOULE FRIES          4.100.8
  AND HAVING HARROWD HELL DIDST BRING AWAY              5.68.3
  LET ALL THE PLAGUES AND HORRID PAINES OF HELL         5.86.5
HELL-DRIVEN                     1
  LET NOT MINE EYES BE HEL-DRIV'N FROM THAT LIGHT       4.48.7
HELLISH                         3
  BY $HELLISH $STYX (BY WHICH THE $THUND'RER
                             SWEARES)                   2.36.5
  OF FORCE OF HEAV'NLY BEAMES, INFUSING
                             HELLISH PAINE              4.6.3
  BETWEENE THE JAWES OF HELLISH $JEALOUSIE              4.78.4
HELM                            1
  JOVE ON HIS HELME THE THUNDERBOLT DID REARE           4.13.8
HELP                           16
  THAT THEY MAY HELPE THEE TO CONSUME OUR DAIES+        1.23.6
  AND IN MY FALL I CRYE FOR HELPE WITH SPEEDE           1.32.9
  TO HELPE HER FLIGHT THROUGHOUT THE FAIREST $ILE       1.43.10
  SINCE THER'S NO HELPE, $COME LET US KISSE
                             AND PART                   2.61.1
  CRYES IN HIS PANGS, $GOD HELPE THE MOTHERLESSE        2.116.18
  WITHOUT THY HELPE, BY ME BE BORNE ALONE               3.36.4
  YOUR SHALLOWEST HELPE WILL HOLD ME UP A FLOATE        3.80.9
  I SICK WITHALL THE HELPE OF BATH DESIRED              3.153.11
  BUT FOUND NO CURE, THE BATH FOR MY HELPE LIES         3.153.13
  USE ALL TO HELPE HIS OTHER CONQUERINGS                4.29.8
  COULD HOPE BY $CUPID'S HELPE ON YOU TO PRAY           4.43.2
  WHO FOR LONG FAITH, THO DAYLY HELPE I CRAVE           4.47.7
  BUT NOW I MEANE NO MORE YOUR HELPE TO TRIE            4.55.9
```

OF $LOVE, NEW-COIND TO HELPE MY BEGGERY   4.62.13
NO WIND, NO SHADE CAN COOLE, WHAT HELPE
                              THEN IN MY CASE   4.76.12
THOU TOLDST MINE EYES SHOULD HELPE THEIR
                              FAMISHT CASE+   4.106.6
HELPLESS   1
  THUS GREAT WITH CHILD TO SPEAKE, AND HELPLESSE
                              IN MY THROWES   4.1.12
HELPS   2
   IT FURTHERS $JUSTICE, BUT HELPES NOT THE DEAD   2.46.14
   YOU TAKE WRONG WAIES, THOSE FAR-FET HELPES
                              BE SUCH   4.15.9
HEMISPHERE   1
   LEAVING MY $HEMISPHERE, LEAVE ME IN NIGHT   4.89.4
HEMS   1
   THAT HEAVENS AYRE IN THIS HUGE RONDURE HEMS   3.21.8
HENCE   8
   AS $IN SOME $COUNTRIES, FARRE REMOTE FROM HENCE   2.50.1
   THEN HENCE TO HEAVEN UNKIND, FOR THY CHILDS
                              PART   2.140.13
   SAVE BREED TO BRAVE HIM, WHEN HE TAKES
                              THEE HENCE   3.12.14
   BY PRAISING HIM HERE WHO DOTH HENCE REMAINE   3.39.14
   FROM HENCE YOUR MEMORY DEATH CANNOT TAKE   3.81.3
   YOUR NAME FROM HENCE IMMORTALL LIFE SHALL HAVE   3.81.5
   TO MAKE HIM SEEME LONG HENCE, AS HE SHOWES NOW   3.101.14
   HENCE, THOU SUBBORND $INFORMER, A TREW SOULE   3.125.13
HENCEFORTH   3
   EVER HENCEFORTH MY $BOSOME BE YOUR $HEARSE   2.45.7
   HENCEFORTH TOO RASHLY ON THAT GUILEFULL NET   5.37.10
   DARE NOT HENCEFORTH ABOVE THE BOUNDS OF DEWTIE   5.61.3
HERALD   2
   AND ONLY HERAULD TO THE GAUDY SPRING   3.1.10
   FRESH SPRING THE HERALD OF LOVES MIGHTY KING   5.70.1
HERALDS   1
   SERVE HIM WITH SHOT, HER LIPS HIS HERALDS ARRE   4.29.10
HERBS   1
   OF HERBES OR BEASTES, WHICH $INDE OR $AFRIKE HOLD   4.3.8
HERCULES   2
   BUT FIND SOME $HERCULES TO BEARE, IN STEED   4.51.7
   FAR PASSING THOSE WHICH $HERCULES CAME BY   5.77.7
HERD   1
   WHICH ERST FROM HEAT DID CANOPIE THE HERD   3.12.6
HEREAFTER   2
   AND $QUEENES HEREAFTER SHALL BE GLAD TO LIVE   2.6.7
   THAT IT HEREAFTER MAY YOU NOT REPENT   5.73.13
HEREBY   1
   BUT YET, WHAT COMFORTS SHALL I HEREBY GAINE+   1.52.13
HEREIN   1
   HEREIN LIVES WISDOME, BEAUTY, AND INCREASE   3.11.5
HERESY   1
   YET HERESY NOR TREASON DIDST CONSPIRE   5.48.7
HERETIC   1
   IT FEARES NOT POLICY THAT $HERITICKE   3.124.9
HERETICS   1
   THEN SO BAD END FOR HERETICKS ORDAYNED   5.48.6
HERETOFORE   1
   WHICH HARDLY I ENDURED HERETOFORE   5.63.2
HEROIC   1
   WHICH INWARD SUNNE TO $HEROICKE MINDE DISPLAIES   4.25.8

HERSELF   3
  FORGOT HERSELFE, AND THOUGHT SHE HAD BEEN
                     DROWNED   2.109.4
   THREW IN HERSELFE, TO SAVE HERSELFE BY DROWNING   2.109.12
   THREW IN HERSELFE, TO SAVE HERSELFE BY DROWNING   2.109.12
HESPERUS   1
  O $EYES, BEHOLD YOUR HAPPY $HESPERUS   2.129.1
HID   8
  FOR PRECIOUS FRIENDS HID IN DEATHS DATELES NIGHT   3.30.6
  SHALL TIMES BEST $JEWELL FROM TIMES CHEST
                LIE HID+   3.65.10
  WHO LIKE A THEEFE, HID IN DARKE BUSH DOTH LY   4.20.3
  WHILE THAT BLACKE HUE FROM ME THE BAD GUEST HID   4.20.11
  YET WERE THE HID AND MEANER BEAUTIES PARCHT   4.22.12
  NOR IN HID WAYES TO GUIDE $PHILOSOPHIE   4.28.10
  WHEN $SUN IS HID, CAN STARRES SUCH BEAMES
               DISPLAY+   4.88.6
  YOUR MORALL NOTES STRAIGHT MY HID MEANING TEARE   4.104.12
HIDDEN   4
  TOLDE THE DUMBE MESSAGE OF MY HIDDEN GRIEFE   1.8.6
  BUT THINGS REMOV'D THAT HIDDEN IN THERE LIE   3.31.8
  A WICKED AMBUSH WHICH LAY HIDDEN LONG   5.12.6
  THROUGH HIDDEN PERILS ROUND ABOUT ME PLAST   5.34.8
HIDE   12
  ILE HIDE HER SINNE AND SAY IT WAS MY LOT   1.30.10
  ILE MONE MY SELFE, AND HIDE THE WRONG I HAVE   1.59.10
  AND FROM THE FOR-LORNE WORLD HIS VISAGE HIDE   3.33.7
  THAT SOME-TIMES ANGER THRUSTS INTO HIS HIDE   3.50.10
  OR AS THE WARD-ROBE WHICH THE ROBE DOTH HIDE   3.52.10
  NOT ONCE VOUCHSAFE TO HIDE MY WILL IN THINE   3.135.6
  IF THOU DOOST SEEKE TO HAVE WHAT THOU
              DOOST HIDE   3.142.13
  FROM THAT FOE'S WOUNDS THEIR TENDER SKINNES
              TO HIDE   4.22.8
  BUT YET IF IN YOUR HARDNED BREST YE HIDE   5.25.9
  THAT FROM THE FOOLISH FISH THEYR BAYTS DOE HYDE   5.47.4
  THE $PANTHER KNOWING THAT HIS SPOTTED HYDE   5.53.1
  WITHIN A BUSH HIS DREADFULL HEAD DOTH HIDE   5.53.3
HIDEOUS   3
  TO HIDIOUS WINTER AND CONFOUNDS HIM THERE   3.5.6
  AND SEE THE BRAVE DAY SUNCK IN HIDIOUS NIGHT   3.12.2
  BUT THEN FROM HEAVEN MOST HIDEOUS STORMES
              ARE SENT   5.46.3
HIDES   2
  HYDES IN THOSE CHRISTALL QUIVERS OF HER EYES   2.126.10
  WHICH HIDES YOUR LIFE, AND SHEWES NOT
              HALFE YOUR PARTS   3.17.4
HIDING   2
  HIDING THY BRAV'RY IN THEIR ROTTEN SMOKE   3.34.4
  YET HIDING ROYALL BLOUD FULL OFT IN RURALL VAINE   4.6.8
HIE   2
  OR FOR SOME BRAWLE, WHICH IN THAT CHAMBER HIE   4.26.7
  BUT FAILST THOU NOT IN PHRASE SO HEAV'NLY HIE+   4.67.6
HIED   1
  AND THETHER HIED A SAD DISTEMPERD GUEST   3.153.12
HIGH   35
  THAT MAKES ME FALL FROM OFF MY HIE DESIRE   1.32.8
  THE MOUNTING VENTER FOR A HIGH DELIGHT   1.35.3
  SUFFICE THAT HIGH ATTEMPTS HAVE NEVER SHAME   1.35.9
  RAISING MY HOPES ON HILLS OF HIGH DESIRE   1.36.1

```
MY SLENDER MEANES PRESUM'D TOO HIGH A PART              1.36.3
YET I PROTEST MY HIGH DESIRING WILL                     1.36.9
WHICH WELL THE REACH OF THEIR HIGH WITS RECORDS         1.55.4
ON MY HEART-STRINGS HIGH TUN'D UNTO HER FAME            1.57.4
ELIZIUM IS TOO HIGH A SEATE FOR $ME                     2.39.5
IN $PRIDE OF $WIT, WHEN HIGH DESIRE OF $FAME            2.47.1
NOW, OR BY CHAUNCE, OR HEAVENS HIE PROVIDENCE           2.116.9
OR MY SWIFT-WINGED $MUSE TYRED BY TOO
                         HIE FLYING                     2.117.10
ELIZIA IS TOO HIE A SEATE FOR MEE                       2.118.5
IF IT WERE FILD WITH YOUR MOST HIGH DESERTS+            3.17.2
THINE EYES, THAT TAUGHT THE DUMBE ON HIGH TO SING       3.78.5
AS HIGH AS LEARNING, MY RUDE IGNORANCE                  3.78.14
THY LOVE IS BITTER THEN HIGH BIRTH TO ME                3.91.9
(EXIL'D FOR AY FROM THOSE HIGH TREASURES, WHICH         4.24.13
AND KNOW THOSE $BODIES HIGH RAIGNE ON THE LOW           4.26.11
TH'INDIFFERENT $JUDGE BETWEENE THE HIGH AND LOW         4.39.4
WRACKES $TRIUMPHS BE, WHICH $LOVE (HIGH
                         SET) DOTH BREED                4.42.14
FOR LATE WITH HEART MOST HIGH, WITH EYES MOST LOW       4.63.5
HEAV'NS ENVY NOT AT MY HIGH TRIUMPHING                  4.63.10
O JOY, TOO HIGH FOR MY LOW STILE TO SHOW                4.69.1
OF HER HIGH HEART GIV'N ME THE MONARCHIE                4.69.10
TREBLES SING HIGH, AS WELL AS BASES DEEPE               4.70.6
THAT CONVERSATION SWEET, WHERE SUCH HIGH
                         COMFORTS BE                    4.77.10
WHAT, DOTH HIGH PLACE AMBITIOUS THOUGHTS AUGMENT+       4.83.9
AND THAT HIGH LOOK, WITH WHICH SHE DOTH
                         COMPTROLL                      5.10.10
BUT YE HIGH HEVENS, THAT ALL THIS SOROWE SEE            5.46.9
NOT EARTH., FOR HER HIGH THOGHTS MORE
                         HEAVENLY ARE                   5.55.5
AND EKE HER MIND IS PURE IMMORTALL HYE                  5.55.12
HIGH TIME IT IS, THIS WARRE NOW ENDED WERE              5.57.2
YEE WHOSE HIGH WORTHS SURPASSING PARAGON                5.66.5
SHALL LIFT YOU UP UNTO AN HIGH DEGREE                   5.82.14
HIGHER                   2
SHE BUILDS HER FAME ON HIGHER SEATED PRAISE             4.81.10
MY SPIRIT TO AN HIGHER PITCH WILL RAYSE                 5.80.12
HIGHEST                  7
WHICH $NAME MY $MUSE TO HIGHEST $HEAV'NS
                         SHALL RAYSE                    2.54.13
WHICH NAME MY $MUSE TO HIGHEST HEAVEN
                         SHAL RAISE                     2.101.13
IN HIGHEST WAY OF HEAV'N THE $SUNNE DID RIDE            4.22.1
UNSEENE, UNHEARD, WHILE THOUGHT TO HIGHEST PLACE        4.27.13
OF HIGHEST WISH, I WISH YOU SO MUCH BLISSE              4.84.13
LET HONOR SELFE TO THEE GRAUNT HIGHEST PLACE            4.103.14
AND HE THAT STANDETH ON THE HYGHEST STAYRE              5.58.11
HIGHMOST                 1
BUT WHEN FROM HIGH-MOST PICH WITH WERY CAR              3.7.9
HIGHWAY                  1
HIGHWAY SINCE YOU MY CHIEFE $PERNASSUS BE               4.84.1
HILL                     3
O CLEERE-EYDE $RECTOR OF THE HOLY $HILL                 1.4.10
AND HAVING CLIMB'D THE STEEPE UP HEAVENLY HILL          3.7.5
I RATHER WISHT THEE CLIME THE $MUSES' HILL              4.10.3
HILLS                    2
RAISING MY HOPES ON HILLS OF HIGH DESIRE                1.36.1
I FIND OLD $POETS HYLLS AND FLOODS ADMIRE               2.120.2
```

HIMSELF   10
  KEPT FOR HIMSELFE, DEFENDED FROM ALL HARMES   1.53.12
  TILL HE HIMSELFE THYS $EAGLES ART HAD TAUGHT   2.122.8
  THAT ON HIMSELFE SUCH MURDROUS SHAME COMMITS   3.9.14
  OR HEART IN LOVE WITH SIGHES HIMSELFE
                             DOTH SMOTHER   3.47.4
  AT LENGTH HE PERCH'D HIMSELF IN $STELLA'S
                             JOYFULL FACE   4.8.8
  THERE HIMSELFE WITH HIS SHOT HE CLOSE DOTH LAY   4.20.8
  SINCE TO HIMSELFE HE DOTH YOUR GIFTS APPLY   4.43.3
  THAT VOYCE, WHICH MAKES THE SOULE PLANT
                             HIMSELFE IN THE EARES   4.77.9
  THOUGH OFT HIMSELFE MY MATE-IN-ARMES HE SWARE   4.95.8
  BY $LOVE HIMSELFE AND IN HIS GARDEN PLASTE   5.77.12
HIND   1
  LYKE A YOUNG FAWNE THAT LATE HATH LOST THE HYND   5.78.2
HINDERED   1
  BY SUCH UNSUTED SPEECH SHOULD HINDRED BE   4.51.14
HINDERS   1
  THAT HINDERS HEAVENLY THOUGHTS WITH DROSSY SLIME   5.13.12
HINDMOST   1
  (THOUGH WORDS COME HIND-MOST) HOLDS HIS
                             RANKE BEFORE   3.85.12
HIRE   3
  GOE HYRE THY SELFE SOME BUNGLING $HARPERS $BOY   2.48.10
  WELL WORTHY THOU TO HAVE FOUND BETTER HYRE   5.48.5
  UPON THEE FALL FOR THINE ACCURSED HYRE   5.86.6
HISTORY   3
  IN MANIES LOOKES, THE FALCE HEARTS HISTORY   3.93.7
  A $PROPHET OFT, AND OFT AN HISTORIE   4.32.3
  THINE EYES MY PRIDE, THY LIPS MY HISTORY   4.90.3
HIT   1
  SO SWEETE SOUNDS STRAIGHT MINE EARE AND
                             HEART DO HIT   4.55.13
HITHERWARD   1
  'SCHOLLER,' SAITH $LOVE, 'BEND HITHERWARD
                             YOUR WIT'   4.19.14
HITS   2
  MY DEEPEST SENCE, HOW HARD TRUE SORROW HITS   3.120.10
  FROM HEAVENLY STANDING HITS EACH MORTALL WIGHT   4.97.4
HOARSE   2
  GROWNE HOARCE WITH CRYING MERCY, MERCY GIVE   1.16.6
  HOARCE SOUNDS THE VOYCE THAT PRAYSETH
                             NOT HER NAME   1.57.10
HOISTED   1
  THAT I HAVE HOYSTED SAILE TO AL THE WINDES   3.117.7
HOLD   28
  TO CRAVE REDRESSE, YET HOLD AFFLICTION DEARE   1.20.7
  AND STILL MUST HOLD HER DEARE TILL AFTER DEATH   1.21.11
  I HOLD THAT VILE, WHICH $VULGAR WIT AFFORDS   2.4.11
  THEN, SWEET $DESPAIRE, AWHILE HOLD UP THY HEAD   2.26.13
  IN EV'RY THING I HOLD THIS $MAXIM STILL   2.28.13
  STRIVING TO HOLD IT STRONGLY IN THE $DEEPE   2.58.10
  THEN SWEET $DISPAIRE, AWHILE HOLD UP THY HEAD   2.137.13
  SO SHOULD THAT BEAUTY WHICH YOU HOLD IN LEASE   3.13.5
  HOW WITH THIS RAGE SHALL BEAUTIE HOLD A PLEA   3.65.3
  O HOW SHALL SUMMERS HUNNY BREATH HOLD OUT   3.65.5
  OR WHAT STRONG HAND CAN HOLD HIS SWIFT
                             FOOTE BACK   3.65.11
  AND FOR THE PEACE OF YOU I HOLD SUCH STRIFE   3.75.3

```
YOUR SHALLOWEST HELPE WILL HOLD ME UP A FLOATE        3.80.9
FOR HOW DO I HOLD THEE BUT BY THY GRANTING            3.87.5
THEREFORE LIKE HER, I SCME-TIME HOLD MY TONGUE        3.102.13
THAT POORE RETENTICN COULD NOT SO MUCH HOLD           3.122.9
DOEST HOULD TIMES FICKLE GLASSE, HIS SICKLE,
                                       HOWER          3.126.2
FOR NOTHING HOLD ME, SO IT PLEASE THEE HOLD           3.136.11
FOR NOTHING HOLD ME, SO IT PLEASE THEE HOLD           3.136.11
NO WANT OF CONSCIENCE HCLD IT THAT I CALL             3.151.13
OF HERBES OR BEASTES, WHICH $INDE OR $AFRIKE HOLD      4.3.8
AS WHAT THEIR HANDS DO HOLD, THEIR HEADS CO KNOW       4.24.6
'FOOLE,' ANSWERS HE, 'NC $INDES SUCH TREASURES
                                       HOLD           4.32.12
AND LOVE DOTH HOLD MY HAND, AND MAKES ME WRITE        4.90.14
WHICH HOLD MY LIFE IN THEIR DEAD DOING MIGHT          5.1.2
SHALL HANDLE YOU ANC HOLD IN LOVES SOFT BANDS         5.1.3
SITH ALL YOUR TEMPESTS CANNOT HOLD ME BACKE           5.46.10
AND CATCHING HOLD CN THINE OWNE WICKED HED            5.86.10
HOLDETH                  1
THAT WHILST WITH $MARS SHE HOLDETH HER OLD $WAY       2.48.13
HOLDS                   12
HOLDES IN HER FAIREST HAND WHAT DEAREST IS            1.12.10
THAT HOLDS, THAT BURNES, THAT WOUNDS ME
                      IN THIS SORT                    1.14.8
YET CANNOT LEAVE HER LOVE THAT HOLDS ME HATEFULL      1.18.5
HOLDS IN PERFECTICN BUT A LITTLE MOMENT               3.15.2
MY TOUNG-TIDE $MUSE IN MANNERS HOLDS HER STILL        3.85.1
(THOUGH WORDS COME HIND-MOST) HOLDS HIS
                      RANKE BEFORE                    3.85.12
NOR HIS OWNE VISICN HOULDS WHAT IT DOTH CATCH         3.113.8
WHILST HER NEGLECTED CHILD HOLDS HER IN CHACE         3.143.5
HOLDS MY YOUNG BRAINE CAPTIV'D IN GOLDEN CAGE         4.23.11
THAT HAND, WHICH WITHOUT TOUCH HOLDS MORE
                      THEN $ATLAS MIGHT               4.77.5
PLEASINGST CONSORT, WHERE EACH SENCE HOLCS A PART     4.79.3
SLOW HEAVINESSE IN BOTH HOLDS ONE DEGREE              4.96.6
HOLLAND                  1
HOW $HOLLAND HEARTS, NOW SO GOOD TOWNES BE LCST       4.30.7
HOLY                    16
O CLEERE-EYDE $RECTCR OF THE HOLY $HILL               1.4.10
A HAPPY CONVOY TO A HOLY $LAND                        1.46.6
MY HOLY $THOUGHTS, THEY BE THE $VESTALL FLAME         2.30.10
CARLEGION $CHESTER VAUNTS HER HOLY $DEE               2.32.5
CHASTE HOLY $VOWES FOR MY $SOULES SACRIFICE           2.55.10
CHASTE HOLY VOWES FCR MY SOULES SACRIFICE             2.102.10
SINCE HOLY $VESTALL LAWES HAVE BEEN NEGLECTED         2.105.1
AND RACKE HER WITH A THCUSAND HOLY WISHES             2.115.14
CARLEGION $CHESTER, VAUNTS HER HOLY $DEE              2.124.5
HOW MANY A HOLY AND OBSEQUIOUS TEARE                  3.31.5
IN HIM THOSE HOLY ANTIQUE HOWERS ARE SEENE            3.68.9
SWEET BEAUTY HATH NC NAME NO HOLY BOURE               3.127.7
WHICH BORROWD FROM THIS HOLIE FIRE OF LOVE            3.153.5
MUSES, I OFT INVOKED YOUR HOLY AYDE                   4.55.1
THIS HOLY SEASON FIT TO FAST AND PRAY                 5.22.1
THEREFORE, I LYKEWISE ON SO HOLY DAY                  5.22.3
HOMAGE                   2
IF I HAVE DONE DUE HOMAGE TO HER EYES                 1.15.9
DOTH HOMAGE TO HIS NEW APPEARING SIGHT                3.7.3
HOME                     5
IN $WARRES AT HOME, OR WHEN FOR $CONQUESTS BCUND      2.58.2
```

```
    TILL THEY RETURN'D.. $HOME WHEN THEY NEVER CAME      2.58.6
    SO FARRE FROM HOME INTO MY DEEDS TO PRYE             3.61.6
    COMES HOME AGAINE, ON BETTER JUDGEMENT MAKING        3.87.12
    THAT IS MY HOME OF LOVE, IF I HAVE RANG'D            3.109.5
HOMEWARD                2
    SHALT BEND THY WRINCKLES HOMEWARD TO THE EARTH       1.50.10
    SO OFT AS HOMEWARD I FROM HER DEPART                 5.52.1
HONEST                  3
    HAPS TO LEND SOME TO ONE TRUE HONEST $FRIEND         2.10.8
    THEN HONEST $PEOPLE, BEARE WITH $LOVE AND $ME        2.22.2
    AND ALL MY HONEST FAITH IN THEE IS LOST             3.152.8
HONEY                   2
    AND HER DISDAINES ARE $GALL, HER FAVOURS $HUNNY      1.6.4
    O HOW SHALL SUMMERS HUNNY BREATH HOLD OUT            3.65.5
HONEYED                 1
    O HONIED SIGHS, WHICH FROM THAT BREAST DO RISE       4.100.5
HONOR                   40
    A MODEST $MAIDE, DECKT WITH A BLUSH OF HONOR         1.6.5
    AFFECT NO HONOR BUT WHAT SHE CAN GIVE                1.12.6
    IF ON HER LOVE MY LIFE AND HONOUR LYES               1.15.11
    SUCH HONOUR UNTO CRUELTY TO GIVE+                    1.17.8
    TO $THETIS GIVE THE HONOUR OF THY FEETE              1.19.8
    DID MAKE THE HONOUR OF THE FALL THE MORE             1.35.4
    DANGER HATH HONOR, GREAT DESIGNES THEIR FAME         1.35.6
    LIVES WITHOUT HONOUR, DIES WITHOUT A NAME            1.35.11
    THE IMAGE OF THY BLUSH AND $SOMMERS HONOR            1.39.2
    JOYES IN THAT HONOR WHICH HER EYES HAVE WONNE        1.53.7
    HIS ERROR WAS HIS HONOUR AND RENOWNE                 1.56.2
    AND SINNE OF FROWNES BRING HONOUR TO THE FACE        1.56.12
    WHOSE DUE REPORTS GIVE HONOR TO HER EYES             1.57.8
    WHAT THOUGH MY $MUSE NO HONOR GET THEREBY            1.59.13
    WHERE $VERTUE, $HONOUR, $WIT, AND $BEAUTIE LAY       2.14.10
    THAT $GOLD NOR $HONOUR NE'R HAD POW'R TO MOVE        2.15.4
    THEN FOR A $MONARCH WILL I HONOUR THEE               2.115.4
    WHICH SCORNE THE HONOR THAT IS DONE TO THEE          2.123.10
    OF ALL THINE HONOUR SHEE HATH ROBBED THEE            2.126.4
    WORDS, THOUGHTS, AND DEEDS, DEVOTED TO HER HONOR     2.138.6
    WHICH HUSBANDRY IN HONOUR MIGHT UPHOLD               3.13.10
    OF PUBLIKE HONOUR AND PROUD TITLES BOST              3.25.2
    UNLOOKT FOR JOY IN THAT I HONOUR MOST                3.25.4
    IS FROM THE BOOKE OF HONOUR RASED QUITE              3.25.11
    NOR THOU WITH PUBLIKE KINDNESSE HONOUR ME            3.36.11
    UNLESSE THOU TAKE THAT HONOUR FROM THY NAME          3.36.12
    AND GILDED HONOR SHAMEFULLY MISPLAST                 3.66.5
    TO HONOR ALL THEIR DEATHS, WHO FOR HER BLEED         4.7.14
    HONOUR IS HONOUR'D, THAT THOU DOEST POSSESSE         4.35.9
    THEN SERVANT'S WRACKE, WHERE NEW DOUBTS
                                HONOR BRINGS             4.45.11
    SERVICE AND $HONOR, WONDER WITH DELIGHT              4.72.9
    THE HEIGHT OF HONOR IN THE KINDLY BADGE
                                OF SHAME+                4.102.3
    LET HONOR SELFE TO THEE GRAUNT HIGHEST PLACE         4.103.14
    SUCH PRIDE IS PRAISE, SUCH PORTLINESSE IS HONOR      5.5.9
    SUCH LIFE SHOULD BE THE HONOR OF YOUR LIGHT          5.7.13
    BUT MONGST THEM ALL, WHICH DID $LOVES HONOR RAYSE    5.19.9
    I HONOR AND ADMIRE THE MAKERS ART                    5.24.4
    MOTE HAVE YOUR LIFE IN HONOUR LONG MAINTAYNED        5.36.12
    ADORN'D WITH HONOUR, LOVE, AND CHASTITY              5.69.8
    THAT HONOUR AND LARGE RICHESSE TO ME LENT            5.74.8
```

```
BUT THAT I HOPE SOME GOOD CONCEIPT OF THINE          3.26.7
WISHING ME LIKE TO ONE MORE RICH IN HOPE             3.29.5
BEING HAD TO TRYUMPH, BEING LACKT TO HOPE            3.52.14
AND YET TO TIMES IN HOPE, MY VERSE SHALL STAND       3.60.13
BUT HOPE OF $ORPHANS, AND UN-FATHERED FRUITE         3.97.10
BUT IF THOU CATCH THY HOPE TURNE BACK TO ME          3.143.11
AND AH WHAT HOPE, THAT HOPE SHOULD ONCE SEE DAY      4.35.7
AND AH WHAT HOPE, THAT HOPE SHOULD ONCE SEE DAY      4.35.7
COULD HOPE BY $CUPID'S HELPE ON YOU TO PRAY          4.43.2
OF $HOPE, WHICH MAKES IT SEEME FAIRE TO THE EYE      4.49.8
TO WITLESSE THINGS, THEN $LOVE I HOPE (SINCE WIT     4.59.13
NOR HOPE, NOR WISHE ANOTHER COURSE TO FRAME          4.64.12
AND DO I SEE SOME CAUSE A HOPE TO FEEDE              4.66.1
AND YET AMID ALL FEARES A HOPE THERE IS              4.66.9
HOPE, ART THOU TRUE, OR DOEST THOU FLATTER ME+       4.67.1
CHIEFE GOOD, WHERETO MY HOPE DOTH ONLY ASPIRE        4.68.3
WHO SEEKE, WHO HOPE, WHO LOVE, WHO LIVE BUT THEE     4.90.2
SEEING HOPE YEELD WHEN THIS WO STRAKE HIM FURST      4.95.6
FALSE FLATTERING HOPE, THAT WITH SO FAIRE A FACE     4.106.2
DOTH SEEME TO PROMISE HOPE OF NEW DELIGHT            5.4.2
TWIXT FEARE AND HOPE DEPENDING DOUBTFULLY+           5.25.4
GIVES ME GREAT HOPE OF YOUR RELENTING MYND           5.28.2
YET HOPE I WELL, THAT WHEN THIS STORME IS PAST       5.34.9
WITHOUT HOPE OF ASWAGEMENT OR RELEASE+               5.36.4
SO DOE I HOPE HER STUBBORNE HART TO BEND             5.51.11
IN WHICH I HOPE ERE LONG FOR TO ARRYVE               5.63.6
AND WHEN I HOPE TO SEE THEYR TREW OBJECT             5.78.11
HOPED                  3
AND THUS BY THOSE OF WHOM I HOP'D FOR AYD            2.29.13
WHAT CAN BE HOPED MY HARVEST TIME WILL BE+           4.21.11
A PRETY CASE- I HOPED HER TO BRING                   4.57.12
HOPELESS                2
NOT THAT THEY FEARE THE HOPE-LESSE $MAN TO KILL      2.50.10
MY $HART IMPRISONED IN A HOPELES $ILE                2.122.1
HOPES                  20
BUT MY DEGRADED HOPES, WITH SUCH DISGRACE            1.7.11
MY HOPES DOE REST IN LIMITS OF HER GRACE             1.12.7
MY LAST $RESORT WHERETO MY HOPES APPEALE             1.22.2
THUS SHE RETURNES MY HOPES SO FRUITLESSE EVER        1.24.13
HOPES ARE UNSURE, WHEN CERTAINE IS MY PAINE          1.25.14
NO LIGHTNING LOOKES WHICH FALLING HOPES ERECT        1.31.10
RAISING MY HOPES ON HILLS OF HIGH DESIRE             1.36.1
WHEN SHALL MY INTERDICTED HOPES RETURNE              1.49.3
THE LEVELL OF MY HOPES DESIRED MOST                  1.53.4
ALL OTHER HONORS DOE MY HOPES REFUSE                 1.58.3
BASELY ATTENDING ON THE HOPES OF MEN                 1.58.8
MY $HOPES REVIV'D, WHICH LONG IN $GRAVE HAD LYNE     2.35.12
I BUILD MY $HOPES A WORLD ABOVE THE $SKIE            2.62.9
MY HOPES REVIV'D WHICH LONG IN GRAVE HAD LYNE        2.112.12
I BUILD MY HOPES, A WORLD ABOVE THE SKYE             2.150.9
APPLYING FEARES TO HOPES, AND HOPES TO FEARES        3.119.3
APPLYING FEARES TO HOPES, AND HOPES TO FEARES        3.119.3
OF HOPES BEGOT BY FEARE, OF WOT NOT WHAT DESIRES     4.6.2
SHE OFT HATH DRUNKE MY TEARES, NOW HOPES TO ENJOY    4.70.3
THEN THOSE BLEST EYES, WHERE ALL MY HOPES
                              DO DWELL                4.86.13
HOPE'S                  5
YET MY $HOPES $WINGS ARE LADEN SO WITH $FEARE        2.26.6
AS THEY CANNOT ASCEND TO MY $HOPES $SPHERE           2.26.7
YET MY HOPES WINGS ARE LODEN SO WITH FEARE           2.137.6
```

```
AS THEY CANNOT ASCEND TO MY HOPES SPHEARE          2.137.7
POORE HOPE'S FIRST WEALTH, OSTAGE OF PROMIST
                            WEALE                   4.79.12
HOPING                      2
  HOPING THEREBY TO FREE MY BETTER PART             1.27.4
  HOPING THAT WHEN THEY MIGHT FIND $STELLA ALONE    4.57.5
HORNED                      1
  THE HORNED $RAM DOTH IN HIS COURSE AWAKE          2.147.2
HORNS                       2
  TO FILL HIS HORNES THIS YEARE ON $CHRISTIAN COAST 4.30.2
  IS IT NOT EVILL THAT SUCH A $DEVILL WANTS
                            HORNES+                 4.78.14
HORRID                      1
  LET ALL THE PLAGUES AND HORRID PAINES OF HELL     5.86.5
HORROR                      3
  MY PLEASURES HORROR, $MUSICKE TRAGICKE NOTES      1.9.11
  WHEN MY $HEART IS THE VERY $DEN OF $HORROR        2.41.2
  WHEN MY HART IS THE VERY $DEN OF HORROR           2.143.2
HORRORS                     2
  LANGUISHT WITH HORRORS OF THE SILENT NIGHT        4.89.8
  WHILE THE BLACKE HORRORS OF THE SILENT NIGHT      4.98.9
HORROR'S                    1
  IN HORRORS SABLE CLOWDES SETS MY LIVES SUNNE      1.30.2
HORSE                       7
  THEN CAN NO HORSE WITH MY DESIRE KEEPE PACE       3.51.9
  SOME IN THEIR $HAWKES AND $HOUNDS, SOME
                            IN THEIR $HORSE         3.91.4
  HAVING THIS DAY MY HORSE, MY HAND, MY LAUNCE      4.41.1
  I ON MY HORSE, AND $LOVE ON ME DOTH TRIE          4.49.1
  A HORSMAN TO MY HORSE, A HORSE TO $LOVE           4.49.3
  A HORSMAN TO MY HORSE, A HORSE TO $LOVE           4.49.3
  MY HORSE, HE SPURRES WITH SHARPE DESIRE MY HART   4.49.11
HORSEBACK                   1
  ON HORSEBACKE MET HIM IN HIS FURIOUS RACE         4.22.6
HORSEMAN                    1
  A HORSMAN TO MY HORSE, A HORSE TO $LOVE           4.49.3
HORSEMEN                    1
  HORSEMEN MY SKILL IN HORSMANSHIP ADVAUNCE         4.41.5
HORSES                      1
  OF MORE DELIGHT THEN $HAWKES OR $HORSES BEE       3.91.11
HORSES'                     1
  TEMPERS HER WORDS TO TRAMPLING HORSES FEET        4.84.3
HORSMANSHIP                 1
  HORSEMEN MY SKILL IN HORSMANSHIP ADVAUNCE         4.41.5
HORSMANSHIPS                1
  OUR HORSMANSHIPS, WHILE BY STRANGE WORKE I PROVE  4.49.2
HOST                        3
  THE LEAST ABLE TO KYLL AN HOSTE OF $KINGS         2.126.8
  HOW $POLES' RIGHT KING MEANES, WITHOUT
                            LEAVE OF HOAST          4.30.3
  BUT HIM HER HOST THAT UNKIND GUEST HAD SLAINE     4.38.14
HOSTAGE                     2
  MY $HEART FOR $HOSTAGE THAT IT SHALL REMAINE      2.63.6
  POORE HOPE'S FIRST WEALTH, OSTAGE OF PROMIST
                            WEALE                   4.79.12
HOSTAGES                    1
  AND HOSTAGES DOE OFFER FOR MY TRUTH               5.11.2
HOT                         7
  YOUR $BEAUTIE IS THE HOT AND SPLEND'ROUS $SUNNE   2.16.5
  MY $LOVE MAKES HOTE THE FIRE WHOSE HEAT IS SPENT  2.127.1
```

SOMETIME TOO HOT THE EYE OF HEAVEN SHINES   3.18.5
THREE $APRILL PERFUMES IN THREE HOT $JUNES
                              BURN'D   3.104.7
AND SO THE $GENERALL OF HOT DESIRE   3.154.7
TILL WITHOUT FEWELL YOU CAN MAKE HOT FIRE   4.46.14
IS NOT DISSOLV'D THROUGH MY SO HOT DESYRE   5.30.3
HOTTEST   1
I FEELE THE FLAMES OF HOTTEST SOMMER DAY   4.89.14
HOUND   1
NOR CHASTE BY HOUND, NOR FORC'D BY $HUNTERS ARTE 2.135.3
HOUNDS   3
MY THOUGHTS (LIKE $HOUNDES) PURSUE ME TO MY DEATH 1.5.12
SOME IN THEIR $HAWKES AND $HOUNDS, SOME
                    IN THEIR $HORSE   3.91.4
WITH PANTING HOUNDS BEGUILED OF THEIR PRAY   5.67.4
HOUR   7
BY CURING ME, AND KILLING ME EACH $HOW'R   2.50.13
BUT OUT ALACK, HE WAS BUT ONE HOURE MINE   3.33.11
THE WHICH HE WILL NOT EV'RY HOWER SURVAY   3.52.3
NOR DARE I CHIDE THE WORLD WITHOUT END HOURE   3.57.5
DOEST HOULD TIMES FICKLE GLASSE, HIS SICKLE,
                              HOWER   3.126.2
FOR LUSTY SPRING NOW IN HIS TIMELY HOWRE   5.4.9
IN ONE SHORT HOURE I FIND BY HER UNDONNE   5.23.8
HOURS   19
AND PRODIGALL OF HOWERS AND YEARES BETRAIES   1.23.11
SWIFT SPEEDY $TIME, FEATHRED WITH FLYING HOURES   1.39.11
SHEW'D IN THESE LINES, THE WORKE OF CAREFULL
                              HOURES   1.59.7
AND THUS DIVIDING OF MY FATALL $HOURES   2.3.5
AND THUS DEVIDING OF MY FATALL HOWRES   2.110.5
WHY LENGTHNEST THOU THY DARKEST HOWRES SO   2.145.3
THOSE HOWERS THAT WITH GENTLE WORKE DID FRAME   3.5.1
NOW STAND YOU ON THE TOP OF HAPPIE HOURES   3.16.5
O CARVE NOT WITH THY HOWERS MY LOVES FAIRE BROW   3.19.9
YET DOTH IT STEALE SWEET HOURES FROM LOVES
                              DELIGHT   3.36.8
UPON THE HOURES, AND TIMES OF YOUR DESIRE+   3.57.2
OR AT YOUR HAND TH'ACCOUNT OF HOURES TO CRAVE   3.58.3
TO FIND OUT SHAMES AND IDLE HOURES IN ME   3.61.7
WHEN HOURES HAVE DREIND HIS BLOOD AND
                    FILD HIS BROW   3.63.3
IN HIM THOSE HOLY ANTIQUE HOWERS ARE SEENE   3.68.9
LOVE ALTERS NOT WITH HIS BREEFE HOURES
                    AND WEEKES   3.116.11
WHICH WORKES ON LEASES OF SHORT NUMBRED HOWERS   3.124.10
BUY TEARMES DIVINE IN SELLING HOURES OF CROSSE   3.146.11
BUT JOYOUS HOURES DOO FLY AWAY TOO FAST   5.87.14
HOUSE   2
WHO LETS SO FAIRE A HOUSE FALL TO DECAY   3.13.9
I SEE THE HOUSE, MY HEART THY SELFE CONTAINE   4.85.1
HOUSEWIFE   1
LOE AS A CAREFULL HUSWIFE RUNNES TO CATCH   3.143.1
HOVE   1
NE JOY OF OUGHT THAT UNDER HEAVEN DOTH HOVE   5.89.9
HOVERS   1
MY SPOTLESSE LOVE HOVERS WITH PUREST WINGS   1.12.1
HOWEVER   1
BY THIS I SEE, HOW-EVER THINGS BE PAST   2.2.13

HUE   20
   NOR ARE MY PASSIONS LIMND FOR OUTWARD HEW   1.4.5
   WHICH, THEN PRESENTS HER WINTER-WITHERED HEW   1.38.10
   THE HEW WHICH THOU SO CAREFULLY DOST NORISH   1.50.7
   A MAN IN HEW ALL $HEWS IN HIS CONTROWLING   3.20.7
   AND STEALE DEAD SEEING CF HIS LIVING HEW+   3.67.6
   THOU ART AS FAIRE IN KNOWLEDGE AS IN HEW   3.82.5
   OF DIFFERENT FLOWERS IN CDOR AND IN HEW   3.98.6
   SO YOUR SWEETE HEW, WHICH ME THINKES STILL
                              DOTH STAND   3.104.11
   OR DID SHE ELSE THAT SOBER HUE DEVISE   4.7.5
   WHILE THAT BLACKE HUE FROM ME THE BAD GUEST HID 4.20.11
   THAT SKIN, WHOSE PASSE-PRAISE HUE SCORNS
                      THIS POORE TERME OF WHITE   4.77.7
   TAKES IN THAT SAD HUE, WHICH WITH TH'INWARD NIGHT 4.99.7
   THAT HUE, WHOSE FCRCE MY HART STILL UNTO
                              THRALDOME TIES+   4.102.8
   AT WONDROUS SIGHT CF SO CELESTIALL HEW   5.3.8
   FOR WHEN YE MILDLY LOOKE WITH LOVELY HEW   5.7.5
   THROUGH SWEET ALLUREMENT OF HER LOVELY HEW   5.31.10
   THE FAYRE $IDEA OF YOUR CELESTIALL HEW   5.45.7
   FOR WITH THE GOODLY SEMBLANT OF HER HEW   5.53.6
   SHALL TURNE TO NOUGHT AND LOOSE THAT GLORIOUS HEW 5.79.6
   THE CONTEMPLATION CF WHCSE HEAVENLY HEW   5.80.11
HUES   1
   A MAN IN HEW ALL $HEWS IN HIS CONTROWLING   3.20.7
HUGE   4
   THAT THIS HUGE STAGE PRESENTETH NOUGHT BUT SHOWES 3.15.3
   THAT HEAVENS AYRE IN THIS HUGE RONDURE HEMS   3.21.8
   THAT BEING NOW WITH HER HUGE BRIGTNESSE DAZED   5.3.5
   THE HUGE MASSACRES WHICH HER EYES DO MAKE   5.10.6
HUGELY   1
   BUT ALL ALONE STANDS HUGELY POLLITICK   3.124.11
HUMAN   2
   IN PERFECT HUMANE SHAPE, ALL HEAV'NLY $BLISSE   2.17.12
   AND THUS IF THOU BE NOT OF HUMAINE KINDE   2.140.9
HUMBLE   5
   MY HUMBLE ACCENTS BEARE THE $OLIVE BOUGH   1.4.11
   THE HUMBLE AS THE PROUDEST SAILE DOTH BEARE   3.80.6
   THE HUMBLE SALVE, WHICH WOUNDED BOSOMES FITS   3.120.12
   O EYES, WHERE HUMBLE LOCKES MOST GLORIOUS PROVE 4.42.5
   SWEET, IT WAS SAUCIE $LCVE, NOT HUMBLE I   4.73.8
HUMBLED   5
   ARE HUMBLED THOUGHTS, WHICH BIT OF $REVERENCE
                              MOVE   4.49.6
   AND HUMBLED HARTS BRINGS CAPTIVES UNTO THEE   5.10.7
   AND DOE MYNE HUMBLED HART BEFORE HER POURE   5.20.2
   TO BE SO CRUELL TC AN HUMBLED FOE+   5.41.2
   BUT HIM THAT AT YCUR FOOTSTOOLE HUMBLED LIES   5.49.11
HUMBLENESS   1
   AND $HUMBLENESSE GROWES CNE WITH $MAJESTIE   4.48.4
HUMBLER   1
   ANOTHER HUMBLER WIT TO SHEPHEARD'S PIPE RETIRES 4.6.7
HUMBLESS   2
   AND WITH MEEKE HUMBLESSE AND AFFLICTED MOOD   5.2.11
   MYLD HUMBLESSE MIXT WITH AWFULL MAJESTY   5.13.5
HUMILITY   1
   AND EKE MINE EIES WITH MEEKE HUMILITY   5.43.11
HUMOR   5
   LOVE, IN A $HUMOR, PLAY'D THE $PRODIGALL   2.7.1

```
SOME SAY, $THAT IN MY $HUMOR I EXCELL              2.42.4
SOME SAY THAT IN MY HUMOR I EXCELL                2.128.4
AND EVERY HUMOR HATH HIS ADJUNCT PLEASURE         3.91.5
THEN THAT, WHICH ON THY HUMOR DOTH DEPEND         3.92.8
HUMORS                      1
A $POET EKE, AS HUMOURS FLY OR CREEPE             4.32.4
HUNDRED                     2
EVEN OF FIVE HUNDRETH COURSES OF THE $SUNNE       3.59.6
AN HUNDRED $GRACES AS IN SHADE TO SIT             5.40.4
HUNDREDS                    1
HUNDREDS OF YEARES YOU $STELLA'S FEET MAY KISSE   4.84.14
HUNG                        2
WHICH LIKE A JEWELL (HUNGE IN GASTLY NIGHT)       3.27.11
HUNG WITH THE TROPHEIS OF MY LOVERS GON           3.31.10
HUNGER                      2
PINED WITH $HUNGER, RISING FROM A $FEAST          2.62.4
PYNED WITH HUNGER, RYSING FROM A FEAST            2.150.4
HUNGER-STARVED              1
WHOSE $SENSES, LIKE POORE $PRIS'NERS,
                    HUNGER-STARV'D                2.49.7
HUNGER-STARVEN             2
IF HUNGER-STARVEN THOUGHTS SO LONG RETAINED       1.15.3
WHERE HUNGER-STARVEN, WANTING LOOKES TO LIVE      2.116.13
HUNGRY                      6
YET MUST THAT BLISSE MY HUNGRY THOUGHTS APPEASE   1.24.12
THY HUNGRIE EIES, EVEN TILL THEY WINCK
                    WITH FULNESSE                 3.56.6
WHEN I HAVE SEENE THE HUNGRY $OCEAN GAINE         3.64.5
I CAUGHT AT ONE OF THEM A HUNGRIE BIT             4.82.11
MY HUNGRY EYES THROUGH GREEDY COVETIZE            5.35.1
MY HUNGRY EYES, THROUGH GREEDY COVETIZE           5.83.1
HUNTED                      1
PAST REASON HUNTED, AND NO SOONER HAD             3.129.6
HUNTER'S                    1
NOR CHASTE BY HOUND, NOR FORC'D BY $HUNTERS ARTE  2.135.3
HUNTS                       1
HUNTS AFTER BLOUD, WHEN HE BY CHANCE DOTH FIND    5.56.3
HUNTSMAN                    1
LYKE AS A HUNTSMAN AFTER WEARY CHACE              5.67.1
HURT                        5
THE FAULT IS HERS, THOUGH MINE THE HURT MUST BE   1.15.14
HURT IN THE $EMBRYON, MAKES MY JOYES ABHORTIVE    2.141.4
THEY THAT HAVE POWRE TO HURT, AND WILL DOE NONE   3.94.1
I THOUGHT THOSE BABES OF SOME PINNE'S
                    HURT DID WHINE                4.16.7
WHO HIS OWNE JOY TO HIS OWNE HURT APPLIES         4.78.7
HURTS                       1
THAT ALL THY HURTS IN MY HART'S WRACKE I REECE    4.93.13
HUSBAND                     4
THAT FOR HER LATE DECEASED $HUSBAND DY'D          2.15.8
MARKE HOW ONE STRING SWEET HUSBAND TO AN OTHER    3.8.9
LIKE A DECEIVED HUSBAND, SO LOVES FACE            3.93.2
AND HUSBAND NATURES RITCHES FROM EXPENCE          3.94.6
HUSBANDRY                   2
DISDAINES THE TILLAGE OF THY HUSBANDRY+           3.3.6
WHICH HUSBANDRY IN HONOUR MIGHT UPHOLD            3.13.10
HUSBAND'S                   1
BY CHILDRENS EYES, HER HUSBANDS SHAPE IN MINDE    3.9.8
HUSH                        1
THEN WHEN HER MOURNEFULL HIMNS DID HUSH
                    THE NIGHT                     3.102.10
```

```
HYACINTH                           1
  AND YOU ARE CHANG'D, BUT NOT T'A $HIACINT        1.37.13
HYDRA                              1
  AND YET THE $HYDRA CF MY CARES RENUES            1.16.9
HYMN                               1
  TO EVERY $HIMNE THAT ABLE SPIRIT AFFORDS         3.85.7
HYMNS                              2
  FROM SULLEN EARTH SINGS HIMNS AT $HEAVENS GATE   3.29.12
  THEN WHEN HER MOURNEFULL HIMNS DID HUSH
                            THE NIGHT              3.102.10
HYPASIS                            1
  SOME WHIR-POOLE $PO, AND SLYDING $HYPASIS        2.120.10
HYRCAN                             1
  TO $HYRCAN $TYGRES, AND TO RUTHLES $BEARES       1.19.12
ICE                                8
  SHALL REST IN $ISE, WHEN THINE IS GRAV'D
                            IN $MARBLE             1.44.8
  TO BREAKE THE $ISE THAT HATH CONGEALD HER HEART+ 1.49.8
  BURN'D IN A $SEA OF YCE, AND DROWN'D AMIDST
                            A FIRE                 2.62.14
  DISDAYNE $ICE TO MY LIFE, IS TO MY SOULE A FIRE  2.132.3
  BURN'D IN A $SEA CF $ICE, AND DROWN'D
                            AMIDST A FIRE          2.150.14
  MY LOVE IS LYKE TC YSE, AND I TO FYRE            5.30.1
  THAT FIRE WHICH ALL THING MELTS, SHOULD
                            HARDEN YSE             5.30.10
  AND YSE WHICH IS CCNGEALD WITH SENCELESSE COLD   5.30.11
IDEA                               13
  THAT FAIRE $IDEA ONELY LIVES BY THEE             2.32.14
  ONELY I CALL ON MY DIVINE $IDEA                  2.39.14
  MY $SOULE-SHRIN'D $SAINT, MY FAIRE $IDEA LIES    2.53.2
  MY SOULE-SHRINDE $SAINT, MY FAIRE $IDEA LYES     2.113.2
  VERTUES $IDEA IN VIRGINITIE                      2.116.1
  BUT EVER CALL UPON DIVINE $IDEA                  2.118.14
  THYS, PURE $IDEA, VERTUES RIGHT $IDEA            2.119.9
  THYS, PURE $IDEA, VERTUES RIGHT $IDEA            2.119.9
  A FOOLES THINKE I, HAD YOU $IDEA SEENE           2.120.13
  THAT FAYRE $IDEA SHEE DCTH LIVE BY THEE          2.124.14
  WHOSE PURE $IDEA NEVER TONGUE EXPREST            2.139.13
  THE FAYRE $IDEA OF YOUR CELESTIALL HEW           5.45.7
  OF WHICH BEHOLDING THE $IDAEA PLAYNE             5.88.9
IDIOTS                             1
  AND $IDEOTS STILL ARE RUNNING AFTER $BOYES       2.22.7
IDLE                               6
  LYKE IDLE $ECCHOES EVER AUNSWERING.. SO          2.141.7
  TO FIND OUT SHAMES AND IDLE HOURES IN ME         3.61.7
  WHICH SHALL ABOVE THAT IDLE RANCKE REMAINE       3.122.3
  WITH IDLE PAINES, AND MISSING AYME, DO GUESSE    4.23.4
  AND DOTH HIS YDLE MESSAGE SET AT NOUGHT          5.19.12
  AND THAT SAME GLORIOUS BEAUTIES YDLE BOAST       5.41.9
IDLER                              1
  'WHAT IDLER THING, THEN SPEAKE AND NOT BE HARD+' 4.34.9
IDLY                               5
  THUS TALKING IDLY IN THIS $BEDLAM FIT            2.9.9
  IN GENTLE NUMBERS TIME SO IDELY SPENT            3.100.6
  BUT THAT MY WEALTH I HAVE MOST IDLY SPENT        4.18.8
  MY LOVE LYKE THE $SPECTATOR YDLY SITS            5.54.2
  THEY YDLY BACK RETURNE TO ME AGAYNE              5.78.10
IDOL                               6
  THOUGH MY SOULES $IDOLL SCORNETH ALL MY VOWES    1.11.10
```

```
     CUPID, DUMBE $IDOLL, PEEVISH $SAINT OF LOVE        2.126.1
     NO MORE SHALT THOU NOR $SAINT NOR $IDOLL BE        2.126.2
     NOR MY BELOVED AS AN $IDOLL SHOW                   3.105.2
     THAT GOODLY $IDOLL NOW SO GAY BESEENE              5.27.5
     MY SOVERAYNE SAYNT, THE $IDOLL OF MY THOUGHT       5.61.2
IDOLATRY                    1
     LET NOT MY LOVE BE CAL'D $IDOLATRIE                3.105.1
IGNORANCE                   2
     AND HEAVIE IGNORANCE ALOFT TO FLIE                 3.78.6
     AS HIGH AS LEARNING, MY RUDE IGNORANCE             3.78.14
IGNORANT                    1
     WOULD $GOD I WERE AS IGNORANT AS THEY              2.43.11
ILIADS                      1
     THE WAILING $ILIADS OF MY TRAGICKE WOE             1.47.2
ILL                        33
     AND BY THAT HAND WHOM SUCH DEEDS ILL BECOME        1.31.14
     ILE TELL THE WORLD THAT I DESERV'D BUT ILL         1.33.11
     AND OF BOTH, WRONGFULL DEEMES, AND ILL CONCEIVES   1.52.8
     THE SHIPWRACKE OF MY ILL ADVENTRED YOUTH           1.54.6
     WHICH CEASETH NOT TO TEMPT $ME TO EACH $ILL        2.20.3
     THE $CIRCUMSTANCE DOTH MAKE IT GOOD, OR ILL        2.28.14
     TO THEIR GROSSE $SENSE APPLY HER SELFE SO ILL      2.43.10
     EV'N SO MY $MISTRES WORKES UPON MY $ILL            2.50.12
     AS TENDER NURSE HER BABE FROM FARING ILL           3.22.12
     AND THEY ARE RITCH, AND RANSOME ALL ILL DEEDS      3.34.14
     LASCIVIOUS GRACE, IN WHOM ALL IL WEL SHOWES        3.40.13
     (THOUGH YOU DOE ANY THING) HE THINKES NO ILL       3.57.14
     NOT BLAME YOUR PLEASURE BE IT ILL OR WELL          3.58.14
     AND CAPTIVE-GOOD ATTENDING $CAPTAINE ILL           3.66.12
     IF SOME SUSPECT OF ILL MASKT NOT THY SHOW          3.70.13
     THOU CANST NOT (LOVE) DISGRACE ME HALFE SO ILL     3.89.5
     SOME IN THEIR GARMENTS THOUGH NEW-FANGLED ILL      3.91.3
     NAMING THY NAME, BLESSES AN ILL REPORT             3.95.8
     THE HARDEST KNIFE ILL US'D DOTH LOOSE HIS EDGE     3.95.14
     FOR WHAT CARE I WHO CALLES ME WELL OR ILL          3.112.3
     WHICH RANCKE OF GOODNESSE WOULD BY ILL BE CURED    3.118.12
     O BENEFIT OF ILL, NOW I FIND TRUE                  3.119.9
     AND IN MY MADNESSE MIGHT SPEAKE ILL OF THEE        3.140.10
     NOW THIS ILL WRESTING WORLD IS GROWNE SO BAD       3.140.11
     THE WORSER SPIRIT A WOMAN COLLOUR'D IL             3.144.4
     FEEDING ON THAT WHICH DOTH PRESERVE THE ILL        3.147.3
     WHENCE HAST THOU THIS BECOMMING OF THINGS IL       3.150.5
     AND SWEET IS $MOLY, BUT HIS ROOT IS ILL            5.26.8
     BUT DID SHE KNOW HOW ILL THESE TWO ACCORD          5.31.13
     AND SPEAKE HER GOOD, THOUGH SHE REQUITE IT ILL     5.48.14
     THEN NOT ON HIM THAT NEVER THOUGHT YOU ILL         5.49.7
     GOOD SHAMES TO BE TO ILL AN INSTRUMENT             5.53.12
     WITHOUT CONSTRAYNT OR DREAD OF ANY ILL             5.65.6
ILL-ACCEPTED                1
     UNHAPPY $PEN, AND ILL-ACCEPTED LINES               1.59.1
ILL-MADE                    1
     TO WARME WITH ILL-MADE FIRE COLD $MOSCOVY          4.30.4
ILLS                        2
     THE ILLS THAT WERE, NOT GREW TO FAULTS ASSURED     3.118.10
     AND GAINE BY ILLS THRISE MORE THEN I HAVE SPENT    3.119.14
ILLUSION                    1
     THROUGH SWEET ILLUSION OF HER LOOKES DELIGHT       5.16.4
IMAGE                      22
     PRESENT THE $IMAGE OF THE CARES I PROVE            1.2.3
     THE IMAGE OF THY BLUSH AND $SOMMERS HONOR          1.39.2
```

```
PAYNTED THE BLACKEST $IMAGE OF MY WOE              2.114.11
AND IN THYS $IMAGE HIS DARKE CLOWDY EYES           2.114.13
CELESTIALL $IMAGE, $LOAD-STONE OF DESIRE           2.123.6
THOU $SABLE SHADOW, $IMAGE OF DISPAYRE             2.145.5
THE LIVELY $IMAGE CF $DIVINITIE                    2.146.14
DIE SINGLE AND THINE $IMAGE DIES WITH THEE         3.3.14
TO FINDE WHERE YOUR TRUE $IMAGE PICTUR'D LIES      3.24.6
SHOW ME YOUR IMAGE IN SOME ANTIQUE BOOKE           3.59.7
IS IT THY WIL, THY $IMAGE SHOULD KEEPE OPEN        3.61.1
AN IMAGE IS, WHICH FOR CUR SELVES WE CARVE         4.5.6
SWEET $STELLA'S IMAGE I DO STEALE TO MEE'          4.32.14
UNTO MY MIND, IS $STELLA'S IMAGE, WROUGHT          4.38.6
LIVELIER THEN ELSE-WHERE, $STELLA'S IMAGE SEE      4.39.14
OF EVERIE IMAGE, WHICH MAY COMFORT SHOW+           4.66.4
RESEMBLE TH'YMAGE CF THEIR GOODLY LIGHT            5.9.4
IN WHICH HER GLORICUS YMAGE PLACED IS              5.22.6
THE GOODLY YMAGE CF YOUR VISNOMY                   5.45.11
THE GLORIOUS IMAGE CF THE MAKERS BEAUTIE           5.61.1
WHOSE YMAGE YET I CARRY FRESH IN MYND              5.78.4
BUT TH'ONELY IMAGE CF THAT HEAVENLY RAY            5.88.7
IMAGED                    1
ALAS, IF $FANCY DRAWNE BY IMAG'D THINGS            4.45.9
IMAGES                    3
CEASE DREAMES, TH'$IMAGES OF DAY DESIRES           1.54.9
THEIR IMAGES I LOV'D, I VIEW IN THEE               3.31.13
DOE I NOT SEE THAT FAYREST YMAGES                  5.51.1
IMAGINARY                 2
PAINT SHADOWES IN IMAGINARY LINES                  1.55.3
SAVE THAT MY SOULES IMAGINARY SIGHT                3.27.9
IMBRUED                   1
WITH MURTHERING HANDS IMBRUD IN MINE OWN BLOCD     2.114.12
IMITATE                   3
MY WORDS MIGHT IMITATE MY DEEREST THOUGHTS
                         DIRECTION                 2.117.7
WHY SHOULD FALSE PAINTING IMMITATE HIS CHEEKE      3.67.5
OR DO YOU CUTTED $SPARTANES IMITATE+               4.92.3
IMITATED                  1
IS POORELY IMMITATED AFTER YOU                     3.53.6
IMMORTAL                 14
THEN SHOULDST THOU LIVE IN AN IMMORTALL STILE      1.43.12
STILL TO SURVIVE IN MY IMMORTALL $SONG             2.6.14
THE $SOULE OF $MAN IMMORTALL AND DIVINE            2.12.2
BUT YOU BROKE INTC $HEAV'NS IMMORTALL STCRE        2.14.9
THE $SUN-BEAMES SMCTHERED WITH IMMORTALL $SMCKE    2.55.6
THE $SUN-BEAMES SMCTHERED WITH IMMORTALL SMOKE     2.102.6
WHOSE GLORIOUS HAND IMMCRTALL HATH ENROLC THEE     2.129.12
WITH TEARES, SIGHES, AND DISDAINE, SHALL
                         HAVE IMMORTAL STRIFE      2.132.14
YOUR NAME FROM HENCE IMMCRTALL LIFE SHALL HAVE     3.81.5
ON THOSE FAYRE EYES MY LCVES IMMORTALL LIGHT       5.16.2
BUT THAT WHICH SHAL YOU MAKE IMMORTALL, CHERISH    5.27.14
AND EKE HER MIND IS PURE IMMORTALL HYE             5.55.12
SHALL BE THEREOF IMMORTALL MONIMENT                5.69.10
IN SETTING YOUR IMMCRTALL PRAYSES FORTH            5.82.12
IMMORTALIZE               2
OR MAKE MY PEN HER NAME IMORTALIZE                 2.123.11
A MORTALL THING SC TO IMMORTALIZE                  5.75.6
IMMORTALLY                1
AND EVERY PART REMAINES IMMORTALLY                 5.45.8
```

IMMURED   1
  IN WHOSE CONFINE IMMURED IS THE STORE   3.84.3
IMP   1
  ALTHOUGH LESSE GIFTS IMPE FEATHERS OFT ON $FAME   4.75.4
IMPAIR   1
  FOR I IMPAIRE NOT BEAUTIE BEING MUTE   3.83.11
IMPANELED   1
  TO SIDE THIS TITLE IS IMPANNELLED   3.46.9
IMPARADISE   1
  FOR SHE THAT CAN MY HEART IMPARADIZE   1.12.9
IMPART   7
  AND MUST THEIR GLORY TO THE WORLD IMPART   1.10.12
  REVEALE THE TREASURE WHICH HER SMILES IMPART+   1.49.6
  THEN NIGARD TRUTH WOULD WILLINGLY IMPART   3.72.8
  YET TO THOSE FOOLES HEAV'N SUCH WIT DOTH IMPART   4.24.5
  BUT MORE I CRIE, LESSE GRACE SHE DOTH IMPART   4.44.6
  MOST RICH, WHEN MOST HIS RICHES IT IMPART   4.79.7
  O KISSE, WHICH DOEST THOSE RUDDIE GEMMES IMPART   4.81.1
IMPARTING   1
  SLEEPES WONDER $BEAUTY, WONDERS TO WORLDS
                          IMPARTING   2.136.4
IMPEACHED   1
  WHEN MOST IMPEACHT, STANDS LEAST IN THY
                          CONTROULE   3.125.14
IMPEDIMENTS   1
  ADMIT IMPEDIMENTS, LOVE IS NOT LOVE   3.116.2
IMPERFECT   1
  WHEN IN DEAD NIGHT THEIR FAIRE IMPERFECT SHADE   3.43.11
IMPERIOUS   1
  TO SHEW THE POWRE OF YOUR IMPERIOUS EYES   5.49.6
IMPIETY   1
  AND WITH HIS PRESENCE GRACE IMPIETIE   3.67.2
IMPLIED   1
  FOR IN THOSE LOFTY LOOKES IS CLOSE IMPLIDE   5.5.5
IMPORT   1
  WERE TO IMPORT FORGETFULNESSE IN MEE   3.122.14
IMPORTS   1
  WHICH TELLS THE WORLD HOW MUCH MY GRIEFE IMPORTS   1.60.4
IMPORTUNE   3
  PRESSE TO HER EYES, IMPORTUNE ME SOME GOOD   1.2.11
  WHOME THINE EYES WOOE AS MINE IMPORTUNE THEE   3.142.10
  TH'IMPORTUNE SUIT OF MY DESIRE TO SHONNE   5.23.6
IMPOSED   1
  THE $STARRE OF MY MISHAP IMPOS'D THIS PAINE   1.32.1
IMPOST   2
  NOR PAYD THE IMPOST OF HIS WAVES MORE TRULY   1.48.7
  LO HERE THE IMPOST CF A FAITH ENTIRE   1.60.1
IMPREGNABLE   1
  WHEN ROCKS IMPREGNABLE ARE NOT SO STOUTE   3.65.7
IMPRESSED   1
  SINCE $SONNETS THUS IN $BUNDLES ARE IMPREST   2.31.9
IMPRESSION   2
  TH'IMPRESSION OF HER EYES DO PEARCE SO DEEPE   1.26.7
  YOUR LOVE AND PITTIE DOTH TH'IMPRESSION FILL   3.112.1
IMPRINT   1
  THE VACANT LEAVES THY MINDES IMPRINT WILL BEARE   3.77.3
IMPRINTED   1
  IMPRINTED IN MY TEARES BY LOOKING STILL ON THEE   2.114.7
IMPRISONED   8
  PINES IN HER GRIEFE, IMPRISONED IN HER NEST   1.29.3

```
AND THUS AM I IMPRISON'D IN THE $AIRE                    2.26.12
MY WOFULL $HEART, IMPRISON'D IN MY $BREST                2.33.2
MY $HART IMPRISONED IN A HOPELES $ILE                    2.122.1
MY WOFULL HART IMPRISOND IN MY BREAST                    2.133.2
AND THUS AM I IMPRISOND IN THE AYRE                      2.137.12
BY NEW UNFOULDING HIS IMPRISON'D PRIDE                   3.52.12
TH'IMPRISON'D ABSENCE OF YOUR LIBERTIE                   3.58.6
IMPURE                      1
  THEIR LOOSER LOOKES THAT STIR UP LUSTES IMPURE         5.21.8
IMPUTE                      2
  THIS SILENCE FOR MY SINNE YOU DID IMPUTE               3.83.9
  SOME LUCKIE WITS IMPUTE IT BUT TO CHAUNCE              4.41.8
INBENT                      1
  FROM OUT THY HEAVY MOULD, THAT INBENT EYES             4.94.3
INCAPABLE                   1
  INCAPABLE OF MORE REPLEAT, WITH YOU                    3.113.13
INCENSE                     4
  HAST SENT THE INCENSE OF THY SIGHS TO HEAVEN           1.8.2
  SERVE AS AN INCENSE TO A CRUELL $DAME                  1.47.10
  RECEIVE THE $INCENSE WHICH I OFFER HERE                2.54.9
  RECEAVE THE INCENSE WHICH I OFFER HEERE                2.101.9
INCERTAINTIES               1
  INCERTENTIES NOW CROWNE THEM-SELVES ASSUR'DE           3.107.7
INCERTAINTY                 1
  WHEN I WAS CERTAINE ORE IN-CERTAINTY                   3.115.11
INCESSANT                   2
  AND LAY INCESSANT BATTERY TO HER HEART                 5.14.10
  NE YOUR INCESSANT BATTRY MORE TO BEARE                 5.57.4
INCESSANTLY                 1
  BUT ON HER NAME INCESSANTLY TO CRIE                    4.55.11
INCISION                    1
  FIRST MAKE INCISION ON EACH MAST'RING $VEINE           2.50.6
INCLINE                     1
  MY BOILING SPRITES DID THITHER SOONE INCLINE           4.16.3
INCLINED                    2
  MEN TO DEVOTION OUGHT TO BE INCLYND                    5.22.2
  YE BEARING IT DOE SEEME TO ME INCLIND                  5.28.4
INCLUDES                    1
  MY $BREST'S THE $VESSELL, WHICH INCLUDES
                             THE SAME                    2.30.12
INCLUDING                   2
  MY $BREST THE $FORGE, INCLUDING ALL THE HEATE          2.40.3
  BY BREAST THE FORGE, INCLUDING ALL THE HEATE           2.144.3
INCONSTANT                  2
  THEN THE CONCEIT OF THIS INCONSTANT STAY               3.15.9
  THOU CANST NOT VEX ME WITH INCONSTANT MINDE            3.92.9
INCREASE                   10
  BUT THEIR $EXPERIENCE TO INCREASE THE MORE             2.50.11
  FROM FAIREST CREATURES WE DESIRE INCREASE              3.1.1
  HEREIN LIVES WISDOME, BEAUTY, AND INCREASE             3.11.5
  WHEN I PERCEIVE THAT MEN AS PLANTS INCREASE            3.15.5
  THE TEEMING $AUTUMNE BIG WITH RITCH INCREASE           3.97.6
  HER FLAMIE GLISTRING LIGHTS INCREASE WITH
                             TIME AND PLACE              4.76.10
  WHERE THOSE RED CHEEKS, WHICH OFT WITH
                       FAIRE ENCREASE DID FRAME          4.102.2
  BUT THAT THEIR CRUELTY DOTH STILL INCREACE             5.36.7
  AND TAKE DELIGHT T'ENCREASE A WRETCHES WOE             5.41.7
  THE MORE I FYND THEIR MALICE TO INCREACE               5.44.14
```

INCREASED   1
  WITH MY REFLEX YOURS SHALL ENCREASED BE   5.66.14
INCREASETH   2
  MY $SIGHES THE $BELLOWES, WHICH THE $FLAME
                            ENCREASETH   2.40.5
  MY SIGHES, THE BELLOWES WHICH THE FLAME
                            INCREASETH   2.144.5
INCREASING   3
  AGAINE INCREASING, AS YOU ARE CONSUMING   2.16.11
  AND STIL INCREASING AS THOU ART CONSUMING   2.106.11
  INCREASING STORE WITH LOSSE, AND LOSSE WITH STORE   3.64.8
IN-DARKENED   1
  THAT MY LIVES LIGHT WHOLY IN-DARKNED IS   1.21.4
INDE   1
  OF HERBES OR BEASTES, WHICH $INDE OR $AFRIKE HOLD   4.3.8
INDEED   9
  ONCE LET HER LOVE INDEED, OR ELS EYE ME NEVER   1.24.14
  SOME WISE IN SHEW, MORE $FOOLES INDEED THEN THEY   2.22.14
  BUT WHEN MY GLASSE SHEWES ME MY SELFE INDEED   3.62.9
  TRUE, THAT TRUE $BEAUTIE $VERTUE IS INDEED   4.5.9
  BE $LOVE'S INDEED, IN $STELLA'S SELFE HE MAY   4.52.10
  THEY LOVE INDEED, WHO QUAKE TO SAY THEY LOVE   4.54.14
  THAT WHO INDEED INFELT AFFECTION BEARES   4.61.5
  YET SIGHS, DEERE SIGHS, INDEEDE TRUE FRIENDS
                            YOU ARE   4.95.1
  THAT CAN EXPRESSE THE LIFE OF THINGS INDEED   5.17.14
INDENTURES   1
  THE GLOBE OF WEALE, LIPS $LOVE'S INDENTURES MAKE   4.85.13
INDES   1
  'FOOLE,' ANSWERS HE, 'NO $INDES SUCH TREASURES
                            HOLD   4.32.12
INDIAN   1
  BE YOUR WORDS MADE (GOOD $SIR) OF $INDIAN WARE   4.92.1
INDIAS   1
  AND BOTH THE $INDIAS OF THEIR TREASURES SPOILE   5.15.3
INDIFFERENT   1
  TH'INDIFFERENT $JUDGE BETWEENE THE HIGH AND LOW   4.39.4
INDIGEST   1
  TO MAKE OF MONSTERS, AND THINGS INDIGEST   3.114.5
INDIRECTLY   1
  WHY SHOULD POORE BEAUTIE INDIRECTLY SEEKE   3.67.7
INDITE   1
  OR ELSE $LOVE WERE UNABLE TO INDITE   2.38.4
INDUS   1
  NOW BROAD-BRYMD $INDUS, THEN OF $PINDUS HEIGHT   2.120.5
INFANCY   2
  AS THE $WORLDS $BEAUTIE IN HIS $INFANCIE   2.17.7
  BEHOLD WORLDS $BEAUTIE IN HER INFANCIE   2.107.7
INFANT   1
  TO M'INFANT STILE THE $CRADLE, AND THE $GRAVE   1.59.12
INFANTS   1
  GOE WAILING $VERSE, THE $INFANTS OF MY LOVE   1.2.1
INFANT'S   1
  NOT PRIZING HER POORE INFANTS DISCONTENT   3.143.8
INFECTED   1
  INFECTED BY THOSE VAPOURS, WHICH ARISE   4.78.2
INFECTION   3
  AH WHEREFORE WITH INFECTION SHOULD HE LIVE   3.67.1
  BUT IF THAT FLOWRE WITH BASE INFECTION MEETE   3.94.11
  POTIONS OF $EYSELL GAINST MY STRONG INFECTION   3.111.10

```
INFELT                       1
  THAT WHO INDEED INFELT AFFECTION BEARES          4.61.5
INFERIOR                     1
  MY SAWSIE BARKE (INFERICR FARRE TC HIS)          3.80.7
INFERNAL                     4
  WHEN SHE WAS RAPT TC THE INFERNALL $BOWER        2.36.8
  WITH ALL HIS $TORMENTS AND $INFERNALL TERROR+    2.41.4
  WITH ALL HIS TORMENTS AND INFERNALL TERRCR       2.143.4
  TILL NOW, WRAPT IN A MOST INFERNALL NIGHT        4.33.3
INFIDEL                      1
  SOME $ATHIEST OR VILE $INFIDELL IN LOVE          2.112.1
INFINITE                     2
  AND IN HER EYES OF ARROWES INFINIT               4.17.11
  WHERE $NATURE DCTH WITH INFINITE AGREE+          4.35.4
INFLAME                      2
  IF THIS HER WORST, HOW SHOULD HER BEST INFLAME+  1.17.11
  THE $SPIRIT, WHEN IT TO $GOD-WARD DCTH INFLAME   2.12.12
INFLAMING                    1
  LAID BY HIS SIDE HIS HEART INFLAMING BRAND       3.154.2
INFLUENCE                    5
  WHOSE INFLUENCE RULE THE $ORBE OF MY POORE HART+ 1.34.10
  (FEARING THE STARS PRESAGED INFLUENCE)           2.116.11
  WHEREON THE $STARS IN SECRET INFLUENCE CCMMENT   3.15.4
  WHOSE INFLUENCE IS THINE, AND BORNE OF THEE      3.78.10
  THOU CANST VOUCHSAFE THE INFLUENCE OF A THOUGHT  4.40.6
INFORMER                     1
  HENCE, THOU SUBBORND $INFORMER, A TREW SCULE     3.125.13
INFUSING                     1
  OF FORCE OF HEAV'NLY BEAMES, INFUSING
                              HELLISH PAINE        4.6.3
INFUSION                     1
  WITH SWEET INFUSICN, AND PUT YOU IN MIND         5.28.7
INHABIT                      1
  OR DURST INHABIT CN A LIVING BROW                3.68.4
INHEARSE                     1
  THAT DID MY RIPE THCUGHTS IN MY BRAINE INHEARCE  3.86.3
INHERIT                      1
  THEY RIGHTLY DO INHERRIT HEAVENS GRACES          3.94.5
INHERITORS                   1
  SHALL WORMES INHERITORS CF THIS EXCESSE          3.146.7
INIQUITY                     1
  SELFE, SO SELFE LCVING WERE INIQUITY             3.62.12
INJURIES                     2
  THE INJURIES THAT TC MY SELFE I DOE              3.88.11
  THAT THEY ELSE-WHERE MIGHT DART THEIR INJURIES   3.139.12
INJURIOUS                    3
  INJURIOUS $DELIA YET I LCVE THEE STILL           1.33.9
  INJURIOUS DISTANCE SHOULD NOT STOP MY WAY        3.44.2
  WITH TIMES INJURICUS HAND CHRUSHT AND ORE-WORNE  3.63.2
INJURY                       4
  TO BEARE LOVES WRCNG, THEN HATES KNOWNE INJURY   3.40.12
  WITHOUT ACCUSING YCU OF INJURY                   3.58.8
  WAIGHES NOT THE DUST AND INJURY OF AGE           3.108.10
  AND ONELY CHERISH DCTH WITH INJURIE              4.78.8
INK                          8
  PAPER AND $INKE CAN PAINT BUT NAKED $WORDS       2.13.5
  PAPER AND YNCKE, CAN PAYNT BUT NAKED WORDS       2.121.5
  THAT IN BLACK INCK MY LCVE MAY STILL SHINE
                              BRIGHT               3.65.14
  WHAT'S IN THE BRAINE THAT $INCK MAY CHARACTER    3.108.1
```

```
    WHILE TEARES POWRE OUT HIS INKE, AND SIGHS
                        BREATHE OUT HIS WORDS        4.6.10
    MY VERIE INKE TURNES STRAIGHT TO $STELLA'S NAME  4.19.6
    WHAT INKE IS BLACKE INOUGH TO PAINT MY WO+       4.93.3
    WHILE BEAUTIE'S REDDEST INKE $VENUS FOR
                        HIM DOTH STURRE              4.102.14
INK'S                        1
    MY HARMES ON $INK'S POORE LOSSE, PERHAPS
                        SOME FIND                    4.34.13
INN                          2
  AS $LOVE AND I, LATE HARBOUR'D IN ONE $INNE        2.59.1
  THE $INNE OF CARE, THE $NURSE OF DRERY SORROW      2.145.2
INNATED                      1
  AND ALL IN VAINE, HER PRIDE IS SO INNATED          1.18.11
INNER                        1
  BREAKE FORTH AT LENGTH OUT OF THE INNER PART       5.2.5
INNOCENCE                    2
  AND $INNOCENCE IS CLOSING UP HIS $EYES             2.61.12
  THAT BOLDNED INNOCENCE BEARES IN HIR EIES          5.5.10
INNOCENT                     1
  INNOCENT PAPER WHOM TOO CRUELL HAND                5.48.1
INNUMERABLE                  2
  I FINDE, MY $GRIEFES INNUMERABLE GROWE             2.3.3
  I WELL PERCEIVE MY GRIEFE INNUMERABLE GROWES       2.110.3
INQUIRE                      3
  BUT $O, SEE, SEE, WE NEED INQUIRE NO FURTHER       2.2.9
  NE ANY THEN SHALL AFTER IT INQUIRE                 5.27.9
  THEN NEEDS ANOTHER $ELEMENT INQUIRE                5.55.9
INSEPERATE                   1
  AND JOY, WHICH IS INSEPERATE FROM THOSE EYES       4.101.7
INSIDE                       1
  OR SEEKE HEAVN'S COURSE, OR HEAVN'S INSIDE TO SEE  4.10.5
INSIGHT                      1
  WHILES DIVING DEEPE THROUGH AMOROUS INSIGHT        5.76.7
INSPIRATION                  1
  BY INSPIRATION, CAME CONCEAV'D WITH THOUGHT        2.116.2
INSPIRE                      2
  LET IT LYKEWISE YOUR GENTLE BREST INSPIRE          5.28.6
  THAT ME WITH HEAVENLY FURY DOTH INSPIRE            5.85.11
INSPIRED                     2
  MY LIPS ARE SWEET, INSPIRED WITH $STELLA'S KISSE   4.74.14
  THEN IS MY SOULE WITH LIFE AND LOVE INSPIRED       5.7.6
INSPIRES                     1
  THEIR SWEET APPEARING STILL SUCH POWER INSPIRES    1.34.7
INSPIRING                    2
  AND BY INSPIRING, GLORIFIDE MY QUILL               2.104.11
  UNTILL BY YOUR INSPIRING I MIGHT KNOW              4.55.7
INSTANT                      1
  TO MAKE SOME SPECIALL INSTANT SPECIALL BLEST       3.52.11
INSTAR                       1
  AND MUST INSTARRE THE $NEEDLE, AND THE $RAILE      1.45.12
INSTINCT                     1
  AS IF BY SOME INSTINCT THE WRETCH DID KNOW         3.50.7
INSTRUMENT                   1
  GOOD SHAMES TO BE TO ILL AN INSTRUMENT             5.53.12
INSUFFICIENCY                1
  WITH INSUFFICIENCY MY HEART TO SWAY                3.150.2
INSULTS                      1
  WHILE HE INSULTS ORE DULL AND SPEACHLESSE
                        TRIBES                       3.107.12
```

```
INTELLECTUAL                1
  AS INTELLECTUALL, IT IS $MEMORIE                    2.12.8
INTELLIGENCE                1
  WHICH NIGHTLY GULLS HIM WITH INTELLIGENCE           3.86.10
INTEND                      1
  INTEND A ZELOUS PILGRIMAGE TO THEE                  3.27.6
INTENERAT                   1
  INTENERAT THAT HEART THAT SETS SO LIGHT             1.10.7
INTENT                      2
  BUT GREEDILY HER FELL INTENT POURSEWTH              5.11.7
  A CLOSE INTENT AT LAST TO SHEW ME GRACE             5.25.10
INTENTS                     1
  TAN SACRED BEAUTIE, BLUNT THE SHARP'ST INTENTS      3.115.7
INTERCESSION                1
  OF INTERCESSION BUT TO MOVE HER WILL                1.4.12
INTERCHANGE                 1
  WHEN I HAVE SEENE SUCH INTERCHANGE OF STATE         3.64.9
INTERDICTED                 1
  WHEN SHALL MY INTERDICTED HOPES RETURNE             1.49.3
INTEREST                    2
  AS INTEREST OF THE DEAD, WHICH NOW APPEARE          3.31.7
  MY LIFE HATH IN THIS LINE SOME INTEREST             3.74.3
INTERIM                     1
  LET THIS SAD $INTRIM LIKE THE $OCEAN BE             3.56.9
INTERLACE                   1
  MARBLE MIXT RED AND WHITE DO ENTERLACE              4.9.8
INTERLINED                  2
  WITH MY $LIFE'S $SORROW INTERLINED SO               2.54.3
  WITH MY LIVES SOROW ENTERLYNED SO                   2.101.3
INTERMIXED                  1
  BUT BEST IS BEST, IF NEVER INTERMIXT                3.101.8
INTERPRET                   1
  WELL, HOW SO THOU INTERPRET THE CONTENTS            4.67.12
INTERRUPTED                 1
  WITH INTERRUPTED ACCENTS OF DESPAIRE                1.2.6
INTIMATE                    1
  THAT INTIMATE IN VAINE MY CHASTE DESIRE             1.59.2
INTREAT                     1
  BUT SINCE YE ARE MY SCOURGE I WILL INTREAT          5.24.13
INTREATY                    1
  AND LONG INTREATY SOFTEN HER HARD HART              5.18.6
INURE                       1
  WITH SUCH STRANGE TERMES HER EYES SHE DOTH INURE    5.21.9
INURED                      1
  SUCH HAUGHTY MYNDS ENUR'D TO HARDY FIGHT            5.14.7
INVADE                      2
  IN $ME'S THAT $FAITH WHICH $TIME CANNOT INVADE      2.4.12
  I $STELLA'S EYES ASSAYLL, INVADE HER EARES          4.61.3
INVAIL                      1
  WHICH THEN SHALL MOST INVAILE AND SHADOW MOST       1.40.12
INVENT                      7
  STRAIGHT TAXETH $REASON, WANTING TO INVENT          2.38.7
  STRAIGHT TAXETH $REASON, WANTING TO INVENT          2.131.7
  HOW CAN MY $MUSE WANT SUBJECT TO INVENT             3.38.1
  YET WHAT OF THEE THY $POET DOTH INVENT              3.79.7
  MY BEST WITS STILL THEIR OWNE DISGRACE INVENT       4.19.5
  THEN BY THAT COUNT, WHICH LOVERS BOOKS INVENT       5.60.9
  IN THIS AS IN THE REST, YE MOTE INVENT              5.82.6
INVENTION                   13
  WHY IN THIS SORT I WREST $INVENTION SO              2.9.2
```

POWR'D OUT WHAT FIRST FRCM QUICKE $INVENTION CAME	2.21.6
THAT EV'RY $DUDGEN LOW $INVENTION GOES+	2.31.8
THEN POSSIBLY $INVENTION CAN EXTEND	2.34.11
WERE NOT $INVENTICN STAULD, TREADING $INVENTIONS MAZE	2.117.9
INVENTION AND MY $MUSE, PERFECTION AND HER LCVE	2.117.13
AND LET $INVENTION CF HER BEAUTY VAUNT	2.151.9
WHEN THOU THY SELFE DOST GIVE INVENTION LIGHT+	3.38.8
WHICH LABORING FOR INVENTION BEARE AMISSE	3.59.3
AND KEEPE INVENTICN IN A NOTED WEED	3.76.6
THAT OVER-GOES MY BLUNT INVENTION QUITE	3.103.7
AND IN THIS CHANGE IS MY INVENTION SPENT	3.105.11
INVENTION, $NATURE'S CHILD, FLED STEP-DAME $STUDIE'S BLOWES	4.1.10

INVENTIONS   1
STUDYING INVENTIONS FINE, HER WITS TO ENTERTAINE	4.1.6

INVENTION'S   2
WERE NOT $INVENTICN STAULD, TREADING $INVENTIONS MAZE	2.117.9
BUT WORDS CAME HALTING FORTH, WANTING $INVENTION'S STAY	4.1.9

INVESTS   1
ANGER INVESTS WITH SUCH A LOVELY GRACE	4.73.13

INVIOLATE   1
YET AM I STILL INVICLATE TO $YOU	2.51.14

INVITE   2
PROMISING WONDERS, WONDER TO INVITE	4.26.4
FOR THAT AT LENGTH YET DCTH INVITE SOME REST	4.96.13

INVITED   1
NOR TASTE, NOR SMELL, DESIRE TO BE INVITED	3.141.7

INVITES   1
INVITES MY $HEART TC BE THE CHIEFEST $GHEST	2.7.4

INVITEST   1
WITH SWEETE SOFT SHADES THOU OFT INVITEST ME	4.98.5

INVITING   1
WHERETO TH'INVITING TIME OUR FASHION CALLS	3.124.8

INVOCATE   3
SOME CALL ON $HEAVEN, SCME INVOCATE ON $HELL	2.39.3
SOME INVOCATE THE $GODS, SOME SPIRITS OF $HELL	2.118.3
THEN THOSE OLD NINE WHICH RIMERS INVOCATE	3.38.10

INVOKED   2
SO OFT HAVE I INVCK'D THEE FOR MY $MUSE	3.78.1
MUSES, I OFT INVOKEC YOUR HOLY AYDE	4.55.1

INWARD   16
DO FEELE MINE INWARD HEAT AS GREAT (I KNCW IT)	1.43.6
YOU BEST DISCERN'D CF MY $MINDS INWARD $EYES	2.57.1
NEITHER IN INWARD WCRTH NOR OUTWARD FAIRE	3.16.11
AND MY HEARTS RIGHT, THEIR INWARD LOVE OF HEART	3.46.14
IT IS SO GROUNDED INWARD IN MY HEART	3.62.4
TO KISSE THE TENDER INWARD OF THY HAND	3.128.6
THE INWARD LIGHT.. AND THAT THE HEAVENLY PART	4.5.2
AS DO BEWRAY A WANT OF INWARD TUCH	4.15.10
WHICH INWARD SUNNE TO $HEROICKE MINDE DISPLAIES	4.25.8
MY MIND BEMONES HIS SENSE OF INWARD SMART	4.44.2
THAT INWARD SUNNE IN THINE EYES SHINETH SC	4.71.8
MY $ORPHAN SENCE FLIES TC THE INWARD SIGHT	4.88.10
TAKES IN THAT SAD HUE, WHICH WITH TH'INWARD NIGHT	4.99.7
OF TH'INWARD BALE CF MY LOVE PINED HART	5.2.2
AND IN MY SELFE, MY INWARD SELFE I MEANE	5.45.3
THE INWARD LANGUOR CF MY WOUNDED HART	5.50.10

```
IO                          1
  SING THEN MY $MUSE, NOW $IO $PEAN SING            4.63.9
IRE                         4
  WILL BUILDE AN ALTAR TO APPEASE HER YRE           5.22.10
  FOR WHICH THE GODS IN THEYR REVENGEFULL YRE       5.28.11
  DID MAKE THE MATTER TO AVENGE HER YRE             5.48.2
  IN MY TRUE LOVE DID STIRRE UP COLES OF YRE        5.86.8
IRISH                       1
  AND LET THE $BARDS WITHIN THAT $IRISH $ILE        2.25.9
IRKED                       1
  AND IS EVEN IRKT THAT SO SWEET $COMEDIE           4.51.13
IRKSOME                     1
  NOW THAT OF ABSENCE THE MOST IRKSOME NIGHT        4.89.1
IRON                        4
  BY IRON LAWES OF DUTY TO DEPART                   4.87.4
  WHOM IRON DOORES DO KEEPE FROM USE OF DAY+        4.108.11
  THE HARDEST YRON SOON DOTH MOLLIFY                5.32.2
  HER HART MORE HARDE THEN YRON SOFT AWHIT          5.32.6
ISIS                        2
  COTSWOLD COMMENDS HER $ISIS TO THE $TAME          2.32.9
  COTSWOOLD COMMENDS HER $ISIS AND HER $TAME        2.124.9
ISLAND                      1
  OR IN THIS $ILAND ALT'RETH WITH THE $FASHIONS+    2.27.4
ISLANDS                     1
  WHICH THOSE FAYRE $ILANDS OF THY LOOKES AFFOORD   2.134.6
ISLE                        4
  TO HELPE HER FLIGHT THROUGHOUT THE FAIREST $ILE   1.43.10
  TH'ETERNALL WONDER OF OUR HAPPY $ILE              1.53.8
  AND LET THE $BARDS WITHIN THAT $IRISH $ILE        2.25.9
  MY $HART IMPRISONED IN A HOPELES $ILE             2.122.1
ISSUE                       3
  AND CANNOT ISSUE FORTH TO SEEKE HER GOOD          1.29.4
  WHEN YOUR SWEET ISSUE YOUR SWEET FORME
                          SHOULD BEARE              3.13.8
  YET THIS ABOUNDANT ISSUE SEEM'D TO ME             3.97.9
ISSUELESS                   1
  AH., IF THOU ISSULESSE SHALT HAP TO DIE           3.9.3
ISTER                       1
  SOME $GANGES, $ISTER, AND OF $TAGUS TELL          2.120.9
ITCH                        1
  MY TONGUE DOTH ITCH, MY THOUGHTS IN LABOUR BE     4.37.2
IVORY                       6
  YIELD THY HANDS PRIDE UNTO TH' $IVORY WHITE       1.19.5
  THAT LOVELY, ARCHED, YVORIE, POLLISH'D $BROW      2.8.5
  WHENCE HAST THOU $IVORIE, $RUBIES, PEARLE
                          AND GOLD                  4.32.10
  IF $YVORIE, HER FORHEAD YVORY WEENE               5.15.10
  IF $YVORIE, HER FORHEAD YVORY WEENE               5.15.10
  A GOODLY TABLE OF PURE YVORY                      5.77.2
IXION                       2
  AND TURNE THE $WHEELE WITH DAMNED $IXION          2.40.14
  AND TURNE THE WHEELE WITH DAMNED $IXION           2.144.14
JACKS                       2
  DO I ENVIE THOSE $JACKES THAT NIMBLE LEAPE        3.128.5
  SINCE SAUSIE $JACKES SO HAPPY ARE IN THIS         3.128.13
JADE                        1
  BUT LOVE, FOR LOVE, THUS SHALL EXCUSE MY JADE     3.51.12
JAIL                        1
  THOU CANST NOT THEN USE RIGOR IN MY $JAILE        3.133.12
```

```
JANUS'                         1
  NEW YEARE FORTH LOOKING OUT OF JANUS GATE           5.4.1
JAR                            1
  THRUGH STUBBORN PRIDE AMONGST THEMSELVES DID JAR    5.44.2
JASMINE                        1
  HER NIPPLES LYKE YONG BLOSSOMD $JESSEMYNES          5.64.12
JAWS                           2
  PLUCKE THE KEENE TEETH FROM THE FIERCE
                              $TYGERS YAWES           3.19.3
  BETWEENE THE JAWES OF HELLISH $JEALOUSIE            4.78.4
JEALOUS                        3
  PEOPLED WITH $ARMIES OF PALE JEALOUS EYES           2.122.2
  NOR DARE I QUESTICN WITH MY JEALIOUS THOUGHT        3.57.9
  DEERE, THEREFORE BE NOT JEALOUS OVER ME             4.91.12
JEALOUSY                       2
  THE SKOPE AND TENURE OF THY $JELOUSIE+              3.61.8
  BETWEENE THE JAWES CF HELLISH $JEALOUSIE            4.78.4
JEER                           1
  ME $THINKES I SEE SOME CROOKED $MIMICKE JEERE       2.31.1
JEST                           1
  I LAUGH AT $FORTUNE, AS IN JEST TO DIE              2.24.14
JETS                           1
  OR SEEING JETS, BLACKE, BUT IN BLACKNESSE BRIGHT    4.91.8
JEWEL                          5
  WHICH LIKE A JEWELL (HUNGE IN GASTLY NIGHT)         3.27.11
  SHALL TIMES BEST $JEWELL FROM TIMES CHEST
                              LIE HID+                3.65.10
  THE BASEST $JEWELL WIL BE WELL ESTEEM'D             3.96.6
  THOU ART THE FAIREST AND MOST PRECIOUS $JEWELL      3.131.4
  THEN KNOW, THAT MERCY IS THE MIGHTIES JEWELL        5.49.3
JEWELS                         2
  BUT THOU, TO WHOM MY JEWELS TRIFLES ARE             3.48.5
  OR CAPTAINE $JEWELLS IN THE CARCONET                3.52.8
JOIN                           1
  JOYNE WITH THE SPIGHT OF FORTUNE, MAKE ME BOW       3.90.3
JOINED                         1
  HIS $SIRE'S REVENGE, JOYN'D WITH A KINGDOME'S
                              GAINE                   4.75.6
JOLLITY                        1
  AND NEEDIE $NOTHING TRIMD IN JOLLITIE               3.66.3
JOT                            4
  (YET HIS DULL $SPIRIT HER NOT ONE JOT COULD MOVE)   2.21.2
  NOR SHALL MY $SPIRIT ONE JOT OF VIGOUR LCSE         2.31.6
  THAT $WE ONE JOT CF FORMER $LOVE RETEYNE            2.61.8
  THAT WONDER IS HOW I SHOULD LIVE A JOT              5.57.6
JOURNEY                        3
  BUT THEN BEGINS A JOURNY IN MY HEAD                 3.27.3
  HOW HEAVIE DOE I JOURNEY ON THE WAY                 3.50.1
  WITH WHAT PASTIME, TIME'S JOURNEY SHE BEGUILCE      4.92.12
JOVE                           5
  CONDEMN'D BY $JOVE TO ENDLESSE $TORMENT BEE         2.14.2
  SOME ONE HIS SONG IN $JCVE, AND $JOVE'S
                              STRANGE TALES ATTIRES   4.6.5
  PHOEBUS WAS $JUDGE BETWEENE $JOVE, $MARS,
                              AND $LOVE               4.13.1
  JOVE ON HIS HELME THE THUNDERBOLT DID REARE         4.13.8
  WITH WHICH SHE WONTS TO TEMPER ANGRY $JOVE          5.39.3
JOVE'S                         3
  SOME ONE HIS SONG IN $JCVE, AND $JOVE'S
                              STRANGE TALES ATTIRES   4.6.5
```

```
JOVES GOLDEN SHIELD DID $EAGLE SABLES BEARE        4.13.3
NECTAR OF $MIRTH, SINCE I $JOVE'S CUP DO KEEPE      4.70.4
JOY                63
THAT NEVER DEIGNES TO GIVE ME JOY TO LIVE+         1.17.6
I WHO DID NEVER JOY IN OTHER $SUN                  1.33.5
NOW JOY THY TIME BEFORE THY SWEET BE DONE          1.40.7
THEN I WOULD JOY THE FAIREST SHE THAT LIVES        1.48.12
SENSELESSE WITH TOO MUCH $JOY, EACH OTHER SEEING   2.11.7
MY NEVER-CERTAINE $JOY BREEDS EVER-CERTAINE
                              $FEARES              2.26.4
WHY DOE I SPEAKE OF $JOY, OR WRITE OF $LOVE        2.41.1
SO MAY'ST THOU LIVE, TO THY FAIRE $MOTHERS $JOY    2.48.12
RAVISH'D WITH $JOY AMID'ST A HELL OF $WOE          2.62.7
AND HEAVEN MAY JOY TO THINK ON PAST WORLDS
                              BLISSE               2.107.12
TWIXT JOY AND GRIEFE, YET WITH A SMYLING
                              FROWNING             2.109.9
OR EVER JOY EXPRESSE, WHAT PERFECT JOY
                              HATH TAUGHT          2.117.3
OR EVER JOY EXPRESSE, WHAT PERFECT JOY
                              HATH TAUGHT          2.117.3
THEN WONDER, TONGUE, THEN JOY, MIGHT WEL
                              REPORT A WONDER      2.117.4
RARE BEAUTY, $NATURES JOY, PERFECTIONS $MOTHER     2.123.2
LAUGHING FOR JOY UPON MY LOVELY FAYRE              2.125.14
MY NEVER CERTAINE JOY, BREEDS EVER-CERTAINE
                              FEARES               2.137.4
DIE, DIE, MY SOULE, AND NEVER TASTE OF JOY         2.139.1
WHY DOE I SPEAKE OF JOY, OR WRITE OF LOVE          2.143.1
THE GRAVE OF JOY, PRYSON OF DAYES DELIGHT          2.145.10
RAVISHT WITH JOY, AMIDST A HELL OF WOE             2.150.7
SWEETS WITH SWEETS WARRE NOT, JOY DELIGHTS IN JOY   3.8.2
SWEETS WITH SWEETS WARRE NOT, JOY DELIGHTS IN JOY   3.8.2
UNLOOKT FOR JOY IN THAT I HONOUR MOST              3.25.4
BUT HERE'S THE JOY, MY FRIEND AND I ARE ONE        3.42.13
THIS TOLD, I JOY, BUT THEN NO LONGER GLAD          3.45.13
MY GREEFE LIES ONWARD AND MY JOY BEHIND            3.50.14
WHEREIN IT FINDES A JOY ABOVE THE REST             3.91.6
BEFORE A JOY PROPOSD BEHIND A DREAME               3.129.12
O HOW FOR JOY HE LEAPES, O HOW HE CROWES           4.17.12
AND JOY THEREIN, THOUGH $NATIONS COUNT IT SHAME    4.28.8
SOULE'S JOY, BEND NOT THOSE MORNING STARRES
                              FROM ME              4.48.1
O THINKE I THEN, WHAT PARADISE OF JOY              4.68.13
O JOY, TOO HIGH FOR MY LOW STILE TO SHOW           4.69.1
MY $MUSE MAY WELL GRUDGE AT MY HEAV'NLY JOY        4.70.1
SHALL PAINT OUT JOY, THOUGH BUT IN BLACKE
                              AND WHITE            4.70.11
THE ONELY LIGHT OF JOY, THE ONELY WARMTH OF $LOVE  4.76.4
THOSE LOOKES, WHOSE BEAMES BE JOY, WHOSE
                              MOTION IS DELIGHT    4.77.1
WHO HIS OWNE JOY TO HIS OWNE HURT APPLIES          4.78.7
LEAST JOY, BY $NATURE APT SPRITES TO ENLARGE       4.85.3
YET SWAM IN JOY, SUCH LOVE IN HER WAS SEENE        4.87.11
FAINT COWARD JOY NO LONGER TARRY DARE              4.95.5
HER SELFE (TO SHEW NO OTHER JOY HATH PLACE)        4.97.7
BUT WO IS ME, THOUGH JOY IT SELFE WERE SHE         4.97.12
SHE COULD NOT SHEW MY BLIND BRAINE WAIES OF JOY    4.97.13
SUCH TEARES, SIGHS, PLAINTS, NO SORROW
                              IS, BUT JOY          4.100.12
```

```
AND JOY, WHICH IS INSEPERATE FROM THOSE EYES          4.101.7
THE BOTE FOR JOY COULD NOT TO DAUNCE FORBEARE         4.103.5
THERE SHINES A JOY FROM THEE MY ONLY LIGHT            4.108.4
THAT IN MY WOES FOR THEE THOU ART MY JOY              4.108.13
SEE HOW THE $TYRANNESSE DOTH JOY TO SEE               5.10.5
WHYLEST RAPT WITH JOY RESEMBLING HEAVENLY MADNES      5.39.9
BUT JOY HER THRALL FOR EVER TO REMAYNE                5.42.7
BUT HAVING HER, MY JOY WIL BE THE GREATER             5.51.14
THERE LET NO THOUGHT OF JOY OR PLEASURE VAINE         5.52.9
SOMETIMES I JOY WHEN GLAD OCCASION FITS               5.54.5
SOONE AFTER WHEN MY JOY TO SORROW FLITS               5.54.7
THE BUD OF JOY, THE BLOSSOME OF THE MORNE             5.61.9
THEN SHALL THE NEW YEARES JOY FORTH FRESHLY SEND      5.62.9
THIS JOYOUS DAY, DEARE $LORD, WITH JOY BEGIN          5.68.5
I JOY TO SEE HOW IN YOUR DRAWEN WORK                  5.71.1
JOY OF MY LIFE, FULL OFT FOR LOVING YOU               5.82.1
NE JOY OF OUGHT THAT UNDER HEAVEN DOTH HOVE           5.89.9
```

JOYED   5
```
BUT HAPPY HE THAT JOY'D HIS STONE AND ART             1.13.13
LOTHSOME THEIR DAIES, WHOM NO SUN EVER JOYD           1.26.6
A WORLD TO SEE, YET HOW HE JOYD TO HEARE              2.125.7
A LYFE, THAT NEVER JOYD BUT IN HER LOVE               2.138.9
I JOYED, BUT STRAIGHT THUS WATRED WAS MY WINE         4.62.5
```

JOYFUL   2
```
MY JOYFULL $NORTH, WHERE ALL MY FORTUNE LIES          1.53.3
AT LENGTH HE PERCH'D HIMSELF IN $STELLA'S
                    JOYFULL FACE                      4.8.8
```

JOYOUS   6
```
THE JOYOUS SAFETY OF SO SWEET A REST                  5.63.10
THIS JOYOUS DAY, DEARE $LORD, WITH JOY BEGIN          5.68.5
TELL HER THE JOYOUS TIME WIL NOT BE STAID             5.70.7
THERE FILL YOUR SELFE WITH THOSE MOST
                    JOYOUS SIGHTS                      5.84.9
BUT JOYOUS HOURES DOO FLY AWAY TOO FAST               5.87.14
CAN COMFORT ME, BUT HER OWNE JOYOUS SIGHT             5.89.10
```

JOYS   20
```
MY JOYS BUT SHADOWES, TOUCH OF TRUTH, MY ANGUISH      1.16.3
THERE MY SOULES TYRANT JOYES HER, IN THE SACK         1.47.7
JOYES IN THAT HONOR WHICH HER EYES HAVE WONNE         1.53.7
MY JOYES ABORTIVE, PERISH IN THEIR BYRTH              1.60.11
DEFINE MY $WEALE, AND TELL THE JOYES OF $HEAVEN       2.60.1
UNTO THE WORLD HAD ALL MY JOYES BEEN MUTE             2.104.3
TH'ARERAGE OF MY JOYES, DIRECTS ME TO MY LOSSE        2.110.8
THUS MIDST A THOUSAND WOES, TEN THOUSAND
                    JOYES ARISE                        2.114.8
YET IN THESE JOYES, THE SHADOWES OF MY GOOD           2.114.9
THE PASSIONS OF DISPAIRE, BUT JOYES TO MY DESIRE      2.127.8
HURT IN THE $EMBRYON, MAKES MY JOYES ABHORTIVE        2.141.4
DEFINE MY LOVE, AND TELL THE JOYES OF HEAVEN          2.149.1
LET HIM, DEPRIVED OF SWEET BUT UNFELT JOYES           4.24.12
WHOSE BEAMES BE JOYES, WHOSE JOYES ALL VERTUES BE     4.42.2
WHOSE BEAMES BE JOYES, WHOSE JOYES ALL VERTUES BE     4.42.2
ARE METAMORPHOSD STRAIGHT TO TUNES OF JOYES           4.44.14
THAT HEAV'N OF JOYES THROWES ONELY DOWNE ON ME        4.60.3
NEAST OF YOUNG JOYES, SCHOOLMASTER OF DELIGHT         4.79.8
AND IN MY JOYES FOR THEE MY ONLY ANNOY                4.108.14
NO EIES BUT JOYES, IN WHICH AL POWERS CONSPIRE        5.8.3
```

JOY'S   3
```
MY $JOYES ARRERAGE LEADES ME TO MY LOSSE              2.3.8
AH BED, THE FIELD WHERE JOYE'S PEACE SOME DO SEE      4.98.1
```

UPON THY CHEEREFULL FACE, JOYE'S LIVERY WEARE   4.103.3
JUDGE   11
  YOU BEST CAN JUDGE THE WRONGS THAT SHE HATH DONE   1.3.12
  I KNOW HER HEART CANNOT BUT JUDGE WITH ME   1.49.13
  THEN JUDGE THE WORLD HER BEAUTY GIVES THE SAME   1.57.12
  O, JUDGE NOT RASHLY (GENTLE $SIR) I PRAY   2.24.4
  PHOEBUS WAS $JUDGE BETWEENE $JOVE, $MARS,
                          AND $LOVE   4.13.1
  BUT HARDER $JUDGES JUDGE AMBITION'S RAGE   4.23.9
  CAN JUDGE OF $LOVE, THOU FEEL'ST A $LOVER'S CASE   4.31.6
  TH'INDIFFERENT $JUDGE BETWEENE THE HIGH AND LOW   4.39.4
  TOWNE-FOLKES MY STRENGTH., A DAINTIER
                          JUDGE APPLIES   4.41.6
  NOW JUDGE BY THIS.. IN PIERCING PHRASES LATE   4.58.9
  OR IF I NEEDS (SWEET $JUDGE) MUST TORMENTS HAVE   4.86.11
JUDGED   1
  NOR GRAVER BROWES HAVE JUDG'D MY $MUSE SC VAINE   1.7.6
JUDGES   2
  BUT HARDER $JUDGES JUDGE AMBITION'S RAGE   4.23.9
  THOSE SCARLET JUDGES, THREATNING BLOUDY PAINE+   4.73.11
JUDGING   2
  IN JUDGING, $REASCN ONELY IS HER $NAME   2.12.9
  BY MY LOVE JUDGING WHAT $LOVE'S PAINE MIGHT BE   4.16.8
JUDGMENT   11
  UP, TO MY $PITCH, NC COMMON $JUDGEMENT FLYES   2.31.13
  HAVING THE $JUDGEMENT DUE TO HIS $OFFENCE   2.50.3
  AND SINCE THE WORLD TO JUDGEMENT DOTH DECLYNE   2.119.7
  NOT FROM THE STARS DO I MY JUDGEMENT PLUCKE   3.14.1
  SO TIL THE JUDGEMENT THAT YOUR SELFE ARISE   3.55.13
  COMES HOME AGAINE, CN BETTER JUDGEMENT MAKING   3.87.12
  YET THEN MY JUDGEMENT KNEW NO REASON WHY   3.115.3
  WHERETO THE JUDGEMENT OF MY HEART IS TIDE+   3.137.8
  OR IF THEY HAVE, WHERE IS MY JUDGMENT FLED   3.148.3
  BOTH BY THE JUDGEMENT OF THE $ENGLISH EYES   4.41.3
  MAKES ME IN MY BEST THOUGHTS AND QUIETST
                          JUDGEMENT SEE   4.77.12
JUDGMENTS   1
  THEIR JUDGEMENTS HACKNEY ON, THE FAULT
                          ON SICKNESSE LAY   4.102.10
JUDGMENT'S   1
  THY BLACKE IS FAIREST IN MY JUDGEMENTS PLACE   3.131.12
JUMP   1
  FOR NIMBLE THOUGHT CAN JUMPE BOTH SEA AND LAND   3.44.7
JUNCATS   1
  ALL SPRED WITH JUNCATS, FIT TO ENTERTAYNE   5.77.3
JUNES   1
  THREE $APRILL PERFUMES IN THREE HOT $JUNES
                          BURN'D   3.104.7
JUNIPER   1
  SWEET IS THE $JUNIPERE, BUT SHARPE HIS BOUGH   5.26.2
JUST   11
  AND SEE HOW JUST I RECKCN WITH THINE EIES   1.1.10
  AND OF JUST LENGTH CUR NIGHT AND DAY DOTH MAKE   2.147.3
  JUST TO THE TIME, NCT WITH THE TIME EXCHANG'D   3.109.7
  AND ON JUST PROOFE SURMISE, ACCUMILATE   3.117.10
  AND THE JUST PLEASURE LCST, WHICH IS SO DEEMED   3.121.3
  THE MORE I HEARE AND SEE JUST CAUSE OF HATE   3.150.10
  AND BY JUST COUNTS MY SELFE A BANCKROUT KNOW   4.18.3
  ONLY LOV'D $TYRANTS, JUST IN CRUELTY   4.42.6
  THAT GIV'ST NO BETTER EARE TO MY JUST CRIES   4.65.2

```
     NE IF I WOULD, COULD I JUST TITLE MAKE            4.90.9
     WILL TEACH TO SPEAKE, AND MY JUST CAUSE TO PLEAD  5.43.10
JUSTICE                4
     MY FAITH SHOULD WIN, IF $JUSTICE MIGHT HAVE PLACE 1.8.12
     IT FURTHERS $JUSTICE, BUT HELPES NOT THE DEAD     2.46.14
     IN JUSTICE PAINES COME NOT TILL FAULTS DO CALL    4.86.10
     AGAINST YOUR EIES THAT JUSTICE I MAY GAINE        5.12.14
JUSTIFY                1
     O CALL NOT ME TO JUSTIFIE THE WRONG               3.139.1
JUSTLY                 1
     MAY JUSTLY PRAISE, AND BLAME MY LOVELESSE $FAIRE  1.2.8
KALENDS                1
     THE DATE OF $AGE, THE $KALENDS OF OUR DEATH       1.50.12
KEEN                   2
     PLUCKE THE KEENE TEETH FROM THE FIERCE
                            $TYGERS YAWES              3.19.3
     LIKE AS TO MAKE OUR APPETITES MORE KEENE          3.118.1
KEEP                  26
     WHAT 'TIS TO KEEPE A $DRUNKARD COMPANIE           2.7.14
     IN MOST DISTRACTION THEY KEEPE THAT IN $MINDE     2.9.8
     WHAT WILL $YOU KEEPE A MEANE THEN BETWIXT EITHER+ 2.19.7
     THINK'ST THOU, MY $WIT SHALL KEEPE THE
                            PACK-$HORSE $WAY           2.31.7
     NIGHT WAS ORDAYN'D, TOGETHER $FRIENDS TO KEEPE    2.37.4
     TO KEEPE $THEE FROM $OBLIVION AND THE $GRAVE      2.44.10
     GAVE IT TO KEEPE TO $SPIRITS WITHIN THE $GROUND   2.58.4
     WITH THOSE RICH $BEAUTIES $HEAV'N GIVES
                            YOU TO KEEPE               2.58.12
     WHEN EVERY PRIVAT WIDDOW WELL MAY KEEPE           3.9.7
     BEARING THY HEART WHICH I WILL KEEPE SO CHARY     3.22.11
     AND KEEPE MY DROOPING EYE-LIDS OPEN WIDE          3.27.7
     THEN CAN NO HORSE WITH MY DESIRE KEEPE PACE       3.51.9
     IS IT THY WIL, THY $IMAGE SHOULD KEEPE OPEN       3.61.1
     AND KEEPE INVENTION IN A NOTED WEED               3.76.6
     TO KEEPE AN ADJUNCKT TO REMEMBER THEE             3.122.13
     SHE MAY DETAINE, BUT NOT STILL KEEPE HER
                            TRESURE                    3.126.10
     WHILST MANY $NYMPHES THAT VOU'D CHAST
                            LIFE TO KEEP               3.154.3
     TO KEEPE THE PACE OF THEIR FIRST LOVING STATE     4.17.4
     TO KEEPE THEMSELVES AND THEIR CHIEF CITIES FREE   4.29.2
     TO KEEPE IT SELFE IN LIFE AND LIBERTY             4.29.6
     SINCE THOU IN ME SO SURE A POWER DOEST KEEPE      4.32.5
     KEEPE STILL MY $ZENITH, EVER SHINE ON ME          4.42.8
     NECTAR OF $MIRTH, SINCE I $JOVE'S CUP DO KEEPE    4.70.4
     WHILE CRAFTILY YOU SEEM'D YOUR CUT TO KEEPE       4.83.3
     CANNOT HEAVN'S FOOD, ONCE FELT, KEEPE
                            STOMAKES FREE              4.88.7
     WHOM IRON DOORES DO KEEPE FROM USE OF DAY+        4.108.11
KEEPEST                1
     O CUNNING LOVE, WITH TEARES THOU KEEPST
                            ME BLINDE                  3.148.13
KEEPETH                1
     THE VOLUMES OF $RELIGIONS LAWES SHEE KEEPETH      2.105.11
KEEPS                  9
     THE MEANE OBSERVER (WHOM BASE SAFETY KEEPS)       1.35.10
     TO GIVE AWAY YOUR SELFE, KEEPS YOUR SELFE STILL   3.16.13
     SO IS THE TIME THAT KEEPES YOU AS MY CHEST        3.52.9
     IT IS MY LOVE THAT KEEPES MINE EIE AWAKE          3.61.10
     SHE KEEPES THEE TO THIS PURPOSE, THAT HER SKILL   3.126.7
```

```
WHO ERE KEEPES ME, LET MY HEART BE HIS GARDE        3.133.11
SWEET GARD'N $NYMPH, WHICH KEEPES THE
                          $CHERRIE TREE               4.82.5
OF HIS MAZDE POWERS KEEPES PERFIT HARMONY             4.99.8
THE RAGING WAVES AND KEEPES HER COURSE ARIGHT         5.59.6
KENT                2
AND $KENT WILL SAY, HER $MEDWAY DOTH EXCELL           2.32.8
AND $KENT WILL SAY, HER $MEDWAY DOTH EXCELL           2.124.8
KEPT                7
KEPT FOR HIMSELFE, DEFENDED FROM ALL HARMES           1.53.12
AND KEPT UNUSDE THE USER SO DESTROYES IT              3.9.12
WHICH THREE TILL NOW, NEVER KEPT SEATE IN ONE         3.105.14
ANGRY THAT HIS PRESCRIPTIONS ARE NOT KEPT             3.147.6
MY STILL KEPT COURSE, WHILE OTHERS SLEEPE,
                          TO MONE                     4.40.4
HAVE EVER SINCE ME KEPT IN CRUELL BANDS               5.12.12
AMONGST THY DEEREST RELICKS TO BE KEPT                5.22.14
KEY                 2
SO AM I AS THE RICH WHOSE BLESSED KEY                 3.52.1
A DOUBLE KEY, WHICH OPENS TO THE HEART                4.79.6
KEYS                1
HE YEELDS $LOVE UP THE $KEYES UNTO MY $HEART          2.29.11
KILL               13
WHO WHILST I LOVE, DOTH KILL ME WITH DISDAINE         1.3.14
UPON THIS HEART, WHOM CRUELTY WILL KILL               1.33.8
FRAM'D MY DESIRES FIT FOR HER EYES TO KILL            1.36.14
NOT THAT THEY FEARE THE HOPE-LESSE $MAN TO KILL       2.50.10
THE LEAST ABLE TO KYLL AN HOSTE OF $KINGS             2.126.8
KILL ME WITH SPIGHTS YET WE MUST NOT BE FOES          3.40.14
TOO MORROW SEE AGAINE, AND DOE NOT KILL               3.56.7
MAY TIME DISGRACE, AND WRETCHED MYNUIT KILL           3.126.8
LET NO UNKINDE, NO FAIRE BESEECHERS KILL              3.135.13
KILL ME OUT-RIGHT WITH LOOKES, AND RID MY PAINE       3.139.14
LABOUR TO KILL IN ME THIS KILLING CARE                4.68.12
IS IT BECAUSE YOUR EYES HAVE POWRE TO KILL+           5.49.2
AND KILL WITH LOOKS, AS $COCKATRICES DOO              5.49.10
KILLED              2
WITH BEAUTITS TREASURE ERE IT BE SELFE KIL'D          3.6.4
WHAT SIGHES STOLNE OUT, OR KILD BEFORE
                          FULL BORNE+                 4.67.9
KILLER              1
DEARE $KILLER, SPARE NOT THY SWEET CRUELL SHOT        4.48.13
KILLING             2
BY CURING ME, AND KILLING ME EACH $HOW'R              2.50.13
LABOUR TO KILL IN ME THIS KILLING CARE                4.68.12
KILLS               4
UNTO THE TYRANT, WHOSE UNKINDNES KILS                 1.24.4
BUT AH, THOUGHT KILLS ME THAT I AM NOT THOUGHT        3.44.9
KILS HIS OWNE CHILDREN, TEARES, FINDING
                          THAT THEY                   4.95.10
WHOME BEING CAUGHT SHE KILLS WITH CRUELL PRYDE        5.47.7
KIN                 1
THAT I PERHAPS AM SOMEWHAT KINNE TO THEE              4.65.12
KIND               36
SHE MAY BECOME MORE KINDE TO THEE OR ME               1.23.14
SLEW HIS DEARE $FRIEND, MY KIND AND TRUEST $HEART     2.7.12
RETAYNING $KNOWLEDGE, STILL THE SAME IN KIND          2.12.7
THE $FIRE HE STOLE, ALTHOUGH OF $HEAV'NLY KIND        2.14.5
OF THE $BIRDS KIND, THE $PHOENIX IS ALONE             2.16.2
A CRIPPLE $HAND TO WRITE, YET LAME BY $KIND           2.35.7
```

```
THAT EV'RY $CREATURE TO HIS KIND DO'ST CALL          2.37.11
HEAV'NS ARE NOT KIND TO THEM, THAT KNOW
                            THEM MOST                 2.43.14
IF IT WERE OF THAT $KINGLY KIND, OR NO               2.56.4
IF THEY WERE OF THE $EAGLES KINDE OR NO              2.103.4
TO SHEW THEIR KINDE, BEGAN TO CLIME THE SKIES        2.103.10
BY THY RARE PLUME THY KIND IS EASLY KNOWNE           2.106.3
A CRIPPLE HAND TO WRITE, YET LAME BY KIND            2.112.7
KINDE WORDS UNKINDEST MEATE I CAN DEVISE             2.115.11
AND THUS IF THOU BE NOT OF HUMAINE KINDE             2.140.9
BE AS THY PRESENCE IS GRACIOUS AND KIND              3.10.11
OR TO THY SELFE AT LEAST KIND HARTED PROVE           3.10.12
THEN CHURLS THEIR THOUGHTS (ALTHOUGH THEIR
                            EIES WERE KIND)          3.69.11
CANNOT DISPRAISE, BUT IN A KINDE OF PRAISE           3.95.7
KINDE IS MY LOVE TO DAY, TO MORROW KINDE             3.105.5
KINDE IS MY LOVE TO DAY, TO MORROW KINDE             3.105.5
FAIRE, KINDE, AND TRUE, IS ALL MY ARGUMENT           3.105.9
FAIRE, KINDE AND TRUE, VARRYING TO OTHER WORDS       3.105.10
FAIRE, KINDE, AND TRUE, HAVE OFTEN LIV'D ALONE       3.105.13
AND SICKE OF WEL-FARE FOUND A KIND OF MEETNESSE      3.118.7
FOR THOU ART COVETOUS, AND HE IS KINDE               3.134.6
AND PLAY THE MOTHERS PART KISSE ME, BE KIND          3.143.12
IN TRUTH, O $LOVE, WITH WHAT A BOYISH KIND           4.11.1
HER HEART, SWEETE HEART, IS OF NO $TYGRE'S KIND      4.44.4
A KIND OF GRACE IT IS TO SLAY WITH SPEED             4.48.14
SINCE KIND OR CHANCE GIVES BOTH ONE LIVERIE          4.96.2
SUCH LOVE NOT LYKE TO LUSTS OF BASER KYND            5.6.3
THAT IT CAN ALTER ALL THE COURSE OF KYND             5.30.14
THE FIRST MY BEING TO ME GAVE BY KIND                5.74.5
THE SECOND IS MY SOVEREIGNE $QUEENE MOST KIND        5.74.7
OF THAT SELFE KYND WITH WHICH THE $FURIES FELL       5.86.2
```
KINDER   1
```
KINDER THEN SHE WHOM I SO LONG HAVE LOVED            2.45.14
```
KINDLE   6
```
AND THOSE BRIGHT RAIES THAT KINDLE ALL THIS FIRE     1.38.3
THOSE TEARES WHICH QUENCH MY HOPE, STILL
                            KINDLE MY DESIRE          2.132.1
SO HARD IT IS TO KINDLE NEW DESIRE                   5.6.9
MAY KINDLE LIVING FIRE WITHIN MY BREST               5.7.12
SHOULD KINDLE FYRE BY WONDERFULL DEVYSE+             5.30.12
THE SPARKES WHEREOF LET KINDLE THINE OWN FYRE        5.86.9
```
KINDLED   5
```
WHICH BEING KINDLED BY THAT HEAV'NLY FIRE            2.16.7
THE $FUELL KINDLED WITH $CELESTIALL $HEAT            2.30.8
FED BY THY WORTH, AND KINDLED BY THY SIGHT+          4.68.8
THE LIGHT WHEROF HATH KINDLED HEAVENLY FYRE          5.3.3
KINDLED ABOVE UNTO THE MAKER NEERE                   5.8.2
```
KINDLING   2
```
WITH THINE EYES KINDLING THAT $CELESTIAL FLAME       2.105.7
IS LONG ERE IT CONCEIVE THE KINDLING FYRE            5.6.6
```
KINDLY   2
```
SOME, WHO NOT KINDLY RELLISH MY $CONCEIT             2.42.5
THE HEIGHT OF HONOR IN THE KINDLY BADGE
                            OF SHAME+                 4.102.3
```
KINDNESS   5
```
FALSE $FRIENDS THY KINDNESSE, BORNE BUT
                            TO DECEIVE $THEE          2.10.10
AND KINDNES, BE UNKINDNES IN MY LOVE                 2.139.4
STRONG LOCKE OF KINDNESSE, $CLOSET OF
                            LOVES STORE               2.146.5
```

```
NOR THOU WITH PUBLIKE KINDNESSE HONOUR ME          3.36.11
FOR I HAVE SWORNE DEEPE OTHES OF THY DEEPE
                              KINDNESSE             3.152.9
KINDS                 1
  ALL FRAILTIES THAT BESIEGE ALL KINDES OF BLOOD    3.109.10
KING                  7
  (THE $KING OF $SENCES, GREATER THEN THE REST)     2.29.10
  AND ALL THOSE BEAUTIES WHEREOF NOW HE'S $KING      3.63.6
  IN SLEEPE A $KING, BUT WAKING NO SUCH MATTER       3.87.14
  OUGHT TO BE KING, FROM WHOSE RULES WHO DO SWERVE   4.5.3
  HOW $POLES' RIGHT KING MEANES, WITHOUT
                     LEAVE OF HOAST                 4.30.3
  THAT WARNES AL LOVERS WAYT UPON THEIR KING         5.19.3
  FRESH SPRING THE HERALD OF LOVES MIGHTY KING       5.70.1
KINGDOM               1
  ADVANTAGE ON THE $KINGDOME OF THE SHOARE           3.64.6
KINGDOMS              1
  THEN THOU ALONE KINGDOMES OF HEARTS SHOULDST OWE   3.70.14
KINGDOM'S             1
  HIS $SIRE'S REVENGE, JOYN'D WITH A KINGDOME'S
                              GAINE                 4.75.6
KINGLY                4
  IF IT WERE OF THAT $KINGLY KIND, OR NO             2.56.4
  AND THAT THEY CAME OF THIS RARE KINGLIE BROOD      2.103.8
  AND MY GREAT MINDE MOST KINGLY DRINKES IT UP       3.114.10
  THOU BUT OF ALL THE KINGLY $TRIBUTE TAKE           4.85.14
KINGS                 6
  THE LEAST ABLE TO KYLL AN HOSTE OF $KINGS          2.126.8
  THAT THEN I SKORNE TO CHANGE MY STATE
                     WITH $KINGS                    3.29.14
  CREEPE IN TWIXT VOWES, AND CHANGE DECREES
                     OF $KINGS                      3.115.6
  LIKE SOME WEAKE $LORDS, NEIGHBORD BY MIGHTY KINGS  4.29.1
  NO KINGS BE CROWN'D BUT THEY SOME COVENANTS MAKE   4.69.14
  OF ALL THE KINGS THAT EVER HERE DID RAIGNE         4.75.1
KING'S                1
  THIS $KINGS FAIRE $ENTRANCE, AND OUR $PEACE
                     WITH $SPAINE                   2.51.8
KISS                  20
  SINCE THER'S NO HELPE, $COME LET US KISSE
                     AND PART                       2.61.1
  HIS STONE-COLD LIPS DOTH KISSE THE BLESSED
                     SHAFT                          2.135.14
  TO KISSE THE TENDER INWARD OF THY HAND            3.128.6
  GIVE THEM THEIR FINGERS, ME THY LIPS TO KISSE     3.128.14
  AND PLAY THE MOTHERS PART KISSE ME, BE KIND       3.143.12
  THE $SUNNE WHICH OTHERS BURN'D, DID HER
                     BUT KISSE                      4.22.14
  WITH EITHER LIP HE DOTH THE OTHER KISSE           4.43.11
  AND YET MY $STARRE, BECAUSE A SUGRED KISSE        4.73.5
  THAT $ANGER' SELFE I NEEDS MUST KISSE AGAINE      4.73.14
  MY LIPS ARE SWEET, INSPIRED WITH $STELLA'S KISSE  4.74.14
  THOSE LIPS, WHICH MAKE DEATH'S PAY A MEANE
                     PRICE FOR A KISSE              4.77.6
  SWEET KISSE, THY SWEETS I FAINE WOULD
                     SWEETLY ENDITE                 4.79.1
  CEASE WE TO PRAISE, NOW PRAY WE FOR A KISSE       4.79.14
  SWEET LIP, YOU TEACH MY MOUTH WITH ONE
                     SWEET KISSE                    4.80.14
  O KISSE, WHICH DOEST THOSE RUDDIE GEMMES IMPART   4.81.1
```

```
    O KISSE, WHICH SOULES, EVEN SOULES TOGETHER TIES      4.81.5
    I WILL BUT KISSE, I NEVER MORE WILL BITE              4.82.14
    HUNDREDS OF YEARES YOU $STELLA'S FEET MAY KISSE       4.84.14
    FIRST DID WITH PUFFING KISSE THOSE LOCKES
                                 DISPLAY                  4.103.11
    COMMING TO KISSE HER LYPS, (SUCH GRACE I FOUND)        5.64.1
KISSES                2
    AND THAT WHICH GAVE ME WOUNDS, $ILE GIVE
                               IT KISSES                  1.46.12
    ILE EXECUTE HER WITH A THOUSAND KISSES               2.115.16
KISSING               2
    KISSING WITH GOLDEN FACE THE MEDDOWES GREENE           3.33.3
    STOP YOU MY MOUTH WITH STILL STILL KISSING ME         4.81.14
KISS-WORTHY           1
    O HEAV'NLY FOOLE, THY MOST KISSE-WORTHIE FACE         4.73.12
KNEELEDST             1
    REASON THOU KNEEL'DST, AND OFFEREDST STRAIGHT
                               TO PROVE                   4.10.13
KNEELING              1
    WHEN $FAITH IS KNEELING BY HIS BED OF $DEATH          2.61.11
KNEW                  3
    THAT YET THE WORLD UNWORTHY NEVER KNEWE              2.139.12
    YET THEN MY JUDGEMENT KNEW NO REASON WHY              3.115.3
    AS IF THEY KNEW THE MEANING OF THEIR LAYES            5.19.8
KNIFE                 5
    BY KNIFE, BY LIQUOR, OR BY SALVE TO DEALE             1.14.11
    AGAINST CONFOUNDING $AGES CRUELL KNIFE                3.63.10
    THE COWARD CONQUEST OF A WRETCHES KNIFE               3.74.11
    THE HARDEST KNIFE ILL US'D DOTH LOOSE HIS EDGE        3.95.14
    SO THOU PREVENST HIS SIETH, AND CROOKED KNIFE        3.100.14
KNIGHT                1
    BUT ONLY FOR THIS WORTHY KNIGHT DURST PROVE           4.75.13
KNIGHTS               2
    LET OTHERS SING OF $KNIGHTS AND $PALLADINES           1.55.1
    IN PRAISE OF $LADIES DEAD, AND LOVELY $KNIGHTS        3.106.4
KNIT                  3
    THY MERRIT HATH MY DUTIE STRONGLY KNIT                3.26.2
    IN OBJECT BEST TO KNIT AND STRENGTH OUR SIGHT         4.7.6
    TO KNIT THE KNOT, THAT EVER SHALL REMAINE             5.6.14
KNOCK                 1
    KNOCKE AT THAT HARD HART, BEGGE TILL YOU
                               HAVE MOV'D HER             1.2.13
KNOT                  2
    COME SLEEPE, O SLEEPE, THE CERTAINE KNOT OF PEACE     4.39.1
    TO KNIT THE KNOT, THAT EVER SHALL REMAINE             5.6.14
KNOW                  55
    ONCE LET HER KNOW, SH'HATH DONE ENOUGH
                               TO PROVE ME                1.10.13
    TH'$ELISIAN GHOSTS SHALL NEVER KNOW THE SAME          1.30.14
    DO FEELE MINE INWARD HEAT AS GREAT (I KNOW IT)        1.43.6
    I KNOW HER HEART CANNOT BUT JUDGE WITH ME             1.49.13
    HEAV'NS ARE NOT KIND TO THEM, THAT KNOW
                               THEM MOST                  2.43.14
    CUPID, I HATE THEE, WHICH $I'DE HAVE THEE KNOW        2.48.1
    FOR THAT THE VERTUE I THEREOF WOULD KNOW              2.56.2
    AND FOR THEIR VERTUES I DESIERD TO KNOW               2.103.2
    SHOULD TEACH THE WORLD TO KNOW THE WONDER
                               THAT I PROVE               2.117.14
    I FEELE, YOU KNOW, THE HEAVENS CAN TELL
                               THE REST                  2.139.14
```

```
O NONE BUT UNTHRIFTS, DEARE MY LOVE YOU KNOW          3.13.13
THEY DRAW BUT WHAT THEY SEE, KNOW NOT THE HART        3.24.14
AS IF BY SOME INSTINCT THE WRETCH DID KNOW            3.50.7
IN WINGED SPEED NO MOTION SHALL I KNOW                3.51.8
AND YOU IN EVERY BLESSED SHAPE WE KNOW                3.53.12
O KNOW SWEET LOVE I ALWAIES WRITE OF YOU              3.76.9
THOU BY THY DYALS SHADY STEALTH MAIST KNOW            3.77.7
THOU MAIST BE FALCE, AND YET I KNOW IT NOT            3.92.14
THEREFORE IN THAT I CANNOT KNOW THY CHANGE            3.93.6
TO KNOW MY SHAMES AND PRAISES FROM YOUR TOUNGE        3.112.6
I LOVE TO HEARE HER SPEAKE, YET WELL I KNOW           3.130.9
THEY KNOW WHAT BEAUTIE IS, SEE WHERE IT LYES          3.137.3
I DO BELEEVE HER THOUGH I KNOW SHE LYES               3.138.2
NO NEWES BUT HEALTH FROM THEIR $PHISITIONS KNOW       3.140.8
YET THIS SHAL I NERE KNOW BUT LIVE IN DOUBT           3.144.13
BUT LOVE HATE ON FOR NOW I KNOW THY MINDE             3.149.13
LOVE IS TOO YOUNG TO KNOW WHAT CONSCIENCE IS          3.151.1
PLEASURE MIGHT CAUSE HER READE, READING
                            MIGHT MAKE HER KNOW        4.1.3
FOR ME IN SOOTH, NO $MUSE BUT ONE I KNOW              4.3.9
AS WHO BY BEING POISOND DOTH POISON KNOW              4.16.14
AND BY JUST COUNTS MY SELFE A BANCKROUT KNOW          4.18.3
SOME THAT KNOW HOW MY SPRING I DID ADDRESSE           4.23.5
AS WHAT THEIR HANDS DO HOLD, THEIR HEADS DO KNOW      4.24.6
FOR ME, I DO $NATURE UNIDLE KNOW                      4.26.9
AND KNOW GREAT CAUSES, GREAT EFFECTS PROCURE          4.26.10
AND KNOW THOSE $BODIES HIGH RAIGNE ON THE LOW         4.26.11
BUT KNOW THAT I IN PURE SIMPLICITIE                   4.28.12
BUT KNOW NOT HOW, FOR STILL I THINKE OF YOU           4.30.14
MY WORDS I KNOW DO WELL SET FORTH MY MIND             4.44.1
NOT THOUGH THEREOF THE CAUSE HER SELFE SHE KNOW       4.45.4
AND THINKE SO STILL, SO $STELLA KNOW MY MIND          4.54.9
UNTILL BY YOUR INSPIRING I MIGHT KNOW                 4.55.7
HER GRAUNT TO ME, BY HER OWNE VERTUE KNOW             4.63.4
WHO WILL IN FAIREST BOOKE OF $NATURE KNOW             4.71.1
SO AMPLE EARES AS NEVER GOOD NEWES KNOW               4.78.13
AND THAT YOU KNOW, I ENVY YOU NO LOT                  4.84.12
I WOULD KNOW WHETHER SHE DID SIT OR WALKE             4.92.9
I HAVE (LIVE I AND KNOW THIS) HARMED THEE             4.93.10
I WOULD KNOW BY WHAT RIGHT THIS PALENESSE
                            OVERCAME                   4.102.7
AND WHEN I SIGH, SHE SAYES I KNOW THE ART             5.18.11
AND KNOW NO END OF HER OWNE MYSERY                    5.25.2
BUT DID SHE KNOW HOW ILL THESE TWO ACCORD             5.31.13
THE HEAVENS KNOW BEST WHAT IS THE BEST FOR ME         5.46.6
THEN KNOW, THAT MERCY IS THE MIGHTIES JEWELL          5.49.3
ALL THAT THEY KNOW NOT, ENVY OR ADMYRE                5.85.6
KNOWEST                     4
THOU DOOST LOVE HER, BECAUSE THOU KNOWST
                            I LOVE HER                 3.42.6
AND LIKE ENOUGH THOU KNOWST THY ESTIMATE              3.87.2
FOR WELL THOU KNOW'ST TO MY DEARE DOTING HART         3.131.3
IN LOVING THEE THOU KNOW'ST I AM FORSWORNE            3.152.1
KNOWING                     8
AND KNOWING MORE THEN EVER HATH BEENE TAUGHT          2.34.3
KNOWING A BETTER SPIRIT DOTH USE YOUR NAME            3.80.2
THY SELFE THOU GAV'ST, THY OWNE WORTH
                            THEN NOT KNOWING           3.87.9
AS ILE MY SELFE DISGRACE, KNOWING THY WIL             3.89.7
KNOWING THY HEART TORMENT ME WITH DISDAINE            3.132.2
```

AND KNOWING, LOVE, AND LOVING, LAY APART   4.24.7
KNOWING WORLDS PASSE, ERE SHE ENOUGH CAN FIND   4.101.13
THE $PANTHER KNOWING THAT HIS SPOTTED HYDE   5.53.1
KNOWLEDGE   8
THIS CRUELL KNOWLEDGE OF THESE CONTRARIES   1.20.13
RETAYNING $KNOWLEDGE, STILL THE SAME IN KIND   2.12.7
BUT FROM THINE EIES MY KNOWLEDGE I DERIVE   3.14.9
WITHIN THE KNOWLEDGE OF MINE OWNE DESART   3.49.10
THOU ART AS FAIRE IN KNOWLEDGE AS IN HEW   3.82.5
KNOWLEDGE MIGHT PITIE WINNE, AND PITIE
                          GRACE OBTAINE   4.1.4
MY YOUTH DOTH WASTE, MY KNOWLEDGE BRINGS
                          FORTH TOYES   4.18.9
DEEME THAT MY $MUSE SOME FRUIT OF KNOWLEDGE PLIES 4.23.6
KNOWN   13
MY $MUSE HAD SLEPT, AND NONE HAD KNOWNE MY MINDE 1.6.14
THE WORLD HAD NEVER KNOWNE WHAT I DOE FINDE   1.7.3
SO $DELIA, HATH MINE ERROR MADE ME KNOWNE   1.56.5
NOR SEEKES IT TO BE KNOWNE UNTO THE $GREAT   1.58.10
WHICH BEST BY YOU, OF LIVING $THINGS, IS KNOWNE   2.16.3
MAKE KNOWNE THE $FAITH, THAT $FORTUNE
                          COULD NOT MOVE   2.60.5
NOR MY HART KNOWNE THE POWER OF THY NAME   2.104.6
BY THY RARE PLUME THY KIND IS EASLY KNOWNE   2.106.3
MAKE KNOWNE THAT FAYTH, UNKINDNES COULD NOT MOVE 2.149.5
TO BEARE LOVES WRONG, THEN HATES KNOWNE INJURY   3.40.12
BUT KNOWNE WORTH DID IN MINE OF TIME PROCEED   4.2.3
OF $LOVERS NEVER KNOWNE, A GRIEVOUS CASE   4.45.6
DESPOYLD OF WARLIKE ARMES AND KNOWEN SHIELD   5.52.4
KNOWS   14
NOR YET WISE $REASON ABSOLUTELY KNOWES   2.46.4
THOUGH YET HEAVEN KNOWES IT IS BUT AS A TOMBE   3.17.3
AND YET LOVE KNOWES IT IS A GREATER GRIEFE   3.40.11
MINE EIE WELL KNOWES WHAT WITH HIS GUST
                          IS GREEING   3.114.11
WHICH IS NOT MIXT WITH SECONDS, KNOWS NO ART   3.125.11
ALL THIS THE WORLD WELL KNOWES YET NONE
                          KNOWES WELL   3.129.13
ALL THIS THE WORLD WELL KNOWES YET NONE
                          KNOWES WELL   3.129.13
AND WILL THY SOULE KNOWES IS ADMITTED THERE   3.136.3
WHICH MY HEART KNOWES THE WIDE WORLDS
                          COMMON PLACE+   3.137.10
ALTHOUGH SHE KNOWES MY DAYES ARE PAST THE BEST   3.138.6
LET ME EXCUSE THEE, AH MY LOVE WELL KNOWES   3.139.9
YET WHO KNOWES NOT CONSCIENCE IS BORNE OF LOVE   3.151.2
HE KNOWES NOT) GROW IN ONLY FOLLIE RICH   4.24.14
WHERE WELL HE KNOWES, NO MAN TO HIM CAN COME   4.43.14
LABOR   8
TOYLING WITH $PAINE, MY $LABOUR NEVER CEASETH   2.40.7
LABOUR IS LIGHT, WHERE $LOVE (QUOTH I) DOTH PAY   2.59.9
TOYLING WITH PAINE, MY LABOUR NEVER CEASETH   2.144.7
MY TONGUE DOTH ITCH, MY THOUGHTS IN LABOUR BE   4.37.2
LET ME NO STEPS BUT OF LOST LABOUR TRACE   4.64.6
LABOUR TO KILL IN ME THIS KILLING CARE   4.68.12
SUCH LABOUR LIKE THE $SPYDERS WEB I FYND   5.23.13
GOTTEN AT LAST WITH LABOUR AND LONG TOYLE   5.69.14
LABORING   2
GAVE $LIFE AND $COURAGE TO MY LAB'RING $PEN   2.47.2
WHICH LABORING FOR INVENTION BEARE AMISSE   3.59.3

```
LACE                      1
  AND LACE IT SELFE WITH HIS SOCIETIE+                    3.67.4
LACK                      7
  IN $LOVE THERE IS NO LACK, THUS I BEGIN                 2.59.3
  I SIGH THE LACKE OF MANY A THING I SOUGHT               3.30.3
  HAVE EYES TO WONDER, BUT LACK TOUNGS TO PRAISE          3.106.14
  OF BIRD, OF FLOWRE, OR SHAPE WHICH IT DOTH LACK         3.113.6
  AT SUCH WHO NOT BORNE FAIRE NO BEAUTY LACK              3.127.11
  AND ALL THEY FOULE THAT THY COMPLEXION LACKE            3.132.14
  I SWEARE BY HER I LOVE AND LACKE, THAT I                4.105.5
LACKED                    4
  BEING HAD TO TRYUMPH, BEING LACKT TO HOPE               3.52.14
  THEN LACKT I MATTER, THAT INFEEBLED MINE                3.86.14
  MY SOULES LONG LACKED FOODE, MY HEAVENS BLIS            5.1.12
  SINCE I HAVE LACKT THE COMFORT OF THAT LIGHT            5.88.1
LACKING                   4
  WHICH I BY LACKING HAVE SUPPOSED DEAD                   3.31.2
  FOR LACKING IT THEY CANNOT LYFE SUSTAYNE                5.35.5
  LACKYNG MY LOVE I GO FROM PLACE TO PLACE                5.78.1
  FOR LACKING IT, THEY CANNOT LYFE SUSTAYNE               5.83.5
LADEN                     3
  YET MY $HOPES $WINGS ARE LADEN SO WITH $FEARE           2.26.6
  SEE WHERE SHEE FLOTES, LADEN WITH PUREST LOVE           2.134.5
  FAYRE WHEN HER BREST LYKE A RICH LADEN BARKE            5.81.5
LADIES                    4
  LADIES AND $TYRANTS, NEVER LAWES RESPECT                1.31.12
  IN PRAISE OF $LADIES DEAD, AND LOVELY $KNIGHTS          3.106.4
  WHEN SOME FAIRE $LADIES, BY HARD PROMISE TIED           4.22.5
  BUT HEERE I DO STORE OF FAIRE $LADIES MEETE             4.106.9
LADY                      3
  EVEN SO (ALAS) A $LADY $DIAN'S PEERE                    4.97.9
  SO $LADIE NOW TO YOU I DOO COMPLAINE                    5.12.13
  LEAVE LADY IN YOUR GLASSE OF CHRISTALL CLENE            5.45.1
LAID                      6
  WHERE, WITH SWEET $WOOD, LAYD CURIOUSLY BY $ART         2.30.5
  OR LAYD GREAT BASES FOR ETERNITY                        3.125.3
  ON PURPOSE LAYD TO MAKE THE TAKER MAD                   3.129.8
  $CUPID LAID BY HIS BRAND AND FELL A SLEEPE              3.153.1
  LAID BY HIS SIDE HIS HEART INFLAMING BRAND              3.154.2
  GOE TO MY LOVE, WHERE SHE IS CARELESSE LAYD             5.70.5
LAIR                      1
  ROUZ'D FROM MY BREAST, HIS SURE AND SAFEST LAYRE        2.135.2
LAMB                      2
  IF LIKE A $LAMBE HE COULD HIS LOOKES TRANSLATE          3.96.10
  THE SILLY LAMBE THAT TO HIS MIGHT DOTH YIELD            5.20.8
LAMBS                     1
  HOW MANY $LAMBS MIGHT THE STERNE $WOLFE BETRAY          3.96.9
LAME                      5
  A CRIPPLE $HAND TO WRITE, YET LAME BY $KIND             2.35.7
  A CRIPPLE HAND TO WRITE, YET LAME BY KIND               2.112.7
  SO I, MADE LAME BY $FORTUNES DEAREST SPIGHT             3.37.3
  SO THEN I AM NOT LAME, POORE, NOR DISPIS'D              3.37.9
  MY WITS, QUICKE IN VAINE THOUGHTS, IN VERTUE LAME       4.21.4
LAMENESS                  1
  SPEAKE OF MY LAMENESSE, AND I STRAIGHT WILL HALT        3.89.3
LAMENTABLE                1
  WHICH HERE I YEELD I LAMENTABLE WISE                    1.57.6
LAMENTEST                 1
  LAMENT'ST MY DEATH, WITH TEARES OF THY DISDAINE         2.130.14
```

LAMP   2
  ATTENDS THAT $LAMPE WITH EYE WHICH NEVER
                SLEEPETH   2.105.10
  O $LAMPE OF VERTUE, SUN-BRIGHT, EVER SHYNING   2.129.6
LAMPING   1
  THOSE LAMPING EYES WILL DEIGNE SOMETIMES TO LOOK   5.1.6
LAMPS   1
  AND FOOLES CAN THINKE THOSE $LAMPES OF
                PUREST LIGHT   4.26.2
LANCE   1
  HAVING THIS DAY MY HORSE, MY HAND, MY LAUNCE   4.41.1
LAND   5
  A HAPPY CONVOY TO A HOLY $LAND   1.46.6
  AS TO THE $ROMAN THAT WOULD FREE HIS $LAND   1.56.1
  OUR $LAWES ALOW NO $LAND TO BASTERDY   2.140.11
  FOR NIMBLE THOUGHT CAN JUMPE BOTH SEA AND LAND   3.44.7
  THROUGH $FAERY LAND, WHICH THOSE SIX BOOKS
                COMPILE   5.80.2
LANGUISH   6
  IF A SWEET LANGUISH WITH A CHAST DESIRE   1.15.2
  HAPPY IN SLEEPE, WAKING CONTENT TO LANGUISH   1.16.1
  WHERE LOE I LANGUISH IN SO HEAVY SMART   1.36.6
  AND YET I'D RATHER LANGUISH FOR HER LOVE   1.48.11
  RELIEVE MY LANGUISH, AND RESTORE THE LIGHT   1.54.3
  YET WHILE I LANGUISH, HIM THAT BOSOME CLIPS   4.59.9
LANGUISHED   4
  TO ME THAT LANGUISHT FOR HER SAKE   3.145.3
  I READE IT IN THY LOOKES, THY LANGUISHT GRACE   4.31.7
  MY LIFE FORGETS TO NOURISH LANGUISHT SPRITES   4.42.10
  LANGUISHT WITH HORRORS OF THE SILENT NIGHT   4.89.8
LANGUISHING   1
  LONG LANGUISHING IN DOUBLE MALADY   5.50.1
LANGUISHMENT   1
  WHICH I HAVE WASTED IN LONG LANGUISHMENT   5.60.11
LANGUOR   3
  BUT AL MY DAYES IN PINING LANGUOR SPEND   5.36.3
  THE INWARD LANGUOR OF MY WOUNDED HART   5.50.10
  LONGWHILE ALONE IN LANGUOR TO REMAINE   5.52.8
LAP   6
  NOW WHILST THY $MAY HATH FILD THY LAP
                WITH FLOWERS   1.40.2
  AND LEAVES HIS $MOTHERS LAP TO SPORT HIM THERE   2.4.8
  OR FROM THEIR PROUD LAP PLUCK THEM WHERE
                THEY GREW   3.98.8
  BUT SHE IN CHAFE HIM FROM HER LAP DID SHOVE   4.17.7
  THAT LAP DOTH LAP, NAY LETS, IN SPITE OF SPITE   4.59.10
  THAT LAP DOTH LAP, NAY LETS, IN SPITE OF SPITE   4.59.10
LARGE   9
  YET THIS LARGE $ROOME IS BOUNDED WITH $DESPAIRE   2.26.9
  YET THYS LARGE ROOME IS BOUNDED WITH DYSPAIRE   2.137.9
  TO LEAPE LARGE LENGTHS OF MILES WHEN THOU
                ART GONE   3.44.10
  TAKE HEED (DEARE HEART) OF THIS LARGE PRIVILEDGE   3.95.13
  WILT THOU WHOSE WILL IS LARGE AND SPATIOUS   3.135.5
  ONE WILL OF MINE TO MAKE THY LARGE $WILL MORE   3.135.12
  WHY SO LARGE COST HAVING SO SHORT A LEASE   3.146.5
  AND THINKE I SHOULD NOT YOUR LARGE PRECEPTS
                MISSE+   4.56.4
  THAT HONOUR AND LARGE RICHESSE TO ME LENT   5.74.8

```
LARGESS                    1
  THE BOUNTIOUS LARGESSE GIVEN THEE TO GIVE+           3.4.6
LARK                       1
  (LIKE TO THE $LARKE AT BREAKE OF DAYE ARISING)       3.29.11
LASCIVIOUS                 2
  LASCIVIOUS GRACE, IN WHOM ALL IL WEL SHOWES          3.40.13
  (MAKING LASCIVIOUS COMMENTS ON THY SPORT)            3.95.6
LAST                      21
  MY LAST $RESORT WHERETO MY HOPES APPEALE             1.22.2
  AND SEE MY FORTUNE EVER LIKE TO LAST                 1.28.11
  YET $HEAV'N WILL STILL HAVE $MURTHER OUT AT LAST     2.2.14
  WHAT THEY LAST THOUGHT OF, WHEN THE $BRAINE
                          GREW SICKE                   2.9.7
  YET READE AT LAST THE STORIE OF MY $WOE              2.54.1
  NOW AT THE LAST GASPE, OF $LOVES LATEST $BREATH      2.61.9
  IN DAIES LONG SINCE, BEFORE THESE LAST SO BAD        3.67.14
  IF THOU WILT LEAVE ME, DO NOT LEAVE ME LAST          3.90.9
  TO BLAZE THESE LAST, AND SWARE DEVOUTLY THEN         4.13.13
  BUT THIS AT LAST IS HER SWEET BREATH'D DEFENCE       4.61.4
  STOLNE TO MY HEART, SINCE LAST FAIRE NIGHT,
                          NAY DAY                      4.66.10
  AND SHEW THE LAST ENSAMPLE OF YOUR PRIDE             5.25.6
  A CLOSE INTENT AT LAST TO SHEW ME GRACE              5.25.10
  THAT GREATER MEEDE AT LAST MAY TURNE TO MEE          5.25.14
  WILL SHINE AGAIN, AND LOOKE ON ME AT LAST            5.34.11
  SHE MEANES AT LAST TO MAKE HER PITEOUS SPOYLE        5.41.12
  MOST HAPPY HE THAT CAN AT LAST ATCHYVE               5.63.9
  GOTTEN AT LAST WITH LABOUR AND LONG TOYLE            5.69.14
  THE THIRD MY LOVE, MY LIVES LAST ORNAMENT            5.74.9
  AND SEEKE EACH WHERE, WHERE LAST I SAWE HER FACE     5.78.3
  SO SORROW STILL DOTH SEEME TOO LONG TO LAST          5.87.13
LASTING                    2
  THIS MAY REMAINE THY LASTING MONUMENT                1.42.9
  FULL CHARACTERD WITH LASTING MEMORY                  3.122.2
LASTLY                     2
  THUS TO MY AID, I LASTLY CONJURE THEE                2.36.4
  LASTLY, MINE $EYES AMAZEDLY HAVE SEENE               2.51.5
LATE                      21
  SHE THEN IS SCORND THAT LATE ADORND THE $FAYRE       1.39.7
  THAT FOR HER LATE DECEASED $HUSBAND DY'D             2.15.8
  AS $LOVE AND I, LATE HARBOUR'D IN ONE $INNE          2.59.1
  BARE RN'WD QUIERS, WHERE LATE THE SWEET
                          BIRDS SANG                   3.73.4
  LOVE BORNE IN $GREECE, OF LATE FLED FROM
                          HIS NATIVE PLACE             4.8.1
  HIS MOTHER DEARE $CUPID OFFENDED LATE                4.17.1
  VERTUE OF LATE, WITH VERTUOUS CARE TO STER           4.25.9
  YET HEARING LATE A FABLE, WHICH DID SHOW             4.45.5
  NOW JUDGE BY THIS.. IN PIERCING PHRASES LATE         4.58.9
  LATE TYR'D WITH WO, EVEN READY FOR TO PINE           4.62.1
  FOR LATE WITH HEART MOST HIGH, WITH EYES MOST LOW    4.63.5
  THAT $BALLANCE WEIGH'D WHAT SWORD DID
                          LATE OBTAINE                 4.75.8
  ADMITTED LATE BY YOUR BEST-GRACED GRACE              4.82.10
  YOU SAY FORSOOTH, YOU LEFT HER WELL OF LATE          4.92.7
  RETOURNE AGAYNE MY FORCES LATE DISMAYD               5.14.1
  FOR WHEN ON ME THOU SHINEDST LATE IN SADNESSE        5.39.6
  COMES FORTH AFRESH CUT OF THEIR LATE DISMAY          5.40.11
  LYKE A YOUNG FAWNE THAT LATE HATH LOST THE HYND      5.78.2
  I SEEKE THE FIELDS WITH HER LATE FOOTING SYND        5.78.5
```

```
     I SEEKE HER BOWRE WITH HER LATE PRESENCE CECKT        5.78.6
     FOR HIS RETURNE THAT SEEMES TO LINGER LATE            5.89.4
LATER                     1
     OUR LOVE SHALL LIVE, AND LATER LIFE RENEW             5.75.14
LATEST                    2
     NOW AT THE LAST GASPE, CF $LOVES LATEST $BREATH       2.61.9
     WHILST THUS HE PANTETH FCR HIS LATEST BREATH          2.135.10
LAUD                      1
     THAT ANY LAUD TC ME THEREOF SHOULD GROW               4.90.10
LAUGH                     5
     YOU THAT BEHOLD US, LAUGH US NOT TO SCORNE            2.22.11
     I LAUGH AT $FORTUNE, AS IN JEST TO DIE                2.24.14
     THAT I MAY LAUGH AT HER IN EQUALL SORT                5.10.13
     AS SHE DOTH LAUGH AT ME AND MAKES MY PAIN
                                       HER SPORT           5.10.14
     BUT WHEN I LAUGH SHE MOCKS, AND WHEN I CRY            5.54.11
LAUGHED                   1
     THAT HEAVIE $SATURNE LAUGHT AND LEAPT WITH HIM        3.98.4
LAUGHETH                  2
     DESPITETH $LOVE, AND LAUGHETH AT HER $FOLLY           2.38.10
     DISPIGHTETH $LOVE, AND LAUGHETH AT HER FOLLY          2.131.10
LAUGHING                  1
     LAUGHING FOR JOY UPCN MY LOVELY FAYRE                 2.125.14
LAUGHS                    1
     SHE LAUGHES, AND HARDENS EVERMORE HER HART            5.54.12
LAUGHTER                  2
     LAUGHTER LOVING $GCDDESSE, WORLDLY PLEASURES
                                       $QUEENE             1.10.6
     AND WHEN I WAILE, SHE TURNES HIR SELFE
                                       TO LAUGHTER         5.18.12
LAUNCHED                  1
     SEEING MY HART THRCUGH LAUNCHED EVERY WHERE           5.57.7
LAURA                     2
     THOUGH THOU A $LAURA HAST NO $PETRARCH FOUND          1.43.3
     FOR THOUGH THAT $LAURA BETTER LIMNED BE               1.43.13
LAUREL                    4
     I IN THE $CIRCUIT FCR THE $LAWRELL STROVE             2.47.6
     A NEST FOR MY YONG PRAISE IN $LAWRELL TREE            4.90.6
     THE LAURELL LEAFE, WHICH YOU THIS DAY DOE WEARE       5.28.1
     DID HER TRANSFORME INTO A LAURELL TREE                5.28.12
LAVISH                    1
     THIS NEW RICH $NOVICE, LAVISH OF HIS CHEST            2.10.5
LAW                       1
     UNRIGHTEOUS $LORD CF LOVE WHAT LAW IS THIS            5.10.1
LAWFUL                    3
     AND GAINST MY SELFE A LAWFULL PLEA COMMENCE           3.35.11
     TO GUARD THE LAWFULL REASONS ON THY PART             3.49.12
     BE IT LAWFULL I LCVE THEE AS THOU LOV'ST THOSE        3.142.9
LAWS                      9
     WHAT BOOTES TO LAWES OF $SUCCOR TO APPEALE+           1.31.11
     LADIES AND $TYRANTS, NEVER LAWES RESPECT              1.31.12
     OR ONELY YOU DOE VICLATE HER $LAWES                   2.27.14
     SINCE HOLY $VESTALL LAWES HAVE BEEN NEGLECTEC         2.105.1
     THE VOLUMES OF $RELIGIONS LAWES SHEE KEEPETH          2.105.11
     OUR $LAWES ALOW NC $LAND TO BASTERDY                  2.140.11
     BY NATURES $LAWES WE THEE A $BASTARD FINDE            2.140.12
     TO LEAVE POORE ME, THOU HAST THE STRENGTH
                                       OF LAWES            3.49.13
     BY IRON LAWES OF DUTY TC DEPART                       4.87.4
```

LAY   16
   WHERE $VERTUE, $HONOUR, $WIT, AND $BEAUTIE LAY   2.14.10
   SATURNE CHIEFE $LORD OF THE $ASCENDANT LAY   2.116.7
   AND BOTH FOR MY SAKE LAY ON ME THIS CROSSE   3.42.12
   BEAUTIE NO PENSELL, BEAUTIES TRUTH TO LAY   3.101.7
   TO MY CLOSE HEART, WHERE WHILE SOME FIREBRANDS
                           HE DID LAY   4.8.13
   THERE HIMSELFE WITH HIS SHOT HE CLOSE DOTH LAY   4.20.8
   AND KNOWING, LOVE, AND LOVING, LAY APART   4.24.7
   EACH SOULE DOTH AT $LOVE'S FEET HIS WEAPONS LAY   4.43.7
   ON SILLY ME DO NOT THE BURTHEN LAY   4.51.5
   LET $FORTUNE LAY ON ME HER WORST DISGRACE   4.64.3
   THEIR RAYES TO ME, WHO IN HER TEDIOUS ABSENCE LAY   4.76.2
   TO LAY HIS THEN MARKE WANTING SHAFTS OF SIGHT   4.99.3
   THEIR JUDGEMENTS HACKNEY ON, THE FAULT
                           ON SICKNESSE LAY   4.102.10
   A WICKED AMBUSH WHICH LAY HIDDEN LONG   5.12.6
   AND LAY INCESSANT BATTERY TO HER HEART   5.14.10
   WITH PRETIOUS MERCHANDIZE SHE FORTH DOTH LAY   5.81.6
LAYMAN   1
   POORE $LAYMAN I, FOR SACRED RITES UNFIT   4.74.4
LAYS   8
   AND LAIES TO VIEW MY $VULTUR-GNAWNE HART OPEN   1.15.8
   LAYES DOWNE HIS $QUIVER, WHICH HE ONCE DID BEARE   2.4.6
   BEFORE MY $FACE, IT LAYES DOWNE MY $DESPAIRES   2.20.9
   YET NOR THE LAIES OF BIRDS, NOR THE SWEET SMELL   3.98.5
   SING TO THE EARE THAT DOTH THY LAIES ESTEEME   3.100.7
   WHEN I WAS WONT TO GREET IT WITH MY LAIES   3.102.6
   THAT THY UNKINDNESSE LAYES UPON MY HEART   3.139.2
   AS IF THEY KNEW THE MEANING OF THEIR LAYES   5.19.8
LEA   1
   AND THE OLD $LEA BRAGS OF THE $DANISH $BLOUD   2.32.12
LEAD   6
   YOU BLINDED SOULES WHOM YOUTH AND ERROUR LEADE   1.3.9
   WHO LEAD THEE IN THEIR RYOT EVEN THERE   3.41.11
   HOW MANY GAZERS MIGHST THOU LEAD AWAY   3.96.11
   MELTS DOWNE HIS LEAD INTO MY BOYLING BREST   4.108.2
   BUT $ANGELS COME TO LEAD FRAILE MINDES TO REST   5.8.7
   THE WHICH WAS WONT TO LEAD MY THOUGHTS ASTRAY   5.88.2
LEADEN   2
   THOU $LEADEN $BRAINE, WHICH CENSUR'ST
                           WHAT I WRITE   2.49.1
   SOMEWHAT THY LEAD'N COUNSELS, WHICH I TOOKE   4.56.7
LEADS   5
   FROM CARE TO CARE THAT LEADES A LIFE SO BAD   1.26.2
   MY $JOYES ARRERAGE LEADES ME TO MY LOSSE   2.3.8
   FOR NEVER RESTING TIME LEADS $SUMMER ON   3.5.5
   TO SHUN THE HEAVEN THAT LEADS MEN TO THIS HELL   3.129.14
   BUT WHEN $AURORA LEADES OUT $PHOEBUS' DAUNCE   4.98.12
LEAF   2
   THE LAURELL LEAFE, WHICH YOU THIS DAY DOE WEARE   5.28.1
   BUT IN YOUR BREST HIS LEAFE AND LOVE EMBRACE   5.28.14
LEAGUE   3
   OR ART THOU GROWNE IN LEAGUE WITH THOSE
                           FAIRE EIES   1.23.5
   BETWIXT MINE EYE AND HEART A LEAGUE IS TOOKE   3.47.1
   THE LEAGUE TWIXT THEM, THAT LOYAL LOVE
                           HATH BOUND   5.65.10
LEAN   2
   THY $CHEEKE, NOW FLUSH WITH $ROSES, SUNKE,
                           AND LEANE   2.8.9

LEANE PENURIE WITHIN THAT $PEN DOTH DWELL   3.84.5
LEANDER   1
  SEE THY $LEANDER STRIVING IN THESE WAVES   1.46.2
LEAP   3
  TO LEAPE LARGE LENGTHS OF MILES WHEN THOU
                           ART GONE   3.44.10
  DO I ENVIE THOSE $JACKES THAT NIMBLE LEAPE   3.128.5
  WHICH PANTS AS THOUGH IT STILL SHOULD
                           LEAPE TO THEE   4.107.6
LEAPED   1
  THAT HEAVIE $SATURNE LAUGHT AND LEAPT WITH HIM   3.98.4
LEAPS   1
  O HOW FOR JOY HE LEAPES, O HOW HE CROWES   4.17.12
LEARN   9
  AND LEARNE TO GATHER FLOWERS BEFORE THEY WITHER   1.51.6
  O LEARNE TO READ WHAT SILENT LOVE HATH WRIT   3.23.13
  BUT THENCE I LEARNE AND FIND THE LESSON TRUE   3.118.13
  IF $LOVE LEARNE NOT ALONE TO LOVE AND SEE   4.46.7
  WHERE $LOVE IS CHASTNESSE, $PAINE DOTH
                           LEARNE DELIGHT   4.48.3
  FAR FAR TOO LONG TO LEARNE IT WITHOUT BOOKE   4.56.2
  LET HIM BUT LEARNE OF $LOVE TO READE IN THEE   4.71.3
  WIL SOONE CONCEIVE, AND LEARNE TO CONSTRUE WELL   5.43.14
  PERHAPS HE THERE MAY LEARNE WITH RARE DELIGHT   5.73.11
LEARNED   15
  DELIA MY HART HATH LEARNO OUT OF THOSE EYES   1.20.14
  THAT LEARNED $FATHER, WHICH SO FIRMELY PROVES   2.12.1
  THAT NEVER LEARN'D WHAT $CONSTELLATIONS ARE   2.43.7
  NOR HAD I LEARN'D TO DESCANT ON MY FAIRE   2.104.4
  TO CON MY $CROS-ROWE ERE I LEARN'D TO SPELL   2.111.2
  GAVE MEE SWEET LOCKES WHEN AS I LEARNED WELL   2.111.4
  WHICH BY THEYR NATURE LEARN'D TO MOUNT THE SKYE   2.122.6
  SO MAY THE LEARNED LIKE THE SIMILIE   2.148.4
  HE LEARND BUT SURETIE-LIKE TO WRITE FOR ME   3.134.7
  I NOW HAVE LEARN'D $LOVE RIGHT, AND LEARN'D
                           EVEN SO   4.16.13
  I NOW HAVE LEARN'D $LOVE RIGHT, AND LEARN'D
                           EVEN SO   4.16.13
  THE SCHOOLES WHERE $VENUS HATH LEARN'D $CHASTITIE 4.42.4
  SINCE IN THINE ARMES, IF LEARND FAME TRUTH
                           HATH SPREAD   4.65.13
  AND EKE HIS LEARNED HAND AT PLEASURE GUIDE   5.17.6
  LOVE LEARNED LETTERS TO HER EYES TO READ   5.43.12
LEARNED'S   1
  HAVE ADDED FETHERS TO THE LEARNEDS WING   3.78.7
LEARNING   6
  TO THIS OUR $WORLD, TO $LEARNING, AND TO $HEAVEN 2.18.1
  NINE $MUSES DOE WITH $LEARNING STILL FREQUENT   2.18.6
  UNTO THE $WORLD, TO $LEARNING, AND TO $HEAVEN   2.108.1
  NINE $MUSES DOE WITH LEARNING STILL FREQUENT   2.108.6
  AND OF THIS BOOKE, THIS LEARNING MAIST THOU TASTE 3.77.4
  AS HIGH AS LEARNING, MY RUDE IGNORANCE   3.78.14
LEARNING'S   1
  DIG DEEPE WITH LEARNING'S SPADE, NOW TELL
                           ME THIS   4.21.13
LEARNS   3
  WIT LEARNES IN THEE PERFECTION TO EXPRESSE   4.35.12
  THENCE HIS DESIRES HE LEARNES, HIS LIVE'S
                           COURSE THENCE   4.61.8
  STELLA NOW LEARNES (STRANGE CASE) TO WEEPE
                           IN THEE   4.101.8

LEASE   5
  AND THAT IN $BEAUTIES LEASE EXPIR'D, APPEARES   1.50.11
  SO SHOULD THAT BEAUTY WHICH YOU HOLD IN LEASE   3.13.5
  AND $SOMMERS LEASE HATH ALL TOO SHORT A DATE   3.18.4
  CAN YET THE LEASE CF MY TRUE LOVE CONTROULE   3.107.3
  WHY SO LARGE COST HAVING SO SHORT A LEASE   3.146.5
LEASES   1
  WHICH WORKES ON LEASES CF SHORT NUMBRED HOWERS   3.124.10
LEAST   30
  YET LEAST LONG TRAVAILES BE ABOVE MY STRENGTH   1.14.13
  WHEREIN NO SHEW GAVE CAUSE OF LEAST SUSPECT   1.31.7
  CAN GIVE THE LEAST RELEASE UNTO THY GRIEFE   1.52.10
  THE LEAST ABLE TO KYLL AN HOSTE OF $KINGS   2.126.8
  OR TO THY SELFE AT LEAST KIND HARTED PROVE   3.10.12
  WITH WHAT I MOST INJOY CONTENTED LEAST   3.29.8
  WHEN IN THE LEAST OF THEM MY LIFE HATH END   3.92.6
  OR AT THE LEAST, SO LONG AS BRAINE AND HEART   3.122.5
  WHEN MOST IMPEACHT, STANDS LEAST IN THY CONTROULE 3.125.14
  OR OF THY GIFTS AT LEAST SHADE OUT SOME PART   4.81.8
  THAT DO NOT LEAVE YOUR LEAST FRIEND AT THE WURST 4.95.2
  WHOSE FRUITLESSE WORKE IS BROKEN WITH LEAST WYND 5.23.14
  WHOSE LEAST DELIGHT SUFFICETH TO DEPRIVE   5.63.11
  AFFRAYD OF EVERY DANGERS LEAST DISMAY   5.88.4

  LEAST MY SAD LOOKES BEWRAY ME HOW I FARE   1.29.12
  LEAST MY BEWAILED GUILT SHOULD DO THEE SHAME   3.36.1J
  LEAST THE WISE WORLD SHOULD LOOK INTO YOUR MONE 3.71.13
  O LEAST THE WORLD SHOULD TASKE YOU TO RECITE   3.72.1
  O LEAST YOUR TRUE LOVE MAY SEEME FALCE IN THIS   3.72.9
  LEAST I (TOO MUCH PROPHANE) SHOULD DO IT WRONGE 3.89.11
  LEAST SORROW LEND ME WORDS AND WORDS EXPRESSE   3.140.3
  LEAST EYES WELL SEEING THY FOULE FAULTS
                SHOULD FINDE   3.148.14
  LEAST GUILTY OF MY FAULTS THY SWEET SELFE PROVE 3.151.4
  LEAST IF NO VAILE THOSE BRAVE GLEAMES DID DISGUISE 4.7.7
  NOBLER DESIRES, LEAST ELSE THAT FRIENDLY FOE   4.21.7
  LEAST ONCE SHOULD NOT BE HEARD, TWISE
              SAID, $NO, $NO   4.63.8
  ENVIE, PUT OUT THINE EYES, LEAST THOU DO SEE   4.69.3
  LEAVE THAT SIR $PHIP, LEAST OFF YOUR NECKE
              BE WROONG   4.83.14
  LEAST JOY, BY $NATURE APT SPRITES TO ENLARGE   4.85.3
  LEAST TREMBLING IT HIS WORKMANSHIP SHOULD SPILL 5.17.7
LEAVE   36
  TIS NOT DISDAINE MUST MAKE ME LEAVE TO LOVE   1.8.14
  AND CAUSE HER LEAVE TO TRIUMPH IN THIS WISE   1.10.9
  YET CANNOT LEAVE HER LOVE THAT HOLDS ME HATEFULL 1.18.5
  THEN LEAVE THY GLASSE, AND GAZE THY SELFE ON ME 1.37.9
  YET GOE (FORSAKEN) LEAVE THESE $WOODS,
             THESE PLAINES   1.52.5
  LEAVE HER AND ALL, AND ALL FOR HER THAT LEAVES   1.52.6
  TIME HATH THY $BEAUTIE, WHICH WITH $AGE
             WILL LEAVE THEE   2.10.12
  HER $MARRYNERS DOE LEAVE HER ALL FORLORNE   2.134.11
  WHAT ACCEPTABLE $AUDIT CAN'ST THOU LEAVE+   3.4.12
  WERE IT NOT THY SCURE LEISURE GAVE SWEET LEAVE   3.39.10
  WILL SOURELY LEAVE HER TILL HE HAVE PREVAILED   3.41.8
  TO LEAVE POORE ME, THOU HAST THE STRENGTH
             OF LAWES   3.49.13
  TOWARDS THEE ILE RUN, AND GIVE HIM LEAVE TO GOE 3.51.14

```
SAVE THAT TO DYE, I LEAVE MY LOVE ALONE                3.66.14
TO LOVE THAT WELL, WHICH THOU MUST LEAVE
                                    ERE LONG             3.73.14
IF THOU WILT LEAVE ME, DO NOT LEAVE ME LAST            3.90.9
IF THOU WILT LEAVE ME, DO NOT LEAVE ME LAST            3.90.9
TO LEAVE FOR NOTHING ALL THY SUMME OF GOOD            3.109.12
LEAVE WHAT THOU LIKEST NOT, DEALE NOT THOU WITH IT      4.4.4
LEAVE SENSE, AND THOSE WHICH SENSE'S OBJECTS BE        4.10.7
DEALE THOU WITH POWERS OF THOUGHTS, LEAVE
                                    LOVE TO WILL        4.10.8
HOW $POLES' RIGHT KING MEANES, WITHOUT
                                    LEAVE OF HOAST      4.30.3
TO LEAVE THE SCEPTER OF ALL SUBJECT THINGS             4.38.4
GLAD IF FOR HER HE GIVE THEM LEAVE TO DIE              4.43.8
LEAVE FOLLOWING THAT, WHICH IT IS GAINE TO MISSE      4.47.11
THAT I LOVE NOT, WITHOUT I LEAVE TO LOVE              4.61.14
O GIVE MY PASSIONS LEAVE TO RUN THEIR RACE             4.64.2
LEAVE THAT SIR $PHIP, LEAST OFF YOUR NECKE
                                    BE WROONG          4.83.14
WITH DOING ALL, LEAVE NOTHING DONE BUT PAINE          4.85.8
LEAVING MY $HEMISPHERE, LEAVE ME IN NIGHT             4.89.4
THAT DO NOT LEAVE YOUR LEAST FRIEND AT THE WURST      4.95.2
GREAT SHAME IT IS TO LEAVE LIKE ONE AFRAYD            5.14.3
LEAVE LADY IN YOUR GLASSE OF CHRISTALL CLENE          5.45.1
GIVE LEAVE TO REST ME BEING HALFE FORDONNE            5.80.3
TILL THEN GIVE LEAVE TO ME IN PLEASANT MEW            5.80.9
SINCE I DID LEAVE THE PRESENCE OF MY LOVE             5.87.1
LEAVES                   17
LEAVE HER AND ALL, AND ALL FOR HER THAT LEAVES        1.52.6
AND LEAVES HIS $MOTHERS LAP TO SPORT HIM THERE        2.4.8
LEAVES TO HIS $SONNE ALL HE HAD HEAP'D TOGETHER       2.10.4
SAP CHECKT WITH FROST AND LUSTIE LEAV'S QUITE GON     3.5.7
WHEN LOFTY TREES I SEE BARREN OF LEAVES               3.12.5
GREAT $PRINCES FAVORITES THEIR FAIRE LEAVES
                                    SPREAD             3.25.5
WHEN YELLOW LEAVES, OR NONE, OR FEW DOE HANGE         3.73.2
THE VACANT LEAVES THY MINDES IMPRINT WILL BEARE       3.77.3
THAT LEAVES LOOKE PALE, DREADING THE $WINTERS
                                    NEERE             3.97.14
ONE THING EXPRESSING, LEAVES OUT DIFFERENCE          3.105.8
WHO LEAVES UNSWAI'D THE LIKENESSE OF A MAN           3.141.11
OFT TURNING OTHERS' LEAVES, TO SEE IF
                                    THENCE WOULD FLOW   4.1.7
WITH GUILDED LEAVES OR COLOURD $VELUME PLAYES         4.11.6
HAPPY YE LEAVES WHEN AS THOSE LILLY HANDS             5.1.1
LEAVES, LINES, AND RYMES, SEEKE HER TO
                                    PLEASE ALONE       5.1.13
OF THAT PROUD MAYD, WHOM NOW THOSE LEAVES ATTYRE      5.28.8
HER BREST LYKE LILLYES, ERE THEYR LEAVES BE SHED     5.64.11
LEAVEST                   1
YET OF THAT BEST THOU LEAV'ST THE BEST BEHIND         4.11.4
LEAVING                   4
LEAVING THE $PATH THE GREATER PART DOE GOE            2.9.4
LEAVING THEE LIVING IN POSTERITY+                    3.6.12
LEAVING ME NOUGHT BUT WAILING ELOQUENCE              4.38.11
LEAVING MY $HEMISPHERE, LEAVE ME IN NIGHT            4.89.4
LECTURE                   1
THAT FACE, WHOSE LECTURE SHEWES WHAT PERFECT
                                    BEAUTIE IS         4.77.2
```

```
LED                          5
  WHILST YOUTH AND ERROR LED MY WANDRING MINDE          1.5.1
  SINCE THE FIRST LOCKE THAT LED ME TO THIS ERROR       1.18.1
  BUT WHAT OF THIS+ $SHOULD SHE TO DEATH BE LED         2.46.13
  IS PRISONER LED AWAY WITH HEAVY HART                  5.52.3
  AND MY FRAYLE THOUGHTS TOO RASHLY LED ASTRAY+         5.76.6
LEE                          1
  HOW THY LEE SHORES BY MY SIGHES STORMED BE            4.98.4
LEECH                        2
  THERE CAME TO ME A LEACH THAT WOULD APPLY             5.50.3
  THEN MY LYFES $LEACH DOE YOU YOUR SKILL REVEALE       5.50.13
LEESE                        1
  LEESE BUT THEIR SHOW, THEIR SUBSTANCE
                       STILL LIVES SWEET                3.5.14
LEFT                        14
  PITTIE SO LEFT, TO TH'COLDNESSE OF YOUR $BLOOD        2.58.13
  IN STEED OF TEN, CNE $SIBIL TO US LEFT                2.119.8
  LEFT AS THAT SUNNE ALONE TO COMFORT US                2.129.3
  LEFT TO THE MERCY CF THE WAVES AND WINDE              2.134.4
  AND WALLOWING IN HIS BLCOD, SOME LYFE YET LAFT        2.135.13
  THEN WERE NOT SUMMERS DISTILLATION LEFT               3.5.9
  THAT THOU NO FORME CF THEE HAST LEFT BEHIND           3.9.6
  ART LEFT THE PREY CF EVERY VULGAR THEEFE              3.48.8
  SINCE I LEFT YOU, MINE EYE IS IN MY MINDE             3.113.1
  HATH LEFT ME, AND I DESPERATE NOW APPROOVE            3.147.7
  THE LITLE REASON THAT IS LEFT IN ME                   4.4.10
  THESE THINGS ARE LEFT ME BY MY ONLY $DEARE            4.72.12
  YOU SAY FORSOOTH, YCU LEFT HER WELL OF LATE           4.92.7
  SO I ALONE NOW LEFT DISCONSOLATE                      5.89.5
LEGACY                       3
  A $LEGACIE TO STALE $VIRGINITIE                       2.15.12
  HIS $MOTHER DIED, AND BY HER $LEGACIE                 2.116.10
  UPON THY SELFE THY BEAUTIES LEGACY+                   3.4.2
LEGEA                        1
  AND OLD $LEGEA BRAGS OF $DANISH BLOOD                 2.124.12
LEGIONS                      2
  WHICH MANY $LEGIONS OF TRUE HEARTS HAD WARM'D         3.154.6
  LEGIONS OF LOVES WITH LITTLE WINGS DID FLY            5.16.6
LEGS                         3
  ME THINKES I $FLIE, YET WANT I LEGGES TO $GOE         2.62.5
  MEE THINKS I FLEE, YET WANT I LEGS TO GOE             2.150.5
  HER BREASTS HIS TENTS, LEGS HIS TRIUMPHALL CARRE      4.29.11
LEISURE                      5
  WERE IT NOT THY SOURE LEISURE GAVE SWEET LEAVE        3.39.10
  I MUST ATTEND, TIMES LEASURE WITH MY MONE             3.44.12
  BEING YOUR VASSAIL BOUND TO STAIE YOUR LEISURE        3.58.4
  AND I A TYRANT HAVE NO LEASURE TAKEN                  3.120.7
  THAT TEDIOUS LEASURE MARKS EACH WRINCKLED LINE        4.98.11
LEND                         9
  HAPS TO LEND SOME TC ONE TRUE HONEST $FRIEND          2.10.8
  EACH ONE OF THESE, DOTH AYDE UNTO THE
                       OTHER LENDE                      2.133.14
  NOR $MOONE NOR STARS LEND THEE THEIR SHINING
                       LIGHT                            2.145.12
  NATURES BEQUEST GIVES NCTHING BUT DOTH LEND           3.4.3
  AND YOU BUT ONE, CAN EVERY SHADDOW LEND               3.53.4
  WHAT STRAINED TOUCHES $RHETHORICK CAN LEND            3.82.10
  DARKNING THY POWRE TO LEND BASE SUBJECTS LIGHT        3.100.4
  LEAST SORROW LEND ME WORDS AND WORDS EXPRESSE         3.140.3
  OR LEND YOU ME ANCTHER LIVING BREST                   5.33.14
```

LENDING   1
   BEAUTY HER STRENGTH UNTO SLEEPES WEAKNES
                            LENDING   2.136.10

LENDS   5
   PRAISE HIM WHICH MADE THAT FIRE, WHICH
                     LENDS THAT LIGHT   2.105.14
   AND BEING FRANCK SHE LENDS TO THOSE ARE FREE   3.4.4
   TH'OFFENDERS SORROW LENDS BUT WEAKE RELIEFE   3.34.11
   HE LENDS THEE VERTUE, AND HE STOLE THAT WORD   3.79.9
   THAT TO HIS SUBJECT LENDS NOT SOME SMALL GLORY   3.84.6

LENGTH   14
   GOOD $DELIA LOSE, QUENCH, HEALE ME NOW AT LENGTH   1.14.14
   AND THAT THY BRIGHTNES SETS AT LENGTH TO $WEST   1.40.9
   YET WHICH AT LENGTH THOU MUST BE FORC'D TO LOSE   1.50.8
   WE AND THE $DUTCH AT LENGTH OUR $SELVES TO SEVER   2.51.9
   AND OF JUST LENGTH OUR NIGHT AND DAY DOTH MAKE   2.147.3
   AND NIGHT DOTH NIGHTLY MAKE GREEFES LENGTH
                     SEEME STRONGER   3.28.14
   AT LENGTH TO $LOVE'S DECREES, I FORC'D, AGREED   4.2.7
   AT LENGTH HE PERCH'D HIMSELF IN $STELLA'S
                     JOYFULL FACE   4.8.8
   AND SURE AT LENGTH STOLNE GOODS DO COME TO LIGHT   4.15.11
   BUT YOU FAIRE MAIDES, AT LENGTH THIS TRUE
                     SHALL FIND   4.54.11
   FOR THAT AT LENGTH YET DOTH INVITE SOME REST   4.96.13
   BREAKE FORTH AT LENGTH OUT OF THE INNER PART   5.2.5
   AND SHE TO STONES AT LENGTH ALL FROSEN TURNE+   5.32.14
   I DOE AT LENGTH DESCRY THE HAPPY SHORE   5.63.5

LENGTHENEST   1
   WHY LENGTHNEST THOU THY DARKEST HOWRES SO   2.145.3

LENGTHS   1
   TO LEAPE LARGE LENGTHS OF MILES WHEN THOU
                     ART GONE   3.44.10

LENT   6
   HERE SEE THE GIFTS THAT $GOD AND NATURE LENT THEE   1.42.7
   ONELY THAT LITTLE WHICH TO $ME WAS LENT   2.10.13
   OF ALL THOSE GOODS, WHICH HEAV'N TO ME HATH LENT   4.18.4
   THAT YE YOUR LOVE LENT TO SO MEANE A ONE   5.66.4
   HIM LODGING IN YOUR BOSOME TO HAVE LENT   5.73.14
   THAT HONOUR AND LARGE RICHESSE TO ME LENT   5.74.8

LESS   17
   AND NO REMOVE CAN MAKE THY SORROWES LESSE+   1.52.4
   WHO HAD LESSE $ART THEM LIVELY TO EXPRESSE+   2.27.6
   IS $NATURE GROWNE LESSE POW'RFULL IN THEIR
                     $HEIRES   2.27.7
   BE SCORN'D, LIKE OLD MEN OF LESSE TRUTH
                     THEN TONGUE   3.17.10
   AN EYE MORE BRIGHT THEN THEIRS, LESSE
                     FALSE IN ROWLING   3.20.5
   BOTH GRACE AND FAULTS ARE LOV'D OF MORE AND LESSE   3.96.3
   I LOVE NOT LESSE, THOGH LESSE THE SHOW APPEARE   3.102.2
   I LOVE NOT LESSE, THOGH LESSE THE SHOW APPEARE   3.102.2
   NOT THAT THE SUMMER IS LESSE PLEASANT NOW   3.102.9
   MADE MORE OR LES BY THY CONTINUALL HAST   3.123.12
   BUT MORE I CRIE, LESSE GRACE SHE DOTH IMPART   4.44.6
   'WHAT NOW SIR FOOLE,' SAID HE, 'I WOULD NO LESSE   4.53.7
   I CANNOT BRAG OF WORD, MUCH LESSE OF DEED   4.66.5
   MY WEALTH NO MORE, AND NO WHIT LESSE MY NEED   4.66.7
   'OR SO+' $MUCH LESSE.. '$HOW THEN+' $SURE
                     THUS IT IS   4.74.13

```
  ALTHOUGH LESSE GIFTS IMPE FEATHERS OFT ON $FAME      4.75.4
  NOR NO DAY HATH LESSE QUIET THEN MY NIGHT            4.89.11
LESSER                   2
  OR HAVE OUR $PASSIONS LESSER POW'R THEN THEIRS       2.27.5
  IF IT BE POISON'D, TIS THE LESSER SINNE             3.114.13
LESSON                   6
  AT MY FIRST $LESSON IN THY SACRED NAME               2.111.6
  BUT THENCE I LEARNE AND FIND THE LESSON TRUE        3.118.13
  IN HER SIGHT I A LESSON NEW HAVE SPELD               4.16.12
  FY, SCHOOLE OF $PATIENCE, $FY, YOUR LESSON IS        4.56.1
  WHAT WONDER THEN IF HE HIS LESSON MISSE              4.73.3
  LOVE IS THE LESSON WHICH THE $LORD US TAUGHT         5.68.14
LESSONS                  1
  TO SUCH A SCHOOLE-MISTRESSE, WHOSE LESSONS NEW       4.46.10
LEST                    16 (SEE LEAST)


LET                    124
  LET THEM YET SIGH THEIR OWNE, AND MONE MY WRONGS     1.3.4
  ONCE LET HER KNOW, SH'HATH DONE ENOUGH
                         TO PROVE ME                   1.10.13
  AND LET HER PITTIE IF SHE CANNOT LOVE ME             1.10.14
  LET THIS SUFFICE, THAT ALL THE WORLD MAY SEE         1.15.13
  LET $VENUS HAVE THY GRACES, HER RESIGN'D             1.19.9
  LET HER NOT STILL TRIUMPH OVER THE PRIZE             1.22.13
  YET SPARE HER $TIME, LET HER EXEMPTED BE             1.23.13
  ONCE LET HER LOVE INDEED, OR ELS EYE ME NEVER        1.24.14
  ONCE LET THE $OCEAN OF MY CARES FINDE SHORE          1.46.13
  AND LET HER TELL ME AS SHE IS A WOMAN                1.49.11
  LET LOVE AND YOUTH CONDUCT THY PLEASURES THITHER     1.51.8
  STILL LET DISARMED PEACE DECKE HER AND THEE          1.53.13
  AND LET THE DAY BE TIME ENOUGH TO MOURNE             1.54.5
  LET WAKING EYES SUFFICE TO WAILE THEIR SCORNE        1.54.7
  NEVER LET RISING $SUNNE APPROVE YOU LIERS            1.54.11
  STILL LET ME SLEEPE, IMBRACING CLOUDS IN VAINE       1.54.13
  LET OTHERS SING OF $KNIGHTS AND $PALLADINES          1.55.1
  LET OTHERS STRIVE TO ENTERTAINE WITH $WORDS          2.4.9
  LET WHAT I PRAISE, BE STILL MADE GOOD BY YOU         2.4.13
  AND LET ME TAKE MY SELFE WHAT I DOE CRAVE            2.5.12
  LET $NO AND I, WITH I AND YOU BE SO                  2.5.13
  INTO THE SAME THEN LET A $WOMAN BREATHE              2.15.9
  THERE LET MY $VERSE GET GLORY IN THE $NORTH          2.25.7
  AND LET THE $BARDS WITHIN THAT $IRISH $ILE           2.25.9
  LET $WOLVES AND $BEARES BE CHARMED WITH MY $VERSE    2.25.14
  ARDENS SWEET $ANKOR, LET THY GLORY BEE               2.32.13
  OR $CRUELL, IF THOU CAN'ST NOT., LET US SCORSE       2.52.7
  LET $VERTUE BE THE $TOUCH-STONE OF MY $LOVE          2.60.7
  AND VIEW THE $CROSSES WHICH MY COURSE DOE LET        2.60.10
  SINCE THER'S NO HELPE, $COME LET US KISSE AND PART   2.61.1
  DISCHARGE OUR $FORCES, HERE LET $MALICE CEASE        2.63.7
  LET THE $WORLD SEE THE UTMOST OF THY HATE            2.63.12
  ARDENS SWEET $ANKOR LET THY GLORY BE                 2.124.13
  LET HEAVENS WITHDRAW THEIR SWEET $AMBROZIAN
                         BREATH                        2.145.11
  LET HIM COMPARE IT TO HER HEAVENLY EYE               2.148.2
  LET VERTUE BE THE TUCH-STONE OF MY LOVE              2.149.7
  AND VIEW THE CROSSES WHICH MY COURSE DOTH LET        2.149.10
  AND BY ALL MEANES, LET BLACK UNKINDNES PROVE         2.149.13
  AND LET $INVENTION OF HER BEAUTY VAUNT               2.151.9
  THEN LET NOT WINTERS WRAGGED HAND DEFACE             3.6.1
  LET THOSE WHOM NATURE HATH NOT MADE FOR STORE        3.11.9
```

```
THOU SHOULDST PRINT MORE, NOT LET THAT COPPY DIE        3.11.14
YOU HAD A $FATHER, LET YOUR $SON SAY SO                 3.13.14
O LET ME TRUE IN LOVE BUT TRULY WRITE                   3.21.9
LET THEM SAY MORE THAT LIKE OF HEARE-SAY WELL           3.21.13
O LET MY BOOKS BE THEN THE ELOQUENCE                    3.23.9
LET THOSE WHO ARE IN FAVOR WITH THEIR STARS             3.25.1
TO LET BACE CLOUDES ORE-TAKE ME IN MY WAY               3.34.3
LET ME CONFESSE THAT WE TWO MUST BE TWAINE              3.36.1
AND HE THAT CALLS ON THEE, LET HIM BRING FORTH          3.38.11
EVEN FOR THIS, LET US DEVIDED LIVE                      3.39.5
LET THIS SAD $INTRIM LIKE THE $OCEAN BE                 3.56.9
OH LET ME SUFFER (BEING AT YOUR BECK)                   3.58.5
BUT LET YOUR LOVE EVEN WITH MY LIFE DECAY               3.71.12
LET HIM BUT COPPY WHAT IN YOU IS WRIT                   3.84.9
LET NOT MY LOVE BE CAL'D $IDOLATRIE                     3.105.1
LET ME NOT TO THE MARRIAGE OF TRUE MINDES               3.116.1
NOE, LET ME BE OBSEQUIOUS IN THY HEART                  3.125.9
O LET IT THEN AS WELL BESEEME THY HEART                 3.132.10
BUT THEN MY FRIENDS HEART LET MY POORE
                                 HEART BALE             3.133.10
WHO ERE KEEPES ME, LET MY HEART BE HIS GARDE            3.133.11
LET NO UNKINDE, NO FAIRE BESEECHERS KILL                3.135.13
THEN IN THE NUMBER LET ME PASSE UNTOLD                  3.136.9
LET ME EXCUSE THEE, AH MY LOVE WELL KNOWES              3.139.9
AND LET THAT PINE TO AGGRAVAT THY STORE                 3.146.10
LET DAINTIE WITS CRIE ON THE $SISTERS NINE              4.3.1
OR ELSE LET THEM IN STATELIER GLORIE SHINE              4.3.5
VERTUE ALAS, NOW LET ME TAKE SOME REST                  4.4.1
THEN $LOVE IS SINNE, AND LET ME SINFULL BE              4.14.14
O LET ME PROP MY MIND, YET IN HIS GROWTH                4.19.12
LET HIM, DEPRIVED OF SWEET BUT UNFELT JOYES             4.24.12
COME LET ME WRITE, '$AND TO WHAT END+' $TO EASE         4.34.1
O DO NOT LET THY $TEMPLE BE DESTROYD                    4.40.14
YET $DEARE, LET ME THIS PARDON GET OF YOU               4.46.12
LET HER GO. $SOFT, BUT HERE SHE COMES. $GO TO           4.47.12
WHAT EVER MAY ENSUE, O LET ME BE                        4.48.5
LET NOT MINE EYES BE HEL-DRIV'N FROM THAT LIGHT         4.48.7
O LOOKE, O SHINE, O LET ME DIE AND SEE                  4.48.8
LET $VERTUE HAVE THAT $STELLA'S SELFE., YET THUS        4.52.13
HE CANNOT LOVE.. NO, NO, LET HIM ALONE'                 4.54.8
FOR LET ME BUT NAME HER WHOM I DO LOVE                  4.55.12
WHICH WOULD NOT LET ME, WHOM SHE LOVED, DECLINE         4.62.7
LET $FORTUNE LAY ON ME HER WORST DISGRACE               4.64.3
LET FOLKE ORECHARG'D WITH BRAINE AGAINST ME CRIE        4.64.4
LET CLOUDS BEDIMME MY FACE, BREAKE IN MINE EYE          4.64.5
LET ME NO STEPS BUT OF LOST LABOUR TRACE                4.64.6
LET ALL THE EARTH WITH SCORNE RECOUNT MY CASE           4.64.7
YET LET THIS THOUGHT THY $TYGRISH COURAGE PASSE         4.65.11
COME, COME, AND LET ME POWRE MY SELFE ON THEE           4.69.6
LET HIM BUT LEARNE OF $LOVE TO READE IN THEE            4.71.3
BUT GIVE APT SERVANTS THEIR DUE PLACE, LET EYES         4.85.9
LET EARES HEARE SPEECH, WHICH WIT TO WONDER TIES        4.85.11
LET BREATH SUCKE UP THOSE SWEETES, LET
                              ARMES EMBRACE             4.85.12
LET BREATH SUCKE UP THOSE SWEETES, LET
                              ARMES EMBRACE             4.85.12
HAVE CHANG'D DESERT, LET MINE OWNE CONSCIENCE BE        4.86.2
LET WO GRIPE ON MY HEART, SHAME LOADE MINE EYE          4.86.4
ALL MIRTH FAREWELL, LET ME IN SORROW LIVE               4.100.14
LET HONOR SELFE TO THEE GRAUNT HIGHEST PLACE            4.103.14
```

```
O LET NOT FOOLES IN ME THY WORKES REPROVE        4.107.13
TO FORCE ME LIVE AND WILL NOT LET ME DY          5.11.12
ERE $CUCKOW END, LET HER A REBELL BE             5.19.14
FAYRER THEN FAYREST LET NONE EVER SAY            5.20.13
YET BETTER WERE ATTONCE TO LET ME DIE            5.25.5
LET IT LYKEWISE YOUR GENTLE BREST INSPIRE        5.28.6
LET HER ACCEPT ME AS HER FAITHFULL THRALL        5.29.10
O FAYREST FAYRE LET NEVER IT BE NAMED            5.41.13
LET HER, YF PLEASE HER, BYND WITH ADAMANT CHAYNE 5.42.10
ONELY LET HER ABSTAINE FROM CRUELTY              5.42.13
LET THEM FEELE TH'UTMOST OF YOUR CRUELTYES       5.49.9
NE LET THEYR FAMOUS MONIMENTS TO FADE            5.51.4
THERE LET NO THOUGHT OF JOY OR PLEASURE VAINE    5.52.9
TO LET THEM GAZE WHYLEST HE ON THEM MAY PRAY     5.53.4
BUT LET MY LOVES FAYRE $PLANET SHORT HER WAYES   5.60.13
SO LET US, WHICH THIS CHAUNGE OF WEATHER VEW     5.62.5
THE OLD YEARES SINNES FOREPAST LET US ESCHEW     5.62.7
SO LET US LOVE, DEARE LOVE, LYKE AS WE OUGHT     5.68.13
NOT SO, (QUOD I) LET BASER THINGS DEVIZE         5.75.9
AND LET MY THOUGHTS BEHOLD HER SELFE IN MEE      5.78.14
BUT LET HER PRAYSES YET BE LOW AND MEANE         5.80.13
LET NOT ONE SPARKE OF FILTHY LUSTFULL FYRE       5.84.1
RATHER THEN ENVY LET THEM WONDER AT HER          5.85.7
LET THE WORLD CHOSE TO ENVY OR TO WONDER         5.85.14
LET ALL THE PLAGUES AND HORRID PAINES OF HELL    5.86.5
THE SPARKES WHERECF LET KINDLE THINE OWN FYRE    5.86.9
```

LETS   4
```
CARES NOT FOR THEE, BUT LETS THEE WASTE IN VAINE 1.23.10
YOUR FIRY HEATE LETS NOT HER GLORY PASSE         1.38.13
WHO LETS SO FAIRE A HOUSE FALL TO DECAY          3.13.9
THAT LAP DOTH LAP, NAY LETS, IN SPITE OF SPITE   4.59.10
```

LETTERS   6
```
IN UNKINDE $LETTERS., WROTE SHE CARES NOT HOW    1.10.4
LETTERS AND $LINES WE SEE ARE SOONE DEFACED      2.13.1
LETTERS AND LYNES WE SEE ARE SOONE DEFACED       2.121.1
WHEN I MIGHT READE THOSE LETTERS FAIRE OF BLISSE 4.56.5
LOVE LEARNED LETTERS TO HER EYES TO READ         5.43.12
MOST HAPPY LETTERS FRAM'D BY SKILFULL TRADE      5.74.1
```

LEVEL   4
```
THE LEVELL OF MY HOPES DESIRED MOST              1.53.4
BRING ME WITHIN THE LEVEL OF YOUR FROWNE         3.117.11
NOE, I AM THAT I AM, AND THEY THAT LEVELL        3.121.9
NOR SO FAIRE LEVELL IN SO SECRET STAY            4.20.6
```

LEWIS   1
```
THAT WITTIE $LEWIS TO HIM A TRIBUTE PAID         4.75.11
```

LIARS   1
```
NEVER LET RISING $SUNNE APPROVE YOU LIERS        1.54.11
```

LIBERTIES   1
```
WHEN LOOSING ONE, TWO LIBERTIES YE GAYNE         5.65.3
```

LIBERTY   9
```
WHEREWITH MY LIBERTY THOU DIDST SURPRIZE         1.14.2
AND $LIBERTY DEPRIVES HIM OF HIS $SCOPE          2.26.11
AND LYBERTY DEPRIVES HYM OF HYS SCOPE            2.137.11
THOSE PRETTY WRONGS THAT LIBERTY COMMITS         3.41.1
TH'IMPRISON'D ABSENCE OF YOUR LIBERTIE           3.58.6
NOW EVEN THAT FOOTSTEP OF LOST LIBERTIE          4.2.9
TO KEEPE IT SELFE IN LIFE AND LIBERTY            4.29.6
WHAT, HAVE I THUS BETRAYED MY LIBERTIE+          4.47.1
THAT FONDLY FEARE TO LOOSE YOUR LIBERTY          5.65.2
```

LICENTIOUS   1
   THE WHILES SHE LORDETH IN LICENTIOUS BLISSE   5.10.3
LIDS   2
   IN TOMBE OF LIDS THEN BURIED ARE MINE EYES   4.99.12
   AND TO THE GROUND HER EIE LIDS LOW EMBASETH   5.13.3
LIE   27
   LIE DOWNE TO WAILE, RISE UP TO SIGH AND GRIEVE   1.9.6
   WHO FOR MY LIFE IN SECRETE WAITE DO'ST LYE   2.130.6
   BUT THINGS REMOV'D THAT HIDDEN IN THERE LIE   3.31.8
   MY HEART DOTH PLEAD THAT THOU IN HIM DOUST LYE   3.46.5
   SHALL TIMES BEST $JEWELL FROM TIMES CHEST
                 LIE HID+   3.65.10
   UNLESSE YOU WOULD DEVISE SOME VERTUOUS LYE   3.72.5
   THAT ON THE ASHES CF HIS YOUTH DOTH LYE   3.73.10
   WHEN YOU INTOMBED IN MENS EYES SHALL LYE   3.81.8
   SINCE THAT MY LIFE ON THY REVOLT DOTH LIE   3.92.10
   AS FROM MY SOULE WHICH IN THY BREST DOTH LYE   3.109.4
   THOSE LINES THAT I BEFORE HAVE WRIT DOE LIE   3.115.1
   FOR THY RECORDS, AND WHAT WE SEE DOTH LYE   3.123.11
   THEREFORE I LYE WITH HER, AND SHE WITH ME   3.138.13
   TO MAKE ME GIVE THE LIE TO MY TRUE SIGHT   3.150.3
   TO SWERE AGAINST THE TRUTH SO FOULE A LIE   3.152.14
   WHO LIKE A THEEFE, HID IN DARKE BUSH DOTH LY   4.20.3
   THAT POISON FOULE CF BUBLING PRIDE DOTH LIE   4.27.6
   THAT NEVER I WITH CLOS'D-UP SENSE DO LIE   4.32.6
   AS GOOD TO WRITE AS FOR TO LIE AND GRONE   4.40.1
   DOTH MAKE MY HEART GIVE TO MY TONGUE THE LIE   4.47.14
   I MUST NO MORE IN THY SWEET PASSIONS LIE   4.72.7
   IN SPORT I SUCKT, WHILE SHE ASLEEPE DID LIE   4.73.6
   BUT IF ALL FAITH, LIKE SPOTLESSE $ERMINE LY   4.86.5
   THAT THOUGH IN WRETCHEDNESSE THY LIFE DOTH LIE   4.94.12
   WITH WINDOWES OPE THEN MCST MY MIND DOTH LIE   4.99.5
   COUNTING BUT DUST WHAT IN THE WAY DID LIE   4.105.8
   MONGST WHICH THERE IN A SILVER DISH DID LY   5.77.5
LIED   1
   THAT I MAY NOT BE SC, NCR THOU BE LYDE   3.140.13
LIEN   3
   TO CHECK THE WORLC, HOW THEY INTOMB'D HAVE LIEN   1.45.3
   MY $HOPES REVIV'D, WHICH LONG IN $GRAVE HAD LYNE 2.35.12
   MY HOPES REVIV'D WHICH LCNG IN GRAVE HAD LYNE   2.112.12
LIES   40
   IF ON HER LOVE MY LIFE AND HONOUR LYES   1.15.11
   AND SO SENT BACKE, AND THUS MY FORTUNE LIES   1.25.12
   AND ALL LIES WITHRED THAT WAS HELD SO DEERE   1.42.4
   NOW SHEW THY POWER, AND WHERE THY VERTUE LIES   1.46.7
   MY JOYFULL $NORTH, WHERE ALL MY FORTUNE LIES   1.53.3
   WHEN YET TH'UNBORNE SHALL SAY, $LO WHERE SHE LIES 1.55.7
   THAT ALL THEIR $WEALTH LIES IN THY BEAUTIES
                 $BOOKES   2.3.12
   MY $SOULE-SHRIN'D $SAINT, MY FAIRE $IDEA LIES   2.53.2
   WHOSE DEARE REMEMBRANCE IN MY $BOSOME LYES   2.57.3
   WHEN HIS $PULSE FAYLING, $PASSION SPEECHLESSE
                 LIES   2.61.10
   THAT ALL HER WEALTH LYES IN THY $BEAUTIES
                 BOOKES   2.110.12
   MY SOULE-SHRINDE $SAINT, MY FAIRE $IDEA LYES   2.113.2
   WHERE MY POORE SOULE, THE $BARKE OF SORRCW LYES 2.134.3
   AGAINST THE $FORTE WHERE $BEAUTIES $ARMY LIES   2.142.2
   MY REBELL THOUGHT FCR ME IN $AMBUSHE LYES   2.142.7
   MAKING A FAMINE WHERE ABCUNDANCE LIES   3.1.7

```
THEN BEING ASKT, WHERE ALL THY BEAUTIE LIES          3.2.5
THE AGE TO COME WOULD SAY THIS $POET LIES            3.17.7
TO FINDE WHERE YOUR TRUE $IMAGE PICTUR'D LIES        3.24.6
AND IN THEM-SELVES THEIR PRIDE LIES BURIED           3.25.7
AND SAYES IN HIM THEIR FAIRE APPEARANCE LYES         3.46.8
MY GREEFE LIES ONWARD AND MY JOY BEHIND              3.50.14
EXCUSE NOT SILENCE SO, FOR'T LIES IN THEE            3.101.10
THEY KNOW WHAT BEAUTIE IS, SEE WHERE IT LYES         3.137.3
I DO BELEEVE HER THOUGH I KNOW SHE LYES              3.138.2
AND IN OUR FAULTS BY LYES WE FLATTERED BE            3.138.14
BUT FOUND NO CURE, THE BATH FOR MY HELPE LIES        3.153.13
AND IN HER BREAST BOPEEPE OR COUCHING LYES           4.11.12
THAT IN HER BREAST THY PAP WELL SUGRED LIES          4.12.5
CUPID THEN SMILES, FOR ON HIS CREST THERE LIES       4.13.9
LIES HATCHING STILL THE GOODS WHEREIN THEY FLOW      4.24.2
AND I, BUT FOR BECAUSE MY PROSPECT LIES              4.29.13
AND THERE LONG SINCE, $LOVE THY $LIEUTENANT LIES     4.36.5
FROM OUT THAT NOYSOME GULFE, WHICH GAPING LIES       4.78.3
BEAUTIE'S PLAGUE, $VERTUE'S SCOURGE, SUCCOUR
                             OF LIES                 4.78.6
LOATHING ALL LIES, DOUBTING THIS $FLATTERIE IS       4.80.11
IN $LILLIES' NEAST, WHERE $LOVE'S SELFE
                          LIES ALONG                 4.83.8
STELLA IS SICKE, AND IN THAT SICKE BED LIES          4.101.1
BUT HIM THAT AT YOUR FOOTSTOOLE HUMBLED LIES         5.49.11
THAT WITH FALSE FORGED LYES, WHICH THOU DIDST TEL    5.86.7
LIEUTENANCY              1
AND ON MY THOUGHTS GIVE THY $LIEFTENANCY             4.107.7
LIEUTENANT              1
AND THERE LONG SINCE, $LOVE THY $LIEUTENANT LIES     4.36.5
LIFE                    94
IF ON HER LOVE MY LIFE AND HONOUR LYES               1.15.11
THAT WEARY OF MY LIFE, I LOATH TO LIVE               1.16.8
WHAT IT IS TO BREATHE AND LIVE WITHOUT LIFE          1.20.1
T'AFFECT THIS LIFE, AND YET THIS LIFE DISLEEKE       1.20.11
T'AFFECT THIS LIFE, AND YET THIS LIFE DISLEEKE       1.20.11
FROM CARE TO CARE THAT LEADES A LIFE SO BAD          1.26.2
REIGNE IN MY THOUGHTS, MY LOVE AND LIFE
                         ARE THINE                   1.27.14
ALL MY POORE LIFE BY THEM IS TRODEN DOWNE            1.28.6
THUS SHADES MY LIFE SO LONG AS WANTS ENDURE          1.29.14
IN LIFE AND DEATH $ILE TENDER HER GOOD NAME          1.30.11
MY LIFE NOR DEATH SHAL NEVER BE HER BLOT             1.30.12
THEN THERE I DIE FROM WHENCE MY LIFE SHOULD COME     1.31.13
YOUR $LIFE SO LIKE THE $PHOENIXS BEGUN               2.16.8
GAVE $LIFE AND $COURAGE TO MY LAB'RING $PEN          2.47.2
THOU WHICH HAST SCORNED $LIFE, AND HATED $DEATH      2.49.9
AND ASKE A $WORLD UPON MY $LIFE TO DWELL             2.60.4
FROM $DEATH TO $LIFE, THOU MIGHT'ST HIM
                        YET RECOVER                  2.61.14
SO BY THY DEATH, THY LIFE SHALL BE BEGUNNE           2.106.8
AND YET IN DEATH, SOME HOPE OF LIFE ESPYING          2.109.7
MY LIFE, MY YOUTH, MY LOVE, I HEERE ANOTAMIZE        2.114.14
WHOSE LYFE DOTH SAVE A THOUSAND SOULES
                         FROM HELL                   2.119.12
THAT LIFE (I MEANE) WHICH DOTH $RELIGION TEACH       2.119.13
LOV'D MORE THEN LIFE, YET ONELY ART HIS LOVE         2.129.11
WHO FOR MY LIFE IN SECRETE WAITE DO'ST LYE           2.130.6
DISDAYNE $ICE TO MY LIFE, IS TO MY SOULE A FIRE      2.132.3
WITH MY SOULES FIRE, MY LIFE DISDAINE OUT-WEARES     2.132.7
```

```
DESIRE, MY LOVE, MY SOULE, MY HOPE, HART,
                   AND LIFE CHARMETH              2.132.8
MY LIFE A $PHOENIX IS IN MY SOULES FIRE          2.132.11
DESIRE, MY LOVE, MY SOULE, MY HOPE, MY
                   HART, MY LIFE                  2.132.13
AND WALLOWING IN HIS BLOOD, SOME LYFE YET LAFT   2.135.13
A LYFE, THAT NEVER JOYD BUT IN HER LOVE          2.138.9
THY $MOTHER DYD HER LYFE TO $DEATH RESIGNE       2.140.5
LOE THUS MY LOVE, MY LYFE, MY FORTUNE TRYES      2.142.4
AND ASKE A WORLD UPON MY LIFE TO DWELL           2.149.4
THAT THOU CONSUM'ST THY SELFE IN SINGLE LIFE+    3.9.2
SO SHOULD THE LINES OF LIFE THAT LIFE REPAIRE    3.16.9
SO SHOULD THE LINES OF LIFE THAT LIFE REPAIRE    3.16.9
WHICH HIDES YOUR LIFE, AND SHEWES NOT
                   HALFE YOUR PARTS              3.17.4
SO LONG LIVES THIS, AND THIS GIVES LIFE TO THEE  3.18.14
MY LIFE BEING MADE OF FOURE, WITH TWO ALONE      3.45.7
MY SWEET LOVES BEAUTY, THOUGH MY LOVERS LIFE     3.63.12
TO LIVE A SCOND LIFE ON SECOND HEAD              3.68.7
BUT LET YOUR LOVE EVEN WITH MY LIFE DECAY        3.71.12
MY LIFE HATH IN THIS LINE SOME INTEREST          3.74.3
SO THEN THOU HAST BUT LOST THE DREGS OF LIFE     3.74.9
SO ARE YOU TO MY THOUGHTS AS FOOD TO LIFE        3.75.1
YOUR NAME FROM HENCE IMMORTALL LIFE SHALL HAVE   3.81.5
WHEN OTHERS WOULD GIVE LIFE, AND BRING A TOMBE   3.83.12
THERE LIVES MORE LIFE IN ONE OF YOUR FAIRE EYES  3.83.13
FOR TEARME OF LIFE THOU ART ASSURED MINE         3.92.2
AND LIFE NO LONGER THEN THY LOVE WILL STAY       3.92.3
WHEN IN THE LEAST OF THEM MY LIFE HATH END       3.92.6
SINCE THAT MY LIFE ON THY REVOLT DOTH LIE        3.92.10
GIVE MY LOVE FAME FASTER THEN TIME WASTS LIFE    3.100.13
THAT DID NOT BETTER FOR MY LIFE PROVIDE          3.111.3
AND SAV'D MY LIFE SAYING NOT YOU                 3.145.14
WHILST MANY $NYMPHES THAT VOU'D CHAST
                   LIFE TO KEEP                  3.154.3
THE RICHEST GEMME OF $LOVE AND LIFE ENJOYES      4.24.10
TO KEEPE IT SELFE IN LIFE AND LIBERTY            4.29.6
WITNESSE OF LIFE TO THEM THAT LIVING DIE         4.32.2
FOR OF MY LIFE I MUST A RIDDLE TELL              4.37.4
MY LIFE FORGETS TO NOURISH LANGUISHT SPRITES     4.42.10
MINE EYES, MY LIGHT, MY HEART, MY LIFE, ALAS     4.65.9
LIGHT OF MY LIFE, AND LIFE OF MY DESIRE          4.68.2
LIGHT OF MY LIFE, AND LIFE OF MY DESIRE          4.68.2
BREATHER OF LIFE, AND FASTNER OF DESIRE          4.80.7
THEN SINCE (DEARE LIFE) YOU FAINE WOULD
                   HAVE ME PEACE                 4.81.12
I AM FROM YOU, LIGHT OF MY LIFE, MIS-LED         4.91.2
THAT THOUGH IN WRETCHEDNESSE THY LIFE DOTH LIE   4.94.12
OF ALL THE POWERS WHICH LIFE BESTOWES ON ME      4.107.2
WHICH HOLD MY LIFE IN THEIR DEAD DOING MIGHT     5.1.2
THE WHICH BOTH LYFE AND DEATH FORTH FROM YOU DART 5.7.3
THEN IS MY SOULE WITH LIFE AND LOVE INSPIRED     5.7.6
BUT SINCE THAT LYFE IS MORE THEN DEATH DESYRED   5.7.9
SUCH LIFE SHOULD BE THE HONOR OF YOUR LIGHT      5.7.13
OF MY POORE LIFE TO MAKE UNPITTIED SPOILE        5.11.8
YET MY POORE LIFE, ALL SORROWES TO ASSOYLE       5.11.9
THAT CAN EXPRESSE THE LIFE OF THINGS INDEED      5.17.14
AND TREAD MY LIFE DOWNE IN THE LOWLY FLOURE      5.20.4
THAT WITH ONE LOOKE SHE DOTH MY LIFE DISMAY      5.21.10
HOW LONG SHALL THIS LYKE DYING LYFE ENDURE       5.25.1
```

```
MY $HELICE THE LODESTAR OF MY LYFE                      5.34.10
FOR LACKING IT THEY CANNOT LYFE SUSTAYNE                 5.35.5
BY SLAYING HIM, WHOSE LYFE THOUGH YE DESPYSE            5.36.11
MOTE HAVE YOUR LIFE IN HONOUR LONG MAINTAYNED          5.36.12
ALL CARELESSE HOW MY LIFE FOR HER DECAYSE              5.38.10
BUT AS SHE WILL, WHOSE WILL MY LIFE DOTH SWAY           5.46.7
SO SHALL YOU LIVE BY GIVING LIFE TO ME                 5.49.14
THEN AL THOSE FOURTY WHICH MY LIFE OUTWENT              5.60.8
MOST GLORIOUS $LORD OF LYFE THAT ON THIS DAY            5.68.1
OUR LOVE SHALL LIVE, AND LATER LIFE RENEW              5.75.14
JOY OF MY LIFE, FULL OFT FOR LOVING YOU                 5.82.1
FOR LACKING IT, THEY CANNOT LYFE SUSTAYNE               5.83.5
AND DEAD MY LIFE THAT WANTS SUCH LIVELY BLIS           5.89.14
LIFE'S                    10
IN HORRORS SABLE CLOWDES SETS MY LIVES SUNNE            1.30.2
AND MY $LIVES $HOPE WOULD DIE, BUT FOR $DESPAIRE        2.26.3
WITH MY $LIFE'S $SORROW INTERLINED SO                   2.54.3
WITH MY LIVES SOROW ENTERLYNED SO                      2.101.3
AND MY LIVES HOPE WOULD DIE BUT FOR DYSPAIRE           2.137.3
TO MY LYVES FOE HER $CHIEFTAINE STILL BETRAYING        2.142.8
UNTILL LIVES COMPOSITION BE RECURED                     3.45.9
THENCE HIS DESIRES HE LEARNES, HIS LIVE'S
                         COURSE THENCE                   4.61.8
THEN MY LYFES $LEACH DOE YOU YOUR SKILL REVEALE        5.50.13
THE THIRD MY LOVE, MY LIVES LAST ORNAMENT               5.74.9
LIFT                      2
AND TO THE LIGHT LIFT UP THEYR DROUPING HED            5.40.12
SHALL LIFT YOU UP UNTO AN HIGH DEGREE                  5.82.14
LIFTS                     2
LIFTS UP HIS BURNING HEAD, EACH UNDER EYE               3.7.2
THAT HER CLEARE VOYCE LIFTS THY FAME TO THE SKIES      4.12.8
LIGHT                    70
INTENERAT THAT HEART THAT SETS SO LIGHT                 1.10.7
THAT MY LIVES LIGHT WHOLY IN-DARKNED IS                 1.21.4
MY LIVES SWEET SUNNE, MY DEAREST COMFORTS LIGHT         1.30.3
THE FAIREST FLOWRE THAT EVER SAW THE LIGHT              1.40.6
RELIEVE MY LANGUISH, AND RESTORE THE LIGHT              1.54.3
AND IF WITH $TEARES I FIND THEM ALL TOO LIGHT           2.13.7
THOUGHT IT IN WEIGHT TOO LIGHT BY MANY A $GRAINE       2.38.12
AND ONELY REST CONTENTED WITH THE $LIGHT                2.43.6
WHEN $DARKNESSE HATH OBSCUR'D EACH OTHER $LIGHT        2.55.14
LABOUR IS LIGHT, WHERE $LOVE (QUOTH I) DOTH PAY         2.59.9
(SAITH HE) $LIGHT $BURTHEN'S HEAVY, IF
                         FARRE BORNE                    2.59.10
WHEN DARKNES HATH OBSCUR'D EACH OTHER LIGHT            2.102.14
NO $VIRGINE ONCE ATTENDING ON THAT LIGHT               2.105.3
PRAISE HIM WHICH MADE THAT FIRE, WHICH
                         LENDS THAT LIGHT              2.105.14
AND IF WITH TEARES, I FIND THEM ALL TOO LIGHT          2.121.7
SO $COMET-LIKE EACH STARRE ADVAUNC'D HER LYGHT        2.125.10
THAT LUCKIE $LOAD-STARRE OF ETERNALL LIGHT             2.129.2
THOUGHT HER IN WEIGHT TOO LIGHT BY MANY
                         A GRAINE                      2.131.12
NOR $MOONE NOR STARS LEND THEE THEIR SHINING
                         LIGHT                         2.145.12
WHO LIST TO PRAISE THE DAYES DELICIOUS LYGHT           2.148.1
LOE IN THE $ORIENT WHEN THE GRACIOUS LIGHT             3.7.1
WHEN THOU THY SELFE DOST GIVE INVENTION LIGHT+         3.38.8
TO THE CLEERE DAY WITH THY MUCH CLEERER LIGHT          3.43.7
NATIVITY ONCE IN THE MAINE OF LIGHT                    3.60.5
```

```
WHEN THOU SHALT BE DISPODE TO SET ME LIGHT            3.88.1
DARKNING THY POWRE TO LEND BASE SUBJECTS LIGHT        3.100.4
THE INWARD LIGHT.. AND THAT THE HEAVENLY PART         4.5.2
FRAME DAINTIEST LUSTRE, MIXT OF SHADES AND LIGHT+     4.7.4
DECEIV'D THE QUAKING BOY, WHO THOUGHT
                        FROM SO PURE LIGHT            4.8.10
AND SURE AT LENGTH STOLNE GOODS DO COME TO LIGHT      4.15.11
AND FOOLES CAN THINKE THOSE $LAMPES OF
                        PUREST LIGHT                  4.26.2
A CHAMBER DEAFE TO NOISE, AND BLIND TO LIGHT          4.39.10
LET NOT MINE EYES BE HEL-DRIV'N FROM THAT LIGHT       4.48.7
WHO HARD BY MADE A WINDOW SEND FORTH LIGHT            4.53.9
MINE EYES, MY LIGHT, MY HEART, MY LIFE, ALAS          4.65.9
STELLA, THE ONELY $PLANET OF MY LIGHT                 4.68.1
LIGHT OF MY LIFE, AND LIFE OF MY DESIRE               4.68.2
OF REASON, FROM WHOSE LIGHT THOSE NIGHT-BIRDS
                        FLIE                          4.71.7
THE ONELY LIGHT OF JOY, THE ONELY WARMTH OF $LOVE     4.76.4
SHE COMES WITH LIGHT AND WARMTH, WHICH
                        LIKE $AURORA PROVE            4.76.5
THAT PRESENCE, WHICH DOTH GIVE DARKE HEARTS
                        A LIVING LIGHT                4.77.3
TUSH ABSENCE, WHILE THY MISTES ECLIPSE THAT LIGHT     4.88.9
I AM FROM YOU, LIGHT OF MY LIFE, MIS-LED              4.91.2
IF THIS DARKE PLACE YET SHEW LIKE CANDLE LIGHT        4.91.5
NIGHT BARD FROM $SUN, THOU FROM THY OWNE
                        SUNNE'S LIGHT                 4.96.4
BUT AH POORE $NIGHT, IN LOVE WITH $PHOEBUS' LIGHT     4.97.5
TO WHOM NOR ART NOR NATURE GRAUNTETH LIGHT            4.99.2
SUCH LIGHT IN SENSE, WITH SUCH A DARKNED MIND         4.99.14
THERE SHINES A JOY FROM THEE MY ONLY LIGHT            4.108.4
AND HAPPY LINES, ON WHICH WITH STARRY LIGHT           5.1.5
THE LIGHT WHEROF HATH KINDLED HEAVENLY FYRE           5.3.3
SUCH LIFE SHOULD BE THE HONOR OF YOUR LIGHT           5.7.13
DARK IS THE WORLD, WHERE YOUR LIGHT SHINED NEVER      5.8.13
RESEMBLE TH'YMAGE OF THEIR GOODLY LIGHT               5.9.4
WHOSE LIGHT DOTH LIGHTEN ALL THAT HERE WE SEE         5.9.14
SO FAYRE A PEECE FOR ONE REPULSE SO LIGHT             5.14.4
ON THOSE FAYRE EYES MY LOVES IMMORTALL LIGHT          5.16.2
WITH LOVELY LIGHT TO CLEARE MY CLOUDY GRIEF           5.34.12
AND TO THE LIGHT LIFT UP THEYR DROUPING HED           5.40.12
NOT AYRE., FOR SHE IS NOT SO LIGHT OR RARE            5.55.7
THE BEAME OF LIGHT, WHOM MORTAL EYES ADMYRE           5.61.10
FOR NOW YOUR LIGHT DOTH MORE IT SELFE DILATE          5.66.11
YET SINCE YOUR LIGHT HATH ONCE ENLUMIND ME            5.66.13
RESEMBLING HEAVENS GLORY IN HER LIGHT                 5.72.6
HER GOODLY LIGHT WITH SMILES SHE DRIVES AWAY          5.81.8
NE ONE LIGHT GLANCE OF SENSUALL DESYRE                5.84.3
AND WHEN AS NIGHT HATH US OF LIGHT FORLORNE           5.87.7
SINCE I HAVE LACKT THE COMFORT OF THAT LIGHT          5.88.1
WITH LIGHT THEREOF I DOE MY SELFE SUSTAYNE            5.88.11
DARK IS MY DAY, WHYLES HER FAYRE LIGHT I MIS          5.89.13
```

LIGHTEN   3
```
LIGHTEN FOORTH SMILES TO CLEERE THE CLOUDED AIRE      1.51.9
THOSE POWREFULL EIES, WHICH LIGHTEN MY
                        DARK SPRIGHT                  5.9.2
WHOSE LIGHT DOTH LIGHTEN ALL THAT HERE WE SEE         5.9.14
```

LIGHTENED   1
```
WHICH MY $HEART, LIGHTNED BY THY $LOVE, DOTH SEE      2.12.14
```

LIGHTLY   1
  WHO CAN SHEW ALL HIS LOVE, DOTH LOVE BUT LIGHTLY   1.1.14
LIGHTNESS   1
  THEN HAD NO FINGER POINTED AT MY LIGHTNESSE   1.7.2
LIGHTNING   10
  HER SMILES ARE LIGHTNING, THOUGH HER PRICE
                     DESPAIRE   1.6.3
  NO LIGHTNING LOOKES WHICH FALLING HOPES ERECT   1.31.10
  WITH FLAMES AND LIGHTNING THEIR EXORDIUMS PAYNT 2.118.2
  LIGHTNING THE WORLD, ECLIPSED BY HIS SET   2.125.4
  SLEEPE LIGHTNING $BEAUTY, $BEAUTY SLEEPES
                    DARKNES CLEERETH   2.136.3
  WOUNDED WITH $ARROWES FROM THY LIGHTNING EYES 2.142.5
  BUT STRAIGHT I SAW MOTIONS OF LIGHTNING GRACE 4.20.12
  SHE LIGHTNING $LOVE, DISPLAYING $VENUS' SKIES   4.63.7
  THEN DOE I DIE, AS ONE WITH LIGHTNING FYRED   5.7.8
  NOR TO THE LIGHTNING.. FOR THEY STILL PERSEVER   5.9.9
LIGHTNINGS   2
  WITH $FLAMES AND $LIGHTNINGS THEIR $EXORDIUMS
                    PAINT   2.39.2
  THUNDRED DISDAINES AND LIGHTNINGS OF DISGRACE   4.60.4
LIGHTS   6
  WHERE BLAZE THOSE LIGHTS FAIREST OF EARTHLY
                    THINGS   1.12.3
  THY BLESSED $EYES, THE $SUNNE WHICH LIGHTS
                    THIS $FIRE   2.30.9
  AT WHOSE PURE $EYES, $LOVE LIGHTS HIS
                    HALLOW'D $FIRE   2.57.8
  WHICH DARE CLAIME FROM THOSE LIGHTS THE
                    NAME OF BEST   4.9.11
  AND IF FROM $MAJESTIE OF SACRED LIGHTS   4.42.12
  HER FLAMIE GLISTRING LIGHTS INCREASE WITH
                    TIME AND PLACE   4.76.10
LIGHT'S   1
  FEED'ST THY LIGHTS FLAME WITH SELFE SUBSTANTIALL
                    FEWELL   3.1.6
LIKE   133
  COME TO THEIR VIEW, WHO LIKE AFFLICTED ARE   1.3.3
  MY THOUGHTS (LIKE $HOUNDES) PURSUE ME TO MY DEATH 1.5.12
  MY HEAVY FORTUNE IS MUCH LIKE THE SAME   1.13.3
  BEING MERCILES LIKE THEE THAT NO MAN WEIES+   1.23.8
  AND SEE MY FORTUNE EVER LIKE TO LAST   1.28.11
  LIKE AS THE SPOTLESSE $ERMELIN DISTREST   1.29.1
  BEAUTIE (SWEET $LOVE) IS LIKE THE MORNING DEW   1.50.1
  WHEN EVERY PLACE PRESENTS LIKE FACE OF WOE   1.52.3
  LIKE AS THE $LUTE DELIGHTS OR ELS DISLIKES   1.57.1
  LIKE AN ADVENTUROUS $SEA-FARER AM I   2.1.1
  LIKE GRIZZLED $MOSSE UPON SOME AGED $TREE   2.8.8
  NONE LIKE TO THAT, NONE LIKE TO YOU IS FOUND   2.16.4
  NONE LIKE TO THAT, NONE LIKE TO YOU IS FOUND   2.16.4
  YOUR $LIFE SO LIKE THE $PHOENIXS BEGUN   2.16.8
  THAT SHE IS GONE, HER LIKE AGAINE TO SEE   2.17.14
  MUCH LIKE HIS $WIT, THAT WAS TO USE THE SAME   2.21.8
  AND LIKE A $WANTON, SPORTS WITH EV'RY $FETHER   2.22.6
  I, LIKE A $MAN DEVOUT, AND CHARITABLE   2.23.5
  THAT IT, LIKE THOSE, BY LOOKING MIGHT BE BLEST 2.33.4
  LIKE THEY THAT $LUST, I CARE NOT, I WILL NONE   2.39.8
  SOME $MEN THERE BE, WHICH LIKE MY $METHOD WELL 2.42.1
  WHILST I LIKE $ORPHEUS SING TO $TREES
                    AND $STONES   2.45.12

BUT THOU, WHOSE $PEN HATH LIKE A $PACKE-$HORSE SERV'D	2.49.5
WHOSE $SENSES, LIKE POORE $PRIS'NERS, HUNGER-STARV'D	2.49.7
WHEN LIKE AN $EAGLET I FIRST FOUND MY $LOVE	2.56.1
IT AFTER THEE, IS LIKE AN $EAGLET FLOWNE	2.56.14
SHE WAS, THE LIKE THAT NEVER WAS, NOR NEVER MORE SHALBE	2.107.14
FOR I WAS APT A SCHOLLER LIKE TO PROVE	2.111.3
I LYKE NOT $LIMBO, NOR BLACKE $ACHERON	2.118.8
SOME WITS THERE BE, WHICH LYKE MY METHOD WELL	2.128.1
AND LIKE A $TYRANT MAK'ST MY GRIEFE THY GAME	2.130.12
LYKE IDLE $ECCHOES EVER AUNSWERING.. SO	2.141.7
AND $BEDLAM LIKE THUS RAVING IN MY GRIEFE	2.143.10
DEATH LIKE TO THEE, SO LYVE THOU STILL IN DEATH	2.145.9
SO MAY THE LEARNED LIKE THE SIMILIE	2.148.4
LIKE FEEBLE AGE HE REELETH FROM THE DAY	3.7.10
THE WORLD WILL WAILE THEE LIKE A MAKELESSE WIFE	3.9.4
BE SCORN'D, LIKE OLD MEN OF LESSE TRUTH THEN TONGUE	3.17.10
LET THEM SAY MORE THAT LIKE OF HEARE-SAY WELL	3.21.13
WHICH LIKE A JEWELL (HUNGE IN GASTLY NIGHT)	3.27.11
WISHING ME LIKE TO ONE MORE RICH IN HOPE	3.29.5
FEATUR'D LIKE HIM, LIKE HIM WITH FRIENDS POSSEST	3.29.6
FEATUR'D LIKE HIM, LIKE HIM WITH FRIENDS POSSEST	3.29.6
(LIKE TO THE $LARKE AT BREAKE OF DAYE ARISING)	3.29.11
LIKE STONES OF WORTH THEY THINLY PLACED ARE	3.52.7
BUT YOU LIKE NONE, NONE YOU FOR CONSTANT HEART	3.53.14
LET THIS SAD $INTRIM LIKE THE $OCEAN BE	3.56.9
BUT LIKE A SAD SLAVE STAY AND THINKE OF NOUGHT	3.57.11
LIKE AS THE WAVES MAKE TOWARDS THE PIBLED SHORE	3.60.1
WHILE SHADOWES LIKE TO THEE DO MOCKE MY SIGHT+	3.61.4
AND LIKE UNLETTERED CLARKE STILL CRIE $AMEN	3.85.6
AND LIKE ENOUGH THOU KNOWST THY ESTIMATE	3.87.2
LIKE A DECEIVED HUSBAND, SO LOVES FACE	3.93.2
HOW LIKE $EAVES APPLE DOTH THY BEAUTY GROW	3.93.13
WHICH LIKE A CANKER IN THE FRAGRANT $ROSE	3.95.2
IF LIKE A $LAMBE HE COULD HIS LOOKES TRANSLATE	3.96.10
HOW LIKE A $WINTER HATH MY ABSENCE BEENE	3.97.1
LIKE WIDDOWED WOMBES AFTER THEIR $LORDS DECEASE	3.97.8
THEREFORE LIKE HER, I SOME-TIME HOLD MY TONGUE	3.102.13
AH YET DOTH BEAUTY LIKE A $DYALL HAND	3.104.9
NOTHING SWEET BOY, BUT YET LIKE PRAYERS DIVINE	3.108.5
LIKE HIM THAT TRAVELS I RETURNE AGAINE	3.109.6
TO WHAT IT WORKES IN, LIKE THE $DYERS HAND	3.111.7
WHILST LIKE A WILLING PACIENT I WILL DRINKE	3.111.9
LIKE AS TO MAKE OUR APPETITES MORE KEENE	3.118.1
MY $MISTRES EYES ARE NOTHING LIKE THE $SUNNE	3.130.1
AND SUTE THY PITTY LIKE IN EVERY PART	3.132.12
WHICH LIKE TWO SPIRITS DO SUGJEST ME STILL	3.144.2
DOTH FOLLOW NIGHT WHO LIKE A FIEND	3.145.11
IS GONE, AND NOW LIKE SLAVE-BORNE $MUSCOVITE	4.2.10
WOULD SHE IN BEAMIE BLACKE, LIKE PAINTER WISE	4.7.3
WHOSE FAIRE SKIN, BEAMY EYES, LIKE MORNING SUN ON SNOW	4.8.9
FOR LIKE A CHILD THAT SOME FAIRE BOOKE DOTH FIND	4.11.5
THOU COUNTEST $STELLA THINE, LIKE THOSE WHOSE POWERS	4.12.9
IN NATURE APT TO LIKE WHEN I DID SEE	4.16.1
AND STRAIGHT THEREWITH, LIKE WAGS NEW GOT TO PLAY	4.17.13

```
THAT UNTO ME, WHO FARE LIKE HIM THAT BOTH              4.19.10
WHO LIKE A THEEFE, HID IN DARKE BUSH DOTH LY           4.20.3
THAT MINE OWNE WRITINGS LIKE BAD SERVANTS SHOW         4.21.3
EITHER TO DO LIKE HIM, WHICH OPEN SHONE                4.22.10
LIKE SOME WEAKE $LORDS, NEIGHBORD BY MIGHTY KINGS      4.29.1
TO ME THAT FEELE THE LIKE, THY STATE DESCRIES          4.31.8
WHERE TRUTH IT SELFE MUST SPEAKE LIKE FLATTERIE+       4.35.2
THAT I WELL FIND NO ELOQUENCE LIKE IT                  4.55.14
HAST THOU FOUND SUCH AND SUCH LIKE ARGUMENTS+          4.67.10
SHE COMES WITH LIGHT AND WARMTH, WHICH
                            LIKE $AURORA PROVE         4.76.5
NOR DO LIKE $LORDS, WHOSE WEAKE CONFUSED BRAINE        4.85.5
BUT IF ALL FAITH, LIKE SPOTLESSE $ERMINE LY            4.86.5
IF THIS DARKE PLACE YET SHEW LIKE CANDLE LIGHT         4.91.5
LOVE MOVES THY PAINE, AND LIKE A FAITHFULL PAGE        4.101.9
LYKE CAPTIVES TREMBLING AT THE VICTORS SIGHT           5.1.4
IN WHICH THOU LURKEST LYKE TO VIPERS BROOD             5.2.6
AND HER FAIRE COUNTENANCE LIKE A GOODLY BANNER         5.5.11
SUCH LOVE NOT LYKE TO LUSTS OF BASER KYND              5.6.3
GREAT SHAME IT IS TO LEAVE LIKE ONE AFRAYD             5.14.3
THE SWEET EYE-GLAUNCES, THAT LIKE ARROWES GLIDE        5.17.9
LYKE SACRED PRIESTS THAT NEVER THINKE AMISSE           5.22.8
SUCH LABOUR LIKE THE $SPYDERS WEB I FYND               5.23.13
HOW LONG SHALL THIS LYKE DYING LYFE ENDURE             5.25.1
MY LOVE IS LYKE TO YSE, AND I TO FYRE                  5.30.1
LYKE AS A SHIP THAT THROUGH THE $OCEAN WYDE            5.34.1
IN THEIR AMAZEMENT LYKE $NARCISSUS VAINE               5.35.7
BUT LOTHE THE THINGS WHICH THEY DID LIKE BEFORE        5.35.11
BUT LIKE A STUPID STOCK IN SILENCE DIE                 5.43.8
MOST LIVELY LYKE BEHOLD YOUR SEMBLANT TREW             5.45.4
FOR THEY ARE LYKE BUT UNTO GOLDEN HOOKES               5.47.3
I GOE LYKE ONE THAT HAVING LOST THE FIELD              5.52.2
MY LOVE LYKE THE $SPECTATOR YDLY SITS                  5.54.2
AND MASK IN MYRTH LYKE TO A $COMEDY                    5.54.6
NOT WATER., FOR HER LOVE DOTH BURNE LIKE FYRE          5.55.6
BE LYKE IN MERCY AS IN ALL THE REST                    5.55.14
LIKE A VAINE BUBBLE BLOWEN UP WITH AYRE                5.58.6
BUT LIKE A STEDDY SHIP DOTH STRONGLY PART              5.59.5
HER LIPS DID SMELL LYKE UNTO $GILLYFLOWERS             5.64.5
HER RUDDY CHEEKES LYKE UNTO $ROSES RED                 5.64.6
HER SNOWY BROWES LYKE BUDDED $BELLAMOURES              5.64.7
HER LOVELY EYES LYKE $PINCKS BUT NEWLY SPRED           5.64.8
HER GOODLY BOSOME LYKE A $STRAWBERRY BED               5.64.9
HER NECK LYKE TO A BOUNCH OF $COLLAMBYNES              5.64.10
HER BREST LYKE LILLYES, ERE THEYR LEAVES BE SHED       5.64.11
HER NIPPLES LYKE YONG BLOSSOMD $JESSEMYNES             5.64.12
LYKE AS A HUNTSMAN AFTER WEARY CHACE                   5.67.1
AND FOR THY SAKE THAT ALL LYKE DEARE DIDST BUY         5.68.11
SO LET US LOVE, DEARE LOVE, LYKE AS WE OUGHT           5.68.13
LYKE AS A BYRD THAT IN ONES HAND DOTH SPY              5.73.5
FOR I MY SELVE SHALL LYKE TO THIS DECAY                5.75.7
AND TWIXT HER PAPS LIKE EARLY FRUIT IN $MAY            5.76.9
LYKE A YOUNG FAWNE THAT LATE HATH LOST THE HYND        5.78.2
ALL OTHER FAYRE LYKE FLOWRES UNTYMELY FADE             5.79.14
FAYRE WHEN HER BREST LYKE A RICH LADEN BARKE           5.81.5
IN THEYR AMAZEMENT LYKE $NARCISSUS VAYNE               5.83.7
BUT LOATH THE THINGS WHICH THEY DID LIKE BEFORE        5.83.11
LYKE AS THE $CULVER ON THE BARED BOUGH                 5.89.1
```

LIKED   2

```
I SAW AND LIKED, I LIKED BUT LOVED NOT                 4.2.5
```

```
         I SAW AND LIKED, I LIKED BUT LOVED NOT              4.2.5
LIKELY                     1
         WHO+ CAN HE LOVE+ A LIKELY THING, THEY SAY          2.24.2
LIKEN                      1
         AND TELL ME WHERETO CAN YE LYKEN IT                 5.40.2
LIKENED                    1
         THEN SITH TO HEAVEN YE LYKENED ARE THE BEST         5.55.13
LIKENESS                   1
         WHO LEAVES UNSWAI'D THE LIKENESSE OF A MAN          3.141.11
LIKER                      1
         MUCH LIKER THEN YOUR PAINTED COUNTERFEIT            3.16.8
LIKES                      1
         HOW $ULSTER LIKES OF THAT SAME GOLDEN BIT           4.30.9
LIKEST                     4
         LEAVE WHAT THOU LIKEST NOT, DEALE NOT THOU WITH IT  4.4.4
         THOUGHT WITH GOOD CAUSE THOU LIKEST SO
                                   WELL THE NIGHT            4.96.1
         THEN TO THE $MAKER SELFE THEY LIKEST BE             5.9.13
         LYKEST IT SEEMETH IN MY SIMPLE WIT                  5.40.5
LIKEWISE                   7
         AND SO LIKEWISE, RENOWMED IS THY BLAME              1.56.9
         THEREFORE, I LYKEWISE ON SO HOLY DAY                5.22.3
         LET IT LYKEWISE YOUR GENTLE BREST INSPIRE           5.28.6
         SO MY STORME BEATEN HART LIKEWISE IS CHEARED        5.40.13
         SO LIKEWISE LOVE CHEARE YOU YOUR HEAVY SPRIGHT      5.62.13
         MAY LIKEWISE LOVE THEE FOR THE SAME AGAINE          5.68.10
         AND EEK MY NAME BEE WYPED OUT LYKEWIZE              5.75.8
LIKING                     1
         WITHIN WHAT BOUNDS CAN ONE HIS LIKING STAY          4.35.3
LILIES                     4
         LILLIES THAT FESTER, SMELL FAR WORSE THEN WEEDS     3.94.14
         NOR DID I WONDER AT THE $LILLIES WHITE              3.98.9
         MAKING THOSE $LILLIES AND THOSE $ROSES GROW         4.100.2
         HER BREST LYKE LILLYES, ERE THEYR LEAVES BE SHED    5.64.11
LILIES'                    1
         IN $LILLIES' NEAST, WHERE $LOVE'S SELFE
                                   LIES ALONG                4.83.8
LILY                       2
         THE $LILLIE I CONDEMNED FOR THY HAND                3.99.6
         HAPPY YE LEAVES WHEN AS THOSE LILLY HANDS           5.1.1
LIMBECKS                   1
         DISTIL'D FROM $LYMBECKS FOULE AS HELL WITHIN        3.119.2
LIMBO                      1
         I LYKE NOT $LIMBO, NOR BLACKE $ACHERON              2.118.8
LIMBS                      2
         THE DEARE REPOSE FOR LIMS WITH TRAVAILL TIRED       3.27.2
         LOE THUS BY DAY MY LIMS, BY NIGHT MY MIND           3.27.13
LIMIT                      1
         FINDING THY WORTH A LIMMIT PAST MY PRAISE           3.82.6
LIMITS                     3
         MY HOPES DOE REST IN LIMITS OF HER GRACE            1.12.7
         FROM LIMITS FARRE REMOTE, WHERE THOU DOOST STAY     3.44.4
         THEE TO THY WRACKE BEYOND THY LIMITS STRAINE        4.85.4
LIMN                       1
         WHAT CURIOUS $PENSILL SERVES TO LIM THEE FORTH+     2.146.3
LIMNED                     4
         NOR ARE MY PASSIONS LIMND FOR OUTWARD HEW           1.4.5
         LIMMED WITH A $PENSILL NOT ALL UNWORTHY             1.42.6
         FOR THOUGH THAT $LAURA BETTER LIMNED BE             1.43.13
         IN THIS FAYRE LIMMED GROUND AS WHITE AS SNOW        2.114.10
```

```
LIMPING                    1
  AND STRENGTH BY LIMPING SWAY DISABLED              3.66.8
LINE                       6
  NAY IF YOU READ THIS LINE, REMEMBER NOT            3.71.5
  MY LIFE HATH IN THIS LINE SOME INTEREST            3.74.3
  BUT WHEN YOUR COUNTINANCE FILD UP HIS LINE         3.86.13
  OR WITH STRANGE SIMILIES ENRICH EACH LINE          4.3.7
  THAT TEDIOUS LEASURE MARKS EACH WRINCKLED LINE     4.98.11
  I SAW THY SELFE WITH MANY A SMILING LINE           4.103.2
LINED                      2
  CLOTH'D WITH FINE TROPES, WITH STRONGEST
                      REASONS LIN'D                  4.58.6
  NOT FOR HIS FAIRE CUTSIDE, NOR WELL LINED BRAINE   4.75.3
LINES                     33
  THESE LINES I USE, T'UNBURTHEN MINE OWNE HART      1.4.13
  THEN HAD NO $CENSORS EYE THESE LINES SURVAID       1.7.5
  IN FEELING HEARTS THAT CAN CONCEIVE THESE LINES    1.43.2
  UNBURIED IN THESE LINES RESERV'D IN PURENES        1.44.10
  LIVES IN MY LINES, AND MUST ETERNALL BEE           1.45.14
  LINES OF DELIGHT, WHERECN HER YOUTH MIGHT SMILE    1.51.2
  PAINT SHADOWES IN IMAGINARY LINES                  1.55.3
  WITH MERCENARY LINES, WITH SERVILE $PEN            1.58.6
  UNHAPPY $PEN, AND ILL-ACCEPTED LINES               1.59.1
  SHEW'D IN THESE LINES, THE WORKE OF CAREFULL
                      HOURES                         1.59.7
  THESE $LINES THAT NCW THOU SCORN'ST, WHICH
                      SHOULD DELIGHT THEE            2.8.13
  LETTERS AND $LINES WE SEE ARE SOONE DEFACED        2.13.1
  ELSE SHOULD MY $LINES GLIDE ON THE $WAVES
                      OF $RHENE                      2.25.3
  AND IN MY $LINES, IF SHE MY LOVE MAY SEE           2.42.12
  AGE RULES MY $LINES WITH $WRINKLES IN MY $FACE     2.44.2
  DROWN'D IN THE $TEARES, EXTORTED BY MY $LINES      2.45.2
  AND SAY'ST, MY $LINES BE DULL, AND DOE NCT MCVE    2.49.2
  COME THOU AND READE, ADMIRE, APPLAUD MY $LINES     2.49.14
  LETTERS AND LYNES WE SEE ARE SOONE DEFACED         2.121.1
  AND IN MY LYNES IF SHEE MY LOVE MAY SEE            2.128.12
  GOE YOU MY LYNES, $EMBASSADORS OF LOVE             2.151.1
  SO SHOULD THE LINES OF LIFE THAT LIFE REPAIRE      3.16.9
  WHEN IN ETERNALL LINES TO TIME THOU GROW'ST        3.18.12
  NOR DRAW NOE LINES THERE WITH THINE ANTIQUE PEN    3.19.10
  THESE POORE RUDE LINES CF THY DECEASED $LOVER      3.32.4
  WITH LINES AND WRINCLES, WHEN HIS YOUTHFULL MORNE  3.63.4
  HIS BEAUTIE SHALL IN THESE BLACKE LINES BE SEENE   3.63.13
  DULLING MY LINES, AND DCING ME DISGRACE            3.103.8
  THOSE LINES THAT I BEFORE HAVE WRIT DOE LIE        3.115.1
  AND NOW MY PEN THESE LINES HAD DASHED QUITE        4.50.12
  STELLA, THOSE FAIRE LINES, WHICH TRUE
                      GOODNESSE SHOW                 4.71.4
  AND HAPPY LINES, CN WHICH WITH STARRY LIGHT        5.1.5
  LEAVES, LINES, AND RYMES, SEEKE HER TO
                      PLEASE ALONE                   5.1.13
LINGER                     2
  TO LINGER OUT A PURPOSD CVER-THROW                 3.90.8
  FOR HIS RETURNE THAT SEEMES TO LINGER LATE         5.89.4
LINKS                      1
  BY LINKES OF $LOVE, AND CNLY $NATURE'S ART         4.81.6
LION                       4
  BAYTING THE $LYON IN HIS FURICUS HEAT              2.147.7
  BUT WHILE I THUS WITH THIS YONG $LYON PLAID        4.16.9
```

```
AND YET THE $LYON THAT IS $LORD OF POWER          5.20.5
THEN EITHER $LYON CR THE $LYONESSE                5.20.10
LIONESS                    1
THEN EITHER $LYON OR THE $LYONESSE                5.20.10
LION'S                     2
DEVOURING TIME BLUNT THOU THE $LYONS PAWES        3.19.1
THOUGH STRONGLY HEDG'D OF BLOUDY $LYON'S PAWES    4.75.10
LIP                        4
OF HAND, OF FOOTE, CF LIP, OF EYE, OF BROW        3.106.6
WITH EITHER LIP HE DOTH THE OTHER KISSE           4.43.11
SWEET SWELLING LIP, WELL MAIST THOU SWELL
                        IN PRIDE                  4.80.1
SWEET LIP, YOU TEACH MY MOUTH WITH ONE
                        SWEET KISSE               4.80.14
LIPS                      34
UPON YOUR $LIPS THE SCARLET DROPS ARE FOUND       2.2.10
THY $LIPS, WITH AGE, AS ANY $WAFER THINNE         2.8.10
MY $TASTE BY HER SWEET $LIPS DRAWNE WITH $DELIGHT 2.29.7
WHICH FROM HER LYPS EXHALD REFINED SWEET          2.125.6
HIS STONE-COLD LIPS DOTH KISSE THE BLESSED
                        SHAFT                     2.135.14
THE MORNINGS $CRIMSCN, TO HER LYPS ALIKE          2.148.5
LOV'S NOT $TIMES FOOLE, THOUGH ROSIE LIPS
                        AND CHEEKS                3.116.9
WHILST MY POORE LIPS WHICH SHOULD THAT
                        HARVEST REAPE             3.128.7
MAKING DEAD WOOD MORE BLEST THEN LIVING LIPS      3.128.12
GIVE THEM THEIR FINGERS, ME THY LIPS TO KISSE     3.128.14
CURRALL IS FARRE MORE RED, THEN HER LIPS RED      3.130.2
OR IF IT DO, NOT FROM THOSE LIPS OF THINE         3.142.5
THOSE LIPS THAT $LOVES OWNE HAND DID MAKE         3.145.1
THAT THOSE LIPS SWELL, SC FULL OF THEE THEY BEE   4.12.3
SERVE HIM WITH SHOT, HER LIPS HIS HERALDS ARRE    4.29.10
TO SHEW HER SKIN, LIPS, TEETH AND HEAD SO WELL+   4.32.11
FAIRE EYES, SWEET LIPS, DEARE HEART, THAT
                        FOOLISH I                 4.43.1
WHEN HE WILL PLAY, THEN IN HER LIPS HE IS         4.43.9
HER EYES, HER LIPS, HER ALL, SAITH $LOVE DO THIS  4.52.3
OF THEM, WHO IN THEIR LIPS $LOVE'S STANDERD BEARE 4.54.6
THIS SOWRE-BREATH'D MATE TAST OF THOSE
                        SUGRED LIPS               4.59.11
MY LIPS ARE SWEET, INSPIRED WITH $STELLA'S KISSE  4.74.14
THOSE LIPS, WHICH MAKE DEATH'S PAY A MEANE
                        PRICE FOR A KISSE         4.77.6
TEACHING DUMBE LIPS A NOBLER EXERCISE             4.81.4
BUT YOU MUST NEEDS WITH THOSE LIPS BILLING BE+    4.83.12
AND THROUGH THOSE LIPS DRINKE $NECTAR
                        FROM THAT TOONG           4.83.13
THE GLOBE OF WEALE, LIPS $LOVE'S INDENTURES MAKE  4.85.13
I SAW THAT SIGHES HER SWEETEST LIPS DID PART      4.87.7
THINE EYES MY PRIDE, THY LIPS MY HISTORY          4.90.3
MILKE HANDS, ROSE CHEEKS, OR LIPS MORE
                        SWEET, MORE RED           4.91.7
IF HER LIPS DAIGND TO SWEETEN MY POORE NAME       4.92.13
IF $RUBIES, LOE HIR LIPS BE $RUBIES SOUND         5.15.8
COMMING TO KISSE HER LYPS, (SUCH GRACE I FOUND)   5.64.1
HER LIPS DID SMELL LYKE UNTO $GILLYFLOWERS        5.64.5
LIQUID                     2
MY LIQUIDS THEN WERE LIQUID CHRISTALL TEARES      2.111.9
A LIQUID PRISONER PENT IN WALLS OF GLASSE         3.5.10
```

```
LIQUIDS                     1
  MY LIQUIDS THEN WERE LIQUID CHRISTALL TEARES        2.111.9
LIQUOR                      1
  BY KNIFE, BY LIQUOR, OR BY SALVE TO DEALE           1.14.11
LIST                        5
  AND LIST NOT SEEKE TO BREAKE, TO QUENCH, TO HEALE   1.14.9
  WHO LIST TO PRAISE THE DAYES DELICIOUS LYGHT        2.148.1
  BE WHERE YOU LIST, YOUR CHARTER IS SO STRONG        3.58.9
  I LIST NOT DIG SO DEEPE FOR BRASEN FAME             4.28.4
  AND FASHION TO WHAT HE IT LIST APPLY                5.32.4
LISTEN                      1
  LISTEN THEN $LORDINGS WITH GOOD EARE TO ME          4.37.3
LITTLE                     19
  ONELY THAT LITTLE WHICH TO $ME WAS LENT             2.10.13
  LITTLE $ILE SAY, BUT THINKE THE $DEVILL'S IN ME     2.15.14
  WITH $SHOWTS AND $CLAPS AT EV'RY LITTLE PAWSE       2.47.9
  HOLDS IN PERFECTICN BUT A LITTLE MOMENT             3.15.2
  THIS LITTLE $LOVE-$GOD LYING ONCE A SLEEPE          3.154.1
  THE LITLE REASON THAT IS LEFT IN ME                4.4.10
  LITLE HE IS, SO LITLE WORTH IS HE                  4.59.5
  LITLE HE IS, SO LITLE WORTH IS HE                  4.59.5
  THEN THINKE NOT LCNG IN TAKING LITLE PAINE          5.6.13
  BUT HER PROUD HART DOE THOU A LITTLE SHAKE          5.10.9
  LEGIONS OF LOVES WITH LITTLE WINGS DID FLY          5.16.6
  MOST SORTS OF MEN DCE SET BUT LITTLE STORE          5.26.12
  WHY THEN SHOULD I ACCOUMPT OF LITTLE PAINE          5.26.13
  HOW EVER NOW THERECF YE LITTLE WEENE                5.27.4
  THEN THINKE HOW LITLE GLCRY YE HAVE GAYNED          5.36.10
  VAYNE MAN (QUOD I) THAT HAST BUT LITTLE PRIEFE      5.50.5
  THAT AL MY WOUNDS WIL HEALE IN LITTLE SPACE         5.57.14
  TO ME YOUR THRALL, IN WHOM IS LITTLE WORTH          5.82.10
  THAT LITTLE THAT I AM, SHALL ALL BE SPENT           5.82.11
LIVE                       69
  LIVE RECONCILED FRIENDS WITHIN HER BROW             1.6.10
  IF THIS BE LOVE, TC LIVE A LIVING DEATH             1.9.13
  THAT WEARY OF MY LIFE, I LOATH TO LIVE              1.16.8
  AND THUS I LIVE BECAUSE I LOVE HER DEERLY           1.16.14
  WHY SHOULD I STRIVE TO MAKE HER LIVE FOR EVER       1.17.5
  THAT NEVER DEIGNES TO GIVE ME JOY TO LIVE+          1.17.6
  WHAT IT IS TO BREATHE AND LIVE WITHOUT LIFE         1.20.1
  SITH I LIVE HATEFULL TC THOSE RUTHLESSE EIES        1.21.7
  THAT THUS I LIVE BCTH DAY AND NIGHT ANNOYD          1.26.8
  BUT ($PHAENIX-LIKE) SHALL MAKE HER LIVE ANEW        1.38.14
  IF THEY REMAINE, THEN THCU SHALT LIVE THEREBY       1.42.13
  THEN SHOULDST THOU LIVE IN AN IMMORTALL STILE       1.43.12
  HOW MANY LIVE, THE GLORY OF WHOSE NAME              1.44.7
  THOU MAIST IN AFTER AGES LIVE ESTEEM'D              1.44.9
  FROM OUT DISPAIRE, WHEREIN THEY LIVE CONFINDE+      1.49.4
  AND HOW I LIVE CAST DOWNE FROM OFF ALL MYRTH        1.60.9
  AND $QUEENES HEREAFTER SHALL BE GLAD TO LIVE        2.6.7
  SO YOU OF $TIME SHALL LIVE BEYOND THE $END          2.16.14
  SO MAY'ST THOU LIVE, TO THY FAIRE $MOTHERS $JOY     2.48.12
  SO MAIST THOU LIVE, PAST WORLD, PAST FAME,
                              PAST END                2.106.14
  WHERE HUNGER-STARVEN, WANTING LOOKES TO LIVE        2.116.13
  THAT FAYRE $IDEA SHEE DCTH LIVE BY THEE             2.124.14
  DEATH LIKE TO THEE, SO LYVE THOU STILL IN DEATH     2.145.9
  BUT IF THOU LIVE REMEMBRED NOT TO BE                3.3.13
  SO GREAT A SUMME CF SUMMES YET CAN'ST NOT LIVE+     3.4.8
  THAT BEAUTY STILL MAY LIVE IN THINE OR THEE         3.10.14
```

NO LONGER YOURS, THEN YOU YOUR SELFE HERE LIVE	3.13.2
CAN MAKE YOU LIVE YCUR SELFE IN EIES OF MEN	3.16.12
AND YOU MUST LIVE DRAWNE BY YOUR OWNE	
SWEET SKILL	3.16.14
YOU SHOULD LIVE TWISE IN IT, AND IN MY RIME	3.17.14
MY LOVE SHALL IN MY VERSE EVER LIVE YOUNG	3.19.14
WHICH IN THY BREST DOTH LIVE, AS THINE IN ME	3.22.7
THOU ART THE GRAVE WHERE BURIED LOVE DOTH LIVE	3.31.9
AND BY A PART OF ALL THY GLORY LIVE	3.37.12
EVEN FOR THIS, LET US DEVIDED LIVE	3.39.5
FOR THAT SWEET ODOR, WHICH DOTH IN IT LIVE	3.54.4
THEY LIVE UNWOO'D, AND UNRESPECTED FADE	3.54.10
YOU LIVE IN THIS, AND DWELL IN LOVERS EIES	3.55.14
AND THEY SHALL LIVE, AND HE IN THEM STILL GREENE	3.63.14
AH WHEREFORE WITH INFECTION SHOULD HE LIVE	3.67.1
WHY SHOULD HE LIVE, NOW NATURE BANCKROUT IS	3.67.9
TO LIVE A SCOND LIFE ON SECOND HEAD	3.68.7
AND LIVE NO MORE TC SHAME NOR ME, NOR YOU	3.72.12
NO PRAISE TO THEE, BUT WHAT IN THEE DOTH LIVE	3.79.12
OR I SHALL LIVE YCUR $EPITAPH TO MAKE	3.81.1
YOU STILL SHALL LIVE (SUCH VERTUE HATH MY $PEN)	3.81.13
SO SHALL I LIVE, SUPPOSING THOU ART TRUE	3.93.1
FOR THEIR CAN LIVE NO HATRED IN THINE EYE	3.93.5
THOUGH TO IT SELFE, IT CNELY LIVE AND DIE	3.94.10
SINCE SPIGHT OF HIM $ILE LIVE IN THIS	
POORE RIME	3.107.11
YET THIS SHAL I NERE KNCW BUT LIVE IN DOUBT	3.144.13
THEN SOULE LIVE THCU UPCN THY SERVANTS LCSSE	3.146.9
THE PRETTIE DEATH, WHILE EACH IN OTHER LIVE	4.79.11
WHO SEEKE, WHO HOPE, WHC LOVE, WHO LIVE BUT THEE	4.90.2
WITH ABSENCE' $VAILE, I LIVE IN $SOROWE'S NIGHT	4.91.4
I HAVE (LIVE I AND KNOW THIS) HARMED THEE	4.93.10
ALL MIRTH FAREWELL, LET ME IN SORROW LIVE	4.100.14
WHICH IF SHE GRAUNT, THEN LIVE AND MY	
LOVE CHERISH	5.2.13
TO FORCE ME LIVE AND WILL NOT LET ME DY	5.11.12
SO DYING LIVE, AND LIVING DO ADORE HER	5.14.14
AND THINCK THEY DY WITH PLEASURE, LIVE	
WITH PAYNE	5.47.14
YET LIVE FOR EVER, THOUGH AGAINST HER WILL	5.48.13
SO SHALL YOU LIVE BY GIVING LIFE TO ME	5.49.14
THAT WONDER IS HOW I SHCULD LIVE A JOT	5.57.6
IN SLAYING HIM THAT WOULD LIVE GLADLY YOURS+	5.57.12
MAY LIVE FOR EVER IN FELICITY	5.68.8
YE THREE $ELIZABETHS FOR EVER LIVE	5.74.13
TO DY IN DUST, BUT YOU SHALL LIVE BY FAME	5.75.10
OUR LOVE SHALL LIVE, AND LATER LIFE RENEW	5.75.14

LIVED   9

STILL HAVE I LIV'D IN GRIEFE, IN HOPE, IN TERROR	1.18.3
SUFFICE, THEY SHEW I LIV'D AND LOV'D THEE DEARE	1.55.14
MY GRIEFES LONG LIV'D, AND CARE SUCCEEDING CARE	1.60.12
THAT THEY SHALL GRIEVE, THEY LIV'D NOT	
IN THESE $TIMES	2.6.11
AND BURNE THE LONG LIV'D $PHAENIX IN HER BLOCD	3.19.4
WHEN BEAUTY LIV'D AND DY'ED AS FLOWERS DC NOW	3.68.2
WHAT MERIT LIV'D IN ME THAT YOU SHOULD LCVE	3.72.2
FAIRE, KINDE, AND TRUE, HAVE OFTEN LIV'D ALONE	3.105.13
WHICH DIE FOR GOODNES, WHO HAVE LIV'D FOR CRIME	3.124.14

LIVELESS   1

OF LIVELESSE $CLODS, US LIVING $MEN TO MAKE	2.14.7

LIVELIER   1
  LIVELIER THEN ELSE-WHERE, $STELLA'S IMAGE SEE   4.39.14
LIVELY   10
  WHO HAD LESSE $ART THEM LIVELY TO EXPRESSE+   2.27.6
  THE LIVELY $IMAGE OF $DIVINITIE   2.146.14
  BEGGERD OF BLOOD TO BLUSH THROUGH LIVELY VAINES   3.67.10
  A DATELESSE LIVELY HEAT STILL TO INDURE   3.153.6
  EFFECTS OF LIVELY HEAT, MUST NEEDS IN NATURE GROW   4.8.11
  MORPHEUS, THE LIVELY SONNE OF DEADLY SLEEPE   4.32.1
  PRINTS HIS OWNE LIVELY FORME IN RUDEST BRAINE   4.58.8
  PAINT WOE'S BLACKE FACE .SO LIVELY TO MY SIGHT   4.98.10
  MOST LIVELY LYKE BEHOLD YOUR SEMBLANT TREW   5.45.4
  AND DEAD MY LIFE THAT WANTS SUCH LIVELY BLIS   5.89.14
LIVERY   5
  THY YOUTHES PROUD LIVERY SO GAZ'D ON NOW   3.2.3
  IN $MARSE'S LIVERIE, PRAUNCING IN THE PRESSE   4.53.6
  GRIEFE BUT $LOVE'S WINTER LIVERIE IS, THE $BOY   4.70.7
  SINCE KIND OR CHANCE GIVES BOTH ONE LIVERIE   4.96.2
  UPON THY CHEEREFULL FACE, JOYE'S LIVERY WEARE   4.103.3
LIVES   15
  BY LOVING HER, THE CRUELST $FAIRE THAT LIVES   1.22.10
  LIVES WITHOUT HONOUR, DIES WITHOUT A NAME   1.35.11
  LIVES IN MY LINES, AND MUST ETERNALL BEE   1.45.14
  THEN I WOULD JOY THE FAIREST SHE THAT LIVES   1.48.12
  THAT FAIRE $IDEA ONELY LIVES BY THEE   2.32.14
  WHICH USED LIVES TH'EXECUTOR TO BE   3.4.14
  LEESE BUT THEIR SHOW, THEIR SUBSTANCE
                      STILL LIVES SWEET   3.5.14
  HEREIN LIVES WISDOME, BEAUTY, AND INCREASE   3.11.5
  SO LONG LIVES THIS, AND THIS GIVES LIFE TO THEE   3.18.14
  AND LOATHSOME CANKER LIVES IN SWEETEST BUD   3.35.4
  THOUGH IN OUR LIVES A SEPERABLE SPIGHT   3.36.6
  AND PROUD OF MANY, LIVES UPON HIS GAINES+   3.67.12
  THERE LIVES MORE LIFE IN ONE OF YOUR FAIRE EYES   3.83.13
  BUT IS PROPHAN'D, IF NOT LIVES IN DISGRACE   3.127.8
  CHAUNGE EEKE OUR MYNDS AND FORMER LIVES AMEND   5.62.6
LIVE'S   6
  ALL MY LIVES SWEET CONSISTS IN HER ALONE   1.12.13
  THAT MY LIVES LIGHT WHOLY IN-DARKNED IS   1.21.4
  MY LIVES SWEET SUNNE, MY DEAREST COMFORTS LIGHT   1.30.3
  MY $LIVES COMPLAINT IN DOLEFULL $ELEGIES   2.54.7
  MY LIVES COMPLAINT IN DOLEFUL $ELEGIES   2.101.7
  MY DOLEFULL $DYPTHONGS WERE MY LIVES DISPAIRES   2.111.11
LIVING   25
  IF THIS BE LOVE, TO LIVE A LIVING DEATH   1.9.13
  IF $HE, FROM $HEAV'N THAT FILCH'D THAT
                      LIVING $FIRE   2.14.1
  OF LIVELESSE $CLODS, US LIVING $MEN TO MAKE   2.14.7
  WHICH BEST BY YOU, OF LIVING $THINGS, IS KNOWNE   2.16.3
  AND CROWNE THE $PIRENS WITH MY LIVING $SONG   2.25.4
  HOW HAPPY ARE ALL OTHER LIVING $THINGS   2.37.5
  THE STRONG-BUILT $TROPHIES TO HER LIVING $FAME   2.45.6
  WHICH ON THE $LIVING WORKE WITHOUT REMORSE   2.50.5
  WHO THEN YET LIVING, DEEMD SHE HAD BEEN DYING   2.109.6
  LEAVING THEE LIVING IN POSTERITY+   3.6.12
  WITH VERTUOUS WISH WOULD BEARE YOUR LIVING
                      FLOWERS   3.16.7
  BY LOOKING ON THEE IN THE LIVING DAY+   3.43.10
  THE LIVING RECORD OF YOUR MEMORY   3.55.8
  AND STEALE DEAD SEEING OF HIS LIVING HEW+   3.67.6

OR DURST INHABIT CN A LIVING BROW   3.68.4
MAKING DEAD WOOD MCRE BLEST THEN LIVING LIPS   3.128.12
OF LIVING DEATHS, CEARE WOUNDS, FAIRE
                         STORMES AND FREESING FIRES 4.6.4
WITNESSE OF LIFE TC THEM THAT LIVING DIE   4.32.2
THAT PRESENCE, WHICH DOTH GIVE DARKE HEARTS
                         A LIVING LIGHT   4.77.3
THAT LIVING THUS IN BLACKEST WINTER NIGHT   4.89.13
MAY KINDLE LIVING FIRE WITHIN MY BREST   5.7.12
MORE THEN MOST FAIRE, FULL OF THE LIVING FIRE   5.8.1
SO DYING LIVE, AND LIVING DO ADORE HER   5.14.14
THAT MOTE ENLARGE HER LIVING PRAYSES DEAC   5.33.4
OR LEND YOU ME ANCTHER LIVING BREST   5.33.14
LO   19
  FOR HAPLESSE LOE EVEN WITH MINE OWNE DESIRES   1.13.5
  WHERE LOE I LANGUISH IN SO HEAVY SMART   1.36.6
  WHEN YET TH'UNBORNE SHALL SAY, $LO WHERE SHE LIES 1.55.7
  LO HERE THE IMPOST CF A FAITH ENTIRE   1.60.1
  LOE, HEERE THY $SHEPHEARD SPENT HIS WANDRING
                         YEERES   2.53.10
  LOE, HEERE THY $SHEPHEARD SPENT HIS WANDRING
                         YEERES   2.113.10
  LOE WHERE SHE DROWNES, IN STORMES OF THY
                         DISPLEASURE   2.134.13
  NOW WAS THY PRYME, AND LCE, NOW IS THY WAINE   2.141.13
  LOE THUS MY LOVE, MY LYFE, MY FORTUNE TRYES   2.142.4
  LOE IN THE $ORIENT WHEN THE GRACIOUS LIGHT   3.7.1
  LOE THUS BY DAY MY LIMS, BY NIGHT MY MIND   3.27.13
  LOE AS A CAREFULL HUSWIFE RUNNES TO CATCH   3.143.1
  THEN WITH THOSE EYES HE LOOKES, LO BY AND BY   4.43.6
  BUT LO, WHILE I DC SPEAKE, IT GROWETH
                         NOONE WITH ME   4.76.9
  BREAKEFAST OF $LOVE, BUT LO, LO, WHERE SHE IS   4.79.13
  BREAKEFAST OF $LOVE, BUT LO, LO, WHERE SHE IS   4.79.13
  FOR LOE MY LOVE DCTH IN HER SELFE CONTAINE   5.15.5
  IF $SAPHYRES, LOE HER EIES BE $SAPHYRES PLAINE   5.15.7
  IF $RUBIES, LOE HIR LIPS BE $RUBIES SOUND   5.15.8
LOAD   1
  LET WO GRIPE ON MY HEART, SHAME LOADE MINE EYE   4.86.4
LOADSTONE   1
  CELESTIALL $IMAGE, $LOAC-STONE OF DESIRE   2.123.6
LOAN   1
  WHICH HAPPIES THOSE THAT PAY THE WILLING LONE   3.6.6
LOATHE   3
  THAT WEARY OF MY LIFE, I LOATH TO LIVE   1.16.8
  BUT LOTHE THE THINGS WHICH THEY DID LIKE BEFCRE   5.35.11
  BUT LOATH THE THINGS WHICH THEY DID LIKE BEFCRE   5.83.11
LOATHING   2
  A LOATHING OF ALL LCOSE UNCHASTITIE   4.14.13
  LOATHING ALL LIES, DOUBTING THIS $FLATTERIE IS   4.80.11
LOATHSOME   4
  LOTHSOME THEIR DAIES, WHOM NO SUN EVER JCYD   1.26.6
  CIRCUMPASS'D ROUND WITH FILTH AND LOTHSOME MUD   1.29.2
  AND LOATHSOME CANKER LIVES IN SWEETEST BUD   3.35.4
  TREADING DOWNE EARTH AS LOTHSOME AND FORLORNE   5.13.11
LOCK   2
  STRONG LOCKE OF KINDNESSE, $CLOSET OF
                         LOVES STORE   2.146.5
  RED $PORPHIR IS, WHICH LCCKE OF PEARLE MAKES SURE 4.9.6

LOCKED   1
  THEE HAVE I NOT LOCKT UP IN ANY CHEST   3.48.9
LOCKS   6
    THOSE SNARY LOCKS, ARE THOSE SAME NETS
                          (MY $DEERE)   1.14.1
    THAT FROM HER LOCKES, THY DAY-NETS, NONE
                          SCAPES FREE   4.12.2
    NOR NOURISH SPECIALL LOCKES OF VOWED HAIRE   4.54.3
    FIRST DID WITH PUFFING KISSE THOSE LOCKES
                          DISPLAY   4.103.11
    WHERE RIGROWS EXILE LOCKES UP ALL MY SENSE+   4.104.8
    IF $GOLD, HER LOCKS ARE FINEST GOLD ON GROUND   5.15.11
LODEN   1
  YET MY HOPES WINGS ARE LODEN SO WITH FEARE   2.137.6
LODESTAR   2
    THAT LUCKIE $LOAD-STARRE OF ETERNALL LIGHT   2.129.2
    MY $HELICE THE LODESTAR OF MY LYFE   5.34.10
LODGE   1
    THOUGH HARBENGERS OF DEATH LODGE THERE HIS TRAINE   4.94.8
LODGED   4
    CLOTHED THE $NAKED, LODG'D THIS WAND'RING $GHEST   2.23.6
    SHALL HATE BE FAIRER LOG'D THEN GENTLE LOVE+   3.10.10
    I LODG'D THEE IN MY HEART, AND BEING BLIND   4.65.7
    HOW $VERTUE MAY BEST LODG'D IN BEAUTIE BE   4.71.2
LODGING   3
    AND SET MY $BREST, HIS $LODGING, ON A FIRE   2.23.12
    HIM LODGING IN YOUR BOSOME TO HAVE LENT   5.73.14
    THE NEAST OF LOVE, THE LODGING OF DELIGHT   5.76.2
LODWICK   1
    BUT LODWICK, THIS OF GRACE TO ME AREAD   5.33.5
LOFTY   9
    THE BROKEN TOPS OF LOFTY TREES DECLARE   1.37.5
    AND SAY MY VERSE RUNNES IN A LOFTY VAYNE   2.128.2
    WHEN LOFTY TREES I SEE BARREN OF LEAVES   3.12.5
    WHEN SOMETIME LOFTIE TOWERS I SEE DOWNE RASED   3.64.3
    FOR IN THOSE LOFTY LOOKES IS CLOSE IMPLIDE   5.5.5
    BUT THAT SAME LOFTY COUNTENANCE SEEMES TO SCORNE   5.13.9
    SUCH LOWLINESSE SHALL MAKE YOU LOFTY BE   5.13.14
    THE LOVELY PLEASANCE AND THE LOFTY PRIDE   5.17.11
    WHOSE LOFTY ARGUMENT UPLIFTING ME   5.82.13
LONG   69
    YET LEAST LONG TRAVAILES BE ABOVE MY STRENGTH   1.14.13
    IF HUNGER-STARVEN THOUGHTS SO LONG RETAINED   1.15.3
    LONG ARE THEIR NIGHTS WHOSE CARES DO NEVER SLEEPE   1.26.5
    THUS SHADES MY LIFE SO LONG AS WANTS ENDURE   1.29.14
    THEN FADE THOSE FLOWERS THAT DECKT HER
                          PRIDE SO LONG   1.38.8
    HOW LONG SHALL I IN MINE AFFLICTION MOURNE+   1.49.1
    MY GRIEFES LONG LIV'D, AND CARE SUCCEEDING CARE   1.60.12
    WHO HATH SOME LONG AND DANG'ROUS $VOYAGE BEENE   2.1.2
    WHICH STILL SHALT BE, AS LONG AS THERE IS $SUNNE   2.13.10
    WHERE WITH (ALAS) I HAVE BEENE LONG POSSEST   2.20.2
    MY $HOPES REVIV'D, WHICH LONG IN $GRAVE HAD LYNE   2.35.12
    MY $BRAINE IS DRIE WITH WEEPING ALL TOO LONG   2.41.6
    KINDER THEN SHE WHOM I SO LONG HAVE LOVED   2.45.14
    LONG SINCE DEPARTED (TO THE $WORLD NO MORE)   2.46.10
    ME THINKES 'TIS LONG SINCE FIRST THESE
                          $WARRES BEGUN   2.63.2
    FROM WORLD TO WORLD, THOU LONG HAST SOUGHT
                          TO SEE   2.107.2

```
MY HOPES REVIV'D WHICH LONG IN GRAVE HAD LYNE      2.112.12
SHEE OF WHOM $MERLIN LONG TYME DID FORE-TELL        2.119.10
WHICH STILL SHALT BE AS LONG AS THERE IS $SUNNE     2.121.10
MY BRAYNE IS DRY WITH WEEPING ALL TOO LONG           2.143.6
STILL TO PROLONG MY LONG TYME LOOKT-FOR MORROW+      2.145.4
SO LONG AS MEN CAN BREATH OR EYES CAN SEE            3.18.13
SO LONG LIVES THIS, AND THIS GIVES LIFE TO THEE      3.18.14
AND BURNE THE LONG LIV'D $PHAENIX IN HER BLOOD        3.19.4
SO LONG AS YOUTH AND THOU ARE OF ONE DATE             3.22.2
AND WEEPE A FRESH LOVES LONG SINCE CANCELD WOE        3.30.7
ETERNAL NUMBERS TO OUT-LIVE LONG DATE                3.38.12
SINCE SILDOM COMMING IN THE LONG YEARE SET            3.52.6
IN DAIES LONG SINCE, BEFORE THESE LAST SO BAD        3.67.14
TO LOVE THAT WELL, WHICH THOU MUST LEAVE
                    ERE LONG                         3.73.14
WHERE ART THOU $MUSE THAT THOU FORGETST SO LONG      3.100.1
TO MAKE HIM SEEME LONG HENCE, AS HE SHOWES NOW      3.101.14
OR AT THE LEAST, SO LONG AS BRAINE AND HEART        3.122.5
YOU THAT POORE $PETRARCH'S LONG DECEASED WOES        4.15.7
BEWRAY IT SELFE IN MY LONG SETLED EYES               4.23.2
SURE, IF THAT LONG WITH $LOVE ACQUAINTED EYES        4.31.5
HIM AS THY SLAVE, AND NOW LONG NEEDY $FAME          4.35.10
WHERETO LONG SINCE, THROUGH MY LONG BATTRED EYES     4.36.3
WHERETO LONG SINCE, THROUGH MY LONG BATTRED EYES     4.36.3
AND THERE LONG SINCE, $LOVE THY $LIEUTENANT LIES     4.36.5
LONG SINCE FORC'D BY THY BEAMES, BUT STONE
                    NOR TREE                         4.36.13
UPON A WRETCH, THAT LONG THY GRACE HATH SOUGHT       4.40.7
SO LONG (THOUGH HE FROM BOOKE MYCHE TO DESIRE)      4.46.13
WHO FOR LONG FAITH, THO DAYLY HELPE I CRAVE          4.47.7
FAR FAR TOO LONG TO LEARNE IT WITHOUT BOOKE          4.56.2
NOW I, WIT-BEATEN LONG BY HARDEST $FATE              4.60.9
OR DOTH THE TEDIOUS BURD'N OF LONG WO                4.66.2
BUT WITH SHORT BREATH, LONG LOOKES, STAID
                    FEET AND WALKING HED            4.76.13
GOOD BROTHER $PHILIP, I HAVE BORNE YOU LONG          4.83.1
EACH DAY SEEMES LONG, AND LONGS FOR LONG-STAID
                    NIGHT                            4.89.5
MY SOULES LONG LACKED FOODE, MY HEAVENS BLIS         5.1.12
FRESH LOVE, THAT LONG HATH SLEPT IN CHEERLESSE
                    BOWER                            5.4.6
IS LONG ERE IT CONCEIVE THE KINDLING FYRE            5.6.6
THEN THINKE NOT LONG IN TAKING LITLE PAINE          5.6.13
A WICKED AMBUSH WHICH LAY HIDDEN LONG               5.12.6
AND LONG INTREATY SOFTEN HER HARD HART              5.18.6
FOR WITH ONE LOOKE SHE SPILS THAT LONG I SPONNE    5.23.11
HOW LONG SHALL THIS LYKE DYING LYFE ENDURE          5.25.1
MOTE HAVE YOUR LIFE IN HONOUR LONG MAINTAYNED       5.36.12
AS BEING LONG IN HER LOVES TEMPEST TOST            5.41.11
LONG LANGUISHING IN DOUBLE MALADY                    5.50.1
WHICH I HAVE WASTED IN LONG LANGUISHMENT           5.60.11
AFTER LONG STORMES AND TEMPESTS SAD ASSAY           5.63.1
IN WHICH I HOPE ERE LONG FOR TO ARRYVE              5.63.6
SO AFTER LONG PURSUIT AND VAINE ASSAY               5.67.5
GOTTEN AT LAST WITH LABOUR AND LONG TOYLE          5.69.14
AFTER SO LONG A RACE AS I HAVE RUN                   5.80.1
MANY LONG WEARY DAYES I HAVE OUTWORNE                5.87.2
SO SORROW STILL DOTH SEEME TOO LONG TO LAST         5.87.13
```

LONGED   1
```
NOR AT $FIFTEENE NE'R LONG'D TO BE A $BRIDE          2.15.6
```

```
LONGER                    12
   TH'ANCIENT $WOUNDS NO LONGER CAN CONTAINE              2.46.11
   NO LONGER YOURS, THEN YOU YOUR SELFE HERE LIVE         3.13.2
   BUT DAY DOTH DAILY DRAW MY SORROWES LONGER             3.28.13
   THIS TOLD, I JOY, BUT THEN NO LONGER GLAD              3.45.13
   NOE $LONGER MOURNE FOR ME WHEN I AM DEAD               3.71.1
   AND LIFE NO LONGER THEN THY LOVE WILL STAY             3.92.3
   FOR THAT WHICH LONGER NURSETH THE DISEASE              3.147.2
   FAINT COWARD JOY NO LONGER TARRY DARE                  4.95.5
   FAIRE BE NO LENGER PROUD OF THAT SHALL PERISH          5.27.13
   WHICH I NO LENGER CAN ENDURE TO SUE                    5.57.3
   THE WHICH DOTH LONGER UNTO ME APPEARE                  5.60.7
   THAT SEEMD THE LONGER FOR MY GREATER PAINES            5.60.12
LONGING                   1
   MY LOVE IS AS A FEAVER LONGING STILL                   3.147.1
LONG-LIVING               1
   THE QUIET END OF THAT $LONG-LIVING QUEENE              2.51.7
LONG-LOOKED               1
   AND SO WITH LOOKES, PROLONGS MY LONG-LOOKT EASE        1.24.10
LONGS                     1
   EACH DAY SEEMES LONG, AND LONGS FOR LONG-STAID
                         NIGHT                            4.89.5
LONG-STAYED               1
   EACH DAY SEEMES LONG, AND LONGS FOR LONG-STAID
                         NIGHT                            4.89.5
LONGWHILE                 2
   LONG-WHILE I SOUGHT TO WHAT I MIGHT COMPARE            5.9.1
   LONGWHILE ALONE IN LANGUOR TO REMAINE                  5.52.8
LOOK                      68
   HOW THEY WERE SPENT FOR THEE., LOOKE WHAT THEY ARE     1.1.8
   LOOKE ON THE DEERE EXPENCES OF MY YOUTH                1.1.9
   THE WONDER OF ALL EYES THAT LOOKE UPON HER             1.6.7
   NO DOWNE-CAST LOOKE HAD SIGNIFIED MY MISSE             1.7.10
   SINCE THE FIRST LOOKE THAT LED ME TO THIS ERROR        1.18.1
   SHE THINKES A LOOKE MAY RECOMPENCE MY CARE             1.24.9
   FED WITH SOME PLEASING LOOKE THERE SHALL SHE BE        1.25.11
   LOOKE IN MY GRIEFES, AND BLAME ME NOT TO MOURNE        1.26.1
   WHEN BACKE I LOOKE, I SIGH MY FREEDOME PAST            1.28.9
   LOOKE TO THE HEAVENS., THE HEAVENS YEELDE
                         FORTH NO GRACE                   1.29.6
   AND DOEST NOT RATHER LOCKE ON HIM (ALAS)               1.37.3
   LOOKE $DELIA HOW W'ESTEEME THE HALFE BLOWNE $ROSE      1.39.1
   MOST FAIRE AND LOVELY $MAIDE, LOOKE FROM
                         THE SHORE                        1.46.1
   TIME, LOOKE THOU TOO, IN THIS $TRALUCENT $GLASSE       2.17.5
   I QUAKE TO LOOKE ON $HECAT'S CHARMING $BOOKES          2.39.11
   LOOKE $THOU INTO MY BREST, AND $THOU SHALT SEE         2.55.9
   LOOKE THOU INTO MY BREAST, AND THOU SHALT SEE          2.102.9
   NAY, LOOKE THEE $TIME IN THIS $CELESTIALL GLASSE       2.107.5
   I QUAKE TO LOOKE ON $HECATS CHARMING BOOKES            2.118.11
   WHO IN HER PRIDE SDAYNES ONCE TO LOOKE ON MEE          2.123.12
   TO LOOKE ON HER BY WHOM MINE EYES ARE BLEST            2.133.4
   MY $FAYRE, LOOKE FROM THOSE TURRETS OF
                         THINE EYES                       2.134.1
   LOOKE IN THY GLASSE AND TELL THE FACE THOU VEWEST      3.3.1
   FROM HIS LOW TRACT AND LOOKE AN OTHER WAY              3.7.12
   LOOKE WHAT AN UNTHRIFT IN THE WORLD DOTH SPEND         3.9.9
   LOOKE WHOM SHE BEST INDOW'D, SHE GAVE THE MORE         3.11.11
   THEN LOOK I DEATH MY DAIES SHOULD EXPIATE              3.22.4
   WHO PLEADE FOR LOVE, AND LOOK FOR RECOMPENCE           3.23.11
```

AND LOOKE UPON MY SELFE AND CURSE MY FATE   3.29.4
LOOKE WHAT IS BEST, THAT BEST I WISH IN THEE   3.37.13
BUT WHEN I SLEEPE, IN DREAMES THEY LOOKE ON THEE   3.43.3
WHEN THAT MINE EYE IS FAMISHT FOR A LOOKE   3.47.3
OH THAT RECORD COULD WITH A BACK-WARD LOOKE   3.59.5
THEY LOOKE INTO THE BEAUTY OF THY MIND   3.69.9
O IF (I SAY) YOU LOCKE UPON THIS VERSE   3.71.9
LEAST THE WISE WORLD SHOULD LOOKE INTO YOUR MONE   3.71.13
AND BY AND BY CLEANE STARVED FOR A LOOKE   3.75.10
LOOKE WHAT THY MEMORIE CANNOT CONTAINE   3.77.9
THESE OFFICES, SO OFT AS THOU WILT LOOKE   3.77.13
I WILL ACQUAINTANCE STRANGLE AND LOOKE STRANGE   3.89.8
THAT LEAVES LOOKE PALE, DREADING THE $WINTERS
                            NEERE   3.97.14
LOOKE IN YOUR GLASSE AND THERE APPEARES A FACE   3.103.6
YOUR OWNE GLASSE SHOWES YOU, WHEN YOU
                       LOOKE IN IT   3.103.14
THAT EVERY TOUNG SAIES BEAUTY SHOULD LOOKE SO   3.127.14
'FOOLE,' SAID MY $MUSE TO ME, 'LOOKE IN
                  THY HEART AND WRITE'   4.1.14
LOOKE AT MY HANDS FOR NO SUCH QUINTESSENCE   4.28.11
I START, LOOKE, HEARKE, BUT WHAT IN CLOSDE
                       UP SENCE   4.38.9
O LOOKE, O SHINE, O LET ME DIE AND SEE   4.48.8
LOOKE HERE, I SAY.' I LOCK'D, AND $STELLA SPIDE   4.53.8
WHAT, A WHOLE WEEKE WITHOUT ONE PEECE OF LOOKE   4.56.3
SO DULL AM, THAT I CANNOT LOOKE INTO   4.60.10
LOOKE ON AGAINE, THE FAIRE TEXT BETTER TRIE   4.67.7
THOSE LAMPING EYES WILL DEIGNE SOMETIMES TO LOOK   5.1.6
WHEN YE BEHOLD THAT $ANGELS BLESSED LOOKE   5.1.11
THAT LOOSELY THEY NE DARE TO LOOKE UPON HER   5.5.8
FOR WHEN YE MILDLY LOOKE WITH LOVELY HEW   5.7.5
BUT WHEN YE LOWRE, OR LOOKE ON ME ASKEW   5.7.7
LOOKE EVER LOVELY, AS BECOMES YOU BEST   5.7.10
AND THAT HIGH LOOK, WITH WHICH SHE DOTH
                       COMPTROLL   5.10.10
YET LOWLY STILL VOUCHSAFE TO LOOKE ON ME   5.13.13
OR LOOKE WITH PITTY ON MY PAYNEFUL SMART   5.18.8
THAT WITH ONE LOOKE SHE DOTH MY LIFE DISMAY   5.21.10
FOR WITH ONE LOOKE SHE SPILS THAT LONG I SPONNE   5.23.11
WILL SHINE AGAIN, AND LOOKE ON ME AT LAST   5.34.11
AND CAN NO MORE ENDURE ON THEM TO LOOKE   5.35.12
HER EYES LOOKE LOVELY AND UPON THEM SMYLE   5.47.10
THERE SHE BEHOLDING ME WITH MYLDER LOOKE   5.67.9
AND CAN NO MORE ENDURE ON THEM TO LOOKE   5.83.12
LOOKED   6
AND FOR THEY LOOK'D BUT WITH DEVINING EYES   3.106.11
MOST TRUE IT IS, THAT I HAVE LOOKT ON TRUTH   3.110.5
STELLA LOOKT ON, AND FROM HER HEAVENLY FACE   4.41.13
LOOKE HERE, I SAY.' I LOCK'D, AND $STELLA SPIDE   4.53.8
LOOKING ON ME, WHILE I LOOKT OTHER WAY   4.66.12
HIS WHO TILL DEATH LOOKT IN A WATRIE GLASSE   4.82.3
LOOKED-FOR   1
STILL TO PROLONG MY LONG TYME LOOKT-FOR MORROW+   2.145.4
LOOKERS'   1
SHE TO HER LOVE DOTH LOCKERS EYES ALLURE   5.21.6
LOOKEST   1
STELLA, THOU STRAIGHT LOOKST BABIES IN HER EYES   4.11.10
LOOKING   14
LOOKING ALOFT FROM TURRET OF HER PRIDE   1.47.6

```
THAT IT, LIKE THOSE, BY LOOKING MIGHT BE BLEST        2.33.4
LOOKING INTO THE GLASSE OF MY YOUTHS MISERIES         2.114.1
IMPRINTED IN MY TEARES BY LOOKING STILL ON THEE       2.114.7
THUS SORING STILL, NOT LOOKING ONCE BELOW             2.122.9
AND LOOKING ON THEE, FALLS UPON THE GROUND            2.135.11
WITH ADMIRATION, EVER LOOKING ON HER                  2.138.8
LOOKING ON DARKNES WHICH THE BLIND DOE SEE            3.27.8
BY LOOKING ON THEE IN THE LIVING DAY+                 3.43.10
LOOKING WITH PRETTY RUTH UPON MY PAINE                3.132.4
LOOKING ON ME, WHILE I LOOKT OTHER WAY                4.66.12
BUT LOOKING STILL ON HER I STAND AMAZED               5.3.7
NEW YEARE FORTH LOOKING OUT OF JANUS GATE             5.4.1
FOR LOOKING ON THE EARTH WHENCE SHE WAS BORNE         5.13.6
LOOKS                     48
WITH DOWNEWARD LOOKES, STILL READING ON THE EARTH     1.9.3
AND SO WITH LOOKES, PROLONGS MY LONG-LOOKT EASE       1.24.10
LOOKES FEED MY $HOPE, $HOPE FOSTERS ME IN VAINE       1.25.13
LEAST MY SAD LOOKES BEWRAY ME HOW I FARE              1.29.12
NO LIGHTNING LOOKES WHICH FALLING HOPES ERECT         1.31.10
NO PITTYING EYE LOOKES BACKE UPON MY FEARES           1.32.10
WHICH BY $EXTORTION GAINETH ALL THEIR LOOKES          2.3.10
IN WHOM, $HEAV'N LOOKES IT SELFE AS IN A $GLASSE      2.17.4
SPIGHTFULL $ERINNIS FRIGHTS $ME WITH HER $LOOKES      2.39.9
WHO BY EXTORTION GAINETH ALL THEYR LOOKES             2.110.10
GAVE MEE SWEET LOOKES WHEN AS I LEARNED WELL          2.111.4
WHERE HUNGER-STARVEN, WANTING LOOKES TO LIVE          2.116.13
SPIGHTFULL $ERRINIS FRIGHTS MEE WITH HER LOOKES       2.118.9
MY EYES MADE DIM WITH LOOKES, POURE DOWN
                        A FLOOD OF TEARS               2.133.10
MY DYING LOOKES AND THOUGHTS ARE PEIZ'D
                        IN EQUALL FEARES               2.133.12
WHICH THOSE FAYRE $ILANDS OF THY LOOKES AFFOORD       2.134.6
SEE HOW HEE LOOKES UPON HIS BLEEDING WOUND            2.135.9
SERVING WITH LOOKES HIS SACRED MAJESTY                3.7.4
YET MORTALL LOOKES ADORE HIS BEAUTY STILL             3.7.7
THE $ROSE LOOKES FAIRE, BUT FAIRER WE IT DEEME        3.54.3
THY LOOKES WITH ME, THY HEART IN OTHER PLACE          3.93.4
IN MANIES LOOKES, THE FALCE HEARTS HISTORY            3.93.7
THY LOOKES SHOULD NOTHING THENCE, BUT
                        SWEETNESSE TELL                3.93.12
IF LIKE A $LAMBE HE COULD HIS LOOKES TRANSLATE        3.96.10
MY LOVE LOOKES FRESH, AND DEATH TO ME
                        SUBSCRIBES                     3.107.10
THAT LOOKES ON TEMPESTS AND IS NEVER SHAKEN           3.116.6
IF EYES CORRUPT BY OVER-PARTIALL LOOKES               3.137.5
HER PRETTIE LOOKES HAVE BEENE MINE ENEMIES            3.139.10
KILL ME OUT-RIGHT WITH LOOKES, AND RID MY PAINE       3.139.14
LOOKS OVER THE WORLD, AND CAN FIND NOTHING SUCH       4.9.10
LOOKES TO THE SKIES, AND IN A DITCH DOTH FALL+        4.19.11
WHICH LOOKES TOO OFT IN HIS UNFLATTRING GLASSE        4.27.10
I READE IT IN THY LOOKES, THY LANGUISHT GRACE         4.31.7
O EYES, WHERE HUMBLE LOOKES MOST GLORIOUS PROVE       4.42.5
THEN WITH THOSE EYES HE LOOKES, LO BY AND BY          4.43.6
BUT WITH SHORT BREATH, LONG LOOKES, STAID
                        FEET AND WALKING HED           4.76.13
THOSE LOOKES, WHOSE BEAMES BE JOY, WHOSE
                        MOTION IS DELIGHT              4.77.1
ALAS, WHENCE CAME THIS CHANGE OF LOOKES+ $IF I        4.86.1
AS THY LOOKES STURRE, RUNS UP AND DOWNE TO MAKE       4.101.10
THAT WITH SUCH POYSONOUS CARE MY LOOKES
                        YOU MARKE                      4.104.2
```

```
    FOR IN THOSE LOFTY LOOKES IS CLOSE IMPLICE          5.5.5
    THEIR LOOSER LOOKES THAT STIR UP LJSTES IMPURE      5.21.8
    THUS DOTH SHE TRAINE AND TEACH ME WITH
                          HER LOOKES                    5.21.13
    WITH THAT SUNSHINE WHEN CLOUDY LOOKS ARE CLEARED    5.40.14
    TRUST NOT THE TREASCN OF THOSE SMYLING LOCKES       5.47.1
    AND KILL WITH LOOKS, AS $COCKATRICES DOO            5.49.10
    DOTH PLEASE ALL BEASTS BUT THAT HIS LOOKS
                          THEM FRAY                     5.53.2
    FOR TO THE HEAVEN HER HAUGHTY LOOKES ASPIRE         5.55.11
LOOK'S                        1
    THROUGH SWEET ILLUSION CF HER LOOKES DELIGHT        5.16.4
LOOPHOLES                     1
    ONELY TWO $LOOPE-HCLES, THEN I MIGHT BEHOLD         2.8.4
LOOSE                         2
    A LOATHING OF ALL LCOSE UNCHASTITIE                 4.14.13
    WITH THE LOOSE WYNC YE WAVING CHANCE TO MARKE       5.81.2
LOOSELY                       3
    BECAUSE I LOOSELY TRIFLE IN THIS SORT               2.24.5
    THAT LOOSELY THEY NE DARE TO LOOKE UPON HER         5.5.8
    THEY LOOSELY DID THEYR WANTON WINGES DISPLAY        5.76.11
LOOSER                        1
    THEIR LOOSER LOOKES THAT STIR UP LUSTES IMPURE      5.21.8
LORD                         11
    ARE MADE BY HER TC MURTHER THUS THEIR $LCRD         1.5.14
    FOR WHILST THEY STRIVE WHICH SHALL BE
                          $LORD OF ALL                  1.28.5
    SATURNE CHIEFE $LORD OF THE $ASCENDANT LAY          2.116.7
    LORD OF MY LOVE, TC WHOME IN VASSALAGE              3.26.1
    ACCORDING TO MY $LCRD $LOVE'S OWNE BEHEST           4.50.6
    FORST BY THEIR $LORD, WHO IS ASHAM'D TO FIND        4.99.13
    UNRIGHTEOUS $LORD CF LOVE WHAT LAW IS THIS          5.10.1
    AND YET THE $LYON THAT IS $LORD OF POWER            5.20.5
    MOST GLORIOUS $LORD OF LYFE THAT ON THIS DAY        5.68.1
    THIS JOYOUS DAY, DEARE $LORD, WITH JOY BEGIN        5.68.5
    LOVE IS THE LESSON WHICH THE $LORD US TAUGHT        5.68.14
LORDETH                       1
    THE WHILES SHE LORDETH IN LICENTIOUS BLISSE         5.10.3
LORDINGS                      1
    LISTEN THEN $LORDINGS WITH GOOD EARE TO ME          4.37.3
LORDS                         3
    THEY ARE THE $LORDS AND OWNERS OF THEIR FACES       3.94.7
    LIKE SOME WEAKE $LCRDS, NEIGHBORD BY MIGHTY KINGS   4.29.1
    NOR DO LIKE $LORDS, WHOSE WEAKE CONFUSED BRAINE     4.85.5
LORD'S                        1
    LIKE WIDDOWED WOMBES AFTER THEIR $LORDS CECEASE     3.97.8
LOSE                         19
    I LOSE MY TEARES WHERE I HAVE LOST MY LOVE          1.11.5
    GOOD $DELIA LOSE, QUENCH, HEALE ME NOW AT LENGTH    1.14.14
    YET WHICH AT LENGTH THOU MUST BE FORC'D TO LCSE     1.50.8
    AND I LOSE YOU, FOR ALL MY $WIT AND $PAINES         2.21.14
    NOR SHALL MY $SPIRIT ONE JOT OF VIGOUR LCSE         2.31.6
    NOR LOOSE POSSESSICN OF THAT FAIRE THOU CW'ST       3.18.10
    AND OUR DEARE LOVE LOOSE NAME OF SINGLE CNE         3.39.6
    IF I LOOSE THEE, MY LOSSE IS MY LOVES GAINE         3.42.9
    BOTH FINDE EACH OTHER, AND I LOOSE BOTH TWAINE      3.42.11
    BUT WEEPE TO HAVE, THAT WHICH IT FEARES TO LCOSE    3.64.14
    THE HARDEST KNIFE ILL US'D DOTH LOOSE HIS EDGE      3.95.14
    AND SWEETS GROWNE CCMMON LOOSE THEIR DEARE
                          DELIGHT                       3.102.12
```

```
LOSE ALL, AND MORE BY PAYING TOO MUCH RENT            3.125.6
SO HIM I LOOSE THROUGH MY UNKINDE ABUSE               3.134.12
I SEE MY COURSE TO LOSE MY SELFE DOTH BEND            4.18.12
THEN THAT I LOSE NO MORE FOR $STELLA'S SAKE           4.18.14
TO LOSE HIS $CROWNE, RATHER THEN FAILE HIS $LOVE      4.75.14
THAT FONDLY FEARE TO LOOSE YOUR LIBERTY               5.65.2
SHALL TURNE TO NOUGHT AND LOOSE THAT GLORIOUS HEW     5.79.6
```
LOSING   4
```
AND LOOSING HER, MY FRIEND HATH FOUND THAT LOSSE      3.42.10
THAT THOU IN LOOSING ME, SHALL WIN MUCH GLORY         3.88.8
STILL LOOSING WHEN I SAW MY SELFE TO WIN+             3.119.4
WHEN LOOSING ONE, TWO LIBERTIES YE GAYNE              5.65.3
```
LOSS   13
```
MY $JOYES ARRERAGE LEADES ME TO MY LOSSE              2.3.8
TH'ARERAGE OF MY JOYES, DIRECTS ME TO MY LOSSE        2.110.8
THOUGH THOU REPENT, YET I HAVE STILL THE LOSSE        3.34.10
TO HIM THAT BEARES THE STRONG OFFENSES LOSSE          3.34.12
A LOSSE IN LOVE THAT TOUCHES ME MORE NEERELY          3.42.4
IF I LOOSE THEE, MY LOSSE IS MY LOVES GAINE           3.42.9
AND LOOSING HER, MY FRIEND HATH FOUND THAT LOSSE      3.42.10
INCREASING STORE WITH LOSSE, AND LOSSE WITH STORE     3.64.8
INCREASING STORE WITH LOSSE, AND LOSSE WITH STORE     3.64.8
AND DOE NOT DROP IN FOR AN AFTER LOSSE                3.90.4
COMPAR'D WITH LOSSE OF THEE, WILL NOT SEEME SO        3.90.14
THEN SOULE LIVE THOU UPON THY SERVANTS LOSSE          3.146.9
MY HARMES ON $INK'S POORE LOSSE, PERHAPS
                   SOME FIND                          4.34.13
```
LOSSES   1
```
ALL LOSSES ARE RESTORD, AND SORROWES END              3.30.14
```
LOST   18
```
I LOSE MY TEARES WHERE I HAVE LOST MY LOVE            1.11.5
TIS NINE YEERES NOW SINCE FIRST I LOST MY $WIT        2.9.11
OR HATH IT LOST THE $VERTUE, WITH THE $TIMES          2.27.3
IN YOUR PERFECTIONS SO MUCH AM I LOST                 2.57.14
(QUOTH I) $THE $MAINE LOST, CAST THE $BY AWAY         2.59.11
WHERE MOST I $LOST, THERE MOST OF ALL I $WAN          2.62.3
HER $CABLE BROKE, HER SUREST $ANCHOR LOST             2.134.10
WHERE MOST I LOST, THERE MOST OF ALL I WAN            2.150.3
SO THEN THOU HAST BUT LOST THE DREGS OF LIFE          3.74.9
AND THE JUST PLEASURE LOST, WHICH IS SO DEEMED        3.121.3
HIM HAVE I LOST, THOU HAST BOTH HIM AND ME            3.134.13
AND ALL MY HONEST FAITH IN THEE IS LOST               3.152.8
NOW EVEN THAT FOOTSTEP OF LOST LIBERTIE               4.2.9
HOW $HOLLAND HEARTS, NOW SO GOOD TOWNES BE LOST       4.30.7
LET ME NO STEPS BUT OF LOST LABOUR TRACE              4.64.6
THEN ALL HER NATURES GOODLY GUIFTS ARE LOST           5.41.8
I GOE LYKE ONE THAT HAVING LOST THE FIELD             5.52.2
LYKE A YOUNG FAWNE THAT LATE HATH LOST THE HYND       5.78.2
```
LOT   5
```
ILE HIDE HER SINNE AND SAY IT WAS MY LOT              1.30.10
YET WITH REPINING AT SO PARTIALL LOT                  4.2.8
BUT THAT RICH FOOLE, WHO BY BLIND $FORTUNE'S LOT      4.24.9
AND THAT YOU KNOW, I ENVY YOU NO LOT                  4.84.12
I BLESSE MY LOT, THAT WAS SO LUCKY PLACED             5.82.2
```
LOUD   1
```
IF THOU TURNE BACK AND MY LOUDE CRYING STILL          3.143.14
```
LOVE   497
```
WHICH HERE MY LOVE, MY YOUTH, MY PLAINTS REVEALE      1.1.4
WHO CAN SHEW ALL HIS LOVE, DOTH LOVE BUT LIGHTLY      1.1.14
WHO CAN SHEW ALL HIS LOVE, DOTH LOVE BUT LIGHTLY      1.1.14
```

```
GOE WAILING $VERSE, THE $INFANTS OF MY LOVE              1.2.1
WHO WHILST I LOVE, DOTH KILL ME WITH DISCAINE            1.3.14
MY LOVE AFFECTS NC FAME, NOR STEEMES OF $ART            1.4.14
FAIRE IS MY $LOVE, AND CRUELL AS SHE'S FAIRE            1.6.1
WHOSE FEETE DOE TREAD GREENE PATHS OF
                         YOUTH AND LOVE                 1.6.6
AND YOU MY $VERSE, THE $ADVOCATES OF $LOVE              1.8.9
TIS NOT DISDAINE MUST MAKE ME LEAVE TO LCVE            1.8.14
IF THIS BE LOVE, TC DRAW A WEARIE BREATH               1.9.1
IF THIS BE LOVE, TC WARRE AGAINST MY SOULE             1.9.5
IF THIS BE LOVE, TO CLOATHE ME WITH DARKE THCUGHTS     1.9.9
IF THIS BE LOVE, TC LIVE A LIVING DEATH                1.9.13
THEN DOE I LOVE AND DRAW THIS WEARIE BREATH            1.9.14
THEN DOE I LOVE, AND DRAW THIS WEARIE BREATH           1.10.1
THE TRUEST LOVE THAT EVER YET WAS SEENE                1.10.8
AND LET HER PITTIE IF SHE CANNOT LOVE ME               1.10.14
I LOSE MY TEARES WHERE I HAVE LOST MY LOVE             1.11.5
MY SPOTLESSE LOVE HCVERS WITH PUREST WINGS             1.12.1
SO MUCH I LOVE THE MOST UNLOVING ONE                   1.12.14
UNHAPPY I, TO LOVE A STCNY HART                        1.13.14
LOVE WAS THE FLAME THAT FIRED ME SO NEERE              1.14.3
YET DO I LOVE, ADCRE, AND PRAYSE THE SAME              1.14.7
BEWRAIES MY LOVE, WITH BROKEN WORDS HALFE SPCKEN       1.15.6
IF ON HER LOVE MY LIFE AND HONOUR LYES                 1.15.11
AND THUS I LIVE BECAUSE I LOVE HER DEERLY              1.16.14
WHAT SHOULD HER VERTUES DO, HER SMILES,
                         HER LOVE+                      1.17.10
YET CANNOT LEAVE HER LOVE THAT HOLDS ME HATEFULL       1.18.5
SO TRUE AND LOYALL LOVE NO FAVOUR GAINES ME            1.18.8
OFT HAVE I TOLD HER THAT MY SOULE DID LOVE HER         1.18.13
YEELD $CITHEREAS SCNNE THOSE $ARKES OF LCVE            1.19.2
FROM LOVE OR YEARES UNSUBJECT TO DECAIES               1.23.4
ONCE LET HER LOVE INDEED, OR ELS EYE ME NEVER          1.24.14
TRAITOUR TO ME, AND FAITHFULL TO MY $LOVE              1.25.2
I LOVE TH'EFFECT THE CAUSE BEING OF THIS POWRE         1.26.11
REIGNE IN MY THOUGHTS, MY LOVE AND LIFE
                         ARE THINE                      1.27.14
FOR WELL THOU SAW'ST MY LOVE AND HOW I PIN'D           1.31.8
ONE IN MY LOVE, ANC HER HARD HART STILL CNE            1.33.4
INJURIOUS $DELIA YET I LCVE THEE STILL                 1.33.9
I IN MY LOVE, OR THCU IN THY DISDAINE                  1.33.14
BUT LOVE NOW WHILST THOU MAIST BE LOV'D AGAINE         1.39.14
BUT LOVE WHILST THAT THCU MAIST BE LOV'D AGAINE        1.40.1
I LOVE AS WELL, THCUGH HE COULD BETTER SHOW IT         1.43.8
AND YET I'D RATHER LANGUISH FOR HER LOVE               1.48.11
UNTO HER SELFE, HER SELFE MY LOVE DOTH SCMMON          1.49.9
(IF LOVE IN HER HATH ANY POWER TO MOVE)                1.49.10
WHETHER MY FAITH HATH NCT DESERV'D HER LCVE+           1.49.12
BEAUTIE (SWEET $LOVE) IS LIKE THE MORNING DEW          1.50.1
I MUST NOT GRIEVE MY $LOVE, WHOSE EIES
                         WOULD REEDE                    1.51.1
LET LOVE AND YOUTH CONDUCT THY PLEASURES THITHER       1.51.8
THEE AND THY $LOVE FORLCRNE, AND BOTH DISDAINES        1.52.7
WHICH LOVE DOTH PAY, AND HER DISDAINE EXTORTS          1.60.2
I SEND THOSE EYES THE CABINETS OF LOVE                 1.60.6
THUS IN MY $LOVE, $TIME CALLS ME TO RELATE             2.1.13
THE PAIMENTS OF MY $LOVE, I READ, AND CRCSSE           2.3.6
IN WHOSE DEARE $BOSCME, SWEET DELICIOUS $LOVE          2.4.5
I SAY, I $LOVE, YCU SLEIGHTLY ANSWERE I                2.5.5
I SAY, $YOU $LOVE, YOU PEULE ME OUT A $NC              2.5.6
```

```
LOVE, IN A $HUMOR, PLAY'D THE $PRODIGALL          2.7.1
THY $LOVE, THAT IS ON THE UNWORTHY PLAC'D         2.10.11
THEN IS SHE $LOVE, IMBRACING $CHARITIE            2.12.5
WHICH MY $HEART, LIGHTNED BY THY $LOVE, DOTH SEE  2.12.14
I HAVE A $MED'CINE THAT SHALL CURE MY $LOVE       2.15.2
YOU CANNOT LOVE, MY PRETTIE $HEART, AND WHY+      2.19.1
NOR $LOVE, NOR $HATE, HOW THEN+ WHAT WILL
                            $YOU DOE+             2.19.6
OR WILL $YOU LOVE $ME, AND YET HATE $ME TOO+      2.19.8
YOUR $LOVE AND $HATE IS THIS, I NOW DOE
                            PROVE $YOU            2.19.13
YOU LOVE IN $HATE, BY $HATE TO MAKE $ME
                            LOVE $YOU             2.19.14
YOU LOVE IN $HATE, BY $HATE TO MAKE $ME
                            LOVE $YOU             2.19.14
TO WRITE HIM BUT ONE $SONNET TO HIS $LOVE         2.21.4
YET BY MY $FROTH, THIS $FOOLE HIS $LOVE OBTAINES  2.21.13
THEN HONEST $PEOPLE, BEARE WITH $LOVE AND $ME     2.22.2
LOVE STILL A $BABY, PLAYES WITH $GAWDES
                            AND $TOYES            2.22.5
LOVE BANISH'D $HEAV'N, IN $EARTH WAS HELD
                            IN SCORNE             2.23.1
I $HEARE SOME SAY, THIS $MAN IS NOT IN LOVE       2.24.1
WHO+ CAN HE LOVE+ A LIKELY THING, THEY SAY        2.24.2
I $EVER LOVE, WHERE NEVER $HOPE APPEARES          2.26.1
SO MY $LOVE IS STILL FETT'RED WITH VAINE $HOPE    2.26.10
IS $NOT $LOVE HERE, AS 'TIS IN OTHER $CLYMES      2.27.1
TO $SUCH AS SAY, $THY $LOVE I OVER-PRIZE          2.28.1
WHEN CONQU'RING $LOVE DID FIRST MY $HEART ASSAYLE 2.29.1
HE YEELDS $LOVE UP THE $KEYES UNTO MY $HEART      2.29.11
TO CRUELL $LOVE MY $SOULE WAS FIRST BETRAY'D      2.29.14
THINK'ST THOU MY $LOVE SHALL IN THOSE
                       $RAGGES BE DREST           2.31.11
MARVELL NOT, $LOVE, THOUGH I THY POW'R ADMIRE     2.34.1
MARVELL NOT, $LOVE, THOUGH I THY POW'R ADMIRE     2.34.5
MARVELL NOT, $LOVE, THOUGH I THY POW'R ADMIRE     2.34.9
IF THOU WILT WONDER, HERE'S THE WONDER, $LOVE     2.34.13
SOME MISBELEEVING, AND PROPHANE IN $LOVE          2.35.1
TO MAKE HER LOVE, OR $CUPID BE THOU DAMN'D        2.36.14
AND EACH RETURNES UNTO HIS $LOVE AT $NIGHT+       2.37.8
SITTING ALONE, $LOVE BIDS ME GOE AND WRITE        2.38.1
OR ELSE $LOVE WERE UNABLE TO INDITE               2.38.4
LOVE GROWING ANGRY, VEXED AT THE $SPLEENE         2.38.5
WHERE SHE WITH $LOVE CONVERSING HATH NOT BEENE    2.38.8
DESPITETH $LOVE, AND LAUGHETH AT HER $FOLLY       2.38.10
AND $LOVE CONTEMNING $REASONS REASON WHOLLY       2.38.11
AND $LOVE ALONE PICKS REASON OUT OF LOVE          2.38.14
AND $LOVE ALONE PICKS REASON OUT OF LOVE          2.38.14
LOVE IS THE $FEWELL, WHICH MAINTAINES THE FIRE    2.40.4
WHY DOE I SPEAKE OF $JOY, OR WRITE OF $LOVE       2.41.1
AND IN MY $LINES, IF SHE MY LOVE MAY SEE          2.42.12
WHICH NEVER FELT'ST MY FIERIE TOUCH OF $LOVE      2.49.4
THOU, THUS WHOSE $SPIRIT $LOVE IN HIS
                            FIRE REFINES          2.49.13
CALLING TO MINDE SINCE FIRST MY $LOVE BEGUN       2.51.1
WITH SO PURE $LOVE, AS $TIME COULD NEVER BOAST    2.54.8
BY CHASTE $DESIRE, TRUE $LOVE, AND VERTUOUS
                            $PRAYSE               2.54.14
MY $FAIRE, IF THOU WILT REGISTER MY LOVE          2.55.1
WHEN LIKE AN $EAGLET I FIRST FOUND MY $LOVE       2.56.1
```

```
AT WHOSE PURE $EYES, $LOVE LIGHTS HIS
                    HALLOW'D $FIRE                  2.57.8
AS $LOVE AND I, LATE HARBOUR'D IN ONE $INNE         2.59.1
IN $LOVE THERE IS NO LACK, THUS I BEGIN            2.59.3
LABOUR IS LIGHT, WHERE $LOVE (QUOTH I) DOTH PAY    2.59.9
LET $VERTUE BE THE $TOUCH-STONE OF MY $LOVE        2.60.7
CAN SHEW A $SECOND TO SO PURE A $LOVE              2.60.14
THAT $WE ONE JOT OF FORMER $LOVE RETEYNE           2.61.8
TRUCE, GENTLE $LOVE, A $PARLY NOW I CRAVE          2.63.1
WITH SO PURE LOVE AS TYME COULD NEVER BOAST        2.101.8
BY CHAST DESIRE, TRUE LOVE, AND VERTUES PRAISE     2.101.14
MY $FAYRE, IF THOU WILT REGISTER MY LOVE           2.102.1
MY $THOUGHTS BRED UP WITH $EAGLE-BIRDS OF LOVE     2.103.1
THE PAYMENTS OF MY LOVE I READ, AND READING
                    CROSSE                          2.110.6
THINE EYES TAUGHT MEE THE $ALPHABET OF LOVE        2.111.1
SOME $ATHIEST OR VILE $INFIDELL IN LOVE            2.112.1
MY LIFE, MY YOUTH, MY LOVE, I HEERE ANOTAMIZE      2.114.14
NOW $LOVE, IF THOU WILT PROVE A $CONQUEROR         2.115.1
ILE FETTER HER IN CHAINES OF PUREST LOVE           2.115.6
WHERE FIRST MY $LOVE INTO THE WORLD WAS BROUGHT    2.116.4
WHILST $LOVE (MY $PHOENIX BIRD) IN HER
                    OWN FLAME IS DYING              2.117.12
INVENTION AND MY $MUSE, PERFECTION AND HER LOVE    2.117.13
CUPID, DUMBE $IDOLL, PEEVISH $SAINT OF LOVE        2.126.1
MY $LOVE MAKES HOTE THE FIRE WHOSE HEAT IS SPENT   2.127.1
THIS LOVE, TEARS, SIGHES, MAINTAINE EACH
                    ONE HIS ELEMENT                 2.127.4
THE FIRE, UNTO MY LOVE, COMPARE A PAINTED FIRE     2.127.5
ONELY MY LOVE IS IN THE FIRE INGRAVED              2.127.9
MY LOVE, MY TEARES, MY SIGHES, EXTINGUISHT
                    CANNOT BE                       2.127.14
AND IN MY LYNES IF SHEE MY LOVE MAY SEE            2.128.12
LOV'D MORE THEN LIFE, YET ONELY ART HIS LOVE       2.129.11
SITTING ALONE, LOVE BIDS ME GOE AND WRITE          2.131.1
ELS SENCELES LOVE COULD NEVER ONCE ENDITE          2.131.4
LOVE GROWING ANGRY, VEXED AT THE SPLEENE           2.131.5
WHERE SHEE WITH $LOVE CONVERSING HATH NOT BEENE    2.131.8
DISPIGHTETH $LOVE, AND LAUGHETH AT HER FOLLY       2.131.10
AND $LOVE CONTEMNING $REASONS REASON WHOLY         2.131.11
AND $LOVE ALONE FINDS REASON IN MY LOVE            2.131.14
AND $LOVE ALONE FINDS REASON IN MY LOVE            2.131.14
THOSE SIGHES WHICH COOLE MY HART, ARE
                    COLES UNTO MY LOVE              2.132.2
LOVE HEATS MY HART, MY HART-HEAT MY SIGHES
                    WARMETH                         2.132.6
DESIRE, MY LOVE, MY SOULE, MY HOPE, HART,
                    AND LIFE CHARMETH               2.132.8
MY HART IMBRACETH $LOVE, $LOVE DOTH IMBRACE
                    MY HART                         2.132.10
MY HART IMBRACETH $LOVE, $LOVE DOTH IMBRACE
                    MY HART                         2.132.10
DESIRE, MY LOVE, MY SOULE, MY HOPE, MY
                    HART, MY LIFE                   2.132.13
SEE WHERE SHEE FLOTES, LADEN WITH PUREST LOVE      2.134.5
SLEEPE WITH DELIGHT, $BEAUTY WITH LOVE REWARDING   2.136.8
I $EVER LOVE, WHERE NEVER HOPE APPEARES            2.137.1
SO MY LOVE IS STYLL FETTERED WITH VAINE HOPE       2.137.10
UNFAINED LOVE, IN NAKED SIMPLE TRUTH               2.138.3
A LYFE, THAT NEVER JOYD BUT IN HER LOVE            2.138.9
```

```
AND KINDNES, BE UNKINDNES IN MY LOVE                    2.139.4
THEN WITH UNKINDNES, $LOVE REVENGE THY WRONG            2.139.5
THAT LOVE DIVINE WHICH I HAVE BORNE TO YOU              2.139.10
RARE OF-SPRING OF MY THOUGHTS, MY DEEREST $LOVE         2.141.1
LOE THUS MY LOVE, MY LYFE, MY FORTUNE TRYES             2.142.4
RECORD MY LOVE IN $OCEAN WAVES (UNKIND)                 2.142.9
WHY DOE I SPEAKE OF JOY, OR WRITE OF LOVE               2.143.1
LOVE IS THE FUELL WHICH MAINTAINES THE FIRE             2.144.4
DEFINE MY LOVE, AND TELL THE JOYES OF HEAVEN            2.149.1
LET VERTUE BE THE TUCH-STONE OF MY LOVE                 2.149.7
THE PATIENCE OF SO RARE DIVINE A LOVE                   2.149.14
GOE YOU MY LYNES, $EMBASSADORS OF LOVE                  2.151.1
WHEN $DORUS SINGS HIS SWEET $PAMELAS LOVE               2.151.10
OF HIS SELFE LOVE TO STOP POSTERITY+                    3.3.8
NO LOVE TOWARD OTHERS IN THAT BOSOME SITS               3.9.13
FOR SHAME DENY THAT THOU BEAR'ST LOVE TO ANY            3.10.1
SHALL HATE BE FAIRER LOG'D THEN GENTLE LOVE+            3.10.10
MAKE THEE AN OTHER SELFE FOR LOVE OF ME                 3.10.13
O THAT YOU WERE YOUR SELFE, BUT LOVE YOU ARE            3.13.1
O NONE BUT UNTHRIFTS, DEARE MY LOVE YOU KNOW            3.13.13
AND ALL IN WAR WITH $TIME FOR LOVE OF YOU               3.15.13
MY LOVE SHALL IN MY VERSE EVER LIVE YOUNG               3.19.14
MINE BE THY LOVE AND THY LOVES USE THEIR
                              TREASURE                  3.20.14
O LET ME TRUE IN LOVE BUT TRULY WRITE                   3.21.9
AND THEN BELEEVE ME, MY LOVE IS AS FAIRE                3.21.10
O THEREFORE LOVE BE OF THY SELFE SO WARY                3.22.9
WHO PLEADE FOR LOVE, AND LOOK FOR RECOMPENCE            3.23.11
O LEARNE TO READ WHAT SILENT LOVE HATH WRIT             3.23.13
THEN HAPPY I THAT LOVE AND AM BELOVED                   3.25.13
LORD OF MY LOVE, TO WHOME IN VASSALAGE                  3.26.1
THEN MAY I DARE TO BOAST HOW I DOE LOVE THEE            3.26.13
FOR THY SWEET LOVE REMEMBRED SUCH WELTH BRINGS          3.29.13
AND THERE RAIGNES $LOVE AND ALL $LOVES
                              LOVING PARTS               3.31.3
HATH DEARE RELIGIOUS LOVE STOLNE FROM MINE EYE          3.31.6
THOU ART THE GRAVE WHERE BURIED LOVE DOTH LIVE          3.31.9
RESERVE THEM FOR MY LOVE, NOT FOR THEIR RIME            3.32.7
A DEARER BIRTH THEN THIS HIS LOVE HAD BROUGHT           3.32.11
THEIRS FOR THEIR STILE ILE READ, HIS FOR
                              HIS LOVE                   3.32.14
YET HIM FOR THIS, MY LOVE NO WHIT DISDAINETH            3.33.13
AH BUT THOSE TEARES ARE PEARLE WHICH THY
                              LOVE SHEEDS                3.34.13
SUCH CIVILL WAR IS IN MY LOVE AND HATE                  3.35.12
BUT DOE NOT SO, I LOVE THEE IN SUCH SORT                3.36.13
I MAKE MY LOVE INGRAFTED TO THIS STORE                  3.37.8
AND OUR DEARE LOVE LOOSE NAME OF SINGLE ONE             3.39.6
TO ENTERTAINE THE TIME WITH THOUGHTS OF LOVE            3.39.11
TAKE ALL MY LOVES, MY LOVE, YEA TAKE THEM ALL           3.40.1
NO LOVE, MY LOVE, THAT THOU MAIST TRUE LOVE CALL        3.40.3
NO LOVE, MY LOVE, THAT THOU MAIST TRUE LOVE CALL        3.40.3
NO LOVE, MY LOVE, THAT THOU MAIST TRUE LOVE CALL        3.40.3
THEN IF FOR MY LOVE, THOU MY LOVE RECEIVEST             3.40.5
THEN IF FOR MY LOVE, THOU MY LOVE RECEIVEST             3.40.5
I CANNOT BLAME THEE, FOR MY LOVE THOU USEST             3.40.6
AND YET LOVE KNOWES IT IS A GREATER GRIEFE              3.40.11
A LOSSE IN LOVE THAT TOUCHES ME MORE NEERELY            3.42.4
THOU DOOST LOVE HER, BECAUSE THOU KNOWST
                              I LOVE HER                 3.42.6
```

```
THOU DOOST LOVE HER, BECAUSE THOU KNOWST
                      I LOVE HER                     3.42.6
IN TENDER $EMBASSIE OF LOVE TO THEE                  3.45.6
AND MY HEARTS RIGHT, THEIR INWARD LOVE OF HEART      3.46.14
OR HEART IN LOVE WITH SIGHES HIMSELFE
                      DOTH SMOTHER                   3.47.4
AND IN HIS THOUGHTS OF LOVE DOTH SHARE A PART        3.47.8
SO EITHER BY THY PICTURE OR MY LOVE                  3.47.9
WHEN AS THY LOVE HATH CAST HIS UTMOST SUMME          3.49.3
WHEN LOVE CONVERTED FROM THE THING IT WAS            3.49.7
SINCE WHY TO LOVE, I CAN ALLEDGE NO CAUSE            3.49.14
THUS CAN MY LOVE EXCUSE THE SLOW OFFENCE             3.51.1
THEREFORE DESIRE (OF PERFECTS LOVE BEING MADE)       3.51.10
BUT LOVE, FOR LOVE, THUS SHALL EXCUSE MY JADE        3.51.12
BUT LOVE, FOR LOVE, THUS SHALL EXCUSE MY JADE        3.51.12
SWEET LOVE RENEW THY FORCE, BE IT NOT SAID           3.56.1
SO LOVE BE THOU, ALTHOUGH TOO DAIE THOU FILL         3.56.5
THE SPIRIT OF $LOVE, WITH A PERPETUAL DULNESSE       3.56.8
RETURNE OF LOVE, MORE BLEST MAY BE THE VIEW          3.56.12
SO TRUE A FOOLE IS LOVE, THAT IN YOUR $WILL          3.57.13
O NO, THY LOVE THOUGH MUCH, IS NOT SO GREAT          3.61.9
IT IS MY LOVE THAT KEEPES MINE EIE AWAKE             3.61.10
MINE OWNE TRUE LOVE THAT DOTH MY REST DEFEAT         3.61.11
MINE OWNE SELFE LOVE QUITE CONTRARY I READ           3.62.11
AGAINST MY LOVE SHALL BE AS I AM NOW                 3.63.1
THAT $TIME WILL COME AND TAKE MY LOVE AWAY           3.64.12
THAT IN BLACK INCK MY LOVE MAY STILL SHINE
                      BRIGHT                          3.65.14
SAVE THAT TO DYE, I LEAVE MY LOVE ALONE              3.66.14
FOR $CANKER VICE THE SWEETEST BUDS DOTH LOVE         3.70.7
THE HAND THAT WRIT IT, FOR I LOVE YOU SO             3.71.6
BUT LET YOUR LOVE EVEN WITH MY LIFE DECAY            3.71.12
WHAT MERIT LIV'D IN ME THAT YOU SHOULD LOVE          3.72.2
AFTER MY DEATH (DEARE LOVE) FOR GET ME QUITE         3.72.3
O LEAST YOUR TRUE LOVE MAY SEEME FALCE IN THIS       3.72.9
THAT YOU FOR LOVE SPEAKE WELL OF ME UNTRUE           3.72.10
AND SO SHOULD YOU, TO LOVE THINGS NOTHING WORTH      3.72.14
THIS THOU PERCEV'ST, WHICH MAKES THY LOVE
                      MORE STRONG                    3.73.13
TO LOVE THAT WELL, WHICH THOU MUST LEAVE
                      ERE LONG                       3.73.14
O KNOW SWEET LOVE I ALWAIES WRITE OF YOU             3.76.9
AND YOU AND LOVE ARE STILL MY ARGUMENT               3.76.10
SO IS MY LOVE STILL TELLING WHAT IS TOLD             3.76.14
I GRANT (SWEET LOVE) THY LOVELY ARGUMENT             3.79.5
THE WORST WAS THIS, MY LOVE WAS MY DECAY             3.80.14
AND DO SO LOVE, YET WHEN THEY HAVE DEVISDE           3.82.9
BUT THAT IS IN MY THOUGHT, WHOSE LOVE TO YOU         3.85.11
SUCH IS MY LOVE, TO THEE I SO BELONG                 3.88.13
THOU CANST NOT (LOVE) DISGRACE ME HALFE SO ILL       3.89.5
FOR I MUST NERE LOVE HIM WHOM THOU DOST HATE         3.89.14
THY LOVE IS BITTER THEN HIGH BIRTH TO ME             3.91.9
AND LIFE NO LONGER THEN THY LOVE WILL STAY           3.92.3
FOR IT DEPENDS UPON THAT LOVE OF THINE               3.92.4
HAPPY TO HAVE THY LOVE, HAPPY TO DIE                 3.92.12
MAY STILL SEEME LOVE TO ME, THOUGH ALTER'D NEW       3.93.3
THAT IN THY FACE SWEET LOVE SHOULD EVER DWELL        3.93.10
BUT DOE NOT SO, I LOVE THEE IN SUCH SORT             3.96.13
GIVE MY LOVE FAME FASTER THEN TIME WASTS LIFE        3.100.13
BOTH TRUTH AND BEAUTY ON MY LOVE DEPENDS             3.101.3
```

```
MY LOVE IS STRENGTHNED THOUGH MORE WEAKE
                        IN SEEMING              3.102.1
I LOVE NOT LESSE, THOGH LESSE THE SHOW APPEARE  3.102.2
THAT LOVE IS MARCHANDIZ'D, WHOSE RITCH ESTEEMING 3.102.3
OUR LOVE WAS NEW, AND THEN BUT IN THE SPRING    3.102.5
LET NOT MY LOVE BE CAL'D $IDOLATRIE             3.105.1
KINDE IS MY LOVE TO DAY, TO MORROW KINDE        3.105.5
CAN YET THE LEASE CF MY TRUE LOVE CONTROULE     3.107.3
MY LOVE LOOKES FRESH, AND DEATH TO ME
                        SUBSCRIBES              3.107.10
THAT MAY EXPRESSE MY LOVE, OR THY DEARE MERIT+  3.108.4
SO THAT ETERNALL LCVE IN LOVES FRESH CASE       3.108.9
FINDING THE FIRST CCNCEIT OF LOVE THERE BRED    3.108.13
THAT IS MY HOME OF LOVE, IF I HAVE RANG'D       3.109.5
AND WORSE ESSAIES PROV'D THEE MY BEST OF LOVE   3.110.8
A $GOD IN LOVE, TC WHOM I AM CONFIN'D           3.110.12
YOUR LOVE AND PITTIE DOTH TH'IMPRESSION FILL    3.112.1
AND THAT YOUR LOVE TAUGHT IT THIS $ALCUMIE+     3.114.4
EVEN THOSE THAT SAID I CCULD NOT LOVE YOU DEERER 3.115.2
MIGHT I NOT THEN SAY NCW I LOVE YOU BEST        3.115.10
LOVE IS A $BABE, THEN MIGHT I NOT SAY SO        3.115.13
ADMIT IMPEDIMENTS, LOVE IS NOT LOVE             3.116.2
ADMIT IMPEDIMENTS, LOVE IS NOT LOVE             3.116.2
LOV'S NOT $TIME'S FCOLE, THOUGH ROSIE
                        LIPS AND CHEEKS         3.116.9
LOVE ALTERS NOT WITH HIS BREEFE HOURES
                        AND WEEKES              3.116.11
FORGOT UPON YOUR DEAREST LOVE TO CALL           3.117.3
THE CONSTANCY AND VIRTUE OF YOUR LOVE           3.117.14
THUS POLLICIE IN LCVE T'ANTICIPATE              3.118.9
AND RUIN'D LOVE WHEN IT IS BUILT ANEW           3.119.11
NOR NEED I TALLIES THY DEARE LOVE TO SKORE      3.122.10
YF MY DEARE LOVE WERE BUT THE CHILDE OF STATE   3.124.1
AS SUBJECT TO TIMES LOVE, OR TO TIMES HATE      3.124.3
I LOVE TO HEARE HER SPEAKE, YET WELL I KNOW     3.130.9
AND YET BY HEAVEN I THINKE MY LOVE AS RARE      3.130.13
THY FACE HATH NOT THE PCWER TO MAKE LOVE GRONE  3.131.6
THINE EIES I LOVE, AND THEY AS PITTYING ME      3.132.1
THUS FARRE FOR LOVE, MY LOVE-SUTE SWEET FULLFILL 3.136.4
$WILL, WILL FULFILL THE TREASURE OF THY LOVE    3.136.5
MAKE BUT MY NAME THY LOVE, AND LOVE THAT STILL  3.136.13
MAKE BUT MY NAME THY LOVE, AND LOVE THAT STILL  3.136.13
THOU BLINDE FOOLE LCVE, WHAT DOOST THOU
                        TO MINE EYES            3.137.1
WHEN MY LOVE SWEARES THAT SHE IS MADE OF TRUTH  3.138.1
AND AGE IN LOVE, LCVES NCT T' HAVE YEARES TOLD  3.138.12
LET ME EXCUSE THEE, AH MY LOVE WELL KNOWES      3.139.9
THOUGH NOT TO LOVE, YET LOVE TO TELL ME SO      3.140.6
THOUGH NOT TO LOVE, YET LOVE TO TELL ME SC      3.140.6
IN FAITH I DOE NOT LOVE THEE WITH MINE EYES     3.141.1
LOVE IS MY SINNE, AND THY DEARE VERTUE HATE     3.142.1
AND SEALD FALSE BCNDS OF LOVE AS OFT AS MINE    3.142.7
BE IT LAWFULL I LCVE THEE AS THOU LOV'ST THOSE  3.142.9
MY LOVE IS AS A FEAVER LCNGING STILL            3.147.1
MY REASON THE $PHISITION TO MY LOVE             3.147.5
O ME- WHAT EYES HATH LOVE PUT IN MY HEAD        3.148.1
IF IT BE NOT, THEN LOVE DOTH WELL DENOTE        3.148.7
O CUNNING LOVE, WITH TEARES THOU KEEPST
                        ME BLINDE               3.148.13
CANST THOU $O CRUELL, SAY I LOVE THEE NOT       3.149.1
```

```
BUT LOVE HATE ON FCR NOW I KNOW THY MINDE          3.149.13
WHO TAUGHT THEE HOW TO MAKE ME LOVE THEE MORE       3.150.9
OH THOUGH I LOVE WHAT OTHERS DOE ABHOR             3.150.11
IF THY UNWORTHINESSE RAISD LOVE IN ME              3.150.13
LOVE IS TOO YOUNG TC KNOW WHAT CONSCIENCE IS       3.151.1
YET WHO KNOWES NOT CONSCIENCE IS BORNE OF LOVE     3.151.2
TRIUMPH IN LOVE, FLESH STAIES NO FARTHER REASON    3.151.8
HER LOVE, FOR WHOSE DEARE LOVE I RISE AND FALL     3.151.14
HER LOVE, FOR WHOSE DEARE LOVE I RISE AND FALL     3.151.14
BUT THOU ART TWICE FORSWCRNE TO ME LOVE SWEARING   3.152.2
IN VOWING NEW HATE AFTER NEW LOVE BEARING          3.152.4
OTHES OF THY LOVE, THY TRUTH, THY CONSTANCIE       3.152.10
WHICH BORROWD FROM THIS HOLIE FIRE OF LOVE         3.153.5
LOVES FIRE HEATES WATER, WATER COOLES NOT LOVE     3.154.14
LOVING IN TRUTH, AND FAINE IN VERSE MY
                          LOVE TO SHOW              4.1.1
LOVE GAVE THE WOUND, WHICH WHILE I BREATHE
                          WILL BLEED               4.2.2
I LOVED, BUT STRAIGHT DID NOT WHAT $LOVE DECREED   4.2.6
WHAT $LOVE AND $BEAUTIE BE, THEN ALL MY DEED       4.3.13
IF VAINE LOVE HAVE MY SIMPLE SOULE OPPREST         4.4.3
THAT $VERTUE, THOU THY SELFE SHALT BE IN LOVE      4.4.14
TRUE, AND YET TRUE THAT I MUST $STELLA LCVE        4.5.14
WHEN TREMBLING VOICE BRINGS FORTH THAT
                          I DO $STELLA LCVE         4.6.14
BOTH SO AND THUS, SHE MINDING $LOVE SHOULD BE      4.7.12
LOVE BORNE IN $GREECE, CF LATE FLED FROM
                          HIS NATIVE PLACE          4.8.1
WOULDST BRABLING BE WITH SENCE AND LOVE IN ME      4.10.2
DEALE THOU WITH PCWERS CF THOUGHTS, LEAVE
                          LOVE TO WILL              4.10.8
BUT THOU WOULDST NEEDS FIGHT BOTH WITH
                          LOVE AND SENCE            4.10.9
BY REASON GOOD, GCCD REASON HER TO LOVE            4.10.14
IN TRUTH, O $LOVE, WITH WHAT A BOYISH KIND         4.11.1
PHOEBUS WAS $JUDGE BETWEENE $JOVE, $MARS,
                          AND $LOVE                 4.13.1
WHILE $LOVE ON ME DCTH ALL HIS QUIVER SPEND        4.14.4
THEN $LOVE IS SINNE, AND LET ME SINFULL BE         4.14.14
BUT IF (BOTH FOR YCUR LCVE AND SKILL) YOUR NAME    4.15.12
AND, $LOVE, I THOUGHT THAT I WAS FULL OF THEE      4.16.4
BY MY LOVE JUDGING WHAT $LOVE'S PAINE MIGHT BE     4.16.8
I NOW HAVE LEARN'D $LOVE RIGHT, AND LEARN'D
                          EVEN SO                   4.16.13
BECAUSE THAT $MARS, GROWNE SLACKER IN HER LOVE     4.17.2
'SCHOLLER,' SAITH $LOVE, 'BEND HITHERWARC
                          YOUR WIT'                 4.19.14
MY YOUNG MIND MARDE, WHCM $LOVE DOTH WINDLAS SO    4.21.2
AND KNOWING, LOVE, AND LCVING, LAY APART           4.24.7
THE RICHEST GEMME CF $LCVE AND LIFE ENJOYES        4.24.10
STRANGE FLAMES OF $LOVE IT IN OUR SOULES
                          WOULD RAISE               4.25.4
LOVE OF HER SELFE, TAKES $STELLA'S SHAPE,
                          THAT SHE                  4.25.10
AND FIND TH'EFFECT, FOR I DO BURNE IN LOVE         4.25.14
THE RAINES OF $LOVE I LCVE, THOUGH NEVER SLAKE     4.28.7
THE RAINES OF $LOVE I LCVE, THOUGH NEVER SLAKE     4.28.7
LOVE ONELY READING UNTO ME THIS ART                4.28.14
SO $STELLA'S HEART, FINDING WHAT POWER
                          $LOVE BRINGS              4.29.5
```

```
SURE, IF THAT LONG WITH $LOVE ACQUAINTED EYES          4.31.5
CAN JUDGE OF $LOVE, THOU FEEL'ST A $LOVER'S CASE        4.31.6
IS CONSTANT $LOVE DEEM'D THERE BUT WANT OF WIT+         4.31.10
DO THEY ABOVE LOVE TO BE LOV'D, AND YET                 4.31.12
THOSE $LOVERS SCORNE WHOM THAT $LOVE DOTH
                                    POSSESSE+           4.31.13
AND THERE LONG SINCE, $LOVE THY $LIEUTENANT LIES        4.36.5
WHO WHILE THEY MAKE $LOVE CONQUER, CONQUER $LOVE        4.42.3
WHO WHILE THEY MAKE $LOVE CONQUER, CONQUER $LOVE        4.42.3
WRACKES $TRIUMPHS BE, WHICH $LOVE (HIGH
                          SET) DOTH BREED               4.42.14
WHERE BLUSHING RED, THAT $LOVE'S SELFE
                          THEM DOTH LOVE                4.43.10
HER FACE+ $O $LOVE, A $ROGUE THOU THEN
                          SHOULDST BE                   4.46.6
IF $LOVE LEARNE NOT ALONE TO LOVE AND SEE               4.46.7
IF $LOVE LEARNE NOT ALONE TO LOVE AND SEE               4.46.7
UNKIND, I LOVE YOU NOT.. $O ME, THAT EYE                4.47.13
WHERE $LOVE IS CHASTNESSE, $PAINE DOTH
                          LEARNE DELIGHT                4.48.3
I ON MY HORSE, AND $LOVE ON ME DOTH TRIE                4.49.1
A HORSMAN TO MY HORSE, A HORSE TO $LOVE                 4.49.3
A STRIFE IS GROWNE BETWEENE $VERTUE AND $LOVE           4.52.1
HER EYES, HER LIPS, HER ALL, SAITH $LOVE DO THIS        4.52.3
WELL $LOVE, SINCE THIS DEMURRE OUR SUTE
                          DOTH STAY                     4.52.12
BECAUSE I BREATHE NOT LOVE TO EVERIE ONE                4.54.1
HE CANNOT LOVE.. NO, NO, LET HIM ALONE'                 4.54.8
THEY LOVE INDEED, WHO QUAKE TO SAY THEY LOVE            4.54.14
THEY LOVE INDEED, WHO QUAKE TO SAY THEY LOVE            4.54.14
FOR LET ME BUT NAME HER WHOM I DO LOVE                  4.55.12
IF HE DO LOVE, I BURNE, I BURNE IN LOVE                 4.59.2
IF HE DO LOVE, I BURNE, I BURNE IN LOVE                 4.59.2
TO WITLESSE THINGS, THEN $LOVE I HOPE (SINCE WIT        4.59.13
SHEWES LOVE AND PITIE TO MY ABSENT CASE                 4.60.8
THE GROUND OF THIS FIERCE $LOVE AND LOVELY HATE         4.60.11
NOW SINCE HER CHAST MIND HATES THIS LOVE IN ME          4.61.9
THAT I LOVE NOT, WITHOUT I LEAVE TO LOVE                4.61.14
THAT I LOVE NOT, WITHOUT I LEAVE TO LOVE                4.61.14
WITH RAGE OF $LOVE, I CALD MY $LOVE UNKIND              4.62.2
WITH RAGE OF $LOVE, I CALD MY $LOVE UNKIND              4.62.2
SHE IN WHOSE EYES $LOVE, THOUGH UNFELT,
                          DOTH SHINE                    4.62.3
SWEET SAID THAT I TRUE LOVE IN HER SHOULD FIND          4.62.4
THAT LOVE SHE DID, BUT LOVED A $LOVE NOT BLIND          4.62.6
THAT LOVE SHE DID, BUT LOVED A $LOVE NOT BLIND          4.62.6
WILLD ME THESE TEMPESTS OF VAINE LOVE TO FLIE           4.62.10
OF $LOVE, NEW-COIND TO HELPE MY BEGGERY                 4.62.13
DEARE, LOVE ME NOT, THAT YOU MAY LOVE ME MORE           4.62.14
DEARE, LOVE ME NOT, THAT YOU MAY LOVE ME MORE           4.62.14
SHE LIGHTNING $LOVE, DISPLAYING $VENUS' SKIES           4.63.7
BUT DO NOT WILL ME FROM MY $LOVE TO FLIE                4.64.8
LOVE BY SURE PROOFE I MAY CALL THEE UNKIND              4.65.1
THEY FLED WITH BLUSH, WHICH GUILTIE SEEM'D
                          OF LOVE                       4.66.14
LET HIM BUT LEARNE OF $LOVE TO READE IN THEE            4.71.3
SO WHILE THY BEAUTIE DRAWES THE HEART TO LOVE           4.71.12
AS FAST THY $VERTUE BENDS THAT LOVE TO GOOD             4.71.13
AND OFT SO CLINGS TO MY PURE $LOVE, THAT I              4.72.2
LOVE STILL A BOY, AND OFT A WANTON IS                   4.73.1
```

```
SWEET, IT WAS SAUCIE $LOVE, NOT HUMBLE I            4.73.8
TO LOSE HIS $CROWNE, RATHER THEN FAILE HIS $LOVE    4.75.14
THE ONELY LIGHT OF JOY, THE ONELY WARMTH OF $LOVE   4.76.4
O HOW THE PLEASANT AIRES OF TRUE LOVE BE            4.78.1
BREAKEFAST OF $LOVE, BUT LO, LO, WHERE SHE IS       4.79.13
BY LINKES OF $LOVE, AND ONLY $NATURE'S ART          4.81.6
WHEN IN HER NECKE YOU DID $LOVE DITTIES PEEPE       4.83.6
WITH WINGS OF $LOVE IN AIRE OF WONDER FLIE          4.86.8
YET SWAM IN JOY, SUCH LOVE IN HER WAS SEENE         4.87.11
WHERE MEMORY SETS FOORTH THE BEAMES OF LOVE         4.88.11
IN HART BOTH SIGHT AND LOVE NOW COUPLED BE          4.88.13
WHO SEEKE, WHO HOPE, WHO LOVE, WHO LIVE BUT THEE    4.90.2
AND LOVE DOTH HOLD MY HAND, AND MAKES ME WRITE      4.90.14
NOT THEM, O NO, BUT YOU IN THEM I LOVE              4.91.14
OR IF THY LOVE OF PLAINT YET MINE FORBEARES         4.94.9
BY LOVE WERE MADE APT TO CONSORT WITH ME            4.95.11
BUT AH POORE $NIGHT, IN LOVE WITH $PHOEBUS' LIGHT   4.97.5
LOVE MOVES THY PAINE, AND LIKE A FAITHFULL PAGE     4.101.9
IT IS BUT LOVE, WHICH MAKES HIS PAPER
                              PERFIT WHITE          4.102.12
DO $STELLA LOVE. $FOOLES, WHO DOTH IT DENY+         4.104.14
I SWEARE BY HER I LOVE AND LACKE, THAT I            4.105.5
AND SCORNING SAY, '$SEE WHAT IT IS TO LOVE'         4.107.14
OF TH'INWARD BALE OF MY LOVE PINED HART             5.2.2
WHICH IF SHE GRAUNT, THEN LIVE AND MY
                              LOVE CHERISH          5.2.13
FRESH LOVE, THAT LONG HATH SLEPT IN CHEERLESSE
                              BOWER                 5.4.6
PREPARE YOUR SELFE NEW LOVE TO ENTERTAINE           5.4.14
SUCH LOVE NOT LYKE TO LUSTS OF BASER KYND           5.6.3
THEN IS MY SOULE WITH LIFE AND LOVE INSPIRED        5.7.6
UNRIGHTEOUS $LORD OF LOVE WHAT LAW IS THIS          5.10.1
THOSE ENGINS CAN THE PROUDEST LOVE CONVERT          5.14.12
FOR LOE MY LOVE DOTH IN HER SELFE CONTAINE          5.15.5
THEREFORE $O LOVE, UNLESSE SHE TURNE TO THEE        5.19.13
SHE TO HER LOVE DOTH LOOKERS EYES ALLURE            5.21.6
THEN FLY NO MORE FAYRE LOVE FROM $PHEBUS CHACE      5.28.13
BUT IN YOUR BREST HIS LEAFE AND LOVE EMBRACE        5.28.14
MY LOVE IS LYKE TO YSE, AND I TO FYRE               5.30.1
SUCH IS THE POWRE OF LOVE IN GENTLE MIND            5.30.13
OF A PROUD LOVE, THAT DOTH MY SPIRITE SPOYLE        5.33.12
SWEET SMILE, THE DAUGHTER OF THE $QUEENE OF LOVE    5.39.1
THE LOVE WHICH ME SO CRUELLY TORMENTETH             5.42.1
THE MORE I LOVE AND DOE EMBRACE MY BANE             5.42.4
LOVE LEARNED LETTERS TO HER EYES TO READ            5.43.12
UNTO HER LOVE, AND TEMPTE TO THEYR DECAY            5.47.6
O MIGHTY CHARM WHICH MAKES MEN LOVE THEYR BANE      5.47.13
MY LOVE LYKE THE $SPECTATOR YDLY SITS               5.54.2
NOT WATER., FOR HER LOVE DOTH BURNE LIKE FYRE       5.55.6
BASE THINGS THAT TO HER LOVE TOO BOLD ASPIRE+       5.61.12
SO LIKEWISE LOVE CHEARE YOU YOUR HEAVY SPRIGHT      5.62.13
THE DOUBT WHICH YE MISDEEME, FAYRE LOVE, IS VAINE   5.65.1
SWEET BE THE BANDS, THE WHICH TRUE LOVE DOTH TYE    5.65.5
THE LEAGUE TWIXT THEM, THAT LOYAL LOVE
                              HATH BOUND            5.65.10
THAT YE YOUR LOVE LENT TO SO MEANE A ONE            5.66.4
AND THAT THY LOVE WE WEIGHING WORTHILY              5.68.9
MAY LIKEWISE LOVE THEE FOR THE SAME AGAINE          5.68.10
WITH LOVE MAY ONE ANOTHER ENTERTAYNE                5.68.12
SO LET US LOVE, DEARE LOVE, LYKE AS WE OUGHT        5.68.13
```

SO LET US LOVE, DEARE LOVE, LYKE AS WE OUGHT   5.68.13
LOVE IS THE LESSON WHICH THE $LORD US TAUGHT   5.68.14
ADORN'D WITH HONOUR, LOVE, AND CHASTITY   5.69.8
GOE TO MY LOVE, WHERE SHE IS CARELESSE LAYD   5.70.5
TO WAYT ON LOVE AMONGST HIS LOVELY CREW   5.70.10
MAKE HAST THEREFORE SWEET LOVE, WHILEST
                               IT IS PRIME   5.70.13
OF A DEARE FOE, AND THRALLED TO HIS LOVE   5.71.6
THE THIRD MY LOVE, MY LIVES LAST ORNAMENT   5.74.9
OUR LOVE SHALL LIVE, AND LATER LIFE RENEW   5.75.14
THE NEAST OF LOVE, THE LODGING OF DELIGHT   5.76.2
BY $LOVE HIMSELFE AND IN HIS GARDEN PLASTE   5.77.12
LACKYNG MY LOVE I GO FROM PLACE TO PLACE   5.78.1
FAYRE IS MY LOVE, WHEN HER FAYRE GOLDEN HEARES   5.81.1
OR IN HER EYES THE FYRE OF LOVE DOES SPARKE   5.81.4
THAT ARE SO MUCH BY SO MEANE LOVE EMBASED   5.82.4
IN MY TRUE LOVE DID STIRRE UP COLES OF YRE   5.86.8
SINCE I DID LEAVE THE PRESENCE OF MY LOVE   5.87.1
MOURNE TO MY SELFE THE ABSENCE OF MY LOVE   5.89.6
LOVE-AFFAMISHED   1
AND THEREON FEED MY LOVE-AFFAMISHT HART   5.88.12
LOVED   24
AND TELL TH'UNKINDE, HOW DEARELY I HAVE LOV'D HER   1.2.14
IF I HAVE LOV'D HER DEARER THEN MY BREATH   1.21.9
BUT LOVE NOW WHILST THOU MAIST BE LOV'D AGAINE   1.39.14
BUT LOVE WHILST THAT THOU MAIST BE LOV'D AGAINE   1.40.1
I THAT HAVE LOV'D THEE THUS BEFORE THOU FADST   1.41.7
SUFFICE, THOU SHALT BE LOV'D AS WELL AS SHEE   1.43.14
YET COUNT IT NO DISGRACE THAT I HAVE LOV'D THEE   1.44.14
SUFFICE, THEY SHEW I LIV'D AND LOV'D THEE DEARE   1.55.14
BY THINE OWNE LOVED $PSYCHES, BY THE $FIRES   2.36.9
KINDER THEN SHE WHOM I SO LONG HAVE LOVED   2.45.14
LOV'D MORE THEN LIFE, YET ONELY ART HIS LOVE   2.129.11
THEIR IMAGES I LOV'D, I VIEW IN THEE   3.31.13
AND YET IT MAY BE SAID I LOV'D HER DEERELY   3.42.2
HIS RIDER LOV'D NOT SPEED BEING MADE FROM THEE   3.50.8
BOTH GRACE AND FAULTS ARE LOV'D OF MORE AND LESSE   3.96.3
I NEVER WRIT, NOR NO MAN EVER LOVED   3.116.14
I SAW AND LIKED, I LIKED BUT LOVED NOT   4.2.5
I LOVED, BUT STRAIGHT DID NOT WHAT $LOVE DECREED   4.2.6
DO THEY ABOVE LOVE TO BE LOV'D, AND YET   4.31.12
ONLY LOV'D $TYRANTS, JUST IN CRUELTY   4.42.6
THAT LOVE SHE DID, BUT LOVED A $LOVE NOT BLIND   4.62.6
WHICH WOULD NOT LET ME, WHOM SHE LOVED, DECLINE   4.62.7
THAT WHERE BEFORE HART LOVED AND EYES DID SEE   4.88.12
THEN DARE BE LOV'D BY MEN OF MEANE DEGREE   5.61.14
LOVE-GOD   1
THIS LITTLE $LOVE-$GOD LYING ONCE A SLEEPE   3.154.1
LOVE-KINDLING   1
AND HIS LOVE-KINDLING FIRE DID QUICKLY STEEPE   3.153.3
LOVELESS   1
MAY JUSTLY PRAISE, AND BLAME MY LOVELESSE $FAIRE   1.2.8
LOVELINESS   1
UNTHRIFTY LOVELINESSE WHY DOST THOU SPEND   3.4.1
LOVELY   25
MOST FAIRE AND LOVELY $MAIDE, LOOKE FROM
                              THE SHORE   1.46.1
AND WAST HIM TO THEE WITH THOSE LOVELY EIES   1.46.5
THAT LOVELY, ARCHED, YVORIE, POLLISH'D $BROW   2.8.5
LAUGHING FOR JOY UPON MY LOVELY FAYRE   2.125.14

```
     CALLS BACKE THE LOVELY $APRILL OF HER PRIME          3.3.10
     THE LOVELY GAZE WHERE EVERY EYE DOTH DWELL           3.5.2
     THOU ART MORE LOVELY AND MORE TEMPERATE              3.18.2
     AND SO OF YOU, BEAUTIOUS AND LOVELY YOUTH            3.54.13
     I GRANT (SWEET LOVE) THY LOVELY ARGUMENT             3.79.5
     HOW SWEET AND LOVELY DOST THOU MAKE THE SHAME        3.95.1
     IN PRAISE OF $LADIES DEAD, AND LOVELY $KNIGHTS       3.106.4
     O THOU MY LOVELY $BOY WHO IN THY POWER               3.126.1
     NO LOVELY $PARIS MADE THY $HELLEN HIS                4.33.6
     THE GROUND OF THIS FIERCE $LOVE AND LOVELY HATE      4.60.11
     ANGER INVESTS WITH SUCH A LOVELY GRACE               4.73.13
     FOR WHEN YE MILDLY LOOKE WITH LOVELY HEW             5.7.5
     LOOKE EVER LOVELY, AS BECOMES YOU BEST               5.7.10
     THE LOVELY PLEASANCE AND THE LOFTY PRIDE             5.17.11
     PROUD $DAPHNE SCORNING $PHAEBUS LOVELY FYRE          5.28.9
     THROUGH SWEET ALLUREMENT OF HER LOVELY HEW           5.31.10
     WITH LOVELY LIGHT TO CLEARE MY CLOUDY GRIEF          5.34.12
     HER EYES LOOKE LOVELY AND UPON THEM SMYLE            5.47.10
     HER LOVELY EYES LYKE $PINCKS BUT NEWLY SPRED         5.64.8
     TO WAYT ON LOVE AMONGST HIS LOVELY CREW              5.70.10
     HOW WAS I RAVISHT WITH YOUR LOVELY SIGHT             5.76.5
LOVER                        1
     THESE POORE RUDE LINES OF THY DECEASED $LOVER        3.32.4
LOVERS                       9
     AND THAT MAKES HAPPY $LOVERS EVER DOMBE              1.17.14
     ME THINKES THIS $TIME BECOMMETH $LOVERS BEST         2.37.3
     HUNG WITH THE TROPHEIS OF MY LOVERS GON              3.31.10
     THY LOVERS WITHERING, AS THY SWEET SELFE GROW'ST     3.126.4
     SOME $LOVERS SPEAKE WHEN THEY THEIR $MUSES
                              ENTERTAINE                  4.6.1
     THOSE $LOVERS SCORNE WHOM THAT $LOVE DOTH
                              POSSESSE+                   4.31.13
     OF $LOVERS NEVER KNOWNE, A GRIEVOUS CASE             4.45.6
     DUMBE $SWANNES, NOT CHATRING $PIES, DO
                              $LOVERS PROVE               4.54.13
     THAT WARNES AL LOVERS WAYT UPON THEIR KING           5.19.3
LOVER'S                      4
     MY SWEET LOVES BEAUTY, THOUGH MY LOVERS LIFE         3.63.12
     CAN JUDGE OF $LOVE, THOU FEEL'ST A $LOVER'S CASE     4.31.6
     OF $LOVER'S RUINE SOME SAD $TRAGEDIE                 4.45.13
     WHY THEN DOE I, UNTRAINDE IN LOVERS TRADE            5.51.5
LOVERS'                      4
     BY ALL TRUE $LOVERS $SIGHES, $VOWES, AND
                              $DESIRES                    2.36.11
     YOU LIVE IN THIS, AND DWELL IN LOVERS EIES           3.55.14
     THEN BY THAT COUNT, WHICH LOVERS BOOKS INVENT        5.60.9
     FOR DAMZELS FIT TO DECKE THEIR LOVERS BOWRES         5.64.4
LOVES                       16
     EQUALL WITH HIS, THAT LOVES HIS $MISTRES MOST        2.27.12
     SOME, WHEN IN $RYME, THEY OF THEIR $LOVES
                              DOE TELL                    2.39.1
     SOME WHEN IN RYME THEY OF THEIR $LOVES DOE TELL      2.118.1
     MINE BE THY LOVE AND THY LOVES USE THEIR
                              TREASURE                    3.20.14
     ALTHOUGH OUR UNDEVIDED LOVES ARE ONE                 3.36.2
     IN OUR TWO LOVES THERE IS BUT ONE RESPECT            3.36.5
     TAKE ALL MY LOVES, MY LOVE, YEA TAKE THEM ALL        3.40.1
     SWEETE FLATTERY, THEN SHE LOVES BUT ME ALONE         3.42.14
     THAT MINE EYE LOVES IT AND DOTH FIRST BEGINNE        3.114.14
     AND AGE IN LOVE, LOVES NOT T' HAVE YEARES TOLD       3.138.12
```

```
BUT 'TIS MY HEART THAT LOVES WHAT THEY DISPISE      3.141.3
TWO LOVES I HAVE OF COMFORT AND DISPAIRE            3.144.1
LEGIONS OF LOVES WITH LITTLE WINGS DID FLY          5.16.6
THAT SHE WILL PLAGUE THE MAN THAT LOVES HER MOST    5.41.6
AND FROM ALL WANDRING LOVES WHICH MOTE PERVART      5.42.11
BUT HE MOST HAPPY WHO SUCH ONE LOVES BEST           5.59.14
LOVE'S                59
THESE SAD MEMORIALS OF MY LOVES DISPAIRE            1.9.4
MAY IN HIS $SHADOW MY $LOVES STORIE READ            2.13.14
BUT STILL DISTRACTED IN $LOVES $LUNACIE             2.41.9
NOW AT THE LAST GASPE, OF $LOVES LATEST $BREATH     2.61.9
MY LOVES $SCHOOLE-MISTRIS NOW HATH TAUGHT ME SO     2.111.13
MAY IN HIS SHADOW MY $LOVES STORY READE             2.121.14
LOVES $METHRIDATE, THE PUREST OF PERFECTION         2.123.5
SO IN LOVES DEATH SHALL LOVES PERFECTION PROVE      2.139.9
SO IN LOVES DEATH SHALL LOVES PERFECTION PROVE      2.139.9
THE MOURNFULL ACCENTS OF MY LOVES DISPAYRE          2.141.8
BUT STILL DISTRACTED IN LOVES $LUNACY               2.143.9
STRONG LOCKE OF KINDNESSE, $CLOSET OF
                             LOVES STORE            2.146.5
O CARVE NOT WITH THY HOWERS MY LOVES FAIRE BROW     3.19.9
THE PERFECT CEREMONY OF LOVES RIGHT                 3.23.6
AND IN MINE OWNE LOVES STRENGTH SEEME TO DECAY      3.23.7
ORE-CHARG'D WITH BURTHEN OF MINE OWNE LOVES MIGHT   3.23.8
TO HEARE WIT EIES BELONGS TO LOVES FINE WIHT        3.23.14
AND WEEPE A FRESH LOVES LONG SINCE CANCELD WOE      3.30.7
AND THERE RAIGNES $LOVE AND ALL $LOVES
                             LOVING PARTS           3.31.3
WHICH THOUGH IT ALTER NOT LOVES SOLE EFFECT         3.36.7
YET DOTH IT STEALE SWEET HOURES FROM LOVES
                             DELIGHT                3.36.8
TO BEARE LOVES WRONG, THEN HATES KNOWNE INJURY      3.40.12
IF I LOOSE THEE, MY LOSSE IS MY LOVES GAINE         3.42.9
WITH MY LOVES PICTURE THEN MY EYE DOTH FEAST        3.47.5
MY SWEET LOVES BEAUTY, THOUGH MY LOVERS LIFE        3.63.12
LIKE A DECEIVED HUSBAND, SO LOVES FACE              3.93.2
IF NOT FROM MY LOVES BREATH, THE PURPLE PRIDE       3.99.3
IN MY LOVES VEINES THOU HAST TOO GROSELY DIED       3.99.5
RISE RESTY $MUSE, MY LOVES SWEET FACE SURVAY        3.100.9
SO THAT ETERNALL LOVE IN LOVES FRESH CASE           3.108.9
O LOVES BEST HABIT IS IN SEEMING TRUST              3.138.11
THOSE LIPS THAT $LOVES OWNE HAND DID MAKE           3.145.1
LOVES EYE IS NOT SO TRUE AS ALL MENS.. NO           3.148.8
HOW CAN IT+ $O HOW CAN LOVES EYE BE TRUE            3.148.9
BUT AT MY MISTRES EIE LOVES BRAND NEW FIRED         3.153.9
WHICH FROM LOVES FIRE TOOKE HEAT PERPETUALL         3.154.10
LOVES FIRE HEATES WATER, WATER COOLES NOT LOVE      3.154.14
AT LENGTH TO $LOVE'S DECREES, I FORC'D, AGREED      4.2.7
BY MY LOVE JUDGING WHAT $LOVE'S PAINE MIGHT BE      4.16.8
BY $LOVE'S OWNE SELFE, BUT WITH SO CURIOUS
                             DROUGHT                4.38.7
EACH SOULE DOTH AT $LOVE'S FEET HIS WEAPONS LAY     4.43.7
WHERE BLUSHING RED, THAT $LOVE'S SELFE
                             THEM DOTH LOVE         4.43.10
ACCORDING TO MY $LORD $LOVE'S OWNE BEHEST           4.50.6
BE $LOVE'S INDEED, IN $STELLA'S SELFE HE MAY        4.52.10
OF THEM, WHO IN THEIR LIPS $LOVE'S STANDERD BEARE   4.54.6
AND THEREFORE BY HER $LOVE'S AUTHORITY              4.62.9
GRIEFE BUT $LOVE'S WINTER LIVERIE IS, THE $BOY      4.70.7
IN $LILLIES' NEAST, WHERE $LOVE'S SELFE
                             LIES ALONG             4.83.8
```

```
THE GLOBE OF WEALE, LIPS $LOVE'S INDENTURES MAKE    4.85.13
(SPURD WITH LOVE'S SPUR, THOUGH GALD AND
                        SHORTLY RAIND                 4.98.7
SHALL HANDLE YOU AND HOLD IN LOVES SOFT BANDS         5.1.3
ON THOSE FAYRE EYES MY LOVES IMMORTALL LIGHT          5.16.2
THEIR ANTHEMES SWEET DEVIZED OF LOVES PRAYSE          5.19.6
BUT MONGST THEM ALL, WHICH DID $LOVES HONOR RAYSE     5.19.9
AS BEING LONG IN HER LOVES TEMPEST TOST               5.41.11
BUT LET MY LOVES FAYRE $PLANET SHORT HER WAYES        5.60.13
OF MY LOVES CONQUEST, PEERELESSE BEAUTIES PRISE       5.69.7
FRESH SPRING THE HERALD OF LOVES MIGHTY KING          5.70.1
TO SPORT MY MUSE AND SING MY LOVES SWEET PRAISE       5.80.10
```

LOVEST   6
```
WHY LOV'ST THOU THAT WHICH THOU RECEAVST
                        NOT GLADLY                    3.8.3
BUT THAT THOU NONE LOV'ST IS MOST EVIDENT             3.10.4
AND THEN THOU LOVEST ME FOR MY NAME IS $WILL          3.136.14
TELL ME THOU LOV'ST ELSE-WHERE., BUT IN MY SIGHT      3.139.5
BE IT LAWFULL I LOVE THEE AS THOU LOV'ST THOSE        3.142.9
THOSE THAT CAN SEE THOU LOV'ST, AND I AM BLIND        3.149.14
```

LOVE-SUIT   1
```
THUS FARRE FOR LOVE, MY LOVE-SUTE SWEET FULLFILL      3.136.4
```

LOVING   18
```
LAUGHTER LOVING $GODDESSE, WORLDLY PLEASURES
                        $QUEENE                       1.10.6
BY LOVING HER, THE CRUELST $FAIRE THAT LIVES          1.22.10
HER FOR DISDAINE, AND ME FOR LOVING THUS              1.26.14
O MINE EYES $COMET, SO ADMYR'D BY LOVING              2.129.7
AND PUTS APPARRELL ON MY TOTTERED LOVING              3.26.11
AND THERE RAIGNES $LOVE AND ALL $LOVES
                        LOVING PARTS                  3.31.3
OH THEN VOUTSAFE ME BUT THIS LOVING THOUGHT           3.32.9
LOVING OFFENDORS THUS I WILL EXCUSE YEE               3.42.5
SELFE, SO SELFE LOVING WERE INIQUITY                  3.62.12
FOR BENDING ALL MY LOVING THOUGHTS ON THEE            3.88.10
EVEN TO THY PURE AND MOST MOST LOVING BREST           3.110.14
HAVE PUT ON BLACK, AND LOVING MOURNERS BEE            3.132.3
HATE OF MY SINNE, GROUNDED ON SINFULL LOVING          3.142.2
IN LOVING THEE THOU KNOW'ST I AM FORSWORNE            3.152.1
LOVING IN TRUTH, AND FAINE IN VERSE MY
                        LOVE TO SHOW                  4.1.1
TO KEEPE THE PACE OF THEIR FIRST LOVING STATE         4.17.4
AND KNOWING, LOVE, AND LOVING, LAY APART              4.24.7
JOY OF MY LIFE, FULL OFT FOR LOVING YOU               5.82.1
```

LOW   8
```
THAT EV'RY $DUDGEN LOW $INVENTION GOES+               2.31.8
FROM HIS LOW TRACT AND LOOKE AN OTHER WAY             3.7.12
AND KNOW THOSE $BODIES HIGH RAIGNE ON THE LOW         4.26.11
TH'INDIFFERENT $JUDGE BETWEENE THE HIGH AND LOW       4.39.4
FOR LATE MY HEART MOST HIGH, WITH EYES MOST LOW       4.63.5
O JOY, TOO HIGH FOR MY LOW STILE TO SHOW              4.69.1
AND TO THE GROUND HER EIE LIDS LOW EMBASETH           5.13.3
BUT LET HER PRAYSES YET BE LOW AND MEANE              5.80.13
```

LOWER   3
```
DOTH LOWRE, NAY, CHIDE., NAY, THREAT FOR
                        ONLY THIS                     4.73.7
BUT WHEN YE LOWRE, OR LOOKE ON ME ASKEW               5.7.7
MY LOWER HEAVEN, SO IT PERFORCE MUST BEE              5.46.8
```

LOWEREST   1
```
NAY IF THOU LOWRST ON ME DOE I NOT SPEND              3.149.7
```

```
LOWERS                    1
  NOW USE THE $SOMMER SMILES, ERE $WINTER LOWERS      1.40.4
LOWEST                    1
  FALS LOWEST.. FOR ON EARTH NOUGHT HATH
                              ENDURAUNCE              5.58.12
LOWLINESS                 1
  SUCH LOWLINESSE SHALL MAKE YOU LOFTY BE             5.13.14
LOWLY                     4
  THOU CHANCE TO COME, FALL LOWLY AT HER FEET         5.2.10
  YET LOWLY STILL VOUCHSAFE TO LOOKE ON ME            5.13.13
  AND TREAD MY LIFE DOWNE IN THE LOWLY FLOURE         5.20.4
  WHY DID YE STOUP UNTO SO LOWLY STATE+               5.66.8
LOYAL                     3
  IF THAT A LOYALL HART AND FAITH UNFAINED            1.15.1
  SO TRUE AND LOYALL LOVE NO FAVOUR GAINES ME         1.18.8
  THE LEAGUE TWIXT THEM, THAT LOYAL LOVE
                              HATH BOUND              5.65.10
LUCK                      2
  BUT NOT TO TELL OF GOOD, OR EVIL LUCKE              3.14.3
  YOUTH, LUCKE, AND PRAISE, EVEN FILD MY
                              VEINES WITH PRIDE       4.53.4
LUCKILY                   1
  WHOSE GLORIOUS ACTIONS LUCKILY HAD GAIND            1.45.7
LUCKLESS                  1
  SO LUCKLES WAS MY $BABES NATIVITY                   2.116.6
LUCKY                     3
  THAT LUCKIE $LOAD-STARRE OF ETERNALL LIGHT          2.129.2
  SOME LUCKIE WITS IMPUTE IT BUT TO CHAUNCE           4.41.8
  I BLESSE MY LOT, THAT WAS SO LUCKY PLACED           5.82.2
LUKEWARM                  1
  SALT LUKE-WARME TEARES SHEE FOR HIS DRINKE
                              DID GIVE                2.116.15
LUNACY                    2
  BUT STILL DISTRACTED IN $LOVES $LUNACIE             2.41.9
  BUT STILL DISTRACTED IN LOVES $LUNACY               2.143.9
LUNATIC                   1
  I WILL RESOLVE YOU., I AM $LUNATICKE                2.9.5
LURK                      2
  BUT I MUST PINE, AND IN MY PINING LURKE             1.29.11
  AND ME UNTO THE $SPYDER THAT DOTH LURKE             5.71.3
LURKEST                   1
  IN WHICH THOU LURKEST LYKE TO VIPERS BROOD          5.2.6
LUST                      3
  LIKE THEY THAT $LUST, I CARE NOT, I WILL NONE       2.39.8
  IS LUST IN ACTION, AND TILL ACTION, LUST            3.129.2
  IS LUST IN ACTION, AND TILL ACTION, LUST            3.129.2
LUSTER                    2
  THE SUN-BEAMES TO THAT LUSTRE OF HER SIGHT          2.148.3
  FRAME DAINTIEST LUSTRE, MIXT OF SHADES AND LIGHT+   4.7.4
LUSTFUL                   1
  LET NOT ONE SPARKE OF FILTHY LUSTFULL FYRE          5.84.1
LUSTS                     2
  SUCH LOVE NOT LYKE TO LUSTS OF BASER KYND           5.6.3
  THEIR LOOSER LOOKES THAT STIR UP LUSTES IMPURE      5.21.8
LUSTY                     3
  WHERE ALL THE TREASURE OF THY LUSTY DAIES           3.2.6
  SAP CHECKT WITH FROST AND LUSTIE LEAV'S QUITE GON   3.5.7
  FOR LUSTY SPRING NOW IN HIS TIMELY HOWRE            5.4.9
LUTE                      2
  LIKE AS THE $LUTE DELIGHTS OR ELS DISLIKES          1.57.1
```

```
MY $FAIRE, HAD I NCT ERST ADORND MY $LUTE        2.104.1
LYING                    2
  AND THUS (POORE $CRPHAN) LYING IN DISTRESSE     2.116.17
  THIS LITTLE $LOVE-$GOD LYING ONCE A SLEEPE      3.154.1
LYRE                     1
  WITH VOICE MORE FIT TO WED $AMPHION'S $LYRE       4.68.6
MAD                      10
  AND IN A MOMENT $MAD, $SCBER, $GLAD, AND $SORRIE 2.49.10
  ON PURPOSE LAYD TC MAKE THE TAKER MAD           3.129.8
  FOR IF I SHOULD DISPAIRE I SHOULD GROW MADDE    3.140.9
  MADDE SLANDERERS BY MADDE EARES BELEEVED BE     3.140.12
  MADDE SLANDERERS BY MADDE EARES BELEEVED BE     3.140.12
  AND FRANTICK MADDE WITH EVER-MORE UNREST        3.147.10
  MY THOUGHTS AND MY DISCCURSE AS MAD MENS ARE    3.147.11
  FOR SINCE MAD $MARCH GREAT PROMISE MADE OF ME    4.21.9
  AND GAIN'D BY $MARS, COULD YET MAD $MARS SO TAME 4.75.7
  AND I, MAD WITH DELIGHT, WANT WIT TO CEASE      4.81.13
MADDING                  1
  IN THE DISTRACTION CF THIS MADDING FEVER+       3.119.8
MADE                     63
  ARE MADE BY HER TC MURTHER THUS THEIR $LCRD      1.5.14
  AND MADE THY PASSICNS WITH HER BEAUTIE EVEN      1.8.4
  THIS HEART MADE NCW THE PROSPECTIVE OF CARE      1.22.9
  WHERE MY HARTS THEEFE TC VEXE ME MADE HER CHOICE 1.27.6
  OF HER OWNE SEATE, WHEREOF I MADE HER GUIDE      1.47.8
  WHOSE BEAUTY MADE HIM SPEAKE THAT ELSE WAS DCMBE 1.55.8
  SO $DELIA, HATH MINE ERROR MADE ME KNOWNE        1.56.5
  WHICH PITTY NOT THE WOUNDS MADE BY THEIR MIGHT   1.59.6
  MY $SOULE IS OF A BRAVER $METTLE MADE            2.4.10
  LET WHAT I PRAISE, BE STILL MADE GOOD BY YOU     2.4.13
  NOR OLDER YET, NOR WISER MADE BY YEERES          2.22.3
  A DUMBE-BORNE $MUSE MADE TO EXPRESSE THE $MIND   2.35.6
  WHEN I AM MADE UNHAPPY BY MY SKILL               2.43.12
  THEY THAT ARE BLIND, ARE $MINSTRELS OFTEN MACE   2.48.11
  PRAISE HIM WHICH MADE THAT FIRE, WHICH
                          LENDS THAT LIGHT        2.105.14
  A DUMBE-BORNE $MUSE MADE TO EXPRESSE THE MINC    2.112.6
  MY EYES MADE DIM WITH LCCKES, POURE DOWN
                          A FLOOD OF TEARS        2.133.10
  THIS WERE TO BE NEW MADE WHEN THOU ART OULD      3.2.13
  LET THOSE WHOM NATURE HATH NOT MADE FOR STORE    3.11.9
  SO I, MADE LAME BY $FORTUNES DEAREST SPIGHT      3.37.3
  HOW WOULD (I SAY) MINE EYES BE BLESSED MADE      3.43.9
  MY LIFE BEING MADE CF FCURE, WITH TWO ALCNE      3.45.7
  HIS RIDER LOV'D NCT SPEED BEING MADE FROM THEE   3.50.8
  THEREFORE DESIRE (CF PERFECTS LOVE BEING MADE)   3.51.10
  WHAT IS YOUR SUBSTANCE, WHEREOF ARE YOU MADE     3.53.1
  OF THEIR SWEET DEATHES, ARE SWEETEST ODORS MADE  3.54.12
  THAT $GOD FORBID, THAT MADE ME FIRST YOUR SLAVE  3.58.1
  AND ARTE MADE TUNG-TIDE BY AUTHORITIE            3.66.9
  ERE BEAUTIES DEAD FLEECE MADE ANOTHER GAY        3.68.8
  NOT MAKING WORSE WHAT NATURE MADE SO CLEERE      3.84.10
  AND MADE MY SELFE A MOTLEY TO THE VIEW           3.110.2
  MADE OLD OFFENCES CF AFFECTIONS NEW              3.110.4
  THAT BETTER IS, BY EVIL STILL MADE BETTER        3.119.10
  MADE MORE OR LES BY THY CONTINUALL HAST          3.123.12
  MADE $IN PURSUT AND IN PCSSESSION SO             3.129.9
  WHEN MY LOVE SWEARES THAT SHE IS MADE OF TRUTH   3.138.1
  OR MADE THEM SWERE AGAINST THE THING THEY SEE    3.152.12
  TRUE, THAT ON EARTH WE ARE BUT PILGRIMS MADE     4.5.12
```

```
WHEN $NATURE MADE HER CHIEFE WORKE, $STELLA'S EYES    4.7.1
BUT SHE MOST FAIRE, MOST COLD, MADE HIM
                      THENCE TAKE HIS FLIGHT         4.8.12
OF $STELLA'S BROWES MADE HIM TWO BETTER BOWES        4.17.10
FOR SINCE MAD $MARCH GREAT PROMISE MADE OF ME        4.21.9
WHEREWITH MY FATHER ONCE MADE IT HALFE TAME          4.30.10
NO LOVELY $PARIS MADE THY $HELLEN HIS                4.33.6
MADE MANIFEST BY SUCH A VICTORIE                     4.40.10
SENT FORTH THE BEAMES, WHICH MADE SO FAIRE
                      MY RACE                        4.41.14
WHERE $VERTUE IS MADE STRONG BY $BEAUTIE'S MIGHT     4.48.2
AND NOW HATH MADE ME TO HIS HAND SO RIGHT            4.49.13
WHO HARD BY MADE A WINDOW SEND FORTH LIGHT           4.53.9
WO, HAVING MADE WITH MANY FIGHTS HIS OWNE            4.57.1
NOR THAT HE MADE THE $FLOUREDELUCE SO FRAID          4.75.9
BE YOUR WORDS MADE (GOOD $SIR) OF $INDIAN WARE       4.92.1
GRIEFE FIND THE WORDS, FOR THOU HAST MADE
                      MY BRAINE                      4.94.1
BY LOVE WERE MADE APT TO CONSORT WITH ME             4.95.11
HAVE MADE, BUT FORST BY $NATURE STILL TO FLIE        4.103.10
MADE TO AMAZE WEAKE MENS CONFUSED SKIL               5.17.2
OF HARDEST $MARBLE ARE OF PURPOSE MADE+              5.51.2
MADE FOR TO BE THE WORLDS MOST ORNAMENT              5.53.10
THE WHICH HER MADE ATTONCE SO CRUELL FAIRE           5.55.4
WHEREOF SHE MOTE BE MADE., THAT IS THE SKYE          5.55.10
THE WHICH THREE TIMES THRISE HAPPY HATH ME MADE      5.74.3
BUT CAME THE TYDE, AND MADE MY PAYNES HIS PRAY       5.75.4
HE ONELY FAYRE, AND WHAT HE FAYRE HATH MADE          5.79.13
MADEST                    1
   FRESH SHALT THOU SEE IN ME THE WOUNDS THOU MADST  1.41.5
MADMEN                    1
   AND EVER THIS IN $MAD-MEN YOU SHALL FINDE         2.9.6
MADNESS                   2
   AND IN MY MADNESSE MIGHT SPEAKE ILL OF THEE       3.140.10
   WHYLEST RAPT WITH JOY RESEMBLING HEAVENLY MADNES  5.39.9
MAGIC                     1
   OR HAVE THINE $EYES SUCH $MAGIKE, OR THAT $ART    2.52.3
MAID                     11
   READE IT (SWEET MAIDE) THOUGH IT BE DONE
                      BUT SLEIGHTLY                  1.1.13
   WITH FAIREST HAND, THE SWEET UNKINDEST $MAID      1.5.7
   A MODEST $MAIDE, DECKT WITH A BLUSH OF HONOR      1.6.5
   AND SHE (TH'UNKINDEST MAID) STILL SCORNS
                      THE SAME                       1.15.12
   MOST FAIRE AND LOVELY $MAIDE, LOOKE FROM
                      THE SHORE                      1.46.1
   AH SPORT (SWEET $MAIDE) IN SEASON OF THESE YEARES 1.51.5
   THAT $SOULE (SWEET $MAID) WHICH SO HATH
                      HONOR'D $THEE                  2.55.11
   READE HEERE (SWEET $MAYD) THE STORY OF MY WO      2.101.1
   THAT SOULE (SWEET $MAIDE) WHICH SO HATH
                      HONORED THEE                   2.102.11
   A MAIDE OF $DYANS THIS ADVANTAGE FOUND            3.153.2
   OF THAT PROUD MAYD, WHOM NOW THOSE LEAVES ATTYRE  5.28.8
MAIDEN                    4
   AND MANY MAIDEN GARDENS YET UNSET                 3.16.6
   AND MAIDEN VERTUE RUDELY STRUMPETED               3.66.6
   CAME TRIPPING BY, BUT IN HER MAIDEN HAND          3.154.4
   YET AH, MY $MAYD'N $MUSE DOTH BLUSH TO
                      TELL THE BEST                  4.77.14
```

```
MAIDS                        1
   BUT YOU FAIRE MAIDES, AT LENGTH THIS TRUE
                        SHALL FIND             4.54.11
MAIMED                       3
   AND SCORNING $REASON'S MAYMED $ARGUMENT     2.38.6
   AND SCORNING $REASONS MAYMED $ARGUMENT      2.131.6
   THAT BAD HIS FRIEND, BUT THEN NEW MAIM'D, TO BE   4.106.13
MAIN                         6
   (QUOTH I) $THE $MAINE LOST, CAST THE $BY AWAY   2.59.11
   NATIVITY ONCE IN THE MAINE OF LIGHT         3.60.5
   AND THE FIRME SOILE WIN OF THE WATRY MAINE  3.64.7
   ON YOUR BROAD MAINE DOTH WILFULLY APPEARE   3.80.8
   AS HIS MAINE FORCE, CHOISE SPORT, AND
                        EASEFULL STAY          4.43.4
   NAY SORROW COMES WITH SUCH MAINE RAGE, THAT HE   4.95.9
MAINTAINE                    3
   THIS LOVE, TEARS, SIGHES, MAINTAINE EACH
                        ONE HIS ELEMENT        2.127.4
   UNLESSE THIS GENERALL EVILL THEY MAINTAINE  3.121.13
   I AM RESOLV'D THY ERROUR TO MAINTAINE       4.67.13
MAINTAINED                   1
   MOTE HAVE YOUR LIFE IN HONOUR LONG MAINTAYNED   5.36.12
MAINTAINS                    2
   LOVE IS THE $FEWELL, WHICH MAINTAINES THE FIRE   2.40.4
   LOVE IS THE FUELL WHICH MAINTAINES THE FIRE 2.144.4
MAJESTY                      5
   SERVING WITH LOOKES HIS SACRED MAJESTY      3.7.4
   AND GIVEN GRACE A DOUBLE $MAJESTIE          3.78.8
   AND IF FROM $MAJESTIE OF SACRED LIGHTS      4.42.12
   AND $HUMBLENESSE GROWES ONE WITH $MAJESTIE  4.48.4
   MYLD HUMBLESSE MIXT WITH AWFULL MAJESTY     5.13.5
MAKE                       126
   TIS NOT DISDAINE MUST MAKE ME LEAVE TO LOVE 1.8.14
   THE SWEETEST SACRIFICE MY YOUTH CAN MAKE+   1.17.4
   WHY SHOULD I STRIVE TO MAKE HER LIVE FOR EVER   1.17.5
   MAKE HER THE SENTENCE OF HER WRATH REPEALE  1.22.4
   WHOSE CLOUDED BROW DOTH MAKE MY DAIES SO SAD 1.26.4
   WHILST WE BOTH MAKE THE WORLD ADMIRE AT US  1.26.13
   YET HEAVY HEART TO MAKE SO HARD A CHOISE    1.28.3
   FIXT SURE THEY ARE, BUT WANDRING MAKE ME STRAY   1.34.11
   DID MAKE THE HONOUR OF THE FALL THE MORE    1.35.4
   BUT ($PHAENIX-LIKE) SHALL MAKE HER LIVE ANEW 1.38.14
   MAKE ME TO SAY, WHEN ALL MY GRIEFES ARE GONE 1.51.13
   AND NO REMOVE CAN MAKE THY SORROWES LESSE+  1.52.4
   FOR NO GROUND ELS COULD MAKE THE MUSICKE SUCH 1.57.13
   ANSWERE NO MORE, WITH $SILENCE MAKE REPLY   2.5.11
   THEN WOULD I MAKE THEE READ, BUT TO DESPIGHT THEE   2.8.14
   OF LIVELESSE $CLODS, US LIVING $MEN TO MAKE 2.14.7
   YOU LOVE IN $HATE, BY $HATE TO MAKE $ME
                        LOVE $YOU              2.19.14
   WITH WHAT MIGHT MAKE THE $MISERABLE BLEST   2.23.8
   THE $CIRCUMSTANCE DOTH MAKE IT GOOD, OR ILL 2.28.14
   TO MAKE HER LOVE, OR $CUPID BE THOU DAMN'D  2.36.14
   MEDEA-LIKE, I MAKE THEE YOUNG AGAINE        2.44.6
   FIRST MAKE INCISION ON EACH MAST'RING $VEINE 2.50.6
   FAIRE WORDS MAKE $FOOLES, REPLYETH HE AGAINE 2.59.4
   MAKE KNOWNE THE $FAITH, THAT $FORTUNE
                        COULD NOT MOVE         2.60.5
   HEERE MAKE A $PERIOD $TIME, AND SAIE FOR MEE 2.107.13
   OR MAKE MY PEN HER NAME IMORTALIZE          2.123.11
```

```
THE DAINTY GRASSE MAKE MUSICKE WITH HER FEETE          2.125.8
AND OF JUST LENGTH OUR NIGHT AND DAY DOTH MAKE         2.147.3
MAKE KNOWNE THAT FAYTH, UNKINDNES COULD NOT MOVE       2.149.5
SHALL SUM MY COUNT, AND MAKE MY OLD EXCUSE             3.2.11
MAKE SWEET SOME VIALL., TREASURE THOU SOME PLACE       3.6.3
TO BE DEATHS CONQUEST AND MAKE WORMES THINE HEIRE      3.6.14
MAKE THEE AN OTHER SELFE FOR LOVE OF ME                3.10.13
AND THREESCOORE YEARE WOULD MAKE THE WORLD AWAY        3.11.8
THEN OF THY BEAUTY DO I QUESTION MAKE                  3.12.9
AND NOTHING GAINST $TIMES SIETH CAN MAKE DEFENCE       3.12.13
MAKE WARRE UPPON THIS BLOUDIE TIRANT TIME+             3.16.2
CAN MAKE YOU LIVE YOUR SELFE IN EIES OF MEN            3.16.12
AND MAKE THE EARTH DEVOURE HER OWNE SWEET BROOD        3.19.2
MAKE GLAD AND SORRY SEASONS AS THOU FLEET'ST           3.19.5
MAY MAKE SEEME BARE, IN WANTING WORDS TO SHEW IT       3.26.6
AND NIGHT DOTH NIGHTLY MAKE GREEFES LENGTH
                             SEEME STRONGER            3.28.14
AND MAKE ME TRAVAILE FORTH WITHOUT MY CLOAKE           3.34.2
ALL MEN MAKE FAULTS, AND EVEN I IN THIS                3.35.5
I MAKE MY LOVE INGRAFTED TO THIS STORE                 3.37.8
AND THAT THOU TEACHEST HOW TO MAKE ONE TWAINE          3.39.13
THEN THOU WHOSE SHADDOW SHADDOWES DOTH
                             MAKE BRIGHT               3.43.5
TO MAKE SOME SPECIALL INSTANT SPECIALL BLEST           3.52.11
SAVE WHERE YOU ARE, HOW HAPPY YOU MAKE THOSE           3.57.12
LIKE AS THE WAVES MAKE TOWARDS THE PIBLED SHORE        3.60.1
IF THINKING ON ME THEN SHOULD MAKE YOU WOE             3.71.8
TO MAKE ME TOUNG-TIDE SPEAKING OF YOUR FAME            3.80.4
OR I SHALL LIVE YOUR $EPITAPH TO MAKE                  3.81.1
JOYNE WITH THE SPIGHT OF FORTUNE, MAKE ME BOW          3.90.3
ALL THIS AWAY, AND ME MOST WRETCHED MAKE               3.91.14
HOW SWEET AND LOVELY DOST THOU MAKE THE SHAME          3.95.1
COULD MAKE ME ANY SUMMERS STORY TELL                   3.98.7
AND MAKE TIMES SPOILES DISPISED EVERY WHERE            3.100.12
MAKE ANSWERE $MUSE, WILT THOU NOT HAPLY SAIE           3.101.5
TO MAKE HIM MUCH OUT-LIVE A GILDED TOMBE               3.101.11
TO MAKE HIM SEEME LONG HENCE, AS HE SHOWES NOW         3.101.14
TO MAKE OF MONSTERS, AND THINGS INDIGEST               3.114.5
LIKE AS TO MAKE OUR APPETITES MORE KEENE               3.118.1
AND RATHER MAKE THEM BORNE TO OUR DESIRE               3.123.7
ON PURPOSE LAYD TO MAKE THE TAKER MAD                  3.129.8
AS THOSE WHOSE BEAUTIES PROUDLY MAKE THEM CRUELL       3.131.2
THY FACE HATH NOT THE POWER TO MAKE LOVE GRONE         3.131.6
ONE WILL OF MINE TO MAKE THY LARGE $WILL MORE          3.135.12
MAKE BUT MY NAME THY LOVE, AND LOVE THAT STILL         3.136.13
THOSE LIPS THAT $LOVES OWNE HAND DID MAKE              3.145.1
TO MAKE ME GIVE THE LIE TO MY TRUE SIGHT               3.150.3
WHO TAUGHT THEE HOW TO MAKE ME LOVE THEE MORE          3.150.9
PLEASURE MIGHT CAUSE HER READE, READING
                             MIGHT MAKE HER KNOW       4.1.3
TO MAKE MY SELFE BELEEVE, THAT ALL IS WELL             4.2.13
TILL THAT GOOD $GOD MAKE $CHURCH AND $CHURCHMAN
                             STARVE                    4.5.8
SHE EVEN IN BLACKE DOTH MAKE ALL BEAUTIES FLOW+        4.7.11
WHICH OTHERS SAID DID MAKE THEIR SOULES TO PINE        4.16.6
TO THEM THAT WOULD MAKE SPEECH OF SPEECH ARISE         4.27.4
OF OTHER'S CHILDREN CHANGELINGS USE TO MAKE            4.28.2
WHICH MAKE THE PATENTS OF TRUE WORLDLY BLISSE          4.37.13
O MAKE IN ME THOSE CIVILL WARRES TO CEASE              4.39.7
THINKE $NATURE ME A MAN OF ARMES DID MAKE              4.41.11
```

```
WHO WHILE THEY MAKE $LOVE CONQUER, CONQUER $LOVE      4.42.3
TILL WITHOUT FEWELL YOU CAN MAKE HOT FIRE            4.46.14
DOTH MAKE MY HEART GIVE TO MY TONGUE THE LIE         4.47.14
NO $PATIENCE, IF THOU WILT MY GOOD, THEN MAKE        4.56.12
DEARE, WHY MAKE YOU MORE OF A DOG THEN ME+            4.59.1
NO KINGS BE CROWN'D BUT THEY SOME COVENANTS MAKE     4.69.14
THOSE LIPS, WHICH MAKE DEATH'S PAY A MEANE
                        PRICE FOR A KISSE             4.77.6
THE GLOBE OF WEALE, LIPS $LOVE'S INDENTURES MAKE     4.85.13
NO DOOME SHOULD MAKE ONE'S HEAV'N BECOME
                        HIS HELL                     4.86.14
STELLA WHOSE EYES MAKE ALL MY TEMPESTS CLEERE         4.87.3
UNITED POWERS MAKE EACH THE STRONGER PROVE           4.88.14
NE IF I WOULD, COULD I JUST TITLE MAKE                4.90.9
WHOSE PANTS DO MAKE UNSPILLING CREAME TO FLOW        4.100.6
AS THY LOOKES STURRE, RUNS UP AND DOWNE TO MAKE     4.101.10
WHICH $NATURE' SELFE DID MAKE, AND SELFE
                        ENGRAIND THE SAME+           4.102.6
DOTH MAKE ME MOST TO WISH THY COMFORT NEERE          4.106.8
MAKE IN MY HEAVY MOULD NEW THOUGHTS TO GROW         4.106.11
THE HUGE MASSACRES WHICH HER EYES DO MAKE             5.10.6
ALL THIS WORLDS PRIDE BOW TO A BASER MAKE            5.10.11
OF MY POORE LIFE TO MAKE UNPITTIED SPOILE            5.11.8
TO MAKE A TRUCE AND TERMES TO ENTERTAINE             5.12.2
SUCH LOWLINESSE SHALL MAKE YOU LOFTY BE              5.13.14
DO SEEKE MOST PRETIOUS THINGS TO MAKE YOUR GAIN      5.15.2
IN WHICH THE WORKE THAT SHE ALL DAY DID MAKE         5.23.3
BUT THAT WHICH SHAL YOU MAKE IMMORTALL, CHERISH     5.27.14
BY CONDUCT OF SOME STAR DOTH MAKE HER WAY            5.34.2
OR MAKE AGREEMENT WITH HER THRILLING EYES            5.36.6
THROUGH THE SWEET MUSICK WHICH HIS HARP DID MAKE     5.38.3
SHE MEANES AT LAST TO MAKE HER PITEOUS SPOYLE       5.41.12
THE WHICH MY SELFE AGAINST MY SELFE DOE MAKE         5.44.6
DID MAKE THE MATTER TO AVENGE HER YRE                5.48.2
SUCH MERCY SHAL YOU MAKE ADMYRED TO BE              5.49.13
SO I HER ABSENS WILL MY PENAUNCE MAKE               5.52.13
TO MAKE THE BAYTE HER GAZERS TO EMBREW              5.53.11
I WAILE AND MAKE MY WOES A $TRAGEDY                  5.54.8
BUT GLORY THINKE TO MAKE THESE CRUEL STOURES        5.57.10
MAKE PEACE THEREFORE, AND GRAUNT ME TIMELY GRACE    5.57.13
AND MAKE HIM BOND THAT BONDAGE EARST DYD FLY         5.65.4
DIDST MAKE THY TRIUMPH OVER DEATH AND SIN            5.68.2
BID HER THEREFORE HER SELFE SOONE READY MAKE         5.70.9
WHERE EVERY ONE THAT MISSETH THEN HER MAKE          5.70.11
MAKE HAST THEREFORE SWEET LOVE, WHILEST
                        IT IS PRIME                 5.70.13
DESIRED FOOD, TO IT DOTH MAKE HIS FLIGHT             5.73.6
THROGH WHICH HER WORDS SO WISE DO MAKE THEIR WAY    5.81.11
```

MAKELESS   1
```
THE WORLD WILL WAILE THEE LIKE A MAKELESSE WIFE      3.9.4
```

MAKER   3
```
KINDLED ABOVE UNTO THE MAKER NEERE                   5.8.2
THEN TO THE $MAKER SELFE THEY LIKEST BE             5.9.13
AS IN THEYR MAKER YE THEM BEST MAY SEE             5.53.14
```

MAKER'S   2
```
I HONOR AND ADMIRE THE MAKERS ART                   5.24.4
THE GLORIOUS IMAGE OF THE MAKERS BEAUTIE            5.61.1
```

MAKES   42
```
AND THAT MAKES HAPPY $LOVERS EVER DOMBE             1.17.14
THAT MAKES ME FALL FROM OFF MY HIE DESIRE            1.32.8
```

```
THAT MAKES THE WORLD ADMIRE SO STRANGE EFFECTS        1.34.8
SOONE DOTH IT FADE THAT MAKES THE FAIREST FLORISH     1.50.5
ONE $WOMAN NOW, MAKES THREE ODDE $NUMBERS EVEN        2.18.4
MAKES EVERY $ONE OF THESE THREE $NINES A $TEN         2.18.14
ONE WONDER WOMAN NOW MAKES THREE OD NUMBERS EVEN      2.108.4
MAKES EVERY ONE OF THESE THREE NINES A TEN            2.108.14
MY $LOVE MAKES HOTE THE FIRE WHOSE HEAT IS SPENT      2.127.1
QUENCHLES DESIRE, MAKES HOPE BURNE, DRYES
                   MY TEARES                          2.132.5
HURT IN THE $EMBRYON, MAKES MY JOYES ABHORTIVE        2.141.4
MAKES $SUMMER $WINTER, $AUTUMNE IN THE $SPRING        2.147.11
MAKES BLACKE NIGHT BEAUTIOUS, AND HER
                   OLD FACE NEW                       3.27.12
MAKES $SOMERS WELCOME, THRICE MORE WISH'D,
                   MORE RARE                          3.56.14
THIS THOU PERCEV'ST, WHICH MAKES THY LOVE
                   MORE STRONG                        3.73.13
BEING FOND ON PRAISE, WHICH MAKES YOUR
                   PRAISES WORSE                      3.84.14
BUT MAKES ANTIQUITIE FOR AYE HIS PAGE                 3.108.12
BESHREW THAT HEART THAT MAKES MY HEART TO GROANE      3.133.1
THAT SHE THAT MAKES ME SINNE, AWARDS ME PAINE         3.141.14
SETS DOWNE HER BABE AND MAKES ALL SWIFT DISPATCH      3.143.3
RED $PORPHIR IS, WHICH LOCKE OF PEARLE MAKES SURE      4.9.6
THAT HER SWEETE BREATH MAKES OFT THY FLAMES
                   TO RISE                            4.12.4
THAT HER $GRACE GRACIOUS MAKES THY WRONGS,
                   THAT SHE                           4.12.6
STELLA'S FAIRE HAIRE, HER FACE HE MAKES
                   HIS SHIELD                         4.13.10
AND IF THESE RULES DID FAILE, PROOFE MAKES
                   ME SURE                            4.26.12
THAT MAKES ME OFT MY BEST FRIENDS OVERPASSE           4.27.12
THAT $NOBLENESSE IT SELFE MAKES THUS UNKIND+          4.44.8
OF $HOPE, WHICH MAKES IT SEEME FAIRE TO THE EYE       4.49.8
MAKES ME FALL FROM HER SIGHT, THEN SWEETLY SHE        4.60.6
BUT NO SCUSE SERVES, SHE MAKES HER WRATH APPEARE      4.73.9
THAT VOYCE, WHICH MAKES THE SOULE PLANT
                   HIMSELFE IN THE EARES              4.77.9
MAKES ME IN MY BEST THOUGHTS AND QUIETST
                   JUDGEMENT SEE                      4.77.12
AND LOVE DOTH HOLD MY HAND, AND MAKES ME WRITE        4.90.14
BUT FEELING PROOFE MAKES ME SAY THEY MISTAKE
                   IT FURRE                           4.102.11
IT IS BUT LOVE, WHICH MAKES HIS PAPER
                   PERFIT WHITE                       4.102.12
WITH NO WORSE CURSE THEN ABSENCE MAKES ME TAST        4.105.14
AND MAKES ME THEN BOW DOWNE MY HEAD, AND SAY          4.108.9
GREAT HEAT, AND MAKES HIS FLAMES TO HEAVEN ASPIRE      5.6.8
AS SHE DOTH LAUGH AT ME AND MAKES MY PAIN
                   HER SPORT                          5.10.14
WHOSE EYES HIM STARV'D.. SO PLENTY MAKES ME POORE     5.35.8
O MIGHTY CHARM WHICH MAKES MEN LOVE THEYR BANE        5.47.13
WHOSE EYES HIM STARV'D.. SO PLENTY MAKES ME PORE      5.83.8
MAKEST
            4
AND LIKE A $TYRANT MAK'ST MY GRIEFE THY GAME          2.130.12
AND TENDER CHORLE MAKST WAST IN NIGGARDING            3.1.12
THOU MAKST FAULTS GRACES, THAT TO THEE RESORT         3.96.4
THAT ME THOU MAKEST THUS TORMENTED BE+                5.10.2
```

```
MAKETH                          3
    MY MOST TRUE MINDE THUS MAKETH MINE UNTRUE        3.113.14
    THAT MAKETH IT BE COVETED THE MORE                5.26.10
    AND MAKETH EVERY MINUTE SEEME A MYLE              5.87.12
MAKING                          18
    MAKING MY $SIGHES TO THAW THE $FROZEN $SEAS       2.25.8
    MAKING WITHALL SOME FILTHY $ANTIKE $FACE          2.31.4
    IN MAKING TRYALL CF A $MURTHER WROUGHT            2.46.5
    MAKING THY BREAST THAT SACRED RELIQUES SHRYNE     2.105.12
    MAKING A FAMINE WHERE ABOUNDANCE LIES             3.1.7
    MAKING A COOPELMENT OF PROUD COMPARE              3.21.5
    MAKING NO SUMMER CF AN OTHERS GREENE              3.68.11
    NOT MAKING WORSE WHAT NATURE MADE SO CLEERE       3.84.10
    MAKING HIS STILE ADMIRED EVERY WHERE              3.84.12
    MAKING THEIR TOMBE THE WOMBE WHEREIN THEY GREW+   3.86.4
    COMES HOME AGAINE, ON BETTER JUDGEMENT MAKING     3.87.12
    AGAINST THY REASONS MAKING NO DEFENCE             3.89.4
    (MAKING LASCIVIOUS COMMENTS ON THY SPORT)         3.95.6
    AND BEAUTIE MAKING BEAUTIFULL OLD RIME            3.106.3
    MAKING DEAD WOOD MORE BLEST THEN LIVING LIPS      3.128.12
    TO THY SWEET WILL MAKING ADDITION THUS            3.135.4
    WITH THAT FAIRE BREAST MAKING WOE'S DARKNESSE
                              CLEARE                  4.57.11
    MAKING THOSE $LILLIES AND THOSE $ROSES GROW       4.100.2
MALADIES                        2
    AS TO PREVENT OUR MALLADIES UNSEENE               3.118.3
    AGAINST STRANG MALLADIES A SOVERAIGNE CURE        3.153.8
MALADY                          1
    LONG LANGUISHING IN DOUBLE MALADY                 5.50.1
MALICE                          2
    DISCHARGE OUR $FORCES, HERE LET $MALICE CEASE     2.63.7
    THE MORE I FYND THEIR MALICE TO INCREACE          5.44.14
MAN                             22
    BEING MERCILES LIKE THEE THAT NO MAN WEIES+       1.23.8
    TO ONE $MAN GIVES, DOTH ON ANOTHER SPEND          2.10.6
    THE $SOULE OF $MAN IMMORTALL AND DIVINE           2.12.2
    I, LIKE A $MAN DEVOUT, AND CHARITABLE             2.23.5
    I $HEARE SOME SAY, THIS $MAN IS NOT IN LOVE       2.24.1
    NOT THAT THEY FEARE THE HOPE-LESSE $MAN TO KILL   2.50.10
    EV'N AS A $MAN THAT IN SOME $TRANCE HATH SEENE    2.57.9
    A HASTIE $MAN (QUOTH HE) NE'R WANTED $WOE         2.59.8
    THY FATHER WAS A MAN, THAT WILL I PROVE           2.140.7
    A MAN IN HEW ALL $HEWS IN HIS CONTROWLING         3.20.7
    FOR NO MAN WELL OF SUCH A SALVE CAN SPEAKE        3.34.7
    I NEVER WRIT, NOR NO MAN EVER LOVED               3.116.14
    WHO LEAVES UNSWAI'D THE LIKENESSE OF A MAN        3.141.11
    THE BETTER ANGELL IS A MAN RIGHT FAIRE            3.144.3
    BUT FOR THAT MAN WITH PAINE THIS TRUTH DESCRIES   4.25.5
    THINKE $NATURE ME A MAN OF ARMES DID MAKE         4.41.11
    WHERE WELL HE KNOWES, NO MAN TO HIM CAN COME      4.43.14
    THAT SHE WILL PLAGUE THE MAN THAT LOVES HER MOST  5.41.6
    ENOUGH IT IS FOR ONE MAN TO SUSTAINE              5.46.13
    VAYNE MAN (QUOD I) THAT HAST BUT LITTLE PRIEFE    5.50.5
    VAYNE MAN, SAYD SHE, THAT DOEST IN VAINE ASSAY    5.75.5
    WHOSE SWEET ASPECT BOTH $GOD AND MAN CAN MOVE     5.89.11
MANAGE                          1
    THAT IN THE $MANAGE MYSELFE TAKES DELIGHT         4.49.14
MAN-GOD                         1
    THAT MAN-GOD NOW OF WHOM THEY DYD DIVINE          2.119.5
```

```
MANHOOD                        2
   MY MAN-HOOD DARES NCT WITH FOULE $ATE MELL        2.39.10
   MY MANHOOD DARES NCT WITH FOULE $ATE MELL         2.118.10
MANIFEST                       1
   MADE MANIFEST BY SUCH A VICTORIE                  4.40.10
MANIFOLD                       2
   HER MIND ADORND WITH VERTUES MANIFOLD             5.15.14
   AND FEELE MY FLAMES AUGMENTED MANIFOLD+           5.30.8
MANNER                         3
   THE MANNER OF MY PITTIE WANTING PAINE             3.140.4
   BY NO PRETENCE CLAIME ANY MANER PLACE             4.52.11
   FROM CARELESNESSE CID IN NO MANER GROW            4.93.7
MANNERS                        5
   OH HOW THY WORTH WITH MANNERS MAY I SINGE         3.39.1
   MY TOUNG-TIDE $MUSE IN MANNERS HOLDS HER STILL    3.85.1
   THEN PUBLICK MEANES WHICH PUBLICK MANNERS BREEDS  3.111.4
   IF THAT BE SINNE WHICH DOTH THE MANERS FRAME      4.14.9
   I, CUMBRED WITH GCCD MANERS, ANSWER DO            4.30.13
MAN'S                          7
   AS ANY $MANS, THAT $MEMCRY CAN BOAST              2.27.10
   DESIRING THIS MANS ART, AND THAT MANS SKCPE       3.29.7
   DESIRING THIS MANS ART, AND THAT MANS SKCPE       3.29.7
   RICH IN ALL BEAUTIES WHICH MAN'S EYE CAN SEE      4.37.6
   THE PODRE MAN'S WEALTH, THE PRISONER'S RELEASE    4.39.3
   AND NOW MAN'S WRONGS IN ME, POORE BEAST, DESCRIE  4.49.4
   SUFFICIENT WORKE FCR ONE MANS SIMPLE HEAD         5.33.7
MANSION                        2
   OH WHAT A MANSION HAVE THOSE VICES GOT            3.95.9
   DOST THOU UPON THY FADING MANSION SPEND+          3.146.6
MANTLE                         1
   TO DECKE HIR SELFE, AND HER FAIRE MANTLE WEAVE    5.4.12
MANTLED                        1
   MY FORTUNE MANTLED WITH A CLOWDE S'OBSCURE        1.29.13
MANTLETH                       1
   DOTH BATH IN BLISSE AND MANTLETH MOST AT EASE     5.72.10
MANY                          35
   SO MANY VOWES, AND PRAIERS HAVING SPENT           1.16.7
   HOW MANY LIVE, THE GLORY OF WHOSE NAME            1.44.7
   HOW MANY PALTRY, FCCLISH, PAINTED THINGS          2.6.1
   YORKE MANY $WONDERS OF HER $OWSE CAN TELL         2.32.6
   THOUGHT IT IN WEIGHT TOC LIGHT BY MANY A $GRAINE  2.38.12
   YORKE, MANY WONDERS OF HER $OUSE CAN TELL         2.124.6
   THOUGHT HER IN WEIGHT TCO LIGHT BY MANY
                               A GRAINE             2.131.12
   WHOSE SPEECHLESSE SCNG BEING MANY, SEEMING ONE    3.8.13
   GRAUNT IF THOU WILT, THCU ART BELOV'D OF MANY     3.10.3
   AND MANY MAIDEN GARDENS YET UNSET                 3.16.6
   I SIGH THE LACKE CF MANY A THING I SOUGHT         3.30.3
   AND MOVE TH'EXPENCE OF MANY A VANNISHT SIGHT      3.30.8
   HOW MANY A HOLY AND OBSEQUIOUS TEARE              3.31.5
   THAT DUE OF MANY, NCW IS THINE ALONE              3.31.12
   FULL MANY A GLORICUS MORNING HAVE I SEENE         3.33.1
   AND PROUD OF MANY, LIVES UPON HIS GAINES+         3.67.12
   HOW MANY $LAMBS MIGHT THE STERNE $WOLFE BETRAY    3.96.9
   HOW MANY GAZERS MIGHST THOU LEAD AWAY             3.96.11
   WHILST MANY $NYMPHES THAT VOU'D CHAST
                               LIFE TO KEEP         3.154.3
   WHICH MANY $LEGIONS OF TRUE HEARTS HAD WARM'D     3.154.6
   BEAUTIES, WHICH WERE OF MANIE $CARRETS FINE       4.16.2
   WO, HAVING MADE WITH MANY FIGHTS HIS OWNE         4.57.1
```

```
SO MANIE EYES AY SEEKING THEIR OWNE WOE          4.78.12
I SAW THY SELFE WITH MANY A SMILING LINE         4.103.2
YET MANY WONDROUS THINGS THERE ARE BESIDE        5.17.8
YET CANNOT I WITH MANY A DROPPING TEARE          5.18.5
FOR ALL THAT I IN MANY DAYES DOO WEAVE           5.23.7
THAT MANY NOW MUCH WORSHIP AND ADMIRE            5.27.8
YE SHALL CONDEMNED BE OF MANY A ONE              5.36.14
FOR THAT THEY SHOULD ENDURE THROUGH MANY AGES    5.51.3
WITH MANY DEARE DELIGHTS BEDECKED FYNE           5.71.12
THAT MANY SOUGHT YET NONE COULD EVER TASTE       5.77.10
MANY LONG WEARY DAYES I HAVE OUTWORNE            5.87.2
AND MANY NIGHTS, THAT SLOWLY SEEMD TO MOVE       5.87.3
AND IN HER SONGS SENDS MANY A WISHFULL VOW       5.89.3
MANY'S                         1
IN MANIES LOOKES, THE FALCE HEARTS HISTORY       3.93.7
MAP                            4
WHERE, IN THE $MAP OF ALL MY $MISERIE            2.44.3
THUS IS HIS CHEEKE THE MAP OF DAIES OUT-WORNE    3.68.1
AND HIM AS FOR A MAP DOTH $NATURE STORE          3.68.13
BUT THINKE THAT ALL THE $MAP OF MY STATE
                            I DISPLAY            4.6.13
MAR                            1
TO MARRE THE SUBJECT THAT BEFORE WAS WELL        3.103.10
MARBLE                         6
AND STILL I TOYLE, TO CHANGE THE $MARBLE BREST   1.13.9
YEELD TO THE $MARBLE THY HARD HART AGAINE        1.19.13
SHALL REST IN $ISE, WHEN THINE IS GRAV'D
                            IN $MARBLE           1.44.8
NOT MARBLE, NOR THE GUILDED MONUMENT             3.55.1
MARBLE MIXT RED AND WHITE DO ENTERLACE           4.9.8
OF HARDEST $MARBLE ARE OF PURPOSE MADE+          5.51.2
MARCH                          2
TO MARCH IN RANCKES OF BETTER EQUIPAGE           3.32.12
FOR SINCE MAD $MARCH GREAT PROMISE MADE OF ME    4.21.9
MARCHED                        1
STELLA ALONE WITH FACE UNARMED MARCHT            4.22.9
MARCHETH                       1
BECAUSE IN BRAVE ARRAY HEERE MARCHETH SHE        4.88.3
MARGIN                         1
WHAT BLUSHING NOTES DOEST THOU IN MARGINE SEE+   4.67.8
MARIGOLD                       2
WHERE, IN THE COMPASSE OF A $MARYGOLD            2.151.7
BUT AS THE $MARYGOLD AT THE SUNS EYE             3.25.6
MARINERS                       1
HER $MARRYNERS DOE LEAVE HER ALL FORLORNE        2.134.11
MARJORAM                       1
AND BUDS OF MARJEROM HAD STOLNE THY HAIRE        3.99.7
MARK                           10
MARKE HOW ONE STRING SWEET HUSBAND TO AN OTHER   3.8.9
FOR SLANDERS MARKE WAS EVER YET THE FAIRE        3.70.2
MARKE HOW WITH MY NEGLECT I DOE DISPENCE         3.112.12
O NO, IT IS AN EVER FIXED MARKE                  3.116.5
IS NO FIT MARKE TO PIERCE WITH HIS FINE
                            POINTED DART         4.8.3
WHO MARKE IN THEE WHAT IS IN THEE MOST FAIRE     4.71.11
TO LAY HIS THEN MARKE WANTING SHAFTS OF SIGHT    4.99.3
THAT WITH SUCH POYSONOUS CARE MY LOOKES
                            YOU MARKE            4.104.2
MARK WHEN SHE SMILES WITH AMIABLE CHEARE         5.40.1
WITH THE LOOSE WYND YE WAVING CHANCE TO MARKE    5.81.2
```

```
MARKS                     2
   CAN THOSE BLACKE BEAMES SUCH BURNING MARKES
                              ENGRAVE              4.47.2
   THAT TEDIOUS LEASURE MARKS EACH WRINCKLED LINE  4.98.11
MARRED                    2
   MY YOUNG MIND MARDE, WHOM $LOVE DOTH WINDLAS SO  4.21.2
   PEACE, FOOLISH WIT, WITH WIT MY WIT IS MARD      4.34.11
MARRIAGE                  1
   LET ME NOT TO THE MARRIAGE OF TRUE MINDES        3.116.1
MARRIED                   2
   BY UNIONS MARRIED DO OFFEND THINE EARE           3.8.6
   I GRANT THOU WERT NOT MARRIED TO MY $MUSE        3.82.1
MARS                     11
   AND $MUSE-FOE $MARS, ABROAD FARRE FOSTRED BEE    1.53.14
   THAT WHILST WITH $MARS SHE HOLDETH HER OLD $WAY  2.48.13
   AND TELL THE $GODS, $MARS IS PREDOMINANT         2.151.11
   NOR $MARS HIS SWORD, NOR WARRES QUICK
                              FIRE SHALL BURNE      3.55.7
   PHOEBUS WAS $JUDGE BETWEENE $JOVE, $MARS,
                              AND $LOVE             4.13.1
   BUT IN $VERT FIELD $MARS BARE A GOLDEN SPEARE    4.13.5
   EACH HAD HIS CREAST, $MARS CARIED $VENUS' GLOVE  4.13.7
   BECAUSE THAT $MARS, GROWNE SLACKER IN HER LOVE   4.17.2
   AND GAIN'D BY $MARS, COULD YET MAD $MARS SO TAME 4.75.7
   AND GAIN'D BY $MARS, COULD YET MAD $MARS SO TAME 4.75.7
   AS $MARS IN THREE SCORE YEARES DOTH RUN
                              HIS SPHEARE           5.60.4
MARS'S                    2
   THE BOY REFUSDE FOR FEARE OF $MARSE'S HATE       4.17.5
   IN $MARSE'S LIVERIE, PRAUNCING IN THE PRESSE     4.53.6
MARTIAL                   1
   IN $MARTIALL SPORTS I HAD MY CUNNING TRIDE       4.53.1
MARTYRING                 1
   SUBDUE THYS $TYRANT EVER MARTYRING MEE           2.115.2
MARVEL                   10
   OFT DO I MARVELL, WHETHER $DELIAS EIES           1.34.1
   I GREATLY MARVELL, HOW YOU STILL GOE FREE        2.14.3
   NO MARVELL THEN THOUGH $CHARITIE GROW COLD       2.23.14
   MARVELL NOT, $LOVE, THOUGH I THY POW'R ADMIRE    2.34.1
   MARVELL NOT, $LOVE, THOUGH I THY POW'R ADMIRE    2.34.5
   MARVELL NOT, $LOVE, THOUGH I THY POW'R ADMIRE    2.34.9
   I MARVELL NOT, THOU FEEL'ST NOT MY $DELIGHT      2.49.3
   BUT MY MOST MERVAILE WAS WHEN FROM THE SKYES     2.125.9
   NO MARVAILE THEN THOUGH I MISTAKE MY VIEW        3.148.11
   I MARVAILE OF WHAT SUBSTANCE WAS THE MOULD       5.55.3
MARVELS                   1
   ANOTHER, MERVAILES $SULPHURE $AETNAS FIRE        2.120.4
MASK                      1
   AND MASK IN MYRTH LYKE TO A $COMEDY              5.54.6
MASKED                    4
   THE REGION CLOUDE HATH MASK'D HIM FROM ME NOW    3.33.12
   WHEN SOMMERS BREATH THEIR MASKED BUDS DISCLOSES  3.54.8
   IF SOME SUSPECT OF ILL MASKT NOT THY SHOW        3.70.13
   THAT BRAVELY MASKT, THEIR FANCIES MAY BE TOLD    4.3.2
MASKS                     1
   MY FRIEND, THAT OFT SAW THROUGH ALL MASKES MY WO 4.69.5
MASONRY                   1
   AND BROILES ROOTE OUT THE WORKE OF MASONRY       3.55.6
MASSACRE                  1
   DOE WHAT THOU CANST, RAZE, MASSACRE, AND BURNE   2.63.11
```

```
MASSACRES                    1
  THE HUGE MASSACRES WHICH HER EYES DO MAKE          5.10.6
MASTER                       2
  HASTE THOU THE $MASTER $MISTRIS OF MY PASSION      3.20.2
  EVEN SUCH A BEAUTY AS YOU MAISTER NOW              3.106.8
MASTERING                    1
  FIRST MAKE INCISION ON EACH MAST'RING $VEINE       2.50.6
MASTER'S                     2
  ON SERVANTS' SHAME OFT $MAISTER'S BLAME
                             DOTH SIT                4.107.12
  BUT PLEAD THY MAISTERS CAUSE UNJUSTLY PAYNED       5.48.8
MATCH                        2
  BAD IS THE $MATCH, WHERE NEITHER PARTIE WONNE      2.63.4
  SEEK WITH MY PLAYNTS TO MATCH THAT MOURNFUL DOVE   5.89.8
MATCHABLE                    1
  NE BUT IN HEAVEN MATCHABLE TO NONE                 5.66.7
MATCHED                      1
  THE FIRST, THUS MATCHT, WERE SCARCELY $GENTLEMEN   4.13.14
MATCHETH                     1
  BUT WHY THY ODOR MATCHETH NOT THY SHOW             3.69.13
MATE                         3
  THIS SOWRE-BREATH'D MATE TAST OF THOSE
                             SUGRED LIPS             4.59.11
  COULD NOT ON EARTH HAVE FOUND ONE FIT FOR MATE     5.66.6
  SITS MOURNING FOR THE ABSENCE OF HER MATE          5.89.2
MATE-IN-ARMS                 1
  THOUGH OFT HIMSELFE MY MATE-IN-ARMES HE SWARE      4.95.8
MATRONS                      1
  VIRGINS AND $MATRONS READING THESE MY $RIMES       2.6.9
MATTER                       5
  NO MATTER THEN ALTHOUGH MY FOOTE DID STAND         3.44.5
  THEN LACKT I MATTER, THAT INFEEBLED MINE           3.86.14
  IN SLEEPE A $KING, BUT WAKING NO SUCH MATTER       3.87.14
  DID MAKE THE MATTER TO AVENGE HER YRE              5.48.2
  BUT THEY THAT SKILL NOT OF SO HEAVENLY MATTER      5.85.5
MATTER'S                     1
  THAT FIRE CAN BURNE WHEN ALL THE MATTER'S SPENT    1.41.10
MATURITY                     1
  CRAWLES TO MATURITY, WHEREWITH BEING CROWN'D       3.60.6
MAUGRE                       1
  O VOICE, O FACE, MAUGRE MY SPEECHE'S MIGHT         4.58.12
MAVIS                        1
  SO DOES THE $CUCKOW, WHEN THE $MAVIS SINGS         5.85.3
MAXIM                        1
  IN EV'RY THING I HOLD THIS $MAXIM STILL            2.28.13
MAY                          4
  NOW WHILST THY $MAY HATH FILD THY LAP
                             WITH FLOWERS            1.40.2
  ROUGH WINDES DO SHAKE THE DARLING BUDS OF $MAIE    3.18.3
  IF NOW THE $MAY OF MY YEARES MUCH DECLINE          4.21.10
  AND TWIXT HER PAPS LIKE EARLY FRUIT IN $MAY        5.76.9
MAYR-MAID                    1
  FAIRE-MAYD NO MORE, BUT $MAYR-MAID BE THY NAME     2.130.9
MAZE                         3
  WERE NOT $INVENTION STAULD, TREADING $INVENTIONS
                             MAZE                    2.117.9
  AND TREADING IN THYS NEVER-ENDING MAZE             2.133.7
  MERIDIANIS SITS WITHIN A MAZE                      2.151.8
MAZED                        2
  OF HIS MAZDE POWERS KEEPES PERFIT HARMONY          4.99.8
```

```
    FAYRE EYES, THE MYRROUR OF MY MAZED HART         5.7.1
MAZEFUL                    1
    IN BOTH A MAZEFULL SOLITARINESSE                 4.96.9
MEADOWS                    1
    KISSING WITH GOLDEN FACE THE MEDDOWES GREENE     3.33.3
MEAN                      16
    THE MEANE OBSERVER (WHOM BASE SAFETY KEEPS)      1.35.10
    WHAT WILL $YOU KEEPE A MEANE THEN BETWIXT EITHER+  2.19.7
    WHAT DO'ST THOU MEANE TO $CHEATE ME OF MY $HEART   2.52.1
    THAT LIFE (I MEANE) WHICH DOTH $RELIGION TEACH   2.119.13
    WHEN I SAY '$STELLA', I DO MEANE THE SAME        4.28.5
    MEANE WHILE MY HEART CONFERS WITH $STELLA'S
                            BEAMES                   4.51.12
    BUT NOW I MEANE NO MORE YOUR HELPE TO TRIE       4.55.9
    BUT ($GOD WOT) WOT NOT WHAT THEY MEANE BY IT     4.74.6
    THOSE LIPS, WHICH MAKE DEATH'S PAY A MEANE
                            PRICE FOR A KISSE        4.77.6
    TEACHING THE MEANE, AT ONCE TO TAKE AND GIVE     4.79.9
    OR DO YOU MEANE MY TENDER EARES TO SPARE         4.92.4
    AND IN MY SELFE, MY INWARD SELFE I MEANE         5.45.3
    THEN DARE BE LOV'D BY MEN OF MEANE DEGREE        5.61.14
    THAT YE YOUR LOVE LENT TO SO MEANE A ONE         5.66.4
    BUT LET HER PRAYSES YET BE LOW AND MEANE         5.80.13
    THAT ARE SO MUCH BY SO MEANE LOVE EMBASED        5.82.4
MEANER                     2
    WHICH MEANER PRIZ'D AND MOMENTARY BEE            1.58.4
    YET WERE THE HID AND MEANER BEAUTIES PARCHT      4.22.12
MEANING                    3
    YOUR MORALL NOTES STRAIGHT MY HID MEANING TEARE  4.104.12
    AS IF THEY KNEW THE MEANING OF THEIR LAYES       5.19.8
    MY SIMPLE MEANING WITH DISDAYNFULL SCORNE        5.29.2
MEANS                     13
    MY SLENDER MEANES PRESUM'D TOO HIGH A PART       1.36.3
    DEVISE SOME MEANES, BUT HOW I MAY FORSAKE $YOU   2.11.10
    AND WHEN BY $MEANES, TO DRIVE IT OUT I TRY       2.20.6
    FROM THE STRONG $SPIRIT BY NO MEANES FORCE
                            THE SAME                 2.58.8
    AND BY ALL MEANES, LET BLACK UNKINDNES PROVE     2.149.13
    WITH MEANES MORE BLESSED THEN MY BARREN RIME+    3.16.4
    THEN PUBLICK MEANES WHICH PUBLICK MANNERS BREEDS 3.111.4
    WHAT MEANES THE WORLD TO SAY IT IS NOT SO+       3.148.6
    HOW $POLES' RIGHT KING MEANES, WITHOUT
                            LEAVE OF HOAST           4.30.3
    AS MEANES OF BLISSE I GLADLY WIL EMBRACE         5.25.12
    IS THERE NO MEANES FOR ME TO PURCHACE PEACE      5.36.5
    OUT OF HER BANDS YE BY NO MEANES SHALL GET       5.37.12
    SHE MEANES AT LAST TO MAKE HER PITEOUS SPOYLE    5.41.12
MEANT                      2
    SHE CARV'D THEE FOR HER SEALE, AND MENT THERBY   3.11.13
    AS OF A FRIEND THAT MEANT NOT MUCH AMISSE        4.56.8
MEASURE                    4
    WHO DOTED ON THE $DOLT BEYOND ALL MEASURE        2.21.10
    O RARE EFFECT, TRUE BOND OF FRIENDSHIPS MEASURE  2.146.9
    AND THAT IN GUESSE THEY MEASURE BY THY DEEDS     3.69.10
    BUT THESE PERTICULERS ARE NOT MY MEASURE         3.91.7
MEASURED                   1
    THUS FARRE THE MILES ARE MEASURDE FROM THY FRIEND  3.50.4
MEAT                       2
    KINDE WORDS UNKINDEST MEATE I CAN DEVISE         2.115.11
    MORE SWEET THAN $NECTAR OR $AMBROSIALL MEAT      5.39.13
```

```
MEDEA-LIKE                    1
  MEDEA-LIKE, I MAKE THEE YOUNG AGAINE              2.44.6
MEDICINE                      2
  I HAVE A $MED'CINE THAT SHALL CURE MY $LOVE       2.15.2
  AND BROUGHT TO MEDICINE A HEALTHFULL STATE        3.118.11
MEDICINES                     1
  FIT MEDICINES FOR MY BODIES BEST RELIEFE          5.50.4
MEDITATION                    1
  O FEAREFULL MEDITATION, WHERE ALACK               3.65.9
MEDWAY                        2
  AND $KENT WILL SAY, HER $MEDWAY DOTH EXCELL       2.32.8
  AND $KENT WILL SAY, HER $MEDWAY DOTH EXCELL       2.124.8
MEED                          3
  THAT GREATER MEEDE AT LAST MAY TURNE TO MEE       5.25.14
  THAT OF HER PRESENS I MY MEED MAY TAKE            5.52.14
  SHAME BE THY MEED, AND MISCHIEFE THY REWARD       5.86.13
MEEDS                         1
  YIELDED THEM BY THE VANQUISHT AS THEYR MEEDS      5.29.6
MEEK                          2
  AND WITH MEEKE HUMBLESSE AND AFFLICTED MOOD       5.2.11
  AND EKE MINE EIES WITH MEEKE HUMILITY             5.43.11
MEEKER                        1
  PRAY THAT MY SUNNE GO DOWNE WITH MEEKER
                              BEAMES TO BED         4.76.14
MEEKNESS                      1
  THAT PRIDE AND MEEKNESSE MIXT BY EQUALL PART      5.21.3
MEET                          5
  AND WHEN $WE MEET AT ANY TIME AGAINE              2.61.6
  BUT FLOWERS DISTIL'D THOUGH THEY WITH
                              WINTER MEETE          3.5.13
  BUT IF THAT FLOWRE WITH BASE INFECTION MEETE      3.94.11
  TO HER, WHERE I MY HEART SAFELIEST SHALL MEET     4.84.6
  BUT HEERE I DO STORE OF FAIRE $LADIES MEETE       4.106.9
MEETNESS                      1
  AND SICKE OF WEL-FARE FOUND A KIND OF MEETNESSE   3.118.7
MELANCHOLY                    2
  SINKES DOWNE TO DEATH, OPPREST WITH MELANCHOLIE   3.45.8
  WHENCE THOSE SAME FUMES OF MELANCHOLY RISE        4.23.3
MELL                          2
  MY MAN-HOOD DARES NOT WITH FOULE $ATE MELL        2.39.10
  MY MANHOOD DARES NOT WITH FOULE $ATE MELL         2.118.10
MELODY                        1
  MORE OFT THEN TO A CHAMBER MELODIE                4.84.4
MELTED                        1
  WHICH NOW ARE MELTED BY THINE EYES BRIGHT SUN     1.32.7
MELTING                       1
  A MELTING PLEASANCE RAN THROUGH EVERY PART        5.39.7
MELTS                         3
  FLINT, FROST, DISDAINE, WEARES, MELTES,
                              AND YEELDES WE SEE    1.11.14
  MELTS DOWNE HIS LEAD INTO MY BOYLING BREST        4.108.2
  THAT FIRE WHICH ALL THING MELTS, SHOULD
                              HARDEN YSE            5.30.10
MEMBERS                       1
  AND RULES THE MEMBERS AS IT SELFE DOTH PLEASE+    5.50.8
MEMORIAL                      1
  WHICH FOR MEMORIALL STILL WITH THEE SHALL STAY    3.74.4
MEMORIALS                     3
  THESE SAD MEMORIALS OF MY LOVES DISPAIRE          1.9.4
  THE SAD $MEMORIALLS OF MY $MISERIES               2.54.5
```

```
THE SAD MEMORIALS CF MY MISERIES                    2.101.5
MEMORY                    14
   THE $GODDESSES OF $MEMORY AND $WIT                  2.4.3
   AS INTELLECTUALL, IT IS $MEMORIE                    2.12.8
   AS ANY $MANS, THAT $MEMORY CAN BOAST                2.27.10
   HIS TENDER HEIRE MIGHT BEARE HIS MEMORY             3.1.4
   AND WERE THEIR BRAVE STATE OUT OF MEMORY            3.15.8
   THE LIVING RECORD CF YOUR MEMORY                    3.55.8
   THAT HE SHALL NEVER CUT FROM MEMORY                 3.63.11
   OF MOUTHED GRAVES WILL GIVE THEE MEMORIE            3.77.6
   LOOKE WHAT THY MEMORIE CANNOT CUNTAINE              3.77.9
   FROM HENCE YOUR MEMORY DEATH CANNOT TAKE            3.81.3
   FULL CHARACTERD WITH LASTING MEMORY                 3.122.2
   GIRT FAST BY MEMORIE, AND WHILE I SPURRE            4.49.10
   WHERE MEMORY SETS FCORTH THE BEAMES OF LCVE         4.88.11
   IN WHICH I MAY RECCRD THE MEMORY                    5.69.6
MEN                       39
   MEN DO NOT WEY THE STALKE FOR THAT IT WAS           1.40.13
   WHEN MEN SHALL FIND THY FLOWER, THY GLORY PASSE     1.41.1
   THE SPOYLE OF FAME DESERV'D BY VERTUOUS MEN         1.45.6
   BASELY ATTENDING CN THE HOPES OF MEN                1.58.8
   AS $OTHER $MEN, SO I MY SELFE DOE $MUSE             2.9.1
   WITH $DIET AND $CCRRECTICN, $MEN DISTRAUGHT         2.9.13
   OF LIVELESSE $CLODS, US LIVING $MEN TO MAKE         2.14.7
   IN GREATEST $PERILS SOME $MEN PLEASANT BE           2.24.10
   WHERE OTHER $MEN IN DEPTH OF $PASSION CRIE          2.24.13
   SOME $MEN THERE BE, WHICH LIKE MY $METHOD WELL      2.42.1
   THUS SUNDRY $MEN THEIR SUNDRY $MINDS REPEAT         2.42.8
   I PASSE NOT, I, HCW $MEN AFFECTED BEE               2.42.9
   WONNE GRACE AND CREDIT IN THE $EARES OF $MEN        2.47.4
   NEERER $MEN COME, $THAT FURTHER FLYES AWAY          2.58.9
   NINE WORTHY MEN UNTC THE WORLD WERE GIVEN           2.108.8
   THUS SUNDRY MEN, THEIR SUNDRY MINDS REPEATE         2.128.8
   I PASSE NOT I HOW MEN AFFECTED BE                   2.128.9
   O PUREST MERROR, WHEREIN MEN MAY SEE                2.146.13
   WHEN I PERCEIVE THAT MEN AS PLANTS INCREASE         3.15.5
   CAN MAKE YOU LIVE YCUR SELFE IN EIES OF MEN         3.16.12
   BE SCORN'D, LIKE CLD MEN OF LESSE TRUTH
                       THEN TONGUE                     3.17.10
   SO LONG AS MEN CAN BREATH OR EYES CAN SEE           3.18.13
   FOR BEAUTIES PATTERNE TC SUCCEDING MEN              3.19.12
   EXCEEDED BY THE HIGHT OF HAPPIER MEN                3.32.8
   ALL MEN MAKE FAULTS, AND EVEN I IN THIS             3.35.5
   WHERE BREATH MOST BREATHS, EVEN IN THE
                       MOUTHS OF MEN                   3.81.14
   ALL MEN ARE BAD AND IN THEIR BADNESSE RAIGNE        3.121.14
   TO SHUN THE HEAVEN THAT LEADS MEN TO THIS HELL      3.129.14
   BE ANCHORD IN THE BAYE WHERE ALL MEN RIDE           3.137.6
   SO SHALT THOU FEED CN DEATH, THAT FEEDS CN MEN      3.146.13
   AND GREW A SEETHING BATH WHICH YET MEN PROVE        3.153.7
   FOR MEN DISEASD, BUT I MY $MISTRISSE THRALL         3.154.12
   'BUT WILL NOT WISE MEN THINKE THY WORDS
                       FOND WARE+'                     4.34.7
   MEN TO DEVOTION OUGHT TC BE INCLYND                 5.22.2
   THAT SHE TO WICKED MEN A SCOURGE SHOULD BEE         5.24.11
   MOST SORTS OF MEN DCE SET BUT LITTLE STORE          5.26.12
   O MIGHTY CHARM WHICH MAKES MEN LOVE THEYR BANE      5.47.13
   THEN DARE BE LOV'D BY MEN OF MEANE DEGREE           5.61.14
   MEN CALL YOU FAYRE, AND YOU DOE CREDIT IT           5.79.1
```

MEND   4
    WANT NOTHING THAT THE THOUGHT OF HEARTS CAN MEND   3.69.2
    IN OTHERS WORKES THOU DOOST BUT MEND THE STILE   3.78.11
    WERE IT NOT SINFULL THEN STRIVING TO MEND   3.103.9
    IF NATURE, THEN SHE MAY IT MEND WITH SKILL   5.41.3
MENDED   1
    WHETHER WE ARE MENDED, OR WHERE BETTER THEY   3.59.11
MEN'S   11
    WITH THESE, SHE STEALES MENS HARTS FOR
                              HER RELIEFE   2.126.13
    WHICH STEALES MENS EYES AND WOMENS SOULES AMASETH   3.20.8
    WHEN IN DISGRACE WITH $FORTUNE AND MENS EYES   3.29.1
    WHEN YOU INTOMBED IN MENS EYES SHALL LYE   3.81.8
    AND HAVING THEE, OF ALL MENS PRIDE I BOAST   3.91.12
    MY THOUGHTS AND MY DISCOURSE AS MAD MENS ARE   3.147.11
    LOVES EYE IS NOT SO TRUE AS ALL MENS.. NO   3.148.8
    THE $ORATOUR SO FARRE MEN'S HARTS DOTH BIND   4.58.2
    HOW FAINE WOULD I PAINT THEE TO ALL MEN'S EYES   4.81.7
    MADE TO AMAZE WEAKE MENS CONFUSED SKIL   5.17.2
    IS IT THAT MENS FRAYLE EYES, WHICH GAZE TOO BOLD   5.37.5
MENTION   1
    NE ANY MENTION SHALL THEREOF REMAINE   5.27.10
MERCENARY   1
    WITH MERCENARY LINES, WITH SERVILE $PEN   1.58.6
MERCHANDISE   1
    WITH PRETIOUS MERCHANDIZE SHE FORTH DOTH LAY   5.81.6
MERCHANDISED   1
    THAT LOVE IS MARCHANDIZ'D, WHOSE RITCH ESTEEMING   3.102.3
MERCHANTS   1
    YE TRADEFULL $MERCHANTS THAT WITH WEARY TOYLE   5.15.1
MERCIFUL   1
    WITH MERCIFULL REGARD, GIVE MERCY TOO   5.49.12
MERCILESS   2
    I PRAY IN VAINE, A MERCILESSE TO MOVE   1.11.7
    BEING MERCILES LIKE THEE THAT NO MAN WEIES+   1.23.8
MERCY   12
    GROWNE HOARCE WITH CRYING MERCY, MERCY GIVE   1.16.6
    GROWNE HOARCE WITH CRYING MERCY, MERCY GIVE   1.16.6
    AND NEVER MERCY TO THY MERIT GIVES   1.22.12
    THAT WHICH THY SUCCRING MERCY SHOULD HAVE BLEST   1.31.4
    LEFT TO THE MERCY OF THE WAVES AND WINDE   2.134.4
    STRAIGHT IN HER HEART DID MERCIE COME   3.145.5
    THEN KNOW, THAT MERCY IS THE MIGHTIES JEWELL   5.49.3
    WITH MERCIFULL REGARD, GIVE MERCY TOO   5.49.12
    SUCH MERCY SHAL YOU MAKE ADMYRED TO BE   5.49.13
    AND THEN NO MERCY WILL UNTO ME SHEW   5.53.8
    BUT MERCY DOTH WITH BEAUTIE BEST AGREE   5.53.13
    BE LYKE IN MERCY AS IN ALL THE REST   5.55.14
MERCY-WANTING   1
    THE FURY OF A MERCY-WANTING STORME   1.37.6
MERIDIANIS   1
    MERIDIANIS SITS WITHIN A MAZE   2.151.8
MERIT   8
    AND NEVER MERCY TO THY MERIT GIVES   1.22.12
    THAT ERRORS SHOULD BE GRAC'D THAT MERIT SHAME   1.56.11
    GET NOT ONE GLANCE, TO RECOMPENCE MY $MERIT+   2.43.4
    THY MERRIT HATH MY DUTIE STRONGLY KNIT   3.26.2
    WHAT MERIT LIV'D IN ME THAT YOU SHOULD LOVE   3.72.2
    AND PLACE MY MERRIT IN THE EIE OF SKORNE   3.88.2
    THAT MAY EXPRESSE MY LOVE, OR THY DEARE MERIT+   3.108.4

```
  WHAT MERRIT DO I IN MY SELFE RESPECT              3.149.9
MERITS                 1
  AND THOU SHALT FINDE IT MERRITS NOT REPROOVING    3.142.4
MERLIN                 1
  SHEE OF WHOM $MERLIN LONG TYME DID FORE-TELL      2.119.10
MERRY                  2
  MERY WITH HIM, AND NOT THINKE OF HIS WOE          4.106.14
  THE MERRY $CUCKOW, MESSENGER OF $SPRING           5.19.1
MESSAGE                5
  TOLDE THE DUMBE MESSAGE OF MY HIDDEN GRIEFE       1.8.6
  RECEIVED HAST THIS MESSAGE FROM THY GLASSE        1.41.3
  BEHOLD THE MESSAGE CF A CHAST DESIRE              1.60.3
  AND DOTH HIS YDLE MESSAGE SET AT NOUGHT           5.19.12
  TO BEARE THE MESSAGE OF HER GENTLE SPRIGHT        5.81.12
MESSENGER              2
  MORNE'S MESSENGER, WITH ROSE ENAMELD SKIES        4.99.10
  THE MERRY $CUCKOW, MESSENGER OF $SPRING           5.19.1
MESSENGERS             1
  BY THOSE SWIFT MESSENGERS RETURN'D FROM THEE      3.45.10
MET                    3
  FOOLES AS WE MET, SC $FCOLES AGAINE WE PARTED     2.59.14
  ON HORSEBACKE MET HIM IN HIS FURIOUS RACE         4.22.6
  THAT $VERTUE, IF IT ONCE MET WITH OUR EYES        4.25.3
METAL                  2
  MORE $ARROWES WITH HART-PIERCING METTEL PCYNTED   2.126.11
  ALAS, IF THIS THE CNLY METTALL BE                 4.62.12
METALS                 1
  METALS DOE WASTE, AND FRET WITH $CANKERS $RUST    2.13.2
METAMORPHOSED          1
  ARE METAMORPHOSD STRAIGHT TO TUNES OF JOYES       4.44.14
METAPHORS              1
  AND WHY THESE GIDDY $METAPHORS I USE              2.9.3
METER                  1
  AND STRETCHED MITER OF AN $ANTIQUE SONG           3.17.12
METHOD                 3
  SOME $MEN THERE BE, WHICH LIKE MY $METHOD WELL    2.42.1
  SOME WITS THERE BE, WHICH LYKE MY METHOD WELL     2.128.1
  YOU THAT DO $DICTICNARIE'S METHODE BRING          4.15.5
METHODS                1
  TO NEW FOUND METHCDS, AND TO COMPOUNDS STRANGE+   3.76.4
METHRIDATE             2
  LOVES $METHRIDATE, THE PUREST OF PERFECTION       2.123.5
  HARTS $METHRIDATE, THE SCULES PRESERVATIVE        2.146.6
METTLE                 1
  MY $SOULE IS CF A BRAVER $METTLE MADE             2.4.10
METTLES                1
  METTLES DOE WASTE, AND FRET WITH CANKERS RUST     2.121.2
MEW
  TILL THEN GIVE LEAVE TO ME IN PLEASANT MEW        5.80.9
MIDDLE                 1
  RESEMBLING STRONG YCUTH IN HIS MIDDLE AGE         3.7.6
MIDNIGHT               1
  THEN THERE BE STARRES AT MIDNIGHT IN THE SKYES    2.126.12
MIDST                  1
  THUS MIDST A THOUSAND WCES, TEN THOUSAND
                                   JOYES ARISE      2.114.8
MIGHT                 70
  MY FAITH SHOULD WIN, IF $JUSTICE MIGHT HAVE PLACE 1.8.12
  LINES OF DELIGHT, WHERECN HER YOUTH MIGHT SMILE   1.51.2
  WHICH PITTY NOT THE WOUNDS MADE BY THEIR MIGHT    1.59.6
```

```
THAT $CRUELTY HER SELFE MIGHT GRIEVE TO VIEW          1.60.7
ONELY TWO $LOOPE-HOLES, THEN I MIGHT BEHOLD           2.8.4
DEFAC'D WITH $WRINKLES, THAT I MIGHT BUT SEE          2.8.6
IF IT MIGHT PLEASE $YOU, WOULD TO $GOD $YOU COULD     2.19.4
WITH WHAT MIGHT MAKE THE $MISERABLE BLEST             2.23.8
WHICH MIGHT BE BORROW'D FROM NO $EARTHLY FLAME        2.30.2
ON WHICH THE $SUNNE MIGHT BY REFLECTION BEAT          2.30.6
THAT IT, LIKE THOSE, BY LOOKING MIGHT BE BLEST        2.33.4
IN HEAT OF $BLOUD, A MODEST $MIND MIGHT MOVE          2.47.8
THEN WONDER, TONGUE, THEN JOY, MIGHT WEL
                              REPORT A WONDER         2.117.4
MY WORDS MIGHT IMITATE MY DEEREST THOUGHTS
                              DIRECTION               2.117.7
THAT THEREBY BEAUTIES $ROSE MIGHT NEVER DIE           3.1.2
HIS TENDER HEIRE MIGHT BEARE HIS MEMORY               3.1.4
WHICH HUSBANDRY IN HONOUR MIGHT UPHOLD                3.13.10
ORE-CHARG'D WITH BURTHEN OF MINE OWNE LOVES MIGHT     3.23.8
THAT TO MY USE IT MIGHT UN-USED STAY                  3.48.3
TO MORROW SHARPNED IN HIS FORMER MIGHT                3.56.4
THAT I MIGHT SEE WHAT THE OLD WORLD COULD SAY         3.59.9
O NONE, UNLESSE THIS MIRACLE HAVE MIGHT               3.65.13
AND IN THE PRAISE THEREOF SPENDS ALL HIS MIGHT        3.80.3
AND THEIR GROSSE PAINTING MIGHT BE BETTER US'D        3.82.13
THAT YOU YOUR SELFE BEING EXTANT WELL MIGHT SHOW      3.83.6
AT FIRST THE VERY WORST OF FORTUNES MIGHT             3.90.12
HOW MANY $LAMBS MIGHT THE STERNE $WOLFE BETRAY        3.96.9
TO SPEAKE OF THAT WHICH GIVES THEE ALL
                              THY MIGHT+              3.100.2
AS EASIE MIGHT I FROM MY SELFE DEPART                 3.109.3
MIGHT I NOT THEN SAY NOW I LOVE YOU BEST              3.115.10
LOVE IS A $BABE, THEN MIGHT I NOT SAY SO              3.115.13
O THAT OUR NIGHT OF WO MIGHT HAVE REMEMBRED           3.120.9
THY PYRAMYDS BUYLT UP WITH NEWER MIGHT                3.123.2
IT MIGHT FOR FORTUNES BASTERD BE UNFATHERED           3.124.2
THAT SHE MIGHT THINKE ME SOME UNTUTERD YOUTH          3.138.3
WHAT NEEDST THOU WOUND WITH CUNNING WHEN
                              THY MIGHT               3.139.7
THAT THEY ELSE-WHERE MIGHT DART THEIR INJURIES        3.139.12
IF I MIGHT TEACH THEE WITTE BETTER IT WEARE           3.140.5
AND IN MY MADNESSE MIGHT SPEAKE ILL OF THEE           3.140.10
OH FROM WHAT POWRE HAST THOU THIS POWREFULL
                              MIGHT                   3.150.1
THAT THE DEARE $SHE MIGHT TAKE SOME PLEASURE
                              OF MY PAINE             4.1.2
PLEASURE MIGHT CAUSE HER READE, READING
                              MIGHT MAKE HER KNOW     4.1.3
PLEASURE MIGHT CAUSE HER READE, READING
                              MIGHT MAKE HER KNOW     4.1.3
KNOWLEDGE MIGHT PITIE WINNE, AND PITIE
                              GRACE OBTAINE           4.1.4
WHERE WITH MOST EASE AND WARMTH HE MIGHT
                              EMPLOY HIS ART          4.8.7
BY MY LOVE JUDGING WHAT $LOVE'S PAINE MIGHT BE        4.16.8
TO MORTALL EYES MIGHT SWEETLY SHINE IN HER            4.25.11
I MIGHT, UNHAPPIE WORD, O ME, I MIGHT                 4.33.1
I MIGHT, UNHAPPIE WORD, O ME, I MIGHT                 4.33.1
WHERE $VERTUE IS MADE STRONG BY $BEAUTIE'S MIGHT      4.48.2
MIGHT WINNE SOME GRACE IN YOUR SWEET SKILL ARRAID     4.55.4
UNTILL BY YOUR INSPIRING I MIGHT KNOW                 4.55.7
HOW THEIR BLACKE BANNER MIGHT BE BEST DISPLAID        4.55.8
```

```
WHEN I MIGHT READE THOSE LETTERS FAIRE OF BLISSE       4.56.5
HOPING THAT WHEN THEY MIGHT FIND $STELLA ALONE         4.57.5
O VOICE, O FACE, MAUGRE MY SPEECHE'S MIGHT             4.58.12
THAT HAND, WHICH WITHOUT TOUCH HOLDS MORE
                              THEN $ATLAS MIGHT        4.77.5
THAT IN NO MORE BUT THESE I MIGHT BE FULLY BLEST       4.77.13
STELLA, WHILE NOW BY HONOUR'S CRUELL MIGHT             4.91.1
YET TRUTH (IF $CAITIF'S BREATH MIGHTE
                              CALL THEE) THIS          4.93.5
SILENCE IN BOTH DISPLAIES HIS SULLEN MIGHT             4.96.5
WHEN SORROW (USING MINE OWNE FIER'S MIGHT)             4.108.1
WHICH HOLD MY LIFE IN THEIR DEAD DOING MIGHT           5.1.2
SUCH DEATH THE SAD ENSAMPLE OF YOUR MIGHT              5.7.14
LONG-WHILE I SOUGHT TO WHAT I MIGHT COMPARE            5.9.1
GAYNST SUCH STRONG CASTLES NEEDETH GREATER MIGHT       5.14.5
THE SILLY LAMBE THAT TO HIS MIGHT DOTH YIELD           5.20.8
AND WISH THAT MORE AND GREATER THEY MIGHT BE           5.25.13
BUT IN THE STAY OF HER OWNE STEDFAST MIGHT             5.59.11
NE THINKS OF OTHER HEAVEN, BUT HOW IT MIGHT            5.72.11
MIGHTIER                      1
BUT WHEREFORE DO NOT YOU A MIGHTIER WAIE               3.16.1
MIGHTST                       3
FROM $DEATH TO $LIFE, THOU MIGHT'ST HIM
                              YET RECOVER              2.61.14
AYE ME, BUT YET THOU MIGHST MY SEATE FORBEARE          3.41.9
HOW MANY GAZERS MIGHST THOU LEAD AWAY                  3.96.11
MIGHTY                        5
LIKE SOME WEAKE $LORDS, NEIGHBORD BY MIGHTY KINGS      4.29.1
INTO THE OBJECT OF YOUR MIGHTY VIEW+                   5.7.4
THAT THOU OF THEM MAYST MIGHTIE VENGEANCE TAKE         5.10.8
O MIGHTY CHARM WHICH MAKES MEN LOVE THEYR BANE         5.47.13
FRESH SPRING THE HERALD OF LOVES MIGHTY KING           5.70.1
MIGHTY'S                      1
THEN KNOW, THAT MERCY IS THE MIGHTIES JEWELL           5.49.3
MILD                          4
YET NO MILD COMFORT WOULD THY $BROW REVEALE            1.31.9
MYLD HUMBLESSE MIXT WITH AWFULL MAJESTY                5.13.5
FOR WITH MILD PLEASANCE, WHICH DOTH PRIDE
                              DISPLACE                 5.21.5
WITH SHEW OF MORNING MYLDE HE HATH BEGUN               5.62.3
MILDER                        3
WHAT PASSIONS WOULD HER MILDER FAVOURS MOVE+           1.17.12
STARRES THEN, NOT EYES, MOVE YOU WITH
                              A MILDER VIEW            1.34.13
THERE SHE BEHOLDING ME WITH MYLDER LOOKE               5.67.9
MILDLY                        2
O STARRE OF STARRES, FAYRE $PLANET MILDLY
                              MOOVING                  2.129.5
FOR WHEN YE MILDLY LOOKE WITH LOVELY HEW               5.7.5
MILE                          1
AND MAKETH EVERY MINUTE SEEME A MYLE                   5.87.12
MILES                         2
TO LEAPE LARGE LENGTHS OF MILES WHEN THOU
                              ART GONE                 3.44.10
THUS FARRE THE MILES ARE MEASURDE FROM THY FRIEND      3.50.4
MILK                          1
MILKE HANDS, ROSE CHEEKS, OR LIPS MORE
                              SWEET, MORE RED          4.91.7
MILK-WHITE                    2
O BLESSED $BROOKE, WHOSE MILKE-WHITE $SWANS ADORE      2.53.3
```

```
O BLESSED $BROOKE, WHOSE MILK-WHITE $SWANS ACORE      2.113.3
MILLIONED                          1
BUT RECKENING TIME, WHOSE MILLIOND ACCIDENTS         3.115.5
MILLIONS                           3
  THE RECK'NINGS RISE TO MILLIONS OF $DESPAIRES       2.3.4
  AND STYLL IN RECKONINGS RISE MORE MILLIONS
                           OF DISPAYRES              2.110.4
  THAT MILLIONS OF STRANGE SHADDOWES ON YOU TEND+     3.53.2
MIMIC                            1
  ME $THINKES I SEE SOME CROOKED $MIMICKE JEERE       2.31.1
MIND                          61
  WHILST YOUTH AND ERROR LED MY WANDRING MINDE        1.5.1
  MY $MUSE HAD SLEPT, AND NONE HAD KNOWNE MY MINDE    1.6.14
  BUT YET RESTORE THY FIERCE AND CRUELL MIND          1.19.11
  A BURDEN TO MY SELFE, DISTREST IN MINDE             1.49.2
  THOUGH HAPPIER FAR IF THOU WOULDST CHANGE
                           THY MIND                  1.56.14
  IN MOST DISTRACTION THEY KEEPE THAT IN $MINDE       2.9.8
  MOVING A $WILL IN US, IT IS THE $MIND              2.12.6
  HE DID BESTOW IN TEMPER OF THE $MIND               2.14.8
  A DUMBE-BORNE $MUSE MADE TO EXPRESSE THE $MIND      2.35.6
  IN HEAT OF $BLOUD, A MODEST $MIND MIGHT MOVE        2.47.8
  CALLING TO MINDE SINCE FIRST MY $LOVE BEGUN         2.51.1
  A DUMBE-BORNE $MUSE MADE TO EXPRESSE THE MIND       2.112.6
  INTO THE OCEAN OF A TROUBLED MINDE                 2.134.2
  BY CHILDRENS EYES, HER HUSBANDS SHAPE IN MINCE      3.9.8
  O CHANGE THY THOUGHT, THAT I MAY CHANGE MY MINDE    3.10.9
  TO WORKE MY MIND, WHEN BODDIES WORK'S EXPIRED       3.27.4
  LOE THUS BY DAY MY LIMS, BY NIGHT MY MIND           3.27.13
  FOR THAT SAME GRONE DOTH PUT THIS IN MY MIND        3.50.13
  SINCE MINDE AT FIRST IN CARRECTER WAS DONE          3.59.8
  THEY LOOKE INTO THE BEAUTY OF THY MIND              3.69.9
  TO TAKE A NEW ACQUAINTANCE OF THY MINDE             3.77.12
  THOU CANST NOT VEX ME WITH INCONSTANT MINCE         3.92.9
  SINCE I LEFT YOU, MINE EYE IS IN MY MINDE           3.113.1
  OF HIS QUICK OBJECTS HATH THE MINDE NO PART         3.113.7
  MY MOST TRUE MINDE THUS MAKETH MINE UNTRUE          3.113.14
  OR WHETHER DOTH MY MINDE BEING CROWN'D WITH YOU     3.114.1
  AND MY GREAT MINDE MOST KINGLY DRINKES IT UP        3.114.10
  BUT LOVE HATE ON FOR NOW I KNOW THY MINDE           3.149.13
  THAT IN MY MINDE THY WORST ALL BEST EXCEEDS+        3.150.8
  BUT NEVER HEEDS THE FRUIT OF WRITER'S MIND          4.11.8
  O LET ME PROP MY MIND, YET IN HIS GROWTH            4.19.12
  MY YOUNG MIND MARDE, WHOM $LOVE DOTH WINDLAS SO     4.21.2
  WHICH INWARD SUNNE TO $HEROICKE MINDE DISPLAIES     4.25.8
  STELLA'S GREAT POWRS, THAT SO CONFUSE MY MIND       4.34.14
  UNTO MY MIND, IS $STELLA'S IMAGE, WROUGHT           4.38.6
  THAT HAST MY MIND, NONE OF THE BASEST, BROUGHT      4.40.3
  MY WORDS I KNOW DO WELL SET FORTH MY MIND           4.44.1
  MY MIND BEMONES HIS SENSE OF INWARD SMART           4.44.2
  SO THAT I CANNOT CHUSE BUT WRITE MY MIND            4.50.9
  AND THINKE SO STILL, SO $STELLA KNOW MY MIND        4.54.9
  EACH SENCE OF MINE, EACH GIFT, EACH POWER OF MIND   4.57.2
  OR ELSE PRONOUNCING GRACE, WHEREWITH HIS MIND       4.58.7
  NOW SINCE HER CHAST MIND HATES THIS LOVE IN ME      4.61.9
  WITH CHASTNED MIND, I STRAIGHT MUST SHEW
                           THAT SHE                  4.61.10
  FROM NOBLER COURSE, FIT FOR MY BIRTH AND MIND       4.62.8
  WITH WINDOWES OPE THEN MOST MY MIND DOTH LIE        4.99.5
  SUCH LIGHT IN SENSE, WITH SUCH A DARKNED MIND       4.99.14
```

```
OF SUCH HEAVEN STUFFE, TO CLOATH SO HEAVENLY
                            MYNDE                   4.101.14
BE NOUGHT DISMAYD THAT HER UNMOVED MIND            5.6.1
HER MINDE REMEMBRETH HER MORTALITIE                5.13.7
HER MIND ADORND WITH VERTUES MANIFOLD              5.15.14
HER TEMPLE FAYRE IS BUILT WITHIN MY MIND           5.22.5
GIVES ME GREAT HOPE OF YOUR RELENTING MYND         5.28.2
WITH SWEET INFUSION, AND PUT YOU IN MIND           5.28.7
SUCH IS THE POWRE OF LOVE IN GENTLE MIND           5.30.13
AND EKE HER MIND IS PURE IMMORTALL HYE             5.55.12
IN MIND TO MOUNT UP TO THE PUREST SKY              5.72.2
WITH GUIFTS OF BODY, FORTUNE AND OF MIND           5.74.4
WHOSE YMAGE YET I CARRY FRESH IN MYND              5.78.4
AND VERTUOUS MIND, IS MUCH MORE PRAYSD OF ME       5.79.4
BUT WITH SUCH BRIGHTNESSE WHYLEST I FILL MY MIND   5.88.13
MINDED                  2
IF ALL WERE MINDED SO, THE TIMES SHOULD CEASE      3.11.7
WHETHER THE $TURKISH NEW-MOONE MINDED BE           4.30.1
MINDING                 1
BOTH SO AND THUS, SHE MINDING $LOVE SHOULD BE      4.7.12
MINDS                  10
THUS SUNDRY $MEN THEIR SUNDRY $MINDS REPEAT        2.42.8
THUS SUNDRY MEN, THEIR SUNDRY MINDS REPEATE        2.128.8
DIVERT STRONG MINDES TO TH'COURSE OF ALTRING
                            THINGS                  3.115.8
LET ME NOT TO THE MARRIAGE OF TRUE MINDES          3.116.1
THAT I HAVE FREQUENT BINNE WITH UNKNOWN MINDES     3.117.5
IN WEAKENED MINDS, QUICKE APPREHENDING BREED       4.66.3
THY SELFE, DOEST STRIVE ALL MINDS THAT
                            WAY TO MOVE             4.71.10
BUT $ANGELS COME TO LEAD FRAILE MINDES TO REST     5.8.7
SUCH HAUGHTY MYNDS ENUR'D TO HARDY FIGHT           5.14.7
CHAUNGE EEKE OUR MYNDS AND FORMER LIVES AMEND      5.62.6
MIND'S                  4
YOU BEST DISCERN'D OF MY $MINDS INWARD $EYES       2.57.1
THE VACANT LEAVES THY MINDES IMPRINT WILL BEARE    3.77.3
IN DEEP DISCOVERY OF THE MYNDS DISEASE             5.50.6
ATTEMPT TO WORK HER GENTLE MINDES UNREST           5.84.4
MINE                  163
WHILST BLINDED ONES MINE ERROURS NEVER GESSE       1.3.8
THESE LINES I USE, T'UNBURTHEN MINE OWNE HART      1.4.13
FOR HER NO SOONER HAD MINE EYES BEWRAID            1.5.5
BY MINE OWNE THOUGHTS, SET ON ME BY MY $FAIRE      1.5.11
THOSE THAT I FOSTRED OF MINE OWNE ACCORD           1.5.13
AND YOU MINE EYES, THE AGENTS OF MY HART           1.8.5
TEARES IN MINE EYES, AND SORROW AT MY HART         1.9.12
FOR HAPLESSE LOE EVEN WITH MINE OWNE DESIRES       1.13.5
I FIGURDE ON THE TABLE OF MINE HART                1.13.6
THE FAULT IS HERS, THOUGH MINE THE HURT MUST BE    1.15.14
OF MINE AFFECTIONS TAKEN BY HER EIES               1.22.14
THESE SORROWING SIGHES, THE SMOAKE OF MINE ANNOY   1.24.1
MY CARES DRAW ON MINE EVERLASTING NIGHT            1.30.1
AND WILL WHILST I SHALL DRAW THIS BREATH OF MINE   1.33.10
DO FEELE MINE INWARD HEAT AS GREAT (I KNOW IT)     1.43.6
MY $DELIA HATH THE WATERS OF MINE EIES             1.48.1
THEN MINE UNTO HER CRUELTY HATH BEENE              1.48.8
HOW LONG SHALL I IN MINE AFFLICTION MOURNE+        1.49.1
SO $DELIA, HATH MINE ERROR MADE ME KNOWNE          1.56.5
THEN IF I HAD THE VICTORY MINE OWNE                1.56.7
NONE OTHER FAME MINE UNAMBITIOUS $MUSE             1.58.1
```

```
AND THUS MINE $EIES A DEBTOR TO THINE $EYE          2.3.9
BUT PRECIOUS $TEARES DISTILLING FROM MINE $EYNE     2.7.6
SO MUCH IS $MINE, THAT DOTH WITH $YOU REMAINE       2.11.11
THAT TAKING WHAT IS $MINE, WITH $ME I TAKE $YOU     2.11.12
UNTO MINE AID I SUMMON'D EV'RY $SENSE               2.29.2
MY $HEART SHOULD SUFFER FOR MINE $EYES $OFFENCE     2.29.4
WHILST YET MINE $EYES DOE SURFET WITH $DELIGHT      2.33.1
BUT WHILST MINE $EYES THUS GREEDILY DOE GAZE        2.33.5
BLIND WERE MINE $EYES, TILL THEY WERE
                        SEENE OF THINE              2.35.9
AND MINE $EARES DEAFE, BY THY $FAME HEALED BEE      2.35.10
FILLING MINE $EARES WITH $NOISE, AND $NIGHTLY
                        GRONING                     2.40.6
LASTLY, MINE $EYES AMAZEDLY HAVE SEENE              2.51.5
TO TAKE ALL $MINE, AND GIVE ME NONE AGAINE+         2.52.2
PEN'D IN THE GRIEFE OF MINE AFFLICTED $GHOST        2.54.6
A SECOND $FLOUD, DOWNE RAYNING FROM MINE $EYES      2.55.4
THOU VANQUISHING, THE $CONQUEST IS MINE OWNE        2.63.14
PEND IN THE GRIEFE OF MYNE AFFLICTED GHOST          2.101.6
A SECOND FLOOD DOWNE RAYNING FROM MINE EYES         2.102.4
HAD NOT MINE EYE SEENE THY $CELESTIALL EYE          2.104.5
AND THUS MINE EYES, A DEBTOR TO THINE EYE           2.110.9
BLIND WERE MINE EYES, TILL THEY WERE SEENE
                        OF THINE                    2.112.9
AND MINE EARES DEAFE, BY THY FAME HEALED BE         2.112.10
WITH MURTHERING HANDS IMBRUD IN MINE OWN BLOOD      2.114.12
WITH TEARES OUT OF THE $CHANNELS OF MINE EYES       2.115.9
OR COULD MINE EYE BUT AYME, HER OBJECTS
                        PAST PERFECTION             2.117.6
O MINE EYES $COMET, SO ADMYR'D BY LOVING            2.129.7
WHILST THUS MINE EYES DOE SURFET WITH DELIGHT       2.133.1
TO LOOKE ON HER BY WHOM MINE EYES ARE BLEST         2.133.4
BUT WHILST MINE EYES THUS GREEDILY DOE GAZE         2.133.5
MYNE EYES BEHELD THYS CONFLICT IN THY FACE          2.136.14
MYNE EYES WANT TEARES THUS TO BEWAYLE MY WOE        2.143.5
FILLING MYNE EARES WITH NOYSE AND NIGHTLY
                        GRONING                     2.144.6
MYNE EYES WITH TEARES AGAINST THE FIRE STRYVING     2.144.9
IF THOU COULDST ANSWERE THIS FAIRE CHILD OF MINE    3.2.10
MINE BE THY LOVE AND THY LOVES USE THEIR
                        TREASURE                    3.20.14
PRESUME NOT ON THY HEART WHEN MINE IS SLAINE        3.22.13
AND IN MINE OWNE LOVES STRENGTH SEEME TO DECAY      3.23.7
ORE-CHARG'D WITH BURTHEN OF MINE OWNE LOVES MIGHT   3.23.8
MINE EYE HATH PLAY'D THE PAINTER AND HATH STEELD    3.24.1
MINE EYES HAVE DRAWNE THY SHAPE, AND THINE
                        FOR ME                      3.24.10
DUTY SO GREAT, WHICH WIT SO POORE AS MINE           3.26.5
HATH DEARE RELIGIOUS LOVE STOLNE FROM MINE EYE      3.31.6
BUT OUT ALACK, HE WAS BUT ONE HOURE MINE            3.33.11
AS THOU BEING MINE, MINE IS THY GOOD REPORT         3.36.14
AS THOU BEING MINE, MINE IS THY GOOD REPORT         3.36.14
THE PAINE BE MINE, BUT THINE SHAL BE THE PRAISE     3.38.14
WHAT CAN MINE OWNE PRAISE TO MINE OWNE
                        SELFE BRING                 3.39.3
WHAT CAN MINE OWNE PRAISE TO MINE OWNE
                        SELFE BRING                 3.39.3
AND WHAT IS'T BUT MINE OWNE WHEN I PRAISE THEE      3.39.4
ALL MINE WAS THINE, BEFORE THOU HADST THIS MORE     3.40.4
WHEN MOST I WINKE THEN DOE MINE EYES BEST SEE       3.43.1
```

```
HOW WOULD (I SAY) MINE EYES BE BLESSED MADE        3.43.9
MINE EYE AND HEART ARE AT A MORTALL WARRE          3.46.1
MINE EYE, MY HEART THEIR PICTURES SIGHT
                     WOULD BARRE                   3.46.3
MY HEART, MINE EYE THE FREEEDOME OF THAT RIGHT     3.46.4
AS THUS, MINE EYES DUE IS THEIR OUTWARD PART       3.46.13
BETWIXT MINE EYE AND HEART A LEAGUE IS TOOKE       3.47.1
WHEN THAT MINE EYE IS FAMISHT FOR A LOOKE          3.47.3
AN OTHER TIME MINE EYE IS MY HEARTS GUEST          3.47.7
THOU BEST OF DEEREST, AND MINE ONELY CARE          3.48.7
WITHIN THE KNOWLEDGE OF MINE OWNE DESART           3.49.10
IT IS MY LOVE THAT KEEPES MINE EIE AWAKE           3.61.10
MINE OWNE TRUE LOVE THAT DOTH MY REST DEFEAT       3.61.11
SINNE OF SELFE-LOVE POSSESSETH AL MINE EIE         3.62.1
ME THINKES NO FACE SO GRATIOUS IS AS MINE          3.62.5
AND FOR MY SELFE MINE OWNE WORTH DO DEFINE         3.62.7
MINE OWNE SELFE LOVE QUITE CONTRARY I READ         3.62.11
TO DOE MORE FOR ME THEN MINE OWNE DESERT           3.72.6
THEN LACKT I MATTER, THAT INFEEBLED MINE           3.86.14
WITH MINE OWNE WEAKENESSE BEING BEST ACQUAINTED    3.88.5
FOR TEARME OF LIFE THOU ART ASSURED MINE           3.92.2
AS THOU BEING MINE, MINE IS THY GOOD REPORT        3.96.14
AS THOU BEING MINE, MINE IS THY GOOD REPORT        3.96.14
HATH MOTION, AND MINE EYE MAY BE DECEAVED          3.104.12
NOT MINE OWNE FEARES, NOR THE PROPHETICK SOULE     3.107.1
COUNTING NO OLD THING OLD, THOU MINE, I THINE      3.108.7
GOR'D MINE OWN THOUGHTS, SOLD CHEAP WHAT
                     IS MOST DEARE                 3.110.3
MINE APPETITE I NEVER MORE WILL GRIN'DE            3.110.10
SINCE I LEFT YOU, MINE EYE IS IN MY MINDE          3.113.1
MY MOST TRUE MINDE THUS MAKETH MINE UNTRUE         3.113.14
OR WHETHER SHALL I SAY MINE EIE SAITH TRUE         3.114.3
MINE EIE WELL KNOWES WHAT WITH HIS GUST
                     IS GREEING                    3.114.11
THAT MINE EYE LOVES IT AND DOTH FIRST BEGINNE      3.114.14
HOW HAVE MINE EIES OUT OF THEIR $SPHEARES
                     BENE FITTED                   3.119.7
MINE RANSOMS YOURS, AND YOURS MUST RANSOME MEE     3.120.14
THE WIRY CONCORD THAT MINE EARE CONFOUNDS          3.128.4
MY SELFE $ILE FORFEIT, SO THAT OTHER MINE          3.134.3
ONE WILL OF MINE TO MAKE THY LARGE $WILL MORE      3.135.12
THOU BLINDE FOOLE LOVE, WHAT DOOST THOU
                     TO MINE EYES                  3.137.1
OR MINE EYES SEEING THIS, SAY THIS IS NOT          3.137.11
HER PRETTIE LOOKES HAVE BEENE MINE ENEMIES         3.139.10
IN FAITH I DOE NOT LOVE THEE WITH MINE EYES        3.141.1
NOR ARE MINE EARES WITH THY TOUNGS TUNE
                     DELIGHTED                     3.141.5
O BUT WITH MINE, COMPARE THOU THINE OWNE STATE     3.142.3
AND SEALD FALSE BONDS OF LOVE AS OFT AS MINE       3.142.7
WHOME THINE EYES WOOE AS MINE IMPORTUNE THEE       3.142.10
BUT KNOWNE WORTH DID IN MINE OF TIME PROCEED       4.2.3
WHICH $CUPID'S SELFE FROM $BEAUTIE'S MYNE
                     DID DRAW                      4.9.13
MINE EYES (SHALL I SAY CURST OR BLEST) BEHELD      4.16.10
THAT MINE OWNE WRITINGS LIKE BAD SERVANTS SHOW     4.21.3
SURE YOU SAY WELL, YOUR WISDOME'S GOLDEN MINE      4.21.12
TO HATCH MINE EYES, AND THAT UNBITTED THOUGHT      4.38.2
THAT ONCE COME THERE, THE SOBS OF MINE ANNOYES     4.44.13
LET NOT MINE EYES BE HEL-DRIV'N FROM THAT LIGHT    4.48.7
```

```
PARDON MINE EARES, BOTH I AND THEY DO PRAY            4.51.1
MY HEART THEN QUAK'D, THEN DAZLED WERE MINE EYES      4.53.10
SO SWEETE SOUNDS STRAIGHT MINE EARE AND
                              HEART DO HIT            4.55.13
EACH SENCE OF MINE, EACH GIFT, EACH POWER OF MIND     4.57.2
LET CLOUDS BEDIMME MY FACE, BREAKE IN MINE EYE        4.64.5
BY $NATURE BORNE, I GAVE TO THEE MINE EYES            4.65.8
MINE EYES, MY LIGHT, MY HEART, MY LIFE, ALAS          4.65.9
BUT WHEN MINE EYES BACKE TO THEIR HEAV'N
                              DID MOVE                4.66.13
I, I, O I MAY SAY, THAT SHE IS MINE                   4.69.11
CARE SHINING IN MINE EYES, FAITH IN MY SPRITE         4.72.11
OF GENTLE FORCE, SO THAT MINE EYES DARE
                              GLADLY PLAY             4.76.6
MY HEART CRIES 'AH', IT BURNES, MINE EYES
                              NOW DAZLED BE           4.76.11
HAVE CHANG'D DESERT, LET MINE OWNE CONSCIENCE BE      4.86.2
LET WO GRIPE ON MY HEART, SHAME LOADE MINE EYE        4.86.4
GRAVED IN MINE $EPITAPH A $POET'S NAME                4.90.8
THEY PLEASE I DO CONFESSE, THEY PLEASE MINE EYES      4.91.9
CAN SCARCE DISCERNE THE SHAPE OF MINE OWNE PAINE      4.94.4
OR IF THY LOVE OF PLAINT YET MINE FORBEARES           4.94.9
MINE EYES THEN ONLY WINKE, FOR SPITE PERCHANCE        4.98.13
THAT WORMES SHOULD HAVE THEIR $SUN, AND
                              I WANT MINE             4.98.14
IN TOMBE OF LIDS THEN BURIED ARE MINE EYES            4.99.12
ENVIOUS WITS WHAT HATH BENE MINE OFFENCE              4.104.1
THAT TO EACH WORD, NAY SIGH OF MINE YOU HARKE         4.104.3
IF I BUT STARS UPON MINE ARMOUR BEARE                 4.104.10
BUT CEASE MINE EYES, YOUR TEARES DO WITNESSE
                              WELL                     4.105.9
THOU TOLDST MINE EYES SHOULD HELPE THEIR
                              FAMISHT CASE+            4.106.6
WHEN SORROW (USING MINE OWNE FIER'S MIGHT)            4.108.1
BUT MINE NO PRICE NOR PRAYER MAY SURCEASE             5.11.14
AND DOE MYNE HUMBLED HART BEFORE HER POURE            5.20.2
YET ARE MINE EYES SO FILLED WITH THE STORE            5.35.9
TAKE HEED THEREFORE, MYNE EYES, HOW YE DOE STARE      5.37.9
AND EKE MINE EIES WITH MEEKE HUMILITY                 5.43.11
SHE DOTH ALLURE ME TO MINE OWNE DECAY                 5.53.7
BUT WHEN MYNE EYES I THEREUNTO DIRECT                 5.78.9
CEASSE THEN MYNE EYES, TO SEEKE HER SELFE TO SEE      5.78.13
YET ARE MYNE EYES SO FILLED WITH THE STORE            5.83.9
WHEREOF SOME GLANCE DOTH IN MINE EIE REMAYNE          5.88.8
I STARVE MY BODY AND MINE EYES DOE BLYND              5.88.14
MINERVA                       3
I PASSE NOT FOR $MINERVA, NOR $ASTREA                 2.39.13
I PASSE NOT FOR $MINERVA NOR $ASTRAEA                 2.118.13
WHEN YOU $MINERVA IN THE SUNNE BEHOLD                 2.151.5
MINERVA-LIKE                  1
MINERVA-LIKE, BROUGHT FOORTH WITHOUT A MOTHER         1.2.2
MINERVA'S                     1
SEATED WITH $SOL, AND WEARES $MINERVAS GLOVE          2.151.12
MINION
YET FEAR HER $O THOU MINNION OF HER PLEASURE          3.126.9
MINISTER                      1
TO $WISEDOME'S SELFE TO MINISTER DIRECTION            2.34.7
MINSTRELS                     1
THEY THAT ARE BLIND, ARE $MINSTRELS OFTEN MADE        2.48.11
```

```
MINUTE                   2
    MAY TIME DISGRACE, AND WRETCHED MYNUIT KILL         3.126.8
    AND MAKETH EVERY MINUTE SEEME A MYLE                5.87.12
MINUTES                  3
    NOR CAN I FORTUNE TO BREEFE MYNUITS TELL            3.14.5
    SO DO OUR MINUITES HASTEN TO THEIR END              3.60.2
    THY DYALL HOW THY PRETIOUS MYNUITS WASTE            3.77.2
MINUTE'S                 1
    NOR GIVES $ME ONCE, BUT ONE POORE MINUTES REST      2.20.4
MIRACLE                  3
    THE WORLD SHALL FINDE THIS MYRACLE IN ME            1.41.9
    THIS MIRACLE ON MY POORE $MUSE HAVE TRIED           2.104.10
    O NONE, UNLESSE THIS MIRACLE HAVE MIGHT             3.65.13
MIRACLES                 3
    WHEN I DOE SPEAKE OF $MIRACLES BY THEE              2.35.2
    SEE $MIRACLES, YE UNBELEEVING, SEE                  2.35.5
    SEE MYRACLES, YEE UNBELEEVING SEE                   2.112.5
MIRACULOUS               2
    OR WOULD SHE HER MIRACULOUS POWER SHOW              4.7.9
    WHAT MORE MIRACULOUS THING MAY BE TOLD              5.30.9
MIRE                     1
    DOTH PLUNGE MY WEL-FORM'D SOULE EVEN IN THE MIRE    4.14.7
MIRROR                   5
    THAT $MIRROR SHEWES WHAT POWER IS IN THY FACE       1.37.10
    AND THY $YOUTH PAST, IN THIS PURE $MIRROUR SEE      2.17.6
    AND THY YOUTH PAST, IN THIS FAIRE MIRROR SEE        2.107.6
    O PUREST MERROR, WHEREIN MEN MAY SEE                2.146.13
    FAYRE EYES, THE MYRROUR OF MY MAZED HART            5.7.1
MIRRORS                  1
    THEN IN THESE TEARES, THE MIRRORS OF THESE EYES     2.114.5
MIRTH                    6
    AND HOW I LIVE CAST DOWNE FROM OFF ALL MYRTH        1.60.9
    NECTAR OF $MIRTH, SINCE I $JOVE'S CUP DO KEEPE      4.70.4
    ALL MIRTH FAREWELL, LET ME IN SORROW LIVE           4.100.14
    AND MASK IN MYRTH LYKE TO A $COMEDY                 5.54.6
    DELIGHTS NOT IN MY MERTH NOR RUES MY SMART          5.54.10
    WHAT THEN CAN MOVE HER+ IF NOR MERTH NOR MONE       5.54.13
MISBELIEVING             1
    SOME MISBELEEVING, AND PROPHANE IN $LOVE            2.35.1
MISCALLED                1
    AND SIMPLE-$TRUTH MISCALDE $SIMPLICITIE             3.66.11
MISCHIEF                 1
    SHAME BE THY MEED, AND MISCHIEFE THY REWARD         5.86.13
MISDEEM                  2
    WHY THEN DOE YE PROUD FAYRE, MISDEEME SO FARRE      5.58.13
    THE DOUBT WHICH YE MISDEEME, FAYRE LOVE, IS VAINE   5.65.1
MISER                    1
    AS TWIXT A MISER AND HIS WEALTH IS FOUND            3.75.4
MISERABLE                1
    WITH WHAT MIGHT MAKE THE $MISERABLE BLEST           2.23.8
MISERIES                 4
    THE SAD $MEMORIALLS OF MY $MISERIES                 2.54.5
    THE SAD MEMORIALS OF MY MISERIES                    2.101.5
    LOOKING INTO THE GLASSE OF MY YOUTHS MISERIES       2.114.1
    AND DAYLY MORE AUGMENT MY MISERYES+                 5.36.8
MISERY                   4
    WHERE, IN THE $MAP OF ALL MY $MISERIE               2.44.3
    OR WANT I SENSE TO FEELE MY MISERIE+                4.47.5
    GONE IS THE WINTER OF MY MISERIE                    4.69.7
    AND KNOW NO END OF HER OWNE MYSERY                  5.25.2
```

```
MISFORTUNE                    1
   HATH NO MISFORTUNE, BUT THAT $RICH SHE IS        4.37.14
MISHAP                        2
   THE $STARRE OF MY MISHAP IMPOS'D THIS PAINE      1.32.1
   BUT THEN THE MORE YOUR OWNE MISHAP I REW         5.82.3
MISINTENDED                   1
   THE $DAMZELL BROKE HIS MISINTENDED DART          5.16.12
MISLED                        1
   I AM FROM YOU, LIGHT OF MY LIFE, MIS-LED         4.91.2
MISPLACED                     1
   AND GILDED HONOR SHAMEFULLY MISPLAST             3.66.5
MISPRISION                    1
   SO THY GREAT GUIFT UPON MISPRISION GROWING       3.87.11
MISS                          9
   NO DOWNE-CAST LOOKE HAD SIGNIFIED MY MISSE       1.7.10
   I FIND HOW HEAV'NLY DAY WRETCH I DID MISSE       4.33.4
   THOU NEEDS MUST MISSE, AND SO THOU NEEDS
                          MUST SMART               4.46.11
   LEAVE FOLLOWING THAT, WHICH IT IS GAINE TO MISSE 4.47.11
   AND THINKE I SHOULD NOT YOUR LARGE PRECEPTS
                          MISSE+                   4.56.4
   WHAT WONDER THEN IF HE HIS LESSON MISSE          4.73.3
   THAT GRACE, WHICH $VENUS WEEPES THAT SHE
                          HER SELFE DOTH MISSE      4.77.4
   BUT WIT CONFUS'D WITH TOO MUCH CARE DID MISSE    4.93.8
   DARK IS MY DAY, WHYLES HER FAYRE LIGHT I MIS     5.89.13
MISSES                        1
   THAT HAND THAT DARTS SO RIGHT AND NEVER MISSES   1.46.10
MISSETH                       1
   WHERE EVERY ONE THAT MISSETH THEN HER MAKE       5.70.11
MISSING                       1
   WITH IDLE PAINES, AND MISSING AYME, DO GUESSE    4.23.4
MISSPENT                      1
   THAT FOR MY MIS-SPENT YOUTH THE TEARS
                          FEL FROM MY EYES          2.114.4
MIST                          2
   OF THEE, THY RECORD NEVER CAN BE MIST            3.122.8
   THAT YOU, GUILTLESSE THEREOF, YOUR $NECTAR MIST  4.105.10
MISTAKE                       2
   NO MARVAILE THEN THOUGH I MISTAKE MY VIEW        3.148.11
   BUT FEELING PROOFE MAKES ME SAY THEY MISTAKE
                          IT FURRE                 4.102.11
MISTAKEN                      1
   AND ALL THIS WHILE, I WAS MISTAKEN THERE         2.19.12
MISTAKING                     2
   AND MORE THE FAME OF HIS MISTAKING HAND          1.56.3
   OR MEE TO WHOM THOU GAV'ST IT, ELSE MISTAKING    3.87.10
MISTRESS                      7
   BUT WITH MY $VERSES HE HIS $MISTRES WONNE        2.21.9
   EQUALL WITH HIS, THAT LOVES HIS $MISTRES MOST    2.27.12
   EV'N SO MY $MISTRES WORKES UPON MY $ILL          2.50.12
   HASTE THOU THE $MASTER $MISTRIS OF MY PASSION    3.20.2
   IF $NATURE (SOVERAINE MISTERES OVER WRACK)       3.126.5
   THEN IN THE BREATH THAT FROM MY $MISTRES REEKES  3.130.8
   MY $MISTRES WHEN SHEE WALKES TREADS ON
                          THE GROUND                3.130.12
MISTRESS'                     6
   WHO WRITES MY $MISTRES PRAISE, CAN NEVER
                          WRITE AMISSE              2.128.14
   THEREFORE MY $MISTERSSE EYES ARE $RAVEN BLACKE   3.127.9
```

```
MY $MISTRES EYES ARE NOTHING LIKE THE $SUNNE        3.130.1
BUT AT MY MISTRES EIE LCVES BRAND NEW FIRED         3.153.9
WHERE $CUPID GOT NEW FIRE., MY MISTRES EYE          3.153.14
FOR MEN DISEASD, BUT I MY $MISTRISSE THRALL         3.154.12
```
MISTS   1
```
TUSH ABSENCE, WHILE THY MISTES ECLIPSE THAT LIGHT   4.88.9
```
MISTY   1
```
SO DARKE WITH MISTY VAPORS, WHICH ARISE             4.94.2
```
MISUSE   1
```
FOR ALL MY VOWES ARE OTHES BUT TO MISUSE THEE       3.152.7
```
MIXED   6
```
MIX'D WITH HER $TEARES, THAT NE'R HER
                          TRUE-$LOVE CROST          2.15.5
WHICH IS NOT MIXT WITH SECONDS, KNOWS NO ART        3.125.11
FRAME DAINTIEST LUSTRE, MIXT OF SHADES AND LIGHT+   4.7.4
MARBLE MIXT RED AND WHITE DO ENTERLACE              4.9.8
MYLD HUMBLESSE MIXT WITH AWFULL MAJESTY             5.13.5
THAT PRIDE AND MEEKNESSE MIXT BY EQUALL PART        5.21.3
```
MIXTURE   2
```
WHICH ELEMENTS WITH MORTALL MIXTURE BREEC           4.5.11
WITH SUCH BAD MIXTURE OF MY NIGHT AND DAY           4.89.12
```
MOAN   14
```
LET THEM YET SIGH THEIR CWNE, AND MONE MY WRCNGS    1.3.4
I WORKE ON FLINT, AND THATS THE CAUSE I MCNE        1.13.4
VEXING WITH UNTUN'D MOANE HER DAINTY EARES          1.21.8
ILE MONE MY SELFE, AND HIDE THE WRONG I HAVE        1.59.10
AND MONE TH'EXPENCE OF MANY A VANNISHT SIGHT        3.30.8
THE SAD ACCOUNT OF FORE-BEMONED MONE                3.30.11
I MUST ATTEND, TIMES LEASURE WITH MY MONE           3.44.12
LEAST THE WISE WORLD SHCULD LOOKE INTO YCUR MONE    3.71.13
REVENGE UPON MY SELFE WITH PRESENT MONE+            3.149.8
MY STILL KEPT COURSE, WHILE OTHERS SLEEPE,
                          TO MONE                   4.40.4
THE COURTLY $NYMPHS, ACQUAINTED WITH THE MONE       4.54.5
SHOULD SOONE BE PIERC'D WITH SHARPNESSE
                          OF THE MONE               4.57.8
BUT BY HIS DEATH WHICH SCME PERHAPS WILL MONE       5.36.13
WHAT THEN CAN MOVE HER+ IF NOR MERTH NOR MONE       5.54.13
```
MOANS   1
```
SITH SHE IS DEAFE, AND WILL NOT HEARE MY $MONES     2.45.10
```
MOCK   3
```
WHILE SHADOWES LIKE TO THEE DO MOCKE MY SIGHT+      3.61.4
AND MOCKE YOU WITH ME AFTER I AM GON                3.71.14
AND THE SAD $AUGURS MOCK THEIR OWNE PRESAGE         3.107.6
```
MOCKS   1
```
BUT WHEN I LAUGH SHE MOCKS, AND WHEN I CRY          5.54.11
```
MODEL   1
```
TO MODELL FORTH THE PASSIONS OF THE MORRCW          1.54.10
```
MODELED   1
```
IS MODEL'D OUT THE $WORLD OF MY $DISGRACE           2.44.4
```
MODELS   2
```
BUT WHY+ BECAUSE CF YOU THEY MODELS BE              4.91.10
MODELS SUCH BE WOCD-GLOBES OF GLISTRING SKIES       4.91.11
```
MODERN   1
```
HOW FARRE A MODERNE QUILL DOTH COME TO SHORT        3.83.7
```
MODEST   3
```
A MODEST $MAIDE, DECKT WITH A BLUSH OF HCNOR        1.6.5
IN HEAT OF $BLOUD, A MODEST $MIND MIGHT MOVE        2.47.8
AND MODEST THOUGHTS BREATHD FROM WEL TEMPRED
                          SPRITES                   5.84.6
```

```
MOIETY                          1
  THE CLEERE EYES MOYITIE, AND THE DEARE
                        HEARTS PART                    3.46.12
MOISTURE                        2
  THE WATER, MOYSTURE FROM MY TEARES DERIVETH          2.127.2
  THY TEARES EXPRESSE NIGHT'S NATIVE MOISTURE RIGHT    4.96.8
MOLD                            3
  FROM OUT THY HEAVY MOULD, THAT INBENT EYES           4.94.3
  MAKE IN MY HEAVY MOULD NEW THOUGHTS TO GROW          4.106.11
  I MARVAILE OF WHAT SUBSTANCE WAS THE MOULD           5.55.3
MOLE                            2
  YET WITH THE $MOLE I CREEPE INTO THE $EARTH          2.62.10
  YET WITH THE $MOLE, I CREEPE INTO THE EARTH          2.150.10
MOLEST                          2
  WHY SHOULD I MORE MOLEST THE WORLD WITH CRIES+       1.21.5
  BREAKE OUT, THAT MAY HER SACRED PEACE MOLEST         5.84.2
MOLLIFY                         2
  AND MOLLIFIE THE SLAUGHT'RING $GALLIGLASSE           2.25.12
  THE HARDEST YRON SOON DOTH MOLLIFY                   5.32.2
MOLY                            1
  AND SWEET IS $MOLY, BUT HIS ROOT IS ILL              5.26.8
MOMENT                          2
  AND IN A MOMENT $MAD, $SOBER, $GLAD, AND $SORRIE     2.49.10
  HOLDS IN PERFECTION BUT A LITTLE MOMENT              3.15.2
MOMENTARY                       1
  WHICH MEANER PRIZ'D AND MOMENTARY BEE                1.58.4
MONARCH                         1
  THEN FOR A $MONARCH WILL I HONOUR THEE               2.115.4
MONARCH'S                       1
  DRINKE UP THE MONARKS PLAGUE THIS FLATTERY+          3.114.2
MONARCHY                        1
  OF HER HIGH HEART GIV'N ME THE MONARCHIE             4.69.10
MONGST                          4
  'MONGST ALL THE $CREATURES IN THIS SPACIOUS
                        $ROUND                         2.16.1
  BUT MONGST THEM ALL, WHICH DID $LOVES HONOR RAYSE    5.19.9
  MONGST WHOME THE MORE I SEEKE TO SETTLE PEACE        5.44.13
  MONGST WHICH THERE IN A SILVER DISH DID LY           5.77.5
MONSTER                         1
  A MONSTER, OTHER'S HARME, SELFE-MISERIE              4.78.5
MONSTER-BREEDING                1
  ONE, HE DOTH WONDER MONSTER-BREEDING $NYLE           2.120.3
MONSTERS                        1
  TO MAKE OF MONSTERS, AND THINGS INDIGEST             3.114.5
MONUMENT                        7
  A $MONUMENT THAT WHOSOEVER REEDES                    1.2.7
  THIS MAY REMAINE THY LASTING MONUMENT                1.42.9
  NOT MARBLE, NOR THE GUILDED MONUMENT                 3.55.1
  YOUR MONUMENT SHALL BE MY GENTLE VERSE               3.81.9
  AND THOU IN THIS SHALT FINDE THY MONUMENT            3.107.13
  SHALL BE THEREOF IMMORTALL MONIMENT                  5.69.10
  YOUR GLORIOUS NAME IN GOLDEN MONIMENT                5.82.8
MONUMENTS                       1
  NE LET THEYR FAMOUS MONIMENTS TO FADE                5.51.4
MOOD                            1
  AND WITH MEEKE HUMBLESSE AND AFFLICTED MOOD          5.2.11
MOODS                           1
  IS WRIT IN MOODS AND FROUNES AND WRINCKLES
                        STRANGE                        3.93.8
```

MOON   10
    WHILST $MOONE SHALL SHINE, OR ANY $FIRE
                            SHALL BURNE   2.13.12
    THE WANDRING $MOONE IN EARTHS TRIPLICITIE   2.116.8
    WHILST $MOONE SHALL SHYNE BY NIGHT, OR
                            ANY FIRE SHALL BURNE   2.121.12
    NOR $MOONE NOR STARS LEND THEE THEIR SHINING
                            LIGHT   2.145.12
    WITH $SUNNE AND $MOONE, WITH EARTH AND
                            SEAS RICH GEMS   3.21.6
    CLOUDES AND ECLIPSES STAINE BOTH $MOONE
                            AND $SUNNE   3.35.3
    THE MORTALL $MOONE HATH HER ECLIPSE INDUR'DE   3.107.5
    WITH HOW SAD STEPS, O $MOONE, THOU CLIMB'ST
                            THE SKIES   4.31.1
    THEN EV'N OF FELLOWSHIP, O $MOONE, TELL ME   4.31.9
    NOR TO THE $MOONE.. FOR THEY ARE CHANGED NEVER   5.9.6
MORAL   1
    YOUR MORALL NOTES STRAIGHT MY HID MEANING TEARE   4.104.12
MORE   185
    WHY SHOULD I MORE MOLEST THE WORLD WITH CRIES+   1.21.5
    SHE MAY BECOME MORE KINDE TO THEE OR ME   1.23.14
    WILL RISE NO MORE TO ME, WHOSE DAY IS DUNNE   1.30.4
    DID MAKE THE HONOUR OF THE FALL THE MORE   1.35.4
    HE NEVER HAD MORE FAITH, ALTHOUGH MORE RIME   1.43.7
    HE NEVER HAD MORE FAITH, ALTHOUGH MORE RIME   1.43.7
    AND IF MY PEN COULD MORE ENLARGE THY NAME   1.43.11
    THAT $GRACE WHICH DOTH MORE THEN IN WOMAN THEE   1.45.13
    POORE SOULE QUITE SPENT, WHOSE FORCE CAN
                            DO NO MORE   1.46.3
    THAT THOU BE PLEAS'D, AND I MAY SIGH NO MORE   1.46.14
    TH'$OCEAN NEVER DID ATTEND MORE DULY   1.48.5
    NOR PAYD THE IMPOST OF HIS WAVES MORE TRULY   1.48.7
    BUT AH- NO MORE, THIS MUST NOT BE FORETOLD   1.50.13
    TO ADDE MORE GRIEFE TO AGGRAVATE MY SORROW   1.54.12
    AND MORE THE FAME OF HIS MISTAKING HAND   1.56.3
    AND MY DECEIV'D ATTEMPT, DESERV'D MORE FAME   1.56.6
    I SAY NO MORE, I FEARE I SAYD TOO MUCH   1.60.14
    NO I, AM I, IF I NO MORE CAN HAVE   2.5.10
    ANSWERE NO MORE, WITH $SILENCE MAKE REPLY   2.5.11
    YET MORE TO GRACE THE $COMPANY WITHALL   2.7.3
    AND BID THEM MOURNE, NAY MORE, DESPAIRE
                            WITH THEE   2.17.13
    WITH ONE MORE $ORDER, THESE NINE $ORDERS
                            GLADDETH   2.18.12
    SOME WISE IN SHEW, MORE $FOOLES INDEED THEN THEY   2.22.14
    THOUGH $FEARE GIVES THEM MORE THEN A $HEAV'NLY
                            $SCOPE   2.26.8
    OR IN OUR $FATHERS DID SHE MORE TRANSGRESSE+   2.27.8
    THOUGH I GIVE MORE THEN WELL AFFORDS MY STATE   2.28.5
    AND KNOWING MORE THEN EVER HATH BEENE TAUGHT   2.34.3
    STILL MORE AND MORE IT TO MY TORMENT BURNETH   2.40.12
    STILL MORE AND MORE IT TO MY TORMENT BURNETH   2.40.12
    LONG SINCE DEPARTED (TO THE $WORLD NO MORE)   2.46.10
    WITH THOUSAND $PLAGUES, MORE THEN IN $PURGATORIE   2.49.12
    BUT THEIR $EXPERIENCE TO INCREASE THE MORE   2.50.11
    MORE THEN HIS WOND'RING UTT'RANCE CAN UNFOLD   2.57.10
    NAY, I HAVE DONE.. $YOU GET NO MORE OF $ME   2.61.2
    THEN MORE I $TRAVELD, FURTHER FROM MY $REST   2.62.2
    MORE THEN WORLDS VOLUMES SHALL THEREOF ARISE   2.102.2

```
THAT THEY MAY TEL MORE WORLDS WHAT $TIME
                        HATH SEENE          2.107.11
SHE WAS, THE LIKE THAT NEVER WAS, NOR
                        NEVER MORE SHALBE   2.107.14
WITH ONE MORE ORDER, THESE NINE ORDERS GLADDETH   2.108.12
AND STYLL IN RECKONINGS RISE MORE MILLIONS
                        OF DISPAYRES        2.110.4
NO MORE SHALT THOU NOR $SAINT NOR $IDOLL BE   2.126.2
MORE $ARROWES WITH HART-PIERCING METTEL POYNTED   2.126.11
O CLEEREST DAY-STARRE, NEVER MORE DECLYNING   2.129.8
LOV'D MORE THEN LIFE, YET ONELY ART HIS LOVE   2.129.11
FAIRE-MAYD NO MORE, BUT $MAYR-MAID BE THY NAME   2.130.9
YET FEARE GYVES THEM MORE THEN A HEAVENLY SCOPE   2.137.8
STILL MORE AND MORE UNTO MY TORMENT BURNETH   2.144.12
STILL MORE AND MORE UNTO MY TORMENT BURNETH   2.144.12
THE $GALIXIA, TO HER MORE THEN WHITE   2.148.10
THE MORE I TRAVELL, FURTHER FROM MY REST   2.150.2
HOW MUCH MORE PRAISE DESERV'D THY BEAUTIES USE   3.2.9
LOOKE WHOM SHE BEST INDOW'D, SHE GAVE THE MORE   3.11.11
THOU SHOULDST PRINT MORE, NOT LET THAT COPPY DIE   3.11.14
WITH MEANES MORE BLESSED THEN MY BARREN RIME+   3.16.4
THOU ART MORE LOVELY AND MORE TEMPERATE   3.18.2
THOU ART MORE LOVELY AND MORE TEMPERATE   3.18.2
AN EYE MORE BRIGHT THEN THEIRS, LESSE
                        FALSE IN ROWLING   3.20.5
LET THEM SAY MORE THAT LIKE OF HEARE-SAY WELL   3.21.13
MORE THEN THAT TONGE THAT MORE HATH MORE EXPREST   3.23.12
MORE THEN THAT TONGE THAT MORE HATH MORE EXPREST   3.23.12
MORE THEN THAT TONGE THAT MORE HATH MORE EXPREST   3.23.12
WISHING ME LIKE TO ONE MORE RICH IN HOPE   3.29.5
AND SHALT BY FORTUNE ONCE MORE RE-SURVAY   3.32.3
NO MORE BEE GREEV'D AT THAT WHICH THOU HAST DONE   3.35.1
EXCUSING THEIR SINS MORE THEN THEIR SINS ARE   3.35.8
OR ANY OF THESE ALL, OR ALL, OR MORE   3.37.6
BE THOU THE TENTH $MUSE, TEN TIMES MORE IN WORTH   3.38.9
WHAT HAST THOU THEN MORE THEN THOU HADST BEFORE+   3.40.2
ALL MINE WAS THINE, BEFORE THOU HADST THIS MORE   3.40.4
A LOSSE IN LOVE THAT TOUCHES ME MORE NEERELY   3.42.4
MORE SHARPE TO ME THEN SPURRING TO HIS SIDE   3.50.12
OH HOW MUCH MORE DOTH BEAUTIE BEAUTIOUS SEEME   3.54.1
BUT YOU SHALL SHINE MORE BRIGHT IN THESE CONTENTS   3.55.3
RETURNE OF LOVE, MORE BLEST MAY BE THE VIEW   3.56.12
MAKES $SOMERS WELCOME, THRICE MORE WISH'D,
                        MORE RARE   3.56.14
MAKES $SOMERS WELCOME, THRICE MORE WISH'D,
                        MORE RARE   3.56.14
TO DOE MORE FOR ME THEN MINE OWNE DESERT   3.72.6
AND HANG MORE PRAISE UPON DECEASED I   3.72.7
AND LIVE NO MORE TO SHAME NOR ME, NOR YOU   3.72.12
THIS THOU PERCEV'ST, WHICH MAKES THY LOVE
                        MORE STRONG   3.73.13
THERE LIVES MORE LIFE IN ONE OF YOUR FAIRE EYES   3.83.13
WHO IS IT THAT SAYES MOST, WHICH CAN SAY MORE   3.84.1
AND TO THE MOST OF PRAISE ADDE SOME-THING MORE   3.85.10
THY SWEET BELOVED NAME NO MORE SHALL DWELL   3.89.10
OF MORE DELIGHT THEN $HAWKES OR $HORSES BEE   3.91.11
BOTH GRACE AND FAULTS ARE LOV'D OF MORE AND LESSE   3.96.3
MORE FLOWERS I NOTED, YET I NONE COULD SEE   3.99.14
MY LOVE IS STRENGTHNED THOUGH MORE WEAKE
                        IN SEEMING   3.102.1
```

```
THE ARGUMENT ALL BARE IS OF MORE WORTH              3.103.3
OH BLAME ME NOT IF I NO MORE CAN WRITE              3.103.5
AND MORE, MUCH MORE THEN IN MY VERSE CAN SIT        3.103.13
AND MORE, MUCH MORE THEN IN MY VERSE CAN SIT        3.103.13
MINE APPETITE I NEVER MORE WILL GRIN'DE             3.110.10
INCAPABLE OF MORE REPLEAT, WITH YOU                 3.113.13
LIKE AS TO MAKE OUR APPETITES MORE KEENE            3.118.1
GROWES FAIRER THEN AT FIRST, MORE STRONG,
                              FAR GREATER           3.119.12
AND GAINE BY ILLS THRISE MORE THEN I HAVE SPENT     3.119.14
TO TRUST THOSE TABLES THAT RECEAVE THEE MORE        3.122.12
MADE MORE OR LES BY THY CONTINUALL HAST             3.123.12
WHICH PROVES MORE SHORT THEN WAST OR RUINING+       3.125.4
LOSE ALL, AND MORE BY PAYING TOO MUCH RENT          3.125.6
MAKING DEAD WOOD MORE BLEST THEN LIVING LIPS        3.128.12
CURRALL IS FARRE MORE RED, THEN HER LIPS RED        3.130.2
AND IN SOME PERFUMES IS THERE MORE DELIGHT          3.130.7
THAT $MUSICKE HATH A FARRE MORE PLEASING SOUND      3.130.10
MORE THEN ENOUGH AM I THAT VEXE THEE STILL          3.135.3
ONE WILL OF MINE TO MAKE THY LARGE $WILL MORE       3.135.12
IS MORE THEN MY ORE-PREST DEFENCE CAN BIDE+         3.139.8
WITHIN BE FED, WITHOUT BE RICH NO MORE              3.146.12
AND DEATH ONCE DEAD, THER'S NO MORE DYING THEN      3.146.14
WHO TAUGHT THEE HOW TO MAKE ME LOVE THEE MORE       3.150.9
THE MORE I HEARE AND SEE JUST CAUSE OF HATE         3.150.10
MORE WORTHY I TO BE BELOV'D OF THEE                 3.150.14
FOR I HAVE SWORNE THEE FAIRE.. MORE PERJURDE
                              EYE                   3.152.13
CHURCHES OR SCHOOLES ARE FOR THY SEATE MORE FIT     4.4.6
THEY SUN-LIKE SHOULD MORE DAZLE THEN DELIGHT+       4.7.8
STELLA., NOW SHE IS NAM'D, NEED MORE BE SAID+       4.16.11
THEN THAT I LOSE NO MORE FOR $STELLA'S SAKE         4.18.14
WEALTH BREEDING WANT, MORE BLIST, MORE
                              WRETCHED GROW         4.24.4
WEALTH BREEDING WANT, MORE BLIST, MORE
                              WRETCHED GROW         4.24.4
THAT I HAD BENE MORE FOOLISH OR MORE WISE           4.33.14
THAT I HAD BENE MORE FOOLISH OR MORE WISE           4.33.14
BUT MORE I CRIE, LESSE GRACE SHE DOTH IMPART        4.44.6
THOUGH FALSE, YET WITH FREE SCOPE MORE
                              GRACE DOTH BREED      4.45.10
AND YET TO BREAKE MORE STAVES DID ME ADDRESSE       4.53.2
BUT NOW I MEANE NO MORE YOUR HELPE TO TRIE          4.55.9
BUT AS HE THEM MORE SHORT OR SLACKE DOTH RAINE      4.58.4
DEARE, WHY MAKE YOU MORE OF A DOG THEN ME+          4.59.1
DEARE, LOVE ME NOT, THAT YOU MAY LOVE ME MORE       4.62.14
NO MORE, MY DEARE, NO MORE THESE COUNSELS TRIE      4.64.1
NO MORE, MY DEARE, NO MORE THESE COUNSELS TRIE      4.64.1
MY WEALTH NO MORE, AND NO WHIT LESSE MY NEED        4.66.7
RATHER THEN BY MORE TRUTH TO GET MORE PAINE         4.67.14
RATHER THEN BY MORE TRUTH TO GET MORE PAINE         4.67.14
WITH VOICE MORE FIT TO WED $AMPHION'S $LYRE         4.68.6
I MUST NO MORE IN THY SWEET PASSIONS LIE            4.72.7
THAT HAND, WHICH WITHOUT TOUCH HOLDS MORE
                              THEN $ATLAS MIGHT     4.77.5
THAT IN NO MORE BUT THESE I MIGHT BE FULLY BLEST    4.77.13
PARDON THAT FAULT, ONCE MORE GRAUNT ME THE PLACE    4.82.12
I WILL BUT KISSE, I NEVER MORE WILL BITE            4.82.14
NAY, MORE FOOLE I, OFT SUFFERED YOU TO SLEEPE       4.83.7
MORE OFT THEN TO A CHAMBER MELODIE                  4.84.4
```

```
AND NOTHING THEN THE CAUSE MORE SWEET COULD BE          4.87.13
WHILE NO NIGHT IS MORE DARKE THEN IS MY DAY             4.89.10
MILKE HANDS, ROSE CHEEKS, OR LIPS MORE
                          SWEET, MORE RED              4.91.7
MILKE HANDS, ROSE CHEEKS, OR LIPS MORE
                          SWEET, MORE RED              4.91.7
YET GROWEST MORE WRETCHED THEN THY NATURE BEARES       4.94.13
WHICH AY MOST FAIRE, NOW MORE THEN MOST
                          FAIRE SHOW                   4.100.3
TO WRITE THEREIN MORE FRESH THE STORY
                          OF DELIGHT                   4.102.13
BASE THING I CAN NO MORE ENDURE TO VIEW                5.3.6
BUT SINCE THAT LYFE IS MORE THEN DEATH DESYRED         5.7.9
MORE THEN MOST FAIRE, FULL OF THE LIVING FIRE          5.8.1
NOR TO THE $DIAMOND.. FOR THEY ARE MORE TENDER         5.9.10
BUT SHE MORE CRUELL AND MORE SALVAGE WYLDE             5.20.9
BUT SHE MORE CRUELL AND MORE SALVAGE WYLDE             5.20.9
AND WISH THAT MORE AND GREATER THEY MIGHT BE           5.25.13
THAT MAKETH IT BE COVETED THE MORE                     5.26.10
THEN FLY NO MORE FAYRE LOVE FROM $PHEBUS CHACE         5.28.13
BUT HARDER GROWES THE MORE I HER INTREAT+              5.30.4
BUT THAT I BURNE MUCH MORE IN BOYLING SWEAT            5.30.7
WHAT MORE MIRACULOUS THING MAY BE TOLD                 5.30.9
HER HART MORE HARDE THEN YRON SOFT AWHIT               5.32.6
BUT STILL THE MORE SHE FERVENT SEES MY FIT             5.32.9
THE MORE SHE FRIESETH IN HER WILFULL PRYDE             5.32.10
AND HAVING IT THEY GAZE ON IT THE MORE                 5.35.6
AND CAN NO MORE ENDURE ON THEM TO LOOKE                5.35.12
AND DAYLY MORE AUGMENT MY MISERYES+                    5.36.8
AND FEELING THENCE NO MORE HER SOROWES SADNESSE        5.39.11
MORE SWEET THAN $NECTAR OR $AMBROSIALL MEAT            5.39.13
THAT ALL THE MORE MY SORROW IT AUGMENTETH              5.42.3
THE MORE I LOVE AND DOE EMBRACE MY BANE                5.42.4
THEN DOE I MORE AUGMENT MY FOES DESPIGHT               5.44.10
MONGST WHOME THE MORE I SEEKE TO SETTLE PEACE          5.44.13
THE MORE I FYND THEIR MALICE TO INCREACE               5.44.14
HER HARDNES BLAME WHICH I SHOULD MORE COMMEND+         5.51.6
AND THAT IT THEN MORE STEDFAST WILL ENDURE             5.51.12
ONELY MY PAINES WIL BE THE MORE TO GET HER             5.51.13
OF ALL WORLDS GLADNESSE MORE MY TORMENT FEED           5.52.12
NOT EARTH., FOR HER HIGH THOGHTS MORE
                          HEAVENLY ARE                 5.55.5
NE YOUR INCESSANT BATTRY MORE TO BEARE                 5.57.4
FOR NOW YOUR LIGHT DOTH MORE IT SELFE DILATE           5.66.11
AND VERTUOUS MIND, IS MUCH MORE PRAYSD OF ME           5.79.4
BUT THEN THE MORE YOUR OWNE MISHAP I REW               5.82.3
AND SEEING IT, THEY GAZE ON IT THE MORE                5.83.6
AND CAN NO MORE ENDURE ON THEM TO LOOKE                5.83.12
MORN                    6
EVEN SO MY $SUNNE ONE EARLY MORNE DID SHINE            3.33.9
WITH LINES AND WRINCLES, WHEN HIS YOUTHFULL MORNE      3.63.4
AND YET COULD NOT BY RISING $MORNE FORESEE             4.33.12
WITH SUCH A ROSIE MORNE, WHOSE BEAMES
                          MOST FRESHLY GAY             4.76.7
THE BUD OF JOY, THE BLOSSOME OF THE MORNE              5.61.9
THEYR SAD PROTRACT FROM EVENING UNTILL MORNE           5.87.4
MORNING                 10
AND ($DELIA) THINKE THY MORNING MUST HAVE NIGHT        1.40.8
BEAUTIE (SWEET $LOVE) IS LIKE THE MORNING DEW          1.50.1
SO FAIRE A $MORNING HAD SO FOULE A SET+                2.149.12
```

```
FULL MANY A GLORIOUS MORNING HAVE I SEENE               3.33.1
AND TRULY NOT THE MORNING $SUN OF $HEAVEN               3.132.5
AS THOSE TWO MORNING EYES BECOME THY FACE               3.132.9
WHOSE FAIRE SKIN, BEAMY EYES, LIKE MORNING
                          SUN ON SNOW                   4.8.9
SOULE'S JOY, BEND NOT THOSE MORNING STARRES
                          FROM ME                       4.48.1
WHO HATH THE CRIMSON WEEDS STOLNE FROM
                          MY MORNING SKIES+             4.102.4
WITH SHEW OF MORNING MYLDE HE HATH BEGUN                5.62.3
MORNING'S            1
THE MORNINGS $CRIMSON, TO HER LYPS ALIKE                2.148.5
MORN'S               1
MORNE'S MESSENGER, WITH ROSE ENAMELD SKIES              4.99.10
MORPHEUS             1
MORPHEUS, THE LIVELY SONNE OF DEADLY SLEEPE             4.32.1
MORROW               6
TO MODELL FORTH THE PASSIONS OF THE MORROW              1.54.10
STILL TO PROLONG MY LONG TYME LOOKT-FOR MORROW+         2.145.4
TO MORROW SHARPNED IN HIS FORMER MIGHT                  3.56.4
TOO MORROW SEE AGAINE, AND DOE NOT KILL                 3.56.7
GIVE NOT A WINDY NIGHT A RAINIE MORROW                  3.90.7
KINDE IS MY LOVE TO DAY, TO MORROW KINDE                3.105.5
MORTAL              14
WHERE HEAVEN BEHOLDS HER IN A MORTALL GLASSE            2.107.4
WHAT MORTALL PEN SUFFYCIENTLY CAN PRAYSE THEE+          2.146.2
YET MORTALL LOOKES ADORE HIS BEAUTY STILL               3.7.7
MINE EYE AND HEART ARE AT A MORTALL WARRE               3.46.1
AND BRASSE ETERNALL SLAVE TO MORTALL RAGE               3.64.4
ABOVE A MORTALL PITCH, THAT STRUCK ME DEAD+             3.86.6
THE MORTALL $MOONE HATH HER ECLIPSE INDUR'DE            3.107.5
WHICH ELEMENTS WITH MORTALL MIXTURE BREED               4.5.11
TO MORTALL EYES MIGHT SWEETLY SHINE IN HER              4.25.11
OPPRESSING MORTALL SENSE, MY DEATH PROCEED              4.42.13
FROM HEAVENLY STANDING HITS EACH MORTALL WIGHT          4.97.4
WHEN FAR SPENT NIGHT PERSWADES EACH MORTALL EYE         4.99.1
THE BEAME OF LIGHT, WHOM MORTAL EYES ADMYRE             5.61.10
A MORTALL THING SO TO IMMORTALIZE                       5.75.6
MORTALITY            4
THAT EVER YET COVERED MORTALITY                         1.45.11
BUT SAD MORTALLITY ORE-SWAIES THEIR POWER               3.65.2
HER MINDE REMEMBRETH HER MORTALITIE                     5.13.7
AND CLOGD WITH BURDEN OF MORTALITY                      5.72.4
MORTGAGED            1
AND I MY SELFE AM MORGAG'D TO THY WILL                  3.134.2
MOSS                 1
LIKE GRIZZLED $MOSSE UPON SOME AGED $TREE               2.8.8
MOST               118
SO MUCH I LOVE THE MOST UNLOVING ONE                    1.12.14
NO SUCCOUR FINDE I NOW WHEN MOST I NEEDE                1.32.11
WHICH THEN SHALL MOST INVAILE AND SHADOW MOST           1.40.12
WHICH THEN SHALL MOST INVAILE AND SHADOW MOST           1.40.12
MOST FAIRE AND LOVELY $MAIDE, LOOKE FROM
                          THE SHORE                     1.46.1
THE LEVELL OF MY HOPES DESIRED MOST                     1.53.4
WHERE MOST BECALM'D, WHERE WITH FOULE
                          $WEATHER SPENT                2.1.11
BE YOU MOST WORTHY, WHILST I AM MOST TRUE               2.4.14
BE YOU MOST WORTHY, WHILST I AM MOST TRUE               2.4.14
IN MOST DISTRACTION THEY KEEPE THAT IN $MINDE           2.9.8
```

```
AND TORTURES $ME IN MOST EXTREMITY                    2.20.8
EQUALL WITH HIS, THAT LOVES HIS $MISTRES MOST         2.27.12
IN WHICH EXPENCE, THE MOST SUPPOSE ME VAINE           2.28.6
HEAV'NS ARE NOT KIND TO THEM, THAT KNOW
                                    THEM MOST          2.43.14
MOST OF ALL SHORT, WHEN I SHOULD SHEW YOU MOST        2.57.13
MOST OF ALL SHORT, WHEN I SHOULD SHEW YOU MOST        2.57.13
WHERE MOST I $LOST, THERE MOST OF ALL I $WAN          2.62.3
WHERE MOST I $LOST, THERE MOST OF ALL I $WAN          2.62.3
WHAT MOST I $SEEME, THAT SUREST AM I $NOT             2.62.8
HERE $CHASTITY THAT $VESTALL MOST DIVINE              2.105.9
BUT MY MOST MERVAILE WAS WHEN FROM THE SKYES          2.125.9
O $THOU UNKINDEST FAYRE, MOST FAYREST SHEE            2.140.1
WHERE MOST I LOST, THERE MOST OF ALL I WAN            2.150.3
WHERE MOST I LOST, THERE MOST OF ALL I WAN            2.150.3
WHAT MOST I SEEME, THAT SUREST AM I NOT               2.150.8
BUT THAT THOU NONE LOV'ST IS MOST EVIDENT             3.10.4
SETS YOU MOST RICH IN YOUTH BEFORE MY SIGHT           3.15.10
IF IT WERE FILD WITH YOUR MOST HIGH DESERTS+          3.17.2
BUT I FORBID THEE ONE MOST HAINOUS CRIME              3.19.8
UNLOOKT FOR JOY IN THAT I HONOUR MOST                 3.25.4
WITH WHAT I MOST INJOY CONTENTED LEAST                3.29.8
WHEN MOST I WINKE THEN DOE MINE EYES BEST SEE         3.43.1
MOST WORTHY COMFORT, NOW MY GREATEST GRIEFE           3.48.6
YET BE MOST PROUD OF THAT WHICH I COMPILE             3.78.9
WHERE BREATH MOST BREATHS, EVEN IN THE
                              MOUTHS OF MEN            3.81.14
WHICH SHALL BE MOST MY GLORY BEING DOMBE              3.83.10
WHO IS IT THAT SAYES MOST, WHICH CAN SAY MORE         3.84.1
AND TO THE MOST OF PRAISE ADDE SOME-THING MORE        3.85.10
ALL THIS AWAY, AND ME MOST WRETCHED MAKE              3.91.14
THAT DOE NOT DO THE THING, THEY MOST DO SHOWE         3.94.2
NOW WITH THE DROPS OF THIS MOST BALMIE TIME           3.107.9
GOR'D MINE OWN THOUGHTS, SOLD CHEAP WHAT
                              IS MOST DEARE            3.110.3
MOST TRUE IT IS, THAT I HAVE LOOKT ON TRUTH           3.110.5
EVEN TO THY PURE AND MOST MOST LOVING BREST           3.110.14
EVEN TO THY PURE AND MOST MOST LOVING BREST           3.110.14
THE MOST SWEET-FAVOR OR DEFORMEDST CREATURE           3.113.10
MY MOST TRUE MINDE THUS MAKETH MINE UNTRUE            3.113.14
AND MY GREAT MINDE MOST KINGLY DRINKES IT UP          3.114.10
MY MOST FULL FLAME SHOULD AFTERWARDS BURNE
                              CLEERER                  3.115.4
WHEN MOST IMPEACHT, STANDS LEAST IN THY
                              CONTROULE               3.125.14
THOU ART THE FAIREST AND MOST PRECIOUS $JEWELL       3.131.4
WHEN I BREAKE TWENTY.. I AM PERJUR'D MOST             3.152.6
IT IS MOST TRUE, THAT EYES ARE FORM'D TO SERVE        4.5.1
IT IS MOST TRUE, WHAT WE CALL $CUPID'S DART           4.5.5
WHERE WITH MOST EASE AND WARMTH HE MIGHT
                              EMPLOY HIS ART           4.8.7
BUT SHE MOST FAIRE, MOST COLD, MADE HIM
                       THENCE TAKE HIS FLIGHT          4.8.12
BUT SHE MOST FAIRE, MOST COLD, MADE HIM
                       THENCE TAKE HIS FLIGHT          4.8.12
THOU DOEST PROCEED IN THY MOST SERIOUS WAYES          4.11.2
OR AT THE MOST ON SOME FINE PICTURE STAYES            4.11.7
BUT THAT MY WEALTH I HAVE MOST IDLY SPENT             4.18.8
WHEN MOST I GLORIE, THEN I FEELE MOST SHAME           4.19.3
WHEN MOST I GLORIE, THEN I FEELE MOST SHAME           4.19.3
```

THE WISEST SCHOLLER OF THE WIGHT MOST WISE	4.25.1
IT IS MOST TRUE, FCR SINCE I HER DID SEE	4.25.12
SEEME MOST ALONE IN GREATEST COMPANIE	4.27.2
TILL NOW, WRAPT IN A MOST INFERNALL NIGHT	4.33.3
WHO THOUGH MOST RICH IN THESE AND EVERIE PART	4.37.12
O EYES, WHERE HUMBLE LOOKES MOST GLORIOUS PRCVE	4.42.5
WHOSE CURELESSE WOUNDS EVEN NOW MOST FRESHLY	
BLEED	4.48.11
OF CUNNINGST FISHERS IN MOST TROUBLED STREAMES	4.51.10
SINCE THEY DO WEARE HIS BADGE, MOST FIRMELY PROVE	4.52.4
BUT THEM (SO SWEETE IS SHE) MOST SWEETLY SING	4.57.10
WHICH WOOED WO, MCST RAVISHING DELIGHT	4.58.13
FOR LATE WITH HEART MOST HIGH, WITH EYES MOST LOW	4.63.5
FOR LATE WITH HEART MOST HIGH, WITH EYES MOST LOW	4.63.5
AND ALL IN VAINE, FCR WHILE THY BREATH MCST SWEET	4.68.9
WHO MARKE IN THEE WHAT IS IN THEE MOST FAIRE	4.71.11
O HEAV'NLY FOOLE, THY MCST KISSE-WORTHIE FACE	4.73.12
WITH SUCH A ROSIE MCRNE, WHOSE BEAMES	
MOST FRESHLY GAY	4.76.7
MOST RICH, WHEN MCST HIS RICHES IT IMPART	4.79.7
MOST RICH, WHEN MCST HIS RICHES IT IMPART	4.79.7
MOST SWEET-FAIRE, MCST FAIRE-SWEET, DO NCT ALAS	4.82.7
MOST SWEET-FAIRE, MCST FAIRE-SWEET, DO NCT ALAS	4.82.7
THUS WHILE TH' EFFECT MCST BITTER WAS TO ME	4.87.12
NOW THAT OF ABSENCE THE MOST IRKSOME NIGHT	4.89.1
WITH WINDOWES OPE THEN MCST MY MIND DOTH LIE	4.99.5
WHICH AY MOST FAIRE, NOW MORE THEN MOST	
FAIRE SHOW	4.100.3
WHICH AY MOST FAIRE, NOW MORE THEN MOST	
FAIRE SHOW	4.100.3
DOTH MAKE ME MOST TC WISH THY COMFORT NEERE	4.106.8
MOST RUDE DISPAIRE MY DAILY UNBIDDEN GUEST	4.108.7
THE THING WHICH I DCO MOST IN HER ADMIRE	5.5.3
IS OF THE WORLD UNWCRTHY MOST ENVIDE	5.5.4
MORE THEN MOST FAIRE, FULL OF THE LIVING FIRE	5.8.1
MOST GOODLY TEMPERATURE YE MAY DESCRY	5.13.4
DO SEEKE MOST PRETICUS THINGS TO MAKE YOUR GAIN	5.15.2
NO WORD WAS HEARD CF HER THAT MOST IT OUGHT	5.19.10
IN HIS MOST PRIDE DISDEIGNETH TO DEVOURE	5.20.7
MOST SORTS OF MEN DCE SET BUT LITTLE STORE	5.26.12
TO THAT MOST SACRED $EMPRESSE MY DEAR DRED	5.33.2
THAT SHE WILL PLAGUE THE MAN THAT LOVES HER MOST	5.41.6
MOST LIVELY LYKE BEHOLD YOUR SEMBLANT TREW	5.45.4
BUT THEN FROM HEAVEN MOST HIDEOUS STORMES	
ARE SENT	5.46.3
MADE FOR TO BE THE WORLDS MOST ORNAMENT	5.53.10
THAT SOONEST FALS WHEN AS SHE MOST SUPPOSETH	5.58.3
THAT TO YOUR SELFE YE MCST ASSURED ARRE+	5.58.14
MOST HAPPY SHE THAT MOST ASSURED DOTH REST	5.59.13
MOST HAPPY SHE THAT MOST ASSURED DOTH REST	5.59.13
BUT HE MOST HAPPY WHO SUCH ONE LOVES BEST	5.59.14
MOST HAPPY HE THAT CAN AT LAST ATCHYVE	5.63.9
SUCH FRAGRANT FLOWRES DCE GIVE MOST ODORCUS	
SMELL	5.64.13
MOST GLORIOUS $LORD OF LYFE THAT ON THIS CAY	5.68.1
WHAT TROPHEE THEN SHALL I MOST FIT DEVIZE	5.69.5
DOTH BATH IN BLISSE AND MANTLETH MOST AT EASE	5.72.10
HER HARTS DESIRE WITH MCST CONTENTMENT PLEASE	5.72.12
MOST HAPPY LETTERS FRAM'D BY SKILFULL TRACE	5.74.1
THE SECOND IS MY SCVEREIGNE $QUEENE MOST KINC	5.74.7

```
    OF ALL ALIVE MOST WORTHY TO BE PRAYSED          5.74.12
    THERE FILL YOUR SELFE WITH THOSE MOST
                        JOYOUS SIGHTS                5.84.9
MOTE                    7
    I MOTE PERCEIVE HOW IN HER GLAUNCING SIGHT       5.16.5
    THAT MOTE ENLARGE HER LIVING PRAYSES DEAD        5.33.4
    MOTE HAVE YOUR LIFE IN HONOUR LONG MAINTAYNED    5.36.12
    AND FROM ALL WANDRING LOVES WHICH MOTE PERVART   5.42.11
    MOTE SOFTEN IT AND TO HIS WILL ALLURE            5.51.10
    WHEREOF SHE MOTE BE MADE., THAT IS THE SKYE      5.55.10
    IN THIS AS IN THE REST, YE MOTE INVENT           5.82.6
MOTHER                  7
    MINERVA-LIKE, BROUGHT FOORTH WITHOUT A MOTHER    1.2.2
    HIS $MOTHER DIED, AND BY HER $LEGACIE            2.116.10
    RARE BEAUTY, $NATURES JOY, PERFECTIONS $MOTHER   2.123.2
    THY $MOTHER DYD HER LYFE TO $DEATH RESIGNE       2.140.5
    THOU DOO'ST BEGUILE THE WORLD, UNBLESSE
                        SOME MOTHER                  3.3.4
    RESEMBLING SIER, AND CHILD, AND HAPPY MOTHER     3.8.11
    HIS MOTHER DEARE $CUPID OFFENDED LATE            4.17.1
MOTHERLESS              1
    CRYES IN HIS PANGS, $GOD HELPE THE MOTHERLESSE   2.116.18
MOTHER'S                9
    AND LEAVES HIS $MOTHERS LAP TO SPORT HIM THERE   2.4.8
    BY THY FAIRE $MOTHERS UNAVOIDED $POWER           2.36.6
    SO MAY'ST THOU LIVE, TO THY FAIRE $MOTHERS $JOY  2.48.12
    THOU ART THY MOTHERS GLASSE AND SHE IN THEE      3.3.9
    AS ANY MOTHERS CHILDE, THOUGH NOT SO BRIGHT      3.21.11
    AND PLAY THE MOTHERS PART KISSE ME, BE KIND      3.143.12
    SCHOOL'D ONELY BY HIS MOTHER'S TENDER EYE        4.73.2
    EXPRESSING ALL THY MOTHERS POWREFULL ART         5.39.2
    FROM MOTHERS WOMB DERIV'D BY DEW DESCENT         5.74.6
MOTION                  6
    THESE PRESENT ABSENT WITH SWIFT MOTION SLIDE     3.45.4
    IN WINGED SPEED NO MOTION SHALL I KNOW           3.51.8
    HATH MOTION, AND MINE EYE MAY BE DECEAVED        3.104.12
    UPON THAT BLESSED WOOD WHOSE MOTION SOUNDS       3.128.2
    COMMANDED BY THE MOTION OF THINE EYES            3.149.12
    THOSE LOOKES, WHOSE BEAMES BE JOY, WHOSE
                        MOTION IS DELIGHT            4.77.1
MOTIONS                 2
    STARRES SURE THEY ARE, WHOSE MOTIONS RULE DESIRES 1.34.5
    BUT STRAIGHT I SAW MOTIONS OF LIGHTNING GRACE    4.20.12
MOTIVE                  1
    THAT SHE HATH DONE, THE MOTIVE OF MY PAINE       1.3.13
MOTLEY                  1
    AND MADE MY SELFE A MOTLEY TO THE VIEW           3.110.2
MOUGHT                  1
    NOR UNTO GLASSE.. SUCH BASENESSE MOUGHT
                        OFFEND HER                   5.9.12
MOUNT                   3
    MY $NAME SHALL MOUNT UPON $ETERNITIE             2.44.14
    WHICH BY THEYR NATURE LEARN'D TO MOUNT THE SKYE  2.122.6
    IN MIND TO MOUNT UP TO THE PUREST SKY            5.72.2
MOUNTAIN                2
    FLATTER THE MOUNTAINE TOPS WITH SOVERAINE EIE    3.33.2
    THE MOUNTAINE, OR THE SEA, THE DAY, OR NIGHT     3.113.11
MOUNTED                 1
    THEN SHOULD I SPURRE THOUGH MOUNTED ON THE WIND  3.51.7
```

```
MOUNTING                     4
   THE MOUNTING VENTER FOR A HIGH DELIGHT              1.35.3
   AND RIGHTLY CAME FROM THAT BRAVE MOUNTING $BROOD    2.56.8
   STRAIGHT MOUNTING UP TO THY CELESTIALL EYES         2.103.12
   AND MOUNTING UP, SHALT TO THE HEAVENS ASCEND        2.106.13
MOURN                     9
   IMBRACING CLOUDS BY NIGHT, IN DAY TIME MOURNE       1.16.2
   LOOKE IN MY GRIEFES, AND BLAME ME NOT TO MOURNE     1.26.1
   HOW LONG SHALL I IN MINE AFFLICTION MOURNE+         1.49.1
   AND LET THE DAY BE TIME ENOUGH TO MOURNE            1.54.5
   AND BID THEM MOURNE, NAY MORE, DESPAIRE
                             WITH THEE                 2.17.13
   NOE $LONGER MOURNE FOR ME WHEN I AM DEAD            3.71.1
   YET SO THEY MOURNE BECOMMING OF THEIR WOE           3.127.13
   TO MOURNE FOR ME SINCE MOURNING DOTH THEE GRACE     3.132.11
   MOURNE TO MY SELFE THE ABSENCE OF MY LOVE           5.89.6
MOURNERS                  2
   HER EYES SO SUTED, AND THEY MOURNERS SEEME          3.127.10
   HAVE PUT ON BLACK, AND LOVING MOURNERS BEE          3.132.3
MOURNFUL                  5
   THESE FATALL $ANTHEAMES, SAD AND MORNEFULL $SONGS   1.3.2
   MY $MUSE SHOULD SOUND THY PRAISE WITH
                        MOURNFULL WARBLE                1.44.6
   THE MOURNFULL ACCENTS OF MY LOVES DISPAYRE          2.141.8
   THEN WHEN HER MOURNEFULL HIMNS DID HUSH
                             THE NIGHT                 3.102.10
   SEEK WITH MY PLAYNTS TO MATCH THAT MOURNFUL COVE    5.89.8
MOURNING                  6
   NO $BAYES I SEEKE TO DECKE MY MOURNING BROW         1.4.9
   PORTRAITE OF HELL, THE AYRES BLACK MOURNING WEED    2.145.6
   TO MOURNE FOR ME SINCE MOURNING DOTH THEE GRACE     3.132.11
   PLACED EVER THERE, GAVE HIM THIS MOURNING WEED      4.7.13
   SILENT AND SAD IN MOURNING WEEDES DOTH DIGHT        4.97.8
   SITS MOURNING FOR THE ABSENCE OF HER MATE           5.89.2
MOUTH                     7
   MY MOUTH TOO TENDER IS FOR THY HARD BIT             4.4.8
   MY MOUTH DOTH WATER, AND MY BREAST DOTH SWELL       4.37.1
   THUS MUCH MY HEART COMPELD MY MOUTH TO SAY          4.80.9
   BUT NOW SPITE OF MY HEART MY MOUTH WILL STAY        4.80.10
   SWEET LIP, YOU TEACH MY MOUTH WITH ONE
                          SWEET KISSE                  4.80.14
   STOP YOU MY MOUTH WITH STILL STILL KISSING ME       4.81.14
   AND MY GLAD MOUTH WITH HER SWEET PRAYSES FILL       5.85.12
MOUTHED                   1
   OF MOUTHED GRAVES WILL GIVE THEE MEMORIE            3.77.6
MOUTHS                    1
   WHERE BREATH MOST BREATHS, EVEN IN THE
                          MOUTHS OF MEN                3.81.14
MOVE                     37
   OF INTERCESSION BUT TO MOVE HER WILL                1.4.12
   YET THOUGH I SEE, THAT NOUGHT WE DOE, CAN MOVE      1.8.13
   I PRAY IN VAINE, A MERCILESSE TO MOVE               1.11.7
   WHAT PASSIONS WOULD HER MILDER FAVOURS MOVE+        1.17.12
   (AND THAT WITH TEARES) YET ALL THIS WILL
                             NOT MOVE HER              1.18.14
   STARRES THEN, NOT EYES, MOVE YOU WITH
                          A MILDER VIEW                1.34.13
   YET NOUGHT THE ROCKE OF THAT HARD HEART CAN MOVE    1.48.9
   (IF LOVE IN HER HATH ANY POWER TO MOVE)             1.49.10
   TH'AFFLICTION HER UNKIND DISDAINE DOTH MOVE         1.60.8
```

```
THAT $GOLD NOR $HONOUR NE'R HAD POW'R TO MOVE      2.15.4
(YET HIS DULL $SPIRIT HER NOT ONE JOT COULD MOVE)  2.21.2
IN HEAT OF $BLOUD, A MODEST $MIND MIGHT MOVE       2.47.8
AND SAY'ST, MY $LINES BE DULL, AND DOE NOT MOVE    2.49.2
MAKE KNOWNE THE $FAITH, THAT $FORTUNE
                          COULD NOT MOVE           2.60.5
THIS PUNISHMENT THE PITTILESSE MAY MOVE            2.115.8
A FAYTH, THAT TIME NOR FORTUNE COULD NOT MOVE      2.138.11
IF SIGHES, NOR TEARES, NOR VOWES, NOR
                     PRAYERS CAN MOVE              2.139.2
MAKE KNOWNE THAT FAYTH, UNKINDNES COULD NOT MOVE   2.149.5
FROM WHENCE, IF YOU ONE TEARE OF PITTY MOVE        2.151.3
FOR THOU NOR FARTHER THEN MY THOUGHTS CANST MOVE   3.47.11
AND SHOULD IN SOULE UP TO OUR COUNTREY MOVE        4.5.13
HIS PAPER, PALE DISPAIRE, AND PAINE HIS
                          PEN DOTH MOVE            4.6.11
WITH PRICKING SHOT HE DID NOT THROUGHLY MOVE       4.17.3
MOVE NOT THY HEAVY GRACE, THOU SHALT IN ME         4.39.13
O EYES, WHICH DO THE $SPHEARES OF BEAUTIE MOVE     4.42.1
ARE HUMBLED THOUGHTS, WHICH BIT OF $REVERENCE
                          MOVE                     4.49.6
NOT THIS FAIRE OUTSIDE, WHICH OUR HEARTS
                          DOTH MOVE                4.52.8
IF HE WAITE WELL, I NEVER THENCE WOULD MOVE        4.59.3
BUT WHEN MINE EYES BACKE TO THEIR HEAV'N
                          DID MOVE                 4.66.13
THY SELFE, DOEST STRIVE ALL MINDS THAT
                          WAY TO MOVE              4.71.10
SHE COMES, AND STREIGHT THEREWITH HER
                          SHINING TWINS DO MOVE    4.76.1
IF YOU HEARE THAT THEY SEEME MY HART TO MOVE       4.91.13
NOR MOVE THE $DOLPHIN FROM HER STUBBORNE WILL      5.38.8
WHAT THEN CAN MOVE HER+ IF NOR MERTH NOR MONE      5.54.13
BEGAN IN ME TO MOVE, ONE YEARE IS SPENT            5.60.6
AND MANY NIGHTS, THAT SLOWLY SEEMD TO MOVE         5.87.3
WHOSE SWEET ASPECT BOTH $GOD AND MAN CAN MOVE      5.89.11
MOVED                     4
KNOCKE AT THAT HARD HART, BEGGE TILL YOU
                          HAVE MOV'D HER           1.2.13
ALTHOUGH MY CAREFULL ACCENTS NEVER MOOV'D THEE     1.44.13
WHICH WITH MY PLAINT SEEME YET WITH PITTIE MOVED   2.45.13
NE WILBE MOOV'D WITH REASON OR WITH REWTH          5.11.5
MOVES                     3
AND THAT ALL THIS MOOVES NOT HER THOUGHTS A WHIT   1.21.12
GIVES HER THAT $NAME, AS SHE THE $BODY MOVES       2.12.4
LOVE MOVES THY PAINE, AND LIKE A FAITHFULL PAGE    4.101.9
MOVING                    4
MOVING A $WILL IN US, IT IS THE $MIND              2.12.6
O STARRE OF STARRES, FAYRE $PLANET MILDLY
                          MOOVING                  2.129.5
TIL WHATSOEVER STAR THAT GUIDES MY MOVING          3.26.9
WHO MOVING OTHERS, ARE THEMSELVES AS STONE         3.94.3
MOW                       1
AND NOTHING STANDS BUT FOR HIS SIETH TO MOW        3.60.12
MUCH                      50
SO MUCH I LOVE THE MOST UNLOVING ONE               1.12.14
MY HEAVY FORTUNE IS MUCH LIKE THE SAME             1.13.3
SO MUCH I PLEASE TO PERISH IN MY WOE               1.14.12
WHY SHOULD M'AFFLICTED $MUSE SO MUCH ENDEVOUR      1.17.7
HOW TO THINKE MUCH, AND HAVE NO WORDS TO SPEAKE    1.20.6
```

TO VIEW YOUR FORME TOO MUCH, MAY DANGER BEE	1.37.11
WHICH TELLS THE WORLD HOW MUCH MY GRIEFE IMPORTS	1.60.4
I SAY NO MORE, I FEARE I SAYD TOO MUCH	1.60.14
SHALL BE SO MUCH DELIGHTED WITH THY STORY	2.6.10
SENSELESSE WITH TOO MUCH $JOY, EACH OTHER SEEING	2.11.7
SO MUCH IS $MINE, THAT DOTH WITH $YOU REMAINE	2.11.11
MUCH LIKE HIS $WIT, THAT WAS TO USE THE SAME	2.21.8
AND I GIVE MUCH, BECAUSE I GAINE THEREBY	2.28.10
AND MUCH COMMEND THE STRANGENESSE OF MY $VAINE	2.42.2
IN YOUR PERFECTIONS SO MUCH AM I LOST	2.57.14
HOW MUCH MORE PRAISE DESERV'D THY BEAUTIES USE	3.2.9
BE NOT SELFE-WILD FOR THOU ART MUCH TOO FAIRE	3.6.13
MUCH LIKER THEN YOUR PAINTED COUNTERFEIT	3.16.8
OR SOME FIERCE THING REPLEAT WITH TOO MUCH RAGE	3.23.3
TO THE CLEERE DAY WITH THY MUCH CLEERER LIGHT	3.43.7
BUT THAT SO MUCH OF EARTH AND WATER WROUGHT	3.44.11
OH HOW MUCH MORE DOTH BEAUTIE BEAUTIOUS SEEME	3.54.1
O NO, THY LOVE THOUGH MUCH, IS NOT SO GREAT	3.61.9
DO NOT SO MUCH AS MY POORE NAME REHERSE	3.71.11
SHALL PROFIT THEE, AND MUCH INRICH THY BOOKE	3.77.14
THAT THOU IN LOOSING ME, SHALL WIN MUCH GLORY	3.88.8
LEAST I (TOO MUCH PROPHANE) SHOULD DO IT WRONGE	3.89.11
TO MAKE HIM MUCH OUT-LIVE A GILDED TOMBE	3.101.11
AND MORE, MUCH MORE THEN IN MY VERSE CAN SIT	3.103.13
THAT POORE RETENTION COULD NOT SO MUCH HOLD	3.122.9
LOSE ALL, AND MORE BY PAYING TOO MUCH RENT	3.125.6
MY TOUNG-TIDE PATIENCE WITH TOO MUCH DISDAINE	3.140.2
I CAN SPEAKE WHAT I FEELE, AND FEELE AS MUCH AS THEY	4.6.12
IF NOW THE $MAY OF MY YEARES MUCH DECLINE	4.21.10
WHILE TOO MUCH WIT (FORSOOTH) SO TROUBLED ME	4.33.10
O $STELLA DEARE, HOW MUCH THY POWER HATH WROUGHT	4.40.2
I MUCH DO GUESSE, YET FIND NO TRUTH SAVE THIS	4.44.9
AS OF A FRIEND THAT MEANT NOT MUCH AMISSE	4.56.8
I CANNOT BRAG OF WORD, MUCH LESSE OF DEED	4.66.5
'OR SO+' $MUCH LESSE.. '$HOW THEN+' $SURE THUS IT IS	4.74.13
THUS MUCH MY HEART COMPELD MY MOUTH TO SAY	4.80.9
OF HIGHEST WISH, I WISH YOU SO MUCH BLISSE	4.84.13
BUT WIT CONFUS'D WITH TOO MUCH CARE DID MISSE	4.93.8
SURE THEY PREVAILE AS MUCH WITH ME, AS HE	4.106.12
THAT MANY NOW MUCH WORSHIP AND ADMIRE	5.27.8
BUT THAT I BURNE MUCH MORE IN BOYLING SWEAT	5.30.7
BUT YE THEREBY MUCH GREATER GLORY GATE	5.66.9
AND VERTUOUS MIND, IS MUCH MORE PRAYSD OF ME	5.79.4
THAT ARE SO MUCH BY SO MEANE LOVE EMBASED	5.82.4
FOR HAD THE EQUALL HEVENS SO MUCH YOU GRACED	5.82.5

MUD   2
CIRCUMPASS'D ROUND WITH FILTH AND LOTHSOME MUD	1.29.2
ROSES HAVE THORNES, AND SILVER FOUNTAINES MUD	3.35.2

MURDER   5
ARE MADE BY HER TO MURTHER THUS THEIR $LORD	1.5.14
WHO SHOULD I THINKE THE $MURTHER SHOULD COMMIT+	2.2.2
AND IN YOUR $EYE, THE $BOY THAT DID THE $MURTHER	2.2.11
YET $HEAV'N WILL STILL HAVE $MURTHER OUT AT LAST	2.2.14
IN MAKING TRYALL OF A $MURTHER WROUGHT	2.46.5

MURDEREST   1
AND MURTHER'ST $VERTUE WITH THY COY DISDAINE	2.44.8

MURDERING   5
WHOSE STATE BEST SHEWES THE FORCE OF MURDERING EIES+	1.37.4

```
    BUT ONELY I, GUILTLESSE OF MURTH'RING IT              2.2.4
    WITH MURTHERING HANDS IMBRUD IN MINE OWN BLOOD      2.114.12
    IN THINE EYES TRYUMPH MURTHERING MY POORE HART      2.140.2
    SEE THERE THAT BOY, THAT MURTHRING BOY I SAY         4.20.2
MURDEROUS                 3
    THAT ON HIMSELFE SUCH MURDROUS SHAME COMMITS         3.9.14
    FOR THOU ART SO POSSEST WITH MURDROUS HATE           3.10.5
    IS PERJURD, MURDROUS, BLOUDDY FULL OF BLAME         3.129.3
MUSCOVITE                 1
    IS GONE, AND NOW LIKE SLAVE-BORNE $MUSCOVITE         4.2.10
MUSCOVY                   1
    TO WARME WITH ILL-MADE FIRE COLD $MOSCOVY            4.30.4
MUSE                      54
    MY $MUSE HAD SLEPT, AND NONE HAD KNOWNE MY MINDE     1.6.14
    NOR GRAVER BROWES HAVE JUDG'D MY $MUSE SO VAINE      1.7.6
    WHY SHOULD M'AFFLICTED $MUSE SO MUCH ENDEVOUR        1.17.7
    MY $MUSE SHOULD SOUND THY PRAISE WITH
                        MOURNFULL WARBLE                 1.44.6
SO SOUNDS MY $MUSE ACCORDING AS SHE STRIKES             1.57.3
ELSE HARSH MY STILE, UNTUNABLE MY $MUSE                 1.57.9
NONE OTHER FAME MINE UNAMBITIOUS $MUSE                  1.58.1
WHAT THOUGH MY $MUSE NO HONOR GET THEREBY              1.59.13
AS $OTHER $MEN, SO I MY SELFE DOE $MUSE                 2.9.1
AND MY FAIRE $MUSE, ONE $MUSE UNTO THE $NINE           2.18.10
AND MY FAIRE $MUSE, ONE $MUSE UNTO THE $NINE           2.18.10
MY $MUSE, MY $WORTHY, AND MY $ANGEL THEN               2.18.13
TO WHOM MY $MUSE WITH FIERIE $WINGS SHALL PASSE        2.25.10
AND TAXE MY $MUSE WITH THIS FANTASTICKE $GRACE          2.31.2
A DUMBE-BORNE $MUSE MADE TO EXPRESSE THE $MIND          2.35.6
WHICH $NAME MY $MUSE TO HIGHEST $HEAV'NS
                        SHALL RAYSE                     2.54.13
WHICH NAME MY $MUSE TO HIGHEST HEAVEN
                        SHAL RAISE                     2.101.13
NOR MY $MUSE BEEN THE TRUMPET OF THY FAME              2.104.8
THIS MIRACLE ON MY POORE $MUSE HAVE TRIED             2.104.10
AND MY FAIRE $MUSE, ONE $MUSE UNTO THE NINE           2.108.10
AND MY FAIRE $MUSE, ONE $MUSE UNTO THE NINE           2.108.10
MY $MUSE, MY $WORTHY, AND MY $ANGELL THEN             2.108.13
A DUMBE-BORNE $MUSE MADE TO EXPRESSE THE MIND         2.112.6
OR MY SWIFT-WINGED $MUSE TYRED BY TOO
                        HIE FLYING                     2.117.10
INVENTION AND MY $MUSE, PERFECTION AND HER LOVE       2.117.13
A $MUSE, THAT UNTO HEAVEN HATH RAISD HER FAME         2.138.12
WHAT $MUSE HATH POWER, ABOVE THY HEIGHT
                        TO RAISE THEE+                  2.146.4
SO IS IT NOT WITH ME AS WITH THAT $MUSE                3.21.1
HAD MY FRIENDS $MUSE GROWNE WITH THIS
                        GROWING AGE                     3.32.10
HOW CAN MY $MUSE WANT SUBJECT TO INVENT                3.38.1
BE THOU THE TENTH $MUSE, TEN TIMES MORE IN WORTH       3.38.9
IF MY SLIGHT $MUSE DOE PLEASE THESE CURIOUS
                        DAIES                           3.38.13
SO OFT HAVE I INVOK'D THEE FOR MY $MUSE                3.78.1
AND MY SICK $MUSE DOTH GIVE AN OTHER PLACE             3.79.4
I GRANT THOU WERT NOT MARRIED TO MY $MUSE              3.82.1
MY TOUNG-TIDE $MUSE IN MANNERS HOLDS HER STILL         3.85.1
WHERE ART THOU $MUSE THAT THOU FORGETST SO LONG       3.100.1
RETURNE FORGETFULL $MUSE, AND STRAIGHT REDEEME        3.100.5
RISE RESTY $MUSE, MY LOVES SWEET FACE SURVAY          3.100.9
OH TRUANT $MUSE WHAT SHALBE THY AMENDS                3.101.1
```

```
MAKE ANSWERE $MUSE, WILT THOU NOT HAPLY SAIE       3.101.5
THEN DO THY OFFICE $MUSE, I TEACH THEE HOW         3.101.13
ALACK WHAT POVERTY MY $MUSE BRINGS FORTH           3.103.1
'FOOLE,' SAID MY $MUSE TO ME, 'LOOKE IN
                          THY HEART AND WRITE'     4.1.14
FOR ME IN SOOTH, NO $MUSE BUT ONE I KNOW           4.3.9
DEEME THAT MY $MUSE SOME FRUIT OF KNOWLEDGE PLIES  4.23.6
SING THEN MY $MUSE, NOW $IO $PEAN SING             4.63.9
MY $MUSE MAY WELL GRUDGE AT MY HEAV'NLY JOY        4.70.1
COME THEN MY $MUSE, SHEW THOU HEIGHT OF DELIGHT    4.70.9
CEASE EAGER $MUSE, PEACE PEN, FOR MY SAKE STAY     4.70.12
YET AH, MY $MAYD'N $MUSE DOTH BLUSH TO
                          TELL THE BEST            4.77.14
AND THAT MY $MUSE TO SOME EARES NOT UNSWEET        4.84.2
MY $MUSE AND I MUST YOU OF DUTIE GREET             4.84.7
TO SPORT MY MUSE AND SING MY LOVES SWEET PRAISE    5.80.10
MUSED            1
SOME MUZ'D TO SEE THE EARTH ENVY THE AYRE          2.125.5
MUSE-FOE         1
AND $MUSE-FOE $MARS, ABROAD FARRE FOSTRED BEE      1.53.14
MUSES            11
NINE $MUSES DOE WITH $LEARNING STILL FREQUENT      2.18.6
THE THRICE-THREE $MUSES BUT TOO WANTON BE          2.39.7
MUSES WHICH SADLY SIT ABOUT MY $CHAYRE             2.45.1
NINE $MUSES DOE WITH LEARNING STILL FREQUENT       2.108.6
THE $MUSES NICE, THE $FURIES CRUELL BE             2.118.7
SOME OLD $PERNASSUS, WHERE THE $MUSES DWELL        2.120.11
AND PRECIOUS PHRASE BY ALL THE $MUSES FIL'D        3.85.4
SOME $LOVERS SPEAKE WHEN THEY THEIR $MUSES
                          ENTERTAINE               4.6.1
MUSES, I OFT INVOKED YOUR HOLY AYDE                4.55.1
AND $MUSES SCORNE WITH VULGAR BRAINES TO DWELL     4.74.3
THE NEW $PERNASSUS, WHERE THE $MUSES BIDE          4.80.5
MUSES'           2
I RATHER WISHT THEE CLIME THE $MUSES' HILL         4.10.3
WITH WORDS, WHEREIN THE $MUSES' TREASURES BE       4.60.7
MUSIC            15
MY PLEASURES HORROR, $MUSICKE TRAGICKE NOTES       1.9.11
FOR NO GROUND ELS COULD MAKE THE MUSICKE SUCH      1.57.13
INCLOSE MY $MUSIKE, YOU POORE SENSELESSE $WALLS    2.45.9
THE DAINTY GRASSE MAKE MUSICKE WITH HER FEETE      2.125.8
MUSICK TO HEARE, WHY HEAR'ST THOU MUSICK SADLY     3.8.1
MUSICK TO HEARE, WHY HEAR'ST THOU MUSICK SADLY     3.8.1
BUT THAT WILD MUSICK BURTHENS EVERY BOW            3.102.11
HOW OFT WHEN THOU MY MUSIKE MUSIKE PLAYST          3.128.1
HOW OFT WHEN THOU MY MUSIKE MUSIKE PLAYST          3.128.1
THAT $MUSICKE HATH A FARRE MORE PLEASING SOUND     3.130.10
WISE SILENCE IS BEST MUSICKE UNTO BLISSE           4.70.14
SWEETNER OF MUSICKE, WISEDOME'S BEAUTIFIER         4.80.6
WHILE SOBD OUT WORDS A PERFECT $MUSIKE GIVE        4.100.11
THROUGH THE SWEET MUSICK WHICH HIS HARP DID MAKE   5.38.3
BUT MY RUDE MUSICK, WHICH WAS WONT TO PLEASE       5.38.5
MUST             78
TIS NOT DISDAINE MUST MAKE ME LEAVE TO LOVE        1.8.14
AND MUST THEIR GLORY TO THE WORLD IMPART           1.10.12
THE FAULT IS HERS, THOUGH MINE THE HURT MUST BE    1.15.14
STILL MUST I WHET MY YONG DESIRES ABATED           1.18.9
AND STILL MUST HOLD HER DEARE TILL AFTER DEATH     1.21.11
YET SURE SHE CANNOT BUT MUST THINKE A PART         1.21.13
YET MUST THAT BLISSE MY HUNGRY THOUGHTS APPEASE    1.24.12
```

```
YET SOONE AGAINE I MUST HER BACKE RECALL              1.25.7
YET MY SOULES SOVERAIGNE, SINCE I MUST RESIGNE        1.27.13
BUT I MUST PINE, AND IN MY PINING LURKE               1.29.11
MY HEATES MUST DROWNE IN TH'$OCEAN OF MY TEARES       1.32.12
WHICH STILL MUST BEARE THE TITLE OF MY WRONG          1.32.13
AND HAVE NO STARS BUT THOSE, THAT MUST FULFILL        1.33.6
MUST YEELD UP ALL TO TYRANT $TIMES DESIRE             1.38.7
AND ($DELIA) THINKE THY MORNING MUST HAVE NIGHT       1.40.8
AND MUST INSTARRE THE $NEEDLE, AND THE $RAILE         1.45.12
LIVES IN MY LINES, AND MUST ETERNALL BEE              1.45.14
YET WHICH AT LENGTH THOU MUST BE FORC'D TO LOSE       1.50.8
BUT AH- NO MORE, THIS MUST NOT BE FORETOLD            1.50.13
FOR WOMEN GRIEVE TO THINKE THEY MUST BE OLD           1.50.14
I MUST NOT GRIEVE MY $LOVE, WHOSE EIES
                              WOULD REEDE             1.51.1
AND SHE IS YONG, AND NOW MUST SPORT THE WHILE         1.51.4
PITTY AND SMILES MUST ONELY YEELD THEE PRAISE         1.51.12
BEARING THE WOUND, I NEEDES MUST FEELE THE PAINE      1.52.14
BUT I MUST SING OF THEE, AND THOSE FAIRE EIES         1.55.5
AND THESE THY SACRED VERTUES MUST PROTECT             1.55.11
MUST $WOE AND I, HAVE NAUGHT BUT $NO AND I+           2.5.9
REASON AND I (YOU MUST CONCEIVE) ARE TWAINE           2.9.10
OR $NATURE MUST BE PARTIALL IN MY $CAUSE              2.27.13
WHERE, THE FULL $PRAYSE I FREELY MUST CONFESSE        2.47.7
SO MUST YOUR PRAYSE DISTRACTEDLY BE TOLD              2.57.12
THE TIME IS COME DELIVERED SHE MUST BE                2.116.3
MUST PASSE BY AYRE, OR ELSE DYE IN EXILE              2.122.4
A $BASTARD ON BOTH SIDES NEEDES MUST THOU BE          2.140.10
THY UNUS'D BEAUTY MUST BE TOMB'D WITH THEE            3.4.13
THAT THOU AMONG THE WASTES OF TIME MUST GOE           3.12.10
AND YOU MUST LIVE DRAWNE BY YOUR OWNE
                              SWEET SKILL             3.16.14
FOR THROUGH THE $PAINTER MUST YOU SEE HIS SKILL       3.24.5
THAT I AN ACCESSARY NEEDS MUST BE                     3.35.13
LET ME CONFESSE THAT WE TWO MUST BE TWAINE            3.36.1
KILL ME WITH SPIGHTS YET WE MUST NOT BE FOES          3.40.14
I MUST ATTEND, TIMES LEASURE WITH MY MONE             3.44.12
AS THE DEATH BED, WHERECN IT MUST EXPIRE              3.73.11
TO LOVE THAT WELL, WHICH THOU MUST LEAVE
                              ERE LONG                3.73.14
SAVE WHAT IS HAD, OR MUST FROM YOU BE TOOKE           3.75.12
THOUGH I (ONCE GONE) TO ALL THE WORLD MUST DYE        3.81.6
FOR I MUST NERE LOVE HIM WHOM THOU DOST HATE          3.89.14
I MUST EACH DAY SAY ORE THE VERY SAME                 3.108.6
YOU ARE MY $ALL THE WORLD, AND I MUST STRIVE          3.112.5
NEEDES MUST I UNDER MY TRANSGRESSION BOW              3.120.3
MINE RANSOMS YOURS, AND YOURS MUST RANSOME MEE        3.120.14
BY THEIR RANCKE THOUGHTES, MY DEEDES MUST
                              NOT BE SHOWN            3.121.12
HER $AUDITE (THOUGH DELAYD) ANSWER'D MUST BE          3.126.11
BUT SLAVE TO SLAVERY MY SWEET'ST FRIEND MUST BE       3.133.4
THOUGH IN THY STORES ACCOUNT I ONE MUST BE            3.136.10
TRUE, AND YET TRUE THAT I MUST $STELLA LOVE           4.5.14
EFFECTS OF LIVELY HEAT, MUST NEEDS IN NATURE GROW     4.8.11
BUT WITH YOUR $RUBARB WORDS YOW MUST CONTEND          4.14.5
THAT I RESPECTS FOR BOTH OUR SAKES MUST SHOW          4.33.11
WHERE TRUTH IT SELFE MUST SPEAKE LIKE FLATTERIE+      4.35.2
FOR OF MY LIFE I MUST A RIDDLE TELL                   4.37.4
THAT THOU MUST WANT OR FOOD, OR DWELLING PLACE        4.46.4
THOU NEEDS MUST MISSE, AND SO THOU NEEDS
                              MUST SMART              4.46.11
```

```
THOU NEEDS MUST MISSE, AND SO THOU NEEDS
                        MUST SMART              4.46.11
I MAY, I MUST, I CAN, I WILL, I DO              4.47.10
WHILE EACH PRETENDS THAT $STELLA MUST BE HIS    4.52.2
WHILE WITH THE PEOPLE'S SHOUTS I MUST CONFESSE  4.53.3
WITH CHASTNED MIND, I STRAIGHT MUST SHEW
                        THAT SHE                4.61.10
NOW FROM THY FELLOWSHIP I NEEDS MUST PART       4.72.5
I MUST NO MORE IN THY SWEET PASSIONS LIE        4.72.7
VERTUE'S GOLD NOW MUST HEAD MY $CUPID'S DART    4.72.8
THAT $ANGER' SELFE I NEEDS MUST KISSE AGAINE    4.73.14
BUT YOU MUST NEEDS WITH THOSE LIPS BILLING BE+  4.83.12
MY $MUSE AND I MUST YOU OF DUTIE GREET          4.84.7
OR IF I NEEDS (SWEET $JUDGE) MUST TORMENTS HAVE 4.86.11
OR IF SUCH HEAVENLY SIGNES MUST PROVE ANNOY     4.100.13
I MUST BEGIN AND NEVER BRING TO END             5.23.10
MY LOWER HEAVEN, SO IT PERFORCE MUST BEE        5.46.8
MUTE                    4
UNTO THE WORLD HAD ALL MY JOYES BEEN MUTE       2.104.3
MY CARES MY MUTES SO MUTE TO CRAVE RELIEFE      2.111.10
FOR I IMPAIRE NOT BEAUTIE BEING MUTE            3.83.11
AND THOU AWAY, THE VERY BIRDS ARE MUTE          3.97.12
MUTES                   1
MY CARES MY MUTES SO MUTE TO CRAVE RELIEFE      2.111.10
MUTUAL                  3
STRIKES EACH IN EACH BY MUTUALL ORDERING        3.8.10
BUT MUTUALL RENDER, ONELY ME FOR THEE           3.125.12
BUT SIMPLE TRUTH AND MUTUALL GOOD WILL          5.65.11
MUTUALLY                1
THIS TO EACH OTHER MUTUALLY THEY CRAVE          2.33.12
MYCHE                   1
SO LONG (THOUGH HE FROM BOOKE MYCHE TO DESIRE)  4.46.13
MYRRH-BREATHING         2
WHERE SWEET $MYRRH-BREATHING $ZEPHIRE
                        IN THE $SPRING          2.53.5
WHERE SWEET $MYRH-BREATHING $ZEPHYRE IN
                        THE SPRING              2.113.5
MYRTLE                  1
I GOE BEFORE UNTO THE $MIRTLE SHADES            1.30.5
MYSELF                  1
THAT IN THE $MANAGE MYSELFE TAKES DELIGHT       4.49.14
NAKED                   9
PAPER AND $INKE CAN PAINT BUT NAKED $WORDS      2.13.5
CLOTHED THE $NAKED, LODG'D THIS WAND'RING $GHEST 2.23.6
A NAKED $STARVELING EVER MAY'ST THOU BE         2.48.2
PAPER AND YNCKE, CAN PAYNT BUT NAKED WORDS      2.121.5
UNFAINED LOVE, IN NAKED SIMPLE TRUTH            2.138.3
IN THY SOULES THOUGHT (ALL NAKED) WILL BESTOW IT 3.26.8
THAT IT, DESPISDE IN TRUE BUT NAKED SHEW        4.55.3
FOR WHEN, NAK'D BOY, THOU COULDST NO HARBOUR FIND 4.65.5
OR HERS WHOM NAKED THE $TROJAN BOY DID SEE      4.82.4
NAME                    63
AND HAD MY SIGHES STILL TENDING ON HER NAME     1.15.10
WHY SHOULD I OFFER UP UNTO HER NAME             1.17.3
IN LIFE AND DEATH $ILE TENDER HER GOOD NAME     1.30.11
LIVES WITHOUT HONOUR, DIES WITHOUT A NAME       1.35.11
AND IF MY PEN COULD MORE ENLARGE THY NAME       1.43.11
HOW MANY LIVE, THE GLORY OF WHOSE NAME          1.44.7
THE TEMPLE, WHERE HER NAME WAS HONOUR'D STILL   1.47.14
THAT FORTIFIE THY NAME AGAINST OLD AGE          1.55.10
```

```
HOARCE SOUNDS THE VOYCE THAT PRAYSETH
                        NOT HER NAME              1.57.10
GIVES HER THAT $NAME, AS SHE THE $BODY MOVES      2.12.4
IN JUDGING, $REASON ONELY IS HER $NAME            2.12.9
ONE BY THY $NAME, THE OTHER TOUCHING THEE         2.35.8
MY $NAME SHALL MOUNT UPON $ETERNITIE              2.44.14
WHEREIN THE $WORLD SHALL NOW INTOMBE HER $NAME    2.45.8
AND FIRST THE SOUND AND VERTUE OF MY $NAME        2.47.3
MY $SOULE'S $OBLATIONS TO THY SACRED $NAME        2.54.12
WHICH $NAME MY $MUSE TO HIGHEST $HEAV'NS
                        SHALL RAYSE               2.54.13
MY SOULES OBLATIONS TO THY SACRED NAME            2.101.12
WHICH NAME MY $MUSE TO HIGHEST HEAVEN
                        SHAL RAISE                2.101.13
NOR MY HART KNOWNE THE POWER OF THY NAME          2.104.6
WITHIN THE $TEMPLE OF THY SACRED NAME             2.105.6
AT MY FIRST $LESSON IN THY SACRED NAME            2.111.6
ONE BY THY NAME, THE OTHER TOUCHING THEE          2.112.8
OR MAKE MY PEN HER NAME IMORTALIZE                2.123.11
FAIRE-MAYD NO MORE, BUT $MAYR-MAID BE THY NAME    2.130.9
A SOULE, THAT EVER HATH ADOR'D HER NAME           2.138.10
CANCELL MY NAME, AND BLOT IT WITH DISPAYRE        2.142.12
UNLESSE THOU TAKE THAT HONOUR FROM THY NAME       3.36.12
AND OUR DEARE LOVE LOOSE NAME OF SINGLE ONE       3.39.6
DO NOT SO MUCH AS MY POORE NAME REHERSE           3.71.11
MY NAME BE BURIED WHERE MY BODY IS                3.72.11
THAT EVERY WORD DOTH ALMOST FEL MY NAME           3.76.7
KNOWING A BETTER SPIRIT DOTH USE YOUR NAME        3.80.2
YOUR NAME FROM HENCE IMMORTALL LIFE SHALL HAVE    3.81.5
THY SWEET BELOVED NAME NO MORE SHALL DWELL        3.89.10
DOTH SPOT THE BEAUTIE OF THY BUDDING NAME+        3.95.3
NAMING THY NAME, BLESSES AN ILL REPORT            3.95.8
EVEN AS WHEN FIRST I HALLOWED THY FAIRE NAME      3.108.8
THENCE COMES IT THAT MY NAME RECEIVES A BRAND     3.111.5
OR IF IT WEARE IT BORE NOT BEAUTIES NAME          3.127.2
SWEET BEAUTY HATH NO NAME NO HOLY BOURE           3.127.7
MAKE BUT MY NAME THY LOVE, AND LOVE THAT STILL    3.136.13
AND THEN THOU LOVEST ME FOR MY NAME IS $WILL      3.136.14
BUT RYSING AT THY NAME DOTH POINT OUT THEE        3.151.9
WHOSE PORCHES RICH (WHICH NAME OF CHEEKES ENDURE) 4.9.7
WHICH DARE CLAIME FROM THOSE LIGHTS THE
                        NAME OF BEST              4.9.11
BUT IF (BOTH FOR YOUR LOVE AND SKILL) YOUR NAME   4.15.12
MY VERIE INKE TURNES STRAIGHT TO $STELLA'S NAME   4.19.6
DOTH EVEN GROW RICH, NAMING MY STELLA'S NAME      4.35.11
BECAUSE THEIR FOREFRONT BARE SWEET $STELLA'S
                        NAME                      4.50.14
THAT $STELLA (O DEARE NAME) THAT $STELLA IS       4.52.6
BUT ON HER NAME INCESSANTLY TO CRIE               4.55.11
FOR LET ME BUT NAME HER WHOM I DO LOVE            4.55.12
EDWARD NAMED FOURTH, AS FIRST IN PRAISE I NAME    4.75.2
AS CONSTERD IN TRUE SPEECH, THE NAME OF
                        HEAV'N IT BEARES          4.77.11
GRAVED IN MINE $EPITAPH A $POET'S NAME            4.90.8
IF HER LIPS DAIGND TO SWEETEN MY POORE NAME       4.92.13
TO SING YOUR NAME AND PRAYSES OVER ALL            5.73.12
WITH WHICH THAT HAPPY NAME WAS FIRST DESYND       5.74.2
ONE DAY I WROTE HER NAME UPON THE STRAND          5.75.1
AND EEK MY NAME BEE WYPED OUT LYKEWIZE            5.75.8
AND IN THE HEVENS WRYTE YOUR GLORIOUS NAME        5.75.12
```

```
   YOUR GLORIOUS NAME IN GOLDEN MONIMENT              5.82.8
NAMED                    4
   I CONJURE THEE BY ALL THAT I HAVE NAM'D            2.36.13
   STELLA., NOW SHE IS NAM'D, NEED MORE BE SAID+      4.16.11
   EDWARD NAMED FOURTH, AS FIRST IN PRAISE I NAME     4.75.2
   O FAYREST FAYRE LET NEVER IT BE NAMED              5.41.13
NAMES                    1
   BY $HECAT'S $NAMES, BY $PROSERPINE'S SAD $TEARES   2.36.7
NAMING                   4
   STILL NAMING HER, IN NAMING ALL DELIGHT            2.148.12
   STILL NAMING HER, IN NAMING ALL DELIGHT            2.148.12
   NAMING THY NAME, BLESSES AN ILL REPORT             3.95.8
   DOTH EVEN GROW RICH, NAMING MY STELLA'S NAME       4.35.11
NARCISSUS                3
   NARCISSUS CHANG'D T'A FLOWER IN SUCH A CASE        1.37.12
   IN THEIR AMAZEMENT LYKE $NARCISSUS VAINE           5.35.7
   IN THEYR AMAZEMENT LYKE $NARCISSUS VAYNE           5.83.7
NATIONS                  3
   THAT $FORAINE $NATIONS RELLISH NOT OUR $TONGUE     2.25.2
   AND DIFF'RETH IT, AS DOE THE SEV'RALL $NATIONS+    2.27.2
   AND JOY THEREIN, THOUGH $NATIONS COUNT IT SHAME    4.28.8
NATIVE                   2
   LOVE BORNE IN $GREECE, OF LATE FLED FROM
                          HIS NATIVE PLACE            4.8.1
   THY TEARES EXPRESSE NIGHT'S NATIVE MOISTURE RIGHT  4.96.8
NATIVITY                 2
   SO LUCKLES WAS MY $BABES NATIVITY                  2.116.6
   NATIVITY ONCE IN THE MAINE OF LIGHT                3.60.5
NATURE                  47
   FOR HOW COULD $NATURE EVER THUS DEVISE.            1.34.3
   HERE SEE THE GIFTS THAT $GOD AND NATURE LENT THEE  1.42.7
   GIVE $NATURE THANKES, YOU ARE NOT SUCH AS WE       2.22.12
   O, $WHY SHOULD $NATURE NIGGARDLY RESTRAINE         2.25.1
   IS $NATURE GROWNE LESSE POW'RFULL IN THEIR
                          $HEIRES                     2.27.7
   OR $NATURE MUST BE PARTIALL IN MY $CAUSE           2.27.13
   BUT FINDING $NATURE THEIR REQUEST DENYES           2.33.11
   YOU, IN WHOM $NATURE CHOSE HER SELFE TO VIEW       2.57.5
   WHICH BY THEYR NATURE LEARN'D TO MOUNT THE SKYE    2.122.6
   YET FIRE, WATER, AYRE, OF NATURE NOT DEPRIVED      2.127.12
   THE $BASILISKE HIS NATURE TAKES FROM THEE          2.130.5
   CROSSING SWEET NATURE BY UNRULY WILL               2.147.12
   THEN HOW WHEN NATURE CALLS THEE TO BE GONE         3.4.11
   LET THOSE WHOM NATURE HATH NOT MADE FOR STORE      3.11.9
   TILL NATURE AS SHE WROUGHT THEE FELL A DOTINGE     3.20.10
   WHY SHOULD HE LIVE, NOW NATURE BANCKROUT IS        3.67.9
   AND HIM AS FOR A MAP DOTH $NATURE STORE            3.68.13
   NOT MAKING WORSE WHAT NATURE MADE SO CLEERE        3.84.10
   NEVER BELEEVE THOUGH IN MY NATURE RAIGN'D          3.109.9
   AND ALMOST THENCE MY NATURE IS SUBDU'D             3.111.6
   HAVE FACULTIE BY NATURE TO SUBSIST                 3.122.6
   IF $NATURE (SOVERAINE MISTERES OVER WRACK)         3.126.5
   BUT $COPYING IS, WHAT IN HER $NATURE WRITES        4.3.14
   REBELS TO $NATURE, STRIVE FOR THEIR OWNE SMART     4.5.4
   WHEN $NATURE MADE HER CHIEFE WORKE, $STELLA'S EYES 4.7.1
   EFFECTS OF LIVELY HEAT, MUST NEEDS IN NATURE GROW  4.8.11
   IN NATURE APT TO LIKE WHEN I DID SEE               4.16.1
   TILL THAT HIS GRANDAME $NATURE PITTYING IT         4.17.9
   AND NOT IN $NATURE FOR BEST FRUITS UNFIT           4.19.13
   FOR ME, I DO $NATURE UNIDLE KNOW                   4.26.9
```

```
WHERE $NATURE DOTH WITH INFINITE AGREE+              4.35.4
WITH SO SWEETE VOICE, AND BY SWEETE $NATURE SO       4.36.9
THINKE $NATURE ME A MAN CF ARMES DID MAKE            4.41.11
THE HEAV'NLY NATURE OF THAT PLACE IS SUCH            4.44.12
BY $NATURE BORNE, I GAVE TO THEE MINE EYES           4.65.8
WHO WILL IN FAIREST BOOKE OF $NATURE KNOW            4.71.1
LEAST JOY, BY $NATURE APT SPRITES TO ENLARGE         4.85.3
YET GROWEST MORE WRETCHED THEN THY NATURE BEARES     4.94.13
TO WHOM NOR ART NCR NATURE GRAUNTETH LIGHT           4.99.2
NATURE WITH CARE SWEATES FOR HER DARLING'S SAKE      4.101.12
WHICH $NATURE' SELFE DID MAKE, AND SELFE
                        ENGRAIND THE SAME+           4.102.6
HAVE MADE, BUT FORST BY $NATURE STILL TO FLIE        4.103.10
WAS IT THE WORKE CF NATURE OR OF $ART                5.21.1
AH WHY HATH NATURE TO SC HARD A HART                 5.31.1
IS IT HER NATURE CR IS IT HER WILL                   5.41.1
IF NATURE, THEN SHE MAY IT MEND WITH SKILL           5.41.3
BUT IF HER NATURE AND HER WIL BE SO                  5.41.5
NATURE'S                20
WITH HEAVENLY COLCURS DIDE, WITH NATURES
                        WONDER CROUND                2.106.4
RARE BEAUTY, $NATURES JCY, PERFECTIONS $MOTHER       2.123.2
BY NATURES $LAWES WE THEE A $BASTARD FINDE           2.140.12
NATURES BEQUEST GIVES NCTHING BUT DOTH LEND          3.4.3
BY CHANCE, OR NATURES CHANGING COURSE UNTRIM'D       3.18.8
A $WOMANS FACE WITH NATURES OWNE HAND PAINTED        3.20.1
FEEDES ON THE RARITIES CF NATURES TRUTH              3.60.11
AND HUSBAND NATURES RITCHES FROM EXPENCE             3.94.6
FOR SINCE EACH HAND HATH PUT ON $NATURES POWER       3.127.5
INVENTION, $NATURE'S CHILD, FLED STEP-DAME
                        $STUDIE'S BLOWES             4.1.10
PREPAR'D BY $NATURE'S CHIEFEST FURNITURE             4.9.2
OR REACH THE FRUITE OF $NATURE'S CHOISEST TREE       4.10.4
SO WHEN THOU SAW'ST IN $NATURE'S CABINET             4.11.9
UNABLE QUITE TO PAY EVEN $NATURE'S RENT              4.18.5
WHO SINCE HE HATH, BY $NATURE'S SPECIALL GRACE       4.78.9
NATURE'S PRAISE, $VERTUE'S STALL, $CUPID'S
                        COLD FIRE                    4.80.3
BY LINKES OF $LOVE, AND CNLY $NATURE'S ART           4.81.6
OF NATURES SKILL THE ONELY COMPLEMENT                5.24.3
THEN ALL HER NATURES GOODLY GUIFTS ARE LOST          5.41.8
THE REST BE WORKS CF NATURES WONDERMENT              5.81.13
NAUGHT                  5
MUST $WOE AND I, HAVE NAUGHT BUT $NO AND I+          2.5.9
THAT THIS HUGE STAGE PRESENTETH NOUGHT BUT SHOWES    3.15.3
BUT LIKE A SAD SLAVE STAY AND THINKE OF NOUGHT       3.57.11
WITH CHAST AFFECTS, THAT NAUGHT BUT DEATH
                        CAN SEVER                    5.6.12
THAT TO THE WORLD NAUGHT ELSE BE COUNTED DEARE       5.8.4
NAUGHTS                 1
RECEIVING NAUGHTS BY ELEMENTS SO SLOE                3.44.13
NAY                     15
AND BID THEM MOURNE, NAY MORE, DESPAIRE
                        WITH THEE                    2.17.13
WHAT, WILL $YOU HATE+ NAY THAT $YOU WILL
                        NOT NEITHER                  2.19.5
NAY, I HAVE DONE.. $YOU GET NO MORE OF $ME           2.61.2
NAY, LOOKE THEE $TIME IN THIS $CELESTIALL GLASSE     2.107.5
NAY IF YOU READ THIS LINE, REMEMBER NOT              3.71.5
NAY IF THOU LOWRST CN ME DOE I NOT SPEND             3.149.7
```

```
NAY, THAT MAY BREED MY FAME, IT IS SO RARE          4.34.6
THAT LAP DOTH LAP, NAY LETS, IN SPITE OF SPITE      4.59.10
FOR $GRAMMER SAYES (TO $GRAMMER WHO SAYES NAY)      4.63.13
STOLNE TO MY HEART, SINCE LAST FAIRE NIGHT,
                              NAY DAY               4.66.10
DOTH LOWRE, NAY, CHIDE., NAY, THREAT FOR
                              ONLY THIS             4.73.7
DOTH LOWRE, NAY, CHIDE., NAY, THREAT FOR
                              ONLY THIS             4.73.7
NAY, MORE FOOLE I, CFT SUFFERED YOJ TO SLEEPE       4.83.7
NAY SORROW COMES WITH SUCH MAINE RAGE, THAT HE      4.95.9
THAT TO EACH WORD, NAY SIGH OF MINE YOU HARKE       4.104.3
```
NE   20
```
NE IF I WOULD, COULD I JUST TITLE MAKE              4.90.9
THAT LOOSELY THEY NE DARE TO LOOKE UPON HER         5.5.8
NE WILBE MOOV'D WITH REASON OR WITH REWTH           5.11.5
NE ANY THEN SHALL AFTER IT INQUIRE                  5.27.9
NE ANY MENTION SHALL THEREOF REMAINE                5.27.10
NE ALL THE PLAYNTS AND PRAYERS WITH WHICH I         5.32.7
NE DOE I WISH (FOR WISHING WERE BUT VAINE)          5.42.5
NE LET THEYR FAMOUS MONIMENTS TO FADE               5.51.4
NE OUGHT SO HARD, BUT HE THAT WOULD ATTEND          5.51.9
NE YOUR INCESSANT BATTRY MORE TO BEARE              5.57.4
NE NONE SO RICH OR WISE, SO STRONG OR FAYRE         5.58.9
NE FEARD WITH WORSE TO ANY CHAUNCE TO START         5.59.4
NE OUGHT FOR TEMPEST DOTH FROM IT DEPART            5.59.7
NE OUGHT FOR FAYRER WEATHERS FALSE DELIGHT          5.59.8
OF GRUDGING FOES, NE FAVOUR SEEK OF FRIENDS         5.59.10
NE BUT IN HEAVEN MATCHABLE TO NONE                  5.66.7
NE THINKS OF OTHER HEAVEN, BUT HOW IT MIGHT         5.72.11
NE ONE LIGHT GLANCE OF SENSUALL DESYRE              5.84.3
NE OUGHT I SEE, THOUGH IN THE CLEAREST DAY          5.88.5
NE JOY OF OUGHT THAT UNDER HEAVEN DOTH HOVE         5.89.9
```
NEAR   19
```
LOVE WAS THE FLAME THAT FIRED ME SO NEERE           1.14.3
HOW TO BE BOLD FAR CFF, AND BASHFULL NEARE          1.20.5
AND FROST OF AGE HATH NIPT THY BEAUTIES NEERE       1.42.2
NEERE THE DEAD $BCDY HAPPILY BE BROUGHT             2.46.7
SHE COMMING NEERE, THAT MY POORE $HEART
                              HATH SLAINE           2.46.9
SO NEERE THYNE EYES CELESTIALL SUNNE ASPYRED        2.122.10
FROM ME FARRE OF, WITH CTHERS ALL TO NEERE          3.61.14
THAT LEAVES LOOKE PALE, DREADING THE $WINTERS
                              NEERE                 3.97.14
IF THY SOULE CHECK THEE THAT I COME SO NEERE        3.136.1
YET DO NOT SO, BUT SINCE I AM NEERE SLAINE          3.139.13
AS TESTIE SICK-MEN WHEN THEIR DEATHS BE NEERE       3.140.7
NEARE THERABOUT, INTO YCUR $POESIE WRING            4.15.4
HOW FAIRE A DAY WAS NEARE, O PUNISHT EYES           4.33.13
IN $BEAUTIE'S THRCNE, SEE NOW WHO DARES
                              COME NEARE            4.73.10
FROM COMMING NEARE THOSE $CHERRIES BANISH ME        4.82.8
SO NEERE, IN SO GCCD TIME, SO FREE A PLACE+         4.105.2
DOTH MAKE ME MOST TC WISH THY COMFORT NEERE         4.106.8
KINDLED ABOVE UNTC THE MAKER NEERE                  5.8.2
SWEET IS THE $EGLANTINE, BUT PRICKETH NERE          5.26.3
```
NEARER   1
```
NEERER $MEN COME, $THAT FURTHER FLYES AWAY          2.58.9
```
NEARLY   2
```
THIS IS MY STATE, MY GRIEFES DO TOUCH SO NEERLY     1.16.13
```

```
      A LOSSE IN LOVE THAT TOUCHES ME MORE NEERELY          3.42.4
NECESSARY                    1
      NOR GIVES TO NECESSARY WRINCKLES PLACE                3.108.11
NECK                         6
      ONE ON ANOTHERS NECKE DO WITNESSE BEARE               3.131.11
      WHOSE NECKE BECOMES SUCH YOKE OF TYRANNY+             4.47.4
      WHEN IN HER NECKE YOU DID $LOVE DITTIES PEEPE         4.83.6
      LEAVE THAT SIR $PHIP, LEAST OFF YOUR NECKE
                              BE WROONG                     4.83.14
      THE WHILES HER FOOT SHE IN MY NECKE DOTH PLACE        5.20.3
      HER NECK LYKE TO A BOUNCH OF $CULLAMBYNES             5.64.10
NECTAR                       5
      THE $WELL OF $NECTAR, PAV'D WITH PEARLE
                              AND GOLD                      2.109.13
      NECTAR OF $MIRTH, SINCE I $JOVE'S CUP DO KEEPE        4.70.4
      AND THROUGH THOSE LIPS DRINKE $NECTAR
                              FROM THAT TOONG               4.83.13
      THAT YOU, GUILTLESSE THEREOF, YOUR $NECTAR MIST       4.105.10
      MORE SWEET THAN $NECTAR OR $AMBROSIALL MEAT           5.39.13
NECTAR-DROPPING              2
      GENTLY DISTILLS HIS $NECTAR-DROPPING SHOWRES          2.53.6
      GENTLY DISTILS HIS $NECTAR-DROPPING SHOWERS           2.113.6
NEED                        14
      NO SUCCOUR FINDE I NOW WHEN MOST I NEEDE              1.32.11
      BUT $O, SEE, SEE, WE NEED INQUIRE NO FURTHER          2.2.9
      WAND'RING ABROAD IN $NEED AND $BEGGERIE               2.23.2
      TILL I RETURNE OF POSTING IS NOE NEED                 3.51.4
      WHERE CHEEKES NEED BLOOD, IN THEE IT IS ABUS'D        3.82.14
      I NEVER SAW THAT YOU DID PAINTING NEED                3.83.1
      THEN NEED I NOT TO FEARE THE WORST OF WRONGS          3.92.5
      NOR NEED I TALLIES THY DEARE LOVE TO SKORE            3.122.10
      STELLA., NOW SHE IS NAM'D, NEED MORE BE SAID+         4.16.11
      TO THEM THAT DO SUCH ENTERTAINMENT NEED               4.51.3
      MY WEALTH NO MORE, AND NO WHIT LESSE MY NEED          4.66.7
      A GREATER CRAFTESMANS HAND THERETO DOTH NEEDE         5.17.13
      SUCH SELFE ASSURANCE NEED NOT FEARE THE SPIGHT        5.59.9
      HART NEED NOT WISH NONE OTHER HAPPINESSE              5.72.13
NEEDEST                      1
      WHAT NEEDST THOU WOUND WITH CUNNING WHEN
                              THY MIGHT                     3.139.7
NEEDETH                      2
      GAYNST SUCH STRONG CASTLES NEEDETH GREATER MIGHT      5.14.5
      WHAT NEEDETH YOU TO SEEKE SO FARRE IN VAINE+          5.15.4
NEEDFUL                      1
      READY TO STORE THEIR CAMPES OF NEEDFULL THINGS        4.29.4
NEEDING                      1
      TO BE DISEAS'D ERE THAT THERE WAS TRUE NEEDING        3.118.8
NEEDLE                       1
      AND MUST INSTARRE THE $NEEDLE, AND THE $RAILE         1.45.12
NEEDS                       19
      BEARING THE WOUND, I NEEDES MUST FEELE THE PAINE      1.52.14
      A $BASTARD ON BOTH SIDES NEEDES MUST THOU BE          2.140.10
      THAT I AN ACCESSARY NEEDS MUST BE                     3.35.13
      TRUTH NEEDS NO COLLOUR WITH HIS COLLOUR FIXT          3.101.6
      BECAUSE HE NEEDS NO PRAISE, WILT THOU BE DUMB+        3.101.1
      NEEDES MUST I UNDER MY TRANSGRESSION BOW              3.120.3
      THE BOY FOR TRIALL NEEDES WOULD TOUCH MY BREST        3.153.10
      BUT IF THAT NEEDS THOU WILT USURPING BE               4.4.9
      EFFECTS OF LIVELY HEAT, MUST NEEDS IN NATURE GROW     4.8.11
      BUT THOU WOULDST NEEDS FIGHT BOTH WITH
                              LOVE AND SENCE                4.10.9
```

THOU NEEDS MUST MISSE, AND SO THOU NEEDS
                MUST SMART   4.46.11
THOU NEEDS MUST MISSE, AND SO THOU NEEDS
                MUST SMART   4.46.11
NOW FROM THY FELLOWSHIP I NEEDS MUST PART   4.72.5
THAT $ANGER' SELFE I NEEDS MUST KISSE AGAINE   4.73.14
BUT YOU MUST NEEDS WITH THOSE LIPS BILLING BE+ 4.83.12
OR IF I NEEDS (SWEET $JUDGE) MUST TORMENTS HAVE 4.86.11
TO THIS GREAT CAUSE, WHICH NEEDS BOTH
                USE AND ART   4.107.8
BUT SITH SHE WILL THE CONQUEST CHALLENG NEEDS   5.29.9
THEN NEEDS ANOTHER $ELEMENT INQUIRE   5.55.9
NEEDSLY   1
DOE WHAT I COULD, IT NEEDSLY WOULD ASPIRE   2.56.11
NEEDY   2
AND NEEDIE $NOTHING TRIMD IN JOLLITIE   3.66.3
HIM AS THY SLAVE, AND NOW LONG NEEDY $FAME   4.35.10
NE'ER   9
THAT $GOLD NOR $HONOUR NE'R HAD POW'R TO MOVE   2.15.4
MIX'D WITH HER $TEARES, THAT NE'R HER
                TRUE-$LOVE CROST   2.15.5
NOR AT $FIFTEENE NE'R LONG'D TO BE A $BRIDE   2.15.6
A HASTIE $MAN (QUOTH HE) NE'R WANTED $WOE   2.59.8
MY SOULE HAD NE'R FELT THY $DIVINITIE   2.104.7
SUCH HEAVENLY TOUCHES NERE TOUCHT EARTHLY FACES 3.17.8
FOR I MUST NERE LOVE HIM WHOM THOU DOST HATE 3.89.14
EVEN SO BEING FULL OF YOUR NERE CLOYING
                SWEETNESSE   3.118.5
YET THIS SHAL I NERE KNOW BUT LIVE IN DOUBT 3.144.13
NEGATIVES   1
THAT IN ONE SPEECH TWO $NEGATIVES AFFIRME   4.63.14
NEGLECT   2
FOR THY NEGLECT OF TRUTH IN BEAUTY DI'D+   3.101.2
MARKE HOW WITH MY NEGLECT I DOE DISPENCE   3.112.12
NEGLECTED   3
THESE SAD NEGLECTED NOTES FOR HER DEARE SAKE+ 1.17.2
SINCE HOLY $VESTALL LAWES HAVE BEEN NEGLECTED 2.105.1
WHILST HER NEGLECTED CHILD HOLDS HER IN CHACE 3.143.5
NEIGH   1
SHALL NAIGH NOE DULL FLESH IN HIS FIERY RACE 3.51.11
NEIGHBORED   1
LIKE SOME WEAKE $LORDS, NEIGHBORD BY MIGHTY KINGS 4.29.1
NEITHER   8
WHAT, WILL $YOU HATE+ NAY THAT $YOU WILL
                NOT NEITHER   2.19.5
BAD IS THE $MATCH, WHERE NEITHER PARTIE WONNE 2.63.4
NEITHER IN INWARD WORTH NOR OUTWARD FAIRE   3.16.11
NO, NEITHER HE, NOR HIS COMPIERS BY NIGHT   3.86.7
OF ALL MY THOUGHTS HATH NEITHER STOP NOR START 4.23.13
THAT NETHER I MAY SPEAKE NOR THINKE AT ALL   5.43.7
THAT NETHER WILL FOR BETTER BE ALLURED   5.59.3
NETHER TO ONE HER SELFE NOR OTHER BENDS   5.59.12
NEPHEWS   1
SAY TO OUR $NEPHEWES, THAT THOU ONCE HAST SEENE 2.17.11
NEPTUNE'S   1
NEPTUNES BEST DARLING, HELD BETWEENE HIS ARMES 1.53.10
NERVES   1
UNLESSE MY $NERVES WERE BRASSE OR HAMMERED
                STEELE   3.120.4

NEST   8
  PINES IN HER GRIEFE, IMPRISONED IN HER NEST   1.29.3
  UPON THE $NEST I SET IT FORTH, TO PROVE   2.56.3
  UPON THE NEST I SET THEM, FORTH TO PROVE   2.103.3
  NEAST OF YOUNG JOYES, SCHOOLMASTER OF DELIGHT   4.79.8
  IN $LILLIES' NEAST, WHERE $LOVE'S SELFE
                           LIES ALONG   4.83.8
  A NEST FOR MY YONG PRAISE IN $LAWRELL TREE   4.90.6
  AND MY YONG SOULE FLUTTERS TO THEE HIS NEST   4.108.6
  THE NEAST OF LOVE, THE LODGING OF DELIGHT   5.76.2
NESTOR'S   1
  WHAT $NESTOR'S COUNSELL CAN MY FLAMES ALAY   4.35.5
NET   3
  STRONG IS THE NET, AND FERVENT IS THE FLAME   1.14.5
  SHE DOTH ATTYRE UNDER A NET OF GOLD   5.37.2
  HENCEFORTH TOO RASHLY ON THAT GUILEFULL NET   5.37.10
NETS   1
  THOSE SNARY LOCKS, ARE THOSE SAME NETS
                           (MY $DEERE)   1.14.1
NEVER   96
  WHILST BLINDED ONES MINE ERROURS NEVER GESSE   1.3.8
  THE WORLD HAD NEVER KNOWNE WHAT I DOE FINDE   1.7.3
  GRIEFES EVER SPRINGING, COMFORTS NEVER BORNE   1.16.4
  THAT NEVER DEIGNES TO GIVE ME JOY TO LIVE+   1.17.6
  THE CIRCLE OF MY SORROWES NEVER ENDING   1.18.4
  NEVER TO FINDE, AND EVERMORE TO SEEKE   1.20.9
  AND NEVER MERCY TO THY MERIT GIVES   1.22.12
  ONCE LET HER LOVE INDEED, OR ELS EYE ME NEVER   1.24.14
  YET NEVER ANY TRUE EFFECT I PROVE   1.25.4
  LONG ARE THEIR NIGHTS WHOSE CARES DO NEVER SLEEPE   1.26.5
  AND THERE PREPARE HER FLOWRES THAT NEVER FADES   1.30.7
  MY LIFE NOR DEATH SHAL NEVER BE HER BLOT   1.30.12
  TH'$ELISIAN GHOSTS SHALL NEVER KNOW THE SAME   1.30.14
  LADIES AND $TYRANTS, NEVER LAWES RESPECT   1.31.12
  I WHO DID NEVER JOY IN OTHER $SUN   1.33.5
  SUFFICE THAT HIGH ATTEMPTS HAVE NEVER SHAME   1.35.9
  WHEN DARKE SHALL SEEME THY DAY THAT NEVER CLEARES   1.42.3
  HE NEVER HAD MORE FAITH, ALTHOUGH MORE RIME   1.43.7
  ALTHOUGH MY CAREFULL ACCENTS NEVER MOOV'D THEE   1.44.13
  YET NEVER FOUND THAT BARBAROUS HAND ATTAIND   1.45.5
  THAT HAND THAT DARTS SO RIGHT AND NEVER MISSES   1.46.10
  THAT NEVER FALL TO EBBE, BUT EVER RISE   1.48.3
  FOR TO THEIR FLOW SHE NEVER GRANTS AN END   1.48.4
  TH'$OCEAN NEVER DID ATTEND MORE DULY   1.48.5
  AND STRAIGHT TIS GONE AS IT HAD NEVER BEENE   1.50.4
  NEVER LET RISING $SUNNE APPROVE YOU LIERS   1.54.11
  AND NEVER WAKE TO FEELE THE DAYES DISDAINE   1.54.14
  SINCE $YOU ONE WERE, I NEVER SINCE WAS ONE   2.11.3
  NOR WHILST THE $WORLD IS, NEVER SHALL BE DONE   2.13.11
  THAT BEING CHID, DID NEVER WORD REPLIE   2.15.10
  NOR NEVER STOOD ONE WORD THEREOF TO BLOT   2.21.7
  I $EVER LOVE, WHERE NEVER $HOPE APPEARES   2.26.1
  TOYLING WITH $PAINE, MY $LABOUR NEVER CEASETH   2.40.7
  THAT NEVER LEARN'D WHAT $CONSTELLATIONS ARE   2.43.7
  WHICH NEVER FELT'ST MY FIERIE TOUCH OF $LOVE   2.49.4
  WITH SO PURE $LOVE, AS $TIME COULD NEVER BOAST   2.54.8
  TILL THEY RETURN'D.. $HOME WHEN THEY NEVER CAME   2.58.6
  WITH SO PURE LOVE AS TYME COULD NEVER BOAST   2.101.8
  ATTENDS THAT $LAMPE WITH EYE WHICH NEVER
                           SLEEPETH   2.105.10

```
SHE WAS, THE LIKE THAT NEVER WAS, NOR
                      NEVER MORE SHALBE              2.107.14
SHE WAS, THE LIKE THAT NEVER WAS, NOR
                      NEVER MORE SHALBE              2.107.14
NOR WHILST THE WORLD IS, NEVER SHALL BE DONE        2.121.11
YET THERE HE BURNES, IN FIRE THATS NEVER
                      QUENCHED                       2.122.14
WHO WRITES MY $MISTRES PRAISE, CAN NEVER
                      WRITE AMISSE                   2.128.14
O CLEEREST DAY-STARRE, NEVER MORE DECLYNING         2.129.8
ELS SENCELES LOVE COULD NEVER ONCE ENDITE           2.131.4
FROM THENCE (THEY VOW) THEY NEVER WILL DEPART       2.132.12
I $EVER LOVE, WHERE NEVER HOPE APPEARES             2.137.1
MY NEVER CERTAINE JOY, BREEDS EVER-CERTAINE
                      FEARES                         2.137.4
A LYFE, THAT NEVER JOYD BUT IN HER LOVE             2.138.9
DIE, DIE, MY SOULE, AND NEVER TASTE OF JOY          2.139.1
THAT YET THE WORLD UNWORTHY NEVER KNEWE             2.139.12
WHOSE PURE $IDEA NEVER TONGUE EXPREST               2.139.13
SO SHALL I BE, AS I HAD NEVER BEENE                 2.142.13
TOYLING WITH PAINE, MY LABOUR NEVER CEASETH         2.144.7
THAT THEREBY BEAUTIES $ROSE MIGHT NEVER DIE         3.1.2
FOR NEVER RESTING TIME LEADS $SUMMER ON             3.5.5
(A CLOSET NEVER PEARST WITH CHRISTALL EYES)         3.46.6
THAT HE SHALL NEVER CUT FROM MEMORY                 3.63.11
I NEVER SAW THAT YOU DID PAINTING NEED              3.83.1
BUT BEST IS BEST, IF NEVER INTERMIXT                3.101.8
TO ME FAIRE FRIEND YOU NEVER CAN BE OLD             3.104.1
WHICH THREE TILL NOW, NEVER KEPT SEATE IN ONE       3.105.14
O NEVER SAY THAT I WAS FALSE OF HEART               3.109.1
NEVER BELEEVE THOUGH IN MY NATURE RAIGN'D           3.109.9
MINE APPETITE I NEVER MORE WILL GRIN'DE             3.110.10
THAT LOOKES ON TEMPESTS AND IS NEVER SHAKEN         3.116.6
I NEVER WRIT, NOR NO MAN EVER LOVED                 3.116.14
WHILST IT HATH THOUGHT IT SELFE SO BLESSED
                      NEVER+                         3.119.6
OF THEE, THY RECORD NEVER CAN BE MIST               3.122.8
I GRAUNT I NEVER SAW A GODDESSE GOE                 3.130.11
BUT NEVER HEEDS THE FRUIT OF WRITER'S MIND          4.11.8
THE RAINES OF $LOVE I LOVE, THOUGH NEVER SLAKE      4.28.7
THAT NEVER I WITH CLOS'D-UP SENSE DO LIE            4.32.6
FOR THOUGH I NEVER SEE THEM, BUT STRAIGHT WAYES     4.42.9
OF $LOVERS NEVER KNOWNE, A GRIEVOUS CASE            4.45.6
IF HE WAITE WELL, I NEVER THENCE WOULD MOVE         4.59.3
I NEVER DRANKE OF $AGANIPPE WELL                    4.74.1
SO AMPLE EARES AS NEVER GOOD NEWES KNOW             4.78.13
I WILL BUT KISSE, I NEVER MORE WILL BITE            4.82.14
WAS NEVER IN THIS WORLD OUGHT WORTHY TRICE          5.5.13
DARK IS THE WORLD, WHERE YOUR LIGHT SHINED NEVER    5.8.13
NOR TO THE $MOONE.. FOR THEY ARE CHANGED NEVER      5.9.6
SUCH ART OF EYES I NEVER READ IN BOOKES             5.21.14
LYKE SACRED PRIESTS THAT NEVER THINKE AMISSE        5.22.8
I MUST BEGIN AND NEVER BRING TO END                 5.23.10
AND BE FORGOT AS IT HAD NEVER BEENE                 5.27.7
BUT WHAT THIS VERSE, THAT NEVER SHALL EXPYRE        5.27.11
OR SHALL THEIR RUTHLESSE TORMENT NEVER CEASE        5.36.2
O FAYREST FAYRE LET NEVER IT BE NAMED               5.41.13
THE WHICH THAT IT FROM HER MAY NEVER START          5.42.9
THEN NOT ON HIM THAT NEVER THOUGHT YOU ILL          5.49.7
SITH NEVER OUGHT WAS EXCELLENT ASSAYDE              5.51.7
```

```
    SO FIRMELY, THAT YE NEVER MAY REMOVE               5.71.8
    WHICH OFT I WISHT, YET NEVER WAS SO BLEST           5.76.14
    THE WHICH MY SELFE COULD NEVER YET ATTAYNE          5.84.10
NEVER-CERTAIN              1
    MY NEVER-CERTAINE $JOY BREEDS EVER-CERTAINE
                                $FEARES                 2.26.4
NEVER-ENDING              1
    AND TREADING IN THYS NEVER-ENDING MAZE              2.133.7
NEVER-HOPING              2
    YET $HOPE DRAWES ON MY NEVER-HOPING $CARE           2.26.2
    YET HOPE DRAWES ON MY NEVER-HOPING CARE             2.137.2
NEVER-RESTING             1
    THE NEVER-RESTING STONE CF $CARE TO ROULE           1.9.7
NEW                      48
    STILL NEW BORNE SORROWES OF HER FRESH DISDAINE      1.16.10
    THIS NEW RICH $NOVICE, LAVISH OF HIS CHEST          2.10.5
    THIS WERE TO BE NEW MADE WHEN THOU ART OULD         3.2.13
    DOTH HOMAGE TO HIS NEW APPEARING SIGHT              3.7.3
    AS HE TAKES FROM YCU, I INGRAFT YOU NEW             3.15.14
    MAKES BLACKE NIGHT BEAUTIOUS, AND HER
                                OLD FACE NEW            3.27.12
    AND WITH OLD WOES NEW WAILE MY DEARE TIMES WASTE    3.30.4
    WHICH I NEW PAY AS IF NCT PAYD BEFORE               3.30.12
    BY NEW UNFOULDING HIS IMPRISON'D PRIDE              3.52.12
    AND YOU IN $GRECIAN TIRES ARE PAINTED NEW           3.53.8
    WHICH PARTS THE SHCRE, WHERE TWO CONTRACTED NEW     3.56.10
    IF THEIR BEE NOTHING NEW, BUT THAT WHICH IS         3.59.1
    ROBBING NO OULD TO DRESSE HIS BEAUTY NEW            3.68.12
    WHY IS MY VERSE SO BARREN OF NEW PRIDE+             3.76.1
    TO NEW FOUND METHODS, AND TO COMPOUNDS STRANGE+     3.76.4
    SO ALL MY BEST IS DRESSING OLD WORDS NEW            3.76.11
    FOR AS THE $SUN IS DAILY NEW AND OLD                3.76.13
    TO TAKE A NEW ACQUAINTANCE OF THY MINDE             3.77.12
    MAY STILL SEEME LOVE TO ME, THOUGH ALTER'D NEW      3.93.3
    OUR LOVE WAS NEW, AND THEN BUT IN THE SPRING        3.102.5
    WHAT'S NEW TO SPEAKE, WHAT NOW TO REGISTER          3.108.3
    MADE OLD OFFENCES CF AFFECTIONS NEW                 3.110.4
    AND TOUGHT IT THUS A NEW TO GREETE                  3.145.8
    IN ACT THY BED-VOW BROAKE AND NEW FAITH TORNE       3.152.3
    IN VOWING NEW HATE AFTER NEW LOVE BEARING           3.152.4
    IN VOWING NEW HATE AFTER NEW LOVE BEARING           3.152.4
    BUT AT MY MISTRES EIE LCVES BRAND NEW FIRED         3.153.9
    WHERE $CUPID GOT NEW FIRE., MY MISTRES EYE          3.153.14
    ENNOBLING NEW FOUND $TROPES WITH PROBLEMES OLD      4.3.6
    IN HER SIGHT I A LESSON NEW HAVE SPELD              4.16.12
    AND STRAIGHT THEREWITH, LIKE WAGS NEW
                                GOT TO PLAY             4.17.13
    STELLA, WHENCE DOTH THIS NEW ASSAULT ARISE          4.36.1
    BUT WILT NEW WARRE UPON THINE OWNE BEGIN+           4.36.8
    THEN SERVANT'S WRACKE, WHERE NEW DOUBTS
                                HONOR BRINGS            4.45.11
    TO SUCH A SCHOOLE-MISTRESSE, WHOSE LESSONS NEW      4.46.10
    SO MAY YOU STILL HAVE SCMEWHAT NEW TO SAY           4.51.4
    THE NEW $PERNASSUS, WHERE THE $MUSES BIDE           4.80.5
    MAKE IN MY HEAVY MCULD NEW THOUGHTS TO GROW         4.106.11
    THAT BAD HIS FRIEND, BUT THEN NEW MAIM'D, TO BE     4.106.13
    NEW YEARE FORTH LCCKING CUT OF JANUS GATE           5.4.1
    DOTH SEEME TO PROMISE HCPE OF NEW DELIGHT           5.4.2
    PREPARE YOUR SELFE NEW LCVE TO ENTERTAINE           5.4.14
    SO HARD IT IS TO KINDLE NEW DESIRE                  5.6.9
```

```
I THINKE THAT I A NEW $PANDORA SEE              5.24.8
THE NEW BEGINS HIS COMPAST COURSE ANEW          5.62.2
THEN SHALL THE NEW YEARES JOY FORTH FRESHLY SEND  5.62.9
AND CHAUNGE OLD YEARES ANNOY TO NEW DELIGHT     5.62.14
AND GATHER TO MY SELFE NEW BREATH AWHILE        5.80.4
NEWBORN                      1
WITH NEW-BORNE SIGHES AND DENISEND WIT DO SING  4.15.8
NEW-COINED                   1
OF $LOVE, NEW-COIND TO HELPE MY BEGGERY         4.62.13
NEWER                        2
ON NEWER PROOFE, TO TRIE AN OLDER FRIEND        3.110.11
THY PYRAMYDS BUYLT UP WITH NEWER MIGHT          3.123.2
NEWFANGLED                   1
SOME IN THEIR GARMENTS THOUGH NEW-FANGLED ILL   3.91.3
NEW-FOUND                    1
OR GEMMES, OR FRUTES OF NEW-FOUND $PARADISE     4.81.2
NEWLY                        1
HER LOVELY EYES LYKE $PINCKS BUT NEWLY SPRED    5.64.8
NEW-MOON                     1
WHETHER THE $TURKISH NEW-MOONE MINDED BE        4.30.1
NEWS                         2
NO NEWES BUT HEALTH FROM THEIR $PHISITIONS KNOW 3.140.8
SO AMPLE EARES AS NEVER GOOD NEWES KNOW         4.78.13
NEXT                         5
YET SERVES NOT $THIS.. WHAT NEXT, WHAT
                    OTHER $SHIFT+               2.19.9
MY CONSONANTS THE NEXT WHEN I HAD DONE          2.111.7
THEN GIVE ME WELCOME, NEXT MY HEAVEN THE BEST   3.110.13
AND MY NEXT SELFE THOU HARDER HAST INGROSSED    3.133.6
THINKING TO QUENCH HER THIRST AT THE NEXT BROOKE  5.67.8
NICE                         1
THE $MUSES NICE, THE $FURIES CRUELL BE          2.118.7
NIGGARD                      2
THEN BEAUTIOUS NIGARD WHY DOOST THOU ABUSE        3.4.5
THEN NIGARD TRUTH WOULD WILLINGLY IMPART         3.72.8
NIGGARDING                   1
AND TENDER CHORLE MAKST WAST IN NIGGARDING       3.1.12
NIGGARDLY                    1
O, $WHY SHOULD $NATURE NIGGARDLY RESTRAINE       2.25.1
NIGHT                       69
THOU POWRE THAT RUL'ST THE CONFINES OF THE NIGHT  1.10.5
IMBRACING CLOUDS BY NIGHT, IN DAY TIME MOURNE    1.16.2
THAT THUS I LIVE BOTH DAY AND NIGHT ANNOYD       1.26.8
MY CARES DRAW ON MINE EVERLASTING NIGHT          1.30.1
AND ($DELIA) THINKE THY MORNING MUST HAVE NIGHT  1.40.8
CARE-CHARMER $SLEEPE, SCNNE OF THE SABLE NIGHT   1.54.1
WHEN NOW THE $NIGHT DOTH SUMMON ALL TO SLEEPE+   2.37.2
NIGHT WAS ORDAYN'D, TOGETHER $FRIENDS TO KEEPE   2.37.4
AND EACH RETURNES UNTO HIS $LOVE AT $NIGHT+      2.37.8
WHY SHOULD'ST THOU, $NIGHT, ABUSE ME ONELY THUS  2.37.10
IF WHEN $NIGHT COMES, YOU BID ME GOE AWAY        2.37.14
WHERE BLESSED $ANGELS SINGING DAY AND NIGHT      2.105.13
WHILST $MOONE SHALL SHYNE BY NIGHT, OR
                    ANY FIRE SHALL BURNE         2.121.12
BLACKE PYTCHY $NIGHT, COMPANYON OF MY WOE        2.145.1
AND OF JUST LENGTH OUR NIGHT AND DAY DOTH MAKE   2.147.3
AND SEE THE BRAVE DAY SUNCK IN HIDIOUS NIGHT     3.12.2
TO CHANGE YOUR DAY OF YOUTH TO SULLIED NIGHT     3.15.12
WHICH LIKE A JEWELL (HUNGE IN GASTLY NIGHT)      3.27.11
MAKES BLACKE NIGHT BEAUTIOUS, AND HER
                    OLD FACE NEW                 3.27.12
```

```
LOE THUS BY DAY MY LIMS, BY NIGHT MY MIND          3.27.13
WHEN DAIES OPPRESSION IS NOT EAZD BY NIGHT         3.28.3
BUT DAY BY NIGHT AND NIGHT BY DAY OPREST           3.28.4
BUT DAY BY NIGHT AND NIGHT BY DAY OPREST           3.28.4
SO FLATTER I THE SWART COMPLEXIOND NIGHT           3.28.11
AND NIGHT DOTH NIGHTLY MAKE GREEFES LENGTH
                        SEEME STRONGER             3.28.14
FOR PRECIOUS FRIENDS HID IN DEATHS DATELES NIGHT   3.30.6
WHEN IN DEAD NIGHT THEIR FAIRE IMPERFECT SHADE     3.43.11
MY HEAVY EIELIDS TO THE WEARY NIGHT+               3.61.2
HATH TRAVAILD ON TO $AGES STEEPIE NIGHT            3.63.5
WHICH BY AND BY BLACKE NIGHT DOTH TAKE AWAY        3.73.7
NO, NEITHER HE, NOR HIS COMPIERS BY NIGHT          3.86.7
GIVE NOT A WINDY NIGHT A RAINIE MORROW             3.90.7
THEN WHEN HER MOURNEFULL HIMNS DID HUSH
                        THE NIGHT                  3.102.10
THE MOUNTAINE, OR THE SEA, THE DAY, OR NIGHT       3.113.11
O THAT OUR NIGHT OF WO MIGHT HAVE REMEMBRED        3.120.9
DOTH FOLLOW NIGHT WHO LIKE A FIEND                 3.145.11
WHO ART AS BLACK AS HELL, AS DARKE AS NIGHT        3.147.14
BUT FOR TO SPANGLE THE BLACKE WEEDS OF NIGHT       4.26.6
TILL NOW, WRAPT IN A MOST INFERNALL NIGHT          4.33.3
THIS NIGHT WHILE SLEEPE BEGINS WITH HEAVY WINGS    4.38.1
STOLNE TO MY HEART, SINCE LAST FAIRE NIGHT,
                        NAY DAY                     4.66.10
NOW THAT OF ABSENCE THE MOST IRKSOME NIGHT         4.89.1
LEAVING MY $HEMISPHERE, LEAVE ME IN NIGHT          4.89.4
EACH DAY SEEMES LONG, AND LONGS FOR LONG-STAID
                        NIGHT                       4.89.5
THE NIGHT AS TEDIOUS, WOOES TH'APPROCH OF DAY      4.89.6
LANGUISHT WITH HORRORS OF THE SILENT NIGHT         4.89.8
SUFFERING THE EVILS BOTH OF THE DAY AND NIGHT      4.89.9
WHILE NO NIGHT IS MORE DARKE THEN IS MY DAY        4.89.10
NOR NO DAY HATH LESSE QUIET THEN MY NIGHT          4.89.11
WITH SUCH BAD MIXTURE OF MY NIGHT AND DAY          4.89.12
THAT LIVING THUS IN BLACKEST WINTER NIGHT          4.89.13
WITH ABSENCE' $VAILE, I LIVE IN $SOROWE'S NIGHT    4.91.4
THOUGHT WITH GOOD CAUSE THOU LIKEST SO
                        WELL THE NIGHT             4.96.1
NIGHT BARD FROM $SUN, THOU FROM THY OWNE
                        SUNNE'S LIGHT              4.96.4
IN NIGHT OF SPRITES THE GASTLY POWERS STUR         4.96.10
DIAN THAT FAINE WOULD CHEARE HER FRIEND
                        THE $NIGHT                 4.97.1
BUT AH POORE $NIGHT, IN LOVE WITH $PHOEBUS' LIGHT  4.97.5
WHILE THE BLACKE HORRORS OF THE SILENT NIGHT       4.98.9
WHEN FAR SPENT NIGHT PERSWADES EACH MORTALL EYE    4.99.1
TAKES IN THAT SAD HUE, WHICH WITH TH'INWARD NIGHT  4.99.7
CURST BE THE NIGHT WHICH DID YOUR STRIFE RESIST    4.105.12
CLIPS STREIGHT MY WINGS, STREIGHT WRAPS
                        ME IN HIS NIGHT            4.108.8
AND CALLING FORTH OUT OF SAD $WINTERS NIGHT        5.4.5
NOT TO THE $SUN.. FOR THEY DOO SHINE BY NIGHT      5.9.5
ON WHICH MY THOUGHTS DOO DAY AND NIGHT ATTEND      5.22.7
THE SAME AT NIGHT SHE DID AGAINE UNREAVE           5.23.4
I WISH THAT NIGHT THE NOYOUS DAY WOULD END         5.87.6
AND WHEN AS NIGHT HATH US OF LIGHT FORLORNE        5.87.7
I WANDER AS IN DARKNESSE OF THE NIGHT              5.88.3
NIGHT-BIRDS                1
OF REASON, FROM WHOSE LIGHT THOSE NIGHT-BIRDS
                        FLIE                       4.71.7
```

NIGHTINGALES   2
  WHERE $NIGHTINGALES IN $ARDEN SIT AND SING   2.53.7
  WHERE $NIGHTINGALS IN $ARDEN SIT AND SING   2.113.7
NIGHTLY   4
  FILLING MINE $EARES WITH $NOISE, AND $NIGHTLY
                               GRONING   2.40.6
  FILLING MYNE EARES WITH NOYSE AND NIGHTLY
                               GRONING   2.144.6
  AND NIGHT DOTH NIGHTLY MAKE GREEFES LENGTH
                          SEEME STRONGER   3.28.14
  WHICH NIGHTLY GULLS HIM WITH INTELLIGENCE   3.86.10
NIGHTS   3
  LONG ARE THEIR NIGHTS WHOSE CARES DO NEVER SLEEPE   1.26.5
  ALL DAYES ARE NIGHTS TO SEE TILL I SEE THEE   3.43.13
  AND MANY NIGHTS, THAT SLOWLY SEEMD TO MOVE   5.87.3
NIGHT'S   5
  UPON HIS SOVEREIGNES COURSE, THE NIGHTS
                          PALE $QUEENE   1.48.6
  WITHOUT THE TORMENT OF THE NIGHTS UNTRUTH   1.54.8
  AND NIGHTS BRIGHT DAIES WHEN DREAMS DO
                        SHEW THEE ME   3.43.14
  THY TEARES EXPRESSE NIGHT'S NATIVE MOISTURE RIGHT   4.96.8
  BUT, BUT (ALAS) NIGHT'S SIDE THE ODS HATH FUR   4.96.12
NILE   1
  ONE, HE DOTH WONDER MONSTER-BREEDING $NYLE   2.120.3
NIMBLE   3
  FOR NIMBLE THOUGHT CAN JUMPE BOTH SEA AND LAND   3.44.7
  DO I ENVIE THOSE $JACKES THAT NIMBLE LEAPE   3.128.5
  SO NIMBLE FEET AS STIRRE STILL, THOUGH
                        ON THORNES   4.78.11
NINE   17
  TIS NINE YEERES NOW SINCE FIRST I LOST MY $WIT   2.9.11
  THREE $NINES THERE ARE, TO EVERY ONE A $NINE   2.18.2
  NINE ORDERS FIRST OF $ANGELS BE IN $HEAVEN   2.18.5
  NINE $MUSES DOE WITH $LEARNING STILL FREQUENT   2.18.6
  NINE WORTHIE $WOMEN TO THE $WORLD WERE GIVEN   2.18.8
  MY WORTHY, $ONE TO THESE $NINE $WORTHIES ADDETH   2.18.9
  AND MY FAIRE $MUSE, ONE $MUSE UNTO THE $NINE   2.18.10
  WITH ONE MORE $ORDER, THESE NINE $ORDERS
                        GLADDETH   2.18.12
  THREE NINES THERE ARE, TO EVERIE ONE A NINE   2.108.2
  NINE ORDERS FIRST OF $ANGELS BE IN HEAVEN   2.108.5
  NINE $MUSES DOE WITH LEARNING STILL FREQUENT   2.108.6
  NINE WORTHY MEN UNTO THE WORLD WERE GIVEN   2.108.8
  MY $WORTHIE, ONE TO THESE NINE $WORTHIES, ADDETH 2.108.9
  AND MY FAIRE $MUSE, ONE $MUSE UNTO THE NINE   2.108.10
  WITH ONE MORE ORDER, THESE NINE ORDERS GLADDETH 2.108.12
  THEN THOSE OLD NINE WHICH RIMERS INVOCATE   3.38.10
  LET DAINTIE WITS CRIE ON THE $SISTERS NINE   4.3.1
NINES   4
  THREE $NINES THERE ARE, TO EVERY ONE A $NINE   2.18.2
  MAKES EVERY $ONE OF THESE THREE $NINES A $TEN   2.18.14
  THREE NINES THERE ARE, TO EVERIE ONE A NINE   2.108.2
  MAKES EVERY ONE OF THESE THREE NINES A TEN   2.108.14
NIPPED   1
  AND FROST OF AGE HATH NIPT THY BEAUTIES NEERE   1.42.2
NIPPLES   1
  HER NIPPLES LYKE YONG BLOSSOMD $JESSEMYNES   5.64.12
NO   246
  FOR THAT NO COLOURS CAN DEPAINT MY SORROWES   1.4.6

```
NO $BAYES I SEEKE TC DECKE MY MOURNING BROW          1.4.9
MY LOVE AFFECTS NC FAME, NOR STEEMES OF $ART         1.4.14
FOR HER NO SOONER HAD MINE EYES BEWRAID              1.5.5
THEN HAD NO FINGER POINTED AT MY LIGHTNESSE          1.7.2
THEN HAD NO $CENSCRS EYE THESE LINES SURVAIC         1.7.5
NO $SUNNE MY BLUSH AND ERROR HAD BEWRAID             1.7.7
NO DOWNE-CAST LOOKE HAD SIGNIFIED MY MISSE           1.7.10
NO FAVOUR THOUGH, THE CRUELL FAIRE ALLOWES           1.11.12
AFFECT NO HONOR BUT WHAT SHE CAN GIVE                1.12.6
I WEIGH NO COMFORT UNLESSE SHE RELIEVE               1.12.8
FINDING NO END NOR PERICD OF MY PAINE                1.16.12
SO TRUE AND LOYALL LOVE NO FAVOUR GAINES ME          1.18.8
SHE YEELDS NO PLACE AT ALL FOR PITTIES DWELLING      1.18.12
HOW TO THINKE MUCH, AND HAVE NO WORDS TO SPEAKE      1.20.6
THAT PITTY SHINES NC COMFORT TO MY BLIS              1.21.2
BEING MERCILES LIKE THEE THAT NO MAN WEIES+          1.23.8
OFT WHEN I FINDE IN HER NO TRUTH AT ALL              1.25.5
LOTHSOME THEIR DAIES, WHCM NO SUN EVER JCYD          1.26.6
LOOKE TO THE HEAVENS., THE HEAVENS YEELDE
                         FORTH NO GRACE              1.29.6
WILL RISE NO MORE TC ME, WHOSE DAY IS DUNNE          1.30.4
NO PRIVILEDGE OF FAITH COULD IT PROTECT              1.31.5
WHEREIN NO SHEW GAVE CAUSE OF LEAST SUSPECT          1.31.7
YET NO MILD COMFORT WOULD THY $BROW REVEALE          1.31.9
NO LIGHTNING LOOKES WHICH FALLING HOPES ERECT        1.31.10
WITH STILL FRESH CARES, SUPPLIDE WITH NO RELIEFE     1.32.4
NO PITTYING EYE LCCKES BACKE UPON MY FEARES          1.32.10
NO SUCCOUR FINDE I NOW WHEN MOST I NEEDE             1.32.11
AND HAVE NO STARS BLT THOSE, THAT MUST FULFILL       1.33.6
AND THEREFORE $DELIA, TIS TO ME NO BLOT              1.35.13
NO SOONER SPREADS HER GLORY IN THE AYRE              1.39.5
NO $APRILL CAN REVIVE THY WITHERED FLOWRES           1.39.9
THOUGH THOU A $LAURA HAST NO $PETRARCH FOUND         1.43.3
YET COUNT IT NO DISGRACE THAT I HAVE LOV'C THEE      1.44.14
POORE SOULE QUITE SPENT, WHOSE FORCE CAN
                         DO NO MORE                  1.46.3
THAT THOU BE PLEAS'C, AND I MAY SIGH NO MORE         1.46.14
BUT AH- NO MORE, THIS MUST NOT BE FORETOLD           1.50.13
AND NO REMOVE CAN MAKE THY SORROWES LESSE+           1.52.4
FOR NO GROUND ELS CCULD MAKE THE MUSICKE SUCH        1.57.13
NO, NO, MY $VERSE RESPECTS NOT $THAMES
                         NOR $THEATERS               1.58.9
NO, NO, MY $VERSE RESPECTS NOT $THAMES
                         NOR $THEATERS               1.58.9
NO CTHER PROUDER $BROOKES SHALL HEARE MY WRONG       1.58.14
WHAT THOUGH MY $MLSE NO HONOR GET THEREBY            1.59.13
I SAY NO MORE, I FEARE I SAYD TOO MUCH               1.60.14
SINCE, BUT YOUR SELFE, THERE WAS NO $CREATURE BY     2.2.3
BUT $0, SEE, SEE, WE NEED INQUIRE NO FURTHER         2.2.9
NOTHING BUT $NO AND I, AND I AND $NO                 2.5.1
NOTHING BUT $NO AND I, AND I AND $NO                 2.5.1
WITH THIS AFFIRMING $NO, DENYING I                   2.5.4
I SAY, $YOU $LOVE, YOU PEULE ME OUT A $NC            2.5.6
SAVE MEE I $CRIE, YCU SIGH ME OUT A $NO              2.5.8
MUST $WOE AND I, HAVE NAUGHT BUT $NO AND I+          2.5.9
NO I, AM I, IF I NC MORE CAN HAVE                    2.5.10
NO I, AM I, IF I NC MORE CAN HAVE                    2.5.10
ANSWERE NO MORE, WITH $SILENCE MAKE REPLY            2.5.11
LET $NO AND I, WITH I AND YOU BE SO                  2.5.13
THEN ANSWERE $NO AND I, AND I AND $NO                2.5.14
```

THEN ANSWERE $NO AND I, AND I AND $NO	2.5.14
SHALL BE FORGOTTEN, WHOM NO $POET SINGS	2.6.3
NO OTHER $DRINKE WOULD SERVE THIS $GLUTTONS TURNE	2.7.5
NO WISER I, THEN WHEN AS YOUNG AS HE	2.22.10
NO MARVELL THEN THOUGH $CHARITIE GROW COLD	2.23.14
WHICH MIGHT BE BORROW'D FROM NO $EARTHLY FLAME	2.30.2
I FEARE NO CENSURE, NOR WHAT THOU CANST SAY	2.31.5
UP, TO MY $PITCH, NO COMMON $JUDGEMENT FLYES	2.31.13
THAT THIS TO ME DOTH YET NO WONDER PROVE	2.34.14
LONG SINCE DEPARTED (TO THE $WORLD NO MORE)	2.46.10
TH'ANCIENT $WOUNDS NO LONGER CAN CONTAINE	2.46.11
NO PUBLIKE $GLORIE VAINELY I PURSUE	2.47.13
IF IT WERE OF THAT $KINGLY KIND, OR NO	2.56.4
BUT IT NO SOONER SAW MY $SUNNE APPEARE	2.56.5
FROM THE STRONG $SPIRIT BY NO MEANES FORCE	
THE SAME	2.58.8
IN $LOVE THERE IS NO LACK, THUS I BEGIN	2.59.3
SINCE THER'S NO HELPE, $COME LET US KISSE	
AND PART	2.61.1
NAY, I HAVE DONE.. $YOU GET NO MORE OF $ME	2.61.2
OR IF NO THING BUT $DEATH WILL SERVE THY TURNE	2.63.9
IF THEY WERE OF THE $EAGLES KINDE OR NO	2.103.4
BUT THEY NO SOONER SAW MY $SUNNE APPEARE	2.103.5
NO $VIRGINE ONCE ATTENDING ON THAT LIGHT	2.105.3
POORE $BROOKES AND $BANKS HAD NO SUCH	
WONDERS BEENE	2.120.14
NO CLOWDE WAS SEENE, BUT CHRISTALINE THE AYRE	2.125.13
NO MORE SHALT THOU NOR $SAINT NOR $IDOLL BE	2.126.2
NO $GOD ART THOU, A $GODDESSE SHEE DOTH PROVE	2.126.3
FAIRE-MAYD NO MORE, BUT $MAYR-MAID BE THY NAME	2.130.9
OUR $LAWES ALOW NO $LAND TO BASTERDY	2.140.11
A HEAVEN ON EARTH, ON EARTH NO HEAVEN BUT THIS	2.151.14
NOR IT NOR NOE REMEMBRANCE WHAT IT WAS	3.5.12
THAT THOU NO FORME OF THEE HAST LEFT BEHIND	3.9.6
NO LOVE TOWARD OTHERS IN THAT BOSOME SITS	3.9.13
NO LONGER YOURS, THEN YOU YOUR SELFE HERE LIVE	3.13.2
FIND NO DETERMINATION, THEN YOU WERE	3.13.6
NOR DRAW NOE LINES THERE WITH THINE ANTIQUE PEN	3.19.10
FOR THEE, AND FOR MY SELFE, NOE QUIET FINDE	3.27.14
YET HIM FOR THIS, MY LOVE NO WHIT DISDAINETH	3.33.13
FOR NO MAN WELL OF SUCH A SALVE CAN SPEAKE	3.34.7
NO MORE BEE GREEV'D AT THAT WHICH THOU HAST DONE	3.35.1
NO LOVE, MY LOVE, THAT THOU MAIST TRUE LOVE CALL	3.40.3
NO MATTER THEN ALTHOUGH MY FOOTE DID STAND	3.44.5
THIS TOLD, I JOY, BUT THEN NO LONGER GLAD	3.45.13
SINCE WHY TO LOVE, I CAN ALLEDGE NO CAUSE	3.49.14
TILL I RETURNE OF POSTING IS NOE NEED	3.51.4
IN WINGED SPEED NO MOTION SHALL I KNOW	3.51.8
THEN CAN NO HORSE WITH MY DESIRE KEEPE PACE	3.51.9
SHALL NAIGH NOE DULL FLESH IN HIS FIERY RACE	3.51.11
I HAVE NO PRECIOUS TIME AT AL TO SPEND	3.57.3
(THOUGH YOU DOE ANY THING) HE THINKES NO ILL	3.57.14
O NO, THY LOVE THOUGH MUCH, IS NOT SO GREAT	3.61.9
AND FOR THIS SINNE THERE IS NO REMEDIE	3.62.3
ME THINKES NO FACE SO GRATIOUS IS AS MINE	3.62.5
NO SHAPE SO TRUE, NO TRUTH OF SUCH ACCOUNT	3.62.6
NO SHAPE SO TRUE, NO TRUTH OF SUCH ACCOUNT	3.62.6
WHOSE ACTION IS NO STRONGER THEN A FLOWER+	3.65.4
FOR SHE HATH NO EXCHECKER NOW BUT HIS	3.67.11
MAKING NO SUMMER OF AN OTHERS GREENE	3.68.11

```
ROBBING NO OULD TO DRESSE HIS BEAUTY NEW            3.68.12
NOE $LONGER MOURNE FOR ME WHEN I AM DEAD            3.71.1
AND LIVE NO MORE TO SHAME NOR ME, NOR YOU           3.72.12
POSSESSING OR PURSUING NO DELIGHT                   3.75.11
NO PRAISE TO THEE, BUT WHAT IN THEE DOTH LIVE       3.79.12
AND THEREFORE TO YOUR FAIRE NO PAINTING SET         3.83.2
NO, NEITHER HE, NOR HIS COMPIERS BY NIGHT           3.86.7
IN SLEEPE A $KING, BUT WAKING NO SUCH MATTER        3.87.14
AGAINST THY REASONS MAKING NO DEFENCE               3.89.4
THY SWEET BELOVED NAME NO MORE SHALL DWELL          3.89.10
AND LIFE NO LONGER THEN THY LOVE WILL STAY          3.92.3
BUT WHATS SO BLESSED FAIRE THAT FEARES NO BLOT      3.92.13
FOR THEIR CAN LIVE NO HATRED IN THINE EYE           3.93.5
TRUTH NEEDS NO COLLOUR WITH HIS COLLOUR FIXT        3.101.6
BEAUTIE NO PENSELL, BEAUTIES TRUTH TO LAY           3.101.7
BECAUSE HE NEEDS NO PRAISE, WILT THOU BE DUMB+      3.101.9
OH BLAME ME NOT IF I NO MORE CAN WRITE              3.103.5
FOR TO NO OTHER PASSE MY VERSES TEND                3.103.11
STEALE FROM HIS FIGURE, AND NO PACE PERCEIV'D       3.104.10
COUNTING NO OLD THING OLD, THOU MINE, I THINE       3.108.7
NOW ALL IS DONE, HAVE WHAT SHALL HAVE NO END        3.110.9
NO BITTERNESSE THAT I WILL BITTER THINKE            3.111.11
FOR IT NO FORME DELIVERS TO THE HEART               3.113.5
OF HIS QUICK OBJECTS HATH THE MINDE NO PART         3.113.7
YET THEN MY JUDGEMENT KNEW NO REASON WHY            3.115.3
O NO, IT IS AN EVER FIXED MARKE                     3.116.5
I NEVER WRIT, NOR NO MAN EVER LOVED                 3.116.14
AND I A TYRANT HAVE NO LEASURE TAKEN                3.120.7
NOE, I AM THAT I AM, AND THEY THAT LEVELL           3.121.9
NO- $TIME, THOU SHALT NOT BOST THAT I DOE CHANGE    3.123.1
NO IT WAS BUYLDED FAR FROM ACCIDENT                 3.124.5
NOE, LET ME BE OBSEQUIOUS IN THY HEART              3.125.9
WHICH IS NOT MIXT WITH SECONDS, KNOWS NO ART        3.125.11
SWEET BEAUTY HATH NO NAME NO HOLY BOURE             3.127.7
SWEET BEAUTY HATH NO NAME NO HOLY BOURE             3.127.7
AT SUCH WHO NOT BORNE FAIRE NO BEAUTY LACK          3.127.11
INJOYD NO SOONER BUT DISPISED STRAIGHT              3.129.5
PAST REASON HUNTED, AND NO SOONER HAD               3.129.6
BUT NO SUCH $ROSES SEE I IN HER CHEEKES             3.130.6
AND IN MY WILL NO FAIRE ACCEPTANCE SHINE            3.135.8
LET NO UNKINDE, NO FAIRE BESEECHERS KILL            3.135.13
LET NO UNKINDE, NO FAIRE BESEECHERS KILL            3.135.13
NO NEWES BUT HEALTH FROM THEIR $PHISITIONS KNOW     3.140.8
WITHIN BE FED, WITHOUT BE RICH NO MORE              3.146.12
AND DEATH ONCE DEAD, THER'S NO MORE DYING THEN      3.146.14
WHICH HAVE NO CORRESPONDENCE WITH TRUE SIGHT        3.148.2
LOVES EYE IS NOT SO TRUE AS ALL MENS.. NO           3.148.8
NO MARVAILE THEN THOUGH I MISTAKE MY VIEW           3.148.11
TRIUMPH IN LOVE, FLESH STAIES NO FARTHER REASON     3.151.8
NO WANT OF CONSCIENCE HOLD IT THAT I CALL           3.151.13
BUT FOUND NO CURE, THE BATH FOR MY HELPE LIES       3.153.13
FOR ME IN SOOTH, NO $MUSE BUT ONE I KNOW            4.3.9
LEAST IF NO VAILE THOSE BRAVE GLEAMES DID DISGUISE  4.7.7
IS NO FIT MARKE TO PIERCE WITH HIS FINE
                          POINTED DART              4.8.3
O NO, HER HEART IS SUCH A $CITTADELL                4.12.12
AND WHICH IS WORSE, NO GOOD EXCUSE CAN SHOW         4.18.7
I SEE AND YET NO GREATER SOROW TAKE                 4.18.13
THEN THAT I LOSE NO MORE FOR $STELLA'S SAKE         4.18.14
SO $TYRAN HE NO FITTER PLACE COULD SPIE             4.20.5
```

```
HAVING NO SCARFE OF CLOWDS BEFORE HIS FACE        4.22.3
TO HAVE FOR NO CAUSE BIRTHRIGHT IN THE SKIE       4.26.5
I BEG NO SUBJECT TO USE ELOQUENCE                 4.28.9
LOOKE AT MY HANDS FOR NO SUCH QUINTESSENCE        4.28.11
'FOOLE,' ANSWERS HE, 'NO $INDES SUCH TREASURES
                                           HOLD   4.32.12
NO LOVELY $PARIS MADE THY $HELLEN HIS             4.33.6
NO FORCE, NO FRAUD, ROBD THEE OF THY DELIGHT      4.33.7
NO FORCE, NO FRAUD, ROBD THEE OF THY DELIGHT      4.33.7
HATH NO MISFORTUNE, BUT THAT $RICH SHE IS         4.37.14
WHERE WELL HE KNOWES, NO MAN TO HIM CAN COME      4.43.14
HER HEART, SWEETE HEART, IS OF NO $TYGRE'S KIND   4.44.4
AND YET SHE HEARES, YET I NO PITTY FIND           4.44.5
I MUCH DO GUESSE, YET FIND NO TRUTH SAVE THIS     4.44.9
MAY GET NO ALMES BUT SCORNE OF BEGGERIE           4.47.8
BY NO PRETENCE CLAIME ANY MANER PLACE             4.52.11
'WHAT NOW SIR FOOLE,' SAID HE, 'I WOULD NO LESSE  4.53.7
HE CANNOT LOVE.. NO, NO, LET HIM ALONE'           4.54.8
HE CANNOT LOVE.. NO, NO, LET HIM ALONE'           4.54.8
BUT NOW I MEANE NO MORE YOUR HELPE TO TRIE        4.55.9
THAT I WELL FIND NO ELOQUENCE LIKE IT             4.55.14
NO $PATIENCE, IF THOU WILT MY GOOD, THEN MAKE     4.56.12
THAT NO PACE ELSE THEIR GUIDED STEPS CAN FIND     4.58.3
LEAST ONCE SHOULD NOT BE HEARD, TWISE
                             SAID, $NO, $NO       4.63.8
LEAST ONCE SHOULD NOT BE HEARD, TWISE
                             SAID, $NO, $NO       4.63.8
NO MORE, MY DEARE, NO MORE THESE COUNSELS TRIE    4.64.1
NO MORE, MY DEARE, NO MORE THESE COUNSELS TRIE    4.64.1
LET ME NO STEPS BUT OF LOST LABOUR TRACE          4.64.6
THAT GIV'ST NO BETTER EARE TO MY JUST CRIES       4.65.2
FOR WHEN, NAK'D BOY, THOU COULDST NO HARBOUR FIND 4.65.5
MY WEALTH NO MORE, AND NO WHIT LESSE MY NEED      4.66.7
MY WEALTH NO MORE, AND NO WHIT LESSE MY NEED      4.66.7
NO KINGS BE CROWN'D BUT THEY SOME COVENANTS MAKE  4.69.14
I MUST NO MORE IN THY SWEET PASSIONS LIE          4.72.7
BUT NO SCUSE SERVES, SHE MAKES HER WRATH APPEARE  4.73.9
I AM NO PICK-PURSE OF ANOTHER'S WIT               4.74.8
GUESSE WE THE CAUSE.. '$WHAT, IS IT THUS+'
                                         $FIE NO  4.74.12
NO WIND, NO SHADE CAN COOLE, WHAT HELPE
                             THEN IN MY CASE      4.76.12
NO WIND, NO SHADE CAN COOLE, WHAT HELPE
                             THEN IN MY CASE      4.76.12
THAT IN NO MORE BUT THESE I MIGHT BE FULLY BLEST  4.77.13
AND NO SPURRE CAN HIS RESTY RACE RENEW            4.80.12
BY NO ENCROCHMENT WRONGD, NOR TIME FORGOT         4.84.10
AND THAT YOU KNOW, I ENVY YOU NO LOT              4.84.12
NO DOOME SHOULD MAKE ONE'S HEAV'N BECOME
                                      HIS HELL    4.86.14
WHILE NO NIGHT IS MORE DARKE THEN IS MY DAY       4.89.10
NOR NO DAY HATH LESSE QUIET THEN MY NIGHT         4.89.11
NOT THEM, O NO, BUT YOU IN THEM I LOVE            4.91.14
FROM CARELESNESSE DID IN NO MANER GROW            4.93.7
FAINT COWARD JOY NO LONGER TARRY DARE             4.95.5
HER SELFE (TO SHEW NO OTHER JOY HATH PLACE)       4.97.7
O TEARES, NO TEARES, BUT RAINE FROM BEAUTIE'S
                                        SKIES     4.100.1
SUCH TEARES, SIGHS, PLAINTS, NO SORROW
                             IS, BUT JOY          4.100.12
```

```
WITH NO WORSE CURSE THEN ABSENCE MAKES ME TAST      4.105.14
BASE THING I CAN NC MORE ENDURE TO VIEW                5.3.6
NO EIES BUT JOYES, IN WHICH AL POWERS CONSPIRE         5.8.3
BUT MINE NO PRICE NCR PRAYER MAY SURCEASE             5.11.14
NO WORD WAS HEARD CF HER THAT MOST IT OUGHT           5.19.10
AND KNOW NO END OF HER CWNE MYSERY                     5.25.2
FAIRE BE NO LENGER PROUD OF THAT SHALL PERISH         5.27.13
THEN FLY NO MORE FAYRE LCVE FROM $PHEBUS CHACE        5.28.13
WITH NO CONTENTMENT CAN THEMSELVES SUFFIZE            5.35.3
AND CAN NO MORE ENCURE CN THEM TO LOOKE               5.35.12
IS THERE NO MEANES FOR ME TO PURCHACE PEACE            5.36.5
OUT OF HER BANDS YE BY NC MEANES SHALL GET            5.37.12
AND FEELING THENCE NO MCRE HER SOROWES SADNESSE       5.39.11
NO SKILL CAN STINT NOR REASON CAN ASLAKE              5.44.8
THERE LET NO THOUGHT OF JOY OR PLEASURE VAINE          5.52.9
AND THEN NO MERCY WILL UNTO ME SHEW                    5.53.8
SHE IS NO WOMAN, BUT A SENCELESSE STONE               5.54.14
WHICH I NO LENGER CAN ENDURE TO SUE                    5.57.3
THE GENTLE BIRDE FEELES NO CAPTIVITY                   5.65.7
WITH NO CONTENTMENT CAN THEMSELVES SUFFIZE            5.83.3
AND CAN NO MORE ENCURE CN THEM TO LOOKE               5.83.12
BUT SPEAKE NO WORD TO HER OF THESE SAD PLIGHTS        5.84.11
```

NOBLE   2
```
SEEKING TO QUENCH IN ME THE NOBLE FIRE                 4.68.7
WHEN THOSE RENOUMED NOBLE $PERES OF $GREECE            5.44.1
```

NOBLENESS   1
```
THAT $NOBLENESSE IT SELFE MAKES THUS UNKIND+           4.44.8
```

NOBLER   5
```
MY NOBLER PART TO MY GRCSE BODIES TREASON             3.151.6
NOBLER DESIRES, LEAST ELSE THAT FRIENDLY FOE           4.21.7
FROM NOBLER COURSE, FIT FOR MY BIRTH AND MINC          4.62.8
O BLISSE, FIT FOR A NOBLER STATE THEN ME               4.69.2
TEACHING DUMBE LIPS A NCBLER EXERCISE                  4.81.4
```

NOBLEST   1
```
YET NOBLEST $CONQUERORS DO WRECKES AVOID              4.40.11
```

NOISE   4
```
FILLING MINE $EARES WITH $NOISE, AND $NIGHTLY
                    GRONING                            2.40.6
FILLING MYNE EARES WITH NOYSE AND NIGHTLY
                    GRONING                           2.144.6
A CHAMBER DEAFE TC NOISE, AND BLIND TO LIGHT          4.39.10
WITH NOYSE WHEREOF THE QUYRE OF $BYRDS RESOUNDED       5.19.5
```

NOISOME   1
```
FROM OUT THAT NOYSCME GULFE, WHICH GAPING LIES         4.78.3
```

NONE   36
```
AH YOU, AND NONE BUT YOU MY SORROWES REACE             1.3.11
MY $MUSE HAD SLEPT, AND NONE HAD KNOWNE MY MINDE       1.6.14
STILL TO COMPLAINE MY GRIEFES, WHILST NONE RELIEVE     1.9.8
NONE OTHER FAME MINE UNAMBITIOUS $MUSE                  1.58.1
MY $HEART WAS SLAINE, AND NONE BUT YOU AND I           2.2.1
NONE LIKE TO THAT, NONE LIKE TO YOU IS FCUND           2.16.4
NONE LIKE TO THAT, NONE LIKE TO YOU IS FCUND           2.16.4
LIKE THEY THAT $LUST, I CARE NOT, I WILL NONE          2.39.8
TO TAKE ALL $MINE, AND GIVE ME NONE AGAINE+            2.52.2
WHAT TALKE I OF A $HEART, WHEN THOU HAST NONE+        2.52.13
SINGS THIS TO THEE THOU SINGLE WILT PROVE NONE         3.8.14
BUT THAT THOU NONE LOV'ST IS MOST EVIDENT              3.10.4
O NONE BUT UNTHRIFTS, DEARE MY LOVE YOU KNOW          3.13.13
BUT YOU LIKE NONE, NONE YOU FOR CONSTANT HEART        3.53.14
BUT YOU LIKE NONE, NONE YOU FOR CONSTANT HEART        3.53.14
```

```
O NONE, UNLESSE THIS MIRACLE HAVE MIGHT              3.65.13
WHEN YELLOW LEAVES, OR NONE, OR FEW DOE HANGE        3.73.2
THEY THAT HAVE POWRE TO HURT, AND WILL DCE NONE      3.94.1
MORE FLOWERS I NOTED, YET I NONE COULD SEE           3.99.14
NONE ELSE TO ME, NOR I TO NONE ALIVE                 3.112.7
NONE ELSE TO ME, NOR I TO NONE ALIVE                 3.112.7
ALL THIS THE WORLD WELL KNOWES YET NONE
                             KNOWES WELL             3.129.13
AMONG A NUMBER ONE IS RECKON'D NONE                  3.136.8
THAT FROM HER LOCKES, THY DAY-NETS, NONE
                             SCAPES FREE             4.12.2
THEN BE THEY CLOSE, AND SO NONE SHALL DISPLEASE      4.34.8
THAT HAST MY MIND, NONE CF THE BASEST, BROUGHT       4.40.3
AS I MAY WELL RECCUNT, BUT NONE CAN PRIZE            4.65.4
WHOM IF YE PLEASE, I CARE FOR OTHER NONE             5.1.14
FAYRER THEN FAYREST LET NONE EVER SAY                5.20.13
HER GLORIES PRIDE THAT NONE MAY IT REPAYRE           5.58.8
NE NONE SO RICH OR WISE, SO STRONG OR FAYRE          5.58.9
NE BUT IN HEAVEN MATCHABLE TO NONE                   5.66.7
FOR NONE CAN CALL AGAINE THE PASSED TIME             5.70.14
HART NEED NOT WISH NONE CTHER HAPPINESSE             5.72.13
MY HART, WHOM NONE WITH SERVILE BANDS CAN TYE        5.73.2
THAT MANY SOUGHT YET NONE COULD EVER TASTE           5.77.10
NOON                    2
SO THOU, THY SELFE CUT-GCING IN THY NOON             3.7.13
BUT LO, WHILE I DC SPEAKE, IT GROWETH
                             NOONE WITH ME           4.76.9
NORTH                   5
MY JOYFULL $NORTH, WHERE ALL MY FORTUNE LIES         1.53.3
FLORISH FAIRE $ALBICN, GLORY OF THE $NORTH           1.53.9
WHEN $EAST, WHEN $WEST, WHEN $SOUTH, AND
                             WHEN BY $NORTH          2.1.7
THERE LET MY $VERSE GET GLORY IN THE $NORTH          2.25.7
BUT FINDING THESE $NORTH CLYMES DO COLDLY
                             HIM EMBRACE             4.8.5
NORTHERN                1
OUR $NORTHERNE $BCRDERS BOAST OF $TWEEDS
                             FAIRE $FLOUD           2.32.10
NOSE                    1
THAT WHEN THOU FEED'ST, THY $NOSE SHALL
                             TOUCH THY $CHINNE      2.8.12
NOTE                    6
CLEERE-SIGHTED YOU, SOONE NOTE WHAT IS AWRIE         1.3.7
NOTE BUT MY $SIGHES, AND THINE $EYES SHALL BEHOLD    2.55.5
NOTE BUT MY SIGHES, AND THINE EYES SHAL BEHOLD       2.102.5
WHO ALL IN ONE, ONE PLEASING NOTE DO SING            3.8.12
FOR THEY IN THEE A THOUSAND ERRORS NOTE              3.141.2
BEGIN HIS WITLESSE NOTE APACE TO CLATTER             5.85.4
NOTED                   2
AND KEEPE INVENTICN IN A NOTED WEED                  3.76.6
MORE FLOWERS I NOTED, YET I NONE COULD SEE           3.99.14
NOTES                   5
MY PLEASURES HORROR, $MUSICKE TRAGICKE NCTES         1.9.11
THESE SAD NEGLECTEC NOTES FOR HER DEARE SAKE+        1.17.2
WHAT BLUSHING NOTES DOEST THOU IN MARGINE SEE+       4.67.8
IN WELL RAISDE NOTES, MY PEN THE BEST IT MAY         4.70.10
YOUR MORALL NOTES STRAIGHT MY HID MEANING TEARE      4.104.12
NOTHERN                 1
OUR $NORTHERN BORDERS BCAST OF $TWEEDS
                             FAIRE FLOOD            2.124.10
```

NOTHING   33
    NOTHING BUT $NO AND I, AND I AND $NO   2.5.1
    WHEN NOTHING ELSE REMAYNETH OF THESE DAYES   2.6.6
    THERE'S NOTHING GRIEVES ME, BUT THAT $AGE
                          SHOULD HASTE   2.8.1
    TO $NOTHING FITTER CAN I $THEE COMPARE   2.10.1
    SINCE TO OBTAINE THEE, NOTHING ME WILL STED   2.15.1
    WHICH YEELDS THEM NOTHING, AT THE EASIEST RATE   2.28.7
    AS THOUGH TO ME IT NOTHING DID BELONG   2.47.12
    NATURES BEQUEST GIVES NOTHING BUT DOTH LEND   3.4.3
    AND NOTHING GAINST $TIMES SIETH CAN MAKE DEFENCE   3.12.13
    BY ADDING ONE THING TO MY PURPOSE NOTHING   3.20.12
    IF THEIR BEE NOTHING NEW, BUT THAT WHICH IS   3.59.1
    AND NOTHING STANDS BUT FOR HIS SIETH TO MOW   3.60.12
    AND NEEDIE $NOTHING TRIMD IN JOLLITIE   3.66.3
    WANT NOTHING THAT THE THOUGHT OF HEARTS CAN MEND   3.69.2
    FOR YOU IN ME CAN NOTHING WORTHY PROVE   3.72.4
    AND SO SHOULD YOU, TO LOVE THINGS NOTHING WORTH   3.72.14
    THY LOOKES SHOULD NOTHING THENCE, BUT
                          SWEETNESSE TELL   3.93.12
    NOTHING SWEET BOY, BUT YET LIKE PRAYERS DIVINE   3.108.5
    TO LEAVE FOR NOTHING ALL THY SUMME OF GOOD   3.109.12
    FOR NOTHING THIS WIDE $UNIVERSE I CALL   3.109.13
    TO ME ARE NOTHING NOVELL, NOTHING STRANGE   3.123.3
    TO ME ARE NOTHING NOVELL, NOTHING STRANGE   3.123.3
    MY $MISTRES EYES ARE NOTHING LIKE THE $SUNNE   3.130.1
    IN NOTHING ART THOU BLACKE SAVE IN THY DEEDS   3.131.13
    FOR NOTHING HOLD ME, SO IT PLEASE THEE HOLD   3.136.11
    THAT NOTHING ME, A SOME-THING SWEET TO THEE   3.136.12
    LOOKS OVER THE WORLD, AND CAN FIND NOTHING SUCH   4.9.10
    WITH DOING ALL, LEAVE NOTHING DONE BUT PAINE   4.85.8
    AND NOTHING THEN THE CAUSE MORE SWEET COULD BE   4.87.13
    FOR NOTHING FROM MY WIT OR WILL DOTH FLOW   4.90.12
    OF THAT FAIRE SIGHT, THAT NOTHING ELSE
                          THEY BROOKE   5.35.10
    ALL PAINES ARE NOTHING IN RESPECT OF THIS   5.63.13
    OF THAT FAYRE SIGHT, THAT NOTHING ELSE
                          THEY BROOKE   5.83.10
NOUGHT   14
    YET THOUGH I SEE, THAT NOUGHT WE DOE, CAN MOVE   1.8.13
    T'HAVE PEACE ABROAD, AND NOUGHT WITHIN BUT STRIFE   1.20.3
    AND YEELD ME NOUGHT THAT GIVES THEM THEIR RENOWNE   1.28.8
    YET NOUGHT THE ROCKE OF THAT HARD HEART CAN MOVE   1.48.9
    READIE OF WIT AND FEARING NOUGHT BUT SHAME   4.14.11
    THAT $PLATO I READ FOR NOUGHT, BUT IF HE TAME   4.21.5
    LEAVING ME NOUGHT BUT WAILING ELOQUENCE   4.38.11
    BE NOUGHT DISMAYD THAT HER UNMOVED MIND   5.6.1
    YET FIND I NOUGHT ON EARTH TO WHICH I DARE   5.9.3
    NOR UNTO $CHRISTALL.. FOR NOUGHT MAY THEM SEVER   5.9.11
    AND DOTH HIS YDLE MESSAGE SET AT NOUGHT   5.19.12
    HER SELFE ASSURD, AND IS OF NOUGHT AFFRAYD   5.58.4
    FALS LOWEST.. FOR ON EARTH NOUGHT HATH
                          ENDURAUNCE   5.58.12
    SHALL TURNE TO NOUGHT AND LOOSE THAT GLORIOUS HEW   5.79.6
NOURISH   3
    THE HEW WHICH THOU SO CAREFULLY DOST NORISH   1.50.7
    MY LIFE FORGETS TO NOURISH LANGUISHT SPRITES   4.42.10
    NOR NOURISH SPECIALL LOCKES OF VOWED HAIRE   4.54.3
NOURISHED   1
    CONSUM'D WITH THAT WHICH IT WAS NURRISHT BY   3.73.12

```
NOVEL                        1
    TO ME ARE NOTHING NOVELL, NOTHING STRANGE           3.123.3
NOVICE                       1
    THIS NEW RICH $NOVICE, LAVISH OF HIS CHEST           2.10.5
NOYOUS                       1
    I WISH THAT NIGHT THE NOYOUS DAY WOULD END           5.87.6
NUMBER                       5
    ONE NUMBER OF THE $EARTH, THE OTHER BOTH $DIVINE     2.18.3
    ONE NUMBER OF THE EARTH, THE OTHER BOTH DIVINE       2.108.3
    AND IN FRESH NUMBERS NUMBER ALL YOUR GRACES          3.17.6
    AMONG A NUMBER ONE IS RECKON'D NONE                  3.136.8
    THEN IN THE NUMBER LET ME PASSE UNTOLD               3.136.9
NUMBERED                     1
    WHICH WORKES ON LEASES OF SHORT NUMBRED HOWERS       3.124.10
NUMBERS                      8
    ONE $WOMAN NOW, MAKES THREE ODDE $NUMBERS EVEN       2.18.4
    AND WHEN MY FLOWING $NUMBERS THEY REHEARSE           2.25.13
    ONE WONDER WOMAN NOW MAKES THREE OD NUMBERS EVEN     2.108.4
    AND IN FRESH NUMBERS NUMBER ALL YOUR GRACES          3.17.6
    ETERNAL NUMBERS TO OUT-LIVE LONG DATE                3.38.12
    BUT NOW MY GRACIOUS NUMBERS ARE DECAYDE              3.79.3
    IN GENTLE NUMBERS TIME SO IDELY SPENT                3.100.6
    WHOSE NUMBERS, WAYES, GREATNESSE, ETERNITIE          4.26.3
NURSE                        3
    THE $INNE OF CARE, THE $NURSE OF DRERY SORROW        2.145.2
    AS TENDER NURSE HER BABE FROM FARING ILL             3.22.12
    YOU SEEKE TO NURSE AT FULLEST BREASTS OF $FAME       4.15.13
NURSED                       2
    THOSE CHILDREN NURST, DELIVERD FROM THY BRAINE       3.77.11
    BUT AS YOU WITH MY BREAST I OFT HAVE NURST           4.95.3
NURSETH                      1
    FOR THAT WHICH LONGER NURSETH THE DISEASE            3.147.2
NUT                          1
    SWEET IS THE NUT, BUT BITTER IS HIS PILL             5.26.6
NYMPH                        5
    AND IN THESE $SHADES, DEARE $NYMPH, HE
                            OFT HATH BEENE               2.53.11
    AND IN THESE SHADES (DEER $NIMPHE) HE
                            OFT HATH BEEN                2.113.11
    TOWARDES $AURORA'S $COURT A $NYMPH DOTH DWELL        4.37.5
    NYMPH OF THE GARD'N, WHERE ALL BEAUTIES BE           4.82.1
    SWEET GARD'N $NYMPH, WHICH KEEPES THE
                            $CHERRIE TREE                4.82.5
NYMPH-LIKE                   1
    A THOUSAND $NIMPH-LIKE AND INAMOR'D $GRACES          2.4.2
NYMPHS                       3
    WHILST MANY $NYMPHES THAT VOU'D CHAST
                            LIFE TO KEEP                 3.154.3
    THE COURTLY $NYMPHS, ACQUAINTED WITH THE MONE        4.54.5
    BRINGING WITH HER THOSE STARRY $NIMPHS,
                            WHOSE CHACE                  4.97.3
O                          119
    O CLEERE-EYDE $RECTOR OF THE HOLY $HILL              1.4.10
    THY CRUELTY, THY GLORY., $O STRANGE CASE             1.56.10
    BUT $O, SEE, SEE, WE NEED INQUIRE NO FURTHER         2.2.9
    O $GOD FROM $YOU, THAT I COULD PRIVATE BE            2.11.2
    YOU DOE BEWITCH $ME, $O THAT I COULD FLIE            2.11.13
    O SWEETEST $SHADOW, HOW THOU SERV'ST MY TURNE        2.13.9
    O, JUDGE NOT RASHLY (GENTLE $SIR) I PRAY             2.24.4
    O, $WHY SHOULD $NATURE NIGGARDLY RESTRAINE           2.25.1
```

```
WITH HOW SAD STEPS, O $MOONE, THOU CLIMB'ST
                        THE SKIES              4.31.1
THEN EV'N OF FELLOWSHIP, O $MOONE, TELL ME     4.31.9
I MIGHT, UNHAPPIE WORD, O ME, I MIGHT          4.33.1
HOW FAIRE A DAY WAS NEARE, O PUNISHT EYES      4.33.13
COME SLEEPE, O SLEEPE, THE CERTAINE KNOT OF PEACE  4.39.1
O MAKE IN ME THOSE CIVILL WARRES TO CEASE      4.39.7
O $STELLA DEARE, HOW MUCH THY POWER HATH WROUGHT   4.40.2
O DO NOT LET THY $TEMPLE BE DESTROYD           4.40.14
O EYES, WHICH DO THE $SPHEARES OF BEAUTIE MOVE  4.42.1
O EYES, WHERE HUMBLE LOCKES MOST GLORIOUS PROVE  4.42.5
DO NOT, O DO NOT FROM POORE ME REMOVE          4.42.7
YET STILL ON ME, O EYES, DART DOWNE YOUR RAYES  4.42.11
HER FACE+ $O $LOVE, A $ROGUE THOU THEN
                        SHOULDST BE            4.46.6
UNKIND, I LOVE YOU NOT.. $O ME, THAT EYE       4.47.13
WHAT EVER MAY ENSUE, O LET ME BE               4.48.5
O LOOKE, O SHINE, O LET ME DIE AND SEE         4.48.8
O LOOKE, O SHINE, O LET ME DIE AND SEE         4.48.8
O LOOKE, O SHINE, O LET ME DIE AND SEE         4.48.8
THAT $STELLA (O DEARE NAME) THAT $STELLA IS    4.52.6
O VOICE, O FACE, MAUGRE MY SPEECHE'S MIGHT     4.58.12
O VOICE, O FACE, MAUGRE MY SPEECHE'S MIGHT     4.58.12
O $DOCTOR $CUPID, THOU FOR ME REPLY            4.61.12
O $GRAMMER RULES, O NOW YOUR VERTUES SHOW      4.63.1
O $GRAMMER RULES, O NOW YOUR VERTUES SHOW      4.63.1
FOR $GRAMMER SAYES (O THIS DEARE $STELLA WEIGHE)  4.63.12
O GIVE MY PASSIONS LEAVE TO RUN THEIR RACE     4.64.2
O THINKE I THEN, WHAT PARADISE OF JOY          4.68.13
O JOY, TOO HIGH FOR MY LOW STILE TO SHOW       4.69.1
O BLISSE, FIT FOR A NOBLER STATE THEN ME       4.69.2
MY SPRING APPEARES, O SEE WHAT HERE DOTH GROW  4.69.8
I, I, O I MAY SAY, THAT SHE IS MINE            4.69.11
O HEAV'NLY FOOLE, THY MOST KISSE-WORTHIE FACE  4.73.12
O HOW THE PLEASANT AIRES OF TRUE LOVE BE       4.78.1
O KISSE, WHICH DOEST THOSE RUDDIE GEMMES IMPART  4.81.1
O KISSE, WHICH SOULES, EVEN SOULES TOGETHER TIES  4.81.5
O EASE YOUR HAND, TREATE NOT SO HARD YOUR SLAVE  4.86.9
NOT THEM, O NO, BUT YOU IN THEM I LOVE         4.91.14
O $GOD, THINKE YOU THAT SATISFIES MY CARE+     4.92.8
O FATE, O FAULT, O CURSE, CHILD OF MY BLISSE   4.93.1
O FATE, O FAULT, O CURSE, CHILD OF MY BLISSE   4.93.1
O FATE, O FAULT, O CURSE, CHILD OF MY BLISSE   4.93.1
O TEARES, NO TEARES, BUT RAINE FROM BEAUTIE'S
                        SKIES                  4.100.1
O HONIED SIGHS, WHICH FROM THAT BREAST DO RISE  4.100.5
O PLAINTS CONSERV'D IN SUCH A SUGRED PHRAISE   4.100.9
O HAPPIE $TEMS, THAT DIDST MY $STELLA BEARE    4.103.1
THEY DID THEMSELVES (O SWEETEST PRISON) TWINE  4.103.8
WITH SIGHT THEREOF CRIDE OUT., O FAIRE DISGRACE  4.103.13
O ABSENT PRESENCE $STELLA IS NOT HERE          4.106.1
O LET NOT FOOLES IN ME THY WORKES REPROVE      4.107.13
THEREFORE $O LOVE, UNLESSE SHE TURNE TO THEE   5.19.13
THE WHICH VOUCHSAFE $O GODDESSE TO ACCEPT      5.22.13
O FAYREST FAYRE LET NEVER IT BE NAMED          5.41.13
O MIGHTY CHARM WHICH MAKES MEN LOVE THEYR BANE  5.47.13
OAK                     1
THE DUREFULL $OAKE, WHOSE SAP IS NOT YET DRIDE  5.6.5
OATHS                   4
BUT WHY OF TWO OTHES BREACH DOE I ACCUSE THEE  3.152.5
```

```
    FOR ALL MY VOWES ARE OTHES BUT TO MISUSE THEE        3.152.7
    FOR I HAVE SWORNE DEEPE OTHES OF THY DEEPE
                              KINDNESSE                   3.152.9
    OTHES OF THY LOVE, THY TRUTH, THY CONSTANCIE          3.152.10
OBEY                  2
    O, WHY SHOULD $BEAUTIE ($CUSTOME TO OBEY)            2.43.9
    WHOM THEN SHALL I CR HEAVEN OR HER OBAY+             5.46.5
OBJECT                8
    GILDING THE OBJECT WHERE-UPON IT GAZETH             3.20.6
    IN OBJECT BEST TO KNIT AND STRENGTH OUR SIGHT       4.7.6
    (AS HIS SOLE OBJECT OF FELICITIE)                  4.86.7
    DEAD GLASSE, DOOST THOU THY OBJECT SO IMBRACE      4.105.3
    INTO THE OBJECT OF YOUR MIGHTY VIEW+              5.7.4
    STILL TO BEHOLD THE OBJECT OF THEIR PAINE         5.35.2
    AND WHEN I HOPE TC SEE THEYR TREW OBJECT          5.78.11
    STILL TO BEHOLD THE OBJECT OF THEYR PAYNE         5.83.2
OBJECTS               6
    FINDING THEIR $OBJECTS CVER-SOONE DEPART          2.33.6
    OR COULD MINE EYE BLT AYME, HER OBJECTS
                              PAST PERFECTION          2.117.6
    BEHOLD, THEIR OBJECTS OVER-SOONE DEPART           2.133.6
    OF HIS QUICK OBJECTS HATH THE MINDE NO PART       3.113.7
    AS FAST AS OBJECTS TO HIS BEAMES ASSEMBLE         3.114.8
    LEAVE SENSE, AND THCSE WHICH SENSE'S OBJECTS BE   4.10.7
OBLATION              1
    AND TAKE THOU MY CBLACICN, POORE BUT FREE         3.125.10
OBLATIONS             2
    MY $SOULE'S $OBLATICNS TC THY SACRED $NAME        2.54.12
    MY SOULES OBLATIONS TO THY SACRED NAME            2.101.12
OBLIVION              2
    TO KEEPE $THEE FROM $OBLIVION AND THE $GRAVE      2.44.10
    TIL EACH TO RAZ'D CBLIVICN YEELD HIS PART         3.122.7
OBLIVIOUS             1
    GAINST DEATH, AND ALL OBLIVIOUS EMNITY            3.55.9
OBSCURE               2
    AND CLOUDS OBSCURE HAD SHADED STILL HER
                              BRIGHTNESSE              1.7.4
    MY FORTUNE MANTLED WITH A CLOWDE S'OBSCURE        1.29.13
OBSCURED              2
    WHEN $DARKNESSE HATH OBSCUR'D EACH OTHER $LIGHT   2.55.14
    WHEN DARKNES HATH CBSCUR'D EACH OTHER LIGHT       2.102.14
OBSCURENESS           1
    ME FROM THE VULGAR, THEE FROM ALL OBSCURENES      1.44.12
OBSCURITY             1
    THY $GIFTS THOU IN $OBSCURITIE DOEST WASTE        2.10.9
OBSEQUIOUS            2
    HOW MANY A HOLY AND OBSEQUIOUS TEARE              3.31.5
    NOE, LET ME BE OBSEQUIOUS IN THY HEART            3.125.9
OBSERVER              1
    THE MEANE OBSERVER (WHOM BASE SAFETY KEEPS)       1.35.10
OBSTINATE             1
    FAYRE BE YE SURE, BUT HARD AND OBSTINATE          5.56.9
OBTAIN                5
    WHAT SHOULD I DO THEN, IF I SHOULD OBTAINE+       1.48.14
    SINCE TO OBTAINE THEE, NOTHING ME WILL STED       2.15.1
    AND MY SOULE THEN CBTAINE WHICH SO MY
                              SOULE DESIRETH           2.117.8
    KNOWLEDGE MIGHT PITIE WINNE, AND PITIE
                              GRACE OBTAINE            4.1.4
    THAT $BALLANCE WEIGH'D WHAT SWORD DID
                              LATE OBTAINE             4.75.8
```

```
OBTAINED                        1
  GUIDED SO WELL, THAT I OBTAIN'D THE PRIZE          4.41.2
OBTAINS                         1
  YET BY MY $FROTH, THIS $FOOLE HIS $LOVE OBTAINES   2.21.13
OCCASION                        1
  SOMETIMES I JOY WHEN GLAD OCCASION FITS            5.54.5
OCEAN                          11
  UNTO THE BOUNDLESSE $OCEAN OF THY BEAUTIE          1.1.1
  MY HEATES MUST DROWNE IN TH'$OCEAN OF MY TEARES    1.32.12
  ONCE LET THE $OCEAN OF MY CARES FINDE SHORE        1.46.13
  TH'$OCEAN NEVER DID ATTEND MORE DULY               1.48.5
  DOWNE FELL HE IN THY $BEAUTIES $OCEAN DRENCHED     2.122.13
  INTO THE OCEAN OF A TROUBLED MINDE                 2.134.2
  RECORD MY LOVE IN $OCEAN WAVES (UNKIND)            2.142.9
  LET THIS SAD $INTRIM LIKE THE $OCEAN BE            3.56.9
  WHEN I HAVE SEENE THE HUNGRY $OCEAN GAINE          3.64.5
  BUT SINCE YOUR WORTH (WIDE AS THE $OCEAN IS)       3.80.5
  LYKE AS A SHIP THAT THROUGH THE $OCEAN WYDE        5.34.1
OCEANS                          3
  THE WATER, TO MY TEARES, AS DROPS TO $OCEANS BE    2.127.6
  ONELY MY TEARES BY $OCEANS MAY BE GESSED           2.127.10
  WHAT $OCEANS OF DELIGHT IN ME DO FLOW              4.69.4
ODD                             2
  ONE $WOMAN NOW, MAKES THREE ODDE $NUMBERS EVEN     2.18.4
  ONE WONDER WOMAN NOW MAKES THREE OD NUMBERS EVEN   2.108.4
ODDS                            1
  BUT, BUT (ALAS) NIGHT'S SIDE THE ODS HATH FUR      4.96.12
ODOR                            4
  FOR THAT SWEET ODOR, WHICH DOTH IN IT LIVE         3.54.4
  BUT WHY THY ODOR MATCHETH NOT THY SHOW             3.69.13
  OF DIFFERENT FLOWERS IN ODOR AND IN HEW            3.98.6
  BUT HER SWEET ODOUR DID THEM ALL EXCELL            5.64.14
ODOROUS                         1
  SUCH FRAGRANT FLOWRES DOE GIVE MOST ODOROUS
                                           SMELL     5.64.13
ODORS                           4
  T'$ARABIAN ODORS GIVE THY BREATHING SWEETE         1.19.6
  THE PRECIOUS $ODORS BE MY CHASTE $DESIRE           2.30.11
  OF THEIR SWEET DEATHES, ARE SWEETEST ODORS MADE    3.54.12
  THAT DAINTY ODOURS FROM THEM THREW AROUND          5.64.3
O'ER                            6
  AND SABLE CURLS OR SILVER'D ORE WITH WHITE         3.12.4
  AND HEAVILY FROM WOE TO WOE TELL ORE               3.30.10
  WHILE HE INSULTS ORE DULL AND SPEACHLESSE
                                           TRIBES    3.107.12
  I MUST EACH DAY SAY ORE THE VERY SAME              3.108.6
  WHEN I WAS CERTAINE ORE IN-CERTAINTY               3.115.11
  ORE WHOME THEIR FINGERS WALKE WITH GENTLE GATE     3.128.11
O'ERCHARGED                     2
  ORE-CHARG'D WITH BURTHEN OF MINE OWNE LOVES MIGHT  3.23.8
  LET FOLKE ORECHARG'D WITH BRAINE AGAINST ME CRIE   4.64.4
O'ERCOME                        1
  WHERE, IN HIS $CUPS O'RCOME WITH FOULE $EXCESSE    2.7.9
O'ER-GREEN                      1
  SO YOU ORE-GREENE MY BAD, MY GOOD ALOW+            3.112.4
O'ERLOOK                        1
  AND THEREFORE MAIEST WITHOUT ATTAINT ORE-LOOKE     3.82.2
O'ER-PRESSED                    1
  IS MORE THEN MY ORE-PREST DEFENCE CAN BIDE+        3.139.8
```

O'ER-READ   1
  WHICH EYES NOT YET CREATED SHALL ORE-REAC   3.81.10
O'ER-SNOWED   1
  BEAUTY ORE-SNOW'D AND BARENES EVERY WHERE   3.5.8
O'ER-SWAYS   1
  BUT SAD MORTALLITY ORE-SWAIES THEIR POWER   3.65.2
O'ERTAKE   1
  TO LET BACE CLOUDES ORE-TAKE ME IN MY WAY   3.34.3
O'ER-WORN   1
  WITH TIMES INJURICUS HAND CHRUSHT AND ORE-WORNE   3.63.2
OFF   5
  HOW TO BE BOLD FAR CFF, AND BASHFULL NEARE   1.20.5
  THAT MAKES ME FALL FROM CFF MY HIE DESIRE   1.32.8
  AND HOW I LIVE CAST DOWNE FROM OFF ALL MYRTH   1.60.9
  HOW FAR I TOYLE, STILL FARTHER OFF FROM THEE   3.28.8
  LEAVE THAT SIR $PHIP, LEAST OFF YOUR NECKE
                                 BE WROONG   4.83.14
OFFENCE   3
  MY $HEART SHOULD SUFFER FOR MINE $EYES $CFFENCE   2.29.4
  HAVING THE $JUDGEMENT DUE TO HIS $OFFENCE   2.50.3
  ENVIOUS WITS WHAT HATH BENE MINE OFFENCE   4.104.1
OFFEND   5
  BY UNIONS MARRIED DC OFFEND THINE EARE   3.8.6
  FEARE TO OFFEND, WILL WCRTHIE TO APPEARE   4.72.10
  NOR UNTO GLASSE.. SUCH BASENESSE MOUGHT
                                 OFFEND HER   5.9.12
  FOR ALL THEIR FAULTS WITH WHICH THEY DID OFFEND   5.24.12
  AND FLY THE FAULTS WITH WHICH WE DID OFFEND   5.62.8
OFFENDED   1
  HIS MOTHER DEARE $CUPID CFFENDED LATE   4.17.1
OFFENDERS   1
  LOVING OFFENDORS THUS I WILL EXCUSE YEE   3.42.5
OFFENDER'S   1
  TH'OFFENDERS SORRCW LENDS BUT WEAKE RELIEFE   3.34.11
OFFENDS   2
  TO WRITE WITH $BLCUD, CF FORCE UFFENDS THE $SIGHT   2.13.6
  TO WRITE WITH BLOCD, CF FORCE OFFENDS THE SIGHT   2.121.6
OFFENSE   2
  THUS CAN MY LOVE EXCUSE THE SLOW OFFENCE   3.51.1
  AND I WILL COMMENT UPON THAT CFFENCE   3.89.2
OFFENSES   1
  MADE OLD OFFENCES CF AFFECTIONS NEW   3.110.4
OFFENSE'S   1
  TO HIM THAT BEARES THE STRONG OFFENSES LCSSE   3.34.12
OFFER   6
  WHY SHOULD I OFFER LP UNTO HER NAME   1.17.3
  RECEIVE THE $INCENSE WHICH I OFFER HERE   2.54.9
  I OFFER FREE $CONDITIONS OF FAIRE $PEACE   2.63.5
  RECEAVE THE INCENSE WHICH I OFFER HEERE   2.101.9
  THAT IN MY HEART I CFFER STILL TO THEE   4.40.13
  AND HOSTAGES DOE CFFER FCR MY TRUTH   5.11.2
OFFERED   1
  THE SACRIFICE HERE CFFRED TO HER SIGHT   1.59.8
OFFEREDST   1
  REASON THOU KNEEL'DST, AND OFFEREDST STRAIGHT
                                 TO PRUVE   4.10.13
OFFICE   2
  THEN DO THY OFFICE $MUSE, I TEACH THEE HCW   3.101.13
  WHILE EVERIE OFFICE THEMSELVES WILL DISCHARGE   4.85.7

```
OFFICES                    2
  AND DOTH THE SEV'RALL $OFFICES DEFINE              2.12.3
  THESE OFFICES, SO OFT AS THOU WILT LOOKE           3.77.13
OFFSPRING                  2
  IF SO IT HAP, THIS OF-SPRING OF MY CARE            1.3.1
  RARE OF-SPRING OF MY THOUGHTS, MY DEEREST $LOVE    2.141.1
OFT                       56
  AND OFT WITH CAREFULL TURNES, WITH SILENT $ART     1.8.7
  OFT HAVE I TOLD HER THAT MY SOULE DID LOVE HER     1.18.13
  OFT WHEN I FINDE IN HER NO TRUTH AT ALL            1.25.5
  OFT AND IN VAINE MY REBEL THOUGHTS HAVE VENTRED    1.27.1
  OFT DO I MARVELL, WHETHER $DELIAS EIES             1.34.1
  AND THOUGH TH'EVENT OFT ANSWERS NOT THE SAME       1.35.8
  OFT 'T'ATH BEEN PROV'D, THE BREATHLESSE
                          $COARSE WILL BLEED         2.46.8
  TH'INCERTAINE $TIMES OFT VARYING IN THEIR $COURSE  2.51.2
  AND IN THESE $SHADES, DEARE $NYMPH, HE
                          OFT HATH BEENE             2.53.11
  OFT TAKING PEN IN HAND, WITH WORDS TO
                          CAST MY WOES               2.110.1
  AND IN THESE SHADES (DEER $NIMPHE) HE
                          OFT HATH BEEN              2.113.11
  BY OFT PREDICT THAT I IN HEAVEN FINDE              3.14.8
  THESE OFFICES, SO OFT AS THOU WILT LOOKE           3.77.13
  SO OFT HAVE I INVOK'D THEE FOR MY $MUSE            3.78.1
  HOW OFT WHEN THOU MY MUSIKE MUSIKE PLAYST          3.128.1
  AND SEALD FALSE BONDS OF LOVE AS OFT AS MINE       3.142.7
  OFT TURNING OTHERS' LEAVES, TO SEE IF
                          THENCE WOULD FLOW          4.1.7
  YET HIDING ROYALL BLOUD FULL OFT IN RURALL VAINE   4.6.8
  THAT HER SWEETE BREATH MAKES OFT THY FLAMES
                          TO RISE                    4.12.4
  WHO OFT FORE-JUDGE MY AFTER-FOLLOWING RACE         4.26.13
  BECAUSE I OFT IN DARKE ABSTRACTED GUISE            4.27.1
  WHICH LOOKES TOO OFT IN HIS UNFLATTRING GLASSE     4.27.10
  THAT MAKES ME OFT MY BEST FRIENDS OVERPASSE        4.27.12
  A $PROPHET OFT, AND OFT AN HISTORIE                4.32.3
  A $PROPHET OFT, AND OFT AN HISTORIE                4.32.3
  OFT CRUELL FIGHTS WELL PICTURED FORTH DO PLEASE    4.34.4
  STELLA OFT SEES THE VERIE FACE OF WO               4.45.1
  I CURST THEE OFT, I PITIE NOW THY CASE             4.46.1
  FOR THOUGH I OFT MY SELFE OF THEM BEMONE           4.48.9
  MUSES, I OFT INVOKED YOUR HOLY AYDE                4.55.1
  AND OFT WHOLE TROUPES OF SADDEST WORDS I STAID     4.55.5
  HE BARKS, MY SONGS THINE OWNE VOYCE OFT
                          DOTH PROVE                 4.59.6
  OFT WITH TRUE SIGHES, OFT WITH UNCALLED TEARES     4.61.1
  OFT WITH TRUE SIGHES, OFT WITH UNCALLED TEARES     4.61.1
  MY FRIEND, THAT OFT SAW THROUGH ALL MASKES MY WO   4.69.5
  SHE OFT HATH DRUNKE MY TEARES, NOW HOPES TO ENJOY  4.70.3
  AND OFT SO CLINGS TO MY PURE $LOVE, THAT I         4.72.2
  LOVE STILL A BOY, AND OFT A WANTON IS              4.73.1
  ALTHOUGH LESSE GIFTS IMPE FEATHERS OFT ON $FAME    4.75.4
  NAY, MORE FOOLE I, OFT SUFFERED YOU TO SLEEPE      4.83.7
  MORE OFT THEN TO A CHAMBER MELODIE                 4.84.4
  THAT TO WIN ME, OFT SHEWES A PRESENT PAY+          4.88.4
  BUT AS YOU WITH MY BREAST I OFT HAVE NURST         4.95.3
  THOUGH OFT HIMSELFE MY MATE-IN-ARMES HE SWARE      4.95.8
  SHEWES HER OFT AT THE FULL HER FAIREST FACE        4.97.2
  WITH SWEETE SOFT SHADES THOU OFT INVITEST ME       4.98.5
```

```
    SWEETNESSE, THAT BREATHES AND PANTS AS
                        OFT AS SHE              4.101.2
    WHERE THOSE RED CHEEKS, WHICH OFT WITH
                        FAIRE ENCREASE DID FRAME  4.102.2
    ON SERVANTS' SHAME CFT $MAISTER'S BLAME
                        DOTH SIT                4.107.12
    THE POWRE THEREOF, WHICH OFTE IN ME I FIND   5.28.5
    SO OFT AS HOMEWARD I FRCM HER DEPART         5.52.1
    SO OFT AS I HER BEAUTY DOE BEHOLD            5.55.1
    OFT WHEN MY SPIRIT DOTH SPRED HER BOLDER WINGES  5.72.1
    WHICH OFT I WISHT, YET NEVER WAS SO BLEST    5.76.14
    FAYRE WHEN THAT CLCUD OF PRYDE, WHICH
                        OFT DOTH DARK           5.81.7
    JOY OF MY LIFE, FULL OFT FOR LOVING YOU      5.82.1
OFTEN               7
    THUS OFTEN AS I CHASE MY HOPE FROM ME        1.25.9
    THEY THAT ARE BLIND, ARE $MINSTRELS OFTEN MACE  2.48.11
    AND OFTEN IS HIS GCLD CCMPLEXION DIMM'D      3.18.6
    FAIRE, KINDE, AND TRUE, HAVE OFTEN LIV'D ALONE  3.105.13
    WHEREOF, WITH WHOM, HOW OFTEN DID SHE TALKE  4.92.11
    THE ROLLING WHEELE THAT RUNNETH OFTEN ROUND  5.18.1
    AND DRIZLING DROPS THAT CFTEN DOE REDOUNC    5.18.3
OFT-VARYING             1
    MY TEDIOUS $TRAVELS, AND OFT-VARYING $FATE   2.1.14
OH                  16
    OH THEN VOUTSAFE ME BUT THIS LOVING THOUGHT  3.32.9
    OH GIVE THY SELFE THE THANKES IF OUGHT IN ME  3.38.5
    OH HOW THY WORTH WITH MANNERS MAY I SINGE    3.39.1
    OH ABSENCE WHAT A TCRMENT WOULDST THOU PROVE  3.39.9
    OH HOW MUCH MORE DCTH BEAUTIE BEAUTIOUS SEEME  3.54.1
    OH LET ME SUFFER (BEING AT YOUR BECK)        3.58.5
    OH THAT RECORD COULD WITH A BACK-WARD LOCKE  3.59.5
    OH SURE I AM THE WITS OF FORMER DAIES        3.59.13
    OH WHAT A HAPPY TITLE DC I FINDE             3.92.11
    OH IN WHAT SWEETS DCEST THOU THY SINNES INCLCSE  3.95.4
    OH WHAT A MANSION HAVE THOSE VICES GOT       3.95.9
    OH TRUANT $MUSE WHAT SHALBE THY AMENDS       3.101.1
    OH BLAME ME NOT IF I NO MORE CAN WRITE       3.103.5
    OH TIS THE FIRST, TIS FLATRY IN MY SEEING    3.114.9
    OH FROM WHAT POWRE HAST THOU THIS POWREFULL
                        MIGHT                   3.150.1
    OH THOUGH I LOVE WHAT OTHERS DOE ABHOR       3.150.11
OLD                 44
    I SHALL FORGET OLD WRONGS, MY GRIEFES
                        SHALL CEASE             1.46.11
    FOR WOMEN GRIEVE TC THINKE THEY MUST BE CLD  1.50.14
    THAT FORTIFIE THY NAME AGAINST OLD AGE       1.55.10
    THAT IN MY DAYES I MAY NOT SEE THEE OLD      2.8.2
    YET OLD $PROMETHEUS PUNISH'D FOR HIS $RAPE   2.14.13
    AND THE OLD $LEA BRAGS CF THE $DANISH $BLOUD  2.32.12
    THAT WHILST WITH $MARS SHE HOLDETH HER OLD $WAY  2.48.13
    I FIND OLD $POETS HYLLS AND FLOODS ADMIRE    2.120.2
    PELION AND $OSSA, FROSTY $CAUCASE OLD        2.120.6
    SOME OLD $PERNASSUS, WHERE THE $MUSES DWELL  2.120.11
    AND OLD $LEGEA BRAGS OF $DANISH BLOOD        2.124.12
    THY $BOWE HALFE BRCKE, IS PEEC'D WITH
                        OLDE DESIRE             2.126.5
    FOR THOU ALONE RENEW'ST THAT OLDE DESIRE     2.145.13
    SHALL SUM MY COUNT, AND MAKE MY OLD EXCUSE   3.2.11
    THIS WERE TO BE NEW MADE WHEN THOU ART OULD  3.2.13
```

```
BE SCORN'D, LIKE OLD MEN OF LESSE TRUTH
                       THEN TONGUE              3.17.10
YET DOE THY WORST OULD $TIME DISPIGHT THY WRONG  3.19.13
MY GLASSE SHALL NOT PERSWADE ME I AM OULD      3.22.1
MAKES BLACKE NIGHT BEAUTIOUS, AND HER
                       OLD FACE NEW            3.27.12
AND WITH OLD WOES NEW WAILE MY DEARE TIMES WASTE  3.30.4
THEN THOSE OLD NINE WHICH RIMERS INVOCATE      3.38.10
THAT I MIGHT SEE WHAT THE OLD WORLD COULD SAY   3.59.9
ROBBING NO OULD TO DRESSE HIS BEAUTY NEW       3.68.12
SO ALL MY BEST IS DRESSING OLD WORDS NEW       3.76.11
FOR AS THE $SUN IS DAILY NEW AND OLD           3.76.13
AND HAPLIE OF OUR OLD ACQUAINTANCE TELL        3.89.12
WHAT OLD $DECEMBERS BARENESSE EVERY WHERE+     3.97.4
TO ME FAIRE FRIEND YOU NEVER CAN BE OLD        3.104.1
AND BEAUTIE MAKING BEAUTIFULL OLD RIME         3.106.3
COUNTING NO OLD THING OLD, THOU MINE, I THINE  3.108.7
COUNTING NO OLD THING OLD, THOU MINE, I THINE  3.108.7
MADE OLD OFFENCES OF AFFECTIONS NEW            3.110.4
WHAT THOU DOST FOYST UPON US THAT IS OULD      3.123.6
IN THE OULD AGE BLACKE WAS NOT COUNTED FAIRE   3.127.1
AND WHEREFORE SAY NOT I THAT I AM OLD+         3.138.10
ENNOBLING NEW FOUND $TROPES WITH PROBLEMES OLD  4.3.6
THY SCEPTER USE IN SOME OLD $CATOE'S BREST     4.4.5
WHICH FROM THE RIBS OF OLD $PARNASSUS FLOWES   4.15.2
IN THIS OLD WORLD, GROWNE NOW SO TOO TOO WISE  4.65.6
DESIRE, THOUGH THOU MY OLD COMPANION ART       4.72.1
AND BIDDING TH'OLD $ADIEU, HIS PASSED DATE     5.4.3
BIDS ALL OLD THOUGHTS TO DIE IN DUMPISH SPRIGHT  5.4.4
THE OLD YEARES SINNES FOREPAST LET US ESCHEW   5.62.7
AND CHAUNGE OLD YEARES ANNOY TO NEW DELIGHT    5.62.14
OLDER                  2
NOR OLDER YET, NOR WISER MADE BY YEERES        2.22.3
ON NEWER PROOFE, TO TRIE AN OLDER FRIEND       3.110.11
OLIVE                  1
MY HUMBLE ACCENTS BEARE THE $OLIVE BOUGH       1.4.11
OLIVES                 1
AND PEACE PROCLAIMES $OLIVES OF ENDLESSE AGE   3.107.8
OLYMPUS                1
THE $DELIAN $CYNTHUS, THEN $OLYMPUS WEIGHT     2.120.7
ONCE                  39
ONCE LET HER KNOW, SH'HATH DONE ENOUGH
                       TO PROVE ME            1.10.13
WHOSE ROWLING GRACE DEIGNE ONCE A TURNE OF BLIS  1.12.12
CAUSE ONCE THE DATE OF HER DISDAINE T'EXPIRE   1.22.3
ONCE LET HER LOVE INDEED, OR ELS EYE ME NEVER  1.24.14
I ONCE MAY SEE WHEN YEARES SHALL WRECK MY WRONG  1.38.1
WHEN ONCE THEY FIND HER FLOWRE HER GLORY PAS   1.40.14
ONCE LET THE $OCEAN OF MY CARES FINDE SHORE    1.46.13
LAYES DOWNE HIS $QUIVER, WHICH HE ONCE DID BEARE  2.4.6
THE $DIAMOND SHALL ONCE CONSUME TO $DUST       2.13.3
SAY TO OUR $NEPHEWES, THAT THOU ONCE HAST SEENE  2.17.11
NOR GIVES $ME ONCE, BUT ONE POORE MINUTES REST  2.20.4
NO $VIRGINE ONCE ATTENDING ON THAT LIGHT       2.105.3
NOR YET THOSE HEAVENLY SECRETS ONCE RESPECTED  2.105.4
THE $DIAMOND SHALL ONCE CONSUME TO DUST        2.121.3
THUS SORING STILL, NOT LOOKING ONCE BELOW      2.122.9
WHO IN HER PRIDE SDAYNES ONCE TO LOOKE ON MEE  2.123.12
ELS SENCELES LOVE COULD NEVER ONCE ENDITE      2.131.4
AFTER A THOUSAND VICTORIES ONCE FOILD          3.25.10
```

```
AND SHALT BY FORTUNE ONCE MORE RE-SURVAY              3.32.3
WHEN YOU HAVE BID YCUR SERVANT ONCE ADIEUE            3.57.8
NATIVITY ONCE IN THE MAINE OF LIGHT                   3.60.5
THOUGH I (ONCE GONE) TO ALL THE WORLD MUST DYE        3.81.6
THAT YOU WERE ONCE UNKIND BE-FRIENDS MEE NOW          3.120.1
TO WAIGH HOW ONCE I SUFFERED IN YOUR CRIME            3.120.8
NOT ONCE VOUCHSAFE TO HIDE MY WILL IN THINE           3.135.6
AND DEATH ONCE DEAD, THER'S NO MORE DYING THEN        3.146.14
THIS LITTLE $LOVE-$GOD LYING ONCE A SLEEPE            3.154.1
THAT $VERTUE, IF IT ONCE MET WITH OUR EYES            4.25.3
WHEREWITH MY FATHER ONCE MADE IT HALFE TAME           4.30.10
AND AH WHAT HOPE, THAT HOPE SHOULD ONCE SEE CAY       4.35.7
THAT ONCE COME THERE, THE SOBS OF MINE ANNOYES        4.44.13
LEAST ONCE SHOULD NCT BE HEARD, TWISE
                         SAID, $NO, $NO               4.63.8
BUT THAT WHICH ONCE MAY WIN THY CRUELL HART           4.64.13
TEACHING THE MEANE, AT CNCE TO TAKE AND GIVE          4.79.9
PARDON THAT FAULT, CNCE MORE GRAUNT ME THE PLACE      4.82.12
CANNOT HEAVN'S FOOD, ONCE FELT, KEEPE
                         STOMAKES FREE                4.88.7
BUT WHEN IT ONCE DCTH BURNE, IT DOTH DIVIDE           5.6.7
THAT SHE WILL ONCE VOUCHSAFE MY PLAINT TC HEARE       5.18.7
YET SINCE YOUR LIGHT HATH ONCE ENLUMIND ME            5.66.13
ONE            139
SO MUCH I LOVE THE MOST UNLOVING ONE                  1.12.14
AS ONE THAT DIES WITHOUT HER COMPANY                  1.25.8
WITH THEE SUCH POWERS TC PLAGUE ONE SILLY HARTE       1.27.12
STILL IN THE TRACE CF CNE PERPLEXED THOUGHT           1.33.1
ONE IN MY LOVE, AND HER HARD HART STILL CNE           1.33.4
ONE IN MY LOVE, AND HER HARD HART STILL CNE           1.33.4
BUT I MAY ADDE CNE FEATHER TO THY FAME                1.43.9
HAPPY THE HEART THAT SIGH'D FOR SUCH A ONE            1.51.14
TO ONE $MAN GIVES, DOTH CN ANOTHER SPEND              2.10.6
HAPS TO LEND SOME TC ONE TRUE HONEST $FRIEND          2.10.8
SINCE $YOU ONE WERE, I NEVER SINCE WAS ONE            2.11.3
SINCE $YOU ONE WERE, I NEVER SINCE WAS ONE            2.11.3
WITH ONE THRICE-MARRY'D'S $PRAY'RS, THAT
                         DID BEQUEATH                 2.15.11
ONE, IN WHOM ALL THE $EXCELLENCIES BE                 2.17.3
THREE $NINES THERE ARE, TO EVERY ONE A $NINE          2.18.2
ONE NUMBER OF THE $EARTH, THE OTHER BOTH $DIVINE      2.18.3
ONE $WOMAN NOW, MAKES THREE ODDE $NUMBERS EVEN        2.18.4
MY WORTHY, $ONE TC THESE $NINE $WORTHIES ADCETH       2.18.9
AND MY FAIRE $MUSE, ONE $MUSE UNTO THE $NINE          2.18.10
WITH ONE MORE $ORDER, THESE NINE $ORDERS
                         GLADDETH                     2.18.12
MAKES EVERY $ONE CF THESE THREE $NINES A $TEN         2.18.14
NOR GIVES $ME ONCE, BUT CNE POORE MINUTES REST        2.20.4
(YET HIS DULL $SPIRIT HER NOT ONE JOT COULD MOVE)     2.21.2
TO WRITE HIM BUT CNE $SCNNET TO HIS $LOVE             2.21.4
NOR NEVER STOOD ONE WORD THEREOF TO BLOT              2.21.7
AS ONE THAT FAINE HIS $SORROWES WOULD BEGUILE         2.24.6
NOR SHALL MY $SPIRIT ONE JOT OF VIGOUR LCSE           2.31.6
THAT SINCE THE ONE CANNCT THE OTHER BEE               2.33.13
ONE BY THY $NAME, THE OTHER TOUCHING THEE             2.35.8
GET NOT ONE GLANCE, TO RECOMPENCE MY $MERIT+          2.43.4
AND FOR ONE PIECE OF $THINE, MY WHOLE HEART TAKE      2.52.4
OR IF THOU HAST, IT IS A FLINTY ONE                   2.52.14
AS $LOVE AND I, LATE HARBOUR'D IN ONE $INNE           2.59.1
THAT $WE ONE JOT CF FORMER $LOVE RETEYNE              2.61.8
```

```
IN $ONE WHOLE WORLD IS BUT ONE $PHOENIX FOUND         2.106.1
IN $ONE WHOLE WORLD IS BUT ONE $PHOENIX FOUND         2.106.1
THREE NINES THERE ARE, TO EVERIE ONE A NINE           2.108.2
ONE NUMBER OF THE EARTH, THE OTHER BOTH DIVINE        2.108.3
ONE WONDER WOMAN NOW MAKES THREE OD NUMBERS EVEN      2.108.4
MY $WORTHIE, ONE TO THESE NINE $WORTHIES, ADDETH      2.108.9
AND MY FAIRE $MUSE, ONE $MUSE UNTO THE NINE           2.108.10
WITH ONE MORE ORDER, THESE NINE ORDERS GLADDETH       2.108.12
MAKES EVERY ONE OF THESE THREE NINES A TEN            2.108.14
ONE BY THY NAME, THE OTHER TOUCHING THEE              2.112.8
IN STEED OF TEN, CNE $SIBIL TO US LEFT                2.119.8
ONE, HE DOTH WONDER MONSTER-BREEDING $NYLE            2.120.3
THIS LOVE, TEARS, SIGHES, MAINTAINE EACH
                      ONE HIS ELEMENT                 2.127.4
EACH ONE OF THESE, DOTH AYDE UNTO THE
                      OTHER LENDE                     2.133.14
FROM WHENCE, IF YOU ONE TEARE OF PITTY MOVE           2.151.3
OR TEN TIMES HAPPIER BE IT TEN FOR ONE                3.6.8
MARKE HOW ONE STRING SWEET HUSBAND TO AN OTHER        3.8.9
WHO ALL IN ONE, ONE PLEASING NOTE DO SING             3.8.12
WHO ALL IN ONE, ONE PLEASING NOTE DO SING             3.8.12
WHOSE SPEECHLESSE SCNG BEING MANY, SEEMING ONE        3.8.13
IN ONE OF THINE, FROM THAT WHICH THOU DEPARTEST       3.11.2
BUT I FORBID THEE CNE MOST HAINOUS CRIME              3.19.8
BY ADDING ONE THING TO MY PURPOSE NOTHING             3.20.12
SO LONG AS YOUTH AND THCU ARE OF ONE DATE             3.22.2
THE ONE BY TOYLE, THE OTHER TO COMPLAINE              3.28.7
WISHING ME LIKE TC CNE MORE RICH IN HOPE              3.29.5
EVEN SO MY $SUNNE CNE EARLY MORNE DID SHINE           3.33.9
BUT OUT ALACK, HE WAS BUT ONE HOURE MINE              3.33.11
ALTHOUGH OUR UNDEVIDED LOVES ARE ONE                  3.36.2
IN OUR TWO LOVES THERE IS BUT ONE RESPECT             3.36.5
AND OUR DEARE LOVE LOOSE NAME OF SINGLE CNE           3.39.6
AND THAT THOU TEACHEST HOW TO MAKE ONE TWAINE         3.39.13
BUT HERE'S THE JOY, MY FRIEND AND I ARE CNE           3.42.13
SINCE EVERY ONE, HATH EVERY ONE, ONE SHADE            3.53.3
SINCE EVERY ONE, HATH EVERY ONE, ONE SHADE            3.53.3
SINCE EVERY ONE, HATH EVERY ONE, ONE SHADE            3.53.3
AND YOU BUT ONE, CAN EVERY SHADDOW LEND               3.53.4
THE ONE DOTH SHADDOW OF YOUR BEAUTIE SHOW             3.53.10
WHY WRITE I STILL ALL ONE, EVER THE SAME              3.76.5
THERE LIVES MORE LIFE IN ONE OF YOUR FAIRE EYES       3.83.13
ALL THESE I BETTER IN ONE GENERALL BEST               3.91.8
TO ONE, OF ONE, STILL SUCH, AND EVER SO               3.105.4
TO ONE, OF ONE, STILL SUCH, AND EVER SO               3.105.4
ONE THING EXPRESSING, LEAVES OUT DIFFERENCE           3.105.8
THREE THEAMS IN ONE, WHICH WONDROUS SCOPE
                      AFFORDS                         3.105.12
WHICH THREE TILL NCW, NEVER KEPT SEATE IN ONE         3.105.14
ONE ON ANOTHERS NECKE DC WITNESSE BEARE               3.131.11
ONE WILL OF MINE TC MAKE THY LARGE $WILL MORE         3.135.12
THINKE ALL BUT ONE, AND ME IN THAT ONE $WILL          3.135.14
THINKE ALL BUT ONE, AND ME IN THAT ONE $WILL          3.135.14
I FILL IT FULL WITH WILS, AND MY WILL ONE             3.136.6
AMONG A NUMBER ONE IS RECKON'D NONE                   3.136.8
THOUGH IN THY STORES ACCCUNT I ONE MUST BE            3.136.10
DISWADE ONE FOOLISH HEART FROM SERVING THEE           3.141.10
ONE OF HER FETHERED CREATURES BROAKE AWAY             3.143.2
I GESSE ONE ANGEL IN AN OTHERS HEL                    3.144.12
TILL MY BAD ANGEL FIRE MY GOOD ONE OUT                3.144.14
```

```
FOR ME IN SOOTH, NO $MUSE BUT ONE I KNOW              4.3.9
I SWEARE, MY HEART SUCH ONE SHALL SHEW TO THEE        4.4.12
SOME ONE HIS SONG IN $JOVE, AND $JOVE'S
                       STRANGE TALES ATTIRES          4.6.5
BUT ONE WORSE FAULT, $AMBITION, I CONFESSE            4.27.11
IF $FRENCH CAN YET THREE PARTS IN ONE AGREE           4.30.5
WITHIN WHAT BOUNDS CAN ONE HIS LIKING STAY            4.35.3
AND $HUMBLENESSE GROWES ONE WITH $MAJESTIE            4.48.4
ONE HAND FORGOTT TO RULE, TH'OTHER TO FIGHT           4.53.11
BECAUSE I BREATHE NOT LOVE TO EVERIE ONE              4.54.1
WHAT, A WHOLE WEEKE WITHOUT ONE PEECE OF LOOKE        4.56.3
THAT IN ONE SPEECH TWO $NEGATIVES AFFIRME             4.63.14
FORTUNE WHEELES STILL WITH ME IN ONE SORT SLOW        4.66.6
ONE FROM THE OTHER SCARCELY CAN DESCRIE               4.72.3
SWEET LIP, YOU TEACH MY MOUTH WITH ONE
                       SWEET KISSE                    4.80.14
I CAUGHT AT ONE OF THEM A HUNGRIE BIT                 4.82.11
SINCE KIND OR CHANCE GIVES BOTH ONE LIVERIE           4.96.2
SLOW HEAVINESSE IN BOTH HOLDS ONE DEGREE              4.96.6
THEN DOE I DIE, AS ONE WITH LIGHTNING FYRED           5.7.8
ONE DAY I SOUGHT WITH HER HART-THRILLING EIES         5.12.1
GREAT SHAME IT IS TO LEAVE LIKE ONE AFRAYD            5.14.3
SO FAYRE A PEECE FOR ONE REPULSE SO LIGHT             5.14.4
ONE DAY AS I UNWARILY DID GAZE                        5.16.1
ONE OF THOSE ARCHERS CLOSELY I DID SPY                5.16.9
THAT WITH ONE LOOKE SHE DOTH MY LIFE DISMAY           5.21.10
IN ONE SHORT HOURE I FIND BY HER UNDONNE              5.23.8
FOR WITH ONE LOOKE SHE SPILS THAT LONG I SPONNE       5.23.11
AND WITH ONE WORD MY WHOLE YEARS WORK DOTH REND       5.23.12
BUT MY PROUD ONE DOTH WORKE THE GREATER SCATH         5.31.9
SUFFICIENT WORKE FOR ONE MANS SIMPLE HEAD             5.33.7
SINS THAT THIS ONE IS TOST WITH TROUBLOUS FIT         5.33.11
YE SHALL CONDEMNED BE OF MANY A ONE                   5.36.14
YET WITH ONE WORD SHE CAN IT SAVE OR SPILL            5.38.11
ENOUGH IT IS FOR ONE MAN TO SUSTAINE                  5.46.13
AND WITH ONE SALVE BOTH HART AND BODY HEALE           5.50.14
I GOE LYKE ONE THAT HAVING LOST THE FIELD             5.52.2
YE CRUELL ONE, WHAT GLORY CAN BE GOT                  5.57.11
NETHER TO ONE HER SELFE NOR OTHER BENDS               5.59.12
BUT HE MOST HAPPY WHO SUCH ONE LOVES BEST             5.59.14
BEGAN IN ME TO MOVE, ONE YEARE IS SPENT               5.60.6
WHEN LOOSING ONE, TWO LIBERTIES YE GAYNE              5.65.3
THIS ONE DISPARAGEMENT THEY TO YOU GAVE               5.66.3
THAT YE YOUR LOVE LENT TO SO MEANE A ONE              5.66.4
COULD NOT ON EARTH HAVE FOUND ONE FIT FOR MATE        5.66.6
WITH LOVE MAY ONE ANOTHER ENTERTAYNE                  5.68.12
WHERE EVERY ONE THAT MISSETH THEN HER MAKE            5.70.11
ONE DAY I WROTE HER NAME UPON THE STRAND              5.75.1
LET NOT ONE SPARKE OF FILTHY LUSTFULL FYRE            5.84.1
NE ONE LIGHT GLANCE OF SENSUALL DESYRE                5.84.3
ONES                   1
WHILST BLINDED ONES MINE ERROURS NEVER GESSE          1.3.8
ONE'S                  2
NO DOOME SHOULD MAKE ONE'S HEAV'N BECOME
                       HIS HELL                       4.86.14
LYKE AS A BYRD THAT IN ONES HAND DOTH SPY             5.73.5
ONLY                   77
I ONELY SOUGHT THE BLISSE TO HAVE HER SIGHT           1.36.12
PITTY AND SMILES MUST ONELY YEELD THEE PRAISE         1.51.12
PENSIVE ALONE, ONELY BUT WITH $DISPAIRE               1.60.10
```

```
BUT ONELY I, GUILTLESSE OF MURTH'RING IT              2.2.4
TO HAVE SEENE THEE, THEIR $SEXES ONELY GLORY          2.6.12
ONELY TWO $LOOPE-HOLES, THEN I MIGHT BEHOLD           2.8.4
ONELY THAT LITTLE WHICH TO $ME WAS LENT               2.10.13
AND ONELY ABSENT, WHEN $WEE ARE TOGETHER              2.11.8
IN JUDGING, $REASON ONELY IS HER $NAME                2.12.9
ONELY BY DYING, BORNE THE VERY SAME                   2.16.12
WHERE $FAME BY $DEATH IS ONELY TO BE GOT              2.24.11
OR ONELY YOU DOE VIOLATE HER $LAWES                   2.27.14
THY HALLOW'D $TEMPLE ONELY IS MY $HEART               2.30.14
THAT FAIRE $IDEA ONELY LIVES BY THEE                  2.32.14
THAT I AM ONELY STARV'D IN MY DESIRE                  2.34.4
THAT I AM ONELY STARV'D IN MY DESIRE                  2.34.8
AND YET AM ONELY STARV'D IN MY DESIRE                 2.34.12
WHO ONELY WRITE, MY SKILL IN $VERSE TO PROVE          2.35.4
ONELY BY $VERTUE THAT PROCEEDS FROM THEE              2.35.14
WHY SHOULD'ST THOU, $NIGHT, ABUSE ME ONELY THUS       2.37.10
AND YET 'TIS THOU DO'ST ONELY SEVER US+               2.37.12
ONELY I CALL ON MY DIVINE $IDEA                       2.39.14
ONELY MY COMFORT STILL CONSISTS IN THIS               2.42.13
AND ONELY REST CONTENTED WITH THE $LIGHT              2.43.6
ONELY COMPELL'D ON THIS POORE GOOD TO BOAST           2.43.13
ONELY TO SHEW HER $BEAUTIES $SOV'RAIGNE $POW'R        2.50.14
AND ONELY WRITE, MY SKILL IN VERSE TO PROVE           2.112.4
AND IN THY HEAVEN, THERE ONELY IS MY HELL             2.123.14
ONELY MY LOVE IS IN THE FIRE INGRAVED                 2.127.9
ONELY MY TEARES BY $OCEANS MAY BE GESSED              2.127.10
ONELY MY SIGHES ARE BY THE AYRE EXPRESSED             2.127.11
LOV'D MORE THEN LIFE, YET ONELY ART HIS LOVE          2.129.11
UNTO HER VEYNES, THE ONELY $PHOENIX PLUME             2.148.8
FOR ALL MY WOES, THAT ONELY SHALL SUFFISE             2.151.4
AND ONLY HERAULD TO THE GAUDY SPRING                  3.1.10
THOU BEST OF DEEREST, AND MINE ONELY CARE             3.48.7
BUT FOR THEIR VIRTUE ONLY IS THEIR SHOW               3.54.9
THOUGH TO IT SELFE, IT ONELY LIVE AND DIE             3.94.10
BUT MUTUALL RENDER, ONELY ME FOR THEE                 3.125.12
ONELY MY PLAGUE THUS FARRE I COUNT MY GAINE           3.141.13
BUT ONLY $STELLA'S EYES AND $STELLA'S HART            4.23.14
HE KNOWES NOT) GROW IN ONLY FOLLIE RICH               4.24.14
BY ONLY THOSE TWO STARRES IN $STELLA'S FACE           4.26.14
SO IN MY SWELLING BREAST THAT ONLY I                  4.27.7
PRINCESSE OF $BEAUTIE, FOR WHOSE ONLY SAKE            4.28.6
LOVE ONELY READING UNTO ME THIS ART                   4.28.14
THAT SHE, ME THINKS, NOT ONELY SHINES BUT SINGS       4.38.8
ONLY LOV'D $TYRANTS, JUST IN CRUELTY                  4.42.6
SHE HEARD MY PLAINTS, AND DID NOT ONLY HEARE          4.57.9
ALAS, IF YOU GRAUNT ONLY SUCH DELIGHT                 4.59.12
THAT HEAV'N OF JOYES THROWES ONELY DOWNE ON ME        4.60.3
ALAS, IF THIS THE ONLY METTALL BE                     4.62.12
STELLA, THE ONELY $PLANET OF MY LIGHT                 4.68.1
CHIEFE GOOD, WHERETO MY HOPE DOTH ONLY ASPIRE         4.68.3
THESE THINGS ARE LEFT ME BY MY ONLY $DEARE            4.72.12
SCHOOL'D ONELY BY HIS MOTHER'S TENDER EYE             4.73.2
DOTH LOWRE, NAY, CHIDE., NAY, THREAT FOR
                                ONLY THIS             4.73.7
BUT ONLY FOR THIS WORTHY KNIGHT DURST PROVE           4.75.13
THE ONELY LIGHT OF JOY, THE ONELY WARMTH OF $LOVE     4.76.4
THE ONELY LIGHT OF JOY, THE ONELY WARMTH OF $LOVE     4.76.4
SCORTCH NOT, BUT ONELY DO DARKE CHILLING
                                SPRITES REMOVE        4.76.8
```

AND ONELY CHERISH DOTH WITH INJURIE   4.78.8
BY LINKES OF $LOVE, AND ONLY $NATURE'S ART   4.81.6
SAFE IN MY SOULE, WHICH ONLY DOTH TO THEE   4.86.6
ONLY WITH PAINES MY PAINES THUS EASED BE   4.93.12
ONLY TRUE SIGHS, YOU DO NOT GO AWAY   4.95.12
MINE EYES THEN ONLY WINKE, FOR SPITE PERCHANCE   4.98.13
ONELY UNTO THE HEAV'N OF $STELLA'S FACE   4.105.7
THERE SHINES A JOY FROM THEE MY ONLY LIGHT   4.108.4
AND IN MY JOYES FOR THEE MY ONLY ANNOY   4.108.14
OF NATURES SKILL THE ONELY COMPLEMENT   5.24.3
ONELY LET HER ABSTAINE FROM CRUELTY   5.42.13
ONELY MY PAINES WIL BE THE MORE TO GET HER   5.51.13
BUT ONELY THAT IS PERMANENT AND FREE   5.79.7
HE ONELY FAYRE, AND WHAT HE FAYRE HATH MADE   5.79.13
ONELY BEHOLD HER RARE PERFECTION   5.84.13
BUT TH'ONELY IMAGE OF THAT HEAVENLY RAY   5.88.7
ONSET   1
BUT IN THE ONSET COME, SO STALL I TASTE   3.90.11
ONWARD   2
MY GREEFE LIES ONWARD AND MY JOY BEHIND   3.50.14
NOW BLESSED YOU, BEARE ONWARD BLESSED ME   4.84.5
ONWARDS   1
AS THOU GOEST ONWARDS STILL WILL PLUCKE
                          THEE BACKE   3.126.6
OPE   1
WITH WINDOWES OPE THEN MOST MY MIND DOTH LIE   4.99.5
OPEN   6
AND LAIES TO VIEW MY $VULTUR-GNAWNE HART OPEN   1.15.8
BUT ON HER $RAYES WITH OPEN $EYES IT STOOD   2.56.6
CAST MY DESARTS INTO THE OPEN AYRE   2.142.10
AND KEEPE MY DROOPING EYE-LIDS OPEN WIDE   3.27.7
IS IT THY WIL, THY $IMAGE SHOULD KEEPE OPEN   3.61.1
EITHER TO DO LIKE HIM, WHICH OPEN SHONE   4.22.10
OPENED   1
WAS HELD, IN OPEND SENSE IT FLIES AWAY   4.38.10
OPENS   2
AN OTHER PASSAGE OPENS AT HER VOICE   1.27.8
A DOUBLE KEY, WHICH OPENS TO THE HEART   4.79.6
OPINION   1
BEAUTY AND YOUTH T'OPINION AND DISDAINE   1.23.12
OPPOSE   1
I THUS OPPOSE MY $REASONS FORCES WHOLLY   2.28.4
OPPOSED   1
BEING STEDFASTLY OPPOSED TO THE SAME   2.30.4
OPPRESS   1
A FEEBLE BEAST, DOTH FELLY HIM OPPRESSE   5.56.4
OPPRESSED   6
MY FENCE OPPRESS'D, HAD FAILD, AND HEART
                          HAD BROKEN   1.7.14
BUT DAY BY NIGHT AND NIGHT BY DAY OPREST   3.28.4
SINKES DOWNE TO DEATH, OPPREST WITH MELANCHOLIE   3.45.8
IF VAINE LOVE HAVE MY SIMPLE SOULE OPPREST   4.4.3
THROUGH THAT DARKE FORNACE TO MY HART OPPREST   4.108.3
REMEMBRANCE OF ALL PAINES WHICH HIM OPPREST   5.63.12
OPPRESSING   1
OPPRESSING MORTALL SENSE, MY DEATH PROCEED   4.42.13
OPPRESSION   1
WHEN DAIES OPPRESSION IS NOT EAZD BY NIGHT   3.28.3
ORANGE   1
TRUST IN THE SHADE OF PLEASING $ORANGE TREE   4.30.8

```
ORATOR                    1
   THE $ORATOUR SO FARRE MEN'S HARTS DOTH BIND        4.58.2
ORB                       1
   WHOSE INFLUENCE RULE THE $ORBE OF MY POORE HART+   1.34.10
ORCADES                   1
   THENCE TAKE YOU $WING UNTO THE $ORCADES            2.25.6
ORDAINED                  2
   NIGHT WAS ORDAYN'D, TOGETHER $FRIENDS TO KEEPE     2.37.4
   THEN SO BAD END FOR HERETICKS ORDAYNED             5.48.6
ORDER                     3
   WHICH THERE IN ORDER TAKE THEIR SEVERALL PLACES    2.4.4
   WITH ONE MORE $ORDER, THESE NINE $ORDERS
                          GLADDETH                    2.18.12
   WITH ONE MORE ORDER, THESE NINE ORDERS GLADDETH    2.108.12
ORDERING                  1
   STRIKES EACH IN EACH BY MUTUALL ORDERING           3.8.10
ORDERS                    4
   NINE ORDERS FIRST OF $ANGELS BE IN $HEAVEN         2.18.5
   WITH ONE MORE $ORDER, THESE NINE $ORDERS
                          GLADDETH                    2.18.12
   NINE ORDERS FIRST OF $ANGELS BE IN HEAVEN          2.108.5
   WITH ONE MORE ORDER, THESE NINE ORDERS GLADDETH    2.108.12
ORE                       1
   RESTORE THY TRESSES TO THE GOLDEN $ORE             1.19.1
ORIENT                    2
   AND TO TH'$ORIENT DO THY $PEARLES REMOVE           1.19.4
   LOE IN THE $ORIENT WHEN THE GRACIOUS LIGHT         3.7.1
ORNAMENT                  7
   THOU THAT ART NOW THE WORLDS FRESH ORNAMENT        3.1.9
   WHO HEAVEN IT SELFE FOR ORNAMENT DOTH USE          3.21.3
   BY THAT SWEET ORNAMENT WHICH TRUTH DOTH GIVE       3.54.2
   WITHOUT ALL ORNAMENT, IT SELFE AND TRUE            3.68.10
   THE ORNAMENT OF BEAUTY IS SUSPECT                  3.70.3
   MADE FOR TO BE THE WORLDS MOST ORNAMENT            5.53.10
   THE THIRD MY LOVE, MY LIVES LAST ORNAMENT          5.74.9
ORNAMENTS                 2
   THAT HAVE PROPHAN'D THEIR SCARLET ORNAMENTS        3.142.6
   AND ALL THOSE PRETIOUS ORNAMENTS DEFACE            5.31.4
ORPHAN                    4
   TH'$ORPHAN OF $FORTUNE, BORNE TO BE HER SCORNE     1.26.3
   AND THUS (POORE $ORPHAN) LYING IN DISTRESSE        2.116.17
   MY $ORPHAN SENCE FLIES TO THE INWARD SIGHT         4.88.10
   BARE ME IN HAND, THAT IN THIS $ORPHANE PLACE       4.106.3
ORPHANS                   1
   BUT HOPE OF $ORPHANS, AND UN-FATHERED FRUITE       3.97.10
ORPHEUS                   2
   WHILST I LIKE $ORPHEUS SING TO $TREES
                          AND $STONES                 2.45.12
   THEN $ORPHEUS WITH HIS HARP THEYR STRIFE DID BAR   5.44.4
OSSA                      1
   PELION AND $OSSA, FROSTY $CAUCASE OLD              2.120.6
OTHER                     68
   WITNESSE YOUR $FATHERS GRIEFE EXCEEDES ALL OTHER   1.2.4
   AN OTHER PASSAGE OPENS AT HER VOICE                1.27.8
   I WHO DID NEVER JOY IN OTHER $SUN                  1.33.5
   NOR OTHER HAND COULD GIVE SO TRUE A TOUCH          1.57.14
   NONE OTHER FAME MINE UNAMBITIOUS $MUSE             1.58.1
   ALL OTHER HONORS DOE MY HOPES REFUSE               1.58.3
   NO OTHER PROUDER $BROOKES SHALL HEARE MY WRONG     1.58.14
   NO OTHER $DRINKE WOULD SERVE THIS $GLUTTONS TURNE  2.7.5
```

```
AS $OTHER $MEN, SO I MY SELFE DOE $MUSE                    2.9.1
SENSELESSE WITH TOO MUCH $JOY, EACH OTHER SEEING          2.11.7
ONE NUMBER OF THE $EARTH, THE OTHER BOTH $DIVINE          2.18.3
YET SERVES NOT $THIS.. WHAT NEXT, WHAT
                        OTHER $SHIFT+                     2.19.9
WHERE OTHER $MEN IN DEPTH OF $PASSION CRIE                2.24.13
IS $NOT $LOVE HERE, AS 'TIS IN OTHER $CLYMES              2.27.1
AND TELLS THE OTHER, HOW THEY SHOULD BE BLEST             2.29.12
THIS TO EACH OTHER MUTUALLY THEY CRAVE                    2.33.12
THAT SINCE THE ONE CANNOT THE OTHER BEE                   2.33.13
ONE BY THY $NAME, THE OTHER TOUCHING THEE                 2.35.8
HOW HAPPY ARE ALL OTHER LIVING $THINGS                    2.37.5
WHEN $DARKNESSE HATH OBSCUR'D EACH OTHER $LIGHT           2.55.14
WITH $PROVERBS THUS EACH OTHER INTERTAINE                 2.59.2
AND HAVING THUS AWHILE EACH OTHER THWARTED                2.59.13
WHEN DARKNES HATH OBSCUR'D EACH OTHER LIGHT              2.102.14
ONE NUMBER OF THE EARTH, THE OTHER BOTH DIVINE           2.108.3
ONE BY THY NAME, THE OTHER TOUCHING THEE                 2.112.8
WHEREIN EACH FAYREST PART EXCELLETH OTHER                2.123.4
EACH ONE OF THESE, DOTH AYDE UNTO THE
                        OTHER LENDE                      2.133.14
NOW IS THE TIME THAT FACE SHOULD FORME AN OTHER           3.3.2
THAT'S FOR THY SELFE TO BREED AN OTHER THEE               3.6.7
FROM HIS LOW TRACT AND LOOKE AN OTHER WAY                 3.7.12
MARKE HOW ONE STRING SWEET HUSBAND TO AN OTHER           3.8.9
MAKE THEE AN OTHER SELFE FOR LOVE OF ME                  3.10.13
AND YOUR SWEET SEMBLANCE TO SOME OTHER GIVE              3.13.4
THE ONE BY TOYLE, THE OTHER TO COMPLAINE                 3.28.7
BOTH FINDE EACH OTHER, AND I LOOSE BOTH TWAINE           3.42.11
THE OTHER TWO, SLIGHT AYRE, AND PURGING FIRE             3.45.1
THE FIRST MY THOUGHT, THE OTHER MY DESIRE                3.45.3
AND EACH DOTH GOOD TURNES NOW UNTO THE OTHER             3.47.2
AN OTHER TIME MINE EYE IS MY HEARTS GUEST                3.47.7
THE OTHER AS YOUR BOUNTIE DOTH APPEARE                   3.53.11
AS I ALL OTHER IN ALL WORTHS SURMOUNT                    3.62.8
IN OTHER ACCENTS DOE THIS PRAISE CONFOUND                3.69.7
AND MY SICK $MUSE DOTH GIVE AN OTHER PLACE               3.79.4
I THINKE GOOD THOUGHTS, WHILST OTHER WRITE
                        GOOD WORDES                      3.85.5
WHEN OTHER PETTIE GRIEFES HAVE DONE THEIR SPIGHT        3.90.10
AND OTHER STRAINES OF WOE, WHICH NOW SEEME WOE          3.90.13
THY LOOKES WITH ME, THY HEART IN OTHER PLACE             3.93.4
OUR BLUSHING SHAME, AN OTHER WHITE DISPAIRE              3.99.9
FOR TO NO OTHER PASSE MY VERSES TEND                    3.103.11
FAIRE, KINDE AND TRUE, VARRYING TO OTHER WORDS          3.105.10
THESE BLENCHES GAVE MY HEART AN OTHER YOUTH             3.110.7
MY SELFE $ILE FORFEIT, SO THAT OTHER MINE               3.134.3
USE ALL TO HELPE HIS OTHER CONQUERINGS                   4.29.8
WITH EITHER LIP HE DOTH THE OTHER KISSE                  4.43.11
ONE HAND FORGOTT TO RULE, TH'OTHER TO FIGHT              4.53.11
NOR OTHER SUGRING OF MY SPEECH TO PROVE                  4.55.10
LOOKING ON ME, WHILE I LOOKT OTHER WAY                   4.66.12
ONE FROM THE OTHER SCARCELY CAN DESCRIE                  4.72.3
THE PRETTIE DEATH, WHILE EACH IN OTHER LIVE              4.79.11
IF THOU PRAISE NOT, ALL OTHER PRAISE IS SHAME            4.90.4
HER SELFE (TO SHEW NO OTHER JOY HATH PLACE)              4.97.7
WHOM IF YE PLEASE, I CARE FOR OTHER NONE                 5.1.14
WHOSE PRYDE DEPRAVES EACH OTHER BETTER PART              5.31.3
SITH TO ALL OTHER BEASTES OF BLOODY RACE                 5.31.5
NETHER TO ONE HER SELFE NOR OTHER BENDS                  5.59.12
```

```
NE THINKS OF OTHER HEAVEN, BUT HOW IT MIGHT         5.72.11
HART NEED NOT WISH NONE OTHER HAPPINESSE            5.72.13
ALL OTHER FAYRE LYKE FLOWRES UNTYMELY FADE          5.79.14
OTHERS                  22
LET OTHERS SING OF $KNIGHTS AND $PALLADINES         1.55.1
LET OTHERS STRIVE TO ENTERTAINE WITH $WORDS         2.4.9
AS COVETOUS THE OTHERS USE TO HAVE                  2.33.10
NOT TO AVAILE YOU, NOR DOE OTHERS GOOD              2.58.14
NO LOVE TOWARD OTHERS IN THAT BOSOME SITS           3.9.13
AND DIE AS FAST AS THEY SEE OTHERS GROW             3.12.12
FROM ME FARRE OF, WITH OTHERS ALL TO NEERE          3.61.14
WHEN OTHERS WOULD GIVE LIFE, AND BRING A TOMBE      3.83.12
THEN OTHERS, FOR THE BREATH OF WORDS RESPECT        3.85.13
WHO MOVING OTHERS, ARE THEMSELVES AS STONE          3.94.3
OTHERS, BUT STEWARDS OF THEIR EXCELLENCE            3.94.8
NOT BY OUR FEELING, BUT BY OTHERS SEEING            3.121.4
SHALL WILL IN OTHERS SEEME RIGHT GRACIOUS           3.135.7
OH THOUGH I LOVE WHAT OTHERS DOE ABHOR              3.150.11
WITH OTHERS THOU SHOULDST NOT ABHOR MY STATE        3.150.12
WHICH OTHERS SAID DID MAKE THEIR SOULES TO PINE     4.16.6
THE $SUNNE WHICH OTHERS BURN'D, DID HER
                                     BUT KISSE      4.22.14
OTHERS, BECAUSE THE $PRINCE MY SERVICE TRIES        4.23.7
FAWNE ON MY SELF, AND OTHERS TO DESPISE             4.27.8
MY STILL KEPT COURSE, WHILE OTHERS SLEEPE,
                                     TO MONE        4.40.4
OTHERS, BECAUSE OF BOTH SIDES I DO TAKE             4.41.9
WHEN OTHERS GAZE UPON THEYR SHADOWES VAYNE          5.88.6
OTHER'S                 13
THESE NOW THE OTHERS $HAPPINESSE DOE PRAYSE         2.33.7
COMPARE MY $WORTH WITH OTHERS BASE $DESERT          2.60.6
AND WHILST MY HART AND EYE, ENVY EACH
                              OTHERS PRAISE         2.133.11
YET OTHERS FORCE, THE OTHERS FORCE REVIVING         2.136.12
YET OTHERS FORCE, THE OTHERS FORCE REVIVING         2.136.12
AND OTHERS FOE, THE OTHERS FOE IMBRACE              2.136.13
AND OTHERS FOE, THE OTHERS FOE IMBRACE              2.136.13
COMPARE MY WORTH WITH OTHERS BASE DESERT            2.149.6
MAKING NO SUMMER OF AN OTHERS GREENE                3.68.11
I GESSE ONE ANGEL IN AN OTHERS HEL                  3.144.12
OF OTHER'S CHILDREN CHANGELINGS USE TO MAKE         4.28.2
A MONSTER, OTHER'S HARME, SELFE-MISERIE             4.78.5
SEEKES WITH SWEET PEACE TO SALVE EACH
                              OTHERS WOUND          5.65.12
IN OTHERS WORKES THOU DOOST BUT MEND THE STILE      3.78.11
OF OTHERS VOYCES, THAT MY $ADDERS SENCE             3.112.10
FOR WHY SHOULD OTHERS FALSE ADULTERAT EYES          3.121.5
ROBD OTHERS BEDS REVENUES OF THEIR RENTS            3.142.8
OFT TURNING OTHERS' LEAVES, TO SEE IF
                          THENCE WOULD FLOW         4.1.7
AND OTHERS' FEETE STILL SEEM'D BUT STRANGERS
                               IN MY WAY            4.1.11
WITHOUT MY PLUMES FROM OTHERS' WINGS I TAKE         4.90.11
IN HER OWNE POWRE, AND SCORNETH OTHERS AYDE         5.58.2
OUGHT                   19
SO RARE A FAITH OUGHT BETTER BE REWARDED            1.11.8
OH GIVE THY SELFE THE THANKES IF OUGHT IN ME        3.38.5
WER'T OUGHT TO ME I BORE THE CANOPY                 3.125.1
OUGHT TO BE KING, FROM WHOSE RULES WHO DO SWERVE    4.5.3
HATH THIS WORLD OUGHT SO FAIRE AS $STELLA IS+       4.21.14
```

NOR OUGHT DO CARE, THOUGH SOME ABOVE ME SIT	4.64.11
THAT ERE BY THEM OUGHT UNDERTAKEN BE	4.107.3
WAS NEVER IN THIS WORLD OUGHT WORTHY TRIDE	5.5.13
NO WORD WAS HEARD OF HER THAT MOST IT OUGHT	5.19.10
MEN TO DEVOTION OUGHT TO BE INCLYND	5.22.2
SITH NEVER OUGHT WAS EXCELLENT ASSAYDE	5.51.7
NE OUGHT SO HARD, BUT HE THAT WOULD ATTEND	5.51.9
NE OUGHT FOR TEMPEST DOTH FROM IT DEPART	5.59.7
NE OUGHT FOR FAYRER WEATHERS FALSE DELIGHT	5.59.8
T'ACCUSE OF PRIDE, OR RASHLY BLAME FOR OUGHT	5.61.4
SUCH HEAVENLY FORMES OUGHT RATHER WORSHIPT BE	5.61.13
SO LET US LOVE, DEARE LOVE, LYKE AS WE OUGHT	5.68.13
NE OUGHT I SEE, THOUGH IN THE CLEAREST DAY	5.88.5
NE JOY OF OUGHT THAT UNDER HEAVEN DOTH HOVE	5.89.9

OURS   1

CRIE, '$VICTORIE, THIS FAIRE DAY ALL IS OURS'	4.12.11

OUSE   2

YORKE MANY $WONDERS OF HER $OWSE CAN TELL	2.32.6
YORKE, MANY WONDERS OF HER $OUSE CAN TELL	2.124.6

OUT   72

SIGH OUT A $STORIE OF HER CRUELL DEEDES	1.2.5
DID FORCE ME GRONE OUT GRIEFES, AND UTTER THIS	1.7.12
DELIA MY HART HATH LEARND OUT OF THOSE EYES	1.20.14
TO SAVE THINE OWNE, STRETCH OUT THE FAIREST HAND	1.46.8
STRETCH OUT THE FAIREST HAND, A PLEDGE OF PEACE	1.46.9
FROM OUT DISPAIRE, WHEREIN THEY LIVE CONFINDE+	1.49.4
SEEKE OUT SOME PLACE, AND SEE IF ANY PLACE	1.52.9
YET $HEAV'N WILL STILL HAVE $MURTHER OUT AT LAST	2.2.14
HOW FALS IT OUT SO STRANGELY YOU REPLY+	2.5.2
I SAY, $YOU $LOVE, YOU PEULE ME OUT A $NO	2.5.6
SAVE MEE I $CRIE, YOU SIGH ME OUT A $NO	2.5.8
THY $PEARLY $TEETH OUT OF THY $HEAD SO CLEANE	2.8.11
SINCE $YOU IN $ME, MY SELFE SINCE OUT OF $ME	2.11.4
AND WHEN BY $MEANES, TO DRIVE IT OUT I TRY	2.20.6
POWR'D OUT WHAT FIRST FROM QUICKE $INVENTION CAME	2.21.6
ALL UNCLEANE $THOUGHTS, FOULE $SPIRITS	
CAST OUT IN MEE	2.35.13
REASON PUT BACK, DOTH OUT OF SIGHT REMOVE	2.38.13
AND $LOVE ALONE PICKS REASON OUT OF LOVE	2.38.14
AND IN BARE WORDS PAINT OUT MY $PASSIONS PAINE	2.42.7
IS MODEL'D OUT THE $WORLD OF MY $DISGRACE	2.44.4
ALL UNCLEANE THOUGHTS, FOULE SPIRITS CAST	
OUT IN MEE	2.112.13
WITH TEARES OUT OF THE $CHANNELS OF MINE EYES	2.115.9
AND IN BARE WORDS PAYNT OUT MY PASSIONS PAYNE	2.128.7
WHEN OUR WORLDS SUNNE IS VANISHT OUT OF SIGHT	2.129.4
REASON PUT BACK, DOTH OUT OF SIGHT REMOVE	2.131.13
AND WERE THEIR BRAVE STATE OUT OF MEMORY	3.15.8
BUT SINCE SHE PRICKT THEE OUT FOR WOMENS	
PLEASURE	3.20.13
BUT OUT ALACK, HE WAS BUT ONE HOURE MINE	3.33.11
AND BROILES ROOTE OUT THE WORKE OF MASONRY	3.55.6
THAT WEARE THIS WORLD OUT TO THE ENDING DOOME	3.55.12
TO FIND OUT SHAMES AND IDLE HOURES IN ME	3.61.7
ARE VANISHING, OR VANISHT OUT OF SIGHT	3.63.7
O HOW SHALL SUMMERS HUNNY BREATH HOLD OUT	3.65.5
WITH OUT ALL BAYLE SHALL CARRY ME AWAY	3.74.2
TO LINGER OUT A PURPOSD OVER-THROW	3.90.8
WHICH FOR THEIR HABITATION CHOSE OUT THEE	3.95.10
ONE THING EXPRESSING, LEAVES OUT DIFFERENCE	3.105.8

```
SEEMES SEEING, BUT EFFECTUALLY IS OUT              3.113.4
BUT BEARES IT OUT EVEN TO THE EDGE OF DOOME        3.116.12
HOW HAVE MINE EIES OUT CF THEIR $SPHEARES
                         BENE FITTED               3.119.7
TILL MY BAD ANGEL FIRE MY GOOD UNE OUT             3.144.14
BUT RYSING AT THY NAME DOTH POINT OUT THEE         3.151.9
WHILE TEARES POWRE CUT HIS INKE, AND SIGHS
                  BREATHE OUT HIS WORDS            4.6.10
WHILE TEARES POWRE CUT HIS INKE, AND SIGHS
                  BREATHE OUT HIS WORDS            4.6.10
BREATHE OUT THE FLAMES WHICH BURNE WITHIN
                  MY HEART                         4.28.13
WITH SHIELD OF PROOFE SHIELD ME FROM OUT
                  THE PREASE                       4.39.5
AND CANNOT CHUSE BUT PUT OUT WHAT I WRITE          4.50.10
GROWNE NOW HIS SLAVES, HE FORST THEM OUT TO FIND   4.57.3
WHAT SIGHES STOLNE CUT, OR KILD BEFORE
                  FULL BORNE+                      4.67.9
ENVIE, PUT OUT THINE EYES, LEAST THOU DO SEE       4.69.3
SHALL PAINT OUT JOY, THOUGH BUT IN BLACKE
                  AND WHITE                        4.70.11
FROM OUT THAT NOYSOME GULFE, WHICH GAPING LIES     4.78.3
OR OF THY GIFTS AT LEAST SHADE OUT SOME PART       4.81.8
OUT TRAYTOUR ABSENCE, DAREST THOU COUNSELL ME      4.88.1
FROM OUT THY HEAVY MOULD, THAT INBENT EYES         4.94.3
WOULD FAINE DRIVE CLOUDES FROM OUT MY
                  HEAVY CHEERE                     4.97.11
BUT WHEN $AURORA LEADES CUT $PHOEBUS' DAUNCE       4.98.12
WHILE SOBD OUT WORDS A PERFECT $MUSIKE GIVE        4.100.11
WITH SIGHT THEREOF CRIDE OUT., O FAIRE DISGRACE    4.103.13
FROM OUT MY RIBS, AND PUFFING PROVE THAT I         4.104.13
BREAKE FORTH AT LENGTH OUT OF THE INNER PART       5.2.5
NEW YEARE FORTH LOCKING OUT OF JANUS GATE          5.4.1
AND CALLING FORTH CUT OF SAD $WINTERS NIGHT        5.4.5
SHOOT OUT HIS DARTS TO BASE AFFECTIONS WOUND+      5.8.6
THAT DEATH OUT OF THEYR SHINY BEAMES DOE DART      5.24.7
OUT OF HER COURSE DOTH WANDER FAR ASTRAY           5.34.4
OUT OF HER BANDS YE BY NO MEANES SHALL GET         5.37.12
COMES FORTH AFRESH CUT CF THEIR LATE DISMAY        5.40.11
BY WHOM MY SPIRIT CUT OF DUST WAS RAYSED           5.74.10
AND EEK MY NAME BEE WYPED OUT LYKEWIZE             5.75.8
OUT OF MY PRISON I WILL BREAKE ANEW                5.80.6
BREAKE OUT, THAT MAY HER SACRED PEACE MOLEST       5.84.2
OUTBRAVES               1
   THE BASEST WEED OUT-BRAVES HIS DIGNITY          3.94.12
OUTCAST                 2
   YOU OUT-CAST $EAGLETS, DAZELED WITH YOUR $SUNNE 1.3.10
   I ALL ALONE BEWEEPE MY OUT-CAST STATE           3.29.2
OUTGOING                1
   SO THOU, THY SELFE OUT-GOING IN THY NOON        3.7.13
OUTLIVE                 3
   ETERNAL NUMBERS TO OUT-LIVE LONG DATE           3.38.12
   OF $PRINCES SHALL CUT-LIVE THIS POWREFULL RIME  3.55.2
   TO MAKE HIM MUCH OUT-LIVE A GILDED TOMBE        3.101.11
OUTRIGHT                1
   KILL ME OUT-RIGHT WITH LOOKES, AND RID MY PAINE 3.139.14
OUTSIDE                 2
   NOT THIS FAIRE OUTSIDE, WHICH OUR HEARTS
                  DOTH MOVE                        4.52.8
   NOT FOR HIS FAIRE CUTSIDE, NOR WELL LINED BRAINE 4.75.3
```

OUTSTRIPPED   1
  AND THOUGH THEY BE OUT-STRIPT BY EVERY PEN   3.32.6
OUTWARD   9
  NOR ARE MY PASSIONS LIMND FOR OUTWARD HEW   1.4.5
  NEITHER IN INWARD WORTH NOR OUTWARD FAIRE   3.16.11
  AS THUS, MINE EYES DUE IS THEIR OUTWARD PART   3.46.13
  THEIR OUTWARD THUS WITH OUTWARD PRAISE IS CROWND   3.69.5
  THEIR OUTWARD THUS WITH OUTWARD PRAISE IS CROWND   3.69.5
  WHERE TIME AND OUTWARD FORME WOULD SHEW IT DEAD   3.108.14
  WITH MY EXTERN THE OUTWARD HONORING   3.125.2
  PAINTING THY OUTWARD WALLS SO COSTLIE GAY+   3.146.4
  PLAYING AND SHINING IN EACH OUTWARD PART   4.11.13
OUTWARDLY   1
  AND YET YOUR $GRACES OUTWARDLY $DIVINE   2.57.2
OUTWEARS   1
  WITH MY SOULES FIRE, MY LIFE DISDAINE OUT-WEARES   2.132.7
OUTWENT   1
  THEN AL THOSE FOURTY WHICH MY LIFE OUTWENT   5.60.8
OUTWORN   3
  THE RICH PROUD COST OF OUTWORNE BURIED AGE   3.64.2
  THUS IS HIS CHEEKE THE MAP OF DAIES OUT-WORNE   3.68.1
  MANY LONG WEARY DAYES I HAVE OUTWORNE   5.87.2
OVER   10
  LET HER NOT STILL TRIUMPH OVER THE PRIZE   1.22.13
  NOW IF THOU WOULD'ST, WHEN ALL HAVE GIVEN
           HIM OVER   2.61.13
  THEN SO TO CAST HER $BALLAST OVER BOORD   2.134.8
  IF $NATURE (SOVERAINE MISTERES OVER WRACK)   3.126.5
  LOOKS OVER THE WORLD, AND CAN FIND NOTHING SUCH   4.9.10
  DEERE, THEREFORE BE NOT JEALOUS OVER ME   4.91.12
  AND REIGNETH OVER EVERY BEAST IN FIELD   5.20.6
  I MAY IN TRUMP OF FAME BLAZE OVER ALL   5.29.12
  DIDST MAKE THY TRIUMPH OVER DEATH AND SIN   5.68.2
  TO SING YOUR NAME AND PRAYSES OVER ALL   5.73.12
OVERCAME   1
  I WOULD KNOW BY WHAT RIGHT THIS PALENESSE
           OVERCAME   4.102.7
OVERCAST   1
  ME TO DIRECT, WITH CLOUDES IS OVERCAST   5.34.6
OVERCOME   2
  FAVOURS (I THINKE) WOULD SENCE QUITE OVERCOME   1.17.13
  WITH DARKEST SHADE DOTH OVERCOME MY DAY   4.89.2
OVERFLOWING   1
  OR CHOKED BE WITH OVERFLOWING GALL   5.43.4
OVER-GOES   1
  THAT OVER-GOES MY BLUNT INVENTION QUITE   3.103.7
OVERGROWN   1
  AND VAPOURS OF DISDAINE SO OVERGROWNE   1.21.3
OVER-PARTIAL   1
  IF EYES CORRUPT BY OVER-PARTIALL LOOKES   3.137.5
OVERPASS   1
  THAT MAKES ME OFT MY BEST FRIENDS OVERPASSE   4.27.12
OVERPLUS   1
  AND $WILL TOO BOOTE, AND $WILL IN OVER-PLUS   3.135.2
OVER-PRIZE   1
  TO $SUCH AS SAY, $THY $LOVE I OVER-PRIZE   2.28.1
OVER-SOON   2
  FINDING THEIR $OBJECTS OVER-SOONE DEPART   2.33.6
  BEHOLD, THEIR OBJECTS OVER-SOONE DEPART   2.133.6

```
OVERSPREAD              1
  AND THAT FAIRE YOU MY $SUNNE, THUS OVERSPRED       4.91.3
OVERTHROW              3
  THEN IF HE HAD THE TYRANT OVER-THROWNE             1.56.4
  TO LINGER OUT A PURPOSD OVER-THROW                 3.90.8
  THERE SHALL HE FIND ALL VICES' OVERTHROW           4.71.5
OVERTHROWN             2
  I SEND DEFIANCE, SINCE IF OVERTHROWNE              2.63.13
  WEIGH THEN HOW I BY THEE AM OVERTHROWNE            4.40.8
OVERTHWART             1
  ALAS, WHAT CAUSE IS THERE SO OVERTHWART            4.44.7
OVERTURN               1
  WHEN WASTEFULL WARRE SHALL $STATUES OVER-TURNE     3.55.5
OVER-WISE              1
  O FOOLES, OR OVER-WISE, ALAS THE RACE              4.23.12
OWE                    3
  THEN THOU ALONE KINGDOMES OF HEARTS SHOULDST OWE   3.70.14
  WHICH UNTO IT BY BIRTHRIGHT I DO OW                4.18.6
  SUCH COLTISH GYRES, THAT TO MY BIRTH I OWE         4.21.6
OWES                   1
  SINCE WHAT HE OWES THEE, THOU THY SELFE
                              DOOST PAY              3.79.14
OWEST                  1
  NOR LOOSE POSSESSION OF THAT FAIRE THOU OW'ST      3.18.10
OWN                   83
  LET THEM YET SIGH THEIR OWNE, AND MONE MY WRONGS    1.3.4
  THESE LINES I USE, T'UNBURTHEN MINE OWNE HART       1.4.13
  BY MINE OWNE THOUGHTS, SET ON ME BY MY $FAIRE       1.5.11
  THOSE THAT I FOSTRED OF MINE OWNE ACCORD            1.5.13
  FOR HAPLESSE LOE EVEN WITH MINE OWNE DESIRES        1.13.5
  TO SAVE THINE OWNE, STRETCH OUT THE FAIREST HAND    1.46.8
  OF HER OWNE SEATE, WHEREOF I MADE HER GUIDE         1.47.8
  TO GOE FROM SORROW, AND THINE OWNE DISTRESSE+       1.52.2
  STEALE FROM THY SELFE, AND BE THY CARES
                              OWNE THIEFE            1.52.12
  THEN IF I HAD THE VICTORY MINE OWNE                1.56.7
  FROM MY $SELFE $YOU, OR FROM YOUR OWNE $SELFE I     2.11.14
  BY THINE OWNE LOVED $PSYCHES, BY THE $FIRES         2.36.9
  WHEN SHE HER OWNE PERFECTION WOULD ADMIRE           2.57.6
  THOU VANQUISHING, THE $CONQUEST IS MINE OWNE        2.63.14
  HEAPE THINE OWN VERTUES SEASONED BY THEIR SUNNE     2.106.5
  WITH THINE OWNE SWEETNES AL THE HEAVENS
                              PERFUMING              2.106.10
  AT HER OWN RARE PERFECTIONS SO AMAZED              2.109.8
  AND SHEE ON HER OWNE DESTINY DIVINING              2.109.11
  WITH MURTHERING HANDS IMBRUD IN MINE OWN BLOOD      2.114.12
  WHILST $LOVE (MY $PHOENIX BIRD) IN HER
                              OWN FLAME IS DYING     2.117.12
  THUS WAS THE WANTON CAUSE OF HYS OWNE WOE          2.122.12
  BUT THOU CONTRACTED TO THINE OWNE BRIGHT EYES       3.1.5
  WITHIN THINE OWNE BUD BURIEST THY CONTENT           3.1.11
  TO SAY WITHIN THINE OWNE DEEPE SUNKEN EYES          3.2.7
  AND YOU MUST LIVE DRAWNE BY YOUR OWNE
                              SWEET SKILL            3.16.14
  AND MAKE THE EARTH DEVOURE HER OWNE SWEET BROOD     3.19.2
  A $WOMANS FACE WITH NATURES OWNE HAND PAINTED       3.20.1
  WHOSE STRENGTHS ABONDANCE WEAKENS HIS OWNE HEART    3.23.4
  AND IN MINE OWNE LOVES STRENGTH SEEME TO DECAY      3.23.7
  ORE-CHARG'D WITH BURTHEN OF MINE OWNE LOVES MIGHT   3.23.8
  THINE OWNE SWEET ARGUMENT, TO EXCELLENT            3.38.3
```

```
WHAT CAN MINE OWNE PRAISE TO MINE OWNE
                    SELFE BRING                  3.39.3
WHAT CAN MINE OWNE PRAISE TO MINE OWNE
                    SELFE BRING                  3.39.3
AND WHAT IS'T BUT MINE OWNE WHEN I PRAISE THEE   3.39.4
WITHIN THE KNOWLEDGE OF MINE OWNE DESART         3.49.10
MINE OWNE TRUE LOVE THAT DOTH MY REST DEFEAT     3.61.11
AND FOR MY SELFE MINE OWNE WORTH DO DEFINE       3.62.7
MINE OWNE SELFE LOVE QUITE CONTRARY I READ       3.62.11
BUT THOSE SAME TOUNGS THAT GIVE THEE SO
                    THINE OWNE                   3.69.6
TO DOE MORE FOR ME THEN MINE OWNE DESERT         3.72.6
THY SELFE THOU GAV'ST, THY OWNE WORTH
                    THEN NOT KNOWING             3.87.9
WITH MINE OWNE WEAKENESSE BEING BEST ACQUAINTED  3.88.5
YOUR OWNE GLASSE SHOWES YOU, WHEN YOU
                    LOOKE IN IT                  3.103.14
NOT MINE OWNE FEARES, NOR THE PROPHETICK SOULE   3.107.1
AND THE SAD $AUGURS MOCK THEIR OWNE PRESAGE      3.107.6
GOR'D MINE OWN THOUGHTS, SOLD CHEAP WHAT
                    IS MOST DEARE                3.110.3
NOR HIS OWNE VISION HOULDS WHAT IT DOTH CATCH    3.113.8
AND GIVEN TO TIME YOUR OWNE DEARE PURCHAS'D
                    RIGHT                        3.117.6
AT MY ABUSES, RECKON UP THEIR OWNE               3.121.10
O BUT WITH MINE, COMPARE THOU THINE OWNE STATE   3.142.3
THOSE LIPS THAT $LOVES OWNE HAND DID MAKE        3.145.1
REBELS TO $NATURE, STRIVE FOR THEIR OWNE SMART   4.5.4
MY BEST WITS STILL THEIR OWNE DISGRACE INVENT    4.19.5
THAT MINE OWNE WRITINGS LIKE BAD SERVANTS SHOW   4.21.3
OR CARELESSE OF THE WEALTH BECAUSE HER OWNE      4.22.11
AND DAMNING THEIR OWNE SELVES TO $TANTAL'S SMART 4.24.3
BUT WILT NEW WARRE UPON THINE OWNE BEGIN+        4.36.8
BY $LOVE'S OWNE SELFE, BUT WITH SO CURIOUS
                    DROUGHT                      4.38.7
ACCORDING TO MY $LORD $LOVE'S OWNE BEHEST        4.50.6
WO, HAVING MADE WITH MANY FIGHTS HIS OWNE        4.57.1
PRINTS HIS OWNE LIVELY FORME IN RUDEST BRAINE    4.58.8
HE BARKS, MY SONGS THINE OWNE VOYCE OFT
                    DOTH PROVE                   4.59.6
HER GRAUNT TO ME, BY HER OWNE VERTUE KNOW        4.63.4
WHO HIS OWNE JOY TO HIS OWNE HURT APPLIES        4.78.7
WHO HIS OWNE JOY TO HIS OWNE HURT APPLIES        4.78.7
SO MANIE EYES AY SEEKING THEIR OWNE WOE          4.78.12
HAVE CHANG'D DESERT, LET MINE OWNE CONSCIENCE BE 4.86.2
CAN SCARCE DISCERNE THE SHAPE OF MINE OWNE PAINE 4.94.4
KILS HIS OWNE CHILDREN, TEARES, FINDING
                    THAT THEY                    4.95.10
NIGHT BARD FROM $SUN, THOU FROM THY OWNE
                    SUNNE'S LIGHT                4.96.4
TILL IT HAVE WROUGHT WHAT THY OWNE WILL ATTENDS  4.107.11
WHEN SORROW (USING MINE OWNE FIER'S MIGHT)       4.108.1
AND KNOW NO END OF HER OWNE MYSERY               5.25.2
SHE DOTH ALLURE ME TO MINE OWNE DECAY            5.53.7
IN HER OWNE POWRE, AND SCORNETH OTHERS AYDE      5.58.2
BUT FAYLETH TRUSTING ON HIS OWNE ASSURANCE       5.58.10
BUT IN THE STAY OF HER OWNE STEDFAST MIGHT       5.59.11
AND WITH HER OWNE GOODWILL HIR FYRMELY TYDE      5.67.12
SO GOODLY WONNE WITH HER OWNE WILL BEGUYLD       5.67.14
BUT THEN THE MORE YOUR OWNE MISHAP I REW         5.82.3
```

THE SPARKES WHEREOF LET KINDLE THINE OWN FYRE   5.86.9
AND CATCHING HOLD ON THINE OWNE WICKED HED   5.86.10
CAN COMFORT ME, BUT HER OWNE JOYOUS SIGHT   5.89.10
OWNERS   1
THEY ARE THE $LORDS AND OWNERS OF THEIR FACES   3.94.7
OWNER'S   1
THE OWNERS TONGUE DOTH PUBLISH EVERY WHERE   3.102.4
PACE   5
THEN CAN NO HORSE WITH MY DESIRE KEEPE PACE   3.51.9
SHALL YOU PACE FORTH, YOUR PRAISE SHALL
                          STIL FINDE ROOME   3.55.10
STEALE FROM HIS FIGURE, AND NO PACE PERCEIV'D   3.104.10
TO KEEPE THE PACE OF THEIR FIRST LOVING STATE   4.17.4
THAT NO PACE ELSE THEIR GUIDED STEPS CAN FIND   4.58.3
PACIFY   1
I WOULD HER YIELD, HER WRATH TO PACIFY   5.11.10
PACK-HORSE   2
THINK'ST THOU, MY $WIT SHALL KEEPE THE
                          PACK-$HORSE $WAY   2.31.7
BUT THOU, WHOSE $PEN HATH LIKE A $PACKE-$HORSE
                          SERV'D   2.49.5
PAGE   4
BUT MAKES ANTIQUITIE FOR AYE HIS PAGE   3.108.12
WHERE $CUPID IS SWORNE PAGE TO $CHASTITY+   4.35.8
LOVE MOVES THY PAINE, AND LIKE A FAITHFULL PAGE   4.101.9
CURST BE THE PAGE FROM WHOME THE BAD TORCH FELL   4.105.11
PAGEANT'S   1
BEHOLDING ME THAT ALL THE PAGEANTS PLAY   5.54.3
PAID   5
NOR PAYD THE IMPOST OF HIS WAVES MORE TRULY   1.48.7
MY HEART HATH PAID SUCH GRIEVOUS $USURIE   2.3.11
MY HART HATH PAYD SUCH GRIEVOUS USURY   2.110.11
WHICH I NEW PAY AS IF NOT PAYD BEFORE   3.30.12
THAT WITTIE $LEWIS TO HIM A TRIBUTE PAID   4.75.11
PAIN   44
THAT SHE HATH DONE, THE MOTIVE OF MY PAINE   1.3.13
FINDING NO END NOR PERIOD OF MY PAINE   1.16.12
SO SHALT THOU CEASE TO PLAGUE, AND I TO PAINE   1.19.14
HOPES ARE UNSURE, WHEN CERTAINE IS MY PAINE   1.25.14
THE $STARRE OF MY MISHAP IMPOS'D THIS PAINE   1.32.1
AND THREW ME DOWNE TO PAINE IN ALL THIS FIRE   1.36.5
BEARING THE WOUND, I NEEDES MUST FEELE THE PAINE   1.52.14
TOYLING WITH $PAINE, MY $LABOUR NEVER CEASETH   2.40.7
AND IN BARE WORDS PAINT OUT MY $PASSIONS PAINE   2.42.7
AND IN BARE WORDS PAYNT OUT MY PASSIONS PAYNE   2.128.7
THUS DO I FEELE THE PAINE, THE CAUSE,
                          YET CANNOT SEE   2.130.8
MY TONGUE IN PAYNE, MY HARTS COUNSELS BEWRAYING   2.142.6
TOYLING WITH PAINE, MY LABOUR NEVER CEASETH   2.144.7
THE PAINE BE MINE, BUT THINE SHAL BE THE PRAISE   3.38.14
LOOKING WITH PRETTY RUTH UPON MY PAINE   3.132.4
KILL ME OUT-RIGHT WITH LOOKES, AND RID MY PAINE   3.139.14
THE MANNER OF MY PITTIE WANTING PAINE   3.140.4
THAT SHE THAT MAKES ME SINNE, AWARDS ME PAINE   3.141.14
THAT THE DEARE $SHE MIGHT TAKE SOME PLEASURE
                          OF MY PAINE   4.1.2
OF FORCE OF HEAV'NLY BEAMES, INFUSING
                          HELLISH PAINE   4.6.3
HIS PAPER, PALE DISPAIRE, AND PAINE HIS
                          PEN DOTH MOVE   4.6.11

```
THAT TO WIN IT, IS ALL THE SKILL AND PAINE        4.12.14
ALAS HAVE I NOT PAINE ENOUGH MY FRIEND            4.14.1
BY MY LOVE JUDGING WHAT $LOVE'S PAINE MIGHT BE    4.16.8
BUT FOR THAT MAN WITH PAINE THIS TRUTH DESCRIES   4.25.5
WHERE $LOVE IS CHASTNESSE, $PAINE DOTH
                          LEARNE DELIGHT          4.48.3
RATHER THEN BY MORE TRUTH TO GET MORE PAINE       4.67.14
THOSE SCARLET JUDGES, THREATNING BLOUDY PAINE+    4.73.11
WITH DOING ALL, LEAVE NOTHING DONE BUT PAINE      4.85.8
CAN SCARCE DISCERNE THE SHAPE OF MINE OWNE PAINE  4.94.4
LOVE MOVES THY PAINE, AND LIKE A FAITHFULL PAGE   4.101.9
ALL FOLKES PREST AT THY WILL THY PAINE
                          TO 'SWAGE               4.101.11
THEN THINKE NOT LONG IN TAKING LITLE PAINE        5.6.13
AS SHE DOTH LAUGH AT ME AND MAKES MY PAIN
                          HER SPORT               5.10.14
ALL PAINE HATH END AND EVERY WAR HATH PEACE       5.11.13
YET AS IT WAS, I HARDLY SCAP'T WITH PAINE         5.16.14
WHY THEN SHOULD I ACCOUMPT OF LITTLE PAINE        5.26.13
SHALL TO YOU PURCHAS WITH HER THANKLES PAINE      5.27.12
STILL TO BEHOLD THE OBJECT OF THEIR PAINE         5.35.2
SO PLEASING IS IN MY EXTREAMEST PAINE             5.42.2
AND DYING DOE THEM SELVES OF PAYNE BEGUYLE        5.47.12
AND THINCK THEY DY WITH PLEASURE, LIVE
                          WITH PAYNE              5.47.14
TO SORROW AND TO SOLITARY PAINE                   5.52.6
STILL TO BEHOLD THE OBJECT OF THEYR PAYNE         5.83.2
PAINED                    1
BUT PLEAD THY MAISTERS CAUSE UNJUSTLY PAYNED      5.48.8
PAINFUL                   3
THE PAINEFULL WARRIER FAMOSED FOR WORTH           3.25.9
OR LOOKE WITH PITTY ON MY PAYNEFUL SMART          5.18.8
THE PAYNEFULL SMITH WITH FORCE OF FERVENT HEAT    5.32.1
PAINS                     18
AND I LOSE YOU, FOR ALL MY $WIT AND $PAINES       2.21.14
AND IN MY $SOULE THE PAINES OF $HELL I PROVE      2.41.3
EXPRESSE MY $WOES, AND SHEW THE PAINES OF $HELL   2.60.2
AND IN MY SOULE THE PAYNES OF HELL I PROVE        2.143.3
EXPRESSE MY WOES, AND SHEW THE PAYNES OF HELL     2.149.2
WITH IDLE PAINES, AND MISSING AYME, DO GUESSE     4.23.4
WITH ME THOSE PAINES FOR $GOD'S SAKE DO NOT TAKE  4.28.3
SO SWEETS MY PAINES, THAT MY PAINES ME REJOYCE    4.57.14
SO SWEETS MY PAINES, THAT MY PAINES ME REJOYCE    4.57.14
IN JUSTICE PAINES COME NOT TILL FAULTS DO CALL    4.86.10
ONLY WITH PAINES MY PAINES THUS EASED BE          4.93.12
ONLY WITH PAINES MY PAINES THUS EASED BE          4.93.12
ONELY MY PAINES WIL BE THE MORE TO GET HER        5.51.13
THAT SEEMD THE LONGER FOR MY GREATER PAINES       5.60.12
REMEMBRANCE OF ALL PAINES WHICH HIM OPPREST       5.63.12
ALL PAINES ARE NOTHING IN RESPECT OF THIS         5.63.13
BUT CAME THE TYDE, AND MADE MY PAYNES HIS PRAY    5.75.4
LET ALL THE PLAGUES AND HORRID PAINES OF HELL     5.86.5
PAINT                     14
TO PAINT ON FLOODS, TILL THE SHORE CRIE TO TH'AIRE 1.9.2
PAINT SHADOWES IN IMAGINARY LINES                 1.55.3
PAPER AND $INKE CAN PAINT BUT NAKED $WORDS        2.13.5
WITH $FLAMES AND $LIGHTNINGS THEIR $EXORDIUMS
                          PAINT                   2.39.2
AND IN BARE WORDS PAINT OUT MY $PASSIONS PAINE    2.42.7
WITH FLAMES AND LIGHTNING THEIR EXORDIUMS PAYNT   2.118.2
```

PAPER AND YNCKE, CAN PAYNT BUT NAKED WORDS `2.121.5
AND IN BARE WORDS PAYNT OUT MY PASSIONS PAYNE 2.128.7
I SOUGHT FIT WORDS TO PAINT THE BLACKEST
        FACE OF WOE 4.1.5
WHILE WITH A FEELING SKILL I PAINT MY HELL 4.2.14
SHALL PAINT OUT JOY, THOUGH BUT IN BLACKE
        AND WHITE 4.70.11
HOW FAINE WOULD I PAINT THEE TO ALL MEN'S EYES 4.81.7
WHAT INKE IS BLACKE INOUGH TO PAINT MY WO+ 4.93.3
PAINT WOE'S BLACKE FACE SO LIVELY TO MY SIGHT 4.98.10
PAINTED   11
AND IF A BROW WITH CARES CHARACTERS PAINTED 1.15.5
DRAWNE WITH MY BLOOD, AND PAINTED WITH MY CARES 1.47.3
HOW MANY PALTRY, FOOLISH, PAINTED THINGS 2.6.1
PAYNTED THE BLACKEST $IMAGE OF MY WOE 2.114.11
THE FIRE, UNTO MY LOVE, COMPARE A PAINTED FIRE 2.127.5
MUCH LIKER THEN YOUR PAINTED COUNTERFEIT 3.16.8
A $WOMANS FACE WITH NATURES OWNE HAND PAINTED 3.20.1
STIRD BY A PAINTED BEAUTY TO HIS VERSE 3.21.2
AND TO THE PAINTED BANQUET BIDS MY HEART 3.47.6
AND YOU IN $GRECIAN TIRES ARE PAINTED NEW 3.53.8
PAINTED IN MY BECLOWDED STORMIE FACE 4.45.2
PAINTER   3
MINE EYE HATH PLAY'D THE PAINTER AND HATH STEELD 3.24.1
FOR THROUGH THE $PAINTER MUST YOU SEE HIS SKILL 3.24.5
WOULD SHE IN BEAMIE BLACKE, LIKE PAINTER WISE 4.7.3
PAINTER'S   1
AND PERSPECTIVE IT IS BEST $PAINTERS ART 3.24.4
PAINTING   7
PAINTING MY $PASSIONS IN THESE SAD $DESIGNES 2.45.4
PAINTING MY AGE WITH BEAUTY OF THY DAIES 3.62.14
WHY SHOULD FALSE PAINTING IMMITATE HIS CHEEKE 3.67.5
AND THEIR GROSSE PAINTING MIGHT BE BETTER US'D 3.82.13
I NEVER SAW THAT YOU DID PAINTING NEED 3.83.1
AND THEREFORE TO YOUR FAIRE NO PAINTING SET 3.83.2
PAINTING THY OUTWARD WALLS SO COSTLIE GAY+ 3.146.4
PALADINS   1
LET OTHERS SING OF $KNIGHTS AND $PALLADINES 1.55.1
PALATE   2
AND TO HIS PALLAT DOTH PREPARE THE CUP 3.114.12
WITH EAGER COMPOUNDS WE CUR PALLAT URGE 3.118.2
PALE   7
HOW TO BE PALE WITH ANGUISH, RED WITH FEARE 1.20.2
UPON HIS SOVEREIGNES COURSE, THE NIGHTS
        PALE $QUEENE 1.48.6
YOUR $CHEEKES YET PALE, SINCE FIRST HE
        GAVE THE $WOUND 2.2.12
PEOPLED WITH $ARMIES OF PALE JEALOUS EYES 2.122.2
GUILDING PALE STREAMES WITH HEAVENLY ALCUMY 3.33.4
THAT LEAVES LOOKE PALE, DREADING THE $WINTERS
        NEERE 3.97.14
HIS PAPER, PALE DISPAIRE, AND PAINE HIS
        PEN DOTH MOVE 4.6.11
PALENESS   2
THAT IN THAT PALENESSE BEAUTIE'S WHITE WE SEE 4.101.6
I WOULD KNOW BY WHAT RIGHT THIS PALENESSE
        OVERCAME 4.102.7
PALFREYS   1
TROTTING HIS SUN-STEEDS TILL THE $PALFRAYS SWEAT 2.147.6

```
PALTRY                      1
   HOW MANY PALTRY, FOOLISH, PAINTED THINGS         2.6.1
PAMELA'S                    1
   WHEN $DORUS SINGS HIS SWEET $PAMELAS LOVE        2.151.10
PANDORA                     1
   I THINKE THAT I A NEW $PANDORA SEE               5.24.8
PANGS                       1
   CRYES IN HIS PANGS, $GOD HELPE THE MOTHERLESSE   2.116.18
PANTETH                     1
   WHILST THUS HE PANTETH FOR HIS LATEST BREATH     2.135.10
PANTHER                     1
   THE $PANTHER KNOWING THAT HIS SPOTTED HYDE       5.53.1
PANTING                     2
   CANNOT BE STAID WITHIN MY PANTING BREAST         4.50.2
   WITH PANTING HOUNDS BEGUILED OF THEIR PRAY       5.67.4
PANTS                       3
   WHOSE PANTS DO MAKE UNSPILLING CREAME TO FLOW    4.100.6
   SWEETNESSE, THAT BREATHES AND PANTS AS
                              OFT AS SHE            4.101.2
   WHICH PANTS AS THOUGH IT STILL SHOULD
                              LEAPE TO THEE         4.107.6
PAP                         1
   THAT IN HER BREAST THY PAP WELL SUGRED LIES      4.12.5
PAPER                       6
   PAPER AND $INKE CAN PAINT BUT NAKED $WORDS       2.13.5
   PAPER AND YNCKE, CAN PAYNT BUT NAKED WORDS       2.121.5
   FOR EVERY VULGAR PAPER TO REHEARSE               3.38.4
   HIS PAPER, PALE DISPAIRE, AND PAINE HIS
                              PEN DOTH MOVE         4.6.11
   IT IS BUT LOVE, WHICH MAKES HIS PAPER
                              PERFIT WHITE          4.102.12
   INNOCENT PAPER WHOM TOO CRUELL HAND              5.48.1
PAPERS                      4
   BE NOT DISPLEASD THAT THESE MY PAPERS SHOULD     1.44.1
   FOR $GOD FORBID I SHOULD MY $PAPERS BLOT         1.58.5
   TURNING MY $PAPERS, ASKES, $WHAT HAVE WE HEERE+  2.31.3
   SO SHOULD MY PAPERS (YELLOWED WITH THEIR AGE)    3.17.9
PAPS                        1
   AND TWIXT HER PAPS LIKE EARLY FRUIT IN $MAY      5.76.9
PARADISE                    5
   SINCE HE THAT BLESSED $PARADISE DID PROVE        2.4.7
   O THINKE I THEN, WHAT PARADISE OF JOY            4.68.13
   OR GEMMES, OR FRUTES OF NEW-FOUND $PARADISE      4.81.2
   THE BOWRE OF BLISSE, THE PARADICE OF PLEASURE    5.76.3
   SWEET FRUIT OF PLEASURE BROUGHT FROM PARADICE    5.77.11
PARAGON                     1
   YEE WHOSE HIGH WORTHS SURPASSING PARAGON         5.66.5
PARALLELS                   1
   AND DELVES THE PARALELS IN BEAUTIES BROW         3.60.10
PARCHED                     2
   WHOSE $GRIEFE HATH PARCH'D THY $BODY,
                              DRY'D THY $BLOOD      2.49.8
   YET WERE THE HID AND MEANER BEAUTIES PARCHT      4.22.12
PARDON                      6
   YOUR SELFE TO PARDON OF SELFE-DOING CRIME        3.58.12
   I DO CONFESSE, PARDON A FAULT CONFEST            4.4.7
   YET $DEARE, LET ME THIS PARDON GET OF YOU        4.46.12
   PARDON MINE EARES, BOTH I AND THEY DO PRAY       4.51.1
   PARDON THAT FAULT, ONCE MORE GRAUNT ME THE PLACE 4.82.12
   PARDON FOR THEE, AND GRACE FOR ME INTREAT        5.2.12
```

```
PARIS                        1
  NO LOVELY $PARIS MADE THY $HELLEN HIS              4.33.6
PARLEY                       1
  TRUCE, GENTLE $LOVE, A $PARLY NOW I CRAVE          2.63.1
PARNASSUS                    4
  SOME OLD $PERNASSUS, WHERE THE $MUSES DWELL       2.120.11
  WHICH FROM THE RIBS OF OLD $PARNASSUS FLOWES       4.15.2
  THE NEW $PERNASSUS, WHERE THE $MUSES BIDE          4.80.5
  HIGHWAY SINCE YOU MY CHIEFE $PERNASSUS BE          4.84.1
PART                        53
  YET SURE SHE CANNOT BUT MUST THINKE A PART         1.21.13
  HER PRAISE FROM MY COMPLAINT I MAY NOT PART        1.26.10
  HOPING THEREBY TO FREE MY BETTER PART              1.27.4
  IN ENDLES ERRORS, WHENCE I CANNOT PART             1.34.12
  MY SLENDER MEANES PRESUM'D TOO HIGH A PART         1.36.3
  STRAIGHTWAYES HE PLAY'S A SWAGG'RING $RUFFINS
                       PART                          2.7.10
  LEAVING THE $PATH THE GREATER PART DOE GOE         2.9.4
  BUT WHEN MY $TOUCHING CAME TO PLAY HIS PART        2.29.9
  RECEIVING STRENGTH FROM EV'RY SECRET PART          2.30.7
  WHERE I INTOMB'D, MY BETTER PART SHALL SAVE        2.44.12
  SINCE THER'S NO HELPE, $COME LET US KISSE
                       AND PART                      2.61.1
  WHEREIN EACH FAYREST PART EXCELLETH OTHER          2.123.4
  NOW DOE I SWEARE BY HEAVENS, BEFORE WE PART        2.140.3
  THEN HENCE TO HEAVEN UNKIND, FOR THY CHILDS
                       PART                          2.140.13
  WHO WITH HIS FEARE IS PUT BESIDES HIS PART         3.23.2
  AND BY A PART OF ALL THY GLORY LIVE                3.37.12
  WHEN THOU ART ALL THE BETTER PART OF ME+           3.39.2
  THE CLEERE EYES MCYITIE, AND THE DEARE
                       HEARTS PART                   3.46.12
  AS THUS, MINE EYES DUE IS THEIR OUTWARD PART       3.46.13
  AND IN HIS THOUGHTS OF LOVE DOTH SHARE A PART      3.47.8
  FROM WHENCE AT PLEASURE THOU MAIST COME AND PART   3.48.12
  TO GUARD THE LAWFULL REASONS ON THY PART           3.49.12
  IN ALL EXTERNALL GRACE YOU HAVE SOME PART          3.53.13
  AND ALL MY SOULE, AND AL MY EVERY PART             3.62.2
  THE VERY PART WAS CONSECRATE TO THEE               3.74.6
  MY SPIRIT IS THINE THE BETTER PART OF ME           3.74.8
  ALTHOUGH IN ME EACH PART WILL BE FORGOTTEN         3.81.4
  UPON THY PART I CAN SET DOWNE A STORY              3.88.6
  DOTH PART HIS FUNCTION, AND IS PARTLY BLIND        3.113.3
  OF HIS QUICK OBJECTS HATH THE MINDE NO PART        3.113.7
  TIL EACH TO RAZ'D OBLIVION YEELD HIS PART          3.122.7
  AND SUTE THY PITTY LIKE IN EVERY PART              3.132.12
  AND PLAY THE MOTHERS PART KISSE ME, BE KIND        3.143.12
  MY NOBLER PART TO MY GROSE BODIES TREASON          3.151.6
  THE INWARD LIGHT.. AND THAT THE HEAVENLY PART      4.5.2
  NOT USDE TO FROZEN CLIPS, HE STRAVE TO
                       FIND SOME PART                4.8.6
  PLAYING AND SHINING IN EACH OUTWARD PART           4.11.13
  WHO THOUGH MOST RICH IN THESE AND EVERIE PART      4.37.12
  NOW FROM THY FELLOWSHIP I NEEDS MUST PART          4.72.5
  PLEASINGST CONSORT, WHERE EACH SENCE HOLDS A PART  4.79.3
  OR OF THY GIFTS AT LEAST SHADE OUT SOME PART       4.81.8
  I SAW THAT SIGHES HER SWEETEST LIPS DID PART       4.87.7
  THANKE MAY YOU HAVE FOR SUCH A THANKFULL PART      4.95.13
  THEY FIRST RESORT UNTO THAT SOUERAIGNE PART        4.107.4
  BREAKE FORTH AT LENGTH OUT OF THE INNER PART       5.2.5
```

```
BUT WHEN I PLEADE, SHE BIDS ME PLAY MY PART          5.18.9
THAT PRIDE AND MEEKNESSE MIXT BY EQUALL PART         5.21.3
AND RARE PERFECTION OF EACH GOODLY PART              5.24.2
WHOSE PRYDE DEPRAVES EACH OTHER BETTER PART          5.31.3
A MELTING PLEASANCE RAN THROUGH EVERY PART           5.39.7
AND EVERY PART REMAINES IMMORTALLY                   5.45.8
BUT LIKE A STEDDY SHIP DOTH STRONGLY PART            5.59.5
THROUGH CONTEMPLATICN OF MY PUREST PART              5.88.10
PARTAKE                        1
WHEN I AGAINST MY SELFE WITH THEE PERTAKE            3.149.2
PARTED                         1
FOOLES AS WE MET, SC $FCOLES AGAINE WE PARTED        2.59.14
PARTIAL                        2
OR $NATURE MUST BE PARTIALL IN MY $CAUSE             2.27.13
YET WITH REPINING AT SO PARTIALL LOT                 4.2.8
PARTICULARS                    1
BUT THESE PERTICULERS ARE NOT MY MEASURE             3.91.7
PARTLY                         1
DOTH PART HIS FUNCTION, AND IS PARTLY BLIND          3.113.3
PARTS                         12
OUR $WESTERNE $PARTS EXTOLL THEIR $WILIS $FAME       2.32.11
OUR $WESTERNE PARTS EXTCLL THEYR $WILYS FAME         2.124.11
IN SINGLENESSE THE PARTS THAT THOU SHOULD'ST BEARE   3.8.8
WHICH HIDES YOUR LIFE, AND SHEWES NOT
                            HALFE YOUR PARTS         3.17.4
AND THERE RAIGNES $LOVE AND ALL $LOVES
                            LOVING PARTS             3.31.3
WHO ALL THEIR PARTS OF ME TO THEE DID GIVE           3.31.11
INTITLED IN THEIR PARTS, DO CROWNED SIT              3.37.7
WHICH PARTS THE SHORE, WHERE TWO CONTRACTED NEW      3.56.10
THOSE PARTS OF THEE THAT THE WORLDS EYE DOTH VIEW    3.69.1
IF $FRENCH CAN YET THREE PARTS IN ONE AGREE          4.30.5
DEEPE IS THE WOUND, THAT DINTS THE PARTS ENTIRE      5.6.11
DEEPE IN THE CLOSET OF MY PARTS ENTYRE               5.85.9
PARTY                          2
BAD IS THE $MATCH, WHERE NEITHER PARTIE WONNE        2.63.4
THY ADVERSE PARTY IS THY $ADVOCATE                   3.35.10
PASS                          23
YOUR FIRY HEATE LETS NOT HER GLORY PASSE             1.38.13
WHEN ONCE THEY FIND HER FLOWRE HER GLORY PAS         1.40.14
WHEN MEN SHALL FIND THY FLOWER, THY GLORY PASSE      1.41.1
STAY, SPEEDY $TIME, BEHCLD, BEFORE THOU PASSE        2.17.1
PASSE ON, AND TO $PCSTERITIE TELL THIS               2.17.9
TO WHOM MY $MUSE WITH FIERIE $WINGS SHALL PASSE      2.25.10
I PASSE NOT FOR $MINERVA, NOR $ASTREA                2.39.13
I PASSE NOT, I, HCW $MEN AFFECTED BEE                2.42.9
STAY, STAY, SWEET $TIME, BEHOLD OR ERE
                            THOU PASSE               2.107.1
NOW PASSE ON $TIME, TO AFTER-WORLDS TELL THIS        2.107.9
I PASSE NOT FOR $MINERVA NOR $ASTRAEA                2.118.13
MUST PASSE BY AYRE, OR ELSE DYE IN EXILE             2.122.4
I PASSE NOT I HOW MEN AFFECTED BE                    2.128.9
AGAINST THAT TIME WHEN THOU SHALT STRANGELY PASSE    3.49.5
FOR TO NO OTHER PASSE MY VERSES TEND                 3.103.11
THEN IN THE NUMBER LET ME PASSE UNTOLD               3.136.9
FOR THOUGH SHE PASSE ALL THINGS, YET WHAT IS ALL     4.19.9
POORE PASSENGER, PASSE NOW THEREBY I DID             4.20.9
YET LET THIS THOUGHT THY $TYGRISH COURAGE PASSE      4.65.11
BEAUTIES WHICH DO IN EXCELLENCIE PASSE               4.82.2
KNOWING WORLDS PASSE, ERE SHE ENOUGH CAN FIND        4.101.13
```

```
  BUT IF I BY A HAPPY WINDOW PASSE                    4.104.9
  BUT SUCH SWEET CORDIALLS PASSE $PHYSITIONS ART      5.50.12
PASSAGE               3
  TO STOP THE PASSAGE OF MY VANQUISHT HART            1.27.2
  AN OTHER PASSAGE OPENS AT HER VOICE                 1.27.8
  MY SIGHES SHALL STOP THE PASSAGE OF THE AYRE        2.115.7
PASSED                3
  YET CRAV'D THE $ALMES OF SUCH AS PASSED BY          2.23.4
  AND BIDDING TH'OLD $ADIEU, HIS PASSED DATE          5.4.3
  FOR NONE CAN CALL AGAINE THE PASSED TIME            5.70.14
PASSENGER             1
  POORE PASSENGER, PASSE NOW THEREBY I DID            4.20.9
PASSING               5
  SOME SAY, I HAVE A PASSING PLEASING $STRAINE        2.42.3
  PASSING BY THAT CLEERE FOUNTAINE OF THINE EYE       2.109.2
  SOME SAY I HAVE A PASSING PLEASING STRAINE          2.128.3
  AT EVERY RASH BEHOLDER PASSING BY                   5.16.8
  FAR PASSING THOSE WHICH $HERCULES CAME BY           5.77.7
PASSION               5
  WHERE OTHER $MEN IN DEPTH OF $PASSION CRIE          2.24.13
  WHEN HIS $PULSE FAYLING, $PASSION SPEECHLESSE
                               LIES                   2.61.10
  HASTE THOU THE $MASTER $MISTRIS OF MY PASSION       3.20.2
  YOU CALME THE STORME THAT PASSION DID BEGIN         5.8.11
  THE PITEOUS PASSION OF HIS DYING SMART              5.48.12
PASSIONS             15
  NOR ARE MY PASSIONS LIMND FOR OUTWARD HEW           1.4.5
  AND MADE THY PASSIONS WITH HER BEAUTIE EVEN         1.8.4
  WHAT PASSIONS WOULD HER MILDER FAVOURS MOVE+        1.17.12
  TO MODELL FORTH THE PASSIONS OF THE MORROW          1.54.10
  THESE TRIBUTARY PASSIONS, BEAUTIES DUE              1.60.5
  OR HAVE OUR $PASSIONS LESSER POW'R THEN THEIRS      2.27.5
  IN GRIEVOUS $PASSIONS, MY $WOES STILL BEMONING      2.40.8
  PAINTING MY $PASSIONS IN THESE SAD $DESIGNES        2.45.4
  THE PASSIONS OF DISPAIRE, BUT JOYES TO MY DESIRE    2.127.8
  IN GREEVOUS PASSIONS MY WOES STYLL BEMONING         2.144.8
  MY WIT DOTH STRIVE THOSE PASSIONS TO DEFEND         4.18.10
  O GIVE MY PASSIONS LEAVE TO RUN THEIR RACE          4.64.2
  I MUST NO MORE IN THY SWEET PASSIONS LIE            4.72.7
  WHILEST MY WEAK POWRES OF PASSIONS WARREID ARRE     5.44.7
  AND GRIEFE RENEW, AND PASSIONS DOE AWAKE            5.44.11
PASSION'S             2
  AND IN BARE WORDS PAINT OUT MY $PASSIONS PAINE      2.42.7
  AND IN BARE WORDS PAYNT OUT MY PASSIONS PAYNE       2.128.7
PASS-PRAISE           1
  THAT SKIN, WHOSE PASSE-PRAISE HUE SCORNS
                     THIS POORE TERME OF WHITE  4.77.7
PAST                 24
  WHEN BACKE I LOOKE, I SIGH MY FREEDOME PAST         1.28.9
  THE $GULPHES AND $STRAITS, THAT STRANGELY
                               HE HAD PAST            2.1.10
  BY THIS I SEE, HOW-EVER THINGS BE PAST              2.2.13
  (NOT TOO FARRE PAST) MAY TO THEIR $WITS
                               BE BROUGHT             2.9.14
  AND THY $YOUTH PAST, IN THIS PURE $MIRROUR SEE      2.17.6
  SO MAIST THOU LIVE, PAST WORLD, PAST FAME,
                     PAST END                         2.106.14
  SO MAIST THOU LIVE, PAST WORLD, PAST FAME,
                     PAST END                         2.106.14
  SO MAIST THOU LIVE, PAST WORLD, PAST FAME,
                     PAST END                         2.106.14
```

```
AND THY YOUTH PAST, IN THIS FAIRE MIRROR SEE          2.107.6
AND HEAVEN MAY JOY TO THINK ON PAST WORLDS
                                  BLISSE              2.107.12
COULD ALL CONCEITE CONCLUDE, WHICH PAST
                        CONCEITE ADMIRETH             2.117.5
OR COULD MINE EYE BUT AYME, HER OBJECTS
                        PAST PERFECTION               2.117.6
WHEN I BEHOLD THE VIOLET PAST PRIME                   3.12.3
I SOMMON UP REMEMBRANCE OF THINGS PAST                3.30.2
THOU HAST PAST BY THE AMBUSH OF YOUNG DAIES           3.70.9
FINDING THY WORTH A LIMMIT PAST MY PRAISE             3.82.6
AS I BY YOURS, Y'HAVE PAST A HELL OF $TIME            3.120.6
NOT WONDRING AT THE PRESENT, NOR THE PAST             3.123.10
PAST REASON HUNTED, AND NO SOONER HAD                 3.129.6
PAST REASON HATED AS A SWOLLOWED BAYT                 3.129.7
ALTHOUGH SHE KNOWES MY DAYES ARE PAST THE BEST        3.138.6
PAST CURE I AM, NOW $REASON IS PAST CARE              3.147.9
PAST CURE I AM, NOW $REASON IS PAST CARE              3.147.9
YET HOPE I WELL, THAT WHEN THIS STORME IS PAST        5.34.9
```

PASTIME   1
```
WITH WHAT PASTIME, TIME'S JOURNEY SHE BEGUILCE        4.92.12
```
PATENT   1
```
AND SO MY PATTENT BACK AGAINE IS SWERVING             3.87.8
```
PATENTS   1
```
WHICH MAKE THE PATENTS OF TRUE WORLDLY BLISSE         4.37.13
```
PATH   1
```
LEAVING THE $PATH THE GREATER PART DOE GOE            2.9.4
```
PATHS   2
```
WHOSE FEETE DOE TREAD GREENE PATHS OF
                        YOUTH AND LOVE                1.6.6
HAUNTING UNTRODDEN PATHS TO WAILE APART               1.9.10
```
PATIENCE   7
```
THE PATIENCE OF SO RARE DIVINE A LOVE                 2.149.14
AND PATIENCE TAME, TO SUFFERANCE BIDE EACH CHECK      3.58.7
MY TOUNG-TIDE PATIENCE WITH TOO MUCH DISDAINE         3.140.2
FY, SCHOOLE OF $PATIENCE, $FY, YOUR LESSON IS         4.56.1
NO $PATIENCE, IF THOU WILT MY GOOD, THEN MAKE         4.56.12
HER COME, AND HEARE WITH PATIENCE MY DESIRE           4.56.13
AND THEN WITH PATIENCE BID ME BEARE MY FIRE           4.56.14
```
PATIENT   1
```
WHILST LIKE A WILLING PACIENT I WILL DRINKE           3.111.9
```
PATTERN   2
```
FOR BEAUTIES PATTERNE TO SUCCEDING MEN                3.19.12
DRAWNE AFTER YOU, YOU PATTERNE OF ALL THOSE           3.98.12
```
PAUSE   1
```
WITH $SHOWTS AND $CLAPS AT EV'RY LITTLE PAWSE         2.47.9
```
PAVED   1
```
THE $WELL OF $NECTAR, PAV'D WITH PEARLE
                        AND GOLD                      2.109.13
```
PAWN   1
```
POORE $ROGUE, GOE PAWNE THY $FASCIA AND THY $BOW      2.48.3
```
PAWS   3
```
DEVOURING TIME BLUNT THOU THE $LYONS PAWES            3.19.1
THOUGH STRONGLY HEDG'D OF BLOUDY $LYON'S PAWES        4.75.10
SO PIERCING PAWES, AS SPOYLE WHEN THEY EMBRACE        4.78.10
```
PAY   11
```
ARE THOSE DUE TRIBUTES THAT MY FAITH DOTH PAY         1.24.3
WHICH LOVE DOTH PAY, AND HER DISDAINE EXTORTS         1.60.2
LABOUR IS LIGHT, WHERE $LOVE (QUOTH I) DOTH PAY       2.59.9
TILL THOU ALONE TO PAY THE HEAVENS THEIR DUTIE        2.105.5
```

```
WHICH HAPPIES THOSE THAT PAY THE WILLING LONE        3.6.6
WHICH I NEW PAY AS IF NOT PAYD BEFORE               3.30.12
SINCE WHAT HE OWES THEE, THOU THY SELFE
                              DOOST PAY            3.79.14
UNABLE QUITE TO PAY EVEN $NATURE'S RENT             4.18.5
I WILL GOOD TRIBUTE PAY IF THOU DO SO               4.39.8
THOSE LIPS, WHICH MAKE DEATH'S PAY A MEANE
                    PRICE FOR A KISSE               4.77.6
THAT TO WIN ME, OFT SHEWES A PRESENT PAY+           4.88.4
PAYING                  1
LOSE ALL, AND MORE BY PAYING TOO MUCH RENT         3.125.6
PAYMENTS                2
THE PAIMENTS OF MY $LOVE, I READ, AND CROSSE        2.3.6
THE PAYMENTS OF MY LOVE I READ, AND READING
                         CROSSE                    2.110.6
PAYS                    2
HE ROBS THEE OF, AND PAYES IT THEE AGAINE           3.79.8
HE PAIES THE WHOLE, AND YET AM I NOT FREE         3.134.14
PEACE                  25
T'HAVE PEACE ABROAD, AND NOUGHT WITHIN BUT STRIFE   1.20.3
STRETCH OUT THE FAIREST HAND, A PLEDGE OF PEACE     1.46.9
STILL LET DISARMED PEACE DECKE HER AND THEE        1.53.13
ESSEX GREAT FALL, $TYRONE HIS $PEACE TO GAINE       2.51.6
THIS $KINGS FAIRE $ENTRANCE, AND OUR $PEACE
                       WITH $SPAINE                 2.51.8
I OFFER FREE $CONDITIONS OF FAIRE $PEACE            2.63.5
AND FOR THE PEACE OF YOU I HOLD SUCH STRIFE         3.75.3
AND PEACE PROCLAIMES $OLIVES OF ENDLESSE AGE       3.107.8
AND PLEASD WITH OUR SOFT PEACE, STAID
                 HERE HIS FLYING RACE               4.8.4
PEACE, FOOLISH WIT, WITH WIT MY WIT IS MARD        4.34.11
COME SLEEPE, O SLEEPE, THE CERTAINE KNOT OF PEACE   4.39.1
CEASE EAGER $MUSE, PEACE PEN, FOR MY SAKE STAY     4.70.12
THEN SINCE (DEARE LIFE) YOU FAINE WOULD
                    HAVE ME PEACE                  4.81.12
AH BED, THE FIELD WHERE JOYE'S PEACE SOME DO SEE    4.98.1
DAYLY WHEN I DO SEEKE AND SEW FOR PEACE             5.11.1
ALL PAINE HATH END AND EVERY WAR HATH PEACE        5.11.13
IS THERE NO MEANES FOR ME TO PURCHACE PEACE         5.36.5
MONGST WHOME THE MORE I SEEKE TO SETTLE PEACE      5.44.13
SWEET WARRIOUR WHEN SHALL I HAVE PEACE WITH YOU+    5.57.1
MAKE PEACE THEREFORE, AND GRAUNT ME TIMELY GRACE   5.57.13
BETOKENING PEACE AND PLENTY TO ENSEW                5.62.4
SEEKES WITH SWEET PEACE TO SALVE EACH
                       OTHERS WOUND                5.65.12
AND ALL THENSFORTH ETERNALL PEACE SHALL SEE        5.71.13
BREAKE OUT, THAT MAY HER SACRED PEACE MOLEST        5.84.2
IN MY SWEET PEACE SUCH BREACHES TO HAVE BRED       5.86.12
PEAK                    2
THE $PEAKE HER $DOVE, WHOSE $BANKES SO FERTILE BE   2.32.7
THE $PEAKE HER $DOVE, WHOSE BANCKS SO
                       FERTILL BEE                 2.124.7
PEAN                    1
SING THEN MY $MUSE, NOW $IO $PEAN SING              4.63.9
PEARL                   4
THE $WELL OF $NECTAR, PAV'D WITH PEARLE
                        AND GOLD                   2.109.13
AH BUT THOSE TEARES ARE PEARLE WHICH THY
                        LOVE SHEEDS                3.34.13
RED $PORPHIR IS, WHICH LOCKE OF PEARLE MAKES SURE   4.9.6
```

```
        WHENCE HAST THOU $IVORIE, $RUBIES, PEARLE
                         AND GOLD                        4.32.10
PEARLS                   5
   AND TO TH'$ORIENT DO THY $PEARLES REMOVE              1.19.4
   FOR ME, I WEPT TO SEE PEARLES SCATTERED SO            4.87.9
   IF $PEARLES, HIR TEETH BE PEARLES BOTH
                         PURE AND ROUND                  5.15.9
   IF $PEARLES, HIR TEETH BE PEARLES BOTH
                         PURE AND ROUND                  5.15.9
   THE GATE WITH PEARLES AND RUBYES RICHLY DIGHT         5.81.10
PEARLY                   1
   THY $PEARLY $TEETH CUT OF THY $HEAD SO CLEANE         2.8.11
PEBBLED                  1
   LIKE AS THE WAVES MAKE TOWARDS THE PIBLED SHORE       3.60.1
PEEP                     2
   DELIGHTS TO PEEPE, TO GAZE THEREIN ON THEE            3.24.12
   WHEN IN HER NECKE YOU DID $LOVE DITTIES PEEPE         4.83.6
PEER                     2
   EVEN SO (ALAS) A $LADY $DIAN'S PEERE                  4.97.9
   THEN HAD YE SORTED WITH A PRINCES PERE                5.66.10
PEERLESS                 1
   OF MY LOVES CONQUEST, PEERELESSE BEAUTIES PRISE       5.69.7
PEERS                    1
   WHEN THOSE RENOUMED NOBLE $PERES OF $GREECE           5.44.1
PEEVISH                  1
   CUPID, DUMBE $IDOLL, PEEVISH $SAINT OF LOVE           2.126.1
PEIZED                   1
   MY DYING LOOKES AND THOUGHTS ARE PEIZ'D
                         IN EQUALL FEARES                2.133.12
PELION                   1
   PELION AND $OSSA, FROSTY $CAUCASE OLD                 2.120.6
PEN                      30
   AND IF MY PEN COULD MORE ENLARGE THY NAME             1.43.11
   TH'ETERNALL $ANNALS OF A HAPPY PEN                    1.45.8
   WITH MERCENARY LINES, WITH SERVILE $PEN               1.58.6
   UNHAPPY $PEN, AND ILL-ACCEPTED LINES                  1.59.1
   TAKING MY $PENNE, WITH $WORDS TO CAST MY $WOE         2.3.1
   WHEN I, AS FAST AS E'R MY $PENNE COULD TROT           2.21.5
   WHILST THUS MY $PEN STRIVES TO ETERNIZE THEE          2.44.1
   GAVE $LIFE AND $COURAGE TO MY LAB'RING $PEN           2.47.2
   BUT THOU, WHOSE $PEN HATH LIKE A $PACKE-$HORSE
                         SERV'D                          2.49.5
   OFT TAKING PEN IN HAND, WITH WORDS TO
                         CAST MY WOES                    2.110.1
   OR MAKE MY PEN HER NAME IMORTALIZE                    2.123.11
   WHAT MORTALL PEN SUFFYCIENTLY CAN PRAYSE THEE+        2.146.2
   WHICH THIS ($TIMES PENSEL OR MY PUPILL PEN)           3.16.10
   NOR DRAW NOE LINES THERE WITH THINE ANTIQUE PEN       3.19.10
   AND THOUGH THEY BE CUT-STRIPT BY EVERY PEN            3.32.6
   AS EVERY $ALIEN PEN HATH GOT MY USE                   3.78.3
   DESERVES THE TRAVAILE OF A WORTHIER PEN               3.79.6
   YOU STILL SHALL LIVE (SUCH VERTUE HATH MY $PEN)       3.81.13
   LEANE PENURIE WITHIN THAT $PEN DOTH DWELL             3.84.5
   IN POLISHT FORME OF WELL REFINED PEN                  3.85.8
   AND GIVES THY PEN BOTH SKILL AND ARGUMENT             3.100.8
   I SEE THEIR ANTIQUE $PEN WOULD HAVE EXPREST           3.106.7
   BITING MY TREWAND PEN, BEATING MY SELFE FOR SPITE     4.1.13
   HIS PAPER, PALE DISPAIRE, AND PAINE HIS
                         PEN DOTH MOVE                   4.6.11
   AND YET MY WORDS, AS THEM MY PEN DOTH FRAME           4.19.7
```

```
AND NOW MY PEN THESE LINES HAD DASHED QUITE          4.50.12
IN WELL RAISDE NOTES, MY PEN THE BEST IT MAY         4.70.10
CEASE EAGER $MUSE, PEACE PEN, FOR MY SAKE STAY       4.70.12
AND WHEN MY PEN WOULD WRITE HER TITLES TRUE          5.3.11
WHAT PEN, WHAT PENCILL CAN EXPRESSE HER FILL+        5.17.4
PENANCE                   3
NOR DOUBLE PENNANCE TO CORRECT CORRECTION            3.111.12
SO I HER ABSENS WILL MY PENAUNCE MAKE                5.52.13
SHALL BE BY HIM AMEARST WITH PENANCE DEW             5.70.12
PENCIL                    5
LIMMED WITH A $PENSILL NOT ALL UNWORTHY              1.42.6
WHAT CURIOUS $PENSILL SERVES TO LIM THEE FORTH+      2.146.3
WHICH THIS ($TIMES PENSEL OR MY PUPILL PEN)          3.16.10
BEAUTIE NO PENSELL, BEAUTIES TRUTH TO LAY            3.101.7
WHAT PEN, WHAT PENCILL CAN EXPRESSE HER FILL+        5.17.4
PENELOPE                  1
$PENELOPE FOR HER $ULISSES SAKE                      5.23.1
PENNED                    2
PEN'D IN THE GRIEFE OF MINE AFFLICTED $GHOST         2.54.6
PEND IN THE GRIEFE OF MYNE AFFLICTED GHOST           2.101.6
PENNY-FATHER              1
THEN TO THE $SONNE OF SOME RICH $PENNY-FATHER        2.10.2
PENSIVE                   1
PENSIVE ALONE, ONELY BUT WITH $DISPAIRE              1.60.10
PENSIVENESS               2
THE CURIOUS WITS, SEEING DULL PENSIVENESSE           4.23.1
IN SECRET SOROW AND SAD PENSIVENESSE                 5.34.14
PENT                      2
A LIQUID PRISONER PENT IN WALLS OF GLASSE            3.5.10
AND YET THOU WILT, FOR I BEING PENT IN THEE          3.133.13
PENURY                    3
IN $PLENTY I AM STARV'D WITH $PENURIE                2.62.11
IN PLENTY, AM I STARV'D WITH PENURY                  2.150.11
LEANE PENURIE WITHIN THAT $PEN DOTH DWELL            3.84.5
PEOPLE                    1
THEN HONEST $PEOPLE, BEARE WITH $LOVE AND $ME        2.22.2
PEOPLED                   1
PEOPLED WITH $ARMIES OF PALE JEALOUS EYES            2.122.2
PEOPLE'S                  1
WHILE WITH THE PEOPLE'S SHOUTS I MUST CONFESSE       4.53.3
PERCEIVE                  4
I SEE $YOUR CRAFT, NOW I PERCEIVE $YOUR DRIFT        2.19.11
I WELL PERCEIVE MY GRIEFE INNUMERABLE GROWES         2.110.3
WHEN I PERCEIVE THAT MEN AS PLANTS INCREASE          3.15.5
I MOTE PERCEIVE HOW IN HER GLAUNCING SIGHT           5.16.5
PERCEIVED                 1
STEALE FROM HIS FIGURE, AND NO PACE PERCEIV'D        3.104.10
PERCEIVEST                1
THIS THOU PERCEV'ST, WHICH MAKES THY LOVE
                         MORE STRONG                 3.73.13
PERCHANCE                 1
MINE EYES THEN ONLY WINKE, FOR SPITE PERCHANCE       4.98.13
PERCHED                   1
AT LENGTH HE PERCH'D HIMSELF IN $STELLA'S
                         JOYFULL FACE                4.8.8
PERFECT                   9
IN PERFECT HUMANE SHAPE, ALL HEAV'NLY $BLISSE        2.17.12
OR EVER JOY EXPRESSE, WHAT PERFECT JOY
                         HATH TAUGHT                 2.117.3
THE PERFECT CEREMONY OF LOVES RIGHT                  3.23.6
```

```
CREATING EVERY BAD A PERFECT BEST                          3.114.7
THAT FACE, WHOSE LECTURE SHEWES WHAT PERFECT
                              BEAUTIE IS                    4.77.2
OF HIS MAZDE POWERS KEEPES PERFIT HARMONY                  4.99.8
WHILE SOBD OUT WORDS A PERFECT $MUSIKE GIVE                4.100.11
IT IS BUT LOVE, WHICH MAKES HIS PAPER
                              PERFIT WHITE                  4.102.12
AND PERFECT BEAUTY DID AT FIRST PROCEED                    5.79.12
PERFECTION                  15
AYMING AT THINGS EXCEEDING ALL PERFECTION                  2.34.6
WHEN SHE HER OWNE PERFECTION WOULD ADMIRE                  2.57.6
OR COULD MINE EYE BUT AYME, HER OBJECTS
                              PAST PERFECTION               2.117.6
DID NOT PERFECTION STILL ON HER PERFECTION GAZE            2.117.11
DID NOT PERFECTION STILL ON HER PERFECTION GAZE            2.117.11
INVENTION AND MY $MUSE, PERFECTION AND HER LOVE            2.117.13
LOVES $METHRIDATE, THE PUREST OF PERFECTION                2.123.5
SO IN LOVES DEATH SHALL LOVES PERFECTION PROVE             2.139.9
IN WHOM ALL PURENES WITH PERFECTION STROVE                 2.141.3
AT HER PERFECTION STAND YOU THEN AND GAZE                  2.151.6
HOLDS IN PERFECTION BUT A LITTLE MOMENT                    3.15.2
AND RIGHT PERFECTION WRONGFULLY DISGRAC'D                  3.66.7
WIT LEARNES IN THEE PERFECTION TO EXPRESSE                 4.35.12
AND RARE PERFECTION OF EACH GOODLY PART                    5.24.2
ONELY BEHOLD HER RARE PERFECTION                           5.84.13
PERFECTIONS                  3
IN YOUR PERFECTIONS SO MUCH AM I LOST                      2.57.14
BUT THY DIVINE PERFECTIONS BY THEIR SKILL                  2.104.9
AT HER OWN RARE PERFECTIONS SO AMAZED                      2.109.8
PERFECTION'S                 2
RARE BEAUTY, $NATURES JOY, PERFECTIONS $MOTHER             2.123.2
AND NOT CONTENT TO BE $PERFECTION'S HEIRE                  4.71.9
PERFECTS                     1
THEREFORE DESIRE (CF PERFECTS LOVE BEING MADE)             3.51.10
PERFORCE                     2
PERFORCE AM THINE AND ALL THAT IS IN ME                   3.133.14
MY LOWER HEAVEN, SO IT PERFORCE MUST BEE                   5.46.8
PERFUME                      1
THE SWEET OF $EDEN, TO HER BREATHES PERFUME                2.148.6
PERFUMED                     1
AS THE PERFUMED TINCTURE OF THE $ROSES                     3.54.6
PERFUMES                     2
THREE $APRILL PERFUMES IN THREE HOT $JUNES
                              BURN'D                        3.104.7
AND IN SOME PERFUMES IS THERE MORE DELIGHT                3.130.7
PERFUMING                    2
WITH SO RARE SWEETNESSE ALL THE $HEAV'NS
                              PERFUMING                     2.16.10
WITH THINE OWNE SWEETNES AL THE HEAVENS
                              PERFUMING                     2.106.10
PERHAPS                      7
WHEN I (PERHAPS) COMPOUNDED AM WITH CLAY                   3.71.10
AND EVERIE FLOURE, NOT SWEET PERHAPS,
                              WHICH GROWES                  4.15.3
MY HARMES ON $INK'S POORE LOSSE, PERHAPS
                              SOME FIND                     4.34.13
BID'N, PERHAPS HE FETCHETH THEE A GLOVE                    4.59.7
THAT I PERHAPS AM SOMEWHAT KINNE TO THEE                   4.65.12
BUT BY HIS DEATH WHICH SOME PERHAPS WILL MONE              5.36.13
PERHAPS HE THERE MAY LEARNE WITH RARE DELIGHT              5.73.11
```

PERIL   1
  AND ON WHAT $ROCKS IN PERILL TO BE CAST+   2.1.12
PERILS   2
  IN GREATEST $PERILS SOME $MEN PLEASANT BE   2.24.10
  THROUGH HIDDEN PERILS RCUND ABOUT ME PLAST   5.34.8
PERIOD   2
  FINDING NO END NOR PERIOD OF MY PAINE   1.16.12
  HEERE MAKE A $PERICD $TIME, AND SAIE FOR MEE   2.107.13
PERISH   8
  AND SO DID PERISH BY MY PROPER ART   1.13.8
  SO MUCH I PLEASE TC PERISH IN MY WOE   1.14.12
  THESE MAY REMAINE WHEN THOU AND I SHALL PERISH   1.42.12
  MY JOYES ABORTIVE, PERISH IN THEIR BYRTH   1.60.11
  AND THOUGH IN YOUTH, MY $YOUTH UNTIMELY PERISH   2.44.9
  HARSH, FEATURELESSE, AND RUDE, BARRENLY PERRISH   3.11.10
  IF NOT, DIE SOONE, AND I WITH THEE WILL PERISH   5.2.14
  FAIRE BE NO LENGER PROUD OF THAT SHALL PERISH   5.27.13
PERJURED   3
  IS PERJURD, MURDRCUS, BLOUDDY FULL OF BLAME   3.129.3
  WHEN I BREAKE TWENTY.. I AM PERJUR'D MOST   3.152.6
  FOR I HAVE SWORNE ,THEE FAIRE.. MORE PERJURDE
                          EYE   3.152.13
PERMANENT   1
  BUT ONELY THAT IS PERMANENT AND FREE   5.79.7
PERMIT   1
  ANON PERMIT THE BASEST CLOUDES TO RIDE   3.33.5
PERNICIOUS   1
  THE WEEPING $CROCCDILE.. THESE VILE PERNICIOUS
                          THREE   2.130.4
PERPETUAL   2
  THE SPIRIT OF $LOVE, WITH A PERPETUAL DULNESSE   3.56.8
  WHICH FROM LOVES FIRE TCCKE HEAT PERPETUALL   3.154.10
PERPLEXED   1
  STILL IN THE TRACE CF ONE PERPLEXED THOUGHT   1.33.1
PERPLEXITY   1
  THAT FULL OF DOUBTS, THCU OF PERPLEXITY   4.96.7
PERSEVERE   2
  NOR TO THE LIGHTNING.. FCR THEY STILL PERSEVER   5.9.9
  BUT IN HER PRIDE SHE DOCTH PERSEVER STILL   5.38.9
PERSIST   1
  DOTH STILL PERSIST IN HER REBELLIOUS PRIDE   5.6.2
PERSPECTIVE   1
  AND PERSPECTIVE IT IS BEST $PAINTERS ART   3.24.4
PERSUADE   1
  MY GLASSE SHALL NCT PERSWADE ME I AM OULD   3.22.1
PERSUADES   2
  WHAT WORDS SO ERE SHE SPEAKES PERSWADES FOR THEE 4.12.7
  WHEN FAR SPENT NIGHT PERSWADES EACH MORTALL EYE   4.99.1
PERSUASIONS   1
  AND STILL TH'EFFECT OF THY PERSWASIONS PROVE   4.4.11
PERUSAL   1
  WORTHY PERUSAL STAND AGAINST THY SIGHT   3.38.6
PERVERT   1
  AND FROM ALL WANDRING LCVES WHICH MOTE PERVART   5.42.11
PETRARCH   1
  THOUGH THOU A $LAURA HAST NO $PETRARCH FCUND   1.43.3
PETRARCH'S   1
  YOU THAT POORE $PETRARCH'S LONG DECEASED WOES   4.15.7
PETTY   1
  WHEN OTHER PETTIE GRIEFES HAVE DONE THEIR SPIGHT 3.90.10

PEULE   1
  I SAY, $YOU $LOVE, YOU PEULE ME OUT A $NO   2.5.6
PHILIP   1
  GOOD BROTHER $PHILIP, I HAVE BORNE YOU LCNG   4.83.1
PHILOMEL   1
  AS $PHILOMELL IN SUMMERS FRONT DOTH SINGE   3.102.7
PHILOSOPHY   1
  NOR IN HID WAYES TC GUIDE $PHILOSOPHIE   4.28.10
PHIP   1
  LEAVE THAT SIR $PHIP, LEAST OFF YOUR NECKE
                       BE WROONG   4.83.14
PHLEGETHON   2
  I WILL NOT COME IN $STIX OR $PHLEGETON   2.39.6
  I WYLL NOT COME IN $STIXE NOR $PHLEGITON   2.118.6
PHLEGMATIC   1
  IN THY COLD STUFFE A FLEGMATIKE DELIGHT+   4.56.11
PHOEBUS   2
  PHOEBUS WAS $JUDGE BETWEENE $JOVE, $MARS,
                     AND $LOVE   4.13.1
  PHOEBUS DREW WIDE THE CURTAINES OF THE SKIES   4.13.12
PHOEBUS'   6
  BY $PHOEBUS' DOOME, WITH SUGRED SENTENCE SAYES   4.25.2
  BUT AH POORE $NIGHT, IN LOVE WITH $PHOEBUS' LIGHT 4.97.5
  BUT WHEN $AURORA LEADES CUT $PHOEBUS' DAUNCE   4.98.12
  AH WHAT DOTH $PHOEBUS' GOLD THAT WRETCH AVAILE   4.108.10
  PROUD $DAPHNE SCORNING $PHAEBUS LOVELY FYRE   5.28.9
  THEN FLY NO MORE FAYRE LOVE FROM $PHEBUS CHACE   5.28.13
PHOENIX   9
  OF THE $BIRDS KIND, THE $PHOENIX IS ALONE   2.16.2
  IN $ONE WHOLE WORLD IS BUT ONE $PHOENIX FOUND   2.106.1
  A $PHOENIX THOU, THIS $PHOENIX THEN ALONE   2.106.2
  A $PHOENIX THOU, THIS $PHOENIX THEN ALONE   2.106.2
  WHILST $LOVE (MY $PHOENIX BIRD) IN HER
               OWN FLAME IS DYING 2.117.12
  MY LIFE A $PHOENIX IS IN MY SOULES FIRE   2.132.11
  UNTO HER VEYNES, THE ONELY $PHOENIX PLUME   2.148.8
  AND BURNE THE LONG LIV'D $PHAENIX IN HER BLOOD   3.19.4
  WHEN I DEMAUND OF $PHENIX $STELLA'S STATE   4.92.6
PHOENIX-LIKE   1
  BUT ($PHAENIX-LIKE) SHALL MAKE HER LIVE ANEW   1.38.14
PHOENIX'S   1
  YOUR $LIFE SO LIKE THE $PHOENIXS BEGUN   2.16.8
PHRASE   4
  BUT SEE, FOR YOU TC $HEAV'N FOR $PHRAZE I RUNNE   2.21.11
  AND PRECIOUS PHRASE BY ALL THE $MUSES FIL'D   3.85.4
  BUT FAILST THOU NCT IN PHRASE SO HEAV'NLY HIE+   4.67.6
  O PLAINTS CONSERV'D IN SUCH A SUGRED PHRAISE   4.100.9
PHRASES   3
  OR $PINDARE'S $APES, FLAUNT THEY IN PHRASES FINE   4.3.3
  PHRASES AND $PROBLEMES FROM MY REACH DO GROW   4.3.10
  NOW JUDGE BY THIS.. IN PIERCING PHRASES LATE   4.58.9
PHYSIC   3
  THEN $POYSON, AND WITH $PHYSIKE HIM RESTCRE   2.50.9
  NOR CAN THY SHAME GIVE PHISICKE TC MY GRIEFE   3.34.9
  DESIRE IS DEATH, WHICH $PHISICK DID EXCEPT   3.147.8
PHYSICIAN   1
  MY REASON THE $PHISITION TO MY LOVE   3.147.5
PHYSICIANS   1
  NO NEWES BUT HEALTH FROM THEIR $PHISITIONS KNOW   3.140.8

```
PHYSICIAN'S                     1
   BUT SUCH SWEET CORDIALLS PASSE $PHYSITIONS ART          5.50.12
PICK-PURSE                      1
   I AM NO PICK-PURSE CF ANCTHER'S WIT                     4.74.8
PICKS                           1
   AND $LOVE ALONE PICKS REASON OUT OF LOVE                2.38.14
PICTURE                         5
   THEN TAKE THIS PICTURE WHICH I HERE PRESENT THEE        1.42.5
   WITH MY LOVES PICTURE THEN MY EYE DOTH FEAST            3.47.5
   SO EITHER BY THY PICTURE OR MY LOVE                     3.47.9
   OR IF THEY SLEEPE, THY PICTURE IN MY SIGHT              3.47.13
   OR AT THE MOST ON SCME FINE PICTURE STAYES              4.11.7
PICTURED                        2
   TO FINDE WHERE YOUR TRUE $IMAGE PICTUR'D LIES           3.24.6
   OFT CRUELL FIGHTS WELL PICTURED FORTH DO PLEASE         4.34.4
PICTURES                        1
   MINE EYE, MY HEART THEIR PICTURES SIGHT
                              WOULD BARRE                  3.46.3
PIECE                           4
   AND FOR ONE PIECE CF $THINE, MY WHOLE HEART TAKE        2.52.8
   WHAT, A WHOLE WEEKE WITHCUT ONE PEECE OF LOOKE          4.56.3
   SOME BEAUTIE'S PEECE, AS AMBER COLOURD HED              4.91.6
   SO FAYRE A PEECE FCR ONE REPULSE SO LIGHT               5.14.4
PIECED                          1
   THY $BOWE HALFE BRCKE, IS PEEC'D WITH
                              OLDE DESIRE                  2.126.5
PIED                            2
   WHEN PROUD PIDE $APRILL (DREST IN ALL HIS TRIM)         3.98.2
   ENAM'LING WITH PIED FLOWERS THEIR THOUGHTS OF GOLD      4.3.4
PIERCE                          2
   TH'IMPRESSION OF HER EYES DO PEARCE SO DEEPE            1.26.7
   IS NO FIT MARKE TC PIERCE WITH HIS FINE
                              POINTED DART                 4.8.3
PIERCED                         3
   (A CLOSET NEVER PEARST WITH CHRISTALL EYES)             3.46.6
   BUT ERE I COULD FLIE THENCE, IT PIERC'D MY HEART        4.20.14
   SHOULD SOONE BE PIERC'D WITH SHARPNESSE
                              OF THE MONE                  4.57.8
PIERCING                        3
   INTO HIS HART THE PIERCING $ARROW FLYES                 2.135.8
   NOW JUDGE BY THIS.. IN PIERCING PHRASES LATE            4.58.9
   SO PIERCING PAWES, AS SPOYLE WHEN THEY EMBRACE          4.78.10
PIES                            1
   DUMBE $SWANNES, NCT CHATRING $PIES, DO
                              $LOVERS PROVE                4.54.13
PILGRIMAGE                      2
   ATTENDING ON HIS GCULDEN PILGRIMAGE                     3.7.8
   INTEND A ZELOUS PILGRIMAGE TO THEE                      3.27.6
PILGRIMS                        1
   TRUE, THAT ON EARTH WE ARE BUT PILGRIMS MADE            4.5.12
PILL                            1
   SWEET IS THE NUT, BUT BITTER IS HIS PILL                5.26.6
PILLOWS                         1
   TAKE THOU OF ME SMCCTH PILLOWES, SWEETEST BED           4.39.9
PINDAR'S                        1
   OR $PINDARE'S $APES, FLAUNT THEY IN PHRASES FINE        4.3.3
PINDUS'                         1
   NOW BROAD-BRYMD $INDUS, THEN OF $PINDUS HEIGHT          2.120.5
PINE                            9
   THE CRUELST $FAYRE THAT SEES I PINE FOR HER             1.22.11
```

BUT I MUST PINE, AND IN MY PINING LURKE	1.29.11
THUS DO I PINE AND SURFET DAY BY DAY	3.75.13
WHY DOST THOU PINE WITHIN AND SUFFER DEARTH	3.146.3
AND LET THAT PINE TO AGGRAVAT THY STORE	3.146.10
WHICH OTHERS SAID DID MAKE THEIR SOULES TO PINE	4.16.6
LATE TYR'D WITH WO, EVEN READY FOR TO PINE	4.62.1
BUT HAVING PINE AND HAVING NOT COMPLAINE	5.35.4
BUT HAVING PINE, AND HAVING NOT COMPLAYNE	5.83.4

PINED   5

FOR WELL THOU SAW'ST MY LOVE AND HOW I PIN'D	1.31.8
PINED WITH $HUNGER, RISING FROM A $FEAST	2.62.4
STILL EMPTY GORG'D, WITH CARES CONSUMPTION PYNDE	2.116.14
PYNED WITH HUNGER, RYSING FROM A FEAST	2.150.4
OF TH'INWARD BALE OF MY LOVE PINED HART	5.2.2

PINES   1

PINES IN HER GRIEFE, IMPRISONED IN HER NEST	1.29.3

PINING   2

BUT I MUST PINE, AND IN MY PINING LURKE	1.29.11
BUT AL MY DAYES IN PINING LANGUOR SPEND	5.36.3

PINIONS   2

TO PROVE THE $PYNIONS, IT ASCENDS THE $SKYES	2.56.10
THAT WITH THE RAYES HIS WAFTING PYNEONS FIRED	2.122.11

PINKS   1

HER LOVELY EYES LYKE $PINCKS BUT NEWLY SPRED	5.64.8

PIN'S   1

I THOUGHT THOSE BABES OF SOME PINNE'S HURT DID WHINE	4.16.7

PIPE   2

AND STOPS HIS PIPE IN GROWTH OF RIPER DAIES	3.102.8
ANOTHER HUMBLER WIT TO SHEPHEARD'S PIPE RETIRES	4.6.7

PIREN'S   1

AND CROWNE THE $PIRENS WITH MY LIVING $SONG	2.25.4

PIT   1

IN HER CHEEKES PIT THOU DIDST THY PITFOULD SET	4.11.11

PITCH   4

UP, TO MY $PITCH, NO COMMON $JUDGEMENT FLYES	2.31.13
BUT WHEN FROM HIGH-MOST PICH WITH WERY CAR	3.7.9
ABOVE A MORTALL PITCH, THAT STRUCK ME DEAD+	3.86.6
MY SPIRIT TO AN HIGHER PITCH WILL RAYSE	5.80.12

PITCHY   1

BLACKE PYTCHY $NIGHT, COMPANYON OF MY WOE	2.145.1

PITEOUS   3

DOTH $STELLA NOW BEGIN WITH PITEOUS EYE	4.67.2
SHE MEANES AT LAST TO MAKE HER PITEOUS SPOYLE	5.41.12
THE PITEOUS PASSION OF HIS DYING SMART	5.48.12

PITFOULD   1

IN HER CHEEKES PIT THOU DIDST THY PITFOULD SET	4.11.11

PITIED   1

THY PITTY MAY DESERVE TO PITTIED BEE	3.142.12

PITIFUL   1

PITTIFULL THRIVORS IN THEIR GAZING SPENT	3.125.8

PITILESS   2

THIS PUNISHMENT THE PITTILESSE MAY MOVE	2.115.8
FAYRE BE YE SURE, BUT PROUD AND PITTILESSE	5.56.5

PITY   36

WAKEN HER SLEEPING PITTY WITH YOUR CRYING	1.2.12
AND HAD SHE PITTY TO CONJOYNE WITH THOSE	1.6.11
AND LET HER PITTIE IF SHE CANNOT LOVE ME	1.10.14
THAT PITTY SHINES NO COMFORT TO MY BLIS	1.21.2

```
POWRE FROM THOSE EYES, WHICH PITTY CANNOT SPARE       1.22.6
NOW SEND FORTH HOPE, FOR NOW CALME PITTY SAVES        1.46.4
PITTY AND SMILES DCE BEST BECOME THE FAIRE            1.51.11
PITTY AND SMILES MUST ONELY YEELD THEE PRAISE         1.51.12
WHICH PITTY NOT THE WOUNDS MADE BY THEIR MIGHT        1.59.6
WHICH WITH MY PLAINT SEEME YET WITH PITTIE MCVED      2.45.13
BUT WHAT OF $PITTY DOE I SPEAKE TO $THEE              2.52.9
THEY $HEAVEN AND $EARTH TO PITTY SHALL PROVCKE        2.55.8
PITTIE SO LEFT, TC TH'COLDNESSE OF YOUR $BLCCD        2.58.13
THEY HEAVEN AND EARTH TC PITTY SHALL PROVCKE          2.102.8
FROM WHENCE, IF YCU ONE TEARE OF PITTY MOVE           2.151.3
PITTY THE WORLD, CR ELSE THIS GLUTTON BE              3.1.13
PITTY ME THEN, AND WISH I WERE RENU'DE                3.111.8
PITTIE ME THEN DEARE FRIEND, AND I ASSURE YEE         3.111.13
EVEN THAT YOUR PITTIE IS ENOUGH TO CURE MEE           3.111.14
YOUR LOVE AND PITTIE DOTH TH'IMPRESSION FILL          3.112.1
AND SUTE THY PITTY LIKE IN EVERY PART                 3.132.12
THE MANNER OF MY PITTIE WANTING PAINE                 3.140.4
ROOTE PITTIE IN THY HEART THAT WHEN IT GROWES         3.142.11
THY PITTY MAY DESERVE TC PITTIED BEE                  3.142.12
KNOWLEDGE MIGHT PITIE WINNE, AND PITIE
                         GRACE OBTAINE                4.1.4
KNOWLEDGE MIGHT PITIE WINNE, AND PITIE
                         GRACE OBTAINE                4.1.4
SUCH SMART MAY PITIE CLAIME OF ANY HART               4.44.3
AND YET SHE HEARES, YET I NO PITTY FIND               4.44.5
BUT CANNOT SKILL TC PITIE MY DISGRACE                 4.45.3
PITIE THEREOF GATE IN HER BREAST SJCH PLACE           4.45.7
I AM NOT I, PITIE THE TALE OF ME                      4.45.14
I CURST THEE OFT, I PITIE NOW THY CASE                4.46.1
SHEWES LOVE AND PITIE TC MY ABSENT CASE               4.60.8
WHILE GRACEFULL PITTY BEAUTY BEAUTIFIES               4.100.4
OR LOOKE WITH PITTY ON MY PAYNEFUL SMART              5.18.8
TO SPILL WERE PITTY, BUT TO SAVE WERE PRAYSE          5.38.12
PITYING                3
NO PITTYING EYE LCCKES BACKE UPON MY FEARES           1.32.10
THINE EIES I LOVE, AND THEY AS PITTYING ME            3.132.1
TILL THAT HIS GRANDAME $NATURE PITTYING IT            4.17.9
PITY'S                 2
SHE YEELDS NO PLACE AT ALL FOR PITTIES DWELLING       1.18.12
REBATE THY $SPLEENE, IF BUT FCR $PITTIES SAKE         2.52.6
PLACE                  48
BUT WITH DISDAINE TC SEE ME IN THAT PLACE             1.5.6
MY FAITH SHOULD WIN, IF $JUSTICE MIGHT HAVE PLACE     1.8.12
SHE YEELDS NO PLACE AT ALL FCR PITTIES DWELLING       1.18.12
WHEN EVERY PLACE PRESENTS LIKE FACE OF WCE            1.52.3
SEEKE OUT SOME PLACE, AND SEE IF ANY PLACE            1.52.9
SEEKE OUT SOME PLACE, AND SEE IF ANY PLACE            1.52.9
AS HOW THE $POLE TC EV'RY PLACE WAS REAR'C            2.1.8
WHILST I IN DARKENESSE, IN THE SELFE-SAME PLACE       2.43.3
THEN ON A PLACE PREPARED FOR HER THERE                2.115.15
WHY SHOULD'ST THOU PLACE THY $TROPHIES
                         IN THOSE EYES                2.123.9
MAKE SWEET SOME VIALL., TREASURE THOU SOME PLACE      3.6.3
SHIFTS BUT HIS PLACE, FCR STILL THE WORLC
                         INJOYES IT                   3.9.10
AS SOONE AS THINKE THE PLACE WHERE HE WOULD BE        3.44.8
EACH CHANGING PLACE WITH THAT WHICH GOES BEFCRE       3.60.3
AND MY SICK $MUSE DCTH GIVE AN UTHER PLACE            3.79.4
AND PLACE MY MERRIT IN THE EIE UF SKORNE              3.88.2
```

```
THY LOOKES WITH ME, THY HEART IN OTHER PLACE        3.93.4
NOR GIVES TO NECESSARY WRINCKLES PLACE              3.108.11
THY BLACKE IS FAIREST IN MY JUDGEMENTS PLACE        3.131.12
WHICH MY HEART KNOWES THE WIDE WORLDS
                        COMMON PLACE+                3.137.10
LOVE BORNE IN $GREECE, OF LATE FLED FROM
                        HIS NATIVE PLACE             4.8.1
GOLD IS THE COVERING OF THAT STATELY PLACE           4.9.4
SO $TYRAN HE NO FITTER PLACE COULD SPIE              4.20.5
AND STAID PLEASD WITH THE PROSPECT OF THE PLACE      4.20.10
PROGRESSING THEN FROM FAIRE TWINNES' GOLD'N PLACE    4.22.2
SCOURGE OF IT SELFE, STILL CLIMING SLIPPRIE
                        PLACE                        4.23.10
UNSEENE, UNHEARD, WHILE THOUGHT TO HIGHEST PLACE     4.27.13
WHAT, MAY IT BE THAT EVEN IN HEAV'NLY PLACE          4.31.3
THE BAITING PLACE OF WIT, THE BALME OF WOE           4.39.2
THE HEAV'NLY NATURE OF THAT PLACE IS SUCH            4.44.12
PITIE THEREOF GATE IN HER BREAST SUCH PLACE          4.45.7
THAT THOU MUST WANT OR FOOD, OR DWELLING PLACE       4.46.4
BY NO PRETENCE CLAIME ANY MANER PLACE                4.52.11
WHEN MY GOOD $ANGELL GUIDES ME TO THE PLACE          4.60.1
HER FLAMIE GLISTRING LIGHTS INCREASE WITH
                        TIME AND PLACE               4.76.10
PARDON THAT FAULT, ONCE MORE GRAUNT ME THE PLACE     4.82.12
WHAT, DOTH HIGH PLACE AMBITIOUS THOUGHTS AUGMENT+    4.83.9
BUT GIVE APT SERVANTS THEIR DUE PLACE, LET EYES      4.85.9
IF THIS DARKE PLACE YET SHEW LIKE CANDLE LIGHT       4.91.5
HER SELFE (TO SHEW NO OTHER JOY HATH PLACE)          4.97.7
LET HONOR SELFE TO THEE GRAUNT HIGHEST PLACE         4.103.14
SO NEERE, IN SO GOOD TIME, SO FREE A PLACE+          4.105.2
BARE ME IN HAND, THAT IN THIS $ORPHANE PLACE         4.106.3
THE WHILES HER FOOT SHE IN MY NECKE DOTH PLACE       5.20.3
SITS DOWNE TO REST HIM IN SOME SHADY PLACE           5.67.3
AND THERE TO REST THEMSELVES DID BOLDLY PLACE        5.76.12
LACKYNG MY LOVE I GO FROM PLACE TO PLACE             5.78.1
LACKYNG MY LOVE I GO FROM PLACE TO PLACE             5.78.1
PLACED                  10
THAT WHERE THOSE TWO CLEARE SPARKLING
                        $EYES ARE PLAC'D             2.8.3
THY $LOVE, THAT IS ON THE UNWORTHY PLAC'D            2.10.11
PLAC'D IN THE FORLORNE HOPE OF ALL DISPAYRE          2.142.1
LIKE STONES OF WORTH THEY THINLY PLACED ARE          3.52.7
PLACED EVER THERE, GAVE HIM THIS MOURNING WEED       4.7.13
BY BEING PLACED IN SUCH A WRETCH AS I                4.94.14
IN WHICH HER GLORIOUS YMAGE PLACED IS                5.22.6
THROUGH HIDDEN PERILS ROUND ABOUT ME PLAST           5.34.8
BY $LOVE HIMSELFE AND IN HIS GARDEN PLASTE           5.77.12
I BLESSE MY LOT, THAT WAS SO LUCKY PLACED            5.82.2
PLACES                  1
WHICH THERE IN ORDER TAKE THEIR SEVERALL PLACES      2.4.4
PLAGUE                  9
SO SHALT THOU CEASE TO PLAGUE, AND I TO PAINE        1.19.14
WITH THEE SUCH POWERS TO PLAGUE ONE SILLY HARTE      1.27.12
THUS $ILE PLAGUE HER WHICH SO HATH PLAGUED MEE       2.115.18
DRINKE UP THE MONARKS PLAGUE THIS FLATTERY+          3.114.2
AND TO THIS FALSE PLAGUE ARE THEY NOW
                        TRANSFERRED                  3.137.14
ONELY MY PLAGUE THUS FARRE I COUNT MY GAINE          3.141.13
BEAUTIE'S PLAGUE, $VERTUE'S SCOURGE, SUCCOUR
                        OF LIES                       4.78.6
```

```
A STILL FELT PLAGUE, TO SELFE CONDEMNING ME          4.86.3
THAT SHE WILL PLAGUE THE MAN THAT LOVES HER MOST     5.41.6
PLAGUED              1
THUS $ILE PLAGUE HER WHICH SO HATH PLAGUED MEE       2.115.18
PLAGUES              3
WITH THOUSAND $PLAGUES, MORE THEN IN $PURGATORIE     2.49.12
OF PLAGUES, OF DEARTHS, OR SEASONS QUALLITY          3.14.4
LET ALL THE PLAGUES AND HORRID PAINES OF HELL        5.86.5
PLAIN                5
IN TRUE PLAINE WORDS, BY THY TRUE TELLING FRIEND     3.82.12
IF $SAPHYRES, LOE HER EIES BE $SAPHYRES PLAINE       5.15.7
BUT IF YOUR SELFE IN ME YE PLAYNE WILL SEE           5.45.13
WAS IT A DREAME, OR DID I SEE IT PLAYNE              5.77.1
OF WHICH BEHOLDING THE $IDAEA PLAYNE                 5.88.9
PLAINLY              1
AND URG'D THAT TITLE WHICH DOTH PLAINELY PROVE       1.8.11
PLAIN-PATHED         1
PLAINE-PATH'D $EXPERIENCE, TH'UNLEARNEDS GUIDE       2.46.1
PLAINS               1
YET GOE (FORSAKEN) LEAVE THESE $WOODS,
                            THESE PLAINES            1.52.5
PLAINT               4
WHICH WITH MY PLAINT SEEME YET WITH PITTIE MOVED     2.45.13
TO SOME A SWEETEST PLAINT, A SWEETEST
                            STILE AFFORDS            4.6.9
OR IF THY LOVE OF PLAINT YET MINE FORBEARES          4.94.9
THAT SHE WILL ONCE VOUCHSAFE MY PLAINT TO HEARE      5.18.7
PLAINTIVE            1
THESE PLAINTIVE $VERSE, THE $POSTES OF MY DESIRE     1.4.1
PLAINTS              10
WHICH HERE MY LOVE, MY YOUTH, MY PLAINTS REVEALE     1.1.4
THEN WHO HAD HEARD THE PLAINTS I UTTER NOW+          1.6.12
IT PLEASETH ME IF I MY PLAINTS REHEARSE              2.128.11
SHE HEARD MY PLAINTS, AND DID NOT ONLY HEARE         4.57.9
O PLAINTS CONSERV'D IN SUCH A SUGRED PHRAISE         4.100.9
SUCH TEARES, SIGHS, PLAINTS, NO SORROW
                            IS, BUT JOY              4.100.12
PLAYNTS, PRAYERS, VOWES, RUTH, SORROW,
                            AND DISMAY               5.14.11
NE ALL THE PLAYNTS AND PRAYERS WITH WHICH I          5.32.7
WITH ALL THE PLAYNTS WHICH TO HER BE APPLYDE         5.32.12
SEEK WITH MY PLAYNTS TO MATCH THAT MOURNFUL COVE     5.89.8
PLANET               6
O STARRE OF STARRES, FAYRE $PLANET MILDLY
                            MOOVING                  2.129.5
BUT MY FAIRE $PLANET, WHO DIRECTS ME STILL           2.147.9
STELLA, THE ONELY $PLANET OF MY LIGHT                4.68.1
TO EVERY PLANET POINT HIS SUNDRY YEARE               5.60.2
SO SINCE THE WINGED $GOD HIS PLANET CLEARE           5.60.5
BUT LET MY LOVES FAYRE $PLANET SHORT HER WAYES       5.60.13
PLANETS              1
WHILE THOSE FAIRE PLANETS ON THY STREAMES
                            DID SHINE                4.103.4
PLANT                1
THAT VOYCE, WHICH MAKES THE SOULE PLANT
                            HIMSELFE IN THE EARES    4.77.9
PLANTS               1
WHEN I PERCEIVE THAT MEN AS PLANTS INCREASE          3.15.5
PLATO                1
THAT $PLATO I READ FOR NOUGHT, BUT IF HE TAME        4.21.5
```

PLAY   18
  YET $FOOLES AND $CHILDREN SOMETIMES TELL IN PLAY   2.22.13
  BUT WHEN MY $TOUCHING CAME TO PLAY HIS PART   2.29.9
  THOU, HER BLIND $SCNNE, MAY'ST SIT BY
                          THEM, AND PLAY   2.48.14
  PLAY NOT THE $TYRANT, BUT TAKE SOME $REMCRSE   2.52.5
  EV'N AS THIS $SPIRIT, SC YOU ALONE DOE PLAY   2.58.11
  WILL PLAY THE TIRANTS TC THE VERY SAME   3.5.3
  HANG ON SUCH THORNES, AND PLAY AS WANTONLY   3.54.7
  TO PLAIE THE WATCH-MAN EVER FOR THY SAKE   3.61.12
  AS WITH YOUR SHADDOW I WITH THESE DID PLAY   3.98.14
  AND PLAY THE MOTHERS PART KISSE ME, BE KIND   3.143.12
  AND STRAIGHT THEREWITH, LIKE WAGS NEW
                          GOT TO PLAY   4.17.13
  WHEN HE WILL PLAY, THEN IN HER LIPS HE IS   4.43.9
  WHEN FOR SO SOFT A ROD DEARE PLAY HE TRIE+   4.73.4
  OF GENTLE FORCE, SC THAT MINE EYES DARE
                          GLADLY PLAY   4.76.6
  BUT WHEN I PLEADE, SHE BIDS ME PLAY MY PART   5.18.9
  THAT THEY TAKE PLEASURE IN HER CRUELL PLAY   5.47.11
  RIGHT SO MY CRUELL FAYRE WITH ME DOTH PLAY   5.53.5
  BEHOLDING ME THAT ALL THE PAGEANTS PLAY   5.54.3
PLAYED   4
  LOVE, IN A $HUMOR, PLAY'D THE $PRODIGALL   2.7.1
  HAST PLAYD THE THIEFE, AND STOLNE MY HART
                          FROM ME   2.130.11
  MINE EYE HATH PLAY'D THE PAINTER AND HATH STEELD   3.24.1
  BUT WHILE I THUS WITH THIS YONG $LYON PLAID   4.16.9
PLAYEST   1
  HOW OFT WHEN THOU MY MUSIKE MUSIKE PLAYST   3.128.1
PLAYING   1
  PLAYING AND SHINING IN EACH OUTWARD PART   4.11.13
PLAYS   4
  AS IS HIS ART THAT PLAYES UPON THE SAME   1.57.2
  STRAIGHTWAYES HE PLAY'S A SWAGG'RING $RUFFINS
                          PART   2.7.10
  LOVE STILL A $BABY, PLAYES WITH $GAWDES
                          AND $TOYES   2.22.5
  WITH GUILDED LEAVES OR CCLOURD $VELUME PLAYES   4.11.6
PLEA   3
  AND GAINST MY SELFE A LAWFULL PLEA COMMENCE   3.35.11
  BUT THE DEFENDANT DCTH THAT PLEA DENY   3.46.7
  HOW WITH THIS RAGE SHALL BEAUTIE HOLD A PLEA   3.65.3
PLEAD   6
  WHO PLEADE FOR LOVE, AND LOOK FOR RECOMPENCE   3.23.11
  MY HEART DOTH PLEAD THAT THOU IN HIM DOOST LYE   3.46.5
  BUT WHEN I PLEADE, SHE BIDS ME PLAY MY PART   5.18.9
  SO DOE I WEEPE, AND WAYLE, AND PLEADE IN VAINE   5.18.13
  WILL TEACH TO SPEAKE, AND MY JUST CAUSE TO PLEAD   5.43.10
  BUT PLEAD THY MAISTERS CAUSE UNJUSTLY PAYNED   5.48.8
PLEASANCE   4
  THE LOVELY PLEASANCE AND THE LOFTY PRIDE   5.17.11
  FOR WITH MILD PLEASANCE, WHICH DOTH PRIDE
                          DISPLACE   5.21.5
  A MELTING PLEASANCE RAN THROUGH EVERY PART   5.39.7
  IN HER UNSPOTTED PLEASAUNS TO DELIGHT   5.89.12
PLEASANT   4
  IN GREATEST $PERILS SOME $MEN PLEASANT BE   2.24.10
  NOT THAT THE SUMMER IS LESSE PLEASANT NOW   3.102.9
  O HOW THE PLEASANT AIRES OF TRUE LOVE BE   4.78.1

```
    TILL THEN GIVE LEAVE TO ME IN PLEASANT MEW          5.80.9
PLEASE                  20
    SO MUCH I PLEASE TO PERISH IN MY WOE                1.14.12
    IF IT MIGHT PLEASE $YOU, WOULD TO $GOD $YOU COULD   2.19.4
    AND PLEASE YOUR SELFE WITH THIS $CONCEIT
                                THE WHILE               2.24.8
    AS'T PLEASE THE $FATES, BY THEIR RESISTLESSE
                                FORCE                   2.51.4
    I TELL THE $DAY TO PLEASE HIM THOU ART BRIGHT       3.28.9
    IF MY SLIGHT $MUSE DOE PLEASE THESE CURIOUS
                                DAIES                   3.38.13
    FOR NOTHING HOLD ME, SO IT PLEASE THEE HOLD         3.136.11
    TH'UNCERTAINE SICKLIE APPETITE TO PLEASE            3.147.4
    THEY SHOULD STILL DAUNCE TO PLEASE A GAZER'S
                                SIGHT                   4.26.8
    OFT CRUELL FIGHTS WELL PICTURED FORTH DO PLEASE     4.34.4
    IN VERSE, AND THAT MY VERSE BEST WITS
                                DOTH PLEASE+            4.74.11
    THEY PLEASE I DO CONFESSE, THEY PLEASE MINE EYES    4.91.9
    THEY PLEASE I DO CONFESSE, THEY PLEASE MINE EYES    4.91.9
    LEAVES, LINES, AND RYMES, SEEKE HER TO
                                PLEASE ALONE            5.1.13
    WHOM IF YE PLEASE, I CARE FOR OTHER NONE            5.1.14
    BUT MY RUDE MUSICK, WHICH WAS WONT TO PLEASE        5.38.5
    LET HER, YF PLEASE HER, BYND WITH ADAMANT CHAYNE    5.42.10
    AND RULES THE MEMBERS AS IT SELFE DOTH PLEASE+      5.50.8
    DOTH PLEASE ALL BEASTS BUT THAT HIS LOOKS
                                THEM FRAY               5.53.2
    HER HARTS DESIRE WITH MOST CONTENTMENT PLEASE      5.72.12
PLEASED                 4
    THAT THOU BE PLEAS'D, AND I MAY SIGH NO MORE        1.46.14
    WHO IN DISPIGHT OF VIEW IS PLEASD TO DOTE           3.141.4
    AND PLEASD WITH OUR SOFT PEACE, STAID
                            HERE HIS FLYING RACE        4.8.4
    AND STAID PLEASD WITH THE PROSPECT OF THE PLACE     4.20.10
PLEASETH                2
    IT PLEASETH ME, IF I MY $WOES REHEARSE              2.42.11
    IT PLEASETH ME IF I MY PLAINTS REHEARSE             2.128.11
PLEASING                9
    FED WITH SOME PLEASING LOOKE THERE SHALL SHE BE     1.25.11
    IF ANY PLEASING RELISH HERE I USE                  1.57.11
    SOME SAY, I HAVE A PASSING PLEASING $STRAINE        2.42.3
    SOME SAY I HAVE A PASSING PLEASING STRAINE          2.128.3
    WHO ALL IN ONE, ONE PLEASING NOTE DO SING          3.8.12
    THAT $MUSICKE HATH A FARRE MORE PLEASING SOUND     3.130.10
    TRUST IN THE SHADE OF PLEASING $ORANGE TREE         4.30.8
    WING'D WITH WHOSE BREATH, SO PLEASING
                                $ZEPHIRES BLOW          4.100.7
    SO PLEASING IS IN MY EXTREAMEST PAINE               5.42.2
PLEASINGST              1
    PLEASINGST CONSORT, WHERE EACH SENCE HOLDS A PART   4.79.3
PLEASURE                24
    AND IF I FINDE SUCH PLEASURE TO COMPLAINE           1.48.13
    OR ELSE RECEAV'ST WITH PLEASURE THINE ANNOY+        3.8.4
    BUT SINCE SHE PRICKT THEE OUT FOR WOMENS
                                PLEASURE                3.20.13
    FROM WHENCE AT PLEASURE THOU MAIST COME AND PART    3.48.12
    FOR BLUNTING THE FINE POINT OF SELDOME PLEASURE     3.52.4
    I SHOULD IN THOUGHT CONTROULE YOUR TIMES
                                OF PLEASURE             3.58.2
```

```
NOT BLAME YOUR PLEASURE BE IT ILL OR WELL        3.58.14
THEN BETTERD THAT THE WORLD MAY SEE MY PLEASURE  3.75.8
AND EVERY HUMOR HATH HIS ADJUNCT PLEASURE        3.91.5
FROM THEE, THE PLEASURE OF THE FLEETING YEARE+   3.97.2
AND THE JUST PLEASURE LOST, WHICH IS SO DEEMED   3.121.3
YET FEAR HER $0 THOU MINNION OF HER PLEASURE     3.126.9
THAT THE DEARE $SHE MIGHT TAKE SOME PLEASURE
                             OF MY PAINE         4.1.2
PLEASURE MIGHT CAUSE HER READE, READING
                        MIGHT MAKE HER KNOW      4.1.3
AND EKE HIS LEARNED HAND AT PLEASURE GUIDE       5.17.6
THAT ENDLESSE PLEASURE SHALL UNTO ME GAINE+      5.26.14
AND FEEDS AT PLEASURE ON THE WRETCHED PRAY       5.47.8
THAT THEY TAKE PLEASURE IN HER CRUELL PLAY       5.47.11
AND THINCK THEY DY WITH PLEASURE, LIVE
                        WITH PAYNE               5.47.14
BUT IF IT BE YOUR PLEASURE AND PROUD WILL        5.49.5
THERE LET NO THOUGHT OF JOY OR PLEASURE VAINE    5.52.9
AND SPOTLESSE PLEASURE BUILDS HER SACRED BOWRE   5.65.14
THE BOWRE OF BLISSE, THE PARADICE OF PLEASURE    5.76.3
SWEET FRUIT OF PLEASURE BROUGHT FROM PARADICE    5.77.11
PLEASURES                    2
LET LOVE AND YOUTH CONDUCT THY PLEASURES THITHER 1.51.8
FOR $SOMMER AND HIS PLEASURES WAITE ON THEE      3.97.11
PLEASURE'S                   3
MY PLEASURES HORROR, $MUSICKE TRAGICKE NOTES     1.9.11
LAUGHTER LOVING $GODDESSE, WORLDLY PLEASURES
                        $QUEENE                  1.10.6
DRAWNE WITH SWEET PLEASURES BAYT, IT BACK
                        DOTH FLY                 5.72.7
PLEDGE                       4
STRETCH OUT THE FAIREST HAND, A PLEDGE OF PEACE  1.46.9
SO FOR MY $PLEDGE THOU GIVE ME $PLEDGE AGAINE    2.63.8
SO FOR MY $PLEDGE THOU GIVE ME $PLEDGE AGAINE    2.63.8
AND YIELD FOR PLEDGE MY POORE CAPTYVED HART      5.42.8
PLENTEOUS                    1
WITH PLENTEOUS HAND BY HEAVEN UPON YOU THROWN    5.66.2
PLENTY                       5
IN $PLENTY I AM STARV'D WITH $PENURIE            2.62.11
IN PLENTY, AM I STARV'D WITH PENURY              2.150.11
WHOSE EYES HIM STARV'D.. SO PLENTY MAKES ME POORE 5.35.8
BETOKENING PEACE AND PLENTY TO ENSEW             5.62.4
WHOSE EYES HIM STARV'D.. SO PLENTY MAKES ME PORE 5.83.8
PLIES                        1
DEEME THAT MY $MUSE SOME FRUIT OF KNOWLEDGE PLIES 4.23.6
PLIGHT                       1
HOW CAN I THEN RETURNE IN HAPPY PLIGHT           3.28.1
PLIGHTS                      1
BUT SPEAKE NO WORD TO HER OF THESE SAD PLIGHTS   5.84.11
PLODS                        1
PLODS DULY ON, TO BEARE THAT WAIGHT IN ME        3.50.6
PLOT                         1
WHY SHOULD MY HEART THINKE THAT A SEVERALL PLOT  3.137.9
PLOWMAN                      1
SO DOTH THE $PLOW-MAN GAZE THE WAND'RING $STARRE 2.43.5
PLOWS                        1
WITHIN THEMSELVES, AND ON THEM PLOUGHS HAVE EAR'D 1.45.4
PLUCK                        4
NOT FROM THE STARS DO I MY JUDGEMENT PLUCKE      3.14.1
PLUCKE THE KEENE TEETH FROM THE FIERCE $TYGERS YAWES 3.19.3
```

```
AS WHO BY BEING POISOND DOTH POISON KNOW          4.16.14
THAT POISON FOULE OF BUBLING PRIDE DOTH LIE       4.27.6
POISONED                  3
  IF IT BE POISON'D, TIS THE LESSER SINNE         3.114.13
  AS WHO BY BEING POISOND DOTH POISON KNOW        4.16.14
  OF POYSONED WORDS AND SPITEFULL SPEECHES WELL   5.86.4
POISONOUS                 1
  THAT WITH SUCH POYSONOUS CARE MY LOOKES
                              YOU MARKE           4.104.2
POLE                      1
  AS HOW THE $POLE TO EV'RY PLACE WAS REAR'D      2.1.8
POLES'                    1
  HOW $POLES' RIGHT KING MEANES, WITHOUT
                              LEAVE OF HOAST      4.30.3
POLICY                    2
  THUS POLLICIE IN LOVE T'ANTICIPATE              3.118.9
  IT FEARES NOT POLICY THAT $HERITICKE            3.124.9
POLISHED                  2
  THAT LOVELY, ARCHED, YVORIE, POLLISH'D $BROW    2.8.5
  IN POLISHT FORME OF WELL REFINED PEN            3.85.8
POLITIC                   1
  BUT ALL ALONE STANDS HUGELY POLLITICK           3.124.11
POMP                      2
  BUT STRAIGHT HER WIDE BLOWNE POMP COMES
                              TO DECLINE          1.39.6
  IT SUFFERS NOT IN SMILINGE POMP, NOR FALLS      3.124.6
POMPOUS                   1
  THE GREATEST $PRINCE WITH POMPOUS ROIALTY+      5.77.4
POOR                     62
  RUNNES THIS POORE $RIVER, CHARG'D WITH
                              STREAMES OF ZEALE   1.1.2
  THOU POORE HEART SACRIFIZ'D UNTO THE FAIREST    1.8.1
  UPON THE PROSTRATE SPOYLE OF THAT POORE HART    1.10.10
  WITH THIS POORE HEART CONSUMED WITH DISPAIRE    1.22.8
  OF SUCH AS SPOILE THY POORE AFFLICTED STATE     1.28.4
  ALL MY POORE LIFE BY THEM IS TRODEN DOWNE       1.28.6
  WHILST BY THY EIES PURSU'D, MY POORE HEART FLEW 1.31.1
  WHOSE INFLUENCE RULE THE $ORBE OF MY POORE HART+ 1.34.10
  HER PRIDE BROOK'D NOT POORE SOULES SHOULD
                              SO ASPIRE           1.36.8
  POORE SOULE QUITE SPENT, WHOSE FORCE CAN
                              DO NO MORE          1.46.3
  AND WHITHER (POORE FORSAKEN) WILT THOU GOE      1.52.1
  BUT $AVON RICH IN FAME, THOUGH POORE IN WATERS  1.58.11
  THUS POORE $THEEVES SUFFER, WHEN THE GREATER
                              SCAPE               2.14.14
  NOR GIVES $ME ONCE, BUT ONE POORE MINUTES REST  2.20.4
  ONELY COMPELL'D ON THIS POORE GOOD TO BOAST     2.43.13
  INCLOSE MY $MUSIKE, YOU POORE SENSELESSE $WALLS 2.45.9
  SHE COMMING NEERE, THAT MY POORE $HEART
                              HATH SLAINE         2.46.9
  POORE $ROGUE, GOE PAWNE THY $FASCIA AND THY $BOW 2.48.3
  WHOSE $SENSES, LIKE POORE $PRIS'NERS,
                              HUNGER-STARV'D      2.49.7
  TOO RICH A $RELIQUE FOR SO POORE A $SHRINE      2.57.4
  THIS MIRACLE ON MY POORE $MUSE HAVE TRIED       2.104.10
  AND THUS (POORE $ORPHAN) LYING IN DISTRESSE     2.116.17
  POORE $BROOKES AND $BANKS HAD NO SUCH
                              WONDERS BEENE       2.120.14
  WHERE MY POORE SOULE, THE $BARKE OF SORROW LYES 2.134.3
```

IN THINE EYES TRYUMPH MURTHERING MY POORE HART	2.140.2
DUTY SO GREAT, WHICH WIT SO POORE AS MINE	3.26.5
THESE POORE RUDE LINES OF THY DECEASED $LOVER	3.32.4
SO THEN I AM NOT LAME, POORE, NOR DISPIS'D	3.37.9
TO LEAVE POORE ME, THOU HAST THE STRENGTH OF LAWES	3.49.13
O WHAT EXCUSE WILL MY POORE BEAST THEN FIND	3.51.5
WHY SHOULD POORE BEAUTIE INDIRECTLY SEEKE	3.67.7
DO NOT SO MUCH AS MY POORE NAME REHERSE	3.71.11
SINCE SPIGHT OF HIM $ILE LIVE IN THIS POORE RIME	3.107.11
THAT POORE RETENTICN COULD NOT SO MUCH HOLD	3.122.9
AND TAKE THOU MY OBLACICN, POORE BUT FREE	3.125.10
WHILST MY POORE LIPS WHICH SHOULD THAT HARVEST REAPE	3.128.7
BUT THEN MY FRIENDS HEART LET MY POORE HEART BALE	3.133.10
NOT PRIZING HER POORE INFANTS DISCONTENT	3.143.8
POORE SOULE THE CENTER OF MY SINFULL EARTH	3.146.1
HE IS CONTENTED THY POORE DRUDGE TO BE	3.151.11
AND STRANGE THINGS COST TOO DEARE FOR MY POORE SPRITES	4.3.11
OF TOUCH THEY ARE, AND POORE I AM THEIR STRAW	4.9.14
YOU THAT POORE $PETRARCH'S LONG DECEASED WOES	4.15.7
POORE PASSENGER, PASSE NOW THEREBY I DID	4.20.9
MY HARMES ON $INK'S POORE LOSSE, PERHAPS SOME FIND	4.34.13
THE POORE MAN'S WEALTH, THE PRISONER'S RELEASE	4.39.3
DO NOT, O DO NOT FROM POORE ME REMOVE	4.42.7
ALAS POORE WAG, THAT NOW A SCHOLLER ART	4.46.9
AND NOW MAN'S WRONGS IN ME, POORE BEAST, DESCRIE	4.49.4
WHILE THOSE POORE BABES THEIR DEATH IN BIRTH DO FIND	4.50.11
POORE $LAYMAN I, FOR SACRED RITES JNFIT	4.74.4
THAT SKIN, WHOSE PASSE-PRAISE HUE SCORNS THIS POORE TERME OF WHITE	4.77.7
POORE HOPE'S FIRST WEALTH, OSTAGE OF PROMIST WEALE	4.79.12
IF HER LIPS DAIGND TO SWEETEN MY POORE NAME	4.92.13
FOR MY POORE SOULE, WHICH NOW THAT SICKNESSE TRIES	4.94.6
BUT AH POORE $NIGHT, IN LOVE WITH $PHOEBUS' LIGHT	4.97.5
OF MY POORE LIFE TO MAKE UNPITTIED SPOILE	5.11.8
YET MY POORE LIFE, ALL SORROWES TO ASSOYLE	5.11.9
OF SUCH POORE THRALLS HER CRUELL HANDS EMBREW	5.31.12
WHOSE EYES HIM STARV'D.. SO PLENTY MAKES ME POORE	5.35.8
AND YIELD FOR PLEDGE MY POORE CAPTYVED HART	5.42.8
WHOSE EYES HIM STARV'D.. SO PLENTY MAKES ME PORE	5.83.8

POORLY   1

IS POORELY IMMITATED AFTER YOU	3.53.6

PORCHES   1

WHOSE PORCHES RICH (WHICH NAME OF CHEEKES ENDURE)	4.9.7

PORPHIR   1

RED $PORPHIR IS, WHICH LOCKE OF PEARLE MAKES SURE	4.9.6

PORT   2

PROCEEDING FROM THE $PORT WHENCE HE PUT FORTH	2.1.5
IN THAT PROUD PORT, WHICH HER SO GOODLY GRACETH	5.13.1

PORTLINESS   1

SUCH PRIDE IS PRAISE, SUCH PORTLINESSE IS HONOR	5.5.9

PORTLY   1
  IN FINDING FAULT WITH HER TOO PORTLY PRIDE   5.5.2
PORTRAIT   3
  PORTRAITE OF HELL, THE AYRES BLACK MOURNING WEED   2.145.6
  TO PORTRAIT THAT WHICH IN THIS WORLD IS BEST   4.50.8
  THE GLORIOUS POURTRAICT OF THAT $ANGELS FACE   5.17.1
POSSESS   4
  POSSESSE ME WHOLE, MY HEARTS TRIUMVIRATE   1.28.2
  YET PRIDE I THINKE DOTH NOT MY SOULE POSSESSE   4.27.9
  THOSE $LOVERS SCORNE WHOM THAT $LOVE DOTH
                     POSSESSE+   4.31.13
  HONOUR IS HONOUR'D, THAT THOU DOEST POSSESSE   4.35.9
POSSESSED   3
  WHERE WITH (ALAS) I HAVE BEENE LONG POSSEST   2.20.2
  FOR THOU ART SO POSSEST WITH MURDROUS HATE   3.10.5
  FEATUR'D LIKE HIM, LIKE HIM WITH FRIENDS POSSEST   3.29.6
POSSESSETH   1
  SINNE OF SELFE-LOVE POSSESSETH AL MINE EIE   3.62.1
POSSESSING   2
  POSSESSING OR PURSUING NO DELIGHT   3.75.11
  FAREWELL THOU ART TOO DEARE FOR MY POSSESSING   3.87.1
POSSESSION   2
  NOR LOOSE POSSESSION OF THAT FAIRE THOU OW'ST   3.18.10
  MADE $IN PURSUT AND IN POSSESSION SO   3.129.9
POSSIBLY   1
  THEN POSSIBLY $INVENTION CAN EXTEND   2.34.11
POSTERITY   6
  WHICH HAPPILY POSTERITY MAY CHERRISH   1.42.10
  PASSE ON, AND TO $POSTERITIE TELL THIS   2.17.9
  OF HIS SELFE LOVE TO STOP POSTERITY+   3.3.8
  LEAVING THEE LIVING IN POSTERITY+   3.6.12
  EVEN IN THE EYES OF ALL POSTERITY   3.55.11
  AND TELL HER PRAYSE TO ALL POSTERITY   5.69.11
POSTING   1
  TILL I RETURNE OF POSTING IS NOE NEED   3.51.4
POSTS   1
  THESE PLAINTIVE $VERSE, THE $POSTES OF MY DESIRE   1.4.1
POTIONS   2
  POTIONS OF $EYSELL GAINST MY STRONG INFECTION   3.111.10
  WHAT POTIONS HAVE I DRUNKE OF $SYREN TEARES   3.119.1
POUR   3
  MY EYES MADE DIM WITH LOOKES, POURE DOWN
                   A FLOOD OF TEARS   2.133.10
  WHILE TEARES POWRE OUT HIS INKE, AND SIGHS
                  BREATHE OUT HIS WORDS   4.6.10
  AND DOE MYNE HUMBLED HART BEFORE HER POURE   5.20.2
POURED   1
  POWR'D OUT WHAT FIRST FROM QUICKE $INVENTION CAME   2.21.6
POUREST   1
  WHILE THOU DOST BREATH THAT POOR'ST INTO MY VERSE   3.38.2
POVERTY   2
  ALTHOUGH THOU STEALE THEE ALL MY POVERTY   3.40.10
  ALACK WHAT POVERTY MY $MUSE BRINGS FORTH   3.103.1
POWDER   1
  THE POWDER OF HER $HEART DRY'D, WHEN SHE IS DEAD   2.15.3
POWDERED   1
  BROADRED WITH BULS AND SWANS, POWDRED
                 WITH GOLDEN RAINE   4.6.6
POWER   43
  THOU POWRE THAT RUL'ST THE CONFINES OF THE NIGHT   1.10.5

```
POWRE FROM THOSE EYES, WHICH PITTY CANNOT SPARE        1.22.6
AND YET THOU SEEST THY POWRE SHE DISOBAYES             1.23.9
I LOVE TH'EFFECT THE CAUSE BEING OF THIS POWRE         1.26.11
THEIR SWEET APPEARING STILL SUCH POWER INSPIRES        1.34.7
THAT $MIRROR SHEWES WHAT POWER IS IN THY FACE          1.37.10
NOW SHEW THY POWER, AND WHERE THY VERTUE LIES          1.46.7
BECAUSE THEIR POWER SERVE TO EXACT THE SAME            1.47.12
(IF LOVE IN HER HATH ANY POWER TO MOVE)                1.49.10
THAT $GOLD NOR $HONOUR NE'R HAD POW'R TO MOVE          2.15.4
IF THIS $RECEIT HAVE NOT THE POW'R TO WINNE ME         2.15.13
OR HAVE OUR $PASSIONS LESSER POW'R THEN THEIRS         2.27.5
MARVELL NOT, $LOVE, THOUGH I THY POW'R ADMIRE          2.34.1
MARVELL NOT, $LOVE, THOUGH I THY POW'R ADMIRE          2.34.5
MARVELL NOT, $LOVE, THOUGH I THY POW'R ADMIRE          2.34.9
BY THY FAIRE $MOTHERS UNAVOIDED $POWER                 2.36.6
ONELY TO SHEW HER $BEAUTIES $SOV'RAIGNE $POW'R         2.50.14
NOR MY HART KNOWNE THE POWER OF THY NAME               2.104.6
BY THY GREAT POWER, AND BY STRONG FAYTH IN THEE        2.112.14
WHAT $MUSE HATH POWER, ABOVE THY HEIGHT
                          TO RAISE THEE+               2.146.4
BUT SAD MORTALLITY CRE-SWAIES THEIR POWER              3.65.2
THEY THAT HAVE POWRE TO HURT, AND WILL DOE NONE        3.94.1
DARKNING THY POWRE TO LEND BASE SUBJECTS LIGHT         3.100.4
O THOU MY LOVELY $BOY WHO IN THY POWER                 3.126.1
FOR SINCE EACH HAND HATH PUT ON $NATURES POWER         3.127.5
THY FACE HATH NOT THE POWER TO MAKE LOVE GRONE         3.131.6
USE POWER WITH POWER, AND SLAY ME NOT BY $ART          3.139.4
USE POWER WITH POWER, AND SLAY ME NOT BY $ART          3.139.4
OH FROM WHAT POWRE HAST THOU THIS POWREFULL
                          MIGHT                        3.150.1
OR WOULD SHE HER MIRACULOUS POWER SHOW                 4.7.9
SO $STELLA'S HEART, FINDING WHAT POWER
                          $LOVE BRINGS                 4.29.5
SINCE THOU IN ME SO SURE A POWER DOEST KEEPE           4.32.5
O $STELLA DEARE, HOW MUCH THY POWER HATH WROUGHT       4.40.2
EACH SENCE OF MINE, EACH GIFT, EACH POWER OF MIND      4.57.2
COME, COME, AND LET ME POWRE MY SELFE ON THEE          4.69.6
HIS WANTON WINGS AND DARTS OF DEADLY POWER             5.4.8
AND YET THE $LYON THAT IS $LORD OF POWER               5.20.5
TO PROVE YOUR POWRE, WHICH I TOO WEL HAVE TRIDE        5.25.8
THE POWRE THEREOF, WHICH OFTE IN ME I FIND             5.28.5
SUCH IS THE POWRE OF LOVE IN GENTLE MIND               5.30.13
IS IT BECAUSE YOUR EYES HAVE POWRE TO KILL+            5.49.2
TO SHEW THE POWRE OF YOUR IMPERIOUS EYES               5.49.6
IN HER OWNE POWRE, AND SCORNETH OTHERS AYDE            5.58.2
POWERFUL                 5
IS $NATURE GROWNE LESSE POW'RFULL IN THEIR
                          $HEIRES                      2.27.7
OF $PRINCES SHALL OUT-LIVE THIS POWREFULL RIME         3.55.2
OH FROM WHAT POWRE HAST THOU THIS POWREFULL
                          MIGHT                        3.150.1
THOSE POWREFULL EIES, WHICH LIGHTEN MY
                          DARK SPRIGHT                 5.9.2
EXPRESSING ALL THY MOTHERS POWREFULL ART               5.39.2
POWERS                  15
WITH THEE SUCH POWERS TO PLAGUE ONE SILLY HARTE        1.27.12
CELESTIALL FIRE, AND UNRESPECTING POWRES               1.59.5
MY SINFULL EARTH THESE REBBELL POWRES
                          THAT THEE ARRAY              3.146.2
DEALE THOU WITH POWERS OF THOUGHTS, LEAVE
                          LOVE TO WILL                 4.10.8
```

```
THOU COUNTEST $STELLA THINE, LIKE THOSE
                    WHOSE POWERS               4.12.9
BENDS ALL HIS POWERS, EVEN UNTO $STELLA'S GRACE   4.27.14
STELLA'S GREAT POWRS, THAT SO CONFUSE MY MIND     4.34.14
DOTH FALL TO STRAY, AND MY CHIEFE POWRES
                    ARE BROUGHT                 4.38.3
UNITED POWERS MAKE EACH THE STRONGER PROVE        4.88.14
IN NIGHT OF SPRITES THE GASTLY POWERS STUR        4.96.10
OF HIS MAZDE POWERS KEEPES PERFIT HARMONY         4.99.8
OF ALL THE POWERS WHICH LIFE BESTOWES ON ME       4.107.2
NO EIES BUT JOYES, IN WHICH AL POWERS CONSPIRE    5.8.3
WHILEST MY WEAK POWRES OF PASSIONS WARREID ARRE   5.44.7
SO WEAKE MY POWRES, SO SORE MY WOUNDS APPEARE     5.57.5
PRACTICE                  1
PRACTISE THY $QUIVER, AND TURNE $CROW-KEEPER      2.48.8
PRACTISED                 1
AND WITH THE SAME HE PRACTISED TO FLYE            2.122.7
PRAISE                   75
MAY JUSTLY PRAISE, AND BLAME MY LOVELESSE $FAIRE  1.2.8
YET DO I LOVE, ADORE, AND PRAYSE THE SAME         1.14.7
HER PRAISE FROM MY COMPLAINT I MAY NOT PART       1.26.10
ILE PRAISE HER FACE, AND BLAME HER FLINTY HEART   1.26.12
MY $MUSE SHOULD SOUND THY PRAISE WITH
                    MOURNFULL WARBLE            1.44.6
PITTY AND SMILES MUST ONELY YEELD THEE PRAISE     1.51.12
LET WHAT I PRAISE, BE STILL MADE GOOD BY YOU      2.4.13
UPON THE $ALMES OF THY SUPERFLUOUS PRAYSE         2.6.8
THESE NOW THE OTHERS $HAPPINESSE DOE PRAYSE       2.33.7
WRITING HER PRAYSE, I CANNOT WRITE AMISSE         2.42.14
WHERE, THE FULL $PRAYSE I FREELY MUST CONFESSE    2.47.7
MY $ZEALE, MY $HOPE, MY $VOWES, MY $PRAYSE,
                    MY $PRAY'R                  2.54.11
BY CHASTE $DESIRE, TRUE $LOVE, AND VERTUOUS
                    $PRAYSE                     2.54.14
SO MUST YOUR PRAYSE DISTRACTEDLY BE TOLD          2.57.12
MY ZEALE, MY HOPE, MY VOWES, MY PRAISE,
                    MY PRAYER                   2.101.11
BY CHAST DESIRE, TRUE LOVE, AND VERTUES PRAISE    2.101.14
PRAISE HIM WHICH MADE THAT FIRE, WHICH
                    LENDS THAT LIGHT            2.105.14
WHO WRITES MY $MISTRES PRAISE, CAN NEVER
                    WRITE AMISSE                2.128.14
AND WHILST MY HART AND EYE, ENVY EACH
                    OTHERS PRAISE               2.133.11
AND PRAISE HER STILL TO THY UNTIMELY GRAVE        2.139.8
WHAT MORTALL PEN SUFFYCIENTLY CAN PRAYSE THEE+    2.146.2
WHO LIST TO PRAISE THE DAYES DELICIOUS LYGHT      2.148.1
WERE AN ALL-EATING SHAME, AND THRIFTLESSE PRAISE  3.2.8
HOW MUCH MORE PRAISE DESERV'D THY BEAUTIES USE    3.2.9
I WILL NOT PRAYSE THAT PURPOSE NOT TO SELL        3.21.14
THE PAINE BE MINE, BUT THINE SHAL BE THE PRAISE   3.38.14
WHAT CAN MINE OWNE PRAISE TO MINE OWNE
                    SELFE BRING                 3.39.3
AND WHAT IS'T BUT MINE OWNE WHEN I PRAISE THEE    3.39.4
SHALL YOU PACE FORTH, YOUR PRAISE SHALL
                    STIL FINDE ROOME            3.55.10
TO SUBJECTS WORSE HAVE GIVEN ADMIRING PRAISE      3.59.14
T'IS THEE (MY SELFE) THAT FOR MY SELFE I PRAISE   3.62.13
THEIR OUTWARD THUS WITH OUTWARD PRAISE IS CROWND  3.69.5
IN OTHER ACCENTS DOE THIS PRAISE CONFOUND         3.69.7
```

```
YET THIS THY PRAISE CANNCT BE SOE THY PRAISE        3.70.11
YET THIS THY PRAISE CANNOT BE SOE THY PRAISE        3.70.11
AND HANG MORE PRAISE UPCN DECEASED I                3.72.7
NO PRAISE TO THEE, BUT WHAT IN THEE DOTH LIVE       3.79.12
AND IN THE PRAISE THERECF SPENDS ALL HIS MIGHT      3.80.3
FINDING THY WORTH A LIMMIT PAST MY PRAISE           3.82.6
THEN BOTH YOUR $PCETS CAN IN PRAISE DEVISE          3.83.14
THEN THIS RICH PRAISE, THAT YOU ALONE, ARE YCU      3.84.2
BEING FOND ON PRAISE, WHICH MAKES YOUR
                          PRAISES WORSE             3.84.14
WHILE COMMENTS OF YCUR PRAISE RICHLY COMPIL'C       3.85.2
AND TO THE MOST OF PRAISE ADDE SOME-THING MORE      3.85.10
CANNOT DISPRAISE, BUT IN A KINDE OF PRAISE          3.95.7
NOR PRAISE THE DEEPE VERMILLION IN THE $ROSE        3.98.10
BECAUSE HE NEEDS NC PRAISE, WILT THOU BE DUMB+      3.101.9
THEN WHEN IT HATH MY ADDED PRAISE BESIDE            3.103.4
IN PRAISE OF $LADIES DEAD, AND LOVELY $KNIGHTS      3.106.4
HAVE EYES TO WONDER, BUT LACK TOUNGS TO PRAISE      3.106.14
I CALL IT PRAISE TC SUFFER $TYRANNIE                4.2.11
NOT THOU BY PRAISE, BUT PRAISE IN THEE IS RAISDE    4.35.13
NOT THOU BY PRAISE, BUT PRAISE IN THEE IS RAISDE    4.35.13
IT IS A PRAISE TO PRAISE, WHEN THOU ART PRAISDE     4.35.14
IT IS A PRAISE TO PRAISE, WHEN THOU ART PRAISDE     4.35.14
ABASE HER PRAISE, SAYING SHE DOTH EXCELL            4.37.8
HIS PRAISE TO SLEIGHT, WHICH FROM GOOD
                          USE DOTH RISE             4.41.7
YOUTH, LUCKE, AND PRAISE, EVEN FILD MY
                          VEINES WITH PRIDE         4.53.4
EDWARD NAMED FOURTH, AS FIRST IN PRAISE I NAME      4.75.2
CEASE WE TO PRAISE, NOW PRAY WE FOR A KISSE         4.79.14
NATURE'S PRAISE, $VERTUE'S STALL, $CUPID'S
                          COLD FIRE                 4.80.3
WITHOUT HOW FARRE THIS PRAISE IS SHORT OF YOU       4.80.13
SHE BUILDS HER FAME ON HIGHER SEATED PRAISE         4.81.10
IF THOU PRAISE NOT, ALL CTHER PRAISE IS SHAME       4.90.4
IF THOU PRAISE NOT, ALL CTHER PRAISE IS SHAME       4.90.4
A NEST FOR MY YONG PRAISE IN $LAWRELL TREE          4.90.6
THAT ELOQUENCE IT SELFE ENVIES YOUR PRAISE          4.100.10
SUCH PRIDE IS PRAISE, SUCH PORTLINESSE IS HONOR     5.5.9
THEIR ANTHEMES SWEET DEVIZED OF LOVES PRAYSE        5.19.6
AND FILL THE WORLD WITH HER VICTORIOUS PRAYSE       5.29.14
TO SPILL WERE PITTY, BUT TO SAVE WERE PRAYSE        5.38.12
AND TELL HER PRAYSE TO ALL POSTERITY                5.69.11
TO SPEAKE HER PRAYSE AND GLORY EXCELLENT            5.74.11
TO SPORT MY MUSE AND SING MY LOVES SWEET PRAISE     5.80.10
WHEN I DOE PRAISE HER, SAY I DOE BUT FLATTER        5.85.2
PRAISED                   9
AND STATELY $SEVERNE FOR HER $SHOARE IS PRAYSED     2.32.2
AND STATELY $SEVERNE, FCR HER SHORES IS PRAISED     2.124.2
HEARING YOU PRAISD, I SAY 'TIS SO, 'TIS TRUE        3.85.9
AND TO BE PRAISD CF AGES YET TO BE                  3.101.12
IT IS A PRAISE TO PRAISE, WHEN THOJ ART PRAISDE     4.35.14
WITNESSE THE WORLD HOW WCRTHY TO BE PRAYZED         5.3.2
CHOSE RATHER TO BE PRAYSD FOR DOOING GOOD           5.38.13
OF ALL ALIVE MOST WCRTHY TO BE PRAYSED              5.74.12
AND VERTUOUS MIND, IS MUCH MORE PRAYSD OF ME        5.79.4
PRAISES                   11
AND DOE NOT STICKE TO TERME MY $PRAYSES FOLLY       2.28.2
BEING FOND ON PRAISE, WHICH MAKES YOUR
                          PRAISES WORSE             3.84.14
```

```
    SINCE ALL ALIKE MY SONGS AND PRAISES BE          3.105.3
    SO ALL THEIR PRAISES ARE BUT PROPHESIES          3.106.9
    TO KNOW MY SHAMES AND PRAISES FROM YOUR TOUNGE   3.112.6
    SO WHEN MY TOUNG WOULD SPEAK HER PRAISES DEW        5.3.9
    THAT MOTE ENLARGE HER LIVING PRAYSES DEAD          5.33.4
    TO SING YOUR NAME AND PRAYSES OVER ALL            5.73.12
    BUT LET HER PRAYSES YET BE LOW AND MEANE          5.80.13
    IN SETTING YOUR IMMORTALL PRAYSES FORTH           5.82.12
    AND MY GLAD MOUTH WITH HER SWEET PRAYSES FILL     5.85.12
PRAISETH                        1
    HOARCE SOUNDS THE VOYCE THAT PRAYSETH
                          NOT HER NAME               1.57.10
PRAISING                        4
    PRAISING VERTUES IN THEM THAT HAVE THEM NOT        1.58.7
    PRAYSING THE FAYREST, COMPARE IT TO MY FAIRE     2.148.11
    BY PRAISING HIM HERE WHO DOTH HENCE REMAINE       3.39.14
    PRAISING THY WORTH, DISPIGHT HIS CRUELL HAND      3.60.14
PRANCING                        1
    IN $MARSE'S LIVERIE, PRAUNCING IN THE PRESSE       4.53.6
PRAY                            8
    I PRAY IN VAINE, A MERCILESSE TO MOVE             1.11.7
    YET WILL I WEEPE, VOW, PRAY TO CRUELL SHEE       1.11.13
    O, JUDGE NOT RASHLY (GENTLE $SIR) I PRAY          2.24.4
    SO WILL I PRAY THAT THOU MAIST HAVE THY $WILL    3.143.13
    PARDON MINE EARES, BOTH I AND THEY DO PRAY        4.51.1
    PRAY THAT MY SUNNE GO DOWNE WITH MEEKER
                          BEAMES TO BED              4.76.14
    CEASE WE TO PRAISE, NOW PRAY WE FOR A KISSE      4.79.14
    THIS HOLY SEASON FIT TO FAST AND PRAY             5.22.1
PRAYER                          4
    WHOSE $BREST IS PROOFE AGAINST $COMPLAINT
                          OR $PRAYER+                2.52.10
    MY $ZEALE, MY $HOPE, MY $VOWES, MY $PRAYSE,
                          MY $PRAY'R                 2.54.11
    MY ZEALE, MY HOPE, MY VOWES, MY PRAISE,
                          MY PRAYER                 2.101.11
    BUT MINE NO PRICE NOR PRAYER MAY SURCEASE        5.11.14
PRAYERS                        12
    TEARES, VOWES, AND PRAYERS, WINNE THE
                          HARDEST HART               1.11.1
    TEARES, VOWES, AND PRAYERS, HAVE I SPENT IN VAINE 1.11.2
    PRAYERS PREVAILE NOT WITH A QUAINT DISDAINE       1.11.4
    THOUGH ALL MY PRAYERS BE TO SO DEAFE EARES       1.11.11
    SO MANY VOWES, AND PRAIERS HAVING SPENT           1.16.7
    WITH ONE THRICE-MARRY'D'S $PRAY'RS, THAT
                          DID BEQUEATH              2.15.11
    AND IF BY $THEE MY $PRAYERS MAY BE ENROL'D        2.55.7
    AND IF BY THEE MY PRAYERS MAY BE ENROLD          2.102.7
    IF SIGHES, NOR TEARES, NOR VOWES, NOR
                          PRAYERS CAN MOVE           2.139.2
    NOTHING SWEET BOY, BUT YET LIKE PRAYERS DIVINE   3.108.5
    PLAYNTS, PRAYERS, VOWES, RUTH, SORROW,
                          AND DISMAY                5.14.11
    NE ALL THE PLAYNTS AND PRAYERS WITH WHICH I       5.32.7
PREACH                          1
    AND BY EXAMPLE, TRUE REPENTANCE PREACH          2.119.14
PREACHEST                       1
    IN SECRET SILENCE, WHICH SUCH WONDERS PREACHEST 2.146.12
```

```
PREASE                        1
  WITH SHIELD OF PROOFE SHIELD ME FROM OUT
                        THE PREASE              4.39.5
PRECEPT                       1
  BUT SHE HIS PRECEPT PROUDLY DISOBAYES        5.19.11
PRECEPTS                      2
  AND THINKE I SHOULD NOT YOUR LARGE PRECEPTS
                        MISSE+                  4.56.4
  AS MY YOUNG $DOVE MAY IN YOUR PRECEPTS WISE  4.63.3
PRECIOUS                     12
  BUT PRECIOUS $TEARES DISTILLING FROM MINE $EYNE  2.7.6
  THE PRECIOUS $SPICES BE YOUR CHASTE $DESIRE  2.16.6
  THE PRECIOUS $ODORS BE MY CHASTE $DESIRE     2.30.11
  FOR PRECIOUS FRIENDS HID IN DEATHS DATELES NIGHT  3.30.6
  I HAVE NO PRECIOUS TIME AT AL TO SPEND       3.57.3
  THY DYALL HOW THY PRETIOUS MYNUITS WASTE     3.77.2
  AND PRECIOUS PHRASE BY ALL THE $MUSES FIL'D  3.85.4
  BOUND FOR THE PRIZE OF (ALL TO PRECIOUS) YOU 3.86.2
  THOU ART THE FAIREST AND MOST PRECIOUS $JEWELL  3.131.4
  DO SEEKE MOST PRETICUS THINGS TO MAKE YOUR GAIN  5.15.2
  AND ALL THOSE PRETICUS ORNAMENTS DEFACE      5.31.4
  WITH PRETIOUS MERCHANDIZE SHE FORTH DOTH LAY 5.81.6
PREDICT                       1
  BY OFT PREDICT THAT I IN HEAVEN FINDE        3.14.8
PREDOMINANT                   1
  AND TELL THE $GODS, $MARS IS PREDOMINANT     2.151.11
PREFER                        1
  TO SOME BASE $RUSTICK DOE THY SELFE PREFERRE 2.48.6
PREFIGURING                   1
  OF THIS OUR TIME, ALL YOU PREFIGURING        3.106.10
PREFIXED                      1
  WHEN MY ABODES PREFIXED TIME IS SPENT        5.46.1
PRENTICE                      1
  SONETS BE NOT BOUND PRENTISE TO ANNOY        4.70.5
PREPARE                       5
  AND THERE PREPARE HER FLOWRES THAT NEVER FADES  1.30.7
  AGAINST THIS CUMMING END YOU SHOULD PREPARE  3.13.3
  AND TO HIS PALLAT DOTH PREPARE THE CUP       3.114.12
  BEFORE SHE COULD PREPARE TO BE UNKIND        4.57.6
  PREPARE YOUR SELFE NEW LOVE TO ENTERTAINE    5.4.14
PREPARED                      4
  THEN ON A PLACE PREPARED FOR HER THERE       2.115.15
  PREPAR'D BY $NATURE'S CHIEFEST FURNITURE     4.9.2
  YET EACH PREPAR'D, WITH FANNE'S WEL-SHADING GRACE  4.22.7
  DEW TO THY SELFE THAT IT FOR ME PREPARD      5.86.14
PREPOSTEROUSLY                1
  THAT IT COULD SO PREPOSTEROUSLIE BE STAIN'D  3.109.11
PRESAGE                       1
  AND THE SAD $AUGURS MOCK THEIR OWNE PRESAGE  3.107.6
PRESAGED                      1
  (FEARING THE STARS PRESAGED INFLUENCE)       2.116.11
PRESAGERS                     1
  AND DOMB PRESAGERS OF MY SPEAKING BREST      3.23.10
PRESCRIPTIONS                 1
  ANGRY THAT HIS PRESCRIPTIONS ARE NOT KEPT    3.147.6
PRESENCE                     13
  TO ATTEND THE PRESENCE OF MY WORLDS $DEERE   1.30.6
  BE AS THY PRESENCE IS GRACIOUS AND KIND      3.10.11
  AND WITH HIS PRESENCE GRACE IMPIETIE         3.67.2
```

```
     WHOSE PRESENCE, ABSENCE, ABSENCE PRESENCE IS        4.60.13
     THAT PRESENCE, WHICH DOTH GIVE DARKE HEARTS
                              A LIVING LIGHT             4.77.3
     O ABSENT PRESENCE $STELLA IS NOT HERE               4.106.1
     AND AS A $QUEENE, WHO FROM HER PRESENCE SENDS        4.107.9
     BUT IF IN PRESENCE CF THAT FAYREST PROUD             5.2.9
     FROM PRESENCE OF MY DEAREST DEARE EXYLDE             5.52.7
     THAT OF HER PRESENS I MY MEED MAY TAKE               5.52.14
     I SEEKE HER BOWRE WITH HER LATE PRESENCE DECKT       5.78.6
     SINCE I DID LEAVE THE PRESENCE OF MY LOVE            5.87.1
PRESENT                   12
     PRESENT THE $IMAGE CF THE CARES I PROVE              1.2.3
     WISH TO BE PRESENT, AND YET SHUN T'APPEARE           1.20.4
     AND WAILE THE STATE WHEREIN I PRESENT STAND          1.28.10
     THEN TAKE THIS PICTURE WHICH I HERE PRESENT THEE     1.42.5
     THOUGH EITHER DISTANT, PRESENT YET TO EITHER         2.11.6
     THESE PRESENT ABSENT WITH SWIFT MOTION SLIDE         3.45.4
     THY SEIFE AWAY, ARE PRESENT STILL WITH ME            3.47.10
     FOR WE WHICH NOW BEHOLD THESE PRESENT DAYES          3.106.13
     CROWNING THE PRESENT, DCUBTING OF THE REST           3.115.12
     NOT WONDRING AT THE PRESENT, NOR THE PAST            3.123.10
     REVENGE UPON MY SELFE WITH PRESENT MONE+             3.149.8
     THAT TO WIN ME, OFT SHEWES A PRESENT PAY+            4.88.4
PRESENTEST                1
     AND THOU PRESENT'ST A PURE UNSTAYINED PRIME          3.70.8
PRESENTETH                1
     THAT THIS HUGE STAGE PRESENTETH NOUGHT BUT SHOWES    3.15.3
PRESENTS                  3
     WHICH, THEN PRESENTS HER WINTER-WITHERED HEW         1.38.10
     WHEN EVERY PLACE PRESENTS LIKE FACE OF WOE           1.52.3
     PRESENTS THEIR SHADDOE TO MY SIGHTLES VIEW           3.27.10
PRESERVATIVE              1
     HARTS $METHRIDATE, THE SOULES PRESERVATIVE           2.146.6
PRESERVE                  3
     PRESERVE MY $TEARES, AND THOU THY $SELFE
                              SHALT PROVE                 2.55.3
     PRESERVE MY TEARES, AND THOU THY SELFE
                              SHALT PROVE                 2.102.3
     FEEDING ON THAT WHICH DCTH PRESERVE THE ILL          3.147.3
PRESS                     4
     PRESSE TO HER EYES, IMPCRTUNE ME SOME GOOD           1.2.11
     WITH THOSE THE THRCNGED $THEATERS THAT PRESSE        2.47.5
     BE WISE AS THOU ART CRUELL, DO NOT PRESSE            3.140.1
     IN $MARSE'S LIVERIE, PRAUNCING IN THE PRESSE         4.53.6
PRESSED                   1
     ALL FOLKES PREST AT THY WILL THY PAINE
                              TO 'SWAGE                   4.101.11
PRESUME                   1
     PRESUME NOT ON THY HEART WHEN MINE IS SLAINE         3.22.13
PRESUMED                  1
     MY SLENDER MEANES PRESUM'D TOO HIGH A PART           1.36.3
PRESUMING                 2
     BUT THESE WEAKE WHINGS PRESUMING TO ASPIRE           1.32.6
     OR BLAME TH'ATTEMPT PRESUMING SO TO SORE             1.35.2
PRETENCE                  1
     BY NO PRETENCE CLAIME ANY MANER PLACE                4.52.11
PRETENDS                  1
     WHILE EACH PRETENDS THAT $STELLA MJST BE HIS         4.52.2
PRETTY                    6
     YOU CANNOT LOVE, MY PRETTIE $HEART, AND WHY+         2.19.1
```

```
THOSE PRETTY WRONGS THAT LIBERTY COMMITS          3.41.1
LOOKING WITH PRETTY RUTH UPON MY PAINE            3.132.4
HER PRETTIE LOOKES HAVE BEENE MINE ENEMIES        3.139.10
A PRETY CASE- I HOPED HER TO BRING                4.57.12
THE PRETTIE DEATH, WHILE EACH IN OTHER LIVE       4.79.11
PREVAIL             4
PRAYERS PREVAILE NOT WITH A QUAINT DISDAINE       1.11.4
DOUBTING, IF THAT PROUD $TYRANT SHOULD PREVAYLE   2.29.3
SURE THEY PREVAILE AS MUCH WITH ME, AS HE         4.106.12
SO STRANGELY (ALAS) THY WORKS IN ME PREVAILE      4.108.12
PREVAILED           1
WILL SOURELY LEAVE HER TILL HE HAVE PREVAILED     3.41.8
PREVENT             1
AS TO PREVENT OUR MALLADIES UNSEENE               3.118.3
PREVENTEST          1
SO THOU PREVENST HIS SIETH, AND CROOKED KNIFE     3.100.14
PREY               11
ART LEFT THE PREY OF EVERY VULGAR THEEFE          3.48.8
THE PRAY OF WORMES, MY BODY BEING DEAD            3.74.10
TILL BLOUDIE BULLET GET HIM WRONGFULL PRAY        4.20.4
COULD HOPE BY $CUPID'S HELPE ON YOU TO PRAY       4.43.2
FROM BASE DESIRE ON EARTHLY CATES TO PRAY+        4.88.8
THAT YE WERE BLOODED IN A YEELDED PRAY            5.20.14
AND FEEDS AT PLEASURE ON THE WRETCHED PRAY        5.47.8
TO LET THEM GAZE WHYLEST HE ON THEM MAY PRAY      5.53.4
WITH PANTING HOUNDS BEGUILED OF THEIR PRAY        5.67.4
BUT CAME THE TYDE, AND MADE MY PAYNES HIS PRAY    5.75.4
ON THE SWEET SPOYLE OF BEAUTIE THEY DID PRAY      5.76.8
PREYED              1
DEVOURING TYME AND CHANGEFUL CHANCE HAVE PRAYD    5.58.7
PRICE               5
YET AT THIS PRICE RETURNES ME TREBLE GAINE        2.28.8
THOSE LIPS, WHICH MAKE DEATH'S PAY A MEANE
                            PRICE FOR A KISSE      4.77.6
BUT MINE NO PRICE NOR PRAYER MAY SURCEASE         5.11.14
OF MY LOVES CONQUEST, PEERELESSE BEAUTIES PRISE   5.69.7
TWOO GOLDEN APPLES OF UNVALEWD PRICE              5.77.6
PRICKED             1
BUT SINCE SHE PRICKT THEE OUT FOR WOMENS
                            PLEASURE              3.20.13
PRICKETH            1
SWEET IS THE $EGLANTINE, BUT PRICKETH NERE        5.26.3
PRICKING            1
WITH PRICKING SHOT HE DID NOT THROUGHLY MOVE      4.17.3
PRIDE              44
HER SMILES ARE LIGHTNING, THOUGH HER PRIDE
                            DESPAIRE              1.6.3
AND ALL IN VAINE, HER PRIDE IS SO INNATED         1.18.11
YEELD THY HANDS PRIDE UNTO TH'$IVORY WHITE        1.19.5
HER PRIDE BROOK'D NOT POORE SOULES SHOULD
                            SO ASPIRE             1.36.8
THEN FADE THOSE FLOWERS THAT DECKT HER
                            PRIDE SO LONG         1.38.8
LOOKING ALOFT FROM TURRET OF HER PRIDE            1.47.6
IN $PRIDE OF $WIT, WHEN HIGH DESIRE OF $FAME      2.47.1
WHO IN HER PRIDE SDAYNES ONCE TO LOOKE ON MEE     2.123.12
AND IN THEM-SELVES THEIR PRIDE LIES BURIED        3.25.7
BY NEW UNFOULDING HIS IMPRISON'D PRIDE            3.52.12
WHY IS MY VERSE SO BARREN OF NEW PRIDE+           3.76.1
```

HE OF TALL BUILDING, AND OF GOODLY PRIDE	3.80.12
AND HAVING THEE, OF ALL MENS PRIDE I BOAST	3.91.12
IF NOT FROM MY LOVES BREATH, THE PURPLE PRIDE	3.99.3
BUT FOR HIS THEFT IN PRIDE OF ALL HIS GROWTH	3.99.12
THAT HAVING SUCH A SKOPE TO SHOW HER PRICE	3.103.2
HAVE FROM THE FORRESTS SHOOKE THREE SUMMERS PRIDE	3.104.4
WOOING HIS PURITY WITH HER FOWLE PRIDE	3.144.8
AS HIS TRIUMPHANT PRIZE, PROUD OF THIS PRIDE	3.151.10
BUT SHINING FORTH OF HEATE IN HIS CHIEFE PRIDE	4.22.4
THAT POISON FOULE OF BUBLING PRIDE DOTH LIE	4.27.6
YET PRIDE I THINKE DOTH NOT MY SOULE POSSESSE	4.27.9
YOUTH, LUCKE, AND PRAISE, EVEN FILD MY VEINES WITH PRIDE	4.53.4
SWEET SWELLING LIP, WELL MAIST THOU SWELL IN PRIDE	4.80.1
THINE EYES MY PRIDE, THY LIPS MY HISTORY	4.90.3
IN FINDING FAULT WITH HER TOO PORTLY PRIDE	5.5.2
SUCH PRIDE IS PRAISE, SUCH PORTLINESSE IS HONOR	5.5.9
WITHOUT SOME SPARK OF SUCH SELF-PLEASING PRICE	5.5.14
DOTH STILL PERSIST IN HER REBELLIOUS PRIDE	5.6.2
ALL THIS WORLDS PRIDE BOW TO A BASER MAKE	5.10.11
THE LOVELY PLEASANCE AND THE LOFTY PRIDE	5.17.11
IN HIS MOST PRIDE DISDEIGNETH TO DEVOURE	5.20.7
THAT PRIDE AND MEEKNESSE MIXT BY EQUALL PART	5.21.3
FOR WITH MILD PLEASANCE, WHICH DOTH PRIDE DISPLACE	5.21.5
AND SHEW THE LAST ENSAMPLE OF YOUR PRIDE	5.25.6
WHOSE PRYDE DEPRAVES EACH OTHER BETTER PART	5.31.3
THE MORE SHE FRIESETH IN HER WILFULL PRYDE	5.32.10
BUT IN HER PRIDE SHE DOOTH PERSEVER STILL	5.38.9
THRUGH STUBBORN PRIDE AMONGST THEMSELVES DID JAR	5.44.2
WHOME BEING CAUGHT SHE KILLS WITH CRUELL PRYDE	5.47.7
HER GLORIES PRIDE THAT NONE MAY IT REPAYRE	5.58.8
T'ACCUSE OF PRIDE, OR RASHLY BLAME FOR OUGHT	5.61.4
THERE PRIDE DARE NOT APPROCH, NOR DISCORD SPILL	5.65.9
FAYRE WHEN THAT CLOUD OF PRYDE, WHICH OFT DOTH DARK	5.81.7

PRIEFE   1
VAYNE MAN (QUOD I) THAT HAST BUT LITTLE PRIEFE	5.50.5

PRIESTS   2
THOSE $PRIESTS WHICH FIRST THE $VESTALL $FIRE BEGUN	2.30.1
LYKE SACRED PRIESTS THAT NEVER THINKE AMISSE	5.22.8

PRIME   6
NOW WAS THY PRYME, AND LOE, NOW IS THY WAINE	2.141.13
CALLS BACKE THE LOVELY $APRILL OF HER PRIME	3.3.10
WHEN I BEHOLD THE VIOLET PAST PRIME	3.12.3
AND THOU PRESENT'ST A PURE UNSTAYINED PRIME	3.70.8
BEARING THE WANTON BURTHEN OF THE PRIME	3.97.7
MAKE HAST THEREFORE SWEET LOVE, WHILEST IT IS PRIME	5.70.13

PRINCE   2
OTHERS, BECAUSE THE $PRINCE MY SERVICE TRIES	4.23.7
THE GREATEST $PRINCE WITH POMPOUS ROIALTY+	5.77.4

PRINCES   2
OR SAY WITH $PRINCES IF IT SHAL GO WEL	3.14.7
OF $PRINCES SHALL OUT-LIVE THIS POWREFULL RIME	3.55.2

PRINCES'   1
GREAT $PRINCES FAVORITES THEIR FAIRE LEAVES SPREAD	3.25.5

```
PRINCESS                      3
  PRINCESSE OF $BEAUTIE, FOR WHOSE ONLY SAKE        4.28.6
  STELLA SINCE THOU SC RIGHT A $PRINCESSE ART       4.107.1
  THEN HAD YE SORTED WITH A PRINCES PERE            5.66.10
PRINT                         1
  THOU SHOULDST PRINT MORE, NOT LET THAT COPPY DIE  3.11.14
PRINTS                        1
  PRINTS HIS OWNE LIVELY FORME IN RUDEST BRAINE     4.58.8
PRISON                        7
  MY HART SHALL BE THE PRISON FOR MY FAYRE          2.115.5
  THE GRAVE OF JOY, PRYSON OF DAYES DELIGHT         2.145.10
  PRISON MY HEART IN THY STEELE BOSOMES WARDE       3.133.9
  THEY DID THEMSELVES (O SWEETEST PRISON) TWINE     4.103.8
  SO SWEET YOUR PRISCN YOU IN TIME SHALL PROVE      5.71.11
  BREAKING HIS PRISCN FORTH TO YOU DOTH FLY         5.73.4
  OUT OF MY PRISON I WILL BREAKE ANEW               5.80.6
PRISONER                      3
  A LIQUID PRISONER PENT IN WALLS OF GLASSE         3.5.10
  IS PRISONER LED AWAY WITH HEAVY HART              5.52.3
  SO DOE I NOW MY SELFE A PRISONER YEELD            5.52.5
PRISONERS                     1
  WHOSE $SENSES, LIKE POORE $PRIS'NERS,
                    HUNGER-STARV'D                  2.49.7
PRISONER'S                    1
  THE POORE MAN'S WEALTH, THE PRISONER'S RELEASE    4.39.3
PRIVATE                       2
  O $GOD FROM $YOU, THAT I COULD PRIVATE BE         2.11.2
  WHEN EVERY PRIVAT WIDDOW WELL MAY KEEPE           3.9.7
PRIVILEGE                     4
  NO PRIVILEDGE OF FAITH COULD IT PROTECT           1.31.5
  THAT YOU YOUR SELFE MAY PRIVILEDGE YOUR TIME      3.58.10
  TAKE HEED (DEARE HEART) OF THIS LARGE PRIVILEDGE  3.95.13
  BY SENCE'S PRIVILEDGE, CAN SCAPE FROM THEE        4.36.14
PRIZE                         7
  LET HER NOT STILL TRIUMPH OVER THE PRIZE          1.22.13
  WHOSE WORTHY PRIZE SHOULD HAVE ENRITCHT
                    THY TREASURE                    2.134.14
  FOR TRUTH PROOVES THEEVISH FOR A PRIZE SC DEARE   3.48.14
  BOUND FOR THE PRIZE OF (ALL TO PRECIOUS) YOU      3.86.2
  AS HIS TRIUMPHANT PRIZE, PROUD OF THIS PRIDE      3.151.10
  GUIDED SO WELL, THAT I OBTAIN'D THE PRIZE         4.41.2
  AS I MAY WELL RECCUNT, BUT NONE CAN PRIZE         4.65.4
PRIZED                        1
  WHICH MEANER PRIZ'D AND MOMENTARY BEE             1.58.4
PRIZING                       1
  NOT PRIZING HER POORE INFANTS DISCONTENT          3.143.8
PROBLEMS                      2
  ENNOBLING NEW FOUND $TROPES WITH PROBLEMES OLD    4.3.6
  PHRASES AND $PROBLEMES FROM MY REACH DO GROW      4.3.10
PROCEED                       8
  THAT EV'RY THING WHENCE $SHADOW DOTH PROCEED      2.13.13
  THAT EVERY THING WHENCE SHADOW DOTH PROCEEDE      2.121.13
  SHEWING THEIR BIRTH, AND WHERE THEY DID PROCEED+  3.76.8
  BUT KNOWNE WORTH DID IN MINE OF TIME PROCEED      4.2.3
  THOU DOEST PROCEED IN THY MOST SERIOUS WAYES      4.11.2
  OPPRESSING MORTALL SENSE, MY DEATH PROCEED        4.42.13
  SO MAY YOUR TONGUE STILL FLUENTLY PROCEED         4.51.2
  AND PERFECT BEAUTY DID AT FIRST PROCEED           5.79.12
PROCEEDING                    1
  PROCEEDING FROM THE $PORT WHENCE HE PUT FORTH     2.1.5
```

PROCEEDS   2
  ONELY BY $VERTUE THAT PROCEEDS FROM THEE   2.35.14
  AND THENCE THIS SLAUNDER AS I THINKE PROCEEDS   3.131.14
PROCESS   2
  HAVE FOLLOWED HARD THE $PROCESSE OF MY CASE   1.8.10
  IN PROCESSE OF THE SEASONS HAVE I SEENE   3.104.6
PROCLAIMS   1
  AND PEACE PROCLAIMES $OLIVES OF ENDLESSE AGE   3.107.8
PROCURE   1
  AND KNOW GREAT CAUSES, GREAT EFFECTS PROCURE   4.26.10
PRODIGAL   2
  AND PRODIGALL OF HOWERS AND YEARES BETRAIES   1.23.11
  LOVE, IN A $HUMOR, PLAY'D THE $PRODIGALL   2.7.1
PROFANE   2
  SOME MISBELEEVING, AND PROPHANE IN $LOVE   2.35.1
  LEAST I (TOO MUCH PROPHANE) SHOULD DO IT WRONGE   3.89.11
PROFANED   2
  BUT IS PROPHAN'D, IF NOT LIVES IN DISGRACE   3.127.8
  THAT HAVE PROPHAN'D THEIR SCARLET ORNAMENTS   3.142.6
PROFESS   1
  PROFESSE IN DEED I DO NOT $CUPID'S ART   4.54.10
PROFIT   1
  SHALL PROFIT THEE, AND MUCH INRICH THY BOOKE   3.77.14
PROFITLESS   1
  PROFITLES USERER WHY DOOST THOU USE   3.4.7
PROFOUND   1
  IN SO PROFOUND $ABISME I THROW ALL CARE   3.112.9
PROGNOSTICATE   1
  OR ELSE OF THEE THIS I PROGNOSTICATE   3.14.13
PROGRESS   1
  TIMES THEEVISH PROGRESSE TO ETERNITIE   3.77.8
PROGRESSING   1
  PROGRESSING THEN FROM FAIRE TWINNES' GOLD'N PLACE 4.22.2
PROLONG   1
  STILL TO PROLONG MY LONG TYME LOOKT-FOR MORROW+   2.145.4
PROLONGS   2
  AND SO WITH LOOKES, PROLONGS MY LONG-LOOKT EASE   1.24.10
  FALSE $HOPE PROLONGS MY EVER CERTAINE GRIEFE   1.25.1
PROMETHEUS   2
  THAT FARRE BEYOND $PROMETHEUS DID ASPIRE   2.14.4
  YET OLD $PROMETHEUS PUNISH'D FOR HIS $RAPE   2.14.13
PROMISE   4
  WHY DIDST THOU PROMISE SUCH A BEAUTIOUS DAY   3.34.1
  FOR SINCE MAD $MARCH GREAT PROMISE MADE OF ME   4.21.9
  WHEN SOME FAIRE $LADIES, BY HARD PROMISE TIED   4.22.5
  DOTH SEEME TO PROMISE HOPE OF NEW DELIGHT   5.4.2
PROMISED   2
  A THOUSAND TIMES IT PROMIS'D ME RELIEFE   1.25.3
  POORE HOPE'S FIRST WEALTH, OSTAGE OF PROMIST
                              WEALE   4.79.12
PROMISING   1
  PROMISING WONDERS, WONDER TO INVITE   4.26.4
PRONE   1
  NOR TENDER FEELING TO BASE TOUCHES PRONE   3.141.6
PRONOUNCING   1
  OR ELSE PRONOUNCING GRACE, WHEREWITH HIS MIND   4.58.7
PROOF   10
  TH'EVIDENCE SO GREAT A PROOFE DOTH CARRIE   2.2.8
  WHOSE $BREST IS PROOFE AGAINST $COMPLAINT
                              OR $PRAYER+   2.52.10

```
ON NEWER PROOFE, TO TRIE AN OLDER FRIEND          3.110.11
AND ON JUST PROOFE SURMISE, ACCUMILATE            3.117.10
A BLISSE IN PROOFE AND PROUD AND VERY WO          3.129.11
FORC'D BY A TEDIOUS PROOFE, THAT $TURKISH
                          HARDNED HART              4.8.2
AND IF THESE RULES DID FAILE, PROOFE MAKES
                          ME SURE                  4.26.12
WITH SHIELD OF PROOFE SHIELD ME FROM OUT
                          THE PREASE                4.39.5
LOVE BY SURE PROOFE I MAY CALL THEE UNKIND          4.65.1
BUT FEELING PROOFE MAKES ME SAY THEY MISTAKE
                          IT FURRE                 4.102.11
PROP                        1
O LET ME PROP MY MIND, YET IN HIS GROWTH           4.19.12
PROPER                      2
AND CARVE HIS PROPER GRIEFE UPON A STONE            1.13.2
AND SO DID PERISH BY MY PROPER ART                 1.13.8
PROPHECIES                  1
SO ALL THEIR PRAISES ARE BUT PROPHESIES            3.106.9
PROPHESIED                  1
WHO PROPHECIED OF $CHRIST OR ERE HE CAME           2.119.3
PROPHET                     1
A $PROPHET OFT, AND OFT AN HISTORIE                4.32.3
PROPHETIC                   1
NOT MINE OWNE FEARES, NOR THE PROPHETICK SOULE     3.107.1
PROPHETS                    1
THIS EARTH OF THOSE SWEET $PROPHETS HATH BEREFT    2.119.6
PROPORTION                  1
WITH SAD EYES I THEIR WEAKE PROPORTION SEE         4.50.7
PROPOSED                    1
BEFORE A JOY PROPOSD BEHIND A DREAME               3.129.12
PROSERPINE'S                1
BY $HECAT'S $NAMES, BY $PROSERPINE'S SAD $TEARES   2.36.7
PROSPECT                    2
AND STAID PLEASD WITH THE PROSPECT OF THE PLACE    4.20.10
AND I, BUT FOR BECAUSE MY PROSPECT LIES            4.29.13
PROSPECTIVE                 1
THIS HEART MADE NOW THE PROSPECTIVE OF CARE        1.22.9
PROSTRATE                   2
UPON THE PROSTRATE SPOYLE OF THAT POORE HART       1.10.10
AS IS A STORME, THAT ALL THINGS DOTH PROSTRATE     5.56.6
PROTECT                     2
NO PRIVILEDGE OF FAITH COULD IT PROTECT            1.31.5
AND THESE THY SACRED VERTUES MUST PROTECT          1.55.11
PROTEST                     1
YET I PROTEST MY HIGH DESIRING WILL                1.36.9
PROTESTS                    2
FOR SHE PROTESTS TO BANISH THEE HER FACE           4.46.5
DELIGHT PROTESTS HE IS NOT FOR THE ACCURST         4.95.7
PROTRACT                    1
THEYR SAD PROTRACT FROM EVENING UNTILL MORNE       5.87.4
PROUD                      35
AT HER PROUD FEETE, AND SHE RESPECTS NOT IT        1.24.6
HAVE SEENE THOSE WALLS WHICH PROUD AMBITION
                          REAR'D                    1.45.2
DOUBTING, IF THAT PROUD $TYRANT SHOULD PREVAYLE    2.29.3
WHEN THE PROUD $ROUND ON EV'RY SIDE HATH RUNG      2.47.10
FROM THAT PROUD $BEAUTY, WHICH WAS MY BETRAYER+    2.52.12
THY YOUTHES PROUD LIVERY SO GAZ'D ON NOW           3.2.3
MAKING A COOPELMENT OF PROUD COMPARE               3.21.5
```

```
OF PUBLIKE HONOUR AND PROUD TITLES BOST          3.25.2
THE RICH PROUD COST OF CUTWORNE BURIED AGE       3.64.2
AND PROUD OF MANY, LIVES UPON HIS GAINES+        3.67.12
NOW PROUD AS AN INJOYER, AND ANON                3.75.5
YET BE MOST PROUD OF THAT WHICH I COMPILE        3.78.9
WAS IT THE PROUD FULL SAILE OF HIS GREAT VERSE   3.86.1
WHEN PROUD PIDE $APRILL (DREST IN ALL HIS TRIM)  3.98.2
OR FROM THEIR PROUD LAP PLUCK THEM WHERE
                                   THEY GREW     3.98.8
A BLISSE IN PROOFE AND PROUD AND VERY WO         3.129.11
BEARE THINE EYES STRAIGHT, THOUGH THY
                         PROUD HEART GOE WIDE     3.140.14
THY PROUD HEARTS SLAVE AND VASSALL WRETCH TO BE  3.141.12
THAT IS SO PROUDE THY SERVICE TO DISPISE         3.149.10
AS HIS TRIUMPHANT PRIZE, PROUD OF THIS PRIDE     3.151.10
ARE $BEAUTIES THERE AS PROUD AS HERE THEY BE+    4.31.11
BUT IF IN PRESENCE CF THAT FAYREST PROUD         5.2.9
BUT HER PROUD HART DOE THOU A LITTLE SHAKE       5.10.9
IN THAT PROUD PORT, WHICH HER SO GOODLY GRACETH  5.13.1
FAIRE PROUD NOW TELL ME WHY SHOULD FAIRE BE PROUD 5.27.1
FAIRE PROUD NOW TELL ME WHY SHOULD FAIRE BE PROUD 5.27.1
FAIRE BE NO LENGER PROUD OF THAT SHALL PERISH    5.27.13
OF THAT PROUD MAYD, WHOM NOW THOSE LEAVES ATTYRE 5.28.8
PROUD $DAPHNE SCORNING $PHAEBUS LOVELY FYRE      5.28.9
BUT MY PROUD ONE DCTH WORKE THE GREATER SCATH    5.31.9
OF A PROUD LOVE, THAT DCTH MY SPIRITE SPOYLE     5.33.12
AND EKE MY TOUNG WITH PROUD RESTRAINT TO TIE+    5.43.6
BUT IF IT BE YOUR PLEASURE AND PROUD WILL        5.49.5
FAYRE BE YE SURE, BUT PROUD AND PITTILESSE       5.56.5
WHY THEN DOE YE PROUD FAYRE, MISDEEME SO FARRE   5.58.13
PROUDER                2
NO OTHER PROUDER $BROOKES SHALL HEARE MY WRONG   1.58.14
RICHER THEN WEALTH, PROUDER THEN GARMENTS COST   3.91.10
PROUDEST               3
ABOUT THE $TEMPLE CF THE PROUDEST FRAME          1.12.2
THE HUMBLE AS THE PROUDEST SAILE DOTH BEARE      3.80.6
THOSE ENGINS CAN THE PROUDEST LOVE CONVERT       5.14.12
PROUDLY                3
PROUDLY THOU SCORN'ST MY $WORLD-OUT-WEARING
                              $RIMES             2.44.7
AS THOSE WHOSE BEAUTIES PROUDLY MAKE THEM CRUELL 3.131.2
BUT SHE HIS PRECEPT PROUDLY DISOBAYES            5.19.11
PROVE                  58
PRESENT THE $IMAGE CF THE CARES I PROVE          1.2.3
AND URG'D THAT TITLE WHICH DOTH PLAINELY PROVE   1.8.11
ONCE LET HER KNOW, SH'HATH DONE ENOUGH
                              TO PROVE ME        1.10.13
YET NEVER ANY TRUE EFFECT I PROVE                1.25.4
SINCE HE THAT BLESSED $PARADISE DID PROVE        2.4.7
YOUR $LOVE AND $HATE IS THIS, I NOW DOE
                         PROVE $YOU              2.19.13
READE BUT HIS $VERSE, AND IT WILL EAS'LY PROVE   2.24.3
THAT THIS TO ME DCTH YET NO WONDER PROVE         2.34.14
WHO ONELY WRITE, MY SKILL IN $VERSE TO PROVE     2.35.4
AND IN MY $SOULE THE PAINES OF $HELL I PROVE     2.41.3
THOUGH $HEAVEN AND $EARTH, PROVE BOTH
                              TO ME UNTRUE       2.51.13
PRESERVE MY $TEARES, AND THOU THY $SELFE
                              SHALT PROVE        2.55.3
UPON THE $NEST I SET IT FORTH, TO PROVE          2.56.3
```

```
TO PROVE THE $PYNICNS, IT ASCENDS THE $SKYES        2.56.10
AND SEE IF $TIME (IF HE WOULD STRIVE TO PROVE)      2.60.13
PRESERVE MY TEARES, AND THOU THY SELFE
                              SHALT PROVE            2.102.3
UPON THE NEST I SET THEM, FORTH TO PROVE            2.103.3
FOR I WAS APT A SCHOLLER LIKE TO PROVE              2.111.3
AND ONELY WRITE, MY SKILL IN VERSE TO PROVE         2.112.4
NOW $LOVE, IF THOU WILT PROVE A $CONQUEROR          2.115.1
SHOULD TEACH THE WORLD TO KNOW THE WONDER
                              THAT I PROVE           2.117.14
NO $GOD ART THOU, A $GODDESSE SHEE DOTH PROVE       2.126.3
I PROVE MY VERSE AUTENTIQUE STILL IN THYS           2.128.13
WITH TEARES, SIGHES, AND DISDAINE, THYS
                          CONTRARY I PROVE           2.132.4
DESIRING YET A THOUSAND DEATHS TO PROVE             2.134.7
SO IN LOVES DEATH SHALL LOVES PERFECTION PROVE      2.139.9
THY FATHER WAS A MAN, THAT WILL I PROVE             2.140.7
AND IN MY SOULE THE PAYNES OF HELL I PROVE          2.143.3
AND BY ALL MEANES, LET BLACK UNKINDNES PROVE        2.149.13
SINGS THIS TO THEE THOU SINGLE WILT PROVE NONE      3.8.14
OR TO THY SELFE AT LEAST KIND HARTED PROVE          3.10.12
TIL THEN, NOT SHOW MY HEAD WHERE THOU
                          MAIST PROVE ME             3.26.14
BUT SINCE HE DIED AND $POETS BETTER PROVE           3.32.13
OH ABSENCE WHAT A TORMENT WOULDST THOU PROVE        3.39.9
FOR YOU IN ME CAN NOTHING WORTHY PROVE              3.72.4
AND PROVE THEE VIRTUOUS, THOUGH THOU ART
                              FORSWORNE              3.88.4
SINCE MY APPEALE SAIES I DID STRIVE TO PROOVE       3.117.13
IN THINGS OF GREAT RECEIT WITH EASE WE PROOVE       3.136.7
LEAST GUILTY OF MY FAULTS THY SWEET SELFE PROVE     3.151.4
AND GREW A SEETHING BATH WHICH YET MEN PROVE        3.153.7
CAME THERE FOR CURE AND THIS BY THAT I PROVE        3.154.13
AND STILL TH'EFFECT OF THY PERSWASIONS PROVE        4.4.11
REASON THOU KNEEL'DST, AND OFFEREDST STRAIGHT
                              TO PROVE               4.10.13
WHO THREATNED STRIPES, IF HE HIS WRATH DID PROVE    4.17.6
VERTUE'S GREAT BEAUTIE IN THAT FACE I PROVE         4.25.13
O EYES, WHERE HUMBLE LOCKES MOST GLORIOUS PROVE     4.42.5
OUR HORSMANSHIPS, WHILE BY STRANGE WORKE I PROVE    4.49.2
SINCE THEY DO WEARE HIS BADGE, MOST FIRMELY PROVE   4.52.4
DUMBE $SWANNES, NOT CHATRING $PIES, DO
                          $LOVERS PROVE              4.54.13
NOR OTHER SUGRING CF MY SPEECH TO PROVE             4.55.10
HE BARKS, MY SONGS THINE OWNE VOYCE OFT
                          DOTH PROVE                 4.59.6
BUT ONLY FOR THIS WORTHY KNIGHT DURST PROVE         4.75.13
SHE COMES WITH LIGHT AND WARMTH, WHICH
                          LIKE $AURORA PROVE         4.76.5
UNITED POWERS MAKE EACH THE STRONGER PROVE          4.88.14
OR IF SUCH HEAVENLY SIGNES MUST PROVE ANNOY         4.100.13
FROM OUT MY RIBS, AND PUFFING PROVE THAT I          4.104.13
TO PROVE YOUR POWRE, WHICH I TOO WEL HAVE TRICE     5.25.8
SO SWEET YOUR PRISON YOU IN TIME SHALL PROVE        5.71.11
PROVED                   5
WELL, WELL, I FEARE IT WILL BE PROV'D BY YOU        2.2.7
OFT 'T'ATH BEEN PROV'D, THE BREATHLESSE
                      $COARSE WILL BLEED             2.46.8
WHICH PROOV'D MY BIRDS DELIGHTED IN THE AYRE        2.103.7
AND WORSE ESSAIES PROV'D THEE MY BEST OF LOVE       3.110.8
```

```
                                                                    IF THIS BE ERROR AND UPON ME PROVED              3.116.13
PROVERBS                    1
   WITH $PROVERBS THUS EACH OTHER INTERTAINE                        2.59.2
PROVES                      3
   THAT LEARNED $FATHER, WHICH SO FIRMELY PROVES                    2.12.1
   FOR TRUTH PROOVES THEEVISH FOR A PRIZE SO DEARE                  3.48.14
   WHICH PROVES MORE SHORT THEN WAST OR RUINING+                    3.125.4
PROVIDE                     1
   THAT DID NOT BETTER FOR MY LIFE PROVIDE                          3.111.3
PROVIDENCE                  1
   NOW, OR BY CHAUNCE, OR HEAVENS HIE PROVIDENCE                    2.116.9
PROVING                     1
   PROOVING HIS BEAUTIE BY SUCCESSION THINE                        3.2.12
PROVOKE                     3
   THEY $HEAVEN AND $EARTH TO PITTY SHALL PROVOKE                   2.55.8
   THEY HEAVEN AND EARTH TO PITTY SHALL PROVOKE                     2.102.8
   THE BLOODY SPURRE CANNOT PROVOKE HIM ON                         3.50.9
PROVOKED                    1
   THUS AM I STILL PROVOK'D, TO EVERY $EVILL                       2.20.13
PRY                         1
   SO FARRE FROM HOME INTO MY DEEDS TO PRYE                        3.61.6
PSYCHE'S                    1
   BY THINE OWNE LOVED $PSYCHES, BY THE $FIRES                      2.36.9
PUBLIC                      6
   NO PUBLIKE $GLORIE VAINELY I PURSUE                             2.47.13
   OF PUBLIKE HONOUR AND PROUD TITLES BOST                         3.25.2
   NOR THOU WITH PUBLIKE KINDNESSE HONOUR ME                        3.36.11
   THEN PUBLICK MEANES WHICH PUBLICK MANNERS BREEDS                 3.111.4
   THEN PUBLICK MEANES WHICH PUBLICK MANNERS BREEDS                 3.111.4
   BE YOU STILL FAIRE, HONOURD BY PUBLIKE HEED                      4.84.9
PUBLISH                     2
   THE OWNERS TONGUE DOTH PUBLISH EVERY WHERE                      3.102.4
   'ART NOT ASHAM'D TO PUBLISH THY DISEASE+'                        4.34.5
PUFFING                     2
   FIRST DID WITH PUFFING KISSE THOSE LOCKES
                                 DISPLAY                            4.103.11
   FROM OUT MY RIBS, AND PUFFING PROVE THAT I                      4.104.13
PULSE                       1
   WHEN HIS $PULSE FAYLING, $PASSION SPEECHLESSE
                                 LIES                               2.61.10
PUNISHED                    2
   YET OLD $PROMETHEUS PUNISH'D FOR HIS $RAPE                       2.14.13
   HOW FAIRE A DAY WAS NEARE, O PUNISHT EYES                        4.33.13
PUNISHMENT                  1
   THIS PUNISHMENT THE PITTILESSE MAY MOVE                          2.115.8
PUPIL                       1
   WHICH THIS ($TIMES PENSEL OR MY PUPILL PEN)                      3.16.10
PURBLIND                    1
   THOU PURBLIND $BOY, SINCE THOU HAST BEENE
                                 SO SLACKE                          2.36.1
PURCHASE                    3
   SHALL TO YOU PURCHAS WITH HER THANKLES PAINE                     5.27.12
   IS THERE NO MEANES FOR ME TO PURCHACE PEACE                      5.36.5
   THE HAPPY PURCHASE OF MY GLORIOUS SPOILE                         5.69.13
PURCHASED                   2
   IF HER DEFECTS HAVE PURCHAST HER THIS FAME                       1.17.9
   AND GIVEN TO TIME YOUR OWNE DEARE PURCHAS'D
                                 RIGHT                              3.117.6
PURE                        20
   AND THY $YOUTH PAST, IN THIS PURE $MIRROUR SEE                   2.17.6
```

```
WITH SO PURE $LOVE, AS $TIME COULD NEVER BOAST          2.54.8
AT WHOSE PURE $EYES, $LOVE LIGHTS HIS
                              HALLOW'D $FIRE             2.57.8
CAN SHEW A $SECOND TO SO PURE A $LOVE                   2.60.14
WITH SO PURE LOVE AS TYME COULD NEVER BOAST             2.101.8
THE $GODS PURE FIRE HATH BEEN EXTINGUISHT QUITE         2.105.2
THYS, PURE $IDEA, VERTUES RIGHT $IDEA                   2.119.9
IF $CHASTE AND PURE DEVOTION OF MY YOUTH                2.138.1
WHOSE PURE $IDEA NEVER TONGUE EXPREST                   2.139.13
AND THOU PRESENT'ST A PURE UNSTAYINED PRIME             3.70.8
EVEN TO THY PURE AND MOST MOST LOVING BREST             3.110.14
DECEIV'D THE QUAKING BOY, WHO THOUGHT
                              FROM SO PURE LIGHT         4.8.10
HATH HIS FRONT BUILT OF $ALABASTER PURE                 4.9.3
BUT KNOW THAT I IN PURE SIMPLICITIE                     4.28.12
AND OFT SO CLINGS TO MY PURE $LOVE, THAT I              4.72.2
IF $PEARLES, HIR TEETH BE PEARLES BOTH
                              PURE AND ROUND             5.15.9
BURNING IN FLAMES OF PURE AND CHAST DESYRE              5.22.12
AND EKE HER MIND IS PURE IMMORTALL HYE                  5.55.12
A GOODLY TABLE OF PURE YVORY                            5.77.2
BUT PURE AFFECTIONS BRED IN SPOTLESSE BREST             5.84.5
PURENESS                    2
UNBURIED IN THESE LINES RESERV'D IN PURENES             1.44.10
IN WHOM ALL PURENES WITH PERFECTION STROVE              2.141.3
PURER                       1
NOR TO THE $STARRES.. FOR THEY HAVE PURER SIGHT         5.9.7
PUREST                      10
MY SPOTLESSE LOVE HOVERS WITH PUREST WINGS              1.12.1
ILE FETTER HER IN CHAINES OF PUREST LOVE                2.115.6
LOVES $METHRIDATE, THE PUREST OF PERFECTION             2.123.5
OF PUREST GOLD, TEMPRED WITH VERTUES FIRE               2.126.7
SEE WHERE SHEE FLOTES, LADEN WITH PUREST LOVE           2.134.5
O PUREST MERROR, WHEREIN MEN MAY SEE                    2.146.13
AND PUREST FAITH UNHAPPILY FORSWORNE                    3.66.4
AND FOOLES CAN THINKE THOSE $LAMPES OF
                              PUREST LIGHT              4.26.2
IN MIND TO MOUNT UP TO THE PUREST SKY                   5.72.2
THROUGH CONTEMPLATION OF MY PUREST PART                 5.88.10
PURGATORY                   1
WITH THOUSAND $PLAGUES, MORE THEN IN $PURGATORIE        2.49.12
PURGE                       1
WE SICKEN TO SHUN SICKNESSE WHEN WE PURGE               3.118.4
PURGING                     1
THE OTHER TWO, SLIGHT AYRE, AND PURGING FIRE            3.45.1
PURITY                      1
WOOING HIS PURITY WITH HER FOWLE PRIDE                  3.144.8
PURLING                     1
YOU THAT DO SEARCH FOR EVERIE PURLING SPRING            4.15.1
PURLOIN                     1
FOR FEARE THAT SOME THEIR $TREASURES SHOULD
                              PURLOYNE                   2.58.3
PURPLE                      1
IF NOT FROM MY LOVES BREATH, THE PURPLE PRIDE           3.99.3
PURPOSE                     6
BY ADDING ONE THING TO MY PURPOSE NOTHING               3.20.12
I WILL NOT PRAYSE THAT PURPOSE NOT TO SELL              3.21.14
YOU ARE SO STRONGLY IN MY PURPOSE BRED                  3.112.13
SHE KEEPES THEE TO THIS PURPOSE, THAT HER SKILL         3.126.7
ON PURPOSE LAYD TO MAKE THE TAKER MAD                   3.129.8
```

```
  OF HARDEST $MARBLE ARE CF PURPOSE MADE+              5.51.2
PURPOSED              1
  TO LINGER OUT A PURPOSD CVER-THROW                   3.90.8
PURSUE                2
  MY THOUGHTS (LIKE $HOUNDES) PURSUE ME TO MY DEATH    1.5.12
  NO PUBLIKE $GLORIE VAINELY I PURSUE                  2.47.13
PURSUED               1
  WHILST BY THY EIES PURSU'D, MY POORE HEART FLEW      1.31.1
PURSUES               1
  AND STILL MY HOPE THE $SOMMER WINDES PURSUES         1.16.11
PURSUETH              1
  BUT GREEDILY HER FELL INTENT POURSEWTH               5.11.7
PURSUING              1
  POSSESSING OR PURSUING NO DELIGHT                    3.75.11
PURSUIT               3
  MADE $IN PURSUT AND IN PCSSESSION SO                 3.129.9
  IN PURSUIT OF THE THING SHE WOULD HAVE STAY          3.143.4
  SO AFTER LONG PURSUIT AND VAINE ASSAY                5.67.5
PUT                  13
  PROCEEDING FROM THE $PORT WHENCE HE PUT FORTH        2.1.5
  REASON PUT BACK, DCTH OUT OF SIGHT REMOVE            2.38.13
  REASON PUT BACK, DCTH OUT OF SIGHT REMOVE            2.131.13
  WHO WITH HIS FEARE IS PUT BESIDES HIS PART           3.23.2
  FOR THAT SAME GRONE DOTH PUT THIS IN MY MIND         3.50.13
  HATH PUT A SPIRIT CF YOUTH IN EVERY THING            3.98.3
  FOR SINCE EACH HAND HATH PUT ON $NATURES POWER       3.127.5
  HAVE PUT ON BLACK, AND LCVING MOURNERS BEE           3.132.3
  TO PUT FAIRE TRUTH UPON SO FOULE A FACE              3.137.12
  O ME- WHAT EYES HATH LOVE PUT IN MY HEAD             3.148.1
  AND CANNOT CHUSE BUT PUT OUT WHAT I WRITE            4.50.10
  ENVIE, PUT OUT THINE EYES, LEAST THOU DO SEE         4.69.3
  WITH SWEET INFUSICN, ANC PUT YOU IN MIND             5.28.7
PUTEST                1
  THOU USURER THAT PUT'ST FORTH ALL TO USE             3.134.10
PUTS                  2
  FOR WHO GETS WEALTH THAT PUTS NOT FROM THE SHORE+    1.35.5
  AND PUTS APPARRELL CN MY TOTTERED LOVING             3.26.11
PYGMALION             1
  BEHOLD WHAT HAP $PIGMALICN HAD TO FRAME              1.13.1
PYRAMIDS              1
  THY PYRAMYDS BUYLT UP WITH NEWER MIGHT               3.123.2
QUAFFING              1
  QUAFFING $CAROWSES IN THIS COSTLY $WINE              2.7.8
QUAINT                1
  PRAYERS PREVAILE NCT WITH A QUAINT DISDAINE          1.11.4
QUAKE                 3
  I QUAKE TO LOOKE CN $HECAT'S CHARMING $BCOKES        2.39.11
  I QUAKE TO LOOKE CN $HECATS CHARMING BOOKES          2.118.11
  THEY LOVE INDEED, WHO QUAKE TO SAY THEY LOVE         4.54.14
QUAKED                1
  MY HEART THEN QUAK'D, THEN DAZLED WERE MINE EYES     4.53.10
QUAKING               1
  DECEIV'D THE QUAKING BOY, WHO THOUGHT
                      FROM SO PURE LIGHT                4.8.10
QUALIFY               1
  THOUGH ABSENCE SEEN'D MY FLAME TO QUALLIFIE          3.109.2
QUALITY               1
  OF PLAGUES, OF DEARTHS, OR SEASONS QUALLITY          3.14.4
QUEEN                12
  LAUGHTER LOVING $GCDDESSE, WORLDLY PLEASURES
                      $QUEENE                           1.10.6
```

```
UPON HIS SOVEREIGNES COURSE, THE NIGHTS
                         PALE $QUEENE              1.48.6
THE QUIET END OF THAT $LONG-LIVING QUEENE        2.51.7
SAY THUS FAIRE $BROOKE, WHEN THOU SHALT
                         SEE THY QUEENE           2.53.9
SAY THUS FAYRE $BROOKE WHEN THOU SHALT
                         SEE THY $QUEENE          2.113.9
AS ON THE FINGER OF A THRONED $QUEENE            3.96.5
QUEENE $VERTUE'S COURT, WHICH SOME CALL
                         $STELLA'S FACE           4.9.1
AND AS A $QUEENE, WHO FROM HER PRESENCE SENDS     4.107.9
NOT FINISHING HER $QUEENE OF FAERY               5.33.3
SWEET SMILE, THE DAUGHTER OF THE $QUEENE OF LOVE  5.39.1
THE SECOND IS MY SOVEREIGNE $QUEENE MOST KIND    5.74.7
FIT FOR THE HANDMAYD OF THE $FAERY $QUEENE        5.80.14
QUEENS                   1
AND $QUEENES HEREAFTER SHALL BE GLAD TO LIVE      2.6.7
QUENCH                   6
  AND LIST NOT SEEKE TO BREAKE, TO QUENCH, TO HEALE  1.14.9
  GOOD $DELIA LOSE, QUENCH, HEALE ME NOW AT LENGTH   1.14.14
  SHE'ST QUENCH HER THIRST AS DULY AS THEY FALL      2.115.10
  THOSE TEARES WHICH QUENCH MY HOPE, STILL
                         KINDLE MY DESIRE         2.132.1
  SEEKING TO QUENCH IN ME THE NOBLE FIRE          4.68.7
  THINKING TO QUENCH HER THIRST AT THE NEXT BROOKE  5.67.8
QUENCHED                 2
  YET THERE HE BURNES, IN FIRE THATS NEVER
                         QUENCHED                 2.122.14
  THIS BRAND SHE QUENCHED IN A COOLE $WELL BY      3.154.9
QUENCHLESS               1
  QUENCHLES DESIRE, MAKES HOPE BURNE, DRYES
                         MY TEARES                2.132.5
QUEST                    2
  A QUEST OF THOUGHTS, ALL TENNANTS TO THE HEART   3.46.10
  HAD, HAVING, AND IN QUEST, TO HAVE EXTREAME      3.129.10
QUESTION                 2
  THEN OF THY BEAUTY DO I QUESTION MAKE            3.12.9
  NOR DARE I QUESTION WITH MY JEALIOUS THOUGHT     3.57.9
QUESTIONS                2
  THESE QUESTIONS BUSIE WITS TO ME DO FRAME        4.30.12
  THAT TO MY QUESTIONS YOU SO TOTALL ARE+          4.92.5
QUICK                    6
  POWR'D OUT WHAT FIRST FROM QUICKE $INVENTION CAME  2.21.6
  NOR $MARS HIS SWORD, NOR WARRES QUICK
                         FIRE SHALL BURNE         3.55.7
  SO FAR FROM VARIATION OR QUICKE CHANGE+          3.76.2
  OF HIS QUICK OBJECTS HATH THE MINDE NO PART      3.113.7
  MY WITS, QUICKE IN VAINE THOUGHTS, IN VERTUE LAME  4.21.4
  IN WEAKENED MINDS, QUICKE APPREHENDING BREED     4.66.3
QUICKER                  1
  FOR WHEN THESE QUICKER $ELEMENTS ARE GONE        3.45.5
QUICKLY                  2
  AND HIS LOVE-KINDLING FIRE DID QUICKLY STEEPE    3.153.3
  SHALL QUICKLY ME FROM WHAT SHE HATES REMOVE      4.61.11
QUIET                    4
  THE QUIET $EV'NING YET TOGETHER BRINGS           2.37.7
  THE QUIET END OF THAT $LONG-LIVING QUEENE        2.51.7
  FOR THEE, AND FOR MY SELFE, NOE QUIET FINDE      3.27.14
  NOR NO DAY HATH LESSE QUIET THEN MY NIGHT        4.89.11
```

```
QUIETEST                    1
  MAKES ME IN MY BEST THOUGHTS AND QUIETST
                          JUDGEMENT SEE            4.77.12
QUIET'S                     1
  BUT WHEN HE WILL FCR QUIET'S SAKE REMOVE         4.43.12
QUIETUS                     1
  AND HER $QUIETUS IS TO RENDER THEE               3.126.12
QUILL                       4
  AND BY INSPIRING, GLORIFIDE MY QUILL             2.104.11
  HOW FARRE A MODERNE QUILL DOTH COME TO SHORT     3.83.7
  RESERVE THEIR $CHARACTER WITH GOULDEN QUILL      3.85.3
  HER WORTH IS WRITTEN WITH A GOLDEN QUILL         5.85.10
QUINTESSENCE                2
  LOOKE AT MY HANDS FCR NC SUCH QUINTESSENCE       4.28.11
  THOSE WORDS, WHICH DO SUBLIME THE QUINTESSENCE
                          OF BLISSE                4.77.8
QUIT                        2
  DOE QUIT THE DEAD, AND ME NOT ACCESSARIE         2.2.6
  THO WORLDS QUITE ME, SHALL I MY SELFE FORGIVE+   4.93.11
QUITE                       17
  FAVOURS (I THINKE) WOULD SENCE QUITE OVERCOME    1.17.13
  POORE SOULE QUITE SPENT, WHOSE FORCE CAN
                          DO NO MORE               1.46.3
  AND I A $BANKRUPT, QUITE UNDONE BY $THEE         2.3.14
  THE $GODS PURE FIRE HATH BEEN EXTINGUISHT QUITE  2.105.2
  AND I A $BANCKRUPT QUITE UNDONE BY THEE          2.110.14
  SAP CHECKT WITH FRCST AND LUSTIE LEAV'S QUITE GON  3.5.7
  IS FROM THE BOOKE CF HONCUR RASED QUITE          3.25.11
  MINE OWNE SELFE LCVE QUITE CONTRARY I READ       3.62.11
  AFTER MY DEATH (DEARE LCVE) FOR GET ME QUITE     3.72.3
  THAT OVER-GOES MY BLUNT INVENTION QUITE          3.103.7
  UNABLE QUITE TO PAY EVEN $NATURE'S RENT          4.18.5
  WITH DEARTH OF WORDS, OR ANSWERS QUITE AWRIE     4.27.3
  AND NOW MY PEN THESE LINES HAD DASHED QUITE      4.50.12
  UNTO THE SIEGE BY YCU ABANDON'D QUITE            5.14.2
  ACCOUMPTS MY SELFE HER CAPTIVE QUITE FORLORNE    5.29.4
  MY SOULE WAS RAVISHT QUITE AS IN A TRAUNCE       5.39.10
  CONSUME THEE QUITE, THAT DIDST WITH GUILE
                          CONSPIRE                 5.86.11
QUIVER                      3
  LAYES DOWNE HIS $QUIVER, WHICH HE ONCE DID BEARE  2.4.6
  PRACTISE THY $QUIVER, AND TURNE $CROW-KEEPER     2.48.8
  WHILE $LOVE ON ME DCTH ALL HIS QUIVER SPEND      4.14.4
QUIVERS                     2
  HYDES IN THOSE CHRISTALL QUIVERS OF HER EYES     2.126.10
  CLOS'D WITH THEIR CUIVERS IN SLEEP'S ARMCRY      4.99.4
QUOTE                       2
  VAYNE MAN (QUOD I) THAT HAST BUT LITTLE PRIEFE   5.50.5
  NOT SO, (QUOD I) LET BASER THINGS DEVIZE         5.75.9
QUOTH                       5
  WHO SPARES TO SPEAKE, DCTH SPARE TO SPEEC
                          (QUOTH I)                2.59.5
  A HASTIE $MAN (QUCTH HE) NE'R WANTED $WOE        2.59.8
  LABOUR IS LIGHT, WHERE $LOVE (QUOTH I) DCTH PAY  2.59.9
  (QUOTH I) $THE $MAINE LCST, CAST THE $BY AWAY    2.59.11
  THE BAY (QUOTH SHE) IS CF THE VICTOURS BCRNE     5.29.5
RACE                        13
  SHALL NAIGH NOE DULL FLESH IN HIS FIERY RACE     3.51.11
  AND PLEASD WITH OUR SOFT PEACE, STAID
                          HERE HIS FLYING RACE     4.8.4
```

ON HORSEBACKE MET HIM IN HIS FURIOUS RACE   4.22.6
O FOOLES, OR OVER-WISE, ALAS THE RACE   4.23.12
WHO OFT FORE-JUDGE MY AFTER-FOLLOWING RACE   4.26.13
SENT FORTH THE BEAMES, WHICH MADE SO FAIRE
                                MY RACE   4.41.14
BUT WHEN THE RUGGEDST STEP OF $FORTUNE'S RACE   4.60.5
O GIVE MY PASSIONS LEAVE TO RUN THEIR RACE   4.64.2
AND NO SPURRE CAN HIS RESTY RACE RENEW   4.80.12
WAS NOT IN FAULT, WHO BENT THY DAZLING RACE   4.105.6
SITH TO ALL OTHER BEASTES OF BLOODY RACE   5.31.5
THE WEARY YEARE HIS RACE NOW HAVING RUN   5.62.1
AFTER SO LONG A RACE AS I HAVE RUN   5.80.1
RACK   2
AND RACKE HER WITH A THOUSAND HOLY WISHES   2.115.14
WITH OUGLY RACK ON HIS CELESTIALL FACE   3.33.6
RADIANT   1
ARE EYES, OR ELS TWO RADIANT STARRES THAT SHINE   1.34.2
RAGE   9
AGAINST THE DARKE AND TIMES CONSUMING RAGE   1.55.12
AND BARREN RAGE OF DEATHS ETERNALL COLD+   3.13.12
AND YOUR TRUE RIGHTS BE TERMD A $POETS RAGE   3.17.11
OR SOME FIERCE THING REPLEAT WITH TOO MUCH RAGE   3.23.3
AND BRASSE ETERNALL SLAVE TO MORTALL RAGE   3.64.4
HOW WITH THIS RAGE SHALL BEAUTIE HOLD A PLEA   3.65.3
BUT HARDER $JUDGES JUDGE AMBITION'S RAGE   4.23.9
WITH RAGE OF $LOVE, I CALD MY $LOVE UNKIND   4.62.2
NAY SORROW COMES WITH SUCH MAINE RAGE, THAT HE   4.95.9
RAGGED   1
THEN LET NOT WINTERS WRAGGED HAND DEFACE   3.6.1
RAGING   2
AS IS A ROCKE AMIDST THE RAGING FLOODS   5.56.10
THE RAGING WAVES AND KEEPES HER COURSE ARIGHT   5.59.6
RAGS   2
THINK'ST THOU MY $LOVE SHALL IN THOSE
                          $RAGGES BE DREST   2.31.11
FOR SOME FEW $RAGGES, WHEREWITH TO COVER THEE   2.48.4
RAIL   3
AND MUST INSTARRE THE $NEEDLE, AND THE $RAILE   1.45.12
NOW RAILE UPON HER $HAIRE, THEN ON HER $EYE   2.41.11
NOW RAYLE UPON HER HAYRE, NOW ON HER EYE   2.143.11
RAIMENT   1
IS BUT THE SEEMELY RAYMENT OF MY HEART   3.22.6
RAIN   7
POINTING TO EACH HIS THUNDER, RAINE AND WINDE   3.14.6
TO DRY THE RAINE ON MY STORME-BEATEN FACE   3.34.6
THE SEA ALL WATER, YET RECEIVES RAINE STILL   3.135.9
BROADRED WITH BULS AND SWANS, POWDRED
                        WITH GOLDEN RAINE   4.6.6
O TEARES, NO TEARES, BUT RAINE FROM BEAUTIE'S
                                SKIES   4.100.1
THEN YOU FAIRE FLOWRE, IN WHOM FRESH YOUTH
                             DOTH RAINE   5.4.13
THE STORMES, WHICH SHE ALONE ON ME DOTH RAINE   5.46.14
RAINING   2
A SECOND $FLOUD, DOWNE RAYNING FROM MINE $EYES   2.55.4
A SECOND FLOOD DOWNE RAYNING FROM MINE EYES   2.102.4
RAINY   1
GIVE NOT A WINDY NIGHT A RAINIE MORROW   3.90.7
RAISE   8
AND CALME THE TEMPEST WHICH MY SIGHS DOO RAISE   1.51.10

```
      WHICH $NAME MY $MUSE TO HIGHEST $HEAV'NS
                           SHALL RAYSE              2.54.13
      WHICH NAME MY $MUSE TO HIGHEST HEAVEN
                           SHAL RAISE               2.101.13
      MY HART SURCHARG'D WITH THOUGHTS, SIGHES
                           IN ABUNDANCE RAISE       2.133.9
      WHAT $MUSE HATH POWER, ABOVE THY HEIGHT
                           TO RAISE THEE+           2.146.4
      STRANGE FLAMES OF $LOVE IT IN OUR SOULES
                           WOULD RAISE              4.25.4
      BUT MONGST THEM ALL, WHICH DID $LOVES HONOR RAYSE   5.19.9
      MY SPIRIT TO AN HIGHER PITCH WILL RAYSE      5.80.12
RAISED                        9
      AND $AVONS $FAME, TO $ALBIONS $CLIFFES IS RAYSED   2.32.4
      AND $AVONS FAME, TO $ALBYONS $CLIVES IS RAYSED    2.124.4
      A $MUSE, THAT UNTO HEAVEN HATH RAISD HER FAME   2.138.12
      IF THY UNWORTHINESSE RAISD LOVE IN ME        3.150.13
      NOT THOU BY PRAISE, BUT PRAISE IN THEE IS RAISDE   4.35.13
      MY FORCES RAZDE, THY BANNERS RAISD WITHIN    4.36.6
      IN WELL RAISDE NOTES, MY PEN THE BEST IT MAY   4.70.10
      IN MY FRAILE SPIRIT BY HER FROM BASENESSE RAYSED   5.3.4
      BY WHOM MY SPIRIT OUT OF DUST WAS RAYSED     5.74.10
RAISING                       1
      RAISING MY HOPES ON HILLS OF HIGH DESIRE     1.36.1
RAM                           1
      THE HORNED $RAM DOTH IN HIS COURSE AWAKE     2.147.2
RAN                           1
      A MELTING PLEASANCE RAN THROUGH EVERY PART   5.39.7
RANDOM                        1
      AT RANDON FROM THE TRUTH VAINELY EXPREST     3.147.12
RANGE                         1
      AND SET MY THOUGHTS IN HEEDLESSE WAYES TO RANGE   1.5.2
RANGED                        1
      THAT IS MY HOME OF LOVE, IF I HAVE RANG'D    3.109.5
RANK                          5
      TO THY FAIRE FLOWER AD THE RANCKE SMELL OF WEEDS   3.69.12
      (THOUGH WORDS COME HIND-MOST) HOLDS HIS
                           RANKE BEFORE            3.85.12
      WHICH RANCKE OF GOODNESSE WOULD BY ILL BE CURED   3.118.12
      BY THEIR RANCKE THOUGHTES, MY DEEDES MUST
                           NOT BE SHOWN            3.121.12
      WHICH SHALL ABOVE THAT IDLE RANCKE REMAINE   3.122.3
RANKS                         1
      TO MARCH IN RANCKES OF BETTER EQUIPAGE       3.32.12
RANSACK                       1
      AND RANSACKE ALL $APOLLOS GOLDEN $TREASURE   2.21.12
RANSACKED                     1
      A CONQUERD, YELDEN, RANSACKT HEART TO WINNE+   4.36.2
RANSOM                        2
      AND THEY ARE RITCH, AND RANSOME ALL ILL DEEDS   3.34.14
      MINE RANSOMS YOURS, AND YOURS MUST RANSOME MEE   3.120.14
RANSOMS                       1
      MINE RANSOMS YOURS, AND YOURS MUST RANSOME MEE   3.120.14
RAPE                          1
      YET OLD $PROMETHEUS PUNISH'D FOR HIS $RAPE   2.14.13
RAPT                          2
      WHEN SHE WAS RAPT TO THE INFERNALL $BOWER    2.36.8
      WHYLEST RAPT WITH JOY RESEMBLING HEAVENLY MADNES   5.39.9
RARE                         23
      SO RARE A FAITH OUGHT BETTER BE REWARDED     1.11.8
```

```
AS SHORT THAT BLISSE, SO IS THE COMFORT RARE          1.24.11
RAIGNE IN MY THOUGHTS FAIRE HAND, SWEETE
                          EYE, RARE VOICE               1.28.1
WITH SO RARE SWEETNESSE ALL THE $HEAV'NS
                          PERFUMING                     2.16.10
AND THAT THEY CAME OF THIS RARE KINGLIE BROOD           2.103.8
BY THY RARE PLUME THY KIND IS EASLY KNOWNE              2.106.3
AT HER OWN RARE PERFECTIONS SO AMAZED                   2.109.8
RARE BEAUTY, $NATURES JOY, PERFECTIONS $MOTHER          2.123.2
RARE OF-SPRING OF MY THOUGHTS, MY DEEREST $LOVE         2.141.1
O RARE EFFECT, TRUE BOND OF FRIENDSHIPS MEASURE         2.146.9
THE PATIENCE OF SO RARE DIVINE A LOVE                   2.149.14
WITH $APRILLS FIRST BORNE FLOWERS AND
                          ALL THINGS RARE               3.21.7
THEREFORE ARE FEASTS SO SOLLEMNE AND SO RARE            3.52.5
MAKES $SOMERS WELCOME, THRICE MORE WISH'D,
                          MORE RARE                     3.56.14
AND YET BY HEAVEN I THINKE MY LOVE AS RARE              3.130.13
NAY, THAT MAY BREED MY FAME, IT IS SO RARE              4.34.6
WITH CHOISEST WORDS, THY WORDS WITH REASONS RARE        4.68.10
AND RARE PERFECTION OF EACH GOODLY PART                 5.24.2
NOT AYRE., FOR SHE IS NOT SO LIGHT OR RARE              5.55.7
THAT MAY ADMIRE SUCH WORLDS RARE WONDERMENT             5.69.12
PERHAPS HE THERE MAY LEARNE WITH RARE DELIGHT           5.73.11
MY VERSE YOUR VERTUES RARE SHALL ETERNIZE               5.75.11
ONELY BEHOLD HER RARE PERFECTION                        5.84.13
RAREST                    1
WITH CHOISE DELIGHTS AND RAREST COMPANY                 4.97.10
RARITIES                  1
FEEDES ON THE RARITIES OF NATURES TRUTH                 3.60.11
RASH                      2
THRETNING RASH EIES WHICH GAZE ON HER SO WIDE           5.5.7
AT EVERY RASH BEHOLDER PASSING BY                       5.16.8
RASHLY                    4
O, JUDGE NOT RASHLY (GENTLE $SIR) I PRAY                2.24.4
HENCEFORTH TOO RASHLY ON THAT GUILEFULL NET             5.37.10
T'ACCUSE OF PRIDE, OR RASHLY BLAME FOR OUGHT            5.61.4
AND MY FRAYLE THOUGHTS TOO RASHLY LED ASTRAY+           5.76.6
RATE                      2
WHICH YEELDS THEM NOTHING, AT THE EASIEST RATE          2.28.7
THAT YOU ALLOW ME THEM BY SO SMALL RATE+                4.92.2
RATHER                    9
AND DOEST NOT RATHER LOOKE ON HIM (ALAS)                1.37.3
AND YET I'D RATHER LANGUISH FOR HER LOVE                1.48.11
AND RATHER MAKE THEM BORNE TO OUR DESIRE                3.123.7
I RATHER WISHT THEE CLIME THE $MUSES' HILL              4.10.3
RATHER THEN BY MORE TRUTH TO GET MORE PAINE             4.67.14
TO LOSE HIS $CROWNE, RATHER THEN FAILE HIS $LOVE        4.75.14
CHOSE RATHER TO BE PRAYSD FOR DOOING GOOD               5.38.13
SUCH HEAVENLY FORMES OUGHT RATHER WORSHIPT BE           5.61.13
RATHER THEN ENVY LET THEM WONDER AT HER                 5.85.7
RATTLING                  1
INTO YOUR RIMES, RUNNING IN RATLING ROWES               4.15.6
RAVEN                     1
THEREFORE MY $MISTERSSE EYES ARE $RAVEN BLACKE          3.127.9
RAVING                    2
AND $BEDLAM-LIKE, THUS RAVING IN MY $GRIEFE             2.41.10
AND $BEDLAM LIKE THUS RAVING IN MY GRIEFE               2.143.10
RAVISHED                  7
RAVISH'D A $WORLD BEYOND THE FARTHEST $THOUGHT          2.34.2
```

```
RAVISH'D WITH $JOY AMID'ST A HELL OF $WOE            2.62.7
RAVISHT WITH JOY, AMIDST A HELL OF WOE               2.150.7
RAVISHT, STAID NOT, TILL IN HER GOLDEN HAIRE         4.103.7
IT RAVISHT IS WITH FANCIES WONDERMENT                5.3.12
MY SOULE WAS RAVISHT QUITE AS IN A TRAUNCE           5.39.10
HOW WAS I RAVISHT WITH YOUR LOVELY SIGHT             5.76.5
```
RAVISHING   1
```
WHICH WOOED WO, MOST RAVISHING DELIGHT               4.58.13
```
RAY   4
```
SO I WHOSE STAR, THAT WENT WITH HER BRIGHT RAY       5.34.5
THRUGH THE BROAD WORLD DOTH SPRED HIS GOODLY RAY     5.40.8
INTO THE GLOOMING WORLD HIS GLADSOME RAY             5.62.10
BUT TH'ONELY IMAGE OF THAT HEAVENLY RAY              5.88.7
```
RAYS   9
```
AND THOSE BRIGHT RAIES THAT KINDLE ALL THIS FIRE     1.38.3
DISPERSE THEIR $RAYES ON EV'RY VULGAR $SPIRIT        2.43.2
BUT ON HER $RAYES WITH OPEN $EYES IT STOOD           2.56.6
BUT ON HER RAYES WITH GAZING EYES THEY STOOD         2.103.6
THAT WITH THE RAYES HIS WAFTING PYNEONS FIRED        2.122.11
WHILST FROM THEYR RAYES BY $CUPIDS SKILFULL HAND     2.135.7
FOR SOONE AS THEY STRAKE THEE WITH $STELLA'S
                            RAYES                     4.10.12
YET STILL ON ME, O EYES, DART DOWNE YOUR RAYES       4.42.11
THEIR RAYES TO ME, WHO IN HER TEDIOUS ABSENCE LAY    4.76.2
```
RAZE   1
```
DOE WHAT THOU CANST, RAZE, MASSACRE, AND BURNE       2.63.11
```
RAZED   4
```
IS FROM THE BOOKE OF HONOUR RASED QUITE              3.25.11
WHEN SOMETIME LOFTIE TOWERS I SEE DOWNE RASED        3.64.3
TIL EACH TO RAZ'D OBLIVION YEELD HIS PART            3.122.7
MY FORCES RAZDE, THY BANNERS RAISD WITHIN            4.36.6
```
REACH   5
```
WHICH WELL THE REACH OF THEIR HIGH WITS RECORDS      1.55.4
SOME, WHO REACH NOT THE HEIGHT OF MY CONCEITE        2.128.5
PHRASES AND $PROBLEMES FROM MY REACH DO GROW         4.3.10
OR REACH THE FRUITE OF $NATURE'S CHOISEST TREE       4.10.4
BEAUTIES SO FARRE FROM REACH OF WORDS, THAT WE       4.37.7
```
READ   35
```
READE IT (SWEET MAIDE) THOUGH IT BE DONE
                      BUT SLEIGHTLY                  1.1.13
AH YOU, AND NONE BUT YOU MY SORROWES REACE           1.3.11
HERE READ THY SELFE, AND WHAT I SUFFRED FOR THEE     1.42.8
READ IN MY FACE, A VOLUME OF DISPAIRES               1.47.1
I MUST NOT GRIEVE MY $LOVE, WHOSE EIES
                      WOULD REEDE                    1.51.1
THE PAIMENTS OF MY $LOVE, I READ, AND CROSSE         2.3.6
THEN WOULD I MAKE THEE READ, BUT TO DESPIGHT THEE    2.8.14
MAY IN HIS $SHADOW MY $LOVES STORIE READ             2.13.14
READE BUT HIS $VERSE, AND IT WILL EAS'LY PROVE       2.24.3
COME THOU AND READE, ADMIRE, APPLAUD MY $LINES       2.49.14
YET READE AT LAST THE STORIE OF MY $WOE              2.54.1
SO MAY THE $HEAVENS READ WONDERS IN MY $HEART        2.60.8
READE HEERE (SWEET $MAYD) THE STORY OF MY WO         2.101.1
THE PAYMENTS OF MY LOVE I READ, AND READING
                            CROSSE                   2.110.6
THAT I CAN READE A STORY OF MY WOE                   2.111.14
MAY IN HIS SHADOW MY $LOVES STORY READE              2.121.14
SO MAY THE HEAVENS READE WONDERS IN MY HART          2.149.8
AND CONSTANT STARS IN THEM I READ SUCH ART           3.14.10
O LEARNE TO READ WHAT SILENT LOVE HATH WRIT          3.23.13
```

```
THEIRS FOR THEIR STILE ILE READ, HIS FOR
                      HIS LOVE                         3.32.14
MINE OWNE SELFE LOVE QUITE CONTRARY I READ             3.62.11
NAY IF YOU READ THIS LINE, REMEMBER NOT                3.71.5
PLEASURE MIGHT CAUSE HER READE, READING
                      MIGHT MAKE HER KNOW              4.1.3
HOW THEN+ EVEN THUS.. IN $STELLA'S FACE I REED         4.3.12
THAT $PLATO I READ FOR NOUGHT, BUT IF HE TAME          4.21.5
I READE IT IN THY LOOKES, THY LANGUISHT GRACE          4.31.7
THEN THINKE MY DEARE, THAT YOU IN ME DO REED           4.45.12
WHEN I MIGHT READE THOSE LETTERS FAIRE OF BLISSE       4.56.5
STELLA'S SWEETE BREATH THE SAME TO ME DID REED         4.58.11
SO CHILDREN STILL READE YOU WITH AWFULL EYES           4.63.2
LET HIM BUT LEARNE OF $LOVE TO READE IN THEE           4.71.3
THAT ALL THY HURTS IN MY HART'S WRACKE I REEDE         4.93.13
AND READE THE SORROWES OF MY DYING SPRIGHT             5.1.7
SUCH ART OF EYES I NEVER READ IN BOOKES                5.21.14
LOVE LEARNED LETTERS TO HER EYES TO READ               5.43.12
READING                 6
WITH DOWNEWARD LOCKES, STILL READING ON THE EARTH      1.9.3
VIRGINS AND $MATRONS READING THESE MY $RIMES           2.6.9
THE PAYMENTS OF MY LOVE I READ, AND READING
                      CROSSE                           2.110.6
READING SOMETYME, MY SORROWES TO BEGUILE               2.120.1
PLEASURE MIGHT CAUSE HER READE, READING
                      MIGHT MAKE HER KNOW              4.1.3
LOVE ONELY READING UNTO ME THIS ART                    4.28.14
READS                   1
A $MONUMENT THAT WHOSOEVER REEDES                      1.2.7
READY                   6
THE READY HANDMAYDS ON HER GRACE T'ATTEND              1.48.2
READIE OF WIT AND FEARING NOUGHT BUT SHAME             4.14.11
READY TO STORE THEIR CAMPES OF NEEDFULL THINGS         4.29.4
LATE TYR'D WITH WO, EVEN READY FOR TO PINE             4.62.1
IS READY TO COME FORTH HIM TO RECEIVE                  5.4.10
BID HER THEREFORE HER SELFE SOONE READY MAKE           5.70.9
REALM                   1
THIS REALME OF BLISSE, WHILE VERTUOUS
                      COURSE I TAKE                    4.69.13
REAP                    1
WHILST MY POORE LIPS WHICH SHOULD THAT
                      HARVEST REAPE                    3.128.7
REAR                    1
JOVE ON HIS HELME THE THUNDERBOLT DID REARE            4.13.8
REARED                  2
HAVE SEENE THOSE WALLS WHICH PROUD AMBITION
                      REAR'D                           1.45.2
AS HOW THE $POLE TO EV'RY PLACE WAS REAR'D             2.1.8
REARS                   1
WHILES HER FAIRE FACE SHE REARES UP TO THE SKIE        5.13.2
REARWARD                1
COME IN THE REREWARD OF A CONQUERD WOE                 3.90.6
REASCEND                1
I WISH THAT DAY WOULD SHORTLY REASCEND                 5.87.8
REASON                  31
REASON AND I (YOU MUST CONCEIVE) ARE TWAINE            2.9.10
IN JUDGING, $REASON ONELY IS HER $NAME                 2.12.9
REASON PLUCKS BACK, COMMANDING ME TO STAY              2.38.2
STRAIGHT TAXETH $REASON, WANTING TO INVENT             2.38.7
REASON REPROCHED WITH THIS COY $DISDAINE               2.38.9
```

```
AND $LOVE CONTEMNING $REASONS REASON WHOLLY          2.38.11
REASON PUT BACK, DOTH OUT OF SIGHT REMOVE            2.38.13
AND $LOVE ALONE PICKS REASON OUT OF LOVE             2.38.14
NOR YET WISE $REASCN ABSOLUTELY KNOWES                2.46.4
REASON PLUCKS BACKE, COMMAUNDING ME TO STAY         2.131.2
STRAIGHT TAXETH $REASON, WANTING TO INVENT          2.131.7
REASON REPROCHED WITH THIS COY DISDAINE             2.131.9
AND $LOVE CONTEMNING $REASONS REASON WHOLY         2.131.11
REASON PUT BACK, DOTH OUT OF SIGHT REMOVE          2.131.13
AND $LOVE ALONE FINDS REASON IN MY LOVE            2.131.14
WHOSE THWARTING COURSE, DEPRIVES THE WORLD
                                   OF REASON        2.147.14
YET THEN MY JUDGEMENT KNEW NO REASON WHY            3.115.3
PAST REASON HUNTED, AND NO SOONER HAD                3.129.6
PAST REASON HATED AS A SWOLLOWED BAYT                3.129.7
MY REASON THE $PHISITION TO MY LOVE                  3.147.5
PAST CURE I AM, NCW $REASON IS PAST CARE             3.147.9
TRIUMPH IN LOVE, FLESH STAIES NO FARTHER REASON      3.151.8
THE LITLE REASON THAT IS LEFT IN ME                   4.4.10
REASON, IN FAITH THOU ART WELL SERV'D, THAT STILL     4.10.1
REASON THOU KNEEL'DST, AND OFFEREDST STRAIGHT
                                   TO PROVE          4.10.13
BY REASON GOOD, GOOD REASON HER TO LOVE              4.10.14
BY REASON GOOD, GOOD REASON HER TO LOVE              4.10.14
OF REASON, FROM WHCSE LIGHT THOSE NIGHT-BIRDS
                                      FLIE            4.71.7
NE WILBE MOOV'D WITH REASON OR WITH REWTH             5.11.5
NO SKILL CAN STINT NOR REASON CAN ASLAKE              5.44.8
WHAT REASON IS IT THEN BUT SHE SHOULD SCORNE         5.61.11
REASONS                  6
SHALL REASONS FINDE OF SETLED GRAVITIE                3.49.8
TO GUARD THE LAWFULL REASONS ON THY PART             3.49.12
AGAINST THY REASONS MAKING NO DEFENCE                 3.89.4
CLOTH'D WITH FINE TROPES, WITH STRONGEST
                         REASONS LIN'D                4.58.6
WITH CHOISEST WORDS, THY WORDS WITH REASONS RARE     4.68.10
THY REASONS FIRMLY SET ON $VERTUE'S FEET             4.68.11
REASON'S                 7
I THUS OPPOSE MY $REASONS FORCES WHOLLY               2.28.4
AND SCORNING $REASON'S MAYMED $ARGUMENT               2.38.6
AND $LOVE CONTEMNING $REASONS REASON WHOLLY          2.38.11
AND SCORNING $REASONS MAYMED $ARGUMENT              2.131.6
AND $LOVE CONTEMNING $REASONS REASON WHOLY         2.131.11
WHEN INTO $REASON'S AUDITE I DO GO                   4.18.2
SINCE $REASON'S SELFE DOTH BLOW THE COLE IN ME+      4.35.6
REBATE                   1
REBATE THY $SPLEENE, IF BUT FOR $PITTIES SAKE        2.52.6
REBEL                    4
OFT AND IN VAINE MY REBEL THOUGHTS HAVE VENTRED       1.27.1
MY REBELL THOUGHT FOR ME IN $AMBUSHE LYES            2.142.7
MY SINFULL EARTH THESE REBBELL POWRES
                         THAT THEE ARRAY             3.146.2
ERE $CUCKOW END, LET HER A REBELL BE                 5.19.14
REBELLING                1
UPON THE FLINT OF SUCH A HART REBELLING             1.18.10
REBELLIOUS               1
DOTH STILL PERSIST IN HER REBELLIOUS PRIDE            5.6.2
REBELS                   2
CALL BACKE THE STIFFE-NECK'D $REBELS FROM $EXILE     2.25.11
REBELS TO $NATURE, STRIVE FOR THEIR OWNE SMART        4.5.4
```

REBOUNDED   1
  THAT ALL THE WOODS THEYR ECCHOES BACK REBOUNDED   5.19.7
REBUKED   1
  SO I RETURNE REBUKT TO MY CONTENT   3.119.13
RECALL   1
  YET SOONE AGAINE I MUST HER BACKE RECALL   1.25.7
RECEIPT   2
  IF THIS $RECEIT HAVE NOT THE POW'R TO WINNE ME   2.15.13
  IN THINGS OF GREAT RECEIT WITH EASE WE PROOVE   3.136.7
RECEIVE   5
  DEVIS'D A $VESSELL TO RECEIVE THE $SUNNE   2.30.3
  RECEIVE THE $INCENSE WHICH I OFFER HERE   2.54.9
  RECEAVE THE INCENSE WHICH I OFFER HEERE   2.101.9
  TO TRUST THOSE TABLES THAT RECEAVE THEE MORE   3.122.12
  IS READY TO COME FORTH HIM TO RECEIVE   5.4.10
RECEIVED   1
  RECEIVED HAST THIS MESSAGE FROM THY GLASSE   1.41.3
RECEIVES   3
  THENCE COMES IT THAT MY NAME RECEIVES A BRAND   3.111.5
  WHEN NOT TO BE, RECEIVES REPROACH OF BEING   3.121.2
  THE SEA ALL WATER, YET RECEIVES RAINE STILL   3.135.9
RECEIVEST   3
  WHY LOV'ST THOU THAT WHICH THOU RECEAVST
                              NOT GLADLY   3.8.3
  OR ELSE RECEAV'ST WITH PLEASURE THINE ANNOY+   3.8.4
  THEN IF FOR MY LOVE, THOU MY LOVE RECEIVEST   3.40.5
RECEIVING   2
  RECEIVING STRENGTH FROM EV'RY SECRET PART   2.30.7
  RECEIVING NAUGHTS BY ELEMENTS SO SLOE   3.44.13
RECITE   1
  O LEAST THE WORLD SHOULD TASKE YOU TO RECITE   3.72.1
RECKON   2
  AND SEE HOW JUST I RECKON WITH THINE EIES   1.1.10
  AT MY ABUSES, RECKON UP THEIR OWNE   3.121.10
RECKONED   1
  AMONG A NUMBER ONE IS RECKON'D NONE   3.136.8
RECKONING   1
  BUT RECKENING TIME, WHOSE MILLIOND ACCIDENTS   3.115.5
RECKONINGS   2
  THE RECK'NINGS RISE TO MILLIONS OF $DESPAIRES   2.3.4
  AND STYLL IN RECKONINGS RISE MORE MILLIONS
                              OF DISPAYRES   2.110.4
RECOMPENSE   3
  SHE THINKES A LOOKE MAY RECOMPENCE MY CARE   1.24.9
  GET NOT ONE GLANCE, TO RECOMPENCE MY $MERIT+   2.43.4
  WHO PLEADE FOR LOVE, AND LOOK FOR RECOMPENCE   3.23.11
RECONCILED   1
  LIVE RECONCILED FRIENDS WITHIN HER BROW   1.6.10
RECORD   6
  AND WITH THE $SWAN RECORD THY DYING SONG   2.139.7
  RECORD MY LOVE IN $OCEAN WAVES (UNKIND)   2.142.9
  THE LIVING RECORD OF YOUR MEMORY   3.55.8
  OH THAT RECORD COULD WITH A BACK-WARD LOOKE   3.59.5
  OF THEE, THY RECORD NEVER CAN BE MIST   3.122.8
  IN WHICH I MAY RECORD THE MEMORY   5.69.6
RECORDER   1
  RECORDER OF REVENGE, REMEMBRANCER OF CARE   2.145.7
RECORDS   3
  WHICH WELL THE REACH OF THEIR HIGH WITS RECORDS   1.55.4
  FOR THY RECORDS, AND WHAT WE SEE DOTH LYE   3.123.11

```
    IN WHICH THEY WOULD THE RECORDS HAVE ENROLD        5.69.3
RECOUNT                      2
  LET ALL THE EARTH WITH SCORNE RECOUNT MY CASE        4.64.7
  AS I MAY WELL RECOUNT, BUT NONE CAN PRIZE            4.65.4
RECOUNTING                   1
  OF THEIR FAIRE HEALTH, RECOUNTING IT TO ME           3.45.12
RECOVER                      1
  FROM $DEATH TO $LIFE, THOU MIGHT'ST HIM
                             YET RECOVER               2.61.14
RECTOR                       1
  O CLEERE-EYDE $RECTOR OF THE HOLY $HILL              1.4.10
RECURE                       2
  AND WITH THEIR $BALMES RECURE THE $WOUNDS AGAINE     2.50.8
  AND WITH ANOTHER DOTH IT STREIGHT RECURE             5.21.11
RECURED                      1
  UNTILL LIVES COMPOSITION BE RECURED                  3.45.9
RED                         12
  HOW TO BE PALE WITH ANGUISH, RED WITH FEARE          1.20.2
  A THIRD NOR RED, NOR WHITE, HAD STOLNE OF BOTH       3.99.10
  CURRALL IS FARRE MORE RED, THEN HER LIPS RED         3.130.2
  CURRALL IS FARRE MORE RED, THEN HER LIPS RED         3.130.2
  I HAVE SEENE $ROSES DAMASKT, RED AND WHITE           3.130.5
  RED $PORPHIR IS, WHICH LOCKE OF PEARLE MAKES SURE    4.9.6
  MARBLE MIXT RED AND WHITE DO ENTERLACE               4.9.8
  WHERE BLUSHING RED, THAT $LOVE'S SELFE
                             THEM DOTH LOVE            4.43.10
  MILKE HANDS, ROSE CHEEKS, OR LIPS MORE
                             SWEET, MORE RED           4.91.7
  WHERE THOSE RED CHEEKS, WHICH OFT WITH
                             FAIRE ENCREASE DID FRAME  4.102.2
  HER RUDDY CHEEKES LYKE UNTO $ROSES RED               5.64.6
  FAYRE WHEN THE ROSE IN HER RED CHEEKES APPEARES      5.81.3
REDDEST                      1
  WHILE BEAUTIE'S REDDEST INKE $VENUS FOR
                             HIM DOTH STURRE           4.102.14
REDEEM                       1
  RETURNE FORGETFULL $MUSE, AND STRAIGHT REDEEME       3.100.5
REDEEMED                     1
  THESE SHALL INTOMBE THOSE EIES, THAT HAVE
                             REDEEM'D                  1.44.11
REDOUBLING                   1
  REDOUBLING SIGHES THE ACCENTS OF MY GRIEFE           2.111.12
REDOUND                      1
  AND DRIZLING DROPS THAT OFTEN DUE REDOUND            5.18.3
REDRESS                      2
  TO CRAVE REDRESSE, YET HOLD AFFLICTION DEARE         1.20.7
  THINKE THAT I THINKE STATE ERROURS TO REDRESSE       4.23.8
REEKS                        1
  THEN IN THE BREATH THAT FROM MY $MISTRES REEKES      3.130.8
REEL                         1
  THUS THE $WORLD DOTH, AND EVERMORE SHALL $REELE      2.51.10
REELETH                      1
  LIKE FEEBLE AGE HE REELETH FROM THE DAY              3.7.10
REFIGURED                    1
  IF TEN OF THINE TEN TIMES REFIGUR'D THEE             3.6.10
REFINED                      4
  THY $CRISTALL STREAME REFINED BY HER $EYES           2.53.4
  THAT CHRISTALL STREAME REFINED BY HER EYES           2.113.4
  WHICH FROM HER LYPS EXHALD REFINED SWEET             2.125.6
  IN POLISHT FORME OF WELL REFINED PEN                 3.85.8
```

```
REFINES                        1
  THOU, THUS WHOSE $SPIRIT $LOVE IN HIS
                        FIRE REFINES            2.49.13
REFLECTING                     1
  BY THOSE REFLECTING $SUN-BEAMES OF THY BEAUTIE   2.105.8
REFLECTION                     1
  ON WHICH THE $SUNNE MIGHT BY REFLECTION BEAT     2.30.6
REFLEX                         1
  WITH MY REFLEX YOURS SHALL ENCREASED BE          5.66.14
REFRESH                        2
  WHOSE SHORT REFRESH UPON THE TENDER GREENE       1.50.2
  AS CAN REFRESH THE HELL WHERE MY SOULE FRIES     4.100.8
REFRESHED                      1
  THEN AS A STEED REFRESHED AFTER TOYLE            5.80.5
REFUGE                         1
  INTO THE SACRED $REFUGE OF THY BREST             1.31.2
REFUSE                         3
  ALL OTHER HONORS DOE MY HOPES REFUSE             1.58.3
  I THAT THUS TAKE, OR THEY THAT THUS REFUSE       2.28.11
  THAT IN THE VERY REFUSE OF THY DEEDS             3.150.6
REFUSED                        1
  THE BOY REFUSDE FOR FEARE OF $MARSE'S HATE       4.17.5
REFUSEST                       1
  BY WILFULL TASTE OF WHAT THY SELFE REFUSEST      3.40.8
REGARD                         2
  WHICH HASTE FOR SUCCOUR TO HER SLOW REGARD       1.4.2
  WITH MERCIFULL REGARD, GIVE MERCY TOO            5.49.12
REGARDED                       1
  I VOW MY FAITH, WHERE FAITH IS NOT REGARDED      1.11.6
REGION                         1
  THE REGION CLOUDE HATH MASK'D HIM FROM ME NOW    3.33.12
REGIONS                        1
  IF $THOSE TEN $REGIONS REGISTRED BY $FAME        2.119.1
REGISTER                       3
  MY $FAIRE, IF THOU WILT REGISTER MY LOVE         2.55.1
  MY $FAYRE, IF THOU WILT REGISTER MY LOVE         2.102.1
  WHAT'S NEW TO SPEAKE, WHAT NOW TO REGISTER       3.108.3
REGISTERED                     1
  IF $THOSE TEN $REGIONS REGISTRED BY $FAME        2.119.1
REGISTERS                      1
  THY REGISTERS AND THEE I BOTH DEFIE              3.123.9
REHEARSE                       7
  AND WHEN MY FLOWING $NUMBERS THEY REHEARSE       2.25.13
  IT PLEASETH ME, IF I MY $WOES REHEARSE           2.42.11
  IT PLEASETH ME IF I MY PLAINTS REHEARSE          2.128.11
  AND EVERY FAIRE WITH HIS FAIRE DOTH REHERSE      3.21.4
  FOR EVERY VULGAR PAPER TO REHEARSE               3.38.4
  DO NOT SO MUCH AS MY POORE NAME REHERSE          3.71.11
  AND TOUNGS TO BE, YOUR BEEING SHALL REHEARSE     3.81.11
REIGN                          6
  REIGNE IN MY THOUGHTS, MY LOVE AND LIFE
                        ARE THINE                 1.27.14
  RAIGNE IN MY THOUGHTS FAIRE HAND, SWEETE
                        EYE, RARE VOICE           1.28.1
  AND EACH (THOUGH ENIMES TO ETHERS RAIGNE)        3.28.5
  ALL MEN ARE BAD AND IN THEIR BADNESSE RAIGNE     3.121.14
  AND KNOW THOSE $BODIES HIGH RAIGNE ON THE LOW    4.26.11
  OF ALL THE KINGS THAT EVER HERE DID RAIGNE       4.75.1
REIGNED                        1
  NEVER BELEEVE THOUGH IN MY NATURE RAIGN'D        3.109.9
```

REIGNETH   1
  AND REIGNETH OVER EVERY BEAST IN FIELD   5.20.6
REIGNS   1
  AND THERE RAIGNES $LOVE AND ALL $LOVES
                          LOVING PARTS   3.31.3
REIN   1
  BUT AS HE THEM MORE SHORT OR SLACKE DOTH RAINE   4.58.4
REINED   2
  FINDING ME RAIN'D WITH SUCH A HEAVY HAND   1.28.12
  (SPURD WITH LOVE'S SPUR, THOUGH GALD AND
                          SHORTLY RAIND   4.98.7
REINS   2
  THE RAINES OF $LOVE I LOVE, THOUGH NEVER SLAKE   4.28.7
  THE RAINES WHEREWITH MY $RIDER DOTH ME TIE   4.49.5
REJOICE   1
  SO SWEETS MY PAINES, THAT MY PAINES ME REJOYCE   4.57.14
RELATE   1
  THUS IN MY $LOVE, $TIME CALLS ME TO RELATE   2.1.13
RELEASE   3
  CAN GIVE THE LEAST RELEASE UNTO THY GRIEFE   1.52.10
  THE POORE MAN'S WEALTH, THE PRISONER'S RELEASE   4.39.3
  WITHOUT HOPE OF ASWAGEMENT OR RELEASE+   5.36.4
RELEASING   1
  THE $CHARTER OF THY WORTH GIVES THEE RELEASING   3.87.3
RELENT   2
  AND STILL EXPECTING WHEN SHE WILL RELENT   1.16.5
  BUT SINCE YE DEIGND SO GOODLY TO RELENT   5.82.9
RELENTING   1
  GIVES ME GREAT HOPE OF YOUR RELENTING MYND   5.28.2
RELIC   1
  TOO RICH A $RELIQUE FOR SO POORE A $SHRINE   2.57.4
RELICS   1
  AMONGST THY DEEREST RELICKS TO BE KEPT   5.22.14
RELIC'S   1
  MAKING THY BREAST THAT SACRED RELIQUES SHRYNE   2.105.12
RELIEF   7
  DID TREATE THE CRUELL FAIRE TO YEELD RELIEFE   1.8.8
  A THOUSAND TIMES IT PROMIS'D ME RELIEFE   1.25.3
  WITH STILL FRESH CARES, SUPPLIDE WITH NO RELIEFE   1.32.4
  MY CARES MY MUTES SO MUTE TO CRAVE RELIEFE   2.111.10
  WITH THESE, SHE STEALES MENS HARTS FOR
                          HER RELIEFE   2.126.13
  TH'OFFENDERS SORROW LENDS BUT WEAKE RELIEFE   3.34.11
  FIT MEDICINES FOR MY BODIES BEST RELIEFE   5.50.4
RELIEVE   3
  STILL TO COMPLAINE MY GRIEFES, WHILST NONE RELIEVE   1.9.8
  I WEIGH NO COMFORT UNLESSE SHE RELIEVE   1.12.8
  RELIEVE MY LANGUISH, AND RESTORE THE LIGHT   1.54.3
RELIGION   1
  THAT LIFE (I MEANE) WHICH DOTH $RELIGION TEACH   2.119.13
RELIGION'S   1
  THE VOLUMES OF $RELIGIONS LAWES SHEE KEEPETH   2.105.11
RELIGIOUS   1
  HATH DEARE RELIGIOUS LOVE STOLNE FROM MINE EYE   3.31.6
RELISH   3
  IF ANY PLEASING RELISH HERE I USE   1.57.11
  THAT $FORAINE $NATIONS RELLISH NOT OUR $TONGUE   2.25.2
  SOME, WHO NOT KINDLY RELLISH MY $CONCEIT   2.42.5
REMAIN   16
  THIS MAY REMAINE THY LASTING MONUMENT   1.42.9

THESE MAY REMAINE WHEN THOU AND I SHALL PERISH	1.42.12
IF THEY REMAINE, THEN THOU SHALT LIVE THEREBY	1.42.13
THEY WILL REMAINE, AND SO THOU CANST NOT DIE	1.42.14
SO MUCH IS $MINE, THAT DOTH WITH $YOU REMAINE	2.11.11
MY $HEART FOR $HOSTAGE THAT IT SHALL REMAINE	2.63.6
SO SHALL THOSE BLOTS THAT DO WITH ME REMAINE	3.36.3
BY PRAISING HIM HERE WHO DOTH HENCE REMAINE	3.39.14
WHICH SHALL ABOVE THAT IDLE RANCKE REMAINE	3.122.3
TO KNIT THE KNOT, THAT EVER SHALL REMAINE	5.6.14
SO AS I THEN DISARMED DID REMAINE	5.12.5
WHILES SHE AS STEELE AND FLINT DOTH STILL REMAYNE	5.18.14
NE ANY MENTION SHALL THEREOF REMAINE	5.27.10
BUT JOY HER THRALL FOR EVER TO REMAYNE	5.42.7
LONGWHILE ALONE IN LANGUOR TO REMAINE	5.52.8
WHEREOF SOME GLANCE DOTH IN MINE EIE REMAYNE	5.88.8
REMAINED 1	
HER SOVERAIGNTY SHOULD HAVE REMAINED STILL	1.36.11
REMAINETH 1	
WHEN NOTHING ELSE REMAYNETH OF THESE DAYES	2.6.6
REMAINING 1	
THOUGH SPENT THY FLAME, IN ME THE HEAT REMAINING	1.41.6
REMAINS 5	
WHAT SHOULD I SAY+ WHAT YET REMAINES TO DOE+	2.41.5
WHERE SHEE REMAINES FOR ALL EYES TO BEHOLD	2.109.14
AND THAT IS THIS, AND THIS WITH THEE REMAINES	3.74.14
WHAT THEN REMAINES BUT I TO ASHES BURNE	5.32.13
AND EVERY PART REMAINES IMMORTALLY	5.45.8
REMEDY 2	
AND FOR THIS SINNE THERE IS NO REMEDIE	3.62.3
GROWING A BATH AND HEALTHFULL REMEDY	3.154.11
REMEMBER 2	
NAY IF YOU READ THIS LINE, REMEMBER NOT	3.71.5
TO KEEPE AN ADJUNCKT TO REMEMBER THEE	3.122.13
REMEMBERED 4	
BUT IF THOU LIVE REMEMBRED NOT TO BE	3.3.13
FOR THY SWEET LOVE REMEMBRED SUCH WELTH BRINGS	3.29.13
TO BASE OF THEE TO BE REMEMBRED	3.74.12
O THAT OUR NIGHT OF WO MIGHT HAVE REMEMBRED	3.120.9
REMEMBRANCE 4	
WHOSE DEARE REMEMBRANCE IN MY $BOSOME LYES	2.57.3
NOR IT NOR NOE REMEMBRANCE WHAT IT WAS	3.5.12
I SOMMON UP REMEMBRANCE OF THINGS PAST	3.30.2
REMEMBRANCE OF ALL PAINES WHICH HIM OPPREST	5.63.12
REMEMBRANCER 1	
RECORDER OF REVENGE, REMEMBRANCER OF CARE	2.145.7
REMEMBRETH 1	
HER MINDE REMEMBRETH HER MORTALITIE	5.13.7
REMNANT 1	
AND NOW EMPLOY THE REMNANT OF MY WIT	4.2.12
REMORSE 2	
WHICH ON THE $LIVING WORKE WITHOUT REMORSE	2.50.5
PLAY NOT THE $TYRANT, BUT TAKE SOME $REMORSE	2.52.5
REMOTE 2	
AS $IN SOME $COUNTRIES, FARRE REMOTE FROM HENCE	2.50.1
FROM LIMITS FARRE REMOTE, WHERE THOU DOOST STAY	3.44.4
REMOVE 12	
AND TO TH'$ORIENT DO THY $PEARLES REMOVE	1.19.4
AND NO REMOVE CAN MAKE THY SORROWES LESSE+	1.52.4
REASON PUT BACK, DOTH OUT OF SIGHT REMOVE	2.38.13

```
REASON PUT BACK, DOTH OUT OF SIGHT REMOVE          2.131.13
WHERE I MAY NOT REMOVE, NOR BE REMOVED             3.25.14
OR BENDS WITH THE REMOVER TO REMOVE                3.116.4
DO NOT, O DO NOT FROM POORE ME REMOVE              4.42.7
BUT WHEN HE WILL FOR QUIET'S SAKE REMOVE           4.43.12
SHALL QUICKLY ME FROM WHAT SHE HATES REMOVE        4.61.11
SCORTCH NOT, BUT ONELY DO DARKE CHILLING
                            SPRITES REMOVE         4.76.8
REMOVE THE CAUSE BY WHICH YOUR FAYRE BEAMES
                            DARKNED BE             5.45.14
SO FIRMELY, THAT YE NEVER MAY REMOVE               5.71.8
REMOVED                    4
WHERE I MAY NOT REMOVE, NOR BE REMOVED             3.25.14
BUT THINGS REMOV'D THAT HIDDEN IN THERE LIE        3.31.8
UPON THE FARTHEST EARTH REMOOV'D FROM THEE         3.44.6
AND YET THIS TIME REMOV'D WAS SOMMERS TIME         3.97.5
REMOVER                    1
OR BENDS WITH THE REMOVER TO REMOVE                3.116.4
REND                       1
AND WITH ONE WORD MY WHOLE YEARS WORK DOTH REND    5.23.12
RENDER                     2
BUT MUTUALL RENDER, ONELY ME FOR THEE              3.125.12
AND HER $QUIETUS IS TO RENDER THEE                 3.126.12
RENEW                      5
SWEET LOVE RENEW THY FORCE, BE IT NOT SAID         3.56.1
AND NO SPURRE CAN HIS RESTY RACE RENEW             4.80.12
AND IF I SPEAKE, HER WRATH RENEW I SHALL           5.43.2
AND GRIEFE RENEW, AND PASSIONS DOE AWAKE           5.44.11
OUR LOVE SHALL LIVE, AND LATER LIFE RENEW          5.75.14
RENEWED                    1
PITTY ME THEN, AND WISH I WERE RENU'DE             3.111.8
RENEWEST                   2
FOR THOU ALONE RENEW'ST THAT OLDE DESIRE           2.145.13
WHOSE FRESH REPAIRE IF NOW THOU NOT RENEWEST       3.3.3
RENEWETH                   1
TO BATTELL, AND THE WEARY WAR RENEW'TH             5.11.4
RENEWS                     1
AND YET THE $HYDRA OF MY CARES RENUES              1.16.9
RENOWN                     3
AND YEELD ME NOUGHT THAT GIVES THEM THEIR RENOWNE  1.28.8
HIS ERROR WAS HIS HONOUR AND RENOWNE               1.56.2
RICH IN THE TREASURE OF DESERV'D RENOWNE           4.37.9
RENOWNED                   4
AND SO LIKEWISE, RENOWMED IS THY BLAME             1.56.9
THE $CRYSTALL $TRENT, FOR $FOORDS AND
                            $FISH RENOWNED         2.32.3
THE CHRISTALL $TRENT, FOR $FOORDS AND
                            FISHE RENOWNED         2.124.3
WHEN THOSE RENOUMED NOBLE $PERES OF $GREECE        5.44.1
RENT                       4
SEE HOW HER SAYLES BE RENT, HER TACKLINGS WORNE    2.134.9
LOSE ALL, AND MORE BY PAYING TOO MUCH RENT         3.125.6
UNABLE QUITE TO PAY EVEN $NATURE'S RENT            4.18.5
HART RENT THY SELFE, THOU DOEST THY SELFE
                            BUT RIGHT              4.33.5
RENTS                      1
ROBD OTHERS BEDS REVENUES OF THEIR RENTS           3.142.8
REPAIR                     4
WHOSE FRESH REPAIRE IF NOW THOU NOT RENEWEST       3.3.3
WHICH TO REPAIRE SHOULD BE THY CHIEFE DESIRE       3.10.8
```

```
SO SHOULD THE LINES OF LIFE THAT LIFE REPAIRE          3.16.9
HER GLORIES PRIDE THAT NONE MAY IT REPAYRE             5.58.8
REPAIREST            1
AND STILL AGAINST HER FROWNES FRESH VOWES
                              REPAIREST                 1.8.3
REPAY               1
WHEREIN I SHOULD YOUR GREAT DESERTS REPAY             3.117.2
REPEAL              1
MAKE HER THE SENTENCE OF HER WRATH REPEALE            1.22.4
REPEAT              2
THUS SUNDRY $MEN THEIR SUNDRY $MINDS REPEAT           2.42.8
THUS SUNDRY MEN, THEIR SUNDRY MINDS REPEATE         2.128.8
REPENT              5
AND THAT THOU WAST UNKINDE, THOU MAYST REPENT       1.41.12
THOU MAIST REPENT THAT THOU HAST SCORND
                              MY TEARES               1.41.13
THOUGH THOU REPENT, YET I HAVE STILL THE LOSSE        3.34.10
I WILLING RUN, YET WHILE I RUN, REPENT                4.19.4
THAT IT HEREAFTER MAY YOU NOT REPENT                  5.73.13
REPENTANCE          1
AND BY EXAMPLE, TRUE REPENTANCE PREACH              2.119.14
REPINING            1
YET WITH REPINING AT SO PARTIALL LOT                  4.2.8
REPLETE             2
OR SOME FIERCE THING REPLEAT WITH TOO MUCH RAGE       3.23.3
INCAPABLE OF MORE REPLEAT, WITH YOU                  3.113.13
REPLIES             1
YOU HAVE SPUNNE A FAIRE $THRED, HE REPLYES
                              IN SCORNE               2.59.12
REPLY               5
HOW FALS IT OUT SO STRANGELY YOU REPLY+               2.5.2
ANSWERE NO MORE, WITH $SILENCE MAKE REPLY             2.5.11
THAT BEING CHID, DID NEVER WORD REPLIE                2.15.10
FORTUNE ASSISTS THE BOLDEST, I REPLY                  2.59.7
O $DOCTOR $CUPID, THOU FOR ME REPLY                   4.61.12
REPLYETH            1
FAIRE WORDS MAKE $FOOLES, REPLYETH HE AGAINE          2.59.4
REPORT              8
BEARE NOT REPORT OF ANY SLENDER FIRE                  1.4.3
DEEPE IS THE WOUND MY SIGHES CAN WELL REPORT          1.14.6
IF EVER WONDER COULD REPORT A WONDER                  2.117.1
THEN WONDER, TONGUE, THEN JOY, MIGHT WEL
                              REPORT A WONDER          2.117.4
AS THOU BEING MINE, MINE IS THY GOOD REPORT           3.36.14
AND THEREFORE HAVE I SLEPT IN YOUR REPORT             3.83.5
NAMING THY NAME, BLESSES AN ILL REPORT                3.95.8
AS THOU BEING MINE, MINE IS THY GOOD REPORT           3.96.14
REPORTS             1
WHOSE DUE REPORTS GIVE HONOR TO HER EYES              1.57.8
REPOSE              2
THE DEARE REPOSE FOR LIMS WITH TRAVAILL TIRED         3.27.2
DOTH TEACH THAT EASE AND THAT REPOSE TO SAY           3.50.3
REPOSETH            1
WEAKE IS TH'ASSURANCE THAT WEAKE FLESH REPOSETH       5.58.1
REPREHEND           1
AND YET I CANNOT REPREHEND THE FLIGHT                 1.35.1
REPROACH            1
WHEN NOT TO BE, RECEIVES REPROACH OF BEING           3.121.2
REPROACHED          2
REASON REPROCHED WITH THIS COY $DISDAINE              2.38.9
```

```
    REASON REPROCHED WITH THIS COY DISDAINE          2.131.9
REPROVE                    1
    O LET NOT FOOLES IN ME THY WORKES REPROVE        4.107.13
REPROVING                  1
    AND THOU SHALT FINDE IT MERRITS NOT REPROOVING   3.142.4
REPULSE                    1
    SO FAYRE A PEECE FOR ONE REPULSE SO LIGHT        5.14.4
REQUEST                    1
    BUT FINDING $NATURE THEIR REQUEST DENYES         2.33.11
REQUIRE                    1
    NOR SERVICES TO DOE TIL YOU REQUIRE              3.57.4
REQUITE                    1
    AND SPEAKE HER GOOD, THOUGH SHE REQUITE IT ILL   5.48.14
RESEMBLE                   3
    THREE SORTS OF $SERPENTS DOE RESEMBLE THEE       2.130.1
    SUCH CHERUBINES AS YOUR SWEET SELFE RESEMBLE     3.114.6
    RESEMBLE TH'YMAGE OF THEIR GOODLY LIGHT          5.9.4
RESEMBLING                 4
    RESEMBLING STRONG YOUTH IN HIS MIDDLE AGE        3.7.6
    RESEMBLING SIER, AND CHILD, AND HAPPY MOTHER     3.8.11
    WHYLEST RAPT WITH JOY RESEMBLING HEAVENLY MADNES 5.39.9
    RESEMBLING HEAVENS GLORY IN HER LIGHT            5.72.6
RESERVE                    2
    RESERVE THEM FOR MY LOVE, NOT FOR THEIR RIME     3.32.7
    RESERVE THEIR $CHARACTER WITH GOULDEN QUILL      3.85.3
RESERVED                   1
    UNBURIED IN THESE LINES RESERV'D IN PURENES      1.44.10
RESIDENT                   2
    THESE WITH THE $GODS ARE EVER RESIDENT           2.18.7
    THESE WITH THE $GODS ARE EVER RESIDENT           2.108.7
RESIGN                     2
    YET MY SOULES SOVERAIGNE, SINCE I MUST RESIGNE   1.27.13
    THY $MOTHER DYD HER LYFE TO $DEATH RESIGNE       2.140.5
RESIGNED                   1
    LET $VENUS HAVE THY GRACES, HER RESIGN'D         1.19.9
RESIST                     1
    CURST BE THE NIGHT WHICH DID YOUR STRIFE RESIST  4.105.12
RESISTLESS                 1
    AS'T PLEASE THE $FATES, BY THEIR RESISTLESSE
                            FORCE                    2.51.4
RESOLUTE                   1
    THEY RESOLUTE+ SO STANDS THE CASE WITH ME        2.24.12
RESOLVE                    1
    I WILL RESOLVE YOU., I AM $LUNATICKE             2.9.5
RESOLVED                   1
    I AM RESOLV'D THY ERROUR TO MAINTAINE            4.67.13
RESORT                     3
    MY LAST $RESORT WHERETO MY HOPES APPEALE         1.22.2
    THOU MAKST FAULTS GRACES, THAT TO THEE RESORT    3.96.4
    THEY FIRST RESORT UNTO THAT SOUERAIGNE PART      4.107.4
RESOUNDED                  1
    WITH NOYSE WHEREOF THE QUYRE OF $BYRDS RESOUNDED 5.19.5
RESPECT                    6
    LADIES AND $TYRANTS, NEVER LAWES RESPECT         1.31.12
    TO SHOW ME WORTHY OF THEIR SWEET RESPECT         3.26.12
    IN OUR TWO LOVES THERE IS BUT ONE RESPECT        3.36.5
    THEN OTHERS, FOR THE BREATH OF WORDS RESPECT     3.85.13
    WHAT MERRIT DO I IN MY SELFE RESPECT             3.149.9
    ALL PAINES ARE NOTHING IN RESPECT OF THIS        5.63.13
```

```
RESPECTED                    1
  NOR YET THOSE HEAVENLY SECRETS ONCE RESPECTED        2.105.4
RESPECTS                     5
  AT HER PROUD FEETE, AND SHE RESPECTS NOT IT          1.24.6
  NO, NO, MY $VERSE RESPECTS NOT $THAMES
                    NOR $THEATERS                       1.58.9
  AND MY $RESPECTS AND $SERVICES TO YOU                2.27.11
  CAULD TO THAT AUDITE BY ADVIS'D RESPECTS             3.49.4
  THAT I RESPECTS FOR BOTH OUR SAKES MUST SHOW         4.33.11
RESPITE                      2
  SWEETE, FOR A WHILE GIVE RESPITE TO MY HART          4.107.5
  TO GRAUNT SMALL RESPIT TO MY RESTLESSE TOILE         5.11.6
REST                        37
  MY HOPES DOE REST IN LIMITS OF HER GRACE             1.12.7
  YET CANNOT FINDE HER BREATHE UNTO MY REST            1.13.11
  SHALL REST IN $ISE, WHEN THINE IS GRAV'D
                    IN $MARBLE                          1.44.8
  THEN HEERE HE RIOTS, YET AMONGST THE REST            2.10.7
  I GIVE $THEE BACKE, WHEN ALL THE REST IS SPENT       2.10.14
  NOR GIVES $ME ONCE, BUT ONE POORE MINUTES REST       2.20.4
  AMONGST THE REST OF $FOCLES AND $CHILDREN BE         2.22.4
  (THE $KING OF $SENCES, GREATER THEN THE REST)        2.29.10
  DEARE, WHY SHOULD YOU COMMAND ME TO MY $REST         2.37.1
  AND ONELY REST CONTENTED WITH THE $LIGHT             2.43.6
  THEN MORE I $TRAVELD, FURTHER FROM MY $REST          2.62.2
  I FEELE, YOU KNOW, THE HEAVENS CAN TELL
                    THE REST                            2.139.14
  THE MORE I TRAVELL, FURTHER FROM MY REST             2.150.2
  AND ALL THE REST FORGOT FOR WHICH HE TOILD           3.25.12
  THAT AM DEBARD THE BENIFIT OF REST+                  3.28.2
  MINE OWNE TRUE LOVE THAT DOTH MY REST DEFEAT         3.61.11
  DEATHS SECOND SELFE THAT SEALS UP ALL IN REST        3.73.8
  WHEREIN IT FINDES A JOY ABOVE THE REST               3.91.6
  CROWNING THE PRESENT, DOUBTING OF THE REST           3.115.12
  VERTUE ALAS, NOW LET ME TAKE SOME REST               4.4.1
  FOR THAT AT LENGTH YET DOTH INVITE SOME REST         4.96.13
  TO STEALE SOME REST, BUT WRETCH I AM CONSTRAIND      4.98.6
  BUT $ANGELS COME TO LEAD FRAILE MINDES TO REST       5.8.7
  THAT WITH THEYR TERROUR AL THE REST MAY CHACE        5.31.7
  ALL WERE IT AS THE REST BUT RUDELY WRIT              5.33.8
  CEASSE THEN, TILL SHE VOUCHSAFE TO GRAWNT
                    ME REST                             5.33.13
  BE LYKE IN MERCY AS IN ALL THE REST                  5.55.14
  MOST HAPPY SHE THAT MOST ASSURED DOTH REST           5.59.13
  THE JOYOUS SAFETY OF SO SWEET A REST                 5.63.10
  SITS DOWNE TO REST HIM IN SOME SHADY PLACE           5.67.3
  AND THERE TO REST THEMSELVES DID BOLDLY PLACE        5.76.12
  SWEET THOUGHTS I ENVY YOUR SO HAPPY REST             5.76.13
  FOR ALL THE REST, HOW EVER FAYRE IT BE               5.79.5
  GIVE LEAVE TO REST ME BEING HALFE FORDONNE           5.80.3
  THE REST BE WORKS OF NATURES WONDERMENT              5.81.13
  IN THIS AS IN THE REST, YE MOTE INVENT               5.82.6
  GOE VISIT HER IN HER CHAST BOWRE OF REST             5.84.7
RESTFUL                      1
  TYR'D WITH ALL THESE FOR RESTFULL DEATH I CRY        3.66.1
RESTING                      1
  FOR NEVER RESTING TIME LEADS $SUMMER ON              3.5.5
RESTLESS                     2
  BUT FINDING NOT THOSE RESTLESSE FLAMES IN ME         4.16.5
  TO GRAUNT SMALL RESPIT TO MY RESTLESSE TOILE         5.11.6
```

RESTORE   6
  RESTORE THY TRESSES TO THE GOLDEN $ORE   1.19.1
  RESTORE THY BLUSH UNTO $AURORA BRIGHT   1.19.7
  BUT YET RESTORE THY FIERCE AND CRUELL MIND   1.19.11
  RELIEVE MY LANGUISH, AND RESTORE THE LIGHT   1.54.3
  THEN $POYSON, AND WITH $PHYSIKE HIM RESTORE   2.50.9
  THOU WILT RESTORE TO BE MY COMFORT STILL   3.134.4
RESTORED   1
  ALL LOSSES ARE RESTORD, AND SORROWES END   3.30.14
RESTRAIN   2
  O, $WHY SHOULD $NATURE NIGGARDLY RESTRAINE   2.25.1
  HIS SAFE ASSURANCE, STRONGLY IT RESTRAYNE   5.42.12
RESTRAINT   1
  AND EKE MY TOUNG WITH PROUD RESTRAINT TO TIE+   5.43.6
RESTS   1
  BUT SINCE SHE WEIGHS THEM NOT, THIS RESTS FOR ME   1.59.9
RESTY   2
  RISE RESTY $MUSE, MY LOVES SWEET FACE SURVAY   3.100.9
  AND NO SPURRE CAN HIS RESTY RACE RENEW   4.80.12
RESURVEY   1
  AND SHALT BY FORTUNE ONCE MORE RE-SURVAY   3.32.3
RETAIN   2
  THAT WHAT $THEY GET, $THEY EVER DOE RETAINE   2.52.4
  THAT $WE ONE JOT OF FORMER $LOVE RETEYNE   2.61.8
RETAINED   1
  IF HUNGER-STARVEN THOUGHTS SO LONG RETAINED   1.15.3
RETAINING   1
  RETAYNING $KNOWLEDGE, STILL THE SAME IN KIND   2.12.7
RETEERE   1
  TILL $VIRGINS SMYLES DOE SOUND HIS SWEET RETEERE   2.147.8
RETENTION   1
  THAT POORE RETENTION COULD NOT SO MUCH HOLD   3.122.9
RETIRE   1
  HER THUNDER OF DISDAINE FORST ME RETIRE   1.36.4
RETIRES   1
  ANOTHER HUMBLER WIT TO SHEPHEARD'S PIPE RETIRES   4.6.7
RETRAIT   1
  BEST CHARGE, AND BRAVEST RETRAIT IN $CUPID'S
                FIGHT   4.79.5
RETURN   12
  WHEN SHALL MY INTERDICTED HOPES RETURNE   1.49.3
  WITH DARKE FORGETTING OF MY CARE RETURNE   1.54.4
  HOW CAN I THEN RETURNE IN HAPPY PLIGHT   3.28.1
  TILL I RETURNE OF POSTING IS NOE NEED   3.51.4
  RETURNE OF LOVE, MORE BLEST MAY BE THE VIEW   3.56.12
  RETURNE FORGETFULL $MUSE, AND STRAIGHT REDEEME   3.100.5
  LIKE HIM THAT TRAVELS I RETURNE AGAINE   3.109.6
  SO I RETURNE REBUKT TO MY CONTENT   3.119.13
  WHAT SO IS FAYREST SHALL TO EARTH RETURNE   5.13.8
  RETOURNE AGAYNE MY FORCES LATE DISMAYD   5.14.1
  THEY YDLY BACK RETURNE TO ME AGAYNE   5.78.10
  FOR HIS RETURNE THAT SEEMES TO LINGER LATE   5.89.4
RETURNED   3
  TILL THEY RETURN'D.. $HOME WHEN THEY NEVER CAME   2.58.6
  BY THOSE SWIFT MESSENGERS RETURN'D FROM THEE   3.45.10
  THE GENTLE DEARE RETURND THE SELFE-SAME WAY   5.67.7
RETURNING   1
  RETURNING THEE THE TRIBUTE OF MY DUTIE   1.1.3
RETURNS   3
  THUS SHE RETURNES MY HOPES SO FRUITLESSE EVER   1.24.13

```
YET AT THIS PRICE RETURNES ME TREBLE GAINE          2.28.8
AND EACH RETURNES UNTO HIS $LOVE AT $NIGHT+          2.37.8
REVEAL                4
  WHICH HERE MY LOVE, MY YOUTH, MY PLAINTS REVEALE   1.1.4
  YET NO MILD COMFORT WOULD THY $BROW REVEALE        1.31.9
  REVEALE THE TREASURE WHICH HER SMILES IMPART+      1.49.6
  THEN MY LYFES $LEACH DOE YOU YOUR SKILL REVEALE    5.50.13
REVENGE                6
  THEN WITH UNKINDNES, $LOVE REVENGE THY WRONG       2.139.5
  O SWEET'ST REVENGE THAT ERE THE HEAVENS GAVE       2.139.6
  MY HALFE-SLAINE HART SHALL TAKE REVENGE ON THEE    2.140.4
  RECORDER OF REVENGE, REMEMBRANCER OF CARE          2.145.7
  REVENGE UPON MY SELFE WITH PRESENT MONE+           3.149.8
  HIS $SIRE'S REVENGE, JOYN'D WITH A KINGDOME'S
                                        GAINE        4.75.6
REVENGEFUL                 1
  FOR WHICH THE GODS IN THEYR REVENGEFULL YRE        5.28.11
REVENUES                   1
  ROBD OTHERS BEDS REVENUES OF THEIR RENTS           3.142.8
REVERENCE                  1
  ARE HUMBLED THOUGHTS, WHICH BIT OF $REVERENCE
                                        MOVE         4.49.6
REVIEW                     1
  WHEN THOU REVEWEST THIS, THOU DOEST REVEW          3.74.5
REVIEWEST                  1
  WHEN THOU REVEWEST THIS, THOU DOEST REVEW          3.74.5
REVIVE                     1
  NO $APRILL CAN REVIVE THY WITHERED FLOWRES         1.39.9
REVIVED                    3
  MY $HOPES REVIV'D, WHICH LONG IN $GRAVE HAD LYNE   2.35.12
  MY HOPES REVIV'D WHICH LONG IN GRAVE HAD LYNE      2.112.12
  AND ME REVIVED WITH HART ROBBING GLADNESSE         5.39.8
REVIVETH                   1
  AND MY STRONG SIGHES, THE AYRES WEAKE
                          FORCE REVIVETH             2.127.3
REVIVING                   4
  BUT WITH THOSE $DROPS, THE $FLAME AGAINE
                          REVIVING                   2.40.11
  SUNNE OF THE WORLD, THOU HART REVYVING FIRE        2.123.8
  YET OTHERS FORCE, THE OTHERS FORCE REVIVING        2.136.12
  BUT WITH THOSE DROPS THE COLES AGAINE REVYVING     2.144.11
REVOLT                     1
  SINCE THAT MY LIFE ON THY REVOLT DOTH LIE          3.92.10
REVOLUTION                 1
  OR WHETHER REVOLUTION BE THE SAME                  3.59.12
REWARD                6
  FORGING A GRIEFE TO WINNE A FAMES REWARD           1.4.4
  SEE WHAT REWARD HE HATH THAT SERVES THE
                               UNGRATEFULL           1.18.7
  OR CAN I THINKE WHAT MY $REWARD SHALL BE           2.52.11
  WHICH FOR REWARD SPOILE IT WITH VAINE ANNOYES      4.18.11
  IS SAWCINESSE REWARD OF CURTESIE+                  4.83.10
  SHAME BE THY MEED, AND MISCHIEFE THY REWARD        5.86.13
REWARDED                   1
  SO RARE A FAITH OUGHT BETTER BE REWARDED           1.11.8
REWARDING                  1
  SLEEPE WITH DELIGHT, $BEAUTY WITH LOVE REWARDING   2.136.8
RHENE                      1
  ELSE SHOULD MY $LINES GLIDE ON THE $WAVES
                          OF $RHENE                  2.25.3
```

RHETORIC   1
  WHAT STRAINED TOUCHES $RHETHORICK CAN LEND   3.82.10
RHUBARB   1
  BUT WITH YOUR $RUBARB WORDS YOW MUST CONTEND   4.14.5
RHYME   9
  HE NEVER HAD MORE FAITH, ALTHOUGH MORE RIME   1.43.7
  SOME, WHEN IN $RYME, THEY OF THEIR $LOVES
                  DOE TELL   2.39.1
  SOME WHEN IN RYME THEY OF THEIR $LOVES DOE TELL   2.118.1
  WITH MEANES MORE BLESSED THEN MY BARREN RIME+   3.16.4
  YOU SHOULD LIVE TWISE IN IT, AND IN MY RIME   3.17.14
  RESERVE THEM FOR MY LOVE, NOT FOR THEIR RIME   3.32.7
  OF $PRINCES SHALL CUT-LIVE THIS POWREFULL RIME   3.55.2
  AND BEAUTIE MAKING BEAUTIFULL OLD RIME   3.106.3
  SINCE SPIGHT OF HIM $ILE LIVE IN THIS
              POORE RIME   3.107.11
RHYMERS   1
  THEN THOSE OLD NINE WHICH RIMERS INVOCATE   3.38.10
RHYMES   7
  VIRGINS AND $MATRONS READING THESE MY $RIMES   2.6.9
  PROUDLY THOU SCORN'ST MY $WORLD-OUT-WEARING
              $RIMES   2.44.7
  ENSUING $AGES YET MY $RIMES SHALL CHERISH   2.44.11
  INTO YOUR RIMES, RUNNING IN RATLING ROWES   4.15.6
  IF STILL I FORCE HER IN SAD RIMES TO CREEPE   4.70.2
  AND HAPPY RYMES BATH'D IN THE SACRED BROOKE   5.1.9
  LEAVES, LINES, AND RYMES, SEEKE HER TO
              PLEASE ALONE   5.1.13
RIBS   2
  WHICH FROM THE RIBS OF OLD $PARNASSUS FLOWES   4.15.2
  FROM OUT MY RIBS, AND PUFFING PROVE THAT I   4.104.13
RICH   30
  BUT $AVON RICH IN FAME, THOUGH POORE IN WATERS   1.58.11
  THEN TO THE $SONNE OF SOME RICH $PENNY-FATHER   2.10.2
  THIS NEW RICH $NOVICE, LAVISH OF HIS CHEST   2.10.5
  TOO RICH A $RELIQUE FOR SO POORE A $SHRINE   2.57.4
  WITH THOSE RICH $BEAUTIES $HEAV'N GIVES
              YOU TO KEEPE   2.58.12
  SETS YOU MOST RICH IN YOUTH BEFORE MY SIGHT   3.15.10
  WITH $SUNNE AND $MOONE, WITH EARTH AND
              SEAS RICH GEMS   3.21.6
  WISHING ME LIKE TO ONE MORE RICH IN HOPE   3.29.5
  AND THEY ARE RITCH, AND RANSOME ALL ILL DEEDS   3.34.14
  SO AM I AS THE RICH WHOSE BLESSED KEY   3.52.1
  THE RICH PROUD COST OF OUTWORNE BURIED AGE   3.64.2
  THEN THIS RICH PRAISE, THAT YOU ALONE, ARE YOU 3.84.2
  THE TEEMING $AUTUMNE BIG WITH RITCH INCREASE   3.97.6
  THAT LOVE IS MARCHANDIZ'D, WHOSE RITCH ESTEEMING 3.102.3
  SO THOU BEEING RICH IN $WILL ADDE TO THY $WILL 3.135.11
  WITHIN BE FED, WITHOUT BE RICH NO MORE   3.146.12
  WHOSE PORCHES RICH (WHICH NAME OF CHEEKES ENDURE) 4.9.7
  RICH FOOLES THERE BE, WHOSE BASE AND FILTHY HART 4.24.1
  BUT THAT RICH FOOLE, WHO BY BLIND $FORTUNE'S LOT 4.24.9
  HE KNOWES NOT) GROW IN ONLY FOLLIE RICH   4.24.14
  DOTH EVEN GROW RICH, NAMING MY STELLA'S NAME 4.35.11
  RICH IN ALL BEAUTIES WHICH MAN'S EYE CAN SEE   4.37.6
  RICH IN THE TREASURE OF DESERV'D RENOWNE   4.37.9
  RICH IN THE RICHES OF A ROYALL HART   4.37.10
  RICH IN THOSE GIFTS WHICH GIVE TH'ETERNALL
              CROWNE   4.37.11

```
WHO THOUGH MOST RICH IN THESE AND EVERIE PART        4.37.12
HATH NO MISFORTUNE, BUT THAT $RICH SHE IS            4.37.14
MOST RICH, WHEN MOST HIS RICHES IT IMPART            4.79.7
NE NONE SO RICH OR WISE, SO STRONG OR FAYRE          5.58.9
FAYRE WHEN HER BREST LYKE A RICH LADEN BARKE         5.81.5
RICHER                       1
RICHER THEN WEALTH, PROUDER THEN GARMENTS COST       3.91.10
RICHES                       7
AND FOR THAT RITCHES WHERE IS MY DESERVING+          3.87.6
AND HUSBAND NATURES RITCHES FROM EXPENCE             3.94.6
RICH IN THE RICHES OF A ROYALL HART                  4.37.10
COPARTNER OF THE RICHES OF THAT SIGHT                4.48.6
MOST RICH, WHEN MOST HIS RICHES IT IMPART            4.79.7
ALL THIS WORLDS RICHES THAT MAY FARRE BE FOUND       5.15.6
THAT HONOUR AND LARGE RICHESSE TO ME LENT            5.74.8
RICHEST                      3
O RICHEST $CASKET OF ALL HEAVENLY TREASURE           2.146.11
THE RICHEST GEMME OF $LOVE AND LIFE ENJOYES          4.24.10
FAYRE BOSOME FRAUGHT WITH VERTUES RICHEST TRESURE    5.76.1
RICHLY                       4
WHILE COMMENTS OF YOUR PRAISE RICHLY COMPIL'D        3.85.2
IN WHOSE COTE ARMOUR RICHLY ARE DISPLAYD             5.70.2
HER BREST THAT TABLE WAS SO RICHLY SPREDD            5.77.13
THE GATE WITH PEARLES AND RUBYES RICHLY DIGHT        5.81.10
RID                          1
KILL ME OUT-RIGHT WITH LOOKES, AND RID MY PAINE      3.139.14
RIDDLE                       1
FOR OF MY LIFE I MUST A RIDDLE TELL                  4.37.4
RIDE                         4
ANON PERMIT THE BASEST CLOUDES TO RIDE               3.33.5
WHILST HE UPON YOUR SOUNDLESSE DEEPE DOTH RIDE       3.80.10
BE ANCHORD IN THE BAYE WHERE ALL MEN RIDE            3.137.6
IN HIGHEST WAY OF HEAV'N THE $SUNNE DID RIDE         4.22.1
RIDER                        2
HIS RIDER LOV'D NOT SPEED BEING MADE FROM THEE       3.50.8
THE RAINES WHEREWITH MY $RIDER DOTH ME TIE           4.49.5
RIGHT                       29
WAS NOT TO DISPOSSESSE HER OF HER RIGHT              1.36.10
THAT HAND THAT DARTS SO *RIGHT AND NEVER MISSES      1.46.10
IN $RIGHT OR $WRONG, THEY CALL HER $CONSCIENCE       2.12.11
THYS, PURE $IDEA, VERTUES RIGHT $IDEA                2.119.9
YET SEE HOW RIGHT HE COMES UNTO MY FAYRE             2.135.4
THE PERFECT CEREMONY OF LOVES RIGHT                  3.23.6
MY HEART, MINE EYE THE FREEEDOME OF THAT RIGHT       3.46.4
AND MY HEARTS RIGHT, THEIR INWARD LOVE OF HEART      3.46.14
AND RIGHT PERFECTION WRONGFULLY DISGRAC'D            3.66.7
THE RIGHT OF SEPULCHERS, WERE SHORNE AWAY            3.68.6
THAT FOR THY RIGHT, MY SELFE WILL BEARE
                        ALL WRONG                    3.88.14
THAT MY STEEL'D SENCE OR CHANGES RIGHT OR WRONG      3.112.8
AND GIVEN TO TIME YOUR OWNE DEARE PURCHAS'D
                        RIGHT                        3.117.6
SHALL WILL IN OTHERS SEEME RIGHT GRACIOUS            3.135.7
IN THINGS RIGHT TRUE MY HEART AND EYES
                        HAVE ERRED                   3.137.13
THE BETTER ANGELL IS A MAN RIGHT FAIRE               3.144.3
I NOW HAVE LEARN'D $LOVE RIGHT, AND LEARN'D
                        EVEN SO                      4.16.13
YOUR WORDS MY FRIEND (RIGHT HEALTHFULL
                        CAUSTIKS) BLAME              4.21.1
```

```
HOW $POLES' RIGHT KING MEANES, WITHOUT
                        LEAVE OF HOAST          4.30.3
HART RENT THY SELFE, THOU DOEST THY SELFE
                        BUT RIGHT              4.33.5
AND IF THESE THINGS, AS BEING THINE BY RIGHT   4.39.12
AND NOW HATH MADE ME TO HIS HAND SO RIGHT      4.49.13
THAT HIS RIGHT BADGE IS BUT WORNE IN THE HART  4.54.12
WHICH, COUPLING $DOVES, GUIDES $VENUS'
                        CHARIOT RIGHT          4.79.4
THY TEARES EXPRESSE NIGHT'S NATIVE MOISTURE RIGHT  4.96.8
I WOULD KNOW BY WHAT RIGHT THIS PALENESSE
                        OVERCAME               4.102.7
STELLA SINCE THOU SO RIGHT A $PRINCESSE ART    4.107.1
RIGHT SO MY CRUELL FAYRE WITH ME DOTH PLAY     5.53.5
RIGHT SO YOUR SELFE WERE CAUGHT IN CUNNING SNARE  5.71.5
RIGHTLY               2
AND RIGHTLY CAME FROM THAT BRAVE MOUNTING $BROOD  2.56.8
THEY RIGHTLY DO INHERRIT HEAVENS GRACES        3.94.5
RIGHTS                1
AND YOUR TRUE RIGHTS BE TERMD A $POETS RAGE    3.17.11
RIGOR                 3
THY RIGOR IN THAT $SANCTUARY SLEW              1.31.3
THE WORKE OF RIGOR, FATALLY BEGUN              1.33.7
THOU CANST NOT THEN USE RIGOR IN MY $JAILE     3.133.12
RIGOROUS              2
WHERE RIGROWS EXILE LOCKES UP ALL MY SENSE+    4.104.8
WHO ME CAPTIVING STREIGHT WITH RIGOROUS WRONG  5.12.11
RIND                  2
HER SOULE, ARM'D BUT WITH SUCH A DAINTY RIND   4.57.7
SWEET IS THE $CYPRESSE, BUT HIS RYND IS TOUGH  5.26.5
RIOT                  1
WHO LEAD THEE IN THEIR RYOT EVEN THERE         3.41.11
RIOTS                 1
THEN HEERE HE RIOTS, YET AMONGST THE REST      2.10.7
RIPE                  1
THAT DID MY RIPE THOUGHTS IN MY BRAINE INHEARCE  3.86.3
RIPER                 2
BUT AS THE RIPER SHOULD BY TIME DECEASE        3.1.3
AND STOPS HIS PIPE IN GROWTH OF RIPER DAIES    3.102.8
RISE                  12
LIE DOWNE TO WAILE, RISE UP TO SIGH AND GRIEVE  1.9.6
WILL RISE NO MORE TO ME, WHOSE DAY IS DUNNE    1.30.4
THERE DO THESE SMOAKES THAT FROM AFFLICTION RISE  1.47.9
THAT NEVER FALL TO EBBE, BUT EVER RISE         1.48.3
THE RECK'NINGS RISE TO MILLIONS OF $DESPAIRES  2.3.4
AND STYLL IN RECKONINGS RISE MORE MILLIONS
                        OF DISPAYRES           2.110.4
RISE RESTY $MUSE, MY LOVES SWEET FACE SURVAY   3.100.9
HER LOVE, FOR WHOSE DEARE LOVE I RISE AND FALL  3.151.14
THAT HER SWEETE BREATH MAKES OFT THY FLAMES
                        TO RISE                4.12.4
WHENCE THOSE SAME FUMES OF MELANCHOLY RISE     4.23.3
HIS PRAISE TO SLEIGHT, WHICH FROM GOOD
                        USE DOTH RISE          4.41.7
O HONIED SIGHS, WHICH FROM THAT BREAST DO RISE  4.100.5
RISING                7
AND WHILST THOU SPREADST UNTO THE RISING SUNNE  1.40.5
NEVER LET RISING $SUNNE APPROVE YOU LIERS      1.54.11
SO $FAIRE A RISING, HAD SO $FOULE A SET        2.60.12
PINED WITH $HUNGER, RISING FROM A $FEAST       2.62.4
```

```
   PYNED WITH HUNGER, RYSING FROM A FEAST           2.150.4
   BUT RYSING AT THY NAME DOTH POINT OUT THEE       3.151.9
   AND YET COULD NOT BY RISING $MORNE FORESEE       4.33.12
RITES               1
   POORE $LAYMAN I, FOR SACRED RITES UNFIT          4.74.4
RIVER               1
   RUNNES THIS POORE $RIVER, CHARG'D WITH
                         STREAMES OF ZEALE          1.1.2
ROB                 2
   ROB HER FAIRE $BROW, BREAKE IN ON $BEAUTY, STEALE  1.22.5
   THE CHARMING SMILES, THAT ROB SENCE FROM
                         THE HART                   5.17.10
ROBBED              4
   OF ALL THINE HONOUR SHEE HATH ROBBED THEE        2.126.4
   YET HAPPY HE THATS ROBD OF SUCH A THIEFE         2.126.14
   ROBD OTHERS BEDS REVENUES OF THEIR RENTS         3.142.8
   NO FORCE, NO FRAUD, ROBD THEE OF THY DELIGHT     4.33.7
ROBBERY             2
   I DOE FORGIVE THY ROBB'RIE GENTLE THEEFE         3.40.9
   AND TO HIS ROBBRY HAD ANNEXT THY BREATH          3.99.11
ROBBING             2
   ROBBING NO OULD TO DRESSE HIS BEAUTY NEW         3.68.12
   AND ME REVIVED WITH HART ROBBING GLADNESSE       5.39.8
ROBE                1
   OR AS THE WARD-ROBE WHICH THE ROBE DOTH HIDE      3.52.10
ROBS                2
   TO THAT SWEET THEEFE WHICH SOURELY ROBS FROM ME  3.35.14
   HE ROBS THEE OF, AND PAYES IT THEE AGAINE        3.79.8
ROCK                2
   YET NOUGHT THE ROCKE OF THAT HARD HEART CAN MOVE  1.48.9
   AS IS A ROCKE AMIDST THE RAGING FLOODS           5.56.10
ROCKS               2
   AND ON WHAT $ROCKS IN PERILL TO BE CAST+         2.1.12
   WHEN ROCKS IMPREGNABLE ARE NOT SO STOUTE         3.65.7
ROD                 1
   WHEN FOR SO SOFT A ROD DEARE PLAY HE TRIE+       4.73.4
ROGUE               2
   POORE $ROGUE, GOE PAWNE THY $FASCIA AND THY $BOW  2.48.3
   HER FACE+ $O $LOVE, A $ROGUE THOU THEN
                         SHOULDST BE                4.46.6
ROLL                2
   WITH $SISIPHUS THUS DOE I ROLE THE STONE         2.40.13
   WITH $SISIPHUS THUS DOE I ROLE THE STONE         2.144.13
ROLLING             3
   WHOSE ROWLING GRACE DEIGNE ONCE A TURNE OF BLIS  1.12.12
   AN EYE MORE BRIGHT THEN THEIRS, LESSE
                         FALSE IN ROWLING           3.20.5
   THE ROLLING WHEELE THAT RUNNETH OFTEN ROUND      5.18.1
ROMAN               1
   AS TO THE $ROMAN THAT WOULD FREE HIS $LAND       1.56.1
ROME                1
   FROM ALL THE WORLD, HER HEART IS THEN HIS ROME   4.43.13
RONDURE             1
   THAT HEAVENS AYRE IN THIS HUGE RONDURE HEMS      3.21.8
ROOF                1
   SEEKING THAT BEAUTIOUS ROOFE TO RUINATE          3.10.7
ROOM                3
   YET THIS LARGE $ROOME IS BOUNDED WITH $DESPAIRE  2.26.9
   YET THYS LARGE ROOME IS BOUNDED WITH DYSPAIRE    2.137.9
   SHALL YOU PACE FORTH, YOUR PRAISE SHALL
                         STIL FINDE ROOME           3.55.10
```

ROOT   4
    BUT SINCE THE SWEETEST ROOTE YEELDS FRUITE
                          SO SOWRE   1.26.9
    AND BROILES ROOTE CUT THE WORKE OF MASONRY   3.55.6
    ROOTE PITTIE IN THY HEART THAT WHEN IT GROWES   3.142.11
    AND SWEET IS $MOLY, BUT HIS ROOT IS ILL   5.26.8
ROSE   12
    LOOKE $DELIA HOW W'ESTEEME THE HALFE BLOWNE $ROSE   1.39.1
    SHORT IS THE GLORY OF THE BLUSHING $ROSE   1.50.6
    THAT THEREBY BEAUTIES $ROSE MIGHT NEVER DIE   3.1.2
    THE $ROSE LOOKES FAIRE, BUT FAIRER WE IT DEEME   3.54.3
    $ROSES OF SHADDOW, SINCE HIS $ROSE IS TRUE+   3.67.8
    WHICH LIKE A CANKER IN THE FRAGRANT $ROSE   3.95.2
    NOR PRAISE THE DEEPE VERMILLION IN THE $ROSE   3.98.10
    SAVE THOU MY $ROSE, IN IT THOU ART MY ALL   3.109.14
    MILKE HANDS, ROSE CHEEKS, OR LIPS MORE
                          SWEET, MORE RED   4.91.7
    MORNE'S MESSENGER, WITH ROSE ENAMELD SKIES   4.99.10
    SWEET IS THE $ROSE, BUT GROWES UPON A BRERE   5.26.1
    FAYRE WHEN THE ROSE IN HER RED CHEEKES APPEARES   5.81.3
ROSES   13
    SO FADE THE $ROSES OF THOSE CHEEKS OF THINE   1.39.8
    THY $CHEEKE, NOW FLUSH WITH $ROSES, SUNKE,
                          AND LEANE   2.8.9
    ROSES HAVE THORNES, AND SILVER FOUNTAINES MUD   3.35.2
    AS THE PERFUMED TINCTURE OF THE $ROSES   3.54.6
    DIE TO THEMSELVES. $SWEET $ROSES DOE NOT SO   3.54.11
    $ROSES OF SHADDOW, SINCE HIS $ROSE IS TRUE+   3.67.8
    THE $ROSES FEAREFULLY ON THORNES DID STAND   3.99.8
    I HAVE SEENE $ROSES DAMASKT, RED AND WHITE   3.130.5
    BUT NO SUCH $ROSES SEE I IN HER CHEEKES   3.130.6
    WHERE ROSES GUEULS ARE BORNE IN SILVER FIELD   4.13.11
    MAKING THOSE $LILLIES AND THOSE $ROSES GROW   4.100.2
    WHERE BE THOSE $ROSES GONE, WHICH SWEETNED
                          SO OUR EYES+   4.102.1
    HER RUDDY CHEEKES LYKE UNTO $ROSES RED   5.64.6
ROSY   3
    LOV'S NOT $TIMES FOOLE, THOUGH ROSIE LIPS
                          AND CHEEKS   3.116.9
    A ROSIE GARLAND, AND A WEARIE HED   4.39.11
    WITH SUCH A ROSIE MORNE, WHOSE BEAMES
                          MOST FRESHLY GAY   4.76.7
ROTTEN   2
    HIDING THY BRAV'RY IN THEIR ROTTEN SMOKE   3.34.4
    OR YOU SURVIVE WHEN I IN EARTH AM ROTTEN   3.81.2
ROUGH   2
    ROUGH WINDES DO SHAKE THE DARLING BUDS OF $MAIE   3.18.3
    SWEET IS THE FIRBLOOME, BUT HIS BRAUNCHES ROUGH   5.26.4
ROUND   6
    CIRCUMPASS'D ROUND WITH FILTH AND LOTHSOME MUD   1.29.2
    'MONGST ALL THE $CREATURES IN THIS SPACIOUS
                          $ROUND   2.16.1
    WHEN THE PROUD $ROUND ON EV'RY SIDE HATH RUNG   2.47.10
    IF $PEARLES, HIR TEETH BE PEARLES BOTH
                          PURE AND ROUND   5.15.9
    THE ROLLING WHEELE THAT RUNNETH OFTEN ROUND   5.18.1
    THROUGH HIDDEN PERILS ROUND ABOUT ME PLAST   5.34.8
ROUSED   1
    ROUZ'D FROM MY BREAST, HIS SURE AND SAFEST LAYRE   2.135.2

```
ROWS                        1
   INTO YOUR RIMES, RUNNING IN RATLING ROWES              4.15.6
ROYAL                       2
   YET HIDING ROYALL BLOUD FULL OFT IN RURALL VAINE        4.6.8
   RICH IN THE RICHES CF A ROYALL HART                     4.37.10
ROYALTY                     1
   THE GREATEST $PRINCE WITH POMPOUS ROIALTY+              5.77.4
RUBIES                      4
   WHENCE HAST THOU $IVORIE, $RUBIES, PEARLE
                                AND GOLD                   4.32.10
   IF $RUBIES, LOE HIR LIPS BE $RUBIES SOUND               5.15.8
   IF $RUBIES, LOE HIR LIPS BE $RUBIES SOUND               5.15.8
   THE GATE WITH PEARLES AND RUBYES RICHLY DIGHT           5.81.10
RUDDY                       2
   O KISSE, WHICH DOEST THCSE RUDDIE GEMMES IMPART         4.81.1
   HER RUDDY CHEEKES LYKE UNTO $ROSES RED                  5.64.6
RUDE                        7
   HARSH, FEATURELESSE, AND RUDE, BARRENLY PERRISH         3.11.10
   THESE POORE RUDE LINES CF THY DECEASED $LOVER           3.32.4
   AS HIGH AS LEARNING, MY RUDE IGNORANCE                  3.78.14
   SAVAGE, EXTREAME, RUDE, CRUELL, NOT TO TRUST            3.129.4
   NOT BY RUDE FORCE, BUT SWEETEST SOVERAIGNTIE            4.71.6
   MOST RUDE DISPAIRE MY DAILY UNBIDDEN GUEST              4.108.7
   BUT MY RUDE MUSICK, WHICH WAS WONT TO PLEASE            5.38.5
RUDELY                      3
   AND MAIDEN VERTUE RUDELY STRUMPETED                     3.66.6
   RUDELY THOU WRONGEST MY DEARE HARTS DESIRE              5.5.1
   ALL WERE IT AS THE REST BUT RUDELY WRIT                 5.33.8
RUDEST                      2
   FOR IF IT SEE THE RUD'ST OR GENTLEST SIGHT              3.113.9
   PRINTS HIS OWNE LIVELY FCRME IN RUDEST BRAINE           4.58.8
RUE                         1
   BUT THEN THE MORE YCUR CWNE MISHAP I REW                5.82.3
RUES                        1
   DELIGHTS NOT IN MY MERTH NOR RUES MY SMART              5.54.10
RUFFIN'S                    1
   STRAIGHTWAYES HE PLAY'S A SWAGG'RING $RUFFINS
                                PART                       2.7.10
RUGGEDEST                   1
   BUT WHEN THE RUGGEDST STEP OF $FORTUNE'S RACE           4.60.5
RUIN                        4
   RUINE HATH TAUGHT ME THUS TO RUMINATE                   3.64.11
   OF SINFULL THOUGHTS, WHICH DO IN RUINE END+             4.14.8
   OF $LOVER'S RUINE SCME SAD $TRAGEDIE                    4.45.13
   WHOM YE DOE WRECK, DOE RUINE, AND DESTROY               5.56.14
RUINATE                     2
   SEEKING THAT BEAUTICUS RCOFE TO RUINATE                 3.10.7
   BEATS ON IT STRONGLY IT TO RUINATE                      5.56.8
RUINED                      2
   BARE RN'WD QUIERS, WHERE LATE THE SWEET
                                BIRDS SANG                 3.73.4
   AND RUIN'D LOVE WHEN IT IS BUILT ANEW                   3.119.11
RUINING                     1
   WHICH PROVES MORE SHORT THEN WAST OR RUINING+           3.125.4
RUINS                       2
   THUS RUINES SHE (TO SATISFIE HER WILL)                  1.47.13
   THE RUINES OF HER CCNQUEST TO ESPIE                     4.67.3
RULE                        4
   THE NEVER-RESTING STONE CF $CARE TO ROULE               1.9.7
   STARRES SURE THEY ARE, WHOSE MOTIONS RULE DESIRES       1.34.5
```

```
          WHOSE INFLUENCE RULE THE $ORBE OF MY POORE HART+      1.34.10
          ONE HAND FORGOTT TO RULE, TH'OTHER TO FIGHT           4.53.11
RULES                        6
          AGE RULES MY $LINES WITH $WRINKLES IN MY $FACE         2.44.2
          OUGHT TO BE KING, FROM WHOSE RULES WHO DO SWERVE       4.5.3
          AND IF THESE RULES DID FAILE, PROOFE MAKES
                                          ME SURE                4.26.12
          RULES WITH A BECKE, SO TYRANNIZETH THEE                4.46.3
          O $GRAMMER RULES, O NOW YOUR VERTUES SHOW              4.63.1
          AND RULES THE MEMBERS AS IT SELFE DOTH PLEASE+         5.50.8
RULEST                       1
          THOU POWRE THAT RUL'ST THE CONFINES OF THE NIGHT      1.10.5
RUMINATE                     1
          RUINE HATH TAUGHT ME THUS TO RUMINATE                 3.64.11
RUMOR                        1
          THEY DEEME, AND OF THEIR DOOME THE RUMOUR FLIES       4.27.5
RUN                         11
          MY CEASLES CARES CONTINUALLY RUN ON                   1.33.2
          BUT SEE, FOR YOU TO $HEAV'N FOR $PHRAZE I RUNNE        2.21.11
          HOW $THINGS STILL UNEXPECTEDLY HAVE RUNNE             2.51.3
          TOWARDS THEE ILE RUN, AND GIVE HIM LEAVE TO GOE        3.51.14
          I WILLING RUN, YET WHILE I RUN, REPENT                4.19.4
          I WILLING RUN, YET WHILE I RUN, REPENT                4.19.4
          O GIVE MY PASSIONS LEAVE TO RUN THEIR RACE            4.64.2
          FROM MY DEARE $CAPTAINNESSE TO RUN AWAY+              4.88.2
          AS $MARS IN THREE SCORE YEARES DOTH RUN
                                          HIS SPHEARE            5.60.4
          THE WEARY YEARE HIS RACE NOW HAVING RUN               5.62.1
          AFTER SO LONG A RACE AS I HAVE RUN                    5.80.1
RUNG                         1
          WHEN THE PROUD $ROUND ON EV'RY SIDE HATH RUNG         2.47.10
RUNNEST                      1
          SO RUNST THOU AFTER THAT WHICH FLIES FROM THEE        3.143.9
RUNNETH                      1
          THE ROLLING WHEELE THAT RUNNETH OFTEN ROUND           5.18.1
RUNNING                      2
          AND $IDEOTS STILL ARE RUNNING AFTER $BOYES            2.22.7
          INTO YOUR RIMES, RUNNING IN RATLING ROWES             4.15.6
RUNS                         4
          RUNNES THIS POORE $RIVER, CHARG'D WITH
                                  STREAMES OF ZEALE             1.1.2
          AND SAY MY VERSE RUNNES IN A LOFTY VAYNE              2.128.2
          LOE AS A CAREFULL HUSWIFE RUNNES TO CATCH             3.143.1
          AS THY LOOKES STURRE, RUNS UP AND DOWNE TO MAKE       4.101.10
RURAL                        1
          YET HIDING ROYALL BLOUD FULL OFT IN RURALL VAINE       4.6.8
RUST                         2
          METALS DOE WASTE, AND FRET WITH $CANKERS $RUST        2.13.2
          METTLES DOE WASTE, AND FRET WITH CANKERS RUST         2.121.2
RUSTIC                       1
          TO SOME BASE $RUSTICK DOE THY SELFE PREFERRE          2.48.6
RUTH                         3
          LOOKING WITH PRETTY RUTH UPON MY PAINE                3.132.4
          NE WILBE MOOV'D WITH REASON OR WITH REWTH             5.11.5
          PLAYNTS, PRAYERS, VOWES, RUTH, SORROW,
                                          AND DISMAY             5.14.11
RUTHLESS                     3
          TO $HYRCAN $TYGRES, AND TO RUTHLES $BEARES             1.19.12
          SITH I LIVE HATEFULL TO THOSE RUTHLESSE EIES          1.21.7
          OR SHALL THEIR RUTHLESSE TORMENT NEVER CEASE          5.36.2
```

```
I SEND THEM BACK AGAINE AND STRAIGHT GROW SAD        3.45.14
LET THIS SAD $INTRIM LIKE THE $OCEAN BE              3.56.9
BUT LIKE A SAD SLAVE STAY AND THINKE OF NOUGHT       3.57.11
BUT SAD MORTALLITY ORE-SWAIES THEIR POWER            3.65.2
AND THE SAD $AUGURS MOCK THEIR OWNE PRESAGE          3.107.6
AND THETHER HIED A SAD DISTEMPERD GUEST              3.153.12
WITH HOW SAD STEPS, O $MOONE, THOU CLIMB'ST
                                 THE SKIES           4.31.1
OF $LOVER'S RUINE SOME SAD $TRAGEDIE                 4.45.13
WITH SAD EYES I THEIR WEAKE PROPORTION SEE           4.50.7
EVEN THOSE SAD WORDS EVEN IN SAD ME DID BREED        4.58.14
EVEN THOSE SAD WORDS EVEN IN SAD ME DID BREED        4.58.14
IF STILL I FORCE HER IN SAD RIMES TO CREEPE          4.70.2
AND HER SAD WORDS MY SADDED SENCE DID HEARE          4.87.8
SILENT AND SAD IN MOURNING WEEDES DOTH DIGHT         4.97.8
TAKES IN THAT SAD HUE, WHICH WITH TH'INWARD NIGHT    4.99.7
AND CALLING FORTH OUT OF SAD $WINTERS NIGHT          5.4.5
SUCH DEATH THE SAD ENSAMPLE OF YOUR MIGHT            5.7.14
IN SECRET SOROW AND SAD PENSIVENESSE                 5.34.14
BUT SUDDEN DUMPS AND DRERY SAD DISDAYNE              5.52.11
AFTER LONG STORMES AND TEMPESTS SAD ASSAY            5.63.1
BUT SPEAKE NO WORD TO HER OF THESE SAD PLIGHTS       5.84.11
THEYR SAD PROTRACT FROM EVENING UNTILL MORNE         5.87.4
SADDED                     1
AND HER SAD WORDS MY SADDED SENCE DID HEARE          4.87.8
SADDEST                    1
AND OFT WHOLE TROUPES OF SADDEST WORDS I STAID       4.55.5
SADDLE                     1
THE $WAND IS $WILL, THOU $FANCIE $SADDLE ART         4.49.9
SADLY                      4
MUSES WHICH SADLY SIT ABOUT MY $CHAYRE               2.45.1
SADLY I SIT, UNMOV'D WITH THE $APPLAUSE              2.47.11
MUSICK TO HEARE, WHY HEAR'ST THOU MUSICK SADLY       3.8.1
BOTH SADLY BLACKE, BOTH BLACKLY DARKNED BE           4.96.3
SADNESS                    2
FOR WHEN ON ME THOU SHINEDST LATE IN SADNESSE        5.39.6
AND FEELING THENCE NO MORE HER SOROWES SADNESSE      5.39.11
SAFE                       2
SAFE IN MY SOULE, WHICH ONLY DOTH TO THEE            4.86.6
HIS SAFE ASSURANCE, STRONGLY IT RESTRAYNE            5.42.12
SAFELIEST                  1
TO HER, WHERE I MY HEART SAFELIEST SHALL MEET        4.84.6
SAFEST                     1
ROUZ'D FROM MY BREAST, HIS SURE AND SAFEST LAYRE     2.135.2
SAFETY                     2
THE MEANE OBSERVER (WHOM BASE SAFETY KEEPS)          1.35.10
THE JOYOUS SAFETY OF SO SWEET A REST                 5.63.10
SAID                       13
I SAY NO MORE, I FEARE I SAYD TOO MUCH               1.60.14
AND YET IT MAY BE SAID I LOV'D HER DEERELY           3.42.2
SWEET LOVE RENEW THY FORCE, BE IT NOT SAID           3.56.1
EVEN THOSE THAT SAID I COULD NOT LOVE YOU DEERER     3.115.2
BREATH'D FORTH THE SOUND THAT SAID I HATE            3.145.2
'FOOLE,' SAID MY $MUSE TO ME, 'LOOKE IN
                          THY HEART AND WRITE'       4.1.14
WHICH OTHERS SAID DID MAKE THEIR SOULES TO PINE      4.16.6
STELLA., NOW SHE IS NAM'D, NEED MORE BE SAID+        4.16.11
'WHAT NOW SIR FOOLE,' SAID HE, 'I WOULD NO LESSE     4.53.7
SWEET SAID THAT I TRUE LOVE IN HER SHOULD FIND       4.62.4
LEAST ONCE SHOULD NOT BE HEARD, TWISE
                          SAID, $NO, $NO             4.63.8
```

```
  SAY ALL, AND ALL WELL SAYD, STILL SAY THE SAME        4.92.14
  VAYNE MAN, SAYD SHE, THAT DOEST IN VAINE ASSAY         5.75.5
SAIL                3
  THE HUMBLE AS THE PROUDEST SAILE DOTH BEARE            3.80.6
  WAS IT THE PROUD FULL SAILE OF HIS GREAT VERSE         3.86.1
  THAT I HAVE HOYSTED SAILE TO AL THE WINDES             3.117.7
SAILED                      1
  HOW FARRE HE SAYL'D, WHAT $COUNTRIES HE HAD SEENE       2.1.4
SAILS                       2
  SEE HOW HER SAYLES BE RENT, HER TACKLINGS WORNE        2.134.9
  BEWARE FULL SAILES DROWNE NOT THY TOTTRING BARGE       4.85.2
SAINT               9
  SACRED ON EARTH, DESIGN'D A $SAINT ABOVE                1.6.8
  MY $SOULE-SHRIN'D $SAINT, MY FAIRE $IDEA LIES          2.53.2
  MY SOULE-SHRINDE $SAINT, MY FAIRE $IDEA LYES           2.113.2
  CUPID, DUMBE $IDOLL, PEEVISH $SAINT OF LCVE            2.126.1
  NO MORE SHALT THOU NOR $SAINT NOR $IDOLL BE            2.126.2
  AND WOULD CORRUPT MY SAINT TO BE A DIVEL               3.144.7
  SO CAPTIVES TO HIS $SAINT BOTH SOULE AND SENCE         4.61.6
  FOR MY SWEET $SAYNT SOME SERVICE FIT WILL FIND         5.22.4
  MY SOVERAYNE SAYNT, THE $IDOLL OF MY THOUGHT           5.61.2
SAINTED                     1
  TO HER THAT SITS IN MY THOUGHTS $TEMPLE SAINTED        1.15.7
SAINTS                      1
  AND WITH THE CREW CF BLESSED $SAYNTS UPBROUGHT         5.61.7
SAITH                       1
  OR WHETHER SHALL I SAY MINE EIE SAITH TRUE             3.114.3
SAKE                18
  THESE SAD NEGLECTED NOTES FOR HER DEARE SAKE+          1.17.2
  REBATE THY $SPLEENE, IF BUT FOR $PITTIES SAKE          2.52.6
  AND FOR MY SAKE EVEN SO DOTH SHE ABUSE ME              3.42.7
  SUFFRING MY FRIEND FOR MY SAKE TO APPROOVE HER         3.42.8
  AND BOTH FOR MY SAKE LAY ON ME THIS CROSSE             3.42.12
  TO PLAIE THE WATCH-MAN EVER FOR THY SAKE               3.61.12
  O FOR MY SAKE DOE YCU WISH FORTUNE CHIDE               3.111.1
  AND SUE A FRIEND, CAME DEBTER FOR MY SAKE              3.134.11
  TO ME THAT LANGUISHT FOR HER SAKE                      3.145.3
  AM OF MY SELFE, ALL TIRANT FOR THY SAKE+               3.149.4
  THEN THAT I LOSE NC MORE FOR $STELLA'S SAKE            4.18.14
  WITH ME THOSE PAINES FOR $GOD'S SAKE DO NCT TAKE       4.28.3
  PRINCESSE OF $BEAUTIE, FOR WHOSE ONLY SAKE             4.28.6
  BUT WHEN HE WILL FCR QUIET'S SAKE REMOVE               4.43.12
  CEASE EAGER $MUSE, PEACE PEN, FOR MY SAKE STAY         4.70.12
  NATURE WITH CARE SWEATES FOR HER DARLING'S SAKE        4.101.12
  $PENELOPE FOR HER $ULISSES SAKE                        5.23.1
  AND FOR THY SAKE THAT ALL LYKE DEARE DIDST BUY         5.68.11
SAKES                       1
  THAT I RESPECTS FCR BOTH OUR SAKES MUST SHOW           4.33.11
SALT                        1
  SALT LUKE-WARME TEARES SHEE FOR HIS DRINKE
                              DID GIVE                   2.116.15
SALUTATION                  1
  GIVE SALUTATION TO MY SPCRTIVE BLOOD+                  3.121.6
SALUTE                      1
  CALS EACH WIGHT TC SALUTE THE FLOURE OF BLISSE         4.99.11
SALVAGE                     1
  BUT SHE MORE CRUELL AND MORE SALVAGE WYLCE             5.20.9
SALVE               5
  BY KNIFE, BY LIQUCR, OR BY SALVE TO DEALE              1.14.11
  FOR NO MAN WELL OF SUCH A SALVE CAN SPEAKE             3.34.7
```

THE HUMBLE SALVE, WHICH WOUNDED BOSOMES FITS	3.120.12
AND WITH ONE SALVE BOTH HART AND BODY HEALE	5.50.14
SEEKES WITH SWEET PEACE TO SALVE EACH	
OTHERS WOUND	5.65.12

SALVING   1

MY SELFE CORRUPTING SALVING THY AMISSE	3.35.7

SAME   43

MY HEAVY FORTUNE IS MUCH LIKE THE SAME	1.13.3
THOSE SNARY LOCKS, ARE THOSE SAME NETS	
(MY $DEERE)	1.14.1
YET DO I LOVE, ADORE, AND PRAYSE THE SAME	1.14.7
AND SHE (TH'UNKINDEST MAID) STILL SCORNS	
THE SAME	1.15.12
TH'$ELISIAN GHOSTS SHALL NEVER KNOW THE SAME	1.30.14
AND THOUGH TH'EVENT OFT ANSWERS NOT THE SAME	1.35.8
AND THINKE THE SAME BECOMES THY FADING BEST	1.40.11
BECAUSE THEIR POWER SERVE TO EXACT THE SAME	1.47.12
AND THY HARD HEART HAD YEELDED UP THE SAME	1.56.8
AS IS HIS ART THAT PLAYES UPON THE SAME	1.57.2
THEN JUDGE THE WORLD HER BEAUTY GIVES THE SAME	1.57.12
RETAYNING $KNOWLEDGE, STILL THE SAME IN KIND	2.12.7
INTO THE SAME THEN LET A $WOMAN BREATHE	2.15.9
ONELY BY DYING, BORNE THE VERY SAME	2.16.12
BUT NOW AGAINE $YOU WILL THE SAME DENIE	2.19.3
MUCH LIKE HIS $WIT, THAT WAS TO USE THE SAME	2.21.8
BEING STEDFASTLY OPPOSED TO THE SAME	2.30.4
MY $BREST'S THE $VESSELL, WHICH INCLUDES	
THE SAME	2.30.12
SUCH AS BY $ART TO GET THE SAME HAVE TRY'D	2.58.7
FROM THE STRONG $SPIRIT BY NO MEANES FORCE	
THE SAME	2.58.8
THEN WITH THY BEAUTIE SET THE SAME ON FIRE	2.106.7
AND WITH THE SAME HE PRACTISED TO FLYE	2.122.7
WILL PLAY THE TIRANTS TO THE VERY SAME	3.5.3
FOR THAT SAME GRONE DOTH PUT THIS IN MY MIND	3.50.13
OR WHETHER REVOLUTION BE THE SAME	3.59.12
BUT THOSE SAME TOUNGS THAT GIVE THEE SO	
THINE OWNE	3.69.6
WHY WRITE I STILL ALL ONE, EVER THE SAME	3.76.5
I MUST EACH DAY SAY ORE THE VERY SAME	3.108.6
THAT SEE MY WRACKE, AND YET EMBRACE THE SAME+	4.19.2
WHENCE THOSE SAME FUMES OF MELANCHOLY RISE	4.23.3
WHEN I SAY '$STELLA', I DO MEANE THE SAME	4.28.5
HOW $ULSTER LIKES OF THAT SAME GOLDEN BIT	4.30.9
BUT THAT THEY STOPT HIS FURIE FROM THE SAME	4.50.13
STELLA'S SWEETE BREATH THE SAME TO ME DID REED	4.58.11
AND I DO SWEARE EVEN BY THE SAME DELIGHT	4.82.13
SAY ALL, AND ALL WELL SAYD, STILL SAY THE SAME	4.92.14
WHICH $NATURE' SELFE DID MAKE, AND SELFE	
ENGRAIND THE SAME+	4.102.6
BUT THAT SAME LOFTY COUNTENANCE SEEMES TO SCORNE	5.13.9
AND ON THE SAME MY HART WILL SACRIFISE	5.22.11
THE SAME AT NIGHT SHE DID AGAINE UNREAVE	5.23.4
AND THAT SAME GLORIOUS BEAUTIES YDLE BOAST	5.41.9
THAT SHIP, THAT TREE, AND THAT SAME BEAST AM I	5.56.13
MAY LIKEWISE LOVE THEE FOR THE SAME AGAINE	5.68.10

SANCTUARY   1

THY RIGOR IN THAT $SANCTUARY SLEW	1.31.3

SANG   1

BARE RN'WD QUIERS, WHERE LATE THE SWEET	
BIRDS SANG	3.73.4

```
SAP                       3
   SAP CHECKT WITH FROST AND LUSTIE LEAV'S QUITE GON    3.5.7
   VAUNT IN THEIR YOUTHFULL SAP, AT HEIGHT DECREASE     3.15.7
   THE DUREFULL $OAKE, WHOSE SAP IS NOT YET DRIDE       5.6.5
SAPPHIRES                 2
   IF $SAPHYRES, LOE HER EIES BE $SAPHYRES PLAINE       5.15.7
   IF $SAPHYRES, LOE HER EIES BE $SAPHYRES PLAINE       5.15.7
SAT                       1
   BRAKE BOW, BRAKE SHAFTS, WHILE $CUPID
                          WEEPING SATE                  4.17.8
SATIATE                   1
   AND EV'RY $DRUDGE DOTH DULL OUR SATIATE $EARE        2.31.10
SATIRE                    1
   IF ANY, BE A $SATIRE TO DECAY                        3.100.11
SATISFIES                 1
   O $GOD, THINKE YOU THAT SATISFIES MY CARE+           4.92.8
SATISIFY                  1
   THUS RUINES SHE (TO SATISFIE HER WILL)               1.47.13
SATURN                    2
   SATURNE CHIEFE $LORD OF THE $ASCENDANT LAY           2.116.7
   THAT HEAVIE $SATURNE LAUGHT AND LEAPT WITH HIM       3.98.4
SAUCES                    1
   TO BITTER SAWCES DID I FRAME MY FEEDING              3.118.6
SAUCINESS                 1
   IS SAWCINESSE REWARD OF CURTESIE+                    4.83.10
SAUCY                     3
   MY SAWSIE BARKE (INFERIOR FARRE TO HIS)              3.80.7
   SINCE SAUSIE $JACKES SO HAPPY ARE IN THIS            3.128.13
   SWEET, IT WAS SAUCIE $LOVE, NOT HUMBLE I             4.73.8
SAVAGE                    1
   SAVAGE, EXTREAME, RUDE, CRUELL, NOT TO TRUST         3.129.4
SAVE                      17
   TO SAVE THINE OWNE, STRETCH OUT THE FAIREST HAND     1.46.8
   SAVE MEE I $CRIE, YOU SIGH ME OUT A $NO              2.5.8
   WHERE I INTOMB'D, MY BETTER PART SHALL SAVE          2.44.12
   THREW IN HERSELFE, TO SAVE HERSELFE BY DROWNING      2.109.12
   WHOSE LYFE DOTH SAVE A THOUSAND SOULES
                          FROM HELL                     2.119.12
   SAVE BREED TO BRAVE HIM, WHEN HE TAKES
                          THEE HENCE                    3.12.14
   SAVE THAT MY SOULES IMAGINARY SIGHT                  3.27.9
   SAVE WHERE THOU ART NOT, THOUGH I FEELE THOU ART     3.48.10
   SAVE WHERE YOU ARE, HOW HAPPY YOU MAKE THOSE         3.57.12
   SAVE THAT TO DYE, I LEAVE MY LOVE ALONE              3.66.14
   SAVE WHAT IS HAD, OR MUST FROM YOU BE TOCKE          3.75.12
   SAVE THOU MY $ROSE, IN IT THOU ART MY ALL            3.109.14
   IN NOTHING ART THOU BLACKE SAVE IN THY DEEDS         3.131.13
   I MUCH DO GUESSE, YET FIND NO TRUTH SAVE THIS        4.44.9
   YET WITH ONE WORD SHE CAN IT SAVE OR SPILL           5.38.11
   TO SPILL WERE PITTY, BUT TO SAVE WERE PRAYSE         5.38.12
   AND GREATER GLORY THINKE TO SAVE, THEN SPILL         5.49.4
SAVED                     1
   AND SAV'D MY LIFE SAYING NOT YOU                     3.145.14
SAVES                     1
   NOW SEND FORTH HOPE, FOR NOW CALME PITTY SAVES       1.46.4
SAVING                    2
   AND ALL THEIR SHOWES BUT SHADOWES SAVING SHE         5.35.14
   AND ALL THEYR SHEWES BUT SHADOWES SAVING SHE         5.83.14
SAVOR                     1
   FOR COMPOUND SWEET., $FORGOING SIMPLE SAVOR          3.125.7
```

SAW   15
    THE FAIREST FLOWRE THAT EVER SAW THE LIGHT   1.40.6
    BUT IT NO SOONER SAW MY $SUNNE APPEARE   2.56.5
    BUT THEY NO SOONER SAW MY $SUNNE APPEARE   2.103.5
    I NEVER SAW THAT YOU DID PAINTING NEED   3.83.1
    SINCE FIRST I SAW YOU FRESH WHICH YET ARE GREENE   3.104.8
    STILL LOOSING WHEN I SAW MY SELFE TO WIN+   3.119.4
    I GRAUNT I NEVER SAW A GODDESSE GOE   3.130.11
    BUT WHEN SHE SAW MY WOFULL STATE   3.145.4
    I SAW AND LIKED, I LIKED BUT LOVED NOT   4.2.5
    BUT STRAIGHT I SAW MOTIONS OF LIGHTNING GRACE   4.20.12
    MY FRIEND, THAT OFT SAW THROUGH ALL MASKES MY WO   4.69.5
    I SAW THAT TEARES DID IN HER EYES APPEARE   4.87.6
    I SAW THAT SIGHES HER SWEETEST LIPS DID PART   4.87.7
    I SAW THY SELFE WITH MANY A SMILING LINE   4.103.2
    AND SEEKE EACH WHERE, WHERE LAST I SAWE HER FACE   5.78.3
SAWEST   2
    FOR WELL THOU SAW'ST MY LOVE AND HOW I PIN'D   1.31.8
    SO WHEN THOU SAW'ST IN $NATURE'S CABINET   4.11.9
SAY   78
    SAY HER DISDAINE HATH DRYED UP MY BLOOD   1.2.9
    ILE HIDE HER SINNE AND SAY IT WAS MY LOT   1.30.10
    MAKE ME TO SAY, WHEN ALL MY GRIEFES ARE GONE   1.51.13
    WHEN YET TH'UNBORNE SHALL SAY, $LO WHERE SHE LIES   1.55.7
    I SAY NO MORE, I FEARE I SAYD TOO MUCH   1.60.14
    I SAY, I $LOVE, YOU SLEIGHTLY ANSWERE I   2.5.5
    I SAY, $YOU $LOVE, YOU PEULE ME OUT A $NO   2.5.6
    I SAY, I $DIE, YOU $ECCHO ME WITH I   2.5.7
    LITTLE $ILE SAY, BUT THINKE THE $DEVILL'S IN ME   2.15.14
    SAY TO OUR $NEPHEWES, THAT THOU ONCE HAST SEENE   2.17.11
    I $HEARE SOME SAY, THIS $MAN IS NOT IN LOVE   2.24.1
    WHO+ CAN HE LOVE+ A LIKELY THING, THEY SAY   2.24.2
    TO $SUCH AS SAY, $THY $LOVE I OVER-PRIZE   2.28.1
    I FEARE NO CENSURE, NOR WHAT THOU CANST SAY   2.31.5
    AND $KENT WILL SAY, HER $MEDWAY DOTH EXCELL   2.32.8
    MAY SAY, THAT THOU ART FLATTERED BY MEE   2.35.3
    WHAT SHOULD I SAY+ WHAT YET REMAINES TO DOE+   2.41.5
    SOME SAY, I HAVE A PASSING PLEASING $STRAINE   2.42.3
    SOME SAY, $THAT IN MY $HUMOR I EXCELL   2.42.4
    THEY SAY ($AS $POETS DOE) I USE TO FAINE   2.42.6
    SAY THUS FAIRE $BROOKE, WHEN THOU SHALT
                          SEE THY QUEENE   2.53.9
    HEERE MAKE A $PERIOD $TIME, AND SAIE FOR MEE   2.107.13
    MAY BLASPHEME THUS, AND SAY, I FLATTER THEE   2.112.3
    SAY THUS FAYRE $BROOKE WHEN THOU SHALT
                          SEE THY $QUEENE   2.113.9
    AND $KENT WILL SAY, HER $MEDWAY DOTH EXCELL   2.124.8
    AND SAY MY VERSE RUNNES IN A LOFTY VAYNE   2.128.2
    SOME SAY I HAVE A PASSING PLEASING STRAINE   2.128.3
    SOME SAY THAT IN MY HUMOR I EXCELL   2.128.4
    THEY SAY, (AS $POETS DOE) I USE TO FAYNE   2.128.6
    TO SAY WITHIN THINE OWNE DEEPE SUNKEN EYES   3.2.7
    YOU HAD A $FATHER, LET YOUR $SON SAY SO   3.13.14
    OR SAY WITH $PRINCES IF IT SHAL GO WEL   3.14.7
    THE AGE TO COME WOULD SAY THIS $POET LIES   3.17.7
    LET THEM SAY MORE THAT LIKE OF HEARE-SAY WELL   3.21.13
    SO I FOR FEARE OF TRUST, FORGET TO SAY   3.23.5
    HOW WOULD (I SAY) MINE EYES BE BLESSED MADE   3.43.9
    DOTH TEACH THAT EASE AND THAT REPOSE TO SAY   3.50.3
    THAT I MIGHT SEE WHAT THE OLD WORLD COULD SAY   3.59.9

O IF (I SAY) YOU LOOKE UPON THIS VERSE	3.71.9
THEN THANKE HIM NOT FOR THAT WHICH HE DOTH SAY	3.79.13
WHO IS IT THAT SAYES MOST, WHICH CAN SAY MORE	3.84.1
HEARING YOU PRAISD, I SAY 'TIS SO, 'TIS TRUE	3.85.9
SAY THAT THOU DIDST FORSAKE MEE FOR SOME FALT	3.89.1
SOME SAY THY FAULT IS YOUTH, SOME WANTONESSE	3.96.1
SOME SAY THY GRACE IS YOUTH AND GENTLE SPORT	3.96.2
MAKE ANSWERE $MUSE, WILT THOU NOT HAPLY SAIE	3.101.5
I MUST EACH DAY SAY ORE THE VERY SAME	3.108.6
O NEVER SAY THAT I WAS FALSE OF HEART	3.109.1
OR WHETHER SHALL I SAY MINE EIE SAITH TRUE	3.114.3
MIGHT I NOT THEN SAY NOW I LOVE YOU BEST	3.115.10
LOVE IS A $BABE, THEN MIGHT I NOT SAY SO	3.115.13
YET IN GOOD FAITH SOME SAY THAT THEE BEHOLD	3.131.5
TO SAY THEY ERRE, I DARE NOT BE SO BOLD	3.131.7
OR MINE EYES SEEING THIS, SAY THIS IS NOT	3.137.11
AND WHEREFORE SAY NOT I THAT I AM OLD+	3.138.10
WHAT MEANES THE WORLD TO SAY IT IS NOT SO+	3.148.6
CANST THOU $O CRUELL, SAY I LOVE THEE NOT	3.149.1
MINE EYES (SHALL I SAY CURST OR BLEST) BEHELD	4.16.10
SEE THERE THAT BOY, THAT MURTHRING BOY I SAY	4.20.2
SURE YOU SAY WELL, YOUR WISDOME'S GOLDEN MINE	4.21.12
WHEN I SAY '$STELLA', I DO MEANE THE SAME	4.28.5
WHAT MAY WORDS SAY, OR WHAT MAY WORDS NOT SAY	4.35.1
WHAT MAY WORDS SAY, OR WHAT MAY WORDS NOT SAY	4.35.1
SO MAY YOU STILL HAVE SOMEWHAT NEW TO SAY	4.51.4
LOOKE HERE, I SAY.' I LOOK'D, AND $STELLA SPIDE	4.53.8
'WHAT HE+' SAY THEY OF ME, 'NOW I DARE SWEARE	4.54.7
THEY LOVE INDEED, WHO QUAKE TO SAY THEY LOVE	4.54.14
I, I, O I MAY SAY, THAT SHE IS MINE	4.69.11
THUS MUCH MY HEART COMPELD MY MOUTH TO SAY	4.80.9
YOU SAY FORSOOTH, YOU LEFT HER WELL OF LATE	4.92.7
SAY ALL, AND ALL WELL SAYD, STILL SAY THE SAME	4.92.14
SAY ALL, AND ALL WELL SAYD, STILL SAY THE SAME	4.92.14
BUT FEELING PROOFE MAKES ME SAY THEY MISTAKE IT FURRE	4.102.11
STELLA, I SAY MY $STELLA, SHOULD APPEARE	4.106.4
AND SCORNING SAY, '$SEE WHAT IT IS TO LOVE'	4.107.14
AND MAKES ME THEN BOW DOWNE MY HEAD, AND SAY	4.108.9
FAYRER THEN FAYREST LET NONE EVER SAY	5.20.13
WHEN I DOE PRAISE HER, SAY I DOE BUT FLATTER	5.85.2

SAYEST   2

AND SAY'ST, MY $LINES BE DULL, AND DOE NOT MOVE	2.49.2
WHAT SAIST THOU NOW, WHERE IS THAT DAINTY CHEERE	4.106.5

SAYETH   4

AS WELL (SAYTH HE) TOO FORWARD, AS TOO SLOW	2.59.6
(SAITH HE) $LIGHT $BURTHEN'S HEAVY, IF FARRE BORNE	2.59.10
'SCHOLLER,' SAITH $LOVE, 'BEND HITHERWARD YOUR WIT'	4.19.14
HER EYES, HER LIPS, HER ALL, SAITH $LOVE DO THIS	4.52.3

SAYING   3

AND SAV'D MY LIFE SAYING NOT YOU	3.145.14
TO GRIEVE ME WORSE, IN SAYING THAT $DESIRE	4.14.6
ABASE HER PRAISE, SAYING SHE DOTH EXCELL	4.37.8

SAYS   13

THAT TELLS THE TRUTH, AND SAYES THAT ALL IS GONE	1.41.4
AND SAYES IN HIM THEIR FAIRE APPEARANCE LYES	3.46.8
WHO IS IT THAT SAYES MOST, WHICH CAN SAY MORE	3.84.1
SINCE MY APPEALE SAIES I DID STRIVE TO PROOVE	3.117.13

```
THAT EVERY TOUNG SAIES BEAUTY SHOULD LOOKE SC      3.127.14
BUT WHEREFORE SAYES SHE NOT SHE IS UNJUST+         3.138.9
BY $PHOEBUS' DOOME, WITH SUGRED SENTENCE SAYES      4.25.2
FOR $GRAMMER SAYES (O THIS DEARE $STELLA WEIGHE)   4.63.12
FOR $GRAMMER SAYES (TO $GRAMMER WHO SAYES NAY)     4.63.13
FOR $GRAMMER SAYES (TO $GRAMMER WHO SAYES NAY)     4.63.13
BUT SHE FORBIDS, WITH BLUSHING WORDS, SHE SAYES     4.81.9
AND WHEN I WEEP, SHE SAYES TEARES ARE BUT WATER    5.18.10
AND WHEN I SIGH, SHE SAYES I KNOW THE ART          5.18.11
SCALE                         1
THINKING TO SCALE THE HEAVEN OF HER HART            1.36.2
SCANDAL                       1
WHICH VULGAR SCANDALL STAMPT UPON MY BROW          3.112.2
SCANT                         1
I SEARCH THE EARTH, THE EARTH I FINDE AS SKANT      1.29.7
SCANTED                       1
ACCUSE ME THUS, THAT I HAVE SCANTED ALL            3.117.1
SCAPE                         2
THUS POORE $THEEVES SUFFER, WHEN THE GREATER
                           SCAPE                    2.14.14
BY SENCE'S PRIVILEDGE, CAN SCAPE FROM THEE          4.36.14
SCAPED                        2
AH DOE NOT, WHEN MY HEART HATH SCAPTE THIS SORROW   3.90.5
YET AS IT WAS, I HARDLY SCAP'T WITH PAINE          5.16.14
SCAPES                        1
THAT FROM HER LOCKES, THY DAY-NETS, NONE
                           SCAPES FREE              4.12.2
SCARABIES                     1
I SCORNE ALL $EARTHLY $DUNG-BRED $SCARABIES         2.31.14
SCARCE                        2
CAN SCARCE DISCERNE THE SHAPE OF MINE OWNE PAINE    4.94.4
THAT WHICH IS GOLD OR HEARE, MAY SCARSE BE TOLD+    5.37.4
SCARCELY                      5
SOMETIMES WHAT $SCHOOLE-MEN SCARCELY CAN DECIDE     2.46.3
AND SCARCELY GREETE ME WITH THAT SUNNE THINE EYE    3.49.6
THE FIRST, THUS MATCHT, WERE SCARCELY $GENTLEMEN   4.13.14
ONE FROM THE OTHER SCARCELY CAN DESCRIE            4.72.3
THENCE, SO FARRE THENCE, THAT SCARCELY
                           ANY SPARKE              4.104.6
SCARF                         1
HAVING NO SCARFE OF CLOWDS BEFORE HIS FACE          4.22.3
SCARLET                       3
UPON YOUR $LIPS THE SCARLET DROPS ARE FOUND         2.2.10
THAT HAVE PROPHAN'D THEIR SCARLET ORNAMENTS        3.142.6
THOSE SCARLET JUDGES, THREATNING BLOUDY PAINE+    4.73.11
SCATH                         1
BUT MY PROUD ONE DOTH WORKE THE GREATER SCATH      5.31.9
SCATTERED                     1
FOR ME, I WEPT TO SEE PEARLES SCATTERED SO          4.87.9
SCEPTER                       2
THY SCEPTER USE IN SOME OLD $CATOE'S BREST          4.4.5
TO LEAVE THE SCEPTER OF ALL SUBJECT THINGS          4.38.4
SCHOLAR                       4
FOR I WAS APT A SCHOLLER LIKE TO PROVE             2.111.3
'SCHOLLER,' SAITH $LOVE, 'BEND HITHERWARD
                           YOUR WIT'
                                                  4.19.14
THE WISEST SCHOLLER OF THE WIGHT MOST WISE          4.25.1
ALAS POORE WAG, THAT NOW A SCHOLLER ART             4.46.9
SCHOOL                        1
FY, SCHOOLE OF $PATIENCE, $FY, YOUR LESSON IS       4.56.1
```

SCHOOLED   1
  SCHOOL'D ONELY BY HIS MOTHER'S TENDER EYE   4.73.2
SCHOOLMASTER   1
  NEAST OF YOUNG JOYES, SCHOOLMASTER OF DELIGHT   4.79.8
SCHOOLMEN   1
  SOMETIMES WHAT $SCHOOLE-MEN SCARCELY CAN DECIDE   2.46.3
SCHOOLMISTRESS   2
  MY LOVES $SCHOOLE-MISTRIS NOW HATH TAUGHT ME SO   2.111.13
  TO SUCH A SCHOOLE-MISTRESSE, WHOSE LESSONS NEW   4.46.10
SCHOOLS   2
  CHURCHES OR SCHOOLES ARE FOR THY SEATE MORE FIT   4.4.6
  THE SCHOOLES WHERE $VENUS HATH LEARN'D $CHASTITIE 4.42.4
SCOPE   10
  THOUGH $FEARE GIVES THEM MORE THEN A $HEAV'NLY
                              $SCOPE   2.26.8
  AND $LIBERTY DEPRIVES HIM OF HIS $SCOPE   2.26.11
  YET FEARE GYVES THEM MORE THEN A HEAVENLY SCOPE   2.137.8
  AND LYBERTY DEPRIVES HYM OF HYS SCOPE   2.137.11
  DESIRING THIS MANS ART, AND THAT MANS SKOPE   3.29.7
  BLESSED ARE YOU WHOSE WORTHINESSE GIVES SKOPE   3.52.13
  THE SKOPE AND TENURE OF THY $JELOUSIE+   3.61.8
  THAT HAVING SUCH A SKOPE TO SHOW HER PRIDE   3.103.2
  THREE THEAMS IN ONE, WHICH WONDROUS SCOPE
                              AFFORDS   3.105.12
  THOUGH FALSE, YET WITH FREE SCOPE MORE
                              GRACE DOTH BREED   4.45.10
SCORCH   1
  SCORTCH NOT, BUT ONELY DO DARKE CHILLING
                              SPRITES REMOVE   4.76.8
SCORCHING   2
  WHOSE SCORCHING GLEED, MY HEART TO $CINDERS
                              TURNETH   2.40.10
  WITH SCORCHING GLEED MY HART TO CYNDERS TURNETH   2.144.10
SCORE   2
  NOR NEED I TALLIES THY DEARE LOVE TO SKORE   3.122.10
  AS $MARS IN THREE SCORE YEARES DOTH RUN
                              HIS SPHEARE   5.60.4
SCORN   18
  TH'$ORPHAN OF $FORTUNE, BORNE TO BE HER SCORNE   1.26.3
  LET WAKING EYES SUFFICE TO WAILE THEIR SCORNE   1.54.7
  YOU THAT BEHOLD US, LAUGH US NOT TO SCORNE   2.22.11
  LOVE BANISH'D $HEAV'N, IN $EARTH WAS HELD
                              IN SCORNE   2.23.1
  I SCORNE ALL $EARTHLY $DUNG-BRED $SCARABIES   2.31.14
  YOU HAVE SPUNNE A FAIRE $THRED, HE REPLYES
                              IN SCORNE   2.59.12
  WHICH SCORNE THE HONOR THAT IS DONE TO THEE   2.123.10
  THAT THEN I SKORNE TO CHANGE MY STATE
                              WITH $KINGS   3.29.14
  AND PLACE MY MERRIT IN THE EIE OF SKORNE   3.88.2
  THOUGH DUSTIE WITS DARE SCORNE $ASTROLOGIE   4.26.1
  THOSE $LOVERS SCORNE WHOM THAT $LOVE DOTH
                              POSSESSE+   4.31.13
  MAY GET NO ALMES BUT SCORNE OF BEGGERIE   4.47.8
  LET ALL THE EARTH WITH SCORNE RECOUNT MY CASE   4.64.7
  AND $MUSES SCORNE WITH VULGAR BRAINES TO DWELL   4.74.3
  SCORN OF BASE THINGS, AND SDEIGNE OF FOULE
                              DISHONOR   5.5.6
  BUT THAT SAME LOFTY COUNTENANCE SEEMES TO SCORNE   5.13.9
  MY SIMPLE MEANING WITH DISDAYNFULL SCORNE   5.29.2

```
WHAT REASON IS IT THEN BUT SHE SHOULD SCORNE          5.61.11
SCORNED              5
   SHE THEN IS SCORND THAT LATE ADORND THE $FAYRE       1.39.7
   THOU MAIST REPENT THAT THOU HAST SCORND
                              MY TEARES                  1.41.13
   THOU WHICH HAST SCORNED $LIFE, AND HATED $DEATH       2.49.9
   BE SCORN'D, LIKE OLD MEN OF LESSE TRUTH
                              THEN TONGUE                3.17.10
   IF SO GREAT SERVICES MAY SCORNED BE                   4.65.10
SCORNEST             2
   THESE $LINES THAT NOW THOU SCORN'ST, WHICH
                         SHOULD DELIGHT THEE             2.8.13
   PROUDLY THOU SCORN'ST MY $WORLD-OUT-WEARING
                              $RIMES                     2.44.7
SCORNETH             2
   THOUGH MY SOULES $IDOLL SCORNETH ALL MY VOWES         1.11.10
   IN HER OWNE POWRE, AND SCORNETH OTHERS AYDE           5.58.2
SCORNING             5
   AND SCORNING $REASON'S MAYMED $ARGUMENT               2.38.6
   AND SCORNING $REASONS MAYMED $ARGUMENT                2.131.6
   AND SCORNING SAY, '$SEE WHAT IT IS TO LOVE'           4.107.14
   OF HER FREEWILL, SCORNING BOTH THEE AND ME            5.10.4
   PROUD $DAPHNE SCORNING $PHAEBUS LOVELY FYRE           5.28.9
SCORNS
   AND SHE (TH'UNKINDEST MAID) STILL SCORNS
                              THE SAME                   1.15.12
   THAT SKIN, WHOSE PASSE-PRAISE HUE SCORNS
                         THIS POORE TERME OF WHITE       4.77.7
SCORSE               1
   OR $CRUELL, IF THOU CAN'ST NOT., LET US SCORSE        2.52.7
SCOTLAND             1
   BUT BOUNDED THUS, TO $SCOTLAND GET YOU FORTH          2.25.5
SCOTTISH             1
   IF IN THE $SCOTTISHE $COURT BE WELTRING YET           4.30.11
SCOURGE              4
   SCOURGE OF IT SELFE, STILL CLIMING SLIPPRIE
                              PLACE                      4.23.10
   BEAUTIE'S PLAGUE, $VERTUE'S SCOURGE, SUCCOUR
                              OF LIES                    4.78.6
   THAT SHE TO WICKED MEN A SCOURGE SHOULD BEE           5.24.11
   BUT SINCE YE ARE MY SCOURGE I WILL INTREAT            5.24.13
SCUSE                2
   BUT NO SCUSE SERVES, SHE MAKES HER WRATH APPEARE      4.73.9
   AND DO I THEN MY SELFE THIS VAINE SCUSE GIVE+         4.93.9
SCYTH                1
   AS IF SHE WERE EXEMPT FROM $SYETH OR $BOW             1.23.3
SCYTHE               4
   AND NOTHING GAINST $TIMES SIETH CAN MAKE DEFENCE      3.12.13
   AND NOTHING STANDS BUT FOR HIS SIETH TO MOW           3.60.12
   SO THOU PREVENST HIS SIETH, AND CROOKED KNIFE         3.100.14
   I WILL BE TRUE DISPIGHT THY SYETH AND THEE            3.123.14
SDAINS               1
   WHO IN HER PRIDE SDAYNES ONCE TO LOOKE ON MEE         2.123.12
SEA                  7
   BURN'D IN A $SEA OF YCE, AND DROWN'D AMIDST
                              A FIRE                     2.62.14
   BURN'D IN A $SEA OF $ICE, AND DROWN'D
                              AMIDST A FIRE              2.150.14
   FOR NIMBLE THOUGHT CAN JUMPE BOTH SEA AND LAND        3.44.7
   SINCE BRASSE, NOR STONE, NOR EARTH, NOR
                              BOUNDLESSE SEA             3.65.1
```

```
THE MOUNTAINE, OR THE SEA, THE DAY, OR NIGHT      3.113.11
THE SEA ALL WATER, YET RECEIVES RAINE STILL       3.135.9
THAT, FROM THAT SEA DERIV'D, TEARS' SPRING
                              DID FLOW             4.45.8
SEA-FARER                    1
  LIKE AN ADVENTUROUS $SEA-FARER AM I              2.1.1
SEAL                         1
  SHE CARV'D THEE FOR HER SEALE, AND MENT THERBY   3.11.13
SEALED                       1
  AND SEALD FALSE BONDS OF LOVE AS OFT AS MINE     3.142.7
SEALS                        1
  DEATHS SECOND SELFE THAT SEALS UP ALL IN REST    3.73.8
SEARCH                       2
  I SEARCH THE EARTH, THE EARTH I FINDE AS SKANT   1.29.7
  YOU THAT DO SEARCH FOR EVERIE PURLING SPRING     4.15.1
SEAS                         2
  MAKING MY $SIGHES TO THAW THE $FROZEN $SEAS      2.25.8
  HE FORTH WAS THROWN INTO THE GREEDY SEAS         5.38.2
SEA'S                        1
  WITH $SUNNE AND $MOONE, WITH EARTH AND
                       SEAS RICH GEMS              3.21.6
SEASON                       3
  AH SPORT (SWEET $MAIDE) IN SEASON OF THESE YEARES 1.51.5
  SUCH IS THE SUNNE, WHO GUIDES MY YOUTHFULL
                       SEASON                      2.147.13
  THIS HOLY SEASON FIT TO FAST AND PRAY            5.22.1
SEASONED                     2
  HEAPE THINE OWN VERTUES SEASONED BY THEIR SUNNE  2.106.5
  OR AS SWEET SEASON'D SHEWERS ARE TO THE GROUND   3.75.2
SEASONS                      2
  MAKE GLAD AND SORRY SEASONS AS THOU FLEET'ST     3.19.5
  IN PROCESSE OF THE SEASONS HAVE I SEENE          3.104.6
SEASONS'                     1
  OF PLAGUES, OF DEARTHS, OR SEASONS QUALLITY      3.14.4
SEAT                         7
  OF HER OWNE SEATE, WHEREOF I MADE HER GUIDE      1.47.8
  SHALL HAVE MY $SONG, WHERE $DELIA HATH HER SEAT  1.58.12
  ELIZIUM IS TOO HIGH A SEATE FOR $ME              2.39.5
  ELIZIA IS TOO HIE A SEATE FOR MEE                2.118.5
  AYE ME, BUT YET THOU MIGHST MY SEATE FORBEARE    3.41.9
  WHICH THREE TILL NOW, NEVER KEPT SEATE IN ONE    3.105.14
  CHURCHES OR SCHOOLES ARE FOR THY SEATE MORE FIT  4.4.6
SEATED                       2
  SEATED WITH $SOL, AND WEARES $MINERVAS GLOVE     2.151.12
  SHE BUILDS HER FAME ON HIGHER SEATED PRAISE      4.81.10
SECOND                       10
  A SECOND $FLOUD, DOWNE RAYNING FROM MINE $EYES   2.55.4
  CAN SHEW A $SECOND TO SO PURE A $LOVE            2.60.14
  A SECOND FLOOD DOWNE RAYNING FROM MINE EYES      2.102.4
  THE SECOND BURTHEN OF A FORMER CHILD+            3.59.4
  TO LIVE A SCOND LIFE ON SECOND HEAD              3.68.7
  TO LIVE A SCOND LIFE ON SECOND HEAD              3.68.7
  DEATHS SECOND SELFE THAT SEALS UP ALL IN REST    3.73.8
  THE SECOND IS MY SOVEREIGNE $QUEENE MOST KIND    5.74.7
  AGAYNE I WROTE IT WITH A SECOND HAND             5.75.3
  AND STOUTLY WILL THAT SECOND WORKE ASSOYLE       5.80.7
SECONDS                      1
  WHICH IS NOT MIXT WITH SECONDS, KNOWS NO ART     3.125.11
SECRECY                      1
  SWEET SECRECIE, WHAT TONGUE CAN TELL THY WORTH+  2.146.1
```

```
SECRET                          7
    RECEIVING STRENGTH FROM EV'RY SECRET PART            2.30.7
    THE SHORES BESET WITH THOUSAND SECRET SPYES          2.122.3
    WHO FOR MY LIFE IN SECRETE WAITE DO'ST LYE           2.130.6
    IN SECRET SILENCE, WHICH SUCH WONDERS PREACHEST      2.146.12
    WHEREON THE $STARS IN SECRET INFLUENCE COMMENT       3.15.4
    NOR SO FAIRE LEVELL IN SO SECRET STAY                4.20.6
    IN SECRET SOROW AND SAD PENSIVENESSE                 5.34.14
SECRETLY                        1
    YET I MY HART WITH SILENCE SECRETLY                  5.43.9
SECRETS                         1
    NOR YET THOSE HEAVENLY SECRETS ONCE RESPECTED        2.105.4
SEE                           144
    AND SEE HOW JUST I RECKON WITH THINE EIES            1.1.10
    BUT WITH DISDAINE TO SEE ME IN THAT PLACE            1.5.6
    YET THOUGH I SEE, THAT NOUGHT WE DOE, CAN MOVE       1.8.13
    FLINT, FROST, DISDAINE, WEARES, MELTES,
                             AND YEELDES WE SEE          1.11.14
    LET THIS SUFFICE, THAT ALL THE WORLD MAY SEE         1.15.13
    SEE WHAT REWARD HE HATH THAT SERVES THE
                             UNGRATEFULL                 1.18.7
    AND SEE MY FORTUNE EVER LIKE TO LAST                 1.28.11
    SEE THEN WHO SINNES THE GREATER OF US TWAINE         1.33.13
    HER SIGHT CONTENTED THUS TO SEE ME SPILL             1.36.13
    I ONCE MAY SEE WHEN YEARES SHALL WRECK MY WRONG      1.38.1
    FRESH SHALT THOU SEE IN ME THE WOUNDS THOU MADST     1.41.5
    THEN WHAT MY FAITH HATH BENE THY SELFE SHALL SEE     1.41.11
    HERE SEE THE GIFTS THAT $GOD AND NATURE LENT THEE    1.42.7
    SEE THY $LEANDER STRIVING IN THESE WAVES             1.46.2
    SEEKE OUT SOME PLACE, AND SEE IF ANY PLACE           1.52.9
    BUT $O, SEE, SEE, WE NEED INQUIRE NO FURTHER         2.2.9
    BUT $O, SEE, SEE, WE NEED INQUIRE NO FURTHER         2.2.9
    BY THIS I SEE, HOW-EVER THINGS BE PAST               2.2.13
    A GENTLE WARNING ($FRIENDS) THUS MAY YOU SEE         2.7.13
    THAT IN MY DAYES I MAY NOT SEE THEE OLD              2.8.2
    DEFAC'D WITH $WRINKLES, THAT I MIGHT BUT SEE         2.8.6
    WHICH MY $HEART, LIGHTNED BY THY $LOVE, DOTH SEE     2.12.14
    LETTERS AND $LINES WE SEE ARE SOONE DEFACED          2.13.1
    FROM $AGE TO $AGE, WHAT THOU HAST SOUGHT TO SEE      2.17.2
    AND THY $YOUTH PAST, IN THIS PURE $MIRROUR SEE       2.17.6
    YET SEE THOU TELL, BUT TRULY, WHAT HATH BEENE        2.17.10
    THAT SHE IS GONE, HER LIKE AGAINE TO SEE             2.17.14
    I SEE $YOUR CRAFT, NOW I PERCEIVE $YOUR DRIFT        2.19.11
    BUT SEE, FOR YOU TO $HEAV'N FOR $PHRAZE I RUNNE      2.21.11
    YEE SHALLOW $CENSURES, SOMETIME SEE YEE NOT          2.24.9
    ME $THINKES I SEE SOME CROOKED $MIMICKE JEERE        2.31.1
    THAT $EYES COULD THINKE OF THAT MY $HEART
                             COULD SEE                   2.33.14
    SEE $MIRACLES, YE UNBELEEVING, SEE                   2.35.5
    SEE $MIRACLES, YE UNBELEEVING, SEE                   2.35.5
    AND IN MY $LINES, IF SHE MY LOVE MAY SEE             2.42.12
    SAY THUS FAIRE $BROOKE, WHEN THOU SHALT
                             SEE THY QUEENE              2.53.9
    LOOKE $THOU INTO MY BREST, AND $THOU SHALT SEE       2.55.9
    AND SEE IF $TIME (IF HE WOULD STRIVE TO PROVE)       2.60.13
    LET THE $WORLD SEE THE UTMOST OF THY HATE            2.63.12
    LOOKE THOU INTO MY BREAST, AND THOU SHALT SEE        2.102.9
    FROM WORLD TO WORLD, THOU LONG HAST SOUGHT
                             TO SEE                      2.107.2
    AND THY YOUTH PAST, IN THIS FAIRE MIRROR SEE         2.107.6
```

```
SEE MYRACLES, YEE UNBELEEVING SEE                        2.112.5
SEE MYRACLES, YEE UNBELEEVING SEE                        2.112.5
SAY THUS FAYRE $BROCKE WHEN THOU SHALT
                           SEE THY $QUEENE               2.113.9
I SEE THE UGLY FACE OF MY DEFORMED CARES                 2.114.2
THY FAYREST YOUTH AND $BEAUTIE DOE I SEE                 2.114.6
LETTERS AND LYNES WE SEE ARE SOONE DEFACED               2.121.1
SOME MUZ'D TO SEE THE EARTH ENVY THE AYRE                2.125.5
A WORLD TO SEE, YET HOW HE JOYD TO HEARE                 2.125.7
AND IN MY LYNES IF SHEE MY LOVE MAY SEE                  2.128.12
THUS DO I FEELE THE PAINE, THE CAUSE,
                           YET CANNOT SEE                2.130.8
SEE WHERE SHEE FLOTES, LADEN WITH PUREST LOVE            2.134.5
SEE HOW HER SAYLES BE RENT, HER TACKLINGS WORNE          2.134.9
SEE CHASTE $DIANA, WHERE MY HARMLES HART                 2.135.1
YET SEE HOW RIGHT HE COMES UNTO MY FAYRE                 2.135.4
SEE HOW MY $DEERE COMES TO THY $BEAUTIES STAND           2.135.5
SEE HOW HEE LOOKES UPON HIS BLEEDING WOUND               2.135.9
O PUREST MERROR, WHEREIN MEN MAY SEE                     2.146.13
AND SEE THY BLOOD WARME WHEN THOU FEEL'ST
                           IT COULD                      3.2.14
SO THOU THROUGH WINDOWES OF THINE AGE SHALT SEE          3.3.11
AND SEE THE BRAVE DAY SUNCK IN HIDIOUS NIGHT             3.12.2
WHEN LOFTY TREES I SEE BARREN OF LEAVES                  3.12.5
AND DIE AS FAST AS THEY SEE OTHERS GROW                  3.12.12
SO LONG AS MEN CAN BREATH OR EYES CAN SEE                3.18.13
FOR THROUGH THE $PAINTER MUST YOU SEE HIS SKILL          3.24.5
NOW SEE WHAT GOOD-TURNES EYES FOR EIES HAVE DONE         3.24.9
THEY DRAW BUT WHAT THEY SEE, KNOW NOT THE HART           3.24.14
LOOKING ON DARKNES WHICH THE BLIND DOE SEE               3.27.8
TO SEE HIS ACTIVE CHILDE DO DEEDS OF YOUTH               3.37.2
WHEN MOST I WINKE THEN DOE MINE EYES BEST SEE            3.43.1
ALL DAYES ARE NIGHTS TO SEE TILL I SEE THEE             3.43.13
ALL DAYES ARE NIGHTS TO SEE TILL I SEE THEE             3.43.13
WHEN I SHALL SEE THEE FROWNE ON MY DEFECTS               3.49.2
TOO MORROW SEE AGAINE, AND DOE NOT KILL                  3.56.7
COME DAILY TO THE BANCKES, THAT WHEN THEY SEE            3.56.11
THAT I MIGHT SEE WHAT THE OLD WORLD COULD SAY            3.59.9
WHEN SOMETIME LOFTIE TOWERS I SEE DOWNE RASED            3.64.3
THEN BETTERD THAT THE WORLD MAY SEE MY PLEASURE          3.75.8
I SEE, A BETTER STATE TO ME BELONGS                      3.92.7
AND ALL THINGS TURNES TO FAIRE, THAT EIES
                           CAN SEE                       3.95.12
MORE FLOWERS I NOTED, YET I NONE COULD SEE               3.99.14
I SEE DISCRIPTIONS OF THE FAIREST WIGHTS                 3.106.2
I SEE THEIR ANTIQUE $PEN WOULD HAVE EXPREST              3.106.7
FOR IF IT SEE THE RUD'ST OR GENTLEST SIGHT               3.113.9
FOR THY RECORDS, AND WHAT WE SEE DOTH LYE                3.123.11
BUT NO SUCH $ROSES SEE I IN HER CHEEKES                  3.130.6
THAT THEY BEHOLD AND SEE NOT WHAT THEY SEE               3.137.2
THAT THEY BEHOLD AND SEE NOT WHAT THEY SEE               3.137.2
THEY KNOW WHAT BEAUTIE IS, SEE WHERE IT LYES             3.137.3
THAT CENSURES FALSELY WHAT THEY SEE ARIGHT+              3.148.4
THOSE THAT CAN SEE THOU LOV'ST, AND I AM BLIND           3.149.14
THE MORE I HEARE AND SEE JUST CAUSE OF HATE              3.150.10
OR MADE THEM SWERE AGAINST THE THING THEY SEE            3.152.12
OFT TURNING OTHERS' LEAVES, TO SEE IF
                           THENCE WOULD FLOW             4.1.7
OR SEEKE HEAVN'S COURSE, OR HEAVN'S INSIDE TO SEE        4.10.5
IN NATURE APT TO LIKE WHEN I DID SEE                     4.16.1
```

```
I SEE MY COURSE TO LOSE MY SELFE DOTH BEND          4.18.12
I SEE AND YET NO GREATER SOROW TAKE                 4.18.13
THAT SEE MY WRACKE, AND YET EMBRACE THE SAME+        4.19.2
SEE THERE THAT BOY, THAT MURTHRING BOY I SAY         4.20.2
IT IS MOST TRUE, FOR SINCE I HER DID SEE            4.25.12
AND THEN WOULD NOT, OR COULD NOT SEE MY BLISSE       4.33.2
AND AH WHAT HOPE, THAT HOPE SHOULD ONCE SEE DAY      4.35.7
RICH IN ALL BEAUTIES WHICH MAN'S EYE CAN SEE         4.37.6
LIVELIER THEN ELSE-WHERE, $STELLA'S IMAGE SEE       4.39.14
FOR THOUGH I NEVER SEE THEM, BUT STRAIGHT WAYES      4.42.9
FOR WHEN HE WILL SEE WHO DARE HIM GAINESAY           4.43.5
IF $LOVE LEARNE NOT ALONE TO LOVE AND SEE            4.46.7
O LOOKE, O SHINE, O LET ME DIE AND SEE               4.48.8
WITH SAD EYES I THEIR WEAKE PROPORTION SEE           4.50.7
TILL THAT HER BLUSH TAUGHT ME MY SHAME TO SEE       4.53.14
WHERE ALL MY GOOD I DO IN $STELLA SEE                4.60.2
AND DO I SEE SOME CAUSE A HOPE TO FEEDE              4.66.1
WHAT BLUSHING NOTES DOEST THOU IN MARGINE SEE+       4.67.8
ENVIE, PUT OUT THINE EYES, LEAST THOU DO SEE         4.69.3
MY SPRING APPEARES, O SEE WHAT HERE DOTH GROW        4.69.8
IN $BEAUTIE'S THRONE, SEE NOW WHO DARES
                         COME NEARE                 4.73.10
MAKES ME IN MY BEST THOUGHTS AND QUIETST
                         JUDGEMENT SEE              4.77.12
OR HERS WHOM NAKED THE $TROJAN BOY DID SEE           4.82.4
I SEE THE HOUSE, MY HEART THY SELFE CONTAINE         4.85.1
SEE $BEAUTIE'S TOTALL SUMME SUMM'D IN HER FACE      4.85.10
FOR ME, I WEPT TO SEE PEARLES SCATTERED SO           4.87.9
THAT WHERE BEFORE HART LOVED AND EYES DID SEE       4.88.12
AH BED, THE FIELD WHERE JOYE'S PEACE SOME DO SEE     4.98.1
THAT IN THAT PALENESSE BEAUTIE'S WHITE WE SEE       4.101.6
AND SCORNING SAY, '$SEE WHAT IT IS TO LOVE'        4.107.14
WHOSE LIGHT DOTH LIGHTEN ALL THAT HERE WE SEE        5.9.14
SEE HOW THE $TYRANNESSE DOTH JOY TO SEE              5.10.5
SEE HOW THE $TYRANNESSE DOTH JOY TO SEE              5.10.5
I THINKE THAT I A NEW $PANDORA SEE                   5.24.8
SEE HOW THE STUBBORNE DAMZELL DOTH DEPRAVE           5.29.1
BUT IF YOUR SELFE IN ME YE PLAYNE WILL SEE          5.45.13
BUT YE HIGH HEVENS, THAT ALL THIS SOROWE SEE         5.46.9
DOE I NOT SEE THAT FAYREST YMAGES                    5.51.1
AS IN THEYR MAKER YE THEM BEST MAY SEE              5.53.14
STRANGE THING ME SEEMD TO SEE A BEAST SO WYLD       5.67.13
I JOY TO SEE HOW IN YOUR DRAWEN WORK                 5.71.1
AND ALL THENSFORTH ETERNALL PEACE SHALL SEE         5.71.13
WAS IT A DREAME, OR DID I SEE IT PLAYNE              5.77.1
AND WHEN I HOPE TO SEE THEYR TREW OBJECT            5.78.11
CEASSE THEN MYNE EYES, TO SEEKE HER SELFE TO SEE    5.78.13
FOR THAT YOUR SELFE YE DAYLY SUCH DOE SEE            5.79.2
NE OUGHT I SEE, THOUGH IN THE CLEAREST DAY           5.88.5
```

SEED   2
```
FLOWERS HAVE A TIME BEFORE THEY COME TO SEEDE        1.51.3
TO BE DIVINE AND BORNE OF HEAVENLY SEED             5.79.10
```

SEEING   15
```
SENSELESSE WITH TOO MUCH $JOY, EACH OTHER SEEING     2.11.7
AND STEALE DEAD SEEING OF HIS LIVING HEW+            3.67.6
BY SEEING FARTHER THEN THE EYE HATH SHOWNE           3.69.8
SEEMES SEEING, BUT EFFECTUALLY IS OUT               3.113.4
OH TIS THE FIRST, TIS FLATRY IN MY SEEING           3.114.9
NOT BY OUR FEELING, BUT BY OTHERS SEEING            3.121.4
OR MINE EYES SEEING THIS, SAY THIS IS NOT          3.137.11
```

```
LEAST EYES WELL SEEING THY FOULE FAULTS
                          SHOULD FINDE            3.148.14
THE CURIOUS WITS, SEEING DULL PENSIVENESSE        4.23.1
I, SEEING BETTER SIGHTS IN SIGHT'S DECAY          4.38.12
OR SEEING JETS, BLACKE, BUT IN BLACKNESSE BRIGHT  4.91.8
SEEING HOPE YEELD WHEN THIS WO STRAKE HIM FURST   4.95.6
SEEING MY HART THROUGH LAUNCHED EVERY WHERE       5.57.7
SEEING THE GAME FROM HIM ESCAPT AWAY              5.67.2
AND SEEING IT, THEY GAZE ON IT THE MORE           5.83.6
SEEK                    29
NO $BAYES I SEEKE TO DECKE MY MOURNING BROW        1.4.9
AND LIST NOT SEEKE TO BREAKE, TO QUENCH, TO HEALE  1.14.9
NEVER TO FINDE, AND EVERMORE TO SEEKE              1.20.9
AND SEEKE THAT WHICH I DARE NOT HOPE TO FINDE      1.20.10
AND CANNOT ISSUE FORTH TO SEEKE HER GOOD           1.29.4
SEEKE OUT SOME PLACE, AND SEE IF ANY PLACE         1.52.9
ALL THAT I SEEKE, IS TO ETERNIZE YOU               2.47.14
WHEN WHAT I SEEKE (MY WEARIE TRAVELS END)          3.50.2
WHY SHOULD POORE BEAUTIE INDIRECTLY SEEKE          3.67.7
AND THEREFORE ART INFORC'D TO SEEKE ANEW           3.82.7
IF THOU DOOST SEEKE TO HAVE WHAT THOU
                          DOOST HIDE             3.142.13
OR SEEKE HEAVN'S COURSE, OR HEAVN'S INSIDE TO SEE  4.10.5
YOU SEEKE TO NURSE AT FULLEST BREASTS OF $FAME     4.15.13
STELLA THINKE NOT THAT I BY VERSE SEEKE FAME       4.90.1
WHO SEEKE, WHO HOPE, WHO LOVE, WHO LIVE BUT THEE   4.90.2
LEAVES, LINES, AND RYMES, SEEKE HER TO
                          PLEASE ALONE            5.1.13
AND SEEKE SOME SUCCCUR BOTH TO EASE MY SMART       5.2.7
DAYLY WHEN I DO SEEKE AND SEW FOR PEACE            5.11.1
DO SEEKE MOST PRETICUS THINGS TO MAKE YOUR GAIN    5.15.2
WHAT NEEDETH YOU TO SEEKE SO FARRE IN VAINE+       5.15.4
IN VAINE I SEEKE AND SEW TO HER FOR GRACE          5.20.1
MONGST WHOME THE MORE I SEEKE TO SETTLE PEACE      5.44.13
THEN WITH SOME CORDIALLS SEEKE FIRST TO APPEASE    5.50.9
OF GRUDGING FOES, NE FAVOUR SEEK OF FRIENDS        5.59.10
AND SEEKE EACH WHERE, WHERE LAST I SAWE HER FACE   5.78.3
I SEEKE THE FIELDS WITH HER LATE FOOTING SYND      5.78.5
I SEEKE HER BOWRE WITH HER LATE PRESENCE DECKT     5.78.6
CEASSE THEN MYNE EYES, TO SEEKE HER SELFE TO SEE   5.78.13
SEEK WITH MY PLAYNTS TO MATCH THAT MOURNFUL DOVE   5.89.8
SEEKEST                  1
BUT, FOOLE, SEEKST NOT TO GET INTO HER HART        4.11.14
SEEKING                  4
SEEKING IN VAINE WHAT I HAVE EVER SOUGHT           1.33.3
SEEKING THAT BEAUTICUS ROOFE TO RUINATE            3.10.7
SEEKING TO QUENCH IN ME THE NOBLE FIRE             4.68.7
SO MANIE EYES AY SEEKING THEIR OWNE WOE            4.78.12
SEEKS                    3
NOR SEEKES IT TO BE KNOWNE UNTO THE $GREAT         1.58.10
BUT THEN SHE SEEKES WITH TORMENT AND TURMOYLE      5.11.11
SEEKES WITH SWEET PEACE TO SALVE EACH
                          OTHERS WOUND            5.65.12
SEEM                    25
ALTHOUGH THIS WORLD MAY SEEME HER DEEDE TO BLAME   1.30.13
WHEN DARKE SHALL SEEME THY DAY THAT NEVER CLEARES  1.42.3
THOUGH MY $CONCEIT I FURTHER SEEME TO BEND         2.34.10
WHICH WITH MY PLAINT SEEME YET WITH PITTIE MOVED   2.45.13
WHAT MOST I $SEEME, THAT SUREST AM I $NOT          2.62.8
WHAT MOST I SEEME, THAT SUREST AM I NOT            2.150.8
```

AND IN MINE OWNE LOVES STRENGTH SEEME TO DECAY   3.23.7
MAY MAKE SEEME BARE, IN WANTING WORDS TO SHEW IT   3.26.6
AND NIGHT DOTH NIGHTLY MAKE GREEFES LENGTH
                        SEEME STRONGER   3.28.14
WHEN SWIFT EXTREMITY CAN SEEME BUT SLOW   3.51.6
OH HOW MUCH MORE DOTH BEAUTIE BEAUTIOUS SEEME   3.54.1
O LEAST YOUR TRUE LOVE MAY SEEME FALCE IN THIS   3.72.9
AND OTHER STRAINES OF WOE, WHICH NOW SEEME WOE   3.90.13
COMPAR'D WITH LOSSE OF THEE, WILL NOT SEEME SO   3.90.14
MAY STILL SEEME LOVE TO ME, THOUGH ALTER'D NEW   3.93.3
TO MAKE HIM SEEME LONG HENCE, AS HE SHOWES NOW   3.101.14
HER EYES SO SUTED, AND THEY MOURNERS SEEME   3.127.10
SHALL WILL IN OTHERS SEEME RIGHT GRACIOUS   3.135.7
SEEME MOST ALONE IN GREATEST COMPANIE   4.27.2
OF $HOPE, WHICH MAKES IT SEEME FAIRE TO THE EYE   4.49.8
IF YOU HEARE THAT THEY SEEME MY HART TO MOVE   4.91.13
DOTH SEEME TO PROMISE HOPE OF NEW DELIGHT   5.4.2
YE BEARING IT DOE SEEME TO ME INCLIND   5.28.4
AND MAKETH EVERY MINUTE SEEME A MYLE   5.87.12
SO SORROW STILL DOTH SEEME TOO LONG TO LAST   5.87.13
SEEMED   12
YET THIS ABOUNDANT ISSUE SEEM'D TO ME   3.97.9
YET SEEM'D IT $WINTER STILL, AND YOU AWAY   3.98.13
THOUGH ABSENCE SEEM'D MY FLAME TO QUALLIFIE   3.109.2
AND OTHERS' FEETE STILL SEEM'D BUT STRANGERS
                        IN MY WAY   4.1.11
THEY FLED WITH BLUSH, WHICH GUILTIE SEEM'D
                        OF LOVE   4.66.14
WHILE CRAFTILY YOU SEEM'D YOUR CUT TO KEEPE   4.83.3
SEEMD EVERY BIT, WHICH THENCEFORTH I DID EAT   5.39.14
THAT SEEMD THE LONGER FOR MY GREATER PAINES   5.60.12
ME SEEMD I SMELT A GARDIN OF SWEET FLOWRES   5.64.2
STRANGE THING ME SEEMD TO SEE A BEAST SO WYLD   5.67.13
WHOSE HARVEST SEEMD TO HASTEN NOW APACE   5.76.10
AND MANY NIGHTS, THAT SLOWLY SEEMD TO MOVE   5.87.3
SEEMETH   3
ALL THIS WORLDS GLORY SEEMETH VAYNE TO ME   5.35.13
LYKEST IT SEEMETH IN MY SIMPLE WIT   5.40.5
ALL THIS WORLDS GLORY SEEMETH VAYNE TO ME   5.83.13
SEEMING   3
WHOSE SPEECHLESSE SONG BEING MANY, SEEMING ONE   3.8.13
MY LOVE IS STRENGTHNED THOUGH MORE WEAKE
                        IN SEEMING   3.102.1
O LOVES BEST HABIT IS IN SEEMING TRUST   3.138.11
SEEMLY   1
IS BUT THE SEEMELY RAYMENT OF MY HEART   3.22.6
SEEMS   8
SUCH SEEMES YOUR BEAUTIE STILL.. $THREE
                        $WINTERS COLDE   3.104.3
SEEMES SEEING, BUT EFFECTUALLY IS OUT   3.113.4
THAT WHEREAS BLACKE SEEMES $BEAUTIE'S CONTRARY   4.7.10
EACH DAY SEEMES LONG, AND LONGS FOR LONG-STAID
                        NIGHT   4.89.5
BUT THAT SAME LOFTY COUNTENANCE SEEMES TO SCORNE   5.13.9
FAYRE SOYLE IT SEEMES FROM FAR AND FRAUGHT
                        WITH STORE   5.63.7
THAT FURTHER SEEMES HIS TERME STILL TO EXTEND   5.87.11
FOR HIS RETURNE THAT SEEMES TO LINGER LATE   5.89.4
SEEN   27
THE TRUEST LOVE THAT EVER YET WAS SEENE   1.10.8

```
HAVE SEENE THOSE WALLS WHICH PROUD AMBITION
                        REAR'D                           1.45.2
HOW FARRE HE SAYL'D, WHAT $COUNTRIES HE HAD SEENE        2.1.4
TO HAVE SEENE THEE, THEIR $SEXES ONELY GLORY             2.6.12
SAY TO OUR $NEPHEWES, THAT THOU ONCE HAST SEENE          2.17.11
BLIND WERE MINE $EYES, TILL THEY WERE
                        SEENE OF THINE                   2.35.9
LASTLY, MINE $EYES AMAZEDLY HAVE SEENE                   2.51.5
EV'N AS A $MAN THAT IN SOME $TRANCE HATH SEENE           2.57.9
BE IT NOT SEENE IN EITHER OF OUR $BROWES                 2.61.7
HAD NOT MINE EYE SEENE THY $CELESTIALL EYE               2.104.5
THAT THEY MAY TEL MORE WORLDS WHAT $TIME
                        HATH SEENE                       2.107.11
BLIND WERE MINE EYES, TILL THEY WERE SEENE
                        OF THINE                         2.112.9
A FOOLES THINKE I, HAD YOU $IDEA SEENE                   2.120.13
NO CLOWDE WAS SEENE, BUT CHRISTALINE THE AYRE            2.125.13
NOR MY DISGRACES TO THE WORLD BE SEENE                   2.142.14
FULL MANY A GLORIOUS MORNING HAVE I SEENE                3.33.1
HIS BEAUTIE SHALL IN THESE BLACKE LINES BE SEENE         3.63.13
WHEN I HAVE SEENE BY TIMES FELL HAND DEFACED             3.64.1
WHEN I HAVE SEENE THE HUNGRY $OCEAN GAINE                3.64.5
WHEN I HAVE SEENE SUCH INTERCHANGE OF STATE              3.64.9
IN HIM THOSE HOLY ANTIQUE HOWERS ARE SEENE               3.68.9
SO ARE THOSE ERRORS THAT IN THEE ARE SEENE               3.96.7
WHAT FREEZINGS HAVE I FELT, WHAT DARKE
                        DAIES SEENE+                     3.97.3
IN PROCESSE OF THE SEASONS HAVE I SEENE                  3.104.6
HAVE I NOT SEENE DWELLERS ON FORME AND FAVOR             3.125.5
I HAVE SEENE $ROSES DAMASKT, RED AND WHITE               3.130.5
YET SWAM IN JOY, SUCH LOVE IN HER WAS SEENE              4.87.11
SEES                    5
THE CRUELST $FAYRE THAT SEES I PINE FOR HER              1.22.11
THE SUNNE IT SELFE SEES NOT, TILL HEAVEN
                        CLEERES                          3.148.12
STELLA OFT SEES THE VERIE FACE OF WO                     4.45.1
AS WHAT MY HART STILL SEES THOU CANST NOT SPIE+          4.105.4
BUT STILL THE MORE SHE FERVENT SEES MY FIT               5.32.9
SEEST                   3
AND YET THOU SEEST THY POWRE SHE DISOBAYES               1.23.9
IN ME THOU SEEST THE TWI-LIGHT OF SUCH DAY               3.73.5
IN ME THOU SEEST THE GLOWING OF SUCH FIRE                3.73.9
SEETHING                1
AND GREW A SEETHING BATH WHICH YET MEN PROVE             3.153.7
SELDOM                  2
FOR BLUNTING THE FINE POINT OF SELDOME PLEASURE          3.52.4
SINCE SILDOM COMMING IN THE LONG YEARE SET               3.52.6
SELF                    218
DELIA HER SELFE, AND ALL THE WORLD MAY VIEW              1.4.7
GRATEFULL T'ANOTHER, TO MY SELFE UNKINDE                 1.20.12
I VIEW MY SELFE, MY SELFE IN WOFULL CASE                 1.29.8
I VIEW MY SELFE, MY SELFE IN WOFULL CASE                 1.29.8
HEAVEN NOR EARTH WILL NOT, MY SELFE CANNOT WAKE          1.29.9
AND BLAME MY SELFE T'EXCUSE THAT HEART OF THINE          1.33.12
UPON MY SELFE THOU BEST MAYST FINDE THE FORME            1.37.8
THEN LEAVE THY GLASSE, AND GAZE THY SELFE ON ME          1.37.9
THEN WHAT MY FAITH HATH BENE THY SELFE SHALL SEE         1.41.11
HERE READ THY SELFE, AND WHAT I SUFFRED FOR THEE         1.42.8
A BURDEN TO MY SELFE, DISTREST IN MINDE                  1.49.2
UNTO HER SELFE, HER SELFE MY LOVE DOTH SOMMON            1.49.9
```

```
UNTO HER SELFE, HER SELFE MY LOVE DOTH SOMMON        1.49.9
STEALE FROM THY SELFE, AND BE THY CARES
                          OWNE THIEFE                1.52.12
ILE MONE MY SELFE, AND HIDE THE WRONG I HAVE         1.59.10
EACH $BIRD SINGS TO HER SELFE, AND SO WILL I         1.59.14
THAT $CRUELTY HER SELFE MIGHT GRIEVE TO VIEW         1.60.7
SINCE, BUT YOUR SELFE, THERE WAS NO $CREATURE BY     2.2.3
IT SLEW IT SELFE., THE $VERDICT ON THE VIEW          2.2.5
AND LET ME TAKE MY SELFE WHAT I DOE CRAVE            2.5.12
AS $OTHER $MEN, SO I MY SELFE DOE $MUSE              2.9.1
SINCE $YOU IN $ME, MY SELFE SINCE OUT OF $ME         2.11.4
TRANSPORTED FROM MY $SELFE, INTO $YOUR BEING         2.11.5
GIVE $ME MY $SELFE, AND TAKE YOUR $SELFE AGAINE      2.11.9
GIVE $ME MY $SELFE, AND TAKE YOUR $SELFE AGAINE      2.11.9
FROM MY $SELFE $YOU, OR FROM YOUR OWNE $SELFE I      2.11.14
FROM MY $SELFE $YOU, OR FROM YOUR OWNE $SELFE I      2.11.14
YOUR SELFE THUS BURNED IN THAT SACRED FLAME          2.16.9
IN WHOM, $HEAV'N LOCKES IT SELFE AS IN A $GLASSE     2.17.4
NOW TEMPTING $ME, TO DROWNE MY $SELFE IN TEARES      2.20.11
AND PLEASE YOUR SELFE WITH THIS $CONCEIT
                          THE WHILE                  2.24.8
TO $WISEDOME'S SELFE TO MINISTER DIRECTION           2.34.7
TO THEIR GROSSE $SENSE APPLY HER SELFE SO ILL        2.43.10
TO SOME BASE $RUSTICK DOE THY SELFE PREFERRE         2.48.6
GOE HYRE THY SELFE SOME BUNGLING $HARPERS $BOY       2.48.10
PRESERVE MY $TEARES, AND THOU THY $SELFE
                          SHALT PROVE                2.55.3
YOU, IN WHOM $NATURE CHOSE HER SELFE TO VIEW         2.57.5
THAT THUS SO CLEANLY, I MY $SELFE CAN FREE           2.61.4
PRESERVE MY TEARES, AND THOU THY SELFE
                          SHALT PROVE                2.102.3
AND IN MY VERSE THY SELFE ART DEIFIED                2.104.12
THUS FROM THY SELFE THE CAUSE IS THUS DERIVED        2.104.13
THY SELFE THUS BURNED IN THIS SACRED FLAME           2.106.9
FEED'ST THY LIGHTS FLAME WITH SELFE SUBSTANTIALL
                          FEWELL                     3.1.6
THY SELFE THY FOE, TO THY SWEET SELFE TOO CRUELL     3.1.8
THY SELFE THY FOE, TO THY SWEET SELFE TOO CRUELL     3.1.8
OF HIS SELFE LOVE TO STOP POSTERITY+                 3.3.8
UPON THY SELFE THY BEAUTIES LEGACY+                  3.4.2
FOR HAVING TRAFFIKE WITH THY SELFE ALONE             3.4.9
THOU OF THY SELFE THY SWEET SELFE DOST DECEAVE       3.4.10
THOU OF THY SELFE THY SWEET SELFE DOST DECEAVE       3.4.10
WITH BEAUTITS TREASURE ERE IT BE SELFE KIL'D         3.6.4
THAT'S FOR THY SELFE TO BREED AN OTHER THEE          3.6.7
TEN TIMES THY SELFE WERE HAPPIER THEN THOU ART       3.6.9
SO THOU, THY SELFE CUT-GOING IN THY NOON             3.7.13
THAT THOU CONSUM'ST THY SELFE IN SINGLE LIFE+        3.9.2
WHO FOR THY SELFE ART SO UNPROVIDENT                 3.10.2
THAT GAINST THY SELFE THOU STICKST NOT
                          TO CONSPIRE                3.10.6
OR TO THY SELFE AT LEAST KIND HARTED PROVE           3.10.12
MAKE THEE AN OTHER SELFE FOR LOVE OF ME              3.10.13
O THAT YOU WERE YOUR SELFE, BUT LOVE YOU ARE         3.13.1
NO LONGER YOURS, THEN YOU YOUR SELFE HERE LIVE       3.13.2
YOU SELFE AGAIN AFTER YOUR SELFES DECEASE            3.13.7
IF FROM THY SELFE, TO STORE THOU WOULDST CONVERT     3.14.12
AND FORTIFIE YOUR SELFE IN YOUR DECAY                3.16.3
CAN MAKE YOU LIVE YOUR SELFE IN EIES OF MEN          3.16.12
TO GIVE AWAY YOUR SELFE, KEEPS YOUR SELFE STILL      3.16.13
```

TO GIVE AWAY YOUR SELFE, KEEPS YOUR SELFE STILL   3.16.13
WHO HEAVEN IT SELFE FOR ORNAMENT DOTH USE   3.21.3
O THEREFORE LOVE BE OF THY SELFE SO WARY   3.22.9
AS I NOT FOR MY SELFE, BUT FOR THEE WILL   3.22.10
FOR THEE, AND FOR MY SELFE, NOE QUIET FINDE   3.27.14
AND LOOKE UPON MY SELFE AND CURSE MY FATE   3.29.4
YET IN THESE THOUGHTS MY SELFE ALMOST DESPISING   3.29.9
MY SELFE CORRUPTING SALVING THY AMISSE   3.35.7
AND GAINST MY SELFE A LAWFULL PLEA COMMENCE   3.35.11
OH GIVE THY SELFE THE THANKES IF OUGHT IN ME   3.38.5
WHEN THOU THY SELFE DOST GIVE INVENTION LIGHT+   3.38.8
WHAT CAN MINE OWNE PRAISE TO MINE OWNE
                  SELFE BRING   3.39.3
BUT YET BE BLAM'D, IF THOU THIS SELFE DECEAVEST   3.40.7
BY WILFULL TASTE OF WHAT THY SELFE REFUSEST   3.40.8
THY SEIFE AWAY, ARE PRESENT STILL WITH ME   3.47.10
AND THIS MY HAND, AGAINST MY SELFE UPREARE   3.49.11
SO TIL THE JUDGEMENT THAT YOUR SELFE ARISE   3.55.13
THAT YOU YOUR SELFE MAY PRIVILEDGE YOUR TIME   3.58.10
YOUR SELFE TO PARDON OF SELFE-DOING CRIME   3.58.12
AND FOR MY SELFE MINE OWNE WORTH DO DEFINE   3.62.7
BUT WHEN MY GLASSE SHEWES ME MY SELFE INDEED   3.62.9
MINE OWNE SELFE LOVE QUITE CONTRARY I READ   3.62.11
SELFE, SO SELFE LOVING WERE INIQUITY   3.62.12
SELFE, SO SELFE LOVING WERE INIQUITY   3.62.12
T'IS THEE (MY SELFE) THAT FOR MY SELFE I PRAISE   3.62.13
T'IS THEE (MY SELFE) THAT FOR MY SELFE I PRAISE   3.62.13
OR STATE IT SELFE CONFOUNDED, TO DECAY   3.64.10
AND LACE IT SELFE WITH HIS SOCIETIE+   3.67.4
WITHOUT ALL ORNAMENT, IT SELFE AND TRUE   3.68.10
DEATHS SECOND SELFE THAT SEALS UP ALL IN REST   3.73.8
SINCE WHAT HE OWES THEE, THOU THY SELFE
                  DOOST PAY   3.79.14
THAT YOU YOUR SELFE BEING EXTANT WELL MIGHT SHOW   3.83.6
THY SELFE THOU GAV'ST, THY OWNE WORTH
                  THEN NOT KNOWING   3.87.9
UPON THY SIDE, AGAINST MY SELFE ILE FIGHT   3.88.3
THE INJURIES THAT TO MY SELFE I DOE   3.88.11
THAT FOR THY RIGHT, MY SELFE WILL BEARE
                  ALL WRONG   3.88.14
AS ILE MY SELFE DISGRACE, KNOWING THY WIL   3.89.7
FOR THEE, AGAINST MY SELFE ILE VOW DEBATE   3.89.13
BUT DOE THY WORST TO STEALE THY SELFE AWAY   3.92.1
THOUGH TO IT SELFE, IT ONELY LIVE AND DIE   3.94.10
AS EASIE MIGHT I FROM MY SELFE DEPART   3.109.3
SO THAT MY SELFE BRING WATER FOR MY STAINE   3.109.8
AND MADE MY SELFE A MOTLEY TO THE VIEW   3.110.2
SUCH CHERUBINES AS YOUR SWEET SELFE RESEMBLE   3.114.6
STILL LOOSING WHEN I SAW MY SELFE TO WIN+   3.119.4
WHILST IT HATH THOUGHT IT SELFE SO BLESSED
                  NEVER+   3.119.6
THY LOVERS WITHERING, AS THY SWEET SELFE GROW'ST   3.126.4
ALTHOUGH I SWEARE IT TO MY SELFE ALONE   3.131.8
THEN WILL I SWEARE BEAUTY HER SELFE IS BLACKE   3.132.13
ME FROM MY SELFE THY CRUELL EYE HATH TAKEN   3.133.5
AND MY NEXT SELFE THOU HARDER HAST INGROSSED   3.133.6
OF HIM, MY SELFE, AND THEE I AM FORSAKEN   3.133.7
AND I MY SELFE AM MORGAG'D TO THY WILL   3.134.2
MY SELFE $ILE FORFEIT, SO THAT OTHER MINE   3.134.3
BY SELFE EXAMPLE MAI'ST THOU BE DENIDE   3.142.14

```
THE SUNNE IT SELFE SEES NOT, TILL HEAVEN
                        CLEERES                         3.148.12
WHEN I AGAINST MY SELFE WITH THEE PERTAKE               3.149.2
AM OF MY SELFE, ALL TIRANT FOR THY SAKE+               3.149.4
REVENGE UPON MY SELFE WITH PRESENT MONE+               3.149.8
WHAT MERRIT DO I IN MY SELFE RESPECT                    3.149.9
LEAST GUILTY OF MY FAULTS THY SWEET SELFE PROVE         3.151.4
BITING MY TREWAND PEN, BEATING MY SELFE FOR SPITE       4.1.13
TO MAKE MY SELFE BELEEVE, THAT ALL IS WELL              4.2.13
THAT $VERTUE, THOU THY SELFE SHALT BE IN LOVE           4.4.14
WHICH $CUPID'S SELFE FROM $BEAUTIE'S MYNE
                        DID DRAW                        4.9.13
WITH WHAT SHARPE CHECKES I IN MY SELFE AM SHENT         4.18.1
AND BY JUST COUNTS MY SELFE A BANCKROUT KNOW            4.18.3
I SEE MY COURSE TO LOSE MY SELFE DOTH BEND              4.18.12
BEWRAY IT SELFE IN MY LONG SETLED EYES                  4.23.2
SCOURGE OF IT SELFE, STILL CLIMING SLIPPRIE
                        PLACE                           4.23.10
LOVE OF HER SELFE, TAKES $STELLA'S SHAPE,
                        THAT SHE                        4.25.10
FAWNE ON MY SELF, AND OTHERS TO DESPISE                 4.27.8
TO KEEPE IT SELFE IN LIFE AND LIBERTY                   4.29.6
HART RENT THY SELFE, THOU DOEST THY SELFE
                        BUT RIGHT                       4.33.5
HART RENT THY SELFE, THOU DOEST THY SELFE
                        BUT RIGHT                       4.33.5
BUT TO MY SELFE MY SELFE DID GIVE THE BLOW              4.33.9
BUT TO MY SELFE MY SELFE DID GIVE THE BLOW              4.33.9
WHERE TRUTH IT SELFE MUST SPEAKE LIKE FLATTERIE+        4.35.2
SINCE $REASON'S SELFE DOTH BLOW THE COLE IN ME+         4.35.6
BY $LOVE'S OWNE SELFE, BUT WITH SO CURIOUS
                        DROUGHT                         4.38.7
WHERE BLUSHING RED, THAT $LOVE'S SELFE
                        THEM DOTH LOVE                  4.43.10
THAT $NOBLENESSE IT SELFE MAKES THUS UNKIND+            4.44.8
NOT THOUGH THEREOF THE CAUSE HER SELFE SHE KNOW         4.45.4
FOR THOUGH I OFT MY SELFE OF THEM BEMONE                4.48.9
BE $LOVE'S INDEED, IN $STELLA'S SELFE HE MAY            4.52.10
LET $VERTUE HAVE THAT $STELLA'S SELFE., YET THUS        4.52.13
THE THOROWEST WORDS, FIT FOR WOE'S SELFE TO GRONE       4.57.4
AND ANCHOR FAST MY SELFE ON $VERTUE'S SHORE             4.62.11
COME, COME, AND LET ME POWRE MY SELFE ON THEE           4.69.6
THY SELFE, DOEST STRIVE ALL MINDS THAT
                        WAY TO MOVE                     4.71.10
THAT $ANGER' SELFE I NEEDS MUST KISSE AGAINE            4.73.14
THAT GRACE, WHICH $VENUS WEEPES THAT SHE
                        HER SELFE DOTH MISSE            4.77.4
IN $LILLIES' NEAST, WHERE $LOVE'S SELFE
                        LIES ALONG                      4.83.8
CANNOT SUCH GRACE YOUR SILLY SELFE CONTENT              4.83.11
I SEE THE HOUSE, MY HEART THY SELFE CONTAINE            4.85.1
A STILL FELT PLAGUE, TO SELFE CONDEMNING ME             4.86.3
AND DO I THEN MY SELFE THIS VAINE SCUSE GIVE+           4.93.9
THO WORLDS QUITE ME, SHALL I MY SELFE FORGIVE+          4.93.11
WHICH EVEN TO SENCE, SENCE OF IT SELFE DENIES           4.94.7
YET WAILE THY SELFE, AND WAILE WITH CAUSEFULL
                        TEARES                          4.94.11
HER SELFE (TO SHEW NO OTHER JOY HATH PLACE)             4.97.7
BUT WO IS ME, THOUGH JOY IT SELFE WERE SHE              4.97.12
THAT ELOQUENCE IT SELFE ENVIES YOUR PRAISE              4.100.10
```

```
THAT SICKENESSE BRAGS IT SELFE BEST GRACED TO BE        4.101.4
WHICH $NATURE' SELFE DID MAKE, AND SELFE
                      ENGRAIND THE SAME+                  4.102.6
WHICH $NATURE' SELFE DID MAKE, AND SELFE
                      ENGRAIND THE SAME+                  4.102.6
I SAW THY SELFE WITH MANY A SMILING LINE                4.103.2
LET HONOR SELFE TO THEE GRAUNT HIGHEST PLACE            4.103.14
BUT THOU ART GONE, NOW THAT SELFE FELT DISGRACE         4.106.7
AND ALSO TO SUSTAYNE THY SELFE WITH FOOD                  5.2.8
TO DECKE HIR SELFE, AND HER FAIRE MANTLE WEAVE           5.4.12
PREPARE YOUR SELFE NEW LOVE TO ENTERTAINE                5.4.14
THEN TO THE $MAKER SELFE THEY LIKEST BE                  5.9.13
SHE CRUELL WARRIOUR DOTH HER SELFE ADDRESSE              5.11.3
WAS FORST TO YEELD MY SELFE INTO THEIR HANDS            5.12.10
FOR LOE MY LOVE DOTH IN HER SELFE CONTAINE               5.15.5
AND WHEN I WAILE, SHE TURNES HIR SELFE
                      TO LAUGHTER                        5.18.12
AND IN THE SHADE OF DEATH IT SELFE SHALL SHROUD          5.27.3
ACCOUMPTS MY SELFE HER CAPTIVE QUITE FORLORNE            5.29.4
SWEET IS THY VERTUE AS THY SELFE SWEET ART               5.39.5
THE WHICH MY SELFE AGAINST MY SELFE DOE MAKE             5.44.6
THE WHICH MY SELFE AGAINST MY SELFE DOE MAKE             5.44.6
TO BATTAILE FRESH AGAINST MY SELFE TO FIGHT             5.44.12
YOUR GOODLY SELFE FOR EVERMORE TO VEW                    5.45.2
AND IN MY SELFE, MY INWARD SELFE I MEANE                 5.45.3
AND IN MY SELFE, MY INWARD SELFE I MEANE                 5.45.3
BUT IF YOUR SELFE IN ME YE PLAYNE WILL SEE              5.45.13
AND RULES THE MEMBERS AS IT SELFE DOTH PLEASE+           5.50.8
SO DOE I NOW MY SELFE A PRISONER YEELD                   5.52.5
DOTH SUFFER WRECK BOTH OF HER SELFE AND GOODS           5.56.12
HER SELFE ASSURD, AND IS OF NOUGHT AFFRAYD               5.58.4
THAT TO YOUR SELFE YE MOST ASSURED ARRE+                5.58.14
UNTO HER SELFE AND SETLED SO IN HART                     5.59.2
SUCH SELFE ASSURANCE NEED NOT FEARE THE SPIGHT           5.59.9
NETHER TO ONE HER SELFE NOR OTHER BENDS                 5.59.12
FOR NOW YOUR LIGHT DOTH MORE IT SELFE DILATE            5.66.11
BID HER THEREFORE HER SELFE SOONE READY MAKE             5.70.9
YOUR SELFE UNTO THE $BEE YE DOE COMPARE                  5.71.2
RIGHT SO YOUR SELFE WERE CAUGHT IN CUNNING SNARE         5.71.5
BEING MY SELFE CAPTYVED HERE IN CARE                     5.73.1
FOR I MY SELVE SHALL LYKE TO THIS DECAY                  5.75.7
I FYND MY SELFE BUT FED WITH FANCIES VAYNE              5.78.12
CEASSE THEN MYNE EYES, TO SEEKE HER SELFE TO SEE        5.78.13
AND LET MY THOUGHTS BEHOLD HER SELFE IN MEE             5.78.14
FOR THAT YOUR SELFE YE DAYLY SUCH DOE SEE                5.79.2
AND GATHER TO MY SELFE NEW BREATH AWHILE                 5.80.4
THERE FILL YOUR SELFE WITH THOSE MOST
                      JOYOUS SIGHTS                       5.84.9
THE WHICH MY SELFE COULD NEVER YET ATTAYNE              5.84.10
OF THAT SELFE KYND WITH WHICH THE $FURIES FELL           5.86.2
DEW TO THY SELFE THAT IT FOR ME PREPARD                 5.86.14
WITH LIGHT THEREOF I DOE MY SELFE SUSTAYNE              5.88.11
MOURNE TO MY SELFE THE ABSENCE OF MY LOVE                5.89.6
SELF-DOING               1
YOUR SELFE TO PARDON OF SELFE-DOING CRIME               3.58.12
SELF-LOVE                1
SINNE OF SELFE-LOVE POSSESSETH AL MINE EIE               3.62.1
SELF-MISERY              1
A MONSTER, OTHER'S HARME, SELFE-MISERIE                  4.78.5
```

SELFNESS   1
  THAT WHOLLY HERS, ALL SELFNESSE HE FORBEARES   4.61.7
SELF-PLEASING   1
  WITHOUT SOME SPARK OF SUCH SELF-PLEASING PRIDE   5.5.14
SELF'S   1
  YOU SELFE AGAIN AFTER YOUR SELFES DECEASE   3.13.7
SELFSAME   3
  WHILST I IN DARKENESSE, IN THE SELFE-SAME PLACE   2.43.3
  CHEARED AND CHECKT EVEN BY THE SELFE-SAME SKIE   3.15.6
  THE GENTLE DEARE RETURND THE SELFE-SAME WAY   5.67.7
SELF-WILLED   1
  BE NOT SELFE-WILD FOR THOU ART MUCH TOO FAIRE   3.6.13
SELL   1
  I WILL NOT PRAYSE THAT PURPOSE NOT TO SELL   3.21.14
SELLING   1
  BUY TEARMES DIVINE IN SELLING HOURES OF CROSSE   3.146.11
SELVES   5
  SOFTEN YOUR SELVES WITH EV'RY $TEARE THAT FALLS   2.45.11
  WE AND THE $DUTCH AT LENGTH OUR $SELVES TO SEVER   2.51.9
  AN IMAGE IS, WHICH FOR OUR SELVES WE CARVE   4.5.6
  AND DAMNING THEIR OWNE SELVES TO $TANTAL'S SMART   4.24.3
  AND DYING DOE THEM SELVES OF PAYNE BEGUYLE   5.47.12
SEMBLANCE   1
  AND YOUR SWEET SEMBLANCE TO SOME OTHER GIVE   3.13.4
SEMBLANT   2
  MOST LIVELY LYKE BEHOLD YOUR SEMBLANT TREW   5.45.4
  FOR WITH THE GOODLY SEMBLANT OF HER HEW   5.53.6
SEND   8
  NOW SEND FORTH HOPE, FOR NOW CALME PITTY SAVES   1.46.4
  I SEND THOSE EYES THE CABINETS OF LOVE   1.60.6
  I SEND DEFIANCE, SINCE IF OVERTHROWNE   2.63.13
  TO THEE I SEND THIS WRITTEN AMBASSAGE   3.26.3
  I SEND THEM BACK AGAINE AND STRAIGHT GROW SAD   3.45.14
  WHO HARD BY MADE A WINDOW SEND FORTH LIGHT   4.53.9
  INTO THIS SINFULL WORLD FROM HEAVEN TO SEND   5.24.10
  THEN SHALL THE NEW YEARES JOY FORTH FRESHLY SEND   5.62.9
SENDEST   2
  AND TO MY HART SEND'ST POYSON FROM THINE EYE   2.130.7
  IS IT THY SPIRIT THAT THOU SEND'ST FROM THEE   3.61.5
SENDS   2
  AND AS A $QUEENE, WHO FROM HER PRESENCE SENDS   4.107.9
  AND IN HER SONGS SENDS MANY A WISHFULL VOW   5.89.3
SENSE   28
  MY SENCE OPPRESS'D, HAD FAILD, AND HEART
                            HAD BROKEN   1.7.14
  FAVOURS (I THINKE) WOULD SENCE QUITE OVERCOME   1.17.13
  IN SPEEDIE APPREHENSION, IT IS $SENSE   2.12.10
  UNTO MINE AID I SUMMON'D EV'RY $SENSE   2.29.2
  TO THEIR GROSSE $SENCE APPLY HER SELFE SO ILL   2.43.10
  FOR TO THY SENSUALL FAULT I BRING IN SENCE   3.35.9
  THAT MY STEEL'D SENCE OR CHANGES RIGHT OR WRONG   3.112.8
  OF OTHERS VOYCES, THAT MY $ADDERS SENCE   3.112.10
  MY DEEPEST SENCE, HOW HARD TRUE SORROW HITS   3.120.10
  WOULDST BRABLING BE WITH SENCE AND LOVE IN ME   4.10.2
  LEAVE SENSE, AND THOSE WHICH SENSE'S OBJECTS BE   4.10.7
  BUT THOU WOULDST NEEDS FIGHT BOTH WITH
                            LOVE AND SENCE   4.10.9
  THAT NEVER I WITH CLOS'D-UP SENSE DO LIE   4.32.6
  I START, LOOKE, HEARKE, BUT WHAT IN CLOSDE
                            UP SENCE   4.38.9

```
WAS HELD, IN OPEND SENSE IT FLIES AWAY              4.38.10
OPPRESSING MORTALL SENSE, MY DEATH PROCEED          4.42.13
MY MIND BEMONES HIS SENSE OF INWARD SMART           4.44.2
OR WANT I SENSE TO FEELE MY MISERIE+                4.47.5
EACH SENCE OF MINE, EACH GIFT, EACH POWER OF MIND   4.57.2
SO CAPTIVES TO HIS $SAINT BOTH SOULE AND SENCE      4.61.6
PLEASINGST CONSORT, WHERE EACH SENCE HOLDS A PART   4.79.3
AND HER SAD WORDS MY SADDED SENCE DID HEARE         4.87.8
MY $ORPHAN SENCE FLIES TO THE INWARD SIGHT          4.88.10
WHICH EVEN TO SENCE, SENCE OF IT SELFE DENIES       4.94.7
WHICH EVEN TO SENCE, SENCE OF IT SELFE DENIES       4.94.7
SUCH LIGHT IN SENSE, WITH SUCH A DARKNED MIND       4.99.14
WHERE RIGROWS EXILE LOCKES UP ALL MY SENSE+         4.104.8
THE CHARMING SMILES, THAT ROB SENCE FROM
                         THE HART                   5.17.10
```

SENSELESS   5
```
  SENSELESSE WITH TOO MUCH $JOY, EACH OTHER SEEING   2.11.7
  INCLOSE MY $MUSIKE, YOU POORE SENSELESSE $WALLS    2.45.9
  ELS SENCELES LOVE COULD NEVER ONCE ENDITE          2.131.4
  AND YSE WHICH IS CONGEALD WITH SENCELESSE COLD     5.30.11
  SHE IS NO WOMAN, BUT A SENCELESSE STONE            5.54.14
```
SENSES   4
```
  AND BAD MY $SENSES TO A SOLEMNE $FEAST             2.7.2
  (THE $KING OF $SENCES, GREATER THEN THE REST)      2.29.10
  WHOSE $SENSES, LIKE POORE $PRIS'NERS,
                         HUNGER-STARV'D              2.49.7
  BUT MY FIVE WITS, NOR MY FIVE SENCES CAN           3.141.9
```
SENSE'S   4
```
  THE SOULES DELIGHT, THE SENCES TRUE DIRECTION      2.123.7
  LEAVE SENSE, AND THOSE WHICH SENSE'S OBJECTS BE    4.10.7
  WHILE HE EACH THING IN SENSE'S BALLANCE WAYES      4.25.6
  BY SENCE'S PRIVILEDGE, CAN SCAPE FROM THEE         4.36.14
```
SENSUAL   3
```
  FOR TO THY SENSUALL FAULT I BRING IN SENCE         3.35.9
  TO ANY SENSUALL FEAST WITH THEE ALONE              3.141.8
  NE ONE LIGHT GLANCE OF SENSUALL DESYRE             5.84.3
```
SENT   6
```
  HAST SENT THE INCENSE OF THY SIGHS TO HEAVEN       1.8.2
  AND SO SENT BACKE, AND THUS MY FORTUNE LIES        1.25.12
  AND OF SOME SENT FROM THAT SWEET ENEMIE $FRAUNCE   4.41.4
  SENT FORTH THE BEAMES, WHICH MADE SO FAIRE
                         MY RACE                     4.41.14
  STELLA'S EYES SENT TO ME THE BEAMES OF BLISSE      4.66.11
  BUT THEN FROM HEAVEN MOST HIDEOUS STORMES
                         ARE SENT                    5.46.3
```
SENTENCE   3
```
  I WRITTEN FINDE THE SENTENCE OF MY DEATH           1.10.3
  MAKE HER THE SENTENCE OF HER WRATH REPEALE         1.22.4
  BY $PHOEBUS' DOOME, WITH SUGRED SENTENCE SAYES     4.25.2
```
SEPARABLE   1
```
  THOUGH IN OUR LIVES A SEPERABLE SPIGHT             3.36.6
```
SEPARATION   1
```
  THAT BY THIS SEPERATION I MAY GIVE                 3.39.7
```
SEPULCHERS   1
```
  THE RIGHT OF SEPULCHERS, WERE SHORNE AWAY          3.68.6
```
SEQUENT   1
```
  IN SEQUENT TOILE ALL FORWARDS DO CONTEND           3.60.4
```
SERIOUS   1
```
  THOU DOEST PROCEED IN THY MOST SERIOUS WAYES       4.11.2
```

SERPENTS   1
  THREE SORTS OF $SERPENTS DUE RESEMBLE THEE   2.130.1
SERVANT   1
  WHEN YOU HAVE BID YCUR SERVANT ONCE ADIEUE   3.57.8
SERVANTS   2
  THAT MINE OWNE WRITINGS LIKE BAD SERVANTS SHCW   4.21.3
  BUT GIVE APT SERVANTS THEIR DUE PLACE, LET EYES   4.85.9
SERVANT'S   2
  THEN SOULE LIVE THCU UPCN THY SERVANTS LCSSE   3.146.9
  THEN SERVANT'S WRACKE, WHERE NEW DOUBTS
                   HONOR BRINGS   4.45.11
SERVANTS'   1
  ON SERVANTS' SHAME CFT $MAISTER'S BLAME DOTH SIT   4.107.12
SERVE   7
  AND SERVE ALL THREE, AND YET THEY SPOILE ME TOO   1.28.14
  SERVE AS AN INCENSE TO A CRUELL $DAME   1.47.10
  BECAUSE THEIR POWER SERVE TO EXACT THE SAME   1.47.12
  NO OTHER $DRINKE WCULD SERVE THIS $GLUTTONS TURNE 2.7.5
  OR IF NO THING BUT $DEATH WILL SERVE THY TURNE   2.63.9
  IT IS MOST TRUE, THAT EYES ARE FORM'D TO SERVE   4.5.1
  SERVE HIM WITH SHCT, HER LIPS HIS HERALDS ARRE   4.29.10
SERVED   2
  BUT THOU, WHOSE $PEN HATH LIKE A $PACKE-$HORSE
                   SERV'D   2.49.5
  REASON, IN FAITH THCU ART WELL SERV'D, THAT STILL   4.10.1
SERVES   5
  THAT SERVES A $TRCPHEY TC HER CONQUERING EIES   1.10.11
  SEE WHAT REWARD HE HATH THAT SERVES THE
                   UNGRATEFULL   1.18.7
  YET SERVES NOT $THIS.. WHAT NEXT, WHAT
                   OTHER $SHIFT+ 2.19.9
  WHAT CURIOUS $PENSILL SERVES TO LIM THEE FORTH+   2.146.3
  BUT NO SCUSE SERVES, SHE MAKES HER WRATH APPEARE   4.73.9
SERVEST   2
  O SWEETEST $SHADOW, HOW THOU SERV'ST MY TURNE   2.13.9
  O SWEETEST SHADOW, HOW THOU SERV'ST MY TURNE   2.121.9
SERVICE   5
  OR IF A WORLD OF FAITHFULL SERVICE DONE   2.138.5
  THAT IS SO PROUDE THY SERVICE TU DISPISE   3.149.10
  OTHERS, BECAUSE THE $PRINCE MY SERVICE TRIES   4.23.7
  SERVICE AND $HONOR, WONDER WITH DELIGHT   4.72.9
  FOR MY SWEET $SAYNT SOME SERVICE FIT WILL FIND   5.22.4
SERVICES   3
  AND MY $RESPECTS AND $SERVICES TO YOU   2.27.11
  NOR SERVICES TO DOE TIL YOU REQUIRE   3.57.4
  IF SO GREAT SERVICES MAY SCORNED BE   4.65.10
SERVILE   2
  WITH MERCENARY LINES, WITH SERVILE $PEN   1.58.6
  MY HART, WHOM NONE WITH SERVILE BANDS CAN TYE   5.73.2
SERVING   2
  SERVING WITH LOCKES HIS SACRED MAJESTY   3.7.4
  DISWADE ONE FOOLISH HEART FROM SERVING THEE   3.141.10
SESSIONS   1
  WHEN TO THE $SESSICNS OF SWEET SILENT THCUGHT   3.30.1
SET   25
  AND SET MY THCUGHTS IN HEEDLESSE WAYES TC RANGE   1.5.2
  BY MINE OWNE THOUGHTS, SET ON ME BY MY $FAIRE   1.5.11
  SUBSTRACTING, SET MY $SWEETS UNTO MY $SOWRES   2.3.7
  AND SET MY $BREST, HIS $LODGING, ON A FIRE   2.23.12
  UPON THE $NEST I SET IT FORTH, TO PROVE   2.56.3

```
  SO $FAIRE A RISING, HAD SO $FOULE A SET              2.60.12
  UPON THE NEST I SET THEM, FORTH TO PROVE             2.103.3
  THEN WITH THY BEAUTIE SET THE SAME ON FIRE           2.106.7
  AND IN SUBSTRACTING, SET MY SWEETS UNTO
                            MY SOWRES                   2.110.7
  LIGHTNING THE WORLD, ECLIPSED BY HIS SET             2.125.4
  SO FAIRE A $MORNING HAD SO FOULE A SET+              2.149.12
  SINCE SILDOM COMMING IN THE LONG YEARE SET            3.52.6
  ON $HELLENS CHEEKE ALL ART OF BEAUTIE SET             3.53.7
  TIME DOTH TRANSFIXE THE FLORISH SET ON YOUTH          3.60.9
  AND THEREFORE TO YOUR FAIRE NO PAINTING SET           3.83.2
  WHEN THOU SHALT BE DISPODE TO SET ME LIGHT            3.88.1
  UPON THY PART I CAN SET DOWNE A STORY                 3.88.6
  TO SET A FORME UPON DESIRED CHANGE                    3.89.6
  IN HER CHEEKES PIT THOU DIDST THY PITFOULD SET        4.11.11
  WRACKES $TRIUMPHS BE, WHICH $LOVE (HIGH
                            SET) DOTH BREED             4.42.14
  MY WORDS I KNOW DO WELL SET FORTH MY MIND             4.44.1
  NOR DO NOT USE SET COLOURS FOR TO WEARE               4.54.2
  THY REASONS FIRMLY SET ON $VERTUE'S FEET              4.68.11
  AND DOTH HIS YDLE MESSAGE SET AT NOUGHT               5.19.12
  MOST SORTS OF MEN DOE SET BUT LITTLE STORE            5.26.12
SETS                6
  INTENERAT THAT HEART THAT SETS SO LIGHT               1.10.7
  IN HORRORS SABLE CLOWDES SETS MY LIVES SUNNE          1.30.2
  AND THAT THY BRIGHTNES SETS AT LENGTH TO $WEST        1.40.9
  SETS YOU MOST RICH IN YOUTH BEFORE MY SIGHT           3.15.10
  SETS DOWNE HER BABE AND MAKES ALL SWIFT DISPATCH      3.143.3
  WHERE MEMORY SETS FOORTH THE BEAMES OF LOVE           4.88.11
SETST               1
  THOU SETST A BATE BETWEENE MY WILL AND WIT            4.4.2
SETTING             2
  DECLYNING WITH THE SETTING OF MY SUNNE               2.141.10
  IN SETTING YOUR IMMORTALL PRAYSES FORTH               5.82.12
SETTLE              1
  MONGST WHOME THE MORE I SEEKE TO SETTLE PEACE         5.44.13
SETTLED             3
  SHALL REASONS FINDE OF SETLED GRAVITIE                3.49.8
  BEWRAY IT SELFE IN MY LONG SETLED EYES                4.23.2
  UNTO HER SELFE AND SETLED SO IN HART                  5.59.2
SEVER               4
  AND YET 'TIS THOU DO'ST ONELY SEVER US+              2.37.12
  WE AND THE $DUTCH AT LENGTH OUR $SELVES TO SEVER      2.51.9
  WITH CHAST AFFECTS, THAT NAUGHT BUT DEATH
                            CAN SEVER                   5.6.12
  NOR UNTO $CHRISTALL.. FOR NOUGHT MAY THEM SEVER       5.9.11
SEVERAL             6
  WHICH THERE IN ORDER TAKE THEIR SEVERALL PLACES       2.4.4
  AND DOTH THE SEV'RALL $OFFICES DEFINE                 2.12.3
  THESE OF THE $SOULE THE SEV'RALL $FUNCTIONS BEE       2.12.13
  AND DIFF'RETH IT, AS DOE THE SEV'RALL $NATIONS+       2.27.2
  WHICH THOUGH THE $DAY DIS-JOYNE BY SEV'RALL
                            FLIGHT                      2.37.6
  WHY SHOULD MY HEART THINKE THAT A SEVERALL PLOT       3.137.9
SEVERN              2
  AND STATELY $SEVERNE FOR HER $SHOARE IS PRAYSED       2.32.2
  AND STATELY $SEVERNE, FOR HER SHORES IS PRAISED       2.124.2
SEX'S               1
  TO HAVE SEENE THEE, THEIR $SEXES ONELY GLORY          2.6.12
```

SHADE   12
  NOR SHALL DEATH BRAG THOU WANDR'ST IN HIS SHADE   3.18.11
  WHEN TO UN-SEEING EYES THY SHADE SHINES SO+   3.43.8
  WHEN IN DEAD NIGHT THEIR FAIRE IMPERFECT SHADE   3.43.11
  SINCE EVERY ONE, HATH EVERY ONE, ONE SHADE   3.53.3
  WHEREOF THIS $BEAUTIE CAN BE BUT A SHADE   4.5.10
  TRUST IN THE SHADE OF PLEASING $ORANGE TREE   4.30.8
  NOR EVER DID IN SHADE OF $TEMPE SIT   4.74.2
  NO WIND, NO SHADE CAN COOLE, WHAT HELPE
                 THEN IN MY CASE   4.76.12
  OR OF THY GIFTS AT LEAST SHADE OUT SOME PART   4.81.8
  WITH DARKEST SHADE DOTH OVERCOME MY DAY   4.89.2
  AND IN THE SHADE OF DEATH IT SELFE SHALL SHROUD   5.27.3
  AN HUNDRED $GRACES AS IN SHADE TO SIT   5.40.4
SHADED   1
  AND CLOUDS OBSCURE HAD SHADED STILL HER
                 BRIGHTNESSE   1.7.4
SHADES   7
  HER BROW SHADES FROWNES, ALTHOUGH HER
                 EYES ARE SUNNY   1.6.2
  THUS SHADES MY LIFE SO LONG AS WANTS ENDURE   1.29.14
  I GOE BEFORE UNTO THE $MIRTLE SHADES   1.30.5
  AND IN THESE $SHADES, DEARE $NYMPH, HE
                 OFT HATH BEENE   2.53.11
  AND IN THESE SHADES (DEER $NIMPHE) HE
                 OFT HATH BEEN   2.113.11
  FRAME DAINTIEST LUSTRE, MIXT OF SHADES AND LIGHT+   4.7.4
  WITH SWEETE SOFT SHADES THOU OFT INVITEST ME   4.98.5
SHADOW   17
  WHICH THEN SHALL MOST INVAILE AND SHADOW MOST   1.40.12
  O SWEETEST $SHADOW, HOW THOU SERV'ST MY TURNE   2.13.9
  THAT EV'RY THING WHENCE $SHADOW DOTH PROCEED   2.13.13
  MAY IN HIS $SHADOW MY $LOVES STORIE READ   2.13.14
  O SWEETEST SHADOW, HOW THOU SERV'ST MY TURNE   2.121.9
  THAT EVERY THING WHENCE SHADOW DOTH PROCEEDE   2.121.13
  MAY IN HIS SHADOW MY $LOVES STORY READE   2.121.14
  AND THOU $CONCEITE, THE SHADOW OF MY BLISSE   2.141.9
  THOU $SABLE SHADOW, $IMAGE OF DISPAYRE   2.145.5
  THE SHADOW AND THE VAILE OF EVERY SINFULL DEED   2.145.8
  PRESENTS THEIR SHADDOE TO MY SIGHTLES VIEW   3.27.10
  WHILST THAT THIS SHADOW DOTH SUCH SUBSTANCE GIVE   3.37.10
  THEN THOU WHOSE SHADOW SHADDOWES DOTH
                 MAKE BRIGHT   3.43.5
  AND YOU BUT ONE, CAN EVERY SHADDOW LEND   3.53.4
  THE ONE DOTH SHADDOW OF YOUR BEAUTIE SHOW   3.53.10
  $ROSES OF SHADDOW, SINCE HIS $ROSE IS TRUE+   3.67.8
  AS WITH YOUR SHADDOW I WITH THESE DID PLAY   3.98.14
SHADOWS   9
  MY JOYS BUT SHADOWES, TOUCH OF TRUTH, MY ANGUISH   1.16.3
  PAINT SHADOWES IN IMAGINARY LINES   1.55.3
  YET IN THESE JOYES, THE SHADOWES OF MY GOOD   2.114.9
  THEN THOU WHOSE SHADOW SHADDOWES DOTH
                 MAKE BRIGHT   3.43.5
  THAT MILLIONS OF STRANGE SHADDOWES ON YOU TEND+   3.53.2
  WHILE SHADOWES LIKE TO THEE DO MOCKE MY SIGHT+   3.61.4
  AND ALL THEIR SHOWES BUT SHADOWES SAVING SHE   5.35.14
  AND ALL THEYR SHEWES BUT SHADOWES SAVING SHE   5.83.14
  WHEN OTHERS GAZE UPON THEYR SHADOWES VAYNE   5.88.6
SHADOW'S   1
  HOW WOULD THY SHADOWES FORME, FORME HAPPY SHOW   3.43.6

SHADY   2
  THOU BY THY DYALS SHADY STEALTH MAIST KNOW   3.77.7
  SITS DOWNE TO REST HIM IN SOME SHADY PLACE   5.67.3
SHAFT   1
  HIS STONE-COLD LIPS DOTH KISSE THE BLESSED
                    SHAFT   2.135.14
SHAFTS   3
  THY SHAFTS BE SPENT, AND SHEE (TO WARRE
                APPOINTED)   2.126.9
  BRAKE BOW, BRAKE SHAFTS, WHILE $CUPID
                WEEPING SATE   4.17.8
  TO LAY HIS THEN MARKE WANTING SHAFTS OF SIGHT   4.99.3
SHAKE   5
  SHAKE HANDS FOR EVER, $CANCELL ALL OUR $VOWES   2.61.5
  ROUGH WINDES DO SHAKE THE DARLING BUDS OF $MAIE   3.18.3
  DOE IN CONSENT SHAKE HANDS TO TORTURE ME   3.28.6
  UPON THOSE BOUGHES WHICH SHAKE AGAINST THE COULD   3.73.3
  BUT HER PROUD HART DOE THOU A LITTLE SHAKE   5.10.9
SHAKEN   2
  THAT LOOKES ON TEMPESTS AND IS NEVER SHAKEN   3.116.6
  FOR IF YOU WERE BY MY UNKINDNESSE SHAKEN   3.120.5
SHALLOW   1
  YEE SHALLOW $CENSURES, SOMETIME SEE YEE NOT   2.24.9
SHALLOWEST   1
  YOUR SHALLOWEST HELPE WILL HOLD ME UP A FLOATE   3.80.9
SHAME   25
  SUFFICE THAT HIGH ATTEMPTS HAVE NEVER SHAME   1.35.9
  THINKE NOT (SWEET $DELIA) THIS SHALL BE THY SHAME   1.44.5
  THAT ERRORS SHOULD BE GRAC'D THAT MERIT SHAME   1.56.11
  WERE AN ALL-EATING SHAME, AND THRIFTLESSE PRAISE   3.2.8
  THAT ON HIMSELFE SUCH MURDROUS SHAME COMMITS   3.9.14
  FOR SHAME DENY THAT THOU BEAR'ST LOVE TO ANY   3.10.1
  NOR CAN THY SHAME GIVE PHISICKE TO MY GRIEFE   3.34.9
  LEAST MY BEWAILED GUILT SHOULD DO THEE SHAME   3.36.10
  AND LIVE NO MORE TO SHAME NOR ME, NOR YOU   3.72.12
  HOW SWEET AND LOVELY DOST THOU MAKE THE SHAME   3.95.1
  OUR BLUSHING SHAME, AN OTHER WHITE DISPAIRE   3.99.9
  AND $BEAUTIE SLANDERD WITH A BASTARD SHAME   3.127.4
  TH'EXPENCE OF $SPIRIT IN A WASTE OF SHAME   3.129.1
  READIE OF WIT AND FEARING NOUGHT BUT SHAME   4.14.11
  WHEN MOST I GLORIE, THEN I FEELE MOST SHAME   4.19.3
  GREAT EXPECTATION, WEARE A TRAINE OF SHAME   4.21.8
  AND JOY THEREIN, THOUGH $NATIONS COUNT IT SHAME   4.28.8
  TILL THAT HER BLUSH TAUGHT ME MY SHAME TO SEE   4.53.14
  LET WO GRIPE ON MY HEART, SHAME LOADE MINE EYE   4.86.4
  IF THOU PRAISE NOT, ALL OTHER PRAISE IS SHAME   4.90.4
  THE HEIGHT OF HONOR IN THE KINDLY BADGE
                OF SHAME+   4.102.3
  ON SERVANTS' SHAME OFT $MAISTER'S BLAME
                DOTH SIT   4.107.12
  GREAT SHAME IT IS TO LEAVE LIKE ONE AFRAYD   5.14.3
  GREAT SHAME IT IS, THING SO DIVINE IN VIEW   5.53.9
  SHAME BE THY MEED, AND MISCHIEFE THY REWARD   5.86.13
SHAMED   3
  FOR I AM SHAMD BY THAT WHICH I BRING FORTH   3.72.13
  NOR BLAM'D FOR BLOUD, NOR SHAM'D FOR SINFULL
                DEED   4.84.11
  THAT SO FAYRE BEAUTY WAS SO FOWLY SHAMED   5.41.14
SHAMEFULLY   1
  AND GILDED HONOR SHAMEFULLY MISPLAST   3.66.5

SHAMES   4
  TO FIND OUT SHAMES AND IDLE HOURES IN ME   3.61.7
  TO KNOW MY SHAMES AND PRAISES FROM YOUR TOUNGE   3.112.6
  SHAMES NOT TO BE WITH GUILTLESSE BLOUD DEFYLDE   5.20.11
  GOOD SHAMES TO BE TO ILL AN INSTRUMENT   5.53.12
SHAPE   9
  IN PERFECT HUMANE SHAPE, ALL HEAV'NLY $BLISSE   2.17.12
  BY CHILDRENS EYES, HER HUSBANDS SHAPE IN MINDE   3.9.8
  MINE EYES HAVE DRAWNE THY SHAPE, AND THINE
                              FOR ME   3.24.10
  AND YOU IN EVERY BLESSED SHAPE WE KNOW   3.53.12
  NO SHAPE SO TRUE, NO TRUTH OF SUCH ACCOUNT   3.62.6
  OF BIRD, OF FLOWRE, OR SHAPE WHICH IT DOTH LACK   3.113.6
  LOVE OF HER SELFE, TAKES $STELLA'S SHAPE,
                              THAT SHE   4.25.10
  CAN SCARCE DISCERNE THE SHAPE OF MINE OWNE PAINE   4.94.4
  VIEWING THE SHAPE OF DARKNESSE AND DELIGHT   4.99.6
SHAPES   1
  THE $CROE, OR $DOVE, IT SHAPES THEM TO
                              YOUR FEATURE   3.113.12
SHARE   1
  AND IN HIS THOUGHTS OF LOVE DOTH SHARE A PART   3.47.8
SHARP   5
  MORE SHARPE TO ME THEN SPURRING TO HIS SIDE   3.50.12
  WITH WHAT SHARPE CHECKES I IN MY SELFE AM SHENT   4.18.1
  THAT BUSIE ARCHER HIS SHARPE ARROWES TRIES+   4.31.4
  MY HORSE, HE SPURRES WITH SHARPE DESIRE MY HART   4.49.11
  SWEET IS THE $JUNIPERE, BUT SHARPE HIS BOUGH   5.26.2
SHARPENED   1
  TO MORROW SHARPNED IN HIS FORMER MIGHT   3.56.4
SHARPEST   1
  TAN SACRED BEAUTIE, BLUNT THE SHARP'ST INTENTS   3.115.7
SHARPLY   1
  YET SHOOT YE SHARPELY STILL, AND SPARE ME NOT   5.57.9
SHARPNESS   1
  SHOULD SOONE BE PIERC'D WITH SHARPNESSE
                              OF THE MONE   4.57.8
SHEAVES   1
  AND $SOMMERS GREENE ALL GIRDED UP IN SHEAVES   3.12.7
SHED   1
  HER BREST LYKE LILLYES, ERE THEYR LEAVES BE SHED   5.64.11
SHEDS   1
  AH BUT THOSE TEARES ARE PEARLE WHICH THY
                              LOVE SHEEDS   3.34.13
SHEEN   1
  IF SILVER, HER FAIRE HANDS ARE SILVER SHEENE   5.15.12
SHEET   1
  ERE THEY BE WELL WRAP'D IN THEIR WINDING $SHEET+   2.6.4
SHENT   1
  WITH WHAT SHARPE CHECKES I IN MY SELFE AM SHENT   4.18.1
SHEPHERD   2
  LOE, HEERE THY $SHEPHEARD SPENT HIS WANDRING
                              YEERES   2.53.10
  LOE, HEERE THY $SHEPHEARD SPENT HIS WANDRING
                              YEERES   2.113.10
SHEPHERD'S   1
  ANOTHER HUMBLER WIT TO SHEPHEARD'S PIPE RETIRES   4.6.7
SHIELD   5
  JOVES GOLDEN SHIELD DID $EAGLE SABLES BEARE   4.13.3
  STELLA'S FAIRE HAIRE, HER FACE HE MAKES
                              HIS SHIELD   4.13.10

```
   WITH SHIELD OF PROOFE SHIELD ME FROM OUT
                          THE PREASE              4.39.5
   WITH SHIELD OF PROOFE SHIELD ME FROM OUT
                          THE PREASE              4.39.5
   DESPOYLD OF WARLIKE ARMES AND KNOWEN SHIELD    5.52.4
SHIFT                      1
   YET SERVES NOT $THIS.. WHAT NEXT, WHAT
                          OTHER $SHIFT+           2.19.9
SHIFTING                   1
   WITH SHIFTING CHANGE AS IS FALSE WOMENS FASHION  3.20.4
SHIFTS                     1
   SHIFTS BUT HIS PLACE, FOR STILL THE WORLD
                          INJOYES IT             3.9.10
SHINE                     16
   ARE EYES, OR ELS TWO RADIANT STARRES THAT SHINE  1.34.2
   WHILST $MOONE SHALL SHINE, OR ANY $FIRE
                          SHALL BURNE            2.13.12
   WHILST $MOONE SHALL SHYNE BY NIGHT, OR
                          ANY FIRE SHALL BURNE   2.121.12
   EVEN SO MY $SUNNE ONE EARLY MORNE DID SHINE    3.33.9
   BUT YOU SHALL SHINE MORE BRIGHT IN THESE CONTENTS  3.55.3
   THAT IN BLACK INCK MY LOVE MAY STILL SHINE
                          BRIGHT                 3.65.14
   AND IN MY WILL NO FAIRE ACCEPTANCE SHINE       3.135.8
   OR ELSE LET THEM IN STATELIER GLORIE SHINE     4.3.5
   TO MORTALL EYES MIGHT SWEETLY SHINE IN HER     4.25.11
   KEEPE STILL MY $ZENITH, EVER SHINE ON ME       4.42.8
   O LOOKE, O SHINE, O LET ME DIE AND SEE         4.48.8
   SHE IN WHOSE EYES $LOVE, THOUGH UNFELT,
                          DOTH SHINE             4.62.3
   FOR $STELLA HATH WITH WORDS WHERE FAITH
                          DOTH SHINE             4.69.9
   WHILE THOSE FAIRE PLANETS ON THY STREAMES
                          DID SHINE              4.103.4
   NOT TO THE $SUN.. FOR THEY DOO SHINE BY NIGHT  5.9.5
   WILL SHINE AGAIN, AND LOOKE ON ME AT LAST      5.34.11
SHINED                     1
   DARK IS THE WORLD, WHERE YOUR LIGHT SHINED NEVER  5.8.13
SHINEDST                   1
   FOR WHEN ON ME THOU SHINEDST LATE IN SADNESSE  5.39.6
SHINES                     7
   THAT PITTY SHINES NO COMFORT TO MY BLIS        1.21.2
   IN BASE ATTIRE, YET CLEERLY $BEAUTY SHINES     1.43.4
   MY CHASTE DESIRE, WHICH FROM DARKE SORROW SHINES  1.59.3
   SOMETIME TOO HOT THE EYE OF HEAVEN SHINES      3.18.5
   WHEN TO UN-SEEING EYES THY SHADE SHINES SO+    3.43.8
   THAT SHE, ME THINKS, NOT ONELY SHINES BUT SINGS  4.38.8
   THERE SHINES A JOY FROM THEE MY ONLY LIGHT     4.108.4
SHINEST                    1
   CUPID, BECAUSE THOU SHIN'ST IN $STELLAS EYES   4.12.1
SHINETH                    1
   THAT INWARD SUNNE IN THINE EYES SHINETH SO     4.71.8
SHINING                    9
   THOSE $EYES TO MY $HEART SHINING EVER BRIGHT   2.55.13
   THOSE EYES TO MY HART SHINING EVER BRIGHT      2.102.13
   THE GLORIOUS SUN-BEAMES OF HER EYES BRIGHT
                          SHINING                2.109.10
   O $LAMPE OF VERTUE, SUN-BRIGHT, EVER SHYNING   2.129.6
   NOR $MOONE NOR STARS LEND THEE THEIR SHINING
                          LIGHT                  2.145.12
```

```
  PLAYING AND SHINING IN EACH OUTWARD PART          4.11.13
  BUT SHINING FORTH CF HEATE IN HIS CHIEFE PRICE     4.22.4
  CARE SHINING IN MINE EYES, FAITH IN MY SPRITE      4.72.11
  SHE COMES, AND STREIGHT THEREWITH HER
                       SHINING TWINS DC MCVE         4.76.1
SHINY                   1
  THAT DEATH OUT OF THEYR SHINY BEAMES DOE DART      5.24.7
SHIP                    4
  LYKE AS A SHIP THAT THRCUGH THE $OCEAN WYDE        5.34.1
  GAYNST WHICH A SHIP OF SUCCOUR DESOLATE            5.56.11
  THAT SHIP, THAT TREE, AND THAT SAME BEAST AM I     5.56.13
  BUT LIKE A STEDDY SHIP DOTH STRONGLY PART          5.59.5
SHIPS                   2
  OUR $FLOUDS-$QUEEN $THAMES, FOR $SHIPS
                       AND $SWANS IS CROWNED         2.32.1
  OUR FLOODS-$QUEENE $THAMES, FOR SHYPS
                       AND $SWANS IS CROWNED         2.124.1
SHIPWRACK               1
  THE SHIPWRACKE OF MY ILL ADVENTRED YOUTH           1.54.6
SHONE                   1
  EITHER TO DO LIKE HIM, WHICH OPEN SHONE            4.22.10
SHOOK                   1
  HAVE FROM THE FORRESTS SHOOKE THREE SUMMERS
                       PRIDE                         3.104.4
SHOOT                   4
  BUT SHOOTE NOT AT ME IN YOUR WAKENED HATE          3.117.12
  HOW FARRE THEY SHOCTE AWRIE- THE TRUE CAUSE IS     4.41.12
  SHOOT OUT HIS DARTS TO BASE AFFECTIONS WOUND+      5.8.6
  YET SHOOT YE SHARPELY STILL, AND SPARE ME NOT      5.57.9
SHOP                    1
  WHICH IN MY BOSOMES SHOP IS HANGING STIL           3.24.7
SHORE                  13
  TO PAINT ON FLOODS, TILL THE SHORE CRIE TC TH'AIRE 1.9.2
  FOR WHO GETS WEALTH THAT PUTS NOT FROM THE SHORE+  1.35.5
  MOST FAIRE AND LOVELY $MAIDE, LOOKE FROM
                       THE SHORE                     1.46.1
  ONCE LET THE $OCEAN OF MY CARES FINDE SHCRE        1.46.13
  AND STATELY $SEVERNE FOR HER $SHOARE IS PRAYSED    2.32.2
  CLEERE $ANKOR, ON WHOSE $SILVER-SANDED SHORE       2.53.1
  CLEERE $ANKOR, ON WHOSE SILVER-SANDED SHORE        2.113.1
  WHICH PARTS THE SHCRE, WHERE TWO CONTRACTED NEW    3.56.10
  LIKE AS THE WAVES MAKE TCWARDS THE PIBLED SHORE    3.60.1
  ADVANTAGE ON THE $KINGDCME OF THE SHOARE           3.64.6
  AND ANCHOR FAST MY SELFE ON $VERTUE'S SHORE        4.62.11
  ON THE $THESSALIAN SHORE FROM HIM DID FLEE         5.28.10
  I DOE AT LENGTH DESCRY THE HAPPY SHORE             5.63.5
SHORES                  3
  THE SHORES BESET WITH THOUSAND SECRET SPYES        2.122.3
  AND STATELY $SEVERNE, FCR HER SHORES IS PRAISED    2.124.2
  HOW THY LEE SHORES BY MY SIGHES STORMED BE         4.98.4
SHORN                   1
  THE RIGHT OF SEPULCHERS, WERE SHORNE AWAY          3.68.6
SHORT                  16
  AS SHORT THAT BLISSE, SC IS THE COMFORT RARE       1.24.11
  WHOSE SHORT REFRESH UPON THE TENDER GREENE         1.50.2
  SHORT IS THE GLORY CF THE BLUSHING $ROSE           1.50.6
  MOST OF ALL SHORT, WHEN I SHOULD SHEW YOU MOST     2.57.13
  AND $SOMMERS LEASE HATH ALL TOO SHORT A CATE       3.18.4
  HOW FARRE A MODERNE QUILL DOTH COME TO SHORT       3.83.7
  WHICH WORKES ON LEASES CF SHORT NUMBRED HOWERS     3.124.10
```

WHICH PROVES MORE SHORT THEN WAST OR RUINING+   3.125.4
WHY SO LARGE COST HAVING SO SHORT A LEASE   3.146.5
BUT AS HE THEM MORE SHORT OR SLACKE DOTH RAINE   4.58.4
BUT WITH SHORT BREATH, LONG LOOKES, STAID
       FEET AND WALKING HED   4.76.13
WITHOUT HOW FARRE THIS PRAISE IS SHORT OF YOU   4.80.13
IN ONE SHORT HOURE I FIND BY HER UNDONNE   5.23.8
BUT LET MY LOVES FAYRE $PLANET SHORT HER WAYES   5.60.13
THIS YEARE ENSUING, OR ELSE SHORT MY DAYES   5.60.14
ALL SORROWES SHORT THAT GAINE ETERNALL BLISSE   5.63.14
SHORTLY   3
(SPURD WITH LOVE'S SPUR, THOUGH GALD AND
       SHORTLY RAIND   4.98.7
AND THEN MY BODY SHALL HAVE SHORTLY EASE   5.50.11
I WISH THAT DAY WOULD SHORTLY REASCEND   5.87.8
SHOT   6
NOT AT FIRST SIGHT, NOR WITH A DRIBBED SHOT   4.2.1
WITH PRICKING SHOT HE DID NOT THROUGHLY MOVE   4.17.3
THERE HIMSELFE WITH HIS SHOT HE CLOSE DOTH LAY   4.20.8
SERVE HIM WITH SHOT, HER LIPS HIS HERALDS ARRE   4.29.10
DEARE $KILLER, SPARE NOT THY SWEET CRUELL SHOT   4.48.13
WITH THOUSAND ARROWES, WHICH YOUR EIES HAVE SHOT   5.57.8
SHOUTS   2
WITH $SHOWTS AND $CLAPS AT EV'RY LITTLE PAWSE   2.47.9
WHILE WITH THE PEOPLE'S SHOUTS I MUST CONFESSE   4.53.3
SHOVE   2
WHICH THROUGH A BLEEDING HEART HIS POINT
       DID SHOVE   4.13.6
BUT SHE IN CHAFE HIM FROM HER LAP DID SHOVE   4.17.7
SHOW   65
WHO CAN SHEW ALL HIS LOVE, DOTH LOVE BUT LIGHTLY   1.1.14
WHEREIN NO SHEW GAVE CAUSE OF LEAST SUSPECT   1.31.7
I LOVE AS WELL, THOUGH HE COULD BETTER SHOW IT   1.43.8
NOW SHEW THY POWER, AND WHERE THY VERTUE LIES   1.46.7
CHEERES FOR A TIME, BUT TILL THE $SUNNE DOTH SHEW   1.50.3
SUFFICE, THEY SHEW I LIV'D AND LOV'D THEE DEARE   1.55.14
SOME WISE IN SHEW, MORE $FOOLES INDEED THEN THEY   2.22.14
ONELY TO SHEW HER $BEAUTIES $SOV'RAIGNE $POW'R   2.50.14
TO SHEW, THAT I HAD HATCH'D IT FOR THE $AYRE   2.56.7
MOST OF ALL SHORT, WHEN I SHOULD SHEW YOU MOST   2.57.13
EXPRESSE MY $WOES, AND SHEW THE PAINES OF $HELL   2.60.2
CAN SHEW A $SECOND TO SO PURE A $LOVE   2.60.14
TO SHEW THEIR KINDE, BEGAN TO CLIME THE SKIES   2.103.10
EXPRESSE MY WOES, AND SHEW THE PAYNES OF HELL   2.149.2
LEESE BUT THEIR SHOW, THEIR SUBSTANCE
       STILL LIVES SWEET   3.5.14
TO WITNESSE DUTY, NOT TO SHEW MY WIT   3.26.4
MAY MAKE SEEME BARE, IN WANTING WORDS TO SHEW IT   3.26.6
TO SHOW ME WORTHY OF THEIR SWEET RESPECT   3.26.12
TIL THEN, NOT SHOW MY HEAD WHERE THOU
       MAIST PROVE ME   3.26.14
HOW WOULD THY SHADOWES FORME, FORME HAPPY SHOW   3.43.6
AND NIGHTS BRIGHT DAIES WHEN DREAMS DO
       SHEW THEE ME   3.43.14
THE ONE DOTH SHADDOW OF YOUR BEAUTIE SHOW   3.53.10
BUT FOR THEIR VIRTUE ONLY IS THEIR SHOW   3.54.9
SHOW ME YOUR IMAGE IN SOME ANTIQUE BOOKE   3.59.7
O HIM SHE STORES, TO SHOW WHAT WELTH SHE HAD   3.67.13
TO SHEW FAULSE $ART WHAT BEAUTY WAS OF YORE   3.68.14
BUT WHY THY ODOR MATCHETH NOT THY SHOW   3.69.13

```
IF SOME SUSPECT OF ILL MASKT NOT THY SHOW          3.70.13
THY GLASSE WILL SHEW THEE HOW THY BEAUTIES WERE     3.77.1
THE WRINCKLES WHICH THY GLASSE WILL TRULY SHOW      3.77.5
THAT YOU YOUR SELFE BEING EXTANT WELL MIGHT SHOW    3.83.6
IF THY SWEET VERTUE ANSWERE NOT THY SHOW           3.93.14
THAT DOE NOT DO THE THING, THEY MOST DO SHOWE       3.94.2
I LOVE NOT LESSE, THOGH LESSE THE SHOW APPEARE      3.102.2
THAT HAVING SUCH A SKOPE TO SHOW HER PRIDE          3.103.2
NOR MY BELOVED AS AN $IDOLL SHOW                    3.105.2
WHERE TIME AND OUTWARD FORME WOULD SHEW IT DEAD    3.108.14
LOVING IN TRUTH, AND FAINE IN VERSE MY
                             LOVE TO SHOW             4.1.1
I SWEARE, MY HEART SUCH ONE SHALL SHEW TO THEE      4.4.12
OR WOULD SHE HER MIRACULOUS POWER SHOW               4.7.9
AND WHICH IS WORSE, NO GOOD EXCUSE CAN SHOW         4.18.7
THAT MINE OWNE WRITINGS LIKE BAD SERVANTS SHOW      4.21.3
AS SACRED THINGS, FAR FROM ALL DAUNGER'S SHOW       4.24.8
TO SHEW HER SKIN, LIPS, TEETH AND HEAD SO WELL+     4.32.11
THAT I RESPECTS FOR BOTH OUR SAKES MUST SHOW        4.33.11
IN ALL SWEETE STRATAGEMS SWEETE $ARTE CAN SHOW      4.36.11
YET HEARING LATE A FABLE, WHICH DID SHOW            4.45.5
THAT IT, DESPISDE IN TRUE BUT NAKED SHEW            4.55.3
WITH CHASTNED MIND, I STRAIGHT MUST SHEW
                             THAT SHE               4.61.10
O $GRAMMER RULES, O NOW YOUR VERTUES SHOW           4.63.1
OF EVERIE IMAGE, WHICH MAY COMFORT SHOW+            4.66.4
O JOY, TOO HIGH FOR MY LOW STILE TO SHOW            4.69.1
COME THEN MY $MUSE, SHEW THOU HEIGHT OF DELIGHT     4.70.9
STELLA, THOSE FAIRE LINES, WHICH TRUE
                             GOODNESSE SHOW          4.71.4
IF THIS DARKE PLACE YET SHEW LIKE CANDLE LIGHT      4.91.5
WHAT SOBS CAN GIVE WORDS GRACE MY GRIEFE TO SHOW+   4.93.2
HER SELFE (TO SHEW NO OTHER JOY HATH PLACE)         4.97.7
SHE COULD NOT SHEW MY BLIND BRAINE WAIES OF JOY     4.97.13
WHICH AY MOST FAIRE, NOW MORE THEN MOST
                             FAIRE SHOW             4.100.3
AND SHEW THE LAST ENSAMPLE OF YOUR PRIDE            5.25.6
A CLOSE INTENT AT LAST TO SHEW ME GRACE             5.25.10
WITHIN MY HART, THOUGH HARDLY IT CAN SHEW           5.45.5
TO SHEW THE POWRE OF YOUR IMPERIOUS EYES            5.49.6
AND THEN NO MERCY WILL UNTO ME SHEW                 5.53.8
WITH SHEW OF MORNING MYLDE HE HATH BEGUN            5.62.3
SHOWED                       3
OR THAT MY WITS HAVE SHEWED THE BEST THEY COULD     1.44.3
SHEW'D IN THESE LINES, THE WORKE OF CAREFULL
                             HOURES                  1.59.7
BUT WHEN YE HAVE SHEWED ALL EXTREMITYES             5.36.9
SHOWERS                      5
GENTLY DISTILLS HIS $NECTAR-DROPPING SHOWRES        2.53.6
GENTLY DISTILS HIS $NECTAR-DROPPING SHOWERS         2.113.6
OR AS SWEET SEASON'D SHEWERS ARE TO THE GROUND      3.75.2
THAT IT NOR GROWES WITH HEAT, NOR DROWNES
                             WITH SHOWRES          3.124.12
SOME FRESH AND FRUITFULL SHOWERS UPON
                     MY SUNNE-BURN'D BRAINE          4.1.8
SHOWEST                      2
WHEN THOU WILT CLOSE UP THAT WHICH NOW
                             THOU SHOW'ST          1.40.10
WHO HAST BY WAYNING GROWNE, AND THEREIN SHOU'ST    3.126.3
```

```
SHOWING                    1
  SHEWING THEIR BIRTH, AND WHERE THEY DID PROCEED+      3.76.8
SHOWN                      2
  BY SEEING FARTHER THEN THE EYE HATH SHOWNE            3.69.8
  BY THEIR RANCKE THOUGHTES, MY DEEDES MUST
                          NOT BE SHOWN                  3.121.12
SHOWS                     16
  WHOSE STATE BEST SHEWES THE FORCE OF MURDERING
                          EIES+                         1.37.4
  THAT $MIRROR SHEWES WHAT POWER IS IN THY FACE         1.37.10
  SHEWES BY HIS $COMPASSE, HOW HIS $COURSE
                          HE STEER'D                    2.1.6
  HER SIMPLE $FOLLOWERS EVIDENTLY SHEWES                2.46.2
  THAT THIS HUGE STAGE PRESENTETH NOUGHT BUT SHOWES     3.15.3
  WHICH HIDES YOUR LIFE, AND SHEWES NOT
                          HALFE YOUR PARTS              3.17.4
  LASCIVIOUS GRACE, IN WHOM ALL IL WEL SHOWES           3.40.13
  BUT WHEN MY GLASSE SHEWES ME MY SELFE INDEED          3.62.9
  TO MAKE HIM SEEME LONG HENCE, AS HE SHOWES NOW        3.101.14
  YOUR OWNE GLASSE SHOWES YOU, WHEN YOU
                          LOOKE IN IT                   3.103.14
  SHEWES LOVE AND PITIE TO MY ABSENT CASE               4.60.8
  THAT FACE, WHOSE LECTURE SHEWES WHAT PERFECT
                          BEAUTIE IS                    4.77.2
  THAT TO WIN ME, OFT SHEWES A PRESENT PAY+             4.88.4
  SHEWES HER OFT AT THE FULL HER FAIREST FACE           4.97.2
  AND ALL THEIR SHOWES BUT SHADOWES SAVING SHE          5.35.14
  AND ALL THEYR SHEWES BUT SHADOWES SAVING SHE          5.83.14
SHREWD                     1
  FALS TO SHREWD TURNES, AND I WAS IN HIS WAY           4.17.14
SHRILL                     2
  HIS TROMPET SHRILL HATH THRISE ALREADY SOUNDED        5.19.2
  WHICH WHEN AS FAME IN HER SHRILL TRUMP
                          SHAL THUNDER                  5.85.13
SHRINE                     2
  TOO RICH A $RELIQUE FOR SO POORE A $SHRINE            2.57.4
  MAKING THY BREAST THAT SACRED RELIQUES SHRYNE         2.105.12
SHRINES                    1
  THAT SHRINES IN FLESH SO TRUE A $DEITIE               4.4.13
SHROUD                     1
  AND IN THE SHADE OF DEATH IT SELFE SHALL SHROUD       5.27.3
SHUN                       5
  WISH TO BE PRESENT, AND YET SHUN T'APPEARE            1.20.4
  WE SICKEN TO SHUN SICKNESSE WHEN WE PURGE             3.118.4
  TO SHUN THE HEAVEN THAT LEADS MEN TO THIS HELL        3.129.14
  TH'IMPORTUNE SUIT OF MY DESIRE TO SHONNE              5.23.6
  AND WARNE TO SHUN THE DAUNGER OF THEYR WRATH          5.31.8
SHUT                       1
  AND SHUT THOSE WAIES MY FRIENDLY FOE FIRST ENTRED     1.27.3
SIBYL                      1
  IN STEED OF TEN, ONE $SIBIL TO US LEFT                2.119.8
SIBYLS                     1
  BY THEYR TEN $SIBILS HAVE THE WORLD CONTROLD          2.119.2
SICK                      12
  WHAT THEY LAST THOUGHT OF, WHEN THE $BRAINE
                          GREW SICKE                    2.9.7
  AND MY SICK $MUSE DOTH GIVE AN OTHER PLACE            3.79.4
  I WAS NOT SICK OF ANY FEARE FROM THENCE               3.86.12
  AND SICKE OF WEL-FARE FOUND A KIND OF MEETNESSE       3.118.7
  DRUGS POYSON HIM THAT SO FELL SICKE OF YOU            3.118.14
```

```
    I SICK WITHALL THE HELPE OF BATH DESIRED           3.153.11
    STELLA IS SICKE, AND IN THAT SICKE BED LIES        4.101.1
    STELLA IS SICKE, AND IN THAT SICKE BED LIES        4.101.1
    AND GRACE, SICKE TCC, SUCH FINE CONCLUSICNS
                                    TRIES              4.101.3
    BEAUTY IS SICKE, BUT SICKE IN SO FAIRE GUISE       4.101.5
    BEAUTY IS SICKE, BUT SICKE IN SO FAIRE GUISE       4.101.5
    SICKE, THIRSTY, GLAD (THOUGH BUT OF EMPTY
                                    GLASSE)            4.104.11
SICKEN                          1
    WE SICKEN TO SHUN SICKNESSE WHEN WE PURGE          3.118.4
SICKLE                          1
    DOEST HOULD TIMES FICKLE GLASSE, HIS SICKLE,
                                    HOWER              3.126.2
SICKLE'S                        1
    WITHIN HIS BENDING SICKLES COMPASSE COME           3.116.10
SICKLY                          1
    TH'UNCERTAINE SICKLIE APPETITE TO PLEASE           3.147.4
SICK-MEN                        1
    AS TESTIE SICK-MEN WHEN THEIR DEATHS BE NEERE      3.140.7
SICKNESS                        4
    WE SICKEN TO SHUN SICKNESSE WHEN WE PURGE          3.118.4
    FOR MY POORE SOULE, WHICH NOW THAT SICKNESSE
                                    TRIES              4.94.6
    THAT SICKENESSE BRAGS IT SELFE BEST GRACED TC BE   4.101.4
    THEIR JUDGEMENTS HACKNEY ON, THE FAULT
                                    ON SICKNESSE LAY   4.102.10
SIDE                            8
    WHEN THE PROUD $RCUND ON EV'RY SIDE HATH RUNG      2.47.10
    TO SIDE THIS TITLE IS IMPANNELLED                  3.46.9
    MORE SHARPE TO ME THEN SPURRING TO HIS SICE        3.50.12
    UPON THY SIDE, AGAINST MY SELFE ILE FIGHT          3.88.3
    TO STAND IN THY AFFAIRES, FALL BY THY SIDE         3.151.12
    LAID BY HIS SIDE HIS HEART INFLAMING BRAND         3.154.2
    IN MY FREE SIDE+ CR AM I BORNE A SLAVE             4.47.3
    BUT, BUT (ALAS) NIGHT'S SIDE THE ODS HATH FUR      4.96.12
SIDES                           3
    A $BASTARD ON BOTH SIDES NEEDES MUST THOU BE       2.140.10
    ON BOTH SIDES THUS IS SIMPLE TRUTH SUPPREST        3.138.8
    OTHERS, BECAUSE OF BOTH SIDES I DO TAKE            4.41.9
SIEGE                           2
    AGAINST THE WRACKFULL SIEDGE OF BATTRING DAYES     3.65.6
    UNTO THE SIEGE BY YCU ABANDON'D QUITE              5.14.2
SIGH                            9
    SIGH OUT A $STORIE CF HER CRUELL DEEDES            1.2.5
    LET THEM YET SIGH THEIR CWNE, AND MONE MY WRCNGS   1.3.4
    LIE DOWNE TO WAILE, RISE UP TO SIGH AND GRIEVE     1.9.6
    WHEN BACKE I LOOKE, I SIGH MY FREEDOME PAST        1.28.9
    THAT THOU BE PLEAS'C, AND I MAY SIGH NO MORE       1.46.14
    SAVE MEE I $CRIE, YCU SIGH ME OUT A $NO            2.5.8
    I SIGH THE LACKE CF MANY A THING I SOUGHT          3.30.3
    THAT TO EACH WORD, NAY SIGH OF MINE YOU HARKE      4.104.3
    AND WHEN I SIGH, SHE SAYES I KNOW THE ART          5.18.11
SIGHED                          3
    HAPPY THE HEART THAT SIGH'D FOR SUCH A ONE         1.51.14
    I SIGHD HER SIGHES, AND WAILED FOR HER WC          4.87.10
    HOW CLOTH'D, HOW WAITED ON, SIGHD SHE OR SMILDE    4.92.10
SIGHING                         2
    AND THEN IN SIGHING, TO GIVE UP MY BREATH          2.20.12
    MY SIGHES BE SPENT WITH GRIEFE AND SIGHING SC      2.143.7
```

SIGHS   56
  HERE HAVE I SUMM'D MY SIGHS, HERE I INROLE   1.1.7
  HAST SENT THE INCENSE OF THY SIGHS TO HEAVEN   1.8.2
  DEEPE IS THE WOUND MY SIGHES CAN WELL REPORT   1.14.6
  AND HAD MY SIGHES STILL TENDING ON HER NAME   1.15.10
  THE AYRE WITH SIGHES, THE EARTH BELOW
                    WITH TEARES+   1.21.6
  THESE SORROWING SIGHES, THE SMOAKE OF MINE ANNOY   1.24.1
  AND CALME THE TEMPEST WHICH MY SIGHS DOO RAISE   1.51.10
  WHICH WITH MY $SIGHES THIS $EPICURE DOTH BURNE   2.7.7
  AND $SIGHES AND $SIGNES A SILLY $HOPE AFFORDS   2.13.8
  BOYL'D WITH HER $SIGHES, IN GIVING UP THE $GHOST   2.15.7
  WITH $SIGHES AND $TEARES STILL FURNISHING
                    HIS $TABLE   2.23.7
  MAKING MY $SIGHES TO THAW THE $FROZEN $SEAS   2.25.8
  I AM SURE MY $SIGHES COME FROM A $HEART AS TRUE   2.27.9
  BY ALL TRUE $LOVERS $SIGHES, $VOWES, AND
                    $DESIRES   2.36.11
  MY $SIGHES THE $BELLOWES, WHICH THE $FLAME
                    ENCREASETH   2.40.5
  MY $SIGHES BE SPENT IN UTT'RING OF MY $WOE   2.41.7
  WITH HEAVIE $SIGHES WHILST THUS I BREAKE
                    THE $AYRE   2.45.3
  SMOAK'D WITH MY $SIGHES, AND BLOTTED WITH
                    MY $TEARES   2.54.4
  NOTE BUT MY $SIGHES, AND THINE $EYES SHALL BEHOLD   2.55.5
  SMOK'D WITH MY SIGHES, AND BLOTTED WITH
                    MY TEARES   2.101.4
  NOTE BUT MY SIGHES, AND THINE EYES SHAL BEHOLD   2.102.5
  REDOUBLING SIGHES THE ACCENTS OF MY GRIEFE   2.111.12
  MY SIGHES SHALL STOP THE PASSAGE OF THE AYRE   2.115.7
  AND EVER-MORE WITH SIGHES HE SUPT AND DYNDE   2.116.16
  AND SIGHES AND SIGNES A SILLY HOPE AFFOORDS   2.121.8
  AND MY STRONG SIGHES, THE AYRES WEAKE
                    FORCE REVIVETH   2.127.3
  THIS LOVE, TEARS, SIGHES, MAINTAINE EACH
                    ONE HIS ELEMENT   2.127.4
  THE AYRE, UNTO MY SIGHES, AS $EAGLE TO THE FLIE   2.127.7
  ONELY MY SIGHES ARE BY THE AYRE EXPRESSED   2.127.11
  MY LOVE, MY TEARES, MY SIGHES, EXTINGUISHT
                    CANNOT BE   2.127.14
  THOSE SIGHES WHICH COOLE MY HART, ARE
                    COLES UNTO MY LOVE   2.132.2
  WITH TEARES, SIGHES, AND DISDAINE, THYS
                    CONTRARY I PROVE   2.132.4
  LOVE HEATS MY HART, MY HART-HEAT MY SIGHES
                    WARMETH   2.132.6
  WITH TEARES, SIGHES, AND DISDAINE, SHALL
                    HAVE IMMORTAL STRIFE   2.132.14
  MY HART SURCHARG'D WITH THOUGHTS, SIGHES
                    IN ABUNDANCE RAISE   2.133.9
  AND THUS WHILST SIGHES AND TEARES TOGETHER
                    DOE CONTENDE   2.133.13
  A THOUSAND VOWES, A THOUSAND SIGHES AND TEARES   2.138.4
  IF SIGHES, NOR TEARES, NOR VOWES, NOR
                    PRAYERS CAN MOVE   2.139.2
  AND YOU MY SIGHES, $SYMTOMAS OF MY WOE   2.141.5
  MY SIGHES BE SPENT WITH GRIEFE AND SIGHING SO   2.143.7
  MY SIGHES, THE BELLOWES WHICH THE FLAME
                    INCREASETH   2.144.5

```
OR HEART IN LOVE WITH SIGHES HIMSELFE
                         DOTH SMOTHER          3.47.4
WHILE TEARES POWRE OUT HIS INKE, AND SIGHS
                         BREATHE OUT HIS WORDS 4.6.10
WITH NEW-BORNE SIGHES AND DENISEND WIT DO SING  4.15.8
OFT WITH TRUE SIGHES, OFT WITH UNCALLED TEARES  4.61.1
WHAT SIGHES STOLNE OUT, OR KILD BEFORE
                         FULL BORNE+           4.67.9
I SAW THAT SIGHES HER SWEETEST LIPS DID PART    4.87.7
I SIGHD HER SIGHES, AND WAILED FOR HER WO       4.87.10
I CRY THY SIGHS., MY DEERE, THY TEARES I BLEEDE 4.93.14
YET SIGHS, DEERE SIGHS, INDEEDE TRUE FRIENDS
                         YOU ARE               4.95.1
YET SIGHS, DEERE SIGHS, INDEEDE TRUE FRIENDS
                         YOU ARE               4.95.1
ONLY TRUE SIGHS, YOU DO NOT GO AWAY             4.95.12
HOW THY LEE SHORES BY MY SIGHES STORMED BE      4.98.4
O HONIED SIGHS, WHICH FROM THAT BREAST DO RISE  4.100.5
SUCH TEARES, SIGHS, PLAINTS, NO SORROW
                         IS, BUT JOY           4.100.12
AND SITHENS HAVE WITH SIGHES AND SORROWES FED   5.2.3
```

SIGHT   57

```
I ONELY SOUGHT THE BLISSE TO HAVE HER SIGHT     1.36.12
HER SIGHT CONTENTED THUS TO SEE ME SPILL        1.36.13
THE SACRIFICE HERE OFFRED TO HER SIGHT          1.59.8
TO WRITE WITH $BLOUD, OF FORCE OFFENDS THE $SIGHT 2.13.6
BUT HE WITH $BEAUTIE FIRST CORRUPTED $SIGHT     2.29.5
WISHETH TO BE TRANSFORMED TO MY $SIGHT          2.33.3
REASON PUT BACK, DOTH OUT OF SIGHT REMOVE       2.38.13
BEYOND THE BENT OF HIS UNKNOWING $SIGHT         2.43.8
TO WRITE WITH BLOOD, OF FORCE OFFENDS THE SIGHT 2.121.6
AND SUMMOND $ANGELS TO THYS BLESSED SIGHT       2.125.12
WHEN OUR WORLDS SUNNE IS VANISHT OUT OF SIGHT   2.129.4
REASON PUT BACK, DOTH OUT OF SIGHT REMOVE       2.131.13
WISHING TO BE TRANS-FORMD INTO MY SIGHT         2.133.3
THE SUN-BEAMES TO THAT LUSTRE OF HER SIGHT      2.148.3
DOTH HOMAGE TO HIS NEW APPEARING SIGHT          3.7.3
SETS YOU MOST RICH IN YOUTH BEFORE MY SIGHT     3.15.10
SAVE THAT MY SOULES IMAGINARY SIGHT             3.27.9
AND MONE TH'EXPENCE OF MANY A VANNISHT SIGHT    3.30.8
WORTHY PERUSAL STAND AGAINST THY SIGHT          3.38.6
HOW TO DEVIDE THE CONQUEST OF THY SIGHT         3.46.2
MINE EYE, MY HEART THEIR PICTURES SIGHT
                         WOULD BARRE           3.46.3
OR IF THEY SLEEPE, THY PICTURE IN MY SIGHT      3.47.13
WHILE SHADOWES LIKE TO THEE DO MOCKE MY SIGHT+  3.61.4
ARE VANISHING, OR VANISHT OUT OF SIGHT          3.63.7
SOME-TIME ALL FUL WITH FEASTING ON YOUR SIGHT   3.75.9
FOR IF IT SEE THE RUD'ST OR GENTLEST SIGHT      3.113.9
WHICH SHOULD TRANSPORT ME FARTHEST FROM
                         YOUR SIGHT            3.117.8
THEY ARE BUT DRESSINGS OF A FORMER SIGHT        3.123.4
TELL ME THOU LOV'ST ELSE-WHERE., BUT IN MY SIGHT 3.139.5
TEMPTETH MY BETTER ANGEL FROM MY SIGHT          3.144.6
WHICH HAVE NO CORRESPONDENCE WITH TRUE SIGHT    3.148.2
TO MAKE ME GIVE THE LIE TO MY TRUE SIGHT        3.150.3
NOT AT FIRST SIGHT, NOR WITH A DRIBBED SHOT     4.2.1
IN OBJECT BEST TO KNIT AND STRENGTH OUR SIGHT   4.7.6
IN HER SIGHT I A LESSON NEW HAVE SPELD          4.16.12
THEY SHOULD STILL DAUNCE TO PLEASE A GAZER'S
                         SIGHT                 4.26.8
```

```
COPARTNER OF THE RICHES OF THAT SIGHT                   4.48.6
BUT NOW THAT I, ALAS, DO WANT HER SIGHT                 4.56.9
MAKES ME FALL FROM HER SIGHT, THEN SWEETLY SHE          4.60.6
FED BY THY WORTH, AND KINDLED BY THY SIGHT+             4.68.8
MY $ORPHAN SENCE FLIES TO THE INWARD SIGHT              4.88.10
IN HART BOTH SIGHT AND LOVE NOW COUPLED BE              4.88.13
WHILE I DISPAIRE BY $SUNNE'S SIGHT TO ENJOY             4.97.14
PAINT WOE'S BLACKE FACE SO LIVELY TO MY SIGHT           4.98.10
TO LAY HIS THEN MARKE WANTING SHAFTS OF SIGHT           4.99.3
WITH SIGHT THEREOF CRIDE OUT., O FAIRE DISGRACE         4.103.13
UNHAPPIE SIGHT, AND HATH SHE VANISHT BY                 4.105.1
LYKE CAPTIVES TREMBLING AT THE VICTORS SIGHT            5.1.4
AT WONDROUS SIGHT OF SO CELESTIALL HEW                  5.3.8
NOR TO THE $STARRES.. FOR THEY HAVE PURER SIGHT         5.9.7
I MOTE PERCEIVE HOW IN HER GLAUNCING SIGHT              5.16.5
OF THAT FAIRE SIGHT, THAT NOTHING ELSE
                          THEY BROOKE                   5.35.10
AT SIGHT WHEREOF EACH BIRD THAT SITS ON SPRAY           5.40.9
TO FEED HIS FILL, FLYES BACKE UNTO YOUR SIGHT           5.73.8
HOW WAS I RAVISHT WITH YOUR LOVELY SIGHT                5.76.5
OF THAT FAYRE SIGHT, THAT NOTHING ELSE
                          THEY BROOKE                   5.83.10
CAN COMFORT ME, BUT HER OWNE JOYOUS SIGHT               5.89.10
SIGHTLESS                 2
PRESENTS THEIR SHADDOE TO MY SIGHTLES VIEW              3.27.10
THROUGH HEAVY SLEEPE ON SIGHTLESSE EYES
                          DOTH STAY+                    3.43.12
SIGHTS                    2
I, SEEING BETTER SIGHTS IN SIGHT'S DECAY                4.38.12
THERE FILL YOUR SELFE WITH THOSE MOST
                          JOYOUS SIGHTS                 5.84.9
SIGHT'S                   1
I, SEEING BETTER SIGHTS IN SIGHT'S DECAY                4.38.12
SIGNED                    2
FAITH BEING WITH BLOOD, AND FIVE YEARES
                          WITNES SIGN'D                 1.31.6
I SEEKE THE FIELDS WITH HER LATE FOOTING SYNC           5.78.5
SIGNIFIED                 1
NO DOWNE-CAST LOOKE HAD SIGNIFIED MY MISSE              1.7.10
SIGNS                     4
AND $SIGHES AND $SIGNES A SILLY $HOPE AFFORDS           2.13.8
AND SIGHES AND SIGNES A SILLY HOPE AFFOORDS             2.121.8
BEFORE THESE BASTARD SIGNES OF FAIRE WERE BORNE         3.68.3
OR IF SUCH HEAVENLY SIGNES MUST PROVE ANNOY             4.100.13
SILENCE                   9
ANSWERE NO MORE, WITH $SILENCE MAKE REPLY               2.5.11
IN SECRET SILENCE, WHICH SUCH WONDERS PREACHEST         2.146.12
THIS SILENCE FOR MY SINNE YOU DID IMPUTE                3.83.9
AS VICTORS OF MY SILENCE CANNOT BOAST                   3.86.11
EXCUSE NOT SILENCE SO, FOR'T LIES IN THEE               3.101.10
WISE SILENCE IS BEST MUSICKE UNTO BLISSE                4.70.14
SILENCE IN BOTH DISPLAIES HIS SULLEN MIGHT              4.96.5
BUT LIKE A STUPID STOCK IN SILENCE DIE                  5.43.8
YET I MY HART WITH SILENCE SECRETLY                     5.43.9
SILENT                    10
AND OFT WITH CAREFULL TURNES, WITH SILENT $ART          1.8.7
BROTHER TO DEATH, IN SILENT DARKNES BORNE               1.54.2
O LEARNE TO READ WHAT SILENT LOVE HATH WRIT             3.23.13
WHEN TO THE $SESSIONS OF SWEET SILENT THOUGHT           3.30.1
BUT MY HEART BURNES, I CANNOT SILENT BE                 4.81.11
```

```
  LANGUISHT WITH HORRORS OF THE SILENT NIGHT        4.89.8
  SILENT AND SAD IN MOURNING WEEDES DOTH DIGHT      4.97.8
  WHILE THE BLACKE HORRORS OF THE SILENT NIGHT      4.98.9
  SHALL I THEN SILENT BE OR SHALL I SPEAKE+         5.43.1
  AND IF I SILENT BE, MY HART WILL BREAKE           5.43.3
SILENTLY                  1
  HOW SILENTLY, AND WITH HOW WANNE A FACE           4.31.2
SILLY                     7
  WITH THEE SUCH POWERS TO PLAGUE ONE SILLY HARTE   1.27.12
  AND $SIGHES AND $SIGNES A SILLY $HOPE AFFORDS     2.13.8
  AND SIGHES AND SIGNES A SILLY HOPE AFFOORDS       2.121.8
  ON SILLY ME DO NOT THE BURTHEN LAY                4.51.5
  CANNOT SUCH GRACE YOUR SILLY SELFE CONTENT        4.83.11
  THE SILLY LAMBE THAT TO HIS MIGHT DOTH YIELD      5.20.8
  WITH WHICH MY SILLY BARKE WAS TOSSED SORE         5.63.4
SILVER                    6
  WHEN GOLDEN HAIRES SHALL CHANGE TO SILVER WIER    1.38.2
  ROSES HAVE THORNES, AND SILVER FOUNTAINES MUD     3.35.2
  WHERE ROSES GUEULS ARE BORNE IN SILVER FIELD      4.13.11
  IF SILVER, HER FAIRE HANDS ARE SILVER SHEENE      5.15.12
  IF SILVER, HER FAIRE HANDS ARE SILVER SHEENE      5.15.12
  MONGST WHICH THERE IN A SILVER DISH DID LY        5.77.5
SILVERED                  1
  AND SABLE CURLS OR SILVER'D ORE WITH WHITE        3.12.4
SILVER-SANDED             2
  CLEERE $ANKOR, ON WHOSE $SILVER-SANDED SHORE      2.53.1
  CLEERE $ANKOR, ON WHOSE SILVER-SANDED SHORE       2.113.1
SIMILE                    1
  SO MAY THE LEARNED LIKE THE SIMILIE               2.148.4
SIMILES                   1
  OR WITH STRANGE SIMILIES ENRICH EACH LINE         4.3.7
SIMOIS                    1
  SOME $HELYCON, AND SOME FAIRE $SIMOIS             2.120.12
SIMPLE                    9
  HER SIMPLE $FOLLOWERS EVIDENTLY SHEWES            2.46.2
  UNFAINED LOVE, IN NAKED SIMPLE TRUTH              2.138.3
  FOR COMPOUND SWEET., $FORGOING SIMPLE SAVOR       3.125.7
  ON BOTH SIDES THUS IS SIMPLE TRUTH SUPPREST       3.138.8
  IF VAINE LOVE HAVE MY SIMPLE SOULE OPPREST        4.4.3
  MY SIMPLE MEANING WITH DISDAYNFULL SCORNE         5.29.2
  SUFFICIENT WORKE FOR ONE MANS SIMPLE HEAD         5.33.7
  LYKEST IT SEEMETH IN MY SIMPLE WIT                5.40.5
  BUT SIMPLE TRUTH AND MUTUALL GOOD WILL            5.65.11
SIMPLE-TRUTH              1
  AND SIMPLE-$TRUTH MISCALDE $SIMPLICITIE           3.66.11
SIMPLICITY                2
  AND SIMPLE-$TRUTH MISCALDE $SIMPLICITIE           3.66.11
  BUT KNOW THAT I IN PURE SIMPLICITIE               4.28.12
SIMPLY                    1
  SIMPLY I CREDIT HER FALSE SPEAKING TONGUE         3.138.7
SIN                      15
  ILE HIDE HER SINNE AND SAY IT WAS MY LOT          1.30.10
  AND SINNE OF FROWNES BRING HONOUR TO THE FACE     1.56.12
  SINNE OF SELFE-LOVE POSSESSETH AL MINE EIE        3.62.1
  AND FOR THIS SINNE THERE IS NO REMEDIE            3.62.3
  THAT SINNE BY HIM ADVANTAGE SHOULD ATCHIVE        3.67.3
  THIS SILENCE FOR MY SINNE YOU DID IMPUTE          3.83.9
  IF IT BE POISON'D, TIS THE LESSER SINNE           3.114.13
  THAT SHE THAT MAKES ME SINNE, AWARDS ME PAINE     3.141.14
  LOVE IS MY SINNE, AND THY DEARE VERTUE HATE       3.142.1
```

HATE OF MY SINNE, GROUNDED ON SINFULL LOVING   3.142.2
IF THAT BE SINNE WHICH DOTH THE MANERS FRAME   4.14.9
IF THAT BE SINNE WHICH IN FIXT HEARTS DOTH BREED   4.14.12
THEN $LOVE IS SINNE, AND LET ME SINFULL BE   4.14.14
DIDST MAKE THY TRIUMPH OVER DEATH AND SIN   5.68.2
BEING WITH THY DEARE BLOOD CLENE WASHT FROM SIN   5.68.7
SINCE   85
   SINCE THE FIRST LOOKE THAT LED ME TO THIS ERROR   1.18.1
   BUT SINCE THE SWEETEST ROOTE YEELDS FRUITE
                             SO SOWRE   1.26.9
YET MY SOULES SOVERAIGNE, SINCE I MUST RESIGNE   1.27.13
BUT SINCE SHE WEIGHS THEM NOT, THIS RESTS FOR ME   1.59.9
SINCE, BUT YOUR SELFE, THERE WAS NO $CREATURE BY   2.2.3
YOUR $CHEEKES YET PALE, SINCE FIRST HE
                             GAVE THE $WOUND   2.2.12
SINCE HE THAT BLESSED $PARADISE DID PROVE   2.4.7
TIS NINE YEERES NOW SINCE FIRST I LOST MY $WIT   2.9.11
SINCE $YOU ONE WERE, I NEVER SINCE WAS ONE   2.11.3
SINCE $YOU ONE WERE, I NEVER SINCE WAS ONE   2.11.3
SINCE $YOU IN $ME, MY SELFE SINCE OUT OF $ME   2.11.4
SINCE $YOU IN $ME, MY SELFE SINCE OUT OF $ME   2.11.4
SINCE TO OBTAINE THEE, NOTHING ME WILL STED   2.15.1
SINCE $SONNETS THUS IN $BUNDLES ARE IMPREST   2.31.9
THAT SINCE THE ONE CANNOT THE OTHER BEE   2.33.13
THOU PURBLIND $BOY, SINCE THOU HAST BEENE
                             SO SLACKE   2.36.1
SINCE SHE DISDAINES TO BLESSE MY HAPPIE $VERSE   2.45.5
LONG SINCE DEPARTED (TO THE $WORLD NO MORE)   2.46.10
CALLING TO MINDE SINCE FIRST MY $LOVE BEGUN   2.51.1
TELL $ME, IF EVER SINCE THE $WORLD BEGUNNE   2.60.11
SINCE THER'S NO HELPE, $COME LET US KISSE
                             AND PART   2.61.1
ME THINKES 'TIS LONG SINCE FIRST THESE
                             $WARRES BEGUN   2.63.2
I SEND DEFIANCE, SINCE IF OVERTHROWNE   2.63.13
SINCE HOLY $VESTALL LAWES HAVE BEEN NEGLECTED   2.105.1
AND SINCE THE WORLD TO JUDGEMENT DOTH DECLYNE   2.119.7
TELL MEE, IF EVER SINCE THE WORLD BEGUNNE   2.149.11
SINCE SWEETS AND BEAUTIES DO THEM-SELVES FORSAKE   3.12.11
BUT SINCE SHE PRICKT THEE OUT FOR WOMENS
                             PLEASURE   3.20.13
AND WEEPE A FRESH LOVES LONG SINCE CANCELD WOE   3.30.7
BUT SINCE HE DIED AND $POETS BETTER PROVE   3.32.13
SINCE WHY TO LOVE, I CAN ALLEDGE NO CAUSE   3.49.14
SINCE FROM THEE GOING, HE WENT WILFULL SLOW   3.51.13
SINCE SILDOM COMMING IN THE LONG YEARE SET   3.52.6
SINCE EVERY ONE, HATH EVERY ONE, ONE SHADE   3.53.3
SINCE MINDE AT FIRST IN CARRECTER WAS DONE   3.59.8
SINCE BRASSE, NOR STONE, NOR EARTH, NOR
                             BOUNDLESSE SEA   3.65.1
$ROSES OF SHADDOW, SINCE HIS $ROSE IS TRUE+   3.67.8
IN DAIES LONG SINCE, BEFORE THESE LAST SO BAD   3.67.14
SINCE WHAT HE OWES THEE, THOU THY SELFE
                             DOOST PAY   3.79.14
BUT SINCE YOUR WORTH (WIDE AS THE $OCEAN IS)   3.80.5
SINCE THAT MY LIFE ON THY REVOLT DOTH LIE   3.92.10
SINCE FIRST I SAW YOU FRESH WHICH YET ARE GREENE   3.104.8
SINCE ALL ALIKE MY SONGS AND PRAISES BE   3.105.3
SINCE SPIGHT OF HIM $ILE LIVE IN THIS
                             POORE RIME   3.107.11

```
SINCE I LEFT YOU, MINE EYE IS IN MY MINDE            3.113.1
SINCE MY APPEALE SAIES I DID STRIVE TO PROOVE        3.117.13
FOR SINCE EACH HAND HATH PUT ON $NATURES POWER       3.127.5
SINCE SAUSIE $JACKES SO HAPPY ARE IN THIS            3.128.13
TO MOURNE FOR ME SINCE MOURNING DOTH THEE GRACE      3.132.11
YET DO NOT SO, BUT SINCE I AM NEERE SLAINE           3.139.13
FOR SINCE MAD $MARCH GREAT PROMISE MADE OF ME        4.21.9
IT IS MOST TRUE, FOR SINCE I HER DID SEE             4.25.12
SINCE THOU IN ME SO SURE A POWER DOEST KEEPE         4.32.5
SINCE $REASON'S SELFE DOTH BLOW THE COLE IN ME+      4.35.6
WHERETO LONG SINCE, THROUGH MY LONG BATTRED EYES     4.36.3
AND THERE LONG SINCE, $LOVE THY $LIEUTENANT LIES     4.36.5
LONG SINCE FORC'D BY THY BEAMES, BUT STONE
                              NOR TREE               4.36.13
SINCE THEN THOU HAST SO FARRE SUBDUED ME             4.40.12
SINCE TO HIMSELFE HE DOTH YOUR GIFTS APPLY           4.43.3
BLIND-HITTING BOY, SINCE SHE THAT THEE AND ME        4.46.2
YET SINCE MY DEATH-WOUND IS ALREADY GOT              4.48.12
SINCE THEY DO WEARE HIS BADGE, MOST FIRMELY PROVE    4.52.4
WELL $LOVE, SINCE THIS DEMURRE OUR SUTE
                              DOTH STAY              4.52.12
TO WITLESSE THINGS, THEN $LOVE I HOPE (SINCE WIT     4.59.13
NOW SINCE HER CHAST MIND HATES THIS LOVE IN ME       4.61.9
SINCE IN THINE ARMES, IF LEARND FAME TRUTH
                              HATH SPREAD            4.65.13
STOLNE TO MY HEART, SINCE LAST FAIRE NIGHT,
                              NAY DAY                4.66.10
NECTAR OF $MIRTH, SINCE I $JOVE'S CUP DO KEEPE       4.70.4
WHO SINCE HE HATH, BY $NATURE'S SPECIALL GRACE       4.78.9
SINCE BEST WITS THINKE IT WIT THEE TO ADMIRE         4.80.2
THEN SINCE (DEARE LIFE) YOU FAINE WOULD
                              HAVE ME PEACE          4.81.12
HIGHWAY SINCE YOU MY CHIEFE $PERNASSUS BE            4.84.1
SINCE $STELLA'S EYES, WONT TO GIVE ME MY DAY         4.89.3
SINCE ALL MY WORDS THY BEAUTY DOTH ENDITE            4.90.13
SINCE KIND OR CHANCE GIVES BOTH ONE LIVERIE          4.96.2
STELLA SINCE THOU SO RIGHT A $PRINCESSE ART          4.107.1
BUT SINCE THAT LYFE IS MORE THEN DEATH DESYRED       5.7.9
HAVE EVER SINCE ME KEPT IN CRUELL BANDS              5.12.12
BUT SINCE YE ARE MY SCOURGE I WILL INTREAT           5.24.13
FOR SINCE IT IS THE BADG WHICH I DOE BEARE           5.28.3
SO SINCE THE WINGED $GOD HIS PLANET CLEARE           5.60.5
YET SINCE YOUR LIGHT HATH ONCE ENLUMIND ME           5.66.13
BUT SINCE YE DEIGND SO GOODLY TO RELENT              5.82.9
SINCE I DID LEAVE THE PRESENCE OF MY LOVE            5.87.1
SINCE I HAVE LACKT THE COMFORT OF THAT LIGHT         5.88.1
```

SINFUL   10
```
THE SHADOW AND THE VAILE OF EVERY SINFULL DEED       2.145.8
WERE IT NOT SINFULL THEN STRIVING TO MEND            3.103.9
HATE OF MY SINNE, GROUNDED ON SINFULL LOVING         3.142.2
POORE SOULE THE CENTER OF MY SINFULL EARTH           3.146.1
MY SINFULL EARTH THESE REBBELL POWRES
                              THAT THEE ARRAY        3.146.2
OF SINFULL THOUGHTS, WHICH DO IN RUINE END+          4.14.8
THEN $LOVE IS SINNE, AND LET ME SINFULL BE           4.14.14
NOR BLAM'D FOR BLOUD, NOR SHAM'D FOR SINFULL
                              DEED                   4.84.11
INTO THIS SINFULL WORLD FROM HEAVEN TO SEND          5.24.10
EXCEEDING SWEET, YET VOYD OF SINFULL VICE            5.77.9
```

```
SING                      21
   WHY SHOULD I SING IN VERSE, WHY SHOULD I FRAME        1.17.1
   LET OTHERS SING OF $KNIGHTS AND $PALLADINES           1.55.1
   BUT I MUST SING OF THEE, AND THOSE FAIRE EIES         1.55.5
   WHILST I LIKE $ORPHEUS SING TO $TREES
                            AND $STONES                  2.45.12
   WHERE $NIGHTINGALES IN $ARDEN SIT AND SING            2.53.7
   WHERE $NIGHTINGALS IN $ARDEN SIT AND SING             2.113.7
   WHO ALL IN ONE, ONE PLEASING NOTE DO SING             3.8.12
   OH HOW THY WORTH WITH MANNERS MAY I SINGE             3.39.1
   THINE EYES, THAT TAUGHT THE DUMBE ON HIGH TO SING     3.78.5
   OR IF THEY SING, TIS WITH SO DULL A CHEERE            3.97.13
   SING TO THE EARE THAT DOTH THY LAIES ESTEEME          3.100.7
   AS $PHILOMELL IN SUMMERS FRONT DOTH SINGE             3.102.7
   THEY HAD NOT STILL ENOUGH YOUR WORTH TO SING          3.106.12
   WITH NEW-BORNE SIGHES AND DENISEND WIT DO SING        4.15.8
   BUT THEM (SO SWEETE IS SHE) MOST SWEETLY SING         4.57.10
   SING THEN MY $MUSE, NOW $IO $PEAN SING                4.63.9
   SING THEN MY $MUSE, NOW $IO $PEAN SING                4.63.9
   TREBLES SING HIGH, AS WELL AS BASES DEEPE             4.70.6
   TO SING THE GLORY OF THEIR FAMOUS DEEDES              5.29.8
   TO SING YOUR NAME AND PRAYSES OVER ALL                5.73.12
   TO SPORT MY MUSE AND SING MY LOVES SWEET PRAISE       5.80.10
SINGING                   1
   WHERE BLESSED $ANGELS SINGING DAY AND NIGHT           2.105.13
SINGLE                    4
   DIE SINGLE AND THINE $IMAGE DIES WITH THEE            3.3.14
   SINGS THIS TO THEE THOU SINGLE WILT PROVE NONE        3.8.14
   THAT THOU CONSUM'ST THY SELFE IN SINGLE LIFE+         3.9.2
   AND OUR DEARE LOVE LOOSE NAME OF SINGLE ONE           3.39.6
SINGLENESS                1
   IN SINGLENESSE THE PARTS THAT THOU SHOULD'ST BEARE    3.8.8
SINGS                     9
   WHO WHILST I BURNE, SHE SINGS AT MY SOULES WRACK      1.47.5
   EACH $BIRD SINGS TO HER SELFE, AND SO WILL I          1.59.14
   SHALL BE FORGOTTEN, WHOM NO $POET SINGS               2.6.3
   WHEN $DORUS SINGS HIS SWEET $PAMELAS LOVE             2.151.10
   SINGS THIS TO THEE THOU SINGLE WILT PROVE NONE        3.8.14
   FROM SULLEN EARTH SINGS HIMNS AT $HEAVENS GATE        3.29.12
   THAT SHE, ME THINKS, NOT ONELY SHINES BUT SINGS       4.38.8
   WITHIN HER CAGE, BUT SINGES AND FEEDS HER FILL        5.65.8
   SO DOES THE $CUCKOW, WHEN THE $MAVIS SINGS            5.85.3
SINKS                     1
   SINKES DOWNE TO DEATH, OPPREST WITH MELANCHOLIE       3.45.8
SINS                      6
   SEE THEN WHO SINNES THE GREATER OF US TWAINE          1.33.13
   EXCUSING THEIR SINS MORE THEN THEIR SINS ARE          3.35.8
   EXCUSING THEIR SINS MORE THEN THEIR SINS ARE          3.35.8
   OH IN WHAT SWEETS DOEST THOU THY SINNES INCLOSE       3.95.4
   SINS THAT THIS ONE IS TOST WITH TROUBLOUS FIT         5.33.11
   THE OLD YEARES SINNES FOREPAST LET US ESCHEW          5.62.7
SIR                       4
   O, JUDGE NOT RASHLY (GENTLE $SIR) I PRAY              2.24.4
   'WHAT NOW SIR FOOLE,' SAID HE, 'I WOULD NO LESSE      4.53.7
   LEAVE THAT SIR $PHIP, LEAST OFF YOUR NECKE
                            BE WROONG                    4.83.14
   BE YOUR WORDS MADE (GOOD $SIR) OF $INDIAN WARE        4.92.1
SIRE                      2
   RESEMBLING SIER, AND CHILD, AND HAPPY MOTHER          3.8.11
   BUT FROM THY HEART, WHILE MY SIRE CHARMETH THEE       4.32.13
```

```
SIREN                    2
  TH'INCHAUNTING $SYREN, WHICH DOTH SO ENTICE       2.130.3
  WHAT POTIONS HAVE I DRUNKE OF $SYREN TEARES       3.119.1
SIRE'S                   1
  HIS $SIRE'S REVENGE, JOYN'D WITH A KINGDOME'S
                          GAINE                     4.75.6
SISTERS                  1
  LET DAINTIE WITS CRIE ON THE $SISTERS NINE        4.3.1
SISYPHUS                 2
  WITH $SISIPHUS THUS DOE I ROLE THE STONE          2.40.13
  WITH $SISIPHUS THUS DOE I ROLE THE STONE          2.144.13
SIT                     13
  BRIGHT STARRE OF $BEAUTY, ON WHOSE EYE-LIDS SIT   2.4.1
  MUSES WHICH SADLY SIT ABOUT MY $CHAYRE            2.45.1
  SADLY I SIT, UNMOV'D WITH THE $APPLAUSE           2.47.11
  THOU, HER BLIND $SONNE, MAY'ST SIT BY
                          THEM, AND PLAY            2.48.14
  WHERE $NIGHTINGALES IN $ARDEN SIT AND SING        2.53.7
  WHERE $NIGHTINGALS IN $ARDEN SIT AND SING         2.113.7
  INTITLED IN THEIR PARTS, DO CROWNED SIT           3.37.7
  AND MORE, MUCH MORE THEN IN MY VERSE CAN SIT      3.103.13
  NOR OUGHT DO CARE, THOUGH SOME ABOVE ME SIT       4.64.11
  NOR EVER DID IN SHADE OF $TEMPE SIT               4.74.2
  I WOULD KNOW WHETHER SHE DID SIT OR WALKE         4.92.9
  ON SERVANTS' SHAME OFT $MAISTER'S BLAME
                          DOTH SIT                  4.107.12
  AN HUNDRED $GRACES AS IN SHADE TO SIT             5.40.4
SITH                     8
  SITH I LIVE HATEFULL TO THOSE RUTHLESSE EIES      1.21.7
  SITH SHE IS DEAFE, AND WILL NOT HEARE MY $MONES   2.45.10
  SITH ALL WORLDS GLORIE IS BUT DROSSE UNCLEANE     5.27.2
  BUT SITH SHE WILL THE CONQUEST CHALLENG NEEDS     5.29.9
  SITH TO ALL OTHER BEASTES OF BLOODY RACE          5.31.5
  SITH ALL YOUR TEMPESTS CANNOT HOLD ME BACKE       5.46.10
  SITH NEVER OUGHT WAS EXCELLENT ASSAYDE            5.51.7
  THEN SITH TO HEAVEN YE LYKENED ARE THE BEST       5.55.13
SITHENS                  1
  AND SITHENS HAVE WITH SIGHES AND SORROWES FED     5.2.3
SITS                     8
  TO HER THAT SITS IN MY THOUGHTS $TEMPLE SAINTED   1.15.7
  MERIDIANIS SITS WITHIN A MAZE                     2.151.8
  NO LOVE TOWARD OTHERS IN THAT BOSOME SITS         3.9.13
  HE SITS ME FAST, HOW EVER I DO STURRE             4.49.12
  AT SIGHT WHEREOF EACH BIRD THAT SITS ON SPRAY     5.40.9
  MY LOVE LYKE THE $SPECTATOR YDLY SITS             5.54.2
  SITS DOWNE TO REST HIM IN SOME SHADY PLACE        5.67.3
  SITS MOURNING FOR THE ABSENCE OF HER MATE         5.89.2
SITTING                  3
  AND THOU WITH CAREFULL BROW SITTING ALONE         1.41.2
  SITTING ALONE, $LOVE BIDS ME GOE AND WRITE        2.38.1
  SITTING ALONE, LOVE BIDS ME GOE AND WRITE         2.131.1
SITUATION                1
  AND SITUATION WITH THOSE DANCING CHIPS            3.128.10
SIX                      1
  THROUGH $FAERY LAND, WHICH THOSE SIX BOOKS
                          COMPILE                   5.80.2
SKIES                   15
  GAZING THY BEAUTY DEIGN'D THEE BY THE SKIES       1.37.2
  TO PROVE THE $PYNIONS, IT ASCENDS THE $SKYES      2.56.10
  TO SHEW THEIR KINDE, BEGAN TO CLIME THE SKIES     2.103.10
```

```
BUT MY MOST MERVAILE WAS WHEN FROM THE SKYES          2.125.9
THEN THERE BE STARRES AT MIDNIGHT IN THE SKYES       2.126.12
THAT HER CLEARE VOYCE LIFTS THY FAME TO THE SKIES      4.12.8
PHOEBUS DREW WIDE THE CURTAINES OF THE SKIES          4.13.12
LOOKES TO THE SKIES, AND IN A DITCH DOTH FALL+        4.19.11
AND SO NOR WILL, NOR CAN, BEHOLD THOSE SKIES           4.25.7
WITH HOW SAD STEPS, O $MOONE, THOU CLIMB'ST
                          THE SKIES                    4.31.1
SHE LIGHTNING $LOVE, DISPLAYING $VENUS' SKIES          4.63.7
MODELS SUCH BE WOOD-GLOBES OF GLISTRING SKIES          4.91.11
MORNE'S MESSENGER, WITH ROSE ENAMELD SKIES             4.99.10
O TEARES, NO TEARES, BUT RAINE FROM BEAUTIE'S
                          SKIES                        4.100.1
WHO HATH THE CRIMSON WEEDS STOLNE FROM
                          MY MORNING SKIES+            4.102.4
SKILL                    26
WHO ONELY WRITE, MY SKILL IN $VERSE TO PROVE           2.35.4
WHEN I AM MADE UNHAPPY BY MY SKILL                     2.43.12
BUT THY DIVINE PERFECTIONS BY THEIR SKILL              2.104.9
AND ONELY WRITE, MY SKILL IN VERSE TO PROVE            2.112.4
AND YOU MUST LIVE DRAWNE BY YOUR OWNE
                          SWEET SKILL                  3.16.14
FOR THROUGH THE $PAINTER MUST YOU SEE HIS SKILL        3.24.5
AND $FOLLY ($DOCTOR-LIKE) CONTROULING SKILL            3.66.10
SOME GLORY IN THEIR BIRTH, SOME IN THEIR SKILL         3.91.1
AND GIVES THY PEN BOTH SKILL AND ARGUMENT              3.100.8
SHE KEEPES THEE TO THIS PURPOSE, THAT HER SKILL        3.126.7
THERE IS SUCH STRENGTH AND WARRANTISE OF SKILL         3.150.7
WHILE WITH A FEELING SKILL I PAINT MY HELL             4.2.14
THAT TO WIN IT, IS ALL THE SKILL AND PAINE             4.12.14
BUT IF (BOTH FOR YOUR LOVE AND SKILL) YOUR NAME        4.15.12
HORSEMEN MY SKILL IN HORSMANSHIP ADVAUNCE              4.41.5
BUT CANNOT SKILL TO PITIE MY DISGRACE                  4.45.3
MIGHT WINNE SOME GRACE IN YOUR SWEET SKILL ARRAID      4.55.4
MADE TO AMAZE WEAKE MENS CONFUSED SKIL                 5.17.2
OF NATURES SKILL THE ONELY COMPLEMENT                  5.24.3
THAT HER GREAT TRIUMPH WHICH MY SKILL EXCEEDS          5.29.11
AND WITH SLY SKILL SO CUNNINGLY THEM DRESSES           5.37.3
SOME DAINTY EARES, CANNOT WITH ANY SKILL               5.38.6
IF NATURE, THEN SHE MAY IT MEND WITH SKILL             5.41.3
NO SKILL CAN STINT NOR REASON CAN ASLAKE               5.44.8
THEN MY LYFES $LEACH DOE YOU YOUR SKILL REVEALE        5.50.13
BUT THEY THAT SKILL NOT OF SO HEAVENLY MATTER          5.85.5
SKILLED                   2
IN SWEETEST STRENGTH, SO SWEETLY SKILD WITHALL         4.36.10
THEY THAT IN COURSE OF HEAVENLY SPHEARES
                          ARE SKILD                    5.60.1
SKILLFUL                  2
WHILST FROM THEYR RAYES BY $CUPIDS SKILFULL HAND       2.135.7
MOST HAPPY LETTERS FRAM'D BY SKILFULL TRADE            5.74.1
SKIN                      4
WHOSE FAIRE SKIN, BEAMY EYES, LIKE MORNING
                          SUN ON SNOW                  4.8.9
HER FLESH HIS FOOD, HER SKIN HIS ARMOUR BRAVE          4.29.12
TO SHEW HER SKIN, LIPS, TEETH AND HEAD SO WELL+        4.32.11
THAT SKIN, WHOSE PASSE-PRAISE HUE SCORNS
                          THIS POORE TERME OF WHITE    4.77.7
SKINS                     1
FROM THAT FOE'S WOUNDS THEIR TENDER SKINNES
                          TO HIDE                      4.22.8
```

```
SKY                             8
   I BUILD MY $HOPES A WORLD ABOVE THE $SKIE          2.62.9
   WHICH BY THEYR NATURE LEARN'D TO' MOUNT THE SKYE   2.122.6
   I BUILD MY HOPES, A WORLD ABOVE THE SKYE           2.150.9
   CHEARED AND CHECKT EVEN BY THE SELFE-SAME SKIE     3.15.6
   TO HAVE FOR NO CAUSE BIRTHRIGHT IN THE SKIE        4.26.5
   WHILES HER FAIRE FACE SHE REARES UP TO THE SKIE    5.13.2
   WHEREOF SHE MOTE BE MADE., THAT IS THE SKYE        5.55.10
   IN MIND TO MOUNT UP TO THE PUREST SKY              5.72.2
SLACK                           2
   THOU PURBLIND $BOY, SINCE THOU HAST BEENE
                          SO SLACKE                   2.36.1
   BUT AS HE THEM MORE SHORT OR SLACKE DOTH RAINE     4.58.4
SLACKER                         1
   BECAUSE THAT $MARS, GROWNE SLACKER IN HER LOVE     4.17.2
SLAIN                           8
   MY $HEART WAS SLAINE, AND NONE BUT YOU AND I       2.2.1
   SHE COMMING NEERE, THAT MY POORE $HEART
                          HATH SLAINE                 2.46.9
   THOU $CROCODILE, WHO WHEN THOU HAST ME SLAINE      2.130.13
   NOW WAST THOU BORNE, NOW IN THY CRADLE SLAYNE      2.141.14
   PRESUME NOT ON THY HEART WHEN MINE IS SLAINE       3.22.13
   YET DO NOT SO, BUT SINCE I AM NEERE SLAINE         3.139.13
   BUT HIM HER HOST THAT UNKIND GUEST HAD SLAINE      4.38.14
   HAD SHE NOT SO DOON, SURE I HAD BENE SLAYNE        5.16.13
SLAKE                           1
   THE RAINES OF $LOVE I LOVE, THOUGH NEVER SLAKE     4.28.7
SLANDER                         2
   SO THOU BE GOOD, SLANDER DOTH BUT APPROVE          3.70.5
   AND THENCE THIS SLAUNDER AS I THINKE PROCEEDS      3.131.14
SLANDERED                       1
   AND $BEAUTIE SLANDERD WITH A BASTARD SHAME         3.127.4
SLANDERERS                      1
   MADDE SLANDERERS BY MADDE EARES BELEEVED BE        3.140.12
SLANDERING                      1
   SLANDRING $CREATION WITH A FALSE ESTEEME           3.127.12
SLANDER'S                       1
   FOR SLANDERS MARKE WAS EVER YET THE FAIRE          3.70.2
SLAUGHTERING                    1
   AND MOLLIFIE THE SLAUGHT'RING $GALLIGLASSE         2.25.12
SLAVE                          11
   BEING YOUR SLAVE WHAT SHOULD I DOE BUT TEND        3.57.1
   BUT LIKE A SAD SLAVE STAY AND THINKE OF NOUGHT     3.57.11
   THAT $GOD FORBID, THAT MADE ME FIRST YOUR SLAVE    3.58.1
   AND BRASSE ETERNALL SLAVE TO MORTALL RAGE          3.64.4
   BUT SLAVE TO SLAVERY MY SWEET'ST FRIEND MUST BE    3.133.4
   THY PROUD HEARTS SLAVE AND VASSALL WRETCH TO BE    3.141.12
   UPON THAT COAST, AM GIV'N UP FOR A SLAVE           4.29.14
   HIM AS THY SLAVE, AND NOW LONG NEEDY $FAME         4.35.10
   IN MY FREE SIDE+ OR AM I BORNE A SLAVE             4.47.3
   WHEN $CUPID, HAVING ME HIS SLAVE DESCRIDE          4.53.5
   O EASE YOUR HAND, TREATE NOT SO HARD YOUR SLAVE    4.86.9
SLAVE-BORN                      1
   IS GONE, AND NOW LIKE SLAVE-BORNE $MUSCOVITE       4.2.10
SLAVERY                         1
   BUT SLAVE TO SLAVERY MY SWEET'ST FRIEND MUST BE    3.133.4
SLAVES                          1
   GROWNE NOW HIS SLAVES, HE FORST THEM OUT TO FIND   4.57.3
SLAY                            3
   USE POWER WITH POWER, AND SLAY ME NOT BY $ART      3.139.4
```

```
A KIND OF GRACE IT IS TC SLAY WITH SPEED          4.48.14
YET EVEN WHYLST HER BLOCDY HANDS THEM SLAY        5.47.9
SLAYING                   2
  BY SLAYING HIM, WHOSE LYFE THOUGH YE DESPYSE     5.36.11
  IN SLAYING HIM THAT WOULD LIVE GLADLY YOURS+     5.57.12
SLEDGE                    1
  THAT WITH HIS HEAVY SLEDGE HE CAN IT BEAT        5.32.3
SLEEP                    31
  HAPPY IN SLEEPE, WAKING CONTENT TO LANGUISH      1.16.1
  LONG ARE THEIR NIGHTS WHOSE CARES DO NEVER SLEEPE 1.26.5
  CARE-CHARMER $SLEEPE, SCNNE OF THE SABLE NIGHT   1.54.1
  STILL LET ME SLEEPE, IMBRACING CLOUDS IN VAINE   1.54.13
  IN $ME IT SPEAKES, WHETHER I $SLEEPE OR $WAKE    2.20.5
  WHEN NOW THE $NIGHT DOTH SUMMCN ALL TO SLEEPE+   2.37.2
  SWEETE SLEEPE SO ARM'D WITH $BEAUTIES
                          ARROWES DARTING          2.136.1
  SLEEPE IN THY $BEAUTY, $BEAUTY IN SLEEPE
                          APPEARETH                2.136.2
  SLEEPE IN THY $BEAUTY, $BEAUTY IN SLEEPE
                          APPEARETH                2.136.2
  SLEEPE LIGHTNING $BEAUTY, $BEAUTY SLEEPES
                          DARKNES CLEERETH         2.136.3
  SLEEP WATCHING $BEAUTY, $BEAUTY WAKING,
                          SLEEPE GUARDING          2.136.5
  SLEEP WATCHING $BEAUTY, $BEAUTY WAKING,
                          SLEEPE GUARDING          2.136.5
  BEAUTY IN SLEEPE, SLEEPE IN $BEAUTY CHARMED      2.136.6
  BEAUTY IN SLEEPE, SLEEPE IN $BEAUTY CHARMED      2.136.6
  SLEEPE WITH DELIGHT, $BEAUTY WITH LOVE REWARDING 2.136.8
  SLEEPE AND $BEAUTY, WITH EQUALL FORCES STRYVING  2.136.9
  SLEEPE WITH $BEAUTY, $BEAUTY WITH SLEEPE
                          CONTENDING               2.136.11
  SLEEPE WITH $BEAUTY, $BEAUTY WITH SLEEPE
                          CONTENDING               2.136.11
  BUT WHEN I SLEEPE, IN DREAMES THEY LOOKE ON THEE 3.43.3
  THROUGH HEAVY SLEEPE ON SIGHTLESSE EYES
                          DOTH STAY+               3.43.12
  OR IF THEY SLEEPE, THY PICTURE IN MY SIGHT       3.47.13
  IN SLEEPE A $KING, BUT WAKING NO SUCH MATTER     3.87.14
  $CUPID LAID BY HIS BRAND AND FELL A SLEEPE       3.153.1
  THIS LITTLE $LOVE-$GOD LYING ONCE A SLEEPE       3.154.1
  MORPHEUS, THE LIVELY SONNE OF DEADLY SLEEPE      4.32.1
  THIS NIGHT WHILE SLEEPE BEGINS WITH HEAVY WINGS  4.38.1
  CALD IT ANEW, AND WOOED SLEEPE AGAINE            4.38.13
  COME SLEEPE, O SLEEPE, THE CERTAINE KNOT OF PEACE 4.39.1
  COME SLEEPE, O SLEEPE, THE CERTAINE KNOT OF PEACE 4.39.1
  MY STILL KEPT COURSE, WHILE OTHERS SLEEPE,
                          TO MONE                  4.40.4
  NAY, MORE FOOLE I, CFT SUFFERED YOU TO SLEEPE    4.83.7
SLEEPETH                  1
  ATTENDS THAT $LAMPE WITH EYE WHICH NEVER
                          SLEEPETH                 2.105.10
SLEEPING                  2
  WAKEN HER SLEEPING PITTY WITH YOUR CRYING        1.2.12
  WAS SLEEPING BY A $VIRGIN HAND DISARM'D          3.154.8
SLEEPS                    2
  AND IN ETERNALL DARKNESSE EVER SLEEPS            1.35.12
  SLEEPE LIGHTNING $BEAUTY, $BEAUTY SLEEPES
                          DARKNES CLEERETH         2.136.3
```

SLEEP'S   4
  SLEEPES WONDER $BEAUTY, WONDERS TO WORLDS
                              IMPARTING   2.136.4
  SLEEPES AGED COLDNES, WITH $BEAUTIES FIRE WARMED   2.136.7
  BEAUTY HER STRENGTH UNTO SLEEPES WEAKNES
                              LENDING   2.136.10
  CLOS'D WITH THEIR QUIVERS IN SLEEP'S ARMORY   4.99.4
SLEIGHT   1
  HIS PRAISE TO SLEIGHT, WHICH FROM GOOD
                              USE DOTH RISE   4.41.7
SLENDER   2
  BEARE NOT REPORT OF ANY SLENDER FIRE   1.4.3
  MY SLENDER MEANES PRESUM'D TOO HIGH A PART   1.36.3
SLEPT   3
  MY $MUSE HAD SLEPT, AND NONE HAD KNOWNE MY MINDE   1.6.14
  AND THEREFORE HAVE I SLEPT IN YOUR REPORT   3.83.5
  FRESH LOVE, THAT LONG HATH SLEPT IN CHEERLESSE
                              BOWER   5.4.6
SLEW   3
  THY RIGOR IN THAT $SANCTUARY SLEW   1.31.3
  IT SLEW IT SELFE., THE $VERDICT ON THE VIEW   2.2.5
  SLEW HIS DEARE $FRIEND, MY KIND AND TRUEST $HEART   2.7.12
SLIDE   2
  THESE PRESENT ABSENT WITH SWIFT MOTION SLIDE   3.45.4
  WHENCE WORDS, NOT WORDS, BUT HEAV'NLY
                              GRACES SLIDE   4.80.4
SLIDING   1
  SOME WHIR-POOLE $PO, AND SLYDING $HYPASIS   2.120.10
SLIGHT   2
  IF MY SLIGHT $MUSE DOE PLEASE THESE CURIOUS
                              DAIES   3.38.13
  THE OTHER TWO, SLIGHT AYRE, AND PURGING FIRE   3.45.1
SLIGHTLY   2
  READE IT (SWEET MAIDE) THOUGH IT BE DONE
                              BUT SLEIGHTLY   1.1.13
  I SAY, I $LOVE, YOU SLEIGHTLY ANSWERE I   2.5.5
SLIME   1
  THAT HINDERS HEAVENLY THOUGHTS WITH DROSSY SLIME   5.13.12
SLIPPERY   1
  SCOURGE OF IT SELFE, STILL CLIMING SLIPPRIE
                              PLACE   4.23.10
SLOW   11
  WHICH HASTE FOR SUCCOUR TO HER SLOW REGARD   1.4.2
  AS WELL (SAYTH HE) TOO FORWARD, AS TOO SLOW   2.59.6
  SLOW $ARRER, FRANTICK $GALLUS, $CYDNUS COLD   2.120.8
  RECEIVING NAUGHTS BY ELEMENTS SO SLOE   3.44.13
  THUS CAN MY LOVE EXCUSE THE SLOW OFFENCE   3.51.1
  WHEN SWIFT EXTREMITY CAN SEEME BUT SLOW   3.51.6
  SINCE FROM THEE GOING, HE WENT WILFULL SLOW   3.51.13
  UNMOOVED, COULD, AND TO TEMPTATION SLOW   3.94.4
  NOW WITH SLOW WORDS, NOW WITH DUMBE ELOQUENCE   4.61.2
  FORTUNE WHEELES STILL WITH ME IN ONE SORT SLOW 4.66.6
  SLOW HEAVINESSE IN BOTH HOLDS ONE DEGREE   4.96.6
SLOWLY   1
  AND MANY NIGHTS, THAT SLOWLY SEEMD TO MOVE   5.87.3
SLUMBERS   1
  DOST THOU DESIRE MY SLUMBERS SHOULD BE BROKEN   3.61.3
SLUTTISH   1
  THEN UNSWEPT STONE, BESMEER'D WITH SLUTTISH TIME   3.55.4

SLY   1
   AND WITH SLY SKILL SO CUNNINGLY THEM DRESSES   5.37.3
SMALL   6
   WIL BE A TOTTER'D WEED OF SMAL WORTH HELD   3.2.4
   THAT TO HIS SUBJECT LENDS NOT SOME SMALL GLORY   3.84.6
   NOR THIS, NOR THAT, NOR ANY SUCH SMALL CAUSE   4.75.12
   THAT YOU ALLOW ME THEM BY SO SMALL RATE+   4.92.2
   TO GRAUNT SMALL RESPIT TO MY RESTLESSE TOILE   5.11.6
   THEN THOSE SMALL FORTS WHICH YE WERE WONT BELAY   5.14.6
SMART   14
   WHERE LOE I LANGUISH IN SO HEAVY SMART   1.36.6
   REBELS TO $NATURE, STRIVE FOR THEIR OWNE SMART   4.5.4
   AND DAMNING THEIR OWNE SELVES TO $TANTAL'S SMART   4.24.3
   WHAT HARDER THING THEN SMART, AND NOT TO SPEAKE+   4.34.10
   MY MIND BEMONES HIS SENSE OF INWARD SMART   4.44.2
   SUCH SMART MAY PITIE CLAIME OF ANY HART   4.44.3
   THOU NEEDS MUST MISSE, AND SO THOU NEEDS
                               MUST SMART   4.46.11
   ALAS I FOUND, THAT SHE WITH ME DID SMART   4.87.5
   AND SEEKE SOME SUCCOUR BOTH TO EASE MY SMART   5.2.7
   OR LOOKE WITH PITTY ON MY PAYNEFUL SMART   5.18.8
   BUT WHEN I FEELE THE BITTER BALEFULL SMART   5.24.5
   TO BE ACQUIT FRO MY CONTINUALL SMART   5.42.6
   THE PITEOUS PASSION OF HIS DYING SMART   5.48.12
   DELIGHTS NOT IN MY MERTH NOR RUES MY SMART   5.54.10
SMELL   6
   TO THY FAIRE FLOWER AD THE RANCKE SMELL OF WEEDS   3.69.12
   LILLIES THAT FESTER, SMELL FAR WORSE THEN WEEDS   3.94.14
   YET NOR THE LAIES OF BIRDS, NOR THE SWEET SMELL   3.98.5
   NOR TASTE, NOR SMELL, DESIRE TO BE INVITED   3.141.7
   HER LIPS DID SMELL LYKE UNTO $GILLYFLOWERS   5.64.5
   SUCH FRAGRANT FLOWRES DOE GIVE MOST ODOROUS
                               SMELL   5.64.13
SMELLED   1
   ME SEEMD I SMELT A GARDIN OF SWEET FLOWRES   5.64.2
SMELLING   1
   MY $SMELLING WONNE WITH HER $BREATHS $SPICERIE   2.29.8
SMELLS   1
   SWEET THEEFE WHENCE DIDST THOU STEALE
                               THY SWEET THAT SMELS   3.99.2
SMILE   7
   LINES OF DELIGHT, WHEREON HER YOUTH MIGHT SMILE   1.51.2
   DECKT WITH HER YOUTH WHEREON THE WORLD DOTH SMILE   1.53.6
   TEACHING BLIND EYES BOTH HOW TO SMILE AND WEEPE   4.32.8
   HATH CHEEKES TO SMILE, AS WELL AS EYES TO WEEPE   4.70.8
   HER SMILE ME DRAWES, HER FROWNE ME DRIVES AWAY   5.21.12
   SWEET SMILE, THE DAUGHTER OF THE $QUEENE OF LOVE   5.39.1
   HER EYES LOOKE LOVELY AND UPON THEM SMYLE   5.47.10
SMILED   1
   HOW CLOTH'D, HOW WAITED ON, SIGHD SHE OR SMILDE   4.92.10
SMILES   13
   HER SMILES ARE LIGHTNING, THOUGH HER PRIDE
                               DESPAIRE   1.6.3
   WHAT SHOULD HER VERTUES DO, HER SMILES,
                               HER LOVE+   1.17.10
   NOW USE THE $SOMMER SMILES, ERE $WINTER LOWERS   1.40.4
   REVEALE THE TREASURE WHICH HER SMILES IMPART+   1.49.6
   LIGHTEN FOORTH SMILES TO CLEERE THE CLOUDED AIRE   1.51.9
   PITTY AND SMILES DOE BEST BECOME THE FAIRE   1.51.11
   PITTY AND SMILES MUST ONELY YEELD THEE PRAISE   1.51.12

```
          TILL $VIRGINS SMYLES DOE SOUND HIS SWEET RETEERE    2.147.8
          CUPID THEN SMILES, FOR ON HIS CREST THERE LIES      4.13.9
          THE CHARMING SMILES, THAT ROB SENCE FROM
                                      THE HART                5.17.10
          MARK WHEN SHE SMILES WITH AMIABLE CHEARE            5.40.1
          SO SHE WITH FLATTRING SMYLES WEAKE HARTS
                                      DOTH GUYDE              5.47.5
          HER GOODLY LIGHT WITH SMILES SHE DRIVES AWAY        5.81.8
SMILING                   5
          TWIXT JOY AND GRIEFE, YET WITH A SMYLING
                                      FROWNING                2.109.9
          SMYLING, AS THOUGH HE GLORIED IN HIS DEATH          2.135.12
          IT SUFFERS NOT IN SMILINGE POMP, NOR FALLS          3.124.6
          I SAW THY SELFE WITH MANY A SMILING LINE            4.103.2
          TRUST NOT THE TREASON OF THOSE SMYLING LOOKES       5.47.1
SMITE                     1
          AND HARDER GROWES THE HARDER SHE IS SMIT            5.32.11
SMITH                     1
          THE PAYNEFULL SMITH WITH FORCE OF FERVENT HEAT      5.32.1
SMOKE                     5
          FED BUT WITH SMOKE, AND CHERISHT BUT WITH FIRE      1.15.4
          THESE SORROWING SIGHES, THE SMOAKE OF MINE ANNOY    1.24.1
          THE $SUN-BEAMES SMOTHERED WITH IMMORTALL $SMOKE     2.55.6
          THE $SUN-BEAMES SMOTHERED WITH IMMORTALL SMOKE      2.102.6
          HIDING THY BRAV'RY IN THEIR ROTTEN SMOKE            3.34.4
SMOKED                    2
          SMOAK'D WITH MY $SIGHES, AND BLOTTED WITH
                                      MY $TEARES              2.54.4
          SMOK'D WITH MY SIGHES, AND BLOTTED WITH
                                      MY TEARES               2.101.4
SMOKES                    1
          THERE DO THESE SMOAKES THAT FROM AFFLICTION RISE    1.47.9
SMOOTH                    2
          TAKE THOU OF ME SMOOTH PILLOWES, SWEETEST BED       4.39.9
          HOW FALLES IT THEN, THAT WITH SO SMOOTH AN EASE     4.74.9
SMOTHER                   1
          OR HEART IN LOVE WITH SIGHES HIMSELFE
                                      DOTH SMOTHER            3.47.4
SMOTHERED                 2
          THE $SUN-BEAMES SMOTHERED WITH IMMORTALL $SMOKE     2.55.6
          THE $SUN-BEAMES SMOTHERED WITH IMMORTALL SMOKE      2.102.6
SNAKY                     1
          THEYR SNAKY HEADS DOE COMBE, FROM WHICH A SPRING    5.86.3
SNARE                     2
          SHE MAY ENTANGLE IN THAT GOLDEN SNARE               5.37.6
          RIGHT SO YOUR SELFE WERE CAUGHT IN CUNNING SNARE    5.71.5
SNARY                     1
          THOSE SNARY LOCKS, ARE THOSE SAME NETS
                                      (MY $DEERE)             1.14.1
SNOW                      3
          IN THIS FAYRE LIMMED GROUND AS WHITE AS SNOW        2.114.10
          IF SNOW BE WHITE, WHY THEN HER BRESTS ARE DUN       3.130.3
          WHOSE FAIRE SKIN, BEAMY EYES, LIKE MORNING
                                      SUN ON SNOW             4.8.9
SNOWS                     2
          WHEN WINTER SNOWES UPON THY SABLE HAIRES            1.41.14
          WHEN WINTER SNOWES UPON THY SABLE HAIRES            1.42.1
SNOWY                     1
          HER SNOWY BROWES LYKE BUDDED $BELLAMOURES           5.64.7
```

```
SOAR                     1
  OR BLAME TH'ATTEMPT PRESUMING SO TO SORE            1.35.2
SOARING                  1
  THUS SORING STILL, NOT LOOKING ONCE BELOW           2.122.9
SOBBED                   1
  WHILE SOBD OUT WORDS A PERFECT $MUSIKE GIVE         4.100.11
SOBER                    3
  AND IN A MOMENT $MAD, $SOBER, $GLAD, AND $SORRIE    2.49.10
  DOTH HALFE THAT GLORY TO THE SOBER $WEST            3.132.8
  OR DID SHE ELSE THAT SOBER HUE DEVISE               4.7.5
SOBS                     2
  THAT ONCE COME THERE, THE SOBS OF MINE ANNOYES      4.44.13
  WHAT SOBS CAN GIVE WORDS GRACE MY GRIEFE TO SHOW+   4.93.2
SOCIETY                  1
  AND LACE IT SELFE WITH HIS SOCIETIE+                3.67.4
SOFT                     8
  WHICH ON THY SOFT CHEEKE FOR COMPLEXION DWELLS+     3.99.4
  AND PLEASD WITH OUR SOFT PEACE, STAID
                       HERE HIS FLYING RACE           4.8.4
  LET HER GO. $SOFT, BUT HERE SHE COMES. $GO TO       4.47.12
  WHEN FOR SO SOFT A ROD DEARE PLAY HE TRIE+          4.73.4
  AS THOUGH THAT FAIRE SOFT HAND DID YOU
                       GREAT WRONG                    4.83.4
  WITH SWEETE SOFT SHADES THOU OFT INVITEST ME        4.98.5
  SHALL HANDLE YOU AND HOLD IN LOVES SOFT BANDS       5.1.3
  HER HART MORE HARDE THEN YRON SOFT AWHIT            5.32.6
SOFTEN                   4
  TEARES CANNOT SOFTEN FLINT, NOR VOWES CONVART       1.11.3
  SOFTEN YOUR SELVES WITH EV'RY $TEARE THAT FALLS     2.45.11
  AND LONG INTREATY SOFTEN HER HARD HART              5.18.6
  MOTE SOFTEN IT AND TO HIS WILL ALLURE               5.51.10
SOIL                     4
  AND THE FIRME SOILE WIN OF THE WATRY MAINE          3.64.7
  THE SOLYE IS THIS, THAT THOU DOEST COMMON GROW      3.69.14
  WHY SHOULDST THOU TOYLE OUR THORNIE SOILE
                       TO TILL+                       4.10.6
  FAYRE SOYLE IT SEEMES FROM FAR AND FRAUGHT
                       WITH STORE                     5.63.7
SOL                      1
  SEATED WITH $SOL, AND WEARES $MINERVAS GLOVE        2.151.12
SOLACE                   1
  DARE TO APPROCH, THAT MAY MY SOLACE BREED           5.52.10
SOLD                     1
  GOR'D MINE OWN THOUGHTS, SOLD CHEAP WHAT
                       IS MOST DEARE                  3.110.3
SOLE                     2
  WHICH THOUGH IT ALTER NOT LOVES SOLE EFFECT         3.36.7
  (AS HIS SOLE OBJECT OF FELICITIE)                   4.86.7
SOLEMN                   2
  AND BAD MY $SENSES TO A SOLEMNE $FEAST              2.7.2
  THEREFORE ARE FEASTS SO SOLLEMNE AND SO RARE        3.52.5
SOLITARINESS             1
  IN BOTH A MAZEFULL SOLITARINESSE                    4.96.9
SOLITARY                 1
  TO SORROW AND TO SOLITARY PAINE                     5.52.6
SOME                   121
  PRESSE TO HER EYES, IMPORTUNE ME SOME GOOD          1.2.11
  FED WITH SOME PLEASING LOOKE THERE SHALL SHE BE     1.25.11
  SEEKE OUT SOME PLACE, AND SEE IF ANY PLACE          1.52.9
  WHO HATH SOME LONG AND DANG'ROUS $VOYAGE BEENE      2.1.2
```

```
LIKE GRIZZLED $MOSSE UPCN SOME AGED $TREE              2.8.8
THEN TO THE $SONNE CF SCME RICH $PENNY-FATHER          2.10.2
HAPS TO LEND SOME TC ONE TRUE HONEST $FRIEND           2.10.8
DEVISE SOME MEANES, BUT HOW I MAY FORSAKE $YCU         2.11.10
SOME WISE IN SHEW, MORE $FOOLES INDEED THEN THEY       2.22.14
I $HEARE SOME SAY, THIS $MAN IS NOT IN LCVE            2.24.1
IN GREATEST $PERILS SOME $MEN PLEASANT BE              2.24.10
ME $THINKES I SEE SCME CROOKED $MIMICKE JEERE          2.31.1
MAKING WITHALL SOME FILTHY $ANTIKE $FACE               2.31.4
SOME MISBELEEVING, AND PROPHANE IN $LOVE               2.35.1
SOME, WHEN IN $RYME, THEY OF THEIR $LOVES
                            DOE TELL                   2.39.1
SOME CALL ON $HEAVEN, SCME INVOCATE ON $HELL           2.39.3
SOME CALL ON $HEAVEN, SCME INVOCATE ON $HELL           2.39.3
SOME $MEN THERE BE, WHICH LIKE MY $METHOC WELL         2.42.1
SOME SAY, I HAVE A PASSING PLEASING $STRAINE           2.42.3
SOME SAY, $THAT IN MY $HUMOR I EXCELL                  2.42.4
SOME, WHO NOT KINDLY RELLISH MY $CONCEIT               2.42.5
FOR SOME FEW $RAGGES, WHEREWITH TO COVER THEE          2.48.4
TO SOME BASE $RUSTICK DCE THY SELFE PREFERRE           2.48.6
GOE HYRE THY SELFE SOME BUNGLING $HARPERS $BOY         2.48.10
AS $IN SOME $COUNTRIES, FARRE REMOTE FRUM HENCE        2.50.1
PLAY NOT THE $TYRANT, BUT TAKE SOME $REMORSE           2.52.5
EV'N AS A $MAN THAT IN SCME $TRANCE HATH SEENE         2.57.9
FOR FEARE THAT SOME THEIR $TREASURES SHOULD
                            PURLOYNE                   2.58.3
AND YET IN DEATH, SCME HOPE OF LIFE ESPYING            2.109.7
SOME $ATHIEST OR VILE $INFIDELL IN LOVE                2.112.1
SOME WHEN IN RYME THEY CF THEIR $LOVES DCE TELL        2.118.1
SOME INVOCATE THE $GODS, SOME SPIRITS OF $HELL         2.118.3
SOME INVOCATE THE $GODS, SOME SPIRITS OF $HELL         2.118.3
SOME $GANGES, $ISTER, AND OF $TAGUS TELL               2.120.9
SOME WHIR-POOLE $PO, AND SLYDING $HYPASIS              2.120.10
SOME OLD $PERNASSUS, WHERE THE $MUSES DWELL            2.120.11
SOME $HELYCON, AND SOME FAIRE $SIMOIS                  2.120.12
SOME $HELYCON, AND SOME FAIRE $SIMOIS                  2.120.12
SOME MUZ'D TO SEE THE EARTH ENVY THE AYRE              2.125.5
SOME WITS THERE BE, WHICH LYKE MY METHOD WELL          2.128.1
SOME SAY I HAVE A PASSING PLEASING STRAINE             2.128.3
SOME SAY THAT IN MY HUMCR I EXCELL                     2.128.4
SOME, WHO REACH NOT THE HEIGHT OF MY CONCEITE          2.128.5
AND WALLOWING IN HIS BLCOD, SCME LYFE YET LAFT         2.135.13
THOU DOO'ST BEGUILE THE WORLD, UNBLESSE
                            SOME MOTHER                3.3.4
MAKE SWEET SOME VIALL., TREASURE THOU SOME PLACE       3.6.3
MAKE SWEET SOME VIALL., TREASURE THOJ SOME PLACE       3.6.3
AND YOUR SWEET SEMBLANCE TO SOME OTHER GIVE            3.13.4
BUT WERE SOME CHILDE OF YOURS ALIVE THAT TIME          3.17.13
OR SOME FIERCE THING REPLEAT WITH TOO MUCH RAGE        3.23.3
BUT THAT I HOPE SCME GOOD CONCEIPT OF THINE            3.26.7
AS IF BY SOME INSTINCT THE WRETCH DID KNOW             3.50.7
TO MAKE SOME SPECIALL INSTANT SPECIALL BLEST           3.52.11
IN ALL EXTERNALL GRACE YOU HAVE SOME PART              3.53.13
SHOW ME YOUR IMAGE IN SCME ANTIQUE BOOKE               3.59.7
IF SOME SUSPECT OF ILL MASKT NOT THY SHOW              3.70.13
UNLESSE YOU WOULD DEVISE SOME VERTUOUS LYE             3.72.5
MY LIFE HATH IN THIS LINE SOME INTEREST                3.74.3
SOME FRESHER STAMPE OF THE TIME BETTERING DAYES        3.82.8
THAT TO HIS SUBJECT LENDS NOT SOME SMALL GLORY         3.84.6
SAY THAT THOU DIDST FORSAKE MEE FOR SOME FALT          3.89.1
```

```
SOME GLORY IN THEIR BIRTH, SOME IN THEIR SKILL          3.91.1
SOME GLORY IN THEIR BIRTH, SOME IN THEIR SKILL          3.91.1
SOME IN THEIR WEALTH, SOME IN THEIR BODIES FORCE        3.91.2
SOME IN THEIR WEALTH, SOME IN THEIR BODIES FORCE        3.91.2
SOME IN THEIR GARMENTS THOUGH NEW-FANGLED ILL           3.91.3
SOME IN THEIR $HAWKES AND $HOUNDS, SOME
                         IN THEIR $HORSE                3.91.4
SOME IN THEIR $HAWKES AND $HOUNDS, SOME
                         IN THEIR $HORSE                3.91.4
SOME SAY THY FAULT IS YOUTH, SOME WANTONESSE            3.96.1
SOME SAY THY FAULT IS YOUTH, SOME WANTONESSE            3.96.1
SOME SAY THY GRACE IS YOUTH AND GENTLE SPORT            3.96.2
SPENDST THOU THY FURIE ON SOME WORTHLESSE SONGE         3.100.3
AND IN SOME PERFUMES IS THERE MORE DELIGHT              3.130.7
YET IN GOOD FAITH SOME SAY THAT THEE BEHOLD             3.131.5
THAT SHE MIGHT THINKE ME SOME UNTUTERD YOUTH            3.138.3
THAT THE DEARE $SHE MIGHT TAKE SOME PLEASURE
                         OF MY PAINE                    4.1.2
SOME FRESH AND FRUITFULL SHOWERS UPON
                         MY SUNNE-BURN'D BRAINE         4.1.8
VERTUE ALAS, NOW LET ME TAKE SOME REST                  4.4.1
THY SCEPTER USE IN SOME OLD $CATOE'S BREST              4.4.5
SOME $LOVERS SPEAKE WHEN THEY THEIR $MUSES
                         ENTERTAINE                     4.6.1
SOME ONE HIS SONG IN $JOVE, AND $JOVE'S
                         STRANGE TALES ATTIRES          4.6.5
TO SOME A SWEETEST PLAINT, A SWEETEST
                         STILE AFFORDS                  4.6.9
NOT USDE TO FROZEN CLIPS, HE STRAVE TO
                         FIND SOME PART                 4.8.6
TO MY CLOSE HEART, WHERE WHILE SOME FIREBRANDS
                         HE DID LAY                     4.8.13
QUEENE $VERTUE'S COURT, WHICH SOME CALL
                         $STELLA'S FACE                 4.9.1
FOR LIKE A CHILD THAT SOME FAIRE BOOKE DOTH FIND        4.11.5
OR AT THE MOST ON SOME FINE PICTURE STAYES              4.11.7
I THOUGHT THOSE BABES OF SOME PINNE'S
                         HURT DID WHINE                 4.16.7
WHEN SOME FAIRE $LADIES, BY HARD PROMISE TIED           4.22.5
SOME THAT KNOW HOW MY SPRING I DID ADDRESSE             4.23.5
DEEME THAT MY $MUSE SOME FRUIT OF KNOWLEDGE PLIES       4.23.6
OR FOR SOME BRAWLE, WHICH IN THAT CHAMBER HIE           4.26.7
LIKE SOME WEAKE $LORDS, NEIGHBORD BY MIGHTY KINGS       4.29.1
MY HARMES ON $INK'S POORE LOSSE, PERHAPS
                         SOME FIND                      4.34.13
AND OF SOME SENT FROM THAT SWEET ENEMIE $FRAUNCE        4.41.4
SOME LUCKIE WITS IMPUTE IT BUT TO CHAUNCE               4.41.8
OF $LOVER'S RUINE SOME SAD $TRAGEDIE                    4.45.13
BUT FIND SOME $HERCULES TO BEARE, IN STEED              4.51.7
MIGHT WINNE SOME GRACE IN YOUR SWEET SKILL ARRAID       4.55.4
THEN SOME GOOD BODY TELL ME HOW I DO                    4.60.12
NOR OUGHT DO CARE, THOUGH SOME ABOVE ME SIT             4.64.11
AND DO I SEE SOME CAUSE A HOPE TO FEEDE                 4.66.1
NO KINGS BE CROWN'D BUT THEY SOME COVENANTS MAKE        4.69.14
'BUT AH,' $DESIRE STILL CRIES, 'GIVE ME
                         SOME FOOD'                     4.71.14
SOME DO I HEARE OF $POETS' FURIE TELL                   4.74.5
OR OF THY GIFTS AT LEAST SHADE OUT SOME PART            4.81.8
AND THAT MY $MUSE TO SOME EARES NOT UNSWEET             4.84.2
SOME BEAUTIE'S PEECE, AS AMBER COLOURD HED              4.91.6
```

```
          FOR THAT AT LENGTH YET DOTH INVITE SOME REST        4.96.13
          AH BED, THE FIELD WHERE JOYE'S PEACE SOME DO SEE    4.98.1
          TO STEALE SOME REST, BUT WRETCH I AM CONSTRAIND     4.98.6
          AND SEEKE SUCCCUR BOTH TO EASE MY SMART             5.2.7
          WITHOUT SOME SPARK OF SUCH SELF-PLEASING PRIDE      5.5.14
          FOR MY SWEET $SAYNT SOME SERVICE FIT WILL FIND      5.22.4
          BY CONDUCT OF SOME STAR DOTH MAKE HER WAY           5.34.2
          BUT BY HIS DEATH WHICH SOME PERHAPS WILL MONE       5.36.13
          SOME DAINTY EARES, CANNOT WITH ANY SKILL            5.38.6
          THEN WITH SOME CORDIALLS SEEKE FIRST TO APPEASE     5.50.9
          SITS DOWNE TO REST HIM IN SOME SHADY PLACE          5.67.3
          SOM HEVENLY WIT, WHOSE VERSE COULD HAVE ENCHASED    5.82.7
          WHEREOF SOME GLANCE DOTH IN MINE EIE REMAYNE        5.88.8
SOMETHING               3
          AND TO THE MOST OF PRAISE ADDE SOME-THING MORE      3.85.10
          THAT NOTHING ME, A SOME-THING SWEET TO THEE         3.136.12
          USE SOMETHING ELSE TO CHAST'N ME WITHALL            4.86.12
SOMETIME                9
          YEE SHALLOW $CENSURES, SOMETIME SEE YEE NOT         2.24.9
          BEAUTY SOMETIME IN ALL HER GLORY CROWNED            2.109.1
          READING SOMETYME, MY SORROWES TO BEGUILE            2.120.1
          SOMETIME TOO HOT THE EYE OF HEAVEN SHINES           3.18.5
          AND EVERY FAIRE FROM FAIRE SOME-TIME DECLINES       3.18.7
          WHEN I AM SOME-TIME ABSENT FROM THY HEART           3.41.2
          WHEN SOMETIME LOFTIE TOWERS I SEE DOWNE RASED       3.64.3
          SOME-TIME ALL FUL WITH FEASTING ON YOUR SIGHT       3.75.9
          THEREFORE LIKE HER, I SOME-TIME HOLD MY TONGUE      3.102.13
SOMETIMES               6
          YET $FOOLES AND $CHILDREN SOMETIMES TELL IN PLAY    2.22.13
          SOMETIMES WHAT $SCHOOLE-MEN SCARCELY CAN DECIDE     2.46.3
          THAT SOME-TIMES ANGER THRUSTS INTO HIS HIDE         3.50.10
          THE DOORE BY WHICH SOMETIMES COMES FORTH
                              HER $GRACE                      4.9.5
          THOSE LAMPING EYES WILL DEIGNE SOMETIMES TO LOOK    5.1.6
          SOMETIMES I JOY WHEN GLAD OCCASION FITS             5.54.5
SOMEWHAT                3
          SO MAY YOU STILL HAVE SOMEWHAT NEW TO SAY           4.51.4
          SOMEWHAT THY LEAD'N COUNSELS, WHICH I TOOKE         4.56.7
          THAT I PERHAPS AM SOMEWHAT KINNE TO THEE            4.65.12
SON                     9
          YEELD $CITHEREAS SONNE THOSE $ARKES OF LOVE         1.19.2
          CARE-CHARMER $SLEEPE, SONNE OF THE SABLE NIGHT      1.54.1
          THEN TO THE $SONNE OF SOME RICH $PENNY-FATHER       2.10.2
          LEAVES TO HIS $SONNE ALL HE HAD HEAP'D TOGETHER     2.10.4
          THOU, HER BLIND $SONNE, MAY'ST SIT BY
                              THEM, AND PLAY                  2.48.14
          UNLOK'D ON DIEST UNLESSE THOU GET A SONNE           3.7.14
          YOU HAD A $FATHER, LET YOUR $SON SAY SO             3.13.14
          AND WHEN A WOMAN WOES, WHAT WOMANS SONNE            3.41.7
          MORPHEUS, THE LIVELY SONNE OF DEADLY SLEEPE         4.32.1
SONG                    12
          THEN BEAUTY (NOW THE BURTHEN OF MY SONG)            1.38.5
          SHALL HAVE MY $SONG, WHERE $DELIA HATH HER SEAT     1.58.12
          AVON SHALL BE MY $THAMES, AND SHE MY $SONG          1.58.13
          STILL TO SURVIVE IN MY IMMORTALL $SONG              2.6.14
          AND CROWNE THE $PIRENS WITH MY LIVING $SONG         2.25.4
          AND WITH THE $SWAN RECORD THY DYING SONG            2.139.7
          WHOSE SPEECHLESSE SONG BEING MANY, SEEMING ONE      3.8.13
          AND STRETCHED MITER OF AN $ANTIQUE SONG             3.17.12
          SPENDST THOU THY FURIE ON SOME WORTHLESSE SONGE     3.100.3
```

```
  BECAUSE I WOULD NOT DULL YOU WITH MY SONGE          3.102.14
  SOME ONE HIS SONG IN $JOVE, AND $JOVE'S
                          STRANGE TALES ATTIRES          4.6.5
  I BARE (WITH $ENVIE) YET I BARE YOUR SONG             4.83.5
SONGS             4
  THESE FATALL $ANTHEAMES, SAD AND MORNEFULL $SONGS      1.3.2
  SINCE ALL ALIKE MY SONGS AND PRAISES BE              3.105.3
  HE BARKS, MY SONGS THINE OWNE VOYCE OFT
                          DOTH PROVE                      4.59.6
  AND IN HER SONGS SENDS MANY A WISHFULL VOW            5.89.3
SONNET            1
  TO WRITE HIM BUT ONE $SONNET TO HIS $LOVE             2.21.4
SONNETS           2
  SINCE $SONNETS THUS IN $BUNDLES ARE IMPREST           2.31.9
  SONETS BE NOT BOUND PRENTISE TO ANNOY                 4.70.5
SONS              1
  GALLEIN'S ADOPTIVE SONNES, WHO BY A BEATEN WAY       4.102.9
SOON             22
  CLEERE-SIGHTED YOU, SOONE NOTE WHAT IS AWRIE           1.3.7
  YET SOONE AGAINE I MUST HER BACKE RECALL              1.25.7
  IF ANY ASKE ME WHY SO SOONE I CAME                    1.30.9
  SOONE DOTH IT FADE THAT MAKES THE FAIREST FLORISH     1.50.5
  LETTERS AND $LINES WE SEE ARE SOONE DEFACED           2.13.1
  LETTERS AND LYNES WE SEE ARE SOONE DEFACED           2.121.1
  AS SOONE AS THINKE THE PLACE WHERE HE WOULD BE        3.44.8
  AND SOONE TO YOU, AS YOU TO ME THEN TENDRED         3.120.11
  TO WIN ME SOONE TO HELL MY FEMALL EVILL              3.144.5
  FOR SOONE AS THEY STRAKE THEE WITH $STELLA'S
                          RAYES                          4.10.12
  MY BOILING SPRITES DID THITHER SOONE INCLINE          4.16.3
  AND YET AS SOONE AS THEY SO FORMED BE                 4.50.5
  SHOULD SOUNE BE PIERC'D WITH SHARPNESSE
                          OF THE MONE                     4.57.8
  BECOMES A CLOG) WILL SOONE EASE ME OF IT             4.59.14
  BUT SOONE AS THOUGHT OF THEE BREEDS MY DELIGHT       4.108.5
  IF NOT, DIE SOONE, AND I WITH THEE WILL PERISH        5.2.14
  WILS HIM AWAKE, AND SOONE ABOUT HIM DIGHT             5.4.7
  SUCH CRUELTY SHE WOULD HAVE SOONE ABHORD             5.31.14
  THE HARDEST YRON SOON DOTH MOLLIFY                    5.32.2
  WIL SOONE CONCEIVE, AND LEARNE TO CONSTRUE WELL      5.43.14
  SOONE AFTER WHEN MY JOY TO SORROW FLITS               5.54.7
  BID HER THEREFORE HER SELFE SOONE READY MAKE          5.70.9
SOONER            6
  FOR HER NO SOONER HAD MINE EYES BEWRAID               1.5.5
  NO SOONER SPREADS HER GLORY IN THE AYRE              1.39.5
  BUT IT NO SOONER SAW MY $SUNNE APPEARE               2.56.5
  BUT THEY NO SOONER SAW MY $SUNNE APPEARE            2.103.5
  INJOYD NO SOONER BUT DISPISED STRAIGHT              3.129.5
  PAST REASON HUNTED, AND NO SOONER HAD              3.129.6
SOONEST           1
  THAT SOONEST FALS WHEN AS SHE MOST SUPPOSETH         5.58.3
SOOTH             1
  FOR ME IN SOOTH, NO $MUSE BUT ONE I KNOW              4.3.9
SOPHISTRY         1
  DRIV'N ELSE TO GRAUNT BY $ANGEL'S SOPHISTRIE         4.61.13
SORE              2
  SO WEAKE MY POWRES, SO SORE MY WOUNDS APPEARE        5.57.5
  WITH WHICH MY SILLY BARKE WAS TOSSED SORE            5.63.4
SORELY            1
  WILL BOTH TOGETHER ME TOO SORELY WRACK              5.46.12
```

SORROW   28
    TEARES IN MINE EYES, AND SORROW AT MY HART   1.9.12
    TO GOE FROM SORROW, AND THINE OWNE DISTRESSE+   1.52.2
    TO ADDE MORE GRIEFE TO AGGRAVATE MY SORROW   1.54.12
    MY CHASTE DESIRE, WHICH FROM DARKE SORROW SHINES   1.59.3
    OR ALL MY $HOPE FOR $SORROW WILL BE DEAD   2.26.14
    WITH MY $LIFE'S $SORROW INTERLINED SO   2.54.3
    WITH MY LIVES SORCW ENTERLYNED SO   2.101.3
    WHERE MY POORE SOULE, THE $BARKE OF SORRCW LYES   2.134.3
    OR ALL MY HOPE FOR SORRCW WILL BE DEAD   2.137.14
    THE $INNE OF CARE, THE $NURSE OF DRERY SCRROW   2.145.2
    TH'OFFENDERS SORRCW LENDS BUT WEAKE RELIEFE   3.34.11
    AH DOE NOT, WHEN MY HEART HATH SCAPTE THIS SCRROW 3.90.5
    AND FOR THAT SORRCW, WHICH I THEN DIDDE FEELE   3.120.2
    MY DEEPEST SENCE, HCW HARD TRUE SORROW HITS   3.120.10
    LEAST SORROW LEND ME WORDS AND WORDS EXPRESSE   3.140.3
    I SEE AND YET NO GREATER SOROW TAKE   4.18.13
    NAY SORROW COMES WITH SUCH MAINE RAGE, THAT HE   4.95.9
    SUCH TEARES, SIGHS, PLAINTS, NO SORROW
                           IS, BUT JOY   4.100.12
    ALL MIRTH FAREWELL, LET ME IN SORROW LIVE   4.100.14
    WHEN SORROW (USING NINE CWNE FIER'S MIGHT)   4.108.1
    PLAYNTS, PRAYERS, VCWES, RUTH, SORROW,
                           AND DISMAY   5.14.11
    IN SECRET SOROW AND SAD PENSIVENESSE   5.34.14
    THAT ALL THE MORE MY SORROW IT AUGMENTETH   5.42.3
    WITH SORROW DIMMED AND DEFORMD IT WERE   5.45.10
    BUT YE HIGH HEVENS, THAT ALL THIS SOROWE SEE   5.46.9
    TO SORROW AND TO SCLITARY PAINE   5.52.6
    SOONE AFTER WHEN MY JOY TO SORROW FLITS   5.54.7
    SO SORROW STILL DCTH SEEME TOO LONG TO LAST   5.87.13
SORROWING   1
    THESE SORROWING SIGHES, THE SMOAKE OF MINE ANNOY   1.24.1
SORROWS   13
    AH YOU, AND NONE BUT YOU MY SORROWES REACE   1.3.11
    FOR THAT NO COLOURS CAN DEPAINT MY SORROWES   1.4.6
    STILL NEW BORNE SCRROWES OF HER FRESH DISCAINE   1.16.10
    THE CIRCLE OF MY SCRROWES NEVER ENDING   1.18.4
    AND NO REMOVE CAN MAKE THY SORROWES LESSE+   1.52.4
    AS ONE THAT FAINE HIS $SORROWES WOJLD BEGUILE   2.24.6
    READING SOMETYME, MY SORROWES TO BEGUILE   2.120.1
    BUT DAY DOTH DAILY CRAW MY SORROWES LONGER   3.28.13
    ALL LOSSES ARE RESTCRD, AND SORROWES END   3.30.14
    AND READE THE SORRCWES CF MY DYING SPRIGHT   5.1.7
    AND SITHENS HAVE WITH SIGHES AND SORROWES FED   5.2.3
    YET MY POORE LIFE, ALL SCRROWES TO ASSOYLE   5.11.9
    ALL SORROWES SHORT THAT GAINE ETERNALL BLISSE   5.63.14
SORROW'S   3
    WITH ABSENCE' $VAILE, I LIVE IN $SOROWE'S NIGHT   4.91.4
    AS GRUDGING ME MY SCRROWE'S ELOQUENCE+   4.104.4
    AND FEELING THENCE NO MCRE HER SOROWES SADNESSE   5.39.11
SORRY   2
    AND IN A MOMENT $MAD, $SOBER, $GLAD, AND $SORRIE   2.49.10
    MAKE GLAD AND SORRY SEASONS AS THOJ FLEET'ST   3.19.5
SORT   7
    THAT HOLDS, THAT BURNES, THAT WOUNDS ME
                           IN THIS SORT   1.14.8
    WHY IN THIS SORT I WREST $INVENTION SO   2.9.2
    BECAUSE I LOOSELY TRIFLE IN THIS SORT   2.24.5
    BUT DOE NOT SO, I LCVE THEE IN SUCH SORT   3.36.13

```
    BUT DOE NOT SO, I LOVE THEE IN SUCH SORT          3.96.13
    FORTUNE WHEELES STILL WITH ME IN ONE SORT SLOW     4.66.6
    THAT I MAY LAUGH AT HER IN EQUALL SORT             5.10.13
SORTED                    1
    THEN HAD YE SORTED WITH A PRINCES PERE             5.66.10
SORTS                     3
    THREE SORTS OF $SERPENTS DOE RESEMBLE THEE         2.130.1
    MOST SORTS OF MEN DOE SET BUT LITTLE STORE         5.26.12
    ALL SORTS OF FLOWERS THE WHICH ON EARTH DO SPRING  5.70.3
SOT                       2
    WISE IN $CONCEIT, IN $ACT A VERY SOT              2.62.6
    WISE IN CONCEITE, IN ACTE A VERY SOT              2.150.6
SOUGHT                   12
    SEEKING IN VAINE WHAT I HAVE EVER SOUGHT           1.33.3
    I ONELY SOUGHT THE BLISSE TO HAVE HER SIGHT        1.36.12
    FROM $AGE TO $AGE, WHAT THOU HAST SOUGHT TO SEE    2.17.2
    FROM WORLD TO WORLD, THOU LONG HAST SOUGHT
                              TO SEE                   2.107.2
    I SIGH THE LACKE OF MANY A THING I SOUGHT          3.30.3
    I SOUGHT FIT WORDS TO PAINT THE BLACKEST
                              FACE OF WOE              4.1.5
    UPON A WRETCH, THAT LONG THY GRACE HATH SOUGHT     4.40.7
    LONG-WHILE I SOUGHT TO WHAT I MIGHT COMPARE        5.9.1
    ONE DAY I SOUGHT WITH HER HART-THRILLING EIES      5.12.1
    WHICH SOUGHT ME TO ENTRAP IN TREASONS TRAINE       5.12.4
    SOUGHT NOT TO FLY, BUT FEARELESSE STILL DID BIDE   5.67.10
    THAT MANY SOUGHT YET NONE COULD EVER TASTE         5.77.10
SOUL                     51
    HERE I UNCLASPE THE $BOOKE OF MY CHARG'D SOULE     1.1.5
    IF THIS BE LOVE, TO WARRE AGAINST MY SOULE         1.9.5
    OFT HAVE I TOLD HER THAT MY SOULE DID LOVE HER     1.18.13
    A WAY THROUGH WANT TO FREE MY SOULE FROM CARE      1.29.10
    POORE SOULE QUITE SPENT, WHOSE FORCE CAN
                              DO NO MORE               1.46.3
    MY $SOULE IS OF A BRAVER $METTLE MADE              2.4.10
    THE $SOULE OF $MAN IMMORTALL AND DIVINE            2.12.2
    THESE OF THE $SOULE THE SEV'RALL $FUNCTIONS BEE    2.12.13
    AND MY GOOD $ANGELL (IN MY $SOULE DIVINE)          2.18.11
    TO CRUELL $LOVE MY $SOULE WAS FIRST BETRAY'D       2.29.14
    AND IN MY $SOULE THE PAINES OF $HELL I PROVE       2.41.3
    THAT $SOULE (SWEET $MAID) WHICH SO HATH
                              HONOR'D $THEE            2.55.11
    THAT SOULE (SWEET $MAIDE) WHICH SO HATH
                              HONORED THEE             2.102.11
    MY SOULE HAD NE'R FELT THY $DIVINITIE              2.104.7
    AND MY GOOD $ANGELL IN MY SOULE DIVINE             2.108.11
    AND MY SOULE THEN OBTAINE WHICH SO MY
                              SOULE DESIRETH           2.117.8
    AND MY SOULE THEN OBTAINE WHICH SO MY
                              SOULE DESIRETH           2.117.8
    DISDAYNE $ICE TO MY LIFE, IS TO MY SOULE A FIRE    2.132.3
    DESIRE, MY LOVE, MY SOULE, MY HOPE, HART,
                              AND LIFE CHARMETH        2.132.8
    DESIRE, MY LOVE, MY SOULE, MY HOPE, MY
                              HART, MY LIFE            2.132.13
    WHERE MY POORE SOULE, THE $BARKE OF SORROW LYES    2.134.3
    A SOULE, THAT EVER HATH ADOR'D HER NAME            2.138.10
    DIE, DIE, MY SOULE, AND NEVER TASTE OF JOY         2.139.1
    AND IN MY SOULE THE PAYNES OF HELL I PROVE         2.143.3
    AND ALL MY SOULE, AND AL MY EVERY PART             3.62.2
```

```
NOT MINE OWNE FEARES, NOR THE PROPHETICK SOULE        3.107.1
AS FROM MY SOULE WHICH IN THY BREST DOTH LYE          3.109.4
HENCE, THOU SUBBORND $INFORMER, A TREW SCULE          3.125.13
IF THY SOULE CHECK THEE THAT I COME SO NEERE          3.136.1
SWEARE TO THY BLIND SOULE THAT I WAS THY $WILL        3.136.2
AND WILL THY SOULE KNOWES IS ADMITTED THERE           3.136.3
POORE SOULE THE CENTER CF MY SINFULL EARTH            3.146.1
THEN SOULE LIVE THOU UPCN THY SERVANTS LOSSE          3.146.9
MY SOULE DOTH TELL MY BODY THAT HE MAY                3.151.7
IF VAINE LOVE HAVE MY SIMPLE SOULE OPPREST            4.4.3
AND SHOULD IN SOULE UP TO OUR COUNTREY MCVE           4.5.13
DOTH PLUNGE MY WEL-FORM'D SOULE EVEN IN THE MIRE      4.14.7
YET PRIDE I THINKE DOTH NOT MY SOULE POSSESSE         4.27.9
THAT NOT MY SOULE, WHICH AT THY FOOT DID FALL         4.36.12
EACH SOULE DOTH AT $LOVE'S FEET HIS WEAPONS LAY       4.43.7
THAT VERTUOUS SOULE, SURE HEIRE OF HEAV'NLY
                              BLISSE                   4.52.7
HER SOULE, ARM'D BUT WITH SUCH A DAINTY RIND          4.57.7
BUT I UNBID, FETCH EVEN MY SOULE TO THEE              4.59.8
SO CAPTIVES TO HIS $SAINT BOTH SOULE AND SENCE        4.61.6
THAT VOYCE, WHICH MAKES THE SOULE PLANT
                 HIMSELFE IN THE EARES                4.77.9
SAFE IN MY SOULE, WHICH ONLY DOTH TO THEE             4.86.6
FOR MY POORE SOULE, WHICH NOW THAT SICKNESSE
                              TRIES                    4.94.6
AS CAN REFRESH THE HELL WHERE MY SOULE FRIES          4.100.8
AND MY YONG SOULE FLUTTERS TO THEE HIS NEST           4.108.6
THEN IS MY SOULE WITH LIFE AND LOVE INSPIRED          5.7.6
MY SOULE WAS RAVISHT QUITE AS IN A TRAUNCE            5.39.10
SOULS                      9
YOU BLINDED SOULES WHOM YOUTH AND ERROUR LEADE        1.3.9
HER PRIDE BROOK'D NCT POORE SOULES SHOULD
                      SO ASPIRE                        1.36.8
WHOSE LYFE DOTH SAVE A THOUSAND SOULES
                      FROM HELL                        2.119.12
WHICH STEALES MENS EYES AND WOMENS SOULES AMASETH     3.20.8
ALL TOUNGS (THE VCICE OF SOULES) GIVE
                 THEE THAT END                        3.69.3
WHICH OTHERS SAID DID MAKE THEIR SOULES TO PINE       4.16.6
STRANGE FLAMES OF $LOVE IT IN OUR SOULES
                 WOULD RAISE                          4.25.4
O KISSE, WHICH SOULES, EVEN SOULES TOGETHER TIES      4.81.5
O KISSE, WHICH SOULES, EVEN SOULES TOGETHER TIES      4.81.5
SOUL'S                     18
THOUGH MY SOULES $IDOLL SCORNETH ALL MY VOWES         1.11.10
YET MY SOULES SOVERAIGNE, SINCE I MUST RESIGNE        1.27.13
WHO WHILST I BURNE, SHE SINGS AT MY SOULES WRACK      1.47.5
THERE MY SOULES TYRANT JOYES HER, IN THE SACK         1.47.7
MY $SOULE'S $OBLATICNS TO THY SACRED $NAME            2.54.12
CHASTE HOLY $VOWES FOR MY $SOULES SACRIFICE           2.55.10
TO MY $SOULES $SUNNE, THOSE TWO $CELESTIALL
                          $EYES                        2.56.12
MY SOULES OBLATIONS TO THY SACRED NAME                2.101.12
CHASTE HOLY VOWES FCR MY SOULES SACRIFICE             2.102.10
THE SOULES DELIGHT, THE SENCES TRUE DIRECTION         2.123.7
WHEN MY SOULES SUNNE FRCM HER FAYRE $CABYNET          2.125.2
WITH MY SOULES FIRE, MY LIFE DISDAINE OUT-WEARES      2.132.7
MY LIFE A $PHOENIX IS IN MY SOULES FIRE               2.132.11
HARTS $METHRIDATE, THE SCULES PRESERVATIVE            2.146.6
IN THY SOULES THOUGHT (ALL NAKED) WILL BESTOW IT      3.26.8
```

```
SAVE THAT MY SOULES IMAGINARY SIGHT                    3.27.9
SOULE'S JOY, BEND NCT THOSE MORNING STARRES
                               FROM ME                 4.48.1
MY SOULES LONG LACKED FCCDE, MY HEAVENS BLIS           5.1.12
SOUL-SHRINED            2
MY $SOULE-SHRIN'D $SAINT, MY FAIRE $IDEA LIES          2.53.2
MY SOULE-SHRINDE $SAINT, MY FAIRE $IDEA LYES           2.113.2
SOUND                   8
MY $MUSE SHOULD SCUND THY PRAISE WITH
                          MOURNFULL WARBLE             1.44.6
HER TOUCH DOTH CAUSE THE WARBLE OF THE SCUND           1.57.5
AND FIRST THE SOUND AND VERTUE OF MY $NAME             2.47.3
TILL $VIRGINS SMYLES DOE SOUND HIS SWEET RETEERE       2.147.8
THAT $MUSICKE HATH A FARRE MORE PLEASING SOUND         3.130.10
BREATH'D FORTH THE SOUND THAT SAID I HATE              3.145.2
NOR TRUMPETS SOUND I HEARD, NOR FRIENDLY CRIES         4.53.12
IF $RUBIES, LOE HIR LIPS BE $RUBIES SOUND              5.15.8
SOUNDED                 1
HIS TROMPET SHRILL HATH THRISE ALREADY SCUNDED         5.19.2
SOUNDING                1
WORDS CONSONANT, AND SOUNDING TO THY FAME              2.111.8
SOUNDLESS               1
WHILST HE UPON YOUR SOUNDLESSE DEEPE DOTH RIDE         3.80.10
SOUNDS                  5
SO SOUNDS MY $MUSE ACCORDING AS SHE STRIKES            1.57.3
HOARCE SOUNDS THE VCYCE THAT PRAYSETH
                          NOT HER NAME                 1.57.10
IF THE TRUE CONCORD OF WELL TUNED SOUNDS               3.8.5
UPON THAT BLESSED WCOD WHOSE MOTION SOUNDS             3.128.2
SO SWEETE SOUNDS STRAIGHT MINE EARE AND
                          HEART DO HIT                 4.55.13
SOUR                    5
BUT SINCE THE SWEETEST RCOTE YEELDS FRUITE
                          SO SOWRE                     1.26.9
WERE IT NOT THY SCURE LEISURE GAVE SWEET LEAVE         3.39.10
NOR THINKE THE BITTERNESSE OF ABSENCE SOWRE            3.57.7
SWEET IS THE BROOME-FLOWRE, BUT YET SOWRE ENCUGH       5.26.7
SO EVERY SWEET WITH SOURE IS TEMPRED STILL             5.26.9
SOUR-BREATHED           1
THIS SOWRE-BREATH'D MATE TAST OF THOSE
                          SUGRED LIPS                  4.59.11
SOUREST                 1
FOR SWEETEST THINGS TURNE SOWREST BY THEIR
                          DEEDES                       3.94.13
SOURLY                  2
TO THAT SWEET THEEFE WHICH SOURELY ROBS FROM ME        3.35.14
WILL SOURELY LEAVE HER TILL HE HAVE PREVAILED          3.41.8
SOURS                   2
SUBSTRACTING, SET MY $SWEETS UNTO MY $SOWRES           2.3.7
AND IN SUBSTRACTING, SET MY SWEETS UNTO
                          MY SOWRES                    2.110.7
SOUTH                   1
WHEN $EAST, WHEN $WEST, WHEN $SOUTH, AND
                          WHEN BY $NORTH               2.1.7
SOVEREIGN               12
YET MY SOULES SOVERAIGNE, SINCE I MUST RESIGNE         1.27.13
WHY SHOULD YOUR FAIRE $EYES WITH SUCH
                          SOV'RAIGNE GRACE             2.43.1
ONELY TO SHEW HER $BEAUTIES $SOV'RAIGNE $POW'R         2.50.14
FLATTER THE MOUNTAINE TCPS WITH SOVERAINE EIE          3.33.2
```

```
WHILST I (MY SOVERAINE) WATCH THE CLOCK FOR YOU      3.57.6
IF $NATURE (SOVERAINE MISTERES OVER WRACK)           3.126.5
AGAINST STRANG MALLADIES A SOVERAIGNE CURE           3.153.8
THEY FIRST RESORT UNTO THAT SOUERAIGNE PART          4.107.4
THE SOVERAYNE BEAUTY WHICH I DOO ADMYRE              5.3.1
MY SOVERAYNE SAYNT, THE $IDOLL OF MY THOUGHT         5.61.2
WHERE WHEN THAT SOVERAYNE BEAUTY IT DOTH SPY         5.72.5
THE SECOND IS MY SOVEREIGNE $QUEENE MOST KIND        5.74.7
```
SOVEREIGN'S   2
```
  UPON HIS SOVEREIGNES COURSE, THE NIGHTS
                          PALE $QUEENE                1.48.6
  BEQUEATH'D HIS WARDSHIP TO MY SOVERAIGNES EYE       2.116.12
```
SOVEREIGNTY   3
```
  HER SOVERAIGNTY SHOULD HAVE REMAINED STILL          1.36.11
  WHETHER WITH WORDS THIS SOVERAIGNTY HE GAINE        4.58.5
  NOT BY RUDE FORCE, BUT SWEETEST SOVERAIGNTIE        4.71.6
```
SOWN   1
```
  AND WHEN $CORNE'S SOWNE, OR GROWNE INTO THE $EARE   2.48.7
```
SPACE   2
```
  FOR THEN DISPIGHT CF SPACE I WOULD BE BROUGHT       3.44.3
  THAT AL MY WOUNDS WIL HEALE IN LITTLE SPACE         5.57.14
```
SPACIOUS   2
```
  'MONGST ALL THE $CREATURES IN THIS SPACIOUS
                          $ROUND                      2.16.1
  WILT THOU WHOSE WILL IS LARGE AND SPATIOUS          3.135.5
```
SPADE   1
```
  DIG DEEPE WITH LEARNING'S SPADE, NOW TELL
                          ME THIS                     4.21.13
```
SPAIN   1
```
  THIS $KINGS FAIRE $ENTRANCE, AND OUR $PEACE
                          WITH $SPAINE                2.51.8
```
SPANGLE   1
```
  BUT FOR TO SPANGLE THE BLACKE WEEDS OF NIGHT        4.26.6
```
SPARE   7
```
  POWRE FROM THOSE EYES, WHICH PITTY CANNOT SPARE     1.22.6
  OR DOST THOU SPARE HER FOR HER CRUELTIES            1.23.7
  YET SPARE HER $TIME, LET HER EXEMPTED BE            1.23.13
  WHO SPARES TO SPEAKE, DOTH SPARE TO SPEED
                          (QUOTH I)                   2.59.5
  DEARE $KILLER, SPARE NOT THY SWEET CRUELL SHOT      4.48.13
  OR DO YOU MEANE MY TENDER EARES TO SPARE            4.92.4
  YET SHOOT YE SHARPELY STILL, AND SPARE ME NOT       5.57.9
```
SPARES   1
```
  WHO SPARES TO SPEAKE, DOTH SPARE TO SPEED
                          (QUOTH I)                   2.59.5
```
SPARK   4
```
  THENCE, SO FARRE THENCE, THAT SCARCELY
                          ANY SPARKE                  4.104.6
  WITHOUT SOME SPARK CF SUCH SELF-PLEASING PRIDE      5.5.14
  OR IN HER EYES THE FYRE OF LOVE DOES SPARKE         5.81.4
  LET NOT ONE SPARKE CF FILTHY LUSTFULL FYRE          5.84.1
```
SPARKLING   2
```
  THAT WHERE THOSE TWO CLEARE SPARKLING
                          $EYES ARE PLAC'D            2.8.3
  WHEN SPARKLING STARS TWIRE NOT THOU GUIL'ST
                          TH'EAVEN                    3.28.12
```
SPARKS   1
```
  THE SPARKES WHERECF LET KINDLE THINE OWN FYRE       5.86.9
```
SPARTANS   1
```
  OR DO YOU CUTTED $SPARTANES IMITATE+                4.92.3
```

SPEAK   35
   HOW TO THINKE MUCH, AND HAVE NO WORDS TO SPEAKE   1.20.6
   WHOSE BEAUTY MADE HIM SPEAKE THAT ELSE WAS DCMBE   1.55.8
   WHEN I DOE SPEAKE CF $MIRACLES BY THEE   2.35.2
   WHY DOE I SPEAKE CF $JOY, OR WRITE OF $LCVE   2.41.1
   BUT WHAT OF $PITTY DOE I SPEAKE TO $THEE   2.52.9
   WHO SPARES TO SPEAKE, DCTH SPARE TO SPEEC
                            (QUOTH I)   2.59.5
   WHEN I DOE SPEAKE CF THY DIVINITIE   2.112.2
   WHY DOE I SPEAKE CF JOY, OR WRITE OF LOVE   2.143.1
   FOR NO MAN WELL OF SUCH A SALVE CAN SPEAKE   3.34.7
   SPEAKE OF THE SPRING, AND FOYZON OF THE YEARE   3.53.9
   THAT YOU FOR LOVE SPEAKE WELL OF ME UNTRUE   3.72.10
   SPEAKE OF MY LAMENESSE, AND I STRAIGHT WILL HALT   3.89.3
   TO SPEAKE OF THAT WHICH GIVES THEE ALL
                            THY MIGHT+   3.100.2
   WHAT'S NEW TO SPEAKE, WHAT NOW TO REGISTER   3.108.3
   I LOVE TO HEARE HER SPEAKE, YET WELL I KNCW   3.130.9
   AND IN MY MADNESSE MIGHT SPEAKE ILL OF THEE   3.140.10
   THUS GREAT WITH CHILD TC SPEAKE, AND HELPLESSE
                            IN MY THROWES   4.1.12
   SOME $LOVERS SPEAKE WHEN THEY THEIR $MUSES
                            ENTERTAINE   4.6.1
   I CAN SPEAKE WHAT I FEELE, AND FEELE AS
                            MUCH AS THEY   4.6.12
   'WHAT IDLER THING, THEN SPEAKE AND NOT BE HARD+'   4.34.9
   WHAT HARDER THING THEN SMART, AND NOT TO SPEAKE+   4.34.10
   WHERE TRUTH IT SELFE MUST SPEAKE LIKE FLATTERIE+   4.35.2
   MY THOUGHTS I SPEAKE, AND WHAT I SPEAKE
                            DOTH FLOW   4.74.10
   MY THOUGHTS I SPEAKE, AND WHAT I SPEAKE
                            DOTH FLOW   4.74.10
   BUT LO, WHILE I DC SPEAKE, IT GROWETH
                            NOONE WITH ME   4.76.9
   SO WHEN MY TOUNG WCULD SPEAK HER PRAISES CEW   5.3.9
   YET IN MY HART I THEN BCTH SPEAKE AND WRITE   5.3.13
   YOU STOP MY TOUNG, AND TEACH MY HART TO SPEAKE   5.8.10
   SHALL I THEN SILENT BE CR SHALL I SPEAKE+   5.43.1
   AND IF I SPEAKE, HER WRATH RENEW I SHALL   5.43.2
   THAT NETHER I MAY SPEAKE NOR THINKE AT ALL   5.43.7
   WILL TEACH TO SPEAKE, AND MY JUST CAUSE TO PLEAD   5.43.10
   AND SPEAKE HER GOCD, THCUGH SHE REQUITE IT ILL   5.48.14
   TO SPEAKE HER PRAYSE AND GLORY EXCELLENT   5.74.11
   BUT SPEAKE NO WORD TO HER OF THESE SAD PLIGHTS   5.84.11
SPEAKING   5
   AND DOMB PRESAGERS CF MY SPEAKING BREST   3.23.10
   TO MAKE ME TOUNG-TIDE SPEAKING OF YOUR FAME   3.80.4
   SPEAKING OF WORTH, WHAT WORTH IN YOU DOTH GROW   3.83.8
   ME FOR MY DOMBE THCUGHTS, SPEAKING IN EFFECT   3.85.14
   SIMPLY I CREDIT HER FALSE SPEAKING TONGUE   3.138.7
SPEAKS   2
   IN $ME IT SPEAKES, WHETHER I $SLEEPE OR $WAKE   2.20.5
   WHAT WORDS SO ERE SHE SPEAKES PERSWADES FOR THEE   4.12.7
SPEAR   1
   BUT IN $VERT FIELD $MARS BARE A GOLDEN SPEARE   4.13.5
SPECIAL   4
   TO MAKE SOME SPECIALL INSTANT SPECIALL BLEST   3.52.11
   TO MAKE SOME SPECIALL INSTANT SPECIALL BLEST   3.52.11
   NOR NOURISH SPECIALL LOCKES OF VOWED HAIRE   4.54.3
   WHO SINCE HE HATH, BY $NATURE'S SPECIALL GRACE   4.78.9

```
SPECTATOR                        1
  MY LOVE LYKE THE $SPECTATOR YDLY SITS              5.54.2
SPEECH                           9
  TO THEM THAT WOULD MAKE SPEECH OF SPEECH ARISE     4.27.4
  TO THEM THAT WOULD MAKE SPEECH OF SPEECH ARISE     4.27.4
  BY SUCH UNSUTED SPEECH SHOULD HINDRED BE           4.51.14
  NOR GIVE EACH SPEECH A FULL POINT OF A GRONE       4.54.4
  WITH CHOISEST FLOWERS MY SPEECH TO ENGARLAND SO    4.55.2
  NOR OTHER SUGRING CF MY SPEECH TO PROVE            4.55.10
  THAT IN ONE SPEECH TWO $NEGATIVES AFFIRME          4.63.14
  AS CONSTERD IN TRUE SPEECH, THE NAME OF
                        HEAV'N IT BEARES             4.77.11
  LET EARES HEARE SPEECH, WHICH WIT TO WONDER TIES   4.85.11
SPEECHES                         1
  OF POYSONED WORDS AND SPITEFULL SPEECHES WELL      5.86.4
SPEECHLESS                       3
  WHEN HIS $PULSE FAYLING, $PASSION SPEECHLESSE
                        LIES                         2.61.10
  WHOSE SPEECHLESSE SONG BEING MANY, SEEMING ONE     3.8.13
  WHILE HE INSULTS ORE DULL AND SPEACHLESSE
                        TRIBES                       3.107.12
SPEECH'S                         1
  O VOICE, O FACE, MAUGRE MY SPEECHE'S MIGHT         4.58.12
SPEED                            6
  AND IN MY FALL I CRYE FOR HELPE WITH SPEEDE        1.32.9
  WHO SPARES TO SPEAKE, DOTH SPARE TO SPEED
                        (QUOTH I)                    2.59.5
  HIS RIDER LOV'D NOT SPEED BEING MADE FROM THEE     3.50.8
  OF MY DULL BEARER, WHEN FROM THEE I SPEED          3.51.2
  IN WINGED SPEED NO MOTION SHALL I KNOW             3.51.8
  A KIND OF GRACE IT IS TO SLAY WITH SPEED           4.48.14
SPEEDY                           3
  SWIFT SPEEDY $TIME, FEATHRED WITH FLYING HOURES    1.39.11
  IN SPEEDIE APPREHENSION, IT IS $SENSE              2.12.10
  STAY, SPEEDY $TIME, BEHOLD, BEFORE THOU PASSE      2.17.1
SPELL                            2
  TO CON MY $CROS-ROWE ERE I LEARN'D TO SPELL        2.111.2
  WHICH HER DEEP WIT, THAT TRUE HARTS THOUGHT
                        CAN SPEL                     5.43.13
SPELLED                          1
  IN HER SIGHT I A LESSON NEW HAVE SPELD             4.16.12
SPEND                            11
  TO SPEND THE $APRILL OF MY YEARES IN GRIEFE        1.32.2
  TO ONE $MAN GIVES, DOTH ON ANOTHER SPEND           2.10.6
  UNTHRIFTY LOVELINESSE WHY DOST THOU SPEND          3.4.1
  LOOKE WHAT AN UNTHRIFT IN THE WORLD DOTH SPEND     3.9.9
  I HAVE NO PRECIOUS TIME AT AL TO SPEND             3.57.3
  DOST THOU UPON THY FADING MANSION SPEND+           3.146.6
  NAY IF THOU LOWRST ON ME DOE I NOT SPEND           3.149.7
  WHILE $LOVE ON ME DOTH ALL HIS QUIVER SPEND        4.14.4
  WHY DOEST THOU SPEND THE TREASURES OF THY SPRITE   4.68.5
  BUT AL MY DAYES IN PINING LANGUOR SPEND            5.36.3
  THUS I THE TIME WITH EXPECTATION SPEND             5.87.9
SPENDEST                         1
  SPENDST THOU THY FURIE ON SOME WORTHLESSE SONGE    3.100.3
SPENDING                         1
  SPENDING AGAINE WHAT IS ALREADY SPENT              3.76.12
SPENDS                           1
  AND IN THE PRAISE THEREOF SPENDS ALL HIS MIGHT     3.80.3
```

SPENT   28
  HOW THEY WERE SPENT FOR THEE., LOOKE WHAT THEY ARE   1.1.8
  TEARES, VOWES, AND PRAYERS. HAVE I SPENT IN VAINE   1.11.2
  SO MANY VOWES, AND PRAIERS HAVING SPENT   1.16.7
  THOUGH SPENT THY FLAME, IN ME THE HEAT REMAINING   1.41.6
  THAT FIRE CAN BURNE WHEN ALL THE MATTER'S SPENT   1.41.10
  THESE COLOURS WITH THY FADING ARE NOT SPENT   1.42.11
  POORE SOULE QUITE SPENT, WHOSE FORCE CAN
                          DO NO MORE   1.46.3
  WHERE MOST BECALM'D, WHERE WITH FOULE
                          $WEATHER SPENT   2.1.11
  I GIVE $THEE BACKE, WHEN ALL THE REST IS SPENT   2.10.14
  SPENT ON THINE $ALTARS, FLAMING UP TO $HEAV'N   2.36.10
  MY $SIGHES BE SPENT IN UTT'RING OF MY $WOE   2.41.7
  LOE, HEERE THY $SHEPHEARD SPENT HIS WANDRING
                          YEERES   2.53.10
  LOE, HEERE THY $SHEPHEARD SPENT HIS WANDRING
                          YEERES   2.113.10
  THY SHAFTS BE SPENT, AND SHEE (TO WARRE
                          APPOINTED)   2.126.9
  MY $LOVE MAKES HOTE THE FIRE WHOSE HEAT IS SPENT   2.127.1
  MY SIGHES BE SPENT WITH GRIEFE AND SIGHING SO   2.143.7
  SPENDING AGAINE WHAT IS ALREADY SPENT   3.76.12
  IN GENTLE NUMBERS TIME SO IDELY SPENT   3.100.6
  AND IN THIS CHANGE IS MY INVENTION SPENT   3.105.11
  WHEN TYRANTS CRESTS AND TOMBS OF BRASSE
                          ARE SPENT   3.107.14
  AND GAINE BY ILLS THRISE MORE THEN I HAVE SPENT   3.119.14
  PITTIFULL THRIVORS IN THEIR GAZING SPENT   3.125.8
  BUT THAT MY WEALTH I HAVE MOST IDLY SPENT   4.18.8
  AVISE THEMSELVES THAT THEY ARE VAINELY SPENT   4.19.8
  WHEN FAR SPENT NIGHT PERSWADES EACH MORTALL EYE   4.99.1
  WHEN MY ABODES PREFIXED TIME IS SPENT   5.46.1
  BEGAN IN ME TO MOVE, ONE YEARE IS SPENT   5.60.6
  THAT LITTLE THAT I AM, SHALL ALL BE SPENT   5.82.11
SPHERE   4
  AS THEY CANNOT ASCEND TO MY $HOPES $SPHERE   2.26.7
  AS THEY CANNOT ASCEND TO MY HOPES SPHEARE   2.137.7
  AS $MARS IN THREE SCORE YEARES DOTH RUN
                          HIS SPHEARE   5.60.4
  THE SPHEARE OF $CUPID FOURTY YEARES CONTAINES   5.60.10
SPHERES   4
  AND THY SWEET VOICE GIVE BACK UNTO THE $SPHEARES   1.19.10
  HOW HAVE MINE EIES OUT OF THEIR $SPHEARES
                          BENE FITTED   3.119.7
  O EYES, WHICH DO THE $SPHEARES OF BEAUTIE MOVE   4.42.1
  THEY THAT IN COURSE OF HEAVENLY SPHEARES
                          ARE SKILD   5.60.1
SPICERY   1
  MY $SMELLING WONNE WITH HER $BREATHS $SPICERIE   2.29.8
SPICES   1
  THE PRECIOUS $SPICES BE YOUR CHASTE $DESIRE   2.16.6
SPIDER   2
  AND ME UNTO THE $SPYDER THAT DOTH LURKE   5.71.3
  BETWEENE THE $SPYDER AND THE GENTLE $BEE   5.71.14
SPIDER'S   1
  SUCH LABOUR LIKE THE $SPYDERS WEB I FYND   5.23.13
SPIED   1
  LOOKE HERE, I SAY.' I LOOK'D, AND $STELLA SPIDE   4.53.8

```
SPIES                         2
   THE SHORES BESET WITH THOUSAND SECRET SPYES        2.122.3
   OR ON MY FRAILTIES WHY ARE FRAILER SPIES           3.121.7
SPIGHT                        1
   SUCH SELFE ASSURANCE NEED NOT FEARE THE SPIGHT     5.59.9
SPILL                         6
   HER SIGHT CONTENTED THUS TO SEE ME SPILL           1.36.13
   LEAST TREMBLING IT HIS WORKMANSHIP SHOULD SPILL    5.17.7
   YET WITH ONE WORD SHE CAN IT SAVE OR SPILL         5.38.11
   TO SPILL WERE PITTY, BUT TO SAVE WERE PRAYSE       5.38.12
   AND GREATER GLORY THINKE TO SAVE, THEN SPILL       5.49.4
   THERE PRIDE DARE NOT APPROCH, NOR DISCORD SPILL    5.65.9
SPILLING                      1
   THEN TO BE BLAM'D FOR SPILLING GUILTLESSE BLOOD    5.38.14
SPILLS                        1
   FOR WITH ONE LOOKE SHE SPILS THAT LONG I SPONNE    5.23.11
SPIRIT                       26
   THE $SPIRIT, WHEN IT TO $GOD-WARD DOTH INFLAME     2.12.12
   AN $EVILL SPIRIT YOUR BEAUTIE HAUNTS $ME STILL     2.20.1
   BY THIS GOOD WICKED $SPIRIT, SWEET $ANGELL
                                         $DEVILL     2.20.14
   (YET HIS DULL $SPIRIT HER NOT ONE JOT COULD MOVE)  2.21.2
   NOR SHALL MY $SPIRIT ONE JOT OF VIGOUR LOSE        2.31.6
   DISPERSE THEIR $RAYES ON EV'RY VULGAR $SPIRIT      2.43.2
   THOU, THUS WHOSE $SPIRIT $LOVE IN HIS
                                    FIRE REFINES     2.49.13
   THAT RAPT IN $SPIRIT, IN BETTER $WORLDS
                                     HATH BEENE      2.57.11
   FROM THE STRONG $SPIRIT BY NO MEANES FORCE
                                     THE SAME        2.58.8
   EV'N AS THIS $SPIRIT, SO YOU ALONE DOE PLAY        2.58.11
   THE SPIRIT OF $LOVE, WITH A PERPETUAL DULNESSE     3.56.8
   IS IT THY SPIRIT THAT THOU SEND'ST FROM THEE       3.61.5
   MY SPIRIT IS THINE THE BETTER PART OF ME           3.74.8
   KNOWING A BETTER SPIRIT DOTH USE YOUR NAME         3.80.2
   TO EVERY $HIMNE THAT ABLE SPIRIT AFFORDS           3.85.7
   WAS IT HIS SPIRIT, BY SPIRITS TAUGHT TO WRITE      3.86.5
   HATH PUT A SPIRIT OF YOUTH IN EVERY THING          3.98.3
   WHICH HATH NOT FIGUR'D TO THEE MY TRUE SPIRIT      3.108.2
   TH'EXPENCE OF $SPIRIT IN A WASTE OF SHAME          3.129.1
   THE WORSER SPIRIT A WOMAN COLLOUR'D IL             3.144.4
   IN MY FRAILE SPIRIT BY HER FROM BASENESSE RAYSED   5.3.4
   OF A PROUD LOVE, THAT DOTH MY SPIRITE SPOYLE       5.33.12
   OFT WHEN MY SPIRIT DOTH SPRED HER BOLDER WINGES    5.72.1
   BY WHOM MY SPIRIT OUT OF DUST WAS RAYSED           5.74.10
   DERIV'D FROM THAT FAYRE $SPIRIT, FROM
                                   WHOM AL TRUE       5.79.11
   MY SPIRIT TO AN HIGHER PITCH WILL RAYSE            5.80.12
SPIRITED                      1
   IN THEE OR SPRITES OR SPIRITED GASTLINESSE         4.96.11
SPIRITS                       6
   ALL UNCLEANE $THOUGHTS, FOULE $SPIRITS
                                   CAST OUT IN MEE    2.35.13
   GAVE IT TO KEEPE TO $SPIRITS WITHIN THE $GROUND    2.58.4
   ALL UNCLEANE THOUGHTS, FOULE SPIRITS CAST
                                    OUT IN MEE        2.112.13
   SOME INVOCATE THE $GODS, SOME SPIRITS OF $HELL     2.118.3
   WAS IT HIS SPIRIT, BY SPIRITS TAUGHT TO WRITE      3.86.5
   WHICH LIKE TWO SPIRITS DO SUGJEST ME STILL         3.144.2
```

SPITE   10
  THOUGH IN OUR LIVES A SEPERABLE SPIGHT   3.36.6
  SO I, MADE LAME BY $FORTUNES DEAREST SPIGHT   3.37.3
  JOYNE WITH THE SPIGHT OF FORTUNE, MAKE ME BOW   3.90.3
  WHEN OTHER PETTIE GRIEFES HAVE DONE THEIR SPIGHT   3.90.10
  SINCE SPIGHT OF HIM $ILE LIVE IN THIS
                            POORE RIME   3.107.11
  BITING MY TREWAND PEN, BEATING MY SELFE FOR SPITE 4.1.13
  THAT LAP DOTH LAP, NAY LETS, IN SPITE OF SPITE   4.59.10
  THAT LAP DOTH LAP, NAY LETS, IN SPITE OF SPITE   4.59.10
  BUT NOW SPITE OF MY HEART MY MOUTH WILL STAY   4.80.10
  MINE EYES THEN ONLY WINKE, FOR SPITE PERCHANCE   4.98.13
SPITEFUL   3
  SPIGHTFULL $ERINNIS FRIGHTS $ME WITH HER $LOOKES   2.39.9
  SPIGHTFULL $ERRINIS FRIGHTS MEE WITH HER LOOKES   2.118.9
  OF POYSONED WORDS AND SPITEFULL SPEECHES WELL   5.86.4
SPITES   1
  KILL ME WITH SPIGHTS YET WE MUST NOT BE FOES   3.40.14
SPLEEN   3
  LOVE GROWING ANGRY, VEXED AT THE $SPLEENE   2.38.5
  REBATE THY $SPLEENE, IF BUT FOR $PITTIES SAKE   2.52.6
  LOVE GROWING ANGRY, VEXED AT THE SPLEENE   2.131.5
SPLENDOR   1
  WITH ALL TRIUMPHANT SPLENDOR ON MY BROW   3.33.10
SPLENDOROUS   1
  YOUR $BEAUTIE IS THE HOT AND SPLEND'ROUS $SUNNE   2.16.5
SPOIL   14
  UPON THE PROSTRATE SPOYLE OF THAT POORE HART   1.10.10
  OF SUCH AS SPOILE THY POORE AFFLICTED STATE   1.28.4
  AND SERVE ALL THREE, AND YET THEY SPOILE ME TOO   1.28.14
  THE SPOYLE OF FAME DESERV'D BY VERTUOUS MEN   1.45.6
  THOUGH TIME DO SPOYLE THEE OF THE FAIREST VAILE   1.45.10
  OR WHO HIS SPOILE OR BEAUTIE CAN FORBID+   3.65.12
  WHICH FOR REWARD SPOILE IT WITH VAINE ANNOYES   4.18.11
  SO PIERCING PAWES, AS SPOYLE WHEN THEY EMBRACE   4.78.10
  OF MY POORE LIFE TO MAKE UNPITTIED SPOILE   5.11.8
  AND BOTH THE $INDIAS OF THEIR TREASURES SPOILE   5.15.3
  OF A PROUD LOVE, THAT DOTH MY SPIRITE SPOYLE   5.33.12
  SHE MEANES AT LAST TO MAKE HER PITEOUS SPOYLE   5.41.12
  THE HAPPY PURCHASE OF MY GLORIOUS SPOILE   5.69.13
  ON THE SWEET SPOYLE OF BEAUTIE THEY DID PRAY   5.76.8
SPOILS   1
  AND MAKE TIMES SPOILES DISPISED EVERY WHERE   3.100.12
SPOKEN   2
  FOR BEING FULL, SHOULD I NOT THEN HAVE SPOKEN   1.7.13
  BEWRAIES MY LOVE, WITH BROKEN WORDS HALFE SPOKEN   1.15.6
SPORT   11
  WHICH TURN'D MY SPORT INTO A $HARTS DISPAIRE   1.5.9
  AND SHE IS YONG, AND NOW MUST SPORT THE WHILE   1.51.4
  AH SPORT (SWEET $MAIDE) IN SEASON OF THESE YEARES 1.51.5
  AND LEAVES HIS $MOTHERS LAP TO SPORT HIM THERE   2.4.8
  YOU NOW SUPPOSE ME ALL THIS TIME IN SPORT   2.24.7
  (MAKING LASCIVIOUS COMMENTS ON THY SPORT)   3.95.6
  SOME SAY THY GRACE IS YOUTH AND GENTLE SPORT   3.96.2
  AS HIS MAINE FORCE, CHOISE SPORT, AND
                            EASEFULL STAY   4.43.4
  IN SPORT I SUCKT, WHILE SHE ASLEEPE DID LIE   4.73.6
  AS SHE DOTH LAUGH AT ME AND MAKES MY PAIN
                            HER SPORT   5.10.14
  TO SPORT MY MUSE AND SING MY LOVES SWEET PRAISE   5.80.10

SPORTIVE   1
  GIVE SALUTATION TO MY SPORTIVE BLOOD+   3.121.6
SPORTS   2
  AND LIKE A $WANTON, SPORTS WITH EV'RY $FETHER   2.22.6
  IN $MARTIALL SPORTS I HAD MY CUNNING TRICE   4.53.1
SPOT   1
  DOTH SPOT THE BEAUTIE OF THY BUDDING NAME+   3.95.3
SPOTLESS   5
  MY SPOTLESSE LOVE HOVERS WITH PUREST WINGS   1.12.1
  LIKE AS THE SPOTLESSE $ERMELIN DISTREST   1.29.1
  BUT IF ALL FAITH, LIKE SPOTLESSE $ERMINE LY   4.86.5
  AND SPOTLESSE PLEASURE BUILDS HER SACRED BOWRE   5.65.14
  BUT PURE AFFECTIONS BRED IN SPOTLESSE BREST   5.84.5
SPOTTED   1
  THE $PANTHER KNOWING THAT HIS SPOTTED HYDE   5.53.1
SPRAY   1
  AT SIGHT WHEREOF EACH BIRD THAT SITS ON SPRAY   5.40.9
SPREAD   7
  GREAT $PRINCES FAVORITES THEIR FAIRE LEAVES
                        SPREAD   3.25.5
  SINCE IN THINE ARMES, IF LEARND FAME TRUTH
                        HATH SPREAD   4.65.13
  THRUGH THE BROAD WORLD DOTH SPRED HIS GOODLY RAY   5.40.8
  HER LOVELY EYES LYKE $PINCKS BUT NEWLY SPRED   5.64.8
  OFT WHEN MY SPIRIT DOTH SPRED HER BOLDER WINGES   5.72.1
  ALL SPRED WITH JUNCATS, FIT TO ENTERTAYNE   5.77.3
  HER BREST THAT TABLE WAS SO RICHLY SPREDD   5.77.13
SPREADEST   1
  AND WHILST THOU SPREADST UNTO THE RISING SUNNE   1.40.5
SPREADS   2
  NO SOONER SPREADS HER GLORY IN THE AYRE   1.39.5
  SPREDS IN DEFIANCE OF ALL ENEMIES   5.5.12
SPRING   19
  AND $WINTER WOES, FOR SPRING OF YOUTH UNFIT   1.24.8
  WHERE SWEET $MYRRH-BREATHING $ZEPHIRE
                        IN THE $SPRING   2.53.5
  SHALT SPRING AGAINE FROM TH'ASHES OF THY FAME   2.106.12
  WHERE SWEET $MYRH-BREATHING $ZEPHYRE IN
                        THE SPRING   2.113.5
  MAKES $SUMMER $WINTER, $AUTUMNE IN THE $SPRING   2.147.11
  AND ONLY HERAULD TO THE GAUDY SPRING   3.1.10
  SPEAKE OF THE SPRING, AND FOYZON OF THE YEARE   3.53.9
  STEALING AWAY THE TREASURE OF HIS $SPRING   3.63.8
  FROM YOU HAVE I BEENE ABSENT IN THE SPRING   3.98.1
  OUR LOVE WAS NEW, AND THEN BUT IN THE SPRING   3.102.5
  YOU THAT DO SEARCH FOR EVERIE PURLING SPRING   4.15.1
  SOME THAT KNOW HOW MY SPRING I DID ADDRESSE   4.23.5
  THAT, FROM THAT SEA DERIV'D, TEARS' SPRING
                        DID FLOW   4.45.8
  MY SPRING APPEARES, O SEE WHAT HERE DOTH GROW   4.69.8
  FOR LUSTY SPRING NOW IN HIS TIMELY HOWRE   5.4.9
  THE MERRY $CUCKOW, MESSENGER OF $SPRING   5.19.1
  FRESH SPRING THE HERALD OF LOVES MIGHTY KING   5.70.1
  ALL SORTS OF FLOWERS THE WHICH ON EARTH DO SPRING   5.70.3
  THEYR SNAKY HEADS OOE COMBE, FROM WHICH A SPRING   5.86.3
SPRINGING   3
  GRIEFES EVER SPRINGING, COMFORTS NEVER BORNE   1.16.4
  WHOSE SPRINGING GRACE ADORNS THY GLORY NOW   1.39.10
  SPRINGING WITH THAT, AND FADING STRAIGHT
                        WITH THIS   2.141.11

SPRINGS   1
  THREE BEAUTIOUS SPRINGS TO YELLOW $AUTUMNE
                  TURN'D   3.104.5
SPRITE   9
  OR SPRITE, DISDAINE OF SUCH DISDAINE TO HAVE+   4.47.6
  WHY DOEST THOU SPEND THE TREASURES OF THY SPRITE   4.68.5
  CARE SHINING IN MINE EYES, FAITH IN MY SPRITE   4.72.11
  AND READE THE SORROWES OF MY DYING SPRIGHT   5.1.7
  BIDS ALL OLD THOUGHTS TO DIE IN DUMPISH SPRIGHT   5.4.4
  THOSE POWREFULL EIES, WHICH LIGHTEN MY
                DARK SPRIGHT   5.9.2
  SO LIKEWISE LOVE CHEARE YOU YOUR HEAVY SPRIGHT   5.62.13
  THE SACRED HARBOUR OF THAT HEVENLY SPRIGHT   5.76.4
  TO BEARE THE MESSAGE OF HER GENTLE SPRIGHT   5.81.12
SPRITES   8
  AND STRANGE THINGS COST TOO DEARE FOR
                MY POORE SPRITES   4.3.11
  MY BOILING SPRITES DID THITHER SOONE INCLINE   4.16.3
  MY LIFE FORGETS TO NOURISH LANGUISHT SPRITES   4.42.10
  SCORTCH NOT, BUT ONELY DO DARKE CHILLING
                SPRITES REMOVE   4.76.8
  LEAST JOY, BY $NATURE APT SPRITES TO ENLARGE   4.85.3
  IN NIGHT OF SPRITES THE GASTLY POWERS STUR   4.96.10
  IN THEE OR SPRITES OR SPIRITED GASTLINESSE   4.96.11
  AND MODEST THOUGHTS BREATHD FROM WEL TEMPRED
                SPRITES   5.84.6
SPRUNG   2
  MY $VICES CUR'D, BY $VERTUES SPRUNG FROM THEE   2.35.11
  MY VICES CUR'D, BY VERTUES SPRUNG FROM THEE   2.112.11
SPUN   2
  YOU HAVE SPUNNE A FAIRE $THRED, HE REPLYES
                IN SCORNE   2.59.12
  FOR WITH ONE LOOKE SHE SPILS THAT LONG I SPONNE   5.23.11
SPUR   5
  THE BLOODY SPURRE CANNOT PROVOKE HIM ON   3.50.9
  THEN SHOULD I SPURRE THOUGH MOUNTED ON THE WIND   3.51.7
  GIRT FAST BY MEMORIE, AND WHILE I SPURRE   4.49.10
  AND NO SPURRE CAN HIS RESTY RACE RENEW   4.80.12
  (SPURD WITH LOVE'S SPUR, THOUGH GALD AND
                SHORTLY RAIND   4.98.7
SPURRED   1
  (SPURD WITH LOVE'S SPUR, THOUGH GALD AND
                SHORTLY RAIND   4.98.7
SPURRING   1
  MORE SHARPE TO ME THEN SPURRING TO HIS SIDE   3.50.12
SPURS   1
  MY HORSE, HE SPURRES WITH SHARPE DESIRE MY HART   4.49.11
SPY   5
  SO $TYRAN HE NO FITTER PLACE COULD SPIE   4.20.5
  AS WHAT MY HART STILL SEES THOU CANST NOT SPIE+   4.105.4
  ONE OF THOSE ARCHERS CLOSELY I DID SPY   5.16.9
  WHERE WHEN THAT SOVERAYNE BEAUTY IT DOTH SPY   5.72.5
  LYKE AS A BYRD THAT IN ONES HAND DOTH SPY   5.73.5
STAGE   2
  THAT THIS HUGE STAGE PRESENTETH NOUGHT BUT SHOWES 3.15.3
  AS AN UNPERFECT ACTOR ON THE STAGE   3.23.1
STAIN   5
  NOW WHILST THY BEAUTY BEARES WITHOUT A STAINE   1.40.3
  SUNS OF THE WORLD MAY STAINE, WHEN HEAVENS
                SUN STAINTEH   3.33.14

```
CLOUDES AND ECLIPSES STAINE BOTH $MOONE
                        AND $SUNNE          3.35.3
  SO THAT MY SELFE BRING WATER FOR MY STAINE   3.109.8
  SCORN OF BASE THINGS, AND SDEIGNE OF FOULE
                        DISHONOR            5.5.6
STAINED              2
  THAT IT COULD SO PREPOSTEROUSLIE BE STAIN'D   3.109.11
  HOW IS THY GRACE BY MY STRANGE FORTUNE STAINE   4.98.3
STAINETH             1
  SUNS OF THE WORLD MAY STAINE, WHEN HEAVENS
                        SUN STAINTEH        3.33.14
STAINS               2
  AND FRESHEST $COLOURS WITH FOULE STAYNES
                        DISGRACED           2.13.4
  AND FRESHEST COLOURS WITH FOULE STAINES
                        DISGRACED           2.121.4
STAIR                1
  AND HE THAT STANDETH ON THE HYGHEST STAYRE    5.58.11
STALE                2
  A $LEGACIE TO STALE $VIRGINITIE           2.15.12
  THEN DID ON HIM WHO FIRST STALE DOWNE THE FIRE   4.14.3
STALK                1
  MEN DO NOT WEY THE STALKE FOR THAT IT WAS    1.40.13
STALL                1
  NATURE'S PRAISE, $VERTUE'S STALL, $CUPID'S
                        COLD FIRE           4.80.3
STALLED              1
  WERE NOT $INVENTION STAULD, TREADING $INVENTIONS
                        MAZE                2.117.9
STAMP                1
  SOME FRESHER STAMPE OF THE TIME BETTERING DAYES   3.82.8
STAMPED              1
  WHICH VULGAR SCANDALL STAMPT UPON MY BROW    3.112.2
STANCH               1
  THEN STANCH THE BLEEDING, THEN TRANS-PIERCE
                        THE $COARSE         2.50.7
STAND                13
  AND WAILE THE STATE WHEREIN I PRESENT STAND   1.28.10
  YET STAND AS FREE AS ERE YOU DID BEFORE     2.14.12
  SEE HOW MY $DEERE COMES TO THY $BEAUTIES STAND   2.135.5
  AT HER PERFECTION STAND YOU THEN AND GAZE    2.151.6
  NOW STAND YOU ON THE TOP OF HAPPIE HOURES    3.16.5
  WORTHY PERUSAL STAND AGAINST THY SIGHT      3.38.6
  NO MATTER THEN ALTHOUGH MY FOOTE DID STAND   3.44.5
  AND YET TO TIMES IN HOPE, MY VERSE SHALL STAND   3.60.13
  THE $ROSES FEAREFULLY ON THORNES DID STAND   3.99.8
  SO YOUR SWEETE HEW, WHICH ME THINKES STILL
                        DOTH STAND          3.104.11
  AT THE WOODS BOULDNES BY THEE BLUSHING STAND   3.128.8
  TO STAND IN THY AFFAIRES, FALL BY THY SIDE   3.151.12
  BUT LOOKING STILL ON HER I STAND AMAZED     5.3.7
STANDARD             1
  OF THEM, WHO IN THEIR LIPS $LOVE'S STANDERD BEARE   4.54.6
STANDETH             1
  AND HE THAT STANDETH ON THE HYGHEST STAYRE    5.58.11
STANDING             1
  FROM HEAVENLY STANDING HITS EACH MORTALL WIGHT   4.97.4
STANDS               5
  THEY RESOLUTE+ SO STANDS THE CASE WITH ME    2.24.12
  AND THERE STANDS GAZING ON THOSE DARTING EYES   2.135.6
```

AND NOTHING STANDS BUT FOR HIS SIETH TO MOW	3.60.12
BUT ALL ALONE STANDS HUGELY POLLITICK	3.124.11
WHEN MOST IMPEACHT, STANDS LEAST IN THY CONTROULE	3.125.14

STAR   11

THE $STARRE OF MY MISHAP IMPOS'D THIS PAINE	1.32.1
BRIGHT STARRE OF $BEAUTY, ON WHOSE EYE-LIDS SIT	2.4.1
SO DOTH THE $PLOW-MAN GAZE THE WAND'RING $STARRE	2.43.5
SO $COMET-LIKE EACH STARRE ADVAUNC'D HER LYGHT	2.125.10
O STARRE OF STARRES, FAYRE $PLANET MILDLY MOOVING	2.129.5
TIL WHATSOEVER STAR THAT GUIDES MY MOVING	3.26.9
IT IS THE STAR TO EVERY WANDRING BARKE	3.116.7
NOR THAT FULL $STARRE THAT USHERS IN THE $EAVEN	3.132.7
AND YET MY $STARRE, BECAUSE A SUGRED KISSE	4.73.5
BY CONDUCT OF SOME STAR DOTH MAKE HER WAY	5.34.2
SO I WHOSE STAR, THAT WENT WITH HER BRIGHT RAY	5.34.5

STARE   1

TAKE HEED THEREFORE, MYNE EYES, HOW YE DOE STARE	5.37.9

STARRY   2

BRINGING WITH HER THOSE STARRY $NIMPHS, WHOSE CHACE	4.97.3
AND HAPPY LINES, ON WHICH WITH STARRY LIGHT	5.1.5

STARS   22

BEQUEATH THE HEAVENS THE STARRES THAT I ADORE	1.19.3
AND HAVE NO STARS BUT THOSE, THAT MUST FULFILL	1.33.6
ARE EYES, OR ELS TWO RADIANT STARRES THAT SHINE	1.34.2
STARRES SURE THEY ARE, WHOSE MOTIONS RULE DESIRES	1.34.5
YET WHETHER FIXT OR WANDRING STARRES ARE THEY	1.34.9
STARRES THEN, NOT EYES, MOVE YOU WITH A MILDER VIEW	1.34.13
AND WING'D BY $FAME, YOU TO THE $STARRES ASCEND	2.16.13
DECLARE WHAT $FATE UNLUCKY $STARRES HAVE GIVEN	2.60.3
THEN THERE BE STARRES AT MIDNIGHT IN THE SKYES	2.126.12
O STARRE OF STARRES, FAYRE $PLANET MILDLY MOOVING	2.129.5
NOR $MOONE NOR STARS LEND THEE THEIR SHINING LIGHT	2.145.12
DECLARE WHAT FATE UNLUCKY STARRES HAVE GIVEN	2.149.3
NOT FROM THE STARS DO I MY JUDGEMENT PLUCKE	3.14.1
AND CONSTANT STARS IN THEM I READ SUCH ART	3.14.10
WHEREON THE $STARS IN SECRET INFLUENCE COMMENT	3.15.4
LET THOSE WHO ARE IN FAVOR WITH THEIR STARS	3.25.1
WHEN SPARKLING STARS TWIRE NOT THOU GUIL'ST TH'EAVEN	3.28.12
BY ONLY THOSE TWO STARRES IN $STELLA'S FACE	4.26.14
SOULE'S JOY, BEND NOT THOSE MORNING STARRES FROM ME	4.48.1
WHEN $SUN IS HID, CAN STARRES SUCH BEAMES DISPLAY+	4.88.6
IF I BUT STARS UPON MINE ARMOUR BEARE	4.104.10
NOR TO THE $STARRES.. FOR THEY HAVE PURER SIGHT	5.9.7

STARS'   1

(FEARING THE STARS PRESAGED INFLUENCE)	2.116.11

START   4

OF ALL MY THOUGHTS HATH NEITHER STOP NOR START	4.23.13
I START, LOOKE, HEARKE, BUT WHAT IN CLOSDE UP SENCE	4.38.9
THE WHICH THAT IT FROM HER MAY NEVER START	5.42.9
NE FEARD WITH WORSE TO ANY CHAUNCE TO START	5.59.4

STARVE   2
   TILL THAT GOOD $GOD MAKE $CHURCH AND $CHURCHMAN
                       STARVE   4.5.8
   I STARVE MY BODY AND MINE EYES DOE BLYND   5.88.14
STARVED   9
   AND STARVED YOU, IN SUCCOURS STILL DENYING   1.2.10
   THAT I AM ONELY STARV'D IN MY DESIRE   2.34.4
   THAT I AM ONELY STARV'D IN MY DESIRE   2.34.8
   AND YET AM ONELY STARV'D IN MY DESIRE   2.34.12
   IN $PLENTY I AM STARV'D WITH $PENURIE   2.62.11
   IN PLENTY, AM I STARV'D WITH PENURY   2.150.11
   AND BY AND BY CLEANE STARVED FOR A LOOKE   3.75.10
   WHOSE EYES HIM STARV'D.. SO PLENTY MAKES ME POORE 5.35.8
   WHOSE EYES HIM STARV'D.. SO PLENTY MAKES ME PORE   5.83.8
STARVELING   1
   A NAKED $STARVELING EVER MAY'ST THOU BE   2.48.2
STATE   28
   THIS IS MY STATE, MY GRIEFES DO TOUCH SO NEERLY 1.16.13
   OF SUCH AS SPOILE THY POORE AFFLICTED STATE   1.28.4
   AND WAILE THE STATE WHEREIN I PRESENT STAND   1.28.10
   WHOSE STATE BEST SHEWES THE FORCE OF MURDERING
                      EIES+   1.37.4
   THIS IS MY STATE, AND $DELIAS HEART IS SUCH   1.60.13
   THOUGH I GIVE MORE THEN WELL AFFORDS MY STATE   2.28.5
   STILL THIRSTING FOR SUBVERSION OF MY STATE   2.63.10
   AND WERE THEIR BRAVE STATE OUT OF MEMORY   3.15.8
   I ALL ALONE BEWEEPE MY OUT-CAST STATE   3.29.2
   HAPLYE I THINKE ON THEE, AND THEN MY STATE   3.29.10
   THAT THEN I SKORNE TO CHANGE MY STATE
                 WITH $KINGS   3.29.14
   WHEN I HAVE SEENE SUCH INTERCHANGE OF STATE   3.64.9
   OR STATE IT SELFE CONFOUNDED, TO DECAY   3.64.10
   I SEE, A BETTER STATE TO ME BELONGS   3.92.7
   IF THOU WOULDST USE THE STRENGTH OF ALL
                THY STATE+   3.96.12
   AND BROUGHT TO MEDICINE A HEALTHFULL STATE   3.118.11
   YF MY DEARE LOVE WERE BUT THE CHILDE OF STATE   3.124.1
   TO BE SO TIKLED THEY WOULD CHANGE THEIR STATE   3.128.9
   O BUT WITH MINE, COMPARE THOU THINE OWNE STATE   3.142.3
   BUT WHEN SHE SAW MY WOFULL STATE   3.145.4
   WITH OTHERS THOU SHOULDST NOT ABHOR MY STATE   3.150.12
   BUT THINKE THAT ALL THE $MAP OF MY STATE
               I DISPLAY   4.6.13
   TO KEEPE THE PACE OF THEIR FIRST LOVING STATE   4.17.4
   THINKE THAT I THINKE STATE ERROURS TO REDRESSE   4.23.8
   TO ME THAT FEELE THE LIKE, THY STATE DESCRIES   4.31.8
   O BLISSE, FIT FOR A NOBLER STATE THEN ME   4.69.2
   WHEN I DEMAUND OF $PHENIX $STELLA'S STATE   4.92.6
   WHY DID YE STOUP UNTO SO LOWLY STATE+   5.66.8
STATELIER   1
   OR ELSE LET THEM IN STATELIER GLORIE SHINE   4.3.5
STATELY   4
   AND STATELY $SEVERNE FOR HER $SHOARE IS PRAYSED 2.32.2
   AND STATELY $SEVERNE, FOR HER SHORES IS PRAISED 2.124.2
   GOLD IS THE COVERING OF THAT STATELY PLACE   4.9.4
   USED $TROPHEES TO ERECT IN STATELY WIZE   5.69.2
STATUES   1
   WHEN WASTEFULL WARRE SHALL $STATUES OVER-TURNE   3.55.5
STATUTE   1
   THE STATUTE OF THY BEAUTY THOU WILT TAKE   3.134.9

```
STAVES                    1
   AND YET TO BREAKE MORE STAVES DID ME ADDRESSE        4.53.2
STAY                     25
   STAY, SPEEDY $TIME, BEHOLD, BEFORE THOU PASSE        2.17.1
   REASON PLUCKS BACK, COMMANDING ME TO STAY            2.38.2
   STAY, STAY, SWEET $TIME, BEHOLD OR ERE
                         THOU PASSE                     2.107.1
   STAY, STAY, SWEET $TIME, BEHOLD OR ERE
                         THOU PASSE                     2.107.1
   REASON PLUCKS BACKE, COMMAUNDING ME TO STAY          2.131.2
   THEN THE CONCEIT OF THIS INCONSTANT STAY             3.15.9
   THROUGH HEAVY SLEEPE ON SIGHTLESSE EYES
                         DOTH STAY+                     3.43.12
   FROM LIMITS FARRE REMOTE, WHERE THOU DOOST STAY      3.44.4
   THAT TO MY USE IT MIGHT UN-USED STAY                 3.48.3
   BUT LIKE A SAD SLAVE STAY AND THINKE OF NOUGHT       3.57.11
   BEING YOUR VASSAIL BOUND TO STAIE YOUR LEISURE       3.58.4
   WHICH FOR MEMORIALL STILL WITH THEE SHALL STAY       3.74.4
   AND LIFE NO LONGER THEN THY LOVE WILL STAY           3.92.3
   IN PURSUIT OF THE THING SHE WOULD HAVE STAY          3.143.4
   BUT WORDS CAME HALTING FORTH, WANTING
                         $INVENTION'S STAY              4.1.9
   NOR SO FAIRE LEVELL IN SO SECRET STAY                4.20.6
   WITHIN WHAT BOUNDS CAN ONE HIS LIKING STAY           4.35.3
   AS HIS MAINE FORCE, CHOISE SPORT, AND
                         EASEFULL STAY                  4.43.4
   WELL $LOVE, SINCE THIS DEMURRE OUR SUTE
                         DOTH STAY                      4.52.12
   CEASE EAGER $MUSE, PEACE PEN, FOR MY SAKE STAY       4.70.12
   BUT NOW SPITE OF MY HEART MY MOUTH WILL STAY         4.80.10
   AND FAINE THOSE $AECLS' YOUTHES THERE
                         WOULD THEIR STAY               4.103.9
   AS WILLING ME AGAINST HER WILL TO STAY               5.46.4
   OF THIS WORLDS $THEATRE IN WHICH WE STAY             5.54.1
   BUT IN THE STAY OF HER OWNE STEDFAST MIGHT           5.59.11
STAYED                    8
   AND PLEASD WITH OUR SOFT PEACE, STAID
                         HERE HIS FLYING RACE           4.8.4
   WELL STAID WITH TRUTH IN WORD AND FAITH OF DEED      4.14.10
   AND STAID PLEASD WITH THE PROSPECT OF THE PLACE      4.20.10
   CANNOT BE STAID WITHIN MY PANTING BREAST             4.50.2
   AND OFT WHOLE TROUPES OF SADDEST WORDS I STAID       4.55.5
   BUT WITH SHORT BREATH, LONG LOOKES, STAID
                         FEET AND WALKING HED           4.76.13
   RAVISHT, STAID NOT, TILL IN HER GOLDEN HAIRE         4.103.7
   TELL HER THE JOYOUS TIME WIL NOT BE STAID            5.70.7
STAYS                     3
   WHICH CONQUERS ALL BUT THEE, AND THEE TOO STAIES     1.23.2
   TRIUMPH IN LOVE, FLESH STAIES NO FARTHER REASON      3.151.8
   OR AT THE MOST ON SOME FINE PICTURE STAYES           4.11.7
STEAD                     3
   SINCE TO OBTAINE THEE, NOTHING ME WILL STED          2.15.1
   IN STEED OF TEN, ONE $SIBIL TO US LEFT               2.119.8
   BUT FIND SOME $HERCULES TO BEARE, IN STEED           4.51.7
STEADFAST                 2
   AND THAT IT THEN MORE STEDFAST WILL ENDURE           5.51.12
   BUT IN THE STAY OF HER OWNE STEDFAST MIGHT           5.59.11
STEADFASTLY               1
   BEING STEDFASTLY OPPOSED TO THE SAME                 2.30.4
```

STEADY   1
  BUT LIKE A STEDDY SHIP DOTH STRONGLY PART   5.59.5
STEAL   12
  ROB HER FAIRE $BROW, BREAKE IN ON $BEAUTY, STEALE   1.22.5
  STEALE FROM THY SELFE, AND BE THY CARES
                         OWNE THIEFE   1.52.12
  WHO GAVE CONSENT TO STEALE AWAY MY $HEART   2.23.11
  YET DOTH IT STEALE SWEET HOURES FROM LOVES
                         DELIGHT   3.36.8
  ALTHOUGH THOU STEALE THEE ALL MY POVERTY   3.40.10
  AND STEALE DEAD SEEING OF HIS LIVING HEW+   3.67.6
  DOUBTING THE FILCHING AGE WILL STEALE
                         HIS TREASURE   3.75.6
  BUT DOE THY WORST TO STEALE THY SELFE AWAY   3.92.1
  SWEET THEEFE WHENCE DIDST THOU STEALE
                         THY SWEET THAT SMELS 3.99.2
  STEALE FROM HIS FIGURE, AND NO PACE PERCEIV'D   3.104.10
  SWEET $STELLA'S IMAGE I DO STEALE TO MEE'   4.32.14
  TO STEALE SOME REST, BUT WRETCH I AM CONSTRAIND   4.98.6
STEALING   2
  STEALING UNSEENE TO WEST WITH THIS DISGRACE   3.33.8
  STEALING AWAY THE TREASURE OF HIS $SPRING   3.63.8
STEALS   2
  WITH THESE, SHE STEALES MENS HARTS FOR
                         HER RELIEFE   2.126.13
  WHICH STEALES MENS EYES AND WOMENS SOULES AMASETH 3.20.8
STEALTH   1
  THOU BY THY DYALS SHADY STEALTH MAIST KNOW   3.77.7
STEED   1
  THEN AS A STEED REFRESHED AFTER TOYLE   5.80.5
STEEL   5
  NOR GATES OF STEELE SO STRONG BUT TIME DECAYES+   3.65.8
  UNLESSE MY $NERVES WERE BRASSE OR HAMMERED
                         STEELE   3.120.4
  PRISON MY HEART IN THY STEELE BOSOMES WARDE   3.133.9
  THE HARDEST STEELE IN TRACT OF TIME DOTH TEARE   5.18.2
  WHILES SHE AS STEELE AND FLINT DOTH STILL
                         REMAYNE   5.18.14
STEELED   1
  THAT MY STEEL'D SENCE OR CHANGES RIGHT OR WRONG   3.112.8
STEEMS   1
  MY LOVE AFFECTS NO FAME, NOR STEEMES OF $ART   1.4.14
STEEP   2
  AND HAVING CLIMB'D THE STEEPE UP HEAVENLY HILL   3.7.5
  AND HIS LOVE-KINDLING FIRE DID QUICKLY STEEPE   3.153.3
STEEPY   1
  HATH TRAVAILD ON TO $AGES STEEPIE NIGHT   3.63.5
STEERED   1
  SHEWES BY HIS $COMPASSE, HOW HIS $COURSE
                         HE STEER'D   2.1.6
STELLA   41
  TRUE, AND YET TRUE THAT I MUST $STELLA LOVE   4.5.14
  WHEN TREMBLING VOICE BRINGS FORTH THAT
                         I DO $STELLA LOVE   4.6.14
  STELLA, THOU STRAIGHT LOOKST BABIES IN HER EYES   4.11.10
  THOU COUNTEST $STELLA THINE, LIKE THOSE
                         WHOSE POWERS   4.12.9
  STELLA BEHOLD, AND THEN BEGIN TO ENDITE   4.15.14
  STELLA., NOW SHE IS NAM'D, NEED MORE BE SAID+   4.16.11
  HATH THIS WORLD OUGHT SO FAIRE AS $STELLA IS+   4.21.14

```
STELLA ALONE WITH FACE UNARMED MARCHT                  4.22.9
WHEN I SAY '$STELLA', I DO MEANE THE SAME              4.28.5
BUT BY THY WORKE MY $STELLA I DESCRIE                  4.32.7
STELLA, WHENCE DOTH THIS NEW ASSAULT ARISE            4.36.1
O $STELLA DEARE, HOW MUCH THY POWER HATH WROUGHT      4.40.2
STELLA LOOKT ON, AND FROM HER HEAVENLY FACE           4.41.13
STELLA OFT SEES THE VERIE FACE OF WO                  4.45.1
STELLA, THE FULNESSE OF MY THOUGHTS OF THEE           4.50.1
WHILE EACH PRETENDS THAT $STELLA MUST BE HIS          4.52.2
THAT $STELLA (O DEARE NAME) THAT $STELLA IS           4.52.6
THAT $STELLA (O DEARE NAME) THAT $STELLA IS           4.52.6
LOOKE HERE, I SAY.' I LOOK'D, AND $STELLA SPIDE       4.53.8
AND THINKE SO STILL, SO $STELLA KNOW MY MIND          4.54.9
HOPING THAT WHEN THEY MIGHT FIND $STELLA ALONE        4.57.5
WHERE ALL MY GOOD I DO IN $STELLA SEE                 4.60.2
FOR $GRAMMER SAYES (O THIS DEARE $STELLA WEIGHE)      4.63.12
DOTH $STELLA NOW BEGIN WITH PITEOUS EYE               4.67.2
STELLA, THE ONELY $PLANET OF MY LIGHT                 4.68.1
FOR $STELLA HATH WITH WORDS WHERE FAITH
                         DOTH SHINE                   4.69.9
STELLA, THOSE FAIRE LINES, WHICH TRUE
                         GOODNESSE SHOW               4.71.4
WHEN I WAS FORST FROM $STELLA EVER DEERE              4.87.1
STELLA FOOD OF MY THOUGHTS, HART OF MY HART           4.87.2
STELLA WHOSE EYES MAKE ALL MY TEMPESTS CLEERE         4.87.3
STELLA THINKE NOT THAT I BY VERSE SEEKE FAME          4.90.1
STELLA, WHILE NOW BY HONOUR'S CRUELL MIGHT            4.91.1
THROUGH ME, WRETCH ME, EVEN $STELLA VEXED IS          4.93.4
STELLA IS SICKE, AND IN THAT SICKE BED LIES           4.101.1
STELLA NOW LEARNES (STRANGE CASE) TO WEEPE
                         IN THEE                      4.101.8
O HAPPIE $TEMS, THAT DIDST MY $STELLA BEARE           4.103.1
DO $STELLA LOVE. $FCOLES, WHO DOTH IT DENY+           4.104.14
O ABSENT PRESENCE $STELLA IS NOT HERE                 4.106.1
STELLA, I SAY MY $STELLA, SHOULD APPEARE              4.106.4
STELLA, I SAY MY $STELLA, SHOULD APPEARE              4.106.4
STELLA SINCE THOU SO RIGHT A $PRINCESSE ART           4.107.1
STELLA'S                 33
HOW THEN+ EVEN THUS.. IN $STELLA'S FACE I REED        4.3.12
WHEN $NATURE MADE HER CHIEFE WORKE, $STELLA'S EYES    4.7.1
AT LENGTH HE PERCH'D HIMSELF IN $STELLA'S
                         JOYFULL FACE                 4.8.8
QUEENE $VERTUE'S COURT, WHICH SOME CALL
                         $STELLA'S FACE               4.9.1
FOR SOONE AS THEY STRAKE THEE WITH $STELLA'S
                         RAYES                        4.10.12
CUPID, BECAUSE THOU SHIN'ST IN $STELLAS EYES          4.12.1
STELLA'S FAIRE HAIRE, HER FACE HE MAKES
                         HIS SHIELD                   4.13.10
OF $STELLA'S BROWES MADE HIM TWO BETTER BOWES         4.17.10
THEN THAT I LOSE NO MORE FOR $STELLA'S SAKE           4.18.14
MY VERIE INKE TURNES STRAIGHT TO $STELLA'S NAME       4.19.6
BUT ONLY $STELLA'S EYES AND $STELLA'S HART            4.23.14
BUT ONLY $STELLA'S EYES AND $STELLA'S HART            4.23.14
LOVE OF HER SELFE, TAKES $STELLA'S SHAPE,
                         THAT SHE                     4.25.10
BY ONLY THOSE TWO STARRES IN $STELLA'S FACE           4.26.14
BENDS ALL HIS POWERS, EVEN UNTO $STELLA'S GRACE       4.27.14
SO $STELLA'S HEART, FINDING WHAT POWER
                         $LOVE BRINGS                 4.29.5
```

```
SWEET $STELLA'S IMAGE I DO STEALE TO MEE'        4.32.14
STELLA'S GREAT POWRS, THAT SO CONFUSE MY MIND    4.34.14
DOTH EVEN GROW RICH, NAMING MY STELLA'S NAME     4.35.11
UNTO MY MIND, IS $STELLA'S IMAGE, WROUGHT         4.38.6
LIVELIER THEN ELSE-WHERE, $STELLA'S IMAGE SEE    4.39.14
BECAUSE THEIR FOREFRONT BARE SWEET $STELLA'S
                              NAME               4.50.14
MEANE WHILE MY HEART CONFERS WITH $STELLA'S
                              BEAMES             4.51.12
BE $LOVE'S INDEED, IN $STELLA'S SELFE HE MAY     4.52.10
LET $VERTUE HAVE THAT $STELLA'S SELFE., YET THUS 4.52.13
STELLA'S SWEETE BREATH THE SAME TO ME DID REED   4.58.11
I $STELLA'S EYES ASSAYLL, INVADE HER EARES        4.61.3
STELLA'S EYES SENT TO ME THE BEAMES OF BLISSE    4.66.11
MY LIPS ARE SWEET, INSPIRED WITH $STELLA'S KISSE 4.74.14
HUNDREDS OF YEARES YOU $STELLA'S FEET MAY KISSE  4.84.14
SINCE $STELLA'S EYES, WONT TO GIVE ME MY DAY      4.89.3
WHEN I DEMAUND OF $PHENIX $STELLA'S STATE         4.92.6
ONELY UNTO THE HEAV'N OF $STELLA'S FACE          4.105.7
STELLED                       1
MINE EYE HATH PLAY'D THE PAINTER AND HATH STEELD  3.24.1
STEP                          1
BUT WHEN THE RUGGEDST STEP OF $FORTUNE'S RACE      4.60.5
STEP-DAME                     1
INVENTION, $NATURE'S CHILD, FLED STEP-DAME
                    $STUDIE'S BLOWES             4.1.10
STEPS                         3
WITH HOW SAD STEPS, O $MOONE, THOU CLIMB'ST
                    THE SKIES                     4.31.1
THAT NO PACE ELSE THEIR GUIDED STEPS CAN FIND     4.58.3
LET ME NO STEPS BUT OF LOST LABOUR TRACE          4.64.6
STERN                         2
HOW MANY $LAMBS MIGHT THE STERNE $WOLFE BETRAY    3.96.9
AND WITH STERNE COUNTENANCE BACK AGAIN DOTH CHACE 5.21.7
STEWARDS                      1
OTHERS, BUT STEWARDS OF THEIR EXCELLENCE          3.94.8
STICK                         1
AND DOE NOT STICKE TO TERME MY $PRAYSES FOLLY     2.28.2
STICKEST                      1
THAT GAINST THY SELFE THOU STICKST NOT
                    TO CONSPIRE                   3.10.6
STIFF-NECKED                  1
CALL BACKE THE STIFFE-NECK'D $REBELS FROM $EXILE 2.25.11
STIFFNESS                     1
WHICH HER TOO CONSTANT STIFFENESSE DOTH
                    CONSTRAYN                     5.84.12
STILL                        164
AND STARVED YOU, IN SUCCOURS STILL DENYING       1.2.10
WHICH STILL IS CHAC'D, WHILE I HAVE ANY BREATH   1.5.10
AND CLOUDS OBSCURE HAD SHADED STILL HER
                    BRIGHTNESSE                   1.7.4
AND STILL AGAINST HER FROWNES FRESH VOWES
                    REPAIREST                     1.8.3
WITH DOWNEWARD LOCKES, STILL READING ON THE EARTH 1.9.3
STILL TO COMPLAINE MY GRIEFES, WHILST NONE RELIEVE 1.9.8
AND STILL I TOYLE, TO CHANGE THE $MARBLE BREST   1.13.9
AND HAD MY SIGHES STILL TENDING ON HER NAME      1.15.10
AND SHE (TH'UNKINDEST MAID) STILL SCORNS
                    THE SAME                      1.15.12
AND STILL EXPECTING WHEN SHE WILL RELENT          1.16.5
```

```
STILL NEW BORNE SORROWES OF HER FRESH DISDAINE        1.16.10
AND STILL MY HOPE THE $SOMMER WINDES PURSUES          1.16.11
STILL HAVE I LIV'D IN GRIEFE, IN HOPE, IN TERROR      1.18.3
STILL MUST I WHET MY YONG DESIRES ABATED              1.18.9
AND STILL MUST HOLD HER DEARE TILL AFTER DEATH        1.21.11
LET HER NOT STILL TRIUMPH OVER THE PRIZE              1.22.13
WITH STILL FRESH CARES, SUPPLIDE WITH NO RELIEFE      1.32.4
WHICH STILL MUST BEARE THE TITLE OF MY WRONG          1.32.13
STILL IN THE TRACE OF ONE PERPLEXED THOUGHT           1.33.1
ONE IN MY LOVE, AND HER HARD HART STILL ONE           1.33.4
INJURIOUS $DELIA YET I LOVE THEE STILL                1.33.9
THEIR SWEET APPEARING STILL SUCH POWER INSPIRES       1.34.7
HER SOVERAIGNTY SHOULD HAVE REMAINED STILL            1.36.11
THE TEMPLE, WHERE HER NAME WAS HONOUR'D STILL         1.47.14
STILL LET DISARMED PEACE DECKE HER AND THEE           1.53.13
STILL LET ME SLEEPE, IMBRACING CLOUDS IN VAINE        1.54.13
YET $HEAV'N WILL STILL HAVE $MURTHER OUT AT LAST      2.2.14
LET WHAT I PRAISE, BE STILL MADE GOOD BY YOU          2.4.13
STILL TO SURVIVE IN MY IMMORTALL $SONG                2.6.14
YOU NOT ALONE, WHEN $YOU ARE STILL ALONE              2.11.1
RETAYNING $KNOWLEDGE, STILL THE SAME IN KIND          2.12.7
WHICH STILL SHALT BE, AS LONG AS THERE IS $SUNNE      2.13.10
I GREATLY MARVELL, HOW YOU STILL GOE FREE             2.14.3
NINE $MUSES DOE WITH $LEARNING STILL FREQUENT         2.18.6
AN $EVILL SPIRIT YOUR BEAUTIE HAUNTS $ME STILL        2.20.1
THUS AM I STILL PROVOK'D, TO EVERY $EVILL             2.20.13
LOVE STILL A $BABY, PLAYES WITH $GAWDES
                           AND $TOYES                 2.22.5
AND $IDEOTS STILL ARE RUNNING AFTER $BOYES            2.22.7
HE STILL AS YOUNG AS WHEN HE FIRST WAS BORNE          2.22.9
WITH $SIGHES AND $TEARES STILL FURNISHING
                           HIS $TABLE                 2.23.7
SO MY $LOVE IS STILL FETT'RED WITH VAINE $HOPE        2.26.10
IN EV'RY THING I HOLD THIS $MAXIM STILL               2.28.13
BOASTING, THAT SHE DOTH STILL DIRECT THE WAY          2.38.3
I STILL FEARE $BUG-BEARES IN $APOLLO'S $CELL          2.39.12
IN GRIEVOUS $PASSIONS, MY $WOES STILL BEMONING        2.40.8
STILL MORE AND MORE IT TO MY TORMENT BURNETH          2.40.12
BUT STILL DISTRACTED IN $LOVES $LUNACIE               2.41.9
ONELY MY COMFORT STILL CONSISTS IN THIS               2.42.13
HOW $THINGS STILL UNEXPECTEDLY HAVE RUNNE             2.51.3
YET AM I STILL INVIOLATE TO $YOU                      2.51.14
STILL THIRSTING FOR SUBVERSION OF MY STATE            2.63.10
AND STIL INCREASING AS THOU ART CONSUMING             2.106.11
NINE $MUSES DOE WITH LEARNING STILL FREQUENT          2.108.6
AND STYLL IN RECKONINGS RISE MORE MILLIONS
                           OF DISPAYRES               2.110.4
IMPRINTED IN MY TEARES BY LOOKING STILL ON THEE       2.114.7
STILL EMPTY GORG'D, WITH CARES CONSUMPTION
                           PYNDE                       2.116.14
DID NOT PERFECTION STILL ON HER PERFECTION GAZE       2.117.11
I STYLL FEARE BUGBEARES IN $APOLLOS $CELL             2.118.12
WHICH STILL SHALT BE AS LONG AS THERE IS $SUNNE       2.121.10
THUS SORING STILL, NOT LOOKING ONCE BELOW             2.122.9
I PROVE MY VERSE AUTENTIQUE STILL IN THYS             2.128.13
BOASTING THAT SHEE DOTH STILL DIRECT THE WAY          2.131.3
THOSE TEARES WHICH QUENCH MY HOPE, STILL
                           KINDLE MY DESIRE           2.132.1
SO MY LOVE IS STYLL FETTERED WITH VAINE HOPE          2.137.10
AND PRAISE HER STILL TO THY UNTIMELY GRAVE            2.139.8
```

```
TO MY LYVES FOE HER $CHIEFTAINE STILL BETRAYING        2.142.8
BUT STILL DISTRACTED IN LOVES $LUNACY                  2.143.9
IN GREEVOUS PASSIONS MY WOES STYLL BEMONING            2.144.8
STILL MORE AND MORE UNTO MY TORMENT BURNETH            2.144.12
STILL TO PROLONG MY LONG TYME LOOKT-FOR MORROW+        2.145.4
DEATH LIKE TO THEE, SO LYVE THOU STILL IN DEATH        2.145.9
WHICH STILL TORMENTS ME IN DAYES BURNING FIRE          2.145.14
BUT MY FAIRE $PLANET, WHO DIRECTS ME STILL             2.147.9
STILL NAMING HER, IN NAMING ALL DELIGHT                2.148.12
LEESE BUT THEIR SHOW, THEIR SUBSTANCE
                         STILL LIVES SWEET             3.5.14
YET MORTALL LOOKES ADORE HIS BEAUTY STILL              3.7.7
THE WORLD WILBE THY WIDDOW AND STILL WEEPE             3.9.5
SHIFTS BUT HIS PLACE, FOR STILL THE WORLD
                         INJOYES IT                    3.9.10
THAT BEAUTY STILL MAY LIVE IN THINE OR THEE            3.10.14
TO GIVE AWAY YOUR SELFE, KEEPS YOUR SELFE STILL        3.16.13
WHICH IN MY BOSOMES SHOP IS HANGING STIL               3.24.7
HOW FAR I TOYLE, STILL FARTHER OFF FROM THEE           3.28.8
THOUGH THOU REPENT, YET I HAVE STILL THE LOSSE         3.34.10
FOR STILL TEMPTATION FOLLOWES WHERE THOU ART           3.41.4
THY SEIFE AWAY, ARE PRESENT STILL WITH ME              3.47.10
AND I AM STILL WITH THEM, AND THEY WITH THEE           3.47.12
SHALL YOU PACE FORTH, YOUR PRAISE SHALL
                         STIL FINDE ROOME              3.55.10
AND THEY SHALL LIVE, AND HE IN THEM STILL GREENE       3.63.14
THAT IN BLACK INCK MY LOVE MAY STILL SHINE
                         BRIGHT                        3.65.14
WHICH FOR MEMORIALL STILL WITH THEE SHALL STAY         3.74.4
WHY WRITE I STILL ALL ONE, EVER THE SAME               3.76.5
AND YOU AND LOVE ARE STILL MY ARGUMENT                 3.76.10
SO IS MY LOVE STILL TELLING WHAT IS TOLD               3.76.14
YOU STILL SHALL LIVE (SUCH VERTUE HATH MY $PEN)        3.81.13
MY TOUNG-TIDE $MUSE IN MANNERS HOLDS HER STILL         3.85.1
AND LIKE UNLETTERED CLARKE STILL CRIE $AMEN            3.85.6
MAY STILL SEEME LOVE TO ME, THOUGH ALTER'D NEW         3.93.3
YET SEEM'D IT $WINTER STILL, AND YOU AWAY              3.98.13
SUCH SEEMES YOUR BEAUTIE STILL.. $THREE
                         $WINTERS COLDE                3.104.3
SO YOUR SWEETE HEW, WHICH ME THINKES STILL
                         DOTH STAND                    3.104.11
TO ONE, OF ONE, STILL SUCH, AND EVER SO                3.105.4
STILL CONSTANT IN A WONDROUS EXCELLENCE                3.105.6
THEY HAD NOT STILL ENOUGH YOUR WORTH TO SING           3.106.12
TO GIVE FULL GROWTH TO THAT WHICH STILL
                         DOTH GROW                     3.115.14
STILL LOOSING WHEN I SAW MY SELFE TO WIN+              3.119.4
THAT BETTER IS, BY EVIL STILL MADE BETTER              3.119.10
AS THOU GOEST ONWARDS STILL WILL PLUCKE
                         THEE BACKE                    3.126.6
SHE MAY DETAINE, BUT NOT STILL KEEPE HER
                         TRESURE                       3.126.10
THOU WILT RESTORE TO BE MY COMFORT STILL               3.134.4
MORE THEN ENOUGH AM I THAT VEXE THEE STILL             3.135.3
THE SEA ALL WATER, YET RECEIVES RAINE STILL            3.135.9
MAKE BUT MY NAME THY LOVE, AND LOVE THAT STILL         3.136.13
IF THOU TURNE BACK AND MY LOUDE CRYING STILL           3.143.14
WHICH LIKE TWO SPIRITS DO SUGJEST ME STILL             3.144.2
MY LOVE IS AS A FEAVER LONGING STILL                   3.147.1
A DATELESSE LIVELY HEAT STILL TO INDURE                3.153.6
```

```
AND OTHERS' FEETE STILL SEEM'D BUT STRANGERS
                              IN MY WAY            4.1.11
AND STILL TH'EFFECT OF THY PERSWASIONS PROVE      4.4.11
REASON, IN FAITH THOU ART WELL SERV'D, THAT STILL  4.10.1
MY BEST WITS STILL THEIR OWNE DISGRACE INVENT     4.19.5
SCOURGE OF IT SELFE, STILL CLIMING SLIPPRIE
                              PLACE               4.23.10
LIES HATCHING STILL THE GOODS WHEREIN THEY FLOW   4.24.2
THEY SHOULD STILL DAUNCE TO PLEASE A GAZER'S
                              SIGHT               4.26.8
BUT KNOW NOT HOW, FOR STILL I THINKE OF YOU       4.30.14
MY STILL KEPT COURSE, WHILE OTHERS SLEEPE,
                              TO MONE             4.40.4
THAT IN MY HEART I OFFER STILL TO THEE            4.40.13
KEEPE STILL MY $ZENITH, EVER SHINE ON ME          4.42.8
YET STILL ON ME, O EYES, DART DOWNE YOUR RAYES    4.42.11
SO MAY YOUR TONGUE STILL FLUENTLY PROCEED         4.51.2
SO MAY YOU STILL HAVE SOMEWHAT NEW TO SAY         4.51.4
AND THINKE SO STILL, SO $STELLA KNOW MY MIND      4.54.9
SO CHILDREN STILL READE YOU WITH AWFULL EYES      4.63.2
FORTUNE WHEELES STILL WITH ME IN ONE SORT SLOW    4.66.6
DESIRE STILL ON THE STILTS OF FEARE DOTH GO       4.66.8
IF STILL I FORCE HER IN SAD RIMES TO CREEPE       4.70.2
'BUT AH,' $DESIRE STILL CRIES, 'GIVE ME
                              SOME FOOD'          4.71.14
LOVE STILL A BOY, AND OFT A WANTON IS             4.73.1
SO NIMBLE FEET AS STIRRE STILL, THOUGH
                              ON THORNES          4.78.11
STOP YOU MY MOUTH WITH STILL STILL KISSING ME     4.81.14
STOP YOU MY MOUTH WITH STILL STILL KISSING ME     4.81.14
BE YOU STILL FAIRE, HONOURD BY PUBLIKE HEED       4.84.9
A STILL FELT PLAGUE, TO SELFE CONDEMNING ME       4.86.3
SAY ALL, AND ALL WELL SAYD, STILL SAY THE SAME    4.92.14
THOU THOUGH STILL TIRED, YET STILL DOOST
                              IT DETEST           4.96.14
THOU THOUGH STILL TIRED, YET STILL DOOST
                              IT DETEST           4.96.14
THAT HUE, WHOSE FORCE MY HART STILL UNTO
                              THRALDOME TIES+      4.102.8
HAVE MADE, BUT FORST BY $NATURE STILL TO FLIE     4.103.10
AS WHAT MY HART STILL SEES THOU CANST NOT SPIE+   4.105.4
WHICH PANTS AS THOUGH IT STILL SHOULD
                              LEAPE TO THEE        4.107.6
BUT LOOKING STILL ON HER I STAND AMAZED           5.3.7
DOTH STILL PERSIST IN HER REBELLIOUS PRIDE        5.6.2
NOR TO THE LIGHTNING.. FOR THEY STILL PERSEVER    5.9.9
YET LOWLY STILL VOUCHSAFE TO LOOKE ON ME          5.13.13
WHILES SHE AS STEELE AND FLINT DOTH STILL
                              REMAYNE             5.18.14
SO EVERY SWEET WITH SOURE IS TEMPRED STILL        5.26.9
BUT STILL THE MORE SHE FERVENT SEES MY FIT        5.32.9
STILL TO BEHOLD THE OBJECT OF THEIR PAINE         5.35.2
BUT THAT THEIR CRUELTY DOTH STILL INCREACE        5.36.7
BUT IN HER PRIDE SHE DOOTH PERSEVER STILL         5.38.9
YET SHOOT YE SHARPELY STILL, AND SPARE ME NOT     5.57.9
SOUGHT NOT TO FLY, BUT FEARELESSE STILL DID BIDE  5.67.10
STILL TO BEHOLD THE OBJECT OF THEYR PAYNE         5.83.2
THAT FURTHER SEEMES HIS TERME STILL TO EXTEND     5.87.11
SO SORROW STILL DOTH SEEME TOO LONG TO LAST       5.87.13
```

```
STILTS                        1
  DESIRE STILL ON THE STILTS OF FEARE DOTH GO        4.66.8
STING                         1
  VENEMOUS TOUNG TIPT WITH VILE ADDERS STING         5.86.1
STINT                         1
  NO SKILL CAN STINT NOR REASON CAN ASLAKE           5.44.8
STIR                          8
  VERTUE OF LATE, WITH VERTUOUS CARE TO STER         4.25.9
  HE SITS ME FAST, HOW EVER I DO STURRE              4.49.12
  SO NIMBLE FEET AS STIRRE STILL, THOUGH
                          ON THURNES                 4.78.11
  IN NIGHT OF SPRITES THE GASTLY POWERS STUR         4.96.10
  AS THY LOOKES STURRE, RUNS UP AND DOWNE TO MAKE    4.101.10
  WHILE BEAUTIE'S REDDEST INKE $VENUS FOR
                          HIM DOTH STURRE            4.102.14
  THEIR LOOSER LOOKES THAT STIR UP LUSTES IMPURE     5.21.8
  IN MY TRUE LOVE DID STIRRE UP COLES OF YRE         5.86.8
STIRRED                       1
  STIRD BY A PAINTED BEAUTY TO HIS VERSE             3.21.2
STOCK                         1
  BUT LIKE A STUPID STOCK IN SILENCE DIE             5.43.8
STOLE                         2
  THE $FIRE HE STOLE, ALTHOUGH OF $HEAV'NLY KIND     2.14.5
  HE LENDS THEE VERTUE, AND HE STOLE THAT WORD       3.79.9
STOLEN                       11
  WITH THOSE SWEET STRINGS STOLNE FROM THY
                          GOLDEN HAYRE               2.104.2
  HAST PLAYD THE THIEFE, AND STOLNE MY HART
                          FROM ME                    2.130.11
  HATH DEARE RELIGIOUS LOVE STOLNE FROM MINE EYE     3.31.6
  AND EVEN THENCE THOU WILT BE STOLNE I FEARE        3.48.13
  AND BUDS OF MARJEROM HAD STOLNE THY HAIRE          3.99.7
  A THIRD NOR RED, NOR WHITE, HAD STOLNE OF BOTH     3.99.10
  BUT SWEET, OR CULLER IT HAD STOLNE FROM THEE       3.99.15
  AND SURE AT LENGTH STOLNE GOODS DO COME TO LIGHT   4.15.11
  STOLNE TO MY HEART, SINCE LAST FAIRE NIGHT,
                          NAY DAY                    4.66.10
  WHAT SIGHES STOLNE OUT, OR KILD BEFORE
                          FULL BORNE+                4.67.9
  WHO HATH THE CRIMSON WEEDS STOLNE FROM
                          MY MORNING SKIES+          4.102.4
STOMACH                       1
  WHOSE $STOMACK UNTO $GALL HATH TURN'D THY $FOOD    2.49.6
STOMACHS                      1
  CANNOT HEAVN'S FOOD, ONCE FELT, KEEPE
                          STOMAKES FREE              4.88.7
STONE                        10
  THE NEVER-RESTING STONE OF $CARE TO ROULE          1.9.7
  AND CARVE HIS PROPER GRIEFE UPON A STONE           1.13.2
  BUT HAPPY HE THAT JOY'D HIS STONE AND ART          1.13.13
  WITH $SISIPHUS THUS DOE I ROLE THE STONE           2.40.13
  WITH $SISIPHUS THUS DOE I ROLE THE STONE           2.144.13
  THEN UNSWEPT STONE, BESMEER'D WITH SLUTTISH TIME   3.55.4
  SINCE BRASSE, NOR STONE, NOR EARTH, NOR
                          BOUNDLESSE SEA             3.65.1
  WHO MOVING OTHERS, ARE THEMSELVES AS STONE         3.94.3
  LONG SINCE FORC'D BY THY BEAMES, BUT STONE
                          NOR TREE                   4.36.13
  SHE IS NO WOMAN, BUT A SENCELESSE STONE            5.54.14
```

STONE-COLD   1
  HIS STONE-COLD LIPS DOTH KISSE THE BLESSED
                            SHAFT   2.135.14
STONES   3
  WHILST I LIKE $ORPHEUS SING TO $TREES
                      AND $STONES   2.45.12
   LIKE STONES OF WORTH THEY THINLY PLACED ARE   3.52.7
   AND SHE TO STONES AT LENGTH ALL FROSEN TURNE+   5.32.14
STONISHT   1
  THE WHILES MY STONISHT HART STOOD IN AMAZE   5.16.3
STONY   1
  UNHAPPY I, TO LOVE A STONY HART   1.13.14
STOOD   4
  NOR NEVER STOOD ONE WORD THEREOF TO BLOT   2.21.7
  BUT ON HER $RAYES WITH OPEN $EYES IT STOOD   2.56.6
  BUT ON HER RAYES WITH GAZING EYES THEY STOOD   2.103.6
  THE WHILES MY STONISHT HART STOOD IN AMAZE   5.16.3
STOOP   1
  WHY DID YE STOUP UNTO SO LOWLY STATE+   5.66.8
STOP   7
  TO STOP THE PASSAGE OF MY VANQUISHT HART   1.27.2
  MY SIGHES SHALL STOP THE PASSAGE OF THE AYRE   2.115.7
  OF HIS SELFE LOVE TO STOP POSTERITY+   3.3.8
  INJURIOUS DISTANCE SHOULD NOT STOP MY WAY   3.44.2
  OF ALL MY THOUGHTS HATH NEITHER STOP NOR START   4.23.13
  STOP YOU MY MOUTH WITH STILL STILL KISSING ME   4.81.14
  YOU STOP MY TOUNG, AND TEACH MY HART TO SPEAKE   5.8.10
STOPPED   3
  TO CRYTTICK AND TO FLATTERER STOPPED ARE   3.112.11
  BUT THAT THEY STOPT HIS FURIE FROM THE SAME   4.50.13
  IT STOPPED IS WITH THOUGHTS ASTONISHMENT   5.3.10
STOPS   1
  AND STOPS HIS PIPE IN GROWTH OF RIPER DAIES   3.102.8
STORE   18
  BUT YOU BROKE INTO $HEAV'NS IMMORTALL STORE   2.14.9
  IN $FORMER TIMES, SUCH AS HAD STORE OF $COYNE   2.58.1
  STRONG LOCKE OF KINDNESSE, $CLOSET OF
                      LOVES STORE   2.146.5
  LET THOSE WHOM NATURE HATH NOT MADE FOR STORE   3.11.9
  IF FROM THY SELFE, TO STORE THOU WOULDST CONVERT 3.14.12
  I MAKE MY LOVE INGRAFTED TO THIS STORE   3.37.8
  INCREASING STORE WITH LOSSE, AND LOSSE WITH STORE 3.64.8
  INCREASING STORE WITH LOSSE, AND LOSSE WITH STORE 3.64.8
  AND HIM AS FOR A MAP DOTH $NATURE STORE   3.68.13
  IN WHOSE CONFINE IMMURED IS THE STORE   3.84.3
  AND IN ABUNDANCE ADDETH TO HIS STORE   3.135.10
  AND LET THAT PINE TO AGGRAVAT THY STORE   3.146.10
  READY TO STORE THEIR CAMPES OF NEEDFULL THINGS   4.29.4
  BUT HEERE I DO STORE OF FAIRE $LADIES MEETE   4.106.9
  MOST SORTS OF MEN DOE SET BUT LITTLE STORE   5.26.12
  YET ARE MINE EYES SO FILLED WITH THE STORE   5.35.9
  FAYRE SOYLE IT SEEMES FROM FAR AND FRAUGHT
                    WITH STORE   5.63.7
  YET ARE MYNE EYES SO FILLED WITH THE STORE   5.83.9
STORED   1
  SO FORTIFIED WITH WIT, STOR'D WITH DISDAINE   4.12.13
STORES   2
  O HIM SHE STORES, TO SHOW WHAT WELTH SHE HAD   3.67.13
  THOUGH IN THY STORES ACCOUNT I ONE MUST BE   3.136.10

```
STORM                          7
    THE FURY OF A MERCY-WANTING STORME                        1.37.6
    YOU CALME THE STORME THAT PASSION DID BEGIN               5.8.11
    WHENAS A STORME HATH DIMD HER TRUSTY GUYDE                5.34.3
    YET HOPE I WELL, THAT WHEN THIS STORME IS PAST            5.34.9
    THAT WHEN A DREADFULL STORME AWAY IS FLIT                 5.40.7
    SO MY STORME BEATEN HART LIKEWISE IS CHEARED              5.40.13
    AS IS A STORME, THAT ALL THINGS DOTH PROSTRATE            5.56.6
STORM-BEATEN                   1
    TO DRY THE RAINE ON MY STORME-BEATEN FACE                 3.34.6
STORMED                        1
    HOW THY LEE SHORES BY MY SIGHES STORMED BE                4.98.4
STORMS                         7
    LOE WHERE SHE DROWNES, IN STORMES OF THY
                              DISPLEASURE                     2.134.13
    OF LIVING DEATHS, DEARE WOUNDS, FAIRE
                              STORMES AND FREESING FIRES      4.6.4
    BUT THEN FROM HEAVEN MOST HIDEOUS STORMES
                              ARE SENT                        5.46.3
    ASWAGE YOUR STORMES, OR ELSE BOTH YOU AND SHE             5.46.11
    THE STORMES, WHICH SHE ALONE ON ME DOTH RAINE             5.46.14
    AND ALL THESE STORMES WHICH NOW HIS BEAUTY BLEND          5.62.11
    AFTER LONG STORMES AND TEMPESTS SAD ASSAY                 5.63.1
STORMY                         2
    AGAINST THE STORMY GUSTS OF WINTERS DAY                   3.13.11
    PAINTED IN MY BECLOWDED STORMIE FACE                      4.45.2
STORY                         12
    SIGH OUT A $STORIE CF HER CRUELL DEEDES                   1.2.5
    SHALL BE SO MUCH DELIGHTED WITH THY STORY                 2.6.10
    MAY IN HIS $SHADOW MY $LOVES STORIE READ                  2.13.14
    YET READE AT LAST THE STORIE OF MY $WOE                   2.54.1
    READE HEERE (SWEET $MAYD) THE STORY OF MY WO              2.101.1
    THAT I CAN READE A STORY OF MY WOE                        2.111.14
    MAY IN HIS SHADOW MY $LOVES STORY READE                   2.121.14
    THAT YOU ARE YOU, SC DIGNIFIES HIS STORY                  3.84.8
    UPON THY PART I CAN SET DOWNE A STORY                     3.88.6
    THAT TONGUE THAT TELLS THE STORY OF THY DAIES             3.95.5
    COULD MAKE ME ANY SUMMERS STORY TELL                      3.98.7
    TO WRITE THEREIN MORE FRESH THE STORY
                              OF DELIGHT                      4.102.13
STOURES                        1
    BUT GLORY THINKE TC MAKE THESE CRUEL STOURES              5.57.10
STOUT                          1
    WHEN ROCKS IMPREGNABLE ARE NOT SO STOUTE                  3.65.7
STOUTLY                        1
    AND STOUTLY WILL THAT SECOND WORKE ASSOYLE                5.80.7
STRAIGHT                      33
    BUT STRAIGHT HER WIDE BLOWNE POMP COMES
                              TO DECLINE                      1.39.6
    AND STRAIGHT TIS GONE AS IT HAD NEVER BEENE               1.50.4
    STRAIGHT TAXETH $REASON, WANTING TO INVENT                2.38.7
    STRAIGHT MOUNTING UP TO THY CELESTIALL EYES               2.103.12
    STRAIGHT TAXETH $REASON, WANTING TO INVENT                2.131.7
    SPRINGING WITH THAT, AND FADING STRAIGHT
                              WITH THIS                       2.141.11
    I SEND THEM BACK AGAINE AND STRAIGHT GROW SAD             3.45.14
    SPEAKE OF MY LAMENESSE, AND I STRAIGHT WILL HALT          3.89.3
    RETURNE FORGETFULL $MUSE, AND STRAIGHT REDEEME            3.100.5
    I MAY BE STRAIGHT THOUGH THEY THEM-SELVES
                              BE BEVEL                        3.121.11
```

```
INJOYD NO SOONER BUT DISPISED STRAIGHT            3.129.5
BEARE THINE EYES STRAIGHT, THOUGH THY
                      PROUD HEART GOE WIDE         3.140.14
STRAIGHT IN HER HEART DID MERCIE COME             3.145.5
I LOVED, BUT STRAIGHT DID NOT WHAT $LOVE DECREED   4.2.6
REASON THOU KNEEL'DST, AND OFFEREDST STRAIGHT
                      TO PROVE                     4.10.13
STELLA, THOU STRAIGHT LOOKST BABIES IN HER EYES   4.11.10
AND STRAIGHT THEREWITH, LIKE WAGS NEW
                      GOT TO PLAY                  4.17.13
MY VERIE INKE TURNES STRAIGHT TO $STELLA'S NAME    4.19.6
BUT STRAIGHT I SAW MOTIONS OF LIGHTNING GRACE     4.20.12
THE FIRST THAT STRAIGHT MY FANCIE'S ERROR BRINGS   4.38.5
FOR THOUGH I NEVER SEE THEM, BUT STRAIGHT WAYES    4.42.9
ARE METAMORPHOSD STRAIGHT TO TUNES OF JOYES       4.44.14
SO SWEETE SOUNDS STRAIGHT MINE EARE AND
                      HEART DO HIT                 4.55.13
WITH CHASTNED MIND, I STRAIGHT MUST SHEW
                      THAT SHE                     4.61.10
I JOYED, BUT STRAIGHT THUS WATRED WAS MY WINE      4.62.5
SHE COMES, AND STREIGHT THEREWITH HER
                      SHINING TWINS DO MOVE        4.76.1
YOUR MORALL NOTES STRAIGHT MY HID MEANING TEARE   4.104.12
CLIPS STREIGHT MY WINGS, STREIGHT WRAPS
                      ME IN HIS NIGHT              4.108.8
CLIPS STREIGHT MY WINGS, STREIGHT WRAPS
                      ME IN HIS NIGHT              4.108.8
WHO ME CAPTIVING STREIGHT WITH RIGOROUS WRONG     5.12.11
AND WITH ANOTHER DOTH IT STREIGHT RECURE          5.21.11
MY CRUELL FAYRE STREIGHT BIDS ME WEND MY WAY       5.46.2
IN WHOSE STREIGHT BANDS YE NOW CAPTIVED ARE        5.71.7
STRAIGHTWAY              1
STRAIGHT-WAY SHE HASTS HER UNTO $DELIAS EIES      1.25.10
STRAIGHTWAYS            1
STRAIGHTWAYES HE PLAY'S A SWAGG'RING $RUFFINS
                      PART                         2.7.10
STRAIN                 3
SOME SAY, I HAVE A PASSING PLEASING $STRAINE       2.42.3
SOME SAY I HAVE A PASSING PLEASING STRAINE        2.128.3
THEE TO THY WRACKE BEYOND THY LIMITS STRAINE       4.85.4
STRAINED               1
WHAT STRAINED TOUCHES $RHETHORICK CAN LEND        3.82.10
STRAINS                1
AND OTHER STRAINES OF WOE, WHICH NOW SEEME WOE    3.90.13
STRAITS                1
THE $GULPHES AND $STRAITS, THAT STRANGELY
                      HE HAD PAST                  2.1.10
STRAKE                 2
FOR SOONE AS THEY STRAKE THEE WITH $STELLA'S
                      RAYES                        4.10.12
SEEING HOPE YEELD WHEN THIS WO STRAKE HIM FURST    4.95.6
STRAND                 1
ONE DAY I WROTE HER NAME UPON THE STRAND           5.75.1
STRANGE               17
THAT MAKES THE WORLD ADMIRE SO STRANGE EFFECTS     1.34.8
THY CRUELTY, THY GLORY., $O STRANGE CASE          1.56.10
THAT MILLIONS OF STRANGE SHADDOWES ON YOU TEND+    3.53.2
TO NEW FOUND METHODS, AND TO COMPOUNDS STRANGE+    3.76.4
I WILL ACQUAINTANCE STRANGLE AND LOOKE STRANGE     3.89.8
IS WRIT IN MOODS AND FROUNES AND WRINCKLES
                      STRANGE                      3.93.8
```

TO ME ARE NOTHING NOVELL, NOTHING STRANGE   3.123.3
AGAINST STRANG MALLADIES A SOVERAIGNE CURE   3.153.8
OR WITH STRANGE SIMILIES ENRICH EACH LINE   4.3.7
AND STRANGE THINGS COST TOO DEARE FOR
                              MY POORE SPRITES   4.3.11
SOME ONE HIS SONG IN $JOVE, AND $JOVE'S
                              STRANGE TALES ATTIRES   4.6.5
STRANGE FLAMES OF $LOVE IT IN OUR SOULES
                              WOULD RAISE   4.25.4
OUR HORSMANSHIPS, WHILE BY STRANGE WORKE I PROVE   4.49.2
HOW IS THY GRACE BY MY STRANGE FORTUNE STAIND   4.98.3
STELLA NOW LEARNES (STRANGE CASE) TO WEEPE
                              IN THEE   4.101.8
WITH SUCH STRANGE TERMES HER EYES SHE DOTH INURE   5.21.9
STRANGE THING ME SEEMD TO SEE A BEAST SO WYLD   5.67.13
STRANGELY   5
THE $GULPHES AND $STRAITS, THAT STRANGELY
                              HE HAD PAST   2.1.10
HOW FALS IT OUT SO STRANGELY YOU REPLY+   2.5.2
AGAINST THAT TIME WHEN THOU SHALT STRANGELY PASSE   3.49.5
ASCONCE AND STRANGELY.. $BUT BY ALL ABOVE   3.110.6
SO STRANGELY (ALAS) THY WORKS IN ME PREVAILE   4.108.12
STRANGENESS   1
AND MUCH COMMEND THE STRANGENESSE OF MY $VAINE   2.42.2
STRANGERS   1
AND OTHERS' FEETE STILL SEEM'D BUT STRANGERS
                              IN MY WAY   4.1.11
STRANGLE   1
I WILL ACQUAINTANCE STRANGLE AND LOOKE STRANGE   3.89.8
STRATAGEMS   1
IN ALL SWEETE STRATAGEMS SWEETE $ARTE CAN SHOW   4.36.11
STRAVE   1
NOT USDE TO FROZEN CLIPS, HE STRAVE TO
                              FIND SOME PART   4.8.6
STRAW   1
OF TOUCH THEY ARE, AND POORE I AM THEIR STRAW   4.9.14
STRAWBERRY   1
HER GOODLY BOSOME LYKE A $STRAWBERRY BED   5.64.9
STRAY   2
FIXT SURE THEY ARE, BUT WANDRING MAKE ME STRAY   1.34.11
DOTH FALL TO STRAY, AND MY CHIEFE POWRES
                              ARE BROUGHT   4.38.3
STRAYING   2
AND CHIDE THY BEAUTY, AND THY STRAYING YOUTH   3.41.10
OF STRAYING WAYES, WHEN VALIANT ERROUR GUIDES   4.51.11
STREAM   2
THY $CRISTALL STREAME REFINED BY HER $EYES   2.53.4
THAT CHRISTALL STREAME REFINED BY HER EYES   2.113.4
STREAMS   4
RUNNES THIS POORE $RIVER, CHARG'D WITH
                              STREAMES OF ZEALE   1.1.2
GUILDING PALE STREAMES WITH HEAVENLY ALCUMY   3.33.4
OF CUNNINGST FISHERS IN MOST TROUBLED STREAMES   4.51.10
WHILE THOSE FAIRE PLANETS ON THY STREAMES
                              DID SHINE   4.103.4
STREET   1
THAT NOW IN $COACHES TROUBLE EV'RY $STREET   2.6.2
STRENGTH   12
YET LEAST LONG TRAVAILES BE ABOVE MY STRENGTH   1.14.13
RECEIVING STRENGTH FROM EV'RY SECRET PART   2.30.7

```
BEAUTY HER STRENGTH UNTO SLEEPES WEAKNES
                         LENDING              2.136.10
AND IN MINE OWNE LOVES STRENGTH SEEME TO DECAY    3.23.7
TO LEAVE POORE ME, THOU HAST THE STRENGTH
                         OF LAWES              3.49.13
AND STRENGTH BY LIMPING SWAY DISABLED          3.66.8
IF THOU WOULDST USE THE STRENGTH OF ALL
                         THY STATE+            3.96.12
THERE IS SUCH STRENGTH AND WARRANTISE OF SKILL  3.150.7
IN OBJECT BEST TO KNIT AND STRENGTH OUR SIGHT    4.7.6
IN SWEETEST STRENGTH, SO SWEETLY SKILD WITHALL  4.36.10
TOWNE-FOLKES MY STRENGTH., A DAINTIER
                         JUDGE APPLIES          4.41.6
  ALL FLESH IS FRAYLE, AND ALL HER STRENGTH UNSTAYD  5.58.5
STRENGTHENED          1
  MY LOVE IS STRENGTHNED THOUGH MORE WEAKE
                         IN SEEMING            3.102.1
STRENGTH'S             1
  WHOSE STRENGTHS ABONDANCE WEAKENS HIS OWNE HEART  3.23.4
STRETCH               2
   TO SAVE THINE OWNE, STRETCH OUT THE FAIREST HAND  1.46.8
   STRETCH OUT THE FAIREST HAND, A PLEDGE OF PEACE   1.46.9
STRETCHED             1
  AND STRETCHED MITER OF AN $ANTIQUE SONG      3.17.12
STRIFE                6
   T'HAVE PEACE ABROAD, AND NOUGHT WITHIN BUT STRIFE  1.20.3
  WITH TEARES, SIGHES, AND DISDAINE, SHALL
                       HAVE IMMORTAL STRIFE   2.132.14
  AND FOR THE PEACE OF YOU I HOLD SUCH STRIFE    3.75.3
  A STRIFE IS GROWNE BETWEENE $VERTUE AND $LOVE   4.52.1
  CURST BE THE NIGHT WHICH DID YOUR STRIFE RESIST  4.105.12
  THEN $ORPHEUS WITH HIS HARP THEYR STRIFE DID BAR   5.44.4
STRIKES               2
  SO SOUNDS MY $MUSE ACCORDING AS SHE STRIKES    1.57.3
  STRIKES EACH IN EACH BY MUTUALL ORDERING      3.8.10
STRING                1
  MARKE HOW ONE STRING SWEET HUSBAND TO AN OTHER    3.8.9
STRINGS               2
  WITH THOSE SWEET STRINGS STOLNE FROM THY
                       GOLDEN HAYRE           2.104.2
  HER $BOWE IS BEAUTY, WITH TEN THOUSAND STRINGS   2.126.6
STRIPES               1
  WHO THREATNED STRIPES, IF HE HIS WRATH DID PROVE   4.17.6
STRIVE                9
  WHY SHOULD I STRIVE TO MAKE HER LIVE FOR EVER   1.17.5
  FOR WHILST THEY STRIVE WHICH SHALL BE
                       $LORD OF ALL           1.28.5
  LET OTHERS STRIVE TO ENTERTAINE WITH $WORDS     2.4.9
  AND SEE IF $TIME (IF HE WOULD STRIVE TO PROVE)  2.60.13
  YOU ARE MY $ALL THE WORLD, AND I MUST STRIVE   3.112.5
  SINCE MY APPEALE SAIES I DID STRIVE TO PROOVE  3.117.13
  REBELS TO $NATURE, STRIVE FOR THEIR OWNE SMART   4.5.4
  MY WIT DOTH STRIVE THOSE PASSIONS TO DEFEND    4.18.10
  THY SELFE, DOEST STRIVE ALL MINDS THAT
                       WAY TO MOVE            4.71.10
STRIVES               1
  WHILST THUS MY $PEN STRIVES TO ETERNIZE THEE    2.44.1
STRIVING              7
   SEE THY $LEANDER STRIVING IN THESE WAVES      1.46.2
  MY $EYES WITH $TEARES AGAINST THE FIRE STRIVING  2.40.9
```

```
STRIVING TO HOLD IT STRONGLY IN THE $DEEPE          2.58.10
SLEEPE AND $BEAUTY, WITH EQUALL FORCES STRYVING     2.136.9
MYNE EYES WITH TEARES AGAINST THE FIRE STRYVING     2.144.9
WERE IT NOT SINFULL THEN STRIVING TO MEND           3.103.9
STRIVING ABROAD A FORAGING TO GO                    4.55.6
STRONG                      25
STRONG IS THE NET, AND FERVENT IS THE FLAME         1.14.5
TO HAVE AFFECTION STRONG, A BODY WEAKE              1.20.8
CAUS'D BY THOSE CRUELL BEAMES THAT WERE
                      SO STRONG                      1.32.14
SHALL FAILE IN FORCE, THEIR WORKING NOT SO STRONG   1.38.4
BE MY STRONG $FAITH ASCENDING TO THY $FAME          2.54.10
FROM THE STRONG $SPIRIT BY NO MEANES FORCE
                      THE SAME                       2.58.8
BY MY STRONG FAYTH ASCENDING TO THY FAME            2.101.10
BY THY GREAT POWER, AND BY STRONG FAYTH IN THEE     2.112.14
AND MY STRONG SIGHES, THE AYRES WEAKE
                      FORCE REVIVETH                 2.127.3
STRONG LOCKE OF KINDNESSE, $CLOSET OF
                      LOVES STORE                    2.146.5
RESEMBLING STRONG YOUTH IN HIS MIDDLE AGE           3.7.6
TO HIM THAT BEARES THE STRONG OFFENSES LOSSE        3.34.12
BE WHERE YOU LIST, YOUR CHARTER IS SO STRONG        3.58.9
NOR GATES OF STEELE SO STRONG BUT TIME DECAYES+     3.65.8
OR WHAT STRONG HAND CAN HOLD HIS SWIFT
                      FOOTE BACK                     3.65.11
THIS THOU PERCEV'ST, WHICH MAKES THY LOVE
                      MORE STRONG                    3.73.13
POTIONS OF $EYSELL GAINST MY STRONG INFECTION       3.111.10
DIVERT STRONG MINDES TO TH'COURSE OF ALTRING
                      THINGS                         3.115.8
GROWES FAIRER THEN AT FIRST, MORE STRONG,
                      FAR GREATER                    3.119.12
WHERE $VERTUE IS MADE STRONG BY $BEAUTIE'S MIGHT    4.48.2
STRONG THRUGH YOUR CAUSE, BUT BY YOUR VERTUE WEAK   5.8.12
TOO FEEBLE I T'ABIDE THE BRUNT SO STRONG            5.12.9
GAYNST SUCH STRONG CASTLES NEEDETH GREATER MIGHT    5.14.5
NE NONE SO RICH OR WISE, SO STRONG OR FAYRE         5.58.9
WITH STRONG ENDEVOUR AND ATTENTION DEW              5.80.8
STRONG-BUILT                 1
THE STRONG-BUILT $TROPHIES TO HER LIVING $FAME      2.45.6
STRONGER                     3
AND NIGHT DOTH NIGHTLY MAKE GREEFES LENGTH
                      SEEME STRONGER                 3.28.14
WHOSE ACTION IS NO STRONGER THEN A FLOWER+          3.65.4
UNITED POWERS MAKE EACH THE STRONGER PROVE          4.88.14
STRONGEST                    1
CLOTH'D WITH FINE TROPES, WITH STRONGEST
                      REASONS LIN'D                  4.58.6
STRONGLY                     8
AND TO ATTEND IT, THEM AS STRONGLY TY'D             2.58.5
STRIVING TO HOLD IT STRONGLY IN THE $DEEPE          2.58.10
THY MERRIT HATH MY DUTIE STRONGLY KNIT              3.26.2
YOU ARE SO STRONGLY IN MY PURPOSE BRED              3.112.13
THOUGH STRONGLY HEDG'D OF BLOUDY $LYON'S PAWES      4.75.10
HIS SAFE ASSURANCE, STRONGLY IT RESTRAYNE           5.42.12
BEATS ON IT STRONGLY IT TO RUINATE                  5.56.8
BUT LIKE A STEDDY SHIP DOTH STRONGLY PART           5.59.5
STROVE                       2
I IN THE $CIRCUIT FOR THE $LAWRELL STROVE           2.47.6
```

```
  IN WHOM ALL PURENES WITH PERFECTION STROVE        2.141.3
STRUCK                  1
  ABOVE A MORTALL PITCH, THAT STRUCK ME DEAD+        3.86.6
STRUGGLE                1
  BUT THEY DO SWELL AND STRUGGLE FORTH OF ME         4.50.3
STRUMPETED              1
  AND MAIDEN VERTUE RUDELY STRUMPETED                3.66.6
STUBBORN                5
  SEE HOW THE STUBBORNE DAMZELL DOTH DEPRAVE         5.29.1
  DOE BEAT ON TH'ANDUYLE OF HER STUBBERNE WIT        5.32.8
  NOR MOVE THE $DOLPHIN FROM HER STUBBORNE WILL      5.38.8
  THRUGH STUBBORN PRIDE AMONGST THEMSELVES DID JAR   5.44.2
  SO DOE I HOPE HER STUBBORNE HART TO BEND           5.51.11
STUDYING                1
  STUDYING INVENTIONS FINE, HER WITS TO ENTERTAINE   4.1.6
STUDY'S                 1
  INVENTION, $NATURE'S CHILD, FLED STEP-DAME
                       $STUDIE'S BLOWES              4.1.10
STUFF                   2
  IN THY COLD STUFFE A FLEGMATIKE DELIGHT+           4.56.11
  OF SUCH HEAVEN STUFFE, TO CLOATH SO HEAVENLY
                       MYNDE                         4.101.14
STUMBLING               1
  WITNESSE WITH ME, THAT MY FOULE STUMBLING SO       4.93.6
STUPID                  1
  BUT LIKE A STUPID STOCK IN SILENCE DIE             5.43.8
STYLE                   8
  THEN SHOULDST THOU LIVE IN AN IMMORTALL STILE      1.43.12
  ELSE HARSH MY STILE, UNTUNABLE MY $MUSE            1.57.9
  TO M'INFANT STILE THE $CRADLE, AND THE $GRAVE      1.59.12
  THEIRS FOR THEIR STILE ILE READ, HIS FOR
                       HIS LOVE                      3.32.14
  IN OTHERS WORKES THOU DOOST BUT MEND THE STILE     3.78.11
  MAKING HIS STILE ADMIRED EVERY WHERE               3.84.12
  TO SOME A SWEETEST PLAINT, A SWEETEST
                       STILE AFFORDS                 4.6.9
  O JOY, TOO HIGH FOR MY LOW STILE TO SHOW           4.69.1
STYX                    3
  BY $HELLISH $STYX (BY WHICH THE $THUND'RER
                       SWEARES)                      2.36.5
  I WILL NOT COME IN $STIX OR $PHLEGETON             2.39.6
  I WYLL NOT COME IN $STIXE NOR $PHLEGITON           2.118.6
'SUAGE                  1
  ALL FOLKES PREST AT THY WILL THY PAINE
                       TO 'SWAGE                     4.101.11
SUBDUE                  3
  TIME, CRUELL TIME, COME AND SUBDUE THAT $BROW      1.23.1
  SUBDUE THYS $TYRANT EVER MARTYRING MEE             2.115.2
  WHERE WHENAS DEATH SHALL ALL THE WORLD SUBDEW      5.75.13
SUBDUED                 2
  AND ALMOST THENCE MY NATURE IS SUBDU'D             3.111.6
  SINCE THEN THOU HAST SO FARRE SUBDUED ME           4.40.12
SUBJECT                 7
  HOW CAN MY $MUSE WANT SUBJECT TO INVENT            3.38.1
  OF THEIR FAIRE SUBJECT, BLESSING EVERY BOOKE       3.82.4
  THAT TO HIS SUBJECT LENDS NOT SOME SMALL GLORY     3.84.6
  TO MARRE THE SUBJECT THAT BEFORE WAS WELL          3.103.10
  AS SUBJECT TO TIMES LOVE, OR TO TIMES HATE         3.124.3
  I BEG NO SUBJECT TO USE ELOQUENCE                  4.28.9
  TO LEAVE THE SCEPTER OF ALL SUBJECT THINGS         4.38.4
```

```
UPON THE FLINT OF SUCH A HART REBELLING              1.18.10
WITH THEE SUCH POWERS TO PLAGUE ONE SILLY HARTE      1.27.12
OF SUCH AS SPOILE THY POORE AFFLICTED STATE          1.28.4
FINDING ME RAIN'D WITH SUCH A HEAVY HAND             1.28.12
AND BY THAT HAND WHOM SUCH DEEDS ILL BECOME          1.31.14
THEIR SWEET APPEARING STILL SUCH POWER INSPIRES      1.34.7
NARCISSUS CHANG'D T'A FLOWER IN SUCH A CASE          1.37.12
THEN DO NOT THOU SUCH TREASURE WAST IN VAINE         1.39.13
AND IF I FINDE SUCH PLEASURE TO COMPLAINE            1.48.13
HAPPY THE HEART THAT SIGH'D FOR SUCH A ONE           1.51.14
FOR NO GROUND ELS COULD MAKE THE MUSICKE SUCH        1.57.13
THIS IS MY STATE, AND $DELIAS HEART IS SUCH          1.60.13
MY HEART HATH PAID SUCH GRIEVOUS $USURIE             2.3.11
GIVE $NATURE THANKES, YOU ARE NOT SUCH AS WE         2.22.12
YET CRAV'D THE $ALMES OF SUCH AS PASSED BY           2.23.4
TO $SUCH AS SAY, $THY $LOVE I OVER-PRIZE             2.28.1
WHY SHOULD YOUR FAIRE $EYES WITH SUCH
                          SOV'RAIGNE GRACE           2.43.1
OR HAVE THINE $EYES SUCH $MAGIKE, OR THAT $ART       2.52.3
IN $FORMER TIMES, SUCH AS HAD STORE OF $COYNE        2.58.1
SUCH AS BY $ART TO GET THE SAME HAVE TRY'D           2.58.7
MY HART HATH PAYD SUCH GRIEVOUS USURY                2.110.11
POORE $BROOKES AND $BANKS HAD NO SUCH
                          WONDERS BEENE              2.120.14
YET HAPPY HE THATS ROBD OF SUCH A THIEFE             2.126.14
IN SECRET SILENCE, WHICH SUCH WONDERS PREACHEST      2.146.12
UNKINDLY, SUCH DISTEMPRATURE DOTH BRING              2.147.10
SUCH IS THE SUNNE, WHO GUIDES MY YOUTHFULL
                          SEASON                     2.147.13
THAT ON HIMSELFE SUCH MURDROUS SHAME COMMITS         3.9.14
AND CONSTANT STARS IN THEM I READ SUCH ART           3.14.10
SUCH HEAVENLY TOUCHES NERE TOUCHT EARTHLY FACES      3.17.8
WHILST I WHOME FORTUNE OF SUCH TRYUMPH BARS          3.25.3
FOR THY SWEET LOVE REMEMBRED SUCH WELTH BRINGS       3.29.13
WHY DIDST THOU PROMISE SUCH A BEAUTIOUS DAY          3.34.1
FOR NO MAN WELL OF SUCH A SALVE CAN SPEAKE           3.34.7
SUCH CIVILL WAR IS IN MY LOVE AND HATE               3.35.12
BUT DOE NOT SO, I LOVE THEE IN SUCH SORT             3.36.13
WHILST THAT THIS SHADOW DOTH SUCH SUBSTANCE GIVE     3.37.10
HANG ON SUCH THORNES, AND PLAY AS WANTONLY           3.54.7
NO SHAPE SO TRUE, NO TRUTH OF SUCH ACCOUNT           3.62.6
FOR SUCH A TIME DO I NOW FORTIFIE                    3.63.9
WHEN I HAVE SEENE SUCH INTERCHANGE OF STATE          3.64.9
IN ME THOU SEEST THE TWI-LIGHT OF SUCH DAY           3.73.5
IN ME THOU SEEST THE GLOWING OF SUCH FIRE            3.73.9
AND FOR THE PEACE OF YOU I HOLD SUCH STRIFE          3.75.3
AND FOUND SUCH FAIRE ASSISTANCE IN MY VERSE          3.78.2
YOU STILL SHALL LIVE (SUCH VERTUE HATH MY $PEN)      3.81.13
AND SUCH A COUNTER-PART SHALL FAME HIS WIT           3.84.11
IN SLEEPE A $KING, BUT WAKING NO SUCH MATTER         3.87.14
SUCH IS MY LOVE, TO THEE I SO BELONG                 3.88.13
BUT DOE NOT SO, I LOVE THEE IN SUCH SORT             3.96.13
THAT HAVING SUCH A SKOPE TO SHOW HER PRIDE           3.103.2
SUCH SEEMES YOUR BEAUTIE STILL.. $THREE
                          $WINTERS COLDE             3.104.3
TO ONE, OF ONE, STILL SUCH, AND EVER SO             3.105.4
EVEN SUCH A BEAUTY AS YOU MAISTER NOW                3.106.8
SUCH CHERUBINES AS YOUR SWEET SELFE RESEMBLE         3.114.6
AT SUCH WHO NOT BORNE FAIRE NO BEAUTY LACK           3.127.11
BUT NO SUCH $ROSES SEE I IN HER CHEEKES              3.130.6
```

```
THERE IS SUCH STRENGTH AND WARRANTISE OF SKILL      3.150.7
I SWEARE, MY HEART SUCH ONE SHALL SHEW TO THEE        4.4.12
LOOKS OVER THE WORLD, AND CAN FIND NOTHING SUCH       4.9.10
O NO, HER HEART IS SUCH A $CITTADELL                 4.12.12
YOU TAKE WRONG WAIES, THOSE FAR-FET HELPES
                                        BE SUCH       4.15.9
SUCH COLTISH GYRES, THAT TO MY BIRTH I OWE            4.21.6
YET TO THOSE FOOLES HEAV'N SUCH WIT DOTH IMPART       4.24.5
AND CAN WITH FOULE ABUSE SUCH BEAUTIES BLOT          4.24.11
LOOKE AT MY HANDS FOR NO SUCH QUINTESSENCE           4.28.11
'FOOLE,' ANSWERS HE, 'NO $INDES SUCH TREASURES
                                        HOLD         4.32.12
MADE MANIFEST BY SUCH A VICTORIE                     4.40.10
SUCH SMART MAY PITIE CLAIME OF ANY HART               4.44.3
THE HEAV'NLY NATURE OF THAT PLACE IS SUCH            4.44.12
PITIE THEREOF GATE IN HER BREAST SUCH PLACE           4.45.7
TO SUCH A SCHOOLE-MISTRESSE, WHOSE LESSONS NEW       4.46.10
CAN THOSE BLACKE BEAMES SUCH BURNING MARKES
                                        ENGRAVE       4.47.2
WHOSE NECKE BECOMES SUCH YOKE OF TYRANNY+             4.47.4
OR SPRITE, DISDAINE OF SUCH DISDAINE TO HAVE+         4.47.6
TO THEM THAT DO SUCH ENTERTAINMENT NEED               4.51.3
BY SUCH UNSUTED SPEECH SHOULD HINDRED BE             4.51.14
HER SOULE, ARM'D BUT WITH SUCH A DAINTY RIND          4.57.7
ALAS, IF YOU GRAUNT ONLY SUCH DELIGHT                4.59.12
THOU WHOM TO ME SUCH MY GOOD TURNES SHOULD BIND       4.65.3
HAST THOU FOUND SUCH AND SUCH LIKE ARGUMENTS+        4.67.10
HAST THOU FOUND SUCH AND SUCH LIKE ARGUMENTS+        4.67.10
ANGER INVESTS WITH SUCH A LOVELY GRACE               4.73.13
NOR THIS, NOR THAT, NOR ANY SUCH SMALL CAUSE         4.75.12
WITH SUCH A ROSIE MORNE, WHOSE BEAMES
                              MOST FRESHLY GAY        4.76.7
THAT CONVERSATION SWEET, WHERE SUCH HIGH
                              COMFORTS BE            4.77.10
IS IT NOT EVILL THAT SUCH A $DEVILL WANTS
                              HORNES+               4.78.14
CANNOT SUCH GRACE YOUR SILLY SELFE CONTENT           4.83.11
YET SWAM IN JOY, SUCH LOVE IN HER WAS SEENE          4.87.11
IS FAITH SO WEAKE+ $OR IS SUCH FORCE IN THEE+         4.88.5
WHEN $SUN IS HID, CAN STARRES SUCH BEAMES
                              DISPLAY+               4.88.6
WITH SUCH BAD MIXTURE OF MY NIGHT AND DAY            4.89.12
MODELS SUCH BE WOOD-GLOBES OF GLISTRING SKIES        4.91.11
BY BEING PLACED IN SUCH A WRETCH AS I                4.94.14
NAY SORROW COMES WITH SUCH MAINE RAGE, THAT HE        4.95.9
THANKE MAY YOU HAVE FOR SUCH A THANKFULL PART        4.95.13
SUCH LIGHT IN SENSE, WITH SUCH A DARKNED MIND        4.99.14
SUCH LIGHT IN SENSE, WITH SUCH A DARKNED MIND        4.99.14
O PLAINTS CONSERV'D IN SUCH A SUGRED PHRAISE         4.100.9
SUCH TEARES, SIGHS, PLAINTS, NO SORROW
                              IS, BUT JOY           4.100.12
OR IF SUCH HEAVENLY SIGNES MUST PROVE ANNOY         4.100.13
AND GRACE, SICKE TOO, SUCH FINE CONCLUSIONS
                              TRIES                 4.101.3
OF SUCH HEAVEN STUFFE, TO CLOATH SO HEAVENLY
                              MYNDE                 4.101.14
THAT WITH SUCH POYSONOUS CARE MY LOOKES
                              YOU MARKE             4.104.2
SUCH PRIDE IS PRAISE, SUCH PORTLINESSE IS HONOR       5.5.9
SUCH PRIDE IS PRAISE, SUCH PORTLINESSE IS HONOR       5.5.9
```

WITHOUT SOME SPARK OF SUCH SELF-PLEASING PRIDE	5.5.14
SUCH LOVE NOT LYKE TO LUSTS OF BASER KYND	5.6.3
SUCH LIFE SHOULD BE THE HONOR OF YOUR LIGHT	5.7.13
SUCH DEATH THE SAD ENSAMPLE OF YOUR MIGHT	5.7.14
NOR UNTO GLASSE.. SUCH BASENESSE MOUGHT	
OFFEND HER	5.9.12
SUCH LOWLINESSE SHALL MAKE YOU LOFTY BE	5.13.14
GAYNST SUCH STRONG CASTLES NEEDETH GREATER MIGHT	5.14.5
SUCH HAUGHTY MYNDS ENUR'D TO HARDY FIGHT	5.14.7
WITH SUCH STRANGE TERMES HER EYES SHE DOTH INURE	5.21.9
SUCH ART OF EYES I NEVER READ IN BOOKES	5.21.14
SUCH SUBTILE CRAFT MY $DAMZELL DOTH CONCEAVE	5.23.5
SUCH LABOUR LIKE THE $SPYDERS WEB I FYND	5.23.13
SUCH IS THE POWRE OF LOVE IN GENTLE MIND	5.30.13
OF SUCH POORE THRALLS HER CRUELL HANDS EMBREW	5.31.12
SUCH CRUELTY SHE WOULD HAVE SOONE ABHORD	5.31.14
IS BUT A BAYT SUCH WRETCHES TO BEGJILE	5.41.10
SUCH MERCY SHAL YOU MAKE ADMYRED TO BE	5.49.13
BUT SUCH SWEET CORDIALLS PASSE $PHYSITIONS ART	5.50.12
SUCH SELFE ASSURANCE NEED NOT FEARE THE SPIGHT	5.59.9
BUT HE MOST HAPPY WHO SUCH ONE LOVES BEST	5.59.14
SUCH HEAVENLY FORMES OUGHT RATHER WORSHIPT BE	5.61.13
COMMING TO KISSE HER LYPS, (SUCH GRACE I FOUND)	5.64.1
SUCH FRAGRANT FLOWRES DOE GIVE MOST ODORCUS	
SMELL	5.64.13
THAT MAY ADMIRE SUCH WORLDS RARE WONDERMENT	5.69.12
BUT HERE ON EARTH TO HAVE SUCH HEVENS BLISSE	5.72.14
THAT THREE SUCH GRACES DID UNTO ME GIVE	5.74.14
FOR THAT YOUR SELFE YE DAYLY SUCH DOE SEE	5.79.2
IN MY SWEET PEACE SUCH BREACHES TO HAVE BRED	5.86.12
BUT WITH SUCH BRIGHTNESSE WHYLEST I FILL MY MIND	5.88.13
AND DEAD MY LIFE THAT WANTS SUCH LIVELY BLIS	5.89.14

SUCK   1
LET BREATH SUCKE UP THOSE SWEETES, LET	
ARMES EMBRACE	4.85.12

SUCKED   1
IN SPORT I SUCKT, WHILE SHE ASLEEPE DID LIE	4.73.6

SUDDEN   3
(DIANA-LIKE) TO WORKE MY SUDDEN CHANGE	1.5.4
AND HASTES $ME ON UNTO A SUDDEN $DEATH	2.20.10
BUT SUDDEN DUMPS AND DRERY SAD DISDAYNE	5.52.11

SUDDENLY   1
WHEN SUDDENLY WITH TWINCLE OF HER EYE	5.16.11

SUE   4
AND SUE A FRIEND, CAME DEBTER FOR MY SAKE	3.134.11
DAYLY WHEN I DO SEEKE AND SEW FOR PEACE	5.11.1
IN VAINE I SEEKE AND SEW TO HER FOR GRACE	5.20.1
WHICH I NO LENGER CAN ENDURE TO SUE	5.57.3

SUFFER   6
THUS POORE $THEEVES SUFFER, WHEN THE GREATER	
SCAPE	2.14.14
MY $HEART SHOULD SUFFER FOR MINE $EYES $OFFENCE	2.29.4
OH LET ME SUFFER (BEING AT YOUR BECK)	3.58.5
WHY DOST THOU PINE WITHIN AND SUFFER DEARTH	3.146.3
I CALL IT PRAISE TO SUFFER $TYRANNIE	4.2.11
DOTH SUFFER WRECK BOTH OF HER SELFE AND GOODS	5.56.12

SUFFERANCE   1
AND PATIENCE TAME, TO SUFFERANCE BIDE EACH CHECK	3.58.7

SUFFERED   4
HERE READ THY SELFE, AND WHAT I SUFFRED FOR THEE	1.42.8

```
   AND SUFF'RED HER TO GLORY IN MY $WRACKE            2.36.3
   TO WAIGH HOW ONCE I SUFFERED IN YOUR CRIME         3.120.8
   NAY, MORE FOOLE I, OFT SUFFERED YOU TO SLEEPE      4.83.7
SUFFERING                   2
   SUFFRING MY FRIEND FOR MY SAKE TO APPROOVE HER     3.42.8
   SUFFERING THE EVILS BOTH OF THE DAY AND NIGHT      4.89.9
SUFFERS                     1
   IT SUFFERS NOT IN SMILINGE POMP, NOR FALLS         3.124.6
SUFFICE                     9
   LET THIS SUFFICE, THAT ALL THE WORLD MAY SEE       1.15.13
   SUFFICE THAT HIGH ATTEMPTS HAVE NEVER SHAME        1.35.9
   SUFFICE, THOU SHALT BE 'LOV'D AS WELL AS SHEE      1.43.14
   LET WAKING EYES SUFFICE TO WAILE THEIR SCORNE      1.54.7
   SUFFICE, THEY SHEW I LIV'D AND LOV'D THEE DEARE    1.55.14
   FOR ALL MY WOES, THAT ONELY SHALL SUFFISE          2.151.4
   OF CONQUEST, DO NOT THESE EFFECTS SUFFICE          4.36.7
   WITH NO CONTENTMENT CAN THEMSELVES SUFFIZE         5.35.3
   WITH NO CONTENTMENT CAN THEMSELVES SUFFIZE         5.83.3
SUFFICED                    1
   THAT I IN THY ABUNDANCE AM SUFFIC'D                3.37.11
SUFFICETH                   1
   WHOSE LEAST DELIGHT SUFFICETH TO DEPRIVE           5.63.11
SUFFICIENT                  1
   SUFFICIENT WORKE FOR ONE MANS SIMPLE HEAD          5.33.7
SUFFICIENTLY                1
   WHAT MORTALL PEN SUFFYCIENTLY CAN PRAYSE THEE+     2.146.2
SUGARED                     5
   THAT IN HER BREAST THY PAP WELL SUGRED LIES        4.12.5
   BY $PHOEBUS' DOOME, WITH SUGRED SENTENCE SAYES     4.25.2
   THIS SOWRE-BREATH'D MATE TAST OF THOSE
                            SUGRED LIPS               4.59.11
   AND YET MY $STARRE, BECAUSE A SUGRED KISSE         4.73.5
   O PLAINTS CONSERV'D IN SUCH A SUGRED PHRAISE       4.100.9
SUGARING                    1
   NOR OTHER SUGRING OF MY SPEECH TO PROVE            4.55.10
SUGGEST                     1
   WHICH LIKE TWO SPIRITS DO SUGJEST ME STILL         3.144.2
SUIT                        3
   AND SUTE THY PITTY LIKE IN EVERY PART              3.132.12
   WELL $LOVE, SINCE THIS DEMURRE OUR SUTE
                            DOTH STAY                 4.52.12
   TH'IMPORTUNE SUIT OF MY DESIRE TO SHONNE           5.23.6
SUITED                      1
   HER EYES SO SUTED, AND THEY MOURNERS SEEME         3.127.10
SULLEN                      3
   FROM SULLEN EARTH SINGS HIMNS AT $HEAVENS GATE     3.29.12
   THEN YOU SHALL HEARE THE SURLY SULLEN BELL         3.71.2
   SILENCE IN BOTH DISPLAIES HIS SULLEN MIGHT         4.96.5
SULLIED                     1
   TO CHANGE YOUR DAY OF YOUTH TO SULLIED NIGHT       3.15.12
SULPHUR                     1
   ANOTHER, MERVAILES $SULPHURE $AETNAS FIRE          2.120.4
SUM                         7
   DUELY TO COUNT THE SUMME OF ALL MY CARES           2.3.2
   BEGINNING TO ACCOUNT THE SUM OF ALL MY CARES       2.110.2
   SHALL SUM MY COUNT, AND MAKE MY OLD EXCUSE         3.2.11
   SO GREAT A SUMME OF SUMMES YET CAN'ST NOT LIVE+    3.4.8
   WHEN AS THY LOVE HATH CAST HIS UTMOST SUMME        3.49.3
   TO LEAVE FOR NOTHING ALL THY SUMME OF GOOD         3.109.12
   SEE $BEAUTIE'S TOTALL SUMME SUMM'D IN HER FACE     4.85.10
```

SUMMED   4
  HERE HAVE I SUMM'D MY SIGHS, HERE I INROLE   1.1.7
  AND WHEN THE $PLUMES WERE SUMM'D WITH
                          SWEET DESIRE   2.56.9
  BUT NOW THEIR PLUMES FULL SUMD WITH SWEET DESIRE   2.103.9
  SEE $BEAUTIE'S TOTALL SUMME SUMM'D IN HER FACE   4.85.10
SUMMER   12
  AND STILL MY HOPE THE $SOMMER WINDES PURSUES   1.16.11
  NOW USE THE $SOMMER SMILES, ERE $WINTER LOWERS   1.40.4
  MAKES $SUMMER $WINTER, $AUTUMNE IN THE $SPRING   2.147.11
  FOR NEVER RESTING TIME LEADS $SUMMER ON   3.5.5
  IN THEE THY SUMMER ERE THOU BE DISTIL'D   3.6.2
  BUT THY ETERNALL $SOMMER SHALL NOT FADE   3.18.9
  MAKING NO SUMMER OF AN OTHERS GREENE   3.68.11
  THE SOMMERS FLOWRE IS TO THE SOMMER SWEET   3.94.9
  FOR $SOMMER AND HIS PLEASURES WAITE ON THEE   3.97.11
  NOT THAT THE SUMMER IS LESSE PLEASANT NOW   3.102.9
  ERE YOU WERE BORNE WAS BEAUTIES SUMMER DEAD   3.104.14
  I FEELE THE FLAMES OF HOTTEST SOMMER DAY   4.89.14
SUMMER'S   14
  THE IMAGE OF THY BLUSH AND $SOMMERS HONOR   1.39.2
  THEN WERE NOT SUMMERS DISTILLATION LEFT   3.5.9
  AND $SOMMERS GREENE ALL GIRDED UP IN SHEAVES   3.12.7
  SHALL I COMPARE THEE TO A $SUMMERS DAY+   3.18.1
  AND $SOMMERS LEASE HATH ALL TOO SHORT A DATE   3.18.4
  WHEN SOMMERS BREATH THEIR MASKED BUDS DISCLOSES   3.54.8
  MAKES $SOMERS WELCOME, THRICE MORE WISH'D,
                          MORE RARE   3.56.14
  O HOW SHALL SUMMERS HUNNY BREATH HOLD OUT   3.65.5
  THE SOMMERS FLOWRE IS TO THE SOMMER SWEET   3.94.9
  AND YET THIS TIME REMOV'D WAS SOMMERS TIME   3.97.5
  COULD MAKE ME ANY SUMMERS STORY TELL   3.98.7
  AS $PHILOMELL IN SUMMERS FRONT DOTH SINGE   3.102.7
  HAVE FROM THE FORRESTS SHOOKE THREE SUMMERS
                          PRIDE   3.104.4
  UNTO THE FAYRE SUNSHINE IN SOMERS DAY   5.40.6
SUMMON   3
  UNTO HER SELFE, HER SELFE MY LOVE DOTH SOMMON   1.49.9
  WHEN NOW THE $NIGHT DOTH SUMMON ALL TO SLEEPE+   2.37.2
  I SOMMON UP REMEMBRANCE OF THINGS PAST   3.30.2
SUMMONED   2
  UNTO MINE AID I SUMMON'D EV'RY $SENSE   2.29.2
  AND SUMMOND $ANGELS TO THYS BLESSED SIGHT   2.125.12
SUMS   2
  AND CROSSE MY CARES ERE GREATER SUMMES ARISE   1.1.12
  SO GREAT A SUMME OF SUMMES YET CAN'ST NOT LIVE+   3.4.8
SUN   56
  YOU OUT-CAST $EAGLETS, DAZELED WITH YOUR $SUNNE   1.3.10
  NO $SUNNE MY BLUSH AND ERROR HAD BEWRAID   1.7.7
  LOTHSOME THEIR DAIES, WHOM NO SUN EVER JOYD   1.26.6
  IN HORRORS SABLE CLOWDES SETS MY LIVES SUNNE   1.30.2
  MY LIVES SWEET SUNNE, MY DEAREST COMFORTS LIGHT   1.30.3
  WHICH NOW ARE MELTED BY THINE EYES BRIGHT SUN   1.32.7
  I WHO DID NEVER JOY IN OTHER $SUN   1.33.5
  AND WHILST THOU SPREADST UNTO THE RISING SUNNE   1.40.5
  CHEERES FOR A TIME, BUT TILL THE $SUNNE DOTH SHEW   1.50.3
  THERE WHERE MY $DELIA FAIRER THEN THE $SUNNE   1.53.5
  NEVER LET RISING $SUNNE APPROVE YOU LIERS   1.54.11
  WHICH STILL SHALT BE, AS LONG AS THERE IS $SUNNE   2.13.10
  YOUR $BEAUTIE IS THE HOT AND SPLEND'ROUS $SUNNE   2.16.5

```
DEVIS'D A $VESSELL TO RECEIVE THE $SUNNE                2.30.3
ON WHICH THE $SUNNE MIGHT BY REFLECTION BEAT            2.30.6
THY BLESSED $EYES, THE $SUNNE WHICH LIGHTS
                              THIS $FIRE                 2.30.9
BUT IT NO SOONER SAW MY $SUNNE APPEARE                  2.56.5
TO MY $SOULES $SUNNE, THOSE TWO $CELESTIALL
                              $EYES                      2.56.12
BEHOLD THE $CLOUDS WHICH HAVE ECLIPS'D MY $SUNNE        2.60.9
BUT THEY NO SOONER SAW MY $SUNNE APPEARE                2.103.5
HEAPE THINE OWN VERTUES SEASONED BY THEIR SUNNE         2.106.5
WHICH STILL SHALT BE AS LONG AS THERE IS $SUNNE         2.121.10
SO NEERE THYNE EYES CELESTIALL SUNNE ASPYRED            2.122.10
SUNNE OF THE WORLD, THOU HART REVYVING FIRE             2.123.8
THE GLORIOUS SUNNE WENT BLUSHING TO HIS BED             2.125.1
WHEN MY SOULES SUNNE FROM HER FAYRE $CABYNET            2.125.2
LEFT AS THAT SUNNE ALONE TO COMFORT US                  2.129.3
WHEN OUR WORLDS SUNNE IS VANISHT OUT OF SIGHT           2.129.4
OR EYES THAT HAVE BEHELD HER AS THEYR SUNNE             2.138.7
DECLYNING WITH THE SETTING OF MY SUNNE                  2.141.10
THE GOLDEN $SUNNE UPON HIS FIERY WHEELES                2.147.1
SUCH IS THE SUNNE, WHO GUIDES MY YOUTHFULL
                              SEASON                     2.147.13
BEHOLD THE $CLOWDES WHICH HAVE ECLIPS'D MY SUNNE        2.149.9
WHEN YOU $MINERVA IN THE SUNNE BEHOLD                   2.151.5
WITH $SUNNE AND $MOONE, WITH EARTH AND
                              SEAS RICH GEMS             3.21.6
ARE WINDOWES TO MY BREST, WHERE-THROUGH THE $SUN        3.24.11
EVEN SO MY $SUNNE ONE EARLY MORNE DID SHINE             3.33.9
SUNS OF THE WORLD MAY STAINE, WHEN HEAVENS
                              SUN STAINTEH               3.33.14
CLOUDES AND ECLIPSES STAINE BOTH $MOONE
                              AND $SUNNE                 3.35.3
AND SCARCELY GREETE ME WITH THAT SUNNE THINE EYE        3.49.6
EVEN OF FIVE HUNDRETH COURSES OF THE $SUNNE             3.59.6
FOR AS THE $SUN IS DAILY NEW AND OLD                    3.76.13
MY $MISTRES EYES ARE NOTHING LIKE THE $SUNNE            3.130.1
AND TRULY NOT THE MORNING $SUN OF $HEAVEN               3.132.5
THE SUNNE IT SELFE SEES NOT, TILL HEAVEN
                              CLEERES                    3.148.12
WHOSE FAIRE SKIN, BEAMY EYES, LIKE MORNING
                              SUN ON SNOW                4.8.9
IN HIGHEST WAY OF HEAV'N THE $SUNNE DID RIDE            4.22.1
THE $SUNNE WHICH OTHERS BURN'D, DID HER
                              BUT KISSE                  4.22.14
WHICH INWARD SUNNE TO $HEROICKE MINDE DISPLAIES         4.25.8
THAT INWARD SUNNE IN THINE EYES SHINETH SO              4.71.8
PRAY THAT MY SUNNE GO DOWNE WITH MEEKER
                              BEAMES TO BED              4.76.14
WHEN $SUN IS HID, CAN STARRES SUCH BEAMES
                              DISPLAY+                   4.88.6
AND THAT FAIRE YOU MY $SUNNE, THUS OVERSPRED            4.91.3
NIGHT BARD FROM $SUN, THOU FROM THY OWNE
                              SUNNE'S LIGHT              4.96.4
THAT WORMES SHOULD HAVE THEIR $SUN, AND
                              I WANT MINE                4.98.14
NOT TO THE $SUN.. FOR THEY DOO SHINE BY NIGHT           5.9.5
SUNBEAMS                      5
   THE $SUN-BEAMES SMOTHERED WITH IMMORTALL $SMOKE       2.55.6
   THE $SUN-BEAMES SMOTHERED WITH IMMORTALL SMOKE        2.102.6
   BY THOSE REFLECTING $SUN-BEAMES OF THY BEAUTIE        2.105.8
```

```
SUPPRESSED                    1
  ON BOTH SIDES THUS IS SIMPLE TRUTH SUPPREST        3.138.8
SURCEASE                      1
  BUT MINE NO PRICE NOR PRAYER MAY SURCEASE          5.11.14
SURCHARGED                    2
  WHEN THOU SURCHARG'D WITH BURTHEN OF THY YEERES    1.50.9
  MY HART SURCHARG'D WITH THOUGHTS, SIGHES
                          IN ABUNDANCE RAISE         2.133.9
SURE                         23
  YET SURE SHE CANNOT BUT MUST THINKE A PART         1.21.13
  STARRES SURE THEY ARE, WHOSE MOTIONS RULE DESIRES  1.34.5
  FIXT SURE THEY ARE, BUT WANDRING MAKE ME STRAY     1.34.11
  I AM SURE MY $SIGHES COME FROM A $HEART AS TRUE     2.27.9
  ROUZ'D FROM MY BREAST, HIS SURE AND SAFEST LAYRE   2.135.2
  GOE $BASTARD GOE, FOR SURE OF THENCE THOU ART       2.140.14
  FROM HANDS OF FALSEHOOD, IN SURE WARDS OF TRUST+    3.48.4
  OH SURE I AM THE WITS OF FORMER DAIES              3.59.13
  AND TO BE SURE THAT IS NOT FALSE I SWEARE          3.131.9
  RED $PORPHIR IS, WHICH LOCKE OF PEARLE MAKES SURE  4.9.6
  AND SURE AT LENGTH STOLNE GOODS DO COME TO LIGHT   4.15.11
  SURE YOU SAY WELL, YOUR WISDOME'S GOLDEN MINE      4.21.12
  AND IF THESE RULES DID FAILE, PROOFE MAKES
                          ME SURE                    4.26.12
  SURE, IF THAT LONG WITH $LOVE ACQUAINTED EYES      4.31.5
  SINCE THOU IN ME SO SURE A POWER DOEST KEEPE       4.32.5
  THAT VERTUOUS SOULE, SURE HEIRE OF HEAV'NLY
                          BLISSE                     4.52.7
  LOVE BY SURE PROOFE I MAY CALL THEE UNKIND         4.65.1
  'OR SO+' $MUCH LESSE.. '$HOW THEN+' $SURE
                          THUS IT IS                 4.74.13
  SURE THEY PREVAILE AS MUCH WITH ME, AS HE          4.106.12
  HAD SHE NOT SO DOON, SURE I HAD BENE SLAYNE        5.16.13
  FAYRE YE BE SURE, BUT CRUELL AND UNKIND            5.56.1
  FAYRE BE YE SURE, BUT PROUD AND PITTILESSE         5.56.5
  FAYRE BE YE SURE, BUT HARD AND OBSTINATE           5.56.9
SUREST                        3
  WHAT MOST I $SEEME, THAT SUREST AM I $NOT          2.62.8
  HER $CABLE BROKE, HER SUREST $ANCHOR LOST          2.134.10
  WHAT MOST I SEEME, THAT SUREST AM I NOT            2.150.8
SURETY-LIKE                   1
  HE LEARND BUT SURETIE-LIKE TO WRITE FOR ME         3.134.7
SURFEIT                       5
  WHILST YET MINE $EYES DOE SURFET WITH $DELIGHT     2.33.1
  AND YET I $SURFET IN THE GREATEST $DEARTH          2.62.12
  WHILST THUS MINE EYES DOE SURFET WITH DELIGHT      2.133.1
  AND YET I SURFET IN THE GREATEST DEARTH            2.150.12
  THUS DO I PINE AND SURFET DAY BY DAY               3.75.13
SURGEONS                      1
  BY $SURGEONS BEG'D, THEIR $ART ON HIM TO TRIE      2.50.4
SURLY                         1
  THEN YOU SHALL HEARE THE SURLY SULLEN BELL         3.71.2
SURMISE                       1
  AND ON JUST PROOFE SURMISE, ACCUMILATE             3.117.10
SURMOUNT                      1
  AS I ALL OTHER IN ALL WORTHS SURMOUNT              3.62.8
SURPASS                       1
  WHOSE FRUIT DOTH FARRE TH'$ESPERIAN TAST SURPASSE  4.82.6
SURPASSING                    1
  YEE WHOSE HIGH WORTHS SURPASSING PARAGON           5.66.5
```

SURPRISE   1
  WHEREWITH MY LIBERTY THOU DIDST SURPRIZE   1.14.2
SURVEY   2
  THE WHICH HE WILL NOT EV'RY HOWER SURVAY   3.52.3
  RISE RESTY $MUSE, MY LOVES SWEET FACE SURVAY   3.100.9
SURVEYED   1
  THEN HAD NO $CENSORS EYE THESE LINES SURVAID   1.7.5
SURVIVE   3
  STILL TO SURVIVE IN MY IMMORTALL $SONG   2.6.14
  IF THOU SURVIVE MY WELL CONTENTED DAIE   3.32.1
  OR YOU SURVIVE WHEN I IN EARTH AM ROTTEN   3.81.2
SURVIVED   1
  THAT BY THY FAME ALL FAME SHALL BE SURVIVED   2.104.14
SUSPECT   4
  WHEREIN NO SHEW GAVE CAUSE OF LEAST SUSPECT   1.31.7
  THE ORNAMENT OF BEAUTY IS SUSPECT   3.70.3
  IF SOME SUSPECT OF ILL MASKT NOT THY SHOW   3.70.13
  SUSPECT I MAY, YET NOT DIRECTLY TELL   3.144.10
SUSTAIN   5
  AND ALSO TO SUSTAYNE THY SELFE WITH FOOD   5.2.8
  FOR LACKING IT THEY CANNOT LYFE SUSTAYNE   5.35.5
  ENOUGH IT IS FOR ONE MAN TO SUSTAINE   5.46.13
  FOR LACKING IT, THEY CANNOT LYFE SUSTAYNE   5.83.5
  WITH LIGHT THEREOF I DOE MY SELFE SUSTAYNE   5.88.11
SWAGGERING   1
  STRAIGHTWAYES HE PLAY'S A SWAGG'RING $RUFFINS
                            PART   2.7.10
SWALLOWED   1
  PAST REASON HATED AS A SWOLLOWED BAYT   3.129.7
SWAM   1
  YET SWAM IN JOY, SUCH LOVE IN HER WAS SEENE   4.87.11
SWAN   1
  AND WITH THE $SWAN RECORD THY DYING SONG   2.139.7
SWANS   6
  OUR $FLOUDS-$QUEEN $THAMES, FOR $SHIPS
                      AND $SWANS IS CROWNED   2.32.1
  O BLESSED $BROOKE, WHOSE MILKE-WHITE $SWANS ADORE 2.53.3
  O BLESSED $BROOKE, WHOSE MILK-WHITE $SWANS ADORE   2.113.3
  OUR FLOODS-$QUEENE $THAMES, FOR SHYPS
                      AND $SWANS IS CROWNED   2.124.1
  BROADRED WITH BULS AND SWANS, POWDRED
                      WITH GOLDEN RAINE   4.6.6
  DUMBE $SWANNES, NOT CHATRING $PIES, DO
                      $LOVERS PROVE   4.54.13
SWART   1
  SO FLATTER I THE SWART COMPLEXIOND NIGHT   3.28.11
SWAY   4
  AND STRENGTH BY LIMPING SWAY DISABLED   3.66.8
  WITH INSUFFICIENCY MY HEART TO SWAY   3.150.2
  OF $ATLAS TYR'D, YOUR WISEDOME'S HEAV'NLY SWAY   4.51.8
  BUT AS SHE WILL, WHOSE WILL MY LIFE DOTH SWAY   5.46.7
SWAYEST   1
  WITH THY SWEET FINGERS WHEN THOU GENTLY SWAYST   3.128.3
SWEAR   16
  NOW DOE I SWEARE BY HEAVENS, BEFORE WE PART   2.140.3
  ALTHOUGH I SWEARE IT TO MY SELFE ALONE   3.131.8
  AND TO BE SURE THAT IS NOT FALSE I SWEARE   3.131.9
  THEN WILL I SWEARE BEAUTY HER SELFE IS BLACKE   3.132.13
  SWEARE TO THY BLIND SOULE THAT I WAS THY $WILL   3.136.2
  AND SWERE THAT BRIGHTNESSE DOTH NOT GRACE
                      THE DAY+   3.150.4

OR MADE THEM SWERE AGAINST THE THING THEY SEE	3.152.12
TO SWERE AGAINST THE TRUTH SO FOULE A LIE	3.152.14
I SWEARE, MY HEART SUCH CNE SHALL SHEW TC THEE	4.4.12
TO BLAZE THESE LAST, AND SWARE DEVOUTLY THEN	4.13.13
'WHAT HE+' SAY THEY OF ME, 'NOW I DARE SWEARE	4.54.7
AND THIS I SWEARE BY BLACKEST BROOKE OF HELL	4.74.7
AND I DO SWEARE EVEN BY THE SAME DELIGHT	4.82.13
IN TRUTH I SWEARE, I WISH NOT THERE SHOULD BE	4.90.7
THOUGH OFT HIMSELFE MY MATE-IN-ARMES HE SWARE	4.95.8
I SWEARE BY HER I LCVE AND LACKE, THAT I	4.105.5

SWEARING 1

BUT THOU ART TWICE FORSWCRNE TO ME LOVE SWEARING	3.152.2

SWEARS 2

BY $HELLISH $STYX (BY WHICH THE $THUND'RER SWEARES)	2.36.5
WHEN MY LOVE SWEARES THAT SHE IS MADE OF TRUTH	3.138.1

SWEAT 2

TROTTING HIS SUN-STEEDS TILL THE $PALFRAYS SWEAT	2.147.6
BUT THAT I BURNE MUCH MCRE IN BOYLING SWEAT	5.30.7

SWEATS 1

NATURE WITH CARE SWEATES FOR HER DARLING'S SAKE	4.101.12

SWEET 179

READE IT (SWEET MAIDE) THOUGH IT BE DONE BUT SLEIGHTLY	1.1.13
WITH FAIREST HAND, THE SWEET UNKINDEST $MAID	1.5.7
ALL MY LIVES SWEET CONSISTS IN HER ALONE	1.12.13
IF A SWEET LANGUISH WITH A CHAST DESIRE	1.15.2
T'$ARABIAN ODORS GIVE THY BREATHING SWEETE	1.19.6
AND THY SWEET VOICE GIVE BACK UNTO THE $SPHEARES	1.19.10
RAIGNE IN MY THOUGHTS FAIRE HAND, SWEETE EYE, RARE VOICE	1.28.1
MY LIVES SWEET SUNNE, MY DEAREST COMFORTS LIGHT	1.30.3
THEIR SWEET APPEARING STILL SUCH POWER INSPIRES	1.34.7
YOUR SWEET ASPECT CN HIM THAT HONOURS YOU	1.34.14
NOW JOY THY TIME BEFORE THY SWEET BE DONE	1.40.7
THINKE NOT (SWEET $DELIA) THIS SHALL BE THY SHAME	1.44.5
BEAUTIE (SWEET $LCVE) IS LIKE THE MORNING DEW	1.50.1
AH SPORT (SWEET $MAIDE) IN SEASON OF THESE YEARES	1.51.5
IN WHOSE DEARE $BCSOME, SWEET DELICIOUS $LOVE	2.4.5
BY THIS GOOD WICKED $SPIRIT, SWEET $ANGELL $DEVILL	2.20.14
THEN, SWEET $DESPAIRE, AWHILE HOLD UP THY HEAD	2.26.13
MY $TASTE BY HER SWEET $LIPS DRAWNE WITH $DELIGHT	2.29.7
WHERE, WITH SWEET $WOOD, LAYD CURIOUSLY BY $ART	2.30.5
ARDENS SWEET $ANKCR, LET THY GLORY BEE	2.32.13
WHERE SWEET $MYRRH-BREATHING $ZEPHIRE IN THE $SPRING	2.53.5
AND THOU, SWEET $ANKOR, ART MY $HELICON	2.53.14
THAT $SOULE (SWEET $MAID) WHICH SO HATH HONOR'D $THEE	2.55.11
AND WHEN THE $PLUMES WERE SUMM'D WITH SWEET DESIRE	2.56.9
READE HEERE (SWEET $MAYD) THE STORY OF MY WO	2.101.1
THAT SOULE (SWEET $MAIDE) WHICH SO HATH HONORED THEE	2.102.11
BUT NOW THEIR PLUMES FULL SUMD WITH SWEET DESIRE	2.103.9
WITH THOSE SWEET STRINGS STOLNE FROM THY GOLDEN HAYRE	2.104.2
STAY, STAY, SWEET $TIME, BEHOLD OR ERE THOU PASSE	2.107.1

```
GAVE MEE SWEET LOOKES WHEN AS I LEARNED WELL          2.111.4
WHERE SWEET $MYRH-BREATHING $ZEPHYRE IN
                              THE SPRING               2.113.5
AND THOU SWEET $ANKOR ART MY $HELICON                 2.113.14
MY SWEET, MY FAIRE, MY GOOD, MY BEST OF ALL           2.115.12
THIS EARTH OF THOSE SWEET $PROPHETS HATH BEREFT       2.119.6
ARDENS SWEET $ANKOR LET THY GLORY BE                  2.124.13
WHICH FROM HER LYPS EXHALD REFINED SWEET              2.125.6
THAT I MAY BLESSE MEE AT THY SWEET ARISE              2.129.14
WHO WITH THY SWEET ALURING HARMONY                    2.130.10
SWEETE SLEEPE SO ARM'D WITH $BEAUTIES
                              ARROWES DARTING          2.136.1
THEN SWEET $DISPAIRE, AWHILE HOLD UP THY HEAD         2.137.13
BEGOT BY FANCY, ON SWEET HOPE EXHORTIVE               2.141.2
LET HEAVENS WITHDRAW THEIR SWEET $AMBROZIAN
                              BREATH                   2.145.11
SWEET SECRECIE, WHAT TONGUE CAN TELL THY WORTH+       2.146.1
TILL $VIRGINS SMYLES DOE SOUND HIS SWEET RETEERE      2.147.8
CROSSING SWEET NATURE BY UNRULY WILL                  2.147.12
THE SWEET OF $EDEN, TO HER BREATHES PERFUME           2.148.6
WHEN $DORUS SINGS HIS SWEET $PAMELAS LOVE             2.151.10
THY SELFE THY FOE, TO THY SWEET SELFE TOO CRUELL      3.1.8
THOU OF THY SELFE THY SWEET SELFE DOST DECEAVE        3.4.10
LEESE BUT THEIR SHOW, THEIR SUBSTANCE
                         STILL LIVES SWEET             3.5.14
MAKE SWEET SOME VIALL., TREASURE THOU SOME PLACE      3.6.3
MARKE HOW ONE STRING SWEET HUSBAND TO AN OTHER        3.8.9
AND YOUR SWEET SEMBLANCE TO SOME OTHER GIVE           3.13.4
WHEN YOUR SWEET ISSUE YOUR SWEET FORME
                         SHOULD BEARE                  3.13.8
WHEN YOUR SWEET ISSUE YOUR SWEET FORME
                         SHOULD BEARE                  3.13.8
AND YOU MUST LIVE DRAWNE BY YOUR OWNE
                         SWEET SKILL                   3.16.14
AND MAKE THE EARTH DEVOURE HER OWNE SWEET BROOD       3.19.2
TO SHOW ME WORTHY OF THEIR SWEET RESPECT              3.26.12
FOR THY SWEET LOVE REMEMBRED SUCH WELTH BRINGS        3.29.13
WHEN TO THE $SESSIONS OF SWEET SILENT THOUGHT         3.30.1
TO THAT SWEET THEEFE WHICH SOURELY ROBS FROM ME       3.35.14
YET DOTH IT STEALE SWEET HOURES FROM LOVES
                         DELIGHT                       3.36.8
THINE OWNE SWEET ARGUMENT, TO EXCELLENT               3.38.3
WERE IT NOT THY SOURE LEISURE GAVE SWEET LEAVE        3.39.10
SWEETE FLATTERY, THEN SHE LOVES BUT ME ALONE          3.42.14
CAN BRING HIM TO HIS SWEET UP-LOCKED TREASURE         3.52.2
BY THAT SWEET ORNAMENT WHICH TRUTH DOTH GIVE          3.54.2
FOR THAT SWEET ODOR, WHICH DOTH IN IT LIVE            3.54.4
DIE TO THEMSELVES. $SWEET $ROSES DOE NOT SO           3.54.11
OF THEIR SWEET DEATHES, ARE SWEETEST ODORS MADE       3.54.12
SWEET LOVE RENEW THY FORCE, BE IT NOT SAID            3.56.1
MY SWEET LOVES BEAUTY, THOUGH MY LOVERS LIFE          3.63.12
THAT I IN YOUR SWEET THOUGHTS WOULD BE FORGOT         3.71.7
BARE RN'WD QUIERS, WHERE LATE THE SWEET
                         BIRDS SANG                    3.73.4
OR AS SWEET SEASON'D SHEWERS ARE TO THE GROUND        3.75.2
O KNOW SWEET LOVE I ALWAIES WRITE OF YOU              3.76.9
AND $ARTS WITH THY SWEETE GRACES GRACED BE            3.78.12
I GRANT (SWEET LOVE) THY LOVELY ARGUMENT              3.79.5
THY SWEET BELOVED NAME NO MORE SHALL DWELL            3.89.10
THAT IN THY FACE SWEET LOVE SHOULD EVER DWELL         3.93.10
```

```
IF THY SWEET VERTUE ANSWERE NOT THY SHOW            3.93.14
THE SOMMERS FLOWRE IS TO THE SOMMER SWEET           3.94.9
HOW SWEET AND LOVELY DOST THOU MAKE THE SHAME       3.95.1
YET NOR THE LAIES OF BIRDS, NOR THE SWEET SMELL     3.98.5
THEY WEARE BUT SWEET, BUT FIGURES OF DELIGHT        3.98.11
SWEET THEEFE WHENCE DIDST THOU STEALE
                        THY SWEET THAT SMELS         3.99.2
SWEET THEEFE WHENCE DIDST THOU STEALE
                        THY SWEET THAT SMELS         3.99.2
BUT SWEET, OR CULLER IT HAD STOLNE FROM THEE        3.99.15
RISE RESTY $MUSE, MY LOVES SWEET FACE SURVAY        3.100.9
SO YOUR SWEETE HEW, WHICH ME THINKES STILL
                        DOTH STAND                  3.104.11
THEN IN THE BLAZON OF SWEET BEAUTIES BEST           3.106.5
NOTHING SWEET BOY, BUT YET LIKE PRAYERS DIVINE      3.108.5
SUCH CHERUBINES AS YOUR SWEET SELFE RESEMBLE        3.114.6
FOR COMPOUND SWEET., $FORGOING SIMPLE SAVOR         3.125.7
THY LOVERS WITHERING, AS THY SWEET SELFE GROW'ST    3.126.4
SWEET BEAUTY HATH NO NAME NO HOLY BOURE             3.127.7
WITH THY SWEET FINGERS WHEN THOU GENTLY SWAYST      3.128.3
TO THY SWEET WILL MAKING ADDITION THUS              3.135.4
THUS FARRE FOR LOVE, MY LOVE-SUTE SWEET FULLFILL    3.136.4
THAT NOTHING ME, A SOME-THING SWEET TO THEE         3.136.12
CHIDING THAT TONGUE THAT EVER SWEET                 3.145.6
LEAST GUILTY OF MY FAULTS THY SWEET SELFE PROVE     3.151.4
THAT HER SWEETE BREATH MAKES OFT THY FLAMES
                        TO RISE                      4.12.4
AND EVERIE FLOURE, NOT SWEET PERHAPS,
                        WHICH GROWES                 4.15.3
AS THAT SWEETE BLACKE WHICH VAILES THE
                        HEAV'NLY EYE                 4.20.7
LET HIM, DEPRIVED OF SWEET BUT UNFELT JOYES         4.24.12
SWEET $STELLA'S IMAGE I DO STEALE TO MEE'           4.32.14
WITH SO SWEETE VOICE, AND BY SWEETE $NATURE SO      4.36.9
WITH SO SWEETE VOICE, AND BY SWEETE $NATURE SO      4.36.9
IN ALL SWEETE STRATAGEMS SWEETE $ARTE CAN SHOW      4.36.11
IN ALL SWEETE STRATAGEMS SWEETE $ARTE CAN SHOW      4.36.11
AND OF SOME SENT FROM THAT SWEET ENEMIE $FRAUNCE    4.41.4
FAIRE EYES, SWEET LIPS, DEARE HEART, THAT
                        FOOLISH I                    4.43.1
HER HEART, SWEETE HEART, IS OF NO $TYGRE'S KIND     4.44.4
DEARE $KILLER, SPARE NOT THY SWEET CRUELL SHOT      4.48.13
BECAUSE THEIR FOREFRONT BARE SWEET $STELLA'S
                        NAME                         4.50.14
AND IS EVEN IRKT THAT SO SWEET $COMEDIE             4.51.13
MIGHT WINNE SOME GRACE IN YOUR SWEET SKILL ARRAID   4.55.4
SO SWEETE SOUNDS STRAIGHT MINE EARE AND
                        HEART DO HIT                 4.55.13
BUT THEM (SO SWEETE IS SHE) MOST SWEETLY SING       4.57.10
STELLA'S SWEETE BREATH THE SAME TO ME DID REED      4.58.11
BUT THIS AT LAST IS HER SWEET BREATH'D DEFENCE      4.61.4
SWEET SAID THAT I TRUE LOVE IN HER SHOULD FIND      4.62.4
BUT $GRAMMER'S FORCE WITH SWEET SUCCESSE
                        CONFIRME                     4.63.11
AND ALL IN VAINE, FOR WHILE THY BREATH MOST SWEET   4.68.9
I MUST NO MORE IN THY SWEET PASSIONS LIE            4.72.7
SWEET, IT WAS SAUCIE $LOVE, NOT HUMBLE I            4.73.8
MY LIPS ARE SWEET, INSPIRED WITH $STELLA'S KISSE    4.74.14
THAT CONVERSATION SWEET, WHERE SUCH HIGH
                        COMFORTS BE                  4.77.10
```

```
SWEET KISSE, THY SWEETS I FAINE WOULD
                        SWEETLY ENDITE                4.79.1
SWEET SWELLING LIP, WELL MAIST THOU SWELL
                        IN PRIDE                      4.80.1
SWEET LIP, YOU TEACH MY MOUTH WITH ONE
                        SWEET KISSE                   4.80.14
SWEET LIP, YOU TEACH MY MOUTH WITH ONE
                        SWEET KISSE                   4.80.14
SWEET GARD'N $NYMPH, WHICH KEEPES THE
                        $CHERRIE TREE                 4.82.5
OR IF I NEEDS (SWEET $JUDGE) MUST TORMENTS HAVE       4.86.11
AND NOTHING THEN THE CAUSE MORE SWEET COULD BE        4.87.13
MILKE HANDS, ROSE CHEEKS, OR LIPS MORE
                        SWEET, MORE RED               4.91.7
WITH SWEETE SOFT SHADES THOU OFT INVITEST ME          4.98.5
BUT WHEN BIRDS CHARME, AND THAT SWEETE
                        AIRE, WHICH IS                4.99.9
WHO MAY WITH CHARME OF CONVERSATION SWEETE            4.106.10
SWEETE, FOR A WHILE GIVE RESPITE TO MY HART           4.107.5
THROUGH SWEET ILLUSION CF HER LOOKES DELIGHT          5.16.4
THE SWEET EYE-GLAUNCES, THAT LIKE ARROWES GLIDE       5.17.9
THEIR ANTHEMES SWEET DEVIZED OF LOVES PRAYSE          5.19.6
FOR MY SWEET $SAYNT SOME SERVICE FIT WILL FIND        5.22.4
SWEET IS THE $ROSE, BUT GROWES UPON A BRERE           5.26.1
SWEET IS THE $JUNIPERE, BUT SHARPE HIS BOUGH          5.26.2
SWEET IS THE $EGLANTINE, BUT PRICKETH NERE            5.26.3
SWEET IS THE FIRBLCOME, BUT HIS BRAUNCHES ROUGH       5.26.4
SWEET IS THE $CYPRESSE, BUT HIS RYND IS TOUGH         5.26.5
SWEET IS THE NUT, BUT BITTER IS HIS PILL              5.26.6
SWEET IS THE BROOME-FLOWRE, BUT YET SOWRE ENCUGH      5.26.7
AND SWEET IS $MOLY, BUT HIS ROOT IS ILL               5.26.8
SO EVERY SWEET WITH SOURE IS TEMPRED STILL            5.26.9
WITH SWEET INFUSION, AND PUT YOU IN MIND              5.28.7
THROUGH SWEET ALLUREMENT OF HER LOVELY HEW            5.31.10
THROUGH THE SWEET MUSICK WHICH HIS HARP DID MAKE      5.38.3
SWEET SMILE, THE DAUGHTER OF THE $QUEENE OF LOVE      5.39.1
SWEET IS THY VERTUE AS THY SELFE SWEET ART            5.39.5
SWEET IS THY VERTUE AS THY SELFE SWEET ART            5.39.5
MORE SWEET THAN $NECTAR OR $AMBROSIALL MEAT           5.39.13
BUT SUCH SWEET CORDIALLS PASSE $PHYSITIONS ART        5.50.12
SWEET WARRIOUR WHEN SHALL I HAVE PEACE WITH YOU+      5.57.1
THE JOYOUS SAFETY CF SO SWEET A REST                  5.63.10
ME SEEMD I SMELT A GARDIN OF SWEET FLOWRES            5.64.2
BUT HER SWEET ODOUR DID THEM ALL EXCELL               5.64.14
SWEET BE THE BANDS, THE WHICH TRUE LOVE COTH TYE      5.65.5
SEEKES WITH SWEET PEACE TO SALVE EACH
                        OTHERS WOUND                  5.65.12
MAKE HAST THEREFORE SWEET LOVE, WHILEST
                        IT IS PRIME                   5.70.13
SO SWEET YOUR PRISCN YOU IN TIME SHALL PROVE          5.71.11
DRAWNE WITH SWEET PLEASURES BAYT, IT BACK
                        DOTH FLY                      5.72.7
ON THE SWEET SPOYLE OF BEAUTIE THEY DID PRAY          5.76.8
SWEET THOUGHTS I ENVY YCUR SO HAPPY REST              5.76.13
EXCEEDING SWEET, YET VOYD OF SINFULL VICE             5.77.9
SWEET FRUIT OF PLEASURE BROUGHT FROM PARADICE         5.77.11
TO SPORT MY MUSE AND SING MY LOVES SWEET PRAISE       5.80.10
AND MY GLAD MOUTH WITH HER SWEET PRAYSES FILL         5.85.12
IN MY SWEET PEACE SUCH BREACHES TO HAVE BRED          5.86.12
WHOSE SWEET ASPECT BOTH $GOD AND MAN CAN MOVE         5.89.11
```

```
SWEETEN                    1
   IF HER LIPS DAIGND TO SWEETEN MY POORE NAME        4.92.13
SWEETENED                  1
   WHERE BE THOSE $ROSES GONE, WHICH SWEETNED
                           SO OUR EYES+                4.102.1
SWEETENER                  2
   WHICH EVEN OF SWEETNESSE SWEETEST SWEETNER ART      4.79.2
   SWEETNER OF MUSICKE, WISEDOME'S BEAUTIFIER          4.80.6
SWEETENING                 1
   BREATHING ALL BLISSE AND SWEETNING TO THE HEART     4.81.3
SWEETEST                   22
   OF HER, WHOSE SWEETEST GRACE I DO ADORE             1.13.10
   THE SWEETEST SACRIFICE MY YOUTH CAN MAKE+           1.17.4
   BUT SINCE THE SWEETEST ROOTE YEELDS FRUITE
                           SO SOWRE                    1.26.9
   AND WHERE THE SWEETEST BLOSSOMES FIRST APPEARES     1.51.7
   A WAYLING DESCANT ON THE SWEETEST GROUND            1.57.7
   O SWEETEST $SHADOW, HOW THOU SERV'ST MY TURNE       2.13.9
   O SWEETEST SHADOW, HOW THOU SERV'ST MY TURNE        2.121.9
   O SWEET'ST REVENGE THAT ERE THE HEAVENS GAVE        2.139.6
   AND LOATHSOME CANKER LIVES IN SWEETEST BUD          3.35.4
   OF THEIR SWEET DEATHES, ARE SWEETEST ODORS MADE     3.54.12
   A $CROW THAT FLIES IN HEAVENS SWEETEST AYRE         3.70.4
   FOR $CANKER VICE THE SWEETEST BUDS DOTH LOVE        3.70.7
   FOR SWEETEST THINGS TURNE SOWREST BY THEIR
                           DEEDES                      3.94.13
   BUT SLAVE TO SLAVERY MY SWEET'ST FRIEND MUST BE     3.133.4
   TO SOME A SWEETEST PLAINT, A SWEETEST
                           STILE AFFORDS               4.6.9
   TO SOME A SWEETEST PLAINT, A SWEETEST
                           STILE AFFORDS               4.6.9
   IN SWEETEST STRENGTH, SO SWEETLY SKILD WITHALL      4.36.10
   TAKE THOU OF ME SMOOTH PILLOWES, SWEETEST BED       4.39.9
   NOT BY RUDE FORCE, BUT SWEETEST SOVERAIGNTIE        4.71.6
   WHICH EVEN OF SWEETNESSE SWEETEST SWEETNER ART      4.79.2
   I SAW THAT SIGHES HER SWEETEST LIPS DID PART        4.87.7
   THEY DID THEMSELVES (O SWEETEST PRISON) TWINE       4.103.8
SWEET-FAIR                 1
   MOST SWEET-FAIRE, MOST FAIRE-SWEET, DO NOT ALAS     4.82.7
SWEET-FAVOR                1
   THE MOST SWEET-FAVOR OR DEFORMEDST CREATURE         3.113.10
SWEETLY                    8
   THEY DO BUT SWEETLY CHIDE THEE, WHO CONFOUNDS       3.8.7
   WHICH TIME AND THOUGHTS SO SWEETLY DOST DECEIVE     3.39.12
   TO MORTALL EYES MIGHT SWEETLY SHINE IN HER          4.25.11
   IN SWEETEST STRENGTH, SO SWEETLY SKILD WITHALL      4.36.10
   BUT THEM (SO SWEETE IS SHE) MOST SWEETLY SING       4.57.10
   MAKES ME FALL FROM HER SIGHT, THEN SWEETLY SHE      4.60.6
   SWEET KISSE, THY SWEETS I FAINE WOULD
                           SWEETLY ENDITE              4.79.1
   WHEN ON EACH EYELID SWEETLY DOE APPEARE             5.40.3
SWEETNESS                  6
   WITH SO RARE SWEETNESSE ALL THE $HEAV'NS
                           PERFUMING                   2.16.10
   WITH THINE OWNE SWEETNES AL THE HEAVENS
                           PERFUMING                   2.106.10
   THY LOOKES SHOULD NOTHING THENCE, BUT
                           SWEETNESSE TELL             3.93.12
   EVEN SO BEING FULL OF YOUR NERE CLOYING
                           SWEETNESSE                  3.118.5
```

```
WHICH EVEN OF SWEETNESSE SWEETEST SWEETNER ART     4.79.2
SWEETNESSE, THAT BREATHES AND PANTS AS
                             OFT AS SHE              4.101.2
SWEETS                    11
   SUBSTRACTING, SET MY $SWEETS UNTO MY $SOWRES      2.3.7
   AND IN SUBSTRACTING, SET MY SWEETS UNTO
                             MY SOWRES               2.110.7
   SWEETS WITH SWEETS WARRE NOT, JOY DELIGHTS IN JOY  3.8.2
   SWEETS WITH SWEETS WARRE NOT, JOY DELIGHTS IN JOY  3.8.2
   SINCE SWEETS AND BEAUTIES DO THEM-SELVES FORSAKE  3.12.11
   TO THE WIDE WORLD AND ALL HER FADING SWEETS       3.19.7
   OH IN WHAT SWEETS DOEST THOU THY SINNES INCLOSE   3.95.4
   AND SWEETS GROWNE COMMON LOOSE THEIR DEARE
                             DELIGHT                 3.102.12
   SO SWEETS MY PAINES, THAT MY PAINES ME REJOYCE    4.57.14
   SWEET KISSE, THY SWEETS I FAINE WOULD
                             SWEETLY ENDITE          4.79.1
   LET BREATH SUCKE UP THOSE SWEETES, LET
                             ARMES EMBRACE           4.85.12
SWELL                     4
   THAT THOSE LIPS SWELL, SO FULL OF THEE THEY BEE   4.12.3
   MY MOUTH DOTH WATER, AND MY BREAST DOTH SWELL     4.37.1
   BUT THEY DO SWELL AND STRUGGLE FORTH OF ME        4.50.3
   SWEET SWELLING LIP, WELL MAIST THOU SWELL
                             IN PRIDE                4.80.1
SWELLING                  2
   SO IN MY SWELLING BREAST THAT ONLY I              4.27.7
   SWEET SWELLING LIP, WELL MAIST THOU SWELL
                             IN PRIDE                4.80.1
SWERVE                    1
   OUGHT TO BE KING, FROM WHOSE RULES WHO DO SWERVE  4.5.3
SWERVING                  1
   AND SO MY PATTENT BACK AGAINE IS SWERVING         3.87.8
SWIFT                     6
   SWIFT SPEEDY $TIME, FEATHRED WITH FLYING HOURES   1.39.11
   THESE PRESENT ABSENT WITH SWIFT MOTION SLIDE      3.45.4
   BY THOSE SWIFT MESSENGERS RETURN'D FROM THEE      3.45.10
   WHEN SWIFT EXTREMITY CAN SEEME BUT SLOW           3.51.6
   OR WHAT STRONG HAND CAN HOLD HIS SWIFT
                             FOOTE BACK              3.65.11
   SETS DOWNE HER BABE AND MAKES ALL SWIFT DISPATCH  3.143.3
SWIFT-FOOTED              1
   AND DO WHAT ERE THOU WILT SWIFT-FOOTED TIME       3.19.6
SWIFT-WINGED              1
   OR MY SWIFT-WINGED $MUSE TYRED BY TOO
                             HIE FLYING              2.117.10
SWORD                     3
   NOR $MARS HIS SWORD, NOR WARRES QUICK
                             FIRE SHALL BURNE        3.55.7
   WITH SWORD OF WIT, GIVING WOUNDS OF DISPRAISE     4.10.10
   THAT $BALLANCE WEIGH'D WHAT SWORD DID
                             LATE OBTAINE            4.75.8
SWORN                     4
   FOR I HAVE SWORNE THEE FAIRE, AND THOUGHT
                             THEE BRIGHT             3.147.13
   FOR I HAVE SWORNE DEEPE OTHES OF THY DEEPE
                             KINDNESSE               3.152.9
   FOR I HAVE SWORNE THEE FAIRE.. MORE PERJURDE
                             EYE                     3.152.13
   WHERE $CUPID IS SWORNE PAGE TO $CHASTITY+         4.35.8
```

SYMPATHIZED   1
   THOU TRULY FAIRE, WERT TRULY SIMPATHIZDE   3.82.11
SYMTOMAS   1
   AND YOU MY SIGHES, $SYMTOMAS OF MY WOE   2.141.5
TABLE   5
   I FIGURDE ON THE TABLE OF MINE HART   1.13.6
   WITH $SIGHES AND $TEARES STILL FURNISHING
                  HIS $TABLE   2.23.7
   THY BEAUTIES FORME IN TABLE OF MY HEART   3.24.2
   A GOODLY TABLE OF PURE YVORY   5.77.2
   HER BREST THAT TABLE WAS SO RICHLY SPREDD   5.77.13
TABLES   2
   TTHY GUIFT,, THY TABLES, ARE WITHIN MY BRAINE   3.122.1
   TO TRUST THOSE TABLES THAT RECEAVE THEE MORE   3.122.12
TACKLINGS   1
   SEE HOW HER SAYLES BE RENT, HER TACKLINGS WORNE 2.134.9
TAGUS   1
   SOME $GANGES, $ISTER, AND OF $TAGUS TELL   2.120.9
TAKE   48
   THEN TAKE THIS PICTURE WHICH I HERE PRESENT THEE   1.42.5
   WHICH THERE IN ORDER TAKE THEIR SEVERALL PLACES   2.4.4
   AND LET ME TAKE MY SELFE WHAT I DOE CRAVE   2.5.12
   GIVE $ME MY $SELFE, AND TAKE YOUR $SELFE AGAINE   2.11.9
   THAT TAKING WHAT IS $MINE, WITH $ME I TAKE $YOU   2.11.12
   WHICH FROM ABOVE HE CRAFTILY DID TAKE   2.14.6
   WITH GREATER $TORMENTS, THEN IT $ME DOTH TAKE   2.20.7
   THENCE TAKE YOU $WING UNTO THE $ORCADES   2.25.6
   I THAT THUS TAKE, OR THEY THAT THUS REFUSE   2.28.11
   TO TAKE ALL $MINE, AND GIVE ME NONE AGAINE+   2.52.2
   PLAY NOT THE $TYRANT, BUT TAKE SOME $REMORSE   2.52.5
   AND FOR ONE PIECE OF $THINE, MY WHOLE HEART TAKE   2.52.8
   MY HALFE-SLAINE HART SHALL TAKE REVENGE ON THEE   2.140.4
   UNLESSE THOU TAKE THAT HONOUR FROM THY NAME   3.36.12
   TAKE ALL MY COMFORT OF THY WORTH AND TRUTH   3.37.4
   TAKE ALL MY LOVES, MY LOVE, YEA TAKE THEM ALL   3.40.1
   TAKE ALL MY LOVES, MY LOVE, YEA TAKE THEM ALL   3.40.1
   THAT $TIME WILL COME AND TAKE MY LOVE AWAY   3.64.12
   WHICH BY AND BY BLACKE NIGHT DOTH TAKE AWAY   3.73.7
   TO TAKE A NEW ACQUAINTANCE OF THY MINDE   3.77.12
   FROM HENCE YOUR MEMORY DEATH CANNOT TAKE   3.81.3
   WRETCHED IN THIS ALONE, THAT THOU MAIST TAKE   3.91.13
   TAKE HEED (DEARE HEART) OF THIS LARGE PRIVILEDGE   3.95.13
   AND TAKE THOU MY OBLACION, POORE BUT FREE   3.125.10
   THE STATUTE OF THY BEAUTY THOU WILT TAKE   3.134.9
   YET WHAT THE BEST IS, TAKE THE WORST TO BE   3.137.4
   THAT THE DEARE $SHE MIGHT TAKE SOME PLEASURE
                  OF MY PAINE   4.1.2
   VERTUE ALAS, NOW LET ME TAKE SOME REST   4.4.1
   BUT SHE MOST FAIRE, MOST COLD, MADE HIM
             THENCE TAKE HIS FLIGHT   4.8.12
   YOU TAKE WRONG WAIES, THOSE FAR-FET HELPES
                  BE SUCH   4.15.9
   I SEE AND YET NO GREATER SOROW TAKE   4.18.13
   WITH ME THOSE PAINES FOR $GOD'S SAKE DO NOT TAKE   4.28.3
   TAKE THOU OF ME SMOOTH PILLOWES, SWEETEST BED   4.39.9
   OTHERS, BECAUSE OF BOTH SIDES I DO TAKE   4.41.9
   WHAT, DOST THOU THINKE THAT I CAN EVER TAKE   4.56.10
   WILL SHE TAKE TIME, BEFORE ALL WRACKED BE+   4.67.4
   THIS REALME OF BLISSE, WHILE VERTUOUS
                  COURSE I TAKE   4.69.13

```
TEACHING THE MEANE, AT ONCE TO TAKE AND GIVE          4.79.9
THOU BUT OF ALL THE KINGLY $TRIBUTE TAKE              4.85.14
WITHOUT MY PLUMES FROM OTHERS' WINGS I TAKE           4.90.11
THAT THOU OF THEM MAYST MIGHTIE VENGEANCE TAKE        5.10.8
TAKE HEED THEREFORE, MYNE EYES, HOW YE DOE STARE      5.37.9
AND TAKE DELIGHT T'ENCREASE A WRETCHES WOE            5.41.7
BUT WHEN IN HAND MY TUNELESSE HARP I TAKE             5.44.9
THAT THEY TAKE PLEASURE IN HER CRUELL PLAY            5.47.11
THAT OF HER PRESENS I MY MEED MAY TAKE                5.52.14
UNLESSE SHE DOE HIM BY THE FORELOCK TAKE              5.70.8
DOE YOU HIM TAKE, AND IN YOUR BOSOME BRIGHT           5.73.9
```
TAKEN   4
```
OF MINE AFFECTIONS TAKEN BY HER EIES                  1.22.14
WHOSE WORTHS UNKNOWNE, ALTHOUGH HIS HIGTH
                                    BE TAKEN          3.116.8
AND I A TYRANT HAVE NO LEASURE TAKEN                  3.120.7
ME FROM MY SELFE THY CRUELL EYE HATH TAKEN            3.133.5
```
TAKER   1
```
ON PURPOSE LAYD TO MAKE THE TAKER MAD                 3.129.8
```
TAKES   8
```
THE $BASILISKE HIS NATURE TAKES FROM THEE             2.130.5
THEN TO THE $TROPICKE TAKES HIS FULL $CAREERE         2.147.5
SAVE BREED TO BRAVE HIM, WHEN HE TAKES
                                    THEE HENCE        3.12.14
AS HE TAKES FROM YOU, I INGRAFT YOU NEW               3.15.14
AS A DECREPIT FATHER TAKES DELIGHT                    3.37.1
LOVE OF HER SELFE, TAKES $STELLA'S SHAPE,
                                    THAT SHE          4.25.10
THAT IN THE $MANAGE MYSELFE TAKES DELIGHT             4.49.14
TAKES IN THAT SAD HUE, WHICH WITH TH'INWARD NIGHT     4.99.7
```
TAKETH   1
```
BUT TAKETH GLORY IN HER CRUELNESSE                    5.20.12
```
TAKING   5
```
TAKING MY $PENNE, WITH $WORDS TO CAST MY $WOE         2.3.1
THAT TAKING WHAT IS $MINE, WITH $ME I TAKE $YOU       2.11.12
WHICH TAKING THENCE, YOU HAVE ESCAP'D AWAY            2.14.11
OFT TAKING PEN IN HAND, WITH WORDS TO
                                    CAST MY WOES      2.110.1
THEN THINKE NOT LONG IN TAKING LITLE PAINE            5.6.13
```
TALE   1
```
I AM NOT I, PITIE THE TALE OF ME                      4.45.14
```
TALENTS   1
```
WHOSE TALENTS HELD YOUNG $GANIMED ABOVE               4.13.4
```
TALES   1
```
SOME ONE HIS SONG IN $JOVE, AND $JOVE'S
                          STRANGE TALES ATTIRES       4.6.5
```
TALK   2
```
WHAT TALKE I OF A $HEART, WHEN THOU HAST NONE+        2.52.13
WHEREOF, WITH WHOM, HOW OFTEN DID SHE TALKE           4.92.11
```
TALKING   1
```
THUS TALKING IDLY IN THIS $BEDLAM FIT                 2.9.9
```
TALL   1
```
HE OF TALL BUILDING, AND OF GOODLY PRIDE              3.80.12
```
TALLIES   1
```
NOR NEED I TALLIES THY DEARE LOVE TO SKORE            3.122.10
```
TAME   6
```
COTSWOLD COMMENDS HER $ISIS TO THE $TAME              2.32.9
COTSWOOLD COMMENDS HER $ISIS AND HER $TAME            2.124.9
AND PATIENCE TAME, TO SUFFERANCE BIDE EACH CHECK      3.58.7
THAT $PLATO I READ FOR NOUGHT, BUT IF HE TAME         4.21.5
```

WHEREWITH MY FATHER ONCE MADE IT HALFE TAME   4.30.10
AND GAIN'D BY $MARS, COULD YET MAD $MARS SO TAME   4.75.7
TAN   1
TAN SACRED BEAUTIE, BLUNT THE SHARP'ST INTENTS   3.115.7
TANNED   1
BEATED AND CHOPT WITH TAND ANTIQUITIE   3.62.10
TANTAL'S   1
AND DAMNING THEIR OWNE SELVES TO $TANTAL'S SMART   4.24.3
TARRY   1
FAINT COWARD JOY NO LONGER TARRY DARE   4.95.5
TASK   1
O LEAST THE WORLD SHOULD TASKE YOU TO RECITE   3.72.1
TASTE   10
MY $TASTE BY HER SWEET $LIPS DRAWNE WITH $DELIGHT   2.29.7
DIE, DIE, MY SOULE, AND NEVER TASTE OF JOY   2.139.1
BY WILFULL TASTE OF WHAT THY SELFE REFUSEST   3.40.8
AND OF THIS BOOKE, THIS LEARNING MAIST THOU TASTE   3.77.4
BUT IN THE ONSET COME, SO STALL I TASTE   3.90.11
NOR TASTE, NOR SMELL, DESIRE TO BE INVITED   3.141.7
THIS SOWRE-BREATH'D MATE TAST OF THOSE
                              SUGRED LIPS   4.59.11
WHOSE FRUIT DOTH FARRE TH'$ESPERIAN TAST SURPASSE   4.82.6
WITH NO WORSE CURSE THEN ABSENCE MAKES ME TAST   4.105.14
THAT MANY SOUGHT YET NONE COULD EVER TASTE   5.77.10
TAUGHT   14
AND KNOWING MORE THEN EVER HATH BEENE TAUGHT   2.34.3
THINE EYES TAUGHT MEE THE $ALPHABET OF LOVE   2.111.1
MY LOVES $SCHOOLE-MISTRIS NOW HATH TAUGHT ME SO   2.111.13
OR EVER JOY EXPRESSE, WHAT PERFECT JOY
                              HATH TAUGHT   2.117.3
TILL HE HIMSELFE THYS $EAGLES ART HAD TAUGHT   2.122.8
RUINE HATH TAUGHT ME THUS TO RUMINATE   3.64.11
THINE EYES, THAT TAUGHT THE DUMBE ON HIGH TO SING   3.78.5
WAS IT HIS SPIRIT, BY SPIRITS TAUGHT TO WRITE   3.86.5
AND THAT YOUR LOVE TAUGHT IT THIS $ALCUMIE+   3.114.4
AND TOUGHT IT THUS A NEW TO GREETE   3.145.8
WHO TAUGHT THEE HOW TO MAKE ME LOVE THEE MORE   3.150.9
TILL THAT HER BLUSH TAUGHT ME MY SHAME TO SEE   4.53.14
VENUS IS TAUGHT WITH $DIAN'S WINGS TO FLIE   4.72.6
LOVE IS THE LESSON WHICH THE $LORD US TAUGHT   5.68.14
TAX   1
AND TAXE MY $MUSE WITH THIS FANTASTICKE $GRACE   2.31.2
TAXETH   2
STRAIGHT TAXETH $REASON, WANTING TO INVENT   2.38.7
STRAIGHT TAXETH $REASON, WANTING TO INVENT   2.131.7
TEACH   10
SHOULD TEACH THE WORLD TO KNOW THE WONDER
                              THAT 1 PROVE   2.117.14
THAT LIFE (I MEANE) WHICH DOTH $RELIGION TEACH   2.119.13
DOTH TEACH THAT EASE AND THAT REPOSE TO SAY   3.50.3
THEN DO THY OFFICE $MUSE, I TEACH THEE HOW   3.101.13
IF I MIGHT TEACH THEE WITTE BETTER IT WEARE   3.140.5
WHICH IN HER FACE TEACH VERTUE, I COULD BROOKE   4.56.6
SWEET LIP, YOU TEACH MY MOUTH WITH ONE
                              SWEET KISSE   4.80.14
YOU STOP MY TOUNG, AND TEACH MY HART TO SPEAKE   5.8.10
THUS DOTH SHE TRAINE AND TEACH ME WITH
                              HER LOOKES   5.21.13
WILL TEACH TO SPEAKE, AND MY JUST CAUSE TO PLEAD   5.43.10

```
TEACHEST                    2
  CONCEITE OF $ANGELS, WHICH ALL WISDOM TEACHEST        2.146.10
  AND THAT THOU TEACHEST HOW TO MAKE ONE TWAINE         3.39.13
TEACHING                    3
  TEACHING BLIND EYES BOTH HOW TO SMILE AND WEEPE       4.32.8
  TEACHING THE MEANE, AT CNCE TO TAKE AND GIVE          4.79.9
  TEACHING DUMBE LIPS A NCBLER EXERCISE                 4.81.4
TEAR                        6
  SOFTEN YOUR SELVES WITH EV'RY $TEARE THAT FALLS       2.45.11
  FROM WHENCE, IF YCU ONE TEARE OF PITTY MCVE           2.151.3
  HOW MANY A HOLY AND OBSEQUIOUS TEARE                  3.31.5
  YOUR MORALL NOTES STRAIGHT MY HID MEANING TEARE       4.104.12
  THE HARDEST STEELE IN TRACT OF TIME DOTH TEARE        5.18.2
  YET CANNOT I WITH MANY A DROPPING TEARE               5.18.5
TEARS                      69
  TEARES IN MINE EYES, AND SORROW AT MY HART            1.9.12
  TEARES, VOWES, AND PRAYERS, WINNE THE
                            HARDEST HART                1.11.1
  TEARES, VOWES, AND PRAYERS. HAVE I SPENT IN VAINE     1.11.2
  TEARES CANNOT SOFTEN FLINT, NOR VOWES CONVART         1.11.3
  I LOSE MY TEARES WHERE I HAVE LOST MY LOVE            1.11.5
  YET, THOUGH I CANNOT WINNE HER WILL WITH TEARES       1.11.9
  (AND THAT WITH TEARES) YET ALL THIS WILL
                            NOT MOVE HER                1.18.14
  THE AYRE WITH SIGHES, THE EARTH BELOW
                            WITH TEARES+                1.21.6
  THESE TEARES, WHICH HEATE OF SACRED FLAME DISTILS     1.24.2
  MY FLOWER UNTIMELY'S WITHRED WITH MY TEARES           1.24.7
  MY HEATES MUST DRCWNE IN TH'$OCEAN OF MY TEARES       1.32.12
  THOU MAIST REPENT THAT THOU HAST SCORND
                            MY TEARES                   1.41.13
  WHERE BEAT THESE TEARES WITH ZEALE, AND
                            FURY DRIVES                 1.48.10
  BUT PRECIOUS $TEARES DISTILLING FROM MINE $EYNE       2.7.6
  AND IF WITH $TEARES I FIND THEM ALL TOO LIGHT         2.13.7
  MIX'D WITH HER $TEARES, THAT NE'R HER
                            TRUE-$LOVE CROST            2.15.5
  NOW TEMPTING $ME, TO DRCWNE MY $SELFE IN TEARES       2.20.11
  WITH $SIGHES AND $TEARES STILL FURNISHING
                            HIS $TABLE                  2.23.7
  BY $HECAT'S $NAMES, BY $PROSERPINE'S SAD $TEARES      2.36.7
  MY $EYES WITH $TEARES AGAINST THE FIRE STRIVING       2.40.9
  DROWN'D IN THE $TEARES, EXTORTED BY MY $LINES         2.45.2
  AND HEERE TO $THEE HE SACRIFIC'D HIS $TEARES          2.53.12
  SMOAK'D WITH MY $SIGHES, AND BLOTTED WITH
                            MY $TEARES                  2.54.4
  PRESERVE MY $TEARES, AND THOU THY $SELFE
                            SHALT PROVE                 2.55.3
  SMOK'D WITH MY SIGHES, AND BLOTTED WITH
                            MY TEARES                   2.101.4
  PRESERVE MY TEARES, AND THOU THY SELFE
                            SHALT PROVE                 2.102.3
  MY LIQUIDS THEN WERE LIQUID CHRISTALL TEARES          2.111.9
  AND HEERE TO THEE HE SACRIFIZ'D HIS TEARES            2.113.12
  THAT FOR MY MIS-SPENT YCUTH THE TEARS
                            FEL FROM MY EYES            2.114.4
  THEN IN THESE TEARES, THE MIRRORS OF THESE EYES       2.114.5
  IMPRINTED IN MY TEARES BY LOOKING STILL CN THEE       2.114.7
  WITH TEARES OUT OF THE $CHANNELS OF MINE EYES         2.115.9
  SALT LUKE-WARME TEARES SHEE FOR HIS DRINKE
                            DID GIVE                    2.116.15
```

```
AND IF WITH TEARES, I FIND THEM ALL TOO LIGHT        2.121.7
THE WATER, MOYSTURE FROM MY TEARES DERIVETH          2.127.2
THIS LOVE, TEARS, SIGHES, MAINTAINE EACH
                        ONE HIS ELEMENT              2.127.4
THE WATER, TO MY TEARES, AS DROPS TO $OCEANS BE      2.127.6
ONELY MY TEARES BY $OCEANS MAY BE GESSED             2.127.10
MY LOVE, MY TEARES, MY SIGHES, EXTINGUISHT
                        CANNOT BE                    2.127.14
LAMENT'ST MY DEATH, WITH TEARES OF THY DISDAINE      2.130.14
THOSE TEARES WHICH QUENCH MY HOPE, STILL
                        KINDLE MY DESIRE             2.132.1
WITH TEARES, SIGHES, AND DISDAINE, THYS
                        CONTRARY I PROVE             2.132.4
QUENCHLES DESIRE, MAKES HOPE BURNE, DRYES
                        MY TEARES                    2.132.5
WITH TEARES, SIGHES, AND DISDAINE, SHALL
                        HAVE IMMORTAL STRIFE         2.132.14
MY EYES MADE DIM WITH LOCKES, POURE DOWN
                        A FLOOD OF TEARS             2.133.10
AND THUS WHILST SIGHES AND TEARES TOGETHER
                        DOE CONTENDE                 2.133.13
A THOUSAND VOWES, A THOUSAND SIGHES AND TEARES       2.138.4
IF SIGHES, NOR TEARES, NOR VOWES, NOR
                        PRAYERS CAN MOVE             2.139.2
MYNE EYES WANT TEARES THUS TO BEWAYLE MY WOE         2.143.5
MYNE EYES WITH TEARES AGAINST THE FIRE STRYVING      2.144.9
AH BUT THOSE TEARES ARE PEARLE WHICH THY
                        LOVE SHEEDS                  3.34.13
BUT HEAVIE TEARES, BADGES OF EITHERS WOE             3.44.14
WHAT POTIONS HAVE I DRUNKE OF $SYREN TEARES          3.119.1
THAT IS SO VEXT WITH WATCHING AND WITH TEARES+       3.148.10
O CUNNING LOVE, WITH TEARES THOU KEEPST
                        ME BLINDE                    3.148.13
WHILE TEARES POWRE OUT HIS INKE, AND SIGHS
                        BREATHE OUT HIS WORDS        4.6.10
OFT WITH TRUE SIGHES, OFT WITH UNCALLED TEARES       4.61.1
SHE OFT HATH DRUNKE MY TEARES, NOW HOPES TO ENJOY    4.70.3
I SAW THAT TEARES DID IN HER EYES APPEARE            4.87.6
I CRY THY SIGHS., MY DEERE, THY TEARES I BLEEDE      4.93.14
YET WAILE THY SELFE, AND WAILE WITH CAUSEFULL
                        TEARES                       4.94.11
KILS HIS OWNE CHILDREN, TEARES, FINDING
                        THAT THEY                    4.95.10
THY TEARES EXPRESSE NIGHT'S NATIVE MOISTURE RIGHT    4.96.8
O TEARES, NO TEARES, BUT RAINE FROM BEAUTIE'S
                        SKIES                        4.100.1
O TEARES, NO TEARES, BUT RAINE FROM BEAUTIE'S
                        SKIES                        4.100.1
SUCH TEARES, SIGHS, PLAINTS, NO SORROW
                        IS, BUT JOY                  4.100.12
BUT CEASE MINE EYES, YOUR TEARES DO WITNESSE
                        WELL                         4.105.9
WRITTEN WITH TEARES IN HARTS CLOSE BLEEDING BOOK     5.1.8
AND WHEN I WEEP, SHE SAYES TEARES ARE BUT WATER      5.18.10
TEARS'                  1
THAT, FROM THAT SEA DERIV'D, TEARS' SPRING
                        DID FLOW                     4.45.8
TEDIOUS                 7
MY TEDIOUS $TRAVELS, AND OFT-VARYING $FATE           2.1.14
FORC'D BY A TEDIOUS PROOFE, THAT $TURKISH
                        HARDNED HART                 4.8.2
```

```
OR DOTH THE TEDIOUS BURD'N OF LONG WO                 4.66.2
THEIR RAYES TO ME, WHO IN HER TEDIOUS ABSENCE LAY     4.76.2
THE NIGHT AS TEDIOUS, WOOES TH'APPROCH OF DAY         4.89.6
THAT TEDIOUS LEASURE MARKS EACH WRINCKLED LINE        4.98.11
THINCK EVER TO ENDURE SO TAEDIOUS TOYLE+              5.33.10
```

TEEMING   1
```
THE TEEMING $AUTUMNE BIG WITH RITCH INCREASE          3.97.6
```
TEETH   4
```
THY $PEARLY $TEETH CUT OF THY $HEAD SO CLEANE         2.8.11
PLUCKE THE KEENE TEETH FROM THE FIERCE
                         $TYGERS YAWES                3.19.3
TO SHEW HER SKIN, LIPS, TEETH AND HEAD SO WELL+       4.32.11
IF $PEARLES, HIR TEETH BE PEARLES BOTH
                    PURE AND ROUND                    5.15.9
```
TELL   55
```
AND TELL TH'UNKINDE, HOW DEARELY I HAVE LOV'D HER     1.2.14
ILE TELL THE WORLD THAT I DESERV'D BUT ILL            1.33.11
GOE YOU MY VERSE, GO TELL HER WHAT SHE WAS            1.38.11
AND LET HER TELL ME AS SHE IS A WOMAN                 1.49.11
AND CALL'D TO TELL OF HIS $DISCOVERIE                 2.1.3
I TELL YEE ($FAIRE) ILE NOT BE ANSWERED SO            2.5.3
PASSE ON, AND TO $POSTERITIE TELL THIS                2.17.9
YET SEE THOU TELL, BUT TRULY, WHAT HATH BEENE         2.17.10
YET $FOOLES AND $CHILDREN SOMETIMES TELL IN PLAY      2.22.13
YORKE MANY $WONDERS OF HER $OWSE CAN TELL             2.32.6
SOME, WHEN IN $RYME, THEY OF THEIR $LOVES
                         DOE TELL                     2.39.1
AND I WANT WORDS, WHEREWITH TO TELL MY $WRONG         2.41.8
DEFINE MY $WEALE, AND TELL THE JOYES OF $HEAVEN       2.60.1
TELL $ME, IF EVER SINCE THE $WORLD BEGUNNE            2.60.11
NOW PASSE ON $TIME, TO AFTER-WORLDS TELL THIS         2.107.9
TELL TRUELIE $TIME WHAT IN THY TIME HATH BEENE        2.107.10
THAT THEY MAY TEL MORE WORLDS WHAT $TIME
                         HATH SEENE                   2.107.11
OR TONGUE OF WONDER WORTH COULD TELL A
                         WONDER THOUGHT               2.117.2
SOME WHEN IN RYME THEY OF THEIR $LOVES DOE TELL       2.118.1
SOME $GANGES, $ISTER, AND OF $TAGUS TELL              2.120.9
YORKE, MANY WONDERS OF HER $OUSE CAN TELL             2.124.6
I FEELE, YOU KNOW, THE HEAVENS CAN TELL
                         THE REST                     2.139.14
SWEET SECRECIE, WHAT TONGUE CAN TELL THY WORTH+       2.146.1
DEFINE MY LOVE, AND TELL THE JOYES OF HEAVEN          2.149.1
TELL MEE, IF EVER SINCE THE WORLD BEGUNNE             2.149.11
AND TELL THE $GODS, $MARS IS PREDOMINANT              2.151.11
AND TELL THE WORLD, THAT IN THE WORLD THERE IS        2.151.13
LOOKE IN THY GLASSE AND TELL THE FACE THOU VEWEST     3.3.1
BUT NOT TO TELL OF GOOD, OR EVIL LUCKE                3.14.3
NOR CAN I FORTUNE TO BREEFE MYNUITS TELL              3.14.5
I TELL THE $DAY TO PLEASE HIM THOU ART BRIGHT         3.28.9
AND HEAVILY FROM WOE TO WOE TELL ORE                  3.30.10
THAT EVERY WORD DOTH ALMOST FEL MY NAME               3.76.7
BUT HE THAT WRITES OF YOU, IF HE CAN TELL             3.84.7
AND HAPLIE OF OUR OLD ACQUAINTANCE TELL               3.89.12
THY LOOKES SHOULD NOTHING THENCE, BUT
                         SWEETNESSE TELL              3.93.12
COULD MAKE ME ANY SUMMERS STORY TELL                  3.98.7
THEN OF YOUR GRACES AND YOUR GIFTS TO TELL            3.103.12
TELL ME THOU LOV'ST ELSE-WHERE., BUT IN MY SIGHT      3.139.5
THOUGH NOT TO LOVE, YET LOVE TO TELL ME SO            3.140.6
```

```
    SUSPECT I MAY, YET NOT DIRECTLY TELL                    3.144.10
    MY SOULE DOTH TELL MY BODY THAT HE MAY                  3.151.7
    DIG DEEPE WITH LEARNING'S SPADE, NOW TELL
                               ME THIS                      4.21.13
    THEN EV'N OF FELLOWSHIP, O $MOONE, TELL ME              4.31.9
    VOUCHSAFE OF ALL ACQUAINTANCE THIS TO TELL              4.32.9
    FOR OF MY LIFE I MUST A RIDDLE TELL                     4.37.4
    THEN SOME GOOD BODY TELL ME HOW I DO                    4.60.12
    SOME DO I HEARE OF $POETS' FURIE TELL                   4.74.5
    YET AH, MY $MAYD'N $MUSE DOTH BLUSH TO
                               TELL THE BEST                4.77.14
    FAIRE PROUD NOW TELL ME WHY SHOULD FAIRE BE PROUD       5.27.1
    TELL ME WHEN SHALL THESE WEARIE WOES HAVE END           5.36.1
    AND TELL ME WHERETO CAN YE LYKEN IT                     5.40.2
    AND TELL HER PRAYSE TO ALL POSTERITY                    5.69.11
    TELL HER THE JOYOUS TIME WIL NOT BE STAID               5.70.7
    THAT WITH FALSE FORGED LYES, WHICH THOU DIDST TEL       5.86.7
TELLING                        2
    SO IS MY LOVE STILL TELLING WHAT IS TOLD                3.76.14
    IN TRUE PLAINE WORDS, BY THY TRUE TELLING FRIEND        3.82.12
TELLS                          5
    THAT TELLS THE TRUTH, AND SAYES THAT ALL IS GONE        1.41.4
    WHICH TELLS THE WORLD HOW MUCH MY GRIEFE IMPORTS        1.60.4
    AND TELLS THE OTHER, HOW THEY SHOULD BE BLEST           2.29.12
    WHEN I DOE COUNT THE CLOCK THAT TELS THE TIME           3.12.1
    THAT TONGUE THAT TELLS THE STORY OF THY DAIES           3.95.5
TEMPE                          3
    FAIRE $ARDEN, THOU MY $TEMPE ART ALONE                  2.53.13
    FAYRE $ARDEN, THOU MY $TEMPE ART ALONE                  2.113.13
    NOR EVER DID IN SHADE OF $TEMPE SIT                     4.74.2
TEMPER                         2
    HE DID BESTOW IN TEMPER OF THE $MIND                    2.14.8
    WITH WHICH SHE WONTS TO TEMPER ANGRY $JOVE              5.39.3
TEMPERATE                      1
    THOU ART MORE LOVELY AND MORE TEMPERATE                 3.18.2
TEMPERATURE                    1
    MOST GOODLY TEMPERATURE YE MAY DESCRY                   5.13.4
TEMPERED                       4
    OF PUREST GOLD, TEMPRED WITH VERTUES FIRE               2.126.7
    WHICH TEMPRED SO THE FEATURE OF HER FACE                5.21.2
    SO EVERY SWEET WITH SOURE IS TEMPRED STILL              5.26.9
    AND MODEST THOUGHTS BREATHD FROM WEL TEMPRED
                               SPRITES                      5.84.6
TEMPERS                        1
    TEMPERS HER WORDS TO TRAMPLING HORSES FEET              4.84.3
TEMPEST                        5
    AND CALME AND TEMPEST FOLLOW THEIR ASPECTS              1.34.6
    AND CALME THE TEMPEST WHICH MY SIGHS DOO RAISE          1.51.10
    THE DREADFULL TEMPEST OF HER WRATH APPEASE              5.38.7
    AS BEING LONG IN HER LOVES TEMPEST TOST                 5.41.11
    NE OUGHT FOR TEMPEST DOTH FROM IT DEPART                5.59.7
TEMPESTS                       4
    THAT LOOKES ON TEMPESTS AND IS NEVER SHAKEN             3.116.6
    WILLD ME THESE TEMPESTS OF VAINE LOVE TO FLIE           4.62.10
    STELLA WHOSE EYES MAKE ALL MY TEMPESTS CLEERE           4.87.3
    SITH ALL YOUR TEMPESTS CANNOT HOLD ME BACKE             5.46.10
TEMPEST'S                      2
    ARION, WHEN THROUGH TEMPESTS CRUEL WRACKE               5.38.1
    AFTER LONG STORMES AND TEMPESTS SAD ASSAY               5.63.1
```

TEMPLE   8
  ABOUT THE $TEMPLE CF THE PROUDEST FRAME   1.12.2
  TO HER THAT SITS IN MY THOUGHTS $TEMPLE SAINTED 1.15.7
  THE TEMPLE, WHERE HER NAME WAS HONOUR'D STILL 1.47.14
  THY HALLOW'D $TEMPLE ONELY IS MY $HEART   2.30.14
  WITHIN THE $TEMPLE CF THY SACRED NAME   2.105.6
  AND, FOOLES, ADORE IN TEMPLE OF OUR HART   4.5.7
  O DO NOT LET THY $TEMPLE BE DESTROYD   4.40.14
  HER TEMPLE FAYRE IS BUILT WITHIN MY MIND   5.22.5
TEMPT   2
  WHICH CEASETH NOT TC TEMPT $ME TO EACH $ILL 2.20.3
  UNTO HER LOVE, AND TEMPTE TO THEYR DECAY   5.47.6
TEMPTATION   2
  FOR STILL TEMPTATICN FOLLOWES WHERE THOU ART 3.41.4
  UNMOOVED, COULD, AND TO TEMPTATION SLOW   3.94.4
TEMPTETH   1
  TEMPTETH MY BETTER ANGEL FROM MY SIGHT   3.144.6
TEMPTING   2
  NOW TEMPTING $ME, TC DRCWNE MY $SELFE IN TEARES 2.20.11
  HERS BY THY BEAUTY TEMPTING HER TO THEE   3.41.13
TEN   14
  MAKES EVERY $ONE CF THESE THREE $NINES A $TEN 2.18.14
  MAKES EVERY ONE OF THESE THREE NINES A TEN   2.108.14
  THUS MIDST A THOUSAND WCES, TEN THOUSAND
                     JOYES ARISE   2.114.8
  IF $THOSE TEN $REGICNS REGISTRED BY $FAME   2.119.1
  BY THEYR TEN $SIBILS HAVE THE WORLD CONTRCLD 2.119.2
  IN STEED OF TEN, CNE $SIBIL TO US LEFT   2.119.8
  HER $BOWE IS BEAUTY, WITH TEN THOUSAND STRINGS 2.126.6
  OR TEN TIMES HAPPIER BE IT TEN FOR ONE   3.6.8
  OR TEN TIMES HAPPIER BE IT TEN FOR ONE   3.6.8
  TEN TIMES THY SELFE WERE HAPPIER THEN THOU ART 3.6.9
  IF TEN OF THINE TEN TIMES REFIGUR'D THEE   3.6.10
  IF TEN OF THINE TEN TIMES REFIGUR'D THEE   3.6.10
  THIS WISH I HAVE, THEN TEN TIMES HAPPY ME   3.37.14
  BE THOU THE TENTH $MUSE, TEN TIMES MORE IN WCRTH 3.38.9
TENANTS   1
  A QUEST OF THOUGHTS, ALL TENNANTS TO THE HEART 3.46.10
TEND   3
  THAT MILLIONS OF STRANGE SHADDOWES ON YOU TEND+ 3.53.2
  BEING YOUR SLAVE WHAT SHOULD I DOE BUT TEND 3.57.1
  FOR TO NO OTHER PASSE MY VERSES TEND   3.103.11
TENDER   15
  IN LIFE AND DEATH $ILE TENDER HER GOOD NAME 1.30.11
  WHILST YET HER TENDER BUD DOTH UNDISCLOSE   1.39.3
  WHOSE SHORT REFRESH UPON THE TENDER GREENE   1.50.2
  HIS TENDER HEIRE MIGHT BEARE HIS MEMORY   3.1.4
  AND TENDER CHORLE MAKST WAST IN NIGGARDING   3.1.12
  AS TENDER NURSE HER BABE FROM FARING ILL   3.22.12
  IN TENDER $EMBASSIE OF LCVE TO THEE   3.45.6
  THE BARREN TENDER CF A $POETS DEBT   3.83.4
  TO KISSE THE TENDER INWARD OF THY HAND   3.128.6
  NOR TENDER FEELING TO BASE TOUCHES PRONE   3.141.6
  MY MOUTH TOO TENDER IS FOR THY HARD BIT   4.4.8
  FROM THAT FOE'S WCUNDS THEIR TENDER SKINNES
                     TO HIDE   4.22.8
  SCHOOL'D ONELY BY HIS MCTHER'S TENDER EYE   4.73.2
  OR DO YOU MEANE MY TENDER EARES TO SPARE   4.92.4
  NOR TO THE $DIAMOND.. FCR THEY ARE MORE TENDER 5.9.10

```
TENDERED                      1
  AND SOONE TO YOU, AS YOU TO ME THEN TENDRED         3.120.11
TENDING                       2
  AND HAD MY SIGHES STILL TENDING ON HER NAME         1.15.10
  TO THIS THOUGHTS-MAZE, TO MY CONFUSION TENDING      1.18.2
TENTH                         1
  BE THOU THE TENTH $MUSE, TEN TIMES MORE IN WORTH    3.38.9
TENTS                         1
  HER BREASTS HIS TENTS, LEGS HIS TRIUMPHALL CARRE    4.29.11
TENURE                        1
  THE SKOPE AND TENURE OF THY $JELOUSIE+              3.61.8
TERM                          4
  AND DOE NOT STICKE TO TERME MY $PRAYSES FOLLY        2.28.2
  FOR TEARME OF LIFE THOU ART ASSURED MINE            3.92.2
  THAT SKIN, WHOSE PASSE-PRAISE HUE SCORNS
                       THIS POORE TERME OF WHITE  4.77.7
  THAT FURTHER SEEMES HIS TERME STILL TO EXTEND       5.87.11
TERMED                        1
  AND YOUR TRUE RIGHTS BE TERMD A $POETS RAGE         3.17.11
TERMS                         4
  BUY TEARMES DIVINE IN SELLING HOURES OF CROSSE      3.146.11
  TO MAKE A TRUCE AND TERMES TO ENTERTAINE            5.12.2
  WITH SUCH STRANGE TERMES HER EYES SHE DOTH INURE    5.21.9
  BUT WAST AND WEARE AWAY IN TERMES UNSURE            5.25.3
TERROR                        4
  STILL HAVE I LIV'D IN GRIEFE, IN HOPE, IN TERROR    1.18.3
  WITH ALL HIS $TORMENTS AND $INFERNALL TERROR+       2.41.4
  WITH ALL HIS TORMENTS AND INFERNALL TERROR          2.143.4
  THAT WITH THEYR TERROUR AL THE REST MAY CHACE       5.31.7
TESTY                         1
  AS TESTIE SICK-MEN WHEN THEIR DEATHS BE NEERE       3.140.7
TEXT                          1
  LOOKE ON AGAINE, THE FAIRE TEXT BETTER TRIE         4.67.7
THAMES                        5
  NO, NO, MY $VERSE RESPECTS NOT $THAMES
                            NOR $THEATERS             1.58.9
  AVON SHALL BE MY $THAMES, AND SHE MY $SONG          1.58.13
  OUR $FLOUDS-$QUEEN $THAMES, FOR $SHIPS
                       AND $SWANS IS CROWNED          2.32.1
  OUR FLOODS-$QUEENE $THAMES, FOR SHYPS
                       AND $SWANS IS CROWNED          2.124.1
  O HAPPIE $TEMS, THAT DIDST MY $STELLA BEARE         4.103.1
THAN                        103
  IF I HAVE LOV'D HER DEARER THEN MY BREATH           1.21.9
  THAT $GRACE WHICH DOTH MORE THEN IN WOMAN THEE      1.45.13
  THEN MINE UNTO HER CRUELTY HATH BEENE               1.48.8
  THEN I WOULD JOY THE FAIREST SHE THAT LIVES         1.48.12
  THERE WHERE MY $DELIA FAIRER THEN THE $SUNNE        1.53.5
  THEN IF HE HAD THE TYRANT OVER-THROWNE              1.56.4
  THEN IF I HAD THE VICTORY MINE OWNE                 1.56.7
  THEN TO THE $SONNE OF SOME RICH $PENNY-FATHER       2.10.2
  WITH GREATER $TORMENTS, THEN IT $ME DOTH TAKE       2.20.7
  NO WISER I, THEN WHEN AS YOUNG AS HE                2.22.10
  SOME WISE IN SHEW, MORE $FOOLES INDEED THEN THEY    2.22.14
  THOUGH $FEARE GIVES THEM MORE THEN A $HEAV'NLY
                            $SCOPE                    2.26.8
  OR HAVE OUR $PASSIONS LESSER POW'R THEN THEIRS      2.27.5
  THOUGH I GIVE MORE THEN WELL AFFORDS MY STATE       2.28.5
  (THE $KING OF $SENCES, GREATER THEN THE REST)       2.29.10
  AND KNOWING MORE THEN EVER HATH BEENE TAUGHT        2.34.3
```

THEN POSSIBLY $INVENTION CAN EXTEND	2.34.11
KINDER THEN SHE WHOM I SO LONG HAVE LOVED	2.45.14
WITH THOUSAND $PLAGUES, MORE THEN IN $PURGATORIE	2.49.12
MORE THEN HIS WOND'RING UTT'RANCE CAN UNFOLD	2.57.10
MORE THEN WORLDS VOLUMES SHALL THEREOF ARISE	2.102.2
THEN THERE BE STARRES AT MIDNIGHT IN THE SKYES	2.126.12
LOV'D MORE THEN LIFE, YET ONELY ART HIS LOVE	2.129.11
YET FEARE GYVES THEM MORE THEN A HEAVENLY SCOPE	2.137.8
TEN TIMES THY SELFE WERE HAPPIER THEN THOU ART	3.6.9
SHALL HATE BE FAIRER LOG'D THEN GENTLE LOVE+	3.10.10
NO LONGER YOURS, THEN YOU YOUR SELFE HERE LIVE	3.13.2
WITH MEANES MORE BLESSED THEN MY BARREN RIME+	3.16.4
MUCH LIKER THEN YOUR PAINTED COUNTERFEIT	3.16.8
BE SCORN'D, LIKE OLD MEN OF LESSE TRUTH THEN TONGUE	3.17.10
AN EYE MORE BRIGHT THEN THEIRS, LESSE FALSE IN ROWLING	3.20.5
HOW CAN I THEN BE ELDER THEN THOU ART+	3.22.8
MORE THEN THAT TONGE THAT MORE HATH MORE EXPREST	3.23.12
A DEARER BIRTH THEN THIS HIS LOVE HAD BROUGHT	3.32.11
EXCUSING THEIR SINS MORE THEN THEIR SINS ARE	3.35.8
WHAT HAST THOU THEN MORE THEN THOU HADST BEFORE+	3.40.2
TO BEARE LOVES WRONG, THEN HATES KNOWNE INJURY	3.40.12
FOR THOU NOR FARTHER THEN MY THOUGHTS CANST MOVE	3.47.11
THEN UNSWEPT STONE, BESMEER'D WITH SLUTTISH TIME	3.55.4
THY EDGE SHOULD BLUNTER BE THEN APETITE	3.56.2
WHOSE ACTION IS NO STRONGER THEN A FLOWER+	3.65.4
BY SEEING FARTHER THEN THE EYE HATH SHOWNE	3.69.8
TO DOE MORE FOR ME THEN MINE OWNE DESERT	3.72.6
THEN NIGARD TRUTH WOULD WILLINGLY IMPART	3.72.8
THEN BOTH YOUR $POETS CAN IN PRAISE DEVISE	3.83.14
THEN THIS RICH PRAISE, THAT YOU ALONE, ARE YOU	3.84.2
THY LOVE IS BITTER THEN HIGH BIRTH TO ME	3.91.9
RICHER THEN WEALTH, PROUDER THEN GARMENTS COST	3.91.10
RICHER THEN WEALTH, PROUDER THEN GARMENTS COST	3.91.10
OF MORE DELIGHT THEN $HAWKES OR $HORSES BEE	3.91.11
AND LIFE NO LONGER THEN THY LOVE WILL STAY	3.92.3
THEN THAT, WHICH ON THY HUMOR DOTH DEPEND	3.92.8
LILLIES THAT FESTER, SMELL FAR WORSE THEN WEEDS	3.94.14
GIVE MY LOVE FAME FASTER THEN TIME WASTS LIFE	3.100.13
THEN WHEN HER MOURNEFULL HIMNS DID HUSH THE NIGHT	3.102.10
THEN WHEN IT HATH MY ADDED PRAISE BESIDE	3.103.4
THEN OF YOUR GRACES AND YOUR GIFTS TO TELL	3.103.12
AND MORE, MUCH MORE THEN IN MY VERSE CAN SIT	3.103.13
THEN PUBLICK MEANES WHICH PUBLICK MANNERS BREEDS	3.111.4
GROWES FAIRER THEN AT FIRST, MORE STRONG, FAR GREATER	3.119.12
AND GAINE BY ILLS THRISE MORE THEN I HAVE SPENT	3.119.14
TIS BETTER TO BE VILE THEN VILE ESTEEMED	3.121.1
MAKING DEAD WOOD MORE BLEST THEN LIVING LIPS	3.128.12
CURRALL IS FARRE MORE RED, THEN HER LIPS RED	3.130.2
THEN IN THE BREATH THAT FROM MY $MISTRES REEKES	3.130.8
MORE THEN ENOUGH AM I THAT VEXE THEE STILL	3.135.3
IS MORE THEN MY ORE-PREST DEFENCE CAN BIDE+	3.139.8
THEY SUN-LIKE SHOULD MORE DAZLE THEN DELIGHT+	4.7.8
THEN DID ON HIM WHO FIRST STALE DOWNE THE FIRE	4.14.3
THEN THAT I LOSE NO MORE FOR $STELLA'S SAKE	4.18.14
'WHAT IDLER THING, THEN SPEAKE AND NOT BE HARD+'	4.34.9
WHAT HARDER THING THEN SMART, AND NOT TO SPEAKE+	4.34.10

```
LIVELIER THEN ELSE-WHERE, $STELLA'S IMAGE SEE        4.39.14
THEN SERVANT'S WRACKE, WHERE NEW DOUBTS
                          HONOR BRINGS               4.45.11
DEARE, WHY MAKE YOU MORE OF A DOG THEN ME+            4.59.1
RATHER THEN BY MORE TRUTH TO GET MORE PAINE          4.67.14
O BLISSE, FIT FOR A NOBLER STATE THEN ME             4.69.2
TO LOSE HIS $CROWNE, RATHER THEN FAILE HIS $LOVE     4.75.14
THAT HAND, WHICH WITHOUT TOUCH HOLDS MORE
                          THEN $ATLAS MIGHT          4.77.5
MORE OFT THEN TO A CHAMBER MELODIE                   4.84.4
THEN THOSE BLEST EYES, WHERE ALL MY HOPES
                          DO DWELL                   4.86.13
WHILE NO NIGHT IS MORE DARKE THEN IS MY DAY          4.89.10
NOR NO DAY HATH LESSE QUIET THEN MY NIGHT            4.89.11
YET GROWEST MORE WRETCHED THEN THY NATURE BEARES     4.94.13
WHICH AY MOST FAIRE, NOW MORE THEN MOST
                          FAIRE SHOW                 4.100.3
WITH NO WORSE CURSE THEN ABSENCE MAKES ME TAST       4.105.14
TILL GREATER THEN MY WOMBE THOU WOXEN ART            5.2.4
BUT SINCE THAT LYFE IS MORE THEN DEATH DESYRED       5.7.9
MORE THEN MOST FAIRE, FULL OF THE LIVING FIRE        5.8.1
THEN THOSE SMALL FORTS WHICH YE WERE WONT BELAY      5.14.6
THEN EITHER $LYON OR THE $LYONESSE                   5.20.10
FAYRER THEN FAYREST LET NONE EVER SAY                5.20.13
THEN TO TORMENT ME THUS WITH CRUELTY                 5.25.7
HER HART MORE HARDE THEN YRON SOFT AWHIT             5.32.6
THEN TO BE BLAM'D FOR SPILLING GUILTLESSE BLOOD      5.38.14
MORE SWEET THAN $NECTAR OR $AMBROSIALL MEAT          5.39.13
CLEARER THEN CHRISTALL WOULD THEREIN APPERE          5.45.12
THEN SO BAD END FOR HERETICKS ORDAYNED               5.48.6
AND GREATER GLORY THINKE TO SAVE, THEN SPILL         5.49.4
THEN AL THOSE FOURTY WHICH MY LIFE OUTWENT           5.60.8
THEN DARE BE LOV'D BY MEN OF MEANE DEGREE            5.61.14
THEN HAD YE SORTED WITH A PRINCES PERE               5.66.10
RATHER THEN ENVY LET THEM WONDER AT HER              5.85.7
THANK                        2
THEN THANKE HIM NOT FOR THAT WHICH HE DOTH SAY       3.79.13
THANKE MAY YOU HAVE FOR SUCH A THANKFULL PART        4.95.13
THANKFUL                     1
THANKE MAY YOU HAVE FOR SUCH A THANKFULL PART        4.95.13
THANKFULLY                   1
WITH THANKES AND WISHES, WISHING THANKFULLY          4.84.8
THANKLESS                    1
SHALL TO YOU PURCHAS WITH HER THANKLES PAINE         5.27.12
THANKS                       3
GIVE $NATURE THANKES, YOU ARE NOT SUCH AS WE         2.22.12
OH GIVE THY SELFE THE THANKES IF OUGHT IN ME         3.38.5
WITH THANKES AND WISHES, WISHING THANKFULLY          4.84.8
THANK-WORTHIEST              1
THANKE-WORTHIEST YET WHEN YOU SHALL BREAKE
                          MY HART                    4.95.14
THAW                         1
MAKING MY $SIGHES TO THAW THE $FROZEN $SEAS          2.25.8
THEATER                      1
OF THIS WORLDS $THEATRE IN WHICH WE STAY             5.54.1
THEATERS                     2
NO, NO, MY $VERSE RESPECTS NOT $THAMES
                          NOR $THEATERS              1.58.9
WITH THOSE THE THRONGED $THEATERS THAT PRESSE        2.47.5
```

THEFT   1
  BUT FOR HIS THEFT IN PRIDE OF ALL HIS GROWTH   3.99.12
THEMES   1
  THREE THEAMS IN ONE, WHICH WONDROUS SCOPE
                              AFFORDS   3.105.12
THEMSELVES   17
  WITHIN THEMSELVES, AND CN THEM PLOJGHS HAVE EAR'D   1.45.4
  AGAINST THESE $FOLKES, THAT THINKE THEMSELVES
                              SO WISE   2.28.3
  WISHING THEMSELVES, THAT THEY HAD BEENE MY $HEART   2.33.8
  SINCE SWEETS AND BEAUTIES DO THEM-SELVES FORSAKE   3.12.11
  AND IN THEM-SELVES THEIR PRIDE LIES BURIED   3.25.7
  DIE TO THEMSELVES. $SWEET $ROSES DOE NOT SO   3.54.11
  WHO MOVING OTHERS, ARE THEMSELVES AS STONE   3.94.3
  INCERTENTIES NOW CRCWNE THEM-SELVES ASSUR'DE   3.107.7
  I MAY BE STRAIGHT THOUGH THEY THEM-SELVES
                              BE BEVEL   3.121.11
  AVISE THEMSELVES THAT THEY ARE VAINELY SPENT   4.19.8
  TO KEEPE THEMSELVES AND THEIR CHIEF CITIES FREE   4.29.2
  WHILE EVERIE OFFICE THEMSELVES WILL DISCHARGE   4.85.7
  THEY DID THEMSELVES (O SWEETEST PRISON) TWINE   4.103.8
  WITH NO CONTENTMENT CAN THEMSELVES SUFFIZE   5.35.3
  THRUGH STUBBORN PRIDE AMONGST THEMSELVES DID JAR   5.44.2
  AND THERE TO REST THEMSELVES DID BOLDLY PLACE   5.76.12
  WITH NO CONTENTMENT CAN THEMSELVES SUFFIZE   5.83.3
THENCE   24
  WHICH TAKING THENCE, YOU HAVE ESCAP'D AWAY   2.14.11
  THENCE TAKE YOU $WING UNTO THE $ORCADES   2.25.6
  FROM THENCE (THEY VCW) THEY NEVER WILL DEPART   2.132.12
  GOE $BASTARD GOE, FCR SURE OF THENCE THOU ART   2.140.14
  AND EVEN THENCE THCU WILT BE STOLNE I FEARE   3.48.13
  FROM WHERE THOU ART, WHY SHOULLD I HAST ME THENCE   3.51.3
  I WAS NOT SICK OF ANY FEARE FROM THENCE   3.86.12
  THY LOOKES SHOULD NCTHING THENCE, BUT
                              SWEETNESSE TELL   3.93.12
  THENCE COMES IT THAT MY NAME RECEIVES A BRANC   3.111.5
  AND ALMOST THENCE MY NATURE IS SUBDU'D   3.111.6
  BUT THENCE I LEARNE AND FIND THE LESSON TRUE   3.118.13
  AND THENCE THIS SLAUNDER AS I THINKE PROCEEDS   3.131.14
  OFT TURNING OTHERS' LEAVES, TO SEE IF
                              THENCE WOULD FLOW   4.1.7
  BUT SHE MOST FAIRE, MOST COLD, MADE HIM
                              THENCE TAKE HIS FLIGHT   4.8.12
  BUT ERE I COULD FLIE THENCE, IT PIERC'D MY HEART   4.20.14
  IF HE WAITE WELL, I NEVER THENCE WOULD MCVE   4.59.3
  THENCE HIS DESIRES HE LEARNES, HIS LIVE'S
                              COURSE THENCE   4.61.8
  THENCE HIS DESIRES HE LEARNES, HIS LIVE'S
                              COURSE THENCE   4.61.8
  AH, IS IT NOT ENOUGH, THAT I AM THENCE   4.104.5
  THENCE, SO FARRE THENCE, THAT SCARCELY
                              ANY SPARKE   4.104.6
  THENCE, SO FARRE THENCE, THAT SCARCELY
                              ANY SPARKE   4.104.6
  THENCE BREAKING FCRTH DID THICK ABOUT ME THRCNG   5.12.8
  AND FEELING THENCE NO MCRE HER SUROWES SADNESSE   5.39.11
  CAPTIVITY THENCE CAPTIVE US TO WIN   5.68.4
THENCEFORTH   2
  SEEMD EVERY BIT, WHICH THENCEFORTH I DID EAT   5.39.14
  AND ALL THENSFORTH ETERNALL PEACE SHALL SEE   5.71.13

```
THEREABOUT                       1
  NEARE THERABOUT, INTO YOUR $POESIE WRING              4.15.4
THEREBY                          9
  HOPING THEREBY TO FREE MY BETTER PART                 1.27.4
  BUT AH, WHAT GLORIE CAN SHE GET THEREBY               1.27.11
  IF THEY REMAINE, THEN THOU SHALT LIVE THEREBY         1.42.13
  WHAT THOUGH MY $MUSE NO HONOR GET THEREBY             1.59.13
  AND I GIVE MUCH, BECAUSE I GAINE THEREBY              2.28.10
  THAT THEREBY BEAUTIES $ROSE MIGHT NEVER DIE           3.1.2
  SHE CARV'D THEE FOR HER SEALE, AND MENT THERBY        3.11.13
  POORE PASSENGER, PASSE NOW THEREBY I DID              4.20.9
  BUT YE THEREBY MUCH GREATER GLORY GATE                5.66.9
THEREFORE                       30
  HARD IS HER HART, AND WOE IS ME THEREFORE             1.13.12
  AND THEREFORE $DELIA, TIS TO ME NO BLOT               1.35.13
  AND THEREFORE GRIEVE NOT IF THY BEAUTIES DIE          1.45.9
  O THEREFORE LOVE BE OF THY SELFE SO WARY              3.22.9
  GENTLE THOU ART, AND THEREFORE TO BE WONNE            3.41.5
  BEAUTIOUS THOU ART, THEREFORE TO BE ASSAILED          3.41.6
  THEREFORE DESIRE (OF PERFECTS LOVE BEING MADE)        3.51.10
  THEREFORE ARE FEASTS SO SOLLEMNE AND SO RARE          3.52.5
  AND THEREFORE MAIEST WITHOUT ATTAINT ORE-LOOKE        3.82.2
  AND THEREFORE ART INFORC'D TO SEEKE ANEW              3.82.7
  AND THEREFORE TO YOUR FAIRE NO PAINTING SET           3.83.2
  AND THEREFORE HAVE I SLEPT IN YOUR REPORT             3.83.5
  THEREFORE IN THAT I CANNOT KNOW THY CHANGE            3.93.6
  THEREFORE LIKE HER, I SOME-TIME HOLD MY TONGUE        3.102.13
  THEREFORE MY VERSE TO CONSTANCIE CONFIN'DE            3.105.7
  THEREFORE TO GIVE THEM FROM ME WAS I BOLD             3.122.11
  OUR DATES ARE BREEFE, AND THEREFOR WE ADMIRE          3.123.5
  THEREFORE MY $MISTERSSE EYES ARE $RAVEN BLACKE        3.127.9
  THEREFORE I LYE WITH HER, AND SHE WITH ME             3.138.13
  AND THEREFORE FROM MY FACE SHE TURNES MY FOES         3.139.11
  AND THEREFORE, THOUGH HER BEAUTIE AND HER GRACE       4.52.9
  AND THEREFORE BY HER $LOVE'S AUTHORITY                4.62.9
  DEERE, THEREFORE BE NOT JEALOUS OVER ME               4.91.12
  BRING THEREFORE ALL THE FORCES THAT YE MAY            5.14.9
  THEREFORE $O LOVE, UNLESSE SHE TURNE TO THEE          5.19.13
  THEREFORE, I LYKEWISE ON SO HOLY DAY                  5.22.3
  TAKE HEED THEREFORE, MYNE EYES, HOW YE DOE STARE      5.37.9
  MAKE PEACE THEREFORE, AND GRAUNT ME TIMELY GRACE      5.57.13
  BID HER THEREFORE HER SELFE SOONE READY MAKE          5.70.9
  MAKE HAST THEREFORE SWEET LOVE, WHILEST
                               IT IS PRIME              5.70.13
THEREIN                          6
  DELIGHTS TO PEEPE, TO GAZE THEREIN ON THEE            3.24.12
  SO DOST THOU TOO, AND THEREIN DIGNIFI'D               3.101.4
  WHO HAST BY WAYNING GROWNE, AND THEREIN SHOU'ST       3.126.3
  AND JOY THEREIN, THOUGH $NATIONS COUNT IT SHAME       4.28.8
  TO WRITE THEREIN MORE FRESH THE STORY
                               OF DELIGHT               4.102.13
  CLEARER THEN CHRISTALL WOULD THEREIN APPERE           5.45.12
THEREOF                         15
  NOR NEVER STOOD ONE WORD THEREOF TO BLOT              2.21.7
  A $WORLD OF $VOLUMES SHALL THEREOF ARISE              2.55.2
  FOR THAT THE VERTUE I THEREOF WOULD KNOW              2.56.2
  MORE THEN WORLDS VOLUMES SHALL THEREOF ARISE          2.102.2
  AND IN THE PRAISE THEREOF SPENDS ALL HIS MIGHT        3.80.3
  NOT THOUGH THEREOF THE CAUSE HER SELFE SHE KNOW       4.45.4
  PITIE THEREOF GATE IN HER BREAST SUCH PLACE           4.45.7
```

```
THAT ANY LAUD TO ME THEREOF SHOULD GROW              4.90.10
WITH SIGHT THEREOF CRIDE OUT., O FAIRE DISGRACE      4.103.13
THAT YOU, GUILTLESSE THEREOF, YOUR $NECTAR MIST      4.105.10
HOW EVER NOW THEREOF YE LITTLE WEENE                  5.27.4
NE ANY MENTION SHALL THEREOF REMAINE                 5.27.10
THE POWRE THEREOF, WHICH OFTE IN ME I FIND            5.28.5
SHALL BE THEREOF IMMORTALL MONIMENT                  5.69.10
WITH LIGHT THEREOF I DOE MY SELFE SUSTAYNE           5.88.11
```
THEREON   2
```
MY THOUGHTS THE GUESTS, WHICH WOULD THEREON
                          HAVE FEDD                  5.77.14
AND THEREON FEED MY LOVE-AFFAMISHT HART              5.88.12
```
THERETO   1
```
A GREATER CRAFTESMANS HAND THERETO DOTH NEEDE        5.17.13
```
THEREUNTO   1
```
BUT WHEN MYNE EYES I THEREUNTO DIRECT                 5.78.9
```
THEREWITH   4
```
AND STRAIGHT THEREWITH, LIKE WAGS NEW
                          GOT TO PLAY                4.17.13
SHE COMES, AND STREIGHT THEREWITH HER
                          SHINING TWINS DO MOVE       4.76.1
AND THEY THEREWITH DOE POETES HEADS ADORNE            5.29.7
AND THEREWITH DOE HER CRUELTY COMPARE                 5.55.2
```
THESSALIAN   1
```
ON THE $THESSALIAN SHORE FROM HIM DID FLEE           5.28.10
```
THETIS   1
```
TO $THETIS GIVE THE HONOUR OF THY FEETE              1.19.8
```
THICK   1
```
THENCE BREAKING FORTH DID THICK ABOUT ME THRONG      5.12.8
```
THIEF   11
```
WHERE MY HARTS THEEFE TO VEXE ME MADE HER CHOICE     1.27.6
STEALE FROM THY SELFE, AND BE THY CARES
                          OWNE THIEFE                1.52.12
NOW CALL HER $GODDESSE, THEN I CALL HER $THIEFE      2.41.12
YET HAPPY HE THATS ROBD OF SUCH A THIEFE            2.126.14
HAST PLAYD THE THIEFE, AND STOLNE MY HART
                          FROM ME                    2.130.11
NOW CALL HER $GODDESSE, THEN I CALL HER THIEFE      2.143.12
TO THAT SWEET THEEFE WHICH SOURELY ROBS FROM ME      3.35.14
I DOE FORGIVE THY ROBB'RIE GENTLE THEEFE             3.40.9
ART LEFT THE PREY OF EVERY VULGAR THEEFE             3.48.8
SWEET THEEFE WHENCE DIDST THOU STEALE
                          THY SWEET THAT SMELS        3.99.2
WHO LIKE A THEEFE, HID IN DARKE BUSH DOTH LY         4.20.3
```
THIEVES   1
```
THUS POORE $THEEVES SUFFER, WHEN THE GREATER
                          SCAPE                      2.14.14
```
THIEVISH   2
```
FOR TRUTH PROOVES THEEVISH FOR A PRIZE SO DEARE      3.48.14
TIMES THEEVISH PROGRESSE TO ETERNITIE                3.77.8
```
THIN   1
```
THY $LIPS, WITH AGE, AS ANY $WAFER THINNE            2.8.10
```
THING   30
```
THAT EV'RY THING WHENCE $SHADOW DOTH PROCEED        2.13.13
WHO+ CAN HE LOVE+ A LIKELY THING, THEY SAY           2.24.2
IN EV'RY THING I HOLD THIS $MAXIM STILL             2.28.13
OR IF NO THING BUT $DEATH WILL SERVE THY TURNE       2.63.9
THAT EVERY THING WHENCE SHADOW DOTH PROCEEDE       2.121.13
WHEN I CONSIDER EVERY THING THAT GROWES              3.15.1
BY ADDING ONE THING TO MY PURPOSE NOTHING           3.20.12
```

```
OR SOME FIERCE THING REPLEAT WITH TOO MUCH RAGE          3.23.3
I SIGH THE LACKE OF MANY A THING I SOUGHT                3.30.3
WHEN LOVE CONVERTED FROM THE THING IT WAS                3.49.7
(THOUGH YOU DOE ANY THING) HE THINKES NO ILL             3.57.14
THAT DOE NOT DO THE THING, THEY MOST DO SHOWE            3.94.2
HATH PUT A SPIRIT OF YOUTH IN EVERY THING                3.98.3
ONE THING EXPRESSING, LEAVES OUT DIFFERENCE              3.105.8
COUNTING NO OLD THING OLD, THOU MINE, I THINE            3.108.7
IN PURSUIT OF THE THING SHE WOULD HAVE STAY              3.143.4
OR MADE THEM SWERE AGAINST THE THING THEY SEE            3.152.12
WHILE HE EACH THING IN SENSE'S BALLANCE WAYES            4.25.6
'WHAT IDLER THING, THEN SPEAKE AND NOT BE HARD+'         4.34.9
WHAT HARDER THING THEN SMART, AND NOT TO SPEAKE+         4.34.10
I CRAV'D THE THING WHICH EVER SHE DENIES                 4.63.6
BASE THING I CAN NO MORE ENDURE TO VIEW                  5.3.6
THE THING WHICH I DOO MOST IN HER ADMIRE                 5.5.3
BASE THING, AND THINKE HOW SHE TO HEAVEN
                                     MAY CLIME           5.13.10
WHAT MORE MIRACULOUS THING MAY BE TOLD                   5.30.9
THAT FIRE WHICH ALL THING MELTS, SHOULD
                                   HARDEN YSE            5.30.10
THING SO DIVINE TO VEW OF EARTHLY EYE                    5.45.6
GREAT SHAME IT IS, THING SO DIVINE IN VIEW               5.53.9
STRANGE THING ME SEEMD TO SEE A BEAST SO WYLD            5.67.13
A MORTALL THING SO TO IMMORTALIZE                        5.75.6
```

THINGS   44
```
WHERE BLAZE THOSE LIGHTS FAIREST OF EARTHLY
                                   THINGS               1.12.3
AND ALL THINGS FIT AGAINST HER COMMING THERE             1.30.8
BY THIS I SEE, HOW-EVER THINGS BE PAST                   2.2.13
HOW MANY PALTRY, FOOLISH, PAINTED THINGS                 2.6.1
WHICH BEST BY YOU, OF LIVING $THINGS, IS KNOWNE          2.16.3
AYMING AT THINGS EXCEEDING ALL PERFECTION                2.34.6
HOW HAPPY ARE ALL OTHER LIVING $THINGS                   2.37.5
HOW $THINGS STILL UNEXPECTEDLY HAVE RUNNE                2.51.3
CHEEFE GOOD, FROM WHOM ALL GOOD THINGS WE DERIVE         2.146.8
WITH $APRILLS FIRST BORNE FLOWERS AND
                              ALL THINGS RARE            3.21.7
I SOMMON UP REMEMBRANCE OF THINGS PAST                   3.30.2
BUT THINGS REMOV'D THAT HIDDEN IN THERE LIE              3.31.8
FOR ALL THE DAY THEY VIEW THINGS UNRESPECTED             3.43.2
AND SO SHOULD YOU, TO LOVE THINGS NOTHING WORTH          3.72.14
FOR SWEETEST THINGS TURNE SOWREST BY THEIR
                                    DEEDES               3.94.13
AND ALL THINGS TURNES TO FAIRE, THAT EIES
                                   CAN SEE               3.95.12
TO TRUTHS TRANSLATED, AND FOR TRUE THINGS DEEM'D         3.96.8
OF THE WIDE WORLD, DREAMING ON THINGS TO COME            3.107.2
TO MAKE OF MONSTERS, AND THINGS INDIGEST                 3.114.5
DIVERT STRONG MINDES TO TH'COURSE OF ALTRING
                                   THINGS               3.115.8
IN THINGS OF GREAT RECEIT WITH EASE WE PROOVE            3.136.7
IN THINGS RIGHT TRUE MY HEART AND EYES
                              HAVE ERRED                 3.137.13
WHENCE HAST THOU THIS BECOMMING OF THINGS IL             3.150.5
AND STRANGE THINGS COST TOO DEARE FOR
                              MY POORE SPRITES           4.3.11
FOR THOUGH SHE PASSE ALL THINGS, YET WHAT IS ALL         4.19.9
AS SACRED THINGS, FAR FROM ALL DAUNGER'S SHOW            4.24.8
READY TO STORE THEIR CAMPES OF NEEDFULL THINGS           4.29.4
```

```
TO LEAVE THE SCEPTER OF ALL SUBJECT THINGS          4.38.4
AND IF THESE THINGS, AS BEING THINE BY RIGHT        4.39.12
ALAS, IF $FANCY DRAWNE BY IMAG'D THINGS             4.45.9
TO WITLESSE THINGS, THEN $LOVE I HOPE (SINCE WIT    4.59.13
THESE THINGS ARE LEFT ME BY MY ONLY $DEARE          4.72.12
SCORN OF BASE THINGS, AND SDEIGNE OF FOULE
                            DISHONOR                5.5.6
DO SEEKE MOST PRETIOUS THINGS TO MAKE YOUR GAIN     5.15.2
YET MANY WONDROUS THINGS THERE ARE BESIDE           5.17.8
THAT CAN EXPRESSE THE LIFE OF THINGS INDEED         5.17.14
FOR EASIE THINGS THAT MAY BE GOT AT WILL            5.26.11
BUT LOTHE THE THINGS WHICH THEY DID LIKE BEFORE     5.35.11
AS IS A STORME, THAT ALL THINGS DOTH PROSTRATE      5.56.6
BASE THINGS THAT TO HER LOVE TOO BOLD ASPIRE+       5.61.12
IT DOWN IS WEIGHD WITH THOGHT OF EARTHLY THINGS     5.72.3
NOT SO, (QUOD I) LET BASER THINGS DEVIZE            5.75.9
BUT LOATH THE THINGS WHICH THEY DID LIKE BEFORE     5.83.11
THE WORLD THAT CANNOT DEEME OF WORTHY THINGS        5.85.1
THINK                    59
FAVOURS (I THINKE) WOULD SENCE QUITE OVERCOME       1.17.13
HOW TO THINKE MUCH, AND HAVE NO WORDS TO SPEAKE     1.20.6
YET SURE SHE CANNOT BUT MUST THINKE A PART          1.21.13
AND ($DELIA) THINKE THY MORNING MUST HAVE NIGHT     1.40.8
AND THINKE THE SAME BECOMES THY FADING BEST         1.40.11
THINKE NOT (SWEET $DELIA) THIS SHALL BE THY SHAME   1.44.5
FOR WOMEN GRIEVE TO THINKE THEY MUST BE OLD         1.50.14
WHO SHOULD I THINKE THE $MURTHER SHOULD COMMIT+     2.2.2
LITTLE $ILE SAY, BUT THINKE THE $DEVILL'S IN ME     2.15.14
AGAINST THESE $FOLKES, THAT THINKE THEMSELVES
                            SO WISE                 2.28.3
THAT $EYES COULD THINKE OF THAT MY $HEART
                            COULD SEE               2.33.14
OR CAN I THINKE WHAT MY $REWARD SHALL BE            2.52.11
AND HEAVEN MAY JOY TO THINK ON PAST WORLDS
                            BLISSE                  2.107.12
A FOOLES THINKE I, HAD YOU $IDEA SEENE              2.120.13
HAPLYE I THINKE ON THEE, AND THEN MY STATE          3.29.10
BUT IF THE WHILE I THINKE ON THEE (DEARE FRIEND)    3.30.13
AS SOONE AS THINKE THE PLACE WHERE HE WOULD BE      3.44.8
NOR THINKE THE BITTERNESSE OF ABSENCE SOWRE         3.57.7
BUT LIKE A SAD SLAVE STAY AND THINKE OF NOUGHT      3.57.11
I THINKE GOOD THOUGHTS, WHILST OTHER WRITE
                            GOOD WORDES             3.85.5
NO BITTERNESSE THAT I WILL BITTER THINKE            3.111.11
WHICH IN THEIR WILS COUNT BAD WHAT I THINK GOOD+    3.121.8
THEN THINKE THAT WE BEFORE HAVE HEARD THEM TOULD    3.123.8
AND YET BY HEAVEN I THINKE MY LOVE AS RARE          3.130.13
AND THENCE THIS SLAUNDER AS I THINKE PROCEEDS       3.131.14
THINKE ALL BUT ONE, AND ME IN THAT ONE $WILL        3.135.14
WHY SHOULD MY HEART THINKE THAT A SEVERALL PLOT     3.137.9
THAT SHE MIGHT THINKE ME SOME UNTUTERD YOUTH        3.138.3
DOE I NOT THINKE ON THEE WHEN I FORGOT              3.149.3
BUT THINKE THAT ALL THE $MAP OF MY STATE
                            I DISPLAY               4.6.13
THINKE THAT I THINKE STATE ERROURS TO REDRESSE      4.23.8
THINKE THAT I THINKE STATE ERROURS TO REDRESSE      4.23.8
AND FOOLES CAN THINKE THOSE $LAMPES OF
                            PUREST LIGHT            4.26.2
YET PRIDE I THINKE DOTH NOT MY SOULE POSSESSE       4.27.9
BUT KNOW NOT HOW, FOR STILL I THINKE OF YOU         4.30.14
```

```
'BUT WILL NOT WISE MEN THINKE THY WORDS
                  FOND WARE+'                       4.34.7
AND THEN, THINKE THUS, ALTHOUGH THY BEAUTIE BE      4.40.9
THINKE $NATURE ME A MAN OF ARMES DID MAKE           4.41.11
THEN THINKE MY DEARE, THAT YOU IN ME DO REED        4.45.12
AND THINKE SO STILL, SO $STELLA KNOW MY MIND        4.54.9
AND THINKE I SHOULD NOT YOUR LARGE PRECEPTS
                  MISSE+                            4.56.4
WHAT, DOST THOU THINKE THAT I CAN EVER TAKE         4.56.10
O THINKE I THEN, WHAT PARADISE OF JOY               4.68.13
SINCE BEST WITS THINKE IT WIT THEE TO ADMIRE        4.80.2
STELLA THINKE NOT THAT I BY VERSE SEEKE FAME        4.90.1
O $GOD, THINKE YOU THAT SATISFIES MY CARE+          4.92.8
MERY WITH HIM, AND NOT THINKE OF HIS WOE            4.106.14
THEN THINKE NOT LONG IN TAKING LITLE PAINE          5.6.13
BASE THING, AND THINKE HOW SHE TO HEAVEN
                  MAY CLIME                         5.13.10
LYKE SACRED PRIESTS THAT NEVER THINKE AMISSE        5.22.8
SO WHEN I THINKE TO END THAT I BEGONNE              5.23.9
I THINKE THAT I A NEW $PANDORA SEE                  5.24.8
DOE YE NOT THINCK TH'ACCOMPLISHMENT OF IT           5.33.6
THINCK EVER TO ENDURE SO TAEDIOUS TOYLE+            5.33.10
THEN THINKE HOW LITLE GLORY YE HAVE GAYNED          5.36.10
THAT NETHER I MAY SPEAKE NOR THINKE AT ALL          5.43.7
AND THINCK THEY DY WITH PLEASURE, LIVE
                  WITH PAYNE                        5.47.14
AND GREATER GLORY THINKE TO SAVE, THEN SPILL        5.49.4
BUT GLORY THINKE TO MAKE THESE CRUEL STOURES        5.57.10
THINKEST              2
THINK'ST THOU, MY $WIT SHALL KEEPE THE
                  PACK-$HORSE $WAY                  2.31.7
THINK'ST THOU MY $LOVE SHALL IN THOSE
                  $RAGGES BE DREST                  2.31.11
THINKING              5
THINKING TO SCALE THE HEAVEN OF HER HART            1.36.2
IF THINKING ON ME THEN SHOULD MAKE YOU WOE          3.71.8
A THOUSAND GRONES BUT THINKING ON THY FACE          3.131.10
THUS VAINELY THINKING THAT SHE THINKES ME YOUNG     3.138.5
THINKING TO QUENCH HER THIRST AT THE NEXT BROOKE    5.67.8
THINKS               14
SHE THINKES A LOOKE MAY RECOMPENCE MY CARE          1.24.9
ME $THINKES I SEE SOME CROOKED $MIMICKE JEERE       2.31.1
ME THINKES THIS $TIME BECOMMETH $LOVERS BEST        2.37.3
ME THINKES I $FLIE, YET WANT I LEGGES TO $GOE       2.62.5
ME THINKES 'TIS LONG SINCE FIRST THESE
                  $WARRES BEGUN                     2.63.2
MEE THINKS I FLEE, YET WANT I LEGS TO GOE           2.150.5
AND YET ME THINKES I HAVE $ASTRONOMY                3.14.2
(THOUGH YOU DOE ANY THING) HE THINKES NO ILL        3.57.14
ME THINKES NO FACE SO GRATIOUS IS AS MINE           3.62.5
SO YOUR SWEETE HEW, WHICH ME THINKES STILL
                  DOTH STAND                        3.104.11
THAT ALL THE WORLD BESIDES ME THINKES
                  Y'ARE DEAD                        3.112.14
THUS VAINELY THINKING THAT SHE THINKES ME YOUNG     3.138.5
THAT SHE, ME THINKS, NOT ONELY SHINES BUT SINGS     4.38.8
NE THINKS OF OTHER HEAVEN, BUT HOW IT MIGHT         5.72.11
THINLY               1
LIKE STONES OF WORTH THEY THINLY PLACED ARE         3.52.7
```

```
THIRD                    2
   A THIRD NOR RED, NOR WHITE, HAD STOLNE OF BOTH       3.99.10
   THE THIRD MY LOVE, MY LIVES LAST ORNAMENT             5.74.9
THIRST                   2
   SHE'ST QUENCH HER THIRST AS DULY AS THEY FALL        2.115.10
   THINKING TO QUENCH HER THIRST AT THE NEXT BROOKE      5.67.8
THIRSTING                1
   STILL THIRSTING FOR SUBVERSION OF MY STATE           2.63.10
THIRSTY                  1
   SICKE, THIRSTY, GLAD (THOUGH BUT OF EMPTY
                            GLASSE)                      4.104.11
THITHER                  4
   AND THETHER ALL MY FORCES DOE TRANSPORTE             1.27.7
   LET LOVE AND YOUTH CONDUCT THY PLEASURES THITHER     1.51.8
   AND THETHER HIED A SAD DISTEMPERD GUEST              3.153.12
   MY BOILING SPRITES DID THITHER SOONE INCLINE         4.16.3
THORNS                   4
   ROSES HAVE THORNES, AND SILVER FOUNTAINES MUD        3.35.2
   HANG ON SUCH THORNES, AND PLAY AS WANTONLY           3.54.7
   THE $ROSES FEAREFULLY ON THORNES DID STAND           3.99.8
   SO NIMBLE FEET AS STIRRE STILL, THOUGH
                            ON THORNES                   4.78.11
THORNY                   1
   WHY SHOULDST THOU TOYLE OUR THORNIE SOILE
                            TO TILL+                     4.10.6
THOROUGHEST              1
   THE THOROWEST WORDS, FIT FOR WOE'S SELFE TO GRONE    4.57.4
THOUGHT                 44
   STILL IN THE TRACE OF ONE PERPLEXED THOUGHT          1.33.1
   CONVAY THEE FROM THE THOUGHT OF THY DISGRACE         1.52.11
   WHAT THEY LAST THOUGHT OF, WHEN THE $BRAINE
                            GREW SICKE                   2.9.7
   RAVISH'D A $WORLD BEYOND THE FARTHEST $THOUGHT       2.34.2
   THOUGHT IT IN WEIGHT TOO LIGHT BY MANY A $GRAINE     2.38.12
   FORGOT HERSELFE, AND THOUGHT SHE HAD BEEN
                            DROWNED                      2.109.4
   BY INSPIRATION, CAME CONCEAV'D WITH THOUGHT          2.116.2
   OR TONGUE OF WONDER WORTH COULD TELL A
                            WONDER THOUGHT               2.117.2
   HE FRAMD HIM WINGS WITH FEATHERS OF HIS THOUGHT      2.122.5
   THOUGHT HER IN WEIGHT TOO LIGHT BY MANY
                            A GRAINE                     2.131.12
   MY REBELL THOUGHT FOR ME IN $AMBUSHE LYES            2.142.7
   O CHANGE THY THOUGHT, THAT I MAY CHANGE MY MINDE     3.10.9
   IN THY SOULES THOUGHT (ALL NAKED) WILL BESTOW IT     3.26.8
   WHEN TO THE $SESSIONS OF SWEET SILENT THOUGHT        3.30.1
   AND ALL THOSE FRIENDS WHICH I THOUGHT BURIED         3.31.4
   OH THEN VOUTSAFE ME BUT THIS LOVING THOUGHT          3.32.9
   IF THE DULL SUBSTANCE OF MY FLESH WERE THOUGHT       3.44.1
   FOR NIMBLE THOUGHT CAN JUMPE BOTH SEA AND LAND       3.44.7
   BUT AH, THOUGHT KILLS ME THAT I AM NOT THOUGHT       3.44.9
   BUT AH, THOUGHT KILLS ME THAT I AM NOT THOUGHT       3.44.9
   THE FIRST MY THOUGHT, THE OTHER MY DESIRE            3.45.3
   NOR DARE I QUESTION WITH MY JEALIOUS THOUGHT         3.57.9
   I SHOULD IN THOUGHT CONTROULE YOUR TIMES
                            OF PLEASURE                  3.58.2
   THIS THOUGHT IS AS A DEATH WHICH CANNOT CHOOSE       3.64.13
   WANT NOTHING THAT THE THOUGHT OF HEARTS CAN MEND     3.69.2
   I FOUND (OR THOUGHT I FOUND) YOU DID EXCEED          3.83.3
   BUT THAT IS IN MY THOUGHT, WHOSE LOVE TO YOU         3.85.11
```

```
WHILST IT HATH THOUGHT IT SELFE SO BLESSED
                         NEVER+                           3.119.6
FOR I HAVE SWORNE THEE FAIRE, AND THOUGHT
                         THEE BRIGHT                      3.147.13
DECEIV'D THE QUAKING BOY, WHO THOUGHT
                         FROM SO PURE LIGHT               4.8.10
AND, $LOVE, I THOUGHT THAT I WAS FULL OF THEE            4.16.4
I THOUGHT THOSE BABES OF SOME PINNE'S
                         HURT DID WHINE                   4.16.7
UNSEENE, UNHEARD, WHILE THOUGHT TO HIGHEST PLACE         4.27.13
TO HATCH MINE EYES, AND THAT UNBITTED THOUGHT           4.38.2
THOU CANST VOUCHSAFE THE INFLUENCE OF A THOUGHT         4.40.6
YET LET THIS THOUGHT THY $TYGRISH COURAGE PASSE         4.65.11
THOUGHT WITH GOOD CAUSE THOU LIKEST SO
                         WELL THE NIGHT                   4.96.1
BUT SOONE AS THOUGHT OF THEE BREEDS MY DELIGHT          4.108.5
UNQUIET THOUGHT, WHOM AT THE FIRST I BRED               5.2.1
WHICH HER DEEP WIT, THAT TRUE HARTS THOUGHT
                         CAN SPEL                         5.43.13
THEN NOT ON HIM THAT NEVER THOUGHT YOU ILL              5.49.7
THERE LET NO THOUGHT OF JOY OR PLEASURE VAINE           5.52.9
MY SOVERAYNE SAYNT, THE $IDOLL OF MY THOUGHT            5.61.2
IT DOWN IS WEIGHD WITH THOGHT OF EARTHLY THINGS         5.72.3
THOUGHTS                 68
AND SET MY THOUGHTS IN HEEDLESSE WAYES TO RANGE         1.5.2
BY MINE OWNE THOUGHTS, SET ON ME BY MY $FAIRE           1.5.11
MY THOUGHTS (LIKE $HOUNDES) PURSUE ME TO MY DEATH       1.5.12
IF THIS BE LOVE, TO CLOATHE ME WITH DARKE THOUGHTS      1.9.9
M'AMBITIOUS THOUGHTS CONFINED IN HER FACE               1.12.5
IF HUNGER-STARVEN THOUGHTS SO LONG RETAINED             1.15.3
AND THAT ALL THIS MOOVES NOT HER THOUGHTS A WHIT        1.21.12
YET MUST THAT BLISSE MY HUNGRY THOUGHTS APPEASE         1.24.12
OFT AND IN VAINE MY REBEL THOUGHTS HAVE VENTRED         1.27.1
REIGNE IN MY THOUGHTS, MY LOVE AND LIFE
                         ARE THINE                        1.27.14
RAIGNE IN MY THOUGHTS FAIRE HAND, SWEETE
                         EYE, RARE VOICE                  1.28.1
INTIC'D MY $THOUGHTS, AGAINST ME TO CONSPIRE            2.23.10
MY HOLY $THOUGHTS, THEY BE THE $VESTALL FLAME           2.30.10
ALL UNCLEANE $THOUGHTS, FOULE $SPIRITS
                         CAST OUT IN MEE                  2.35.13
MY $HEART THE $ANVILE, WHERE MY $THOUGHTS
                         DOE BEATE                        2.40.1
THOU WHICH HAST BANN'D THY $THOUGHTS,
                         AND CURST THY $BIRTH             2.49.11
MY $THOUGHTS BRED UP WITH $EAGLE-BIRDS OF LOVE          2.103.1
AND THUS (MY FAIRE) MY THOUGHTS AWAY BE FLOWNE          2.103.13
ALL UNCLEANE THOUGHTS, FOULE SPIRITS CAST
                         OUT IN MEE                       2.112.13
MY HART SURCHARG'D WITH THOUGHTS, SIGHES
                         IN ABUNDANCE RAISE               2.133.9
MY DYING LOOKES AND THOUGHTS ARE PEIZ'D
                         IN EQUALL FEARES                 2.133.12
WORDS, THOUGHTS, AND DEEDS, DEVOTED TO HER HONOR        2.138.6
RARE OF-SPRING OF MY THOUGHTS, MY DEEREST $LOVE         2.141.1
MY $HART THE $ANVILE WHERE MY THOUGHTS DOE BEATE        2.144.1
FOR THEN MY THOUGHTS (FROM FAR WHERE I ABIDE)           3.27.5
YET IN THESE THOUGHTS MY SELFE ALMOST DESPISING         3.29.9
TO ENTERTAINE THE TIME WITH THOUGHTS OF LOVE            3.39.11
WHICH TIME AND THOUGHTS SO SWEETLY DOST DECEIVE         3.39.12
```

```
A QUEST OF THOUGHTS, ALL TENNANTS TO THE HEART        3.46.10
AND IN HIS THOUGHTS OF LOVE DOTH SHARE A PART          3.47.8
FOR THOU NOR FARTHER THEN MY THOUGHTS CANST MOVE       3.47.11
THEN CHURLS THEIR THOUGHTS (ALTHOUGH THEIR
                          EIES WERE KIND)              3.69.11
THAT I IN YOUR SWEET THOUGHTS WOULD BE FORGOT          3.71.7
SO ARE YOU TO MY THOUGHTS AS FOOD TO LIFE              3.75.1
I THINKE GOOD THOUGHTS, WHILST OTHER WRITE
                          GOOD WORDES                  3.85.5
ME FOR MY DOMBE THOUGHTS, SPEAKING IN EFFECT           3.85.14
THAT DID MY RIPE THOUGHTS IN MY BRAINE INHEARCE        3.86.3
FOR BENDING ALL MY LOVING THOUGHTS ON THEE             3.88.10
WHAT ERE THY THOUGHTS, OR THY HEARTS WORKINGS BE       3.93.11
GOR'D MINE OWN THOUGHTS, SOLD CHEAP WHAT
                          IS MOST DEARE                3.110.3
BY THEIR RANCKE THOUGHTES, MY DEEDES MUST
                          NOT BE SHOWN                 3.121.12
MY THOUGHTS AND MY DISCOURSE AS MAD MENS ARE           3.147.11
ENAM'LING WITH PIED FLOWERS THEIR THOUGHTS OF GOLD     4.3.4
DEALE THOU WITH POWERS OF THOUGHTS, LEAVE
                          LOVE TO WILL                 4.10.8
OF SINFULL THOUGHTS, WHICH DO IN RUINE END+            4.14.8
MY WITS, QUICKE IN VAINE THOUGHTS, IN VERTUE LAME      4.21.4
OF ALL MY THOUGHTS HATH NEITHER STOP NOR START         4.23.13
MY TONGUE DOTH ITCH, MY THOUGHTS IN LABOUR BE          4.37.2
ARE HUMBLED THOUGHTS, WHICH BIT OF $REVERENCE
                          MOVE                         4.49.6
STELLA, THE FULNESSE OF MY THOUGHTS OF THEE            4.50.1
MY THOUGHTS I SPEAKE, AND WHAT I SPEAKE
                          DOTH FLOW                    4.74.10
MAKES ME IN MY BEST THOUGHTS AND QUIETST
                          JUDGEMENT SEE                4.77.12
WHAT, DOTH HIGH PLACE AMBITIOUS THOUGHTS AUGMENT+      4.83.9
STELLA FOOD OF MY THOUGHTS, HART OF MY HART            4.87.2
THE FIELD WHERE ALL MY THOUGHTS TO WARRE
                          BE TRAIND                    4.98.2
MAKE IN MY HEAVY MOULD NEW THOUGHTS TO GROW            4.106.11
AND ON MY THOUGHTS GIVE THY $LIEFTENANCY               4.107.7
BIDS ALL OLD THOUGHTS TO DIE IN DUMPISH SPRIGHT        5.4.4
YOU FRAME MY THOUGHTS AND FASHION ME WITHIN            5.8.9
THAT HINDERS HEAVENLY THOUGHTS WITH DROSSY SLIME       5.13.12
ON WHICH MY THOUGHTS DOO DAY AND NIGHT ATTEND          5.22.7
NOT EARTH., FOR HER HIGH THOGHTS MORE
                          HEAVENLY ARE                 5.55.5
AND MY FRAYLE THOUGHTS TOO RASHLY LED ASTRAY+          5.76.6
SWEET THOUGHTS I ENVY YOUR SO HAPPY REST               5.76.13
MY THOUGHTS THE GUESTS, WHICH WOULD THEREON
                          HAVE FEDD                    5.77.14
AND LET MY THOUGHTS BEHOLD HER SELFE IN MEE            5.78.14
AND MODEST THOUGHTS BREATHD FROM WEL TEMPRED
                          SPRITES                      5.84.6
THE WHICH WAS WONT TO LEAD MY THOUGHTS ASTRAY          5.88.2
THOUGHT'S                 3
TO HER THAT SITS IN MY THOUGHTS $TEMPLE SAINTED        1.15.7
MY WORDS MIGHT IMITATE MY DEEREST THOUGHTS
                          DIRECTION                    2.117.7
IT STOPPED IS WITH THOUGHTS ASTONISHMENT               5.3.10
THOUGHTS-MAZE             1
TO THIS THOUGHTS-MAZE, TO MY CONFUSION TENDING         1.18.2
```

THOUSAND   17
  A THOUSAND TIMES IT PROMIS'D ME RELIEFE   1.25.3
  A THOUSAND $NIMPH-LIKE AND INAMOR'D $GRACES   2.4.2
  WITH THOUSAND $PLAGUES, MORE THEN IN $PURGATORIE   2.49.12
  THUS MIDST A THOUSAND WOES, TEN THOUSAND
                           JOYES ARISE   2.114.8
  THUS MIDST A THOUSAND WOES, TEN THOUSAND
                           JOYES ARISE   2.114.8
  AND RACKE HER WITH A THOUSAND HOLY WISHES   2.115.14
  ILE EXECUTE HER WITH A THOUSAND KISSES   2.115.16
  WHOSE LYFE DOTH SAVE A THOUSAND SOULES
                           FROM HELL   2.119.12
  THE SHORES BESET WITH THOUSAND SECRET SPYES   2.122.3
  HER $BOWE IS BEAUTY, WITH TEN THOUSAND STRINGS   2.126.6
  DESIRING YET A THOUSAND DEATHS TO PROVE   2.134.7
  A THOUSAND VOWES, A THOUSAND SIGHES AND TEARES   2.138.4
  A THOUSAND VOWES, A THOUSAND SIGHES AND TEARES   2.138.4
  AFTER A THOUSAND VICTORIES ONCE FOILD   3.25.10
  A THOUSAND GRONES BUT THINKING ON THY FACE   3.131.10
  FOR THEY IN THEE A THOUSAND ERRORS NOTE   3.141.2
  WITH THOUSAND ARROWES, WHICH YOUR EIES HAVE SHOT   5.57.8
THRALL   6
  FOR MEN DISEASD, BUT I MY $MISTRISSE THRALL   3.154.12
  LET HER ACCEPT ME AS HER FAITHFULL THRALL   5.29.10
  BUT JOY HER THRALL FOR EVER TO REMAYNE   5.42.7
  WHAT TYRANNY IS THIS BOTH MY HART TO THRALL   5.43.5
  GENTLY ENCAGE, THAT HE MAY BE YOUR THRALL   5.73.10
  TO ME YOUR THRALL, IN WHOM IS LITTLE WORTH   5.82.10
THRALLDOM   1
  THAT HUE, WHOSE FORCE MY HART STILL UNTO
                           THRALDOME TIES+   4.102.8
THRALLED   2
  UNDER THE BLOW OF THRALLED DISCONTENT   3.124.7
  OF A DEARE FOE, AND THRALLED TO HIS LOVE   5.71.6
THRALLS   1
  OF SUCH POORE THRALLS HER CRUELL HANDS EMBREW   5.31.12
THREAD   1
  YOU HAVE SPUNNE A FAIRE $THRED, HE REPLYES
                           IN SCORNE   2.59.12
THREAT   1
  DOTH LOWRE, NAY, CHIDE., NAY, THREAT FOR
                           ONLY THIS   4.73.7
THREATENED   1
  WHO THREATNED STRIPES, IF HE HIS WRATH DID PROVE   4.17.6
THREATENING   2
  THOSE SCARLET JUDGES, THREATNING BLOUDY PAINE+   4.73.11
  THREINING RASH EIES WHICH GAZE ON HER SO WIDE   5.5.7
THREATS   1
  WHEN ALL THE GODS HE THREATS WITH THUNDRING DART   5.39.4
THREE   21
  AND SERVE ALL THREE, AND YET THEY SPOILE ME TOO   1.28.14
  THREE $NINES THERE ARE, TO EVERY ONE A $NINE   2.18.2
  ONE $WOMAN NOW, MAKES THREE ODDE $NUMBERS EVEN   2.18.4
  MAKES EVERY $ONE OF THESE THREE $NINES A $TEN   2.18.14
  THREE NINES THERE ARE, TO EVERIE ONE A NINE   2.108.2
  ONE WONDER WOMAN NOW MAKES THREE OD NUMBERS EVEN   2.108.4
  MAKES EVERY ONE OF THESE THREE NINES A TEN   2.108.14
  THREE SORTS OF $SERPENTS DOE RESEMBLE THEE   2.130.1
  THE WEEPING $CROCCODILE.. THESE VILE PERNICIOUS
                           THREE   2.130.4

```
SUCH SEEMES YOUR BEAUTIE STILL.. $THREE
                    $WINTERS COLDE                    3.104.3
HAVE FROM THE FORRESTS SHOOKE THREE SUMMERS
                    PRIDE                             3.104.4
THREE BEAUTIOUS SPRINGS TO YELLOW $AUTUMNE
                    TURN'D                            3.104.5
THREE $APRILL PERFUMES IN THREE HOT $JUNES
                    BURN'D                            3.104.7
THREE $APRILL PERFUMES IN THREE HOT $JUNES
                    BURN'D                            3.104.7
THREE THEAMS IN ONE, WHICH WONDROUS SCOPE
                    AFFORDS                           3.105.12
WHICH THREE TILL NOW, NEVER KEPT SEATE IN ONE         3.105.14
OF THOSE THREE GODS, WHOSE ARMES THE FAIREST WERE     4.13.2
IF $FRENCH CAN YET THREE PARTS IN ONE AGREE           4.30.5
THE WHICH THREE TIMES THRISE HAPPY HATH ME MADE       5.74.3
YE THREE $ELIZABETHS FOR EVER LIVE                    5.74.13
THAT THREE SUCH GRACES DID UNTO ME GIVE               5.74.14
THREEFOLD                    1
A TORMENT THRICE THREE-FOLD THUS TO BE CROSSED        3.133.8
THREESCORE                   2
  AND THREESCOORE YEARE WOULD MAKE THE WORLD AWAY     3.11.8
  AS $MARS IN THREE SCORE YEARES DOTH RUN
                    HIS SPHEARE                       5.60.4
THREW                        4
  AND THREW ME DOWNE TO PAINE IN ALL THIS FIRE        1.36.5
  THREW IN HERSELFE, TO SAVE HERSELFE BY DROWNING     2.109.12
  I HATE, FROM HATE AWAY SHE THREW                    3.145.13
  THAT DAINTY ODOURS FROM THEM THREW AROUND           5.64.3
THRICE                       7
  THRICE HAPPY BE THOSE EYES WHICH MAY BEHOLD
                    THEE                              2.129.10
  MAKES $SOMERS WELCOME, THRICE MORE WISH'D,
                    MORE RARE                         3.56.14
  AND GAINE BY ILLS THRISE MORE THEN I HAVE SPENT     3.119.14
  A TORMENT THRICE THREE-FOLD THUS TO BE CROSSED      3.133.8
  HIS TROMPET SHRILL HATH THRISE ALREADY SOUNDED      5.19.2
  THRISE HAPPIE SHE, THAT IS SO WELL ASSURED          5.59.1
  THE WHICH THREE TIMES THRISE HAPPY HATH ME MADE     5.74.3
THRICE-GRATEFUL              1
  A SACRIFICE THRICE-GRATEFULL TO HER EIES            1.47.11
THRICE-MARRIED'S            1
  WITH ONE THRICE-MARRY'D'S $PRAY'RS, THAT
                    DID BEQUEATH                      2.15.11
THRICE-THREE                1
  THE THRICE-THREE $MUSES BUT TOO WANTON BE           2.39.7
THRIFTLESS                  1
  WERE AN ALL-EATING SHAME, AND THRIFTLESSE PRAISE    3.2.8
THRILLING                   1
  OR MAKE AGREEMENT WITH HER THRILLING EYES           5.36.6
THRIVE                      2
  AS TRUTH AND BEAUTIE SHAL TOGETHER THRIVE           3.14.11
  THEN $IF HE THRIVE AND I BE CAST AWAY               3.80.13
THRIVERS                    1
  PITTIFULL THRIVORS IN THEIR GAZING SPENT            3.125.8
THROES                      1
  THUS GREAT WITH CHILD TO SPEAKE, AND HELPLESSE
                    IN MY THROWES                     4.1.12
THRONE                      2
  ALAS, IF FROM THE HEIGHT OF $VERTUE'S THRONE        4.40.5
```

```
      IN $BEAUTIE'S THRONE, SEE NOW WHO DARES
                       COME NEARE              4.73.10
THRONED                  1
   AS ON THE FINGER CF A THRONED $QUEENE        3.96.5
THRONG                   2
   SO SHALT THOU FLYE ABOVE THE VULGAR $THRONG  2.6.13
   THENCE BREAKING FCRTH DID THICK ABOUT ME THRONG  5.12.8
THRONGED                 1
   WITH THOSE THE THRONGED $THEATERS THAT PRESSE  2.47.5
THROUGH                 36
   A WAY THROUGH WANT TO FREE MY SOULE FROM CARE  1.29.10
   SO THOU THROUGH WINDOWES OF THINE AGE SHALT SEE  3.3.11
   FOR THROUGH THE $PAINTER MUST YOU SEE HIS SKILL  3.24.5
   TIS NOT ENOUGH THAT THROUGH THE CLOUDE
                       THOU BREAKE            3.34.5
THROUGH HEAVY SLEEPE ON SIGHTLESSE EYES
                       DOTH STAY+             3.43.12
BEGGERD OF BLOOD TO BLUSH THROUGH LIVELY VAINES  3.67.10
SO HIM I LOOSE THROUGH MY UNKINDE ABUSE         3.134.12
THE WINDOWES NOW THROUGH WHICH THIS HEAV'NLY GUEST  4.9.9
WHICH THROUGH A BLEEDING HEART HIS POINT
                       DID SHOVE              4.13.6
WHERETO LONG SINCE, THROUGH MY LONG BATTRED EYES  4.36.3
THAT THROUGH MY HEART THEIR BEAMIE DARTS BE GONE  4.48.10
MY FRIEND, THAT OFT SAW THROUGH ALL MASKES MY WO  4.69.5
AND THROUGH THOSE LIPS DRINKE $NECTAR
                       FROM THAT TOONG        4.83.13
THROUGH ME, WRETCH ME, EVEN $STELLA VEXED IS    4.93.4
THROUGH THAT DARKE FORNACE TO MY HART OPPREST   4.108.3
THRUGH YOUR BRIGHT BEAMS DOTH NOT THE
                       BLINDED GUEST          5.8.5
STRONG THRUGH YOUR CAUSE, BUT BY YOUR VERTUE WEAK  5.8.12
THROUGH SWEET ILLUSION CF HER LOOKES DELIGHT    5.16.4
IS NOT DISSOLV'D THROUGH MY SO HOT DESYRE       5.30.3
THROUGH SWEET ALLUREMENT OF HER LOVELY HEW      5.31.10
LYKE AS A SHIP THAT THROUGH THE $OCEAN WYDE     5.34.1
THROUGH HIDDEN PERILS ROUND ABOUT ME PLAST      5.34.8
MY HUNGRY EYES THROUGH GREEDY COVETIZE          5.35.1
ARION, WHEN THROUGH TEMPESTS CRUEL WRACKE       5.38.1
THROUGH THE SWEET MUSICK WHICH HIS HARP DID MAKE  5.38.3
A MELTING PLEASANCE RAN THROUGH EVERY PART      5.39.7
THRUGH THE BROAD WORLD DOTH SPRED HIS GOODLY RAY  5.40.8
THRUGH STUBBORN PRIDE AMONGST THEMSELVES DID JAR  5.44.2
AND WERE IT NOT THAT THROUGH YOUR CRUELTY       5.45.9
FOR THAT THEY SHOULD ENDURE THROUGH MANY AGES   5.51.3
SEEING MY HART THROUGH LAUNCHED EVERY WHERE     5.57.7
WHILES DIVING DEEPE THROUGH AMOROUS INSIGHT     5.76.7
THROUGH $FAERY LAND, WHICH THOSE SIX BOOKS
                       COMPILE                5.80.2
THROGH WHICH HER WORDS SO WISE DO MAKE THEIR WAY  5.81.11
MY HUNGRY EYES, THROUGH GREEDY COVETIZE         5.83.1
THROUGH CONTEMPLATION OF MY PUREST PART         5.88.10
THROUGHLY                1
   WITH PRICKING SHOT HE DID NOT THROUGHLY MOVE  4.17.3
THROUGHOUT               1
   TO HELPE HER FLIGHT THROUGHOUT THE FAIREST $ILE  1.43.10
THROW                    2
   IN SO PROFOUND $ABISME I THROW ALL CARE      3.112.9
   OF THOSE FIERCE DARTS, DISPAIRE AT ME DOTH THROW  4.39.6
```

THROWN   2
  HE FORTH WAS THROWN INTO THE GREEDY SEAS   5.38.2
  WITH PLENTEOUS HAND BY HEAVEN UPON YOU THROWN   5.66.2
THROWS   1
  THAT HEAV'N OF JOYES THROWES ONELY DOWNE ON ME   4.60.3
THRUST   1
  EACH TRIFLE UNDER TRUEST BARRES TO THRUST   3.48.2
THRUSTS   1
  THAT SOME-TIMES ANGER THRUSTS INTO HIS HIDE   3.50.10
THUNDER   3
  HER THUNDER OF DISDAINE FORST ME RETIRE   1.36.4
  POINTING TO EACH HIS THUNDER, RAINE AND WINDE   3.14.6
  WHICH WHEN AS FAME IN HER SHRILL TRUMP
                          SHAL THUNDER   5.85.13
THUNDERBOLT   1
  JOVE ON HIS HELME THE THUNDERBOLT DID REARE   4.13.8
THUNDERED   1
  THUNDRED DISDAINES AND LIGHTNINGS OF DISGRACE   4.60.4
THUNDERER   1
  BY $HELLISH $STYX (BY WHICH THE $THUND'RER
                          SWEARES)   2.36.5
THUNDERING   1
  WHEN ALL THE GODS HE THREATS WITH THUNDRING DART   5.39.4
THWARTED   1
  AND HAVING THUS AWHILE EACH OTHER THWARTED   2.59.13
THWARTING   1
  WHOSE THWARTING COURSE, DEPRIVES THE WORLD
                          OF REASON   2.147.14
TICKLED   1
  TO BE SO TIKLED THEY WOULD CHANGE THEIR STATE   3.128.9
TIDE   1
  BUT CAME THE TYDE, AND MADE MY PAYNES HIS PRAY   5.75.4
TIDES   1
  FOR ME, WHILE YOU DISCOURSE OF COURTLY TIDES   4.51.9
TIE   6
  TO TYE UP ENVY, EVERMORE INLARGED   3.70.12
  WHERETO AL BONDS DO TIE ME DAY BY DAY   3.117.4
  THE RAINES WHEREWITH MY $RIDER DOTH ME TIE   4.49.5
  AND EKE MY TOUNG WITH PROUD RESTRAINT TO TIE+   5.43.6
  SWEET BE THE BANDS, THE WHICH TRUE LOVE DOTH TYE   5.65.5
  MY HART, WHOM NONE WITH SERVILE BANDS CAN TYE   5.73.2
TIED   4
  AND TO ATTEND IT, THEM AS STRONGLY TY'D   2.58.5
  WHERETO THE JUDGEMENT OF MY HEART IS TIDE+   3.137.8
  WHEN SOME FAIRE $LADIES, BY HARD PROMISE TIED   4.22.5
  AND WITH HER OWNE GOODWILL HIR FYRMELY TYDE   5.67.12
TIES   3
  O KISSE, WHICH SOULES, EVEN SOULES TOGETHER TIES   4.81.5
  LET EARES HEARE SPEECH, WHICH WIT TO WONDER TIES   4.85.11
  THAT HUE, WHOSE FORCE MY HART STILL UNTO
                          THRALDOME TIES+   4.102.8
TIGER   1
  AS IS A $TYGRE THAT WITH GREEDINESSE   5.56.2
TIGERISH   1
  YET LET THIS THOUGHT THY $TYGRISH COURAGE PASSE   4.65.11
TIGERS   1
  TO $HYRCAN $TYGRES, AND TO RUTHLES $BEARES   1.19.12
TIGER'S   2
  PLUCKE THE KEENE TEETH FROM THE FIERCE
                          $TYGERS YAWES   3.19.3

```
                HER HEART, SWEETE HEART, IS OF NO $TYGRE'S KIND        4.44.4
TILL                        43
         KNOCKE AT THAT HARD HART, BEGGE TILL YOU
                             HAVE MOV'D HER                            1.2.13
         TO PAINT ON FLOODS, TILL THE SHORE CRIE TO TH'AIRE           1.9.2
         AND STILL MUST HOLD HER DEARE TILL AFTER DEATH               1.21.11
         CHEERES FOR A TIME, BUT TILL THE $SUNNE DOTH SHEW            1.50.3
         BLIND WERE MINE $EYES, TILL THEY WERE
                             SEENE OF THINE                            2.35.9
         TILL THEY RETURN'D.. $HOME WHEN THEY NEVER CAME              2.58.6
         TILL THOU ALONE TO PAY THE HEAVENS THEIR DUTIE               2.105.5
         BLIND WERE MINE EYES, TILL THEY WERE SEENE
                                OF THINE                               2.112.9
         TILL HE HIMSELFE THYS $EAGLES ART HAD TAUGHT                 2.122.8
         TROTTING HIS SUN-STEEDS TILL THE $PALFRAYS SWEAT             2.147.6
         TILL $VIRGINS SMYLES DOE SOUND HIS SWEET RETEERE             2.147.8
         TILL NATURE AS SHE WROUGHT THEE FELL A DOTINGE               3.20.10
         TIL WHATSOEVER STAR THAT GUIDES MY MOVING                    3.26.9
         TIL THEN, NOT SHOW MY HEAD WHERE THOU
                             MAIST PROVE ME                            3.26.14
         WILL SOURELY LEAVE HER TILL HE HAVE PREVAILED                3.41.8
         ALL DAYES ARE NIGHTS TO SEE TILL I SEE THEE                  3.43.13
         TILL I RETURNE OF POSTING IS NOE NEED                        3.51.4
         SO TIL THE JUDGEMENT THAT YOUR SELFE ARISE                   3.55.13
         THY HUNGRIE EIES, EVEN TILL THEY WINCK
                             WITH FULNESSE                             3.56.6
         NOR SERVICES TO DOE TIL YOU REQUIRE                          3.57.4
         WHICH THREE TILL NOW, NEVER KEPT SEATE IN ONE                3.105.14
         TIL EACH TO RAZ'D OBLIVION YEELD HIS PART                    3.122.7
         IS LUST IN ACTION, AND TILL ACTION, LUST                     3.129.2
         TILL MY BAD ANGEL FIRE MY GOOD ONE OUT                       3.144.14
         THE SUNNE IT SELFE SEES NOT, TILL HEAVEN
                             CLEERES                                   3.148.12
         TILL BY DEGREES IT HAD FULL CONQUEST GOT                     4.2.4
         TILL THAT GOOD $GOD MAKE $CHURCH AND $CHURCHMAN
                             STARVE                                    4.5.8
         TILL DOWNE-RIGHT BLOWES DID FOYLE THY
                             CUNNING FENCE                             4.10.11
         TILL THAT HIS GRANDAME $NATURE PITTYING IT                   4.17.9
         TILL BLOUDIE BULLET GET HIM WRONGFULL PRAY                   4.20.4
         TILL NOW, WRAPT IN A MOST INFERNALL NIGHT                    4.33.3
         TILL WITHOUT FEWELL YOU CAN MAKE HOT FIRE                    4.46.14
         TILL THAT IN WORDS THY FIGURE BE EXPREST                     4.50.4
         TILL THAT HER BLUSH TAUGHT ME MY SHAME TO SEE                4.53.14
         HIS WHO TILL DEATH LOOKT IN A WATRIE GLASSE                  4.82.3
         IN JUSTICE PAINES COME NOT TILL FAULTS DO CALL               4.86.10
         RAVISHT, STAID NOT, TILL IN HER GOLDEN HAIRE                 4.103.7
         TILL IT HAVE WROUGHT WHAT THY OWNE WILL ATTENDS              4.107.11
         TILL GREATER THEN MY WOMBE THOU WOXEN ART                    5.2.4
         CEASSE THEN, TILL SHE VOUCHSAFE TO GRAWNT
                             ME REST                                   5.33.13
         TILL THEN I WANDER CAREFULL COMFORTLESSE                     5.34.13
         TILL I IN HAND HER YET HALFE TREMBLING TOOKE                 5.67.11
         TILL THEN GIVE LEAVE TO ME IN PLEASANT MEW                   5.80.9
TILL                        1
         WHY SHOULDST THOU TOYLE OUR THORNIE SOIL TO TILL+            4.10.6
TILLAGE                     1
         DISDAINES THE TILLAGE OF THY HUSBANDRY+
                                                                      3.3.6
TILLED                      1
         BEST IN MY FACE, HOW CARES HAVE TILD DEEPE
                             FORROWES
                                                                      1.4.8
```

TIME   106

IMBRACING CLOUDS BY NIGHT, IN DAY TIME MOURNE	1.16.2
COME $TIME THE ANCHOR-HOLD OF MY DESIRE	1.22.1
TIME, CRUELL TIME, COME AND SUBDUE THAT $BROW	1.23.1
TIME, CRUELL TIME, COME AND SUBDUE THAT $BROW	1.23.1
YET SPARE HER $TIME, LET HER EXEMPTED BE	1.23.13
THAT FULL OF BEAUTY, TIME BESTOWES UPON HER	1.39.4
SWIFT SPEEDY $TIME, FEATHRED WITH FLYING HOURES	1.39.11
NOW JOY THY TIME BEFORE THY SWEET BE DONE	1.40.7
THOUGH TIME DO SPOYLE THEE OF THE FAIREST VAILE	1.45.10
CHEERES FOR A TIME, BUT TILL THE $SUNNE DOTH SHEW	1.50.3
FLOWERS HAVE A TIME BEFORE THEY COME TO SEEDE	1.51.3
AND LET THE DAY BE TIME ENOUGH TO MOURNE	1.54.5
AUTENTIQUE SHALL MY VERSE IN TIME TO COME	1.55.6
THUS IN MY $LOVE, $TIME CALLS ME TO RELATE	2.1.13
IN $ME'S THAT $FAITH WHICH $TIME CANNOT INVADE	2.4.12
TIME HATH THY $BEAUTIE, WHICH WITH $AGE WILL LEAVE THEE	2.10.12
SO YOU OF $TIME SHALL LIVE BEYOND THE $END	2.16.14
STAY, SPEEDY $TIME, BEHOLD, BEFORE THOU PASSE	2.17.1
TIME, LOOKE THOU TOO, IN THIS $TRALUCENT $GLASSE	2.17.5
THERE WAS A TIME, $YOU TOLD $ME THAT YOU WOULD	2.19.2
YOU NOW SUPPOSE ME ALL THIS TIME IN SPORT	2.24.7
ME THINKES THIS $TIME BECOMMETH $LOVERS BEST	2.37.3
WITH SO PURE $LOVE, AS $TIME COULD NEVER BOAST	2.54.8
AND SEE IF $TIME (IF HE WOULD STRIVE TO PROVE)	2.60.13
AND WHEN $WE MEET AT ANY TIME AGAINE	2.61.6
WITH SO PURE LOVE AS TYME COULD NEVER BOAST	2.101.8
STAY, STAY, SWEET $TIME, BEHOLD OR ERE THOU PASSE	2.107.1
NAY, LOOKE THEE $TIME IN THIS $CELESTIALL GLASSE	2.107.5
NOW PASSE ON $TIME, TO AFTER-WORLDS TELL THIS	2.107.9
TELL TRUELIE $TIME WHAT IN THY TIME HATH BEENE	2.107.10
TELL TRUELIE $TIME WHAT IN THY TIME HATH BEENE	2.107.10
THAT THEY MAY TEL MORE WORLDS WHAT $TIME HATH SEENE	2.107.11
HEERE MAKE A $PERIOD $TIME, AND SAIE FOR MEE	2.107.13
THE TIME IS COME DELIVERED SHE MUST BE	2.116.3
SHEE OF WHOM $MERLIN LONG TYME DID FORE-TELL	2.119.10
A FAYTH, THAT TIME NOR FORTUNE COULD NOT MOVE	2.138.11
STILL TO PROLONG MY LONG TYME LOOKT-FOR MORROW+	2.145.4
BUT AS THE RIPER SHOULD BY TIME DECEASE	3.1.3
NOW IS THE TIME THAT FACE SHOULD FORME AN OTHER	3.3.2
DISPIGHT OF WRINKLES THIS THY GOULDEN TIME	3.3.12
FOR NEVER RESTING TIME LEADS $SUMMER ON	3.5.5
WHEN I DOE COUNT THE CLOCK THAT TELS THE TIME	3.12.1
THAT THOU AMONG THE WASTES OF TIME MUST GOE	3.12.10
WHERE WASTFULL TIME DEBATETH WITH DECAY	3.15.11
AND ALL IN WAR WITH $TIME FOR LOVE OF YOU	3.15.13
MAKE WARRE UPPON THIS BLOUDIE TIRANT TIME+	3.16.2
WHO WILL BELEEVE MY VERSE IN TIME TO COME	3.17.1
BUT WERE SOME CHILDE OF YOURS ALIVE THAT TIME	3.17.13
WHEN IN ETERNALL LINES TO TIME THOU GROW'ST	3.18.12
DEVOURING TIME BLUNT THOU THE $LYONS PAWES	3.19.1
AND DO WHAT ERE THOU WILT SWIFT-FOOTED TIME	3.19.6
YET DOE THY WORST CULD $TIME DISPIGHT THY WRONG	3.19.13
COMPARE THEM WITH THE BETT'RING OF THE TIME	3.32.5
TO ENTERTAINE THE TIME WITH THOUGHTS OF LOVE	3.39.11
WHICH TIME AND THOUGHTS SO SWEETLY DOST DECEIVE	3.39.12
AN OTHER TIME MINE EYE IS MY HEARTS GUEST	3.47.7

AGAINST THAT TIME (IF EVER THAT TIME COME)   3.49.1
AGAINST THAT TIME (IF EVER THAT TIME COME)   3.49.1
AGAINST THAT TIME WHEN THOU SHALT STRANGELY PASSE   3.49.5
AGAINST THAT TIME DO I INSCONCE ME HERE   3.49.9
SO IS THE TIME THAT KEEPES YOU AS MY CHEST   3.52.9
THEN UNSWEPT STONE, BESMEER'D WITH SLUTTISH TIME   3.55.4
I HAVE NO PRECIOUS TIME AT AL TO SPEND   3.57.3
THAT YOU YOUR SELFE MAY PRIVILEDGE YOUR TIME   3.58.10
AND TIME THAT GAVE, DOTH NOW HIS GIFT CONFOUND   3.60.8
TIME DOTH TRANSFIXE THE FLORISH SET ON YOUTH   3.60.9
FOR SUCH A TIME DO I NOW FORTIFIE   3.63.9
THAT $TIME WILL COME AND TAKE MY LOVE AWAY   3.64.12
NOR GATES OF STEELE SO STRONG BUT TIME DECAYES+   3.65.8
THEIR WORTH THE GREATER BEEING WOO'D OF TIME   3.70.6
THAT TIME OF YEEARE THOU MAIST IN ME BEHOLD   3.73.1
WHY WITH THE TIME DO I NOT GLANCE ASIDE   3.76.3
SOME FRESHER STAMPE OF THE TIME BETTERING DAYES   3.82.8
AND YET THIS TIME REMOV'D WAS SUMMERS TIME   3.97.5
AND YET THIS TIME REMOV'D WAS SUMMERS TIME   3.97.5
IN GENTLE NUMBERS TIME SO IDELY SPENT   3.100.6
IF TIME HAVE ANY WRINCLE GRAVEN THERE   3.100.10
GIVE MY LOVE FAME FASTER THEN TIME WASTS LIFE   3.100.13
WHEN IN THE $CHRONICLE OF WASTED TIME   3.106.1
OF THIS OUR TIME, ALL YOU PREFIGURING   3.106.10
NOW WITH THE DROPS OF THIS MOST BALMIE TIME   3.107.9
WHERE TIME AND OUTWARD FORME WOULD SHEW IT DEAD   3.108.14
JUST TO THE TIME, NOT WITH THE TIME EXCHANG'D   3.109.7
JUST TO THE TIME, NOT WITH THE TIME EXCHANG'D   3.109.7
BUT RECKENING TIME, WHOSE MILLIOND ACCIDENTS   3.115.5
AND GIVEN TO TIME YOUR OWNE DEARE PURCHAS'D
                                       RIGHT   3.117.6
AS I BY YOURS, Y'HAVE PAST A HELL OF $TIME   3.120.6
NO- $TIME, THOU SHALT NOT BOST THAT I DOE CHANGE   3.123.1
WHERETO TH'INVITING TIME OUR FASHION CALLS   3.124.8
TO THIS I WITNES CALL THE FOLES OF TIME   3.124.13
MAY TIME DISGRACE, AND WRETCHED MYNUIT KILL   3.126.8
BUT KNOWNE WORTH DID IN MINE OF TIME PROCEED   4.2.3
WHAT CAN BE HOPED MY HARVEST TIME WILL BE+   4.21.11
WILL SHE TAKE TIME, BEFORE ALL WRACKED BE+   4.67.4
HER FLAMIE GLISTRING LIGHTS INCREASE WITH
                                TIME AND PLACE   4.76.10
BY NO ENCROCHMENT WRONGD, NOR TIME FORGOT   4.84.10
SO NEERE, IN SO GOOD TIME, SO FREE A PLACE+   4.105.2
THE HARDEST STEELE IN TRACT OF TIME DOTH TEARE   5.18.2
AND DOE ME NOT BEFORE MY TIME TO DY   5.42.14
WHEN MY ABODES PREFIXED TIME IS SPENT   5.46.1
HIGH TIME IT IS, THIS WARRE NOW ENDED WERE   5.57.2
DEVOURING TYME AND CHANGEFUL CHANCE HAVE PRAYD   5.58.7
TELL HER THE JOYOUS TIME WIL NOT BE STAID   5.70.7
FOR NONE CAN CALL AGAINE THE PASSED TIME   5.70.14
SO SWEET YOUR PRISON YOU IN TIME SHALL PROVE   5.71.11
THUS I THE TIME WITH EXPECTATION SPEND   5.87.9

TIMELY   3
FOR LUSTY SPRING NOW IN HIS TIMELY HOWRE   5.4.9
MAKE PEACE THEREFORE, AND GRAUNT ME TIMELY GRACE   5.57.13
SHALL TURNE TO CAULMES AND TYMELY CLEARE AWAY   5.62.12

TIMES   17
A THOUSAND TIMES IT PROMIS'D ME RELIEFE   1.25.3
THAT THEY SHALL GRIEVE, THEY LIV'D NOT
                              IN THESE $TIMES   2.6.11

OR HATH IT LOST THE $VERTUE, WITH THE $TIMES   2.27.3
WHILST IN DESPITE OF TYRANNIZING $TIMES   2.44.5
TH'INCERTAINE $TIMES OFT VARYING IN THEIR $COURSE   2.51.2
IN $FORMER TIMES, SUCH AS HAD STORE OF $COYNE   2.58.1
OR TEN TIMES HAPPIER BE IT TEN FOR ONE   3.6.8
TEN TIMES THY SELFE WERE HAPPIER THEN THOU ART   3.6.9
IF TEN OF THINE TEN TIMES REFIGUR'D THEE   3.6.10
IF ALL WERE MINDED SO, THE TIMES SHOULD CEASE   3.11.7
AND WITH OLD WOES NEW WAILE MY DEARE TIMES WASTE   3.30.4
THIS WISH I HAVE, THEN TEN TIMES HAPPY ME   3.37.14
BE THOU THE TENTH $MUSE, TEN TIMES MORE IN WORTH   3.38.9
UPON THE HOURES, AND TIMES OF YOUR DESIRE+   3.57.2
I SHOULD IN THOUGHT CONTROULE YOUR TIMES
                             OF PLEASURE   3.58.2
AND YET TO TIMES IN HOPE, MY VERSE SHALL STAND   3.60.13
THE WHICH THREE TIMES THRISE HAPPY HATH ME MADE   5.74.3
TIME'S   18
MUST YEELD UP ALL TO TYRANT $TIMES DESIRE   1.38.7
AGAINST THE DARKE AND TIMES CONSUMING RAGE   1.55.12
AND NOTHING GAINST $TIMES SIETH CAN MAKE DEFENCE   3.12.13
WHICH THIS ($TIMES PENSEL OR MY PUPILL PEN)   3.16.10
BUT WHEN IN THEE TIMES FORRWES I BEHOULD   3.22.3
I MUST ATTEND, TIMES LEASURE WITH MY MONE   3.44.12
WITH TIMES INJURIOUS HAND CHRUSHT AND ORE-WORNE   3.63.2
WHEN I HAVE SEENE BY TIMES FELL HAND DEFACED   3.64.1
SHALL TIMES BEST $JEWELL FROM TIMES CHEST
                             LIE HID+   3.65.10
SHALL TIMES BEST $JEWELL FROM TIMES CHEST
                             LIE HID+   3.65.10
TIMES THEEVISH PROGRESSE TO ETERNITIE   3.77.8
AND MAKE TIMES SPOILES DISPISED EVERY WHERE   3.100.12
ALAS WHY FEARING OF TIMES TIRANIE   3.115.9
LOV'S NOT $TIMES FOOLE, THOUGH ROSIE LIPS
                             AND CHEEKS   3.116.9
AS SUBJECT TO TIMES LOVE, OR TO TIMES HATE   3.124.3
AS SUBJECT TO TIMES LOVE, OR TO TIMES HATE   3.124.3
DOEST HOULD TIMES FICKLE GLASSE, HIS SICKLE,
                             HOWER   3.126.2
WITH WHAT PASTIME, TIME'S JOURNEY SHE BEGUILDE   4.92.12
TINCTURE   1
AS THE PERFUMED TINCTURE OF THE $ROSES   3.54.6
TIPPED   1
VENEMOUS TOUNG TIPT WITH VILE ADDERS STING   5.86.1
TIRE   1
UPON WHOSE BREAST A FIERCER $GRIPE DOTH TIRE   4.14.2
TIRED   9
OR MY SWIFT-WINGED $MUSE TYRED BY TOO
                             HIE FLYING   2.117.10
THE DEARE REPOSE FOR LIMS WITH TRAVAILL TIRED   3.27.2
THE BEAST THAT BEARES ME, TIRED WITH MY WOE   3.50.5
TYR'D WITH ALL THESE FOR RESTFULL DEATH I CRY   3.66.1
TYR'D WITH ALL THESE, FROM THESE WOULD I BE GONE   3.66.13
OF $ATLAS TYR'D, YOUR WISEDOME'S HEAV'NLY SWAY   4.51.8
LATE TYR'D WITH WO, EVEN READY FOR TO PINE   4.62.1
TIRED WITH THE DUSTY TOILES OF BUSIE DAY   4.89.7
THOU THOUGH STILL TIRED, YET STILL DOOST
                             IT DETEST   4.96.14
TIRES   1
AND YOU IN $GRECIAN TIRES ARE PAINTED NEW   3.53.8

TITLE   6
   AND URG'D THAT TITLE WHICH DOTH PLAINELY PROVE   1.8.11
   WHICH STILL MUST BEARE THE TITLE OF MY WRONG   1.32.13
   TO SIDE THIS TITLE IS IMPANNELLED   3.46.9
   OH WHAT A HAPPY TITLE DO I FINDE   3.92.11
   BUT $VERTUE THUS THAT TITLE DOTH DISPROVE   4.52.5
   NE IF I WOULD, COULD I JUST TITLE MAKE   4.90.9
TITLES   2
   OF PUBLIKE HONOUR AND PROUD TITLES BOST   3.25.2
   AND WHEN MY PEN WOULD WRITE HER TITLES TRUE   5.3.11
TOGETHER   9
   LEAVES TO HIS $SONNE ALL HE HAD HEAP'D TOGETHER   2.10.4
   AND ONELY ABSENT, WHEN $WEE ARE TOGETHER   2.11.8
   THEN $FOOLES AND $CHILDREN FITT'ST TO
                             GOE TOGETHER   2.22.8
   NIGHT WAS ORDAYN'D, TOGETHER $FRIENDS TO KEEPE   2.37.4
   THE QUIET $EV'NING YET TOGETHER BRINGS   2.37.7
   AND THUS WHILST SIGHES AND TEARES TOGETHER
                             DOE CONTENDE   2.133.13
   AS TRUTH AND BEAUTIE SHAL TOGETHER THRIVE   3.14.11
   O KISSE, WHICH SOULES, EVEN SOULES TOGETHER TIES   4.81.5
   WILL BOTH TOGETHER ME TOO SORELY WRACK   5.46.12
TOIL   11
   AND STILL I TOYLE, TO CHANGE THE $MARBLE BREST   1.13.9
   WEARY WITH TOYLE, I HAST ME TO MY BED   3.27.1
   THE ONE BY TOYLE, THE OTHER TO COMPLAINE   3.28.7
   HOW FAR I TOYLE, STILL FARTHER OFF FROM THEE   3.28.8
   IN SEQUENT TOILE ALL FORWARDS DO CONTEND   3.60.4
   WHY SHOULDST THOU TOYLE OUR THORNIE SOILE
                             TO TILL+   4.10.6
   TO GRAUNT SMALL RESPIT TO MY RESTLESSE TOILE   5.11.6
   YE TRADEFULL $MERCHANTS THAT WITH WEARY TOYLE   5.15.1
   THINCK EVER TO ENDURE SO TAEDIOUS TOYLE+   5.33.10
   GOTTEN AT LAST WITH LABOUR AND LONG TOYLE   5.69.14
   THEN AS A STEED REFRESHED AFTER TOYLE   5.80.5
TOILED   1
   AND ALL THE REST FORGOT FOR WHICH HE TOILD   3.25.12
TOILING   2
   TOYLING WITH $PAINE, MY $LABOUR NEVER CEASETH   2.40.7
   TOYLING WITH PAINE, MY LABOUR NEVER CEASETH   2.144.7
TOILS   1
   TIRED WITH THE DUSTY TOILES OF BUSIE DAY   4.89.7
TOLD   11
   TOLDE THE DUMBE MESSAGE OF MY HIDDEN GRIEFE   1.8.6
   OFT HAVE I TOLD HER THAT MY SOULE DID LOVE HER   1.18.13
   THERE WAS A TIME, $YOU TOLD $ME THAT YOU WOULD   2.19.2
   SO MUST YOUR PRAYSE DISTRACTEDLY BE TOLD   2.57.12
   THIS TOLD, I JOY, BUT THEN NO LONGER GLAD   3.45.13
   SO IS MY LOVE STILL TELLING WHAT IS TOLD   3.76.14
   THEN THINKE THAT WE BEFORE HAVE HEARD THEM TOULD   3.123.8
   AND AGE IN LOVE, LOVES NOT T' HAVE YEARES TOLD   3.138.12
   THAT BRAVELY MASKT, THEIR FANCIES MAY BE TOLD   4.3.2
   WHAT MORE MIRACULOUS THING MAY BE TOLD   5.30.9
   THAT WHICH IS GOLD OR HEARE, MAY SCARSE BE TOLD+   5.37.4
TOLDST   1
   THOU TOLDST MINE EYES SHOULD HELPE THEIR
                             FAMISHT CASE+   4.106.6
TOMB   6
   OR WHO IS HE SO FOND WILL BE THE TOMBE   3.3.7
   THOUGH YET HEAVEN KNOWES IT IS BUT AS A TOMBE   3.17.3

WHEN OTHERS WOULD GIVE LIFE, AND BRING A TOMBE 3.83.12
MAKING THEIR TOMBE THE WOMBE WHEREIN THEY GREW+ 3.86.4
TO MAKE HIM MUCH OUT-LIVE A GILDED TOMBE 3.101.11
IN TOMBE OF LIDS THEN BURIED ARE MINE EYES 4.99.12
TOMBED 1
THY UNUS'D BEAUTY MUST BE TOMB'D WITH THEE 3.4.13
TOMBS 1
WHEN TYRANTS CRESTS AND TOMBS OF BRASSE
ARE SPENT 3.107.14
TONGUE 25
THAT $FORAINE $NATIONS RELLISH NOT OUR $TONGUE 2.25.2
OR TONGUE OF WONDER WORTH COULD TELL A
WONDER THOUGHT 2.117.2
THEN WONDER, TONGUE, THEN JOY, MIGHT WEL
REPORT A WONDER 2.117.4
WHOSE PURE $IDEA NEVER TONGUE EXPREST 2.139.13
MY TONGUE IN PAYNE, MY HARTS COUNSELS BEWRAYING 2.142.6
SWEET SECRECIE, WHAT TONGUE CAN TELL THY WORTH+ 2.146.1
BE SCORN'D, LIKE OLD MEN OF LESSE TRUTH
THEN TONGUE 3.17.10
MORE THEN THAT TONGE THAT MORE HATH MORE EXPREST 3.23.12
BE ABSENT FROM THY WALKES AND IN MY TONGUE 3.89.9
THAT TONGUE THAT TELLS THE STORY OF THY DAIES 3.95.5
THE OWNERS TONGUE DOTH PUBLISH EVERY WHERE 3.102.4
THEREFORE LIKE HER, I SOME-TIME HOLD MY TONGUE 3.102.13
TO KNOW MY SHAMES AND PRAISES FROM YOUR TOUNGE 3.112.6
THAT EVERY TOUNG SAIES BEAUTY SHOULD LOOKE SO 3.127.14
SIMPLY I CREDIT HER FALSE SPEAKING TONGUE 3.138.7
WOUND ME NOT WITH THINE EYE BUT WITH THY TOUNG 3.139.3
CHIDING THAT TONGUE THAT EVER SWEET 3.145.6
MY TONGUE DOTH ITCH, MY THOUGHTS IN LABOUR BE 4.37.2
DOTH MAKE MY HEART GIVE TO MY TONGUE THE LIE 4.47.14
SO MAY YOUR TONGUE STILL FLUENTLY PROCEED 4.51.2
AND THROUGH THOSE LIPS DRINKE $NECTAR
FROM THAT TOONG 4.83.13
SO WHEN MY TOUNG WOULD SPEAK HER PRAISES DEW 5.3.9
YOU STOP MY TOUNG, AND TEACH MY HART TO SPEAKE 5.8.10
AND EKE MY TOUNG WITH PROUD RESTRAINT TO TIE+ 5.43.6
VENEMOUS TOUNG TIPT WITH VILE ADDERS STING 5.86.1
TONGUES 4
ALL TOUNGS (THE VOICE OF SOULES) GIVE
THEE THAT END 3.69.3
BUT THOSE SAME TOUNGS THAT GIVE THEE SO
THINE OWNE 3.69.6
AND TOUNGS TO BE, YOUR BEEING SHALL REHEARSE 3.81.11
HAVE EYES TO WONDER, BUT LACK TOUNGS TO PRAISE 3.106.14
TONGUE'S 2
MY $HEARING BRIB'D WITH HER $TONGUES $HARMONIE 2.29.6
NOR ARE MINE EARES WITH THY TOUNGS TUNE
DELIGHTED 3.141.5
TONGUE-TIED 4
AND ARTE MADE TUNG-TIDE BY AUTHORITIE 3.66.9
TO MAKE ME TOUNG-TIDE SPEAKING OF YOUR FAME 3.80.4
MY TOUNG-TIDE $MUSE IN MANNERS HOLDS HER STILL 3.85.1
MY TOUNG-TIDE PATIENCE WITH TOO MUCH DISDAINE 3.140.2
TOOK 7
BETWIXT MINE EYE AND HEART A LEAGUE IS TOOKE 3.47.1
HOW CAREFULL WAS I WHEN I TOOKE MY WAY 3.48.1
SAVE WHAT IS HAD, OR MUST FROM YOU BE TOCKE 3.75.12
THE FAYREST VOTARY TOOKE UP THAT FIRE 3.154.5

WHICH FROM LOVES FIRE TOOKE HEAT PERPETUALL	3.154.10
SOMEWHAT THY LEAD'N COUNSELS, WHICH I TOOKE	4.56.7
TILL I IN HAND HER YET HALFE TREMBLING TOOKE	5.67.11

TOP   2

ON HEAVENLIE TOP CF THY DIVINE DESIRE	2.106.6
NOW STAND YOU ON THE TOP OF HAPPIE HOURES	3.16.5

TOPS   2

THE BROKEN TOPS OF LOFTY TREES DECLARE	1.37.5
FLATTER THE MOUNTAINE TCPS WITH SOVERAINE EIE	3.33.2

TORCH   1

CURST BE THE PAGE FROM WHOME THE BAD TORCH FELL	4.105.11

TORMENT   11

WITHOUT THE TORMENT OF THE NIGHTS JNTRUTH	1.54.8
CONDEMN'D BY $JOVE TO ENDLESSE $TORMENT BEE	2.14.2
STILL MORE AND MORE IT TC MY TORMENT BURNETH	2.40.12
STILL MORE AND MORE UNTC MY TORMENT BURNETH	2.144.12
OH ABSENCE WHAT A TCRMENT WOULDST THOU PROVE	3.39.9
KNOWING THY HEART TCRMENT ME WITH DISDAINE	3.132.2
A TORMENT THRICE THREE-FCLD THUS TO BE CRCSSED	3.133.8
BUT THEN SHE SEEKES WITH TORMENT AND TURMOYLE	5.11.11
THEN TO TORMENT ME THUS WITH CRUELTY	5.25.7
OR SHALL THEIR RUTHLESSE TORMENT NEVER CEASE	5.36.2
OF ALL WORLDS GLADNESSE MORE MY TORMENT FEED	5.52.12

TORMENTED   1

THAT ME THOU MAKEST THUS TORMENTED BE+	5.10.2

TORMENTETH   1

THE LOVE WHICH ME SC CRUELLY TORMENTETH	5.42.1

TORMENTOR   1

AND BUT APPOINT ME FOR HER $TORMENTOR	2.115.3

TORMENTS   5

WITH GREATER $TORMENTS, THEN IT $ME DOTH TAKE	2.20.7
WITH ALL HIS $TORMENTS AND $INFERNALL TERROR+	2.41.4
WITH ALL HIS TORMENTS AND INFERNALL TERRCR	2.143.4
WHICH STILL TORMENTS ME IN DAYES BURNING FIRE	2.145.14
OR IF I NEEDS (SWEET $JUDGE) MUST TORMENTS HAVE	4.86.11

TORN   1

IN ACT THY BED-VOW BROAKE AND NEW FAITH TORNE	3.152.3

TORN-TRESSED   1

ILE BINDE HER THEN WITH MY TORNE-TRESSED HAIRE	2.115.13

TORTURE   2

DOE IN CONSENT SHAKE HANDS TO TCRTURE ME	3.28.6
I'ST NOT YNOUGH TC TORTURE ME ALONE	3.133.3

TORTURES   1

AND TORTURES $ME IN MOST EXTREMITY	2.20.8

TOSS   1

WITH CARE'S HARD HAND) TC TURNE AND TOSSE IN THEE	4.98.8

TOSSED   3

SINS THAT THIS ONE IS TCST WITH TROUBLOUS FIT	5.33.11
AS BEING LONG IN HER LOVES TEMPEST TOST	5.41.11
WITH WHICH MY SILLY BARKE WAS TOSSED SORE	5.63.4

TOTAL   2

SEE $BEAUTIE'S TOTALL SUMME SUMM'D IN HER FACE	4.85.10
THAT TO MY QUESTICNS YOU SO TOTALL ARE+	4.92.5

TOTTERED   2

WIL BE A TOTTER'D WEED CF SMAL WORTH HELD	3.2.4
AND PUTS APPARRELL CN MY TOTTERED LOVING	3.26.11

TOTTERING   1

BEWARE FULL SAILES DROWNE NOT THY TOTTRING BARGE	4.85.2

TOUCH   14

MY JOYS BUT SHADOWES, TCUCH OF TRUTH, MY ANGUISH	1.16.3

THIS IS MY STATE, MY GRIEFES DO TOUCH SO NEERLY   1.16.13
HER TOUCH DOTH CAUSE THE WARBLE OF THE SOUND   1.57.5
NOR OTHER HAND COULD GIVE SO TRUE A TOUCH   1.57.14
THAT WHEN THOU FEED'ST, THY $NOSE SHALL
                             TOUCH THY $CHINNE   2.8.12
WHICH NEVER FELT'ST MY FIERIE TOUCH OF $LOVE   2.49.4
THE BOY FOR TRIALL NEEDES WOULD TOUCH MY BREST   3.153.10
OF TOUCH THEY ARE THAT WITHOUT TOUCH DOTH TOUCH   4.9.12
OF TOUCH THEY ARE THAT WITHOUT TOUCH DOTH TOUCH   4.9.12
OF TOUCH THEY ARE THAT WITHOUT TOUCH DOTH TOUCH   4.9.12
OF TOUCH THEY ARE, AND POORE I AM THEIR STRAW   4.9.14
AS DO BEWRAY A WANT OF INWARD TUCH   4.15.10
THAT WHEN THE BREATH OF MY COMPLAINTS DOTH TUCH   4.44.10
THAT HAND, WHICH WITHOUT TOUCH HOLDS MORE
                             THEN $ATLAS MIGHT   4.77.5
TOUCHED   2
MY TOUCHT HEART TURNES IT TO THAT HAPPY COST   1.53.2
SUCH HEAVENLY TOUCHES NERE TOUCHT EARTHLY FACES   3.17.8
TOUCHES   4
SUCH HEAVENLY TOUCHES NERE TOUCHT EARTHLY FACES   3.17.8
A LOSSE IN LOVE THAT TOUCHES ME MORE NEERELY   3.42.4
WHAT STRAINED TOUCHES $RHETHORICK CAN LEND   3.82.10
NOR TENDER FEELING TO BASE TOUCHES PRONE   3.141.6
TOUCHING   3
BUT WHEN MY $TOUCHING CAME TO PLAY HIS PART   2.29.9
ONE BY THY $NAME, THE OTHER TOUCHING THEE   2.35.8
ONE BY THY NAME, THE OTHER TOUCHING THEE   2.112.8
TOUCHSTONE   2
LET $VERTUE BE THE $TOUCH-STONE OF MY $LOVE   2.60.7
LET VERTUE BE THE TUCH-STONE OF MY LOVE   2.149.7
TOUGH   1
SWEET IS THE $CYPRESSE, BUT HIS RYND IS TOUGH   5.26.5
TOWARD   1
NO LOVE TOWARD OTHERS IN THAT BOSOME SITS   3.9.13
TOWARDS   4
YET HOW SHEE BENDS TOWARDS THAT BLESSED $COAST   2.134.12
TOWARDS THEE ILE RUN, AND GIVE HIM LEAVE TO GOE   3.51.14
LIKE AS THE WAVES MAKE TOWARDS THE PIBLED SHORE   3.60.1
TOWARDES $AURORA'S $COURT A $NYMPH DOTH DWELL   4.37.5
TOWER   1
THERE FAYTH DOTH FEARLESSE DWELL IN BRASEN TOWRE   5.65.13
TOWERS   1
WHEN SOMETIME LOFTIE TOWERS I SEE DOWNE RASED   3.64.3
TOWN-FOLKS   1
TOWNE-FOLKES MY STRENGTH., A DAINTIER
                             JUDGE APPLIES   4.41.6
TOWNS   1
HOW $HOLLAND HEARTS, NOW SO GOOD TOWNES BE LOST   4.30.7
TOY   1
IF FAYTH AND ZEALE BE BUT ESTEEMD A TOY   2.139.3
TOYS   2
LOVE STILL A $BABY, PLAYES WITH $GAWDES
                             AND $TOYES   2.22.5
MY YOUTH DOTH WASTE, MY KNOWLEDGE BRINGS
                             FORTH TOYES   4.18.9
TRACE   2
STILL IN THE TRACE OF ONE PERPLEXED THOUGHT   1.33.1
LET ME NO STEPS BUT OF LOST LABOUR TRACE   4.64.6
TRACT   2
FROM HIS LOW TRACT AND LOOKE AN OTHER WAY   3.7.12

```
     THE HARDEST STEELE IN TRACT OF TIME DOTH TEARE      5.18.2
TRADE                      3
  OR BEING $BLIND (AS FITTEST FOR THE $TRADE)            2.48.9
  WHY THEN DOE I, UNTRAINDE IN LOVERS TRADE              5.51.5
  MOST HAPPY LETTERS FRAM'D BY SKILFULL TRADE            5.74.1
TRADEFUL                   1
  YE TRADEFULL $MERCHANTS THAT WITH WEARY TOYLE          5.15.1
TRAFFIC                    1
  FOR HAVING TRAFFIKE WITH THY SELFE ALONE               3.4.9
TRAGEDY                    2
  OF $LOVER'S RUINE SOME SAD $TRAGEDIE                   4.45.13
  I WAILE AND MAKE MY WOES A $TRAGEDY                    5.54.8
TRAGIC                     2
  MY PLEASURES HORROR, $MUSICKE TRAGICKE NOTES           1.9.11
  THE WAILING $ILIADS OF MY TRAGICKE WOE                 1.47.2
TRAIN                      4
  GREAT EXPECTATION, WEARE A TRAINE OF SHAME             4.21.8
  THOUGH HARBENGERS OF DEATH LODGE THERE HIS TRAINE      4.94.8
  WHICH SOUGHT ME TO ENTRAP IN TREASONS TRAINE           5.12.4
  THUS DOTH SHE TRAINE AND TEACH ME WITH
                          HER LOOKES                     5.21.13
TRAINED                                  1
  THE FIELD WHERE ALL MY THOUGHTS TO WARRE
                          BE TRAIND                      4.98.2
TRAINS                                   1
  UNTILL YE HAVE THEYR GUYLEFULL TRAYNES WELL TRYDE      5.47.2
TRAITOR                    2
  TRAITOUR TO ME, AND FAITHFULL TO MY $LOVE              1.25.2
  OUT TRAYTOUR ABSENCE, DAREST THOU COUNSELL ME          4.88.1
TRALUCENT                                1
  TIME, LOOKE THOU TOO, IN THIS $TRALUCENT $GLASSE       2.17.5
TRAMPLING                                1
  TEMPERS HER WORDS TO TRAMPLING HORSES FEET             4.84.3
TRANCE                     2
  EV'N AS A $MAN THAT IN SOME $TRANCE HATH SEENE         2.57.9
  MY SOULE WAS RAVISHT QUITE AS IN A TRAUNCE             5.39.10
TRANSFERRED                              1
  AND TO THIS FALSE PLAGUE ARE THEY NOW
                          TRANSFERRED                    3.137.14
TRANSFIX                                 1
  TIME DOTH TRANSFIXE THE FLORISH SET ON YOUTH           3.60.9
TRANSFORM                                1
  DID HER TRANSFORME INTO A LAURELL TREE                 5.28.12
TRANSFORMED                3
  WISHETH TO BE TRANSFORMED TO MY $SIGHT                 2.33.3
  WISHING TO BE TRANS-FORMD INTO MY SIGHT                2.133.3
  WISH NOW TO BE TRANS-FORMD INTO MY HART                2.133.8
TRANSGRESS                               1
  OR IN OUR $FATHERS DID SHE MORE TRANSGRESSE+           2.27.8
TRANSGRESSION                            1
  NEEDES MUST I UNDER MY TRANSGRESSION BOW               3.120.3
TRANSLATE                                1
  IF LIKE A $LAMBE HE COULD HIS LOOKES TRANSLATE         3.96.10
TRANSLATED                 2
  TO TRUTHS TRANSLATED, AND FOR TRUE THINGS DEEM'D       3.96.8
  HER EYE'S-SPEECH IS TRANSLATED THUS BY THEE            4.67.5
TRANSPIERCE                              1
  THEN STANCH THE BLEEDING, THEN TRANS-PIERCE
                          THE $COARSE                    2.50.7
```

```
TRANSPIERCING                    1
   THE $DART TRANSPEARSING, WERE THOSE $CHRISTALL
                               EIES                    1.14.4
TRANSPORT                        2
   AND THETHER ALL MY FORCES DOE TRANSPORTE            1.27.7
   WHICH SHOULD TRANSPORT ME FARTHEST FROM
                               YOUR SIGHT              3.117.8
TRANSPORTED                      1
   TRANSPORTED FROM MY $SELFE, INTO $YOUR BEING        2.11.5
TRAVAIL                          2
   THE DEARE REPOSE FOR LIMS WITH TRAVAILL TIRED       3.27.2
   DESERVES THE TRAVAILE OF A WORTHIER PEN             3.79.6
TRAVAILS                         1
   YET LEAST LONG TRAVAILES BE ABOVE MY STRENGTH       1.14.13
TRAVEL                           2
   THE MORE I TRAVELL, FURTHER FROM MY REST            2.150.2
   AND MAKE ME TRAVAILE FORTH WITHOUT MY CLOAKE        3.34.2
TRAVELED                         2
   THEN MORE I $TRAVELD, FURTHER FROM MY $REST         2.62.2
   HATH TRAVAILD ON TO $AGES STEEPIE NIGHT             3.63.5
TRAVELS                          3
   MY TEDIOUS $TRAVELS, AND OFT-VARYING $FATE          2.1.14
   WHEN WHAT I SEEKE (MY WEARIE TRAVELS END)           3.50.2
   LIKE HIM THAT TRAVELS I RETURNE AGAINE              3.109.6
TREACHERY                        1
   I BANISH HER, AND BLAME HER TRECHERY                1.25.6
TREAD                            2
   WHOSE FEETE DOE TREAD GREENE PATHS OF
                               YOUTH AND LOVE          1.6.6
   AND TREAD MY LIFE DOWNE IN THE LOWLY FLOURE         5.20.4
TREADING                         3
   WERE NOT $INVENTION STAULD, TREADING $INVENTIONS
                               MAZE                    2.117.9
   AND TREADING IN THYS NEVER-ENDING MAZE              2.133.7
   TREADING DOWNE EARTH AS LOTHSOME AND FORLORNE       5.13.11
TREADS                           1
   MY $MISTRES WHEN SHEE WALKES TREADS ON
                               THE GROUND              3.130.12
TREASON                          3
   MY NOBLER PART TO MY GROSE BODIES TREASON           3.151.6
   TRUST NOT THE TREASON OF THOSE SMYLING LOOKES       5.47.1
   YET HERESY NOR TREASON DIDST CONSPIRE               5.48.7
TREASON'S                        1
   WHICH SOUGHT ME TO ENTRAP IN TREASONS TRAINE        5.12.4
TREASURE                        16
   THEN DO NOT THOU SUCH TREASURE WAST IN VAINE        1.39.13
   REVEALE THE TREASURE WHICH HER SMILES IMPART+       1.49.6
   AND RANSACKE ALL $APOLLOS GOLDEN $TREASURE          2.21.12
   WHOSE WORTHY PRIZE SHOULD HAVE ENRITCHT
                               THY TREASURE            2.134.14
   O RICHEST $CASKET OF ALL HEAVENLY TREASURE          2.146.11
   WHERE ALL THE TREASURE OF THY LUSTY DAIES           3.2.6
   MAKE SWEET SOME VIALL., TREASURE THOU SOME PLACE    3.6.3
   WITH BEAUTITS TREASURE ERE IT BE SELFE KIL'D        3.6.4
   MINE BE THY LOVE AND THY LOVES USE THEIR
                               TREASURE                3.20.14
   CAN BRING HIM TO HIS SWEET UP-LOCKED TREASURE       3.52.2
   STEALING AWAY THE TREASURE OF HIS $SPRING           3.63.8
   DOUBTING THE FILCHING AGE WILL STEALE
                               HIS TREASURE            3.75.6
```

SHE MAY DETAINE, BUT NOT STILL KEEPE HER
                                    TRESURE   3.126.10
$WILL, WILL FULFILL THE TREASURE OF THY LOVE   3.136.5
RICH IN THE TREASURE OF DESERV'D RENOWNE   4.37.9
FAYRE BOSOME FRAUGHT WITH VERTUES RICHEST TRESURE   5.76.1
TREASURES   6
FOR FEARE THAT SOME THEIR $TREASURES SHOULD
                                    PURLOYNE   2.58.3
(EXIL'D FOR AY FRCM THOSE HIGH TREASURES, WHICH   4.24.13
'FOOLE,' ANSWERS HE, 'NO $INDES SUCH TREASURES
                                    HOLD   4.32.12
WITH WORDS, WHEREIN THE $MUSES' TREASURES BE   4.60.7
WHY DOEST THOU SPEND THE TREASURES OF THY SPRITE   4.68.5
AND BOTH THE $INDIAS OF THEIR TREASURES SPOILE   5.15.3
TREAT   2
DID TREATE THE CRUELL FAIRE TO YEELD RELIEFE   1.8.8
O EASE YOUR HAND, TREATE NOT SO HARD YOUR SLAVE   4.86.9
TREBLE   1
YET AT THIS PRICE RETURNES ME TREBLE GAINE   2.28.8
TREBLES   1
TREBLES SING HIGH, AS WELL AS BASES DEEPE   4.70.6
TREE   9
LIKE GRIZZLED $MOSSE UPCN SOME AGED $TREE   2.8.8
OR REACH THE FRUITE OF $NATURE'S CHOISEST TREE   4.10.4
TRUST IN THE SHADE CF PLEASING $ORANGE TREE   4.30.8
LONG SINCE FORC'D BY THY BEAMES, BUT STONE
                                    NOR TREE   4.36.13
SWEET GARD'N $NYMPH, WHICH KEEPES THE
                                    $CHERRIE TREE   4.82.5
A NEST FOR MY YONG PRAISE IN $LAWRELL TREE   4.90.6
DID HER TRANSFORME INTO A LAURELL TREE   5.28.12
FINDING A TREE ALONE ALL COMFORTLESSE   5.56.7
THAT SHIP, THAT TREE, AND THAT SAME BEAST AM I   5.56.13
TREES   3
THE BROKEN TOPS OF LOFTY TREES DECLARE   1.37.5
WHILST I LIKE $ORPHEUS SING TO $TREES
                                    AND $STONES   2.45.12
WHEN LOFTY TREES I SEE BARREN OF LEAVES   3.12.5
TREMBLING   4
WHEN TREMBLING VOICE BRINGS FORTH THAT
                                    I DO $STELLA LOVE   4.6.14
LYKE CAPTIVES TREMBLING AT THE VICTORS SIGHT   5.1.4
LEAST TREMBLING IT HIS WORKMANSHIP SHOULD SPILL   5.17.7
TILL I IN HAND HER YET HALFE TREMBLING TOOKE   5.67.11
TRENCHES   1
AND DIGGE DEEP TRENCHES IN THY BEAUTIES FIELD   3.2.2
TRENT   2
THE $CRYSTALL $TRENT, FCR $FOORDS AND
                                    $FISH RENOWNED   2.32.3
THE CHRISTALL $TRENT, FCR $FOORDS AND
                                    FISHE RENOWNED   2.124.3
TRESPASS   2
AUTHORIZING THY TRESPAS WITH COMPARE   3.35.6
BUT THAT YOUR TRESPASSE NOW BECOMES A FEE   3.120.13
TRESSED   1
THE $ANGELS TRESSES, TO HER TRESSED HAYRE   2.148.9
TRESSES   5
RESTORE THY TRESSES TO THE GOLDEN $ORE   1.19.1
THE $ANGELS TRESSES, TO HER TRESSED HAYRE   2.148.9
BEFORE THE GOULDEN TRESSES OF THE DEAD   3.68.5

```
WHAT GUYLE IS THIS, THAT THOSE HER GOLDEN TRESSES    5.37.1
BUT THE FAYRE TRESSES OF YOUR GOLDEN HAYRE           5.73.3
TRIAL                    2
IN MAKING TRYALL CF A $MURTHER WROUGHT               2.46.5
THE BOY FOR TRIALL NEEDES WOULD TOUCH MY BREST       3.153.10
TRIBES                   1
WHILE HE INSULTS CRE DULL AND SPEACHLESSE
                         TRIBES                      3.107.12
TRIBUTARY                1
THESE TRIBUTARY PASSIONS, BEAUTIES DUE               1.60.5
TRIBUTE                  5
RETURNING THEE THE TRIBUTE OF MY DUTIE               1.1.3
WITH MY HARTS TRYBUTE TC HER CONQUERING EYES         2.151.2
I WILL GOOD TRIBUTE PAY IF THOU DO SO                4.39.8
THAT WITTIE $LEWIS TO HIM A TRIBUTE PAID             4.75.11
THOU BUT OF ALL THE KINGLY $TRIBUTE TAKE             4.85.14
TRIBUTES                 1
ARE THOSE DUE TRIBUTES THAT MY FAITH DOTH PAY        1.24.3
TRIED                    6
SUCH AS BY $ART TC GET THE SAME HAVE TRY'D           2.58.7
THIS MIRACLE ON MY POORE $MUSE HAVE TRIED            2.104.10
IN $MARTIALL SPORTS I HAD MY CUNNING TRIDE           4.53.1
WAS NEVER IN THIS WCRLD OUGHT WORTHY TRIDE           5.5.13
TO PROVE YOUR POWRE, WHICH I TOO WEL HAVE TRICE      5.25.8
UNTILL YE HAVE THEYR GUYLEFULL TRAYNES WELL TRYDE    5.47.2
TRIES                    5
LOE THUS MY LOVE, MY LYFE, MY FORTUNE TRYES          2.142.4
OTHERS, BECAUSE THE $PRINCE MY SERVICE TRIES         4.23.7
THAT BUSIE ARCHER HIS SHARPE ARROWES TRIES+          4.31.4
FOR MY POORE SOULE, WHICH NOW THAT SICKNESSE
                         TRIES                       4.94.6
AND GRACE, SICKE TCO, SUCH FINE CONCLUSICNS
                         TRIES                       4.101.3
TRIFLE                   2
BECAUSE I LOOSELY TRIFLE IN THIS SORT                2.24.5
EACH TRIFLE UNDER TRUEST BARRES TO THRUST            3.48.2
TRIFLES                  1
BUT THOU, TO WHOM MY JEWELS TRIFLES ARE              3.48.5
TRIM                     1
WHEN PROUD PIDE $APRILL (DREST IN ALL HIS TRIM)      3.98.2
TRIMMED                  1
AND NEEDIE $NOTHING TRIMD IN JOLLITIE                3.66.3
TRINITY                  1
THE WORKE OF THAT UNITED $TRINITIE                   2.123.3
TRIPLICITY               1
THE WANDRING $MOONE IN EARTHS TRIPLICITIE            2.116.8
TRIPPING                 1
CAME TRIPPING BY, BUT IN HER MAIDEN HAND             3.154.4
TRIUMPH                  8
AND CAUSE HER LEAVE TO TRIUMPH IN THIS WISE          1.10.9
LET HER NOT STILL TRIUMPH OVER THE PRIZE             1.22.13
IN THINE EYES TRYUMPH MURTHERING MY POORE HART       2.140.2
WHILST I WHOME FORTUNE CF SUCH TRYUMPH BARS          3.25.3
BEING HAD TO TRYUMPH, BEING LACKT TO HOPE            3.52.14
TRIUMPH IN LOVE, FLESH STAIES NO FARTHER REASON      3.151.8
THAT HER GREAT TRIUMPH WHICH MY SKILL EXCEEDS        5.29.11
DIDST MAKE THY TRIUMPH CVER DEATH AND SIN            5.68.2
TRIUMPHAL                1
HER BREASTS HIS TENTS, LEGS HIS TRIUMPHALL CARRE     4.29.11
```

```
TRIUMPHANT                        2
   WITH ALL TRIUMPHANT SPLENDOR ON MY BROW          3.33.10
   AS HIS TRIUMPHANT PRIZE, PROUD OF THIS PRIDE      3.151.10
TRIUMPHING                        1
   HEAV'NS ENVY NOT AT MY HIGH TRIUMPHING            4.63.10
TRIUMPHS                          1
   WRACKES $TRIUMPHS BE, WHICH $LOVE (HIGH
                          SET) DOTH BREED            4.42.14
TRIUMVIRATE                       1
   POSSESSE ME WHOLE, MY HEARTS TRIUMVIRATE          1.28.2
TRODDEN                           1
   ALL MY POORE LIFE BY THEM IS TRODEN DOWNE         1.28.6
TROJAN                            1
   OR HERS WHOM NAKED THE $TROJAN BOY DID SEE        4.82.4
TROPES                            2
   ENNOBLING NEW FOUND $TROPES WITH PROBLEMES OLD    4.3.6
   CLOTH'D WITH FINE TROPES, WITH STRONGEST
                          REASONS LIN'D              4.58.6
TROPHIES                          8
   THEY ALL ERECT THEIR $TROPHIES ON MY FALL         1.28.7
   THESE ARE THE $ARKES, THE $TROPHIES I ERECT       1.55.9
   THE STRONG-BUILT $TROPHIES TO HER LIVING $FAME    2.45.6
   ERECTING $TROPHIES TO THY $SACRED $EYES           2.55.12
   ERECTING $TROPHIES TO THY SACRED EYES             2.102.12
   WHY SHOULD'ST THOU PLACE THY $TROPHIES
                          IN THOSE EYES              2.123.9
   HUNG WITH THE TROPHEIS OF MY LOVERS GON           3.31.10
   USED $TROPHEES TO ERECT IN STATELY WIZE           5.69.2
TROPHY                            2
   THAT SERVES A $TROPHEY TO HER CONQUERING EIES     1.10.11
   WHAT TROPHEE THEN SHALL I MOST FIT DEVIZE         5.69.5
TROPIC                            1
   THEN TO THE $TROPICKE TAKES HIS FULL $CAREERE     2.147.5
TROT                              1
   WHEN I, AS FAST AS E'R MY $PENNE COULD TROT       2.21.5
TROTTING                          1
   TROTTING HIS SUN-STEEDS TILL THE $PALFRAYS SWEAT  2.147.6
TROUBLE                           2
   THAT NOW IN $COACHES TROUBLE EV'RY $STREET        2.6.2
   AND TROUBLE DEAFE HEAVEN WITH MY BOOTLESSE CRIES  3.29.3
TROUBLED                          6
   WHEN SHAL HER TROUBLED BROW CHARG'D WITH DISCAINE 1.49.5
   BEARE WITH $ME THEN, THOUGH TROUBLED BE
                          MY $BRAINE                 2.9.12
   INTO THE OCEAN OF A TROUBLED MINDE                2.134.2
   WHILE TOO MUCH WIT (FORSOOTH) SO TROUBLED ME      4.33.10
   OF CUNNINGST FISHERS IN MOST TROUBLED STREAMES    4.51.10
   DISGUYSING DIVERSLY MY TROUBLED WITS              5.54.4
TROUBLOUS                         1
   SINS THAT THIS ONE IS TOST WITH TROUBLOUS FIT     5.33.11
TROUPES                           1
   AND OFT WHOLE TROUPES OF SADDEST WORDS I STAID    4.55.5
TRUANT                            2
   OH TRUANT $MUSE WHAT SHALBE THY AMENDS            3.101.1
   BITING MY TREWAND PEN, BEATING MY SELFE FOR SPITE 4.1.13
TRUCE                             2
   TRUCE, GENTLE $LOVE, A $PARLY NOW I CRAVE         2.63.1
   TO MAKE A TRUCE AND TERMES TO ENTERTAINE          5.12.2
TRUE                             81
   SO TRUE AND LOYALL LOVE NO FAVOUR GAINES ME       1.18.8
```

```
SHE DOTH ME WRONG, TO GRIEVE SO TRUE A HEART          1.21.14
YET NEVER ANY TRUE EFFECT I PROVE                     1.25.4
NOR OTHER HAND COULD GIVE SO TRUE A TOUCH             1.57.14
BE YOU MOST WORTHY, WHILST I AM MOST TRUE             2.4.14
HAPS TO LEND SOME TO ONE TRUE HONEST $FRIEND          2.10.8
I AM SURE MY $SIGHES COME FROM A $HEART AS TRUE       2.27.9
BY ALL TRUE $LOVERS $SIGHES, $VOWES, AND
                               $DESIRES              2.36.11
BY CHASTE $DESIRE, TRUE $LOVE, AND VERTUOUS
                               $PRAYSE              2.54.14
BY CHAST DESIRE, TRUE LOVE, AND VERTUES PRAISE       2.101.14
AND BY EXAMPLE, TRUE REPENTANCE PREACH               2.119.14
THE SOULES DELIGHT, THE SENCES TRUE DIRECTION        2.123.7
O RARE EFFECT, TRUE BOND OF FRIENDSHIPS MEASURE      2.146.9
IF THE TRUE CONCORD OF WELL TUNED SOUNDS             3.8.5
AND YOUR TRUE RIGHTS BE TERMD A $POETS RAGE          3.17.11
O LET ME TRUE IN LOVE BUT TRULY WRITE                3.21.9
TO FINDE WHERE YOUR TRUE $IMAGE PICTUR'D LIES        3.24.6
NO LOVE, MY LOVE, THAT THOU MAIST TRUE LOVE CALL     3.40.3
SO TRUE A FOOLE IS LOVE, THAT IN YOUR $WILL          3.57.13
MINE OWNE TRUE LOVE THAT DOTH MY REST DEFEAT         3.61.11
NO SHAPE SO TRUE, NO TRUTH OF SUCH ACCOUNT           3.62.6
$ROSES OF SHADDOW, SINCE HIS $ROSE IS TRUE+          3.67.8
WITHOUT ALL ORNAMENT, IT SELFE AND TRUE              3.68.10
O LEAST YOUR TRUE LOVE MAY SEEME FALCE IN THIS       3.72.9
IN TRUE PLAINE WORDS, BY THY TRUE TELLING FRIEND     3.82.12
IN TRUE PLAINE WORDS, BY THY TRUE TELLING FRIEND     3.82.12
HEARING YOU PRAISD, I SAY 'TIS SO, 'TIS TRUE         3.85.9
SO SHALL I LIVE, SUPPOSING THOU ART TRUE             3.93.1
TO TRUTHS TRANSLATED, AND FOR TRUE THINGS DEEM'D     3.96.8
FAIRE, KINDE, AND TRUE, IS ALL MY ARGUMENT           3.105.9
FAIRE, KINDE AND TRUE, VARRYING TO OTHER WORDS       3.105.10
FAIRE, KINDE, AND TRUE, HAVE OFTEN LIV'D ALONE       3.105.13
CAN YET THE LEASE OF MY TRUE LOVE CONTROULE          3.107.3
WHICH HATH NOT FIGUR'D TO THEE MY TRUE SPIRIT        3.108.2
ALAS 'TIS TRUE, I HAVE GONE HERE AND THERE           3.110.1
MOST TRUE IT IS, THAT I HAVE LOOKT ON TRUTH          3.110.5
MY MOST TRUE MINDE THUS MAKETH MINE UNTRUE           3.113.14
OR WHETHER SHALL I SAY MINE EIE SAITH TRUE           3.114.3
LET ME NOT TO THE MARRIAGE OF TRUE MINDES            3.116.1
TO BE DISEAS'D ERE THAT THERE WAS TRUE NEEDING       3.118.8
BUT THENCE I LEARNE AND FIND THE LESSON TRUE         3.118.13
O BENEFIT OF ILL, NOW I FIND TRUE                    3.119.9
MY DEEPEST SENCE, HOW HARD TRUE SORROW HITS          3.120.10
I WILL BE TRUE DISPIGHT THY SYETH AND THEE           3.123.14
HENCE, THOU SUBBORND $INFORMER, A TREW SOULE         3.125.13
IN THINGS RIGHT TRUE MY HEART AND EYES
                               HAVE ERRED            3.137.13
WHICH HAVE NO CORRESPONDENCE WITH TRUE SIGHT         3.148.2
LOVES EYE IS NOT SO TRUE AS ALL MENS.. NO            3.148.8
HOW CAN IT+ $O HOW CAN LOVES EYE BE TRUE             3.148.9
TO MAKE ME GIVE THE LIE TO MY TRUE SIGHT             3.150.3
WHICH MANY $LEGIONS OF TRUE HEARTS HAD WARM'D        3.154.6
THAT SHRINES IN FLESH SO TRUE A $DEITIE              4.4.13
IT IS MOST TRUE, THAT EYES ARE FORM'D TO SERVE       4.5.1
IT IS MOST TRUE, WHAT WE CALL $CUPID'S DART          4.5.5
TRUE, THAT TRUE $BEAUTIE $VERTUE IS INDEED           4.5.9
TRUE, THAT TRUE $BEAUTIE $VERTUE IS INDEED           4.5.9
TRUE, THAT ON EARTH WE ARE BUT PILGRIMS MADE         4.5.12
TRUE, AND YET TRUE THAT I MUST $STELLA LOVE          4.5.14
```

```
TRUE, AND YET TRUE THAT I MUST $STELLA LOVE           4.5.14
IT IS MOST TRUE, FOR SINCE I HER DID SEE              4.25.12
WHICH MAKE THE PATENTS OF TRUE WORLDLY BLISSE         4.37.13
HOW FARRE THEY SHOOTE AWRIE- THE TRUE CAUSE IS        4.41.12
BUT YOU FAIRE MAIDES, AT LENGTH THIS TRUE
                            SHALL FIND                4.54.11
THAT IT, DESPISDE IN TRUE BUT NAKED SHEW              4.55.3
OFT WITH TRUE SIGHES, OFT WITH UNCALLED TEARES        4.61.1
SWEET SAID THAT I TRUE LOVE IN HER SHOULD FIND        4.62.4
HOPE, ART THOU TRUE, OR DOEST THOU FLATTER ME+        4.67.1
STELLA, THOSE FAIRE LINES, WHICH TRUE
                            GOODNESSE SHOW            4.71.4
AS CONSTERD IN TRUE SPEECH, THE NAME OF
                            HEAV'N IT BEARES          4.77.11
O HOW THE PLEASANT AIRES OF TRUE LOVE BE              4.78.1
YET SIGHS, DEERE SIGHS, INDEEDE TRUE FRIENDS
                            YOU ARE                   4.95.1
ONLY TRUE SIGHS, YOU DO NOT GO AWAY                   4.95.12
AND WHEN MY PEN WOULD WRITE HER TITLES TRUE           5.3.11
WHICH HER DEEP WIT, THAT TRUE HARTS THOUGHT
                            CAN SPEL                  5.43.13
MOST LIVELY LYKE BEHOLD YOUR SEMBLANT TREW            5.45.4
SWEET BE THE BANDS, THE WHICH TRUE LOVE DOTH TYE      5.65.5
AND WHEN I HOPE TO SEE THEYR TREW OBJECT              5.78.11
BUT THE TREW FAYRE, THAT IS THE GENTLE WIT            5.79.3
THAT IS TRUE BEAUTIE.. THAT DOTH ARGUE YOU            5.79.9
DERIV'D FROM THAT FAYRE $SPIRIT, FROM
                            WHOM AL TRUE              5.79.11
IN MY TRUE LOVE DID STIRRE UP COLES OF YRE            5.86.8
TRUE-LOVE                    1
MIX'D WITH HER $TEARES, THAT NE'R HER
                            TRUE-$LOVE CROST          2.15.5
TRUEST                       3
THE TRUEST LOVE THAT EVER YET WAS SEENE               1.10.8
SLEW HIS DEARE $FRIEND, MY KIND AND TRUEST $HEART     2.7.12
EACH TRIFLE UNDER TRUEST BARRES TO THRUST             3.48.2
TRULL                        1
THAT EV'RY $DOWDY, EV'RY $TRULL DOTH WEARE+           2.31.12
TRULY                        8
NOR PAYD THE IMPOST OF HIS WAVES MORE TRULY           1.48.7
YET SEE THOU TELL, BUT TRULY, WHAT HATH BEENE         2.17.10
TELL TRUELIE $TIME WHAT IN THY TIME HATH BEENE        2.107.10
O LET ME TRUE IN LOVE BUT TRULY WRITE                 3.21.9
THE WRINCKLES WHICH THY GLASSE WILL TRULY SHOW        3.77.5
THOU TRULY FAIRE, WERT TRULY SIMPATHIZDE              3.82.11
THOU TRULY FAIRE, WERT TRULY SIMPATHIZDE              3.82.11
AND TRULY NOT THE MORNING $SUN OF $HEAVEN             3.132.5
TRUMP                        2
I MAY IN TRUMP OF FAME BLAZE OVER ALL                 5.29.12
WHICH WHEN AS FAME IN HER SHRILL TRUMP
                            SHAL THUNDER              5.85.13
TRUMPET                      2
NOR MY $MUSE BEEN THE TRUMPET OF THY FAME             2.104.8
HIS TROMPET SHRILL HATH THRISE ALREADY SOUNDED        5.19.2
TRUMPETS'                    1
NOR TRUMPETS SOUND I HEARD, NOR FRIENDLY CRIES        4.53.12
TRUST                        7
SO I FOR FEARE OF TRUST, FORGET TO SAY                3.23.5
FROM HANDS OF FALSEHOOD, IN SURE WARDS OF TRUST+      3.48.4
TO TRUST THOSE TABLES THAT RECEAVE THEE MORE          3.122.12
```

SAVAGE, EXTREAME, RUDE, CRUELL, NOT TO TRUST	3.129.4
O LOVES BEST HABIT IS IN SEEMING TRUST	3.138.11
TRUST IN THE SHADE OF PLEASING $ORANGE TREE	4.30.8
TRUST NOT THE TREASON OF THOSE SMYLING LOOKES	5.47.1

TRUSTING   1

BUT FAYLETH TRUSTING ON HIS OWNE ASSURANCE	5.58.10

TRUSTY   1

WHENAS A STORME HATH DIMD HER TRUSTY GUYDE	5.34.3

TRUTH   40

EXAMINE WELL THY BEAUTIE WITH MY TRUTH	1.1.11
MY JOYS BUT SHADOWES, TOUCH OF TRUTH, MY ANGUISH	1.16.3
OFT WHEN I FINDE IN HER NO TRUTH AT ALL	1.25.5
THAT TELLS THE TRUTH, AND SAYES THAT ALL IS GONE	1.41.4
UNFAINED LOVE, IN NAKED SIMPLE TRUTH	2.138.3
AS TRUTH AND BEAUTIE SHAL TOGETHER THRIVE	3.14.11
BE SCORN'D, LIKE OLD MEN OF LESSE TRUTH THEN TONGUE	3.17.10
TAKE ALL MY COMFORT OF THY WORTH AND TRUTH	3.37.4
WHERE THOU ART FORST TO BREAKE A TWO-FOLD TRUTH	3.41.12
FOR TRUTH PROOVES THEEVISH FOR A PRIZE SO DEARE	3.48.14
BY THAT SWEET ORNAMENT WHICH TRUTH DOTH GIVE	3.54.2
WHEN THAT SHALL VADE, BY VERSE DISTILS YOUR TRUTH	3.54.14
FEEDES ON THE RARITIES OF NATURES TRUTH	3.60.11
NO SHAPE SO TRUE, NO TRUTH OF SUCH ACCOUNT	3.62.6
UTTRING BARE TRUTH, EVEN SO AS FOES $COMMEND	3.69.4
THEN NIGARD TRUTH WOULD WILLINGLY IMPART	3.72.8
FOR THY NEGLECT OF TRUTH IN BEAUTY DI'D+	3.101.2
BOTH TRUTH AND BEAUTY ON MY LOVE DEPENDS	3.101.3
TRUTH NEEDS NO COLLOUR WITH HIS COLLOUR FIXT	3.101.6
BEAUTIE NO PENSELL, BEAUTIES TRUTH TO LAY	3.101.7
MOST TRUE IT IS, THAT I HAVE LOOKT ON TRUTH	3.110.5
TO PUT FAIRE TRUTH UPON SO FOULE A FACE	3.137.12
WHEN MY LOVE SWEARES THAT SHE IS MADE OF TRUTH	3.138.1
ON BOTH SIDES THUS IS SIMPLE TRUTH SUPPREST	3.138.8
AT RANDON FROM THE TRUTH VAINELY EXPREST	3.147.12
OTHES OF THY LOVE, THY TRUTH, THY CONSTANCIE	3.152.10
TO SWERE AGAINST THE TRUTH SO FOULE A LIE	3.152.14
LOVING IN TRUTH, AND FAINE IN VERSE MY LOVE TO SHOW	4.1.1
IN TRUTH, O $LOVE, WITH WHAT A BOYISH KIND	4.11.1
WELL STAID WITH TRUTH IN WORD AND FAITH OF DEED	4.14.10
BUT FOR THAT MAN WITH PAINE THIS TRUTH DESCRIES	4.25.5
WHERE TRUTH IT SELFE MUST SPEAKE LIKE FLATTERIE+	4.35.2
I MUCH DO GUESSE, YET FIND NO TRUTH SAVE THIS	4.44.9
SINCE IN THINE ARMES, IF LEARND FAME TRUTH HATH SPREAD	4.65.13
RATHER THEN BY MORE TRUTH TO GET MORE PAINE	4.67.14
I GIVE YOU HERE MY HAND FOR TRUTH OF THIS	4.70.13
IN TRUTH I SWEARE, I WISH NOT THERE SHOULD BE	4.90.7
YET TRUTH (IF $CAITIF'S BREATH MIGHTE CALL THEE) THIS	4.93.5
AND HOSTAGES DOE OFFER FOR MY TRUTH	5.11.2
BUT SIMPLE TRUTH AND MUTUALL GOOD WILL	5.65.11

TRUTHS   1

TO TRUTHS TRANSLATED, AND FOR TRUE THINGS DEEM'D	3.96.8

TRUTH'S   1

THY END IS $TRUTHES AND $BEAUTIES DOOME AND DATE	3.14.14

TRY   8

AND WHEN BY $MEANES, TO DRIVE IT OUT I TRY	2.20.6

```
BY $SURGEONS BEG'D, THEIR $ART ON HIM TO TRIE        2.50.4
ON NEWER PROOFE, TO TRIE AN OLDER FRIEND             3.110.11
I ON MY HORSE, AND $LOVE ON ME DOTH TRIE             4.49.1
BUT NOW I MEANE NO MORE YOUR HELPE TO TRIE           4.55.9
NO MORE, MY DEARE, NO MORE THESE COUNSELS TRIE       4.64.1
LOOKE ON AGAINE, THE FAIRE TEXT BETTER TRIE          4.67.7
WHEN FOR SO SOFT A ROD DEARE PLAY HE TRIE+           4.73.4
```
TUNE   1
```
NOR ARE MINE EARES WITH THY TOUNGS TUNE
                         DELIGHTED                   3.141.5
```
TUNED   2
```
ON MY HEART-STRINGS HIGH TUN'D UNTO HER FAME         1.57.4
IF THE TRUE CONCORD OF WELL TUNED SOUNDS             3.8.5
```
TUNELESS   1
```
BUT WHEN IN HAND MY TUNELESSE HARP I TAKE            5.44.9
```
TUNES   1
```
ARE METAMORPHOSD STRAIGHT TO TUNES OF JOYES          4.44.14
```
TURKISH   2
```
FORC'D BY A TEDIOUS PROOFE, THAT $TURKISH
                         HARDNED HART                4.8.2
WHETHER THE $TURKISH NEW-MOONE MINDED BE             4.30.1
```
TURMOIL   1
```
BUT THEN SHE SEEKES WITH TORMENT AND TURMOYLE        5.11.11
```
TURN   18
```
WHOSE ROWLING GRACE DEIGNE ONCE A TURNE OF BLIS      1.12.12
NO OTHER $DRINKE WOULD SERVE THIS $GLUTTONS TURNE    2.7.5
O SWEETEST $SHADOW, HOW THOU SERV'ST MY TURNE        2.13.9
AND TURNE THE $WHEELE WITH DAMNED $IXION             2.40.14
PRACTISE THY $QUIVER, AND TURNE $CROW-KEEPER         2.48.8
HOW E'RE BLIND $FORTUNE TURNE HER GIDDIE $WHEELE     2.51.12
OR IF NO THING BUT $DEATH WILL SERVE THY TURNE       2.63.9
O SWEETEST SHADOW, HOW THOU SERV'ST MY TURNE         2.121.9
AND TURNE THE WHEELE WITH DAMNED $IXION              2.144.14
FOR SWEETEST THINGS TURNE SOWREST BY THEIR
                         DEEDES                      3.94.13
BUT IF THOU CATCH THY HOPE TURNE BACK TO ME          3.143.11
IF THOU TURNE BACK AND MY LOUDE CRYING STILL         3.143.14
WITH CARE'S HARD HAND) TO TURNE AND TOSSE IN THEE    4.98.8
THEREFORE $O LOVE, UNLESSE SHE TURNE TO THEE         5.19.13
THAT GREATER MEEDE AT LAST MAY TURNE TO MEE          5.25.14
AND SHE TO STONES AT LENGTH ALL FROSEN TURNE+        5.32.14
SHALL TURNE TO CAULMES AND TYMELY CLEARE AWAY        5.62.12
SHALL TURNE TO NOUGHT AND LOOSE THAT GLORIOUS HEW    5.79.6
```
TURNED   5
```
WHICH TURN'D MY SPORT INTO A $HARTS DISPAIRE         1.5.9
I FEARE YOUR EYE HATH TURND YOUR HEART TO FLINT      1.37.14
WHOSE $STOMACK UNTO $GALL HATH TURN'D THY $FOOD      2.49.6
THREE BEAUTIOUS SPRINGS TO YELLOW $AUTUMNE
                         TURN'D                      3.104.5
AND WHETHER THAT MY ANGEL BE TURN'D FINDE            3.144.9
```
TURNETH   2
```
WHOSE SCORCHING GLEED, MY HEART TO $CINDERS
                         TURNETH                     2.40.10
WITH SCORCHING GLEED MY HART TO CYNDERS TURNETH      2.144.10
```
TURNING   2
```
TURNING MY $PAPERS, ASKES, $WHAT HAVE WE HEERE+      2.31.3
OFT TURNING OTHERS' LEAVES, TO SEE IF
                         THENCE WOULD FLOW           4.1.7
```
TURNS   9
```
AND OFT WITH CAREFULL TURNES, WITH SILENT $ART       1.8.7
```

```
MY TOUCHT HEART TURNES IT TO THAT HAPPY COST        1.53.2
AND EACH DOTH GOOD TURNES NOW UNTO THE OTHER        3.47.2
AND ALL THINGS TURNES TO FAIRE, THAT EIES
                                    CAN SEE         3.95.12
AND THEREFORE FROM MY FACE SHE TURNES MY FOES       3.139.11
FALS TO SHREWD TURNES, AND I WAS IN HIS WAY         4.17.14
MY VERIE INKE TURNES STRAIGHT TO $STELLA'S NAME     4.19.6
THOU WHOM TO ME SUCH MY GOOD TURNES SHOULD BIND     4.65.3
AND WHEN I WAILE, SHE TURNES HIR SELFE
                                    TO LAUGHTER     5.18.12
TURRET                      1
  LOOKING ALOFT FROM TURRET OF HER PRIDE            1.47.6
TURRETS                     1
  MY $FAYRE, LOOKE FROM THOSE TURRETS OF
                                    THINE EYES      2.134.1
TUSH                        1
  TUSH ABSENCE, WHILE THY MISTES ECLIPSE THAT LIGHT 4.88.9
TWAIN                       5
  SEE THEN WHO SINNES THE GREATER OF US TWAINE      1.33.13
  REASON AND I (YOU MUST CONCEIVE) ARE TWAINE       2.9.10
  LET ME CONFESSE THAT WE TWO MUST BE TWAINE        3.36.1
  AND THAT THOU TEACHEST HOW TO MAKE ONE TWAINE     3.39.13
  BOTH FINDE EACH OTHER, AND I LOOSE BOTH TWAINE    3.42.11
TWEED'S                     2
  OUR $NORTHERNE $BORDERS BOAST OF $TWEEDS
                                    FAIRE $FLOUD    2.32.10
  OUR $NORTHERN BORDERS BOAST OF $TWEEDS
                                    FAIRE FLOOD     2.124.10
TWENTY                      1
  WHEN I BREAKE TWENTY.. I AM PERJUR'D MOST         3.152.6
TWICE                       3
  YOU SHOULD LIVE TWISE IN IT, AND IN MY RIME       3.17.14
  BUT THOU ART TWICE FORSWORNE TO ME LOVE SWEARING  3.152.2
  LEAST ONCE SHOULD NOT BE HEARD, TWISE
                                    SAID, $NO, $NO  4.63.8
TWILIGHT                    1
  IN ME THOU SEEST THE TWI-LIGHT OF SUCH DAY        3.73.5
TWINE                       1
  THEY DID THEMSELVES (O SWEETEST PRISON) TWINE     4.103.8
TWINKLE                     1
  WHEN SUDDENLY WITH TWINCLE OF HER EYE             5.16.11
TWINS                       1
  SHE COMES, AND STREIGHT THEREWITH HER
                                    SHINING TWINS DO MOVE  4.76.1
TWIN'S                      1
  PROGRESSING THEN FROM FAIRE TWINNES' GOLD'N PLACE 4.22.2
TWIRE                       1
  WHEN SPARKLING STARS TWIRE NOT THOU GUIL'ST
                                    TH'EAVEN        3.28.12
TWIXT                       7
  TWIXT JOY AND GRIEFE, YET WITH A SMYLING
                                    FROWNING        2.109.9
  WHILST FIRE, WATER, AYRE, TWIXT HEAVEN
                                    AND EARTH SHAL BE  2.127.13
  AS TWIXT A MISER AND HIS WEALTH IS FOUND          3.75.4
  CREEPE IN TWIXT VOWES, AND CHANGE DECREES
                                    OF $KINGS       3.115.6
  TWIXT FEARE AND HOPE DEPENDING DOUBTFULLY+        5.25.4
  THE LEAGUE TWIXT THEM, THAT LOYAL LOVE
                                    HATH BOUND      5.65.10
```

```
AND TWIXT HER PAPS LIKE EARLY FRUIT IN $MAY            5.76.9
TWO                      19
  ARE EYES, OR ELS TWO RADIANT STARRES THAT SHINE      1.34.2
  THAT WHERE THOSE TWO CLEARE SPARKLING
                            $EYES ARE PLAC'D            2.8.3
  ONELY TWO $LOOPE-HOLES, THEN I MIGHT BEHOLD           2.8.4
  TO MY $SOULES $SUNNE, THOSE TWO $CELESTIALL
                            $EYES                       2.56.12
  LET ME CONFESSE THAT WE TWO MUST BE TWAINE            3.36.1
  IN OUR TWO LOVES THERE IS BUT ONE RESPECT             3.36.5
  THE OTHER TWO, SLIGHT AYRE, AND PURGING FIRE          3.45.1
  MY LIFE BEING MADE OF FOURE, WITH TWO ALONE           3.45.7
  WHICH PARTS THE SHORE, WHERE TWO CONTRACTED NEW       3.56.10
  AS THOSE TWO MORNING EYES BECOME THY FACE             3.132.9
  TWO LOVES I HAVE OF COMFORT AND DISPAIRE              3.144.1
  WHICH LIKE TWO SPIRITS DO SUGGEST ME STILL            3.144.2
  BUT WHY OF TWO OTHES BREACH DOE I ACCUSE THEE         3.152.5
  OF $STELLA'S BROWES MADE HIM TWO BETTER BOWES         4.17.10
  BY ONLY THOSE TWO STARRES IN $STELLA'S FACE           4.26.14
  THAT IN ONE SPEECH TWO $NEGATIVES AFFIRME             4.63.14
  BUT DID SHE KNOW HOW ILL THESE TWO ACCORD             5.31.13
  WHEN LOOSING ONE, TWO LIBERTIES YE GAYNE              5.65.3
  TWOO GOLDEN APPLES OF UNVALEWD PRICE                  5.77.6
TWOFOLD                  1
  WHERE THOU ART FORST TO BREAKE A TWO-FOLD TRUTH       3.41.12
TYRAN                    1
  SO $TYRAN HE NO FITTER PLACE COULD SPIE               4.20.5
TYRANNESS                1
  SEE HOW THE $TYRANNESSE DOTH JOY TO SEE               5.10.5
TYRANNIZETH              1
  RULES WITH A BECKE, SO TYRANNIZETH THEE               4.46.3
TYRANNIZING              1
  WHILST IN DESPITE OF TYRANNIZING $TIMES               2.44.5
TYRANNOUS                1
  THOU ART AS TIRANOUS, SO AS THOU ART                  3.131.1
TYRANNY                  4
  ALAS WHY FEARING OF TIMES TIRANIE                     3.115.9
  I CALL IT PRAISE TO SUFFER $TYRANNIE                  4.2.11
  WHOSE NECKE BECOMES SUCH YOKE OF TYRANNY+             4.47.4
  WHAT TYRANNY IS THIS BOTH MY HART TO THRALL           5.43.5
TYRANT                   11
  UNTO THE TYRANT, WHOSE UNKINDNES KILS                 1.24.4
  MUST YEELD UP ALL TO TYRANT $TIMES DESIRE             1.38.7
  THERE MY SOULES TYRANT JOYES HER, IN THE SACK         1.47.7
  THEN IF HE HAD THE TYRANT OVER-THROWNE                1.56.4
  DOUBTING, IF THAT PROUD $TYRANT SHOULD PREVAYLE       2.29.3
  PLAY NOT THE $TYRANT, BUT TAKE SOME $REMORSE          2.52.5
  SUBDUE THYS $TYRANT EVER MARTYRING MEE                2.115.2
  AND LIKE A $TYRANT MAK'ST MY GRIEFE THY GAME          2.130.12
  MAKE WARRE UPPON THIS BLOUDIE TIRANT TIME+            3.16.2
  AND I A TYRANT HAVE NO LEASURE TAKEN                  3.120.7
  AM OF MY SELFE, ALL TIRANT FOR THY SAKE+              3.149.4
TYRANTS                  4
  MY FREEDOMES TYRANTS CONQUERING ALL BY ARTE           1.27.10
  LADIES AND $TYRANTS, NEVER LAWES RESPECT              1.31.12
  WILL PLAY THE TIRANTS TO THE VERY SAME                3.5.3
  ONLY LOV'D $TYRANTS, JUST IN CRUELTY                  4.42.6
TYRANTS'                 1
  WHEN TYRANTS CRESTS AND TOMBS OF BRASSE
                            ARE SPENT                   3.107.14
```

```
TYRONE                       1
  ESSEX GREAT FALL, $TYRONE HIS $PEACE TO GAINE        2.51.6
UGLY                         2
  I SEE THE UGLY FACE OF MY DEFORMED CARES             2.114.2
  WITH OUGLY RACK ON HIS CELESTIALL FACE               3.33.6
ULSTER                       1
  HOW $ULSTER LIKES OF THAT SAME GOLDEN BIT            4.30.9
ULYSSES'                     1
  $PENELOPE FOR HER $ULISSES SAKE                      5.23.1
UNABLE                       2
  OR ELSE $LOVE WERE UNABLE TO INDITE                  2.38.4
  UNABLE QUITE TO PAY EVEN $NATURE'S RENT              4.18.5
UNAFFECTED                   1
  BUT UNTOUCHT HEARTS, WITH UNAFFECTED EIE             1.3.5
UNAMBITIOUS                  1
  NONE OTHER FAME MINE UNAMBITIOUS $MUSE               1.58.1
UNARMED                      1
  STELLA ALONE WITH FACE UNARMED MARCHT                4.22.9
UNAVOIDED                    1
  BY THY FAIRE $MOTHERS UNAVOIDED $POWER               2.36.6
UNAWARE                      1
  IN CLOSE AWAYT TO CATCH HER UNAWARE                  5.71.4
UNAWARES                     1
  ALL UNAWARES, A $GODDESSE CHASTE I FINDE             1.5.3
UNBELIEVING                  2
  SEE $MIRACLES, YE UNBELEEVING, SEE                   2.35.5
  SEE MYRACLES, YEE UNBELEEVING SEE                    2.112.5
UNBID                        1
  BUT I UNBID, FETCH EVEN MY SOULE TO THEE             4.59.8
UNBIDDEN                     1
  MOST RUDE DISPAIRE MY DAILY UNBIDDEN GUEST           4.108.7
UNBITTED                     1
  TO HATCH MINE EYES, AND THAT UNBITTED THOUGHT        4.38.2
UNBLESS                      1
  THOU DOO'ST BEGUILE THE WORLD, UNBLESSE
                             SOME MOTHER               3.3.4
UNBORN                       1
  WHEN YET TH'UNBORNE SHALL SAY, $LO WHERE SHE LIES    1.55.7
UNBRED                       1
  FOR FEARE OF WHICH, HEARE THIS THOU AGE UNBRED       3.104.13
UNBURDEN                     1
  THESE LINES I USE, T'UNBURTHEN MINE OWNE HART        1.4.13
UNBURIED                     1
  UNBURIED IN THESE LINES RESERV'D IN PURENES          1.44.10
UNCALLED                     1
  OFT WITH TRUE SIGHES, OFT WITH UNCALLED TEARES       4.61.1
UNCERTAIN                    3
  UNCERTAINE $DREAD GIVES $WINGS UNTO MY $HOPE         2.26.5
  TH'INCERTAINE $TIMES OFT VARYING IN THEIR $COURSE    2.51.2
  TH'UNCERTAINE SICKLIE APPETITE TO PLEASE             3.147.4
UNCERTAIN-DREAD              1
  UNCERTAINE-DREAD, GYVES WINGS UNTO MY HOPE           2.137.5
UNCHASTITY                   1
  A LOATHING OF ALL LOOSE UNCHASTITIE                  4.14.13
UNCLASP                      1
  HERE I UNCLASPE THE $BOOKE OF MY CHARG'D SOULE       1.1.5
UNCLEAN                      3
  ALL UNCLEANE $THOUGHTS, FOULE $SPIRITS
                             CAST OUT IN MEE           2.35.13
  ALL UNCLEANE THOUGHTS, FOULE SPIRITS CAST
                             OUT IN MEE                2.112.13
```

```
      SITH ALL WORLDS GLORIE IS BUT DROSSE UNCLEANE       5.27.2
UNDER              8
  LIFTS UP HIS BURNING HEAD, EACH UNDER EYE               3.7.2
  EACH TRIFLE UNDER TRUEST BARRES TO THRUST               3.48.2
  AND UNDER THEE THEIR POESIE DISPERSE                    3.78.4
  NEEDES MUST I UNDER MY TRANSGRESSION BOW                3.120.3
  UNDER THE BLOW OF THRALLED DISCONTENT                   3.124.7
  UNDER THAT BOND THAT HIM AS FAST DOTH BINDE             3.134.8
  SHE DOTH ATTYRE UNDER A NET OF GOLD                     5.37.2
  NE JOY OF OUGHT THAT UNDER HEAVEN DOTH HOVE             5.89.9
UNDERCHARGE                1
  NOT POINTING TO FIT FOLKES EACH UNDERCHARGE             4.85.6
UNDERSTAND                 1
  AND ERE SHE COULD THY CAUSE WEL UNDERSTAND              5.48.3
UNDERTAKEN                 1
  THAT ERE BY THEM OUGHT UNDERTAKEN BE                    4.107.3
UNDISCLOSE                 1
  WHILST YET HER TENDER BUD DOTH UNDISCLOSE               1.39.3
UNDIVIDED                  1
  ALTHOUGH OUR UNDEVIDED LOVES ARE ONE                    3.36.2
UNDONE                     3
  AND I A $BANKRUPT, QUITE UNDONE BY $THEE                2.3.14
  AND I A $BANCKRUPT QUITE UNDONE BY THEE                 2.110.14
  IN ONE SHORT HOURE I FIND BY HER UNDONNE                5.23.8
UN-EARED                   1
  FOR WHERE IS SHE SO FAIRE WHOSE UN-EARD WOMBE           3.3.5
UNEXPECTEDLY               1
  HOW $THINGS STILL UNEXPECTEDLY HAVE RUNNE               2.51.3
UNFAINED                   2
  IF THAT A LOYALL HART AND FAITH UNFAINED                1.15.1
  UNFAINED LOVE, IN NAKED SIMPLE TRUTH                    2.138.3
UNFAIR                     1
  AND THAT UNFAIRE WHICH FAIRELY DOTH EXCELL              3.5.4
UNFATHERED                 2
  BUT HOPE OF $ORPHANS, AND UN-FATHERED FRUITE            3.97.10
  IT MIGHT FOR FORTUNES BASTERD BE UNFATHERED             3.124.2
UNFELT                     2
  LET HIM, DEPRIVED OF SWEET BUT UNFELT JOYES             4.24.12
  SHE IN WHOSE EYES $LOVE, THOUGH UNFELT,
                              DOTH SHINE                  4.62.3
UNFIT                      3
  AND $WINTER WOES, FOR SPRING OF YOUTH UNFIT             1.24.8
  AND NOT IN $NATURE FOR BEST FRUITS UNFIT                4.19.13
  POORE $LAYMAN I, FOR SACRED RITES UNFIT                 4.74.4
UNFLATTERING               1
  WHICH LOOKES TOO OFT IN HIS UNFLATTRING GLASSE          4.27.10
UNFOLD                     1
  MORE THEN HIS WOND'RING UTT'RANCE CAN UNFOLD            2.57.10
UNFOLDING                  1
  BY NEW UNFOULDING HIS IMPRISON'D PRIDE                  3.52.12
UNGRATEFUL                 2
  SEE WHAT REWARD HE HATH THAT SERVES THE
                              UNGRATEFULL                 1.18.7
  BUT THIS UNGRATEFULL, FOR MY GOOD DESERT                2.23.9
UNGRATEFULNESS             1
  DO THEY CALL $VERTUE THERE UNGRATEFULNESSE+             4.31.14
UNHAPPILY                  1
  AND PUREST FAITH UNHAPPILY FORSWORNE                    3.66.4
UNHAPPY                    7
  UNHAPPY I, TO LOVE A STONY HART                         1.13.14
```

UNHAPPY $PEN, AND ILL-ACCEPTED LINES	1.59.1
WHEN I AM MADE UNHAPPY BY MY SKILL	2.43.12
UNHAPPY $BORNE, OF ALL UNHAPPY DAY	2.116.5
UNHAPPY $BORNE, OF ALL UNHAPPY DAY	2.116.5
I MIGHT, UNHAPPIE WORD, O ME, I MIGHT	4.33.1
UNHAPPIE SIGHT, AND HATH SHE VANISHT BY	4.105.1

UNHEARD   1
UNSEENE, UNHEARD, WHILE THOUGHT TO HIGHEST PLACE	4.27.13

UNIDLE   1
FOR ME, I DO $NATURE UNIDLE KNOW	4.26.9

UNIONS   1
BY UNIONS MARRIED DO OFFEND THINE EARE	3.8.6

UNITED   2
THE WORKE OF THAT UNITED $TRINITIE	2.123.3
UNITED POWERS MAKE EACH THE STRONGER PROVE	4.88.14

UNIVERSE   1
FOR NOTHING THIS WIDE $UNIVERSE I CALL	3.109.13

UNJUST   1
BUT WHEREFORE SAYES SHE NOT SHE IS UNJUST+	3.138.9

UNJUSTLY   1
BUT PLEAD THY MAISTERS CAUSE UNJUSTLY PAYNED	5.48.8

UNKIND   21
AND TELL TH'UNKINDE, HOW DEARELY I HAVE LOV'D HER	1.2.14
FOR HAD SHE NOT BEENE FAIRE AND THUS UNKINDE	1.6.13
FOR HAD SHE NOT BEENE FAIRE AND THUS UNKINDE	1.7.1
IN UNKINDE $LETTERS., WROTE SHE CARES NOT HOW	1.10.4
GRATEFULL T'ANOTHER, TO MY SELFE UNKINDE	1.20.12
AND THAT THOU WAST UNKINDE, THOU MAYST REPENT	1.41.12
YET HAPPY $DELIA THAT THOU WAST UNKIND	1.56.13
TH'AFFLICTION HER UNKIND DISDAINE DOTH MOVE	1.60.8
YET FAIRE UNKINDE, TO GOOD TO BE DISGRACED	2.138.14
THEN HENCE TO HEAVEN UNKIND, FOR THY CHILDS PART	2.140.13
RECORD MY LOVE IN $OCEAN WAVES (UNKIND)	2.142.9
THAT YOU WERE ONCE UNKIND BE-FRIENDS MEE NOW	3.120.1
SO HIM I LOOSE THROUGH MY UNKINDE ABUSE	3.134.12
LET NO UNKINDE, NO FAIRE BESEECHERS KILL	3.135.13
BUT HIM HER HOST THAT UNKIND GUEST HAD SLAINE	4.38.14
THAT $NOBLENESSE IT SELFE MAKES THUS UNKIND+	4.44.8
UNKIND, I LOVE YOU NOT.. $O ME, THAT EYE	4.47.13
BEFORE SHE COULD PREPARE TO BE UNKIND	4.57.6
WITH RAGE OF $LOVE, I CALD MY $LOVE UNKIND	4.62.2
LOVE BY SURE PROOFE I MAY CALL THEE UNKIND	4.65.1
FAYRE YE BE SURE, BUT CRUELL AND UNKIND	5.56.1

UNKINDEST   4
WITH FAIREST HAND, THE SWEET UNKINDEST $MAID	1.5.7
AND SHE (TH'UNKINDEST MAID) STILL SCORNS THE SAME	1.15.12
KINDE WORDS UNKINDEST MEATE I CAN DEVISE	2.115.11
O $THOU UNKINDEST FAYRE, MOST FAYREST SHEE	2.140.1

UNKINDLY   1
UNKINDLY, SUCH DISTEMPRATURE DOTH BRING	2.147.10

UNKINDNESS   7
UNTO THE TYRANT, WHOSE UNKINDNES KILS	1.24.4
AND KINDNES, BE UNKINDNES IN MY LOVE	2.139.4
THEN WITH UNKINDNES, $LOVE REVENGE THY WRONG	2.139.5
MAKE KNOWNE THAT FAYTH, UNKINDNES COULD NOT MOVE	2.149.5
AND BY ALL MEANES, LET BLACK UNKINDNES PROVE	2.149.13
FOR IF YOU WERE BY MY UNKINDNESSE SHAKEN	3.120.5
THAT THY UNKINDNESSE LAYES UPON MY HEART	3.139.2

```
UNKNOWING                          1
  BEYOND THE BENT OF HIS UNKNOWING $SIGHT          2.43.8
UNKNOWN                            2
  WHOSE WORTHS UNKNOWNE, ALTHOUGH HIS HIGTH
                              BE TAKEN              3.116.8
  THAT I HAVE FREQUENT BINNE WITH UNKNOWN MINDES   3.117.5
UNLEARNED                          1
  UNLEARNED IN THE WORLDS FALSE SUBTILTIES         3.138.4
UNLEARNED'S                        1
  PLAINE-PATH'D $EXPERIENCE, TH'UNLEARNEDS GUIDE   2.46.1
UNLESS                             9
  I WEIGH NO COMFORT UNLESSE SHE RELIEVE           1.12.8
  UNLOK'D ON DIEST UNLESSE THOU GET A SONNE        3.7.14
  UNLESSE THOU TAKE THAT HONOUR FROM THY NAME      3.36.12
  O NONE, UNLESSE THIS MIRACLE HAVE MIGHT          3.65.13
  UNLESSE YOU WOULD DEVISE SOME VERTUOUS LYE       3.72.5
  UNLESSE MY $NERVES WERE BRASSE OR HAMMERED
                              STEELE                3.120.4
  UNLESSE THIS GENERALL EVILL THEY MAINTAINE       3.121.13
  THEREFORE $O LOVE, UNLESSE SHE TURNE TO THEE     5.19.13
  UNLESSE SHE DOE HIM BY THE FORELOCK TAKE         5.70.8
UNLETTERED                         1
  AND LIKE UNLETTERED CLARKE STILL CRIE $AMEN      3.85.6
UNLOOKED                           2
  UNLOK'D ON DIEST UNLESSE THOU GET A SONNE        3.7.14
  UNLOOKT FOR JOY IN THAT I HONOUR MOST            3.25.4
UNLOVING                           1
  SO MUCH I LOVE THE MOST UNLOVING ONE             1.12.14
UNLUCKY                            2
  DECLARE WHAT $FATE UNLUCKY $STARRES HAVE GIVEN   2.60.3
  DECLARE WHAT FATE UNLUCKY STARRES HAVE GIVEN     2.149.3
UNMOVED                            3
  SADLY I SIT, UNMOV'D WITH THE $APPLAUSE          2.47.11
  UNMOOVED, COULD, AND TO TEMPTATION SLOW          3.94.4
  BE NOUGHT DISMAYD THAT HER UNMOVED MIND          5.6.1
UNPERFECT                          1
  AS AN UNPERFECT ACTOR ON THE STAGE               3.23.1
UNPITIED                           1
  OF MY POORE LIFE TO MAKE UNPITTIED SPOILE        5.11.8
UNPROVIDENT                        1
  WHO FOR THY SELFE ART SO UNPROVIDENT             3.10.2
UNQUIET                            1
  UNQUIET THOUGHT, WHOM AT THE FIRST I BRED        5.2.1
UNREAVE                            1
  THE SAME AT NIGHT SHE DID AGAINE UNREAVE         5.23.4
UNRESPECTED                        2
  FOR ALL THE DAY THEY VIEW THINGS UNRESPECTED     3.43.2
  THEY LIVE UNWOO'D, AND UNRESPECTED FADE          3.54.10
UNRESPECTING                       1
  CELESTIALL FIRE, AND UNRESPECTING POWRES         1.59.5
UNREST                             2
  AND FRANTICK MADDE WITH EVER-MORE UNREST         3.147.10
  ATTEMPT TO WORK HER GENTLE MINDES UNREST         5.84.4
UNRIGHTEOUS                        1
  UNRIGHTEOUS $LORD OF LOVE WHAT LAW IS THIS       5.10.1
UNRULY                             1
  CROSSING SWEET NATURE BY UNRULY WILL             2.147.12
UNSEEING                           1
  WHEN TO UN-SEEING EYES THY SHADE SHINES SO+      3.43.8
```

```
UNSEEN                        3
  STEALING UNSEENE TO WEST WITH THIS DISGRACE        3.33.8
  AS TO PREVENT OUR MALLADIES UNSEENE                3.118.3
  UNSEENE, UNHEARD, WHILE THOUGHT TO HIGHEST PLACE   4.27.13
UNSET                         1
  AND MANY MAIDEN GARDENS YET UNSET                  3.16.6
UNSKILLFUL                    1
  THEY VALUE NOT, UNSKILFULL HOW TO USE              2.28.9
UNSPILLING                    1
  WHOSE PANTS DO MAKE UNSPILLING CREAME TO FLOW      4.100.6
UNSPOTTED                     1
  IN HER UNSPOTTED PLEASAUNS TO DELIGHT              5.89.12
UNSTAINED                     1
  AND THOU PRESENT'ST A PURE UNSTAYINED PRIME        3.70.8
UNSTAYED                      1
  ALL FLESH IS FRAYLE, AND ALL HER STRENGTH UNSTAYD  5.58.5
UNSUBJECT                     1
  FROM LOVE OR YEARES UNSUBJECT TO DECAIES           1.23.4
UNSUITED                      1
  BY SUCH UNSUTED SPEECH SHOULD HINDRED BE           4.51.14
UNSURE                        2
  HOPES ARE UNSURE, WHEN CERTAINE IS MY PAINE        1.25.14
  BUT WAST AND WEARE AWAY IN TERMES UNSURE           5.25.3
UNSWAYED                      1
  WHO LEAVES UNSWAI'D THE LIKENESSE OF A MAN         3.141.11
UNSWEET                       1
  AND THAT MY $MUSE TO SOME EARES NOT UNSWEET        4.84.2
UNSWEPT                       1
  THEN UNSWEPT STONE, BESMEER'D WITH SLUTTISH TIME   3.55.4
UNTAINTED                     1
  HIM IN THY COURSE UNTAINTED DOE ALLOW              3.19.11
UNTHRIFT                      1
  LOOKE WHAT AN UNTHRIFT IN THE WORLD DOTH SPEND     3.9.9
UNTHRIFTS                     1
  O NONE BUT UNTHRIFTS, DEARE MY LOVE YOU KNOW       3.13.13
UNTHRIFTY                     1
  UNTHRIFTY LOVELINESSE WHY DOST THOU SPEND          3.4.1
UNTIL                         4
  UNTILL LIVES COMPOSITION BE RECURED                3.45.9
  UNTILL BY YOUR INSPIRING I MIGHT KNOW              4.55.7
  UNTILL YE HAVE THEYR GUYLEFULL TRAYNES WELL TRYDE  5.47.2
  THEYR SAD PROTRACT FROM EVENING UNTILL MORNE       5.87.4
UNTIMELY                      5
  MY FLOWER UNTIMELY'S WITHRED WITH MY TEARES        1.24.7
  IN AGED ACCENTS, AND UNTIMELY WORDS                1.55.2
  AND THOUGH IN YOUTH, MY $YOUTH UNTIMELY PERISH     2.44.9
  AND PRAISE HER STILL TO THY UNTIMELY GRAVE         2.139.8
  ALL OTHER FAYRE LYKE FLOWRES UNTYMELY FADE         5.79.14
UNTO                         78
  UNTO THE BOUNDLESSE $OCEAN OF THY BEAUTIE          1.1.1
  THOU POORE HEART SACRIFIZ'D UNTO THE FAIREST       1.8.1
  YET CANNOT FINDE HER BREATHE UNTO MY REST          1.13.11
  WHY SHOULD I OFFER UP UNTO HER NAME                1.17.3
  SUCH HONOUR UNTO CRUELTY TO GIVE+                  1.17.8
  YEELD THY HANDS PRIDE UNTO TH'$IVORY WHITE         1.19.5
  RESTORE THY BLUSH UNTO $AURORA BRIGHT              1.19.7
  AND THY SWEET VOICE GIVE BACK UNTO THE $SPHEARES   1.19.10
  UNTO THE TYRANT, WHOSE UNKINDNES KILS              1.24.4
  STRAIGHT-WAY SHE HASTS HER UNTO $DELIAS EIES       1.25.10
  I GOE BEFORE UNTO THE $MIRTLE SHADES               1.30.5
```

```
AND WHILST THOU SPREADST UNTO THE RISING SUNNE          1.40.5
BEWRAY UNTO THE WORLD HOW FAIRE THOU ART                1.44.2
THEN MINE UNTO HER CRUELTY HATH BEENE                   1.48.8
UNTO HER SELFE, HER SELFE MY LOVE DOTH SOMMON           1.49.9
CAN GIVE THE LEAST RELEASE UNTO THY GRIEFE              1.52.10
ON MY HEART-STRINGS HIGH TUN'D UNTO HER FAME            1.57.4
NOR SEEKES IT TO BE KNOWNE UNTO THE $GREAT              1.58.10
SUBSTRACTING, SET MY $SWEETS UNTO MY $SOWRES            2.3.7
AND MY FAIRE $MUSE, ONE $MUSE UNTO THE $NINE            2.18.10
AND HASTES $ME ON UNTO A SUDDEN $DEATH                  2.20.10
THENCE TAKE YOU $WING UNTO THE $ORCADES                 2.25.6
UNCERTAINE $DREAD GIVES $WINGS UNTO MY $HOPE            2.26.5
UNTO MINE AID I SUMMON'D EV'RY $SENSE                   2.29.2
HE YEELDS $LOVE UP THE $KEYES UNTO MY $HEART            2.29.11
AND EACH RETURNES UNTO HIS $LOVE AT $NIGHT+             2.37.8
WHOSE $STOMACK UNTO $GALL HATH TURN'D THY $FOOD         2.49.6
UNTO THE WORLD HAD ALL MY JOYES BEEN MUTE               2.104.3
UNTO THE $WORLD, TO $LEARNING, AND TO $HEAVEN           2.108.1
NINE WORTHY MEN UNTO THE WORLD WERE GIVEN               2.108.8
AND MY FAIRE $MUSE, ONE $MUSE UNTO THE NINE             2.108.10
AND IN SUBSTRACTING, SET MY SWEETS UNTO
                            MY SOWRES                   2.110.7
THE FIRE, UNTO MY LOVE, COMPARE A PAINTED FIRE          2.127.5
THE AYRE, UNTO MY SIGHES, AS $EAGLE TO THE FLIE         2.127.7
THOSE SIGHES WHICH COOLE MY HART, ARE
                            COLES UNTO MY LOVE          2.132.2
EACH ONE OF THESE, DOTH AYDE UNTO THE
                            OTHER LENDE                 2.133.14
YET SEE HOW RIGHT HE COMES UNTO MY FAYRE                2.135.4
BEAUTY HER STRENGTH UNTO SLEEPES WEAKNES
                            LENDING                     2.136.10
UNCERTAINE-DREAD, GYVES WINGS UNTO MY HOPE              2.137.5
A $MUSE, THAT UNTO HEAVEN HATH RAISD HER FAME           2.138.12
COMMIT MY WORDS UNTO THE FLEETING WIND                  2.142.11
STILL MORE AND MORE UNTO MY TORMENT BURNETH             2.144.12
UNTO HER VEYNES, THE ONELY $PHOENIX PLUME               2.148.8
AND EACH DOTH GOOD TURNES NOW UNTO THE OTHER            3.47.2
WHICH UNTO IT BY BIRTHRIGHT I DO OW                     4.18.6
THAT UNTO ME, WHO FARE LIKE HIM THAT BOTH               4.19.10
BENDS ALL HIS POWERS, EVEN UNTO $STELLA'S GRACE         4.27.14
LOVE ONELY READING UNTO ME THIS ART                     4.28.14
UNTO MY MIND, IS $STELLA'S IMAGE, WROUGHT               4.38.6
THOSE DAINTIE DORES UNTO THE $COURT OF BLISSE           4.44.11
WISE SILENCE IS BEST MUSICKE UNTO BLISSE                4.70.14
THAT HUE, WHOSE FORCE MY HART STILL UNTO
                            THRALDOME TIES+             4.102.8
ONELY UNTO THE HEAV'N OF $STELLA'S FACE                 4.105.7
THEY FIRST RESORT UNTO THAT SOUERAIGNE PART             4.107.4
KINDLED ABOVE UNTO THE MAKER NEERE                      5.8.2
NOR UNTO $CHRISTALL.. FOR NOUGHT MAY THEM SEVER         5.9.11
NOR UNTO GLASSE.. SUCH BASENESSE MOUGHT
                            OFFEND HER                  5.9.12
AND HUMBLED HARTS BRINGS CAPTIVES UNTO THEE             5.10.7
UNTO THE SIEGE BY YOU ABANDON'D QUITE                   5.14.2
DISDAYNE TO YIELD UNTO THE FIRST ASSAY                  5.14.8
THAT ENDLESSE PLEASURE SHALL UNTO ME GAINE+             5.26.14
AND BY THE BAY WHICH I UNTO HER GAVE                    5.29.3
UNTO THE FAYRE SUNSHINE IN SOMERS DAY                   5.40.6
FOR THEY ARE LYKE BUT UNTO GOLDEN HOOKES                5.47.3
UNTO HER LOVE, AND TEMPTE TO THEYR DECAY                5.47.6
```

```
DID SACRIFIZE UNTO THE GREEDY FYRE                        5.48.4
AND THEN NO MERCY WILL UNTO ME SHEW                        5.53.8
UNTO HER SELFE AND SETLED SO IN HART                      5.59.2
THE WHICH DOTH LONGER UNTO ME APPEARE                      5.60.7
HER LIPS DID SMELL LYKE UNTO $GILLYFLOWERS                 5.64.5
HER RUDDY CHEEKES LYKE UNTO $ROSES RED                     5.64.6
WHY DID YE STOUP UNTO SO LOWLY STATE+                      5.66.8
YOUR SELFE UNTO THE $BEE YE DOE COMPARE                    5.71.2
AND ME UNTO THE $SPYDER THAT DOTH LURKE                    5.71.3
AND UNTO HEAVEN FORGETS HER FORMER FLIGHT                  5.72.8
TO FEED HIS FILL, FLYES BACKE UNTO YOUR SIGHT              5.73.8
THAT THREE SUCH GRACES DID UNTO ME GIVE                   5.74.14
SHALL LIFT YOU UP UNTO AN HIGH DEGREE                     5.82.14
UNTOLD                      1
THEN IN THE NUMBER LET ME PASSE UNTOLD                    3.136.9
UNTOUCHED                   1
BUT UNTOUCHT HEARTS, WITH UNAFFECTED EIE                   1.3.5
UNTRAINED                   1
WHY THEN DOE I, UNTRAINDE IN LOVERS TRADE                 5.51.5
UNTRIMMED                   1
BY CHANCE, OR NATURES CHANGING COURSE UNTRIM'D            3.18.8
UNTRODDEN                   1
HAUNTING UNTRODDEN PATHS TO WAILE APART                   1.9.10
UNTRUE                      3
THOUGH $HEAVEN AND $EARTH, PROVE BOTH
                      TO ME UNTRUE                        2.51.13
THAT YOU FOR LOVE SPEAKE WELL OF ME UNTRUE                3.72.10
MY MOST TRUE MINDE THUS MAKETH MINE UNTRUE               3.113.14
UNTRUTH                     1
WITHOUT THE TORMENT OF THE NIGHTS UNTRUTH                 1.54.8
UNTUNABLE                   1
ELSE HARSH MY STILE, UNTUNABLE MY $MUSE                   1.57.9
UNTUNED                     1
VEXING WITH UNTUN'D MOANE HER DAINTY EARES                1.21.8
UNTUTORED                   1
THAT SHE MIGHT THINKE ME SOME UNTUTERD YOUTH              3.138.3
UNUSED                      4
THY UNUS'D BEAUTY MUST BE TOMB'D WITH THEE                3.4.13
AND KEPT UNUSDE THE USER SO DESTROYES IT                  3.9.12
THEN CAN I DROWNE AN EYE (UN-US'D TO FLOW)                3.30.5
THAT TO MY USE IT MIGHT UN-USED STAY                      3.48.3
UNVALUED                    1
TWOO GOLDEN APPLES OF UNVALEWD PRICE                      5.77.6
UNWARES                     2
HE BURNT UNWARES HIS WINGS, AND CANNOT FLY AWAY           4.8.14
WHICH HER FAYRE EYES UNWARES DOE WORKE IN MEE             5.24.6
UNWARILY                    1
ONE DAY AS I UNWARILY DID GAZE                            5.16.1
UNWOOED                     1
THEY LIVE UNWOO'D, AND UNRESPECTED FADE                   3.54.10
UNWORTHINESS                1
IF THY UNWORTHINESSE RAISD LOVE IN ME                    3.150.13
UNWORTHY                    4
LIMMED WITH A $PENSILL NOT ALL UNWORTHY                   1.42.6
THY $LOVE, THAT IS ON THE UNWORTHY PLAC'D                 2.10.11
THAT YET THE WORLD UNWORTHY NEVER KNEWE                  2.139.12
IS OF THE WORLD UNWORTHY MOST ENVIDE                      5.5.4
UP                         47
SAY HER DISDAINE HATH DRYED UP MY BLOOD                   1.2.9
LIE DOWNE TO WAILE, RISE UP TO SIGH AND GRIEVE            1.9.6
```

```
WHY SHOULD I OFFER UP UNTO HER NAME              1.17.3
MUST YEELD UP ALL TO TYRANT $TIMES DESIRE        1.38.7
WHEN THOU WILT CLOSE UP THAT WHICH NOW
                        THOU SHOW'ST             1.40.10
AND THY HARD HEART HAD YEELDED UP THE SAME       1.56.8
BOYL'D WITH HER $SIGHES, IN GIVING UP THE $GHOST 2.15.7
AND THEN IN SIGHING, TO GIVE UP MY BREATH        2.20.12
THEN, SWEET $DESPAIRE, AWHILE HOLD UP THY HEAD   2.26.13
HE YEELDS $LOVE UP THE $KEYES UNTO MY $HEART     2.29.11
UP, TO MY $PITCH, NO COMMON $JUDGEMENT FLYES     2.31.13
SPENT ON THINE $ALTARS, FLAMING UP TO $HEAV'N    2.36.10
AND $INNOCENCE IS CLOSING UP HIS $EYES           2.61.12
MY $THOUGHTS BRED UP WITH $EAGLE-BIRDS OF LOVE   2.103.1
STRAIGHT MOUNTING UP TO THY CELESTIALL EYES      2.103.12
AND MOUNTING UP, SHALT TO THE HEAVENS ASCEND     2.106.13
THEN SWEET $DISPAIRE, AWHILE HOLD UP THY HEAD    2.137.13
LIFTS UP HIS BURNING HEAD, EACH UNDER EYE        3.7.2
AND HAVING CLIMB'D THE STEEPE UP HEAVENLY HILL   3.7.5
AND $SOMMERS GREENE ALL GIRDED UP IN SHEAVES     3.12.7
I SOMMON UP REMEMBRANCE OF THINGS PAST           3.30.2
THEE HAVE I NOT LOCKT UP IN ANY CHEST            3.48.9
TO TYE UP ENVY, EVERMORE INLARGED                3.70.12
DEATHS SECOND SELFE THAT SEALS UP ALL IN REST    3.73.8
YOUR SHALLOWEST HELPE WILL HOLD ME UP A FLOATE   3.80.9
BUT WHEN YOUR COUNTINANCE FILD UP HIS LINE       3.86.13
A VENGFULL CANKER EATE HIM UP TO DEATH           3.99.13
DRINKE UP THE MONARKS PLAGUE THIS FLATTERY+      3.114.2
AND MY GREAT MINDE MOST KINGLY DRINKES IT UP     3.114.10
AT MY ABUSES, RECKON UP THEIR OWNE               3.121.10
THY PYRAMYDS BUYLT UP WITH NEWER MIGHT           3.123.2
EATE UP THY CHARGE+ IS THIS THY BODIES END+      3.146.8
THE FAYREST VOTARY TOOKE UP THAT FIRE            3.154.5
AND SHOULD IN SOULE UP TO OUR COUNTREY MOVE      4.5.13
HAVING GOT UP A BREACH BY FIGHTING WELL          4.12.10
UPON THAT COAST, AM GIV'N UP FOR A SLAVE         4.29.14
I START, LOOKE, HEARKE, BUT WHAT IN CLOSDE
                        UP SENCE                 4.38.9
LET BREATH SUCKE UP THOSE SWEETES, LET
                        ARMES EMBRACE            4.85.12
AS THY LOOKES STURRE, RUNS UP AND DOWNE TO MAKE  4.101.10
WHERE RIGROWS EXILE LOCKES UP ALL MY SENSE+      4.104.8
WHILES HER FAIRE FACE SHE REARES UP TO THE SKIE  5.13.2
THEIR LOOSER LOOKES THAT STIR UP LUSTES IMPURE   5.21.8
AND TO THE LIGHT LIFT UP THEYR DROJPING HED      5.40.12
LIKE A VAINE BUBBLE BLOWEN UP WITH AYRE          5.58.6
IN MIND TO MOUNT UP TO THE PUREST SKY            5.72.2
SHALL LIFT YOU UP UNTO AN HIGH DEGREE            5.82.14
IN MY TRUE LOVE DID STIRRE UP COLES OF YRE       5.86.8
UPBROUGHT            1
  AND WITH THE CREW OF BLESSED $SAYNTS UPBROUGHT 5.61.7
UPHOLD               1
  WHICH HUSBANDRY IN HONOUR MIGHT UPHOLD         3.13.10
UPLIFTING            1
  WHOSE LOFTY ARGUMENT UPLIFTING ME              5.82.13
UP-LOCKED            1
  CAN BRING HIM TO HIS SWEET UP-LOCKED TREASURE  3.52.2
UPON                 75
  CAST WATER-COLD $DISDAINE UPON MY FACE         1.5.8
  THE WONDER OF ALL EYES THAT LOOKE UPON HER     1.6.7
  UPON THE PROSTRATE SPOYLE OF THAT POORE HART   1.10.10
```

AND CARVE HIS PROPER GRIEFE UPON A STONE	1.13.2
UPON THE FLINT OF SUCH A HART REBELLING	1.18.10
NO PITTYING EYE LOCKES BACKE UPON MY FEARES	1.32.10
UPON THIS HEART, WHOM CRUELTY WILL KILL	1.33.8
UPON MY SELFE THOU BEST MAYST FINDE THE FORME	1.37.8
THAT FULL OF BEAUTY, TIME BESTOWES UPON HER	1.39.4
WHEN WINTER SNOWES UPON THY SABLE HAIRES	1.41.14
WHEN WINTER SNOWES UPON THY SABLE HAIRES	1.42.1
UPON HIS SOVEREIGNES COURSE, THE NIGHTS PALE $QUEENE	1.48.6
WHOSE SHORT REFRESH UPON THE TENDER GREENE	1.50.2
AS IS HIS ART THAT PLAYES UPON THE SAME	1.57.2
UPON YOUR $LIPS THE SCARLET DROPS ARE FOUND	2.2.10
UPON THE $ALMES OF THY SUPERFLUOUS PRAYSE	2.6.8
LIKE GRIZZLED $MOSSE UPON SOME AGED $TREE	2.8.8
NOW RAILE UPON HER $HAIRE, THEN ON HER $EYE	2.41.11
MY $NAME SHALL MOUNT UPON $ETERNITIE	2.44.14
EV'N SO MY $MISTRES WORKES UPON MY $ILL	2.50.12
UPON THE $NEST I SET IT FORTH, TO PROVE	2.56.3
AND ASKE A $WORLD UPON MY $LIFE TO DWELL	2.60.4
UPON THE NEST I SET THEM, FORTH TO PROVE	2.103.3
BUT EVER CALL UPON DIVINE $IDEA	2.118.14
LAUGHING FOR JOY UPON MY LOVELY FAYRE	2.125.14
SEE HOW HEE LOOKES UPON HIS BLEEDING WOUND	2.135.9
AND LOOKING ON THEE, FALLS UPON THE GROUND	2.135.11
NOW RAYLE UPON HER HAYRE, NOW ON HER EYE	2.143.11
THE GOLDEN $SUNNE UPON HIS FIERY WHEELES	2.147.1
AND ASKE A WORLD UPON MY LIFE TO DWELL	2.149.4
UPON THY SELFE THY BEAUTIES LEGACY+	3.4.2
MAKE WARRE UPPON THIS BLOUDIE TIRANT TIME+	3.16.2
AND LOOKE UPON MY SELFE AND CURSE MY FATE	3.29.4
UPON THE FARTHEST EARTH REMOOV'D FROM THEE	3.44.6
UPON THE HOURES, AND TIMES OF YOUR DESIRE+	3.57.2
AND PROUD OF MANY, LIVES UPON HIS GAINES+	3.67.12
O IF (I SAY) YOU LOCKE UPON THIS VERSE	3.71.9
AND HANG MORE PRAISE UPON DECEASED I	3.72.7
UPON THOSE BOUGHES WHICH SHAKE AGAINST THE COULD	3.73.3
WHILST I ALONE DID CALL UPON THY AYDE	3.79.1
WHILST HE UPON YOUR SOUNDLESSE DEEPE DOTH RIDE	3.80.10
SO THY GREAT GUIFT UPON MISPRISION GROWING	3.87.11
UPON THY SIDE, AGAINST MY SELFE ILE FIGHT	3.88.3
UPON THY PART I CAN SET DOWNE A STORY	3.88.6
AND I WILL COMMENT UPON THAT OFFENCE	3.89.2
TO SET A FORME UPON DESIRED CHANGE	3.89.6
FOR IT DEPENDS UPON THAT LOVE OF THINE	3.92.4
WHICH VULGAR SCANDALL STAMPT UPON MY BROW	3.112.2
IF THIS BE ERROR AND UPON ME PROVED	3.116.13
FORGOT UPON YOUR DEAREST LOVE TO CALL	3.117.3
WHAT THOU DOST FOYST UPON US THAT IS OULD	3.123.6
UPON THAT BLESSED WOOD WHOSE MOTION SOUNDS	3.128.2
LOOKING WITH PRETTY RUTH UPON MY PAINE	3.132.4
TO PUT FAIRE TRUTH UPON SO FOULE A FACE	3.137.12
THAT THY UNKINDNESSE LAYES UPON MY HEART	3.139.2
DOST THOU UPON THY FADING MANSION SPEND+	3.146.6
THEN SOULE LIVE THOU UPON THY SERVANTS LOSSE	3.146.9
ON WHOM FROUN'ST THOU THAT I DOE FAUNE UPON	3.149.6
REVENGE UPON MY SELFE WITH PRESENT MONE+	3.149.8
SOME FRESH AND FRUITFULL SHOWERS UPON MY SUNNE-BURN'D BRAINE	4.1.8
UPON WHOSE BREAST A FIERCER $GRIPE DOTH TIRE	4.14.2

UPON THAT COAST, AM GIV'N UP FOR A SLAVE   4.29.14
BUT WILT NEW WARRE UPON THINE OWNE BEGIN+   4.36.8
UPON A WRETCH, THAT LONG THY GRACE HATH SOUGHT   4.40.7
SO GRATEFULL NOW YOU WAITE UPON MY CARE   4.95.4
UPON THY CHEEREFULL FACE, JOYE'S LIVERY WEARE   4.103.3
IF I BUT STARS UPON MINE ARMOUR BEARE   4.104.10
THAT LOOSELY THEY NE DARE TO LOOKE UPON HER   5.5.8
THAT WARNES AL LOVERS WAYT UPON THEIR KING   5.19.3
SWEET IS THE $ROSE, BUT GROWES UPON A BRERE   5.26.1
HER EYES LOOKE LOVELY AND UPON THEM SMYLE   5.47.10
WITH PLENTEOUS HAND BY HEAVEN UPON YOU THROWN   5.66.2
ONE DAY I WROTE HER NAME UPON THE STRAND   5.75.1
UPON THEE FALL FOR THINE ACCURSED HYRE   5.86.6
WHEN OTHERS GAZE UPON THEYR SHADOWES VAYNE   5.88.6
UPREAR   1
AND THIS MY HAND, AGAINST MY SELFE UPREARE   3.49.11
URGE   2
WITH EAGER COMPOUNDS WE OUR PALLAT URGE   3.118.2
THEN GENTLE CHEATER URGE NOT MY AMISSE   3.151.3
URGED   1
AND URG'D THAT TITLE WHICH DOTH PLAINELY PROVE   1.8.11
USE   31
THESE LINES I USE, T'UNBURTHEN MINE OWNE HART   1.4.13
NOW USE THE $SOMMER SMILES, ERE $WINTER LOWERS   1.40.4
IF ANY PLEASING RELISH HERE I USE   1.57.11
AND WHY THESE GIDDY $METAPHORS I USE   2.9.3
MUCH LIKE HIS $WIT, THAT WAS TO USE THE SAME   2.21.8
THEY VALUE NOT, UNSKILFULL HOW TO USE   2.28.9
AS COVETOUS THE OTHERS USE TO HAVE   2.33.10
THEY SAY ($AS $POETS DOE) I USE TO FAINE   2.42.6
THEY SAY, (AS $POETS DOE) I USE TO FAYNE   2.128.6
HOW MUCH MORE PRAISE DESERV'D THY BEAUTIES USE   3.2.9
PROFITLES USERER WHY DOOST THOU USE   3.4.7
THAT USE IS NOT FORBIDDEN USERY   3.6.5
MINE BE THY LOVE AND THY LOVES USE THEIR
                             TREASURE   3.20.14
WHO HEAVEN IT SELFE FOR ORNAMENT DOTH USE   3.21.3
THAT TO MY USE IT MIGHT UN-USED STAY   3.48.3
AS EVERY $ALIEN PEN HATH GOT MY USE   3.78.3
KNOWING A BETTER SPIRIT DOTH USE YOUR NAME   3.80.2
THE DEDICATED WORDS WHICH WRITERS USE   3.82.3
IF THOU WOULDST USE THE STRENGTH OF ALL
                             THY STATE+   3.96.12
THOU CANST NOT THEN USE RIGOR IN MY $JAILE   3.133.12
THOU USURER THAT PUT'ST FORTH ALL TO USE   3.134.10
USE POWER WITH POWER, AND SLAY ME NOT BY $ART   3.139.4
THY SCEPTER USE IN SOME OLD $CATOE'S BREST   4.4.5
OF OTHER'S CHILDREN CHANGELINGS USE TO MAKE   4.28.2
I BEG NO SUBJECT TO USE ELOQUENCE   4.28.9
USE ALL TO HELPE HIS OTHER CONQUERINGS   4.29.8
HIS PRAISE TO SLEIGHT, WHICH FROM GOOD
                             USE DOTH RISE   4.41.7
NOR DO NOT USE SET COLOURS FOR TO WEARE   4.54.2
USE SOMETHING ELSE TO CHAST'N ME WITHALL   4.86.12
TO THIS GREAT CAUSE, WHICH NEEDS BOTH
                             USE AND ART   4.107.8
WHOM IRON DOORES DO KEEPE FROM USE OF DAY+   4.108.11
USED   6
WHICH USED LIVES TH'EXECUTOR TO BE   3.4.14
AND THEIR GROSSE PAINTING MIGHT BE BETTER US'D   3.82.13

THE HARDEST KNIFE ILL US'D DOTH LOOSE HIS EDGE	3.95.14
WAS USDE IN GIVING GENTLE DOME	3.145.7
NOT USDE TO FROZEN CLIPS, HE STRAVE TO FIND SOME PART	4.8.6
USED $TROPHEES TO ERECT IN STATELY WIZE	5.69.2

USER   1

AND KEPT UNUSDE THE USER SO DESTROYES IT	3.9.12

USEST   1

I CANNOT BLAME THEE, FOR MY LOVE THOU USEST	3.40.6

USHERS   1

NOR THAT FULL $STARRE THAT USHERS IN THE $EAVEN	3.132.7

USING   1

WHEN SORROW (USING NINE OWNE FIER'S MIGHT)	4.108.1

USURER   2

PROFITLES USERER WHY DOOST THOU USE	3.4.7
THOU USURER THAT PUT'ST FORTH ALL TO USE	3.134.10

USURPING   1

BUT IF THAT NEEDS THOU WILT USURPING BE	4.4.9

USURY   3

MY HEART HATH PAID SUCH GRIEVOUS $USURIE	2.3.11
MY HART HATH PAYD SUCH GRIEVOUS USURY	2.110.11
THAT USE IS NOT FORBIDDEN USERY	3.6.5

UTMOST   3

LET THE $WORLD SEE THE UTMOST OF THY HATE	2.63.12
WHEN AS THY LOVE HATH CAST HIS UTMOST SUMME	3.49.3
LET THEM FEELE TH'UTMOST OF YOUR CRUELTYES	5.49.9

UTTER   3

THEN WHO HAD HEARD THE PLAINTS I UTTER NOW+	1.6.12
DID FORCE ME GRONE OUT GRIEFES, AND UTTER THIS	1.7.12
TO UTTER FORTH THE ANGUISH OF HIS HART	5.48.10

UTTERANCE   1

MORE THEN HIS WOND'RING UTT'RANCE CAN UNFOLD	2.57.10

UTTERING   2

MY $SIGHES BE SPENT IN UTT'RING OF MY $WOE	2.41.7
UTTRING BARE TRUTH, EVEN SO AS FOES $COMMEND	3.69.4

VACANT   1

THE VACANT LEAVES THY MINDES IMPRINT WILL BEARE	3.77.3

VADE   2

WHEN THAT SHALL VADE, BY VERSE DISTILS YOUR TRUTH	3.54.14
HOW DOTH THE COLOUR VADE OF THOSE VERMILLION DIES	4.102.5

VAIN   37

NOR GRAVER BROWES HAVE JUDG'D MY $MUSE SO VAINE	1.7.6
TEARES, VOWES, AND PRAYERS. HAVE I SPENT IN VAINE	1.11.2
I PRAY IN VAINE, A MERCILESSE TO MOVE	1.11.7
AND ALL IN VAINE, HER PRIDE IS SO INNATED	1.18.11
CARES NOT FOR THEE, BUT LETS THEE WASTE IN VAINE	1.23.10
LOOKES FEED MY $HOPE, $HOPE FOSTERS ME IN VAINE	1.25.13
OFT AND IN VAINE MY REBEL THOUGHTS HAVE VENTRED	1.27.1
SEEKING IN VAINE WHAT I HAVE EVER SOUGHT	1.33.3
THEN DO NOT THOU SUCH TREASURE WAST IN VAINE	1.39.13
STILL LET ME SLEEPE, IMBRACING CLOUDS IN VAINE	1.54.13
THAT INTIMATE IN VAINE MY CHASTE DESIRE	1.59.2
SO MY $LOVE IS STILL FETT'RED WITH VAINE $HOPE	2.26.10
IN WHICH EXPENCE, THE MOST SUPPOSE ME VAINE	2.28.6
SO MY LOVE IS STYLL FETTERED WITH VAINE HOPE	2.137.10
IF VAINE LOVE HAVE MY SIMPLE SOULE OPPREST	4.4.3
WHICH FOR REWARD SPOILE IT WITH VAINE ANNOYES	4.18.11
MY WITS, QUICKE IN VAINE THOUGHTS, IN VERTUE LAME	4.21.4

```
WILLD ME THESE TEMPESTS OF VAINE LOVE TO FLIE        4.62.10
AND ALL IN VAINE, FOR WHILE THY BREATH MOST SWEET     4.68.9
AND DO I THEN MY SELFE THIS VAINE SCUSE GIVE+         4.93.9
WHAT NEEDETH YOU TO SEEKE SO FARRE IN VAINE+          5.15.4
SO DOE I WEEPE, AND WAYLE, AND PLEADE IN VAINE        5.18.13
IN VAINE I SEEKE AND SEW TO HER FOR GRACE             5.20.1
IN THEIR AMAZEMENT LYKE $NARCISSUS VAINE              5.35.7
ALL THIS WORLDS GLORY SEEMETH VAYNE TO ME             5.35.13
NE DOE I WISH (FOR WISHING WERE BUT VAINE)            5.42.5
VAYNE MAN (QUOD I) THAT HAST BUT LITTLE PRIEFE        5.50.5
THERE LET NO THOUGHT OF JOY OR PLEASURE VAINE         5.52.9
LIKE A VAINE BUBBLE BLOWEN UP WITH AYRE               5.58.6
THE DOUBT WHICH YE MISDEEME, FAYRE LOVE, IS VAINE     5.65.1
SO AFTER LONG PURSUIT AND VAINE ASSAY                 5.67.5
VAYNE MAN, SAYD SHE, THAT DOEST IN VAINE ASSAY        5.75.5
VAYNE MAN, SAYD SHE, THAT DOEST IN VAINE ASSAY        5.75.5
I FYND MY SELFE BUT FED WITH FANCIES VAYNE            5.78.12
IN THEYR AMAZEMENT LYKE $NARCISSUS VAYNE              5.83.7
ALL THIS WORLDS GLORY SEEMETH VAYNE TO ME             5.83.13
WHEN OTHERS GAZE UPON THEYR SHADOWES VAYNE            5.88.6
VAINLY                        4
NO PUBLIKE $GLORIE VAINELY I PURSUE                   2.47.13
THUS VAINELY THINKING THAT SHE THINKES ME YOUNG       3.138.5
AT RANDON FROM THE TRUTH VAINELY EXPREST              3.147.12
AVISE THEMSELVES THAT THEY ARE VAINELY SPENT          4.19.8
VALIANT                       1
OF STRAYING WAYES, WHEN VALIANT ERROUR GUIDES         4.51.11
VALLEY-FOUNTAIN               1
IN A COULD VALLIE-FOUNTAINE OF THAT GROUND            3.153.4
VALOROUS                      1
OF THEYR GREAT DEEDS AND VALAROUS EMPRIZE             5.69.4
VALUE                         1
THEY VALUE NOT, UNSKILFULL HOW TO USE                 2.28.9
VANISHED                      4
WHEN OUR WORLDS SUNNE IS VANISHT OUT OF SIGHT         2.129.4
AND MONE TH'EXPENCE OF MANY A VANNISHT SIGHT          3.30.8
ARE VANISHING, OR VANISHT OUT OF SIGHT                3.63.7
UNHAPPIE SIGHT, AND HATH SHE VANISHT BY               4.105.1
VANISHING                     1
ARE VANISHING, OR VANISHT OUT OF SIGHT                3.63.7
VANQUISHED                    2
TO STOP THE PASSAGE OF MY VANQUISHT HART              1.27.2
YIELDED THEM BY THE VANQUISHT AS THEYR MEEDS          5.29.6
VANQUISHING                   1
THOU VANQUISHING, THE $CONQUEST IS MINE OWNE          2.63.14
VANTAGE                       2
DOING THEE VANTAGE, DUBLE VANTAGE ME                  3.88.12
DOING THEE VANTAGE, DUBLE VANTAGE ME                  3.88.12
VAPORS                        3
AND VAPOURS OF DISDAINE SO OVERGROWNE                 1.21.3
INFECTED BY THOSE VAPOURS, WHICH ARISE                4.78.2
SO DARKE WITH MISTY VAPORS, WHICH ARISE               4.94.2
VARIATION                     1
SO FAR FROM VARIATION OR QUICKE CHANGE+               3.76.2
VARYING                       2
TH'INCERTAINE $TIMES OFT VARYING IN THEIR $COURSE     2.51.2
FAIRE, KINDE AND TRUE, VARRYING TO OTHER WORDS        3.105.10
VASSAL                        2
BEING YOUR VASSAIL BOUND TO STAIE YOUR LEISURE        3.58.4
THY PROUD HEARTS SLAVE AND VASSALL WRETCH TO BE       3.141.12
```

VASSALAGE   1
   LORD OF MY LOVE, TC WHOME IN VASSALAGE   3.26.1
VAUNT   2
   AND LET $INVENTION CF HER BEAUTY VAUNT   2.151.9
   VAUNT IN THEIR YOUTHFULL SAP, AT HEIGHT DECREASE 3.15.7
VAUNTS   2
   CARLEGION $CHESTER VAUNTS HER HOLY $DEE   2.32.5
   CARLEGION $CHESTER, VAUNTS HER HOLY $DEE   2.124.5
VEIL   6
   THOUGH TIME DO SPCYLE THEE OF THE FAIREST VAILE   1.45.10
   O BLESSED FAYRE, NCW VAILE THOSE HEAVENLY EYES   2.129.13
   THE SHADOW AND THE VAILE OF EVERY SINFULL DEED   2.145.8
   WHERE BEAUTIES VAILE DOTH COVER EVERY BLCT   3.95.11
   LEAST IF NO VAILE THOSE BRAVE GLEAMES DID DISGUISE 4.7.7
   WITH ABSENCE' $VAILE, I LIVE IN $SOROWE'S NIGHT   4.91.4
VEILS   1
   AS THAT SWEETE BLACKE WHICH VAILES THE
                          HEAV'NLY EYE   4.20.7
VEIN   4
   AND MUCH COMMEND THE STRANGENESSE OF MY $VAINE   2.42.2
   FIRST MAKE INCISICN ON EACH MAST'RING $VEINE   2.50.6
   AND SAY MY VERSE RUNNES IN A LOFTY VAYNE   2.128.2
   YET HIDING ROYALL BLOUD FULL OFT IN RURALL VAINE 4.6.8
VEINS   4
   UNTO HER VEYNES, THE ONELY $PHOENIX PLUME   2.148.8
   BEGGERD OF BLOOD TC BLUSH THROUGH LIVELY VAINES   3.67.10
   IN MY LOVES VEINES THOU HAST TOU GROSELY DIED   3.99.5
   YOUTH, LUCKE, AND PRAISE, EVEN FILD MY
                          VEINES WITH PRIDE   4.53.4
VELUME   1
   WITH GUILDED LEAVES OR CCLOURD $VELUME PLAYES   4.11.6
VENGEANCE   1
   THAT THOU OF THEM MAYST MIGHTIE VENGEANCE TAKE   5.10.8
VENGEFUL   1
   A VENGFULL CANKER EATE HIM UP TO DEATH   3.99.13
VENOMOUS   1
   VENEMOUS TOUNG TIPT WITH VILE ADDERS STING   5.86.1
VENTURE   1
   THE MOUNTING VENTER FOR A HIGH DELIGHT   1.35.3
VENTURED   1
   OFT AND IN VAINE MY REBEL THOUGHTS HAVE VENTRED   1.27.1
VENUS   5
   LET $VENUS HAVE THY GRACES, HER RESIGN'D   1.19.9
   THE SCHOOLES WHERE $VENUS HATH LEARN'D $CHASTITIE 4.42.4
   VENUS IS TAUGHT WITH $DIAN'S WINGS TO FLIE   4.72.6
   THAT GRACE, WHICH $VENUS WEEPES THAT SHE
                          HER SELFE DOTH MISSE   4.77.4
   WHILE BEAUTIE'S REDDEST INKE $VENUS FOR
                          HIM DOTH STURRE   4.102.14
VENUS'   3
   EACH HAD HIS CREAST, $MARS CARIED $VENUS' GLCVE   4.13.7
   SHE LIGHTNING $LOVE, DISPLAYING $VENUS' SKIES   4.63.7
   WHICH, COUPLING $DCVES, GUIDES $VENUS'
                          CHARIOT RIGHT   4.79.4
VERDICT   2
   IT SLEW IT SELFE., THE $VERDICT ON THE VIEW   2.2.5
   AND BY THEIR VERDICT IS DETERMINED   3.46.11
VERMILION   2
   NOR PRAISE THE DEEPE VERMILLION IN THE $ROSE   3.98.10
   HOW DOTH THE COLOUR VADE OF THOSE VERMILLION
                          DIES   4.102.5

VERSE   41
  GOE WAILING $VERSE, THE $INFANTS OF MY LOVE   1.2.1
  THESE PLAINTIVE $VERSE, THE $POSTES OF MY DESIRE   1.4.1
  AND YOU MY $VERSE, THE $ADVOCATES OF $LOVE   1.8.9
  WHY SHOULD I SING IN VERSE, WHY SHOULD I FRAME   1.17.1
  GOE YOU MY VERSE, GO TELL HER WHAT SHE WAS   1.38.11
  AUTENTIQUE SHALL MY VERSE IN TIME TO COME   1.55.6
  NO, NO, MY $VERSE RESPECTS NOT $THAMES
                              NOR $THEATERS   1.58.9
  READE BUT HIS $VERSE, AND IT WILL EAS'LY PROVE   2.24.3
  THERE LET MY $VERSE GET GLORY IN THE $NORTH   2.25.7
  LET $WOLVES AND $BEARES BE CHARMED WITH
                              MY $VERSE   2.25.14
  WHO ONELY WRITE, MY SKILL IN $VERSE TO PROVE   2.35.4
  NOR WHO COMMENDS, OR DISCOMMENDS MY $VERSE   2.42.10
  SINCE SHE DISDAINES TO BLESSE MY HAPPIE $VERSE   2.45.5
  AND IN MY VERSE THY SELFE ART DEIFIED   2.104.12
  AND ONELY WRITE, MY SKILL IN VERSE TO PROVE   2.112.4
  AND SAY MY VERSE RUNNES IN A LOFTY VAYNE   2.128.2
  NOR WHO COMMEND OR DISCOMMEND MY VERSE   2.128.10
  I PROVE MY VERSE AUTENTIQUE STILL IN THYS   2.128.13
  WHO WILL BELEEVE MY VERSE IN TIME TO COME   3.17.1
  MY LOVE SHALL IN MY VERSE EVER LIVE YOUNG   3.19.14
  STIRD BY A PAINTED BEAUTY TO HIS VERSE   3.21.2
  WHILE THOU DOST BREATH THAT POOR'ST INTO MY VERSE   3.38.2
  WHEN THAT SHALL VADE, BY VERSE DISTILS
                              YOUR TRUTH   3.54.14
  AND YET TO TIMES IN HOPE, MY VERSE SHALL STAND   3.60.13
  O IF (I SAY) YOU LOCKE UPON THIS VERSE   3.71.9
  WHY IS MY VERSE SO BARREN OF NEW PRIDE+   3.76.1
  AND FOUND SUCH FAIRE ASSISTANCE IN MY VERSE   3.78.2
  MY VERSE ALONE HAD ALL THY GENTLE GRACE   3.79.2
  YOUR MONUMENT SHALL BE MY GENTLE VERSE   3.81.9
  WAS IT THE PROUD FULL SAILE OF HIS GREAT VERSE   3.86.1
  GIVING HIM AYDE, MY VERSE ASTONISHED   3.86.8
  AND MORE, MUCH MORE THEN IN MY VERSE CAN SIT   3.103.13
  THEREFORE MY VERSE TO CONSTANCIE CONFIN'DE   3.105.7
  LOVING IN TRUTH, AND FAINE IN VERSE MY
                              LOVE TO SHOW   4.1.1
  IN VERSE, AND THAT MY VERSE BEST WITS
                              DOTH PLEASE+   4.74.11
  IN VERSE, AND THAT MY VERSE BEST WITS
                              DOTH PLEASE+   4.74.11
  STELLA THINKE NOT THAT I BY VERSE SEEKE FAME   4.90.1
  BUT WHAT THIS VERSE, THAT NEVER SHALL EXPYRE   5.27.11
  EVEN THIS VERSE VOWD TO ETERNITY   5.69.9
  MY VERSE YOUR VERTUES RARE SHALL ETERNIZE   5.75.11
  SOM HEVENLY WIT, WHOSE VERSE COULD HAVE ENCHASED   5.82.7
VERSES   2
  BUT WITH MY $VERSES HE HIS $MISTRES WONNE   2.21.9
  FOR TO NO OTHER PASSE MY VERSES TEND   3.103.11
VERT   1
  BUT IN $VERT FIELD $MARS BARE A GOLDEN SPEARE   4.13.5
VERY   15
  ONELY BY DYING, BORNE THE VERY SAME   2.16.12
  WHEN MY $HEART IS THE VERY $DEN OF $HORROR   2.41.2
  WISE IN $CONCEIT, IN $ACT A VERY SOT   2.62.6
  WHEN MY HART IS THE VERY $DEN OF HORROR   2.143.2
  WISE IN CONCEITE, IN ACTE A VERY SOT   2.150.6
  WILL PLAY THE TIRANTS TO THE VERY SAME   3.5.3

```
THE VERY PART WAS CONSECRATE TO THEE                    3.74.6
AT FIRST THE VERY WORST OF FORTUNES MIGHT               3.90.12
AND THOU AWAY, THE VERY BIRDS ARE MUTE                  3.97.12
I MUST EACH DAY SAY ORE THE VERY SAME                   3.108.6
A BLISSE IN PROOFE AND PROUD AND VERY WO                3.129.11
THAT IN THE VERY REFUSE OF THY DEEDS                    3.150.6
MY VERIE INKE TURNES STRAIGHT TO $STELLA'S NAME         4.19.6
STELLA OFT SEES THE VERIE FACE OF WO                    4.45.1
AYMING HIS ARROW AT MY VERY HART                        5.16.10
VESSEL                  2
DEVIS'D A $VESSELL TO RECEIVE THE $SUNNE                2.30.3
MY $BREST'S THE $VESSELL, WHICH INCLUDES
                         THE SAME                       2.30.12
VESTA                   1
THOU ART MY $VESTA, THOU MY $GODDESSE ART               2.30.13
VESTAL                  4
THOSE $PRIESTS WHICH FIRST THE $VESTALL
                     $FIRE BEGUN                        2.30.1
MY HOLY $THOUGHTS, THEY BE THE $VESTALL FLAME           2.30.10
SINCE HOLY $VESTALL LAWES HAVE BEEN NEGLECTED           2.105.1
HERE $CHASTITY THAT $VESTALL MOST DIVINE                2.105.9
VEX                     3
WHERE MY HARTS THEEFE TO VEXE ME MADE HER CHOICE        1.27.6
THOU CANST NOT VEX ME WITH INCONSTANT MINDE             3.92.9
MORE THEN ENOUGH AM I THAT VEXE THEE STILL              3.135.3
VEXED                   6
LOVE GROWING ANGRY, VEXED AT THE $SPLEENE               2.38.5
LOVE GROWING ANGRY, VEXED AT THE SPLEENE                2.131.5
THAT IS SO VEXT WITH WATCHING AND WITH TEARES+          3.148.10
I HAD BENE VEXT, IF VEXT I HAD NOT BEENE                4.87.14
I HAD BENE VEXT, IF VEXT I HAD NOT BEENE                4.87.14
THROUGH ME, WRETCH ME, EVEN $STELLA VEXED IS            4.93.4
VEXING                  2
VEXING WITH UNTUN'D MOANE HER DAINTY EARES              1.21.8
THE GLASSES OF THY DAYLY VEXING CARE+'                  4.34.3
VIAL                    1
MAKE SWEET SOME VIALL., TREASURE THOU SOME PLACE        3.6.3
VICE                    2
FOR $CANKER VICE THE SWEETEST BUDS DOTH LOVE            3.70.7
EXCEEDING SWEET, YET VOYD OF SINFULL VICE               5.77.9
VICES                   3
MY $VICES CUR'D, BY $VERTUES SPRUNG FROM THEE           2.35.11
MY VICES CUR'D, BY VERTUES SPRUNG FROM THEE             2.112.11
OH WHAT A MANSION HAVE THOSE VICES GOT                  3.95.9
VICE'S                  1
THERE SHALL HE FIND ALL VICES' OVERTHROW                4.71.5
VICTOR                  1
EITHER NOT ASSAYLD, OR VICTOR BEEING CHARG'D            3.70.10
VICTORIES               1
AFTER A THOUSAND VICTORIES ONCE FOILD                   3.25.10
VICTORIOUS              1
AND FILL THE WORLD WITH HER VICTORIOUS PRAYSE           5.29.14
VICTORS                 2
AS VICTORS OF MY SILENCE CANNOT BOAST                   3.86.11
THE BAY (QUOTH SHE) IS OF THE VICTOURS BORNE            5.29.5
VICTOR'S                1
LYKE CAPTIVES TREMBLING AT THE VICTORS SIGHT            5.1.4
VICTORY                 3
THEN IF I HAD THE VICTORY MINE OWNE                     1.56.7
CRIE, '$VICTORIE, THIS FAIRE DAY ALL IS OURS'           4.12.11
```

```
     MADE MANIFEST BY SUCH A VICTORIE                    4.40.10
VIEW                    25
     COME TO THEIR VIEW, WHO LIKE AFFLICTED ARE             1.3.3
     DELIA HER SELFE, AND ALL THE WORLD MAY VIEW            1.4.7
     AND LAIES TO VIEW MY $VULTUR-GNAWNE HART OPEN          1.15.8
     I VIEW MY SELFE, MY SELFE IN WOFULL CASE               1.29.8
     STARRES THEN, NOT EYES, MOVE YOU WITH
                              A MILDER VIEW                1.34.13
     TO VIEW YOUR FORME TOO MUCH, MAY DANGER BEE           1.37.11
     THAT $CRUELTY HER SELFE MIGHT GRIEVE TO VIEW          1.60.7
     IT SLEW IT SELFE., THE $VERDICT ON THE VIEW           2.2.5
     YOU, IN WHOM $NATURE CHOSE HER SELFE TO VIEW          2.57.5
     AND VIEW THE $CROSSES WHICH MY COURSE DOE LET         2.60.10
     AND VIEW THE CROSSES WHICH MY COURSE DOTH LET        2.149.10
     PRESENTS THEIR SHADDOE TO MY SIGHTLES VIEW           3.27.10
     THEIR IMAGES I LOV'D, I VIEW IN THEE                 3.31.13
     FOR ALL THE DAY THEY VIEW THINGS UNRESPECTED          3.43.2
     RETURNE OF LOVE, MORE BLEST MAY BE THE VIEW          3.56.12
     THOSE PARTS OF THEE THAT THE WORLDS EYE DOTH VIEW     3.69.1
     AND MADE MY SELFE A MOTLEY TO THE VIEW              3.110.2
     WHO IN DISPIGHT OF VIEW IS PLEASD TO DOTE           3.141.4
     NO MARVAILE THEN THOUGH I MISTAKE MY VIEW          3.148.11
     BASE THING I CAN NO MORE ENDURE TO VIEW              5.3.6
     INTO THE OBJECT OF YOUR MIGHTY VIEW+                  5.7.4
     YOUR GOODLY SELFE FOR EVERMORE TO VEW               5.45.2
     THING SO DIVINE TO VEW OF EARTHLY EYE               5.45.6
     GREAT SHAME IT IS, THING SO DIVINE IN VIEW          5.53.9
     SO LET US, WHICH THIS CHAUNGE OF WEATHER VEW        5.62.5
VIEWEST                  1
     LOOKE IN THY GLASSE AND TELL THE FACE THOU VEWEST     3.3.1
VIEWING                  1
     VIEWING THE SHAPE OF DARKNESSE AND DELIGHT            4.99.6
VIGOR                    1
     NOR SHALL MY $SPIRIT ONE JOT OF VIGOUR LOSE          2.31.6
VILE                     8
     I HOLD THAT VILE, WHICH $VULGAR WIT AFFORDS          2.4.11
     IF THE VILE ACTORS OF THE HEYNOUS DEED               2.46.6
     SOME $ATHIEST OR VILE $INFIDELL IN LOVE             2.112.1
     THE WEEPING $CROCCODILE.. THESE VILE PERNICIOUS
                              THREE                      2.130.4
     FROM THIS VILE WORLD WITH VILDEST WORMES TO DWELL    3.71.4
     TIS BETTER TO BE VILE THEN VILE ESTEEMED           3.121.1
     TIS BETTER TO BE VILE THEN VILE ESTEEMED           3.121.1
     VENEMOUS TOUNG TIPT WITH VILE ADDERS STING          5.86.1
VILEST                   1
     FROM THIS VILE WORLD WITH VILDEST WORMES TO DWELL    3.71.4
VIOLATE                  1
     OR ONELY YOU DOE VIOLATE HER $LAWES                2.27.14
VIOLET                   2
     WHEN I BEHOLD THE VIOLET PAST PRIME                 3.12.3
     THE FORWARD VIOLET THUS DID I CHIDE                 3.99.1
VIPER'S                  1
     IN WHICH THOU LURKEST LYKE TO VIPERS BROOD           5.2.6
VIRGIN                   2
     NO $VIRGINE ONCE ATTENDING ON THAT LIGHT           2.105.3
     WAS SLEEPING BY A $VIRGIN HAND DISARM'D            3.154.8
VIRGINITY                2
     A $LEGACIE TO STALE $VIRGINITIE                    2.15.12
     VERTUES $IDEA IN VIRGINITIE                        2.116.1
```

VIRGINS   1
   VIRGINS AND $MATRONS READING THESE MY $RIMES   2.6.9
VIRGINS'   1
   TILL $VIRGINS SMYLES DOE SOUND HIS SWEET RETEERE 2.147.8
VIRTUE   41
   NOW SHEW THY POWER, AND WHERE THY VERTUE LIES   1.46.7
   DRAWNE WITH TH'ATRACTIVE VERTUE OF HER EYES   1.53.1
   WHERE $VERTUE, $HONCUR, $WIT, AND $BEAUTIE LAY   2.14.10
   OR HATH IT LOST THE $VERTUE, WITH THE $TIMES   2.27.3
   ONELY BY $VERTUE THAT PROCEEDS FROM THEE   2.35.14
   AND MURTHER'ST $VERTUE WITH THY COY DISDAINE   2.44.8
   AND FIRST THE SOUND AND VERTUE OF MY $NAME   2.47.3
   FOR THAT THE VERTUE I THEREOF WOULD KNOW   2.56.2
   LET $VERTUE BE THE $TOUCH-STONE OF MY $LCVE   2.60.7
   O $LAMPE OF VERTUE, SUN-BRIGHT, EVER SHYNING   2.129.6
   O VERTUE, WHICH ALL VERTUES DOE ADORE   2.146.7
   LET VERTUE BE THE TUCH-STONE OF MY LOVE   2.149.7
   BUT FOR THEIR VIRTUE ONLY IS THEIR SHOW   3.54.9
   AND MAIDEN VERTUE RUDELY STRUMPETED   3.66.6
   HE LENDS THEE VERTUE, AND HE STOLE THAT WORD   3.79.9
   YOU STILL SHALL LIVE (SUCH VERTUE HATH MY $PEN) 3.81.13
   IF THY SWEET VERTUE ANSWERE NOT THY SHOW   3.93.14
   THE CONSTANCY AND VIRTUE OF YOUR LOVE   3.117.14
   LOVE IS MY SINNE, AND THY DEARE VERTUE HATE   3.142.1
   VERTUE ALAS, NOW LET ME TAKE SOME REST   4.4.1
   THAT $VERTUE, THOU THY SELFE SHALT BE IN LOVE   4.4.14
   TRUE, THAT TRUE $BEAUTIE $VERTUE IS INDEED   4.5.9
   MY WITS, QUICKE IN VAINE THOUGHTS, IN VERTUE LAME 4.21.4
   THAT $VERTUE, IF IT ONCE MET WITH OUR EYES   4.25.3
   VERTUE OF LATE, WITH VERTUOUS CARE TO STER   4.25.9
   DO THEY CALL $VERTUE THERE UNGRATEFULNESSE+   4.31.14
   VERTUE AWAKE, $BEAUTIE BUT BEAUTIE IS   4.47.9
   WHERE $VERTUE IS MADE STRONG BY $BEAUTIE'S MIGHT 4.48.2
   A STRIFE IS GROWNE BETWEENE $VERTUE AND $LOVE   4.52.1
   BUT $VERTUE THUS THAT TITLE DOTH DISPROVE   4.52.5
   LET $VERTUE HAVE THAT $STELLA'S SELFE., YET THUS 4.52.13
   THAT $VERTUE BUT THAT BODY GRAUNT TO US   4.52.14
   WHICH IN HER FACE TEACH VERTUE, I COULD BROOKE   4.56.6
   HER GRAUNT TO ME, BY HER OWNE VERTUE KNOW   4.63.4
   THOU ART MY $WIT, AND THOU MY $VERTUE ART   4.64.14
   IT IS, SO FAIRE A $VERTUE TO ENJOY   4.68.14
   HOW $VERTUE MAY BEST LODG'D IN BEAUTIE BE   4.71.2
   AS FAST THY $VERTUE BENDS THAT LOVE TO GOOD   4.71.13
   WHAT WONDROUS VERTUE IS CONTAYND IN YOU   5.7.2
   STRONG THRUGH YOUR CAUSE, BUT BY YOUR VERTUE WEAK 5.8.12
   SWEET IS THY VERTUE AS THY SELFE SWEET ART   5.39.5
VIRTUES   12
   WHAT SHOULD HER VERTUES DO, HER SMILES,
                      HER LOVE+   1.17.10
   AND THESE THY SACRED VERTUES MUST PROTECT   1.55.11
   PRAISING VERTUES IN THEM THAT HAVE THEM NOT   1.58.7
   MY $VICES CUR'D, BY $VERTUES SPRUNG FROM THEE   2.35.11
   AND FOR THEIR VERTUES I DESIERD TO KNOW   2.103.2
   HEAPE THINE OWN VERTUES SEASONED BY THEIR SUNNE 2.106.5
   MY VICES CUR'D, BY VERTUES SPRUNG FROM THEE   2.112.11
   O VERTUE, WHICH ALL VERTUES DOE ADORE   2.146.7
   WHOSE BEAMES BE JOYES, WHOSE JOYES ALL VERTUES BE 4.42.2
   O $GRAMMER RULES, O NOW YOUR VERTUES SHOW   4.63.1
   HER MIND ADORND WITH VERTUES MANIFOLD   5.15.14
   MY VERSE YOUR VERTUES RARE SHALL ETERNIZE   5.75.11

```
VIRTUE'S                    13
   BY CHAST DESIRE, TRUE LOVE, AND VERTUES PRAISE    2.101.14
   VERTUES $IDEA IN VIRGINITIE                       2.116.1
   THYS, PURE $IDEA, VERTUES RIGHT $IDEA             2.119.9
   OF PUREST GOLD, TEMPRED WITH VERTUES FIRE         2.126.7
   QUEENE $VERTUE'S COURT, WHICH SOME CALL
                         $STELLA'S FACE              4.9.1
   VERTUE'S GREAT BEAUTIE IN THAT FACE I PROVE       4.25.13
   ALAS, IF FROM THE HEIGHT OF $VERTUE'S THRONE      4.40.5
   AND ANCHOR FAST MY SELFE ON $VERTUE'S SHORE       4.62.11
   THY REASONS FIRMLY SET ON $VERTUE'S FEET          4.68.11
   VERTUE'S GOLD NOW MUST HEAD MY $CUPID'S DART      4.72.8
   BEAUTIE'S PLAGUE, $VERTUE'S SCOURGE, SUCCOUR
                         OF LIES                     4.78.6
   NATURE'S PRAISE, $VERTUE'S STALL, $CUPID'S
                         COLD FIRE                   4.80.3
   FAYRE BOSOME FRAUGHT WITH VERTUES RICHEST TRESURE 5.76.1
VIRTUOUS                    9
   THE SPOYLE OF FAME DESERV'D BY VERTUOUS MEN       1.45.6
   BY CHASTE $DESIRE, TRUE $LOVE, AND VERTUOUS
                         $PRAYSE                     2.54.14
   WITH VERTUOUS WISH WOULD BEARE YOUR LIVING
                         FLOWERS                     3.16.7
   UNLESSE YOU WOULD DEVISE SOME VERTUOUS LYE        3.72.5
   AND PROVE THEE VIRTUOUS, THOUGH THOU ART
                         FORSWORNE                   3.88.4
   VERTUE OF LATE, WITH VERTUOUS CARE TO STER        4.25.9
   THAT VERTUOUS SOULE, SURE HEIRE OF HEAV'NLY
                         BLISSE                      4.52.7
   THIS REALME OF BLISSE, WHILE VERTUOUS
                         COURSE I TAKE               4.69.13
   AND VERTUOUS MIND, IS MUCH MORE PRAYSD OF ME      5.79.4
VISAGE                      1
   AND FROM THE FOR-LORNE WORLD HIS VISAGE HIDE      3.33.7
VISION                      1
   NOR HIS OWNE VISION HOULDS WHAT IT DOTH CATCH     3.113.8
VISIT                       1
   GOE VISIT HER IN HER CHAST BOWRE OF REST          5.84.7
VISNOMY                     1
   THE GOODLY YMAGE OF YOUR VISNOMY                  5.45.11
VOICE                      14
   AND THY SWEET VOICE GIVE BACK UNTO THE $SPHEARES  1.19.10
   AN OTHER PASSAGE OPENS AT HER VOICE               1.27.8
   HER VOYCE BETRAIES ME TO HER HAND AND EYE         1.27.9
   RAIGNE IN MY THOUGHTS FAIRE HAND, SWEETE
                         EYE, RARE VOICE             1.28.1
   HOARCE SOUNDS THE VOYCE THAT PRAYSETH
                         NOT HER NAME                1.57.10
   ALL TOUNGS (THE VOICE OF SOULES) GIVE
                         THEE THAT END               3.69.3
   WHEN TREMBLING VOICE BRINGS FORTH THAT
                         I DO $STELLA LOVE           4.6.14
   THAT HER CLEARE VOYCE LIFTS THY FAME TO THE SKIES 4.12.8
   WITH SO SWEETE VOICE, AND BY SWEETE $NATURE SO    4.36.9
   TO FEELE MY GRIEFES, AND SHE WITH FACE AND VOICE  4.57.13
   O VOICE, O FACE, MAUGRE MY SPEECHE'S MIGHT        4.58.12
   HE BARKS, MY SONGS THINE OWNE VOYCE OFT
                         DOTH PROVE                  4.59.6
   WITH VOICE MORE FIT TO WED $AMPHION'S $LYRE       4.68.6
   THAT VOYCE, WHICH MAKES THE SOULE PLANT
                         HIMSELFE IN THE EARES       4.77.9
```

```
VOICES                      1
   OF OTHERS VOYCES, THAT MY $ADDERS SENCE          3.112.10
VOID                        1
   EXCEEDING SWEET, YET VOYD OF SINFULL VICE         5.77.9
VOLUME                      1
   READ IN MY FACE, A VOLUME OF DISPAIRES            1.47.1
VOLUMES                     3
   A $WORLD OF $VOLUMES SHALL THEREOF ARISE          2.55.2
   MORE THEN WORLDS VOLUMES SHALL THEREOF ARISE      2.102.2
   THE VOLUMES OF $RELIGIONS LAWES SHEE KEEPETH      2.105.11
VOTARY                      1
   THE FAYREST VOTARY TOOKE UP THAT FIRE            3.154.5
VOUCHSAFE                   8
   OH THEN VOUTSAFE ME BUT THIS LOVING THOUGHT       3.32.9
   NOT ONCE VOUCHSAFE TO HIDE MY WILL IN THINE       3.135.6
   VOUCHSAFE OF ALL ACQUAINTANCE THIS TO TELL        4.32.9
   THOU CANST VOUCHSAFE THE INFLUENCE OF A THOUGHT   4.40.6
   YET LOWLY STILL VOUCHSAFE TO LOOKE ON ME          5.13.13
   THAT SHE WILL ONCE VOUCHSAFE MY PLAINT TO HEARE   5.18.7
   THE WHICH VOUCHSAFE $O GODDESSE TO ACCEPT         5.22.13
   CEASSE THEN, TILL SHE VOUCHSAFE TO GRAWNT
                                       ME REST       5.33.13
VOW                         6
   I VOW MY FAITH, WHERE FAITH IS NOT REGARDED       1.11.6
   YET WILL I WEEPE, VOW, PRAY TO CRUELL SHEE        1.11.13
   FROM THENCE (THEY VOW) THEY NEVER WILL DEPART     2.132.12
   FOR THEE, AGAINST MY SELFE ILE VOW DEBATE         3.89.13
   THIS I DOE VOW AND THIS SHALL EVER BE             3.123.13
   AND IN HER SONGS SENDS MANY A WISHFULL VOW        5.89.3
VOWED                       3
   WHILST MANY $NYMPHES THAT VOU'D CHAST
                                LIFE TO KEEP         3.154.3
   NOR NOURISH SPECIALL LOCKES OF VOWED HAIRE        4.54.3
   EVEN THIS VERSE VOWD TO ETERNITY                  5.69.9
VOWELS                      1
   VOWES WERE MY VOWELS WHEN I THEN BEGUN            2.111.5
VOWING                      1
   IN VOWING NEW HATE AFTER NEW LOVE BEARING         3.152.4
VOWS                       18
   AND STILL AGAINST HER FROWNES FRESH VOWES
                                  REPAIREST          1.8.3
   TEARES, VOWES, AND PRAYERS, WINNE THE
                                  HARDEST HART       1.11.1
   TEARES, VOWES, AND PRAYERS. HAVE I SPENT IN VAINE 1.11.2
   TEARES CANNOT SOFTEN FLINT, NOR VOWES CONVART     1.11.3
   THOUGH MY SOULES $IDOLL SCORNETH ALL MY VOWES     1.11.10
   SO MANY VOWES, AND PRAIERS HAVING SPENT           1.16.7
   BY ALL TRUE $LOVERS $SIGHES, $VOWES, AND
                                  $DESIRES           2.36.11
   MY $ZEALE, MY $HOPE, MY $VOWES, MY $PRAYSE,
                                  MY $PRAY'R         2.54.11
   CHASTE HOLY $VOWES FOR MY $SOULES SACRIFICE       2.55.10
   SHAKE HANDS FOR EVER, $CANCELL ALL OUR $VOWES     2.61.5
   MY ZEALE, MY HOPE, MY VOWES, MY PRAISE,
                                  MY PRAYER          2.101.11
   CHASTE HOLY VOWES FOR MY SOULES SACRIFICE         2.102.10
   VOWES WERE MY VOWELS WHEN I THEN BEGUN            2.111.5
   A THOUSAND VOWES, A THOUSAND SIGHES AND TEARES    2.138.4
   IF SIGHES, NOR TEARES, NOR VOWES, NOR
                                PRAYERS CAN MOVE     2.139.2
```

```
CREEPE IN TWIXT VOWES, AND CHANGE DECREES
                        OF $KINGS            3.115.6
FOR ALL MY VOWES ARE OTHES BUT TO MISUSE THEE   3.152.7
PLAYNTS, PRAYERS, VOWES, RUTH, SORROW,
                        AND DISMAY           5.14.11
```

VOYAGE   2
```
WHO HATH SOME LONG AND DANG'ROUS $VOYAGE BEENE    2.1.2
IN WHICH HER CIRCLES VOYAGE IS FULFILD           5.60.3
```

VULGAR   8
```
ME FROM THE VULGAR, THEE FROM ALL OBSCURENES      1.44.12
I HOLD THAT VILE, WHICH $VULGAR WIT AFFORDS       2.4.11
SO SHALT THOU FLYE ABOVE THE VULGAR $THRONG       2.6.13
DISPERSE THEIR $RAYES ON EV'RY VULGAR $SPIRIT     2.43.2
FOR EVERY VULGAR PAPER TO REHEARSE                3.38.4
ART LEFT THE PREY OF EVERY VULGAR THEEFE          3.48.8
WHICH VULGAR SCANDALL STAMPT UPON MY BROW         3.112.2
AND $MUSES SCORNE WITH VULGAR BRAINES TO DWELL    4.74.3
```

VULTURE-GNAWN   1
```
AND LAIES TO VIEW MY $VULTUR-GNAWNE HART OPEN     1.15.8
```

WAFER   1
```
THY $LIPS, WITH AGE, AS ANY $WAFER THINNE         2.8.10
```

WAFTING   1
```
THAT WITH THE RAYES HIS WAFTING PYNEONS FIRED     2.122.11
```

WAG   1
```
ALAS POORE WAG, THAT NOW A SCHOLLER ART           4.46.9
```

WAGS   1
```
AND STRAIGHT THEREWITH, LIKE WAGS NEW
                        GOT TO PLAY          4.17.13
```

WAIL   11
```
LIE DOWNE TO WAILE, RISE UP TO SIGH AND GRIEVE    1.9.6
HAUNTING UNTRODDEN PATHS TO WAILE APART           1.9.10
AND WAILE THE STATE WHEREIN I PRESENT STAND       1.28.10
LET WAKING EYES SUFFICE TO WAILE THEIR SCORNE     1.54.7
THE WORLD WILL WAILE THEE LIKE A MAKELESSE WIFE   3.9.4
AND WITH OLD WOES NEW WAILE MY DEARE TIMES WASTE  3.30.4
YET WAILE THY SELFE, AND WAILE WITH CAUSEFULL
                        TEARES               4.94.11
YET WAILE THY SELFE, AND WAILE WITH CAUSEFULL
                        TEARES               4.94.11
AND WHEN I WAILE, SHE TURNES HIR SELFE
                        TO LAUGHTER          5.18.12
SO DOE I WEEPE, AND WAYLE, AND PLEADE IN VAINE    5.18.13
I WAILE AND MAKE MY WOES A $TRAGEDY               5.54.8
```

WAILED   1
```
I SIGHD HER SIGHES, AND WAILED FOR HER WO         4.87.10
```

WAILING   5
```
GOE WAILING $VERSE, THE $INFANTS OF MY LOVE       1.2.1
THE WAILING $ILIADS OF MY TRAGICKE WOE            1.47.2
A WAYLING DESCANT ON THE SWEETEST GROUND          1.57.7
THAT SHE HATH THEE IS OF MY WAYLING CHEEFE        3.42.3
LEAVING ME NOUGHT BUT WAILING ELOQUENCE           4.38.11
```

WAIT   7
```
WHO FOR MY LIFE IN SECRETE WAITE DO'ST LYE        2.130.6
I AM TO WAITE, THOUGH WAITING SO BE HELL          3.58.13
FOR $SOMMER AND HIS PLEASURES WAITE ON THEE       3.97.11
IF HE WAITE WELL, I NEVER THENCE WOULD MOVE       4.59.3
SO GRATEFULL NOW YOU WAITE UPON MY CARE           4.95.4
THAT WARNES AL LOVERS WAYT UPON THEIR KING        5.19.3
TO WAYT ON LOVE AMONGST HIS LOVELY CREW           5.70.10
```

WAITED   1
  HOW CLOTH'D, HOW WAITED ON, SIGHD SHE, OR SMILDE   4.92.10
WAITING   1
  I AM TO WAITE, THOUGH WAITING SO BE HELL   3.58.13
WAKE   4
  HEAVEN NOR EARTH WILL NOT, MY SELFE CANNOT WAKE   1.29.9
  AND NEVER WAKE TO FEELE THE DAYES DISDAINE   1.54.14
  IN $ME IT SPEAKES, WHETHER I $SLEEPE OR $WAKE   2.20.5
  FOR THEE WATCH I, WHILST THOU DOST WAKE
                                    ELSEWHERE   3.61.13
WAKEN   1
  WAKEN HER SLEEPING PITTY WITH YOUR CRYING   1.2.12
WAKENED   1
  BUT SHOOTE NOT AT ME IN YOUR WAKENED HATE   3.117.12
WAKING   4
  HAPPY IN SLEEPE, WAKING CONTENT TO LANGUISH   1.16.1
  LET WAKING EYES SUFFICE TO WAILE THEIR SCORNE   1.54.7
  SLEEP WATCHING $BEAUTY, $BEAUTY WAKING,
                            SLEEPE GUARDING   2.136.5
  IN SLEEPE A $KING, BUT WAKING NO SUCH MATTER   3.87.14
WALK   2
  ORE WHOME THEIR FINGERS WALKE WITH GENTLE GATE   3.128.11
  I WOULD KNOW WHETHER SHE DID SIT OR WALKE   4.92.9
WALKED   1
  THEN HAD I WALKT WITH BOLD ERECTED FACE   1.7.9
WALKING   1
  BUT WITH SHORT BREATH, LONG LOOKES, STAID
                            FEET AND WALKING HED   4.76.13
WALKS   2
  BE ABSENT FROM THY WALKES AND IN MY TONGUE   3.89.9
  MY $MISTRES WHEN SHEE WALKES TREADS ON
                            THE GROUND   3.130.12
WALLOWING   1
  AND WALLOWING IN HIS BLOOD, SOME LYFE YET LAFT   2.135.13
WALLS   4
  HAVE SEENE THOSE WALLS WHICH PROUD AMBITION
                                    REAR'D   1.45.2
  INCLOSE MY $MUSIKE, YOU POORE SENSELESSE $WALLS   2.45.9
  A LIQUID PRISONER PENT IN WALLS OF GLASSE   3.5.10
  PAINTING THY OUTWARD WALLS SO COSTLIE GAY+   3.146.4
WAN   3
  WHERE MOST I $LOST, THERE MOST OF ALL I $WAN   2.62.3
  WHERE MOST I LOST, THERE MOST OF ALL I WAN   2.150.3
  HOW SILENTLY, AND WITH HOW WANNE A FACE   4.31.2
WAND   1
  THE $WAND IS $WILL, THOU $FANCIE $SADDLE ART   4.49.9
WANDER   4
  OUT OF HER COURSE DOTH WANDER FAR ASTRAY   5.34.4
  DOE WANDER NOW IN DARKNESSE AND DISMAY   5.34.7
  TILL THEN I WANDER CAREFULL COMFORTLESSE   5.34.13
  I WANDER AS IN DARKNESSE OF THE NIGHT   5.88.3
WANDEREST   1
  NOR SHALL DEATH BRAG THOU WANDR'ST IN HIS SHADE   3.18.11
WANDERING   12
  WHILST YOUTH AND ERROR LED MY WANDRING MINDE   1.5.1
  YET WHETHER FIXT OR WANDRING STARRES ARE THEY   1.34.9
  FIXT SURE THEY ARE, BUT WANDRING MAKE ME STRAY   1.34.11
  WAND'RING ABROAD IN $NEED AND $BEGGERIE   2.23.2
  CLOTHED THE $NAKED, LODG'D THIS WAND'RING $GHEST   2.23.6
  SO DOTH THE $PLOW-MAN GAZE THE WAND'RING $STARRE   2.43.5

```
    LOE, HEERE THY $SHEPHEARD SPENT HIS WANDRING
                            YEERES                       2.53.10
    LOE, HEERE THY $SHEPHEARD SPENT HIS WANDRING
                            YEERES                       2.113.10
    THE WANDRING $MOONE IN EARTHS TRIPLICITIE            2.116.8
    IT IS THE STAR TO EVERY WANDRING BARKE               3.116.7
    AND FROM ALL WANDRING LOVES WHICH MOTE PERVART       5.42.11
    AND WANDRING HERE AND THERE ALL DESOLATE             5.89.7
WANE                        3
    FINDING MY FORTUNE EVER IN THE WAINE                 1.32.3
    NOW WAS THY PRYME, AND LOE, NOW IS THY WAINE         2.141.13
    AS FAST AS THOU SHALT WANE SO FAST THOU GROW'ST      3.11.1
WANING                      2
    MY FAITH SHALL WAXE, WHEN THOU ARE IN THY WAINING    1.41.8
    WHO HAST BY WAYNING GROWNE, AND THEREIN SHOU'ST      3.126.3
WANT                        21
    SO I INVIRON'D WITH A HATEFULL WANT                  1.29.5
    A WAY THROUGH WANT TO FREE MY SOULE FROM CARE        1.29.10
    AND I WANT WORDS, WHEREWITH TO TELL MY $WRONG        2.41.8
    ME THINKES I $FLIE, YET WANT I LEGGES TO $GOE        2.62.5
    I HAVE, I WANT, $DESPAIRE, AND YET $DESIRE           2.62.13
    MYNE EYES WANT TEARES THUS TO BEWAYLE MY WOE         2.143.5
    AND I WANT WORDS FOR TO EXPRESSE MY WRONG            2.143.8
    MEE THINKS I FLEE, YET WANT I LEGS TO GOE            2.150.5
    I HAVE, I WANT, DISPAYRE, AND YET DESIRE             2.150.13
    YET EYES THIS CUNNING WANT TO GRACE THEIR ART        3.24.13
    HOW CAN MY $MUSE WANT SUBJECT TO INVENT              3.38.1
    WANT NOTHING THAT THE THOUGHT OF HEARTS CAN MEND     3.69.2
    NO WANT OF CONSCIENCE HOLD IT THAT I CALL            3.151.13
    AS DO BEWRAY A WANT OF INWARD TUCH                   4.15.10
    WEALTH BREEDING WANT, MORE BLIST, MORE
                            WRETCHED GROW                4.24.4
    IS CONSTANT $LOVE DEEM'D THERE BUT WANT OF WIT+      4.31.10
    THAT THOU MUST WANT OR FOOD, OR DWELLING PLACE       4.46.4
    OR WANT I SENSE TO FEELE MY MISERIE+                 4.47.5
    BUT NOW THAT I, ALAS, DO WANT HER SIGHT              4.56.9
    AND I, MAD WITH DELIGHT, WANT WIT TO CEASE           4.81.13
    THAT WORMES SHOULD HAVE THEIR $SUN, AND
                            I WANT MINE                  4.98.14
WANTED                      1
    A HASTIE $MAN (QUOTH HE) NE'R WANTED $WOE            2.59.8
WANTING                     9
    AND WANTING $FRIENDS, THOUGH OF A $GODDESSE BORNE    2.23.3
    STRAIGHT TAXETH $REASON, WANTING TO INVENT           2.38.7
    WHERE HUNGER-STARVEN, WANTING LOOKES TO LIVE         2.116.13
    STRAIGHT TAXETH $REASON, WANTING TO INVENT           2.131.7
    MAY MAKE SEEME BARE, IN WANTING WORDS TO SHEW IT     3.26.6
    THE CAUSE OF THIS FAIRE GUIFT IN ME IS WANTING       3.87.7
    THE MANNER OF MY PITTIE WANTING PAINE                3.140.4
    BUT WORDS CAME HALTING FORTH, WANTING
                            $INVENTION'S STAY            4.1.9
    TO LAY HIS THEN MARKE WANTING SHAFTS OF SIGHT        4.99.3
WANTON                      8
    AND LIKE A $WANTON, SPORTS WITH EV'RY $FETHER        2.22.6
    THE THRICE-THREE $MUSES BUT TOO WANTON BE            2.39.7
    THUS WAS THE WANTON CAUSE OF HYS OWNE WOE            2.122.12
    BEARING THE WANTON BURTHEN OF THE PRIME              3.97.7
    LOVE STILL A BOY, AND OFT A WANTON IS                4.73.1
    WHILE WANTON WINDS WITH BEAUTIES SO DEVINE           4.103.6
    HIS WANTON WINGS AND DARTS OF DEADLY POWER           5.4.8
```

```
THEY LOOSELY DID THEYR WANTON WINGES DISPLAY          5.76.11
WANTONLY                    1
  HANG ON SUCH THORNES, AND PLAY AS WANTONLY          3.54.7
WANTONNESS                  1
  SOME SAY THY FAULT IS YOUTH, SOME WANTONESSE        3.96.1
WANTS                       3
  THUS SHADES MY LIFE SO LONG AS WANTS ENDURE         1.29.14
  IS IT NOT EVILL THAT SUCH A $DEVILL WANTS
                              HORNES+                  4.78.14
  AND DEAD MY LIFE THAT WANTS SUCH LIVELY BLIS        5.89.14
WAR                        14
  IF THIS BE LOVE, TO WARRE AGAINST MY SOULE          1.9.5
  THY SHAFTS BE SPENT, AND SHEE (TO WARRE
                              APPOINTED)               2.126.9
  SWEETS WITH SWEETS WARRE NOT, JOY DELIGHTS IN JOY   3.8.2
  AND ALL IN WAR WITH $TIME FOR LOVE OF YOU           3.15.13
  MAKE WARRE UPPON THIS BLOUDIE TIRANT TIME+          3.16.2
  SUCH CIVILL WAR IS IN MY LOVE AND HATE              3.35.12
  MINE EYE AND HEART ARE AT A MORTALL WARRE           3.46.1
  WHEN WASTEFULL WARRE SHALL $STATUES OVER-TURNE      3.55.5
  BUT WILT NEW WARRE UPON THINE OWNE BEGIN+           4.36.8
  THE FIELD WHERE ALL MY THOUGHTS TO WARRE
                              BE TRAIND                4.98.2
  TO BATTELL, AND THE WEARY WAR RENEW'TH              5.11.4
  ALL PAINE HATH END AND EVERY WAR HATH PEACE         5.11.13
  BUT THIS CONTINUALL CRUELL CIVILL WARRE             5.44.5
  HIGH TIME IT IS, THIS WARRE NOW ENDED WERE          5.57.2
WARBLE                      2
  MY $MUSE SHOULD SOUND THY PRAISE WITH
                              MOURNFULL WARBLE         1.44.6
  HER TOUCH DOTH CAUSE THE WARBLE OF THE SOUND        1.57.5
WARD                        1
  PRISON MY HEART IN THY STEELE BOSOMES WARDE         3.133.9
WARDROBE                    1
  OR AS THE WARD-ROBE WHICH THE ROBE DOTH HIDE        3.52.10
WARDS                       1
  FROM HANDS OF FALSEHOOD, IN SURE WARDS OF TRUST+    3.48.4
WARDSHIP                    1
  BEQUEATH'D HIS WARDSHIP TO MY SOVERAIGNES EYE       2.116.12
WARE                        2
  'BUT WILL NOT WISE MEN THINKE THY WORDS
                              FOND WARE+'              4.34.7
  BE YOUR WORDS MADE (GOOD $SIR) OF $INDIAN WARE      4.92.1
WARLIKE                     1
  DESPOYLD OF WARLIKE ARMES AND KNOWEN SHIELD         5.52.4
WARM                        2
  AND SEE THY BLOOD WARME WHEN THOU FEEL'ST
                              IT COULD                 3.2.14
  TO WARME WITH ILL-MADE FIRE COLD $MOSCOVY           4.30.4
WARMED                      3
  (THE CHASTEST FLAME THAT EVER WARMED HART)          1.44.4
  SLEEPES AGED COLDNES, WITH $BEAUTIES FIRE WARMED    2.136.7
  WHICH MANY $LEGIONS OF TRUE HEARTS HAD WARM'D       3.154.6
WARMETH                     1
  LOVE HEATS MY HART, MY HART-HEAT MY SIGHES
                              WARMETH                  2.132.6
WARMTH                      3
  WHERE WITH MOST EASE AND WARMTH HE MIGHT
                              EMPLOY HIS ART           4.8.7
  THE ONELY LIGHT OF JOY, THE ONELY WARMTH OF $LOVE   4.76.4
```

```
                    SHE COMES WITH LIGHT AND WARMTH, WHICH
                              LIKE $AURORA PROVE              4.76.5
WARN                 1
       AND WARNE TO SHUN THE DAUNGER OF THEYR WRATH          5.31.8
WARNING              2
       A GENTLE WARNING ($FRIENDS) THUS MAY YOU SEE          2.7.13
       GIVE WARNING TO THE WORLD THAT I AM FLED              3.71.3
WARNS                2
       AND WARNES THE $EARTH WITH DIVERS COLORD FLOWRE       5.4.11
       THAT WARNES AL LOVERS WAYT UPON THEIR KING            5.19.3
WARRANTISE           1
       THERE IS SUCH STRENGTH AND WARRANTISE OF SKILL        3.150.7
WARREID              1
       WHILEST MY WEAK POWRES OF PASSIONS WARREID ARRE       5.44.7
WARRIOR              3
       THE PAINEFULL WARRIER FAMOSED FOR WORTH               3.25.9
       SHE CRUELL WARRIOUR DOTH HER SELFE ADDRESSE           5.11.3
       SWEET WARRIOUR WHEN SHALL I HAVE PEACE WITH YOU+      5.57.1
WARRIORS             1
       THE FAMOUS WARRIORS OF THE ANTICKE WORLD              5.69.1
WARS                 3
       IN $WARRES AT HOME, OR WHEN FOR $CONQUESTS BOUND      2.58.2
       ME THINKES 'TIS LONG SINCE FIRST THESE
                              $WARRES BEGUN                  2.63.2
       O MAKE IN ME THOSE CIVILL WARRES TO CEASE             4.39.7
WAR'S                1
       NOR $MARS HIS SWORD, NOR WARRES QUICK
                              FIRE SHALL BURNE               3.55.7
WARY                 1
       O THEREFORE LOVE BE OF THY SELFE SO WARY              3.22.9
WASHED               2
       BEING WITH THY DEARE BLOOD CLENE WASHT FROM SIN       5.68.7
       BUT CAME THE WAVES AND WASHED IT AWAY                 5.75.2
WASTE                13
       CARES NOT FOR THEE, BUT LETS THEE WASTE IN VAINE      1.23.10
       THY $GIFTS THOU IN $OBSCURITIE DOEST WASTE            2.10.9
       METALS DOE WASTE, AND FRET WITH $CANKERS $RUST        2.13.2
       METTLES DOE WASTE, AND FRET WITH CANKERS RUST         2.121.2
       AND TENDER CHORLE MAKST WAST IN NIGGARDING            3.1.12
       BUT BEAUTIES WASTE HATH IN THE WORLD AN END           3.9.11
       AND WITH OLD WOES NEW WAILE MY DEARE TIMES WASTE      3.30.4
       THY DYALL HOW THY PRETIOUS MYNUITS WASTE              3.77.2
       COMMIT TO THESE WASTE BLACKS, AND THOU
                              SHALT FINDE                    3.77.10
       WHICH PROVES MORE SHORT THEN WAST OR RUINING+         3.125.4
       TH'EXPENCE OF $SPIRIT IN A WASTE OF SHAME             3.129.1
       MY YOUTH DOTH WASTE, MY KNOWLEDGE BRINGS
                              FORTH TOYES                    4.18.9
       BUT WAST AND WEARE AWAY IN TERMES UNSURE              5.25.3
WASTED               2
       WHEN IN THE $CHRONICLE OF WASTED TIME                 3.106.1
       WHICH I HAVE WASTED IN LONG LANGUISHMENT              5.60.11
WASTEFUL             2
       WHERE WASTFULL TIME DEBATETH WITH DECAY               3.15.11
       WHEN WASTEFULL WARRE SHALL $STATUES OVER-TURNE        3.55.5
WASTES               2
       THAT THOU AMONG THE WASTES OF TIME MUST GOE           3.12.10
       GIVE MY LOVE FAME FASTER THEN TIME WASTS LIFE         3.100.13
WATCH                2
       WHILST I (MY SOVERAINE) WATCH THE CLOCK FOR YOU       3.57.6
```

```
    FOR THEE WATCH I, WHILST THOU DOST WAKE
                              ELSEWHERE              3.61.13
WATCHING                       2
    SLEEP WATCHING $BEAUTY, $BEAUTY WAKING,
                              SLEEPE GUARDING        2.136.5
    THAT IS SO VEXT WITH WATCHING AND WITH TEARES+   3.148.10
WATCHMAN                       1
    TO PLAIE THE WATCH-MAN EVER FOR THY SAKE         3.61.12
WATER                         12
    THE WATER, MOYSTURE FROM MY TEARES DERIVETH      2.127.2
    THE WATER, TO MY TEARES, AS DROPS TO $OCEANS BE  2.127.6
    YET FIRE, WATER, AYRE, OF NATURE NOT DEPRIVED    2.127.12
    WHILST FIRE, WATER, AYRE, TWIXT HEAVEN
                              AND EARTH SHAL BE      2.127.13
    BUT THAT SO MUCH OF EARTH AND WATER WROUGHT      3.44.11
    SO THAT MY SELFE BRING WATER FOR MY STAINE       3.109.8
    THE SEA ALL WATER, YET RECEIVES RAINE STILL      3.135.9
    LOVES FIRE HEATES WATER, WATER COOLES NOT LOVE   3.154.14
    LOVES FIRE HEATES WATER, WATER COOLES NOT LOVE   3.154.14
    MY MOUTH DOTH WATER, AND MY BREAST DOTH SWELL    4.37.1
    AND WHEN I WEEP, SHE SAYES TEARES ARE BUT WATER  5.18.10
    NOT WATER., FOR HER LOVE DOTH BURNE LIKE FYRE    5.55.6
WATER-COLD                     1
    CAST WATER-COLD $DISDAINE UPON MY FACE           1.5.8
WATERED                        1
    I JOYED, BUT STRAIGHT THUS WATRED WAS MY WINE    4.62.5
WATERS                         2
    MY $DELIA HATH THE WATERS OF MINE EIES           1.48.1
    BUT $AVON RICH IN FAME, THOUGH POORE IN WATERS   1.58.11
WATERY                         2
    AND THE FIRME SOILE WIN OF THE WATRY MAINE       3.64.7
    HIS WHO TILL DEATH LOOKT IN A WATRIE GLASSE      4.82.3
WAVES                          8
    SEE THY $LEANDER STRIVING IN THESE WAVES         1.46.2
    NOR PAYD THE IMPOST OF HIS WAVES MORE TRULY      1.48.7
    ELSE SHOULD MY $LINES GLIDE ON THE $WAVES
                              OF $RHENE              2.25.3
    LEFT TO THE MERCY OF THE WAVES AND WINDE         2.134.4
    RECORD MY LOVE IN $OCEAN WAVES (UNKIND)          2.142.9
    LIKE AS THE WAVES MAKE TOWARDS THE PIBLED SHORE  3.60.1
    THE RAGING WAVES AND KEEPES HER COURSE ARIGHT    5.59.6
    BUT CAME THE WAVES AND WASHED IT AWAY            5.75.2
WAVING                         1
    WITH THE LOOSE WYND YE WAVING CHANCE TO MARKE    5.81.2
WAX                            1
    MY FAITH SHALL WAXE, WHEN THOU ARE IN THY WAINING 1.41.8
WAY                           22
    A WAY THROUGH WANT TO FREE MY SOULE FROM CARE    1.29.10
    THINK'ST THOU, MY $WIT SHALL KEEPE THE
                              PACK-$HORSE $WAY       2.31.7
    BOASTING, THAT SHE DOTH STILL DIRECT THE WAY     2.38.3
    THAT WHILST WITH $MARS SHE HOLDETH HER OLD $WAY  2.48.13
    BOASTING THAT SHEE DOTH STILL DIRECT THE WAY     2.131.3
    FROM HIS LOW TRACT AND LOOKE AN OTHER WAY        3.7.12
    BUT WHEREFORE DO NOT YOU A MIGHTIER WAIE         3.16.1
    TO LET BACE CLOUDES ORE-TAKE ME IN MY WAY        3.34.3
    INJURIOUS DISTANCE SHOULD NOT STOP MY WAY        3.44.2
    HOW CAREFULL WAS I WHEN I TOOKE MY WAY           3.48.1
    HOW HEAVIE DOE I JOURNEY ON THE WAY              3.50.1
    AND OTHERS' FEETE STILL SEEM'D BUT STRANGERS
                              IN MY WAY              4.1.11
```

```
FALS TO SHREWD TURNES, AND I WAS IN HIS WAY          4.17.14
IN HIGHEST WAY OF HEAV'N THE $SUNNE DID RIDE          4.22.1
LOOKING ON ME, WHILE I LOOKT OTHER WAY               4.66.12
THY SELFE, DOEST STRIVE ALL MINDS THAT
                              WAY TO MOVE             4.71.10
GALLEIN'S ADOPTIVE SONNES, WHO BY A BEATEN WAY        4.102.9
COUNTING BUT DUST WHAT IN THE WAY DID LIE             4.105.8
BY CONDUCT OF SOME STAR DOTH MAKE HER WAY             5.34.2
MY CRUELL FAYRE STREIGHT BIDS ME WEND MY WAY          5.46.2
THE GENTLE DEARE RETURND THE SELFE-SAME WAY           5.67.7
THROGH WHICH HER WORDS SO WISE DO MAKE THEIR WAY      5.81.11
```

WAYS   10

```
AND SET MY THOUGHTS IN HEEDLESSE WAYES TO RANGE       1.5.2
AND SHUT THOSE WAIES MY FRIENDLY FOE FIRST ENTRED     1.27.3
THOU DOEST PROCEED IN THY MOST SERIOUS WAYES          4.11.2
YOU TAKE WRONG WAIES, THOSE FAR-FET HELPES
                              BE SUCH                 4.15.9
WHOSE NUMBERS, WAYES, GREATNESSE, ETERNITIE           4.26.3
NOR IN HID WAYES TO GUIDE $PHILOSOPHIE                4.28.10
FOR THOUGH I NEVER SEE THEM, BUT STRAIGHT WAYES       4.42.9
OF STRAYING WAYES, WHEN VALIANT ERROUR GUIDES         4.51.11
SHE COULD NOT SHEW MY BLIND BRAINE WAIES OF JOY       4.97.13
BUT LET MY LOVES FAYRE $PLANET SHORT HER WAYES        5.60.13
```

WEAK   17

```
TO HAVE AFFECTION STRONG, A BODY WEAKE                1.20.8
BUT THESE WEAKE WHINGS PRESUMING TO ASPIRE            1.32.6
AND MY STRONG SIGHES, THE AYRES WEAKE
                              FORCE REVIVETH          2.127.3
TH'OFFENDERS SORROW LENDS BUT WEAKE RELIEFE           3.34.11
MY LOVE IS STRENGTHNED THOUGH MORE WEAKE
                              IN SEEMING              3.102.1
LIKE SOME WEAKE $LORDS, NEIGHBORD BY MIGHTY KINGS     4.29.1
WITH SAD EYES I THEIR WEAKE PROPORTION SEE            4.50.7
NOR DO LIKE $LORDS, WHOSE WEAKE CONFUSED BRAINE       4.85.5
IS FAITH SO WEAKE+ $OR IS SUCH FORCE IN THEE+         4.88.5
THAT YOUR BRIGHT BEAMS OF MY WEAK EIES ADMYRED        5.7.11
STRONG THRUGH YOUR CAUSE, BUT BY YOUR VERTUE WEAK     5.8.12
MADE TO AMAZE WEAKE MENS CONFUSED SKIL                5.17.2
WHILEST MY WEAK POWRES OF PASSIONS WARREID ARRE       5.44.7
SO SHE WITH FLATTRING SMYLES WEAKE HARTS
                              DOTH GUYDE              5.47.5
SO WEAKE MY POWRES, SO SORE MY WOUNDS APPEARE         5.57.5
WEAKE IS TH'ASSURANCE THAT WEAKE FLESH REPOSETH       5.58.1
WEAKE IS TH'ASSURANCE THAT WEAKE FLESH REPOSETH       5.58.1
```

WEAKENED   1

```
IN WEAKENED MINDS, QUICKE APPREHENDING BREED          4.66.3
```

WEAKENS   1

```
WHOSE STRENGTHS ABONDANCE WEAKENS HIS OWNE HEART      3.23.4
```

WEAKER   1

```
THEYR WEAKER HARTS, WHICH ARE NOT WEL AWARE+          5.37.8
```

WEAKNESS   2

```
BEAUTY HER STRENGTH UNTO SLEEPES WEAKNES
                              LENDING                 2.136.10
WITH MINE OWNE WEAKENESSE BEING BEST ACQUAINTED       3.88.5
```

WEAL   3

```
DEFINE MY $WEALE, AND TELL THE JOYES OF $HEAVEN       2.60.1
POORE HOPE'S FIRST WEALTH, OSTAGE OF PROMIST
                              WEALE                   4.79.12
THE GLOBE OF WEALE, LIPS $LOVE'S INDENTURES MAKE      4.85.13
```

WEALTH   16
  FOR WHO GETS WEALTH THAT PUTS NOT FROM THE SHORE+   1.35.5
  THAT ALL THEIR $WEALTH LIES IN THY BEAUTIES
                $BOOKES   2.3.12
  THAT ALL HER WEALTH LYES IN THY $BEAUTIES
                BOOKES   2.110.12
  FOR THY SWEET LOVE REMEMBRED SUCH WELTH BRINGS   3.29.13
  FOR WHETHER BEAUTY, BIRTH, OR WEALTH, OR WIT   3.37.5
  O HIM SHE STORES, TO SHOW WHAT WELTH SHE HAD   3.67.13
  AS TWIXT A MISER AND HIS WEALTH IS FOUND   3.75.4
  SOME IN THEIR WEALTH, SOME IN THEIR BODIES FORCE 3.91.2
  RICHER THEN WEALTH, PROUDER THEN GARMENTS COST   3.91.10
  BUT THAT MY WEALTH I HAVE MOST IDLY SPENT   4.18.8
  OR CARELESSE OF THE WEALTH BECAUSE HER OWNE   4.22.11
  WEALTH BREEDING WANT, MORE BLIST, MORE
                WRETCHED GROW   4.24.4
  THE POORE MAN'S WEALTH, THE PRISONER'S RELEASE   4.39.3
  MY WEALTH NO MORE, AND NO WHIT LESSE MY NEED   4.66.7
  WORLD OF MY WEALTH, AND HEAV'N OF MY DELIGHT   4.68.4
  POORE HOPE'S FIRST WEALTH, OSTAGE OF PROMIST
                WEALE   4.79.12
WEAPONS   1
  EACH SOULE DOTH AT $LOVE'S FEET HIS WEAPONS LAY 4.43.7
WEAR   10
  THAT EV'RY $DOWDY, EV'RY $TRULL DOTH WEARE+   2.31.12
  THAT WEARE THIS WORLD OUT TO THE ENDING DOOME   3.55.12
  IF I MIGHT TEACH THEE WITTE BETTER IT WEARE   3.140.5
  GREAT EXPECTATION, WEARE A TRAINE OF SHAME   4.21.8
  SINCE THEY DO WEARE HIS BADGE, MOST FIRMELY PROVE 4.52.4
  NOR DO NOT USE SET COLOURS FOR TO WEARE   4.54.2
  UPON THY CHEEREFULL FACE, JOYE'S LIVERY WEARE   4.103.3
  THE FIRMEST FLINT DOTH IN CONTINUANCE WEARE   5.18.4
  BUT WAST AND WEARE AWAY IN TERMES UNSURE   5.25.3
  THE LAURELL LEAFE, WHICH YOU THIS DAY DOE WEARE 5.28.1
WEARS   2
  FLINT, FROST, DISDAINE, WEARES, MELTES,
                AND YEELDES WE SEE   1.11.14
  SEATED WITH $SOL, AND WEARES $MINERVAS GLOVE   2.151.12
WEARY   16
  IF THIS BE LOVE, TO DRAW A WEARIE BREATH   1.9.1
  THEN DOE I LOVE AND DRAW THIS WEARIE BREATH   1.9.14
  THEN DOE I LOVE, AND DRAW THIS WEARIE BREATH   1.10.1
  THAT WEARY OF MY LIFE, I LOATH TO LIVE   1.16.8
  BUT WHEN FROM HIGH-MOST PICH WITH WERY CAR   3.7.9
  WEARY WITH TOYLE, I HAST ME TO MY BED   3.27.1
  WHEN WHAT I SEEKE (MY WEARIE TRAVELS END)   3.50.2
  MY HEAVY EIELIDS TO THE WEARY NIGHT+   3.61.2
  A ROSIE GARLAND, AND A WEARIE HED   4.39.11
  TO BATTELL, AND THE WEARY WAR RENEW'TH   5.11.4
  YE TRADEFULL $MERCHANTS THAT WITH WEARY TOYLE   5.15.1
  TELL ME WHEN SHALL THESE WEARIE WOES HAVE END   5.36.1
  THE WEARY YEARE HIS RACE NOW HAVING RUN   5.62.1
  LYKE AS A HUNTSMAN AFTER WEARY CHACE   5.67.1
  WHEN I ALL WEARY HAD THE CHACE FORSOOKE   5.67.6
  MANY LONG WEARY DAYES I HAVE OUTWORNE   5.87.2
WEATHER   2
  WHERE MOST BECALM'D, WHERE WITH FOULE
                $WEATHER SPENT   2.1.11
  SO LET US, WHICH THIS CHAUNGE OF WEATHER VEW   5.62.5

WEATHER'S   1
  NE OUGHT FOR FAYRER WEATHERS FALSE DELIGHT   5.59.8
WEAVE   2
  TO DECKE HIR SELFE, AND HER FAIRE MANTLE WEAVE   5.4.12
  FOR ALL THAT I IN MANY DAYES DOO WEAVE   5.23.7
WEB   2
  DEVIZ'D A $WEB HER WOOERS TO DECEAVE   5.23.2
  SUCH LABOUR LIKE THE $SPYDERS WEB I FYND   5.23.13
WED   1
  WITH VOICE MORE FIT TO WED $AMPHION'S $LYRE   4.68.6
WEED   5
  PORTRAITE OF HELL, THE AYRES BLACK MOURNING WEED   2.145.6
  WIL BE A TOTTER'D WEED OF SMAL WORTH HELD   3.2.4
  AND KEEPE INVENTION IN A NOTED WEED   3.76.6
  THE BASEST WEED OUT-BRAVES HIS DIGNITY   3.94.12
  PLACED EVER THERE, GAVE HIM THIS MOURNING WEED   4.7.13
WEEDS   7
  TO THY FAIRE FLOWER AD THE RANCKE SMELL OF WEEDS   3.69.12
  LILLIES THAT FESTER, SMELL FAR WORSE THEN WEEDS   3.94.14
  WEEDS AMONG WEEDS, OR FLOWERS WITH FLOWERS
                      GATHERD   3.124.4
  WEEDS AMONG WEEDS, OR FLOWERS WITH FLOWERS
                      GATHERD   3.124.4
  BUT FOR TO SPANGLE THE BLACKE WEEDS OF NIGHT   4.26.6
  SILENT AND SAD IN MOURNING WEEDES DOTH DIGHT   4.97.8
  WHO HATH THE CRIMSON WEEDS STOLNE FROM
                MY MORNING SKIES+   4.102.4
WEEK   1
  WHAT, A WHOLE WEEKE WITHOUT ONE PEECE OF LOOKE   4.56.3
WEEKS   1
  LOVE ALTERS NOT WITH HIS BREEFE HOURES
                AND WEEKES   3.116.11
WEEN   2
  IF $YVORIE, HER FORHEAD YVORY WEENE   5.15.10
  HOW EVER NOW THEREOF YE LITTLE WEENE   5.27.4
WEEP   9
  YET WILL I WEEPE, VOW, PRAY TO CRUELL SHEE   1.11.13
  THE WORLD WILBE THY WIDDOW AND STILL WEEPE   3.9.5
  AND WEEPE A FRESH LOVES LONG SINCE CANCELD WOE   3.30.7
  BUT WEEPE TO HAVE, THAT WHICH IT FEARES TO LOOSE   3.64.14
  TEACHING BLIND EYES BOTH HOW TO SMILE AND WEEPE   4.32.8
  HATH CHEEKES TO SMILE, AS WELL AS EYES TO WEEPE   4.70.8
  STELLA NOW LEARNES (STRANGE CASE) TO WEEPE
                IN THEE   4.101.8
  AND WHEN I WEEP, SHE SAYES TEARES ARE BUT WATER   5.18.10
  SO DOE I WEEPE, AND WAYLE, AND PLEADE IN VAINE   5.18.13
WEEPING   4
  MY $BRAINE IS DRIE WITH WEEPING ALL TOO LONG   2.41.6
  THE WEEPING $CROCODILE.. THESE VILE PERNICIOUS
                THREE   2.130.4
  MY BRAYNE IS DRY WITH WEEPING ALL TOO LONG   2.143.6
  BRAKE BOW, BRAKE SHAFTS, WHILE $CUPID
                WEEPING SATE   4.17.8
WEEPS   1
  THAT GRACE, WHICH $VENUS WEEPES THAT SHE
                HER SELFE DOTH MISSE   4.77.4
WEIGH   5
  I WEIGH NO COMFORT UNLESSE SHE RELIEVE   1.12.8
  MEN DO NOT WEY THE STALKE FOR THAT IT WAS   1.40.13
  TO WAIGH HOW ONCE I SUFFERED IN YOUR CRIME   3.120.8

WEIGH THEN HOW I BY THEE AM OVERTHROWNE   4.40.8
FOR $GRAMMER SAYES (O THIS DEARE $STELLA WEIGHE)   4.63.12
WEIGHED   2
  THAT $BALLANCE WEIGH'D WHAT SWORD DID
                LATE OBTAINE   4.75.8
  IT DOWN IS WEIGHD WITH THOGHT OF EARTHLY THINGS   5.72.3
WEIGHING   1
  AND THAT THY LOVE WE WEIGHING WORTHILY   5.68.9
WEIGHS   4
  BEING MERCILES LIKE THEE THAT NO MAN WEIES+   1.23.8
  BUT SINCE SHE WEIGHS THEM NOT, THIS RESTS FOR ME   1.59.9
  WAIGHES NOT THE DUST AND INJURY OF AGE   3.108.10
  WHILE HE EACH THING IN SENSE'S BALLANCE WAYES   4.25.6
WEIGHT   4
  THOUGHT IT IN WEIGHT TOO LIGHT BY MANY A $GRAINE   2.38.12
  THE $DELIAN $CYNTHUS, THEN $OLYMPUS WEIGHT   2.120.7
  THOUGHT HER IN WEIGHT TOO LIGHT BY MANY
               A GRAINE   2.131.12
  PLODS DULY ON, TO BEARE THAT WAIGHT IN ME   3.50.6
WELCOME   2
  MAKES $SOMERS WELCOME, THRICE MORE WISH'D,
              MORE RARE   3.56.14
  THEN GIVE ME WELCOME, NEXT MY HEAVEN THE BEST   3.110.13
WELFARE   1
  AND SICKE OF WEL-FARE FOUND A KIND OF MEETNESSE   3.118.7
WELL   85
  EXAMINE WELL THY BEAUTIE WITH MY TRUTH   1.1.11
  DEEPE IS THE WOUND MY SIGHES CAN WELL REPORT   1.14.6
  FOR WELL THOU SAW'ST MY LOVE AND HOW I PIN'D   1.31.8
  I LOVE AS WELL, THOUGH HE COULD BETTER SHOW IT   1.43.8
  SUFFICE, THOU SHALT BE LOV'D AS WELL AS SHEE   1.43.14
  WHICH WELL THE REACH OF THEIR HIGH WITS RECORDS   1.55.4
  WELL, WELL, I FEARE IT WILL BE PROV'D BY YOU   2.2.7
  WELL, WELL, I FEARE IT WILL BE PROV'D BY YOU   2.2.7
  ERE THEY BE WELL WRAP'D IN THEIR WINDING $SHEET+   2.6.4
  WELL, WELL, MY $FRIENDS, WHEN $BEGGERS
              GROW THUS BOLD   2.23.13
  WELL, WELL, MY $FRIENDS, WHEN $BEGGERS
              GROW THUS BOLD   2.23.13
  THOUGH I GIVE MORE THEN WELL AFFORDS MY STATE   2.28.5
  WELL COULD I WISH, IT WOULD BE EVER $DAY   2.37.13
  SOME $MEN THERE BE, WHICH LIKE MY $METHOD WELL   2.42.1
  AS WELL (SAYTH HE) TOO FORWARD, AS TOO SLOW   2.59.6
  THE $WELL OF $NECTAR, PAV'D WITH PEARLE
              AND GOLD   2.109.13
  I WELL PERCEIVE MY GRIEFE INNUMERABLE GROWES   2.110.3
  GAVE MEE SWEET LOCKES WHEN AS I LEARNED WELL   2.111.4
  THEN WONDER, TONGUE, THEN JOY, MIGHT WEL
              REPORT A WONDER   2.117.4
  SOME WITS THERE BE, WHICH LYKE MY METHOD WELL   2.128.1
  IF THE TRUE CONCORD OF WELL TUNED SOUNDS   3.8.5
  WHEN EVERY PRIVAT WIDDOW WELL MAY KEEPE   3.9.7
  OR SAY WITH $PRINCES IF IT SHAL GO WEL   3.14.7
  LET THEM SAY MORE THAT LIKE OF HEARE-SAY WELL   3.21.13
  IF THOU SURVIVE MY WELL CONTENTED DAIE   3.32.1
  FOR NO MAN WELL OF SUCH A SALVE CAN SPEAKE   3.34.7
  LASCIVIOUS GRACE, IN WHOM ALL IL WEL SHOWES   3.40.13
  THY BEAUTIE, AND THY YEARES FULL WELL BEFITS   3.41.3
  NOT BLAME YOUR PLEASURE BE IT ILL OR WELL   3.58.14
  THAT YOU FOR LOVE SPEAKE WELL OF ME UNTRUE   3.72.10

```
TO LOVE THAT WELL, WHICH THOU MUST LEAVE
                        ERE LONG                    3.73.14
THAT YOU YOUR SELFE BEING EXTANT WELL MIGHT SHOW     3.83.6
IN POLISHT FORME OF WELL REFINED PEN                 3.85.8
THE BASEST $JEWELL WIL BE WELL ESTEEM'D              3.96.6
TO MARRE THE SUBJECT THAT BEFORE WAS WELL            3.103.10
FOR WHAT CARE I WHO CALLES ME WELL OR ILL            3.112.3
MINE EIE WELL KNOWES WHAT WITH HIS GUST
                        IS GREEING                   3.114.11
ALL THIS THE WORLD WELL KNOWES YET NONE
                        KNOWES WELL                  3.129.13
ALL THIS THE WORLD WELL KNOWES YET NONE
                        KNOWES WELL                  3.129.13
I LOVE TO HEARE HER SPEAKE, YET WELL I KNOW          3.130.9
FOR WELL THOU KNOW'ST TO MY DEARE DOTING HART        3.131.3
O LET IT THEN AS WELL BESEEME THY HEART              3.132.10
LET ME EXCUSE THEE, AH MY LOVE WELL KNOWES           3.139.9
IF IT BE NOT, THEN LOVE DOTH WELL DENOTE             3.148.7
LEAST EYES WELL SEEING THY FOULE FAULTS
                        SHOULD FINDE                 3.148.14
THIS BRAND SHE QUENCHED IN A COOLE $WELL BY          3.154.9
TO MAKE MY SELFE BELEEVE, THAT ALL IS WELL           4.2.13
REASON, IN FAITH THOU ART WELL SERV'D, THAT STILL    4.10.1
THAT IN HER BREAST THY PAP WELL SUGRED LIES          4.12.5
HAVING GOT UP A BREACH BY FIGHTING WELL              4.12.10
WELL STAID WITH TRUTH IN WORD AND FAITH OF DEED      4.14.10
SURE YOU SAY WELL, YOUR WISDOME'S GOLDEN MINE        4.21.12
TO SHEW HER SKIN, LIPS, TEETH AND HEAD SO WELL+      4.32.11
OFT CRUELL FIGHTS WELL PICTURED FORTH DO PLEASE      4.34.4
GUIDED SO WELL, THAT I OBTAIN'D THE PRIZE            4.41.2
WHERE WELL HE KNOWES, NO MAN TO HIM CAN COME         4.43.14
MY WORDS I KNOW DO WELL SET FORTH MY MIND            4.44.1
WELL $LOVE, SINCE THIS DEMURRE OUR SUTE
                        DOTH STAY                    4.52.12
THAT I WELL FIND NO ELOQUENCE LIKE IT                4.55.14
IF HE WAITE WELL, I NEVER THENCE WOULD MOVE          4.59.3
AS I MAY WELL RECOUNT, BUT NONE CAN PRIZE            4.65.4
WELL, HOW SO THOU INTERPRET THE CONTENTS             4.67.12
MY $MUSE MAY WELL GRUDGE AT MY HEAV'NLY JOY          4.70.1
TREBLES SING HIGH, AS WELL AS BASES DEEPE            4.70.6
HATH CHEEKES TO SMILE, AS WELL AS EYES TO WEEPE      4.70.8
IN WELL RAISDE NOTES, MY PEN THE BEST IT MAY         4.70.10
I NEVER DRANKE OF $AGANIPPE WELL                     4.74.1
NOT FOR HIS FAIRE OUTSIDE, NOR WELL LINED BRAINE     4.75.3
SWEET SWELLING LIP, WELL MAIST THOU SWELL
                        IN PRIDE                     4.80.1
YOU SAY FORSOOTH, YOU LEFT HER WELL OF LATE          4.92.7
SAY ALL, AND ALL WELL SAYD, STILL SAY THE SAME       4.92.14
THOUGHT WITH GOOD CAUSE THOU LIKEST SO
                        WELL THE NIGHT               4.96.1
BUT CEASE MINE EYES, YOUR TEARES DO WITNESSE
                        WELL                         4.105.9
WELL IS HE BORNE, THAT MAY BEHOLD YOU EVER           5.8.14
TO PROVE YOUR POWRE, WHICH I TOO WEL HAVE TRIDE      5.25.8
YET HOPE I WELL, THAT WHEN THIS STORME IS PAST       5.34.9
THEYR WEAKER HARTS, WHICH ARE NOT WEL AWARE+         5.37.8
WIL SOONE CONCEIVE, AND LEARNE TO CONSTRUE WELL      5.43.14
UNTILL YE HAVE THEYR GUYLEFULL TRAYNES WELL TRYDE    5.47.2
AND ERE SHE COULD THY CAUSE WEL UNDERSTAND           5.48.3
WELL WORTHY THOU TO HAVE FOUND BETTER HYRE           5.48.5
```

```
THRISE HAPPIE SHE, THAT IS SO WELL ASSURED            5.59.1
YET IN HER WINTERS BOWRE NOT WELL AWAKE               5.70.6
AND MODEST THOUGHTS BREATHD FROM WEL TEMPRED
                              SPRITES                 5.84.6
OF POYSONED WORDS AND SPITEFULL SPEECHES WELL         5.86.4
WELL-FORMED               1
  DOTH PLUNGE MY WEL-FORM'D SOULE EVEN IN THE MIRE    4.14.7
WELL-SHADING              1
  YET EACH PREPAR'D, WITH FANNE'S WEL-SHADING GRACE   4.22.7
WELTERING                 1
  IF IN THE $SCOTTISHE $COURT BE WELTRING YET         4.30.11
WENCH                     1
  A $WITLESSE $GALLANT, A YOUNG $WENCH THAT WOO'D     2.21.1
WEND                      1
  MY CRUELL FAYRE STREIGHT BIDS ME WEND MY WAY        5.46.2
WENT                      3
  THE GLORIOUS SUNNE WENT BLUSHING TO HIS BED         2.125.1
  SINCE FROM THEE GOING, HE WENT WILFULL SLOW         3.51.13
  HER DAINTIEST BARE WENT FREE., THE CAUSE
                              WAS THIS                4.22.13
WEPT                      1
  FOR ME, I WEPT TO SEE PEARLES SCATTERED SO          4.87.9
WEST                      5
  AND THAT THY BRIGHTNES SETS AT LENGTH TO $WEST      1.40.9
  WHEN $EAST, WHEN $WEST, WHEN $SOUTH, AND
                          WHEN BY $NORTH              2.1.7
  STEALING UNSEENE TO WEST WITH THIS DISGRACE         3.33.8
  AS AFTER $SUN-SET FADETH IN THE $WEST               3.73.6
  DOTH HALFE THAT GLORY TO THE SOBER $WEST            3.132.8
WESTERN                   2
  OUR $WESTERNE $PARTS EXTOLL THEIR $WILIS $FAME      2.32.11
  OUR $WESTERNE PARTS EXTOLL THEYR $WILYS FAME        2.124.11
WET                       1
  IS IT FOR FEARE TO WET A WIDDOWES EYE               3.9.1
WHATSOEVER                1
  TIL WHATSOEVER STAR THAT GUIDES MY MOVING           3.26.9
WHEEL                     4
  AND TURNE THE $WHEELE WITH DAMNED $IXION            2.40.14
  HOW E'RE BLIND $FORTUNE TURNE HER GIDDIE $WHEELE    2.51.12
  AND TURNE THE WHEELE WITH DAMNED $IXION             2.144.14
  THE ROLLING WHEELE THAT RUNNETH OFTEN ROUND         5.18.1
WHEELS                    3
  MY FORTUNES WHEELES THE CIRCLE OF HER EIES          1.12.11
  THE GOLDEN $SUNNE UPON HIS FIERY WHEELES            2.147.1
  FORTUNE WHEELES STILL WITH ME IN ONE SORT SLOW      4.66.6
WHENAS                    2
  WHENAS A STORME HATH DIMD HER TRUSTY GUYDE          5.34.3
  WHERE WHENAS DEATH SHALL ALL THE WORLD SUBDEW       5.75.13
WHENCE                    16
  THEN THERE I DIE FROM WHENCE MY LIFE SHOULD COME    1.31.13
  IN ENDLES ERRORS, WHENCE I CANNOT PART              1.34.12
  PROCEEDING FROM THE $PORT WHENCE HE PUT FORTH       2.1.5
  THAT EV'RY THING WHENCE $SHADOW DOTH PROCEED        2.13.13
  THAT EVERY THING WHENCE SHADOW DOTH PROCEEDE        2.121.13
  FROM WHENCE, IF YOU ONE TEARE OF PITTY MOVE         2.151.3
  FROM WHENCE AT PLEASURE THOU MAIST COME AND PART    3.48.12
  SWEET THEEFE WHENCE DIDST THOU STEALE
                          THY SWEET THAT SMELS        3.99.2
  WHENCE HAST THOU THIS BECOMMING OF THINGS IL        3.150.5
  WHENCE THOSE SAME FUMES OF MELANCHOLY RISE          4.23.3
```

```
   WHENCE HAST THOU $IVORIE, $RUBIES, PEARLE
                    AND GOLD                          4.32.10
   STELLA, WHENCE DOTH THIS NEW ASSAULT ARISE         4.36.1
   WHENCE WORDS, NOT WORDS, BUT HEAV'NLY
                    GRACES SLIDE                       4.80.4
   ALAS, WHENCE CAME THIS CHANGE OF LOOKES+ $IF I      4.86.1
   OF $HELICON WHENCE SHE DERIVED IS                   5.1.10
   FOR LOOKING ON THE EARTH WHENCE SHE WAS BORNE       5.13.6
WHEREAS                   1
   THAT WHEREAS BLACKE SEEMES $BEAUTIE'S CONTRARY      4.7.10
WHEREFORE                 4
   BUT WHEREFORE DO NOT YOU A MIGHTIER WAIE            3.16.1
   AH WHEREFORE WITH INFECTION SHOULD HE LIVE          3.67.1
   BUT WHEREFORE SAYES SHE NOT SHE IS UNJUST+          3.138.9
   AND WHEREFORE SAY NOT I THAT I AM OLD+              3.138.10
WHEREIN                  14
   AND WAILE THE STATE WHEREIN I PRESENT STAND         1.28.10
   WHEREIN NO SHEW GAVE CAUSE OF LEAST SUSPECT         1.31.7
   FROM OUT DISPAIRE, WHEREIN THEY LIVE CONFINDE+      1.49.4
   WHEREIN THE $WORLD SHALL NOW INTOMBE HER $NAME      2.45.8
   THAT WONDER NOW WHEREIN ALL WONDERS BE              2.107.3
   WHEREIN EACH FAYREST PART EXCELLETH OTHER           2.123.4
   O PUREST MERROR, WHEREIN MEN MAY SEE                2.146.13
   MY BODY IS THE FRAME WHEREIN TI'S HELD              3.24.3
   MAKING THEIR TOMBE THE WOMBE WHEREIN THEY GREW+     3.86.4
   OF FAULTS CONCEALD, WHEREIN I AM ATTAINTED          3.88.7
   WHEREIN IT FINDES A JOY ABOVE THE REST              3.91.6
   WHEREIN I SHOULD YOUR GREAT DESERTS REPAY           3.117.2
   LIES HATCHING STILL THE GOODS WHEREIN THEY FLOW     4.24.2
   WITH WORDS, WHEREIN THE $MUSES' TREASURES BE        4.60.7
WHEREOF                  11
   OF HER OWNE SEATE, WHEREOF I MADE HER GUIDE         1.47.8
   WHAT IS YOUR SUBSTANCE, WHEREOF ARE YOU MADE        3.53.1
   AND ALL THOSE BEAUTIES WHEREOF NOW HE'S $KING       3.63.6
   WHEREOF THIS $BEAUTIE CAN BE BUT A SHADE            4.5.10
   WHEREOF, WITH WHOM, HOW OFTEN DID SHE TALKE         4.92.11
   THE LIGHT WHEROF HATH KINDLED HEAVENLY FYRE         5.3.3
   WITH NOYSE WHEREOF THE QUYRE OF $BYRDS RESOUNDED    5.19.5
   AT SIGHT WHEREOF EACH BIRD THAT SITS ON SPRAY       5.40.9
   WHEREOF SHE MOTE BE MADE., THAT IS THE SKYE         5.55.10
   THE SPARKES WHEREOF LET KINDLE THINE OWN FYRE       5.86.9
   WHEREOF SOME GLANCE DOTH IN MINE EIE REMAYNE        5.88.8
WHEREON                   5
   LINES OF DELIGHT, WHEREON HER YOUTH MIGHT SMILE     1.51.2
   DECKT WITH HER YOUTH WHEREON THE WORLD DOTH SMILE   1.53.6
   WHEREON THE $STARS IN SECRET INFLUENCE COMMENT      3.15.4
   AS THE DEATH BED, WHEREON IT MUST EXPIRE            3.73.11
   IF THAT BE FAIRE WHEREON MY FALSE EYES DOTE         3.148.5
WHERETHROUGH              1
   ARE WINDOWES TO MY BREST, WHERE-THROUGH THE $SUN    3.24.11
WHERETO                   7
   MY LAST $RESORT WHERETO MY HOPES APPEALE            1.22.2
   WHERETO AL BONDS DO TIE ME DAY BY DAY               3.117.4
   WHERETO TH'INVITING TIME OUR FASHION CALLS          3.124.8
   WHERETO THE JUDGEMENT OF MY HEART IS TIDE+          3.137.8
   WHERETO LONG SINCE, THROUGH MY LONG BATTRED EYES    4.36.3
   CHIEFE GOOD, WHERETO MY HOPE DOTH ONLY ASPIRE       4.68.3
   AND TELL ME WHERETO CAN YE LYKEN IT                 5.40.2
WHEREUPON                 1
   GILDING THE OBJECT WHERE-UPON IT GAZETH             3.20.6
```

WHEREWITH   7
  WHEREWITH MY LIBERTY THOU DIDST SURPRIZE   1.14.2
  AND I WANT WORDS, WHEREWITH TO TELL MY $WRONG   2.41.8
  FOR SOME FEW $RAGGES, WHEREWITH TO COVER THEE   2.48.4
  CRAWLES TO MATURITY, WHEREWITH BEING CROWN'D   3.60.6
  WHEREWITH MY FATHER ONCE MADE IT HALFE TAME   4.30.10
  THE RAINES WHEREWITH MY $RIDER DOTH ME TIE   4.49.5
  OR ELSE PRONOUNCING GRACE, WHEREWITH HIS MIND 4.58.7
WHET   1
  STILL MUST I WHET MY YONG DESIRES ABATED   1.18.9
WHETHER   14
  OFT DO I MARVELL, WHETHER $DELIAS EIES   1.34.1
  YET WHETHER FIXT OR WANDRING STARRES ARE THEY 1.34.9
  WHETHER MY FAITH HATH NOT DESERV'D HER LOVE+   1.49.12
  IN $ME IT SPEAKES, WHETHER I $SLEEPE OR $WAKE 2.20.5
  WHETHER ARE THESE DECEIVED THEN, OR I+   2.28.12
  FOR WHETHER BEAUTY, BIRTH, OR WEALTH, OR WIT   3.37.5
  WHETHER WE ARE MENDED, OR WHERE BETTER THEY   3.59.11
  OR WHETHER REVOLUTION BE THE SAME   3.59.12
  OR WHETHER DOTH MY MINDE BEING CROWN'D WITH YOU 3.114.1
  OR WHETHER SHALL I SAY MINE EIE SAITH TRUE   3.114.3
  AND WHETHER THAT MY ANGEL BE TURN'D FINDE   3.144.9
  WHETHER THE $TURKISH NEW-MOONE MINDED BE   4.30.1
  WHETHER WITH WORDS THIS SOVERAIGNTY HE GAINE   4.58.5
  I WOULD KNOW WHETHER SHE DID SIT OR WALKE   4.92.9
WHILE   57
  WHICH STILL IS CHAC'D, WHILE I HAVE ANY BREATH 1.5.10
  AND SHE IS YONG, AND NOW MUST SPORT THE WHILE 1.51.4
  AND ALL THIS WHILE, I WAS MISTAKEN THERE   2.19.12
  AND PLEASE YOUR SELFE WITH THIS $CONCEIT
                         THE WHILE   2.24.8
  BUT IF THE WHILE I THINKE ON THEE (DEARE FRIEND) 3.30.13
  WHILE THOU DOST BREATH THAT POOR'ST INTO MY VERSE 3.38.2
  WHILE SHADOWES LIKE TO THEE DO MOCKE MY SIGHT+ 3.61.4
  WHILE COMMENTS OF YOUR PRAISE RICHLY COMPIL'D 3.85.2
  NOW WHILE THE WORLD IS BENT MY DEEDS TO CROSSE 3.90.2
  WHILE HE INSULTS ORE DULL AND SPEACHLESSE
                         TRIBES   3.107.12
  LOVE GAVE THE WOUND, WHICH WHILE I BREATHE
                         WILL BLEED   4.2.2
  WHILE WITH A FEELING SKILL I PAINT MY HELL   4.2.14
  WHILE TEARES POWRE OUT HIS INKE, AND SIGHS
                  BREATHE OUT HIS WORDS   4.6.10
  TO MY CLOSE HEART, WHERE WHILE SOME FIREBRANDS
                       HE DID LAY   4.8.13
  WHILE $LOVE ON ME DOTH ALL HIS QUIVER SPEND   4.14.4
  BUT WHILE I THUS WITH THIS YONG $LYON PLAID   4.16.9
  BRAKE BOW, BRAKE SHAFTS, WHILE $CUPID
                      WEEPING SATE   4.17.8
  I WILLING RUN, YET WHILE I RUN, REPENT   4.19.4
  WHILE THAT BLACKE HUE FROM ME THE BAD GUEST HID 4.20.11
  WHILE HE EACH THING IN SENSE'S BALLANCE WAYES 4.25.6
  UNSEENE, UNHEARD, WHILE THOUGHT TO HIGHEST PLACE 4.27.13
  BUT FROM THY HEART, WHILE MY SIRE CHARMETH THEE 4.32.13
  WHILE TOO MUCH WIT (FORSOOTH) SO TROUBLED ME   4.33.10
  THUS WRITE I WHILE I DOUBT TO WRITE, AND WREAKE 4.34.12
  THIS NIGHT WHILE SLEEPE BEGINS WITH HEAVY WINGS 4.38.1
  MY STILL KEPT COURSE, WHILE OTHERS SLEEPE,
                       TO MONE   4.40.4
  WHO WHILE THEY MAKE $LOVE CONQUER, CONQUER $LOVE 4.42.3

```
    OUR HORSMANSHIPS, WHILE BY STRANGE WORKE I PROVE      4.49.2
    GIRT FAST BY MEMORIE, AND WHILE I SPURRE              4.49.10
    WHILE THOSE POORE BABES THEIR DEATH IN
                            BIRTH DO FIND                 4.50.11
    FOR ME, WHILE YOU DISCOURSE OF COURTLY TIDES          4.51.9
    MEANE WHILE MY HEART CONFERS WITH $STELLA'S
                            BEAMES                        4.51.12
    WHILE EACH PRETENDS THAT $STELLA MUST BE HIS          4.52.2
    WHILE WITH THE PEOPLE'S SHOUTS I MUST CONFESSE        4.53.3
    YET WHILE I LANGUISH, HIM THAT BOSOME CLIPS           4.59.9
    LOOKING ON ME, WHILE I LOOKT OTHER WAY                4.66.12
    AND ALL IN VAINE, FOR WHILE THY BREATH MOST SWEET     4.68.9
    THIS REALME OF BLISSE, WHILE VERTUOUS
                            COURSE I TAKE                 4.69.13
    SO WHILE THY BEAUTIE DRAWES THE HEART TO LOVE         4.71.12
    WHILE EACH DOTH BLOW THE FIER OF MY HART              4.72.4
    IN SPORT I SUCKT, WHILE SHE ASLEEPE DID LIE           4.73.6
    BUT LO, WHILE I DO SPEAKE, IT GROWETH
                            NOONE WITH ME                 4.76.9
    THE PRETTIE DEATH, WHILE EACH IN OTHER LIVE           4.79.11
    WHILE CRAFTILY YOU SEEM'D YOUR CUT TO KEEPE           4.83.3
    WHILE EVERIE OFFICE THEMSELVES WILL DISCHARGE         4.85.7
    THUS WHILE TH' EFFECT MOST BITTER WAS TO ME           4.87.12
    TUSH ABSENCE, WHILE THY MISTES ECLIPSE THAT LIGHT     4.88.9
    WHILE NO NIGHT IS MORE DARKE THEN IS MY DAY           4.89.10
    STELLA, WHILE NOW BY HONOUR'S CRUELL MIGHT            4.91.1
    WHILE I DISPAIRE BY $SUNNE'S SIGHT TO ENJOY           4.97.14
    WHILE THE BLACKE HORRORS OF THE SILENT NIGHT          4.98.9
    WHILE GRACEFULL PITTY BEAUTY BEAUTIFIES               4.100.4
    WHILE SOBD OUT WORDS A PERFECT $MUSIKE GIVE           4.100.11
    WHILE BEAUTIE'S REDDEST INKE $VENUS FOR
                            HIM DOTH STURRE               4.102.14
    WHILE THOSE FAIRE PLANETS ON THY STREAMES
                            DID SHINE                     4.103.4
    WHILE WANTON WINDS WITH BEAUTIES SO DEVINE            4.103.6
    SWEETE, FOR A WHILE GIVE RESPITE TO MY HART           4.107.5
WHILES                  7
    THE WHILES SHE LORDETH IN LICENTIOUS BLISSE           5.10.3
    WHILES HER FAIRE FACE SHE REARES UP TO THE SKIE       5.13.2
    THE WHILES MY STONISHT HART STOOD IN AMAZE            5.16.3
    WHILES SHE AS STEELE AND FLINT DOTH STILL
                            REMAYNE                       5.18.14
    THE WHILES HER FOOT SHE IN MY NECKE DOTH PLACE        5.20.3
    WHILES DIVING DEEPE THROUGH AMOROUS INSIGHT           5.76.7
    DARK IS MY DAY, WHYLES HER FAYRE LIGHT I MIS          5.89.13
WHILEST                 5
    WHYLEST RAPT WITH JOY RESEMBLING HEAVENLY MADNES      5.39.9
    WHILEST MY WEAK POWRES OF PASSIONS WARREID ARRE       5.44.7
    TO LET THEM GAZE WHYLEST HE ON THEM MAY PRAY          5.53.4
    MAKE HAST THEREFORE SWEET LOVE, WHILEST
                            IT IS PRIME                   5.70.13
    BUT WITH SUCH BRIGHTNESSE WHYLEST I FILL MY MIND      5.88.13
WHILST                  53
    WHILST BLINDED ONES MINE ERROURS NEVER GESSE          1.3.8
    WHO WHILST I LOVE, DOTH KILL ME WITH DISDAINE         1.3.14
    WHILST YOUTH AND ERROR LED MY WANDRING MINDE          1.5.1
    STILL TO COMPLAINE MY GRIEFES, WHILST NONE RELIEVE    1.9.8
    WHILST WE BOTH MAKE THE WORLD ADMIRE AT US            1.26.13
    AND WHILST I GARDE THESE WINDOWES OF THIS FORTE       1.27.5
    FOR WHILST THEY STRIVE WHICH SHALL BE
                            $LORD OF ALL                  1.28.5
```

```
WHILST BY THY EIES PURSU'D, MY POORE HEART FLEW        1.31.1
AND WILL WHILST I SHALL DRAW THIS BREATH OF MINE       1.33.10
WHILST YET HER TENDER BUD DOTH UNDISCLOSE              1.39.3
BUT LOVE NOW WHILST THOU MAIST BE LOV'D AGAINE         1.39.14
BUT LOVE WHILST THAT THCU MAIST BE LOV'D AGAINE        1.40.1
NOW WHILST THY $MAY HATH FILD THY LAP
                            WITH FLOWERS               1.40.2
NOW WHILST THY BEAUTY BEARES WITHOUT A STAINE          1.40.3
AND WHILST THOU SPREADST UNTO THE RISING SUNNE         1.40.5
THOU CANST NOT DIE WHILST ANY ZEALE ABOUND             1.43.1
WHO WHILST I BURNE, SHE SINGS AT MY SOULES WRACK       1.47.5
BE YOU MOST WORTHY, WHILST I AM MOST TRUE              2.4.14
NOR WHILST THE $WORLD IS, NEVER SHALL BE DONE          2.13.11
WHILST $MOONE SHALL SHINE, OR ANY $FIRE
                            SHALL BURNE                2.13.12
WHILST YET MINE $EYES DCE SURFET WITH $DELIGHT         2.33.1
BUT WHILST MINE $EYES THUS GREEDILY DOE GAZE           2.33.5
WHILST I IN DARKENESSE, IN THE SELFE-SAME PLACE        2.43.3
WHILST THUS MY $PEN STRIVES TO ETERNIZE THEE           2.44.1
WHILST IN DESPITE CF TYRANNIZING $TIMES                2.44.5
WITH HEAVIE $SIGHES WHILST THUS I BREAKE
                            THE $AYRE                  2.45.3
WHILST I LIKE $ORPHEUS SING TO $TREES
                            AND $STONES                2.45.12
THAT WHILST WITH $MARS SHE HOLDETH HER OLD $WAY        2.48.13
AND THUS WHILST $BEAUTIE ON HER BEAUTY GAZED           2.109.5
WHILST $LOVE (MY $PHOENIX BIRD) IN HER
                            OWN FLAME IS DYING         2.117.12
NOR WHILST THE WORLD IS, NEVER SHALL BE DONE           2.121.11
WHILST $MOONE SHALL SHYNE BY NIGHT, OR
                            ANY FIRE SHALL BURNE       2.121.12
WHILST FIRE, WATER, AYRE, TWIXT HEAVEN
                            AND EARTH SHAL BE          2.127.13
WHILST THUS MINE EYES DCE SURFET WITH DELIGHT          2.133.1
BUT WHILST MINE EYES THUS GREEDILY DOE GAZE            2.133.5
AND WHILST MY HART AND EYE, ENVY EACH
                            OTHERS PRAISE              2.133.11
AND THUS WHILST SIGHES AND TEARES TOGETHER
                            DOE CONTENDE               2.133.13
WHILST FROM THEYR RAYES BY $CUPIDS SKILFULL HAND       2.135.7
WHILST THUS HE PANTETH FOR HIS LATEST BREATH           2.135.10
WHILST I WHOME FORTUNE CF SUCH TRYUMPH BARS            3.25.3
WHILST THAT THIS SHADOW DOTH SUCH SUBSTANCE GIVE       3.37.10
WHILST I (MY SOVERAINE) WATCH THE CLOCK FOR YOU        3.57.6
FOR THEE WATCH I, WHILST THOU DOST WAKE
                            ELSEWHERE                  3.61.13
WHILST I ALONE DID CALL UPON THY AYDE                  3.79.1
WHILST HE UPON YOUR SOUNDLESSE DEEPE DOTH RIDE         3.80.10
I THINKE GOOD THOUGHTS, WHILST OTHER WRITE
                            GOOD WORDES                3.85.5
WHILST LIKE A WILLING PACIENT I WILL DRINKE            3.111.9
WHILST IT HATH THOUGHT IT SELFE SO BLESSED
                            NEVER+                     3.119.6
WHILST MY POORE LIPS WHICH SHOULD THAT
                            HARVEST REAPE              3.128.7
WHILST HER NEGLECTED CHILD HOLDS HER IN CHACE          3.143.5
WHILST I THY BABE CHACE THEE A FARRE BEHIND            3.143.10
WHILST MANY $NYMPHES THAT VOU'D CHAST
                            LIFE TO KEEP               3.154.3
YET EVEN WHYLST HER BLOODY HANDS THEM SLAY             5.47.9
```

WHINE   1
  I THOUGHT THOSE BABES OF SOME PINNE'S
                         HURT DID WHINE   4.16.7
WHIR-POOL   1
  SOME WHIR-POOLE $PO, AND SLYDING $HYPASIS   2.120.10
WHIT   3
  AND THAT ALL THIS MOOVES NOT HER THOUGHTS A WHIT   1.21.12
  YET HIM FOR THIS, MY LOVE NO WHIT DISDAINETH   3.33.13
  MY WEALTH NO MORE, AND NO WHIT LESSE MY NEED   4.66.7
WHITE   15
  YEELD THY HANDS PRIDE UNTO TH'$IVORY WHITE   1.19.5
  IN THIS FAYRE LIMMED GROUND AS WHITE AS SNOW   2.114.10
  THE $GALIXIA, TO HER MORE THEN WHITE   2.148.10
  AND SABLE CURLS OR SILVER'D ORE WITH WHITE   3.12.4
  BORNE ON THE BEARE WITH WHITE AND BRISTLY BEARD   3.12.8
  NOR DID I WONDER AT THE $LILLIES WHITE   3.98.9
  OUR BLUSHING SHAME, AN OTHER WHITE DISPAIRE   3.99.9
  A THIRD NOR RED, NOR WHITE, HAD STOLNE OF BOTH   3.99.10
  IF SNOW BE WHITE, WHY THEN HER BRESTS ARE DUN   3.130.3
  I HAVE SEENE $ROSES DAMASKT, RED AND WHITE   3.130.5
  MARBLE MIXT RED AND WHITE DO ENTERLACE   4.9.8
  SHALL PAINT OUT JOY, THOUGH BUT IN BLACKE
                         AND WHITE   4.70.11
  THAT SKIN, WHOSE PASSE-PRAISE HUE SCORNS
               THIS POORE TERME OF WHITE 4.77.7
  THAT IN THAT PALENESSE BEAUTIE'S WHITE WE SEE   4.101.6
  IT IS BUT LOVE, WHICH MAKES HIS PAPER
                     PERFIT WHITE   4.102.12
WHITHER   1
  AND WHITHER (POORE FORSAKEN) WILT THOU GOE   1.52.1
WHOLE   8
  POSSESSE ME WHOLE, MY HEARTS TRIUMVIRATE   1.28.2
  AND FOR ONE PIECE OF $THINE, MY WHOLE HEART TAKE   2.52.8
  IN $ONE WHOLE WORLD IS BUT ONE $PHOENIX FOUND   2.106.1
  HE PAIES THE WHOLE, AND YET AM I NOT FREE   3.134.14
  WHOLE ARMIES OF THY BEAUTIES ENTRED IN   4.36.4
  AND OFT WHOLE TROUPES OF SADDEST WORDS I STAID   4.55.5
  WHAT, A WHOLE WEEKE WITHOUT ONE PEECE OF LOOKE   4.56.3
  AND WITH ONE WORD MY WHOLE YEARS WORK DOTH REND   5.23.12
WHOLLY   5
  THAT MY LIVES LIGHT WHOLY IN-DARKNED IS   1.21.4
  I THUS OPPOSE MY $REASONS FORCES WHOLLY   2.28.4
  AND $LOVE CONTEMNING $REASONS REASON WHOLLY   2.38.11
  AND $LOVE CONTEMNING $REASONS REASON WHOLY   2.131.11
  THAT WHOLLY HERS, ALL SELFNESSE HE FORBEARES   4.61.7
WHOSOEVER   1
  A $MONUMENT THAT WHOSOEVER REEDES   1.2.7
WICKED   4
  BY THIS GOOD WICKED $SPIRIT, SWEET $ANGELL
                         $DEVILL   2.20.14
  A WICKED AMBUSH WHICH LAY HIDDEN LONG   5.12.6
  THAT SHE TO WICKED MEN A SCOURGE SHOULD BEE   5.24.11
  AND CATCHING HOLD ON THINE OWNE WICKED HED   5.86.10
WIDE   11
  BUT STRAIGHT HER WIDE BLOWNE POMP COMES
                       TO DECLINE   1.39.6
  TO THE WIDE WORLD AND ALL HER FADING SWEETS   3.19.7
  AND KEEPE MY DROOPING EYE-LIDS OPEN WIDE   3.27.7
  BUT SINCE YOUR WORTH (WIDE AS THE $OCEAN IS)   3.80.5
  OF THE WIDE WORLD, DREAMING ON THINGS TO COME   3.107.2

```
FOR NOTHING THIS WIDE $UNIVERSE I CALL              3.109.13
WHICH MY HEART KNOWES THE WIDE WORLDS
                        COMMON PLACE+               3.137.10
BEARE THINE EYES STRAIGHT, THOUGH THY
                        PROUD HEART GOE WIDE        3.140.14
PHOEBUS DREW WIDE THE CURTAINES OF THE SKIES        4.13.12
THRETNING RASH EIES WHICH GAZE ON HER SO WIDE       5.5.7
LYKE AS A SHIP THAT THROUGH THE $OCEAN WYDE         5.34.1
WIDOW                 2
  THE WORLD WILBE THY WIDDOW AND STILL WEEPE        3.9.5
  WHEN EVERY PRIVAT WIDDOW WELL MAY KEEPE           3.9.7
WIDOWED               1
  LIKE WIDDOWED WOMBES AFTER THEIR $LORDS DECEASE   3.97.8
WIDOW'S               1
  IS IT FOR FEARE TO WET A WIDDOWES EYE             3.9.1
WIFE                  1
  THE WORLD WILL WAILE THEE LIKE A MAKELESSE WIFE   3.9.4
WIGHT                 3
  THE WISEST SCHOLLER OF THE WIGHT MOST WISE        4.25.1
  FROM HEAVENLY STANDING HITS EACH MORTALL WIGHT    4.97.4
  CALS EACH WIGHT TO SALUTE THE FLOURE OF BLISSE    4.99.11
WIGHTS                1
  I SEE DISCRIPTIONS OF THE FAIREST WIGHTS          3.106.2
WILD                  3
  BUT THAT WILD MUSICK BURTHENS EVERY BOW           3.102.11
  BUT SHE MORE CRUELL AND MORE SALVAGE WYLDE        5.20.9
  STRANGE THING ME SEEMD TO SEE A BEAST SO WYLD     5.67.13
WILIS'                2
  OUR $WESTERNE $PARTS EXTOLL THEIR $WILIS $FAME    2.32.11
  OUR $WESTERNE PARTS EXTOLL THEYR $WILYS FAME      2.124.11
WILL                  48
  OF INTERCESSION BUT TO MOVE HER WILL              1.4.12
  YET, THOUGH I CANNOT WINNE HER WILL WITH TEARES   1.11.9
  YET I PROTEST MY HIGH DESIRING WILL               1.36.9
  THUS RUINES SHE (TO SATISFIE HER WILL)            1.47.13
  MOVING A $WILL IN US, IT IS THE $MIND             2.12.6
  YOU $WILL, AND $WILL NOT, WHAT A COYLE IS HERE+   2.19.10
  LIKE THEY THAT $LUST, I CARE NOT, I WILL NONE     2.39.8
  CROSSING SWEET NATURE BY UNRULY WILL             2.147.12
  SO TRUE A FOOLE IS LOVE, THAT IN YOUR $WILL       3.57.13
  TO WHAT YOU WILL, TO YOU IT DOTH BELONG           3.58.11
  IS IT THY WIL, THY $IMAGE SHOULD KEEPE OPEN       3.61.1
  AS ILE MY SELFE DISGRACE, KNOWING THY WIL         3.89.7
  AND I MY SELFE AM MORGAG'D TO THY WILL            3.134.2
  WHO EVER HATH HER WISH, THOU HAST THY $WILL       3.135.1
  AND $WILL TOO BOOTE, AND $WILL IN OVER-PLUS       3.135.2
  TO THY SWEET WILL MAKING ADDITION THUS            3.135.4
  WILT THOU WHOSE WILL IS LARGE AND SPATIOUS        3.135.5
  NOT ONCE VOUCHSAFE TO HIDE MY WILL IN THINE       3.135.6
  SHALL WILL IN OTHERS SEEME RIGHT GRACIOUS         3.135.7
  AND IN MY WILL NO FAIRE ACCEPTANCE SHINE          3.135.8
  SO THOU BEEING RICH IN $WILL ADDE TO THY $WILL    3.135.11
  ONE WILL OF MINE TO MAKE THY LARGE $WILL MORE     3.135.12
  THINKE ALL BUT ONE, AND ME IN THAT ONE $WILL      3.135.14
  SWEARE TO THY BLIND SOULE THAT I WAS THY $WILL    3.136.2
  AND WILL THY SOULE KNOWES IS ADMITTED THERE       3.136.3
  WILL, WILL FULFILL THE TREASURE OF THY LOVE       3.136.5
  I FILL IT FULL WITH WILS, AND MY WILL ONE         3.136.6
  AND THEN THOU LOVEST ME FOR MY NAME IS $WILL      3.136.14
  SO WILL I PRAY THAT THOU MAIST HAVE THY $WILL     3.143.13
```

```
THOU SETST A BATE BETWEENE MY WILL AND WIT          4.4.2
DEALE THOU WITH POWERS OF THOUGHTS, LEAVE
                          LOVE TO WILL            4.10.8
THE $WAND IS $WILL, THOU $FANCIE $SADDLE ART       4.49.9
FOR NOTHING FROM MY WIT OF WILL DOTH FLOW          4.90.12
ALL FOLKES PREST AT THY WILL THY PAINE
                          TO 'SWAGE              4.101.11
TILL IT HAVE WROUGHT WHAT THY OWNE WILL ATTENDS   4.107.11
FOR THOUGH HE COLOURS COULD DEVIZE AT WILL         5.17.5
FOR EASIE THINGS THAT MAY BE GOT AT WILL           5.26.11
NOR MOVE THE $DOLPHIN FROM HER STUBBORNE WILL      5.38.8
IS IT HER NATURE OR IS IT HER WILL                 5.41.1
IF WILL, THEN SHE AT WILL MAY WILL FORGOE          5.41.4
BUT IF HER NATURE AND HER WIL BE SO                5.41.5
AS WILLING ME AGAINST HER WILL TO STAY             5.46.4
BUT AS SHE WILL, WHOSE WILL MY LIFE DOTH SWAY      5.46.7
YET LIVE FOR EVER, THOUGH AGAINST HER WILL         5.48.13
BUT IF IT BE YOUR PLEASURE AND PROUD WILL          5.49.5
MOTE SOFTEN IT AND TO HIS WILL ALLURE              5.51.10
BUT SIMPLE TRUTH AND MUTUALL GOOD WILL             5.65.11
SO GOODLY WONNE WITH HER OWNE WILL BEGUYLD         5.67.14
WILLED                    1
WILLD ME THESE TEMPESTS OF VAINE LOVE TO FLIE      4.62.10
WILLFUL                   3
BY WILFULL TASTE OF WHAT THY SELFE REFUSEST        3.40.8
SINCE FROM THEE GOING, HE WENT WILFULL SLOW        3.51.13
THE MORE SHE FRIESETH IN HER WILFULL PRYDE         5.32.10
WILLFULLY                 1
ON YOUR BROAD MAINE DOTH WILFULLY APPEARE          3.80.8
WILLFULNESS               1
BOOKE BOTH MY WILFULNESSE AND ERRORS DOWNE         3.117.9
WILLING                   5
WHICH HAPPIES THOSE THAT PAY THE WILLING LONE       3.6.6
WHILST LIKE A WILLING PACIENT I WILL DRINKE        3.111.9
I WILLING RUN, YET WHILE I RUN, REPENT             4.19.4
DOTH WILLING GRAUNT, THAT IN THE FRONTIERS HE      4.29.7
AS WILLING ME AGAINST HER WILL TO STAY             5.46.4
WILLINGLY                 1
THEN NIGARD TRUTH WOULD WILLINGLY IMPART           3.72.8
WILLS                     3
WHICH IN THEIR WILS COUNT BAD WHAT I THINK GOOD+   3.121.8
I FILL IT FULL WITH WILS, AND MY WILL ONE          3.136.6
WILS HIM AWAKE, AND SOONE ABOUT HIM DIGHT          5.4.7
WIN                      16
FORGING A GRIEFE TO WINNE A FAMES REWARD           1.4.4
MY FAITH SHOULD WIN, IF $JUSTICE MIGHT HAVE PLACE  1.8.12
TEARES, VOWES, AND PRAYERS, WINNE THE
                          HARDEST HART            1.11.1
YET, THOUGH I CANNOT WINNE HER WILL WITH TEARES    1.11.9
IF THIS $RECEIT HAVE NOT THE POW'R TO WINNE ME     2.15.13
AND THE FIRME SOILE WIN OF THE WATRY MAINE         3.64.7
THAT THOU IN LOOSING ME, SHALL WIN MUCH GLORY      3.88.8
STILL LOOSING WHEN I SAW MY SELFE TO WIN+          3.119.4
TO WIN ME SOONE TO HELL MY FEMALL EVILL            3.144.5
KNOWLEDGE MIGHT PITIE WINNE, AND PITIE
                          GRACE OBTAINE            4.1.4
THAT TO WIN IT, IS ALL THE SKILL AND PAINE         4.12.14
A CONQUERD, YELDEN, RANSACKT HEART TO WINNE+       4.36.2
MIGHT WINNE SOME GRACE IN YOUR SWEET SKILL ARRAID  4.55.4
BUT THAT WHICH ONCE MAY WIN THY CRUELL HART        4.64.13
```

THAT TO WIN ME, OFT SHEWES A PRESENT PAY+   4.88.4
CAPTIVITY THENCE CAPTIVE US TO WIN   5.68.4
WIND   7
LEFT TO THE MERCY OF THE WAVES AND WINDE   2.134.4
COMMIT MY WORDS UNTO THE FLEETING WIND   2.142.11
POINTING TO EACH HIS THUNDER, RAINE AND WINDE   3.14.6
THEN SHOULD I SPURRE THOUGH MOUNTED ON THE WIND 3.51.7
NO WIND, NO SHADE CAN COOLE, WHAT HELPE
                            THEN IN MY CASE   4.76.12
WHOSE FRUITLESSE WORKE IS BROKEN WITH LEAST WYND 5.23.14
WITH THE LOOSE WYND YE WAVING CHANCE TO MARKE   5.81.2
WINDING   1
ERE THEY BE WELL WRAP'D IN THEIR WINDING $SHEET+ 2.6.4
WINDLASS   1
MY YOUNG MIND MARDE, WHOM $LOVE DOTH WINDLAS SO 4.21.2
WINDOW   3
WHO HARD BY MADE A WINDOW SEND FORTH LIGHT   4.53.9
SHE SO DISCHEVELD, BLUSHT., FROM WINDOW I   4.103.12
BUT IF I BY A HAPPY WINDOW PASSE   4.104.9
WINDOWS   6
AND WHILST I GARDE THESE WINDOWES OF THIS FORTE 1.27.5
SO THOU THROUGH WINDOWES OF THINE AGE SHALT SEE 3.3.11
THAT HATH HIS WINDOWES GLAZED WITH THINE EYES   3.24.8
ARE WINDOWES TO MY BREST, WHERE-THROUGH THE $SUN 3.24.11
THE WINDOWES NOW THROUGH WHICH THIS HEAV'NLY GUEST 4.9.9
WITH WINDOWES OPE THEN MOST MY MIND DOTH LIE   4.99.5
WINDS   4
AND STILL MY HOPE THE $SOMMER WINDES PURSUES   1.16.11
ROUGH WINDES DO SHAKE THE DARLING BUDS OF $MAIE 3.18.3
THAT I HAVE HOYSTED SAILE TO AL THE WINDES   3.117.7
WHILE WANTON WINDS WITH BEAUTIES SO DEVINE   4.103.6
WINDY   1
GIVE NOT A WINDY NIGHT A RAINIE MORROW   3.90.7
WINE   2
QUAFFING $CAROWSES IN THIS COSTLY $WINE   2.7.8
I JOYED, BUT STRAIGHT THUS WATRED WAS MY WINE   4.62.5
WING   2
THENCE TAKE YOU $WING UNTO THE $ORCADES   2.25.6
HAVE ADDED FETHERS TO THE LEARNEDS WING   3.78.7
WINGED   4
AND WING'D BY $FAME, YOU TO THE $STARRES ASCEND 2.16.13
IN WINGED SPEED NO MOTION SHALL I KNOW   3.51.8
WING'D WITH WHOSE BREATH, SO PLEASING
                          $ZEPHIRES BLOW   4.100.7
SO SINCE THE WINGED $GOD HIS PLANET CLEARE   5.60.5
WINGS   18
MY SPOTLESSE LOVE HOVERS WITH PUREST WINGS   1.12.1
BUT THESE WEAKE WHINGS PRESUMING TO ASPIRE   1.32.6
TO WHOM MY $MUSE WITH FIERIE $WINGS SHALL PASSE 2.25.10
UNCERTAINE $DREAD GIVES $WINGS UNTO MY $HOPE   2.26.5
YET MY $HOPES $WINGS ARE LADEN SO WITH $FEARE   2.26.6
HE FRAMD HIM WINGS WITH FEATHERS OF HIS THOUGHT 2.122.5
UNCERTAINE-DREAD, GYVES WINGS UNTO MY HOPE   2.137.5
YET MY HOPES WINGS ARE LODEN SO WITH FEARE   2.137.6
HE BURNT UNWARES HIS WINGS, AND CANNOT FLY AWAY 4.8.14
THIS NIGHT WHILE SLEEPE BEGINS WITH HEAVY WINGS 4.38.1
VENUS IS TAUGHT WITH $DIAN'S WINGS TO FLIE   4.72.6
WITH WINGS OF $LOVE IN AIRE OF WONDER FLIE   4.86.8
WITHOUT MY PLUMES FROM OTHERS' WINGS I TAKE   4.90.11
CLIPS STREIGHT MY WINGS, STREIGHT WRAPS
                          ME IN HIS NIGHT   4.108.8

```
HIS WANTON WINGS AND DARTS OF DEADLY POWER          5.4.8
LEGIONS OF LOVES WITH LITTLE WINGS DID FLY          5.16.6
OFT WHEN MY SPIRIT DOTH SPRED HER BOLDER WINGES     5.72.1
THEY LOOSELY DID THEYR WANTON WINGES DISPLAY        5.76.11
WINK                     3
  WHEN MOST I WINKE THEN DOE MINE EYES BEST SEE     3.43.1
  THY HUNGRIE EIES, EVEN TILL THEY WINCK
                            WITH FULNESSE            3.56.6
  MINE EYES THEN ONLY WINKE, FOR SPITE PERCHANCE    4.98.13
WINTER                   13
  AND $WINTER WOES, FOR SPRING OF YOUTH UNFIT       1.24.8
  NOW USE THE $SOMMER SMILES, ERE $WINTER LOWERS    1.40.4
  WHEN WINTER SNOWES UPON THY SABLE HAIRES          1.41.14
  WHEN WINTER SNOWES UPON THY SABLE HAIRES          1.42.1
  MAKES $SUMMER $WINTER, $AUTUMNE IN THE $SPRING    2.147.11
  TO HIDIOUS WINTER AND CONFOUNDS HIM THERE         3.5.6
  BUT FLOWERS DISTIL'D THOUGH THEY WITH
                            WINTER MEETE             3.5.13
  AS CAL IT $WINTER, WHICH BEING FUL OF CARE        3.56.13
  HOW LIKE A $WINTER HATH MY ABSENCE BEENE          3.97.1
  YET SEEM'D IT $WINTER STILL, AND YOU AWAY         3.98.13
  GONE IS THE WINTER OF MY MISERIE                  4.69.7
  GRIEFE BUT $LOVE'S WINTER LIVERIE IS, THE $BOY    4.70.7
  THAT LIVING THUS IN BLACKEST WINTER NIGHT         4.89.13
WINTERS                  3
  WHEN FORTIE $WINTERS SHALL BESEIGE THY BROW       3.2.1
  THAT LEAVES LOOKE PALE, DREADING THE $WINTERS
                            NEERE                    3.97.14
  SUCH SEEMES YOUR BEAUTIE STILL.. $THREE
                            $WINTERS COLDE           3.104.3
WINTER'S                 4
  THEN LET NOT WINTERS WRAGGED HAND DEFACE          3.6.1
  AGAINST THE STORMY GUSTS OF WINTERS DAY           3.13.11
  AND CALLING FORTH OUT OF SAD $WINTERS NIGHT       5.4.5
  YET IN HER WINTERS BOWRE NOT WELL AWAKE           5.70.6
WINTER-WITHERED          1
  WHICH, THEN PRESENTS HER WINTER-WITHERED HEW      1.38.10
WIPED                    1
  AND EEK MY NAME BEE WYPED OUT LYKEWIZE            5.75.8
WIRE                     1
  WHEN GOLDEN HAIRES SHALL CHANGE TO SILVER WIER    1.38.2
WIRES                    2
  IF HAIRES BE WIERS, BLACK WIERS GROW ON HER HEAD  3.130.4
  IF HAIRES BE WIERS, BLACK WIERS GROW ON HER HEAD  3.130.4
WIRY                     1
  THE WIRY CONCORD THAT MINE EARE CONFOUNDS         3.128.4
WISDOM                   2
  CONCEITE OF $ANGELS, WHICH ALL WISDOM TEACHEST    2.146.10
  HEREIN LIVES WISDOME, BEAUTY, AND INCREASE        3.11.5
WISDOM'S                 4
  TO $WISEDOME'S SELFE TO MINISTER DIRECTION        2.34.7
  SURE YOU SAY WELL, YOUR WISDOME'S GOLDEN MINE     4.21.12
  OF $ATLAS TYR'D, YOUR WISEDOME'S HEAV'NLY SWAY    4.51.8
  SWEETNER OF MUSICKE, WISEDOME'S BEAUTIFIER        4.80.6
WISE                     19
  AND CAUSE HER LEAVE TO TRIUMPH IN THIS WISE       1.10.9
  WHICH HERE I YEELD I LAMENTABLE WISE              1.57.6
  SOME WISE IN SHEW, MORE $FOOLES INDEED THEN THEY  2.22.14
  AGAINST THESE $FOLKES, THAT THINKE THEMSELVES
                            SO WISE                 2.28.3
```

```
NOR YET WISE $REASON ABSOLUTELY KNOWES              2.46.4
WISE IN $CONCEIT, IN $ACT A VERY SOT                2.62.6
WISE IN CONCEITE, IN ACTE A VERY SOT                2.150.6
LEAST THE WISE WORLD SHOULD LOOKE INTO YOUR MONE    3.71.13
BE WISE AS THOU ART CRUELL, DO NOT PRESSE           3.140.1
WOULD SHE IN BEAMIE BLACKE, LIKE PAINTER WISE       4.7.3
THE WISEST SCHOLLER OF THE WIGHT MOST WISE          4.25.1
THAT I HAD BENE MORE FOOLISH OR MORE WISE           4.33.14
'BUT WILL NOT WISE MEN THINKE THY WORDS
                            FOND WARE+'              4.34.7
AS MY YOUNG $DOVE MAY IN YOUR PRECEPTS WISE         4.63.3
IN THIS OLD WORLD, GROWNE NOW SO TOO TOO WISE       4.65.6
WISE SILENCE IS BEST MUSICKE UNTO BLISSE            4.70.14
NE NONE SO RICH OR WISE, SO STRONG OR FAYRE         5.58.9
USED $TROPHEES TO ERECT IN STATELY WIZE             5.69.2
THROGH WHICH HER WORDS SO WISE DO MAKE THEIR WAY    5.81.11
WISER                       2
NOR OLDER YET, NOR WISER MADE BY YEERES             2.22.3
NO WISER I, THEN WHEN AS YOUNG AS HE                2.22.10
WISEST                      1
THE WISEST SCHOLLER OF THE WIGHT MOST WISE          4.25.1
WISE-VALIANT                1
NOR THAT HE COULD YOUNG-WISE, WISE-VALIANT FRAME    4.75.5
WISH                        19
WISH TO BE PRESENT, AND YET SHUN T'APPEARE          1.20.4
WELL COULD I WISH, IT WOULD BE EVER $DAY            2.37.13
WISH NOW TO BE TRANS-FORMD INTO MY HART             2.133.8
WITH VERTUOUS WISH WOULD BEARE YOUR LIVING
                            FLOWERS                  3.16.7
LOOKE WHAT IS BEST, THAT BEST I WISH IN THEE        3.37.13
THIS WISH I HAVE, THEN TEN TIMES HAPPY ME           3.37.14
O FOR MY SAKE DOE YOU WISH FORTUNE CHIDE            3.111.1
PITTY ME THEN, AND WISH I WERE RENJ'DE              3.111.8
WHO EVER HATH HER WISH, THOU HAST THY $WILL         3.135.1
NOR HOPE, NOR WISHE ANOTHER COURSE TO FRAME         4.64.12
OF HIGHEST WISH, I WISH YOU SO MUCH BLISSE          4.84.13
OF HIGHEST WISH, I WISH YOU SO MUCH BLISSE          4.84.13
IN TRUTH I SWEARE, I WISH NOT THERE SHOULD BE       4.90.7
DOTH MAKE ME MOST TO WISH THY COMFORT NEERE         4.106.8
AND WISH THAT MORE AND GREATER THEY MIGHT BE        5.25.13
NE DOE I WISH (FOR WISHING WERE BUT VAINE)          5.42.5
HART NEED NOT WISH NONE OTHER HAPPINESSE            5.72.13
I WISH THAT NIGHT THE NOYOUS DAY WOULD END          5.87.6
I WISH THAT DAY WOULD SHORTLY REASCEND              5.87.8
WISHED                      4
INTREATED ME, AS E'R I WISH'D HIS GOOD              2.21.3
MAKES $SOMERS WELCOME, THRICE MORE WISH'D,
                            MORE RARE                3.56.14
I RATHER WISHT THEE CLIME THE $MUSES' HILL          4.10.3
WHICH OFT I WISHT, YET NEVER WAS SO BLEST           5.76.14
WISHES                      2
AND RACKE HER WITH A THOUSAND HOLY WISHES           2.115.14
WITH THANKES AND WISHES, WISHING THANKFULLY         4.84.8
WISHETH                     1
WISHETH TO BE TRANSFORMED TO MY $SIGHT              2.33.3
WISHFUL                     1
AND IN HER SONGS SENDS MANY A WISHFULL VOW          5.89.3
WISHING                     5
WISHING THEMSELVES, THAT THEY HAD BEENE MY $HEART   2.33.8
WISHING TO BE TRANS-FORMD INTO MY SIGHT             2.133.3
```

```
        WISHING ME LIKE TO ONE MORE RICH IN HOPE                3.29.5
        WITH THANKES AND WISHES, WISHING THANKFULLY             4.84.8
        NE DOE I WISH (FOR WISHING WERE BUT VAINE)              5.42.5
WIT                   50
        THE $GODDESSES OF $MEMORY AND $WIT                      2.4.3
        I HOLD THAT VILE, WHICH $VULGAR WIT AFFORDS             2.4.11
        TIS NINE YEERES NOW SINCE FIRST I LOST MY $WIT          2.9.11
        WHERE $VERTUE, $HONOUR, $WIT, AND $BEAUTIE LAY          2.14.10
        MUCH LIKE HIS $WIT, THAT WAS TO USE THE SAME            2.21.8
        AND I LOSE YOU, FOR ALL MY $WIT AND $PAINES             2.21.14
        THINK'ST THOU, MY $WIT SHALL KEEPE THE
                                PACK-$HORSE $WAY                2.31.7
        IN $PRIDE OF $WIT, WHEN HIGH DESIRE OF $FAME            2.47.1
        TO HEARE WIT EIES BELONGS TO LOVES FINE WIHT            3.23.14
        TO HEARE WIT EIES BELONGS TO LOVES FINE WIHT            3.23.14
        TO WITNESSE DUTY, NOT TO SHEW MY WIT                    3.26.4
        DUTY SO GREAT, WHICH WIT SO POORE AS MINE               3.26.5
        FOR WHETHER BEAUTY, BIRTH, OR WEALTH, OR WIT            3.37.5
        AND SUCH A COUNTER-PART SHALL FAME HIS WIT              3.84.11
        IF I MIGHT TEACH THEE WITTE BETTER IT WEARE             3.140.5
        AND NOW EMPLOY THE REMNANT OF MY WIT                    4.2.12
        THOU SETST A BATE BETWEENE MY WILL AND WIT              4.4.2
        ANOTHER HUMBLER WIT TO SHEPHEARD'S PIPE RETIRES         4.6.7
        WITH SWORD OF WIT, GIVING WOUNDS OF DISPRAISE           4.10.10
        SO FORTIFIED WITH WIT, STOR'D WITH DISDAINE             4.12.13
        READIE OF WIT AND FEARING NOUGHT BUT SHAME              4.14.11
        WITH NEW-BORNE SIGHES AND DENISEND WIT DO SING          4.15.8
        MY WIT DOTH STRIVE THOSE PASSIONS TO DEFEND             4.18.10
        'SCHOLLER,' SAITH $LOVE, 'BEND HITHERWARD
                                YOUR WIT'                       4.19.14
        YET TO THOSE FOOLES HEAV'N SUCH WIT DOTH IMPART         4.24.5
        IS CONSTANT $LOVE DEEM'D THERE BUT WANT OF WIT+         4.31.10
        WHILE TOO MUCH WIT (FORSOOTH) SO TROUBLED ME            4.33.10
        PEACE, FOOLISH WIT, WITH WIT MY WIT IS MARD             4.34.11
        PEACE, FOOLISH WIT, WITH WIT MY WIT IS MARD             4.34.11
        PEACE, FOOLISH WIT, WITH WIT MY WIT IS MARD             4.34.11
        WIT LEARNES IN THEE PERFECTION TO EXPRESSE              4.35.12
        THE BAITING PLACE OF WIT, THE BALME OF WOE              4.39.2
        TO WITLESSE THINGS, THEN $LOVE I HOPE (SINCE WIT        4.59.13
        I DO NOT ENVIE $ARISTOTLE'S WIT                         4.64.9
        THOU ART MY $WIT, AND THOU MY $VERTUE ART               4.64.14
        I AM NO PICK-PURSE OF ANOTHER'S WIT                     4.74.8
        SINCE BEST WITS THINKE IT WIT THEE TO ADMIRE            4.80.2
        AND I, MAD WITH DELIGHT, WANT WIT TO CEASE              4.81.13
        FOR THOUGH FULL OF DESIRE, EMPTIE OF WIT                4.82.9
        LET EARES HEARE SPEECH, WHICH WIT TO WONDER TIES        4.85.11
        FOR NOTHING FROM MY WIT OR WILL DOTH FLOW               4.90.12
        BUT WIT CONFUS'D WITH TOO MUCH CARE DID MISSE           4.93.8
        WHOM SHE IMPLOYES, DISMISSE FROM THEE MY WIT            4.107.10
        THE WONDER THAT MY WIT CANNOT ENDITE                    5.3.14
        DOE BEAT ON TH'ANDUYLE OF HER STUBBERNE WIT             5.32.8
        HOW THEN SHOULD I WITHOUT ANOTHER WIT                   5.33.9
        LYKEST IT SEEMETH IN MY SIMPLE WIT                      5.40.5
        WHICH HER DEEP WIT, THAT TRUE HARTS THOUGHT
                                CAN SPEL                        5.43.13
        BUT THE TREW FAYRE, THAT IS THE GENTLE WIT              5.79.3
        SOM HEVENLY WIT, WHOSE VERSE COULD HAVE ENCHASED        5.82.7
WIT-BEATEN                 1
        NOW I, WIT-BEATEN LONG BY HARDEST $FATE                 4.60.9
```

```
WITHAL                          6
  YET MORE TO GRACE THE $COMPANY WITHALL            2.7.3
  MAKING WITHALL SOME FILTHY $ANTIKE $FACE          2.31.4
  AND I AM GLAD, YEA GLAD WITHALL MY HEART          2.61.3
  I SICK WITHALL THE HELPE OF BATH DESIRED          3.153.11
  IN SWEETEST STRENGTH, SC SWEETLY SKILD WITHALL    4.36.10
  USE SOMETHING ELSE TO CHAST'N ME WITHALL          4.86.12
WITHDRAW                        1
  LET HEAVENS WITHDRAW THEIR SWEET $AMBROZIAN
                                    BREATH          2.145.11
WITHER                          1
  AND LEARNE TO GATHER FLCWERS BEFORE THEY WITHER   1.51.6
WITHERED                        4
  MY FLOWER UNTIMELY'S WITHRED WITH MY TEARES       1.24.7
  NO $APRILL CAN REVIVE THY WITHERED FLOWRES        1.39.9
  AND ALL LIES WITHRED THAT WAS HELD SO DEERE       1.42.4
  WITH WITHERED BROWES, ALL WRINCKLED WITH
                                    DISPAIRES       2.114.3
WITHERING                       1
  THY LOVERS WITHERING, AS THY SWEET SELFE GROW'ST  3.126.4
WITHIN                          31
  LIVE RECONCILED FRIENDS WITHIN HER BROW           1.6.10
  FOR HER THE CRUELL $FAIRE, WITHIN WHOSE BROW      1.10.2
  T'HAVE PEACE ABROAD, AND NOUGHT WITHIN BUT STRIFE 1.20.3
  AND I (THOUGH BORNE WITHIN A COLDER CLIME)        1.43.5
  WITHIN THEMSELVES, AND CN THEM PLOUGHS HAVE EAR'D 1.45.4
  AND LET THE $BARDS WITHIN THAT $IRISH $ILE        2.25.9
  GAVE IT TO KEEPE TC $SPIRITS WITHIN THE $GROUND   2.58.4
  WITHIN THE $TEMPLE CF THY SACRED NAME             2.105.6
  IT IS THY HEAVEN WITHIN HER FACE TO DWELL         2.123.13
  MERIDIANIS SITS WITHIN A MAZE                     2.151.8
  WITHIN THINE OWNE BUD BURIEST THY CONTENT         3.1.11
  TO SAY WITHIN THINE OWNE DEEPE SUNKEN EYES        3.2.7
  WITHIN THE GENTLE CLOSURE OF MY BREST             3.48.11
  WITHIN THE KNOWLEDGE OF MINE OWNE DESART          3.49.10
  LEANE PENURIE WITHIN THAT $PEN DOTH DWELL         3.84.5
  WITHIN HIS BENDING SICKLES COMPASSE COME          3.116.10
  BRING ME WITHIN THE LEVEL OF YOUR FROWNE          3.117.11
  DISTIL'D FROM $LYMBECKS FOULE AS HELL WITHIN      3.119.2
  TTHY GUIFT,, THY TABLES, ARE WITHIN MY BRAINE     3.122.1
  WHY DOST THOU PINE WITHIN AND SUFFER DEARTH       3.146.3
  WITHIN BE FED, WITHCUT BE RICH NO MORE            3.146.12
  BREATHE OUT THE FLAMES WHICH BURNE WITHIN
                                    MY HEART        4.28.13
  WITHIN WHAT BOUNDS CAN CNE HIS LIKING STAY        4.35.3
  MY FORCES RAZDE, THY BANNERS RAISD WITHIN         4.36.6
  CANNOT BE STAID WITHIN MY PANTING BREAST          4.50.2
  MAY KINDLE LIVING FIRE WITHIN MY BREST            5.7.12
  YOU FRAME MY THOUGHTS AND FASHION ME WITHIN       5.8.9
  HER TEMPLE FAYRE IS BUILT WITHIN MY MIND          5.22.5
  WITHIN MY HART, THCUGH HARDLY IT CAN SHEW         5.45.5
  WITHIN A BUSH HIS DREADFULL HEAD DOTH HIDE        5.53.3
  WITHIN HER CAGE, BUT SINGES AND FEEDS HER FILL    5.65.8
WITHOUT                         30
  MINERVA-LIKE, BROUGHT FCORTH WITHOUT A MOTHER     1.2.2
  WHAT IT IS TO BREATHE AND LIVE WITHOUT LIFE       1.20.1
  AS ONE THAT DIES WITHOUT HER COMPANY              1.25.8
  LIVES WITHOUT HONCUR, DIES WITHOUT A NAME         1.35.11
  LIVES WITHOUT HONCUR, DIES WITHOUT A NAME         1.35.11
  NOW WHILST THY BEAUTY BEARES WITHOUT A STAINE     1.40.3
```

```
WITHOUT THE TORMENT OF THE NIGHTS UNTRUTH            1.54.8
WHICH ON THE $LIVING WORKE WITHOUT REMORSE           2.50.5
WITHOUT THIS FOLLIE, AGE, AND COULD DECAY            3.11.6
AND MAKE ME TRAVAILE FORTH WITHOUT MY CLOAKE         3.34.2
WITHOUT THY HELPE, BY ME BE BORNE ALONE              3.36.4
NOR DARE I CHIDE THE WORLD WITHOUT END HOURE         3.57.5
WITHOUT ACCUSING YCU OF INJURY                       3.58.8
WITHOUT ALL ORNAMENT, IT SELFE AND TRUE              3.68.10
AND THEREFORE MAIEST WITHOUT ATTAINT ORE-LOOKE       3.82.2
WITHIN BE FED, WITHOUT BE RICH NO MORE               3.146.12
OF TOUCH THEY ARE THAT WITHOUT TOUCH DOTH TOUCH      4.9.12
HOW $POLES' RIGHT KING MEANES, WITHOUT
                          LEAVE OF HOAST             4.30.3
WITHOUT DESIRE TO FEED CF FURTHER GRACE              4.46.8
TILL WITHOUT FEWELL YOU CAN MAKE HOT FIRE            4.46.14
FAR FAR TOO LONG TO LEARNE IT WITHOUT BOOKE          4.56.2
WHAT, A WHOLE WEEKE WITHOUT ONE PEECE OF LOOKE       4.56.3
THAT I LOVE NOT, WITHOUT I LEAVE TO LOVE             4.61.14
THAT HAND, WHICH WITHOUT TOUCH HOLDS MORE
                          THEN $ATLAS MIGHT          4.77.5
WITHOUT HOW FARRE THIS PRAISE IS SHORT OF YOU        4.80.13
WITHOUT MY PLUMES FROM CTHERS' WINGS I TAKE          4.90.11
WITHOUT SOME SPARK CF SUCH SELF-PLEASING PRIDE       5.5.14
HOW THEN SHOULD I WITHOUT ANOTHER WIT                5.33.9
WITHOUT HOPE OF ASWAGEMENT OR RELEASE+               5.36.4
WITHOUT CONSTRAYNT CR DREAD OF ANY ILL               5.65.6
```

WITLESS   3
```
A $WITLESSE $GALLANT, A YOUNG $WENCH THAT WOO'D      2.21.1
TO WITLESSE THINGS, THEN $LOVE I HOPE (SINCE WIT     4.59.13
BEGIN HIS WITLESSE NOTE APACE TO CLATTER             5.85.4
```

WITNESS   10
```
WITNESSE YOUR $FATHERS GRIEFE EXCEEDES ALL OTHER     1.2.4
MY BREATH THAT CALLS THE HEAVENS TO WITNES IT        1.21.10
FAITH BEING WITH BLCOD, AND FIVE YEARES
                          WITNES SIGN'D              1.31.6
TO WITNESSE DUTY, NCT TC SHEW MY WIT                 3.26.4
TO THIS I WITNES CALL THE FOLES OF TIME              3.124.13
ONE ON ANOTHERS NECKE DC WITNESSE BEARE              3.131.11
WITNESSE OF LIFE TC THEM THAT LIVING DIE             4.32.2
WITNESSE WITH ME, THAT MY FOULE STUMBLING SO         4.93.6
BUT CEASE MINE EYES, YOUR TEARES DO WITNESSE
                          WELL                       4.105.9
WITNESSE THE WORLC HOW WCRTHY TO BE PRAYZED          5.3.2
```

WITS   18
```
OR THAT MY WITS HAVE SHEWED THE BEST THEY COULD      1.44.3
WHICH WELL THE REACH OF THEIR HIGH WITS RECORDS      1.55.4
(NOT TOO FARRE PAST) MAY TO THEIR $WITS
                          BE BROUGHT                 2.9.14
SOME WITS THERE BE, WHICH LYKE MY METHOD WELL        2.128.1
OH SURE I AM THE WITS OF FORMER DAIES                3.59.13
BUT MY FIVE WITS, NCR MY FIVE SENCES CAN             3.141.9
STUDYING INVENTIONS FINE, HER WITS TO ENTERTAINE     4.1.6
LET DAINTIE WITS CRIE ON THE $SISTERS NINE           4.3.1
MY BEST WITS STILL THEIR OWNE DISGRACE INVENT        4.19.5
MY WITS, QUICKE IN VAINE THOUGHTS, IN VERTUE LAME    4.21.4
THE CURIOUS WITS, SEEING DULL PENSIVENESSE           4.23.1
THOUGH DUSTIE WITS DARE SCORNE $ASTROLOGIE           4.26.1
THESE QUESTIONS BUSIE WITS TO ME DO FRAME            4.30.12
SOME LUCKIE WITS IMPUTE IT BUT TO CHAUNCE            4.41.8
IN VERSE, AND THAT MY VERSE BEST WITS
                          DOTH PLEASE+               4.74.11
```

```
SINCE BEST WITS THINKE IT WIT THEE TO ADMIRE          4.80.2
ENVIOUS WITS WHAT HATH BENE MINE OFFENCE              4.104.1
DISGUYSING DIVERSLY MY TROUBLED WITS                  5.54.4
```
WITTY   1
```
THAT WITTIE $LEWIS TO HIM A TRIBUTE PAID              4.75.11
```
WOE   47
```
HARD IS HER HART, AND WOE IS ME THEREFORE             1.13.12
SO MUCH I PLEASE TC PERISH IN MY WOE                  1.14.12
THE WAILING $ILIADS OF MY TRAGICKE WOE                1.47.2
WHEN EVERY PLACE PRESENTS LIKE FACE OF WOE            1.52.3
TAKING MY $PENNE, WITH $WORDS TO CAST MY $WOE         2.3.1
MUST $WOE AND I, HAVE NAUGHT BUT $NO AND I+           2.5.9
MY $SIGHES BE SPENT IN UTT'RING OF MY $WOE            2.41.7
YET READE AT LAST THE STCRIE OF MY $WOE               2.54.1
A HASTIE $MAN (QUOTH HE) NE'R WANTED $WOE             2.59.8
RAVISH'D WITH $JOY AMID'ST A HELL OF $WOE             2.62.7
READE HEERE (SWEET $MAYD) THE STORY OF MY WO          2.101.1
THAT I CAN READE A STORY OF MY WOE                    2.111.14
PAYNTED THE BLACKEST $IMAGE OF MY WOE                 2.114.11
THUS WAS THE WANTCN CAUSE OF HYS OWNE WOE             2.122.12
AND YOU MY SIGHES, $SYMTCMAS OF MY WOE                2.141.5
MYNE EYES WANT TEARES THUS TO BEWAYLE MY WOE          2.143.5
BLACKE PYTCHY $NIGHT, CCMPANYON OF MY WOE             2.145.1
RAVISHT WITH JOY, AMIDST A HELL OF WOE                2.150.7
AND WEEPE A FRESH LCVES LONG SINCE CANCELD WOE        3.30.7
AND HEAVILY FROM WOE TO WOE TELL ORE                  3.30.10
AND HEAVILY FROM WOE TO WOE TELL ORE                  3.30.10
BUT HEAVIE TEARES, BADGES OF EITHERS WOE              3.44.14
THE BEAST THAT BEARES ME, TIRED WITH MY WOE           3.50.5
IF THINKING ON ME THEN SHOULD MAKE YOU WOE            3.71.8
COME IN THE REREWARD OF A CONQUERD WOE                3.90.6
AND OTHER STRAINES CF WOE, WHICH NOW SEEME WOE        3.90.13
AND OTHER STRAINES CF WOE, WHICH NOW SEEME WOE        3.90.13
O THAT OUR NIGHT CF WO MIGHT HAVE REMEMBRED           3.120.9
YET SO THEY MOURNE BECCMMING OF THEIR WOE             3.127.13
A BLISSE IN PROOFE AND PROUD AND VERY WO              3.129.11
I SOUGHT FIT WORDS TO PAINT THE BLACKEST
                         FACE OF WOE                  4.1.5
THE BAITING PLACE CF WIT, THE BALME OF WOE            4.39.2
STELLA OFT SEES THE VERIE FACE OF WO                  4.45.1
WO, HAVING MADE WITH MANY FIGHTS HIS OWNE             4.57.1
WHICH WOOED WO, MOST RAVISHING DELIGHT                4.58.13
LATE TYR'D WITH WO, EVEN READY FOR TO PINE            4.62.1
OR DOTH THE TEDIOUS BURD'N OF LONG WO                 4.66.2
MY FRIEND, THAT OFT SAW THROUGH ALL MASKES MY WO      4.69.5
BENIGHTED IN COLD WO, BUT NOW APPEARES MY DAY         4.76.3
SO MANIE EYES AY SEEKING THEIR OWNE WOE               4.78.12
LET WO GRIPE ON MY HEART, SHAME LOADE MINE EYE        4.86.4
I SIGHD HER SIGHES, AND WAILED FOR HER WO             4.87.10
WHAT INKE IS BLACKE INOUGH TO PAINT MY WC+            4.93.3
SEEING HOPE YEELD WHEN THIS WO STRAKE HIM FURST       4.95.6
BUT WO IS ME, THOUGH JOY IT SELFE WERE SHE            4.97.12
MERY WITH HIM, AND NOT THINKE OF HIS WOE              4.106.14
AND TAKE DELIGHT T'ENCREASE A WRETCHES WOE            5.41.7
```
WOEFUL   4
```
I VIEW MY SELFE, MY SELFE IN WOFULL CASE              1.29.8
MY WOFULL $HEART, IMPRISON'D IN MY $BREST             2.33.2
MY WOFULL HART IMPRISOND IN MY BREAST                 2.133.2
BUT WHEN SHE SAW MY WOFULL STATE                      3.145.4
```

WOES   19
    AND $WINTER WOES, FCR SPRING OF YOUTH UNFIT   1.24.8
    AND $FATES AND $FURIES, WITH THEIR WOES ACQUAINT   2.39.4
    IN GRIEVOUS $PASSICNS, MY $WOES STILL BEMONING   2.40.8
    IT PLEASETH ME, IF I MY $WOES REHEARSE   2.42.11
    EXPRESSE MY $WOES, AND SHEW THE PAINES OF $HELL   2.60.2
    OFT TAKING PEN IN HAND, WITH WORDS TO
                          CAST MY WOES   2.110.1
    THUS MIDST A THOUSAND WCES, TEN THOUSAND
                          JOYES ARISE   2.114.8
    AND HEAVEN, AND EARTH, DOE WITH THEIR
                          WOES ACQUAINT   2.118.4
    IN GREEVOUS PASSICNS MY WOES STYLL BEMONING   2.144.8
    EXPRESSE MY WOES, AND SHEW THE PAYNES OF HELL   2.149.2
    FOR ALL MY WOES, THAT ONELY SHALL SUFFISE   2.151.4
    AND WITH OLD WOES NEW WAILE MY DEARE TIMES WASTE   3.30.4
    AND WHEN A WOMAN WCES, WHAT WOMANS SONNE   3.41.7
    YOU THAT POORE $PETRARCH'S LONG DECEASED WOES   4.15.7
    TH' ANATOMY OF ALL MY WCES I WRATE   4.58.10
    THAT IN MY WOES FCR THEE THOU ART MY JOY   4.108.13
    THEN ALL THE WOES AND WRECKS WHICH I ABICE   5.25.11
    TELL ME WHEN SHALL THESE WEARIE WOES HAVE END   5.36.1
    I WAILE AND MAKE MY WOES A $TRAGEDY   5.54.8
WOE'S   3
    THE THOROWEST WORDS, FIT FOR WOE'S SELFE TO GRONE   4.57.4
    WITH THAT FAIRE BREAST MAKING WOE'S DARKNESSE
                          CLEARE   4.57.11
    PAINT WOE'S BLACKE FACE SO LIVELY TO MY SIGHT   4.98.10
WOLF   1
    HOW MANY $LAMBS MIGHT THE STERNE $WOLFE BETRAY   3.96.9
WOLVES   1
    LET $WOLVES AND $BEARES BE CHARMED WITH
                          MY $VERSE   2.25.14
WOMAN   9
    THAT $GRACE WHICH DOTH MORE THEN IN WOMAN THEE   1.45.13
    AND LET HER TELL ME AS SHE IS A WOMAN   1.49.11
    INTO THE SAME THEN LET A $WOMAN BREATHE   2.15.9
    ONE $WOMAN NOW, MAKES THREE ODDE $NUMBERS EVEN   2.18.4
    ONE WONDER WOMAN NCW MAKES THREE OD NUMBERS EVEN   2.108.4
    AND FOR A WOMAN WERT THCU FIRST CREATED   3.20.9
    AND WHEN A WOMAN WCES, WHAT WOMANS SONNE   3.41.7
    THE WORSER SPIRIT A WOMAN COLLOUR'D IL   3.144.4
    SHE IS NO WOMAN, BUT A SENCELESSE STONE   5.54.14
WOMAN'S   3
    A $WOMANS FACE WITH NATURES OWNE HAND PAINTED   3.20.1
    A WOMANS GENTLE HART BUT NOT ACQUAINTED   3.20.3
    AND WHEN A WOMAN WCES, WHAT WOMANS SONNE   3.41.7
WOMB   4
    FOR WHERE IS SHE SC FAIRE WHOSE UN-EARD WOMBE   3.3.5
    MAKING THEIR TOMBE THE WOMBE WHEREIN THEY GREW+   3.86.4
    TILL GREATER THEN MY WOMBE THOU WOXEN ART   5.2.4
    FROM MOTHERS WOMB DERIV'D BY DEW DESCENT   5.74.6
WOMBS   1
    LIKE WIDDOWED WOMBES AFTER THEIR $LORDS DECEASE   3.97.8
WOMEN   2
    FOR WOMEN GRIEVE TC THINKE THEY MUST BE OLD   1.50.14
    NINE WORTHIE $WOMEN TO THE $WORLD WERE GIVEN   2.18.8
WOMEN'S   3
    WITH SHIFTING CHANGE AS IS FALSE WOMENS FASHION   3.20.4
    WHICH STEALES MENS EYES AND WOMENS SOULES AMASETH   3.20.8

```
BUT SINCE SHE PRICKT THEE OUT FOR WOMENS
                              PLEASURE                3.20.13
WON                 8
   JOYES IN THAT HONOR WHICH HER EYES HAVE WONNE      1.53.7
   BUT WITH MY $VERSES HE HIS $MISTRES WONNE          2.21.9
   MY $SMELLING WONNE WITH HER $BREATHS $SPICERIE     2.29.8
   WONNE GRACE AND CREDIT IN THE $EARES OF $MEN       2.47.4
   BAD IS THE $MATCH, WHERE NEITHER PARTIE WONNE      2.63.4
   GENTLE THOU ART, AND THEREFORE TO BE WONNE         3.41.5
   THE HARDER WONNE, THE FIRMER WILL ABIDE            5.6.4
   SO GOODLY WONNE WITH HER OWNE WILL BEGUYLD         5.67.14
WONDER              31
   THE WONDER OF ALL EYES THAT LOOKE UPON HER         1.6.7
   TH'ETERNALL WONDER OF OUR HAPPY $ILE               1.53.8
   IF THOU WILT WONDER, HERE'S THE WONDER, $LOVE      2.34.13
   IF THOU WILT WONDER, HERE'S THE WONDER, $LOVE      2.34.13
   THAT THIS TO ME DOTH YET NO WONDER PROVE           2.34.14
   WITH HEAVENLY COLOURS DIDE, WITH NATURES
                              WONDER CROUND            2.106.4
   THAT WONDER NOW WHEREIN ALL WONDERS BE             2.107.3
   ONE WONDER WOMAN NOW MAKES THREE OD NUMBERS EVEN   2.108.4
   IF EVER WONDER COULD REPORT A WONDER               2.117.1
   IF EVER WONDER COULD REPORT A WONDER               2.117.1
   OR TONGUE OF WONDER WORTH COULD TELL A
                              WONDER THOUGHT           2.117.2
   OR TONGUE OF WONDER WORTH COULD TELL A
                              WONDER THOUGHT           2.117.2
   THEN WONDER, TONGUE, THEN JOY, MIGHT WEL
                              REPORT A WONDER          2.117.4
   THEN WONDER, TONGUE, THEN JOY, MIGHT WEL
                              REPORT A WONDER          2.117.4
   SHOULD TEACH THE WORLD TO KNOW THE WONDER
                              THAT I PROVE             2.117.14
   ONE, HE DOTH WONDER MONSTER-BREEDING $NYLE         2.120.3
   WONDER OF $HEAVEN, GLASSE OF DIVINITIE             2.123.1
   O OUR WORLDS WONDER, CROWNE OF HEAVEN ABOVE        2.129.9
   SLEEPES WONDER $BEAUTY, WONDERS TO WORLDS
                              IMPARTING                2.136.4
   TO THIS COMPOSED WONDER OF YOUR FRAME              3.59.10
   NOR DID I WONDER AT THE $LILLIES WHITE             3.98.9
   HAVE EYES TO WONDER, BUT LACK TOUNGS TO PRAISE     3.106.14
   PROMISING WONDERS, WONDER TO INVITE                4.26.4
   SERVICE AND $HONOR, WONDER WITH DELIGHT            4.72.9
   WHAT WONDER THEN IF HE HIS LESSON MISSE            4.73.3
   LET EARES HEARE SPEECH, WHICH WIT TO WONDER TIES   4.85.11
   WITH WINGS OF $LOVE IN AIRE OF WONDER FLIE         4.86.8
   THE WONDER THAT MY WIT CANNOT ENDITE               5.3.14
   THAT WONDER IS HOW I SHOULD LIVE A JOT             5.57.6
   RATHER THEN ENVY LET THEM WONDER AT HER            5.85.7
   LET THE WORLD CHOSE TO ENVY OR TO WONDER           5.85.14
WONDERFUL           1
   SHOULD KINDLE FYRE BY WONDERFULL DEVYSE+           5.30.12
WONDERING           2
   MORE THEN HIS WOND'RING UTT'RANCE CAN UNFOLD       2.57.10
   NOT WONDRING AT THE PRESENT, NOR THE PAST          3.123.10
WONDERMENT          4
   IT RAVISHT IS WITH FANCIES WONDERMENT              5.3.12
   WHEN I BEHOLD THAT BEAUTIES WONDERMENT             5.24.1
   THAT MAY ADMIRE SUCH WORLDS RARE WONDERMENT        5.69.12
   THE REST BE WORKS OF NATURES WONDERMENT            5.81.13
```

```
WONDERS                        9
   YORKE MANY $WONDERS OF HER $OWSE CAN TELL          2.32.6
   SO MAY THE $HEAVENS READ WONDERS IN MY $HEART      2.60.8
   THAT WONDER NOW WHEREIN ALL WONDERS BE             2.107.3
   POORE $BROOKES AND $BANKS HAD NO SUCH
                           WONDERS BEENE              2.120.14
   YORKE, MANY WONDERS OF HER $OUSE CAN TELL          2.124.6
   SLEEPES WONDER $BEAUTY, WONDERS TO WORLDS
                           IMPARTING                  2.136.4
   IN SECRET SILENCE, WHICH SUCH WONDERS PREACHEST    2.146.12
   SO MAY THE HEAVENS READE WONDERS IN MY HART        2.149.8
   PROMISING WONDERS, WONDER TO INVITE                4.26.4
WONDROUS                       5
   STILL CONSTANT IN A WONDROUS EXCELLENCE            3.105.6
   THREE THEAMS IN ONE, WHICH WONDROUS SCOPE
                           AFFORDS                    3.105.12
   AT WONDROUS SIGHT CF SO CELESTIALL HEW             5.3.8
   WHAT WONDROUS VERTUE IS CONTAYND IN YOU            5.7.2
   YET MANY WONDROUS THINGS THERE ARE BESIDE          5.17.8
WONT                           7
   WHEN I WAS WONT TC GREET IT WITH MY LAIES          3.102.6
   SINCE $STELLA'S EYES, WONT TO GIVE ME MY DAY       4.89.3
   THEN THOSE SMALL FCRTS WHICH YE WERE WONT BELAY    5.14.6
   SO I WHOSE STAR, THAT WCNT WITH HER BRIGHT RAY     5.34.5
   BUT MY RUDE MUSICK, WHICH WAS WONT TO PLEASE       5.38.5
   EVEN SO MY HART, THAT WCNT ON YOUR FAYRE EYE       5.73.7
   THE WHICH WAS WONT TO LEAD MY THOUGHTS ASTRAY      5.88.2
WONTS                          1
   WITH WHICH SHE WONTS TO TEMPER ANGRY $JOVE         5.39.3
WOO                            1
   WHOME THINE EYES WCOE AS MINE IMPORTUNE THEE       3.142.10
WOOD                           3
   WHERE, WITH SWEET $WOOD, LAYD CURIOUSLY BY $ART    2.30.5
   UPON THAT BLESSED WCOD WHOSE MOTION SOUNDS         3.128.2
   MAKING DEAD WOOD MCRE BLEST THEN LIVING LIPS       3.128.12
WOODBIND                       1
   WITH WOODBYND FLOWERS AND FRAGRANT $EGLANTINE      5.71.10
WOOD-GLOBES                    1
   MODELS SUCH BE WOOD-GLOBES OF GLISTRING SKIES      4.91.11
WOODS                          2
   YET GOE (FORSAKEN) LEAVE THESE $WOODS,
                           THESE PLAINES              1.52.5
   THAT ALL THE WOODS THEYR ECCHOES BACK REBCUNCED    5.19.7
WOOD'S                         1
   AT THE WOODS BOULDNES BY THEE BLUSHING STAND       3.128.8
WOOED                          4
   A $WITLESSE $GALLANT, A YOUNG $WENCH THAT WOO'D    2.21.1
   THEIR WORTH THE GREATER BEEING WOO'D OF TIME       3.70.6
   CALD IT ANEW, AND WCOED SLEEPE AGAINE              4.38.13
   WHICH WOOED WO, MCST RAVISHING DELIGHT             4.58.13
WOOERS                         1
   DEVIZ'D A $WEB HER WOOERS TO DECEAVE               5.23.2
WOOING                         1
   WOOING HIS PURITY WITH HER FOWLE PRIDE             3.144.8
WOOS                           1
   THE NIGHT AS TEDIOUS, WCOES TH'APPROCH OF DAY      4.89.6
WORD                           12
   THAT BEING CHID, DID NEVER WORD REPLIE             2.15.10
   NOR NEVER STOOD ONE WORD THEREOF TO BLOT           2.21.7
   THAT EVERY WORD DCTH ALMOST FEL MY NAME            3.76.7
```

```
HE LENDS THEE VERTUE, AND HE STOLE THAT WORD        3.79.9
WELL STAID WITH TRUTH IN WORD AND FAITH OF DEED     4.14.10
I MIGHT, UNHAPPIE WORD, O ME, I MIGHT               4.33.1
I CANNOT BRAG OF WORD, MUCH LESSE OF DEED           4.66.5
THAT TO EACH WORD, NAY SIGH OF MINE YOU HARKE       4.104.3
NO WORD WAS HEARD OF HER THAT MOST IT OUGHT         5.19.10
AND WITH ONE WORD MY WHOLE YEARS WORK DOTH REND     5.23.12
YET WITH ONE WORD SHE CAN IT SAVE OR SPILL          5.38.11
BUT SPEAKE NO WORD TO HER OF THESE SAD PLIGHTS      5.84.11
WORDS            67
BEWRAIES MY LOVE, WITH BROKEN WORDS HALFE SPOKEN    1.15.6
HOW TO THINKE MUCH, AND HAVE NO WORDS TO SPEAKE     1.20.6
IN AGED ACCENTS, AND UNTIMELY WORDS                 1.55.2
TAKING MY $PENNE, WITH $WORDS TO CAST MY $WOE       2.3.1
LET OTHERS STRIVE TO ENTERTAINE WITH $WORDS         2.4.9
PAPER AND $INKE CAN PAINT BUT NAKED $WORDS          2.13.5
MY $WORDS THE $HAMMERS, FASHIONING MY DESIRE        2.40.2
AND I WANT WORDS, WHEREWITH TO TELL MY $WRONG       2.41.8
AND IN BARE WORDS PAINT OUT MY $PASSIONS PAINE      2.42.7
FAIRE WORDS MAKE $FOOLES, REPLYETH HE AGAINE        2.59.4
OFT TAKING PEN IN HAND, WITH WORDS TO
                           CAST MY WOES             2.110.1
WORDS CONSONANT, AND SOUNDING TO THY FAME           2.111.8
KINDE WORDS UNKINDEST MEATE I CAN DEVISE            2.115.11
MY WORDS MIGHT IMITATE MY DEEREST THOUGHTS
                           DIRECTION                2.117.7
PAPER AND YNCKE, CAN PAYNT BUT NAKED WORDS          2.121.5
AND IN BARE WORDS PAYNT OUT MY PASSIONS PAYNE       2.128.7
WORDS, THOUGHTS, AND DEEDS, DEVOTED TO HER HONOR    2.138.6
COMMIT MY WORDS UNTO THE FLEETING WIND              2.142.11
AND I WANT WORDS FOR TO EXPRESSE MY WRONG           2.143.8
MY WORDS THE HAMMERS, FASHIONING MY DESIRES         2.144.2
MAY MAKE SEEME BARE, IN WANTING WORDS TO SHEW IT    3.26.6
SO ALL MY BEST IS DRESSING OLD WORDS NEW            3.76.11
THE DEDICATED WORDS WHICH WRITERS USE               3.82.3
IN TRUE PLAINE WORDS, BY THY TRUE TELLING FRIEND    3.82.12
I THINKE GOOD THOUGHTS, WHILST OTHER WRITE
                           GOOD WORDES              3.85.5
(THOUGH WORDS COME HIND-MOST) HOLDS HIS
                           RANKE BEFORE             3.85.12
THEN OTHERS, FOR THE BREATH OF WORDS RESPECT        3.85.13
FAIRE, KINDE AND TRUE, VARRYING TO OTHER WORDS      3.105.10
LEAST SORROW LEND ME WORDS AND WORDS EXPRESSE       3.140.3
LEAST SORROW LEND ME WORDS AND WORDS EXPRESSE       3.140.3
I SOUGHT FIT WORDS TO PAINT THE BLACKEST
                           FACE OF WOE              4.1.5
BUT WORDS CAME HALTING FORTH, WANTING
                           $INVENTION'S STAY        4.1.9
WHILE TEARES POWRE OUT HIS INKE, AND SIGHS
                           BREATHE OUT HIS WORDS    4.6.10
WHAT WORDS SO ERE SHE SPEAKES PERSWADES FOR THEE    4.12.7
BUT WITH YOUR $RUBARB WORDS YOW MUST CONTEND        4.14.5
AND YET MY WORDS, AS THEM MY PEN DOTH FRAME         4.19.7
YOUR WORDS MY FRIEND (RIGHT HEALTHFULL
                           CAUSTIKS) BLAME          4.21.1
WITH DEARTH OF WORDS, OR ANSWERS QUITE AWRIE        4.27.3
A BURTHNED HART. '$HOW CAN WORDS EASE, WHICH ARE    4.34.2
'BUT WILL NOT WISE MEN THINKE THY WORDS
                           FOND WARE+'              4.34.7
WHAT MAY WORDS SAY, OR WHAT MAY WORDS NOT SAY       4.35.1
```

```
WHAT MAY WORDS SAY, OR WHAT MAY WORDS NOT SAY        4.35.1
BEAUTIES SO FARRE FROM REACH OF WORDS, THAT WE       4.37.7
MY WORDS I KNOW DO WELL SET FORTH MY MIND            4.44.1
TILL THAT IN WORDS THY FIGURE BE EXPREST             4.50.4
AND OFT WHOLE TROUPES OF SADDEST WORDS I STAID       4.55.5
THE THOROWEST WORDS, FIT FOR WOE'S SELFE TO GRONE    4.57.4
WHETHER WITH WORDS THIS SOVERAIGNTY HE GAINE         4.58.5
EVEN THOSE SAD WORDS EVEN IN SAD ME DID BREED        4.58.14
WITH WORDS, WHEREIN THE $MUSES' TREASURES BE         4.60.7
NOW WITH SLOW WORDS, NOW WITH DUMBE ELOQUENCE        4.61.2
WITH CHOISEST WORDS, THY WORDS WITH REASONS RARE     4.68.10
WITH CHOISEST WORDS, THY WORDS WITH REASONS RARE     4.68.10
FOR $STELLA HATH WITH WORDS WHERE FAITH
                         DOTH SHINE                  4.69.9
THOSE WORDS, WHICH DO SUBLIME THE QUINTESSENCE
                         OF BLISSE                   4.77.8
WHENCE WORDS, NOT WORDS, BUT HEAV'NLY
                         GRACES SLIDE                4.80.4
WHENCE WORDS, NOT WORDS, BUT HEAV'NLY
                         GRACES SLIDE                4.80.4
BUT SHE FORBIDS, WITH BLUSHING WORDS, SHE SAYES      4.81.9
TEMPERS HER WORDS TO TRAMPLING HORSES FEET           4.84.3
AND HER SAD WORDS MY SADDED SENCE DID HEARE          4.87.8
SINCE ALL MY WORDS THY BEAUTY DOTH ENDITE            4.90.13
BE YOUR WORDS MADE (GOOD $SIR) OF $INDIAN WARE       4.92.1
WHAT SOBS CAN GIVE WORDS GRACE MY GRIEFE TO SHOW+    4.93.2
GRIEFE FIND THE WORDS, FOR THOU HAST MADE
                         MY BRAINE                   4.94.1
WHILE SOBD OUT WORDS A PERFECT $MUSIKE GIVE          4.100.11
THROGH WHICH HER WORDS SO WISE DO MAKE THEIR WAY     5.81.11
OF POYSONED WORDS AND SPITEFULL SPEECHES WELL        5.86.4
```
WORK   24
```
(DIANA-LIKE) TO WORKE MY SUDDEN CHANGE               1.5.4
I WORKE ON FLINT, AND THATS THE CAUSE I MONE         1.13.4
THE WORKE OF RIGOR, FATALLY BEGUN                    1.33.7
SHEW'D IN THESE LINES, THE WORKE OF CAREFULL
                         HOURES                      1.59.7
WHICH ON THE $LIVING WORKE WITHOUT REMORSE           2.50.5
THE WORKE OF THAT UNITED $TRINITIE                   2.123.3
THOSE HOWERS THAT WITH GENTLE WORKE DID FRAME        3.5.1
TO WORKE MY MIND, WHEN BODDIES WORK'S EXPIRED        3.27.4
AND BROILES ROOTE CUT THE WORKE OF MASONRY           3.55.6
WHEN $NATURE MADE HER CHIEFE WORKE, $STELLA'S EYES   4.7.1
BUT BY THY WORKE MY $STELLA I DESCRIE                4.32.7
OUR HORSMANSHIPS, WHILE BY STRANGE WORKE I PROVE     4.49.2
WAS IT THE WORKE OF NATURE OR OF $ART                5.21.1
IN WHICH THE WORKE THAT SHE ALL DAY DID MAKE         5.23.3
AND WITH ONE WORD MY WHOLE YEARS WORK DOTH REND      5.23.12
WHOSE FRUITLESSE WORKE IS BROKEN WITH LEAST WYND     5.23.14
WHICH HER FAYRE EYES UNWARES DOE WORKE IN MEE        5.24.6
BUT MY PROUD ONE DOTH WORKE THE GREATER SCATH        5.31.9
SUFFICIENT WORKE FOR ONE MANS SIMPLE HEAD            5.33.7
I JOY TO SEE HOW IN YOUR DRAWEN WORK                 5.71.1
BUT AS YOUR WORKE IS WOVEN ALL ABOVE                 5.71.9
AND STOUTLY WILL THAT SECOND WORKE ASSOYLE           5.80.7
BUT THIS THE WORKE OF HARTS ASTONISHMENT             5.81.14
ATTEMPT TO WORK HER GENTLE MINDES UNREST             5.84.4
```
WORKING   1
```
SHALL FAILE IN FORCE, THEIR WORKING NOT SO STRONG    1.38.4
```

WORKINGS   1
  WHAT ERE THY THOUGHTS, OR THY HEARTS WORKINGS BE   3.93.11
WORKMANSHIP   1
  LEAST TREMBLING IT HIS WORKMANSHIP SHOULD SPILL   5.17.7
WORKS   8
  EV'N SO MY $MISTRES WORKES UPON MY $ILL   2.50.12
  TO WORKE MY MIND, WHEN BODDIES WORK'S EXPIRED   3.27.4
  IN OTHERS WORKES THOU DOOST BUT MEND THE STILE   3.78.11
  TO WHAT IT WORKES IN, LIKE THE $DYERS HAND   3.111.7
  WHICH WORKES ON LEASES OF SHORT NUMBRED HOWERS   3.124.10
  O LET NOT FOOLES IN ME THY WORKES REPROVE   4.107.13
  SO STRANGELY (ALAS) THY WORKS IN ME PREVAILE   4.108.12
  THE REST BE WORKS OF NATURES WONDERMENT   5.81.13
WORLD   104
  DELIA HER SELFE, AND ALL THE WORLD MAY VIEW   1.4.7
  THE WORLD HAD NEVER KNOWNE WHAT I DOE FINDE   1.7.3
  NOR YET THE WORLD HAVE HEARD OF SUCH DISDAINE   1.7.8
  AND MUST THEIR GLORY TO THE WORLD IMPART   1.10.12
  WHICH CLEERE OUR CLOUDED WORLD WITH BRIGHTEST
              FLAME   1.12.4
  THE FAIREST FORME, THAT ALL THE WORLD ADMIRES   1.13.7
  LET THIS SUFFICE, THAT ALL THE WORLD MAY SEE   1.15.13
  WHY SHOULD I MORE MOLEST THE WORLD WITH CRIES+   1.21.5
  WHILST WE BOTH MAKE THE WORLD ADMIRE AT US   1.26.13
  ALTHOUGH THIS WORLD MAY SEEME HER DEEDE TO BLAME   1.30.13
  ILE TELL THE WORLD THAT I DESERV'D BUT ILL   1.33.11
  THAT MAKES THE WORLD ADMIRE SO STRANGE EFFECTS   1.34.8
  WHOSE GLORIOUS BLAZE THE WORLD DOTH SO ADMIRE   1.38.6
  THE WORLD SHALL FINDE THIS MYRACLE IN ME   1.41.9
  BEWRAY UNTO THE WORLD HOW FAIRE THOU ART   1.44.2
  TO CHECK THE WORLD, HOW THEY INTOMB'D HAVE LIEN   1.45.3
  DECKT WITH HER YOUTH WHEREON THE WORLD DOTH SMILE   1.53.6
  DIVIDED FROM THE WORLD, AS BETTER WORTH   1.53.11
  THEN JUDGE THE WORLD HER BEAUTY GIVES THE SAME   1.57.12
  WHICH TELLS THE WORLD HOW MUCH MY GRIEFE IMPORTS   1.60.4
  NOR WHILST THE $WORLD IS, NEVER SHALL BE DONE   2.13.11
  TO THIS OUR $WORLD, TO $LEARNING, AND TO $HEAVEN   2.18.1
  NINE WORTHIE $WOMEN TO THE $WORLD WERE GIVEN   2.18.8
  RAVISH'D A $WORLD BEYOND THE FARTHEST $THOUGHT   2.34.2
  IS MODEL'D OUT THE $WORLD OF MY $DISGRACE   2.44.4
  WHEREIN THE $WORLD SHALL NOW INTOMBE HER $NAME   2.45.8
  LONG SINCE DEPARTED (TO THE $WORLD NO MORE)   2.46.10
  THUS THE $WORLD DOTH, AND EVERMORE SHALL $REELE   2.51.10
  A $WORLD OF $VOLUMES SHALL THEREOF ARISE   2.55.2
  AND ASKE A $WORLD UPON MY $LIFE TO DWELL   2.60.4
  TELL $ME, IF EVER SINCE THE $WORLD BEGUNNE   2.60.11
  I BUILD MY $HOPES A WORLD ABOVE THE $SKIE   2.62.9
  LET THE $WORLD SEE THE UTMOST OF THY HATE   2.63.12
  UNTO THE WORLD HAD ALL MY JOYES BEEN MUTE   2.104.3
  IN $ONE WHOLE WORLD IS BUT ONE $PHOENIX FOUND   2.106.1
  SO MAIST THOU LIVE, PAST WORLD, PAST FAME,
              PAST END   2.106.14
  FROM WORLD TO WORLD, THOU LONG HAST SOUGHT
              TO SEE   2.107.2
  FROM WORLD TO WORLD, THOU LONG HAST SOUGHT
              TO SEE   2.107.2
  UNTO THE $WORLD, TO $LEARNING, AND TO $HEAVEN   2.108.1
  NINE WORTHY MEN UNTO THE WORLD WERE GIVEN   2.108.8
  WHERE FIRST MY $LOVE INTO THE WORLD WAS BROUGHT   2.116.4
  SHOULD TEACH THE WORLD TO KNOW THE WONDER
              THAT I PROVE   2.117.14

```
BY THEYR TEN $SIBILS HAVE THE WORLD CONTROLD        2.119.2
AND SINCE THE WORLD TO JUDGEMENT DOTH DECLYNE       2.119.7
NOR WHILST THE WORLD IS, NEVER SHALL BE DONE        2.121.11
SUNNE OF THE WORLD, THOU HART REVYVING FIRE         2.123.8
LIGHTNING THE WORLD, ECLIPSED BY HIS SET           2.125.4
A WORLD TO SEE, YET HOW HE JOYD TO HEARE           2.125.7
OR IF A WORLD OF FAITHFULL SERVICE DONE            2.138.5
THAT YET THE WORLD UNWORTHY NEVER KNEWE            2.139.12
NOR MY DISGRACES TO THE WORLD BE SEENE            2.142.14
WHOSE THWARTING COURSE, DEPRIVES THE WORLD
                                OF REASON          2.147.14
AND ASKE A WORLD UPON MY LIFE TO DWELL             2.149.4
TELL MEE, IF EVER SINCE THE WORLD BEGUNNE          2.149.11
I BUILD MY HOPES, A WORLD ABOVE THE SKYE           2.150.9
AND TELL THE WORLD, THAT IN THE WORLD THERE IS     2.151.13
AND TELL THE WORLD, THAT IN THE WORLD THERE IS     2.151.13
PITTY THE WORLD, OR ELSE THIS GLUTTON BE           3.1.13
THOU DOO'ST BEGUILE THE WORLD, UNBLESSE
                                SOME MOTHER        3.3.4
THE WORLD WILL WAILE THEE LIKE A MAKELESSE WIFE    3.9.4
THE WORLD WILBE THY WIDDOW AND STILL WEEPE         3.9.5
LOOKE WHAT AN UNTHRIFT IN THE WORLD DOTH SPEND     3.9.9
SHIFTS BUT HIS PLACE, FOR STILL THE WORLD
                                INJOYES IT         3.9.10
BUT BEAUTIES WASTE HATH IN THE WORLD AN END        3.9.11
AND THREESCOORE YEARE WOULD MAKE THE WORLD AWAY    3.11.8
TO THE WIDE WORLD AND ALL HER FADING SWEETS        3.19.7
AND FROM THE FOR-LORNE WORLD HIS VISAGE HIDE       3.33.7
SUNS OF THE WORLD MAY STAINE, WHEN HEAVENS
                                SUN STAINTEH       3.33.14
THAT WEARE THIS WORLD OUT TO THE ENDING DOOME      3.55.12
NOR DARE I CHIDE THE WORLD WITHOUT END HOURE       3.57.5
THAT I MIGHT SEE WHAT THE OLD WORLD COULD SAY      3.59.9
GIVE WARNING TO THE WORLD THAT I AM FLED           3.71.3
FROM THIS VILE WORLD WITH VILDEST WORMES TO DWELL  3.71.4
LEAST THE WISE WORLD SHOULD LOOKE INTO YOUR MONE   3.71.13
O LEAST THE WORLD SHOULD TASKE YOU TO RECITE       3.72.1
THEN BETTERD THAT THE WORLD MAY SEE MY PLEASURE    3.75.8
THOUGH I (ONCE GONE) TO ALL THE WORLD MUST DYE     3.81.6
WHEN ALL THE BREATHERS OF THIS WORLD ARE DEAD      3.81.12
NOW WHILE THE WORLD IS BENT MY DEEDS TO CROSSE     3.90.2
OF THE WIDE WORLD, DREAMING ON THINGS TO COME      3.107.2
YOU ARE MY $ALL THE WORLD, AND I MUST STRIVE       3.112.5
THAT ALL THE WORLD BESIDES ME THINKES
                                Y'ARE DEAD         3.112.14
ALL THIS THE WORLD WELL KNOWES YET NONE
                                KNOWES WELL        3.129.13
NOW THIS ILL WRESTING WORLD IS GROWNE SO BAD       3.140.11
WHAT MEANES THE WORLD TO SAY IT IS NOT SO+         3.148.6
LOOKS OVER THE WORLD, AND CAN FIND NOTHING SUCH    4.9.10
HATH THIS WORLD OUGHT SO FAIRE AS $STELLA IS+      4.21.14
FROM ALL THE WORLD, HER HEART IS THEN HIS ROME     4.43.13
TO PORTRAIT THAT WHICH IN THIS WORLD IS BEST       4.50.8
IN THIS OLD WORLD, GROWNE NOW SO TOO TOO WISE      4.65.6
WORLD OF MY WEALTH, AND HEAV'N OF MY DELIGHT       4.68.4
WITNESSE THE WORLD HOW WORTHY TO BE PRAYZED        5.3.2
IS OF THE WORLD UNWORTHY MOST ENVIDE              5.5.4
WAS NEVER IN THIS WORLD OUGHT WORTHY TRIDE         5.5.13
THAT TO THE WORLD NAUGHT ELSE BE COUNTED DEARE     5.8.4
DARK IS THE WORLD, WHERE YOUR LIGHT SHINED NEVER   5.8.13
```

```
INTO THIS SINFULL WORLD FROM HEAVEN TO SEND          5.24.10
AND FILL THE WORLD WITH HER VICTORIOUS PRAYSE        5.29.14
THRUGH THE BROAD WORLD DOTH SPRED HIS GOODLY RAY     5.40.8
INTO THE GLOOMING WORLD HIS GLADSOME RAY             5.62.10
THE FAMOUS WARRIORS OF THE ANTICKE WORLD             5.69.1
WHERE WHENAS DEATH SHALL ALL THE WORLD SUBDEW        5.75.13
THE WORLD THAT CANNOT DEEME OF WORTHY THINGS         5.85.1
LET THE WORLD CHOSE TO ENVY OR TO WONDER             5.85.14
```
WORLDLY   2
```
  LAUGHTER LOVING $GODDESSE, WORLDLY PLEASURES
                         $QUEENE                     1.10.6
  WHICH MAKE THE PATENTS OF TRUE WORLDLY BLISSE      4.37.13
```
WORLD-OUT-WEARING   1
```
  PROUDLY THOU SCORN'ST MY $WORLD-OUT-WEARING
                         $RIMES                      2.44.7
```
WORLDS   5
```
  THAT RAPT IN $SPIRIT, IN BETTER $WORLDS
                         HATH BEENE                  2.57.11
  THAT THEY MAY TEL MORE WORLDS WHAT $TIME
                         HATH SEENE                  2.107.11
  SLEEPES WONDER $BEAUTY, WONDERS TO WORLDS
                         IMPARTING                   2.136.4
  THO WORLDS QUITE ME, SHALL I MY SELFE FORGIVE+     4.93.11
  KNOWING WORLDS PASSE, ERE SHE ENOUGH CAN FIND      4.101.13
```
WORLD'S   22
```
  TO ATTEND THE PRESENCE OF MY WORLDS $DEERE         1.30.6
  AS THE $WORLDS $BEAUTIE IN HIS $INFANCIE           2.17.7
  MORE THEN WORLDS VOLUMES SHALL THEREOF ARISE       2.102.2
  BEHOLD WORLDS $BEAUTIE IN HER INFANCIE             2.107.7
  AND HEAVEN MAY JOY TO THINK ON PAST WORLDS
                         BLISSE                      2.107.12
  WHEN OUR WORLDS SUNNE IS VANISHT OUT OF SIGHT      2.129.4
  O OUR WORLDS WONDER, CROWNE OF HEAVEN ABOVE        2.129.9
  THOU THAT ART NOW THE WORLDS FRESH ORNAMENT        3.1.9
  TO EATE THE WORLDS DUE, BY THE GRAVE AND THEE      3.1.14
  THOSE PARTS OF THEE THAT THE WORLDS EYE DOTH VIEW  3.69.1
  WHICH MY HEART KNOWES THE WIDE WORLDS
                         COMMON PLACE+               3.137.10
  UNLEARNED IN THE WORLDS FALSE SUBTILTIES           3.138.4
  ALL THIS WORLDS PRIDE BOW TO A BASER MAKE          5.10.11
  ALL THIS WORLDS RICHES THAT MAY FARRE BE FOUND     5.15.6
  AND THIS WORLDS WORTHLESSE GLORY TO EMBASE         5.17.3
  SITH ALL WORLDS GLORIE IS BUT DROSSE UNCLEANE      5.27.2
  ALL THIS WORLDS GLORY SEEMETH VAYNE TO ME          5.35.13
  OF ALL WORLDS GLADNESSE MORE MY TORMENT FEED       5.52.12
  MADE FOR TO BE THE WORLDS MOST ORNAMENT            5.53.10
  OF THIS WORLDS $THEATRE IN WHICH WE STAY           5.54.1
  THAT MAY ADMIRE SUCH WORLDS RARE WONDERMENT        5.69.12
  ALL THIS WORLDS GLORY SEEMETH VAYNE TO ME          5.83.13
```
WORMS   5
```
  TO BE DEATHS CONQUEST AND MAKE WORMES THINE HEIRE  3.6.14
  FROM THIS VILE WORLD WITH VILDEST WORMES TO DWELL  3.71.4
  THE PRAY OF WORMES, MY BODY BEING DEAD             3.74.10
  SHALL WORMES INHERITORS OF THIS EXCESSE            3.146.7
  THAT WORMES SHOULD HAVE THEIR $SUN, AND
                         I WANT MINE                 4.98.14
```
WORN   2
```
  SEE HOW HER SAYLES BE RENT, HER TACKLINGS WORNE    2.134.9
  THAT HIS RIGHT BADGE IS BUT WORNE IN THE HART      4.54.12
```

WORSE   10
  TO SUBJECTS WORSE HAVE GIVEN ADMIRING PRAISE   3.59.14
  NOT MAKING WORSE WHAT NATURE MADE SO CLEERE   3.84.10
  BEING FOND ON PRAISE, WHICH MAKES YOUR
                PRAISES WORSE   3.84.14
  LILLIES THAT FESTER, SMELL FAR WORSE THEN WEEDS   3.94.14
  AND WORSE ESSAIES PROV'D THEE MY BEST OF LOVE   3.110.8
  TO GRIEVE ME WORSE, IN SAYING THAT $DESIRE   4.14.6
  AND WHICH IS WORSE, NO GOOD EXCUSE CAN SHOW   4.18.7
  BUT ONE WORSE FAULT, $AMBITION, I CONFESSE   4.27.11
  WITH NO WORSE CURSE THEN ABSENCE MAKES ME TAST   4.105.14
  NE FEARD WITH WORSE TO ANY CHAUNCE TO START   5.59.4
WORSER   1
  THE WORSER SPIRIT A WOMAN COLLOUR'D IL   3.144.4
WORSHIP   2
  WHEN ALL MY BEST DOTH WORSHIP THY DEFECT   3.149.11
  THAT MANY NOW MUCH WORSHIP AND ADMIRE   5.27.8
WORSHIPPED   1
  SUCH HEAVENLY FORMES OUGHT RATHER WORSHIPT BE   5.61.13
WORST   10
  IF THIS HER WORST, HOW SHOULD HER BEST INFLAME+   1.17.11
  YET DOE THY WORST OULD $TIME DISPIGHT THY WRONG   3.19.13
  THE WORST WAS THIS, MY LOVE WAS MY DECAY   3.80.14
  AT FIRST THE VERY WORST OF FORTUNES MIGHT   3.90.12
  BUT DOE THY WORST TO STEALE THY SELFE AWAY   3.92.1
  THEN NEED I NOT TO FEARE THE WORST OF WRONGS   3.92.5
  YET WHAT THE BEST IS, TAKE THE WORST TO BE   3.137.4
  THAT IN MY MINDE THY WORST ALL BEST EXCEEDS+   3.150.8
  LET $FORTUNE LAY ON ME HER WORST DISGRACE   4.64.3
  THAT DO NOT LEAVE YOUR LEAST FRIEND AT THE WURST   4.95.2
WORTH   30
  DIVIDED FROM THE WORLD, AS BETTER WORTH   1.53.11
  COMPARE MY $WORTH WITH OTHERS BASE $DESERT   2.60.6
  OR TONGUE OF WONDER WORTH COULD TELL A
                WONDER THOUGHT   2.117.2
  SWEET SECRECIE, WHAT TONGUE CAN TELL THY WORTH+   2.146.1
  COMPARE MY WORTH WITH OTHERS BASE DESERT   2.149.6
  WIL BE A TOTTER'D WEED OF SMAL WORTH HELD   3.2.4
  NEITHER IN INWARD WORTH NOR OUTWARD FAIRE   3.16.11
  THE PAINEFULL WARRIER FAMOSED FOR WORTH   3.25.9
  TAKE ALL MY COMFORT OF THY WORTH AND TRUTH   3.37.4
  BE THOU THE TENTH $MUSE, TEN TIMES MORE IN WORTH   3.38.9
  OH HOW THY WORTH WITH MANNERS MAY I SINGE   3.39.1
  LIKE STONES OF WORTH THEY THINLY PLACED ARE   3.52.7
  PRAISING THY WORTH, DISPIGHT HIS CRUELL HAND   3.60.14
  AND FOR MY SELFE MINE OWNE WORTH DO DEFINE   3.62.7
  THEIR WORTH THE GREATER BEEING WOO'D OF TIME   3.70.6
  AND SO SHOULD YOU, TO LOVE THINGS NOTHING WORTH   3.72.14
  THE WORTH OF THAT, IS THAT WHICH IT CONTAINES   3.74.13
  BUT SINCE YOUR WORTH (WIDE AS THE $OCEAN IS)   3.80.5
  FINDING THY WORTH A LIMMIT PAST MY PRAISE   3.82.6
  SPEAKING OF WORTH, WHAT WORTH IN YOU DOTH GROW   3.83.8
  SPEAKING OF WORTH, WHAT WORTH IN YOU DOTH GROW   3.83.8
  THE $CHARTER OF THY WORTH GIVES THEE RELEASING   3.87.3
  THY SELFE THOU GAV'ST, THY OWNE WORTH
                THEN NOT KNOWING   3.87.9
  THE ARGUMENT ALL BARE IS OF MORE WORTH   3.103.3
  THEY HAD NOT STILL ENOUGH YOUR WORTH TO SING   3.106.12
  BUT KNOWNE WORTH DID IN MINE OF TIME PROCEED   4.2.3
  LITLE HE IS, SO LITLE WORTH IS HE   4.59.5

```
FED BY THY WORTH, AND KINDLED BY THY SIGHT+            4.68.8
TO ME YOUR THRALL, IN WHOM IS LITTLE WORTH             5.82.10
HER WORTH IS WRITTEN WITH A GOLDEN QUILL               5.85.10
WORTHIER                1
DESERVES THE TRAVAILE OF A WORTHIER PEN                3.79.6
WORTHIES                2
MY WORTHY, $ONE TO THESE $NINE $WORTHIES ADDETH        2.18.9
MY $WORTHIE, ONE TO THESE NINE $WORTHIES, ADDETH       2.108.9
WORTHILY                1
AND THAT THY LOVE WE WEIGHING WORTHILY                 5.68.9
WORTHINESS              1
BLESSED ARE YOU WHOSE WORTHINESSE GIVES SKOPE          3.52.13
WORTHLESS               3
OR (BEING WRACKT) I AM A WORTHLESSE BOTE               3.80.11
SPENDST THOU THY FURIE ON SOME WORTHLESSE SONGE        3.100.3
AND THIS WORLDS WORTHLESSE GLORY TO EMBASE             5.17.3
WORTHS                  3
AS I ALL OTHER IN ALL WORTHS SURMOUNT                  3.62.8
WHOSE WORTHS UNKNOWNE, ALTHOUGH HIS HIGTH
                                  BE TAKEN             3.116.8
YEE WHOSE HIGH WORTHS SURPASSING PARAGON               5.66.5
WORTHY                 21
BE YOU MOST WORTHY, WHILST I AM MOST TRUE              2.4.14
NINE WORTHIE $WOMEN TO THE $WORLD WERE GIVEN           2.18.8
MY WORTHY, $ONE TO THESE $NINE $WORTHIES ADDETH        2.18.9
MY $MUSE, MY $WORTHY, AND MY $ANGEL THEN               2.18.13
NINE WORTHY MEN UNTO THE WORLD WERE GIVEN              2.108.8
MY $WORTHIE, ONE TO THESE NINE $WORTHIES, ADDETH       2.108.9
MY $MUSE, MY $WORTHY, AND MY $ANGELL THEN              2.108.13
WHOSE WORTHY PRIZE SHOULD HAVE ENRITCHT
                               THY TREASURE            2.134.14
TO SHOW ME WORTHY OF THEIR SWEET RESPECT               3.26.12
WORTHY PERUSAL STAND AGAINST THY SIGHT                 3.38.6
MOST WORTHY COMFORT, NOW MY GREATEST GRIEFE            3.48.6
FOR YOU IN ME CAN NOTHING WORTHY PROVE                 3.72.4
MORE WORTHY I TO BE BELOV'D OF THEE                    3.150.14
FEARE TO OFFEND, WILL WORTHIE TO APPEARE               4.72.10
BUT ONLY FOR THIS WORTHY KNIGHT DURST PROVE            4.75.13
AS OF A CAITIFE WORTHY SO TO DIE                       4.94.10
WITNESSE THE WORLD HOW WORTHY TO BE PRAYZED            5.3.2
WAS NEVER IN THIS WORLD OUGHT WORTHY TRICE             5.5.13
WELL WORTHY THOU TO HAVE FOUND BETTER HYRE             5.48.5
OF ALL ALIVE MOST WORTHY TO BE PRAYSED                 5.74.12
THE WORLD THAT CANNOT DEEME OF WORTHY THINGS           5.85.1
WOT                     3
OF HOPES BEGOT BY FEARE, OF WOT NOT WHAT DESIRES       4.6.2
BUT ($GOD WOT) WOT NOT WHAT THEY MEANE BY IT           4.74.6
BUT ($GOD WOT) WOT NOT WHAT THEY MEANE BY IT           4.74.6
WOUND                  17
DEEPE IS THE WOUND MY SIGHES CAN WELL REPORT           1.14.6
THE BOND, THE FLAME, THE WOUND THAT FESTRETH SO        1.14.10
BEARING THE WOUND, I NEEDES MUST FEELE THE PAINE       1.52.14
YOUR $CHEEKES YET PALE, SINCE FIRST HE
                               GAVE THE $WOUND         2.2.12
TO WOUND HER $HEART, WHOSE $EYES HAVE WOUNDED ME       2.36.2
SEE HOW HEE LOOKES UPON HIS BLEEDING WOUND             2.135.9
THAT HEALES THE WOUND, AND CURES NOT THE DISGRACE      3.34.8
FOR THAT DEEPE WOUND IT GIVES MY FRIEND AND ME         3.133.2
WOUND ME NOT WITH THINE EYE BUT WITH THY TOUNG         3.139.3
WHAT NEEDST THOU WOUND WITH CUNNING WHEN
                               THY MIGHT               3.139.7
```

```
LOVE GAVE THE WOUND, WHICH WHILE I BREATHE
                        WILL BLEED                      4.2.2
FLIE, FLY, MY FRIENDS, I HAVE MY DEATH
                        WOUND., FLY                     4.20.1
THE FRIENDLY FRAY, WHERE BLOWES BOTH WOUND
                        AND HEALE                       4.79.10
DEEPE IS THE WOUND, THAT DINTS THE PARTS ENTIRE         5.6.11
SHOOT OUT HIS DARTS TO BASE AFFECTIONS WOUND+           5.8.6
OF MY HARTS WOUND AND OF MY BODIES GRIEFE               5.50.2
SEEKES WITH SWEET PEACE TO SALVE EACH
                        OTHERS WOUND                    5.65.12
WOUNDED                         4
 TO WOUND HER $HEART, WHOSE $EYES HAVE WOUNDED ME       2.36.2
WOUNDED WITH $ARROWES FROM THY LIGHTNING EYES           2.142.5
THE HUMBLE SALVE, WHICH WOUNDED BOSOMES FITS            3.120.12
THE INWARD LANGUOR OF MY WOUNDED HART                   5.50.10
WOUNDING                        1
AND OF WHAT FORCE THY WOUNDING GRACES ARE               1.37.7
WOUNDS                         13
THAT HOLDS, THAT BURNES, THAT WOUNDS ME
                        IN THIS SORT                    1.14.8
FRESH SHALT THOU SEE IN ME THE WOUNDS THOU MADST        1.41.5
AND THAT WHICH GAVE ME WOUNDS, $ILE GIVE
                        IT KISSES                       1.46.12
WHICH PITTY NOT THE WOUNDS MADE BY THEIR MIGHT          1.59.6
BY ALL THE $WOUNDS THAT EVER THOU HAST GIV'N            2.36.12
TH'ANCIENT $WOUNDS NO LONGER CAN CONTAINE               2.46.11
AND WITH THEIR $BALMES RECURE THE $WOUNDS AGAINE        2.50.8
OF LIVING DEATHS, DEARE WOUNDS, FAIRE
                        STORMES AND FREESING FIRES      4.6.4
WITH SWORD OF WIT, GIVING WOUNDS OF DISPRAISE           4.10.10
FROM THAT FOE'S WOUNDS THEIR TENDER SKINNES
                        TO HIDE                         4.22.8
WHOSE CURELESSE WOUNDS EVEN NOW MOST FRESHLY
                        BLEED                           4.48.11
SO WEAKE MY POWRES, SO SORE MY WOUNDS APPEARE           5.57.5
THAT AL MY WOUNDS WIL HEALE IN LITTLE SPACE             5.57.14
WOVEN                           1
BUT AS YOUR WORKE IS WOVEN ALL ABOVE                    5.71.9
WOXEN                           1
TILL GREATER THEN MY WOMBE THOU WOXEN ART               5.2.4
WRACK                           9
WHO WHILST I BURNE, SHE SINGS AT MY SOULES WRACK        1.47.5
AND SUFF'RED HER TO GLORY IN MY $WRACKE                 2.36.3
IF $NATURE (SOVERAINE MISTERES OVER WRACK)              3.126.5
THAT SEE MY WRACKE, AND YET EMBRACE THE SAME+           4.19.2
THEN SERVANT'S WRACKE, WHERE NEW DOUBTS
                        HONOR BRINGS                    4.45.11
THEE TO THY WRACKE BEYOND THY LIMITS STRAINE            4.85.4
THAT ALL THY HURTS IN MY HART'S WRACKE I REEDE          4.93.13
ARION, WHEN THROUGH TEMPESTS CRUEL WRACKE               5.38.1
WILL BOTH TOGETHER ME TOO SORELY WRACK                  5.46.12
WRACKED                         2
OR (BEING WRACKT) I AM A WORTHLESSE BOTE                3.80.11
WILL SHE TAKE TIME, BEFORE ALL WRACKED BE+              4.67.4
WRACKFUL                        1
AGAINST THE WRACKFULL SIEDGE OF BATTRING DAYES          3.65.6
WRACKS                          1
WRACKES $TRIUMPHS BE, WHICH $LOVE (HIGH
                        SET) DOTH BREED                 4.42.14
```

WRAPPED   4
   ERE THEY BE WELL WRAP'D IN THEIR WINDING $SHEET+   2.6.4
   THAT RAPT IN $SPIRIT, IN BETTER $WORLDS
                HATH BEENE   2.57.11
   IN COLOUR BLACKE, WHY WRAPT SHE BEAMES SO BRIGHT+   4.7.2
   TILL NOW, WRAPT IN A MOST INFERNALL NIGHT   4.33.3
WRAPS   1
   CLIPS STREIGHT MY WINGS, STREIGHT WRAPS
               ME IN HIS NIGHT   4.108.8
WRATE   1
   TH' ANATOMY OF ALL MY WOES I WRATE   4.58.10
WRATH   7
   MAKE HER THE SENTENCE OF HER WRATH REPEALE   1.22.4
   WHO THREATNED STRIPES, IF HE HIS WRATH DID PROVE   4.17.6
   BUT NO SCUSE SERVES, SHE MAKES HER WRATH APPEARE   4.73.9
   I WOULD HER YIELD, HER WRATH TO PACIFY   5.11.10
   AND WARNE TO SHUN THE DAUNGER OF THEYR WRATH   5.31.8
   THE DREADFULL TEMPEST OF HER WRATH APPEASE   5.38.7
   AND IF I SPEAKE, HER WRATH RENEW I SHALL   5.43.2
WREAK   1
   THUS WRITE I WHILE I DOUBT TO WRITE, AND WREAKE   4.34.12
WRECK   3
   I ONCE MAY SEE WHEN YEARES SHALL WRECK MY WRONG   1.38.1
   DOTH SUFFER WRECK BOTH OF HER SELFE AND GOODS   5.56.12
   WHOM YE DOE WRECK, DOE RUINE, AND DESTROY   5.56.14
WRECKS   2
   YET NOBLEST $CONQUEROURS DO WRECKES AVOID   4.40.11
   THEN ALL THE WOES AND WRECKS WHICH I ABIDE   5.25.11
WREST   1
   WHY IN THIS SORT I WREST $INVENTION SO   2.9.2
WRESTING   1
   NOW THIS ILL WRESTING WORLD IS GROWNE SO BAD   3.140.11
WRETCH   8
   AS IF BY SOME INSTINCT THE WRETCH DID KNOW   3.50.7
   THY PROUD HEARTS SLAVE AND VASSALL WRETCH TO BE   3.141.12
   I FIND HOW HEAV'NLY DAY WRETCH I DID MISSE   4.33.4
   UPON A WRETCH, THAT LONG THY GRACE HATH SOUGHT   4.40.7
   THROUGH ME, WRETCH ME, EVEN $STELLA VEXED IS   4.93.4
   BY BEING PLACED IN SUCH A WRETCH AS I   4.94.14
   TO STEALE SOME REST, BUT WRETCH I AM CONSTRAIND   4.98.6
   AH WHAT DOTH $PHOEBUS' GOLD THAT WRETCH AVAILE   4.108.10
WRETCHED   8
   THE WRETCHED $CREATURE, DESTINED TO DIE   2.50.2
   WRETCHED IN THIS ALONE, THAT THOU MAIST TAKE   3.91.13
   ALL THIS AWAY, AND ME MOST WRETCHED MAKE   3.91.14
   WHAT WRETCHED ERRORS HATH MY HEART COMMITTED   3.119.5
   MAY TIME DISGRACE, AND WRETCHED MYNUIT KILL   3.126.8
   WEALTH BREEDING WANT, MORE BLIST, MORE
               WRETCHED GROW   4.24.4
   YET GROWEST MORE WRETCHED THEN THY NATURE BEARES   4.94.13
   AND FEEDS AT PLEASURE ON THE WRETCHED PRAY   5.47.8
WRETCHEDNESS   1
   THAT THOUGH IN WRETCHEDNESSE THY LIFE DOTH LIE   4.94.12
WRETCHES   1
   IS BUT A BAYT SUCH WRETCHES TO BEGUILE   5.41.10
WRETCH'S   2
   THE COWARD CONQUEST OF A WRETCHES KNIFE   3.74.11
   AND TAKE DELIGHT T'ENCREASE A WRETCHES WOE   5.41.7
WRING   1
   NEARE THERABOUT, INTO YOUR $POESIE WRING   4.15.4

```
WRINKLE                      1
   IF TIME HAVE ANY WRINCLE GRAVEN THERE            3.100.10
WRINKLED                     2
   WITH WITHERED BROWES, ALL WRINCKLED WITH
                              DISPAIRES              2.114.3
   THAT TEDIOUS LEASURE MARKS EACH WRINCKLED LINE   4.98.11
WRINKLES                     8
   SHALT BEND THY WRINCKLES HOMEWARD TO THE EARTH   1.50.10
   DEFAC'D WITH $WRINKLES, THAT I MIGHT BUT SEE      2.8.6
   AGE RULES MY $LINES WITH $WRINCKLES IN MY $FACE   2.44.2
   DISPIGHT OF WRINKLES THIS THY GOULDEN TIME        3.3.12
   WITH LINES AND WRINCLES, WHEN HIS YOUTHFULL MORNE 3.63.4
   THE WRINCKLES WHICH THY GLASSE WILL TRULY SHOW    3.77.5
   IS WRIT IN MOODS AND FROWNES AND WRINCKLES
                              STRANGE                3.93.8
   NOR GIVES TO NECESSARY WRINCKLES PLACE           3.108.11
WRIT                         7
   O LEARNE TO READ WHAT SILENT LOVE HATH WRIT      3.23.13
   THE HAND THAT WRIT IT, FOR I LOVE YOU SO          3.71.6
   LET HIM BUT COPPY WHAT IN YOU IS WRIT             3.84.9
   IS WRIT IN MOODS AND FROWNES AND WRINCKLES
                              STRANGE                3.93.8
   THOSE LINES THAT I BEFORE HAVE WRIT DOE LIE      3.115.1
   I NEVER WRIT, NOR NO MAN EVER LOVED              3.116.14
   ALL WERE IT AS THE REST BUT RUDELY WRIT           5.33.8
WRITE                       36
   TO WRITE WITH $BLOUD, OF FORCE OFFENDS THE $SIGHT 2.13.6
   TO WRITE HIM BUT ONE $SONNET TO HIS $LOVE         2.21.4
   WHO ONELY WRITE, MY SKILL IN $VERSE TO PROVE      2.35.4
   A CRIPPLE $HAND TO WRITE, YET LAME BY $KIND       2.35.7
   SITTING ALONE, $LOVE BIDS ME GOE AND WRITE        2.38.1
   WHY DOE I SPEAKE OF $JOY, OR WRITE OF $LOVE       2.41.1
   WRITING HER PRAYSE, I CANNOT WRITE AMISSE         2.42.14
   THOU $LEADEN $BRAINE, WHICH CENSUR'ST
                              WHAT I WRITE            2.49.1
   AND ONELY WRITE, MY SKILL IN VERSE TO PROVE       2.112.4
   A CRIPPLE HAND TO WRITE, YET LAME BY KIND         2.112.7
   TO WRITE WITH BLOOD, OF FORCE OFFENDS THE SIGHT   2.121.6
   WHO WRITES MY $MISTRES PRAISE, CAN NEVER
                              WRITE AMISSE           2.128.14
   SITTING ALONE, LOVE BIDS ME GOE AND WRITE         2.131.1
   WHY DOE I SPEAKE OF JOY, OR WRITE OF LOVE         2.143.1
   IF I COULD WRITE THE BEAUTY OF YOUR EYES          3.17.5
   O LET ME TRUE IN LOVE BUT TRULY WRITE             3.21.9
   FOR WHO'S SO DUMBE THAT CANNOT WRITE TO THEE      3.38.7
   WHY WRITE I STILL ALL ONE, EVER THE SAME          3.76.5
   O KNOW SWEET LOVE I ALWAIES WRITE OF YOU          3.76.9
   O HOW I FAINT WHEN I OF YOU DO WRITE              3.80.1
   I THINKE GOOD THOUGHTS, WHILST OTHER WRITE
                              GOOD WORDES            3.85.5
   WAS IT HIS SPIRIT, BY SPIRITS TAUGHT TO WRITE     3.86.5
   OH BLAME ME NOT IF I NO MORE CAN WRITE           3.103.5
   HE LEARND BUT SURETIE-LIKE TO WRITE FOR ME       3.134.7
   'FOOLE,' SAID MY $MUSE TO ME, 'LOOKE IN
                              THY HEART AND WRITE'    4.1.14
   COME LET ME WRITE, '$AND TO WHAT END+' $TO EASE   4.34.1
   THUS WRITE I WHILE I DOUBT TO WRITE, AND WREAKE   4.34.12
   THUS WRITE I WHILE I DOUBT TO WRITE, AND WREAKE   4.34.12
   AS GOOD TO WRITE AS FOR TO LIE AND GRONE          4.40.1
   SO THAT I CANNOT CHUSE BUT WRITE MY MIND          4.50.9
```

```
AND CANNOT CHUSE BUT PUT OUT WHAT I WRITE          4.50.10
AND LOVE DOTH HOLD MY HAND, AND MAKES ME WRITE     4.90.14
TO WRITE THEREIN MORE FRESH THE STORY
                              OF DELIGHT           4.102.13
AND WHEN MY PEN WOULD WRITE HER TITLES TRUE        5.3.11
YET IN MY HART I THEN BOTH SPEAKE AND WRITE        5.3.13
AND IN THE HEVENS WRYTE YOUR GLORIOUS NAME         5.75.12
```
WRITERS   1
```
THE DEDICATED WORDS WHICH WRITERS USE              3.82.3
```
WRITER'S   1
```
BUT NEVER HEEDS THE FRUIT OF WRITER'S MIND         4.11.8
```
WRITES   3
```
WHO WRITES MY $MISTRES PRAISE, CAN NEVER
                           WRITE AMISSE            2.128.14
BUT HE THAT WRITES OF YOU, IF HE CAN TELL          3.84.7
BUT $COPYING IS, WHAT IN HER $NATURE WRITES        4.3.14
```
WRITING   1
```
WRITING HER PRAYSE, I CANNOT WRITE AMISSE          2.42.14
```
WRITINGS   1
```
THAT MINE OWNE WRITINGS LIKE BAD SERVANTS SHOW     4.21.3
```
WRITTEN   4
```
I WRITTEN FINDE THE SENTENCE OF MY DEATH           1.10.3
TO THEE I SEND THIS WRITTEN AMBASSAGE              3.26.3
WRITTEN WITH TEARES IN HARTS CLOSE BLEEDING BOOK   5.1.8
HER WORTH IS WRITTEN WITH A GOLDEN QUILL           5.85.10
```
WRONG   19
```
SHE DOTH ME WRONG, TO GRIEVE SO TRUE A HEART       1.21.14
WHICH STILL MUST BEARE THE TITLE OF MY WRONG       1.32.13
I ONCE MAY SEE WHEN YEARES SHALL WRECK MY WRONG    1.38.1
NO OTHER PROUDER $BROOKES SHALL HEARE MY WRONG     1.58.14
ILE MONE MY SELFE, AND HIDE THE WRONG I HAVE       1.59.10
IN $RIGHT OR $WRONG, THEY CALL HER $CONSCIENCE     2.12.11
AND I WANT WORDS, WHEREWITH TO TELL MY $WRONG      2.41.8
THEN WITH UNKINDNES, $LOVE REVENGE THY WRONG       2.139.5
AND I WANT WORDS FOR TO EXPRESSE MY WRONG          2.143.8
YET DOE THY WORST OULD $TIME DISPIGHT THY WRONG    3.19.13
TO BEARE LOVES WRONG, THEN HATES KNOWNE INJURY     3.40.12
THAT FOR THY RIGHT, MY SELFE WILL BEARE
                           ALL WRONG               3.88.14
LEAST I (TOO MUCH PROPHANE) SHOULD DO IT WRONGE    3.89.11
THAT MY STEEL'D SENCE OR CHANGES RIGHT OR WRONG    3.112.8
O CALL NOT ME TO JUSTIFIE THE WRONG                3.139.1
YOU TAKE WRONG WAIES, THOSE FAR-FET HELPES
                           BE SUCH                 4.15.9
AS THOUGH THAT FAIRE SOFT HAND DID YOU
                           GREAT WRONG             4.83.4
WHO ME CAPTIVING STREIGHT WITH RIGOROUS WRONG      5.12.11
GREAT WRONG I DOE, I CAN IT NOT DENY               5.33.1
```
WRONGED   1
```
BY NO ENCROCHMENT WRONGD, NOR TIME FORGOT          4.84.10
```
WRONGEST   1
```
RUDELY THOU WRONGEST MY DEARE HARTS DESIRE         5.5.1
```
WRONGFUL   2
```
AND OF BOTH, WRONGFULL DEEMES, AND ILL CONCEIVES   1.52.8
TILL BLOUDIE BULLET GET HIM WRONGFULL PRAY         4.20.4
```
WRONGFULLY   1
```
AND RIGHT PERFECTION WRONGFULLY DISGRAC'D          3.66.7
```
WRONGS   7
```
LET THEM YET SIGH THEIR OWNE, AND MONE MY WRONGS   1.3.4
YOU BEST CAN JUDGE THE WRONGS THAT SHE HATH DONE   1.3.12
```

```
    I SHALL FORGET OLD WRONGS, MY GRIEFES
                              SHALL CEASE          1.46.11
    THOSE PRETTY WRONGS THAT LIBERTY COMMITS       3.41.1
    THEN NEED I NOT TO FEARE THE WORST OF WRCNGS   3.92.5
    THAT HER $GRACE GRACIOUS MAKES THY WRONGS,
                              THAT SHE             4.12.6
    AND NOW MAN'S WRONGS IN ME, POORE BEAST, DESCRIE  4.49.4
WROTE               3
    IN UNKINDE $LETTERS., WROTE SHE CARES NOT HOW  1.10.4
    ONE DAY I WROTE HER NAME UPON THE STRAND       5.75.1
    AGAYNE I WROTE IT WITH A SECOND HAND           5.75.3
WROUGHT             8
    WROUGHT BY HER HAND THAT I HAVE HONOUR'D SO    1.47.4
    IN MAKING TRYALL CF A $MURTHER WROUGHT         2.46.5
    TILL NATURE AS SHE WROUGHT THEE FELL A DOTINGE 3.20.10
    BUT THAT SO MUCH CF EARTH AND WATER WROUGHT    3.44.11
    UNTO MY MIND, IS $STELLA'S IMAGE, WROUGHT      4.38.6
    O $STELLA DEARE, HCW MUCH THY POWER HATH WROUGHT  4.40.2
    TILL IT HAVE WROUGHT WHAT THY OWNE WILL ATTENDS  4.107.11
    FOR BEING AS SHE IS DIVINELY WROUGHT           5.61.5
WRUNG               1
    LEAVE THAT SIR $PHIP, LEAST OFF YOUR NECKE
                              BE WROONG            4.83.14
YEA                 2
    AND I AM GLAD, YEA GLAD WITHALL MY HEART       2.61.3
    TAKE ALL MY LOVES, MY LCVE, YEA TAKE THEM ALL  3.40.1
YEAR                11
    AND THREESCOORE YEARE WCULD MAKE THE WORLD AWAY  3.11.8
    SINCE SILDOM COMMING IN THE LONG YEARE SET     3.52.6
    SPEAKE OF THE SPRING, AND FOYZON OF THE YEARE  3.53.9
    THAT TIME OF YEEARE THOU MAIST IN ME BEHOLD    3.73.1
    FROM THEE, THE PLEASURE CF THE FLEETING YEARE+ 3.97.2
    TO FILL HIS HORNES THIS YEARE ON $CHRISTIAN COAST  4.30.2
    NEW YEARE FORTH LCCKING OUT OF JANUS GATE      5.4.1
    TO EVERY PLANET PCINT HIS SUNDRY YEARE         5.60.2
    BEGAN IN ME TO MOVE, ONE YEARE IS SPENT        5.60.6
    THIS YEARE ENSUING, OR ELSE SHORT MY DAYES     5.60.14
    THE WEARY YEARE HIS RACE NOW HAVING RUN        5.62.1
YEARS               18
    FROM LOVE OR YEARES UNSUBJECT TO DECAIES       1.23.4
    AND PRODIGALL OF HCWERS AND YEARES BETRAIES    1.23.11
    I SACRIFISE MY YOUTH, AND BLOOMING YEARES      1.24.5
    TO SPEND THE $APRILL OF MY YEARES IN GRIEFE    1.32.2
    I ONCE MAY SEE WHEN YEARES SHALL WRECK MY WRCNG  1.38.1
    WHEN THOU SURCHARG'D WITH BURTHEN OF THY YEERES  1.50.9
    AH SPORT (SWEET $MAIDE) IN SEASON OF THESE YEARES  1.51.5
    TIS NINE YEERES NCW SINCE FIRST I LOST MY $WIT  2.9.11
    NOR OLDER YET, NOR WISER MADE BY YEERES        2.22.3
    LOE, HEERE THY $SHEPHEARD SPENT HIS WANDRING
                              YEERES               2.53.10
    LOE, HEERE THY $SHEPHEARD SPENT HIS WANDRING
                              YEERES               2.113.10
    OR GLORIE OF MY $APRILL-SPRINGING YEERES       2.138.2
    THY BEAUTIE, AND THY YEARES FULL WELL BEFITS   3.41.3
    AND AGE IN LOVE, LCVES NCT T' HAVE YEARES TOLD 3.138.12
    IF NOW THE $MAY OF MY YEARES MUCH DECLINE      4.21.10
    HUNDREDS OF YEARES YOU $STELLA'S FEET MAY KISSE  4.84.14
    AS $MARS IN THREE SCORE YEARES DOTH RUN
                              HIS SPHEARE          5.60.4
    THE SPHEARE OF $CUPID FCURTY YEARES CONTAINES  5.60.10
```

```
YEAR'S                    5
   FAITH BEING WITH BLOOD, AND FIVE YEARES
                       WITNES SIGN'D              1.31.6
   AND WITH ONE WORD MY WHOLE YEARS WORK DOTH REND   5.23.12
   THE OLD YEARES SINNES FOREPAST LET US ESCHEW      5.62.7
   THEN SHALL THE NEW YEARES JOY FORTH FRESHLY SEND  5.62.9
   AND CHAUNGE OLD YEARES ANNOY TO NEW DELIGHT       5.62.14
YELLOW                    2
   WHEN YELLOW LEAVES, OR NONE, OR FEW DOE HANGE     3.73.2
   THREE BEAUTIOUS SPRINGS TO YELLOW $AUTUMNE
                       TURN'D                     3.104.5
YELLOWED                  1
   SO SHOULD MY PAPERS (YELLOWED WITH THEIR AGE)    3.17.9
YIELD                    21
   DID TREATE THE CRUELL FAIRE TO YEELD RELIEFE     1.8.8
   YEELD $CITHEREAS SONNE THOSE $ARKES OF LOVE      1.19.2
   YEELD THY HANDS PRIDE UNTO TH'$IVORY WHITE       1.19.5
   YEELD TO THE $MARBLE THY HARD HART AGAINE        1.19.13
   AND YEELD ME NOUGHT THAT GIVES THEM THEIR RENOWNE  1.28.8
   WHAT CAN I DO BUT YEELD+ AND YEELD I DOO         1.28.13
   WHAT CAN I DO BUT YEELD+ AND YEELD I DOO         1.28.13
   LOOKE TO THE HEAVENS.., THE HEAVENS YEELDE
                       FORTH NO GRACE            1.29.6
   MUST YEELD UP ALL TO TYRANT $TIMES DESIRE        1.38.7
   PITTY AND SMILES MUST ONELY YEELD THEE PRAISE    1.51.12
   WHICH HERE I YEELD I LAMENTABLE WISE             1.57.6
   THE EARTH CAN YEELD ME BUT A COMMON GRAVE        3.81.7
   TIL EACH TO RAZ'D OBLIVION YEELD HIS PART        3.122.7
   DO EASLY YEELD, THAT ALL THEIR COASTS MAY BE     4.29.3
   SEEING HOPE YEELD WHEN THIS WO STRAKE HIM FURST  4.95.6
   I WOULD HER YIELD, HER WRATH TO PACIFY           5.11.10
   WAS FORST TO YEELD MY SELFE INTO THEIR HANDS     5.12.10
   DISDAYNE TO YIELD UNTO THE FIRST ASSAY           5.14.8
   THE SILLY LAMBE THAT TO HIS MIGHT DOTH YIELD     5.20.8
   AND YIELD FOR PLEDGE MY POORE CAPTYVED HART      5.42.8
   SO DOE I NOW MY SELFE A PRISONER YEELD           5.52.5
YIELDED                   3
   AND THY HARD HEART HAD YEELDED UP THE SAME       1.56.8
   THAT YE WERE BLOODED IN A YEELDED PRAY           5.20.14
   YIELDED THEM BY THE VANQUISHT AS THEYR MEEDS     5.29.6
YIELDEN                   1
   A CONQUERD, YELDEN, RANSACKT HEART TO WINNE+     4.36.2
YIELDS                    5
   FLINT, FROST, DISDAINE, WEARES, MELTES,
                       AND YEELDES WE SEE        1.11.14
   SHE YEELDS NO PLACE AT ALL FOR PITTIES DWELLING  1.18.12
   BUT SINCE THE SWEETEST ROOTE YEELDS FRUITE
                       SO SOWRE                  1.26.9
   WHICH YEELDS THEM NOTHING, AT THE EASIEST RATE   2.28.7
   HE YEELDS $LOVE UP THE $KEYES UNTO MY $HEART     2.29.11
YOKE                      1
   WHOSE NECKE BECOMES SUCH YOKE OF TYRANNY+        4.47.4
YORE                      1
   TO SHEW FAULSE $ART WHAT BEAUTY WAS OF YORE      3.68.14
YORK                      2
   YORKE MANY $WONDERS OF HER $OWSE CAN TELL        2.32.6
   YORKE, MANY WONDERS OF HER $OUSE CAN TELL        2.124.6
YOUNG                    20
   STILL MUST I WHET MY YONG DESIRES ABATED        1.18.9
   AND SHE IS YONG, AND NOW MUST SPORT THE WHILE    1.51.4
```

A $WITLESSE $GALLANT, A YOUNG $WENCH THAT WOO'D   2.21.1
HE STILL AS YOUNG AS WHEN HE FIRST WAS BORNE   2.22.9
NO WISER I, THEN WHEN AS YOUNG AS HE   2.22.10
MEDEA-LIKE, I MAKE THEE YOUNG AGAINE   2.44.6
MY LOVE SHALL IN MY VERSE EVER LIVE YOUNG   3.19.14
THOU HAST PAST BY THE AMBUSH OF YOUNG DAIES   3.70.9
THUS VAINELY THINKING THAT SHE THINKES ME YOUNG   3.138.5
LOVE IS TOO YOUNG TO KNOW WHAT CONSCIENCE IS   3.151.1
WHOSE TALENTS HELD YOUNG $GANIMED ABOVE   4.13.4
BUT WHILE I THUS WITH THIS YONG $LYON PLAID   4.16.9
MY YOUNG MIND MARDE, WHOM $LOVE DOTH WINGLAS SO   4.21.2
HOLDS MY YOUNG BRAINE CAPTIV'D IN GOLDEN CAGE   4.23.11
AS MY YOUNG $DOVE MAY IN YOUR PRECEPTS WISE   4.63.3
NEAST OF YOUNG JOYES, SCHOOLMASTER OF DELIGHT   4.79.8
A NEST FOR MY YONG PRAISE IN $LAWRELL TREE   4.90.6
AND MY YONG SOULE FLUTTERS TO THEE HIS NEST   4.108.6
HER NIPPLES LYKE YONG BLOSSOMD $JESSEMYNES   5.64.12
LYKE A YOUNG FAWNE THAT LATE HATH LOST THE HYND   5.78.2
YOUNGLY   1
AND THAT FRESH BLOUD WHICH YONGLY THOU BESTOW'ST   3.11.3
YOUNG-WISE   1
NOR THAT HE COULD YOUNG-WISE, WISE-VALIANT FRAME   4.75.5
YOUTH   40
WHICH HERE MY LOVE, MY YOUTH, MY PLAINTS REVEALE   1.1.4
LOOKE ON THE DEERE EXPENCES OF MY YOUTH   1.1.9
YOU BLINDED SOULES WHOM YOUTH AND ERROUR LEADE   1.3.9
WHILST YOUTH AND ERROR LED MY WANDRING MINDE   1.5.1
WHOSE FEETE DOE TREAD GREENE PATHS OF
                         YOUTH AND LOVE   1.6.6
THE SWEETEST SACRIFICE MY YOUTH CAN MAKE+   1.17.4
BEAUTY AND YOUTH T'OPINION AND DISDAINE   1.23.12
I SACRIFISE MY YOUTH, AND BLOOMING YEARES   1.24.5
AND $WINTER WOES, FOR SPRING OF YOUTH UNFIT   1.24.8
LINES OF DELIGHT, WHEREON HER YOUTH MIGHT SMILE   1.51.2
LET LOVE AND YOUTH CONDUCT THY PLEASURES THITHER   1.51.8
DECKT WITH HER YOUTH WHEREON THE WORLD DOTH SMILE   1.53.6
THE SHIPWRACKE OF MY ILL ADVENTRED YOUTH   1.54.6
THOUGH TH'ERROR OF MY YOUTH IN THEM APPEARE   1.55.13
AND THY $YOUTH PAST, IN THIS PURE $MIRROUR SEE   2.17.6
AND THOUGH IN YOUTH, MY $YOUTH UNTIMELY PERISH   2.44.9
AND THOUGH IN YOUTH, MY $YOUTH UNTIMELY PERISH   2.44.9
AND THY YOUTH PAST, IN THIS FAIRE MIRROR SEE   2.107.6
THAT FOR MY MIS-SPENT YOUTH THE TEARS
                         FEL FROM MY EYES   2.114.4
THY FAYREST YOUTH AND $BEAUTIE DOE I SEE   2.114.6
MY LIFE, MY YOUTH, MY LOVE, I HEERE ANOTAMIZE   2.114.14
IF $CHASTE AND PURE DEVOTION OF MY YOUTH   2.138.1
RESEMBLING STRONG YOUTH IN HIS MIDDLE AGE   3.7.6
THOU MAIST CALL THINE, WHEN THOU FROM
                         YOUTH CONVERTEST   3.11.4
SETS YOU MOST RICH IN YOUTH BEFORE MY SIGHT   3.15.10
TO CHANGE YOUR DAY OF YOUTH TO SULLIED NIGHT   3.15.12
SO LONG AS YOUTH AND THOU ARE OF ONE DATE   3.22.2
TO SEE HIS ACTIVE CHILDE DO DEEDS OF YOUTH   3.37.2
AND CHIDE THY BEAUTY, AND THY STRAYING YOUTH   3.41.10
AND SO OF YOU, BEAUTIOUS AND LOVELY YOUTH   3.54.13
TIME DOTH TRANSFIXE THE FLORISH SET ON YOUTH   3.60.9
THAT ON THE ASHES OF HIS YOUTH DOTH LYE   3.73.10
SOME SAY THY FAULT IS YOUTH, SOME WANTONESSE   3.96.1
SOME SAY THY GRACE IS YOUTH AND GENTLE SPORT   3.96.2

```
HATH PUT A SPIRIT OF YOUTH IN EVERY THING          3.98.3
THESE BLENCHES GAVE MY HEART AN OTHER YOUTH        3.110.7
THAT SHE MIGHT THINKE ME SOME UNTUTERD YOUTH       3.138.3
MY YOUTH DOTH WASTE, MY KNOWLEDGE BRINGS
                            FORTH TOYES            4.18.9
YOUTH, LUCKE, AND PRAISE, EVEN FILD MY
                            VEINES WITH PRIDE      4.53.4
THEN YOU FAIRE FLOWRE, IN WHOM FRESH YOUTH
                            DOTH RAINE             5.4.13
YOUTHFUL                        3
  SUCH IS THE SUNNE, WHO GUIDES MY YOUTHFULL
                            SEASON                 2.147.13
  VAUNT IN THEIR YOUTHFULL SAP, AT HEIGHT DECREASE 3.15.7
  WITH LINES AND WRINCLES, WHEN HIS YOUTHFULL MORNE 3.63.4
YOUTHS                          1
  AND FAINE THOSE $AEOLS' YOUTHES THERE
                            WOULD THEIR STAY       4.103.9
YOUTH'S                         2
  LOOKING INTO THE GLASSE OF MY YOUTHS MISERIES    2.114.1
  THY YOUTHES PROUD LIVERY SO GAZ'D ON NOW         3.2.3
ZEAL                            6
  RUNNES THIS POORE $RIVER, CHARG'D WITH
                            STREAMES OF ZEALE      1.1.2
  THOU CANST NOT DIE WHILST ANY ZEALE ABOUND       1.43.1
  WHERE BEAT THESE TEARES WITH ZEALE, AND
                            FURY DRIVES            1.48.10
  MY $ZEALE, MY $HOPE, MY $VOWES, MY $PRAYSE,
                            MY $PRAY'R             2.54.11
  MY ZEALE, MY HOPE, MY VOWES, MY PRAISE,
                            MY PRAYER              2.101.11
  IF FAYTH AND ZEALE BE BUT ESTEEMD A TOY          2.139.3
ZEALOUS                         1
  INTEND A ZELOUS PILGRIMAGE TO THEE               3.27.6
ZENITH                          1
  KEEPE STILL MY $ZENITH, EVER SHINE ON ME         4.42.8
ZEPHYR                          2
  WHERE SWEET $MYRRH-BREATHING $ZEPHIRE
                            IN THE $SPRING         2.53.5
  WHERE SWEET $MYRH-BREATHING $ZEPHYRE IN
                            THE SPRING             2.113.5
```

LISTINGS OF WORDS BY FREQUENCIES

SAMUEL DANIEL, 'DELIA'

Word	Freq	Word	Freq	Word	Freq	Word	Freq
THE	262	HATH	18	BLAME	9	DAY	6
MY	233	THEIR	18	DESIRE	9	ELSE	6
AND	224	UNTO	18	EARTH	9	FLOWERS	6
TO	174	CAN	17	FACE	9	FORTH	6
HER	169	EVER	17	HAPPY	9	I'LL	6
OF	143	LET	17	LIKE	9	LEAVE	6
I	139	MORE	17	MOVE	9	LIES	6
THAT	126	NOW	17	NAME	9	LIVES	6
IN	95	SELF	17	PITY	9	LOOKS	6
THY	77	WHILST	17	POWER	9	MAID	6
WITH	74	BEAUTY	16	THINE	9	MAYEST	6
A	66	FIND	16	ANY	8	MOST	6
ME	56	LIVE	16	BREATH	8	NIGHT	6
SO	56	MAY	16	DEAR	8	OFT	6
LOVE	54	YOU	16	DEATH	8	PLACE	6
NOT	47	DELIA	15	DONE	8	PRAISE	6
HAVE	44	SEE	15	GRIEFS	8	PRIDE	6
NO	44	SUCH	15	HARD	8	SEEK	6
SHE	44	THUS	15	HIGH	8	SHOW	6
FOR	43	FAITH	14	HOPE	8	STARS	6
YET	43	HONOR	14	LOVED	8	UP	6
THOU	42	SWEET	14	MADE	8	VOWS	6
BUT	41	UPON	14	MUCH	8	WELL	6
HEART	41	WHERE	14	MUSE	8	WOULD	6
BE	40	YOUTH	14	ONE	8	AGAINST	5
THIS	40	CARES	13	THEM	8	ALTHOUGH	5
ALL	39	FAIREST	13	UNKIND	8	BACK	5
EYES	38	HAND	13	WHO	8	BEEN	5
WHICH	36	LOOK	13	WHY	8	BETTER	5
IS	35	MAKE	13	YEARS	8	BLISS	5
SHALL	32	OR	13	YOUR	8	BORN	5
THEE	32	TEARS	13	COULD	7	CHASTE	5
IF	31	TIME	13	DESPAIR	7	CRUELTY	5
THESE	28	WILL	12	DID	7	DARK	5
DO	27	AT	12	ERROR	7	DESIRES	5
NEVER	27	BROW	12	EYE	7	DRAW	5
MUST	26	CANNOT	12	FIRE	7	FALL	5
STILL	26	GLORY	12	FLAME	7	FLINT	5
WHEN	25	LIFE	12	FORTUNE	7	FLOWER	5
FROM	24	NOR	12	GO	7	FORCE	5
HAD	24	POOR	12	GRACE	7	HE	5
THOSE	24	WAS	12	GRIEVE	7	LANGUISH	5
ARE	23	CARE	11	LONG	7	LIGHT	5
ON	23	CRUEL	11	ONCE	7	MIND	5
THEN	23	GIVE	11	OTHER	7	PART	5
WHAT	23	GRIEF	11	OUT	7	PASSIONS	5
AS	22	HERE	11	PAIN	7	PRAYERS	5
THOUGH	22	HIS	11	SIGHS	7	READ	5
BY	21	HOPES	11	SMILES	7	SAD	5
MINE	21	SAME	11	SPENT	7	SAY	5
SHOULD	21	SUN	11	THAN	7	SHALT	5
FAIR	20	THOUGHTS	11	THERE	7	SIGH	5
WHOSE	20	VAIN	11	THINK	7	SORROWS	5
WORLD	20	YIELD	11	VERSE	7	SOUL	5
DISDAIN	19	BEST	10	VIEW	7	SPOIL	5
HOW	19	FAME	10	WITHOUT	7	STATE	5
IT	19	LINES	10	BEFORE	6	SUFFICE	5
THEY	19	OWN	10	CAUSE	6	SWEETEST	5
DOTH	18	ART	9	COME	6	TOO	5

Word		Word		Word		Word	
VOICE	5	SINCE	4	FREE	3	ADD	2
WERE	5	SLEEP	4	GIVES	3	AFFECT	2
WHOM	5	SOON	4	GONE	3	AFTER	2
WITHIN	5	SORROW	4	HAIRS	3	ANGUISH	2
WRONG	5	SOUL'S	4	HATEFUL	3	APPEAL	2
ACCENTS	4	STRONG	4	HEART'S	3	APPEAR	2
AFFLICTION	4	TELL	4	HEAVEN	3	APPEARS	2
AGAIN	4	THEREBY	4	HELP	3	APRIL	2
AH	4	TILL	4	HOLDS	3	ARKS	2
AIR	4	TIS	4	HOURS	3	ASPIRE	2
AN	4	TOUCH	4	HUE	3	ATTAINED	2
BEING	4	TRUE	4	JUDGE	3	AVON	2
BLUSH	4	TRUTH	4	KILL	3	BASE	2
BOTH	4	TYRANT	4	LENGTH	3	BEARS	2
CAREFUL	4	WAIL	4	LIMNED	3	BEAUTIES	2
CASE	4	WAST	4	LIVED	3	BEAUTY'S	2
CHANGE	4	WE	4	LOSE	3	BETRAYS	2
CLOUDED	4	WEARY	4	LOVING	3	BEWRAY	2
CLOUDS	4	WIN	4	MARBLE	3	BEWRAYED	2
COMFORT	4	WINTER	4	MESSAGE	3	BLAZE	2
DESERVED	4	WOE	4	NEAR	3	BLINDED	2
DIE	4	WORK	4	OFF	3	BLOWN	2
DOST	4	WOUNDS	4	OLD	3	BOLD	2
DOWN	4	ABOVE	3	ONLY	3	BREAST	2
DUE	4	ADMIRE	3	PASS	3	BRIGHTNESS	2
ETERNAL	4	ADORE	3	PEACE	3	BURN	2
FAR	4	AFFLICTED	3	RARE	3	CANST	2
FRESH	4	AGE	3	RELIEF	3	CELESTIAL	2
FROWNS	4	ALONE	3	RELIEVE	3	CERTAIN	2
GLASS	4	ATTEMPT	3	REST	3	CHANGED	2
GOOD	4	ATTEND	3	REVEAL	3	CHEEKS	2
GREAT	4	BEAR	3	RULE	3	CHOICE	2
HAST	4	BECAUSE	3	SERVE	3	CIRCLE	2
HEAT	4	BECOME	3	SETS	3	CLEAR	2
HEAVENS	4	BEHOLD	3	SHADES	3	COLORS	2
HEAVY	4	BLOOD	3	SHAME	3	COMPLAIN	2
HIM	4	BLOT	3	SHINES	3	CONFINED	2
ILL	4	BREAK	3	SHORT	3	CONQUERING	2
JOY	4	BRIGHT	3	SIGHT	3	CONTENT	2
JOYS	4	BROKEN	3	SING	3	CRUELEST	2
KNOW	4	BURDEN	3	SOME	3	CRY	2
KNOWN	4	CALM	3	SONG	3	CRYING	2
LEAST	4	CAST	3	SPARE	3	DAINTY	2
LO	4	CEASE	3	SPORT	3	DANGER	2
MAKES	4	CHARGED	3	STONE	3	DARKNESS	2
MEN	4	COMFORTS	3	STYLE	3	DATE	2
MERCY	4	DAYS	3	SUCCOR	3	DEAREST	2
MIGHT	4	DEAL	3	SURE	3	DEARLY	2
MOAN	4	DECKED	3	TEMPLE	3	DECK	2
MOURN	4	DEEP	3	TENDER	3	DEEDS	2
NONE	4	DELIA'S	3	THEREFORE	3	DELIGHT	2
NOUGHT	4	DISDAINS	3	USE	3	DIES	2
OCEAN	4	DISGRACE	3	VIRTUES	3	DISTRESS	2
OUR	4	DUMB	3	WAILING	3	DISTRESSED	2
PEN	4	ERECT	3	WANDERING	3	DRAWN	2
PERISH	4	ERRORS	3	WHEREIN	3	EARS	2
PRESENT	4	FADE	3	WHETHER	3	EFFECT	2
PROVE	4	FAVORS	3	WITHERED	3	EMBRACING	2
REMAIN	4	FEAR	3	WITNESS	3	END	2
RESTORE	4	FEEL	3	WORDS	3	ENOUGH	2
RISE	4	FEET	3	WOUND	3	ERE	2
SABLE	4	FINDING	3	WRONGS	3	EVEN	2
SACRED	4	FIRST	3	YIELDS	3	EXACT	2
SACRIFICE	4	FORM	3	ZEAL	3	FADING	2
SHORE	4	FRAME	3	ABROAD	3	FAVOR	2

FED	2	NATURE	2	SOONER	2	ACCORDING	1
FIT	2	NIGHT'S	2	SOUGHT	2	ACCOUNTS	1
FIXED	2	NORTH	2	SOULS	2	ACTIONS	1
FLIGHT	2	NOTES	2	SOUND	2	ADMIRES	1
FLOURISH	2	O	2	SOUNDS	2	ADMIRETH	1
FOLLOW	2	OBSCURE	2	SPEAK	2	ADORNED	1
FORCED	2	PAINT	2	SPOKEN	2	ADORNS	1
FORSAKEN	2	PAINTED	2	SPOTLESS	2	ADVENTURED	1
FOSTERED	2	PALE	2	SPRINGING	2	ADVERSARIES	1
FOUND	2	PAPERS	2	STEAL	2	ADVOCATES	1
FROST	2	PASSAGE	2	STRAIGHT	2	AFFECTED	1
FULL	2	PATHS	2	STRANGE	2	AFFECTION	1
FURY	2	PAY	2	STRETCH	2	AFFECTIONS	1
GAVE	2	PINE	2	STRIVE	2	AFFECTS	1
GAZE	2	PLAGUE	2	SUMMER	2	AGED	1
GET	2	PLAINTS	2	TELLS	2	AGENTS	1
GLORIOUS	2	PLEASING	2	TEMPEST	2	AGES	1
GOD	2	PLEASURES	2	TENDING	2	AGGRAVATE	1
GODDESS	2	POWERS	2	THAMES	2	ALAS	1
GOLDEN	2	PRAY	2	THIEF	2	ALBION	1
GRACES	2	PRESENTS	2	THINGS	2	ALLOWS	1
GREATER	2	PRESUMING	2	THITHER	2	ALOFT	1
GREEN	2	PROLONGS	2	THOUGHT	2	AMBITION	1
GROUND	2	PROPER	2	TIMES	2	AMBITIOUS	1
GROWN	2	PROTECT	2	TITLE	2	ANCHOR-HOLD	1
HALF	2	PROUD	2	TOLD	2	ANEW	1
HAP	2	QUEEN	2	TRAGIC	2	ANNALS	1
HEAL	2	QUENCH	2	TREASURE	2	ANNOY	1
HEARD	2	QUITE	2	TRIUMPH	2	ANNOYED	1
HEARTS	2	RATHER	2	TROPHIES	2	ANOTHER	1
HELD	2	REIGN	2	TURNED	2	ANSWERS	1
HIDE	2	REMOVE	2	TURNS	2	ANTHEMS	1
HOARSE	2	RENOWN	2	TYRANTS	2	APART	1
HOLD	2	REPENT	2	UNHAPPY	2	APPEARING	1
HOLY	2	REPORT	2	UNKINDEST	2	APPEASE	1
HONORED	2	RESPECTS	2	UNTIMELY	2	APPROACH	1
HONORS	2	RETURN	2	US	2	APPROVE	1
ICE	2	REWARD	2	UTTER	2	ARABIAN	1
IMAGE	2	RIGHT	2	VIRTUE	2	ARISE	1
IMPART	2	RIGOR	2	VOW	2	ARMS	1
IMPOST	2	RISING	2	WAKE	2	ASK	1
INCENSE	2	ROSE	2	WAKING	2	ASPECT	1
INTO	2	RUTHLESS	2	WANT	2	ASPECTS	1
ISLE	2	SCORN	2	WARBLE	2	ATTAIN	1
JOYED	2	SCORNED	2	WATERS	2	ATTEMPTED	1
LAND	2	SEAT	2	WAVES	2	ATTEMPTS	1
LAST	2	SEEM	2	WAYS	2	ATTENDING	1
LAURA	2	SEEN	2	WEAK	2	ATTIRE	1
LAWS	2	SEND	2	WEIGH	2	ATTRACTIVE	1
LED	2	SENSE	2	WEIGHS	2	AURORA	1
LETS	2	SENT	2	WHENCE	2	AUTHENTIC	1
LIGHTNING	2	SENTENCE	2	WHEREON	2	AWRY	1
LOATHSOME	2	SERVES	2	WHILE	2	BAD	1
LORD	2	SET	2	WILT	2	BANISH	1
LOVELY	2	SHADOWS	2	WINGS	2	BARBAROUS	1
LOYAL	2	SHOWED	2	WISE	2	BASELY	1
MANY	2	SHOWS	2	WITS	2	BASHFUL	1
MERCILESS	2	SILENT	2	WOMAN	2	BAYS	1
MERIT	2	SIN	2	WONDER	2	BEAMS	1
MILDER	2	SINGS	2	YOUNG	2	BEARING	1
MONUMENT	2	SLENDER	2	ABATED	1	BEAT	1
MORNING	2	SMILE	2	ABORTIVE	1	BECOMES	1
MOURNFUL	2	SMOKE	2	ABOUND	1	BEG	1
MOVED	2	SNOWS	2	ABOUT	1	BEGUN	1
MUSIC	2	SON	2	ACCORD	1	BELOW	1

Word		Word		Word		Word	
GRAVE	1	INFLUENCE	1	LOCKS	1	NEW	1
GRAVED	1	INJURIOUS	1	LOFTY	1	NIGHTS	1
GRAVER	1	INNATED	1	LONG-LOOKED	1	NIPPED	1
GROAN	1	INSPIRES	1	LOOKING	1	NOTE	1
GUARD	1	INSTAR	1	LOST	1	NOURISH	1
GUESS	1	INTENERAT	1	LOT	1	OBSCURENESS	1
GUIDE	1	INTERCESSION	1	LOVE'S	1	OBSERVER	1
HAND'S	1	INTERDICTED	1	LOVELESS	1	OBTAIN	1
HANDMAIDS	1	INTERRUPTED	1	LOVERS	1	ODORS	1
HAPLESS	1	INTIMATE	1	LOWERS	1	OFFER	1
HAPPIER	1	INVAIL	1	LUCKILY	1	OFFERED	1
HAPPILY	1	INWARD	1	LURK	1	OFFSPRING	1
HAPPINESS	1	ISSUE	1	LUTE	1	OFTEN	1
HARDEST	1	IVORY	1	MADEST	1	OLIVE	1
HARMS	1	JOYFUL	1	MAN	1	ONES	1
HARSH	1	JUDGED	1	MANTLED	1	OPEN	1
HASTE	1	JUST	1	MARS	1	OPENS	1
HASTES	1	JUSTICE	1	MARVEL	1	OPINION	1
HAUNTING	1	JUSTLY	1	MATTER'S	1	OPPRESSED	1
HAVING	1	KALENDS	1	MEAN	1	ORB	1
HEAR	1	KEEPS	1	MEANER	1	ORE	1
HEART-ST		KEPT	1	MEANS	1	ORIENT	1
RINGS	1	KILLS	1	MELTED	1	ORPHAN	1
HEATS	1	KIND	1	MELTS	1	OTHERS	1
HEEDLESS	1	KINDLE	1	MEMORIALS	1	OUGHT	1
HEREBY	1	KISSES	1	MERCENARY	1	OUTCAST	1
HERS	1	KNIFE	1	MERCY-WA		OUTWARD	1
HIDDEN	1	KNIGHTS	1	NTING	1	OVER	1
HILL	1	KNOCK	1	MILD	1	OVERCOME	1
HILLS	1	KNOWLEDGE	1	MINERVA-LIKE	1	OVERGROWN	1
HIMSELF	1	LADIES	1	MIRACLE	1	OVERTHROW	1
HOMAGE	1	LAMENTABLE	1	MIRROR	1	PAID	1
HOMEWARD	1	LAP	1	MIRTH	1	PALADINS	1
HONEY	1	LASTING	1	MISHAP	1	PAST	1
HOPING	1	LATE	1	MISS	1	PEARLS	1
HORROR	1	LAUGHTER	1	MISSES	1	PENCIL	1
HORROR'S	1	LAYS	1	MISTAKING	1	PENSIVE	1
HOUNDS	1	LEAD	1	MODEL	1	PERIOD	1
HOVERS	1	LEADS	1	MODEST	1	PERPLEXED	1
HUMBLE	1	LEAGUE	1	MOLEST	1	PETRARCH	1
HUNGER-S		LEANDER	1	MOMENTARY	1	PHOENIX-LIKE	1
TARVEN	1	LEARN	1	MORROW	1	PICTURE	1
HUNGRY	1	LEARNED	1	MORTALITY	1	PIERCE	1
HURT	1	LEASE	1	MOTHER	1	PINED	1
HYACINTH	1	LEAVES	1	MOTIONS	1	PINES	1
HYDRA	1	LENT	1	MOTIVE	1	PINING	1
HYRCAN	1	LESS	1	MOUNTING	1	PITY'S	1
I'D	1	LETTERS	1	MOURNING	1	PITYING	1
IDOL	1	LEVEL	1	MOVES	1	PLAINLY	1
ILIADS	1	LIARS	1	MUD	1	PLAINS	1
ILL-ACCEPTED	1	LIBERTY	1	MURDER	1	PLAINTIVE	1
IMAGES	1	LIE	1	MURDERING	1	PLAYS	1
IMAGINARY	1	LIEN	1	MUSE-FOE	1	PLEASE	1
IMMORTAL	1	LIFE'S	1	MYRTLE	1	PLEASED	1
IMPARADISE	1	LIGHTEN	1	NARCISSUS	1	PLEASURE	1
IMPORTS	1	LIGHTLY	1	NEARLY	1	PLEASURE'S	1
IMPORTUNE	1	LIGHTNESS	1	NEED	1	PLEDGE	1
IMPOSED	1	LIGHTS	1	NEEDLE	1	PLOWS	1
IMPRESSION	1	LIKEWISE	1	NEEDS	1	POINTED	1
IMPRISONED	1	LIMITS	1	NEGLECTED	1	POMP	1
IN-DARKENED	1	LIQUOR	1	NEPTUNE'S	1	POSSESS	1
INDEED	1	LIST	1	NEST	1	POSTERITY	1
INFANT	1	LIVE'S	1	NET	1	POSTS	1
INFANTS	1	LIVING	1	NETS	1	PRAISETH	1
INFLAME	1	LOATHE	1	NEVER-RESTING	1		

Word		Word		Word		Word	
PRAISING	1	REPORTS	1	SIGNED	1	SUPPLIED	1
PREPARE	1	REPREHEND	1	SIGNIFIED	1	SURCHARGED	1
PRESENCE	1	RESERVED	1	SILLY	1	SURPRISE	1
PRESS	1	RESIGN	1	SILVER	1	SURVEYED	1
PRESUMED	1	RESIGNED	1	SINS	1	SUSPECT	1
PREVAIL	1	RESORT	1	SITH	1	SWIFT	1
PRIVILEGE	1	RESPECT	1	SITS	1	TABLE	1
PRIZE	1	RESTS	1	SITTING	1	TAKE	1
PRIZED	1	RETAINED	1	SKIES	1	TAKEN	1
PROCESS	1	RETIRE	1	SLEEPING	1	TERROR	1
PRODIGAL	1	RETURNING	1	SLEEPS	1	THEATERS	1
PROMISED	1	RETURNS	1	SLEPT	1	THEMSELVES	1
PROSPECTIVE	1	REVIVE	1	SLEW	1	THETIS	1
PROSTRATE	1	REWARDED	1	SLIGHTLY	1	THINKING	1
PROTEST	1	RHYME	1	SLOW	1	THINKS	1
PROUDER	1	RICH	1	SMART	1	THOUGHT'S	1
PROUDEST	1	RIVER	1	SMOKES	1	THOUGHTS	
PURCHASED	1	ROB	1	SNARY	1	-MAZE	1
PURENESS	1	ROCK	1	SOAR	1	THOUSAND	1
PUREST	1	ROLLING	1	SOFTEN	1	THREE	1
PURSUE	1	ROMAN	1	SONGS	1	THREW	1
PURSUED	1	ROOT	1	SORROWING	1	THRICE-G	
PURSUES	1	ROSES	1	SORT	1	RATEFUL	1
PUTS	1	ROUND	1	SOUR	1	THROUGH	1
PYGMALION	1	RUINS	1	SOVEREIGN	1	THROUGHOUT	1
QUAINT	1	RULEST	1	SOVEREIGN'S	1	THUNDER	1
RADIANT	1	RUN	1	SOVEREIGNTY	1	TIGERS	1
RAGE	1	RUNS	1	SPEED	1	TILLED	1
RAIL	1	SACK	1	SPEEDY	1	TIME'S	1
RAISE	1	SACRIFICED	1	SPEND	1	TOIL	1
RAISING	1	SAFETY	1	SPHERES	1	TOPS	1
RANGE	1	SAID	1	SPILL	1	TORMENT	1
RAYS	1	SAINT	1	SPREADEST	1	TOUCHED	1
REACH	1	SAINTED	1	SPREADS	1	TRACE	1
READING	1	SAKE	1	SPRING	1	TRAITOR	1
READS	1	SALVE	1	STAIN	1	TRANSPIE	
READY	1	SANCTUARY	1	STALK	1	RCING	1
REARED	1	SATISIFY	1	STAND	1	TRANSPORT	1
REBEL	1	SAVE	1	STAR	1	TRAVAILS	1
REBELLING	1	SAVES	1	STARVED	1	TREACHERY	1
RECALL	1	SAW	1	STAYS	1	TREAD	1
RECEIVED	1	SAWEST	1	STEEMS	1	TREAT	1
RECKON	1	SAYS	1	STONY	1	TREES	1
RECOMPENSE	1	SCALE	1	STOP	1	TRESSES	1
RECONCILED	1	SCANT	1	STORM	1	TRIBUTARY	1
RECORDS	1	SCORNETH	1	STORY	1	TRIBUTE	1
RECTOR	1	SCORNS	1	STRAIGHTWAY	1	TRIBUTES	1
RED	1	SCYTH	1	STRAY	1	TRIUMVIRATE	1
REDEEMED	1	SEARCH	1	STREAMS	1	TRODDEN	1
REDRESS	1	SEASON	1	STRENGTH	1	TROPHY	1
REFRESH	1	SEED	1	STRIFE	1	TROUBLED	1
REFUGE	1	SEEKING	1	STRIKES	1	TRUEST	1
REFUSE	1	SEEKS	1	STRIVING	1	TRULY	1
REGARD	1	SEES	1	SUBDUE	1	TUNED	1
REGARDED	1	SEEST	1	SUBSTANCE	1	TURN	1
REINED	1	SERVILE	1	SUCCEEDING	1	TURRET	1
RELEASE	1	SHADED	1	SUCCORING	1	TWAIN	1
RELENT	1	SHADOW	1	SUCCORS	1	TWO	1
RELISH	1	SHINE	1	SUDDEN	1	UNAFFECTED	1
REMAINED	1	SHIPWRACK	1	SUFFERED	1	UNAMBITIOUS	1
REMAINING	1	SHOULDST	1	SUMMED	1	UNAWARES	1
RENEWS	1	SHOWEST	1	SUMMER'S	1	UNBORN	1
RENOWNED	1	SHUN	1	SUMMON	1	UNBURDEN	1
REPAIREST	1	SHUT	1	SUMS	1	UNBURIED	1
REPEAL	1	SIGHED	1	SUNNY	1	UNCLASP	1

Word		Word		Word		Word	
UNDISCLOSE	1	VENUS	1	WEARS	1	WOEFUL	1
UNFAINED	1	VEX	1	WEEP	1	WOES	1
UNFIT	1	VEXING	1	WEST	1	WOMEN	1
UNGRATEFUL	1	VICTORY	1	WHEELS	1	WON	1
UNKINDNESS	1	VIRTUOUS	1	WHEREOF	1	WOODS	1
UNLESS	1	VOLUME	1	WHERETO	1	WORKING	1
UNLOVING	1	VULGAR	1	WHEREWITH	1	WORLD'S	1
UNRESPECTING	1	VULTURE-GNAWN	1	WHET	1	WORLDLY	1
UNSUBJECT	1	WAKEN	1	WHIT	1	WORST	1
UNSURE	1	WALKED	1	WHITE	1	WORTH	1
UNTOUCHED	1	WALLS	1	WHITHER	1	WOULDST	1
UNTRODDEN	1	WANE	1	WHOLE	1	WOUNDING	1
UNTRUTH	1	WANING	1	WHOLLY	1	WRACK	1
UNTUNABLE	1	WANTS	1	WHOSOEVER	1	WRATH	1
UNTUNED	1	WAR	1	WIDE	1	WRECK	1
UNWORTHY	1	WARMED	1	WINDOWS	1	WRINKLES	1
URGED	1	WASTE	1	WINDS	1	WRITTEN	1
VANQUISHED	1	WATER-COLD	1	WINTER-WITHERED	1	WRONGFUL	
VAPORS	1	WAX	1	WIRE	1	WROTE	1
VEIL	1	WAY	1	WISH	1	WROUGHT	1
VENTURE	1	WEALTH	1	WITHER	1	YIELDED	1
VENTURED	1						

MICHAEL DRAYTON, 'IDEA'

Word		Word		Word		Word	
THE	229	THEY	30	OTHER	15	EACH	9
MY	224	ON	28	THOUGH	15	GIVE	9
AND	201	SHALL	28	WHOSE	15	GOOD	9
I	183	HAVE	27	CAN	14	HERE	9
TO	182	FROM	26	OUR	14	MAY	9
IN	134	ONE	26	AGAIN	13	O	9
WITH	104	THEN	26	DID	13	REASON	9
THAT	102	EYES	25	EVER	13	SAME	9
OF	96	IF	25	HEAVEN	13	THEM	9
YOU	72	SOME	25	MOST	13	UNTO	9
A	68	STILL	25	OUT	13	WELL	9
ME	65	SEE	24	THAN	13	WHY	9
LOVE	64	ONLY	23	THERE	13	ALONE	8
BY	59	YOUR	23	WORLD	13	FAME	8
BE	57	NOW	22	FIRE	12	FOOLS	8
IS	55	THEIR	22	SIGHS	12	GO	8
THOU	53	WHERE	22	TIME	12	HAST	8
THY	50	WILL	22	TOO	12	HATE	8
AS	48	DOTH	21	WOULD	12	HOPE	8
HER	47	SELF	21	ART	11	KEEP	8
NOT	46	ARE	19	BEEN	11	KIND	8
IT	45	EVERY	19	COULD	11	LINES	8
WHEN	45	HATH	19	MAKE	11	LONG	8
WHICH	45	SINCE	19	PROVE	11	MIGHT	8
BUT	44	MORE	18	TAKE	11	MUSE	8
HIS	43	AM	17	TEARS	11	NAME	8
SO	42	AT	17	WHILST	11	NINE	8
THIS	42	LIKE	17	WHO	11	POOR	8
YET	39	NOR	17	DESIRE	10	POWER	8
ALL	37	WAS	17	HAD	10	PRAISE	8
WHAT	37	FAIR	16	MEN	10	REST	8
DO	33	FIRST	16	NEVER	10	SUCH	8
OR	33	MINE	16	SPIRIT	10	SUN	8
NO	32	SAY	16	SWEET	10	THINE	8
THUS	32	SHE	16	TELL	10	UPON	8
HE	31	SHOULD	16	THOSE	10	WIT	8
THEE	31	THESE	16	WE	10	WRITE	8
FOR	30	HOW	15	WERE	10	BREAST	7
HEART	30	LET	15	BEAUTY	9	CALL	7

Word		Word		Word		Word	
DEATH	7	SIGHT	5	WANDERING	4	MUSES	3
FEAR	7	SIT	5	WISE	4	NAKED	3
HIM	7	SPENT	5	WOES	4	NAY	3
LIVING	7	THINK	5	WON	4	OFT	3
MAN	7	THOUGHTS	5	WORTHY	4	OTHERS	3
MUCH	7	TIMES	5	YE	4	PAINS	3
NOTHING	7	TIS	5	YOUNG	4	PAINT	3
READ	7	TOGETHER	5	ABOVE	3	PASSIONS	3
SEEN	7	TRUE	5	AFFORDS	3	PEACE	3
SOUL	7	USE	5	AID	3	PLEASE	3
UP	7	AGAINST	4	AIR	3	PRECIOUS	3
US	7	AN	4	AMONGST	3	PROUD	3
VIRTUE	7	ANY	4	ANCHOR	3	REASON'S	3
WHOM	7	BACK	4	ANGEL	3	RHYMES	3
WORDS	7	BOAST	4	ANSWER	3	SACRED	3
AGE	6	BODY	4	BEAR	3	SAD	3
BLESSED	6	BORN	4	BEST	3	SEEM	3
FOUL	6	BRAIN	4	BETTER	3	SENSE	3
GET	6	CAME	4	BOSOM	3	SENSES	3
GIVES	6	CAST	4	BOY	3	SHADOW	3
INTO	6	CHASTE	4	BROUGHT	3	SON	3
LIGHT	6	CHILDREN	4	BURN	3	SOUL'S	3
MADE	6	CONCEIT	4	CANST	3	STORY	3
MARVEL	6	DELIGHT	4	CARE	3	TAKING	3
MIND	6	DOST	4	COURSE	3	THEREOF	3
NATURE	6	EITHER	4	CRAVE	3	THOUGHT	3
NONE	6	ELSE	4	CREATURE	3	THREE	3
PART	6	EVEN	4	DOWN	3	TWO	3
SHOW	6	FAITH	4	DULL	3	VERY	3
THINGS	6	FORTUNE	4	E'ER	3	VIEW	3
TURN	6	FREE	4	EARS	3	VULGAR	3
VERSE	6	FURTHER	4	EARTHLY	3	WANT	3
WOE	6	GAVE	4	END	3	WAY	3
ADMIRE	5	GIVEN	4	EXPRESS	3	WINGS	3
AWAY	5	GLAD	4	EYE	3	WITHAL	3
BEFORE	5	GODDESS	4	FACE	3	WONDER	3
BEGUN	5	GRACE	4	FIND	3	WOUNDS	3
BEHOLD	5	GREATER	4	FLY	3	YEARS	3
BEING	5	HEAVENLY	4	FORCE	3	YOUTH	3
BEYOND	5	HEAVENS	4	FORTH	3	AFTER	2
BLIND	5	HELL	4	FOUND	3	ALMS	2
BLOOD	5	HOLD	4	GAIN	3	AMIDST	2
CANNOT	5	ILL	4	GENTLE	3	APOLLO'S	2
COME	5	IMMORTAL	4	GOD	3	ARDEN	2
DEAD	5	INVENTION	4	GRIEF	3	ASCEND	2
DEAR	5	LAST	4	GROW	3	ASPIRE	2
DESPAIR	5	LIES	4	HAVING	3	AWHILE	2
DIE	5	MURDER	4	HEAT	3	BAD	2
DIVINE	5	NE'ER	4	HOLY	3	BASE	2
EARTH	5	OLD	4	IDEA	3	BEARS	2
FAR	5	ONCE	4	JOT	3	BEAT	2
FLAME	5	OWN	4	KNOW	3	BEAUTY'S	2
FRIENDS	5	PAST	4	LIPS	3	BECAUSE	2
GLORY	5	PITY	4	LITTLE	3	BID	2
JOY	5	PURE	4	LIVE	3	BLEEDING	2
LIFE	5	QUOTH	4	LOOK	3	BLESS	2
LOST	5	REPLY	4	LOOKS	3	BOOKS	2
MOVE	5	RICH	4	LOVE'S	3	BOTH	2
MUST	5	SCORN	4	MAKING	3	BOUNDED	2
NIGHT	5	SET	4	MANY	3	BREATH	2
PASS	5	SPEAK	4	MAYST	3	BRIGHT	2
PEN	5	STARVED	4	MEANS	3	BROOK	2
PLAY	5	THING	4	MEMORY	3	BURNED	2
SEVERAL	5	THINKS	4	MISTRESS	3	CARES	2
SHALT	5	VOWS	4	MOTHER'S	3	CEASETH	2

CELESTIAL	2	GRACES	2	PRAYERS	2	THENCE	2
CHARITY	2	GRAVE	2	PROMETHEUS	2	THINKEST	2
CLEAR	2	GREAT	2	PROOF	2	THOUSAND	2
COMMENDS	2	GREATEST	2	PROVED	2	TILL	2
COMPANY	2	GRIEVOUS	2	PUT	2	TOLD	2
COMPARE	2	GROWN	2	QUEEN	2	TORMENT	2
COMPLAINT	2	GUEST	2	QUIET	2	TORMENTS	2
CONFESS	2	HAIR	2	QUIVER	2	TOUCH	2
CONJURE	2	HALLOWED	2	RAGS	2	TOUCHING	2
CORSE	2	HAPPY	2	RAVISHED	2	TROPHIES	2
COUNTRIES	2	HEAD	2	RAYS	2	TRY	2
COY	2	HEAR	2	RECEIVE	2	TYRANT	2
CRUEL	2	HEAVY	2	REHEARSE	2	UNCERTAIN	2
CRY	2	HECATE'S	2	RELISH	2	VAIN	2
CRYSTAL	2	HIGH	2	REMAIN	2	VEIN	2
CUPID	2	HOME	2	REMORSE	2	VESSEL	2
DAINTY	2	HONEST	2	RETAIN	2	VESTAL	2
DAMNED	2	HONOR	2	RETURNS	2	VILE	2
DARKNESS	2	HOPE'S	2	RISING	2	WANTING	2
DAY	2	HOPES	2	ROUND	2	WANTON	2
DAYS	2	HUMOR	2	RUN	2	WARS	2
DEAF	2	I'LL	2	SADLY	2	WASTE	2
DEFACED	2	IMPRISONED	2	SAVE	2	WHEEL	2
DEFINE	2	INFERNAL	2	SAYETH	2	WHENCE	2
DENY	2	JUDGMENT	2	SCOPE	2	WHEREWITH	2
DESERT	2	KINDLED	2	SCORNEST	2	WHETHER	2
DESPAIRS	2	KNOWN	2	SECOND	2	WHILE	2
DESPITE	2	LABOR	2	SELVES	2	WHOLLY	2
DEVIL	2	LASTLY	2	SENSELESS	2	WILT	2
DISDAIN	2	LATE	2	SERVE	2	WISER	2
DONE	2	LAUGH	2	SEVER	2	WITHIN	2
DRIED	2	LAYS	2	SHORE	2	WOMAN	2
DROPS	2	LEARNED	2	SHOWS	2	WONDERS	2
DROWNED	2	LEARNING	2	SING	2	WORD	2
DUE	2	LEAVES	2	SKILL	2	WOUND	2
EAGLET	2	LESS	2	SLAIN	2	WRAPPED	2
EAR	2	LIFE'S	2	SLEEP	2	WRINKLES	2
ENDLESS	2	LIGHTS	2	SLEW	2	WRONG	2
ENTERTAIN	2	LIVES	2	SOMETIMES	2	YIELDS	2
ERE	2	LOSE	2	SONG	2	ABOUT	1
ETERNITY	2	LOVED	2	SORROW	2	ABROAD	1
ETERNIZE	2	LOVES	2	SORT	2	ABSENT	1
EVIL	2	MAKES	2	SOVEREIGN	2	ABSOLUTELY	1
EXCEL	2	MEAN	2	SPEEDY	2	ABSTRACTS	1
EXPERIENCE	2	MIRACLES	2	SPIRITS	2	ABUSE	1
FAIN	2	NATIONS	2	SPLEEN	2	ACCESSORY	1
FALL	2	NEAR	2	SPORT	2	ACQUAINT	1
FALLS	2	NEED	2	STAR	2	ACT	1
FATE	2	NEITHER	2	STARS	2	ACTORS	1
FATES	2	NINES	2	STATE	2	ADDETH	1
FEAST	2	NORTH	2	STAY	2	ADORE	1
FIERY	2	NUMBERS	2	STOOD	2	ADVENTUROUS	1
FINDING	2	OFFENCE	2	STORE	2	AFFECTED	1
FITTEST	2	OFFER	2	STRANGELY	2	AFFIRMING	1
FLIES	2	ORDER	2	STRIVE	2	AFFLICTED	1
FLOOD	2	ORDERS	2	STRIVING	2	AGED	1
FOLLY	2	PACK-HORSE	2	STRONG	2	AGES	1
FORCES	2	PAIN	2	STRONGLY	2	AIMING	1
FORMER	2	PASSION	2	STYX	2	ALAS	1
FRIEND	2	PERFECTION	2	SUFFER	2	ALBION'S	1
FUEL	2	PLACE	2	SUNDRY	2	ALTARS	1
GAZE	2	PLACED	2	SUPPOSE	2	ALTERETH	1
GHOST	2	PLAYS	2	SURFEIT	2	ALTHOUGH	1
GIDDY	2	PLEDGE	2	SWANS	2	AMAZEDLY	1
GLASS	2	PRAYER	2	THEMSELVES	2	AMISS	1

Word		Word		Word		Word	
ANCIENT	1	BIRTH	1	CHIEFEST	1	CREDIT	1
ANGELS	1	BLEED	1	CHIN	1	CREEP	1
ANGRY	1	BLISS	1	CHOSE	1	CRIPPLE	1
ANOTHER	1	BLOT	1	CINDERS	1	CRISPED	1
ANSWERED	1	BLOTTED	1	CIRCUIT	1	CROOKED	1
ANTIC	1	BOASTING	1	CIRCUMSTANCE	1	CROSS	1
ANVIL	1	BOILED	1	CLAPS	1	CROSSED	1
APPEAR	1	BOLD	1	CLEAN	1	CROSSES	1
APPEARS	1	BOLDEST	1	CLEANLY	1	CROW-KEEPER	1
APPLAUD	1	BORDERS	1	CLIFFS	1	CROWN	1
APPLAUSE	1	BORNE	1	CLIMES	1	CROWNED	1
APPLY	1	BORROWED	1	CLODS	1	CUPS	1
APPREHENSION	1	BOUND	1	CLOSING	1	CURE	1
ARCHED	1	BOW	1	CLOTHED	1	CURED	1
ARCHERY	1	BOWER	1	CLOUDS	1	CURING	1
ARDEN'S	1	BOYS	1	COACHES	1	CURIOUSLY	1
ARGUMENT	1	BRAGS	1	COIL	1	CURLED	1
ARISE	1	BRAVE	1	COIN	1	CURSE	1
ARREARAGE	1	BRAVER	1	COLD	1	CURSED	1
ASCENDING	1	BREAK	1	COLDNESS	1	CUSTOM	1
ASCENDS	1	BREATH'S	1	COLORS	1	DANGEROUS	1
ASK	1	BREATHE	1	COMES	1	DANISH	1
ASKS	1	BREATHLESS	1	COMFORT	1	DARES	1
ASSAIL	1	BRED	1	COMING	1	DEARTH	1
ASSISTS	1	BREEDS	1	COMMAND	1	DEBTOR	1
ASTRAEA	1	BRIBED	1	COMMANDING	1	DECEASED	1
ATE	1	BRIDE	1	COMMEND	1	DECEIVE	1
ATTEND	1	BRINGS	1	COMMIT	1	DECEIVED	1
AVAIL	1	BROKE	1	COMMON	1	DECIDE	1
AVON'S	1	BROOD	1	COMPASS	1	DECLARE	1
BABY	1	BROW	1	COMPELLED	1	DEE	1
BALMS	1	BROWS	1	CONCEIVE	1	DEED	1
BANISHED	1	BUGBEARS	1	CONDEMNED	1	DEEP	1
BANKRUPT	1	BUILD	1	CONDEMNING	1	DEFIANCE	1
BANKS	1	BUNDLES	1	CONDITIONS	1	DELICIOUS	1
BANNED	1	BUNGLING	1	CONQUERING	1	DELIGHTED	1
BANQUET	1	BURDEN	1	CONQUEST	1	DEN	1
BARDS	1	BURNETH	1	CONQUESTS	1	DENIES	1
BARE	1	CALLED	1	CONSCIENCE	1	DENYING	1
BEAUTIES	1	CALLING	1	CONSENT	1	DEPART	1
BECALMED	1	CALLS	1	CONSISTS	1	DEPARTED	1
BECOMETH	1	CANCEL	1	CONSPIRE	1	DEPRIVES	1
BED	1	CANKER'S	1	CONSTANT	1	DEPTH	
BEDLAM	1	CAPES	1	CONSTELL		DESIGNS	
BEDLAM-LIKE	1	CARLEGION	1	ATIONS	1	DESIRES	1
BEGAN	1	CAROUSES	1	CONSUME	1	DESPITETH	1
BEGGARS	1	CARRY	1	CONSUMING	1	DESTINED	1
BEGGARY	1	CASE	1	CONTAIN	1	DEVISE	1
BEGGED	1	CAUSE	1	CONTENTED	1	DEVISED	1
BEGIN	1	CEASE	1	CONTINENT	1	DEVOUT	1
BEGUILE	1	CELL	1	CONVERSING	1	DEW-EMPE	
BELLOWS	1	CENSURE	1	CORN	1	ARLED	1
BELONG	1	CENSURES	1	CORRECTION	1	DIAMOND	1
BEMOANING	1	CENSUREST	1	CORRUPTED	1	DIED	1
BEND	1	CHAIR	1	COSTLY	1	DIET	1
BENT	1	CHARITABLE	1	COTSWOLD	1	DIFFERETH	1
BEQUEATH	1	CHARMED	1	COUNT	1	DIRECT	1
BESTOW	1	CHARMING	1	COURAGE	1	DIRECTION	1
BESTOWING	1	CHEAT	1	COURTEOUS	1	DISCERNED	1
BETRAYED	1	CHEEK	1	COVER	1	DISCHARGE	1
BETRAYER	1	CHEEKS	1	COVETOUS	1	DISCOMMENDS	1
BETWIXT	1	CHERISH	1	CRAFT	1	DISCOVERY	1
BEWITCH	1	CHEST	1	CRAFTILY	1	DISCRETION	1
BIDS	1	CHESTER	1	CRAVED	1	DISDAINS	1
BIRD'S	1	CHID	1	CREATURES	1	DISGRACE	1

IRISH	1	LO	1	MODELED	1	ORDAINED	1
ISIS	1	LODGED	1	MODEST	1	ORPHEUS	1
ISLAND	1	LODGING	1	MOLE	1	OTHER'S	1
ISLE	1	LONG-LIVING	1	MOLLIFY	1	OTHERS'	1
IVORY	1	LONGED	1	MOMENT	1	OUSE	1
IXION	1	LONGER	1	MONGST	1	OUTWARDLY	1
JEER	1	LOOKING	1	MOON	1	OVER	1
JEST	1	LOOPHOLES	1	MOSS	1	OVER-PRIZE	1
JOVE	1	LOOSELY	1	MOUNT	1	OVER-SOON	1
JOY'S	1	LOSS	1	MOUNTING	1	OVERTHROWN	1
JOYS	1	LOVELY	1	MOURN	1	PAID	1
JUDGE	1	LOVERS	1	MOVED	1	PAINTED	1
JUDGING	1	LOVERS'	1	MOVES	1	PAINTING	1
JUSTICE	1	LOW	1	MOVING	1	PALE	1
KENT	1	LUNACY	1	MURDEREST	1	PALTRY	1
KEYS	1	LUNATIC	1	MURDERING	1	PAPER	1
KILL	1	LUST	1	MUSIC	1	PAPERS	1
KILLING	1	MAD	1	MUTUALLY	1	PARADISE	1
KINDER	1	MADMEN	1	MYRRH-BR	1	PARCHED	1
KINDLY	1	MAGIC	1	EATHING	1	PARLEY	1
KINDNESS	1	MAID	1	NAMED	1	PARTED	1
KING	1	MAIMED	1	NAMES	1	PARTIAL	1
KING'S	1	MAIN	1	NAUGHT	1	PARTS	1
KINGLY	1	MAINTAINS	1	NEARER	1	PARTY	1
KISS	1	MALICE	1	NECTAR-D	1	PASSED	1
KNEELING	1	MAN'S	1	ROPPING	1	PASSING	1
KNOWING	1	MANHOOD	1	NEEDSLY	1	PASSION'S	1
KNOWLEDGE	1	MAP	1	NEPHEWS	1	PATH	1
KNOWS	1	MARS	1	NEST	1	PAUSE	1
LABORING	1	MASSACRE	1	NEVER-CE	1	PAWN	1
LACK	1	MASTERING	1	RTAIN	1	PAY	1
LADEN	1	MATCH	1	NEVER-HOPING	1	PAYMENTS	1
LAID	1	MATRONS	1	NEW	1	PEAK	1
LAME	1	MAXIM	1	NEXT	1	PEARLY	1
LAP	1	MEASURE	1	NIGGARDLY	1	PENNED	1
LARGE	1	MEDEA-LIKE	1	NIGHTINGALES	1	PENNY-FATHER	1
LATEST	1	MEDICINE	1	NIGHTLY	1	PENURY	1
LAUGHETH	1	MEDWAY	1	NOISE	1	PEOPLE	1
LAUREL	1	MEET	1	NORTHERN	1	PERCEIVE	1
LAVISH	1	MELL	1	NOSE	1	PERFECT	1
LAWS	1	MEMORIALS	1	NOTE	1	PERFECTIONS	1
LAY	1	MERIT	1	NOVICE	1	PERFUMING	1
LEA	1	MET	1	NUMBER	1	PERIL	1
LEADEN	1	METALS	1	NYMPH	1	PERILS	1
LEADS	1	METAPHORS	1	NYMPH-LIKE	1	PERISH	1
LEAN	1	METHOD	1	O'ERCOME	1	PEULE	1
LEAVE	1	METTLE	1	OBEY	1	PHLEGETHON	1
LEAVING	1	MIGHTST	1	OBJECTS	1	PHOENIX	1
LED	1	MILK-WHITE	1	OBLATIONS	1	PHOENIX'S	1
LEFT	1	MILLIONS	1	OBLIVION	1	PHRASE	1
LEGACY	1	MIMIC	1	OBSCURED	1	PHYSIC	1
LEGS	1	MIND'S	1	OBSCURITY	1	PICKS	1
LEND	1	MINDS	1	OBTAIN	1	PIECE	1
LENGTH	1	MINERVA	1	OBTAINS	1	PINED	1
LENT	1	MINISTER	1	ODD	1	PINIONS	1
LESSER	1	MINSTRELS	1	ODORS	1	PIREN'S	1
LETTERS	1	MINUTE'S	1	OFFENDS	1	PITCH	1
LIBERTY	1	MIRROR	1	OFFICES	1	PITY'S	1
LIEN	1	MISBELIEVING	1	OFT-VARYING	1	PLACES	1
LIGHTENED	1	MISERABLE	1	OFTEN	1	PLAGUES	1
LIGHTNINGS	1	MISERIES	1	OLDER	1	PLAIN-PATHED	1
LIKELY	1	MISERY	1	OPEN	1	PLAINT	1
LIVED	1	MISTAKEN	1	OPPOSE	1	PLAYED	1
LIVELESS	1	MIXED	1	OPPOSED	1	PLEASANT	1
LIVELY	1	MOANS	1	ORCADES	1	PLEASETH	1

PLEASING	1	RASHLY	1	SAINT	1	SLOW	1
PLENTY	1	RATE	1	SAKE	1	SMELLING	1
PLOWMAN	1	RAVING	1	SATIATE	1	SMOKE	1
PLUCKS	1	RAZE	1	SAW	1	SMOKED	1
PLUMES	1	READING	1	SAYEST	1	SMOTHERED	1
POET	1	REARED	1	SCAPE	1	SOBER	1
POETS	1	REBATE	1	SCARABIES	1	SOFTEN	1
POISON	1	REBELS	1	SCARCELY	1	SOLEMN	1
POLE	1	RECEIPT	1	SCARLET	1	SOMETIME	1
POLISHED	1	RECEIVING	1	SCHOOLMEN	1	SONNET	1
PORT	1	RECKONINGS	1	SCORCHING	1	SONNETS	1
POSSESSED	1	RECOMPENSE	1	SCORNED	1	SOON	1
POSSIBLY	1	RECOVER	1	SCORNING	1	SOONER	1
POSTERITY	1	RECURE	1	SCORSE	1	SORROWS	1
POURED	1	REEL	1	SCOTLAND	1	SORRY	1
POWDER	1	REFINED	1	SEA	1	SOT	1
POWERFUL	1	REFINES	1	SEA-FARER	1	SOUGHT	1
PRACTICE	1	REFLECTION	1	SEAS	1	SOUL-SHRINED	1
PRAISED	1	REFUSE	1	SEAT	1	SOUND	1
PRAISES	1	REGISTER	1	SECRET	1	SOURS	1
PRAY	1	RELATE	1	SEEING	1	SOUTH	1
PREFER	1	RELIC	1	SEEK	1	SOWN	1
PRESENT	1	REMAINETH	1	SELFSAME	1	SPACIOUS	1
PRESERVE	1	REMAINS	1	SEND	1	SPAIN	1
PRESS	1	REMEMBRANCE	1	SERVED	1	SPARE	1
PRETTY	1	REMOTE	1	SERVES	1	SPARES	1
PREVAIL	1	REMOVE	1	SERVEST	1	SPARKLING	1
PRICE	1	RENOWNED	1	SERVICES	1	SPEAKS	1
PRIDE	1	REPEAT	1	SEVERN	1	SPEECHLESS	1
PRIESTS	1	REPLIES	1	SEX'S	1	SPEED	1
PRISONERS	1	REPLYETH	1	SHADES	1	SPEND	1
PRIVATE	1	REPROACHED	1	SHAKE	1	SPHERE	1
PROCEED	1	REQUEST	1	SHALLOW	1	SPICERY	1
PROCEEDING	1	RESIDENT	1	SHAPE	1	SPICES	1
PROCEEDS	1	RESISTLESS	1	SHEET	1	SPITEFUL	1
PRODIGAL	1	RESOLUTE	1	SHEPHERD	1	SPLENDOROUS	1
PROFANE	1	RESOLVE	1	SHIFT	1	SPORTS	1
PROSERPINE'S	1	RESPECTS	1	SHINE	1	SPRING	1
PROUDLY	1	RESTORE	1	SHINING	1	SPRUNG	1
PROVERBS	1	RESTRAIN	1	SHIPS	1	SPUN	1
PROVES	1	RETAINING	1	SHORT	1	STAINS	1
PROVOKE	1	RETURNED	1	SHOULDST	1	STALE	1
PROVOKED	1	REVIVED	1	SHOUTS	1	STANCH	1
PSYCHE'S	1	REVIVING	1	SHOWERS	1	STAND	1
PUBLIC	1	REWARD	1	SHRINE	1	STANDS	1
PULSE	1	RHENE	1	SICK	1	STARVELING	1
PUNISHED	1	RHYME	1	SIDE	1	STATELY	1
PURBLIND	1	RIGHT	1	SIGH	1	STEAD	1
PURGATORY	1	RIGHTLY	1	SIGHING	1	STEADFASTLY	1
PURLOIN	1	RIOTS	1	SIGNS	1	STEAL	1
PURSUE	1	RISE	1	SILENCE	1	STEERED	1
QUAFFING	1	ROCKS	1	SILLY	1	STICK	1
QUAKE	1	ROGUE	1	SILVER-S		STIFF-NECKED	1
QUEENS	1	ROLL	1	ANDED	1	STOLE	1
QUICK	1	ROOM	1	SIMPLE	1	STOMACH	1
QUIT	1	ROSES	1	SINGS	1	STONE	1
QUITE	1	RUFFIN'S	1	SIR	1	STONES	1
RAIL	1	RULES	1	SISYPHUS	1	STRAIGHT	1
RAINING	1	RUNG	1	SITH	1	STRAIGHTWAYS	1
RAISE	1	RUNNING	1	SITTING	1	STRAIN	1
RAISED	1	RUST	1	SKIES	1	STRAITS	1
RANSACK	1	RUSTIC	1	SKY	1	STRANGENESS	1
RAPE	1	SACRIFICE	1	SLACK	1	STREAM	1
RAPT	1	SACRIFICED	1	SLAUGHTERING	1	STREET	1
RARE	1	SAILED	1	SLIGHTLY	1	STRENGTH	1

STRIVES	1	THIEVES	1	TYRANNIZING	1	WEAR	1
STRONG-BUILT	1	THIN	1	TYRONE	1	WEATHER	1
STROVE	1	THIRSTING	1	UNABLE	1	WEEPING	1
SUBTRACTING	1	THOU'LT	1	UNAVOIDED	1	WEIGHT	1
SUBVERSION	1	THREAD	1	UNBELIEVING	1	WENCH	1
SUDDEN	1	THRICE-M		UNCLEAN	1	WEST	1
SUFFERED	1	ARRIED'S	1	UNDONE	1	WESTERN	1
SUM	1	THRICE-THREE	1	UNEXPECTEDLY	1	WHEREIN	1
SUMMED	1	THRONG	1	UNFOLD	1	WHOLE	1
SUMMON	1	THRONGED	1	UNGRATEFUL	1	WICKED	1
SUMMONED	1	THUNDERER	1	UNHAPPY	1	WILIS'	1
SUNBEAMS	1	THWARTED	1	UNKNOWING	1	WIN	1
SUNK	1	TIED	1	UNLEARNED'S	1	WINDING	1
SUPERFLUOUS	1	TOILING	1	UNLUCKY	1	WINE	1
SURE	1	TONGUE	1	UNMOVED	1	WING	1
SUREST	1	TONGUE'S	1	UNSKILLFUL	1	WINGED	1
SURGEONS	1	TORTURES	1	UNTIMELY	1	WISDOM'S	1
SURVIVE	1	TOUCHSTONE	1	UNTRUE	1	WISH	1
SWAGGERING	1	TOYS	1	UNWORTHY	1	WISHED	1
SWEARS	1	TRADE	1	USURY	1	WISHETH	1
SWEETEST	1	TRALUCENT	1	UTMOST	1	WISHING	1
SWEETNESS	1	TRANCE	1	UTTERANCE	1	WITHOUT	1
SWEETS	1	TRANSFORMED	1	UTTERING	1	WITLESS	1
TABLE	1	TRANSGRESS	1	VAINLY	1	WITS	1
TALK	1	TRANSPIERCE	1	VALUE	1	WOEFUL	1
TALKING	1	TRANSPORTED	1	VANQUISHING	1	WOLVES	1
TAME	1	TRAVELED	1	VARYING	1	WOMEN	1
TASTE	1	TRAVELS	1	VAUNTS	1	WONDERING	1
TAUGHT	1	TREASURE	1	VERDICT	1	WOOD	1
TAX	1	TREASURES	1	VERSES	1	WOOED	1
TAXETH	1	TREBLE	1	VESTA	1	WORK	1
TEAR	1	TREE	1	VEXED	1	WORKS	1
TEDIOUS	1	TREES	1	VICES	1	WORLD-OU	
TEETH	1	TRENT	1	VIGOR	1	T-WEARING	1
TELLS	1	TRIAL	1	VIOLATE	1	WORLD'S	1
TEMPE	1	TRIED	1	VIRGINITY	1	WORLDS	1
TEMPER	1	TRIFLE	1	VIRGINS	1	WORTH	1
TEMPLE	1	TROT	1	VIRTUES	1	WORTHIES	1
TEMPT	1	TROUBLE	1	VIRTUOUS	1	WOULDST	1
TEMPTING	1	TROUBLED	1	VOLUMES	1	WOUNDED	1
TEN	1	TRUCE	1	VOYAGE	1	WRACK	1
TERM	1	TRUE-LOVE	1	WAFER	1	WREST	1
TERROR	1	TRUEST	1	WAKE	1	WRETCHED	1
THAMES	1	TRULL	1	WALLS	1	WRITING	1
THANKS	1	TRULY	1	WAN	1	WROUGHT	1
THAW	1	TURNED	1	WANTED	1	YEA	1
THEATERS	1	TURNETH	1	WARNING	1	YORK	1
THEIRS	1	TURNING	1	WAVES	1	ZEAL	1
THEREBY	1	TWAIN	1	WEAL	1	ZEPHYR	1
THIEF	1	TWEED'S	1	WEALTH	1		

MICHAEL DRAYTON, 'IDEA'S MIRROUR'

MY	254	LOVE	54	YET	29	SHE	25
THE	198	THAT	51	FAIR	28	BEAUTY	24
AND	161	BY	49	FOR	28	ME	24
OF	142	BE	40	ON	27	THIS	24
TO	114	EYES	37	THEN	27	WORLD	24
IN	112	THOU	36	THUS	27	STILL	23
WITH	100	HIS	35	FROM	26	SWEET	23
HER	86	ALL	34	HEART	26	BUT	22
I	75	IS	33	TEARS	26	DO	22
THY	69	SO	33	THEE	26	FIRE	22
A	67	WHICH	32	NOW	25	NOR	22

Word	Count	Word	Count	Word	Count	Word	Count
SIGHS	22	LIKE	9	FIRST	5	OTHERS'	4
OR	21	WHOSE	9	GO	5	PAIN	4
SEE	20	ALONE	8	IMAGE	8	REVENGE	4
THEIR	19	ARE	8	IT	8	SELF	4
AS	18	BLESSED	8	LEARNED	8	SHINING	4
DOTH	18	HOW	8	LIES	8	SORROW	4
HATH	18	IDEA	8	LOOKING	8	SPENT	4
HEAVEN	18	LOOKS	8	MAKE	8	STARS	4
NEVER	18	ONLY	8	MOVE	8	STRONG	4
SHALL	18	PERFECTION	8	OTHER	8	SUNBEAMS	4
WHERE	18	PRAISE	8	CUT	8	TAUGHT	4
HE	17	SAY	8	PASS	8	THAN	4
LIFE	17	THOUGHTS	8	POOR	8	TRUE	4
MINE	17	UPON	8	PURE	8	UNKINDNESS	4
NOT	17	WERE	8	PUREST	8	UP	4
THOSE	17	WILL	8	READ	8	VIRTUE'S	4
HAD	16	WOE	8	SET	8	VIRTUES	4
HOPE	16	YOU	8	THREE	8	WANT	4
IF	16	AT	7	TILL	7	WATER	4
SOME	16	GRIEF	7	TONGUE	7	WE	4
UNTO	16	HEAVENLY	7	TOO	7	WORTHY	4
MORE	15	HELL	7	VERSE	7	AGAIN	3
O	15	HERE	7	VOWS	7	AM	3
ONE	15	JOYS	7	WELL	7	ANGEL	3
SUN	15	LET	7	WHOM	7	ARISE	3
THINE	15	NINE	7	YOUTH	7	ARROWS	3
WHEN	15	OUR	7	ANCHOR	7	BASTARD	3
MAY	14	OWN	7	ANGELS	7	CALL	3
PROVE	14	PAST	7	BEGUN	7	CAME	3
THESE	14	RARE	7	BLACK	7	CANNOT	3
THEY	14	REASON	7	BLOOD	7	CAUSE	3
WONDER	14	SHALT	7	CARE	7	COURSE	3
DESIRE	13	SOUL'S	7	CARES	7	CROWNED	3
TELL	13	BEAUTY'S	6	CAST	6	DAY	3
WHO	13	BREAST	6	CHASTE	6	DAY'S	3
BEEN	12	CELESTIAL	6	COMPARE	6	DESPAIRS	3
EVER	12	CONCEIT	6	CRYSTAL	6	DOLEFUL	3
FAME	12	DISDAIN	6	DIE	6	DOWN	3
JOY	12	EACH	6	DIVINITY	6	DWELL	3
SLEEP	12	GOOD	6	DONE	6	FIND	3
SOUL	12	KIND	6	DYING	6	FLOOD	3
TIME	12	LONG	6	EVERY	6	FOE	3
WAS	12	LOOK	6	EXPRESS	6	GAZE	3
AIR	11	LOVE'S	6	FACE	6	GLORIOUS	3
ART	11	MAKES	6	FAIREST	6	GLORY	3
EYE	11	MOST	6	FEAR	6	GODDESS	3
HAVE	11	OLD	6	FLAME	6	GODS	3
MUSE	11	ONCE	6	FORCE	6	GOLDEN	3
THERE	11	PHOENIX	6	FOUL	6	GRAVE	3
WHAT	11	SACRED	6	GLASS	6	HAPPY	3
WHILST	11	SEEN	6	HAIR	6	HEART'S	3
DIVINE	10	SHADOW	6	HAND	6	HEAT	3
INTO	10	SIGHT	6	HAST	6	HEIGHT	3
NAME	10	SUCH	6	HIM	6	HERSELF	3
NO	10	TEN	6	HOLY	6	HIGH	3
THOUSAND	10	THOUGHT	6	HONOR	6	IMMORTAL	3
WORDS	10	WOES	6	I'LL	6	IMPRISONED	3
BEHOLD	9	WONDERS	6	LAWS	6	INVENTION	3
CAN	9	WORLD'S	6	LEFT	6	KNOW	3
COULD	9	WRITE	6	LIGHTNING	6	KNOWN	3
DEATH	9	ABOVE	5	LIVE	5	LIFE'S	3
DESPAIR	9	DELIGHT	5	LO	5	LINES	3
EARTH	9	DID	5	MEN	5	LIPS	3
HEAVENS	9	ERE	5	NATURE	5	LOVES	3
LIGHT	9	FAITH	5	NIGHT	5	MADE	3

MAZE	3	COMES	2	MINERVA	2	THENCE	2
MOON	3	CROCODILE	2	MIRROR	2	THINK	2
MOTHER	3	CRUEL	2	MISERIES	2	TORMENTS	2
MUSES	3	DAINTY	2	MORTAL	2	TRANSFORMED	2
MUST	3	DARKNESS	2	MOUNTING	2	TREADING	2
NATURE'S	3	DARTING	2	MURDERING	2	TREASURE	2
OCEAN	3	DEAREST	2	MUTE	2	TROPHIES	2
PAINT	3	DECLINING	2	NAKED	2	TURN	2
PART	3	DEPART	2	NAMING	2	TWIXT	2
PEN	3	DEPRIVES	2	NINES	2	TYRANT	2
POWER	3	DIRECTION	2	OBJECTS	2	UNHAPPY	2
RAISE	3	DIRECTS	2	OCEANS	2	UNKINDEST	2
RAYS	3	DISGRACED	2	OFT	2	US	2
REVIVING	3	DREARY	2	ORDERS	2	VEIL	2
SAINT	3	DROPS	2	PAINS	2	VERY	2
SECRET	3	DROWNED	2	PAINTED	2	VESTAL	2
SINCE	3	EAGLE'S	2	PASSING	2	VILE	2
SKIES	3	EARS	2	PASSIONS	2	VOLUMES	2
SLEEP'S	3	ECLIPSED	2	PERFECTIONS	2	WANDERING	2
SPRING	3	ELIZIA	2	PINED	2	WANTING	2
STAY	3	ELSE	2	PITY	2	WAST	2
STORY	3	EMBRACE	2	PLACE	2	WAVES	2
STRAIGHT	3	END	2	PLANET	2	WEEPING	2
THEM	3	ENDLESS	2	PLUME	2	WEIGHT	2
THIEF	3	ENROLLED	2	POETS	2	WHENCE	2
THOUGH	3	ENVY	2	PRAYERS	2	WHITE	2
UNKIND	3	EQUAL	2	PRISON	2	WILT	2
VIRTUE	3	EXCEL	2	QUENCH	2	WIND	2
WHEREIN	3	EXPRESSED	2	QUITE	2	WOULD	2
WHY	3	EXTINGUISHED	2	RAISED	2	WRONG	2
WINGS	3	EYE'S	2	READING	2	YEARS	2
WITHIN	3	FEARS	2	REASON'S	2	ZEAL	2
WORTH	3	FEEL	2	RECORD	2	'ST	1
ACCENTS	2	FELL	2	REFINED	2	ABLE	1
ADORE	2	FLY	2	RELIEF	2	ABORTIVE	1
AGAINST	2	FORLORN	2	REPORT	2	ABSTRACTS	1
AIR'S	2	FORTH	2	REST	2	ABUNDANCE	1
AMIDST	2	FORTUNE	2	RIGHT	2	ACCOUNT	1
AN	2	FULL	2	ROBBED	2	ACHERON	1
ARDEN	2	GAVE	2	SAME	2	ACQUAINT	1
ARMED	2	GAZING	2	SAVE	2	ACT	1
ASCEND	2	GIVEN	2	SCOPE	2	ADDETH	1
BACK	2	GIVES	2	SHORES	2	ADMIRATION	1
BANKS	2	GOD	2	SHOULD	2	ADMIRE	1
BEFORE	2	GOLD	2	SHOW	2	ADMIRED	1
BEGAN	2	GRIEVOUS	2	SKILL	2	ADMIRETH	1
BEHELD	2	GROUND	2	SKY	2	ADORED	1
BLESS	2	HELICON	2	SLAIN	2	ADORNED	1
BLISS	2	HOPE'S	2	SMILING	2	ADVANCED	1
BOAST	2	HOPES	2	SOMETIME	2	AETNA'S	1
BOOKS	2	HOURS	2	SPEAK	2	AFFECTED	1
BORN	2	ICE	2	SPIRITS	2	AFFLICTED	1
BOTH	2	IDOL	2	STAND	2	AFFORD	1
BOW	2	JOYED	2	STAR	2	AFFORDS	1
BREATH	2	KINDNESS	2	STOLEN	2	AFTER-WORLDS	1
BRIGHT	2	LAMP	2	STRINGS	2	AGED	1
BROKE	2	LEARNING	2	STRIVING	2	AID	1
BROOK	2	LEND	2	SUNDRY	2	AIM	1
BURN	2	LIVES	2	SURE	2	ALBION'S	1
BURNED	2	LOST	2	SUREST	2	ALIKE	1
CHIEF	2	MAID	2	SURFEIT	2	ALLOW	1
CLEAR	2	MANY	2	SWANS	2	ALLURING	1
COALS	2	METHRIDATE	2	SWEETEST	2	ALPHABET	1
COLORS	2	MIGHT	2	TAKES	2	AMAZED	1
COME	2	MIND	2	TEACH	2	AMBASSADORS	1

AMBROSIAN	1	BEHOLDS	1	CHARMING	1	CROWN	1
AMBUSH	1	BELLOWS	1	CHASED	1	CRUCIFY	1
AMISS	1	BELOW	1	CHASTITY	1	CRYSTALLINE	1
AMONGST	1	BEMOANING	1	CHEEK	1	CUMAEA	1
ANATOMIZE	1	BENDS	1	CHESTER	1	CUPID	1
ANGEL'S	1	BEQUEATHED	1	CHIEFTAIN	1	CUPID'S	1
ANGRY	1	BEREFT	1	CHILD'S	1	CURED	1
ANOTHER	1	BESET	1	CHRIST	1	CURIOUS	1
ANSWERING	1	BEST	1	CINDERS	1	CURSE	1
ANTHEMS	1	BETRAYING	1	CLEAREST	1	CYDNUS	1
ANVIL	1	BEWAIL	1	CLEARETH	1	CYNTHUS	1
ANY	1	BEWRAYING	1	CLIMB	1	DAMNED	1
APOLLO'S	1	BIDS	1	CLIVES	1	DANGEROUS	1
APPEAR	1	BIND	1	CLOSET	1	DANISH	1
APPEARETH	1	BIRD	1	CLOUD	1	DARES	1
APPEARS	1	BIRDS	1	CLOUDS	1	DARK	1
APPOINT	1	BIRTH	1	CLOUDY	1	DARKEST	1
APPOINTED	1	BLACKEST	1	COAST	1	DAY-STAR	1
APRIL-SP		BLASPHEME	1	COCKATRICE	1	DEAD	1
RINGING	1	BLEEDING	1	COLD	1	DEAF	1
APT	1	BLIND	1	COLDNESS	1	DEAR	1
ARDEN'S	1	BLOT	1	COMET	1	DEARTH	1
ARGUMENT	1	BLOTTED	1	COMET-LIKE	1	DEATHS	1
ARMIES	1	BLUSHING	1	COMFORT	1	DEBTOR	1
ARMY	1	BOARD	1	COMMANDING	1	DECLARE	1
ARREARAGE	1	BOASTING	1	COMMEND	1	DECLINE	1
ARRER	1	BOND	1	COMMENDS	1	DEE	1
ARROW	1	BORDERS	1	COMMIT	1	DEED	1
ASCENDANT	1	BORNE	1	COMPANION	1	DEEDS	1
ASCENDING	1	BOUNDED	1	COMPARISON	1	DEEMED	1
ASHES	1	BRAGS	1	COMPASS	1	DEER	1
ASK	1	BRAIN	1	COMPLAINT	1	DEFACED	1
ASPIRE	1	BREATH'S	1	CON	1	DEFINE	1
ASPIRED	1	BRED	1	CONCEALED	1	DEFORMED	1
ASSAILED	1	BREEDS	1	CONCEIVED	1	DEIFIED	1
ASTRAEA	1	BRING	1	CONCLUDE	1	DELIAN	1
ATE	1	BROAD-BR		CONDEMNING	1	DELICIOUS	1
ATHEIST	1	IMMED	1	CONFESS	1	DELIGHTED	1
ATTENDING	1	BROOD	1	CONFLICT	1	DELIVERED	1
ATTENDS	1	BROOKS	1	CONQUERING	1	DELPHOS	1
AUTHENTIQUE	1	BROUGHT	1	CONQUEROR	1	DEN	1
AUTUMN	1	BROWS	1	CONSONANT	1	DENY	1
AVON'S	1	BUGBEARS	1	CONSONANTS	1	DEPRIVED	1
AWAKE	1	BUILD	1	CONSUME	1	DERIVE	1
AWAKED	1	BURNETH	1	CONSUMING	1	DERIVED	1
AWAY	1	BURNING	1	CONSUMPTION	1	DERIVETH	1
AWHILE	1	BURNS	1	CONTEND	1	DESCANT	1
BABE'S	1	CABINET	1	CONTENDING	1	DESERT	1
BACKWARD	1	CABLE	1	CONTRARY	1	DESERTS	1
BAITING	1	CANCEL	1	CONTROLLED	1	DESERVE	1
BALLAST	1	CANKER'S	1	CONVERSING	1	DESIRED	1
BANKRUPT	1	CARE'S	1	COOL	1	DESIRES	1
BARE	1	CAREER	1	COTSWOLD	1	DESIRETH	1
BARK	1	CARLEGION	1	COUNSELS	1	DESIRING	1
BASE	1	CASKET	1	COY	1	DESPITETH	1
BASILISK	1	CAUCASE	1	CRADLE	1	DESTINY	1
BASTARDY	1	CEASETH	1	CRAVE	1	DEVISE	1
BEAMS	1	CELL	1	CREEP	1	DEVOTED	1
BEAT	1	CERTAIN	1	CRIES	1	DEVOTION	1
BECOMES	1	CHAINS	1	CRIMSON	1	DEW-EMPE	
BED	1	CHANCE	1	CRIPPLE	1	ARLED	1
BEDLAM	1	CHANCING	1	CROSS	1	DIAMOND	1
BEGINNING	1	CHANNELS	1	CROSS-ROW	1	DIANA	1
BEGOT	1	CHARMED	1	CROSSES	1	DIED	1
BEGUILE	1	CHARMETH	1	CROSSING	1	DIM	1

Word		Word		Word		Word	
DINED	1	EXECUTE	1	FRIEND	1	HONORED	1
DIPHTHONGS	1	EXHALED	1	FRIENDSHIP'S	1	HOPELESS	1
DIRECT	1	EXHORTIVE	1	FRIGHTS	1	HORNED	1
DISCOMMEND	1	EXILE	1	FROSTY	1	HORROR	1
DISCOVERED	1	EXORDIUMS	1	FROWNING	1	HOST	1
DISGRACES	1	EXTOL	1	FUEL	1	HOT	1
DISPLEASURE	1	EXTORTION	1	FURIES	1	HOUND	1
DISTEMPE		EYE-KILLING	1	FURIOUS	1	HUMAN	1
RATURE	1	EYES'	1	FURTHER	1	HUMOR	1
DISTILLS	1	FADING	1	GAINETH	1	HUNGER	1
DISTRACTED	1	FAIN	1	GALIXIA	1	HUNGER-S	
DISTRESS	1	FAIR-MAID	1	GALLUS	1	TARVEN	1
DIVIDING	1	FAIRER	1	GAME	1	HUNTER'S	1
DIVINING	1	FAITHFUL	1	GANGES	1	HURT	1
DOOM	1	FALL	1	GAZED	1	HYPASIS	1
DORUS	1	FALLS	1	GENTLY	1	IDLE	1
DOST	1	FANCY	1	GHASTLY	1	IMBRUED	1
DOVE	1	FASHIONING	1	GHOST	1	IMITATE	1
DRAWS	1	FATAL	1	GIVE	1	IMMORTALIZE	1
DRENCHED	1	FATE	1	GLADDETH	1	IMPARTING	1
DRIES	1	FATHER	1	GLEED	1	IMPRINTED	1
DRINK	1	FEARING	1	GLORIED	1	INCENSE	1
DROWNING	1	FEAST	1	GLORIFIED	1	INCLUDING	1
DROWNS	1	FEATHERS	1	GLOVE	1	INCREASETH	1
DRY	1	FEET	1	GODS'	1	INCREASING	1
DUE	1	FELT	1	GONE	1	INDUS	1
DULY	1	FERTILE	1	GORGED	1	INFANCY	1
DUMB	1	FETTER	1	GRACE	1	INFERNAL	1
DUMB-BORN	1	FETTERED	1	GRAIN	1	INFIDEL	1
DUST	1	FIERY	1	GRASS	1	INFLUENCE	1
DUTY	1	FILLING	1	GREAT	1	INK	1
DYED	1	FINDS	1	GREATEST	1	INN	1
EAGLE	1	FIRED	1	GREEDILY	1	INNUMERABLE	1
EAGLE-BIRDS	1	FISH	1	GROANING	1	INSPIRATION	1
EAGLETS	1	FISHES	1	GROWING	1	INSPIRING	1
EARTH'S	1	FLAMES	1	GROWS	1	INTERLINED	1
EASILY	1	FLATTER	1	GUARDING	1	INVENT	1
ECHOES	1	FLEE	1	GUESSED	1	INVENTION'S	1
EDEN	1	FLEETING	1	GUIDES	1	INVOCATE	1
EFFECT	1	FLIES	1	HALF	1	ISIS	1
ELEGIES	1	FLINGING	1	HALF-SLAIN	1	ISLANDS	1
ELEMENT	1	FLOATS	1	HAMMERS	1	ISLE	1
EMBRACED	1	FLOOD'S-		HANDS	1	ISTER	1
EMBRACETH	1	QUEEN	1	HARMLESS	1	IXION	1
EMBRYON	1	FLOODS	1	HARMONY	1	JEALOUS	1
EMPTY	1	FLOWERS	1	HEAD	1	JUDGMENT	1
ENCHANTING	1	FLOWN	1	HEALED	1	JUST	1
ENDED	1	FLYING	1	HEAP	1	KEEPETH	1
ENDITE	1	FOLLY	1	HEAR	1	KENT	1
ENGRAVED	1	FOOL'S	1	HEART-HEAT	1	KILL	1
ENRICHED	1	FORCED	1	HEART-PI		KINDLE	
ENTICE	1	FORCES	1	ERCING	1	KINDLING	1
ERECTING	1	FORDS	1	HEARTS	1	KINGLY	1
ERINYS	1	FORETELL	1	HEATS	1	KINGS	1
ERST	1	FORETOLD	1	HEAVEN'S	1	KISS	1
ESPY	1	FORGE	1	HECATE'S	1	KISSES	1
ESPYING	1	FORGOT	1	HEELS	1	KNEW	1
ESTEEMED	1	FORT	1	HELP	1	LABOR	1
ETERNAL	1	FOUND	1	HENCE	1	LADEN	1
EVEN	1	FOUNTAIN	1	HESPERUS	1	LAIR	1
EVER-CERTAIN	1	FRAMED	1	HIDES	1	LAME	1
EVERMORE	1	FRANTIC	1	HIGHEST	1	LAMENTEST	1
EXAMPLE	1	FREQUENT	1	HILLS	1	LAND	1
EXCELLETH	1	FRESHEST	1	HIMSELF	1	LARGE	1
EXCELLING	1	FRET	1	HOLD	1	LATEST	1

LAUGHETH	1	MELL	1	OBTAIN	1	POINTED	1
LAUGHING	1	MEMORIALS	1	ODD	1	POISON	1
LAY	1	MEN'S	1	OFFENDS	1	PORTRAIT	1
LEAST	1	MERCY	1	OFFER	1	POUR	1
LEAVE	1	MERIDIANIS	1	OFFSPRING	1	PRACTISED	1
LEGACY	1	MERLIN	1	OLYMPUS	1	PRAISED	1
LEGEA	1	METAL	1	OPEN	1	PRAISING	1
LEGS	1	METHOD	1	ORDER	1	PRAYER	1
LENDING	1	METTLES	1	ORPHAN	1	PREACH	1
LENDS	1	MIDNIGHT	1	OSSA	1	PREACHEST	1
LENGTH	1	MIDST	1	OTHER'S	1	PREDOMINANT	1
LENGTHENEST	1	MILDLY	1	OTHERS	1	PREPARED	1
LESSON	1	MILK-WHITE	1	OUSE	1	PRESAGED	1
LETTERS	1	MILLIONS	1	OUTWEARS	1	PRESERVATIVE	1
LIBERTY	1	MINDS	1	OVER	1	PRESERVE	1
LIE	1	MINERVA'S	1	OVER-SOON	1	PRIDE	1
LIEN	1	MIRACLE	1	PAID	1	PRIME	1
LIMBO	1	MIRACLES	1	PALE	1	PRIZE	1
LIMN	1	MIRRORS	1	PALFREYS	1	PROCEED	1
LIMNED	1	MISSPENT	1	PAMELA'S	1	PROLONG	1
LION	1	MISTRESS'	1	PANGS	1	PROPHESIED	1
LIQUID	1	MOISTURE	1	PANTETH	1	PROPHETS	1
LIQUIDS	1	MOLE	1	PAPER	1	PROVED	1
LIST	1	MONARCH	1	PARNASSUS	1	PROVIDENCE	1
LIVELY	1	MONSTER-		PARTS	1	PROVOKE	1
LIVING	1	BREEDING	1	PASSAGE	1	PUNISHMENT	1
LOADSTONE	1	MORNING	1	PASSION'S	1	PURENESS	1
LOCK	1	MORNING'S	1	PATIENCE	1	PUT	1
LODEN	1	MORROW	1	PAVED	1	QUAKE	1
LODESTAR	1	MOTHERLESS	1	PAY	1	QUEEN	1
LOFTY	1	MOUNT	1	PAYMENTS	1	QUENCHED	1
LOOKED-FOR	1	MOURNFUL	1	PEAK	1	QUENCHLESS	1
LORD	1	MOURNING	1	PEARL	1	QUILL	1
LOSS	1	MOVING	1	PEEVISH	1	QUIVERS	1
LOVED	1	MUSED	1	PEIZED	1	RACK	1
LOVELY	1	MUSIC	1	PELION	1	RAIL	1
LOVING	1	MUTES	1	PENCIL	1	RAINING	1
LUCKLESS	1	MYRRH-BR		PENNED	1	RAM	1
LUCKY	1	EATHING	1	PENURY	1	RAVING	1
LUKEWARM	1	NATIVITY	1	PEOPLED	1	RAVISHED	1
LUNACY	1	NAY	1	PERCEIVE	1	REACH	1
LUSTER	1	NE'ER	1	PERFECT	1	REBEL	1
LUTE	1	NEAR	1	PERFECTION'S	1	RECEIVE	1
LYING	1	NECTAR	1	PERFUME	1	RECKONINGS	1
MAIMED	1	NECTAR-D		PERFUMING	1	RECORDER	1
MAINTAIN	1	ROPPING	1	PERIOD	1	REDOUBLING	1
MAINTAINS	1	NEEDS	1	PERNICIOUS	1	REFLECTING	1
MAKEST	1	NEGLECTED	1	PHLEGETHON	1	REGIONS	1
MAKING	1	NEST	1	PIECED	1	REGISTER	1
MAN	1	NEVER-ENDING	1	PIERCING	1	REGISTERED	1
MAN-GOD	1	NEVER-HOPING	1	PINDUS'	1	REHEARSE	1
MANHOOD	1	NEXT	1	PINIONS	1	RELIC'S	1
MARIGOLD	1	NICE	1	PITCHY	1	RELIGION	1
MARINERS	1	NIGHTINGALES	1	PITILESS	1	RELIGION'S	1
MARS	1	NIGHTLY	1	PLACED	1	REMAINS	1
MARTYRING	1	NILE	1	PLAGUE	1	REMEMBRANCER	1
MARVEL	1	NOISE	1	PLAGUED	1	REMOVE	1
MARVELS	1	NOTE	1	PLAINTS	1	RENEWEST	1
MAYR-MAID	1	NOTHERN	1	PLAYED	1	RENOWNED	1
MAYST	1	NUMBER	1	PLEASETH	1	RENT	1
MEAN	1	NUMBERS	1	PLEASING	1	REPEAT	1
MEANS	1	NURSE	1	PLENTY	1	REPENTANCE	1
MEASURE	1	NYMPH	1	PLUCKS	1	REPROACHED	1
MEAT	1	OBLATIONS	1	PLUMES	1	RESEMBLE	1
MEDWAY	1	OBSCURED	1	PO	1	RESIDENT	1

Word		Word		Word		Word	
RESIGN	1	SIGNS	1	STRENGTH	1	TRIBUTE	1
RESPECTED	1	SILENCE	1	STRIFE	1	TRIED	1
RETEERE	1	SILLY	1	STROVE	1	TRIES	1
REVIVED	1	SILVER-S		STYX	1	TRINITY	1
REVIVETH	1	ANDED	1	SUBDUE	1	TRIPLICITY	1
REWARDING	1	SIMILE	1	SUBTRACTING	1	TRIUMPH	1
RHYME	1	SIMOIS	1	SUFFICE	1	TROPIC	1
RICHEST	1	SIMPLE	1	SUFFICIENTLY	1	TROTTING	1
RISE	1	SINFUL	1	SULPHUR	1	TROUBLED	1
RISING	1	SING	1	SUM	1	TRULY	1
ROLL	1	SINGING	1	SUMMED	1	TRUMPET	1
ROOM	1	SINGS	1	SUMMER	1	TRUTH	1
ROUSED	1	SIREN	1	SUMMONED	1	TURNETH	1
RUNS	1	SISYPHUS	1	SUN-BRIGHT	1	TURRETS	1
RUST	1	SIT	1	SUN-STEEDS	1	TWEED'S	1
SABLE	1	SITS	1	SUNSHINE	1	UGLY	1
SACRIFICE	1	SITTING	1	SUPERLATIVE	1	UNBELIEVING	1
SACRIFICED	1	SKILLFUL	1	SUPPED	1	UNCERTAI	
SAD	1	SLEEPETH	1	SURCHARGED	1	N-DREAD	1
SAFEST	1	SLEEPS	1	SURVIVED	1	UNCLEAN	1
SAILS	1	SLIDING	1	SWAN	1	UNDONE	1
SALT	1	SLOW	1	SWEAR	1	UNFAINED	1
SATURN	1	SMILES	1	SWEAT	1	UNITED	1
SAW	1	SMOKE	1	SWEETNESS	1	UNKINDLY	1
SCHOLAR	1	SMOKED	1	SWEETS	1	UNLUCKY	1
SCHOOLMI		SMOTHERED	1	SWIFT-WINGED	1	UNRULY	1
STRESS	1	SNOW	1	SYMTOMAS	1	UNTIMELY	1
SCORCHING	1	SOARING	1	TACKLINGS	1	UNWORTHY	1
SCORN	1	SOL	1	TAGUS	1	USE	1
SCORNING	1	SONG	1	TAKE	1	USURY	1
SDAINS	1	SOON	1	TAKING	1	VAIN	1
SEA	1	SOONER	1	TAME	1	VANISHED	1
SEASON	1	SORROWS	1	TASTE	1	VAUNT	1
SEASONED	1	SORTS	1	TAXETH	1	VAUNTS	1
SEAT	1	SOT	1	TEACHEST	1	VEIN	1
SEATED	1	SOUGHT	1	TEAR	1	VEINS	1
SECOND	1	SOUL-SHRINED	1	TEMPE	1	VEXED	1
SECRECY	1	SOULS	1	TEMPERED	1	VICES	1
SECRETS	1	SOUND	1	TEMPLE	1	VIEW	1
SEEM	1	SOUNDING	1	TERROR	1	VIRGIN	1
SENDEST	1	SOURS	1	THAMES	1	VIRGINITY	1
SENSE'S	1	SOVEREIGN'S	1	THEREOF	1	VIRGINS'	1
SENSELESS	1	SPELL	1	THING	1	VOW	1
SERPENTS	1	SPHERE	1	THINGS	1	VOWELS	1
SERVES	1	SPIES	1	THINKS	1	WAFTING	1
SERVEST	1	SPITEFUL	1	THIRST	1	WAIT	1
SERVICE	1	SPLEEN	1	THOUGHT'S	1	WAKING	1
SETTING	1	SPRINGING	1	THREW	1	WALLOWING	1
SEVERN	1	SPRUNG	1	THRICE	1	WAN	1
SHADES	1	STAINS	1	THWARTING	1	WANE	1
SHADOWS	1	STALLED	1	TIRED	1	WANTON	1
SHAFT	1	STANDS	1	TOGETHER	1	WAR	1
SHAFTS	1	STARS'	1	TOILING	1	WARDSHIP	1
SHALBE	1	STARVED	1	TOP	1	WARMED	1
SHEPHERD	1	STATELY	1	TORMENT	1	WARMETH	1
SHINE	1	STEAD	1	TORMENTOR	1	WASTE	1
SHIPS	1	STEALS	1	TORN-TRESSED	1	WATCHING	1
SHORE	1	STONE	1	TOUCHING	1	WAY	1
SHOULDST	1	STONE-COLD	1	TOUCHSTONE	1	WEAK	1
SHOWERS	1	STOOD	1	TOWARDS	1	WEAKNESS	1
SHRINE	1	STOP	1	TOY	1	WEALTH	1
SIBYL	1	STORE	1	TRAVEL	1	WEARS	1
SIBYLS	1	STORMS	1	TRENT	1	WEED	1
SIDES	1	STRAIN	1	TRESSED	1	WENT	1
SIGHING	1	STREAM	1	TRESSES	1	WESTERN	1

WHEEL	1	WISE	1	WOMAN	1	WRITES	1
WHEELS	1	WISH	1	WORK	1	YE	1
WHIR-POOL	1	WISHES	1	WORLDS	1	YORK	1
WHOLE	1	WISHING	1	WORN	1	YOUR	1
WHOLLY	1	WITHDRAW	1	WORTHIES	1	YOUTH'S	1
WILIS'	1	WITHERED	1	WOUND	1	YOUTHFUL	1
WINTER	1	WITS	1	WOUNDED	1	ZEPHYR	1
WISDOM	1	WOEFUL	1	WRINKLED	1		

WILLIAM SHAKESPEARE, 'SONNETS'

AND	490	EYES	51	LOVE'S	25	NEVER	16
THE	442	HEART	51	OTHER	25	OH	16
TO	417	HER	51	WHY	25	TOO	16
MY	392	YET	51	EVEN	24	UP	16
OF	370	ART	49	SINCE	24	AGE	15
I	344	NOW	46	BEST	23	BEFORE	15
IN	323	CAN	44	LIFE	23	COME	15
THAT	322	FAIR	44	SHOW	23	EACH	15
THY	272	HE	44	DEAR	22	POOR	15
THOU	235	SHOULD	44	LOOK	22	PROUD	15
IS	182	THAN	44	NIGHT	22	TELL	15
WITH	180	THINE	44	OLD	22	THINK	15
FOR	172	WHERE	44	THUS	22	TIME'S	15
A	169	HATH	43	TRUTH	22	VERSE	15
ME	168	MAKE	43	MUST	21	WE	15
NOT	166	ONE	42	THESE	21	YOUTH	15
LOVE	165	STILL	42	WORTH	21	EVER	14
BUT	163	HOW	40	WOULD	21	FRIEND	14
THEE	161	EYE	39	MADE	20	GENTLE	14
SO	145	HIM	38	PART	20	MEN	14
BE	140	TRUE	38	ALONE	19	STATE	14
AS	122	AM	35	FACE	19	THINGS	14
ALL	118	SEE	35	FALSE	19	TILL	14
IT	115	LIKE	34	ILL	19	WILT	14
YOU	112	O	34	NOTHING	19	BEAR	13
HIS	108	SHE	33	OUR	19	BLACK	13
WHICH	108	THOSE	33	WHOSE	19	COULD	13
THIS	107	THOUGH	33	AGAINST	18	DIE	13
WHEN	106	BEING	32	AWAY	18	FIRST	13
YOUR	100	WHO	32	BEAUTY'S	18	FULL	13
BY	93	EVERY	31	BETTER	18	GOOD	13
DOTH	87	SOME	31	HAND	18	HEAVEN	13
SELF	85	SUCH	31	SIGHT	18	HOLD	13
DO	84	WERE	31	THERE	18	LEAST	13
FROM	82	DOST	30	THOUGHT	18	LIE	13
OR	81	OWN	30	THOUGHTS	18	MANY	13
ON	80	LIVE	29	BOTH	17	NONE	13
THEIR	80	MAY	29	DAYS	17	TAKE	13
NO	79	UPON	29	FAR	17	USE	13
THEN	78	WAS	29	HAST	17	WHILST	13
HAVE	77	DAY	28	KNOW	17	CHANGE	12
WHAT	75	PRAISE	28	MUCH	17	EARTH	12
ARE	71	SAY	28	NAME	17	END	12
IF	68	WORLD	28	OUT	17	HOURS	12
MORE	64	AN	27	THEM	17	KIND	12
MINE	63	GIVE	27	THEREFORE	17	LIES	12
WILL	63	MOST	27	DEAD	16	LONG	12
SHALL	58	DID	26	DEATH	16	LOOKS	12
SWEET	55	LET	26	FIND	16	MAKING	12
TIME	54	MIGHT	26	HAD	16	MAYST	12
NOR	53	NEW	26	HATE	16	PROVE	12
THEY	53	WELL	26	MIND	16	SEEM	12
BEAUTY	52	AT	25	MUSE	16	SUMMER'S	12

Word		Word		Word		Word	
THING	12	BRING	8	WIT	7	WISH	6
TIS	12	BROW	8	WORST	7	WRIT	6
WHOM	12	CHILD	8	ARGUMENT	6	WRONG	6
WOE	12	CRUEL	8	BEEN	6	ABSENCE	5
AFTER	11	DEEP	8	BLIND	6	ANGEL	5
ANY	11	DELIGHT	8	BOOK	6	ANTIQUE	5
BLESSED	11	DISGRACE	8	CARE	6	BARREN	5
BRIGHT	11	FAULTS	8	COMPARE	6	BASE	5
DESIRE	11	FEAR	8	DESPITE	6	BELOVED	5
FORM	11	FLOWERS	8	DULL	6	BIRTH	5
GRACE	11	FRESH	8	DUMB	6	BOAST	5
HAPPY	11	GIVES	8	DWELL	6	BRAIN	5
KNOWS	11	GLORY	8	ENOUGH	6	BRAND	5
OTHERS	11	GROW	8	ETERNAL	6	BURIED	5
PLEASURE	11	HELL	8	FEARS	6	CALLS	5
PRIDE	11	JOY	8	FORTUNE	6	CANKER	5
RICH	11	LEAVES	8	GAINST	6	CHEEK	5
RIGHT	11	LINES	8	GO	6	CHIDE	5
SEEN	11	LOVELY	8	HAVING	6	CURE	5
SHALT	11	MAKES	8	HEAD	6	DATE	5
SUN	11	MEMORY	8	HEAR	6	DONE	5
TONGUE	11	SAKE	8	HEAVEN'S	6	DOOM	5
WITHIN	11	SAVE	8	HEAVY	6	DOWN	5
AGAIN	10	SIN	8	HENCE	6	DUE	5
CALL	10	SPEAK	8	HOPE	6	ELSE	5
CANNOT	10	STAND	8	JUDGMENT	6	FAIREST	5
DEEDS	10	SUMMER	8	LIGHT	6	FAITH	5
FIRE	10	THENCE	8	LONGER	6	FAST	5
FOUND	10	VIEW	8	LOVEST	6	FELL	5
GLASS	10	WITHOUT	8	MAD	6	FLOWER	5
GREAT	10	AH	7	MEN'S	6	GAVE	5
LEAVE	10	BAD	7	MUSIC	6	GIFT	5
LOSS	10	BEHOLD	7	NATURE'S	6	GOLDEN	5
LOVING	10	BREAST	7	O'ER	6	GRACES	5
NATURE	10	CANST	7	ONLY	6	GRACIOUS	5
ONCE	10	EXCUSE	7	PAINTING	6	GREEN	5
PAST	10	FORTH	7	PRECIOUS	6	GREW	5
PEN	10	FOUL	7	PRESENT	6	GRIEF	5
PLACE	10	HEART'S	7	REASON	6	HERE	5
SHAME	10	HONOR	7	REST	6	HIDE	5
SOUL	10	I'LL	7	RETURN	6	HOLDS	5
SPIRIT	10	LESS	7	RHYME	6	HUE	5
TIMES	10	LIPS	7	ROSE	6	INTO	5
WORDS	10	LIVING	7	SAME	6	INVENTION	5
WRITE	10	OUTWARD	7	SHOULDEST	6	KEEPS	5
ALTHOUGH	9	PARTS	7	SHOWS	6	KILL	5
BACK	9	PUT	7	SLAVE	6	LACK	5
BEAUTEOUS	9	ROSES	7	SLEEP	6	LARGE	5
DECAY	9	SAD	7	SOMETIME	6	LEFT	5
ERE	9	SEEING	7	SPENT	6	LEND	5
GONE	9	SET	7	STRANGE	6	LIVED	5
KEEP	9	SHADOW	7	SWEETEST	6	LOVED	5
LIVES	9	SING	7	SWEETS	6	MAN	5
LOSE	9	SKILL	7	TAUGHT	6	MERIT	5
LOVES	9	STEAL	7	THEMSELVES	6	MISTRESS'	5
PITY	9	STRAIGHT	7	THINKS	6	MOAN	5
POWER	9	SWEAR	7	THROUGH	6	MORTAL	5
STAY	9	TEN	7	UNDER	6	MOTION	5
STORE	9	TENDER	7	UNLESS	6	NEAR	5
STRONG	9	THREE	7	WAR	6	NEED	5
TREASURE	9	VERY	7	WAY	6	NEEDS	5
TWO	9	VIRTUE	7	WEALTH	6	OFT	5
BLOOD	8	WASTE	7	WHETHER	6	ORNAMENT	5
BORN	8	WHITE	7	WHILE	6	PAIN	5
BREATH	8	WIDE	7	WINTER	6	PAINTED	5

Word		Word		Word		Word	
PLAY	5	CRIME	4	SHADE	4	CLEAR	3
PURPOSE	5	CROWNED	4	SHINE	4	COLOR	3
QUITE	5	DARE	4	SINFUL	4	COMPLEXION	3
RAGE	5	DEATH'S	4	SINGLE	4	CONCEIT	3
RANK	5	ERRORS	4	SMELL	4	CONFINED	3
READ	5	EVIL	4	SONG	4	CONFOUNDS	3
SAW	5	FARTHER	4	SOVEREIGN	4	CONQUEST	3
SAYS	5	FORGOT	4	STORY	4	CONSCIENCE	3
SCOPE	5	FORMER	4	SUBSTANCE	4	CONSTANCY	3
SHAPE	5	FORSWORN	4	SUM	4	CONSTANT	3
SHORT	5	FRAME	4	TASTE	4	CONTROL	3
SICK	5	FREE	4	THIEF	4	COST	3
SIDE	5	FRIENDS	4	TIRED	4	COURSE	3
SLOW	5	GAIN	4	TOIL	4	COVER	3
SORROW	5	GIVEN	4	TOLD	4	CUNNING	3
SPEAKING	5	GRANT	4	TONGUE-TIED	4	DAILY	3
SPEND	5	GROAN	4	TONGUES	4	DARK	3
SPITE	5	GROWN	4	TOUCHES	4	DEAREST	3
SPRING	5	GROWS	4	UNUSED	4	DECEASE	3
STARS	5	HEARTS	4	USED	4	DEFENSE	3
STOLEN	5	HEAT	4	WANT	4	DESERT	3
STRENGTH	5	HELP	4	WEARY	4	DESPAIR	3
SUBJECT	5	HIGH	4	WEEDS	4	DESPISED	3
SWIFT	5	HOLY	4	WHEREFORE	4	DIDST	3
TEARS	5	HOUR	4	WIN	4	DIED	3
TOMB	5	IMAGE	4	WORK	4	DISTILLED	3
TOOK	5	INCREASE	4	WORMS	4	DOUBLE	3
TRULY	5	INWARD	4	WOUND	4	DRAW	3
TRUST	5	JEWEL	4	WRETCHED	4	DRAWN	3
WATER	5	JUST	4	YE	4	DUTY	3
WHEREIN	5	KNIFE	4	YOUNG	4	EAR	3
WORLD'S	5	KNOWEST	4	ABUSE	4	EAT	3
WORSE	5	KNOWING	4	ACQUAINTANCE	3	EDGE	3
WORTHY	5	LAID	4	ACTION	3	EFFECT	3
WRINKLES	5	LAYS	4	ADVANTAGE	3	ELSEWHERE	3
YEAR	5	LEASE	4	ALACK	3	ETERNITY	3
YOURS	5	LEISURE	4	ALMOST	3	EVERMORE	3
ABOVE	4	LENDS	4	AMISS	3	EXPENSE	3
ABSENT	4	LOST	4	AMONG	4	EXPRESSED	3
ABUNDANCE	4	MARK	4	ANSWER	4	EYE'S	3
ACCOUNT	4	MISTRESS	4	APPETITE	4	FAIRER	3
ADD	4	MORROW	4	APPROVE	4	FALL	3
AIR	4	NE'ER	4	APRIL	4	FAME	3
APPEAR	4	NUMBERS	4	AUDIT	4	FAULT	3
ASSURED	4	OATHS	4	BASEST	4	FEEDING	3
BABE	4	OTHERS'	4	BASTARD	4	FILL	3
BARE	4	PLEASE	4	BEARING	4	FILLED	3
BATH	4	PLUCK	4	BEARS	4	FINGERS	3
BEAUTIES	4	PRAISES	4	BECAUSE	4	FIVE	3
BEHIND	4	PRIME	4	BIRDS	3	FIXED	3
BELIEVE	4	PUBLIC	4	BITTER	3	FLAME	3
BLAME	4	RARE	4	BLOODY	4	FLATTER	3
BODY	4	RED	4	BLOT	4	FLATTERY	3
BODY'S	4	REHEARSE	4	BLUNT	4	FLESH	3
BRASS	4	REMEMBERED	4	BONDS	4	FLIES	3
BREAK	4	REMOVED	4	BOY	4	FOES	3
BUDS	4	REPORT	4	BRAVE	4	FOOL	3
CATCH	4	RESPECT	4	BRIEF	4	FOOT	3
CHEEKS	4	RUDE	4	BROUGHT	4	FORBID	3
CLOUDS	4	SAID	4	BURDEN	4	FORTUNE'S	3
COLD	4	SCYTHE	4	BURN	4	FROWN	3
COMFORT	4	SEA	4	CAME	4	GAVEST	3
COMMON	4	SECOND	4	CAUSE	4	GENERAL	3
CONTENTED	4	SEEK	4	CHARACTER	3	GILDED	3
COUNT	4	SENSE	4	CHEST	3	GOT	3

GRAVE	3	RECEIVEST	3	ADDITION	2	CHECK	2
GREATER	3	RECORD	3	ADJUNCT	2	CHECKED	2
GREET	3	REMAIN	3	AFFAIRS	2	CHIEF	2
GROUND	3	REPAIR	3	AFFORDS	2	CHURL	2
GROWEST	3	RIDE	3	AGE'S	2	CLEARER	2
GROWING	3	SAIL	3	AID	2	CLOCK	2
GROWTH	3	SEEMED	3	ALAS	2	CLOUD	2
HALF	3	SEEMING	3	ALCHEMY	2	COMES	2
HANG	3	SHADOWS	3	ALIVE	2	COMING	2
HAPLY	3	SHAKE	3	ALLOW	2	COMMENT	2
HAPPIER	3	SHORE	3	ALTERED	2	COMMENTS	2
HASTE	3	SILENCE	3	ALTERS	2	COMMITS	2
HEAVENLY	3	SINS	3	ANEW	2	COMPOUNDS	2
HEIGHT	3	SON	3	ANON	2	CONCORD	2
HEIR	3	SOON	3	ANTIQUITY	2	CONFOUND	2
HOME	3	SPEED	3	ASIDE	2	CONTENT	2
HOT	3	STAIN	3	ASSAILED	2	CONTRACTED	2
HUSBAND	3	STANDS	3	ATTENDING	2	CONTROLLING	2
INFECTION	3	STAR	3	AUTUMN	2	CONVERTED	2
INJURY	3	STEEL	3	AYE	2	COPY	2
KEPT	3	STONE	3	BAIL	2	CORRUPT	2
KISS	3	STYLE	3	BARENESS	2	COUNTERFEIT	2
KNOWLEDGE	3	SURE	3	BARK	2	COUNTING	2
LAWFUL	3	SUSPECT	3	BARS	2	CREATED	2
LINE	3	SWORN	3	BEAST	2	CREATION	2
LO	3	TAKEN	3	BECOMES	2	CREATURES	2
LOOKING	3	TAKES	3	BECOMING	2	CRIES	2
LOSING	3	TEACH	3	BED	2	CROOKED	2
MAIDEN	3	TEND	3	BELONG	2	CROSS	2
MAIN	3	THEREIN	3	BELONGS	2	CROW	2
MANNERS	3	THINKING	3	BENDING	2	CRY	2
MASKED	3	THORNS	3	BENEFIT	2	CUPID	2
MATTER	3	THOUSAND	3	BENT	2	CURSE	2
MEANS	3	THRICE	3	BESIDES	2	DATELESS	2
MEND	3	TORMENT	3	BESIEGE	2	DEARER	2
MINDS	3	TRIUMPH	3	BETRAY	2	DEATHS	2
MINUTES	3	TURN	3	BETTERING	2	DECEASED	2
MOCK	3	TURNS	3	BIDE	2	DECEIVE	2
MONUMENT	3	TWAIN	3	BITTERNESS	2	DECEIVED	2
MOON	3	TYRANT	3	BLAMED	2	DEEMED	2
MORNING	3	UNKIND	3	BLUSHING	2	DEFECT	2
MOTHER'S	3	VILE	3	BOLD	2	DELIGHTS	2
MOURN	3	VIRTUOUS	3	BORE	2	DENY	2
MURDEROUS	3	VULGAR	3	BORNE	2	DEPART	2
NUMBER	3	WANTING	3	BORROWED	2	DEPENDS	2
OCEAN	3	WEED	3	BOSOM	2	DESERTS	2
ODOR	3	WEEP	3	BOSOM'S	2	DESIRED	2
OUTLIVE	3	WERT	3	BOUND	2	DESPISE	2
PACE	3	WEST	3	BOUNTEOUS	2	DEVISE	2
PASS	3	WHENCE	3	BOUNTY	2	DIAL	2
PAY	3	WHEREON	3	BOW	2	DISCONTENT	2
PERJURED	3	WHERETO	3	BRED	2	DISDAIN	2
PICTURE	3	WINDOWS	3	BREED	2	DISEASED	2
PINE	3	WITNESS	3	BRINGS	2	DIVINE	2
PLAGUE	3	WOMAN	3	BROKE	2	DOING	2
PLEA	3	WOMAN'S	3	BUD	2	DOTE	2
POSTERITY	3	WOMEN'S	3	BUILT	2	DOTING	2
PRETTY	3	WONDER	3	CALLED	2	DOUBTING	2
PRIZE	3	WORKS	3	CANOPY	2	DREAM	2
PROOF	3	WOULDST	3	CAPTAIN	2	DREAMS	2
QUICK	3	ABHOR	2	CAREFUL	2	DRINK	2
RAIN	3	ABIDE	2	CAST	2	DUST	2
RAZED	3	ACCUSE	2	CHANGING	2	EARS	2
REASONS	3	ACQUAINTED	2	CHARTER	2	EASE	2
RECEIVES	3	ADDED	2	CHASE	2	ECLIPSES	2

746

EITHER	2	HEALTHFUL	2	MIGHTST	2	PRIVILEGE	2
EITHER'S	2	HEAVILY	2	MILES	2	PROFANED	2
ELEMENTS	2	HELD	2	MORN	2	PROVED	2
ENEMIES	2	HID	2	MOTHER	2	PROVES	2
ENVY	2	HIDEOUS	2	MOUNTAIN	2	PURE	2
ESTEEM	2	HIMSELF	2	MOURNERS	2	PURSUIT	2
ESTEEMED	2	HOPES	2	MOVING	2	QUEST	2
EXAMPLE	2	HORSE	2	MUTE	2	QUESTION	2
EXCELLENCE	2	HUGE	2	MUTUAL	2	QUILL	2
EXPRESS	2	HUMBLE	2	NAUGHT	2	RANSOM	2
EXTREME	2	HUMOR	2	NAY	2	REIGN	2
EYELIDS	2	HUNG	2	NEGLECT	2	REMEDY	2
FACES	2	HUNGRY	2	NEITHER	2	REMEMBER	2
FADE	2	HUSBANDRY	2	NEWER	2	REMEMBRANCE	2
FADING	2	HYMNS	2	NEXT	2	REMOVE	2
FALSEHOOD	2	IDLE	2	NIGGARD	2	RENDER	2
FARTHEST	2	IGNORANCE	2	NIGHTLY	2	REPLETE	2
FASHION	2	ILLS	2	NIGHTS	2	REPOSE	2
FATHER	2	IMPRISONED	2	NIMBLE	2	RESEMBLING	2
FAVOR	2	INCONSTANT	2	NOTE	2	RESERVE	2
FEAST	2	INFLUENCE	2	NOTED	2	RICHES	2
FEEDS	2	INJURIES	2	OBJECTS	2	RIPER	2
FEEL	2	INJURIOUS	2	OBSEQUIOUS	2	RISE	2
FEELING	2	INK	2	OFFENSE	2	ROBBERY	2
FEVER	2	INTEREST	2	OFTEN	2	ROBS	2
FIEND	2	INVENT	2	OPEN	2	ROOT	2
FIERCE	2	ISSUE	2	OPPRESSED	2	ROTTEN	2
FIGHT	2	JACKS	2	OTHER'S	2	RUINED	2
FINDING	2	JEWELS	2	OUGHT	2	SACRED	2
FINDS	2	JOURNEY	2	OUTWORN	2	SALVE	2
FINE	2	KEEN	2	PAINTER	2	SAP	2
FLED	2	KINDNESS	2	PALATE	2	SAUCY	2
FOLLOW	2	KING	2	PALE	2	SCORN	2
FOLLY	2	KINGS	2	PATIENCE	2	SEASONS	2
FOND	2	LACKED	2	PATTERN	2	SEAT	2
FORBEAR	2	LAME	2	PAYS	2	SEEMS	2
FORCE	2	LASCIVIOUS	2	PEACE	2	SEEST	2
FORFEIT	2	LAST	2	PENCIL	2	SELDOM	2
FORGET	2	LAY	2	PENT	2	SEND	2
FORSAKE	2	LEAD	2	PERFECT	2	SENSUAL	2
FORTIFY	2	LEADS	2	PERFECTION	2	SERVING	2
FRAILTIES	2	LEAP	2	PERFUMES	2	SETS	2
FULFILL	2	LEARN	2	PERPETUAL	2	SHAKEN	2
GARMENTS	2	LEARNING	2	PHYSIC	2	SHAMES	2
GATE	2	LEVEL	2	PILGRIMAGE	2	SHINES	2
GAY	2	LIBERTY	2	PITCH	2	SHOWERS	2
GAZE	2	LILIES	2	PLEAD	2	SHOWN	2
GILDING	2	LIMBS	2	PLEASING	2	SHUN	2
GIVING	2	LITTLE	2	POET	2	SIGHTLESS	2
GLAD	2	LIVELY	2	POET'S	2	SILENT	2
GLANCE	2	LOFTY	2	POETS	2	SIMPLE	2
GOD	2	LOOKED	2	POINT	2	SINGS	2
GODDESS	2	LOVER'S	2	POLICY	2	SIT	2
GOLD	2	LUST	2	POSSESSED	2	SLAIN	2
GOODNESS	2	LUSTY	2	POSSESSING	2	SLANDER	2
GROSS	2	MAJESTY	2	POSSESSION	2	SLIGHT	2
GROUNDED	2	MAKEST	2	POTIONS	2	SMALL	2
GUARD	2	MALADIES	2	POVERTY	2	SOIL	2
GUESS	2	MAN'S	2	POWERFUL	2	SOMETHING	2
GUEST	2	MANSION	2	PRAISED	2	SOONER	2
GUILTY	2	MAP	2	PRAISING	2	SORROWS	2
HADST	2	MARRIED	2	PRAY	2	SORT	2
HANDS	2	MASTER	2	PREPARE	2	SOUL'S	2
HAWKS	2	MEASURE	2	PRESENCE	2	SOULS	2
HEALTH	2	MEET	2	PRINCES	2	SOUND	2

SOUNDS	2	VOWS	2	ADONIS	1	ATTEND	1
SOUR	2	WAIL	2	ADORE	1	AUGURS	1
SOURLY	2	WAIT	2	ADULTERATE	1	AUTHORITY	1
SPECIAL	2	WALKS	2	ADVANCE	1	AUTHORIZING	1
SPEECHLESS	2	WALLS	2	ADVERSE	1	AWAKE	1
SPIRITS	2	WASTEFUL	2	ADVISED	1	AWAKES	1
SPORT	2	WASTES	2	ADVOCATE	1	AWARDS	1
SPUR	2	WATCH	2	AFFABLE	1	BACKWARD	1
STAGE	2	WEAK	2	AFFECTIONS	1	BADGES	1
STEALING	2	WEAR	2	AFFORD	1	BADNESS	1
STEEP	2	WELCOME	2	AFTERWARDS	1	BAIT	1
STOP	2	WHEREOF	2	AGES	1	BALMY	1
STORES	2	WIDOW	2	AGGRAVATE	1	BANKRUPT	1
STRANGELY	2	WILLFUL	2	ALIEN	1	BANKS	1
STRIVE	2	WILLING	2	ALIKE	1	BANQUET	1
STRONGER	2	WILLS	2	ALL-EATING	1	BAR	1
STRONGLY	2	WIND	2	ALLAYED	1	BARRENLY	1
SUBJECTS	2	WINDS	2	ALLEGE	1	BASES	1
SUFFER	2	WINK	2	ALOFT	1	BATTERING	1
SULLEN	2	WINTER'S	2	ALREADY	1	BAY	1
SUPPOSED	2	WINTERS	2	ALTER	1	BEAMS	1
SURVEY	2	WIRES	2	ALTERATION	1	BEARD	1
SURVIVE	2	WISE	2	ALTERING	1	BEARER	1
SWAY	2	WITS	2	ALWAYS	1	BEAREST	1
SWEETLY	2	WOES	2	AMAZETH	1	BEATED	1
SWEETNESS	2	WOMB	2	AMBUSH	1	BEAUTIFUL	1
TABLES	2	WONDROUS	2	AMEN	1	BECK	1
TATTERED	2	WOOD	2	AMENDS	1	BECOME	1
TELLING	2	WORD	2	ANCHORED	1	BED-VOW	1
TELLS	2	WORTHLESS	2	ANGER	1	BEDS'	1
TEMPTATION	2	WRETCH	2	ANGRY	1	BEFITS	1
THEIRS	2	WRONGS	2	ANNEXED	1	BEFRIENDS	1
THEREBY	2	WROUGHT	2	ANNOY	1	BEGGAR	1
THIEVISH	2	YEARS	2	ANOTHER	1	BEGGARED	1
THRIVE	2	YELLOW	2	ANOTHER'S	1	BEGIN	1
TIE	2	YIELD	2	ANSWERED	1	BEGINS	1
TITLE	2	YOUTHFUL	2	ANSWERS	1	BEGUILE	1
TORTURE	2	ABLE	1	ANTICIPATE	1	BEGUILED	1
TOWARDS	2	ABOUT	1	APPAREL	1	BEHAVIOR	1
TRAVAIL	2	ABUNDANT	1	APPEAL	1	BELIED	1
TRAVELS	2	ABUSED	1	APPEARANCE	1	BELIEVED	1
TRESPASS	2	ABUSES	1	APPEARING	1	BELL	1
TRIUMPHANT	2	ABYSM	1	APPEARS	1	BENDS	1
TURNED	2	ACCENTS	1	APPETITES	1	BEQUEST	1
TWICE	2	ACCEPTABLE	1	APPLE	1	BEREFT	1
TWIXT	2	ACCEPTANCE	1	APPLYING	1	BESEECHERS	1
UNFATHERED	2	ACCESSORY	1	APRIL'S	1	BESEEM	1
UNKINDNESS	2	ACCIDENT	1	ARIGHT	1	BESHREW	1
UNKNOWN	2	ACCIDENTS	1	ARISE	1	BESIDE	1
UNLOOKED	2	ACCUMULATE	1	ARISING	1	BESMEARED	1
UNRESPECTED	2	ACCUSING	1	ARRAY	1	BESTOW	1
UNSEEN	2	ACHIEVE	1	ARREST	1	BESTOWEST	1
UNTRUE	2	ACKNOWLEDGE	1	ART'S	1	BETRAYING	1
URGE	2	ACT	1	ARTS	1	BETTERED	1
US	2	ACTIVE	1	ASHES	1	BETWIXT	1
USURER	2	ACTOR	1	ASKANCE	1	BEVEL	1
VAINLY	2	ADDER'S	1	ASKED	1	BEWAILED	1
VANISHED	2	ADDETH	1	ASPECT	1	BEWEEP	1
VANTAGE	2	ADDING	1	ASSEMBLE	1	BEYOND	1
VASSAL	2	ADIEU	1	ASSISTANCE	1	BID	1
VEINS	2	ADMIRE	1	ASSURE	1	BIDS	1
VEX	2	ADMIRED	1	ASTONISHED	1	BIG	1
VIOLET	2	ADMIRING	1	ASTRONOMY	1	BIND	1
VOUCHSAFE	2	ADMIT	1	ATTAINT	1	BIRD	1
VOW	2	ADMITTED	1	ATTAINTED	1	BLACKS	1

DISDAINETH	1	EMNITY	1	FAMINE	1	FOREGONE	1
DISDAINS	1	ENCLOSE	1	FAMISHED	1	FORESTS	1
DISEASE	1	ENDEARED	1	FAMOUSED	1	FORGED	1
DISGRACED	1	ENDING	1	FAREWELL	1	FORGETFUL	1
DISPATCH	1	ENDLESS	1	FARING	1	FORGETFU	
DISPENSE	1	ENDOWED	1	FASTER	1	LNESS	1
DISPERSE	1	ENDURE	1	FATE	1	FORGETST	1
DISPOSED	1	ENDURED	1	FAVORITES	1	FORGIVE	1
DISPRAISE	1	ENFEEBLED	1	FAWN	1	FORGOING	1
DISSUADE	1	ENFORCED	1	FEARFUL	1	FORGOTTEN	1
DISTANCE	1	ENGRAFT	1	FEARFULLY	1	FORLORN	1
DISTEMPERED	1	ENGRAFTED	1	FEARING	1	FORSAKEN	1
DISTILLATION	1	ENGROSSED	1	FEASTING	1	FORTY	1
DISTILLS	1	ENJOY	1	FEASTS	1	FORWARD	1
DISTRACTION	1	ENJOYED	1	FEATHERED	1	FORWARDS	1
DIVERT	1	ENJOYER	1	FEATHERS	1	FOUNTAINS	1
DIVIDE	1	ENJOYS	1	FEATURE	1	FOUR	1
DIVIDED	1	ENLARGED	1	FEATURED	1	FRAGRANT	1
DIVINING	1	ENLIGHTEN	1	FEATURELESS	1	FRAILER	1
DOCTOR-LIKE	1	ENRICH	1	FED	1	FRANK	1
DOUBT	1	ENSCONCE	1	FEE	1	FRANTIC	1
DOVE	1	ENTERTAIN	1	FEEBLE	1	FREEDOM	1
DRAINED	1	ENTITLED	1	FEED	1	FREEZINGS	1
DREADING	1	ENTOMBED	1	FEEDEST	1	FREQUENT	1
DREAMING	1	EPITAPH	1	FEELEST	1	FRESHER	1
DREGS	1	EQUAL	1	FELT	1	FRIEND'S	1
DRESS	1	EQUIPAGE	1	FEMALE	1	FRONT	1
DRESSED	1	ERR	1	FESTER	1	FROST	1
DRESSING	1	ERRED	1	FEW	1	FROWNEST	1
DRESSINGS	1	ERROR	1	FICKLE	1	FROWNS	1
DRINKS	1	ERST	1	FIELD	1	FRUIT	1
DROOPING	1	ESSAYS	1	FIERY	1	FUEL	1
DROP	1	ESTEEMING	1	FIGURE	1	FULLNESS	1
DROPS	1	ESTIMATE	1	FIGURED	1	FUNCTION	1
DROSS	1	EVE'S	1	FIGURES	1	FURROWS	1
DROWN	1	EVIDENT	1	FILCHING	1	FURY	1
DROWNS	1	EXCEED	1	FILED	1	GAINER	1
DRUDGE	1	EXCEEDED	1	FINGER	1	GAINS	1
DRUGS	1	EXCEEDS	1	FIRED	1	GARDENS	1
DRUNK	1	EXCEL	1	FIRM	1	GATES	1
DRY	1	EXCELLENT	1	FITS	1	GATHERED	1
DULLING	1	EXCEPT	1	FITTED	1	GAUDY	1
DULLNESS	1	EXCESS	1	FLATTERED	1	GAZED	1
DULY	1	EXCHANGED	1	FLATTERER	1	GAZERS	1
DUN	1	EXCHEQUER	1	FLEECE	1	GAZETH	1
DURST	1	EXCUSING	1	FLEETEST	1	GAZING	1
DUTEOUS	1	EXECUTOR	1	FLEETING	1	GEMS	1
DWELLERS	1	EXPIATE	1	FLOAT	1	GENTLEST	1
DWELLS	1	EXPIRE	1	FLOURISH	1	GENTLY	1
DYED	1	EXPIRED	1	FLOW	1	GET	1
DYER'S	1	EXPRESSING	1	FLOWN	1	GHASTLY	1
DYING	1	EXTANT	1	FLY	1	GHOST	1
EAGER	1	EXTERN	1	FOE	1	GIFTS	1
EARLY	1	EXTERNAL	1	FOILED	1	GILDEST	1
EARTHLY	1	EXTREMITY	1	FOISON	1	GIRDED	1
EASED	1	EYED	1	FOIST	1	GLADLY	1
EAST	1	EYES'	1	FOLLOWED	1	GLAZED	1
EASY	1	FACULTY	1	FOLLOWS	1	GLORIOUS	1
ECLIPSE	1	FADETH	1	FOOD	1	GLOWING	1
EFFECTUALLY	1	FAINT	1	FOOLISH	1	GLUTTON	1
EISEL	1	FAIRING	1	FOOLS	1	GLUTTONING	1
ELDER	1	FAIRLY	1	FORBIDDEN	1	GOES	1
ELOQUENCE	1	FALLS	1	FORCED	1	GOEST	1
EMBASSAGE	1	FALSELY	1	FORE	1	GOING	1
EMBASSY	1	FAMILIAR	1	FOREBEMOANED	1	GOOD-TURNS	1

Word		Word		Word		Word	
GOODLY	1	HIDING	1	INSTINCT	1	LENGTH	1
GORED	1	HIED	1	INSUFFIC		LENGTHS	1
GOVERNS	1	HIGHMOST	1	IENCY	1	LESSER	1
GRACED	1	HILL	1	INSULTS	1	LESSON	1
GRACIOUSLY	1	HINDMOST	1	INTELLIGENCE	1	LETS	1
GRANTING	1	HISTORY	1	INTEND	1	LIED	1
GRAVEN	1	HITS	1	INTENTS	1	LIFE'S	1
GRAVES	1	HOISTED	1	INTERCHANGE	1	LIFTS	1
GRAVITY	1	HOMAGE	1	INTERIM	1	LIGHT'S	1
GRAY	1	HONEST	1	INTERMIXED	1	LIKENESS	1
GREATEST	1	HONEY	1	INVITED	1	LIKER	1
GRECIAN	1	HONORING	1	INVITING	1	LILY	1
GREEING	1	HOOKS	1	INVOCATE	1	LIMBECKS	1
GRIEF'S	1	HORSES	1	INVOKED	1	LIMIT	1
GRIEFS	1	HOUNDS	1	ISSUELESS	1	LIMITS	1
GRIEVANCES	1	HOUSE	1	JADE	1	LIMPING	1
GRIEVE	1	HOUSEWIFE	1	JAIL	1	LINGER	1
GRIEVED	1	HUES	1	JAWS	1	LION'S	1
GRIND	1	HUGELY	1	JEALOUS	1	LIP	1
GROANS	1	HUNDRED	1	JEALOUSY	1	LIQUID	1
GROSSLY	1	HUNTED	1	JOIN	1	LIST	1
GUIDES	1	HURT	1	JOLLITY	1	LIVERY	1
GUILT	1	HUSBAND'S	1	JUDGMENT'S	1	LOAN	1
GULLS	1	HUSH	1	JUMP	1	LOATHSOME	1
GUST	1	HYMN	1	JUNES	1	LOCKED	1
GUSTS	1	IDLY	1	JUSTIFY	1	LODGED	1
HABIT	1	IDOL	1	KEEPEST	1	LONGING	1
HABITATION	1	IDOLATRY	1	KEY	1	LORD	1
HAIR	1	IMAGES	1	KILLED	1	LORD'S	1
HAIRS	1	IMAGINARY	1	KILLS	1	LORDS	1
HALLOWED	1	IMITATE	1	KINDS	1	LOSSES	1
HALT	1	IMITATED	1	KINGDOM	1	LOUD	1
HAMMERED	1	IMMORTAL	1	KINGDOMS	1	LOVE-GOD	1
HANGING	1	IMMURED	1	KINGLY	1	LOVE-KIN	
HAP	1	IMPAIR	1	KISSING	1	DLING	1
HAPPIES	1	IMPANELED	1	KNEW	1	LOVE-SUIT	1
HARD	1	IMPART	1	KNIGHTS	1	LOVELINESS	1
HARDER	1	IMPEACHED	1	KNIT	1	LOVER	1
HARDEST	1	IMPEDIMENTS	1	KNOWN	1	LOVERS	1
HARMFUL	1	IMPERFECT	1	LABORING	1	LOVERS'	1
HARSH	1	IMPIETY	1	LACE	1	LOW	1
HARVEST	1	IMPORT	1	LACKING	1	LOWEREST	1
HASTEN	1	IMPORTUNE	1	LADIES	1	LUCK	1
HATE'S	1	IMPREGNABLE	1	LAMB	1	LYING	1
HATED	1	IMPRESSION	1	LAMBS	1	MADDING	1
HATETH	1	IMPRINT	1	LAMENESS	1	MADNESS	1
HATRED	1	IMPUTE	1	LAND	1	MAID	1
HEALS	1	INCAPABLE	1	LANGUISHED	1	MAINTAIN	1
HEARD	1	INCERTAI		LAP	1	MAKELESS	1
HEAREST	1	NTIES	1	LARGESS	1	MAKETH	1
HEARING	1	INCERTAINTY	1	LARK	1	MANNER	1
HEARSAY	1	INCREASING	1	LASTING	1	MANY'S	1
HEARTED	1	INDEED	1	LATE	1	MAR	1
HEATS	1	INDIGEST	1	LAUGHED	1	MARBLE	1
HEED	1	INDIRECTLY	1	LAWS	1	MARCH	1
HEINOUS	1	INFANT'S	1	LEAGUE	1	MARIGOLD	1
HELEN'S	1	INFERIOR	1	LEAN	1	MARJORAM	1
HEMS	1	INFLAMING	1	LEAPED	1	MARRIAGE	1
HERALD	1	INFORMER	1	LEARNED	1	MARS	1
HERD	1	INHABIT	1	LEARNED'S	1	MARVEL	1
HEREIN	1	INHEARSE	1	LEASES	1	MASONRY	1
HERETIC	1	INHERIT	1	LEAVING	1	MATCHETH	1
HERS	1	INHERITORS	1	LEESE	1	MATURITY	1
HIDDEN	1	INIQUITY	1	LEGACY	1	MEADOWS	1
HIDES	1	INSTANT	1	LEGIONS	1	MEANT	1

Word	Count	Word	Count	Word	Count	Word	Count
MEASURED	1	NINE	1	PARDON	1	POUREST	1
MEDICINE	1	NOBLER	1	PARTAKE	1	POWERS	1
MEDITATION	1	NOON	1	PARTICULARS	1	PRAYERS	1
MEETNESS	1	NOURISHED	1	PARTLY	1	PREDICT	1
MELANCHOLY	1	NOVEL	1	PARTY	1	PREFIGURING	1
MEMORIAL	1	NUMBERED	1	PASSED	1	PREPOSTE	
MENDED	1	NURSE	1	PASSION	1	ROUSLY	1
MERCHANDISED	1	NURSED	1	PATENT	1	PRESAGE	1
MERCY	1	NURSETH	1	PATIENT	1	PRESAGERS	1
MERITS	1	NYMPHS	1	PAWS	1	PRESCRIP	
MESSENGERS	1	O'ER-GREEN	1	PAYING	1	TIONS	1
METER	1	O'ER-PRESSED	1	PEARL	1	PRESENTEST	1
METHODS	1	O'ER-READ	1	PEBBLED	1	PRESENTETH	1
MIDDLE	1	O'ER-SNOWED	1	PEEP	1	PRESENTS	1
MIGHTIER	1	O'ER-SWAYS	1	PENANCE	1	PRESERVE	1
MILLIONED	1	O'ER-WORN	1	PENURY	1	PRESS	1
MILLIONS	1	O'ERCHARGED	1	PERCEIVE	1	PRESUME	1
MIND'S	1	O'ERLOOK	1	PERCEIVED	1	PREVAILED	1
MINDED	1	O'ERTAKE	1	PERCEIVEST	1	PREVENT	1
MINION	1	OBJECT	1	PERFECTS	1	PREVENTEST	1
MINUTE	1	OBLATION	1	PERFORCE	1	PREY	1
MIRACLE	1	OBLIVION	1	PERFUMED	1	PRICKED	1
MISCALLED	1	OBLIVIOUS	1	PERHAPS	1	PRINCES'	1
MISER	1	ODORS	1	PERISH	1	PRINT	1
MISPLACED	1	OFF	1	PERMIT	1	PRISON	1
MISPRISION	1	OFFEND	1	PERSPECTIVE	1	PRISONER	1
MIST	1	OFFENDER'S	1	PERSUADE	1	PRIVATE	1
MISTAKE	1	OFFENDERS	1	PERUSAL	1	PRIZING	1
MISTAKING	1	OFFENSE'S	1	PETTY	1	PROCEED	1
MISUSE	1	OFFENSES	1	PHILOMEL	1	PROCEEDS	1
MIXED	1	OFFICE	1	PHOENIX	1	PROCESS	1
MODERN	1	OFFICES	1	PHRASE	1	PROCLAIMS	1
MOIETY	1	OLDER	1	PHYSICIAN	1	PROFANE	1
MOMENT	1	OLIVES	1	PHYSICIANS	1	PROFIT	1
MONARCH'S	1	ONSET	1	PICTURED	1	PROFITLESS	1
MONSTERS	1	ONWARD	1	PICTURES	1	PROFOUND	1
MOODS	1	ONWARDS	1	PIED	1	PROGNOST	
MORTALITY	1	OPPRESSION	1	PIERCED	1	ICATE	1
MORTGAGED	1	ORDERING	1	PIPE	1	PROGRESS	1
MOTLEY	1	ORIENT	1	PITIED	1	PROMISE	1
MOUNTED	1	ORNAMENTS	1	PITIFUL	1	PRONE	1
MOURNFUL	1	ORPHANS	1	PITYING	1	PROPHECIES	1
MOURNING	1	OUTBRAVES	1	PLACED	1	PROPHETIC	1
MOUTHED	1	OUTCAST	1	PLAGUES	1	PROPOSED	1
MOUTHS	1	OUTGOING	1	PLAIN	1	PROUDER	1
MOVE	1	OUTRIGHT	1	PLANTS	1	PROUDEST	1
MOW	1	OUTSTRIPPED	1	PLAYED	1	PROUDLY	1
MUD	1	OVER	1	PLAYEST	1	PROVIDE	1
MUSES	1	OVER-GOES	1	PLEASANT	1	PROVING	1
NAKED	1	OVER-PARTIAL	1	PLEASED	1	PROVOKE	1
NAMING	1	OVERPLUS	1	PLEASURES	1	PRY	1
NATIVITY	1	OVERTHROW	1	PLIGHT	1	PUBLISH	1
NAUGHTS	1	OVERTURN	1	PLODS	1	PUPIL	1
NEARLY	1	OWE	1	PLOT	1	PURCHASED	1
NECESSARY	1	OWES	1	POESY	1	PUREST	1
NECK	1	OWEST	1	POINTING	1	PURGE	1
NEEDEST	1	OWNER'S	1	POINTS	1	PURGING	1
NEEDING	1	OWNERS	1	POISON	1	PURITY	1
NEEDY	1	PAGE	1	POISONED	1	PURPLE	1
NEGLECTED	1	PAID	1	POLISHED	1	PURPOSED	1
NEIGH	1	PAINFUL	1	POLITIC	1	PURSUING	1
NERVES	1	PAINTER'S	1	POMP	1	PUTEST	1
NEWFANGLED	1	PAPER	1	POORLY	1	PUTS	1
NEWS	1	PAPERS	1	POSSESSETH	1	PYRAMIDS	1
NIGGARDING	1	PARALLELS	1	POSTING	1	QUALIFY	1

QUALITY	1	RESPECTS	1	SCARLET	1	SIGH	1
QUEEN	1	RESTFUL	1	SCORE	1	SIGHS	1
QUENCHED	1	RESTING	1	SCORNED	1	SIGNS	1
QUICKER	1	RESTORE	1	SEA'S	1	SILVER	1
QUICKLY	1	RESTORED	1	SEAL	1	SILVERED	1
QUIET	1	RESTY	1	SEALED	1	SIMPLE-TRUTH	1
QUIETUS	1	RESURVEY	1	SEALS	1	SIMPLICITY	1
RACE	1	RETENTION	1	SEASONED	1	SIMPLY	1
RACK	1	RETURNED	1	SEASONS'	1	SINGLENESS	1
RAGGED	1	REVENGE	1	SECONDS	1	SINKS	1
RAIMENT	1	REVENUES	1	SECRET	1	SIRE	1
RAINY	1	REVIEW	1	SEEKING	1	SIREN	1
RAISED	1	REVIEWEST	1	SEEMLY	1	SITS	1
RANDOM	1	REVOLT	1	SEES	1	SITUATION	1
RANGED	1	REVOLUTION	1	SEETHING	1	SKY	1
RANKS	1	RHETORIC	1	SELF-DOING	1	SLANDER'S	1
RANSOMS	1	RHYMERS	1	SELF-LOVE	1	SLANDERED	1
RARITIES	1	RICHER	1	SELF-WILLED	1	SLANDERERS	1
RATHER	1	RICHLY	1	SELF'S	1	SLANDERING	1
RAVEN	1	RID	1	SELFSAME	1	SLAVERY	1
REAP	1	RIDER	1	SELL	1	SLAY	1
REARWARD	1	RIGHTLY	1	SELLING	1	SLEEPING	1
REBEL	1	RIGHTS	1	SEMBLANCE	1	SLEPT	1
REBUKED	1	RIGOR	1	SENDEST	1	SLIDE	1
RECEIPT	1	RIOT	1	SENSES	1	SLUMBERS	1
RECEIVE	1	RIPE	1	SEPARABLE	1	SLUTTISH	1
RECEIVING	1	RISING	1	SEPARATION	1	SMELLS	1
RECITE	1	ROBBED	1	SEPULCHERS	1	SMILING	1
RECKON	1	ROBBING	1	SEQUENT	1	SMOKE	1
RECKONED	1	ROBE	1	SERVANT	1	SMOTHER	1
RECKONING	1	ROCKS	1	SERVANT'S	1	SNOW	1
RECOMPENSE	1	ROLLING	1	SERVICE	1	SOBER	1
RECORDS	1	RONDURE	1	SERVICES	1	SOCIETY	1
RECOUNTING	1	ROOF	1	SESSIONS	1	SOFT	1
RECURED	1	ROOM	1	SETTLED	1	SOLD	1
REDEEM	1	ROSY	1	SEVERAL	1	SOLE	1
REEKS	1	ROUGH	1	SHADOW'S	1	SOLEMN	1
REELETH	1	RUDELY	1	SHADY	1	SOMETIMES	1
REFIGURED	1	RUDEST	1	SHALBE	1	SONGS	1
REFINED	1	RUIN	1	SHALLOWEST	1	SORRY	1
REFUSE	1	RUINATE	1	SHAMED	1	SOUGHT	1
REFUSEST	1	RUINING	1	SHAMEFULLY	1	SOUNDLESS	1
REGION	1	RUMINATE	1	SHAPES	1	SOUREST	1
REGISTER	1	RUN	1	SHARE	1	SPACE	1
REGISTERS	1	RUNNEST	1	SHARP	1	SPACIOUS	1
REIGNED	1	RUNS	1	SHARPENED	1	SPARKLING	1
REIGNS	1	RUTH	1	SHARPEST	1	SPENDEST	1
RELEASING	1	SABLE	1	SHEAVES	1	SPENDING	1
RELIEF	1	SADLY	1	SHEDS	1	SPENDS	1
RELIGIOUS	1	SAINT	1	SHIFTING	1	SPHERES	1
REMAINS	1	SAITH	1	SHIFTS	1	SPIES	1
REMOTE	1	SALUTATION	1	SHOOK	1	SPITES	1
REMOVER	1	SALVING	1	SHOOT	1	SPLENDOR	1
RENEW	1	SANG	1	SHOP	1	SPOIL	1
RENEWED	1	SATIRE	1	SHORN	1	SPOILS	1
RENEWEST	1	SATURN	1	SHOWEST	1	SPORTIVE	1
RENT	1	SAUCES	1	SHOWING	1	SPOT	1
RENTS	1	SAVAGE	1	SICK-MEN	1	SPREAD	1
REPAY	1	SAVED	1	SICKEN	1	SPRINGS	1
REPENT	1	SAVOR	1	SICKLE	1	SPURRING	1
REPROACH	1	SAYING	1	SICKLE'S	1	STAINED	1
REPROVING	1	SCANDAL	1	SICKLY	1	STAINETH	1
REQUIRE	1	SCANTED	1	SICKNESS	1	STAMP	1
RESEMBLE	1	SCAPED	1	SIDES	1	STAMPED	1
RESORT	1	SCARCELY	1	SIEGE	1	STARVED	1

STATUES	1	SURMISE	1	TOMBED	1	UNPERFECT	1
STATUTE	1	SURMOUNT	1	TOMBS	1	UNPROVIDENT	1
STAYS	1	SWALLOWED	1	TONGUE'S	1	UNREST	1
STEALS	1	SWART	1	TOP	1	UNSEEING	1
STEALTH	1	SWAYEST	1	TOPS	1	UNSET	1
STEELED	1	SWEARING	1	TORN	1	UNSTAINED	1
STEEPY	1	SWEARS	1	TOUCH	1	UNSWAYED	1
STELLED	1	SWEET-FAVOR	1	TOUCHED	1	UNSWEPT	1
STERN	1	SWERVING	1	TOWARD	1	UNTAINTED	1
STEWARDS	1	SWIFT-FOOTED	1	TOWERS	1	UNTHRIFT	1
STICKEST	1	SWORD	1	TRACT	1	UNTHRIFTS	1
STIRRED	1	SYMPATHIZED	1	TRAFFIC	1	UNTHRIFTY	1
STOLE	1	TABLE	1	TRANSFERRED	1	UNTIL	1
STONES	1	TAKER	1	TRANSFIX	1	UNTO	1
STOPPED	1	TALL	1	TRANSGRE		UNTOLD	
STOPS	1	TALLIES	1	SSION	1	UNTRIMMED	1
STORM-BEATEN	1	TAME	1	TRANSLATE	1	UNTUTORED	1
STORMY	1	TAN	1	TRANSLATED	1	UNWOOED	1
STOUT	1	TANNED	1	TRANSPORT	1	UNWORTHINESS	1
STRAINED	1	TASK	1	TRAVEL	1	UP-LOCKED	1
STRAINS	1	TEACHEST	1	TRAVELED	1	UPHOLD	1
STRANGLE	1	TEAR	1	TREADS	1	UPREAR	1
STRAYING	1	TEEMING	1	TREASON	1	USER	1
STREAMS	1	TEETH	1	TREES	1	USEST	1
STRENGTH'S	1	TEMPERATE	1	TRENCHES	1	USHERS	1
STRENGTHENED	1	TEMPESTS	1	TRESSES	1	USURY	1
STRETCHED	1	TEMPTETH	1	TRIAL	1	UTMOST	1
STRIFE	1	TEMPTING	1	TRIBES	1	UTTERING	1
STRIKES	1	TENANTS	1	TRIFLE	1	VACANT	1
STRING	1	TENDERED	1	TRIFLES	1	VADE	1
STRIVING	1	TENTH	1	TRIM	1	VALLEY-F	
STRUCK	1	TENURE	1	TRIMMED	1	OUNTAIN	1
STRUMPETED	1	TERM	1	TRIPPING	1	VANISHING	1
SUBDUED	1	TERMED	1	TROPHIES	1	VARIATION	1
SUBORNED	1	TERMS	1	TROUBLE	1	VARYING	1
SUBSCRIBES	1	TESTY	1	TRUANT	1	VASSALAGE	1
SUBSIST	1	THANK	1	TRUEST	1	VAUNT	1
SUBSTANTIAL	1	THANKS	1	TRUTH'S	1	VEIL	1
SUBTLETIES	1	THEFT	1	TRUTHS	1	VENGEFUL	1
SUCCEEDING	1	THEMES	1	TRY	1	VERDICT	1
SUCCESSION	1	THEREOF	1	TUNE	1	VERMILION	1
SUCCESSIVE	1	THINLY	1	TUNED	1	VERSES	1
SUE	1	THIRD	1	TWENTY	1	VEXED	1
SUFFERANCE	1	THITHER	1	TWILIGHT	1	VIAL	1
SUFFERED	1	THRALL	1	TWIRE	1	VICE	1
SUFFERING	1	THRALLED	1	TWOFOLD	1	VICES	1
SUFFERS	1	THREEFOLD	1	TYRANNOUS	1	VICTOR	1
SUFFICED	1	THREESCORE	1	TYRANNY	1	VICTORIES	1
SUGGEST	1	THREW	1	TYRANTS	1	VICTORS	1
SUIT	1	THRIFTLESS	1	TYRANTS'	1	VIEWEST	1
SUITED	1	THRIVERS	1	UGLY	1	VILEST	1
SULLIED	1	THRONED	1	UN-EARED	1	VIRGIN	1
SUMMON	1	THROW	1	UNBLESS	1	VISAGE	1
SUMS	1	THRUST	1	UNBRED	1	VISION	1
SUN'S	1	THRUSTS	1	UNCERTAIN	1	VOICE	1
SUNK	1	THUNDER	1	UNDIVIDED	1	VOICES	1
SUNKEN	1	TICKLED	1	UNFAIR	1	VOTARY	1
SUNS	1	TIED	1	UNFOLDING	1	VOWED	1
SUNSET	1	TIGER'S	1	UNHAPPILY	1	VOWING	1
SUPPOSE	1	TILLAGE	1	UNIONS	1	WAILING	1
SUPPOSING	1	TINCTURE	1	UNIVERSE	1	WAITING	1
SUPPRESSED	1	TIRES	1	UNJUST	1	WAKE	1
SURETY-LIKE	1	TITLES	1	UNLEARNED	1	WAKENED	1
SURFEIT	1	TOGETHER	1	UNLETTERED	1	WAKING	1
SURLY	1	TOILED	1	UNMOVED	1	WALK	1

Word		Word		Word		Word	
WANDEREST	1	WEAKENS	1	WILLFULNESS	1	WORSER	1
WANDERING	1	WEAKNESS	1	WILLINGLY	1	WORSHIP	1
WANE	1	WEEKS	1	WINDY	1	WORTHIER	1
WANING	1	WEIGH	1	WING	1	WORTHINESS	1
WANTON	1	WEIGHS	1	WINGED	1	WORTHS	1
WANTONLY	1	WEIGHT	1	WIRY	1	WOUNDED	1
WANTONNESS	1	WELFARE	1	WISDOM	1	WRACK	1
WAR'S	1	WENT	1	WISHED	1	WRACKED	1
WARD	1	WET	1	WISHING	1	WRACKFUL	1
WARDROBE	1	WHATSOEVER	1	WITHAL	1	WRESTING	1
WARDS	1	WHERETHROUGH	1	WITHERING	1	WRETCH'S	1
WARM	1	WHEREUPON	1	WOEFUL	1	WRINKLE	1
WARMED	1	WHEREWITH	1	WOLF	1	WRITERS	1
WARNING	1	WHIT	1	WOMBS	1	WRITES	1
WARRANTISE	1	WHOLE	1	WON	1	WRITTEN	1
WARRIOR	1	WIDOW'S	1	WONDERING	1	WRONGFULLY	1
WARY	1	WIDOWED	1	WONT	1	YEA	1
WASTED	1	WIFE	1	WOO	1	YELLOWED	1
WATCHING	1	WIGHTS	1	WOOD'S	1	YORE	1
WATCHMAN	1	WILD	1	WOOED	1	YOUNGLY	1
WATERY	1	WILLBE	1	WOOING	1	YOUTH'S	1
WAVES	1	WILLFULLY	1	WORKINGS	1	ZEALOUS	1

SIR PHILIP SIDNEY, 'ASTROPHEL AND STELLA'

Word		Word		Word		Word	
MY	298	AS	53	FACE	27	ALAS	18
OF	291	NOW	53	MAKE	27	DAY	18
TO	276	OR	53	WELL	27	GIVE	18
I	257	THIS	53	SINCE	26	LIPS	18
THAT	249	THEE	49	GRACE	25	MADE	18
AND	247	YET	49	NIGHT	25	OUT	18
IN	246	SELF	48	WILL	24	SENSE	18
THE	228	WHILE	47	EVEN	23	THERE	18
WITH	169	IF	46	HIM	23	THINK	18
BUT	150	SUCH	46	LIGHT	23	WOULD	18
ME	141	THEN	44	PLACE	23	HEAVENLY	17
A	117	ON	43	THUS	23	LONG	17
LOVE	108	STELLA	41	ART	22	MAKES	17
SO	103	THEY	41	AT	22	ONE	17
HER	102	SWEET	39	DEAR	22	PRAISE	17
IS	97	MOST	38	EACH	22	BEAUTY	16
DO	93	WHO	38	GOOD	22	POOR	16
FOR	93	WHEN	37	HAVE	22	STRAIGHT	16
THY	93	FAIR	36	KNOW	22	WOE	16
NOT	92	HOW	36	MIGHT	22	BLACK	15
WHICH	91	SOME	36	SHOW	22	BLISS	15
BE	88	THEIR	36	FIND	21	PROVE	15
DOTH	87	MINE	35	HATH	21	SIGHT	15
HIS	85	MORE	35	JOY	21	SOUL	15
BY	79	WORDS	35	LIKE	21	THOUGHTS	15
THOU	76	YOUR	35	MUST	21	AM	14
FROM	64	LET	34	OWN	21	KISS	14
YOU	62	WHERE	34	TRUE	21	PAIN	14
DID	61	NOR	33	BOTH	20	TAKE	14
SHE	61	OFT	33	NATURE	20	TILL	14
NO	60	SEE	33	THEM	20	BEAMS	13
WHAT	60	STELLA'S	33	ARE	19	BECAUSE	13
HEART	59	STILL	33	BEST	19	COULD	13
IT	59	CAN	32	DELIGHT	19	DESIRE	13
EYES	58	ONLY	30	MIND	19	HOPE	13
ALL	56	THOUGH	30	SAY	19	LEAVE	13
HE	55	WHOSE	30	SHOULD	19	LIFE	13
O	55	MAY	28	THAN	19	LOVE'S	13
THOSE	54	WIT	28	VIRTUE	19	NAME	13

Word		Word		Word		Word	
OUR	13	RACE	9	SHINE	7	BORN	5
SIGHS	13	SAD	9	SLEEP	7	BRINGS	5
WAS	13	SAME	9	SMART	7	CEASE	5
BREAST	12	SHAME	9	SPRITES	7	COLD	5
CAUSE	12	SPEAK	9	STAYED	7	COMES	5
COME	12	SPEECH	9	STRANGE	7	DART	5
DOST	12	THENCE	9	TELL	7	DEED	5
FLY	12	THINGS	9	TOUCH	7	EMBRACE	5
MOVE	12	THOUGHT	9	UP	7	ENVY	5
MUCH	12	USE	9	WAY	7	FAST	5
RICH	12	WRITE	9	WAYS	7	FEAR	5
TEARS	12	ABSENCE	8	WEALTH	7	FOOD	5
THESE	12	AH	8	WERE	7	FORTUNE	5
BEAUTIES	11	BREATH	8	WISE	7	GET	5
BEAUTY'S	11	BREED	8	BARE	6	GOLD	5
CANNOT	11	CUPID'S	8	BLIND	6	GONE	5
FAR	11	ELSE	8	CHIEF	6	HAST	5
FORTH	11	FIT	8	CRY	6	HAVING	5
FULL	11	FLOW	8	CURSED	6	HEARTS	5
HEAVEN	11	HAD	8	DEATH	6	HEAVY	5
HIGH	11	LEAST	8	DISGRACE	6	HIMSELF	5
LIE	11	LOOK	8	EASE	6	HORSE	5
LIES	11	NATURE'S	8	ELOQUENCE	6	HUE	5
LOOKS	11	STAY	8	EVERY	6	IMAGE	5
NEW	11	SWEAR	8	FAULT	6	INDEED	5
RIGHT	11	SWEETEST	8	FLAMES	6	LENGTH	5
SHALL	11	THINE	8	HARD	6	LIVE	5
TRUTH	11	THROUGH	8	HEAR	6	MORTAL	5
WHOM	11	UPON	8	HID	6	OLD	5
WITS	11	VIRTUE'S	8	HONOR	6	PLEASE	5
CARE	10	VOICE	8	INTO	6	PRESENCE	5
FAME	10	WANT	8	MARS	6	PROOF	5
FIRST	10	WE	8	MOUTH	6	RED	5
GREAT	10	YOUNG	8	NEAR	6	SAYS	5
GROW	10	BEAR	7	OTHERS	6	SCORN	5
HAND	10	CALL	7	PAINT	6	SET	5
HERE	10	COURSE	7	PASS	6	SHOT	5
LATE	10	CUPID	7	PEACE	6	SING	5
MUSE	10	DARE	7	PEN	6	SLAVE	5
NEEDS	10	DOWN	7	POWER	6	SOFT	5
PART	10	EARS	7	PRAY	6	SORROW	5
PITY	10	FAIN	7	PRIDE	6	SPITE	5
READ	10	FAITH	7	REASON	6	SUGARED	5
SKIES	10	FEEL	7	SAKE	6	SWEETLY	5
SUN	10	FEET	7	SAW	6	TEDIOUS	5
SURE	10	FINE	7	SHADE	6	THEREOF	5
TOO	10	FIRE	7	SICK	6	TREE	5
UNTO	10	FOOL	7	SKILL	6	TRY	5
WITHOUT	10	FOOLS	7	SOON	6	WHENCE	5
BOY	9	FORCED	7	STATE	6	WHITE	5
BRAIN	9	FREE	7	STIR	6	WHY	5
CASE	9	FRIEND	7	TIME	6	WISH	5
DARK	9	GO	7	UNKIND	6	WONDER	5
EVER	9	GRANT	7	VAIN	6	ABOVE	4
EYE	9	HEAD	7	WIN	6	APPEAR	4
FORCE	9	HELP	7	WINGS	6	APT	4
FRAME	9	INWARD	7	WORLD	6	ARISE	4
GOLDEN	9	JOYS	7	WRETCH	6	ARMS	4
KEEP	9	JUDGE	7	ALONE	5	AWAY	4
LAY	9	LESS	7	ANY	5	BED	4
NAY	9	LOVED	7	BAD	5	BEING	4
NEVER	9	MEAN	7	BEEN	5	BETTER	4
ONCE	9	MISS	7	BEFORE	5	BIT	4
OTHER	9	PAINS	7	BETWEEN	5	BLEED	4
POWERS	9	SAID	7	BLESSED	5	BLOW	4

Word		Word		Word		Word	
BLUSH	4	SEEING	4	CURSE	3	LOVING	3
BOOK	4	SEEK	4	DAILY	3	MAD	3
BREATHE	4	SHIELD	4	DANCE	3	MAN	3
BURN	4	SHINING	4	DAZZLED	3	MAN'S	3
CHEEKS	4	SHOWS	4	DEEP	3	MOAN	3
CHILD	4	SILENT	4	DESCRY	3	MORNING	3
COMFORT	4	SIT	4	DESIRES	3	MUSIC	3
CONFESS	4	SKIN	4	DISDAIN	3	NAKED	3
COURT	4	SOULS	4	DISPLAY	3	NECK	3
CRIES	4	SPRING	4	DISPLAYS	3	NECTAR	3
CRUEL	4	STARS	4	DOOM	3	NEED	3
DAINTY	4	STOLEN	4	DUMB	3	NOTES	3
DESPAIR	4	SWELL	4	DWELL	3	NOUGHT	3
DIE	4	TENDER	4	EAR	3	NYMPH	3
ENOUGH	4	THEMSELVES	4	EFFECT	3	OBJECT	3
ERE	4	THING	4	EFFECTS	3	OTHERS'	3
FALL	4	TIRED	4	ENDITE	3	PAGE	3
FIELD	4	TONGUE	4	ENJOY	3	PANTS	3
FINDING	4	TREASURES	4	ERROR	3	PARNASSUS	3
FRUIT	4	TRIES	4	FAIREST	3	PASSIONS	3
GIFTS	4	VENUS	4	FELT	3	PHRASES	3
GLASS	4	VERSE	4	FIE	3	PLAINTS	3
GOT	4	WEAK	4	FIGHT	3	POSSESS	3
GRAMMAR	4	WEAR	4	FLED	3	QUITE	3
GROWN	4	WITHIN	4	FLIES	3	RAGE	3
GUEST	4	WOES	4	FOOLISH	3	RAISED	3
HELL	4	WORD	4	FOUL	3	RATHER	3
HIGHEST	4	WORSE	4	FOUND	3	RAYS	3
HOLD	4	WOUNDS	4	FRIENDLY	3	REACH	3
HOLDS	4	WRACK	4	FRIENDS	3	READY	3
IMPART	4	AGAIN	3	GAIN	3	REASONS	3
INK	4	AIR	3	GAVE	3	REST	3
JUST	4	AN	3	GLISTERING	3	RICHES	3
KIND	4	ANNOY	3	GOD	3	ROSES	3
LEARN	4	AYE	3	GOODS	3	SACRED	3
LEARNED	4	BADGE	3	GRIEF	3	SCARCELY	3
LIVELY	4	BEAMY	3	GROAN	3	SCHOLAR	3
LIVERY	4	BEARS	3	GUESS	3	SEEM	3
LIVING	4	BEGIN	3	GUIDES	3	SEEMED	3
LO	4	BEND	3	HAIR	3	SENSE'S	3
LOCKS	4	BIRTH	3	HANDS	3	SENT	3
LOOKED	4	BLACKEST	3	HEARD	3	SHAPE	3
LOVERS	4	BLOOD	3	HEAVEN'S	3	SHARP	3
LOW	4	BLOODY	3	HEIGHT	3	SHORT	3
MANY	4	BLOWS	3	HOPES	3	SICKNESS	3
MARK	4	BLUSHING	3	JOVE	3	SIN	3
MUSES	4	BOW	3	JOVE'S	3	SINFUL	3
NEST	4	BRAVE	3	KINGS	3	SIR	3
NOBLER	4	BREAK	3	KNOWLEDGE	3	SLOW	3
NONE	4	BUSY	3	LABOR	3	SOMEWHAT	3
NOTHING	4	CAME	3	LANGUISHED	3	SPENT	3
OUGHT	4	CANST	3	LAP	3	SPRITE	3
PARDON	4	CHAMBER	3	LAST	3	SPUR	3
PATIENCE	4	CHEER	3	LEARNS	3	STEPS	3
PAY	4	CHILDREN	3	LEFT	3	STRENGTH	3
PERFECT	4	CHOICEST	3	LESSON	3	STRIVE	3
PERHAPS	4	CLAIM	3	LIBERTY	3	SWEETS	3
PHOEBUS'	4	CLEAR	3	LIGHTS	3	TAKES	3
PLAY	4	CLIPS	3	LINE	3	TAME	3
PROCEED	4	CLOSE	3	LIP	3	TASTE	3
PURE	4	CLOUDS	3	LITTLE	3	TEACHING	3
REMOVE	4	CONQUEST	3	LOSE	3	THEREFORE	3
RISE	4	CONTENT	3	LOST	3	TIES	3
RULES	4	CREEP	3	LOT	3	TRIBUTE	3
RUN	4	CURIOUS	3	LOVELY	3	TURNS	3

TWO	3	BROOK	2	FIGHTS	2	LIKED	2
VENUS'	3	BROUGHT	2	FIRMLY	2	LIKEST	2
VEXED	3	BURDEN	2	FLATTERY	2	LINED	2
VIRTUOUS	3	BURNS	2	FLESH	2	LINES	2
WARMTH	3	CALLED	2	FLIGHT	2	LOATHING	2
WEEDS	3	CHANCE	2	FLOWER	2	LODGED	2
WEEP	3	CHARM	2	FLOWERS	2	LORD	2
WHEREWITH	3	CHASTITY	2	FOE	2	LORDS	2
WHETHER	3	CHOICE	2	FOLKS	2	LOVER'S	2
WHOLE	3	CHOOSE	2	FORBEARS	2	MAIN	2
WIGHT	3	CLOSED	2	FORGOT	2	MAJESTY	2
WILT	3	CLOTHED	2	FORMED	2	MAKING	2
WINDOW	3	COAST	2	FORSOOTH	2	MANNER	2
WINTER	3	COLOR	2	FORTUNE'S	2	MANNERS	2
WISDOM'S	3	COLORED	2	FRESH	2	MARKS	2
WITNESS	3	COMPANY	2	FRESHLY	2	MARRED	2
WORK	3	CONFUSED	2	FRUITS	2	MARS'S	2
WORTH	3	CONQUER	2	FUR	2	MEET	2
WORTHY	3	CONSORT	2	FURY	2	MEMORY	2
WOT	3	CONVERSATION	2	GARDEN	2	MEN'S	2
WOULDST	3	COUNSEL	2	GEMS	2	MET	2
WOUND	3	COUNSELS	2	GIVEN	2	MINDS	2
WRONG	3	COURTLY	2	GLAD	2	MIRTH	2
WROUGHT	3	CREST	2	GLORY	2	MISERY	2
ABSENT	2	CROWN	2	GLOVE	2	MIXED	2
ACQUAINTED	2	CUNNING	2	GRIPE	2	MIXTURE	2
ADDRESS	2	DAINTIEST	2	GROWS	2	MODELS	2
AGREE	2	DARKENED	2	GUIDED	2	MOLD	2
ALTHOUGH	2	DARKNESS	2	GUISE	2	MOON	2
AMBITIOUS	2	DARTS	2	HAPPY	2	MORN	2
ANGER	2	DEAL	2	HARDER	2	MOURNING	2
ANNOYS	2	DEATHS	2	HARK	2	MUSES'	2
ANOTHER	2	DECLINE	2	HATE	2	NAMED	2
ANSWERS	2	DEEM	2	HATES	2	NATIVE	2
APPEARS	2	DENIES	2	HEAT	2	NIGHT'S	2
APPLIES	2	DESCRIED	2	HEIR	2	NOURISH	2
ARMOR	2	DESCRIES	2	HELD	2	NYMPHS	2
ARROW	2	DIAN'S	2	HELLISH	2	OBTAIN	2
ARROWS	2	DIDST	2	HERS	2	OPPRESSED	2
ASHAMED	2	DIG	2	HIE	2	ORPHAN	2
ASPIRE	2	DOG	2	HISTORY	2	OTHER'S	2
ATLAS	2	DOORS	2	HONOR'S	2	OUTSIDE	2
AURORA	2	DOUBT	2	HONORED	2	OVER	2
AWRY	2	DOUBTS	2	HOPED	2	OWE	2
BABES	2	DRIVE	2	HORNS	2	PACE	2
BALANCE	2	DULL	2	HORRORS	2	PALENESS	2
BANISH	2	DUSTY	2	HOST	2	PAPER	2
BASE	2	DUTY	2	HUMBLE	2	PARADISE	2
BECOMES	2	EARTH	2	HURT	2	PAWS	2
BEGGARY	2	EITHER	2	INCREASE	2	PEARL	2
BEHOLD	2	EMPLOY	2	INFINITE	2	PERSUADES	2
BENDS	2	EMPTY	2	INVITE	2	PHOEBUS	2
BENT	2	END	2	IRON	2	PHRASE	2
BEWRAY	2	ENTERTAIN	2	JOY'S	2	PIECE	2
BIND	2	EXCEL	2	JUDGES	2	PIERCED	2
BIRTHRIGHT	2	EXPRESS	2	JUDGMENT	2	PIERCING	2
BLAME	2	FAIL	2	KEEPS	2	PINE	2
BLEEDING	2	FALLS	2	KING	2	PLACED	2
BLISSED	2	FALSE	2	KNOWING	2	PLAGUE	2
BODY	2	FANCY	2	KNOWN	2	PLAINT	2
BOILING	2	FATE	2	KNOWS	2	PLEASED	2
BRAKE	2	FEED	2	LADIES	2	PLEASING	2
BREASTS	2	FEELING	2	LEAVES	2	PLEASURE	2
BRIGHT	2	FELLOWSHIP	2	LEAVING	2	POINT	2
BRING	2	FIERCE	2	LIGHTNING	2	POISON	2

PRECEPTS	2	SPEND	2	WRETCHED	2	ASLEEP	1
PREPARED	2	SPOIL	2	WRONGS	2	ASSAIL	1
PRETTY	2	SPORT	2	YEARS	2	ASSAULT	1
PREVAIL	2	SPY	2	YIELD	2	ASTROLOGY	1
PRINCESS	2	START	2	YOUTH	2	ATTENDS	1
PRIZE	2	STEAL	2	'SUAGE	1	ATTIRES	1
PROBLEMS	2	STOP	2	ABASE	1	AUDIT	1
PROMISE	2	STORE	2	ABROAD	1	AUGMENT	1
PROSPECT	2	STRAKE	2	ABSTRACTED	1	AURORA'S	1
PROTESTS	2	STREAMS	2	ABUSE	1	AUTHOR	1
PUFFING	2	STRIFE	2	ACCORDING	1	AUTHORITY	1
PUT	2	STUFF	2	ACCURST	1	AVAIL	1
QUEEN	2	STYLE	2	ACQUAINTANCE	1	AVISE	1
QUESTIONS	2	SUBJECT	2	ADMIRE	1	AVOID	1
QUICK	2	SUN'S	2	ADMITTED	1	AWAKE	1
QUINTESSENCE	2	SWANS	2	ADOPTIVE	1	AWFUL	1
RAIN	2	SWEETENER	2	ADORE	1	BABIES	1
RARE	2	SWEETNESS	2	ADVANCE	1	BACK	1
READING	2	SWELLING	2	AEOLS'	1	BAITING	1
REASON'S	2	SWORD	2	AFFECTION	1	BALM	1
RECOUNT	2	TAUGHT	2	AFFIRM	1	BANISHED	1
REIGN	2	TEACH	2	AFFORDS	1	BANKROUT	1
REINS	2	TEMPESTS	2	AFRIKE	1	BANNER	1
RENT	2	TEMPLE	2	AFTER-FO		BANNERS	
REWARD	2	THEREIN	2	LLOWING	1	BARD	1
RHYMES	2	THEREWITH	2	AGAINST	1	BARGE	1
RIBS	2	THREE	2	AGANIPPE	1	BARKS	1
ROSE	2	THRONE	2	AGREED	1	BASES	1
ROSY	2	TITLE	2	AID	1	BASEST	1
ROYAL	2	TOTAL	2	AIM	1	BATE	1
RUDE	2	TRAIN	2	AIRS	1	BATTERED	1
RUIN	2	TROPES	2	ALABASTER	1	BEAREST	1
SAYETH	2	TROUBLED	2	ALLAY	1	BEAST	1
SAYING	2	TURKISH	2	ALLEGORY'S	1	BEASTS	1
SCEPTER	2	TYRANNY	2	ALLOW	1	BEAT	1
SCHOOLS	2	UNFELT	2	ALMS	1	BEATEN	1
SCOURGE	2	UNFIT	2	ALONG	1	BEATING	1
SCUSE	2	UNHAPPY	2	ALREADY	1	BEAUTIFIER	1
SEEKING	2	VAPORS	2	AMBER	1	BEAUTIFIES	1
SEEMS	2	VEIL	2	AMBITION	1	BECK	1
SEES	2	VERY	2	AMBITION'S	1	BECLOUDED	1
SELVES	2	VICTORY	2	AMID	1	BECOME	1
SERVANTS	2	VIRTUES	2	AMISS	1	BEDIM	1
SERVE	2	VOUCHSAFE	2	AMPHION'S	1	BEG	1
SERVICE	2	WAIL	2	AMPLE	1	BEGINS	1
SHADES	2	WAIT	2	ANATOMY	1	BEGOT	1
SHAFTS	2	WANTING	2	ANCHOR	1	BEGUILED	1
SHALT	2	WANTON	2	ANEW	1	BEHELD	1
SHINES	2	WAR	2	ANGEL	1	BEHEST	1
SHOULDST	2	WARE	2	ANGEL'S	1	BEHIND	1
SHOVE	2	WEAL	2	ANOTHER'S	1	BELIEVE	1
SIDE	2	WEIGH	2	ANSWER	1	BEMOAN	1
SIGHED	2	WHEREIN	2	APART	1	BEMOANS	1
SILENCE	2	WHEREOF	2	APES	1	BENIGHTED	1
SILLY	2	WHERETO	2	APPLY	1	BEST-GRACED	1
SMALL	2	WILLING	2	APPREHENDING	1	BESTOWS	1
SMILE	2	WINDOWS	2	APPROACH	1	BETRAYED	1
SMOOTH	2	WITHAL	2	ARCHER	1	BEWARE	1
SOBS	2	WOE'S	2	ARGUMENTS	1	BEYOND	1
SONG	2	WOOED	2	ARISTOTLE'S	1	BID	1
SORROW'S	2	WORKS	2	ARMED	1	BIDDEN	1
SOUGHT	2	WORLDS	2	ARMIES	1	BIDE	1
SOVEREIGNTY	2	WORST	2	ARMORY	1	BILLING	1
SPARE	2	WRAPPED	2	ARRAY	1	BIRDS	1
SPECIAL	2	WRATH	2	ARRAYED	1	BITE	1

Word		Word		Word		Word	
BITING	1	CARE'S	1	CONDEMNING	1	DEAF	1
BITTER	1	CARELESS	1	CONDITIONLY	1	DEARTH	1
BLACKLY	1	CARELESSNESS	1	CONFERS	1	DEATH-WOUND	1
BLACKNESS	1	CARRIED	1	CONFESSED	1	DEATH'S	1
BLAMED	1	CARVE	1	CONFIRM	1	DECAY	1
BLAZE	1	CATES	1	CONFUSE	1	DECEASED	1
BLIND-HI		CATO'S	1	CONQUERED	1	DECEIVED	1
TTING	1	CAUGHT	1	CONQUERINGS	1	DECREED	1
BLOT	1	CAUSEFUL	1	CONQUERORS	1	DECREES	1
BLUSHED	1	CAUSES	1	CONSCIENCE	1	DEEMED	1
BOAST	1	CAUSTICS	1	CONSERVED	1	DEFENCE	1
BOAT	1	CERTAIN	1	CONSTANT	1	DEFEND	1
BODIES	1	CHAFE	1	CONSTERD	1	DEGREE	1
BOPEEPE	1	CHAIN	1	CONSTRAINED	1	DEGREES	1
BORNE	1	CHANGE	1	CONTAIN	1	DEIGNED	1
BOSOM	1	CHANGED	1	CONTEND	1	DEITY	1
BOSS	1	CHANGELINGS	1	CONTENTS	1	DELIGHTS	1
BOUND	1	CHARGE	1	CONTRARY	1	DEMAND	1
BOUNDS	1	CHARIOT	1	COOL	1	DEMUR	1
BOWS	1	CHARMETH	1	COPARTNER	1	DENIZENED	1
BOYISH	1	CHASE	1	COPYING	1	DENY	1
BRABBLING	1	CHASTE	1	COST	1	DEPART	1
BRAG	1	CHASTEN	1	COUCHING	1	DEPRIVED	1
BRAGS	1	CHASTENED	1	COULDST	1	DERIVED	1
BRAINS	1	CHASTENESS	1	COUNT	1	DESERT	1
BRAVELY	1	CHATTERING	1	COUNTEST	1	DESERVED	1
BRAVEST	1	CHECKS	1	COUNTING	1	DESPAIRING	1
BRAWL	1	CHEEK'S	1	COUNTRY	1	DESPISE	1
BRAZEN	1	CHEERFUL	1	COUNTS	1	DESPISED	1
BREACH	1	CHERISH	1	COUPLED	1	DESTROYED	1
BREAKFAST	1	CHERRIES	1	COUPLING	1	DETEST	1
BREATHED	1	CHERRY	1	COURAGE	1	DEVIL	1
BREATHER	1	CHIDE	1	COURTESY	1	DEVISE	1
BREATHES	1	CHIEFEST	1	COVENANTS	1	DEVOUTLY	1
BREATHING	1	CHILLING	1	COVERING	1	DIAN	1
BREEDING	1	CHRISTIAN	1	COWARD	1	DICTIONARY'S	1
BREEDS	1	CHURCH	1	CRAFTILY	1	DIETS	1
BRINGING	1	CHURCHES	1	CRAVE	1	DIGHT	1
BROADERED	1	CHURCHMAN	1	CRAVED	1	DISCERN	1
BROTHER	1	CITADEL	1	CREAM	1	DISCHARGE	1
BROWS	1	CITIES	1	CRIED	1	DISCOURSE	1
BUBBLING	1	CIVIL	1	CRIMSON	1	DISDAINS	1
BUILDS	1	CLIMB	1	CROWNED	1	DISEASE	1
BUILT	1	CLIMBEST	1	CROWS	1	DISGUISE	1
BULLET	1	CLIMBING	1	CRUELTY	1	DISHEVELED	1
BULLS	1	CLIMES	1	CUMBERED	1	DISMISS	1
BURDENED	1	CLINGS	1	CUNNINGEST	1	DISPLAYED	1
BURIED	1	CLOG	1	CUP	1	DISPLAYING	1
BURNED	1	CLOSED-UP	1	CURBED	1	DISPLEASE	1
BURNING	1	CLOTHE	1	CURELESS	1	DISPRAISE	1
BURNT	1	COACHMAN	1	CURTAINS	1	DISPROVE	1
BUSH	1	COAL	1	CUT	1	DITCH	1
CABINET	1	COASTS	1	CUTTED	1	DITTIES	1
CAESAR'S	1	COLDLY	1	DAINTIER	1	DIVINE	1
CAGE	1	COLORS	1	DAMNING	1	DOCTOR	1
CAITIFF	1	COLTISH	1	DANGER'S	1	DOING	1
CAITIFF'S	1	COMEDY	1	DARES	1	DONE	1
CALLS	1	COMFORTS	1	DAREST	1	DOOR	1
CAMPS	1	COMING	1	DARKEST	1	DOUBLE	1
CANDLE	1	COMPANION	1	DARLING'S	1	DOUBTING	1
CAPTAINNESS	1	COMPELLED	1	DASHED	1	DOVE	1
CAPTIVED	1	COMPLAIN	1	DAY-NETS	1	DOVES	1
CAPTIVES	1	COMPLAINTS	1	DAZZLE	1	DOWNRIGHT	1
CAR	1	CONCEITS	1	DEAD	1	DRANK	1
CARATS	1	CONCLUSIONS	1	DEADLY	1	DRAW	1

HIT	1	ITCH	1	LIKES	1	MIGHTY	1
HITHERWARD	1	IVORY	1	LIKING	1	MILK	1
HITS	1	JAWS	1	LILIES	1	MINDED	1
HOLLAND	1	JEALOUS	1	LILIES'	1	MINDING	1
HOLY	1	JEALOUSY	1	LIMITS	1	MIRACULOUS	1
HONEYED	1	JETS	1	LINKS	1	MIRE	1
HOPE'S	1	JOINED	1	LION	1	MISFORTUNE	1
HOPING	1	JOURNEY	1	LION'S	1	MISLED	1
HORSEBACK	1	JOYED	1	LIST	1	MISSING	1
HORSEMAN	1	JOYFUL	1	LISTEN	1	MIST	1
HORSEMEN	1	JUDGING	1	LIVELIER	1	MISTAKE	1
HORSES'	1	JUDGMENTS	1	LOAD	1	MISTS	1
HORSMANSHIP	1	JUSTICE	1	LOCK	1	MISTY	1
HORSMANSHIPS	1	KEPT	1	LODGE	1	MOISTURE	1
HOSTAGE	1	KEY	1	LONG-STAYED	1	MONARCHY	1
HOT	1	KILL	1	LONGER	1	MONSTER	1
HOTTEST	1	KILLED	1	LONGS	1	MORAL	1
HOUSE	1	KILLER	1	LOOKEST	1	MORN'S	1
HUMBLED	1	KILLING	1	LOOKING	1	MORPHEUS	1
HUMBLENESS	1	KILLS	1	LOOSE	1	MOTHER	1
HUMBLER	1	KIN	1	LORDINGS	1	MOTHER'S	1
HUMORS	1	KINDLED	1	LOSS	1	MOTION	1
HUNDREDS	1	KINDLY	1	LOWER	1	MOTIONS	1
HUNGRY	1	KINGDOM'S	1	LUCK	1	MOVES	1
HURTS	1	KINGLY	1	LUCKY	1	MURDERING	1
IDLE	1	KISS-WORTHY	1	LUSTER	1	MUSCOVITE	1
IDLER	1	KISSING	1	LYRE	1	MUSCOVY	1
IDLY	1	KNEELEDST	1	MAIDEN	1	MYCHE	1
ILL-MADE	1	KNIGHT	1	MAIDS	1	MYSELF	1
IMAGED	1	KNIT	1	MAIMED	1	NAMING	1
IMITATE	1	KNOT	1	MAINTAIN	1	NATIONS	1
IMP	1	LACK	1	MANAGE	1	NE	1
IMPUTE	1	LADY	1	MANIFEST	1	NEEDFUL	1
INBENT	1	LAME	1	MAP	1	NEEDY	1
INCESSANTLY	1	LAMPS	1	MARBLE	1	NEGATIVES	1
INCLINE	1	LANCE	1	MARCH	1	NEIGHBORED	1
INDE	1	LANGUISH	1	MARCHED	1	NEITHER	1
INDENTURES	1	LARGE	1	MARCHETH	1	NESTOR'S	1
INDES	1	LAUD	1	MARGIN	1	NEW-COINED	1
INDIAN	1	LAUREL	1	MARTIAL	1	NEW-FOUND	1
INDIFFERENT	1	LAWS	1	MASKED	1	NEW-MOON	1
INFECTED	1	LAYMAN	1	MASKS	1	NEWBORN	1
INFELT	1	LEAD	1	MASTER'S	1	NEWS	1
INFERNAL	1	LEADEN	1	MATCHED	1	NIGHT-BIRDS	1
INFLUENCE	1	LEADS	1	MATE	1	NIMBLE	1
INFUSING	1	LEAP	1	MATE-IN-ARMS	1	NINE	1
INJURY	1	LEAPS	1	MAUGRE	1	NOBLE	1
INK'S	1	LEARNING'S	1	MAYST	1	NOBLENESS	1
INSEPERATE	1	LEAVEST	1	MAZED	1	NOBLEST	1
INSIDE	1	LECTURE	1	MAZEFUL	1	NOISE	1
INSPIRED	1	LEE	1	MEANER	1	NOISOME	1
INSPIRING	1	LEGS	1	MEANING	1	NOON	1
INTERLACE	1	LEISURE	1	MEANS	1	NORTH	1
INTERPRET	1	LENT	1	MEANT	1	NUMBERS	1
INVADE	1	LESSONS	1	MEEKER	1	NURSE	1
INVENT	1	LETS	1	MELANCHOLY	1	NURSED	1
INVENTION	1	LETTERS	1	MELODY	1	O'ERCHARGED	1
INVENTION'S	1	LEVEL	1	MELTS	1	OBJECTS	1
INVENTIONS	1	LEWIS	1	MEN	1	OBTAINED	1
INVESTS	1	LIDS	1	MERRY	1	OCEANS	1
INVITEST	1	LIEUTENANCY	1	MESSENGER	1	ODDS	1
INVOKED	1	LIEUTENANT	1	METAL	1	OFF	1
IO	1	LIFE'S	1	METAMORP		OFFENCE	1
IRKED	1	LIFTS	1	HOSED	1	OFFEND	1
IRKSOME	1	LIGHTNINGS	1	METHOD	1	OFFENDED	1

OFFER	1	PIPE	1	QUAKING	1	RULE	1
OFFEREDST	1	PIT	1	QUENCH	1	RUMOR	1
OFFICE	1	PITEOUS	1	QUICKLY	1	RUNNING	1
OFTEN	1	PITFOULD	1	QUIET	1	RUNS	1
ONE'S	1	PITYING	1	QUIET'S	1	RURAL	1
ONWARD	1	PLANET	1	QUIETEST	1	SABLES	1
OPE	1	PLANETS	1	QUIT	1	SADDED	1
OPEN	1	PLANT	1	QUIVER	1	SADDEST	1
OPENED	1	PLATO	1	QUIVERS	1	SADDLE	1
OPENS	1	PLAYED	1	RAISE	1	SADLY	1
OPPRESSING	1	PLAYING	1	RANSACKED	1	SAFE	1
ORANGE	1	PLAYS	1	RAREST	1	SAFELIEST	1
ORATOR	1	PLEASANT	1	RATE	1	SAILS	1
OURS	1	PLEASINGST	1	RATTLING	1	SAINT	1
OUTWARD	1	PLIES	1	RAVISHED	1	SAKES	1
OVER-WISE	1	PLUMES	1	RAVISHING	1	SALUTE	1
OVERCAME	1	PLUNGE	1	RAZED	1	SAT	1
OVERCOME	1	POESY	1	REALM	1	SATISFIES	1
OVERPASS	1	POET	1	REAR	1	SAUCINESS	1
OVERSPREAD	1	POET'S	1	REBELS	1	SAUCY	1
OVERTHROW	1	POETS'	1	REDDEST	1	SAVE	1
OVERTHROWN	1	POINTED	1	REDRESS	1	SAWEST	1
OVERTHWART	1	POINTING	1	REFRESH	1	SAYEST	1
PAID	1	POISONED	1	REFUSED	1	SCAPE	1
PAINTED	1	POISONOUS	1	REIN	1	SCAPES	1
PAINTER	1	POLES'	1	REINED	1	SCARCE	1
PALE	1	PORCHES	1	REJOICE	1	SCARF	1
PANTING	1	PORPHIR	1	RELEASE	1	SCARLET	1
PAP	1	PORTRAIT	1	REMNANT	1	SCATTERED	1
PARCHED	1	POUR	1	RENEW	1	SCHOOL	1
PARIS	1	POWDERED	1	RENOWN	1	SCHOOLED	1
PARTIAL	1	PRAISED	1	REPENT	1	SCHOOLMASTER	1
PARTS	1	PRANCING	1	REPINING	1	SCHOOLMI	
PASS-PRAISE	1	PREASE	1	REPLY	1	STRESS	1
PASSENGER	1	PRENTICE	1	REPROVE	1	SCOPE	1
PASTIME	1	PREPARE	1	RESIST	1	SCORCH	1
PATENTS	1	PRESENT	1	RESOLVED	1	SCORNED	1
PEAN	1	PRESS	1	RESORT	1	SCORNING	1
PEARLS	1	PRESSED	1	RESPECTS	1	SCORNS	1
PEEP	1	PRETENCE	1	RESPITE	1	SCOTTISH	1
PEER	1	PRETENDS	1	RESTLESS	1	SEA	1
PENSIVENESS	1	PRICE	1	RESTY	1	SEARCH	1
PEOPLE'S	1	PRICKING	1	RETIRES	1	SEAT	1
PERCHANCE	1	PRINCE	1	RETRAIT	1	SEATED	1
PERCHED	1	PRINTS	1	REVENGE	1	SECRET	1
PERFECTION	1	PRISON	1	REVERENCE	1	SEEKEST	1
PERFECTION'S	1	PRISONER'S	1	RHUBARB	1	SEEN	1
PERPLEXITY	1	PRIVILEGE	1	RICHEST	1	SELF-MISERY	1
PERSUASIONS	1	PROCURE	1	RIDDLE	1	SELFNESS	1
PETRARCH'S	1	PROFESS	1	RIDE	1	SEND	1
PHILIP	1	PROGRESSING	1	RIDER	1	SENDS	1
PHILOSOPHY	1	PROMISED	1	RIGOROUS	1	SENTENCE	1
PHIP	1	PROMISING	1	RIND	1	SERIOUS	1
PHLEGMATIC	1	PRONOUNCING	1	RISING	1	SERVANT'S	1
PHOENIX	1	PROP	1	RITES	1	SERVANTS'	1
PICK-PURSE	1	PROPHET	1	ROBBED	1	SERVED	1
PICTURE	1	PROPORTION	1	ROD	1	SERVES	1
PICTURED	1	PROUD	1	ROGUE	1	SERVICES	1
PIED	1	PUBLIC	1	ROME	1	SETS	1
PIERCE	1	PUBLISH	1	ROWS	1	SETST	1
PIES	1	PUNISHED	1	RUBIES	1	SETTLED	1
PILGRIMS	1	PUREST	1	RUDDY	1	SHAMED	1
PILLOWS	1	PURLING	1	RUDEST	1	SHARPNESS	1
PIN'S	1	QUAKE	1	RUGGEDEST	1	SHENT	1
PINDAR'S	1	QUAKED	1	RUINS	1	SHEPHERD'S	1

SHINEST	1	SPANGLE	1	SUFFERED	1	TIGERISH	1
SHINETH	1	SPARK	1	SUFFERING	1	TIME'S	1
SHONE	1	SPARTANS	1	SUFFICE	1	TIRE	1
SHOOT	1	SPEAKS	1	SUGARING	1	TOGETHER	1
SHORE	1	SPEAR	1	SUIT	1	TOIL	1
SHORES	1	SPEECH'S	1	SULLEN	1	TOILS	1
SHORTLY	1	SPEED	1	SUM	1	TOLD	1
SHOUTS	1	SPELLED	1	SUMMED	1	TOLDST	1
SHOWERS	1	SPHERES	1	SUMMER	1	TOMB	1
SHREWD	1	SPIED	1	SUN-LIKE	1	TOOK	1
SHRINES	1	SPIRITED	1	SUNBURNED	1	TORCH	1
SIDES	1	SPORTS	1	SURPASS	1	TORMENTS	1
SIGH	1	SPOTLESS	1	SWAM	1	TOSS	1
SIGHT'S	1	SPREAD	1	SWAY	1	TOTTERING	1
SIGHTS	1	SPURRED	1	SWEATS	1	TOWARDS	1
SIGNS	1	SPURS	1	SWEET-FAIR	1	TOWN-FOLKS	1
SILENTLY	1	STAINED	1	SWEETEN	1	TOWNS	1
SILVER	1	STALE	1	SWEETENED	1	TOYS	1
SIMILES	1	STALL	1	SWEETENING	1	TRACE	1
SIMPLE	1	STANDARD	1	SWERVE	1	TRAGEDY	1
SIMPLICITY	1	STANDING	1	SWORN	1	TRAINED	1
SINGS	1	STAR	1	TALE	1	TRAITOR	1
SIRE	1	STARRY	1	TALENTS	1	TRAMPLING	1
SIRE'S	1	STARVE	1	TALES	1	TRANSLATED	1
SISTERS	1	STATELIER	1	TALK	1	TREASURE	1
SITS	1	STATELY	1	TANTAL'S	1	TREAT	1
SKILLED	1	STAVES	1	TARRY	1	TREBLES	1
SKINS	1	STAYS	1	TEAR	1	TREMBLING	1
SKY	1	STEAD	1	TEARS'	1	TRIED	1
SLACK	1	STEP	1	TEETH	1	TRIUMPHAL	1
SLACKER	1	STEP-DAME	1	TEMPE	1	TRIUMPHING	1
SLAIN	1	STILTS	1	TEMPERS	1	TRIUMPHS	1
SLAKE	1	STOMACHS	1	TENTS	1	TROJAN	1
SLAVE-BORN	1	STONE	1	TERM	1	TROUPES	1
SLAVES	1	STOPPED	1	TEXT	1	TRUANT	1
SLAY	1	STORED	1	THAMES	1	TRUMPETS'	1
SLEEP'S	1	STORMED	1	THANK	1	TRUST	1
SLEIGHT	1	STORMS	1	THANK-WO		TUNES	1
SLIDE	1	STORMY	1	RTHIEST	1	TURN	1
SLIPPERY	1	STORY	1	THANKFUL	1	TURNING	1
SMILED	1	STRAIN	1	THANKFULLY	1	TUSH	1
SMILES	1	STRANGELY	1	THANKS	1	TWICE	1
SMILING	1	STRANGERS	1	THEREABOUT	1	TWIN'S	1
SNOW	1	STRATAGEMS	1	THEREBY	1	TWINE	1
SOBBED	1	STRAVE	1	THIEF	1	TWINS	1
SOBER	1	STRAW	1	THINKS	1	TYRAN	1
SOIL	1	STRAY	1	THIRSTY	1	TYRANNIZETH	1
SOLE	1	STRAYING	1	THITHER	1	TYRANTS	1
SOLITARINESS	1	STRIPES	1	THORNS	1	ULSTER	1
SOMETHING	1	STRIVING	1	THORNY	1	UNABLE	1
SOMETIMES	1	STRONG	1	THOROUGHEST	1	UNARMED	1
SON	1	STRONGER	1	THRALLDOM	1	UNBID	1
SONGS	1	STRONGEST	1	THREAT	1	UNBIDDEN	1
SONNETS	1	STRONGLY	1	THREATENED	1	UNBITTED	1
SONS	1	STRUGGLE	1	THREATENING	1	UNCALLED	1
SOOTH	1	STUDY'S	1	THROES	1	UNCHASTITY	1
SOPHISTRY	1	STUDYING	1	THROUGHLY	1	UNDERCHARGE	1
SORT	1	STUMBLING	1	THROW	1	UNDERTAKEN	1
SOUL'S	1	SUBDUED	1	THROWS	1	UNFLATTERING	1
SOUND	1	SUBLIME	1	THUNDERBOLT	1	UNGRATEF	
SOUNDS	1	SUCCESS	1	THUNDERED	1	ULNESS	1
SOUR-BRE		SUCCOR	1	TIDES	1	UNHEARD	1
ATHED	1	SUCK	1	TIE	1	UNIDLE	1
SOVEREIGN	1	SUCKED	1	TIED	1	UNITED	1
SPADE	1	SUFFER	1	TIGER'S	1	UNSEEN	1

UNSPILLING	1	WAILED	1	WELTERING	1	WOOD-GLOBES	1
UNSUITED	1	WAILING	1	WENT	1	WOOS	1
UNSWEET	1	WAITED	1	WEPT	1	WORLDLY	1
UNTIL	1	WALK	1	WHEELS	1	WORMS	1
UNWARES	1	WALKING	1	WHEREAS	1	WORN	1
US	1	WAN	1	WHINE	1	WRACKED	1
USED	1	WAND	1	WHIT	1	WRACKS	1
USING	1	WANTS	1	WHOLLY	1	WRAPS	1
USURPING	1	WARM	1	WIDE	1	WRATE	1
VADE	1	WARS	1	WILLED	1	WREAK	1
VAINLY	1	WASTE	1	WIND	1	WRECKS	1
VALIANT	1	WATER	1	WINDLASS	1	WRETCHEDNESS	1
VANISHED	1	WATERED	1	WINDS	1	WRING	1
VEILS	1	WATERY	1	WINE	1	WRINKLED	1
VEIN	1	WEAKENED	1	WINGED	1	WRITER'S	1
VEINS	1	WEAPONS	1	WINK	1	WRITES	1
VELUME	1	WEARY	1	WISE-VALIANT	1	WRITINGS	1
VERMILION	1	WED	1	WISEST	1	WRONGED	1
VERT	1	WEED	1	WISHED	1	WRONGFUL	1
VEXING	1	WEEK	1	WISHES	1	YEAR	1
VICE'S	1	WEEPING	1	WISHING	1	YIELDEN	1
VIEWING	1	WEEPS	1	WIT-BEATEN	1	YOKE	1
VOWED	1	WEIGHED	1	WITLESS	1	YOUNG-WISE	1
VULGAR	1	WEIGHS	1	WITTY	1	YOUTHS	1
WAG	1	WELL-FORMED	1	WONDERS	1	ZENITH	1
WAGS	1	WELL-SHADING	1	WONT	1	ZEPHYRS	1

EDMUND SPENSER, 'AMORETTI'

THE	311	LIKE	43	HOW	19	GLORY	13
AND	275	ON	43	LONG	19	JOY	13
TO	270	SELF	43	NE	19	MIND	13
HER	231	DID	39	NOR	19	WORLD	13
OF	216	MAY	39	PRIDE	19	LIVE	12
THAT	208	SWEET	38	THEM	19	OUGHT	12
MY	179	YOU	38	WHOSE	19	OUT	12
IN	164	EYES	37	CRUEL	18	PAIN	12
WITH	159	MORE	36	GOODLY	18	SHOULD	12
I	155	HEART	35	HE	18	THINGS	12
BUT	128	YET	34	NOW	18	THINK	12
WHICH	105	THEY	33	SEE	17	WELL	12
IS	103	BY	32	THAN	17	WERE	12
SO	93	SUCH	32	VAIN	17	WORK	12
FOR	86	THIS	32	WHOM	17	BEAUTY	11
ME	83	AT	31	EVER	16	DEAR	11
ALL	82	ONE	31	HATH	16	DEATH	11
DOTH	81	OR	31	LOOK	16	DIE	11
SHE	81	FROM	29	NEVER	16	GREATER	11
IT	79	HAVE	28	DAY	15	LITTLE	11
BE	69	MOST	28	FIRE	15	MANY	11
A	68	ARE	27	HEAVENLY	15	MINE	11
YOUR	67	CAN	27	REST	15	OWN	11
DO	64	MAKE	27	STILL	15	PEACE	11
WHEN	54	LET	25	THY	15	THOU	11
YE	54	LIFE	24	FORTH	14	THOUGHTS	11
FAIR	52	UNTO	24	HAPPY	14	AWAY	10
HIS	52	IF	23	HEAVEN	14	BEHOLD	10
LOVE	52	WAS	23	PROUD	14	BEING	10
THEN	50	LIGHT	21	SEEK	14	BREAST	10
AS	47	NO	21	THERE	14	DELIGHT	10
NOT	47	THROUGH	21	TOO	14	EARTH	10
THEIR	47	HIM	20	WOULD	14	FIT	10
WILL	47	THOSE	20	BOTH	13	GLORIOUS	10
SHALL	44	WHAT	20	EVERY	13	GOLDEN	10

Word	Count	Word	Count	Word	Count	Word	Count
LAST	10	SAD	7	BODY	5	BREAK	4
LOVELY	10	SOON	7	BRIGHT	5	BRING	4
PLEASURE	10	THEREFORE	7	CAUSE	5	BROOK	4
SIGHT	10	THOUGH	7	CHANCE	5	BURN	4
SOME	10	UP	7	CHASE	5	CAME	4
SPEAK	10	WEARY	7	CLOSE	5	CHASTE	4
WORLD'S	10	WHILES	7	COURSE	5	COUNTENANCE	4
ART	9	WHY	7	DEEP	5	DARK	4
BLISS	9	WIT	7	DOWN	5	DART	4
CANNOT	9	AGAINST	6	DYING	5	DAYS	4
END	9	AN	6	ELSE	5	DREADFUL	4
ENDURE	9	APPEAR	6	ERE	5	DUE	4
FIND	9	BACK	6	FED	5	EASE	4
GENTLE	9	BANDS	6	FLOWERS	5	ENTERTAIN	4
HAVING	9	COULD	6	FRESH	5	ENVY	4
LOVE'S	9	CRUELTY	6	GAIN	5	FACE	4
NEW	9	DARE	6	GIVE	5	FAMOUS	4
NONE	9	DIDST	6	GRANT	5	FAULTS	4
PART	9	DISMAY	6	GRIEF	5	FIELD	4
SINCE	9	EKE	6	HANDS	5	FLAMES	4
SKILL	9	EYE	6	HEAD	5	FOUND	4
THING	9	FAR	6	IMMORTAL	5	FULL	4
TIME	9	FIRST	6	KIND	5	GIFTS	4
TRUE	9	HAD	6	LEAVE	5	GO	4
AFTER	8	HEART'S	6	LIVING	5	GOLD	4
AGAIN	8	ILL	6	LOFTY	5	GOOD	4
BEST	8	IMAGE	6	LORD	5	GREEDY	4
BOWER	8	INTO	6	MAKES	5	HARDER	4
DESIRE	8	JOYOUS	6	MAN	5	HEAVENS	4
FLY	8	KNOW	6	MEAN	5	HERE	4
GRACE	8	LIKEWISE	6	MOVE	5	HIDE	4
GREAT	8	MEN	6	NATURE	5	HOLD	4
HAND	8	MERCY	6	PLACE	5	HUMBLED	4
HOPE	8	MUCH	6	PRESENCE	5	IRE	4
LOOKS	8	NAME	6	PREY	5	KINDLE	4
MADE	8	PAINS	6	PURE	5	LEAST	4
MIGHT	8	POOR	6	SOUGHT	5	LEAVES	4
POWER	8	PRAISES	6	SPILL	5	LONGER	4
PRAISE	8	RARE	6	SPREAD	5	LOVES	4
SORROW	8	SACRED	6	SPRING	5	LOWLY	4
TAKE	8	SAME	6	STORMS	5	MEANS	4
THEE	8	SEEMED	6	STRONG	5	MIGHTY	4
UPON	8	SHOW	6	STUBBORN	5	O	4
WEAK	8	SITH	6	SUSTAIN	5	OBJECT	4
WHERE	8	SMART	6	THEREOF	5	OLD	4
ADMIRE	7	SPIRIT	6	THRALL	5	OVER	4
ANY	7	SPOIL	6	TILL	5	PLACED	4
EACH	7	SPRITE	6	TOIL	5	PLAIN	4
FAIREST	7	STORM	6	TURN	5	PLAINTS	4
FILL	7	TELL	6	WHILEST	5	PLAY	4
FRAIL	7	THESE	6	WISH	5	PLEAD	4
GAZE	7	THOUGHT	6	WONT	5	PLEASANCE	4
HARD	7	US	6	WORTHY	5	PRAISED	4
HIGH	7	VIEW	6	YEAR	5	QUEEN	4
HONOR	7	WE	6	ADORN	4	QUITE	4
HUE	7	WHEREOF	6	ASPIRE	4	RAY	4
LATE	7	WITHIN	6	ASSAY	4	RETURN	4
MOTE	7	YIELD	6	ASSURANCE	4	SCORN	4
NIGHT	7	ALONE	5	ASSURED	4	SEEM	4
NOUGHT	7	ANOTHER	5	BEAMS	4	SEEMS	4
OFT	7	BASE	5	BEGIN	4	SHIP	4
ONLY	7	BEAST	5	BEHOLDING	4	SHORT	4
OTHER	7	BEAUTY'S	5	BLOOD	4	SIMPLE	4
PLEASE	7	BEFORE	5	BORN	4	SITS	4
REMAIN	7	BETTER	5	BOSOM	4	SMILES	4

Word		Word		Word		Word	
SORROWS	4	DEAD	3	ONCE	3	AFFECTIONS	2
SOVEREIGN	4	DECAY	3	PEARLS	3	AGREE	2
STORE	4	DECK	3	PLANET	3	AIR	2
STRAIGHT	4	DELIGHTS	3	PLENTY	3	ALIVE	2
SURE	4	DERIVED	3	POWERS	3	ALLURED	2
THEMSELVES	4	DEVISE	3	PRECIOUS	3	AM	2
THUS	4	DIVINE	3	PRICE	3	AMAZE	2
TONGUE	4	DREAD	3	PRISON	3	AMAZEMENT	2
TORMENT	4	EMBRACE	3	PURCHASE	3	ANEW	2
VERSE	4	ENEMIES	3	RACE	3	ANGEL'S	2
VOUCHSAFE	4	EQUAL	3	RASHLY	3	ANGELS	2
WANDER	4	EVEN	3	RATHER	3	APACE	2
WAR	4	FAIRY	3	RAVISHED	3	APPLY	2
WAY	4	FALL	3	READ	3	APPROACH	2
WINGS	4	FALSE	3	REASON	3	ASPECT	2
WITHOUT	4	FAME	3	RENEW	3	ASSOIL	2
WONDER	4	FEAR	3	RICHLY	3	ASTONISHMENT	2
WONDERMENT	4	FEARLESS	3	ROUND	3	ATTEND	2
WORD	4	FEED	3	RUBIES	3	ATTONCE	2
WOUND	4	FEEL	3	RUN	3	AUGMENT	2
WRATH	4	FLESH	3	SAVE	3	BANE	2
YEAR'S	4	FLOWER	3	SECOND	3	BARK	2
ABIDE	3	FOOD	3	SEEING	3	BASENESS	2
ABOUT	3	FORCE	3	SEEMETH	3	BATH	2
ABOVE	3	FORLORN	3	SHADOWS	3	BATTERY	2
ABSENCE	3	GATE	3	SHAME	3	BATTLE	2
AFRAID	3	GAVE	3	SILVER	3	BAY	2
ALLURE	3	GLANCE	3	SING	3	BEASTS	2
AMONGST	3	GODS	3	SKY	3	BEE	2
APPEASE	3	GROWS	3	SMILE	3	BEEN	2
ARROWS	3	GUIDE	3	SPARK	3	BEGUILED	2
ASTRAY	3	GUILEFUL	3	SPENT	3	BEND	2
ATTIRE	3	HARDEST	3	SPY	3	BITTER	2
AWAKE	3	HARDLY	3	STAY	3	BLAME	2
BAIT	3	HARP	3	STRONGLY	3	BLESS	2
BASER	3	HEARTS	3	SUE	3	BODY'S	2
BEAR	3	HEAT	3	TEACH	3	BOLD	2
BEAT	3	HEAVEN'S	3	TEMPERED	3	BOOK	2
BEGUILE	3	HEAVY	3	TEMPEST	3	BOUGH	2
BIDS	3	ICE	3	TERMS	3	BOUND	2
BIRD	3	INCREASE	3	THENCE	3	BREAKING	2
BLESSED	3	INWARD	3	THINE	3	BRIGHTNESS	2
BLOODY	3	IVORY	3	THREE	3	BROOD	2
BOOKS	3	LACKING	3	THRICE	3	CALL	2
BRED	3	LANGUOR	3	TIE	3	CAPTIVE	2
CAPTIVED	3	LAUGH	3	TIMELY	3	CAPTIVES	2
CARELESS	3	LAY	3	TOSSED	3	CAPTIVITY	2
CAUGHT	3	LENGTH	3	TREE	3	CARE	2
CEASE	3	LENT	3	TREMBLING	3	CELESTIAL	2
CHANGE	3	LIPS	3	TRIED	3	CHEEKS	2
CLEAR	3	LO	3	TWIXT	3	CHEER	2
COLD	3	LOOKING	3	TWO	3	CHERISH	2
COME	3	LOST	3	VIRTUE	3	CHOOSE	2
COMES	3	LOVERS'	3	WAIL	3	CLEAN	2
COMPARE	3	MAKER	3	WEAR	3	CLOUDY	2
COMPLAIN	3	MEED	3	WHO	3	COLORS	2
CONCEIVE	3	MILD	3	WICKED	3	COMFORT	2
CONSPIRE	3	MINDS	3	WISE	3	COMFORTLESS	2
CONTENTMENT	3	MIRTH	3	WOES	3	COMING	2
CRYSTAL	3	MONGST	3	WONDROUS	3	CONQUEST	2
CUCKOO	3	NATURE'S	3	WRITE	3	CONSTANT	2
DAILY	3	NEED	3	ACCEPT	3	CONSUME	2
DAINTY	3	NEITHER	3	ACHIEVE	2	CONTEMPL	
DAMSEL	3	NOTHING	3	ADMIRED	2	ATION	2
DARKNESS	3	OFFEND	3	ADORNED	2	CONTINUAL	2

CORDIALS	2	GENTLY	2	LONGWHILE	2	RASH	2
COVETIZE	2	GET	2	LOOSELY	2	READY	2
CREW	2	GIVEN	2	LOSE	2	RED	2
DARTS	2	GLAD	2	LOW	2	REMAINS	2
DEADLY	2	GLADLY	2	LOWER	2	REMOVE	2
DEAREST	2	GLADNESS	2	LUSTS	2	RESEMBLING	2
DEEDS	2	GLASS	2	MAKER'S	2	RHYMES	2
DEEM	2	GOD	2	MAKETH	2	RICH	2
DEGREE	2	GOT	2	MANIFOLD	2	RICHES	2
DEPART	2	GRACES	2	MARK	2	RIGHT	2
DESCRY	2	GROUND	2	MATE	2	ROSE	2
DESIRED	2	GUILE	2	MATTER	2	RUDELY	2
DESOLATE	2	GUILTLESS	2	MEANING	2	RUTH	2
DEVISED	2	HAIR	2	MEEK	2	SACRIFICE	2
DIGHT	2	HALF	2	MEN'S	2	SADNESS	2
DIMMED	2	HAUGHTY	2	MESSAGE	2	SAINT	2
DIRECT	2	HEADS	2	MIND'S	2	SAKE	2
DISDAIN	2	HEAL	2	MISDEEM	2	SALVE	2
DISMAYED	2	HEAR	2	MIXED	2	SAPPHIRES	2
DISPLAY	2	HELL	2	MOAN	2	SAVING	2
DOES	2	HENCEFORTH	2	MONUMENT	2	SAY	2
DOING	2	HIDDEN	2	MORN	2	SAYS	2
DOLPHIN	2	HIRE	2	MORTAL	2	SCORNING	2
DRAWN	2	HOLY	2	MORTALITY	2	SCOURGE	2
DRIVES	2	HOUR	2	MOTHER'S	2	SEEKS	2
DUST	2	HUGE	2	MUSIC	2	SEMBLANT	2
EARTHLY	2	HUMBLESS	2	MUST	2	SEND	2
EGLANTINE	2	HUNGRY	2	NARCISSUS	2	SENSELESS	2
EMBREW	2	IDEA	2	NAUGHT	2	SET	2
ENOUGH	2	IDLE	2	NEAR	2	SEVER	2
ENSAMPLE	2	IDLY	2	NECK	2	SHADE	2
ENSUE	2	IDOL	2	NEEDETH	2	SHAMES	2
ENTIRE	2	INCESSANT	2	NEEDS	2	SHINE	2
ENTREAT	2	INCLINED	2	NET	2	SHOOT	2
ETERNAL	2	INQUIRE	2	OFTEN	2	SHORE	2
EVERMORE	2	INSPIRE	2	ORNAMENT	2	SHORTLY	2
EXCEEDING	2	INTENT	2	OUR	2	SHOWS	2
EXCELLENT	2	INVENT	2	PAINFUL	2	SHRILL	2
EXPRESS	2	IRON	2	PARADISE	2	SHUN	2
FADE	2	KEPT	2	PARTS	2	SILENCE	2
FAIRER	2	KILL	2	PASSED	2	SILENT	2
FALLS	2	KINDLED	2	PASSING	2	SILLY	2
FASHION	2	KING	2	PASSION	2	SIN	2
FAST	2	LABOR	2	PASSIONS	2	SINFUL	2
FEEBLE	2	LACKED	2	PEN	2	SINGS	2
FEEDS	2	LADY	2	PENANCE	2	SINS	2
FELL	2	LAUREL	2	PERFECTION	2	SLAYING	2
FERVENT	2	LEAD	2	PERHAPS	2	SMALL	2
FIGHT	2	LEAF	2	PERISH	2	SMELL	2
FILLED	2	LEARN	2	PERSEVERE	2	SNARE	2
FINDING	2	LEARNED	2	PHOEBUS'	2	SOFT	2
FIRMLY	2	LED	2	PINE	2	SOFTEN	2
FLIGHT	2	LEECH	2	PITEOUS	2	SOMETIMES	2
FLINT	2	LETTERS	2	PITY	2	SORE	2
FOE	2	LIES	2	POWERFUL	2	SORTS	2
FORCES	2	LIFE'S	2	PRAY	2	SOUL	2
FORMER	2	LIFT	2	PRAYERS	2	SOUR	2
FORTY	2	LIGHTEN	2	PRISONER	2	SPEND	2
FRAGRANT	2	LIGHTNING	2	PROVE	2	SPHERE	2
FRAUGHT	2	LIKEST	2	PUREST	2	SPIDER	2
FREE	2	LINES	2	QUOTE	2	SPORT	2
FROZEN	2	LION	2	RAGING	2	SPOTLESS	2
FRUIT	2	LIVELY	2	RAIN	2	STAR	2
GAINST	2	LOATHE	2	RAISE	2	START	2
GARDEN	2	LODGING	2	RAISED	2	STARVED	2

STEADFAST	2	ACCOMPLISHMENT	1	ATTENTION	1	BONDAGE	1
STEEL	2	ACCORD	1	AUGMENTED	1	BORNE	1
STIR	2	ACCOUMPT	1	AUGMENTETH	1	BORROWED	1
STRANGE	2	ACCOUMPTS	1	AUTHOR	1	BOUNDS	1
SUCCOR	2	ACCURSED	1	AVENGE	1	BOW	1
SUFFICE	2	ACCUSE	1	AWAIT	1	BOWERS	1
SUNSHINE	2	ACQUIT	1	AWARE	1	BRANCHES	1
TABLE	2	ADAMANT	1	AWFUL	1	BRAZEN	1
TEAR	2	ADDER'S	1	AWHILE	1	BREACHES	1
TEARS	2	ADDRESS	1	AWHIT	1	BREATH	1
TEMPESTS	2	ADIEU	1	BAD	1	BREATHED	1
THENCEFORTH	2	ADORE	1	BADGE	1	BREED	1
THEREON	2	AFFECTS	1	BAITS	1	BRIAR	1
THEREWITH	2	AFFLICTED	1	BALE	1	BRINGS	1
THROWN	2	AFRESH	1	BALEFUL	1	BROAD	1
TOLD	2	AGES	1	BANNER	1	BROKE	1
TRADE	2	AGREEMENT	1	BAR	1	BROKEN	1
TRAIN	2	AH	1	BARED	1	BROOM-FLOWER	1
TREASON	2	AID	1	BATHED	1	BROUGHT	1
TRESSES	2	AIMING	1	BAYS	1	BROWS	1
TRIUMPH	2	ALLUREMENT	1	BEAM	1	BRUNT	1
TRUMP	2	ALREADY	1	BEARING	1	BUBBLE	1
TRUTH	2	ALSO	1	BEARS	1	BUD	1
UNDER	2	ALTAR	1	BEATEN	1	BUDDED	1
UNLESS	2	ALTER	1	BEATS	1	BUILD	1
UNTIL	2	AMAZED	1	BECAUSE	1	BUILDS	1
VIRTUES	2	AMBROSIAL	1	BECOMES	1	BUILT	1
WAIT	2	AMBUSH	1	BED	1	BUNCH	1
WANDERING	2	AMEND	1	BEDECKED	1	BURDEN	1
WANTON	2	AMERCED	1	BEGAN	1	BURNING	1
WARNS	2	AMIABLE	1	BEGINS	1	BUSH	1
WARRIOR	2	AMIDST	1	BEGONE	1	BUY	1
WASHED	2	AMISS	1	BEGUN	1	CAGE	1
WATER	2	AMOROUS	1	BEHOLDER	1	CALLING	1
WAVES	2	ANGELIC	1	BELAY	1	CALM	1
WEAVE	2	ANGRY	1	BELLAMOURES	1	CALMS	1
WEB	2	ANGUISH	1	BENDS	1	CAPTIVING	1
WEEN	2	ANNOY	1	BESEEN	1	CAREFUL	1
WEEP	2	ANTHEMS	1	BESIDE	1	CARRY	1
WHENAS	2	ANTIQUE	1	BETOKENING	1	CASTLES	1
WHENCE	2	ANVIL	1	BETWEEN	1	CATCH	1
WIDE	2	APPEARS	1	BID	1	CATCHING	1
WILD	2	APPLES	1	BIDDING	1	CHAIN	1
WIND	2	APPLIED	1	BIDE	1	CHALLENGE	1
WINTER'S	2	ARCHERS	1	BIND	1	CHANGED	1
WOMB	2	AREAD	1	BIRDS	1	CHANGEFUL	1
WON	2	ARGUE	1	BIT	1	CHANGES	1
WORDS	2	ARGUMENT	1	BLACK	1	CHARM	1
WORTH	2	ARIGHT	1	BLAMED	1	CHARMING	1
WOUNDS	2	ARION	1	BLAZE	1	CHASTITY	1
WRACK	2	ARMOR	1	BLEEDING	1	CHEERED	1
WRECK	2	ARMS	1	BLEND	1	CHEERFUL	1
WRITTEN	2	AROUND	1	BLESSINGS	1	CHEERLESS	1
WRONG	2	ARRAYED	1	BLIND	1	CHIEF	1
WROTE	2	ARRIVE	1	BLINDED	1	CHOIR	1
YEARS	2	ARROW	1	BLOODED	1	CHOKED	1
YIELDED	2	ASHES	1	BLOSSOM	1	CIRCLE'S	1
YOUNG	2	ASKEW	1	BLOSSOMED	1	CIVIL	1
YOURS	2	ASLAKE	1	BLOWN	1	CLATTER	1
ABANDONED	1	ASSAYED	1	BOAST	1	CLEARED	1
ABHORRED	1	ASSUAGE	1	BOILING	1	CLEARER	1
ABODE'S	1	ASSUAGEMENT	1	BOLDENED	1	CLEAREST	1
ABSTAIN	1	ATALANTA	1	BOLDER	1	CLIMB	1
ACCOMPANIED	1	ATTAIN	1	BOLDLY	1	CLOGGED	1
		ATTEMPT	1	BOND	1	CLOSELY	1

Word		Word		Word		Word	
CLOSET	1	DEFIANCE	1	DROPS	1	FAINT	1
CLOUD	1	DEFILED	1	DROSS	1	FAITH	1
CLOUDS	1	DEFORMED	1	DROSSY	1	FAITHFUL	1
COALS	1	DEIGN	1	DUMPISH	1	FANCIES	1
COAT	1	DEIGNED	1	DUMPS	1	FANCY	1
COCKATRICES	1	DELAYED	1	DUREFUL	1	FANCY'S	1
COLORED	1	DEN	1	DUTY	1	FAULT	1
COLUMBINES	1	DENY	1	DWELL	1	FAVOR	1
COMB	1	DEPENDING	1	EARLY	1	FAWN	1
COMEDY	1	DEPRAVE	1	EARS	1	FEARED	1
COMMEND	1	DEPRAVES	1	EASY	1	FEATURE	1
COMPASSED	1	DEPRIVE	1	EAT	1	FEELING	1
COMPILE	1	DESCENT	1	ECHOES	1	FEELS	1
COMPLAINED	1	DESERT	1	EITHER	1	FEET	1
COMPLEMENT	1	DESIGNED	1	ELECTION	1	FELICITY	1
COMPTROL	1	DESIRES	1	ELEMENT	1	FELLY	1
CONDEMNED	1	DESPISE	1	ELIZABETHS	1	FETTERS	1
CONDUCT	1	DESPITE	1	EMBASE	1	FEW	1
CONFUSED	1	DESPOILED	1	EMBASED	1	FIELDS	1
CONGEALED	1	DESTROY	1	EMBASETH	1	FIERCE	1
CONSTRAIN	1	DEVICE	1	EMPRESS	1	FIERY	1
CONSTRAINED	1	DEVOTION	1	EMPRISE	1	FILTHY	1
CONSTRAINT	1	DEVOUR	1	ENCAGE	1	FINE	1
CONSTRUE	1	DEVOURING	1	ENCHASED	1	FINEST	1
CONTAIN	1	DEW	1	ENDEAVOR	1	FINISHING	1
CONTAINED	1	DIAMOND	1	ENDED	1	FIRBLOOM	1
CONTAINS	1	DIDDEST	1	ENDITE	1	FIRED	1
CONTINUANCE	1	DILATE	1	ENDLESS	1	FIRMER	1
CONVERT	1	DINTS	1	ENDURANCE	1	FIRMEST	1
CORRUPTION	1	DISARMED	1	ENDURED	1	FISH	1
COUNCIL	1	DISCONSOLATE	1	ENFOLD	1	FITS	1
COUNT	1	DISCORD	1	ENGINES	1	FLATTER	1
COUNTED	1	DISCOVERY	1	ENLARGE	1	FLATTERING	1
COVERT	1	DISDAINETH	1	ENLUMINED	1	FLED	1
COVET	1	DISDAINFUL	1	ENROLL	1	FLEE	1
COVETED	1	DISEASE	1	ENROLLED	1	FLEECE	1
CRAFT	1	DISGUISING	1	ENSUING	1	FLESH'S	1
CRAFTILY	1	DISH	1	ENTANGLE	1	FLIES	1
CRAFTSMAN'S	1	DISHONOR	1	ENTICE	1	FLIT	1
CREDIT	1	DISOBEYS	1	ENTRAP	1	FLITS	1
CROWNED	1	DISPARAG		ENTRAPPED	1	FLOODS	1
CRUELLY	1	EMENT	1	ENVIED	1	FOE'S	1
CRUELNESS	1	DISPLACE	1	ERECT	1	FOES	1
CRUELTIES	1	DISPLAYED	1	ERST	1	FONDLY	1
CRY	1	DISSOLVED	1	ESCAPED	1	FONDNESS	1
CULVER	1	DIVERS	1	ESCHEW	1	FOOLISH	1
CUNNING	1	DIVERSELY	1	ETERNITY	1	FOOT	1
CUNNINGLY	1	DIVIDE	1	ETERNIZE	1	FOOTING	1
CUPID	1	DIVINELY	1	EVENING	1	FOOTSTOOL	1
CYPRESS	1	DIVING	1	EXCEEDS	1	FORCED	1
DAMSELS	1	DOEST	1	EXCEL	1	FOREDONE	1
DANGER	1	DOFF	1	EXILED	1	FOREHEAD	1
DANGER'S	1	DONE	1	EXPECTATION	1	FORELOCK	1
DANGEROUS	1	DOUBLE	1	EXPIRE	1	FOREPAST	1
DAPHNE	1	DOUBT	1	EXPRESSED	1	FORGED	1
DARKENED	1	DOUBTFULLY	1	EXPRESSING	1	FORGETFUL	1
DARTING	1	DOVE	1	EXTEND	1	FORGETS	1
DATE	1	DRAWS	1	EXTREMEST	1	FORGO	1
DAUGHTER	1	DREAM	1	EXTREMITIES	1	FORGOT	1
DAZED	1	DREARY	1	EYE-GLANCES	1	FORMS	1
DECAYS	1	DRESSES	1	EYELID	1	FORSOOK	1
DECEIVE	1	DRIED	1	EYEN	1	FORTS	1
DECKED	1	DRIZZLING	1	FAIL	1	FORTUNE	1
DEER	1	DROOPING	1	FAILETH	1	FORTUNE'S	1
DEFACE	1	DROPPING	1	FAIN	1	FOUL	1

FOULLY	1	HEED	1	KNIT	1	MALADY	1
FRAME	1	HELICE	1	KNOT	1	MALICE	1
FRAMED	1	HELICON	1	KNOWING	1	MAN'S	1
FRAY	1	HERALD	1	KNOWN	1	MANTLE	1
FREEWILL	1	HERCULES	1	LADEN	1	MANTLETH	1
FREEZE	1	HEREAFTER	1	LAID	1	MARBLE	1
FREEZETH	1	HERESY	1	LAMB	1	MARS	1
FRESHLY	1	HERETICS	1	LAMPING	1	MARVEL	1
FRIENDS	1	HERETOFORE	1	LAND	1	MASK	1
FRO	1	HIDEOUS	1	LANGUISHING	1	MASSACRES	1
FROWN	1	HIGHER	1	LANGUISHMENT	1	MASTER'S	1
FRUITLESS	1	HIGHEST	1	LARGE	1	MATCH	1
FRY	1	HIMSELF	1	LATER	1	MATCHABLE	1
FULFILLED	1	HIND	1	LAUGHS	1	MAVIS	1
FULLNESS	1	HINDERS	1	LAUGHTER	1	MAYST	1
FURIES	1	HOMEWARD	1	LAUNCHED	1	MAZED	1
FURTHER	1	HOOKS	1	LAW	1	MEAT	1
FURY	1	HORRID	1	LAYS	1	MEDICINES	1
GAINED	1	HOSTAGES	1	LEAGUE	1	MEEDS	1
GALL	1	HOT	1	LEFT	1	MEEKNESS	1
GAME	1	HOUNDS	1	LEGIONS	1	MELTING	1
GARLAND	1	HOURS	1	LEND	1	MELTS	1
GATHER	1	HOVE	1	LESSON	1	MEMBERS	1
GAY	1	HUMILITY	1	LIBERTIES	1	MEMORY	1
GAZERS	1	HUNDRED	1	LIBERTY	1	MEND	1
GILLYFLOWERS	1	HUNTS	1	LICENTIOUS	1	MENTION	1
GIVES	1	HUNTSMAN	1	LIDS	1	MERCHANDISE	1
GIVING	1	ILLUSION	1	LIE	1	MERCHANTS	1
GLADSOME	1	IMAGES	1	LIKEN	1	MERCIFUL	1
GLANCING	1	IMMORTALIZE	1	LIKENED	1	MERRY	1
GLIDE	1	IMMORTALLY	1	LILIES	1	MESSENGER	1
GLOOMING	1	IMPERIOUS	1	LILY	1	MEW	1
GLORIOUSLY	1	IMPLIED	1	LINGER	1	MIGHTY'S	1
GLORY'S	1	IMPORTUNE	1	LIONESS	1	MILDER	1
GODDESS	1	IMPURE	1	LIST	1	MILDLY	1
GOODS	1	INCREASED	1	LIVES	1	MILE	1
GOODWILL	1	INDEED	1	LOATHSOME	1	MINUTE	1
GOTTEN	1	INDIAS	1	LOCKS	1	MIRACULOUS	1
GRACED	1	INFUSION	1	LODESTAR	1	MIRROR	1
GRACETH	1	INNER	1	LODWICK	1	MISCHIEF	1
GREATEST	1	INNOCENCE	1	LOOK'S	1	MISERIES	1
GREECE	1	INNOCENT	1	LOOKERS'	1	MISERY	1
GREEDILY	1	INSIGHT	1	LOOSE	1	MISHAP	1
GREEDINESS	1	INSPIRED	1	LOOSER	1	MISINTENDED	1
GRUDGING	1	INSTRUMENT	1	LORDETH	1	MISS	1
GUEST	1	INTREAT	1	LOSING	1	MISSETH	1
GUESTS	1	INTREATY	1	LOT	1	MOCKS	1
HAIRS	1	INURE	1	LOVE-AFF		MODEST	
HANDLE	1	INURED	1	AMISHED	1	MOLD	1
HANDMAID	1	JANUS'	1	LOVED	1	MOLEST	1
HAPPINESS	1	JAR	1	LOVERS	1	MOLLIFY	1
HARBOR	1	JASMINE	1	LOVING	1	MOLY	1
HARDEN	1	JEWEL	1	LOWEST	1	MONUMENTS	1
HARDENED	1	JOT	1	LOWLINESS	1	MOOD	1
HARDENS	1	JOVE	1	LOYAL	1	MOON	1
HARDNESS	1	JOYS	1	LUCKY	1	MORNING	1
HARDY	1	JUNCATS	1	LURK	1	MOUGHT	1
HARROWED	1	JUNIPER	1	LURKEST	1	MOUNT	1
HARVEST	1	JUST	1	LUSTFUL	1	MOURN	1
HAST	1	JUSTICE	1	LUSTY	1	MOURNFUL	1
HASTE	1	KEEPS	1	MADNESS	1	MOURNING	1
HASTEN	1	KILLS	1	MAID	1	MOUTH	1
HEARD	1	KINDLING	1	MAINTAINED	1	MOVED	1
HEART-TH		KISS	1	MAJESTY	1	MUSE	1
RILLING	1	KNEW	1	MAKEST	1	MUTUAL	1

Word		Word		Word		Word	
SPHERES	1	TAKETH	1	TROPHIES	1	VOYAGE	1
SPIDER'S	1	TAKING	1	TROPHY	1	WANTS	1
SPIGHT	1	TASTE	1	TROUBLED	1	WARLIKE	1
SPILLING	1	TAUGHT	1	TROUBLOUS	1	WARN	1
SPILLS	1	TEDIOUS	1	TRUCE	1	WARREID	1
SPITEFUL	1	TEETH	1	TRUMPET	1	WARRIORS	1
SPOTTED	1	TEMPER	1	TRUST	1	WASTE	1
SPRAY	1	TEMPERATURE	1	TRUSTING	1	WASTED	1
SPREADS	1	TEMPEST'S	1	TRUSTY	1	WAVING	1
SPRITES	1	TEMPLE	1	TUNELESS	1	WAYS	1
SPUN	1	TEMPT	1	TURMOIL	1	WEAKER	1
STAIN	1	TENDER	1	TURNS	1	WEATHER	1
STAIR	1	TERM	1	TWINKLE	1	WEATHER'S	1
STAND	1	TERROR	1	TYRANNESS	1	WEIGHED	1
STANDETH	1	THANKLESS	1	TYRANNY	1	WEIGHING	1
STARE	1	THEATER	1	ULYSSES'	1	WEND	1
STARRY	1	THEREBY	1	UNAWARE	1	WHEEL	1
STARS	1	THEREIN	1	UNCLEAN	1	WHERETO	1
STARVE	1	THERETO	1	UNDERSTAND	1	WHILST	1
STATE	1	THEREUNTO	1	UNDONE	1	WHOLE	1
STATELY	1	THESSALIAN	1	UNJUSTLY	1	WILLBE	1
STAYED	1	THICK	1	UNKIND	1	WILLFUL	1
STEADY	1	THINKING	1	UNMOVED	1	WILLING	1
STEED	1	THINKS	1	UNPITIED	1	WILLS	1
STERN	1	THIRD	1	UNQUIET	1	WIN	1
STIFFNESS	1	THIRST	1	UNREAVE	1	WINGED	1
STING	1	THOUGHT'S	1	UNREST	1	WIPED	1
STINT	1	THOUSAND	1	UNRIGHTEOUS	1	WISHED	1
STOCK	1	THRALLED	1	UNSPOTTED	1	WISHFUL	1
STONE	1	THRALLS	1	UNSTAYED	1	WISHING	1
STONES	1	THREATENING	1	UNSURE	1	WITLESS	1
STONISHT	1	THREATS	1	UNTIMELY	1	WITNESS	1
STOOD	1	THREESCORE	1	UNTRAINED	1	WITS	1
STOOP	1	THREW	1	UNVALUED	1	WOE	1
STOP	1	THRILLING	1	UNWARES	1	WOMAN	1
STOPPED	1	THRONG	1	UNWARILY	1	WONDERFUL	1
STOURES	1	THUNDER	1	UNWORTHY	1	WONTS	1
STOUTLY	1	THUNDERING	1	UPBROUGHT	1	WOODBIND	1
STRAND	1	TIDE	1	UPLIFTING	1	WOODS	1
STRAWBERRY	1	TIED	1	USED	1	WOOERS	1
STRENGTH	1	TIGER	1	UTMOST	1	WORKMANSHIP	1
STRIFE	1	TIMES	1	UTTER	1	WORKS	1
STUPID	1	TIPPED	1	VALOROUS	1	WORSE	1
SUBDUE	1	TITLES	1	VANQUISHED	1	WORSHIP	1
SUBSTANCE	1	TOGETHER	1	VENGEANCE	1	WORSHIPPED	1
SUBTLE	1	TOOK	1	VENOMOUS	1	WORTHILY	1
SUDDEN	1	TORMENTED	1	VERY	1	WORTHLESS	1
SUDDENLY	1	TORMENTETH	1	VICE	1	WORTHS	1
SUFFER	1	TOUGH	1	VICTOR'S	1	WOUNDED	1
SUFFICETH	1	TOWER	1	VICTORIOUS	1	WOVEN	1
SUFFICIENT	1	TRACT	1	VICTORS	1	WOXEN	1
SUIT	1	TRADEFUL	1	VILE	1	WRECKS	1
SUMMER'S	1	TRAGEDY	1	VIPER'S	1	WRETCH'S	1
SUN	1	TRAINS	1	VIRTUE'S	1	WRETCHED	1
SUNDRY	1	TRANCE	1	VIRTUOUS	1	WRETCHES	1
SUPPOSETH	1	TRANSFORM	1	VISIT	1	WRIT	1
SURCEASE	1	TREAD	1	VISNOMY	1	WRONGEST	1
SURPASSING	1	TREADING	1	VOID	1	WROUGHT	1
SWAY	1	TREASON'S	1	VOW	1		
SWEAT	1	TREASURE	1	VOWED	1		
SWEETLY	1	TREASURES	1	VOWS	1		